Webster's
New American
Dictionary

Webster's
New American
Dictionary

Created in Cooperation with the Editors of
MERRIAM-WEBSTER

SMITHMARK
REFERENCE

This edition published in 1995 by
SMITHMARK Publishers, Inc., 16 East 32nd Street,
New York, NY 10016.

SMITHMARK books are available for bulk purchase for sales
promotion and premium use. For details write or call the
manager of special sales, SMITHMARK Publishers Inc.,
16 East 32nd Street, New York, NY 10016.

Library of Congress Cataloging-in-Publication Data

Webster's new American dictionary.
p.   cm.
ISBN 0-8317-9165-9
1. English language—Dictionaries.   I. Title: Merriam-Webster
dictionary.
PE1628.W5568   1995
423—dc20   95-2048
                                                           CIP

Printed in the United States of America

10 9 8 7 6 5 4 3 2 1

Contents

Preface

Webster's New American Dictionary is a dictionary designed to meet the day-to-day needs of dictionary users in the home, office, and classroom. It emphasizes practicality and ease of use and offers a range of material.

The heart of this book is the A-Z vocabulary. This vocabulary is a compilation of the words most likely to be looked up by any person searching for a meaning, pronunciation, or end-of-line division point.

The A-Z vocabulary is followed by several sections that dictionary users have long found helpful. These sections are listed on the Contents page.

The A-Z vocabulary is preceded by a section of Explanatory Notes that should be read carefully by every user of the dictionary. Following these notes is a page that lists and explains the pronunciation symbols used in this dictionary.

Webster's New American Dictionary was created in cooperation with the editors of Merriam-Webster Inc., a company that has been publishing dictionaries for nearly 150 years.

Explanatory Notes

Entries

A boldface letter or a combination of such letters, including punctuation marks and diacritics where needed, that is set flush with the left-hand margin of each column of type is a main entry. The main entry may consist of letters set solid, of letters joined by a hyphen or a diagonal, or of letters separated by one or more spaces:

> **alone** . . . *adj*
> **avant–garde** . . . *n*
> **and/or** . . . *conj*
> **assembly language** . . . *n*

The material in lightface type that follows each main entry on the same line and on succeeding indented lines presents information about the main entry.

The main entries follow one another in alphabetical order letter by letter: *bill of health* follows *billion; Day of Atonement* follows *daylight saving time*. Those containing an Arabic numeral are alphabetized as if the numeral were spelled out: *4-H* comes between *fourfold* and *Four Hundred; 3-D* comes between *three* and *three-dimensional*. Those that often begin with the abbreviation *St.* in common usage have the abbreviation spelled out: *Saint Valentine's Day*.

A pair of guide words is printed at the top of each page. These indicate that the entries falling alphabetically between the words at the top of the outer column of each page are found on that page.

The guide words are usually the alphabetically first and the alphabetically last entries on the page:

airfield ● albatross

Occasionally the last printed entry is not the alphabetically last entry. On page 42, for example, *bassoon* is the last main entry, but *bassos*, an inflected form at *basso*, is the alphabetically last entry and is therefore the second guide word. The alphabetically last entry is not used, however, if it follows alphabetically the first guide word on the succeeding page. Thus on page 49 *biggest* is not a guide word because it follows alphabetically the entry *bigamist* which is the first guide word on page 50.

Any boldface word—a main entry with definition, a variant, an inflected form, a defined or undefined run-on, or a run-in entry—may be used as a guide word.

When one main entry has exactly the same written form as another, the two are distinguished by superscript numerals preceding each word:

> [1]**melt** . . . *vb*   [1]**pine** . . . *n*
> [2]**melt** *n*   [2]**pine** *vb*

Full words come before parts of words made up of the same letters; solid compounds come before hyphenated compounds; hyphenated compounds come before open compounds; and lowercase entries come before those with an initial capital:

> [2]**super** . . . *adj*
> **super-** . . . *prefix*
> **run·down** . . . *n*
> **run–down** . . . *adj*
> **run down** *vb*
> **dutch** . . . *adv*
> **Dutch** . . . *n*

The centered dots within entry words indicate division points at which a hyphen may be put at the end of a line of print or writing. Thus the noun *cap·puc·ci·no* may be ended on one line and continued on the next in this manner:

> cap-
> puccino
>
> cappuc-
> cino
>
> cappucci-
> no

Centered dots are not shown after a single initial letter or before a single terminal letter because typesetters seldom cut off a single letter:

> **abyss** . . . *n*
> **flighty** . . . *adj*
> **idea** . . . *n*

Nor are they usually shown at the second and succeeding homographs unless they differ among themselves:

> [1]**sig·nal** . . . *n*
> [2]**signal** *vb*
> [3]**signal** *adj*
> [1]**min·ute** . . . *n*
> [2]**mi·nute** . . . *adj*

There are acceptable alternative end-of-line divisions just as there are acceptable variant spellings and pronunciations, but no more than one division is shown for any entry in this dictionary.

A double hyphen at the end of a line in this dictionary (as in the definition at **ant lion**) stands for a hyphen that is retained when the word is written as a unit on one line. This kind of fixed hyphen is always represented in boldface words in this dictionary with an en dash.

When a main entry is followed by the word *or* and another spelling, the two spellings are equal variants. Both are standard, and either one may be used according to personal inclination:

ocher *or* **ochre**

If two variants joined by *or* are out of alphabetical order, they remain equal variants. The one printed first is, however, slightly more common than the second:

¹plow *or* **plough**

When another spelling is joined to the main entry by the word *also*, the spelling after *also* is a secondary variant and occurs less frequently than the first:

absinthe *also* **absinth**

Secondary variants belong to standard usage and may be used according to personal inclination. Once the word *also* is used to signal a secondary variant, all following variants are joined by *or*:

²wool·ly *also* **wool·ie** *or* **wooly**

Variants whose spelling puts them alphabetically more than a column away from the main entry are entered at their own alphabetical places and usually not at the main entry:

li·chee *var of* LITCHI

Variants having a usage label appear only at their own alphabetical places:

me·tre . . . *chiefly Brit var of* METER

To show all the stylings that are found for English compounds would require space that can be better used for other information. So this dictionary limits itself to a single styling for a compound:

peace·mak·er

pell–mell

boom box

When a compound is widely used and one styling predominates, that styling is shown. When a compound is uncommon or when the evidence indicates that two or three stylings are approximately equal in frequency, the styling shown is based on the comparison of other similar compounds.

A main entry may be followed by one or more derivatives or by a homograph with a different functional label. These are run-on entries. Each is introduced by a boldface dash and each has a functional label. They are not defined, however, since their meanings are readily understood from the meaning of the root word:

fear·less . . . *adj* . . . — **fear·less·ly** *adv*
 — **fear·less·ness** *n*

hic·cup . . . *n* . . . — **hiccup** *vb*

A main entry may be followed by one or more phrases containing the entry word or an inflected form of it. These are also run-on entries. Each is introduced by a boldface dash but there is no functional label. They are, however, defined since their meanings are more than the sum of the meanings of their elements:

¹set . . . *vb* . . . — **set sail** : . . .

¹hand . . . *n* . . . — **at hand** : . . .

Defined phrases of this sort are run on at the entry defining the first major word in the phrase. When there are variants, however, the run-on appears at the entry defining the first major word which is invariable in the phrase:

¹seed . . . *n* . . . — **go to seed** *or* **run
to seed 1** : . . .

Boldface words that appear within parentheses (as **co·ca** at **co·caine** and **jet engine** and **jet propulsion** at **jet–propelled**) are run-in entries.

Attention is called to the definition of *vocabulary entry* on page 585. The term *dictionary entry* includes all vocabulary entries as well as all boldface entries in the section headed "Foreign Words and Phrases."

Pronunciation

The matter between a pair of reversed virgules \ \ following the entry word indicates the pronunciation. The symbols used are explained in the chart printed inside the back cover.

A hyphen is used in the pronunciation to show syllabic division. These hyphens sometimes coincide with the centered dots in the entry word that indicate end-of-line division:

ab·sen·tee \ˌab-sən-ˈtē\

Sometimes they do not:

met·ric \ˈme-trik\

A high-set mark " indicates major (primary) stress or accent; a low-set mark ₁ indicates minor (secondary) stress or accent:

heart·beat \ˈhärt-ˌbēt\

The stress mark stands at the beginning of the syllable that receives the stress.

A syllable with neither a high-set mark nor a low-set mark is unstressed:

¹**struc·ture** \ˈstrək-chər\

The presence of variant pronunciations indicates that not all educated speakers pronounce words the same way. A second-place variant is not to be regarded as less acceptable than the pronunciation that is given first. It may, in fact, be used by as many educated speakers as the first variant, but the requirements of the printed page are such that one must precede the other:

apri·cot \ˈa-prə-ˌkät, ˈā-\
pro·vost \ˈprō-ˌvōst, ˈprä-vəst\

Symbols enclosed by parentheses represent elements that are present in the pronunciation of some speakers but are absent from the pronunciation of other speakers, or elements that are present in some but absent from other utterances of the same speaker:

¹**om·ni·bus** \ˈäm-ni-(ˌ)bəs\
ad·di·tion·al \ə-ˈdi-sh(ə-)nəl\

Thus, the above parentheses indicate that some people say \ˈäm-ni-ˌbəs\ and others say \ˈäm-ni-bəs\; some \ə-ˈdi-shə-nəl\, others \ə-ˈdi-shnəl\.

When a main entry has less than a full pronunciation, the missing part is to be supplied from a pronunciation in a preceding entry or within the same pair of reversed virgules:

cham·pi·on·ship \-ˌship\
pa·la·ver \pə-ˈla-vər, -ˈlä-\

The pronunciation of the first three syllables of *championship* is found at the main entry *champion*. The hyphens before and after \ˈlä\ in the pronunciation of *palaver* indicate that both the first and the last parts of the pronunciation are to be taken from the immediately preceding pronunciation.

In general, no pronunciation is indicated for open compounds consisting of two or more English words that have own-place entry:

witch doctor *n*

Only the first entry in a sequence of numbered homographs is given a pronunciation if their pronunciations are the same:

¹**re·ward** \ri-ˈwȯrd\ *vb*
²**reward** *n*

The absent but implied pronunciation of derivatives and compounds run on after a main entry is a combination of the pronunciation at the main entry and the pronunciation of the other element as given at its alphabetical place in the vocabulary:

— **quick·ness** *n*
— **hold forth**

Thus, the pronunciation of *quickness* is the sum of the pronunciations given at *quick* and *-ness;* that of *hold forth*, the sum of the pronunciations of the two elements that make up the phrase.

Functional Labels

An italic label indicating a part of speech or another functional classification follows the pronunciation or, if no pronunciation is given, the main entry. The eight traditional parts of speech are indicated as follows:

bold . . . *adj*
forth·with . . . *adv*
¹**but** . . . *conj*
ge·sund·heit . . . *interj*
bo·le·ro . . . *n*
²**un·der** . . . *prep*
¹**it** . . . *pron*
slap . . . *vb*

Other italicized labels used to indicate functional classifications that are not traditional parts of speech include:

ATM *abbr*
self- *comb form*
un- . . . *prefix*
-ial *adj suffix*
²**-ly** *adv suffix*
²**-er** . . . *n suffix*
-ize . . . *vb suffix*
Fe *symbol*
may . . . *verbal auxiliary*

Functional labels are sometimes combined:

afloat . . . *adj or adv*

Inflected Forms

Nouns

The plurals of nouns are shown in this dictionary when suffixation brings about a change of final -*y* to -*i*-, when the noun ends in a consonant plus -*o* or in -*ey*, when the noun ends in -*oo*, when the noun has an irregular plural or a zero plural or a foreign plural, when the noun is a compound that pluralizes any element but the last, when a final consonant is doubled, when the noun has variant plurals, and when it is believed that the dictionary user might have reasonable doubts about the spelling of the plural or when the plural is spelled in a way contrary to what is expected:

> ²spy *n, pl* spies
> si·lo . . . *n, pl* silos
> val·ley . . . *n, pl* valleys
> ²shampoo *n, pl* shampoos
> ¹quiz . . . *n, pl* quiz·zes
> ¹fish . . . *n, pl* fish *or* fishes
> mouse . . . *n, pl* mice
> moose . . . *n, pl* moose
> cri·te·ri·on . . . *n, pl* -ria
> son–in–law . . . *n, pl* sons–in–law
> pi . . . *n, pl* pis
> ³dry *n, pl* drys

Cutback inflected forms are used when the noun has three or more syllables:

> ame·ni·ty . . . *n, pl* -ties

The plurals of nouns are usually not shown when the base word is unchanged by suffixation, when the noun is a compound whose second element is readily recognizable as a regular free form entered at its own place, or when the noun is unlikely to occur in the plural:

> night . . . *n*
> fore·foot . . . *n*
> mo·nog·a·my . . . *n*

Nouns that are plural in form and that regularly occur in plural construction are labeled *n pl*:

> munch·ies . . . *n pl*

Nouns that are plural in form but that are not always construed as plurals are appropriately labeled:

> lo·gis·tics . . . *n sing or pl*

Verbs

The principal parts of verbs are shown in this dictionary when suffixation brings about a doubling of a final consonant or an elision of a final -*e* or a change of final -*y* to -*i*-, when final -*c* changes to -*ck* in suffixation, when the verb ends in -*ey*, when the inflection is irregular,

when there are variant inflected forms, and when it is believed that the dictionary user might have reasonable doubts about the spelling of an inflected form or when the inflected form is spelled in a way contrary to what is expected:

> ²snag *vb* snagged; snag·ging
> ¹move . . . *vb* moved; mov·ing
> ¹cry . . . *vb* cried; cry·ing
> ¹frol·ic . . . *vb* frol·icked; frol·ick·ing
> sur·vey . . . *vb* sur·veyed; sur·vey·ing
> ¹drive . . . *vb* drove . . .; driv·en . . .; driv·ing
> ²bus *vb* bused *or* bussed; bus·ing *or* bus·sing
> ²visa *vb* vi·saed . . .; vi·sa·ing
> ²chagrin *vb* cha·grined . . .; cha·grin·ing

The principal parts of a regularly inflected verb are shown when it is desirable to indicate the pronunciation of one of the inflected forms:

> learn . . . *vb* learned \'lərnd, 'lərnt\; learn·ing
> ¹al·ter \'ȯl-tər\ *vb* al·tered; al·ter·ing \-t(ə-)riŋ\

Cutback inflected forms are usually used when the verb has three or more syllables, when it is a two-syllable word that ends in -*l* and has variant spellings, and when it is a compound whose second element is readily recognized as an irregular verb:

> elim·i·nate . . . *vb* -nated; -nat·ing
> ²quarrel *vb* -reled *or* -relled; -rel·ing *or* -rel·ling
> ¹re·take . . . *vb* -took . . .; -tak·en . . .; -tak·ing

The principal parts of verbs are usually not shown when the base word is unchanged by suffixation or when the verb is a compound whose second element is readily recognizable as a regular free form entered at its own place:

> ¹jump . . . *vb*
> pre·judge . . . *vb*

Another inflected form of English verbs is the third person singular of the present tense, which is regularly formed by the addition of -*s* or -*es* to the base form of the verb. This inflected form is not shown except at a handful of entries (as *have* and *do*) for which it is in some way anomalous.

Adjectives & Adverbs

The comparative and superlative forms of adjectives and adverbs are shown in this dictionary when suffixation brings about a doubling of a final consonant or an elision of a final -*e* or a change of final -*y* to -*i*-, when the word ends in -*ey*, when the inflection is irregular, and when there are variant inflected forms:

> ¹red . . . *adj* red·der; red·dest

¹tame . . . *adj* **tam·er; tam·est**

¹kind·ly . . . *adj* **kind·li·er; -est**

hors·ey *or* **horsy** . . . *adj* **hors·i·er; -est**

¹good . . . *adj* **bet·ter** . . .; **best**

¹far . . . *adv* **far·ther** . . . *or* **fur·ther** . . .;
    far·thest *or* **fur·thest**

The superlative forms of adjectives and adverbs of two or more syllables are usually cut back:

³**fancy** *adj* **fan·ci·er; -est**

¹**ear·ly** . . . *adv* **ear·li·er; -est**

The comparative and superlative forms of regularly inflected adjectives and adverbs are shown when it is desirable to indicate the pronunciation of the inflected forms:

¹**young** \\ᵖyəŋ\ *adj* **youn·ger** \ᵖyəŋ-gər\; **youn·gest**
   \ᵖyəŋ-gəst\

The inclusion of inflected forms in *-er* and *-est* at adjective and adverb entries means nothing more about the use of *more* and *most* with these adjectives and adverbs than that their comparative and superlative degrees may be expressed in either way: *lazier* or *more lazy; laziest* or *most lazy.*
    At a few adjective entries only the superlative form is shown:

²**mere** *adj, superlative* **mer·est**

The absence of the comparative form indicates that there is no evidence of its use.
    The comparative and superlative forms of adjectives and adverbs are usually not shown when the base word is unchanged by suffixation, when the inflected forms of the word are identical with those of a preceding homograph, or when the word is a compound whose second element is readily recognizable as a regular free form entered at its own place:

¹**near** *adv*

³**good** *adv*

un·wor·thy . . . *adj*

Inflected forms are not shown at undefined run-ons.

Capitalization

Most entries in this dictionary begin with a lowercase letter. A few of these have an italicized label *often cap,* which indicates that the word is as likely to be capitalized as not and that it is as acceptable with an uppercase initial as it is with one in lowercase. Some entries begin with an uppercase letter, which indicates that the word is usually capitalized. The absence of an initial capital or of an *often cap* label indicates that the word is not ordinarily capitalized:

salm·on . . . *n*

gar·gan·tuan . . . *adj, often cap*

Mo·hawk . . . *n*

The capitalization of entries that are open or hyphenated compounds is similarly indicated by the form of the entry or by an italicized label:

dry goods . . . *n pl*

french fry *vb, often cap 1st F*

un–Amer·i·can . . . *adj*

Par·kin·son's disease . . . *n*

lazy Su·san . . . *n*

Jack Frost *n*

A word that is capitalized in some senses and lowercase in others shows variations from the form of the main entry by the use of italicized labels at the appropriate senses:

Trin·i·ty . . . *n* . . . **2** *not cap*

To·ry . . . *n* . . . **3** *often not cap*

ti·tan . . . *n* **1** *cap*

re·nais·sance . . . *n* . . . **1** *cap* . . . **2** *often cap*

Etymology

This dictionary gives the etymologies for a number of the vocabulary entries. These etymologies are in boldface square brackets preceding the definition. Meanings given in roman type within these brackets are not definitions of the entry, but are meanings of the Middle English, Old English, or non-English words within the brackets.
    The etymology gives the language from which words borrowed into English have come. It also gives the form of the word in that language or a representation of the word in our alphabet if the form in that language differs from that in English:

philo·den·dron . . . [NL, fr. Gk, neut. of *philo-dendros* loving trees . . .]

¹**sav·age** . . . [ME *sauvage,* fr. MF, fr. ML *salvaticus,* alter. of L *silvaticus* of the woods, wild . . .]

An etymology beginning with the name of a language (including ME or OE) and not giving the foreign (or Middle English or Old English) form indicates that this form is the same as the form of the entry word:

le·gume . . . [F]
¹jour·ney . . . [ME, fr. OF . . .]

An etymology beginning with the name of a language (including ME or OE) and not giving the foreign (or Middle English or Old English) meaning indicates that this meaning is the same as the meaning expressed in the first definition in the entry:

ug·ly . . . *adj* . . . [ME, fr. ON *uggligr* . . .] **1** : FRIGHTFUL, DIRE

Usage

Three types of status labels are used in this dictionary—temporal, regional, and stylistic—to signal that a word or a sense of a word is not part of the standard vocabulary of English.

The temporal label *obs* for "obsolete" means that there is no evidence of use since 1755:

³**post** *n* **1** *obs*

The label *obs* is a comment on the word being defined. When a thing, as distinguished from the word used to designate it, is obsolete, appropriate orientation is usually given in the definition:

cat·a·pult . . . *n* **1** : an ancient military machine for hurling missiles

The temporal label *archaic* means that a word or sense once in common use is found today only sporadically or in special contexts:

¹**mete** . . . *vb* . . . **1** *archaic*
¹**thou** . . . *pron, archaic*

A word or sense limited in use to a specific region of the U.S. has an appropriate label. The adverb *chiefly* precedes a label when the word has some currency outside the specified region, and a double label is used to indicate considerable currency in each of two specific regions:

²**wash** *n* . . . **5** *West*
do·gie . . . *n, chiefly West*
crul·ler . . . *n* . . . **2** *Northern & Midland*

Words current in all regions of the U.S. have no label.

A word or sense limited in use to one of the other countries of the English-speaking world has an appropriate regional label:

chem·ist . . . *n* . . . **2** *Brit*
loch . . . *n, Scot*
²**wireless** *n* . . . **2** *chiefly Brit*

The label *dial* for "dialect" indicates that the pattern of use of a word or sense is too complex for summary labeling: it usually includes several regional varieties of American English or of American and British English:

²**mind** *vb* **1** *chiefly dial*

The stylistic label *slang* is used with words or senses that are especially appropriate in contexts of extreme informality:

³**can** . . . *vb* . . . **2** *slang*
²**grand** *n, slang*

There is no satisfactory objective test for slang, especially with reference to a word out of context. No word, in fact, is invariably slang, and many standard words can be given slang applications.

Definitions are sometimes followed by verbal illustrations that show a typical use of the word in context. These illustrations are enclosed in angle brackets, and the word being illustrated is usually replaced by a lightface swung dash. The swung dash stands for the boldface entry word, and it may be followed by an italicized suffix:

¹**jump** . . . *vb* . . . **5** . . . ⟨~ the gun⟩
all–around . . . *adj* **1** . . . ⟨best ~ performance⟩
¹**can·on** . . . *n* . . . **3** . . . ⟨the ~*s* of good taste⟩
en·joy . . . *vb* . . . **2** . . . ⟨~*ed* the concert⟩

The swung dash is not used when the form of the boldface entry word is changed in suffixation, and it is not used for open compounds:

²**deal** *vb* . . . **2** . . . ⟨*dealt* him a blow⟩
drum up *vb* **1** . . . ⟨*drum up* business⟩

Definitions are sometimes followed by usage notes that give supplementary information about such matters as idiom, syntax, and semantic relationship. A usage note is introduced by a lightface dash:

²**cry** *n* . . . **5** . . . — usu. used in the phrase *a far cry*

²**drum** *vb* . . . **4** . . . — usu. used with *out*

¹**jaw** . . . *n* . . . **2** . . . — usu. used in pl.

¹**ada·gio** . . . *adv or adj* . . . — used as a direction in music

hajji . . . *n* . . . — often used as a title

Sometimes a usage note is used in place of a definition. Some function words (as conjunctions and prepositions) have chiefly grammatical meaning and little or no lexical meaning; most interjections express feelings but are otherwise untranslatable into lexical meaning; and some other words (as honorific titles) are more amenable to comment than to definition:

or . . . *conj* — used as a function word to indicate an alternative

¹at . . . *prep* **1** — used to indicate a point in time or space

auf Wie•der•seh•en . . . *interj* . . . — used to express farewell

sir . . . *n* . . . **2** — used as a usu. respectful form of address

Sense Division

A boldface colon is used in this dictionary to introduce a definition:

equine . . . *adj* . . . : of or relating to the horse

It is also used to separate two or more definitions of a single sense:

no•ti•fy . . . *vb* . . . **1** : to give notice of : report the occurrence of

Boldface Arabic numerals separate the senses of a word that has more than one sense:

add . . . *vb* **1** : to join something else so as to increase in number or amount **2** : to say further . . . **3** : to combine (numbers) into one sum

A particular semantic relationship between senses is sometimes suggested by the use of one of the two italic sense dividers *esp* or *also*.

The sense divider *esp* (for *especially*) is used to introduce the most common meaning included in the more general preceding definition:

crys•tal . . . *n* . . . **2** : something resembling crystal (as in transparency); *esp* : a clear glass used for table articles

The sense divider *also* is used to introduce a meaning related to the preceding sense by an easily understood extension of that sense:

chi•na . . . *n* : porcelain ware; *also* : domestic pottery in general

The order of senses is historical: the sense known to have been first used in English is entered first. This is not to be taken to mean, however, that each sense of a multisense word developed from the immediately preceding sense. It is altogether possible that sense 1 of a word has given rise to sense 2 and sense 2 to sense 3, but frequently sense 2 and sense 3 may have developed independently of one another from sense 1.

When an italicized label follows a boldface numeral, the label applies only to that specific numbered sense. It does not apply to any other boldface numbered senses:

craft . . . *n* . . . **3** *pl usu* **craft**

¹fa•ther . . . *n* . . . **2** *cap* . . . **5** *often cap*

dul•ci•mer . . . *n* . . . **2** *or* **dul•ci•more** \-ₘmōr\

²lift *n* . . . **5** *chiefly Brit*

At *craft* the *pl* label applies to sense **3** but to none of the other numbered senses. At *father* the *cap* label applies only to sense **2** and the *often cap* label only to sense **5**. At *dulcimer* the variant spelling and pronunciation apply only to sense **2**, and the *chiefly Brit* label at *lift* applies only to sense **5**.

Cross-Reference

Four different kinds of cross-references are used in this dictionary: directional, synonymous, cognate, and inflectional. In each instance the cross-reference is readily recognized by the lightface small capitals in which it is printed.

A cross-reference following a lightface dash and beginning with *see* is a directional cross-reference. It directs the dictionary user to look elsewhere for further information:

ri•al . . . *n* — see MONEY table

A cross-reference following a boldface colon is a synonymous cross-reference. It may stand alone as the only definition for an entry or for a sense of an entry; it may follow an analytical definition; it may be one of two or more synonymous cross-references separated by commas:

pa•pa . . . *n* : FATHER

¹par•tic•u•lar . . . *adj* . . . **4** : attentive to details : PRECISE

²main *adj* **1** : CHIEF, PRINCIPAL

¹fig•ure . . . *n* . . . **6** : SHAPE, FORM, OUTLINE

A synonymous cross-reference indicates that an entry, a definition at the entry, or a specific sense at the entry cross-referred to can be substituted as a definition for the entry or the sense in which the cross-reference appears.

A cross-reference following an italic *var of* ("variant of") is a cognate cross-reference:

pick•a•back . . . *var of* PIGGYBACK

Occasionally a cognate cross-reference has a limiting label preceding *var of* as an indication that the variant is not standard English:

aero•plane . . . *chiefly Brit var of* AIRPLANE

A cross-reference following an italic label that identifies an entry as an inflected form (as of a noun or verb) is an inflectional cross-reference:

calves *pl of* CALF

woven *past part of* WEAVE

Inflectional cross-references appear only when the inflected form falls at least a column away from the entry cross-referred to.

Synonyms

A boldface **syn** near the end of an entry introduces words that are synonymous with the word being defined:

alone . . . *adj* . . . **syn** lonely, lonesome, lone, solitary

Synonyms are not definitions although they may often be substituted for each other in context.

Combining Forms, Prefixes, & Suffixes

An entry that begins or ends with a hyphen is a word element that forms part of an English compound:

-wise . . . *adv comb form* . . . ⟨slant*wise*⟩

ex- . . . *prefix* . . . ⟨*ex*-president⟩

-let . . . *n suffix* **1** . . . ⟨book*let*⟩

Combining forms, prefixes, and suffixes are entered in this dictionary for two reasons: to make understandable the meaning of many undefined run-ons and to make recognizable the meaningful elements of words that are not entered in the dictionary.

Lists of Undefined Words

Lists of undefined words occur after the entries *anti-*, *in-*, *non-*, *over-*, *re-*, *self-*, *semi-*, *sub-*, *super-*, and *un-*. These words are undefined because they are self-explanatory: their meanings are simply the sum of a meaning of the prefix or combining form and a meaning of the root word.

Abbreviations & Symbols

Abbreviations and symbols for chemical elements are included as main entries in the vocabulary:

RSVP *abbr* . . . please reply

Ca *symbol* calcium

Abbreviations have been normalized to one form. In practice, however, there is considerable variation in the use of periods and in capitalization (as *vhf*, *v.h.f.*, *VHF*, and *V.H.F.*), and stylings other than those given in this dictionary are often acceptable.

Symbols that are not capable of being alphabetized are included in a separate section of the back matter headed "Signs and Symbols."

Abbreviations Used in This Work

ab	about	*Aram*	Aramaic
abbr	abbreviation	*B.C.*	before Christ
abl	ablative	*Brit*	British
acc	accusative	*C*	Celsius
A.D.	anno Domini	*Calif*	California
adj	adjective	*CanF*	Canadian French
adv	adverb	*cap*	capital, capitalized
alter	alteration	*Celt*	Celtic
Am	American	*cent*	century
AmerF	American French	*Chin*	Chinese
AmerInd	American Indian	*comb*	combining
AmerSp	American Spanish	*compar*	comparative
Ar	Arabic	*conj*	conjunction

D	Dutch	*Norw*	Norwegian
Dan	Danish	*n pl*	noun plural
dat	dative	*obs*	obsolete
deriv	derivative	*OE*	Old English
dial	dialect	*OF*	Old French
dim	diminutive	*OIt*	Old Italian
E	English	*ON*	Old Norse
Egypt	Egyptian	*OPer*	Old Persian
Eng	English	*OProv*	Old Provençal
esp	especially	*orig*	originally
F	Fahrenheit, French	*part*	participle
fem	feminine	*Per*	Persian
fr	from	*perh*	perhaps
G	German	*Pg*	Portuguese
Gk	Greek	*pl*	plural
Gmc	Germanic	*Pol*	Polish
Heb	Hebrew	*pp*	past participle
Hung	Hungarian	*prep*	preposition
Icel	Icelandic	*pres*	present
imit	imitative	*prob*	probably
imper	imperative	*pron*	pronoun, pronunciation
interj	interjection		
Ir	Irish	*Prov*	Provençal
irreg	irregular	*prp*	present participle
It, Ital	Italian	*Russ*	Russian
Jp	Japanese	*Sc*	Scotch, Scots
K	Kelvin	*Scand*	Scandinavian
L	Latin	*ScGael*	Scottish Gaelic
LaF	Louisiana French	*Scot*	Scottish
LG	Low German	*sing*	singular
LGk	Late Greek	*Skt*	Sanskrit
LHeb	Late Hebrew	*Slav*	Slavic
lit	literally	*So*	South
LL	Late Latin	*Sp*	Spanish
masc	masculine	*St*	Saint
MD	Middle Dutch	*superl*	superlative
ME	Middle English	*Sw*	Swedish
MexSp	Mexican Spanish	*syn*	synonym, synonymy
MF	Middle French	*trans*	translation
MGk	Middle Greek	*Turk*	Turkish
ML	Medieval Latin	*US*	United States
modif	modification	*USSR*	Union of Soviet Socialist Republics
MS	manuscript		
n	noun	*usu*	usually
neut	neuter	*var*	variant
NewEng	New England	*vb*	verb
NGk	New Greek	*vi*	verb intransitive
NHeb	New Hebrew	*VL*	Vulgar Latin
NL	New Latin	*vt*	verb transitive
No	North	*W*	Welsh

Pronunciation Symbols

ə . . . . . abut, collect, suppose

ˈə, ˌə . . . humdrum

ᵊ . . . . . (in ᵊl, ᵊn) battle, cotton; (in lᵊ, mᵊ, rᵊ) French table, prisme, titre

ər . . . . operation, further

a . . . . . map, patch

ā . . . . . day, fate

ä . . . . . bother, cot, father

à . . . . . a sound between \a\ and \ä\, as in an Eastern New England pronunciation of aunt, ask

au̇ . . . . now, out

b . . . . . baby, rib

ch . . . . chin, catch

d . . . . . did, adder

e . . . . . set, red

ē . . . . . beat, easy

f . . . . . fifty, cuff

g . . . . . go, big

h . . . . . hat, ahead

hw . . . . whale

i . . . . . tip, banish

ī . . . . . site, buy

j . . . . . job, edge

k . . . . . kin, cook

k̲ . . . . . German Bach, Scots loch

l . . . . . lily, cool

m . . . . murmur, dim

n . . . . . nine, own

ⁿ . . . . . indicates that a preceding vowel is pronounced through both nose and mouth, as in French bon \bōⁿ\

ŋ . . . . . sing, singer, finger, ink

ō . . . . . bone, hollow

ȯ . . . . . saw

œ . . . . French bœuf, German Hölle

œ̄ . . . . French feu, German Höhle

ȯi . . . . toy

p . . . . . pepper, lip

r . . . . . rarity

s . . . . . source, less

sh . . . . shy, mission

t . . . . . tie, attack

th . . . . thin, ether

t̲h̲ . . . . then, either

ü . . . . . boot, few \ˈfyü\

u̇ . . . . . put, pure \ˈpyu̇r\

ᵫ . . . . German füllen

ᵫ̄ . . . . French rue, German fühlen

v . . . . . vivid, give

w . . . . we, away

y . . . . . yard, cue \ˈkyü\

ʸ . . . . . indicates that a preceding \l\, \n\, or \w\ is modified by having the tongue approximate the position for \y\, as in French digne \dēnʸ\

z . . . . . zone, raise

zh . . . . vision, pleasure

\ . . . . . slant line used in pairs to mark the beginning and end of a transcription: \ˈpen\

ˈ . . . . . mark at the beginning of a syllable that has primary (strongest) stress: \ˈshəf-əl-ˌbōrd\

ˌ . . . . . mark at the beginning of a syllable that has secondary (next-strongest) stress: \ˈshəf-əl-ˌbōrd\

- . . . . . mark of a syllable division in pronunciations (the mark of end-of-line division in boldface entries is a centered dot ·)

( ) . . . . indicate that what is symbolized between sometimes occurs and sometimes does not occur in the pronunciation of the word: bakery \ˈbā-k(ə-)rē\ = \ˈbā-kə-rē, ˈbā-krē\

A

¹**a** \'ā\ *n, pl* **a's** *or* **as** \'āz\ *often cap* **1** : the 1st letter of the English alphabet **2** : a grade rating a student's work as superior

²**a** \ə, (')ā\ *indefinite article* : ONE, SOME — used to indicate an unspecified or unidentified individual ⟨there's ∼ man outside⟩

³**a** *abbr, often cap* **1** absent **2** acre **3** alto **4** answer **5** are **6** area

AA *abbr* **1** Alcoholics Anonymous **2** antiaircraft **3** associate in arts

AAA *abbr* American Automobile Association

A and M *abbr* agricultural and mechanical

A and R *abbr* artists and repertory

aard•vark \'ärd-ˌvärk\ *n* [obs. Afrikaans, fr. Afrikaans *aard* earth + *vark* pig] : a large burrowing African ungulate mammal that feeds on ants and termites with its sticky tongue

ab *abbr* about

AB *abbr* **1** able-bodied seaman **2** airman basic **3** [NL *artium baccalaureus*] bachelor of arts

ABA *abbr* American Bar Association

aback \ə-'bak\ *adv* : by surprise ⟨taken ∼⟩

aba•cus \'a-bə-kəs\ *n, pl* **aba•ci** \-ˌsī, -ˌkē\ *or* **aba•cus•es** : an instrument for making calculations by sliding counters along rods or grooves

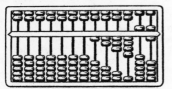

abacus

¹**abaft** \ə-'baft\ *prep* : to the rear of

²**abaft** *adv* : toward or at the stern : AFT

ab•a•lo•ne \ˌa-bə-'lō-nē, 'a-bə-ˌ\ *n* : a large edible sea mollusk with a flattened slightly spiral shell with holes along the edge

¹**aban•don** \ə-'ban-dən\ *vb* [ME *abandounen*, fr. MF *abandoner*, fr. *abandon*, n., surrender, fr. *a bandon* in one's power] : to give up completely : FORSAKE, DESERT — **aban•don•ment** *n*

²**abandon** *n* : a thorough yielding to natural impulses; *esp* : EXUBERANCE

aban•doned \ə-'ban-dənd\ *adj* : morally unrestrained **syn** profligate, dissolute, reprobate

abase \ə-'bās\ *vb* **abased; abas•ing** : HUMBLE, DEGRADE — **abase•ment** *n*

abash \ə-'bash\ *vb* : to destroy the composure of : EMBARRASS — **abash•ment** *n*

abate \ə-'bāt\ *vb* **abat•ed; abat•ing 1** : to put an end to ⟨∼ a nuisance⟩ **2** : to decrease in amount, number, or degree

abate•ment \ə-'bāt-mənt\ *n* **1** : DECREASE **2** : an amount abated; *esp* : a deduction from a tax

ab•at•toir \'a-bə-ˌtwär\ *n* [F] : SLAUGHTERHOUSE

ab•ba•cy \'a-bə-sē\ *n, pl* **-cies** : the office or term of office of an abbot or abbess

ab•bé \a-'bā, 'a-ˌ\ *n* : a member of the French secular clergy — used as a title

ab•bess \'a-bəs\ *n* : the superior of a convent for nuns

ab•bey \'a-bē\ *n, pl* **abbeys 1** : MONASTERY **2** : CONVENT **3** : an abbey church

ab•bot \'a-bət\ *n* [ME *abbod*, fr. OE, fr. LL *abbat-, abbas*, fr. LGk *abbas*, fr. Aramaic *abbā* father] : the superior of a monastery for men

abbr *abbr* abbreviation

ab•bre•vi•ate \ə-'brē-vē-ˌāt\ *vb* **-at•ed; -at•ing** : SHORT-

EN, CURTAIL; *esp* : to reduce to an abbreviation

ab•bre•vi•a•tion \ə-ˌbrē-vē-'ā-shən\ *n* **1** : the act or result of abbreviating **2** : a shortened form of a word or phrase used for brevity esp. in writing

¹**ABC** \ˌā-(ˌ)bē-'sē\ *n, pl* **ABC's** *or* **ABCs** \-'sēz\ **1** : ALPHABET — usu. used in pl. **2** : RUDIMENTS

²**ABC** *abbr* American Broadcasting Company

Ab•di•as \ab-'dī-əs\ *n* : OBADIAH

ab•di•cate \'ab-di-ˌkāt\ *vb* **-cat•ed; -cat•ing** : to give up (as a throne) formally — **ab•di•ca•tion** \ˌab-di-'kā-shən\ *n*

ab•do•men \'ab-də-mən, ab-'dō-\ *n* **1** : the cavity in or area of the body between the chest and the pelvis **2** : the part of the body posterior to the thorax in an arthropod — **ab•dom•i•nal** \ab-'dä-mən-ᵊl\ *adj* — **ab•dom•i•nal•ly** *adv*

ab•duct \ab-'dəkt\ *vb* : to take away (a person) by force : KIDNAP — **ab•duc•tion** \-'dək-shən\ *n* — **ab•duc•tor** \-tər\ *n*

abeam \ə-'bēm\ *adv or adj* : on a line at right angles to a ship's keel

abed \ə-'bed\ *adv or adj* : in bed

Abe•na•ki \ˌa-bə-'nä-kē\ *n, pl* **Abenaki** *or* **Abenakis** : a member of a group of American Indian peoples of northern New England and southern Quebec

ab•er•ra•tion \ˌa-bə-'rā-shən\ *n* **1** : deviation esp. from a moral standard or normal state **2** : failure of a mirror or lens to produce exact point-to-point correspondence between an object and its image **3** : unsoundness of mind : DERANGEMENT — **ab•er•rant** \a-'ber-ənt\ *adj*

abet \ə-'bet\ *vb* **abet•ted; abet•ting** [ME *abetten*, fr. MF *abeter*, fr. OF *beter* to bait] **1** : INCITE, ENCOURAGE **2** : to assist or support in the achievement of a purpose — **abet•tor** *or* **abet•ter** \-'be-tər\ *n*

abey•ance \ə-'bā-əns\ *n* : a condition of suspended activity

ab•hor \ab-'hȯr, ab-\ *vb* **ab•horred; ab•hor•ring** [ME *abhorren*, fr. L *abhorrēre*, fr. *ab-* + *horrēre* to shudder] : LOATHE, DETEST — **ab•hor•rence** \-əns\ *n*

ab•hor•rent \-ənt\ *adj* : LOATHSOME, DETESTABLE

abide \ə-'bīd\ *vb* **abode** \-'bōd\ *or* **abid•ed; abid•ing 1** : BEAR, ENDURE **2** : DWELL, REMAIN, LAST

abil•i•ty \ə-'bi-lə-tē\ *n, pl* **-ties** : the quality of being able : POWER, SKILL

-ability *also* **-ibility** *n suffix* : capacity, fitness, or tendency to act or be acted on in a (specified) way ⟨flammability⟩

ab•ject \'ab-ˌjekt, ab-'jekt\ *adj* : low in spirit or hope : CRINGING — **ab•jec•tion** \ab-'jek-shən\ *n* — **ab•ject•ly** *adv* — **ab•ject•ness** *n*

ab•jure \ab-'jūr\ *vb* **ab•jured; ab•jur•ing 1** : to renounce solemnly : RECANT **2** : to abstain from — **ab•ju•ra•tion** \ˌab-jə-'rā-shən\ *n*

abl *abbr* ablative

ab•late \a-'blāt\ *vb* **ab•lat•ed; ab•lat•ing** : to remove or become removed esp. by cutting, abrading, or vaporizing

ab•la•tion \a-'blā-shən\ *n* **1** : surgical cutting and removal **2** : loss of a part (as the outside of a nose cone) by melting or vaporization

ab•la•tive \'ab-lə-tiv\ *adj* : of, relating to, or constituting a grammatical case (as in Latin) expressing typically the relation of separation and source — **ablative** *n*

ablaze \ə-'blāz\ *adj or adv* : being on fire : BLAZING

able \'ā-bəl\ *adj* **abler** \-b(ə-)lər\; **ablest** \-b(ə-)ləst\ **1** : having sufficient power, skill, or resources to accomplish an object **2** : marked by skill or efficiency — **ably** \-blē\ *adv*

-able *also* **-ible** *adj suffix* **1** : capable of, fit for, or worthy of (being so acted upon or toward) ⟨break*able*⟩

⟨collect*ible*⟩ **2** : tending, given, or liable to ⟨knowl-edge*able*⟩ ⟨perish*able*⟩

able-bod·ied \ˌā-bəl-ˈbä-dēd\ *adj* : having a sound strong body

abloom \ə-ˈblüm\ *adj* : BLOOMING

ab·lu·tion \ə-ˈblü-shən, a-\ *n* : the washing of one's body or part of it

ABM \ˌā-(ˌ)bē-ˈem\ *n*, *pl* **ABM's** *or* **ABMs** : ANTIBAL-LISTIC MISSILE

Ab·na·ki \ab-ˈnä-kē\ *var of* ABENAKI

ab·ne·gate \ˈab-ni-ˌgāt\ *vb* **-gat·ed; -gat·ing 1** : DENY, RENOUNCE **2** : SURRENDER, RELINQUISH — **ab·ne·ga·tion** \ˌab-ni-ˈgā-shən\ *n*

ab·nor·mal \ab-ˈnȯr-məl\ *adj* : deviating from the normal or average — **ab·nor·mal·i·ty** \ˌab-nȯr-ˈma-lə-tē\ *n* — **ab·nor·mal·ly** *adv*

¹aboard \ə-ˈbȯrd\ *adv* **1** : ALONGSIDE **2** : on, onto, or within a car, ship, or aircraft **3** : in or into a group or association ⟨welcome new workers ∼⟩

²aboard *prep* : ON, ONTO, WITHIN

abode \ə-ˈbōd\ *n* **1** : STAY, SOJOURN **2** : HOME, RESI-DENCE

abol·ish \ə-ˈbä-lish\ *vb* : to do away with : ANNUL — **ab·o·li·tion** \ˌa-bə-ˈli-shən\ *n*

ab·o·li·tion·ism \ˌa-bə-ˈli-shə-ˌni-zəm\ *n* : advocacy of the abolition of slavery — **ab·o·li·tion·ist** \-ˈli-sh(ə-)nist\ *n or adj*

A–bomb \ˈā-ˌbäm\ *n* : ATOMIC BOMB — **A–bomb** *vb*

abom·i·na·ble \ə-ˈbä-mə-nə-bəl\ *adj* : ODIOUS, LOATH-SOME, DETESTABLE

abominable snow·man \-ˈsnō-mən, -ˌman\ *n*, *often cap A&S* : a mysterious creature with human or ape-like characteristics reported to exist in the high Hi-malayas

abom·i·nate \ə-ˈbä-mə-ˌnāt\ *vb* **-nat·ed; -nat·ing** [L *abominari*, lit., to deprecate as an ill omen, fr. *ab-* away + *omen* omen] : LOATHE, DETEST

abom·i·na·tion \ə-ˌbä-mə-ˈnā-shən\ *n* **1** : something abominable **2** : DISGUST, LOATHING

ab·orig·i·nal \ˌa-bə-ˈri-jə-nəl\ *adj* : ORIGINAL, INDIGE-NOUS, PRIMITIVE

ab·orig·i·ne \ˌa-bə-ˈri-jə-nē\ *n* : a member of the orig-inal race of inhabitants of a region : NATIVE

aborn·ing \ə-ˈbȯr-niŋ\ *adv* : while being born or pro-duced

¹abort \ə-ˈbȯrt\ *vb* **1** : to cause or undergo abortion **2** : to terminate prematurely ⟨∼ a spaceflight⟩ — **abor·tive** \-ˈbȯr-tiv\ *adj*

²abort *n* : the premature termination of a mission of or a procedure relating to an aircraft or spacecraft

abor·tion \ə-ˈbȯr-shən\ *n* : the spontaneous or induced termination of a pregnancy after, accompanied by, resulting in, or closely followed by the death of the embryo or fetus

abor·tion·ist \-sh(ə-)nist\ *n* : one who induces abor-tions

abound \ə-ˈbaund\ *vb* **1** : to be plentiful : TEEM **2** : to be fully supplied

¹about \ə-ˈbaut\ *adv* **1** : reasonably close to; *also* : on the verge of ⟨∼ to join the army⟩ **2** : on all sides **3** : NEARBY

²about *prep* **1** : on every side of **2** : near to **3** : CON-CERNING

about–face \-ˈfās\ *n* : a reversal of direction or attitude — **about–face** *vb*

¹above \ə-ˈbəv\ *adv* **1** : in the sky; *also* : in or to heaven **2** : in or to a higher place; *also* : higher on the same page or on a preceding page

²above *prep* **1** : in or to a higher place than : OVER ⟨storm clouds ∼ the bay⟩ **2** : superior to ⟨he thought her far ∼ him⟩ **3** : more than : EXCEEDING **4** : as dis-tinct from ⟨∼ the noise⟩

above·board \-ˌbōrd\ *adv or adj* : without conceal-ment or deception : OPENLY

abp *abbr* archbishop

abr *abbr* abridged; abridgment

ab·ra·ca·dab·ra \ˌa-brə-kə-ˈda-brə\ *n* **1** : a magical charm or incantation against calamity **2** : GIBBERISH

abrade \ə-ˈbrād\ *vb* **abrad·ed; abrad·ing 1** : to wear away by friction **2** : to wear down in spirit : IRRITATE — **abra·sion** \-ˈbrā-zhən\ *n*

¹abra·sive \ə-ˈbrā-siv\ *n* : a substance (as pumice) for abrading, smoothing, or polishing

²abrasive *adj* : tending to abrade : causing irritation ⟨∼ relationships⟩ — **abra·sive·ly** *adv* — **abra·sive·ness** *n*

abreast \ə-ˈbrest\ *adv or adj* **1** : side by side **2** : up to a standard or level esp. of knowledge

abridge \ə-ˈbrij\ *vb* **abridged; abridg·ing** [ME *abre-gen*, fr. MF *abregier*, fr. LL *abbreviare*, fr. L *ad* to + *brevis* short] : to lessen in length or extent : SHORTEN — **abridg·ment** *or* **abridge·ment** *n*

abroad \ə-ˈbrȯd\ *adv or adj* **1** : over a wide area **2** : away from one's home **3** : outside one's country

ab·ro·gate \ˈa-brə-ˌgāt\ *vb* **-gat·ed; -gat·ing** : ANNUL, REVOKE — **ab·ro·ga·tion** \ˌa-brə-ˈgā-shən\ *n*

abrupt \ə-ˈbrəpt\ *adj* **1** : broken or as if broken off **2** : SUDDEN, HASTY **3** : so quick as to seem rude **4** : DIS-CONNECTED **5** : STEEP — **abrupt·ly** *adv*

abs *abbr* absolute

ab·scess \ˈab-ˌses\ *n*, *pl* **ab·scess·es** [L *abscessus*, lit., act of going away, fr. *abscedere* to go away, fr. *abs-*, *ab-* away + *cedere* to go] : a localized collection of pus surrounded by inflamed tissue — **ab·scessed** \-ˌsest\ *adj*

ab·scis·sa \ab-ˈsi-sə\ *n*, *pl* **abscissas** *also* **ab·scis·sae** \-ˈsi-(ˌ)sē\ : the horizontal coordinate of a point in a plane coordinate system obtained by measuring par-allel to the x-axis

ab·scis·sion \ab-ˈsi-zhən\ *n* **1** : the act or process of cutting off **2** : the natural separation of flowers, fruits, or leaves from plants — **ab·scise** \ab-ˈsīz\ *vb*

ab·scond \ab-ˈskänd\ *vb* : to depart secretly and hide oneself

ab·sence \ˈab-səns\ *n* **1** : the state or time of being ab-sent **2** : WANT, LACK **3** : INATTENTION

¹ab·sent \ˈab-sənt\ *adj* **1** : not present **2** : LACKING **3** : INATTENTIVE

²ab·sent \ab-ˈsent\ *vb* : to keep (oneself) away

³ab·sent \ˈab-sənt\ *prep* : in the absence of : WITHOUT

ab·sen·tee \ˌab-sən-ˈtē\ *n* : one that is absent or keeps away

absentee ballot *n* : a ballot submitted (as by mail) in advance of an election by a voter who is unable to be present at the polls

ab·sen·tee·ism \ˌab-sən-ˈtē-ˌi-zəm\ *n* : chronic ab-sence (as from work or school)

ab·sent–mind·ed \ˌab-sənt-ˈmīn-dəd\ *adj* : unaware of one's surroundings or actions : INATTENTIVE — **ab·sent·mind·ed·ly** *adv* — **ab·sent·mind·ed·ness** *n*

ab·sinthe *also* **ab·sinth** \ˈab-ˌsinth\ *n* [F] : a liqueur flavored esp. with wormwood and anise

ab·so·lute \ˈab-sə-ˌlüt, ˌab-sə-ˈlüt\ *adj* **1** : free from imperfection or mixture **2** : free from control, restric-tion, or qualification **3** : lacking grammatical connec-tion with any other word in a sentence ⟨∼ construction⟩ **4** : POSITIVE ⟨∼ proof⟩ **5** : relating to the fundamental units of length, mass, and time **6** : FUN-DAMENTAL, ULTIMATE — **ab·so·lute·ly** *adv*

absolute pitch *n* **1** : the position of a tone in a standard scale independently determined by its rate of vibra-tion **2** : the ability to sing a note asked for or to name a note heard

absolute value *n* : the numerical value of a real num-ber that for a positive number or zero is equal to the number itself and for a negative number is equal to the positive number which when added to it is equal to zero

absolute zero *n* : a theoretical temperature marked by a complete absence of heat and equivalent to exactly −273.15°C or −459.67°F

ab·so·lu·tion \ˌab-sə-ˈlü-shən\ *n* : the act of absolving;

esp : a remission of sins pronounced by a priest in the sacrament of reconciliation

ab•so•lut•ism \'ab-sə-¸lü-¸ti-zəm\ *n* **1** : the theory that a ruler or government should have unlimited power **2** : government by an absolute ruler or authority

ab•solve \əb-'zälv, -'sälv\ *vb* **ab•solved; ab•solv•ing** : to set free from an obligation or the consequences of guilt

ab•sorb \əb-'sȯrb, -'zȯrb\ *vb* **1** : to take in and make part of an existent whole **2** : to suck up or take in in the manner of a sponge **3** : to engage (one's attention) : ENGROSS **4** : to receive without recoil or echo (a ceiling that ~*s* sound) **5** : ASSUME, BEAR (~ all costs) **6** : to transform (radiant energy) into a different form usu. with a resulting rise in temperature — **ab•sorb•ing** *adj* — **ab•sorb•ing•ly** *adv*

ab•sor•bent *also* **ab•sor•bant** \əb-'sȯr-bənt, '-zȯr-\ *adj* : able to absorb (~ cotton) — **ab•sor•ben•cy** \-bən-sē\ *n* — **absorbent** *also* **absorbant** *n*

ab•sorp•tion \əb-'sȯrp-shən, -'zȯrp-\ *n* **1** : a process of absorbing or being absorbed **2** : concentration of attention — **ab•sorp•tive** \-tiv\ *adj*

ab•stain \əb-'stān\ *vb* : to refrain from an action or practice — **ab•stain•er** *n* — **ab•sten•tion** \-'sten-chən\ *n*

ab•ste•mi•ous \ab-'stē-mē-əs\ *adj* : sparing in use of food or drink : TEMPERATE — **ab•ste•mi•ous•ly** *adv* — **ab•ste•mi•ous•ness** *n*

ab•sti•nence \'ab-stə-nəns\ *n* : voluntary refraining esp. from eating certain foods or drinking liquor — **ab•sti•nent** \-nənt\ *adj*

abstr *abbr* abstract

¹ab•stract \ab-'strakt, 'ab-¸strakt\ *adj* **1** : considered apart from a particular instance **2** : expressing a quality apart from an object (*whiteness* is an ~ word) **3** : having only intrinsic form with little or no pictorial representation (~ painting) — **ab•stract•ly** *adv* — **ab•stract•ness** *n*

²ab•stract \'ab-¸strakt; *2 also* ab-'strakt\ *n* **1** : SUMMARY, EPITOME **2** : an abstract thing or state

³ab•stract \ab-'strakt, 'ab-¸strakt; *2 usu* 'ab-¸strakt\ *vb* **1** : REMOVE, SEPARATE **2** : to make an abstract of : SUMMARIZE **3** : to draw away the attention of **4** : STEAL — **ab•stract•ed•ly** \ab-'strak-təd-lē, 'ab-¸strak-\ *adv*

abstract expressionism *n* : art that expresses the artist's attitudes and emotions through abstract forms — **abstract expressionist** *n*

ab•strac•tion \ab-'strak-shən\ *n* **1** : the act of abstracting : the state of being abstracted **2** : an abstract idea **3** : an abstract work of art

ab•struse \ab-'strüs\ *adj* : hard to understand : RECONDITE — **ab•struse•ly** *adv* — **ab•struse•ness** *n*

ab•surd \əb-'sərd, -'zərd\ *adj* [MF *absurde,* fr. L *absurdus,* fr. *ab-* from + *surdus* deaf, stupid] : RIDICULOUS, UNREASONABLE — **ab•sur•di•ty** \-'sər-də-tē, -'zər-\ *n* — **ab•surd•ly** *adv*

abun•dant \ə-'bən-dənt\ *adj* [ME, fr. MF, fr. L *abundant-, abundans,* prp. of *abundare* to abound, fr. *ab-* from + *unda* wave] : more than enough : amply sufficient **syn** copious, plentiful, ample, bountiful — **abun•dance** \-dəns\ *n* — **abun•dant•ly** *adv*

¹abuse \ə-'byüs\ *n* **1** : a corrupt practice **2** : MISUSE (drug ~) **3** : coarse and insulting speech **4** : MISTREATMENT (child ~)

²abuse \ə-'byüz\ *vb* **abused; abus•ing 1** : to put to a wrong use : MISUSE **2** : MISTREAT **3** : to attack in words : REVILE — **abus•er** *n* — **abu•sive** \-'byü-siv\ *adj* — **abu•sive•ly** *adv* — **abu•sive•ness** *n*

abut \ə-'bət\ *vb* **abut•ted; abut•ting** : to touch along a border : border on

abut•ment \ə-'bət-mənt\ *n* : the part of a structure (as a bridge) that supports weight or withstands lateral pressure

abut•ter \ə-'bə-tər\ *n* : one that abuts; *esp* : the owner of a contiguous property

abys•mal \ə-'biz-məl\ *adj* **1** : immeasurably deep : BOTTOMLESS **2** : absolutely wretched (~ living conditions of the poor) — **abys•mal•ly** *adv*

abyss \ə-'bis\ *n* **1** : the bottomless pit in old accounts of the universe **2** : an immeasurable depth

abys•sal \ə-'bi-səl\ *adj* : of or relating to the bottom waters of the ocean depths

ac *abbr* account

-ac *n suffix* : one affected with (hypochondri*ac*)

Ac *symbol* actinium

AC *abbr* **1** air-conditioning **2** alternating current **3** [L *ante Christum*] before Christ **4** [L *ante cibum*] before meals **5** area code

aca•cia \ə-'kā-shə\ *n* : any of numerous leguminous trees or shrubs with round white or yellow flower clusters and often fernlike leaves

acad *abbr* academic; academy

ac•a•deme \'a-kə-¸dēm, ¸a-kə-'\ *n* : SCHOOL; *also* : academic environment

¹ac•a•dem•ic \¸a-kə-'de-mik\ *n* : a person who is academic in background, outlook, or methods

²academic *adj* **1** : of, relating to, or associated with schools or colleges **2** : literary or general rather than technical **3** : theoretical rather than practical — **ac•a•dem•i•cal•ly** \-mi-k(ə-)lē\ *adv*

ac•a•de•mi•cian \¸a-kə-də-'mi-shən, ə-¸ka-də-\ *n* **1** : a member of a society of scholars or artists **2** : ACADEMIC

ac•a•dem•i•cism \¸a-kə-'de-mə-¸si-zəm\ *also* **acad•e•mism** \ə-'ka-də-¸mi-zəm\ *n* **1** : a formal academic quality **2** : purely speculative thinking

acad•e•my \ə-'ka-də-mē\ *n, pl* **-mies** [Gk *Akadēmeia,* school of philosophy founded by Plato, fr. *Akadēmeia,* gymnasium where Plato taught, fr. *Akadēmos* Greek mythological hero] **1** : a school above the elementary level; *esp* : a private high school **2** : a society of scholars or artists

acan•thus \ə-'kan-thəs\ *n, pl* **acanthus 1** : any of a genus of prickly herbs of the Mediterranean region **2** : an ornamentation (as on a column) representing the leaves of the acanthus

a cap•pel•la *also* **a ca•pel•la** \¸ä-kə-'pe-lə\ *adv or adj* [It *a cappella* in chapel style] : without instrumental accompaniment

acc *abbr* accusative

ac•cede \ak-'sēd\ *vb* **ac•ced•ed; ac•ced•ing 1** : to become a party to an agreement **2** : to express approval **3** : to enter upon an office **syn** agree, acquiesce, assent, consent, subscribe

ac•cel•er•ate \ik-'se-lə-¸rāt, ak-\ *vb* **-at•ed; -at•ing 1** : to bring about earlier **2** : to speed up : QUICKEN — **ac•cel•er•a•tion** \-¸se-lə-'rā-shən\ *n*

ac•cel•er•a•tor \ik-'se-lə-¸rā-tər, ak-\ *n* **1** : one that accelerates **2** : a pedal for controlling the speed of a motor-vehicle engine **3** : an apparatus for imparting high velocities to charged particles

ac•cel•er•om•e•ter \ik-¸se-lə-'rä-mə-tər, ak-\ *n* : an instrument for measuring acceleration or vibrations

¹ac•cent \'ak-¸sent, ak-'sent\ *vb* : STRESS, EMPHASIZE

²ac•cent \'ak-¸sent\ *n* **1** : a distinctive manner of pronunciation (a foreign ~) **2** : prominence given to one syllable of a word esp. by stress **3** : a mark (as ´, `, ^) over a vowel used usu. to indicate a difference in pronunciation from a vowel not so marked — **ac•cen•tu•al** \ak-'sen-chə-wəl\ *adj*

ac•cen•tu•ate \ak-'sen-chə-¸wāt\ *vb* **-at•ed; -at•ing** : ACCENT — **ac•cen•tu•a•tion** \-¸sen-chə-'wā-shən\ *n*

ac•cept \ik-'sept, ak-\ *vb* **1** : to receive willingly **2** : to agree to **3** : to assume an obligation to pay

ac•cept•able \ik-'sep-tə-bəl, ak-\ *adj* : capable or worthy of being accepted — **ac•cept•abil•i•ty** \ik-¸sep-tə-'bi-lə-tē, ak-\ *n*

ac•cep•tance \ik-'sep-təns, ak-\ *n* **1** : the act of accepting **2** : the state of being accepted or acceptable **3** : an accepted bill of exchange

ac·cep·ta·tion \ˌak-ˌsep-ˈtā-shən\ *n* : the generally understood meaning of a word

¹**ac·cess** \ˈak-ˌses\ *n* **1** : capacity to enter or approach **2** : a way of approach : ENTRANCE

²**access** *vb* : to get at : gain access to

ac·ces·si·ble \ik-ˈse-sə-bəl, ak-, ek-\ *adj* **1** : capable of being reached ⟨∼ by train⟩ **2** : capable of being used, seen, or known : OBTAINABLE ⟨∼ information⟩ — **ac·ces·si·bil·i·ty** \-ˌse-sə-ˈbi-lə-tē\ *n*

ac·ces·sion \ik-ˈse-shən, ak-\ *n* **1** : increase by something added **2** : something added **3** : the act of coming to a high office or position

ac·ces·so·ry *also* **ac·ces·sa·ry** \ik-ˈse-sə-rē, ak-\ *n, pl* **-ries** **1** : a person who though not present abets or assists in the commission of an offense **2** : something helpful but not essential **syn** appurtenance, adjunct, appendage, appendix — **accessory** *adj*

ac·ci·dent \ˈak-sə-dənt\ *n* **1** : an event occurring by chance or unintentionally **2** : CHANCE ⟨met by ∼⟩ **3** : a nonessential property

¹**ac·ci·den·tal** \ˌak-sə-ˈdent-əl\ *adj* **1** : happening unexpectedly or by chance **2** : happening without intent or through carelessness **syn** casual, fortuitous, incidental, chance — **ac·ci·den·tal·ly** \-ˈdent-ə-lē\ *also* **ac·ci·dent·ly** \-ˈdent-lē\ *adv*

²**accidental** *n* : a musical note foreign to a key indicated by a signature

ac·claim \ə-ˈklām\ *vb* **1** : APPLAUD, PRAISE **2** : to declare by acclamation **syn** extol, laud, commend, hail — **acclaim** *n*

ac·cla·ma·tion \ˌa-klə-ˈmā-shən\ *n* **1** : loud eager applause **2** : an overwhelming affirmative vote by shouting or applause rather than by ballot

ac·cli·mate \ˈa-klə-ˌmāt, ə-ˈklī-mət\ *vb* **-mat·ed; -mat·ing** : ACCLIMATIZE — **ac·cli·ma·tion** \ˌa-klə-ˈmā-shən, -ˌklī-\ *n*

ac·cli·ma·tize \ə-ˈklī-mə-ˌtīz\ *vb* **-tized; -tiz·ing** : to accustom or become accustomed to a new climate or situation — **ac·cli·ma·ti·za·tion** \-ˌklī-mə-tə-ˈzā-shən\ *n*

ac·cliv·i·ty \ə-ˈkli-və-tē\ *n, pl* **-ties** : an ascending slope

ac·co·lade \ˈa-kə-ˌlād\ *n* [F, fr. *accoler* to embrace, fr. L *ad-* to + *collum* neck] : an expression of praise : AWARD

ac·com·mo·date \ə-ˈkä-mə-ˌdāt\ *vb* **-dat·ed; -dat·ing 1** : to make fit or suitable : ADAPT, ADJUST **2** : HARMONIZE, RECONCILE **3** : to provide with something needed **4** : to hold without crowding **5** : to undergo visual accommodation

ac·com·mo·dat·ing *adj* : OBLIGING

ac·com·mo·da·tion \ə-ˌkä-mə-ˈdā-shən\ *n* **1** : something supplied to satisfy a need; *esp* : LODGINGS — usu. used in pl. **2** : the act of accommodating : ADJUSTMENT **3** : the automatic adjustment of the eye for seeing at different distances

ac·com·pa·ni·ment \ə-ˈkəm-pə-nē- mənt, -ˈkəmp-nē-\ *n* : something that accompanies another; *esp* : subordinate music to support a principal voice or instrument

ac·com·pa·ny \-nē\ *vb* **-nied; -ny·ing 1** : to go or occur with : ATTEND **2** : to play an accompaniment for — **ac·com·pa·nist** \-nist\ *n*

ac·com·plice \ə-ˈkäm-pləs, -ˈkəm-\ *n* : an associate in crime

ac·com·plish \ə-ˈkäm-plish, -ˈkəm-\ *vb* : to bring to completion **syn** achieve, effect, execute, perform — **ac·com·plish·er** *n*

ac·com·plished *adj* **1** : EXPERT, SKILLED **2** : established beyond doubt

ac·com·plish·ment \ə-ˈkäm-plish-mənt, -ˈkəm-\ *n* **1** : COMPLETION **2** : something completed or effected **3** : an acquired excellence or skill

¹**ac·cord** \ə-ˈkord\ *vb* [ME, fr. OF *acorder*, fr. L *ad-* to + *cord-*, *cor* heart] **1** : GRANT, CONCEDE **2** : AGREE, HARMONIZE — **ac·cor·dant** \-ˈkord-ənt\ *adj*

²**accord** *n* **1** : AGREEMENT, HARMONY **2** : willingness to act ⟨gave of their own ∼⟩

ac·cor·dance \ə-ˈkord-əns\ *n* **1** : ACCORD **2** : the act of granting

ac·cord·ing·ly \ə-ˈkor-diŋ-lē\ *adv* **1** : in accordance **2** : CONSEQUENTLY, SO

according to *prep* **1** : in conformity with ⟨paid *according to* ability⟩ **2** : as stated or attested by ⟨*according to* you⟩

¹**ac·cor·di·on** \ə-ˈkor-dē-ən\ *n* [G *Akkordion*, fr. *Akkord* chord] : a portable keyboard instrument with a bellows and reeds — **ac·cor·di·on·ist** \-ə-nist\ *n*

accordion

²**accordion** *adj* : folding like the bellows of an accordion ⟨∼ pleats⟩

ac·cost \ə-ˈkost\ *vb* [MF *accoster*, ultim. fr. L *ad-* to + *costa* rib, side] : to approach and speak to esp. aggressively

¹**ac·count** \ə-ˈkaunt\ *n* **1** : a statement of business transactions **2** : an arrangement with a vendor to supply credit **3** : a statement of reasons, causes, or motives **4** : VALUE, IMPORTANCE **5** : a sum of money deposited in a bank and subject to withdrawal by the depositor — **on account of** : BECAUSE OF — **on no account** : under no circumstances — **on one's own account** : on one's own behalf

²**account** *vb* **1** : CONSIDER ⟨I ∼ him lucky⟩ **2** : to give an explanation — used with *for*

ac·count·able \ə-ˈkaun-tə-bəl\ *adj* **1** : ANSWERABLE, RESPONSIBLE **2** : EXPLICABLE — **ac·count·abil·i·ty** \-ˌkaun-tə-ˈbi-lə-tē\ *n*

ac·coun·tant \ə-ˈkaunt-ənt\ *n* : a person skilled in accounting — **ac·coun·tan·cy** \-ən-sē\ *n*

account executive *n* : a business executive in charge of a client's account

ac·count·ing \ə-ˈkaun-tiŋ\ *n* : the art or system of keeping and analyzing financial records

ac·cou·tre *or* **ac·cou·ter** \ə-ˈkü-tər\ *vb* **-cou·tred** *or* **-cou·tered; -cou·tring** *or* **-cou·ter·ing** \-ˈkü-t(ə-)riŋ\ : EQUIP, OUTFIT

ac·cou·tre·ment *or* **ac·cou·ter·ment** \ə-ˈkü-trə-mənt, -ˈkü-tər-\ *n* [F] **1** : an accessory item — usu. used in pl. **2** : an identifying characteristic

ac·cred·it \ə-ˈkre-dət\ *vb* **1** : to endorse or approve officially **2** : CREDIT — **ac·cred·i·ta·tion** \-ˌkre-də-ˈtā-shən\ *n*

ac·cre·tion \ə-ˈkrē-shən\ *n* **1** : growth or enlargement esp. by addition from without **2** : a product of accretion

ac·crue \ə-ˈkrü\ *vb* **ac·crued; ac·cru·ing 1** : to come by way of increase **2** : to be added by periodic growth — **ac·cru·al** \-əl\ *n*

acct *abbr* account; accountant

ac·cul·tur·a·tion \ə-ˌkəl-chə-ˈrā-shən\ *n* : cultural modification of an individual or group by borrowing and adapting traits from another culture

ac·cu·mu·late \ə-ˈkyü-myə-ˌlāt\ *vb* **-lat·ed; -lat·ing** [L *accumulare*, fr. *ad-* to + *cumulare* to heap up] : to heap or pile up **syn** amass, gather, collect, stockpile — **ac·cu·mu·la·tion** \-ˌkyü-myə-ˈlā-shən\ n — **ac·cu·mu·la·tive** \-ˈkyü-myə-lə-tiv\ adj — **ac·cu·mu·la·tor** \-ˈkyü-myəˌlā-tər\ n

ac·cu·rate \ˈa-kyə-rət\ adj : free from error : EXACT, PRECISE — **ac·cu·ra·cy** \-rə-sē\ n — **ac·cu·rate·ly** adv — **ac·cu·rate·ness** n

ac·cursed \ə-ˈkərst, -ˈkər-səd\ or **ac·curst** \ə-ˈkərst\ adj 1 : being under a curse 2 : DAMNABLE, EXECRABLE

ac·cus·al \ə-ˈkyü-zəl\ n : ACCUSATION

ac·cu·sa·tive \ə-ˈkyü-zə-tiv\ adj : of, relating to, or being a grammatical case marking the direct object of a verb or the object of a preposition — **accusative** n

ac·cuse \ə-ˈkyüz\ vb **ac·cused; ac·cus·ing** : to charge with an offense : BLAME — **ac·cu·sa·tion** \ˌa-kyə-ˈzā-shən\ n — **ac·cus·er** n

ac·cused \ə-ˈkyüzd\ n, pl **accused** : the defendant in a criminal case

ac·cus·tom \ə-ˈkəs-təm\ vb : to make familiar through use or experience

ac·cus·tomed \ə-ˈkəs-təmd\ adj : USUAL, CUSTOMARY

¹**ace** \ˈās\ n [ME as a die face marked with one spot, fr. OF, fr. L, unit, a copper coin] 1 : a playing card bearing a single large pip in its center 2 : a point (as in tennis) won on a serve that goes untouched 3 : a golf score of one stroke on a hole 4 : a combat pilot who has downed five or more enemy planes 5 : one that excels

²**ace** vb **aced; ac·ing** 1 : to score an ace against (an opponent) or on (a golf hole) 2 : to defeat decisively

³**ace** adj : of first rank or quality

acer·bic \ə-ˈsər-bik, a-\ adj : acid in temper, mood, or tone

acer·bi·ty \ə-ˈsər-bə-tē\ n, pl **-ties** : SOURNESS, BITTERNESS

acet·amin·o·phen \ə-ˌsē-tə-ˈmi-nə-fən\ n : a crystalline compound used in chemical synthesis and in medicine to relieve pain and fever

ac·e·tate \ˈa-sə-ˌtāt\ n 1 : a salt or ester of acetic acid 2 : a textile fiber made from cellulose and acetic acid; also : a fabric or plastic made of this fiber

ace·tic acid \ə-ˈsē-tik-\ n : a colorless pungent liquid acid that is the chief acid of vinegar and is used esp. in making chemical compounds

ac·e·tone \ˈa-sə-ˌtōn\ n : a volatile flammable fragrant liquid compound used in making other chemical compounds and as a solvent

ace·tyl·cho·line \ə-ˌsēt-ᵊl-ˈkō-ˌlēn\ n : a compound that is released at nerve endings of the autonomic nervous system and is active in the transmission of nerve impulses

acet·y·lene \ə-ˈset-ᵊl-ən, -ᵊl-ˌēn\ n : a colorless flammable gas used as a fuel (as in welding and soldering)

ace·tyl·sal·i·cyl·ic acid \ə-ˈsēt-ᵊl-ˌsa-lə-ˈsi-lik-\ n : ASPIRIN 1

ache \ˈāk\ vb **ached; ach·ing** 1 : to suffer a usu. dull persistent pain 2 : LONG, YEARN — **ache** n

achieve \ə-ˈchēv\ vb **achieved; achiev·ing** [ME acheven, fr. MF achever to finish, fr. a- to (fr. L ad-) + chief end, head, fr. L caput] : to gain by work or effort **syn** accomplish, attain, realize — **achiev·able** \-ˈchē-və-bəl\ adj — **achieve·ment** n — **achiev·er** n

Achil·les' heel \ə-ˌki-lēz-\ n [fr. the story that the Greek warrior Achilles was vulnerable only in the heel] : a vulnerable point

Achil·les tendon \ə-ˌki-lēz-\ n : the tendon joining the muscles in the calf of the leg to the bone of the heel

ach·ro·mat·ic \ˌa-krə-ˈma-tik\ adj : giving an image almost free from extraneous colors ⟨~ lens⟩

achy \ˈā-kē\ adj **ach·i·er; ach·i·est** : afflicted with aches — **ach·i·ness** n

¹**ac·id** \ˈa-səd\ adj 1 : sour or biting to the taste; also : sharp or sour in manner 2 : of or relating to an acid — **acid·i·ty** \ə-ˈsi-də-tē\ n — **acid·ly** adv

²**acid** n 1 : a sour substance 2 : a usu. water-soluble chemical compound that has a sour taste, re-

acts with a base to form a salt, and reddens litmus 3 : LSD — **acid·ic** \ə-ˈsi-dik\ adj

acid·i·fy \ə-ˈsi-də-ˌfī\ vb **-fied; -fy·ing** 1 : to make or become acid 2 : to change into an acid — **acid·i·fi·ca·tion** \-ˌsi-də-fə-ˈkā-shən\ n

ac·i·do·sis \ˌa-sə-ˈdō-səs\ n, pl **-do·ses** \-ˌsēz\ : an abnormal state of reduced alkalinity of the blood and body tissues

acid precipitation n : precipitation with above normal acidity that is caused esp. by atmospheric pollutants

acid rain n : acid precipitation in the form of rain

acid test n : a severe or crucial test

acid·u·lous \ə-ˈsi-jə-ləs\ adj : somewhat acid or harsh in taste or manner

ack abbr acknowledge; acknowledgment

ac·knowl·edge \ik-ˈnä-lij, ak-\ vb **-edged; -edg·ing** 1 : to recognize the rights or authority of 2 : to admit as true 3 : to express thanks for; also : to report receipt of 4 : to recognize as valid — **ac·knowl·edg·ment** or **ac·knowl·edge·ment** n

ACLU abbr American Civil Liberties Union

ac·me \ˈak-mē\ n [Gk akmē] : the highest point

ac·ne \ˈak-nē\ n [Gk aknē, MS var. of akmē, lit., point] : a skin disorder marked by inflammation of skin glands and hair follicles and by pimple formation esp. on the face

ac·o·lyte \ˈa-kə-ˌlīt\ n 1 : one who assists a member of the clergy in a liturgical service 2 : FOLLOWER

ac·o·nite \ˈa-kə-ˌnīt\ n 1 : MONKSHOOD 2 : a drug obtained from a common Old World monkshood

acorn \ˈā-ˌkȯrn, -kərn\ n : the nut of the oak

acorn squash n : an acorn-shaped dark green winter squash with a ridged surface

acous·tic \ə-ˈkü-stik\ or **acous·ti·cal** \-sti-kəl\ adj : of or relating to the sense or organs of hearing, to sound, or to the science of sounds 2 : deadening sound ⟨~ tile⟩ 3 : operated by or utilizing sound waves — **acous·ti·cal·ly** \-k(ə-)lē\ adv

acous·tics \ə-ˈkü-stiks\ n sing or pl 1 : the science of sound 2 : the qualities in a room that make it easy or hard for a person in it to hear distinctly

ac·quaint \ə-ˈkwānt\ vb [ME, ultim. fr. L ad- + cognoscere to know] 1 : to cause to know personally 2 : INFORM

ac·quain·tance \ə-ˈkwānt-ᵊns\ n 1 : personal knowledge 2 : a person with whom one is acquainted — **ac·quain·tance·ship** n

ac·qui·esce \ˌa-kwē-ˈes\ vb **-esced; -esc·ing** : to accept, comply, or submit without open opposition **syn** consent, agree, assent, accede — **ac·qui·es·cence** \-ˈes-ᵊns\ n — **ac·qui·es·cent** \-ᵊnt\ adj — **ac·qui·es·cent·ly** adv

ac·quire \ə-ˈkwīr\ vb **ac·quired; ac·quir·ing** : to gain possession of : GET — **ac·quir·able** \-ˈkwī-rə-bəl\ adj

ac·quired \ə-ˈkwīrd\ adj 1 : gained by or as a result of effort or experience 2 : caused by environmental forces and not passed from parent to offspring in the genes ⟨~ characteristics⟩

acquired immune deficiency syndrome n : AIDS

acquired immunodeficiency syndrome n : AIDS

ac·quire·ment n 1 : ATTAINMENT, ACCOMPLISHMENT 2 : the act of acquiring

ac·qui·si·tion \ˌa-kwə-ˈzi-shən\ n 1 : ACQUIREMENT 2 : something acquired

ac·quis·i·tive \ə-ˈkwi-zə-tiv\ adj : eager to acquire : GREEDY — **ac·quis·i·tive·ly** adv — **ac·quis·i·tive·ness** n

ac·quit \ə-ˈkwit\ vb **ac·quit·ted; ac·quit·ting** 1 : to pronounce not guilty 2 : to conduct (oneself) usu. satisfactorily — **ac·quit·tal** \-ᵊl\ n

acre \ˈā-kər\ n 1 pl : LANDS, ESTATE 2 — see WEIGHT table

acre·age \ˈā-k(ə-)rij\ n : area in acres

ac·rid \ˈa-krəd\ adj 1 : sharp and biting in taste or odor 2 : deeply bitter : CAUSTIC — **acrid·i·ty** \a-ˈkri-də-tē\ n — **ac·rid·ly** adv — **ac·rid·ness** n

ac·ri·mo·ny \'a-krə-ˌmō-nē\ *n, pl* **-nies** : harsh or biting sharpness of language or feeling — **ac·ri·mo·ni·ous** \ˌa-krə-'mō-nē-əs\ *adj* — **ac·ri·mo·ni·ous·ly** *adv* — **ac·ri·mo·ni·ous·ness** *n*

ac·ro·bat \'a-krə-ˌbat\ *n* [F *acrobate*, fr. Gk *akrobatēs*, fr. *akros* topmost + *bainein* to go] : a performer of gymnastic feats — **ac·ro·bat·ic** \ˌa-krə-'ba-tik\ *adj* — **ac·ro·bat·i·cal·ly** \-ti-k(ə-)lē\ *adv*

ac·ro·bat·ics \ˌa-krə-'ba-tiks\ *n sing or pl* : the performance of an acrobat

ac·ro·nym \'a-krə-ˌnim\ *n* : a word (as *radar*) formed from the initial letter or letters of each of the successive parts or major parts of a compound term

ac·ro·pho·bia \ˌa-krə-'fō-bē-ə\ *n* : abnormal dread of being at a great height

acrop·o·lis \ə-'krä-pə-ləs\ *n* [Gk *akropolis*, fr. *akros* topmost + *polis* city] : the upper fortified part of an ancient Greek city

¹**across** \ə-'krós\ *adv* **1** : to or on the opposite side **2** : so as to be understandable ⟨get the point ∼⟩

²**across** *prep* **1** : to or on the opposite side of ⟨ran ∼ the street⟩ **2** : on so as to cross or pass at an angle ⟨a log ∼ the road⟩

across–the–board *adj* **1** : placed to win if a competitor wins, places, or shows ⟨an ∼ bet⟩ **2** : including all classes or categories ⟨an ∼ wage increase⟩

acros·tic \ə-'krós-tik\ *n* : a composition usu. in verse in which the initial or final letters of the lines taken in order form a word or phrase — **acrostic** *adj*

acryl·ic \ə-'kri-lik\ *n* **1** : ACRYLIC RESIN **2** : a paint in which the vehicle is acrylic resin **3** : a quick-drying synthetic textile fiber

acrylic resin *n* : a glassy thermoplastic used for cast and molded parts or as coatings and adhesives

¹**act** \'akt\ *n* **1** : a thing done : DEED **2** : STATUTE, DECREE **3** : a main division of a play; *also* : an item on a variety program **4** : an instance of insincere behavior : PRETENSE

²**act** *vb* **1** : to perform by action esp. on the stage; *also* : FEIGN, SIMULATE, PRETEND **2** : to take action **3** : to conduct oneself : BEHAVE **4** : to perform a specified function **5** : to produce an effect

³**act** *abbr* **1** active **2** actual

ACT *abbr* Australian Capital Territory

actg *abbr* acting

ACTH \ˌā-(ˌ)sē-(ˌ)tē-'āch\ *n* : a protein hormone of the pituitary gland that stimulates the adrenal cortex

act·ing \'ak-tiŋ\ *adj* : doing duty temporarily or for another ⟨∼ president⟩

ac·tin·i·um \ak-'ti-nē-əm\ *n* : a radioactive metallic chemical element — see ELEMENT table

ac·tion \'ak-shən\ *n* **1** : a legal proceeding **2** : the manner or method of performing **3** : ACTIVITY **4** : ACT, DEED **5** : the accomplishment of a thing usu. over a period of time, in stages, or with the possibility of repetition **6** *pl* : CONDUCT **7** : COMBAT, BATTLE **8** : the events of a literary plot **9** : an operating mechanism ⟨the ∼ of a gun⟩; *also* : the way it operates ⟨stiff ∼⟩

ac·tion·able \'ak-sh(ə-)nə-bəl\ *adj* : affording ground for an action or suit at law — **ac·tion·ably** \-blē\ *adv*

ac·ti·vate \'ak-tə-ˌvāt\ *vb* **-vat·ed; -vat·ing 1** : to spur into action; *also* : to make active, reactive, or radioactive **2** : to treat (as carbon) so as to improve adsorptive properties **3** : to set up (a military unit) formally; *also* : to call to active duty — **ac·ti·va·tion** \ˌak-tə-'vā-shən\ *n* — **ac·ti·va·tor** \'ak-tə-ˌvā-tər\ *n*

ac·tive \'ak-tiv\ *adj* **1** : causing or involving action or change **2** : asserting that the grammatical subject performs the action represented by the verb ⟨∼ voice⟩ **3** : BRISK, LIVELY **4** : erupting or likely to erupt ⟨∼ volcano⟩ **5** : presently in operation or use **6** : tending to progress or to cause degeneration ⟨∼ tuberculosis⟩ — **active** *n* — **ac·tive·ly** *adv* — **ac·tive·ness** *n*

ac·tiv·ism \'ak-ti-ˌvi-zəm\ *n* : a doctrine or practice that emphasizes vigorous action for political ends — **ac·tiv·ist** \-vist\ *n or adj*

ac·tiv·i·ty \ak-'ti-və-tē\ *n, pl* **-ties 1** : the quality or state of being active **2** : forceful or energetic action **3** : an occupation in which one is engaged

ac·tor \'ak-tər\ *n* : a person who acts in a play or motion picture

ac·tress \'ak-trəs\ *n* : a woman who is an actor

Acts \'akts\ *or* **Acts of the Apostles** *n* — see BIBLE table

ac·tu·al \'ak-chə-wəl, -shə-\ *adj* : really existing : REAL — **ac·tu·al·i·ty** \ˌak-chə-'wa-lə-tē, -shə-\ *n* — **ac·tu·al·iza·tion** \ˌak-chə-wə-lə-'zā-shən, -shə-\ *n* — **ac·tu·al·ize** \'ak-chə-wə-ˌlīz, -shə-\ *vb*

ac·tu·al·ly \'ak-chə-wə-lē, -shə-\ *adv* : in fact or in truth : REALLY

ac·tu·ary \'ak-chə-ˌwer-ē, -shə-\ *n, pl* **-ar·ies** : a person who calculates insurance risks and premiums — **ac·tu·ar·i·al** \ˌak-chə-'wer-ē-əl, -shə-\ *adj*

ac·tu·ate \'ak-chə-ˌwāt\ *vb* **-at·ed; -at·ing 1** : to put into action **2** : to move to action — **ac·tu·a·tion** \ˌak-chə-'wā-shən, -shə-\ *n* — **ac·tu·a·tor** \'ak-chə-ˌwā-tər, -shə-\ *n*

act up *vb* **1** : MISBEHAVE **2** : to function improperly

acu·ity \ə-'kyü-ə-tē\ *n, pl* **-ities** : keenness of perception

acu·men \ə-'kyü-mən\ *n* : mental keenness and penetration **syn** discernment, insight, percipience, perspicacity

acu·pres·sure \'a-kyu̇-ˌpre-shər\ *n* : SHIATSU

acu·punc·ture \-ˌpəŋk-chər\ *n* : an orig. Chinese practice of puncturing the body (as with needles) at specific points to cure disease or relieve pain — **acu·punc·tur·ist** \ˌa-kyu̇-'pəŋk-chə-rist\ *n*

acute \ə-'kyüt\ *adj* **acut·er; acut·est** [L *acutus*, pp. of *acuere* to sharpen, fr. *acus* needle] **1** : SHARP, POINTED **2** : containing less than 90 degrees ⟨an ∼ angle⟩ **3** : sharply perceptive; *esp* : mentally keen **4** : SEVERE ⟨∼ distress⟩; *also* : having a sudden onset, sharp rise, and short duration ⟨∼ inflammation⟩ **5** : of, marked by, or being an accent mark having the form ´ — **acute·ly** *adv* — **acute·ness** *n*

acy·clo·vir \(ˌ)ā-'sī-klō-ˌvir\ *n* : a drug used esp. to treat the genital form of herpes simplex

ad \'ad\ *n* : ADVERTISEMENT

AD *abbr* **1** after date **2** [L *anno Domini*] in the year of our Lord — often printed in small capitals and often punctuated **3** assistant director **4** athletic director

ad·age \'a-dij\ *n* : an old familiar saying : PROVERB, MAXIM

¹**ada·gio** \ə-'dä-j(ē-ˌ)ō, -zh(ē-ˌ)ō\ *adv or adj* [It] : at a slow tempo — used as a direction in music

²**adagio** *n, pl* **-gios 1** : an adagio movement **2** : a ballet duet or trio displaying feats of lifting and balancing

¹**ad·a·mant** \'a-də-mənt, -ˌmant\ *n* [ME, fr. OF, fr. L *adamant-, adamas* hardest metal, diamond, fr. Gk] : a stone believed to be impenetrably hard — **ad·a·man·tine** \ˌa-də-'man-ˌtēn, -ˌtīn\ *adj*

²**adamant** *adj* : INFLEXIBLE, UNYIELDING — **ad·a·mant·ly** *adv*

Ad·am's apple \'a-dəmz-\ *n* : the projection in front of the neck formed by the largest cartilage of the larynx

adapt \ə-'dapt\ *vb* : to make suitable or fit (as for a new use or for different conditions) **syn** adjust, accommodate, conform — **adapt·abil·i·ty** \ə-ˌdap-tə-'bi-lə-tē\ *n* — **adapt·able** *adj* — **ad·ap·ta·tion** \ˌa-ˌdap-'tā-shən\ *n* — **ad·ap·ta·tion·al** \-sh(ə-)nəl\ *adj* — **adap·tive** \ə-'dap-tiv\ *adj* — **ad·ap·tiv·i·ty** \ˌa-ˌdap-'ti-və-tē\ *n*

adapt·er *also* **adap·tor** \ə-'dap-tər\ *n* **1** : one that adapts **2** : a device for connecting two dissimilar parts of an apparatus **3** : an attachment for adapting apparatus for uses not orig. intended

ADC *abbr* **1** aide-de-camp **2** Aid to Dependent Children

add \'ad\ *vb* **1** : to join to something else so as to increase in number or amount **2** : to say further ⟨let me ∼ this⟩ **3** : to combine (numbers) into one sum

ad·dend \'a-ˌdend\ *n* : a number to be added to another

ad·den·dum \ə-'den-dəm\ *n, pl* -da \-də\ [L] : something added; *esp* : a supplement to a book

¹ad·der \'a-dər\ *n* **1** : a poisonous European viper or a related snake **2** : any of various harmless No. American snakes (as the hognose snake)

²add·er \'a-dər\ *n* : one that adds; *esp* : a device that performs addition

¹ad·dict \ə-'dikt\ *vb* **1** : to devote or surrender (oneself) to something habitually or excessively **2** : to cause addiction to a substance in (as a person) — **ad·dic·tive** \-'dik-tiv\ *adj*

²ad·dict \'a-(ˌ)dikt\ *n* : one who is addicted to a substance

ad·dic·tion \ə-'dik-shən\ *n* **1** : the quality or state of being addicted **2** : compulsive need for and use of a habit-forming substance (as heroin, nicotine, or alcohol) characterized by well-defined physiological symptoms upon withdrawal; *also* : persistent compulsive use of a substance known by the user to be harmful

ad·di·tion \ə-'di-shən\ *n* **1** : the act or process of adding; *also* : something added **2** : the operation of combining numbers to obtain their sum **syn** accretion, increment, accession, augmentation

ad·di·tion·al \ə-'di-sh(ə-)nəl\ *adj* : coming by way of addition : ADDED, EXTRA

ad·di·tion·al·ly \ə-'di-sh(ə-)nə-lē\ *adv* : in or by way of addition : FURTHERMORE

¹ad·di·tive \'a-də-tiv\ *adj* **1** : of, relating to, or characterized by addition **2** : produced by addition — **ad·di·tiv·i·ty** \ˌa-də-'ti-və-tē\ *n*

²additive *n* : a substance added to another in small quantities to effect a desired change in properties ⟨food ∼s⟩

ad·dle \'ad-ᵊl\ *vb* **ad·dled; ad·dling 1** : to throw into confusion : MUDDLE **2** : to become rotten ⟨addled eggs⟩

addn *abbr* addition

addnl *abbr* additional

add–on \'ad-ˌon, -ˌän\ *n* : something (as a feature or accessory) added esp. as an enhancement

¹ad·dress \ə-'dres\ *vb* **1** : to direct the attention of (oneself) **2** : to direct one's remarks to : deliver an address to **3** : to mark directions for delivery on **4** : to identify (as a memory location) by an address

²ad·dress \ə-'dres, 'a-ˌdres\ *n* **1** : skillful management **2** : a formal speech : LECTURE **3** : the place where a person or organization may be communicated with **4** : the directions for delivery placed on mail **5** : a location (as in a computer's memory) where particular data is stored

ad·dress·ee \ˌa-ˌdre-'sē, ə-ˌdre-'sē\ *n* : one to whom something is addressed

ad·duce \ə-'düs, -'dyüs\ *vb* **ad·duced; ad·duc·ing** : to offer as argument, reason, or proof **syn** advance, allege, cite, submit — **ad·duc·er** *n*

-ade *n suffix* **1** : act : action ⟨blockade⟩ **2** : product; *esp* : sweet drink ⟨limeade⟩

ad·e·nine \'ad-ᵊn-ˌēn\ *n* : one of the purine bases that make up the genetic code of DNA and RNA

ad·e·noid \'ad-ˌnȯid, -ᵊn-ˌȯid\ *n* : an enlarged mass of tissue near the opening of the nose into the throat — usu. used in pl. — **adenoid** *or* **ad·e·noi·dal** \ˌad-'nȯi-dəl, -ᵊn-'ȯi-\ *adj*

aden·o·sine tri·phos·phate \ə-'de-nə-ˌsēn-trī-'fäs-ˌfāt\ *n* : ATP

¹ad·ept \'a-ˌdept\ *n* : EXPERT

²adept \ə-'dept\ *adj* : highly skilled : EXPERT — **adept·ly** *adv* — **adept·ness** *n*

ad·e·quate \'a-di-kwət\ *adj* : equal to or sufficient for a specific requirement — **ad·e·qua·cy** \-kwə-sē\ *n* — **ad·e·quate·ly** *adv* — **ad·e·quate·ness** *n*

ad·here \ad-'hir\ *vb* **ad·hered; ad·her·ing 1** : to give support : maintain loyalty **2** : to stick fast : CLING —

ad·her·ence \-'hir-əns\ *n* — **ad·her·ent** \-ənt\ *adj or n*

ad·he·sion \ad-'hē-zhən\ *n* **1** : the act or state of adhering **2** : the union of bodily tissues abnormally grown together after inflammation; *also* : the newly formed uniting tissue **3** : the molecular attraction between the surfaces of bodies in contact

¹ad·he·sive \-'hē-siv, -ziv\ *adj* **1** : tending to adhere : STICKY **2** : prepared for adhering

²adhesive *n* : an adhesive substance

adhesive tape *n* : tape coated on one side with an adhesive mixture; *esp* : one used for covering wounds

¹ad hoc \'ad-'häk, -'hōk\ *adv* [L, for this] : for the case at hand apart from other applications

²ad hoc *adj* : concerned with or formed for a particular purpose ⟨an ad hoc committee⟩ ⟨ad hoc solutions⟩

adi·a·bat·ic \ˌa-dē-ə-'ba-tik\ *adj* : occurring without loss or gain of heat — **adi·a·bat·i·cal·ly** \-ti-k(ə-)lē\ *adv*

adieu \ə-'dü, -'dyü\ *n, pl* **adieus** *or* **adieux** \ə-'düz, -'dyüz\ : FAREWELL — often used interjectionally

ad in·fi·ni·tum \ˌad-ˌin-fə-'nī-təm\ *adv or adj* : without end or limit

ad in·ter·im \ad-'in-tə-rəm, -ˌrim\ *adv* : for the intervening time — **ad interim** *adj*

adi·os \ˌa-dē-'ōs, ˌä-\ *interj* [Sp adiós, lit., to God] — used to express farewell

ad·i·pose \'a-də-ˌpōs\ *adj* : of or relating to animal fat : FATTY

adj *abbr* **1** adjective **2** adjutant

ad·ja·cent \ə-'jās-ᵊnt\ *adj* : situated near or next **syn** adjoining, contiguous, abutting, juxtaposed, conterminous — **ad·ja·cent·ly** *adv*

ad·jec·tive \'a-jik-tiv\ *n* : a word that typically serves as a modifier of a noun — **ad·jec·ti·val** \ˌa-jik-'tī-vəl\ *adj* — **ad·jec·ti·val·ly** *adv*

ad·join \ə-'jȯin\ *vb* : to be situated next to

ad·join·ing *adj* : touching or bounding at a point or line

ad·journ \ə-'jərn\ *vb* **1** : to suspend indefinitely or until a stated time **2** : to transfer to another place — **ad·journ·ment** *n*

ad·judge \ə-'jəj\ *vb* **ad·judged; ad·judg·ing 1** : JUDGE, ADJUDICATE **2** : to hold or pronounce to be : DEEM **3** : to award by judicial decision

ad·ju·di·cate \ə-'jü-di-ˌkāt\ *vb* **-cat·ed; -cat·ing** : to settle judicially — **ad·ju·di·ca·tion** \ə-ˌjü-di-'kā-shən\ *n*

ad·junct \'a-ˌjəŋkt\ *n* : something joined or added to another but not essentially a part of it **syn** appendage, appurtenance, accessory, appendix

ad·jure \ə-'jür\ *vb* **ad·jured; ad·jur·ing** : to command solemnly : urge earnestly **syn** beg, beseech, implore — **ad·ju·ra·tion** \ˌa-jə-'rā-shən\ *n*

ad·just \ə-'jəst\ *vb* **1** : to bring to agreement : SETTLE **2** : to cause to conform : ADAPT, FIT **3** : REGULATE ⟨∼ a watch⟩ — **ad·just·able** *adj* — **ad·just·er** *also* **ad·jus·tor** \ə-'jəs-tər\ *n* — **ad·just·ment** \ə-'jəst-mənt\ *n*

ad·ju·tant \'a-jə-tənt\ *n* : one who assists; *esp* : an officer who assists a commanding officer by handling correspondence and keeping records

ad·ju·vant \'a-jə-vənt\ *n* : one that helps or facilitates; *esp* : something that enhances the effectiveness of medical treatment — **adjuvant** *adj*

¹ad–lib \'ad-'lib\ *vb* **ad–libbed; ad–lib·bing** : IMPROVISE — **ad–lib** *n*

²ad–lib *adj* : spoken, composed, or performed without preparation

ad lib \'ad-'lib\ *adv* [NL ad libitum] **1** : at one's pleasure **2** : without limit

adm *abbr* administration; administrative

ADM *abbr* admiral

ad·man \'ad-ˌman\ *n* : one who writes, solicits, or places advertisements

admin *abbr* administration; administrative

ad·min·is·ter \əd-'mi-nə-stər\ *vb* **1** : MANAGE, SUPERINTEND **2** : to mete out : DISPENSE **3** : to give ritually or remedially ⟨∼ quinine for malaria⟩ **4** : to perform the office of administrator — **ad·min·is·tra·ble** \-strə-bəl\ *adj* — **ad·min·is·trant** \-strənt\ *n*

ad·min·is·tra·tion \ad-ˌmi-nə-ˈstrā-shən\ *n* 1 : the act or process of administering 2 : MANAGEMENT 3 : the officials directing the government of a country 4 : the term of office of an administrative officer or body — **ad·min·is·tra·tive** \ad-ˈmi-nə-ˌstrā-tiv\ *adj* — **ad·min·is·tra·tive·ly** *adv*

ad·min·is·tra·tor \ad-ˈmi-nə-ˌstrā-tər\ *n* : one that administers; *esp* : one who settles an intestate estate

ad·mi·ra·ble \ˈad-m(ə)rə-bəl\ *adj* : worthy of admiration : EXCELLENT — **ad·mi·ra·bil·i·ty** \ˌad-m(ə)rə-ˈbi-lə-tē\ *n* — **ad·mi·ra·ble·ness** *n* — **ad·mi·ra·bly** \-blē\ *adv*

ad·mi·ral \ˈad-m(ə)rəl\ *n* [ME, ultim. fr. Ar *amīr-al-* commander of the (as in *amīr-al-baḥr* commander of the sea)] : a commissioned officer in the navy ranking next below a fleet admiral

ad·mi·ral·ty \ˈad-m(ə)rəl-tē\ *n* 1 *cap* : a British government department formerly having authority over naval affairs 2 : the court having jurisdiction over questions of maritime law

ad·mire \əd-ˈmīr\ *vb* **ad·mired**; **ad·mir·ing** [MF *admirer*, fr. L *admirari*, fr. *ad-* to + *mirari* to wonder] : to regard with high esteem — **ad·mi·ra·tion** \ˌad-mə-ˈrā-shən\ *n* — **ad·mir·er** *n* — **ad·mir·ing·ly** \-ˈmī-riŋ-lē\ *adv*

ad·mis·si·ble \əd-ˈmi-sə-bəl\ *adj* : that can be or is worthy to be admitted or allowed : ALLOWABLE ⟨∼ evidence⟩ — **ad·mis·si·bil·i·ty** \-ˌmi-sə-ˈbi-lə-tē\ *n*

ad·mis·sion \əd-ˈmi-shən\ *n* 1 : the act of admitting 2 : the privilege of being admitted 3 : a fee paid for admission 4 : the granting of an argument 5 : the acknowledgment of a fact

ad·mit \əd-ˈmit\ *vb* **ad·mit·ted**; **ad·mit·ting** 1 : PERMIT, ALLOW 2 : to recognize as genuine or valid 3 : to allow to enter

ad·mit·tance \əd-ˈmit-ᵊns\ *n* : permission to enter

ad·mit·ted·ly \əd-ˈmi-təd-lē\ *adv* 1 : as has been or must be admitted 2 : it must be admitted

ad·mix \ad-ˈmiks\ *vb* : to mix in

ad·mix·ture \ad-ˈmiks-chər\ *n* 1 : something added in mixing 2 : MIXTURE

ad·mon·ish \ad-ˈmä-nish\ *vb* : to warn gently : reprove with a warning **syn** chide, reproach, rebuke, reprimand, reprove — **ad·mon·ish·er** *n* — **ad·mon·ish·ing·ly** *adv* — **ad·mon·ish·ment** *n* — **ad·mo·ni·tion** \ˌad-mə-ˈni-shən\ *n* — **ad·mon·i·to·ry** \ad-ˈmä-nə-ˌtōr-ē\ *adj*

ad nau·se·am \ad-ˈnȯ-zē-əm\ *adv* [L] : to a sickening or excessive degree

ado \ə-ˈdü\ *n* 1 : bustling excitement : FUSS 2 : TROUBLE

ado·be \ə-ˈdō-bē\ *n* 1 : sun-dried brick; *also* : clay for making such bricks 2 : a structure made of adobe bricks

ad·o·les·cence \ˌad-ᵊl-ˈes-ᵊns\ *n* : the process or period of growth between childhood and maturity — **ad·o·les·cent** \-ᵊnt\ *adj or n*

adopt \ə-ˈdäpt\ *vb* 1 : to take (a child of other parents) as one's own child 2 : to take up and practice as one's own 3 : to accept formally and put into effect — **adopt·able** \-ˈdäp-tə-bəl\ *adj* — **adopt·er** *n* — **adop·tion** \-ˈdäp-shən\ *n*

adop·tive \ə-ˈdäp-tiv\ *adj* : made or acquired by adoption ⟨∼ father⟩ — **adop·tive·ly** *adv*

ador·able \ə-ˈdȯr-ə-bəl\ *adj* 1 : worthy of adoration 2 : extremely charming — **ador·able·ness** *n* — **ador·ably** \-blē\ *adv*

adore \ə-ˈdȯr\ *vb* **adored**; **ador·ing** [ME *adouren*, fr. MF *adorer*, fr. L *adorare*, fr. *ad-* to + *orare* to speak, pray] 1 : WORSHIP 2 : to regard with loving admiration 3 : to be extremely fond of — **ad·o·ra·tion** \ˌa-də-ˈrā-shən\ *n*

adorn \ə-ˈdȯrn\ *vb* : to enhance the appearance of esp. with ornaments — **adorn·ment** *n*

ad·re·nal \ə-ˈdrēn-ᵊl\ *adj* : of, relating to, or being a pair of endocrine organs (**adrenal glands**) that are located near the kidneys and produce several hormones and esp. epinephrine

adren·a·line \ə-ˈdren-ᵊl-ən\ *n* : EPINEPHRINE

adrift \ə-ˈdrift\ *adv or adj* 1 : afloat without motive power or moorings 2 : without guidance or purpose

adroit \ə-ˈdrȯit\ *adj* [F, fr. OF, fr. *a-* to + *droit* right] 1 : dexterous with one's hands 2 : SHREWD, RESOURCEFUL **syn** canny, clever, cunning, ingenious — **adroit·ly** *adv* — **adroit·ness** *n*

ad·sorb \ad-ˈsȯrb, -ˈzȯrb\ *vb* : to take up (as molecules of gases) and hold on the surface of a solid or liquid — **ad·sorp·tion** \-ˈsȯrp-shən, -ˈzȯrp-\ *n*

ad·u·late \ˈa-jə-ˌlāt\ *vb* **-lat·ed**; **-lat·ing** : to flatter or admire excessively — **ad·u·la·tion** \ˌa-jə-ˈlā-shən\ *n* — **ad·u·la·tor** \ˈa-jə-ˌlā-tər\ *n* — **ad·u·la·to·ry** \-lə-ˌtōr-ē\ *adj*

¹**adult** \ə-ˈdəlt, ˈa-ˌ\ *adj* [L *adultus*, pp. of *adolescere* to grow up, fr. *ad-* to + *alescere* to grow] : fully developed and mature — **adult·hood** *n*

²**adult** *n* : one that is adult; *esp* : a human being after an age (as 18) specified by law

adul·ter·ant \ə-ˈdəl-tə-rənt\ *n* : something used to adulterate another

adul·ter·ate \ə-ˈdəl-tə-ˌrāt\ *vb* **-at·ed**; **-at·ing** [L *adulterare*, fr. *ad-* to + *alter* other] : to make impure by mixing in a foreign or inferior substance — **adul·ter·a·tion** \-ˌdəl-tə-ˈrā-shən\ *n*

adul·tery \ə-ˈdəl-t(ə-)rē\ *n, pl* **-ter·ies** : sexual unfaithfulness of a married person — **adul·ter·er** \-tər-ər\ *n* — **adul·ter·ess** \-t(ə-)rəs\ *n* — **adul·ter·ous** \-t(ə-)rəs\ *adj*

ad·um·brate \ˈa-dəm-ˌbrāt\ *vb* **-brat·ed**; **-brat·ing** 1 : to foreshadow vaguely : INTIMATE 2 : to suggest or disclose partially 3 : SHADE, OBSCURE — **ad·um·bra·tion** \ˌa-dəm-ˈbrā-shən\ *n*

adv *abbr* 1 adverb 2 advertisement

ad va·lor·em \ˌad-və-ˈlȯr-əm\ *adj* [L, according to the value] : imposed at a percentage of the value ⟨an *ad valorem* tax⟩

¹**ad·vance** \əd-ˈvans\ *vb* **ad·vanced**; **ad·vanc·ing** 1 : to assist the progress of 2 : to bring or move forward 3 : to promote in rank 4 : to make earlier in time 5 : PROPOSE 6 : LEND 7 : to raise in rate : INCREASE — **ad·vance·ment** *n*

²**advance** *n* 1 : a forward movement 2 : IMPROVEMENT 3 : a rise esp. in price or value 4 : OFFER — **in advance** : BEFOREHAND

³**advance** *adj* : made, sent, or furnished ahead of time

ad·van·tage \əd-ˈvan-tij\ *n* 1 : superiority of position 2 : BENEFIT, GAIN 3 : the 1st point won in tennis after deuce — **ad·van·ta·geous** \ˌad-van-ˈtā-jəs\ *adj* — **ad·van·ta·geous·ly** *adv*

ad·vent \ˈad-ˌvent\ *n* 1 *cap* : a penitential period beginning four Sundays before Christmas 2 *cap* : the coming of Christ 3 : a coming into being or use

ad·ven·ti·tious \ˌad-vən-ˈti-shəs\ *adj* 1 : ACCIDENTAL, INCIDENTAL 2 : arising or occurring sporadically or in other than the usual location ⟨∼ buds⟩ — **ad·ven·ti·tious·ly** *adv*

¹**ad·ven·ture** \əd-ˈven-chər\ *n* 1 : a risky undertaking 2 : a remarkable and exciting experience — **ad·ven·tur·ous** \-ch(ə-)rəs\ *adj*

²**adventure** *vb* **-ven·tured**; **-ven·tur·ing** \-ˈven-ch(ə-)riŋ\ : RISK, HAZARD

ad·ven·tur·er \əd-ˈven-ch(ə-)rər\ *n* 1 : a person who engages in new and risky undertakings 2 : a person who follows a military career for adventure or profit 3 : a person who tries to gain wealth by questionable means

ad·ven·ture·some \əd-ˈven-chər-səm\ *adj* : inclined to take risks

ad·ven·tur·ess \əd-ˈven-ch(ə-)rəs\ *n* : a female adventurer

ad·verb \ˈad-ˌvərb\ *n* : a word that typically serves as

a modifier of a verb, an adjective, or another adverb
— **ad·ver·bi·al** \ad-'vər-bē-əl\ *adj* — **ad·ver·bi·al·ly** *adv*

¹**ad·ver·sary** \'ad-vər-₁ser-ē\ *n, pl* **-sar·ies** : FOE

²**adversary** *adj* : involving antagonistic parties or interests

ad·verse \ad-'vərs, 'ad-₁vərs\ *adj* **1** : acting against or in a contrary direction **2** : UNFAVORABLE — **ad·verse·ly** *adv*

ad·ver·si·ty \ad-'vər-sə-tē\ *n, pl* **-ties** : hard times : MISFORTUNE

ad·vert \ad-'vərt\ *vb* : REFER

ad·ver·tise \'ad-vər-₁tīz\ *vb* **-tised; -tis·ing 1** : INFORM, NOTIFY **2** : to call public attention to esp. in order to sell — **ad·ver·tis·er** *n*

ad·ver·tise·ment \₁ad-vər-'tīz-mənt; əd-'vər-təs-mənt\ *n* **1** : the act of advertising **2** : a public notice intended to advertise something

ad·ver·tis·ing \'ad-vər-₁tī-ziŋ\ *n* : the business of preparing advertisements

ad·vice \əd-'vīs\ *n* **1** : recommendation with regard to a course of action : COUNSEL **2** : INFORMATION, REPORT

ad·vis·able \əd-'vī-zə-bəl\ *adj* : proper to be done : EXPEDIENT — **ad·vis·abil·i·ty** \-₁vī-zə-'bi-lə-tē\ *n*

ad·vise \əd-'vīz\ *vb* **ad·vised; ad·vis·ing 1** : to give advice to : COUNSEL **2** : INFORM, NOTIFY **3** : CONSULT, CONFER — **ad·vis·er** *or* **ad·vi·sor** \-'vī-zər\ *n*

ad·vised \əd-'vīzd\ *adj* : thought out : CONSIDERED ⟨well-*advised*⟩ — **ad·vis·ed·ly** \-'vī-zəd-lē\ *adv*

ad·vise·ment \əd-'vīz-mənt\ *n* **1** : careful consideration **2** : the act of advising

ad·vi·so·ry \əd-'vī-zə-rē\ *adj* **1** : having or exercising power to advise **2** : containing advice

¹**ad·vo·cate** \'ad-və-kət, -₁kāt\ *n* [ultim. fr. L *advocare* to summon, fr. *ad-* to + *vocare* to call] **1** : one who pleads another's cause **2** : one who argues or pleads for a cause or proposal — **ad·vo·ca·cy** \-və-kə-sē\ *n*

²**ad·vo·cate** \-₁kāt\ *vb* **-cat·ed; -cat·ing** : to plead in favor of — **ad·vo·ca·tion** \₁ad-və-'kā-shən\ *n*

advt *abbr* advertisement

adze *also* **adz** \'adz\ *n* : a tool with a curved blade set at right angles to the handle that is used in shaping wood

adze

AEC *abbr* Atomic Energy Commission

ae·gis \'ē-jəs\ *n* **1** : SHIELD, PROTECTION **2** : PATRONAGE, SPONSORSHIP

ae·o·li·an harp \ē-'ō-lē-ən-\ *n* : a box with strings that produce musical sounds when the wind blows on them

ae·on \'ē-ən, -₁än\ *n* : an indefinitely long time : AGE

aer·ate \'a(-ə)r-₁āt\ *vb* **aer·at·ed; aer·at·ing 1** : to supply (blood) with oxygen by respiration **2** : to supply, impregnate, or combine with a gas and esp. air — **aer·a·tion** \₁a(-ə)r-'ā-shən\ *n* — **aer·a·tor** \'a(-ə)r-₁ā-tər\ *n*

¹**aer·i·al** \'ar-ē-əl\ *adj* **1** : inhabiting, occurring in, or done in the air **2** : AIRY **3** : of or relating to aircraft

²**aer·i·al** \'ar-ē-əl\ *n* : ANTENNA 2

aer·i·al·ist \'ar-ē-ə-list\ *n* : a performer of feats above the ground esp. on a trapeze

ae·rie \'ar-ē, 'ir-ē\ *n* : a highly placed nest (as of an eagle)

aer·o·bat·ics \₁ar-ə-'ba-tiks\ *n sing or pl* : spectacular flying feats and maneuvers

aer·o·bic \₁a(-ə)r-'rō-bik\ *adj* **1** : living or active only in the presence of oxygen ⟨∼ bacteria⟩ **2** : of or relating to aerobics — **aer·o·bi·cal·ly** \-bi-k(ə-)lē\ *adv*

aer·o·bics \-biks\ *n sing or pl* : strenuous exercises that produce a marked temporary increase in respiration and heart rate; *also* : a system of physical conditioning involving these

aero·drome \'ar-ə-₁drōm\ *n, chiefly Brit* : AIRPORT

aero·dy·nam·ics \₁ar-ō-dī-'na-miks\ *n* : the science dealing with the forces acting on bodies in motion in a gas (as air) — **aero·dy·nam·ic** \-mik\ *also* **aero·dy·nam·i·cal** \-mi-kəl\ *adj* — **aero·dy·nam·i·cal·ly** \-mi-k(ə-)lē\ *adv*

aero·naut \'ar-ə-₁nȯt\ *n* : one who operates or travels in an airship or balloon

aero·nau·tics \₁ar-ə-'nȯ-tiks\ *n* : the science of aircraft operation — **aero·nau·ti·cal** \-ti-kəl\ *also* **aero·nau·tic** \-tik\ *adj*

aero·plane \'ar-ə-₁plān\ *chiefly Brit var of* AIRPLANE

aero·sol \'ar-ə-₁säl, -₁sȯl\ *n* **1** : a suspension of fine solid or liquid particles in a gas **2** : a substance (as an insecticide) dispensed from a pressurized container as an aerosol

aero·space \'ar-ō-₁spās\ *n* : the earth's atmosphere and the space beyond — **aerospace** *adj*

aery \'ar-ē\ *adj* **aer·i·er; -est** : having an aerial quality : ETHEREAL

aes·thete \'es-₁thēt\ *n* : a person having or affecting sensitivity to beauty esp. in art

aes·thet·ic \es-'the-tik\ *adj* **1** : of or relating to aesthetics : ARTISTIC **2** : appreciative of the beautiful — **aes·thet·i·cal·ly** \-ti-k(ə-)lē\ *adv*

aes·thet·ics \-tiks\ *n* : a branch of philosophy dealing with the nature, creation, and appreciation of beauty

AF *abbr* **1** air force **2** audio frequency

¹**afar** \ə-'fär\ *adv* : from, at, or to a great distance

²**afar** *n* : a great distance

AFB *abbr* air force base

AFC *abbr* **1** American Football Conference **2** automatic frequency control

AFDC *abbr* Aid to Families with Dependent Children

af·fa·ble \'a-fə-bəl\ *adj* : courteous and agreeable in conversation — **af·fa·bil·i·ty** \₁a-fə-'bi-lə-tē\ *n* — **af·fa·bly** \'a-fə-blē\ *adv*

af·fair \ə-'far\ *n* [ME *affaire*, fr. MF, fr. *a faire* to do] **1** : something that relates to or involves one : CONCERN **2** : a romantic or sexual attachment of limited duration

¹**af·fect** \ə-'fekt, a-\ *vb* **1** : to be fond of using or wearing **2** : SIMULATE, ASSUME, PRETEND

²**affect** *vb* : to produce an effect on : INFLUENCE

af·fec·ta·tion \₁a-fek-'tā-shən\ *n* : an attitude or behavior that is assumed by a person but not genuinely felt

af·fect·ed \ə-'fek-təd\ *adj* **1** : given to affectation **2** : artificially assumed to impress others — **af·fect·ed·ly** *adv*

af·fect·ing \ə-'fek-tiŋ\ *adj* : arousing pity, sympathy, or sorrow ⟨an ∼ story⟩ — **af·fect·ing·ly** *adv*

af·fec·tion \ə-'fek-shən\ *n* : tender attachment — **af·fec·tion·ate** \-sh(ə-)nət\ *adj* — **af·fec·tion·ate·ly** *adv*

af·fer·ent \'a-fə-rənt, -₁fer-ənt\ *adj* : bearing or conducting inward toward a more central part and esp. a nerve center (as the brain or spinal cord)

af·fi·ance \ə-'fī-əns\ *vb* **-anced; -anc·ing** : BETROTH, ENGAGE

af·fi·da·vit \₁a-fə-'dā-vət\ *n* [ML, he has made an oath] : a sworn statement in writing

¹**af·fil·i·ate** \ə-'fi-lē-₁āt\ *vb* **-at·ed; -at·ing** : to associate as a member or branch — **af·fil·i·a·tion** \-₁fi-lē-'ā-shən\ *n*

²**af·fil·i·ate** \ə-'fi-lē-ət\ *n* : an affiliated person or organization

af·fin·i·ty \ə-'fi-nə-tē\ *n, pl* **-ties 1** : KINSHIP, RELATIONSHIP **2** : attractive force : ATTRACTION, SYMPATHY

af·firm \ə-'fərm\ *vb* **1** : CONFIRM **2** : to assert positively **3** : to make a solemn and formal declaration or assertion in place of an oath **syn** aver, avow, avouch, declare, assert — **af·fir·ma·tion** \a-fər-'mā-shən\ *n*

¹af·fir·ma·tive \ə-'fər-mə-tiv\ *adj* : asserting that the fact is so : POSITIVE

²affirmative *n* **1** : an expression of affirmation or assent **2** : the side that upholds the proposition stated in a debate

affirmative action *n* : an active effort to improve the employment or educational opportunities of members of minority groups and women

¹af·fix \ə-'fiks\ *vb* : ATTACH, ADD

²af·fix \'a-ˌfiks\ *n* : one or more sounds or letters attached to the beginning or end of a word that produce a derivative word or an inflectional form

af·fla·tus \ə-'flā-təs\ *n* : divine inspiration

af·flict \ə-'flikt\ *vb* **1** : to cause pain and distress to **syn** rack, try, torment, torture — **af·flic·tion** \-'flik-shən\ *n*

af·flic·tive \ə-'flik-tiv\ *adj* : causing affliction : DISTRESSING — **af·flic·tive·ly** *adv*

af·flu·ence \'a-ˌflü-ən(t)s, a-'flü-\ *n* : abundant supply; *also* : WEALTH, RICHES — **af·flu·ent** \-ənt\ *adj*

af·ford \ə-'ford\ *vb* **1** : to manage to bear or bear the cost of without serious harm or loss **2** : PROVIDE, FURNISH

af·for·es·ta·tion \a-ˌfor-ə-'stā-shən\ *n* : the act or process of establishing a forest — **af·for·est** \a-'for-əst, -'fär-\ *vb*

af·fray \ə-'frā\ *n* : FIGHT, FRAY

af·fright \ə-'frīt\ *vb* : FRIGHTEN, ALARM — **affright** *n*

af·front \ə-'frənt\ *vb* **1** : INSULT **2** : CONFRONT — **affront** *n*

af·ghan \'af-ˌgan\ *n* **1** *cap* : a native or inhabitant of Afghanistan **2** : a blanket or shawl of colored wool knitted or crocheted in sections — **Afghan** *adj*

Afghan hound *n* : any of a breed of tall slim swift hunting dogs with a coat of silky thick hair and a long silky top knot

af·gha·ni \af-'ga-nē\ *n* — see MONEY table

afi·cio·na·do \ə-ˌfi-sh(ē-)ə-'nä-dō, -sē-ə-\ *n, pl* **-dos** [Sp, fr. pp. of *aficionar* to inspire affection] : DEVOTEE, FAN

afield \ə-'fēld\ *adv or adj* **1** : to, in, or on the field **2** : away from home **3** : out of the way : ASTRAY

afire \ə-'fīr\ *adj or adv* : being on fire : BURNING

AFL *abbr* American Football League

aflame \ə-'flām\ *adj or adv* : FLAMING

AFL–CIO *abbr* American Federation of Labor and Congress of Industrial Organizations

afloat \ə-'flōt\ *adj or adv* **1** : borne on or as if on the water **2** : CIRCULATING ⟨rumors were ∼⟩ **3** : ADRIFT

aflut·ter \ə-'flə-tər\ *adj* **1** : FLUTTERING **2** : nervously excited

afoot \ə-'fut\ *adv or adj* **1** : on foot **2** : in action : in progress

afore·men·tioned \ə-'for-'men-chənd\ *adj* : mentioned previously

afore·said \-ˌsed\ *adj* : said or named before

afore·thought \-ˌthot\ *adj* : PREMEDITATED ⟨with malice ∼⟩

a for·ti·o·ri \ˌä-ˌfor-tē-'or-ē\ *adv* [NL, lit., from the stronger (argument)] : with even greater reason

afoul of \ə-'faul-əv\ *prep* **1** : in or into conflict with **2** : in or into collision or entanglement with

Afr *abbr* Africa; African

afraid \ə-'frād\ *adj* : FRIGHTENED, FEARFUL

A–frame \'ā-ˌfrām\ *n* : a building having triangular front and rear walls with the roof reaching to the ground

afresh \ə-'fresh\ *adv* : ANEW, AGAIN

Af·ri·can \'a-fri-kən\ *n* **1** : a native or inhabitant of Africa **2** : a person of African ancestry — **African** *adj*

A·fri·can–Amer·i·can \-ə-'mer-ə-kən\ *n* : AFROAMERICAN — **African–American** *adj*

Af·ri·can·ized bee \'a-fri-kə-ˌnīzd-\ *n* : a highly aggressive hybrid honeybee accidentally produced from Brazilian and African stocks that has spread from So. America into Mexico and the southern U.S.

Africanized honeybee *n* : AFRICANIZED BEE

African violet *n* : a tropical African plant widely grown indoors for its velvety fleshy leaves and showy purple, pink, or white flowers

Af·ri·kaans \ˌa-fri-'käns\ *n* : a language developed from 17th century Dutch that is one of the official languages of the Republic of So. Africa

¹Af·ro \'a-frō\ *adj* : having the hair shaped into a round bushy mass

²Afro *n, pl* **Afros** : an Afro hairstyle

Af·ro–Amer·i·can \ˌa-frō-ə-'mer-ə-kən\ *n* : an American of African and esp. of black African descent — **Afro–American** *adj*

aft \'aft\ *adv* : near, toward, or in the stern of a ship or the tail of an aircraft

AFT *abbr* American Federation of Teachers

¹af·ter \'af-tər\ *adv* : AFTERWARD, SUBSEQUENTLY

²after *prep* **1** : behind in place **2** : later than **3** : in pursuit or search of ⟨he's ∼ your job⟩

³after *conj* : following the time when

⁴after *adj* **1** : LATER **2** : located toward the rear

af·ter·birth \'af-tər-ˌbərth\ *n* : the placenta and membranes of the fetus that are expelled after childbirth

af·ter·burn·er \-ˌbər-nər\ *n* : a device incorporated in the tail pipe of a turbojet engine for injecting fuel into the hot exhaust gases and burning it to provide extra thrust

af·ter·care \-ˌker\ *n* : the care, nursing, or treatment of a convalescent patient

af·ter·deck \-ˌdek\ *n* : the rear half of the deck of a ship

af·ter·ef·fect \-ə-ˌfekt\ *n* : an effect that follows its cause after an interval

af·ter·glow \-ˌglō\ *n* : a glow remaining where a light has disappeared

af·ter·im·age \-ˌim-ij\ *n* : a usu. visual sensation continuing after the stimulus causing it has ended

af·ter·life \-ˌlīf\ *n* : an existence after death

af·ter·math \-ˌmath\ *n* **1** : a second-growth crop esp. of hay **2** : CONSEQUENCES, EFFECTS **syn** aftereffect, upshot, result, outcome

af·ter·noon \ˌaf-tər-'nün\ *n* : the time between noon and evening

af·ter·shave \'af-tər-ˌshāv\ *n* : a usu. scented lotion for the face after shaving

af·ter·taste \-ˌtāst\ *n* : a sensation (as of flavor) continuing after the stimulus causing it has ended

af·ter–tax \'af-tər-'taks\ *adj* : remaining after payment of taxes and esp. of income tax ⟨an ∼ profit⟩

af·ter·thought \-ˌthot\ *n* : a later thought; *also* : something thought of later

af·ter·ward \-wərd\ *or* **af·ter·wards** \-wərdz\ *adv* : at a later time

Ag *symbol* [L *argentum*] silver

AG *abbr* **1** adjutant general **2** attorney general

again \ə-'gen, -'gin\ *adv* **1** : once more : ANEW **2** : on the other hand **3** : in addition : BESIDES

against \ə-'genst\ *prep* **1** : in opposition to **2** : directly opposite to : FACING **3** : as defense from **4** : so as to touch or strike ⟨threw him ∼ the wall⟩; *also* : TOUCHING

¹aga·pe \ä-'gä-pā, 'ä-gə-ˌpā\ *n* [Gk, lit., love] : unselfish unconditional love for another

²agape \ə-'gāp\ *adj or adv* : having the mouth open in wonder or surprise : GAPING

agar \'ä-ˌgär\ *n* **1** : a jellylike substance extracted from a red alga and used esp. as a gelling and stabilizing agent in foods **2** : a culture medium containing agar

agar–agar \ˌä-ˌgär-'ä-ˌgär\ *n* : AGAR

ag·ate \'a-gət\ *n* **1** : a striped or clouded quartz **2** : a playing marble of agate or of glass

aga·ve \ə-'gä-vē\ *n* : any of a genus of spinyleaved plants (as a century plant) related to the amaryllis

agcy *abbr* agency

¹age \'āj\ *n* **1** : the length of time during which a being or thing has lived or existed **2** : the time of life at which some particular qualification is achieved; *esp* : MAJORITY **3** : the latter part of life **4** : a long time **5** : a period in history

²age *vb* **aged; ag·ing** *or* **age·ing 1** : to grow old or cause to grow old **2** : to become or cause to become mature or mellow

-age *n suffix* **1** : aggregate : collection ⟨track*age*⟩ **2** : action : process ⟨haul*age*⟩ **3** : cumulative result of ⟨break*age*⟩ **4** : rate of ⟨dos*age*⟩ **5** : house or place of ⟨orphan*age*⟩ **6** : state : rank ⟨vassal*age*⟩ **7** : fee : charge ⟨post*age*⟩

aged \'ā-jəd *for 1;* 'ājd *for 2*\ *adj* **1** : of advanced age **2** : having attained a specified age ⟨a man ∼ 40 years⟩

age·less \'āj-ləs\ *adj* **1** : not growing old or showing the effects of age **2** : TIMELESS, ETERNAL ⟨∼ truths⟩

agen·cy \'ā-jən-sē\ *n, pl* **-cies 1** : one through which something is accomplished : INSTRUMENTALITY **2** : the office or function of an agent **3** : an establishment doing business for another **4** : an administrative division (as of a government) **syn** means, medium, vehicle

agen·da \ə-'jen-də\ *n* : a list of things to be done : PROGRAM

agent \'ā-jənt\ *n* **1** : one that acts **2** : MEANS, INSTRUMENT **3** : a person acting or doing business for another **syn** attorney, deputy, proxy, delegate

Agent Orange *n* : an herbicide widely used in the Vietnam War that is composed of 2,4-D and 2,4,5-T and contains a toxic contaminant

agent pro·vo·ca·teur \'ä-ˌzhäⁿ-prō-ˌvä-kə-ˌtər, 'ā-jənt-\ *n, pl* **agents provocateurs** \'ä-ˌzhäⁿ-prō-ˌväk-ə-'tər, 'ā-jənts-prō-\ [F] : a person hired to infiltrate a group and incite its members to illegal action

age of consent : the age at which one is legally competent to give consent esp. to marriage or to sexual intercourse

age–old \'āj-'ōld\ *adj* : having existed for ages : ANCIENT

ag·er·a·tum \ˌa-jə-'rā-təm\ *n, pl* **-tum** *also* **-tums** : any of a large genus of tropical American plants that are related to the daisies and have small showy heads of blue or white flowers

Ag·ge·us \a-'gē-əs\ *n* : HAGGAI

¹ag·glom·er·ate \ə-'glä-mə-ˌrāt\ *vb* **-at·ed; -at·ing** [L *agglomerare* to heap up, join, fr. *ad-* to + *glomer-*, *glomus* ball] : to gather into a mass : CLUSTER — **ag·glom·er·a·tion** \-ˌglä-mə-'rā-shən\ *n*

²ag·glom·er·ate \-rət\ *n* : rock composed of volcanic fragments

ag·glu·ti·nate \ə-'glüt-ᵊn-ˌāt\ *vb* **-nat·ed; -nat·ing 1** : to cause to adhere : gather into a group or mass **2** : to cause (as red blood cells or bacteria) to collect into clumps — **ag·glu·ti·na·tion** \-ˌglüt-ᵊn-'ā-shən\ *n*

ag·gran·dize \ə-'gran-ˌdīz, 'a-grən-\ *vb* **-dized; -diz·ing** : to make great or greater — **ag·gran·dize·ment** \ə-'gran-dəz-mənt, -ˌdīz-; ˌa-grən-'dīz-\ *n*

ag·gra·vate \'a-grə-ˌvāt\ *vb* **-vat·ed; -vat·ing 1** : to make more severe : INTENSIFY **2** : IRRITATE — **ag·gra·va·tion** \ˌa-grə-'vā-shən\ *n*

¹ag·gre·gate \'a-gri-gət\ *adj* : formed by the gathering of units into one mass

²ag·gre·gate \-ˌgāt\ *vb* **-gat·ed; -gat·ing** : to collect into one mass

³ag·gre·gate \-gət\ *n* : a mass or body of units or parts somewhat loosely associated with one another; *also* : the whole amount

ag·gre·ga·tion \ˌa-gri-'gā-shən\ *n* **1** : a group, body, or mass composed of many distinct parts **2** : the collecting of units or parts into a mass or whole

ag·gres·sion \ə-'gre-shən\ *n* **1** : an unprovoked attack **2** : the practice of making attacks **3** : hostile, injurious, or destructive behavior or outlook esp. when caused by frustration — **ag·gres·sor** \-'gre-sər\ *n*

ag·gres·sive \ə-'gre-siv\ *adj* **1** : tending toward or exhibiting aggression; *esp* : marked by combative readiness **2** : marked by driving energy or initiative : ENTERPRISING **3** : more intensive or comprehensive esp. in dosage or extent — **ag·gres·sive·ly** *adv* — **ag·gres·sive·ness** *n*

ag·grieve \ə-'grēv\ *vb* **ag·grieved; ag·griev·ing 1** : to cause grief to **2** : to inflict injury on : WRONG

aghast \ə-'gast\ *adj* : struck with amazement or horror

ag·ile \'a-jəl\ *adj* : able to move quickly and easily — **agil·i·ty** \ə-'ji-lə-tē\ *n*

ag·i·tate \'a-jə-ˌtāt\ *vb* **-tat·ed; -tat·ing 1** : to move with an irregular rapid motion **2** : to stir up : EXCITE **3** : to discuss earnestly **4** : to attempt to arouse public feeling — **ag·i·ta·tion** \ˌa-jə-'tā-shən\ *n* — **ag·i·ta·tor** \'a-jə-ˌtā-tər\ *n*

ag·it·prop \'a-jət-ˌpräp\ *n* [Russ] : political propaganda promulgated esp. through the arts

agleam \ə-'glēm\ *adj* : GLEAMING

aglit·ter \ə-'gli-tər\ *adj* : GLITTERING

aglow \ə-'glō\ *adj* : GLOWING

ag·nos·tic \ag-'näs-tik\ *adj* [Gk *agnōstos* unknown, unknowable, fr. *a-* un- + *gnōstos* known] : of or relating to the belief that the existence of any ultimate reality (as God) is unknown and prob. unknowable — **agnostic** *n* — **ag·nos·ti·cism** \-'näs-tə-ˌsi-zəm\ *n*

ago \ə-'gō\ *adj or adv* : earlier than the present time

agog \ə-'gäg\ *adj* [MF *en gogues* in mirth] : full of excitement : EAGER

a–go–go \ä-'gō-ˌgō\ *adj* [*Whisky à Gogo,* café and disco in Paris, France, fr. F *à gogo* galore] : GO-GO

ag·o·nize \'a-gə-ˌnīz\ *vb* **-nized; -niz·ing** : to suffer or cause to suffer agony — **ag·o·niz·ing·ly** *adv*

ag·o·ny \'a-gə-nē\ *n, pl* **-nies** [ME *agonie,* fr. L *agonia,* fr. Gk *agōnia* struggle, anguish, fr. *agōn* gathering, contest for a prize] : extreme pain of mind or body **syn** suffering, distress, misery

ago·ra \ˌä-gə-'rä\ *n, pl* **ago·rot** \-'rōt\ — see *shekel* at MONEY table

ag·o·ra·pho·bia \ˌa-gə-rə-'fō-bē-ə\ *n* : abnormal fear of being in a helpless, embarrassing, or inescapable situation characterized esp. by avoidance of open or public places — **ag·o·ra·pho·bic** \-'fō-bik, -'fä-\ *adj or n*

agr *abbr* agricultural; agriculture

agrar·i·an \ə-'grer-ē-ən\ *adj* **1** : of or relating to land or its ownership ⟨∼ reforms⟩ **2** : of or relating to farmers or farming interests — **agrarian** *n* — **agrar·i·an·ism** *n*

agree \ə-'grē\ *vb* **agreed; agree·ing 1** : ADMIT, CONCEDE **2** : to be similar : CORRESPOND **3** : to express agreement or approval **4** : to be in harmony **5** : to settle by common consent **6** : to be fitting or healthful : SUIT

agree·able \ə-'grē-ə-bəl\ *adj* **1** : PLEASING, PLEASANT **2** : ready to consent **3** : being in harmony : CONSONANT — **agree·able·ness** *n* — **agree·ably** \-blē\ *adv*

agree·ment \ə-'grē-mənt\ *n* **1** : harmony of opinion or action **2** : mutual understanding or arrangement; *also* : a document containing such an arrangement

ag·ri·busi·ness \'a-grə-ˌbiz-nəs, -ˌnəz\ *n* : an industry engaged in the manufacture and sale of farm equipment and supplies and in the production, processing, storage, and sale of farm commodities

agric *abbr* agricultural; agriculture

ag·ri·cul·ture \'a-gri-ˌkəl-chər\ *n* : FARMING, HUSBANDRY — **ag·ri·cul·tur·al** \ˌa-gri-'kəl-ch(ə-)rəl\ *adj* — **ag·ri·cul·tur·ist** \-ch(ə-)rist\ *or* **ag·ri·cul·tur·al·ist** \-ch(ə-)rə-list\ *n*

agron·o·my \ə-'grä-nə-mē\ *n* : a branch of agriculture that deals with the raising of crops and the care of the soil — **ag·ro·nom·ic** \ˌa-grə-'nä-mik\ *adj* — **agron·o·mist** \ə-'grä-nə-mist\ *n*

aground \ə-'graúnd\ *adv or adj* : on or onto the bottom or shore ⟨ran ∼⟩

agt *abbr* agent

ague \'ā-gyü\ *n* : a fever (as malaria) with recurrent chills and sweating

ahead \ə-'hed\ *adv or adj* **1** : in or toward the front **2** : into or for the future ⟨plan ∼⟩ **3** : in or toward a more advantageous position

ahead of *prep* **1** : in front or advance of **2** : in excess of : ABOVE

AHL *abbr* American Hockey League

ahoy \ə-'hói\ *interj* — used in hailing ⟨ship ∼⟩

AI *abbr* artificial intelligence

¹**aid** \'ād\ *vb* : to provide with what is useful in achieving an end : ASSIST

²**aid** *n* **1** : ASSISTANCE **2** : ASSISTANT

AID *abbr* Agency for International Development

aide \'ād\ *n* : a person who acts as an assistant; *esp* : a military officer assisting a superior

aide–de–camp \,ād-di-'kamp, -'käⁿ\ *n*, *pl* **aides–de–camp** \,ādz-di-\ [F] : AIDE

AIDS \'ādz\ *n* [*acquired immunodeficiency syndrome*] : a serious disease of the human immune system that is caused by infection with HIV, that is characterized by severe reduction in the numbers of helper T cells, that in modern industrialized nations occurs esp. in intravenous users of illicit drugs and in homosexual and bisexual men, and that is transmitted esp. in blood and bodily secretions (as semen)

AIDS–related complex *n* : a group of symptoms (as fever, weight loss, and lymphadenopathy) that is associated with the presence of antibodies to HIV and is followed by the development of AIDS in a certain proportion of cases

AIDS virus *n* : HIV

ai·grette \ā-'gret, 'ā-,\ *n* [F, plume, egret] : a plume or decorative tuft for the head

ail \'āl\ *vb* **1** : to be the matter with : TROUBLE **2** : to be unwell

ai·lan·thus \ā-'lan-thəs\ *n* : any of a genus of Asian trees or shrubs with pinnate leaves and ill-scented greenish flowers

ai·le·ron \'ā-lə-,rän\ *n* : a movable part of an airplane wing used in banking

ail·ment \'āl-mənt\ *n* : a bodily disorder

¹**aim** \'ām\ *vb* [ME, fr. MF *aesmer & esmer*; MF *aesmer*, fr. OF, fr. *a-* to (fr. L *ad-*) + *esmer* to estimate, fr. L *aestimare*] **1** : to point a weapon at an object **2** : to direct one's efforts : ASPIRE **3** : to direct to or toward a specified object or goal

²**aim** *n* **1** : the pointing of a weapon at an object **2** : the ability to hit a target **3** : OBJECT, PURPOSE — **aim·less** \-ləs\ *adj* — **aim·less·ly** *adv* — **aim·less·ness** *n*

AIM *abbr* American Indian Movement

ain't \'ānt\ **1** : are not **2** : is not **3** : am not — though disapproved by many and more common in less educated speech, used orally in most parts of the U.S. by many educated speakers esp. in the phrase *ain't I*

Ai·nu \'ī-nü\ *n*, *pl* **Ainu** *or* **Ainus 1** : a member of an indigenous people of northern Japan **2** : the language of the Ainu people

¹**air** \'ar\ *n* **1** : the gaseous mixture surrounding the earth **2** : a light breeze **3** : MELODY, TUNE **4** : the outward appearance of a person or thing : MANNER **5** : an artificial manner **6** : COMPRESSED AIR ⟨∼ sprayer⟩ **7** : AIRCRAFT ⟨∼ patrol⟩ **8** : AVIATION ⟨∼ safety⟩ **9** : the medium of transmission of radio waves; *also* : RADIO, TELEVISION

²**air** *vb* **1** : to expose to the air **2** : to expose to public view

air bag *n* : a bag designed to inflate automatically to protect automobile occupants in case of collision

air·boat \'ar-,bōt\ *n* : a shallow-draft boat driven by an airplane propeller

air·borne \-,bórn\ *adj* : done or being in the air

air brake *n* **1** : a brake operated by a piston driven by compressed air **2** : a surface projected into the airflow to lower an airplane's speed

air·brush \'ar-,brəsh\ *n* : a device for applying a fine spray (as of paint) by compressed air — **airbrush** *vb*

air–con·di·tion \,ar-kən-'di-shən\ *vb* : to equip with an apparatus for filtering air and controlling its humidity and temperature — **air con·di·tion·er** \-'di-sh(ə-)nər\ *n*

air·craft \'ar-,kraft\ *n*, *pl* **aircraft** : a vehicle for traveling through the air

aircraft carrier *n* : a warship with a deck on which airplanes can be launched and landed

air·drop \'ar-,dräp\ *n* : delivery of cargo or personnel by parachute from an airplane in flight — **air·drop** *vb*

Aire·dale terrier \'ar-,dāl-\ *n* : any of a breed of large terriers with a hard wiry coat

air·fare \'ar-,far\ *n* : fare for travel by airplane

air·field \-,fēld\ *n* : AIRPORT

air·flow \-,flō\ *n* : the motion of air relative to a body in it

air·foil \-,fóil\ *n* : an airplane surface designed to produce reaction forces from the air through which it moves

air force *n* : the military organization of a nation for air warfare

air·frame \'ar-,frām\ *n* : the structure of an aircraft, rocket, or missile without the power plant

air·freight \-'frāt\ *n* : freight transport by aircraft in volume; *also* : the charge for this service

air gun *n* **1** : a gun operated by compressed air **2** : a hand tool that works by compressed air; *esp* : AIR-BRUSH

air·head \'ar-,hed\ *n* : a mindless or stupid person

air lane *n* : AIRWAY 1

air·lift \'ar-,lift\ *n* : transportation (as of supplies or passengers) by aircraft — **airlift** *vb*

air·line \-,līn\ *n* : a transportation system using airplanes

air·lin·er \-,lī-nər\ *n* : a large passenger airplane operated by an airline

air lock *n* : an airtight chamber separating areas of different pressure

air·mail \'ar-,māl\ *n* : the system of transporting mail by aircraft; *also* : mail so transported — **airmail** *vb*

air·man \-mən\ *n* **1** : AVIATOR, PILOT **2** : an enlisted man in the air force in one of the three ranks below sergeant

airman basic *n* : an enlisted man of the lowest rank in the air force

airman first class *n* : an enlisted man in the air force with a rank just below that of sergeant

air mass *n* : a large horizontally homogeneous body of air

air·mo·bile \'ar-,mō-bəl, -,bēl\ *adj* : of, relating to, or being a military unit whose members are transported to combat areas usu. by helicopter

air·plane \-,plān\ *n* : a powered heavier-than-air aircraft that has fixed wings from which it derives lift

air·play \-,plā\ *n* : the playing of a musical recording on the air by a radio station

air pocket *n* : a condition of the atmosphere that causes an airplane to drop suddenly

air police *n* : the military police of an air force

air·port \'ar-,pórt\ *n* : a place from which aircraft operate that usu. has paved runways and a terminal

air raid *n* : an attack by armed airplanes on a surface target

air·ship \'ar-,ship\ *n* : a lighter-than-air aircraft having propulsion and steering systems

air·sick \-,sik\ *adj* : affected with motion sickness associated with flying — **air·sick·ness** *n*

air·space \-,spās\ *n* : the space above a nation and under its jurisdiction

air·speed \-,spēd\ *n* : the speed of an object (as an airplane) with relation to the surrounding air

air·strip \-,strip\ *n* : a runway without normal airport facilities

air·tight \'ar-'tīt\ *adj* **1** : so tightly sealed that no air can enter or escape **2** : leaving no opening for attack

air–to–air *adj* : launched from one airplane in flight at another; *also* : involving aircraft in flight

air·waves \'ar-ˌwāvz\ *n pl* : AIR 9

air·way \-ˌwā\ *n* **1** : a regular route for airplanes **2** : AIRLINE

air·wor·thy \-ˌwər-<u>the</u>̄\ *adj* : fit for operation in the air ⟨an ∼ plane⟩ — **air·wor·thi·ness** *n*

airy \'ar-ē\ *adj* **air·i·er; -est** **1** : LOFTY **2** : lacking in reality : EMPTY **3** : DELICATE **4** : BREEZY

aisle \'īl\ *n* [ME *ile*, fr. MF *ele* wing, fr. L *ala*] **1** : the side of a church nave separated by piers from the nave proper **2** : a passage between sections of seats

ajar \ə-'jär\ *adj or adv* : partly open

AK *abbr* Alaska

aka *abbr* also known as

AKC *abbr* American Kennel Club

akim·bo \ə-'kim-bō\ *adj or adv* : having the hand on the hip and the elbow turned outward

akin \ə-'kin\ *adj* **1** : related by blood **2** : similar in kind

Al *symbol* aluminum

AL *abbr* **1** Alabama **2** American League **3** American Legion

¹-al *adj suffix* : of, relating to, or characterized by ⟨directional⟩

²-al *n suffix* : action : process ⟨rehearsal⟩

Ala *abbr* Alabama

al·a·bas·ter \'a-lə-ˌbas-tər\ *n* **1** : a compact fine⸗textured usu. white and translucent gypsum often carved into objects (as vases) **2** : a hard translucent calcite

à la carte \ˌa-lə-'kärt, ˌä-\ *adv or adj* [F] : with a separate price for each item on the menu

alac·ri·ty \ə-'la-krə-tē\ *n* : cheerful readiness : BRISKNESS

à la mode \ˌa-lə-'mōd, ˌä-\ *adj* [F, according to the fashion] **1** : FASHIONABLE, STYLISH **2** : topped with ice cream

¹alarm \ə-'lärm\ *also* **ala·rum** \ə-'lär-əm, -'lar-\ *n* [ME *alarme*, fr. MF, fr. OIt *all'arme*, lit., to the weapon] **1** : a warning signal or device **2** : the terror caused by sudden danger

²alarm *also* **alarum** *vb* **1** : to warn of danger **2** : FRIGHTEN

alarm·ist \ə-'lär-mist\ *n* : a person who alarms others esp. needlessly

alas \ə-'las\ *interj* — used to express unhappiness, pity, or concern

al·ba·core \'al-bə-ˌkōr\ *n, pl* **-core** *or* **-cores** : a large tuna that is a source of canned tuna

Al·ba·nian \al-'bā-nē-ən\ *n* : a native or inhabitant of Albania

al·ba·tross \'al-bə-ˌtrȯs, -ˌträs\ *n, pl* **-tross** *or* **-tross·es** : any of a family of large web-footed seabirds

al·be·do \al-'bē-(ˌ)dō\ *n, pl* **-dos** : the fraction of incident radiation that is reflected by a body or surface

al·be·it \ȯl-'bē-ət, al-\ *conj* : even though : ALTHOUGH

al·bi·no \al-'bī-nō\ *n, pl* **-nos** : a person or nonhuman mammal lacking coloring matter in the skin, hair, and eyes — **al·bi·nism** \'al-bə-ˌni-zəm\ *n*

al·bum \'al-bəm\ *n* **1** : a book with blank pages used for making a collection (as of stamps) **2** : one or more recordings (as on tape or disk) produced as a single unit

al·bu·men \al-'byü-mən\ *n* **1** : the white of an egg **2** : ALBUMIN

al·bu·min \al-'byü-mən\ *n* : any of numerous water⸗soluble proteins of blood, milk, egg white, and plant and animal tissues

al·bu·min·ous \al-'byü-mə-nəs\ *adj* : containing or resembling albumen or albumin

alc *abbr* alcohol

al·cal·de \al-'käl-dē\ *n* : the chief administrative and judicial officer of a Spanish or Spanish-American town

al·ca·zar \al-'kä-zər, -'ka-\ *n* [Sp *alcázar*, fr. Ar *al-qaṣr* the castle] : a Spanish fortress or palace

al·che·my \'al-kə-mē\ *n* : medieval chemistry chiefly concerned with efforts to turn base metals into gold — **al·che·mist** \'al-kə-mist\ *n*

al·co·hol \'al-kə-ˌhȯl\ *n* [NL, fr. ML, powdered antimony, fr. Sp, fr. Ar *al-kuḥul* the powdered antimony] **1** : a colorless flammable liquid that is the intoxicating agent in fermented and distilled liquors **2** : any of various carbon compounds similar to alcohol **3** : beverages containing alcohol

¹al·co·hol·ic \ˌal-kə-'hȯ-lik, -'hä-\ *adj* **1** : of, relating to, caused by, or containing alcohol **2** : affected with alcoholism — **al·co·hol·i·cal·ly** \-li-k(ə-)lē\ *adv*

²alcoholic *n* : a person affected with alcoholism

al·co·hol·ism \'al-kə-ˌhȯ-ˌli-zəm\ *n* : continued excessive and usu. uncontrollable use of alcoholic drinks; *also* : a complex chronic psychological and nutritional disorder associated with such use

al·cove \'al-ˌkōv\ *n* **1** : a nook or small recess opening off a larger room **2** : a niche or arched opening (as in a wall)

ald *abbr* alderman

al·der \'ȯl-dər\ *n* : a tree or shrub related to the birches and growing in wet areas

al·der·man \'ȯl-dər-mən\ *n* : a member of a city legislative body

ale \'āl\ *n* : an alcoholic beverage brewed from malt and hops that is usu. more bitter than beer

ale·a·tor·ic \ˌā-lē-ə-'tȯr-ik\ *adj* : characterized by chance or random elements ⟨∼ music⟩

ale·a·to·ry \'ā-lē-ə-ˌtȯr-ē\ *adj* : ALEATORIC

alee \ə-'lē\ *adv* : on or toward the lee

ale·house \'āl-ˌhaús\ *n* : a place where ale is sold to be drunk on the premises

¹alert \ə-'lərt\ *adj* [It *all' erta*, lit., on the ascent] **1** : watchful against danger **2** : quick to perceive and act — **alert·ly** *adv* — **alert·ness** *n*

²alert *n* **1** : ALARM 1 **2** : the period during which an alert is in effect

³alert *vb* **1** : WARN **2** : to make aware of

Aleut \ˌa-lē-'üt, ə-'lüt\ *n* **1** : a member of a people of the Aleutian and Shumagin islands and the western part of Alaska peninsula **2** : the language of the Aleuts

ale·wife \'āl-ˌwīf\ *n* : a food fish of the herring family abundant esp. on the Atlantic coast

Al·ex·an·dri·an \ˌa-lig-'zan-drē-ən\ *adj* **1** : of or relating to Alexander the Great **2** : HELLENISTIC

al·ex·an·drine \-'zan-drən\ *n, often cap* : a line of six iambic feet

al·fal·fa \al-'fal-fə\ *n* : a leguminous plant widely grown for hay and forage

al·fres·co \al-'fres-kō\ *adj or adv* [It] : taking place in the open air

alg *abbr* algebra

al·ga \'al-gə\ *n, pl* **al·gae** \'al-(ˌ)jē\ : any of a group of lower plants having chlorophyll but no vascular system and including seaweeds and related freshwater plants — **al·gal** \-gəl\ *adj*

al·ge·bra \'al-jə-brə\ *n* [ML, fr. Ar *al-jabr*] : a branch of mathematics using symbols (as letters) to explore the relationships between numbers and the operations used to work with them — **al·ge·bra·ic** \ˌal-jə-'brā-ik\ *adj* — **al·ge·bra·i·cal·ly** \-'brā-ə-k(ə-)lē\ *adv*

Al·ge·ri·an \al-'jir-ē-ən\ *n* : a native or inhabitant of Algeria — **Algerian** *adj*

Al·gon·quin \al-'gän-kwən, -'gäŋ-\ *n* : a member of an American Indian people of the Ottawa River valley

al·go·rithm \'al-gə-ˌri-<u>th</u>əm\ *n* : a procedure for solving a problem esp. in mathematics or computing — **al·go·rith·mic** \ˌal-gə-'ri<u>th</u>-mik\ *adj* — **al·go·rith·mi·cal·ly** \-mi-k(ə-)lē\ *adv*

¹alias \'ā-lē-əs, 'āl-yəs\ *adv* [L, otherwise, fr. *alius* other] : otherwise called

²alias *n* : an assumed name

¹al·i·bi \'a-lə-ˌbī\ *n* [L, elsewhere, fr. *alius* other] **1** : a plea offered by an accused person of not having been at the scene of an offense **2** : an excuse (as for failure)

²alibi *vb* **-bied; -bi·ing 1** : to furnish an excuse for **2** : to offer an excuse

¹alien \'ā-lē-ən, 'āl-yən\ *adj* : belonging to another : FOREIGN

²alien *n* **1** : a foreign-born resident who has not been naturalized **2** : EXTRATERRESTRIAL

alien·able \'āl-yə-nə-bəl, 'ā-lē-ə-nə-\ *adj* : transferable to the ownership of another ⟨~ property⟩

alien·ate \'ā-lē-ə-ˌnāt, 'āl-yə-\ *vb* **-at·ed; -at·ing 1** : to make hostile : ESTRANGE **2** : to transfer (property) to another — **alien·ation** \ˌā-lē-ə-'nā-shən, ˌāl-yə-\ *n*

alien·ist \'ā-lē-ə-nist, 'āl-yə-\ *n* : PSYCHIATRIST

¹alight \ə-'līt\ *vb* **alight·ed** *also* **alit** \ə-'lit\ **alight·ing 1** : to get down (as from a vehicle) **2** : to come to rest from the air **syn** settle, land, perch

²alight *adj* : lighted up

align *also* **aline** \ə-'līn\ *vb* **1** : to bring into line **2** : to array on the side of or against a cause — **align·er** *n* — **align·ment** *also* **aline·ment** *n*

¹alike \ə-'līk\ *adv* : EQUALLY

²alike *adj* : LIKE **syn** akin, analogous, similar, comparable

al·i·ment \'a-lə-mənt\ *n* : NOURISHMENT 1 — **aliment** *vb*

al·i·men·ta·ry \ˌa-lə-'men-t(ə-)rē\ *adj* : of, relating to, or functioning in nourishment or nutrition

alimentary canal *n* : the tube that extends from the mouth to the anus and functions in the digestion and absorption of food and the elimination of residues

al·i·mo·ny \'a-lə-ˌmō-nē\ *n, pl* **-nies** [L *alimonia* sustenance, fr. *alere* to nourish] : an allowance made to one spouse by the other for support pending or after legal separation or divorce

A–line \'ā-ˌlīn\ *adj* : having a flared bottom and a close-fitting top ⟨an ~ skirt⟩

alive \ə-'līv\ *adj* **1** : having life **2** : being in force or operation **3** : SENSITIVE ⟨~ to the danger⟩ **4** : ALERT, BRISK **5** : ANIMATED ⟨streets ~ with traffic⟩ — **alive·ness** *n*

alk *abbr* alkaline

al·ka·li \'al-kə-ˌlī\ *n, pl* **-lies** *or* **-lis 1** : a substance (as a hydroxide) that has a bitter taste and neutralizes acids **2** : a mixture of salts in the soil of some dry regions in such amount as to make ordinary farming impossible — **al·ka·line** \-kə-lən, -ˌlīn\ *adj* — **al·ka·lin·i·ty** \ˌal-kə-'li-nə-tē\ *n*

al·ka·loid \'al-kə-ˌlȯid\ *n* : any of various usu. basic and bitter organic compounds found esp. in seed plants

al·kane \'al-ˌkān\ *n* : a hydrocarbon in which each carbon atom is bonded to 4 other atoms

al·kyd \'al-kəd\ *n* : any of numerous synthetic resins used esp. for protective coatings and in paint

¹all \'ȯl\ *adj* **1** : the whole of **2** : every member of **3** : EVERY ⟨~ manner of problems⟩ **4** : any whatever ⟨beyond ~ doubt⟩ **5** : nothing but ⟨~ ears⟩ **6** : being more than one person or thing ⟨who ~ is coming⟩

²all *adv* **1** : WHOLLY **2** : selected as the best — used in combination ⟨*all*-state champs⟩ **3** : so much ⟨~ the better for it⟩ **4** : for each side ⟨the score is two ~⟩

³all *pron* **1** : the whole number, quantity, or amount ⟨~ of it is gone⟩ **2** : EVERYBODY, EVERYTHING ⟨that is ~⟩

⁴all *n* : the whole of one's resources ⟨gave his ~⟩

Al·lah \'ä-lä, 'a-; ä-'lä\ *n* [Ar] : GOD 1 — used in Islam

all along *adv* : all the time ⟨knew it *all along*⟩

all–Amer·i·can \ˌȯl-ə-'mer-ə-kən\ *adj* **1** : selected as the best in the U.S. **2** : composed wholly of American elements **3** : typical of the U.S. — **all–American** *n*

all–around \ˌȯl-ə-'raúnd\ *adj* **1** : considered in all aspects ⟨best ~ performance⟩ **2** : competent in many fields : VERSATILE ⟨an ~ athlete⟩

al·lay \ə-'lā\ *vb* **1** : ALLEVIATE **2** : CALM **syn** lighten, relieve, ease, assuage

all clear *n* : a signal that a danger has passed

al·lege \ə-'lej\ *vb* **al·leged; al·leg·ing 1** : to assert without proof **2** : to offer as a reason — **al·le·ga·tion** \ˌa-li-'gā-shən\ *n* — **al·leg·ed·ly** \ə-'le-jəd-lē\ *adv*

al·le·giance \ə-'lē-jəns\ *n* **1** : loyalty owed by a citizen to a government **2** : loyalty to a person or cause

al·le·go·ry \'a-lə-ˌgȯr-ē\ *n, pl* **-ries** : the expression through symbolism of truths or generalizations about human experience — **al·le·gor·i·cal** \ˌa-lə-'gȯr-i-kəl\ *adj* — **al·le·gor·i·cal·ly** \-k(ə-)lē\ *adv*

¹al·le·gro \ə-'le-grō, -'lā-\ *n, pl* **-gros** : an allegro movement

²allegro *adv or adj* [It, merry] : at a brisk lively tempo — used as a direction in music

al·le·lu·ia \ˌa-lə-'lü-yə\ *interj* : HALLELUJAH

Al·len wrench \'a-lən-\ *n* [*Allen* Manufacturing Company, Hartford, Conn.] : an L-shaped hexagonal metal bar of which either end fits the socket of a screw or bolt

al·ler·gen \'a-lər-jən\ *n* : something that causes allergy — **al·ler·gen·ic** \ˌa-lər-'je-nik\ *adj*

al·ler·gist \'a-lər-jist\ *n* : a specialist in allergies

al·ler·gy \'a-lər-jē\ *n, pl* **-gies** [G *Allergie*, fr. Gk *allos* other + *ergon* work] : exaggerated or abnormal reaction (as by sneezing) to substances or situations harmless to most people — **al·ler·gic** \ə-'lər-jik\ *adj*

al·le·vi·ate \ə-'lē-vē-ˌāt\ *vb* **-at·ed; -at·ing** : RELIEVE, LESSEN **syn** lighten, mitigate, allay — **al·le·vi·a·tion** \ə-ˌlē-vē-'ā-shən\ *n*

al·ley \'a-lē\ *n, pl* **alleys 1** : a garden or park walk **2** : a place for bowling **3** : a narrow passageway esp. between buildings

al·ley–oop \ˌa-lē-'yüp\ *n* : a basketball play in which a player catches a pass above the basket and immediately dunks the ball

al·ley·way \'a-lē-ˌwā\ *n* : ALLEY 3

All·hal·lows \ȯl-'ha-lōz\ *n, pl* **Allhallows** : ALL SAINTS' DAY

al·li·ance \ə-'lī-əns\ *n* : a union to promote common interests **syn** league, coalition, confederacy, federation

al·li·ga·tor \'a-lə-ˌgā-tər\ *n* [Sp *el lagarto* the lizard] : either of two large short-legged reptiles resembling crocodiles but having a shorter and broader snout

alligator

alligator pear *n* : AVOCADO

al·lit·er·ate \ə-'li-tə-ˌrāt\ *vb* **-at·ed; -at·ing 1** : to form an alliteration **2** : to arrange so as to make alliteration

al·lit·er·a·tion \ə-ˌli-tə-'rā-shən\ *n* : the repetition of initial sounds in adjacent words or syllables — **al·lit·er·a·tive** \-'li-tə-ˌrā-tiv\ *adj*

al·lo·cate \'a-lə-ˌkāt\ *vb* **-cat·ed; -cat·ing** : ALLOT, ASSIGN — **al·lo·ca·tion** \ˌa-lə-'kā-shən\ *n*

al·lot \ə-'lät\ *vb* **al·lot·ted; al·lot·ting** : to distribute as a share **syn** assign, apportion, allocate — **al·lot·ment** *n*

all–out \'ȯl-'aút\ *adj* : made with maximum effort

all over *adv* : EVERYWHERE

al·low \ə-'laú\ *vb* **1** : to assign as a share ⟨~ time for rest⟩ **2** : to count as a deduction **3** : to make allowance ⟨~ for expansion⟩ **4** : ADMIT, CONCEDE **5** : PERMIT ⟨~s the dog to roam⟩ — **al·low·able** *adj*

al·low·ance \-əns\ *n* **1** : an allotted share **2** : money given regularly for expenses **3** : a taking into account of extenuating circumstances

al·loy \'a-ˌlȯi, ə-'lȯi\ *n* **1** : a substance composed of metals melted together **2** : an admixture that lessens value — **alloy** \ə-'lȯi, 'a-ˌlȯi\ *vb*

all right *adv* **1** : very well ⟨*all right*, let's go⟩ **2** : beyond doubt **3** : SATISFACTORILY — **all right** *adj*

All Saints' Day *n* : a Christian feast on November 1 in honor of all the saints

All Souls' Day *n* : a day of prayer observed by some Christian churches on November 2 for the souls of the faithful departed

all·spice \'ȯl-ˌspīs\ *n* : the berry of a West Indian tree related to the European myrtle; *also* : the mildly pungent and aromatic spice made from it

all–star \'ȯl-ˌstär\ *n* : a member of a team of star performers — **all–star** *adj*

all told *adv* : with everything counted

al·lude \ə-'lüd\ *vb* **al·lud·ed; al·lud·ing** [L *alludere*, lit., to play with] : to refer indirectly — **al·lu·sion** \-'lü-zhən\ *n* — **al·lu·sive** \-'lü-siv\ *adj* — **al·lu·sive·ly** *adv* — **al·lu·sive·ness** *n*

al·lure \ə-'lu̇r\ *vb* **al·lured; al·lur·ing** : CHARM, ENTICE — **allure** *n* — **al·lur·ing·ly** *adv*

al·lu·vi·um \ə-'lü-vē-əm\ *n*, *pl* **-vi·ums** *or* **-via** \-vē-ə\ : soil material (as clay) deposited by running water — **al·lu·vi·al** \-vē-əl\ *adj or n*

al·ly \ə-'lī, 'a-ˌlī\ *vb* **al·lied; al·ly·ing** : to enter into an alliance — **al·ly** \'a-ˌlī, ə-'lī\ *n*

-ally *adv suffix* : ²-LY ⟨specific*ally*⟩

al·ma ma·ter \ˌal-mə-'mä-tər\ *n* [L, fostering mother] **1** : an educational institute that one has attended **2** : the song or hymn of an alma mater

al·ma·nac \'ȯl-mə-ˌnak, 'al-\ *n* **1** : a publication esp. of astronomical and meteorological data **2** : a usu. annual publication of miscellaneous information

al·man·dite \'al-mən-ˌdīt\ *n* : a deep red garnet

al·mighty \ȯl-'mī-tē\ *adj* **1** *often cap* : having absolute power over all ⟨*Almighty* God⟩ **2** : relatively unlimited in power — **al·might·i·ness** *n*

Almighty *n* : GOD 1

al·mond \'ä-mənd, 'a-; 'al-\ *n* : a small tree related to the peach; *also* : the edible nutlike kernel of the fruit

al·mo·ner \'al-mə-nər, 'ä-mə-\ *n* : a person who distributes alms

al·most \'ȯl-ˌmōst, ȯl-'mōst\ *adv* : very nearly but not exactly

alms \'ämz, 'älmz\ *n*, *pl* **alms** [ME *almesse*, *almes*, fr. OE *ælmesse*, *ælms*, fr. L *eleemosyna* alms, fr. Gk *eleēmosynē* pity, alms, fr. *eleēmōn* merciful] : something given freely to relieve the poor

alms·house \-ˌhau̇s\ *n* : POORHOUSE

al·oe \'a-lō\ *n* **1** : any of a large genus of succulent chiefly southern African plants related to the lilies **2** *pl* : the dried juice of the leaves of an aloe used esp. formerly as a laxative

aloft \ə-'lȯft\ *adv* **1** : high in the air **2** : in flight

alo·ha \ə-'lō-ə, ä-'lō-hä\ *interj* [Hawaiian] — used to greet or bid farewell

alone \ə-'lōn\ *adj* **1** : separated from others **2** : not including anyone or anything else : ONLY **syn** lonely, lonesome, lone, solitary — **alone** *adv*

¹along \ə-'lȯŋ\ *prep* **1** : in line with the direction of ⟨sail ∼ the coast⟩ **2** : at a point on or during ⟨stopped ∼ the way⟩

²along *adv* **1** : FORWARD, ON **2** : as a companion ⟨bring her ∼⟩ **3** : at an advanced point ⟨plans are far ∼⟩

along·shore \ə-'lȯŋ-'shōr\ *adv or adj* : along the shore or coast

¹along·side \-'sīd\ *adv* : along or by the side

²alongside *prep* **1** : along or by the side of **2** : in association with

alongside of *prep* : ALONGSIDE

aloof \ə-'lüf\ *adj* : removed or distant physically or emotionally — **aloof·ness** *n*

al·o·pe·cia \ˌa-lə-'pē-sh(ē-)ə\ *n* : BALDNESS

aloud \ə-'lau̇d\ *adv* : with a loud voice

alp \'alp\ *n* : a high rugged mountain

al·paca \al-'pa-kə\ *n* : a domesticated mammal esp. of Peru that is related to the llama; *also* : its woolly hair or cloth made from this

al·pha \'al-fə\ *n* **1** : the 1st letter of the Greek alphabet — A or α **2** : something first : BEGINNING

al·pha·bet \'al-fə-ˌbet\ *n* : the set of letters or characters used in writing a language

al·pha·bet·i·cal \ˌal-fə-'be-ti-kəl\ *or* **al·pha·bet·ic** \-'be-tik\ *adj* **1** : arranged in the order of the letters of the alphabet **2** : of or employing an alphabet — **al·pha·bet·i·cal·ly** \-ti-k(ə-)lē\ *adv*

al·pha·bet·ize \'al-fə-bə-ˌtīz\ *vb* **-ized; -iz·ing** : to arrange in alphabetical order — **al·pha·bet·iz·er** *n*

al·pha·nu·mer·ic \ˌal-fə-nu̇-'mer-ik, -nyu̇-\ *adj* : consisting of letters and numbers and often other symbols ⟨an ∼ code⟩; *also* : being a character in an alphanumeric system

alpha particle *n* : a positively charged particle identical with the nucleus of a helium atom that is ejected at high speed in certain radioactive transformations

alpha rhythm *n* : ALPHA WAVE

alpha wave *n* : an electrical rhythm of the brain often associated with a state of wakeful relaxation

Al·pine \'al-ˌpīn\ *adj* **1** : relating to, located in, or resembling the Alps mountains **2** *often not cap* : of, relating to, or growing on upland slopes above timberline **3** : of or relating to competitive ski events consisting of slalom and downhill racing

al·ready \ȯl-'re-dē\ *adv* : by this time : PREVIOUSLY

al·right \ȯl-'rīt\ *adv* : ALL RIGHT

al·so \'ȯl-sō\ *adv* : in addition : TOO

al·so-ran \-ˌran\ *n* **1** : a horse or dog that finishes out of the money in a race **2** : a contestant that does not win

alt *abbr* **1** alternate **2** altitude

Alta *abbr* Alberta

al·tar \'ȯl-tər\ *n* **1** : a structure on which sacrifices are offered or incense is burned **2** : a table used as a center of ritual or worship

altar boy *n* : a boy who assists the celebrant at a church service

¹al·ter \'ȯl-tər\ *vb* **al·tered; al·ter·ing** \-t(ə-)riŋ\ **1** : to make or become different **2** : CASTRATE, SPAY — **al·ter·a·tion** \ˌȯl-tə-'rā-shən\ *n*

²alter *abbr* alteration

al·ter·ca·tion \ˌȯl-tər-'kā-shən\ *n* : a noisy or angry dispute

alter ego \ˌȯl-tər-'ē-gō\ *n* [L, lit., second I] : a second self; *esp* : a trusted friend

¹al·ter·nate \'ȯl-tər-nət, 'al-\ *adj* **1** : arranged or succeeding by turns **2** : every other **3** : being an alternative ⟨an ∼ route⟩ — **al·ter·nate·ly** *adv*

²al·ter·nate \-ˌnāt\ *vb* **-nat·ed; -nat·ing** : to occur or cause to occur by turns — **al·ter·na·tion** \ˌȯl-tər-'nā-shən, ˌal-\ *n*

³alternate *n* : SUBSTITUTE

alternating current *n* : an electric current that reverses its direction at regular intervals

al·ter·na·tive \ȯl-'tər-nə-tiv, al-\ *adj* : offering a choice — **alternative** *n*

al·ter·na·tor \'ȯl-tər-ˌnā-tər, 'al-\ *n* : an electric generator for producing alternating current

al·though *also* **al·tho** \ȯl-'thō\ *conj* : in spite of the fact that : even though

al·tim·e·ter \al-'ti-mə-tər, 'al-tə-ˌmē-tər\ *n* : an instrument for measuring altitude

al·ti·tude \'al-tə-ˌtüd, -ˌtyüd\ *n* **1** : angular distance above the horizon **2** : vertical distance : HEIGHT **3** : the perpendicular distance in a geometric figure from the vertex to the base, from the vertex of an angle to the side opposite, or from the base to a parallel side or face

al·to \'al-tō\ *n*, *pl* **altos** [It, lit., high, fr. L *altus*] : the lower female voice part in a 4-part chorus; *also* : a singer having this voice or part

¹al·to·geth·er \ˌȯl-tə-'ge-thər\ *adv* **1** : WHOLLY **2** : in all **3** : on the whole

²altogether *n* : NUDE ⟨posed in the ∼⟩

al·tru·ism \'al-trü-ˌi-zəm\ *n* : unselfish interest in the welfare of others — **al·tru·ist** \-ist\ *n* — **al·tru·is·tic** \ˌal-trü-ʹis-tik\ *adj* — **al·tru·is·ti·cal·ly** \-ti-k(ə-)lē\ *adv*

al·um \ʹa-ləm\ *n* : either of two colorless crystalline aluminum-containing compounds used esp. as an emetic or as an astringent and styptic

alu·mi·na \ə-ʹlü-mə-nə\ *n* : the oxide of aluminum occurring in nature as corundum and in bauxite

al·u·min·i·um \ˌal-yə-ʹmi-nē-əm\ *n, chiefly Brit* : ALUMINUM

alu·mi·nize \ə-ʹlü-mə-ˌnīz\ *vb* **-nized; -niz·ing** : to treat with aluminum

alu·mi·num \ə-ʹlü-mə-nəm\ *n* : a silver-white malleable ductile light metallic element that is the most abundant metal in the earth's crust — see ELEMENT table

alum·na \ə-ʹləm-nə\ *n, pl* **-nae** \-(ˌ)nē\ : a woman graduate or former student of a college or school

alum·nus \ə-ʹləm-nəs\ *n, pl* **-ni** \-ˌnī\ [L, foster son, pupil, fr. *alere* to nourish] : a graduate or former student of a college or school

al·ways \ʹȯl-wēz, -wəz, -(ˌ)wāz\ *adv* **1** : at all times : INVARIABLY **2** : FOREVER

Alz·hei·mer's disease \ʹälts-ˌhī-mərz-, ʹalts-\ *n* : a degenerative disease of the central nervous system characterized esp. by premature senile mental deterioration

am *pres 1st sing of* BE

¹Am *abbr* America; American

²Am *symbol* americium

¹AM \ʹā-ˌem\ *n* : a broadcasting system using amplitude modulation; *also* : a radio receiver for broadcasts made by such a system

²AM *abbr* **1** ante meridiem — often not cap. and often punctuated **2** [NL *artium magister*] master of arts

AMA *abbr* American Medical Association

amah \ʹä-(ˌ)mä\ *n* : an Oriental female servant; *esp* : a Chinese nurse

amain \ə-ʹmān\ *adv, archaic* : with full force or speed

amal·gam \ə-ʹmal-gəm\ *n* **1** : an alloy of mercury with another metal used in making dental cements **2** : a mixture of different elements

amal·gam·ate \ə-ʹmal-gə-ˌmāt\ *vb* **-at·ed; -at·ing** : to unite or merge into one body — **amal·ga·ma·tion** \-ˌmal-gə-ʹmā-shən\ *n*

aman·u·en·sis \ə-ˌman-yə-ʹwen-səs\ *n, pl* **-en·ses** \-ˌsēz\ : one employed to write from dictation or to copy what another has written : SECRETARY

am·a·ranth \ʹa-mə-ˌranth\ *n* **1** : any of a large genus of coarse herbs sometimes grown for their showy flowers **2** : a flower that never fades

am·a·ran·thine \ˌa-mə-ʹran-thən, -ˌthīn\ *adj* **1** : relating to or resembling an amaranth **2** : UNDYING

am·a·ryl·lis \ˌa-mə-ʹri-ləs\ *n* : any of various plants related to the lilies; *esp* : any of several African herbs having bulbs and grown for their clusters of large showy flowers

amass \ə-ʹmas\ *vb* : ACCUMULATE

am·a·teur \ʹa-mə-(ˌ)tər, -ˌtūr, -ˌtyūr, -ˌchūr, -chər\ *n* [F, fr. L *amator* lover, fr. *amare* to love] **1** : a person who engages in a pursuit for pleasure and not as a profession **2** : a person who is not expert — **am·a·teur·ish** \ˌa-mə-ʹtər-ish, -ʹtūr-, -ʹtyūr-, -ʹchūr-, -ʹchər-\ *adj* — **am·a·teur·ism** \ʹa-mə-(ˌ)tər-i- zəm, -ˌtūr-, -ˌtyūr-, -ˌchūr-, -ˌchər-\ *n*

am·a·tive \ʹa-mə-tiv\ *adj* : indicative of love : AMOROUS — **am·a·tive·ly** *adv* — **am·a·tive·ness** *n*

am·a·to·ry \ʹa-mə-ˌtōr-ē\ *adj* : of or expressing sexual love

amaze \ə-ʹmāz\ *vb* **amazed; amaz·ing** : to fill with wonder : ASTOUND **syn** astonish, surprise, dumbfound — **amaze·ment** *n* — **amaz·ing·ly** *adv*

am·a·zon \ʹa-mə-ˌzän, -zən\ *n* **1** *cap* : a member of a race of female warriors of Greek mythology **2** : a tall strong often masculine woman — **am·a·zo·ni·an** \ˌa-mə-ʹzō-nē-ən\ *adj, often cap*

amb *abbr* ambassador

am·bas·sa·dor \am-ʹba-sə-dər\ *n* : a representative esp. of a government — **am·bas·sa·do·ri·al** \-ˌba-sə-ʹdȯr-ē-əl\ *adj* — **am·bas·sa·dor·ship** *n*

am·ber \ʹam-bər\ *n* : a yellowish or brownish fossil resin used esp. for ornamental objects; *also* : the color of this resin

am·ber·gris \ʹam-bər-ˌgris, -ˌgrēs\ *n* : a waxy substance from the sperm whale used in making perfumes

am·bi·dex·trous \ˌam-bi-ʹdek-strəs\ *adj* : using both hands with equal ease — **am·bi·dex·trous·ly** *adv*

am·bi·ence *or* **am·bi·ance** \ʹam-bē-əns, äⁿ-ʹbyäⁿs\ *n* : a pervading atmosphere

am·bi·ent \ʹam-bē-ənt\ *adj* : existing on all sides

am·big·u·ous \am-ʹbi-gyə-wəs\ *adj* : capable of being understood in more than one way — **am·bi·gu·i·ty** \ˌam-bə-ʹgyü-ə-tē\ *n* — **am·big·u·ous·ly** *adv*

am·bi·tion \am-ʹbi-shən\ *n* [ME, fr. MF or L; MF, fr. L *ambition-, ambitio*, lit., act of soliciting for votes, fr. *ambire* to go around] : eager desire for success or power

am·bi·tious \-shəs\ *adj* : characterized by ambition — **am·bi·tious·ly** *adv*

am·biv·a·lence \am-ʹbi-və-ləns\ *n* : simultaneous attraction toward and repulsion from a person, object, or action — **am·biv·a·lent** \-lənt\ *adj*

¹am·ble \ʹam-bəl\ *vb* **am·bled; am·bling** \-b(ə-)liŋ\ : to go at an amble

²amble *n* : an easy gait esp. of a horse

am·bro·sia \am-ʹbrō-zh(ē-)ə\ *n* : the food of the Greek and Roman gods — **am·bro·sial** \-zh(ē-)əl\ *adj*

am·bu·lance \ʹam-byə-ləns\ *n* : a vehicle equipped for carrying the injured or sick

am·bu·lant \ʹam-byə-lənt\ *adj* : AMBULATORY

¹am·bu·la·to·ry \ʹam-byə-lə-ˌtōr-ē\ *adj* **1** : of, relating to, or adapted to walking **2** : able to walk or move about

²ambulatory *n, pl* **-ries** : a sheltered place (as in a cloister) for walking

am·bus·cade \ʹam-bə-ˌskād\ *n* : AMBUSH

am·bush \ʹam-ˌbúsh\ *n* : a trap in which concealed persons wait to attack by surprise — **ambush** *vb*

amdt *abbr* amendment

ame·ba, ame·boid *var of* AMOEBA, AMOEBOID

ame·lio·rate \ə-ʹmēl-yə-ˌrāt\ *vb* **-rat·ed; -rat·ing** : to make or grow better : IMPROVE — **ame·lio·ra·tion** \-ˌmēl-yə-ʹrā-shən\ *n*

amen \(ˌ)ā-ʹmen, (ˌ)ä-\ *interj* — used esp. at the end of prayers to affirm or express approval

ame·na·ble \ə-ʹmē-nə-bəl, -ʹme-\ *adj* **1** : ANSWERABLE **2** : COMPLIANT

amend \ə-ʹmend\ *vb* **1** : to change for the better : IMPROVE **2** : to alter formally in phraseology — **amend·able** \-ʹmen-də-bəl\ *adj*

amend·ment \ə-ʹmend-mənt\ *n* **1** : correction of faults **2** : the process of amending a parliamentary motion or a constitution; *also* : the alteration so proposed or made

amends \ə-ʹmendz\ *n sing or pl* : compensation for injury or loss

ame·ni·ty \ə-ʹme-nə-tē, -ʹmē-\ *n, pl* **-ties 1** : AGREEABLENESS **2** : a gesture observed in social relationships **3** : something that serves as a comfort or convenience

Amer *abbr* America; American

amerce \ə-ʹmərs\ *vb* **amerced; amerc·ing 1** : to penalize by a fine determined by the court **2** : PUNISH — **amerce·ment** *n*

Amer·i·can \ə-ʹmer-ə-kən\ *n* **1** : a native or inhabitant of No. or So. America **2** : a citizen of the U.S. — **American** *adj* — **Amer·i·can·ism** \-ə-kə-ˌni-zəm\ *n* — **Amer·i·can·iza·tion** \ə-ˌmer-ə-kə-nə-ʹzā-shən\ *n* — **Amer·i·can·ize** \ə-ʹmer-ə-kə-ˌnīz\ *vb* — **Amer·i·can·ness** *n*

Amer·i·ca·na \ə-ˌmer-ə-ʹka-nə, -ʹkä-\ *n pl* : materials concerning or characteristic of America, its civilization, or its culture

American Indian *n* : a member of any of the aboriginal peoples of No. and So. America except the Eskimos

American plan *n* : a hotel plan whereby the daily rates cover the cost of room and three meals

American Sign Language *n* : a sign language for the deaf in which meaning is conveyed by a system of hand gestures and placement

am·er·i·ci·um \₁am-ə-'rish-ē-əm, -'ris-\ *n* : a radioactive metallic chemical element produced artificially from plutonium — see ELEMENT table

AmerInd *abbr* American Indian

Am·er·in·di·an \₁a-mə-'rin-dē-ən\ *n* : AMERICAN INDIAN — **Amerindian** *adj*

am·e·thyst \'a-mə-thəst\ *n* [ME *amatiste*, fr. OF & L; OF, fr. L *amethystus*, fr. Gk *amethystos*, lit., remedy against drunkenness, fr. *a-* not + *methyein* to be drunk, fr. *methy* wine] : a gemstone consisting of clear purple or bluish violet quartz

ami·a·ble \'ā-mē-ə-bəl\ *adj* **1** : AGREEABLE **2** : having a friendly and sociable disposition — **ami·a·bil·i·ty** \₁ā-mē-ə-'bi-lə-tē\ *n* — **ami·a·ble·ness** *n* — **ami·a·bly** \'ā-mē-ə-blē\ *adv*

am·i·ca·ble \'a-mi-kə-bəl\ *adj* : FRIENDLY, PEACEABLE — **am·i·ca·bil·i·ty** \₁a-mi-kə-'bi-lə-tē\ *n* — **am·i·ca·bly** \'a-mi-kə-blē\ *adv*

amid \ə-'mid\ *or* **amidst** \-'midst\ *prep* : in or into the middle of : AMONG

amid·ships \ə-'mid-₁ships\ *adv* : in or near the middle of a ship

ami·no acid \ə-'mē-nō-\ *n* : any of numerous nitrogen-containing acids that include some which are used by cells to build proteins

¹**amiss** \ə-'mis\ *adv* **1** : WRONGLY **2** : ASTRAY **3** : IMPERFECTLY

²**amiss** *adj* **1** : WRONG **2** : out of place

am·i·ty \'a-mə-tē\ *n, pl* **-ties** : FRIENDSHIP; *esp* : friendly relations between nations

am·me·ter \'a-₁mē-tər\ *n* : an instrument for measuring electric current in amperes

am·mo \'a-mō\ *n* : AMMUNITION

am·mo·nia \ə-'mō-nyə\ *n* [NL, fr. L *sal ammoniacus* sal ammoniac (ammonium chloride), lit., salt of Ammon, fr. Gk *ammōniakos* of Ammon, fr. *Ammōn* Ammon, Amen, an Egyptian god near one of whose temples it was prepared] **1** : a colorless gaseous compound of nitrogen and hydrogen used in refrigeration and in the making of fertilizers and explosives **2** : a solution (**ammonia water**) of ammonia in water

am·mo·ni·um \ə-'mō-nē-əm\ *n* : an ion or chemical group derived from ammonia by combination with hydrogen

ammonium chloride *n* : a white crystalline volatile salt used in batteries and as an expectorant

am·mu·ni·tion \₁am-yə-'ni-shən\ *n* **1** : projectiles fired from guns **2** : explosive items used in war **3** : material for use in attack or defense

Amn *abbr* airman

am·ne·sia \am-'nē-zhə\ *n* **1** : abnormal loss of memory **2** : the selective overlooking of events or acts not favorable to one's purpose — **am·ne·si·ac** \-zhē-₁ak, -zē-\ *or* **am·ne·sic** \-zik, -sik\ *adj or n*

am·nes·ty \'am-nə-stē\ *n, pl* **-ties** : an act granting a pardon to a group of individuals — **amnesty** *vb*

am·nio·cen·te·sis \₁am-nē-ō-₁sen-'tē-səs\ *n, pl* **-te·ses** \-₁sēz\ : the surgical insertion of a hollow needle through the abdominal wall and uterus of a pregnant female esp. to obtain fluid used to check the fetus for chromosomal abnormality and to determine sex

amoe·ba \ə-'mē-bə\ *n, pl* **-bas** *or* **-bae** \-(₁)bē\ : any of various tiny one-celled protozoans that lack permanent cell organs and occur esp. in water and soil — **amoe·bic** \-bik\ *adj*

amoe·boid \-₁bȯid\ *adj* : resembling an amoeba esp. in moving or readily changing shape

amok \ə-'mək, -'mäk\ *or* **amuck** \-'mək\ *adv* : in a violent, frenzied, or uncontrolled manner ⟨run ∼⟩

among \ə-'məŋ\ *also* **amongst** \-'məŋst\ *prep* **1** : in or through the midst of **2** : in the number, class, or company of **3** : in shares to each of **4** : by common action of

amon·til·la·do \ə-₁män-tə-'lä-dō\ *n, pl* **-dos** [Sp] : a medium dry sherry

amor·al \ā-'mȯr-əl\ *adj* **1** : neither moral nor immoral; *esp* : being outside the sphere to which moral judgments apply **2** : lacking moral sensibility — **amor·al·ly** *adv*

am·o·rous \'a-mə-rəs\ *adj* **1** : inclined to love **2** : being in love **3** : of or indicative of love — **am·o·rous·ly** *adv* — **am·o·rous·ness** *n*

amor·phous \ə-'mȯr-fəs\ *adj* **1** : SHAPELESS, FORMLESS **2** : not crystallized

am·or·tize \'a-mər-₁tīz, ə-'mȯr-\ *vb* **-tized; -tiz·ing** : to extinguish (as a mortgage) usu. by payment on the principal at the time of each periodic interest payment — **amor·ti·za·tion** \₁a-mər-tə-'zā-shən, ə-₁mȯr-\ *n*

Amos \'ā-məs\ — see BIBLE table

¹**amount** \ə-'maunt\ *vb* **1** : to be equivalent **2** : to reach a total : add up

²**amount** *n* **1** : the total number or quantity **2** : a principal sum plus the interest on it

amour \ə-'mùr, ä-, a-\ *n* **1** : a love affair esp. when illicit **2** : LOVER

amour pro·pre \₁a-₁mùr-'prȯprᵊ, ₁ä-, -'prȯprᵊ\ *n* [F] : SELF-ESTEEM

¹**amp** \'amp\ *n* : AMPLIFIER; *also* : a unit consisting of an electronic amplifier and a loudspeaker

²**amp** *abbr* ampere

am·per·age \'am-p(ə-)rij\ *n* : the strength of a current of electricity expressed in amperes

am·pere \'am-₁pir\ *n* : a unit of electric current equivalent to a steady current produced by one volt applied across a resistance of one ohm

am·per·sand \'am-pər-₁sand\ *n* [alter. of *and per se and*, spoken form of the phrase *& per se and*, lit., (the character) *&* by itself (stands for the word) *and*] : a character *&* used for the word *and*

am·phet·amine \am-'fe-tə-₁mēn, -mən\ *n* : a compound or one of its derivatives that stimulates the central nervous system and is used esp. to treat hyperactive children and to suppress appetite

am·phib·i·an \am-'fi-bē-ən\ *n* **1** : an amphibious organism; *esp* : any of a class of animals (as frogs and salamanders) intermediate between fishes and reptiles **2** : an airplane that can land on and take off from either land or water

am·phib·i·ous \am-'fi-bē-əs\ *adj* [Gk *amphibios*, lit., living a double life, fr. *amphi-* on both sides + *bios* mode of life] **1** : able to live both on land and in water **2** : adapted for both land and water **3** : made by joint action of land, sea, and air forces invading from the sea; *also* : trained for such action

am·phi·bole \'am-fə-₁bōl\ *n* : any of a group of rock-forming minerals of similar crystal structure

am·phi·the·ater \'am-fə-₁thē-ə-tər\ *n* **1** : an oval or circular structure with rising tiers of seats around an arena **2** : a very large auditorium

am·pho·ra \'am-fə-rə\ *n, pl* **-rae** \-₁rē\ *or* **-ras** : an ancient Greek jar or vase with two handles that rise almost to the level of the mouth

am·ple \'am-pəl\ *adj* **am·pler** \-plər\ **am·plest** \-pləst\ **1** : LARGE, CAPACIOUS **2** : enough to satisfy : ABUNDANT — **am·ply** \-plē\ *adv*

am·pli·fy \'am-plə-₁fī\ *vb* **-fied; -fy·ing 1** : to expand by extended treatment **2** : to increase in magnitude or strength; *esp* : to make louder — **am·pli·fi·ca·tion** \₁am-plə-fə-'kā-shən\ *n* — **am·pli·fi·er** \'am-plə-₁fī(-ə)r\ *n*

am·pli·tude \-ₜtüd, -ₜtyüd\ *n* **1** : ample extent : FULL-NESS **2** : the extent of a vibratory movement (as of a pendulum) or of an oscillation (as of an alternating current or a radio wave)

amplitude modulation *n* : modulation of the ampli-tude of a radio carrier wave in accordance with the strength of the signal; *also* : a broadcasting system using such modulation

am·poule *or* **am·pule** *also* **am·pul** \'am-ₜpyül, -ₜpül\ *n* : a small sealed bulbous glass vessel used to hold a solution for hypodermic injection

am·pu·tate \'am-pyə-ₜtāt\ *vb* **-tat·ed; -tat·ing** : to cut off ⟨~ a leg⟩ — **am·pu·ta·tion** \ₜam-pyə-'tā-shən\ *n*

am·pu·tee \ₜam-pyə-'tē\ *n* : one who has had a limb amputated

AMSLAN *abbr* American Sign Language

amt *abbr* amount

amuck \ə-'mək\ *var of* AMOK

am·u·let \'am-yə-lət\ *n* : an ornament worn as a charm against evil

amuse \ə-'myüz\ *vb* **amused; amus·ing** : to entertain in a light or playful manner : DIVERT — **amuse·ment** *n*

AM·VETS \'am-ₜvets\ *abbr* American Veterans (of World War II)

am·y·lase \'a-mə-ₜlās, -ₜlāz\ *n* : any of several en-zymes that accelerate the breakdown of starch and glycogen

an \ən, (')an\ *indefinite article* : A — used before words beginning with a vowel sound

¹-an *or* **-ian** *also* **-ean** *n suffix* **1** : one that belongs to ⟨American⟩ ⟨crustacean⟩ **2** : one skilled in or special-izing in ⟨phonetician⟩

²-an *or* **-ian** *also* **-ean** *adj suffix* **1** : of or belonging to ⟨American⟩ **2** : characteristic of : resembling ⟨Mozartean⟩

AN *abbr* airman (Navy)

an·a·bol·ic steroid \ₜa-nə-'bä-lik-\ *n* : any of a group of synthetic steroid hormones sometimes abused by athletes in training to increase temporarily the size of their muscles

anach·ro·nism \ə-'na-krə-ₜni-zəm\ *n* **1** : the error of placing a person or thing in the wrong period **2** : one that is chronologically out of place — **anach·ro·nis·tic** \ə-ₜna-krə-'nis-tik\ *adj* — **anach·ro·nous** \-'na-krə-nəs\ *adj*

an·a·con·da \ₜa-nə-'kän-də\ *n* : a large So. American snake that suffocates and kills its prey by constriction

anae·mia, anae·mic *chiefly Brit var of* ANEMIA, ANE-MIC

an·aer·obe \'a-nə-ₜrōb\ *n* : an anaerobic organism

an·aer·o·bic \ₜa-nə-'rō-bik\ *adj* : living, active, occur-ring, or existing in the absence of free oxygen

an·aes·the·sia, an·aes·thet·ic *chiefly Brit var of* ANES-THESIA, ANESTHETIC

ana·gram \'a-nə-ₜgram\ *n* : a word or phrase made by transposing the letters of another word or phrase

¹anal \'ān-ᵊl\ *adj* **1** : of, relating to, or situated near the anus **2** : of, relating to, or characterized by the stage of psychosexual development in psychoanalytic the-ory during which one is concerned esp. with feces **3** : of, relating to, or characterized by personality traits (as parsimony and ill humor) considered typical of fixation at the anal stage of development — **anal·ly** *adv*

²anal *abbr* **1** analogy **2** analysis; analytic

an·al·ge·sia \ₜan-ᵊl-'jē-zhə\ *n* : insensibility to pain — **an·al·ge·sic** \-'jē-zik, -sik\ *adj*

an·al·ge·sic \-'jē-zik, -sik\ *n* : an agent for producing analgesia

analog computer \'an-ᵊl-ₜög-, -ₜäg-\ *n* : a computer that operates with numbers represented by directly measurable quantities (as voltages)

anal·o·gous \ə-'na-lə-gəs\ *adj* : similar in one or more respects

an·a·logue *or* **an·a·log** \'an-ᵊl-ₜög, -ₜag\ *n* **1** : some-

thing that is analogous to something else **2** : an organ similar in function to one of another animal or plant but different in structure or origin

anal·o·gy \ə-'na-lə-jē\ *n, pl* **-gies 1** : inference that if two or more things agree in some respects they will probably agree in others **2** : a likeness in one or more ways between things otherwise unlike — **an·a·log·i·cal** \ₜan-ᵊl-'ä-ji-kəl\ *adj* — **an·a·log·i·cal·ly** \-k(ə-)lē\ *adv*

an·a·lyse *chiefly Brit var of* ANALYZE

anal·y·sis \ə-'na-lə-səs\ *n, pl* **-y·ses** \-ₜsēz\ [NL, fr. Gk, fr. *analyein* to break up, fr. *ana-* up + *lyein* to loosen] **1** : separation of a thing into the parts or elements of which it is composed **2** : an examination of a thing to determine its parts or elements; *also* : a statement showing the results of such an examination **3** : PSY-CHOANALYSIS — **an·a·lyst** \'an-ᵊl-ist\ *n* — **an·a·lyt·ic** \ₜan-ᵊl-'i-tik\ *or* **an·a·lyt·i·cal** \-ti-kəl\ *adj* — **an·a·lyt·i·cal·ly** *adv*

an·a·lyze \'an-ᵊl-ₜīz\ *vb* **-lyzed; -lyz·ing** : to make an analysis of

an·a·pest \'a-nə-ₜpest\ *n* : a metrical foot of two unac-cented syllables followed by one accented syllable — **an·a·pes·tic** \ₜa-nə-'pes-tik\ *adj or n*

an·ar·chism \'a-nər-ₜki-zəm\ *n* : the theory that all government is undesirable — **an·ar·chist** \-kist\ *n or adj* — **an·ar·chis·tic** \ₜa-nər-'kis-tik\ *adj*

an·ar·chy \'an-ər-kē\ *n* **1** : a social structure without government or law and order **2** : utter confusion — **an·ar·chic** \a-'när-kik\ *adj* — **an·ar·chi·cal·ly** \-ki-k(ə-)lē\ *adv*

anas·to·mo·sis \ə-ₜnas-tə-'mō-səs\ *n, pl* **-mo·ses** \-ₜsēz\ **1** : the union of parts or branches (as of blood vessels) **2** : NETWORK

anat *abbr* anatomical; anatomy

anath·e·ma \ə-'na-thə-mə\ *n* **1** : a solemn curse **2** : a person or thing accursed; *also* : one intensely disliked

anath·e·ma·tize \-ₜtīz\ *vb* **-tized; -tiz·ing** : to pro-nounce an anathema against : CURSE

anat·o·mize \ə-'na-tə-ₜmīz\ *vb* **-mized; -miz·ing** : to dissect so as to examine the structure and parts; *also* : ANALYZE

anat·o·my \ə-'na-tə-mē\ *n, pl* **-mies** [LL *anatomia* dis-section, fr. Gk *anatomē*, fr. *anatemnein* to dissect, fr. *ana-* up + *temnein* to cut] **1** : a branch of science dealing with the structure of organisms **2** : structural makeup esp. of an organism or any of its parts **3** : a separating into parts for detailed study : ANALYSIS — **an·a·tom·ic** \ₜa-nə-'tä-mik\ *or* **an·a·tom·i·cal** \-mi-kəl\ *adj* — **an·a·tom·i·cal·ly** \-mi-k(ə-)lē\ *adv* — **anat·o·mist** \ə-'na-tə-mist\ *n*

anc *abbr* ancient

-ance *n suffix* **1** : action or process ⟨further*ance*⟩ : in-stance of an action or process ⟨perform*ance*⟩ **2** : qual-ity or state : instance of a quality or state ⟨protuber*ance*⟩ **3** : amount or degree ⟨conduct*ance*⟩

an·ces·tor \'an-ₜses-tər\ *n* [ME *ancestre*, fr. OF, fr. L *antecessor* predecessor, fr. *antecedere* to go before, fr. *ante-* before + *cedere* to go] : one from whom an individual is descended

an·ces·tress \'an-ₜses-trəs\ *n* : a female ancestor

an·ces·try \'an-ₜses-trē\ *n* **1** : line of descent : LINEAGE **2** : ANCESTORS — **an·ces·tral** \an-'ses-trəl\ *adj*

¹an·chor \'aŋ-kər\ *n* **1** : a heavy metal device attached to a ship that catches hold of the bottom and holds the ship in place **2** : ANCHORPERSON

²anchor *vb* : to hold or become held in place by or as if by an anchor

an·chor·age \'aŋ-k(ə-)rij\ *n* : a place suitable for ships to anchor

an·cho·rite \'aŋ-kə-ₜrīt\ *n* : HERMIT

an·chor·man \'aŋ-kər-ₜman\ *n* **1** : the member of a team who competes last **2** : an anchorperson who is a man

an·chor·per·son \-ₜpər-sən\ *n* : a broadcaster who

reads the news and introduces the reports of other broadcasters

an·chor·wom·an \-ˌwu̇-mən\ *n* **1** : a woman who competes last **2** : an anchorperson who is a woman

an·cho·vy \ˈan-ˌchō-vē, an-ˈchō-\ *n, pl* **-vies** *or* **-vy** : a small herringlike fish used esp. for sauces and relishes

an·cien ré·gime \ˌän̄s-yaⁿ-rā-ˈzhēm\ *n* **1** : the political and social system of France before the Revolution of 1789 **2** : a system no longer prevailing

¹an·cient \ˈān-shənt\ *adj* **1** : having existed for many years **2** : belonging to times long past; *esp* : belonging to the period before the Middle Ages

²ancient *n* **1** : an aged person **2** *pl* : the peoples of ancient Greece and Rome; *esp* : the classical authors of Greece and Rome

an·cil·lary \ˈan-sə-ˌler-ē\ *adj* **1** : SUBORDINATE, SUBSIDIARY **2** : AUXILIARY, SUPPLEMENTARY — **ancillary** *n*

-ancy *n suffix* : quality or state ⟨flamboy*ancy*⟩

and \ənd, (ˈ)and\ *conj* **1** — used to indicate connection or addition esp. of items within the same class or type or to join words or phrases of the same grammatical rank or function **2** — used to join one finite verb to another so that together they are equivalent to an infinitive of purpose ⟨come ∼ see me⟩

¹an·dan·te \än-ˈdän-ˌtā, -tē\ *adv or adj* [It., lit., going, prp. of *andare* to go] : moderately slow — used as a direction in music

²andante *n* : an andante movement

and·iron \ˈan-ˌdī-(ə)rn\ *n* : one of a pair of metal supports for firewood in a fireplace

and/or \ˈand-ˈȯr\ *conj* — used to indicate that either *and* or *or* may apply ⟨men ∼ women means men *and* women or men *or* women⟩

An·dor·ran \an-ˈdȯr-ən\ *n* : a native or inhabitant of Andorra

an·dro·gen \ˈan-drə-jən\ *n* : a male sex hormone

an·drog·y·nous \an-ˈdrä-jə-nəs\ *adj* **1** : having the characteristics of both male and female **2** : suitable for either sex ⟨∼ clothing⟩

an·droid \ˈan-ˌdrȯid\ *n* : a mobile robot usu. with a human form

an·ec·dot·al \ˌa-nik-ˈdōt-ᵊl\ *adj* **1** : relating to or consisting of anecdotes **2** : based on reports of an unscientific nature — **an·ec·dot·al·ly** *adv*

an·ec·dote \ˈan-ik-ˌdōt\ *n, pl* **-dotes** *also* **-dota** \ˌa-nik-ˈdō-tə\ [F, fr. Gk *anekdota* unpublished items, fr. *a-* not + *ekdidonai* to publish] : a brief story of an interesting, amusing, or biographical incident

ane·mia \ə-ˈnē-mē-ə\ *n* **1** : a condition in which blood is deficient in quantity, in red blood cells, or in hemoglobin and which is marked by pallor, weakness, and irregular heart action **2** : lack of vitality — **ane·mic** \ə-ˈnē-mik\ *adj*

an·e·mom·e·ter \ˌa-nə-ˈmä-mə-tər\ *n* : an instrument for measuring the force or speed of the wind

anem·o·ne \ə-ˈne-mə-nē\ *n* : any of a large genus of herbs related to the buttercups that have showy flowers without petals but with conspicuous often colored sepals

anent \ə-ˈnent\ *prep* : CONCERNING

an·es·the·sia \ˌa-nəs-ˈthē-zhə\ *n* : loss of bodily sensation

an·es·the·si·ol·o·gy \-ˌthē-zē-ˈä-lə-jē\ *n* : a branch of medical science dealing with anesthesia and anesthetics — **an·es·the·si·ol·o·gist** \-jist\ *n*

¹an·es·thet·ic \ˌa-nəs-ˈthe-tik\ *adj* : of, relating to, or capable of producing anesthesia

²anesthetic *n* : an agent that produces anesthesia — **anes·the·tist** \ə-ˈnes-thə-tist\ *n* — **anes·the·tize** \-thə-ˌtīz\ *vb*

anew \ə-ˈnü, -ˈnyü\ *adv* **1** : over again **2** : in a new form

an·gel \ˈān-jəl\ *n* [ME, fr. OF *angele*, fr. L *angelus*, fr. Gk *angelos*, lit., messenger] **1** : a spiritual being superior to man **2** : an attendant spirit **3** : a winged figure of human form in art **4** : MESSENGER, HARBINGER **5** : a person held to resemble an angel **6** : a financial backer — **an·gel·ic** \an-ˈje-lik\ *or* **an·gel·i·cal** \-li-kəl\ *adj* — **an·gel·i·cal·ly** \-k(ə-)lē\ *adv*

an·gel·fish \ˈān-jəl-ˌfish\ *n* : any of several bright-colored tropical fishes that are flattened from side to side

an·gel·i·ca \an-ˈje-li-kə\ *n* : a biennial herb related to the carrot whose roots and fruit furnish a flavoring oil

¹an·ger \ˈaŋ-gər\ *vb* : to make angry

²anger *n* [ME, affliction, anger, fr. ON *angr* grief] : a strong feeling of displeasure **syn** wrath, ire, rage, fury, indignation

an·gi·na \an-ˈjī-nə\ *n* : a disorder (as of the heart) marked by attacks of intense pain; *esp* : ANGINA PECTORIS — **an·gi·nal** \an-ˈjīn-ᵊl\ *adj*

angina pec·to·ris \-ˈpek-t(ə-)rəs\ *n* : a heart disease marked by brief attacks of sharp chest pain caused by deficient oxygenation of heart muscles

an·gio·gram \ˈan-jē-ə-ˌgram\ *n* : an X-ray photograph made by angiography

an·gi·og·ra·phy \ˌan-jē-ˈä-grə-fē\ *n* : the use of X rays to make blood vessels visible (as by photography) after injection of a substance opaque to radiation

an·gio·plas·ty \ˈan-jē-ə-ˌplas-tē\ *n* : surgical repair of a blood vessel esp. by using an inflatable catheter to unblock arteries clogged by atherosclerotic deposits

an·gio·sperm \-ˌspərm\ *n* : FLOWERING PLANT

¹an·gle \ˈaŋ-gəl\ *n* **1** : a sharp projecting corner **2** : the figure formed by the meeting of two lines in a point **3** : a point of view **4** : a special technique or plan : GIMMICK — **an·gled** *adj*

angle 2: *1* obtuse, *2* right, *3* acute

²angle *vb* **an·gled; an·gling** \-g(ə-)liŋ\ : to turn, move, or direct at an angle

³angle *vb* **an·gled; an·gling** \-g(ə-)liŋ\ : to fish with a hook and line — **an·gler** \-glər\ *n* — **an·gling** \-gliŋ\ *n*

an·gle·worm \ˈaŋ-gəl-ˌwərm\ *n* : EARTHWORM

An·gli·can \ˈaŋ-gli-kən\ *adj* **1** : of or relating to the established episcopal Church of England **2** : of or relating to England or the English nation — **Anglican** *n* — **An·gli·can·ism** \-kə-ˌni-zəm\ *n*

an·gli·cize \ˈaŋ-glə-ˌsīz\ *vb* **-cized; -ciz·ing** *often cap* **1** : to make English (as in habits, speech, character, or outlook) **2** : to borrow (a foreign word or phrase) into English without changing form or spelling and sometimes without changing pronunciation — **an·gli·ci·za·tion** \ˌaŋ-glə-sə-ˈzā-shən\ *n, often cap*

An·glo \ˈaŋ-glō\ *n, pl* **Anglos** : a non-Hispanic white inhabitant of the U.S.; *esp* : one of English origin and descent

An·glo–French \ˌaŋ-glō-ˈfrench\ *n* : the French language used in medieval England

An·glo·phile \ˈaŋ-glə-ˌfīl\ *also* **An·glo·phil** \-ˌfil\ *n* : one who greatly admires England and things English

An·glo·phobe \ˈaŋ-glə-ˌfōb\ *n* : one who is averse to England and things English

An·glo–Sax·on \ˌaŋ-glō-ˈsak-sən\ *n* **1** : a member of any of the Germanic peoples who invaded England in the 5th century A.D. **2** : a member of the English people **3** : Old English — **Anglo–Saxon** *adj*

an·go·ra \aŋ-ˈgȯr-ə, an-\ *n* **1** : yarn or cloth made from the hair of an Angora goat or rabbit **2** *cap* : any of a breed of cats, goats, or rabbits with a long silky coat

an·gry \ˈaŋ-grē\ *adj* **an·gri·er; -est** : feeling or showing

anger syn enraged, wrathful, irate, indignant, mad —
an·gri·ly \-grə-lē\ adv
angst \ˈäŋst\ n [G] : a feeling of anxiety
ang·strom \ˈaŋ-strəm\ n : a unit of length equal to one
ten-billionth of a meter
an·guish \ˈaŋ-gwish\ n : extreme pain or distress esp.
of mind — **an·guished** \-gwisht\ adj
an·gu·lar \ˈaŋ-gyə-lər\ adj 1 : sharp-cornered 2 : having one or more angles 3 : being thin and bony — **an·
gu·lar·i·ty** \ˌaŋ-gyə-ˈlar-ə-tē\ n
An·gus \ˈaŋ-gəs\ n : any of a breed of usu. black horn-
less beef cattle originating in Scotland
an·hy·drous \an-ˈhī-drəs\ adj : free from water
an·i·line \ˈan-ᵊl-ən\ n : an oily poisonous liquid used in
making dyes, medicines, and explosives
an·i·mad·vert \ˌa-nə-ˌmad-ˈvərt\ vb : to remark critically : express censure — **an·i·mad·ver·sion** \-ˈvər-
zhən\ n
¹an·i·mal \ˈa-nə-məl\ n 1 : any of a kingdom of living
things typically differing from plants in capacity for
active movement, in rapid response to stimulation,
and in lack of cellulose cell walls 2 : a lower animal
as distinguished from human beings; also : MAMMAL
²animal adj 1 : of, relating to, or derived from animals
2 : of or relating to the physical as distinguished from
the mental or spiritual syn carnal, fleshly, sensual
an·i·mal·cule \ˌa-nə-ˈmal-kyül\ n : a tiny animal usu.
invisible to the naked eye
¹an·i·mate \ˈa-nə-mət\ adj : having life
²an·i·mate \-ˌmāt\ vb **-mat·ed; -mat·ing** 1 : to impart
life to 2 : to give spirit and vigor to 3 : to make appear
to move ⟨~ a cartoon for motion pictures⟩ — **an·
i·mat·ed** adj
an·i·ma·tion \ˌa-nə-ˈmā-shən\ n 1 : VIVACITY, LIVELI-
NESS 2 : a motion picture made from a series of drawings simulating motions by means of slight
progressive changes
an·i·mism \ˈa-nə-ˌmi-zəm\ n : attribution of conscious
life to objects in and phenomena of nature or to inanimate objects — **an·i·mist** \-mist\ n — **an·i·mis·
tic** \ˌa-nə-ˈmis-tik\ adj
an·i·mos·i·ty \ˌa-nə-ˈmä-sə-tē\ n, pl **-ties** : ILL WILL,
RESENTMENT
an·i·mus \ˈa-nə-məs\ n : deep-seated resentment and
hostility
an·ion \ˈa-ˌnī-ən, -ˌnī-än\ n : a negatively charged ion
an·ise \ˈa-nəs\ n : an herb related to the carrot with aromatic seeds (**aniseed** \-ˌsēd\) used in flavoring
an·is·ette \ˌa-nə-ˈset, -ˈzet\ n [F] : a usu. colorless
sweet liqueur flavored with aniseed
ankh \ˈäŋk\ n : a cross having a loop for its upper vertical arm and serving esp. in ancient Egypt as an emblem of life
an·kle \ˈaŋ-kəl\ n : the joint or region between the foot
and the leg
an·kle·bone \ˈaŋ-kəl-ˌbōn\ n : the bone that in human
beings bears the weight of the body and with the tibia
and fibula forms the ankle joint
an·klet \ˈaŋ-klət\ n 1 : something (as an ornament)
worn around the ankle 2 : a short sock reaching
slightly above the ankle
ann abbr 1 annals 2 annual
an·nals \ˈan-ᵊlz\ n pl 1 : a record of events in chronological order 2 : historical records — **an·nal·ist** \-ᵊl-
ist\ n
an·neal \ə-ˈnēl\ vb 1 : to make (as glass or steel) less
brittle by heating and then cooling 2 : STRENGTHEN,
TOUGHEN
¹an·nex \ə-ˈneks, ˈa-ˌneks\ vb 1 : to attach as an addition 2 : to incorporate (as a territory) within a political domain — **an·nex·a·tion** \ˌa-ˌnek-ˈsā-shən\ n
²an·nex \ˈa-ˌneks, -niks\ n : a subsidiary or supplementary structure
an·nexe chiefly Brit var of ANNEX
an·ni·hi·late \ə-ˈnī-ə-ˌlāt\ vb **-lat·ed; -lat·ing** : to de-

stroy completely — **an·ni·hi·la·tion** \-ˌnī-ə-ˈlā-shən\
n
an·ni·ver·sa·ry \ˌa-nə-ˈvər-sə-rē\ n, pl **-ries** : the annual return of the date of a notable event and esp. a
wedding
an·no Do·mi·ni \ˌa-nō-ˈdä-mə-nē, -ˈdō-, -ˌnī\ adv, often cap A [ML, in the year of the Lord] — used to
indicate that a time division falls within the Christian
era
an·no·tate \ˈa-nə-ˌtāt\ vb **-tat·ed; -tat·ing** : to furnish
with notes — **an·no·ta·tion** \ˌa-nə-ˈtā-shən\ n — **an·
no·ta·tor** \ˈa-nə-ˌtā-tər\ n
an·nounce \ə-ˈnaůns\ vb **an·nounced; an·nounc·ing** 1
: to make known publicly 2 : to give notice of the arrival or presence of — **an·nounce·ment** n
an·nounc·er \ə-ˈnaůn-sər\ n : a person who introduces
radio or television programs, makes commercial announcements, or gives station identification
an·noy \ə-ˈnòi\ vb : to disturb or irritate esp. by repeated acts : VEX syn irk, bother, pester, tease, harass — **an·noy·ing·ly** adv
an·noy·ance \ə-ˈnòi-əns\ n 1 : the act of annoying 2
: the state of being annoyed 3 : NUISANCE
¹an·nu·al \ˈan-yə-wəl\ adj 1 : covering the period of a
year 2 : occurring once a year : YEARLY 3 : completing the life cycle in one growing season ⟨~ plants⟩ —
an·nu·al·ly adv
²annual n 1 : a publication appearing once a year 2 : an
annual plant
annual ring n : the layer of wood produced by a single
year's growth of a woody plant
an·nu·i·tant \ə-ˈnü-ə-tənt, -ˈnyü-\ n : a beneficiary of
an annuity
an·nu·i·ty \ə-ˈnü-ə-tē, -ˈnyü-\ n, pl **-i·ties** : an amount
payable annually; also : the right to receive such a
payment
an·nul \ə-ˈnəl\ vb **an·nulled; an·nul·ling** : to make legally void — **an·nul·ment** n
an·nu·lar \ˈan-yə-lər\ adj : ring-shaped
an·nun·ci·ate \ə-ˈnən-sē-ˌāt\ vb **-at·ed; -at·ing** : AN-
NOUNCE
an·nun·ci·a·tion \ə-ˌnən-sē-ˈā-shən\ n 1 : ANNOUNCE-
MENT 2 cap : March 25 observed as a church festival
commemorating the announcement of the Incarnation
an·nun·ci·a·tor \ə-ˈnən-sē-ˌā-tər\ n : one that annuncia-
tes; specif : a usu. electrically controlled signal
board or indicator
an·ode \ˈa-ˌnōd\ n 1 : the positive electrode of an electrolytic cell 2 : the negative terminal of a battery 3
: the electron-collecting electrode of an electron tube
— **an·od·ic** \a-ˈnä-dik\ also **an·od·al** \-ˈnōd-ᵊl\ adj
an·od·ize \ˈa-nə-ˌdīz\ vb **-ized; -iz·ing** : to subject (a
metal) to electrolytic action as the anode of a cell in
order to coat with a protective or decorative film
an·o·dyne \ˈa-nə-ˌdīn\ n : something that relieves pain
: a soothing agent
anoint \ə-ˈnòint\ vb 1 : to apply oil to esp. as a sacred
rite 2 : CONSECRATE — **anoint·ment** n
anom·a·lous \ə-ˈnä-mə-ləs\ adj : deviating from a general rule : ABNORMAL
anom·a·ly \ə-ˈnä-mə-lē\ n, pl **-lies** : something anomalous : IRREGULARITY
¹anon \ə-ˈnän\ adv, archaic : SOON
²anon abbr anonymous; anonymously
anon·y·mous \ə-ˈnä-nə-məs\ adj : of unknown or un-
declared origin or authorship — **an·o·nym·i·ty** \ˌa-nə-
ˈni-mə-tē\ n — **anon·y·mous·ly** adv
anoph·e·les \ə-ˈnä-fə-ˌlēz\ n [NL, genus name, fr. Gk
anōphelēs useless, fr. a- not + ophelos advantage,
help] : any of a genus of mosquitoes that includes all
mosquitoes which transmit malaria to human beings
an·o·rec·tic \ˌa-nə-ˈrek-tik\ adj : ANOREXIC — **anorec-
tic** n
an·orex·ia \ˌa-nə-ˈrek-sē-ə\ n 1 : loss of appetite esp.
when prolonged 2 : ANOREXIA NERVOSA

anorexia ner·vo·sa \-nər-'vō-sə\ *n* : a serious disorder in eating behavior marked esp. by a pathological fear of weight gain leading to faulty eating patterns, malnutrition, and usu. excessive weight loss

an·orex·ic \ˌa-nə-'rek-sik\ *adj* **1** : lacking or causing loss of appetite **2** : affected with or as if with anorexia nervosa — **anorexic** *n*

¹an·oth·er \ə-'nə-thər\ *adj* **1** : some other **2** : being one in addition : one more

²another *pron* **1** : an additional one : one more **2** : one that is different from the first or present one

ans *abbr* answer

¹an·swer \'an-sər\ *n* **1** : something spoken or written in reply to a question **2** : a solution of a problem

²answer *vb* **1** : to speak or write in reply to **2** : to be responsible **3** : to be adequate — **an·swer·er** *n*

an·swer·able \'an-sə-rə-bəl\ *adj* **1** : subject to taking blame or responsibility **2** : capable of being refuted

answering machine *n* : a machine that receives telephone calls by playing a recorded message and usu. by recording messages from callers

answering service *n* : a commercial service that answers telephone calls for its clients

¹ant \'ant\ *n* : any of a family of small social insects related to the bees and living in communities usu. in earth or wood

²ant *abbr* antonym

Ant *abbr* Antarctica

ant- — see ANTI-

¹-ant *n suffix* **1** : one that performs or promotes (a specified action) ⟨cool*ant*⟩ **2** : thing that is acted upon (in a specified manner) ⟨inhal*ant*⟩

²-ant *adj suffix* **1** : performing (a specified action) or being (in a specified condition) ⟨propell*ant*⟩ **2** : promoting (a specified action or process) ⟨expector*ant*⟩

ant·ac·id \ant-'a-səd\ *n* : an agent that counteracts acidity — **antacid** *adj*

an·tag·o·nism \an-'ta-gə-ˌni-zəm\ *n* **1** : active opposition or hostility **2** : opposition in physiological action — **an·tag·o·nis·tic** \-ˌta-gə-'nis-tik\ *adj*

an·tag·o·nist \-nist\ *n* : ADVERSARY, OPPONENT

an·tag·o·nize \an-'ta-gə-ˌnīz\ *vb* **-nized; -niz·ing** : to provoke the hostility of

ant·arc·tic \ant-'ärk-tik, -'är-tik\ *adj, often cap* : of or relating to the south pole or the region near it

antarctic circle *n, often cap A&C* : the parallel of latitude that is approximately 66½ degrees south of the equator

¹an·te \'an-tē\ *n* : a poker stake put up before the deal to build the pot; *also* : an amount paid : PRICE

²ante *vb* **an·ted; an·te·ing 1** : to put up (an ante) **2** : PAY

ant·eat·er \'ant-ˌē-tər\ *n* : any of several mammals (as an aardvark) that feed mostly on ants or termites

an·te·bel·lum \ˌan-ti-'be-ləm\ *adj* : existing before a war; *esp* : existing before the U.S. Civil War of 1861-65

an·te·ced·ent \ˌan-tə-'sēd-ᵊnt\ *n* **1** : a noun, pronoun, phrase, or clause referred to by a personal or relative pronoun **2** : a preceding event or cause **3** *pl* : the significant conditions of one's earlier life **4** *pl* : ANCESTORS — **antecedent** *adj*

an·te·cham·ber \'an-ti-ˌchām-bər\ *n* : ANTEROOM

an·te·date \'an-ti-ˌdāt\ *vb* **1** : to date (a paper) as of an earlier day than that on which the actual writing or signing is done **2** : to precede in time

an·te·di·lu·vi·an \ˌan-ti-də-'lü-vē-ən, -dī-\ *adj* **1** : of the period before the biblical flood **2** : ANTIQUATED

an·te·lope \'ant-ᵊl-ˌōp\ *n, pl* **-lope** *or* **-lopes** [ME, fabulous heraldic beast, prob. fr. MF *antelop* savage animal with sawlike horns, fr. ML *anthalopus*, fr. LGk *antholops*] **1** : any of various Old World cud-chewing mammals related to the oxen but with smaller lighter bodies and horns that extend upward and backward **2** : PRONGHORN

an·te me·ri·di·em \'an-ti-mə-ˌri-dē-əm\ *adj* [L] : being before noon

an·ten·na \an-'te-nə\ *n, pl* **-nae** \-(ˌ)nē\ *or* **-nas** [ML, fr. L, sail yard] **1** : one of the long slender paired segmented sensory organs on the head of an arthropod (as an insect or crab) **2** *pl usu* **-nas** : a metallic device (as a rod or wire) for sending out or receiving radio waves

an·te·pe·nult \ˌan-ti-'pē-ˌnəlt\ *also* **an·te·pen·ul·ti·ma** \-pi-'nəl-tə-mə\ *n* : the 3d syllable of a word counting from the end — **an·te·pen·ul·ti·mate** \-pi-'nəl-tə-mət\ *adj or n*

an·te·ri·or \an-'tir-ē-ər\ *adj* **1** : situated before or toward the front **2** : situated near or nearer to the head **3** : coming before in time **syn** preceding, previous, prior, antecedent

an·te·room \'an-ti-ˌrüm, -ˌrùm\ *n* : a room forming the entrance to another and often used as a waiting room

an·them \'an-thəm\ *n* **1** : a sacred vocal composition **2** : a song or hymn of praise or gladness

an·ther \'an-thər\ *n* : the part of a stamen of a seed plant that produces and contains pollen

ant·hill \'ant-ˌhil\ *n* : a mound thrown up by ants or termites in digging their nest

an·thol·o·gy \an-'thä-lə-jē\ *n, pl* **-gies** [NL *anthologia* collection of epigrams, fr. MGk, fr. Gk, flower gathering, fr. *anthos* flower + *logia* collecting, fr. *legein* to gather] : a collection of literary selections — **an·thol·o·gist** \-jist\ *n* — **an·thol·o·gize** \-ˌjīz\ *vb*

an·thra·cite \'an-thrə-ˌsīt\ *n* : a hard glossy coal that burns without much smoke

an·thrax \'an-ˌthraks\ *n* : an infectious and usu. fatal bacterial disease of warm-blooded animals (as cattle and sheep) that is transmissible to humans; *also* : a bacterium causing anthrax

an·thro·po·cen·tric \ˌan-thrə-pə-'sen-trik\ *adj* : interpreting or regarding the world in terms of human values and experiences

an·thro·poid \'an-thrə-ˌpòid\ *n* **1** : any of several large tailless apes (as a gorilla) **2** : a person resembling an ape — **anthropoid** *adj*

an·thro·pol·o·gy \ˌan-thrə-'pä-lə-jē\ *n* : the science of human beings and esp. of their physical characteristics, their origin and the distribution of races, their environment and social relations, and their culture — **an·thro·po·log·i·cal** \-pə-'lä-ji-kəl\ *adj* — **an·thro·pol·o·gist** \-'pä-lə-jist\ *n*

an·thro·po·mor·phism \ˌan-thrə-pə-'mòr-ˌfi-zəm\ *n* : an interpretation of what is not human or personal in terms of human or personal characteristics : HUMANIZATION — **an·thro·po·mor·phic** \-fik\ *adj*

an·ti- \ˌan-ˌtī, -tē\ *n, pl* **antis** : one who is opposed

anti- \ˌan-ti, -tē, -ˌtē\ *or* **ant-** *or* **anth-** *prefix* **1** : opposite in kind, position, or action **2** : opposing : hostile toward **3** : counteractive **4** : preventive of : curative of

antiaging	antigovernment
anti-AIDS	anti-imperialism
antiaircraft	anti-imperialist
antialcohol	antiknock
anti-American	antilabor
antiapartheid	antimalarial
antibacterial	antimicrobial
anticapitalist	antinausea
anti-Catholic	antipoverty
anticholesterol	antislavery
anticlerical	antispasmodic
anticolonial	antistatic
anticommunism	antisubmarine
anticommunist	antitank
antidemocratic	antitumor
antiestablishment	antiviral
antifascist	

an·ti·abor·tion \ˌan-tē-ə-'bòr-shən, ˌan-ˌtī-\ *adj* : opposed to abortion

an·ti·bal·lis·tic missile \ˌan-ti-bə-'lis-tik-, ˌan-ˌtī-\ *n* : a missile for intercepting and destroying ballistic missiles

an·ti·bi·ot·ic \-bī-'ä-tik, -bē-\ *n* : a substance produced by or derived by chemical alteration of a substance produced by a microorganism (as a fungus or bacterium) that in dilute solution inhibits or kills another microorganism — **antibiotic** *adj*

an·ti·body \'an-ti-ˌbä-dē\ *n* : any of a large number of proteins of high molecular weight produced normally by specialized B cells after stimulation by an antigen and acting specifically against the antigen in an immune response

¹**an·tic** \'an-tik\ *n* : an often wildly playful or funny act or action

²**antic** *adj* [It *antico* ancient, fr. L *antiquus*] **1** *archaic* : GROTESQUE **2** : PLAYFUL

an·ti·can·cer \ˌan-ti-'kan-sər, ˌan-ˌtī-\ *adj* : used against or tending to arrest cancer ⟨∼ drugs⟩

An·ti·christ \'an-ti-ˌkrīst\ *n* **1** : one who denies or opposes Christ **2** : a false Christ

an·tic·i·pate \an-'ti-sə-ˌpāt\ *vb* **-pat·ed; -pat·ing 1** : to foresee and provide for beforehand **2** : to look forward to — **an·tic·i·pa·tion** \-ti-sə-'pā-shən\ *n* — **an·tic·i·pa·to·ry** \-'ti-sə-pə-ˌtōr-ē\ *adj*

an·ti·cli·max \ˌan-ti-'klī-ˌmaks\ *n* : something closing a series that is strikingly less important than what has preceded it — **an·ti·cli·mac·tic** \-klī-'mak-tik\ *adj*

an·ti·cline \'an-ti-ˌklīn\ *n* : an arch of layers of rock in the earth's crust

an·ti·co·ag·u·lant \ˌan-ti-kō-'a-gyə-lənt\ *n* : a substance that hinders the clotting of blood — **anticoagulant** *adj*

an·ti·cy·clone \ˌan-ti-'sī-ˌklōn\ *n* : a system of winds that rotates about a center of high atmospheric pressure — **an·ti·cy·clon·ic** \-sī-'klä-nik\ *adj*

¹**an·ti·de·pres·sant** \ˌan-ti-di-'pres-ᵊnt, ˌan-ˌtī-\ *adj* : used or tending to relieve psychic depression ⟨∼ drugs⟩

²**antidepressant** *n* : an antidepressant drug

an·ti·dote \'an-ti-ˌdōt\ *n* : a remedy to counteract the effects of poison

an·ti·drug \'an-ˌtī-ˌdrəg\ *adj* : acting against or opposing illicit drugs

an·ti·fer·til·i·ty \ˌan-ti-fər-'ti-lə-tē\ *adj* : tending to control excess or unwanted fertility : CONTRACEPTIVE ⟨∼ agents⟩

an·ti·freeze \'an-ti-ˌfrēz\ *n* : a substance added to a liquid to lower its freezing temperature

an·ti·gen \'an-ti-jən\ *n* : a usu. protein or carbohydrate substance (as a toxin or an enzyme) capable of stimulating an immune response — **an·ti·gen·ic** \ˌan-ti-'je-nik\ *adj* — **an·ti·ge·nic·i·ty** \-jə-'ni-sə-tē\ *n*

an·ti·grav·i·ty \ˌan-ti-'gra-və-tē, ˌan-ˌtī-\ *adj* : reducing or canceling the effect of gravity

an·ti·he·ro \'an-ti-ˌhē-rō, 'an-ˌtī-\ *n* : a protagonist who is notably lacking in heroic qualities (as courage)

an·ti·his·ta·mine \ˌan-ti-'his-tə-ˌmēn, ˌan-ˌtī-, -mən\ *n* : any of various drugs used in treating allergies and colds

an·ti·hy·per·ten·sive \-ˌhī-pər-'ten-siv\ *n* : a substance that is effective against high blood pressure — **antihypertensive** *adj*

an·ti–in·flam·ma·to·ry \-in-'fla-mə-ˌtōr-ē\ *adj* : counteracting inflammation — **anti–inflammatory** *n*

an·ti–in·tel·lec·tu·al \-ˌint-ᵊl-'ek-chə-wəl\ *adj* : opposing or hostile to intellectuals or to an intellectual view or approach

an·ti·lock \'an-ti-ˌläk, 'an-ˌtī-\ *adj* : being a braking system designed to prevent the wheels from locking

an·ti·log·a·rithm \ˌan-ti-'lo-gə-ˌri-thəm, ˌan-ˌtī-, -'lä-\ *n* : the number corresponding to a given logarithm

an·ti·ma·cas·sar \ˌan-ti-mə-'ka-sər\ *n* : a cover to protect the back or arms of furniture

an·ti·mat·ter \'an-ti-ˌma-tər, 'an-ˌtī-\ *n* : matter composed of antiparticles

an·ti·mo·ny \'an-tə-ˌmō-nē\ *n* : a brittle silvery white metallic chemical element used esp. in alloys — see ELEMENT table

an·ti·neu·tron \ˌan-ti-'nü-ˌträn, ˌan-ˌtī-, -'nyü-\ *n* : the antiparticle of the neutron

an·ti·no·mi·an \ˌan-ti-'nō-mē-ən\ *n* : one who denies the validity of moral laws

an·tin·o·my \an-'ti-nə-mē\ *n, pl* **-mies** : a contradiction between two seemingly true statements

an·ti·nov·el \'an-ti-ˌnä-vəl, 'an-ˌtī-\ *n* : a work of fiction that lacks all or most of the traditional features of the novel

an·ti·nu·cle·ar \ˌan-ti-'nü-klē-ər, -'nyü-\ *adj* : opposing the use or production of nuclear power plants

an·ti·ox·i·dant \ˌan-tē-'äk-sə-dənt, ˌan-ˌtī-\ *n* : a substance that inhibits oxidation — **antioxidant** *adj*

an·ti·par·ti·cle \'an-ti-ˌpär-ti-kəl, 'an-ˌtī-\ *n* : a subatomic particle identical to another subatomic particle in mass but opposite to it in electric and magnetic properties

an·ti·pas·to \ˌan-ti-'pas-tō, ˌän-ti-'päs-\ *n, pl* **-ti** \-(ˌ)tē\ : any of various typically Italian hors d'oeuvres

an·tip·a·thy \an-'ti-pə-thē\ *n, pl* **-thies 1** : settled aversion or dislike **2** : an object of aversion — **an·ti·pa·thet·ic** \ˌan-ti-pə-'the-tik\ *adj*

an·ti·per·son·nel \ˌan-ti-ˌpərs-ᵊn-'el, ˌan-ˌtī-\ *adj* : designed for use against military personnel ⟨∼ mine⟩

an·ti·per·spi·rant \-'pər-spə-rənt\ *n* : a preparation used to check perspiration

an·tiph·o·nal \an-'ti-fən-ᵊl\ *adj* : performed by two alternating groups — **an·tiph·o·nal·ly** *adv*

an·ti·pode \'an-tə-ˌpōd\ *n, pl* **an·tip·o·des** \an-'ti-pə-ˌdēz\ [ME *antipodes*, pl., persons dwelling at opposite points on the globe, fr. L, fr. Gk, fr. pl. of *antipod-, antipous* with feet opposite, fr. *anti-* against + *pod-, pous* foot] : the parts of the earth diametrically opposite — usu. used in pl. — **an·tip·o·dal** \an-'ti-pəd-ᵊl\ *adj* — **an·tip·o·de·an** \(ˌ)an-ˌti-pə-'dē-ən\ *adj*

an·ti·pol·lu·tion \ˌan-ti-pə-'lü-shən\ *adj* : designed to prevent, reduce, or eliminate pollution ⟨∼ laws⟩

an·ti·pope \'an-ti-ˌpōp\ *n* : one elected or claiming to be pope in opposition to the pope canonically chosen

an·ti·pro·ton \ˌan-ti-'prō-ˌtän\ *n* : the antiparticle of the proton

an·ti·quar·i·an \ˌan-tə-'kwer-ē-ən\ *adj* **1** : of or relating to antiquities **2** : dealing in old books — **antiquarian** *n* — **an·ti·quar·i·an·ism** *n*

an·ti·quary \'an-tə-ˌkwer-ē\ *n, pl* **-quar·ies** : a person who collects or studies antiquities

an·ti·quat·ed \'an-tə-ˌkwā-təd\ *adj* : OUT-OF-DATE, OLD-FASHIONED

¹**an·tique** \an-'tēk\ *n* : an object made in a bygone period

²**antique** *adj* **1** : belonging to antiquity **2** : OLD-FASHIONED **3** : of a bygone style or period

³**antique** *vb* **-tiqued; -tiqu·ing 1** : to finish or refinish in antique style : give an appearance of age to **2** : to shop around for antiques — **an·tiqu·er** *n*

an·tiq·ui·ty \an-'ti-kwə-tē\ *n, pl* **-ties 1** : ancient times **2** : great age **3** *pl* : relics of ancient times **4** *pl* : matters relating to ancient culture

an·tis *pl of* ANTI

an·ti–Sem·i·tism \ˌan-ti-'se-mə-ˌti-zəm, ˌan-ˌtī-\ *n* : hostility toward Jews as a religious or social minority — **an·ti–Se·mit·ic** \-sə-'mi-tik\ *adj*

an·ti·sep·tic \ˌan-tə-'sep-tik\ *adj* **1** : killing or checking the growth of germs that cause decay or infection **2** : scrupulously clean : ASEPTIC — **antiseptic** *n* — **an·ti·sep·ti·cal·ly** *adv*

an·ti·se·rum \'an-ti-ˌsir-əm, 'an-ˌtī-\ *n* : a serum containing antibodies

an·ti·so·cial \ˌan-ti-'sō-shəl\ *adj* **1** : disliking the society of others **2** : contrary or hostile to the well-being of society ⟨crime is ∼⟩ — **an·ti·so·cial·ly** *adv*

an·tith·e·sis \an-'ti-thə-səs\ *n, pl* **-e·ses** \-ˌsēz\ **1** : the opposition or contrast of ideas **2** : the direct opposite

an·ti·thet·i·cal \ˌan-tə-'the-ti-kəl\ *also* **an·ti·thet·ic**

\-tik\ *adj* : constituting or marked by antithesis — **an-ti-thet-i-cal-ly** \-ti-k(ə-)lē\ *adv*

an-ti-tox-in \,an-ti-'täk-sən\ *n* : an antibody that is able to neutralize a particular toxin or disease-causing agent; *also* : an antiserum containing an antitoxin

an-ti-trust \,an-ti-'trəst\ *adj* : of or relating to legislation against trusts; *also* : consisting of laws to protect trade and commerce from unlawful restraints and monopolies or unfair business practices

an-ti-ven-in \-'ve-nən\ *n* : an antitoxin to a venom; *also* : a serum containing such antitoxin

ant-ler \'ant-lər\ *n* [ME *aunteler*, fr. MF *antoillier*, fr. (assumed) VL *anteocularis* located before the eye, fr. L *ante-* before + *oculus* eye] : one of the paired deciduous solid bone processes on the head of a deer; *also* : a branch of this — **ant-lered** \-lərd\ *adj*

ant lion *n* : any of various insects having a long-jawed larva that digs a conical pit in which it lies in wait for insects (as ants) on which it feeds

an-to-nym \'an-tə-,nim\ *n* : a word of opposite meaning

anus \'ā-nəs\ *n* [L] : the lower or posterior opening of the alimentary canal

an-vil \'an-vəl\ *n* 1 : a heavy iron block on which metal is shaped 2 : INCUS

anx-i-ety \aŋ-'zī-ə-tē\ *n, pl* **-et-ies** 1 : painful uneasiness of mind usu. over an anticipated ill 2 : abnormal apprehension and fear often accompanied by physiological signs (as sweating and increased pulse), by doubt about the nature and reality of the threat itself, and by self-doubt

anx-ious \'aŋk-shəs\ *adj* 1 : uneasy in mind : WORRIED 2 : earnestly wishing : EAGER — **anx-ious-ly** *adv*

¹any \'e-nē\ *adj* 1 : one chosen at random 2 : of whatever number or quantity

²any *pron* 1 : any one or ones ⟨take ∼ of the books you like⟩ 2 : any amount ⟨∼ of the money not used is to be returned⟩

³any *adv* : to any extent or degree : AT ALL ⟨could not walk ∼ farther⟩

any-body \-,bä-dē, -bə-\ *pron* : ANYONE

any-how \-,haû\ *adv* 1 : in any way 2 : NEVERTHELESS; *also* : in any case

any-more \,e-nē-'mōr\ *adv* 1 : any longer 2 : at the present time

any-one \'e-nē-(,)wən\ *pron* : any person

any-place \-,plās\ *adv* : ANYWHERE

any-thing \-,thiŋ\ *pron* : any thing whatever

any-time \'e-nē-,tīm\ *adv* : at any time whatever

any-way \-,wā\ *adv* : ANYHOW

any-where \-,hwer\ *adv* : in or to any place

any-wise \-,wīz\ *adv* : in any way whatever

A–OK \,ā-ō-'kā\ *adv or adj* : very definitely OK

A1 \'ā-'wən\ *adj* : of the finest quality

aor-ta \ā-'òr-tə\ *n, pl* **-tas** *or* **-tae** \-tē\ : the main artery that carries blood from the heart — **aor-tic** \-tik\ *adj*

ap *abbr* 1 apostle 2 apothecaries'

AP *abbr* 1 American plan 2 Associated Press

apace \ə-'pās\ *adv* : SWIFTLY

Apache \ə-'pa-chē\ *n, pl* **Apache** *or* **Apach-es** \-'pa-chēz, -'pa-shəz\ : a member of an American Indian people of the southwestern U.S.; *also* : any of the languages of the Apache people — **Apach-e-an** \ə-'pa-chē-ən\ *adj or n*

ap-a-nage *var of* APPANAGE

apart \ə-'pärt\ *adv* 1 : separately in place or time 2 : ASIDE 3 : in two or more parts : to pieces

apart-heid \ə-'pär-,tāt, -,tīt\ *n* [Afrikaans] : a policy of racial segregation practiced in the Republic of So. Africa

apart-ment \ə-'pärt-mənt\ *n* : a room or set of rooms occupied as a dwelling; *also* : a building divided into individual dwelling units

ap-a-thy \'a-pə-thē\ *n* 1 : lack of emotion 2 : lack of interest : INDIFFERENCE — **ap-a-thet-ic** \,a-pə-'the-tik\ *adj* — **ap-a-thet-i-cal-ly** \-ti-k(ə-)lē\ *adv*

ap-a-tite \'a-pə-,tīt\ *n* : any of a group of minerals that are phosphates of calcium and occur esp. in phosphate rock and in bones and teeth

APB *abbr* all points bulletin

¹ape \'āp\ *n* 1 : any of the larger tailless primates (as a baboon or gorilla); *also* : MONKEY 2 : MIMIC, IMITATOR; *also* : a large uncouth person

²ape *vb* **aped; ap-ing** : IMITATE, MIMIC

ape–man \'āp-,man\ *n* : a primate intermediate in character between Homo sapiens and the higher apes

aper-çu \,à-per-sūē, ,a-pər-'sü\ *n, pl* **aperçus** \-sūē(z), -'süz\ : an immediate impression; *esp* : INSIGHT

aper-i-tif \,ä-,per-ə-'tēf\ *n* : an alcoholic drink taken as an appetizer

ap-er-ture \'a-pər-,chùr, -chər\ *n* : OPENING, HOLE

apex \'ā-,peks\ *n, pl* **apex-es** *or* **api-ces** \'ā-pə-,sēz, 'a-\ : the highest point : PEAK

apha-sia \ə-'fā-zh(ē-)ə\ *n* : loss or impairment of the power to use or comprehend words — **apha-sic** \-zik\ *adj or n*

aph-elion \a-'fēl-yən\ *n, pl* **-elia** \-yə\ [NL, fr. *apo-* away from + Gk *hēlios* sun] : the point in an object's orbit most distant from the sun

aphid \'ā-fəd\ *n* : any of numerous small insects that suck the juices of plants

aphis \'ā-fəs, 'ā-\ *n, pl* **aphi-des** \-fə-,dēz\ : APHID

aph-o-rism \'a-fə-,ri-zəm\ *n* : a short saying stating a general truth : MAXIM — **aph-o-ris-tic** \,a-fə-'ris-tik\ *adj*

aph-ro-di-si-ac \,a-frə-'di-zē-,ak, -'dē-zē-\ *n* : an agent that excites sexual desire — **aphrodisiac** *adj*

api-ary \'ā-pē-,er-ē\ *n, pl* **-ar-ies** : a place where bees are kept — **api-a-rist** \-pē-ə-rist\ *n*

api-cal \'ā-pi-kəl, 'a-\ *adj* : of, relating to, or situated at an apex — **api-cal-ly** \-k(ə-)lē\ *adv*

apiece \ə-'pēs\ *adv* : for each one

aplen-ty \ə-'plen-tē\ *adj* : being in plenty or abundance

aplomb \ə-'pläm, -'pləm\ *n* [F, lit., perpendicularity, fr. MF, fr. *a plomb*, lit., according to the plummet] : complete composure or self-assurance

APO *abbr* army post office

Apoc *abbr* 1 Apocalypse 2 Apocrypha

apoc-a-lypse \ə-'pä-kə-,lips\ *n* 1 : a writing prophesying a cataclysm in which evil forces are destroyed 2 *cap* — see BIBLE table — **apoc-a-lyp-tic** \-,pä-kə-'lip-tik\ *also* **apoc-a-lyp-ti-cal** \-ti-kəl\ *adj*

Apoc-ry-pha \ə-'pä-krə-fə\ *n* 1 *not cap* : writings of dubious authenticity 2 : books included in the Septuagint and Vulgate but excluded from the Jewish and Protestant canons of the Old Testament — see BIBLE table 3 : early Christian writings not included in the New Testament

apoc-ry-phal \-fəl\ *adj* 1 : not canonical : SPURIOUS 2 *often cap* : of or resembling the Apocrypha — **apocry-phal-ly** *adv* — **apoc-ry-phal-ness** *n*

apo-gee \'a-pə-(,)jē\ *n* [F *apogée*, fr. NL *apogaeum*, fr. Gk *apogaion*, fr. *apo* away from + *gē* earth] : the point at which an orbiting object is farthest from the body being orbited

apo-lit-i-cal \,ā-pə-'li-ti-kəl\ *adj* 1 : having an aversion for or no interest in political affairs 2 : having no political significance — **apo-lit-i-cal-ly** \-k(ə-)lē\ *adv*

apol-o-get-ic \ə-,pä-lə-'je-tik\ *adj* : expressing apology — **apol-o-get-i-cal-ly** \-ti-k(ə-)lē\ *adv*

ap-o-lo-gia \,a-pə-'lō-j(ē-)ə\ *n* : APOLOGY; *esp* : an argument in support or justification

apol-o-gize \ə-'pä-lə-,jīz\ *vb* **-gized; -giz-ing** : to make an apology : express regret — **apol-o-gist** \-jist\ *n*

apol-o-gy \ə-'pä-lə-jē\ *n, pl* **-gies** 1 : a formal justification : DEFENSE 2 : an expression of regret for a wrong

ap-o-plexy \'a-pə-,plek-sē\ *n* : STROKE 3 — **ap-o-plec-tic** \,a-pə-'plek-tik\ *adj*

aport \ə-'pōrt\ *adv* : on or toward the left side of a ship

apos-ta-sy \ə-'päs-tə-sē\ *n, pl* **-sies** : a renunciation or abandonment of a former loyalty (as to a religion) — **apos-tate** \ə-'päs-,tāt, -tət\ *adj or n*

a pos·te·ri·o·ri \ˌä-pō-ˌstir-ē-'ōr-ē\ *adj* [L, lit., from the latter] : relating to or derived by reasoning from observed facts — **a posteriori** *adv*

apos·tle \ə-'pä-səl\ *n* **1** : one of the group composed of Jesus' 12 original disciples and Paul **2** : the first prominent missionary to a region or group **3** : a person who initiates or first advocates a great reform — **apos·tle·ship** *n*

ap·os·tol·ic \ˌa-pə-'stä-lik\ *adj* **1** : of or relating to an apostle or to the New Testament apostles **2** : of or relating to a succession of spiritual authority from the apostles **3** : PAPAL

¹apos·tro·phe \ə-'päs-trə-(ˌ)fē\ *n* : the rhetorical addressing of a usu. absent person or a usu. personified thing (as in "O grave, where is thy victory?")

²apostrophe *n* : a punctuation mark ' used esp. to indicate the possessive case or the omission of a letter or figure

apos·tro·phize \ə-'päs-trə-ˌfīz\ *vb* **-phized; -phiz·ing** : to address as if present or capable of understanding

apothecaries' weight *n* : a system of weights based on the troy pound and ounce and used chiefly by pharmacists — see WEIGHT table

apoth·e·cary \ə-'pä-thə-ˌker-ē\ *n, pl* **-car·ies** [ME *apothecarie,* fr. ML *apothecarius,* fr. LL, shopkeeper, fr. L *apotheca* storehouse, fr. Gk *apothēkē,* fr. *apotithenai* to put away] : DRUGGIST

ap·o·thegm \'a-pə-ˌthem\ *n* : APHORISM

apo·the·o·sis \ə-ˌpä-thē-'ō-səs, ˌa-pə-'thē-ə-səs\ *n, pl* **-o·ses** \-ˌsēz\ **1** : DEIFICATION **2** : the perfect example

app *abbr* **1** apparatus **2** appendix

ap·pall *also* **ap·pal** \ə-'pȯl\ *vb* **ap·palled; ap·pall·ing** : to overcome with horror : DISMAY

Ap·pa·loo·sa \ˌa-pə-'lü-sə\ *n* : any of a breed of saddle horses developed in western No. America and usu. having a white or solid-colored coat with small spots

Appaloosa

ap·pa·nage \'a-pə-nij\ *n* **1** : provision (as a grant of land) made by a sovereign or legislative body for dependent members of the royal family **2** : a rightful adjunct

ap·pa·ra·tus \ˌa-pə-'ra-təs, -'rä-\ *n, pl* **-tus·es** *or* **-tus** [L] **1** : a set of materials or equipment for a particular use **2** : a complex machine or device : MECHANISM **3** : the organization of a political party or underground movement

¹ap·par·el \ə-'par-əl\ *vb* **-eled** *or* **-elled; -el·ing** *or* **-el·ling** **1** : CLOTHE **2** : ADORN

²apparel *n* : CLOTHING, DRESS

ap·par·ent \ə-'par-ənt\ *adj* **1** : open to view : VISIBLE **2** : EVIDENT, OBVIOUS **3** : appearing as real or true : SEEMING

ap·par·ent·ly \-lē\ *adv* : it seems apparent

ap·pa·ri·tion \ˌa-pə-'ri-shən\ *n* : a supernatural appearance : GHOST

ap·peal \ə-'pēl\ *vb* **1** : to take steps to have (a case) reheard in a higher court **2** : to plead for help, corroboration, or decision **3** : to arouse a sympathetic response — **appeal** *n*

ap·pear \ə-'pir\ *vb* **1** : to become visible **2** : to come formally before an authority **3** : SEEM **4** : to become evident **5** : to come before the public

ap·pear·ance \ə-'pir-əns\ *n* **1** : outward aspect : LOOK **2** : the act of appearing **3** : PHENOMENON

ap·pease \ə-'pēz\ *vb* **ap·peased; ap·peas·ing** **1** : to cause to subside : ALLAY **2** : PACIFY, CONCILIATE; *esp* : to buy off by concessions — **ap·pease·ment** *n* — **ap·peas·able** \-'pē-zə-bəl\ *adj*

ap·pel·lant \ə-'pe-lənt\ *n* : one who appeals esp. from a judicial decision

ap·pel·late \ə-'pe-lət\ *adj* : having power to review decisions of a lower court

ap·pel·la·tion \ˌa-pə-'lā-shən\ *n* : NAME, DESIGNATION

ap·pel·lee \ˌa-pə-'lē\ *n* : one against whom an appeal is taken

ap·pend \ə-'pend\ *vb* : to attach esp. as something additional : AFFIX

ap·pend·age \ə-'pen-dij\ *n* **1** : something appended to a principal or greater thing **2** : a projecting part of the body (as an antenna) esp. when paired with one on each side **syn** accessory, adjunct, appendix, appurtenance

ap·pen·dec·to·my \ˌa-pən-'dek-tə-mē\ *n, pl* **-mies** : surgical removal of the intestinal appendix

ap·pen·di·ci·tis \ə-ˌpen-də-'sī-təs\ *n* : inflammation of the intestinal appendix

ap·pen·dix \ə-'pen-diks\ *n, pl* **-dix·es** *or* **-di·ces** \-də-ˌsēz\ [L] **1** : supplementary matter added at the end of a book **2** : a narrow blind tube usu. about three or four inches long that extends from the cecum in the lower right-hand part of the abdomen

ap·per·tain \ˌa-pər-'tān\ *vb* : to belong as a rightful part or privilege

ap·pe·tite \'a-pə-ˌtīt\ *n* [ME *apetit,* fr. MF, fr. L *appetitus,* fr. *appetere* to strive after, fr. *ad-* to + *petere* to go to] **1** : natural desire for satisfying some want or need esp. for food **2** : TASTE, PREFERENCE

ap·pe·tiz·er \'a-pə-ˌtī-zər\ *n* : a food or drink taken just before a meal to stimulate the appetite

ap·pe·tiz·ing \-ziŋ\ *adj* : tempting to the appetite — **ap·pe·tiz·ing·ly** *adv*

appl *abbr* applied

ap·plaud \ə-'plȯd\ *vb* : to show approval esp. by clapping

ap·plause \ə-'plȯz\ *n* : approval publicly expressed (as by clapping)

ap·ple \'a-pəl\ *n* : a rounded fruit with firm white flesh and a seedy core; *also* : a tree that bears this fruit

ap·ple·jack \-ˌjak\ *n* : a liquor distilled from fermented cider

ap·pli·ance \ə-'plī-əns\ *n* **1** : INSTRUMENT, DEVICE **2** : a piece of household equipment (as a stove or toaster) operated by gas or electricity

ap·pli·ca·ble \'a-pli-kə-bəl, ə-'pli-kə-\ *adj* : capable of being applied : RELEVANT — **ap·pli·ca·bil·i·ty** \ˌa-pli-kə-'bi-lə-tē, ə-ˌpli-kə-\ *n*

ap·pli·cant \'a-pli-kənt\ *n* : one who applies

ap·pli·ca·tion \ˌa-plə-'kā-shən\ *n* **1** : the act of applying **2** : assiduous attention **3** : REQUEST; *also* : a form used in making a request **4** : something placed or spread on a surface **5** : capacity for use

ap·pli·ca·tor \'a-plə-ˌkā-tər\ *n* : a device for applying a substance (as medicine or polish)

ap·plied \ə-'plīd\ *adj* : put to practical use ⟨~ art⟩

ap·pli·qué \ˌa-plə-'kā\ *n* [F] : a fabric decoration cut out and fastened to a larger piece of material — **ap·pliqué** *vb*

ap·ply \ə-'plī\ *vb* **ap·plied; ap·ply·ing** **1** : to put to practical use **2** : to place in contact : put or spread on a surface **3** : to employ with close attention **4** : to have reference or connection **5** : to submit a request

ap·point \ə-'pȯint\ *vb* **1** : to fix or set officially ⟨~ a day for trial⟩ **2** : to name officially **3** : to fit out : EQUIP

ap·point·ee \ə-ˌpȯin-'tē, ˌa-\ *n* : a person appointed

ap·point·ive \ə-'pȯin-tiv\ *adj* : subject to appointment

ap·point·ment \ə-'pȯint-mənt\ *n* **1** : the act of appointing **2** : an arrangement for a meeting **3** *pl* : FURNISHINGS, EQUIPMENT **4** : a nonelective office or position

ap·por·tion \ə-'pōr-shən\ *vb* : to distribute proportionately : ALLOT — **ap·por·tion·ment** *n*

ap·po·site \'a-pə-zət\ *adj* : APPROPRIATE, RELEVANT — **ap·po·site·ly** *adv* — **ap·po·site·ness** *n*

ap·po·si·tion \₁a-pə-'zi-shən\ *n* : a grammatical construction in which a noun or pronoun is followed by another that has the same referent (as *the poet* and *Burns* in "a biography of the poet Burns")

ap·pos·i·tive \ə-'pä-zə-tiv, a-\ *adj* : of, relating to, or standing in grammatical apposition — **appositive** *n*

ap·praise \ə-'prāz\ *vb* **ap·praised; ap·prais·ing** : to set a value on — **ap·prais·al** \-'prā-zəl\ *n* — **ap·prais·er** *n*

ap·pre·cia·ble \ə-'prē-shə-bəl\ *adj* : large enough to be recognized and measured — **ap·pre·cia·bly** *adv*

ap·pre·ci·ate \ə-'prē-shē-₁āt\ *vb* **-at·ed; -at·ing** 1 : to value justly 2 : to be aware of 3 : to be grateful for 4 : to increase in value — **ap·pre·ci·a·tion** \-₁prē-shē-'ā-shən\ *n*

ap·pre·cia·tive \ə-'prē-shə-tiv, -shē-₁āt-\ *adj* : having or showing appreciation — **ap·pre·cia·tive·ly** *adv*

ap·pre·hend \₁a-pri-'hend\ *vb* 1 : ARREST 2 : to become aware of 3 : to look forward to with dread 4 : UNDERSTAND — **ap·pre·hen·sion** \-'hen-chən\ *n*

ap·pre·hen·sive \-'hen-siv\ *adj* : viewing the future with anxiety — **ap·pre·hen·sive·ly** *adv* — **ap·pre·hen·sive·ness** *n*

¹ap·pren·tice \ə-'pren-təs\ *n* 1 : a person learning a craft under a skilled worker 2 : BEGINNER — **ap·pren·tice·ship** *n*

²apprentice *vb* **-ticed; -tic·ing** : to bind or set at work as an apprentice

ap·prise \ə-'prīz\ *vb* **ap·prised; ap·pris·ing** : INFORM

ap·proach \ə-'prōch\ *vb* 1 : to move nearer to 2 : to be almost the same as 3 : to make advances to esp. for the purpose of creating a desired result 4 : to take preliminary steps toward — **approach** *n* — **ap·proach·able** *adj*

ap·pro·ba·tion \₁a-prə-'bā-shən\ *n* : APPROVAL

¹ap·pro·pri·ate \ə-'prō-prē-₁āt\ *vb* **-at·ed; -at·ing** 1 : to take possession of 2 : to set apart for a particular use

²ap·pro·pri·ate \ə-'prō-prē-ət\ *adj* : fitted to a purpose or use : SUITABLE **syn** proper, fit, apt, befitting — **ap·pro·pri·ate·ly** *adv* — **ap·pro·pri·ate·ness** *n*

ap·pro·pri·a·tion \ə-₁prō-prē-'ā-shən\ *n* : something (as money) set aside by formal action for a specific use

ap·prov·al \ə-'prü-vəl\ *n* : an act of approving — **on approval** : subject to a prospective buyer's acceptance or refusal

ap·prove \ə-'prüv\ *vb* **ap·proved; ap·prov·ing** 1 : to have or express a favorable opinion of 2 : to accept as satisfactory : RATIFY

approx *abbr* approximate; approximately

¹ap·prox·i·mate \ə-'präk-sə-mət\ *adj* : nearly correct or exact — **ap·prox·i·mate·ly** *adv*

²ap·prox·i·mate \-₁māt\ *vb* **-mat·ed; -mat·ing** : to come near : APPROACH — **ap·prox·i·ma·tion** \ə-₁präk-sə-'mā-shən\ *n*

appt *abbr* appoint; appointed; appointment

ap·pur·te·nance \ə-'pərt-nəns, -ᵊn-əns\ *n* : something that belongs to or goes with another thing **syn** accessory, adjunct, appendage, appendix — **ap·pur·te·nant** \ə-'pərt-nənt, -ᵊn-ənt\ *adj*

Apr *abbr* April

APR *abbr* annual percentage rate

apri·cot \'a-prə-₁kät, 'ā-\ *n* [deriv. of Ar *al-birqûq*] : an oval orange-colored fruit resembling the related peach and plum in flavor; *also* : a tree bearing apricots

April \'ā-prəl\ *n* [ME, fr. OF & L; OF *avrill*, fr. L *Aprilis*] : the 4th month of the year having 30 days

a pri·o·ri \₁ä-prē-'ōr-ē\ *adj* [L, from the former] 1 : characterized by or derived by reasoning from self-evident propositions 2 : independent of experience — **a priori** *adv*

apron \'ā-prən\ *n* [ME, alter. (resulting fr. misdivision of *a napron*) of *napron*, fr. MF *naperon*, dim. of *nape* cloth, modif. of L *mappa* napkin] 1 : a garment tied over the front of the body to protect the clothes 2 : a paved area for parking or handling airplanes — **aproned** *adj*

¹ap·ro·pos \₁a-prə-'pō, 'a-prə-₁pō\ *adv* [F *à propos*, lit., to the purpose] 1 : OPPORTUNELY 2 : in passing : INCIDENTALLY

²apropos *adj* : being to the point

apropos of *prep* : with regard to

apse \'aps\ *n* : a projecting usu. semicircular and vaulted part of a building (as a church)

¹apt \'apt\ *adj* 1 : well adapted : SUITABLE 2 : having an habitual tendency : LIKELY 3 : quick to learn — **apt·ly** *adv* — **apt·ness** \'apt-nəs\ *n*

²apt *abbr* 1 apartment 2 aptitude

ap·ti·tude \'ap-tə-₁tüd, -₁tyüd\ *n* 1 : natural ability : TALENT 2 : capacity for learning 3 : APPROPRIATENESS

aqua \'a-kwə, 'ä-\ *n* : a light greenish blue color

aqua·cul·ture *also* **aqui·cul·ture** \'a-kwə-₁kəl-chər, 'ä-\ *n* : the cultivation of aquatic plants or animals (as fish or shellfish) for human use

aqua·ma·rine \₁a-kwə-mə-'rēn, ₁ä-\ *n* 1 : a bluish green gem 2 : a pale blue to light greenish blue

aqua·naut \'a-kwə-₁nòt, 'ä-\ *n* : a person who lives in an underwater shelter for an extended period

aqua·plane \-₁plān\ *n* : a board towed behind a motorboat and ridden by a person standing on it — **aquaplane** *vb*

aqua re·gia \₁a-kwə-'rē-j(ē-)ə\ *n* [NL, lit., royal water] : a mixture of nitric and hydrochloric acids that dissolves gold or platinum

aquar·i·um \ə-'kwar-ē-əm\ *n, pl* **-i·ums** *or* **-ia** \-ē-ə\ 1 : a container (as a glass tank) in which living aquatic animals or plants are kept 2 : a place where aquatic animals and plants are kept and shown

Aquar·i·us \ə-'kwar-ē-əs\ *n* [L, lit., water carrier] 1 : a zodiacal constellation between Capricorn and Pisces usu. pictured as a man pouring water 2 : the 11th sign of the zodiac in astrology; *also* : one born under this sign

¹aquat·ic \ə-'kwä-tik, -'kwa-\ *adj* 1 : growing or living in or frequenting water 2 : performed in or on water

²aquatic *n* : an aquatic animal or plant

aqua·vit \'ä-kwə-₁vēt\ *n* : a clear liquor flavored with caraway seeds

aqua vi·tae \₁a-kwə-'vī-tē, ₁ä-\ *n* [ME, fr. ML, lit., water of life] : a strong alcoholic liquor (as brandy)

aq·ue·duct \'a-kwə-₁dəkt\ *n* 1 : a conduit for carrying running water 2 : a structure carrying a canal over a river or hollow 3 : a passage in a bodily part

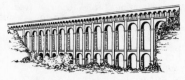

aqueduct 1

aque·ous \'ā-kwē-əs, 'a-\ *adj* 1 : WATERY 2 : made of, by, or with water

aqueous humor *n* : a clear fluid occupying the space between the lens and the cornea of the eye

aqui·fer \'a-kwə-fər, 'ä-\ *n* : a water-bearing stratum of permeable rock, sand, or gravel

aq·ui·line \'a-kwə-₁līn, -lən\ *adj* 1 : of or resembling an eagle 2 : hooked like an eagle's beak ⟨an ∼ nose⟩

ar *abbr* arrival; arrive

Ar *symbol* argon

AR *abbr* Arkansas

-ar *adj suffix* : of or relating to ⟨molecul*ar*⟩ : being ⟨spectacul*ar*⟩ : resembling ⟨oracul*ar*⟩

Ar·ab \'ar-əb\ *n* **1** : a member of a Semitic people of the Arabian peninsula in southwestern Asia **2** : a member of an Arabic-speaking people — **Arab** *adj* — **Ara·bi·an** \ə-'rā-bē-ən\ *adj or n*

ar·a·besque \ar-ə-'besk\ *n* : a design of interlacing lines forming figures of flowers, foliage, and sometimes animals — **arabesque** *adj*

¹Ar·a·bic \'ar-ə-bik\ *n* : a Semitic language of southwestern Asia and northern Africa

²Arabic *adj* **1** : of or relating to the Arabs, Arabic, or the Arabian peninsula in southwestern Asia **2** : expressed in or making use of Arabic numerals

Arabic numeral *n* : any of the number symbols 0, 1, 2, 3, 4, 5, 6, 7, 8, 9

ar·a·ble \'ar-ə-bəl\ *adj* : fit for or used for the growing of crops

arach·nid \ə-'rak-nəd\ *n* : any of a class of usu. 8-legged arthropods comprising the spiders, scorpions, mites, and ticks — **arachnid** *adj*

Ar·a·ma·ic \ar-ə-'mā-ik\ *n* : an ancient Semitic language

ar·a·mid \'ar-ə-məd, -mid\ *n* : any of several light but very strong heat-resistant synthetic materials used esp. in textiles and plastics

Arap·a·ho *or* **Arap·a·hoe** \ə-'ra-pə-hō\ *n, pl* **-ho** *or* **-hos** *or* **-hoe** *or* **-hoes** : a member of an American Indian people of the western U.S.

ar·bi·ter \'är-bə-tər\ *n* : one having power to decide : JUDGE

ar·bi·trage \'är-bə-träzh\ *n* [F, fr. MF, arbitration] : the purchase and sale of the same or equivalent securities in different markets in order to profit from price discrepancies

ar·bi·tra·geur \är-bə-(,)trä-'zhər\ *or* **ar·bi·trag·er** \'är-bə-trä-zhər\ *n* : one who practices arbitrage

ar·bit·ra·ment \är-'bi-trə-mənt\ *n* **1** : the act of deciding a dispute **2** : the judgment given by an arbitrator

ar·bi·trary \'är-bə-trer-ē\ *adj* **1** : AUTOCRATIC, DESPOTIC **2** : determined by will or caprice : selected at random — **ar·bi·trari·ly** \är-bə-'trer-ə-lē\ *adv* — **ar·bi·trari·ness** \'är-bə-trer-ē-nəs\ *n*

ar·bi·trate \'är-bə-trāt\ *vb* **-trat·ed; -trat·ing** **1** : to act as arbitrator **2** : to act on as arbitrator **3** : to submit for decision to an arbitrator — **ar·bi·tra·tion** \är-bə-'trā-shən\ *n*

ar·bi·tra·tor \'är-bə-trā-tər\ *n* : one chosen to settle differences between two parties in a controversy

ar·bor \'är-bər\ *n* [ME *erber* plot of grass, arbor, fr. OF *herbier* plot of grass, fr. *herbe* herb, grass] : a shelter formed of or covered with vines or branches

ar·bo·re·al \är-'bōr-ē-əl\ *adj* **1** : of, relating to, or resembling a tree **2** : living in trees ⟨~ monkeys⟩

ar·bo·re·tum \är-bə-'rē-təm\ *n, pl* **-retums** *or* **-re·ta** \-tə\ [L, plantation of trees, fr. *arbor* tree] : a place where trees and plants are grown for scientific and educational purposes

ar·bor·vi·tae \är-bər-'vī-tē\ *n* : any of various evergreen trees and shrubs with scalelike leaves that are related to the cypresses

ar·bour *chiefly Brit var of* ARBOR

ar·bu·tus \är-'byü-təs\ *n* : TRAILING ARBUTUS

¹arc \'ärk\ *n* **1** : a sustained luminous discharge of electricity (as between two electrodes) **2** : a continuous portion of a curved line (as part of the circumference of a circle)

²arc *vb* **arced** \'ärkt\; **arc·ing** \'är-kiŋ\ : to form an electric arc

ARC *abbr* **1** AIDS-related complex **2** American Red Cross

ar·cade \är-'kād\ *n* **1** : an arched or covered passageway; *esp* : one lined with shops **2** : a row of arches with their supporting columns

ar·cane \är-'kān\ *adj* : SECRET, MYSTERIOUS

¹arch \'ärch\ *n* **1** : a curved structure spanning an open-

ing (as a door) **2** : something resembling an arch **3** : ARCHWAY

²arch *vb* **1** : to cover with an arch **2** : to form or bend into an arch

³arch *adj* **1** : CHIEF, EMINENT **2** : ROGUISH, MISCHIEVOUS — **arch·ly** *adv* — **arch·ness** *n*

⁴arch *abbr* architect; architectural; architecture

ar·chae·ol·o·gy *or* **ar·che·ol·o·gy** \är-kē-'ä-lə-jē\ *n* : the study of past human life as revealed by relics left by ancient peoples — **ar·chae·o·log·i·cal** \-ə-'lä-ji-kəl\ *adj* — **ar·chae·ol·o·gist** \-'ä-lə-jist\ *n*

ar·cha·ic \är-'kā-ik\ *adj* **1** : having the characteristics of the language of the past and surviving chiefly in specialized uses ⟨~ words⟩ **2** : belonging to an earlier time : ANTIQUATED — **ar·cha·i·cal·ly** \-i-k(ə-)lē\ *adv*

arch·an·gel \'ärk-kān-jəl\ *n* : a chief angel

arch·bish·op \ärch-'bi-shəp\ *n* : a bishop of high rank

arch·bish·op·ric \-ə-(,)prik\ *n* : the jurisdiction or office of an archbishop

arch·con·ser·va·tive \(,)ärch-kən-'sər-və-tiv\ *n* : an extreme conservative — **archconservative** *adj*

arch·dea·con \-'dē-kən\ *n* : a church official who assists a diocesan bishop in ceremonial or administrative functions

arch·di·o·cese \-'dī-ə-səs, -sēz\ *n* : the diocese of an archbishop

arch·duke \-'dük, -'dyük\ *n* **1** : a sovereign prince **2** : a prince of the imperial family of Austria

Ar·che·an \är-'kē-ən\ *adj* : of, relating to, or being the earliest eon of geologic history — **Archean** *n*

arch·en·e·my \ärch-'e-nə-mē\ *n, pl* **-mies** : a principal enemy

Ar·cheo·zo·ic \är-kē-ə-'zō-ik\ *adj* : ARCHEAN — **Archeozoic** *n*

ar·chery \'är-chə-rē\ *n* : the art or practice of shooting with bow and arrows — **ar·cher** \'är-chər\ *n*

ar·che·type \'är-ki-tīp\ *n* : the original pattern or model of all things of the same type

arch·fiend \ärch-'fēnd\ *n* : a chief fiend; *esp* : SATAN

ar·chi·epis·co·pal \är-kē-ə-'pis-kə-pəl\ *adj* : of or relating to an archbishop

ar·chi·man·drite \är-kə-'man-drīt\ *n* : a dignitary in an Eastern church ranking below a bishop

ar·chi·pel·a·go \är-kə-'pe-lə-gō, är-chə-\ *n, pl* **-goes** *or* **-gos** : a group of islands

ar·chi·tect \'är-kə-tekt\ *n* **1** : a person who plans buildings and oversees their construction **2** : a person who designs and guides a plan or undertaking

ar·chi·tec·ture \'är-kə-tek-chər\ *n* **1** : the art or science of planning and building structures **2** : a method or style of building **3** : the manner in which the elements (as of a design) are arranged or organized — **ar·chi·tec·tur·al** \är-kə-'tek-chə-rəl, -'tek-shrəl\ *adj* — **ar·chi·tec·tur·al·ly** *adv*

ar·chi·trave \'är-kə-trāv\ *n* : the supporting horizontal member just above the columns in a building in the classical style of architecture

ar·chive \'är-kīv\ *n* : a place for keeping public records; *also* : public records — often used in pl.

ar·chi·vist \'är-kə-vist, -kī-\ *n* : a person in charge of archives

ar·chon \'är-kän, -kən\ *n* : a chief magistrate of ancient Athens

arch·way \'ärch-wā\ *n* : a passageway under an arch; *also* : an arch over a passage

arc lamp *n* : a gas-filled electric lamp that produces light when a current arcs between incandescent electrodes

¹arc·tic \'ärk-tik, 'är-tik\ *adj* [ME *artik*, fr. L *arcticus*, fr. Gk *arktikos*, fr. *arktos* bear, Ursa Major, north] **1** *often cap* : of or relating to the north pole or the region near it **2** : FRIGID

²arc·tic \'är-tik, 'ärk-tik\ *n* : a rubber overshoe that reaches to the ankle or above

arctic circle *n, often cap A&C* : the parallel of latitude that is approximately 66½ degrees north of the equator

-ard also **-art** n suffix : one that is characterized by performing some action, possessing some quality, or being associated with some thing esp. conspicuously or excessively ⟨brag*art*⟩ ⟨dull*ard*⟩

ar·dent \'är-dᵊnt\ adj **1** : characterized by warmth of feeling : PASSIONATE **2** : FIERY, HOT **3** : GLOWING — **ar·dent·ly** adv

ar·dor \'är-dər\ n **1** : warmth of feeling : ZEAL **2** : sexual excitement

ar·dour chiefly Brit var of ARDOR

ar·du·ous \'är-jə-wəs, -dyü-wəs\ adj : DIFFICULT, LABORIOUS — **ar·du·ous·ly** adv — **ar·du·ous·ness** n

¹**are** pres 2d sing or pres pl of BE

²**are** \'ar\ n — see METRIC SYSTEM table

ar·ea \'ar-ē-ə\ n **1** : a flat surface or space **2** : the amount of surface included (as within the lines of a geometric figure) **3** : range or extent of some thing or concept **4** : REGION

area code n : a 3-digit number that identifies each telephone service area in a country (as the U.S. or Canada)

are·na \ə-'rē-nə\ n [L harena, arena sand, sandy place] **1** : an enclosed area used for public entertainment **2** : a sphere of activity or competition

Ar·gen·tine \'är-jən-ˌtēn, -ˌtīn\ or **Ar·gen·tin·ean** or **Ar·gen·tin·i·an** \ˌär-jən-'ti-nē-ən\ n : a native or inhabitant of Argentina — **Argentine** or **Argentinean** or **Argentinian** adj

ar·gen·tite \'är-jən-ˌtīt\ n : a dark gray mineral that is an important ore of silver

ar·gon \'är-ˌgän\ n [Gk, neut. of argos idle, lazy, fr. a- not + ergon work; fr. its relative inertness] : a colorless odorless gaseous chemical element found in the air and used for filling electric lamps — see ELEMENT table

ar·go·sy \'är-gə-sē\ n, pl **-sies 1** : a large merchant ship **2** : FLEET

ar·got \'är-gət, -ˌgō\ n : the language of a particular group or class

ar·gu·able \'är-gyü-ə-bəl\ adj : open to argument, dispute, or question

ar·gu·ably \'är-gyü-(ə-)blē\ adv : it can be argued

ar·gue \'är-gyü\ vb **ar·gued; ar·gu·ing 1** : to give reasons for or against something **2** : to contend in words : DISPUTE **3** : DEBATE **4** : to persuade by giving reasons

ar·gu·ment \'är-gyə-mənt\ n **1** : a reason offered in proof **2** : discourse intended to persuade **3** : QUARREL

ar·gu·men·ta·tion \ˌär-gyə-mən-'tā-shən\ n : the art of formal discussion

ar·gu·men·ta·tive \ˌär-gyə-'men-tə-tiv\ adj : inclined to argue

ar·gyle also **ar·gyll** \'är-ˌgīl\ n, often cap : a geometric knitting pattern of varicolored diamonds on a single background color; also : a sock knit in this pattern

aria \'är-ē-ə\ n : an accompanied elaborate vocal solo forming part of a larger work

ar·id \'ar-əd\ adj : very dry; esp : having insufficient rainfall to support agriculture — **arid·i·ty** \ə-'ri-də-tē\ n

Ar·ies \'ar-ˌēz, -ē-ˌēz\ n [L, lit., ram] **1** : a zodiacal constellation between Pisces and Taurus pictured as a ram **2** : the 1st sign of the zodiac in astrology; also : one born under this sign

aright \ə-'rīt\ adv : RIGHT, CORRECTLY

arise \ə-'rīz\ vb **arose** \-'rōz\; **aris·en** \-'riz-ᵊn\; **aris·ing** \-'rī-ziŋ\ **1** : to get up **2** : ORIGINATE **3** : ASCEND syn rise, derive, spring, issue

ar·is·toc·ra·cy \ˌar-ə-'stä-krə-sē\ n, pl **-cies 1** : government by a noble or privileged class; also : a state so governed **2** : the governing class of an aristocracy **3** : UPPER CLASS — **aris·to·crat** \ə-'ris-tə-ˌkrat\ n — **aris·to·crat·ic** \ə-ˌris-tə-'kra-tik\ adj

arith abbr arithmetic; arithmetical

arith·me·tic \ə-'rith-mə-ˌtik\ n **1** : a branch of mathematics that deals with computations usu. with nonnegative real numbers **2** : COMPUTATION, CALCULATION — **ar·ith·met·ic** \ˌar-ith-'me-tik\ or **ar·ith·met·i·cal** \-ti-kəl\ adj — **ar·ith·met·i·cal·ly** \-ti-k(ə-)lē\ adv — **arith·me·ti·cian** \ə-ˌrith-mə-'ti-shən\ n

arithmetic mean n : the sum of a set of numbers divided by the number of numbers in the set

Ariz abbr Arizona

ark \'ärk\ n **1** : a boat held to resemble that of Noah's at the time of the Flood **2** : the sacred chest in a synagogue representing to Hebrews the presence of God; also : the repository for the scrolls of the Torah

Ark abbr Arkansas

¹**arm** \'ärm\ n **1** : a human upper limb; also : a corresponding limb of a lower animal with a backbone **2** : something resembling an arm in shape or position ⟨an ∼ of a chair⟩ **3** : POWER, MIGHT ⟨the ∼ of the law⟩ — **armed** \'ärmd\ adj — **arm·less** adj

²**arm** vb : to furnish with weapons

³**arm** n **1** : WEAPON **2** : a branch of the military forces **3** pl : the hereditary heraldic devices of a family

ar·ma·da \är-'mä-də, -'mā-\ n : a fleet of warships

ar·ma·dil·lo \ˌär-mə-'di-lō\ n, pl **-los** : any of several small burrowing mammals with the head and body protected by an armor of bony plates

armadillo

Ar·ma·ged·don \ˌär-mə-'ged-ᵊn\ n : a final conclusive battle between the forces of good and evil; also : the site or time of this

ar·ma·ment \'är-mə-mənt\ n **1** : military strength **2** : arms and equipment (as of a tank or combat unit) **3** : the process of preparing for war

ar·ma·ture \'är-mə-ˌchur, -chər\ n **1** : a protective covering or structure (as the spines of a cactus) **2** : the rotating part of an electric generator or motor; also : the movable part in an electromagnetic device (as a loudspeaker)

arm·chair \'ärm-ˌcher\ n : a chair with armrests

armed forces n pl : the combined military, naval, and air forces of a nation

Ar·me·nian \är-'mē-nē-ən\ n : a native or inhabitant of Armenia

arm·ful \'ärm-ˌful\ n, pl **armfuls** or **arms·ful** \'ärmz-ˌful\ : as much as the arm or arms can hold

arm·hole \'ärm-ˌhōl\ n : an opening for the arm in a garment

ar·mi·stice \'är-mə-stəs\ n : temporary suspension of hostilities by mutual agreement : TRUCE

arm·let \'ärm-lət\ n : a band worn around the upper arm

ar·mor \'är-mər\ n **1** : protective covering **2** : armored forces and vehicles — **ar·mored** \-mərd\ adj

ar·mor·er \'är-mər-ər\ n **1** : a person who makes arms and armor **2** : a person who services firearms

ar·mo·ri·al \är-'mōr-ē-əl\ adj : of or bearing heraldic arms

ar·mory \'är-mə-rē\ n, pl **ar·mor·ies 1** : a place where arms are stored **2** : a factory where arms are made

ar·mour, ar·moury chiefly Brit var of ARMOR, ARMORY

arm·pit \'ärm-ˌpit\ n : the hollow under the junction of the arm and shoulder

arm·rest \-ˌrest\ n : a support for the arm

ar·my \'är-mē\ n, pl **armies 1** : a body of men organized for war **2** *often cap* : the complete military organization of a country for land warfare **3** : a great number **4** : a body of persons organized to advance a cause

army ant *n* : any of various nomadic social ants

ar·my·worm \\'är-mē-¦wərm\ *n* : any of numerous moths whose larvae move about destroying crops

aro·ma \ə-'rō-mə\ *n* : a usu. pleasing odor : FRA-GRANCE — **ar·o·mat·ic** \¦ar-ə-'ma-tik\ *adj*

aro·ma·ther·a·py \ə-¦rō-mə-¦ther-ə-pē\ *n* : massage with a preparation of fragrant oils extracted from herbs, flowers, and fruits

arose *past of* ARISE

¹around \ə-'raund\ *adv* **1** : in a circle or in circumference ⟨a tree five feet ∼⟩ **2** : in or along a circuit ⟨the road goes ∼ by the lake⟩ **3** : on all sides ⟨nothing for miles ∼⟩ **4** : NEARBY ⟨wait ∼ awhile⟩ **5** : from one place to another ⟨travels ∼ on business⟩ **6** : in an opposite direction ⟨turn ∼⟩

²around *prep* **1** : SURROUNDING ⟨trees ∼ the house⟩ **2** : to or on another side of ⟨∼ the corner⟩ **3** : NEAR ⟨stayed right ∼ home⟩ **4** : along the circuit of ⟨go ∼ the world⟩

arouse \ə-'rauz\ *vb* **aroused; arous·ing 1** : to awaken from sleep **2** : to stir up — **arous·al** \-'rau-zəl\ *n*

ar·peg·gio \är-'pe-jē-¦ō, -'pe-jō\ *n, pl* **-gios** [It fr. *ar-peggiare* to play on the harp, fr. *arpa* harp] : a chord whose notes are performed in succession and not simultaneously

arr *abbr* **1** arranged **2** arrival; arrive

ar·raign \ə-'rān\ *vb* **1** : to call before a court to answer to an indictment **2** : to accuse of wrong or imperfection — **ar·raign·ment** *n*

ar·range \ə-'rānj\ *vb* **ar·ranged; ar·rang·ing 1** : to put in order **2** : to adapt (a musical composition) to voices or instruments other than those for which it was orig. written **3** : to come to an agreement about : SETTLE — **ar·range·ment** *n* — **ar·rang·er** *n*

ar·rant \'ar-ənt\ *adj* : being notoriously without moderation : EXTREME

ar·ras \'ar-əs\ *n, pl* **arras 1** : TAPESTRY **2** : a wall hanging or screen of tapestry

¹ar·ray \ə-'rā\ *vb* **1** : to dress esp. splendidly **2** : to arrange in order

²array *n* **1** : a regular arrangement **2** : rich apparel **3** : an imposing group

ar·rears \ə-'rirz\ *n pl* **1** : a state of being behind in the discharge of obligations ⟨in ∼ with the rent⟩ **2** : overdue debts

¹ar·rest \ə-'rest\ *vb* **1** : STOP, CHECK **2** : to take into legal custody

²arrest *n* **1** : the act of stopping; *also* : the state of being stopped **2** : the taking into custody by legal authority

ar·riv·al \ə-'rī-vəl\ *n* **1** : the act of arriving **2** : one that arrives

ar·rive \ə-'rīv\ *vb* **ar·rived; ar·riv·ing 1** : to reach a destination **2** : to make an appearance ⟨the guests have *arrived*⟩ **3** : to attain success

ar·ro·gant \'ar-ə-gənt\ *adj* : offensively exaggerating one's own importance — **ar·ro·gance** \-gəns\ *n* — **ar·ro·gant·ly** *adv*

ar·ro·gate \-¦gāt\ *vb* **-gat·ed; -gat·ing** : to claim or seize without justification as one's right — **ar·ro·ga·tion** \¦ar-ə-'gā-shən\ *n*

ar·row \'ar-ō\ *n* **1** : a missile shot from a bow and usu. having a slender shaft, a pointed head, and feathers at the butt **2** : a pointed mark used to indicate direction

ar·row·head \'ar-ō-¦hed\ *n* : the pointed end of an arrow

ar·row·root \-¦rüt, -¦rut\ *n* : an edible starch from the roots of any of several tropical American plants; *also* : a plant yielding arrowroot

ar·royo \ə-'rȯi-ə, -ō\ *n, pl* **-royos** [Sp] **1** : a watercourse in a dry region **2** : a water-carved gully or channel

ar·se·nal \'ärs-nəl, 'ärs-²n-əl\ *n* [ultim. fr. Ar *dārṣinā'ah* house of manufacture] **1** : a place for making and storing arms and military equipment **2** : STORE, REPERTORY

ar·se·nic \'ärs-nik, 'ärs-²n-ik\ *n* **1** : a solid brittle poisonous chemical element of grayish metallic luster — see ELEMENT table **2** : a very poisonous oxygen compound of arsenic used in making insecticides

ar·son \'ärs-²n\ *n* : the willful or malicious burning of property — **ar·son·ist** \-ist\ *n*

¹art \'ärt\ *n* **1** : skill acquired by experience or study **2** : a branch of learning; *esp* : one of the humanities **3** : an occupation requiring knowledge or skill **4** : the use of skill and imagination in the production of things of beauty; *also* : works so produced **5** : ART-FULNESS

²art *abbr* **1** article **2** artificial **3** artillery

-art — see -ARD

ar·te·fact *chiefly Brit var of* ARTIFACT

ar·te·ri·al \är-'tir-ē-əl\ *adj* **1** : of or relating to an artery; *also* : relating to or being the oxygenated blood found in most arteries **2** : of, relating to, or being a route for through traffic

ar·te·ri·ole \är-'tir-ē-¦ōl\ *n* : one of the small terminal branches of an artery that ends in capillaries — **ar·te·ri·o·lar** \-¦tir-ē-'ō-lər\ *adj*

ar·te·rio·scle·ro·sis \är-¦tir-ē-ō-sklə-'rō-səs\ *n* : a chronic disease in which arterial walls are abnormally thickened and hardened — **ar·te·rio·scle·rot·ic** \-'rä-tik\ *adj or n*

ar·tery \'är-tə-rē\ *n, pl* **-ter·ies 1** : one of the tubular vessels that carry blood from the heart **2** : a main channel of transportation or communication

ar·te·sian well \är-'tē-zhən-\ *n* : a well from which the water flows to the surface by natural pressure; *also* : a deep well

art·ful \'ärt-fəl\ *adj* **1** : INGENIOUS **2** : CRAFTY — **art·ful·ly** *adv* — **art·ful·ness** *n*

ar·thri·tis \är-'thrī-təs\ *n, pl* **-thri·ti·des** \-'thri-tə-¦dēz\ : inflammation of the joints — **ar·thrit·ic** \-'thri-tik\ *adj or n*

ar·thro·pod \'är-thrə-¦päd\ *n* : any of a phylum of invertebrate animals comprising those (as insects, spiders, or crabs) with segmented bodies and jointed limbs — **arthropod** *adj*

ar·thros·co·py \är-'thräs-kə-pē\ *n, pl* **-pies** : visual examination of the interior of a joint (as the knee) with a special surgical instrument; *also* : joint surgery using arthroscopy — **ar·thro·scope** \'är-thrə-¦skōp\ *n* — **ar·thro·scop·ic** \¦är-thrə-'skä-pik\ *adj*

ar·ti·choke \'är-tə-¦chōk\ *n* [It dial. *articiocco*, ultim. fr. Ar *al-khurshūf*] : a tall herb related to the daisies; *also* : its edible flower head

artichoke

ar·ti·cle \'är-ti-kəl\ *n* [ME, fr. OF, fr. L *articulus* joint, division, dim. of *artus* joint, limb] **1** : a distinct part of a written document **2** : a nonfictional prose composition forming an independent part of a publication **3** : a word (as *an, the*) used with a noun to limit or give definiteness to its application **4** : a member of a class of things; *esp* : COMMODITY

ar·tic·u·lar \är-¹ti-kyə-lər\ *adj* : of or relating to a joint

¹ar·tic·u·late \är-¹ti-kyə-lət\ *adj* **1** : divided into meaningful parts : INTELLIGIBLE **2** : able to speak; *also* : expressing oneself readily and effectively **3** : JOINTED — **ar·tic·u·late·ly** *adv* — **ar·tic·u·late·ness** *n*

²ar·tic·u·late \-ˌlāt\ *vb* **-lat·ed; -lat·ing** **1** : to utter distinctly **2** : to unite by or as if by joints — **ar·tic·u·la·tion** \-ˌti-kyə-¹lā-shən\ *n*

ar·ti·fact \¹är-tə-ˌfakt\ *n* : something made or modified by humans usu. for a purpose; *esp* : an object remaining from another time or culture ⟨prehistoric ∼s⟩

ar·ti·fice \¹är-tə-fəs\ *n* **1** : TRICK; *also* : TRICKERY **2** : an ingenious device; *also* : INGENUITY

ar·ti·fi·cer \är-¹ti-fə-sər, ¹är-tə-fə-sər\ *n* : a skilled worker

ar·ti·fi·cial \ˌär-tə-¹fi-shəl\ *adj* **1** : produced by art rather than nature; *also* : made by humans to imitate nature **2** : not genuine : FEIGNED — **ar·ti·fi·ci·al·i·ty** \-ˌfi-shē-¹a-lə-tē\ *n* — **ar·ti·fi·cial·ly** *adv* — **ar·ti·fi·cial·ness** *n*

artificial insemination *n* : introduction of semen into the uterus or oviduct by other than natural means

artificial intelligence *n* : the capability of a machine to imitate intelligent human behavior

artificial respiration *n* : the rhythmic forcing of air into and out of the lungs of a person whose breathing has stopped

ar·til·lery \är-¹ti-lə-rē\ *n, pl* **-ler·ies** **1** : crew-served mounted firearms (as guns) **2** : a branch of the army armed with artillery — **ar·til·ler·ist** \-rist\ *n*

ar·ti·san \¹är-tə-zən, -sən\ *n* : a skilled manual worker

art·ist \¹är-tist\ *n* **1** : one who practices an art; *esp* : one who creates objects of beauty **2** : ARTISTE

ar·tiste \är-¹tēst\ *n* : a skilled public performer

ar·tis·tic \är-¹tis-tik\ *adj* : showing taste and skill — **ar·tis·ti·cal·ly** \-ti-k(ə-)lē\ *adv*

art·ist·ry \¹är-tə-strē\ *n* : artistic quality or ability

art·less \¹ärt-ləs\ *adj* **1** : lacking art or skill **2** : free from artificiality : NATURAL **3** : free from guile : SINCERE — **art·less·ly** *adv* — **art·less·ness** *n*

art nou·veau \ˌär-nü-¹vō, ˌärt-\ *n, often cap A&N* [F, lit., new art] : a late 19th century design style characterized by sinuous lines and leaf-shaped forms

arty \¹är-tē\ *adj* **art·i·er; -est** : showily or pretentiously artistic — **art·i·ly** \¹ärt-ᵊl-ē\ *adv* — **art·i·ness** *n*

ar·um \¹ar-əm\ *n* : any of a family of plants (as the jack-in-the-pulpit or a skunk cabbage) with flowers in a fleshy enclosed spike

ARV *abbr* American Revised Version

¹-ary *n suffix* : thing or person belonging to or connected with ⟨function*ary*⟩

²-ary *adj suffix* : of, relating to, or connected with ⟨budget*ary*⟩

Ary·an \¹ar-ē-ən, ¹er-; ¹är-yən\ *adj* **1** : INDO-EUROPEAN **2** : NORDIC — **Aryan** *n*

¹as \əz, (ˌ)az\ *adv* **1** : to the same degree or amount : EQUALLY ⟨∼ green as grass⟩ **2** : for instance ⟨various trees, ∼ oak or pine⟩ **3** : when considered in a specified relation ⟨my opinion ∼ distinguished from his⟩

²as *conj* **1** : in the same amount or degree in which ⟨green ∼ grass⟩ **2** : in the same way that ⟨farmed ∼ his father before him had farmed⟩ **3** : WHILE, WHEN ⟨spoke to me ∼ I was leaving⟩ **4** : THOUGH ⟨improbable ∼ it seems⟩ **5** : SINCE, BECAUSE ⟨∼ I'm not wanted, I'll go⟩ **6** : that the result is ⟨so guilty ∼ to leave no doubt⟩

³as *pron* **1** : THAT — used after *same* or *such* ⟨it's the same price ∼ before⟩ **2** : a fact that ⟨he's rich, ∼ you know⟩

⁴as *prep* : in the capacity or character of ⟨this will serve ∼ a substitute⟩

As *symbol* arsenic

AS *abbr* **1** American Samoa **2** Anglo-Saxon **3** associate in science

asa·fet·i·da *or* **asa·foe·ti·da** \ˌa-sə-¹fi-tə-dē, -¹fe-tə-də\ *n* : an ill-smelling plant gum formerly used in medicine

ASAP *abbr* as soon as possible

as·bes·tos \as-¹bes-təs, az-\ *n* : a noncombustible grayish mineral that occurs in fibrous form and has been used as a fireproof material

as·cend \ə-¹send\ *vb* **1** : to move upward : MOUNT, CLIMB **2** : to succeed to : OCCUPY ⟨he ∼ed the throne⟩

as·cen·dan·cy *also* **as·cen·den·cy** \ə-¹sen-dən-sē\ *n* : controlling influence : DOMINATION

¹as·cen·dant *also* **as·cen·dent** \ə-¹sen-dənt\ *n* : a dominant position

²ascendant *also* **ascendent** *adj* **1** : moving upward **2** : DOMINANT

as·cen·sion \ə-¹sen-chən\ *n* : the act or process of ascending

Ascension Day *n* : the Thursday 40 days after Easter observed in commemoration of Christ's ascension into heaven

as·cent \ə-¹sent\ *n* **1** : the act of mounting upward : CLIMB **2** : degree of upward slope

as·cer·tain \ˌas-ər-¹tān\ *vb* : to learn with certainty — **as·cer·tain·able** *adj*

as·cet·ic \ə-¹se-tik\ *adj* : practicing self-denial esp. for spiritual reasons : AUSTERE — **ascetic** *n* — **as·cet·i·cism** \-¹se-tə-ˌsi-zəm\ *n*

ASCII \¹as-kē\ *n* [*A*merican *S*tandard *C*ode for *I*nformation *I*nterchange] : a computer code for representing alphanumeric information

ascor·bic acid \ə-¹skór-bik-\ *n* : VITAMIN C

as·cot \¹as-kət, -ˌkät\ *n* [*Ascot* Heath, racetrack near Ascot, England] : a broad neck scarf that is looped under the chin

as·cribe \ə-¹skrīb\ *vb* **as·cribed; as·crib·ing** : to refer to a supposed cause, source, or author : ATTRIBUTE — **as·crib·able** *adj* — **as·crip·tion** \-¹skrip-shən\ *n*

asep·tic \ā-¹sep-tik\ *adj* : free or freed from disease-causing germs

asex·u·al \ā-¹sek-shə-wəl\ *adj* **1** : lacking sex or functional sex organs **2** : occurring or formed without the production and union of two kinds of germ cells ⟨∼ reproduction⟩ — **asex·u·al·ly** *adv*

as for *prep* : with regard to : CONCERNING ⟨*as for* the others, they were late⟩

¹ash \¹ash\ *n* **1** : any of a genus of trees related to the olive and having winged seeds and bark with grooves and ridges **2** : the tough elastic wood of an ash

²ash *n* **1** : the solid matter left when material is burned **2** : fine mineral particles from a volcano **3** *pl* : the remains of the dead human body after cremation or disintegration

ashamed \ə-¹shāmd\ *adj* **1** : feeling shame **2** : restrained by anticipation of shame ⟨∼ to say anything⟩ — **asham·ed·ly** \-¹shā-məd-lē\ *adv*

ash·en \¹a-shən\ *adj* : resembling ashes (as in color); *esp* : deadly pale

ash·lar \¹ash-lər\ *n* : hewn or squared stone; *also* : masonry of such stone

ashore \ə-¹shōr\ *adv* : on or to the shore

as how *conj* : THAT ⟨allowed *as how* she was glad to be here⟩

ash·ram \¹äsh-rəm\ *n* : a religious retreat esp. of a Hindu sage

ash·tray \¹ash-ˌtrā\ *n* : a receptacle for tobacco ashes

Ash Wednesday *n* : the 1st day of Lent

ashy \¹a-shē\ *adj* **ash·i·er; -est** : ASHEN

Asian \¹ā-zhən\ *adj* : of, relating to, or characteristic of the continent of Asia or its people — **Asian** *n*

Asi·at·ic \ˌā-zhē-¹a-tik\ *adj* : ASIAN — sometimes taken to be offensive — **Asiatic** *n*

¹aside \ə-¹sīd\ *adv* **1** : to or toward the side **2** : out of the way : AWAY

²**aside** *n* : an actor's words heard by the audience but supposedly not by other characters on stage

aside from *prep* **1** : BESIDES ⟨*aside from* being pretty, she's intelligent⟩ **2** : with the exception of ⟨*aside from* one D his grades are excellent⟩

as if *conj* **1** : as it would be if ⟨it's *as if* nothing had changed⟩ **2** : as one would if ⟨he acts *as if* he'd never been away⟩ **3** : THAT ⟨it seems *as if* nothing ever happens around here⟩

as•i•nine \'as-ə-ˌnīn\ *adj* [L *asininus,* fr. *asinus* ass] : STUPID, FOOLISH — **as•i•nin•i•ty** \ˌa-sə-'ni-nə-tē\ *n*

ask \'ask\ *vb* **asked** \'askt\ **ask•ing** **1** : to call on for an answer **2** : UTTER ⟨∼ a question⟩ **3** : to make a request of ⟨∼ him for help⟩ **4** : to make a request for ⟨∼ help of her⟩ **5** : to set as a price ⟨∼ed $800 for the car⟩ **6** : INVITE

askance \ə-'skans\ *adv* **1** : with a side glance **2** : with distrust

askew \ə-'skyü\ *adv or adj* : out of line : AWRY

ASL *abbr* American Sign Language

¹**aslant** \ə-'slant\ *adv or adj* : in a slanting direction

²**aslant** *prep* : over or across in a slanting direction

asleep \ə-'slēp\ *adv or adj* **1** : in or into a state of sleep **2** : DEAD **3** : NUMB **4** : INACTIVE

as long as *conj* **1** : provided that ⟨do as you like *as long as* you get home on time⟩ **2** : INASMUCH AS, SINCE ⟨*as long as* you're up, turn on the light⟩

aso•cial \(ˌ)ā-'sō-shəl\ *adj* : ANTISOCIAL

as of *prep* : AT, DURING, FROM, ON ⟨takes effect *as of* July 1⟩

asp \'asp\ *n* : a small poisonous African snake

as•par•a•gus \ə-'spar-ə-gəs\ *n* : a tall branching perennial herb related to the lilies; *also* : its edible young stalks

as•par•tame \as-'pär-ˌtām\ *n* : a crystalline low-calorie sweetener

ASPCA *abbr* American Society for the Prevention of Cruelty to Animals

as•pect \'as-ˌpekt\ *n* **1** : a position facing a particular direction **2** : APPEARANCE, LOOK **3** : PHASE

as•pen \'as-pən\ *n* : any of several poplars with leaves that flutter in the slightest breeze

as per \'az-ˌpər\ *prep* : in accordance with ⟨*as per* instructions⟩

as•per•i•ty \a-'sper-ə-tē\ *n, pl* **-ties 1** : ROUGHNESS **2** : harshness of temper

as•per•sion \ə-'spər-zhən\ *n* : a slanderous or defamatory remark

as•phalt \'as-ˌfȯlt\ *also* **as•phal•tum** \as-'fȯl-təm\ *n* : a dark substance found in natural beds or obtained as a residue in petroleum refining and used esp. in paving streets

asphalt jungle *n* : a big city or a specified part of a big city

as•pho•del \'as-fə-ˌdel\ *n* : any of several Old World herbs related to the lilies and bearing flowers in long erect spikes

as•phyx•ia \as-'fik-sē-ə\ *n* : a lack of oxygen or excess of carbon dioxide in the body usu. caused by interruption of breathing and causing unconsciousness

as•phyx•i•ate \-sē-ˌāt\ *vb* **-at•ed; -at•ing** : SUFFOCATE — **as•phyx•i•a•tion** \-ˌfik-sē-'ā-shən\ *n*

as•pic \'as-pik\ *n* [F, lit., asp] : a savory meat jelly

as•pi•rant \'as-pə-rənt, ə-'spī-rənt\ *n* : one who aspires **syn** candidate, applicant, seeker

¹**as•pi•rate** \'as-pə-rət\ *n* **1** : an independent sound \h\ or a character (as the letter *h*) representing it **2** : a consonant having aspiration as its final component

²**as•pi•rate** \'as-pə-ˌrāt\ *vb* **-rat•ed; -rat•ing** : to draw, remove, or take up or into by suction

as•pi•ra•tion \ˌas-pə-'rā-shən\ *n* **1** : the pronunciation or addition of an aspirate; *also* : the aspirate or its symbol **2** : a drawing of something in, out, up, or through by or as if by suction **3** : a strong desire to achieve something noble; *also* : an object of this desire

as•pire \ə-'spīr\ *vb* **as•pired; as•pir•ing 1** : to seek to attain or accomplish a particular goal **2** : to rise aloft

as•pi•rin \'as-pə-rən\ *n, pl* **aspirin** *or* **aspirins 1** : a white crystalline drug used to relieve pain and fever **2** : a tablet of aspirin

as regards *also* **as respects** *prep* : in regard to : with respect to

ass \'as\ *n* **1** : any of several long-eared mammals smaller than the related horses; *esp* : one of Africa ancestral to the donkey **2** : a stupid person

as•sail \ə-'sāl\ *vb* : to attack violently — **as•sail•able** *adj* — **as•sail•ant** *n*

as•sas•sin \ə-'sas-ən\ *n* [ML *assassinus,* fr. Ar *ḥashshāshīn,* pl. of *ḥashshāsh* hashish-user, fr. *ḥashīsh* hashish] : a murderer esp. for hire or fanatical reasons

as•sas•si•nate \ə-'sas-ən-ˌāt\ *vb* **-nat•ed; -nat•ing** : to murder by sudden or secret attack — **as•sas•si•na•tion** \-ˌsas-ən-'ā-shən\ *n*

as•sault \ə-'sȯlt\ *n* **1** : a violent attack **2** : an unlawful attempt or threat to do harm to another — **assault** *vb*

assault rifle *n* : a military automatic rifle with a large-capacity magazine

¹**as•say** \'a-ˌsā, a-'sā\ *n* : analysis to determine the quantity of one or more components present in a sample (as of an ore or drug)

²**as•say** \a-'sā, 'a-ˌsā\ *vb* **1** : TRY, ATTEMPT **2** : to subject (as an ore or drug) to an assay **3** : JUDGE 3

as•sem•blage \ə-'sem-blij, *3 & 4 also* ˌas-äm-'bläzh\ *n* **1** : a collection of persons or things : GATHERING **2** : the act of assembling **3** : an artistic composition made from scraps, junk, and odds and ends **4** : the art of making assemblages

as•sem•ble \ə-'sem-bəl\ *vb* **-bled; -bling 1** : to collect into one place : CONGREGATE **2** : to fit together the parts of **3** : to meet together : CONVENE

as•sem•bly \ə-'sem-blē\ *n, pl* **-blies 1** : a gathering of persons : MEETING **2** *cap* : a legislative body; *esp* : the lower house of a legislature **3** : a signal for troops to assemble **4** : the fitting together of parts (as of a machine)

assembly language *n* : a computer language consisting of mnemonic codes corresponding to machine-language instructions

assembly line *n* : an arrangement of machines, equipment, and workers in which work passes from operation to operation in a direct line

as•sem•bly•man \ə-'sem-blē-mən\ *n* : a member of a legislative assembly

as•sem•bly•wom•an \-ˌwù-mən\ *n* : a woman who is a member of an assembly

as•sent \ə-'sent\ *vb* : AGREE, CONCUR — **assent** *n*

as•sert \ə-'sərt\ *vb* **1** : to state positively **2** : to demonstrate the existence of **syn** declare, affirm, protest, avow, claim — **as•ser•tive** \-'sər-tiv\ *adj* — **as•ser•tive•ness** *n*

as•ser•tion \ə-'sər-shən\ *n* : a positive statement

as•sess \ə-'ses\ *vb* **1** : to fix the rate or amount of **2** : to impose (as a tax) at a specified rate **3** : to evaluate for taxation — **as•sess•ment** *n* — **as•ses•sor** \-'se-sər\ *n*

as•set \'a-ˌset\ *n* **1** *pl* : the entire property of a person or company that may be used to pay debts **2** : ADVANTAGE, RESOURCE

as•sev•er•ate \ə-'se-və-ˌrāt\ *vb* **-at•ed; -at•ing** : to assert earnestly — **as•sev•er•a•tion** \-ˌse-və-'rā-shən\ *n*

as•sid•u•ous \ə-'si-jə-wəs\ *adj* : steadily attentive : DILIGENT — **as•si•du•i•ty** \ˌa-sə-'dü-ə-tē, -'dyü-\ *n* — **as•sid•u•ous•ly** *adv* — **as•sid•u•ous•ness** *n*

as•sign \ə-'sīn\ *vb* **1** : to transfer (property) to another **2** : to appoint to or as a duty ⟨∼ a lesson⟩ **3** : FIX, SPECIFY ⟨∼ a limit⟩ **4** : ASCRIBE ⟨∼ a reason⟩ — **as•sign•able** *adj*

as•sig•na•tion \ˌa-sig-'nā-shən\ *n* : an appointment for a meeting; *esp* : TRYST

assigned risk *n* : a poor risk (as an accident-prone motorist) that an insurance company is forced to insure by state law

as·sign·ment \ə-'sīn-mənt\ *n* **1** : the act of assigning **2** : something assigned

as·sim·i·late \ə-'si-mə-ˌlāt\ *vb* **-lat·ed; -lat·ing 1** : to take up and absorb as nourishment; *also* : to absorb into a cultural tradition **2** : COMPREHEND **3** : to make or become similar — **as·sim·i·la·tion** \-ˌsi-mə-'lā-shən\ *n*

¹**as·sist** \ə-'sist\ *vb* : HELP, AID — **as·sis·tance** \-'sis-təns\ *n*

²**assist** *n* **1** : an act of assistance **2** : the action of a player who enables a teammate to make a putout (as in baseball) or score a goal (as in hockey)

as·sis·tant \ə-'sis-tənt\ *n* : a person who assists : HELP-ER

as·size \ə-'sīz\ *n* **1** : a judicial inquest **2** *pl* : the former regular sessions of superior courts in English counties

assn *abbr* association

assoc *abbr* associate; associated; association

¹**as·so·ci·ate** \ə-'sō-shē-ˌāt, -sē-\ *vb* **-at·ed; -at·ing 1** : to join in companionship or partnership **2** : to connect in thought

²**as·so·ci·ate** \-shē-ət, -sē-; -shət\ *n* **1** : a fellow worker : PARTNER **2** : COMPANION **3** *often cap* : a degree conferred esp. by a junior college 〈~ in arts〉 — **associate** *adj*

as·so·ci·a·tion \ə-ˌsō-shē-'ā-shən, -sē-\ *n* **1** : the act of associating **2** : an organization of persons : SOCIETY

as·so·cia·tive \ə-'sō-shē-ˌā-tiv, -sē-; -shə-tiv\ *adj* : of, relating to, or involved in association esp. of ideas or images

as·so·nance \'a-sə-nəns\ *n* : repetition of vowels esp. as an alternative to rhyme in verse — **as·so·nant** \-nənt\ *adj or n*

as soon as *conj* : immediately at or shortly after the time that 〈we'll start *as soon as* they arrive〉

as·sort \ə-'sȯrt\ *vb* **1** : to distribute into like groups : CLASSIFY **2** : HARMONIZE

as·sort·ed \ə-'sȯr-təd\ *adj* : consisting of various kinds

as·sort·ment \-'sȯrt-mənt\ *n* : a collection of assorted things or persons

asst *abbr* assistant

as·suage \ə-'swāj\ *vb* **as·suaged; as·suag·ing 1** : to make (as pain or grief) less : EASE **2** : SATISFY **syn** alleviate, relieve, lighten, mitigate

as·sume \ə-'süm\ *vb* **as·sumed; as·sum·ing 1** : to take upon oneself **2** : to pretend to have or be **3** : to take as granted or true though not proved

as·sump·tion \ə-'səmp-shən\ *n* **1** : the taking up of a person into heaven **2** *cap* : August 15 observed in commemoration of the Assumption of the Virgin Mary **3** : a taking upon oneself **4** : PRETENSION **5** : SUPPOSITION

as·sur·ance \ə-'shùr-əns\ *n* **1** : PLEDGE **2** *chiefly Brit* : INSURANCE **3** : SECURITY **4** : SELF-CONFIDENCE; *also* : AUDACITY

as·sure \ə-'shùr\ *vb* **as·sured; as·sur·ing 1** : INSURE **2** : to give confidence to **3** : to state confidently to **4** : to make certain the coming or attainment of

as·sured \ə-'shùrd\ *n, pl* **assured** *or* **assureds** : IN-SURED

as·ta·tine \'as-tə-ˌtēn\ *n* : an unstable radioactive chemical element — see ELEMENT table

as·ter \'as-tər\ *n* : any of various mostly fall=blooming leafy-stemmed composite herbs with daisy-like purple, white, pink, or yellow flower heads

as·ter·isk \'as-tə-ˌrisk\ *n* [L *asteriscus*, fr. Gk *asteriskos*, lit., little star, dim. of *astēr*] : a character * used as a reference mark or as an indication of the omission of letters or words

astern \ə-'stərn\ *adv or adj* **1** : in, at, or toward the stern **2** : BACKWARD

as·ter·oid \'as-tə-ˌrȯid\ *n* : any of the numerous small celestial bodies found esp. between Mars and Jupiter

asth·ma \'az-mə\ *n* : an often allergic disorder marked by difficulty in breathing and a cough — **asth·mat·ic** \az-'ma-tik\ *adj or n*

as though *conj* : AS IF

astig·ma·tism \ə-'stig-mə-ˌti-zəm\ *n* : a defect in a lens or an eye causing improper focusing — **as·tig·mat·ic** \ˌas-tig-'ma-tik\ *adj*

astir \ə-'stər\ *adj* **1** : being in action : MOVING **2** : being out of bed

as to *prep* **1** : ABOUT, CONCERNING 〈uncertain *as to* what went on〉 **2** : ACCORDING TO 〈graded *as to* size〉

as·ton·ish \ə-'stä-nish\ *vb* : to strike with sudden and usu. great wonder : AMAZE — **as·ton·ish·ing·ly** *adv* — **as·ton·ish·ment** *n*

as·tound \ə-'staùnd\ *vb* : to fill with bewilderment or wonder — **as·tound·ing·ly** *adv*

¹**astrad·dle** \ə-'strad-ᵊl\ *adv* : on or above and extending onto both sides

²**astraddle** *prep* : ASTRIDE

as·tra·khan \'as-trə-kən, -ˌkan\ *n, often cap* **1** : karakul of Russian origin **2** : a cloth with a usu. wool, curled, and looped pile resembling karakul

as·tral \'as-trəl\ *adj* : of, relating to, or coming from the stars

astray \ə-'strā\ *adv or adj* **1** : off the right path or route **2** : into error

¹**astride** \ə-'strīd\ *adv* **1** : with one leg on each side **2** : with legs apart

²**astride** *prep* : with one leg on each side of

¹**as·trin·gent** \ə-'strin-jənt\ *adj* : able or tending to shrink body tissues — **as·trin·gen·cy** \-jən-sē\ *n*

²**astringent** *n* : an astringent agent or substance

astrol *abbr* astrologer; astrology

as·tro·labe \'as-trə-ˌlāb\ *n* : an instrument formerly used for observing the positions of celestial bodies

as·trol·o·gy \ə-'strä-lə-jē\ *n* : divination based on the supposed influence of the stars upon human events — **as·trol·o·ger** \-jər\ *n* — **as·tro·log·i·cal** \ˌas-trə-'lä-ji-kəl\ *adj*

astron *abbr* astronomer; astronomy

as·tro·naut \'as-trə-ˌnȯt\ *n* : a traveler in a spacecraft

as·tro·nau·tics \ˌas-trə-'nȯ-tiks\ *n* : the science of the construction and operation of spacecraft — **as·tro·nau·tic** \-tik\ *or* **as·tro·nau·ti·cal** \-ti-kəl\ *adj*

as·tro·nom·i·cal \ˌas-trə-'nä-mi-kəl\ *also* **as·tro·nom·ic** \-mik\ *adj* **1** : of or relating to astronomy **2** : extremely large 〈an ~ amount of money〉

astronomical unit *n* : a unit of length used in astronomy equal to the mean distance of the earth from the sun or about 93 million miles (150 million kilometers)

as·tron·o·my \ə-'strä-nə-mē\ *n, pl* **-mies** : the science of objects and matter beyond the earth's atmosphere — **as·tron·o·mer** \-mər\ *n*

as·tro·phys·ics \ˌas-trə-'fi-ziks\ *n* : astronomy dealing esp. with the physical properties and dynamic processes of celestial objects — **as·tro·phys·i·cal** \-zi-kəl\ *adj* — **as·tro·phys·i·cist** \-'fi-zə-sist\ *n*

as·tute \ə-'stüt, -'styüt, a-\ *adj* [L *astutus*, fr. *astus* craft] : shrewdly discerning; *also* : WILY — **as·tute·ly** *adv* — **as·tute·ness** *n*

asun·der \ə-'sən-dər\ *adv or adj* **1** : into separate pieces 〈torn ~〉 **2** : separated in position from each other

ASV *abbr* American Standard Version

¹**as well as** *conj* : and in addition : and moreover 〈brave *as well as* loyal〉

²**as well as** *prep* : in addition to : BESIDES 〈the coach, *as well as* the team, is ready〉

asy·lum \ə-'sī-ləm\ *n* [ME, fr. L, fr. Gk *asylon*, neut. of *asylos* inviolable, fr. *a-* not + *sylon* right of seizure] **1** : a place of refuge **2** : protection given to esp. political fugitives **3** : an institution for the care of the needy or sick and esp. of the insane

asym·met·ri·cal \ˌā-sə-'me-tri-kəl\ *or* **asym·met·ric** \-trik\ *adj* : not symmetrical — **asym·me·try** \(ˌ)ā-'si-mə-trē\ *n*

as·ymp·tote \'a-səmp-ˌtōt\ *n* : a straight line that is associated with a curve and tends to approximate it along an infinite branch — **as·ymp·tot·ic** \ˌa-səmp-ˈtä-tik\ *adj* — **as·ymp·tot·i·cal·ly** \-ti-k(ə-)lē\ *adv*

¹**at** \ət, (ˈ)at\ *prep* **1** — used to indicate a point in time or space ⟨be here ∼ 3 o'clock⟩ **2** — used to indicate a goal ⟨swung ∼ the ball⟩ **3** — used to indicate position or condition ⟨∼ rest⟩ **4** — used to indicate means, cause, or manner ⟨sold ∼ auction⟩

²**at** \ˈät\ *n, pl* **at** — see *kip* at MONEY table

At *symbol* astatine

AT *abbr* automatic transmission

at all *adv* : in any way : in any circumstances ⟨not *at all* likely⟩

at·a·vism \ˈa-tə-ˌvi-zəm\ *n* : appearance in an individual of a character typical of an ancestral form; *also* : such an individual or character — **at·a·vis·tic** \ˌa-tə-ˈvis-tik\ *adj*

ate *past of* EAT

¹**-ate** *n suffix* **1** : one acted upon (in a specified way) ⟨distill*ate*⟩ **2** : chemical compound or complex derived from a (specified) compound or element ⟨ace*tate*⟩

²**-ate** *n suffix* **1** : office : function : rank : group of persons holding a (specified) office or rank ⟨episcop*ate*⟩ **2** : state : dominion : jurisdiction ⟨emir*ate*⟩

³**-ate** *adj suffix* **1** : acted on (in a specified way) : being in a (specified) state ⟨temper*ate*⟩ ⟨degener*ate*⟩ **2** : marked by having ⟨vertebr*ate*⟩

⁴**-ate** *vb suffix* : cause to be modified or affected by ⟨pollin*ate*⟩ : cause to become ⟨activ*ate*⟩ : furnish with ⟨aer*ate*⟩

ate·lier \ˌat-ᵊl-ˈyā\ *n* **1** : an artist's or designer's studio **2** : WORKSHOP

athe·ist \ˈā-thē-ist\ *n* : one who denies the existence of God — **athe·ism** \-ˌi-zəm\ *n* — **athe·is·tic** \ˌā-thē-ˈis-tik\ *adj*

ath·e·nae·um *or* **ath·e·ne·um** \ˌa-thə-ˈnē-əm\ *n* : LIBRARY 1

ath·ero·scle·ro·sis \ˌa-thə-rō-sklə-ˈrō-səs\ *n* : arteriosclerosis characterized by the deposition of fatty substances in and the hardening of the inner layer of the arteries — **ath·ero·scle·rot·ic** \-ˈrät-ik\ *adj*

athirst \ə-ˈthərst\ *adj* **1** *archaic* : THIRSTY **2** : EAGER, LONGING

ath·lete \ˈath-ˌlēt\ *n* [ME, fr. L *athleta*, fr. Gk *athlētēs*, fr. *athlein* to contend for a prize, fr. *athlon* prize, contest] : a person who is trained to compete in athletics

athlete's foot *n* : ringworm of the feet

ath·let·ic \ath-ˈle-tik\ *adj* **1** : of or relating to athletes or athletics **2** : VIGOROUS, ACTIVE **3** : STURDY, MUSCULAR

ath·let·ics \ath-ˈle-tiks\ *n sing or pl* : exercises and games requiring physical skill, strength, and endurance

athletic supporter *n* : an elastic pouch used to support the male genitals and worn esp. during athletic activity

¹**athwart** \ə-ˈthwȯrt\ *prep* **1** : ACROSS **2** : in opposition to

²**athwart** *adv* : obliquely across

atilt \ə-ˈtilt\ *adv or adj* **1** : in a tilted position **2** : with lance in hand

-ation *n suffix* : action or process ⟨flirt*ation*⟩ : something connected with an action or process ⟨discolor*ation*⟩

Atl *abbr* Atlantic

at·las \ˈat-ləs\ *n* : a book of maps

atm *abbr* atmosphere; atmospheric

ATM *abbr* automated teller machine

at·mo·sphere \ˈat-mə-ˌsfir\ *n* **1** : the gaseous envelope of a celestial body; *esp* : the mass of air surrounding the earth **2** : a surrounding influence **3** : a unit of pressure equal to the pressure of air at sea level or about 14.7 pounds per square inch (10 newtons per square centimeter) **4** : a dominant effect — **at·mo·spher·ic** \ˌat-mə-ˈsfir-ik, -ˈsfer-\ *adj* — **at·mo·spher·i·cal·ly** \-i-k(ə-)lē\ *adv*

at·mo·spher·ics \ˌat-mə-ˈsfir-iks, -ˈsfer-\ *n pl* : radio noise from atmospheric electrical phenomena

atoll \ˈa-ˌtȯl, -ˌtäl, ˈā-\ *n* : a coral island consisting of a reef surrounding a lagoon

atoll

at·om \ˈa-təm\ *n* [ME, fr. L *atomus*, fr. Gk *atomos*, fr. *atomos* indivisible, fr. a- not + *temnein* to cut] **1** : a tiny particle : BIT **2** : the smallest particle of a chemical element that can exist alone or in combination

atom·ic \ə-ˈtä-mik\ *adj* **1** : of or relating to atoms; *also* : NUCLEAR 2 ⟨∼ energy⟩ **2** : extremely small

atomic bomb *n* : a very destructive bomb utilizing the energy released by splitting the atom

atomic clock *n* : a very precise clock regulated by the natural vibration of atoms or molecules (as of cesium)

atomic number *n* : the number of protons in the nucleus of an element

atomic weight *n* : the mass of one atom of an element

at·om·ize \ˈa-tə-ˌmīz\ *vb* **-ized; -iz·ing** : to reduce to minute particles

at·om·iz·er \ˈa-tə-ˌmī-zər\ *n* : a device for dispensing a liquid (as perfume) as a mist

atom smasher *n* : ACCELERATOR 3

aton·al \ā-ˈtōn-ᵊl\ *adj* : marked by avoidance of traditional musical tonality — **ato·nal·i·ty** \ˌā-tō-ˈna-lə-tē\ *n* — **aton·al·ly** \ā-ˈtōn-ᵊl-ē\ *adv*

atone \ə-ˈtōn\ *vb* **atoned; aton·ing 1** : to make amends **2** : EXPIATE

atone·ment \ə-ˈtōn-mənt\ *n* **1** : the reconciliation of God and man through the death of Jesus Christ **2** : reparation for an offense : SATISFACTION

¹**atop** \ə-ˈtäp\ *prep* : on top of

²**atop** *adv or adj* : on, to, or at the top

ATP \ˌā-ˌtē-ˈpē\ *n* [adenosine *tri*phosphate] : a compound that occurs widely in living tissue and supplies energy for many cellular processes by undergoing enzymatic hydrolysis

atri·um \ˈā-trē-əm\ *n, pl* **atria** \-trē-ə\ *also* **atri·ums 1** : the central room of a Roman house; *also* : an open patio or court in the center of a building (as a hotel) **2** : an anatomical cavity or passage; *esp* : one of the chambers of the heart that receives blood from the veins — **atri·al** \-əl\ *adj*

atro·cious \ə-ˈtrō-shəs\ *adj* **1** : savagely brutal, cruel, or wicked **2** : very bad : ABOMINABLE — **atro·cious·ly** *adv* — **atro·cious·ness** *n*

atroc·i·ty \ə-ˈträ-sə-tē\ *n, pl* **-ties 1** : ATROCIOUSNESS **2** : an atrocious act or object ⟨the *atrocities* of war⟩

at·ro·phy \ˈa-trə-fē\ *n, pl* **-phies** : decrease in size or wasting away of a bodily part or tissue — **atrophy** *vb*

at·ro·pine \ˈa-trə-ˌpēn\ *n* : a drug from belladonna and related plants used esp. to relieve spasms and to dilate the pupil of the eye

att *abbr* **1** attached **2** attention **3** attorney

at·tach \ə-ˈtach\ *vb* **1** : to seize legally in order to force payment of a debt **2** : to bind by personal ties **3** : FASTEN, CONNECT **4** : to be fastened or connected

at·ta·ché \ˌa-tə-ˈshā, ˌa-ˌta-, ˌä-ˌta-\ *n* [F] : a technical expert on the diplomatic staff of an ambassador

at·ta·ché case \ə-ˈta-shā-, ˌa-tə-ˈshā-\ *n* : a small thin suitcase used esp. for carrying business papers; *also* : BRIEFCASE

at·tach·ment \ə-ˈtach-mənt\ *n* **1** : legal seizure of property **2** : connection by ties of affection and regard **3** : a device attached to a machine or implement **4** : a connection by which one thing is attached to another

¹**at·tack** \ə-'tak\ *vb* **1** : to set upon with force or words : ASSAIL, ASSAULT **2** : to set to work on

²**attack** *n* **1** : an offensive action **2** : a fit of sickness

at·tain \ə-'tān\ *vb* **1** : ACHIEVE, ACCOMPLISH **2** : to arrive at : REACH — **at·tain·abil·i·ty** \-'tā-nə-'bi-lə-tē\ *n* — **at·tain·able** *adj*

at·tain·der \ə-'tān-dər\ *n* : extinction of the civil rights of a person upon sentence of death or outlawry

at·tain·ment \ə-'tān-mənt\ *n* **1** : the act of attaining **2** : ACCOMPLISHMENT

at·taint \ə-'tānt\ *vb* : to condemn to loss of civil rights

at·tar \'a-tər\ *n* [Per *'aṭir* perfumed, fr. Ar, fr. *'iṭr* perfume] : a fragrant floral oil

at·tempt \ə-'tempt\ *vb* : to make an effort toward : TRY — **attempt** *n*

at·tend \ə-'tend\ *vb* **1** : to look after : TEND **2** : to be present with **3** : to be present at **4** : to apply oneself **5** : to pay attention **6** : to direct one's attention

at·ten·dance \ə-'ten-dəns\ *n* **1** : the act or fact of attending **2** : the number of persons present; *also* : the number of times a person attends

¹**at·ten·dant** \ə-'ten-dənt\ *n* : one that attends another to render a service

²**attendant** *adj* : ACCOMPANYING ⟨~ circumstances⟩

at·ten·tion \ə-'ten-chən\ *n* **1** : the act or state of applying the mind to an object **2** : CONSIDERATION **3** : an act of courtesy **4** : a position of readiness assumed on command by a soldier — **at·ten·tive** \-'ten-tiv\ *adj* — **at·ten·tive·ly** *adv* — **at·ten·tive·ness** *n*

at·ten·u·ate \ə-'ten-yə-ˌwāt\ *vb* **-at·ed; -at·ing 1** : to make or become thin **2** : WEAKEN — **attenuate** \-wət\ *adj* — **at·ten·u·a·tion** \-ˌten-yə-'wā-shən\ *n*

at·test \ə-'test\ *vb* **1** : to certify as genuine by signing as a witness **2** : MANIFEST **3** : TESTIFY — **at·tes·ta·tion** \ˌa-ˌtes-'tā-shən\ *n*

at·tic \'a-tik\ *n* : the space or room in a building immediately below the roof

¹**at·tire** \ə-'tīr\ *vb* **at·tired; at·tir·ing** : to put garments on : DRESS, ARRAY

²**attire** *n* : DRESS, CLOTHES

at·ti·tude \'a-tə-ˌtüd, -ˌtyüd\ *n* **1** : POSTURE **2** : a mental position or feeling with regard to a fact or state **3** : the position of something in relation to something else

at·ti·tu·di·nize \ˌa-tə-'tüd-ᵊn-ˌīz, -'tyüd-\ *vb* **-nized; -niz·ing** : to assume an affected mental attitude : POSE

attn *abbr* attention

at·tor·ney \ə-'tər-nē\ *n, pl* **-neys** : a legal agent qualified to act for persons in legal proceedings

attorney general *n, pl* **attorneys general** *or* **attorney generals** : the chief legal representative and adviser of a nation or state

at·tract \ə-'trakt\ *vb* **1** : to draw to or toward oneself : cause to approach **2** : to draw by emotional or aesthetic appeal **syn** charm, fascinate, allure, captivate, enchant — **at·trac·tive** \-'trak-tiv\ *adj* — **at·trac·tive·ly** *adv* — **at·trac·tive·ness** *n*

at·trac·tant \ə-'trak-tənt\ *n* : a substance (as a pheromone) used to attract insects or other animals

at·trac·tion \ə-'trak-shən\ *n* **1** : the act or power of attracting; *esp* : personal charm **2** : an attractive quality, object, or feature **3** : a force tending to draw particles together

attrib *abbr* attributive

¹**at·tri·bute** \'a-trə-ˌbyüt\ *n* **1** : an inherent characteristic **2** : a word ascribing a quality; *esp* : ADJECTIVE

²**at·trib·ute** \ə-'tri-ˌbyüt, -byət\ *vb* **-ut·ed; -ut·ing 1** : to explain as to cause or origin ⟨~ the illness to fatigue⟩ **2** : to regard as a characteristic **syn** ascribe, credit, charge, impute — **at·trib·ut·able** *adj* — **at·tri·bu·tion** \ˌa-trə-'byü-shən\ *n*

at·trib·u·tive \ə-'trib-yə-tiv\ *adj* : joined directly to a

modified noun without a linking verb ⟨*red* in *red hair* is an ~ adjective⟩ — **attributive** *n*

at·tri·tion \ə-'tri-shən\ *n* **1** : the act of wearing away by or as if by rubbing **2** : a reduction in numbers as a result of resignation, retirement, or death

at·tune \ə-'tün, -'tyün\ *vb* : to bring into harmony : TUNE — **at·tune·ment** *n*

atty *abbr* attorney

ATV *abbr* all-terrain vehicle

atyp·i·cal \ā-'ti-pi-kəl\ *adj* : not typical : IRREGULAR — **atyp·i·cal·ly** \-k(ə-)lē\ *adv*

Au *symbol* [L *aurum*] gold

au·burn \'ȯ-bərn\ *adj* : reddish brown — **auburn** *n*

au cou·rant \ˌō-ku̇-'räⁿ\ *adj* [F, lit., in the current] : UP-TO-DATE, STYLISH

¹**auc·tion** \'ȯk-shən\ *n* [L *auction-, auctio*, fr. *augēre* to increase] : public sale of property to the highest bidder

²**auction** *vb* **auc·tioned; auc·tion·ing** \-sh(ə-)niŋ\ : to sell at auction

auc·tion·eer \ˌȯk-shə-'nir\ *n* : an agent who conducts an auction

aud *abbr* audit; auditor

au·da·cious \ȯ-'dā-shəs\ *adj* **1** : DARING, BOLD **2** : INSOLENT — **au·da·cious·ly** *adv* — **au·da·cious·ness** *n* — **au·dac·i·ty** \-'da-sə-tē\ *n*

¹**au·di·ble** \'ȯ-də-bəl\ *adj* : capable of being heard — **au·di·bil·i·ty** \ˌȯ-də-'bi-lə-tē\ *n* — **au·di·bly** \'ȯ-də-blē\ *adv*

²**audible** *n* : a play called at the line of scrimmage

au·di·ence \'ȯ-dē-əns\ *n* **1** : a formal interview **2** : an opportunity of being heard **3** : an assembly of listeners or spectators

¹**au·dio** \'ȯ-dē-ˌō\ *adj* **1** : of or relating to frequencies (as of radio waves) corresponding to those of audible sound waves **2** : of or relating to sound or its reproduction and esp. high-fidelity reproduction **3** : relating to or used in the transmission or reception of sound

²**audio** *n* **1** : the transmission, reception, or reproduction of sound **2** : the section of television or motion-picture equipment that deals with sound

au·di·ol·o·gy \ˌȯ-dē-'ä-lə-jē\ *n* : a branch of science dealing with hearing and esp. with the treatment of individuals having trouble with hearing — **au·di·o·log·i·cal** \-ə-'lä-ji-kəl\ *adj* — **au·di·ol·o·gist** \-'ä-lə-jist\ *n*

au·dio·phile \'ȯ-dē-ō-ˌfīl\ *n* : one who is enthusiastic about high-fidelity sound reproduction

au·dio·vi·su·al \ˌȯ-dē-ō-'vi-zhə-wəl\ *adj* : of, relating to, or making use of both hearing and sight

au·dio·vi·su·als \-wəlz\ *n pl* : audiovisual teaching materials (as videotapes)

¹**au·dit** \'ȯ-dət\ *n* : a formal examination and verification of financial accounts

²**audit** *vb* **1** : to perform an audit on or for **2** : to attend (a course) without expecting formal credit

¹**au·di·tion** \ȯ-'di-shən\ *n* : HEARING; *esp* : a trial performance to appraise an entertainer's merits

²**audition** *vb* **-tioned; -tion·ing** \-'di-shə-niŋ\ : to give an audition to; *also* : to give a trial performance

au·di·tor \'ȯ-də-tər\ *n* **1** : LISTENER **2** : a person who audits

au·di·to·ri·um \ˌȯ-də-'tōr-ē-əm\ *n, pl* **-riums** *or* **-ria** \-rē-ə\ **1** : the part of a public building where an audience sits **2** : a hall or building used for public gatherings

au·di·to·ry \'ȯ-də-ˌtōr-ē\ *adj* : of or relating to hearing or to the sense or organs of hearing

auditory tube *n* : EUSTACHIAN TUBE

auf Wie·der·seh·en \au̇f-'vē-dər-ˌzān\ *interj* [G] — used to express farewell

Aug *abbr* August

au·ger \'ȯ-gər\ *n* : a tool for boring

aught \'ȯt, 'ät\ *n* : ZERO, CIPHER

aug·ment \óg-'ment\ *vb* : ENLARGE, INCREASE — **aug·men·ta·tion** \ˌóg-mən-'tā-shən\ *n*

au gra·tin \ō-'grat-ᵊn, ó-, -'grät-\ *adj* [F, lit., with the burnt scrapings from the pan] : covered with bread crumbs or grated cheese and browned

¹**au·gur** \'ó-gər\ *n* : DIVINER, SOOTHSAYER

²**augur** *vb* **1** : to foretell esp. from omens **2** : to give promise of : PRESAGE

au·gu·ry \'ó-gyə-rē, -gə-\ *n, pl* **-ries 1** : divination from omens **2** : OMEN, PORTENT

au·gust \ó-'gəst\ *adj* : marked by majestic dignity or grandeur — **au·gust·ly** *adv* — **au·gust·ness** *n*

Au·gust \'ó-gəst\ *n* [ME, fr. OE, fr. L *Augustus,* fr. *Augustus* Caesar] : the eighth month of the year having 31 days

au jus \ō-'zhü, -'zhüs, -'jüs; ō-zhū̄\ *adj* [F] : served in the juice obtained from roasting

auk \'ók\ *n* : any of several stocky black-and-white diving seabirds that breed in colder parts of the northern hemisphere

auld \'ól, 'óld, 'äl, 'äld\ *adj, chiefly Scot* : OLD

aunt \'ant, 'änt\ *n* **1** : the sister of one's father or mother **2** : the wife of one's uncle

au pair \ō-'par\ *n* [F, on even terms] : a usu. young foreign person who does domestic work for a family in return for room and board and to learn the family's language

au·ra \'ór-ə\ *n* **1** : a distinctive atmosphere surrounding a given source **2** : a luminous radiation

au·ral \'ór-əl\ *adj* : of or relating to the ear or to the sense of hearing

aurar *pl of* EYRIR

au·re·ole \'ór-ē-ˌōl\ *or* **au·re·o·la** \ó-'rē-ə-lə\ *n* : HALO, NIMBUS

au re·voir \ˌō-rə-'vwär\ *n* [F, lit., till seeing again] : GOOD-BYE

au·ri·cle \'ór-i-kəl\ *n* : an atrium of the heart

au·ric·u·lar \ó-'ri-kyə-lər\ *adj* **1** : told privately ⟨∼ confession⟩ **2** : known or recognized by the sense of hearing

au·ro·ra \ə-'rōr-ə\ *n, pl* **auroras** *or* **au·ro·rae** \-(ˌ)ē\ : a luminous phenomenon of streamers or arches of light appearing in the upper atmosphere esp. of a planet's polar regions — **au·ro·ral** \-əl\ *adj*

aurora aus·tra·lis \-ó-'strä-ləs\ *n* : an aurora that occurs in earth's southern hemisphere

aurora bo·re·al·is \-ˌbór-ē-'a-ləs\ *n* : an aurora that occurs in earth's northern hemisphere

AUS *abbr* Army of the United States

aus·pice \'ó-spəs\ *n, pl* **aus·pic·es** \-spə-səz, -ˌsēz\ [L *auspicium,* fr. *auspic-, auspex* diviner by birds, fr. *avis* bird + *specere* to look, look at] **1** : observation of birds by an augur **2** *pl* : kindly patronage and protection **3** : a prophetic sign or omen

aus·pi·cious \ó-'spi-shəs\ *adj* **1** : promising success : PROPITIOUS **2** : FORTUNATE, PROSPEROUS — **aus·pi·cious·ly** *adv* — **aus·pi·cious·ness** *n*

aus·tere \ó-'stir\ *adj* **1** : STERN, SEVERE, STRICT **2** : ABSTEMIOUS **3** : UNADORNED ⟨∼ style⟩ — **aus·tere·ly** *adv* — **aus·ter·i·ty** \-'ster-ə-tē\ *n*

aus·tral \'ós-trəl\ *adj* : SOUTHERN

Aus·tra·lian \ó-'strāl-yən\ *n* : a native or inhabitant of Australia — **Australian** *adj*

Aus·tri·an \'ó-strē-ən\ *n* : a native or inhabitant of Austria — **Austrian** *adj*

Aus·tro·ne·sian \ˌós-trə-'nē-zhən\ *adj* : of, relating to, or constituting a family of languages spoken in the area extending from Madagascar eastward through the Malay Peninsula to Hawaii and Easter Island

auth *abbr* **1** authentic **2** author **3** authorized

au·then·tic \ə-'then-tik, ó-\ *adj* : GENUINE, REAL — **au·then·ti·cal·ly** \-ti-k(ə)lē\ *adv* — **au·then·tic·i·ty** \ˌó-ˌthen-'ti-sə-tē\ *n*

au·then·ti·cate \ə-'then-ti-ˌkāt, ó-\ *vb* **-cat·ed; -cat·ing** : to prove genuine — **au·then·ti·ca·tion** \-ˌthen-ti-'kā-shən\ *n*

au·thor \'ó-thər\ *n* [ME *auctour,* ultim. fr. L *auctor* originator, author, fr. *augēre* to increase] **1** : one that originates or creates **2** : one that writes or composes a literary work

au·thor·ess \'ó-thə-rəs\ *n* : a woman author

au·thor·i·tar·i·an \ó-ˌthär-ə-'ter-ē-ən, ə-, -ˌthór-\ *adj* **1** : characterized by or favoring the principle of blind obedience to authority **2** : characterized by or favoring concentration of political power in an authority not responsible to the people — **authoritarian** *n*

au·thor·i·ta·tive \ə-'thär-ə-ˌtā-tiv, ó-, -'thór-\ *adj* : supported by, proceeding from, or being an authority — **au·thor·i·ta·tive·ly** *adv* — **au·thor·i·ta·tive·ness** *n*

au·thor·i·ty \ə-'thär-ə-tē, ó-, -'thór-\ *n, pl* **-ties 1** : a citation used in support of a statement or in defense of an action; *also* : the source of such a citation **2** : one appealed to as an expert **3** : power to influence thought or behavior **4** : freedom granted : RIGHT **5** : persons in command; *esp* : GOVERNMENT **6** : convincing force

au·tho·rize \'ó-thə-ˌrīz\ *vb* **-rized; -riz·ing 1** : SANCTION **2** : to give legal power to — **au·tho·ri·za·tion** \ˌó-thə-rə-'zā-shən\ *n*

au·thor·ship \'ó-thər-ˌship\ *n* **1** : the state of being an author **2** : the source of a piece of writing, music, or art

au·tism \'ó-ˌti-zəm\ *n* **1** : absorption in self-centered mental activity (as delusions and hallucinations) esp. when accompanied by withdrawal from reality **2** : a mental disorder originating in infancy that is characterized esp. by inability to interact socially, repetitive behavior, and language disorder — **au·tis·tic** \ó-'tis-tik\ *adj*

¹**au·to** \'ó-tō\ *n, pl* **autos** : AUTOMOBILE

²**auto** *abbr* automatic

au·to·bahn \'ó-tō-ˌbän, 'aù-\ *n* : a German, Swiss, or Austrian expressway

au·to·bi·og·ra·phy \ˌó-tə-bī-'ä-grə-fē\ *n* : the biography of a person narrated by that person — **au·to·bi·og·ra·pher** \-fər\ *n* — **au·to·bi·o·graph·i·cal** \-ˌbī-ə-'gra-fi-kəl\ *adj* — **au·to·bi·o·graph·i·cal·ly** \-k(ə-)lē\ *adv*

au·toch·tho·nous \ó-'täk-thə-nəs\ *adj* : INDIGENOUS, NATIVE

au·to·clave \'ó-tō-ˌklāv\ *n* : an apparatus (as for sterilizing) using superheated high-pressure steam

au·toc·ra·cy \ó-'tä-krə-sē\ *n, pl* **-cies** : government by one person having unlimited power — **au·to·crat** \'ó-tə-ˌkrat\ *n* — **au·to·crat·ic** \ˌó-tə-'kra-tik\ *adj* — **au·to·crat·i·cal·ly** \-ti-k(ə-)lē\ *adv*

¹**au·to·graph** \'ó-tə-ˌgraf\ *n* **1** : an original manuscript **2** : a person's signature written by hand

²**autograph** *vb* : to write one's signature on

au·to·im·mune \ˌó-tō-i-'myün\ *adj* : of, relating to, or caused by antibodies or lymphocytes that attack molecules, cells, or tissues of the organism producing them ⟨∼ diseases⟩ — **au·to·im·mu·ni·ty** \-i-'myü-nə-tē\ *n*

au·to·mate \'ó-tə-ˌmāt\ *vb* **-mat·ed; -mat·ing 1** : to operate automatically using mechanical or electronic devices **2** : to convert to automatic operation — **au·to·ma·tion** \ó-tə-'mā-shən\ *n*

automated teller machine *n* : a computer terminal allowing access to one's own bank accounts

¹**au·to·mat·ic** \ˌó-tə-'ma-tik\ *adj* **1** : INVOLUNTARY **2** : made so that certain parts act in a desired manner at the proper time : SELF-ACTING — **au·to·mat·i·cal·ly** \-ti-k(ə-)lē\ *adv*

²**automatic** *n* : an automatic device; *esp* : an automatic firearm

au·tom·a·ton \ó-'tä-mə-tən, -ˌtän\ *n, pl* **-atons** *or* **-a·ta** \-ə-tə, -ə-ˌtä\ **1** : an automatic machine; *esp* : ROBOT **2** : an individual who acts mechanically

au·to·mo·bile \ˌó-tə-mō-ˌbēl, ˌó-tə-mə-ˈbēl\ *n* : a usu. 4-wheeled automotive vehicle for passenger transportation

au·to·mo·tive \ˌó-tə-'mō-tiv\ *adj* **1** : of or relating to automobiles, trucks, or buses **2** : SELF-PROPELLED

au·to·nom·ic nervous system \ˌȯ-tə-ˈnä-mik-\ *n* : a part of the vertebrate nervous system that governs involuntary actions and that consists of the sympathetic nervous system and the parasympathetic nervous system

au·ton·o·mous \ȯ-ˈtä-nə-məs\ *adj* : having the right or power of self-government — **au·ton·o·mous·ly** *adv* — **au·ton·o·my** \-mē\ *n*

au·top·sy \ˈȯ-ˌtäp-sē, ˈȯ-təp-\ *n, pl* **-sies** [Gk *autopsia* act of seeing with one's own eyes, fr. *autos* self + *opsis* sight] : examination of a dead body usu. with dissection sufficient to determine the cause of death or extent of change produced by disease — **autopsy** *vb*

au·tumn \ˈȯ-təm\ *n* : the season between summer and winter — **au·tum·nal** \ȯ-ˈtəm-nəl\ *adj*

aux *abbr* auxiliary

¹**aux·il·ia·ry** \ȯg-ˈzil-yə-rē, -ˈzi-lə-rē\ *adj* **1** : providing help **2** : functioning in a subsidiary capacity **3** : accompanying a verb form to express person, number, mood, or tense ⟨∼ verbs⟩

²**auxiliary** *n, pl* **-ries 1** : an auxiliary person, group, or device **2** : an auxiliary verb

aux·in \ˈȯk-sən\ *n* : a plant hormone that stimulates growth in length

av *abbr* **1** avenue **2** average **3** avoirdupois

AV *abbr* **1** ad valorem **2** audiovisual **3** Authorized Version

¹**avail** \ə-ˈvāl\ *vb* : to be of use or advantage : HELP, BENEFIT

²**avail** *n* : USE ⟨effort was of no ∼⟩

avail·able \ə-ˈvā-lə-bəl\ *adj* **1** : USABLE **2** : ACCESSIBLE — **avail·abil·i·ty** \-ˌvā-lə-ˈbi-lə-tē\ *n*

av·a·lanche \ˈa-və-ˌlanch\ *n* : a mass of snow, ice, earth, or rock sliding down a mountainside

avant–garde \ˌä-ˌvän-ˈgärd, -ˌvänt-\ *n* [F, vanguard] : those esp. in the arts who create or apply new or experimental ideas and techniques — **avant–garde** *adj*

av·a·rice \ˈa-və-rəs\ *n* : excessive desire for wealth : GREED — **av·a·ri·cious** \ˌa-və-ˈri-shəs\ *adj*

avast \ə-ˈvast\ *vb imper* — a nautical command to stop or cease

av·a·tar \ˈa-və-ˌtär\ *n* [Skt *avatāra* descent] : INCARNATION

avaunt \ə-ˈvȯnt\ *adv* : AWAY, HENCE

avdp *abbr* avoirdupois

ave *abbr* avenue

Ave Ma·ria \ˌä-vā-mə-ˈrē-ə\ *n* : HAIL MARY

avenge \ə-ˈvenj\ *vb* **avenged; aveng·ing** : to take vengeance for — **aveng·er** *n*

av·e·nue \ˈa-və-ˌnü, -ˌnyü\ *n* **1** : a way or route to a place or goal : PATH **2** : a broad street

aver \ə-ˈvər\ *vb* **averred; aver·ring** : ALLEGE, ASSERT; *also* : DECLARE

¹**av·er·age** \ˈa-və-rij, ˈa-vrij\ *n* [modif. of MF *avarie* damage to ship or cargo, fr. OIt *avaria*, fr. Ar *ʿawārīyah* damaged merchandise] **1** : ARITHMETIC MEAN **2** : a ratio of successful tries to total tries esp. in athletics ⟨batting ∼ of .303⟩

²**average** *adj* **1** : equaling or approximating an arithmetic mean **2** : being about midway between extremes **3** : not out of the ordinary : COMMON

³**average** *vb* **av·er·aged; av·er·ag·ing 1** : to be at or come to an average **2** : to be, do, or get usually **3** : to find the average of

averse \ə-ˈvərs\ *adj* : having an active feeling of dislike or reluctance ⟨∼ to exercise⟩

aver·sion \ə-ˈvər-zhən\ *n* **1** : a feeling of repugnance for something with a desire to avoid it **2** : something decidedly disliked

avert \ə-ˈvərt\ *vb* **1** : to turn aside or away ⟨∼ the eyes⟩ **2** : to ward off

avg *abbr* average

avi·an \ˈā-vē-ən\ *adj* [L *avis* bird] : of, relating to, or derived from birds

avi·ary \ˈā-vē-ˌer-ē\ *n, pl* **-ar·ies** : a place for keeping birds confined

avi·a·tion \ˌā-vē-ˈā-shən, ˌa-\ *n* **1** : the operation of heavier-than-air aircraft **2** : aircraft manufacture, development, and design

avi·a·tor \ˈā-vē-ˌā-tər, ˈa-\ *n* : an airplane pilot

avi·a·trix \ˌā-vē-ˈā-triks, ˌa-\ *n, pl* **-trix·es** \-trik-səz\ *or* **-tri·ces** \-trə-ˌsēz\ : a woman airplane pilot

av·id \ˈa-vəd\ *adj* **1** : craving eagerly : GREEDY **2** : enthusiastic in pursuit of an interest — **avid·i·ty** \ə-ˈvi-də-tē, a-\ *n* — **av·id·ly** *adv* — **av·id·ness** *n*

avi·on·ics \ˌā-vē-ˈä-niks, ˌa-\ *n pl* : electronics designed for use in aerospace vehicles — **avi·on·ic** \-nik\ *adj*

avo \ˈa-(ˌ)vü\ *n, pl* **avos** — see *pataca* at MONEY table

av·o·ca·do \ˌa-və-ˈkä-dō, ˌä-\ *n, pl* **-dos** *also* **-does** [modif. of Sp *aguacate*, fr. Nahuatl *āhuacatl*, avocado, testicle] : a pulpy green to purple nutty-flavored edible fruit of a tropical American tree; *also* : this tree

av·o·ca·tion \ˌa-və-ˈkā-shən\ *n* : HOBBY

av·o·cet \ˈa-və-ˌset\ *n* : any of several long-legged shorebirds with webbed feet and slender upward-curving bills

avoid \ə-ˈvȯid\ *vb* **1** : to keep away from : SHUN **2** : to prevent the occurrence of **3** : to refrain from — **avoid·able** *adj* — **avoid·ably** *adv* — **avoid·ance** \-ᵊns\ *n*

av·oir·du·pois \ˌa-vər-də-ˈpȯiz\ *n* [ME *avoir de pois* goods sold by weight, fr. OF, lit., goods of weight] **1** : AVOIRDUPOIS WEIGHT **2** : WEIGHT, HEAVINESS; *esp* : personal weight

avoirdupois weight *n* : a system of weights based on a pound of 16 ounces and an ounce of 16 drams (28 grams) — see WEIGHT table

avouch \ə-ˈvaùch\ *vb* **1** : to declare positively : AVER **2** : to vouch for

avow \ə-ˈvaù\ *vb* : to declare openly — **avow·al** \-ˈvaù(-ə)l\ *n*

avun·cu·lar \ə-ˈvəŋ-kyə-lər\ *adj* : of, relating to, or resembling an uncle

await \ə-ˈwāt\ *vb* : to wait for : EXPECT

¹**awake** \ə-ˈwāk\ *vb* **awoke** \-ˈwōk\ *also* **awaked** \-ˈwākt\; **awo·ken** \-ˈwō-kən\ *or* **awaked** *also* **awoke**; **awak·ing** : to bring back to consciousness : wake up

²**awake** *adj* : not asleep; *also* : ALERT

awak·en \ə-ˈwā-kən\ *vb* **awak·ened; awak·en·ing** \-ˈwā-kə-niŋ\ : AWAKE

¹**award** \ə-ˈwȯrd\ *vb* **1** : to give by judicial decision ⟨∼ damages⟩ **2** : to give in recognition of merit or achievement

²**award** *n* **1** : a final decision : JUDGMENT **2** : something awarded : PRIZE

aware \ə-ˈwar\ *adj* : having perception or knowledge : CONSCIOUS, INFORMED — **aware·ness** *n*

awash \ə-ˈwȯsh, -ˈwäsh\ *adj* **1** : washed by waves or tide **2** : AFLOAT **3** : FLOODED

¹**away** \ə-ˈwā\ *adv* **1** : from this or that place ⟨go ∼⟩ **2** : out of the way **3** : in another direction ⟨turn ∼⟩ **4** : out of existence ⟨fade ∼⟩ **5** : from one's possession ⟨give ∼⟩ **6** : without interruption ⟨chatter ∼⟩ **7** : at a distance in space or time ⟨far ∼⟩ ⟨∼ back in 1910⟩

²**away** *adj* **1** : ABSENT **2** : distant in space or time ⟨a lake 10 miles ∼⟩

¹**awe** \ˈȯ\ *n* **1** : profound and reverent dread of the supernatural **2** : respectful fear inspired by authority

²**awe** *vb* **awed; aw·ing** : to inspire with awe

aweigh \ə-ˈwā\ *adj* : just clear of the bottom ⟨anchors ∼⟩

awe·some \ˈȯ-səm\ *adj* **1** : expressive of awe **2** : inspiring awe

awe·struck \-ˌstrək\ *also* **awe·strick·en** \-ˌstri-kən\ *adj* : filled with awe

aw·ful \ˈȯ-fəl\ *adj* **1** : inspiring awe **2** : extremely disagreeable **3** : very great ⟨an ∼ lot of money⟩ — **aw·ful·ly** *adv*

awhile \ə-ˈhwīl\ *adv* : for a while

awhirl \ə-'hwərl\ *adj* : being in a whirl

awk·ward \'ȯ-kwərd\ *adj* **1** : CLUMSY **2** : UNGRACEFUL **3** : difficult to explain : EMBARRASSING **4** : difficult to deal with — **awk·ward·ly** *adv* — **awk·ward·ness** *n*

awl \'ȯl\ *n* : a pointed instrument for making small holes

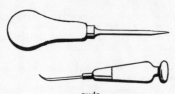

awls

awn·ing \'ȯ-niŋ\ *n* : a rooflike cover (as of canvas) extended over or in front of a place as a shelter

AWOL \'ā-,wȯl, ,ā-,də-bəl-yü-,ō-'el\ *n* : a person who is absent without leave — **AWOL** *adj or adv*

awry \ə-'rī\ *adv or adj* **1** : ASKEW **2** : AMISS

ax *or* **axe** \'aks\ *n* : a chopping or cutting tool with an edged head fitted parallel to a handle

ax·i·al \'ak-sē-əl\ *adj* **1** : of, relating to, or functioning as an axis **2** : situated around, in the direction of, on, or along an axis — **ax·i·al·ly** *adv*

ax·i·om \'ak-sē-əm\ *n* [L *axioma*, fr. Gk *axiōma*, lit., something worthy, fr. *axioun* to think worthy, fr. *axios* worth, worthy] **1** : a statement generally accepted as true : MAXIM **2** : a proposition regarded as a self-evident truth — **ax·i·om·at·ic** \,ak-sē-ə-'ma-tik\ *adj* — **ax·i·om·at·i·cal·ly** \-ti-k(ə-)lē\ *adv*

ax·is \'ak-səs\ *n*, *pl* **ax·es** \-,sēz\ **1** : a straight line around which a body rotates **2** : a straight line or structure with respect to which a body or figure is symmetrical **3** : one of the reference lines of a system of coordinates **4** : an alliance between major powers

ax·le \'ak-səl\ *n* : a shaft on which a wheel revolves

ayah \'ī-ə\ *n* [Hindi *āyā*, fr. Pg *aia*, fr. L *avia* grandmother] : a nurse or maid native to India

aya·tol·lah \,ī-ə-'tō-lə\ *n* [Per, lit., sign of God, fr. Ar *aya* sign, miracle + *allāh* God] : an Islamic religious leader — used as a title of respect

¹aye *also* **ay** \'ā\ *adv* : ALWAYS, EVER

²aye *also* **ay** \'ī\ *adv* : YES

³aye *also* **ay** \'ī\ *n*, *pl* **ayes** : an affirmative vote

AZ *abbr* Arizona

aza·lea \ə-'zāl-yə\ *n* : any of numerous rhododendrons with funnel-shaped blossoms and usu. deciduous leaves

az·i·do·thy·mi·dine \ə-,zi-dō-'thī-mə-,dēn\ *n* : AZT

az·i·muth \'a-zə-məth\ *n* : horizontal direction expressed as an angular distance from a fixed point

AZT \,ā-(,)zē-'tē\ *n* : an antiviral drug used to treat AIDS

Az·tec \'az-,tek\ *n* : a member of a Nahuatl-speaking people that founded the Mexican empire and were conquered by Hernan Cortes in 1519 — **Az·tec·an** *adj*

azure \'a-zhər\ *n* : the blue of the clear sky — **azure** *adj*

B

¹b \'bē\ *n*, *pl* **b's** *or* **bs** \'bēz\ *often cap* **1** : the 2d letter of the English alphabet **2** : a grade rating a student's work as good

²b *abbr*, *often cap* **1** bachelor **2** bass **3** bishop **4** book **5** born

B *symbol* boron

Ba *symbol* barium

BA *abbr* **1** bachelor of arts **2** batting average

bab·bitt \'ba-bət\ *n* : an alloy used for lining bearings; *esp* : one containing tin, copper, and antimony

bab·ble \'ba-bəl\ *vb* **bab·bled; bab·bling 1** : to talk enthusiastically or excessively **2** : to utter meaningless sounds — **babble** *n* — **bab·bler** \-b(ə-)lər\ *n*

babe \'bāb\ *n* **1** : BABY **2** *slang* : GIRL, WOMAN

ba·bel \'bā-bəl, 'ba-\ *n*, *often cap* [fr. the Tower of *Babel*, Gen 11:4–9] : a place or scene of noise and confusion; *also* : a confused sound **syn** hubbub, racket, din, uproar, clamor

ba·boon \ba-'bün\ *n* [ME *babewin*, fr. MF *babouin*, fr. *baboue* grimace] : any of several large apes of Asia and Africa with doglike muzzles

ba·bush·ka \bə-'büsh-kə, -'büsh-\ *n* [Russ, grandmother, dim. of *baba* old woman] : a kerchief for the head

¹ba·by \'bā-bē\ *n*, *pl* **babies 1** : a very young child : INFANT **2** : the youngest or smallest of a group **3** : a childish person — **baby** *adj* — **ba·by·hood** *n* — **ba·by·ish** *adj*

²baby *vb* **ba·bied; ba·by·ing** : to tend or treat often with excessive care

baby's breath *n* : any of a genus of herbs that are related to the pinks and have small delicate flowers

ba·by–sit \'bā-bē-,sit\ *vb* **-sat** \-,sat\; **-sit·ting** : to care for children usu. during a short absence of the parents — **ba·by–sit·ter** *n*

bac·ca·lau·re·ate \,ba-kə-'lȯr-ē-ət\ *n* **1** : the degree of bachelor conferred by colleges and universities **2** : a sermon delivered to a graduating class

bac·ca·rat \,bä-kə-'rä, ,ba-\ *n* : a card game played esp. in European casinos

bac·cha·nal \'ba-kən-ᵊl, ,ba-kə-'nal, ,bä-kə-'näl\ *n* **1** : ORGY **2** : REVELER

bac·cha·na·lia \,ba-kə-'nāl-yə\ *n*, *pl* **bacchanalia** : a drunken orgy — **bac·cha·na·lian** \-'nāl-yən\ *adj or n*

bach·e·lor \'ba-chə-lər\ *n* **1** : a person who has received the usu. lowest degree conferred by a 4-year college **2** : an unmarried man — **bach·e·lor·hood** *n*

bach·e·lor·ette \,ba-chə-lə-'ret\ *n* : a young unmarried woman

bachelor's button *n* : a European plant related to the daisies and having blue, pink, or white flower heads

ba·cil·lus \bə-'si-ləs\ *n*, *pl* **-li** \-,lī\ [NL, fr. ML, small staff, dim. of L *baculus* staff] : any of numerous rod-shaped bacteria; *also* : a disease-producing bacterium — **bac·il·lary** \'ba-sə-,ler-ē\ *adj*

¹back \'bak\ *n* **1** : the rear or dorsal part of the human body; *also* : the corresponding part of a lower animal **2** : the part or surface opposite the front **3** : a player in the backfield in football — **back·less** \-ləs\ *adj*

²back *adv* **1** : to, toward, or at the rear **2** : AGO **3** : so as to be restrained or retarded **4** : to, toward, or in a former place or state **5** : in return or reply

³back *adj* **1** : located at or in the back; *also* : REMOTE **2** : OVERDUE **3** : moving or operating backward **4** : not current

⁴back *vb* **1** : SUPPORT, UPHOLD **2** : to go or cause to go backward or in reverse **3** : to furnish with a back : form the back of

back·ache \'ba-,kāk\ *n* : a pain in the lower back

back–bench·er \-'ben-chər\ *n* : a rank-and-file member of a British legislature

back·bite \-,bīt\ *vb* **-bit** \-,bit\; **-bit·ten** \-,bit-ᵊn\; **-bit·ing** \-,bī-tiŋ\ : to say mean or spiteful things about someone who is absent — **back·bit·er** *n*

back·board \-,bȯrd\ *n* : a board placed at or serving as the back of something

back·bone \-,bōn\ *n* **1** : the bony column in the back of a vertebrate that is the chief support of the trunk and consists of a jointed series of vertebrae enclosing and protecting the spinal cord **2** : firm resolute character

back·drop \'bak-ˌdräp\ *n* : a painted cloth hung across the rear of a stage

back·er \'ba-kər\ *n* : one that supports

back·field \-ˌfēld\ *n* : the football players whose positions are behind the line

[1]**back·fire** \-ˌfīr\ *n* : a loud noise caused by the improperly timed explosion of fuel in the cylinder of an internal combustion engine

[2]**backfire** *vb* 1 : to make or undergo a backfire 2 : to have a result opposite to what was intended

back·gam·mon \'bak-ˌga-mən\ *n* : a game played with pieces on a double board in which the moves are determined by throwing dice

back·ground \'bak-ˌgraund\ *n* 1 : the scenery behind something 2 : the setting within which something takes place; *also* : the sum of a person's experience, training, and understanding

back·hand \'bak-ˌhand\ *n* : a stroke (as in tennis) made with the back of the hand turned in the direction of movement; *also* : the side on which such a stroke is made — **back·hand** *vb*

backhand

back·hand·ed \'bak-'han-dəd\ *adj* 1 : INDIRECT, DEVIOUS; *esp* : SARCASTIC 2 : using or made with a backhand

back·hoe \'bak-ˌhō\ *n* : an excavating machine having a bucket that is drawn toward the machine

back·ing \'ba-kiŋ\ *n* 1 : something forming a back 2 : SUPPORT, AID; *also* : a body of supporters

back·lash \'bak-ˌlash\ *n* 1 : a sudden violent backward movement or reaction 2 : a strong adverse reaction

[1]**back·log** \-ˌlóg, -ˌläg\ *n* 1 : a large log at the back of a hearth fire 2 : an accumulation of tasks unperformed or materials not processed

[2]**backlog** *vb* : to accumulate in reserve

back of *prep* : BEHIND

back out *vb* : to withdraw esp. from a commitment or contest

[1]**back·pack** \'bak-ˌpak\ *n* : a camping pack supported by an aluminum frame and carried on the back

[2]**backpack** *vb* : to hike with a backpack — **back·pack·er** *n*

back·ped·al \'bak-ˌped-ᵊl\ *vb* : RETREAT

back·rest \-ˌrest\ *n* : a rest for the back

back·side \-ˌsīd\ *n* : BUTTOCKS

back·slap \-ˌslap\ *vb* : to display excessive cordiality — **back·slap·per** *n*

back·slide \-ˌslīd\ *vb* -**slid** \-ˌslid\; -**slid** *or* -**slid·den** \-ˌslid-ᵊn\; -**slid·ing** \-ˌslī-diŋ\ : to lapse morally or in religious practice — **back·slid·er** *n*

back·spin \-ˌspin\ *n* : a backward rotary motion of a ball

[1]**back·stage** \'bak-ˌstāj\ *adj* 1 : relating to or occurring in the area behind a stage 2 : of or relating to the private lives of theater people 3 : of or relating to the inner working or operation

[2]**back·stage** \'bak-'stāj\ *adv* 1 : in or to a backstage area 2 : SECRETLY

back·stairs \-ˌstarz\ *adj* : SECRET, FURTIVE; *also* : SORDID, SCANDALOUS

[1]**back·stop** \-ˌstäp\ *n* : something serving as a stop behind something else; *esp* : a screen or fence to keep a ball from leaving the field of play

[2]**backstop** *vb* 1 : SUPPORT 2 : to serve as a backstop to

back·stretch \'bak-'strech\ *n* : the side opposite the homestretch on a racecourse

back·stroke \-ˌstrōk\ *n* : a swimming stroke executed on the back

back talk *n* : impudent, insolent, or argumentative replies

back·track \'bak-ˌtrak\ *vb* 1 : to retrace one's course 2 : to reverse a position or stand

back·up \-ˌəp\ *n* : one that serves as a substitute or alternative

[1]**back·ward** \'bak-wərd\ *or* **back·wards** \-wərdz\ *adv* 1 : toward the back 2 : with the back foremost 3 : in a reverse or contrary direction or way 4 : toward the past; *also* : toward a worse state

[2]**backward** *adj* 1 : directed, turned, or done backward 2 : DIFFIDENT, SHY 3 : retarded in development — **back·ward·ly** *adv* — **back·ward·ness** *n*

back·wash \'bak-ˌwòsh, -ˌwäsh\ *n* : a backward flow or movement (as of water or air) produced by a propelling force (as the motion of oars)

back·wa·ter \-ˌwò-tər, -ˌwä-\ *n* 1 : water held or turned back in its course 2 : an isolated or backward place or condition

back·woods \-'wudz\ *n pl* 1 : wooded or partly cleared areas far from cities 2 : a remote or isolated place

ba·con \'bā-kən\ *n* : salted and smoked meat from the sides or back of a pig

bacteria *pl of* BACTERIUM

bac·te·ri·cid·al \bak-ˌtir-ə-'sīd-ᵊl\ *adj* : destroying bacteria — **bac·te·ri·cide** \-'tir-ə-ˌsīd\ *n*

bac·te·ri·ol·o·gy \bak-ˌtir-ē-'ä-lə-jē\ *n* 1 : a science dealing with bacteria and phenomena 2 : bacterial life and phenomena — **bac·te·ri·o·log·ic** \-ə-'lä-jik\ *or* **bac·te·ri·o·log·i·cal** \-ə-'lä-ji-kəl\ *adj* — **bac·te·ri·ol·o·gist** \-'ä-lə-jist\ *n*

bac·te·rio·phage \bak-'tir-ē-ə-ˌfāj\ *n* : any of various viruses that attack specific bacteria

bac·te·ri·um \bak-'tir-ē-əm\ *n, pl* -**ria** \-ē-ə\ [NL, fr. Gk *baktērion* staff] : any of a class of microscopic plants including some that are disease producers and others that are valued esp. for their chemical effects (as fermentation) — **bac·te·ri·al** \-ē-əl\ *adj*

bad \'bad\ *adj* **worse** \'wərs\; **worst** \'wərst\ 1 : below standard : POOR; *also* : UNFAVORABLE ⟨a ~ report⟩ 2 : SPOILED, DECAYED 3 : WICKED; *also* : not well-behaved : NAUGHTY 4 : DISAGREEABLE ⟨a ~ taste⟩; *also* : HARMFUL 5 : DEFECTIVE, FAULTY ⟨~ wiring⟩; *also* : not valid ⟨a ~ check⟩ 6 : UNWELL, ILL 7 : SORRY, REGRETFUL **syn** evil, wrong, immoral, iniquitous — **bad·ly** *adv* — **bad·ness** *n*

bade *past and past part of* BID

badge \'baj\ *n* : a device or token usu. worn as a sign of status

[1]**bad·ger** \'ba-jər\ *n* : any of several sturdy burrowing mammals with long claws on their forefeet

badger

²**badger** *vb* : to harass or annoy persistently

ba·di·nage \ˌbad-ᵊn-ˈäzh\ *n* [F] : playful talk back and forth : BANTER

bad·land \ˈbad-ˌland\ *n* : a region marked by intricate erosional sculpturing and scanty vegetation — usu. used in pl.

bad·min·ton \ˈbad-ˌmint-ᵊn\ *n* : a court game played with light rackets and a shuttlecock volleyed over a net

Bae·de·ker \ˈbā-di-kər, ˈbe-\ : GUIDEBOOK

¹**baf·fle** \ˈba-fəl\ *vb* **baf·fled; baf·fling** \-fə-liŋ\ : FRUSTRATE, THWART, FOIL; *also* : PERPLEX — **baf·fle·ment** *n*

²**baffle** *n* : a device (as a wall or screen) to deflect, check, or regulate flow (as of liquid or sound) — **baffled** \ˈba-fəld\ *adj*

¹**bag** \ˈbag\ *n* : a flexible usu. closable container (as for storing or carrying)

²**bag** *vb* **bagged; bag·ging 1** : DISTEND, BULGE **2** : to put in a bag **3** : to get possession of; *esp* : to take in hunting **syn** trap, snare, catch, capture, collar

ba·gasse \bə-ˈgas\ *n* [F] : plant residue (as of sugarcane) left after a product (as juice) has been extracted

bag·a·telle \ˌba-gə-ˈtel\ *n* [F] : TRIFLE

ba·gel \ˈbā-gəl\ *n* [Yiddish *beygl*] : a hard glazed doughnut-shaped roll

bag·gage \ˈba-gij\ *n* **1** : the traveling bags and personal belongings of a traveler : LUGGAGE **2** : things that get in the way

bag·gy \ˈba-gē\ *adj* **bag·gi·er; -est** : puffed out or hanging like a bag — **bag·gi·ly** \-gə-lē\ *adv* — **bag·gi·ness** \-gē-nəs\ *n*

bag·man \ˈbag-mən\ *n* : a person who collects or distributes illicitly gained money on behalf of another

ba·gnio \ˈban-yō\ *n, pl* **bagnios** [It *bagno*, lit., public bath] : BROTHEL

bag of waters : a double-walled fluid-filled sac that encloses and protects the fetus in the womb and that breaks releasing its fluid during the process of birth

bag·pipe \ˈbag-ˌpīp\ *n* : a musical wind instrument consisting of a bag, a tube with valves, and sounding pipes — often used in pl.

ba·guette \ba-ˈget\ *n* [F, lit., rod] **1** : a gem having the shape of a narrow rectangle; *also* : the shape itself **2** : a long thin loaf of French bread

Ba·ha·mi·an \bə-ˈhä-mē-ən, -ˈhä-\ *n* : a native or inhabitant of the Bahama Islands

baht \ˈbät\ *n, pl* **baht** *also* **bahts** — see MONEY table

¹**bail** \ˈbāl\ *n* : a container for ladling water out of a boat

²**bail** *vb* : to dip and throw out water from a boat — **bail·er** *n*

³**bail** *n* : security given to guarantee a prisoner's appearance when legally required; *also* : one giving such security or the release secured

⁴**bail** *vb* : to release under bail; *also* : to procure the release of by giving bail — **bail·able** \ˈbā-lə-bəl\ *adj*

⁵**bail** *n* : the arched handle (as of a pail or kettle)

bai·liff \ˈbā-ləf\ *n* **1** : an aide of a British sheriff who serves writs and makes arrests; *also* : a minor officer of a U.S. court **2** : an estate or farm manager esp. in Britain : STEWARD

bai·li·wick \ˈbā-li-ˌwik\ *n* : one's special province or domain **syn** territory, field, sphere

bail·out \ˈbā-ˌlaüt\ *n* : a rescue from financial distress

bairn \ˈbarn\ *n, chiefly Scot* : CHILD

¹**bait** \ˈbāt\ *vb* **1** : to persecute by continued attacks **2** : to harass with dogs usu. for sport ⟨~ a bear⟩ **3** : to furnish (as a hook) with bait **4** : ALLURE, ENTICE **5** : to give food and drink to (as an animal) **syn** badger, heckle, hound

²**bait** *n* **1** : a lure for catching animals (as fish) **2** : LURE, TEMPTATION **syn** snare, trap, decoy, come-on, enticement

bai·za \ˈbī-(ˌ)zä\ *n, pl* **baiza** *or* **baizas** — see *rial* at MONEY table

baize \ˈbāz\ *n* : a coarse feltlike fabric

¹**bake** \ˈbāk\ *vb* **baked; bak·ing 1** : to cook or become cooked in dry heat esp. in an oven **2** : to dry and harden by heat ⟨~ bricks⟩ — **bak·er** *n*

²**bake** *n* : a social gathering featuring baked food

baker's dozen *n* : THIRTEEN

bak·ery \ˈbā-k(ə-)rē\ *n, pl* **-er·ies** : a place for baking or selling baked goods

bake·shop \ˈbāk-ˌshäp\ *n* : BAKERY

baking powder *n* : a powder that consists of a carbonate, an acid, and a starch and that makes the dough rise in baking cakes and biscuits

baking soda *n* : SODIUM BICARBONATE

bak·sheesh \ˈbak-ˌshēsh\ *n* : payment (as a tip or bribe) to expedite service

bal *abbr* balance

bal·a·lai·ka \ˌba-lə-ˈlī-kə\ *n* : a triangular 3-stringed instrument of Russian origin played by plucking or strumming

¹**bal·ance** \ˈba-ləns\ *n* [ME, fr. OF, fr. LL *bilanc-, bilanx* having two scalepans, fr. L *bi* two + *lanc-, lanx* plate] **1** : a weighing device : SCALE **2** : a weight, force, or influence counteracting the effect of another **3** : an oscillating wheel used to regulate a timepiece **4** : a state of equilibrium **5** : REMAINDER, REST; *esp* : an amount in excess esp. on the credit side of an account — **bal·anced** \-lənst\ *adj*

²**balance** *vb* **bal·anced; bal·anc·ing 1** : to compute the balance of an account **2** : to arrange so that one set of elements equals another; *also* : to equal or equalize in weight, number, or proportions **3** : WEIGH **4** : to bring or come to a state or position of balance; *also* : to bring into harmony or proportion

bal·boa \bal-ˈbō-ə\ *n* — see MONEY table

bal·brig·gan \bal-ˈbri-gən\ *n* : a knitted cotton fabric used esp. for underwear

bal·co·ny \ˈbal-kə-nē\ *n, pl* **-nies 1** : a platform projecting from the side of a building and enclosed by a railing **2** : a gallery inside a building

bald \ˈbȯld\ *adj* **1** : lacking a natural or usual covering (as of hair) **2** : UNADORNED, PLAIN **syn** bare, barren, naked, nude — **bald·ly** *adv* — **bald·ness** *n*

bal·da·chin \ˈbȯl-də-kən, ˈbal-\ *or* **bal·da·chi·no** \ˌbal-də-ˈkē-nō\ *n, pl* **-chins** *or* **-chinos** : a canopylike structure over an altar

bald cypress *n* : either of two large swamp trees of the southern U.S. with hard red wood

bald eagle *n* : an eagle of No. America that when mature has white head and neck feathers and a white tail

bal·der·dash \ˈbȯl-dər-ˌdash\ *n* : NONSENSE

bald·ing \ˈbȯl-diŋ\ *adj* : getting bald

bal·dric \ˈbȯl-drik\ *n* : a belt worn over the shoulder to carry a sword or bugle

¹**bale** \ˈbāl\ *n* : a large or closely packed bundle

²**bale** *vb* **baled; bal·ing** : to pack in a bale — **bal·er** *n*

ba·leen \bə-ˈlēn\ *n* : a horny substance attached in plates to the upper jaw of some large whales (**baleen whales**)

bale·ful \ˈbāl-fəl\ *adj* : DEADLY, HARMFUL; *also* : OMINOUS **syn** sinister, malefic, maleficent, malign

¹**balk** \ˈbȯk\ *n* **1** : HINDRANCE, CHECK, SETBACK **2** : an illegal motion of the pitcher in baseball while in position

²**balk** *vb* **1** : BLOCK, THWART **2** : to stop short and refuse to go on **3** : to commit a balk in sports **syn** frustrate, baffle, foil, thwart — **balky** \ˈbȯ-kē\ *adj*

¹**ball** \ˈbȯl\ *n* **1** : a rounded body or mass (as at the base of the thumb or for use as a missile or in a game) **2** : a game played with a ball **3** : a pitched baseball that misses the strike zone and is not swung at by the batter **4** : a hit or thrown ball in various games ⟨foul ~⟩ — **on the ball** : COMPETENT, KNOWLEDGEABLE, ALERT

²**ball** *vb* : to form into a ball

³**ball** *n* : a large formal dance

bal·lad \'ba-ləd\ n 1 : a narrative poem of strongly marked rhythm suitable for singing 2 : a simple song : AIR 3 : a slow romantic song
bal·lad·eer \,ba-lə-'dir\ n : a singer of ballads
¹bal·last \'ba-ləst\ n 1 : heavy material used to stabilize a ship or control a balloon's ascent 2 : crushed stone laid in a railroad bed or used in making concrete
²ballast vb : to provide with ballast **syn** balance, stabilize, steady
ball bearing n : a bearing in which the revolving part turns upon steel balls that roll easily in a groove; also : one of the balls in such a bearing
ball·car·ri·er \'bȯl-,kar-ē-ər\ n : the football player carrying the ball in an offensive play
bal·le·ri·na \,ba-lə-'rē-nə\ n : a female ballet dancer
bal·let \'ba-,lā, ba-'lā\ n 1 : dancing in which fixed poses and steps are combined with light flowing movements often to convey a story; also : a theatrical art form using ballet dancing 2 : a company of ballet dancers
bal·let·o·mane \ba-'le-tə-,mān\ n : a devotee of ballet
bal·lis·tic missile \bə-'lis-tik-\ n : a missile that is guided during ascent and that falls freely during descent
bal·lis·tics \-tiks\ n sing or pl 1 : the science of the motion of projectiles (as bullets) in flight 2 : the flight characteristics of a projectile — **ballistic** adj
ball of fire : an unusually energetic person
¹bal·loon \bə-'lün\ n 1 : a bag filled with gas or heated air so as to rise and float in the atmosphere 2 : a toy consisting of an inflatable bag — **bal·loon·ist** n
²balloon vb 1 : to swell or puff out 2 : to travel in a balloon 3 : to increase rapidly
¹bal·lot \'ba-lət\ n [It ballotta small ball used in secret voting, fr. It dial., dim. of balla ball] 1 : a piece of paper used to cast a vote 2 : the action or a system of voting; also : the right to vote
²ballot vb : to decide by ballot : VOTE
¹ball·park \'bȯl-,pärk\ n : a park in which ball games are played
²ballpark adj : approximately correct ⟨∼ estimate⟩
ball·point \'bȯl-,pȯint\ n : a pen whose writing point is a small rotating metal ball that inks itself from an inner container
ball·room \'bȯl-,rüm, -,rùm\ n : a large room for dances
bal·ly·hoo \'ba-lē-,hü\ n, pl **-hoos** : extravagant statements and claims made for publicity — **ballyhoo** vb
balm \'bäm, 'bälm\ n 1 : a fragrant healing or soothing lotion or ointment 2 : any of several spicy fragrant herbs of the mint family 3 : something that comforts or soothes
balmy \'bä-mē, 'bäl-\ adj **balm·i·er; -est** 1 : gently soothing : MILD 2 : FOOLISH, ABSURD **syn** soft, bland, mild, gentle — **balm·i·ness** n
ba·lo·ney \bə-'lō-nē\ n : NONSENSE
bal·sa \'bȯl-sə\ n : the extremely light strong wood of a tropical American tree; also : the tree
bal·sam \'bȯl-səm\ n 1 : a fragrant aromatic and usu. resinous substance oozing from various plants; also : a preparation containing or smelling like balsam 2 : a balsam-yielding tree (as balsam fir) 3 : a common garden ornamental plant — **bal·sam·ic** \bȯl-'sa-mik\ adj
balsam fir n : a resinous American evergreen tree that is widely used for pulpwood and as a Christmas tree
Bal·ti·more oriole \'bȯl-tə-,mȯr-\ n : a common American oriole in which the male is brightly colored with orange, black, and white
bal·us·ter \'ba-lə-stər\ n [F balustre, fr. It balaustro, fr. balaustra wild pomegranate flower, fr. L balaustium; fr. its shape] : an upright support for a rail (as of a staircase)
bal·us·trade \'ba-lə-,sträd\ n : a row of balusters topped by a rail
bam·boo \bam-'bü\ n, pl **bamboos** : any of various woody mostly tall tropical grasses including some

with strong hollow stems used for building, furniture, or utensils
bamboo curtain n, often cap B&C : a political, military, and ideological barrier in the Orient
bam·boo·zle \bam-'bü-zəl\ vb **-boo·zled; -boo·zling** : TRICK, HOODWINK
¹ban \'ban\ vb **banned; ban·ning** : PROHIBIT, FORBID
²ban n 1 : CURSE 2 : a legal or formal prohibiting
³ban \'bän\ n, pl **ba·ni** \'bä-nē\ — see leu at MONEY table
ba·nal \bə-'näl, -'nal; 'bān-ᵊl\ adj [F] : COMMONPLACE, TRITE — **ba·nal·i·ty** \bā-'na-lə-tē\ n
ba·nana \bə-'na-nə\ n : a treelike tropical plant bearing thick clusters of yellow or reddish finger-shaped fruit; also : this fruit
¹band \'band\ n 1 : something that binds, ties, or goes around 2 : a strip or stripe that can be distinguished (as by color or texture) from nearby matter 3 : a range of wavelengths (as in radio)
²band vb 1 : to tie up, finish, or enclose with a band 2 : to gather together or unite esp. for some common end — **band·er** n
³band n : a group of persons, animals, or things; esp : a group of musicians organized for playing together
¹ban·dage \'ban-dij\ n : a strip of material used esp. in dressing wounds
²bandage vb **ban·daged; ban·dag·ing** : to dress or cover with a bandage
ban·dan·na or **ban·dana** \ban-'da-nə\ n : a large colored figured handkerchief
B and B abbr bed-and-breakfast
band·box \'band-,bäks\ n : a usu. cylindrical box for carrying clothing
band·ed \'ban-dəd\ adj : having or marked with bands
ban·de·role or **ban·de·rol** \'ban-də-,rōl\ n : a long narrow forked flag or streamer
ban·dit \'ban-dət\ n [It bandito, fr. bandire to banish] 1 pl also **ban·dit·ti** \ban-'di-tē\ : an outlaw who lives by plunder; esp : a member of a band of marauders 2 : ROBBER — **ban·dit·ry** \'ban-də-trē\ n
ban·do·lier or **ban·do·leer** \,ban-də-'lir\ n : a belt slung over the shoulder esp. to carry ammunition
band saw n : a saw in the form of an endless steel belt running over pulleys
band·stand \'band-,stand\ n : a usu. roofed platform on which a band or orchestra performs outdoors
b and w abbr black and white
band·wag·on \'band-,wa-gən\ n 1 : a wagon carrying musicians in a parade 2 : a movement that attracts growing support
¹ban·dy \'ban-dē\ vb **ban·died; ban·dy·ing** 1 : to exchange (as blows or quips) esp. in rapid succession 2 : to use in a glib or offhand way
²bandy adj : curved outward ⟨∼ legs⟩
bane \'bān\ n 1 : POISON 2 : WOE, HARM; also : a source of this — **bane·ful** adj
¹bang \'baŋ\ vb 1 : BUMP ⟨fell and ∼ed his knee⟩ 2 : to strike, thrust, or move usu. with a loud noise
²bang n 1 : a resounding blow 2 : a sudden loud noise
³bang adv : DIRECTLY, RIGHT
⁴bang n : a fringe of hair cut short (as across the forehead) — usu. used in pl.
⁵bang vb : to cut a bang in
Ban·gla·deshi \,bäŋ-glə-'de-shē\ n : a native or inhabitant of Bangladesh — **Bangladeshi** adj
ban·gle \'baŋ-gəl\ n : BRACELET; also : a loose-hanging ornament
bang-up \'baŋ-,əp\ adj : FIRST-RATE, EXCELLENT ⟨a ∼ job⟩
bani pl of ³BAN
ban·ish \'ba-nish\ vb 1 : to require by authority to leave a country 2 : to drive out : EXPEL **syn** exile, ostracize, deport, relegate — **ban·ish·ment** n
ban·is·ter \'ba-nə-stər\ n 1 : BALUSTER 2 : a handrail with its supporting posts 3 : HANDRAIL

ban·jo \'ban-₁jō\ *n, pl* **banjos** *also* **banjoes** : a musical instrument with a long neck, a drumlike body, and usu. five strings — **ban·jo·ist** \-ist\ *n*

¹bank \'baŋk\ *n* **1** : a piled-up mass (as of cloud or earth) **2** : an undersea elevation **3** : rising ground bordering a lake, river, or sea **4** : the sideways slope of a surface along a curve or of a vehicle as it rounds a curve

²bank *vb* **1** : to form a bank about **2** : to cover (as a fire) with fuel to keep inactive **3** : to build (a curve) with the roadbed or track inclined laterally upward from the inside edge **4** : to pile or heap in a bank; *also* : to arrange in a tier **5** : to incline (an airplane) laterally

³bank *n* [ME, fr. MF or It; MF *banque*, fr. It *banca*, lit., bench] **1** : an establishment concerned esp. with the custody, loan, exchange, or issue of money, the extension of credit, and the transmission of funds **2** : a stock of or a place for holding something in reserve ⟨a blood ∼⟩

⁴bank *vb* **1** : to conduct the business of a bank **2** : to deposit money or have an account in a bank — **bank·er** *n* — **bank·ing** *n*

⁵bank *n* : a group of objects arranged close together (as in a row or tier) ⟨a ∼ of file drawers⟩

bank·book \'baŋk-₁bùk\ *n* : the depositor's book in which a bank records deposits and withdrawals

bank·card \-₁kärd\ *n* : a credit card issued by a bank

bank·note \-₁nōt\ *n* : a promissory note issued by a bank and circulating as money

bank·roll \-₁rōl\ *n* : supply of money : FUNDS

¹bank·rupt \'baŋ-(₁)krəpt\ *n* : an insolvent person; *esp* : one whose property is turned over by court action to a trustee to be handled for the benefit of his creditors — **bankrupt** *vb*

²bankrupt *adj* **1** : reduced to financial ruin; *esp* : legally declared a bankrupt **2** : wholly lacking in or deprived of some essential ⟨morally ∼⟩ — **bank·rupt·cy** \'baŋ-(₁)krəpt-sē\ *n*

¹ban·ner \'ba-nər\ *n* **1** : a piece of cloth attached to a staff and used by a leader as his standard **2** : FLAG

²banner *adj* : distinguished from all others esp. in excellence ⟨a ∼ year⟩

ban·nock \'ba-nək\ *n* : a flat oatmeal or barley cake usu. cooked on a griddle

banns \'banz\ *n pl* : public announcement esp. in church of a proposed marriage

ban·quet \'baŋ-kwət\ *n* [MF, fr. It *banchetto*, fr. dim. of *banca* bench, bank] : a ceremonial dinner — **banquet** *vb*

ban·quette \baŋ-'ket\ *n* : a long upholstered bench esp. along a wall

ban·shee \'ban-shē\ *n* [Ir *bean sídhe* & ScGael *bean sith*, lit., woman of fairyland] : a female spirit in Gaelic folklore whose wailing warns a family that one of them will soon die

ban·tam \'ban-təm\ *n* **1** : any of numerous small domestic fowls that are often miniatures of standard breeds **2** : a small but pugnacious person

¹ban·ter \'ban-tər\ *vb* : to speak to in a witty and teasing manner

²banter *n* : good-natured witty joking

Ban·tu \'ban-₁tü\ *n, pl* **Bantu** *or* **Bantus** **1** : a member of a group of African peoples of central and southern Africa **2** : a group of African languages spoken by the Bantu

Ban·tu·stan \₁ban-tü-'stan, ₁bän-tü-'stän\ *n* : an all-black enclave in the Republic of So. Africa with a limited degree of self-government

ban·yan \'ban-yən\ *n* [earlier *banyan* Hindu merchant, fr. Hindi *baniyā*; fr. a merchant's pagoda erected under a tree of the species in Iran] : a large East Indian tree whose aerial roots grow downward to the ground and form new trunks

banyan

ban·zai \bän-'zī\ *n* : a Japanese cheer or cry of triumph

bao·bab \'baù-₁bab, 'bā-ə-\ *n* : an Old World tropical tree with short swollen trunk and sour edible gourd-like fruits

bap·tism \'bap-₁ti-zəm\ *n* **1** : a Christian sacrament signifying spiritual rebirth and symbolized by the ritual use of water **2** : an act of baptizing — **bap·tis·mal** \bap-'tiz-məl\ *adj*

baptismal name *n* : GIVEN NAME

Bap·tist \'bap-tist\ *n* : a member of any of several Protestant denominations emphasizing baptism by immersion of believers only

bap·tis·tery *or* **bap·tis·try** \'bap-tə-strē\ *n, pl* **-ter·ies** *or* **-tries** : a place esp. in a church used for baptism

bap·tize \bap-'tīz, 'bap-₁tīz\ *vb* **bap·tized; bap·tiz·ing** [ME, fr. OF *baptiser*, fr. L *baptizare*, fr. Gk *baptizein* to dip, baptize, fr. *baptein* to dip] **1** : to administer baptism to; *also* : CHRISTEN **2** : to purify esp. by an ordeal

¹bar \'bär\ *n* **1** : a long narrow piece of material (as wood or metal) used esp. for a lever, fastening, or support **2** : BARRIER, OBSTACLE **3** : the railing in a law court at which prisoners are stationed; *also* : the legal profession or the whole body of lawyers **4** : a stripe, band, or line much longer than wide **5** : a counter at which food or esp. drink is served; *also* : BARROOM **6** : a vertical line across the musical staff

²bar *vb* **barred; bar·ring** **1** : to fasten, confine, or obstruct with or as if with a bar or bars **2** : to mark with bars : STRIPE **3** : to shut or keep out : EXCLUDE **4** : FORBID, PREVENT

³bar *prep* : EXCEPT

⁴bar *abbr* barometer; barometric

Bar *abbr* Baruch

barb \'bärb\ *n* **1** : a sharp projection extending backward (as from the point of an arrow) **2** : a biting critical remark — **barbed** \'bärbd\ *adj*

bar·bar·ian \bär-'ber-ē-ən\ *adj* **1** : of, relating to, or being a land, culture, or people alien to and usu. believed to be inferior to another's **2** : lacking refinement, learning, or artistic or literary culture — **barbarian** *n*

bar·bar·ic \bär-'bar-ik\ *adj* **1** : BARBARIAN **2** : marked by a lack of restraint : WILD **3** : PRIMITIVE, UNSOPHISTICATED

bar·ba·rism \'bär-bə-₁ri-zəm\ *n* **1** : the social condition of barbarians; *also* : the use or display of barbarian or barbarous acts, attitudes, or ideas **2** : a word or expression that offends standards of correctness or purity

bar·ba·rous \'bär-bə-rəs\ *adj* **1** : lacking culture or refinement **2** : using linguistic barbarisms **3** : mercilessly harsh or cruel — **bar·bar·i·ty** \bär-'bar-ə-tē\ *n* — **bar·ba·rous·ly** *adv*

¹bar·be·cue \'bär-bi-₁kyü\ *n* : a social gathering at which barbecued food is served

²barbecue *vb* **-cued; -cu·ing** **1** : to cook over hot coals or on a revolving spit **2** : to cook in a highly seasoned vinegar sauce

bar·bell \'bär-₁bel\ *n* : a bar with adjustable weights attached to each end used for exercise and in weight-lifting competition

bar·ber \'bär-bər\ *n* [ME, fr. MF *barbeor*, fr. *barbe* beard, fr. L *barba*] : one whose business is cutting and dressing hair and shaving and trimming beards

bar·ber·ry \'bär-ˌber-ē\ *n* : any of a genus of spiny shrubs bearing yellow flowers and oblong red berries

bar·bi·tu·rate \bär-'bi-chə-rət\ *n* : any of various compounds (as a salt or ester) formed from an organic acid (**bar·bi·tu·ric acid** \ˌbär-bə-'tur-ik-, -'tyur-\; *esp* : one used as a sedative or hypnotic

bar·ca·role *or* **bar·ca·rolle** \'bär-kə-ˌrōl\ *n* : a Venetian boat song characterized by a beat suggesting a rowing rhythm; *also* : a piece of music imitating this

bar chart *n* : BAR GRAPH

bar code *n* : a set of printed and variously spaced bars and sometimes numerals that is designed to be scanned to identify the object it labels

bard \'bärd\ *n* : POET

¹bare \'bar\ *adj* **bar·er; bar·est** **1** : NAKED **2** : UNCONCEALED, EXPOSED **3** : EMPTY **4** : leaving nothing to spare : MERE **5** : PLAIN, UNADORNED **syn** nude, bald — **bare·ness** *n*

²bare *vb* **bared; bar·ing** : to make or lay bare : UNCOVER

bare·back \-ˌbak\ *or* **bare·backed** \-'bakt\ *adv or adj* : without a saddle

bare·faced \-'fāst\ *adj* **1** : having the face uncovered; *esp* : BEARDLESS **2** : not concealed : OPEN — **bare·faced·ly** \-'fā-səd-lē, -'fāst-lē\ *adv*

bare·foot \-ˌfut\ *or* **bare·foot·ed** \-'fu-təd\ *adv or adj* : with bare feet

bare–hand·ed \-'han-dəd\ *adv or adj* **1** : without gloves **2** : without tools or weapons

bare·head·ed \-'he-dəd\ *adv or adj* : without a hat

bare·ly \'bar-lē\ *adv* **1** : PLAINLY, MEAGERLY **2** : by a narrow margin : only just ⟨~ enough money⟩

bar·fly \'bär-ˌflī\ *n* : a drinker who frequents bars

¹bar·gain \'bär-gən\ *n* **1** : AGREEMENT **2** : an advantageous purchase **3** : a transaction, situation, or event regarded in the light of its results

²bargain *vb* **1** : to negotiate over the terms of an agreement; *also* : to come to terms **2** : BARTER

bar·gain–base·ment \'bär-gən-'bās-mənt\ *adj* : markedly inexpensive

¹barge \'bärj\ *n* **1** : a broad flat-bottomed boat usu. moved by towing **2** : a motorboat supplied to a flagship (as for an admiral) **3** : a ceremonial boat elegantly furnished — **barge·man** \-mən\ *n*

²barge *vb* **barged; barg·ing** **1** : to carry by barge **2** : to move or thrust oneself clumsily or rudely

bar graph *n* : a graphic technique for comparing amounts by rectangles whose lengths are proportional to the amounts they represent

bari·tone \'bar-ə-ˌtōn\ *n* [F *baryton* or It *baritono*, fr. Gk *barytonos* deep sounding, fr. *barys* heavy + *tonos* tone] : a male voice between bass and tenor; *also* : a man with such a voice

bar·i·um \'bar-ē-əm\ *n* : a silver-white metallic chemical element that occurs only in combination — see ELEMENT table

¹bark \'bärk\ *vb* **1** : to make the short loud cry of a dog **2** : to speak or utter in a curt loud tone : SNAP

²bark *n* : the sound made by a barking dog

³bark *n* : the tough corky outer covering of a woody stem or root

⁴bark *vb* **1** : to strip the bark from **2** : to rub the skin from : ABRADE

⁵bark *n* : a ship of three or more masts with the aft mast fore-and-aft rigged and the others square-rigged

bar·keep \'bär-ˌkēp\ *also* **bar·keep·er** \-ˌkē-pər\ *n* : BARTENDER

bark·er \'bär-kər\ *n* : a person who stands at the entrance esp. to a show and tries to attract customers to it

bar·ley \'bär-lē\ *n* : a cereal grass with seeds used as food and in making malt liquors; *also* : its seed

bar mitz·vah \bär-'mits-və\ *n, often cap B&M* [Heb

bar miṣwāh, lit., son of the (divine) law] **1** : a Jewish boy who at about 13 years of age assumes religious responsibilities **2** : the ceremony recognizing a boy as a bar mitzvah

barn \'bärn\ *n* [ME *bern*, fr. OE *bereærn*, fr. *bere* barley + *ærn* house, store] : a building used esp. for storing hay and grain and for housing livestock or farm equipment

bar·na·cle \'bär-ni-kəl\ *n* : any of numerous small marine crustaceans free-swimming when young but permanently fixed (as to rocks, whales, or ships) when adult

barn·storm \'bärn-ˌstorm\ *vb* : to travel through the country making brief stops to entertain (as with shows or flying stunts) or to campaign for political office

barn·yard \-ˌyärd\ *n* : a usu. fenced area adjoining a barn

baro·graph \'bar-ə-ˌgraf\ *n* : a recording barometer

ba·rom·e·ter \bə-'räm-ə-tər\ *n* : an instrument for measuring atmospheric pressure — **baro·met·ric** \ˌbar-ə-'me-trik\ *adj*

bar·on \'bar-ən\ *n* : a member of the lowest grade of the British peerage — **ba·ro·ni·al** \bə-'rō-nē-əl\ *adj* — **bar·ony** \'bar-ə-nē\ *n*

bar·on·age \'bar-ə-nij\ *n* : PEERAGE

bar·on·ess \'bar-ə-nəs\ *n* **1** : the wife or widow of a baron **2** : a woman holding a baronial title in her own right

bar·on·et \'bar-ə-nət\ *n* : a man holding a rank of honor below a baron but above a knight — **bar·on·et·cy** \-sē\ *n*

ba·roque \bə-'rōk, -'räk\ *adj* : marked by the use of complex forms, bold ornamentation, and the juxtapositioning of contrasting elements

ba·rouche \bə-'rüsh\ *n* [G *Barutsche*, fr. It *biroccio*, ultim. fr. LL *birotus* two-wheeled, fr. L *bi* two + *rota* wheel] : a 4-wheeled carriage with a high driver's seat in front and a folding top

bar·racks \'bar-əks\ *n sing or pl* : a building or group of buildings for lodging soldiers

bar·ra·cu·da \ˌbar-ə-'kü-də\ *n, pl* **-da** *or* **-das** : any of several large predaceous sea fishes including some used for food

bar·rage \bə-'räzh, -'räj\ *n* : a heavy concentration of fire (as of artillery)

barred \'bärd\ *adj* : STRIPED

¹bar·rel \'bar-əl\ *n* **1** : a round bulging cask with flat ends of equal diameter **2** : the amount contained in a barrel **3** : a cylindrical or tubular part ⟨gun ~⟩ — **bar·reled** \-əld\ *adj*

²barrel *vb* **-reled** *or* **-relled; -rel·ing** *or* **-rel·ling** **1** : to pack in a barrel **2** : to travel at high speed

bar·rel·head \-ˌhed\ *n* : the flat end of a barrel — **on the barrelhead** : asking for or granting no credit ⟨paid cash *on the barrelhead*⟩

barrel roll *n* : an airplane maneuver in which a complete revolution about the longitudinal axis is made

¹bar·ren \'bar-ən\ *adj* **1** : STERILE, UNFRUITFUL **2** : unproductive of results ⟨a ~ scheme⟩ **3** : lacking interest or charm **4** : DULL, STUPID — **bar·ren·ness** \-nəs\ *n*

²barren *n* : a tract of barren land

bar·rette \bä-'ret, bə-\ *n* : a clasp or bar for holding the hair in place

¹bar·ri·cade \'bar-ə-ˌkād, ˌbar-ə-'kād\ *vb* **-cad·ed; -cad·ing** : to block, obstruct, or fortify with a barricade

²barricade *n* [F, fr. MF, fr. *barriquer* to barricade, fr. *barrique* barrel] **1** : a hastily thrown-up obstruction or fortification **2** : BARRIER, OBSTACLE

bar·ri·er \'bar-ē-ər\ *n* : something that separates, demarcates, or serves as a barricade ⟨racial ~s⟩

barrier island *n* : a long broad sandy island lying parallel to a shore

barrier reef *n* : a coral reef roughly parallel to a shore and separated from it by a lagoon

bar·ring \\'bär-iŋ\ *prep* : excluding by exception : EXCEPTING

bar·rio \\'bär-ē-ˌō, 'bär-\ *n, pl* **-ri·os 1** : a district of a city or town in a Spanish-speaking country **2** : a Spanish-speaking quarter in a U.S. city

bar·ris·ter \\'bar-ə-stər\ *n* : a British counselor admitted to plead in the higher courts

bar·room \\'bär-ˌrüm, -ˌrüm\ *n* : a room or establishment whose main feature is a bar for the sale of liquor

¹bar·row \\'bar-ō\ *n* : a large burial mound of earth and stones

²barrow *n* **1** : WHEELBARROW **2** : a cart with a boxlike body and two shafts for pushing it

Bart *abbr* baronet

bar·tend·er \\'bär-ˌten-dər\ *n* : one that serves liquor at a bar

bar·ter \\'bär-tər\ *vb* : to trade by exchange of goods — **barter** *n* — **bar·ter·er** *n*

Ba·ruch \\'bär-ˌük, bə-'rük\ *n* — see BIBLE table

bas·al \\'bā-səl\ *adj* **1** : situated at or forming the base **2** : BASIC

basal metabolism *n* : the turnover of energy in a fasting and resting organism using energy solely to maintain vital cellular activity, respiration, and circulation as measured by the rate at which heat is given off

ba·salt \bə-'sȯlt, 'bā-ˌsȯlt\ *n* : a dark fine-grained igneous rock — **ba·sal·tic** \bə-'sȯl-tik\ *adj*

¹base \\'bās\ *n, pl* **bas·es** \\'bā-səz\ **1** : BOTTOM, FOUNDATION **2** : a side or face on which a geometrical figure stands; *also* : the length of a base **3** : a main ingredient or fundamental part **4** : the point of beginning an act or operation **5** : a place on which a force depends for supplies **6** : a number (as 5 in 5⁷) that is raised to a power; *esp* : a number that when raised to a power equal to the logarithm of a number yields the number itself (the logarithm of 100 to ~ 10 is 2 since $10^2 = 100$) **7** : the number of units in a given digit's place of a number system that is required to give the numeral 1 in the next higher place (the decimal system uses a ~ of 10); *also* : such a system using an indicated base (convert from ~ 10 to ~ 2) **8** : any of the four stations at the corners of a baseball diamond **9** : a chemical compound (as lime or ammonia) that reacts with an acid to form a salt, has a bitter taste, and turns litmus blue **syn** basis, ground, groundwork, footing, foundation — **base·man** \\'bās-mən\ *n*

²base *vb* **based; bas·ing 1** : to form or serve as a base for **2** : ESTABLISH

³base *adj* **1** : of inferior quality : DEBASED, ALLOYED **2** : CONTEMPTIBLE, IGNOBLE **3** : MENIAL, DEGRADING **4** : of little value **syn** low, vile, despicable, wretched — **base·ly** *adv* — **base·ness** *n*

base·ball \\'bās-ˌbȯl\ *n* : a game played with a bat and ball by two teams on a field with four bases arranged in a diamond; *also* : the ball used in this game

base·board \-ˌbȯrd\ *n* : a line of boards or molding covering the joint of a wall and the adjoining floor

base·born \-'bȯrn\ *adj* **1** : MEAN, IGNOBLE **2** : of humble birth **3** : of illegitimate birth

base exchange *n* : a post exchange at a naval or air force base

base hit *n* : a hit in baseball that enables the batter to reach base safely with no error made and no base runner forced out

base·less \-ləs\ *adj* : having no base or basis : GROUNDLESS

base·line \\'bās-ˌlīn\ *n* **1** : a line serving as a basis esp. to calculate or locate something **2** : the area within which a baseball player must keep when running between bases

base·ment \-mənt\ *n* **1** : the part of a building that is wholly or partly below ground level **2** : the lowest or fundamental part of something

base on balls : an advance to first base given to a baseball player who receives four balls

base runner *n* : a baseball player who is on base or is attempting to reach a base

¹bash \\'bash\ *vb* **1** : to strike violently : HIT **2** : to smash by a blow **3** : to attack physically or verbally

²bash *n* **1** : a heavy blow **2** : a festive social gathering : PARTY

bash·ful \\'bash-fəl\ *adj* : inclined to shrink from public attention — **bash·ful·ness** *n*

ba·sic \\'bā-sik\ *adj* **1** : of, relating to, or forming the base or essence : FUNDAMENTAL **2** : of, relating to, or having the character of a chemical base **syn** underlying, basal, primary — **ba·sic·i·ty** \bā-'si-sə-tē\ *n*

BA·SIC \\'bā-sik\ *n* [*B*eginner's *A*ll-purpose *S*ymbolic *I*nstruction *C*ode] : a simplified language for programming a computer

ba·si·cal·ly \\'bā-si-k(ə-)lē\ *adv* **1** : at a basic level **2** : for the most part **3** : in a basic manner

ba·sil \\'bā-zəl, 'ba-, -səl\ *n* : any of several mints with fragrant leaves used in cooking

ba·sil·i·ca \bə-'si-li-kə, -'zi-\ *n* [L, fr. Gk *basilikē*, fr. fem. of *basilikos* royal, fr. *basileus* king] **1** : an early Christian church building consisting of nave and aisles with clerestory and apse **2** : a Roman Catholic church given ceremonial privileges

bas·i·lisk \\'ba-sə-lisk, 'ba-zə-\ *n* [ME, fr. L *basiliscus*, fr. Gk *basiliskos*, fr. dim. of *basileus* king] : a legendary reptile with fatal breath and glance

ba·sin \\'bās-ᵊn\ *n* **1** : an open usu. circular vessel with sloping sides for holding liquid (as water) **2** : a hollow or enclosed place containing water; *also* : the region drained by a river

ba·sis \\'bā-səs\ *n, pl* **ba·ses** \-ˌsēz\ **1** : FOUNDATION, BASE **2** : a fundamental principle

bask \\'bask\ *vb* **1** : to expose oneself to comfortable heat **2** : to enjoy something warmly comforting (~*ing* in his friends' admiration)

bas·ket \\'bas-kət\ *n* : a container made of woven material (as twigs or grasses); *also* : any of various lightweight usu. wood containers — **bas·ket·ful** *n*

bas·ket·ball \-ˌbȯl\ *n* : a game played on a court by two teams who try to throw an inflated ball through a raised goal; *also* : the ball used in this game

basket case *n* **1** : a person who has all four limbs amputated **2** : one that is totally incapacitated or inoperative

basket weave *n* : a textile weave resembling the checkered pattern of a plaited basket

bas mitz·vah \bäs-'mits-və\ *n, often cap B&M* [Heb *bath miṣwāh*, lit., daughter of the (divine) law] **1** : a Jewish girl who at about 13 years of age assumes religious responsibilities **2** : the ceremony recognizing a girl as a bas mitzvah

Basque \\'bask\ *n* **1** : a member of a people inhabiting a region bordering on the Bay of Biscay in northern Spain and southwestern France **2** : the language of the Basque people — **Basque** *adj*

bas–re·lief \ˌbä-ri-'lēf\ *n* [F] : a sculpture in relief with the design raised very slightly from the background

¹bass \\'bas\ *n, pl* **bass** *or* **bass·es** : any of numerous sport and food bony fishes (as a striped bass)

²bass \\'bās\ *adj* : of low pitch

³bass \\'bās\ *n* **1** : a deep sound or tone **2** : the lower half of the musical pitch range **3** : the lowest part in a 4-part chorus; *also* : a singer having this voice or part

bas·set hound \\'ba-sət-\ *n* : any of an old breed of short=legged hunting dogs of French origin having long ears and crooked front legs

bas·si·net \ˌba-sə-'net\ *n* : a baby's bed that resembles a basket and often has a hood over one end

bas·so \\'ba-sō, 'bä-\ *n, pl* **bassos** *or* **bas·si** \\'bä-ˌsē\ [It] : a bass singer

bas·soon \bə-'sün\ *n* : a musical wind instrument lower in pitch than the oboe

bass·wood \'bas-ˌwud\ *n* : any of several New World lindens or their wood

bast \'bast\ *n* : BAST FIBER

¹**bas·tard** \'bas-tərd\ *n* **1** : an illegitimate child **2** : an offensive or disagreeable person

²**bastard** *adj* **1** : ILLEGITIMATE **2** : of an inferior or non-typical kind, size, or form; *also* : SPURIOUS — **bas·tardy** *n*

bas·tard·ize \'bas-tər-ˌdīz\ *vb* **-ized; -iz·ing** : to reduce from a higher to a lower state : DEBASE

¹**baste** \'bāst\ *vb* **bast·ed; bast·ing** : to sew with long stitches so as to keep temporarily in place

²**baste** *vb* **bast·ed; bast·ing** : to moisten (as meat) at intervals with liquid while cooking

bast fiber *n* : a strong woody plant fiber obtained chiefly from phloem and used esp. in making ropes

bas·ti·na·do \ˌbas-tə-'nā-dō, -'nä-\ *or* **bas·ti·nade** \ˌbas-tə-'nād, -'näd\ *n, pl* **-na·does** *or* **-nades** **1** : a blow or beating esp. with a stick **2** : a punishment consisting of beating the soles of the feet

bas·tion \'bas-chən\ *n* : a projecting part of a fortification; *also* : a fortified position

¹**bat** \'bat\ *n* **1** : a stout stick : CLUB **2** : a sharp blow **3** : an implement (as of wood) used to hit a ball (as in baseball) **4** : a turn at batting — usu. used with *at*

²**bat** *vb* **bat·ted; bat·ting** : to hit with or as if with a bat

³**bat** *n* : any of an order of night-flying mammals with forelimbs modified to form wings

⁴**bat** *vb* **bat·ted; bat·ting** : WINK, BLINK

batch \'bach\ *n* **1** : a quantity (as of bread) baked at one time **2** : a quantity of material for use at one time or produced at one operation

bate \'bāt\ *vb* **bat·ed; bat·ing** : MODERATE, REDUCE

bath \'bath, 'bath\ *n, pl* **baths** \'ba_th_z, 'baths, 'ba_th_z, 'baths\ **1** : a washing of the body **2** : water for washing the body **3** : a liquid in which objects are immersed so that it can act on them **4** : BATHROOM **5** : a financial loss (took a ∼ in the market)

bathe \'bā_th_\ *vb* **bathed; bath·ing** **1** : to wash in liquid and esp. water; *also* : to apply water or a medicated liquid to ⟨*bathed* her eyes⟩ **2** : to take a bath; *also* : to take a swim **3** : to wash along, over, or against so as to wet **4** : to suffuse with or as if with light — **bath·er** *n*

bath·house \'bath-ˌhaus, 'bath-\ *n* **1** : a building equipped for bathing **2** : a building containing dressing rooms for bathers

bathing suit *n* : SWIMSUIT

ba·thos \'bā-ˌthäs\ *n* [Gk, lit., depth] **1** : the sudden appearance of the commonplace in otherwise elevated matter or style **2** : insincere or overdone pathos — **ba·thet·ic** \bə-'the-tik\ *adj*

bath·robe \'bath-ˌrōb, 'bath-\ *n* : a loose often absorbent robe worn before and after bathing or as a dressing gown

bath·room \-ˌrüm, -ˌrum\ *n* : a room containing a bathtub or shower and usu. a sink and toilet

bath·tub \-ˌtəb\ *n* : a usu. fixed tub for bathing

ba·tik \bə-'tēk, 'ba-tik\ *n* [Javanese *batik*] **1** : an Indonesian method of hand-printing textiles by coating with wax the parts not to be dyed; *also* : a design so executed **2** : a fabric printed by batik

ba·tiste \bə-'tēst\ *n* : a fine sheer fabric of plain weave

bat·man \'bat-mən\ *n* : an orderly of a British military officer

ba·ton \bə-'tän\ *n* : STAFF, ROD; *esp* : a stick with which the leader directs an orchestra or band

bats·man \'bats-mən\ *n* : a batter esp. in cricket

bat·tal·ion \bə-'tal-yən\ *n* **1** : a large body of troops organized to act together : ARMY **2** : a military unit composed of a headquarters and two or more units (as companies)

¹**bat·ten** \'bat-ᵊn\ *vb* **1** : to grow or make fat **2** : THRIVE

²**batten** *n* : a strip of wood used esp. to seal or strengthen a joint

³**batten** *vb* : to fasten with battens

¹**bat·ter** \'ba-tər\ *vb* : to beat or damage with repeated blows

²**batter** *n* : a soft mixture (as for cake) basically of flour and liquid

³**batter** *n* : one that bats; *esp* : the player whose turn it is to bat

battering ram *n* **1** : an ancient military machine for battering down walls **2** : a heavy metal bar with handles used to batter down doors

bat·tery \'ba-tə-rē\ *n, pl* **-ter·ies** **1** : BEATING; *esp* : unlawful beating or use of force on a person **2** : a grouping of artillery pieces for tactical purposes; *also* : the guns of a warship **3** : a group of electric cells for furnishing electric current; *also* : a single electric cell ⟨a flashlight ∼⟩ **4** : a number of similar items grouped or used as a unit ⟨a ∼ of tests⟩ **5** : the pitcher and catcher of a baseball team

bat·ting \'ba-tiŋ\ *n* : layers or sheets of cotton or wool (as for lining quilts)

¹**bat·tle** \'bat-ᵊl\ *n* [ME *batel*, fr. OF *bataille* battle, fortifying tower, battalion, fr. LL *battalia* combat, alter. of *battualia* fencing exercises, fr. L *battuere* to beat] : a general military engagement; *also* : an extended contest or controversy

²**battle** *vb* **bat·tled; bat·tling** : to engage in battle : CONTEND, FIGHT

bat·tle–ax \'bat-ᵊl-ˌaks\ *n* **1** : a long-handled ax formerly used as a weapon **2** : a quarrelsome domineering woman

battle fatigue *n* : COMBAT FATIGUE

bat·tle·field \'bat-ᵊl-ˌfēld\ *n* : a place where a battle is fought

bat·tle·ment \-mənt\ *n* : a decorative or defensive parapet on top of a wall

bat·tle·ship \-ˌship\ *n* : a warship of the most heavily armed and armored class

bat·tle·wag·on \-ˌwa-gən\ *n* : BATTLESHIP

bat·ty \'ba-tē\ *adj* **bat·ti·er; -est** : CRAZY, FOOLISH

bau·ble \'bo-bəl\ *n* : TRINKET

baud \'bod, *Brit* 'bod\ *n, pl* **baud** *also* **bauds** : a unit of data transmission speed

baulk *chiefly Brit var of* BALK

baux·ite \'bok-ˌsīt\ *n* : a clayey mixture that is the chief ore of aluminum

bawd \'bod\ *n* **1** : MADAM **2 2** : PROSTITUTE

bawdy \'bo-dē\ *adj* **bawd·i·er; -est** : OBSCENE, LEWD — **bawd·i·ly** \'bod-ᵊl-ē\ *adv* — **bawd·i·ness** \-dē-nəs\ *n*

¹**bawl** \'bol\ *vb* : to cry or cry out loudly; *also* : to scold harshly

²**bawl** *n* : a long loud cry : BELLOW

¹**bay** \'bā\ *adj* : reddish brown

²**bay** *n* **1** : a bay-colored animal **2** : a reddish brown color

³**bay** *n* **1** : a section or compartment of a building or vehicle **2** : a compartment projecting outward from the wall of a building and containing a window (**bay window**)

⁴**bay** *vb* : to bark with deep long tones

⁵**bay** *n* **1** : the position of one unable to escape and forced to face danger **2** : a baying of dogs

⁶**bay** *n* : an inlet of a body of water (as the sea) usu. smaller than a gulf

⁷**bay** *n* : the European laurel; *also* : a shrub or tree resembling this

bay·ber·ry \'bā-ˌber-ē\ *n* : a hardy deciduous shrub of coastal eastern No. America bearing small hard berries coated with a white wax used for candles; *also* : its fruit

bay leaf *n* : the dried leaf of the European laurel used in cooking

¹**bay·o·net** \'bā-ə-nət, ˌbā-ə-'net\ *n* : a daggerlike weapon made to fit on the muzzle end of a rifle

²**bayonet** *vb* **-net·ed** *also* **-net·ted; -net·ing** *also* **-net·ting** : to use or stab with a bayonet

bay·ou \'bī-yü, -ō\ *n* [Louisiana French, fr. Choctaw *bayuk*] : a marshy or sluggish body of water

bay rum *n* : a fragrant liquid used esp. as a cologne or after-shave lotion

ba·zaar \bə-'zär\ *n* **1** : a group of shops : MARKETPLACE **2** : a fair for the sale of articles usu. for charity

ba·zoo·ka \bə-'zü-kə\ *n* [*bazooka* (a crude musical instrument made of pipes and a funnel)] : a weapon consisting of a tube and launching an explosive rocket able to pierce armor

¹BB \'bē-(ˌ)bē\ *n* : a small round shot pellet

²BB *abbr* base on balls

BBB *abbr* Better Business Bureau

BBC *abbr* British Broadcasting Corporation

bbl *abbr* barrel; barrels

BC *abbr* **1** before Christ — often printed in small capitals and often punctuated **2** British Columbia

B cell *n* [bone-marrow-derived *cell*] : any of the lymphocytes that secrete antibodies when mature

B complex *n* : VITAMIN B COMPLEX

bd *abbr* **1** board **2** bound

bdl *or* **bdle** *abbr* bundle

bdrm *abbr* bedroom

be \'bē\ *vb, past 1st & 3d sing* **was** \'wəz, 'wäz\; *2d sing* **were** \'wər\; *pl* **were**; *past subjunctive* **were**; *past part* **been** \'bin\; *pres part* **be·ing** \'bē-iŋ\; *pres 1st sing* **am** \əm, 'am\; *2d sing* **are** \ər, 'är\; *3d sing* **is** \'iz, əz\; *pl* **are**; *pres subjunctive* **be 1** : to equal in meaning or symbolically ⟨God *is* love⟩; *also* : to have a specified qualification or relationship ⟨leaves *are* green⟩ ⟨this fish *is* a trout⟩ **2** : to have objective existence ⟨I think, therefore I *am*⟩; *also* : to have or occupy a particular place ⟨here *is* your pen⟩ **3** : to take place : OCCUR ⟨the meeting *is* tonight⟩ **4** — used with the past participle of transitive verbs as a passive voice auxiliary ⟨the door *was* opened⟩ **5** — used as the auxiliary of the present participle in expressing continuous action ⟨he *is* sleeping⟩ **6** — used as an auxiliary with the past participle of some intransitive verbs to form archaic perfect tenses **7** — used as an auxiliary with *to* and the infinitive to express futurity, prearrangement, or obligation ⟨you *are* to come when called⟩

Be *symbol* beryllium

¹beach \'bēch\ *n* : a sandy or gravelly part of the shore of an ocean or lake

²beach *vb* : to run or drive ashore

beach buggy *n* : DUNE BUGGY

beach·comb·er \'bēch-ˌkō-mər\ *n* : a person who searches along a shore for something of use or value

beach·head \'bēch-ˌhed\ *n* : a small area on an enemy-held shore occupied in the initial stages of an invasion

bea·con \'bē-kən\ *n* **1** : a signal fire **2** : a guiding or warning signal (as a lighthouse) **3** : a radio transmitter emitting signals for guidance of aircraft

¹bead \'bēd\ *n* [ME *bede* prayer, prayer bead, fr. OE *bed, gebed* prayer] **1** *pl* : a series of prayers and meditations made with a rosary **2** : a small piece of material pierced for threading on a line (as in a rosary) **3** : a small globular body **4** : a narrow projecting rim or band — **bead·ing** *n* — **beady** *adj*

²bead *vb* : to form into a bead

bea·dle \'bēd-ᵊl\ *n* : a usu. English parish officer whose duties include keeping order in church

bea·gle \'bē-gəl\ *n* : a small short-legged smooth-coated hound

beak \'bēk\ *n* : the bill of a bird and esp. of a bird of prey; *also* : a pointed projecting part — **beaked** \'bēkt\ *adj*

bea·ker \'bē-kər\ *n* **1** : a large widemouthed drinking cup **2** : a widemouthed thin-walled laboratory vessel

¹beam \'bēm\ *n* **1** : a large long piece of timber or metal **2** : the bar of a balance from which the scales hang **3** : the breadth of a ship at its widest part **4** : a ray or shaft of light **5** : a collection of nearly parallel rays (as X rays) or particles (as electrons) **6** : a constant radio

beagle

signal transmitted for the guidance of pilots; *also* : the course indicated by this signal

²beam *vb* **1** : to send out light **2** : to aim (a broadcast) by directional antennas **3** : to smile with joy

¹bean \'bēn\ *n* : the edible seed borne in pods by some leguminous plants; *also* : a plant or a pod bearing these

²bean *vb* : to strike on the head with an object

bean·bag \'bēn-ˌbag\ *n* : a cloth bag partially filled typically with dried beans and used as a toy

bean·ball \'bēn-ˌbol\ *n* : a pitch thrown at a batter's head

bean curd *n* : TOFU

bean·ie \'bē-nē\ *n* : a small round tight-fitting skullcap

beano \'bē-nō\ *n, pl* **beanos** : BINGO

¹bear \'bar\ *n, pl* **bears 1** *or pl* **bear** : any of a family of large heavy mammals with shaggy hair and small tails **2** : a gruff or sullen person **3** : one who sells (as securities) in expectation of a price decline — **bear·ish** *adj*

²bear *vb* **bore** \'bōr\; **borne** \'bōrn\ *also* **born** \'bōrn\; **bear·ing 1** : CARRY **2** : to be equipped with **3** : to give as testimony ⟨∼ witness to the facts of the case⟩ **4** : to give birth to; *also* : PRODUCE, YIELD ⟨a tree that ∼s regularly⟩ **5** : ENDURE, SUSTAIN ⟨∼ pain⟩ ⟨*bore* the weight on piles⟩; *also* : to exert pressure or influence **6** : to go in an indicated direction ⟨∼ to the right⟩ — **bear·able** *adj* — **bear·er** *n*

¹beard \'bird\ *n* **1** : the hair that grows on the face of a man **2** : a growth of bristly hairs (as on a goat's chin) — **beard·ed** \'bir-dəd\ *adj* — **beard·less** *adj*

²beard *vb* : to confront boldly

bear·ing \'bar-iŋ\ *n* **1** : manner of carrying oneself : COMPORTMENT **2** : a supporting object, purpose, or point **3** : a machine part in which another part (as an axle or pin) turns **4** : an emblem in a coat of arms **5** : the position or direction of one point with respect to another or to the compass; *also* : a determination of position **6** *pl* : comprehension of one's situation **7** : connection with or influence on something; *also* : SIGNIFICANCE

bear·skin \'bar-ˌskin\ *n* : an article made of the skin of a bear

beast \'bēst\ *n* **1** : ANIMAL 1; *esp* : a 4-footed mammal **2** : a contemptible person

¹beast·ly \'bēst-lē\ *adj* **beast·li·er; -est 1** : BESTIAL **2** : ABOMINABLE, DISAGREEABLE — **beast·li·ness** \-nəs\ *n*

²beastly *adv* : VERY

¹beat \'bēt\ *vb* **beat; beat·en** \'bēt-ᵊn\ *or* **beat; beat·ing 1** : to strike repeatedly **2** : TREAD **3** : to affect or alter by beating ⟨∼ metal into sheets⟩ **4** : to sound (as an alarm) on a drum **5** : OVERCOME; *also* : SURPASS **6** : to act or arrive before ⟨∼ his brother home⟩ **7** : THROB — **beat·er** *n*

²beat *n* **1** : a single stroke or blow esp. of a series; *also* : PULSATION **2** : a rhythmic stress in poetry or music or the rhythmic effect of these **3** : a regularly traversed course

³beat *adj* **1** : EXHAUSTED **2** : of or relating to beatniks
⁴beat *n* : BEATNIK
be·atif·ic \ˌbē-ə-ˈti-fik\ *adj* : giving or indicative of great joy or bliss
be·at·i·fy \bē-ˈa-tə-ˌfī\ *vb* **-fied; -fy·ing 1** : to make supremely happy **2** : to declare to have attained the blessedness of heaven and authorize the title "Blessed" for — **be·at·i·fi·ca·tion** \-ˌa-tə-fə-ˈkā-shən\ *n*
be·at·i·tude \bē-ˈa-tə-ˌtüd, -ˌtyüd\ *n* **1** : a state of utmost bliss **2** : any of the declarations made in the Sermon on the Mount (Mt 5:3–12) beginning "Blessed are"
beat·nik \ˈbēt-nik\ *n* : a person who rejects the mores of established society and indulges in exotic philosophizing and self-expression
beau \ˈbō\ *n, pl* **beaux** \ˈbōz\ *or* **beaus** [F, fr. *beau* beautiful, fr. L *bellus* pretty] **1** : a man of fashion : DANDY **2** : SUITOR, LOVER
beau geste \bō-ˈzhest\ *n, pl* **beaux gestes** *or* **beau gestes** \bō-ˈzhest\ : a graceful or magnanimous gesture
beau ide·al \ˌbō-ī-ˈdē(-ə)l\ *n, pl* **beau ideals** : the perfect type or model
Beau·jo·lais \ˌbō-zhō-ˈlā\ *n* : a French red table wine
beau monde \bō-ˈmänd, -ˈmōⁿd\ *n, pl* **beau mondes** \-ˈmänz, -ˈmändz\ *or* **beaux mondes** \bō-ˈmōⁿd\ : the world of high society and fashion
beau·te·ous \ˈbyü-tē-əs\ *adj* : BEAUTIFUL — **beau·te·ous·ly** *adv*
beau·ti·cian \byü-ˈti-shən\ *n* : COSMETOLOGIST
beau·ti·ful \ˈbyü-ti-fəl\ *adj* : characterized by beauty : LOVELY **syn** pretty, fair, comely — **beau·ti·ful·ly** \-f(ə-)lē\ *adv*
beautiful people *n pl, often cap B&P* : wealthy or famous people whose lifestyle is usu. expensive and well-publicized
beau·ti·fy \ˈbyü-tə-ˌfī\ *vb* **-fied; -fy·ing** : to make more beautiful — **beau·ti·fi·ca·tion** \ˌbyü-tə-fə-ˈkā-shən\ *n* — **beau·ti·fi·er** *n*
beau·ty \ˈbyü-tē\ *n, pl* **beauties** : qualities that give pleasure to the senses or exalt the mind : LOVELINESS; *also* : something having such qualities
beauty shop *n* : an establishment where hairdressing, facials, and manicures are done
beaux arts \bō-ˈzär\ *n pl* [F] : FINE ARTS
bea·ver \ˈbē-vər\ *n, pl* **beavers** : a large fur-bearing herbivorous rodent that builds dams and underwater houses of mud and sticks; *also* : its fur
be·calm \bi-ˈkäm, -ˈkälm\ *vb* : to keep (as a ship) motionless by lack of wind
be·cause \bi-ˈkoz, -ˈkəz\ *conj* : for the reason that
because of *prep* : by reason of
beck \ˈbek\ *n* : a beckoning gesture; *also* : SUMMONS
beck·on \ˈbe-kən\ *vb* : to summon or signal esp. by a nod or gesture; *also* : ATTRACT
be·cloud \bi-ˈklaud\ *vb* : OBSCURE
be·come \bi-ˈkəm\ *vb* **-came** \-ˈkām\; **-come; -coming 1** : to come to be ⟨~ tired⟩ **2** : to suit or be suitable to ⟨her dress ~s her⟩
be·com·ing *adj* : SUITABLE, FIT; *also* : ATTRACTIVE — **be·com·ing·ly** *adv*
¹bed \ˈbed\ *n* **1** : an article of furniture to sleep on **2** : a plot of ground prepared for plants **3** : FOUNDATION, BOTTOM **4** : LAYER, STRATUM
²bed *vb* **bed·ded; bed·ding 1** : to put or go to bed **2** : to fix in a foundation : EMBED **3** : to plant in beds **4** : to lay or lie flat or in layers
bed–and–breakfast *n* : an establishment offering lodging and breakfast
be·daub \bi-ˈdob\ *vb* : SMEAR
be·daz·zle \bi-ˈda-zəl\ *vb* : to confuse by or as if by a strong light; *also* : FASCINATE — **be·daz·zle·ment** *n*
bed·bug \ˈbed-ˌbəg\ *n* : a wingless bloodsucking bug infesting houses and esp. beds
bed·clothes \ˈbed-ˌklōthz\ *n pl* : BEDDING 1

bed·ding \ˈbe-diŋ\ *n* **1** : materials for making up a bed **2** : FOUNDATION
be·deck \bi-ˈdek\ *vb* : ADORN
be·dev·il \bi-ˈde-vəl\ *vb* **1** : HARASS, TORMENT **2** : CONFUSE, MUDDLE
be·dew \bi-ˈdü, -ˈdyü\ *vb* : to wet with or as if with dew
bed·fast \ˈbed-ˌfast\ *adj* : BEDRIDDEN
bed·fel·low \-ˌfe-lō\ *n* **1** : one sharing the bed of another **2** : a close associate : ALLY
be·di·zen \bi-ˈdīz-ᵊn, -ˈdiz-\ *vb* : to dress or adorn with showy or vulgar finery
bed·lam \ˈbed-ləm\ *n* [*Bedlam*, popular name for the Hospital of St. Mary of Bethlehem, London, an insane asylum, fr. ME *Bedlem* Bethlehem] **1** : an insane asylum **2** : a scene of uproar and confusion
bed·ou·in *or* **bed·u·in** \ˈbe-də-wən\ *n, pl* **bedouin** *or* **bedouins** *or* **beduin** *or* **beduins** *often cap* [ME *Bedoyne*, fr. MF *bedoïn*, fr. Ar *badawī* desert dweller] : a nomadic Arab of the Arabian, Syrian, or No. African deserts
bed·pan \ˈbed-ˌpan\ *n* : a shallow vessel used by a bedridden person for urination or defecation
bed·post \-ˌpōst\ *n* : the post of a bed
be·drag·gled \bi-ˈdra-gəld\ *adj* : soiled and disordered as if by being drenched
bed·rid·den \ˈbed-ˌrid-ᵊn\ *adj* : kept in bed by illness or weakness
¹bed·rock \-ˈräk\ *n* : the solid rock underlying surface materials (as soil)
²bedrock *adj* : solidly fundamental, basic, or reliable ⟨traditional ~ values⟩
bed·roll \ˈbed-ˌrōl\ *n* : bedding rolled up for carrying
bed·room \-ˌrüm, -ˌrüm\ *n* : a room containing a bed and used esp. for sleeping
bed·side \-ˌsīd\ *n* : the place beside a bed esp. of a sick or dying person
bed·sore \-ˌsōr\ *n* : an ulceration of tissue deprived of adequate blood supply by prolonged pressure
bed·spread \-ˌspred\ *n* : a usu. ornamental cloth cover for a bed
bed·stead \-ˌsted\ *n* : the framework of a bed
bed·time \-ˌtīm\ *n* : time for going to bed
bed–wet·ting \-ˌwe-tiŋ\ *n* : involuntary discharge of urine esp. in bed during sleep — **bed–wet·ter** *n*
¹bee \ˈbē\ *n* : HONEYBEE; *also* : any of various related insects
²bee *n* : a gathering of people for a specific purpose ⟨quilting ~⟩
beech \ˈbēch\ *n, pl* **beech·es** *or* **beech** : any of a genus of deciduous hardwood trees with smooth gray bark and small sweet triangular nuts; *also* : the wood of a beech — **beech·en** \ˈbē-chən\ *adj*
beech·nut \ˈbēch-ˌnət\ *n* : the nut of a beech
¹beef \ˈbēf\ *n, pl* **beefs** \ˈbēfs\ *or* **beeves** \ˈbēvz\ **1** : the flesh of a steer, cow, or bull; *also* : the dressed carcass of a beef animal **2** : a steer, cow, or bull esp. when fattened for food **3** : MUSCLE, BRAWN **4** *pl* **beefs** : COMPLAINT
²beef *vb* **1** : STRENGTHEN — usu. used with *up* **2** : COMPLAIN
beef·eat·er \ˈbē-ˌfē-tər\ *n* : a yeoman of the guard of an English monarch
beef·steak \-ˌstāk\ *n* : a slice of beef suitable for broiling or frying
beefy \ˈbē-fē\ *adj* **beef·i·er; -est** : THICKSET, BRAWNY
bee·hive \ˈbē-ˌhīv\ *n* : HIVE 1, 3
bee·keep·er \-ˌkē-pər\ *n* : a person who raises bees — **bee·keep·ing** *n*
bee·line \-ˌlīn\ *n* : a straight direct course
been *past part of* BE
beep·er \ˈbē-pər\ *n* : a small radio receiver that beeps when signaled to alert the person carrying it
beer \ˈbir\ *n* : an alcoholic beverage brewed from malt and hops — **beery** *adj*
bees·wax \ˈbēz-ˌwaks\ *n* : WAX 1

beet \'bēt\ *n* : a garden plant with edible leaves and a thick sweet root used as a vegetable, as a source of sugar, or as forage; *also* : its root

¹**bee·tle** \'bēt-ºl\ *n* : any of an order of insects having four wings of which the stiff outer pair covers the membranous inner pair when not in flight

²**beetle** *vb* **bee·tled; bee·tling** : to jut out : PROJECT

be·fall \bi-'fȯl\ *vb* **-fell** \-'fel\; **-fall·en** \-'fȯ-lən\ : to happen to : OCCUR

be·fit \bi-'fit\ *vb* : to be suitable to

be·fog \bi-'fȯg, -'fäg\ *vb* : OBSCURE; *also* : CONFUSE

¹**be·fore** \bi-'fȯr\ *adv or adj* **1** : in front **2** : EARLIER

²**before** *prep* **1** : in front of ⟨stood ∼ him⟩ **2** : earlier than ⟨got there ∼ me⟩ **3** : in a more important category than ⟨put quality ∼ quantity⟩

³**before** *conj* **1** : earlier than the time that ⟨he got here ∼ I did⟩ **2** : more willingly than ⟨she'd starve ∼ she'd steal⟩

be·fore·hand \bi-'fȯr-ˌhand\ *adv or adj* : in advance

be·foul \bi-'faʊl\ *vb* : SOIL

be·friend \bi-'frend\ *vb* : to act as friend to

be·fud·dle \bi-'fəd-ºl\ *vb* : MUDDLE, CONFUSE

beg \'beg\ *vb* **begged; beg·ging 1** : to ask as a charity; *also* : ENTREAT **2** : EVADE; *also* : assume as established, settled, or proved ⟨∼ the question⟩

be·get \bi-'get\ *vb* **-got** \-'gät\, **-got·ten** \-'gät-ºn\ *or* **-got; -get·ting** : to become the father of : SIRE

¹**beg·gar** \'be-gər\ *n* : one that begs; *esp* : a person who begs as a way of life

²**beggar** *vb* : IMPOVERISH

beg·gar·ly \'be-gər-lē\ *adj* **1** : contemptibly mean or inadequate **2** : marked by unrelieved poverty ⟨a ∼ life⟩

beg·gary \'be-gə-rē\ *n* : extreme poverty

be·gin \bi-'gin\ *vb* **be·gan** \-'gan\; **be·gun** \-'gən\; **be·gin·ning 1** : to do the first part of an action : COMMENCE **2** : to come into being : ARISE; *also* : FOUND **3** : ORIGINATE, INVENT — **be·gin·ner** *n*

beg off *vb* : to ask to be excused from something

be·gone \bi-'gȯn\ *vb* : to go away : DEPART — used esp. in the imperative

be·go·nia \bi-'gōn-yə\ *n* : any of a genus of tropical herbs widely grown for their showy leaves and waxy flowers

be·grime \bi-'grīm\ *vb* **be·grimed; be·grim·ing** : to make dirty

be·grudge \bi-'grəj\ *vb* **1** : to give or concede reluctantly **2** : to be reluctant to grant or allow

be·guile \-'gīl\ *vb* **be·guiled; be·guil·ing 1** : DECEIVE **2** : to while away **3** : to engage the interest of by guile

be·guine \bi-'gēn\ *n* [AmerF *béguine*, fr. F *béguin* flirtation] : a vigorous popular dance of the islands of Saint Lucia and Martinique

be·gum \'bā-gəm, 'bē-\ *n* : a Muslim woman of high rank

be·half \bi-'haf, -'háf\ *n* : BENEFIT, SUPPORT, DEFENSE

be·have \bi-'hāv\ *vb* **be·haved; be·hav·ing 1** : to bear, comport, or conduct oneself in a particular and esp. a proper way **2** : to act, function, or react in a particular way

be·hav·ior \bi-'hā-vyər\ *n* : way of behaving; *esp* : personal conduct — **be·hav·ior·al** \-vyə-rəl\ *adj*

be·hav·ior·ism \bi-'hā-vyə-ˌri-zəm\ *n* : a school of psychology concerned with the objective evidence of behavior without reference to conscious experience

be·hav·iour *chiefly Brit var of* BEHAVIOR

be·head \bi-'hed\ *vb* : to cut off the head of

be·he·moth \bi-'hē-məth, 'bē-ə-ˌmäth\ *n* : a huge powerful animal described in Job 40:15–24; *also* : something of monstrous size or power

be·hest \bi-'hest\ *n* **1** : COMMAND **2** : an urgent prompting

¹**be·hind** \bi-'hīnd\ *adv or adj* **1** : BACK, BACKWARD ⟨look ∼ ⟩ **2** : LATE, SLOW

²**behind** *prep* **1** : in or to a place or situation in back of or to the rear of ⟨look ∼ you⟩ ⟨the staff stayed ∼ the troops⟩ **2** : inferior to (as in rank) : BELOW ⟨three

games ∼ the first-place team⟩ **3** : in support of : SUPPORTING ⟨we're ∼ you all the way⟩

be·hind·hand \bi-'hīnd-ˌhand\ *adj* : being in arrears **syn** tardy, late, overdue, belated

be·hold \bi-'hōld\ *vb* **-held** \-'held\; **-hold·ing 1** : to have in sight : SEE **2** — used imperatively to direct the attention **syn** view, observe, notice, espy — **be·hold·er** *n*

be·hold·en \bi-'hōl-dən\ *adj* : OBLIGATED, INDEBTED

be·hoof \bi-'hüf\ *n* : ADVANTAGE, PROFIT

be·hoove \bi-'hüv\ *vb* **be·hooved; be·hoov·ing** : to be necessary, proper, or advantageous for

beige \'bāzh\ *n* : a pale dull yellowish brown — **beige** *adj*

be·ing \'bē-iŋ\ *n* **1** : EXISTENCE; *also* : LIFE **2** : the qualities or constitution of an existent thing **3** : a living thing; *esp* : PERSON

be·la·bor \bi-'lā-bər\ *vb* : to assail (as with words) tiresomely or at length

be·la·bour *chiefly Brit var of* BELABOR

be·lat·ed \bi-'lā-təd\ *adj* : DELAYED, LATE

be·lay \bi-'lā\ *vb* **1** : to wind (a rope) around a pin or cleat in order to hold secure **2** : QUIT, STOP — used in the imperative

belch \'belch\ *vb* **1** : to expel (gas) from the stomach through the mouth **2** : to gush forth ⟨a volcano ∼*ing* lava⟩ — **belch** *n*

bel·dam *or* **bel·dame** \'bel-dəm\ *n* [ME *beldam* grandmother, fr. MF *bel* beautiful + ME *dam* lady, mother] : an old woman

be·lea·guer \bi-'lē-gər\ *vb* **1** : BESIEGE **2** : HARASS ⟨∼*ed* parents⟩

bel·fry \'bel-frē\ *n, pl* **belfries** : a tower for a bell (as on a church); *also* : the part of the tower in which the bell hangs

Belg *abbr* Belgian; Belgium

Bel·gian \'bel-jən\ *n* : a native or inhabitant of Belgium — **Belgian** *adj*

be·lie \bi-'lī\ *vb* **-lied; -ly·ing 1** : MISREPRESENT **2** : to show (something) to be false **3** : to run counter to

be·lief \bə-'lēf\ *n* **1** : CONFIDENCE, TRUST **2** : something (as a tenet or creed) believed **syn** conviction, opinion, persuasion, sentiment

be·lieve \bə-'lēv\ *vb* **be·lieved; be·liev·ing 1** : to have religious convictions **2** : to have a firm conviction about something : accept as true **3** : to hold as an opinion : SUPPOSE — **be·liev·able** *adj* — **be·liev·er** *n*

be·like \bi-'līk\ *adv, archaic* : PROBABLY

be·lit·tle \bi-'lit-ºl\ *vb* **-lit·tled; -lit·tling** : to make seem little or less; *also* : DISPARAGE

¹**bell** \'bel\ *n* **1** : a hollow metallic device that makes a ringing sound when struck **2** : the sounding or stroke of a bell (as on shipboard to tell the time); *also* : time so indicated **3** : something with the flared form of a typical bell

²**bell** *vb* : to provide with a bell

bel·la·don·na \ˌbe-lə-'dä-nə\ *n* [It, lit., beautiful lady; fr. its cosmetic use] : a medicinal extract (as atropine) from a poisonous European herb related to the potato; *also* : this herb

bell–bot·toms \'bel-ˌbä-təmz\ *n pl* : pants with wide flaring bottoms — **bell–bottom** *adj*

bell·boy \'bel-ˌbȯi\ *n* : BELLHOP

belle \'bel\ *n* : an attractive and popular girl or woman

belles let·tres \bel-'letr\ *n pl* [F] : literature that is an end in itself and not practical or purely informative — **bel·le·tris·tic** \ˌbe-lə-'tris-tik\ *adj*

bell·hop \'bel-ˌhäp\ *n* : a hotel or club employee who takes guests to rooms, carries luggage, and runs errands

bel·li·cose \'be-li-ˌkōs\ *adj* : WARLIKE, PUGNACIOUS **syn** belligerent, quarrelsome, combative, contentious — **bel·li·cos·i·ty** \ˌbe-li-'kä-sə-tē\ *n*

bel·lig·er·en·cy \bə-'li-jə-rən-sē\ *n* **1** : the status of a nation engaged in war **2** : BELLIGERENCE, TRUCULENCE

bel·lig·er·ent \-rənt\ *adj* **1** : waging war **2** : TRUCULENT **syn** bellicose, pugnacious, combative, contentious, warlike — **bel·lig·er·ence** \-rəns\ *n* — **belligerent** *n*

bel·low \'be-lō\ *vb* **1** : to make the deep hollow sound characteristic of a bull **2** : to shout in a deep voice — **bellow** *n*

bel·lows \-lōz, -ləz\ *n sing or pl* : a closed device with sides that can be spread apart and then pressed together to draw in air and expel it through a tube

bellows

bell·weth·er \'bel-'we-thər, -'we-\ *n* : one that takes the lead or initiative

¹bel·ly \'be-lē\ *n, pl* **bellies** [ME *bely* bellows, belly, fr. OE *belg* bag, skin] **1** : ABDOMEN; *also* : POTBELLY **2** : the underpart of an animal's body

²belly *vb* **bel·lied; bel·ly·ing** : BULGE

¹bel·ly·ache \'be-lē-ˌāk\ *n* : pain in the abdomen

²bellyache *vb* : COMPLAIN

belly button *n* : the human navel

belly dance *n* : a usu. solo dance emphasizing movement of the belly — **belly dance** *vb* — **belly dancer** *n*

belly laugh *n* : a deep hearty laugh

be·long \bi-'lȯŋ\ *vb* **1** : to be suitable or appropriate; *also* : to be properly situated (shoes ~ in the closet) **2** : to be the property (this ~s to me); *also* : to be attached (as through birth or membership) (~ to a club) **3** : to form an attribute or part (this wheel ~s to the cart) **4** : to be classified (whales ~ among the mammals)

be·long·ings \-'lȯŋ-iŋz\ *n pl* : GOODS, EFFECTS, POSSESSIONS

be·loved \bi-'ləvd, -'lə-vəd\ *adj* : dearly loved — **beloved** *n*

¹be·low \bi-'lō\ *adv* **1** : in or to a lower place or rank **2** : on earth **3** : in hell

²below *prep* **1** : lower than **2** : inferior to (as in rank)

be·low·decks \bi-ˌlō-'deks, -'lō-ˌdeks\ *adv* : inside the superstructure of a boat or down to a lower deck

¹belt \'belt\ *n* **1** : a strip (as of leather) worn about the waist **2** : a flexible continuous band to communicate motion or convey material **3** : a region marked by some distinctive feature; *esp* : one suited to a particular crop

²belt *vb* **1** : to encircle or secure with a belt **2** : to beat with or as if with a belt **3** : to mark with an encircling band **4** : to sing loudly

³belt *n* **1** : a jarring blow : WHACK **2** : DRINK (a ~ of whiskey)

belt–tightening *n* : a reduction in spending

belt·way \'belt-ˌwā\ *n* : a highway around a city

be·lu·ga \bə-'lü-gə\ *n* [Russ] : a white sturgeon of the Black Sea, Caspian Sea, and their tributaries that is a source of caviar; *also* : caviar from beluga roe

bel·ve·dere \'bel-və-ˌdir\ *n* [It, lit., beautiful view] : a structure (as a summerhouse) designed to command a view

be·mire \bi-'mīr\ *vb* : to cover or soil with or sink in mire

be·moan \bi-'mōn\ *vb* : LAMENT, DEPLORE **syn** bewail, grieve, moan, weep

be·muse \bi-'myüz\ *vb* : BEWILDER, CONFUSE

¹bench \'bench\ *n* **1** : a long seat for two or more persons **2** : the seat of a judge in court; *also* : the office or dignity of a judge **3** : COURT; *also* : JUDGES **4** : a

table for holding work and tools (a carpenter's ~)

²bench \'bench\ *vb* **1** : to furnish with benches **2** : to seat on a bench **3** : to remove from or keep out of a game

bench mark *n* **1** : a mark on a permanent object serving as an elevation reference in topographical surveys **2** *usu* **bench·mark** : a point of reference for measurement; *also* : STANDARD

bench press *n* : a press in weight lifting performed by a lifter lying on a bench — **bench–press** *vb*

bench warrant *n* : a warrant issued by a presiding judge or by a court against a person guilty of contempt or indicted for a crime

¹bend \'bend\ *vb* **bent** \'bent\; **bend·ing** **1** : to draw (as a bow) taut **2** : to curve or cause a change of shape in (~ a bar) **3** : to make fast : SECURE **4** : DEFLECT **5** : to turn in a certain direction (*bent* his steps toward town) **6** : APPLY (*bent* themselves to the task) **7** : SUBDUE **8** : to curve downward **9** : YIELD, SUBMIT

²bend *n* **1** : an act or process of bending **2** : something bent; *esp* : CURVE **3** *pl* : a painful and sometimes fatal disorder caused by release of gas bubbles in the tissues upon too rapid decrease in air pressure after a stay in a compressed atmosphere

³bend *n* : a knot by which a rope is fastened (as to another rope)

bend·er \'ben-dər\ *n* : SPREE

¹be·neath \bi-'nēth\ *adv* : BELOW **syn** under, underneath

²beneath *prep* **1** : BELOW, UNDER (stood ~ a tree) **2** : unworthy of (considered such behavior ~ her) **3** : concealed by

bene·dic·tion \ˌbe-nə-'dik-shən\ *n* : the invocation of a blessing esp. at the close of a public worship service

ben·e·fac·tion \-'fak-shən\ *n* : a charitable donation **syn** contribution, alms, beneficence, offering

ben·e·fac·tor \'ben-ə-ˌfak-tər\ *n* : one that confers a benefit and esp. a benefaction

ben·e·fac·tress \-ˌfak-trəs\ *n* : a woman who is a benefactor

ben·e·fice \'be-nə-fəs\ *n* : an ecclesiastical office to which the revenue from an endowment is attached

be·nef·i·cence \bə-'ne-fə-səns\ *n* **1** : beneficent quality **2** : BENEFACTION

be·nef·i·cent \-sənt\ *adj* : doing or producing good (as by acts of kindness or charity); *also* : BENEFICIAL

ben·e·fi·cial \ˌbe-nə-'fi-shəl\ *adj* : being of benefit or help : HELPFUL **syn** advantageous, profitable, favorable, propitious — **ben·e·fi·cial·ly** *adv*

ben·e·fi·cia·ry \ˌbe-nə-'fi-shē-ˌer-ē, -'fi-shə-rē\ *n, pl* **-ries** : one that receives a benefit (as the income of a trust or the proceeds of an insurance)

¹ben·e·fit \'be-nə-fit\ *n* **1** : ADVANTAGE (the ~s of exercise) **2** : useful aid : HELP; *also* : material aid provided or due (as in sickness or unemployment) as a right **3** : a performance or event to raise funds

²benefit *vb* **-fit·ed** \-ˌfi-təd\ *also* **-fit·ted; -fit·ing** *also* **-fit·ting** **1** : to be useful or profitable to **2** : to receive benefit

be·nev·o·lence \bə-'ne-və-ləns\ *n* **1** : charitable nature **2** : an act of kindness : CHARITY — **be·nev·o·lent** \-lənt\ *adj* — **be·nev·o·lent·ly** *adv*

be·night·ed \bi-'nī-təd\ *adj* **1** : overtaken by darkness or night **2** : living in ignorance

be·nign \bi-'nīn\ *adj* [ME *benigne*, fr. MF, fr. L *benignus*] **1** : of a gentle disposition; *also* : showing kindness **2** : of a mild kind; *esp* : not malignant (~ tumors) **syn** benignant, kind, kindly, good-hearted — **be·nig·ni·ty** \-'nig-nə-tē\ *n*

be·nig·nant \-'nig-nənt\ *adj* : BENIGN 1 **syn** kind, kindly, good-hearted

ben·i·son \'be-nə-sən, -zən\ *n* : BLESSING, BENEDICTION

bent \'bent\ *n* **1** : strong inclination or interest; *also* : TALENT **2** : power of endurance **syn** talent, aptitude, gift, flair, knack, genius

ben·thic \'ben-thik\ *adj* : of, relating to, or occurring at the bottom of a body of water

ben·ton·ite \'bent-ᵊn-ˌīt\ *n* : an absorptive clay used esp. as a filler (as in paper)

bent·wood \'bent-ˌwüd\ *adj* : made of wood bent into shape ⟨a ~ rocker⟩

be·numb \bi-'nəm\ *vb* **1** : DULL, DEADEN **2** : to make numb esp. by cold

ben·zene \'ben-ˌzēn\ *n* : a colorless volatile flammable liquid hydrocarbon used in organic synthesis and as a solvent

ben·zine \'ben-ˌzēn\ *n* : any of various flammable petroleum distillates used as solvents or as motor fuels

ben·zo·ate \'ben-zə-ˌwāt\ *n* : a salt or ester of benzoic acid

ben·zo·ic acid \ben-ˌzō-ik-\ *n* : a white crystalline acid used as a preservative and antiseptic and in synthesizing chemicals

ben·zo·in \'ben-zə-wən, -ˌzoin\ *n* : a balsamlike resin from trees of southern Asia used esp. in medicine and perfumes

be·queath \bi-'kwēth, -'kwēth\ *vb* [ME *bequethen*, fr. OE *becwethan*, fr. *be-* + *cwethan* to say] **1** : to leave by will **2** : to hand down

be·quest \bi-'kwest\ *n* **1** : the action of bequeathing **2** : something bequeathed : LEGACY

be·rate \-'rāt\ *vb* : to scold harshly

Ber·ber \'bər-bər\ *n* : a member of any of various peoples living in northern Africa west of Tripoli

ber·ceuse \ber-'sœz, -'süz\ *n, pl* **berceuses** *same or* -'sü-zəz\ [F, fr. *bercer* to rock] **1** : LULLABY **2** : a musical composition that resembles a lullaby

¹be·reaved \bi-'rēvd\ *adj* : suffering the death of a loved one — **be·reave·ment** *n*

²bereaved *n, pl* **bereaved** : one who is bereaved

be·reft \-'reft\ *adj* **1** : deprived of or lacking something — usu. used with *of* **2** : BEREAVED

be·ret \bə-'rā\ *n* : a round soft cap with no visor

berg \'bərg\ *n* : ICEBERG

beri·beri \ˌber-ē-'ber-ē\ *n* : a deficiency disease marked by weakness, wasting, and nerve damage and caused by lack of thiamine

berke·li·um \'bər-klē-əm\ *n* : an artificially prepared radioactive chemical element — see ELEMENT table

berm \'bərm\ *n* : a narrow shelf or path at the top or bottom of a slope; *also* : a mound or bank of earth

Ber·mu·das \bər-'myü-dəz\ *n pl* : BERMUDA SHORTS

Bermuda shorts *n pl* : knee-length walking shorts

ber·ry \'ber-ē\ *n, pl* **berries** **1** : a small pulpy fruit (as a strawberry) **2** : a simple fruit (as a grape, tomato, or banana) with the wall of the ripened ovary thick and pulpy **3** : the dry seed of some plants (as coffee)

ber·serk \bər-'sərk, -'zərk\ *adj* [ON *berserkr* warrior frenzied in battle, fr. *bjǫrn* bear + *serkr* shirt] : FRENZIED, CRAZED — **berserk** *adv*

¹berth \'bərth\ *n* **1** : adequate distance esp. for a ship to maneuver **2** : the place where a ship is anchored or a vehicle rests **3** : ACCOMMODATIONS **4** : JOB, POSITION **syn** post, situation, office, appointment

²berth *vb* **1** : to bring or come into a berth **2** : to allot a berth to

ber·yl \'ber-əl\ *n* : a hard silicate mineral occurring as green, yellow, pink, or white crystals

be·ryl·li·um \bə-'ri-lē-əm\ *n* : a light strong metallic chemical element used as a hardener in alloys — see ELEMENT table

be·seech \bi-'sēch\ *vb* **-sought** \-'sȯt\ *or* **-seeched**; **-seech·ing** : to beg urgently : ENTREAT **syn** implore, plead, supplicate, importune

be·seem \bi-'sēm\ *vb, archaic* : BEFIT

be·set \-'set\ *vb* **1** : TROUBLE, HARASS **2** : ASSAIL; *also* : SURROUND

be·set·ting *adj* : persistently present

¹be·side \bi-'sīd\ *prep* **1** : by the side of ⟨sit ~ me⟩ **2** : BESIDES **3** : not relevant to

²beside *adv, archaic* : BESIDES

¹be·sides \bi-'sīdz\ *prep* **1** : other than **2** : together with

²besides *adv* **1** : as well : ALSO **2** : MOREOVER

be·siege \bi-'sēj\ *vb* : to lay siege to; *also* : to press with requests — **be·sieg·er** *n*

be·smear \-'smir\ *vb* : SMEAR

be·smirch \-'smərch\ *vb* : SMIRCH, SOIL

be·som \'bē-zəm\ *n* : BROOM

be·sot \bi-'sät\ *vb* **be·sot·ted**; **be·sot·ting** **1** : INFATUATE **2** : to make dull esp. by drinking

be·spat·ter \-'spa-tər\ *vb* : SPATTER

be·speak \bi-'spēk\ *vb* **-spoke** \-'spōk\; **-spo·ken** \-'spō-kən\; **-speak·ing** **1** : PREARRANGE **2** : ADDRESS **3** : REQUEST **4** : INDICATE, SIGNIFY **5** : FORETELL

be·sprin·kle \-'spriŋ-kəl\ *vb* : SPRINKLE

¹best \'best\ *adj, superlative of* GOOD **1** : excelling all others **2** : most productive (as of good or satisfaction) **3** : LARGEST, MOST

²best *adv, superlative of* WELL **1** : in the best way **2** : MOST

³best *n* : something that is best

⁴best *vb* : to get the better of : OUTDO

bes·tial \'bes-chəl\ *adj* **1** : of or relating to beasts **2** : resembling a beast esp. in brutality or lack of intelligence

bes·ti·al·i·ty \ˌbes-chē-'a-lə-tē, ˌbēs-\ *n, pl* **-ties** **1** : the condition or status of a lower animal **2** : display or gratification of bestial traits or impulses

bes·ti·ary \'bes-chē-ˌer-ē\ *n, pl* **-ar·ies** : a medieval allegorical or moralizing work on the appearance and habits of animals

be·stir \bi-'stər\ *vb* : to rouse to action

best man *n* : the principal groomsman at a wedding

be·stow \bi-'stō\ *vb* **1** : PUT, PLACE, STOW **2** : to present as a gift — **be·stow·al** *n*

be·stride \bi-'strīd\ *vb* **-strode** \-'strōd\; **-strid·den** \-'strid-ᵊn\; **-strid·ing** : to ride, sit, or stand astride

¹bet \'bet\ *n* **1** : something that is wagered, risked, or pledged usu. between two parties on the outcome of a contest; *also* : the making of such a bet **2** : OPTION ⟨the back road is your best ~⟩

²bet *vb* **bet** *also* **bet·ted**; **bet·ting** **1** : to stake on the outcome of an issue or a contest ⟨*bet* $2 on the race⟩ **2** : to make a bet with **3** : to lay a bet

³bet *abbr* between

be·ta \'bā-tə\ *n* : the 2d letter of the Greek alphabet — B or β

beta block·er \-ˌblä-kər\ *n* : any of a group of drugs that tend to decrease heart action and increase coronary blood flow

be·ta–car·o·tene \-'kar-ə-ˌtēn\ *n* : an isomer of carotene found in dark green and dark yellow vegetables and fruits

be·take \bi-'tāk\ *vb* **-took** \-'tuk\; **-tak·en** \-'tā-kən\; **-tak·ing** : to cause (oneself) to go

beta particle *n* : a high-speed electron; *esp* : one emitted by a radioactive nucleus

beta ray *n* **1** : BETA PARTICLE **2** : a stream of beta particles

be·tel \'bēt-ᵊl\ *n* : a climbing pepper whose leaves are chewed together with lime and betel nut as a stimulant esp. by southern Asians

betel nut *n* : the astringent seed of an Asian palm that is chewed with betel leaves

bête noire \ˌbet-'nwär, ˌbāt-\ *n, pl* **bêtes noires** *same or* -'nwärz\ [F, lit., black beast] : a person or thing strongly disliked or avoided

beth·el \'be-thəl\ *n* [Heb *bēth'ēl* house of God] : a place of worship esp. for seamen

be·think \bi-'thiŋk\ *vb* **-thought** \-'thȯt\; **-think·ing** : REMEMBER; *also* : PONDER

be·tide \bi-'tīd\ *vb* : to happen to

be·times \bi-'tīmz\ *adv* : in good time : EARLY **syn** soon, seasonably, timely

be·to·ken \bi-'tō-kən\ *vb* **1** : PRESAGE **2** : to give evidence of **syn** indicate, attest, bespeak, testify

be·tray \bi-'trā\ *vb* **1** : to lead astray; *esp* : SEDUCE **2**

: to deliver to an enemy **3** : ABANDON **4** : to prove unfaithful to **5** : to reveal unintentionally; *also* : SHOW, INDICATE **syn** mislead, delude, deceive, beguile — **be·tray·al** *n* — **be·tray·er** *n*

be·troth \bi-ˈtrōth, -ˈtroth\ *vb* : to promise to marry — **be·troth·al** *n*

be·trothed *n* : the person to whom one is betrothed

¹bet·ter \ˈbe-tər\ *adj, comparative of* GOOD **1** : greater than half **2** : improved in health **3** : more attractive, favorable, or commendable **4** : more advantageous or effective **5** : improved in accuracy or performance

²better *vb* **1** : to make or become better **2** : SURPASS, EXCEL

³better *adv, comparative of* WELL **1** : in a superior manner **2** : to a higher or greater degree; *also* : MORE

⁴better *n* **1** : something better; *also* : a superior esp. in merit or rank **2** : ADVANTAGE

⁵better *verbal auxiliary* : had better ⟨you ∼ hurry⟩

bet·ter·ment \ˈbe-tər-mənt\ *n* : IMPROVEMENT

bet·tor *or* **bet·ter** \ˈbe-tər\ *n* : one that bets

¹be·tween \bi-ˈtwēn\ *prep* **1** : by the common action of ⟨earned $10,000 ∼ the two of them⟩ **2** : in the interval separating ⟨an alley ∼ two buildings⟩; *also* : in intermediate relation to **3** : in point of comparison of ⟨choose ∼ two cars⟩

²between *adv* : in an intervening space or interval

be·twixt \bi-ˈtwikst\ *adv or prep* : BETWEEN

¹bev·el \ˈbe-vəl\ *n* **1** : a device for adjusting the slant of the surfaces of a piece of work **2** : the angle or slant that one surface or line makes with another when not at right angles

²bevel *vb* **-eled** *or* **-elled; -el·ing** *or* **-el·ling 1** : to cut or shape to a bevel **2** : INCLINE, SLANT

bev·er·age \ˈbev-rij\ *n* : a drinkable liquid

bevy \ˈbe-vē\ *n, pl* **bev·ies 1** : a large group or collection **2** : a group of animals and esp. quail together

be·wail \bi-ˈwāl\ *vb* : LAMENT **syn** deplore, bemoan, grieve, moan, weep

be·ware \-ˈwar\ *vb* : to be on one's guard : be wary of

be·wil·der \bi-ˈwil-dər\ *vb* : PERPLEX, CONFUSE **syn** mystify, distract, puzzle — **be·wil·der·ment** *n*

be·witch \-ˈwich\ *vb* **1** : to affect by witchcraft **2** : CHARM, FASCINATE **syn** enchant, attract, captivate — **be·witch·ment** *n*

bey \ˈbā\ *n* **1** : a former Turkish provincial governor **2** : the former native ruler of Tunis or Tunisia

¹be·yond \bē-ˈänd\ *adv* **1** : FARTHER **2** : BESIDES

²beyond *prep* **1** : on or to the farther side of **2** : out of the reach or sphere of **3** : BESIDES

be·zel \ˈbē-zəl, ˈbe-\ *n* **1** : a rim that holds a transparent covering (as on a watch) **2** : the faceted part of a cut gem that rises above the setting

bf *abbr* boldface

BG *or* **B Gen** *abbr* brigadier general

bhang \ˈbaŋ\ *n* [Hindi *bhāṅg*] : a mildly intoxicating preparation of the leaves and flowering tops of uncultivated hemp

Bi *symbol* bismuth

BIA *abbr* Bureau of Indian Affairs

bi·an·nu·al \(ˌ)bī-ˈan-yə-wəl\ *adj* : occurring twice a year — **bi·an·nu·al·ly** *adv*

¹bi·as \ˈbī-əs\ *n* **1** : a line diagonal to the grain of a fabric **2** : PREJUDICE, BENT

²bias *adv* : on the bias : DIAGONALLY

³bias *vb* **bi·ased** *or* **bi·assed; bi·as·ing** *or* **bi·as·sing** : PREJUDICE

bi·ath·lon \bī-ˈath-lən, -ˌlän\ *n* : a composite athletic contest consisting of cross-country skiing and target shooting with a rifle

¹bib \ˈbib\ *n* : a cloth or plastic shield tied under the chin to protect the clothes while eating

²bib *abbr* Bible; biblical

bi·be·lot \ˈbē-bə-ˌlō\ *n, pl* **bibelots** *same or* -ˌlōz\ : a small household ornament or decorative object

bi·ble \ˈbī-bəl\ *n* [ME, fr. OF, fr. ML *biblia*, fr. Gk, pl. of *biblion* book, fr. *byblos* papyrus, book, fr. *Byblos*,

ancient Phoenician city from which papyrus was exported] **1** *cap* : the sacred scriptures of Christians comprising the Old and New Testaments **2** *cap* : the sacred scriptures of Judaism; *also* : those of some other religion **3** : a publication that is considered authoritative for its subject — **bib·li·cal** \ˈbi-bli-kəl\ *adj* ☞ For table, see next page.

bib·li·og·ra·phy \ˌbi-blē-ˈä-grə-fē\ *n, pl* **-phies 1** : the history or description of writings or publications **2** : a list of writings (as on a subject or of an author) — **bib·li·og·ra·pher** \-fər\ *n* — **bib·li·o·graph·ic** \-ə-ˈgra-fik\ *also* **bib·li·o·graph·i·cal** \-fi-kəl\ *adj*

bib·lio·phile \ˈbi-blē-ə-ˌfīl\ *n* : a lover of books

bib·u·lous \ˈbi-byə-ləs\ *adj* **1** : highly absorbent **2** : fond of alcoholic beverages

bi·cam·er·al \ˈbī-ˈka-mə-rəl\ *adj* : having or consisting of two legislative branches

bicarb \(ˌ)bī-ˈkärb, ˈbī-\ *n* : SODIUM BICARBONATE

bi·car·bon·ate \(ˌ)bī-ˈkär-bə-ˌnāt, -nət\ *n* : an acid carbonate

bicarbonate of soda : SODIUM BICARBONATE

bi·cen·te·na·ry \ˌbī-sen-ˈte-nə-rē, bī-ˈsent-ᵊn-ˌer-ē\ *n* : BICENTENNIAL — **bicentenary** *adj*

bi·cen·ten·ni·al \ˌbī-sen-ˈte-nē-əl\ *n* : a 200th anniversary or its celebration — **bicentennial** *adj*

bi·ceps \ˈbī-ˌseps\ *n, pl* **biceps** *also* **bicepses** [NL, fr. L, two-headed, fr. *bi-* two + *caput* head] : a muscle (as in the front of the upper arm) having two points of origin

¹bick·er \ˈbi-kər\ *n* : ALTERCATION

²bicker *vb* : to engage in a petty quarrel

bi·con·cave \ˌbī-(ˌ)kän-ˈkāv, (ˌ)bī-ˈkän-ˌkāv\ *adj* : concave on both sides

bi·con·vex \ˌbī-(ˌ)kän-ˈveks, (ˌ)bī-ˈkän-ˌveks\ *adj* : convex on both sides

bi·cus·pid \bī-ˈkəs-pəd\ *n* : PREMOLAR

¹bi·cy·cle \ˈbī-ˌsi-kəl\ *n* : a light 2-wheeled vehicle with a steering handle, saddle, and pedals

²bicycle *vb* **-cy·cled; -cy·cling** \-ˌsi-k(ə-)liŋ, -ˌsī-\ : to ride a bicycle — **bi·cy·cler** \-k(ə-)lər\ *n* — **bi·cy·clist** \-k(ə-)list\ *n*

¹bid \ˈbid\ *vb* **bade** \ˈbad, ˈbād\ *or* **bid; bid·den** \ˈbid-ᵊn\ *or* **bid** *also* **bade; bid·ding 1** : COMMAND, ORDER **2** : INVITE **3** : to give expression to **4** : to make a bid : OFFER — **bid·der** *n*

²bid *n* **1** : the act of one who bids; *also* : an offer for something **2** : INVITATION **3** : an announcement in a card game of what a player proposes to accomplish **4** : an attempt to win or gain ⟨a ∼ for mayor⟩

bid·da·ble \ˈbi-də-bəl\ *adj* **1** : OBEDIENT, DOCILE **2** : capable of being bid

bid·dy \ˈbi-dē\ *n, pl* **biddies** : HEN; *also* : a young chicken

bide \ˈbīd\ *vb* **bode** \ˈbōd\ *or* **bid·ed; bided; bid·ing 1** : to wait for **2** : WAIT, TARRY **3** : DWELL

bi·det \bi-ˈdā\ *n* : a bathroom fixture used esp. for bathing the external genitals and the posterior parts of the body

bi·di·rec·tion·al \ˌbī-də-ˈrek-sh(ə-)nəl\ *adj* : involving, moving, or taking place in two usu. opposite directions — **bi·di·rec·tion·al·ly** *adv*

bi·en·ni·al \bī-ˈe-nē-əl\ *adj* **1** : taking place once in two years **2** : lasting two years **3** : producing leaves the first year and fruiting and dying the second year — **biennial** *n* — **bi·en·ni·al·ly** *adv*

bi·en·ni·um \bī-ˈe-nē-əm\ *n, pl* **-niums** *or* **-nia** \-ə-\ [L, fr. *bi-* two + *annus* year] : a period of two years

bier \ˈbir\ *n* : a stand bearing a coffin or corpse

bi·fo·cal \ˈbī-ˌfō-kəl\ *adj* : having two focal lengths

bifocals \-kəlz\ *n pl* : eyeglasses with lenses that have one part that corrects for near vision and one for distant vision

bi·fur·cate \ˈbī-fər-ˌkāt, bī-ˈfər-\ *vb* **-cat·ed; -cat·ing** : to divide into two branches or parts — **bi·fur·ca·tion** \ˌbī-fər-ˈkā-shən\ *n*

big \ˈbig\ *adj* **big·ger; big·gest 1** : large in size,

BOOKS OF THE
OLD TESTAMENT

JEWISH
SCRIPTURE

ROMAN CATHOLIC CANON	PROTESTANT CANON
Genesis	Genesis
Exodus	Exodus
Leviticus	Leviticus
Numbers	Numbers
Deuteronomy	Deuteronomy
Joshua	Joshua
Judges	Judges
Ruth	Ruth
1 & 2 Samuel	1 & 2 Samuel
1 & 2 Kings	1 & 2 Kings
1 & 2 Chronicles	1 & 2 Chronicles
Ezra	Ezra
Nehemiah	Nehemiah
Tobit	
Judith	
Esther	Esther
Job	Job
Psalms	Psalms
Proverbs	Proverbs
Ecclesiastes	Ecclesiastes
Song of Songs	Song of Solomon
Wisdom	
Sirach	
Isaiah	Isaiah
Jeremiah	Jeremiah
Lamentations	Lamentations
Baruch	
Ezekiel	Ezekiel
Daniel	Daniel
Hosea	Hosea
Joel	Joel
Amos	Amos
Obadiah	Obadiah
Jonah	Jonah
Micah	Micah
Nahum	Nahum
Habakkuk	Habakkuk
Zephaniah	Zephaniah
Haggai	Haggai
Zechariah	Zechariah
Malachi	Malachi
1 & 2 Macabees	

Law
Genesis
Exodus
Leviticus
Numbers
Deuteronomy
Prophets
Joshua
Judges
1 & 2 Samuel
1 & 2 Kings
Isaiah
Jeremiah
Ezekiel
Hosea
Joel
Amos
Obadiah
Jonah
Micah
Nahum
Habakkuk
Zephaniah
Haggai
Zechariah
Malachi
Hagiographa
Psalms
Proverbs
Job
Song of Songs
Ruth
Lamentations
Ecclesiastes
Esther
Daniel
Ezra
Nehemiah
1 & 2 Chronicles

PROTESTANT
APOCRYPHA

1 & 2 Esdras
Tobit
Judith
Additions to Esther
Wisdom of Solomon
Ecclesiasticus *or the Wisdom of Jesus Son of Sirach*
Baruch
Prayer of Azariah and the Song of the Three Holy Children
Susanna
Bel and the Dragon
The Prayer of Manasses
1 & 2 Maccabees

BOOKS OF THE
NEW TESTAMENT

Matthew	1 & 2 Thessalonians
Mark	
Luke	1 & 2 Timothy
John	
Acts of the Apostles	Titus
	Philemon
Romans	Hebrews
1 & 2 Corinthians	James
	1 & 2 Peter
Galatians	1, 2, 3 John
Ephesians	Jude
Philippians	Revelation *or* Apocalypse
Colossians	

amount, or scope **2** : PREGNANT; *also* : SWELLING **3** : IMPORTANT, IMPOSING **4** : POPULAR — **big·ness** *n*

big·a·my \'bi-gə-mē\ *n* : the act of marrying one person while still legally married to another — **big·a·mist** \-mist\ *n* — **big·a·mous** \-məs\ *adj*

big bang theory *n* : a theory in astronomy: the universe originated in an explosion (**big bang**) from a single point of nearly infinite energy density

big brother *n* **1** : an older brother **2** : a man who befriends a delinquent or friendless boy **3** *cap both Bs* : the leader of an authoritarian state or movement

Big Dipper *n* : the seven principal stars of Ursa Major in a form resembling a dipper

big·foot \'big-ˌfut\ *n* : SASQUATCH

big·horn \'big-ˌhȯrn\ *n, pl* **bighorn** *or* **bighorns** : a wild sheep of mountainous western No. America

bighorn

bight \'bīt\ *n* **1** : a curve in a coast; *also* : the bay formed by such a curve **2** : a slack part in a rope

big–name \'big-ˈnām\ *adj* : widely popular ⟨a ∼ performer⟩ — **big name** *n*

big·ot \'bi-gət\ *n* : one intolerantly devoted to his or her own prejudices or opinions **syn** fanatic, enthusiast, zealot — **big·ot·ed** \-gə-təd\ *adj* — **big·ot·ry** \-trē\ *n*

big shot \'big-ˌshät\ *n* : an important person

big time \-ˌtīm\ *n* **1** : a high-paying vaudeville circuit requiring only two performances a day **2** : the top rank of an activity or enterprise — **big–tim·er** *n*

big top *n* **1** : the main tent of a circus **2** : CIRCUS

big·wig \'big-ˌwig\ *n* : BIG SHOT

bike \'bīk\ *n* **1** : BICYCLE **2** : MOTORCYCLE

bik·er *n* : MOTORCYCLIST; *esp* : one who is a member of an organized gang

bike·way \'bīk-ˌwā\ *n* : a thoroughfare for bicycles

bi·ki·ni \bə-ˈkē-nē\ *n* : a woman's brief 2-piece bathing suit

bi·lat·er·al \bī-ˈla-tə-rəl\ *adj* **1** : having or involving two sides **2** : affecting reciprocally two sides or parties — **bi·lat·er·al·ly** *adv*

bile \'bīl\ *n* **1** : a bitter greenish fluid secreted by the liver that aids in the digestion of fats **2** : an ill= humored mood

bilge \'bilj\ *n* **1** : the part of a ship that lies between the bottom and the point where the sides go straight up **2** : stale or worthless remarks or ideas

bi·lin·gual \bī-ˈliŋ-gwəl\ *adj* : expressed in, knowing, or using two languages

bil·ious \'bil-yəs\ *adj* **1** : marked by or suffering from disordered liver function **2** : IRRITABLE, ILL-TEMPERED — **bil·ious·ness** *n*

bilk \'bilk\ *vb* : CHEAT, SWINDLE

¹bill \'bil\ *n* : the jaws of a bird together with their horny covering; *also* : a mouth structure (as of a turtle) resembling these — **billed** \'bild\ *adj*

²bill *vb* : to caress fondly

³bill *n* **1** : an itemized statement of particulars; *also*

: INVOICE **2** : a written document or note **3** : a printed advertisement (as a poster) announcing an event **4** : a draft of a law presented to a legislature for enactment **5** : a written statement of a legal wrong suffered or of some breach of law **6** : a piece of paper money

⁴bill vb **1** : to enter in or prepare a bill; also : to submit a bill or account to **2** : to advertise by bills or posters

bill·board \-₁bōrd\ n : a flat surface on which advertising bills are posted

¹bil·let \'bi-lət\ n **1** : an order requiring a person to provide lodging for a soldier; also : quarters assigned by or as if by such an order **2** : POSITION, APPOINTMENT

²billet vb : to assign lodging to by billet

bil·let–doux \₁bi-lā-'dü\ n, pl **billets–doux** \same or -'düz\ [F billet doux, lit., sweet letter] : a love letter

bill·fold \'bil-₁fōld\ n : WALLET

bil·liards \'bil-yərdz\ n : any of several games played on an oblong table by driving balls against each other or into pockets with a cue

bil·lings·gate \'bi-liŋz-₁gāt, Brit usu -git\ n [Billingsgate, old gate and fish market, London, England] : coarsely abusive language

bil·lion \'bil-yən\ n **1** : a thousand millions **2** Brit : a million millions — **billion** adj — **bil·lionth** \-yənth\ adj or n

bill of health : a usu. favorable report following an examination

bill of sale : a legal document transferring ownership of goods

¹bil·low \'bi-lō\ n **1** : WAVE; esp : a great wave **2** : a rolling mass (as of fog or flame) like a great wave — **bil·lowy** \'bi-lə-wē\ adj

²billow vb : to rise and roll in waves; also : to swell out ⟨~ing sails⟩

bil·ly \'bi-lē\ n, pl **billies** : BILLY CLUB

billy club n : a heavy usu. wooden club; esp : a police officer's club

bil·ly goat \'bi-lē-\ n : a male goat

bi·met·al \'bī-₁met-ᵊl\ adj : BIMETALLIC — **bimetal** n

bi·me·tal·lic \₁bī-mə-'ta-lik\ adj : made of two different metals — often used of devices having a bonded expansive part — **bimetallic** n

bi·met·al·lism \bī-'met-ᵊl-₁i-zəm\ n : the use of two metals at fixed ratios to form a standard of value for a monetary system

¹bi·month·ly \bī-'mənth-lē\ adj **1** : occurring every two months **2** : occurring twice a month : SEMIMONTHLY — **bimonthly** adv

²bimonthly n : a bimonthly publication

bin \'bin\ n : a box, crib, or enclosure used for storage

bi·na·ry \'bī-nə-rē, -₁ner-ē\ adj **1** : consisting of two things or parts **2** : relating to, being, or belonging to a system of numbers having 2 as its base ⟨the ~ digits 0 and 1⟩ **3** : involving a choice between or condition of two alternatives only (as on-off, yes-no) — **binary** n

binary star n : a system of two stars revolving around each other

bin·au·ral \bī-'nȯr-əl\ adj : of or relating to sound reproduction involving the use of two separated microphones and two transmission channels to achieve a stereophonic effect

bind \'bīnd\ vb **bound** \'baủnd\; **bind·ing 1** : TIE; also : to restrain as if by tying **2** : to put under an obligation; also : to constrain with legal authority **3** : BANDAGE **4** : to unite into a mass **5** : to compel as if by a pledge ⟨a handshake ~s the deal⟩ **6** : to strengthen or decorate with a band **7** : to fasten together and enclose in a cover ⟨~ books⟩ **8** : to exert a tying, restraining, or compelling effect — **bind·er** n

bind·ing \'bīn-diŋ\ n : something (as a ski fastening, a cover, or an edging fabric) used to bind

¹binge \'binj\ n : SPREE

²binge vb **binged**; **binge·ing** or **bing·ing** : to go on a binge and esp. an eating binge — **bing·er** n

bin·go \'biŋ-gō\ n, pl **bingos** : a game of chance played with cards having numbered squares corresponding

to numbered balls drawn at random and won by covering five squares in a row

bin·na·cle \'bi-ni-kəl\ n [alter. of ME bitakle, fr. Pg or Sp; Pg bitácola & Sp bitácula, fr. L habitaculum dwelling place, fr. habitare to inhabit] : a container holding a ship's compass

¹bin·oc·u·lar \bī-'nä-kyə-lər, bə-\ adj : of, relating to, or adapted to the use of both eyes — **bin·oc·u·lar·ly** adv

²bin·oc·u·lar \bə-'nä-kyə-lər, bī-\ n **1** : a binocular optical instrument (as a microscope) **2** : a hand-held optical instrument composed of two telescopes and a focusing device — usu. used in pl.

bi·no·mi·al \bī-'nō-mē-əl\ n **1** : a mathematical expression consisting of two terms connected by the sign plus (+) or minus (−) **2** : a biological species name consisting of two terms — **binomial** adj

bio·chem·is·try \₁bī-ō-'ke-mə-strē\ n : chemistry that deals with the chemical compounds and processes occurring in living things — **bio·chem·i·cal** \-mi-kəl\ adj or n — **bio·chem·ist** \-mist\ n

bio·de·grad·able \-di-'grā-də-bəl\ adj : capable of being broken down esp. into innocuous products by the actions of living things (as microorganisms) ⟨a ~ detergent⟩ — **bio·de·grad·abil·i·ty** \-₁grā-də-'bi-lə-tē\ n — **bio·deg·ra·da·tion** \-₁de-grə-'dā-shən\ n — **bio·de·grade** \-di-'grād\ vb

bio·di·ver·si·ty \-də-'vər-sə-tē, -dī-\ n : biological diversity in an environment as indicated by numbers of different species of plants and animals

bio·eth·ics \-'e-thiks\ n : the ethics of biological research and its applications esp. in medicine — **bio·eth·i·cal** \-'e-thi-kəl\ adj — **bio·eth·i·cist** \-'e-thə-sist\ n

bio·feed·back \-'fēd-₁bak\ n : the technique of making unconscious or involuntary bodily processes (as heartbeats or brain waves) objectively perceptible to the senses (as by use of an oscilloscope) in order to manipulate them by conscious mental control

biog abbr biographer; biographical; biography

bio·ge·og·ra·phy \₁bī-ō-jē-'ä-grə-fē\ n : a branch of biology that deals with the distribution of plants and animals — **bio·ge·og·ra·pher** n

bi·og·ra·phy \bī-'ä-grə-fē, bē-\ n, pl **-phies** : a written history of a person's life; also : such writings in general — **bi·og·ra·pher** n — **bio·graph·i·cal** \₁bī-ə-'gra-fi-kəl\ also **bio·graph·ic** \-fik\ adj

biol abbr biologic; biological; biologist; biology

bi·o·log·i·cal \₁bī-ə-'lä-ji-kəl\ also **bi·o·log·ic** \-jik\ adj **1** : of, relating to, or produced by biology or life and living processes **2** : related by direct genetic relationship rather than by adoption or marriage ⟨~ parents⟩ — **bi·o·log·i·cal·ly** \-ji-k(ə-)lē\ adv

biological clock n : an inherent timing mechanism inferred to exist in some living systems (as a cell) in order to explain various cyclic physiological and behavioral responses

biological warfare n : warfare in which living organisms (as bacteria) are used as weapons

bi·ol·o·gy \bī-'ä-lə-jē\ n [G Biologie, fr. Gk bios mode of life + logos word] **1** : a science that deals with living beings and life processes **2** : the life processes of an organism or group — **bi·ol·o·gist** \bī-'ä-lə-jist\ n

bio·med·i·cal \₁bī-ō-'me-di-kəl\ adj : of, relating to, or involving biological, medical, and physical science

bi·on·ic \bī-'ä-nik\ adj : having normal biological capability or performance enhanced by or as if by electronic or mechanical devices

bio·phys·ics \₁bī-ō-'fi-ziks\ n : a branch of science concerned with the application of physical principles and methods to biological problems — **bio·phys·i·cal** \-zi-kəl\ adj — **bio·phys·i·cist** \-'fi-zə-sist\ n

bi·op·sy \'bī-₁äp-sē\ n, pl **-sies** : the removal of tissue, cells, or fluids from the living body for examination

bio·rhythm \'bī-ō-₁ri-thəm\ n : an inherent rhythm that appears to control or initiate various biological processes

bio·sphere \'bī-ə-ˌsfir\ n **1** : the part of the world in which life can exist **2** : living beings together with their environment

bio·tech \'bī-ō-ˌtek\ n : BIOTECHNOLOGY

bio·tech·nol·ogy \ˌbī-ō-tek-'nä-lə-jē\ n : biological science when applied esp. in genetic engineering and recombinant DNA technology

bi·ot·ic \bī-'ä-tik\ adj : of or relating to life; esp : caused by living beings

bi·o·tin \'bī-ə-tən\ n : a vitamin of the vitamin B complex found esp. in yeast, liver, and egg yolk and active in growth promotion

bi·o·tite \'bī-ə-ˌtīt\ n : a dark mica containing iron, magnesium, potassium, and aluminum

bi·par·ti·san \bī-'pär-tə-zən\ adj : representing or composed of members of two parties

bi·par·tite \-'pär-ˌtīt\ adj **1** : being in two parts **2** : shared by two ⟨∼ treaty⟩

bi·ped \'bī-ˌped\ n : a 2-footed animal — **bi·ped·al** \(ˌ)bī-'ped-ᵊl\ adj

bi·plane \'bī-ˌplān\ n : an aircraft with two wings placed one above the other

bi·po·lar \bī-'pō-lər\ adj : having or involving the use of two poles — **bi·po·lar·i·ty** \ˌbī-pō-'lar-ə-tē\ n

bi·ra·cial \bī-'rā-shəl\ adj : of, relating to, or involving members of two races

¹**birch** \'bərch\ n **1** : any of a genus of mostly short-lived deciduous shrubs and trees with membranous outer bark and pale close-grained wood; also : this wood **2** : a birch rod or bundle of twigs for flogging — **birch** or **birch·en** \'bər-chən\ adj

²**birch** vb : WHIP, FLOG

¹**bird** \'bərd\ n : any of a class of warm-blooded egg-laying vertebrates having the body feathered and the forelimbs modified to form wings

²**bird** vb : to observe or identify wild birds in their native habitat — **bird·er** n

bird·bath \'bərd-ˌbath, -ˌbáth\ n : a usu. ornamental basin set up for birds to bathe in

bird·house \-ˌhaús\ n : an artificial nesting place for birds; also : AVIARY

bird·ie \'bər-dē\ n : a score of one under par on a hole in golf

bird·lime \-ˌlīm\ n : a sticky substance smeared on twigs to snare small birds

bird of paradise : any of numerous brilliantly colored plumed birds of the New Guinea area

bird of prey : a carnivorous bird that feeds wholly or chiefly on carrion or on meat taken by hunting

bird·seed \'bərd-ˌsēd\ n : a mixture of small seeds (as of hemp or millet) used for feeding birds

bird's-eye \'bərdz-ˌī\ adj **1** : marked with spots resembling birds' eyes ⟨∼ maple⟩ **2** : seen from above as if by a flying bird ⟨∼ view⟩; also : CURSORY

bi·ret·ta \bə-'re-tə\ n : a square cap with three ridges on top worn esp. by Roman Catholic clergymen

birr \'bir, 'bər\ n, pl **birr** — see MONEY table

birth \'bərth\ n **1** : the act or fact of being born or of bringing forth young **2** : LINEAGE, DESCENT **3** : ORIGIN, BEGINNING

birth canal n : the channel formed by the cervix, vagina, and vulva through which the fetus passes during birth

birth control n : control of the number of children born esp. by preventing or lessening the frequency of conception

birth·day \'bərth-ˌdā\ n : the day or anniversary of one's birth

birth defect n : a physical or biochemical defect present at birth and inherited or environmentally induced

birth·mark \'bərth-ˌmärk\ n : an unusual mark or blemish on the skin at birth

birth·place \-ˌplās\ n : place of birth or origin

birth·rate \-ˌrāt\ n : the number of births per number

of individuals in a given area or group during a given time

birth·right \-ˌrīt\ n : a right, privilege, or possession to which one is entitled by birth **syn** legacy, patrimony, heritage, inheritance

birth·stone \-ˌstōn\ n : a gemstone associated symbolically with the month of one's birth

bis·cuit \'bis-kət\ n [ME bisquite, fr. MF bescuit, fr. (pain) bescuit twice-cooked bread] **1** : a crisp flat cake; esp, Brit : CRACKER **2 2** : a small quick bread made from dough that has been rolled and cut or dropped from a spoon

bi·sect \'bī-ˌsekt\ vb : to divide into two usu. equal parts; also : CROSS, INTERSECT — **bi·sec·tion** \'bī-ˌsek-shən\ n — **bi·sec·tor** \-tər\ n

bi·sex·u·al \bī-'sek-shə-wəl\ adj **1** : possessing characters of or having sexual desire for both sexes **2** : of, relating to, or involving both sexes : bisexual n — **bi·sex·u·al·i·ty** \ˌbī-ˌsek-shə-'wal-ə-tē\ n

bish·op \'bi-shəp\ n [ME bisshop, fr. OE bisceop, fr. LL episcopus, fr. Gk episkopos, lit., overseer, fr. epi-on, over + skeptesthai to look] **1** : a member of the clergy ranking above a priest and typically governing a diocese **2** : any of various Protestant church officials who superintend other clergy **3** : a chess piece that can move diagonally across any number of adjoining unoccupied squares

bish·op·ric \'bi-shə-prik\ n **1** : DIOCESE **2** : the office of bishop

bis·muth \'biz-məth\ n : a heavy brittle grayish white metallic chemical element used in alloys and medicine — see ELEMENT table

bi·son \'bīs-ᵊn, 'bīz-\ n, pl **bison** : BUFFALO 2

bisque \'bisk\ n : a thick cream soup

bis·tro \'bēs-trō, 'bis-\ n, pl **bistros** [F] **1** : a small or unpretentious restaurant **2** : BAR; also : NIGHTCLUB

¹**bit** \'bit\ n **1** : the biting or cutting edge or part of a tool **2** : the part of a bridle that is placed in a horse's mouth

²**bit** n **1** : a morsel of food; also : a small piece or quantity of something **2** : a small coin; also : a unit of value equal to 12½ cents **3** : something small or trivial **4** : an indefinite usu. small degree or extent ⟨a ∼ tired⟩

³**bit** n [binary digit] : a unit of computer information equivalent to the result of a choice between two alternatives; also : its physical representation

¹**bitch** \'bich\ n **1** : a female canine; esp : a female dog **2** : a malicious, spiteful, and domineering woman

²**bitch** vb : COMPLAIN

¹**bite** \'bīt\ vb **bit** \'bit\; **bit·ten** \'bit-ᵊn\ also **bit; bit·ing** \'bī-tiŋ\ **1** : to grip with teeth or jaws; also : to wound or sting with or as if with fangs **2** : to cut or pierce with or as if with an edged instrument **3** : to cause to smart or sting **4** : CORRODE **5** : to take bait

²**bite** n **1** : the act or manner of biting **2** : FOOD **3** : a wound made by biting; also : a penetrating effect

bit·ing \'bī-tiŋ\ adj : SHARP, CUTTING

bit·ter \'bi-tər\ adj **1** : being or inducing the one of the basic taste sensations that is acrid, astringent, or disagreeable and is suggestive of hops **2** : marked by intensity or severity (as of distress or hatred) **3** : extremely harsh or cruel — **bit·ter·ly** adv — **bit·ter·ness** n

bit·tern \'bi-tərn\ n : any of various small or medium-sized herons

bit·ters \'bi-tərz\ n sing or pl : a usu. alcoholic solution of bitter and often aromatic plant products used in mixing drinks and as a mild tonic

¹**bit·ter·sweet** \'bi-tər-ˌswēt\ n **1** : a poisonous nightshade with purple flowers and orange-red berries **2** : a woody vine with yellow capsules that open when ripe and disclose scarlet seed coverings

²**bittersweet** adj : being at once both bitter and sweet

bi·tu·mi·nous coal \bə-'tü-mə-nəs-, bī-, -'tyü-\ n : a coal that when heated yields considerable volatile waste matter

bi·valve \\'bī-₁valv\\ *n* : an animal (as a clam) with a shell composed of two separate parts that open and shut — **bivalve** *adj*

¹**biv·ouac** \\'bi-və-₁wak\\ *n* [F, fr. LG *biwacht*, fr. *bi* at + *wacht* guard] : a temporary encampment or shelter

²**bivouac** *vb* **-ouacked; -ouack·ing** : to form a bivouac : CAMP

¹**bi·week·ly** \\₁bī-'wē-klē\\ *adj* **1** : occurring twice a week **2** : occurring every two weeks : FORTNIGHTLY — **biweekly** *adv*

²**biweekly** *n* : a biweekly publication

bi·year·ly \\-'yir-lē\\ *adj* **1** : BIANNUAL **2** : BIENNIAL

bi·zarre \\bə-'zär\\ *adj* : ODD, ECCENTRIC, FANTASTIC — **bi·zarre·ly** *adv*

bk *abbr* **1** bank **2** book

Bk *symbol* berkelium

bkg *abbr* banking

bkgd *abbr* background

bks *abbr* barracks

bkt *abbr* **1** basket **2** bracket

bl *abbr* **1** bale **2** barrel **3** blue

blab \\'blab\\ *vb* **blabbed; blab·bing** : TATTLE, GOSSIP

¹**black** \\'blak\\ *adj* **1** : of the color black; *also* : very dark **2** : SWARTHY **3** : of or relating to various groups of dark-skinned people **4** : of or relating to the Afro-American people or their culture **5** : SOILED, DIRTY **6** : lacking light ⟨a ∼ night⟩ **7** : WICKED, EVIL ⟨∼ magic⟩ **8** : DISMAL, GLOOMY ⟨a ∼ outlook⟩ **9** : SULLEN ⟨a ∼ mood⟩ — **black·ish** *adj* — **black·ly** *adv* — **black·ness** *n*

²**black** *n* **1** : a black pigment or dye; *also* : something (as clothing) that is black **2** : the characteristic color of soot or coal **3** : a person of a dark-skinned race **4** : AFRO-AMERICAN

³**black** *vb* : BLACKEN

black·a·moor \\'bla-kə-₁mur\\ *n* : a dark-skinned person

black–and–blue \\₁bla-kən-'blü\\ *adj* : darkly discolored from blood effused by bruising

black·ball \\'blak-₁ból\\ *vb* **1** : to vote against; *esp* : to exclude from membership by casting a negative vote **2** : OSTRACIZE — **black·ball** *n*

black bass *n* : any of several freshwater sunfishes native to eastern and central No. America

¹**black belt** \\'blak-₁belt\\ *n, often cap both Bs* : an area densely populated by blacks

²**black belt** \\-'belt\\ *n* : one who holds the rating of expert (as in judo or karate); *also* : the rating itself

black·ber·ry \\-₁ber-ē\\ *n* : the usu. black or purple juicy but seedy edible fruit of various brambles; *also* : a plant bearing this fruit

black·bird \\-₁bərd\\ *n* : any of various birds (as the red-winged blackbird) of which the male is largely or wholly black

black·board \\-₁bórd\\ *n* : a smooth usu. dark surface used for writing or drawing on with chalk

black·body \\-'bä-dē\\ *n* : a body or surface that completely absorbs incident radiation with no reflection

black box *n* **1** : a usu. complicated electronic device whose components and workings are unknown or mysterious to the user **2** : a device used in aircraft to record cockpit conversations and flight data

black death *n* : an epidemic of bacterial plague and esp. bubonic plague that spread rapidly in Europe and Asia in the 14th century

black·en \\'bla-kən\\ *vb* **black·ened; black·en·ing** **1** : to make or become black **2** : DEFAME, SULLY

black·ened *adj* : coated with spices and quickly seared in a very hot skillet ⟨∼ swordfish⟩

black eye *n* : a discoloration of the skin around the eye from bruising

black–eyed Su·san \\₁blak-₁īd-'süz-ᵊn\\ *n* : either of two No. American plants that are related to the daisies and have deep yellow to orange flower heads with dark conical centers

Black·foot \\'blak-₁fut\\ *n, pl* **Black·feet** *or* **Blackfoot** : a member of an American Indian people of Montana, Alberta, and Saskatchewan

black·guard \\'bla-gərd, -₁gärd\\ *n* : SCOUNDREL, RASCAL

black·head \\'blak-₁hed\\ *n* : a small usu. dark oily mass plugging the outlet of a skin gland

black hole *n* : a hypothetical celestial object with a gravitational field so strong that light cannot escape from it

black·ing \\'bla-kiŋ\\ *n* : a substance applied to something to make it black

¹**black·jack** \\'blak-₁jak\\ *n* **1** : a leather-covered club with a flexible handle **2** : a card game in which the object is to be dealt cards having a higher count than the dealer but not exceeding 21

²**blackjack** *vb* : to hit with or as if with a blackjack

black light *n* : invisible ultraviolet light

black·list \\'blak-₁list\\ *n* : a list of persons who are disapproved of and are to be punished or boycotted — **blacklist** *vb*

black·mail \\'blak-₁māl\\ *n* : extortion by threats esp. of public exposure; *also* : something so extorted — **blackmail** *vb* — **black·mail·er** *n*

black market *n* : illicit trade in goods; *also* : a place where such trade is carried on

Black Mass *n* : a travesty of the Christian mass ascribed to worshipers of Satan

Black Muslim *n* : a member of a chiefly black group that professes Islamic religious belief

black nationalist *n, often cap B&N* : a member of a group of militant blacks who advocate separatism from whites and the formation of self-governing black communities — **black nationalism** *n, often cap B&N*

black·out \\'bla-₁kaut\\ *n* **1** : a period of darkness due to electrical power failure **2** : a transitory loss or dulling of vision or consciousness **3** : the prohibition or restriction of the telecasting of a sports event — **black out** *vb*

black power *n* : the mobilization of the political and economic power of black Americans esp. to compel respect for their rights and improve their condition

black sheep *n* : a discreditable member of an otherwise respectable group

black·smith \\'blak-₁smith\\ *n* : a smith who forges iron — **black·smith·ing** *n*

black·thorn \\-₁thórn\\ *n* : a European thorny plum

black·top \\'blak-₁täp\\ *n* : a dark tarry material (as asphalt) used esp. for surfacing roads — **blacktop** *vb*

black widow *n* : a venomous New World spider having the female black with an hourglass-shaped red mark on the underside of the abdomen

blad·der \\'bla-dər\\ *n* : a sac in which liquid or gas is stored; *esp* : one in a vertebrate into which urine passes from the kidneys

blade \\'blād\\ *n* **1** : a leaf of a plant and esp. of a grass; *also* : the flat part of a leaf as distinguished from its stalk **2** : something (as the flat part of an oar or an arm of a propeller) resembling the blade of a leaf **3** : the cutting part of an instrument or tool **4** : SWORD; *also* : SWORDSMAN **5** : a dashing fellow ⟨a gay ∼⟩ **6** : the runner of an ice skate — **blad·ed** \\'blā-dəd\\ *adj*

blain \\'blān\\ *n* : an inflammatory swelling or sore

¹**blame** \\'blām\\ *vb* **blamed; blam·ing** [ME, fr. OF *blamer*, fr. L *blasphemare* to blaspheme, fr. Gk *blasphēmein*] **1** : to find fault with **2** : to hold responsible or responsible for **syn** censure, denounce, condemn, criticize — **blam·able** *adj*

²**blame** *n* **1** : CENSURE, REPROOF **2** : responsibility for fault or error **syn** guilt, fault, culpability, onus — **blame·less** *adj* — **blame·less·ly** *adv* — **blame·less·ness** *n*

blame·wor·thy \\-₁wər-t͟hē\\ *adj* : deserving blame — **blame·wor·thi·ness** *n*

blanch \\'blanch\\ *vb* : to make or become white or pale : BLEACH

blanc·mange \blə-'mänj, -'mänzh\ *n* [ME *blancmanger*, fr. MF *blanc manger*, lit., white food] : a dessert made from gelatin or a starchy substance and milk usu. sweetened and flavored

bland \'bland\ *adj* **1** : smooth in manner : SUAVE **2** : gently soothing ⟨a ∼ diet⟩; *also* : INSIPID **syn** gentle, mild, soft, balmy — **bland·ly** *adv* — **bland·ness** *n*

blan·dish·ment \'blan-dish-mənt\ *n* : flattering or coaxing speech or action : CAJOLERY

¹blank \'blaŋk\ *adj* **1** : showing or causing an appearance of dazed dismay; *also* : EXPRESSIONLESS **2** : free from writing or marks; *also* : having spaces to be filled in **3** : DULL, EMPTY ⟨∼ moments⟩ **4** : ABSOLUTE, DOWNRIGHT ⟨a ∼ refusal⟩ **5** : not shaped in final form — **blank·ly** *adv* — **blank·ness** *n*

²blank *n* **1** : an empty space **2** : a form with spaces for the entry of data **3** : an unfinished form (as of a key) **4** : a cartridge with propellant and a seal but no projectile

³blank *vb* **1** : to cover or close up : OBSCURE **2** : to keep from scoring

blank check *n* **1** : a signed check with the amount unspecified **2** : complete freedom of action

¹blan·ket \'blaŋ-kət\ *n* **1** : a heavy woven often woolen covering **2** : a covering layer ⟨a ∼ of snow⟩

²blanket *vb* : to cover with a blanket

³blanket *adj* : covering a group or class ⟨∼ insurance⟩; *also* : applicable in all instances ⟨∼ rules⟩

blank verse *n* : unrhymed iambic pentameter

blare \'blar\ *vb* **blared**; **blar·ing** : to sound loud and harsh; *also* : to proclaim loudly — **blare** *n*

blar·ney \'blär-nē\ *n* [*Blarney stone*, a stone in Blarney Castle, near Cork, Ireland, held to bestow skill in flattery on those who kiss it] : skillful flattery : BLANDISHMENT

bla·sé \blä-'zā\ *adj* [F] : apathetic to pleasure or excitement as a result of excessive indulgence; *also* : SOPHISTICATED

blas·pheme \blas-'fēm, 'blas-₁\ *vb* **blas·phemed**; **blas·phem·ing** **1** : to speak of or address with irreverence **2** : to utter blasphemy — **blas·phem·er** *n*

blas·phe·my \'blas-fə-mē\ *n, pl* **-mies** **1** : the act of expressing lack of reverence for God **2** : irreverence toward something considered sacred — **blas·phe·mous** \-məs\ *adj*

¹blast \'blast\ *n* **1** : a violent gust of wind; *also* : its effect **2** : sound made by a wind instrument **3** : a current of air forced at high pressure through a hole in a furnace (**blast furnace**) **4** : a sudden withering esp. of plants : BLIGHT **5** : EXPLOSION; *also* : the often destructive shock wave of an explosion

²blast *vb* : to shatter by or as if by an explosive

blast off *vb* — TAKE OFF **4** — used esp. of rocket-propelled vehicles — **blast·off** \'blast-₁òf\ *n*

bla·tant \'blāt-ᵊnt\ *adj* : offensively obtrusive : vulgarly showy **syn** vociferous, boisterous, clamorous, obstreperous — **bla·tan·cy** \-ᵊn-sē\ *n* — **bla·tant·ly** *adv*

blath·er \'bla-thər\ *vb* : to talk foolishly at length — **blather** *n*

blath·er·skite \'bla-thər-₁skīt\ *n* : a person who blathers

¹blaze \'blāz\ *n* **1** : FIRE **2** : intense direct light accompanied by heat **3** : something (as a dazzling display or sudden outburst) suggesting fire ⟨a ∼ of autumn leaves⟩ **syn** glare, glow, flame

²blaze *vb* **blazed**; **blaz·ing** **1** : to burn brightly; *also* : to flare up **2** : to be conspicuously bright : GLITTER

³blaze *vb* **blazed**; **blaz·ing** : to make public or conspicuous

⁴blaze *n* **1** : a usu. white stripe on the face of an animal **2** : a trail marker; *esp* : one made on a tree

⁵blaze *vb* **blazed**; **blaz·ing** : to mark (as a tree or trail) with blazes

blaz·er \'blā-zər\ *n* : a sports jacket often with notched collar and pockets that are stitched on

¹bla·zon \'blāz-ᵊn\ *n* **1** : COAT OF ARMS **2** : ostentatious display

²blazon *vb* **1** : to publish widely : PROCLAIM **2** : DECK, ADORN

bldg *abbr* building

bldr *abbr* builder

¹bleach \'blēch\ *vb* : WHITEN, BLANCH

²bleach *n* : a preparation used in bleaching

bleach·ers \'blē-chərz\ *n sing or pl* : a usu. uncovered stand of tiered seats for spectators

bleak \'blēk\ *adj* **1** : desolately barren and often wind-swept **2** : lacking warm or cheering qualities — **bleak·ish** *adj* — **bleak·ly** *adv* — **bleak·ness** *n*

blear \'blir\ *adj* : dim with water or tears ⟨∼ eyes⟩

bleary \'blir-ē\ *adj* **1** : dull or dimmed esp. from fatigue or sleep **2** : poorly outlined or defined

bleat \'blēt\ *n* : the cry of a sheep or goat or a sound like it — **bleat** *vb*

bleed \'blēd\ *vb* **bled** \'bled\; **bleed·ing** **1** : to lose or shed blood **2** : to be wounded; *also* : to feel pain or distress **3** : to flow or ooze from a wounded surface; *also* : to draw fluid from ⟨∼ a tire⟩ **4** : to extort money from

bleed·er \'blē-dər\ *n* : one that bleeds; *esp* : HEMOPHILIAC

bleeding heart *n* **1** : a garden plant related to the poppies that has usu. deep pink drooping heart-shaped flowers **2** : a person who shows extreme sympathy esp. for an object of alleged persecution

¹blem·ish \'ble-mish\ *vb* : to spoil by a flaw : MAR

²blemish *n* : a noticeable flaw

¹blench \'blench\ *vb* [ME, to deceive, blench, fr. OE *blencan* to deceive] : FLINCH, QUAIL **syn** shrink, recoil, wince, start

²blench *vb* : to grow or make pale

¹blend \'blend\ *vb* **blend·ed**; **blend·ing** **1** : to mix thoroughly **2** : to prepare (as coffee) by mixing different varieties **3** : to combine into an integrated whole **4** : HARMONIZE **syn** fuse, merge, mingle, coalesce — **blend·er** *n*

²blend *n* : a product of blending **syn** compound, composite, alloy, mixture

bless \'bles\ *vb* **blessed** \'blest\ *also* **blest** \'blest\; **bless·ing** [ME, fr. OE *blētsian*, fr. *blōd* blood; fr. the use of blood in consecration] **1** : to consecrate by religious rite or word **2** : to sanctify with the sign of the cross **3** : to invoke divine care for **4** : PRAISE, GLORIFY **5** : to confer happiness upon

bless·ed \'ble-səd\ *also* **blest** \'blest\ *adj* **1** : HOLY **2** : BEATIFIED **3** : DELIGHTFUL — **bless·ed·ly** *adv* — **bless·ed·ness** *n*

bless·ing \'ble-siŋ\ *n* **1** : the act or words of one who blesses; *also* : APPROVAL **2** : a thing conducive to happiness **3** : grace said at a meal

blew *past of* BLOW

¹blight \'blīt\ *n* **1** : a plant disease or injury marked by withering; *also* : an organism causing a blight **2** : an impairing or frustrating influence; *also* : a deteriorated condition ⟨urban ∼⟩

²blight *vb* : to affect with or suffer from blight

blimp \'blimp\ *n* : a nonrigid airship

¹blind \'blīnd\ *adj* **1** : lacking or grossly deficient in ability to see; *also* : intended for blind persons **2** : not based on reason, evidence, or knowledge ⟨∼ faith⟩ **3** : not intelligently controlled or directed ⟨∼ chance⟩ **4** : performed solely by using aircraft instruments ⟨a ∼ landing⟩ **5** : hard to discern or make out : HIDDEN ⟨a ∼ seam⟩ **6** : lacking an opening or outlet ⟨a ∼ alley⟩ — **blind·ly** *adv* — **blind·ness** \'blīnd-nəs\ *n*

²blind *vb* **1** : to make blind **2** : DAZZLE **3** : DARKEN; *also* : HIDE

³blind *n* **1** : something (as a shutter) to hinder vision or keep out light **2** : a place of concealment **3** : SUBTERFUGE

blind date *n* : a date between persons who have not previously met; *also* : either of these persons

blind·er \\'blīn-dər\\ *n* : either of two flaps on a horse's bridle to prevent it from seeing to the side

blind·fold \\'blīnd-ˌfōld\\ *vb* : to cover the eyes of with or as if with a bandage — **blindfold** *n*

¹**blink** \\'bliŋk\\ *vb* 1 : WINK 2 : TWINKLE 3 : EVADE, IGNORE

²**blink** *n* 1 : GLIMMER, SPARKLE 2 : a usu. involuntary shutting and opening of the eye

blink·er \\'bliŋ-kər\\ *n* : a blinking light used as a signal

blin·tze \\'blint-sə\\ *or* **blintz** \\'blints\\ *n* [Yiddish *blintse*] : a thin rolled pancake with a filling usu. of cream cheese

blip \\'blip\\ *n* 1 : a spot on a radar screen 2 : ABERRATION 1

bliss \\'blis\\ *n* : complete happiness : JOY **syn** beatitude, blessedness — **bliss·ful** \\-fəl\\ *adj* — **bliss·ful·ly** *adv*

¹**blis·ter** \\'blis-tər\\ *n* 1 : a raised area of skin containing watery fluid; *also* : an agent that causes blisters 2 : something (as a raised spot in paint) suggesting a blister 3 : a disease of plants marked by large swollen patches on the leaves

²**blister** *vb* : to develop a blister; *also* : to cause blisters

blithe \\'blīth, 'blīth\\ *adj* **blith·er; blith·est** : happily lighthearted **syn** merry, jovial, jolly, jocund — **blithe·ly** *adv* — **blithe·some** \\-səm\\ *adj*

blitz \\'blits\\ *n* 1 : an intensive series of air raids 2 : a fast intensive campaign 3 : a rush of the passer by the defensive linebackers in football — **blitz** *vb*

blitz·krieg \\-ˌkrēg\\ *n* [G, lit., lightning war, fr. *Blitz* lightning + *Krieg* war] : a sudden violent enemy attack

bliz·zard \\'bli-zərd\\ *n* : a long severe snowstorm

blk *abbr* 1 black 2 block

bloat \\'blōt\\ *vb* : to swell by or as if by filling with water or air

blob \\'bläb\\ *n* : a small lump or drop of a thick consistency

bloc \\'bläk\\ *n* [F, lit., block] : a combination of individuals or groups (as nations) working for a common purpose

¹**block** \\'bläk\\ *n* 1 : a solid piece of substantial material (as wood or stone) 2 : HINDRANCE, OBSTRUCTION; *also* : interruption of normal function of body or mind ⟨heart ∼⟩ 3 : a frame enclosing one or more pulleys and having a hook or strap by which it may be attached 4 : a piece of material with a hand-cut design on its surface from which copies are to be made 5 : a large building divided into separate units (as apartments or offices) 6 : a row of houses or shops 7 : a city square; *also* : the distance along one of the sides of such a square 8 : a quantity of things considered as a unit ⟨a ∼ of seats⟩

²**block** *vb* 1 : OBSTRUCT, CHECK 2 : to outline roughly ⟨∼ out a design⟩ 3 : to provide or support with a block ⟨∼ up a wheel⟩ **syn** bar, impede, hinder, obstruct

block·ade \\blä-'kād\\ *n* : the isolation of a place usu. by troops or ships — **blockade** *vb* — **block·ad·er** *n*

block·age \\'blä-kij\\ *n* : an act or instance of obstructing : the state of being blocked

block·bust·er \\'bläk-ˌbəs-tər\\ *n* : one that is very large, successful, or violent ⟨a ∼ of a movie⟩

block·head \\'bläk-ˌhed\\ *n* : DOLT, DUNCE

block·house \\-ˌhaus\\ *n* : a small strong building used as a shelter (as from enemy fire) or observation post

¹**blond** *or* **blonde** \\'bländ\\ *adj* : fair in complexion; *also* : of a light or bleached color ⟨∼ mahogany⟩ — **blond·ish** \\'blän-dish\\ *adj*

²**blond** *or* **blonde** *n* : a person having blond hair

blood \\'bləd\\ *n* 1 : a usu. red liquid that circulates in the heart, arteries, and veins of animals 2 : LIFEBLOOD; *also* : LIFE 3 : LINEAGE, STOCK 4 : KINSHIP; *also* : KINDRED 5 : the taking of life 6 : TEMPER, PASSION 7 : DANDY 1 — **blood·less** *adj* — **bloody** *adj*

blood bank *n* : a place where blood or plasma is stored

blood·bath \\'bləd-ˌbath, -ˌbàth\\ *n* : MASSACRE

blood count *n* : the determination of the number of blood cells in a specific volume of blood; *also* : the number of cells so determined

blood·cur·dling \\'bləd-kərd-liŋ, -ˌkər-dᵊl-iŋ\\ *adj* : arousing fright or horror

blood·ed \\'blə-dəd\\ *adj* 1 : having blood of a specified kind ⟨warm-*blooded* animals⟩ 2 : entirely or largely purebred ⟨∼ horses⟩

blood group *n* : one of the classes into which human beings can be separated by the presence or absence in their blood of specific antigens

blood·hound \\'bləd-ˌhaund\\ *n* : any of a breed of large powerful hounds with long drooping ears, a wrinkled face, and keen sense of smell

blood·let·ting \\-ˌle-tiŋ\\ *n* 1 : PHLEBOTOMY 2 : BLOODSHED

blood·line \\-ˌlīn\\ *n* : a sequence of direct ancestors esp. in a pedigree

blood·mo·bile \\-mō-ˌbēl\\ *n* : a motor vehicle equipped for collecting blood from donors

blood poisoning *n* : invasion of the bloodstream by virulent microorganisms from a focus of infection accompanied esp. by chills, fever, and prostration

blood pressure *n* : pressure of the blood on the walls of blood vessels and esp. arteries

blood·root \\'bləd-ˌrüt, -ˌrut\\ *n* : a plant related to the poppy that has a red root and sap, a solitary leaf, and a white flower in early spring

blood·shed \\-ˌshed\\ *n* : wounding or taking of life : CARNAGE, SLAUGHTER

blood·shot \\-ˌshät\\ *adj* : inflamed to redness ⟨∼ eyes⟩

blood·stain \\-ˌstān\\ *n* : a discoloration caused by blood — **blood·stained** \\-ˌstānd\\ *adj*

blood·stone \\-ˌstōn\\ *n* : a green quartz sprinkled with red spots

blood·stream \\-ˌstrēm\\ *n* : the flowing blood in a circulatory system

blood·suck·er \\-ˌsə-kər\\ *n* : an animal that sucks blood; *esp* : LEECH — **blood·suck·ing** *adj*

blood test *n* : a test of the blood; *esp* : one for syphilis

blood·thirsty \\'bləd-ˌthər-stē\\ *adj* : eager to shed blood — **blood·thirst·i·ly** \\-ˌthər-stə-lē\\ *adv* — **blood·thirst·i·ness** \\-stē-nəs\\ *n*

blood type *n* : BLOOD GROUP — **blood–typ·ing** *n*

blood vessel *n* : a vessel (as a vein or artery) in which blood circulates in the body

Bloody Mary \\-'mer-ē\\ *n, pl* **Bloody Marys** : a drink made essentially of vodka and tomato juice

¹**bloom** \\'blüm\\ *n* 1 : FLOWER 1; *also* : flowers or amount of flowers (as of a plant) 2 : the period or state of flowering 3 : a state or time of beauty and vigor 4 : a powdery coating esp. on fruits and leaves 5 : rosy color; *also* : an appearance of freshness or health — **bloomy** *adj*

²**bloom** *vb* 1 : to produce or yield flowers 2 : MATURE 3 : to glow esp. with healthy color **syn** flower, blossom

bloo·mers \\'blü-mərz\\ *n pl* [Amelia *Bloomer* †1894 Am. reformer] : a woman's garment of short loose trousers gathered at the knee

bloop·er \\'blü-pər\\ *n* 1 : a fly ball hit barely beyond a baseball infield 2 : an embarrassing public blunder

¹**blos·som** \\'blä-səm\\ *n* 1 : the flower of a plant 2 : the period or state of flowering

²**blossom** *vb* : FLOWER, BLOOM

¹**blot** \\'blät\\ *n* 1 : SPOT, STAIN ⟨ink ∼s⟩ 2 : BLEMISH **syn** stigma, brand, slur

²**blot** *vb* **blot·ted; blot·ting** 1 : SPOT, STAIN 2 : OBSCURE, ECLIPSE ⟨∼ out the sun⟩ 3 *obs* : MAR; *esp* : DISGRACE 4 : to dry or remove with or as if with an absorbing material 5 : to make a blot

blotch \\'bläch\\ *n* : a usu. large and irregular spot or mark (as of ink or color) — **blotch** *vb* — **blotchy** *adj*

blot·ter \\'blä-tər\\ *n* 1 : a piece of blotting paper 2 : a book for preliminary records (as of sales or arrests)

blot·ting paper *n* : a spongy paper used to absorb ink

blouse \\'blaus, 'blaúz\\ *n* 1 : a loose outer garment like a smock **2** : a usu. loose garment reaching from the neck to about the waist

¹blow \'blō\ *vb* **blew** \'blü\; **blown** \'blōn\; **blow•ing 1** : to move forcibly ⟨the wind *blew*⟩ **2** : to send forth a current of a gas (as air) **3** : to act on with a current of gas or vapor; *esp* : to drive with such a current **4** : to sound or cause to sound ⟨∼ a horn⟩ **5** : PANT, GASP; *also* : to expel moist air in breathing ⟨the whale *blew*⟩ **6** : BOAST; *also* : BLUSTER **7** : MELT — used of an electrical fuse **8** : to shape or form by blown or injected air ⟨∼ glass⟩ **9** : to shatter or destroy by or as if by explosion **10** : to make breathless by exertion **11** : to spend recklessly **12** : to foul up hopelessly ⟨*blew* her lines⟩ — **blow•er** *n*

²blow *n* **1** : a usu. strong blowing of air : GALE **2** : BOASTING, BRAG **3** : an act or instance of blowing

³blow *vb* **blew** \'blü\; **blown** \'blōn\; **blow•ing** : FLOWER, BLOOM

⁴blow *n* **1** : a forcible stroke **2** : COMBAT ⟨come to ∼s⟩ **3** : a severe and usu. unexpected calamity

blow–by–blow *adj* : minutely detailed ⟨∼ account⟩

blow–dry \-ˌdrī\ *vb* : to dry and usu. style hair with a blow-dryer

blow–dryer \-ˌdrī(-ə)r\ *n* : a hand-held hair dryer

blow•fly \'blō-ˌflī\ *n* : any of a family of dipteran flies (as a bluebottle) that deposit their eggs or maggots on meat or in wounds

blow•gun \-ˌgən\ *n* : a tube from which an arrow or a dart may be shot by the force of the breath

blow•out \'blō-ˌaůt\ *n* : a bursting of something (as a tire) because of pressure of the contents (as air)

blow•sy *also* **blow•zy** \'blaů-zē\ *adj* : DISHEVELED, SLOVENLY

blow•torch \'blō-ˌtörch\ *n* : a small portable burner whose flame is made hotter by a blast of air or oxygen

blow•up \'blō-ˌəp\ *n* **1** : EXPLOSION **2** : an outburst of temper **3** : a photographic enlargement

blowy \'blō-ē\ *adj* : WINDY

BLT \ˌbē-el-'tē\ *n* : a bacon, lettuce, and tomato sandwich

¹blub•ber \'blə-bər\ *vb* : to cry noisily

²blubber *n* **1** : the fat of large sea mammals (as whales) **2** : a noisy crying

¹blud•geon \'blə-jən\ *n* : a short often loaded club

²bludgeon *vb* : to strike with or as if with a bludgeon

¹blue \'blü\ *adj* **blu•er; blu•est 1** : of the color blue; *also* : BLUISH **2** : MELANCHOLY; *also* : DEPRESSING **3** : PURITANICAL **4** : INDECENT — **blue•ness** *n*

²blue *n* **1** : a color between green and violet in the spectrum : the color of the clear daytime sky **2** : something (as clothing or the sky) that is blue

blue baby *n* : a baby with bluish skin due to faulty circulation caused by a heart defect

blue•bell \-ˌbel\ *n* : any of various plants with blue bell-shaped flowers

blue•ber•ry \'blü-ˌber-ē, -bə-rē\ *n* : the edible blue or blackish berry of various shrubs of the heath family; *also* : one of these shrubs

blue•bird \-ˌbərd\ *n* : any of several small No. American thrushes that are blue above and reddish-brown or pale blue below

blue•bon•net \'blü-ˌbä-nət\ *n* : either of two low-growing annual lupines of Texas with silky foliage and blue flowers

blue•bot•tle \'blü-ˌbät-ᵊl\ *n* : any of several blowflies with iridescent blue bodies or abdomens

blue cheese *n* : cheese having veins of greenish blue mold

blue–col•lar \'blü-'kä-lər\ *adj* : of, relating to, or being the class of workers whose duties call for work clothes

blue•fish \-ˌfish\ *n* : a marine sport and food fish bluish above and silvery below

blue•grass \-ˌgras\ *n* **1** : KENTUCKY BLUEGRASS **2**

: country music played on stringed instruments having free improvisation and close harmonies

blue jay \-ˌjā\ *n* : a crested bright blue No. American jay

blue jeans *n pl* : pants usu. made of blue denim

blue•nose \'blü-ˌnōz\ *n* : a person who advocates a rigorous moral code

blue•point \-ˌpóint\ *n* : a small oyster typically from the south shore of Long Island, New York

blue•print \-ˌprint\ *n* **1** : a photographic print in white on a blue ground used esp. for copying mechanical drawings and architects' plans **2** : a detailed plan of action — **blueprint** *vb*

blues \'blüz\ *n pl* **1** : MELANCHOLY **2** : music in a style marked by recurrent minor intervals and melancholy lyrics

blue•stock•ing \'blü-ˌstä-kiŋ\ *n* : a woman having intellectual interests

blu•et \'blü-ət\ *n* : a low No. American herb with dainty bluish flowers

blue whale *n* : a very large baleen whale that may reach a weight of 150 tons (135 metric tons) and a length of 100 feet (30 meters)

¹bluff \'bləf\ *adj* **1** : having a broad flattened front **2** : rising steeply with a broad flat front **3** : OUTSPOKEN, FRANK **syn** abrupt, blunt, brusque, curt, gruff

²bluff *n* : a high steep bank : CLIFF

³bluff *vb* : to frighten or deceive by pretense or a mere show of strength

⁴bluff *n* : an act or instance of bluffing; *also* : one who bluffs

blu•ing *or* **blue•ing** \'blü-iŋ\ *n* : a preparation used in laundering to counteract yellowing of white fabrics

blu•ish \'blü-ish\ *adj* : somewhat blue

¹blun•der \'blən-dər\ *vb* **1** : to move clumsily or unsteadily **2** : to make a stupid or needless mistake

²blunder *n* : an avoidable and usu. serious mistake

blun•der•buss \'blən-dər-ˌbəs\ *n* [obs. D *donderbus*, fr. D *donder* thunder + obs. D *bus* gun] : an obsolete short-barreled firearm with a flaring muzzle

blunderbuss

¹blunt \'blənt\ *adj* **1** : not sharp : DULL **2** : lacking in tact : BLUFF **syn** brusque, curt, gruff, abrupt, crusty — **blunt•ly** *adv* — **blunt•ness** *n*

²blunt *vb* : to make or become dull

¹blur \'blər\ *n* **1** : a smear or stain that obscures **2** : something vaguely perceived; *esp* : something moving too quickly to be clearly perceived — **blur•ry** \-ē\ *adj*

²blur *vb* **blurred; blur•ring** : DIM, CLOUD, OBSCURE

blurb \'blərb\ *n* : a short publicity notice (as on a book jacket)

blurt \'blərt\ *vb* : to utter suddenly and impulsively

blush \'bləsh\ *n* : a reddening of the face (as from modesty or confusion) : FLUSH — **blush** *vb* — **blush•ful** *adj*

blus•ter \'bləs-tər\ *vb* **1** : to blow in stormy noisy gusts **2** : to talk or act with noisy swaggering threats — **bluster** *n* — **blus•tery** \-tə-rē\ *adj*

blvd *abbr* boulevard

B lymphocyte *n* : B CELL

BM *abbr* bowel movement

B movie *n* : a cheaply produced motion picture

BO *abbr* **1** best offer **2** body odor **3** box office **4** branch office

boa \'bō-ə\ *n* **1** : a large snake (as the **boa con•stric•tor** \-kən-'strik-tər\ or the related anaconda) that suffocates and kills its prey by constriction **2** : a fluffy scarf usu. of fur or feathers

boar \\'bōr\ *n* : a male swine; *also* : WILD BOAR

¹board \\'bōrd\ *n* **1** : the side of a ship **2** : a thin flat length of sawed lumber; *also* : material (as cardboard) or a piece of material formed as a thin flat firm sheet **3** *pl* : STAGE 1 **4** : a table spread with a meal; *also* : daily meals esp. when furnished for pay **5** : a table at which a council or magistrates sit **6** : a group or association of persons organized for a special responsibility (as the management of a business or institution); *also* : an organized commercial exchange **7** : a sheet of insulating material carrying circuit elements and inserted in an electronic device

²board *vb* **1** : to go or put aboard 〈~ a boat〉 **2** : to cover with boards **3** : to provide or be provided with meals and often lodging — **board·er** *n*

board·ing·house \\'bōr-diŋ-,haus\ *n* : a house at which persons are boarded

board·walk \\'bōrd-,wok\ *n* : a promenade (as of planking) along a beach

boast \\'bōst\ *vb* **1** : to praise oneself **2** : to mention or assert with excessive pride **3** : to prize as a possession; *also* : HAVE (the house ~s a fireplace) — **boast** *n* — **boast·ful** \\-fəl\ *adj* — **boast·ful·ly** *adv*

boat \\'bōt\ *n* : a small vessel for travel on water; *also* : SHIP

boat·er \\'bō-tər\ *n* **1** : one that travels in a boat **2** : a stiff straw hat

boat·man \\'bōt-mən\ *n* : a man who operates, works on, or deals in boats

boat people *n pl* : refugees fleeing by boat

boat·swain \\'bōs-ᵊn\ *n* : a subordinate officer of a ship in charge of the hull and related equipment

¹bob \\'bäb\ *vb* **bobbed; bob·bing** **1** : to move up and down jerkily or repeatedly **2** : to emerge, arise, or appear suddenly or unexpectedly

²bob *n* : a bobbing movement

³bob *n* **1** : a knob, knot, twist, or curl esp. of ribbons, yarn, or hair **2** : a short haircut of a woman or child **3** : FLOAT 2 **4** : a weight hanging from a line

⁴bob *vb* **bobbed; bob·bing** : to cut hair in a bob

⁵bob *n, pl* **bob** *slang Brit* : SHILLING

bob·bin \\'bä-bən\ *n* : a cylinder or spindle for holding or dispensing thread (as in a sewing machine)

bob·ble \\'bä-bəl\ *vb* **bob·bled; bob·bling** : FUMBLE — **bobble** *n*

bob·by \\'bä-bē\ *n, pl* **bobbies** [*Bobby*, nickname for Sir *Robert* Peel, who organized the London police force] *Brit* : a police officer

bobby pin *n* : a flat wire hairpin with prongs that press close together

bob·cat \\'bäb-,kat\ *n* : a small usu. rusty-colored No. American lynx

bob·o·link \\'bä-bə-,liŋk\ *n* : an American migratory songbird related to the meadowlarks

bob·sled \\'bäb-,sled\ *n* **1** : a short sled usu. used as one of a joined pair **2** : a racing sled with two pairs of runners, a steering wheel, and a hand brake — **bob·sled** *vb*

bob·white \(,)bäb-'hwīt\ *n* : any of a genus of quail; *esp* : a popular game bird of the eastern and central U.S.

boc·cie *or* **boc·ci** *or* **boc·ce** \\'bä-chē\ *n* : Italian lawn bowling played on a long narrow court

bock \\'bäk\ *n* : a dark heavy beer usu. sold in early spring

bod \\'bäd\ *n* : BODY

¹bode \\'bōd\ *vb* **bod·ed; bod·ing** : to indicate by signs : PRESAGE

²bode *past of* BIDE

bo·de·ga \bō-'dā-gə\ *n* [Sp, fr. L *apotheca* storehouse] : a store specializing in Hispanic groceries

bod·ice \\'bä-dəs\ *n* [alter. of *bodies*, pl. of *body*] : the usu. close-fitting part of a dress above the waist

bod·i·less \\'bä-di-ləs\ *adj* : lacking a body or material form

¹bod·i·ly \\'bäd-ᵊl-ē\ *adj* : of or relating to the body (~ contact)

²bodily *adv* **1** : in the flesh **2** : as a whole (lifted the crate up ~)

bod·kin \\'bäd-kən\ *n* **1** : DAGGER **2** : a pointed implement for punching holes in cloth **3** : a blunt needle for drawing tape or ribbon through a loop or hem

body \\'bä-dē\ *n, pl* **bod·ies** **1** : the physical whole of a living or dead organism; *also* : the trunk or main mass of an organism as distinguished from its appendages **2** : a human being : PERSON **3** : the main part of something **4** : a mass of matter distinct from other masses **5** : GROUP **6** : VISCOSITY, FIRMNESS **7** : richness of flavor — used esp. of wines — **bod·ied** \\'bä-dēd\ *adj*

body English *n* : bodily motions made in a usu. unconscious effort to influence the movement of a propelled object (as a ball)

body·guard \\'bä-dē-,gärd\ *n* : a personal guard; *also* : RETINUE

body stocking *n* : a sheer close-fitting one-piece garment for the torso that often has sleeves and legs

body·work \\'bä-dē-,wərk\ *n* : the making or repairing of vehicle bodies

Boer \\'bōr, 'bur\ *n* [D, lit., farmer] : a South African of Dutch or Huguenot descent

¹bog \\'bäg, 'bog\ *n* : wet, spongy, poorly drained, and usu. acid ground — **bog·gy** *adj*

²bog *vb* **bogged; bog·ging** : to sink into or as if into a bog

bo·gey *also* **bo·gie** *or* **bo·gy** \\'bu-gē, 'bō- *for 1;* 'bō- *for 2*\ *n, pl* **bogeys** *also* **bogies** **1** : SPECTER, HOBGOBLIN; *also* : a source of fear or annoyance **2** : a score of one over par on a hole in golf

bo·gey·man \\'bu-gē-,man, 'bō-, 'bü-\ *n* : an imaginary monster used in threatening children

bog·gle \\'bä-gəl\ *vb* **bog·gled; bog·gling** : to overwhelm or be overwhelmed with fright or amazement

bo·gus \\'bō-gəs\ *adj* : SPURIOUS, SHAM

Bo·he·mi·an \bō-'hē-mē-ən\ *n* **1** : a native or inhabitant of Bohemia **2** *often not cap* : VAGABOND, WANDERER **3** *often not cap* : a person (as a writer or artist) living an unconventional life — **bohemian** *adj, often cap*

¹boil \\'boil\ *n* : an inflamed swelling on the skin containing pus

²boil *vb* **1** : to heat or become heated to a temperature (**boiling point**) at which vapor is formed and rises in bubbles (water ~s and changes to steam); *also* : to act on or be acted on by a boiling liquid (~ eggs) **2** : to be in a state of seething agitation

³boil *n* : the act or state of boiling

boil·er \\'boi-lər\ *n* **1** : a container in which something is boiled **2** : a strong vessel used in making steam **3** : a tank holding hot water

boil·er·mak·er \\'boi-lər-,mā-kər\ *n* : whiskey with a beer chaser

bois·ter·ous \\'boi-st(ə-)rəs\ *adj* : noisily turbulent or exuberant — **bois·ter·ous·ly** *adv*

bok choy \\'bäk-'choi\ *n* : a Chinese vegetable related to the mustards that forms a loose head of green leaves with long thick white stalks

bo·la \\'bō-lə\ *or* **bo·las** \\-ləs\ *n, pl* **bolas** \\-ləz\ *also* **bo·las·es** [AmerSp *bolas*, fr. Sp *bola* ball] : a cord with weights attached to the ends for hurling at and entangling an animal

☞ For illustration, see next page.

bold \\'bōld\ *adj* **1** : COURAGEOUS, INTREPID **2** : IMPUDENT **3** : STEEP **4** : ADVENTUROUS, FREE (a ~ thinker) **syn** dauntless, brave, valiant — **bold·ly** *adv* — **bold·ness** \\'bōld-nəs\ *n*

bold·face \\'bōld-,fās\ *n* : a heavy-faced type; *also* : printing in boldface — **bold–faced** \\-'fāst\ *adj*

bole \\'bōl\ *n* : the trunk of a tree

bo·le·ro \bə-'ler-ō\ *n, pl* **-ros** **1** : a Spanish dance or its music **2** : a short loose jacket open at the front

bola

bo·li·var \bə-'lē-₁vär, 'bä-lə-vər\ *n, pl* **-va·res** \₁bä-lə-'vär-₁ās, ₁bō-\ *or* **-vars** — see MONEY table

Bo·liv·i·an \bə-'li-vē-ən\ *n* : a native or inhabitant of Bolivia — **Bolivian** *adj*

bo·li·vi·a·no \bə-₁li-vē-'ä-(₁)nō\ *n, pl* **-nos** — see MONEY table

boll \'bōl\ *n* : a seed pod (as of cotton)

boll weevil *n* : a small grayish weevil that infests the cotton plant both as a larva and as an adult

boll·worm \'bōl-₁wərm\ *n* : any of several moths and esp. the corn earworm whose larvae feed on cotton bolls

bo·lo·gna \bə-'lō-nē\ *n* [short for *Bologna sausage*, fr. *Bologna*, Italy] : a large smoked sausage of beef, veal, and pork

Bol·she·vik \'bōl-shə-₁vik\ *n, pl* **Bolsheviks** *also* **Bol·she·vi·ki** \₁bōl-shə-'vi-kē\ [Russ *bol'shevik*, fr. *bol'shiĭ* larger] **1** : a member of the party that seized power in Russia in the revolution of November 1917 **2** : COMMUNIST — **Bolshevik** *adj*

bol·she·vism \'bōl-shə-₁vi-zəm\ *n, often cap* : the doctrine or program of the Bolsheviks advocating violent overthrow of capitalism

¹bol·ster \'bōl-stər\ *n* : a long pillow or cushion

²bolster *vb* : to support with or as if with a bolster; *also* : REINFORCE

¹bolt \'bōlt\ *n* **1** : a missile (as an arrow) for a crossbow or catapult **2** : a flash of lightning : THUNDERBOLT **3** : a sliding bar used to fasten a door **4** : a roll of cloth or wallpaper of specified length **5** : a rod with a head at one end and a screw thread at the other used with a nut to fasten objects together **6** : a metal cylinder that drives the cartridge into the chamber of a firearm

²bolt *vb* **1** : to move suddenly (as in fright or hurry) : START, DASH **2** : to break away (as from association) ⟨~ from a political platform⟩ **3** : to produce seed prematurely **4** : to secure or fasten with a bolt **5** : to swallow hastily or without chewing

³bolt *n* : an act of bolting

bo·lus \'bō-ləs\ *n* **1** : a large pill **2** : a soft mass of chewed food

¹bomb \'bäm\ *n* **1** : a fused explosive device designed to detonate under specified conditions (as impact) **2** : an aerosol or foam dispenser (as of insecticide or hair spray) : SPRAY CAN **3** : a long pass in football

²bomb *vb* : to attack with bombs

bom·bard \bäm-'bärd\ *vb* **1** : to attack esp. with artillery or bombers **2** : to assail persistently **3** : to subject to the impact of rapidly moving particles (as electrons) — **bom·bard·ment** *n*

bom·bar·dier \₁bäm-bər-'dir\ *n* : a bomber-crew member who releases the bombs

bom·bast \'bäm-₁bast\ *n* [ME, cotton padding, fr. MF *bombace*, fr. ML *bombax* cotton, alter. of L *bombyx* silkworm, silk, fr. Gk] : pretentious wordy speech or writing — **bom·bas·tic** \bäm-'bas-tik\ *adj* — **bom·bas·ti·cal·ly** \-ti-k(ə-)lē\ *adv*

bom·ba·zine \₁bäm-bə-'zēn\ *n* **1** : a twilled fabric with silk warp and worsted filling **2** : a silk fabric in twill weave dyed black

bomb·er \'bä-mər\ *n* : one that bombs; *esp* : an airplane for dropping bombs

bomb·proof \'bäm-₁prüf\ *adj* : safe against the explosive force of bombs

bomb·shell \'bäm-₁shel\ *n* **1** : BOMB 1 **2** : one that stuns, amazes, or completely upsets

bona fide \'bō-nə-₁fīd, 'bä-; ₁bō-nə-'fī-dē, -də\ *adj* [L, in good faith] **1** : made in good faith ⟨a *bona fide* agreement⟩ **2** : GENUINE, REAL ⟨a *bona fide* bargain⟩

bo·nan·za \bə-'nan-zə\ *n* [Sp, lit., calm sea, fr. ML *bonacia*, alter. of L *malacia*, fr. Gk *malakia*, lit., softness, fr. *malakos* soft] : something yielding a rich return

bon·bon \'bän-₁bän\ *n* : a candy with a creamy center and a soft covering (as of chocolate)

¹bond \'bänd\ *n* **1** : FETTER **2** : a binding or uniting force or tie ⟨~s of friendship⟩ **3** : an agreement or obligation often made binding by a pledge of money or goods **4** : a person who acts as surety for another **5** : an interest-bearing certificate of public or private indebtedness **6** : the state of goods subject to supervision pending payment of taxes or duties due

²bond *vb* **1** : to assure payment of duties or taxes on (goods) by giving a bond **2** : to insure against losses caused by the acts of ⟨~ a bank teller⟩ **3** : to make or become firmly united as if by bonds ⟨~ iron to copper⟩

bond·age \'bän-dij\ *n* : SLAVERY, SERVITUDE

bond·hold·er \'bänd-₁hōl-dər\ *n* : one that owns a government or corporation bond

bond·ing *n* **1** : the formation of a close personal relationship esp. through frequent or constant association **2** : the attaching of a material (as porcelain) to a tooth surface esp. for cosmetic purposes

bond·man \'bänd-mən\ *n* : SLAVE, SERF

¹bonds·man \'bändz-mən\ *n* : SURETY 3

²bondsman *n* : BONDMAN

bond·wom·an \'bänd-₁wu̇-mən\ *n* : a female slave or serf

¹bone \'bōn\ *n* **1** : a hard largely calcareous tissue forming most of the skeleton of a vertebrate animal; *also* : one of the pieces of bone making up a vertebrate skeleton **2** : a hard animal substance (as ivory or baleen) similar to true bone **3** : something made of bone — **bone·less** *adj* — **bony** *also* **bon·ey** \'bō-nē\ *adj*

²bone *vb* **boned; bon·ing** : to free from bones ⟨~ a chicken⟩

bone black *n* : the black carbon residue from calcined bones used esp. as a pigment

bone meal *n* : crushed or ground bone used esp. as fertilizer or feed

bon·er \'bō-nər\ *n* : a stupid and ridiculous blunder

bone up *vb* **1** : CRAM 3 **2** : to refresh one's memory ⟨*boned up* on the speech before giving it⟩

bon·fire \'bän-₁fīr\ *n* [ME *bonefire* a fire of bones, fr. *bon* bone + *fire*] : a large fire built in the open air

bon·go \'bäŋ-gō\ *n, pl* **bongos** *also* **bongoes** [AmerSp *bongó*] : one of a pair of small tuned drums played with the hands

bon·ho·mie \₁bä-nə-'mē\ *n* [F *bonhomie*, fr. *bonhomme* good-natured man, fr. *bon* good + *homme* man] : good-natured easy friendliness

bo·ni·to \bə-'nē-tō\ *n, pl* **-tos** *or* **-to** : any of several medium-sized tunas

bon mot \bōⁿ-'mō\ *n, pl* **bons mots** \same\ *or* **bon mots** \same *or* -'mō\ [F, lit., good word] : a clever remark

bon·net \'bä-nət\ *n* : a covering (as a cap) for the head; *esp* : a hat for a woman or infant tied under the chin

bon·ny \\'bä-nē\\ *adj* **bon·ni·er; -est** *chiefly Brit* : AT-TRACTIVE, FAIR; *also* : FINE, EXCELLENT

bon·sai \\bōn-'sī\\ *n, pl* **bonsai** [Jp] : a potted plant (as a tree) dwarfed by special methods of culture; *also* : the art of growing such a plant

bo·nus \\'bō-nəs\\ *n* : something in addition to what is expected

bon vi·vant \\,bän-vē-'vänt, ,bōn-vē-'väⁿ\\ *n, pl* **bons vivants** \\,bän-vē-'vänts, ,bōn-vē-'väⁿ\\ *or* **bon vivants** *same*\\ [F, lit., good liver] : a person having cultivated, refined, and sociable tastes esp. in food and drink

bon voy·age \\,bōn-,vói-'äzh, ,bän-; ,bōn-,vwä-'yäzh\\ *n* : FAREWELL — often used as an interjection

bony fish *n* : any of a very large group of fishes (as a salmon or marlin) with a bony rather than a cartilaginous skeleton

bonze \\'bänz\\ *n* : a Buddhist monk

boo \\'bü\\ *n, pl* **boos** : a shout of disapproval or contempt — **boo** *vb*

boo·by \\'bü-bē\\ *n, pl* **boobies** : an awkward foolish person : DOPE

booby hatch *n* : an insane asylum

booby prize *n* : an award for the poorest performance in a contest

booby trap *n* : a trap for the unwary; *esp* : a concealed explosive device set to go off when some harmless-looking object is touched — **booby–trap** *vb*

boo·dle \\'büd-ºl\\ *n* 1 : bribe money 2 : a large amount of money

¹**book** \\'bùk\\ *n* 1 : a set of sheets bound into a volume 2 : a long written or printed narrative or record 3 : a major division of a long literary work 4 *cap* : BIBLE

²**book** *vb* 1 : to engage, reserve, or schedule by or as if by writing in a book ⟨~ seats on a plane⟩ 2 : to enter charges against in a police register

book·case \\-,kās\\ *n* : a piece of furniture consisting of shelves to hold books

book·end \\-,end\\ *n* : a support to hold up a row of books

book·ie \\'bù-kē\\ *n* : BOOKMAKER

book·ish \\'bù-kish\\ *adj* 1 : fond of books and reading 2 : inclined to rely unduly on book knowledge

book·keep·er \\'bùk-,kē-pər\\ *n* : one who records the accounts or transactions of a business — **book·keep·ing** *n*

book·let \\'bùk-lət\\ *n* : PAMPHLET

book·mak·er \\'bùk-,mā-kər\\ *n* : one who determines odds and receives and pays off bets — **book·mak·ing** *n*

book·mark \\-,märk\\ *or* **book·mark·er** \\-,mär-kər\\ *n* : a marker for finding a place in a book

book·mo·bile \\'bùk-mō-,bēl\\ *n* : a truck that serves as a traveling library

book·plate \\'bùk-,plāt\\ *n* : a label pasted in a book to show who owns it

book·sell·er \\'bùk-,se-lər\\ *n* : one who sells books; *esp* : the proprietor of a bookstore

book·shelf \\-,shelf\\ *n* : a shelf for books

book·worm \\'bùk-,wərm\\ *n* : a person unusually devoted to reading and study

¹**boom** \\'büm\\ *vb* 1 : to make a deep hollow sound : RE-SOUND 2 : to grow or cause to grow rapidly esp. in value, esteem, or importance

²**boom** *n* 1 : a booming sound or cry 2 : a rapid expansion or increase esp. of economic activity

³**boom** *n* 1 : a long spar used to extend the bottom of a sail 2 : a line of floating timbers used to obstruct passage or catch floating objects 3 : a beam projecting from the upright pole of a derrick to support or guide the object lifted

boom box *n* : a large portable radio and often tape player

boo·mer·ang \\'bü-mə-,raŋ\\ *n* [Dharuk (an Australian aboriginal language *bumarinʸ*] : a bent or angular club that can be so thrown as to return near the starting point

¹**boon** \\'bün\\ *n* [ME, fr. ON *bōn* petition] : BENEFIT, BLESSING **syn** favor, gift, largess, present

²**boon** *adj* [ME *bon*, fr. MF, good] : CONVIVIAL ⟨a ~ companion⟩

boon·docks \\'bün-,däks\\ *n pl* [Tagalog (language of the Philippines) *bundok* mountain] 1 : rough country filled with dense brush 2 : a rural area

boon·dog·gle \\'bün-,dä-gəl, -,dö-\\ *n* : a useless or wasteful project or activity

boor \\'bùr\\ *n* 1 : YOKEL 2 : a rude or insensitive person **syn** churl, lout, clown, clodhopper — **boor·ish** *adj*

boost \\'büst\\ *vb* 1 : to push up from below 2 : IN-CREASE, RAISE ⟨~ prices⟩ 3 : AID, PROMOTE ⟨voted a bonus to ~ morale⟩ — **boost** *n* — **boost·er** *n*

¹**boot** \\'büt\\ *n, chiefly dial* : something to equalize a trade — **to boot** : BESIDES

²**boot** *vb, archaic* : AVAIL, PROFIT

³**boot** *n* 1 : a covering for the foot and leg 2 : a protective sheath (as of a flower) 3 *Brit* : an automobile trunk 4 : KICK; *also* : a discharge from employment 5 : a navy or marine corps trainee

⁴**boot** *vb* 1 : KICK 2 : to eject or discharge summarily

boot·black \\'büt-,blak\\ *n* : a person who shines shoes

boo·tee *or* **boo·tie** \\'bü-tē\\ *n* : an infant's knitted or crocheted sock

booth \\'büth\\ *n, pl* **booths** \\'büthz, 'büths\\ 1 : a small enclosed stall (as at a fair) 2 : a small enclosure giving privacy for a person ⟨voting ~⟩ ⟨telephone ~⟩ 3 : a restaurant accommodation having a table between backed benches

boot·leg \\'büt-,leg\\ *vb* : to make, transport, or sell (as liquor) illegally — **boot·leg** *adj or n* — **boot·leg·ger** *n*

boot·less \\'büt-ləs\\ *adj* : USELESS **syn** futile, vain, abortive, fruitless — **boot·less·ly** *adv* — **boot·less·ness** *n*

boo·ty \\'bü-tē\\ *n, pl* **booties** : PLUNDER, SPOIL

¹**booze** \\'büz\\ *vb* **boozed; booz·ing** : to drink liquor to excess — **booz·er** *n*

²**booze** *n* : intoxicating liquor — **boozy** *adj*

bop \\'bäp\\ *vb* **bopped; bop·ping** : HIT, SOCK — **bop** *n*

BOQ *abbr* bachelor officers' quarters

bor *abbr* borough

bo·rate \\'bōr-,āt\\ *n* : a salt or ester of boric acid

bo·rax \\'bōr-,aks\\ *n* : a crystalline borate of sodium that occurs as a mineral and is used as a flux and cleanser

bor·del·lo \\bór-'de-lō\\ *n, pl* **-los** [It] : BROTHEL

¹**bor·der** \\'bór-dər\\ *n* 1 : EDGE, MARGIN 2 : BOUNDARY, FRONTIER **syn** rim, brim, brink, fringe, perimeter

²**border** *vb* **bor·dered; bor·der·ing** 1 : to put a border on 2 : ADJOIN 3 : VERGE

bor·der·land \\'bór-dər-,land\\ *n* 1 : territory at or near a border 2 : an outlying or intermediate region often not clearly defined

bor·der·line \\-,līn\\ *adj* : being in an intermediate position or state; *esp* : not quite up to what is standard or expected ⟨~ intelligence⟩

¹**bore** \\'bōr\\ *vb* **bored; bor·ing** 1 : to make a hole in with or as if with a drill 2 : to make (as a well) by boring or digging away material **syn** perforate, drill, prick, puncture — **bor·er** *n*

²**bore** *n* 1 : a hole made by or as if by boring 2 : a cylindrical cavity 3 : the diameter of a hole or tube; *esp* : the interior diameter of a gun barrel or engine cylinder

³**bore** *past of* BEAR

⁴**bore** *n* : a tidal flood with a high abrupt front

⁵**bore** *n* : one that causes boredom

⁶**bore** *vb* **bored; bor·ing** : to weary with tedious dullness

bo·re·al \\'bōr-ē-əl\\ *adj* : of, relating to, or located in northern regions

bore·dom \\'bōr-dəm\\ *n* : the condition of being bored

bo·ric acid \\'bōr-ik-\\ *n* : a white crystalline weak acid that contains boron and is used esp. as an antiseptic

born \\'bórn\\ *adj* 1 : brought into life by birth 2 : NA-

TIVE ⟨American-*born*⟩ **3** : having special natural abilities or character from birth ⟨a ～ leader⟩

born–again *adj* : having experienced a revival of a personal faith or conviction ⟨～ believer⟩ ⟨～ liberal⟩

borne *past part of* BEAR

bo·ron \ˈbȯr-ˌän\ *n* : a chemical element that occurs in nature only in combination (as in borax) — see ELEMENT table

bor·ough \ˈbər-ō\ *n* **1** : a British town that sends one or more members to Parliament; *also* : an incorporated British urban area **2** : an incorporated town or village in some U.S. states; *also* : any of the five political divisions of New York City **3** : a civil division of the state of Alaska corresponding to a county in most other states

bor·row \ˈbär-ō\ *vb* **1** : to take or receive (something) temporarily and with intent to return **2** : to take into possession or use from another source : DERIVE, APPROPRIATE ⟨～ a metaphor⟩

borscht \ˈbȯrsht\ *or* **borsch** \ˈbȯrsh\ *n* [Yiddish *borsht* & Ukrainian & Russ *borshch*] : a soup made mainly from beets

bosh \ˈbäsh\ *n* [Turk *boş* empty] : foolish talk or action : NONSENSE

bosky \ˈbäs-kē\ *adj* : covered with trees or shrubs

¹bos·om \ˈbu̇-zəm, ˈbü-\ *n* **1** : the front of the human chest; *esp* : the female breasts **2** : the seat of secret thoughts and feelings **3** : the part of a garment covering the breast — **bos·omed** \-zəmd\ *adj*

²bosom *adj* : CLOSE, INTIMATE

¹boss \ˈbäs, ˈbȯs\ *n* : a knoblike ornament : STUD

²boss *vb* : to ornament with bosses

³boss \ˈbȯs\ *n* **1** : one (as a foreman or manager) exercising control or supervision **2** : a politician who controls votes or dictates policies — **bossy** *adj*

⁴boss \ˈbȯs\ *vb* : to act as a boss : SUPERVISE

bo·sun \ˈbōs-ᵊn\ *var of* BOATSWAIN

bot *abbr* botanical; botanist; botany

bot·a·ny \ˈbät-ᵊn-ē, ˈbät-nē\ *n, pl* **-nies 1** : a branch of biology dealing with plants and plant life **2** : plant life (as of a given region); *also* : the biology of a plant or plant group — **bo·tan·i·cal** \bə-ˈta-ni-kəl\ *adj* — **bot·a·nist** \ˈbät-ᵊn-ist, ˈbät-nist\ *n* — **bot·a·nize** \-ᵊn-ˌīz\ *vb*

botch \ˈbäch\ *vb* : to foul up hopelessly : BUNGLE — **botch** *n*

¹both \ˈbōth\ *pron* : both ones : the one as well as the other

²both *conj* — used as a function word to indicate and stress the inclusion of each of two or more things specified by coordinated words, phrases, or clauses ⟨～ New York and London⟩

³both *adj* : being the two : affecting the one and the other

both·er \ˈbä-thər\ *vb* : WORRY, PESTER, TROUBLE **syn** vex, annoy, irk, provoke — **bother** *n* — **both·er·some** \-səm\ *adj*

¹bot·tle \ˈbät-ᵊl\ *n* **1** : a container (as of glass) with a narrow neck and usu. no handles **2** : the quantity held by a bottle **3** : intoxicating liquor

²bottle *vb* **bot·tled; bot·tling 1** : to confine as if in a bottle : RESTRAIN **2** : to put into a bottle

bot·tle·neck \ˈbät-ᵊl-ˌnek\ *n* **1** : a narrow passage or point of congestion **2** : something that obstructs or impedes

¹bot·tom \ˈbä-təm\ *n* **1** : an under or supporting surface; *also* : BUTTOCKS **2** : the surface on which a body of water lies **3** : the lowest part or place; *also* : an inferior position ⟨start at the ～⟩ **4** : BOTTOMLAND — **bottom** *adj* — **bot·tom·less** *adj*

²bottom *vb* **1** : to furnish with a bottom **2** : to reach the bottom **3** : to reach a low point before rebounding — usu. used with *out*

bot·tom·land \ˈbä-təm-ˌland\ *n* : low land along a river

bottom line *n* **1** : the essential point : CRUX **2** : the final result : OUTCOME

bot·u·lism \ˈbä-chə-ˌli-zəm\ *n* : an acute paralytic disease caused by a bacterial toxin esp. in food

bou·doir \ˈbü-ˌdwär, ˈbü-, ˌbü-ˈ, ˌbü-ˈ\ *n* [F, fr. *bouder* to pout] : a woman's dressing room or bedroom

bouf·fant \bü-ˈfänt, ˈbü-ˌfänt\ *adj* [F] : puffed out ⟨～ hairdos⟩

bough \ˈbau̇\ *n* : a usu. large or main branch of a tree

bought *past and past part of* BUY

bouil·la·baisse \ˌbü-yə-ˈbās\ *n* : a highly seasoned fish stew made with at least two kinds of fish

bouil·lon \ˈbü-ˌyän; ˈbu̇l-ˌyän, -yən\ *n* : a clear soup made usu. from beef

boul·der \ˈbōl-dər\ *n* : a large detached rounded or worn mass of rock — **boul·dered** \-dərd\ *adj*

bou·le·vard \ˈbu̇-lə-ˌvärd, ˈbü-\ *n* [F, modif. of MD *bolwerc* bulwark] : a broad often landscaped thoroughfare

bounce \ˈbau̇ns\ *vb* **bounced; bounc·ing 1** : to cause to rebound ⟨～ a ball⟩ **2** : to rebound after striking — **bounce** *n* — **bouncy** \ˈbau̇n-sē\ *adj*

bounc·er \ˈbau̇n-sər\ *n* : a person employed in a public place to remove disorderly persons

¹bound \ˈbau̇nd\ *adj* : intending to go

²bound *n* : LIMIT, BOUNDARY — **bound·less** *adj* — **bound·less·ness** *n*

³bound *vb* **1** : to set limits to **2** : to form the boundary of **3** : to name the boundaries of

⁴bound *past and past part of* BIND

⁵bound *adj* **1** : constrained by or as if by bonds : CONFINED, OBLIGED **2** : enclosed in a binding or cover **3** : RESOLVED, DETERMINED; *also* : SURE

⁶bound *n* **1** : LEAP, JUMP **2** : REBOUND, BOUNCE

⁷bound *vb* : SPRING, BOUNCE

bound·ary \ˈbau̇n-drē\ *n, pl* **-aries** : something that marks or fixes a limit (as of territory) **syn** border, frontier, march

bound·en \ˈbau̇n-dən\ *adj* : BINDING

boun·te·ous \ˈbau̇n-tē-əs\ *adj* **1** : GENEROUS **2** : ABUNDANT — **boun·te·ous·ly** *adv* — **boun·te·ous·ness** *n*

boun·ti·ful \ˈbau̇n-ti-fəl\ *adj* **1** : giving freely **2** : PLENTIFUL — **boun·ti·ful·ly** *adv* — **boun·ti·ful·ness** *n*

boun·ty \ˈbau̇n-tē\ *n, pl* **bounties** [ME *bounte* goodness, fr. OF *bonté*, fr. L *bonitas*, fr. *bonus* good] **1** : GENEROSITY **2** : something given liberally **3** : a reward, premium, or subsidy given usu. for doing something

bou·quet \bō-ˈkā, bü-\ *n* [F, fr. MF, thicket, fr. OF *bosc* forest] **1** : flowers picked and fastened together in a bunch **2** : a distinctive aroma (as of wine) **syn** scent, fragrance, perfume, redolence

bour·bon \ˈbər-bən\ *n* : a whiskey distilled from a corn mash

bour·geois \ˈbu̇rzh-ˌwä, bu̇rzh-ˈwä\ *n, pl* **bourgeois** *same or* -ˌwäz, -ˈwäz\ [MF, lit., citizen of a town, fr. *borc* town, borough, fr. L *burgus* fortified place, of Gmc origin] : a middle-class person — **bourgeois** *adj*

bour·geoi·sie \ˌbu̇rzh-ˌwä-ˈzē\ *n* : a social order dominated by bourgeois

bourne *also* **bourn** \ˈbōrn, ˈbu̇rn\ *n* : BOUNDARY; *also* : DESTINATION

bourse \ˈbu̇rs\ *n* : a European stock exchange

bout \ˈbau̇t\ *n* **1** : CONTEST, MATCH **2** : OUTBREAK, ATTACK ⟨a ～ of measles⟩ **3** : SESSION

bou·tique \bü-ˈtēk\ *n* : a small fashionable specialty shop

bou·ton·niere \ˌbüt-ᵊn-ˈir\ *n* : a flower or bouquet worn in a buttonhole

bo·vine \ˈbō-ˌvīn, -ˌvēn\ *adj* **1** : of or relating to oxen or cows **2** : having qualities (as placidity or dullness) characteristic of oxen or cows — **bovine** *n*

¹bow \ˈbau̇\ *vb* **1** : SUBMIT, YIELD **2** : to bend the head or body (as in submission, courtesy, or assent)

²bow *n* : an act or posture of bowing

³bow \ˈbō\ *n* **1** : BEND, ARCH; *esp* : RAINBOW **2** : a weapon for shooting arrows; *also* : ARCHER **3** : a knot formed by doubling a line into two or more loops **4** : a wooden rod strung with horsehairs for playing an instrument of the violin family

⁴**bow** \'bō\ *vb* **1** : BEND, CURVE **2** : to play (an instrument) with a bow

⁵**bow** \'baù\ *n* : the forward part of a ship — **bow** *adj*

bowd·ler·ize \'bōd-lə-₁rīz, 'baùd-\ *vb* **-ized; -iz·ing** : to expurgate by omitting parts considered vulgar

bow·el \'baù(-ə)l\ *n* **1** : INTESTINE; *also* : one of the divisions of the intestine — usu. used in pl. **2** *pl* : the inmost parts ⟨the ~s of the earth⟩

bow·er \'baù(-ə)r\ *n* : a shelter of boughs or vines : ARBOR

¹**bowl** \'bōl\ *n* **1** : a concave vessel used to hold liquids **2** : a drinking vessel **3** : a bowl-shaped part or structure — **bowl·ful** \-₁fùl\ *n*

²**bowl** *n* **1** : a ball for rolling on a level surface in bowling **2** : a cast of the ball in bowling

³**bowl** *vb* **1** : to play a game of bowling; *also* : to roll a ball in bowling **2** : to travel (as in a vehicle) rapidly and smoothly **3** : to strike or knock down with a moving object; *also* : to overwhelm with surprise

bowlder *var of* BOULDER

bow·legged \'bō-₁le-gəd\ *adj* : having legs that bow outward at or below the knee — **bow·leg** \'bō-₁leg\ *n*

¹**bowl·er** \'bō-lər\ *n* : a person who bowls

²**bowl·er** \'bō-lər\ *n* : DERBY 3

bow·line \'bō-lən, -₁līn\ *n* : a knot used to form a loop that neither slips nor jams

bowl·ing \'bō-liŋ\ *n* : any of various games in which balls are rolled on a green or alley at an object or a group of objects; *esp* : TENPINS

bow·man \'bō-mən\ *n* : ARCHER

bow·sprit \'baù-₁sprit\ *n* : a spar projecting forward from the prow of a ship

bow·string \'bō-₁striŋ\ *n* : the cord connecting the two ends of a shooting bow

¹**box** \'bäks\ *n, pl* **box** *or* **box·es** : an evergreen shrub or small tree used esp. for hedges

²**box** *n* **1** : a rigid typically rectangular receptacle often with a cover; *also* : the quantity held by a box **2** : a small compartment (as for a group of theater patrons); *also* : a boxlike receptacle or division **3** : any of six spaces on a baseball diamond where the batter, pitcher, coaches, and catcher stand **4** : PREDICAMENT

³**box** *vb* : to enclose in or as if in a box

⁴**box** *n* : a punch or slap esp. on the ear

⁵**box** *vb* **1** : to strike with the hand **2** : to engage in boxing with

box·car \'bäks-₁kär\ *n* : a roofed freight car usu. with sliding doors in the sides

¹**box·er** \'bäk-sər\ *n* : a person who engages in boxing

²**boxer** *n* : a compact short-haired usu. fawn or brindled dog of a breed of German origin

box·ing \'bäk-siŋ\ *n* : the sport of fighting with the fists

box office *n* : an office (as in a theater) where admission tickets are sold

box·wood \'bäks-₁wùd\ *n* : the tough hard wood of the box; *also* : a box tree or shrub

boy \'bòi\ *n* **1** : a male child : YOUTH **2** : SON — **boy·hood** \-₁hùd\ *n* — **boy·ish** *adj* — **boy·ish·ly** *adv* — **boy·ish·ness** *n*

boy·cott \'bòi-₁kät\ *vb* [Charles C. *Boycott* †1897 Eng. land agent in Ireland who was ostracized for refusing to reduce rents] : to refrain from having any dealings with — **boycott** *n*

boy·friend \'bòi-₁frend\ *n* **1** : a male friend **2** : a frequent or regular male companion of a girl or woman

Boy Scout *n* : a member of any of various national scouting programs (as the Boy Scouts of America)

boy·sen·ber·ry \'bòiz-ₐn-₁ber-ē, 'bòis-\ *n* : a large bramble fruit with a raspberry flavor; *also* : the hybrid plant bearing it developed by crossing blackberries and raspberries

bo·zo \'bō-₁zō\ *n, pl* **bozos** : a foolish or incompetent person

bp *abbr* **1** bishop **2** birthplace

BP *abbr* **1** batting practice **2** blood pressure **3** boiling point

bpl *abbr* birthplace

BPOE *abbr* Benevolent and Protective Order of Elks

br *abbr* **1** branch **2** brass **3** brown

¹**Br** *abbr* Britain; British

²**Br** *symbol* bromine

BR *abbr* bedroom

bra \'brä\ *n* : BRASSIERE

¹**brace** \'brās\ *vb* **braced; brac·ing** **1** *archaic* : to make fast : BIND **2** : to tighten preparatory to use; *also* : to get ready for : prepare oneself **3** : INVIGORATE **4** : to furnish or support with a brace; *also* : STRENGTHEN **5** : to set firmly **6** : to gain courage or confidence

²**brace** *n, pl* **brac·es** **1** *or pl* **brace** : two of a kind ⟨a ~ of dogs⟩ **2** : a crank-shaped device for turning a bit **3** : something (as a tie, prop, or clamp) that distributes, directs, or resists pressure or weight **4** *pl* : SUSPENDERS **5** : an appliance for supporting a body part (as the shoulders) **6** *pl* : dental appliances used to exert pressure to straighten misaligned teeth **7** : one of two marks { } used to connect words or items to be considered together

brace·let \'brā-slət\ *n* [ME, fr. MF, dim. of *bras* arm, fr. L *bracchium*, fr. Gk *brachiōn*] : an ornamental band or chain worn around the wrist

bra·ce·ro \brä-'ser-ō\ *n, pl* **-ros** : a Mexican laborer admitted to the U.S. esp. for seasonal farm work

brack·en \'bra-kən\ *n* : a large coarse fern; *also* : a growth of such ferns

¹**brack·et** \'bra-kət\ *n* **1** : a projecting framework or arm designed to support weight; *also* : a shelf on such framework **2** : one of a pair of punctuation marks [ ] used esp. to enclose interpolated matter **3** : a continuous section of a series; *esp* : one of a graded series of income groups

²**bracket** *vb* **1** : to furnish or fasten with brackets **2** : to place within brackets; *also* : to separate or group with or as if with brackets

brack·ish \'bra-kish\ *adj* : somewhat salty — **brack·ish·ness** *n*

bract \'brakt\ *n* : an often modified leaf on or at the base of a flower stalk

brad \'brad\ *n* : a slender nail with a small head

brae \'brā\ *n, chiefly Scot* : a hillside esp. along a river

brag \'brag\ *vb* **bragged; brag·ging** : to talk or assert boastfully — **brag** *n* — **brag·ger** *n*

brag·ga·do·cio \₁bra-gə-'dō-shē-₁ō, -sē-, -chē-\ *n, pl* **-cios** **1** : BRAGGART, BOASTER **2** : empty boasting **3** : arrogant pretension : COCKINESS

brag·gart \'bra-gərt\ *n* : one who brags

Brah·man *or* **Brah·min** \'brä-mən *for 1;* 'brä-, 'brä-, 'bra- *for 2*\ *n* **1** : a Hindu of the highest caste traditionally assigned to the priesthood **2** : any of a breed of large vigorous humped cattle developed in the southern U.S. from Indian stock **3** *usu* Brahmin : a person of high social standing and cultivated intellect and taste

Brah·man·ism \'brä-mə-₁ni-zəm\ *n* : orthodox Hinduism

¹**braid** \'brād\ *vb* **1** : to form (strands) into a braid : PLAIT; *also* : to make from braids **2** : to ornament with braid

²**braid** *n* **1** : a length of braided hair **2** : a cord or ribbon of three or more interwoven strands

braille \'brāl\ *n, often cap* : a system of writing for the blind that uses characters made up of raised dots ☞ For table, see next page.

¹**brain** \'brān\ *n* **1** : the part of the vertebrate nervous system that is the organ of thought and nervous coordination, is made up of nerve cells and their fibers, and is enclosed in the skull; *also* : a centralized mass of nerve tissue in an invertebrate **2** : INTELLECT, INTELLIGENCE — often used in pl. — **brained** \'brānd\ *adj* — **brain·less** *adj* — **brainy** *adj*

braille alphabet

a	b	c	d	e	f	g	h	i	j
1	2	3	4	5	6	7	8	9	0

k	l	m	n	o	p	q	r	s	t

| u | v | w | x | y | z | Capital Sign | Numeral Sign |

²brain vb **1** : to kill by smashing the skull **2** : to hit on the head

brain·child \\'brān-ˌchīld\ n : a product of one's creative imagination

brain death n : final cessation of activity in the central nervous system esp. as indicated by a flat electroencephalogram — **brain–dead** \-ˌded\ adj

brain drain n : the departure of educated or professional people from one country, sector, or field to another usu. for better pay or living conditions

brain·storm \-ˌstȯrm\ n : a sudden inspiration or idea — **brainstorm** vb

brain·teas·er \-ˌtē-zər\ n : a challenging puzzle

brain·wash·ing \\'brān-ˌwȯ-shing, -ˌwä-\ n **1** : a forcible indoctrination to induce someone to give up basic political, social, or religious beliefs and attitudes and to accept contrasting regimented ideas **2** : persuasion by propaganda or salesmanship — **brain·wash** vb

brain wave n **1** : BRAINSTORM **2** : rhythmic fluctuations of voltage between parts of the brain; also : a current produced by brain waves

braise \\'brāz\ vb **braised; brais·ing** : to cook (meat) slowly in fat and little moisture in a closed pot

¹brake \\'brāk\ n : a common bracken fern

²brake n : rough or wet land heavily overgrown (as with thickets or reeds)

³brake n : a device for slowing or stopping motion esp. by friction — **brake·less** adj

⁴brake vb **braked; brak·ing 1** : to slow or stop by or as if by a brake **2** : to apply a brake

brake·man \\'brāk-mən\ n : a train crew member who inspects the train and assists the conductor

bram·ble \\'bram-bəl\ n : any of a large genus of prickly shrubs (as a blackberry) related to the roses; also : any rough prickly shrub or vine — **bram·bly** \-b(ə-)lē\ adj

bran \\'bran\ n : the edible broken husks of cereal grain sifted from flour or meal

¹branch \\'branch\ n [ME, fr. OF branche, fr. LL branca paw] **1** : a natural subdivision (as a bough or twig) of a plant stem **2** : a division (as of an antler or a river) related to a whole like a plant branch to its stem **3** : a discrete element of a complex system ⟨the executive ∼⟩; esp : a division of a family descended from one ancestor — **branched** \\'brancht\ adj

²branch vb **1** : to develop branches **2** : DIVERGE **3** : to extend activities ⟨the business is ∼ing out⟩

¹brand \\'brand\ n **1** : a piece of charred or burning wood **2** : a mark made (as by burning) usu. to identify; also : a mark of disgrace : STIGMA **3** : a class of goods identified as the product of a particular firm or producer **4** : a distinctive kind ⟨my own ∼ of humor⟩

²brand vb **1** : to mark with a brand **2** : STIGMATIZE

bran·dish \\'bran-dish\ vb : to shake or wave menacingly syn flourish, flash, flaunt

brand–new \\'bran-'nü, -'nyü\ adj : conspicuously new and unused

bran·dy \\'bran-dē\ n, pl **brandies** [short for brandywine, fr. D brandewijn, fr. MD brantwijn, fr. brant distilled + wijn wine] : a liquor distilled from wine or fermented fruit juice — **brandy** vb

brash \\'brash\ adj **1** : IMPETUOUS, AUDACIOUS **2** : aggressively self-assertive

brass \\'bras\ n **1** : an alloy of copper and zinc; also : an object of brass **2** : brazen self-assurance **3** : persons of high rank (as in the military) — **brassy** adj

bras·siere \brə-'zir\ n : a woman's close-fitting undergarment designed to support the breasts

brat \\'brat\ n : an ill-behaved child — **brat·ti·ness** n — **brat·ty** adj

bra·va·do \brə-'vä-dō\ n, pl **-does** or **-dos 1** : blustering swaggering conduct **2** : a show of bravery

¹brave \\'brāv\ adj **brav·er; brav·est** [MF, fr. It & Sp bravo courageous, wild, prob. fr. L barbarus barbarous] **1** : showing courage **2** : EXCELLENT, SPLENDID syn bold, intrepid, courageous, valiant — **brave·ly** adv

²brave vb **braved; brav·ing** : to face or endure bravely

³brave n : an American Indian warrior

brav·ery \\'brā-və-rē\ n, pl **-er·ies** : COURAGE

bra·vo \\'brä-vō\ n, pl **bravos** : a shout of approval — often used as an interjection in applauding

bra·vu·ra \brə-'vyur-ə, -'vur-\ n **1** : a florid brilliant musical style **2** : self-assured brilliant performance — **bravura** adj

brawl \\'brȯl\ n : a noisy quarrel syn fracas, row, rumpus, scrap, fray, melee — **brawl** vb — **brawl·er** n

brawn \\'brȯn\ n : strong muscles; also : muscular strength — **brawn·i·ness** n — **brawny** adj

bray \\'brā\ n : the characteristic harsh cry of a donkey — **bray** vb

braze \\'brāz\ vb **brazed; braz·ing** : to solder with an alloy (as brass) that melts at a lower temperature than the metals being joined — **braz·er** n

¹bra·zen \\'brāz-ᵊn\ adj **1** : made of brass **2** : sounding harsh and loud **3** : of the color of brass **4** : marked by contemptuous boldness — **bra·zen·ly** adv — **bra·zen·ness** n

²brazen vb : to face boldly or defiantly

¹bra·zier \\'brā-zhər\ n : a worker in brass

²brazier n **1** : a vessel holding burning coals (as for heating) **2** : a device on which food is grilled

Bra·zil·ian \brə-'zil-yən\ n : a native or inhabitant of Brazil — **Brazilian** adj

Bra·zil nut \brə-'zil-\ n : a triangular oily edible nut borne in large capsules by a tall So. American tree; also : the tree

¹breach \\'brēch\ n **1** : a breaking of a law, obligation, tie (as of friendship), or standard (as of conduct) **2** : an interruption or opening made by or as if by breaking through syn violation, transgression, infringement, trespass

²breach vb **1** : to make a breach in **2** : to leap out of water ⟨whales ∼ing⟩

¹bread \\'bred\ n **1** : baked food made basically of flour or meal **2** : FOOD

²bread vb : to cover with bread crumbs before cooking

bread·bas·ket \\'bred-ˌbas-kət\ n : a major cereal‑producing region

bread·fruit \-ˌfrüt\ n : a round usu. seedless fruit resembling bread in color and texture when baked; also : a tall tropical tree related to the mulberry and bearing breadfruit

bread·stuff \-ˌstəf\ n : GRAIN, FLOUR

breadth \\'bredth, 'bretth\ n **1** : WIDTH **2** : comprehensive quality : SCOPE ⟨∼ of knowledge⟩

bread·win·ner \\'bred-ˌwi-nər\ n : a member of a family whose wages supply its livelihood

¹break \\'brāk\ vb **broke** \\'brōk\; **bro·ken** \\'brō-kən\; **break·ing 1** : to separate into parts usu. suddenly or violently : come or force apart **2** : TRANSGRESS ⟨∼ a law⟩ **3** : to force a way into, out of, or through **4** : to disrupt the order or unity of ⟨∼ ranks⟩ ⟨∼ up a gang⟩; also : to bring to submission or helplessness **5** : EXCEED, SURPASS ⟨∼ a record⟩ **6** : RUIN **7** : to make known **8** : HALT, INTERRUPT; also : to act or change abruptly (as a course or activity) **9** : to come esp. suddenly into being or notice ⟨as day ∼s⟩ **10** : to fail under stress 11 : HAPPEN, DEVELOP — **break·able** adj or n

²break n 1 : an act of breaking 2 : a result of breaking; esp : an interruption of continuity ⟨coffee ∼⟩ ⟨a ∼ for the commercial⟩ 3 : a stroke of good luck

break·age \'brā-kij\ n 1 : the action of breaking 2 : articles or amount broken 3 : loss due to things broken

break·down \'brāk-₁daủn\ n 1 : functional failure; esp : a physical, mental, or nervous collapse 2 : DISINTE-GRATION 3 : DECOMPOSITION 4 : ANALYSIS, CLASSIFI-CATION — **break down** vb

break·er \'brā-kər\ n 1 : one that breaks 2 : a wave that breaks into foam (as against the shore)

break·fast \'brek-fəst\ n : the first meal of the day — **breakfast** vb

break in vb 1 : to enter a building by force 2 : INTER-RUPT; also : INTRUDE 3 : TRAIN — **break–in** \'brāk-₁in\ n

break·neck \'brāk-'nek\ adj : very fast or dangerous ⟨∼ speed⟩

break out vb 1 : to develop or erupt suddenly or with force 2 : to develop a skin rash

break·through \'brāk-₁thrü\ n 1 : an act or instance of breaking through an obstruction or defensive line 2 : a sudden advance in knowledge or technique

break·up \-₁əp\ n 1 : DISSOLUTION 2 : a division into smaller units — **break up** vb

break·wa·ter \'brāk-₁wỏ-tər, -₁wä-\ n : a structure protecting a harbor or beach from the force of waves

bream \'brim, 'brēm\ n, pl **bream** or **breams** : any of various small freshwater sunfishes

breast \'brest\ n 1 : either of the pair of mammary glands extending from the front of the chest esp. in pubescent and adult human females 2 : the front part of the body between the neck and the abdomen 3 : the seat of emotion and thought

breast·bone \'brest-₁bōn\ n : STERNUM

breast–feed \-₁fēd\ vb : to feed (a baby) from a mother's breast rather than from a bottle

breast·plate \-₁plāt\ n : a metal plate of armor for the breast

breast·stroke \-₁strōk\ n : a swimming stroke executed by extending both arms forward and then sweeping them back with palms out while kicking backward and outward with both legs

breast·work \-₁wərk\ n : a temporary fortification

breath \'breth\ n 1 : the act or power of breathing 2 : a slight breeze 3 : air inhaled or exhaled in breathing 4 : spoken sound 5 : SPIRIT — **breath·less** adj — **breath·less·ly** adv — **breath·less·ness** n — **breathy** \'bre-thē\ adj

breathe \'brēth\ vb **breathed; breath·ing** 1 : to inhale and exhale 2 : LIVE 3 : to halt for rest 4 : to utter softly or secretly — **breath·able** adj

breath·er \'brē-thər\ n 1 : one that breathes 2 : a short rest

breath·tak·ing \'breth-₁tā-kiŋ\ adj 1 : making one out of breath 2 : EXCITING, THRILLING ⟨∼ beauty⟩ — **breath·tak·ing·ly** adv

brec·cia \'bre-chē-ə, -chə\ n : a rock consisting of sharp fragments held in fine-grained material

breech \'brēch\ n 1 pl \ usu \'bri-chəz\: trousers ending near the knee; also : PANTS 2 : BUTTOCKS, RUMP 3 : the part of a firearm at the rear of the barrel

¹breed \'brēd\ vb **bred** \'bred\; **breed·ing** 1 : BEGET; also : ORIGINATE 2 : to propagate sexually; also : MATE 3 : BRING UP, NURTURE 4 : to produce (fissionable material) from material that is not fissionable syn generate, reproduce, procreate, propagate — **breed·er** n

²breed n 1 : a strain of similar and presumably related plants or animals usu. developed in domestication 2 : KIND, SORT, CLASS

breed·ing n 1 : ANCESTRY 2 : training in polite social interaction 3 : sexual propagation of plants or animals

¹breeze \'brēz\ n 1 : a light wind 2 : CINCH, SNAP — **breeze·less** adj

²breeze vb **breezed; breez·ing** : to progress quickly and easily

breeze·way \'brēz-₁wā\ n : a roofed open passage connecting two buildings (as a house and garage)

breezy \'brē-zē\ adj 1 : swept by breezes 2 : briskly informal — **breez·i·ly** \'brē-zə-lē\ adv — **breez·i·ness** \-zē-nəs\ n

breth·ren \'breth-rən, 'bre-thə-; 'bre-thərn\ pl of BROTHER — used esp. in formal or solemn address

Brethren n pl : members of one of several Protestant denominations originating chiefly in a German religious movement and stressing personal religious experience

bre·via·ry \'brē-vyə-rē, -vē-₁er-ē\ n, pl **-ries** often cap : a book of prayers, hymns, psalms, and readings used by Roman Catholic priests

brev·i·ty \'bre-və-tē\ n, pl **-ties** 1 : shortness or conciseness of expression 2 : shortness of duration

brew \'brü\ vb 1 : to prepare (as beer) by steeping, boiling, and fermenting 2 : to prepare (as tea) by steeping in hot water — **brew** n — **brew·er** n — **brew·ery** \'brü-ə-rē, 'brủ(-ə)r-ē\ n

¹bri·ar \'brī-ər\ var of BRIER

²briar n : a tobacco pipe made from the root or stem of a brier

¹bribe \'brīb\ n [ME, something stolen, fr. MF, bread given to a beggar] : something (as money or a favor) given or promised to a person to influence conduct

²bribe vb **bribed; brib·ing** : to influence by offering a bribe — **brib·able** adj — **brib·er** n — **brib·ery** \'brī-bə-rē\ n

bric–a–brac \'bri-kə-₁brak\ n pl [F] : small ornamental articles

¹brick \'brik\ n : a block molded from moist clay and hardened by heat used esp. for building

²brick vb : to close, cover, or pave with bricks

brick·bat \'brik-₁bat\ n 1 : a piece of a hard material (as a brick) esp. when thrown as a missile 2 : an uncomplimentary remark

brick·lay·er \'brik-₁lā-ər\ n : a person who builds or paves with bricks — **brick·lay·ing** n

brid·al \'brīd-ᵊl\ n [ME bridale, fr. OE brȳdealu, fr. brȳd bride + ealu ale] : MARRIAGE, WEDDING

²bridal adj : of or relating to a bride or a wedding

bride \'brīd\ n : a woman just married or about to be married

bride·groom \'brīd-₁grüm, -₁grủm\ n : a man just married or about to be married

brides·maid \'brīdz-₁mād\ n : a woman who attends a bride at her wedding

¹bridge \'brij\ n 1 : a structure built over a depression or obstacle for use as a passageway 2 : something (as the upper part of the nose) resembling a bridge in form or function 3 : a curved piece raising the strings of a musical instrument 4 : the forward part of a ship's superstructure from which it is navigated 5 : an artificial replacement for missing teeth

²bridge vb **bridged; bridg·ing** : to build a bridge over — **bridge·able** adj

³bridge n : a card game for four players developed from whist

bridge·head \-₁hed\ n : an advanced position seized in enemy territory

bridge·work \-₁wərk\ n : dental bridges

¹bri·dle \'brīd-ᵊl\ n 1 : headgear with which a horse is controlled 2 : CURB, RESTRAINT

²bridle vb **bri·dled; bri·dling** 1 : to put a bridle on; also : to restrain with or as if with a bridle 2 : to show hostility or scorn usu. by tossing the head

Brie \'brē\ n : a soft cheese with a whitish rind and a pale yellow interior

¹brief \'brēf\ adj 1 : short in duration or extent 2 : CON-CISE; also : CURT — **brief·ly** adv — **brief·ness** n

²brief n 1 : a concise statement or document; esp : one

summarizing a law client's case or a legal argument **2** *pl* : short snug underpants

³brief *vb* : to give final instructions or essential information to

brief·case \'brēf-ˌkās\ *n* : a flat flexible case for carrying papers

¹bri·er \'brī-(ə)r\ *n* : a plant (as a bramble or rose) with a thorny or prickly woody stem; *also* : a mass or twig of these — **bri·ery** \'brī-(ə)r-ē\ *adj*

²brier *or* **briar** *n* : a heath of southern Europe whose roots and knotted stems are used for making tobacco pipes

¹brig \'brig\ *n* : a 2-masted square-rigged sailing ship

²brig *n* : the place of confinement for offenders on a naval ship

³brig *abbr* brigade

bri·gade \bri-'gād\ *n* **1** : a military unit composed of a headquarters, one or more units of infantry or armored forces, and supporting units **2** : a group organized for a particular purpose (as fire fighting)

brig·a·dier general \ˌbri-gə-ˌdir-\ *n* : a commissioned officer (as in the army) ranking next below a major general

brig·and \'bri-gənd\ *n* : BANDIT — **brig·and·age** \-gən-dij\ *n*

brig·an·tine \'bri-gən-ˌtēn\ *n* : a 2-masted square-rigged ship with a fore-and-aft mainsail

Brig Gen *abbr* brigadier general

bright \'brīt\ *adj* **1** : SHINING, RADIANT **2** : ILLUSTRIOUS, GLORIOUS **3** : INTELLIGENT, CLEVER; *also* : LIVELY, CHEERFUL **syn** brilliant, lustrous, beaming — **bright** *adv* — **bright·ly** *adv* — **bright·ness** *n*

bright·en \'brīt-ᵊn\ *vb* : to make or become bright or brighter — **bright·en·er** *n*

¹bril·liant \'bril-yənt\ *adj* [F *brillant,* prp. of *briller* to shine, fr. It *brillare*] **1** : very bright **2** : STRIKING, DISTINCTIVE **3** : very intelligent **syn** radiant, lustrous, beaming, lucid, bright, lambent — **bril·liance** \-yəns\ *n* — **bril·lian·cy** \-yən-sē\ *n* — **bril·liant·ly** *adv*

²brilliant *n* : a gem cut in a particular form with many facets

¹brim \'brim\ *n* : EDGE, RIM **syn** brink, border, verge, fringe — **brim·less** *adj*

²brim *vb* **brimmed; brim·ming** : to be or become full often to overflowing

brim·ful \-ˈfúl\ *adj* : full to the brim

brim·stone \'brim-ˌstōn\ *n* : SULFUR

brin·dled \'brin-dᵊld\ *adj* : having dark streaks or flecks on a gray or tawny ground (a ~ Great Dane)

brine \'brīn\ *n* **1** : water saturated with salt **2** : OCEAN — **brin·i·ness** *n* — **briny** \'brī-nē\ *adj*

bring \'brin\ *vb* **brought** \'brót\; **bring·ing** \'brin-in\ **1** : to cause to come with one **2** : INDUCE, PERSUADE, LEAD **3** : PRODUCE, EFFECT **4** : to sell for (~ a good price) — **bring·er** *n*

bring about *vb* : to cause to take place

bring up *vb* **1** : to give a parent's fostering care to **2** : to come or bring to a sudden halt **3** : to call to notice

brink \'brink\ *n* **1** : an edge at the top of a steep place **2** : the point of onset

brio \'brē-ō\ *n* : VIVACITY, SPIRIT

bri·quette *or* **bri·quet** \bri-ˈket\ *n* : a compacted often brick-shaped mass of fine material (a charcoal ~)

brisk \'brisk\ *adj* **1** : ALERT, LIVELY **2** : INVIGORATING **syn** agile, spry, nimble — **brisk·ly** *adv* — **brisk·ness** *n*

bris·ket \'bris-kət\ *n* : the breast or lower chest of a quadruped; *also* : a cut of beef from the brisket

bris·ling \'briz-lin, 'bris-\ *n* : SPRAT 1

¹bris·tle \'bris-əl\ *n* : a short stiff coarse hair — **bris·tle·like** \'bris-əl-ˌlīk\ *adj* — **bris·tly** *adj*

²bristle *vb* **bris·tled; bris·tling 1** : to stand stiffly erect **2** : to show angry defiance **3** : to appear as if covered with bristles

Brit *abbr* Britain; British

Bri·tan·nic \bri-ˈta-nik\ *adj* : BRITISH

britch·es \'bri-chəz\ *n pl* : BREECHES, TROUSERS

Brit·ish \'bri-tish\ *n pl* : the people of Great Britain or the Commonwealth — **British** *adj* — **Brit·ish·ness** *n*

British thermal unit *n* : the quantity of heat needed to raise the temperature of one pound of water one degree Fahrenheit

Brit·on \'brit-ᵊn\ *n* **1** : a member of a people inhabiting Britain before the Anglo-Saxon invasion **2** : a native or inhabitant of Great Britain

brit·tle \'brit-ᵊl\ *adj* **brit·tler; brit·tlest** : easily broken : FRAGILE **syn** crisp, crumbly, friable — **brit·tle·ness** *n*

bro *abbr* brother

¹broach \'brōch\ *n* : a pointed tool

²broach *vb* **1** : to pierce (as a cask) in order to draw the contents **2** : to introduce as a topic of conversation

¹broad \'bród\ *adj* **1** : WIDE **2** : SPACIOUS **3** : CLEAR, OPEN **4** : OBVIOUS (a ~ hint) **5** : COARSE, CRUDE (~ stories) **6** : tolerant in outlook **7** : GENERAL **8** : dealing with essential points — **broad·ly** *adv* — **broad·ness** *n*

²broad *n, slang* : WOMAN

¹broad·cast \'bród-ˌkast\ *vb* **broadcast** *also* **broad·cast·ed; broad·cast·ing 1** : to scatter or sow broadcast **2** : to make widely known **3** : to transmit a broadcast — **broad·cast·er** *n*

²broadcast *adv* : to or over a wide area

³broadcast *n* **1** : the transmission of sound or images by radio or television **2** : a single radio or television program

broad·cloth \-ˌklóth\ *n* **1** : a smooth dense woolen cloth **2** : a fine soft cloth of cotton, silk, or synthetic fiber

broad·en \'bród-ᵊn\ *vb* : WIDEN

broad·loom \-ˌlüm\ *adj* : woven on a wide loom esp. in a solid color

broad–mind·ed \-ˈmīn-dəd\ *adj* : tolerant of varied opinions — **broad–mind·ed·ly** *adv* — **broad–mind·ed·ness** *n*

¹broad·side \-ˌsīd\ *n* **1** : a sheet of paper printed usu. on one side (as an advertisement) **2** : all of the guns on one side of a ship; *also* : their simultaneous firing **3** : a volley of abuse or denunciation

²broadside *adv* **1** : with one side forward : SIDEWAYS **2** : from the side (the car was hit ~)

broad–spectrum *adj* : effective against a wide range of organisms (~ antibiotics)

broad·sword \'bród-ˌsórd\ *n* : a broad-bladed sword

broad·tail \-ˌtāl\ *n* : a karakul esp. with flat and wavy fur

bro·cade \brō-ˈkād\ *n* : a usu. silk fabric with a raised design

broc·co·li \'brä-kə-lē\ *n* [It, pl. of *broccolo* flowering top of a cabbage, dim. of *brocco* small nail, sprout, fr. L *broccus* projecting] : the stems and immature usu. green or purple flower heads of either of two garden vegetable plants closely related to the cabbage; *also* : either of the plants

bro·chette \brō-ˈshet\ *n* : SKEWER

bro·chure \brō-ˈshúr\ *n* [F, fr. *brocher* to sew, fr. MF, to prick, fr. OF *brochier,* fr. *broche* pointed tool] : PAMPHLET, BOOKLET

bro·gan \'brō-gən, brō-ˈgan\ *n* : a heavy shoe

brogue \'brōg\ *n* : a dialect or regional pronunciation; *esp* : an Irish accent

broil \'bróil\ *vb* : to cook by exposure to radiant heat : GRILL — **broil** *n*

broil·er \'bró-lər\ *n* **1** : a utensil for broiling **2** : a young chicken fit for broiling

¹broke \'brōk\ *past of* BREAK

²broke *adj* : PENNILESS

¹bro·ken \'brō-kən\ *past part of* BREAK

²broken *adj* **1** : SHATTERED **2** : having gaps or breaks : INTERRUPTED, DISRUPTED **3** : SUBDUED, CRUSHED **4** : BANKRUPT **5** : imperfectly spoken (~ English) — **bro·ken·ly** *adv*

bro·ken·heart·ed \ˌbrō-kən-'här-təd\ adj : overcome by grief or despair

bro·ker \'brō-kər\ n : an agent who negotiates contracts of purchase and sale — **broker** vb

bro·ker·age \'brō-kə-rij\ n 1 : the business of a broker 2 : the fee or commission charged by a broker

bro·mide \'brō-ˌmīd\ n : a compound of bromine and another element or chemical group including some (as potassium bromide) used as sedatives

bro·mid·ic \brō-'mi-dik\ adj : TRITE, UNORIGINAL

bro·mine \'brō-ˌmēn\ n [F brome bromine, fr. Gk brōmos stink] : a deep red liquid corrosive chemical element that gives off an irritating vapor — see ELEMENT table

bronc \'bräŋk\ n : an unbroken or partly broken range horse of western No. America; also : MUSTANG

bron·chi·al \'bräŋ-kē-əl\ adj : of, relating to, or affecting the bronchi or their branches

bron·chi·tis \brän-'kī-təs, bräŋ-\ n : inflammation of the bronchi and their branches — **bron·chit·ic** \-'kitik\ adj

bron·chus \'bräŋ-kəs\ n, pl **bron·chi** \'bräŋ-ˌkī, -ˌkē\ : either of the main divisions of the windpipe each leading to a lung

bron·co \'bräŋ-kō\ n, pl **broncos** [MexSp, fr. Sp, rough, wild] : BRONC

bron·to·sau·rus \ˌbrän-tə-'sor-əs\ also **bron·to·saur** \'brän-tə-ˌsor\ n [NL, fr. Gk brontē thunder + sauros lizard] : any of a genus of large 4-footed and probably herbivorous sauropod dinosaurs of the Jurassic

Bronx cheer \'bräŋks-\ n : RASPBERRY 2

¹**bronze** \'bränz\ vb **bronzed; bronz·ing** : to give the appearance of bronze to

²**bronze** n 1 : an alloy of copper and tin and sometimes other elements; also : something made of bronze 2 : a yellowish brown color — **bronzy** \'brän-zē\ adj

brooch \'brōch, 'brüch\ n : an ornamental clasp or pin

¹**brood** \'brüd\ n : a family of young animals or children and esp. of birds

²**brood** adj : kept for breeding ⟨a ~ mare⟩

³**brood** vb 1 : to sit on eggs to hatch them; also : to shelter (hatched young) with the wings 2 : to think anxiously or gloomily about something — **brood·ing·ly** adv

brood·er \'brü-dər\ n 1 : one that broods 2 : a heated structure for raising young birds

¹**brook** \'bruk\ n : a small natural stream

²**brook** vb : TOLERATE, BEAR

brook·let \'bruk-lət\ n : a small brook

brook trout n : a common speckled cold-water char of No. America

broom \'brüm, 'brum\ n 1 : any of several shrubs of the legume family with long slender branches and usu. yellow flowers 2 : an implement with a long handle (**broom·stick** \-ˌstik\) used for sweeping

bros abbr brothers

broth \'broth\ n, pl **broths** \'broths, 'brothz\ 1 : liquid in which meat or sometimes vegetable food has been cooked 2 : a fluid culture medium

broth·el \'brä-thəl, 'bro-\ n : a house of prostitution

broth·er \'brə-thər\ n, pl **brothers** also **breth·ren** \'breth-rən, 'bre-thə-; 'bre-thərn\ 1 : a male having one or both parents in common with another individual 2 : a man who is a religious but not a priest 3 : KINSMAN; also : SOUL BROTHER — **broth·er·li·ness** \-lē-nəs\ n — **broth·er·ly** adj

broth·er·hood \'brə-thər-ˌhud\ n 1 : the state of being brothers or a brother 2 : ASSOCIATION, FRATERNITY 3 : the whole body of persons in a business or profession

broth·er–in–law \'brə-thə-rən-ˌlo, 'brə-thərn-ˌlo\ n, pl **brothers–in–law** \'brə-thər-zən-\ : the brother of one's spouse; also : the husband of one's sister or of one's spouse's sister

brougham \'brü(-ə)m, 'brō(-ə)m\ n : a light closed horse-drawn carriage with the driver outside in front

brought past and past part of BRING

brou·ha·ha \'brü-ˌhä-ˌhä\ n : HUBBUB, UPROAR

brow \'brau\ n 1 : the eyebrow or the ridge on which it grows; also : FOREHEAD 2 : the projecting upper part of a steep place

brow·beat \'brau-ˌbēt\ vb **-beat; -beat·en** \-'bēt-ᵊn\ or **-beat; -beat·ing** : to intimidate by sternness or arrogance

¹**brown** \'braun\ adj : of the color brown; also : of dark or tanned complexion

²**brown** n : a color like that of coffee or chocolate that is a blend of red and yellow darkened by black — **brown·ish** adj

³**brown** vb : to make or become brown

brown bag·ging \-'ba-giŋ\ n : the practice of carrying one's lunch usu. in a brown bag — **brown bag·ger** n

brown·ie \'brau-nē\ n 1 : a legendary cheerful elf who performs good deeds at night 2 cap : a member of a program of the Girl Scouts for girls in the first through third grades

brown·out \'brau-ˌnaut\ n : a period of reduced voltage of electricity caused esp. by high demand and resulting in reduced illumination

brown rice n : hulled but unpolished rice that retains most of the bran layers

brown·stone \'braun-ˌstōn\ n : a dwelling faced with reddish brown sandstone

¹**browse** \'brauz\ vb **browsed; brows·ing** 1 : to feed on browse; also : GRAZE 2 : to read or look over something in a casual way

²**browse** n : tender shoots, twigs, and leaves fit for food for cattle

bru·in \'brü-ən\ n : BEAR

¹**bruise** \'brüz\ vb **bruised; bruis·ing** 1 : to inflict a bruise on; also : to become bruised 2 : to break down (as leaves or berries) by pounding

²**bruise** n : a surface injury to flesh : CONTUSION

bruis·er \'brü-zər\ n : a big husky man

bruit \'brüt\ vb : to make widely known by common report

brunch \'brənch\ n : a meal that combines a late breakfast and an early lunch

bru·net or **bru·nette** \brü-'net\ adj [F brunet, masc., brunette, fem., brownish, fr. OF, fr. brun brown] : having brown or black hair and usu. a relatively dark complexion — **brunet** or **brunette** n

brunt \'brənt\ n : the main shock, force, or stress esp. of an attack; also : the greater burden

¹**brush** \'brəsh\ n 1 : BRUSHWOOD 2 : scrub vegetation or land covered with it

²**brush** n 1 : a device composed of bristles set in a handle and used esp. for cleaning or painting 2 : a bushy tail (as of a fox) 3 : an electrical conductor that makes contact between a stationary and a moving part (as of a motor) 4 : a quick light touch in passing

³**brush** vb 1 : to treat (as in cleaning or painting) with a brush 2 : to remove with or as if with a brush; also : to dismiss in an offhand manner 3 : to touch gently in passing

⁴**brush** n : SKIRMISH syn encounter, run-in

brush–off \'brəsh-ˌof\ n : a curt offhand dismissal

brush up vb : to renew one's skill

brush·wood \'brəsh-ˌwud\ n 1 : small branches of wood esp. when cut 2 : a thicket of shrubs and small trees

brusque \'brəsk\ adj [F brusque, fr. It brusco, fr. ML bruscus a plant with stiff twigs used for brooms] : CURT, BLUNT, ABRUPT syn gruff, bluff, crusty, short — **brusque·ly** adv

brus·sels sprout \'brəs-əlz-\ n, often cap B : one of the edible small heads borne on the stalk of a plant closely related to the cabbage; also, pl : this plant

bru·tal \'brüt-ᵊl\ adj 1 : befitting a brute : UNFEELING, CRUEL 2 : HARSH, SEVERE ⟨~ weather⟩ 3 : unpleasantly accurate — **bru·tal·i·ty** \brü-'ta-lə-tē\ n — **bru·tal·ly** adv

bru·tal·ize \'brüt-°l-ˌīz\ *vb* **-ized; -iz·ing 1** : to make brutal **2** : to treat brutally

¹brute \'brüt\ *adj* [ME, fr. MF *brut* rough, fr. L *brutus* brutish, lit., heavy] **1** : of or relating to beasts **2** : BRUTAL **3** : UNREASONING; *also* : purely physical ⟨~ strength⟩

²brute *n* **1** : BEAST 1 **2** : a brutal person

brut·ish \'brü-tish\ *adj* **1** : BRUTE 1 **2** : strongly sensual; *also* : showing little intelligence

BS *abbr* bachelor of science

BSA *abbr* Boy Scouts of America

bskt *abbr* basket

Bt *abbr* baronet

btry *abbr* battery

Btu *abbr* British thermal unit

bu *abbr* bushel

¹bub·ble \'bə-bəl\ *n* **1** : a globule of gas in a liquid **2** : a thin film of liquid filled with gas **3** : something lacking firmness or solidity — **bub·bly** *adj*

²bubble *vb* **bub·bled; bub·bling** : to form, rise in, or give off bubbles

bu·bo \'bü-bō, 'byü-\ *n, pl* **buboes** : an inflammatory swelling of a lymph gland

bu·bon·ic plague \bü-'bä-nik-, byü-\ *n* : plague caused by a bacterium transmitted to human beings by flea bites and marked esp. by chills and fever and by buboes usu. in the groin

buc·ca·neer \ˌbə-kə-'nir\ *n* : PIRATE

¹buck \'bək\ *n, pl* **bucks 1** *or pl* **buck** : a male animal (as a deer or antelope) **2** : DANDY **3** : DOLLAR

²buck *vb* **1** : to spring with an arching leap ⟨a ~ing horse⟩ **2** : to charge against something; *also* : to strive for advancement sometimes without regard to ethical behavior

buck·board \-ˌbōrd\ *n* : a 4-wheeled horse-drawn wagon with a floor of long springy boards

buckboard

buck·et \'bə-kət\ *n* **1** : PAIL **2** : an object resembling a bucket in collecting, scooping, or carrying something — **buck·et·ful** *n*

bucket seat *n* : a low separate seat for one person (as in an automobile)

buck·eye \'bə-ˌkī\ *n* : a tree related to the horse chestnut that occurs chiefly in the central U.S.; *also* : its large nutlike seed

buck fever *n* : nervous excitement of an inexperienced hunter at the sight of game

¹buck·le \'bə-kəl\ *n* : a clasp (as on a belt) for two loose ends

²buckle *vb* **buck·led; buck·ling 1** : to fasten with a buckle **2** : to apply oneself with vigor **3** : to crumple up : BEND, COLLAPSE

³buckle *n* : BEND, FOLD, KINK

buck·ler \'bə-klər\ *n* : SHIELD

buck·ram \'bə-krəm\ *n* : a coarse stiff cloth used esp. for binding books

buck·saw \'bək-ˌsò\ *n* : a saw set in a usu. H-shaped frame for sawing wood

buck·shot \'bək-ˌshät\ *n* : lead shot that is from .24 to .33 inch (about 6.1 to 8.4 millimeters) in diameter

buck·skin \-ˌskin\ *n* **1** : the skin of a buck **2** : a soft usu. suede-finished leather — **buckskin** *adj*

buck·tooth \-'tüth\ *n* : a large projecting front tooth — **buck–toothed** \-'tütht\ *adj*

buck·wheat \-ˌhwēt\ *n* : either of two plants grown for their triangular seeds which are used as a cereal grain; *also* : these seeds

bu·col·ic \byü-'kä-lik\ *adj* [L *bucolicus*, fr. Gk *boukolikos*, fr. *boukolos* one who tends cattle, fr. *bous* head of cattle + *-kolos* (akin to L *colere* to cultivate)] : PASTORAL, RURAL

¹bud \'bəd\ *n* **1** : an undeveloped plant shoot (as of a leaf or a flower); *also* : a partly opened flower **2** : an asexual reproductive structure that detaches from the parent and forms a new individual **3** : something not yet fully developed ⟨nipped in the ~⟩

²bud *vb* **bud·ded; bud·ding 1** : to form or put forth buds; *also* : to reproduce by asexual buds **2** : to be or develop like a bud **3** : to reproduce a desired variety (as of peach) by inserting a bud in a plant of a different variety

Bud·dhism \'bü-ˌdi-zəm, 'bù-\ *n* : a religion of eastern and central Asia growing out of the teachings of Gautama Buddha — **Bud·dhist** \'bü-dist, 'bù-\ *n or adj*

bud·dy \'bə-dē\ *n, pl* **buddies 1** : COMPANION; *also* : FRIEND **2** : FELLOW

budge \'bəj\ *vb* **budged; budg·ing** : MOVE, SHIFT; *also* : YIELD

bud·ger·i·gar \'bə-jə-rē-ˌgar\ *n* : a small brightly colored Australian parrot often kept as a pet

¹bud·get \'bə-jət\ *n* [ME *bowgette*, fr. MF *bougette*, dim. of *bouge* leather bag, fr. L *bulga*] **1** : STOCK, SUPPLY **2** : a financial report containing estimates of income and expenses; *also* : a plan for coordinating income and expenses **3** : the amount of money available for a particular use — **bud·get·ary** \'bə-jə-ˌter-ē\ *adj*

²budget *vb* **1** : to allow for in a budget **2** : to draw up a budget

³budget *adj* : INEXPENSIVE

bud·gie \'bə-jē\ *n* : BUDGERIGAR

¹buff \'bəf\ *n* **1** : a yellow to orange yellow color **2** : FAN, ENTHUSIAST

²buff *adj* : of the color buff

³buff *vb* : POLISH, SHINE

buf·fa·lo \'bə-fə-ˌlō\ *n, pl* **-lo** *or* **-loes** *also* **-los 1** : WATER BUFFALO **2** : a large shaggy-maned No. American wild bovine mammal that has short horns and heavy forequarters with a large muscular hump

¹buf·fer \'bə-fər\ *n* : something or someone that protects or shields (as from physical damage or a financial blow)

²buffer *n* : one that buffs

¹buf·fet \'bə-fət\ *n* : BLOW, SLAP

²buffet *vb* **1** : to strike with the hand; *also* : to pound repeatedly **2** : to struggle against or on **syn** beat, batter, drub, pummel, thrash

³buf·fet \(ˌ)bə-'fā, bü-\ *n* **1** : SIDEBOARD **2** : a counter for refreshments; *also* : a meal at which people serve themselves informally

buff leather *n* : a strong supple oil-tanned leather

buf·foon \(ˌ)bə-'fün\ *n* [MF *bouffon*, fr. It *buffone*] : CLOWN **2** — **buf·foon·ery** \-'fü-nə-rē\ *n*

¹bug \'bəg\ *n* **1** : an insect or other creeping or crawling invertebrate animal; *esp* : an insect pest (as a bedbug) **2** : any of an order of insects with sucking mouthparts and incomplete metamorphosis that includes many plant pests **3** : an unexpected flaw or imperfection ⟨a ~ in a computer program⟩ **4** : a disease-producing germ; *also* : a disease caused by it **5** : a concealed listening device

²bug *vb* **bugged; bug·ging 1** : BOTHER, ANNOY **2** : to plant a concealed microphone in

³bug *vb* **bugged; bug·ging** *of the eyes* : PROTRUDE, BULGE

bug·a·boo \'bə-gə-ˌbü\ *n, pl* **-boos** : BOGEY 1

bug·bear \'bəg-ˌbar\ *n* : BOGEY 1; *also* : a source of dread

bug·gy \\'bə-gē\\ *n, pl* **buggies** : a light horse-drawn carriage; *also* : a carriage for a baby

bu·gle \\'byü-gəl\\ *n* [ME, buffalo, instrument made of buffalo horn, bugle, fr. OF, fr. L *buculus,* dim. of *bos* head of cattle] : a valveless brass instrument resembling a trumpet and used esp. for military calls — **bu·gler** *n*

¹**build** \\'bild\\ *vb* **built** \\'bilt\\; **build·ing 1** : to form or have formed by ordering and uniting materials ⟨∼ a house⟩; *also* : to bring into being or develop **2** : to produce or create gradually ⟨∼ an argument on facts⟩ **3** : INCREASE, ENLARGE; *also* : ENHANCE **4** : to engage in building — **build·er** *n*

²**build** *n* : form or mode of structure; *esp* : PHYSIQUE

build·ing \\'bil-diŋ\\ *n* **1** : a usu. roofed and walled structure (as a house) for permanent use **2** : the art or business of constructing buildings

build·up \\'bil-ˌdəp\\ *n* : the act or process of building up; *also* : something produced by this

built–in \\'bil-ˌtin\\ *adj* **1** : forming an integral part of a structure **2** : INHERENT

bulb \\'bəlb\\ *n* **1** : an underground resting stage of a plant (as a lily or an onion) consisting of a short stem base bearing one or more buds enclosed in overlapping leaves; *also* : a fleshy plant structure (as a tuber) resembling a bulb **2** : a plant having or growing from a bulb **3** : a rounded more or less bulb-shaped object or part (as for an electric lamp) — **bul·bous** \\'bəl-bəs\\ *adj*

Bul·gar·i·an \\ˌbəl-'gar-ē-ən, ˌbul-\\ *n* : a native or inhabitant of Bulgaria — **Bulgarian** *adj*

¹**bulge** \\'bəlj\\ *vb* **bulged; bulg·ing** : to become or cause to become protuberant

²**bulge** *n* : a swelling projecting part

bu·li·mia \\bü-'lē-mē-ə, byü-, -'li-\\ *n* **1** : an abnormal and constant craving for food **2** : a serious eating disorder chiefly of females that is characterized by compulsive overeating usu. followed by self-induced vomiting or laxative or diuretic abuse — **bu·lim·ic** \\-'lē-mik, -'li-\\ *adj or n*

¹**bulk** \\'bəlk\\ *n* **1** : MAGNITUDE, VOLUME **2** : material that forms a mass in the intestine; *esp* : FIBER **2 3** : a large mass **4** : the major portion

²**bulk** *vb* **1** : to cause to swell or bulge **2** : to appear as a factor : LOOM

bulk·head \\'bəlk-ˌhed\\ *n* **1** : a partition separating compartments **2** : a structure built to cover a shaft or a cellar stairway

bulky \\'bəl-kē\\ *adj* **bulk·i·er; -est** : having bulk; *esp* : being large and unwieldy

¹**bull** \\'bul\\ *n* **1** : a male bovine animal; *also* : a usu. adult male of various large animals (as the moose, elephant, or whale) **2** : one who buys securities or commodities in expectation of a price increase — **bullish** *adj*

²**bull** *adj* **1** : of, relating to, or suggestive of a bull : MALE **2** : large of its kind

³**bull** *n* [ME *bulle,* fr. ML *bulla,* fr. L, bubble, amulet] **1** : a papal letter **2** : DECREE

⁴**bull** *n, slang* : NONSENSE

⁵**bull** *abbr* bulletin

¹**bull·dog** \\'bul-ˌdog\\ *n* : any of a breed of compact muscular short-haired dogs of English origin

²**bulldog** *vb* : to throw (a steer) by seizing the horns and twisting the neck

bull·doze \\-ˌdōz\\ *vb* **1** : to move, clear, or level with a tractor-driven machine (**bull·doz·er**) having a broad blade for pushing **2** : to force as if by using a bulldozer

bul·let \\'bu-lət\\ *n* [MF *boulette* small ball & *boulet* missile, dims. of *boule* ball] : a missile to be shot from a firearm — **bul·let·proof** \\-ˌprüf\\ *adj*

bul·le·tin \\'bu-lət-ᵊn\\ *n* **1** : a brief public report intended for immediate release on a matter of public interest **2** : a periodical publication (as of a college) — **bulletin** *vb*

bulldog

bull·fight \\'bul-ˌfīt\\ *n* : a spectacle in which people ceremonially fight with and usu. kill bulls in an arena — **bull·fight·er** *n*

bull·frog \\-ˌfrog, -ˌfräg\\ *n* : a large deep-voiced frog

bull·head \\-ˌhed\\ *n* : any of several common freshwater catfishes of the U.S.

bull·head·ed \\-'he-dəd\\ *adj* : stupidly stubborn : HEADSTRONG

bul·lion \\'bul-yən\\ *n* : gold or silver esp. in bars or ingots

bull·ock \\'bu-lək\\ *n* : a young bull; *also* : STEER

bull pen *n* : a place on a baseball field where pitchers warm up; *also* : the relief pitchers of a baseball team

bull session *n* : an informal discussion

bull's–eye \\'bul-ˌzī\\ *n, pl* **bull's–eyes** : the center of a target; *also* : a shot that hits the bull's-eye

¹**bul·ly** \\'bu-lē\\ *n, pl* **bullies** : a person habitually cruel to others who are weaker

²**bully** *adj* : EXCELLENT, FIRST-RATE — often used interjectionally

³**bully** *vb* **bul·lied; bul·ly·ing** : to behave as a bully toward : DOMINEER **syn** browbeat, intimidate, hector

bul·rush \\'bul-ˌrəsh\\ *n* : any of several large rushes or sedges of wetlands

bul·wark \\'bul-(ˌ)wərk, -ˌwork; 'bəl-(ˌ)wərk\\ *n* **1** : a wall-like defensive structure **2** : a strong support or protection

¹**bum** \\'bəm\\ *adj* **1** : of poor quality ⟨∼ advice⟩ **2** : DISABLED ⟨a ∼ knee⟩

²**bum** *vb* **bummed; bum·ming 1** : to spend time unemployed and wandering; *also* : LOAF **2** : to obtain by begging

³**bum** *n* **1** : LOAFER **2** : a devotee of a recreational activity ⟨a ski ∼⟩ **3** : TRAMP

bum·ble·bee \\'bəm-bəl-ˌbē\\ *n* : any of numerous large hairy social bees

bum·mer \\'bə-mər\\ *n* **1** : an unpleasant experience **2** : FAILURE

¹**bump** \\'bəmp\\ *n* **1** : a local bulge; *esp* : a swelling of tissue **2** : a sudden forceful blow or impact — **bumpy** *adj*

²**bump** *vb* **1** : to strike or knock forcibly; *also* : to move by or as if by bumping **2** : to collide with

¹**bum·per** \\'bəm-pər\\ *n* **1** : a cup or glass filled to the brim **2** : something unusually large — **bumper** *adj*

²**bump·er** \\'bəm-pər\\ *n* : a device for absorbing shock or preventing damage; *esp* : a usu. metal bar at either end of an automobile

bump·kin \\'bəmp-kən\\ *n* : an awkward and unsophisticated country person

bump·tious \\'bəmp-shəs\\ *adj* : obtusely and often noisily self-assertive

bun \\'bən\\ *n* : a sweet biscuit or roll

¹**bunch** \\'bənch\\ *n* **1** : SWELLING **2** : CLUSTER, GROUP — **bunchy** *adj*

²**bunch** *vb* : to form into a group or bunch

bun·co *or* **bun·ko** \\'bəŋ-kō\\ *n, pl* **buncos** *or* **bunkos** : a swindling scheme — **bunco** *vb*

¹**bun·dle** \\'bən-dᵊl\\ *n* **1** : several items bunched and fas-

tened together; *also* : something wrapped for carrying 2 : a considerable amount : LOT 3 : a small band of mostly parallel nerve or muscle fibers

²**bundle** *vb* **bun·dled; bun·dling** : to gather or tie in a bundle

bun·dling \'bənd-(ə-)liŋ\ *n* : a former custom of a courting couple's occupying the same bed without undressing

bung \'bəŋ\ *n* : the stopper in the bunghole of a cask

bun·ga·low \'bəŋ-gə-ˌlō\ *n* : a one-storied house with a low-pitched roof

bun·gee cord \'bən-jē-\ *n* : a long elastic cord used esp. in a sport (**bungee jump·ing**) in which it is fastened to a person to arrest a free fall from a high place (as a bridge)

bung·hole \'bəŋ-ˌhōl\ *n* : a hole for emptying or filling a cask

bun·gle \'bəŋ-gəl\ *vb* **bun·gled; bun·gling** : to do badly : BOTCH — **bungle** *n* — **bun·gler** *n*

bun·ion \'bən-yən\ *n* : an inflamed swelling of the first joint of the big toe

¹**bunk** \'bəŋk\ *n* : BED; *esp* : a built-in bed that is often one of a tier

²**bunk** *n* : BUNKUM, NONSENSE

bunk bed *n* : one of two single beds usu. placed one above the other

bun·ker \'bəŋ-kər\ *n* 1 : a bin or compartment for storage (as for coal on a ship) 2 : a protective embankment or dugout 3 : a sand trap or embankment constituting a hazard on a golf course

bun·kum *or* **bun·combe** \'bəŋ-kəm\ *n* [*Buncombe* County, N.C.; fr. a remark made by its congressman, who defended an irrelevant speech by claiming that he was speaking to Buncombe] : insincere or foolish talk

bun·ny \'bə-nē\ *n, pl* **-nies** : RABBIT

Bun·sen burner \'bən-sən-\ *n* : a gas burner usu. consisting of a straight tube with air holes at the bottom

¹**bunt** \'bənt\ *vb* 1 : ¹BUTT 2 : to push or tap a baseball lightly without swinging the bat

²**bunt** *n* : an act or instance of bunting; *also* : a bunted ball

¹**bun·ting** \'bən-tiŋ\ *n* : any of numerous small stout‑billed finches

²**bunting** *n* : a thin fabric used esp. for flags; *also* : FLAGS

¹**buoy** \'bü-ē, 'bȯi\ *n* 1 : a floating object anchored in water to mark something (as a channel) 2 : a float consisting of a ring of buoyant material to support a person who has fallen into the water

²**buoy** *vb* 1 : to mark by a buoy 2 : to keep afloat 3 : to raise the spirits of

buoy·an·cy \'bȯi-ən-sē, 'bü-yən-\ *n* 1 : the tendency of a body to float or rise when submerged in a fluid 2 : the power of a fluid to exert an upward force on a body placed in it 3 : resilience of spirit — **buoy·ant** \-ənt, -yənt\ *adj*

¹**bur** \'bər\ *var of* BURR

²**bur** *abbr* bureau

¹**bur·den** \'bərd-ᵊn\ *n* 1 : LOAD; *also* : CARE, RESPONSIBILITY 2 : something oppressive : ENCUMBRANCE 3 : CARGO; *also* : capacity for cargo

²**burden** *vb* : LOAD, OPPRESS — **bur·den·some** \-səm\ *adj*

³**burden** *n* 1 : REFRAIN, CHORUS 2 : a main theme or idea : GIST

bur·dock \'bər-ˌdäk\ *n* : any of a genus of coarse composite herbs with globe-shaped flower heads surrounded by prickly bracts

bu·reau \'byu̇r-ō\ *n, pl* **bureaus** *also* **bu·reaux** \-ōz\ [F, desk, cloth covering for desks, fr. OF *burel* woolen cloth, ultim. fr. L *burra* shaggy cloth] 1 : a chest of drawers 2 : an administrative unit (as of a government department) 3 : a branch of a publication or wire service in an important news center

bu·reau·cra·cy \byu̇-'rä-krə-sē\ *n, pl* **-cies** 1 : a body of

appointive government officials 2 : government marked by specialization of functions under fixed rules and a hierarchy of authority; *also* : an unwieldy administrative system burdened with excessive complexity and lack of flexibility — **bu·reau·crat** \'byu̇r-ə-ˌkrat\ *n* — **bu·reau·crat·ic** \ˌbyu̇r-ə-'kra-tik\ *adj*

bur·geon \'bər-jən\ *vb* : to put forth fresh growth (as from buds) : grow vigorously : FLOURISH

burgh \'bər-ō\ *n* : a Scottish town

bur·gher \'bər-gər\ *n* 1 : TOWNSMAN 2 : a prosperous solid citizen

bur·glary \'bər-glə-rē\ *n, pl* **-glar·ies** : forcible entry into a building esp. at night with the intent to commit a crime (as theft) — **bur·glar** \-glər\ *n* — **bur·glar·ize** \'bər-glə-ˌrīz\ *vb*

bur·gle \'bər-gəl\ *vb* **bur·gled; bur·gling** : to commit burglary on

bur·go·mas·ter \'bər-gə-ˌmas-tər\ *n* : the chief magistrate of a town in some European countries

bur·gun·dy \'bər-gən-dē\ *n, pl* **-dies** *often cap* 1 : a red or white table wine from the Burgundy region of France 2 : an American red table wine

buri·al \'ber-ē-əl\ *n* : the act or process of burying

burl \'bərl\ *n* : a hard woody often flattened hemispherical outgrowth on a tree

bur·lap \'bər-ˌlap\ *n* : a coarse fabric usu. of jute or hemp used esp. for bags

¹**bur·lesque** \(ˌ)bər-'lesk\ *n* [*burlesque*, adj., comic, droll, fr. F, fr. It *burlesco*, fr. *burla* joke, fr. Sp] 1 : a witty or derisive literary or dramatic imitative work 2 : broadly humorous theatrical entertainment consisting of several items (as songs, skits, or dances)

²**burlesque** *vb* **bur·lesqued; bur·lesqu·ing** : to make ludicrous by burlesque **syn** caricature, parody, travesty

bur·ly \'bər-lē\ *adj* **bur·li·er; -est** : strongly and heavily built : HUSKY **syn** muscular, brawny, beefy, hefty

Bur·mese \ˌbər-'mēz, -'mēs\ *n, pl* **Burmese** : a native or inhabitant of Burma (Myanmar) — **Burmese** *adj*

¹**burn** \'bərn\ *vb* **burned** \'bərnd, 'bərnt\ *or* **burnt** \'bərnt\; **burn·ing** 1 : to be on fire 2 : to feel or look as if on fire 3 : to alter or become altered by or as if by the action of fire or heat 4 : to use as fuel (∼ coal); *also* : to destroy by fire (∼ trash) 5 : to cause or make by fire (∼ a hole); *also* : to affect as if by heat

²**burn** *n* : an injury or effect produced by or as if by burning

burn·er \'bər-nər\ *n* : the part of a fuel-burning or heat‑producing device where the flame or heat is produced

bur·nish \'bər-nish\ *vb* : to make shiny esp. by rubbing : POLISH — **bur·nish·er** *n* — **bur·nish·ing** *adj or n*

bur·noose *or* **bur·nous** \(ˌ)bər-'nüs\ *n* : a hooded cloak worn esp. by Arabs

burn·out \'bər-ˌnau̇t\ *n* 1 : the cessation of operation of a jet or rocket engine 2 : exhaustion of one's physical or emotional strength; *also* : a person suffering from burnout

burp \'bərp\ *n* : an act of belching — **burp** *vb*

burp gun *n* : a small submachine gun

burr \'bər\ *n* 1 *usu* bur : a rough or prickly envelope of a fruit; *also* : a plant that bears burs 2 : roughness left in cutting or shaping metal 3 : WHIR — **bur·ry** *adj*

bur·ri·to \bə-'rē-tō\ *n* [AmerSp, fr. Sp, little donkey, dim. of *burro*] : a flour tortilla rolled around a filling and baked

bur·ro \'bər-ō, 'bu̇r-\ *n, pl* **burros** [Sp] : a usu. small donkey

¹**bur·row** \'bər-ō\ *n* : a hole in the ground made by an animal (as a rabbit)

²**burrow** *vb* 1 : to form by tunneling; *also* : to make a burrow 2 : to progress by or as if by digging — **bur·row·er** *n*

bur·sar \'bər-sər\ *n* : a treasurer esp. of a college

bur·si·tis \(ˌ)bər-'sī-təs\ *n* : inflammation of the serous sac (**bur·sa** \'bər-sə\) of a joint (as the elbow or shoulder)

¹**burst** \'bərst\ *vb* **burst** *or* **burst·ed; burst·ing** 1 : to fly

apart or into pieces **2** : to show one's feelings suddenly; *also* : PLUNGE ⟨∼ into song⟩ **3** : to enter or emerge suddenly : SPRING **4** : to be filled to the breaking point

²burst *n* **1** : a sudden outbreak : SPURT **2** : EXPLOSION **3** : result of bursting

Bu·run·di·an \bu̇-ˈrün-dē-ən\ *n* : a native or inhabitant of Burundi

bury \ˈber-ē\ *vb* **bur·ied; bury·ing 1** : to deposit in the earth; *also* : to inter with funeral ceremonies **2** : CONCEAL, HIDE **3** : SUBMERGE, ENGROSS — usu. used with *in*

¹bus \ˈbəs\ *n, pl* **bus·es** *or* **bus·ses** [short for *omnibus*, fr. F, fr. L, for all, dat. pl. of *omnis* all] : a large motor vehicle for carrying passengers

²bus *vb* **bused** *or* **bussed; bus·ing** *or* **bus·sing 1** : to travel or transport by bus **2** : to work as a busboy

³bus *abbr* business

bus·boy \ˈbəs-ˌbȯi\ *n* : a waiter's helper

bus·by \ˈbəz-bē\ *n, pl* **busbies** : a military full-dress fur hat

bush \ˈbu̇sh\ *n* **1** : SHRUB **2** : rough uncleared country **3** : a thick tuft ⟨a ∼ of hair⟩ — **bushy** *adj*

bushed \ˈbu̇sht\ *adj* : TIRED, EXHAUSTED

bush·el \ˈbu̇-shəl\ *n* — see WEIGHT table

bush·ing \ˈbu̇-shiŋ\ *n* : a usu. removable cylindrical lining for an opening of a mechanical part to limit the size of the opening, resist wear, or serve as a guide

bush·mas·ter \ˈbu̇sh-ˌmas-tər\ *n* : a large venomous tropical American pit viper

bush·whack \-ˌhwak\ *vb* **1** : AMBUSH **2** : to clear a path through esp. by chopping down bushes and branches — **bush·whack·er** *n*

busi·ly \ˈbi-zə-lē\ *adv* : in a busy manner

busi·ness \ˈbiz-nəs, -nəz\ *n* **1** : OCCUPATION; *also* : TASK, MISSION **2** : a commercial or industrial enterprise; *also* : TRADE ⟨∼ is good⟩ **3** : AFFAIR, MATTER **4** : personal concern

busi·ness·man \-ˌman\ *n* : a man engaged in business esp. as an executive

busi·ness·per·son \-ˌpərs-ᵊn\ *n* : a businessman or businesswoman

busi·ness·wom·an \-ˌwu̇-mən\ *n* : a woman engaged in business esp. as an executive

bus·kin \ˈbəs-kən\ *n* **1** : a laced boot reaching halfway to the knee **2** : tragic drama

buss \ˈbəs\ *n* : KISS — **buss** *vb*

¹bust \ˈbəst\ *n* [F *buste*, fr. It *busto*, fr. L *bustum* tomb] **1** : sculpture representing the upper part of the human figure **2** : the part of the human torso between the neck and the waist; *esp* : the breasts of a woman

²bust *vb* **bust·ed** *also* **bust; bust·ing 1** : BREAK, SMASH; *also* : BURST **2** : to ruin financially **3** : TAME **4** : DEMOTE **5** *slang* : ARREST; *also* : RAID

³bust *n* **1** : a drinking session **2** : a complete failure : FLOP **3** : a business depression **4** : PUNCH, SOCK **5** *slang* : a police raid; *also* : ARREST

¹bus·tle \ˈbə-səl\ *vb* **bus·tled; bus·tling** : to move or work in a brisk busy manner

²bustle *n* : briskly energetic activity

³bustle *n* : a pad or frame worn to support the fullness at the back of a woman's skirt

¹busy \ˈbi-zē\ *adj* **busi·er; -est 1** : engaged in action : not idle **2** : being in use ⟨∼ telephones⟩ **3** : full of activity ⟨∼ streets⟩ **4** : MEDDLING

²busy *vb* **bus·ied; busy·ing** : to make or keep busy : OCCUPY

busy·body \ˈbi-zē-ˌbä-dē\ *n* : MEDDLER

busy·work \-ˌwərk\ *n* : work that appears productive but only keeps one occupied

¹but \ˈbət\ *conj* **1** : except for the fact ⟨would have protested ∼ that he was afraid⟩ **2** : THAT ⟨there's no doubt ∼ he won⟩ **3** : without the certainty that ⟨never rains ∼ it pours⟩ **4** : on the contrary ⟨not one, ∼ two job offers⟩ **5** : YET ⟨poor ∼ proud⟩ **6** : with the exception of ⟨none ∼ the strongest attempt it⟩

²but *prep* : other than : EXCEPT ⟨this letter is nothing ∼

an insult⟩; *also* : with the exception of ⟨no one here ∼ me⟩

bu·tane \ˈbyü-ˌtān\ *n* : either of two gaseous hydrocarbons used as a fuel

¹butch·er \ˈbu̇-chər\ *n* [ME *bocher*, fr. OF *bouchier*, fr. *bouc* he-goat] **1** : one who slaughters animals or dresses their flesh; *also* : a dealer in meat **2** : one that kills brutally or needlessly **3** : one that botches — **butch·ery** \-chə-rē\ *n*

²butcher *vb* **1** : to slaughter and dress for meat ⟨∼ hogs⟩ **2** : to kill barbarously **3** : BOTCH

but·ler \ˈbət-lər\ *n* [ME *buteler*, fr. OF *bouteillier* bottle bearer, fr. *bouteille* bottle] : the chief male servant of a household

¹butt \ˈbət\ *vb* : to strike with the head or horns

²butt *n* : a blow or thrust with the head or horns

³butt *n* : a large cask

⁴butt *n* **1** : TARGET **2** : an object of abuse or ridicule

⁵butt *n* : a large, thicker, or bottom end of something

⁶butt *vb* **1** : ABUT **2** : to place or join edge to edge without overlapping

butte \ˈbyüt\ *n* : an isolated steep hill

¹but·ter \ˈbə-tər\ *n* [ME, fr. OE *butere*, fr. L *butyrum* butter, fr. Gk *boutyron*, fr. *bous* cow + *tyros* cheese] **1** : a solid edible emulsion of fat obtained from cream by churning **2** : a substance resembling butter — **buttery** *adj*

²butter *vb* : to spread with or as if with butter

but·ter–and–eggs \ˌbə-tə-rə-ˈnegz\ *n sing or pl* : a common perennial herb related to the snapdragon that has showy yellow and orange flowers

but·ter·cup \ˈbə-tər-ˌkəp\ *n* : any of a genus of herbs having usu. yellow flowers with five petals and sepals

but·ter·fat \-ˌfat\ *n* : the natural fat of milk and chief constituent of butter

but·ter·fin·gered \-ˌfiŋ-gərd\ *adj* : likely to let things fall or slip through the fingers — **but·ter·fin·gers** \-gərz\ *n sing or pl*

but·ter·fly \-ˌflī\ *n* : any of a group of slender day-flying insects with four broad wings covered with bright-colored scales

but·ter·milk \-ˌmilk\ *n* : the liquid remaining after butter is churned

but·ter·nut \-ˌnət\ *n* : the sweet egg-shaped nut of an American tree related to the walnut; *also* : this tree

but·ter·scotch \-ˌskäch\ *n* : a candy made from brown sugar, corn syrup, and water; *also* : the flavor of such candy

but·tock \ˈbə-tək\ *n* **1** : the back of a hip that forms one of the fleshy parts on which a person sits **2** *pl* : the seat of the body : RUMP

¹but·ton \ˈbət-ᵊn\ *n* **1** : a small knob secured to an article (as of clothing) and used as a fastener by passing it through a buttonhole or loop **2** : something that resembles a button **3** : PUSH BUTTON

²button *vb* : to close or fasten with or as if with buttons

¹but·ton·hole \ˈbət-ᵊn-ˌhōl\ *n* : a slit or loop for a button to pass through

²buttonhole *vb* : to detain in conversation by or as if by holding on to the outer garments of

but·tress \ˈbə-trəs\ *n* **1** : a projecting structure to support a wall **2** : PROP, SUPPORT
☞ For illustration, see next page.

²buttress *vb* : PROP, SUPPORT

bu·tut \bu̇-ˈtüt\ *n, pl* **bututs** *or* **butut** — see *dalasi* at MONEY table

bux·om \ˈbək-səm\ *adj* : healthily plump; *esp* : full-bosomed

¹buy \ˈbī\ *vb* **bought** \ˈbȯt\; **buy·ing 1** : to obtain for a price : PURCHASE; *also* : BRIBE **2** : to accept as true — **buy·er** *n*

²buy *n* **1** : PURCHASE 1, 2 **2** : an exceptional value : BARGAIN

¹buzz \ˈbəz\ *vb* **1** : to make a buzz **2** : to fly fast and close to

²buzz *n* : a low humming sound

buttress 1

buz·zard \\'bə-zərd\\ *n* : any of various usu. large birds of prey and esp. the turkey vulture

buzz·er \\'bə-zər\\ *n* : a device that signals with a buzzing sound

buzz saw *n* : CIRCULAR SAW

buzz·word \\'bəz-ˌwərd\\ *n* : a voguish word or phrase often from technical jargon

BV *abbr* Blessed Virgin

BWI *abbr* British West Indies

bx *abbr* box

BX *abbr* base exchange

¹**by** \\'bī, bə\\ *prep* **1** : NEAR ⟨stood ∼ the window⟩ **2** : through or through the medium of : VIA ⟨left ∼ the door⟩ **3** : PAST ⟨drove ∼ the house⟩ **4** : DURING, AT ⟨studied ∼ night⟩ **5** : no later than ⟨get here ∼ 3 p.m.⟩ **6** : through the means or direct agency of ⟨∼ force⟩ **7** : in conformity with; *also* : ACCORDING TO ⟨did it ∼ the book⟩ **8** : with respect to ⟨a vet ∼ profession⟩ **9** : to the amount or extent of ⟨won ∼ a nose⟩ **10** — used to express relationship in multiplication, in division, and in measurements ⟨divide *a* ∼ *b*⟩ ⟨multiply ∼ 6⟩ ⟨15 feet ∼ 20 feet⟩

²**by** \\'bī\\ *adv* **1** : near at hand; *also* : IN ⟨stop ∼⟩ **2** : PAST **3** : ASIDE, APART

bye \\'bī\\ *n* : a position of a participant in a tournament who advances to the next round without playing

by–elec·tion *also* **bye–election** \\'bī-ə-ˌlek-shən\\ *n* : a special election held between regular elections in order to fill a vacancy

by·gone \\'bī-ˌgȯn\\ *adj* : gone by : PAST — **bygone** *n*

by·law *or* **bye·law** \\'bī-ˌlȯ\\ *n* : a rule adopted by an organization for managing its internal affairs

by–line \\'bī-ˌlīn\\ *n* : a line at the beginning of a news story or magazine article giving the writer's name

BYO *abbr* bring your own

BYOB *abbr* bring your own beer; bring your own booze; bring your own bottle

¹**by·pass** \\'bī-ˌpas\\ *n* : a passage to one side or around a blocked or congested area; *also* : a surgical procedure establishing this ⟨a coronary ∼⟩

²**bypass** *vb* : to avoid by means of a bypass

by·path \\-ˌpath, -ˌpȧth\\ *n* : BYWAY

by·play \\'bī-ˌplā\\ *n* : action engaged in on the side (as of a stage) while the main action proceeds

by–prod·uct \\-ˌprä-(ˌ)dəkt\\ *n* : a sometimes unexpected product or result produced in addition to the main product or result

by·stand·er \\-ˌstan-dər\\ *n* : one present but not participating **syn** onlooker, witness, spectator, eyewitness

byte \\'bīt\\ *n* : a group of 8 bits that a computer processes as a unit

by·way \\'bī-ˌwā\\ *n* **1** : a little-traveled side road **2** : a secondary aspect

by·word \\-ˌwərd\\ *n* **1** : PROVERB **2** : one that is noteworthy or notorious

Byz·an·tine \\'biz-ᵊn-ˌtēn, 'bīz-, -ˌtīn; bə-'zan-, bī-\\ *adj* **1** : of, relating to, or characteristic of the ancient city of Byzantium or the the Byzantine Empire **2** *often not cap* : intricately involved and often devious

C

¹**c** \\'sē\\ *n, pl* **c's** *or* **cs** \\'sēz\\ *often cap* **1** : the 3d letter of the English alphabet **2** *slang* : a sum of $100 **3** : a grade rating a student's work as fair

²**c** *abbr, often cap* **1** calorie **2** carat **3** Celsius **4** cent **5** centigrade **6** centimeter **7** century **8** chapter **9** circa **10** cocaine **11** copyright

C *symbol* carbon

ca *abbr* circa

Ca *symbol* calcium

CA *abbr* **1** California **2** chartered accountant **3** chief accountant **4** chronological age

cab \\'kab\\ *n* **1** : a light closed horse-drawn carriage **2** : TAXICAB **3** : the covered compartment for the engineer and controls of a locomotive; *also* : a similar compartment (as on a truck)

CAB *abbr* Civil Aeronautics Board

ca·bal \\kə-'bäl, -'bal\\ *n* [F *cabale*, fr. ML *cabbala* cabala, fr. Heb *qabbālāh*, lit., received (lore)] : a secret group of plotters or political conspirators

ca·ba·la \\'ka-bə-lə, kə-'bä-\\ *n, often cap* **1** : a medieval Jewish mysticism marked by belief in creation through emanation and a cipher method of interpreting Scripture **2** : esoteric or mysterious doctrine

ca·bana \\kə-'ban-yə, -'ba-nə\\ *n* : a shelter at a beach or swimming pool

cab·a·ret \\ˌka-bə-'rā\\ *n* : NIGHTCLUB

cab·bage \\'ka-bij\\ *n* [ME *caboche*, fr. OF, head] : a vegetable related to the mustard with a dense head of leaves

cab·bie *or* **cab·by** \\'ka-bē\\ *n, pl* **cabbies** : a driver of a cab

cab·er·net sau·vi·gnon \\ˌka-bər-'nā-sō-vē-'nyōⁿ\\ *n* : a dry red wine made from a single variety of black grape

cab·in \\'ka-bən\\ *n* **1** : a private room on a ship; *also* : a compartment below deck on a boat for passengers or crew **2** : an aircraft or spacecraft compartment for passengers, crew, or cargo **3** : a small simple one-story house

cabin boy *n* : a boy working as servant on a ship

cabin class *n* : a class of accommodations on a passenger ship superior to tourist class and inferior to first class

cabin cruiser *n* : CRUISER 3

cab·i·net \\'kab-nit\\ *n* **1** : a case or cupboard for holding or displaying articles **2** : the advisory council of a head of state (as a president or sovereign)

cab·i·net·mak·er \\-ˌmā-kər\\ *n* : a woodworker who makes fine furniture — **cab·i·net·mak·ing** *n*

cab·i·net·work \\-ˌwərk\\ *n* : the finished work of a cabinetmaker

¹**ca·ble** \\'kā-bəl\\ *n* **1** : a very strong rope, wire, or chain **2** : a bundle of insulated wires usu. twisted around a central core **3** : CABLEGRAM **4** : CABLE TELEVISION

²**cable** *vb* **ca·bled; ca·bling** : to telegraph by cable

cable car *n* : a vehicle moved by an endless cable

ca·ble·gram \\'kā-bəl-ˌgram\\ *n* : a message sent by a submarine telegraph cable

cable television *n* : a system of television reception in which signals from distant stations are sent by cable to the receivers of paying subscribers

cab·o·chon \\'ka-bə-ˌshän\\ *n* : a gem or bead cut in convex form and highly polished but not given facets; *also* : this style of cutting — **cabochon** *adv*

ca·boose \kə-'büs\ *n* : a car usu. at the rear of a freight train for the use of the train crew and railroad workers

cab·ri·o·let \ˌka-brē-ə-'lā\ *n* [F] **1** : a light 2-wheeled one-horse carriage **2** : a convertible coupe

cab·stand \'kab-ˌstand\ *n* : a place where cabs wait for passengers

ca·cao \kə-'kaů, -'kā-ō\ *n, pl* **cacaos** [Sp] : a So. American tree whose seeds (**cacao beans**) are the source of cocoa and chocolate; *also* : its dried fatty seeds

cac·cia·to·re \ˌkä-chə-'tȯr-ē\ *adj* [It] : cooked with tomatoes and herbs ⟨chicken ∼⟩

cache \'kash\ *n* [F] **1** : a hiding place esp. for preserving provisions; *also* : something hidden or stored in a cache — **cache** *vb*

ca·chet \ka-'shā\ *n* [F] **1** : a seal used esp. as a mark of official approval **2** : a feature or quality conferring prestige; *also* : PRESTIGE **3** : a design, inscription, or advertisement printed or stamped on mail

cack·le \'ka-kəl\ *vb* **cack·led; cack·ling 1** : to make the sharp broken cry characteristic of a hen **2** : to laugh or chatter noisily — **cackle** *n* — **cack·ler** *n*

ca·coph·o·ny \ka-'kä-fə-nē\ *n, pl* **-nies** : harsh or discordant sound — **ca·coph·o·nous** \-nəs\ *adj*

cac·tus \'kak-təs\ *n, pl* **cac·ti** \-ˌtī\ *or* **cac·tus·es** *also* **cactus** : any of a large family of drought-resistant flowering plants with succulent stems and with leaves replaced by scales or prickles

cad \'kad\ *n* : a man who deliberately disregards another's feelings — **cad·dish** \'ka-dish\ *adj* — **cad·dish·ly** *adv* — **cad·dish·ness** *n*

ca·dav·er \kə-'da-vər\ *n* : a dead body

ca·dav·er·ous \kə-'da-və-rəs\ *adj* : suggesting a corpse esp. in gauntness or pallor **syn** wasted, emaciated, gaunt — **ca·dav·er·ous·ly** *adv*

cad·die *or* **cad·dy** \'ka-dē\ *n, pl* **caddies** [F *cadet* military cadet] : a person who assists a golfer esp. by carrying the clubs — **caddie** *or* **caddy** *vb*

cad·dy \'ka-dē\ *n, pl* **caddies** [Malay *kati* a unit of weight] : a small box, can, or chest; *esp* : one to keep tea in

ca·dence \'kād-ᵊns\ *n* : the measure or beat of a rhythmical flow : RHYTHM — **ca·denced** \-ᵊnst\ *adj*

ca·den·za \kə-'den-zə\ *n* [It] : a brilliant sometimes improvised passage usu. toward the close of a musical composition

ca·det \kə-'det\ *n* [F, fr. Prov (Gascony) *capdet* chief, fr. L *capitellum*, fr. L *caput* head] **1** : a younger son or brother **2** : a student in a service academy

Ca·dette \kə-'det\ *n* : a member of a Girl Scout program for girls in sixth through ninth grades

cadge \'kaj\ *vb* **cadged; cadg·ing** : SPONGE, BEG — **cadg·er** *n*

cad·mi·um \'kad-mē-əm\ *n* : a bluish white metallic chemical element used esp. in protective platings — see ELEMENT table

cad·re \'ka-ˌdrā, 'kä-, -drē\ *n* [F] **1** : FRAMEWORK **2** : a central unit esp. of trained personnel able to assume control and train others **3** : a group of indoctrinated leaders active in promoting the interests of a revolutionary party

ca·du·ceus \kə-'dü-sē-əs, -'dyü-, -shəs\ *n, pl* **-cei** \-sē-ˌī\ [L] **1** : the staff of a herald; *esp* : a representation of a staff with two entwined snakes and two wings at the top **2** : an insignia bearing a caduceus and symbolizing a physician

cae·cum *var of* CECUM

Cae·sar \'sē-zər\ *n* **1** : any of the Roman emperors succeeding Augustus Caesar — used as a title **2** *often not cap* : a powerful ruler : AUTOCRAT, DICTATOR; *also* : the civil or temporal power

caesarean *also* **caesarian** *var of* CESAREAN

cae·si·um *chiefly Brit var of* CESIUM

cae·su·ra \si-'zhůr-ə\ *n, pl* **-suras** *or* **-su·rae** \-'zhůr-(ˌ)ē\ : a break in the flow of sound usu. in the middle of a line of verse

ca·fé \ka-'fā\ *n* [F, lit., coffee] **1** : RESTAURANT **2** : BARROOM **3** : NIGHTCLUB

ca·fé au lait \(ˌ)ka-ˌfā-ō-'lā\ *n* : coffee with hot milk in about equal parts

caf·e·te·ria \ˌka-fə-'tir-ē-ə\ *n* [AmerSp *cafetería* coffeehouse] : a restaurant in which the customers serve themselves or are served at a counter

caf·feine \ka-'fēn, 'ka-ˌfēn\ *n* : a stimulating alkaloid found esp. in coffee and tea

caf·tan \kaf-'tan, 'kaf-ˌtan\ *n* [Russ *kaftan*, fr. Turk. fr. Per *qaftān*] : an ankle-length garment with long sleeves worn in countries of the eastern Mediterranean

¹cage \'kāj\ *n* **1** : an openwork enclosure for confining an animal **2** : something resembling a cage

²cage *vb* **caged; cag·ing** : to put or keep in or as if in a cage

ca·gey *also* **ca·gy** \'kā-jē\ *adj* **ca·gi·er; -est** : wary of being trapped or deceived : SHREWD — **ca·gi·ly** \-jə-lē\ *adv* — **ca·gi·ness** \-jē-nəs\ *n*

CAGS *abbr* Certificate of Advanced Graduate Study

ca·hoot \kə-'hüt\ *n* : PARTNERSHIP, LEAGUE — usu. used in pl. ⟨officials in ∼s with the underworld⟩

cai·man \'kā-mən; kā-'man, kī-\ *n* : any of several Central and So. American reptiles closely related to alligators and crocodiles

cairn \'karn\ *n* : a heap of stones serving as a memorial or a landmark

cais·son \'kā-ˌsän, 'kās-ᵊn\ *n* **1** : a usu. 2-wheeled vehicle for artillery ammunition **2** : a watertight chamber used in underwater construction work or as a foundation

caisson disease *n* : ²BEND 3

cai·tiff \'kā-təf\ *adj* [ME *caitif*, fr. OF, captive, vile, fr. L *captivus* captive] : being base, cowardly, or despicable — **caitiff** *n*

ca·jole \kə-'jōl\ *vb* **ca·joled; ca·jol·ing** [F *cajoler*] : to persuade or coax esp. with flattery or false promises — **ca·jole·ment** *n* — **ca·jol·ery** \-'jōl-ə-rē\ *n*

Ca·jun \'kā-jən\ *n* : a Louisianian descended from French-speaking immigrants from Acadia (Nova Scotia) — **Cajun** *adj*

¹cake \'kāk\ *n* **1** : a baked or fried breadlike food usu. in a small flat shape **2** : a sweet baked food made from batter or dough usu. containing flour, sugar, or shortening, and a leaven (as baking powder) **3** : a hardened or compacted substance ⟨a ∼ of soap⟩

²cake *vb* **caked; cak·ing 1** : ENCRUST **2** : to form or harden into a cake

cake·walk \'kāk-ˌwȯk\ *n* **1** : a stage dance typically involving a high prance with backward tilt **2** : a one-sided contest or an easy task

cal *abbr* **1** calendar **2** caliber

Cal *abbr* **1** California **2** calorie

cal·a·bash \'ka-lə-ˌbash\ *n* : the fruit of a gourd; *also* : a utensil made from its hard shell

cal·a·boose \'ka-lə-ˌbüs\ *n* [Sp *calabozo* dungeon] : JAIL

ca·la·di·um \kə-'lā-dē-əm\ *n* : any of a genus of tropical American ornamental plants related to the arums

cal·a·mari \ˌkä-lə-'mär-ē\ *n* [It] : squid used as food

cal·a·mine \'ka-lə-ˌmīn\ *n* : a lotion of oxides of zinc and iron

ca·lam·i·ty \kə-'la-mə-tē\ *n, pl* **-ties 1** : great distress or misfortune **2** : an event causing great harm or loss and affliction : DISASTER — **ca·lam·i·tous** \-təs\ *adj* — **ca·lam·i·tous·ly** *adv* — **ca·lam·i·tous·ness** *n*

calc *abbr* calculate; calculated

cal·car·e·ous \kal-'kar-ē-əs\ *adj* : resembling calcium carbonate in hardness; *also* : containing calcium or calcium carbonate

cal·cif·er·ous \kal-'si-fə-rəs\ *adj* : producing or containing calcium carbonate

cal·ci·fy \'kal-sə-ˌfī\ *vb* **-fied; -fy·ing** : to make or become calcareous — **cal·ci·fi·ca·tion** \ˌkal-sə-fə-'kā-shən\ *n*

cal·ci·mine \'kal-sə-ˌmīn\ *n* : a thin water paint used esp. on plastered surfaces — **calcimine** *vb*

cal·cine \kal-'sīn\ *vb* **cal·cined; cal·cin·ing** : to heat to a high temperature but without fusing to drive off volatile matter and often to reduce to powder — **cal·ci·na·tion** \ˌkal-sə-'nā-shən\ *n*

cal·cite \'kal-ˌsīt\ *n* : a crystalline mineral consisting of calcium carbonate — **cal·cit·ic** \kal-'si-tik\ *adj*

cal·ci·um \'kal-sē-əm\ *n* : a silver-white soft metallic chemical element occurring only in combination — see ELEMENT table

calcium carbonate *n* : a substance found in nature as limestone and marble and in plant ashes, bones, and shells

cal·cu·late \'kal-kyə-ˌlāt\ *vb* **-lat·ed; -lat·ing** [L *calculare,* fr. *calculus* small stone, pebble used in reckoning] **1** : to determine by mathematical processes : COMPUTE **2** : to reckon by exercise of practical judgment : ESTIMATE **3** : to design or adapt for a purpose **4** : COUNT, RELY — **cal·cu·la·ble** \-lə-bəl\ *adj* — **cal·cu·la·tor** \-ˌlā-tər\ *n*

cal·cu·lat·ed \-ˌlā-təd\ *adj* **1** : undertaken after estimating the probability of success or failure ⟨a ~ risk⟩ **2** : planned purposefully : DELIBERATE

cal·cu·lat·ing \-ˌlā-tiŋ\ *adj* : marked by shrewd consideration esp. of self-interest — **cal·cu·lat·ing·ly** *adv*

cal·cu·la·tion \ˌkal-kyə-'lā-shən\ *n* **1** : the process or an act of calculating **2** : the result of an act of calculating **3** : studied care; *also* : cold heartless planning to promote self-interest

cal·cu·lus \'kal-kyə-ləs\ *n, pl* **-li** \-ˌlī\ *also* **-lus·es** [L, pebble (used in reckoning)] **1** : a method of computation or calculation in a special notation (as of logic) **2** : a branch of higher mathematics comprising differential and integral calculus **3** : a concretion usu. of mineral salts esp. in hollow organs or ducts

cal·de·ra \kal-'der-ə, kòl-, -'dir-\ *n* [Sp, lit., caldron] : a large crater usu. formed by the collapse of a volcanic cone

cal·dron *var of* CAULDRON

¹**cal·en·dar** \'ka-lən-dər\ *n* **1** : an arrangement of time into days, weeks, months, and years; *also* : a sheet or folder containing such an arrangement for a period **2** : an orderly list

²**calendar** *vb* : to enter in a calendar

¹**cal·en·der** \'ka-lən-dər\ *vb* : to press (as cloth or paper) between rollers or plates so as to make smooth or glossy or to thin into sheets

²**calender** *n* : a machine for calendering

cal·ends \'ka-ləndz, 'kā-\ *n sing or pl* : the first day of the ancient Roman month

ca·len·du·la \kə-'len-jə-lə\ *n* : any of a genus of yellow-flowered herbs related to the daisies

¹**calf** \'kaf, 'kȧf\ *n, pl* **calves** \'kavz, 'kȧvz\ **1** : the young of the domestic cow; *also* : the young of various large mammals (as the elephant or whale) **2** : CALFSKIN

²**calf** *n, pl* **calves** \'kavz, 'kȧvz\ : the fleshy back of the leg below the knee

calf·skin \'kaf-ˌskin, 'kȧf-\ *n* : leather made of the skin of a calf

cal·i·ber *or* **cal·i·bre** \'ka-lə-bər\ *n* [MF *calibre,* fr. It *calibro,* fr. Ar *qālib* shoemaker's last] **1** : degree of mental capacity, excellence, or importance **2** : the diameter of a projectile **3** : the diameter of the bore of a gun

cal·i·brate \'ka-lə-ˌbrāt\ *vb* **-brat·ed; -brat·ing** : to adjust precisely

cal·i·bra·tion \ˌka-lə-'brā-shən\ *n* : a set of graduated marks indicating values or positions — usu. used in pl.

¹**cal·i·co** \'ka-li-ˌkō\ *n, pl* **-coes** *or* **-cos** : printed cotton fabric

²**calico** *adj* **1** : made of calico **2** : having blotched or spotted markings ⟨a ~ cat⟩

Calif *abbr* California

Cal·i·for·nia poppy \ˌka-lə-'fòr-nyə-\ *n* : a widely cultivated herb with usu. yellow or orange flowers that is related to the poppies

cal·i·for·ni·um \ˌka-lə-'fòr-nē-əm\ *n* : an artificially prepared radioactive chemical element — see ELEMENT table

cal·i·per \'ka-lə-pər\ *n* **1** : any of various instruments having two arms, legs, or jaws used esp. to measure diameter or thickness — usu. used in pl. **2** : a device consisting of two plates lined with a frictional material that press against the sides of a rotating wheel or disk in certain brake systems

ca·liph \'kā-ləf, 'ka-\ *n* : a successor of Muhammad as head of Islam — used as a title — **ca·liph·ate** \-lə-ˌfāt, -fət\ *n*

cal·is·then·ics \ˌka-ləs-'the-niks\ *n sing or pl* [Gk *kalos* beautiful + *sthenos* strength] : bodily exercises usu. done without apparatus — **cal·is·then·ic** *adj*

calk \'kòk\ *var of* CAULK

¹**call** \'kòl\ *vb* **1** : SHOUT, CRY; *also* : to utter a characteristic note or cry **2** : to utter in a loud clear voice **3** : to announce authoritatively **4** : SUMMON **5** : to make a request or demand ⟨~ for an investigation⟩ **6** : to halt (as a baseball game) because of unsuitable conditions **7** : to demand payment of (a loan); *also* : to demand surrender of (as a bond) for redemption **8** : to get or try to get in communication by telephone **9** : to make a brief visit **10** : to speak of or address by name : give a name to **11** : to estimate or consider for practical purposes ⟨~ it ten miles⟩ **12** : to temporarily transfer control of computer processing to (as a subroutine or procedure) — **call·er** *n*

²**call** *n* **1** : SHOUT **2** : the cry of an animal (as a bird) **3** : a request or a command to come or assemble : INVITATION, SUMMONS **4** : DEMAND, CLAIM; *also* : REQUEST **5** : a brief usu. formal visit **6** : an act of calling on the telephone **7** : DECISION ⟨a tough ~⟩ **8** : a temporary transfer of control of computer processing to a particular set of instructions

cal·la lily \'ka-lə-\ *n* : a plant whose flowers form a fleshy yellow spike surrounded by a lilylike usu. white leaf

call·back \'kòl-ˌbak\ *n* : a calling back; *esp* : RECALL 5

call–board \-ˌbòrd\ *n* : a board for posting notices (as of rehearsal calls)

call down *vb* : REPRIMAND

call girl *n* : a prostitute with whom appointments are made by phone

cal·lig·ra·phy \kə-'li-grə-fē\ *n* : artistic or elegant handwriting; *also* : the art of producing such writing — **cal·lig·ra·pher** \-fər\ *n*

call–in \'kòl-ˌin\ *adj* : allowing listeners to engage in broadcast telephone conversations ⟨a ~ show⟩

call in *vb* **1** : to order to return or be returned **2** : to summon to one's aid **3** : to report by telephone

call·ing \'kò-liŋ\ *n* **1** : a strong inner impulse toward a particular course of action **2** : the activity in which one customarily engages as an occupation

cal·li·ope \kə-'lī-ə-(ˌ)pē, 'ka-lē-ˌōp\ *n* [fr. *Calliope,* chief of the Muses, fr. L, fr. Gk *Kalliopē*] : a keyboard musical instrument similar to an organ and made up of a series of whistles

cal·li·per *chiefly Brit var of* CALIPER

call number *n* : a combination of characters assigned to a library book to indicate its place on a shelf

call off *vb* : CANCEL

cal·los·i·ty \ka-'lä-sə-tē\ *n, pl* **-ties** **1** : the quality or state of being callous **2** : CALLUS 1

¹**cal·lous** \'ka-ləs\ *adj* **1** : being thickened and hardened ⟨~ skin⟩ **2** : feeling no emotion or sympathy — **cal·lous·ly** *adv* — **cal·lous·ness** *n*

²**callous** *vb* : to make callous

cal·low \'ka-lō\ *adj* [ME *calu* bald, fr. OE] : lacking adult sophistication ⟨a ~ youth⟩ — **cal·low·ness** *n*

call–up \'kò-ˌləp\ *n* : an order to report for active military service

call up *vb* : to summon for active military duty

cal·lus \'ka-ləs\ *n* **1** : a callous area on skin or bark **2** : tissue that is converted into bone in the healing of a bone fracture — **callus** *vb*

¹calm \'käm, 'kälm\ *n* **1** : a period or a condition free from storms, high winds, or rough water **2** : complete or almost complete absence of wind **3** : a state of tranquillity

²calm *vb* : to make or become calm

³calm *adj* : marked by calm : STILL, UNRUFFLED — **calm·ly** *adv* — **calm·ness** *n*

cal·o·mel \'ka-lə-məl, -₁mel\ *n* : a chloride of mercury used esp. as a fungicide

ca·lor·ic \kə-'lȯ-rik\ *adj* **1** : of or relating to heat **2** : of or relating to calories

cal·o·rie *also* **cal·o·ry** \'ka-lə-rē\ *n, pl* **-ries** : a unit for measuring heat; *esp* : one for measuring the value of foods for producing heat and energy in the human body equivalent to the amount of heat required to raise the temperature of one kilogram of water one degree Celsius

cal·o·rim·e·ter \₁ka-lə-'ri-mə-tər\ *n* : an apparatus for measuring quantities of heat — **cal·o·rim·e·try** \-trē\ *n*

cal·u·met \'kal-yə-₁met, -mət\ *n* : an American Indian ceremonial pipe

ca·lum·ni·ate \kə-'ləm-nē-₁āt\ *vb* **-at·ed; -at·ing** : to make false and malicious statements about **syn** defame, malign, libel, slander, traduce — **ca·lum·ni·a·tion** \-₁ləm-nē-'ā-shən\ *n* — **ca·lum·ni·a·tor** \-'ləm-nē-₁ā-tər\ *n*

cal·um·ny \'ka-ləm-nē\ *n, pl* **-nies** : false and malicious accusation — **ca·lum·ni·ous** \kə-'ləm-nē-əs\ *adj*

calve \'kav, 'käv\ *vb* **calved; calv·ing** : to give birth to a calf

calves *pl of* CALF

Cal·vin·ism \'kal-və-₁ni-zəm\ *n* : the theological system of John Calvin and his followers — **Cal·vin·ist** \-nist\ *n or adj* — **Cal·vin·is·tic** \₁kal-və-'nis-tik\ *adj*

ca·lyp·so \kə-'lip-sō\ *n, pl* **-sos** : a style of music originating in the British West Indies and having lyrics that usu. satirize local personalities and events

ca·lyx \'kā-liks, 'ka-\ *n, pl* **ca·lyx·es** *or* **ca·ly·ces** \'kā-lə-₁sēz, 'ka-\ : the usu. green or leaflike outer part of a flower consisting of sepals

cam \'kam\ *n* : a rotating or sliding piece in a mechanical linkage by which rotary motion is transformed into linear motion or vice versa

ca·ma·ra·de·rie \₁käm-'rä-də-rē, ₁kam-, -'ra-\ *n* [F] : friendly feeling and goodwill among comrades

cam·bi·um \'kam-bē-əm\ *n, pl* **-bi·ums** *or* **-bia** \-bē-ə\ : a thin cellular layer between xylem and phloem of most higher plants from which new tissues develop — **cam·bi·al** \-əl\ *adj*

Cam·bo·di·an \kam-'bō-dē-ən\ *n* : a native or inhabitant of Cambodia — **Cambodian** *adj*

Cam·bri·an \'kam-brē-ən, 'käm-\ *adj* : of, relating to, or being the earliest period of the Paleozoic era — **Cambrian** *n*

cam·bric \'käm-brik\ *n* : a fine thin white linen or cotton fabric

cam·cord·er \'kam-₁kȯr-dər\ *n* : a small portable video camera and recorder

came *past of* COME

cam·el \'ka-məl\ *n* : either of two large hoofed cud-chewing mammals used esp. in desert regions of Asia and Africa for carrying and riding

camel hair *also* **camel's hair** *n* **1** : the hair of a camel or a substitute for it **2** : cloth made of camel hair or of camel hair and wool

ca·mel·lia \kə-'mēl-yə\ *n* : any of a genus of shrubs and trees related to the tea plant and grown in warm regions and greenhouses for their showy roselike flowers

Cam·em·bert \'ka-məm-₁ber\ *n* : a soft cheese with a grayish rind and yellow interior

cam·eo \'ka-mē-₁ō\ *n, pl* **-eos 1** : a gem carved in relief; *also* : a small medallion with a profiled head in relief **2** : a brief appearance esp. by a well-known actor in a play or movie

cam·era \'kam-rə, 'ka-mər-ə\ *n* : a device with a light-proof chamber fitted with a lens through which the image of an object is projected onto a surface for recording (as on film) or for conversion into electrical signals (as for television broadcast) — **cam·era·man** \-₁man, -mən\ *n* — **cam·era·wom·an** *n*

Cam·er·oo·ni·an \₁ka-mə-'rü-nē-ən\ *n* : a native or inhabitant of the Republic of Cameroon or the Cameroons region — **Cameroonian** *adj*

cam·i·sole \'ka-mə-₁sōl\ *n* : a short sleeveless garment for women

camomile *var of* CHAMOMILE

cam·ou·flage \'ka-mə-₁fläzh, -₁fläj\ *n* [F] **1** : the disguising of military equipment with paint, nets, or foliage; *also* : the disguise itself **2** : deceptive behavior — **camouflage** *vb*

¹camp \'kamp\ *n* **1** : a place where tents or buildings are erected for usu. temporary shelter **2** : a collection of tents or other shelters **3** : a body of persons encamped — **camp·ground** \-₁graund\ *n* — **camp·site** \-₁sīt\ *n*

²camp *vb* **1** : to make or occupy a camp **2** : to live in a camp or outdoors

³camp *n* **1** : exaggerated effeminate mannerisms **2** : something so outrageous, inappropriate, or theatrical as to be considered amusing — **camp** *adj* — **camp·i·ly** \'kam-pə-lē\ *adv* — **camp·i·ness** \-pē-nəs\ *n* — **campy** \-pē\ *adj*

⁴camp *vb* : to engage in camp : exhibit the qualities of camp

cam·paign \kam-'pān\ *n* **1** : a series of military operations forming one distinct stage in a war **2** : a series of activities designed to bring about a particular result ⟨advertising ∼⟩ — **campaign** *vb* — **cam·paign·er** *n*

cam·pa·ni·le \₁kam-pə-'nē-lē\ *n, pl* **-ni·les** *or* **-ni·li** \-'nē-lē\ : a usu. freestanding bell tower

cam·pa·nol·o·gy \₁kam-pə-'nä-lə-jē\ *n* : the art of bell ringing — **cam·pa·nol·o·gist** \-jist\ *n*

camp·er \'kam-pər\ *n* **1** : one that camps **2** : a portable dwelling (as a specially equipped vehicle) for use during casual travel and camping

Camp Fire Girl *n* : a member of a national organization of girls from ages 5 to 18

camp follower *n* **1** : a civilian (as a prostitute) who follows a military unit to attend or exploit its personnel **2** : a follower of a group who is not an adherent; *esp* : a politician who joins a movement solely for personal gain

cam·phor \'kam-fər\ *n* : a gummy volatile aromatic compound obtained from an evergreen Asian tree (**camphor tree**) and used esp. in medicine

camp meeting *n* : a series of evangelistic meetings usu. held outdoors

camp·o·ree \₁kam-pə-'rē\ *n* : a gathering of Boy Scouts or Girl Scouts from a given geographic area

cam·pus \'kam-pəs\ *n* [L, plain] : the grounds and buildings of a college or school; *also* : grounds resembling a campus ⟨hospital ∼⟩

cam·shaft \'kam-₁shaft\ *n* : a shaft to which a cam is fastened

¹can \kən, 'kan\ *vb, past* **could** \kəd, 'kud\; *pres sing & pl* **can 1** : be able to **2** : may perhaps ⟨∼ he still be alive⟩ **3** : be permitted by conscience or feeling to ⟨you ∼ hardly blame her⟩ **4** : have permission to ⟨you ∼ go now⟩

²can \'kan\ *n* **1** : a usu. cylindrical container or receptacle ⟨garbage ∼⟩ ⟨coffee ∼⟩ **2** : JAIL **3** : TOILET

³can \'kan\ *vb* **canned; can·ning 1** : to put in a can : preserve by sealing in airtight cans or jars **2** *slang* : to discharge from employment **3** *slang* : to put a stop or an end to — **can·ner** *n*

Can *or* **Canad** *abbr* Canada; Canadian

Can·a·da goose \\'ka-nə-də-\ *n* : a common wild goose of No. America

Ca·na·di·an \kə-'nā-dē-ən\ *n* : a native or inhabitant of Canada — **Canadian** *adj*

ca·naille \kə-'nī, -'nāl\ *n* [F, fr. It *canaglia*, fr. *cane* dog] : RABBLE, RIFFRAFF

ca·nal \kə-'nal\ *n* **1** : a tubular passage in the body : DUCT **2** : an artificial waterway (as for boats or irrigation)

can·a·lize \'kan-ᵊl-ˌīz\ *vb* **-lized; -liz·ing 1** : to provide with a canal or make into or like a channel **2** : to provide with an outlet; *esp* : to direct into preferred channels — **ca·nal·i·za·tion** \ˌkan-ᵊl-ə-'zā-shən\ *n*

can·a·pé \'ka-nə-pē, -ˌpā\ *n* [F, lit., sofa, fr. ML *canopeum, canapeum* mosquito net] : a piece of bread or toast or a cracker topped with a savory food

ca·nard \kə-'närd\ *n* : a false or unfounded report or story

ca·nary \kə-'ner-ē\ *n, pl* **ca·nar·ies** [fr. the *Canary* islands] **1** : a usu. sweet wine similar to Madeira **2** : a usu. yellow or greenish finch often kept in a cage as a pet

ca·nas·ta \kə-'nas-tə\ *n* [Sp, lit., basket] : rummy played with two full decks of cards plus four jokers

canc *abbr* canceled

can·can \'kan-ˌkan\ *n* : a woman's dance of French origin characterized by high kicking

¹can·cel \'kan-səl\ *vb* **-celed** *or* **-celled; -cel·ing** *or* **-cel·ling** [ME *cancellen*, fr. MF *canceller*, fr. LL *cancellare*, fr. L, to make like a lattice, fr. *cancelli* lattice] **1** : to destroy the force or validity of : ANNUL **2** : to match in force or effect : OFFSET **3** : to cross out : DELETE **4** : to remove (a common divisor) from a numerator and denominator; *also* : to remove (equivalents) on opposite sides of an equation or account **5** : to mark (a postage stamp or check) so that it cannot be reused **6** : to neutralize each other's strength or effect — **can·cel·la·tion** \ˌkan-sə-'lā-shən\ *n* — **can·cel·er** *or* **can·cel·ler** *n*

²cancel *n* **1** : CANCELLATION **2** : a deleted part

can·cer \'kan-sər\ *n* [L, lit., crab] **1** *cap* : a zodiacal constellation between Gemini and Leo usu. pictured as a crab **2** *cap* : the 4th sign of the zodiac in astrology; *also* : one born under this sign **3** : a malignant tumor that tends to spread in the body **4** : a malignant evil that spreads destructively — **can·cer·ous** \-sə-rəs\ *adj* — **can·cer·ous·ly** *adv*

can·de·la·bra \ˌkan-də-'lä-brə, -'la-\ *n* : an ornamental branched candlestick or lamp with several lights

candelabra

can·de·la·brum \-brəm\ *n, pl* **-bra** *also* **-brums** : CANDELABRA

can·did \'kan-dəd\ *adj* **1** : FRANK, STRAIGHTFORWARD **2** : relating to photography of subjects acting naturally or spontaneously without being posed — **can·did·ly** *adv* — **can·did·ness** *n*

can·di·da·cy \'kan-də-də-sē\ *n, pl* **-cies** : the state of being a candidate

can·di·date \'kan-də-ˌdāt, 'ka-nə-, -dət\ *n* [L *candidatus*, fr. *candidatus* clothed in white, fr. *candidus* white; fr. the white toga worn by office seekers in ancient Rome] : one who seeks or is proposed for an office, honor, or membership

can·di·da·ture \'kan-də-də-ˌchu̇r, 'ka-nə\ *n, chiefly Brit* : CANDIDACY

can·died \'kan-dēd\ *adj* : preserved in or encrusted with sugar

¹can·dle \'kan-dᵊl\ *n* : a usu. slender mass of tallow or wax molded around a wick that is burned to give light

²candle *vb* **can·dled; can·dling** : to examine (as eggs) by holding between the eye and a light — **can·dler** *n*

can·dle·light \'kan-dᵊl-līt\ *n* **1** : the light of a candle; *also* : any soft artificial light **2** : the time when candles are lit : TWILIGHT

can·dle·lit \-ˌlit\ *adj* : illuminated by candlelight ⟨a ~ dinner⟩

Can·dle·mas \'kan-dᵊl-məs\ *n* : February 2 observed as a church festival in commemoration of the presentation of Christ in the temple

can·dle·stick \-ˌstik\ *n* : a holder with a socket for a candle

can·dle·wick \-ˌwik\ *n* : a soft cotton yarn; *also* : embroidery made with this yarn usu. in tufts

can·dor \'kan-dər\ *n* : FRANKNESS, OUTSPOKENNESS

can·dour *chiefly Brit var of* CANDOR

C and W *abbr* country and western

¹can·dy \'kan-dē\ *n, pl* **candies** : a confection made from sugar often with flavoring and filling

²candy *vb* **can·died; can·dy·ing** : to encrust in sugar often by cooking in a syrup

candy strip·er \-'strī-pər\ *n* : a teenage volunteer worker at a hospital

¹cane \'kān\ *n* **1** : a slender hollow or pithy stem (as of a reed or bramble) **2** : a tall woody grass or reed (as sugarcane) **3** : a walking stick; *also* : a rod for flogging

²cane *vb* **caned; can·ing 1** : to beat with a cane **2** : to weave or make with cane — **can·er** *n*

cane·brake \'kān-ˌbrāk\ *n* : a thicket of cane

¹ca·nine \'kā-ˌnīn\ *n* **1** : a pointed tooth between the outer incisor and the first premolar **2** : a canine mammal (as a domestic dog)

²canine *adj* [L *caninus*, fr. *canis* dog] : of or relating to dogs or to the family to which they belong

can·is·ter \'ka-nə-stər\ *n* **1** : an often cylindrical container

can·ker \'kaŋ-kər\ *n* : a spreading sore that eats into tissue — **can·ker·ous** \-kə-rəs\ *adj*

can·ker·worm \-ˌwərm\ *n* : either of two moths and esp. their larvae that are pests of fruit and shade trees

can·na \'ka-nə\ *n* : any of a genus of tropical herbs with large leaves and racemes of bright-colored flowers

can·na·bis \'ka-nə-bəs\ *n* : any of the psychoactive preparations (as marijuana) or chemicals (as THC) derived from hemp; *also* : HEMP

canned \'kand\ *adj* : prepared in standardized form for general use or wide distribution

can·nery \'ka-nə-rē\ *n, pl* **-ner·ies** : a factory for the canning of foods

can·ni·bal \'ka-nə-bəl\ *n* [NL *Canibalis* a member of a Caribbean Indian people, fr. Sp *Caníbal*] : one that eats the flesh of its own kind — **can·ni·bal·ism** \-bə-ˌli-zəm\ *n* — **can·ni·bal·is·tic** \-bə-'lis-tik\ *adj*

can·ni·bal·ize \'ka-nə-bə-ˌlīz\ *vb* **-ized; -iz·ing 1** : to take usable parts from (as an inoperative machine) to construct or repair another machine **2** : to practice cannibalism

can·non \'ka-nən\ *n, pl* **cannons** *or* **cannon** [MF *canon*, fr. It *cannone*, lit., large tube, fr. *canna* reed, tube, fr. L, cane, reed] : a large heavy gun; *esp* : one mounted on a carriage

can·non·ade \ˌka-nə-'nād\ *n* : a heavy fire of artillery — **cannonade** *vb*

can·non·ball \'ka-nən-ˌbȯl\ *n* : a usu. round solid missile for a cannon

can·non·eer \ˌka-nə-'nir\ *n* : an artillery gunner

can·not \'ka-ˌnät; kə-'nät\ : can not — **cannot but** : to be unable to do otherwise than

can·nu·la \'kan-yə-lə\ *n, pl* **-las** *or* **-lae** \-ˌlē\ : a small tube for insertion into a body cavity or into a duct or vessel

can·ny \'ka-nē\ *adj* **can·ni·er; -est** : PRUDENT, SHREWD — **can·ni·ly** \'kan-əl-ē\ *adv* — **can·ni·ness** \'ka-nē-nəs\ *n*

ca·noe \kə-'nü\ *n* : a light narrow boat with sharp ends and curved sides that is usu. propelled by paddles — **canoe** *vb* — **ca·noe·ist** *n*

canoe

ca·no·la \kə-'nō-lə\ *n* : a rape plant producing seeds that are low in a toxic acid and yield an edible oil (**ca·nola oil**) high in monounsaturated fatty acids; *also* : this oil

¹can·on \'ka-nən\ *n* **1** : a regulation decreed by a church council; *also* : a provision of canon law **2** : an official or authoritative list (as of the saints or the books of the Bible) **3** : an accepted principle ⟨the ∼s of good taste⟩

²canon *n* : a clergyman on the staff of a cathedral

ca·non·i·cal \kə-'nä-ni-kəl\ *adj* **1** : of, relating to, or forming a canon **2** : conforming to a general rule or acceptable procedure : ORTHODOX **3** : of or relating to a clergyman who is a canon — **ca·non·i·cal·ly** \-k(ə-)lē\ *adv*

can·on·ize \'ka-nə-ˌnīz\ *vb* **can·on·ized** \-ˌnīzd\; **can·on·iz·ing 1** : to declare (a deceased person) an officially recognized saint **2** : GLORIFY, EXALT — **can·on·i·za·tion** \ˌka-nə-nə-'zā-shən\ *n*

canon law *n* : the law governing a church

can·o·py \'ka-nə-pē\ *n, pl* **-pies** [ME *canope*, fr. ML *canopeum* mosquito net, fr. L *conopeum*, fr. Gk *kōnōpion*, fr. *kōnōps* mosquito] **1** : an overhanging cover, shelter, or shade **2** : a transparent cover for an airplane cockpit **3** : the fabric part of a parachute — **canopy** *vb*

¹cant \'kant\ *vb* : to give a slant to

²cant *n* **1** : an oblique or slanting surface **2** : TILT, SLANT

³cant *vb* **1** : to beg in a whining manner **2** : to talk hypocritically

⁴cant *n* **1** : the special idiom of a profession or trade : JARGON **2** : insincere speech; *esp* : insincerely pious words or statements

Cant *abbr* Canticle of Canticles

can·ta·bi·le \kän-'tä-bə-ˌlā\ *adv or adj* [It] : in a singing manner — used as a direction in music

can·ta·loupe *also* **can·te·loupe** \'kant-əl-ˌōp\ *n* : MUSKMELON; *esp* : one with orange flesh and rough skin

can·tan·ker·ous \kan-'taŋ-kə-rəs\ *adj* : ILL-NATURED, QUARRELSOME — **can·tan·ker·ous·ly** *adv* — **can·tan·ker·ous·ness** *n*

can·ta·ta \kən-'tä-tə\ *n* [It] : a choral composition usu. sung to instrumental accompaniment

can·teen \kan-'tēn\ *n* [F *cantine* bottle case, canteen (store), fr. It *cantina* wine cellar] **1** : a flask for carrying liquids **2** : a place of recreation and entertainment for military personnel **3** : a small cafeteria or counter at which snacks are served

can·ter \'kan-tər\ *n* : a horse's 3-beat gait resembling but smoother and slower than a gallop — **canter** *vb*

Can·ter·bury bell \'kant-ər-ˌber-ē-\ *n* : any of several plants related to the bluebell that are cultivated for their showy flowers

can·ti·cle \'kan-ti-kəl\ *n* : SONG; *esp* : any of several liturgical songs taken from the Bible

Canticle of Canticles *n* : SONG OF SONGS

¹can·ti·le·ver \'kant-əl-ˌē-vər\ *n* : a projecting beam or structure supported only at one end; *also* : either of a pair of such structures projecting toward each other so that when joined they form a bridge

²cantilever *vb* **1** : to support by a cantilever ⟨a ∼ed shelf⟩ **2** : to build as a cantilever **3** : to project as a cantilever

can·tle \'kant-əl\ *n* : the upwardly projecting rear part of a saddle

can·to \'kan-ˌtō\ *n, pl* **cantos** [It, fr. L *cantus* song] : one of the major divisions of a long poem

can·ton \'kant-ᵊn, 'kan-ˌtän\ *n* : a small territorial division of a country; *esp* : one of the political divisions of Switzerland — **can·ton·al** \'kant-ᵊn-əl, kan-'tän-ᵊl\ *adj*

can·ton·ment \kan-'tōn-mənt, -'tän-\ *n* : usu. temporary quarters for troops

can·tor \'kan-tər\ *n* **1** : a choir leader **2** : a synagogue official who sings liturgical music and leads the congregation in prayer

can·vas *also* **can·vass** \'kan-vəs\ *n* **1** : a strong cloth formerly much used for making tents and sails **2** : a set of sails **3** : a group of tents **4** : a piece of cloth prepared as a surface to receive oil paint; *also* : an oil painting **5** : the canvas-covered floor of a boxing or wrestling ring

can·vas·back \'kan-vəs-ˌbak\ *n* : a No. American wild duck with red head and gray back

¹can·vass *also* **can·vas** \'kan-vəs\ *vb* : to go through (a district) or to (persons) to solicit votes or orders for goods or to determine public opinion or sentiment — **can·vass·er** *n*

²canvass *n* : an act or instance of canvassing

can·yon \'kan-yən\ *n* : a deep narrow valley with high steep sides

¹cap \'kap\ *n* **1** : a covering for the head esp. with a visor and no brim; *also* : something resembling such a covering **2** : a container holding an explosive charge **3** : an upper limit (as on expenditures)

²cap *vb* **capped; cap·ping 1** : to provide or protect with a cap **2** : to form a cap over : CROWN **3** : OUTDO, SURPASS **4** : CLIMAX

³cap *abbr* **1** capacity **2** capital **3** capitalize; capitalized

CAP *abbr* Civil Air Patrol

ca·pa·ble \'kā-pə-bəl\ *adj* : having ability, capacity, or power to do something : ABLE, COMPETENT — **ca·pa·bil·i·ty** \ˌkā-pə-'bi-lə-tē\ *n* — **ca·pa·bly** *adv*

ca·pa·cious \kə-'pā-shəs\ *adj* : able to contain much — **ca·pa·cious·ly** *adv* — **ca·pa·cious·ness** *n*

ca·pac·i·tance \kə-'pa-sə-təns\ *n* : the property of an electric nonconductor that permits the storage of energy

ca·pac·i·tor \kə-'pa-sə-tər\ *n* : an electronic circuit device for temporary storage of electrical energy

¹ca·pac·i·ty \kə-'pa-sə-tē\ *n, pl* **-ties 1** : legal qualification or fitness **2** : the ability to contain, receive, or accommodate **3** : the maximum amount or number that can be contained — see METRIC SYSTEM table, WEIGHT table **4** : ABILITY **5** : position or character assigned or assumed

²capacity *adj* : equaling maximum capacity ⟨a ∼ crowd⟩

cap-a-pie *or* **cap-à-pie** \ˌka-pə-'pē\ *adv* [MF] : from head to foot : at all points

ca·par·i·son \kə-'par-ə-sən\ *n* **1** : an ornamental covering for a horse **2** : TRAPPINGS, ADORNMENT — **caparison** *vb*

¹cape \'kāp\ *n* **1** : a point of land jutting out into water **2** *often cap* : CAPE COD COTTAGE

²cape *n* : a sleeveless garment hanging from the neck over the shoulders

Cape Cod cottage \\'kāp-'käd-\ *n* : a compact rectangular dwelling of one or one-and-a-half stories usu. with a steep gable roof

¹ca·per \\'kā-pər\ *n* : the flower bud or young berry of a Mediterranean shrub pickled for use as a relish; *also* : this shrub

²caper *vb* **ca·pered; ca·per·ing** : to leap about in a playful manner

³caper *n* **1** : a froliclsome leap **2** : a capricious escapade **3** : an illegal or questionable act

cape·skin \\'kāp-ˌskin\ *n* : a light flexible leather made from sheepskins

Cape Verd·ean \-'vər-dē-ən\ *n* : a native or inhabitant of the Republic of Cape Verde

cap·ful \\'kap-ˌfül\ *n, pl* **cap·fuls** *also* **caps·ful** \\'kaps-\ : as much as a cap will hold

cap·il·lar·i·ty \ˌka-pə-'lar-ə-tē\ *n, pl* **-ties** : the action by which the surface of a liquid where it is in contact with a solid (as in a slender tube) is raised or lowered depending on the relative attraction of the molecules of the liquid for each other and for those of the solid

¹cap·il·lary \\'ka-pə-ˌler-ē\ *adj* **1** : resembling a hair **2** : having a very small bore ⟨~ tube⟩ **3** : of or relating to capillaries or to capillarity

²capillary *n, pl* **-lar·ies** : any of the tiny thin-walled blood vessels that carry blood between the smallest arteries and their corresponding veins

¹cap·i·tal \\'ka-pət-ᵊl\ *n* : the top part or piece of an architectural column

²capital *adj* **1** : conforming to the series A, B, C rather than a, b, c ⟨~ letters⟩ ⟨~ G⟩ **2** : punishable by death ⟨a ~ crime⟩ **3** : most serious ⟨a ~ error⟩ **4** : first in importance or position : CHIEF; *also* : being the seat of government ⟨the ~ city⟩ **5** : of or relating to capital ⟨~ expenditures⟩; *esp* : relating to or being assets that add to the long-term net worth of a corporation **6** : FIRST-RATE, EXCELLENT

³capital *n* **1** : accumulated wealth esp. as used to produce more wealth **2** : the total face value of shares of stock issued by a company **3** : persons holding capital **4** : ADVANTAGE, GAIN **5** : a letter larger than the ordinary small letter and often different in form **6** : the capital city of a state or country; *also* : a city preeminent in some activity ⟨the fashion ~⟩

capital gain *n* : the increase in value of an asset (as stock or real estate) between the time it is bought and the time it is sold

capital goods *n pl* : machinery, tools, factories, and commodities used in the production of goods

cap·i·tal·ism \\'ka-pət-ᵊl-ˌi-zəm\ *n* : an economic system characterized by private or corporate ownership of capital goods and by prices, production, and distribution of goods that are determined mainly by competition in a free market

¹cap·i·tal·ist \-ist\ *n* **1** : a person who has capital esp. invested in business **2** : a person of great wealth : PLUTOCRAT **3** : a believer in capitalism

²capitalist *or* **cap·i·tal·is·tic** \ˌka-pət-ᵊl-'is-tik\ *adj* **1** : owning capital **2** : practicing or advocating capitalism **3** : marked by capitalism — **cap·i·tal·is·ti·cal·ly** \-ti-k(ə-)lē\ *adv*

cap·i·tal·iza·tion \ˌka-pət-ᵊl-ə-'zā-shən\ *n* **1** : the act or process of capitalizing **2** : the total amount of money used as capital in a business

cap·i·tal·ize \\'ka-pət-ᵊl-ˌīz\ *vb* **-ized; -iz·ing 1** : to write or print with an initial capital or in capitals **2** : to convert into or use as capital **3** : to supply capital for **4** : to gain by turning something to advantage : PROFIT

cap·i·tal·ly \\'ka-pət-ᵊl-ē\ *adv* : ADMIRABLY, EXCELLENTLY

cap·i·ta·tion \ˌka-pə-'tā-shən\ *n* : a direct uniform tax levied on each person

cap·i·tol \\'ka-pət-ᵊl\ *n* : the building in which a legislature holds its sessions

ca·pit·u·late \kə-'pi-chə-ˌlāt\ *vb* **-lat·ed; -lat·ing 1** : to surrender esp. on conditions agreed upon **2** : to cease

resisting : ACQUIESCE **syn** submit, yield, succumb, cave, defer — **ca·pit·u·la·tion** \-ˌpi-chə-'lā-shən\ *n*

ca·pon \\'kā-ˌpän, -pən\ *n* : a castrated male chicken

cap·puc·ci·no \ˌka-pə-'chē-nō, ˌkä-\ *n* [It, lit., Capuchin; fr. the likeness of its color to that of a Capuchin's habit] : espresso mixed with foamy hot milk or cream and often flavored with cinnamon

ca·pric·cio \kə-'prē-chē-ˌō, -chō\ *n, pl* **-cios** : an instrumental piece in free form usu. lively in tempo and brilliant in style

ca·price \kə-'prēs\ *n* [F, fr. It *capriccio*] **1** : a sudden whim or fancy **2** : an inclination to do things impulsively **3** : CAPRICCIO — **ca·pri·cious** \-'pri-shəs\ *adj* — **ca·pri·cious·ly** *adv* — **ca·pri·cious·ness** *n*

Cap·ri·corn \\'ka-pri-ˌkȯrn\ *n* **1** : a zodiacal constellation between Sagittarius and Aquarius usu. pictured as a goat **2** : the 10th sign of the zodiac in astrology; *also* : one born under this sign

ca·ri·ole \\'ka-prē-ˌōl\ *n* : ³CAPER 1; *also* : an upward leap of a horse with a backward kick at the height of the leap — **capriole** *vb*

caps *abbr* **1** capitals **2** capsule

cap·si·cum \\'kap-si-kəm\ *n* : PEPPER 2

cap·size \\'kap-ˌsīz, kap-'sīz\ *vb* **cap·sized; cap·siz·ing** : UPSET, OVERTURN

cap·stan \\'kap-stən, -ˌstan\ *n* **1** : a machine for moving or raising heavy weights that consists of a vertical drum which can be rotated and around which cable is turned **2** : a rotating shaft that drives recorder tape

cap·su·lar \\'kap-sə-lər\ *adj* : of, relating to, or resembling a capsule

cap·su·lat·ed \-ˌlā-təd\ *adj* : enclosed in a capsule

¹cap·sule \\'kap-səl, -sül\ *n* **1** : a membrane or sac enclosing a body part (as of a joint) **2** : a case bearing spores or seeds **3** : a shell usu. of gelatin that is used for packaging something (as a drug); *also* : such a shell together with its contents **4** : a small pressurized compartment or vehicle (as for space flight)

²capsule *adj* **1** : very brief **2** : very compact

Capt *abbr* captain

¹cap·tain \\'kap-tən\ *n* **1** : a commander of a body of troops **2** : a commissioned officer in the army, air force, or marine corps ranking next below a major **3** : an officer in charge of a ship **4** : a commissioned officer in the navy ranking next below a rear admiral or a commodore **5** : a leader of a side or team **6** : a dominant figure — **cap·tain·cy** *n*

²captain *vb* : to be captain of : LEAD

cap·tion \\'kap-shən\ *n* **1** : a heading esp. of an article or document : TITLE **2** : the explanatory matter accompanying an illustration **3** : a motion-picture subtitle — **cap·tion** *vb*

cap·tious \\'kap-shəs\ *adj* : marked by an inclination to find fault — **cap·tious·ly** *adv* — **cap·tious·ness** *n*

cap·ti·vate \\'kap-tə-ˌvāt\ *vb* **-vat·ed; -vat·ing** : to attract and hold irresistibly by some special charm or art — **cap·ti·va·tion** \ˌkap-tə-'vā-shən\ *n* — **cap·ti·va·tor** \\'kap-tə-ˌvā-tər\ *n*

cap·tive \\'kap-tiv\ *adj* **1** : made prisoner esp. in war **2** : kept within bounds : CONFINED **3** : held under control — **captive** *n* — **cap·tiv·i·ty** \kap-'ti-və-tē\ *n*

cap·tor \\'kap-tər\ *n* : one that captures

¹cap·ture \\'kap-chər\ *n* **1** : the act of capturing **2** : one that has been captured

²capture *vb* **cap·tured; cap·tur·ing 1** : to take captive : WIN, GAIN **2** : to preserve in a relatively permanent form

Ca·pu·chin \\'ka-pyə-shən\ *n* : a member of an austere branch of the order of St. Francis of Assisi engaged in missionary work and preaching

car \\'kär\ *n* **1** : a vehicle moving on wheels **2** : the compartment of an elevator **3** : the part of a balloon or airship that carries passengers or equipment

car·a·cole \\'kar-ə-ˌkōl\ *n* : a half turn to right or left executed by a mounted horse — **caracole** *vb*

car·a·cul \'kar-ə-ˌkəl\ *n* : the pelt of a karakul lamb after the curl begins to loosen

ca·rafe \kə-'raf, -'räf\ *n* : a bottle with a flaring lip used esp. to hold wine

car·am·bo·la \ˌkar-əm-'bō-lə\ *n* **1** : a five-angled green to yellow edible tropical fruit of star-shaped cross section **2** : a tropical tree widely cultivated for carambolas

car·a·mel \'kar-ə-məl, 'kär-məl\ *n* **1** : an amorphous substance obtained by heating sugar and used for flavoring and coloring **2** : a firm chewy candy

car·a·pace \'kar-ə-ˌpās\ *n* : a protective case or shell on the back of some animals (as turtles or crabs)

¹**carat** *var of* KARAT

²**car·at** \'kar-ət\ *n* : a unit of weight for precious stones equal to 200 milligrams

car·a·van \'kar-ə-ˌvan\ *n* **1** : a group of travelers journeying together through desert or hostile regions **2** : a group of vehicles traveling in a file

car·a·van·sa·ry \ˌkar-ə-'van-sə-rē\ *or* **car·a·van·se·rai** \-sə-ˌrī\ *n, pl* **-ries** *or* **-rais** *or* **-rai** [Per *kārwān-sarāī,* fr. *kārwān* caravan + *sarāī* palace, inn] **1** : an inn in eastern countries where caravans rest at night **2** : HOTEL, INN

car·a·vel \'kar-ə-ˌvel\ *n* : a small 15th and 16th century ship with a broad bow, high narrow poop, and usu. three masts

caravel

car·a·way \'kar-ə-ˌwā\ *n* : an aromatic herb related to the carrot with fruits (**caraway seed**) used in seasoning and medicine; *also* : its fruit

car·bide \'kär-ˌbīd\ *n* : a compound of carbon with another element

car·bine \'kär-ˌbēn, -ˌbīn\ *n* : a short-barreled lightweight rifle

car·bo·hy·drate \ˌkär-bō-'hī-ˌdrāt, -drət\ *n* : any of various compounds composed of carbon, hydrogen, and oxygen (as sugars and starches)

car·bol·ic acid \ˌkär-'bä-lik-\ *n* : PHENOL

car·bon \'kär-bən\ *n* **1** : a nonmetallic chemical element occurring in nature esp. as diamond and graphite and as a constituent of coal, petroleum, and limestone — see ELEMENT table **2** : a sheet of carbon paper; *also* : CARBON COPY 1 — **car·bon·less** \-ləs\ *adj*

car·bo·na·ceous \ˌkär-bə-'nā-shəs\ *adj* : relating to, containing, or composed of carbon

¹**car·bon·ate** \'kär-bə-ˌnāt, -nət\ *n* : a salt or ester of carbonic acid

²**car·bon·ate** \-ˌnāt\ *vb* **-at·ed; -at·ing** : to combine or impregnate with carbon dioxide (*carbonated* beverages) — **car·bon·ation** \ˌkär-bə-'nā-shən\ *n*

carbon black *n* : any of various black substances consisting chiefly of carbon and used esp. as pigments

carbon copy *n* **1** : a copy made by carbon paper **2** : DUPLICATE

carbon dating *n* : the determination of the age of old material (as an archaeological specimen) by its content of carbon 14

carbon dioxide *n* : a heavy colorless gas that does not support combustion and is formed in animal respiration and in the combustion and decomposition of organic substances

carbon 14 *n* : a heavy radioactive form of carbon used esp. in dating archaeological materials

car·bon·ic acid \kär-'bä-nik-\ *n* : a weak acid that decomposes readily into water and carbon dioxide

car·bon·if·er·ous \ˌkär-bə-'ni-fə-rəs\ *adj* **1** : producing or containing carbon or coal **2** *cap* : of, relating to, or being the period of the Paleozoic era between the Devonian and the Permian — **Carboniferous** *n*

carbon monoxide *n* : a colorless odorless very poisonous gas formed by the incomplete burning of carbon

carbon paper *n* : a thin paper coated with a pigment and used for making copies

carbon tet·ra·chlo·ride \-ˌte-trə-'klōr-ˌīd\ *n* : a colorless nonflammable toxic liquid used esp. as a solvent

carbon 12 *n* : the most abundant isotope of carbon having a nucleus of 6 protons and 6 neutrons and used as a standard for measurements of atomic weight

car·boy \'kär-ˌbȯi\ *n* [Per *qarāba,* fr. Ar *qarrābah* demijohn] : a large container for liquids

car·bun·cle \'kär-ˌbən-kəl\ *n* : a painful inflammation of the skin and underlying tissue that discharges pus from several openings

car·bu·re·tor \'kär-bə-ˌrā-tər, -byə-\ *n* : an apparatus for supplying an internal combustion engine with an explosive mixture of vaporized fuel and air

car·bu·ret·tor *also* **car·bu·ret·ter** \ˌkär-byə-'re-tər, 'kär-byə-ˌ\ *chiefly Brit var of* CARBURETOR

car·case *Brit var of* CARCASS

car·cass \'kär-kəs\ *n* : a dead body; *esp* : one of an animal dressed for food

car·cin·o·gen \kär-'si-nə-jən\ *n* : an agent causing or inciting cancer — **car·ci·no·gen·ic** \ˌkärs-ᵊn-ō-'je-nik\ *adj* — **car·ci·no·ge·nic·i·ty** \-jə-'ni-sə-tē\ *n*

car·ci·no·ma \ˌkärs-ᵊn-'ō-mə\ *n, pl* **-mas** *or* **-ma·ta** \-tə\ : a malignant tumor of epithelial origin — **car·ci·no·ma·tous** \-təs\ *adj*

¹**card** \'kärd\ *vb* : to comb with a card : cleanse and untangle before spinning — **card·er** *n*

²**card** *n* : an instrument for combing fibers (as wool or cotton)

³**card** *n* **1** : PLAYING CARD **2** *pl* : a game played with playing cards; *also* : card playing **3** : a usu. clownishly amusing person : WAG **4** : a flat stiff usu. small piece of paper, cardboard, or plastic **5** : PROGRAM; *esp* : a sports program

⁴**card** *vb* **1** : to list or schedule on a card **2** : SCORE

⁵**card** *abbr* cardinal

car·da·mom \'kär-də-məm\ *n* : the aromatic capsular fruit of an East Indian herb related to the ginger whose seeds are used as a spice or condiment and in medicine; *also* : this plant

card·board \'kärd-ˌbȯrd\ *n* : PAPERBOARD

card–car·ry·ing \'kärd-ˌkar-ē-iŋ\ *adj* : being a regularly enrolled member of an organized group and esp. of the Communist party

card catalog *n* : a catalog (as of books) in which the entries are arranged systematically on cards

car·di·ac \'kär-dē-ˌak\ *adj* **1** : of, relating to, or located near the heart **2** : of, relating to, or affected with heart disease

car·di·gan \'kär-di-gən\ *n* : a sweater or jacket usu. without a collar and with a full-length opening in the front

¹**car·di·nal** \'kärd-nəl, 'kär-dᵊn-əl\ *n* **1** : an ecclesiastical official of the Roman Catholic Church ranking next below the pope **2** : a crested No. American finch that is nearly completely red in the male

²**cardinal** *adj* [ME, fr. LL *cardinalis,* fr. L serving as a hinge, fr. *cardo* hinge] : of basic importance : CHIEF, MAIN, PRIMARY — **car·di·nal·ly** *adv*

car·di·nal·ate \'kärd-nə-lət, -'kär-dᵊn-ə-let, -ˌlāt\ n : the office, rank, or dignity of a cardinal

cardinal flower n : a No. American plant that bears a spike of brilliant red flowers

cardinal number n : a number (as 1, 5, 82, 357) that is used in simple counting and answers the question "how many?"

cardinal point n : one of the four principal compass points north, south, east, and west

car·di·ol·o·gy \ˌkär-dē-'ä-lə-jē\ n : the study of the heart and its action and diseases — **car·di·ol·o·gist** \-jist\ n

car·dio·pul·mo·nary resuscitation \ˌkär-dē-ō-'pul-mə-ˌner-ē-\ n : a procedure to restore normal breathing after cardiac arrest that includes the clearance of air passages to the lungs, mouth-to-mouth method of artificial respiration, and heart massage by the exertion of pressure on the chest

car·dio·vas·cu·lar \-'vas-kyə-lər\ adj : of or relating to the heart and blood vessels

card·sharp·er \'kärd-ˌshär-pər\ or **card·sharp** \-ˌshärp\ n : a cheater at cards

¹care \'ker\ n 1 : a disquieted state of uncertainty and responsibility : ANXIETY 2 : watchful attention : HEED 3 : CHARGE, SUPERVISION 4 : a person or thing that is an object of anxiety or solicitude

²care vb **cared; car·ing** 1 : to feel anxiety : to feel interest 3 : to give care 4 : to have a liking, fondness, taste, or inclination 5 : to be concerned about ⟨∼ what happens⟩

CARE abbr Cooperative for American Relief to Everywhere

ca·reen \kə-'rēn\ vb 1 : to put (a ship or boat) on a beach esp. in order to clean or repair its hull 2 : to sway from side to side 3 : CAREER

¹ca·reer \kə-'rir\ n [MF carrière, fr. OProv carriera street, fr. ML carraria road for vehicles, fr. L carrus car] 1 : COURSE, PASSAGE; also : speed in a course ⟨ran at full ∼⟩ 2 : an occupation or profession followed as a life's work

²career vb : to go at top speed esp. in a headlong manner

care·free \'ker-ˌfrē\ adj : free from care or worry

care·ful \-fəl\ adj **care·ful·ler; care·ful·lest** 1 : using or taking care : VIGILANT 2 : marked by solicitude, caution, or prudence — **care·ful·ly** adv — **care·ful·ness** n

care·giv·er \-ˌgi-vər\ n : a person who provides direct care (as for children, the disabled, or the chronically ill)

care·less \-ləs\ adj 1 : free from care : UNTROUBLED 2 : UNCONCERNED, INDIFFERENT 3 : not taking care 4 : not showing or receiving care — **care·less·ly** adv — **care·less·ness** n

¹ca·ress \kə-'res\ n : a tender or loving touch or embrace

²caress vb : to touch or stroke tenderly or lovingly — **ca·ress·er** n

car·et \'kar-ət\ n [L, there is lacking, fr. carēre to lack, be without] : a mark ʌ used to indicate the place where something is to be inserted

care·tak·er \'ker-ˌtā-kər\ n 1 : one in charge usu. as occupant in place of an absent owner 2 : one temporarily fulfilling the functions of an office

care·worn \-ˌwōrn\ adj : showing the effects of grief or anxiety

car·fare \'kär-ˌfar\ n : passenger fare (as on a streetcar or bus)

car·go \'kär-gō\ n, pl **cargoes** or **cargos** : the goods carried in a ship, airplane, or vehicle : FREIGHT

Ca·rib·be·an \ˌkar-ə-'bē-ən, kə-'ri-bē-ən\ adj : of or relating to the eastern and southern West Indies or the Caribbean Sea

car·i·bou \'kar-ə-ˌbü\ n, pl **caribou** or **caribous** : a large circumpolar gregarious deer of northern taiga and tundra that usu. has palmate antlers in both sexes — used esp. for one of the New World

car·i·ca·ture \'kar-i-kə-ˌchur\ n 1 : distorted representation to produce a ridiculous effect 2 : a representation esp. in literature or art having the qualities of caricature — **caricature** vb — **car·i·ca·tur·ist** \-ist\ n

car·ies \'kar-ēz\ n, pl **caries** : tooth decay

car·il·lon \'kar-ə-ˌlän\ n : a set of tuned bells sounded by hammers controlled from a keyboard

car·i·ous \'kar-ē-əs\ adj : affected with caries

car·load \'kär-ˌlōd\ n : a load that fills a car

car·mi·na·tive \kär-'mi-nə-tiv\ adj : expelling gas from the alimentary canal — **carminative** n

car·mine \'kär-mən, -ˌmīn\ n : a vivid red

car·nage \'kär-nij\ n : great destruction of life : SLAUGHTER

car·nal \'kärn-ᵊl\ adj [ME, fr. LL carnalis, fr. L carn-, caro flesh] 1 : of or relating to the body 2 : relating to or given to sensual pleasures and appetites — **car·nal·i·ty** \kär-'na-lə-tē\ n — **car·nal·ly** adv

car·na·tion \kär-'nā-shən\ n : a cultivated pink of any of numerous usu. double-flowered varieties derived from an Old World species

car·nau·ba wax \kär-'no-bə-, -'naù-; ˌkär-nə-'ü-bə-\ n : a brittle yellowish wax from a Brazilian palm that is used esp. in polishes

car·ne·lian \kär-'nēl-yən\ n : a hard tough reddish quartz used as a gem

car·ni·val \'kär-nə-vəl\ n [It carnevale, alter. of carnelevare, lit., removal of meat] 1 : a season of merrymaking just before Lent 2 : a boisterous merrymaking 3 : a traveling enterprise offering amusements 4 : an organized program of entertainment

car·niv·o·ra \kär-'ni-və-rə\ n pl : carnivorous mammals

car·ni·vore \'kär-nə-ˌvōr\ n : a flesh-eating animal; esp : any of an order of mammals (as dogs, cats, bears, minks, and seals) feeding mostly on animal flesh

car·niv·o·rous \kär-'ni-və-rəs\ adj 1 : feeding on animal tissues 2 : of or relating to the carnivores — **car·niv·o·rous·ly** adv — **car·niv·o·rous·ness** n

car·ny or **car·ney** or **car·nie** \'kär-nē\ n, pl **carnies** or **carneys** 1 : CARNIVAL 3 2 : one who works with a carnival

car·ol \'kar-əl\ n : a song of joy or devotion — **carol** vb — **car·ol·er** or **car·ol·ler** n

car·om \'kar-əm\ n 1 : a shot in billiards in which the cue ball strikes two other balls 2 : a rebounding esp. at an angle — **carom** vb

car·o·tene \'kar-ə-ˌtēn\ n : any of several orange to red pigments (as beta-carotene) formed esp. in plants and used as a source of vitamin A

ca·rot·id \kə-'rä-təd\ adj : of, relating to, or being the chief artery or pair of arteries that pass up the neck and supply the head — **carotid** n

ca·rous·al \kə-'raù-zəl\ n : CAROUSE

ca·rouse \kə-'raùz\ n [MF carrousse, fr. carous, adv., all out (in boire carous to empty the cup), fr. G garaus] : a drunken revel — **carouse** vb — **ca·rous·er** n

car·ou·sel \ˌkar-ə-'sel, 'kar-ə-ˌsel\ n 1 : MERRY-GO-ROUND 2 : a circular conveyor

¹carp \'kärp\ vb : to find fault : CAVIL, COMPLAIN — **carp** n — **carp·er** n

²carp n, pl **carp** or **carps** : a large variable Asian freshwater fish of sluggish waters often raised for food

¹car·pal \'kär-pəl\ adj : relating to the wrist or the bones of the wrist

²carpal n : a carpal element or bone

carpal tunnel syndrome n : a condition characterized esp. by weakness, pain, and disturbances of sensation (as numbness) in the hand and caused by compression of a nerve in the wrist

car·pe di·em \ˌkär-pe-'dē-ˌem, -'dī-\ n [L, lit., pluck

the day] : enjoyment of the present without concern for the future

car·pel \ˈkär-pəl\ *n* : one of the highly modified leaves that together form the ovary of a flower of a seed plant

car·pen·ter \ˈkär-pən-tər\ *n* : one who builds or repairs wooden structures — **carpenter** *vb* — **car·pen·try** \-trē\ *n*

car·pet \ˈkär-pət\ *n* : a heavy fabric used as a floor covering — **carpet** *vb*

car·pet·bag \-ˌbag\ *n* : a traveling bag common in the 19th century

car·pet·bag·ger \-ˌba-gər\ *n* : a Northerner in the South after the American Civil War usu. seeking private gain under the reconstruction governments

car·pet·ing \ˈkär-pə-tiŋ\ *n* : material for carpets; *also* : CARPETS

car pool *n* : an arrangement in which a group of people commute together by car; *also* : a group having this arrangement — **car·pool** \-ˌpül\ *vb*

car·port \ˈkär-ˌpȯrt\ *n* : an open-sided automobile shelter

car·pus \ˈkär-pəs\ *n* : the wrist or its bones

car·ra·geen·an *or* **car·ra·geen·in** \ˌkar-ə-ˈgē-nən\ *n* : a colloid extracted esp. from a dark purple branching seaweed and used in foods esp. to stabilize and thicken them

car·rel \ˈkar-əl\ *n* : a table often partitioned or enclosed for individual study in a library

car·riage \ˈkar-ij\ *n* 1 : the act of carrying 2 : manner of holding the body 3 : a wheeled vehicle 4 *Brit* : a railway passenger coach 5 : a movable part of a machine for supporting some other moving part ⟨a typewriter ∼⟩

carriage trade *n* : trade from well-to-do or upper-class people

car·ri·er \ˈkar-ē-ər\ *n* 1 : one that carries 2 : a person or organization in the transportation business 3 : AIRCRAFT CARRIER 4 : one whose system carries germs of a disease but who is immune to the disease 5 : an individual having a gene for a trait or condition that is not expressed bodily 6 : an electromagnetic wave whose amplitude or frequency is varied in order to convey a radio or television signal

carrier pigeon *n* : a pigeon used esp. to carry messages

car·ri·on \ˈkar-ē-ən\ *n* : dead and decaying flesh

car·rot \ˈkar-ət\ *n* : the elongated usu. orange root of a common garden plant that is eaten as a vegetable; *also* : this plant

car·rou·sel *var of* CAROUSEL

¹**car·ry** \ˈkar-ē\ *vb* **car·ried; car·ry·ing** 1 : to move while supporting : TRANSPORT, CONVEY, TAKE 2 : to influence by mental or emotional appeal 3 : to get possession or control of : CAPTURE, WIN 4 : to transfer from one place (as a column) to another ⟨∼ a number in adding⟩ 5 : to have or wear on one's person; *also* : to bear within one 6 : INVOLVE, IMPLY 7 : to hold or bear (oneself) in a specified way 8 : to keep in stock for sale 9 : to sustain the weight or burden of : SUPPORT 10 : to prolong in space, time, or degree 11 : to keep on one's books as a debtor 12 : to succeed in (an election) 13 : to win adoption (as in a legislature) 14 : PUBLISH, PRINT 15 : to reach or penetrate to a distance

²**carry** *n* 1 : the range of a gun or projectile or of a struck or thrown ball 2 : PORTAGE 3 : an act or method of carrying ⟨fireman's ∼⟩

car·ry·all \ˈkar-ē-ˌȯl\ *n* : a capacious bag or case

carry away *vb* : to arouse to a high and often excessive degree of emotion

carrying charge *n* : a charge added to the price of merchandise sold on the installment plan

car·ry-on *n* : a piece of luggage suitable for being carried aboard an airplane by a passenger — **carry-on** *adj*

carry on *vb* 1 : CONDUCT, MANAGE 2 : to behave in a foolish, excited, or improper manner 3 : to continue in spite of hindrance or discouragement

carry out *vb* 1 : to put into execution 2 : to bring to a successful conclusion

car·sick \ˈkär-ˌsik\ *adj* : affected with motion sickness esp. in an automobile — **car sickness** *n*

¹**cart** \ˈkärt\ *n* 1 : a heavy 2-wheeled wagon 2 : a small wheeled vehicle

²**cart** *vb* : to convey in or as if in a cart — **cart·er** *n*

cart·age \ˈkär-tij\ *n* : the act of or rate charged for carting

carte blanche \ˈkärt-ˈbläⁿsh\ *n, pl* **cartes blanches** *same or* -ˈbläⁿ-shəz\ [F, lit., blank document] : full discretionary power

car·tel \kär-ˈtel\ *n* : a combination of independent business enterprises designed to limit competition **syn** pool, syndicate, monopoly, trust

car·ti·lage \ˈkärt-əl-ij\ *n* : a usu. translucent somewhat elastic tissue that composes most of the skeleton of young vertebrate embryos and later is mostly converted to bone in higher vertebrates — **car·ti·lag·i·nous** \ˌkärt-əl-ˈa-jə-nəs\ *adj*

cartilaginous fish *n* : any of a class of fishes (as a shark or ray having the skeleton wholly or largely composed of cartilage

car·tog·ra·phy \kär-ˈtä-grə-fē\ *n* : the making of maps — **car·tog·ra·pher** *n*

car·ton \ˈkärt-ᵊn\ *n* : a paperboard box or container

car·toon \kär-ˈtün\ *n* 1 : a preparatory sketch (as for a painting) 2 : a drawing intended as humor, caricature, or satire 3 : COMIC STRIP — **cartoon** *vb* — **car·toon·ist** *n*

car·tridge \ˈkär-trij\ *n* 1 : a tube containing a complete charge for a firearm 2 : a container of material for insertion into an apparatus 3 : a small case containing a phonograph needle and transducer that is attached to a tonearm 4 : a case containing a magnetic tape or disk 5 : a case for holding integrated circuits containing a computer program

cart·wheel \ˈkärt-ˌhwēl\ *n* 1 : a large coin (as a silver dollar) 2 : a lateral handspring with arms and legs extended

carve \ˈkärv\ *vb* **carved; carv·ing** 1 : to cut with care or precision : shape by cutting 2 : to cut into pieces or slices 3 : to slice and serve meat at table — **carv·er** *n*

cary·at·id \ˌkar-ē-ˈa-təd\ *n, pl* **-ids** *or* **-i·des** \-ˈa-tə-ˌdēz\ : a sculptured draped female figure used as an architectural column

CAS *abbr* certificate of advanced study

ca·sa·ba \kə-ˈsä-bə\ *n* : any of several muskmelons with a yellow rind and sweet flesh

¹**cas·cade** \kas-ˈkād\ *n* 1 : a steep usu. small waterfall 2 : something arranged in a series or succession of stages so that each stage derives from or acts upon the product of the preceding

²**cascade** *vb* **cas·cad·ed; cas·cad·ing** : to fall, pass, or connect in or as if in a cascade

cas·cara \kas-ˈkar-ə\ *n* : the dried bark of a small Pacific coastal tree of the U.S. and southern Canada used as a laxative; *also* : this tree

¹**case** \ˈkās\ *n* [ME *cas,* fr. OF, fr. L *casus* fall, chance, fr. *cadere* to fall] 1 : a particular instance or situation 2 : an inflectional form of a noun, pronoun, or adjective indicating its grammatical relation to other words; *also* : such a relation whether indicated by inflection or not 3 : what actually exists or happens : FACT 4 : a suit or action in law : CAUSE 5 : a convincing argument 6 : an instance of disease or injury; *also* : PATIENT 7 : INSTANCE, EXAMPLE — **in case** : as a precaution — **in case of** : in the event of

²**case** *n* [ME *cas,* fr. OF *casse,* fr. L *capsa*] 1 : a box or container for holding something; *also* : a box with its contents 2 : an outer covering 3 : a divided tray for holding printing type 4 : CASING 2

³case *vb* **cased; cas•ing 1 :** to enclose in or cover with a case **2 :** to inspect esp. with intent to rob

ca•sein \ˈkā-ˌsēn, kā-ˈ\ *n* : any of several phosphorus‑containing proteins occurring in or produced from milk

case•ment \ˈkās-mənt\ *n* : a window that opens like a door

case•work \-ˌwərk\ *n* : social work that involves the individual person or family — **case•work•er** *n*

¹cash \ˈkash\ *n* [MF or It; MF *casse* money box, fr. It *cassa*, fr. L *capsa* chest, case] **1 :** ready money **2 :** money or its equivalent paid at the time of purchase or delivery

²cash *vb* : to pay or obtain cash for

ca•shew \ˈka-shü, kə-ˈshü\ *n* : an edible kidney‑shaped nut of a tropical American tree related to the sumacs; *also* : the tree

¹ca•shier \ka-ˈshir\ *vb* : to dismiss from service; *esp* : to dismiss in disgrace

²cash•ier \ka-ˈshir\ *n* **1 :** a bank official responsible for moneys received and paid out **2 :** a person who receives and records payments

cashier's check *n* : a check drawn by a bank upon its own funds and signed by its cashier

cash in *vb* **1 :** to convert into cash ⟨*cash in* bonds⟩ **2 :** to settle accounts and withdraw from a gambling game or business deal **3 :** to obtain financial profit or advantage

cash•mere \ˈkazh-ˌmir, ˈkash-\ *n* : fine wool from the undercoat of an Indian goat (**cashmere goat**) or a yarn spun of this; *also* : a soft twilled fabric orig. woven from this yarn

cash register *n* : a business machine that usu. has a money drawer, indicates each sale, and records the money received

cas•ing \ˈkā-siŋ\ *n* **1 :** something that encases **2 :** the frame of a door or window

ca•si•no \kə-ˈsē-nō\ *n, pl* **-nos** [It, fr. *casa* house] **1 :** a building or room for social amusements; *esp* : one used for gambling **2** *also* **cas•si•no :** a card game in which players win cards by matching those on the table

cask \ˈkask\ *n* : a barrel-shaped container usu. for liquids; *also* : the quantity held by such a container

cas•ket \ˈkas-kət\ *n* **1 :** a small box (as for jewels) **2 :** COFFIN

casque \ˈkask\ *n* : HELMET

cas•sa•va \kə-ˈsä-və\ *n* : any of several tropical spurges with rootstocks yielding a nutritious starch from which tapioca is prepared; *also* : the rootstock or its starch

cas•se•role \ˈka-sə-ˌrōl\ *n* **1 :** a dish in which food may be baked and served **2 :** food cooked and served in a casserole

cas•sette *also* **ca•sette** \kə-ˈset\ *n* **1 :** a lightproof container for photographic plates or film **2 :** a plastic case containing magnetic tape

cas•sia \ˈka-shə\ *n* **1 :** a coarse cinnamon bark **2 :** any of a genus of leguminous herbs, shrubs, and trees of warm regions including several which yield senna

cas•sit•er•ite \kə-ˈsi-tə-ˌrīt\ *n* : a dark mineral that is the chief tin ore

cas•sock \ˈka-sək\ *n* : an ankle-length garment worn esp. by Roman Catholic and Anglican clergy

cas•so•wary \ˈka-sə-ˌwer-ē\ *n, pl* **-war•ies** : any of a genus of large birds closely related to the emu

¹cast \ˈkast\ *vb* **cast; cast•ing 1 :** THROW, FLING **2 :** DIRECT ⟨~ a glance⟩ **3 :** to deposit (a ballot) formally **4 :** to throw off, out, or away : DISCARD, SHED **5 :** COMPUTE; *esp* : to add up **6 :** to assign the parts of (a play) to actors; *also* : to assign to a role or part **7 :** to shape (a substance) by pouring in liquid or plastic form into a mold and letting harden without pressure **8 :** to make (as a knot or stitch) by looping or catching up

²cast *n* **1 :** THROW, FLING **2 :** a throw of dice **3 :** the set of actors in a dramatic production **4 :** something

formed in or as if in a mold; *also* : a rigid surgical dressing (as for protecting and supporting a fractured bone) **5 :** TINGE, HUE **6 :** APPEARANCE, LOOK **7 :** something thrown out or off, shed, or expelled ⟨worm ~s⟩

cas•ta•net \ˌkas-tə-ˈnet\ *n* [Sp *castañeta*, fr. *castaña* chestnut, fr. L *castanea*] : a rhythm instrument consisting of two small wooden, ivory, or plastic shells held in the hand and clicked together

cast•away \ˈkas-tə-ˌwā\ *adj* **1 :** thrown away : REJECTED **2 :** cast adrift or ashore as a survivor of a shipwreck — **castaway** *n*

caste \ˈkast\ *n* [Port *casta*, lit., race, lineage, fr. fem. of *casto* pure, chaste, fr. L *castus*] **1 :** one of the hereditary social classes in Hinduism **2 :** a division of a society based on wealth, inherited rank, or occupation **3 :** social position : PRESTIGE **4 :** a system of rigid social stratification

cas•tel•lat•ed \ˈkas-tə-ˌlā-təd\ *adj* : having battlements like a castle

cast•er \ˈkas-tər\ *n* **1** *or* **cas•tor :** a small container to hold salt or pepper at the table **2 :** a small wheel that turns freely and is used to support and move furniture, trucks, and equipment

cas•ti•gate \ˈkas-tə-ˌgāt\ *vb* **-gat•ed; -gat•ing :** to punish or criticize severely — **cas•ti•ga•tion** \ˌkas-tə-ˈgā-shən\ *n* — **cas•ti•ga•tor** \ˈkas-tə-ˌgā-tər\ *n*

cast•ing \ˈkas-tiŋ\ *n* **1 :** CAST 7 **2 :** something cast in a mold

casting vote *n* : a deciding vote cast by a presiding officer to break a tie

cast iron *n* : a hard brittle alloy of iron, carbon, and silicon cast in a mold

cas•tle \ˈka-səl\ *n* **1 :** a large fortified building or set of buildings **2 :** a large or imposing house **3 :** ³ROOK

castle in the air : an impracticable project

cast–off \ˈkas-ˌtȯf\ *adj* : thrown away or aside — **cast-off** *n*

cas•tor oil \ˈkas-tər-\ *n* : a thick yellowish oil extracted from the poisonous seeds of an herb (**castor–oil plant**) and used as a lubricant and purgative

cas•trate \ˈkas-ˌtrāt\ *vb* **cas•trat•ed; cas•trat•ing :** to deprive of sex glands and esp. testes — **cas•tra•tion** \kas-ˈtrā-shən\ *n* — **cas•tra•tor** \-ər\ *n*

ca•su•al \ˈka-zhə-wəl\ *adj* **1 :** resulting from or occurring by chance **2 :** OCCASIONAL, INCIDENTAL **3 :** OFFHAND, NONCHALANT **4 :** designed for informal use ⟨~ clothing⟩ — **ca•su•al•ly** *adv* — **ca•su•al•ness** *n*

ca•su•al•ty \ˈka-zhəl-tē, ˈka-zhə-wəl-\ *n, pl* **-ties 1 :** serious or fatal accident **2 :** a military person lost through death, injury, sickness, or capture or through being missing in action **3 :** a person or thing injured, lost, or destroyed

ca•su•ist•ry \ˈka-zhə-wə-strē\ *n, pl* **-ries :** specious argument : RATIONALIZATION — **ca•su•ist** \-wist\ *n* — **ca•su•is•tic** \ˌka-zhə-ˈwis-tik\ *or* **ca•su•is•ti•cal** \-ti-kəl\ *adj*

ca•sus bel•li \ˌkä-səs-ˈbe-ˌlē, ˌkā-səs-ˈbe-ˌlī\ *n, pl* **ca•sus belli** \ˌkä-ˌsüs-, ˌkā-\ [NL, occasion of war] : a cause or pretext for a declaration of war

¹cat \ˈkat\ *n* **1 :** a carnivorous mammal long domesticated as a pet and for catching rats and mice **2 :** any of a family of animals (as the lion, lynx, or leopard) including the domestic cat **3 :** a spiteful woman **4 :** GUY

²cat *abbr* catalog

ca•tab•o•lism \kə-ˈta-bə-ˌli-zəm\ *n* : destructive metabolism involving the release of energy and resulting in the breakdown of complex materials — **cat•a•bol•ic** \ˌka-tə-ˈbä-lik\ *adj*

cat•a•clysm \ˈka-tə-ˌkli-zəm\ *n* : a violent change or upheaval — **cat•a•clys•mal** \ˌka-tə-ˈkliz-məl\ *or* **cat•a•clys•mic** \-ˈkliz-mik\ *adj*

cat•a•comb \ˈka-tə-ˌkōm\ *n* : an underground burial place with galleries and recesses for tombs

cat•a•falque \ˈka-tə-ˌfalk, -ˌfȯlk, -ˌfȯk\ *n* : an ornamental structure sometimes used in solemn funerals to hold the body

cat•a•lep•sy \\'ka-tə-ˌlep-sē\ *n, pl* **-sies** : a trancelike nervous condition characterized esp. by loss of voluntary motion — **cat•a•lep•tic** \ˌka-tə-'lep-tik\ *adj or n*

¹**cat•a•log** *or* **cat•a•logue** \\'kat-əl-ˌȯg\ *n* **1** : LIST, REGISTER **2** : a systematic list of items with descriptive details; *also* : a book containing such a list

²**catalog** *or* **catalogue** *vb* **-loged** *or* **-logued; -log•ing** *or* **-logu•ing 1** : to make a catalog of **2** : to enter in a catalog — **cat•a•log•er** *or* **cat•a•logu•er** *n*

ca•tal•pa \kə-'tal-pə\ *n* : a broad-leaved tree with showy flowers and long slim pods

ca•tal•y•sis \kə-'ta-lə-səs\ *n, pl* **-y•ses** \-ˌsēz\ : a change and esp. increase in the rate of a chemical reaction brought about by a substance (**cat•a•lyst** \\'kat-əl-ist\) that is itself unchanged at the end of the reaction — **cat•a•lyt•ic** \ˌkat-əl-'i-tik\ *adj* — **cat•a•lyt•i•cal•ly** \-ti-k(ə-)lē\ *adv*

catalytic converter *n* : an automobile exhaust-system component in which a catalyst changes harmful gases into mostly harmless products

cat•a•lyze \\'kat-əl-ˌīz\ *vb* **-lyzed; -lyz•ing** : to bring about the catalysis of (a chemical reaction)

cat•a•ma•ran \ˌka-tə-mə-'ran\ *n* [Tamil (a language of southern India) *kaṭṭumaram,* fr. *kaṭṭu* to tie + *maram* tree] : a boat with twin hulls

cat•a•mount \\'ka-tə-ˌmaunt\ *n* : COUGAR; *also* : LYNX

cat•a•pult \\'ka-tə-ˌpəlt, -ˌpult\ *n* **1** : an ancient military machine for hurling missiles **2** : a device for launching an airplane (as from an aircraft carrier) — **catapult** *vb*

cat•a•ract \\'ka-tə-ˌrakt\ *n* **1** : a cloudiness of the lens of the eye obstructing vision **2** : a large waterfall; *also* : steep rapids in a river

ca•tarrh \kə-'tär\ *n* : inflammation of a mucous membrane esp. of the nose and throat — **ca•tarrh•al** \-əl\ *adj*

ca•tas•tro•phe \kə-'tas-trə-(ˌ)fē\ *n* [Gk *katastrophē,* fr. *katastrephein* to overturn, fr. *kata-* down + *strephein* to turn] **1** : a great disaster or misfortune **2** : utter failure — **cat•a•stroph•ic** \ˌka-tə-'strä-fik\ *adj* — **cat•a•stroph•i•cal•ly** \-fi-k(ə-)lē\ *adv*

cat•a•ton•ic \ˌka-tə-'tä-nik\ *adj* : of, relating to, or marked by schizophrenia characterized esp. by stupor, negativism, rigidity, purposeless excitement, and abnormal posturing — **catatonic** *n*

cat•bird \\'kat-ˌbərd\ *n* : an American songbird with a catlike mewing call

cat•boat \\'kat-ˌbōt\ *n* : a single-masted sailboat with a single large sail extended by a long boom

cat•call \-ˌkȯl\ *n* : a loud cry made esp. to express disapproval — **catcall** *vb*

¹**catch** \\'kach, 'kech\ *vb* **caught** \\'kȯt\; **catch•ing 1** : to capture esp. after pursuit **2** : TRAP **3** : to discover unexpectedly ⟨*caught* in the act⟩ **4** : to become suddenly aware of **5** : to take hold of : SNATCH ⟨~ at a straw⟩ **6** : INTERCEPT **7** : to get entangled **8** : to become affected with or by ⟨~ fire⟩ ⟨~ cold⟩ **9** : to seize and hold firmly; *also* : FASTEN **10** : OVERTAKE **11** : to be in time for ⟨~ a train⟩ **12** : to take in and retain **13** : to look at or listen to

²**catch** *n* **1** : something caught **2** : the act of catching; *also* : a game consisting of throwing and catching a ball **3** : something that catches or checks or holds immovable ⟨a door ~⟩ **4** : one worth catching esp. as a mate **5** : FRAGMENT, SNATCH **6** : a concealed difficulty or complication

catch•all \\'ka-ˌchȯl, 'ke-\ *n* : something to hold a variety of odds and ends

catch–as–catch–can *adj* : using any means available

catch•er \\'ka-chər, 'ke-\ *n* : one that catches; *esp* : a player positioned behind home plate in baseball

catch•ing *adj* **1** : INFECTIOUS, CONTAGIOUS **2** : ALLURING, CATCHY

catch•ment \\'kach-mənt, 'kech-\ *n* **1** : something that catches water **2** : the action of catching water

catch on *vb* **1** : UNDERSTAND **2** : to become popular

catch•pen•ny \\'kach-ˌpe-nē, 'kech-\ *adj* : using sensationalism or cheapness for appeal ⟨a ~ newspaper⟩

catch–22 \-ˌtwen-tē-'tü\ *n, pl* **catch–22's** *or* **catch–22s** *often cap* C [fr. *Catch-22,* a paradoxical rule found in the novel *Catch-22* (1961) by Joseph Heller] : a problematic situation for which the only solution is denied by a circumstance inherent in the problem or by a rule; *also* : the circumstance or rule that denies a solution

catch•up \\'ke-chəp, 'ka-\ *var of* KETCHUP

catch up *vb* : to travel or work fast enough to overtake or complete

catch•word \\'kach-ˌwərd, 'kech-\ *n* **1** : GUIDE WORD **2** : a word or expression representative of a party, school, or point of view

catchy \\'ka-chē, 'ke-\ *adj* **catch•i•er; -est 1** : likely to catch the interest or attention **2** : TRICKY

cat•e•chism \\'ka-tə-ˌki-zəm\ *n* : a summary or test (as of religious doctrine) usu. in the form of questions and answers — **cat•e•chist** \-ˌkist\ *n* — **cat•e•chize** \-ˌkīz\ *vb*

cat•e•chu•men \ˌka-tə-'kyü-mən\ *n* : a religious convert receiving training before baptism

cat•e•gor•i•cal \ˌka-tə-'gȯr-i-kəl\ *adj* **1** : ABSOLUTE, UNQUALIFIED **2** : of, relating to, or constituting a category — **cat•e•gor•i•cal•ly** \-i-k(ə-)lē\ *adv*

cat•e•go•rize \\'ka-ti-gə-ˌrīz\ *vb* **-rized; -riz•ing** : to put into a category : CLASSIFY — **cat•e•go•ri•za•tion** \ˌka-ti-gə-rə-'zā-shən\ *n*

cat•e•go•ry \\'ka-tə-ˌgȯr-ē\ *n, pl* **-ries** : a division used in classification; *also* : CLASS, GROUP, KIND

ca•ter \\'kā-tər\ *vb* **1** : to provide a supply of food **2** : to supply what is wanted — **ca•ter•er** *n*

cat•er•cor•ner \ˌka-tē-'kȯr-nər, ˌka-tə-, ˌki-tē-\ *or* **cat•er–cor•nered** *adv or adj* [obs. *cater* four + *corner*] : in a diagonal or oblique position

cat•er•pil•lar \\'ka-tər-ˌpi-lər\ *n* [ME *catyrpel,* fr. OF *catepelose,* lit., hairy cat] : a wormlike often hairy insect larva esp. of a butterfly or moth

cat•er•waul \\'ka-tər-ˌwȯl\ *vb* : to make a harsh cry — **caterwaul** *n*

cat•fish \\'kat-ˌfish\ *n* : any of an order of chiefly freshwater stout-bodied fishes with slender tactile processes around the mouth

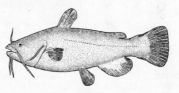

catfish

cat•gut \-ˌgət\ *n* : a tough cord made usu. from sheep intestines

ca•thar•sis \kə-'thär-səs\ *n, pl* **ca•thar•ses** \-ˌsēz\ **1** : an act of purging or purification **2** : elimination of a complex by bringing it to consciousness and affording it expression

¹**ca•thar•tic** \kə-'thär-tik\ *adj* : of, relating to, or producing catharsis

²**cathartic** *n* : PURGATIVE

ca•the•dral \kə-'thē-drəl\ *n* : the principal church of a diocese

cath•e•ter \\'ka-thə-tər\ *n* : a tube for insertion into a bodily passage or cavity usu. for injecting or drawing off material or for keeping a passage open

cath•ode \\'ka-ˌthōd\ *n* **1** : the negative electrode of an electrolytic cell **2** : the positive terminal of a battery **3** : the electron-emitting electrode of an electron tube

— **cath·od·al** \'ka-ˌthō-dəl\ *adj* — **ca·thod·ic** \ka-'thä-dik\ *adj*

cathode—ray tube *n* : a vacuum tube in which a beam of electrons is projected on a fluorescent screen to produce a luminous spot

cath·o·lic \'kath-lik, 'ka-thə-\ *adj* **1** *cap* : of or relating to Catholics and esp. Roman Catholics **2** : GENERAL, UNIVERSAL

Cath·o·lic \'kath-lik, 'ka-thə-\ *n* : a member of a church claiming historical continuity from the ancient undivided Christian church; *esp* : a member of the Roman Catholic Church — **Ca·thol·i·cism** \kə-'thä-lə-ˌsi-zəm\ *n*

cath·o·lic·i·ty \ˌka-thə-'li-sə-tē\ *n, pl* **-ties 1** *cap* : the character of being in conformity with a Catholic church **2** : liberality of sentiments or views **3** : comprehensive range

cat·ion \'kat-ˌī-ən\ *n* : the ion in an electrolyte that migrates to the cathode; *also* : a positively charged ion

cat·kin \'kat-kən\ *n* : a long flower cluster (as of a willow) bearing crowded flowers and prominent bracts

cat·like \-ˌlīk\ *adj* : resembling a cat or its behavior; *esp* : STEALTHY

cat·nap \-ˌnap\ *n* : a very short light nap — **catnap** *vb*

cat·nip \-ˌnip\ *n* : an aromatic mint that is esp. attractive to cats

cat·o'—nine—tails \ˌka-tə-'nīn-ˌtālz\ *n, pl* **cat·o'—nine—tails** : a whip made of usu. nine knotted cords fastened to a handle

CAT scan \'kat-\ *n* [*computerized axial tomography*] : an image made by computed tomography

CAT scanner *n* : a medical instrument consisting of integrated X-ray and computing equipment that is used to make CAT scans

cat's cradle *n* : a game played with a string looped on the fingers in such a way as to resemble a small cradle

cat's—eye \'kats-ˌī\ *n, pl* **cat's—eyes** : any of various iridescent gems

cat's—paw \-ˌpȯ\ *n, pl* **cat's—paws** : a person used by another as a tool

cat·sup \'ke-chəp, 'ka-; 'kat-səp\ *var of* KETCHUP

cat·tail \'kat-ˌtāl\ *n* : a tall reedlike marsh plant with furry brown spikes of tiny flowers

cat·tle \'kat-əl\ *n pl* : LIVESTOCK; *esp* : domestic bovines (as cows, bulls, or calves) — **cat·tle·man** \-mən, -ˌman\ *n*

cat·ty \'ka-tē\ *adj* **cat·ti·er, -est** : slyly spiteful — **cat·ti·ly** \'ka-tᵊl-ē\ *adv* — **cat·ti·ness** *n*

cat·ty—cor·ner *or* **cat·ty—cor·nered** *var of* CATER-CORNER

CATV *abbr* community antenna television

cat·walk \'kat-ˌwȯk\ *n* : a narrow walk (as along a bridge)

Cau·ca·sian \kȯ-'kā-zhən\ *adj* : of or relating to the white race of mankind — **Caucasian** *n* — **Cau·ca·soid** \'kȯ-kə-ˌsȯid\ *adj or n*

cau·cus \'kȯ-kəs\ *n* : a meeting of a group of persons belonging to the same political party or faction usu. to decide upon policies and candidates — **caucus** *vb*

cau·dal \'kȯ-dəl\ *adj* : of, relating to, or located near the tail or the hind end of the body — **cau·dal·ly** *adv*

cau·dil·lo \kaů-'thē-(ˌ)yō, -'thēl-\ *n, pl* **-llos** : a Spanish or Latin-American military dictator

caught \'kȯt\ *past and past part of* CATCH

caul \'kȯl\ *n* : the inner fetal membrane of higher vertebrates esp. when covering the head at birth

caul·dron \'kȯl-drən\ *n* : a large kettle

cau·li·flow·er \'kȯ-li-ˌflaů-(ə)r\ *n* [It *cavolfiore*, fr. *cavolo* cabbage + *fiore* flower] : a garden plant closely related to cabbage and grown for its compact edible head of undeveloped flowers; *also* : this head used as a vegetable

cauliflower ear *n* : an ear deformed from injury and excessive growth of scar tissue

¹caulk \'kȯk\ *vb* [ME, fr. OF *cauquer* to trample, fr. L *calcare*, fr. *calx* heel] : to stop up and make tight against leakage (as a boat or its seams) — **caulk·er** *n*

²caulk *also* **caulk·ing** *n* : material used to caulk

caus·al \'kȯ-zəl\ *adj* **1** : expressing or indicating cause **2** : relating to or acting as a cause — **cau·sal·i·ty** \kȯ-'za-lə-tē\ *n* — **caus·al·ly** *adv*

cau·sa·tion \kȯ-'zā-shən\ *n* **1** : the act or process of causing **2** : the means by which an effect is produced

¹cause \'kȯz\ *n* **1** : REASON, MOTIVE **2** : something that brings about a result; *esp* : a person or thing that is the agent of bringing something about **3** : a suit or action in court : CASE **4** : a question or matter to be decided **5** : a principle or movement earnestly supported — **cause·less** *adj*

²cause *vb* **caused; caus·ing** : to be the cause or occasion of — **caus·a·tive** \'kȯ-zə-tiv\ *adj* — **caus·er** *n*

cause cé·lè·bre \ˌkȯz-sā-'lebrᵊ, ˌkȯz-\ *n, pl* **causes cé·lèbres** *same*\ [F, lit., celebrated case] **1** : a legal case that excites widespread interest **2** : a notorious person, thing, incident, or episode

cau·se·rie \ˌkȯz-'rē, ˌkō-zə-\ *n* [F] **1** : an informal conversation : CHAT **2** : a short informal essay

cause·way \'kȯz-ˌwā\ *n* : a raised way or road across wet ground or water

¹caus·tic \'kȯ-stik\ *adj* **1** : CORROSIVE **2** : SHARP, INCISIVE ⟨~ wit⟩

²caustic *n* **1** : a substance that burns or destroys organic tissue by chemical action **2** : SODIUM HYDROXIDE

cau·ter·ize \'kȯ-tə-ˌrīz\ *vb* **-ized; -iz·ing** : to burn or sear usu. to prevent infection or bleeding — **cau·ter·i·za·tion** \ˌkȯ-tə-rə-'zā-shən\ *n*

¹cau·tion \'kȯ-shən\ *n* **1** : ADMONITION, WARNING **2** : prudent forethought to minimize risk **3** : one that astonishes — **cau·tion·ary** \-shə-ˌner-ē\ *adj*

²caution *vb* : to advise caution to

cau·tious \'kȯ-shəs\ *adj* : marked by or given to caution : CAREFUL — **cau·tious·ly** *adv* — **cau·tious·ness** *n*

cav *abbr* **1** cavalry **2** cavity

cav·al·cade \ˌka-vəl-'kād\ *n* **1** : a procession of riders or carriages; *also* : a procession of vehicles **2** : a dramatic sequence or procession

¹cav·a·lier \ˌka-və-'lir\ *n* [MF, fr. It *cavaliere*, fr. OProv *cavalier*, fr. LL *caballarius* horseman, fr. L *caballus* horse] **1** : a mounted soldier : KNIGHT **2** *cap* : an adherent of Charles I of England **3** : GALLANT

²cavalier *adj* **1** : DEBONAIR **2** : DISDAINFUL, HAUGHTY — **cav·a·lier·ly** *adv*

cav·al·ry \'ka-vəl-rē\ *n, pl* **-ries** : troops mounted on horseback or moving in motor vehicles — **cav·al·ry·man** \-mən, -ˌman\ *n*

¹cave \'kāv\ *n* : a natural underground chamber open to the surface

²cave *vb* **caved; cav·ing** **1** : to collapse or cause to collapse **2** : to cease to resist : SUBMIT — usu. used with *in*

ca·ve·at \'ka-vē-ˌät, -ˌat; 'kä-vē-ˌät\ *n* [L, let him beware] : WARNING

caveat emp·tor \-'emp-tər, -ˌtȯr\ *n* [NL, let the buyer beware] : a principle in commerce: without a warranty the buyer takes a risk

cave—in \'kā-ˌvin\ *n* **1** : the action of caving in **2** : a place where earth has caved in

cave·man \'kāv-ˌman\ *n* **1** : a cave dweller esp. of the Stone Age **2** : a man who acts in a rough or crude manner

cav·ern \'ka-vərn\ *n* : CAVE; *esp* : one of large or unknown size — **cav·ern·ous** *adj* — **cav·ern·ous·ly** *adv*

cav·i·ar *or* **cav·i·are** \'ka-vē-ˌär, 'kä-\ *n* : the salted roe of a large fish (as sturgeon) used as an appetizer

cav·il \'ka-vəl\ *vb* **-iled** *or* **-illed; -il·ing** *or* **-il·ling** : to make frivolous objections or raise trivial objections to — **cavil** *n* — **cav·il·er** *or* **cav·il·ler** *n*

cav·ing \'kā-viŋ\ *n* : the sport of exploring caves : SPELUNKING

cav·i·ta·tion \ˌka-və-ˈtā-shən\ *n* : the formation of partial vacuums in a liquid by a swiftly moving solid body (as a propeller) or by high-intensity sound waves

cav·i·ty \ˈka-və-tē\ *n, pl* **-ties 1** : an unfilled space within a mass : a hollow place **2** : an area of decay in a tooth

ca·vort \kə-ˈvȯrt\ *vb* : PRANCE, CAPER

ca·vy \ˈkā-vē\ *n, pl* **cavies** : GUINEA PIG 1

caw \ˈkȯ\ *vb* : to utter the harsh call of the crow or a similar cry — **caw** *n*

cay \ˈkē, ˈkā\ *n* : ⁴KEY

cay·enne pepper \ˌkī-ˈen-, ˌkā-\ *n* : a condiment consisting of ground dried fruits or seeds of a hot pepper

cay·man *var of* CAIMAN

Ca·yu·ga \kā-ˈü-gə, kī-\ *n, pl* **Cayuga** *or* **Cayugas** : a member of an American Indian people of New York

Cay·use \ˈkī-ˌyüs, kī-ˈ\ *n* **1** *pl* **Cayuse** *or* **Cayuses** : a member of an American Indian people of Oregon and Washington **2** *pl* **cayuses**, *not cap, West* : a native range horse

Cb *symbol* columbium

CB \ˈsē-ˈbē\ *n* : CITIZENS BAND; *also* : the radio set used for citizens-band communications

CBC *abbr* Canadian Broadcasting Corporation

CBD *abbr* cash before delivery

CBS *abbr* Columbia Broadcasting System

CBW *abbr* chemical and biological warfare

cc *abbr* cubic centimeter

CC *abbr* **1** carbon copy **2** community college **3** country club

CCD \ˌsē-ˌsē-ˈdē\ *n* : CHARGE-COUPLED DEVICE

CCTV *abbr* closed-circuit television

CCU *abbr* **1** cardiac care unit **2** coronary care unit **3** critical care unit

ccw *abbr* counterclockwise

cd *abbr* cord

Cd *symbol* cadmium

¹CD \ˌsē-ˈdē\ *n* : COMPACT DISC

²CD *abbr* **1** certificate of deposit **2** Civil Defense

CDR *abbr* commander

CD-ROM \ˌsē-ˌdē-ˈräm\ *n* : a compact disc containing data that can be read by a computer

CDT *abbr* central daylight (saving) time

Ce *symbol* cerium

CE *abbr* **1** chemical engineer **2** civil engineer **3** Corps of Engineers

cease \ˈsēs\ *vb* **ceased; ceas·ing** : to come or bring to an end : STOP

cease–fire \ˈsēs-ˈfīr\ *n* : a suspension of active hostilities

cease·less \ˈsēs-ləs\ *adj* : being without pause or stop : CONTINUOUS — **cease·less·ly** *adv* — **cease·less·ness** *n*

ce·cum \ˈsē-kəm\ *n, pl* **ce·ca** \-kə\ : the blind pouch at the beginning of the large intestine into which the small intestine opens — **ce·cal** \-kəl\ *adj*

ce·dar \ˈsē-dər\ *n* : any of numerous coniferous trees (as a juniper) noted for their fragrant durable wood; *also* : this wood

cede \ˈsēd\ *vb* **ced·ed; ced·ing 1** : to yield or give up esp. by treaty **2** : ASSIGN, TRANSFER — **ced·er** *n*

ce·di \ˈsā-dē\ *n* — see MONEY table

ce·dil·la \si-ˈdi-lə\ *n* : a mark placed under the letter *c* (as ç) to show that the *c* is to be pronounced like *s*

ceil·ing \ˈsē-liŋ\ *n* **1** : the overhead inside lining of a room **2** : the height above the ground of the base of the lowest layer of clouds when over half of the sky is obscured **3** : the greatest height at which an airplane can operate efficiently **4** : a prescribed upper limit ⟨price ∼⟩

cel·an·dine \ˈse-lən-ˌdīn, -ˌdēn\ *n* : a yellow-flowered herb related to the poppies

cel·e·brate \ˈse-lə-ˌbrāt\ *vb* **-brat·ed; -brat·ing 1** : to perform (as a sacrament) with appropriate rites **2** : to honor (as a holiday) by solemn ceremonies or by re-

fraining from ordinary business **3** : to observe a notable occasion with festivities **4** : EXTOL — **cel·e·brant** \-brənt\ *n* — **cel·e·bra·tion** \ˌse-lə-ˈbrā-shən\ *n* — **cel·e·bra·tor** \ˈse-lə-brā-tər\ *n* — **cel·e·bra·to·ry** \-brə-ˌtȯr-ē, -ˌtȯr-; ˌse-lə-ˈbrā-tə-rē\ *adj*

cel·e·brat·ed *adj* : widely known and often referred to **syn** distinguished, renowned, noted, famous, illustrious, notorious

ce·leb·ri·ty \sə-ˈle-brə-tē\ *n, pl* **-ties 1** : the state of being celebrated : RENOWN **2** : a celebrated person

ce·ler·i·ty \sə-ˈler-ə-tē\ *n* : SPEED, RAPIDITY

cel·ery \ˈse-lə-rē\ *n, pl* **-er·ies** : a European herb related to the carrot and widely grown for the crisp edible stems of its leaves

celery cabbage *n* : CHINESE CABBAGE 2

ce·les·ta \sə-ˈles-tə\ *or* **ce·leste** \sə-ˈlest\ *n* : a keyboard instrument with hammers that strike steel plates

ce·les·tial \sə-ˈles-chəl\ *adj* **1** : HEAVENLY, DIVINE **2** : of or relating to the sky — **ce·les·tial·ly** *adv*

celestial navigation *n* : navigation by observation of the positions of stars

celestial sphere *n* : an imaginary sphere of infinite radius against which the celestial bodies appear to be projected

cel·i·ba·cy \ˈse-lə-bə-sē\ *n* **1** : the state of being unmarried; *esp* : abstention by vow from marriage **2** : abstention from sexual intercourse

cel·i·bate \ˈse-lə-bət\ *n* : one who lives in celibacy — **celibate** *adj*

cell \ˈsel\ *n* **1** : a small room (as in a convent or prison) usu. for one person; *also* : a small compartment, cavity, or bounded space **2** : a tiny mass of protoplasm that usu. contains a nucleus, is enclosed by a membrane, and forms the smallest structural unit of living matter capable of functioning independently **3** : a container holding an electrolyte either for generating electricity or for use in electrolysis **4** : a single unit in a device for converting radiant energy into electrical energy — **celled** \ˈseld\ *adj*

cel·lar \ˈse-lər\ *n* **1** : BASEMENT 1 **2** : the lowest position (as in an athletic league) **3** : a stock of wines

cel·lar·ette *or* **cel·lar·et** \ˌse-lə-ˈret\ *n* : a case or cabinet for a few bottles of wine or liquor

cel·lo \ˈche-lō\ *n, pl* **cellos** : a bass member of the violin family tuned an octave below the viola — **cel·list** \-list\ *n*

cel·lo·phane \ˈse-lə-ˌfān\ *n* : a thin transparent material made from cellulose and used as a wrapping

cel·lu·lar \ˈsel-yə-lər\ *adj* **1** : of, relating to, or consisting of cells **2** : of, relating to, or being a radiotelephone system in which a geographical area is divided into small sections each served by a transmitter of limited range

cel·lu·lite \ˈsel-yə-ˌlīt\ *n* : lumpy fat in the thighs, hips, and buttocks of some women

cel·lu·lose \ˈsel-yə-ˌlōs\ *n* : a complex carbohydrate of the cell walls of plants used esp. in making paper or rayon — **cel·lu·los·ic** \ˌsel-yə-ˈlō-sik\ *adj or n*

Cel·si·us \ˈsel-sē-əs\ *adj* : relating to or having a scale for measuring temperature on which the interval between the triple point and the boiling point of water is divided into 99.99 degrees with 0.01° being the triple point and 100.00° the boiling point

Celt \ˈkelt, ˈselt\ *n* : a member of any of a group of peoples (as the Irish or Welsh) of western Europe — **Celt·ic** *adj*

cem·ba·lo \ˈchem-bə-ˌlō\ *n, pl* **-ba·li** \-ˌlē\ *or* **-balos** [It] : HARPSICHORD

¹ce·ment \si-ˈment\ *n* **1** : a powder that is produced from a burned mixture chiefly of clay and limestone and that is used in mortar and concrete; *also* : CONCRETE **2** : a binding element or agency **3** : CEMENTUM; *also* : a substance for filling cavities in teeth

²cement *vb* **1** : to unite by or as if by cement **2** : to cover with concrete — **ce·ment·er** *n*

ce·men·tum \si-ˈmen-təm\ *n* : a specialized external

bony layer covering the dentin of the part of a tooth normally within the gum

cem·e·tery \'se-mə-ˌter-ē\ *n, pl* **-ter·ies** [ME *cimitery*, fr. MF *cimitere*, fr. LL *coemeterium*, fr. Gk *koimētērion* sleeping chamber, burial place, fr. *koiman* to put to sleep] : a burial ground : GRAVEYARD

cen·o·bite \'se-nə-ˌbīt\ *n* : a member of a religious group living together in a monastic community — **cen·o·bit·ic** \ˌse-nə-'bi-tik\ *adj*

ceno·taph \'se-nə-ˌtaf\ *n* [F *cénotaphe*, fr. L *cenotaphium*, fr. Gk *kenotaphion*, fr. *kenos* empty + *taphos* tomb] : a tomb or a monument erected in honor of a person whose body is elsewhere

Ce·no·zo·ic \ˌsē-nə-'zō-ik, ˌse-\ *adj* : of, relating to, or being the era of geologic history that extends from about 65 million years ago to the present — **Cenozoic** *n*

cen·ser \'sen-sər\ *n* : a vessel for burning incense (as in a religious ritual)

¹**cen·sor** \'sen-sər\ *n* **1** : one of two early Roman magistrates whose duties included taking the census **2** : an official who inspects printed matter or sometimes motion pictures with power to suppress anything objectionable — **cen·so·ri·al** \sen-'sōr-ē-əl\ *adj*

²**censor** *vb* : to subject to censorship

cen·so·ri·ous \sen-'sōr-ē-əs\ *adj* : marked by or given to censure : CRITICAL — **cen·so·ri·ous·ly** *adv* — **cen·so·ri·ous·ness** *n*

cen·sor·ship \'sen-sər-ˌship\ *n* **1** : the action of a censor esp. in stopping the transmission or publication of matter considered objectionable **2** : the office of a Roman censor

¹**cen·sure** \'sen-chər\ *n* **1** : the act of blaming or condemning sternly **2** : an official reprimand

²**censure** *vb* **cen·sured; cen·sur·ing** : to find fault with and criticize as blameworthy — **cen·sur·able** *adj* — **cen·sur·er** *n*

cen·sus \'sen-səs\ *n* **1** : a periodic governmental count of population **2** : COUNT, TALLY — **cen·sus** *vb*

¹**cent** \'sent\ *n* [MF, hundred, fr. L *centum*] **1** : a monetary unit equal to ¹⁄₁₀₀ of a basic unit of value — see *birr, dollar, gulden, leone, lilangeni, lira, pound, rand, rupee, shilling* at MONEY table **2** : a coin, token, or note representing one cent

²**cent** *abbr* **1** centigrade **2** central **3** century

cen·taur \'sen-ˌtȯr\ *n* : any of a race of creatures in Greek mythology half man and half horse

¹**cen·ta·vo** \sen-'tä-(ˌ)vō\ *n, pl* **-vos** — see *boliviano, colón, cordoba, lempira, peso, quetzal, sol, sucre* at MONEY table

²**cen·ta·vo** \-'tä-(ˌ)vü, -(ˌ)vō\ *n, pl* **-vos** — see *cruzeiro, escudo, metical* at MONEY table

cen·te·nar·i·an \ˌsent-ᵊn-'er-ē-ən\ *n* : a person who is 100 or more years old

cen·te·nary \sen-'te-nə-rē, 'sent-ᵊn-ˌer-ē\ *n, pl* **-ries** : CENTENNIAL — **cen·tenary** *adj*

cen·ten·ni·al \sen-'te-nē-əl\ *n* : a 100th anniversary or its celebration — **centennial** *adj*

¹**cen·ter** \'sen-tər\ *n* **1** : the point that is equally distant from all points on the circumference of a circle or surface of a sphere; *also* : MIDDLE **1 2** : the point about which an activity concentrates or from which something originates **3** : a region of concentrated population **4** : a middle part **5** *often cap* : political figures holding moderate views esp. between those of conservatives and liberals **6** : a player occupying a middle position (as in football or basketball)

²**center** *vb* **1** : to place or fix at or around a center or central area **2** : to give a central focus or basis : CONCENTRATE **3** : to have a center : FOCUS

cen·ter·board \'sen-tər-ˌbȯrd\ *n* : a retractable keel used esp. in sailboats

cen·ter·piece \-ˌpēs\ *n* **1** : an object in a central position; *esp* : an adornment in the center of a table **2** : one that is of central importance or interest in a larger whole

cen·tes·i·mal \sen-'te-sə-məl\ *adj* : marked by or relating to division into hundredths

¹**cen·tes·i·mo** \chen-'te-zə-ˌmō\ *n, pl* **-mi** \-(ˌ)mē\ — see *lira* at MONEY table

²**cen·tes·i·mo** \sen-'te-sə-ˌmō\ *n, pl* **-mos** — see *balboa, peso* at MONEY table

cen·ti·grade \'sen-tə-ˌgrād, 'sän-\ *adj* : relating to, conforming to, or having a thermometer scale on which the interval between the freezing and boiling points of water is divided into 100 degrees with 0° representing the freezing point and 100° the boiling point ⟨10° ∼⟩

cen·ti·gram \-ˌgram\ *n* — see METRIC SYSTEM table

cen·ti·li·ter \'sen-ti-ˌlē-tər\ *n* — see METRIC SYSTEM table

cen·time \'sän-ˌtēm\ *n* — see *dinar, dirham, franc, gourde* at MONEY table

cen·ti·me·ter \'sen-tə-ˌmē-tər, 'sän-\ *n* — see METRIC SYSTEM table

centimeter–gram–second *adj* : of, relating to, or being a system of units based on the centimeter as the unit of length, the gram as the unit of mass, and the second as the unit of time

cen·ti·mo \'sen-tə-ˌmō\ *n, pl* **-mos** — see *bolivar, colón, dobra, guarani, peseta* at MONEY table

cen·ti·pede \'sen-tə-ˌpēd\ *n* [L *centipeda*, fr. *centum* hundred + *pes* foot] : any of a class of long flattened segmented arthropods with one pair of legs on each segment except the first which has a pair of poison fangs

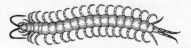

centipede

¹**cen·tral** \'sen-trəl\ *adj* **1** : constituting a center **2** : ESSENTIAL, PRINCIPAL **3** : situated at, in, or near the center **4** : centrally placed and superseding separate units ⟨∼ heating⟩ — **cen·tral·ly** *adv*

²**central** *n* : a central controlling office

cen·tral·ize \'sen-trə-ˌlīz\ *vb* **-ized; -iz·ing** : to bring to a central point or under central control — **cen·tral·i·za·tion** \ˌsen-trə-lə-'zā-shən\ *n* — **cen·tral·iz·er** \'sen-trə-ˌlī-zər\ *n*

central nervous system *n* : the part of the nervous system which integrates nervous function and activity and which in vertebrates consists of the brain and spinal cord

cen·tre *chiefly Brit var of* CENTER

cen·trif·u·gal \sen-'tri-fyə-gəl, -fi-\ *adj* [NL *centrifugus*, fr. *centr-* center + L *fugere* to flee] **1** : proceeding or acting in a direction away from a center or axis **2** : using or acting by centrifugal force

centrifugal force *n* : the force that tends to impel a thing or parts of a thing outward from a center of rotation

cen·tri·fuge \'sen-trə-ˌfyüj\ *n* : a machine using centrifugal force (as for separating substances of different densities or for removing moisture)

cen·trip·e·tal \sen-'tri-pət-ᵊl\ *adj* [NL *centripetus*, fr. *centr-* center + L *petere* seek] : proceeding or acting in a direction toward a center or axis

centripetal force *n* : the force needed to keep an object revolving about a point moving in a circular path

cen·trist \'sen-trist\ *n* **1** *often cap* : a member of a center party **2** : one who holds moderate views

cen·tu·ri·on \sen-'tùr-ē-ən, -'tyùr-\ *n* : an officer commanding a Roman century

cen·tu·ry \'sen-chə-rē\ *n, pl* **-ries** **1** : a subdivision of a Roman legion **2** : a group or sequence of 100 like things **3** : a period of 100 years

century plant *n* : a Mexican agave maturing and flowering only once in many years and then dying

CEO \ˌsē-(ˌ)ē-ˈō\ *n* : the executive with the chief decision-making authority in an organization or business

ce·phal·ic \sə-ˈfa-lik\ *adj* 1 : of or relating to the head 2 : directed toward or situated on or in or near the head

ce·ram·ic \sə-ˈra-mik\ *n* 1 *pl* : the art or process of making articles from a nonmetallic mineral (as clay) by firing 2 : a product produced by ceramics — **ceramic** *adj*

ce·ra·mist \sə-ˈra-mist\ *or* **ce·ram·i·cist** \sə-ˈra-mə-sist\ *n* : one who engages in ceramics

¹**ce·re·al** \ˈsir-ē-əl\ *adj* [L *cerealis*, fr. *Ceres*, the Roman goddess of agriculture] : relating to grain or to the plants that produce it; *also* : made of grain

²**cereal** *n* 1 : a grass (as wheat) yielding grain suitable for food; *also* : its grain 2 : a food and esp. a breakfast food prepared from the grain of a cereal

ce·re·bel·lum \ˌser-ə-ˈbe-ləm\ *n, pl* **-bellums** *or* **-bella** \-lə\ [ML, fr. L, dim. of *cerebrum*] : a part of the brain that projects over the medulla and is concerned esp. with coordination of muscular action and with bodily balance — **cer·e·bel·lar** \-lər\ *adj*

ce·re·bral \sə-ˈrē-brəl, ˈser-ə-\ *adj* 1 : of or relating to the brain, intellect, or cerebrum 2 : appealing to or involving the intellect — **ce·re·bral·ly** *adv*

cerebral cortex *n* : the surface layer of gray matter of the cerebrum that functions chiefly in coordination of sensory and motor information

cerebral palsy *n* : a disorder caused by brain damage usu. before, during, or shortly after birth and marked esp. by defective muscle control

cer·e·brate \ˈser-ə-ˌbrāt\ *vb* **-brat·ed; -brat·ing** : THINK — **cer·e·bra·tion** \ˌser-ə-ˈbrā-shən\ *n*

ce·re·brum \sə-ˈrē-brəm, ˈser-ə-\ *n, pl* **-brums** *or* **-bra** \-brə\ [L] : the enlarged front and upper part of the brain that contains the higher nervous centers

cere·ment \ˈser-ə-mənt, ˈsir-mənt\ *n* : a shroud for the dead

¹**cer·e·mo·ni·al** \ˌser-ə-ˈmō-nē-əl\ *adj* : of, relating to, or forming a ceremony; *also* : stressing careful attention to form and detail — **cer·e·mo·ni·al·ly** *adv*

²**ceremonial** *n* : a ceremonial act or system : RITUAL, FORM

cer·e·mo·ni·ous \ˌser-ə-ˈmō-nē-əs\ *adj* 1 : devoted to forms and ceremony 2 : CEREMONIAL 3 : according to formal usage or procedure 4 : marked by ceremony — **cer·e·mo·ni·ous·ly** *adv* — **cer·e·mo·ni·ous·ness** *n*

cer·e·mo·ny \ˈser-ə-ˌmō-nē\ *n, pl* **-nies** 1 : a formal act or series of acts prescribed by law, ritual, or convention 2 : a conventional act of politeness 3 : a mere outward form with no deeper significance 4 : FORMALITY

ce·re·us \ˈsir-ē-əs\ *n* : any of various cacti of the western U.S. and tropical America

ce·rise \sə-ˈrēs\ *n* [F, lit., cherry] : a moderate red color

ce·ri·um \ˈsir-ē-əm\ *n* : a malleable metallic chemical element used esp. in alloys — see ELEMENT table

cer·met \ˈsər-ˌmet\ *n* : a strong alloy of a heat-resistant compound and a metal used esp. for turbine blades

cert *abbr* certificate; certification; certified; certify

¹**cer·tain** \ˈsərt-ᵊn\ *adj* 1 : FIXED, SETTLED 2 : of a specific but unspecified character ⟨∼ people in authority⟩ 3 : DEPENDABLE, RELIABLE 4 : INDISPUTABLE, UNDENIABLE 5 : assured in mind or action — **cer·tain·ly** *adv*

²**certain** *pron* : certain ones

cer·tain·ty \-tē\ *n, pl* **-ties** 1 : something that is certain 2 : the quality or state of being certain

cer·tif·i·cate \sər-ˈti-fi-kət\ *n* 1 : a document testifying to the truth of a fact 2 : a document testifying that one has fulfilled certain requirements (as of a course or

school) 3 : a document giving evidence of ownership or debt ⟨∼ of deposit⟩

cer·ti·fi·ca·tion \ˌsər-tə-fə-ˈkā-shən\ *n* 1 : the act of certifying : the state of being certified 2 : a certified statement

certified mail *n* : first class mail for which proof of delivery may be secured but no indemnity value is claimed

certified milk *n* : milk produced in dair- ies that operate under the rules and regulations of an authorized medical milk commission

certified public accountant *n* : an accountant who has met the requirements of a state law and has been granted a certificate

cer·ti·fy \ˈsər-tə-ˌfī\ *vb* **-fied; -fy·ing** 1 : VERIFY, CONFIRM 2 : to endorse officially 3 : to guarantee (a bank check) as good by a statement to that effect stamped on its face 4 : to provide with a usu. professional certificate or license **syn** accredit, approve, sanction, endorse — **cer·ti·fi·able** \-ə-bəl\ *adj* — **cer·ti·fi·ably** \-blē\ *adv* — **cer·ti·fi·er** *n*

cer·ti·tude \ˈsər-tə-ˌtüd, -ˌtyüd\ *n* : the state of being or feeling certain

ce·ru·le·an \sə-ˈrü-lē-ən\ *adj* : AZURE

ce·ru·men \sə-ˈrü-mən\ *n* : EARWAX

cer·vi·cal \ˈsər-vi-kəl\ *adj* : of or relating to a neck or cervix

cervical cap *n* : a contraceptive device in the form of a thimble-shaped molded cap that fits over the uterine cervix and blocks sperm from entering the uterus

cer·vix \ˈsər-viks\ *n, pl* **cer·vi·ces** \-və-ˌsēz\ *or* **cervix·es** 1 : NECK; *esp* : the back part of the neck 2 : a constricted portion of an organ or part; *esp* : the narrow outer end of the uterus

ce·sar·e·an *also* **ce·sar·i·an** \si-ˈzar-ē-ən, -ˈzer-\ *n* : CESAREAN SECTION — **cesarean** *also* **cesarian** *adj*

cesarean section *also* **cesarian section** *n* [fr. the belief that Julius Caesar was born this way] : surgical incision of the walls of the abdomen and uterus for delivery of offspring

ce·si·um \ˈsē-zē-əm\ *n* : a silver-white soft ductile chemical element — see ELEMENT table

ces·sa·tion \se-ˈsā-shən\ *n* : a temporary or final ceasing (as of action)

ces·sion \ˈse-shən\ *n* : a yielding (as of rights) to another

cess·pool \ˈses-ˌpül\ *n* : an underground pit or tank for receiving household sewage

ce·ta·cean \si-ˈtā-shən\ *n* : any of an order of aquatic mostly marine mammals that includes whales, porpoises, dolphins, and related forms — **cetacean** *adj*

cf *abbr* [L *confer*] compare

Cf *symbol* californium

CF *abbr* cystic fibrosis

CFC *abbr* chlorofluorocarbon

cg *abbr* centigram

CG *abbr* 1 coast guard 2 commanding general

cgs *abbr* centimeter-gram-second

ch *abbr* 1 chain 2 champion 3 chapter 4 church

CH *abbr* 1 clearinghouse 2 courthouse 3 customhouse

Cha·blis \sha-ˈblē, shə-, shä-; ˈsha-ˌblē\ *n, pl* **Chablis** \-ˈblēz, -(ˌ)blēz\ 1 : a dry sharp white Burgundy wine 2 : a white California wine

cha–cha \ˈchä-ˌchä\ *n* : a fast rhythmic ballroom dance of Latin American origin

Chad·ian \ˈcha-dē-ən\ *n* : a native or inhabitant of Chad — **Chadian** *adj*

chafe \ˈchāf\ *vb* **chafed; chaf·ing** 1 : IRRITATE, VEX 2 : FRET 3 : to warm by rubbing 4 : to rub so as to wear away; *also* : to make sore by rubbing

cha·fer \ˈchā-fər\ *n* : any of various scarab beetles

¹**chaff** \ˈchaf\ *n* 1 : debris (as husks) separated from grain in threshing 2 : something comparatively worthless — **chaffy** *adj*

²**chaff** *n* : light jesting talk : BANTER

³**chaff** *vb* : to tease good-naturedly

chaf·fer \\'cha-fər\ *vb* : BARGAIN, HAGGLE — **chaf·fer·er** *n*

chaf·finch \\'cha-ˌfinch\ *n* : a common European finch with a cheerful song

chaf·ing dish \\'chā-fiŋ-\ *n* : a utensil for cooking food at the table

¹cha·grin \shə-'grin\ *n* : mental uneasiness or annoyance caused by failure, disappointment, or humiliation

²chagrin *vb* **cha·grined** \-'grind\; **cha·grin·ing** : to cause to feel chagrin

¹chain \\'chān\ *n* [ME *cheyne*, fr. MF *chaeine*, fr. L *catena*] **1** : a flexible series of connected links **2** : a chainlike surveying instrument; *also* : a unit of length equal to 66 feet (about 20 meters) **3** *pl* : BONDS, FETTERS **4** : a series of things linked together **syn** train, string, sequence, succession, series

²chain *vb* : to fasten, bind, or connect with a chain; *also* : FETTER

chain gang *n* : a gang of convicts chained together

chain letter *n* : a letter sent to several persons with a request that each send copies to an equal number of persons

chain mail *n* : flexible armor of interlocking metal rings

chain reaction *n* **1** : a series of events in which each event initiates the succeeding one **2** : a chemical or nuclear reaction yielding products that cause further reactions of the same kind

chain saw *n* : a portable power saw that has teeth linked together to form an endless chain — **chain-saw** \\'chān-ˌsò\ *vb*

chain–smoke \\'chān-'smōk\ *vb* : to smoke esp. cigarettes continuously

chain store *n* : any of numerous stores under the same ownership that sell the same lines of goods

¹chair \\'cher\ *n* **1** : a seat with a back for one person **2** : ELECTRIC CHAIR **3** : an official seat; *also* : an office or position of authority or dignity **4** : CHAIRMAN

²chair *vb* : to act as chairman of

chair·lift \\'cher-ˌlift\ *n* : a motor-driven conveyor for skiers consisting of seats hung from a moving cable

chair·man \-mən\ *n* : the presiding officer of a meeting or of a committee — **chair·man·ship** *n*

chair·wom·an \-ˌwu̇-mən\ *n* : a woman who acts as chairman

chaise \\'shāz\ *n* : a 2-wheeled horse-drawn carriage with a folding top

chaise longue \\'shāz-'lóŋ\ *n*, *pl* **chaise longues** *same or* -'lóŋz\ [F *chaise longue*, lit., long chair] : a long reclining chair

chaise lounge \-'lau̇nj\ *n* : CHAISE LONGUE

chal·ced·o·ny \kal-'sed-ᵊn-ē\ *n*, *pl* **-nies** : a translucent pale blue or gray quartz

chal·co·py·rite \ˌkal-kə-'pī-ˌrīt\ *n* : a yellow mineral constituting an important ore of copper

cha·let \sha-'lā\ *n* **1** : a herdsman's cabin in the Swiss mountains **2** : a building in the style of a Swiss cottage with a wide roof overhang

chalet 2

chal·ice \\'cha-ləs\ *n* : a drinking cup; *esp* : the eucharistic cup

¹chalk \\'chòk\ *n* **1** : a soft limestone **2** : chalk or chalky material esp. when used as a crayon — **chalky** *adj*

²chalk *vb* **1** : to rub or mark with chalk **2** : to record with or as if with chalk — usu. used with *up*

chalk·board \\'chòk-ˌbòrd\ *n* : BLACKBOARD

chalk up *vb* **1** : ASCRIBE, CREDIT **2** : ATTAIN, ACHIEVE

¹chal·lenge \\'cha-lənj\ *vb* **chal·lenged; chal·leng·ing** [ME *chalengen* to accuse, fr. OF *chalengier*, fr. L *calumniari* to accuse falsely, fr. *calumnia* calumny] **1** : to order to halt and prove identity **2** : to take exception to : DISPUTE **3** : to issue an invitation to compete against one esp. in single combat : DARE, DEFY — **chal·leng·er** *n*

²challenge *n* **1** : a summons to a duel **2** : an invitation to compete in a sport **3** : a calling into question **4** : an exception taken to a juror **5** : a sentry's command to halt and prove identity **6** : a stimulating or interesting task or problem

chal·lis \\'sha-lē\ *n*, *pl* **chal·lises** \-lēz\ : a lightweight clothing fabric of wool, cotton, or synthetic yarns

cham·ber \\'chām-bər\ *n* **1** : ROOM; *esp* : BEDROOM **2** : an enclosed space or cavity **3** : a hall for meetings of a legislative body **4** : a judge's consultation room — usu. used in pl. **5** : a legislative or judicial body; *also* : a council for a business purpose **6** : the part of a firearm that holds the cartridge or powder charge during firing — **cham·bered** \-bərd\ *adj*

cham·ber·lain \\'chām-bər-lən\ *n* **1** : a chief officer in the household of a king or nobleman **2** : TREASURER

cham·ber·maid \-ˌmād\ *n* : a maid who takes care of bedrooms

chamber music *n* : music intended for performance by a few musicians before a small audience

chamber of commerce : an association of businesspeople for promoting commercial and industrial interests in the community

cham·bray \\'sham-ˌbrā\ *n* : a lightweight clothing fabric of white and colored threads

cha·me·leon \kə-'mēl-yən\ *n* [ME *camelion*, fr. MF, fr. L *chamaeleon*, fr. Gk *chamaileōn*, fr. *chamai* on the ground + *leōn* lion] : a small lizard whose skin changes color esp. according to its surroundings

¹cham·fer \\'cham-fər\ *vb* **1** : to cut a furrow in (as a column) : GROOVE **2** : to make a chamfer on : BEVEL

²chamfer *n* : a beveled edge

cham·ois \\'sha-mē\ *n*, *pl* **cham·ois** *same or* -mēz\ **1** : a small goatlike antelope of Europe and the Caucasus region of Russia **2** *also* **cham·my** \\'sha-mē\ : a soft leather made esp. from the skin of the sheep or goat **3** : a cotton fabric made in imitation of chamois leather

cham·o·mile \\'ka-mə-ˌmīl, -ˌmēl\ *n* : any of a genus of strong-scented herbs related to the daisies and having flower heads that yield a bitter substance used esp. in tonics and teas

¹champ \\'champ, 'chämp\ *vb* **1** : to chew noisily **2** : to show impatience of delay or restraint

²champ \\'champ\ *n* : CHAMPION

cham·pagne \sham-'pān\ *n* : a white effervescent wine

¹cham·pi·on \\'cham-pē-ən\ *n* **1** : a militant advocate or defender **2** : one that wins first prize or place in a contest **3** : one that is acknowledged to be better than all others

²champion *vb* : to protect or fight for as a champion **syn** back, advocate, uphold, support

cham·pi·on·ship \-ˌship\ *n* **1** : the position or title of a champion **2** : the act of championing : DEFENSE **3** : a contest held to determine a champion

¹chance \\'chans\ *n* **1** : something that happens without apparent cause **2** : the unpredictable element in existence : LUCK, FORTUNE **3** : OPPORTUNITY **4** : the likelihood of a particular outcome in an uncertain situation : PROBABILITY **5** : RISK **6** : a raffle ticket — **chance** *adj* — **by chance** : in the haphazard course of events

²chance *vb* **chanced; chanc·ing** **1** : to take place by chance : HAPPEN **2** : to come casually and unexpectedly — used with *upon* **3** : to leave to chance **4** : to accept the risk of

chan·cel \'chan-səl\ *n* : the part of a church including the altar and choir

chan·cel·lery *or* **chan·cel·lory** \'chan- sə-lə-rē\ *n, pl* **-ler·ies** *or* **-lor·ies** **1** : the position or office of a chancellor **2** : the building or room where a chancellor works **3** : the office or staff of an embassy or consulate

chan·cel·lor \'chan-sə-lər\ *n* **1** : a high state official in various countries **2** : the head of a university **3** : a judge in the equity court in various states of the U.S. **4** : the chief minister of state in some European countries — **chan·cel·lor·ship** *n*

chan·cery \'chan-sə-rē\ *n, pl* **-cer·ies** **1** : any of various courts of equity in the U.S. and Britain **2** : a record office for public or diplomatic archives **3** : a chancellor's court or office **4** : the office of an embassy

chan·cre \'shaŋ-kər\ *n* [F, fr. L *cancer*] : a primary sore or ulcer at the site of entry of an infective agent (as of syphilis)

chan·croid \'chaŋ-ıkroid\ *n* : a sexually transmitted disease caused by a bacterium and characterized by chancres that differ from those of syphilis in lacking hardened margins

chancy \'chan-sē\ *adj* **chanc·i·er; -est** **1** *Scot* : AUSPICIOUS **2** : RISKY

chan·de·lier \ıshan-də-'lir\ *n* : a branched lighting fixture suspended from a ceiling

chan·dler \'chand-lər\ *n* [ME *chandeler* a maker or seller of candles, fr. MF *chandelier*, fr. OF, fr. *chandelle* candle, fr. L *candela*] : a dealer in provisions and supplies of a specified kind ⟨ship's ∼⟩ — **chan·dlery** *n*

¹change \'chānj\ *vb* **changed; chang·ing** **1** : to make or become different : ALTER **2** : to replace with another **3** : to give or receive an equivalent sum in notes or coins of usu. smaller denominations or of another currency **4** : to put fresh clothes or covering on ⟨∼ a bed⟩ **5** : to put on different clothes **6** : EXCHANGE — **change·able** *adj* — **chang·er** *n*

²change *n* **1** : the act, process, or result of changing **2** : a fresh set of clothes **3** : money given in exchange for other money of higher denomination **4** : money returned when a payment exceeds the sum due **5** : coins esp. of small denominations — **change·ful** *adj*

change·ling \'chānj-liŋ\ *n* : a child secretly exchanged for another in infancy

change of life : MENOPAUSE

change·over \'chānj-ıō-vər\ *n* : CONVERSION, TRANSITION

change ringing *n* : the art or practice of ringing a set of tuned bells in continually varying order

¹chan·nel \'chan-ᵊl\ *n* **1** : the bed of a stream **2** : the deeper part of a waterway **3** : STRAIT **4** : a means of passage or transmission **5** : a range of frequencies of sufficient width for a single radio or television transmission **6** : a usu. tubular enclosed passage : CONDUIT **7** : a long gutter, groove, or furrow

²channel *vb* **-neled** *or* **-nelled; -neling** *or* **-nel·ling** **1** : to make a channel in **2** : to direct into or through a channel

chan·nel·ize \'chan-ᵊl-ıīz\ *vb* **-ized; -iz·ing** : CHANNEL — **chan·nel·iza·tion** \ıchan-ᵊl-ə-'zā-shən\ *n*

chan·son \shäⁿ-'sōⁿ\ *n, pl* **chan·sons** *same or* -'sōⁿz\ : SONG; *esp* : a cabaret song

¹chant \'chant\ *vb* **1** : SING; *esp* : to sing a chant **2** : to utter or recite in the manner of a chant **3** : to celebrate or praise in song — **chant·er** *n*

²chant *n* **1** : a repetitive melody in which several words are sung to one tone : SONG; *esp* : a liturgical melody **2** : a manner of singing or speaking in musical monotones

chan·teuse \shäⁿ-'tərz, shan-'tüz\ *n, pl* **chan·teuses**

same or -'tər-zəz, -'tü-zəz\ [F] : a woman who is a concert or nightclub singer

chan·tey *or* **chan·ty** \'shan-tē, 'chan-\ *n, pl* **chanteys** *or* **chanties** : a song sung by sailors in rhythm with their work

chan·ti·cleer \ıchan-tə-'klir, ıshan-\ *n* : ROOSTER

Cha·nu·kah \ˌkä-nə-kə, ˈhä-\ *var of* HANUKKAH

cha·os \'kā-ıäs\ *n* **1** *often cap* : the confused unorganized state existing before the creation of distinct forms **2** : the inherent unpredictability in the behavior of a natural system (as the atmosphere or the beating heart) **3** : complete disorder **syn** confusion, jumble, snarl, muddle, disarray — **cha·ot·ic** \kā-'ä-tik\ *adj* — **cha·ot·i·cal·ly** \-ti-k(ə-)lē\ *adv*

¹chap \'chap\ *vb* **chapped; chap·ping** : to dry and crack open usu. from wind and cold ⟨*chapped* lips⟩

²chap *n* : a jaw with its fleshy covering — usu. used in pl.

³chap *n* : FELLOW

⁴chap *abbr* chapter

chap·ar·ral \ısha-pə-'ral\ *n* **1** : a dense impenetrable thicket of shrubs or dwarf trees **2** : an ecological community esp. of southern California composed of shrubby plants

chap·book \'chap-ıbuk\ *n* : a small book of ballads, tales, or tracts

cha·peau \sha-'pō\ *n, pl* **cha·peaus** \-'pōz\ *or* **cha·peaux** \-'pō, -'pōz\ [MF] : HAT

chap·el \'cha-pəl\ *n* [ME, fr. OF *chapele*, fr. ML *cappella*, fr. LL *cappa* cloak; fr. the cloak of St. Martin of Tours preserved as a sacred relic in a chapel built for that purpose] **1** : a private or subordinate place of worship **2** : an assembly at an educational institution usu. including devotional exercises **3** : a place of worship used by a Christian group other than an established church

¹chap·er·on *or* **chap·er·one** \'sha-pə-ırōn\ *n* [F *chaperon*, lit., hood, fr. MF, head covering, fr. *chape* cape, fr. LL *cappa*] **1** : a person (as a matron) who accompanies young unmarried women in public for propriety **2** : an older person who accompanies young people at a social gathering to ensure proper behavior

²chaperon *or* **chaperone** *vb* **-oned; -on·ing** **1** : ESCORT, GUIDE **2** : to act as a chaperon to or for — **chap·er·on·age** \-ırō-nij\ *n*

chap·fall·en \'chap-ıfȯ-lən, 'chäp-\ *adj* **1** : having the lower jaw hanging loosely **2** : DEJECTED, DEPRESSED

chap·lain \'cha-plən\ *n* **1** : a member of the clergy officially attached to a special group (as the army) **2** : a person chosen to conduct religious exercises (as for a club) — **chap·lain·cy** \-sē\ *n*

chap·let \'cha-plət\ *n* **1** : a wreath for the head **2** : a string of beads : NECKLACE

chap·man \'chap-mən\ *n, Brit* : an itinerant dealer : PEDDLER

chaps \'shaps, 'chaps\ *n pl* [MexSp *chaparreras*] : leather leggings resembling trousers without a seat that are worn esp. by western ranch hands

chap·ter \'chap-tər\ *n* **1** : a main division of a book **2** : a body of canons (as of a cathedral) **3** : a local branch of a society or fraternity

¹char \'chär\ *n, pl* **char** *or* **chars** : any of a genus of trouts (as the common brook trout) with small scales

²char *vb* **charred; char·ring** **1** : to burn or become burned to charcoal **2** : SCORCH

³char *vb* **charred; char·ring** : to work as a cleaning woman

char·ac·ter \'kar-ik-tər\ *n* [ME *caracter*, fr. MF *caractère*, fr. L *character* mark, distinctive quality, fr. Gk *charaktēr*, fr. *charassein* to scratch, engrave] **1** : a graphic symbol (as a letter) used in writing or printing **2** : a symbol that represents information; *also* : a representation of such a character that may be accepted by a computer **3** : a distinguishing feature : ATTRIBUTE **4** : the complex of mental and ethical traits marking a person or a group **5** : a person marked by conspicuous often peculiar traits **6** : one of the persons in a novel or play **7** : REPUTATION **8** : moral excellence

¹char·ac·ter·is·tic \ˌkar-ik-tə-ˈris-tik\ *n* : a distinguishing trait, quality, or property

²characteristic *adj* : serving to mark individual character **syn** individual, peculiar, distinctive — **char·ac·ter·is·ti·cal·ly** \-ti-k(ə-)lē\ *adv*

char·ac·ter·ize \ˈkar-ik-tə-ˌrīz\ *vb* **-ized; -iz·ing 1** : to describe the character of **2** : to be a characteristic of — **char·ac·ter·iza·tion** \ˌkar-ik-tə-rə-ˈzā-shən\ *n*

cha·rades \shə-ˈrādz\ *n sing or pl* : a game in which some of the players try to guess a word or phrase from the actions of another player who may not speak

char·coal \ˈchär-ˌkōl\ *n* **1** : a porous carbon prepared from vegetable or animal substances **2** : a piece of fine charcoal used in drawing; *also* : a drawing made with charcoal

chard \ˈchärd\ *n* : SWISS CHARD

char·don·nay \ˌshard-ᵊn-ˈā\ *n, often cap* [F] : a dry white wine made from a single variety of white grape

¹charge \ˈchärj\ *n* **1** : a quantity (as of fuel or ammunition) required to fill something to capacity **2** : a store or accumulation of force **3** : an excess or deficiency of electrons in a body **4** : THRILL, KICK **5** : a task or duty imposed **6** : CARE, RESPONSIBILITY **7** : one given into another's care **8** : instructions from a judge to a jury **9** : COST, EXPENSE, PRICE; *also* : a debit to an account **10** : ACCUSATION, INDICTMENT **11** : ATTACK, ASSAULT

²charge *vb* **charged; charg·ing 1** : to load or fill to capacity **2** : to give an electric charge to; *also* : to restore the activity of (a storage battery) by means of an electric current **3** : to impose a task or responsibility on **4** : COMMAND, ORDER **5** : ACCUSE **6** : to rush against : rush forward in assault **7** : to make liable for payment; *also* : to record a debt or liability against **8** : to fix as a price — **charge·able** *adj*

charge–coupled device *n* : a semiconductor device used esp. as an optical sensor

char·gé d'af·faires \shär-ˌzhā-də-ˈfar\ *n, pl* **chargés d'affaires** \-ˌzhā-, -ˌzhäz-\ [F] : a diplomat who substitutes for an ambassador or minister

¹charg·er \ˈchär-jər\ *n* : a large platter

²charg·er *n* **1** : a device or a workman that charges something **2** : WARHORSE

char·i·ot \ˈchar-ē-ət\ *n* : a 2-wheeled horse-drawn vehicle of ancient times used esp. in war and in races — **char·i·o·teer** \ˌchar-ē-ə-ˈtir\ *n*

cha·ris·ma \kə-ˈriz-mə\ *n* : a personal quality of leadership arousing popular loyalty or enthusiasm — **char·is·mat·ic** \ˌkar-əz-ˈma-tik\ *adj*

char·i·ta·ble \ˈchar-ə-tə-bəl\ *adj* **1** : liberal in giving to needy people **2** : merciful or lenient in judging others **syn** benevolent, philanthropic, altruistic, humanitarian — **char·i·ta·ble·ness** *n* — **char·i·ta·bly** \-blē\ *adv*

char·i·ty \ˈchar-ə-tē\ *n, pl* **-ties 1** : goodwill toward or love of humanity **2** : an act or feeling of generosity **3** : the giving of aid to the poor; *also* : ALMS **4** : an institution engaged in relief of the poor **5** : leniency in judging others **syn** mercy, clemency, lenity

char·la·tan \ˈshär-lə-tən\ *n* : a person making usu. showy pretenses to knowledge or ability : FRAUD, FAKER

Charles·ton \ˈchärl-stən\ *n* : a lively dance in which the knees are swung in and out and the heels are turned sharply outward on each step

char·ley horse \ˈchär-lē-ˌhôrs\ *n* : a muscular pain, cramping, or stiffness from a strain or bruise

¹charm \ˈchärm\ *n* [ME *charme*, fr. MF, fr. L *carmen* song, fr. *canere* to sing] **1** : a practice or expression believed to have magic power **2** : something worn about the person to ward off evil or bring good fortune : AMULET **3** : a trait that fascinates or allures **4**

: physical grace or attraction **5** : a small ornament worn on a bracelet or chain

²charm *vb* **1** : to affect by or as if by a magic spell **2** : to protect by or as if by charms **3** : FASCINATE, ENCHANT **syn** allure, captivate, bewitch, attract — **charm·er** *n*

charm·ing \ˈchär-miŋ\ *adj* : PLEASING, DELIGHTFUL — **charm·ing·ly** *adv*

char·nel house \ˈchärn-ᵊl-\ *n* : a building or chamber in which bodies or bones are deposited

¹chart \ˈchärt\ *n* **1** : MAP **2** : a sheet giving information in the form of a table, list, or diagram; *also* : GRAPH

²chart *vb* **1** : to make a chart of **2** : PLAN

¹char·ter \ˈchär-tər\ *n* **1** : an official document granting rights or privileges (as to a colony, town, or college) from a sovereign or a governing body **2** : CONSTITUTION **3** : a written instrument from a society creating a branch **4** : a mercantile lease of a ship

²charter *vb* **1** : to grant a charter to **2** *Brit* : CERTIFY ⟨~*ed* engineer⟩ **3** : to hire, rent, or lease for temporary use — **char·ter·er** *n*

charter member *n* : an original member of an organization

char·treuse \shär-ˈtrüz, -ˈtrüs\ *n* : a brilliant yellow green

char·wom·an \ˈchär-ˌwu̇-mən\ *n* : a cleaning woman esp. in large buildings

chary \ˈchar-ē\ *adj* **chari·er; -est** [ME, sorrowful, dear, fr. OE *cearig* sorrowful, fr. *caru* sorrow] **1** : CAUTIOUS, CIRCUMSPECT **2** : SPARING — **char·i·ly** \-ə-lē\ *adv*

¹chase \ˈchās\ *n* **1** : PURSUIT; *also* : HUNTING **2** : QUARRY **3** : a tract of unenclosed land used as a game preserve

²chase *vb* **chased; chas·ing 1** : to follow rapidly : PURSUE **2** : HUNT **3** : to seek out ⟨*chasing* down clues⟩ **4** : to cause to depart or flee : drive away **5** : RUSH, HASTEN

³chase *vb* **chased; chas·ing** : to decorate (a metal surface) by embossing or engraving

⁴chase *n* : FURROW, GROOVE

chas·er \ˈchā-sər\ *n* **1** : one that chases **2** : a mild drink (as beer) taken after hard liquor

chasm \ˈka-zəm\ *n* : GORGE 2

chas·sis \ˈcha-sē, ˈsha-sē\ *n, pl* **chas·sis** \-sēz\ : the supporting frame of a structure (as an automobile or television set)

chaste \ˈchāst\ *adj* **chast·er; chast·est 1** : innocent of unlawful sexual intercourse : VIRTUOUS, PURE **2** : CELIBATE **3** : pure in thought : MODEST **4** : severe or simple in design — **chaste·ly** *adv* — **chaste·ness** *n*

chas·ten \ˈchās-ᵊn\ *vb* : to correct through punishment or suffering : DISCIPLINE; *also* : PURIFY — **chas·ten·er** *n*

chas·tise \chas-ˈtīz\ *vb* **chas·tised; chas·tis·ing** [ME *chastisen*, alter. of *chasten*] **1** : to punish esp. bodily **2** : to censure severely : CASTIGATE — **chas·tise·ment** \-mənt, ˈchas-təz-\ *n*

chas·ti·ty \ˈchas-tə-tē\ *n* : the quality or state of being chaste; *esp* : sexual purity

cha·su·ble \ˈcha-zə-bəl, -sə-\ *n* : the outer vestment of the priest at mass

chat \ˈchat\ *n* : light familiar informal talk — **chat** *vb*

châ·teau \sha-ˈtō\ *n, pl* **châ·teaus** \-ˈtōz\ *or* **châ·teaux** \-ˈtō, -ˈtōz\ [F, fr. L *castellum* castle, dim. of *castra* camp] **1** : a feudal castle in France **2** : a large country house **3** : a French vineyard estate

chat·e·laine \ˈshat-ᵊl-ˌān\ *n* **1** : the mistress of a chateau **2** : a clasp or hook for a watch, purse, or keys

chat·tel \ˈchat-ᵊl\ *n* **1** : an item of tangible property other than real estate **2** : SLAVE, BONDMAN

chat·ter \ˈcha-tər\ *vb* **1** : to utter speechlike but meaningless sounds **2** : to talk idly, incessantly, or fast **3** : to click repeatedly or uncontrollably — **chatter** *n* — **chat·ter·er** *n*

chat·ter·box \'cha-tər-ˌbäks\ *n* : one who talks incessantly

chat·ty \'cha-tē\ *adj* **chat·ti·er; -est** : TALKATIVE — **chat·ti·ly** \-tə-lē\ *adv* — **chat·ti·ness** \-tē-nəs\ *n*

¹**chauf·feur** \'shō-fər, shō-'fər\ *n* [F, lit., stoker, fr. *chauffer* to heat] : a person employed to drive an automobile

²**chauffeur** *vb* **chauf·feured; chauf·feur·ing 1** : to do the work of a chauffeur **2** : to transport in the manner of a chauffeur

chaunt \'chȯnt, 'chänt\ *var of* CHANT

chau·vin·ism \'shō-və-ˌni-zəm\ *n* [F *chauvinisme,* fr. Nicolas *Chauvin,* fictional soldier of excessive patriotism and devotion to Napoleon] **1** : excessive or blind patriotism **2** : an attitude of superiority toward members of the opposite sex — **chau·vin·ist** \-nist\ *n or adj* — **chau·vin·is·tic** \ˌshō-və-'nis-tik\ *adj* — **chau·vin·is·ti·cal·ly** \-ti-k(ə-)lē\ *adv*

cheap \'chēp\ *adj* **1** : INEXPENSIVE **2** : costing little effort to obtain **3** : worth little : SHODDY, TAWDRY **4** : worthy of scorn **5** : STINGY — **cheap** *adv* — **cheap·ly** *adv* — **cheap·ness** *n*

cheap·en \'chē-pən\ *vb* **1** : to make or become cheap or cheaper in price or value **2** : to make tawdry

cheap·skate \'chēp-ˌskāt\ *n* : a miserly or stingy person; *esp* : one who tries to avoid paying a fair share of costs

¹**cheat** \'chēt\ *vb* **1** : to deprive of something through fraud or deceit **2** : to practice fraud or trickery **3** : to violate rules (as of a game) dishonestly — **cheat·er** *n*

²**cheat** *n* **1** : the act of deceiving : FRAUD, DECEPTION **2** : one that cheats : a dishonest person

¹**check** \'chek\ *n* **1** : a sudden stoppage of progress **2** : a sudden pause or break **3** : something that stops or restrains **4** : a standard for testing or evaluation **5** : EXAMINATION, INVESTIGATION **6** : the act of testing or verifying **7** : a written order to a bank to pay money **8** : a ticket or token showing ownership or identity **9** : a slip indicating an amount due **10** : a pattern in squares; *also* : a fabric in such a pattern **11** : a mark typically ✔ placed beside an item to show that it has been noted **12** : CRACK, SPLIT

²**check** *vb* **1** : to slow down or stop : BRAKE **2** : to restrain the action or force of : CURB **3** : to compare with a source, original, or authority : VERIFY **4** : to inspect or test for satisfactory condition **5** : to mark with a check as examined **6** : to consign for shipment for one holding a passenger ticket **7** : to mark into squares **8** : to leave or accept for safekeeping in a checkroom **9** : to prove to be consistent or truthful **10** : CRACK, SPLIT

check·book \'chek-ˌbùk\ *n* : a book containing blank checks

¹**check·er** \'che-kər\ *n* : a piece in the game of checkers

²**checker** *vb* **1** : to variegate with different colors or shades **2** : to vary with contrasting elements ⟨a ~ed career⟩ **3** : to mark into squares

³**checker** *n* : one that checks; *esp* : one who checks out purchases in a supermarket

check·er·ber·ry \'che-kər-ˌber-ē\ *n* : WINTERGREEN 1; *also* : the spicy red fruit of this plant

check·er·board \-ˌbȯrd\ *n* : a board of 64 squares of alternate colors used in various games

check·ers \'che-kərz\ *n* : a game for two played on a checkerboard with each player having 12 pieces

check in *vb* : to report one's presence or arrival (as at a hotel)

check·list \'chek-ˌlist\ *n* : a list of things to be checked or done; *also* : a comprehensive list

check·mate \'chek-ˌmāt\ *vb* [ME *chekmaten,* fr. *chekmate,* interj. used to announce checkmate, fr. MF *eschec mat,* fr. Ar *shāh māt,* fr. Per, lit., the king is left unable to escape] **1** : to thwart completely : DEFEAT, FRUSTRATE **2** : to attack (an opponent's king) in chess so that escape is impossible — **checkmate** *n*

check·off \'che-ˌkȯf\ *n* : the deduction of union dues from a worker's paycheck by the employer

check·out \'che-ˌkaùt\ *n* **1** : the action or an instance of checking out **2** : a counter at which checking out is done **3** : the process of examining and testing something as to readiness for intended use

check out *vb* **1** : to settle one's account (as at a hotel) and leave **2** : to total or have totaled the cost of purchases in a store and to make or receive payment for them

check·point \'chek-ˌpȯint\ *n* : a point at which a check is performed

check·room \-ˌrüm, -ˌrùm\ *n* : a room at which baggage, parcels, or clothing is checked

check·up \'che-ˌkəp\ *n* : EXAMINATION; *esp* : a general physical examination

ched·dar \'che-dər\ *n, often cap* : a hard mild to sharp white or yellow cheese of smooth texture

cheek \'chēk\ *n* **1** : the fleshy side part of the face **2** : IMPUDENCE, BOLDNESS, AUDACITY **3** : BUTTOCK 1 — **cheeked** \'chēkt\ *adj*

cheek·bone \'chēk-ˌbōn\ *n* : the bone or bony ridge below the eye

cheeky \'chē-kē\ *adj* **cheek·i·er; -est** : IMPUDENT, SAUCY — **cheek·i·ly** \-kə-lē\ *adv* — **cheek·i·ness** \-kē-nəs\ *n*

cheep \'chēp\ *vb* : to utter faint shrill sounds : PEEP — **cheep** *n*

¹**cheer** \'chir\ *n* [ME *chere* face, cheer, fr. OF, face, fr. ML *cara,* prob. fr. GK *kara* head, face] **1** : state of mind or heart : SPIRIT **2** : ANIMATION, GAIETY **3** : hospitable entertainment : WELCOME **4** : food and drink for a feast **5** : something that gladdens **6** : a shout of applause or encouragement

²**cheer** *vb* **1** : to give hope or courage to : COMFORT **2** : to make glad **3** : to urge on esp. by shouts **4** : to applaud with shouts **5** : to grow or be cheerful — usu. used with *up* — **cheer·er** *n*

cheer·ful \'chir-fəl\ *adj* **1** : having or showing good spirits **2** : conducive to good spirits : pleasant and bright — **cheer·ful·ly** *adv* — **cheer·ful·ness** *n*

cheer·lead·er \'chir-ˌlē-dər\ *n* : a person who directs organized cheering esp. at a sports event

cheer·less \'chir-ləs\ *adj* : BLEAK, DISPIRITING — **cheer·less·ly** *adv* — **cheer·less·ness** *n*

cheery \'chir-ē\ *adj* **cheer·i·er; -est** : CHEERFUL — **cheer·i·ly** \-ə-lē\ *adv* — **cheer·i·ness** \-ē-nəs\ *n*

cheese \'chēz\ *n* : the curd of milk usu. pressed into cakes and cured for use as food

cheese·burg·er \-ˌbər-gər\ *n* : a hamburger topped with cheese

cheese·cake \-ˌkāk\ *n* **1** : a dessert consisting of a creamy filling usu. containing cheese baked in a shell **2** : photographs of shapely scantily clad women

cheese·cloth \-ˌklȯth\ *n* : a lightweight coarse cotton gauze

cheese·par·ing \-ˌpar-iŋ\ *n* : miserly economizing — **cheeseparing** *adj*

cheesy \'chē-zē\ *adj* **chees·i·er; -est** **1** : resembling, suggesting, or containing cheese **2** *slang* : CHEAP **3**

chee·tah \'chē-tə\ *n* [Hindu *cītā* leopard, fr. Skt *citraka,* fr. *citra* bright, variegated] : a large long-legged spotted swift-moving African and formerly Asian cat

cheetah

chef \'shef\ *n* **1** : a cook who manages the kitchen (as of a restaurant) **2** : COOK

chef d'oeu·vre \shā-'dœvr°\ *n, pl* **chefs d'oeuvre** *same* \ : MASTERPIECE

chem *abbr* chemical; chemist; chemistry

¹**chem·i·cal** \'ke-mi-kəl\ *adj* **1** : of, relating to, used in, or produced by chemistry **2** : acting or operated or produced by chemicals — **chem·i·cal·ly** \-k(ə-)lē\ *adv*

²**chemical** *n* : a substance obtained by a chemical process or used for producing a chemical effect

chemical engineering *n* : engineering dealing with the industrial application of chemistry

chemical warfare *n* : warfare using incendiary mixtures, smokes, or irritant, burning, or asphyxiating gases

chemical weapon *n* : a weapon used in chemical warfare

che·mise \shə-'mēz\ *n* **1** : a woman's one-piece undergarment **2** : a loose straight-hanging dress

chem·ist \'ke-mist\ *n* **1** : one trained in chemistry **2** *Brit* : PHARMACIST

chem·is·try \'ke-mə-strē\ *n, pl* **-tries** **1** : the science that deals with the composition, structure, and properties of substances and of the changes they undergo **2** : chemical composition or properties ⟨the ∼ of gasoline⟩ **3** : a strong mutual attraction

che·mo·ther·a·py \,kē-mō-'ther-ə-pē\ *n* : the use of chemicals in the treatment or control of disease — **che·mo·ther·a·peu·tic** \-,ther-ə-'pyü-tik\ *adj*

che·nille \shə-'nēl\ *n* [F, lit., caterpillar, fr. L *canicula*, dim. of *canis* dog] : a fabric with a deep fuzzy pile often used for bedspreads and rugs

cheque \'chek\ *chiefly Brit var of* ¹CHECK 7

che·quer *chiefly Brit var of* CHECKER

cher·ish \'cher-ish\ *vb* **1** : to hold dear : treat with care and affection **2** : to keep deeply in mind — **cher·ish·able** *adj* — **cher·ish·er** *n*

Cher·o·kee \'cher-ə-(,)kē\ *n, pl* **Cherokee** *or* **Cherokees** : a member of an American Indian people orig. of Tennessee and No. Carolina; *also* : their language

che·root \shə-'rüt\ *n* : a cigar cut square at both ends

cher·ry \'cher-ē\ *n, pl* **cherries** [ME *chery*, fr. OF *cherise* (taken as a plural), fr. LL *ceresia*, fr. L *cerasus* cherry tree, fr. Gk *kerasos*] **1** : the small fleshy pale yellow to deep blackish red fruit of a tree related to the roses; *also* : the tree or its wood **2** : a moderate red

chert \'chərt, 'chat\ *n* : a rock resembling flint and consisting essentially of fine crystalline quartz and fibrous chalcedony — **cherty** *adj*

cher·ub \'cher-əb\ *n* **1** *pl* **cher·u·bim** \'cher-ə-,bim\ : an angel of the 2d highest rank **2** *pl* **cherubs** : a chubby rosy person — **che·ru·bic** \chə-'rü-bik\ *adj*

chess \'ches\ *n* : a game for two played on a chessboard with each player having 16 pieces — **chess·man** \-,man, -mən\ *n*

chess·board \'ches-,bōrd\ *n* : a checkerboard used in the game of chess

chest \'chest\ *n* **1** : a box, case, or boxlike receptacle for storage or shipping **2** : the part of the body enclosed by the ribs and sternum — **chest·ed** \'ches-təd\ *adj* — **chest·ful** \'chest-,fûl\ *n*

ches·ter·field \'ches-tər-,fēld\ *n* : an overcoat with a velvet collar

chest·nut \'ches-(,)nət\ *n* **1** : the edible nut of any of a genus of trees related to the beech and oaks; *also* : this tree **2** : a grayish to reddish brown **3** : an old joke or story

chet·rum \'che-trəm\ *n, pl* **chetrums** *or* **chetrum** — see *ngultrum* at MONEY table

che·val glass \shə-'val-\ *n* : a full-length mirror that may be tilted in a frame

che·va·lier \,she-və-'lir, shə-'val-,yā\ *n* : a member of one of various orders of knighthood or of merit

chev·i·ot \'she-vē-ət\ *n, often cap* **1** : a twilled fabric with a rough nap **2** : a sturdy soft-finished cotton fabric

chev·ron \'she-vrən\ *n* : a sleeve badge of one or more V-shaped or inverted V-shaped stripes worn to indicate rank or service (as in the armed forces)

¹**chew** \'chü\ *vb* : to crush or grind with the teeth — **chew·able** *adj* — **chew·er** *n*

²**chew** *n* **1** : an act of chewing **2** : something for chewing

chewy \'chü-ē\ *adj* : requiring much chewing ⟨∼ candy⟩

Chey·enne \shī-'an, -'en\ *n, pl* **Cheyenne** *or* **Cheyennes** [CanF, fr. Dakota *šahíyena*] : a member of an American Indian people of the western plains of the U.S.; *also* : their language

chg *abbr* **1** change **2** charge

chi \'kī\ *n* : the 22d letter of the Greek alphabet — X or χ

Chi·an·ti \kē-'än-tē, -'an-\ *n* : a dry usu. red wine

chiar·oscu·ro \kē-,är-ə-'skur-ō, -'skyur-\ *n, pl* **-ros** [It, fr. *chiaro* clear, light + *oscuro* obscure, dark] **1** : pictorial representation in terms of light and shade without regard to color **2** : the arrangement or treatment of light and dark parts in a pictorial work of art

¹**chic** \'shēk\ *n* : STYLISHNESS

²**chic** *adj* : cleverly stylish : SMART; *also* : currently fashionable

Chi·ca·na \chi-'kä-nə *also* shi-\ *n* : an American woman or girl of Mexican descent — **Chicana** *adj*

chi·cane \shi-'kān\ *n* : CHICANERY

chi·ca·nery \-'ka-nə-rē\ *n, pl* **-ner·ies** : TRICKERY, DECEPTION

Chi·ca·no \chi-'kä-nō\ *n, pl* **-nos** : an American of Mexican descent — **Chicano** *adj*

chi·chi \'shē-(,)shē, 'chē-(,)chē\ *adj* [F] **1** : SHOWY, FRILLY **2** : ARTY, PRECIOUS **3** : CHIC — **chichi** *n*

chick \'chik\ *n* **1** : a young chicken; *also* : a young bird **2** *slang* : a young woman

chick·a·dee \'chi-kə-(,)dē\ *n* : any of several small grayish American birds with black or brown caps

Chick·a·saw \'chi-kə-,sò\ *n, pl* **Chickasaw** *or* **Chickasaws** : a member of an American Indian people of Mississippi and Alabama

¹**chick·en** \'chi-kən\ *n* **1** : a common domestic fowl esp. when young; *also* : its flesh used as food **2** : COWARD

²**chicken** *adj* **1** : COWARDLY **2** *slang* : insistent on petty esp. military discipline

chicken feed *n, slang* : an insignificant sum of money

chick·en·heart·ed \,chi-kən-'här-təd\ *adj* : TIMID, COWARDLY

chicken out *vb* : to lose one's courage

chicken pox *n* : an acute contagious virus disease esp. of children characterized by a low fever and vesicles

chicken wire *n* : a light wire netting of hexagonal mesh

chick–pea \'chik-,pē\ *n* : an Asian leguminous herb cultivated for its short pods with one or two edible seeds; *also* : its seed

chick·weed \'chik-,wēd\ *n* : any of several low-growing small-leaved weeds related to the pinks

chi·cle \'chi-kəl\ *n* : a gum from the latex of a tropical tree used as the chief ingredient of chewing gum

chic·o·ry \'chi-kə-rē\ *n, pl* **-ries** : a usu. blue-flowered herb related to the daisies and grown for its root and for use in salads; *also* : its dried ground root used to flavor or adulterate coffee

chide \'chīd\ *vb* **chid** \'chid\ *or* **chid·ed** \'chī-dəd\; **chid** *or* **chid·den** \'chid-°n\ *or* **chided**; **chid·ing** : to speak disapprovingly to **syn** reproach, reprove, reprimand, admonish, scold, rebuke

¹**chief** \'chēf\ *adj* : highest in rank **2** : most important **syn** principal, main, leading, major — **chief·ly** *adv*

²**chief** *n* **1** : the leader of a body or organization : HEAD **2** : the principal or most valuable part — **chief·dom** *n*

chief master sergeant *n* : a noncommissioned officer of the highest rank in the air force

chief of staff 1 : the ranking officer of a staff in the armed forces **2** : the ranking office of the army or air force

chief of state : the formal head of a national state as

distinguished from the head of the government
chief petty officer *n* : an enlisted man in the navy ranking next below a senior chief petty officer
chief·tain \'chēf-tən\ *n* : a chief esp. of a band, tribe,
or clan — **chief·tain·cy** \-sē\ *n* — **chief·tain·ship** *n*
chief warrant officer *n* : a warrant officer of senior
rank
chif·fon \shi-'fän, 'shi-\ *n* [F, lit., rag, fr. *chiffe* old
rag] : a sheer fabric esp. of silk
chif·fo·nier \ˌshi-fə-'nir\ *n* : a high narrow chest of
drawers
chig·ger \'chi-gər\ *n* : a bloodsucking larval mite that
causes intense itching
chi·gnon \'shēn-ˌyän\ *n* [F, fr. MF *chignon* chain, collar, nape] : a knot of hair worn at the back of the head
Chi·hua·hua \chə-'wä-ˌwä\ *n* : any of a breed of very
small large-eared dogs that originated in Mexico
chil·blain \'chil-ˌblān\ *n* : a sore or inflamed swelling
(as on the feet or hands) caused by exposure to cold
child \'chīld\ *n, pl* **chil·dren** \'chil-drən\ **1** : an unborn
or recently born person **2** : a young person between
the periods of infancy and youth **3** : a male or female
offspring : SON, DAUGHTER **4** : one strongly influenced by another or by a place or state of affairs —
child·ish *adj* — **child·ish·ly** *adv* — **child·ish·ness** *n* —
child·less *adj* — **child·less·ness** *n* — **child·like** *adj*
child·bear·ing \'chīld-ˌbar-iŋ\ *n* : CHILDBIRTH —
childbearing *adj*
child·birth \-ˌbərth\ *n* : the act or process of giving
birth to offspring
child·hood \-ˌhu̇d\ *n* : the state or time of being a child
child·proof \-ˌprüf\ *adj* : made to prevent tampering or
opening by children
child's play *n* : a simple task or act
Chil·ean \'chi-lē-ən, chə-'lā-ən\ *n* : a native or inhabitant of Chile — **Chilean** *adj*
chili *or* **chile** *or* **chil·li** \'chi-lē\ *n, pl* **chil·ies** *or* **chil-
es** *or* **chil·lies** **1** : a pungent pepper related to the tomato **2** : a thick sauce of meat and chilies **3** : CHILI
CON CARNE
chili con car·ne \ˌchi-lē-kän-'kär-nē\ *n* [Sp *chile con
carne* chili with meat] : a spiced stew of ground beef
and chilies or chili powder usu. with beans
chili powder *n* : a seasoning made of ground chilies
and other spices
chili sauce *n* : a spiced tomato sauce usu. made with
red and green peppers
¹chill \'chil\ *n* **1** : a feeling of coldness accompanied by
shivering **2** : moderate coldness **3** : a check to enthusiasm or warmth of feeling
²chill *adj* **1** : moderately cold **2** : COLD, RAW **3** : DIS-
TANT, FORMAL ⟨a ∼ reception⟩ **4** : DEPRESSING, DIS-
PIRITING
³chill *vb* **1** : to make or become cold or chilly **2** : to
make cool esp. without freezing — **chill·er** *n*
chilly \'chi-lē\ *adj* **chill·i·er; -est 1** : noticeably cold **2**
: unpleasantly affected by cold **3** : lacking warmth of
feeling — **chill·i·ness** *n*
¹chime \'chīm\ *n* **1** : a set of bells musically tuned **2** : the
sound of a set of bells — usu. used in pl. **3** : a musical
sound suggesting bells
²chime *vb* **chimed; chim·ing 1** : to make bell=
like sounds **2** : to indicate (as the time of day) by
chiming **3** : to be or act in accord : be in harmony
chime in *vb* : to break into or join in a conversation
chi·me·ra *or* **chi·mae·ra** \kī-'mir-ə, kə-\ *n* [L *chimaera*,
fr. Gk *chimaira* she-goat, chimera] **1** : an imaginary
monster made up of incongruous parts **2** : an illusion
or fabrication of the mind; *esp* : an impossible dream
chi·me·ri·cal \ki-'mer-i-kəl\ *also* **chi·me·ric** \-ik\ *adj* **1**
: FANTASTIC, IMAGINARY **2** : inclined to fantastic
schemes
chim·ney \'chim-nē\ *n, pl* **chimneys 1** : a vertical
structure extending above the roof of a building for
carrying off smoke **2** : a glass tube around a lamp
flame

chimp \'chimp\ *n* : CHIMPANZEE
chim·pan·zee \ˌchim-ˌpan-'zē, chim-'pan-zē\ *n* : an
African ape related to the much larger gorilla
¹chin \'chin\ *n* : the part of the face below the lower lip
including the prominence of the lower jaw — **chin-
less** *adj*
²chin *vb* **chinned; chin·ning** : to raise (oneself) while
hanging by the hands until the chin is level with the
support
chi·na \'chī-nə\ *n* : porcelain ware; *also* : domestic pottery in general
Chi·na·town \-ˌtau̇n\ *n* : the Chinese quarter of a city
chinch bug \'chinch-\ *n* : a small black and white bug
destructive to cereal grasses
chin·chil·la \chin-'chi-lə\ *n* **1** : either of two small So.
American rodents with soft pearl-gray fur; *also* : this
fur **2** : a heavy long-napped woolen cloth

chinchilla 1

chine \'chīn\ *n* : BACKBONE, SPINE; *also* : a cut of meat
including all or part of the backbone
Chi·nese \chī-'nēz, -'nēs\ *n, pl* **Chinese 1** : a native or
inhabitant of China **2** : any of a group of related languages of China — **Chinese** *adj*
Chinese cabbage *n* **1** : BOK CHOY **2** : an Asian garden
plant related to the cabbage and widely grown in the
U.S. for its tight elongate cylindrical heads of pale
green to cream-colored leaves
Chinese checkers *n* : a game in which each player in
turn transfers a set of marbles from a home point to
the opposite point of a pitted 6-pointed star
Chinese gooseberry *n* : a subtropical vine that bears
kiwifruit; *also* : KIWIFRUIT
Chinese lantern *n* : a collapsible translucent cover for
a light
¹chink \'chiŋk\ *n* : a small crack or fissure
²chink *vb* : to fill the chinks of : stop up
³chink *n* : a slight sharp metallic sound
⁴chink *vb* : to make a slight sharp metallic sound
chi·no \'chē-nō\ *n, pl* **chinos 1** : a usu. khaki cotton
twill **2** *pl* : an article of clothing made of chino
Chi·nook \shə-'nu̇k, chə-, -'nük\ *n, pl* **Chinook** *or*
Chinooks : a member of an American Indian people
of Oregon
chintz \'chints\ *n* : a usu. glazed printed cotton cloth
chintzy \'chint-sē\ *adj* **chintz·i·er; -est 1** : decorated
with or as if with chintz **2** : GAUDY, CHEAP **3** : STINGY
chin-up \'chi-ˌnəp\ *n* : the act of chinning oneself
¹chip \'chip\ *n* **1** : a small usu. thin and flat piece (as of
wood) cut or broken off **2** : a thin crisp morsel of food
3 : a counter used in games (as poker) **4** *pl, slang*
: MONEY **5** : a flaw left after a chip is removed **6** : IN-
TEGRATED CIRCUIT **7** : a very small slice of silicon
containing electronic circuits
²chip *vb* **chipped; chip·ping 1** : to cut or break chips
from **2** : to break off in small pieces at the edges **3** : to
play a chip shot
chip in *vb* : CONTRIBUTE
chip·munk \'chip-ˌməŋk\ *n* : any of a genus of small
striped No. American and Asian rodents closely related to the squirrels and marmots
chipped beef \'chipt-\ *n* : smoked dried beef sliced thin
¹chip·per \'chi-pər\ *n* : one that chips
²chipper *adj* : LIVELY, CHEERFUL

Chip·pe·wa \\'chi-pə-ˌwò, -ˌwä, -ˌwä, -wə\ *n, pl* **Chip·pewa** *or* **Chippewas** : OJIBWA

chip shot *n* : a short usu. low shot to the green in golf

chi·rog·ra·phy \kī-'rä-grə-fē\ *n* : HANDWRITING, PENMANSHIP — **chi·ro·graph·ic** \ˌkī-rə-'gra-fik\ *adj*

chi·rop·o·dy \kə-'rä-pə-dē, shə-\ *n* : PODIATRY — **chirop·o·dist** \-dist\ *n*

chi·ro·prac·tic \'kī-rə-ˌprak-tik\ *n* : a system of therapy based esp. on manipulation of body structures — **chi·ro·prac·tor** \-tər\ *n*

chirp \'chərp\ *n* : a short sharp sound characteristic of a small bird or cricket — **chirp** *vb*

¹chis·el \'chi-zəl\ *n* : a metal tool with a sharpened edge at one end used to chip, carve, or cut into a solid material (as wood or stone)

²chisel *vb* **-eled** *or* **-elled; -el·ing** *or* **-el·ling 1** : to work with or as if with a chisel **2** : to obtain by shrewd or often unfair methods; *also* : CHEAT — **chis·el·er** *n*

¹chit \'chit\ *n* [ME *chitte* kitten, cub] **1** : CHILD **2** : a pert young woman

²chit *n* [Hindi *ciṭṭhī* letter, note] : a signed voucher for a small debt

chit·chat \'chit-ˌchat\ *n* : casual or trifling conversation — **chitchat** *vb*

chi·tin \'kīt-ᵊn\ *n* : a sugar polymer that forms part of the hard outer integument esp. of insects — **chi·tin·ous** *adj*

chit·ter·lings *or* **chit·lins** \'chit-lənz\ *n pl* : the intestines of hogs esp. when prepared as food

chi·val·ric \shə-'val-rik\ *adj* : relating to chivalry : CHIVALROUS

chiv·al·rous \'shi-vəl-rəs\ *adj* **1** : of or relating to chivalry **2** : marked by honor, courtesy, and generosity **3** : marked by especial courtesy to women — **chiv·al·rous·ly** *adv* — **chiv·al·rous·ness** *n*

chiv·al·ry \'shi-vəl-rē\ *n, pl* **-ries 1** : mounted men-at-arms **2** : the system or practices of knighthood **3** : the spirit or character of the ideal knight

chive \'chīv\ *n* : an herb related to the onion that has leaves used for flavoring

chla·myd·ia \klə-'mi-dē-ə\ *n, pl* **-i·ae** \-dē-ˌē\ **1** : any of a genus of bacteria that cause various diseases of the eye and urogenital tract **2** : a disease or infection caused by chlamydiae

chlo·ral hydrate \'klòr-əl-\ *n* : a white crystalline compound used as a hypnotic and sedative

chlor·dane \'klòr-ˌdān\ *n* : a highly chlorinated persistent insecticide

chlo·ride \'klòr-ˌīd\ *n* : a compound of chlorine with another element or group

chlo·ri·nate \'klòr-ə-ˌnāt\ *vb* **-nat·ed; -nat·ing** : to treat or combine with chlorine or a chlorine compound — **chlo·ri·na·tion** \ˌklòr-ə-'nā-shən\ *n* — **chlo·ri·na·tor** \'klòr-ə-ˌnā-tər\ *n*

chlo·rine \'klòr-ˌēn\ *n* : a nonmetallic chemical element that is found alone as a strong-smelling greenish yellow irritating gas and is used as a bleach, oxidizing agent, and disinfectant — see ELEMENT table

chlo·rite \'klòr-ˌīt\ *n* : a usu. green mineral found with and resembling mica

chlo·ro·flu·o·ro·car·bon \ˌklòr-ə-'flòr-ə-ˌkär-bən, -'flùr-\ *n* : any of several gaseous compounds that contain carbon, chlorine, fluorine, and sometimes hydrogen and are used esp. as solvents, refrigerants, and aerosol propellants

¹chlo·ro·form \'klòr-ə-ˌfòrm\ *n* : a colorless heavy fluid with etherlike odor used as a solvent and anesthetic

²chloroform *vb* : to treat with chloroform to produce anesthesia or death

chlo·ro·phyll \-ˌfil\ *n* : the green coloring matter of plants that functions in photosynthesis

chm *abbr* chairman

chock \'chäk\ *n* : a wedge for steadying something or for blocking the movement of a wheel — **chock** *vb*

chock·a·block \'chä-kə-ˌbläk\ *adj* : very full : CROWDED

chock–full \'chək-'fùl, 'chäk-\ *adj* : full to the limit : CRAMMED

choc·o·late \'chä-k(ə-)lət, 'chò-\ *n* [Sp, fr. Nahuatl *chocolātl*] **1** : a food prepared from ground roasted cacao beans; *also* : a drink prepared from this **2** : a candy made of or with a coating of chocolate **3** : a dark brown color

Choc·taw \'chäk-ˌtò\ *n, pl* **Choctaw** *or* **Choctaws** : a member of an American Indian people of Mississippi, Alabama, and Louisiana; *also* : their language

¹choice \'chòis\ *n* **1** : the act of choosing : SELECTION **2** : the power or opportunity of choosing : OPTION **3** : the best part **4** : a person or thing selected **5** : a variety offered for selection

²choice *adj* **choic·er; choic·est 1** : worthy of being chosen **2** : selected with care **3** : of high quality

choir \'kwī(-ə)r\ *n* **1** : an organized company of singers (as in a church service) **2** : the part of a church occupied by the singers or by the clergy

choir·boy \'kwī(-ə)r-ˌbòi\ *n* : a boy member of a church choir

choir·mas·ter \-ˌmas-tər\ *n* : the director of a choir (as in a church)

¹choke \'chōk\ *vb* **choked; chok·ing 1** : to hinder breathing (as by obstructing the windpipe) : STRANGLE **2** : to check the growth or action of **3** : CLOG, OBSTRUCT **4** : to enrich the fuel mixture of (a motor) by restricting the carburetor air intake **5** : to perform badly in a critical situation

²choke *n* **1** : the act of choking **2** : a narrowing in size toward the muzzle in the bore of a gun **3** : a valve for choking a gasoline engine

chok·er \'chō-kər\ *n* : something (as a necklace) worn tightly around the neck

cho·ler \'kä-lər, 'kō-\ *n* : a tendency toward anger : IRASCIBILITY

chol·era \'kä-lə-rə\ *n* : a disease marked by severe vomiting and dysentery; *esp* : an often fatal epidemic disease (**Asiatic cholera**) chiefly of southeastern Asia caused by a bacillus

chol·er·ic \'kä-lə-rik, kə-'ler-ik\ *adj* **1** : IRASCIBLE **2** : ANGRY, IRATE

cho·les·ter·ol \kə-'les-tə-ˌròl\ *n* : a physiologically important waxy steroid alcohol found in animal tissues and in high concentrations implicated as a cause of arteriosclerosis

chomp \'chämp, 'chòmp\ *vb* : to chew or bite on something heavily

chon \'chän\ *n, pl* **chon** — see *won* at MONEY table

choose \'chüz\ *vb* **chose** \'chōz\; **cho·sen** \'chōz-ᵊn\; **choos·ing** \'chü-ziŋ\ **1** : to select esp. after consideration **2** : DECIDE **3** : to have a preference for — **chooser** *n*

choosy *or* **choos·ey** \'chü-zē\ *adj* **choos·i·er; -est** : very particular in making choices

¹chop \'chäp\ *vb* **chopped; chop·ping 1** : to cut by repeated blows **2** : to cut into small pieces : MINCE **3** : to strike (a ball) with a short quick downward stroke

²chop *n* **1** : a sharp downward blow or stroke **2** : a small cut of meat often including part of a rib **3** : a short abrupt motion (as of a wave)

³chop *n* **1** : an official seal or stamp **2** : a mark on goods to indicate quality or kind; *also* : QUALITY, GRADE

chop·house \'chäp-ˌhaùs\ *n* : RESTAURANT

chop·per \'chä-pər\ *n* **1** : one that chops **2** *pl, slang* : TEETH **3** : HELICOPTER

chop·pi·ness \'chä-pē-nəs\ *n* : the quality or state of being choppy

¹chop·py \'chä-pē\ *adj* **chop·pi·er; -est 1** : rough with small waves **2** : JERKY, DISCONNECTED — **chop·pi·ly** \-pə-lē\ *adv*

²choppy *adj* **chop·pi·er; -est** : CHANGEABLE, VARIABLE ⟨a ∼ wind⟩

chops \'chäps\ *n pl* : the fleshy covering of the jaws

chop·stick \'chäp-ˌstik\ *n* : one of a pair of sticks used chiefly in oriental countries for lifting food to the mouth

chop su·ey \chäp-'sü-ē\ *n, pl* **chop sueys** : a dish made of vegetables (as bean sprouts, bamboo shoots, water chestnuts, onions, mushrooms) and meat or fish and served with rice

cho·ral \'kōr-əl\ *adj* : of, relating to, or sung by a choir or chorus or in chorus — **cho·ral·ly** *adv*

cho·rale \kə-'ral, -'räl\ *n* **1** : a hymn or psalm sung in church; *also* : a harmonization of a traditional melody **2** : CHORUS, CHOIR

¹chord \'kòrd\ *n* [alter. of ME *cord*, short for *accord*] : three or more musical tones sounded simultaneously

²chord *n* **1** : CORD 2 **2** : a straight line joining two points on a curve

chore \'chōr\ *n* **1** *pl* : the daily light work of a household or farm **2** : a routine task or job **3** : a difficult or disagreeable task

cho·rea \kə-'rē-ə\ *n* : a nervous disorder marked by spasmodic uncontrolled movements

cho·re·og·ra·phy \ˌkōr-ē-'ä-grə-fē\ *n, pl* **-phies** : the art of composing and arranging dances and esp. ballets — **cho·reo·graph** \'kōr-ē-ə-ˌgraf\ *vb* — **cho·re·og·ra·pher** \ˌkōr-ē-'ä-grə-fər\ *n* — **cho·reo·graph·ic** \ˌkōr-ē-ə-'gra-fik\ *adj* — **cho·reo·graph·i·cal·ly** \-fi-k(ə-)lē\ *adv*

cho·ris·ter \'kōr-ə-stər\ *n* : a singer in a choir

chor·tle \'chórt-ᵊl\ *vb* **chor·tled; chor·tling** : to laugh or chuckle esp. in satisfaction or exultation — **chortle** *n*

¹chorus \'kōr-əs\ *n* **1** : an organized company of singers : CHOIR **2** : a group of dancers and singers (as in a musical comedy) **3** : a part of a song repeated at intervals **4** : a composition to be sung by a chorus; *also* : group singing **5** : sounds uttered by a number of persons or animals together ⟨a ∼ of boos⟩

²chorus *vb* : to sing or utter in chorus

chose *past of* CHOOSE

cho·sen \'chōz-ᵊn\ *adj* : selected or marked for special favor or privilege

¹chow \'chaù\ *n* : FOOD

²chow *vb* : EAT — often used with *down*

³chow *n* : CHOW CHOW

chow-chow \'chaù-ˌchaù\ *n* : chopped mixed pickles in mustard sauce

chow chow \'chaù-ˌchaù\ *n* : any of a breed of thick-coated straight-legged muscular dogs of Chinese origin with a blue-black tongue and a short tail curled close to the back

chow·der \'chaù-dər\ *n* : a soup or stew made from seafood or vegetables and containing milk or tomatoes

chow mein \'chaù-'mān\ *n* : a seasoned stew of shredded or diced meat, mushrooms, and vegetables that is usu. served with fried noodles

chrism \'kri-zəm\ *n* : consecrated oil used esp. in baptism, confirmation, and ordination

Christ \'krīst\ *n* [L *Christus*, fr. Gk *Christos*, lit., anointed] : Jesus esp. as the Messiah — **Christ·like** *adj* — **Christ·ly** *adj*

chris·ten \'kris-ᵊn\ *vb* **1** : BAPTIZE **2** : to name at baptism **3** : to name or dedicate (as a ship) by a ceremony suggestive of baptism — **chris·ten·ing** *n*

Chris·ten·dom \'kris-ᵊn-dəm\ *n* **1** : CHRISTIANITY **2** : the part of the world in which Christianity prevails

¹Chris·tian \'kris-chən\ *n* : an adherent of Christianity

²Christian *adj* **1** : of or relating to Christianity **2** : based on or conforming with Christianity **3** : of or relating to a Christian **4** : professing Christianity

chris·ti·a·nia \ˌkris-chē-'a-nē-ə, ˌkris-tē-\ *n* : CHRISTIE

Chris·ti·an·i·ty \ˌkris-chē-'a-nə-tē\ *n* : the religion derived from Jesus Christ, based on the Bible as sacred scripture, and professed by Christians

Chris·tian·ize \'kris-chə-ˌnīz\ *vb* **-ized; -iz·ing** : to make Christian

Christian name *n* : GIVEN NAME

Christian Science *n* : a religion and system of healing founded by Mary Baker Eddy and taught by the Church of Christ, Scientist — **Christian Scientist** *n*

chris·tie *or* **chris·ty** \'kris-tē\ *n, pl* **christies** : a skiing turn made by shifting body weight forward and skidding into a turn with parallel skis

Christ·mas \'kris-məs\ *n* : December 25 celebrated as a church festival in commemoration of the birth of Christ and observed as a legal holiday

Christmas club *n* : a savings account in which regular deposits are made to provide money for Christmas shopping

Christ·mas·tide \'kris-məs-ˌtīd\ *n* : the season of Christmas

chro·mat·ic \krō-'ma-tik\ *adj* **1** : of or relating to color **2** : proceeding by half steps of the musical scale — **chro·mat·i·cism** \-tə-ˌsi-zəm\ *n*

chro·mato·graph \krō-'ma-tə-ˌgraf\ *n* : an instrument used in chromatography

chro·ma·tog·ra·phy \ˌkrō-mə-'tä-grə-fē\ *n* : the separation of a complex mixture into its component compounds as a result of the different rates at which the compounds travel through or over a stationary substance due to differing affinities for the substance — **chro·mato·graph·ic** \krō-ˌma-tə-'gra-fik\ *adj* — **chro·mato·graph·i·cal·ly** \-fi-k(ə-)lē\ *adv*

chrome \'krōm\ *n* **1** : CHROMIUM **2** : a chromium pigment **3** : something plated with an alloy of chromium

chro·mi·um \'krō-mē-əm\ *n* : a bluish white metallic element used esp. in alloys and chrome plating — see ELEMENT table

chro·mo·some \'krō-mə-ˌsōm, -ˌzōm\ *n* : any of the linear or sometimes circular DNA-containing bodies of viruses, bacteria, and the nucleus of higher organisms that contain most or all of the individual's genes — **chro·mo·som·al** \ˌkrō-mə-'sō-məl, -'zō-\ *adj*

chro·mo·sphere \'krō-mə-ˌsfir\ *n* : the lower part of a star's atmosphere

chron *abbr* **1** chronicle **2** chronological; chronology

Chron *abbr* Chronicles

chron·ic \'krä-nik\ *adj* : marked by long duration or frequent recurrence ⟨a ∼ disease⟩; *also* : HABITUAL ⟨a ∼ grumbler⟩ — **chron·i·cal·ly** \-ni-k(ə-)lē\ *adv*

¹chron·i·cle \'krä-ni-kəl\ *n* : HISTORY, NARRATIVE

²chronicle *vb* **-cled; -cling** : to record in or as if in a chronicle — **chron·i·cler** *n*

Chronicles *n* — see BIBLE table

chro·no·graph \'krä-nə-ˌgraf\ *n* : an instrument for measuring and recording time intervals with accuracy — **chro·no·graph·ic** \ˌkrä-nə-'gra-fik\ *adj* — **chro·nog·ra·phy** \krə-'nä-grə-fē\ *n*

chro·nol·o·gy \krə-'nä-lə-jē\ *n, pl* **-gies** **1** : the science that deals with measuring time and dating events **2** : a chronological list or table **3** : arrangement of events in the order of their occurrence — **chron·o·log·i·cal** \ˌkrän-ᵊl-'ä-ji-kəl\ *adj* — **chron·o·log·i·cal·ly** \-k(ə-)lē\ *adv* — **chro·nol·o·gist** \krə-'nä-lə-jist\ *n*

chro·nom·e·ter \krə-'nä-mə-tər\ *n* : a very accurate timepiece

chrys·a·lid \'kri-sə-ləd\ *n* : CHRYSALIS

chrys·a·lis \'kri-sə-ləs\ *n, pl* **chry·sal·i·des** \kri-'sa-lə-ˌdēz\ *or* **chrys·a·lis·es** : an insect pupa in a firm case without a cocoon

chry·san·the·mum \kri-'san-thə-məm\ *n* [L, fr. Gk *chrysanthemon*, fr. *chrysos* gold + *anthemon* flower] : any of various plants related to the daisies including some grown for their showy flowers or for medicinal products or insecticides; *also* : a flower of a chrysanthemum

chub \'chəb\ *n, pl* **chub** *or* **chubs** : any of various small freshwater fishes related to the carp

chub·by \'chə-bē\ *adj* **chub·bi·er; -est** : PLUMP — **chub·bi·ness** *n*

¹chuck \'chək\ *vb* **1** : to give a pat or tap **2** : TOSS **3** : DISCARD; *also* : EJECT **4** : to have done with

²chuck *n* **1** : a light pat under the chin **2** : TOSS

³**chuck** *n* **1** : a cut of beef including most of the neck and the parts around the shoulder blade and the first three ribs **2** : a device for holding work or a tool in a machine (as a lathe)

chuck·hole \'chək-ˌhōl\ *n* : POTHOLE

chuck·le \'chə-kəl\ *vb* **chuck·led; chuck·ling** : to laugh in a quiet hardly audible manner — **chuckle** *n*

chuck wagon *n* : a wagon equipped with a stove and food supplies

¹**chug** \'chəg\ *n* : a dull explosive sound made by or as if by a laboring engine

²**chug** *vb* **chugged; chug·ging** : to move or go with chugs

chuk·ka \'chə-kə\ *n* : a usu. ankle-length leather boot

chuk·ker \'chə-kər\ *also* **chuk·ka** \'chə-kə\ *n* : a playing period of a polo game

¹**chum** \'chəm\ *n* : a close friend

²**chum** *vb* **chummed; chum·ming 1** : to room together **2** : to be a close friend

chum·my \'chə-mē\ *adj* **chum·mi·er; -est** : INTIMATE, SOCIABLE — **chum·mi·ly** \-mə-lē\ *adv* — **chum·mi·ness** \-mē-nəs\ *n*

chump \'chəmp\ *n* : FOOL, BLOCKHEAD

chunk \'chəŋk\ *n* **1** : a short thick piece **2** : a sizable amount

chunky \'chəŋ-kē\ *adj* **chunk·i·er; -est 1** : STOCKY **2** : containing chunks

church \'chərch\ *n* [OE *cirice*, ultim. fr. LGk *kyriakon*, fr. Gk, neut. of *kyriakos* of the lord, fr. *kyrios* lord, master] **1** : a building esp. for Christian public worship **2** : the whole body of Christians **3** : DENOMINATION **4** : CONGREGATION **5** : public divine worship

church·go·er \'chərch-ˌgō(-ə)r\ *n* : one who habitually attends church — **church·go·ing** *adj or n*

church·less \'chərch-ləs\ *adj* : not affiliated with a church

church·man \'chərch-mən\ *n* **1** : CLERGYMAN **2** : a member of a church

church·war·den \'chərch-ˌwȯrd-ᵊn\ *n* : WARDEN 5

church·yard \-ˌyärd\ *n* : a yard that belongs to a church and is often used as a burial ground

churl \'chərl\ *n* **1** : a medieval peasant **2** : RUSTIC **3** : a rude ill-bred person — **churl·ish** *adj* — **churl·ish·ly** *adv* — **churl·ish·ness** *n*

¹**churn** \'chərn\ *n* : a container in which milk or cream is violently stirred in making butter

²**churn** *vb* **1** : to stir in a churn; *also* : to make (butter) by such stirring **2** : to shake around violently

churn out *vb* : to produce mechanically or in large quantity

chute \'shüt\ *n* **1** : an inclined surface, trough, or passage down or through which something may pass ⟨a coal ~⟩ ⟨a mail ~⟩ **2** : PARACHUTE

chut·ney \'chət-nē\ *n, pl* **chutneys** : a thick sauce containing fruits, vinegar, sugar, and spices

chutz·pah \'hu̇t-spə, 'ku̇t-, -(ˌ)spä\ *n* : supreme self-confidence

CIA *abbr* Central Intelligence Agency

cía *abbr* [Sp *compañía*] company

ciao \'chau̇\ *interj* — used to express greeting or farewell

ci·ca·da \sə-'kā-də\ *n* : any of a family of stout-bodied insects related to the aphids and having wide blunt heads and large transparent wings

cicada

ci·ca·trix \'si-kə-ˌtriks\ *n, pl* **ci·ca·tri·ces** \ˌsi-kə-'trī-ˌsēz\ [L] : a scar resulting from formation and contraction of fibrous tissue in a wound

ci·ce·ro·ne \ˌsi-sə-'rō-nē, ˌchē-chə-\ *n, pl* **-ni** \-(ˌ)nē\ : a guide who conducts sightseers

CID *abbr* Criminal Investigation Department

ci·der \'sī-dər\ *n* : juice pressed from fruit (as apples) and used as a beverage, vinegar, or flavoring

cie *abbr* [F *compagnie*] company

ci·gar \si-'gär\ *n* : a roll of tobacco for smoking

cig·a·rette \ˌsi-gə-'ret, 'si-gə-ˌret\ *n* [F, dim. of *cigare* cigar] : a slender roll of cut tobacco enclosed in paper for smoking

cig·a·ril·lo \ˌsi-gə-'ri-lō, -'rē-ō\ *n, pl* **-los** [Sp] **1** : a very small cigar **2** : a cigarette wrapped in tobacco rather than paper

ci·lan·tro \si-'län-trō, -'lan-\ *n* : leaves of coriander used as a flavoring or garnish; *also* : the coriander plant

cil·i·ate \'si-lē-ˌāt\ *n* : any of a group of protozoans characterized by cilia

cil·i·um \'si-lē-əm\ *n, pl* **-ia** \-lē-ə\ **1** : a minute short hairlike process; *esp* : one of a cell **2** : EYELASH

C in C *abbr* commander in chief

cinch \'sinch\ *n* **1** : a girth for a pack or saddle **2** : a sure or an easy thing — **cinch** *vb*

cin·cho·na \siŋ-'kō-nə\ *n* : any of a genus of So. American trees related to the madder; *also* : the bitter quinine-containing bark of a cinchona

cinc·ture \'siŋk-chər\ *n* : BELT, SASH

cin·der \'sin-dər\ *n* **1** : SLAG **2** *pl* : ASHES **3** : a hot piece of partly burned wood or coal **4** : a fragment of lava from an erupting volcano — **cinder** *vb* — **cin·dery** *adj*

cinder block *n* : a building block made of cement and coal cinders

cin·e·ma \'si-nə-mə\ *n* **1** : a motion-picture theater **2** : MOVIES — **cin·e·mat·ic** \ˌsi-nə-'ma-tik\ *adj*

cin·e·ma·theque \ˌsi-nə-mə-'tek\ *n* : a small movie house specializing in avant-garde films

cin·e·ma·tog·ra·phy \ˌsi-nə-mə-'tä-grə-fē\ *n* : motion-picture photography — **cin·e·ma·tog·ra·pher** *n* — **cin·e·mat·o·graph·ic** \-ˌma-tə-'gra-fik\ *adj*

cin·er·ar·i·um \ˌsi-nə-'rer-ē-əm\ *n, pl* **-ia** \-ē-ə\ : a place to receive the ashes of the cremated dead — **cin·er·ary** \'si-nə-ˌrer-ē\ *adj*

cin·na·bar \'si-nə-ˌbär\ *n* : a red mineral that is the only important ore of mercury

cin·na·mon \'si-nə-mən\ *n* : a spice prepared from the highly aromatic bark of any of several trees related to the true laurel; *also* : a tree that yields cinnamon

cinque·foil \'siŋk-ˌfȯil, 'saŋk-\ *n* : any of a genus of plants related to the roses with leaves having five lobes

¹**ci·pher** \'sī-fər\ *n* [ME, fr. MF *cifre*, fr. ML *cifra*, fr. Ar *ṣifr* empty, zero] **1** : ZERO, NAUGHT **2** : a method of secret writing

²**cipher** *vb* : to compute arithmetically

cir *or* **circ** *abbr* circular

cir·ca \'sər-kə\ *prep* : ABOUT ⟨~ 1600⟩

cir·ca·di·an \ˌsər-'kā-dē-ən, ˌsər-kə-'dī-ən\ *adj* : being, having, characterized by, or occurring in approximately 24-hour intervals (as of biological activity)

¹**cir·cle** \'sər-kəl\ *n* **1** : a closed curve every point of which is equally distant from a fixed point within it **2** : something circular **3** : an area of action or influence **4** : CYCLE **5** : a group bound by a common tie

²**circle** *vb* **cir·cled; cir·cling 1** : to enclose in a circle **2** : to move or revolve around; *also* : to move in a circle

cir·clet \'sər-klət\ *n* : a small circle; *esp* : a circular ornament

cir·cuit \'sər-kət\ *n* **1** : a boundary around an enclosed space **2** : a course around a periphery **3** : a regular tour (as by a judge) around an assigned territory **4** : the complete path of an electric current; *also* : an assemblage of electronic components **5** : LEAGUE; *also* : a chain of theaters — **cir·cuit·al** \-ºl\ *adj*

circuit breaker *n* : a switch that automatically interrupts an electric circuit under an abnormal condition

circuit court *n* : a court that sits at two or more places within one judicial district

cir·cu·itous \sər-ʹkyü-ə-təs\ *adj* **1** : having a circular or winding course **2** : not being forthright or direct in language or action

cir·cuit·ry \ʹsər-kə-trē\ *n, pl* **-ries** : the plan or the components of an electric circuit

cir·cu·ity \sər-ʹkyü-ə-tē\ *n, pl* **-ities** : INDIRECTION

¹cir·cu·lar \ʹsər-kyə-lər\ *adj* **1** : having the form of a circle : ROUND **2** : moving in or around a circle **3** : CIRCUITOUS **4** : intended for circulation ⟨a ~ letter⟩ — **cir·cu·lar·i·ty** \ʹsər-kyə-ʹlar-ə-tē\ *n*

²circular *n* : a paper (as a leaflet) intended for wide distribution

cir·cu·lar·ize \ʹsər-kyə-lə-ˌrīz\ *vb* **-ized; -iz·ing 1** : to send circulars to **2** : to poll by questionnaire

circular saw *n* : a power saw with a round cutting blade

cir·cu·late \ʹsər-kyə-ˌlāt\ *vb* **-lat·ed; -lat·ing 1** : to move or cause to move in a circle, circuit, or orbit **2** : to pass from place to place or from person to person — **cir·cu·la·tion** \ˌsər-kyə-ʹlā-shən\ *n*

cir·cu·la·to·ry \ʹsər-kyə-lə-ˌtōr-ē\ *adj* : of or relating to circulation or the circulatory system

circulatory system *n* : the system of blood, blood vessels, lymphatic vessels, and heart concerned with the circulation of the blood and lymph

cir·cum·am·bu·late \ˌsər-kəm-ʹam-byə-ˌlāt\ *vb* **-lat·ed; -lat·ing** : to circle on foot esp. as part of a ritual

cir·cum·cise \ʹsər-kəm-ˌsīz\ *vb* **-cised; -cis·ing** : to cut off the foreskin of — **cir·cum·ci·sion** \ˌsər-kəm-ʹsizhən\ *n*

cir·cum·fer·ence \sər-ʹkəm-f(ə-)rəns\ *n* **1** : the perimeter of a circle **2** : the external boundary or surface of a figure or object

cir·cum·flex \ʹsər-kəm-ˌfleks\ *n* : the mark ˆ over a vowel

cir·cum·lo·cu·tion \ˌsər-kəm-lō-ʹkyü- shən\ *n* : the use of unnecessary words in expressing an idea

cir·cum·lu·nar \-ʹlü-nər\ *adj* : revolving about or surrounding the moon

cir·cum·nav·i·gate \-ʹna-və-ˌgāt\ *vb* : to go completely around (as the earth) esp. by water — **cir·cum·nav·i·ga·tion** \-ˌna-və-ʹgā-shən\ *n*

cir·cum·po·lar \-ʹpō-lər\ *adj* **1** : continually visible above the horizon ⟨a ~ star⟩ **2** : surrounding or found near a pole of the earth

cir·cum·scribe \ʹsər-kəm-ˌskrīb\ *vb* **1** : to constrict the range or activity of **2** : to draw a line around — **cir·cum·scrip·tion** \ˌsər-kəm-ʹskrip-shən\ *n*

cir·cum·spect \ʹsər-kəm-ˌspekt\ *adj* : careful to consider all circumstances and consequences : PRUDENT — **cir·cum·spec·tion** \ˌsər-kəm-ʹspek-shən\ *n*

cir·cum·stance \ʹsər-kəm-ˌstans\ *n* **1** : a fact or event that must be considered along with another fact or event **2** : surrounding conditions **3** : CHANCE, FATE **4** *pl* : situation with regard to wealth **5** : CEREMONY

cir·cum·stan·tial \ˌsər-kəm-ʹstan-chəl\ *adj* **1** : consisting of or depending on circumstances **2** : INCIDENTAL **3** : containing full details — **cir·cum·stan·tial·ly** *adv*

cir·cum·vent \ˌsər-kəm-ʹvent\ *vb* : to check or defeat esp. by stratagem — **cir·cum·ven·tion** \ʹvent-shən\ *n*

cir·cus \ʹsər-kəs\ *n* **1** : a usu. traveling show that features feats of physical skill, wild animal acts, and performances by clowns **2** : a circus performance; *also* : the equipment, livestock, and personnel of a circus

cirque \ʹsərk\ *n* : a deep steep-walled mountain basin usu. forming the blunt end of a valley

cir·rho·sis \sə-ʹrō-səs\ *n, pl* **-rho·ses** \-ˌsēz\ [NL, fr. Gk *kirrhos* orange-colored] : fibrosis of the liver — **cir·rhot·ic** \-ʹrä-tik\ *adj or n*

cir·rus \ʹsir-əs\ *n, pl* **cir·ri** \ʹsir-ˌī\ : a wispy white cloud usu. of minute ice crystals at high altitudes

cis·lu·nar \(ˌ)sis-ʹlü-nər\ *adj* : lying between the earth and the moon or the moon's orbit

cis·tern \ʹsis-tərn\ *n* : an often underground tank for storing water

cit *abbr* **1** citation; cited **2** citizen

cit·a·del \ʹsi-tə-dəl, -ˌdel\ *n* **1** : a fortress commanding a city **2** : STRONGHOLD

ci·ta·tion \sī-ʹtā-shən\ *n* **1** : an official summons to appear (as before a court) **2** : QUOTATION **3** : a formal statement of the achievements of a person; *also* : a specific reference in a military dispatch to meritorious performance of duty

cite \ʹsīt\ *vb* **cit·ed; cit·ing 1** : to summon to appear before a court **2** : QUOTE **3** : to refer to esp. in commendation or praise

cit·i·fied \ʹsi-ti-ˌfīd\ *adj* : of, relating to, or characterized by an urban style of living

cit·i·zen \ʹsi-tə-zən\ *n* **1** : an inhabitant of a city or town **2** : a person who owes allegiance to a government and is entitled to its protection — **cit·i·zen·ship** *n*

cit·i·zen·ry \-rē\ *n, pl* **-ries** : a whole body of citizens

citizens band *n* : a range of radio frequencies set aside for private radio communications

cit·ric acid \ʹsi-trik-\ *n* : a sour organic acid obtained from lemon and lime juices or by fermentation of sugars and used as a flavoring

cit·ron \ʹsi-trən\ *n* **1** : the oval lemonlike fruit of an Asian citrus tree; *also* : the tree **2** : a small hard-fleshed watermelon used esp. in pickles and preserves

cit·ro·nel·la \ˌsi-trə-ʹne-lə\ *n* : an oil obtained from a fragrant grass of southern Asia and used in perfumes and as an insect repellent

cit·rus \ʹsi-trəs\ *n, pl* **citrus** *or* **cit·rus·es** : any of a genus of often thorny evergreen trees or shrubs grown in warm regions for their fruits (as the orange, lemon, lime, and grapefruit); *also* : the fruit

city \ʹsi-tē\ *n, pl* **cit·ies** [ME *citie* large or small town, fr. OF *cité*, fr. ML *civitas*, fr. L, citizenship, state, city of Rome, fr. *civis* citizen] **1** : an inhabited place larger or more important than a town **2** : a municipality in the U.S. governed under a charter granted by the state; *also* : an incorporated municipal unit of the highest class in Canada

city manager *n* : an official employed by an elected council to direct the administration of a city government

city–state \ʹsi-tē-ˌstāt\ *n* : an autonomous state consisting of a city and surrounding territory

civ *abbr* **1** civil; civilian **2** civilization

civ·et \ʹsi-vət\ *n* : a yellowish strong-smelling substance obtained from a catlike mammal (**civet cat**) of Africa or Asia and used in making perfumes

civ·ic \ʹsi-vik\ *adj* : of or relating to a city, citizenship, or civil affairs

civ·ics \-viks\ *n* : a social science dealing with the rights and duties of citizens

civ·il \ʹsi-vəl\ *adj* **1** : of or relating to citizens or to the state as a political body **2** : COURTEOUS, POLITE **3** : of or relating to legal proceedings in connection with private rights and obligations ⟨the ~ code⟩ **4** : of or relating to the general population : not military or ecclesiastical

civil defense *n* : protective measures and emergency relief activities conducted by civilians in case of enemy attack or natural disaster

civil disobedience *n* : refusal to obey governmental commands esp. as a nonviolent means of protest

civil engineer *n* : an engineer whose training or occupation is in the design and construction esp. of public works (as roads or harbors) — **civil engineering** *n*

ci·vil·ian \sə-ʹvil-yən\ *n* : a person not on active duty in a military, police, or fire-fighting force

civ·i·li·sa·tion, civ·i·lise *chiefly Brit var of* CIVILIZA-
TION, CIVILIZE

ci·vil·i·ty \sə-'vi-lə-tē\ *n, pl* **-ties 1** : POLITENESS, COUR-
TESY **2** : a polite act or expression

civ·i·li·za·tion \si-və-lə-'zā-shən\ *n* **1** : a relatively
high level of cultural and technological development
2 : the culture characteristic of a time or place

civ·i·lize \'si-və-,līz\ *vb* **-lized; -liz·ing 1** : to raise from
a primitive state to an advanced and ordered stage of
cultural development **2** : REFINE — **civ·i·lized** *adj*

civil liberty *n* : freedom from arbitrary governmental
interference specifically by denial of governmental
power — usu. used in pl.

civ·il·ly \'si-vəl-lē\ *adv* **1** : in terms of civil rights, matters, or law ⟨∼ dead⟩ **2** : in a civil manner : POLITELY

civil rights *n pl* : the nonpolitical rights of a citizen; *esp*
: those guaranteed by the 13th and 14th amendments
to the Constitution and by acts of Congress

civil servant *n* : a member of a civil service

civil service *n* : the administrative service of a government

civil war *n* : a war between opposing groups of citizens
of the same country

civ·vies \'si-vēz\ *n pl* : civilian clothes as distinguished
from a military uniform

CJ *abbr* chief justice

ck *abbr* **1** cask **2** check

cl *abbr* **1** centiliter **2** class

Cl *symbol* chlorine

¹clack \'klak\ *vb* **1** : CHATTER, PRATTLE **2** : to make or
cause to make a clatter

²clack *n* **1** : rapid continuous talk : CHATTER **2** : a sound
of clacking ⟨the ∼ of a typewriter⟩

clad \'klad\ *adj* **1** : CLOTHED, COVERED **2** : being or
consisting of coins made of outer layers of one metal
bonded to a core of a different metal

¹claim \'klām\ *vb* [ME, fr. MF *clamer*, fr. L *clamare* to
cry out, shout] **1** : to ask for as one's own; *also* : to
take as the rightful owner **2** : to call for : REQUIRE **3**
: to state as a fact : MAINTAIN

²claim *n* **1** : a demand for something due **2** : a right to
something usu. in another's possession **3** : an assertion open to challenge **4** : something claimed (as a
tract of land)

claim·ant \'klā-mənt\ *n* : a person making a claim

clair·voy·ant \klar-'vói-ənt\ *adj* [F, fr. *clair* clear +
voyant seeing] **1** : unusually perceptive **2** : having the
power of discerning objects not present to the senses
— **clair·voy·ance** \-əns\ *n* — **clairvoyant** *n*

clam \'klam\ *n* **1** : any of numerous bivalve mollusks
including many that are edible **2** : DOLLAR

clam·bake \-,bāk\ *n* : a party or gathering (as at the
seashore) at which food is cooked usu. on heated
rocks covered by seaweed

clam·ber \'klam-bər\ *vb* : to climb awkwardly —
clam·ber·er *n*

clam·my \'kla-mē\ *adj* **clam·mi·er; -est** : being damp,
soft, sticky, and usu. cool — **clam·mi·ness** *n*

clam·or \'kla-mər\ *n* **1** : a noisy shouting **2** : a loud continuous noise **3** : insistent public expression (as of
support or protest) — **clamor** *vb* — **clam·or·ous** *adj*

clam·our *chiefly Brit var of* CLAMOR

¹clamp \'klamp\ *n* : a device that holds or presses parts
together firmly

²clamp *vb* : to fasten with or as if with a clamp

clamp down *vb* : to impose restrictions : become repressive — **clamp·down** \'klamp-,daůn\ *n*

clam·shell \'klam-,shel\ *n* : a bucket or grapnel (as on
a dredge) having two hinged jaws

clam up *vb* : to become silent

clan \'klan\ *n* [ME, fr. ScGael *clann* offspring, clan, fr.
Old Irish *cland* plant, offspring, fr. L *planta* plant] : a
group (as in the Scottish Highlands) made up of
households whose heads claim descent from a common ancestor — **clan·nish** *adj* — **clan·nish·ness** *n*

clan·des·tine \klan-'des-tən\ *adj* : held in or conducted
with secrecy

clang \'klaŋ\ *n* : a loud metallic ringing sound — **clang**
vb

clan·gor \'klaŋ-ər, -gər\ *n* : a resounding clang or medley of clangs

clan·gour *chiefly Brit var of* CLANGOR

clank \'klaŋk\ *n* : a sharp brief metallic ringing sound
— **clank** *vb*

¹clap \'klap\ *vb* **clapped; clap·ping 1** : to strike noisily
2 : APPLAUD

²clap *n* **1** : a loud noisy crash **2** : the noise made by clapping the hands

³clap *n* : GONORRHEA

clap·board \'kla-bərd, -,bōrd; 'klap-,bōrd\ *n* : a narrow board thicker at one edge than the other used for
siding — **clap·board** *vb*

clap·per \'kla-pər\ *n* : one that claps; *esp* : the tongue
of a bell

clap·trap \'klap-,trap\ *n* : pretentious nonsense

claque \'klak\ *n* [F, fr. *claquer* to clap] **1** : a group
hired to applaud at a performance **2** : a group of sy-
cophants

clar·et \'klar-ət\ *n* [ME, fr. MF (*vin*) *claret* clear wine]
: a dry red wine

clar·i·fy \'klar-ə-,fī\ *vb* **-fied; -fy·ing** : to make or become clear — **clar·i·fi·ca·tion** \,klar-ə-fə-'kā-shən\ *n*

clar·i·net \,klar-ə-'net\ *n* : a single-reed woodwind instrument in the form of a cylindrical tube with a moderately flaring end — **clar·i·net·ist** *or* **clar·i·net·tist**
\-'ne-tist\ *n*

clarinet

clar·i·on \'klar-ē-ən\ *adj* : brilliantly clear ⟨a ∼ call⟩

clar·i·ty \'klar-ə-tē\ *n* : CLEARNESS

¹clash \'klash\ *vb* **1** : to make or cause to make a clash
2 : CONFLICT, COLLIDE

²clash *n* **1** : a noisy usu. metallic sound of collision **2** : a
hostile encounter; *also* : a conflict of opinion

clasp \'klasp\ *n* **1** : a device (as a hook) for holding objects or parts together **2** : EMBRACE, GRASP — **clasp**
vb

¹class \'klas\ *n* **1** : a group of students meeting regularly
in a course; *also* : a group graduating together **2** : a
course of instruction; *also* : the period when such a
course is taught **3** : social rank; *also* : high quality **4**
: a group of the same general status or nature; *esp* : a
major category in biological classification that is
above the order and below the phylum **5** : a division
or rating based on grade or quality — **class·less** *adj*

²class *vb* : CLASSIFY

class action *n* : a legal action undertaken in behalf of
the plaintiffs and all others having an identical interest in the alleged wrong

¹clas·sic \'kla-sik\ *adj* **1** : serving as a standard of excellence; *also* : TRADITIONAL **2** : CLASSICAL **2 3** : notable esp. as the best example **4** : AUTHENTIC

²classic *n* **1** : a work of enduring excellence and esp. of
ancient Greece or Rome; *also* : its author **2** : a traditional event

clas·si·cal \'kla-si-kəl\ *adj* **1** : CLASSIC **2** : of or relating
to the ancient Greek and Roman classics **3** : of or relating to a form or system of primary significance before modern times ⟨∼ economics⟩ **4** : concerned with
a general study of the arts and sciences — **clas·si·-
cal·ly** \-k(ə-)lē\ *adv*

clas·si·cism \'kla-sə-,si-zəm\ *n* **1** : the principles or
style of the literature or art of ancient Greece and
Rome **2** : adherence to traditional standards believed
to be universally valid — **clas·si·cist** \-sist\ *n*

clas·si·fied \'kla-sə-,fīd\ *adj* : withheld from general
circulation for reasons of national security

clas·si·fy \'kla-sə-ˌfī\ vb **-fied; -fy·ing** : to arrange in or assign to classes — **clas·si·fi·able** adj — **clas·si·fi·ca·tion** \ˌkla-sə-fə-'kā-shən\ n — **clas·si·fi·er** n

class·mate \'klas-ˌmāt\ n : a member of the same class (as in a college)

class·room \-ˌrüm-, -ˌrùm\ n : a place where classes meet

classy \'kla-sē\ adj **class·i·er; -est** : ELEGANT, STYLISH — **class·i·ness** n

clat·ter \'kla-tər\ n : a rattling sound ⟨the ∼ of dishes⟩ — **clatter** vb

clause \'klòz\ n 1 : a group of words having its own subject and predicate but forming only part of a compound or complex sentence 2 : a separate part of an article or document

claus·tro·pho·bia \ˌklò-strə-'fō-bē-ə\ n : abnormal dread of being in closed or narrow spaces — **claus·tro·pho·bic** \-bik\ adj

clav·i·chord \'kla-və-ˌkòrd\ n : an early keyboard instrument in use before the piano

clav·i·cle \'kla-vi-kəl\ n [F clavicule, fr. NL clavicula, fr. L, dim. of L clavis key] : COLLARBONE

cla·vier \klə-'vir; 'klā-vē-ər\ n 1 : the keyboard of a musical instrument 2 : an early keyboard instrument

¹claw \'klò\ n 1 : a sharp usu. curved nail on the toe of an animal 2 : a sharp curved process (as on the foot of an insect); also : a pincerlike organ at the end of a limb of some arthropods (as a lobster) — **clawed** \'klòd\ adj

²claw vb : to rake, seize, or dig with or as if with claws

clay \'klā\ n 1 : an earthy material that is plastic when moist but hard when fired and is used in making pottery; also : finely divided soil consisting largely of such clay 2 : EARTH, MUD 3 : a plastic substance used for modeling 4 : the mortal human body — **clay·ey** \'klā-ē\ adj

clay·more \'klā-ˌmòr\ n : a large 2-edged sword formerly used by Scottish Highlanders

clay pigeon n : a saucer-shaped target thrown from a trap in trapshooting

¹clean \'klēn\ adj 1 : free from dirt or disease 2 : PURE; also : HONORABLE 3 : THOROUGH ⟨made a ∼ sweep⟩ 4 : TRIM ⟨a ship with ∼ lines⟩; also : EVEN 5 : habitually neat — **clean** adv — **clean·ly** \'klēn-lē\ adv — **clean·ness** \-nəs\ n

²clean vb : to make or become clean — **clean·er** n

clean–cut \'klēn-'kət\ adj 1 : cut so that the surface or edge is smooth and even 2 : sharply defined or outlined 3 : giving an effect of wholesomeness

clean·ly \'klen-lē\ adj **clean·li·er; -est** 1 : careful to keep clean 2 : habitually kept clean — **clean·li·ness** n

clean room \'klēn-ˌrüm, -ˌrùm\ n : an uncontaminated room maintained for the manufacture or assembly of objects (as precision parts)

cleanse \'klenz\ vb **cleansed; cleans·ing** : to make clean — **cleans·er** n

¹clean·up \'klē-ˌnəp\ n 1 : an act or instance of cleaning 2 : a very large profit

²cleanup adj : being 4th in the batting order of a baseball team

clean up vb : to make a spectacular business profit

¹clear \'klir\ adj 1 : BRIGHT, LUMINOUS; also : UNTROUBLED, SERENE 2 : CLOUDLESS 3 : CLEAN, PURE; also : TRANSPARENT 4 : easily heard, seen, or understood 5 : capable of sharp discernment; also : free from doubt 6 : INNOCENT 7 : free from restriction, obstruction, or entanglement — **clear** adv — **clear·ness** n

²clear vb 1 : to make or become clear 2 : to go away : DISPERSE 3 : to free from accusation or blame; also : to certify as trustworthy 4 : EXPLAIN 5 : to get free from obstruction 6 : SETTLE 7 : NET 8 : to get rid of : REMOVE 9 : to jump or go by without touching; also : PASS

³clear n : a clear space or part

clear·ance \'klir-əns\ n 1 : an act or process of clearing

2 : the distance by which one object clears another 3 : AUTHORIZATION

clear–cut \'klir-ˌkət\ adj 1 : sharply outlined 2 : DEFINITE, UNEQUIVOCAL

clear–head·ed \-'he-dəd\ adj : having a clear understanding : PERCEPTIVE

clear·ing \'klir-iŋ\ n 1 : a tract of land cleared of wood and brush 2 : the passage of checks and claims through a clearinghouse

clear·ing·house \-ˌhaùs\ n : an institution maintained by banks for making an exchange of checks and claims held by each bank against other banks; also : an informal channel for information or assistance

clear·ly \'klir-lē\ adv 1 : in a clear manner 2 : it is clear

cleat \'klēt\ n : a piece of wood or metal fastened on or projecting from something to give strength, provide a grip, or prevent slipping

cleav·age \'klē-vij\ n 1 : a splitting apart : SPLIT 2 : the depression between a woman's breasts esp. when exposed by a low-cut dress

¹cleave \'klēv\ vb **cleaved** \'klēvd\ or **clove** \'klōv\; **cleaved; cleav·ing** : ADHERE, CLING

²cleave vb **cleaved** \'klēvd\ also **cleft** \'kleft\ or **clove** \'klōv\; **cleaved** also **cleft** or **clo·ven** \'klō-vən\; **cleav·ing** 1 : to divide by force : split asunder 2 : DIVIDE

cleav·er \'klē-vər\ n : a heavy chopping knife for cutting meat

clef \'klef\ n : a sign placed on the staff in music to show what pitch is represented by each line and space

cleft \'kleft\ n : FISSURE, CRACK

cleft palate n : a split in the roof of the mouth that appears as a birth defect

clem·a·tis \'kle-mə-təs; kli-'ma-təs\ n : any of a genus of vines or herbs related to the buttercups that have showy usu. white or purple flowers

clem·en·cy \'kle-mən-sē\ n, pl **-cies** 1 : disposition to be merciful 2 : mildness of weather

clem·ent \'kle-mənt\ adj 1 : MERCIFUL, LENIENT 2 : TEMPERATE, MILD

clench \'klench\ vb 1 : CLINCH 1 2 : to hold fast 3 : to set or close tightly

clere·sto·ry \'klir-ˌstòr-ē\ n : an outside wall of a room or building that rises above an adjoining roof and contains windows

cler·gy \'klər-jē\ n : a body of religious officials authorized to conduct services

cler·gy·man \-mən\ n : a member of the clergy

cler·ic \'kler-ik\ n : a member of the clergy

cler·i·cal \'kler-i-kəl\ adj 1 : of or relating to the clergy 2 : of or relating to a clerk

cler·i·cal·ism \'kler-i-kə-ˌli-zəm\ n : a policy of maintaining or increasing the power of a religious hierarchy

clerk \'klərk, Brit 'klärk\ n 1 : CLERIC 2 : an official responsible for correspondence, records, and accounts; also : a person employed to perform general office work 3 : a store salesperson — **clerk** vb — **clerk·ship** n

clev·er \'kle-vər\ adj 1 : showing skill or resourcefulness 2 : marked by wit or ingenuity — **clev·er·ly** adv — **clev·er·ness** n

clev·is \'kle-vəs\ n : a U-shaped shackle used for fastening

¹clew \'klü\ n 1 : CLUE 2 : a metal loop on a lower corner of a sail

²clew vb : to haul (a sail) up or down by ropes through the clews

cli·ché \kli-'shā\ n [F] : a trite phrase or expression — **cli·chéd** \-'shād\ adj

¹click \'klik\ vb 1 : to make or cause to make a click 2 : to fit or work together smoothly

²click n : a slight sharp noise

cli·ent \'klī-ənt\ n 1 : DEPENDENT 2 : a person who engages the professional services of another; *also* : PA-TRON, CUSTOMER

cli·en·tele \ˌklī-ən-ˈtel, ˌklē-\ *n* : a body of clients and esp. customers

cliff \ˈklif\ *n* : a high steep face of rock, earth, or ice

cliff–hang·er \-ˌhaŋ-ər\ *n* **1** : an adventure serial or melodrama usu. presented in installments each of which ends in suspense **2** : a contest whose outcome is in doubt up to the very end

cli·mac·ter·ic \klī-ˈmak-tə-rik\ *n* **1** : a major turning point or critical stage **2** : MENOPAUSE; *also* : a corresponding period in the male

cli·mate \ˈklī-mət\ *n* [ME *climat*, fr. MF, fr. LL *clima*, fr. Gk *klima* inclination, latitude, climate, fr. *klinein* to lean] **1** : a region having specific climatic conditions **2** : the average weather conditions at a place over a period of years **3** : the prevailing set of conditions (as temperature and humidity) indoors **4** : a prevailing atmosphere or environment ⟨the ∼ of opinion⟩ — **cli·mat·ic** \klī-ˈma-tik\ *adj* — **cli·mat·i·cal·ly** \-ti-k(ə-)lē\ *adv*

cli·ma·tol·o·gy \ˌklī-mə-ˈtä-lə-jē\ *n* : the science that deals with climates — **cli·ma·to·log·i·cal** \-mət-əl-ˈä-ji-kəl\ *adj* — **cli·ma·to·log·i·cal·ly** \-k(ə-)lē\ *adv* — **cli·ma·tol·o·gist** \-mə-ˈtä-lə-jist\ *n*

¹cli·max \ˈklī-ˌmaks\ *n* [L, fr. Gk *klimax* ladder, fr. *klinein* to lean] **1** : a series of ideas or statements so arranged that they increase in force and power from the first to the last; *also* : the last member of such a series **2** : the highest point **3** : ORGASM — **cli·mac·tic** \klī-ˈmak-tik\ *adj*

²climax *vb* : to come or bring to a climax

¹climb \ˈklīm\ *vb* **1** : to rise to a higher point **2** : to go up or down esp. by use of hands and feet; *also* : to ascend in growing — **climb·er** *n*

²climb *n* **1** : a place where climbing is necessary **2** : the act of climbing ; ascent by climbing

clime \ˈklīm\ *n* : CLIMATE

¹clinch \ˈklinch\ *vb* **1** : to turn over or flatten the end of something sticking out ⟨∼ a nail⟩; *also* : to fasten by clinching **2** : to make final : SETTLE **3** : to hold fast or firmly

²clinch *n* **1** : a fastening by means of a clinched nail, rivet, or bolt **2** : an act or instance of clinching in boxing

clinch·er \ˈklin-chər\ *n* : one that clinches; *esp* : a decisive fact, argument, act, or remark

cling \ˈkliŋ\ *vb* **clung** \ˈkləŋ\; **cling·ing** **1** : to adhere as if glued; *also* : to hold or hold on tightly **2** : to have a strong emotional attachment

cling·stone \ˈkliŋ-ˌstōn\ *n* : any of various fruits (as some peaches) whose flesh adheres strongly to the pit

clin·ic \ˈkli-nik\ *n* **1** : a medical class in which patients are examined and discussed **2** : a group meeting for teaching a certain skill and working on individual problems ⟨a reading ∼⟩ **3** : a facility (as of a hospital) for diagnosis and treatment of outpatients

clin·i·cal \ˈkli-ni-kəl\ *adj* **1** : of, relating to, or typical of a clinic; *esp* : involving direct observation of the patient **2** : scientifically dispassionate — **clin·i·cal·ly** \-k(ə-)lē\ *adv*

cli·ni·cian \kli-ˈni-shən\ *n* : a person qualified in the clinical practice of medicine, psychiatry, or psychology as distinguished from one specializing in laboratory or research techniques or in theory

¹clink \ˈkliŋk\ *vb* : to make or cause to make a sharp short metallic sound

²clink *n* : a clinking sound

clin·ker \ˈkliŋ-kər\ *n* : stony matter fused together : SLAG

¹clip \ˈklip\ *vb* **clipped; clip·ping** : to fasten with a clip

²clip *n* **1** : a device that grips, clasps, or hooks **2** : a cartridge holder for a rifle

³clip *vb* **clipped; clip·ping** **1** : to cut or cut off with

shears **2** : CURTAIL, DIMINISH **3** : HIT, PUNCH **4** : to illegally block (an opponent) in football

⁴clip *n* **1** : a 2-bladed instrument for cutting esp. the nails **2** : a sharp blow **3** : a rapid pace

clip·board \ˈklip-ˌbōrd\ *n* : a small writing board with a spring clip at the top for holding papers

clip joint *n, slang* : an establishment (as a nightclub) that makes a practice of defrauding its customers

clip·per \ˈkli-pər\ *n* **1** : an implement for clipping esp. the hair or nails — usu. used in pl. **2** : a fast sailing ship

clip·ping \ˈkli-piŋ\ *n* : a piece clipped from something (as a newspaper)

clique \ˈklēk, ˈklik\ *n* [F] : a small exclusive group of people : COTERIE — **cliqu·ey** \ˈklē-kē, ˈkli-\ *adj* — **cliqu·ish** \-kish\ *adj*

cli·to·ris \ˈkli-tə-rəs\ *n, pl* **cli·to·ri·des** \kli-ˈtòr-ə-ˌdēz\ : a small erectile organ at the anterior or ventral part of the vulva homologous to the penis — **cli·to·ral** \-rəl\ *adj*

clk *abbr* clerk

clo *abbr* clothing

¹cloak \ˈklōk\ *n* **1** : a loose outer garment **2** : something that conceals

²cloak *vb* : to cover or hide with a cloak

cloak–and–dagger *adj* : involving or suggestive of espionage

clob·ber \ˈklä-bər\ *vb* **1** : to pound mercilessly; *also* : to hit with force : SMASH **2** : to defeat overwhelmingly

cloche \ˈklōsh\ *n* [F, lit., bell] : a woman's small close-fitting hat

¹clock \ˈkläk\ *n* : a timepiece not intended to be carried on the person

²clock *vb* **1** : to time (a person or a performance) by a timing device **2** : to register (as speed) on a mechanical recording device — **clock·er** *n*

³clock *n* : an ornamental figure on a stocking or sock

clock·wise \ˈkläk-ˌwīz\ *adv* : in the direction in which the hands of a clock move — **clockwise** *adj*

clock·work \-ˌwərk\ *n* **1** : the machinery that runs a mechanical device (as a clock or toy) **2** : the precision or regularity associated with a clock

clod \ˈkläd\ *n* **1** : a lump esp. of earth or clay **2** : a dull or insensitive person

clod·hop·per \-ˌhä-pər\ *n* **1** : an uncouth rustic **2** : a large heavy shoe

¹clog \ˈkläg\ *n* **1** : a weight so attached as to impede motion **2** : a thick-soled shoe

²clog *vb* **clogged; clog·ging** **1** : to impede with a clog : HINDER **2** : to obstruct passage through **3** : to become filled with extraneous matter

cloi·son·né \ˌklòiz-ən-ˈā\ *adj* : a colored decoration made of enamels poured into the divided areas in a design outlined with wire or metal strips

¹clois·ter \ˈklòi-stər\ *n* [ME *cloistre*, fr. OF, fr. ML *claustrum*, fr. L, bar, bolt, fr. *claudere* to close] **1** : a monastic establishment **2** : a covered usu. colonnaded passage on the side of a court — **clois·tral** \-strəl\ *adj*

²cloister *vb* : to shut away from the world

clone \ˈklōn\ *n* [Gk *klōn* twig, slip] **1** : the offspring produced asexually from an individual (as a plant increased by grafting); *also* : a group of replicas of all or part of a large biological molecule (as DNA) **2** : an individual grown from a single body cell of its parent and genetically identical to the parent **3** : one that appears to be a copy of an original form — **clon·al** \ˈklōn-ᵊl\ *adj* — **clone** *vb*

clop \ˈkläp\ *n* : a sound made by or as if by a hoof or wooden shoe against pavement — **clop** *vb*

¹close \ˈklōz\ *vb* **closed; clos·ing** **1** : to bar passage through : SHUT **2** : to suspend the operations (as of a school) **3** : END, TERMINATE **4** : to bring together the parts or edges of; *also* : to fill up **5** : GRAPPLE ⟨∼ with

the enemy〉 **6** : to enter into an agreement — **clos-able** *or* **close·able** *adj*
²**close** \'klōz\ *n* : CONCLUSION, END
³**close** \'klōs\ *adj* **clos·er; clos·est 1** : having no openings **2** : narrowly restricting or restricted **3** : limited to a privileged class **4** : SECLUDED; *also* : SECRETIVE **5** : RIGOROUS **6** : SULTRY, STUFFY **7** : STINGY **8** : having little space between items or units **9** : fitting tightly; *also* : SHORT 〈~ haircut〉 **10** : NEAR **11** : INTIMATE 〈~ friends〉 **12** : ACCURATE **13** : decided by a narrow margin 〈a ~ game〉 — **close** *adv* — **close·ly** *adv* — **close·ness** *n*
closed–circuit \'klōzd-'sər-kət\ *adj* : used in, shown on, or being a television installation in which the signal is transmitted by wire to a limited number of receivers
closed shop *n* : an establishment having only members of a labor union on the payroll
close·fist·ed \'klōz-'fis-təd, 'klōs-\ *adj* : STINGY
close–knit \'klōs-'nit\ *adj* : closely bound together by social, cultural, economic, or political ties
close·mouthed \'klōz-'mauthd, 'klōs-'mautht\ *adj* : cautious or reticent in speaking
close·out \'klō-₁zaut\ *n* : a sale of a business's entire stock at low prices
close out *vb* **1** : to dispose of by a closeout **2** : to dispose of a business — SELL OUT
¹**clos·et** \'klä-zət, 'klo-\ *n* **1** : a small room for privacy **2** : a small compartment for household utensils or clothing **3** : a state or condition of secrecy 〈came out of the ~〉
²**closet** *vb* : to take into a private room for an interview
close–up \'klō-₁səp\ *n* **1** : a photograph or movie shot taken at close range **2** : an intimate view or examination
clo·sure \'klō-zhər\ *n* **1** : an act of closing : the condition of being closed **2** : something that closes **3** : CLOTURE
clot \'klät\ *n* : a mass formed by a portion of liquid (as blood) thickening and sticking together — **clot** *vb*
cloth \'kloth\ *n, pl* **cloths** \'klothz, 'kloths\ **1** : a pliable fabric made usu. by weaving or knitting natural or synthetic fibers and filaments **2** : TABLECLOTH **3** : distinctive dress of the clergy; *also* : CLERGY
clothe \'kloth\ *vb* **clothed** *or* **clad** \'klad\; **cloth·ing 1** : DRESS **2** : to express by suitably significant language
clothes \'klothz, 'kloz\ *n pl* **1** : CLOTHING **2** : BEDDING 1
clothes·horse \-₁hors\ *n* **1** : a frame on which to hang clothes **2** : a conspicuously dressy person
clothes moth *n* : any of several small pale moths whose larvae eat wool, fur, and feathers
clothes·pin \'klothz-₁pin, 'kloz-\ *n* : a device for fastening clothes on a line
clothes·press \-₁pres\ *n* : a receptacle for clothes
cloth·ier \'kloth-yər, 'klō-thē-ər\ *n* : a maker or seller of clothing
cloth·ing \'klō-thiŋ\ *n* : garments in general
clo·ture \'klō-chər\ *n* : the closing or limitation (as by calling for a vote) of debate in a legislative body
¹**cloud** \'klaud\ *n* [ME, rock, cloud, fr. OE *clūd*] **1** : a visible mass of particles of condensed vapor (as water or ice) suspended in the atmosphere **2** : a usu. visible mass of minute airborne particles; *also* : a mass of obscuring matter in interstellar space **3** : CROWD, SWARM 〈a ~ of mosquitoes〉 **4** : something having a dark or threatening aspect — **cloud·i·ness** \'klaù-dē-nəs\ *n* — **cloud·less** *adj* — **cloudy** *adj*
²**cloud** *vb* **1** : to darken or hide with or as if with a cloud **2** : OBSCURE **3** : TAINT, SULLY
cloud·burst \-₁bərst\ *n* : a sudden heavy rainfall
cloud·let \-lət\ *n* : a small cloud
cloud nine *n* : a feeling of extreme well-being or elation — usu. used with *on*
¹**clout** \'klaut\ *n* **1** : a blow esp. with the hand **2** : PULL, INFLUENCE

²**clout** *vb* : to hit forcefully
¹**clove** \'klōv\ *n* : one of the small bulbs that grows at the base of the scales of a large bulb 〈a ~ of garlic〉
²**clove** *past of* CLEAVE
³**clove** *n* [ME *clowe*, fr. OF *clou* (*de girofle*), lit., nail of clove, fr. L *clavus* nail] : the dried flower bud of an East Indian tree used esp. as a spice
clo·ven \'klō-vən\ *past part of* CLEAVE
cloven foot *n* : CLOVEN HOOF — **cloven–foot·ed** \-'fu-təd\ *adj*
cloven hoof *n* : a foot (as of a sheep) with the front part divided into two parts — **cloven–hoofed** \-'huft, -'huvd\ *adj*
clo·ver \'klō-vər\ *n* : any of a genus of leguminous herbs with usu. 3-parted leaves and dense flower heads
clo·ver·leaf \-₁lēf\ *n, pl* **cloverleafs** \-₁lēfs\ *or* **clo·ver·leaves** \-₁lēvz\ : an interchange between two major highways that from above resembles a four-leaf clover
¹**clown** \'klaun\ *n* **1** : BOOR **2** : a fool or comedian in an entertainment (as a circus) — **clown·ish** *adj* — **clown·ish·ly** *adv* — **clown·ish·ness** *n*
²**clown** *vb* : to act like a clown
cloy \'kloi\ *vb* : to disgust or nauseate with excess of something orig. pleasing — **cloy·ing·ly** *adv*
clr *abbr* clear
¹**club** \'kləb\ *n* **1** : a heavy wooden stick or staff used as a weapon; *also* : BAT **2** : any of a suit of playing cards marked with a black figure resembling a clover leaf **3** : a group of persons associated for a common purpose; *also* : the meeting place of such a group
²**club** *vb* **clubbed; club·bing 1** : to strike with a club **2** : to unite or combine for a common cause
club·foot \'kləb-'fut\ *n* : a misshapen foot twisted out of position from birth; *also* : this deformed condition — **club·foot·ed** \-'fu-təd\ *adj*
club·house \'kləb-₁haus\ *n* **1** : a house occupied by a club **2** : locker rooms used by an athletic team
club sandwich *n* : a sandwich of three slices of bread with two layers of meat (as turkey) and lettuce, tomato, and mayonnaise
club soda *n* : SODA WATER
cluck \'klək\ *n* : the call of a hen esp. to her chicks — **cluck** *vb*
¹**clue** \'klü\ *n* : something that guides through an intricate procedure or maze; *esp* : a piece of evidence leading to the solution of a problem
²**clue** *vb* **clued; clue·ing** *or* **clu·ing** : to provide with a clue; *also* : to give information to 〈~ me in〉
¹**clump** \'kləmp\ *n* **1** : a group of things clustered together **2** : a heavy tramping sound
²**clump** *vb* : to tread clumsily and noisily
clum·sy \'kləm-zē\ *adj* **clum·si·er; -est 1** : lacking dexterity, nimbleness, or grace **2** : not tactful or subtle — **clum·si·ly** \-zə-lē\ *adv* — **clum·si·ness** \-zē-nəs\ *n*
clung *past and past part of* CLING
clunk·er \'kləŋ-kər\ *n* **1** : a dilapidated automobile **2** : a notable failure
¹**clus·ter** \'kləs-tər\ *n* : GROUP, BUNCH
²**cluster** *vb* : to grow or gather in a cluster
¹**clutch** \'kləch\ *vb* : to grasp with or as if with the hand
²**clutch** *n* **1** : the claws or a hand in the act of grasping; *also* : CONTROL, POWER **2** : a device for gripping an object **3** : a coupling used to connect and disconnect a driving and a driven part of a mechanism; *also* : a lever or pedal operating such a coupling **4** : a crucial situation
³**clutch** *adj* : made, done, or successful in a crucial situation
⁴**clutch** *n* **1** : a nest or batch of eggs; *also* : a brood of chicks **2** : GROUP, BUNCH
¹**clut·ter** \'klə-tər\ *vb* : to fill or cover with a disorderly scattering of things
²**clutter** *n* : a crowded mass
cm *abbr* centimeter

Cm *symbol* curium

CM *abbr* [Commonwealth of the Northern Mariana Islands] Northern Mariana Islands

cmdr *abbr* commander

cml *abbr* commercial

CMSgt *abbr* chief master sergeant

CNO *abbr* chief of naval operations

CNS *abbr* central nervous system

co *abbr* 1 company 2 county

Co *symbol* cobalt

CO *abbr* 1 Colorado 2 commanding officer 3 conscientious objector

c/o *abbr* care of

¹**coach** \'kōch\ *n* 1 : a large closed 4-wheeled carriage with an elevated outside front seat for the driver 2 : a railroad passenger car esp. for day travel 3 : BUS 4 : a private tutor; *also* : one who instructs or trains a team of performers

coach 1

²**coach** *vb* : to instruct, direct, or prompt as a coach

coach·man \-mən\ *n* : a man who drives a coach or carriage

co·ad·ju·tor \ˌkō-ə-'jü-tər, kō-'a-jə-tər\ *n* : ASSISTANT; *esp* : an assistant bishop having the right of succession

co·ag·u·lant \kō-'a-gyə-lənt\ *n* : something that produces coagulation

co·ag·u·late \-ˌlāt\ *vb* **-lat·ed; -lat·ing** : CLOT — **co·ag·u·la·tion** \kō-ˌa-gyə-'lā-shən\ *n*

¹**coal** \'kōl\ *n* 1 : EMBER 2 : a black solid combustible mineral used as fuel

²**coal** *vb* 1 : to supply with coal 2 : to take in coal

co·a·lesce \ˌkō-ə-'les\ *vb* **co·a·lesced; co·a·lesc·ing** : to grow together; *also* : FUSE **syn** merge, blend, mingle, mix — **co·a·les·cence** \-²ns\ *n*

coal·field \'kōl-ˌfēld\ *n* : a region rich in coal deposits

coal gas *n* : gas from coal; *esp* : gas distilled from bituminous coal and used for heating

co·a·li·tion \ˌkō-ə-'li-shən\ *n* : UNION; *esp* : a temporary union for a common purpose — **co·a·li·tion·ist** *n*

coal oil *n* : KEROSENE

coal tar *n* : tar distilled from bituminous coal and used in dyes and drugs

co·an·chor \kō-'aŋ-kər\ *n* : a newscaster who shares the duties of head broadcaster

coarse \'kōrs\ *adj* **coars·er; coars·est** 1 : of ordinary or inferior quality 2 : composed of large parts or particles (~ sand) 3 : CRUDE (~ manners) 4 : ROUGH, HARSH — **coarse·ly** *adv* — **coarse·ness** *n*

coars·en \'kōrs-²n\ *vb* : to make or become coarse

¹**coast** \'kōst\ *n* [ME *cost*, fr. MF *coste*, fr. L *costa* rib, side] 1 : SEASHORE 2 : a slide down a slope 3 : the immediate area of view — used in the phrase *the coast is clear* — **coast·al** *adj*

²**coast** *vb* 1 : to sail along the shore 2 : to move (as downhill on a sled) without effort

coast·er *n* 1 : one that coasts 2 : a shallow container or a plate or mat to protect a surface

coaster brake *n* : a brake in the hub of the rear wheel of a bicycle

coast guard *n* : a military force employed in guarding or patrolling a coast — **coast·guards·man** \'kōst-ˌgärdz-mən\ *n*

coast·line \'kōst-ˌlīn\ *n* : the outline or shape of a coast

¹**coat** \'kōt\ *n* 1 : an outer garment for the upper part of the body 2 : an external growth (as of fur or feathers) on an animal 3 : a covering layer — **coat·ed** \'kō-təd\ *adj*

²**coat** *vb* : to cover usu. with a finishing or protective coat

coat·ing \'kō-tiŋ\ *n* : COAT, COVERING

coat of arms : the heraldic bearings (as of a person) usu. depicted on an escutcheon

coat of mail : a garment of metal scales or rings worn as armor

co·au·thor \'kō-'ȯ-thər\ *n* : a joint or associate author — **coauthor** *vb*

coax \'kōks\ *vb* : WHEEDLE; *also* : to gain by gentle urging or flattery

co·ax·i·al \'kō-'ak-sē-əl\ *adj* : having coincident axes — **co·ax·i·al·ly** *adv*

coaxial cable *n* : a cable that consists of a tube of electrically conducting material surrounding a central conductor

cob \'käb\ *n* 1 : a male swan 2 : CORN-COB 3 : a short-legged stocky horse

co·balt \'kō-ˌbȯlt\ *n* [G *Kobalt*, alter. of *Kobold*, lit., goblin; fr. its occurrence in silver ore, believed to be due to goblins] : a tough shiny silver-white magnetic metallic chemical element found with iron and nickel — see ELEMENT table

cob·ble \'kä-bəl\ *vb* **cob·bled; cob·bling** : to make or put together roughly or hastily

cob·bler \'kä-blər\ *n* 1 : a mender or maker of shoes 2 : a deep-dish fruit pie with a thick crust

cob·ble·stone \'kä-bəl-ˌstōn\ *n* : a naturally rounded stone larger than a pebble and smaller than a boulder

co·bra \'kō-brə\ *n* [Pg *cobra* (*de capello*), lit., hooded snake] : any of several venomous snakes of Asia and Africa that when excited expand the skin of the neck into a broad hood

cob·web \'käb-ˌweb\ *n* [ME *coppeweb*, fr. *coppe* spider, fr. OE *ātorcoppe*] 1 : SPIDERWEB; *also* : a thread spun by a spider or insect larva 2 : something flimsy or entangling

co·caine \kō-'kān, 'kō-ˌkān\ *n* : a drug obtained from the leaves of a So. American shrub (**co·ca** \'kō-kə\) that can result in severe psychological dependence and is sometimes used in medicine as a local anesthetic and illegally to stimulate the central nervous system

coc·cus \'kä-kəs\ *n, pl* **coc·ci** \'käk-ˌsī\ : a spherical bacterium

coc·cyx \'käk-siks\ *n, pl* **coc·cy·ges** \'käk-sə-ˌjēz\ *also* **coc·cyx·es** \'käk-sik-səz\ : the end of the spinal column beyond the sacrum esp. in humans

co·chi·neal \'kä-chə-ˌnēl\ *n* : a red dye made from the dried bodies of females of a tropical American insect (**cochineal insect**)

co·chlea \'kō-klē-ə, 'kä-\ *n, pl* **co·chle·as** *or* **co·chle·ae** \-klē-ˌē, -ˌī\ : the usu. spiral part of the inner ear containing nerve endings which carry information about sound to the brain — **co·chle·ar** \-klē-ər\ *adj*

¹**cock** \'käk\ *n* 1 : the adult male of a bird and esp. of the common domestic chicken 2 : VALVE, FAUCET 3 : LEADER 4 : the hammer of a firearm; *also* : the position of the hammer when ready for firing

²**cock** *vb* 1 : to draw back the hammer of a firearm 2 : to set or draw back in readiness for some action (~ your arm to throw) 3 : to turn or tilt usu. to one side

³**cock** *n* : a small pile (as of hay)

cock·ade \kä-'kād\ *n* : an ornament worn on the hat as a badge

cock·a·tiel \ˌkä-kə-'tēl\ *n* : a small crested parrot often kept as a cage bird

cock·a·too \'kä-kə-ˌtü\ *n, pl* **-toos** [D *kaketoe*, fr. Malay *kakatua*] : any of various large noisy Australian crested parrots

cock·a·trice \'kä-kə-trəs, -ˌtrīs\ *n* : a legendary serpent with a deadly glance

cock·crow \'käk-ˌkrō\ *n* : DAWN

cocked hat \'käkt-\ *n* : a hat with the brim turned up on two or three sides

cock·er·el \'kä-kə-rəl\ *n* : a young male domestic chicken

cock·er spaniel \'kä-kər-\ *n* [*cocking* woodcock hunting] : any of a breed of small spaniels with long ears, square muzzle, and silky coat

cock·eyed \'kä-'kīd\ *adj* **1** : turned or tilted to one side **2** : slightly crazy : FOOLISH

cock·fight \'käk-ˌfīt\ *n* : a contest of gamecocks usu. fitted with metal spurs

¹cock·le \'kä-kəl\ *n* : any of several weedy plants related to the pinks

²cockle *n* : a bivalve mollusk with a heart-shaped shell

cock·le·shell \-ˌshel\ *n* **1** : the shell of a cockle **2** : a light flimsy boat

cockleshell 1

cock·ney \'käk-nē\ *n, pl* **cockneys** : a native of London and esp. of the East End of London; *also* : the dialect of a cockney

cock·pit \'käk-ˌpit\ *n* **1** : a pit for cockfights **2** : a space or compartment in a vehicle from which it is steered, piloted, or driven

cock·roach \'käk-ˌrōch\ *n* [Sp *cucaracha*] : any of an order or suborder of active nocturnal insects including some which infest houses and ships

cock·sure \'käk-'shu̇r\ *adj* **1** : perfectly sure : CERTAIN **2** : COCKY

cock·tail \'käk-ˌtāl\ *n* **1** : an iced drink made of liquor and flavoring ingredients **2** : an appetizer (as tomato juice) served as a first course of a meal

cocky \'kä-kē\ *adj* **cock·i·er; -est** : marked by overconfidence : PERT, CONCEITED — **cock·i·ly** \-kə-lē\ *adv* — **cock·i·ness** \-kē-nəs\ *n*

co·coa \'kō-kō\ *n* **1** : CACAO **2** : chocolate deprived of some of its fat and powdered; *also* : a drink made of this heated with water or milk

co·co·nut \'kō-kə-(ˌ)nət\ *n* : a large edible nut produced by a tall tropical palm (**coconut palm**)

co·coon \kə-'kün\ *n* : a case usu. of silk formed by some insect larvae for protection during the pupal stage

cod \'käd\ *n, pl* **cod** *also* **cods** : a bottom-dwelling bony fish of the No. Atlantic that is an important food fish; *also* : a related fish of the Pacific Ocean

COD *abbr* **1** cash on delivery **2** collect on delivery

co·da \'kō-də\ *n* : a closing section in a musical composition that is formally distinct from the main structure

cod·dle \'käd-ᵊl\ *vb* **cod·dled; cod·dling** **1** : to cook slowly in water below the boiling point **2** : PAMPER

¹code \'kōd\ *n* **1** : a systematic statement of a body of law **2** : a system of principles or rules ⟨moral ∼⟩ **3** : a system of signals **4** : a system of symbols (as in secret communication) with special meanings **5** : GENETIC CODE

²code *vb* **cod·ed; cod·ing** : to put into the form or symbols of a code

co·deine \'kō-ˌdēn\ *n* : a narcotic drug obtained from opium and used esp. in cough remedies

co·dex \'kō-ˌdeks\ *n, pl* **co·di·ces** \'kō-də-ˌsēz, 'kä-\ : a manuscript book (as of the Scriptures or classics)

cod·fish \'käd-ˌfish\ *n* : COD

cod·ger \'kä-jər\ *n* : an odd or cranky and usu. elderly fellow

cod·i·cil \'kä-də-səl, -ˌsil\ *n* : a legal instrument modifying an earlier will

cod·i·fy \'kä-də-ˌfī, 'kō-\ *vb* **-fied; -fy·ing** : to arrange in a systematic form — **cod·i·fi·ca·tion** \ˌkä-də-fə-'kā-shən, ˌkō-\ *n*

co·ed \'kō-ˌed\ *n* : a female student in a coeducational institution — **coed** *adj*

co·ed·u·ca·tion \ˌkō-e-jə-'kā-shən\ *n* : the education of male and female students at the same institution — **co·ed·u·ca·tion·al** \-shə-nəl\ *adj* — **co·ed·u·ca·tion·al·ly** *adv*

co·ef·fi·cient \ˌkō-ə-'fi-shənt\ *n* **1** : a constant factor as distinguished from a variable in a mathematical term **2** : a number that serves as a measure of some property (as of a substance, device, or process)

coe·len·ter·ate \si-'len-tə-ˌrāt, -rət\ *n* : any of a phylum of radially symmetrical invertebrate animals including the corals, sea anemones, and jellyfishes

co·equal \kō-'ē-kwəl\ *adj* : equal with another — **coequal** *n* — **co·equal·i·ty** \ˌkō-ē-'kwä-lə-tē\ *n* — **co·equal·ly** *adv*

co·erce \kō-'ərs\ *vb* **co·erced; co·erc·ing** **1** : RESTRAIN, REPRESS **2** : COMPEL **3** : ENFORCE — **co·er·cion** \-'ər-zhən, -shən\ *n* — **co·er·cive** \-'ər-siv\ *adj*

co·e·val \kō-'ē-vəl\ *adj* : of the same age — **coeval** *n*

co·ex·ist \ˌkō-ig-'zist\ *vb* **1** : to exist together or at the same time **2** : to live in peace with each other — **co·ex·is·tence** \-'zis-təns\ *n*

co·ex·ten·sive \ˌkō-ik-'sten-siv\ *adj* : having the same scope or extent in space or time

C of C *abbr* Chamber of Commerce

cof·fee \'ko-fē\ *n* [It & Turk; It *caffè*, fr. Turk *kahve*, fr. Ar *qahwa*] : a drink made from the roasted and ground seeds of a fruit of a tropical shrub or tree; *also* : these seeds (**coffee beans**) or a plant producing them

cof·fee·house \-ˌhau̇s\ *n* : a place where refreshments (as coffee) are sold

coffee klatch \-ˌklach\ *n* : KAFFEE-KLATSCH

cof·fee·pot \-ˌpät\ *n* : a pot for brewing or serving coffee

coffee shop *n* : a small restaurant

coffee table *n* : a low table customarily placed in front of a sofa

cof·fer \'ko-fər\ *n* : a chest or box used esp. for valuables

cof·fer·dam \-ˌdam\ *n* : a watertight enclosure from which water is pumped to expose the bottom of a body of water and permit construction

cof·fin \'ko-fən\ *n* : a box or chest for a corpse to be buried in

C of S *abbr* chief of staff

¹cog \'käg\ *n* : a tooth on the rim of a wheel or gear — **cogged** \'kägd\ *adj*

²cog *abbr* cognate

co·gen·er·a·tion \ˌkō-je-nə-'rā-shən\ *n* : the simultaneous generation of electricity and heat from the same fuel

co·gent \'kō-jənt\ *adj* : having power to compel or constrain : CONVINCING — **co·gen·cy** \-jən-sē\ *n*

cog·i·tate \'kä-jə-ˌtāt\ *vb* **-tat·ed; -tat·ing** : THINK, PONDER — **cog·i·ta·tion** \ˌkä-jə-'tā-shən\ *n* — **cog·i·ta·tive** \'kä-jə-ˌtā-tiv\ *adj*

co·gnac \'kōn-ˌyak\ *n* : a French brandy

cog·nate \'käg-ˌnāt\ *adj* **1** : of the same or similar nature **2** : RELATED; *esp* : related by descent from the same ancestral language — **cognate** *n*

cog·ni·tive \'käg-nə-tiv\ *adj* : of, relating to, or being conscious mental activity (as thinking, remembering, learning, or using language) — **cog·ni·tion** \käg-'ni-shən\ *n*

cog·ni·zance \'käg-nə-zəns\ *n* **1** : apprehension by the mind : AWARENESS **2** : NOTICE, HEED — **cog·ni·zant** \'käg-nə-zənt\ *adj*

cog·no·men \käg-'nō-mən, 'käg-nə-\ *n, pl* **cognomens** *or* **cog·no·mi·na** \käg-'nä-mə-nə, -'nō-\ : NAME; *esp* : NICKNAME

co·gno·scen·te \,kän-yə-'shen-tē\ *n, pl* **-scen·ti** \-tē\ [obs. It] : CONNOISSEUR

cog·wheel \'käg-,hwēl\ *n* : a wheel with cogs or teeth

co·hab·it \kō-'ha-bət\ *vb* : to live together as husband and wife — **co·hab·i·ta·tion** \-,ha-bə-'tā-shən\ *n*

co·here \kō-'hir\ *vb* **co·hered; co·her·ing** : to stick together

co·her·ent \kō-'hir-ənt\ *adj* **1** : having the quality of cohering **2** : logically consistent — **co·her·ence** \-əns\ *n* — **co·her·ent·ly** *adv*

co·he·sion \kō-'hē-zhən\ *n* **1** : a sticking together **2** : molecular attraction by which the particles of a body are united — **co·he·sive** \-siv\ *adj* — **co·he·sive·ly** *adv* — **co·he·sive·ness** *n*

co·ho \'kō-,hō\ *n, pl* **cohos** *or* **coho** : a rather small Pacific salmon with light-colored flesh

co·hort \'kō-,hórt\ *n* **1** : a group of warriors or followers **2** : COMPANION, ACCOMPLICE

coif \'kóif; 2 *usu* 'kwäf\ *n* **1** : a close-fitting hat **2** : COIFFURE

coif·feur \kwä-'fər\ *n* [F] : HAIRDRESSER

coif·feuse \kwä-'fərz, -'fəz, -'füz, -'fyüz\ *n* : a female hairdresser

coif·fure \kwä-'fyúr\ *n* : a manner of arranging the hair

¹coil \'kóil\ *vb* : to wind in a spiral shape

²coil *n* : a series of rings or loops (as of coiled rope, wire, or pipe) : RING, LOOP

¹coin \'kóin\ *n* [ME, fr. MF, wedge, corner, fr. L *cuneus* wedge] **1** : a piece of metal issued by government authority as money **2** : metal money

²coin *vb* **1** : to make (a coin) esp. by stamping : MINT **2** : CREATE, INVENT ⟨∼ a phrase⟩ — **coin·er** *n*

coin·age \'kói-nij\ *n* **1** : the act or process of coining **2** : COINS

co·in·cide \,kō-ən-'sīd, 'kō-ən-,sīd\ *vb* **-cid·ed; -cid·ing** **1** : to occupy the same place in space or time **2** : to correspond or agree exactly

co·in·ci·dence \kō-'in-sə-dəns\ *n* **1** : exact agreement **2** : occurrence together apparently without reason; *also* : an event that so occurs

co·in·ci·dent \-sə-dənt\ *adj* **1** : of similar nature **2** : occupying the same space or time — **co·in·ci·den·tal** \kō-,in-sə-'dent-əl\ *adj*

co·i·tus \'kō-ə-təs\ *n* [L, fr. *coire* to come together] : SEXUAL INTERCOURSE — **co·i·tal** \-əl\ *adj*

¹coke \'kōk\ *n* : a hard gray porous fuel made by heating soft coal to drive off most of its volatile material

²coke *n* : COCAINE

¹col *abbr* **1** colonial; colony **2** column

²col *or* **coll** *abbr* **1** collect, collected, collection **2** college, collegiate

Col *abbr* **1** colonel **2** Colorado **3** Colossians

COL *abbr* **1** colonel **2** cost of living

co·la \'kō-lə\ *n* : a carbonated soft drink usu. containing sugar, caffeine, caramel, and special flavoring

col·an·der \'kə-lən-dər, 'kä-\ *n* : a perforated utensil for draining food

¹cold \'kōld\ *adj* **1** : having a low or decidedly subnormal temperature **2** : lacking warmth of feeling **3** : suffering or uncomfortable from lack of warmth — **cold·ly** *adv* — **cold·ness** *n* — **in cold blood** : with premeditation : DELIBERATELY

²cold *n* **1** : a condition marked by low temperature; *also* : cold weather **2** : a chilly feeling **3** : a bodily disorder popularly associated with chilling; *esp* : COMMON COLD

³cold *adv* : TOTALLY, FINALLY

cold–blood·ed \'kōld-'blə-dəd\ *adj* **1** : lacking normal

human feelings **2** : having a body temperature not internally regulated but close to that of the environment **3** : sensitive to cold

cold feet *n pl* : doubt or fear that prevents action

cold front *n* : an advancing edge of a cold air mass

cold shoulder *n* : cold or unsympathetic behavior — **cold–shoul·der** *vb*

cold sore *n* : a group of blisters appearing in or about the mouth in the oral form of herpes simplex

cold sweat *n* : concurrent perspiration and chill usu. associated with fear, pain, or shock

¹cold turkey *n* : abrupt complete cessation of the use of an addictive drug

²cold turkey *adv* : without a period of adjustment : all at once

cold war *n* : a conflict characterized by the use of means short of sustained overt military action

cole·slaw \'kōl-,slò\ *n* [D *koolsla*, fr. *kool* cabbage + *sla* salad] : a salad made of raw cabbage

col·ic \'kä-lik\ *n* : sharp sudden abdominal pain — **col·icky** \'kä-li-kē\ *adj*

col·i·se·um \,kä-lə-'sē-əm\ *n* : a large structure esp. for athletic contests

col·lab·o·rate \kə-'la-bə-,rāt\ *vb* **-rat·ed; -rat·ing** **1** : to work jointly with others (as in writing a book) **2** : to cooperate with an enemy force occupying one's country — **col·lab·o·ra·tion** \-,la-bə-'rā-shən\ *n* — **col·lab·o·ra·tor** \-'la-bə-,rā-tər\ *n*

col·lage \kə-'läzh\ *n* [F, lit., gluing] : an artistic composition of fragments (as of printed matter) pasted on a surface

¹col·lapse \kə-'laps\ *vb* **col·lapsed; col·laps·ing** **1** : to shrink together abruptly **2** : DISINTEGRATE; *also* : to fall in : give way **3** : to break down physically or mentally; *esp* : to fall helpless or unconscious **4** : to fold down compactly — **col·laps·ible** *adj*

²collapse *n* : BREAKDOWN

¹col·lar \'kä-lər\ *n* **1** : a band, strip, or chain worn around the neck or the neckline of a garment **2** : something resembling a collar — **col·lar·less** *adj*

²collar *vb* : to seize by the collar; *also* : ARREST, GRAB

col·lar·bone \-,bōn\ *n* : the bone of the shoulder that joins the breastbone and the shoulder blade

col·lard \'kä-lərd\ *n* : a stalked smooth-leaved kale — usu. used in pl.

col·late \kə-'lāt; 'kä-,lāt, 'kō-\ *vb* **col·lat·ed; col·lat·ing** **1** : to compare (as two texts) carefully and critically **2** : to assemble in proper order

¹col·lat·er·al \kə-'la-tə-rəl\ *adj* **1** : associated but of secondary importance **2** : descended from the same ancestors but not in the same line **3** : PARALLEL **4** : of, relating to, or being collateral used as security; *also* : secured by collateral

²collateral *n* : property (as stocks) used as security for the repayment of a loan

col·la·tion \kä-'lā-shən, kō-\ *n* **1** : a light meal **2** : the act, process, or result of collating

col·league \'kä-,lēg\ *n* : an associate esp. in a profession

¹col·lect \'kä-likt, -,lekt\ *n* : a short prayer comprising an invocation, petition, and conclusion

²col·lect \kə-'lekt\ *vb* **1** : to bring or come together into one body or place : GATHER **2** : to gain control of ⟨∼ his thoughts⟩ **3** : to receive payment of — **col·lect·ible** *or* **col·lect·able** *adj or n* — **col·lec·tor** \-'lek-tər\ *n*

³col·lect \kə-'lekt\ *adv or adj* : to be paid for by the receiver

col·lect·ed \kə-'lek-təd\ *adj* : SELF-POSSESSED, CALM

col·lec·tion \kə-'lek-shən\ *n* **1** : the act or process of collecting ⟨garbage ∼⟩ **2** : something collected ⟨a stamp ∼⟩ **3** : GROUP, AGGREGATE

¹col·lec·tive \kə-'lek-tiv\ *adj* **1** : of, relating to, or denoting a group of individuals considered as a whole **2** : involving all members of a group as distinct from its individuals **3** : shared or assumed by all members of the group — **col·lec·tive·ly** *adv*

²**collective** *n* **1** : GROUP **2** : a cooperative unit or organization

collective bargaining *n* : negotiation between an employer and a labor union

col·lec·tiv·ism \kə-'lek-ti-₁vi-zəm\ *n* : a political or economic theory advocating collective control esp. over production and distribution

col·lec·tiv·ize \-₁vīz\ *vb* **-ized; -iz·ing** : to organize under collective control — **col·lec·tiv·i·za·tion** \-₁lek-ti-və-'zā-shən\ *n*

col·leen \kä-'lēn, 'kä-₁lēn\ *n* : an Irish girl

col·lege \'kä-lij\ *n* [ME, fr. MF, fr. L *collegium* society, fr. *collega* colleague, fr. *com-* with + *legare* to appoint] **1** : a building used for an educational or religious purpose **2** : an institution of higher learning granting a bachelor's degree; *also* : an institution offering instruction esp. in a vocational or technical field (barber ∼) **3** : an organized body of persons having common interests or duties ⟨∼ of cardinals⟩ — **col·le·giate** \kə-'lē-jət\ *adj*

col·le·gi·al·i·ty \kə-₁lē-jē-'a-lə-tē\ *n* : the relationship of colleagues

col·le·gian \kə-'lē-jən\ *n* : a college student or recent college graduate

col·le·gi·um \kə-'le-gē-əm, -'lā-\ *n, pl* **-gia** \-gē-ə\ *or* **-giums** : a group in which each member has approximately equal power

col·lide \kə-'līd\ *vb* **col·lid·ed; col·lid·ing** **1** : to come together with solid impact **2** : to come into conflict : CLASH

col·lid·er \kə-'lī-dər\ *n* : a particle accelerator in which two beams of particles are made to collide

col·lie \'kä-lē\ *n* : a large dog of a breed with rough⁼ coated and smooth-coated varieties developed in Scotland for herding sheep

collie

col·lier \'käl-yər\ *n* **1** : a coal miner **2** : a ship for carrying coal

col·liery \'käl-yə-rē\ *n, pl* **-lier·ies** : a coal mine and its associated buildings

col·li·mate \'kä-lə-₁māt\ *vb* **-mat·ed; -mat·ing** : to make (as light rays) parallel

col·li·sion \kə-'li-zhən\ *n* : an act or instance of colliding

col·lo·ca·tion \₁kä-lə-'kā-shən\ *n* : the act or result of placing or arranging together; *esp* : a noticeable arrangement or conjoining of linguistic elements (as words)

col·loid \'kä-₁lȯid\ *n* : a substance in the form of submicroscopic particles that when in solution or suspension do not settle out; *also* : such a substance together with the medium in which it is dispersed — **col·loi·dal** \kə-'lȯid-ᵊl\ *adj*

colloq *abbr* colloquial

col·lo·qui·al \kə-'lō-kwē-əl\ *adj* : of, relating to, or characteristic of conversation and esp. of familiar and informal conversation

col·lo·qui·al·ism \-'lō-kwē-ə-₁li-zəm\ *n* : a colloquial expression

col·lo·qui·um \kə-'lō-kwē-əm\ *n, pl* **-qui·ums** *or* **-quia** \-ə\ : CONFERENCE, SEMINAR

col·lo·quy \'kä-lə-kwē\ *n, pl* **-quies** : a usu. formal conversation or conference

col·lu·sion \kə-'lü-zhən\ *n* : secret agreement or cooperation for an illegal or deceitful purpose — **col·lu·sive** \-siv\ *adj*

Colo *abbr* Colorado

co·logne \kə-'lōn\ *n* [*Cologne*, Germany] : a perfumed liquid — **co·logned** \-'lōnd\ *adj*

Co·lom·bi·an \kə-'ləm-bē-ən\ *n* : a native or inhabitant of Colombia — **Colombian** *adj*

¹**co·lon** \'kō-lən\ *n, pl* **colons** *or* **co·la** \-lə\ : the part of the large intestine extending from the cecum to the rectum — **co·lon·ic** \kō-'lä-nik\ *adj*

²**colon** *n, pl* **colons** : a punctuation mark : used esp. to direct attention to following matter (as a list)

co·lón *also* **co·lone** \kə-'lōn\ *n, pl* **co·lo·nes** \-'lō-₁näs\ — see MONEY table

col·o·nel \'kərn-ᵊl\ *n* [alter. of *coronel*, fr. MF, fr. It *colonnello* column of soldiers, colonel, ultim. fr. L *columna*] : a commissioned officer (as in the army) ranking next below a brigadier general

¹**co·lo·nial** \kə-'lō-nē-əl\ *adj* **1** : of, relating to, or characteristic of a colony; *also* : possessing or composed of colonies **2** *often cap* : of or relating to the original 13 colonies forming the U.S.

²**colonial** *n* : a member or inhabitant of a colony

co·lo·nial·ism \-ə-₁li-zəm\ *n* : control by one power over a dependent area or people; *also* : a policy advocating or based on such control — **co·lo·nial·ist** \-list\ *n or adj*

col·o·nist \'kä-lə-nist\ *n* **1** : COLONIAL **2** : one that colonizes or settles in a new country

col·o·nize \'kä-lə-₁nīz\ *vb* **-nized; -niz·ing** **1** : to establish a colony in or on **2** : SETTLE — **col·o·ni·za·tion** \₁kä-lə-nə-'zā-shən\ *n* — **col·o·niz·er** *n*

col·on·nade \₁kä-lə-'nād\ *n* : an evenly spaced row of columns usu. supporting the base of a roof structure

col·o·ny \'kä-lə-nē\ *n, pl* **-nies** **1** : a body of people living in a new territory; *also* : the territory inhabited by these people **2** : a localized population of organisms ⟨a ∼ of bees⟩ **3** : a group with common interests situated in close association ⟨a writers' ∼⟩; *also* : the area occupied by such a group

col·o·phon \'kä-lə-fən, -₁fän\ *n* **1** : an inscription placed at the end of a book with facts relative to its production **2** : a distinctive symbol used by a printer or publisher

¹**col·or** \'kə-lər\ *n* **1** : a phenomenon of light (as red or blue) or visual perception that enables one to differentiate otherwise identical objects; *also* : a hue as contrasted with black, white, or gray **2** : APPEARANCE **3** : complexion tint **4** *pl* : FLAG; *also* : military service ⟨a call to the ∼s⟩ **5** : VIVIDNESS, INTEREST — **col·or·ful** *adj* — **col·or·less** *adj*

²**color** *vb* **1** : to give color to; *also* : to change the color of **2** : BLUSH

Col·o·ra·do potato beetle \₁kä-lə-'ra-dō-, -'rä-\ *n* : a black-and-yellow striped beetle that feeds on the leaves of the potato

col·or·ation \₁kə-lə-'rā-shən\ *n* : use or arrangement of colors

col·or·a·tu·ra \₁kə-lə-rə-'tür-ə, -'tyür-\ *n* **1** : elaborate ornamentation in vocal music **2** : a soprano specializing in coloratura

col·or-blind \'kə-lər-₁blīnd\ *adj* **1** : partially or totally unable to distinguish one or more chromatic colors **2** : not recognizing differences of race — **color blindness** *n*

col·ored \'kə-lərd\ *adj* **1** : having color **2** : SLANTED,

BIASED **3** : of a race other than the white; *esp* : BLACK **4** — sometimes taken to be offensive

col·or·fast \'kə-lər-ˌfast\ *adj* : having color that does not fade or run — **col·or·fast·ness** *n*

co·los·sal \kə-'lä-səl\ *adj* : of very great size or degree

Co·los·sians \kə-'lä-shənz\ *n* — see BIBLE table

co·los·sus \kə-'lä-səs\ *n, pl* **co·los·si** \-ˌsī\ [L] : a gigantic statue; *also* : something of great size or scope

col·our *chiefly Brit var of* COLOR

col·por·teur \'käl-ˌpōr-tər\ *n* [F] : a peddler of religious books

colt \'kōlt\ *n* : FOAL; *also* : a young male horse, ass, or zebra — **colt·ish** *adj*

col·um·bine \'kä-ləm-ˌbīn\ *n* [ME, fr. ML *columbina*, fr. L, fem. of *columbinus* dovelike, fr. *columba* dove] : any of a genus of plants with showy spurred flowers that are related to the buttercups

co·lum·bi·um \kə-'ləm-bē-əm\ *n* : NIOBIUM

Columbus Day \kə-'ləm-bəs-\ *n* : the 2d Monday in October or formerly October 12 observed as a legal holiday in many states in commemoration of the landing of Columbus

col·umn \'kä-ləm\ *n* **1** : one of two or more vertical sections of a printed page; *also* : one in a usu. regular series of articles (as in a newspaper) **2** : a supporting pillar; *esp* : one consisting of a usu. round shaft, a capital, and a base **3** : something resembling a column ⟨a ∼ of water⟩ **4** : a long row (as of soldiers) — **co·lum·nar** \kə-'ləm-nər\ *adj*

col·um·nist \'kä-ləm-nist\ *n* : a person who writes a newspaper or magazine column

com *abbr* **1** comedy; comic **2** comma

co·ma \'kō-mə\ *n* : a state of deep unconsciousness caused by disease, injury, or poison — **co·ma·tose** \'kō-mə-ˌtōs, 'kä-\ *adj*

Co·man·che \kə-'man-chē\ *n, pl* **Comanche** *or* **Comanches** : a member of an American Indian people ranging from Wyoming and Nebraska south into New Mexico and Texas

¹comb \'kōm\ *n* **1** : a toothed instrument for arranging the hair or for separating and cleaning textile fibers **2** : a fleshy crest on the head of a fowl **3** : HONEYCOMB — **comb** *vb* — **combed** \'kōmd\ *adj*

²comb *abbr* combination; combining

com·bat \kəm-'bat, 'käm-ˌbat\ *vb* **-bat·ed** *or* **-batted; -bat·ing** *or* **-bat·ting** **1** : FIGHT, CONTEND **2** : to struggle against: OPPOSE — **com·bat** \'käm-ˌbat\ *n* — **com·bat·ant** \kəm-'bat-ʰnt, 'käm-bə-tənt\ *n* — **com·bat·ive** \kəm-'ba-tiv\ *adj*

combat fatigue *n* : a traumatic neurotic or psychotic reaction occurring under conditions (as wartime combat) that cause intense stress

comb·er \'kō-mər\ *n* **1** : one that combs **2** : a long curling wave of the sea

com·bi·na·tion \ˌkäm-bə-'nā-shən\ *n* **1** : a result or product of combining **2** : a sequence of letters or numbers chosen in setting to lock **3** : the act or process of combining; *also* : the quality or state of being combined

¹com·bine \kəm-'bīn\ *vb* **com·bined; com·bin·ing** : to become one : UNITE

²com·bine \'käm-ˌbīn\ *n* **1** : a combination esp. of business or political interests **2** : a machine that harvests and threshes grain while moving over a field

comb·ings \'kō-miŋz\ *n pl* : loose hairs or fibers removed by a comb

combining form *n* : a linguistic form that occurs only in compounds or derivatives

com·bo \'käm-bō\ *n, pl* **combos** : a small jazz or dance band

com·bus·ti·ble \kəm-'bəs-tə-bəl\ *adj* : capable of being burned — **com·bus·ti·bil·i·ty** \-ˌbəs-tə-'bi-lə-tē\ *n* — **combustible** *n*

com·bus·tion \kəm-'bəs-chən\ *n* **1** : an act or instance of burning **2** : slow oxidation (as in the animal body)

comdg *abbr* commanding

comdr *abbr* commander

comdt *abbr* commandant

come \'kəm\ *vb* **came** \'kām\; **come; com·ing** \'kə-miŋ\ **1** : APPROACH **2** : ARRIVE **3** : to reach the point of being or becoming ⟨∼ to a boil⟩ **4** : AMOUNT ⟨the bill *came* to $10⟩ **5** : to take place **6** : ORIGINATE, ARISE **7** : to be available **8** : REACH, EXTEND — **come clean** : CONFESS — **come into** : ACQUIRE, ACHIEVE — **come to pass** : HAPPEN — **come to terms** : to reach an agreement

come·back \'kəm-ˌbak\ *n* **1** : RETORT **2** : a return to a former position or condition — **come back** *vb*

co·me·di·an \kə-'mē-dē-ən\ *n* **1** : an actor in comedy **2** : a comic person; *esp* : an entertainer specializing in comedy

co·me·di·enne \-ˌmē-dē-'en\ *n* : a woman who is a comedian

come·down \'kəm-ˌdaủn\ *n* : a descent in rank or dignity

com·e·dy \'kä-mə-dē\ *n, pl* **-dies** [ME, fr. MF *comedie*, fr. L *comoedia*, fr. Gk *kōmōidia*, fr. *kōmos* revel + *aeidein* to sing] **1** : a light amusing play with a happy ending **2** : a literary work treating a comic theme or written in a comic style **3** : humorous entertainment

come·ly \'kəm-lē\ *adj* **come·li·er; -est** : ATTRACTIVE, HANDSOME — **come·li·ness** *n*

come off *vb* : SUCCEED

come-on \'kə-ˌmȯn, -ˌmän\ *n* : INDUCEMENT, LURE

come out *vb* **1** : to come into public view **2** : to declare oneself **3** : TURN OUT **5** ⟨everything *came out* all right⟩ — **come out with** : SAY **1**

com·er \'kə-mər\ *n* **1** : one that comes ⟨all ∼s⟩ **2** : a promising beginner

¹co·mes·ti·ble \kə-'mes-tə-bəl\ *adj* : EDIBLE

²comestible *n* : FOOD — usu. used in pl.

com·et \'kä-mət\ *n* [ME *comete*, fr. OE *cometa*, fr. L, fr. Gk *komētēs*, lit., long-haired, fr. *komē* hair] : a small bright celestial body that develops a long tail when near the sun

come to *vb* : to regain consciousness

come·up·pance \kə-'mə-pəns\ *n* : a deserved rebuke or penalty

com·fit \'kəm-fət\ *n* : a candied fruit or nut

¹com·fort \'kəm-fərt\ *vb* **1** : to give strength and hope to **2** : CONSOLE

²comfort *n* **1** : CONSOLATION **2** : freedom from pain, trouble, or anxiety; *also* : something that gives such freedom

com·fort·able \'kəm-fər-tə-bəl, 'kəmf-tər-\ *adj* **1** : providing comfort or security **2** : feeling at ease — **com·fort·ably** \-blē\ *adv*

com·fort·er \'kəm-fər-tər\ *n* **1** : one that comforts **2** : QUILT

com·fy \'kəm-fē\ *adj* : COMFORTABLE

¹com·ic \'kä-mik\ *adj* **1** : relating to comedy or comic strips **2** : provoking laughter or amusement **syn** laughable, funny, farcical — **com·i·cal** *adj*

²comic *n* **1** : COMEDIAN **2** *pl* : the part of a newspaper devoted to comic strips

comic book *n* : a magazine containing sequences of comic strips

comic strip *n* : a group of cartoons in narrative sequence

coming \'kə-miŋ\ *adj* **1** : APPROACHING, NEXT **2** : gaining importance

co·mi·ty \'kä-mə-tē, 'kō-\ *n, pl* **-ties** : friendly civility : COURTESY

coml *abbr* commercial

comm *abbr* **1** command; commander **2** commerce; commercial **3** commission; commissioner **4** committee **5** common **6** commonwealth

com·ma \'kä-mə\ *n* : a punctuation mark , used esp. as a mark of separation within the sentence

¹com·mand \kə-'mand\ *vb* **1** : to direct authoritatively : ORDER **2** : DOMINATE, CONTROL, GOVERN **3** : to overlook from a strategic position

²command *n* **1 :** an order given **2 :** ability to control **: MASTERY 3 :** the act of commanding **4 :** a signal that actuates a device (as a computer); *also* **:** the activation of a device by means of a signal **5 :** a body of troops under a commander; *also* **:** an area or position that one commands **6 :** a position of highest authority

com•man•dant \'kä-mən-₁dant, -₁dänt\ *n* **:** an officer in command

com•man•deer \₁kä-mən-'dir\ *vb* **:** to take possession of by force

com•mand•er \kə-'man-dər\ *n* **1 : LEADER, CHIEF;** *esp* **:** an officer commanding an army or subdivision of an army **2 :** a commissioned officer in the navy ranking next below a captain

commander in chief : the supreme commander of the armed forces

com•mand•ment \kə-'mand-mənt\ *n* **: COMMAND, ORDER;** *esp* **:** any of the Ten Commandments

command module *n* **:** a space vehicle module designed to carry the crew and reentry equipment

com•man•do \kə-'man-dō\ *n, pl* **-dos** *or* **-does** [Afrikaans *kommando,* fr. Dutch *commando* command] **:** a member of a military unit trained for surprise raids

command sergeant major *n* **:** a noncommissioned officer in the army ranking above a first sergeant

com•mem•o•rate \kə-'me-mə-₁rāt\ *vb* **-rat•ed; -rat•ing 1 :** to call or recall to mind **2 :** to serve as a memorial of — **com•mem•o•ra•tion** \-₁me-mə-'rā-shən\ *n*

com•mem•o•ra•tive \kə-'mem-rə-tiv, -'me-mə-₁rā-tiv\ *adj* **:** intended to commemorate an event

com•mence \kə-'mens\ *vb* **com•menced; com•menc•ing : BEGIN, START**

com•mence•ment \-mənt\ *n* **1 :** the act or time of a beginning **2 :** the graduation exercises of a school or college

com•mend \kə-'mend\ *vb* **1 :** to commit to one's care **2 : RECOMMEND 3 : PRAISE** — **com•mend•able** \-'men-də-bəl\ *adj* — **com•mend•ably** \-blē\ *adv* — **com•men•da•tion** \₁kä-mən-'dā-shən, -₁men-\ *n* — **com•mend•er** *n*

com•men•su•ra•ble \kə-'men-sə-rə-bəl\ *adj* **:** having a common measure or a common divisor

com•men•su•rate \kə-'men-sə-rət, -'men-chə-\ *adj* **:** equal in measure or extent; *also* **: PROPORTIONAL, CORRESPONDING** (a job ∼ with her abilities)

com•ment \'kä-₁ment\ *n* **1 :** an expression of opinion **2 :** an explanatory, illustrative, or critical note or observation **: REMARK** — **comment** *vb*

com•men•tary \'kä-mən-₁ter-ē\ *n, pl* **-tar•ies :** a systematic series of comments

com•men•ta•tor \-₁tā-tər\ *n* **:** one who comments; *esp* **:** a person who discusses news events on radio or television

com•merce \'kä-(₁)mərs\ *n* **:** the buying and selling of commodities **: TRADE**

¹com•mer•cial \kə-'mər-shəl\ *adj* **:** having to do with commerce; *also* **:** designed for profit or for mass appeal — **com•mer•cial•ly** *adv*

²commercial *n* **:** an advertisement broadcast on radio or television

com•mer•cial•ism \kə-'mər-shə-₁li-zəm\ *n* **1 :** a spirit, method, or practice characteristic of business **2 :** excessive emphasis on profit

com•mer•cial•ize \-₁līz\ *vb* **-ized; -iz•ing 1 :** to manage on a business basis for profit **2 :** to exploit for profit

com•mi•na•tion \₁kä-mə-'nā-shən\ *n* **: DENUNCIATION** — **com•mi•na•to•ry** \'kä-mə-nə-₁tōr-ē\ *adj*

com•min•gle \kə-'miŋ-gəl\ *vb* **: MINGLE, BLEND**

com•mis•er•ate \kə-'mi-zə-₁rāt\ *vb* **-at•ed; -at•ing :** to feel or express pity **: SYMPATHIZE** — **com•mis•er•a•tion** \-₁mi-zə-'rā-shən\ *n*

com•mis•sar \'kä-mə-₁sär\ *n* [Russ *komissar*] **:** a Communist party official

com•mis•sar•i•at \₁kä-mə-'ser-ē-ət\ *n* **1 :** a system for

supplying troops with food **2 :** a department headed by a commissar

com•mis•sary \'kä-mə-₁ser-ē\ *n, pl* **-sar•ies :** a store for equipment and provisions esp. for military personnel

¹com•mis•sion \kə-'mi-shən\ *n* **1 :** a warrant granting certain powers and imposing certain duties **2 :** a certificate conferring military rank and authority **3 :** authority to act as agent for another; *also* **:** something to be done by an agent **4 :** a body of persons charged with performing a duty **5 :** the doing of some act; *also* **:** the thing done **6 :** the allowance made to an agent for transacting business for another

²commission *vb* **1 :** to give a commission to **2 :** to order to be made **3 :** to put (a ship) into a state of readiness for service

commissioned officer *n* **:** an officer of the armed forces holding rank by a commission from the president

com•mis•sion•er \kə-'mi-shə-nər\ *n* **1 :** a member of a commission **2 :** an official in charge of a department of public service **3 :** the administrative head of a professional sport — **com•mis•sion•er•ship** *n*

com•mit \kə-'mit\ *vb* **com•mit•ted; com•mit•ting 1 :** to put into charge or trust **: ENTRUST 2 :** to put in a prison or mental institution **3 : TRANSFER, CONSIGN 4 :** to carry into action **: PERPETRATE** ⟨∼ a crime⟩ **5 :** to pledge or assign to some particular course or use — **com•mit•ment** *n* — **com•mit•tal** *n*

com•mit•tee \kə-'mi-tē\ *n* **:** a body of persons selected to consider and act or report on some matter — **com•mit•tee•man** \-mən\ *n* — **com•mit•tee•wom•an** \-₁wù-mən\ *n*

commo *abbr* commodore

com•mode \kə-'mōd\ *n* [F, fr. *commode,* adj., suitable, convenient, fr. L *commodus,* fr. *com-* with + *modus* measure] **1 :** a movable washstand with cupboard below **2 : TOILET 3**

com•mo•di•ous \kə-'mō-dē-əs\ *adj* **:** comfortably spacious **: ROOMY**

com•mod•i•ty \kə-'mä-də-tē\ *n, pl* **-ties 1 :** a product of agriculture or mining **2 :** an article of commerce **3 :** something useful or valued ⟨that valuable ∼ patience⟩

com•mo•dore \'kä-mə-₁dōr\ *n* **1 :** a commissioned officer in the navy ranking next below a rear admiral **2 :** an officer commanding a group of merchant ships **3 :** the chief officer of a yacht club

¹com•mon \'kä-mən\ *adj* **1 :** belonging to or serving the community **: PUBLIC 2 :** shared by a number in a group **3 :** widely or generally known, found, or observed **: FAMILIAR** ⟨∼ knowledge⟩ **4 : VERNACULAR 3** ⟨∼ names of plants⟩ **5 :** not above the average esp. in social status **syn** universal, general, generic — **com•mon•ly** *adv*

²common *n* **1** *pl* **:** the common people **2** *pl* **:** a dining hall **3** *pl, cap* **:** the lower house of the British and Canadian parliaments **4 :** a piece of land subject to common use — **in common :** shared together

com•mon•al•ty \'kä-mən-əl-tē\ *n, pl* **-ties :** the common people

common cold *n* **:** a contagious respiratory disease caused by a virus and characterized by a sore, swollen, and inflamed nose and throat, usu. by much mucus, and by coughing and sneezing

common denominator *n* **1 :** a common multiple of the denominators of a number of fractions **2 :** a common trait or theme

common divisor *n* **:** a number or expression that divides two or more numbers or expressions without remainder

com•mon•er \'kä-mə-nər\ *n* **:** one of the common people **:** a person having no rank of nobility

common fraction *n* **:** a fraction in which the numerator and denominator are both integers and are separated by a horizontal or slanted line

common law *n* **:** a group of legal practices and traditions based on judges' decisions and social customs and usu. having the same force as laws passed by legislative bodies

common logarithm *n* : a logarithm whose base is 10

common market *n* : an economic association formed to remove trade barriers among members

common multiple *n* : a multiple of each of two or more numbers or expressions

¹**com·mon·place** \'kä-mən-ˌplās\ *n* : something that is ordinary or trite

²**commonplace** *adj* : ORDINARY

common sense *n* : ordinary good sense and judgment

com·mon·weal \'kä-mən-ˌwēl\ *n* **1** *archaic* : COMMONWEALTH **2** : the general welfare

com·mon·wealth \-ˌwelth\ *n* **1** : the body of people politically organized into a state **2** : STATE; *also* : an association or federation of autonomous states

com·mo·tion \kə-'mō-shən\ *n* **1** : DISTURBANCE, UPRISING **2** : AGITATION

com·mu·nal \kə-'myün-ᵊl, 'käm-yən-ᵊl\ *adj* **1** : of or relating to a commune or community **2** : marked by collective ownership and use of property **3** : shared or used in common

¹**com·mune** \kə-'myün\ *vb* **com·muned; com·mun·ing** : to communicate intimately

²**com·mune** \'käm-ˌyün; kə-'myün\ *n* **1** : the smallest administrative district in some European countries **2** : a community organized on a communal basis

com·mu·ni·ca·ble \kə-'myü-ni-kə-bəl\ *adj* : capable of being communicated ⟨∼ diseases⟩ — **com·mu·ni·ca·bil·i·ty** \-ˌmyü-ni-kə-'bi-lə-tē\ *n*

com·mu·ni·cant \-'myü-ni-kənt\ *n* **1** : a church member entitled to receive Communion **2** : one that communicates; *esp* : INFORMANT

com·mu·ni·cate \kə-'myü-nə-ˌkāt\ *vb* **-cat·ed; -cat·ing 1** : to make known **2** : to pass from one to another : TRANSMIT **3** : to receive Communion **4** : to be in communication **5** : JOIN, CONNECT

com·mu·ni·ca·tion \kə-ˌmyü-nə-'kā-shən\ *n* **1** : an act of transmitting **2** : MESSAGE **3** : exchange of information or opinions **4** : a means of communicating — **com·mu·ni·ca·tive** \-'myü-nə-ˌkā-tiv, -ni-kə-tiv\ *adj*

com·mu·nion \kə-'myü-nyən\ *n* **1** : a sharing of something with others **2** *cap* : a Christian sacrament in which bread and wine are consumed as the substance or symbols of Christ's body and blood in commemoration of the death of Christ **3** : intimate fellowship or rapport **4** : a body of Christians having a common faith and discipline

com·mu·ni·qué \kə-'myü-nə-ˌkā, -ˌmyü-nə-'kā\ *n* : BULLETIN 1

com·mu·nism \'käm-yə-ˌni-zəm\ *n* **1** : social organization in which goods are held in common **2** : a theory of social organization advocating common ownership of means of production and a distribution of products of industry based on need **3** *cap* : a political doctrine based on revolutionary Marxist socialism that was the official ideology of the U.S.S.R. and some other countries; *also* : a system of government in which one party controls state-owned means of production — **com·mu·nist** \-nist\ *n or adj, often cap* — **com·mu·nis·tic** \ˌkäm-yə-'nis-tik\ *adj, often cap*

com·mu·ni·ty \kə-'myü-nə-tē\ *n, pl* **-ties 1** : a body of people living in the same place under the same laws; *also* : a natural population of plants and animals that interact ecologically and live in one place (as a pond) **2** : society at large **3** : joint ownership **4** : SIMILARITY, LIKENESS

community college *n* : a 2-year government-supported college that offers an associate degree

community property *n* : property held jointly by husband and wife

com·mu·ta·tion \ˌkäm-yə-'tā-shən\ *n* : substitution of one form of payment or penalty for another

com·mu·ta·tive \'käm-yə-ˌtā-tiv, kə-'myü-tə-\ *adj* : of, relating to, having, or being the property that a given mathematical operation and set have when the result

obtained using any two elements of the set with the operation does not differ with the order in which the numbers are used — **com·mu·ta·tiv·i·ty** \kə-ˌmyü-tə-'ti-və-tē, ˌkäm-yə-tə-\ *n*

com·mu·ta·tor \'käm-yə-ˌtā-tər\ *n* : a device (as on a generator or motor) for changing the direction of electric current

¹**com·mute** \kə-'myüt\ *vb* **com·mut·ed; com·mut·ing 1** : EXCHANGE **2** : to revoke (a sentence) and impose a milder penalty **3** : to travel back and forth regularly — **com·mut·er** *n*

²**commute** *n* : a trip made in commuting

comp *abbr* **1** comparative; compare **2** compensation **3** compiled; compiler **4** composition; compositor **5** compound **6** comprehensive **7** comptroller

¹**com·pact** \kəm-'pakt, 'käm-ˌpakt\ *adj* **1** : SOLID, DENSE **2** : BRIEF, SUCCINCT **3** : occupying a small volume by efficient use of space ⟨∼ camera⟩ — **com·pact·ly** *adv* — **com·pact·ness** *n*

²**compact** *vb* : to pack together : COMPRESS — **com·pac·tor** \kəm-'pak-tər, 'käm-ˌpak-\ *n*

³**com·pact** \'käm-ˌpakt\ *n* **1** : a small case for cosmetics **2** : a small automobile

⁴**com·pact** \'käm-ˌpakt\ *n* : AGREEMENT, COVENANT

compact disc \'käm-ˌpakt-\ *n* : a small plastic optical disc usu. containing recorded music

¹**com·pan·ion** \kəm-'pan-yən\ *n* [OF *compagnon*, fr. LL *companion-, companio*, fr. L *com-* together + *panis* bread] **1** : an intimate friend or associate : COMRADE **2** : one that is closely connected with something similar — **com·pan·ion·able** *adj* — **com·pan·ion·ship** *n*

²**companion** *n* : COMPANIONWAY

com·pan·ion·way \-ˌwā\ *n* : a ship's stairway from one deck to another

com·pa·ny \'kəm-pə-nē\ *n, pl* **-nies 1** : association with others : FELLOWSHIP; *also* : COMPANIONS **2** : GUESTS **3** : a group of persons or things **4** : an infantry unit consisting of two or more platoons and normally commanded by a captain **5** : a group of musical or dramatic performers **6** : the officers and crew of a ship **7** : an association of persons for carrying on a business **syn** party, band, troop, troupe, corps, outfit

com·pa·ra·ble \'käm-pə-rə-bəl, -prə-\ *adj* : capable of being compared **syn** parallel, similar, like, alike, corresponding — **com·pa·ra·bil·i·ty** \ˌkäm-pə-rə-'bi-lə-tē\ *n*

¹**com·par·a·tive** \kəm-'par-ə-tiv\ *adj* **1** : of, relating to, or constituting the degree of grammatical comparison that denotes increase in quality, quantity, or relation **2** : RELATIVE ⟨a ∼ stranger⟩ — **com·par·a·tive·ly** *adv*

²**comparative** *n* : the comparative degree or form in a language

¹**com·pare** \kəm-'par\ *vb* **com·pared; com·par·ing 1** : to represent as similar : LIKEN **2** : to examine for likenesses and differences **3** : to inflect or modify (an adjective or adverb) according to the degrees of comparison

²**compare** *n* : the possibility of comparing ⟨beauty beyond ∼⟩

com·par·i·son \kəm-'par-ə-sən\ *n* **1** : the act of comparing **2** : change in the form of an adjective or adverb to show different levels of quality, quantity, or relation

com·part·ment \kəm-'pärt-mənt\ *n* **1** : a separate division **2** : a section of an enclosed space : ROOM

com·part·men·tal·ize \kəm-ˌpärt-'ment-ᵊl-ˌīz\ *vb* **-ized; -iz·ing** : to separate into compartments

¹**com·pass** \'kəm-pəs, 'käm-\ *vb* [ME, fr. OF *compasser* to measure, fr. (assumed) VL *compassare* to pace off, fr. L *com-* + *passus* pace] **1** : CONTRIVE, PLOT **2** : ENCIRCLE, ENCOMPASS **3** : BRING ABOUT, ACHIEVE

²**compass** *n* **1** : BOUNDARY, CIRCUMFERENCE **2** : an enclosed space **3** : RANGE, SCOPE **4** : a device for determining direction by means of a magnetic needle swinging freely and pointing to the magnetic north;

also : a nonmagnetic device that indicates direction **5** : an instrument for drawing circles or transferring measurements consisting of two legs joined by a pivot

com·pas·sion \kəm-'pa-shən\ *n* : sympathetic feeling : PITY, MERCY — **com·pas·sion·ate** \-shə-nət\ *adj* — **com·pas·sion·ate·ly** *adv*

com·pat·i·ble \kəm-'pa-tə-bəl\ *adj* : able to exist or act together harmoniously ⟨~ colors⟩ ⟨~ drugs⟩ **syn** consonant, congenial, sympathetic — **com·pat·i·bil·i·ty** \-ˌpa-tə-'bi-lə-tē\ *n*

com·pa·tri·ot \kəm-'pā-trē-ət, -ˌät\ *n* : a fellow countryman

com·peer \'käm-ˌpir\ *n* : EQUAL, PEER

com·pel \kəm-'pel\ *vb* **com·pelled; com·pel·ling** : to drive or urge with force

com·pen·di·ous \kəm-'pen-dē-əs\ *adj* : concise and comprehensive; *also* : COMPREHENSIVE

com·pen·di·um \kəm-'pen-dē-əm\ *n, pl* **-di·ums** *or* **-dia** \-ə\ **1** : a brief summary of a larger work or of a field of knowledge **2** : COLLECTION

com·pen·sate \'käm-pən-ˌsāt\ *vb* **-sat·ed; -sat·ing 1** : to be equivalent to : make up for **2** : PAY, REMUNERATE **syn** balance, offset, counterbalance, counterpoise — **com·pen·sa·tion** \ˌkäm-pən-'sā-shən\ *n* — **com·pen·sa·to·ry** \kəm-'pen-sə-ˌtōr-ē\ *adj*

com·pete \kəm-'pēt\ *vb* **com·pet·ed; com·pet·ing** : CONTEND, VIE

com·pe·tence \'käm-pə-təns\ *n* **1** : adequate means for subsistence **2** : FITNESS, ABILITY

com·pe·ten·cy \-tən-sē\ *n, pl* **-cies** : COMPETENCE

com·pe·tent \-tənt\ *adj* : CAPABLE, FIT, QUALIFIED

com·pe·ti·tion \ˌkäm-pə-'ti-shən\ *n* **1** : the act of competing : RIVALRY **2** : CONTEST, MATCH; *also* : one's competitors — **com·pet·i·tive** \kəm-'pe-tə-tiv\ *adj* — **com·pet·i·tive·ly** *adv* — **com·pet·i·tive·ness** *n*

com·pet·i·tor \kəm-'pe-tə-tər\ *n* : one that competes : RIVAL

com·pile \kəm-'pīl\ *vb* **com·piled; com·pil·ing** [ME, fr. MF *compiler*, fr. L *compilare* to plunder] **1** : to compose out of materials from other documents **2** : to collect and edit into a volume **3** : to translate (a computer program) with a compiler **4** : to build up gradually ⟨~ a record of four wins and two losses⟩ — **com·pi·la·tion** \ˌkäm-pə-'lā-shən\ *n*

com·pil·er \kəm-'pī-lər\ *n* **1** : one that compiles **2** : a computer program that translates any program correctly written in a specific programming language into machine language

com·pla·cence \kəm-'plās-ᵊns\ *n* : SATISFACTION; *esp* : SELF-SATISFACTION — **com·pla·cent** \-ᵊnt\ *adj* — **com·pla·cent·ly** *adv*

com·pla·cen·cy \-ᵊn-sē\ *n, pl* **-cies** : COMPLACENCE

com·plain \kəm-'plān\ *vb* **1** : to express grief, pain, or discontent **2** : to make a formal accusation — **com·plain·ant** *n* — **com·plain·er** *n*

com·plaint \kəm-'plānt\ *n* **1** : expression of grief, pain, or dissatisfaction **2** : a bodily ailment or disease **3** : a formal accusation against a person

com·plai·sance \kəm-'plās-ᵊns, ˌkäm-plā-'zans\ *n* [F] : disposition to please — **com·plai·sant** \-ᵊnt, -'zant\ *adj*

com·pleat \kəm-'plēt\ *adj* : PROFICIENT

com·plect·ed \kəm-'plek-təd\ *adj* : having a specified facial complexion ⟨dark-*complected*⟩

¹com·ple·ment \'käm-plə-mənt\ *n* **1** : something that fills up or completes; *also* : the full quantity, number, or amount that makes a thing complete **2** : an added word by which a predicate is made complete **3** : a group of proteins in blood that combines with antibodies to destroy antigens — **com·ple·men·ta·ry** \ˌkäm-plə-'men-t(ə-)rē\ *adj*

²com·ple·ment \-ˌment\ *vb* : to be complementary to : fill out

¹com·plete \kəm-'plēt\ *adj* **com·plet·er; -est 1** : having all parts or elements **2** : brought to an end **3** : fully carried out; *also* : ABSOLUTE **2** ⟨~ silence⟩ — **com·plete·ly** *adv* — **com·plete·ness** *n* — **com·ple·tion** \-'plē-shən\ *n*

²complete *vb* **com·plet·ed; com·plet·ing 1** : FINISH, CONCLUDE **2** : to make whole or perfect ⟨the hat ~s the outfit⟩

¹com·plex \'käm-ˌpleks\ *n* **1** : a whole made up of or involving intricately interrelated elements **2** : a group of repressed desires and memories that exert a dominating influence on one's personality and behavior ⟨a guilt ~⟩

²com·plex \käm-'pleks, 'käm-ˌpleks\ *adj* **1** : composed of two or more parts **2** : consisting of a main clause and one or more subordinate clauses ⟨~ sentence⟩ **3** : hard to separate, analyze, or solve — **com·plex·i·ty** \käm-'plek-sə-tē\ *n* — **com·plex·ly** *adv*

complex fraction *n* : a fraction with a fraction or mixed number in the numerator or denominator or both

com·plex·ion \kəm-'plek-shən\ *n* **1** : the hue or appearance of the skin esp. of the face **2** : overall appearance — **com·plex·ioned** \-shənd\ *adj*

complex number *n* : a number (as $3 + 4\sqrt{-1}$) formed by adding a real number to the product of a real number and the square root of minus one

com·pli·ance \kəm-'plī-əns\ *n* **1** : the act of complying to a demand or proposal **2** : a disposition to yield — **com·pli·ant** \-ənt\ *adj*

com·pli·cate \'käm-plə-ˌkāt\ *vb* **-cat·ed; -cat·ing** : to make or become complex or intricate

com·pli·cat·ed \'käm-plə-ˌkā-təd\ *adj* **1** : consisting of parts intricately combined **2** : difficult to analyze, understand, or explain — **com·pli·cat·ed·ly** *adv*

com·pli·ca·tion \ˌkäm-plə-'kā-shən\ *n* **1** : the quality or state of being complicated; *also* : a complex feature **2** : a disease or condition that develops during and affects the course of a primary disease or condition

com·plic·i·ty \kəm-'pli-sə-tē\ *n, pl* **-ties** : the state of being an accomplice

¹com·pli·ment \'käm-plə-mənt\ *n* **1** : an expression of approval or admiration; *esp* : a flattering remark **2** *pl* : best wishes : REGARDS

²com·pli·ment \-ˌment\ *vb* : to pay a compliment to

com·pli·men·ta·ry \ˌkäm-plə-'men-t(ə-)rē\ *adj* **1** : containing or expressing a compliment **2** : given free as a courtesy ⟨~ ticket⟩

com·ply \kəm-'plī\ *vb* **com·plied; com·ply·ing** : CONFORM, YIELD

¹com·po·nent \kəm-'pō-nənt, 'käm-ˌpō-\ *n* : a component part **syn** ingredient, element, factor, constituent

²component *adj* : serving to form a part of : CONSTITUENT

com·port \kəm-'pōrt\ *vb* **1** : AGREE, ACCORD **2** : CONDUCT **syn** behave, acquit, deport — **com·port·ment** *n*

com·pose \kəm-'pōz\ *vb* **com·posed; com·pos·ing 1** : to form by putting together : FASHION **2** : to produce (as pages of type) by composition **3** : ADJUST, ARRANGE **4** : CALM, QUIET **5** : to practice composition ⟨~ music⟩ — **com·pos·er** *n*

¹com·pos·ite \käm-'pä-zət\ *adj* **1** : made up of distinct parts or elements **2** : of, relating to, or being a large family of flowering plants (as a daisy or aster) that bear many small flowers united into compact heads resembling single flowers

²composite *n* **1** : something composite **2** : a plant of the composite family **syn** blend, compound, mixture, amalgamation

com·po·si·tion \ˌkäm-pə-'zi-shən\ *n* **1** : the act or process of composing; *esp* : arrangement esp. in artistic form **2** : the arrangement or production of type for printing **3** : general makeup **4** : a product of mixing various elements or ingredients **5** : a literary, musical, or artistic product; *esp* : ESSAY

com·pos·i·tor \kəm-'pä-zə-tər\ *n* : one who sets type

com·post \'käm-ˌpōst\ *n* : a fertilizing material consisting largely of decayed organic matter

com·po·sure \kəm-'pō-zhər\ *n* : CALMNESS, SELF-POSSESSION

com·pote \'käm-ˌpōt\ *n* 1 : fruits cooked in syrup 2 : a bowl (as of glass) usu. with a base and stem for serving esp. fruit or compote

¹**com·pound** \käm-'paund, 'käm-ˌ\ *vb* [ME *compounen*, fr. MF *compondre*, fr. L *componere*, fr. *com-* together + *ponere* to put] 1 : COMBINE 2 : to form by combining parts ⟨∼ a medicine⟩ 3 : SETTLE ⟨∼ a dispute⟩; *also* : to refrain from prosecuting (an offense) in return for a consideration 4 : to increase (as interest) by an amount that can itself vary; *also* : to add to

²**com·pound** \'käm-ˌpaund\ *adj* 1 : made up of individual parts 2 : composed of united similar parts esp. of a kind usu. independent ⟨a ∼ plant ovary⟩ 3 : formed by the combination of two or more otherwise independent elements ⟨∼ sentence⟩

³**com·pound** \'käm-ˌpaund\ *n* 1 : a word consisting of parts that are words 2 : something formed from a union of elements or parts; *esp* : a distinct substance formed by the union of two or more chemical elements **syn** mixture, composite, blend, admixture, alloy

⁴**com·pound** \'käm-ˌpaund\ *n* [by folk etymology fr. Malay *kampung* group of buildings, village] : an enclosure containing buildings

compound interest *n* : interest computed on the sum of an original principal and accrued interest

com·pre·hend \ˌkäm-pri-'hend\ *vb* 1 : UNDERSTAND 2 : INCLUDE — **com·pre·hen·si·ble** \-'hen-sə-bəl\ *adj* — **com·pre·hen·sion** \-'hen-chən\ *n* — **com·pre·hen·sive** \-siv\ *adj*

¹**com·press** \kəm-'pres\ *vb* : to squeeze together **syn** constrict, contract, shrink — **com·pres·sion** \-'pre-shən\ *n* — **com·pres·sor** \-'pre-sər\ *n*

²**com·press** \'käm-ˌpres\ *n* : a folded pad or cloth used to press upon a body part

compressed air *n* : air under pressure greater than that of the atmosphere

com·prise \kəm-'prīz\ *vb* **com·prised; com·pris·ing** 1 : INCLUDE, CONTAIN 2 : to be made up of 3 : COMPOSE, CONSTITUTE

¹**com·pro·mise** \'käm-prə-ˌmīz\ *n* : a settlement of differences reached by mutual concessions

²**compromise** *vb* **-mised; -mis·ing** 1 : to settle by compromise 2 : to expose to suspicion or loss of reputation

comp·trol·ler \kən-'trō-lər, 'kämp-ˌtrō-\ *n* : an official who audits and supervises expenditures and accounts

com·pul·sion \kəm-'pəl-shən\ *n* 1 : an act of compelling 2 : a force that compels 3 : an irresistible impulse **syn** constraint, force, violence, duress — **com·pul·sive** \-siv\ *adj* — **com·pul·so·ry** \-sə-rē\ *adj*

com·punc·tion \kəm-'pəŋk-shən\ *n* : anxiety arising from guilt : REMORSE

com·pute \kəm-'pyüt\ *vb* **com·put·ed; com·put·ing** : CALCULATE, RECKON — **com·pu·ta·tion** \ˌkäm-pyü-'tā-shən\ *n* — **com·pu·ta·tion·al** *adj*

computed tomography *n* : radiography in which a three-dimensional image of a body structure is constructed by computer from a series of plane cross-sectional images made along an axis

com·put·er \kəm-'pyü-tər\ *n* : a programmable electronic device that can store, retrieve, and process data

com·put·er·ise *chiefly Brit var of* COMPUTERIZE

com·put·er·ize \kəm-'pyü-tə-ˌrīz\ *vb* **-ized; -iz·ing** 1 : to carry out, control, or produce by means of a computer 2 : to provide with computers 3 : to store in a computer; *also* : put into a form that a computer can use — **com·put·er·iza·tion** \-ˌpyü-tə-rə-'zā-shən\ *n*

computerized axial tomography *n* : COMPUTED TOMOGRAPHY

com·rade \'käm-ˌrad\ *n* [MF *comarade* group sleeping in one room, roommate, companion, fr. Sp *camarada*, fr. *cámara* room, fr. LL *camera*] : COMPANION, ASSOCIATE — **com·rade·ly** *adj* — **com·rade·ship** *n*

¹**con** \'kän\ *vb* **conned; con·ning** 1 : MEMORIZE 2 : STUDY

²**con** *adv* : in opposition : AGAINST

³**con** *n* : an opposing argument, person, or position ⟨pros and ∼s⟩

⁴**con** *vb* **conned; con·ning** 1 : SWINDLE 2 : PERSUADE, CAJOLE

⁵**con** *n* : CONVICT

conc *abbr* concentrated

con·cat·e·nate \kän-'ka-tə-ˌnāt\ *vb* **-nat·ed; -nat·ing** : to link together in a series or chain — **con·cat·e·na·tion** \(ˌ)kän-ˌka-tə-'nā-shən\ *n*

con·cave \kän-'kāv, 'kän-ˌ\ *adj* : curved or rounded inward like the inside of a bowl — **con·cav·i·ty** \kän-'ka-və-tē\ *n*

con·ceal \kən-'sēl\ *vb* : to place out of sight : HIDE — **con·ceal·ment** *n*

con·cede \kən-'sēd\ *vb* **con·ced·ed; con·ced·ing** 1 : to admit to be true 2 : GRANT, YIELD **syn** allow, acknowledge, avow, confess

con·ceit \kən-'sēt\ *n* 1 : excessively high opinion of one's self or ability : VANITY 2 : an elaborate or strained metaphor — **con·ceit·ed** *adj*

con·ceive \kən-'sēv\ *vb* **con·ceived; con·ceiv·ing** 1 : to become pregnant or pregnant with ⟨∼ a child⟩ 2 : to form an idea of : THINK, IMAGINE — **con·ceiv·able** \-'sē-və-bəl\ *adj* — **con·ceiv·ably** \-blē\ *adv*

con·cel·e·brant \kən-'se-lə-brənt\ *n* : one that jointly participates in celebrating the Eucharist

¹**con·cen·trate** \'kän-sən-ˌtrāt\ *vb* **-trat·ed; -trat·ing** 1 : to gather into one body, mass, or force 2 : to make less dilute 3 : to fix one's powers, efforts, or attentions

²**concentrate** *n* : something concentrated

con·cen·tra·tion \ˌkän-sən-'trā-shən\ *n* 1 : the act or process of concentrating : the state of being concentrated; *esp* : direction of attention on a single object 2 : the amount of a component in a given area or volume

concentration camp *n* : a camp where persons (as prisoners of war or political prisoners) are confined

con·cen·tric \kən-'sen-trik\ *adj* 1 : having a common center ⟨∼ circles⟩ 2 : COAXIAL

con·cept \'kän-ˌsept\ *n* : THOUGHT, NOTION, IDEA — **con·cep·tu·al** \kən-'sep-chə-wəl\ *adj*

con·cep·tion \kən-'sep-shən\ *n* 1 : the process of conceiving or being conceived 2 : the power to form or understand ideas or concepts 3 : IDEA, CONCEPT 4 : the originating of something

con·cep·tu·al·ize \-'sep-chə-wə-ˌlīz\ *vb* **-ized; -iz·ing** : to form a conception of

¹**con·cern** \kən-'sərn\ *vb* 1 : to relate to 2 : to be the business of 3 : INVOLVE, ENGAGE, OCCUPY

²**concern** *n* 1 : INTEREST, ANXIETY 2 : AFFAIR, MATTER 3 : a business organization **syn** care, worry, disquiet, unease

con·cerned *adj* 1 : ANXIOUS, UNEASY 2 : INVOLVED

con·cern·ing *prep* : relating to : REGARDING

con·cern·ment \kən-'sərn-mənt\ *n* 1 : something in which one is concerned 2 : IMPORTANCE, CONSEQUENCE

¹**con·cert** \'kän-(ˌ)sərt\ *n* 1 : agreement in a plan or design 2 : a concerted action 3 : a public performance (as of music)

²**con·cert** \kən-'sərt\ *vb* : to plan together

con·cert·ed \kən-'sər-təd\ *adj* : mutually agreed on; *also* : performed in unison

con·cer·ti·na \ˌkän-sər-'tē-nə\ *n* : an instrument of the accordion family

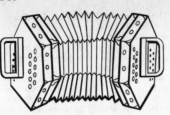

concertina

con·cert·mas·ter \ˈkän-sərt-ˌmas-tər\ *or* **con·cert-meis·ter** \-ˌmī-stər\ *n* : the leader of the first violins of an orchestra and assistant to the conductor

con·cer·to \kən-ˈcher-tō\ *n, pl* **-ti** \-(ˌ)tē\ *or* **-tos** [It] : a piece for one or more solo instruments and orchestra in three movements

con·ces·sion \kən-ˈse-shən\ *n* **1** : an act of conceding or yielding **2** : something yielded **3** : a grant by a government of land or of a right to use it **4** : a grant of a portion of premises for some specific purpose; *also* : the activities or enterprise carried on — **con·ces·sion·ary** \-ˈse-shə-ˌner-ē\ *adj*

con·ces·sion·aire \kən-ˌse-shə-ˈnar, -ˈner\ *n* : one that owns or operates a concession

conch \ˈkäŋk, ˈkänch\ *n, pl* **conchs** \ˈkäŋks\ *or* **conch·es** \ˈkän-chəz\ : a large spiral-shelled marine gastropod mollusk; *also* : its shell

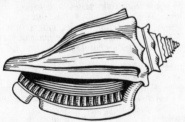

conch

con·cierge \kōⁿ-ˈsyerzh\ *n, pl* **con·cierges** *same or* -ˈsyer-zhəz\ [F] **1** : a resident in an apartment building who performs services for the tenants **2** : a usu. multilingual hotel staff member

con·cil·i·ate \kən-ˈsi-lē-ˌāt\ *vb* **-at·ed; -at·ing 1** : to bring into agreement : RECONCILE **2** : to gain the goodwill of — **con·cil·i·a·tion** \-ˌsi-lē-ˈā-shən\ *n* — **con·cil·i·a·to·ry** \-ˈsi-lē-ə-ˌtōr-ē\ *adj*

con·cise \kən-ˈsīs\ *adj* : expressing much in few words : BRIEF — **con·cise·ly** *adv* — **con·cise·ness** *n*

con·clave \ˈkän-ˌklāv\ *n* [ML, fr. L, room that can be locked, fr. *com-* together + *clavis* key] : a private gathering; *also* : CONVENTION

con·clude \kən-ˈklüd\ *vb* **con·clud·ed; con·clud·ing 1** : to bring to a close : END **2** : DECIDE, JUDGE **3** : to bring about as a result syn close, finish, terminate, complete, halt

con·clu·sion \kən-ˈklü-zhən\ *n* **1** : the logical consequence of a reasoning process **2** : TERMINATION, END **3** : OUTCOME, RESULT — **con·clu·sive** \-siv\ *adj* — **con·clu·sive·ly** *adv*

con·coct \kən-ˈkäkt, kän-\ *vb* **1** : to prepare by combining raw materials **2** : DEVISE — **con·coc·tion** \-ˈkäk-shən\ *n*

con·com·i·tant \-ˈkä-mə-tənt\ *adj* : ACCOMPANYING, ATTENDING — **concomitant** *n*

con·cord \ˈkän-ˌkord, ˈkäŋ-\ *n* : AGREEMENT, HARMONY

con·cor·dance \kən-ˈkor-dᵊns\ *n* **1** : an alphabetical index of words in a book or in an author's works with the passages in which they occur **2** : AGREEMENT, COVENANT

con·cor·dant \-dᵊnt\ *adj* : HARMONIOUS, AGREEING

con·cor·dat \kən-ˈkor-ˌdat\ *n* : CONCORDANCE 2

con·course \ˈkän-ˌkōrs\ *n* **1** : a spontaneous coming together : GATHERING **2** : an open space or hall (as in a bus terminal) where crowds gather

¹con·crete \kän-ˈkrēt, ˈkän-ˌkrēt\ *adj* **1** : naming a real thing or class of things : not abstract **2** : not theoretical : ACTUAL **3** : made of or relating to concrete

²con·crete \ˈkän-ˌkrēt, kän-ˈkrēt\ *vb* **con·cret·ed; con·cret·ing 1** : SOLIDIFY **2** : to cover with concrete

³con·crete \ˈkän-ˌkrēt, kän-ˈkrēt\ *n* : a hard building material made by mixing cement, sand, and gravel with water

con·cre·tion \kän-ˈkrē-shən\ *n* : a hard mass esp. when formed abnormally in the body

con·cu·bine \ˈkäŋ-kyu-ˌbīn\ *n* [ME, fr. MF, fr. L *concubina*, fr. *com-* with + *cubare* to lie] : a woman who is not legally a wife but lives with a man and sometimes has a recognized position in his household; *also* : MISTRESS — **con·cu·bi·nage** \kän-ˈkyü-bə-nij\ *n*

con·cu·pis·cence \kän-ˈkyü-pə-səns\ *n* : ardent sexual desire : LUST

con·cur \kən-ˈkər\ *vb* **con·curred; con·cur·ring 1** : to act together **2** : AGREE **3** : COINCIDE syn unite, combine, cooperate, band, join

con·cur·rence \-ˈkər-əns\ *n* **1** : agreement in action or opinion **2** : occurrence together : CONJUNCTION

con·cur·rent \-ˈkər-ənt\ *adj* **1** : happening or operating at the same time **2** : joint and equal in authority

con·cus·sion \kən-ˈkə-shən\ *n* **1** : a hard blow or collision; *also* : bodily injury (as to the brain) resulting from a sudden jar **2** : AGITATION, SHAKING

con·demn \kən-ˈdem\ *vb* **1** : to declare to be wrong **2** : to convict of guilt **3** : to sentence judicially **4** : to pronounce unfit for use ⟨∼ a building⟩ **5** : to declare forfeited or taken for public use syn denounce, censure, blame, criticize, reprehend — **con·dem·na·tion** \ˌkän-ˌdem-ˈnā-shən\ *n* — **con·dem·na·to·ry** \kən-ˈdem-nə-ˌtōr-ē\ *adj*

con·den·sate \ˈkän-dən-ˌsāt, kən-ˈden-\ *n* : a product of condensation

con·dense \kən-ˈdens\ *vb* **con·densed; con·dens·ing 1** : to make or become more compact or dense : CONCENTRATE **2** : to change from vapor to liquid syn contract, shrink, compress, constrict — **con·den·sa·tion** \ˌkän-den-ˈsā-shən\ *n*

con·dens·er \kən-ˈden-sər\ *n* **1** : one that condenses **2** : CAPACITOR

con·de·scend \ˌkän-di-ˈsend\ *vb* : to assume an air of superiority — **con·de·scend·ing·ly** \-ˈsen-diŋ-lē\ *adv* — **con·de·scen·sion** \-ˈsen-chən\ *n*

con·dign \kən-ˈdīn, ˈkän-ˌdīn\ *adj* : DESERVED, APPROPRIATE ⟨∼ punishment⟩

con·di·ment \ˈkän-də-mənt\ *n* : something used to make food savory; *esp* : a pungent seasoning (as pepper)

¹con·di·tion \kən-ˈdi-shən\ *n* **1** : something essential to the occurrence of some other thing **2** : state of being **3** : social status **4** *pl* : state of affairs : CIRCUMSTANCES **5** : a bodily state in which something is wrong ⟨a heart ∼⟩ **6** : a state of health, fitness, or working order ⟨in good ∼⟩

²condition *vb* **1** : to put into proper condition for action or use **2** : to adapt, modify, or mold to respond in a particular way **3** : to modify so that an act or response previously associated with one stimulus becomes associated with another

con·di·tion·al \kən-ˈdi-shə-nəl\ *adj* : containing, implying, or depending on a condition — **con·di·tion·al·ly** *adv*

con·di·tioned *adj* : determined or established by conditioning

con·do \ˈkän-(ˌ)dō\ *n* : CONDOMINIUM 3

con·dole \kən-ˈdōl\ *vb* **con·doled; con·dol·ing** : to express sympathetic sorrow — **con·do·lence** \kən-ˈdō-ləns\ *n*

con·dom \\'kän-dəm, 'kən-\ *n* : a usu. rubber sheath worn over the penis (as to prevent pregnancy or venereal infection during sexual intercourse)

con·do·min·i·um \\kän-də-'mi-nē-əm\ *n, pl* **-ums** **1** : joint sovereignty (as by two or more nations) **2** : a politically dependent territory under condominium **3** : individual ownership of a unit (as an apartment) in a multiunit structure; *also* : a unit so owned

con·done \kən-'dōn\ *vb* **con·doned; con·don·ing** : to overlook or forgive esp. by treating (an offense) as harmless or trivial **syn** excuse, pardon, forgive, remit — **con·do·na·tion** \\kän-dō-'nā-shən\ *n*

con·dor \\'kän-dər, -₁dȯr\ *n* [Sp *cóndor,* fr. Quechua (a So. American Indian language) *kuntur*] : a very large American vulture of the high Andes; *also* : a related nearly extinct vulture of southern California now resident only in captivity

con·duce \kən-'düs, -'dyüs\ *vb* **con·duced; con·duc·ing** : to lead or contribute to a particular result — **con·du·cive** *adj*

¹con·duct \\'kän-(₁)dəkt\ *n* **1** : MANAGEMENT, DIRECTION **2** : BEHAVIOR

²con·duct \kən-'dəkt\ *vb* **1** : GUIDE, ESCORT **2** : MANAGE, DIRECT **3** : to act as a medium for conveying or transmitting **4** : BEHAVE — **con·duc·tion** \\-'dək-shən\ *n*

con·duc·tance \kən-'dək-təns\ *n* : the readiness with which a conductor transmits an electric current

con·duc·tive \kən-'dək-tiv\ *adj* : having the power to conduct (as heat or electricity) — **con·duc·tiv·i·ty** \\kän-₁dək-'ti-və-tē\ *n*

con·duc·tor \kən-'dək-tər\ *n* **1** : one that conducts; *esp* : a material that permits an electric current to flow easily **2** : a collector of fares in a public conveyance **3** : the leader of a musical ensemble

con·duit \\'kän-₁dü-ət, ₁dyü-, -dwət\ *n* **1** : a channel for conveying fluid **2** : a tube or trough for protecting electric wires or cables **3** : a means of transmitting or distributing

con·dyle \\'kän-₁dīl, -dᵊl\ *n* : an articular prominence of a bone — **con·dy·lar** \\-də-lər\ *adj*

cone \\'kōn\ *n* **1** : the scaly fruit of trees of the pine family **2** : a solid figure formed by rotating a right triangle about one of its legs **3** : a solid figure that slopes evenly to a point from a usu. circular base **4** : any of the conical light-sensitive receptor cells of the retina that function in color vision **5** : something shaped like a cone

Con·es·to·ga wagon \\kä-nə-'stō-gə-\ *n* : a broad= wheeled covered wagon used esp. for transporting freight across the prairies

co·ney \\'kō-nē\ *n, pl* **coneys** **1** : RABBIT; *also* : its fur **2** : PIKA

conf *abbr* **1** conference **2** confidential

con·fab \\'kän-₁fab, kən-'fab\ *n* : CONFABULATION 1

con·fab·u·la·tion \kən-₁fab-yə-'lā-shən\ *n* **1** : CHAT; *also* : CONFERENCE **2** : a filling in of gaps in memory by fabrication

con·fec·tion \kən-'fek-shən\ *n* : a fancy dish or sweet; *also* : CANDY

con·fec·tion·er \\-sh(ə-)nər\ *n* : a maker of or dealer in confections

con·fec·tion·ery \\-shə-₁ner-ē\ *n, pl* **-er·ies** **1** : sweet foods **2** : a confectioner's place of business

Confed *abbr* Confederate

con·fed·er·a·cy \kən-'fe-də-rə-sē\ *n, pl* **-cies** **1** : LEAGUE, ALLIANCE **2** *cap* : the 11 southern states that seceded from the U.S. in 1860 and 1861

¹con·fed·er·ate \kən-'fe-də-rət\ *adj* **1** : united in a league : ALLIED **2** *cap* : of or relating to the Confederacy

²confederate *n* **1** : ALLY, ACCOMPLICE **2** *cap* : an adherent of the Confederacy

³con·fed·er·ate \\-'fe-də-₁rāt\ *vb* **-at·ed; -at·ing** : to unite in a confederacy

con·fed·er·a·tion \kən-₁fe-də-'rā-shən\ *n* **1** : an act of confederating : ALLIANCE **2** : LEAGUE

con·fer \kən-'fər\ *vb* **con·ferred; con·fer·ring** **1** : GRANT, BESTOW **2** : to exchange views : CONSULT — **con·fer·ee** \\kän-fə-'rē\ *n*

con·fer·ence \\'kän-f(ə-)rəns\ *n* **1** : an interchange of views; *also* : a meeting for this purpose **2** : an association of athletic teams

con·fess \kən-'fes\ *vb* **1** : to acknowledge or disclose one's misdeed, fault, or sin **2** : to acknowledge one's sins to God or to a priest **3** : to receive the confession of (a penitent) **syn** admit, own, avow, concede, grant

con·fessed·ly \\-'fe-səd-lē\ *adv* : by confession : ADMITTEDLY

con·fes·sion \\-'fe-shən\ *n* **1** : an act of confessing (as in the sacrament of penance) **2** : an acknowledgment of guilt **3** : a formal statement of religious beliefs **4** : a religious body having a common creed — **con·fes·sion·al** *adj*

con·fes·sion·al \\-'fe-shə-nəl\ *n* : a place where a priest hears confessions

con·fes·sor \kən-'fe-sər\ *n* **1** : one that confesses **2** : a priest who hears confessions

con·fet·ti \kən-'fe-tē\ *n* [It, pl. of *confetto* sweetmeat, fr. ML *confectum,* fr. L, neut. of *confectus,* pp. of *conficere* to prepare] : bits of colored paper or ribbon for throwing (as at weddings)

con·fi·dant \\'kän-fə-₁dänt, -₁dant\ *n* : one to whom secrets are confided

con·fi·dante \\-₁dänt, -₁dant\ *n* : CONFIDANT; *esp* : one who is a woman

con·fide \kən-'fīd\ *vb* **con·fid·ed; con·fid·ing** **1** : to have or show faith : TRUST ⟨∼ in a friend⟩ **2** : to tell confidentially ⟨∼ a secret⟩ **3** : ENTRUST

¹con·fi·dence \\'kän-fə-dəns\ *n* **1** : TRUST, RELIANCE **2** : SELF-ASSURANCE, BOLDNESS **3** : a state of trust or intimacy **4** : SECRET **2** — **con·fi·dent** \\-dənt\ *adj* — **con·fi·dent·ly** *adv*

²confidence *adj* : of or relating to swindling by false promises ⟨a ∼ game⟩

con·fi·den·tial \\kän-fə-'den-chəl\ *adj* **1** : SECRET, PRIVATE **2** : entrusted with confidences ⟨∼ clerk⟩ — **con·fi·den·tial·ly** *adv*

con·fig·u·ra·tion \kən-₁fi-gyə-'rā-shən\ *n* : structural arrangement of parts : SHAPE

con·fig·ure \kən-'fi-gyər\ *vb* **-ured; -ur·ing** : to set up for operation esp. in a particular way

con·fine \kən-'fīn\ *vb* **con·fined; con·fin·ing** **1** : to hold within a location; *also* : IMPRISON **2** : to keep within limits ⟨will ∼ my remarks to one subject⟩ — **con·fine·ment** *n* — **con·fin·er** *n*

con·fines \\'kän-₁fīnz\ *n pl* : BOUNDS, BORDERS

con·firm \kən-'fərm\ *vb* **1** : to give approval to : RATIFY **2** : to make firm or firmer **3** : to administer the rite of confirmation to **4** : VERIFY, CORROBORATE — **con·fir·ma·to·ry** \\-'fər-mə-₁tōr-ē\ *adj*

con·fir·ma·tion \\kän-fər-'mā-shən\ *n* **1** : a religious ceremony admitting a person to full membership in a church or synagogue **2** : an act of ratifying or corroborating; *also* : PROOF

con·fis·cate \\'kän-fə-₁skāt\ *vb* **-cat·ed; -cat·ing** [L *confiscare,* fr. *com-* with + *fiscus* treasury] : to take possession of by or as if by public authority — **con·fis·ca·tion** \\kän-fə-'skā-shən\ *n* — **con·fis·ca·to·ry** \kən-'fis-kə-₁tōr-ē\ *adj*

con·fla·gra·tion \\kän-flə-'grā-shən\ *n* : FIRE; *esp* : a large disastrous fire

¹con·flict \\'kän-₁flikt\ *n* **1** : WAR **2** : a clash between hostile or opposing elements, ideas, or forces

²con·flict \kən-'flikt\ *vb* : to show opposition or irreconcilability : CLASH

con·flu·ence \\'kän-₁flü-əns, kən-'flü-\ *n* **1** : a coming together at one point **2** : the meeting or place of meeting of two or more streams — **con·flu·ent** \\-ənt\ *adj*

con·flux \\'kän-₁fləks\ *n* : CONFLUENCE

con·form \kən-'fȯrm\ *vb* **1** : to be similar or identical; *also* : AGREE **2** : to obey customs or standards; *also* : COMPLY — **con·form·able** *adj*

con·for·mance \kən-'fŏr-məns\ *n* : CONFORMITY

con·for·ma·tion \ˌkän-fŏr-'mā-shən\ *n* : a forming into a whole by arranging parts

con·for·mi·ty \kən-'fŏr-mə-tē\ *n, pl* **-ties 1** : HARMONY, AGREEMENT **2** : COMPLIANCE, OBEDIENCE

con·found \kən-'faůnd, kän-\ *vb* **1** : to throw into disorder or confusion **2** : CONFUSE **2 syn** bewilder, puzzle, perplex, befog

con·fra·ter·ni·ty \ˌkän-frə-'tər-nə-tē\ *n* : a society devoted esp. to a religious or charitable cause

con·frere \'kän-ˌfrer, 'kōⁿ-\ *n* : COLLEAGUE, COMRADE

con·front \kən-'frənt\ *vb* **1** : to face esp. in challenge : OPPOSE; *also* : to deal unflinchingly with ⟨~ed the issue⟩ **2** : to cause to face or meet — **con·fron·ta·tion** \ˌkän-frən-'tā-shən\ *n*

Con·fu·cian \kən-'fyü-shən\ *adj* : of or relating to the Chinese philosopher Confucius or his teachings — **Con·fu·cian·ism** \-shə-ˌni-zəm\ *n*

con·fuse \kən-'fyüz\ *vb* **con·fused; con·fus·ing 1** : to make mentally unclear or uncertain; *also* : to disturb the composure of **2** : to mix up : JUMBLE **syn** muddle, befuddle, addle, fluster — **con·fus·ed·ly** \-'fyü-zəd-lē\ *adv*

con·fu·sion \-'fyü-zhən\ *n* **1** : an act or instance of confusing **2** : the quality or state of being confused

con·fute \kən-'fyüt\ *vb* **con·fut·ed; con·fut·ing** : to overwhelm by argument : REFUTE — **con·fu·ta·tion** \ˌkän-fyü-'tā-shən\ *n*

cong *abbr* congress; congressional

con·ga \'käŋ-gə\ *n* : a Cuban dance of African origin performed by a group usu. in single file

con·geal \kən-'jēl\ *vb* **1** : FREEZE **2** : to make or become hard or thick

con·ge·ner \'kän-jə-nər\ *n* : one related to another; *esp* : a plant or animal of the same taxonomic genus as another — **con·ge·ner·ic** \ˌkän-jə-'ner-ik\ *adj*

con·ge·nial \kən-'jē-nyəl\ *adj* **1** : KINDRED, SYMPATHETIC **2** : suited to one's taste or nature : AGREEABLE — **con·ge·ni·al·i·ty** \-ˌjē-nē-'a-lə-tē\ *n* — **con·ge·nial·ly** *adv*

con·gen·i·tal \kən-'je-nə-tᵊl\ *adj* : existing at or dating from birth **syn** inborn, innate, natural

con·ger eel \'kän-gər-\ *n* : a large edible marine eel of the Atlantic

con·ge·ries \'kän-jə-(ˌ)rēz\ *n, pl* **congeries** : AGGREGATION, COLLECTION

con·gest \kən-'jest\ *vb* **1** : to cause excessive fullness of the blood vessels of (as a lung) **2** : to obstruct by overcrowding — **con·ges·tion** \-'jes-chən\ *n* — **con·ges·tive** \-'jes-tiv\ *adj*

congestive heart failure *n* : heart failure in which the heart is unable to keep enough blood circulating in the tissues or is unable to pump out the blood returned to it by the veins

¹con·glom·er·ate \kən-'glä-mə-rət\ *adj* [L *conglomerare* to roll together, fr. *com-* together + *glomerare* to wind into a ball, fr. *glomer-, glomus* ball] : made up of parts from various sources

²con·glom·er·ate \-ˌrāt\ *vb* **-at·ed; -at·ing** : to form into a mass — **con·glom·er·a·tion** \-ˌglä-mə-'rā-shən\ *n*

³con·glom·er·ate \-rət\ *n* **1** : a mass formed of fragments from various sources; *esp* : a rock composed of fragments varying from pebbles to boulders held together by a cementing material **2** : a widely diversified corporation

Con·go·lese \ˌkäŋ-gə-'lēz, -'lēs\ *n* : a native or inhabitant of Congo — **Congolese** *adj*

con·grat·u·late \kən-'gra-chə-ˌlāt\ *vb* **-lat·ed; -lat·ing** : to express sympathetic pleasure to on account of success or good fortune : FELICITATE — **con·grat·u·la·tion** \-ˌgra-chə-'lā-shən\ *n* — **con·grat·u·la·to·ry** \-'gra-chə-lə-ˌtŏr-ē\ *adj*

con·gre·gate \'käŋ-gri-ˌgāt\ *vb* **-gat·ed; -gat·ing** [ME, fr. L *congregatus*, pp. of *congregare*, fr. *com-* together + *greg-, grex* flock] : ASSEMBLE

con·gre·ga·tion \ˌkäŋ-gri-'gā-shən\ *n* **1** : an assembly of persons met esp. for worship; *also* : a group that habitually so meets **2** : a religious community or order **3** : the act or an instance of congregating

con·gre·ga·tion·al \-shə-nəl\ *adj* **1** : of or relating to a congregation **2** *cap* : observing the faith and practice of certain Protestant churches which recognize the independence of each congregation in church matters — **con·gre·ga·tion·al·ism** \-nə-ˌli-zəm\ *n, often cap* — **con·gre·ga·tion·al·ist** \-list\ *n, often cap*

con·gress \'käŋ-grəs\ *n* **1** : an assembly esp. of delegates for discussion and usu. action on some question **2** : the body of senators and representatives constituting a nation's legislature — **con·gres·sio·nal** \kən-'gre-shə-nəl\ *adj*

con·gress·man \'käŋ-grəs-mən\ *n* : a member of a congress

con·gress·wom·an \-ˌwů-mən\ *n* : a female member of a congress

con·gru·ence \kən-'grü-əns, 'käŋ-grü-\ *n* : the quality of agreeing or coinciding : CONGRUITY — **con·gru·ent** \kən-'grü-ənt, 'käŋ-grü-\ *adj*

con·gru·en·cy \-sē\ *n, pl* **-cies** : CONGRUENCE

con·gru·ity \kän-'grü-ə-tē\ *n, pl* **-ities** : correspondence between things — **con·gru·ous** \'käŋ-grü-əs\ *adj*

con·ic \'kä-nik\ *adj* **1** : of or relating to a cone **2** : CONICAL

con·i·cal \'kä-ni-kəl\ *adj* : resembling a cone esp. in shape

co·ni·fer \'kä-nə-fər, 'kō-\ *n* : any of an order of shrubs or trees (as the pines) that usu. are evergreen and bear cones — **co·nif·er·ous** \kō-'ni-fə-rəs\ *adj*

conj *abbr* conjunction

con·jec·ture \kən-'jek-chər\ *n* : GUESS, SURMISE — **con·jec·tur·al** \-chə-rəl\ *adj* — **conjecture** *vb*

con·join \kən-'jȯin\ *vb* : to join together — **con·joint** \-'jȯint\ *adj*

con·ju·gal \'kän-ji-gəl\ *adj* : of or relating to marriage : MATRIMONIAL

¹con·ju·gate \'kän-ji-gət, -jə-ˌgāt\ *adj* **1** : united esp. in pairs : COUPLED **2** : of kindred origin and meaning ⟨*sing* and *song* are ~⟩ — **con·ju·gate·ly** *adv*

²con·ju·gate \-jə-ˌgāt\ *vb* **-gat·ed; -gat·ing 1** : INFLECT ⟨~ a verb⟩ **2** : to join together : COUPLE

con·ju·ga·tion \ˌkän-jə-'gā-shən\ *n* **1** : an arrangement of the inflectional forms of a verb **2** : the act of conjugating : the state of being conjugated

con·junct \kän-'jəŋkt\ *adj* : JOINED, UNITED

con·junc·tion \kən-'jəŋk-shən\ *n* **1** : COMBINATION **2** : occurrence at the same time **3** : a word that joins together sentences, clauses, phrases, or words

con·junc·ti·va \ˌkän-ˌjəŋk-'tī-və\ *n, pl* **-vas** *or* **-vae** \-(ˌ)vē\ : the mucous membrane lining the inner surface of the eyelids and continuing over the forepart of the eyeball

con·junc·tive \kən-'jəŋk-tiv\ *adj* **1** : CONNECTIVE **2** : CONJUNCT **3** : being or functioning like a conjunction

con·junc·ti·vi·tis \kən-ˌjəŋk-ti-'vī-təs\ *n* : inflammation of the conjunctiva

con·junc·ture \kən-'jəŋk-chər\ *n* **1** : CONJUNCTION, UNION **2** : JUNCTURE **3**

con·jure \'kän-jər, 'kən- *for 1, 2;* kən-'jür *for 3*\ *vb* **con·jured; con·jur·ing 1** : to implore earnestly or solemnly **2** : to practice magic; *esp* : to summon (as a devil) by sorcery **3** : to practice sleight of hand — **con·ju·ra·tion** \ˌkän-jů-'rā-shən, ˌkən-\ *n* — **con·jur·er** *or* **con·ju·ror** \'kän-jər-ər, 'kən-\ *n*

conk \'käŋk\ *vb* : BREAK DOWN; *esp* : STALL ⟨the motor ~ed out⟩

Conn *abbr* Connecticut

con·nect \kə-'nekt\ *vb* **1** : JOIN, LINK **2** : to associate in one's mind — **con·nect·able** *adj* — **con·nec·tor** *n*

con·nec·tion \kə-'nek-shən\ *n* **1** : JUNCTION, UNION **2** : logical relationship : COHERENCE; *esp* : relation of a word to other words in a sentence **3** : family relationship **4** : BOND, LINK **5** : a person related by blood or marriage **6** : relationship in social affairs or in business **7** : an association of persons; *esp* : a religious denomination

¹**con·nec·tive** \kə-ˈnek-tiv\ *adj* : serving to connect — **con·nec·tiv·i·ty** \ˌkä-ˌnek-ˈti-və-tē\ *n*

²**connective** *n* : a word (as a conjunction) that connects words or word groups

con·nex·ion *chiefly Brit var of* CONNECTION

con·ning tower \ˈkä-niŋ-\ *n* : a raised structure on the deck of a submarine

con·nip·tion \kə-ˈnip-shən\ *n* : a fit of rage, hysteria, or alarm

con·nive \kə-ˈnīv\ *vb* **con·nived; con·niv·ing** [F or L; F *conniver*, fr. L *conivēre* to close the eyes, connive] **1** : to pretend ignorance of something one ought to oppose as wrong **2** : to cooperate secretly : give secret aid — **con·niv·ance** *n* — **con·niv·er** *n*

con·nois·seur \ˌkä-nə-ˈsər\ *n* : a critical judge in matters of art or taste

con·no·ta·tion \ˌkä-nə-ˈtā-shən\ *n* : a meaning in addition to or apart from the thing explicitly named or described by a word

con·no·ta·tive \ˈkä-nə-ˌtā-tiv, kə-ˈnō-tə-\ *adj* **1** : connoting or tending to connote **2** : relating to connotation

con·note \kə-ˈnōt\ *vb* **con·not·ed; con·not·ing** : to suggest or mean as a connotation

con·nu·bi·al \kə-ˈnü-bē-əl, -ˈnyü-\ *adj* : of or relating to marriage : CONJUGAL

con·quer \ˈkäŋ-kər\ *vb* **1** : to gain by force of arms : WIN **2** : to get the better of : OVERCOME **syn** defeat, subjugate, subdue, overthrow, vanquish — **con·quer·or** \-ər\ *n*

con·quest \ˈkän-ˌkwest, ˈkäŋ-\ *n* **1** : an act of conquering : VICTORY **2** : something conquered

con·quis·ta·dor \kōŋ-ˈkēs-tə-ˌdȯr, kän-ˈkwis-\ *n, pl* **-do·res** \-ˌkēs-tə-ˈdȯr-ēz, -ˌkwis-\ *or* **-dors** : CONQUEROR; *esp* : a leader in the Spanish conquest of the Americas in the 16th century

cons *abbr* consonant

con·san·guin·i·ty \ˌkän-ˌsan-ˈgwi-nə-tē, -ˌsaŋ-\ *n, pl* **-ties** : blood relationship — **con·san·guin·e·ous** \-nē-əs\ *adj*

con·science \ˈkän-chəns\ *n* : consciousness of the moral right and wrong of one's own acts or motives — **con·science·less** *adj*

con·sci·en·tious \ˌkän-chē-ˈen-chəs\ *adj* : guided by one's own sense of right and wrong **syn** scrupulous, honorable, honest, upright, just — **con·sci·en·tious·ly** *adv*

conscientious objector *n* : a person who refuses to serve in the armed forces or to bear arms on moral or religious grounds

con·scious \ˈkän-chəs\ *adj* **1** : AWARE **2** : known or felt by one's inner self **3** : mentally awake or alert : not asleep or unconscious **4** : INTENTIONAL — **con·scious·ly** *adv* — **con·scious·ness** *n*

con·script \kən-ˈskript\ *vb* : to enroll by compulsion for military or naval service — **conscript** \ˈkän-ˌskript\ *n* — **con·scrip·tion** \kən-ˈskrip-shən\ *n*

con·se·crate \ˈkän-sə-ˌkrāt\ *vb* **-crat·ed; -crat·ing 1** : to induct (as a bishop) into an office with a religious rite **2** : to make or declare sacred ⟨∼ a church⟩ **3** : to devote solemnly to a purpose — **con·se·cra·tion** \ˌkän-sə-ˈkrā-shən\ *n*

con·sec·u·tive \kən-ˈse-kyə-tiv\ *adj* : following in regular order : SUCCESSIVE — **con·sec·u·tive·ly** *adv*

con·sen·su·al \kən-ˈsen-chə-wəl\ *adj* : involving or based on mutual consent

con·sen·sus \kən-ˈsen-səs\ *n* **1** : agreement in opinion, testimony, or belief **2** : collective opinion

¹**con·sent** \kən-ˈsent\ *vb* : to give assent or approval

²**consent** *n* : approval or acceptance of something done or proposed by another

con·se·quence \ˈkän-sə-ˌkwens\ *n* **1** : RESULT **2** : IMPORTANCE **syn** effect, outcome, aftermath, upshot

con·se·quent \-kwənt, -ˌkwent\ *adj* : following as a result or effect

con·se·quen·tial \ˌkän-sə-ˈkwen-chəl\ *adj* **1** : having significant consequences **2** : showing self-importance

con·se·quent·ly \ˈkän-sə-ˌkwent-lē, -kwənt-\ *adv* : as a result : ACCORDINGLY

con·ser·van·cy \kən-ˈsər-vən-sē\ *n, pl* **-cies** : an organization or area designated to conserve natural resources

con·ser·va·tion \ˌkän-sər-ˈvā-shən\ *n* : PRESERVATION; *esp* : planned management of natural resources

con·ser·va·tion·ist \-shə-nist\ *n* : a person who advocates conservation esp. of natural resources

con·ser·va·tism \kən-ˈsər-və-ˌti-zəm\ *n* : disposition to keep to established ways : opposition to change

¹**con·ser·va·tive** \kən-ˈsər-və-tiv\ *adj* **1** : PRESERVATIVE **2** : disposed to maintain existing views, conditions, or institutions **3** : MODERATE, CAUTIOUS — **con·ser·va·tive·ly** *adv*

²**conservative** *n* : a person who is conservative esp. in politics

con·ser·va·tor \kən-ˈsər-və-tər, ˈkän-sər-ˌvā-\ *n* **1** : PROTECTOR, GUARDIAN **2** : one named by a court to protect the interests of an incompetent (as a child)

con·ser·va·to·ry \kən-ˈsər-və-ˌtȯr-ē\ *n, pl* **-ries 1** : GREENHOUSE **2** : a place of instruction in one of the fine arts (as music)

¹**con·serve** \kən-ˈsərv\ *vb* **con·served; con·serv·ing** : to keep from losing or wasting : PRESERVE

²**con·serve** \ˈkän-ˌsərv\ *n* **1** : CONFECTION; *esp* : a candied fruit **2** : PRESERVE; *esp* : one prepared from a mixture of fruits

con·sid·er \kən-ˈsi-dər\ *vb* [ME, fr. MF *considerer*, fr. L *considerare*, fr. *com-* together + *sider-, sidus* heavenly body] **1** : THINK, PONDER **2** : HEED, REGARD **3** : JUDGE, BELIEVE — **con·sid·ered** *adj*

con·sid·er·able \-ˈsi-dər-ə-bəl, -ˈsi-drə-bəl\ *adj* **1** : IMPORTANT **2** : large in extent, amount, or degree — **con·sid·er·ably** \-blē\ *adv*

con·sid·er·ate \kən-ˈsi-də-rət\ *adj* : observant of the rights and feelings of others **syn** thoughtful, attentive

con·sid·er·a·tion \kən-ˌsi-də-ˈrā-shən\ *n* **1** : careful thought : DELIBERATION **2** : a matter taken into account **3** : thoughtful attention **4** : JUDGMENT, OPINION **5** : RECOMPENSE

con·sid·er·ing *prep* : in view of : taking into account

con·sign \kən-ˈsīn\ *vb* **1** : ENTRUST, COMMIT **2** : to deliver formally **3** : to send (goods) to an agent for sale — **con·sign·ee** \ˌkän-sə-ˈnē, -ˌsī-; kən-ˌsī-\ *n* — **con·sign·or** \ˌkän-sə-ˈnȯr, -ˌsī-; kən-ˌsī-\ *n*

con·sign·ment \kən-ˈsīn-mənt\ *n* : something consigned esp. in a single shipment

con·sist \kən-ˈsist\ *vb* **1** : to be inherent : LIE — usu. used with *in* **2** : to be composed or made up — usu. used with *of*

con·sis·tence \kən-ˈsis-təns\ *n* : CONSISTENCY

con·sis·ten·cy \-tən-sē\ *n, pl* **-cies 1** : COHESIVENESS, FIRMNESS **2** : agreement or harmony in parts or of different things **3** : UNIFORMITY ⟨∼ of behavior⟩ — **con·sis·tent** \-tənt\ *adj* — **con·sis·tent·ly** *adv*

con·sis·to·ry \kən-ˈsis-tə-rē\ *n, pl* **-ries** : a solemn assembly (as of Roman Catholic cardinals)

consol *abbr* consolidated

¹**con·sole** \ˈkän-ˌsōl\ *n* **1** : the desklike part of an organ at which the organist sits **2** : the combination of displays and controls of a device or system **3** : a cabinet for a radio or television set resting directly on the floor **4** : a small storage cabinet between bucket seats in an automobile

²**con·sole** \kən-ˈsōl\ *vb* **con·soled; con·sol·ing** : to soothe the grief of : COMFORT, SOLACE — **con·so·la·tion** \ˌkän-sə-ˈlā-shən\ *n* — **con·so·la·to·ry** \kən-ˈsō-lə-ˌtȯr-ē, -ˈsä-\ *adj*

con·sol·i·date \kən-ˈsä-lə-ˌdāt\ *vb* **-dat·ed; -dat·ing 1** : to unite or become united into one whole : COMBINE

2 : to make firm or secure **3** : to form into a compact mass — **con·sol·i·da·tion** \-ˌsä-lə-ˈdā-shən\ *n*

con·som·mé \ˌkän-sə-ˈmā\ *n* [F] : a clear soup made from well-seasoned stock

con·so·nance \ˈkän-sə-nəns\ *n* **1** : AGREEMENT, HARMONY **2** : repetition of consonants esp. as an alternative to rhyme in verse

¹**con·so·nant** \-nənt\ *adj* : having consonance, harmony, or agreement **syn** consistent, compatible, congruous, congenial, sympathetic — **con·so·nant·ly** *adv*

²**consonant** *n* **1** : a speech sound (as \p\, \g\, \n\, \l\, \s\, \r\) characterized by constriction or closure at one or more points in the breath channel **2** : a letter other than *a, e, i, o,* and *u* — **con·so·nan·tal** \ˌkän-sə-ˈnant-ᵊl\ *adj*

¹**con·sort** \ˈkän-ˌsȯrt\ *n* **1** : a ship accompanying another **2** : SPOUSE, MATE

²**con·sort** \kən-ˈsȯrt\ *vb* **1** : to keep company **2** : ACCORD, HARMONIZE

con·sor·tium \kən-ˈsȯr-shəm; -shē-əm, -tē-\ *n, pl* **-sor·tia** \-shə-; -shē-ə, -tē-\ [L, fellowship] : an agreement or combination (as of companies) formed to undertake a large enterprise

con·spec·tus \kən-ˈspek-təs\ *n* **1** : a brief survey or summary **2** : SUMMARY

con·spic·u·ous \kən-ˈspi-kyə-wəs\ *adj* : attracting attention : PROMINENT, STRIKING **syn** noticeable, remarkable, outstanding — **con·spic·u·ous·ly** *adv*

con·spir·a·cy \kən-ˈspir-ə-sē\ *n, pl* **-cies** : an agreement among conspirators : PLOT

con·spire \kən-ˈspīr\ *vb* **conspired; con·spir·ing** [ME, fr. MF *conspirer,* fr. L *conspirare* to be in harmony, conspire, fr. *com-* with + *spirare* to breathe] : to plan secretly an unlawful act : PLOT

con·spir·a·tor \kən-ˈspir-ə-tər\ *n* : one that conspires — **con·spir·a·to·ri·al** \-ˌspir-ə-ˈtȯr-ē-əl\ *adj*

const *abbr* **1** constant **2** constitution; constitutional

con·sta·ble \ˈkän-stə-bəl, ˈkən-\ *n* [ME *conestable,* fr. OF, fr. LL *comes stabuli,* lit., officer of the stable] : a public officer responsible for keeping the peace

con·stab·u·lary \kən-ˈsta-byə-ler-ē\ *n, pl* **-lar·ies 1** : the police of a particular district or country **2** : a police force organized like the military

con·stan·cy \ˈkän-stən-sē\ *n, pl* **-cies 1** : firmness of mind **2** : STABILITY

¹**con·stant** \-stənt\ *adj* **1** : STEADFAST, FAITHFUL **2** : FIXED, UNCHANGING **3** : continually recurring : REGULAR — **con·stant·ly** *adv*

²**constant** *n* : something unchanging

con·stel·la·tion \ˌkän-stə-ˈlā-shən\ *n* : any of 88 groups of stars forming patterns

con·ster·na·tion \ˌkän-stər-ˈnā-shən\ *n* : amazed dismay and confusion

con·sti·pa·tion \ˌkän-stə-ˈpā-shən\ *n* : abnormally difficult or infrequent bowel movements — **con·sti·pate** \ˈkän-stə-ˌpāt\ *vb*

con·stit·u·en·cy \kən-ˈsti-chə-wən-sē\ *n, pl* **-cies** : a body of constituents; *also* : an electoral district

¹**con·stit·u·ent** \-wənt\ *n* **1** : a person entitled to vote for a representative for a district **2** : a component part

²**constituent** *adj* **1** : COMPONENT **2** : having power to create a government or frame or amend a constitution

con·sti·tute \ˈkän-stə-ˌtüt, -ˌtyüt\ *vb* **-tut·ed; -tut·ing 1** : to appoint to an office or duty **2** : SET UP, ESTABLISH ⟨~ a law⟩ **3** : MAKE UP, COMPOSE

con·sti·tu·tion \ˌkän-stə-ˈtü-shən, -ˈtyü-\ *n* **1** : an established law or custom **2** : the physical makeup of the individual **3** : the structure, composition, or makeup of something ⟨~ of the sun⟩ **4** : the basic law in a politically organized body; *also* : a document containing such law

¹**con·sti·tu·tion·al** \-shə-nəl\ *adj* **1** : of or relating to the constitution of body or mind **2** : being in accord with the constitution of a state or society; *also* : of or relating to such a constitution — **con·sti·tu·tion·al·ly** *adv*

²**constitutional** *n* : an exercise (as a walk) taken for one's health

con·sti·tu·tion·al·i·ty \-ˌtü-shə-ˈna-lə-tē, -ˌtyü-\ *n* : the quality or state of being constitutional

con·sti·tu·tive \ˈkän-stə-ˌtü-tiv, -ˌtyü-, kən-ˈsti-chə-tiv\ *adj* **1** : CONSTRUCTIVE **2** : CONSTITUENT, ESSENTIAL

constr *abbr* construction

con·strain \kən-ˈstrān\ *vb* **1** : COMPEL, FORCE **2** : CONFINE **3** : RESTRAIN

con·straint \-ˈstrānt\ *n* **1** : COMPULSION; *also* : RESTRAINT **2** : repression of one's natural feelings

con·strict \kən-ˈstrikt\ *vb* : to draw together : SQUEEZE — **con·stric·tion** \-ˈstrik-shən\ *n* — **con·stric·tive** \-ˈstrik-tiv\ *adj*

con·stric·tor \kən-ˈstrik-tər\ *n* : a snake that kills its prey by crushing it in its coils

con·struct \kən-ˈstrəkt\ *vb* : BUILD, MAKE — **con·struc·tor** \-ˈstrək-tər\ *n*

con·struc·tion \kən-ˈstrək-shən\ *n* **1** : INTERPRETATION **2** : the art, process, or manner of building; *also* : something built, created, or established : STRUCTURE **3** : syntactical arrangement of words in a sentence — **con·struc·tive** \-tiv\ *adj*

con·struc·tion·ist \-shə-nist\ *n* : a person who construes a legal document (as the U.S. Constitution) in a specific way ⟨a strict ~⟩

con·strue \kən-ˈstrü\ *vb* **con·strued; con·stru·ing 1** : to analyze the mutual relations of words in a sentence; *also* : TRANSLATE **2** : EXPLAIN, INTERPRET — **con·stru·able** *adj*

con·sub·stan·ti·a·tion \ˌkän-səb-ˌstan-chē-ˈā-shən\ *n* : the actual substantial presence and combination of the body and blood of Christ with the eucharistic bread and wine

con·sul \ˈkän-səl\ *n* **1** : a chief magistrate of the Roman republic **2** : an official appointed by a government to reside in a foreign country to care for the commercial interests of the appointing government's citizens — **con·sul·ar** \-sə-lər\ *adj* — **con·sul·ate** \-lət\ *n* — **con·sul·ship** *n*

con·sult \kən-ˈsəlt\ *vb* **1** : to ask the advice or opinion of **2** : CONFER — **con·sul·tant** \-ᵊnt\ *n* — **con·sul·ta·tion** \ˌkän-səl-ˈtā-shən\ *n*

con·sume \kən-ˈsüm\ *vb* **con·sumed; con·sum·ing 1** : DESTROY ⟨*consumed* by fire⟩ **2** : to spend wastefully **3** : to eat up : DEVOUR **4** : to absorb the attention of : ENGROSS — **con·sum·able** *adj* — **con·sum·er** *n*

con·sum·er·ism \kən-ˈsü-mə-ˌri-zəm\ *n* : the promotion of consumers' interests (as against false advertising)

consumer price index *n* : an index measuring the change in the cost of widely purchased goods and services from the cost in some base period

¹**con·sum·mate** \ˈkän-sə-mət, kən-ˈsə\ *adj* : PERFECT **syn** finished, accomplished

²**con·sum·mate** \ˈkän-sə-ˌmāt\ *vb* **-mat·ed; -mat·ing** : to make complete : FINISH, ACHIEVE — **con·sum·ma·tion** \ˌkän-sə-ˈmā-shən\ *n*

con·sump·tion \kən-ˈsəmp-shən\ *n* **1** : progressive bodily wasting away; *also* : TUBERCULOSIS **2** : the act of consuming or using up **3** : the use of economic goods

¹**con·sump·tive** \-ˈsəmp-tiv\ *adj* **1** : tending to consume **2** : relating to or affected with consumption

²**consumptive** *n* : a person who has consumption

cont *abbr* **1** containing **2** contents **3** continent; continental **4** continued **5** control

¹**con·tact** \ˈkän-ˌtakt\ *n* **1** : a touching or meeting of bodies **2** : ASSOCIATION, RELATIONSHIP; *also* : CONNECTION, COMMUNICATION **3** : a person serving as a go-between or source of information **4** : CONTACT LENS

²**contact** *vb* **1** : to come or bring into contact : TOUCH **2** : to get in communication with

contact lens *n* : a thin lens fitting over the cornea usu. to correct vision

con·ta·gion \kən-'tā-jən\ *n* **1** : a contagious disease; *also* : the transmission of such a disease **2** : a disease-producing agent (as a virus) **3** : transmission of an influence on the mind or emotions

con·ta·gious \-jəs\ *adj* **1** : transmitted by contact with an infected person, his or her bodily discharges, or something that has touched either **2** : communicated or transmitted like a contagious disease; *esp* : exciting similar emotion or conduct in others

con·tain \kən-'tān\ *vb* **1** : RESTRAIN **2** : to have within : HOLD **3** : COMPRISE, INCLUDE — **con·tain·ment** *n*

con·tain·er \kən-'tā-nər\ *n* : RECEPTACLE; *esp* : one for shipment of goods

con·tam·i·nant \kən-'ta-mə-nənt\ *n* : something that contaminates

con·tam·i·nate \kən-'ta-mə-ˌnāt\ *vb* **-nat·ed; -nat·ing** : to soil, stain, or infect by contact or association — **con·tam·i·na·tion** \-ˌta-mə-'nā-shən\ *n*

contd *abbr* continued

con·temn \kən-'tem\ *vb* : to view or treat with contempt : DESPISE

con·tem·plate \'kän-təm-ˌplāt\ *vb* **-plat·ed; -plat·ing** [L *contemplari,* fr. *com-* with + *templum* space marked out for observation of auguries] **1** : to view or consider with continued attention **2** : INTEND — **con·tem·pla·tion** \ˌkän-təm-'plā-shən\ *n* — **con·tem·pla·tive** \kən-'tem-plə-tiv, 'kän-təm-ˌplā-\ *adj*

con·tem·po·ra·ne·ous \kən-ˌtem-pə-'rā-nē-əs\ *adj* : CONTEMPORARY 1

con·tem·po·rary \kən-'tem-pə-ˌrer-ē\ *adj* **1** : occurring or existing at the same time **2** : marked by characteristics of the present period — **contemporary** *n*

con·tempt \kən-'tempt\ *n* **1** : the act of despising : the state of mind of one who despises **2** : the state of being despised **3** : disobedience to or open disrespect of a court or legislature

con·tempt·ible \kən-'temp-tə-bəl\ *adj* : deserving contempt : DESPICABLE — **con·tempt·ibly** \-blē\ *adv*

con·temp·tu·ous \-'temp-chə-wəs\ *adj* : feeling or expressing contempt — **con·temp·tu·ous·ly** *adv*

con·tend \kən-'tend\ *vb* **1** : to strive against rivals or difficulties **2** : ARGUE **3** : MAINTAIN, ASSERT — **con·tend·er** *n*

¹con·tent \kən-'tent\ *adj* : SATISFIED

²content *vb* : SATISFY; *esp* : to limit (oneself) in requirements or actions

³content *n* : CONTENTMENT

⁴con·tent \'kän-ˌtent\ *n* **1** : something contained ⟨~s of a room⟩ **2** : subject matter or topics treated (as in a book) **3** : MEANING, SIGNIFICANCE **4** : the amount of material contained

con·tent·ed \kən-'ten-təd\ *adj* : SATISFIED — **con·tent·ed·ly** *adv* — **con·tent·ed·ness** *n*

con·ten·tion \kən-'ten-chən\ *n* **1** : CONTEST, STRIFE **2** : an idea or point for which a person argues — **con·ten·tious** \-chəs\ *adj* — **con·ten·tious·ly** *adv*

con·tent·ment \kən-'tent-mənt\ *n* : ease of mind : SATISFACTION

con·ter·mi·nous \kän-'tər-mə-nəs\ *adj* : having the same or a common boundary — **con·ter·mi·nous·ly** *adv*

¹con·test \kən-'test\ *vb* **1** : to engage in strife : FIGHT **2** : CHALLENGE, DISPUTE — **con·tes·tant** \-'tes-tənt\ *n*

²con·test \'kän-ˌtest\ *n* : STRUGGLE, COMPETITION

con·text \'kän-ˌtekst\ *n* [L *contextus* connection of words, coherence, fr. *contexere* to weave together] : the parts of a discourse that surround a word or passage and help to explain its meaning; *also* : the circumstances surrounding an act or event — **con·tex·tu·al·ly** *adv*

con·tig·u·ous \kən-'ti-gyə-wəs\ *adj* : being in contact : TOUCHING; *also* : NEXT, ADJOINING — **con·ti·gu·i·ty** \ˌkän-tə-'gyü-ə-tē\ *n*

con·ti·nence \'känt-ᵊn-əns\ *n* **1** : SELF-RESTRAINT; *esp* : a refraining from sexual intercourse **2** : the ability to retain urine or feces voluntarily

¹con·ti·nent \'känt-ᵊn-ənt\ *adj* : exercising continence

²continent *n* **1** : any of the great divisions of land on the globe **2** *cap* : the continent of Europe

¹con·ti·nen·tal \ˌkän-tə-'nent-ᵊl\ *adj* **1** : of or relating to a continent; *esp, often cap* : of or relating to the continent of Europe **2** *often cap* : of or relating to the colonies later forming the U.S. **3** : of or relating to cuisine based on classical European cooking

²continental *n* **1** *often cap* : a soldier in the Continental army **2** : EUROPEAN

continental drift *n* : a hypothetical slow movement of the continents over a fluid layer deep within the earth

continental shelf *n* : a shallow submarine plain forming a border to a continent

continental slope *n* : a usu. steep slope from a continental shelf to the ocean floor

con·tin·gen·cy \kən-'tin-jən-sē\ *n, pl* **-cies** : a chance or possible event

¹con·tin·gent \-jənt\ *adj* **1** : liable but not certain to happen : POSSIBLE **2** : happening by chance : not planned **3** : dependent on something that may or may not occur **4** : CONDITIONAL **syn** accidental, casual, incidental, odd

²contingent *n* : a quota (as of troops) supplied from an area or group

con·tin·u·al \kən-'tin-yə-wəl\ *adj* **1** : CONTINUOUS, UNBROKEN **2** : steadily recurring — **con·tin·u·al·ly** *adv*

con·tin·u·ance \-yə-wəns\ *n* **1** : unbroken succession **2** : the extent of continuing : DURATION **3** : adjournment of legal proceedings

con·tin·u·a·tion \kən-ˌtin-yə-'wā-shən\ *n* **1** : extension or prolongation of a state or activity **2** : resumption after an interruption; *also* : something that carries on after a pause or break

con·tin·ue \kən-'tin-yü\ *vb* **-tin·ued; -tinu·ing 1** : to maintain without interruption **2** : ENDURE, LAST **3** : to remain in a place or condition **4** : to resume (as a story) after an intermission **5** : EXTEND; *also* : to persist in **6** : to allow to remain **7** : to keep (a legal case) on the calendar or undecided

con·ti·nu·i·ty \ˌkän-tə-'nü-ə-tē, -'nyü-\ *n, pl* **-ties 1** : the state of being continuous **2** : something that has or provides continuity

con·tin·u·ous \kən-'tin-yə-wəs\ *adj* : continuing without interruption — **con·tin·u·ous·ly** *adv*

con·tin·u·um \-yə-wəm\ *n, pl* **-ua** \-yə-wə\ *also* **-ums** : something that is the same throughout or consists of a series of variations or of a sequence of things in regular order

con·tort \kən-'tórt\ *vb* : to twist out of shape — **con·tor·tion** \-'tór-shən\ *n*

con·tor·tion·ist \-'tór-shə-nist\ *n* : an acrobat able to twist the body into unusual postures

con·tour \'kän-ˌtúr\ *n* [F, fr. It *contorno* fr. *contornare* to round off, sketch in outline, fr. L *com-* together + *tornare* to turn in a lathe, fr. *tornus* lathe] **1** : OUTLINE **2** : SHAPE, FORM — often used in pl. ⟨the ~s of a statue⟩

contr *abbr* contract; contraction

con·tra·band \'kän-trə-ˌband\ *n* : goods legally prohibited in trade; *also* : smuggled goods

con·tra·cep·tion \ˌkän-trə-'sep-shən\ *n* : intentional prevention of conception and pregnancy — **con·tra·cep·tive** \-'sep-tive\ *adj or n*

¹con·tract \'kän-ˌtrakt\ *n* **1** : a binding agreement **2** : an undertaking to win a specified number of tricks in bridge — **con·trac·tu·al** \kən-'trak-chə-wəl\ *adj* — **con·trac·tu·al·ly** *adv*

²con·tract \kən-'trakt, 2 usu 'kän-ˌtrakt\ *vb* **1** : to become affected with ⟨~ a disease⟩ **2** : to establish or undertake by contract **3** : SHRINK, LESSEN; *esp* : to draw together esp. so as to shorten ⟨~ a muscle⟩ **4** : to shorten (a word) by omitting letters or sounds in the middle — **con·tract·ible** \kən-'trak-tə-bəl, 'kän-ˌ\ *adj* — **con·trac·tion** \kən-'trak-shən\ *n* — **con·trac·tor** \'kän-ˌtrak-tər, kən-'trak-\ *n*

con·trac·tile \kən-'trakt-ªl\ *adj* : able to contract — **con·trac·til·i·ty** \kän-ıtrak-'ti-lə-tē\ *n*

con·tra·dict \ıkän-trə-'dikt\ *vb* : to assert the contrary of : deny the truth of — **con·tra·dic·tion** \-'dik-shən\ *n* — **con·tra·dic·to·ry** \-'dik-tə-rē\ *adj*

con·tra·dis·tinc·tion \ıkän-trə-dis-'tiŋk-shən\ *n* : distinction by contrast

con·trail \'kän-ıtrāl\ *n* : a streak of condensed water vapor created by an airplane or rocket at high altitudes

con·tra·in·di·ca·tion \ıkän-trə-ıin-də-'kā-shən\ *n* : something (as a symptom or condition) that makes a particular treatment or procedure inadvisable

con·tral·to \kən-'tral-tō\ *n, pl* **-tos** : the lowest female voice; *also* : a singer having such a voice

con·trap·tion \kən-'trap-shən\ *n* : CONTRIVANCE, DEVICE

con·tra·pun·tal \ıkän-trə-'pənt-ªl\ *adj* : of or relating to counterpoint

con·tra·ri·ety \ıkän-trə-'rī-ə-tē\ *n, pl* **-eties** : the state of being contrary : DISAGREEMENT, INCONSISTENCY

con·trari·wise \'kän-ıtrer-ē-ıwīz, kən-'trer-\ *adv* **1** : on the contrary **2** : VICE VERSA

con·trary \'kän-ıtrer-ē; *4 often* kən-'trer-ē\ *adj* **1** : opposite in nature or position **2** : COUNTER, OPPOSED **3** : UNFAVORABLE — used of wind or weather **4** : unwilling to accept control or advice — **con·trari·ly** \-ıtrer-ə-lē, -'trer-\ *adv* — **con·trary** *n is* 'kän-ıtrer-ē, *adv is like adj*\ *n or adv*

¹**con·trast** \kən-'trast\ *vb* [F *contraster*, fr. MF, to oppose, resist, fr. (assumed) VL *contrastare*, fr. L *contra-* against + *stare* to stand] **1** : to show differences when compared **2** : to compare in such a way as to show differences

²**con·trast** \'kän-ıtrast\ *n* **1** : diversity of adjacent parts in color, emotion, tone, or brightness ⟨the ∼ of a photograph⟩ **2** : unlikeness as shown when things are compared : DIFFERENCE

con·tra·vene \ıkän-trə-'vēn\ *vb* **-vened; -ven·ing 1** : to go or act contrary to ⟨∼ a law⟩ **2** : CONTRADICT

con·tre·temps \'kän-trə-ıtän, kōⁿ-trə-'täⁿ\ *n, pl* **con·tre·temps** \-ıtän, -ıtäⁿz\ [F] : an inopportune or embarrassing occurrence

contrib *abbr* contribution; contributor

con·trib·ute \kən-'tri-byət\ *vb* **-ut·ed; -ut·ing** : to give along with others (as to a fund); *also* : HELP, ASSIST — **con·tri·bu·tion** \ıkän-trə-'byü-shən\ *n* — **con·trib·u·tor** \kən-'tri-byə-tər\ *n* — **con·trib·u·to·ry** \-byə-ıtōr-ē\ *adj*

con·trite \'kän-ıtrīt, kən-'trīt\ *adj* : PENITENT, REPENTANT — **con·trite·ly** *adv* — **con·tri·tion** \kən-'tri-shən\ *n*

con·triv·ance \kən-'trī-vəns\ *n* **1** : a mechanical device **2** : SCHEME, PLAN

con·trive \kən-'trīv\ *vb* **con·trived; con·triv·ing 1** : PLAN, DEVISE **2** : FRAME, MAKE **3** : to bring about with difficulty — **con·triv·er** *n*

con·trived \-'trīvd\ *adj* : lacking in natural or spontaneous quality

¹**con·trol** \kən-'trōl\ *vb* **con·trolled; con·trol·ling 1** : to exercise restraining or directing influence over : REGULATE **2** : DOMINATE, RULE

²**control** *n* **1** : power to direct or regulate **2** : RESERVE, RESTRAINT **3** : a device for regulating a mechanism

con·trol·ler \kən-'trō-lər, 'kän-ıtrō-lər\ *n* **1** : COMPTROLLER **2** : one that controls

con·tro·ver·sy \'kän-trə-ıvər-sē\ *n, pl* **-sies** : a clash of opposing views : DISPUTE — **con·tro·ver·sial** \ıkän-trə-'vər-shəl, -sē-əl\ *adj*

con·tro·vert \'kän-trə-ıvərt, ıkän-trə-'vərt\ *vb* : DENY, CONTRADICT — **con·tro·vert·ible** *adj*

con·tu·ma·cious \ıkän-tü-'mā-shəs, -tyü-\ *adj* : stubbornly disobedient **syn** rebellious, insubordinate, seditious — **con·tu·ma·cy** \kän-'tü-mə-sē, -'tyü-; 'kän-tyə-\ *n* — **con·tu·ma·cious·ly** *adv*

con·tu·me·ly \kən-'tü-mə-lē, -'tyü-; 'kän-tə-ımē-lē,

-tyə-\ *n, pl* **-lies** : contemptuous treatment : INSULT

con·tu·sion \kən-'tü-zhən, -'tyü-\ *n* : BRUISE — **con·tuse** \-'tüz, -'tyüz\ *vb*

co·nun·drum \kə-'nən-drəm\ *n* : RIDDLE

conv *abbr* **1** convention **2** convertible

con·va·lesce \ıkän-və-'les\ *vb* **-lesced; -lesc·ing** : to recover health gradually — **con·va·les·cence** \-ªns\ *n* — **con·va·les·cent** \-ªnt\ *adj or n*

con·vec·tion \kən-'vek-shən\ *n* : circulatory motion in a fluid due to warmer portions rising and cooler denser portions sinking; *also* : the transfer of heat by such motion — **con·vec·tion·al** \-shə-nəl\ *adj* — **con·vec·tive** \-'vek-tiv\ *adj*

convection oven *n* : an oven with a fan that circulates hot air uniformly and continuously around the food

con·vene \kən-'vēn\ *vb* **con·vened; con·ven·ing** : ASSEMBLE, MEET

con·ve·nience \kən-'vē-nyəns\ *n* **1** : SUITABLENESS **2** : a laborsaving device **3** : a suitable time ⟨at your ∼⟩ **4** : personal comfort : EASE

con·ve·nient \-nyənt\ *adj* **1** : suited to personal comfort or ease **2** : placed near at hand — **con·ve·nient·ly** *adv*

con·vent \'kän-vənt, -ıvent\ *n* [ME *covent*, fr. OF, fr. ML *conventus*, fr. L, assembly, fr. *convenire* to come together] : a local community or house of a religious order esp. of nuns — **con·ven·tu·al** \kän-'ven-chə-wəl\ *adj*

con·ven·ti·cle \kən-'ven-ti-kəl\ *n* : MEETING; *esp* : a secret meeting for worship

con·ven·tion \kən-'ven-chən\ *n* **1** : an agreement esp. between states on a matter of common concern **2** : MEETING, ASSEMBLY **3** : an assembly of delegates convened for some purpose **4** : generally accepted custom, practice, or belief

con·ven·tion·al \-chə-nəl\ *adj* **1** : sanctioned by general custom **2** : COMMONPLACE, ORDINARY — **con·ven·tion·al·i·ty** \-ıven-chə-'na-lə-tē\ *n* — **con·ven·tion·al·ize** \-'ven-chə-nə-ılīz\ *vb* — **con·ven·tion·al·ly** *adv*

con·verge \kən-'vərj\ *vb* **con·verged; con·verg·ing** : to approach one common center or single point — **con·ver·gence** \kən-'vər-jəns\ *or* **con·ver·gen·cy** \-jən-sē\ *n* — **con·ver·gent** \-jənt\ *adj*

con·ver·sant \kən-'vərs-ªnt\ *adj* : having knowledge and experience — used with *with*

con·ver·sa·tion \ıkän-vər-'sā-shən\ *n* : an informal talking together — **con·ver·sa·tion·al** \-shə-nəl\ *adj* — **con·ver·sa·tion·al·ly** *adv*

con·ver·sa·tion·al·ist \-shə-nªl-ist\ *n* : a person who converses a great deal or who excels in conversation

¹**con·verse** \'kän-ıvərs\ *n* : CONVERSATION

²**con·verse** \kən-'vərs\ *vb* **con·versed; con·vers·ing** : to engage in conversation

³**con·verse** \'kän-ıvərs\ *n* : a statement related to another statement by having its hypothesis and conclusion or its subject and predicate reversed or interchanged

⁴**con·verse** \kən-'vərs, 'kän-ıvers\ *adj* : reversed in order or relation — **con·verse·ly** *adv*

con·ver·sion \kən-'vər-zhən\ *n* **1** : a change in nature or form **2** : an experience associated with a decisive adoption of religion

¹**con·vert** \kən-'vərt\ *vb* **1** : to turn from one belief or party to another **2** : TRANSFORM, CHANGE **3** : MISAPPROPRIATE **4** : EXCHANGE — **con·vert·er** *or* **con·ver·tor** \-'vər-tər\ *n* — **con·vert·ible** *adj*

²**con·vert** \'kän-ıvərt\ *n* : a person who has undergone religious conversion

con·vert·ible \kən-'vər-tə-bəl\ *n* : an automobile with a top that may be lowered or removed

con·vex \kän-'veks, 'kän-ıveks\ *adj* : curved or rounded like the exterior of a sphere or circle — **con·vex·i·ty** \kän-'vek-sə-tē\ *n*

con·vey \kən-'vā\ *vb* **1** : CARRY, TRANSPORT **2** : TRANSMIT, TRANSFER — **con·vey·or** *also* **con·vey·er** \-ər\ *n*

con·vey·ance \-'vā-əns\ *n* **1** : the act of conveying **2** : a legal paper transferring ownership of property **3** : VEHICLE

¹con·vict \kən-ˈvikt\ *vb* : to prove or find guilty

²con·vict \ˈkän-ˌvikt\ *n* : a person serving a prison sentence

con·vic·tion \kən-ˈvik-shən\ *n* **1** : the act of convicting esp. in a court **2** : the state of being convinced : BELIEF

con·vince \kən-ˈvins\ *vb* **con·vinced; con·vinc·ing** : to bring (as by argument) to belief or action — **con·vinc·ing** *adj* — **con·vinc·ing·ly** *adv*

con·viv·ial \kən-ˈvi-vē-əl\ *adj* [LL *convivialis*, fr. L *convivium* banquet, fr. *com-* together + *vivere* to live] : enjoying companionship and the pleasures of feasting and drinking : JOVIAL, FESTIVE — **con·viv·i·al·i·ty** \-ˌvi-vē-ˈa-lə-tē\ *n* — **con·viv·ial·ly** *adv*

con·vo·ca·tion \ˌkän-və-ˈkā-shən\ *n* **1** : a ceremonial assembly (as of the clergy) **2** : the act of convoking

con·voke \kən-ˈvōk\ *vb* **con·voked; con·vok·ing** : to call together to a meeting

con·vo·lut·ed \ˈkän-və-ˌlü-təd\ *adj* **1** : folded in curved or tortuous windings **2** : INVOLVED, INTRICATE

con·vo·lu·tion \ˌkän-və-ˈlü-shən\ *n* : a tortuous or sinuous structure; *esp* : one of the ridges of the brain

¹con·voy \ˈkän-ˌvȯi, kən-ˈvȯi\ *vb* : to accompany for protection

²con·voy \ˈkän-ˌvȯi\ *n* **1** : one that convoys; *esp* : a protective escort (as for ships) **2** : the act of convoying **3** : a group of moving vehicles

con·vulse \kən-ˈvəls\ *vb* **con·vulsed; con·vuls·ing** : to agitate violently

con·vul·sion \kən-ˈvəl-shən\ *n* **1** : an abnormal and violent involuntary contraction or series of contractions of muscle **2** : a violent disturbance — **con·vul·sive** \-siv\ *adj* — **con·vul·sive·ly** *adv*

cony *var of* CONEY

coo \ˈkü\ *n* : a soft low sound made by doves or pigeons; *also* : a sound like this — **coo** *vb*

COO *abbr* chief operating officer

¹cook \ˈkuk\ *n* : a person who prepares food for eating

²cook *vb* **1** : to prepare food for eating **2** : to subject to heat or fire — **cook·er** *n* — **cook·ware** \-ˌwar\ *n*

cook·book \-ˌbuk\ *n* : a book of cooking directions and recipes

cook·ery \ˈku-kə-rē\ *n, pl* **-er·ies** : the art or practice of cooking

cook·ie *or* **cooky** \ˈku-kē\ *n, pl* **cook·ies** : a small sweet flat cake

cook·out \ˈkuk-ˌaut\ *n* : an outing at which a meal is cooked and served in the open

¹cool \ˈkül\ *adj* **1** : moderately cold **2** : not excited : CALM **3** : not friendly **4** : IMPUDENT **5** : protecting from heat **6** *slang* : very good **syn** unflappable, composed, collected, unruffled, nonchalant — **cool·ly** *adv* — **cool·ness** *n*

²cool *vb* : to make or become cool

³cool *n* **1** : a cool time or place **2** : INDIFFERENCE; *also* : SELF-ASSURANCE, COMPOSURE ⟨kept his ∼⟩

cool·ant \ˈkü-lənt\ *n* : a usu. fluid cooling agent

cool·er \ˈkü-lər\ *n* **1** : a container for keeping food or drink cool **2** : JAIL, PRISON **3** : a tall iced drink

coo·lie \ˈkü-lē\ *n* [Hindi *kulī*] : an unskilled laborer usu. in or from the Far East

coon \ˈkün\ *n* : RACCOON

coon·hound \-ˌhaund\ *n* : a sporting dog trained to hunt raccoons

coon·skin \-ˌskin\ *n* : the pelt of a raccoon; *also* : something (as a cap) made of this

¹coop \ˈküp, ˈkup\ *n* : a small enclosure or building usu. for poultry

²coop *vb* : to confine in or as if in a coop — usu. used with *up*

co–op \ˈkō-ˌäp\ *n* : COOPERATIVE

coo·per \ˈkü-pər, ˈku-\ *n* : one who makes or repairs barrels or casks — **cooper** *vb* — **coo·per·age** \-pə-rij\ *n*

co·op·er·ate \kō-ˈä-pə-ˌrāt\ *vb* : to act jointly with another or others — **co·op·er·a·tion** \-ˌä-pə-ˈrā-shən\ *n* — **co·op·er·a·tor** \-ˈä-pə-ˌrā-tər\ *n*

¹co·op·er·a·tive \kō-ˈä-prə-tiv, -ˈä-pə-ˌrā-\ *adj* **1** : willing to work with others **2** : of or relating to an association formed to enable its members to buy or sell to better advantage by eliminating middlemen's profits

²cooperative *n* : a cooperative association

co–opt \kō-ˈäpt\ *vb* **1** : to choose or elect as a colleague **2** : ABSORB, ASSIMILATE; *also* : TAKE OVER

¹co·or·di·nate \kō-ˈȯrd-ᵊn-ət\ *adj* **1** : equal in rank or order **2** : of equal rank in a compound sentence ⟨∼ clause⟩ **3** : joining words or word groups of the same rank — **co·or·di·nate·ly** *adv*

²co·or·di·nate \-ˈȯrd-ᵊn-ˌāt\ *vb* **-nat·ed; -nat·ing 1** : to make or become coordinate **2** : to work or act together harmoniously — **co·or·di·na·tion** \-ˌȯrd-ᵊn-ˈā-shən\ *n* — **co·or·di·na·tor** \-ˈȯrd-ᵊn-ˌā-tər\ *n*

³co·or·di·nate \-ˈȯrd-ᵊn-ət\ *n* **1** : one of a set of numbers used in specifying the location of a point on a surface or in space **2** *pl* : articles (as of clothing) designed to be used together and to attain their effect through pleasing contrast

coot \ˈküt\ *n* **1** : a dark-colored ducklike bird related to the rails **2** : any of several No. American sea ducks **3** : a harmless simple person

coo·tie \ˈkü-tē\ *n* : a body louse

cop \ˈkäp\ *n* : POLICE OFFICER

co–pay·ment \ˈkō-ˌpā-mənt, ˌkō-ˈ\ *n* : a relatively small fixed fee required of a patient by a health insurer (as an HMO) at the time of each outpatient service or filling of a prescription

¹cope \ˈkōp\ *n* : a long cloaklike ecclesiastical vestment

²cope *vb* **coped; cop·ing** : to struggle to overcome problems or difficulties

copi·er \ˈkä-pē-ər\ *n* : one that copies; *esp* : a machine for making copies

co·pi·lot \ˈkō-ˌpī-lət\ *n* : an assistant pilot of an aircraft or spacecraft

cop·ing \ˈkō-piŋ\ *n* : the top layer of a wall

co·pi·ous \ˈkō-pē-əs\ *adj* : LAVISH, ABUNDANT — **co·pi·ous·ly** *adv* — **co·pi·ous·ness** *n*

cop–out \ˈkäp-ˌaut\ *n* : an excuse for copping out; *also* : an act of copping out

cop out *vb* : to back out (as of an unwanted responsibility)

cop·per \ˈkä-pər\ *n* **1** : a malleable reddish metallic chemical element that is one of the best conductors of heat and electricity — see ELEMENT table **2** : a coin or token made of copper — **cop·pery** *adj*

cop·per·head \ˈkä-pər-ˌhed\ *n* : a largely coppery brown pit viper esp. of the eastern and central U.S.

cop·pice \ˈkä-pəs\ *n* : THICKET

co·pra \ˈkō-prə\ *n* : dried coconut meat yielding coconut oil

copse \ˈkäps\ *n* : THICKET

cop·ter \ˈkäp-tər\ *n* : HELICOPTER

cop·u·la \ˈkä-pyə-lə\ *n* : LINKING VERB — **cop·u·la·tive** \-lə-tiv, -ˌlā-\ *adj*

cop·u·late \ˈkä-pyə-ˌlāt\ *vb* **-lat·ed; -lat·ing** : to engage in sexual intercourse — **cop·u·la·tion** \ˌkä-pyə-ˈlā-shən\ *n* — **cop·u·la·to·ry** \ˈkä-pyə-lə-ˌtȯr-ē\ *adj*

¹copy \ˈkä-pē\ *n, pl* **cop·ies 1** : an imitation or reproduction of an original work **2** : material to be set in type **syn** duplicate, reproduction, facsimile, replica

²copy *vb* **cop·ied; copy·ing 1** : to make a copy of **2** : IMITATE — **copy·ist** *n*

copy·book \ˈkä-pē-ˌbuk\ *n* : a book formerly used to teach handwriting containing examples to be copied

copy·boy \-ˌbȯi\ *n* : a person who carries copy and runs errands (as in a newspaper office)

copy·cat \-ˌkat\ *n* : a slavish imitator

copy·desk \-ˌdesk\ *n* : the desk at which newspaper copy is edited

copy editor *n* : one who edits newspaper copy and writes headlines; *also* : one who reads and corrects manuscript copy in a publishing house

copy·read·er \-ˌrē-dər\ *n* : COPY EDITOR

¹copy·right \-ˌrīt\ *n* : the sole right to reproduce, publish, and sell a literary or artistic work

²copyright *vb* : to secure a copyright on

copy·writ·er \ˈkä-pē-ˌrī-tər\ *n* : a writer of advertising copy

co·quet *or* **co·quette** \kō-ˈket\ *vb* **co·quet·ted; co·quet·ting** : FLIRT — **co·quet·ry** \ˈkō-kə-trē, kō-ˈke-trē\ *n*

co·quette \kō-ˈket\ *n* [F, fem. of *coquet*, flirtatious man, dim. of *coq* cock] : FLIRT — **co·quett·ish** *adj*

cor *abbr* corner

Cor *abbr* Corinthians

cor·a·cle \ˈkȯr-ə-kəl\ *n* [W *corwgl*] : a boat made of a frame covered usu. with hide or tarpaulin

cor·al \ˈkȯr-əl\ *n* **1** : a stony or horny material that forms the skeleton of colonies of tiny sea polyps and includes a red form used in jewelry; *also* : a coral= forming polyp or polyp colony **2** : a deep pink color — **coral** *adj*

coral snake *n* : any of several venomous chiefly tropical New World snakes brilliantly banded in red, black, and yellow or white

cor·bel \ˈkȯr-bəl\ *n* : a bracket-shaped architectural member that projects from a wall and supports a weight

¹cord \ˈkȯrd\ *n* **1** : a usu. heavy string consisting of several strands woven or twisted together **2** : a long slender anatomical structure (as a tendon or nerve) **3** : a small flexible insulated electrical cable used to connect an appliance with a receptacle **4** : a cubic measure used esp. for firewood and equal to a stack 4×4×8 feet **5** : a rib or ridge on cloth

²cord *vb* **1** : to tie or furnish with a cord **2** : to pile (wood) in cords

cord·age \ˈkȯr-dij\ *n* : ROPES, CORDS; *esp* : ropes in the rigging of a ship

¹cor·dial \ˈkȯr-jəl\ *adj* [ME, fr. ML *cordialis*, fr. L *cord-, cor* heart] : warmly receptive or welcoming : HEARTFELT, HEARTY — **cor·di·al·i·ty** \ˌkȯr-jē-ˈa-lə-tē, kȯr-ˈja-\ *n* — **cor·dial·ly** *adv*

²cordial *n* **1** : a stimulating medicine or drink **2** : LIQUEUR

cor·dil·le·ra \ˌkȯr-dəl-ˈyer-ə, -də-ˈler-\ *n* [Sp] : a series of parallel mountain ranges

cord·less \ˈkȯrd-ləs\ *adj* : having no cord; *esp* : powered by a battery

cor·do·ba \ˈkȯr-də-bə, -və\ *n* — see MONEY table

cor·don \ˈkȯrd-ᵊn\ *n* **1** : an ornamental cord or ribbon **2** : an encircling line (as of troops or police) — **cordon** *vb*

cor·do·van \ˈkȯr-də-vən\ *n* : a soft fine-grained leather

cor·du·roy \ˈkȯr-də-ˌrȯi\ *n, pl* **-roys** : a heavy ribbed fabric; *also, pl* : trousers of this material

cord·wain·er \ˈkȯrd-ˌwā-nər\ *n* : SHOEMAKER

¹core \ˈkȯr\ *n* **1** : the central usu. inedible part of some fruits (as the apple); *also* : an inmost part of something **2** : GIST, ESSENCE

²core *vb* **cored; cor·ing** : to take out the core of — **cor·er** *n*

CORE \ˈkȯr\ *abbr* Congress of Racial Equality

co·re·spon·dent \ˌkō-ri-ˈspän-dənt\ *n* : a person named as guilty of adultery with the defendant in a divorce suit

co·ri·an·der \ˈkȯr-ē-ˌan-dər\ *n* : an herb related to the carrot; *also* : its aromatic dried fruit used as a flavoring

Cor·in·thi·ans \kə-ˈrin-thē-ənz\ *n* — see BIBLE table

¹cork \ˈkȯrk\ *n* **1** : the tough elastic bark of a European oak (**cork oak**) used esp. for stoppers and insulation; *also* : a stopper of this **2** : a tissue of a woody plant making up most of the bark — **corky** *adj*

²cork *vb* : to furnish with or stop up with cork or a cork

cork·screw \ˈkȯrk-ˌskrü\ *n* : a device for drawing corks from bottles

corm \ˈkȯrm\ *n* : a solid bulblike underground part of a stem (as of the crocus or gladiolus)

cor·mo·rant \ˈkȯr-mə-rənt, -ˌrant\ *n* [ME *cormeraunt*, fr. MF *cormorant*, fr. OF *cormareng*, fr. *corp* raven + *marenc* of the sea, fr. L *marinus*] : any of a family of dark-colored water birds with a long neck, hooked bill, and distensible throat pouch

¹corn \ˈkȯrn\ *n* **1** : the seeds of a cereal grass and esp. of the chief cereal crop of a region (as wheat in Britain and Indian corn in the U.S.); *also* : a cereal grass **2** : sweet corn served as a vegetable

²corn *vb* : to salt (as beef) in brine and preservatives

³corn *n* : a local hardening and thickening of skin (as on a toe)

¹corn·ball \ˈkȯrn-ˌbȯl\ *n* : an unsophisticated person; *also* : something corny

²cornball *adj* : CORNY

corn bread *n* : bread made with cornmeal

corn·cob \-ˌkäb\ *n* : the woody core on which the kernels of Indian corn are arranged

corn·crib \-ˌkrib\ *n* : a crib for storing ears of Indian corn

cor·nea \ˈkȯr-nē-ə\ *n* : the transparent part of the coat of the eyeball covering the iris and the pupil — **cor·ne·al** *adj*

corn ear·worm \-ˈir-ˌwərm\ *n* : a moth whose larva is destructive esp. to Indian corn

¹cor·ner \ˈkȯr-nər\ *n* [ME, fr. OF *cornere*, fr. *corne* horn, corner, fr. L *cornu* horn, point] **1** : the point or angle formed by the meeting of lines, edges, or sides **2** : the place where two streets come together **3** : a quiet secluded place **4** : a position from which retreat or escape is impossible **5** : control of enough of the available supply (as of a commodity) to permit manipulation of the price — **cor·nered** *adj*

²corner *vb* **1** : to drive into a corner **2** : to get a corner on (∼ the wheat market) **3** : to turn a corner

cor·ner·stone \ˈkȯr-nər-ˌstōn\ *n* **1** : a stone forming part of a corner in a wall; *esp* : such a stone laid at a formal ceremony **2** : something of basic importance

cor·net \kȯr-ˈnet\ *n* : a brass band instrument resembling the trumpet

corn flour *n, Brit* : CORNSTARCH

corn·flow·er \ˈkȯrn-ˌflau̇(-ə)r\ *n* : BACHELOR'S BUTTON

cor·nice \ˈkȯr-nəs\ *n* : the horizontal projecting part crowning the wall of a building

corn·meal \ˈkȯrn-ˌmēl\ *n* : meal ground from corn

corn·row \-ˌrō\ *n* : a section of hair braided flat to the scalp in rows — **cornrow** *vb*

corn·stalk \-ˌstȯk\ *n* : a stalk of Indian corn

corn·starch \-ˌstärch\ *n* : a starch made from corn and used in cookery as a thickening agent

corn syrup *n* : a sweet syrup obtained from cornstarch

cor·nu·co·pia \ˌkȯr-nə-ˈkō-pē-ə, -nyə-\ *n* [LL, fr. L *cornu copiae* horn of plenty] : a horn-shaped container filled with fruits and grain emblematic of abundance

cornucopia

corny \ˈkȯr-nē\ *adj* **corn·i·er; -est** : tiresomely simple or sentimental

co·rol·la \kə-ˈrä-lə, -ˈrō-\ *n* : the petals of a flower

cor·ol·lary \ˈkȯr-ə-ˌler-ē\ *n, pl* **-lar·ies 1** : a deduction from a proposition already proved true **2** : CONSE-QUENCE, RESULT

co·ro·na \kə-'rō-nə\ *n* **1** : a colored circle often seen around and close to a luminous body (as the sun or moon) **2** : the outermost part of the atmosphere of a star (as the sun) — **co·ro·nal** \'kȯr-ən-ᵊl, kə-'rōn-ᵊl\ *adj*

cor·o·nal \'kȯr-ən-ᵊl\ *n* : a circlet for the head

¹**cor·o·nary** \'kȯr-ə-ˌner-ē\ *adj* : of or relating to the heart or its blood vessels

²**coronary** *n, pl* **-nar·ies 1** : a coronary blood vessel **2** : CORONARY THROMBOSIS; *also* : HEART ATTACK

coronary thrombosis *n* : the blocking by a thrombus of one of the arteries supplying the heart tissues

cor·o·na·tion \ˌkȯr-ə-'nā-shən\ *n* : the act or ceremony of crowning a monarch

cor·o·ner \'kȯr-ə-nər\ *n* : a public official who investigates causes of deaths possibly not due to natural causes

cor·o·net \ˌkȯr-ə-'net\ *n* **1** : a small crown **2** : an ornamental band worn around the temples

corp *abbr* **1** corporal **2** corporation

¹**cor·po·ral** \'kȯr-p(ə-)rəl\ *adj* : of or relating to the body ⟨~ punishment⟩

²**corporal** *n* : a noncommissioned officer (as in the army) ranking next below a sergeant

cor·po·rate \'kȯr-p(ə-)rət\ *adj* **1** : INCORPORATED; *also* : belonging to an incorporated body **2** : combined into one body

cor·po·ra·tion \ˌkȯr-pə-'rā-shən\ *n* **1** : the municipal authorities of a town or city **2** : a legal creation authorized to act with the rights and liabilities of a person ⟨a business ~⟩

cor·po·re·al \kȯr-'pōr-ē-əl\ *adj* **1** : PHYSICAL, MATERIAL **2** *archaic* : BODILY — **cor·po·re·al·i·ty** \kȯr-ˌpōr-ē-'a-lə-tē\ *n* — **cor·po·re·al·ly** *adv*

corps \'kȯr\ *n, pl* **corps** \'kȯrz\ [F, fr. L *corpus* body] **1** : an organized subdivision of a country's military forces **2** : a group acting under common direction

corpse \'kȯrps\ *n* : a dead body

corps·man \'kȯr-mən, 'kȯrz-\ *n* : an enlisted man trained to give first aid

cor·pu·lence \'kȯr-pyə-ləns\ *n* : excessive fatness : OBESITY

cor·pu·lent \-lənt\ *adj* : OBESE

cor·pus \'kȯr-pəs\ *n, pl* **cor·po·ra** \-pə-rə\ [ME, fr. L] **1** : BODY; *esp* : CORPSE **2** : a body of writings or works

cor·pus·cle \'kȯr-pə-səl, -ˌpə-\ *n* **1** : a minute particle **2** : a living cell (as in blood or cartilage) not aggregated into continuous tissues — **cor·pus·cu·lar** \kȯr-'pəs-kyə-lər\ *adj*

cor·pus de·lic·ti \ˌkȯr-pəs-di-'lik-ˌtī, -tē\ *n, pl* **corpora delicti** [NL, lit., body of the crime] **1** : the substantial fact proving that a crime has been committed **2** : the body of a victim of murder

corr *abbr* **1** correct; corrected; correction **2** correspondence; correspondent; corresponding

cor·ral \kə-'ral\ *n* [Sp] : an enclosure for confining or capturing animals; *also* : an enclosure of wagons for defending a camp — **corral** *vb*

¹**cor·rect** \kə-'rekt\ *vb* **1** : to make right **2** : REPROVE, CHASTISE — **cor·rect·able** \-'rek-tə-bəl\ *adj* — **cor·rec·tion** \-'rek-shən\ *n* — **cor·rec·tion·al** \-'rek-sh(ə-)nəl\ *adj* — **cor·rec·tive** \-'rek-tiv\ *adj*

²**correct** *adj* **1** : conforming to a conventional standard **2** : agreeing with fact or truth — **cor·rect·ly** *adv* — **cor·rect·ness** *n*

cor·re·late \'kȯr-ə-ˌlāt\ *vb* **-lat·ed; -lat·ing** : to connect in a systematic way : establish the mutual relations of — **cor·re·late** \-lət, -ˌlāt\ *n* — **cor·re·la·tion** \ˌkȯr-ə-'lā-shən\ *n*

cor·rel·a·tive \kə-'re-lə-tiv\ *adj* **1** : reciprocally related **2** : regularly used together (as *either* and *or*) — **correlative** *n* — **cor·rel·a·tive·ly** *adv*

cor·re·spond \ˌkȯr-ə-'spänd\ *vb* **1** : to be in agreement

: SUIT, MATCH **2** : to communicate by letter — **cor·re·spond·ing·ly** *adv*

cor·re·spon·dence \-'spän-dəns\ *n* **1** : agreement between particular things **2** : communication by letters; *also* : the letters exchanged

¹**cor·re·spon·dent** \-dənt\ *adj* **1** : SIMILAR **2** : FITTING, CONFORMING

²**correspondent** *n* **1** : something that corresponds **2** : a person with whom one communicates by letter **3** : a person employed to contribute news regularly from a place

cor·ri·dor \'kȯr-ə-dər, -ˌdȯr\ *n* **1** : a passageway into which compartments or rooms open (as in a hotel or school) **2** : a narrow strip of land esp. through foreign-held territory **3** : a densely populated strip of land including two or more major cities

cor·ri·gen·dum \ˌkȯr-ə-'jen-dəm\ *n, pl* **-da** \-də\ [L] : an error in a printed work discovered after printing and shown with its correction on a separate sheet

cor·ri·gi·ble \'kȯr-ə-jə-bəl\ *adj* : CORRECTABLE

cor·rob·o·rate \kə-'rä-bə-ˌrāt\ *vb* **-rat·ed; -rat·ing** [L *corroborare,* fr. *robur* strength] : to support with evidence : CONFIRM — **cor·rob·o·ra·tion** \-ˌrä-bə-'rā-shən\ *n* — **cor·rob·o·ra·tive** \-'rä-bə-ˌrā-tiv, -'rä-brə-\ *adj* — **cor·rob·o·ra·to·ry** \-'rä-bə-rə-ˌtȯr-ē\ *adj*

cor·rode \kə-'rōd\ *vb* **cor·rod·ed; cor·rod·ing** : to wear or be worn away gradually (as by chemical action) — **cor·ro·sion** \-'rō-zhən\ *n* — **cor·ro·sive** \-'rō-siv\ *adj or n*

cor·ru·gate \'kȯr-ə-ˌgāt\ *vb* **-gat·ed; -gat·ing** : to form into wrinkles or ridges and grooves — **cor·ru·gat·ed** *adj* — **cor·ru·ga·tion** \ˌkȯr-ə-'gā-shən\ *n*

¹**cor·rupt** \kə-'rəpt\ *vb* **1** : to make evil : DEPRAVE; *esp* : BRIBE **2** : ROT, SPOIL — **cor·rupt·ible** *adj* — **cor·rup·tion** \-'rəp-shən\ *n*

²**corrupt** *adj* : morally degenerate; *also* : characterized by improper conduct ⟨~ officials⟩

cor·sage \kȯr-'säzh, -'säj\ *n* [F, bust, bodice, fr. OF, bust, fr. *cors* body, fr. L *corpus*] **1** : the waist or bodice of a dress **2** : a bouquet to be worn or carried

cor·sair \'kȯr-ˌsar\ *n* : PIRATE

cor·set \'kȯr-sət\ *n* : a stiffened undergarment worn for support or to give shape to the waist and hips

cor·tege *also* **cor·tège** \kȯr-'tezh, 'kȯr-ˌtezh\ *n* [F] : PROCESSION; *esp* : a funeral procession

cor·tex \'kȯr-ˌteks\ *n, pl* **cor·ti·ces** \'kȯr-tə-ˌsēz\ *or* **cor·tex·es** : an outer or covering layer of an organism or one of its parts ⟨the adrenal ~⟩ ⟨~ of a plant stem⟩; *esp* : the outer layer of gray matter of the brain — **cor·ti·cal** \'kȯr-ti-kəl\ *adj*

cor·ti·sone \'kȯr-tə-ˌsōn, -ˌzōn\ *n* : an adrenal hormone used in treating rheumatoid arthritis

co·run·dum \kə-'rən-dəm\ *n* : a very hard aluminum-containing mineral used as an abrasive or as a gem

cor·us·cate \'kȯr-ə-ˌskāt\ *vb* **-cat·ed; -cat·ing** : FLASH, SPARKLE — **cor·us·ca·tion** \ˌkȯr-ə-'skā-shən\ *n*

cor·vette \kȯr-'vet\ *n* **1** : a naval sailing ship smaller than a frigate **2** : an armed escort ship smaller than a destroyer

co·ry·za \kə-'rī-zə\ *n* : an inflammatory disorder of the upper respiratory tract; *esp* : COMMON COLD

COS *abbr* **1** cash on shipment **2** chief of staff

co·sig·na·to·ry \kō-'sig-nə-ˌtȯr-ē\ *n* : a joint signer

co·sign·er \'kō-ˌsī-nər\ *n* : COSIGNATORY; *esp* : a joint signer of a promissory note

¹**cos·met·ic** \käz-'me-tik\ *adj* [Gk *kosmētikos* skilled in adornment, fr. *kosmein* to arrange, adorn, fr. *kosmos* order, ornament, universe] **1** : intended to beautify the hair or complexion **2** : correcting physical defects esp. to improve appearance ⟨~ dentistry⟩ **3** : SUPERFICIAL

²**cosmetic** *n* : a cosmetic preparation

cos·me·tol·o·gist \ˌkäz-mə-'tä-lə-jist\ *n* : one who gives beauty treatments — **cos·me·tol·o·gy** \-jē\ *n*

cos·mic \'käz-mik\ *also* **cos·mi·cal** \-mi-kəl\ *adj* **1** : of or relating to the cosmos **2** : VAST, GRAND — **cos-mi-cal-ly** *adv*

cosmic ray *n* : a stream of very penetrating atomic nuclei that enter the earth's atmosphere from outer space

cos-mog-o-ny \käz-'mä-gə-nē\ *n, pl* **-nies** : the origin or creation of the world or universe

cos-mol-o-gy \-'mä-lə-jē\ *n, pl* **-gies** : a branch of astronomy dealing with the origin and structure of the universe — **cos-mo-log-i-cal** \ˌkäz-mə-'lä-ji-kəl\ *adj* — **cos-mol-o-gist** \käz-'mä-lə-jist\ *n*

cos-mo-naut \'käz-mə-ˌnȯt\ *n* : a Soviet or Russian astronaut

cos-mo-pol-i-tan \ˌkäz-mə-'pä-lət-ᵊn\ *adj* : belonging to all the world : not local **syn** universal, global, catholic — **cosmopolitan** *n*

cos-mos \'käz-məs, **1** *also* -ˌmōs, -ˌmäs\ *n* **1** : UNIVERSE **2** : a tall garden herb related to the daisies

co-spon-sor \'kō-ˌspän-sər, -'spän-\ *n* : a joint sponsor — **cosponsor** *vb*

cos-sack \'kä-ˌsak, -sək\ *n* [Pol & Ukrainian *kozak,* of Turkic origin] : a member of a group of frontiersmen of southern Russia organized as cavalry in the czarist army

¹**cost** \'kȯst\ *n* **1** : the amount paid or charged for something : PRICE **2** : the loss or penalty incurred in gaining something **3** *pl* : expenses incurred in a law suit

²**cost** *vb* **cost; cost-ing 1** : to require a specified amount in payment **2** : to cause to pay, suffer, or lose

co-star \'kō-ˌstär\ *n* : one of two leading players in a motion picture or play — **co-star** *vb*

Cos-ta Ri-can \ˌkäs-tə-'rē-kən\ *n* : a native or inhabitant of Costa Rica — **Costa Rican** *adj*

cos-tive \'käs-tiv\ *adj* : affected with or causing constipation

cost-ly \'kȯst-lē\ *adj* **cost-li-er; -est** : of great cost or value : not cheap **syn** dear, valuable, expensive — **cost-li-ness** *n*

cos-tume \'käs-ˌtüm, -ˌtyüm\ *n* **1** : the style of attire characteristic of a period or country **2** : a special or fancy dress ⟨Halloween ∼s⟩ — **cos-tum-er** \'käs-ˌtü-mər, -ˌtyü-\ *n*

costume jewelry *n* : inexpensive jewelry

co-sy \'kō-zē\ *var of* COZY

¹**cot** \'kät\ *n* : a small house : COTTAGE

²**cot** *n* : a small often collapsible bed

cote \'kōt, 'kät\ *n* : a small shed or coop (as for sheep or doves)

co-te-rie \'kō-tə-ˌrē, ˌkō-tə-'rē\ *n* [F] : an intimate often exclusive group of persons with a common interest

co-ter-mi-nous \ˌko-'tər-mə-nəs\ *adj* : having the same scope or duration

co-til-lion \kō-'til-yən, kə-\ *n* : a formal ball

cot-tage \'kä-tij\ *n* : a small house — **cot-tag-er** *n*

cottage cheese *n* : a soft uncured cheese made from soured skim milk

cot-ter *or* **cot-tar** \'kä-tər\ *n* : a peasant or farm laborer occupying a cottage and often a small holding

cotter pin *n* : a metal strip bent into a pin whose ends can be spread apart after insertion through a hole or slot

cot-ton \'kät-ᵊn\ *n* [ME *coton,* fr. MF, fr. Ar *quṭun*] **1** : a soft fibrous usu. white substance composed of hairs attached to the seeds of a plant related to the mallow; *also* : this plant **2** : thread or cloth made of cotton — **cot-tony** *adj*

cotton candy *n* : a candy made of spun sugar

cot-ton-mouth \'kät-ᵊn-ˌmau̇th\ *n* : WATER MOCCASIN

cot-ton-seed \-ˌsēd\ *n* : the seed of the cotton plant yielding a protein-rich meal and a fatty oil (**cottonseed oil**) used esp. in cooking

cot-ton-tail \-ˌtāl\ *n* : an American rabbit with a white tufted tail

cot-ton-wood \-ˌwu̇d\ *n* : a poplar having seeds with cottony hairs

cot-y-le-don \ˌkä-tə-'lēd-ᵊn\ *n* : the first leaf or one of the first pair or whorl of leaves developed by a seed plant

¹**couch** \'kau̇ch\ *vb* **1** : to lie or place on a couch **2** : to phrase in a specified manner

²**couch** *n* : a piece of furniture (as a bed or sofa) that one can sit or lie on

couch-ant \'kau̇-chənt\ *adj* : lying down with the head raised ⟨coat of arms with lion ∼⟩

cou-gar \'kü-gər\ *n, pl* **cougars** *also* **cougar** [F *couguar,* fr. NL *cuguacuarana,* modif. of Tupi (a Brazilian Indian language) *siwasuarána,* fr. *siwasú* deer + *-rana* resembling] : a large powerful tawny brown wild American cat

cough \'kȯf\ *vb* : to force air from the lungs with short sharp noises; *also* : to expel by coughing — **cough** *n*

could \kəd, 'ku̇d\ *past of* CAN — used as an auxiliary in the past or as a polite or less forceful alternative to *can* in the present

cou-lee \'kü-lē\ *n* **1** : a small stream **2** : a dry streambed **3** : GULLY

cou-lomb \'kü-ˌläm, -ˌlōm\ *n* : a unit of electric charge equal to the electricity transferred by a current of one ampere in one second

coun-cil \'kau̇n-səl\ *n* **1** : ASSEMBLY, MEETING **2** : an official body of lawmakers ⟨city ∼⟩ — **coun-cil-lor** *or* **coun-cil-or** \-sə-lər\ *n* — **coun-cil-man** \-səl-mən\ *n* — **coun-cil-wom-an** \-ˌwu̇-mən\ *n*

¹**coun-sel** \'kau̇n-səl\ *n* **1** : ADVICE **2** : a plan of action **3** : deliberation together **4** *pl* **counsel** : LAWYER

²**counsel** *vb* **-seled** *or* **-selled; -sel-ing** *or* **-sel-ling 1** : ADVISE **2** : CONSULT

coun-sel-or *or* **coun-sel-lor** \'kau̇n-sə-lər\ *n* **1** : ADVISER **2** : LAWYER **3** : one who has supervisory duties at a summer camp

¹**count** \'kau̇nt\ *vb* [ME *counten,* fr. MF *compter,* fr. L *computare,* fr. *com-* with + *putare* to consider] **1** : to name or indicate one by one in order to find the total number **2** : to recite numbers in order **3** : CONSIDER, ACCOUNT **4** : RELY ⟨you can ∼ on me⟩ **5** : to be of value or account — **count-able** *adj*

²**count** *n* **1** : the act of counting; *also* : the total obtained by counting **2** : a particular charge in an indictment or legal declaration

³**count** *n* [MF *comte,* fr. LL *comes,* fr. L, companion, one of the imperial court, fr. *com-* with + *ire* to go] : a European nobleman whose rank corresponds to that of a British earl

count-down \'kau̇nt-ˌdau̇n\ *n* : a backward counting in fixed units (as seconds) to indicate the time remaining before an event (as the launching of a rocket) — **count down** *vb*

¹**coun-te-nance** \'kau̇nt-ᵊn-əns\ *n* **1** : the human face **2** : FAVOR, APPROVAL

²**countenance** *vb* **-nanced; -nanc-ing** : SANCTION, TOLERATE

¹**count-er** \'kau̇n-tər\ *n* **1** : a piece (as of metal or plastic) used in reckoning or in games **2** : a level surface over which business is transacted, food is served, or work is conducted

²**count-er** *n* : a device for recording a number or amount

³**count-er** *vb* : to act in opposition to

⁴**coun-ter** *adv* : in an opposite direction : CONTRARY

⁵**coun-ter** *n* **1** : OPPOSITE, CONTRARY **2** : an answering or offsetting force or blow

⁶**coun-ter** *adj* : CONTRARY, OPPOSITE

coun-ter-act \ˌkau̇n-tər-'akt\ *vb* : to lessen the force of : OFFSET — **coun-ter-ac-tive** \-'ak-tiv\ *adj*

coun-ter-at-tack \'kau̇n-tər-ə-ˌtak\ *n* : an attack made to oppose an enemy's attack — **counterattack** *vb*

¹**coun-ter-bal-ance** \'kau̇n-tər-ˌba-ləns\ *n* : a weight or influence that balances another

²**counterbalance** \ˌkau̇n-tər-'ba-ləns\ *vb* : to oppose with equal weight or influence

coun-ter-claim \'kau̇n-tər-ˌklām\ *n* : an opposing claim esp. in law

coun·ter·clock·wise \ˌkaún-tər-'kläk-ˌwīz\ *adv* : in a direction opposite to that in which the hands of a clock rotate — **counterclockwise** *adj*

coun·ter·cul·ture \'kaún-tər-ˌkəl-chər\ *n* : a culture esp. of the young with values and mores that run counter to those of established society

coun·ter·es·pi·o·nage \ˌkaún-tər-'es-pē-ə-ˌnäzh, -nij\ *n* : activities intended to discover and defeat enemy espionage

¹coun·ter·feit \'kaún-tər-ˌfit\ *adj* : SHAM, SPURIOUS; *also* : FORGED

²counterfeit *vb* **1** : to copy or imitate in order to deceive **2** : PRETEND, FEIGN — **coun·ter·feit·er** *n*

³counterfeit *n* : something counterfeit : FORGERY **syn** fraud, sham, fake, imposture, deceit, deception

coun·ter·in·sur·gen·cy \ˌkaún-tər-in-'sər-jən-sē\ *n* : military activity designed to deal with insurgents

coun·ter·in·tel·li·gence \-in-'te-lə-jəns\ *n* : organized activities of an intelligence service designed to counter the activities of an enemy's intelligence service

count·er·man \'kaún-tər-ˌman, -mən\ *n* : one who tends a counter

coun·ter·mand \'kaúnt-ər-ˌmand\ *vb* : to withdraw (an order already given) by a contrary order

coun·ter·mea·sure \-ˌme-zhər\ *n* : an action or device designed to counter another

coun·ter·of·fen·sive \-ə-ˌfen-siv\ *n* : a large-scale counterattack

coun·ter·pane \-ˌpān\ *n* : BEDSPREAD

coun·ter·part \-ˌpärt\ *n* : a person or thing very closely like or corresponding to another person or thing

coun·ter·point \-ˌpóint\ *n* : music in which one melody is accompanied by one or more other melodies all woven into a harmonious whole

coun·ter·poise \-ˌpóiz\ *n* : COUNTERBALANCE

coun·ter·rev·o·lu·tion \ˌkaún-tər-ˌre-və-'lü-shən\ *n* : a revolution opposed to a current or earlier one — **coun·ter·rev·o·lu·tion·ary** \-shə-ˌner-ē\ *adj or n*

coun·ter·sign \'kaún-tər-ˌsīn\ *n* **1** : a confirmatory signature added to a writing already signed by another person **2** : a military secret signal that must be given by a person who wishes to pass a guard — **countersign** *vb*

coun·ter·sink \-ˌsiŋk\ *vb* **-sunk** \-ˌsəŋk\; **-sink·ing 1** : to form a funnel-shaped enlargement at the outer end of a drilled hole **2** : to set the head of (as a screw) at or below the surface — **countersink** *n*

coun·ter·spy \-ˌspī\ *n* : a spy engaged in counterespionage

coun·ter·ten·or \-ˌte-nər\ *n* : a tenor with an unusually high range

coun·ter·vail \ˌkaún-tər-'vāl\ *vb* : COUNTERACT

coun·ter·weight \'kaún-tər-ˌwāt\ *n* : COUNTERBALANCE

count·ess \'kaún-təs\ *n* **1** : the wife or widow of a count or an earl **2** : a woman holding the rank of a count or an earl in her own right

count·ing·house \'kaún-tiŋ-ˌhaús\ *n* : a building or office for keeping books and conducting business

count·less \'kaúnt-ləs\ *adj* : INNUMERABLE

coun·tri·fied *also* **coun·try·fied** \'kən-tri-ˌfīd\ *adj* **1** : RURAL, RUSTIC **2** : UNSOPHISTICATED **3** : played or sung in the manner of country music

¹coun·try \'kən-trē\ *n, pl* **countries** [ME *contree*, fr. OF *contrée*, fr. ML *contrata*, fr. L *contra* against, on the opposite side] **1** : REGION, DISTRICT **2** : FATHERLAND **3** : a nation or its territory **4** : rural regions as opposed to towns and cities **5** : COUNTRY MUSIC

²country *adj* **1** : RURAL **2** : of or relating to country music (a ~ singer)

country and western *n* : COUNTRY MUSIC

country club *n* : a suburban club for social life and recreation; *esp* : one having a golf course

coun·try–dance \'kən-trē-ˌdans\ *n* : an English dance in which partners face each other esp. in rows

coun·try·man \'kən-trē-mən, *2 often* -ˌman\ *n* **1** : an inhabitant of a specified country **2** : COMPATRIOT **3** : one raised or living in the country : RUSTIC

country music *n* : music derived from or imitating the folk style of the southern U.S. or of the Western cowboy

coun·try·side \'kən-trē-ˌsīd\ *n* : a rural area or its people

coun·ty \'kaún-tē\ *n, pl* **counties 1** : the domain of a count **2** : a territorial division of a country or state for purposes of local government

coup \'kü\ *n, pl* **coups** \'küz\ [F, blow, stroke] **1** : a brilliant sudden stroke or stratagem **2** : COUP D'ÉTAT

coup de grace \ˌkü-də-'gräs\ *n, pl* **coups de grace** *same*\ [F *coup de grâce*, lit., stroke of mercy] : DEATHBLOW; *also* : a final decisive stroke or event

coup d'état \ˌkü-də-'tä\ *n, pl* **coups d'état** *same or* -'täz\ [F, lit., stroke of state] : a sudden violent overthrow of a government by a small group

cou·pé *or* **coupe** \kü-'pā, *2 often* 'küp\ *n* [F *coupé*, fr. *couper* to cut] **1** : a closed horse-drawn carriage for two persons inside with an outside seat for the driver **2** *usu* **coupe** : a 2-door automobile with an enclosed body

¹cou·ple \'kə-pəl\ *n* **1** : two persons closely associated; *esp* : a man and a woman married or otherwise paired **2** : PAIR **3** : BOND, TIE **4** : an indefinite small number : FEW ⟨a ~ of days ago⟩

²couple *vb* **cou·pled; cou·pling** : to link together

cou·plet \'kə-plət\ *n* : two successive rhyming lines of verse

cou·pling \'kə-pliŋ (*usual for* 2), -pə-liŋ\ *n* **1** : CONNECTION **2** : a device for connecting two parts or things

cou·pon \'kü-ˌpän, 'kyü-\ *n* **1** : a statement attached to a bond showing interest due and designed to be cut off and presented for payment **2** : a form surrendered in order to obtain an article, service, or accommodation **3** : a part of an advertisement to be cut off to use as an order blank or inquiry form or to obtain a discount on merchandise

cour·age \'kər-ij\ *n* : ability to conquer fear or despair : BRAVERY, VALOR — **cou·ra·geous** \kə-'rā-jəs\ *adj* — **cou·ra·geous·ly** *adv*

cou·ri·er \'kúr-ē-ər, 'kər-ē-\ *n* : one who bears messages or information esp. for the diplomatic or military services

¹course \'kōrs\ *n* **1** : PROGRESS, PASSAGE; *also* : direction of progress **2** : the ground or path over which something moves **3** : method of procedure : CONDUCT, BEHAVIOR **4** : an ordered series of acts or proceedings : sequence of events **5** : a series of instruction periods dealing with a subject **6** : the series of studies leading to graduation from a school or college **7** : the part of a meal served at one time — **of course** : as might be expected

²course *vb* **coursed; cours·ing 1** : to hunt with dogs **2** : to run or go speedily

cours·er \'kōr-sər\ *n* : a swift or spirited horse

¹court \'kōrt\ *n* **1** : the residence of a sovereign or similar dignitary **2** : a sovereign's formal assembly of officials and advisers as a governing power **3** : an assembly of the retinue of a sovereign **4** : an open space enclosed by a building or buildings **5** : a space walled or marked off for playing a game (as tennis or basketball) **6** : the place where justice is administered; *also* : a judicial body or a meeting of a judicial body **7** : attention intended to win favor

²court *vb* **1** : to try to gain the favor of **2** : WOO **3** : ATTRACT, TEMPT

cour·te·ous \'kər-tē-əs\ *adj* : marked by respect for others : CIVIL, POLITE — **cour·te·ous·ly** *adv*

cour·te·san \'kōr-tə-zən, -ˌzan\ *n* : PROSTITUTE

cour·te·sy \'kər-tə-sē\ *n, pl* **-sies 1** : courteous behavior : POLITENESS **2** : a favor courteously performed

court·house \'kōrt-ˌhaús\ *n* : a building in which courts of law are held or county offices are located

court·ier \'kōr-tē-ər\ *n* : a person in attendance at a royal court

court·ly \'kōrt-lē\ *adj* **court·li·er; -est** : REFINED, ELEGANT, POLITE *syn* gallant, gracious — **court·li·ness** *n*

court–mar·tial \'kōrt-ˌmär-shəl\ *n, pl* **courts–martial** : a military or naval court for trial of offenses against military or naval law; *also* : a trial by this court — **court–martial** *vb*

court·room \-ˌrüm, -ˌrùm\ *n* : a room in which a court of law is held

court·ship \-ˌship\ *n* : the act of courting : WOOING

court·yard \-ˌyärd\ *n* : an enclosure next to a building

cous·in \'kə-zən\ *n* [ME *cosin*, fr. OF, fr. L *consobrinus*, fr. *com-* with + *sobrinus* second cousin, fr. *soror* sister] : a child of one's uncle or aunt

cou·ture \kü-'tùr, -'tr̄r\ *n* [F] : the business of designing fashionable custom-made women's clothing; *also* : the designers and establishments engaged in this business

cou·tu·ri·er \kü-'tùr-ē-ər, -ē-ˌā\ *n* [F, dressmaker] : the owner of an establishment engaged in couture

cove \'kōv\ *n* : a small sheltered inlet or bay

co·ven \'kə-vən\ *n* : an assembly or band of witches

cov·e·nant \'kə-və-nənt\ *n* : a formal binding agreement : COMPACT — **cov·e·nant** \-nənt, -ˌnant\ *vb*

¹**cov·er** \'kə-vər\ *vb* **1** : to bring or hold within range of a firearm **2** : PROTECT, SHIELD **3** : HIDE, CONCEAL **4** : to place something over or upon **5** : INCLUDE, COMPRISE **6** : to have as one's field of activity ⟨one salesman ∼s the state⟩ **7** : to buy (stocks) in order to have them for delivery on a previous short sale

²**cover** *n* **1** : something that protects or shelters **2** : LID, TOP **3** : CASE, BINDING **4** : TABLECLOTH **5** : a cloth used on a bed **6** : SCREEN, DISGUISE **7** : an envelope or wrapper for mail

cov·er·age \'kə-və-rij\ *n* **1** : the act or fact of covering **2** : the total group covered : SCOPE

cov·er·all \'kə-vər-ˌôl\ *n* : a one-piece outer garment worn to protect one's clothes — usu. used in pl.

cover charge *n* : a charge made by a restaurant or nightclub in addition to the charge for food and drink

cover crop *n* : a crop planted to prevent soil erosion and to provide humus

cov·er·let \'kə-vər-lət\ *n* : BEDSPREAD

¹**co·vert** \'kō-ˌvərt, 'kə-vərt\ *adj* **1** : HIDDEN, SECRET **2** : SHELTERED — **co·vert·ly** *adv*

²**co·vert** \'kə-vərt, 'kō-\ *n* **1** : a secret or sheltered place; *esp* : a thicket sheltering game **2** : a feather covering the bases of the quills of the wings and tail of a bird

cov·er–up \'kə-vər-ˌəp\ *n* **1** : a device for masking or concealing **2** : a usu. concerted effort to keep an illegal or unethical act or situation from being made public

cov·et \'kə-vət\ *vb* : to desire enviously (what belongs to another) — **cov·et·ous** *adj* — **cov·et·ous·ness** *n*

cov·ey \'kə-vē\ *n, pl* **coveys** [ME, fr. MF *covee*, fr. OF, fr. *cover* to sit on, brood over, fr. L *cubare* to lie] **1** : a bird with her brood of young **2** : a small flock (as of quail)

¹**cow** \'kaù\ *n* **1** : the mature female of cattle or of an animal (as the moose, elephant, or whale) of which the male is called *bull* **2** : any domestic bovine animal irrespective of sex or age

²**cow** *vb* : INTIMIDATE, DAUNT, OVERAWE

cow·ard \'kaù-(ə)rd\ *n* [ME, fr. OF *coart*, fr. *coe* tail, fr. L *cauda*] : one who lacks courage or shows shameful fear or timidity — **coward** *adj* — **cow·ard·ice** \'kaù-ər-dəs\ *n* — **cow·ard·ly** *adv or adj*

cow·bird \'kaù-ˌbərd\ *n* : a small No. American bird that lays its eggs in the nests of other birds

cow·boy \-ˌbôi\ *n* : one (as a mounted ranch hand) who tends cattle or horses

cow·er \'kaù-(ə)r\ *vb* : to shrink or crouch down from fear or cold : QUAIL

cow·girl \'kaù-ˌgərl\ *n* : a girl or woman who tends cattle or horses

cow·hand \'kaù-ˌhand\ *n* : COWBOY

cow·hide \-ˌhīd\ *n* **1** : the hide of a cow; *also* : leather made from it **2** : a coarse whip of braided rawhide

cowl \'kaùl\ *n* : a monk's hood

cow·lick \'kaù-ˌlik\ *n* : a turned-up tuft of hair that resists control

cowl·ing \'kaù-liŋ\ *n* : a usu. metal covering for the engine or another part of an airplane

cow·man \'kaù-mən, -ˌman\ *n* : COWBOY; *also* : a cattle owner or rancher

co·work·er \'kō-ˌwər-kər\ *n* : a fellow worker

cow·poke \'kaù-ˌpōk\ *n* : COWBOY

cow pony *n* : a strong and agile horse trained for herding cattle

cow·pox \'kaù-ˌpäks\ *n* : a mild disease of the cow that when communicated to humans protects against smallpox

cow·punch·er \-ˌpən-chər\ *n* : COWBOY

cow·slip \'kaù-ˌslip\ *n* **1** : a yellow-flowered European primrose **2** : MARSH MARIGOLD

cox·comb \'käks-ˌkōm\ *n* : a conceited foolish person : FOP

cox·swain \'käk-sən, -ˌswān\ *n* : the steersman of a ship's boat or a racing shell

coy \'kôi\ *adj* [ME, quiet, shy, fr. MF *coi* calm, fr. L *quietus* quiet] **1** : BASHFUL, SHY **2** : marked by artful playfulness : COQUETTISH — **coy·ly** *adv* — **coy·ness** *n*

coy·ote \'kī-ˌōt, kī-'ō-tē\ *n, pl* **coyotes** *or* **coyote** : a mammal of No. America smaller than the related wolves

coyote

coy·pu \'kôi-pü\ *n* : NUTRIA 2

coz·en \'kəz-ən\ *vb* : CHEAT, DEFRAUD — **coz·en·age** \-ij\ *n* — **coz·en·er** *n*

¹**co·zy** \'kō-zē\ *adj* **co·zi·er; -est** : SNUG, COMFORTABLE — **co·zi·ly** \-zə-lē\ *adv* — **co·zi·ness** \-zē-nəs\ *n*

²**cozy** *n, pl* **co·zies** : a padded covering for a vessel (as a teapot) to keep the contents hot

cp *abbr* **1** compare **2** coupon

CP *abbr* **1** cerebral palsy **2** chemically pure **3** command post **4** communist party

CPA *abbr* certified public accountant

CPB *abbr* Corporation for Public Broadcasting

cpd *abbr* compound

CPI *abbr* consumer price index

Cpl *abbr* corporal

CPO *abbr* chief petty officer

CPOM *abbr* master chief petty officer

CPOS *abbr* senior chief petty officer

CPR *abbr* cardiopulmonary resuscitation

CPT *abbr* captain

CQ *abbr* charge of quarters

cr *abbr* credit; creditor

Cr *symbol* chromium

¹**crab** \'krab\ *n* : any of various crustaceans with a short broad shell and small abdomen

²**crab** n : an ill-natured person

³**crab** vb **crabbed; crab·bing** : COMPLAIN, GROUSE

crab apple n : a small often highly colored sour apple; also : a tree that produces crab apples

crab·bed \'kra-bəd\ adj **1** : MOROSE, PEEVISH **2** : CRAMPED, IRREGULAR

crab·by \'kra-bē\ adj **crab·bi·er; -est** : CROSS, ILL-NATURED

crab·grass \'krab-ˌgras\ n : a weedy grass with creeping or sprawling stems that root freely at the nodes

crab louse n : a louse infesting the pubic region in humans

¹**crack** \'krak\ vb **1** : to break with a sharp sudden sound **2** : to break with or without completely separating into parts **3** : to fail in tone or become harsh ⟨her voice ∼ed⟩ **4** : to subject (as a petroleum oil) to heat for breaking down into lighter products (as gasoline)

²**crack** n **1** : a sudden sharp noise **2** : a witty or sharp remark **3** : a narrow break or opening : FISSURE **4** : a sharp blow **5** : ATTEMPT, TRY **6** : highly purified cocaine in small chips used illicitly usu. for smoking

³**crack** adj : extremely proficient

crack·down \'krak-ˌdau̇n\ n : an act or instance of taking positive disciplinary action ⟨a ∼ on gambling⟩ — **crack down** vb

crack·er \'kra-kər\ n **1** : FIRECRACKER **2** : a dry thin crispy baked bread product made of flour and water

crack·er·jack \-ˌjak\ n : something very excellent — **crackerjack** adj

crack·le \'kra-kəl\ vb **crack·led; crack·ling 1** : to make small sharp snapping noises **2** : to develop fine cracks in a surface — **crackle** n — **crack·ly** \-k(ə-)lē\ adj

crack·pot \'krak-ˌpät\ n : an eccentric person

crack–up \'krak-ˌəp\ n : CRASH, WRECK; also : BREAKDOWN

crack up vb **1** : PRAISE ⟨isn't all it's cracked up to be⟩ **2** : to laugh or cause to laugh out loud **3** : to crash a vehicle

¹**cra·dle** \'krād-°l\ n **1** : a baby's bed or cot **2** : a framework or support (as for a telephone receiver) **3** : INFANCY ⟨from ∼ to the grave⟩ **4** : a place of origin

²**cradle** vb **cra·dled; cra·dling 1** : to place in or as if in a cradle **2** : SHELTER, REAR

craft \'kraft\ n **1** : ART, SKILL; also : an occupation requiring special skill **2** : CUNNING, GUILE **3** pl usu **craft** : a boat esp. of small size; also : AIRCRAFT, SPACECRAFT

crafts·man \'krafts-mən\ n : a skilled artisan — **crafts·man·ship** n

crafty \'kraf-tē\ adj **craft·i·er; -est** : CUNNING, DECEITFUL, SUBTLE — **craft·i·ly** \-tə-lē\ adv — **craft·i·ness** \-tē-nəs\ n

crag \'krag\ n : a steep rugged cliff or rock — **crag·gy** adj

cram \'kram\ vb **crammed; cram·ming 1** : to pack in tight : JAM **2** : to eat greedily **3** : to study rapidly under pressure for an examination

¹**cramp** \'kramp\ n **1** : a sudden painful contraction of muscle **2** : sharp abdominal pain — usu. used in pl.

²**cramp** vb **1** : to affect with a cramp or cramps **2** : to restrain from free action : HAMPER

cran·ber·ry \'kran-ˌber-ē, -bə-rē\ n : the red acid berry of any of several trailing plants related to the heaths; also : one of these plants

¹**crane** \'krān\ n **1** : any of a family of tall wading birds related to the rails; also : any of several herons **2** : a machine for lifting and carrying heavy objects

²**crane** vb **craned; cran·ing** : to stretch one's neck to see better

crane fly n : any of numerous long-legged slender dipteran flies that resemble large mosquitoes but do not bite

cranial nerve n : any of the nerves that arise in pairs from the lower surface of the brain and pass through openings in the skull to the periphery of the body

cra·ni·um \'krā-nē-əm\ n, pl **-ni·ums** or **-nia** \-ə\ : SKULL; esp : the part enclosing the brain — **cra·ni·al** \-əl\ adj

¹**crank** \'kraŋk\ n **1** : a bent part of an axle or shaft or an arm at right angles to the end of a shaft by which circular motion is imparted to or received from it **2** : an eccentric person **3** : a bad-tempered person : GROUCH

²**crank** vb : to start or operate by or as if by turning a crank

crank·case \'kraŋk-ˌkās\ n : the housing of a crankshaft

crank out vb : to produce in a mechanical manner

crank·shaft \'kraŋk-ˌshaft\ n : a shaft turning or driven by a crank

cranky \'kraŋ-kē\ adj **crank·i·er; -est 1** : IRRITABLE **2** : operating uncertainly or imperfectly

cran·ny \'kra-nē\ n, pl **crannies** : CREVICE, CHINK

craps \'kraps\ n : a gambling game played with two dice

crap·shoot·er \'krap-ˌshü-tər\ n : a person who plays craps

¹**crash** \'krash\ vb **1** : to break noisily : SMASH **2** : to damage an airplane in landing **3** : to enter or attend without invitation or without paying ⟨∼ a party⟩

²**crash** n **1** : a loud sound (as of things smashing) **2** : an instance of crashing ⟨a plane ∼⟩; also : COLLISION **3** : a sudden failure (as of a business)

³**crash** adj : marked by concerted effort over the shortest possible time

⁴**crash** n : coarse linen fabric used for towels and draperies

crash–land \'krash-'land\ vb : to land an aircraft or spacecraft under emergency conditions usu. with damage to the craft — **crash landing** n

crass \'kras\ adj : GROSS, INSENSITIVE — **crass·ly** adv

crate \'krāt\ n : a container often of wooden slats — **crate** vb

cra·ter \'krā-tər\ n [L, mixing bowl, crater, fr. Gk kratēr, fr. kerannynai to mix] **1** : the depression around the opening of a volcano **2** : a depression formed by the impact of a meteorite or by the explosion of a bomb or shell

cra·vat \krə-'vat\ n : NECKTIE

crave \'krāv\ vb **craved; crav·ing 1** : to ask for earnestly : BEG **2** : to long for : DESIRE

cra·ven \'krā-vən\ adj : COWARDLY — **craven** n

crav·ing \'krā-viŋ\ n : an urgent or abnormal desire

craw·fish \'kró-ˌfish\ n **1** : CRAYFISH 1 **2** : SPINY LOBSTER

¹**crawl** \'król\ vb **1** : to move slowly by drawing the body along the ground **2** : to advance feebly, cautiously, or slowly **3** : to be swarming with or feel as if swarming with creeping things ⟨a place ∼ing with ants⟩ ⟨her flesh ∼ed⟩

²**crawl** n **1** : a very slow pace **2** : a prone speed swimming stroke

cray·fish \'krā-ˌfish\ n **1** : any of numerous freshwater crustaceans usu. much smaller than the related lobsters **2** : SPINY LOBSTER

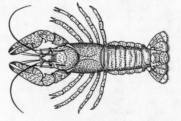

crayfish 1

cray·on \'krā-₁än, -ən\ *n* : a stick of chalk or wax used for writing, drawing, or coloring; *also* : a drawing made with such material — **crayon** *vb*

¹**craze** \'krāz\ *vb* **crazed; craz·ing** [ME *crasen* to crush, craze, of Scand origin] : to make or become insane

²**craze** *n* : FAD, MANIA

cra·zy \'krā-zē\ *adj* **cra·zi·er; -est 1** : mentally disordered : INSANE **2** : wildly impractical; *also* : ERRATIC — **cra·zi·ly** \-zə-lē\ *adv* — **cra·zi·ness** \-zē-nəs\ *n*

CRC *abbr* Civil Rights Commission

creak \'krēk\ *vb* : to make a prolonged squeaking or grating sound — **creak** *n* — **creaky** *adj*

¹**cream** \'krēm\ *n* **1** : the yellowish fat-rich part of milk **2** : a thick smooth sauce, confection, or cosmetic **3** : the choicest part **4** : a pale yellow color — **creamy** *adj*

²**cream** *vb* **1** : to prepare with a cream sauce **2** : to beat or blend into creamy consistency **3** : to defeat decisively

cream cheese *n* : a cheese made from whole milk enriched with cream

cream·ery \'krē-mə-rē\ *n, pl* **-er·ies** : an establishment where butter and cheese are made or milk and cream are prepared for sale

crease \'krēs\ *n* : a mark or line made by or as if by folding — **crease** *vb*

cre·ate \krē-'āt\ *vb* **cre·at·ed; cre·at·ing** : to bring into being : cause to exist : MAKE, PRODUCE — **cre·a·tive** \-'ā-tiv\ *adj* — **cre·a·tiv·i·ty** \₁krē-(₁)ā-'ti-və-tē\ *n*

cre·a·tion \krē-'ā-shən\ *n* **1** : the act of creating or producing (∼ of the world) **2** : something that is created **3** : all created things : WORLD

cre·a·tion·ism \krē-'ā-shə-₁ni-zəm\ *n* : a doctrine or theory holding that matter, the various forms of life, and the world were created by God out of nothing — **cre·a·tion·ist** \-nist\ *n or adj*

cre·a·tor \krē-'ā-tər\ *n* **1** : one that creates : MAKER, AUTHOR **2** *cap* : GOD 1

crea·ture \'krē-chər\ *n* : a lower animal; *also* : a human being

crèche \'kresh\ *n* [F, manger, crib] : a representation of the Nativity scene

cre·dence \'krēd-ᵊns\ *n* : mental acceptance as true or real

cre·den·tial \kri-'den-chəl\ *n* : something that gives a basis for credit or confidence

cre·den·za \kri-'den-zə\ *n* [It, lit., belief, confidence] : a sideboard, buffet, or bookcase usu. without legs

cred·i·ble \'kre-də-bəl\ *adj* : TRUSTWORTHY, BELIEVABLE — **cred·i·bil·i·ty** \₁kre-də-'bi-lə-tē\ *n*

¹**cred·it** \'kre-dət\ *vb* **1** : BELIEVE **2** : to give credit to

²**credit** *n* [MF, fr. It *credito*, fr. L *creditum* something entrusted to another, loan, fr. *credere* to believe, entrust] **1** : the balance (as in a bank) in a person's favor **2** : time given for payment for goods sold on trust **3** : an accounting entry of payment received **4** : BELIEF, FAITH **5** : financial trustworthiness **6** : ESTEEM **7** : a source of honor or distinction **8** : a unit of academic work

cred·it·able \'kre-də-tə-bəl\ *adj* : worthy of esteem or praise — **cred·it·ably** \-blē\ *adv*

credit card *n* : a card authorizing purchases on credit

cred·i·tor \'kre-də-tər\ *n* : a person to whom money is owed

cre·do \'krē-dō, 'krā-\ *n, pl* **credos** [ME, fr. L, I believe] : CREED

cred·u·lous \'kre-jə-ləs\ *adj* : inclined to believe esp. on slight evidence — **cre·du·li·ty** \kri-'dü-lə-tē, -'dyü-\ *n*

Cree \'krē\ *n, pl* **Cree** *or* **Crees** : a member of an American Indian people of Canada

creed \'krēd\ *n* [ME *crede*, fr. OE *crēda*, fr. L *credo* I believe, first word of the Apostles' and Nicene Creeds] : a statement of the essential beliefs of a religious faith

creek \'krēk, 'krik\ *n* **1** *chiefly Brit* : a small inlet **2** : a stream smaller than a river and larger than a brook

Creek \'krēk\ *n* : a member of an American Indian people of Alabama, Georgia, and Florida

creel \'krēl\ *n* : a wicker basket esp. for carrying fish

creep \'krēp\ *vb* **crept** \'krept\; **creep·ing 1** : CRAWL **2** : to feel as though insects were crawling on the skin **3** : to grow over a surface like ivy — **creep** *n* — **creep·er** *n*

creep·ing \'krē-piŋ\ *adj* : developing or advancing by imperceptible degrees

creepy \'krē-pē\ *adj* **creep·i·er; -est** : having or producing a nervous shivery fear

cre·mate \'krē-₁māt\ *vb* **cre·mat·ed; cre·mat·ing** : to reduce (a dead body) to ashes with fire — **cre·ma·tion** \kri-'mā-shən\ *n*

cre·ma·to·ry \'krē-mə-₁tōr-ē, 'kre-\ *n, pl* **-ries** : a furnace for cremating; *also* : a structure containing such a furnace

crème \'krem, 'krēm\ *n, pl* **crèmes** *same or* 'kremz, 'krēmz\ [F, lit., cream] : a sweet liqueur

cren·el·lat·ed *or* **cren·el·at·ed** \'kren-ᵊl-₁ā-təd\ *adj* : having battlements — **cren·el·la·tion** \₁kren-ᵊl-'ā-shən\ *n*

Cre·ole \'krē-₁ōl\ *n* **1** : a descendant of early French or Spanish settlers of the U.S. Gulf states preserving their speech and culture; *also* : a person of mixed French or Spanish and black descent speaking a dialect of French or Spanish **2** *not cap* : a language that has evolved from a pidgin but serves as the native language of a speech community

cre·o·sote \'krē-ə-₁sōt\ *n* : an oily liquid obtained by distillation of coal tar and used in preserving wood

crepe *or* **crêpe** \'krāp\ *n* : a light crinkled fabric of any of various fibers

crêpe su·zette \₁krāp-sü-'zet\ *n, pl* **crêpes suzette** *same or* ₁krāps-\ *or* **crêpe suzettes** \-sü-'zets\ *often cap S* : a thin folded or rolled pancake in a hot orange‑butter sauce that is sprinkled with a liqueur and set ablaze for serving

cre·pus·cu·lar \kri-'pəs-kyə-lər\ *adj* **1** : of, relating to, or resembling twilight **2** : active in the twilight (∼ insects)

cre·scen·do \krə-'shen-dō\ *adv or adj* [It] : increasing in loudness — used as a direction in music — **crescendo** *n*

cres·cent \'kres-ᵊnt\ *n* [ME *cressant*, fr. MF *creissant*, fr. *creistre* to grow, increase, fr. L *crescere*] : the moon at any stage between new moon and first quarter and between last quarter and new moon; *also* : something shaped like the figure of the crescent moon with a convex and a concave edge — **cres·cen·tic** \kre-'sen-tik\ *adj*

cress \'kres\ *n* : any of several salad plants related to the mustards

¹**crest** \'krest\ *n* **1** : a tuft or process on the head of an animal (as a bird) **2** : a heraldic device **3** : an upper part, edge, or limit (the ∼ of a hill) — **crest·ed** \'kres-təd\ *adj* — **crest·less** *adj*

²**crest** *vb* **1** : CROWN **2** : to reach the crest of **3** : to rise to a crest

crest·fall·en \'krest-₁fȯ-lən\ *adj* : DISPIRITED, DEJECTED

Cre·ta·ceous \kri-'tā-shəs\ *adj* : of, relating to, or being the latest period of the Mesozoic era marked by great increase in flowering plants, diversification of mammals, and extinction of the dinosaurs — **Cretaceous** *n*

cre·tin \'krēt-ᵊn\ *n* [F *crétin*, fr. F dial. *cretin*, lit., wretch, innocent victim, fr. L *christianus* Christian] **1** : one affected with cretinism **2** : a stupid person

cre·tin·ism \-₁i-zəm\ *n* : a usu. congenital abnormal condition characterized by physical stunting and mental retardation

cre·tonne \'krē-₁tän\ *n* : a strong unglazed cotton cloth for curtains and upholstery

cre·vasse \kri-'vas\ *n* : a deep fissure esp. in a glacier

crev·ice \'kre-vəs\ *n* : a narrow fissure

¹crew \'krü\ *chiefly Brit past of* CROW

²crew *n* [ME *crue*, lit., reinforcement, fr. MF *creue* increase, fr. *creistre* to grow, fr. L *crescere*] **1** : a body of people trained to work together for certain purposes **2** : a group of people who operate a ship, train, aircraft, or spacecraft **3** : the rowers and coxswain of a racing shell; *also* : the sport of rowing engaged in by a crew — **crew·man** \-mən\ *n*

crew cut *n* : a very short bristly haircut

crew·el \'krü-əl\ *n* : slackly twisted worsted yarn used for embroidery — **crew·el·work** \-,wərk\ *n*

¹crib \'krib\ *n* **1** : a manger for feeding animals **2** : a child's bedstead with high sides **3** : a building or bin for storage (as of grain) **4** : something used for cheating in an exam

²crib *vb* **cribbed; crib·bing 1** : to put in a crib **2** : STEAL, PLAGIARIZE — **crib·ber** *n*

crib·bage \'kri-bij\ *n* : a card game usu. played by two players and scored on a board (**cribbage board**)

crib death *n* : SUDDEN INFANT DEATH SYNDROME

crick \'krik\ *n* : a painful spasm of muscles (as of the neck)

¹crick·et \'kri-kət\ *n* : any of a family of leaping insects related to the grasshoppers and noted for the chirping noises of the male

²cricket *n* : a game played with a bat and ball by two teams on a field centering upon two wickets each defended by a batsman

cri·er \'krī-(ə)r\ *n* : one who calls out proclamations and announcements

crime \'krīm\ *n* : a serious offense against the public law

¹crim·i·nal \'kri-mən-əl\ *adj* **1** : involving or being a crime **2** : relating to crime or its punishment — **crim·i·nal·i·ty** \,kri-mə-'na-lə-tē\ *n* — **crim·i·nal·ly** *adv*

²criminal *n* : one who has committed a crime

crim·i·nol·o·gy \,kri-mə-'nä-lə-jē\ *n* : the scientific study of crime and criminals — **crim·i·nol·o·gist** \,kri-mə-'nä-lə-jist\ *n*

¹crimp \'krimp\ *vb* : to cause to become crinkled, wavy, or bent

²crimp *n* : something (as a curl in hair) produced by or as if by crimping

¹crim·son \'krim-zən\ *n* : a deep purplish red color — **crimson** *adj*

²crimson *vb* : to make or become crimson

cringe \'krinj\ *vb* **cringed; cring·ing** : to shrink in fear : WINCE, COWER

crin·kle \'kriŋ-kəl\ *vb* **crin·kled; crin·kling** : to form many short bends or curves; *also* : WRINKLE — **crin·kle** *n* — **crin·kly** \-kə-lē\ *adj*

crin·o·line \'krin-əl-ən\ *n* **1** : an open-weave cloth used for stiffening and lining **2** : a full stiff skirt or underskirt made of crinoline

¹crip·ple \'kri-pəl\ *n* : a lame or disabled person — sometimes taken to be offensive

²cripple *vb* **crip·pled; crip·pling 1** : to make lame **2** : to make useless or imperfect

cri·sis \'krī-səs\ *n, pl* **cri·ses** \-,sēz\ [L, fr. Gk *krisis*, lit., decision, fr. *krinein* to decide] **1** : the turning point for better or worse in an acute disease or fever **2** : a decisive or critical moment

crisp \'krisp\ *adj* **1** : CURLY, WAVY **2** : BRITTLE **3** : FIRM, FRESH (~ lettuce) **4** : being sharp and clear **5** : LIVELY, SPARKLING **6** : FROSTY, SNAPPY; *also* : INVIGORATING — **crisp** *vb* — **crisp·ly** *adv* — **crisp·ness** *n* — **crispy** *adj*

¹criss·cross \'kris-,kros\ *vb* **1** : to mark with crossed lines **2** : to go or pass back and forth

²crisscross *adj* : marked or characterized by crisscrossing — **crisscross** *adv*

³crisscross *n* : a pattern formed by crossed lines

crit *abbr* critical; criticism

cri·te·ri·on \krī-'tir-ē-ən\ *n, pl* **-ria** \-ē-ə\ : a standard on which a judgment may be based

crit·ic \'kri-tik\ *n* **1** : a person who judges literary or artistic works **2** : one inclined to find fault

crit·i·cal \'kri-ti-kəl\ *adj* **1** : being or relating to a condition or disease involving danger of death **2** : being a crisis **3** : inclined to criticize **4** : relating to criticism or critics **5** : requiring careful judgment **6** : UNCERTAIN — **crit·i·cal·ly** \-k(ə-)lē\ *adv*

crit·i·cism \'kri-tə-,si-zəm\ *n* **1** : the act of criticizing; *esp* : CENSURE **2** : a judgment or review **3** : the art of judging works of literature or art

crit·i·cize \'kri-tə-,sīz\ *vb* **-cized; -ciz·ing 1** : to judge as a critic : EVALUATE **2** : to find fault : express criticism **syn** blame, censure, condemn

cri·tique \krə-'tēk\ *n* : a critical estimate or discussion

crit·ter \'kri-tər\ *n* : CREATURE

croak \'krōk\ *n* : a hoarse harsh cry (as of a frog) — **croak** *vb*

Croat \'krō-,at\ *n* : CROATIAN

Cro·atian \krō-'ā-shən\ *n* : a native or inhabitant of Croatia — **Croatian** *adj*

cro·chet \krō-'shā\ *n* [F, hook, crochet, fr. MF, dim. of *croche* hook] : needlework done with a single thread and hooked needle — **crochet** *vb*

crock \'kräk\ *n* : a thick earthenware pot or jar

crock·ery \'krä-kə-rē\ *n* : EARTHENWARE

croc·o·dile \'krä-kə-,dīl\ *n* [ME & L; ME *cocodrille*, fr. OF, fr. ML *cocodrillus*, alter. of L *crocodilus*, fr. Gk *krokodilos* lizard, crocodile, fr. *krokē* shingle, pebble + *drillos* worm] : any of several thick-skinned long-bodied carnivorous reptiles of tropical and subtropical waters

cro·cus \'krō-kəs\ *n, pl* **cro·cus·es** *also* **crocus** *or* **cro·ci** \-,kī\ : any of a large genus of low herbs related to the irises and having brightly colored flowers borne singly in early spring

crois·sant \krʷä-'säⁿ\ *n, pl* **croissants** *same or* -'sänts, -'säⁿz\ : a rich crescent-shaped roll

Cro-Ma·gnon \krō-'mag-nən, -'man-yən\ *n* : any of a tall erect human race known from skeletal remains found chiefly in southern France and usu. classified as the same species as present-day human beings — **Cro-Magnon** *adj*

crone \'krōn\ *n* : HAG

cro·ny \'krō-nē\ *n, pl* **cronies** : a close friend esp. of long standing

¹crook \'krūk\ *vb* : to curve or bend sharply

²crook *n* **1** : a bent or curved implement **2** : a bent or curved part; *also* : BEND, CURVE **3** : SWINDLER, THIEF

crook·ed \'krū-kəd\ *adj* **1** : having a crook : BENT, CURVED **2** : DISHONEST — **crook·ed·ly** *adv* — **crook·ed·ness** *n*

croon \'krün\ *vb* : to sing or hum in a gentle murmuring voice — **croon·er** *n*

¹crop \'kräp\ *n* **1** : the handle of a whip; *also* : a short riding whip **2** : a pouch in the throat of many birds and insects where food is received **3** : something that can be harvested; *also* : the yield at harvest

²crop *vb* **cropped; crop·ping 1** : to remove the tips of : cut off short; *also* : TRIM **2** : to feed on by cropping **3** : to devote (land) to crops **4** : to appear unexpectedly

crop·land \-,land\ *n* : land devoted to the production of plant crops

crop·per \'krä-pər\ *n* : a raiser of crops; *esp* : SHARE-CROPPER

cro·quet \krō-'kā\ *n* : a game in which mallets are used to drive wooden balls through a series of wickets set out on a lawn

cro·quette \krō-'ket\ *n* [F] : a small often rounded mass of minced meat, fish, or vegetables fried in deep fat

cro·sier \'krō-zhər\ *n* : a staff carried by bishops and abbots

¹cross \'krós\ *n* **1** : a structure consisting of an upright beam and a crossbar used esp. by the ancient Romans for execution **2** : a figure of the cross on which

Christ was crucified used as a Christian symbol **3** : a hybridizing of unlike individuals or strains; *also* : a product of this **4** : a punch delivered with a circular motion over an opponent's lead

²cross *vb* **1** : to lie or place across; *also* : INTERSECT **2** : to cancel by marking a cross on or by lining through **3** : THWART, OBSTRUCT **4** : to go or extend across : TRAVERSE **5** : HYBRIDIZE **6** : to meet and pass on the way

³cross *adj* **1** : lying across **2** : CONTRARY, OPPOSED **3** : marked by bad temper **4** : HYBRID — **cross•ly** *adv*

cross•bar \'kròs-₁bär\ *n* : a transverse bar or piece

cross•bow \-₁bō\ *n* : a short bow mounted crosswise at the end of a wooden stock that shoots short arrows

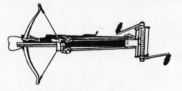

crossbow

cross•breed \'kròs-₁brēd, -'brēd\ *vb* **-bred** \-'bred\; **-breed•ing** : HYBRIDIZE

cross•coun•try \-'kən-trē\ *adj* **1** : extending or moving across a country **2** : proceeding over the countryside (as fields and woods) and not by roads **3** : of or relating to racing or skiing over the countryside instead of over a track or run — **cross–country** *adv*

cross•cur•rent \-'kər-ənt\ *n* **1** : a current running counter to another **2** : a conflicting tendency — usu. used in pl.

¹cross•cut \-₁kət\ *vb* : to cut or saw crosswise esp. of the grain of wood

²crosscut *adj* **1** : made or used for crosscutting (a ~ saw) **2** : cut across the grain

³crosscut *n* : something that cuts through transversely

cross–ex•am•ine \₁kròs-sig-'za-mən\ *vb* : to examine with questions to check the answers to previous questions — **cross–ex•am•i•na•tion** \-₁za-mə-'nā-shən\ *n*

cross–eyed \'kró-₁sīd\ *adj* : having one or both eyes turned inward toward the nose

cross–fer•til•i•za•tion \₁fərt-əl-ə-'zā-shən\ *n* **1** : fertilization between sex cells produced by separate individuals or sometimes by individuals of different kinds; *also* : CROSS-POLLINATION **2** : a broadening or productive interchange (as between cultures) — **cross–fer•til•ize** \-'fərt-əl-₁īz\ *vb*

cross fire *n* **1** : crossing lines of fire in combat **2** : rapid or angry interchange

cross•hair \'kròs-₁har\ *n* : a fine wire or thread in the eyepiece of an optical instrument used as a reference line

cross•hatch \'kròs-₁hach\ *vb* : to mark with two series of parallel lines that intersect — **cross–hatch•ing** *n*

cross•ing \'kró-sig\ *n* **1** : a place or structure for crossing something (as a river) **2** : a point of intersection (as of a street and a railroad track)

cross•over \'kròs-₁ō-vər\ *n* **1** : CROSSING **2** : a member of a political party who votes in the primary of the other party

cross•piece \'kròs-₁pēs\ *n* : a horizontal member

cross–pol•li•na•tion \₁kròs-₁pä-lə-'nā-shən\ *n* : transfer of pollen from one flower to the stigma of another — **cross–pol•li•nate** \'kròs-'pä-lə-₁nāt\ *vb*

cross–pur•pose \'kròs-'pər-pəs\ *n* : a purpose contrary to another purpose (working at ~s)

cross–ques•tion \-'kwes-chən\ *vb* : CROSS-EXAMINE — **cross–question** *n*

cross–re•fer \₁kròs-ri-'fər\ *vb* : to refer by a notation

or direction from one place to another (as in a book or list) — **cross–ref•er•ence** \'kròs-₁re-frəns\ *n*

cross•road \'kròs-₁rōd\ *n* **1** : a road that crosses a main road or runs between main roads **2** : a place where roads meet — usu. used in pl. **3** : a crucial point where a decision must be made

cross section *n* **1** : a section cut across something; *also* : a representation made by or as if by such cutting **2** : a number of persons or things selected from a group that show the general nature of the whole group — **cross–sec•tion•al** *adj*

cross•walk \'kròs-₁wòk\ *n* : a marked path for pedestrians crossing a street

cross•ways \-₁wāz\ *adv* : CROSSWISE

cross•wind \-₁wind\ *n* : a wind not parallel to a course (as of an airplane)

cross•wise \-₁wīz\ *adv* : so as to cross something : ACROSS — **crosswise** *adj*

cross•word \'kròs-₁wərd\ *n* : a puzzle in which words are put into a pattern of numbered squares in answer to clues

crotch \'kräch\ *n* : an angle formed by the parting of two legs, branches, or members

crotch•et \'krä-chət\ *n* : an odd notion : WHIM — **crotch•ety** *adj*

crouch \'kraùch\ *vb* **1** : to stoop or bend low **2** : CRINGE, COWER — **crouch** *n*

croup \'krüp\ *n* : laryngitis esp. of infants marked by a hoarse ringing cough and difficult breathing — **croupy** *adj*

crou•pi•er \'krü-pē-ər, -pē-₁ā\ *n* [F, lit., rider on the rump of a horse, fr. *croupe* rump] : an employee of a gambling casino who collects and pays bets at a gaming table

crou•ton \'krü-₁tän\ *n* [F *croûton*, dim. of *croûte* crust] : a small cube of bread toasted or fried crisp

¹crow \'krō\ *n* **1** : any of various large glossy black birds related to the jays **2** *cap* : a member of an American Indian people of a region in Montana and Wyoming; *also* : the language of the Crow people

²crow *vb* **1** : to make the loud shrill sound characteristic of the cock **2** : to utter a sound expressive of pleasure **3** : EXULT, GLOAT; *also* : BRAG, BOAST

³crow *n* : the cry of the cock

crow•bar \'krō-₁bär\ *n* : a metal bar usu. wedge-shaped at the end for use as a pry or lever

¹crowd \'kraùd\ *vb* **1** : to press close **2** : to collect in numbers : THRONG **3** : CRAM, STUFF

²crowd *n* : a large number of people gathered together at random : THRONG

¹crown \'kraùn\ *n* **1** : a mark of victory or honor; *esp* : the title of a champion in a sport **2** : a royal headdress **3** : the top of the head **4** : the highest part (as of a tree or tooth) **5** *often cap* : sovereign power; *also* : MONARCH **6** : a formerly used British silver coin — **crowned** \'kraùnd\ *adj*

²crown *vb* **1** : to place a crown on **2** : HONOR **3** : TOP, SURMOUNT **4** : to fit (a tooth) with an artificial crown

crown vetch *n* : a European leguminous herb with umbels of pink-and-white flowers and sharp-angled pods

crow's–foot \'krōz-₁fùt\ *n, pl* **crow's–feet** \-₁fēt\ : any of the wrinkles around the outer corners of the eyes — usu. used in pl.

crow's nest *n* : a partly enclosed platform high on a ship's mast for use as a lookout

¹CRT \₁sē-(₁)är-'tē\ *n, pl* **CRTs** *or* **CRT's** : CATHODE-RAY TUBE; *also* : a display device incorporating a cathode-ray tube

²CRT *abbr* carrier route

cru•cial \'krü-shəl\ *adj* : DECISIVE; *also* : IMPORTANT, SIGNIFICANT

cru•ci•ble \'krü-sə-bəl\ *n* : a heat-resistant container in which material can be subjected to great heat

cru•ci•fix \'krü-sə-₁fiks\ *n* : a representation of Christ on the cross

cru·ci·fix·ion \ˌkrü-sə-ˈfik-shən\ n 1 cap : the crucifying of Christ 2 : the act of crucifying

cru·ci·form \ˈkrü-sə-ˌfȯrm\ adj : shaped like a cross

cru·ci·fy \ˈkrü-sə-ˌfī\ vb -fied; -fy·ing 1 : to put to death by nailing or binding the hands and feet to a cross 2 : MORTIFY 1 3 : TORTURE, PERSECUTE

¹**crude** \ˈkrüd\ adj crud·er; crud·est 1 : not refined : RAW ⟨∼ oil⟩ ⟨∼ statistics⟩ 2 : lacking grace, taste, tact, or polish : RUDE — **crude·ly** adv — **cru·di·ty** \ˈkrü-də-tē\ n

²**crude** n : unrefined petroleum

cru·el \ˈkrü-əl\ adj cru·el·er or cru·el·ler; cru·el·est or cru·el·lest : causing pain and suffering to others : MERCILESS — **cru·el·ly** adv — **cru·el·ty** \-tē\ n

cru·et \ˈkrü-ət\ n : a small usu. glass bottle for vinegar, oil, or sauce

cruise \ˈkrüz\ vb cruised; cruis·ing [D kruisen to make a cross, cruise] 1 : to sail about touching at a series of ports 2 : to travel for enjoyment 3 : to travel about the streets at random 4 : to travel at the most efficient operating speed ⟨the cruising speed of an airplane⟩ — **cruise** n

cruis·er \ˈkrü-zər\ n 1 : SQUAD CAR 2 : a large fast moderately armored and gunned warship 3 : a motorboat equipped for living aboard

crul·ler \ˈkrə-lər\ n 1 : a small sweet cake in the form of a twisted strip fried in deep fat 2 Northern & Midland : an unraised doughnut

¹**crumb** \ˈkrəm\ n : a small fragment

²**crumb** vb 1 : to break into crumbs 2 : to cover with crumbs

crum·ble \ˈkrəm-bəl\ vb crum·bled; crum·bling : to break into small pieces : DISINTEGRATE — **crum·bly** adj

crum·my also **crumby** \ˈkrə-mē\ adj crum·mi·er also crumb·i·er; -est 1 : MISERABLE, FILTHY 2 : CHEAP, WORTHLESS

crum·pet \ˈkrəm-pət\ n : a small round unsweetened bread cooked on a griddle

crum·ple \ˈkrəm-pəl\ vb crum·pled; crum·pling 1 : to crush together : RUMPLE 2 : COLLAPSE

¹**crunch** \ˈkrənch\ vb : to chew with a grinding noise; also : to grind or press with a crushing noise

²**crunch** n 1 : an act of or a sound made by crunching 2 : a tight or critical situation — **crunchy** adj

cru·sade \krü-ˈsād\ n 1 cap : any of the expeditions in the 11th, 12th, and 13th centuries undertaken by Christian countries to take the Holy Land from the Muslims 2 : a reforming enterprise undertaken with zeal — **crusade** vb — **cru·sad·er** n

cruse \ˈkrüz, ˈkrüs\ n : a jar for water or oil

¹**crush** \ˈkrəsh\ vb 1 : to squeeze out of shape 2 : HUG, EMBRACE 3 : to grind or pound to small bits 4 : OVERWHELM, SUPPRESS

²**crush** n 1 : an act of crushing 2 : a violent crowding 3 : INFATUATION

crust \ˈkrəst\ n 1 : the outside part of bread; also : a piece of old dry bread 2 : the cover of a pie 3 : a hard surface layer — **crust·al** adj

crus·ta·cean \ˌkrəs-ˈtā-shən\ n : any of a large class of mostly aquatic arthropods (as lobsters or crabs) having a firm crustlike shell — **crustacean** adj

crusty adj crust·i·er; -est 1 : having or being a crust 2 : CROSS, GRUMPY

crutch \ˈkrəch\ n : a supporting device; esp : a support fitting under the armpit for use by the disabled in walking

crux \ˈkrəks, ˈkrüks\ n, pl crux·es 1 : a puzzling or difficult problem 2 : a crucial point

cru·zei·ro \krü-ˈzer-(ˌ)ō, -(ˌ)ü\ n, pl -ros — see MONEY table

¹**cry** \ˈkrī\ vb cried; cry·ing 1 : to call out : SHOUT 2 : to proclaim publicly : ADVERTISE 3 : WEEP

²**cry** n, pl cries 1 : a loud outcry 2 : APPEAL, ENTREATY 3 : a fit of weeping 4 : the characteristic sound uttered by an animal 5 : DISTANCE — usu. used in the phrase a far cry

cry·ba·by \ˈkrī-ˌbā-bē\ n : one who cries easily or often

cryo·gen·ic \ˌkrī-ə-ˈje-nik\ adj : of or relating to the production of very low temperatures; also : involving the use of a very low temperature — **cryo·gen·i·cal·ly** \-ni-k(ə-)lē\ adv

cryo·gen·ics \-niks\ n : a branch of physics that relates to the production and effects of very low temperatures

cryo·lite \ˈkrī-ə-ˌlīt\ n : a usu. white mineral used in making aluminum

crypt \ˈkript\ n : a chamber wholly or partly underground

cryp·tic \ˈkrip-tik\ adj : meant to be puzzling or mysterious

cryp·to·gram \ˈkrip-tə-ˌgram\ n : a communication in cipher or code

cryp·tog·ra·phy \krip-ˈtä-grə-fē\ n : the coding and decoding of secret messages — **cryp·tog·ra·pher** \-fər\ n

crys·tal \ˈkrist-əl\ n [ME cristal, fr. OF, fr. L crystallum, fr. Gk krystallos ice, crystal] 1 : transparent quartz 2 : something resembling crystal (as in transparency); esp : a clear glass used for table articles 3 : a body that is formed by solidification of a substance and has a regular repeating arrangement of atoms and often of external plane faces ⟨a salt ∼⟩ 4 : the transparent cover of a watch dial

crys·tal·line \ˈkris-tə-lən\ adj 1 : made of or resembling crystal 2 : very clear or sparkling

crys·tal·lize \ˈkris-tə-ˌlīz\ vb -lized; -liz·ing 1 : to assume or cause to assume a crystalline form 2 : to take or cause to take a definite form — **crys·tal·li·za·tion** \ˌkris-tə-lə-ˈzā-shən\ n

crys·tal·log·ra·phy \ˌkris-tə-ˈlä-grə-fē\ n : the science dealing with the forms and structures of crystals — **crys·tal·log·ra·pher** n

cs abbr case; cases

Cs symbol cesium

CS abbr 1 civil service 2 county seat

CSA abbr Confederate States of America

CSM abbr command sergeant major

CST abbr central standard time

ct abbr 1 carat 2 cent 3 count 4 county 5 court

CT abbr 1 central time 2 Connecticut

ctn abbr carton

ctr abbr 1 center 2 counter

CT scan \ˌsē-ˈtē-\ n : CAT SCAN

cu abbr cubic

Cu symbol [L cuprum] copper

cub \ˈkəb\ n : a young individual of some animals (as a fox, bear, or lion)

Cu·ban \ˈkyü-bən\ n : a native or inhabitant of Cuba — **Cuban** adj

cub·by·hole \ˈkə-bē-ˌhōl\ n : a snug place (as for storing things)

¹**cube** \ˈkyüb\ n 1 : a solid having 6 equal square sides 2 : the product obtained by taking a number 3 times as a factor ⟨27 is the ∼ of 3⟩

²**cube** vb cubed; cub·ing 1 : to raise to the third power 2 : to form into a cube 3 : to cut into cubes

cube root n : a number whose cube is a given number

cu·bic \ˈkyü-bik\ also **cu·bi·cal** \-bi-kəl\ adj 1 : having the form of a cube 2 : being the volume of a cube whose edge is a specified unit 3 : having length, width, and height

cu·bi·cle \ˈkyü-bi-kəl\ n : a small separate space (as for sleeping or studying)

cubic measure n : a unit (as cubic inch) for measuring volume — see METRIC SYSTEM table, WEIGHT table

cub·ism \ˈkyü-ˌbi-zəm\ n : a style of art characterized by the abstraction of natural forms into fragmented geometric shapes — **cub·ist** \-bist\ n or adj

cu·bit \ˈkyü-bət\ n : an ancient unit of length equal to about 18 inches (46 centimeters)

Cub Scout *n* : a member of the program of the Boy Scouts for boys in the first through fifth grades in school

cuck•old \'kə-kəld, 'kù-\ *n* : a man whose wife is unfaithful — **cuckold** *vb*

¹**cuck•oo** \'kü-kü, 'kù-\ *n, pl* **cuckoos** : a largely grayish brown European bird that lays its eggs in the nests of other birds for them to hatch

²**cuckoo** *adj* : SILLY, FOOLISH

cu•cum•ber \'kyü-(ˌ)kəm-bər\ *n* : the long fleshy many-seeded fruit of a vine of the gourd family that is grown as a garden vegetable; *also* : this vine

cud \'kəd\ *n* : food brought up into the mouth by some animals (as cows) from the rumen to be chewed again

cud•dle \'kəd-ᵊl\ *vb* **cud•dled; cud•dling** : to lie close : SNUGGLE

cud•gel \'kə-jəl\ *n* : a short heavy club — **cudgel** *vb*

¹**cue** \'kyü\ *n* **1** : a word, phrase, or action in a play serving as a signal for the next actor to speak or act **2** : HINT — **cue** *vb*

²**cue** *n* : a tapered rod for striking the balls in billiards or pool

cue ball *n* : the ball a player strikes with a cue in billiards or pool

¹**cuff** \'kəf\ *n* **1** : a part (as of a sleeve or glove) encircling the wrist **2** : the folded hem of a trouser leg

²**cuff** *vb* : to strike esp. with the open hand : SLAP

³**cuff** *n* : a blow with the hand esp. when open

cui•sine \kwi-'zēn\ *n* : style of cooking; *also* : the food prepared

cuke \'kyük\ *n* : CUCUMBER

cul-de-sac \ˌkəl-di-'sak, ˌkùl-\ *n, pl* **culs-de-sac** *same or* \ˌkəlz-, ˌkùlz-\ *also* **cul-de-sacs** \ˌkəl-də-'saks, ˌkùl-\ [F, lit., bottom of the bag] : a street or passage closed at one end

cu•li•nary \'kə-lə-ˌner-ē, 'kyü-\ *adj* : of or relating to the kitchen or cookery

¹**cull** \'kəl\ *vb* : to pick out from a group

²**cull** *n* : something rejected from a group or lot as worthless or inferior

cul•mi•nate \'kəl-mə-ˌnāt\ *vb* **-nat•ed; -nat•ing** : to reach the highest point — **cul•mi•na•tion** \ˌkəl-mə-'nā-shən\ *n*

cu•lotte \'kü-ˌlät, ˌkyü-, kü-ˌlät, kyü-\ *n* [F, breeches, fr. dim. of *cul* backside] : a divided skirt; *also* : a garment having a divided skirt — often used in pl.

cul•pa•ble \'kəl-pə-bəl\ *adj* : deserving blame — **cul•pa•bil•i•ty** \ˌkəl-pə-'bi-lə-tē\ *n*

cul•prit \'kəl-prət\ *n* [Anglo-French (the French of medieval England) *cul.* (abbr. of *culpable* guilty) + *prest, prit* ready (i.e. to prove it), fr. L *praestus*] : one accused or guilty of a crime

cult \'kəlt\ *n* **1** : formal religious veneration **2** : a religious system; *also* : its adherents **3** : faddish devotion; *also* : a group of persons showing such devotion — **cult•ist** *n*

cul•ti•va•ble \'kəl-tə-və-bəl\ *adj* : capable of being cultivated

cul•ti•vate \'kəl-tə-ˌvāt\ *vb* **-vat•ed; -vat•ing 1** : to prepare for the raising of crops **2** : to foster the growth of by tilling or by labor and care ⟨∼ vegetables⟩ **3** : REFINE, IMPROVE **4** : ENCOURAGE, FURTHER — **cul•ti•va•tion** \ˌkəl-tə-'vā-shən\ *n* — **cul•ti•va•tor** \'kəl-tə-ˌvā-tər\ *n*

cul•ture \'kəl-chər\ *n* **1** : TILLAGE, CULTIVATION **2** : the act of developing by education and training **3** : refinement of intellectual and artistic taste **4** : the customary beliefs, social forms, and material traits of a racial, religious, or social group — **cul•tur•al** \'kəl-chə-rəl\ *adj* — **cul•tur•al•ly** *adv* — **cul•tured** \-chərd\ *adj*

cul•vert \'kəl-vərt\ *n* : a drain crossing under a road or railroad

cum *abbr* cumulative

cum•ber \'kəm-bər\ *vb* : to weigh down : BURDEN, HINDER

cum•ber•some \'kəm-bər-səm\ *adj* : hard to handle or manage because of size or weight

cum•brous \'kəm-brəs\ *adj* : CUMBERSOME — **cumbrous•ly** *adv* — **cum•brous•ness** *n*

cum•mer•bund \'kə-mər-ˌbənd, 'kəm-bər-\ *n* [Hindi *kamarband*, fr. Per, fr. *kamar* waist + *band* band] : a broad sash worn as a waistband

cu•mu•la•tive \'kyü-myə-lə-tiv, -ˌlā-\ *adj* : increasing in force or value by successive additions

cu•mu•lo•nim•bus \ˌkyü-myə-lō-'nim-bəs\ *n* : an anvil-shaped cumulus cloud extending to great heights

cu•mu•lus \'kyü-myə-ləs\ *n, pl* **-li** \-ˌlī, -ˌlē\ : a massive cloud having a flat base and rounded outlines

cu•ne•i•form \kyu-'nē-ə-ˌfôrm\ *adj* **1** : wedge-shaped **2** : composed of wedge-shaped characters

cun•ni•lin•gus \ˌkə-ni-'liŋ-gəs\ *also* **cun•ni•linc•tus** \-'liŋk-təs\ *n* : oral stimulation of the vulva or clitoris

¹**cun•ning** \'kə-niŋ\ *adj* **1** : SKILLFUL, DEXTEROUS **2** : marked by wiliness and trickery **3** : CUTE — **cun•ning•ly** *adv*

²**cunning** *n* **1** : SKILL **2** : SLYNESS

¹**cup** \'kəp\ *n* **1** : a small bowl-shaped drinking vessel **2** : the contents of a cup **3** : the consecrated wine of the Communion **4** : something resembling a cup : a small bowl or hollow **5** : a half pint — **cup•ful** *n*

²**cup** *vb* **cupped; cup•ping** : to curve into the shape of a cup

cup•board \'kə-bərd\ *n* : a small closet with shelves for food or dishes

cup•cake \'kəp-ˌkāk\ *n* : a small cake baked in a cuplike mold

cu•pid \'kyü-pəd\ *n* : a winged naked figure of an infant often with a bow and arrow that represents the god Cupid

cu•pid•i•ty \kyu-'pi-də-tē\ *n, pl* **-ties** : excessive desire for money

cu•po•la \'kyü-pə-lə, -ˌlō\ *n* : a small structure on top of a roof or building

¹**cur** \'kər\ *n* : a mongrel dog

²**cur** *abbr* **1** currency **2** current

cu•rate \'kyùr-ət\ *n* **1** : a clergyman in charge of a parish **2** : a member of the clergy who assists a rector or vicar — **cu•ra•cy** \-ə-sē\ *n*

cu•ra•tive \-ə-tiv\ *adj* : relating to or used in the cure of diseases — **curative** *n*

cu•ra•tor \'kyùr-ˌā-tər, kyù-'rā-\ *n* : CUSTODIAN; *esp* : one in charge of a place of exhibit (as a museum or zoo)

¹**curb** \'kərb\ *n* **1** : a bit that exerts pressure on a horse's jaws **2** : CHECK, RESTRAINT **3** : a raised edging (as of stone or concrete) along a paved street

²**curb** *vb* : to hold in or back : RESTRAIN

curb•ing \'kər-biŋ\ *n* **1** : the material for a curb **2** : CURB

curd \'kərd\ *n* : the thick protein-rich part of coagulated milk

cur•dle \'kərd-ᵊl\ *vb* **cur•dled; cur•dling** : to form curds; *also* : SPOIL, SOUR

¹**cure** \'kyùr\ *n* **1** : spiritual care **2** : recovery or relief from disease **3** : a curative agent : REMEDY **4** : a course or period of treatment

²**cure** *vb* **cured; cur•ing 1** : to restore to health : HEAL, REMEDY; *also* : to become cured **2** : to process for storage or use ⟨∼ bacon⟩ — **cur•able** *adj*

cu•ré \kyù-'rā\ *n* [F] : a parish priest

cure-all \'kyùr-ˌ ȯl\ *n* : a remedy for all ills : PANACEA

cu•ret•tage \ˌkyùr-ə-'täzh\ *n* : a surgical scraping or cleaning of a body part (as the uterus)

cur•few \'kər-ˌfyü\ *n* [ME, fr. MF *covrefeu*, signal given to bank the hearth fire, curfew, fr. *covrir* to cover + *feu* fire, fr. L *focus* hearth] : a regulation that specified persons (as children) be off the streets at a set hour of the evening; *also* : the sounding of a signal (as a bell) at this hour

cu•ria \'kyùr-ē-ə, 'kùr-\ *n, pl* **cu•ri•ae** \'kyùr-ē-ˌē, 'kùr-ē-ˌī\ *often cap* : the body of congregations, tribunals, and offices through which the pope governs the Roman Catholic Church

cu·rie \\'kyùr-ē\ *n* : a unit of radioactivity equal to 37 billion disintegrations per second

cu·rio \\'kyúr-ē-ˌō\ *n, pl* **cu·ri·os** : an object or article valued because it is strange or rare

cu·ri·ous \\'kyúr-ē-əs\ *adj* **1** : having a desire to investigate and learn **2** : STRANGE, UNUSUAL, ODD — **cu·ri·os·i·ty** \ˌkyúr-ē-'a-sə-tē\ *n* — **cu·ri·ous·ness** *n*

cu·ri·ous·ly *adv* **1** : in a curious manner **2** : as is curious

cu·ri·um \\'kyúr-ē-əm\ *n* : a metallic radioactive element produced artificially — see ELEMENT table

¹curl \\'kərl\ *vb* **1** : to form into ringlets **2** : CURVE, COIL — **curl·er** *n*

²curl *n* **1** : a lock of hair that coils : RINGLET **2** : something having a spiral or twisted form — **curly** *adj*

cur·lew \\'kər-lü, 'kərl-yü\ *n, pl* **curlews** *or* **curlew** : any of various long-legged brownish birds that have a down-curved bill and are related to the sandpipers and snipes

curli·cue \\'kər-li-ˌkyü\ *n* : a fancifully curved or spiral figure

cur·rant \\'kər-ənt\ *n* **1** : a small seedless raisin **2** : the acid berry of a shrub related to the gooseberry; *also* : this plant

cur·ren·cy \\'kər-ən-sē\ *n, pl* **-cies** **1** : general use or acceptance **2** : something that is in circulation as a medium of exchange : MONEY

¹cur·rent \\'kər-ənt\ *adj* **1** : occurring in or belonging to the present **2** : used as a medium of exchange **3** : generally accepted or practiced

²current *n* **1** : the part of a body of fluid moving continuously in a certain direction; *also* : the swiftest part of a stream **2** : a flow of electric charge; *also* : the rate of such flow

cur·ric·u·lum \kə-'ri-kyə-ləm\ *n, pl* **-la** \-lə\ *also* **-lums** [L, running, course, fr. *currere* to run] : the courses offered by an educational institution

¹cur·ry \\'kər-ē\ *vb* **cur·ried; cur·ry·ing** **1** : to clean the coat of (a horse) with a currycomb **2** : to treat (tanned leather) esp. by incorporating oil or grease — **curry favor** : to seek to gain favor by flattery or attention

²cur·ry *n, pl* **cur·ries** : a powder of pungent spices used in cooking; *also* : a food seasoned with curry

cur·ry·comb \-ˌkōm\ *n* : a comb used esp. to curry horses — **currycomb** *vb*

¹curse \\'kərs\ *n* **1** : a prayer for harm to come upon one **2** : something that is cursed **3** : evil or misfortune coming as if in response to a curse

²curse *vb* **cursed; curs·ing** **1** : to call on divine power to send injury upon **2** : BLASPHEME **3** : AFFLICT **syn** execrate, damn, anathematize, objurgate

cur·sive \\'kər-siv\ *adj* : written with the strokes of the letters joined together and the angles rounded

cur·sor \\'kər-sər\ *n* : a visual cue (as a pointer) on a computer screen that indicates position (as for data entry)

cur·so·ry \\'kər-sə-rē\ *adj* : rapidly and often superficially done : HASTY — **cur·so·ri·ly** \-rə-lē\ *adj*

curt \\'kərt\ *adj* : rudely short or abrupt — **curt·ly** *adv* — **curt·ness** *n*

cur·tail \(ˌ)kər-'tāl\ *vb* : to cut off the end of : SHORTEN — **cur·tail·ment** *n*

cur·tain \\'kərt-ᵊn\ *n* **1** : a hanging screen that can be drawn back esp. at a window **2** : the screen between the stage and auditorium of a theater — **curtain** *vb*

curt·sy *or* **curt·sey** \\'kərt-sē\ *n, pl* **curtsies** *or* **curtseys** : a courteous bow made by women chiefly by bending the knees — **curtsy** *or* **curtsey** *vb*

cur·va·ceous *also* **cur·va·cious** \ˌkər-'vā-shəs\ *adj* : having curves suggestive of a well-proportioned feminine figure

cur·va·ture \\'kər-və-ˌchùr\ *n* : a measure or amount of curving : BEND

¹curve \\'kərv\ *vb* **curved; curv·ing** : to bend from a straight line or course

²curve *n* **1** : a line esp. when curved **2** : something that bends or curves without angles ⟨a ∼ in the road⟩ **3** : a baseball pitch thrown so that it swerves esp. downward and to one side

cur·vet \(ˌ)kər-'vet\ *n* : a prancing leap of a horse — **curvet** *vb*

¹cush·ion \\'kú-shən\ *n* **1** : a soft pillow or pad to rest on or against **2** : the springy pad inside the rim of a billiard table **3** : something soft that prevents discomfort or protects against injury

²cushion *vb* **1** : to provide (as a seat) with a cushion **2** : to soften or lessen the force or shock of

cusp \\'kəsp\ *n* : a pointed end or part (as of a tooth)

cus·pid \\'kəs-pəd\ *n* : a canine tooth

cus·pi·dor \\'kəs-pə-ˌdòr\ *n* : SPITTOON

cus·tard \\'kəs-tərd\ *n* : a sweetened cooked mixture of milk and eggs

cus·to·di·al \ˌkəs-'tō-dē-əl\ *adj* : marked by watching and protecting rather than seeking to cure ⟨∼ care⟩

cus·to·di·an \ˌkəs-'tō-dē-ən\ *n* : one who has custody (as of a building)

cus·to·dy \\'kəs-tə-dē\ *n, pl* **-dies** : immediate charge and control

¹cus·tom \\'kəs-təm\ *n* **1** : habitual course of action : recognized usage **2** *pl* : taxes levied on imports **3** : business patronage

²custom *adj* **1** : made to personal order **2** : doing work only on order

cus·tom·ary \\'kəs-tə-ˌmer-ē\ *adj* **1** : based on or established by custom **2** : commonly practiced or observed : HABITUAL — **cus·tom·ar·i·ly** *adv*

cus·tom–built \\'kəs-təm-'bilt\ *adj* : built to individual order

cus·tom·er \\'kəs-tə-mər\ *n* : BUYER, PURCHASER; *esp* : a regular or frequent buyer

cus·tom·house \\'kəs-təm-ˌhaùs\ *n* : the building where customs are paid

cus·tom·ize \\'kəs-tə-ˌmīz\ *vb* **-ized; -iz·ing** : to build, fit, or alter according to individual specifications

cus·tom–made \\'kəs-təm-'mād\ *adj* : made to individual order

¹cut \\'kət\ *vb* **cut; cut·ting** **1** : to penetrate or divide with a sharp edge : CLEAVE, GASH; *also* : to experience the growth of (a tooth) through the gum **2** : to hurt the feelings of **3** : to strike sharply **4** : SHORTEN, REDUCE **5** : to remove by severing or paring **6** : INTERSECT, CROSS **7** : to divide into parts **8** : to go quickly or change direction abruptly **9** : to cause to stop

²cut *n* **1** : something made by cutting : GASH, CLEFT **2** : SHARE **3** : a segment or section of a meat carcass **4** : an excavated channel or roadway **5** : BAND **4 6** : a sharp stroke or blow **7** : REDUCTION ⟨∼ in wages⟩ **8** : the shape or manner in which a thing is cut

cut–and–dried \ˌkət-ᵊn-'drīd\ *also* **cut–and–dry** \-'drī\ *adj* : according to a plan, set procedure, or formula

cu·ta·ne·ous \kyù-'tā-nē-əs\ *adj* : of, relating to, or affecting the skin

cut·back \\'kət-ˌbak\ *n* **1** : something cut back **2** : REDUCTION

cute \\'kyüt\ *adj* **cut·er; cut·est** [short for *acute*] **1** : CLEVER, SHREWD **2** : daintily attractive : PRETTY

cu·ti·cle \\'kyü-ti-kəl\ *n* **1** : an outer layer (as of skin or a leaf) **2** : dead or horny epidermis esp. around a fingernail — **cu·tic·u·lar** \kyù-'ti-kyə-lər\ *adj*

cut in *vb* **1** : to thrust oneself between others **2** : to interrupt a dancing couple and take one as one's partner

cut·lass \\'kət-ləs\ *n* : a short heavy curved sword

cutlass

cut·ler \\'kət-lər\\ *n* : one who makes, deals in, or repairs cutlery

cut·lery \\'kət-lə-rē\\ *n* : edged or cutting tools; *esp* : implements for cutting and eating food

cut·let \\'kət-lət\\ *n* : a slice of meat (as veal) for broiling or frying

cut·off \\'kət-ıóf\\ *n* **1** : the channel formed when a stream cuts through the neck of an oxbow; *also* : SHORTCUT **2** : a device for cutting off **3** *pl* : shorts orig. made from jeans with the legs cut off at the knees or higher

cut·out \\'kət-ıaút\\ *n* : something cut out or prepared for cutting out from something else ⟨a page of animal ∼s⟩

cut out *vb* **1** : to be all that one can handle ⟨had her work *cut out* for her⟩ **2** : DISCONNECT **3** : to cease operating ⟨the engine *cut out*⟩ **4** : ELIMINATE ⟨*cut out* unnecessary expense⟩

cut–rate \\'kət-'rāt\\ *adj* : relating to or dealing in goods sold at reduced rates

cut·ter \\'kə-tər\\ *n* **1** : a tool or a machine for cutting **2** : a ship's boat for carrying stores and passengers **3** : a small armed vessel in government service **4** : a light sleigh

¹cut·throat \\'kət-ıthrōt\\ *n* : MURDERER

²cutthroat *adj* **1** : MURDEROUS, CRUEL **2** : RUTHLESS ⟨∼ competition⟩

cutthroat trout *n* : a large American trout with a red mark under the jaw

¹cut·ting \\'kə-tiŋ\\ *n* : a piece of a plant able to grow into a new plant

²cutting *adj* **1** : SHARP, EDGED **2** : marked by piercing cold **3** : likely to hurt the feelings : SARCASTIC ⟨a ∼ remark⟩

cut·tle·fish \\'kət-ᵊl-ıfish\\ *n* : a 10-armed mollusk related to the squid with an internal shell (**cut·tle·bone** \\-ıbōn\\) composed of calcium compounds

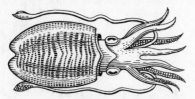

cuttlefish

cut·up \\'kət-ıəp\\ *n* : a person who clowns or acts boisterously — **cut up** *vb*

cut·worm \\-ıwərm\\ *n* : any of various smooth≈bodied moth larvae that feed on plants at night

cw *abbr* clockwise

CWO *abbr* **1** cash with order **2** chief warrant officer

cwt *abbr* hundredweight

-cy \\sē\\ *n suffix* **1** : action : practice ⟨mendican*cy*⟩ **2** : rank : office ⟨chaplain*cy*⟩ **3** : body : class ⟨constituen*cy*⟩ **4** : state : quality ⟨accura*cy*⟩

cy·an \\'sī-ıan, -ən\\ *n* : a greenish blue color

cy·a·nide \\'sī-ə-ınīd, -nəd\\ *n* : a poisonous compound of carbon and nitrogen with another element (as potassium)

cy·ber·net·ics \\ısī-bər-'ne-tiks\\ *n* : the science of communication and control theory that is concerned esp. with the comparative study of automatic control systems — **cy·ber·net·ic** *adj*

cy·cla·men \\'sī-klə-mən\\ *n* : any of a genus of plants related to the primroses and grown for their showy nodding flowers

¹cy·cle \\'sī-kəl\\ *n* **1** : a period of time occupied by a series of events that repeat themselves regularly and in the same order **2** : a recurring round of operations or events **3** : one complete occurrence of a periodic process (as a vibration or current alternation) **4** : a circular or spiral arrangement **5** : a long period of time : AGE **6** : BICYCLE **7** : MOTORCYCLE — **cy·clic** \\'sī-klik, 'si-\\ *or* **cy·cli·cal** \\kli-kəl\\ *adj* — **cy·cli·cal·ly** \\-k(ə-)lē\\ *also* **cy·clic·ly** *adv*

²cy·cle \\'sī-kəl\\ *vb* **cy·cled; cy·cling** : to ride a cycle — **cy·clist** \\'sī-klist, -kə-list\\ *n*

cy·clone \\'sī-ıklōn\\ *n* **1** : a storm or system of winds that rotates about a center of low atmospheric pressure and advances at 20 to 30 miles (about 30 to 50 kilometers) an hour **2** : TORNADO — **cy·clon·ic** \\sī-'klä-nik\\ *adj*

cy·clo·pe·dia *or* **cy·clo·pae·dia** \\ısī-klə-'pē-dē-ə\\ *n* : ENCYCLOPEDIA

cy·clo·tron \\'sī-klə-ıträn\\ *n* : a device for giving high speed to charged particles by magnetic and electric fields

cy·der *Brit var of* CIDER

cyg·net \\'sig-nət\\ *n* : a young swan

cyl *abbr* cylinder

cyl·in·der \\'si-lən-dər\\ *n* : the solid figure formed by turning a rectangle about one side as an axis; *also* : a body or space of this form ⟨an engine ∼⟩ ⟨a bullet in the ∼ of a revolver⟩ — **cy·lin·dri·cal** \\sə-'lin-dri-kəl\\ *adj*

cym·bal \\'sim-bəl\\ *n* : a concave brass plate that produces a brilliant clashing sound

cyn·ic \\'si-nik\\ *n* : one who attributes all actions to selfish motives — **cyn·i·cal** \\-ni-kəl\\ *adj* — **cyn·i·cal·ly** \\-k(ə-)lē\\ *adv* — **cyn·i·cism** \\si-nə-ısi-zəm\\ *n*

cy·no·sure \\'sī-nə-ıshùr, 'si-\\ *n* [MF & L; MF, Ursa Minor, guide, fr. L *cynosura* Ursa Minor, fr. Gk *kynosoura*, fr. *kynos oura* dog's tail] : a center of attraction

CYO *abbr* Catholic Youth Organization

cy·pher *chiefly Brit var of* CIPHER

cy·press \\'sī-prəs\\ *n* **1** : any of a genus of scaly≈ leaved evergreen trees and shrubs **2** : BALD CYPRESS **3** : the wood of a cypress

Cyp·ri·ot \\'si-prē-ət, -ıät\\ *or* **Cyp·ri·ote** \\-ıōt, -ət\\ *n* : a native or inhabitant of Cyprus — **Cypriot** *adj*

cyst \\'sist\\ *n* : an abnormal closed bodily sac usu. containing liquid — **cys·tic** \\'sis-tik\\ *adj*

cystic fibrosis *n* : a common hereditary disease marked esp. by deficiency of pancreatic enzymes, by respiratory symptoms, and by excessive loss of salt in the sweat

cy·tol·o·gy \\sī-'tä-lə-jē\\ *n* : a branch of biology dealing with cells — **cy·to·log·i·cal** \\ısīt-ᵊl-'ä-ji-kəl\\ *or* **cy·to·log·ic** \\-jik\\ *adj* — **cy·tol·o·gist** \\sī-'tä-lə-jist\\ *n*

cy·to·plasm \\'sī-tə-ıpla-zəm\\ *n* : the protoplasm of a cell that lies external to the nucleus — **cy·to·plas·mic** \\ısī-tə-'plaz-mik\\ *adj*

cy·to·sine \\'sī-tə-ısēn\\ *n* : a chemical base that is a pyrimidine coding genetic information in DNA and RNA

CZ *abbr* Canal Zone

czar \\'zär, 'tsär\\ *n* [NL, fr. Russ *tsar'*, ultim. fr. L *Caesar* Caesar] : the ruler of Russia until 1917; *also* : one having great authority — **czar·ist** \\-ist\\ *n or adj*

cza·ri·na \\zä-'rē-nə\\ *n* : the wife of a czar

Czech \\'chek\\ *n* **1** : a native or inhabitant of Czechoslovakia or the Czech Republic **2** : the language of the Czechs — **Czech** *adj*

Czecho·slo·vak \\ıche-kə-'slō-ıväk, -ıvak\\ *or* **Czecho·slo·va·ki·an** \\-slō-'vä-kē-ən, -'va-\\ *adj* : of, relating to, or characteristic of Czechoslovakia or its people — **Czechoslovak** *or* **Czechoslovakian** *n*

D

¹**d** \'dē\ *n, pl* **d's** *or* **ds** \'dēz\ *often cap* **1** : the 4th letter of the English alphabet **2** : a grade rating a student's work as poor

²**d** *abbr, often cap* **1** date **2** daughter **3** day **4** dead **5** deceased **6** degree **7** Democrat **8** [L *denarius, denarii* penny; pence **9** depart; departure **10** diameter

D *symbol* deuterium

DA *abbr* **1** deposit account **2** district attorney **3** don't answer

¹**dab** \'dab\ *n* **1** : a sudden blow or thrust : POKE; *also* : PECK **2** : a gentle touch or stroke : PAT

²**dab** *vb* **dabbed; dab·bing 1** : to strike or touch gently : PAT **2** : to apply lightly or irregularly : DAUB — **dab·ber** *n*

³**dab** *n* **1** : DAUB **2** : a small amount

dab·ble \'da-bəl\ *vb* **dab·bled; dab·bling 1** : to wet by splashing : SPATTER **2** : to paddle or play in or as if in water **3** : to work or involve oneself without serious effort — **dab·bler** *n*

da ca·po \dä-'kä-(ˌ)pō\ *adv or adj* [It] : from the beginning — used as a direction in music to repeat

dace \'dās\ *n, pl* **dace** : any of various small No. American freshwater fishes related to the carp

da·cha \'dä-chə\ *n* [Russ] : a Russian country house

dachs·hund \'däks-ˌhùnt\ *n, pl* **dachshunds** [G, fr. *Dachs* badger + *Hund* dog] : a small dog of a breed of German origin with a long body, short legs, and long drooping ears

dachsund

dac·tyl \'dakt-ᵊl\ *n* [ME *dactile*, fr. L *dactylus*, fr. Gk *daktylos*, lit., finger; fr. the fact that the three syllables have the first one longest like the joints of the finger] : a metrical foot of one accented syllable followed by two unaccented syllables — **dac·tyl·ic** \dak-'ti-lik\ *adj or n*

dad \'dad\ *n* : FATHER 1

Da·da \'dä-(ˌ)dä\ *n* : a movement in art and literature based on deliberate irrationality and negation of traditional artistic values — **da·da·ism** \-ˌi-zəm\ *n, often cap* — **da·da·ist** \-ˌist\ *n or adj, often cap*

dad·dy \'da-dē\ *n, pl* **daddies** : FATHER 1

dad·dy long·legs \ˌda-dē-'lȯn-ˌlegz\ *n, pl* **daddy longlegs** : any of various arachnids resembling the true spiders but having small rounded bodies and long slender legs

dae·mon *var of* DEMON

daf·fo·dil \'da-fə-ˌdil\ *n* : any of a genus of bulbous herbs with usu. large flowers having a trumpetlike center

daf·fy \'da-fē\ *adj* **daf·fi·er; -est** : DAFT

daft \'daft\ *adj* : FOOLISH; *also* : INSANE — **daft·ness** *n*

dag *abbr* dekagram

dag·ger \'da-gər\ *n* **1** : a sharp pointed knife for stabbing **2** : a character † used as a reference mark or to indicate a death date

da·guerre·o·type \də-'ger-(ē-)ə-ˌtīp\ *n* : an early photograph produced on a silver or a silver-covered copper plate

dahl·ia \'dal-yə, 'däl-\ *n* : any of a genus of tuberous herbs related to the daisies and having showy flowers

¹**dai·ly** \'dā-lē\ *adj* **1** : occurring, done, or used every day or every weekday **2** : of or relating to every day ⟨~ visitors⟩ **3** : computed in terms of one day ⟨~ wages⟩ **syn** diurnal, quotidian — **dai·li·ness** \-lē-nəs\ *n* — **daily** *adv*

²**daily** *n, pl* **dailies** : a newspaper published every weekday

daily double *n* : a system of betting on races in which the bettor must pick the winners of two stipulated races in order to win

¹**dain·ty** \'dān-tē\ *n, pl* **dainties** [ME *deinte*, fr. OF *deintié*, fr. L *dignitas* dignity, worth] : something delicious or pleasing to the taste : DELICACY

²**dainty** *adj* **dain·ti·er; -est 1** : pleasing to the taste **2** : delicately pretty **3** : having or showing delicate taste; *also* : FASTIDIOUS **syn** choice, delicate, exquisite, rare, recherché — **dain·ti·ly** \-ti-lē\ *adv* — **dain·ti·ness** \-tē-nəs\ *n*

dai·qui·ri \'dī-kə-rē, 'da-kə-rē\ *n* [*Daiquirí*, Cuba] : a cocktail made of rum, lime juice, and sugar

dairy \'der-ē\ *n, pl* **dair·ies** [ME *deyerie*, fr. *deye* dairymaid, fr. OE *dæge* kneader of bread] **1** : CREAMERY **2** : a farm specializing in milk production

dairy·ing \'der-ē-iŋ\ *n* : the business of operating a dairy

dairy·maid \-ˌmād\ *n* : a woman employed in a dairy

dairy·man \-mən, -ˌman\ *n* : a person who operates a dairy farm or works in a dairy

da·is \'dā-əs\ *n* : a raised platform usu. above the floor of a hall or large room

dai·sy \'dā-zē\ *n, pl* **daisies** [ME *dayeseye*, fr. OE *dægesēage*, fr. *dæg* day + *ēage* eye] : any of numerous composite plants having flower heads in which the marginal flowers resemble petals

daisy wheel *n* : a disk with spokes bearing type that serves as the printing element of an electric typewriter or printer; *also* : a printer that uses such a disk

Da·ko·ta \də-'kō-tə\ *n, pl* **Dakotas** *also* **Dakota** : a member of an American Indian people of the northern Mississippi valley; *also* : their language

dal *abbr* dekaliter

da·la·si \dä-'lä-sē\ *n, pl* **dalasi** *or* **dalasis** — see MONEY table

dale \'dāl\ *n* : VALLEY

dal·ly \'da-lē\ *vb* **dal·lied; dal·ly·ing 1** : to act playfully; *esp* : to play amorously **2** : to waste time **3** : LINGER, DAWDLE **syn** flirt, coquet, toy, trifle — **dal·li·ance** \-lē-əns\ *n*

dal·ma·tian \dal-'mā-shən\ *n, often cap* : any of a breed of medium-sized dogs having a white short=haired coat with black or brown spots

dalmatian

¹**dam** \'dam\ *n* : a female parent — used esp. of a domestic animal

²**dam** *n* : a barrier (as across a stream) to stop the flow of water — **dam** *vb*

³**dam** *abbr* dekameter

¹**dam·age** \'da-mij\ *n* **1** : loss or harm due to injury to persons, property, or reputation **2** *pl* : compensation in money imposed by law for loss or injury ⟨bring a suit for ~*s*⟩

²**damage** *vb* **dam·aged; dam·ag·ing** : to cause damage to

dam·a·scene \'da-mə-ˌsēn\ *vb* **-scened; -scen·ing** : to ornament (as iron or steel) with wavy patterns or with inlaid work of precious metals

dam·ask \'da-məsk\ *n* **1** : a firm lustrous reversible figured fabric used for household linen **2** : a tough steel having decorative wavy lines

dame \'dām\ *n* **1** : a woman of rank, station, or authority **2** : an elderly woman **3** : WOMAN

damn \'dam\ *vb* [ME *dampnen,* fr. OF *dampner,* fr. L *damnare,* fr. *damnum* damage, loss, fine] **1** : to condemn esp. to hell **2** : CURSE — **damned** *adj*

dam·na·ble \'dam-nə-bəl\ *adj* **1** : liable to or deserving punishment **2** : DETESTABLE ⟨~ weather⟩ — **dam·na·bly** \-blē\ *adv*

dam·na·tion \dam-'nā-shən\ *n* **1** : the act of damning **2** : the state of being damned

¹**damp** \'damp\ *n* **1** : a noxious gas **2** : MOISTURE

²**damp** *vb* : DAMPEN

³**damp** *adj* : MOIST — **damp·ness** *n*

damp·en \'dam-pən\ *vb* **1** : to check or diminish in activity or vigor **2** : to make or become damp

damp·er \'dam-pər\ *n* : one that damps; *esp* : a valve or movable plate (as in the flue of a stove, furnace, or fireplace) to regulate the draft

dam·sel \'dam-zəl\ *n* : MAIDEN, GIRL

dam·sel·fly \-ˌflī\ *n* : any of a group of insects that are closely related to the dragonflies but fold their wings above the body when at rest

dam·son \'dam-zən\ *n* : a plum with acid purple fruit; *also* : its fruit

Dan *abbr* Daniel

¹**dance** \'dans\ *vb* **danced; danc·ing** **1** : to glide, step, or move through a set series of movements usu. to music **2** : to move quickly up and down or about **3** : to perform or take part in as a dancer — **danc·er** *n*

²**dance** *n* **1** : an act or instance of dancing **2** : a social gathering for dancing **3** : a piece of music (as a waltz) by which dancing may be guided **4** : the art of dancing

D & C *n* [*d*ilation *and c*urettage] : a surgical procedure used to test for cancer of the uterus or to perform an abortion that involves stretching the opening of the uterus and scraping the inside walls

dan·de·li·on \'dan-də-ˌlī-ən, -dē-\ *n* [MF *dent de lion,* lit., lion's tooth] : any of a genus of common yellow-flowered composite herbs

dan·der \'dan-dər\ *n* : ANGER, TEMPER

dan·di·fy \'dan-di-ˌfī\ *vb* **-fied; -fy·ing** : to cause to resemble a dandy

dan·dle \'dand-ᵊl\ *vb* **dan·dled; dan·dling** : to move up and down in one's arms or on one's knee in affectionate play **syn** caress, fondle, love, pet

dan·druff \'dan-drəf\ *n* : a whitish scurf on the scalp that comes off in small scales — **dan·druffy** \-drə-fē\ *adj*

¹**dan·dy** \'dan-dē\ *n, pl* **dandies** **1** : a man unduly attentive to personal appearance **2** : something excellent in its class **syn** fop, coxcomb, popinjay

²**dandy** *adj* **dan·di·er; -est** : very good : FIRST-RATE

Dane \'dān\ *n* **1** : a native or inhabitant of Denmark **2** : GREAT DANE

dan·ger \'dān-jər\ *n* **1** : exposure or liability to injury, harm, or evil **2** : something that may cause injury or harm **syn** peril, hazard, risk, jeopardy

dan·ger·ous \'dān-jə-rəs\ *adj* **1** : HAZARDOUS, PERILOUS **2** : able or likely to inflict injury — **dan·ger·ous·ly** *adv*

dan·gle \'daŋ-gəl\ *vb* **dan·gled; dan·gling** **1** : to hang loosely esp. with a swinging motion : SWING **2** : to be

a hanger-on or dependent **3** : to be left without proper grammatical connection in a sentence **4** : to keep hanging uncertainly **5** : to offer as an inducement

Dan·iel \'dan-yəl\ *n* — see BIBLE table

Dan·ish \'dā-nish\ *n* : the language of the Danes — **Danish** *adj*

Danish pastry *n* : a pastry made of a rich yeast-raised dough

dank \'daŋk\ *adj* : disagreeably wet or moist : DAMP — **dank·ness** *n*

dan·seuse \dänⁿ-'sərz, -'səz; dän-'süz\ *n* [F] : a female ballet dancer

dap·per \'da-pər\ *adj* **1** : SPRUCE, TRIM **2** : being alert and lively in movement and manners : JAUNTY

dap·ple \'da-pəl\ *vb* **dap·pled; dap·pling** : to mark with different-colored spots

DAR *abbr* Daughters of the American Revolution

¹**dare** \'dar\ *vb* **dared; dar·ing** **1** : to have sufficient courage : be bold enough to **2** : CHALLENGE **3** : to confront boldly

²**dare** *n* : an act or instance of daring : CHALLENGE

dare·dev·il \-ˌde-vəl\ *n* : a recklessly bold person

dar·ing \'dar-iŋ\ *n* : venturesome boldness — **daring** *adj* — **dar·ing·ly** *adv*

¹**dark** \'därk\ *adj* **1** : being without light or without much light **2** : not light in color ⟨a ~ suit⟩ **3** : GLOOMY **4** *often cap* : being a period of stagnation or decline ⟨the *Dark* Ages⟩ **5** : SECRETIVE **syn** dim, dusky, murky, tenebrous — **dark·ly** *adv* — **dark·ness** *n*

²**dark** *n* **1** : absence of light : DARKNESS; *esp* : NIGHT **2** : a dark or deep color — **in the dark 1** : in secrecy **2** : in ignorance

dark·en \'där-kən\ *vb* **1** : to make or grow dark or darker **2** : DIM **3** : BESMIRCH, TARNISH **4** : to make or become gloomy or forbidding

dark horse *n* : a contestant or a political figure whose abilities and chances as a contender are not known

dark·ling \'där-kliŋ\ *adj* **1** : DARK ⟨a ~ plain⟩ **2** : MYSTERIOUS

dark·room \'därk-ˌrüm, -ˌrum\ *n* : a lightproof room in which photographic materials are processed

¹**dar·ling** \'där-liŋ\ *n* **1** : a dearly loved person **2** : FAVORITE

²**darling** *adj* **1** : dearly loved : FAVORITE **2** : very pleasing : CHARMING

darn \'därn\ *vb* : to mend with interlacing stitches — **darn·er** *n*

darning needle *n* **1** : a needle for darning **2** : DRAGONFLY

¹**dart** \'därt\ *n* **1** : a small missile with a point on one end and feathers on the other; *also, pl* : a game in which darts are thrown at a target **2** : something causing a sudden pain **3** : a stitched tapering fold in a garment **4** : a quick movement

²**dart** *vb* **1** : to throw with a sudden movement **2** : to thrust or move suddenly or rapidly **3** : to shoot with a dart containing a usu. tranquilizing drug

dart·er \'där-tər\ *n* : any of numerous small American freshwater fishes related to the perches

Dar·win·ism \'där-wə-ˌni-zəm\ *n* : a theory explaining the origin and continued existence of new species of plants and animals by means of natural selection acting on chance variations — **Dar·win·ist** \-nist\ *n or adj*

¹**dash** \'dash\ *vb* **1** : SMASH **2** : to knock, hurl, or thrust violently **3** : SPLASH, SPATTER **4** : RUIN **5** : DEPRESS, SADDEN **6** : to perform or finish hastily **7** : to move with sudden speed

²**dash** *n* **1** : a sudden burst or splash **2** : a stroke of a pen **3** : a punctuation mark — that is used esp. to indicate a break in the thought or structure of a sentence **4** : a small addition ⟨a ~ of salt⟩ **5** : flashy showiness **6** : animation in style and action **7** : a sudden rush or attempt ⟨made a ~ for the door⟩ **8** : a short foot race **9** : DASHBOARD

dash·board \-ˌbōrd\ *n* : a panel in an automobile or

aircraft below the windshield usu. containing dials and controls

dash·er \'da-shər\ *n* : a device (as in a churn) for agitating something

da·shi·ki \də-'shē-kē\ *or* **dai·shi·ki** \dī-\ *n* [modif. of Yoruba (an African language) *dàŋ́síkí*] : a usu. brightly colored loose-fitting pullover garment

dash·ing \'da-shiŋ\ *adj* **1** : marked by vigorous action **2** : marked by smartness esp. in dress and manners **syn** stylish, chic, fashionable, modish, smart, swank

das·tard \'das-tərd\ *n* **1** : COWARD **2** : a person who acts treacherously — **das·tard·ly** *adj*

dat *abbr* dative

da·ta \'dā-tə, 'da-, 'dä-\ *n sing or pl* [L, pl. of *datum*] : factual information (as measurements or statistics) used as a basis for reasoning, discussion, or calculation

da·ta·base \-ˌbās\ *n* : a usu. large collection of data organized esp. for rapid search and retrieval (as by a computer)

data processing *n* : the action or process of supplying a computer with information and having the computer use it to produce a desired result

¹date \'dāt\ *n* [ME, fr. OF, ultim. fr. L *dactylus*, fr. Gk *daktylos*, lit., finger] : the edible fruit of a tall Old World palm; *also* : this palm

²date *n* [ME, fr. MF, fr. LL *data*, fr. *data* (as in *data Romae* given at Rome), fem. of L *datus*, pp. of *dare* to give] **1** : the day, month, or year of an event **2** : a statement giving the time of execution or making (as of a coin or check) **3** : the period to which something belongs **4** : APPOINTMENT; *esp* : a social engagement between two persons that often has a romantic character **5** : a person with whom one has a usu. romantic date — **to date** : up to the present moment

³date *vb* **dat·ed; dat·ing** **1** : to record the date of or on **2** : to determine, mark, or reveal the date, age, or period of **3** : to make or have a date with **4** : ORIGINATE ⟨~s from ancient times⟩ **5** : EXTEND ⟨dating back to childhood⟩ **6** : to show qualities typical of a past period

dat·ed \'dā-təd\ *adj* **1** : provided with a date **2** : OLD-FASHIONED **syn** antiquated, archaic, old hat, outdated, outmoded, passé

date·less \'dāt-ləs\ *adj* **1** : ENDLESS **2** : having no date **3** : too ancient to be dated **4** : TIMELESS

date·line \'dāt-ˌlīn\ *n* : a line in a publication giving the date and place of composition or issue — **dateline** *vb*

da·tive \'dā-tiv\ *adj* : of, relating to, or constituting a grammatical case marking typically the indirect object of a verb — **dative** *n*

da·tum \'dā-təm, 'da-, 'dä-\ *n, pl* **da·ta** \-tə\ *or* **datums** : a single piece of data : FACT

dau *abbr* daughter

¹daub \'dob\ *vb* **1** : to cover with soft adhesive matter **2** : SMEAR, SMUDGE **3** : to paint crudely — **daub·er** *n*

²daub *n* **1** : something daubed on : SMEAR **2** : a crude picture

daugh·ter \'do-tər\ *n* **1** : a female offspring esp. of human beings **2** : a human female having a specified ancestor or belonging to a group of common ancestry — **daughter** *adj*

daugh·ter–in–law \'do-tə-rən-ˌlo\ *n, pl* **daugh·ters–in–law** \-tər-zən-\ : the wife of one's son

daunt \'dont\ *vb* [ME, fr. OF *danter*, alter. of *donter*, fr. L *domitare* to tame] : to lessen the courage of : INTIMIDATE, OVERWHELM

daunt·less \-ləs\ *adj* : FEARLESS, UNDAUNTED **syn** brave, bold, courageous, lionhearted — **daunt·less·ly** *adv*

dau·phin \'do-fən\ *n, often cap* : the eldest son of a king of France

DAV *abbr* Disabled American Veterans

dav·en·port \'da-vən-ˌpōrt\ *n* : a large upholstered sofa

da·vit \'dā-vət, 'da-\ *n* : a small crane on a ship used in pairs esp. to raise or lower boats

daw·dle \'dod-əl\ *vb* **daw·dled; daw·dling** **1** : to spend time wastefully or idly **2** : LOITER — **daw·dler** *n*

¹dawn \'don\ *vb* **1** : to begin to grow light as the sun rises **2** : to begin to appear or develop **3** : to begin to be understood ⟨the solution ~ed on him⟩

²dawn *n* **1** : the first appearance of light in the morning **2** : a first appearance : BEGINNING ⟨the ~ of a new era⟩

day \'dā\ *n* **1** : the period of light between one night and the next; *also* : DAYLIGHT **2** : the period of rotation of a planet (as earth) or a moon on its axis **3** : a period of 24 hours beginning at midnight **4** : a specified day or date ⟨wedding ~⟩ **5** : a specified time or period : AGE (in olden ~s) **6** : the conflict or contention of the day **7** : the time set apart by usage or law for work ⟨the 8-hour ~⟩

day·bed \'dā-ˌbed\ *n* : a couch that can be converted into a bed

day·book \-ˌbùk\ *n* : DIARY, JOURNAL

day·break \-ˌbrāk\ *n* : DAWN

day care *n* : supervision of and care for children or disabled adults provided during the day; *also* : a program offering day care

day·dream \'dā-ˌdrēm\ *n* : a pleasant reverie — **daydream** *vb*

day·light \'dā-ˌlīt\ *n* **1** : the light of day **2** : DAYTIME **3** : DAWN **4** : understanding of something that has been obscure **5** *pl* : CONSCIOUSNESS; *also* : WITS **6** : an opening or opportunity esp. for action

daylight saving time *n* : time usu. one hour ahead of standard time

Day of Atonement : YOM KIPPUR

day school *n* : a private school without boarding facilities

day student *n* : a student who attends regular classes at a college or preparatory school but does not live there

day·time \'dā-ˌtīm\ *n* : the period of daylight

daze \'dāz\ *vb* **dazed; daz·ing** **1** : to stupefy esp. by a blow **2** : DAZZLE — **daze** *n* — **da·zed·ly** \'dā-zəd-lē\ *adv*

daz·zle \'da-zəl\ *vb* **daz·zled; daz·zling** **1** : to overpower with light **2** : to impress greatly or confound with brilliance — **dazzle** *n*

dB *abbr* decibel

d/b/a *abbr* doing business as

dbl *or* **dble** *abbr* double

DC *abbr* **1** [It *da capo*] from the beginning **2** direct current **3** District of Columbia **4** doctor of chiropractic

DD *abbr* **1** days after date **2** demand draft **3** dishonorable discharge **4** doctor of divinity

D day *n* [*D*, abbr. for *day*] : a day set for launching an operation (as an invasion)

DDS *abbr* doctor of dental surgery

DDT \ˌdē-(ˌ)dē-'tē\ *n* : a persistent insecticide poisonous to many higher animals

DE *abbr* Delaware

dea·con \'dē-kən\ *n* [ME *dekene*, fr. OE *dēacon*, fr. LL *diaconus*, fr. Gk *diakonos*, lit., servant] : a subordinate officer in a Christian church

dea·con·ess \'dē-kə-nəs\ *n* : a woman chosen to assist in the church ministry

de·ac·ti·vate \dē-'ak-tə-ˌvāt\ *vb* : to make inactive or ineffective

¹dead \'ded\ *adj* **1** : LIFELESS **2** : DEATHLIKE, DEADLY (in a ~ faint) **3** : NUMB **4** : very tired **5** : UNRESPONSIVE **6** : EXTINGUISHED ⟨~ coals⟩ **7** : INANIMATE, INERT **8** : no longer active or functioning ⟨a ~ battery⟩ **9** : lacking power, significance, or effect ⟨a ~ custom⟩ **10** : OBSOLETE ⟨a ~ language⟩ **11** : lacking in gaiety or animation ⟨a ~ party⟩ **12** : QUIET, IDLE, UNPRODUCTIVE ⟨~ capital⟩ **13** : lacking elasticity ⟨a ~ tennis ball⟩ **14** : not circulating : STAGNANT ⟨~ air⟩ **15** : lacking warmth, vigor, or taste ⟨~ wine⟩ **16** : absolutely uniform ⟨∼ level⟩ **17** : UNERRING, EXACT ⟨a ∼ shot⟩ **18** : ABRUPT ⟨a ∼ stop⟩ **19** : COMPLETE ⟨a ∼ loss⟩

²**dead** *n, pl* **dead 1** : one that is dead — usu. used collectively ⟨the living and the ∼⟩ **2** : the time of greatest quiet ⟨the ∼ of the night⟩

³**dead** *adv* **1** : UTTERLY ⟨∼ right⟩ **2** : in a sudden and complete manner ⟨stopped ∼⟩ **3** : DIRECTLY ⟨∼ ahead⟩

dead•beat \-₁bēt\ *n* : a person who persistently fails to pay personal debts or expenses

dead duck *n* : GONER

dead•en \'ded-ᵊn\ *vb* **1** : to impair in vigor or sensation : BLUNT ⟨∼ pain⟩ **2** : to lessen the luster or spirit of **3** : to make (as a wall) soundproof

dead end *n* **1** : an end (as of a street) without an exit **2** : a position, situation, or course of action that leads to nothing further — **dead–end** \₁ded-₁end\ *adj*

dead heat *n* : a contest in which two or more contestants tie (as by crossing the finish line simultaneously)

dead letter *n* **1** : something that has lost its force or authority without being formally abolished **2** : a letter that cannot be delivered or returned

dead•line \'ded-₁līn\ *n* : a date or time before which something must be done

dead•lock \'ded-₁läk\ *n* : a stoppage of action because neither faction in a struggle will give in — **deadlock** *vb*

¹**dead•ly** \'ded-lē\ *adj* **dead•li•er; -est 1** : likely to cause or capable of causing death **2** : HOSTILE, IMPLACABLE **3** : very accurate : UNERRING **4** : tending to deprive of force or vitality ⟨a ∼ habit⟩ **5** : suggestive of death **6** : very great : EXTREME — **dead•li•ness** *n*

²**deadly** *adv* **1** : suggesting death ⟨∼ pale⟩ **2** : EXTREMELY ⟨∼ dull⟩

deadly sin *n* : one of seven sins of pride, covetousness, lust, anger, gluttony, envy, and sloth held to be fatal to spiritual progress

¹**dead•pan** \'ded-₁pan\ *adj* : marked by an impassive manner or expression — **deadpan** *vb* — **deadpan** *adv*

²**deadpan** *n* : a completely expressionless face

dead reckoning *n* : the determination of the position of a ship or aircraft solely from the record of the direction and distance of its course

dead•weight \'ded-'wāt\ *n* **1** : the unrelieved weight of an inert mass **2** : a ship's load including the weight of cargo, fuel, crew, and passengers

dead•wood \-₁wùd\ *n* **1** : wood dead on the tree **2** : useless personnel or material

deaf \'def\ *adj* **1** : unable to hear **2** : unwilling to hear or listen ⟨∼ to all suggestions⟩ — **deaf•ness** *n*

deaf•en \'de-fən\ *vb* : to make deaf

deaf–mute \'def-₁myüt\ *n* : a deaf person who has never learned to speak

¹**deal** \'dēl\ *n* **1** : a usu. large or indefinite quantity or degree ⟨a great ∼ of support⟩ **2** : the act or right of distributing cards to players in a card game; *also* : HAND

²**deal** *vb* **dealt** \'delt\; **deal•ing 1** : DISTRIBUTE; *esp* : to distribute playing cards to players in a game **2** : ADMINISTER, DELIVER ⟨*dealt* him a blow⟩ **3** : to concern itself : TREAT ⟨the book ∼s with crime⟩ **4** : to take action in regard to something ⟨∼ with offenders⟩ **5** : TRADE; *also* : to sell or distribute something as a business ⟨∼ in used cars⟩ **6** : to reach a state of acceptance ⟨∼ with her child's death⟩ — **deal•er** *n*

³**deal** *n* **1** : BARGAINING, NEGOTIATION; *also* : TRANSACTION **2** : treatment received ⟨a raw ∼⟩ **3** : an often secret agreement or arrangement for mutual advantage **4** : BARGAIN

⁴**deal** *n* : wood or a board of fir or pine

deal•er•ship \'dē-lər-₁ship\ *n* : an authorized sales agency

deal•ing \'dē-liŋ\ *n* **1** : a way of acting or of doing business **2** *pl* : friendly or business transactions

dean \'dēn\ *n* [ME *deen*, fr. MF *deien*, fr. LL *decanus*, lit., chief of ten, fr. *decem* ten, fr. Gk *dekanos*, fr. *deka* ten] **1** : a clergyman who is head of a group of canons or of joint pastors of a church **2** : the head of a division, faculty, college, or school of a university **3** : a college or secondary school administrator in charge of counseling and disciplining students **4** : DOYEN ⟨the ∼ of a diplomatic corps⟩ — **dean•ship** *n*

dean•ery \'dē-nə-rē\ *n, pl* **-er•ies** : the office, jurisdiction, or official residence of a clerical dean

¹**dear** \'dir\ *adj* **1** : highly valued : PRECIOUS **2** : AFFECTIONATE, FOND **3** : EXPENSIVE **4** : HEARTFELT — **dear•ly** *adv* — **dear•ness** *n*

²**dear** *n* : a loved one : DARLING

Dear John \-'jän\ *n* : a letter (as to a soldier) in which a woman breaks off a marital or romantic relationship

dearth \'dərth\ *n* **1** : SCARCITY, FAMINE

death \'deth\ *n* **1** : the end of life **2** : the cause of loss of life **3** : the state of being dead **4** : DESTRUCTION, EXTINCTION **5** : SLAUGHTER — **death•like** *adj*

death•bed \-₁bed\ *n* **1** : the bed in which a person dies **2** : the last hours of life

death•blow \-₁blō\ *n* : a destructive or killing stroke or event

death•less \-ləs\ *adj* : IMMORTAL, IMPERISHABLE ⟨∼ fame⟩

death•ly \-lē\ *adj* **1** : FATAL **2** : of, relating to, or suggestive of death ⟨a ∼ pallor⟩ — **deathly** *adv*

death rattle *n* : a sound produced by air passing through mucus in the lungs and air passages of a dying person

death's–head \'deths-₁hed\ *n* : a human skull emblematic of death

death•watch \'deth-₁wäch\ *n* : a vigil kept over the dead or dying

deb \'deb\ *n* : DEBUTANTE

de•ba•cle \di-'bä-kəl, -'ba-\ *also* **dé•bâ•cle** \ *same or* dā-'bäk\ *n* [F *débâcle*] : DISASTER, FAILURE, ROUT ⟨stock market ∼⟩

de•bar \di-'bär\ *vb* : to bar from having or doing something : PRECLUDE

de•bark \di-'bärk\ *vb* : DISEMBARK — **de•bar•ka•tion** \₁dē-₁bär-'kā-shən\

de•base \di-'bās\ *vb* : to lower in character, quality, or value **syn** degrade, corrupt, deprave — **de•base•ment** *n*

de•bate \di-'bāt\ *vb* **de•bat•ed; de•bat•ing 1** : to discuss a question by considering opposed arguments **2** : to take part in a debate — **de•bat•able** *adj* — **debate** *n* — **de•bat•er** *n*

de•bauch \di-'bóch\ *vb* : SEDUCE, CORRUPT **syn** debase, demoralize, deprave, pervert — **de•bauch•ery** \-'bó-chə-rē\ *n*

de•ben•ture \di-'ben-chər\ *n* : BOND; *esp* : one secured by the general credit of the issuer rather than a lien on particular assets

de•bil•i•tate \di-'bi-lə-₁tāt\ *vb* **-tat•ed; -tat•ing** : to impair the health or strength of **syn** weaken, disable, enfeeble, undermine

de•bil•i•ty \di-'bi-lə-tē\ *n, pl* **-ties** : an infirm or weakened state

¹**deb•it** \'de-bət\ *vb* : to enter as a debit : charge with or as a debit

²**debit** *n* **1** : an entry in an account showing money paid out or owed **2** : DISADVANTAGE, SHORTCOMING

debit card *n* : a card by which money may be withdrawn or the cost of purchases paid directly from the holder's bank account

deb•o•nair \₁de-bə-'nar\ *adj* [ME *debonere*, fr. OF *debonaire*, fr. *de bon aire* of good family or nature] : SUAVE, URBANE; *also* : LIGHTHEARTED

de•bouch \di-'baùch, -'büsh\ *vb* [F *déboucher*, fr. *dé*- out of + *bouche* mouth] : to come out into an open area : EMERGE

de•brief \di-'brēf\ *vb* : to question (as a pilot back from a mission) in order to obtain useful information

de·bris \də-ˈbrē, dā-; ˈdā-ˌbrē\ *n, pl* **debris** \-ˈbrēz, -ˌbrēz\ **1** : the remains of something broken down or destroyed **2** : an accumulation of rock fragments **3** : RUBBISH

debt \ˈdet\ *n* **1** : SIN, TRESPASS **2** : something owed : OBLIGATION **3** : a condition of owing

debt·or \ˈde-tər\ *n* **1** : one guilty of neglect or violation of duty **2** : one that owes a debt

de·bug \ˌ)dē-ˈbəg\ *vb* : to eliminate errors in

de·bunk \dē-ˈbəŋk\ *vb* : to expose the sham or falseness of ⟨∼ a legend⟩

¹de·but \ˈdā-ˌbyü, dā-ˈbyü\ *n* **1** : a first appearance **2** : a formal entrance into society

²debut *vb* : to make a debut; *also* : INTRODUCE

deb·u·tante \ˈde-byü-ˌtänt\ *n* : a young woman making her formal entrance into society

dec *abbr* **1** deceased **2** decrease

Dec *abbr* December

de·cade \ˈde-ˌkād, de-ˈkād\ *n* : a period of 10 years

dec·a·dence \ˈde-kə-dəns, di-ˈkād-ᵊns\ *n* : DETERIORATION, DECLINE — **dec·a·dent** \ˈde-kə-dənt, di-ˈkād-ᵊnt\ *adj or n*

de·caf \ˈdē-ˌkaf\ *n* : decaffeinated coffee

de·caf·fein·at·ed \ˌ)dē-ˈka-fə-nā-təd\ *adj* : having the caffeine removed ⟨∼ coffee⟩

deca·gon \ˈde-kə-ˌgän\ *n* : a plane polygon of 10 angles and 10 sides

de·cal \ˈdē-ˌkal\ *n* : a picture, design, or label made to be transferred (as to glass) from specially prepared paper

de·cal·co·ma·nia \di-ˌkal-kə-ˈmā-nē-ə\ *n* [F *décalcomanie*, fr. *décalquer* to copy by tracing (fr. *calquer* to trace, fr. It *calcare*, lit., to tread, fr. L) + *manie* mania, fr. LL *mania*] : DECAL

Deca·logue \ˈde-kə-ˌlȯg\ *n* : TEN COMMANDMENTS

de·camp \di-ˈkamp\ *vb* **1** : to break up a camp **2** : to depart suddenly **syn** escape, abscond, flee

de·cant \di-ˈkant\ *vb* : to pour (as wine) gently from one vessel into another

de·cant·er \di-ˈkan-tər\ *n* : an ornamental glass bottle for serving wine

de·cap·i·tate \di-ˈka-pə-ˌtāt\ *vb* **-tat·ed; -tat·ing** : BEHEAD — **de·cap·i·ta·tion** \-ˌka-pə-ˈtā-shən\ *n* — **de·cap·i·ta·tor** \-ˈka-pə-ˌtā-tər\ *n*

deca·syl·lab·ic \ˌde-kə-sə-ˈla-bik\ *adj* : having or composed of verses having 10 syllables — **decasyllabic** *n*

de·cath·lon \di-ˈkath-lən, -ˌlän\ *n* : a 10-event athletic contest

de·cay \di-ˈkā\ *vb* **1** : to decline from a sound or prosperous condition **2** : to cause or undergo decomposition ⟨radium ∼s slowly⟩; *esp* : to break down while spoiling : ROT — **decay** *n*

decd *abbr* deceased

de·cease \di-ˈsēs\ *n* : DEATH

¹de·ceased \-ˈsēst\ *adj* : no longer living; *esp* : recently dead

²deceased *n, pl* **deceased** : a dead person

²de·ce·dent \di-ˈsēd-ᵊnt\ *n* : a deceased person

de·ceit \di-ˈsēt\ *n* **1** : DECEPTION **2** : TRICK **3** : DECEITFULNESS **syn** dissimulation, duplicity, guile

de·ceit·ful \-fəl\ *adj* **1** : practicing or tending to practice deceit **2** : MISLEADING, DECEPTIVE ⟨a ∼ answer⟩ — **de·ceit·ful·ly** *adv* — **de·ceit·ful·ness** *n*

de·ceive \di-ˈsēv\ *vb* **de·ceived; de·ceiv·ing** **1** : to cause to believe an untruth **2** : to use or practice deceit **syn** beguile, betray, delude, mislead — **de·ceiv·er** *n*

de·cel·er·ate \dē-ˈse-lə-ˌrāt\ *vb* **-at·ed; -at·ing** : to slow down

De·cem·ber \di-ˈsem-bər\ *n* [ME *Decembre*, fr. OF, fr. L *December* (tenth month), fr. *decem* ten] : the 12th month of the year having 31 days

de·cen·cy \ˈdēs-ᵊn-sē\ *n, pl* **-cies** **1** : PROPRIETY **2** : conformity to standards of taste, propriety, or quality **3** : standard of propriety — usu. used in pl.

de·cen·ni·al \di-ˈse-nē-əl\ *adj* **1** : consisting of 10 years **2** : happening every 10 years ⟨∼ census⟩

de·cent \ˈdēs-ᵊnt\ *adj* **1** : conforming to standards of propriety, good taste, or morality **2** : modestly clothed **3** : free from immodesty or obscenity **4** : ADEQUATE ⟨∼ housing⟩ — **de·cent·ly** *adv*

de·cen·tral·i·za·tion \dē-ˌsen-trə-lə-ˈzā-shən\ *n* **1** : the distribution of powers from a central authority to regional and local authorities **2** : the redistribution of population and industry from urban centers to outlying areas — **de·cen·tral·ize** \-ˈsen-trə-ˌlīz\ *vb*

de·cep·tion \di-ˈsep-shən\ *n* **1** : the act of deceiving **2** : the fact or condition of being deceived **3** : FRAUD, TRICK — **de·cep·tive** \-ˈsep-tiv\ *adj* — **de·cep·tive·ly** *adv* — **de·cep·tive·ness** *n*

deci·bel \ˈde-sə-ˌbel, -bəl\ *n* : a unit for measuring the relative loudness of sounds

de·cide \di-ˈsīd\ *vb* **de·cid·ed; de·cid·ing** [ME, fr. MF *decider*, fr. L *decidere*, lit., to cut off, fr. *de-* off + *caedere* to cut] **1** : to arrive at a solution that ends uncertainty or dispute about **2** : to bring to a definitive end ⟨one blow *decided* the fight⟩ **3** : to induce to come to a choice **4** : to make a choice or judgment

de·cid·ed \di-ˈsī-dəd\ *adj* **1** : UNQUESTIONABLE **2** : FIRM, DETERMINED — **de·cid·ed·ly** *adv*

de·cid·u·ous \di-ˈsi-jə-wəs\ *adj* **1** : falling off or out usu. at the end of a period of growth or function ⟨∼ leaves⟩ ⟨a ∼ tooth⟩ **2** : having deciduous parts ⟨∼ trees⟩

deci·gram \ˈde-sə-ˌgram\ *n* — see METRIC SYSTEM table

deci·li·ter \-ˌlē-tər\ *n* — see METRIC SYSTEM table

¹dec·i·mal \ˈde-sə-məl\ *adj* : based on the number 10 : reckoning by tens

²decimal *n* : any number expressed in base 10; *esp* : DECIMAL FRACTION

decimal fraction *n* : a fraction (as .25 = $^{25}/_{100}$ or .025 = $^{25}/_{1000}$) or mixed number (as 3.025 = 3 $^{25}/_{1000}$) in which the denominator is a power of 10 usu. expressed by use of the decimal point

decimal point *n* : a period, centered dot, or in some countries a comma at the left of a decimal fraction (as .678) less than one or between a whole number and a decimal fraction in a mixed number (as 3.678)

dec·i·mate \ˈde-sə-ˌmāt\ *vb* **-mat·ed; -mat·ing** **1** : to take or destroy the 10th part of **2** : to destroy a large part of

dec·i·me·ter \ˈde-sə-ˌmē-tər\ *n* — see METRIC SYSTEM table

de·ci·pher \di-ˈsī-fər\ *vb* **1** : DECODE **2** : to make out the meaning of despite indistinctness — **de·ci·pher·able** *adj*

de·ci·sion \di-ˈsi-zhən\ *n* **1** : the act or result of deciding **2** : promptness and firmness in deciding : DETERMINATION

de·ci·sive \-ˈsī-siv\ *adj* **1** : having the power to decide ⟨the ∼ vote⟩ **2** : RESOLUTE, DETERMINED **3** : CONCLUSIVE ⟨a ∼ victory⟩ — **de·ci·sive·ly** *adv* — **de·ci·sive·ness** *n*

¹deck \ˈdek\ *n* **1** : a floorlike platform of a ship; *also* : something resembling the deck of a ship **2** : a pack of playing cards

²deck *vb* **1** : ARRAY **2** : DECORATE **3** : to furnish with a deck **4** : KNOCK DOWN, FLOOR

deck·hand \ˈdek-ˌhand\ *n* : a sailor who performs manual duties

deck·le edge \ˈdek-əl-\ *n* : the rough untrimmed edge of paper — **deck·le-edged** \-ˈejd\ *adj*

de·claim \di-ˈklām\ *vb* : to speak or deliver in the manner of a formal speech — **dec·la·ma·tion** \ˌde-klə-ˈmā-shən\ *n* — **de·clam·a·to·ry** \di-ˈkla-mə-ˌtōr-ē\ *adj*

de·clar·a·tive \di-ˈklar-ə-tiv\ *adj* : making a declaration ⟨∼ sentence⟩

de·clare \di-ˈklar\ *vb* **de·clared; de·clar·ing** **1** : to make known formally, officially, or explicitly : ANNOUNCE ⟨∼ war⟩ **2** : to state emphatically : AFFIRM **3** : to make a full statement of **syn** blazon, broadcast, proclaim, publish — **dec·la·ra·tion** \ˌde-klə-ˈrā-shən\ n — **de·clar·a·to·ry** \di-ˈklar-ə-ˌtōr-ē\ adj — **de·clar·er** n

de·clas·si·fy \dē-ˈkla-sə-ˌfī\ vb : to remove the security classification of — **de·clas·si·fi·ca·tion** \-ˌkla-sə-fə-ˈkā-shən\ n

de·clen·sion \di-ˈklen-chən\ n **1** : the inflectional forms of a noun, pronoun, or adjective **2** : DECLINE, DETERIORATION **3** : DESCENT, SLOPE

¹**de·cline** \di-ˈklīn\ vb **de·clined; de·clin·ing 1** : to slope downward : DESCEND **2** : DROOP **3** : RECEDE **4** : WANE **5** : to withhold consent; also : REFUSE, REJECT **6** : INFLECT **2** ⟨~ a noun⟩ — **de·clin·able** adj — **dec·li·na·tion** \ˌde-klə-ˈnā-shən\ n

²**decline** n **1** : a gradual sinking and wasting away **2** : a change to a lower state or level **3** : the time when something is approaching its end **4** : a descending slope

de·cliv·i·ty \di-ˈkli-və-tē\ n, pl -**ties** : a steep downward slope

de·code \dē-ˈkōd\ vb : to convert (a coded message) into ordinary language — **de·cod·er** n

dé·col·le·té \dā-ˌkäl-ˈtā\ adj [F] **1** : wearing a strapless or low-necked gown **2** : having a low-cut neckline

de·com·mis·sion \ˌdē-kə-ˈmi-shən\ vb : to remove from service

de·com·pose \ˌdē-kəm-ˈpōz\ vb **1** : to separate into constituent parts **2** : to break down in decay : ROT — **de·com·po·si·tion** \dē-ˌkäm-pə-ˈzi-shən\ n

de·com·press \ˌdē-kəm-ˈpres\ vb : to release from pressure or compression — **de·com·pres·sion** \-ˈpre-shən\ n

de·con·ges·tant \ˌdē-kən-ˈjes-tənt\ n : an agent that relieves congestion (as of mucous membranes)

de·con·tam·i·nate \ˌdē-kən-ˈta-mə-ˌnāt\ vb : to rid of contamination (as radioactive material) — **de·con·tam·i·na·tion** \-ˌta-mə-ˈnā-shən\ n

de·con·trol \ˌdē-kən-ˈtrōl\ vb : to end control of ⟨~ prices⟩ — **decontrol** n

de·cor or **dé·cor** \dā-ˈkȯr, ˈdā-ˌkȯr\ n : DECORATION; esp : the style and layout of interior furnishings

dec·o·rate \ˈde-kə-ˌrāt\ vb **-rat·ed; -rat·ing 1** : to furnish with something ornamental ⟨~ a room⟩ **2** : to award a mark of honor (as a medal) to **syn** adorn, beautify, bedeck, garnish, ornament

dec·o·ra·tion \ˌde-kə-ˈrā-shən\ n **1** : the act or process of decorating **2** : ORNAMENT **3** : a badge of honor

dec·o·ra·tive \ˈde-kə-rə-tiv\ adj : ORNAMENTAL

dec·o·ra·tor \ˈde-kə-ˌrā-tər\ n : one that decorates; esp : a person who designs or executes interiors and their furnishings

dec·o·rous \ˈde-kə-rəs, di-ˈkȯr-əs\ adj : PROPER, SEEMLY, CORRECT

de·co·rum \di-ˈkȯr-əm\ n [L] **1** : conformity to accepted standards of conduct **2** : ORDERLINESS, PROPRIETY

¹**de·coy** \ˈdē-ˌkȯi, di-ˈkȯi\ n **1** : something that lures or entices; esp : an artificial bird used to attract live birds within shot **2** : something used to draw attention away from another

²**de·coy** \di-ˈkȯi, ˈdē-ˌkȯi\ vb : to lure by or as if by a decoy : ENTICE

¹**de·crease** \di-ˈkrēs\ vb **de·creased; de·creas·ing** : to grow or cause to grow less : DIMINISH

²**de·crease** \ˈdē-ˌkrēs\ n **1** : the process of decreasing **2** : REDUCTION

¹**de·cree** \di-ˈkrē\ n **1** : ORDER, EDICT **2** : a judicial decision

²**decree** vb **de·creed; de·cree·ing 1** : COMMAND **2** : to determine or order judicially **syn** dictate, ordain, prescribe

dec·re·ment \ˈde-krə-mənt\ n **1** : gradual decrease **2** : the quantity lost by diminution or waste

de·crep·it \di-ˈkre-pət\ adj : broken down with age : WORN-OUT — **de·crep·i·tude** \-pə-ˌtüd, -ˌtyüd\ n

de·cre·scen·do \ˌdā-krə-ˈshen-dō\ adv or adj : with a decrease in volume — used as a direction in music

de·crim·i·nal·ize \dē-ˈkri-mən-ᵊl-ˌīz\ vb : to remove or reduce the criminal status of

de·cry \di-ˈkrī\ vb : to express strong disapproval of

ded·i·cate \ˈde-di-ˌkāt\ vb **-cat·ed; -cat·ing 1** : to devote to the worship of a divine being esp. with sacred rites **2** : to set apart for a definite purpose **3** : to inscribe or address as a compliment — **ded·i·ca·tion** \ˌde-di-ˈkā-shən\ n — **ded·i·ca·tor** \ˈde-di-ˌkā-tər\ n — **ded·i·ca·to·ry** \-kə-ˌtōr-ē\ adj

de·duce \di-ˈdüs, -ˈdyüs\ vb **de·duced; de·duc·ing 1** : to derive by reasoning : INFER **2** : to trace the course of — **de·duc·ible** adj

de·duct \di-ˈdəkt\ vb : SUBTRACT — **de·duct·ible** adj

de·duc·tion \di-ˈdək-shən\ n **1** : SUBTRACTION **2** : something that is or may be subtracted **3** : the deriving of a conclusion by reasoning : the conclusion so reached — **de·duc·tive** \-ˈdək-tiv\ adj — **de·duc·tive·ly** adv

¹**deed** \ˈdēd\ n **1** : something done **2** : FEAT, EXPLOIT **3** : a document containing some legal transfer, bargain, or contract

²**deed** vb : to convey or transfer by deed

dee·jay \ˈdē-ˌjā\ n : DISC JOCKEY

deem \ˈdēm\ vb : THINK, JUDGE **syn** consider, account, reckon, regard, view

de-em·pha·size \dē-ˈem-fə-ˌsīz\ vb : to reduce in relative importance; also : to attach little importance to — **de-em·pha·sis** \-səs\ n

¹**deep** \ˈdēp\ adj **1** : extending far down, back, within, or outward **2** : having a specified extension downward or backward **3** : difficult to understand; also : MYSTERIOUS, OBSCURE ⟨a ~ dark secret⟩ **4** : WISE **5** : ENGROSSED, INVOLVED ⟨~ in thought⟩ **6** : INTENSE, PROFOUND ⟨~ sleep⟩ **7** : dark and rich in color ⟨a ~ red⟩ **8** : having a low musical pitch or range ⟨a ~ voice⟩ **9** : situated well within **10** : covered, enclosed, or filled often to a specified degree — **deep·ly** adv

²**deep** adv **1** : DEEPLY **2** : far on : LATE ⟨~ in the night⟩

³**deep** n **1** : an extremely deep place or part; esp : OCEAN **2** : the middle or most intense part ⟨the ~ of winter⟩

deep·en \ˈdē-pən\ vb : to make or become deep or deeper

deep–freeze \ˈdēp-ˈfrēz\ vb **-froze** \-ˈfrōz\; **-fro·zen** \-ˈfrōz-ᵊn\ : QUICK-FREEZE

deep–fry vb : to cook in enough oil to cover the food being fried

deep–root·ed \-ˈrü-təd, -ˈru̇-\ adj : deeply implanted or established

deep–sea \ˈdēp-ˈsē\ adj : of, relating to, or occurring in the deeper parts of the sea ⟨~ fishing⟩

deep–seat·ed \ˈdēp-ˈsē-təd\ adj **1** : situated far below the surface **2** : firmly established ⟨~ convictions⟩

deer \ˈdir\ n, pl **deer** [ME, deer, animal, fr. OE dēor beast] : any of numerous ruminant mammals with cloven hoofs and usu. antlers esp. in the males

deer·fly \-ˌflī\ n : any of numerous small horseflies

deer·skin \-ˌskin\ n : leather made from the skin of a deer; also : a garment of such leather

de-es·ca·late \dē-ˈes-kə-ˌlāt\ vb : to decrease in extent, volume, or scope : LIMIT — **de-es·ca·la·tion** \-ˌes-kə-ˈlā-shən\ n

def abbr **1** defendant **2** definite **3** definition

de·face \di-ˈfās\ vb : to destroy or mar the face or surface of — **de·face·ment** n — **de·fac·er** n

de fac·to \di-ˈfak-tō, dā-\ adj or adv **1** : actually existing ⟨de facto segregation⟩ **2** : actually exercising power ⟨de facto government⟩

de·fal·ca·tion \ˌdē-fal-ˈkā-shən, -ˈfȯl-; ˌde-fəl-\ n : EMBEZZLEMENT

de·fame \di-ˈfām\ vb **de·famed; de·fam·ing** : to injure or destroy the reputation of by libel or slander **syn** calumniate, denigrate, libel, malign, slander, vilify — **def·a·ma·tion** \ˌde-fə-ˈmā-shən\ n — **de·fam·a·to·ry** \di-ˈfa-mə-ˌtōr-ē\ adj

de·fault \di-ˈfȯlt\ n **1** : failure to do something required by duty or law; also : failure to appear for a legal proceeding **2** : failure to compete in or to finish an appointed contest ⟨lose a race by ∼⟩ — **default** *vb* — **de·fault·er** *n*

¹**de·feat** \di-ˈfēt\ *vb* **1** : FRUSTRATE, NULLIFY **2** : to win victory over : BEAT

²**defeat** *n* **1** : FRUSTRATION **2** : an overthrow of an army in battle **3** : loss of a contest

de·feat·ism \-ˈfē-ˌti-zəm\ *n* : acceptance of or resignation to defeat — **de·feat·ist** \-tist\ *n or adj*

def·e·cate \ˈde-fi-ˌkāt\ *vb* **-cat·ed; -cat·ing 1** : to free from impurity or corruption **2** : to discharge feces from the bowels — **def·e·ca·tion** \ˌde-fi-ˈkā-shən\ *n*

¹**de·fect** \ˈdē-ˌfekt, di-ˈfekt\ *n* : BLEMISH, FAULT, IMPERFECTION

²**defect** \di-ˈfekt\ *vb* : to desert a cause or party esp. in order to espouse another — **de·fec·tion** \-ˈfek-shən\ *n* — **de·fec·tor** \-ˈfek-tər\ *n*

de·fec·tive \di-ˈfek-tiv\ *adj* : FAULTY, DEFICIENT — **defective** *n*

de·fence *chiefly Brit var of* DEFENSE

defend \di-ˈfend\ *vb* [ME, fr. OF *defendre*, fr. L *defendere*, fr. *de-* from + *-fendere* to strike] **1** : to repel danger or attack from **2** : to act as attorney for **3** : to oppose the claim of another in a lawsuit : CONTEST **4** : to maintain against opposition ⟨∼ an idea⟩ — **de·fend·er** *n*

de·fen·dant \di-ˈfen-dənt\ *n* : a person required to make answer in a legal action or suit

defense \di-ˈfens\ *n* **1** : the act of defending : resistance against attack **2** : means, method, or capability of defending **3** : an argument in support **4** : the answer made by the defendant in a legal action **5** : a defending party, group, or team — **de·fense·less** *adj* — **de·fen·si·ble** *adj*

defense mechanism *n* : an often unconscious mental process (as repression) that assists in reaching compromise solutions to personal problems

¹**de·fen·sive** \di-ˈfen-siv\ *adj* **1** : serving or intended to defend or protect **2** : of or relating to the attempt to keep an opponent from scoring (as in a game) — **de·fen·sive·ly** *adv* — **de·fen·sive·ness** *n*

²**defensive** *n* : a defensive position

¹**de·fer** \di-ˈfər\ *vb* **deferred; de·fer·ring** [ME *deferren, differren*, fr. MF *differer*, fr. L *differre* to postpone, be different] : POSTPONE, PUT OFF

²**defer** *vb* **deferred; deferring** [ME *deferren, differren*, fr. MF *deferer, defferer*, fr. LL *deferre*, fr. L, to bring down, bring, fr. *de-* down + *ferre* to carry] : to submit or yield to the opinion or wishes of another

def·er·ence \ˈde-fər-əns\ *n* : courteous, respectful, or ingratiating regard for another's wishes **syn** honor, homage, obeisance, reverence — **def·er·en·tial** \ˌde-fə-ˈren-chəl\ *adj*

de·fer·ment \di-ˈfər-mənt\ *n* : the act of delaying; *esp* : official postponement of military service

de·fi·ance \di-ˈfī-əns\ *n* **1** : CHALLENGE **2** : disposition to resist or contend

de·fi·ant \-ənt\ *adj* : full of defiance : BOLD — **de·fi·ant·ly** *adv*

de·fi·bril·la·tor \dē-ˈfi-brə-ˌlā-tər\ *n* : an electronic device that applies an electric shock to restore the rhythm of a fibrillating heart — **de·fi·bril·late** \-ˌlāt\ *vb* — **de·fi·bril·la·tion** \-ˌfi-brə-ˈlā-shən\ *n*

deficiency disease *n* : a disease (as scurvy or beriberi) caused by a lack of essential dietary elements and esp. a vitamin or mineral

de·fi·cient \di-ˈfi-shənt\ *adj* : lacking in something necessary; *also* : not up to a normal standard — **de·fi·cien·cy** \-shən-sē\ *n*

def·i·cit \ˈde-fə-sət\ *n* : a deficiency in amount; *esp* : an excess of expenditures over revenue

¹**de·file** \di-ˈfīl\ *vb* **de·filed; de·fil·ing 1** : to make filthy **2** : CORRUPT **3** : to violate the chastity of **4** : to violate the sanctity of : DESECRATE **5** : DISHONOR **syn** contaminate, pollute, soil, taint — **de·file·ment** *n*

²**de·file** \di-ˈfīl, ˈdē-ˌfīl\ *n* : a narrow passage or gorge

de·fine \di-ˈfīn\ *vb* **de·fined; de·fin·ing 1** : to set forth the meaning of ⟨∼ a word⟩ **2** : to fix or mark the limits of **3** : to clarify in outline or character — **de·fin·able** *adj* — **de·fin·er** *n*

def·i·nite \ˈde-fə-nət\ *adj* **1** : having distinct limits : FIXED **2** : clear in meaning **3** : typically designating an identified or immediately identifiable person or thing — **def·i·nite·ly** *adv* — **def·i·nite·ness** *n*

def·i·ni·tion \ˌde-fə-ˈni-shən\ *n* **1** : an act of determining or settling **2** : a statement of the meaning of a word or word group; *also* : the action or process of defining **3** : the action or the power of making definite and clear : CLARITY, DISTINCTNESS

de·fin·i·tive \di-ˈfi-nə-tiv\ *adj* **1** : DECISIVE, CONCLUSIVE **2** : authoritative and apparently exhaustive **3** : serving to define or specify precisely

de·flate \di-ˈflāt\ *vb* **de·flat·ed; de·flat·ing 1** : to release air or gas from **2** : to reduce in size, importance, or effectiveness; *also* : to reduce from a state of inflation **3** : to become deflated

de·fla·tion \-ˈflā-shən\ *n* **1** : an act or instance of deflating : the state of being deflated **2** : reduction in the volume of available money or credit resulting in a decline of the general price level

de·flect \di-ˈflekt\ *vb* : to turn aside — **de·flec·tion** \-ˈflek-shən\ *n*

de·flo·ra·tion \ˌde-flə-ˈrā-shən\ *n* : rupture of the hymen

de·flow·er \dē-ˈflau̇(-ə)r\ *vb* : to deprive of virginity

de·fog \dē-ˈfȯg, -ˈfäg\ *vb* : to remove fog or condensed moisture from — **de·fog·ger** *n*

de·fo·li·ant \dē-ˈfō-lē-ənt\ *n* : a chemical spray or dust used to defoliate plants

de·fo·li·ate \-ˌāt\ *vb* : to deprive of leaves esp. prematurely — **de·fo·li·a·tion** \dē-ˌfō-lē-ˈā-shən\ *n* — **de·fo·li·a·tor** \dē-ˈfō-lē-ˌā-tər\ *n*

de·for·es·ta·tion \dē-ˌfȯr-ə-ˈstā-shən\ *n* : the action or process of clearing an area of forests; *also* : the state of having been cleared of forests — **de·for·est** \(ˌ)dē-ˈfȯr-əst, -ˈfär-\ *vb*

de·form \di-ˈfȯrm\ *vb* **1** : DISFIGURE, DEFACE **2** : to make or become misshapen or changed in shape — **de·for·ma·tion** \ˌdē-fȯr-ˈmā-shən, ˌde-fər-\ *n*

de·for·mi·ty \di-ˈfȯr-mə-tē\ *n, pl* **-ties 1** : the state of being deformed **2** : a physical blemish or distortion

de·fraud \di-ˈfrȯd\ *vb* : CHEAT

de·fray \di-ˈfrā\ *vb* : to provide for the payment of : PAY — **de·fray·al** *n*

de·frock \(ˌ)dē-ˈfräk\ *vb* : to deprive (as a priest) of the right to exercise the functions of office

de·frost \di-ˈfrȯst\ *vb* **1** : to thaw out **2** : to free from ice — **de·frost·er** *n*

deft \ˈdeft\ *adj* : quick and neat in action — **deft·ly** *adv* — **deft·ness** *n*

de·funct \di-ˈfəŋkt\ *adj* : DEAD, EXTINCT

de·fuse \dē-ˈfyüz\ *vb* **1** : to remove the fuse from (as a bomb) **2** : to make less harmful, potent, or tense

de·fy \di-ˈfī\ *vb* **de·fied; de·fy·ing** [ME, to renounce faith in, challenge, fr. OF *defier*, fr. *de-* from + *fier* to entrust, ultim. fr. L *fidere* to trust] **1** : CHALLENGE, DARE **2** : to refuse boldly to obey or to yield to : DISREGARD ⟨∼ the law⟩ **3** : WITHSTAND, BAFFLE ⟨a scene that *defies* description⟩

deg *abbr* degree

de·gas \dē-ˈgas\ *vb* : to remove gas from

de·gen·er·a·cy \di-ˈje-nə-rə-sē\ *n, pl* **-cies 1** : the state of being degenerate **2** : the process of becoming degenerate **3** : PERVERSION

¹**de·gen·er·ate** \di-ˈje-nə-rət\ *adj* : fallen or deteriorated from a former, higher, or normal condition — **de·gen·er·a·tion** \-ˌje-nə-ˈrā-shən\ *n* — **de·gen·er·a·tive** \-ˈje-nə-ˌrā-tiv\ *adj*

²**de·gen·er·ate** \di-ˈje-nə-ˌrāt\ *vb* : to undergo deterioration (as in morality, intelligence, structure, or function)

³**de·gen·er·ate** \-rət\ *n* : a degenerate person; *esp* : a sexual pervert

de·grad·able \di-'grā-də-bəl\ *adj* : capable of being chemically degraded

de·grade \di-'grād\ *vb* **1** : to reduce from a higher to a lower rank or degree **2** : DEBASE, CORRUPT **3** : DECOMPOSE — **deg·ra·da·tion** \,de-grə-'dā-shən\ *n*

de·gree \di-'grē\ *n* [ME, fr. OF *degré*, fr. (assumed) VL *degradus*, fr. L *de-* down + *gradus* step, grade] **1** : a step in a series **2** : a rank or grade of official, ecclesiastical, or social position; *also* : the civil condition of a person **3** : the extent, intensity, or scope of something esp. as measured by a graded series **4** : one of the forms or sets of forms used in the comparison of an adjective or adverb **5** : a title conferred upon students by a college, university, or professional school on completion of a program of study **6** : a line or space of the musical staff; *also* : a note or tone of a musical scale **7** : a unit of measure for angles that is equal to an angle with its vertex at the center of a circle and its sides cutting off ¹⁄₃₆₀ of the circumference; *also* : a unit of measure of the arc of a circle equal to the amount of arc cut off by an angle of one degree with its vertex at the center of the circle **8** : any of various units for measuring temperature

de·horn \dē-'hȯrn\ *vb* : to deprive of horns

de·hu·man·ize \dē-'hyü-mə-,nīz\ *vb* : to deprive of human qualities, personality, or spirit — **de·hu·man·i·za·tion** \,dē-,hyü-mə-nə-'zā-shən\ *n*

de·hu·mid·i·fy \,dē-hyü-'mi-də-,fī\ *vb* : to remove moisture from (as the air) — **de·hu·mid·i·fi·er** *n*

de·hy·drate \dē-'hī-,drāt\ *vb* : to remove water from; *also* : to lose liquid — **de·hy·dra·tion** \,dē-hī-'drā-shən\ *n*

de·hy·dro·ge·na·tion \dē-(,)hī-,drä-jə-'nā-shən, -drə-\ *n* : the removal of hydrogen from a chemical compound — **de·hy·dro·ge·nate** \,dē-(,)hī-'drä-jə-,nāt, dē-'hī-drə-jə-\ *vb*

de·ice \dē-'īs\ *vb* : to keep free or rid of ice — **de·ic·er** *n*

de·i·fy \'dē-ə-,fī\ *vb* **-fied; -fy·ing 1** : to make a god of **2** : WORSHIP, GLORIFY — **de·i·fi·ca·tion** \,dē-ə-fə-'kā-shən\ *n*

deign \'dān\ *vb* [ME, fr. OF *deignier*, fr. L *dignare, dignari*, fr. *dignus* worthy] : CONDESCEND

de·ion·ize \dē-'ī-ə-,nīz\ *vb* : to remove ions from

de·ism \'dē-,i-zəm\ *n, often cap* : a system of thought advocating natural religion based on human morality and reason rather than divine revelation — **de·ist** \'dē-ist\ *n, often cap* — **de·is·tic** \dē-'is-tik\ *adj*

de·i·ty \'dē-ə-tē, 'dā-\ *n, pl* **-ties 1** : DIVINITY **2** **2** *cap* : GOD **1** **3** : a god or goddess

dé·jà vu \,dā-,zhä-'vü\ *n* [F, adj., already seen] : the feeling that one has seen or heard something before

de·ject·ed \di-'jek-təd\ *adj* : low in spirits : SAD — **de·ject·ed·ly** *adv*

de·jec·tion \di-'jek-shən\ *n* : lowness of spirits

de jure \dē-'jùr-ē\ *adv or adj* [ML] : by legal right

deka·gram \'de-kə-,gram\ *n* — see METRIC SYSTEM table

deka·li·ter \-,lē-tər\ *n* — see METRIC SYSTEM table

deka·me·ter \-,mē-tər\ *n* — see METRIC SYSTEM table

del *abbr* delegate; delegation

Del *abbr* Delaware

Del·a·ware \'de-lə-,war\ *n, pl* **Delaware** *or* **Delawares** : a member of an American Indian people orig. of the Delaware valley; *also* : their language

¹**de·lay** \di-'lā\ *n* **1** : the act of delaying : the state of being delayed **2** : the time for which something is delayed

²**delay** *vb* **1** : POSTPONE, PUT OFF **2** : to stop, detain, or hinder for a time **3** : to move or act slowly

de·lec·ta·ble \di-'lek-tə-bəl\ *adj* **1** : highly pleasing : DELIGHTFUL **2** : DELICIOUS

de·lec·ta·tion \,dē-,lek-'tā-shən\ *n* : DELIGHT, PLEASURE, DIVERSION

¹**del·e·gate** \'de-li-gət, -,gāt\ *n* **1** : DEPUTY, REPRESENTATIVE **2** : a member of the lower house of the legislature of Maryland, Virginia, or West Virginia

²**del·e·gate** \-,gāt\ *vb* **-gat·ed; -gat·ing 1** : to entrust to another ⟨∼ authority⟩ **2** : to appoint as one's delegate

del·e·ga·tion \,de-li-'gā-shən\ *n* **1** : the act of delegating **2** : one or more persons chosen to represent others

de·lete \di-'lēt\ *vb* **de·let·ed; de·let·ing** [L *delēre* to wipe out, destroy] : to eliminate esp. by blotting out, cutting out, or erasing — **de·le·tion** \-'lē-shən\ *n*

del·e·te·ri·ous \,de-lə-'tir-ē-əs\ *adj* : HARMFUL, NOXIOUS

delft \'delft\ *n* **1** : a Dutch pottery with an opaque white glaze and predominantly blue decoration **2** : glazed pottery esp. when blue and white

delft·ware \-,war\ *n* : DELFT

deli \'de-lē\ *n, pl* **del·is** : DELICATESSEN

¹**de·lib·er·ate** \di-'li-bə-,rāt\ *vb* **-at·ed; -at·ing** : to consider carefully — **de·lib·er·a·tion** \-,li-bə-'rā-shən\ *n* — **de·lib·er·a·tive** \-'li-bə-,rā-tiv, -brə-tiv\ *adj* — **de·lib·er·a·tive·ly** *adv*

²**de·lib·er·ate** \di-'li-bə-rət, -'li-brət\ *adj* [L *deliberare* to consider carefully, fr. *libra* scale, pound] **1** : determined after careful thought **2** : done or said intentionally **3** : UNHURRIED, SLOW — **de·lib·er·ate·ly** *adv* — **de·lib·er·ate·ness** *n*

del·i·ca·cy \'de-li-kə-sē\ *n, pl* **-cies 1** : something pleasing to eat and considered rare or luxurious **2** : FINENESS, DAINTINESS; *also* : FRAILTY **3** : nicety or expressiveness of touch **4** : precise perception and discrimination : SENSITIVITY **5** : sensibility in feeling or conduct; *also* : SQUEAMISHNESS **6** : the quality or state of requiring delicate handling

del·i·cate \'de-li-kət\ *adj* **1** : pleasing to the senses of taste or smell esp. in a mild or subtle way **2** : marked by daintiness or charm : EXQUISITE **3** : FASTIDIOUS, SQUEAMISH, SCRUPULOUS **4** : easily damaged : FRAGILE; *also* : SICKLY **5** : requiring skill or tact **6** : marked by care, skill, or tact **7** : marked by minute precision : very sensitive — **del·i·cate·ly** *adv*

del·i·ca·tes·sen \,de-li-kə-'tes-ᵊn\ *n pl* [G, pl. of *Delicatesse* delicacy, fr. F *délicatesse*] **1** : ready-to-eat food products (as cooked meats and prepared salads) **2** *sing, pl* **delicatessens** : a store where delicatessen are sold

de·li·cious \di-'li-shəs\ *adj* : affording great pleasure : DELIGHTFUL; *esp* : very pleasing to the taste or smell — **de·li·cious·ly** *adv* — **de·li·cious·ness** *n*

¹**de·light** \di-'līt\ *n* **1** : great pleasure or satisfaction : JOY **2** : something that gives great pleasure — **de·light·ful** \-fəl\ *adj* — **de·light·ful·ly** *adv*

²**delight** *vb* **1** : to take great pleasure **2** : to satisfy greatly : PLEASE

de·light·ed *adj* : highly pleased : GRATIFIED — **de·light·ed·ly** *adv*

de·lim·it \di-'li-mət\ *vb* : to fix the limits of

de·lin·eate \di-'li-nē-,āt\ *vb* **-eat·ed; -eat·ing 1** : SKETCH, PORTRAY **2** : to picture in words : DESCRIBE — **de·lin·ea·tion** \-,li-nē-'ā-shən\ *n*

de·lin·quen·cy \di-'liŋ-kwən-sē\ *n, pl* **-cies** : the quality or state of being delinquent

¹**de·lin·quent** \-kwənt\ *n* : a delinquent person

²**delinquent** *adj* **1** : offending by neglect or violation of duty or of law **2** : being overdue in payment

del·i·quesce \,de-li-'kwes\ *vb* **-quesced; -quesc·ing** : MELT, DISSOLVE — **del·i·ques·cent** \-'kwes-ᵊnt\ *adj*

de·lir·i·um \di-'lir-ē-əm\ *n* [L, fr. *delirare* to be crazy, lit., to leave the furrow (in plowing), fr. *de-* from + *lira* furrow] : mental disturbance marked by confusion, disordered speech, and hallucinations; *also* : frenzied excitement — **de·lir·i·ous** \-ē-əs\ *adj* — **de·lir·i·ous·ly** *adv*

delirium tre·mens \-'trē-mənz, -'tre-\ *n* : a violent delirium with tremors that is induced by excessive and prolonged use of alcoholic liquors

de·liv·er \di-'li-vər\ *vb* **-ered; -er·ing 1** : to set free : SAVE **2** : CONVEY, TRANSFER (∼ a letter) **3** : to assist in giving birth or at the birth of; *also* : to give birth to **4** : UTTER, COMMUNICATE **5** : to send to an intended target or destination — **de·liv·er·ance** *n* — **de·liv·er·er** *n*

de·liv·ery \di-'li-və-rē\ *n, pl* **-er·ies** : the act of delivering something; *also* : something delivered — **de·liv·ery·man** \-,man\ *n*

dell \'del\ *n* : a small secluded valley

de·louse \dē-'laůs\ *vb* : to remove lice from

del·phin·i·um \del-'fi-nē-əm\ *n* : any of a genus of mostly perennial herbs related to the buttercups with tall branching spikes of irregular flowers

del·ta \'del-tə\ *n* **1** : the 4th letter of the Greek alphabet — Δ or δ **2** : something shaped like a capital Δ; *esp* : the triangular silt-formed land at the mouth of a river — **del·ta·ic** \del-'tā-ik\ *adj*

de·lude \di-'lüd\ *vb* **de·lud·ed; de·lud·ing** : MISLEAD, DECEIVE, TRICK

¹del·uge \'del-yüj\ *n* **1** : a flooding of land by water **2** : a drenching rain **3** : a great amount or number

²deluge *vb* **del·uged; del·ug·ing 1** : INUNDATE, FLOOD **2** : to overwhelm as if with a deluge

de·lu·sion \di-'lü-zhən\ *n* : a deluding or being deluded; *esp* : a persistent false psychotic belief — **de·lu·sion·al** \-'lü-zhə-nəl\ *adj* — **de·lu·sive** \-'lü-siv\ *adj*

de·luxe \di-'lüks, -'ləks, -'lüks\ *adj* : notably luxurious or elegant

delve \'delv\ *vb* **delved; delv·ing 1** : DIG **2** : to seek laboriously for information

dely *abbr* delivery

Dem *abbr* Democrat; Democratic

de·mag·ne·tize \dē-'mag-nə-,tīz\ *vb* : to cause to lose magnetic properties — **de·mag·ne·ti·za·tion** \dē-,mag-nə-tə-'zā-shən\ *n*

dem·a·gogue *or* **dem·a·gog** \'de-mə-,gäg\ *n* [Gk *dēmagōgos,* fr. *dēmos* people + *agōgos* leading, fr. *agein* to lead] : a person who appeals to the emotions and prejudices of people esp. in order to gain political power — **dem·a·gogu·ery** \-,gä-gə-rē\ *n* — **dem·a·gogy** \-,gä-gē, -,gä-jē\ *n*

¹de·mand \di-'mand\ *n* **1** : an act of demanding; *also* : something claimed as due or just **2** : the ability and desire to buy goods or services; *also* : the quantity of goods wanted at a stated price **3** : a seeking or being sought after : urgent need **4** : a pressing need or requirement

²demand *vb* **1** : to ask for with authority : claim as due or just **2** : to ask earnestly or in the manner of a command **3** : REQUIRE, NEED

de·mar·cate \di-'mär-,kāt, 'dē-,mär-\ *vb* **-cat·ed; -cat·ing 1** : DELIMIT **2** : SEPARATE — **de·mar·ca·tion** \,dē-,mär-'kā-shən\ *n*

dé·marche *or* **de·marche** \dā-'märsh\ *n* : a course of action : MANEUVER

¹de·mean \di-'mēn\ *vb* **de·meaned; de·mean·ing** : to behave or conduct (oneself) usu. in a proper manner

²demean *vb* **de·meaned; de·mean·ing** : DEGRADE, DEBASE

de·mean·or \di-'mē-nər\ *n* : CONDUCT, BEARING

de·mean·our *Brit var of* DEMEANOR

de·ment·ed \di-'men-təd\ *adj* : MAD, INSANE — **de·ment·ed·ly** *adv*

de·men·tia \di-'men-chə\ *n* **1** : mental deterioration **2** : INSANITY

de·mer·it \di-'mer-ət\ *n* **1** : FAULT **2** : a mark placed against a person's record for some fault or offense

de·mesne \di-'mān, -'mēn\ *n* **1** : REALM **2** : manorial land actually possessed by the lord and not held by free tenants **3** : ESTATE **4** : REGION

demi·god \'de-mi-,gäd\ *n* : a mythological being with more power than a mortal but less than a god

demi·john \'de-mi-,jän\ *n* [F *dame-jeanne,* lit., Lady Jane] : a large narrow-necked bottle usu. enclosed in wickerwork

de·mil·i·ta·rize \dē-'mi-lə-tə-,rīz\ *vb* : to strip of military forces, weapons, or fortifications — **de·mil·i·tar·i·za·tion** \dē-,mi-lə-tə-rə-'zā-shən\ *n*

demi·mon·daine \,de-mi-män-'dān\ *n* : a woman of the demimonde

demi·monde \'de-mi-,mänd\ *n* [F *demi-monde,* fr. *demi-* half + *monde* world] **1** : a class of women on the fringes of respectable society supported by wealthy lovers **2** : a group engaged in activity of doubtful legality or propriety

de·min·er·al·ize \dē-'mi-nə-rə-,līz\ *vb* : to remove the mineral matter from — **de·min·er·al·i·za·tion** \-,mi-nə-rə-lə-'zā-shən\ *n*

de·mise \di-'mīz\ *n* **1** : LEASE **2** : transfer of sovereignty to a successor (∼ of the crown) **3** : DEATH **4** : loss of status

demi·tasse \'de-mi-,tas\ *n* : a small cup of black coffee; *also* : the cup used to serve it

de·mo·bi·lize \di-'mō-bə-,līz, dē-\ *vb* **1** : DISBAND **2** : to discharge from military service — **de·mo·bi·li·za·tion** \di-,mō-bə-lə-'zā-shən, dē-\ *n*

de·moc·ra·cy \di-'mä-krə-sē\ *n, pl* **-cies** [MF *democratie,* fr. LL *democratia,* fr. Gk *dēmokratia,* fr. *dēmos* people + *kratos* strength, power] **1** : government by the people; *esp* : rule of the majority **2** : a government in which the supreme power is held by the people **3** : a political unit that has a democratic government **4** *cap* : the principles and policies of the Democratic party in the U.S. **5** : the common people esp. when constituting the source of political authority **6** : the absence of hereditary or arbitrary class distinctions or privileges

dem·o·crat \'de-mə-,krat\ *n* **1** : one who believes in or practices democracy **2** *cap* : a member of the Democratic party of the U.S.

dem·o·crat·ic \,de-mə-'kra-tik\ *adj* **1** : of, relating to, or favoring democracy **2** *often cap* : of or relating to one of the two major political parties in the U.S. associated in modern times with policies of broad social reform and internationalism **3** : relating to or appealing to the common people (∼ art) **4** : not snobbish — **dem·o·crat·i·cal·ly** \-ti-k(ə-)lē\ *adv*

de·moc·ra·tize \di-'mä-krə-,tīz\ *vb* **-tized; -tiz·ing** : to make democratic

dé·mo·dé \,dā-mō-'dā\ *adj* [F] : no longer fashionable : OUT-OF-DATE

de·mo·graph·ics \,de-mə-'gra-fiks, ,dē-\ *n pl* : the statistical characteristics of human populations

de·mog·ra·phy \di-'mä-grə-fē\ *n* : the statistical study of human populations and esp. their size and distribution and the number of births and deaths — **de·mog·ra·pher** \-fər\ *n* — **de·mo·graph·ic** \,de-mə-'gra-fik, ,dē-\ *adj* — **de·mo·graph·i·cal·ly** \-fi-k(ə-)lē\ *adv*

dem·oi·selle \,dem-wə-'zel\ *n* [F] : a young woman

de·mol·ish \di-'mä-lish\ *vb* **1** : to destroy by breaking apart : RAZE **2** : SMASH **3** : to put an end to

de·mo·li·tion \,de-mə-'li-shən, ,dē-\ *n* : the act of demolishing; *esp* : destruction by means of explosives

de·mon *or* **dae·mon** \'dē-mən\ *n* **1** : an evil spirit : DEVIL **2** *usu* **daemon** : an attendant power or spirit **3** : one that has unusual drive or effectiveness

de·mon·e·tize \dē-'mä-nə-,tīz, -'mə-\ *vb* : to stop using as money or as a monetary standard (∼ silver) — **de·mon·e·ti·za·tion** \dē-,mä-nə-tə-'zā-shən, -,mə-\ *n*

de·mo·ni·ac \di-'mō-nē-,ak\ *also* **de·mo·ni·a·cal** \,dē-mə-'nī-ə-kəl\ *adj* **1** : possessed or influenced by a demon **2** : DEVILISH, FIENDISH

de·mon·ic \di-'mä-nik\ *also* **de·mon·i·cal** \-ni-kəl\ *adj* : DEMONIAC **2**

de·mon·ol·o·gy \,dē-mə-'nä-lə-jē\ *n* **1** : the study of demons **2** : belief in demons

de·mon·stra·ble \di-'män-strə-bəl\ *adj* **1** : capable of being demonstrated **2** : APPARENT, EVIDENT — **de·mon·stra·bly** \-blē\ *adv*

dem·on·strate \'de-mən-,strāt\ *vb* **-strat·ed; -strat·ing 1** : to show clearly **2** : to prove or make clear by reasoning or evidence **3** : to explain esp. with many examples **4** : to show publicly ⟨∼ a new car⟩ **5** : to make a public display ⟨∼ in protest⟩ — **dem·on·stra·tion** \‚de-mən-'strä-shən\ *n* — **dem·on·stra·tor** \'de-mən-‚strä-tər\ *n*

¹**de·mon·stra·tive** \di-'män-strə-tiv\ *adj* **1** : demonstrating as real or true **2** : characterized by demonstration **3** : pointing out the one referred to and distinguishing it from others of the same class ⟨∼ pronoun⟩ **4** : marked by display of feeling : EFFUSIVE — **de·mon·stra·tive·ly** *adv* — **de·mon·stra·tive·ness** *n*

²**demonstrative** *n* : a demonstrative word and esp. a pronoun

de·mor·al·ize \di-'mȯr-ə-‚līz\ *vb* **1** : to corrupt in morals **2** : to weaken in discipline or spirit : DISORGANIZE — **de·mor·al·i·za·tion** \di-‚mȯr-ə-lə-'zā-shən\ *n*

de·mote \di-'mōt\ *vb* **de·mot·ed; de·mot·ing** : to reduce to a lower grade or rank — **de·mo·tion** \-'mō-shən\ *n*

de·mot·ic \di-'mä-tik\ *adj* : COMMON, POPULAR

de·mur \di-'mər\ *vb* **de·murred; de·mur·ring** [ME *demeoren* to linger, fr. OF *demorer*, fr. L *demorari*, fr. *morari* to linger, fr. *mora* delay] : to take exception : OBJECT — **demur** *n*

de·mure \di-'myu̇r\ *adj* **1** : quietly modest : DECOROUS **2** : affectedly modest, reserved, or serious : PRIM **syn** shy, bashful, coy, difficult, retiring, unassertive — **de·mure·ly** *adv*

de·mur·rer \di-'mər-ər\ *n* : a claim by the defendant in a legal action that the plaintiff does not have sufficient grounds to proceed

den \'den\ *n* **1** : LAIR **2** : HIDEOUT ⟨a robber's ∼⟩; *also* : a place like a hideout or a center of secret activity ⟨opium ∼⟩ ⟨a ∼ of iniquity⟩ **3** : a cozy private little room

Den *abbr* Denmark

de·na·ture \dē-'nā-chər\ *vb* **de·na·tured; de·na·tur·ing** : to remove the natural qualities of; *esp* : to make (alcohol) unfit for drinking

den·drol·o·gy \den-'drä-lə-jē\ *n* : the study of trees — **den·drol·o·gist** \-jist\ *n*

den·gue \'deŋ-gē, -‚gä\ *n* [Sp] : an acute infectious disease characterized by headache, severe joint pain, and rash

de·ni·al \di-'nī-əl\ *n* **1** : rejection of a request **2** : refusal to admit the truth of a statement or charge; *also* : assertion that something alleged is false **3** : DISAVOWAL **4** : restriction on one's own activity or desires

de·nier \'den-yər\ *n* : a unit of fineness for yarn

den·i·grate \'de-ni-‚grāt\ *vb* **-grat·ed; -grat·ing** [L *denigrare*, fr. *nigrare* to blacken, fr. *niger* black] : to cast aspersions on : DEFAME — **den·i·gra·tion** \‚de-ni-'grā-shən\ *n*

den·im \'de-nəm\ *n* [F (*serge*) *de Nîmes* serge of Nîmes, France] **1** : a firm durable twilled usu. cotton fabric woven with colored warp and white filling threads **2** *pl* : overalls or trousers of usu. blue denim

den·i·zen \'de-nə-zən\ *n* : INHABITANT

de·nom·i·nate \di-'nä-mə-‚nāt\ *vb* : to give a name to : DESIGNATE

de·nom·i·na·tion \di-‚nä-mə-'nā-shən\ *n* **1** : an act of denominating **2** : a value or size of a series of related values (as of money) **3** : NAME, DESIGNATION; *esp* : a general name for a category **4** : a religious organization uniting local congregations in a single body — **de·nom·i·na·tion·al** \-shə-nəl\ *adj*

de·nom·i·na·tor \di-'nä-mə-‚nā-tər\ *n* : the part of a fraction that is below the line indicating division

de·no·ta·tive \'dē-nō-‚tā-tiv, di-'nō-tə-tiv\ *adj* **1** : denoting or tending to denote **2** : relating to denotation

de·note \di-'nōt\ *vb* **1** : to mark out plainly : INDICATE **2** : to make known **3** : MEAN, NAME — **de·no·ta·tion** \‚dē-nō-'tā-shən\ *n*

de·noue·ment \‚dā-‚nü-'mäⁿ\ *n* [F *dénouement*, lit., untying] : the final outcome of the dramatic complications in a literary work

de·nounce \di-'nau̇ns\ *vb* **de·nounced; de·nounc·ing** **1** : to pronounce esp. publicly to be blameworthy or evil **2** : to inform against : ACCUSE **3** : to announce formally the termination of (as a treaty) — **de·nounce·ment** *n*

de no·vo \di-'nō-vō\ *adv or adj* [L] : over again : ANEW

dense \'dens\ *adj* **dens·er; dens·est** **1** : marked by compactness or crowding together of parts : THICK ⟨∼ forest⟩ ⟨a ∼ fog⟩ **2** : DULL, STUPID — **dense·ly** *adv* — **dense·ness** *n*

den·si·ty \'den-sə-tē\ *n, pl* **-ties** **1** : the quality or state of being dense **2** : the quantity of something per unit volume, unit area, or unit length

dent \'dent\ *n* **1** : a small depressed place made by a blow or by pressure **2** : an impression or weakening effect made usu. against resistance **3** : initial progress — **dent** *vb*

den·tal \'dent-ᵊl\ *adj* : of or relating to teeth or dentistry — **den·tal·ly** *adv*

dental floss *n* : a thread used to clean between the teeth

dental hygienist *n* : a person licensed to clean and examine teeth

den·tate \'den-‚tāt\ *adj* : having pointed projections : NOTCHED

den·ti·frice \'den-tə-frəs\ *n* [MF, fr. L *dentifricium*, fr. *dent-, dens* tooth + *fricare* to rub] : a powder, paste, or liquid for cleaning the teeth

den·tin \'dent-ᵊn\ *or* **den·tine** \'den-‚tēn, den-'tēn\ *n* : a calcareous material like bone but harder and denser that composes the principal mass of a tooth

den·tist \'den-tist\ *n* : a person licensed in the care, treatment, and replacement of teeth — **den·tist·ry** *n*

den·ti·tion \den-'ti-shən\ *n* : the number, kind, and arrangement of teeth (as of a person or animal); *also* : TEETH

den·ture \'den-chər\ *n* : a set of teeth; *esp* : a partial or complete set of false teeth

de·nude \di-'nüd, -'nyüd\ *vb* **de·nud·ed; de·nud·ing** : to strip the covering from — **de·nu·da·tion** \‚dē-nü-'dā-shən, -nyü-\ *n*

de·nun·ci·a·tion \di-‚nən-sē-'ā-shən\ *n* : the act of denouncing; *esp* : a public condemnation

de·ny \di-'nī\ *vb* **de·nied; de·ny·ing** **1** : to declare untrue **2** : to refuse to recognize or acknowledge : DISAVOW **3** : to refuse to grant ⟨∼ a request⟩ **4** : to reject as false ⟨∼ a theory⟩

de·o·dar \'dē-ə-‚där\ *n* [Hindi *deodār*, fr. Skt *devadāru*, fr. *deva* god + *dāru* wood] : an East Indian cedar

de·odor·ant \dē-'ō-də-rənt\ *n* : a preparation that gets rid of unpleasant odors

de·odor·ize \dē-'ō-də-‚rīz\ *vb* : to eliminate the offensive odor of

de·ox·i·dize \dē-'äk-sə-‚dīz\ *vb* : to remove oxygen from

de·oxy·ri·bo·nu·cle·ic acid \dē-'äk-si-‚rī-bō-nu̇-‚klē-ik-, -nyü-\ *n* : DNA

de·oxy·ri·bose \dē-‚äk-si-'rī-‚bōs\ *n* : a sugar with five carbon and four oxygen atoms in each molecule that is part of DNA

dep *abbr* **1** depart; departure **2** deposit **3** deputy

de·part \di-'pärt\ *vb* **1** : to go away : go away from : LEAVE **2** : DIE **3** : to turn aside : DEVIATE

de·part·ment \di-'pärt-mənt\ *n* **1** : a distinct sphere or category esp. of an activity or attribute **2** : a functional or division (as of a government, business, or college) — **de·part·men·tal** \di-‚pärt-'ment-ᵊl, ‚dē-\ *adj*

department store *n* : a store selling a wide variety of goods arranged in several departments

de·par·ture \di-'pär-chər\ *n* **1** : the act of going away **2** : a starting out (as on a journey) **3** : DIVERGENCE

de·pend \di-'pend\ *vb* **1** : to be determined, based, or contingent ⟨life ∼s on food⟩ **2** : TRUST, RELY ⟨you can ∼ on me⟩ **3** : to be dependent esp. for financial support **4** : to hang down ⟨a vine ∼*ing* from a tree⟩

de·pend·able \di-'pen-də-bəl\ *adj* : TRUSTWORTHY, RE-LIABLE — **de·pend·abil·i·ty** \-₁pen-də-'bi-lə-tē\ *n*

de·pen·dence *also* **de·pen·dance** \di-'pen-dəns\ *n* **1** : the quality or state of being dependent; *esp* : the quality or state of being influenced by or subject to another **2** : RELIANCE, TRUST **3** : something on which one relies **4** : drug addiction; *also* : HABITUATION 2

de·pen·den·cy \-dən-sē\ *n, pl* **-cies 1** : DEPENDENCE **2** : a territory under the jurisdiction of a nation but not formally annexed by it

¹de·pen·dent \-dənt\ *adj* **1** : hanging down **2** : determined or conditioned by another; *also* : affected with drug dependence **3** : relying on another for support **4** : subject to another's jurisdiction **5** : SUBORDINATE 4

²dependent *also* **de·pen·dant** \-dənt\ *n* : one that is dependent; *esp* : a person who relies on another for support

de·pict \di-'pikt\ *vb* **1** : to represent by a picture **2** : to describe in words — **de·pic·tion** \-'pik-shən\ *n*

de·pil·a·to·ry \di-'pi-lə-₁tōr-ē\ *n, pl* **-ries** : a preparation for removing hair, wool, or bristles

de·plane \dē-'plān\ *vb* : to get out of an airplane

de·plete \di-'plēt\ *vb* **de·plet·ed; de·plet·ing** : to exhaust esp. of strength or resources — **de·ple·tion** \-'plē-shən\ *n*

de·plor·able \di-'plōr-ə-bəl\ *adj* **1** : LAMENTABLE **2** : WRETCHED — **de·plor·ably** *adv*

de·plore \-'plōr\ *vb* **de·plored; de·plor·ing 1** : to feel or express grief for **2** : to regret strongly **3** : to consider unfortunate or deserving of disapproval

de·ploy \di-'plói\ *vb* : to spread out (as troops or ships) in order for battle — **de·ploy·ment** \-mənt\ *n*

de·po·nent \di-'pō-nənt\ *n* : one who gives evidence

de·pop·u·late \dē-'pä-pyə-₁lāt\ *vb* : to reduce greatly the population of — **de·pop·u·la·tion** \-₁pä-pyə-'lā-shən\ *n*

de·port \di-'pōrt\ *vb* **1** : CONDUCT, BEHAVE **2** : BANISH, EXILE — **de·por·ta·tion** \₁dē-₁pōr-'tā-shən\ *n*

de·port·ment \di-'pōrt-mənt\ *n* : BEHAVIOR, BEARING

de·pose \di-'pōz\ *vb* **de·posed; de·pos·ing 1** : to remove from high office (as of king) **2** : to testify under oath or by affidavit

¹de·pos·it \di-'pä-zət\ *vb* **de·pos·it·ed** \-zə-təd\; **de·pos·it·ing 1** : to place for safekeeping or as a pledge; *esp* : to put money in a bank **2** : to lay down : PLACE **3** : to let fall or sink ⟨silt ∼*ed* by a flood⟩ — **de·pos·i·tor** \-zə-tər\ *n*

²deposit *n* **1** : the state of being deposited ⟨money on ∼⟩ **2** : something placed for safekeeping; *esp* : money deposited in a bank **3** : money given as a pledge **4** : an act of depositing **5** : something laid down ⟨a ∼ of silt⟩ **6** : a natural accumulation (as of a mineral)

de·po·si·tion \₁de-pə-'zi-shən, ₁dē-\ *n* **1** : an act of removing from a position of authority **2** : TESTIMONY **3** : the process of depositing **4** : DEPOSIT

de·pos·i·to·ry \di-'pä-zə-₁tōr-ē\ *n, pl* **-ries** : a place where something is deposited esp. for safekeeping

de·pot *1, 2 usu* 'de-pō, *3 usu* 'dē-\ *n* **1** : STOREHOUSE **2** : a place where military supplies or replacements are kept or assembled **3** : a building for railroad or bus passengers

depr *abbr* depreciation

de·prave \di-'prāv\ *vb* **de·praved; de·prav·ing** [ME, fr. MF *depraver*, fr. L *depravare* to pervert, fr. *pravus* crooked, bad] : CORRUPT, PERVERT — **de·praved** *adj* — **de·prav·i·ty** \-'pra-və-tē\ *n*

dep·re·cate \'de-pri-₁kāt\ *vb* **-cat·ed; -cat·ing** [L *deprecari* to avert by prayer, fr. *precari* to pray] **1** : to express disapproval of **2** : BELITTLE — **dep·re·ca·tion** \₁de-pri-'kā-shən\ *n*

dep·re·ca·to·ry \'de-pri-kə-₁tōr-ē\ *adj* **1** : APOLOGETIC **2** : serving to deprecate : DISAPPROVING

de·pre·ci·ate \di-'prē-shē-₁āt\ *vb* **-at·ed; -at·ing** [LL *depretiare*, fr. L *pretium* price] **1** : BELITTLE, DISPAR-

AGE **2** : to lessen in price or value — **de·pre·ci·a·tion** \-₁prē-shē-'ā-shən\ *n*

dep·re·da·tion \₁de-prə-'dā-shən\ *n* : a laying waste or plundering — **dep·re·date** \'de-prə-₁dāt\ *vb*

de·press \di-'pres\ *vb* **1** : to press down : cause to sink to a lower position **2** : to lessen the activity or force of **3** : SADDEN, DISCOURAGE **4** : to lessen in price or value — **de·pres·sor** \-'pre-sər\ *n*

de·pres·sant \di-'pres-ᵊnt\ *n* : one that depresses; *esp* : a chemical substance (as a drug) that reduces bodily functional activity — **depressant** *adj*

de·pressed *adj* **1** : low in spirits; *also* : affected with psychological depression **2** : suffering from economic depression

de·pres·sion \di-'pre-shən\ *n* **1** : an act of depressing : a state of being depressed **2** : a pressing down : LOWERING **3** : a state of feeling sad **4** : a psychological disorder marked esp. by sadness, inactivity, difficulty in thinking and concentration, and feelings of dejection **5** : a depressed area or part **6** : a period of low general economic activity with widespread unemployment

¹de·pres·sive \di-'pre-siv\ *adj* **1** : tending to depress **2** : characterized or affected by psychological depression

²depressive *n* : a person affected with or prone to psychological depression

de·pres·sur·ize \(₁)dē-'pre-shə-₁rīz\ *vb* : to release pressure from

dep·ri·va·tion \₁de-prə-'vā-shən\ *n* **1** : an act or instance of depriving : LOSS **2** : PRIVATION 2

de·prive \di-'prīv\ *vb* **de·prived; de·priv·ing 1** : to take something away from **2** : to stop from having something

de·prived *adj* : marked by deprivation esp. of the necessities of life

de·pro·gram \(₁)dē-'prō-₁gram, -grəm\ *vb* : to dissuade from convictions usu. of a religious nature often by coercive means

dept *abbr* department

depth \'depth\ *n, pl* **depths** \'depths\ **1** : something that is deep; *esp* : the deep part of a body of water **2** : a part that is far from the outside or surface; *also* : the middle or innermost part **3** : ABYSS **4** : a profound or intense state ⟨the ∼*s* of reflection⟩; *also* : the worst part ⟨during the ∼*s* of the depression⟩ **5** : a reprehensibly low condition **6** : the distance from top to bottom or from front to back **7** : the quality of being deep **8** : the degree of intensity

depth charge *n* : an explosive device for use underwater esp. against submarines

dep·u·ta·tion \₁de-pyə-'tā-shən\ *n* **1** : the act of appointing a deputy **2** : DELEGATION

de·pute \di-'pyüt\ *vb* **de·put·ed; de·put·ing** : DELEGATE

dep·u·tize \'de-pyə-₁tīz\ *vb* **-tized; -tiz·ing** : to appoint or act as deputy

dep·u·ty \'de-pyə-tē\ *n, pl* **-ties 1** : a person appointed to act for or in place of another **2** : an assistant empowered to act as a substitute in the absence of a superior **3** : a member of a lower house of a legislative assembly

der *or* **deriv** *abbr* derivation; derivative

de·rail \di-'rāl\ *vb* : to leave or cause to leave the rails — **de·rail·ment** *n*

de·rail·leur \di-'rā-lər\ *n* [F *dérailleur*] : a device for shifting gears on a bicycle by moving the chain from one set of exposed gears to another

de·range \di-'rānj\ *vb* **de·ranged; de·rang·ing 1** : DISARRANGE, UPSET **2** : to make insane — **de·range·ment** *n*

der·by \'dər-bē, *Brit* 'där-\ *n, pl* **derbies 1** : a horse race usu. for three-year-olds held annually **2** : a race or contest open to all **3** : a stiff felt hat with dome-shaped crown and narrow brim

derby 3

de·reg·u·la·tion \(ˌ)dē-ˌre-gyù-ˈlā-shən\ *n* : the act of removing restrictions or regulations — **de·reg·u·late** \-ˈre-gyù-ˌlāt\ *vb*

¹**der·e·lict** \ˈder-ə-ˌlikt\ *adj* 1 : abandoned by the owner or occupant 2 : NEGLIGENT ⟨∼ in his duty⟩

²**derelict** *n* 1 : something voluntarily abandoned; *esp* : a ship abandoned on the high seas 2 : a destitute homeless social misfit : VAGRANT, BUM

der·e·lic·tion \ˌder-ə-ˈlik-shən\ *n* 1 : the act of abandoning : the state of being abandoned 2 : a failure in duty

de·ride \di-ˈrīd\ *vb* **de·rid·ed; de·rid·ing** [L *deridēre,* fr. *ridēre* to laugh] : to laugh at scornfully : RIDICULE

de ri·gueur \də-rē-ˈgər\ *adj* [F] : prescribed or required by fashion, etiquette, or custom : PROPER

de·ri·sion \də-ˈri-zhən\ *n* : RIDICULE — **de·ri·sive** \-ˈrī-siv\ *adj* — **de·ri·sive·ly** *adv* — **de·ri·sive·ness** *n* — **de·ri·so·ry** \-ˈrī-sə-rē\ *adj*

der·i·va·tion \ˌder-ə-ˈvā-shən\ *n* 1 : the formation of a word from an earlier word or root; *also* : an act of ascertaining or stating the derivation of a word 2 : ETYMOLOGY 3 : SOURCE, ORIGIN; *also* : DESCENT 4 : an act or process of deriving

de·riv·a·tive \di-ˈri-və-tiv\ *n* 1 : a word formed by derivation 2 : something derived — **derivative** *adj*

de·rive \di-ˈrīv\ *vb* **de·rived; de·riv·ing** [ME, fr. MF *deriver,* fr. L *derivare,* lit., to draw off (water), fr. *de-* from + *rivus* stream] 1 : to receive or obtain from a source 2 : to obtain from a parent substance 3 : INFER, DEDUCE 4 : to trace the derivation of 5 : to come from a certain source

der·mal \ˈdər-məl\ *adj* : of or relating to the skin : CUTANEOUS

der·ma·ti·tis \ˌdər-mə-ˈtī-təs\ *n* : skin inflammation

der·ma·tol·o·gy \-ˈtä-lə-jē\ *n* : a branch of medical science dealing with the structure, functions, and diseases of the skin — **der·ma·tol·o·gist** \-jist\ *n*

der·mis \ˈdər-məs\ *n* : the sensitive vascular inner layer of the skin

der·o·gate \ˈder-ə-ˌgāt\ *vb* **-gat·ed; -gat·ing** 1 : to cause to seem inferior : DISPARAGE 2 : DETRACT — **der·o·ga·tion** \ˌder-ə-ˈgā-shən\ *n* — **de·rog·a·tive** \di-ˈrä-gə-tiv\ *adj*

de·rog·a·to·ry \di-ˈrä-gə-ˌtōr-ē\ *adj* : intended to lower the reputation of a person or thing : DISPARAGING — **de·rog·a·to·ri·ly** \-ˌrä-gə-ˈtōr-ə-lē\ *adv*

der·rick \ˈder-ik\ *n* [obs. *derrick* hangman, gallows, fr. *Derick,* name of 17th cent. Eng. hangman] 1 : a hoisting apparatus : CRANE 2 : a framework over a drill hole (as for oil) for supporting machinery

der·ri·ere *or* **der·ri·ère** \ˌder-ē-ˈer\ *n* : BUTTOCKS

der·ring-do \ˌder-iŋ-ˈdü\ *n* : DARING

der·rin·ger \ˈder-ən-jər\ *n* : a short-barreled pocket pistol

der·vish \ˈdər-vish\ *n* [Turk *derviş,* lit., beggar, fr. Per *darvīsh*] : a member of a Muslim religious order noted for devotional exercises (as bodily movements leading to a trance)

de·sal·i·nate \dē-ˈsa-lə-ˌnāt\ *vb* **-nat·ed; -nat·ing** : DESALT — **de·sal·i·na·tion** \-ˌsa-lə-ˈnā-shən\ *n*

de·sal·i·nize \dē-ˈsa-lə-ˌnīz\ *vb* **-nized; -niz·ing** : DESALT — **de·sal·i·ni·za·tion** \-ˌsa-lə-nə-ˈzā-shən\ *n*

de·salt \dē-ˈsȯlt\ *vb* : to remove salt from ⟨∼ seawater⟩ — **de·salt·er** *n*

des·cant \ˈdes-ˌkant\ *vb* 1 : to sing or play part music : SING 2 : to discourse or write at length

de·scend \di-ˈsend\ *vb* 1 : to pass from a higher to a lower place or level : pass, move, or climb down or down along 2 : DERIVE ⟨∼ed from royalty⟩ 3 : to pass by inheritance or transmission 4 : to incline, lead, or extend downward 5 : to swoop down or appear suddenly (as in an attack)

¹**de·scen·dant** *or* **de·scen·dent** \di-ˈsen-dənt\ *adj* 1 : DESCENDING 2 : proceeding from an ancestor or source

²**descendant** *or* **descendent** *n* 1 : one descended from another or from a common stock 2 : one deriving directly from a precursor or prototype

de·scent \di-ˈsent\ *n* 1 : ANCESTRY, BIRTH, LINEAGE 2 : the act or process of descending 3 : SLOPE 4 : a descending way (as a downgrade) 5 : a sudden hostile raid or assault 6 : a downward step (as in station or value) : DECLINE

de·scribe \di-ˈskrīb\ *vb* **de·scribed; de·scrib·ing** 1 : to represent or give an account of in words 2 : to trace the outline of — **de·scrib·able** *adj*

de·scrip·tion \di-ˈskrip-shən\ *n* 1 : an account of something; *esp* : an account that presents a picture to a person who reads or hears it 2 : KIND, SORT — **de·scrip·tive** \-ˈskrip-tiv\ *adj*

de·scry \di-ˈskrī\ *vb* **de·scried; de·scry·ing** 1 : to catch sight of 2 : to discover by observation or investigation

des·e·crate \ˈde-si-ˌkrāt\ *vb* **-crat·ed; -crat·ing** : PROFANE — **des·e·cra·tion** \ˌde-si-ˈkrā-shən\ *n*

de·seg·re·gate \dē-ˈse-gri-ˌgāt\ *vb* : to eliminate segregation in; *esp* : to free of any law or practice requiring isolation on the basis of race — **de·seg·re·ga·tion** \-ˌse-gri-ˈgā-shən\ *n*

de·sen·si·tize \dē-ˈsen-sə-ˌtīz\ *vb* : to make (a sensitized or hypersensitive individual) insensitive or nonreactive to a sensitizing agent — **de·sen·si·ti·za·tion** \-ˌsen-sə-tə-ˈzā-shən\ *n*

¹**des·ert** \ˈde-zərt\ *n* : dry land with few plants and little rainfall

²**des·ert** \ˈde-zərt\ *adj* : of, relating to, or resembling a desert; *esp* : being barren and without life ⟨a ∼ island⟩

³**de·sert** \di-ˈzərt\ *n* 1 : deserving of reward or punishment 2 : a just reward or punishment

⁴**de·sert** \di-ˈzərt\ *vb* 1 : to withdraw from 2 : ABANDON, FORSAKE — **de·sert·er** *n* — **de·ser·tion** \-ˈzər-shən\ *n*

de·serve \di-ˈzərv\ *vb* **de·served; de·serv·ing** : to be worthy of : MERIT — **de·serv·ing** *adj*

de·serv·ed·ly \-ˈzər-vəd-lē\ *adv* : according to merit : JUSTLY

des·ic·cate \ˈde-si-ˌkāt\ *vb* **-cat·ed; -cat·ing** : DRY, DEHYDRATE — **des·ic·ca·tion** \ˌde-si-ˈkā-shən\ *n* — **des·ic·ca·tor** \ˈde-si-ˌkā-tər\ *n*

de·sid·er·a·tum \di-ˌsi-də-ˈrä-təm, -ˌzi-, -ˈrā-\ *n, pl* **-ta** \-tə\ [L] : something desired as essential

¹**de·sign** \di-ˈzīn\ *vb* 1 : to conceive and plan out in the mind 2 : INTEND 3 : to devise for a specific function or end 4 : to make a pattern or sketch of 5 : to conceive and draw the plans for

²**design** *n* 1 : a particular purpose : deliberate planning 2 : a mental project or scheme : PLAN 3 : a secret project or scheme : PLOT 4 *pl* : aggressive or evil intent — used with *on* or *against* 5 : a preliminary sketch or plan 6 : an underlying scheme that governs functioning, developing, or unfolding : MOTIF 7 : the arrangement of elements or details in a product or a work of art 8 : a decorative pattern 9 : the art of executing designs

¹**des·ig·nate** \ˈde-zig-ˌnāt, -nət\ *adj* : chosen but not yet installed ⟨ambassador ∼⟩

²**des·ig·nate** \-ˌnāt\ *vb* **-nat·ed; -nat·ing** 1 : to appoint and set apart for a special purpose 2 : to mark or point out : INDICATE; *also* : SPECIFY, STIPULATE 3 : to

call by a name or title — **des·ig·na·tion** \de-zig-'nā-shən\ n

designated hitter n : a baseball player designated at the start of the game to bat in place of the pitcher without causing the pitcher to be removed from the game

de·sign·er \di-'zī-nər\ n 1 : one who creates plans for a project or structure 2 : one who designs and manufactures high-fashion clothing — **designer** adj

de·sign·ing \di-'zī-niŋ\ adj : CRAFTY, SCHEMING

de·sir·able \di-'zī-rə-bəl\ adj 1 : PLEASING, ATTRACTIVE 2 : ADVISABLE ⟨∼ legislation⟩ — **de·sir·abil·i·ty** \-,zī-rə-'bi-lə-tē\ n — **de·sir·able·ness** n

¹**de·sire** \di-'zīr\ vb **de·sired; de·sir·ing** [ME, fr. OF desirer, fr. L desiderare, fr. sider-, sidus heavenly body] 1 : to long or hope for : exhibit or feel desire for 2 : REQUEST

²**desire** n 1 : a strong wish : LONGING, CRAVING 2 : sexual urge or appetite 3 : a usu. formal request for action 4 : something desired

de·sir·ous \di-'zīr-əs\ adj : eagerly wishing : DESIRING

de·sist \di-'zist, -'sist\ vb : to cease to proceed or act

desk \'desk\ n [ME deske, fr. ML desca, fr. OIt desco table, fr. L discus dish, disc] 1 : a table, frame, or case esp. for writing and reading 2 : a counter, stand, or booth at which a person performs duties 3 : a specialized division of an organization (as a newspaper) ⟨city ∼⟩

desk·top publishing \'desk-,täp-\ n : the production of printed matter by means of a microcomputer

¹**des·o·late** \'de-sə-lət, -zə-\ adj 1 : DESERTED, ABANDONED 2 : FORSAKEN, LONELY 3 : DILAPIDATED 4 : BARREN, LIFELESS 5 : CHEERLESS, GLOOMY — **des·o·late·ly** adv — **des·o·late·ness** n

²**des·o·late** \-,lāt\ vb **-lat·ed; -lat·ing** : to make desolate : lay waste : make wretched

des·o·la·tion \,de-sə-'lā-shən, -zə-\ n 1 : the action of desolating 2 : GRIEF, SADNESS 3 : LONELINESS 4 : DEVASTATION, RUIN 5 : barren wasteland

des·oxy·ri·bo·nu·cle·ic acid \de-,zäk-sē-'rī-bō-nù-,klē-ik-, -nyü-\ n : DNA

¹**de·spair** \di-'spar\ vb : to lose all hope or confidence — **de·spair·ing·ly** adv

²**despair** n 1 : utter loss of hope 2 : a cause of hopelessness

des·patch \dis-'pach\ var of DISPATCH

des·per·a·do \,des-pə-'rä-dō, -'rā-\ n, pl **-does** or **-dos** : a bold or reckless criminal

des·per·ate \'des-pə-rət, -prət\ adj 1 : being beyond or almost beyond hope : causing despair 2 : RASH 3 : extremely intense — **des·per·ate·ly** adv — **des·per·ate·ness** n

des·per·a·tion \,des-pə-'rā-shən\ n 1 : a loss of hope and surrender to despair 2 : a state of hopelessness leading to rashness

de·spi·ca·ble \di-'spi-kə-bəl, 'des-pi-\ adj : deserving to be despised — **de·spi·ca·bly** \-blē\ adv

de·spise \di-'spīz\ vb **de·spised; de·spis·ing** 1 : to look down on with contempt or aversion : DISDAIN, DETEST 2 : to regard as negligible, worthless, or distasteful

de·spite \di-'spīt\ prep : in spite of

de·spoil \di-'spóil\ vb : to strip of belongings, possessions, or value — **de·spoil·er** n — **de·spoil·ment** n

de·spo·li·a·tion \di-,spō-lē-'ā-shən\ n : the act of plundering : the state of being despoiled

¹**de·spond** \di-'spänd\ vb : to become discouraged or disheartened

²**despond** n : DESPONDENCY

de·spon·den·cy \-'spän-dən-sē\ n : DEJECTION, HOPELESSNESS — **de·spon·dent** \-dənt\ adj — **de·spon·dent·ly** adv

des·pot \'des-pət, -,pät\ n [MF despote, fr. Gk despotēs master, lord, autocrat] 1 : a ruler with absolute power and authority 2 : a person exercising power tyrannically — **des·pot·ic** \des-'pä-tik\ adj — **des·po·tism** \'des-pə-,ti-zəm\ n

des·sert \di-'zərt\ n : a course of sweet food, fruit, or cheese served at the close of a meal

des·ti·na·tion \,des-tə-'nā-shən\ n 1 : a purpose for which something is destined 2 : an act of appointing, setting aside for a purpose, or predetermining 3 : a place to which one is journeying or to which something is sent

des·tine \'des-tən\ vb **des·tined; des·tin·ing** 1 : to settle in advance 2 : to designate, assign, or dedicate in advance 3 : to direct or set apart for a specific purpose or place

des·ti·ny \'des-tə-nē\ n, pl **-nies** 1 : something to which a person or thing is destined : FATE, FORTUNE 2 : a predetermined course of events

des·ti·tute \'des-tə-,tüt, -,tyüt\ adj 1 : lacking something needed or desirable 2 : suffering extreme poverty — **des·ti·tu·tion** \,des-tə-'tü-shən, -'tyü-\ n

de·stroy \di-'strói\ vb 1 : to put an end to : RUIN 2 : KILL

de·stroy·er \di-'strói-ər\ n 1 : one that destroys 2 : a small speedy warship

de·struc·ti·ble \di-'strək-tə-bəl\ adj : capable of being destroyed — **de·struc·ti·bil·i·ty** \-,strək-tə-'bi-lə-tē\ n

de·struc·tion \di-'strək-shən\ n 1 : RUIN 2 : the action or process of destroying something 3 : a destroying agency

de·struc·tive \di-'strək-tiv\ adj 1 : causing destruction : RUINOUS 2 : designed or tending to destroy — **de·struc·tive·ly** adv — **de·struc·tive·ness** n

de·sue·tude \'de-swi-,tüd, -,tyüd\ n : DISUSE

de·sul·to·ry \'de-səl-,tōr-ē\ adj : passing aimlessly from one thing or subject to another : DISCONNECTED

det abbr 1 detached; detachment 2 detail

de·tach \di-'tach\ vb 1 : to separate esp. from a larger mass 2 : DISENGAGE, WITHDRAW — **de·tach·able** adj

de·tached \di-'tacht\ adj 1 : not joined or connected : SEPARATE 2 : ALOOF, IMPARTIAL ⟨a ∼ attitude⟩

de·tach·ment \di-'tach-mənt\ n 1 : SEPARATION 2 : the dispatching of a body of troops or part of a fleet from the main body for special service; also : the portion so dispatched 3 : a small permanent military unit of special composition 4 : indifference to worldly concerns : ALOOFNESS 5 : IMPARTIALITY

¹**de·tail** \di-'tāl, 'dē-,tāl\ n [F détail, fr. OF detail slice, piece, fr. detaillier to cut in pieces, fr. taillier to cut] 1 : a dealing with something item by item ⟨go into ∼⟩; also : ITEM, PARTICULAR ⟨the ∼s of a story⟩ 2 : selection (as of soldiers) for special duty; also : the persons thus selected

²**detail** vb 1 : to report in particulars : SPECIFY 2 : to assign to a special duty

de·tailed \di-'tāld, 'dē-,tāld\ adj : marked by abundant detail

de·tain \di-'tān\ vb 1 : to hold in or as if in custody 2 : STOP, DELAY

de·tect \di-'tekt\ vb : to discover the nature, existence, presence, or fact of — **de·tect·able** adj — **de·tec·tion** \-'tek-shən\ n — **de·tec·tor** \-'tek-tər\ n

¹**de·tec·tive** \di-'tek-tiv\ adj 1 : fitted or used for detection 2 : of or relating to detectives

²**detective** n : a person employed or engaged in detecting lawbreakers or getting information that is not readily accessible

dé·tente \dā-'tänt\ n [F] : a relaxation of strained relations or tensions (as between nations)

de·ten·tion \di-'ten-chən\ n 1 : the act or fact of detaining : CONFINEMENT; esp : a period of temporary custody prior to disposition by a court 2 : a forced delay

de·ter \di-'tər\ vb **de·terred; de·ter·ring** [L deterrēre, fr. terrēre to frighten] 1 : to turn aside, discourage, or prevent from acting (as by fear) 2 : INHIBIT

de·ter·gent \di-'tər-jənt\ n : a cleansing agent; esp : a chemical product similar to soap in its cleaning ability

de·te·ri·o·rate \di-'tir-ē-ə-,rāt\ vb **-rat·ed; -rat·ing** : to make or become worse in quality or condition — **de-te-ri-o-ra-tion** \-ˌtir-ē-ə-ˈrā-shən\ n

de-ter-min-able \-ˈtər-mə-nə-bəl\ adj : capable of being determined; esp : ASCERTAINABLE

de-ter-mi-nant \-mə-nənt\ n 1 : something that determines or conditions 2 : GENE

de-ter-mi-nate \di-ˈtər-mə-nət\ adj 1 : having fixed limits : DEFINITE 2 : definitely settled — **de-ter-mi-nate-ness** n

de-ter-mi-na-tion \di-ˌtər-mə-ˈnā-shən\ n 1 : the act of coming to a decision; also : the decision or conclusion reached 2 : a fixing of the extent, position, or character of something 3 : accurate measurement (as of length or volume) 4 : firm or fixed purpose

de-ter-mine \di-ˈtər-mən\ vb -mined; -min-ing 1 : to fix conclusively or authoritatively 2 : to come to a decision : SETTLE, RESOLVE 3 : to fix the form or character of beforehand : ORDAIN; also : REGULATE 4 : to find out the limits, nature, dimensions, or scope of ⟨∼ a position at sea⟩ 5 : to bring about as a result

de-ter-mined \-ˈtər-mənd\ adj 1 : firmly resolved 2 : characterized by or showing determination — **de-ter-mined-ly** \-mənd-lē, -mə-nəd-lē\ adv — **de-ter-mined-ness** n

de-ter-min-ism \di-ˈtər-mə-ˌni-zəm\ n : a doctrine that acts of the will, natural events, or social changes are determined by preceding events or natural causes — **de-ter-min-ist** \-nist\ n or adj

de-ter-rence \di-ˈtər-əns\ n : the inhibition of criminal behavior by fear esp. of punishment

de-ter-rent \-ənt\ adj 1 : serving to deter 2 : relating to deterrence — **deterrent** n

de-test \di-ˈtest\ vb [L detestari, lit., to curse while calling a deity to witness, fr. de- from + testari to call to witness] : LOATHE, HATE — **de-test-able** adj — **de-tes-ta-tion** \ˌdē-ˌtes-ˈtā-shən\ n

de-throne \di-ˈthrōn\ vb : to remove from a throne : DEPOSE — **de-throne-ment** n

det-o-nate \ˈdet-ᵊn-ˌāt\ vb -nat-ed; -nat-ing : to explode or cause to explode with violence — **det-o-na-tion** \ˌdet-ᵊn-ˈā-shən\ n

det-o-na-tor \ˈdet-ᵊn-ˌā-tər\ n : a device for detonating an explosive

¹**de-tour** \ˈdē-ˌtu̇r\ n : an indirect way replacing part of a route

²**detour** vb : to go by detour

de-tox \ˈdē-ˌtäks, di-ˈtäks\ n : detoxification from a substance (as alcohol) — **detox** vb

de-tox-i-fy \ˈdē-ˈtäk-sə-ˌfī\ vb -fied; -fy-ing 1 : to remove a poison or toxin or the effect of such from 2 : to free (as a drug user) from an intoxicating or addictive substance or from dependence on it — **de-tox-i-fi-ca-tion** \ˌdē-ˌtäk-sə-fə-ˈkā-shən\ n

de-tract \di-ˈtrakt\ vb 1 : to take away or diminish the value or effect of something 2 : DIVERT — **de-trac-tion** \-ˈtrak-shən\ n — **de-trac-tor** \-ˈtrak-tər\ n

de-train \dē-ˈtrān\ vb : to leave or cause to leave a railroad train

det-ri-ment \ˈde-trə-mənt\ n : INJURY, DAMAGE; also : a cause of injury or damage — **det-ri-men-tal** \ˌde-trə-ˈment-ᵊl\ adj — **det-ri-men-tal-ly** adv

de-tri-tus \di-ˈtrī-təs\ n, pl **de-tri-tus** : fragments resulting from disintegration (as of rocks) : DEBRIS

deuce \ˈdüs, ˈdyüs\ n 1 : a two in cards or dice 2 : a tie in a tennis game with both sides at 40 3 : DEVIL — used chiefly as a mild oath

Deut abbr Deuteronomy

deu-te-ri-um \dü-ˈtir-ē-əm, dyü-\ n : an isotope of hydrogen that has twice the mass of ordinary hydrogen

Deu-ter-on-o-my \ˌdü-tə-ˈrä-nə-mē, ˌdyü-\ n — see BIBLE table

deut-sche mark \ˈdȯi-chə-ˌmärk\ n — see MONEY table

dev abbr deviation

de-val-ue \dē-ˈval-yü\ vb : to reduce the international exchange value of ⟨∼ a currency⟩ — **de-val-u-a-tion** \-ˌval-yə-ˈwā-shən\ n

dev-as-tate \ˈde-və-ˌstāt\ vb -tat-ed; -tat-ing 1 : to bring to ruin 2 : to reduce to chaos or helplessness — **dev-as-ta-tion** \ˌde-və-ˈstā-shən\ n

de-vel-op \di-ˈve-ləp\ vb 1 : to unfold gradually or in detail 2 : to place (exposed photographic material) in chemicals to produce a visible image 3 : to bring out the possibilities of 4 : to make more available or usable ⟨∼ land⟩ 5 : to acquire gradually ⟨∼ a taste for olives⟩ 6 : to go through a natural process of growth, differentiation, or evolution 7 : to come into being gradually — **de-vel-op-er** n — **de-vel-op-ment** n — **de-vel-op-men-tal** \-ˌve-ləp-ˈment-ᵊl\ adj

de-vi-ant \ˈdē-vē-ənt\ adj : deviating esp. from some accepted norm ⟨∼ behavior⟩ — **de-vi-ance** \-əns\ n — **de-vi-an-cy** \-ən-sē\ n — **deviant** n

de-vi-ate \ˈdē-vē-ˌāt\ vb -at-ed; -at-ing [LL deviare, fr. L de- from + via way] : to turn aside from a course, standard, principle, or topic — **de-vi-ate** \-vē-ət, -vē-ˌāt\ n — **de-vi-a-tion** \ˌdē-vē-ˈā-shən\ n

de-vice \di-ˈvīs\ n 1 : SCHEME, STRATAGEM 2 : a piece of equipment or a mechanism for a special purpose 3 : DESIRE, INCLINATION ⟨left to my own ∼s⟩ 4 : an emblematic design

¹**dev-il** \ˈde-vəl\ n [ME devel, fr. OE dēofol, fr. LL diabolus, fr. Gk diabolos, lit., slanderer, fr. diaballein to throw across, slander, fr. dia- across + ballein to throw] 1 often cap : the personal supreme spirit of evil 2 : DEMON 3 : a wicked person 4 : an energetic, reckless, or dashing person 5 : FELLOW ⟨poor ∼⟩ ⟨lucky ∼⟩

²**devil** vb -iled or -illed; -il-ing or -il-ling 1 : to season highly ⟨∼ed eggs⟩ 2 : TEASE, ANNOY

dev-il-ish \ˈde-və-lish\ adj 1 : befitting a devil : EVIL; also : MISCHIEVOUS 2 : EXTREME — **dev-il-ish-ly** adv — **dev-il-ish-ness** n

dev-il-ment \ˈde-vəl-mənt, -ˌment\ n : MISCHIEF

dev-il-ry \-rē\ or **dev-il-try** \-trē\ n, pl **-il-ries** or **-il-tries** 1 : action performed with the help of the devil 2 : MISCHIEF

de-vi-ous \ˈdē-vē-əs\ adj 1 : deviating from a straight line : ROUNDABOUT 2 : ERRANT 3 3 : TRICKY, CUNNING

¹**de-vise** \di-ˈvīz\ vb **de-vised; de-vis-ing** 1 : INVENT 2 : PLOT 3 : to give (real estate) by will

²**devise** n 1 : a disposing of real property by will 2 : a will or clause of a will disposing of real property 3 : property given by will

de-vi-tal-ize \dē-ˈvīt-ᵊl-ˌīz\ vb : to deprive of life or vitality

de-void \di-ˈvȯid\ adj : being without : VOID ⟨a book ∼ of interest⟩

de-voir \də-ˈvwär\ n 1 : DUTY 2 : a formal act of civility or respect

de-volve \di-ˈvälv\ vb **de-volved; de-volv-ing** : to pass (as rights or responsibility) from one to another usu. by succession or transmission — **dev-o-lu-tion** \ˌde-və-ˈlü-shən, ˌdē-\ n

De-vo-ni-an \di-ˈvō-nē-ən\ adj : of, relating to, or being the period of the Paleozoic era between the Silurian and the Mississippian — **Devonian** n

de-vote \di-ˈvōt\ vb **de-vot-ed; de-vot-ing** 1 : to commit to wholly or chiefly 2 : to set apart for a special purpose : DEDICATE

de-vot-ed \-ˈvō-təd\ adj : characterized by loyalty and devotion : FAITHFUL

dev-o-tee \ˌde-və-ˈtē, -ˈtā\ n : an ardent follower, supporter, or enthusiast

de-vo-tion \di-ˈvō-shən\ n 1 : religious fervor 2 : an act of prayer or private worship — usu. used in pl. 3 : a religious exercise for private use 4 : the fact or state of being dedicated and loyal ⟨∼ to music⟩; also : the act of devoting — **de-vo-tion-al** \-shə-nəl\ adj

de-vour \di-ˈvau̇r\ vb 1 : to eat up greedily or ravenously 2 : WASTE, ANNIHILATE 3 : to enjoy avidly ⟨∼ a book⟩ — **de-vour-er** n

de-vout \di-ˈvau̇t\ adj 1 : devoted to religion : PIOUS 2

: expressing devotion or piety **3** : EARNEST, SERIOUS — **de·vout·ly** adv — **de·vout·ness** n

dew \'dü, 'dyü\ n : moisture that condenses on the surfaces of cool bodies at night — **dewy** adj

dew·ber·ry \'dü-ˌber-ē, 'dyü-\ n : any of several sweet edible berries related to and resembling blackberries; also : a trailing bramble bearing these

dew·claw \-ˌklȯ\ n : a digit on the foot of a mammal that does not reach the ground; also : its claw or hoof

dew·lap \-ˌlap\ n : loose skin hanging under the neck of an animal

dew point n : the temperature at which the moisture in the air begins to condense

dex·ter·i·ty \dek-'ster-ə-tē\ n, pl **-ties 1** : mental skill or quickness **2** : readiness and grace in physical activity; esp : skill and ease in using the hands

dex·ter·ous \'dek-strəs\ adj **1** : CLEVER **2** : done with skillfulness **3** : skillful and competent with the hands — **dex·ter·ous·ly** adv

dex·trose \'dek-ˌstrōs\ n : the naturally occurring form of glucose found in plants and blood

DFC abbr Distinguished Flying Cross

dg abbr decigram

DG abbr **1** [LL Dei gratia] by the grace of God **2** director general

DH \ˌdē-'āch\ n : DESIGNATED HITTER

dhow \'daù\ n : an Arab sailing ship usu. having a long overhang forward and a high poop

DI abbr drill instructor

dia abbr diameter

di·a·be·tes \ˌdī-ə-'bē-tēz, -təs\ n : an abnormal state marked by passage of excessive amounts of urine; esp : one (**diabetes mel·li·tus** \-'me-lə-təs\) characterized by deficient insulin, by excess sugar in the blood and urine, and by thirst, hunger, and loss of weight — **di·a·bet·ic** \-'be-tik\ adj or n

di·a·bol·ic \ˌdī-ə-'bä-lik\ or **di·a·bol·i·cal** \-li-kəl\ adj : DEVILISH, FIENDISH — **di·a·bol·i·cal·ly** \-k(ə-)lē\ adv

di·a·crit·ic \ˌdī-ə-'kri-tik\ n : a mark accompanying a letter and indicating a sound value different from that of the same letter when unmarked — **di·a·crit·i·cal** \-ti-kəl\ adj

di·a·dem \'dī-ə-ˌdem\ n : CROWN; esp : a royal headband

di·aer·e·sis \dī-'er-ə-səs\ n, pl **-e·ses** \-ˌsēz\ : a mark ¨ placed over a vowel to show that it is pronounced in a separate syllable (as in naïve)

diag abbr **1** diagonal **2** diagram

di·ag·no·sis \ˌdī-ig-'nō-səs\ n, pl **-no·ses** \-ˌsēz\ : the art or act of identifying a disease from its signs and symptoms; also : the decision reached by diagnosis — **di·ag·nose** \'dī-ig-ˌnōs\ vb — **di·ag·nos·tic** \ˌdī-ig-'näs-tik\ adj — **di·ag·nos·ti·cian** \-ˌnäs-'ti-shən\ n

¹di·ag·o·nal \dī-'a-gə-nəl\ adj **1** : extending from one corner to the opposite corner in a 4-sided figure **2** : running in a slanting direction ⟨∼ stripes⟩ **3** : having slanting markings or parts ⟨a ∼ weave⟩ — **di·ag·o·nal·ly** adv

²diagonal n **1** : a diagonal line **2** : a diagonal row, pattern, or direction **3** : a mark / used esp. to mean "or," "and or," or "per"

¹di·a·gram \'dī-ə-ˌgram\ n : a design and esp. a drawing that makes something easier to understand — **di·a·gram·ma·ble** \-ˌgra-mə-bəl\ adj — **di·a·gram·mat·ic** \ˌdī-ə-grə-'ma-tik\ adj — **di·a·gram·mat·i·cal·ly** \-ti-k(ə-)lē\ adv

²diagram vb **-grammed** or **-gramed** \-ˌgramd\; **-gram·ming** or **-gram·ing** : to represent by a diagram

¹di·al \'dī-(ə)l\ n [ME dyal, fr. ML dialis clock wheel revolving daily, fr. L dies day] **1** : the face of a sundial **2** : the face of a timepiece **3** : a face with a pointer and numbers that indicate something (the ∼ of a gauge) **4** : a device used for making electrical connections or for regulating operation (as of a radio)

²dial vb **di·aled** or **di·alled**; **di·al·ing** or **di·al·ling 1** : to manipulate a dial so as to operate or select **2** : to make a telephone call or connection

³dial abbr dialect

di·a·lect \'dī-ə-ˌlekt\ n : a regional variety of a language

di·a·lec·tic \ˌdī-ə-'lek-tik\ n : the process or art of reasoning by discussion of conflicting ideas; also : the tension between opposing elements

di·a·logue \'dī-ə-ˌlȯg\ n **1** : a conversation between two or more parties **2** : the parts of a literary or dramatic work that represent conversation

di·al·y·sis \dī-'a-lə-səs\ n, pl **-y·ses** \-ˌsēz\ **1** : the separation of substances from solution by means of their unequal diffusion through semipermeable membranes **2** : the medical procedure of removing blood from an artery, purifying it by dialysis, and returning it to a vein

diam abbr diameter

di·am·e·ter \dī-'a-mə-tər\ n [ME diametre, fr. MF, fr. L diametros, fr. Gk, fr. dia- through + metron measure] **1** : a straight line passing through the center of a figure or body; esp : one that divides a circle in half **2** : the length of a diameter

di·a·met·ric \ˌdī-ə-'me-trik\ or **di·a·met·ri·cal** \-tri-kəl\ adj **1** : of, relating to, or constituting a diameter **2** : completely opposed or opposite — **di·a·met·ri·cal·ly** \-k(ə-)lē\ adv

di·a·mond \'dī-mənd, 'dī-ə-\ n **1** : a hard brilliant mineral that consists of crystalline carbon and is used as a gem **2** : a flat figure having four equal sides, two acute angles, and two obtuse angles **3** : any of a suit of playing cards marked with a red diamond **4** : INFIELD; also : the entire playing field in baseball

di·a·mond·back rattlesnake \-ˌbak-\ n : a large and deadly rattlesnake of the southern U.S.

di·an·thus \dī-'an-thəs\ n : ¹PINK 1

di·a·pa·son \ˌdī-ə-'pāz-ᵊn, -'pās-\ n **1** : the organ stop governing the flue pipes that form the primary basis of organ tone **2** : the entire range of musical tones

¹di·a·per \'dī-pər, 'dī-ə-\ n **1** : a cotton or linen fabric woven in a simple geometric pattern **2** : a garment for a baby drawn up between the legs and fastened about the waist

²diaper vb **1** : to ornament with diaper designs **2** : to put a diaper on

di·aph·a·nous \dī-'a-fə-nəs\ adj : of so fine a texture as to be transparent

di·a·pho·ret·ic \ˌdī-ə-fə-'re-tik\ adj : having the power to increase perspiration — **diaphoretic** n

di·a·phragm \'dī-ə-ˌfram\ n **1** : a sheet of muscle between the chest and abdominal cavities of a mammal **2** : a vibrating disk (as in a microphone) **3** : a cup-shaped device usu. of thin rubber fitted over the uterine cervix to act as a mechanical contraceptive barrier — **di·a·phrag·mat·ic** \ˌdī-ə-frag-'ma-tik, -ˌfrag-\ adj

di·a·rist \'dī-ə-rist\ n : one who keeps a diary

di·ar·rhea \ˌdī-ə-'rē-ə\ n : abnormally frequent and watery bowel movements

di·ar·rhoea chiefly Brit var of DIARRHEA

di·a·ry \'dī-ə-rē\ n, pl **-ries** : a daily record esp. of personal experiences; also : a book used as a diary

di·as·to·le \dī-'as-tə-(ˌ)lē\ n : the stretching of the chambers of the heart during which they fill with blood — **di·a·stol·ic** \ˌdī-ə-'stä-lik\ adj

dia·ther·my \'dī-ə-ˌthər-mē\ n : the generation of heat in tissue by electric currents for medical or surgical purposes

di·a·tom \'dī-ə-ˌtäm\ n : any of a class of planktonic one-celled or colonial algae with skeletons of silica

di·atom·ic \ˌdī-ə-'tä-mik\ adj : having two atoms in the molecule

di·a·tribe \'dī-ə-ˌtrīb\ n : biting or abusive speech or writing

dib·ble \'di-bəl\ n : a pointed hand tool for making

holes (as for planting bulbs) in the ground — **dibble** *vb*

¹dice \'dīs\ *n, pl* **dice** : DIE 1

²dice *vb* **diced; dic•ing 1** : to cut into small cubes ⟨∼ carrots⟩ **2** : to play games with dice

di•chot•o•my \dī-'kä-tə-mē\ *n, pl* **-mies** : a division or the process of dividing into two esp. mutually exclusive or contradictory groups — **di•chot•o•mous** \-məs\ *adj*

dick•er \'di-kər\ *vb* : BARGAIN, HAGGLE

dick•ey *or* **dicky** \'di-kē\ *n, pl* **dickeys** *or* **dick•ies** : a small fabric insert worn to fill in the neckline

di•cot•y•le•don \ˌdī-ˌkät-ᵊl-'ēd-ᵊn\ *n* : any of a group of seed plants having an embryo with two cotyledons — **di•cot•y•le•don•ous** *adj*

dict *abbr* dictionary

¹dic•tate \'dik-ˌtāt\ *vb* **dic•tat•ed; dic•tat•ing 1** : to speak or read for a person to transcribe or for a machine to record **2** : COMMAND, ORDER — **dic•ta•tion** \dik-'tā-shən\ *n*

²dic•tate \'dik-ˌtāt\ *n* : an authoritative rule, prescription, or injunction : COMMAND ⟨the ∼s of conscience⟩

dic•ta•tor \'dik-ˌtā-tər\ *n* **1** : a person ruling absolutely and often brutally and oppressively **2** : one that dictates

dic•ta•to•ri•al \ˌdik-tə-'tōr-ē-əl\ *adj* : of, relating to, or characteristic of a dictator or a dictatorship

dic•ta•tor•ship \dik-'tā-tər-ˌship, 'dik-ˌtā-\ *n* **1** : the office of a dictator **2** : autocratic rule, control, or leadership **3** : a government or country in which absolute power is held by a dictator or a small clique

dic•tion \'dik-shən\ *n* **1** : choice of words esp. with regard to correctness, clearness, or effectiveness : WORDING **2** : ENUNCIATION

dic•tio•nary \'dik-shə-ˌner-ē\ *n, pl* **-nar•ies** : a reference book containing words usu. alphabetically arranged along with information about their forms, pronunciations, functions, etymologies, meanings, and syntactical and idiomatic uses

dic•tum \'dik-təm\ *n, pl* **dic•ta** \-tə\ *also* **dictums** : a noteworthy, formal, or authoritative statement or observation

did *past of* DO

di•dac•tic \dī-'dak-tik\ *adj* **1** : intended to instruct, inform, or teach a moral lesson **2** : making moral observations

di•do \'dī-dō\ *n, pl* **didoes** *or* **didos** : a mischievous act : PRANK

¹die \'dī\ *vb* **died; dy•ing** \'dī-iŋ\ **1** : to stop living : EXPIRE **2** : to pass out of existence ⟨a *dying* race⟩ **3** : SUBSIDE **4** ⟨the wind *died* down⟩ **4** : to long keenly ⟨*dying* to go⟩ **5** : STOP ⟨the motor *died*⟩

²die \'dī\ *n 1 pl* **dice** \'dīs\ : a small cube marked on each face with one to six spots and used usu. in pairs in games and gambling **2** *pl* **dies** \'dīz\ : a device used to shape, finish, or impress an object

die-hard \'dī-ˌhärd\ *n* : one who is strongly devoted or determined

die•sel \'dē-zəl, -səl\ *n* **1** : DIESEL ENGINE **2** : a vehicle driven by a diesel engine

diesel engine *n* : an internal combustion engine in whose cylinders air is compressed to a temperature sufficiently high to ignite the fuel

die•sel•ing \'dē-zə-liŋ\ *n* : the continued operation of an internal combustion engine after the ignition has been turned off

¹di•et \'dī-ət\ *n* [ME *diete*, fr. OF, fr. L *diaeta*, fr. Gk *diaita*, lit., manner of living, fr. *diaitasthai* to lead one's life] **1** : food and drink regularly consumed : FARE **2** : an allowance of food prescribed for a special reason (as to lose weight) — **di•e•tary** \-ə-ˌter-ē\ *adj or n*

²diet *vb* : to eat or cause to eat or drink less or according to a prescribed rule — **di•et•er** *n*

di•e•tet•ics \ˌdī-ə-'te-tiks\ *n sing or pl* : the science or

art of applying the principles of nutrition to diet — **di•e•tet•ic** *adj*

di•e•ti•tian *or* **di•e•ti•cian** \ˌdī-ə-'ti-shən\ *n* : a specialist in dietetics

dif *or* **diff** *abbr* difference

dif•fer \'di-fər\ *vb* **dif•fered; dif•fer•ing 1** : to be unlike **2** : VARY **3** : DISAGREE

dif•fer•ence \'di-frəns, 'di-fə-\ *n* **1** : UNLIKENESS ⟨∼ in their looks⟩ **2** : distinction or discrimination in preference **3** : DISAGREEMENT; *also* : an instance or cause of disagreement ⟨unable to settle their ∼s⟩ **4** : the amount by which one number or quantity differs from another

dif•fer•ent \'di-frənt, 'di-fə-\ *adj* **1** : unlike in nature or quality **2** : DISTINCT ⟨∼ age groups⟩; *also* : VARIOUS ⟨∼ members of the club⟩ **3** : ANOTHER ⟨try a ∼ channel⟩ **4** : UNUSUAL, SPECIAL — **dif•fer•ent•ly** *adv*

¹dif•fer•en•tial \ˌdi-fə-'ren-chəl\ *adj* : showing, creating, or relating to a difference

²differential *n* **1** : the amount or degree by which things differ **2** : DIFFERENTIAL GEAR

differential calculus *n* : a branch of mathematics concerned with the study of the rate of change of functions with respect to their variables

differential gear *n* : an arrangement of gears in an automobile that allows one wheel to turn faster than another (as in rounding curves)

dif•fer•en•ti•ate \ˌdi-fə-'ren-chē-ˌāt\ *vb* **-at•ed; -at•ing 1** : to make or become different **2** : to recognize or state the difference ⟨∼ between them⟩ — **dif•fer•en•ti•a•tion** \-ˌren-chē-'ā-shən\ *n*

dif•fi•cult \'di-fi-(ˌ)kəlt\ *adj* **1** : hard to do or make **2** : hard to understand or deal with ⟨∼ reading⟩ ⟨a ∼ child⟩

dif•fi•cul•ty \-(ˌ)kəl-tē\ *n, pl* **-ties 1** : difficult nature ⟨the ∼ of a task⟩ **2** : DISAGREEMENT ⟨settled their *difficulties*⟩ **3** : OBSTACLE ⟨overcome *difficulties*⟩ **4** : TROUBLE ⟨in financial *difficulties*⟩ **syn** hardship, rigor, vicissitude

dif•fi•dent \'di-fə-dənt\ *adj* **1** : lacking confidence **2** : RESERVED 1 — **dif•fi•dence** \-dəns\ *n* — **dif•fi•dent•ly** *adv*

dif•frac•tion \di-'frak-shən\ *n* : the bending or spreading of waves (as of light) esp. when passing through narrow slits

¹dif•fuse \di-'fyüs\ *adj* **1** : VERBOSE, WORDY ⟨∼ writing⟩ **2** : not concentrated or localized ⟨∼ light⟩

²dif•fuse \di-'fyüz\ *vb* **dif•fused; dif•fus•ing 1** : to pour out or spread widely **2** : to undergo or cause to undergo diffusion **3** : to break up light by diffusion

dif•fu•sion \di-'fyü-zhən\ *n* **1** : a diffusing or a being diffused **2** : movement of particles (as of a gas) from a region of high to one of lower concentration **3** : the reflection of light from a rough surface or the passage of light through a translucent material

¹dig \'dig\ *vb* **dug** \'dəg\; **dig•ging 1** : to turn up the soil (as with a spade) **2** : to hollow out or form by removing earth ⟨∼ a hole⟩ **3** : to uncover or seek by turning up earth ⟨∼ potatoes⟩ **4** : DISCOVER ⟨∼ up information⟩ **5** : POKE, THRUST ⟨∼ a person in the ribs⟩ **6** : to work hard **7** : UNDERSTAND, APPRECIATE; *also* : LIKE, ADMIRE

²dig *n* **1** : THRUST, POKE; *also* : a cutting remark : GIBE **2** *pl* : living accommodations

³dig *abbr* digest

¹di•gest \'dī-ˌjest\ *n* : a summarized or shortened version esp. of a literary work

²di•gest \dī-'jest, də-\ *vb* **1** : to think over and arrange in the mind **2** : to convert (food) into simpler forms that can be absorbed by the body **3** : to compress into a short summary — **di•gest•ibil•i•ty** \-ˌjes-tə-'bi-lə-tē\ *n* — **di•gest•ible** *adj* — **di•ges•tion** \-'jes-chən\ *n* — **di•ges•tive** \-'jes-tiv\ *adj*

dig in *vb* **1** : to take a defensive stand esp. by digging trenches **2** : to firmly set to work **3** : to begin eating

dig•it \'di-jət\ *n* [ME, fr. L *digitus* finger, toe] **1** : any

of the Arabic numerals 1 to 9 and usu. the symbol 0
2 : FINGER, TOE
dig·i·tal \'di-jət-əl\ *adj* **1** : of, relating to, or done with
a finger or toe **2** : of, relating to, or using calculation
directly with digits rather than through measurable
physical quantities ⟨a ~ computer⟩ **3** : providing a
readout in numerical digits ⟨a ~ watch⟩ — **dig·i·tal·
ly** *adv*
dig·i·tal·is \ˌdi-jə-'ta-ləs\ *n* : a drug from the common
foxglove that is a powerful heart stimulant; *also*
: FOXGLOVE
dig·ni·fied \'dig-nə-ˌfīd\ *adj* : showing or expressing
dignity
dig·ni·fy \-ˌfī\ *vb* **-fied; -fy·ing** : to give dignity, distinction, or attention to
dig·ni·tary \'dig-nə-ˌter-ē\ *n, pl* **-tar·ies** : a person of
high position or honor
dig·ni·ty \'dig-nə-tē\ *n, pl* **-ties 1** : the quality or state
of being worthy, honored, or esteemed **2** : high rank,
office, or position **3** : formal reserve of manner, language, or appearance
di·graph \'dī-ˌgraf\ *n* : a group of two successive letters whose phonetic value is a single sound (as *ea* in
bread)
di·gress \dī-'gres, də-\ *vb* : to turn aside esp. from the
main subject or argument — **di·gres·sion** \-'gre-shən\
n — **di·gres·sive** \-'gre-siv\ *adj*
dike \'dīk\ *n* : a bank of earth constructed to control
water : LEVEE
dil *abbr* dilute
di·lap·i·dat·ed \də-'la-pə-ˌdā-təd\ *adj* : fallen into partial ruin or decay — **di·lap·i·da·tion** \-ˌla-pə-'dā-
shən\ *n*
di·late \dī-'lāt, 'dī-ˌlāt\ *vb* **di·lat·ed; di·lat·ing**
: SWELL, DISTEND, EXPAND — **dil·a·ta·tion** \ˌdi-lə-'tā-
shən\ *n* — **di·la·tion** \dī-'lā-shən\ *n*
dil·a·to·ry \'di-lə-ˌtōr-ē\ *adj* **1** : DELAYING **2** : TARDY,
SLOW
di·lem·ma \də-'le-mə\ *n* **1** : a usu. undesirable or unpleasant choice; *also* : a situation involving such a
choice **2** : PREDICAMENT
dil·et·tante \ˌdi-lə-'tänt, -'tant\ *n, pl* **-tantes** *or* **-tan·
ti** \-'tän-tē, -'tan-\ [It, fr. prp. of *dilettare* to delight,
fr. L *dilectare*] : a person having a superficial interest
in an art or a branch of knowledge
dil·i·gent \'di-lə-jənt\ *adj* : characterized by steady,
earnest, and energetic effort — PAINSTAKING — **dil·
i·gence** \-jəns\ *n* — **dil·i·gent·ly** *adv*
dill \'dil\ *n* : an herb related to the carrot with aromatic
leaves and seeds used in pickles
dil·ly \'di-lē\ *n, pl* **dil·lies** : one that is remarkable or
outstanding
dil·ly·dal·ly \'di-lē-ˌda-lē\ *vb* : to waste time by loiter-
ing or delaying
¹di·lute \dī-'lüt, də-\ *vb* **di·lut·ed; di·lut·ing** : to lessen
the consistency or strength of by mixing with some-
thing else — **di·lu·tion** \-'lü-shən\ *n*
²dilute *adj* : DILUTED, WEAK
¹dim \'dim\ *adj* **dim·mer; dim·mest 1** : LUSTERLESS,
DULL **2** : not bright or distinct : OBSCURE, FAINT **3**
: not seeing or understanding clearly — **dim·ly** *adv* —
dim·ness *n*
²dim *vb* **dimmed; dim·ming 1** : to make or become dim
or lusterless **2** : to reduce the light from
³dim *abbr* **1** dimension **2** diminished **3** diminutive
dime \'dīm\ *n* [ME, tenth part, tithe, fr. MF, fr. L *dec-
ima*, fr. fem. of *decimus* tenth, fr. *decem* ten] : a U.S.
coin worth ¹/₁₀ dollar
di·men·sion \də-'men-chən, dī-\ *n* **1** : the physical
property of length, breadth, or thickness; *also* : a measure of this **2** : EXTENT, SCOPE, PROPORTIONS — usu.
used in pl. — **di·men·sion·al** \-'men-chə-nəl\ *adj* —
di·men·sion·al·i·ty \-ˌmen-chə-'na-lə-tē\ *n*
di·min·ish \də-'mi-nish\ *vb* **1** : to make less or cause to
appear less **2** : BELITTLE **3** : DWINDLE **4** : TAPER —
dim·i·nu·tion \ˌdi-mə-'nü-shən, -'nyü-\ *n*

di·min·u·en·do \də-ˌmin-yə-'wen-dō\ *adv or adj* : DE-
CRESCENDO
¹di·min·u·tive \də-'min-yə-tiv\ *n* **1** : a diminutive word
or affix **2** : a diminutive individual
²diminutive *adj* **1** : indicating small size and sometimes
the state or quality of being lovable, pitiable, or contemptible ⟨the ~ suffixes *-ette* and *-ling*⟩ **2** : extremely small : TINY
dim·i·ty \'di-mə-tē\ *n, pl* **-ties** : a thin usu. corded cotton fabric
dim·mer \'di-mər\ *n* : a device for controlling the
amount of light from an electric lighting unit
di·mor·phic \(ˌ)dī-'mór-fik\ *adj* : occurring in two dis-
tinct forms — **di·mor·phism** \-ˌfi-zəm\ *n*
¹dim·ple \'dim-pəl\ *n* : a small depression esp. in the
cheek or chin
²dimple *vb* **dim·pled; dim·pling** : to form dimples (as in
smiling)
din \'din\ *n* : a loud confused mixture of noises
di·nar \di-'när\ *n* **1** — see MONEY table **2** — see *rial* at
MONEY table
dine \'dīn\ *vb* **dined; din·ing** [ME, fr. OF *diner*, fr.
(assumed) VL *disjejunare* to break one's fast, ultim.
fr. L *jejunus* fasting] **1** : to eat dinner **2** : to give a dinner to
din·er \'dī-nər\ *n* **1** : one that dines **2** : a railroad dining
car **3** : a restaurant usu. resembling a dining car
di·nette \dī-'net\ *n* : an alcove or small room used for
dining
din·ghy \'diŋ-ē\ *n, pl* **dinghies 1** : a small boat **2** : LIFE
RAFT
din·gle \'diŋ-gəl\ *n* : a small wooded valley
din·go \'diŋ-gō\ *n, pl* **dingoes** : a reddish brown wild
dog of Australia

dingo

din·gus \'diŋ-gəs, -əs\ *n* : DOODAD
din·gy \'din-jē\ *adj* **din·gi·er; -est** : DIRTY, DISCOLORED;
also : SHABBY — **din·gi·ness** *n*
din·ky \'diŋ-kē\ *adj* **din·ki·er; -est** : SMALL, INSIGNIF-
ICANT
din·ner \'di-nər\ *n* : the main meal of the day; *also* : a
formal banquet
din·ner·ware \'di-nər-ˌwar\ *n* : tableware other than
flatware
di·no·fla·gel·late \ˌdī-nō-'fla-jə-lət, -ˌlāt\ *n* : any of an
order of planktonic plantlike unicellular flagellates of
which some cause red tide
di·no·saur \'dī-nə-ˌsòr\ *n* [ultim. fr. Gk *deinos* terrifying + *sauros* lizard] : any of a group of extinct long-
tailed Mesozoic reptiles often of huge size
dint \'dint\ *n* **1** : FORCE ⟨by ~ of sheer grit⟩ **2** : DENT
di·o·cese \'dī-ə-səs, -ˌsēz, -ˌsēs\ *n, pl* **-ces·es** \-sə-səz,
-ˌsē-zəz, -ˌsē-səz\ : the territorial jurisdiction of a
bishop — **di·oc·e·san** \dī-'ä-sə-sən, ˌdī-ə-'sēz-ən\ *adj
or n*
di·ode \'dī-ˌōd\ *n* **1** : an electronic device with two
electrodes or terminals used esp. as a rectifier
di·ox·in \dī-'äk-sən\ *n* : a hydrocarbon that occurs esp.
as a persistent toxic impurity in herbicides (as Agent
Orange)
¹dip \'dip\ *vb* **dipped; dip·ping 1** : to plunge temporarily or partially under the surface (as of a liquid) **2** : to
thrust in a way to suggest immersion **3** : to scoop up

or out : LADLE **4** : to lower and then raise quickly ⟨∼ a flag in salute⟩ **5** : to drop or slope down esp. suddenly ⟨the moon *dipped* below the crest⟩ **6** : to decrease moderately and usu. temporarily ⟨prices *dipped*⟩ **7** : to reach inside or as if inside or below a surface ⟨*dipped* into their savings⟩ **8** : to delve casually into something; *esp* : to read superficially ⟨∼ into a book⟩

²dip *n* **1** : an act of dipping; *esp* : a short swim **2** : inclination downward : DROP **3** : something obtained by or used in dipping **4** : a sauce or soft mixture into which food may be dipped **5** : a liquid into which something may be dipped (as for cleansing or coloring)

diph·the·ria \dif-'thir-ē-ə\ *n* : an acute contagious bacterial disease marked by fever and by coating of the air passages with a membrane that interferes with breathing

diph·thong \'dif-ˌthȯŋ\ *n* : two vowel sounds joined in one syllable to form one speech sound (as *ou* in *out*)

dip·loid \'di-ˌplȯid\ *adj* : having the basic chromosome number doubled — **diploid** *n*

di·plo·ma \də-'plō-mə\ *n, pl* **diplomas** : an official record of graduation from or of a degree conferred by a school

di·plo·ma·cy \də-'plō-mə-sē\ *n* **1** : the art and practice of conducting negotiations between nations **2** : TACT

dip·lo·mat \'di-plə-ˌmat\ *n* : one employed or skilled in diplomacy — **dip·lo·mat·ic** \ˌdi-plə-'ma-tik\ *adj*

di·plo·ma·tist \də-'plō-mə-tist\ *n* : DIPLOMAT

dip·per \'di-pər\ *n* **1** : any of a genus of birds that are related to the thrushes and are skilled in diving **2** : something (as a ladle or scoop) that dips or is used for dipping **3** *cap* : BIG DIPPER **4** *cap* : LITTLE DIPPER

dip·so·ma·nia \ˌdip-sə-'mā-nē-ə\ *n* : an uncontrollable craving for alcoholic liquors — **dip·so·ma·ni·ac** \-nē-ˌak\ *n*

dip·stick \'dip-ˌstik\ *n* : a graduated rod for indicating depth

dip·ter·an \'dip-tə-rən\ *adj* : of, relating to, or being a fly (sense 2) — **dipteran** *n* — **dip·ter·ous** \-rəs\ *adj*

dir *abbr* **1** direction **2** director

dire \'dīr\ *adj* **dir·er; dir·est** **1** : very horrible : DREADFUL **2** : warning of disaster **3** : EXTREME

¹di·rect \də-'rekt, dī-\ *vb* **1** : ADDRESS ⟨∼ a letter⟩; *also* : to impart orally : AIM ⟨∼ a remark to the gallery⟩ **2** : to regulate the activities or course of : guide the supervision, organizing, or performance of **3** : to cause to turn, move, or point or to follow a certain course **4** : to point, extend, or project in a specified line or course **5** : to request or instruct with authority **6** : to show or point out the way

²direct *adj* **1** : stemming immediately from a source ⟨∼ result⟩ **2** : being or passing in a straight line of descent : LINEAL ⟨∼ ancestor⟩ **3** : leading from one point to another in time or space without turn or stop : STRAIGHT **4** : NATURAL, STRAIGHTFORWARD ⟨a ∼ manner⟩ **5** : operating without an intervening agency or step ⟨∼ action⟩ **6** : effected by the action of the people or the electorate and not by representatives ⟨∼ democracy⟩ **7** : consisting of or reproducing the exact words of a speaker or writer — **direct** *adv* — **di·rect·ly** *adv* — **di·rect·ness** *n*

direct current *n* : an electric current flowing in one direction only

di·rec·tion \də-'rek-shən, dī-\ *n* **1** : MANAGEMENT, GUIDANCE **2** : COMMAND, ORDER, INSTRUCTION **3** : the course or line along which something moves, lies, or points **4** : TENDENCY, TREND — **di·rec·tion·al** \-shə-nəl\ *adj*

di·rec·tive \də-'rek-tiv, dī-\ *n* : something that directs and usu. impels toward an action or goal; *esp* : an order issued by a high-level body or official

direct mail *n* : printed matter used for soliciting business or contributions and mailed direct to individuals

di·rec·tor \də-'rek-tər, dī-\ *n* **1** : one that directs : MAN-

AGER, SUPERVISOR, CONDUCTOR **2** : one of a group of persons who direct the affairs of an organized body — **di·rec·to·ri·al** \-ˌrek-'tȯr-ē-əl\ *adj* — **di·rec·tor·ship** *n*

di·rec·tor·ate \-tə-rət\ *n* **1** : the office or position of director **2** : a board of directors; *also* : membership on such a board **3** : an executive staff

di·rec·to·ry \-tə-rē\ *n, pl* **-ries** : an alphabetical or classified list esp. of names and addresses

dire·ful \'dīr-fəl\ *adj* : DREADFUL; *also* : OMINOUS

dirge \'dərj\ *n* : a song of lamentation; *also* : a slow mournful piece of music

dir·ham \'dir-həm\ *n* **1** — see MONEY table **2** — see *dinar, riyal* at MONEY table

di·ri·gi·ble \'dir-ə-jə-bəl, də-'ri-jə-\ *n* : AIRSHIP

dirk \'dərk\ *n* : DAGGER 1

dirndl \'dərnd-ᵊl\ *n* [short for G *Dirndlkleid*, fr. G dial. *Dirndl* girl + G *Kleid* dress] : a full skirt with a tight waistband

dirt \'dərt\ *n* **1** : a filthy or soiling substance (as mud, dust, or grime) **2** : loose or packed earth : SOIL **3** : moral uncleanness **4** : scandalous gossip **5** : embarrassing or incriminating information

¹dirty \'dər-tē\ *adj* **dirt·i·er; -est** **1** : SOILED, FILTHY **2** : INDECENT, SMUTTY ⟨∼ jokes⟩ **3** : BASE, UNFAIR ⟨a ∼ trick⟩ **4** : STORMY, FOGGY ⟨∼ weather⟩ **5** : not clear in color : DULL ⟨a ∼ red⟩ — **dirt·i·ness** *n* — **dirty** *adv*

²dirty *vb* **dirt·ied; dirty·ing** : to make or become dirty

dis·able \di-'sā-bəl\ *vb* **dis·abled; dis·abling** **1** : to disqualify legally **2** : to make unable to perform by or as if by illness, injury, or malfunction — **dis·abil·i·ty** \ˌdi-sə-'bi-lə-tē\ *n*

dis·abled *adj* : incapacitated by illness, injury, or wounds; *also* : physically or mentally impaired

dis·abuse \ˌdi-sə-'byüz\ *vb* : to free from error, fallacy, or misconception

dis·ad·van·tage \ˌdi-səd-'van-tij\ *n* **1** : loss or damage esp. to reputation or finances **2** : an unfavorable, inferior, or prejudicial condition; *also* : HANDICAP — **dis·ad·van·ta·geous** \di-ˌsad-ˌvan-'tā-jəs, -vən-\ *adj*

dis·ad·van·taged \-tijd\ *adj* : lacking in basic resources or conditions believed necessary for an equal position in society

dis·af·fect \ˌdi-sə-'fekt\ *vb* : to alienate the affection or loyalty of — **dis·af·fec·tion** \-'fek-shən\ *n*

dis·agree \ˌdi-sə-'grē\ *vb* **1** : to fail to agree **2** : to differ in opinion **3** : to cause discomfort or distress ⟨fried foods ∼ with her⟩ — **dis·agree·ment** *n*

dis·agree·able \-ə-bəl\ *adj* **1** : causing discomfort : UNPLEASANT, OFFENSIVE **2** : ILL-TEMPERED, PEEVISH — **dis·agree·able·ness** *n* — **dis·agree·ably** \-blē\ *adv*

dis·al·low \ˌdi-sə-'laù\ *vb* : to refuse to admit or recognize : REJECT ⟨∼ a claim⟩ — **dis·al·low·ance** *n*

dis·ap·pear \ˌdi-sə-'pir\ *vb* **1** : to pass out of sight **2** : to cease to be : become lost — **dis·ap·pear·ance** *n*

dis·ap·point \ˌdi-sə-'pȯint\ *vb* : to fail to fulfill the expectation or hope of — **dis·ap·point·ment** *n*

dis·ap·pro·ba·tion \di-ˌsa-prə-'bā-shən\ *n* : DISAPPROVAL

dis·ap·prov·al \ˌdi-sə-'prü-vəl\ *n* : adverse judgment : CENSURE

dis·ap·prove \-'prüv\ *vb* **1** : CONDEMN **2** : to feel or express disapproval ⟨∼s of smoking⟩ **3** : REJECT

dis·arm \di-'särm\ *vb* **1** : to take arms or weapons from **2** : to reduce the size and strength of the armed forces of a country **3** : to make harmless, peaceable, or friendly : win over ⟨a ∼ing smile⟩ — **dis·ar·ma·ment** \-'sär-mə-mənt\ *n*

dis·ar·range \ˌdi-sə-'rānj\ *vb* : to disturb the arrangement or order of — **dis·ar·range·ment** *n*

dis·ar·ray \-'rā\ *n* **1** : DISORDER, CONFUSION **2** : disorderly or careless dress

dis·as·sem·ble \ˌdi-sə-'sem-bəl\ *vb* : to take apart

dis·as·so·ci·ate \-'sō-shē-ˌāt, -sē-\ *vb* : to detach from association

di·sas·ter \di-'zas-tər, -'sas-\ *n* [MF *desastre*, fr. It *disastro,* fr. *astro* star, fr. L *astrum*] : a sudden or great misfortune — **di·sas·trous** \-'zas-trəs\ *adj* — **di·sas·trous·ly** *adv*

dis·avow \di-sə-'vaú\ *vb* : to deny responsibility for : REPUDIATE — **dis·avow·al** \-'vaú-əl\ *n*

dis·band \dis-'band\ *vb* : to break up the organization of : DISPERSE

dis·bar \dis-'bär\ *vb* : to expel from the legal profession — **dis·bar·ment** *n*

dis·be·lieve \dis-bə-'lēv\ *vb* 1 : to hold not worthy of belief : not believe 2 : to withhold or reject belief — **dis·be·lief** \-'lēf\ *n* — **dis·be·liev·er** *n*

dis·bur·den \dis-'bərd-ən\ *vb* : to rid of a burden

dis·burse \dis-'bərs\ *vb* **dis·bursed; dis·burs·ing** 1 : to pay out : EXPEND 2 : DISTRIBUTE — **dis·burse·ment** *n*

¹**disc** *var of* DISK

²**disc** *abbr* discount

dis·card \dis-'kärd, 'dis-ıkärd\ *vb* 1 : to let go a playing card from one's hand; *also* : to play (a card) from a suit other than a trump but different from the one led 2 : to get rid of as unwanted — **dis·card** \'dis-ıkärd\ *n*

disc brake *n* : a brake that operates by the friction of a pair of plates pressing against the sides of a rotating disc

dis·cern \di-'sərn, -'zərn\ *vb* 1 : to detect with the eyes : DISTINGUISH 2 : DISCRIMINATE 3 : to come to know or recognize mentally — **dis·cern·ible** *adj* — **dis·cern·ment** *n*

dis·cern·ing *adj* : revealing insight and understanding

¹**dis·charge** \dis-'chärj, 'dis-ıchärj\ *vb* 1 : to relieve of a charge, load, or burden : UNLOAD; *esp* : to remove the electrical energy from ⟨~ a storage battery⟩ 2 : to let or put off ⟨~ passengers⟩ 3 : SHOOT ⟨~ an arrow⟩ 4 : to set free ⟨~ a prisoner⟩ 5 : to dismiss from service or employment ⟨~ a soldier⟩ 6 : to get rid of by paying or doing ⟨~ a debt⟩ 7 : to give forth fluid ⟨the river ~s into the ocean⟩

²**dis·charge** \'dis-ıchärj, dis-'chärj\ *n* 1 : the act of discharging, unloading, or releasing 2 : something that discharges; *esp* : a certification of release or payment 3 : a firing off (as of a gun) 4 : a flowing out (as of blood from a wound); *also* : something that is emitted ⟨a purulent ~⟩ 5 : release or dismissal esp. from an office or employment; *also* : complete separation from military service 6 : a flow of electricity (as through a gas)

dis·ci·ple \di-'sī-pəl\ *n* 1 : one who accepts and helps to spread the teachings of another; *also* : a convinced adherent 2 *cap* : a member of the Disciples of Christ

dis·ci·pli·nar·i·an \ıdi-sə-plə-'ner-ē-ən\ *n* : one who enforces order

dis·ci·plin·ary \'di-sə-plə-ıner-ē\ *adj* : of or relating to discipline; *also* : CORRECTIVE ⟨take ~ action⟩

¹**dis·ci·pline** \'di-sə-plən\ *n* 1 : PUNISHMENT 2 : a field of study : SUBJECT 3 : training that corrects, molds, or perfects 4 : control gained by obedience or training : orderly conduct 5 : a system of rules governing conduct

²**discipline** *vb* **-plined; -plin·ing** 1 : PUNISH 2 : to train or develop by instruction and exercise esp. in self-control 3 : to bring under control ⟨~ troops⟩; *also* : to impose order upon

disc jockey *n* : an announcer of a radio show of popular recorded music

dis·claim \dis-'klām\ *vb* : DENY, DISAVOW — **dis·claim·er** *n*

dis·close \dis-'klōz\ *vb* : to expose to view — **dis·clo·sure** \-'klō-zhər\ *n*

dis·co \'dis-kō\ *n, pl* **discos** 1 : a nightclub for dancing to live or recorded music 2 : popular dance music characterized by hypnotic rhythm, repetitive lyrics, and electronically produced sounds

dis·col·or \dis-'kə-lər\ *vb* : to alter or change in hue or color esp. for the worse — **dis·col·or·ation** \-ıkə-lə-'rā-shən\ *n*

dis·com·bob·u·late \ıdis-kəm-'bä-byú-ılāt\ *vb* **-lat·ed; -lat·ing** : UPSET, CONFUSE

dis·com·fit \dis-'kəm-fət, *esp Southern* ıdis-kəm-'fit\ *vb* : UPSET, FRUSTRATE — **dis·com·fi·ture** \dis-'kəm-fə-ıchúr\ *n*

¹**dis·com·fort** \dis-'kəm-fərt\ *vb* : to make uncomfortable or uneasy

²**discomfort** *n* : mental or physical uneasiness

dis·com·mode \ıdis-kə-'mōd\ *vb* **-mod·ed; -mod·ing** : INCONVENIENCE, TROUBLE

dis·com·pose \-kəm-'pōz\ *vb* 1 : AGITATE 2 : DISARRANGE — **dis·com·po·sure** \-'pō-zhər\ *n*

dis·con·cert \ıdis-kən-'sərt\ *vb* : CONFUSE, UPSET

dis·con·nect \ıdis-kə-'nekt\ *vb* : to undo the connection of — **dis·con·nec·tion** \-'nek-shən\ *n*

dis·con·nect·ed *adj* : not connected; *also* : INCOHERENT — **dis·con·nect·ed·ly** *adv*

dis·con·so·late \dis-'kän-sə-lət\ *adj* 1 : CHEERLESS 2 : hopelessly sad — **dis·con·so·late·ly** *adv*

dis·con·tent \ıdis-kən-'tent\ *n* : uneasiness of mind : DISSATISFACTION — **dis·con·tent·ed** *adj*

dis·con·tin·ue \ıdis-kən-'tin-yü\ *vb* 1 : to break the continuity of : cease to operate, use, or take 2 : END — **dis·con·tin·u·ance** \-yə-wəns\ *n* — **dis·con·ti·nu·i·ty** \dis-ıkän-tə-'nü-ə-tē, -'nyü-\ *n* — **dis·con·tin·u·ous** \ıdis-kən-'tin-yə-wəs\ *adj*

dis·cord \'dis-ıkórd\ *n* 1 : lack of agreement or harmony : DISSENSION, CONFLICT 2 : a harsh combination of musical sounds 3 : a harsh or unpleasant sound — **dis·cor·dant** \dis-'kórd-ənt\ *adj* — **dis·cor·dant·ly** *adv*

dis·co·theque \'dis-kə-ıtek\ *n* : DISCO 1

¹**dis·count** \'dis-ıkaúnt\ *n* 1 : a reduction made from a regular or list price 2 : a deduction of interest in advance when lending money

²**dis·count** \'dis-ıkaúnt, dis-'kaúnt\ *vb* 1 : to deduct from the amount of a bill, debt, or charge usu. for cash or prompt payment; *also* : to sell or offer for sale at a discount 2 : to lend money after deducting the discount ⟨~ a note⟩ 3 : DISREGARD; *also* : MINIMIZE 4 : to make allowance for bias or exaggeration 5 : to take into account (as a future event) in present calculations — **dis·count·able** *adj* — **dis·count·er** *n*

³**dis·count** \'dis-ıkaúnt\ *adj* : selling goods or services at a discount; *also* : sold at or reflecting a discount

dis·coun·te·nance \dis-'kaúnt-ən-ənts\ *vb* 1 : EMBARRASS, DISCONCERT 2 : to look with disfavor on

dis·cour·age \dis-'kər-ij\ *vb* **-aged; -ag·ing** 1 : to deprive of courage or confidence : DISHEARTEN 2 : to hinder by disfavoring 3 : to attempt to dissuade — **dis·cour·age·ment** *n* — **dis·cour·ag·ing·ly** *adv*

¹**dis·course** \'dis-ıkōrs\ *n* [ME *discours,* fr. ML & LL *discursus;* ML, argument, fr. LL, conversation, fr. L, act of running about, fr. *discurrere* to run about, fr. *currere* to run] 1 : CONVERSATION 2 : formal and usu. extended expression of thought on a subject

²**dis·course** \dis-'kōrs\ *vb* **dis·coursed; dis·cours·ing** 1 : to express oneself in esp. oral discourse 2 : TALK, CONVERSE

dis·cour·te·ous \(ı)dis-'kər-tē-əs\ *adj* : lacking courtesy : UNCIVIL, RUDE — **dis·cour·te·ous·ly** *adv*

dis·cour·te·sy \-'kər-tə-sē\ *n* : RUDENESS; *also* : a rude act

dis·cov·er \dis-'kə-vər\ *vb* 1 : to make known or visible 2 : to obtain sight or knowledge of for the first time; *also* : FIND OUT — **dis·cov·er·er** *n*

dis·cov·ery \dis-'kə-və-rē\ *n, pl* **-er·ies** 1 : the act or process of discovering 2 : something discovered 3 : the disclosure usu. before a civil trial of pertinent facts or documents

¹**dis·cred·it** \(ı)dis-'kre-dət\ *vb* 1 : DISBELIEVE 2 : to cause disbelief in the accuracy or authority of 3 : DISGRACE — **dis·cred·it·able** *adj*

²**discredit** *n* 1 : loss of reputation 2 : lack or loss of belief or confidence

dis·creet \dis-'krēt\ *adj* : showing good judgment; *esp*

: capable of observing prudent silence — **dis·creet·ly** *adv*

dis·crep·an·cy \dis-ˈkre-pən-sē\ *n, pl* **-cies 1** : DIFFERENCE, DISAGREEMENT **2** : an instance of being discrepant

dis·crep·ant \-pənt\ *adj* [ME *discrepaunt*, fr. L *discrepans*, prp. of *discrepare* to sound discordantly, fr. *crepare* to rattle, creak] : being at variance : DISAGREEING

dis·crete \dis-ˈkrēt, ˈdis-ˌkrēt\ *adj* **1** : individually distinct **2** : NONCONTINUOUS

dis·cre·tion \dis-ˈkre-shən\ *n* **1** : the quality of being discreet : PRUDENCE **2** : individual choice or judgment **3** : power of free decision or latitude of choice — **dis·cre·tion·ary** *adj*

dis·crim·i·nate \dis-ˈkri-mə-ˌnāt\ *vb* **-nat·ed; -nat·ing 1** : DISTINGUISH, DIFFERENTIATE **2** : to make a difference in treatment on a basis other than individual merit — **dis·crim·i·na·tion** \-ˌkri-mə-ˈnā-shən\ *n*

dis·crim·i·nat·ing *adj* : marked by discrimination; *esp* : DISCERNING, JUDICIOUS

dis·crim·i·na·to·ry \dis-ˈkri-mə-nə-ˌtōr-ē\ *adj* : marked by esp. unjust discrimination ⟨∼ treatment⟩

dis·cur·sive \dis-ˈkər-siv\ *adj* : passing from one topic to another : RAMBLING — **dis·cur·sive·ly** *adv* — **dis·cur·sive·ness** *n*

dis·cus \ˈdis-kəs\ *n, pl* **dis·cus·es** : a disk that is hurled for distance in a track-and-field contest

dis·cuss \di-ˈskəs\ *vb* [ME, fr. L *discussus*, pp. of *discutere* to disperse, fr. *dis-* apart + *quatere* to shake] **1** : to argue or consider carefully by presenting the various sides **2** : to talk about — **dis·cus·sion** \-ˈskə-shən\ *n*

dis·cus·sant \di-ˈskəs-ᵊnt\ *n* : one who takes part in a formal discussion

¹**dis·dain** \dis-ˈdān\ *n* : CONTEMPT, SCORN — **dis·dain·ful** \-fəl\ *adj* — **dis·dain·ful·ly** *adv*

²**disdain** *vb* **1** : to look on with scorn **2** : to reject or refrain from because of disdain

dis·ease \di-ˈzēz\ *n* : an abnormal bodily condition that impairs functioning and can usu. be recognized by signs and symptoms : SICKNESS — **dis·eased** \-ˈzēzd\ *adj*

dis·em·bark \ˌdi-səm-ˈbärk\ *vb* : to go or put ashore from a ship — **dis·em·bar·ka·tion** \di-ˌsem-ˌbär-ˈkā-shən\ *n*

dis·em·body \ˌdi-səm-ˈbä-dē\ *vb* : to deprive of bodily existence

dis·em·bow·el \-ˈbaú-əl\ *vb* : EVISCERATE 1 — **dis·em·bow·el·ment** *n*

dis·en·chant \ˌdis-ᵊn-ˈchant\ *vb* : DISILLUSION — **dis·en·chant·ment** *n*

dis·en·chant·ed \-ˈchan-təd\ *adj* : DISAPPOINTED, DISSATISFIED

dis·en·cum·ber \ˌdis-ᵊn-ˈkəm-bər\ *vb* : to free from something that burdens

dis·en·fran·chise \ˌdis-ᵊn-ˈfran-ˌchīz\ *vb* : DISFRANCHISE — **dis·en·fran·chise·ment** *n*

dis·en·gage \ˌdis-ᵊn-ˈgāj\ *vb* : RELEASE, EXTRICATE, DISENTANGLE — **dis·en·gage·ment** *n*

dis·en·tan·gle \ˌdis-ᵊn-ˈtaŋ-gəl\ *vb* : to free from entanglement : UNRAVEL

dis·equi·lib·ri·um \di-ˌsē-kwə-ˈli-brē-əm\ *n* : loss or lack of equilibrium

dis·es·tab·lish \ˌdi-sə-ˈsta-blish\ *vb* : to end the establishment of; *esp* : to deprive of the status of an established church — **dis·es·tab·lish·ment** *n*

dis·es·teem \ˌdi-sə-ˈstēm\ *n* : lack of esteem : DISFAVOR, DISREPUTE

dis·fa·vor \(ˌ)dis-ˈfā-vər\ *n* **1** : DISAPPROVAL, DISLIKE **2** : the state or fact of being no longer favored

dis·fig·ure \dis-ˈfi-gyər\ *vb* : to spoil the appearance of ⟨*disfigured* by a scar⟩ — **dis·fig·ure·ment** *n*

dis·fran·chise \dis-ˈfran-ˌchīz\ *vb* : to deprive of a franchise, a legal right, or a privilege; *esp* : to deprive of the right to vote — **dis·fran·chise·ment** *n*

dis·gorge \-ˈgórj\ *vb* : VOMIT; *also* : to discharge forcefully or confusedly

¹**dis·grace** \di-ˈskrās, dis-ˈgrās\ *vb* : to bring reproach or shame to

²**disgrace** *n* **1** : SHAME, DISHONOR; *also* : a cause of shame **2** : the condition of being out of favor : loss of respect — **dis·grace·ful** \-fəl\ *adj* — **dis·grace·ful·ly** *adv*

dis·grun·tle \dis-ˈgrənt-ᵊl\ *vb* **dis·grun·tled; dis·grun·tling** : to put in bad humor

¹**dis·guise** \dis-ˈgīz\ *vb* **dis·guised; dis·guis·ing 1** : to change the appearance of or to conceal the identity or to resemble another **2** : HIDE, CONCEAL

²**disguise** *n* **1** : clothing put on to conceal one's identity or counterfeit another's **2** : an outward appearance that hides what something really is

¹**dis·gust** \dis-ˈgəst\ *n* : AVERSION, REPUGNANCE — **dis·gust·ful** \-fəl\ *adj*

²**disgust** *vb* : to provoke to loathing, repugnance, or aversion : be offensive to — **dis·gust·ed·ly** *adv* — **dis·gust·ing·ly** *adv*

¹**dish** \ˈdish\ *n* [ME, fr. OE *disc* plate, fr. L *discus* quoit, disk, dish, fr. Gk *diskos*, fr. *dikein* to throw] **1** : a vessel used for serving food **2** : the food served in a dish ⟨a ∼ of berries⟩ **3** : food prepared in a particular way **4** : something resembling a dish esp. in being shallow and concave

²**dish** *vb* **1** : to put into a dish **2** : to make concave like a dish

dis·ha·bille \ˌdi-sə-ˈbēl\ *n* [F *déshabillé*] : the state of being dressed in a casual or careless manner

dis·har·mo·ny \(ˌ)dis-ˈhär-mə-nē\ *n* : lack of harmony — **dis·har·mo·ni·ous** \ˌdis-(ˌ)här-ˈmō-nē-əs\ *adj*

dish·cloth \ˈdish-ˌklȯth\ *n* : a cloth for washing dishes

dis·heart·en \dis-ˈhärt-ᵊn\ *vb* : DISCOURAGE, DEJECT

dished \ˈdisht\ *adj* : CONCAVE

di·shev·el \di-ˈshe-vəl\ *vb* **-shev·eled** *or* **-shev·elled; -shev·el·ing** *or* **-shev·el·ling** [ME *discheveled* with disordered hair, fr. MF *deschevelé*, fr. pp. of *descheveler* to disarrange the hair, fr. *chevel* hair, fr. L *capillus*] : to throw into disorder or disarray — **di·shev·eled** *or* **di·shev·elled** *adj*

dis·hon·est \di-ˈsä-nəst\ *adj* : not honest : UNTRUSTWORTHY, DECEITFUL — **dis·hon·est·ly** *adv* — **dis·hon·es·ty** \-nə-stē\ *n*

¹**dis·hon·or** \di-ˈsä-nər\ *vb* **1** : DISGRACE **2** : to refuse to accept or pay ⟨∼ a check⟩

²**dishonor** *n* **1** : lack or loss of honor **2** : SHAME, DISGRACE **3** : a cause of disgrace **4** : the act of dishonoring a negotiable instrument when presented for payment — **dis·hon·or·able** \di-ˈsä-nə-rə-bəl\ *adj* — **dis·hon·or·ably** \-blē\ *adv*

dish out *vb* : to give freely

dish·rag \ˈdish-ˌrag\ *n* : DISHCLOTH

dish·wash·er \-ˌwȯ-shər, -ˌwä-\ *n* : a person or machine that washes dishes

dish·wa·ter \-ˌwȯ-tər, -ˌwä-\ *n* : water used for washing dishes

dis·il·lu·sion \ˌdi-sə-ˈlü-zhən\ *vb* : to leave without illusion or naive faith and trust — **dis·il·lu·sion·ment** *n*

dis·il·lu·sioned *adj* : DISAPPOINTED, DISSATISFIED

dis·in·cli·na·tion \di-ˌsin-klə-ˈnā-shən\ *n* : a preference for avoiding something : slight aversion

dis·in·cline \ˌdis-ᵊn-ˈklīn\ *vb* : to make unwilling

dis·in·clined *adj* : unwilling because of dislike or disapproval

dis·in·fect \ˌdis-ᵊn-ˈfekt\ *vb* : to cleanse of infection-causing germs — **dis·in·fec·tant** \-ˈfek-tənt\ *n* — **dis·in·fec·tion** \-ˈfek-shən\ *n*

dis·in·for·ma·tion \-ˌin-fər-ˈmā-shən\ *n* : false information deliberately and often covertly spread

dis·in·gen·u·ous \ˌdis-ᵊn-ˈjen-yə-wəs\ *adj* : lacking in candor; *also* : giving a false appearance of simple frankness

dis·in·her·it \ˌdis-ᵊn-ˈher-ət\ *vb* : to deprive of the right to inherit

dis·in·te·grate \di-'sin-tə-ˌgrāt\ vb 1 : to break or decompose into constituent parts or small particles 2 : to destroy the unity or integrity of — **dis·in·te·gra·tion** \-ˌsin-tə-'grā-shən\ n

dis·in·ter \ˌdis-ən-'tər\ vb 1 : to take from the grave or tomb 2 : UNEARTH

dis·in·ter·est·ed \(ˌ)dis-'in-tə-rəs-təd, -ˌres-\ adj 1 : not interested 2 : free from selfish motive or interest : UNBIASED — **dis·in·ter·est·ed·ness** n

dis·join \(ˌ)dis-'jȯin\ vb : SEPARATE

dis·joint \(ˌ)dis-'jȯint\ vb : to disturb the orderly arrangement of; also : to separate at the joints

dis·joint·ed adj 1 : DISCONNECTED; esp : INCOHERENT 2 : separated at or as if at the joint

disk or **disc** \'disk\ n 1 : something round and flat; esp : a flat rounded anatomical structure (as the central part of the flower head of a composite plant or a pad of cartilage between vertebrae) 2 usu disc : a phonograph record 3 : a round flat plate coated with a magnetic substance on which data for a computer is stored 4 usu disc : OPTICAL DISK

dis·kette \dis-'ket\ n : FLOPPY DISK

¹**dis·like** \(ˌ)dis-'līk\ n : a feeling of aversion or disapproval

²**dislike** vb : to regard with dislike : DISAPPROVE

dis·lo·cate \'dis-lō-ˌkāt, dis-'lō-\ vb 1 : to put out of place; esp : to displace (a bone or joint) from normal connections ⟨~ a shoulder⟩ 2 : DISRUPT — **dis·lo·ca·tion** \ˌdis-(ˌ)lō-'kā-shən\ n

dis·lodge \(ˌ)dis-'läj\ vb : to force out of a place esp. of rest, hiding, or defense

dis·loy·al \(ˌ)dis-'lȯi-əl\ adj : lacking in loyalty — **dis·loy·al·ty** n

dis·mal \'diz-məl\ adj [ME, fr. dismal, n., days marked as unlucky in medieval calendars, fr. AF, fr ML dies mali, lit., evil days] 1 : showing or causing gloom or depression 2 : lacking merit — **dis·mal·ly** adv

dis·man·tle \(ˌ)dis-'mant-ᵊl\ vb -tled; -tling 1 : to take apart 2 : to strip of furniture and equipment — **dis·man·tle·ment** n

dis·may \dis-'mā\ vb : to cause to lose courage or resolution from alarm or fear : DAUNT — **dismay** n — **dis·may·ing·ly** adv

dis·mem·ber \dis-'mem-bər\ vb 1 : to cut off or separate the limbs or parts of 2 : to break up or tear into pieces — **dis·mem·ber·ment** n

dis·miss \dis-'mis\ vb 1 : to send away 2 : DISCHARGE 5 3 : to put aside or out of mind 4 : to put out of judicial consideration ⟨~ed all charges⟩ — **dis·miss·al** n

dis·mount \dis-'maúnt\ vb 1 : to get down from something (as a horse or bicycle) 2 : UNHORSE 3 : DISASSEMBLE

dis·obe·di·ence \ˌdi-sə-'bē-dē-əns\ n : neglect or refusal to obey — **dis·obe·di·ent** \-ənt\ adj

dis·obey \ˌdi-sə-'bā\ vb : to fail to obey : be disobedient

dis·oblige \ˌdi-sə-'blīj\ vb 1 : to go counter to the wishes of 2 : INCONVENIENCE

¹**dis·or·der** \di-'sȯr-dər\ vb 1 : to disturb the order of 2 : to disturb the regular or normal functions of ⟨a ~ed digestion⟩

²**disorder** n 1 : lack of order : CONFUSION 2 : breach of the peace or public order 3 : an abnormal state of body or mind : AILMENT

dis·or·der·ly \-lē\ adj 1 : offensive to public order 2 : marked by disorder ⟨a ~ desk⟩ — **dis·or·der·li·ness** n

dis·or·ga·nize \di-'sȯr-gə-ˌnīz\ vb : to break up the regular system of : throw into disorder — **dis·or·ga·ni·za·tion** \di-ˌsȯr-gə-nə-'zā-shən\ n

dis·ori·ent \di-'sȯr-ē-ˌent\ vb : to cause to be confused or lost — **dis·ori·en·ta·tion** \di-ˌsȯr-ē-ən-'tā-shən\ n

dis·own \di-'sōn\ vb : REPUDIATE, RENOUNCE, DISCLAIM

dis·par·age \di-'spar-ij\ vb -aged; -ag·ing [ME to degrade by marriage below one's class, disparage, fr. MF desparagier to marry below one's class, fr. OF, fr. parage extraction, lineage, fr. per peer] 1 : to lower in rank or reputation : DEGRADE 2 : BELITTLE — **dis·par·age·ment** n — **dis·par·ag·ing·ly** adv

dis·pa·rate \'dis-pə-rət, dis-'par-ət\ adj : distinct in quality or character — **dis·par·i·ty** \di-'spar-ə-tē\ n

dis·pas·sion·ate \(ˌ)dis-'pa-shə-nət\ adj : not influenced by strong feeling : CALM, IMPARTIAL — **dis·pas·sion** \-'pa-shən\ n — **dis·pas·sion·ate·ly** adv

¹**dis·patch** \di-'spach\ vb 1 : to send off or away with promptness or speed esp. on official business 2 : to put to death 3 : to attend to rapidly or efficiently 4 : DEFEAT — **dis·patch·er** n

²**dis·patch** \di-'spach, 'dis-ˌpach\ n 1 : MESSAGE 2 : a news item sent in by a correspondent to a newspaper 3 : the act of dispatching; esp : SHIPMENT 4 : the act of putting to death 5 : promptness and efficiency in performing a task

dis·pel \di-'spel\ vb **dis·pelled; dis·pel·ling** : to drive away by scattering : DISSIPATE

dis·pens·able \di-'spen-sə-bəl\ adj : capable of being dispensed with

dis·pen·sa·ry \di-'spen-sə-rē\ n, pl -ries : a place where medicine or medical or dental aid is dispensed

dis·pen·sa·tion \ˌdis-pən-'sā-shən\ n 1 : a system of rules for ordering affairs 2 : a particular arrangement or provision esp. of nature 3 : an exemption from a rule or from a vow or oath 4 : the act of dispensing 5 : something dispensed or distributed

dis·pense \di-'spens\ vb **dis·pensed; dis·pens·ing** 1 : to portion out 2 : ADMINISTER ⟨~ justice⟩ 3 : EXEMPT 4 : to make up and give out (remedies) — **dis·pens·er** n — **dispense with** 1 : SUSPEND 2 : to do without

dis·perse \di-'spərs\ vb **dis·persed; dis·pers·ing** : to break up and scatter about : SPREAD — **dis·per·sal** \-'spər-səl\ n — **dis·per·sion** \-'spər-zhən\ n

dis·pir·it \dis-'pir-ət\ vb : DEPRESS, DISCOURAGE, DISHEARTEN

dis·place \dis-'plās\ vb 1 : to remove from the usual or proper place; esp : to expel or force to flee from home or native land ⟨displaced persons⟩ 2 : to move out of position ⟨water displaced by a floating object⟩ 3 : to take the place of : REPLACE

dis·place·ment \-mənt\ n 1 : the act of displacing : the state of being displaced 2 : the volume or weight of a fluid (as water) displaced by a floating body (as a ship) 3 : the difference between the initial position of an object and a later position

¹**dis·play** \di-'splā\ vb : to present to view : make evident

²**display** n 1 : a displaying of something 2 : an electronic device (as a cathode-ray tube) that gives information in visual form; also : the visual information

dis·please \(ˌ)dis-'plēz\ vb 1 : to arouse the disapproval and dislike of 2 : to be offensive to : give displeasure

dis·plea·sure \-'ple-zhər\ n : a feeling of dislike and irritation

dis·port \di-'spōrt\ vb 1 : DIVERT, AMUSE 2 : FROLIC 3 : DISPLAY

dis·pos·able \di-'spō-zə-bəl\ adj 1 : remaining after deduction of taxes ⟨~ income⟩ 2 : designed to be used once and then thrown away ⟨~ diapers⟩ — **dispos·able** n

dis·pos·al \di-'spō-zəl\ n 1 : CONTROL, COMMAND 2 : an orderly arrangement 3 : a getting rid of 4 : MANAGEMENT, ADMINISTRATION 5 : presenting or bestowing something ⟨~ of favors⟩ 6 : a device used to reduce waste matter (as by grinding)

dis·pose \di-'spōz\ vb **dis·posed; dis·pos·ing** 1 : to give a tendency to : INCLINE ⟨disposed to accept⟩ 2 : to put in place : ARRANGE ⟨troops disposed for withdrawal⟩ 3 : SETTLE — **dis·pos·er** n — **dispose of** 1 : to transfer to the control of another **2** : to get rid of **3** : to deal with conclusively

dis·po·si·tion \ˌdis-pə-ˈzi-shən\ *n* **1** : the act or power of disposing : DISPOSAL **2** : RELINQUISHMENT **3** : ARRANGEMENT **4** : TENDENCY, INCLINATION **5** : natural attitude toward things ⟨a cheerful ∼⟩

dis·pos·sess \ˌdis-pə-ˈzes\ *vb* : to put out of possession or occupancy — **dis·pos·ses·sion** \-ˈze-shən\ *n*

dis·praise \(ˌ)dis-ˈprāz\ *vb* : DISPARAGE — **dispraise** *n* — **dis·prais·er** *n*

dis·pro·por·tion \ˌdis-prə-ˈpōr-shən\ *n* : lack of proportion, symmetry, or proper relation — **dis·pro·por·tion·ate** \-shə-nət\ *adj*

dis·prove \(ˌ)dis-ˈprüv\ *vb* : to prove to be false — **dis·proof** \-ˈprüf\ *n*

dis·pu·tant \di-ˈspyüt-ᵊnt, ˈdis-pyə-tənt\ *n* : one that is engaged in a dispute

dis·pu·ta·tion \ˌdis-pyü-ˈtā-shən\ *n* **1** : DEBATE **2** : an oral defense of an academic thesis

dis·pu·ta·tious \-shəs\ *adj* : inclined to dispute : ARGUMENTATIVE

¹dis·pute \di-ˈspyüt\ *vb* **dis·put·ed; dis·put·ing 1** : ARGUE, DEBATE **2** : WRANGLE **3** : to deny the truth or rightness of **4** : to struggle against or over : OPPOSE — **dis·put·able** \di-ˈspyü-tə-bəl, ˈdis-pyə-tə-bəl\ *adj* — **dis·put·er** *n*

²dis·pute *n* **1** : DEBATE **2** : QUARREL

dis·qual·i·fy \(ˌ)dis-ˈkwä-lə-ˌfī\ *vb* : to make or declare unfit or not qualified — **dis·qual·i·fi·ca·tion** \-ˌkwä-lə-fə-ˈkā-shən\ *n*

¹dis·qui·et \(ˌ)dis-ˈkwī-ət\ *vb* : to make uneasy or restless : DISTURB

²disquiet *n* : lack of peace or tranquillity : ANXIETY

dis·qui·etude \(ˌ)dis-ˈkwī-ə-ˌtüd, -ˌtyüd\ *n* : AGITATION, ANXIETY

dis·qui·si·tion \ˌdis-kwə-ˈzi-shən\ *n* : a formal inquiry or discussion

¹dis·re·gard \ˌdis-ri-ˈgärd\ *vb* : to pay no attention to : treat as unworthy of notice or regard

²disregard *n* : the act of disregarding : the state of being disregarded : NEGLECT — **dis·re·gard·ful** *adj*

dis·re·pair \ˌdis-ri-ˈpar\ *n* : the state of being in need of repair

dis·rep·u·ta·ble \dis-ˈre-pyü-tə-bəl\ *adj* : having a bad reputation

dis·re·pute \ˌdis-ri-ˈpyüt\ *n* : lack or decline of reputation : low esteem

dis·re·spect \ˌdis-ri-ˈspekt\ *n* : DISCOURTESY — **dis·re·spect·ful** *adj*

dis·robe \dis-ˈrōb\ *vb* : UNDRESS

dis·rupt \dis-ˈrəpt\ *vb* **1** : to break apart **2** : to throw into disorder **3** : INTERRUPT — **dis·rup·tion** \-ˈrəp-shən\ *n* — **dis·rup·tive** \-ˈrəp-tiv\ *adj*

dis·sat·is·fac·tion \di-ˌsa-təs-ˈfak-shən\ *n* : DISCONTENT

dis·sat·is·fy \di-ˈsa-təs-ˌfī\ *vb* : to fail to satisfy : DISPLEASE

dis·sect \di-ˈsekt\ *vb* **1** : to divide into parts esp. for examination and study **2** : ANALYZE — **dis·sec·tion** \-ˈsek-shən\ *n* — **dis·sec·tor** \-ˈsek-tər\ *n*

dis·sect·ed *adj* : cut deeply into narrow lobes ⟨a ∼ leaf⟩

dis·sem·ble \di-ˈsem-bəl\ *vb* **-bled; -bling 1** : to hide under or put on a false appearance : conceal facts, intentions, or feelings under some pretense **2** : SIMULATE — **dis·sem·bler** *n*

dis·sem·i·nate \di-ˈse-mə-ˌnāt\ *vb* **-nat·ed; -nat·ing** : to spread abroad as if sowing seed ⟨∼ ideas⟩ — **dis·sem·i·na·tion** \-ˌse-mə-ˈnā-shən\ *n*

dis·sen·sion \di-ˈsen-chən\ *n* : disagreement in opinion : DISCORD

¹dis·sent \di-ˈsent\ *vb* **1** : to withhold assent **2** : to differ in opinion

²dissent *n* **1** : difference of opinion; *esp* : religious nonconformity **2** : a written statement in which a justice disagrees with the opinion of the majority

dis·sent·er \di-ˈsen-tər\ *n* **1** : one that dissents **2** *cap* : an English Nonconformist

dis·ser·ta·tion \ˌdi-sər-ˈtā-shən\ *n* : an extended usu. written treatment of a subject; *esp* : one submitted for a doctorate

dis·ser·vice \di-ˈsər-vəs\ *n* : INJURY, HARM, MISCHIEF

dis·sev·er \di-ˈse-vər\ *vb* : SEPARATE, DISUNITE

dis·si·dent \ˈdi-sə-dənt\ *adj* [L *dissidens*, prp. of *dissidēre* to sit apart, disagree, fr. *dis-* apart + *sedēre* to sit] : disagreeing esp. with an established religious or political system, organization, or belief — **dis·si·dence** \-dəns\ *n* — **dissident** *n*

dis·sim·i·lar \di-ˈsi-mə-lər\ *adj* : UNLIKE — **dis·sim·i·lar·i·ty** \di-ˌsi-mə-ˈlar-ə-tē\ *n*

dis·sim·u·late \di-ˈsi-myə-ˌlāt\ *vb* : to hide under a false appearance : DISSEMBLE — **dis·sim·u·la·tion** \di-ˌsi-myə-ˈlā-shən\ *n*

dis·si·pate \ˈdi-sə-ˌpāt\ *vb* **-pat·ed; -pat·ing 1** : to break up and drive off : DISPERSE, SCATTER ⟨the breeze *dissipated* the fog⟩ **2** : SQUANDER **3** : to break up and vanish **4** : to be dissolute; *esp* : to drink alcoholic beverages to excess — **dis·si·pat·ed** *adj* — **dis·si·pa·tion** \ˌdi-sə-ˈpā-shən\ *n*

dis·so·ci·ate \di-ˈsō-shē-ˌāt\ *vb* **-at·ed; -at·ing** : DISCONNECT, DISUNITE — **dis·so·ci·a·tion** \di-ˌso-shē-ˈā-shən\ *n*

dis·so·lute \ˈdi-sə-ˌlüt\ *adj* : loose in morals or conduct — **dis·so·lute·ly** *adv* — **dis·so·lute·ness** *n*

dis·so·lu·tion \ˌdi-sə-ˈlü-shən\ *n* **1** : the action or process of dissolving **2** : separation of a thing into its parts **3** : DECAY; *also* : DEATH **4** : the termination or breaking up of (as an assembly)

dis·solve \di-ˈzälv\ *vb* **1** : to separate into component parts **2** : to pass or cause to pass into solution ⟨sugar ∼s in water⟩ **3** : TERMINATE, DISPERSE ⟨∼ parliament⟩ **4** : to waste or fade away ⟨his courage *dissolved*⟩ **5** : to be overcome emotionally ⟨∼ in tears⟩ **6** : to resolve itself as if by dissolution

dis·so·nance \ˈdi-sə-nəns\ *n* : DISCORD — **dis·so·nant** \-nənt\ *adj*

dis·suade \di-ˈswād\ *vb* **dis·suad·ed; dis·suad·ing** : to advise against a course of action : persuade or try to persuade not to do something — **dis·sua·sion** \-ˈswā-zhən\ *n* — **dis·sua·sive** \-ˈswā-siv\ *adj*

dist *abbr* **1** distance **2** district

¹dis·taff \ˈdis-ˌtaf\ *n, pl* **distaffs** \-ˌtafs, -ˌtavz\ **1** : a staff for holding the flax, tow, or wool in spinning **2** : a woman's work or domain **3** : the female branch or side of a family

²distaff *adj* : MATERNAL, FEMALE

dis·tal \ˈdis-t°l\ *adj* **1** : away from the point of attachment or origin esp. on the body **2** : of, relating to, or being the surface of a tooth that is farthest from the middle of the front of the jaw — **dis·tal·ly** *adv*

¹dis·tance \ˈdis-təns\ *n* **1** : measure of separation in space or time **2** : EXPANSE **3** : the full length ⟨go the ∼⟩ **4** : spatial remoteness **5** : COLDNESS, RESERVE **6** : DIFFERENCE, DISPARITY **7** : a distant point

²distance *vb* **dis·tanced; dis·tanc·ing** : to leave far behind : OUTSTRIP

dis·tant \ˈdis-tənt\ *adj* **1** : separate in space : AWAY **2** : FAR-OFF **3** : far apart or behind **4** : not close in relationship ⟨a ∼ cousin⟩ **5** : different in kind **6** : RESERVED, ALOOF, COLD ⟨∼ politeness⟩ **7** : going a long distance — **dis·tant·ly** *adv* — **dis·tant·ness** *n*

dis·taste \(ˌ)dis-ˈtāst\ *n* : DISINCLINATION, DISLIKE — **dis·taste·ful** *adj*

dis·tem·per \(ˌ)dis-ˈtem-pər\ *n* : a bodily disorder usu. of a domestic animal; *esp* : a contagious often fatal virus disease of dogs

dis·tend \di-ˈstend\ *vb* : EXPAND, SWELL — **dis·ten·si·ble** \-ˈsten-sə-bəl\ *adj* — **dis·ten·sion** *or* **dis·ten·tion** \-chən\ *n*

dis·tich \ˈdis-(ˌ)tik\ *n* : a unit of two lines of poetry

dis·till *also* **dis·til** \di-ˈstil\ *vb* **dis·tilled; dis·till·ing 1** : to fall or let fall in drops **2** : to obtain or purify by

distillation — **dis•till•er** *n* — **dis•till•ery** \-'sti-lə-rē\ *n*
dis•til•late \'dis-tə-ˌlāt, -lət\ *n* : a liquid product condensed from vapor during distillation
dis•til•la•tion \ˌdis-tə-'lā-shən\ *n* : the process of purifying a liquid by successive evaporation and condensation
dis•tinct \di-'stiŋkt\ *adj* **1** : SEPARATE, INDIVIDUAL **2** : presenting a clear unmistakable impression — **dis•tinct•ly** *adv* — **dis•tinct•ness** *n*
dis•tinc•tion \di-'stiŋk-shən\ *n* **1** : the distinguishing of a difference; *also* : the difference distinguished **2** : something that distinguishes **3** : special honor or recognition
dis•tinc•tive \di-'stiŋk-tiv\ *adj* **1** : serving to distinguish **2** : having or giving style or distinction — **dis•tinc•tive•ly** *adv* — **dis•tinc•tive•ness** *n*
dis•tin•guish \di-'stiŋ-gwish\ *vb* [MF *distinguer*, fr. L *distinguere*, lit., to separate by pricking] **1** : to recognize by some mark or characteristic **2** : to hear or see clearly : DISCERN **3** : to make distinctions ⟨∼ between right and wrong⟩ **4** : to give prominence or distinction to; *also* : to take special notice of — **dis•tin•guish•able** *adj*
dis•tin•guished \-gwisht\ *adj* **1** : marked by eminence or excellence **2** : befitting an eminent person
dis•tort \di-'stȯrt\ *vb* **1** : to twist out of the true meaning **2** : to twist out of a natural, normal, or original shape or condition **3** : to cause to be perceived unnaturally — **dis•tor•tion** \-'stȯr-shən\ *n*
distr *abbr* distribute; distribution
dis•tract \di-'strakt\ *vb* **1** : to draw (the attention or mind) to a different object : DIVERT **2** : to stir up or confuse with conflicting emotions or motives — **dis•trac•tion** \-'strak-shən\ *n*
dis•trait \di-'strā\ *adj* : DISTRAUGHT 1
dis•traught \di-'strȯt\ *adj* **1** : agitated with doubt or mental conflict **2** : INSANE
¹dis•tress \di-'stres\ *n* **1** : suffering of body or mind : PAIN, ANGUISH **2** : TROUBLE, MISFORTUNE **3** : a condition of danger or desperate need — **dis•tress•ful** *adj*
²distress *vb* **1** : to subject to great strain or difficulties **2** : UPSET
dis•trib•ute \di-'stri-byüt\ *vb* **-ut•ed; -ut•ing** **1** : to divide among several or many **2** : to spread out : SCATTER; *also* : DELIVER **3** : CLASSIFY — **dis•tri•bu•tion** \ˌdis-trə-'byü-shən\ *n*
dis•trib•u•tive \di-'stri-byù-tiv\ *adj* **1** : of or relating to distribution **2** : being or concerned with a mathematical operation (as multiplication in $a(b + c) = ab + ac$) that produces the same result when operating on a whole mathematical expression as when operating on each part and collecting the results — **dis•trib•u•tive•ly** *adv*
dis•trib•u•tor \di-'stri-byù-tər\ *n* **1** : one that distributes **2** : one that markets goods **3** : a device for directing current to the spark plugs of an engine
dis•trict \'dis-(ˌ)trikt\ *n* **1** : a fixed territorial division (as for administrative or electoral purposes) **2** : an area, region, or section with a distinguishing character
district attorney *n* : the prosecuting attorney of a judicial district
¹dis•trust \dis-'trəst\ *n* : a lack or absence of trust — **dis•trust•ful** \-fəl\ *adj* — **dis•trust•ful•ly** *adv*
²distrust *vb* : to have no trust or confidence in
dis•turb \di-'stərb\ *vb* **1** : to interfere with : INTERRUPT **2** : to alter the position or arrangement of; *also* : to upset the natural and esp. the ecological balance of **3** : to destroy the tranquillity or composure of : make uneasy **4** : to throw into disorder **5** : INCONVENIENCE — **dis•tur•bance** \-'stər-bəns\ *n* — **dis•turb•er** *n*
dis•turbed \-'stərbd\ *adj* : showing symptoms of emotional illness
dis•unite \ˌdis-yü-'nīt\ *vb* : DIVIDE, SEPARATE
dis•uni•ty \dis-'yü-nə-tē\ *n* : lack of unity; *esp* : DISSENSION

dis•use \-'yüs\ *n* : a cessation of use or practice
¹ditch \'dich\ *n* : a long narrow channel or trench dug in the earth
²ditch *vb* **1** : to enclose with a ditch; *also* : to dig a ditch in **2** : to get rid of : DISCARD **3** : to make a forced landing of an airplane on water
dith•er \'di-thər\ *n* : a highly nervous, excited, or agitated state
dit•sy *or* **dit•zy** \'dit-sē\ *adj* **dits•i•er** *or* **ditz•i•er; -est** : eccentrically silly, giddy, or inane
dit•to \'di-tō\ *n, pl* **dittos** [It *ditto, detto*, pp. of *dire* to say, fr. L *dicere*] **1** : a thing mentioned previously or above — used to avoid repeating a word **2** : a mark " or " used as a symbol for the word *ditto*
dit•ty \'di-tē\ *n, pl* **ditties** : a short simple song
di•uret•ic \ˌdī-yə-'re-tik\ *adj* : tending to increase urine flow — **diuretic** *n*
di•ur•nal \dī-'ərn-əl\ *adj* **1** : DAILY **2** : of, relating to, occurring, or active in the daytime
div *abbr* **1** divided **2** dividend **3** division **4** divorced
di•va \'dē-və\ *n, pl* **divas** *or* **di•ve** \-ˌvä\ [It, lit., goddess, fr. L, fem. of *divus* divine, god] : PRIMA DONNA
di•va•gate \'dī-və-ˌgāt\ *vb* **-gat•ed; -gat•ing** : to wander or stray from a course or subject : DIVERGE — **di•va•ga•tion** \ˌdī-və-'gā-shən\ *n*
di•van \'dī-ˌvan, di-'van\ *n* : COUCH, SOFA
¹dive \'dīv\ *vb* **dived** \'dīvd\ *or* **dove** \'dōv\; **dived; div•ing** **1** : to plunge into water headfirst **2** : SUBMERGE **3** : to come or drop down precipitously **4** : to descend in an airplane at a steep angle **5** : to plunge into some matter or activity **6** : DART, LUNGE — **div•er** *n*
²dive *n* **1** : the act or an instance of diving **2** : a sharp decline **3** : a disreputable bar or place of amusement
di•verge \də-'vərj, dī-\ *vb* **di•verged; di•verg•ing** **1** : to move or extend in different directions from a common point : draw apart **2** : to differ in character, form, or opinion **3** : DEVIATE **4** : DEFLECT — **di•ver•gence** \-'vər-jəns\ *n* — **di•ver•gent** \-jənt\ *adj*
di•vers \'dī-vərz\ *adj* : VARIOUS
di•verse \dī-'vərs, də-, 'dī-ˌvərs\ *adj* **1** : UNLIKE **2** : composed of distinct forms or qualities — **di•verse•ly** *adv*
di•ver•si•fy \də-'vər-sə-ˌfī, dī-\ *vb* **-fied; -fy•ing** : to make different or various in form or quality — **di•ver•si•fi•ca•tion** \-ˌvər-sə-fə-'kā-shən\ *n*
di•ver•sion \də-'vər-zhən, dī-\ *n* **1** : a turning aside from a course, activity, or use : DEVIATION **2** : something that diverts or amuses : PASTIME
di•ver•si•ty \də-'vər-sə-tē, dī-\ *n, pl* **-ties** **1** : the condition of being diverse : VARIETY **2** : an instance of being diverse
di•vert \də-'vərt, dī-\ *vb* **1** : to turn from a course or purpose : DEFLECT **2** : DISTRACT **3** : ENTERTAIN, AMUSE
di•vest \dī-'vest, də-\ *vb* **1** : to deprive or dispossess esp. of property, authority, or rights **2** : to strip esp. of clothing, ornament, or equipment
¹di•vide \də-'vīd\ *vb* **di•vid•ed; di•vid•ing** **1** : SEPARATE; *also* : CLASSIFY **2** : CLEAVE, PART **3** : DISTRIBUTE, APPORTION **4** : to possess or make use of in common : share in **5** : to cause to be separate, distinct, or apart from one another **6** : to separate into opposing sides or parties **7** : to mark divisions on **8** : to subject to or use in mathematical division; *also* : to be used as a divisor with respect to **9** : to branch out
²divide *n* : WATERSHED 1
div•i•dend \'di-və-ˌdend\ *n* **1** : an individual share of something distributed **2** : BONUS **3** : a number to be divided **4** : a sum or fund to be divided or distributed
di•vid•er \də-'vī-dər\ *n* **1** : one that divides (as a partition) ⟨room ∼⟩ **2** *pl* : COMPASS 5
div•i•na•tion \ˌdi-və-'nā-shən\ *n* **1** : the art or practice of using omens or magic powers to foretell the future **2** : unusual insight or intuitive perception
¹di•vine \də-'vīn\ *adj* **di•vin•er; -est** **1** : of, relating to,

or being God or a god **2** : supremely good : SUPERB; *also* : HEAVENLY — **di·vine·ly** *adv*
²**divine** *n* **1** : CLERGYMAN **2** : THEOLOGIAN
³**divine** *vb* **di·vined; di·vin·ing 1** : INFER, CONJECTURE **2** : PROPHESY **3** : DOWSE — **di·vin·er** *n*
divining rod *n* : a forked rod believed to reveal the presence of water or minerals by dipping downward when held over a vein
di·vin·i·ty \də-ˈvi-nə-tē\ *n, pl* **-ties 1** : THEOLOGY **2** : the quality or state of being divine **3** : a divine being; *esp* : GOD 1
di·vis·i·ble \də-ˈvi-zə-bəl\ *adj* : capable of being divided — **di·vis·i·bil·i·ty** \-ˌvi-zə-ˈbi-lə-tē\ *n*
di·vi·sion \də-ˈvi-zhən\ *n* **1** : DISTRIBUTION, SEPARATION **2** : one of the parts or groupings into which a whole is divided **3** : DISAGREEMENT, DISUNITY **4** : something that divides or separates **5** : the mathematical operation of finding how many times one number is contained in another **6** : a large self-contained military unit **7** : an administrative or operating unit of a governmental, business, or educational organization — **di·vi·sion·al** \-ˈvi-zhə-nəl\ *adj*
di·vi·sive \də-ˈvī-siv, -ˈvi-ziv\ *adj* : creating disunity or dissension — **di·vi·sive·ly** *adv* — **di·vi·sive·ness** *n*
di·vi·sor \də-ˈvī-zər\ *n* : the number by which a dividend is divided
di·vorce \də-ˈvȯrs\ *n* **1** : an act or instance of legally dissolving a marriage **2** : SEPARATION, SEVERANCE — **divorce** *vb* — **di·vorce·ment** *n*
di·vor·cé \də-ˌvȯr-ˈsā\ *n* [F] : a divorced man
di·vor·cée \də-ˌvȯr-ˈsā, -ˈsē\ *n* : a divorced woman
div·ot \ˈdi-vət\ *n* : a piece of turf dug from a golf fairway in making a stroke
di·vulge \də-ˈvəlj, dī-\ *vb* **di·vulged; di·vulg·ing** : REVEAL, DISCLOSE
Dix·ie·land \ˈdik-sē-ˌland\ *n* : jazz music in duple time played in a style developed in New Orleans
diz·zy \ˈdi-zē\ *adj* **diz·zi·er; -est** [ME *disy,* fr. OE *dysig* stupid] **1** : FOOLISH, SILLY **2** : having a sensation of whirling : GIDDY **3** : causing or caused by giddiness — **diz·zi·ly** \-zə-lē\ *adv* — **diz·zi·ness** \-zē-nəs\ *n*
DJ *n, often not cap* : DISC JOCKEY
dk *abbr* **1** dark **2** deck **3** dock
dl *abbr* deciliter
DLitt *or* **DLit** *abbr* [NL *doctor litterarum*] doctor of letters; doctor of literature
DLO *abbr* dead letter office
dm *abbr* decimeter
DMD *abbr* [NL *dentariae medicinae doctor*] doctor of dental medicine
DMZ *abbr* demilitarized zone
dn *abbr* down
DNA \ˌdē-(ˌ)en-ˈā\ *n* : any of various nucleic acids that are usu. the molecular basis of heredity and are localized esp. in cell nuclei
¹**do** \ˈdü\ *vb* **did** \ˈdid\; **done** \ˈdən\; **do·ing; does** \ˈdəz\ **1** : to bring to pass : ACCOMPLISH **2** : ACT, BEHAVE ⟨∼ as I say⟩ **3** : to be active or busy ⟨up and ∼*ing*⟩ **4** : HAPPEN ⟨what's ∼*ing?*⟩ **5** : to be engaged in the study or practice of : work at ⟨he *does* tailoring⟩ **6** : COOK ⟨steak *done* rare⟩ **7** : to put in order (as by cleaning or arranging) ⟨∼ the dishes⟩ **8** : DECORATE ⟨*did* the hall in blue⟩ **9** : GET ALONG ⟨∼ well in school⟩ **10** : CARRY ON, MANAGE **11** : RENDER ⟨sleep will ∼ you good⟩ **12** : FINISH ⟨when he had *done*⟩ **13** : EXERT ⟨*did* my best⟩ **14** : PRODUCE ⟨*did* a poem⟩ **15** : to play the part of **16** : CHEAT ⟨*did* him out of his share⟩ **17** : TRAVERSE, TOUR **18** : TRAVEL **19** : to spend or serve out a period of time ⟨*did* ten years in prison⟩ **20** : SUFFICE, SUIT **21** : to be fitting or proper **22** : USE ⟨doesn't ∼ drugs⟩ **23** — used as an auxiliary verb (1) before the subject in an interrogatory sentence ⟨*does* he work?⟩ and after some adverbs ⟨never *did* she say so⟩, (2) in a negative statement ⟨I *don't* know⟩, (3) for emphasis ⟨you ∼ know⟩, and (4) as a substitute for a preceding predicate ⟨he works harder than I ∼⟩ —

do·able \ˈdü-ə-bəl\ *adj* — **do away with 1** : to put an end to **2** : DESTROY, KILL — **do by** : to deal with : TREAT ⟨*did* right *by* her⟩ — **do for** : to bring about the death or ruin of — **do the trick** : to produce a desired result
²**do** *n* **1** : AFFAIR, PARTY **2** : a command or entreaty to do something ⟨list of ∼s and don'ts⟩ **3** : HAIRDO
³**do** *abbr* ditto
DOA *abbr* dead on arrival
DOB *abbr* date of birth
dob·bin \ˈdä-bən\ *n* [*Dobbin,* nickname for *Robert*] **1** : a farm horse **2** : a quiet plodding horse
Do·ber·man pin·scher \ˈdō-bər-mən- ˈpin-chər\ *n* : a short-haired medium-sized dog of a breed of German origin
do·bra \ˈdō-brə\ *n* — see MONEY table
¹**doc** \ˈdäk\ *n* : DOCTOR
²**doc** *abbr* document
do·cent \ˈdōs-ᵊnt, dōt-ˈsent\ *n* [obs. G (now *Dozent*), fr. L *docens,* prp. of *docēre* to teach] : TEACHER, LECTURER; *also* : a person who leads a guided tour
doc·ile \ˈdä-səl\ *adj* [L *docilis,* fr. *docēre* to teach] : easily taught, led, or managed : TRACTABLE — **do·cil·i·ty** \dä-ˈsi-lə-tē\ *n*
¹**dock** \ˈdäk\ *n* : any of a genus of coarse weedy herbs related to buckwheat
²**dock** *vb* **1** : to cut off the end of : cut short **2** : to take away a part of : deduct from ⟨∼ a worker's wages⟩
³**dock** *n* **1** : an artificial basin to receive ships **2** : ²SLIP 2 **3** : a wharf or platform for loading or unloading materials
⁴**dock** *vb* **1** : to bring or come into dock **2** : to join (as two spacecraft) mechanically in space
⁵**dock** *n* : the place in a court where a prisoner stands or sits during trial
dock·age \ˈdä-kij\ *n* : docking facilities
dock·et \ˈdä-kət\ *n* **1** : a formal abridged record of the proceedings in a legal action; *also* : a register of such records **2** : a list of legal causes to be tried **3** : a calendar of matters to be acted on : AGENDA **4** : a label attached to a document containing identification or directions — **docket** *vb*
dock·hand \ˈdäk-ˌhand\ *n* : LONGSHOREMAN
dock·work·er \-ˌwər-kər\ *n* : LONGSHOREMAN
dock·yard \-ˌyärd\ *n* : SHIPYARD
¹**doc·tor** \ˈdäk-tər\ *n* [ME *doctour* teacher, doctor, fr. MF & ML; MF, fr. ML *doctor,* fr. L, teacher, fr. *docēre* to teach] **1** : a person holding one of the highest academic degrees (as a PhD) conferred by a university **2** : one skilled in healing arts; *esp* : an academically and legally qualified physician, surgeon, dentist, or veterinarian **3** : a person who restores or repairs things — **doc·tor·al** \-tə-rəl\ *adj*
²**doctor** *vb* **1** : to give medical treatment to **2** : to practice medicine **3** : REPAIR **4** : to adapt or modify for a desired end **5** : to alter deceptively
doc·tor·ate \ˈdäk-tə-rət\ *n* : the degree, title, or rank of a doctor
doc·tri·naire \ˌdäk-trə-ˈnar\ *n* [F] : one who attempts to put an abstract theory into effect without regard to practical difficulties — **doctrinaire** *adj*
doc·trine \ˈdäk-trən\ *n* **1** : something that is taught **2** : DOGMA, TENET — **doc·tri·nal** \-trən-ᵊl\ *adj*
docu·dra·ma \ˈdä-kyə-ˌdrä-mə, -ˌdra-\ *n* : a drama for television, motion pictures, or theater that deals freely with historical events
doc·u·ment \ˈdä-kyə-mənt\ *n* : a paper that furnishes information, proof, or support of something else — **doc·u·ment** \-ˌment\ *vb* — **doc·u·men·ta·tion** \ˌdä-kyə-mən-ˈtā-shən\ *n* — **doc·u·ment·er** *n*
doc·u·men·ta·ry \ˌdä-kyə-ˈmen-tə-rē\ *adj* **1** : consisting of documents; *also* : being in writing ⟨∼ proof⟩ **2** : giving a factual presentation in artistic form ⟨a ∼ movie⟩ — **documentary** *n*
DOD *abbr* Department of Defense
¹**dod·der** \ˈdä-dər\ *n* : any of a genus of leafless elon-

gated wiry parasitic herbs deficient in chlorophyll

²dodder *vb* **dod·dered; dod·der·ing 1** : to tremble or shake usu. from age **2** : to progress feebly and unsteadily

¹dodge \'däj\ *n* **1** : an act of evading by sudden bodily movement **2** : an artful device to evade, deceive, or trick **3** : EXPEDIENT

²dodge *vb* **dodged; dodg·ing 1** : to evade usu. by trickery **2** : to move suddenly aside; *also* : to avoid or evade by so doing — **dodg·er** *n*

do·do \'dō-dō\ *n, pl* **dodoes** *or* **dodos** [Pg *doudo,* fr. *doudo* silly, stupid] **1** : an extinct heavy flightless bird of the island of Mauritius related to the pigeons and larger than a turkey **2** : one hopelessly behind the times; *also* : a stupid person

dodo 1

doe \'dō\ *n, pl* **does** *or* **doe** : an adult female of various mammals (as a deer, rabbit, or kangaroo) of which the male is called *buck*

DOE *abbr* Department of Energy

do·er \'dü-ər\ *n* : one that does

does *pres 3d sing of* DO, *pl of* DOE

doff \'däf\ *vb* [ME, fr. *don* to do + *of* off] **1** : to take off (the hat) in greeting or as a sign of respect **2** : to rid oneself of

¹dog \'dog\ *n* **1** : a flesh-eating domestic mammal related to the wolves; *esp* : a male of this animal **2** : a worthless person **3** : FELLOW, CHAP ⟨you lucky ∼⟩ **4** : a mechanical device for holding something **5** : uncharacteristic or affected stylishness or dignity ⟨put on the ∼⟩ **6** *pl* : RUIN ⟨gone to the ∼s⟩

²dog *vb* **dogged; dog·ging 1** : to hunt or track like a hound **2** : to worry as if by pursuit with dogs : PLAGUE

dog·bane \'dog-ˌbān\ *n* : any of a genus of mostly poisonous herbs with milky juice and often showy flowers

dog·cart \-ˌkärt\ *n* : a light one-horse carriage with two seats back to back

dog·catch·er \-ˌka-chər, -ˌke-\ *n* : a community official assigned to catch and dispose of stray dogs

dog-ear \'dog-ˌgir\ *n* : the turned-down corner of a leaf of a book — **dog-ear** *vb* — **dog-eared** \-ˌgird\ *adj*

dog·fight \'dog-ˌfīt\ *n* : a fight between fighter planes at close range

dog·fish \-ˌfish\ *n* : any of various small sharks

dog·ged \'do-gəd\ *adj* : stubbornly determined : TENACIOUS — **dog·ged·ly** *adv* — **dog·ged·ness** *n*

dog·ger·el \'do-gə-rəl\ *n* : verse that is loosely styled and irregular in measure esp. for comic effect

dog·gie bag *or* **doggy bag** \'do-gē-\ *n* : a container for carrying home leftover food from a restaurant meal

¹dog·gy *or* **dog·gie** \'do-gē\ *n, pl* **doggies** : a small dog

²dog·gy *adj* **dog·gi·er; -est** : of or resembling a dog ⟨a ∼ odor⟩

dog·house \'dog-ˌhaus\ *n* : a shelter for a dog — **in the doghouse** : in a state of disfavor

do·gie \'dō-gē\ *n, chiefly West* : a motherless calf in a range herd

dog·leg \'dog-ˌleg\ *n* : a sharp bend or angle (as in a road) — **dogleg** *vb*

dog·ma \'dog-mə\ *n, pl* **dogmas** *also* **dog·ma·ta** \-mə-tə\ **1** : a tenet or code of tenets **2** : a doctrine or body of doctrines formally proclaimed by a church

dog·ma·tism \'dog-mə-ˌti-zəm\ *n* : positiveness in stating matters of opinion esp. when unwarranted or arrogant — **dog·mat·ic** \dog-'ma-tik\ *adj* — **dog·mat·i·cal·ly** \-ti-k(ə-)lē\ *adv*

do–good·er \'dü-ˌgu̇-dər\ *n* : an earnest often naive humanitarian or reformer

dog·tooth violet \'dog-ˌtüth-\ *n* : any of a genus of wild spring-flowering bulbous herbs related to the lilies

dog·trot \'dog-ˌträt\ *n* : a gentle trot — **dogtrot** *vb*

dog·wood \'dog-ˌwu̇d\ *n* : any of a genus of trees and shrubs having heads of small flowers often with showy white, pink, or red bracts

dogwood

doi·ly \'dȯi-lē\ *n, pl* **doilies** : a small often decorative mat

do in *vb* **1** : RUIN **2** : KILL **3** : TIRE, EXHAUST **4** : CHEAT

do·ings \'dü-iŋz\ *n pl* : GOINGS-ON

do–it–yourself *n* : the activity of doing or making something without professional training or help — **do–it–yourself·er** *n*

dol *abbr* dollar

dol·drums \'dōl-drəmz, 'däl-\ *n pl* **1** : a spell of listlessness or despondency **2** *often cap* : a part of the ocean near the equator known for calms **3** : a state or period of inactivity, stagnation, or slump

¹dole \'dōl\ *n* **1** : a distribution esp. of food, money, or clothing to the needy; *also* : something so distributed **2** : a grant of government funds to the unemployed

²dole *vb* **doled; dol·ing** : to give or distribute as a charity — usu. used with *out*

dole·ful \'dōl-fəl\ *adj* : full of grief : SAD — **dole·ful·ly** *adv*

dole out *vb* **1** : to give or deliver in small portions **2** : DISH OUT

doll \'däl, 'dȯl\ *n* **1** : a small figure of a human being used esp. as a child's plaything **2** : a pretty woman **3** : an attractive person — **doll·ish** \'dä-lish, 'dȯ-\ *adj*

dol·lar \'dä-lər\ *n* [Dutch or LG *daler,* fr. G *Taler,* short for *Joachimstaler,* fr. Sankt *Joachimsthal,* Bohemia, where talers were first made] **1** : any of various basic monetary units (as in the U.S. and Canada) — see MONEY table **2** : a coin, note, or token representing one dollar **3** : RINGGIT

dol·lop \'dä-ləp\ *n* **1** : LUMP, GLOB **2** : PORTION 1 — **dollop** *vb*

doll up *vb* **1** : to dress elegantly or extravagantly **2** : to make more attractive **3** : to get dolled up

dol·ly \'dä-lē\ *n, pl* **dollies** : a small cart or wheeled platform (as for a television or movie camera)

dol·men \'dōl-mən, 'däl-\ *n* : a prehistoric monument consisting of two or more upright stones supporting a horizontal stone slab

do·lo·mite \'dō-lə-ˌmīt, 'dä-\ *n* : a mineral found in broad layers as a compact limestone

do·lor \'dō-lər, 'dä-\ *n* : mental suffering or anguish : SORROW — **do·lor·ous** *adj* — **do·lor·ous·ly** *adv*

dol·phin \'däl-fən\ *n* **1** : any of various small toothed whales with the snout more or less elongated into a beak **2** : either of two active food fishes of tropical and temperate seas

dolt \'dōlt\ *n* : a stupid person — **dolt·ish** \'dōl-tish\ *adj* — **dolt·ish·ness** *n*

dom *abbr* **1** domestic **2** dominant **3** dominion

-dom *n suffix* **1** : dignity : office ⟨duke*dom*⟩ **2** : realm : jurisdiction ⟨king*dom*⟩ **3** : state or fact of being ⟨free*dom*⟩ **4** : those having a (specified) office, occupation, interest, or character ⟨official*dom*⟩

do·main \dō-'mān\ *n* **1** : complete and absolute ownership of land **2** : land completely owned **3** : a territory over which dominion is exercised **4** : a sphere of knowledge, influence, or activity ⟨the ∼ of science⟩

dome \'dōm\ *n* **1** : a large hemispherical roof or ceiling **2** : a structure or natural formation that resembles the dome of a building **3** : a roofed sports stadium — **dome** *vb*

¹do·mes·tic \də-'mes-tik\ *adj* **1** : living near or about human habitations **2** : TAME, DOMESTICATED **3** : relating and limited to one's own country or the country under consideration **4** : of or relating to the household or the family **5** : devoted to home duties and pleasures **6** : INDIGENOUS — **do·mes·ti·cal·ly** \-ti-k(ə-)lē\ *adv*

²domestic *n* : a household servant

do·mes·ti·cate \də-'mes-ti-ˌkāt\ *vb* **-cat·ed; -cat·ing** : to adapt to life in association with and to the use of humans — **do·mes·ti·ca·tion** \-ˌmes-ti-'kā-shən\ *n*

do·mes·tic·i·ty \ˌdō-mes-'tis-ə-tē, də-\ *n, pl* **-ties 1** : the quality or state of being domestic or domesticated **2** : domestic activities or life

do·mi·cile \'dä-mə-ˌsīl, 'dō-; 'dä-mə-səl\ *n* : a dwelling place : HOME — **domicile** *vb* — **dom·i·cil·i·ary** \ˌdä-mə-'si-lē-ˌer-ē, ˌdō-\ *adj*

dom·i·nance \'dä-mə-nəns\ *n* **1** : AUTHORITY, CONTROL **2** : the property of a genetic dominant that prevents expression of a genetic recessive

¹dom·i·nant \-nənt\ *adj* **1** : controlling or prevailing over all others **2** : overlooking from a high position **3** : producing or being a bodily characteristic that is expressed when a contrasting recessive gene or trait is present

²dominant *n* : a dominant gene or trait

dom·i·nate \'dä-mə-ˌnāt\ *vb* **-nat·ed; -nat·ing 1** : RULE, CONTROL **2** : to have a commanding position or controlling power over **3** : to rise high above in a position suggesting power to dominate — **dom·i·na·tor** \-ˌnā-tər\ *n*

dom·i·na·tion \ˌdä-mə-'nā-shən\ *n* **1** : supremacy or preeminence over another **2** : exercise of mastery, ruling power, or preponderant influence

do·mi·na·trix \ˌdä-mə-'nā-triks\ *n, pl* **-trices** \-'nā-trə-ˌsēz, -nə-'trī-sēz\ : a woman who dominates and abuses her sexual partner; *also* : a dominating woman

dom·i·neer \ˌdä-mə-'nir\ *vb* **1** : to rule in an arrogant manner **2** : to be overbearing

Do·min·i·can \də-'mi-ni-kən\ *n* : a native or inhabitant of the Dominican Republic — **Dominican** *adj*

do·mi·nie *l usu* 'dä-mə-nē, *2 usu* 'dō-\ *n* **1** *chiefly Scot* : SCHOOLMASTER **2** : CLERGYMAN

do·min·ion \də-'min-yən\ *n* **1** : DOMAIN **2** : supreme authority : SOVEREIGNTY **3** *often cap* : a self-governing nation of the Commonwealth

dom·i·no \'dä-mə-ˌnō\ *n, pl* **-noes** *or* **-nos 1** : a long loose hooded cloak usu. worn with a half mask as a masquerade costume **2** : a flat rectangular block used as a piece in a game **(dominoes)**

¹don \'dän\ *vb* **donned; don·ning** [ME, fr. *don* to do + *on*] : to put on (as clothes)

²don *n* [Sp, fr. L *dominus* lord, master] **1** : a Spanish nobleman or gentleman — used as a title prefixed to the Christian name **2** : a head, tutor, or fellow in an English university

do·ña \'dō-nya\ *n* : a Spanish woman of rank — used as a title prefixed to the Christian name

do·nate \'dō-ˌnāt\ *vb* **do·nat·ed; do·nat·ing 1** : to make a gift of : CONTRIBUTE **2** : to make a donation

do·na·tion \dō-'nā-shən\ *n* **1** : the making of a gift esp. to a charity **2** : a free contribution : GIFT

¹done \'dən\ *past part of* DO

²done *adj* **1** : doomed to failure, defeat, or death **2** : gone by : OVER ⟨when day is ∼⟩ **3** : cooked sufficiently **4** : conformable to social convention

dong \'dȯŋ, 'däŋ\ *n* — see MONEY table

don·key \'däŋ-kē, 'dəŋ-\ *n, pl* **donkeys 1** : a sturdy and patient domestic mammal classified with the asses **2** : a stupid or obstinate person

don·ny·brook \'dä-nē-ˌbrük\ *n, often cap* [*Donnybrook* Fair, annual Irish event once known for its brawls] : an uproarious brawl

do·nor \'dō-nər\ *n* : one that gives, donates, or presents

donut *var of* DOUGHNUT

doo·dad \'dü-ˌdad\ *n* : an often small article whose common name is unknown or forgotten

doo·dle \'düd-ᵊl\ *vb* **doo·dled; doo·dling** : to draw or scribble aimlessly while occupied with something else — **doodle** *n* — **doo·dler** *n*

doom \'düm\ *n* **1** : JUDGMENT; *esp* : a judicial condemnation or sentence **2** : DESTINY **3** : RUIN, DEATH — **doom** *vb*

dooms·day \'dümz-ˌdā\ *n* : JUDGMENT DAY

door \'dȯr\ *n* **1** : a barrier by which an entry is closed and opened; *also* : a similar part of a piece of furniture **2** : DOORWAY **3** : a means of access or participation : OPPORTUNITY

door·keep·er \-ˌkē-pər\ *n* : a person who tends a door

door·knob \-ˌnäb\ *n* : a knob that when turned releases a door latch

door·man \-ˌman, -mən\ *n* : a usu. uniformed attendant at the door of a building (as a hotel)

door·mat \-ˌmat\ *n* : a mat placed before or inside a door for wiping dirt from the shoes

door·plate \-ˌplāt\ *n* : a nameplate on a door

door·step \-ˌstep\ *n* : a step or series of steps before an outer door

door·way \-ˌwā\ *n* **1** : the opening that a door closes **2** : DOOR **3**

do·pa \'dō-pə\ *n* : a form of an amino acid that is used esp. in the treatment of Parkinson's disease

¹dope \'dōp\ *n* **1** : a preparation for giving a desired quality **2** : a drug esp. when narcotic or addictive and used illegally **3** : a stupid person **4** : INFORMATION

²dope *vb* **doped; dop·ing 1** : to treat with dope; *esp* : to give a narcotic to **2** : FIGURE OUT — usu. used with *out* **3** : to take dope — **dop·er** *n*

dop·ey *also* **dopy** \'dō-pē\ *adj* **dop·i·er; -est 1** : dulled by alcohol or a narcotic **2** : SLUGGISH **3** : STUPID — **dop·i·ness** *n*

Dopp·ler effect \'dä-plər-\ *n* : a change in the frequency at which waves (as of sound) reach an observer from a source in motion with respect to the observer

dork \'dȯrk\ *n, slang* : NERD; *also* : JERK **2**

dorm \'dȯrm\ *n* : DORMITORY

dor·mant \'dȯr-mənt\ *adj* : INACTIVE; *esp* : not actively growing or functioning ⟨∼ buds⟩ — **dor·man·cy** \-mən-sē\ *n*

dor·mer \'dȯr-mər\ *n* [MF *dormeor* dormitory, fr. L *dormitorium*, fr. *dormire* to sleep] : a window built upright in a sloping roof; *also* : the roofed structure containing such a window

dor·mi·to·ry \'dȯr-mə-ˌtōr-ē\ *n, pl* **-ries 1** : a room for sleeping; *esp* : a large room containing a number of beds **2** : a residence hall providing sleeping rooms

dor·mouse \'dȯr-ˌmaus\ *n* : any of numerous Old World squirrellike rodents

dor·sal \'dȯr-səl\ *adj* : of, relating to, or located near or on the surface of the body that in humans is the back but in most other animals is the upper surface — **dor·sal·ly** *adv*

do·ry \'dōr-ē\ *n, pl* **dories** : a flat-bottomed boat with high flaring sides and a sharp bow

DOS *abbr* disk operating system

¹**dose** \'dōs\ *n* [ME, fr. MF, fr. LL *dosis*, fr. Gk, lit., act of giving, fr. *didonai* to give] **1** : a measured quantity (as of medicine) to be taken or administered at one time **2** : the quantity of radiation administered or absorbed — **dos·age** \'dō-sij\ *n*

²**dose** *vb* **dosed**; **dos·ing 1** : to give in doses **2** : to give medicine to

do·sim·e·ter \dō-'si-mə-tər\ *n* : a device for measuring doses of X rays or of radioactivity — **do·sim·e·try** \-mə-trē\ *n*

dos·sier \'dȯs-,yā, 'dȯ-sē-,ā\ *n* [F, bundle of documents labeled on the back, dossier, fr. *dos* back, fr. L *dorsum*] : a file containing detailed records on a particular person or subject

¹**dot** \'dät\ *n* **1** : a small spot : SPECK **2** : a small round mark **3** : a precise point esp. in time ⟨be here on the ∼⟩

²**dot** *vb* **dot·ted**; **dot·ting 1** : to mark with a dot ⟨∼ an *i*⟩ **2** : to cover with or as if with dots — **dot·ter** *n*

DOT *abbr* Department of Transportation

dot·age \'dō-tij\ *n* : feebleness of mind esp. in old age : SENILITY

dot·ard \-tərd\ *n* : a person in dotage

dote \'dōt\ *vb* **dot·ed**; **dot·ing 1** : to be feebleminded esp. from old age **2** : to be lavish or excessive in one's attention, affection, or fondness ⟨*doted* on her niece⟩

dot matrix *n* : a rectangular arrangement of dots from which alphanumeric characters can be formed (as by a computer printer)

Dou·ay Version \dü-'ā-\ *n* : an English translation of the Vulgate used by Roman Catholics

¹**dou·ble** \'də-bəl\ *adj* **1** : TWOFOLD, DUAL **2** : consisting of two members or parts **3** : being twice as great or as many **4** : folded in two **5** : having more than one whorl of petals ⟨∼ roses⟩

²**double** *vb* **dou·bled**; **dou·bling 1** : to make, be, or become twice as great or as many **2** : to make a call in bridge that increases the trick values and penalties of (an opponent's bid) **3** : FOLD **4** : CLENCH **5** : to be or cause to be bent over **6** : to take the place of another **7** : to hit a double **8** : to turn sharply and suddenly; *esp* : to turn back on one's course

³**double** *adv* **1** : DOUBLY **2** : two together

⁴**double** *n* **1** : something twice another in size, strength, speed, quantity, or value **2** : a base hit that enables the batter to reach second base **3** : COUNTERPART, DUPLICATE; *esp* : a person who closely resembles another **4** : UNDERSTUDY, SUBSTITUTE **5** : a sharp turn : REVERSAL **6** : FOLD **7** : a combined bet placed on two different contests **8** *pl* : a game between two pairs of players **9** : an act of doubling in a card game

double bond *n* : a chemical bond in which two atoms in a molecule share two pairs of electrons

double cross *n* : an act of betraying or cheating esp. an associate — **dou·ble-cross** \də-bəl-'krȯs\ *vb* — **dou·ble-cross·er** *n*

dou·ble-deal·ing \də-bəl-'dē-liŋ\ *n* : DUPLICITY — **dou·ble-deal·er** \-'dē-lər\ *n* — **dou·ble-dealing** *adj*

dou·ble-deck·er \-'de-kər\ *n* : something having two decks, levels, or layers — **dou·ble-deck** \-,dek\ *or* **dou·ble-decked** \-,dekt\ *adj*

dou·ble-dig·it \də-bəl-'di-jət\ *adj* : amounting to 10 percent or more

dou·ble en·ten·dre \düb-ᵊl-än-'tänd, də-bəl-, -'tänd-rᵊ\ *n, pl* **double entendres** \same *or* -'tän-drəz\ [obs. F, lit., double meaning] : a word or expression capable of two interpretations with one usu. risqué

dou·ble-head·er \də-bəl-'he-dər\ *n* : two games played consecutively on the same day

double helix *n* : a helix or spiral consisting of two strands (as of DNA) in the surface of a cylinder which coil around its axis

dou·ble-hung \də-bəl-'həŋ\ *adj, of a window* : having an upper and a lower sash that can slide past each other

dou·ble-joint·ed \-'jȯin-təd\ *adj* : having a joint that permits an exceptional degree of freedom of motion of the parts joined ⟨a ∼ finger⟩

double play *n* : a play in baseball by which two players are put out

dou·blet \'də-blət\ *n* **1** : a man's close-fitting jacket worn in Europe esp. in the 16th century **2** : one of two similar or identical things

dou·ble take \'də-bəl-,tāk\ *n* : a delayed reaction to a surprising or significant situation after an initial failure to notice anything unusual

dou·ble-talk \-,tȯk\ *n* : language that appears to be meaningful but in fact is a mixture of sense and nonsense

double up *vb* : to share accommodations designed for one

double whammy *n* : a combination of two usu. adverse forces, circumstances, or effects

dou·bloon \,də-'blün\ *n* : a former gold coin of Spain and Spanish America

dou·bly \'də-blē\ *adv* **1** : in a twofold manner **2** : to twice the degree

¹**doubt** \'daút\ *vb* **1** : to be uncertain about **2** : to lack confidence in : DISTRUST **3** : to consider unlikely — **doubt·able** *adj* — **doubt·er** *n*

²**doubt** *n* **1** : uncertainty of belief or opinion **2** : a condition causing uncertainty, hesitation, or suspense ⟨the outcome was in ∼⟩ **3** : DISTRUST **4** : an inclination not to believe or accept

doubt·ful \'daút-fəl\ *adj* **1** : QUESTIONABLE **2** : UNDECIDED — **doubt·ful·ly** *adv* — **doubt·ful·ness** *n*

¹**doubt·less** \'daút-ləs\ *adv* **1** : without doubt **2** : PROBABLY

²**doubtless** *adj* : free from doubt : CERTAIN — **doubt·less·ly** *adv*

douche \'düsh\ *n* [F] **1** : a jet of fluid (as water) directed against a part or into a cavity of the body; *also* : a cleansing with a douche **2** : a device for giving douches — **douche** *vb*

dough \'dō\ *n* **1** : a mixture that consists of flour or meal and a liquid (as milk or water) and is stiff enough to knead or roll **2** : something resembling dough esp. in consistency **3** : MONEY — **doughy** \'dō-ē\ *adj*

dough·boy \-,bȯi\ *n* : an American infantryman esp. in World War I

dough·nut \-(,)nət\ *n* : a small usu. ring-shaped cake fried in fat

dough·ty \'daú-tē\ *adj* **dough·ti·er**; **-est** : ABLE, STRONG, VALIANT

Doug·las fir \'də-gləs-\ *n* : a tall evergreen timber tree of the western U.S.

do up *vb* **1** : to prepare (as by cleaning) for use **2** : to wrap up **3** : CLOTHE, DECORATE

dour \'daúr, 'dúr\ *adj* [ME, fr. L *durus* hard] **1** : STERN, HARSH **2** : OBSTINATE **3** : SULLEN — **dour·ly** *adv*

douse \'daús, 'daúz\ *vb* **doused**; **dous·ing 1** : to plunge into water **2** : DRENCH **3** : EXTINGUISH

¹**dove** \'dəv\ *n* **1** : any of numerous pigeons; *esp* : a small wild pigeon **2** : an advocate of peace or of a peaceful policy — **dov·ish** \'də-vish\ *adj*

²**dove** \'dōv\ *past of* DIVE

¹**dove·tail** \'dəv-,tāl\ *n* : something that resembles a dove's tail; *esp* : a flaring tenon and a mortise into which it fits tightly

²**dovetail** *vb* **1** : to join by means of dovetails **2** : to fit skillfully together to form a whole ⟨our plans ∼ nicely⟩

dow·a·ger \'daú-i-jər\ *n* **1** : a widow owning property or a title from her deceased husband **2** : a dignified elderly woman

dowdy \'daú-dē\ *adj* **dowd·i·er**; **-est** : lacking neatness and charm : SHABBY, UNTIDY; *also* : lacking smartness

dow·el \'daù-əl\ *n* **1** : a pin used for fastening together two pieces of wood **2** : a round rod (as of wood) — **dowel** *vb*

¹dow·er \'daù-ər\ *n* **1** : the part of a deceased husband's real estate which the law gives for life to his widow **2** : DOWRY

²dower *vb* : to supply with a dower or dowry : ENDOW

dow·itch·er \'daù-i-chər\ *n* : any of several long-billed wading birds related to the sandpipers

¹down \'daùn\ *adv* **1** : toward or in a lower physical position **2** : to a lying or sitting position **3** : toward or to the ground, floor, or bottom **4** : as a down payment ⟨paid $5 ∼⟩ **5** : on paper ⟨put ∼ what he says⟩ **6** : in a direction that is the opposite of up **7** : SOUTH **8** : to or in a lower or worse condition or status **9** : from a past time **10** : to or in a state of less activity **11** : into defeat ⟨voted the motion ∼⟩

²down *prep* : down in, on, along, or through : toward the bottom of

³down *vb* **1** : to go or cause to go or come down **2** : DEFEAT **3** : to cause (a football) to be out of play

⁴down *adj* **1** : occupying a low position; *esp* : lying on the ground **2** : directed or going downward **3** : being in a state of reduced or low activity **4** : DEPRESSED, DEJECTED **5** : SICK ⟨∼ with a cold⟩ **6** : FINISHED, DONE

⁵down *n* **1** : a low or falling period (as in activity, emotional life, or fortunes) **2** : one of a series of attempts to advance a football

⁶down *n* : a rolling usu. treeless upland with sparse soil — usu. used in pl.

⁷down *n* **1** : a covering of soft fluffy feathers; *also* : such feathers **2** : a downlike covering or material

down·beat \'daùn-ˌbēt\ *n* : the downward stroke of a conductor indicating the principally accented note of a measure of music

down·burst \-ˌbərst\ *n* : a powerful downdraft usu. associated with a thunderstorm that is a hazard for low-flying aircraft; *also* : MICROBURST

down·cast \-ˌkast\ *adj* **1** : DEJECTED **2** : directed down ⟨a ∼ glance⟩

down·draft \-ˌdraft\ *n* : a downward current of gas (as air)

down·er \'daù-nər\ *n* **1** : a depressant drug; *esp* : BARBITURATE **2** : someone or something depressing

down·fall \'daùn-ˌfol\ *n* **1** : a sudden fall (as from high rank) **2** : something that causes a downfall — **down·fall·en** \-ˌfo-lən\ *adj*

¹down·grade \'daùn-ˌgrād\ *n* **1** : a downward slope (as of a road) **2** : a decline toward a worse condition

²downgrade *vb* : to lower in quality, value, extent, or status

down·heart·ed \-'här-təd\ *adj* : DEJECTED

down·hill \'daùn-'hil\ *adv* : toward the bottom of a hill — **downhill** \-ˌhil\ *adj*

down·load \-ˌlōd\ *vb* : to transfer (data) from a computer to another device — **down·load·able** \-ˌlō-də-bəl\ *adj*

down payment *n* : a part of the full price paid at the time of purchase or delivery with the balance to be paid later

down·pour \'daùn-ˌpōr\ *n* : a heavy rain

down·range \-'rānj\ *adv* : away from a launching site

¹down·right \-ˌrīt\ *adv* : THOROUGHLY

²downright *adj* **1** : ABSOLUTE, UTTER ⟨a ∼ lie⟩ **2** : PLAIN, BLUNT ⟨a ∼ man⟩

down·shift \-ˌshift\ *vb* : to shift an automotive vehicle into a lower gear

down·size \-ˌsīz\ *vb* : to reduce or undergo reduction in size or numbers

down·spout \-ˌspaùt\ *n* : a vertical pipe used to drain rainwater from a roof

Down's syndrome \'daùnz-\ *or* **Down syndrome** \'daùn-\ *n* : a birth defect characterized by mental retardation, slanting eyes, a broad short skull, broad hands with short fingers, and the presence of an extra chromosome

down·stage \'daùn-'stāj\ *adv or adj* : toward or at the front of a theatrical stage

down·stairs \-'starz\ *adv* : on or to a lower floor and esp. the main or ground floor — **down·stairs** \-ˌstarz\ *adj or n*

down·stream \-'strēm\ *adv or adj* : in the direction of flow of a stream

down·stroke \-ˌstrōk\ *n* : a downward stroke

down·swing \-ˌswiŋ\ *n* **1** : a swing downward **2** : DOWNTURN

down-to-earth *adj* : PRACTICAL, REALISTIC

down·town \'daùn-ˌtaùn\ *n* : the main business district of a town or city — **downtown** \'daùn-'taùn\ *adj or adv*

down·trod·den \'daùn-'träd-ᵊn\ *adj* : suffering oppression

down·turn \-ˌtərn\ *n* : a downward turn esp. in business activity

¹down·ward \'daùn-wərd\ *or* **down·wards** \-wərdz\ *adv* **1** : from a higher to a lower place or condition **2** : from an earlier time **3** : from an ancestor or predecessor

²downward *adj* : directed toward or situated in a lower place or condition

down·wind \'daùn-'wind\ *adv or adj* : in the direction that the wind is blowing

downy \'daù-nē\ *adj* **down·i·er; -est** : resembling or covered with down

downy mildew *n* : any of various parasitic fungi producing whitish masses esp. on the underside of plant leaves; *also* : a plant disease caused by downy mildew

downy woodpecker *n* : a small black-and-white woodpecker of No. America

dow·ry \'daùr-ē\ *n, pl* **dowries** : the property that a woman brings to her husband in marriage

dowse \'daùz\ *vb* **dowsed; dows·ing** : to use a divining rod esp. to find water — **dows·er** *n*

dox·ol·o·gy \däk-'sä-lə-jē\ *n, pl* **-gies** : a usu. short hymn of praise to God

doy·en \'dòi-ən, 'dwä-ˌyaᵐ\ *n* : the senior or most experienced person in a group

doy·enne \dòi-'yen, dwä-'yen\ *n* : a woman who is a doyen

doy·ley *chiefly Brit var of* DOILY

doz *abbr* dozen

doze \'dōz\ *vb* **dozed; doz·ing** : to sleep lightly — **doze** *n*

doz·en \'dəz-ᵊn\ *n, pl* **dozens** *or* **dozen** [ME *dozeine*, fr. OF *dozaine*, fr. *doze* twelve, fr. L *duodecim*, fr. *duo* two + *decem* ten] : a group of twelve — **doz·enth** \-ᵊnth\ *adj*

¹DP \ˌdē-'pē\ *n, pl* **DP's** *or* **DPs** : a displaced person

²DP *abbr* **1** data processing **2** double play

dpt *abbr* department

DPT *abbr* diphtheria-pertussis-tetanus (vaccines)

dr *abbr* **1** debtor **2** dram **3** drive **4** drum

Dr *abbr* doctor

DR *abbr* **1** dead reckoning **2** dining room

drab \'drab\ *adj* **drab·ber; drab·best** **1** : being of a light olive-brown color **2** : DULL, MONOTONOUS, CHEERLESS — **drab·ly** *adv* — **drab·ness** *n*

drach·ma \'drak-mə\ *n, pl* **drach·mas** *or* **drach·mai** \-ˌmī\ *or* **drach·mae** \-(ˌ)mē\ — see MONEY table

dra·co·ni·an \drā-'kō-nē-ən, drə-\ *adj, often cap* : CRUEL; *also* : SEVERE

¹draft \'draft, 'draft\ *n* **1** : the act of drawing or hauling **2** : the act or an instance of drinking or inhaling; *also* : the portion drunk or inhaled in one such act **3** : DOSE, POTION **4** : DELINEATION, PLAN, DESIGN; *also* : a preliminary sketch, outline, or version ⟨a rough ∼ of a speech⟩ **5** : the act of drawing (as from a cask); *also* : a portion of liquid so drawn **6** : the depth of water a ship draws esp. when loaded **7** : a system for or act of selecting persons esp. for compulsory military

service; *also* : the persons so selected **8** : an order for the payment of money drawn by one person or bank on another **9** : a heavy demand : STRAIN **10** : a current of air; *also* : a device to regulate air supply (as in a stove) — **on draft** : ready to be drawn from a receptacle ⟨beer *on draft*⟩
²**draft** *adj* **1** : used or adapted for drawing loads ⟨∼ horses⟩ **2** : being or having been on draft ⟨∼ beer⟩
³**draft** *vb* **1** : to select usu. on a compulsory basis; *esp* : to conscript for military service **2** : to draw the preliminary sketch, version, or plan of **3** : COMPOSE, PREPARE **4** : to draw off or away — **draft·ee** \draf-ˈtē, dràf-\ *n*
drafts·man \ˈdraft-smən, ˈdràft-\ *n* : a person who draws plans (as for buildings or machinery)
drafty \ˈdraf-tē, ˈdràf-\ *adj* **draft·i·er; -est** : exposed to or abounding in drafts of air
¹**drag** \ˈdrag\ *n* **1** : a device pulled along under water for detecting or gathering **2** : something (as a harrow or sledge) that is dragged along over a surface **3** : the act or an instance of dragging **4** : something that hinders progress; *also* : something boring **5** : STREET ⟨the main ∼⟩ **6** : clothing typical of one sex worn by a member of the opposite sex
²**drag** *vb* **dragged; drag·ging 1** : HAUL **2** : to move with painful or undue slowness or difficulty **3** : to force into or out of some situation, condition, or course of action **4** : PROTRACT ⟨∼ a story out⟩ **5** : to hang or lag behind **6** : to explore, search, or fish with a drag **7** : to trail along on the ground **8** : DRAW, PUFF ⟨∼ on a cigarette⟩ — **drag·ger** *n*
drag·net \-ˌnet\ *n* **1** : NET, TRAWL **2** : a network of planned actions for pursuing and catching ⟨a police ∼⟩
drag·o·man \ˈdra-gə-mən\ *n, pl* **-mans** *or* **-men** \-mən\ : an interpreter employed esp. in the Near East
drag·on \ˈdra-gən\ *n* [ME, fr. OF, fr. L *dracon-, draco* serpent, dragon, fr. Gk *drakōn* serpent] : a fabulous animal usu. represented as a huge winged scaly serpent with a crested head and large claws
drag·on·fly \-ˌflī\ *n* : any of a group of large harmless 4-winged insects that hold the wings horizontal and unfolded in repose

dragonfly

¹**dra·goon** \drə-ˈgün, dra-\ *n* [F *dragon* dragon, dragoon, fr. MF] : a heavily armed mounted soldier
²**dragoon** *vb* : to force or attempt to force into submission : COERCE
drag race *n* : an acceleration contest between vehicles
drag strip *n* : a site for drag races
¹**drain** \ˈdrān\ *vb* **1** : to draw off or flow off gradually or completely **2** : to exhaust physically or emotionally **3** : to make or become gradually dry or empty **4** : to carry away the surface water of : discharge surface or surplus water **5** : EMPTY, EXHAUST — **drain·er** *n*
²**drain** *n* **1** : a means (as a channel or sewer) of draining **2** : the act of draining **3** : a gradual outflow; *also* : something causing an outflow ⟨a ∼ on our savings⟩
drain·age \ˈdrā-nij\ *n* **1** : the act or process of draining; *also* : something that is drained off **2** : a means for draining : DRAIN, SEWER **3** : an area drained
drain·pipe \ˈdrān-ˌpīp\ *n* : a pipe for drainage

drake \ˈdrāk\ *n* : a male duck
dram \ˈdram\ *n* **1** — see WEIGHT table **2** : FLUID DRAM **3** : a small drink
dra·ma \ˈdrä-mə, ˈdra-\ *n* [LL, fr. Gk, deed, drama, fr. *dran* to do, act] **1** : a literary composition designed for theatrical presentation **2** : dramatic art, literature, or affairs **3** : a series of events involving conflicting forces — **dra·mat·ic** \drə-ˈma-tik\ *adj* — **dra·mat·i·cal·ly** \-ti-k(ə-)lē\ *adv* — **dra·ma·tist** \ˈdra-mə-tist, ˈdrä-\ *n*
dra·ma·tize \ˈdra-mə-ˌtīz, ˈdrä-\ *vb* **-tized; -tiz·ing 1** : to adapt for or be suitable for theatrical presentation **2** : to present or represent in a dramatic manner — **dram·a·ti·za·tion** \ˌdra-mə-tə-ˈzā-shən, ˌdrä-\ *n*
drank *past and past part of* DRINK
¹**drape** \ˈdrāp\ *vb* **draped; drap·ing 1** : to cover or adorn with or as if with folds of cloth **2** : to cause to hang or stretch out loosely or carelessly **3** : to arrange or become arranged in flowing lines or folds
²**drape** *n* **1** : CURTAIN **2** : arrangement in or of folds **3** : the cut or hang of clothing
drap·er \ˈdrā-pər\ *n, chiefly Brit* : a dealer in cloth and sometimes in clothing and dry goods
drap·ery \ˈdrā-pə-rē\ *n, pl* **-er·ies 1** *Brit* : DRY GOODS **2** : a decorative fabric esp. when hung loosely and in folds; *also* : hangings of heavy fabric used as a curtain
dras·tic \ˈdras-tik\ *adj* : HARSH, RIGOROUS, SEVERE ⟨∼ punishment⟩ — **dras·ti·cal·ly** \-ti-k(ə-)lē\ *adv*
draught \ˈdràft\, **draughty** \ˈdràf-tē\ *chiefly Brit var of* DRAFT, DRAFTY
draughts \ˈdràfts\ *n, Brit* : CHECKERS
draughts·man *chiefly Brit var of* DRAFTSMAN
¹**draw** \ˈdrò\ *vb* **drew** \ˈdrü\; **drawn** \ˈdrón\; **draw·ing 1** : to cause to move toward a force exerted **2** : to cause to go in a certain direction ⟨*drew* him aside⟩ **3** : to move or go steadily or gradually ⟨night ∼s near⟩ **4** : ATTRACT, ENTICE **5** : PROVOKE, ROUSE ⟨*drew* enemy fire⟩ **6** : INHALE ⟨∼ a deep breath⟩ **7** : to bring or pull out ⟨*drew* a gun⟩ **8** : to cause to come out of a container ⟨∼ water for a bath⟩ **9** : EVISCERATE **10** : to require (a specified depth) to float in **11** : ACCUMULATE, GAIN ⟨∼ing interest⟩ **12** : to take money from a place of deposit : WITHDRAW **13** : to receive regularly ⟨∼ a salary⟩ **14** : to take (cards) from a stack or the dealer **15** : to receive or take at random ⟨∼ a winning number⟩ **16** : to bend (a bow) by pulling back the string **17** : WRINKLE, SHRINK **18** : to change shape by or as if by pulling or stretching ⟨a face *drawn* with sorrow⟩ **19** : to leave (a contest) undecided : TIE **20** : DELINEATE, SKETCH **21** : to write out in due form : DRAFT ⟨∼ up a will⟩ **22** : FORMULATE ⟨∼ comparisons⟩ **23** : INFER ⟨∼ a conclusion⟩ **24** : to spread or elongate (metal) by hammering or by pulling through dies **25** : to produce or allow a draft or current of air ⟨the chimney ∼s well⟩ **26** : to swell out in a wind ⟨all sails ∼ing⟩
²**draw** *n* **1** : the act, process, or result of drawing **2** : a lot or chance drawn at random **3** : a contest left undecided or deadlocked : TIE **4** : one that draws attention or patronage
draw·back \ˈdrò-ˌbak\ *n* : DISADVANTAGE 2
draw·bridge \-ˌbrij\ *n* : a bridge made to be raised, lowered, or turned to permit or deny passage
draw·er \ˈdrór, ˈdrò-ər\ *n* **1** : one that draws **2** *pl* : an undergarment for the lower part of the body **3** : a sliding boxlike compartment (as in a table or desk)
draw·ing \ˈdrò-iŋ\ *n* **1** : an act or instance of drawing; *esp* : an occasion when something is decided by drawing lots ⟨tonight's lottery ∼⟩ **2** : the act or art of making a figure, plan, or sketch by means of lines **3** : a representation made by drawing : SKETCH
drawing card *n* : DRAW 4
drawing room *n* : a formal reception room
drawl \ˈdról\ *vb* : to speak or utter slowly with vowels greatly prolonged — **drawl** *n*

draw on *vb* : APPROACH ⟨night *draws on*⟩

draw out *vb* **1** : PROLONG **2** : to cause to speak freely

draw·string \'drȯ-ˌstriŋ\ *n* : a string, cord, or tape for use in closing a bag or controlling fullness in garments or curtains

draw up *vb* **1** : to prepare a draft or version of **2** : to pull oneself erect **3** : to bring or come to a stop

dray \'drā\ *n* : a strong low cart for carrying heavy loads

¹dread \'dred\ *vb* **1** : to fear greatly **2** : to feel extreme reluctance to meet or face

²dread *n* : great fear esp. of some harm to come

³dread *adj* **1** : causing great fear or anxiety **2** : inspiring awe

dread·ful \'dred-fəl\ *adj* **1** : inspiring dread or awe : FRIGHTENING **2** : extremely distasteful, unpleasant, or shocking — **dread·ful·ly** *adv*

dread·locks \'dred-ˌläks\ *n pl* : long braids of hair over the entire head

dread·nought \'dred-ˌnȯt\ *n* : BATTLESHIP

¹dream \'drēm\ *n* [ME *dreem*, fr. OE *drēam* noise, joy, and ON *draumr* dream] **1** : a series of thoughts, images, or emotions occurring during sleep **2** : a dreamlike vision : DAYDREAM, REVERIE **3** : something notable for its beauty, excellence, or enjoyable quality **4** : IDEAL — **dreamy** *adj*

²dream \'drēm\ *vb* **dreamed** \'dremt, 'drēmd\ *or* **dreamt** \'dremt\; **dream·ing 1** : to have a dream of **2** : to indulge in daydreams or fantasies : pass (time) in reverie or inaction **3** : IMAGINE — **dream·er** *n*

dream·land \'drēm-ˌland\ *n* : an unreal delightful country that exists in imagination or in dreams

dream up *vb* : INVENT, CONCOCT

dream·world \-ˌwərld\ *n* : a world of illusion or fantasy

drear \'drir\ *adj* : DREARY

drea·ry \'drir-ē\ *adj* **drea·ri·er; -est** [ME *drery*, fr. OE *drēorig* sad, bloody, fr. *drēor* gore] **1** : DOLEFUL, SAD **2** : DISMAL, GLOOMY — **drea·ri·ly** \-ə-lē\ *adv*

¹dredge \'drej\ *vb* **dredged; dredg·ing** : to gather or search with or as if with a dredge — **dredg·er** *n*

²dredge *n* : a machine or barge for removing earth or silt

³dredge *vb* **dredged; dredg·ing** : to coat (food) by sprinkling (as with flour)

dregs \'dregz\ *n pl* **1** : SEDIMENT 1 **2** : the most undesirable part ⟨the ~ of humanity⟩

drench \'drench\ *vb* : to wet thoroughly

¹dress \'dres\ *vb* **1** : to make or set straight : ALIGN **2** : to prepare for use; *esp* : BUTCHER **3** : TRIM, EMBELLISH ⟨~ a store window⟩ **4** : to put clothes on : CLOTHE; *also* : to put on or wear formal or fancy clothes **5** : to apply dressings or medicine to **6** : to arrange (the hair) by combing, brushing, or curling **7** : to apply fertilizer to **8** : SMOOTH, FINISH ⟨~ leather⟩

²dress *n* **1** : APPAREL, CLOTHING **2** : a garment usu. consisting of a one-piece bodice and skirt — **dress·mak·er** \-ˌmā-kər\ *n* — **dress·mak·ing** \-ˌmā-kiŋ\ *n*

³dress *adj* : suitable for a formal occasion; *also* : requiring formal dress

dres·sage \drə-'säzh\ *n* [F] : the execution by a trained horse of complex movements in response to barely perceptible signals from its rider

dress down *vb* : to scold severely

¹dress·er \'dre-sər\ *n* : a chest of drawers or bureau with a mirror

²dresser *n* : one that dresses

dress·ing \'dre-siŋ\ *n* **1** : the act or process of one who dresses **2** : a sauce for adding to a dish (as a salad) **3** : a seasoned mixture usu. used as stuffing **4** : material used to cover an injury

dressing gown *n* : a loose robe worn esp. while dressing or resting

dressy \'dre-sē\ *adj* **dress·i·er; -est 1** : showy in dress **2** : STYLISH, SMART

drew *past of* DRAW

¹drib·ble \'dri-bəl\ *vb* **drib·bled; drib·bling 1** : to fall or flow in drops : TRICKLE **2** : DROOL **3** : to propel by successive slight taps or bounces

²dribble *n* **1** : a small trickling stream or flow **2** : a drizzling shower **3** : the dribbling of a ball or puck

drib·let \'dri-blət\ *n* **1** : a trifling amount **2** : a drop of liquid

dri·er *or* **dry·er** \'drī-ər\ *n* **1** : a substance that speeds drying (as of paint or ink) **2** *usu* **dryer** : a device for drying

¹drift \'drift\ *n* **1** : the motion or course of something drifting **2** : a mass of matter (as snow or sand) piled up esp. by wind **3** : earth, gravel, and rock deposited by a glacier **4** : a general underlying design or tendency : MEANING

²drift *vb* **1** : to float or be driven along by or as if by a current of water or air **2** : to become piled up by wind or water

drift·er \'drif-tər\ *n* : a person without aim, ambition, or initiative

drift net *n* : a fishing net often miles in extent arranged to drift with the tide or current

drift·wood \'drift-ˌwu̇d\ *n* : wood drifted or floated by water

¹drill \'dril\ *n* **1** : a tool for boring holes **2** : the training of soldiers in marching and the handling of arms **3** : a regularly practiced exercise

²drill *vb* **1** : to instruct and exercise by repetition **2** : to train in or practice military drill **3** : to bore with a drill — **drill·er** *n*

³drill *n* **1** : a shallow furrow or trench in which seed is sown **2** : an agricultural implement for making furrows and dropping seed into them

⁴drill *n* : a firm cotton twilled fabric

drill·mas·ter \'dril-ˌmas-tər\ *n* : an instructor in military drill

drill press *n* : an upright drilling machine in which the drill is pressed to the work usu. by a hand lever

drily *var of* DRYLY

¹drink \'driŋk\ *vb* **drank** \'draŋk\; **drunk** \'drəŋk\ *or* **drank; drink·ing 1** : to swallow liquid : IMBIBE **2** : ABSORB **3** : to take in through the senses ⟨~ in the beautiful scenery⟩ **4** : to give or join in a toast **5** : to drink alcoholic beverages esp. to excess — **drink·able** *adj* — **drink·er** *n*

²drink *n* **1** : BEVERAGE; *also* : an alcoholic beverage **2** : a draft or portion of liquid **3** : excessive consumption of alcoholic beverages

¹drip \'drip\ *vb* **dripped; drip·ping 1** : to fall or let fall in drops **2** : to let fall drops of moisture or liquid ⟨a *dripping* faucet⟩ **3** : to overflow with or as if with moisture

²drip *n* **1** : a falling in drops **2** : liquid that falls, overflows, or is extruded in drops **3** : the sound made by or as if by falling drops

¹drive \'drīv\ *vb* **drove** \'drōv\; **driv·en** \'dri-vən\; **driv·ing 1** : to urge, push, or force onward **2** : to carry through strongly ⟨~ a bargain⟩ **3** : to set or keep in motion or operation **4** : to direct the movement or course of **5** : to convey in a vehicle **6** : to bring into a specified condition ⟨the noise ~s me crazy⟩ **7** : FORCE, COMPEL ⟨*driven* by hunger to steal⟩ **8** : to project, inject, or impress forcefully ⟨*drove* the lesson home⟩ **9** : to produce by opening a way ⟨~ a well⟩ **10** : to progress with strong momentum ⟨a *driving* rain⟩ **11** : to propel an object of play (as a golf ball) by a hard blow — **driv·er** *n*

²drive *n* **1** : a trip in a carriage or automobile **2** : a driving or collecting of animals ⟨a cattle ~⟩ **3** : the guiding of logs downstream to a mill **4** : the act of driving a ball; *also* : the flight of a ball **5** : DRIVEWAY **6** : a public road for driving (as in a park) **7** : the state of being hurried and under pressure **8** : an intensive campaign ⟨membership ~⟩ **9** : the apparatus by which motion is imparted to a machine **10** : an offensive or aggressive move : a military attack **11** : NEED, LONGING **12**

: dynamic quality **13** : a device for reading and writing on magnetic media (as magnetic tape or disks)

drive–in \\'drī-ˌvin\ *adj* : accommodating patrons while they remain in their automobiles — **drive–in** *n*

¹**driv•el** \\'dri-vəl\ *vb* **-eled** *or* **-elled; -el•ing** *or* **-el•ling 1** : DROOL, SLAVER **2** : to talk or utter stupidly, carelessly, or in an infantile way — **driv•el•er** *n*

²**drivel** *n* : NONSENSE

drive•shaft \\'drīv-ˌshaft\ *n* : a shaft that transmits mechanical power

drive•way \-ˌwā\ *n* : a short private road leading from the street to a house, garage, or parking lot

¹**driz•zle** \\'dri-zəl\ *n* : a fine misty rain

²**drizzle** *vb* **driz•zled; driz•zling** : to rain in very small drops

drogue \\'drōg\ *n* : a small parachute for slowing down or stabilizing something (as a space capsule)

droll \\'drōl\ *adj* [F *drôle*, fr. *drôle* scamp, fr. MF *drolle*, fr. MD, imp] : having a humorous, whimsical, or odd quality ⟨a ~ expression⟩ — **droll•ery** \\'drō-lə-rē\ *n* — **drol•ly** *adv*

drom•e•dary \\'drä-mə-ˌder-ē\ *n, pl* **-dar•ies** [ME *dromedarie*, fr. MF *dromedaire*, fr. LL *dromedarius*, fr. L *dromad-, dromas*, fr. Gk, running] : CAMEL; *esp* : a domesticated one-humped camel of western Asia and northern Africa

¹**drone** \\'drōn\ *n* **1** : a male honeybee **2** : one that lives on the labors of others : PARASITE **3** : an unmanned aircraft or ship guided by remote control

²**drone** *vb* **droned; dron•ing** : to sound with a low dull monotonous murmuring sound : speak monotonously

³**drone** *n* : a deep monotonous sound

drool \\'drül\ *vb* **1** : to let liquid flow from the mouth **2** : to talk foolishly

droop \\'drüp\ *vb* **1** : to hang or incline downward **2** : to sink gradually **3** : LANGUISH — **droop** *n* — **droopy** *adj*

¹**drop** \\'dräp\ *n* **1** : the quantity of fluid that falls in one spherical mass **2** *pl* : a dose of medicine measured by drops **3** : a small quantity of drink **4** : the smallest practical unit of liquid measure **5** : something (as a pendant or a small round candy) that resembles a liquid drop **6** : FALL **7** : a decline in quantity or quality **8** : a descent by parachute **9** : the distance through which something drops **10** : a slot into which something is to be dropped **11** : something that drops or has dropped

²**drop** *vb* **dropped; drop•ping 1** : to fall or let fall in drops **2** : to let fall : LOWER ⟨~ a glove⟩ ⟨*dropped* his voice⟩ **3** : SEND ⟨~ me a note⟩ **4** : to let go : DISMISS ⟨~ the subject⟩ **5** : to knock down : cause to fall **6** : to go lower : become less ⟨prices *dropped*⟩ **7** : to come or go unexpectedly or informally ⟨~ in to call⟩ **8** : to pass from one state into a less active one ⟨~ off to sleep⟩ **9** : to move downward or with a current **10** : QUIT ⟨*dropped* out of the race⟩ — **drop back** : to move toward the rear — **drop behind** : to fail to keep up

drop•kick \-ˈkik\ *n* : a kick made by dropping a ball to the ground and kicking it at the moment it starts to rebound — **drop–kick** *vb*

drop•let \\'drä-plət\ *n* : a tiny drop

drop–off \\'dräp-ˌȯf\ *n* **1** : a steep or perpendicular descent **2** : a marked decline ⟨a ~ in attendance⟩

drop off *vb* : to fall asleep

drop out *vb* : to withdraw from participation or membership; *esp* : to leave school before graduation — **drop•out** \\'dräp-ˌaut\ *n*

drop•per \\'drä-pər\ *n* **1** : one that drops **2** : a short glass tube with a rubber bulb used to measure out liquids by drops

drop•pings *n pl* : MANURE, DUNG

drop•sy \\'dräp-sē\ *n* [ME *dropesie*, short for *ydropesie*, fr. OF, fr. L *hydropisis*, fr. Gk *hydrōps*, fr. *hydōr* water] : EDEMA — **drop•si•cal** \-si-kəl\ *adj*

dross \\'dräs\ *n* **1** : the scum that forms on the surface of a molten metal **2** : waste matter : REFUSE

drought \\'draut\ *also* **drouth** \\'drauth\ *n* : a long spell of dry weather

¹**drove** \\'drōv\ *n* **1** : a group of animals driven or moving in a body **2** : a large number : CROWD — usu. used in pl. ⟨tourists arriving in ~s⟩

²**drove** *past of* DRIVE

drov•er \\'drō-vər\ *n* : one that drives domestic animals usu. to market

drown \\'draun\ *vb* **drowned** \\'draund\; **drown•ing 1** : to suffocate by submersion esp. in water **2** : to become drowned **3** : to cover with water **4** : to cause to be muted (as a sound) by a loud noise **5** : OVERPOWER, OVERWHELM

drowse \\'drauz\ *vb* **drowsed; drows•ing** : DOZE — **drowse** *n*

drowsy \\'drau-zē\ *adj* **drows•i•er; -est 1** : ready to fall asleep **2** : making one sleepy — **drows•i•ly** \-zə-lē\ *adv* — **drows•i•ness** \-zē-nəs\ *n*

drub \\'drəb\ *vb* **drubbed; drub•bing 1** : to beat severely **2** : to defeat decisively

drudge \\'drəj\ *vb* **drudged; drudg•ing** : to do hard, menial, or monotonous work — **drudge** *n* — **drudg•ery** \\'drə-jə-rē\ *n*

¹**drug** \\'drəg\ *n* **1** : a substance used as or in medicine **2** : a substance (as heroin or marijuana) that can cause addiction, a marked change in mental status, or psychological dependency

²**drug** *vb* **drugged; drug•ging** : to affect with or as if with drugs; *esp* : to stupefy with a narcotic

drug•gist \\'drə-gist\ *n* : a dealer in drugs and medicines; *also* : PHARMACIST

drug•store \\'drəg-ˌstȯr\ *n* : a retail shop where medicines and miscellaneous articles are sold

dru•id \\'drü-əd\ *n, often cap* : one of an ancient Celtic priesthood appearing in Irish, Welsh, and Christian legends as magicians and wizards

¹**drum** \\'drəm\ *n* **1** : a percussion instrument usu. consisting of a hollow cylinder with a skin or plastic head stretched over one or both ends that is beaten with the hands or with a stick **2** : the sound of a drum; *also* : a similar sound **3** : a drum-shaped object

²**drum** *vb* **drummed; drum•ming 1** : to beat a drum **2** : to sound rhythmically : THROB, BEAT **3** : to summon or enlist by or as if by beating a drum ⟨*drummed* into service⟩ **4** : EXPEL — usu. used with *out* **5** : to drive or force by steady effort ⟨~ the facts into memory⟩ **6** : to strike or tap repeatedly so as to produce rhythmic sounds

drum•beat \\'drəm-ˌbēt\ *n* : a stroke on a drum or its sound

drum major *n* : the leader of a marching band

drum ma•jor•ette \-ˌmā-jə-ˈret\ *n* : a girl or woman who leads a marching band; *also* : a baton twirler who accompanies a marching band

drum•mer \\'drə-mər\ *n* **1** : one that plays a drum **2** : a traveling salesman

drum•stick \\'drəm-ˌstik\ *n* **1** : a stick for beating a drum **2** : the lower segment of a fowl's leg

drum up *vb* **1** : to bring about by persistent effort ⟨*drum up* business⟩ **2** : INVENT, ORIGINATE

¹**drunk** *past part of* DRINK

²**drunk** \\'drəŋk\ *adj* **1** : having the faculties impaired by alcohol ⟨~ drivers⟩ **2** : dominated by an intense feeling ⟨~ with power⟩ **3** : of, relating to, or caused by intoxication

³**drunk** *n* **1** : a period of excessive drinking **2** : a drunken person

drunk•ard \\'drəŋ-kərd\ *n* : one who is habitually drunk

drunk•en \\'drəŋ-kən\ *adj* **1** : DRUNK **2** : given to habitual excessive use of alcohol **3** : of, relating to, or resulting from intoxication **4** : unsteady or lurching as if from intoxication — **drunk•en•ly** *adv* — **drunk•en•ness** *n*

drupe \'drüp\ *n* : a partly fleshy one-seeded fruit (as a plum or cherry) that remains closed at maturity

¹**dry** \'drī\ *adj* **dri·er** \'drī-ər\; **dri·est** \-əst\ **1** : free or freed from water or liquid ⟨~ fruits⟩; *also* : not being in or under water **2** : characterized by lack of water or moisture ⟨~ climate⟩ **3** : lacking freshness : STALE **4** : devoid of natural moisture; *also* : THIRSTY **5** : no longer liquid or sticky ⟨the ink is ~⟩ **6** : not giving milk ⟨a ~ cow⟩ **7** : marked by the absence of alcoholic beverages **8** : prohibiting the making or distributing of alcoholic beverages **9** : not sweet ⟨~ wine⟩ **10** : solid as opposed to liquid ⟨~ groceries⟩ **11** : containing or employing no liquid **12** : SEVERE; *also* : UNINTERESTING, WEARISOME **13** : not productive **14** : marked by a matter-of-fact, ironic, or terse manner of expression ⟨~ humor⟩ — **dry·ly** *adv* — **dry·ness** *n*

²**dry** *vb* **dried; dry·ing** : to make or become dry

³**dry** *n, pl* **drys** : PROHIBITIONIST

dry·ad \'drī-əd, -₁ad\ *n* : WOOD NYMPH

dry cell *n* : a battery whose contents are not spillable

dry–clean \'drī-₁klēn\ *vb* : to clean (fabrics) chiefly with solvents other than water — **dry cleaning** *n*

dry dock \'drī-₁däk\ *n* : a dock that can be kept dry during ship construction or repair

dry·er *var of* DRIER

dry farm·ing *n* : farming without irrigation in areas of limited rainfall — **dry–farm** *vb* — **dry farm·er** *n*

dry goods \'drī-₁gu̇dz\ *n pl* : cloth goods (as fabrics, ribbon, and ready-to-wear clothing)

dry ice *n* : solid carbon dioxide

dry measure *n* : a series of units of capacity for dry commodities — see METRIC SYSTEM table, WEIGHT table

dry run *n* : REHEARSAL, TRIAL

dry·wall \'drī-₁wȯl\ *n* : PLASTERBOARD

DSC *abbr* **1** Distinguished Service Cross **2** doctor of surgical chiropody

DSM *abbr* Distinguished Service Medal

DST *abbr* daylight saving time

DTP *abbr* diphtheria, tetanus, pertussis (vaccines)

d.t.'s \₁dē-'tēz\ *n pl, often cap D&T* : DELIRIUM TREMENS

du·al \'dü-əl, 'dyü-\ *adj* **1** : TWOFOLD, DOUBLE **2** : having a double character or nature — **du·al·ism** \-ə-₁li-zəm\ *n* — **du·al·i·ty** \dü-'a-lə-tē, dyü-\ *n*

¹**dub** \'dəb\ *vb* **dubbed; dub·bing** **1** : to confer knighthood upon **2** : NAME, NICKNAME

²**dub** *n* : a clumsy person : DUFFER

³**dub** *vb* **dubbed; dub·bing** : to add (sound effects) to a motion picture or to a radio or television production

du·bi·ety \dü-'bī-ə-tē, dyü-\ *n, pl* **-eties** : UNCERTAINTY **2** : a matter of doubt

du·bi·ous \'dü-bē-əs, 'dyü-\ *adj* **1** : UNCERTAIN **2** : QUESTIONABLE **3** : feeling doubt : UNDECIDED — **du·bi·ous·ly** *adv* — **du·bi·ous·ness** *n*

du·cal \'dü-kəl, 'dyü-\ *adj* : of or relating to a duke or dukedom

duc·at \'də-kət\ *n* : a gold coin formerly used in various European countries

duch·ess \'də-chəs\ *n* **1** : the wife or widow of a duke **2** : a woman holding the rank of duke in her own right

duchy \'də-chē\ *n, pl* **duch·ies** : the territory of a duke or duchess : DUKEDOM

¹**duck** \'dək\ *n, pl* **ducks** : any of various swimming birds related to but smaller than geese and swans

²**duck** *vb* **1** : to thrust or plunge under water **2** : to lower the head or body suddenly : BOW; *also* : DODGE **3** : to evade a duty, question, or responsibility ⟨~ the issue⟩

³**duck** *n* **1** : a durable closely woven usu. cotton fabric **2** *pl* : light clothes made of duck

duck·bill \'dək-₁bil\ *n* : PLATYPUS

duck·ling \-liŋ\ *n* : a young duck

duck·pin \-₁pin\ *n* **1** : a small bowling pin shorter and wider in the middle than a tenpin **2** *pl but sing in constr* : a bowling game using duckpins

duct \'dəkt\ *n* **1** : a tube or canal for conveying a bodily fluid **2** : a pipe or tube through which a fluid (as air) flows — **duct·less** *adj*

duc·tile \'dəkt-əl\ *adj* **1** : capable of being drawn out (as into wire) or hammered thin **2** : easily led : DOCILE — **duc·til·i·ty** \₁dək-'ti-lə-tē\ *n*

ductless gland *n* : an endocrine gland

dud \'dəd\ *n* **1** *pl* : CLOTHING **2** : one that fails completely; *also* : a bomb or missile that fails to explode

dude \'düd, 'dyüd\ *n* **1** : DANDY 1 **2** : a city dweller; *esp* : an Easterner in the West **3** : FELLOW, GUY

dude ranch *n* : a vacation resort offering activities (as horseback riding) typical of western ranches

dud·geon \'də-jən\ *n* : a fit or state of indignation ⟨in high ~⟩

¹**due** \'dü, 'dyü\ *adj* [ME, fr. MF *deu*, pp. of *devoir* to owe, fr. L *debēre*] **1** : owed or owing as a debt **2** : owed or owing as a right **3** : APPROPRIATE, FITTING **4** : SUFFICIENT, ADEQUATE **5** : REGULAR, LAWFUL ⟨~ process of law⟩ **6** : ATTRIBUTABLE, ASCRIBABLE ⟨~ to negligence⟩ **7** : PAYABLE ⟨a bill ~ today⟩ **8** : SCHEDULED ⟨~ to arrive soon⟩

²**due** *n* **1** : something that rightfully belongs to one ⟨give everyone their ~⟩ **2** : DEBT **3** *pl* : FEES, CHARGES

³**due** *adv* : DIRECTLY, EXACTLY ⟨~ north⟩

du·el \'dü-əl, 'dyü-\ *n* : a combat between two persons; *esp* : one fought with weapons in the presence of witnesses — **duel** *vb* — **du·el·ist** \-ə-list\ *n*

du·en·de \dü-'en-dā\ *n* [Sp dial., charm, fr. Sp, ghost, goblin, fr. *duen de casa*, prob. fr. *dueño de casa* owner of a house] : the power to attract through personal magnetism and charm

du·en·na \dü-'e-nə, dyü-\ *n* **1** : an elderly woman in charge of the younger ladies in a Spanish or Portuguese family **2** : CHAPERON

du·et \dü-'et, dyü-\ *n* : a musical composition for two performers

due to *prep* : BECAUSE OF

duf·fel bag \'də-fəl-\ *n* : a large cylindrical bag for personal belongings

duf·fer \'də-fər\ *n* : an incompetent or clumsy person

dug *past and past part of* DIG

dug·out \'dəg-₁au̇t\ *n* **1** : a boat made by hollowing out a log **2** : a shelter dug in the ground **3** : a low shelter facing a baseball diamond that contains the players' bench

DUI *abbr* driving under the influence

duke \'dük, 'dyük\ *n* **1** : a sovereign ruler of a continental European duchy **2** : a nobleman of the highest rank; *esp* : a member of the highest grade of the British peerage **3** *slang* : FIST 1 ⟨put up your ~s⟩ — **duke·dom** *n*

dul·cet \'dəl-sət\ *adj* **1** : pleasing to the ear **2** : AGREEABLE, SOOTHING

dul·ci·mer \'dəl-sə-mər\ *n* **1** : a stringed instrument of trapezoidal shape played with light hammers held in the hands **2** *or* **dul·ci·more** \-₁mȯr\ : an American folk instrument with three or four strings that is held on the lap and played by plucking or strumming

¹**dull** \'dəl\ *adj* **1** : mentally slow : STUPID **2** : slow in perception or sensibility **3** : LISTLESS **4** : slow in action : SLUGGISH ⟨a ~ market⟩ **5** : lacking intensity; *also* : not resonant or ringing **6** : BLUNT **7** : lacking brilliance or luster **8** : low in saturation and lightness ⟨~ color⟩ **9** : CLOUDY, OVERCAST **10** : TEDIOUS, UNINTERESTING — **dull·ness** *or* **dul·ness** *n* — **dul·ly** *adv*

²**dull** *vb* : to make or become dull

dull·ard \'də-lərd\ *n* : a stupid person

du·ly \'dü-lē, 'dyü-\ *adv* : in a due manner or time

dumb \'dəm\ *adj* **1** : lacking the power of speech **2** : SILENT **3** : STUPID — **dumb·ly** *adv*

dumb·bell \'dəm-₁bel\ *n* **1** : a bar with weights at the end used for exercise **2** : one who is stupid

dumb·found *or* **dum·found** \₁dəm-'fau̇nd\ *vb* : ASTONISH, AMAZE

dumb·wait·er \'dəm-₁wā-tər\ *n* : a small elevator for conveying food and dishes from one floor to another

dum·my \'də-mē\ n, pl **dummies 1** : a person who cannot speak; *also* : a stupid person **2** : the exposed hand in bridge played by the declarer in addition to that player's own hand; *also* : a bridge player whose hand is a dummy **3** : an imitative substitute for something; *also* : MANNEQUIN **4** : one seeming to act alone but really acting for another **5** : a mock-up of matter to be reproduced esp. by printing

¹**dump** \'dəmp\ vb : to let fall in a pile; *also* : to get rid of carelessly

²**dump** n **1** : a place for dumping something (as refuse) **2** : a reserve supply; *also* : a place where such supplies are kept ⟨an ammunition ~⟩ **3** : a messy or objectionable place

dump·ing \'dəm-piŋ\ n : the selling of goods in quantity at below market price

dump·ling \'dəm-pliŋ\ n **1** : a small mass of boiled or steamed dough **2** : a dessert of fruit baked in biscuit dough

dumps \'dəmps\ n pl : a gloomy state of mind : low spirits ⟨in the ~⟩

dump truck n : a truck for transporting and dumping bulk material

dumpy \'dəm-pē\ adj **dump·i·er; -est 1** : short and thick in build **2** : SHABBY

¹**dun** \'dən\ n : a brownish dark gray

²**dun** vb **dunned; dun·ning 1** : to make persistent demands for payment **2** : PLAGUE, PESTER — **dun** n

dunce \'dəns\ n [John *Duns* Scotus, whose once accepted writings were ridiculed in the 16th cent.] : a slow stupid person

dun·der·head \'dən-dər-ˌhed\ n : DUNCE, BLOCKHEAD

dune \'dün, 'dyün\ n : a hill or ridge of sand piled up by the wind

dune buggy n : a motor vehicle with oversize tires for use on sand

¹**dung** \'dəŋ\ n : MANURE

²**dung** vb : to dress (land) with dung

dun·ga·ree \ˌdəŋ-gə-'rē\ n **1** : a heavy coarse cotton twill; *esp* : blue denim **2** pl : clothes made of blue denim

dun·geon \'dən-jən\ n [ME *donjon*, fr. MF, fr. (assumed) VL *domnion-, domnio* keep, mastery, fr. L *dominus* lord] : a dark prison commonly underground

dung·hill \'dəŋ-ˌhil\ n : a manure pile

dunk \'dəŋk\ vb **1** : to dip or submerge temporarily in liquid **2** : to submerge oneself in water **3** : to shoot a basketball into the basket from above the rim

duo \'dü-(ˌ)ō, 'dyü-\ n, pl **du·os 1** : DUET **2** : PAIR **3**

duo·dec·i·mal \ˌdü-ə-'de-sə-məl, ˌdyü-\ adj : of, relating to, or being a system of numbers with a base of 12

du·o·de·num \ˌdü-ə-'dē-nəm, ˌdyü-, dü-'äd-ᵊn-əm, dyü-\ n, pl **-dena** \-'dē-nə, -ᵊn-ə\ or **-denums** : the first part of the small intestine extending from the stomach to the jejunum — **du·o·de·nal** \-'dēn-ᵊl, -ᵊn-əl\ adj

dup abbr **1** duplex **2** duplicate

¹**dupe** \'düp, 'dyüp\ n : one who is easily deceived or cheated : FOOL

²**dupe** vb **duped; dup·ing** : to make a dupe of : DECEIVE, FOOL

du·ple \'dü-pəl, 'dyü-\ adj : having two beats or a multiple of two beats to the measure ⟨~ time⟩

¹**du·plex** \'dü-ˌpleks, 'dyü-\ adj : DOUBLE

²**duplex** n : something duplex; *esp* : a 2-family house

¹**du·pli·cate** \'dü-pli-kət, 'dyü-\ adj **1** : consisting of or existing in two corresponding or identical parts or examples **2** : being the same as another

²**du·pli·cate** \'dü-pli-ˌkāt, 'dyü-\ vb **-cat·ed; -cat·ing 1** : to make double or twofold **2** : to make a copy of — **du·pli·ca·tion** \ˌdü-pli-'kā-shən, ˌdyü-\ n

³**du·pli·cate** \-kət\ n : a thing that exactly resembles another in appearance, pattern, or content : COPY

du·pli·ca·tor \'dü-pli-ˌkā-tər, 'dyü-\ n : COPIER

du·plic·i·ty \dü-'pli-sə-tē, dyü-\ n, pl **-ties** : the disguising of true intentions by deceptive words or action

du·ra·ble \'dur-ə-bəl, 'dyur-\ adj : able to exist for a long time without significant deterioration ⟨~ goods⟩ — **du·ra·bil·i·ty** \ˌdur-ə-'bi-lə-tē, ˌdyur-\ n

du·rance \'dur-əns, 'dyur-\ n : restraint by or as if by physical force ⟨held in ~ vile⟩

du·ra·tion \du-'rā-shən, dyu-\ n : the time during which something exists or lasts

du·ress \du-'res, dyu-\ n : compulsion by threat ⟨confession made under ~⟩

dur·ing \'dur-iŋ, 'dyur-\ prep **1** : THROUGHOUT ⟨swims every day ~ the summer⟩ **2** : at some point in ⟨broke in ~ the night⟩

dusk \'dəsk\ n **1** : the darker part of twilight esp. at night **2** : partial darkness

dusky \'dəs-kē\ adj **dusk·i·er; -est 1** : somewhat dark in color **2** : SHADOWY — **dusk·i·ness** n

¹**dust** \'dəst\ n **1** : fine particles of matter **2** : the particles into which something disintegrates **3** : something worthless **4** : the surface of the ground — **dust·less** adj — **dusty** adj

²**dust** vb **1** : to make free of or remove dust **2** : to sprinkle with fine particles **3** : to sprinkle in the form of dust

dust bowl n : a region suffering from long droughts and dust storms

dust devil n : a small whirlwind containing sand or dust

dust·er \'dəs-tər\ n **1** : one that removes dust **2** : a dress-length housecoat **3** : one that scatters fine particles; *esp* : a device for applying insecticides to crops

dust·pan \'dəst-ˌpan\ n : a flat-ended pan for sweepings

dust storm n : a violent wind carrying dust across a dry region

dutch \'dəch\ adv, often cap : with each person paying his or her own way ⟨go ~⟩

Dutch \'dəch\ n **1 Dutch** pl : the people of the Netherlands **2** : the language of the Netherlands — **Dutch** adj — **Dutch·man** \-mən\ n

Dutch elm disease n : a fungous disease of elms characterized by yellowing of the foliage, defoliation, and death

dutch treat n, often cap D : an entertainment (as a meal) for which each person pays his or her own way — **dutch treat** adv, often cap D

du·te·ous \'dü-tē-əs, 'dyü-\ adj : DUTIFUL, OBEDIENT

du·ti·able \'dü-tē-ə-bəl, 'dyü-\ adj : subject to a duty ⟨~ imports⟩

du·ti·ful \'dü-ti-fəl, 'dyü-\ adj **1** : motivated by a sense of duty ⟨a ~ son⟩ **2** : coming from or showing a sense of duty ⟨~ affection⟩ — **du·ti·ful·ly** adv — **du·ti·ful·ness** n

du·ty \'dü-tē, 'dyü-\ n, pl **duties 1** : conduct or action required by one's occupation or position **2** : assigned service or business; *esp* : active military service **3** : a moral or legal obligation **4** : TAX **5** : the service required (as of a machine) : USE ⟨a heavy-*duty* tire⟩

DV abbr **1** [L *Deo volente*] God willing **2** Douay Version

DVM abbr doctor of veterinary medicine

¹**dwarf** \'dworf\ n, pl **dwarfs** \'dworfs\ or **dwarves** \'dworvz\ : one that is much below normal size — **dwarf·ish** adj

²**dwarf** vb **1** : to restrict the growth or development of : STUNT **2** : to cause to appear smaller ⟨*dwarfed* by comparison⟩

dwell \'dwel\ vb **dwelt** \'dwelt\ or **dwelled** \'dweld, 'dwelt\; **dwell·ing** [ME, fr. OE *dwellan* to go astray, hinder] **1** : ABIDE, REMAIN **2** : RESIDE, EXIST **3** : to keep the attention directed **4** : to write or speak insistently — used with *on* or *upon* — **dwell·er** n

dwell·ing \'dwe-liŋ\ n : RESIDENCE

DWI abbr driving while intoxicated

dwin·dle \'dwind-ᵊl\ vb **dwin·dled; dwin·dling** : to make or become steadily less : DIMINISH

dwt *abbr* pennyweight

Dy *symbol* dysprosium

dyb·buk \\'di-bək\ *n, pl* **dyb·bu·kim** \ˌdi-bù-'kēm\ *also* **dybbuks** : a wandering soul believed in Jewish folklore to enter and possess a person

¹dye \'dī\ *n* **1** : color produced by dyeing **2** : material used for coloring or staining

²dye *vb* **dyed; dye·ing 1** : to impart a new color to esp. by impregnating with a dye **2** : to take up or impart color in dyeing

dye·stuff \'dī-ˌstəf\ *n* : DYE 2

dying *pres part of* DIE

dyke *chiefly Brit var of* DIKE

dy·nam·ic \dī-'na-mik\ *also* **dy·nam·i·cal** \-mi-kəl\ *adj* : of or relating to physical force producing motion : ENERGETIC, FORCEFUL

¹dy·na·mite \'dī-nə-ˌmīt\ *n* : an explosive made of nitroglycerin absorbed in a porous material; *also* : an explosive made without nitroglycerin

²dynamite *vb* **-mit·ed; -mit·ing** : to blow up with dynamite

dy·na·mo \'dī-nə-ˌmō\ *n, pl* **-mos** : an electrical generator

dy·na·mom·e·ter \ˌdī-nə-'mä-mə-tər\ *n* : an instrument for measuring mechanical power (as of an engine)

dy·nas·ty \'dī-nəs-tē, -ˌnas-\ *n, pl* **-ties 1** : a succession of rulers of the same family **2** : a powerful group or family that maintains its position for a long time — **dy·nas·tic** \dī-'nas-tik\ *adj*

dys·en·tery \'dis-ᵊn-ˌter-ē\ *n, pl* **-ter·ies** : a disease marked by diarrhea with blood and mucus in the feces; *also* : DIARRHEA

dys·lex·ia \dis-'lek-sē-ə\ *n* : a disturbance of the ability to read or use language — **dys·lex·ic** \-sik\ *adj or n*

dys·pep·sia \dis-'pep-shə, -sē-ə\ *n* : INDIGESTION — **dys·pep·tic** \-'pep-tik\ *adj or n*

dys·pro·si·um \dis-'prō-zē-əm\ *n* : a metallic chemical element that forms highly magnetic compounds — see ELEMENT table

dys·tro·phy \'dis-trə-fē\ *n, pl* **-phies** : a disorder involving atrophy of muscular tissue; *esp* : MUSCULAR DYSTROPHY

dz *abbr* dozen

E

¹e \'ē\ *n, pl* **e's** *or* **es** \'ēz\ *often cap* **1** : the 5th letter of the English alphabet **2** : the base of the system of natural logarithms having the approximate value 2.71828 **3** : a grade rating a student's work as poor or failing

²e *abbr, often cap* **1** east; eastern **2** error **3** excellent

ea *abbr* each

¹each \'ēch\ *adj* : being one of the class named ⟨∼ man⟩

²each *pron* : every individual one

³each *adv* : APIECE ⟨cost five cents ∼⟩

each other *pron* : each of two or more in reciprocal action or relation ⟨looked at *each other*⟩

ea·ger \'ē-gər\ *adj* : marked by urgent or enthusiastic desire or interest ⟨∼ to learn⟩ **syn** avid, anxious, ardent, keen — **ea·ger·ly** *adv* — **ea·ger·ness** *n*

ea·gle \'ē-gəl\ *n* **1** : a large bird of prey related to the hawks **2** : a score of two under par on a hole in golf

ea·glet \'ē-glət\ *n* : a young eagle

-ean — see -AN

E and OE *abbr* errors and omissions excepted

¹ear \'ir\ *n* **1** : the organ of hearing; *also* : the outer part of this in a vertebrate **2** : something resembling a mammal's ear in shape, position, or function **3** : an ability to understand and appreciate something heard ⟨a good ∼ for music⟩ **4** : sympathetic attention

²ear *n* : the fruiting spike of a cereal (as wheat)

ear·ache \-ˌāk\ *n* : an ache or pain in the ear

ear·drum \-ˌdrəm\ *n* : a thin membrane that receives and transmits sound waves in the ear

eared \'ird\ *adj* : having ears esp. of a specified kind or number ⟨a long-*eared* dog⟩

ear·ful \'ir-ˌfúl\ *n* : a verbal outpouring (as of news, gossip, anger, or complaint)

earl \'ərl\ *n* [ME *erl*, fr. OE *eorl* warrior, nobleman] : a member of the British peerage ranking below a marquess and above a viscount — **earl·dom** \-dəm\ *n*

ear·lobe \'ir-ˌlōb\ *n* : the pendent part of the ear

¹ear·ly \'ər-lē\ *adv* **ear·li·er; -est** : at an early time (as in a period or series)

²early *adj* **ear·li·er; -est 1** : of, relating to, or occurring near the beginning **2** : ANCIENT, PRIMITIVE **3** : occurring before the usual time ⟨an ∼ breakfast⟩; *also* : occurring in the near future

¹ear·mark \'ir-ˌmärk\ *n* : an identification mark (as on the ear of an animal); *also* : a distinguishing mark ⟨∼s of poverty⟩

²earmark *vb* **1** : to mark with an earmark **2** : to designate for a specific purpose

ear·muff \-ˌməf\ *n* : one of a pair of ear coverings worn to protect against cold

earn \'ərn\ *vb* **1** : to receive as a return for service **2** : DESERVE, MERIT **syn** gain, secure, get, obtain, acquire, win

¹ear·nest \'ər-nəst\ *n* : an intensely serious state of mind ⟨spoke in ∼⟩

²earnest *adj* **1** : seriously intent and sober ⟨an ∼ face⟩ ⟨an ∼ attempt⟩ **2** : GRAVE, IMPORTANT **syn** solemn, sedate, staid — **ear·nest·ly** *adv* — **ear·nest·ness** *n*

³earnest *n* **1** : something of value given by a buyer to a seller to bind a bargain **2** : PLEDGE

earn·ings \'ər-niŋz\ *n pl* **1** : something (as wages) earned **2** : the balance of revenue after deduction of costs and expenses

ear·phone \'ir-ˌfōn\ *n* : a device that reproduces sound and is worn over or in the ear

ear·plug \-ˌpləg\ *n* : a protective device for insertion into the opening of the ear

ear·ring \-ˌriŋ\ *n* : an ornament for the earlobe

ear·shot \-ˌshät\ *n* : range of hearing

ear·split·ting \-ˌspli-tiŋ\ *adj* : intolerably loud or shrill

earth \'ərth\ *n* **1** : SOIL, DIRT **2** : LAND, GROUND **3** *often cap* : the planet on which we live that is 3d in order from the sun — see PLANET table

earth·en \'ər-thən\ *adj* : made of earth or baked clay

earth·en·ware \-ˌwar\ *n* : slightly porous opaque pottery fired at low heat

earth·ling \'ərth-liŋ\ *n* : an inhabitant of the earth

earth·ly \'ərth-lē\ *adj* : having to do with the earth esp. as distinguished from heaven — **earth·li·ness** *n*

earth·quake \-ˌkwāk\ *n* : a shaking or trembling of a portion of the earth

earth science *n* : any of the sciences (as geology or meteorology) that deal with the earth or one of its parts

earth·shak·ing \'ərth-ˌshā-kiŋ\ *adj* : of great importance : MOMENTOUS

earth·ward \-wərd\ *also* **earth·wards** \-wərdz\ *adv* : toward the earth

earth·work \'ərth-ˌwərk\ *n* : an embankment or fortification of earth

earth·worm \-ˌwərm\ *n* : a long segmented worm found in damp soil

earthy \'ər-thē\ *adj* **earth·i·er; -est 1** : of, relating to, or consisting of earth; *also* : suggesting earth ⟨∼ flavors⟩ **2** : PRACTICAL **3** : COARSE, GROSS — **earth·i·ness** *n*

ear·wax \'ir-ˌwaks\ *n* : the yellow waxy secretion from the ear

ear·wig \-ˌwig\ *n* : any of numerous insects with slender many-jointed antennae and a pair of appendages resembling forceps at the end of the body

¹ease \'ēz\ *n* **1** : comfort of body or mind **2** : naturalness of manner **3** : freedom from difficulty or effort **syn** relaxation, rest, repose, leisure

²ease *vb* **eased; eas·ing 1** : to relieve from distress **2** : to lessen the pressure or tension of **3** : to make or become less difficult ⟨~ credit⟩

ea·sel \'ē-zəl\ *n* [Dutch *ezel,* lit., ass] : a frame for supporting something (as an artist's canvas)

¹east \'ēst\ *adv* : to or toward the east

²east *adj* **1** : situated toward or at the east **2** : coming from the east

³east *n* **1** : the general direction of sunrise **2** : the compass point directly opposite to west **3** *cap* : regions or countries east of a specified or implied point — **east·er·ly** \'ē-stər-lē\ *adv or adj* — **east·ward** *adv or adj* — **east·wards** *adv*

Eas·ter \'ē-stər\ *n* : a church feast observed on a Sunday in March or April in commemoration of Christ's resurrection

east·ern \'ē-stərn\ *adj* **1** *often cap* : of, relating to, or characteristic of a region designated East **2** *cap* : of, relating to, or being the Christian churches originating in the Church of the Eastern Roman Empire **3** : lying toward or coming from the east — **East·ern·er** *n*

easy \'ē-zē\ *adj* **eas·i·er; -est 1** : marked by ease ⟨an ~ life⟩; *esp* : not causing distress or difficulty ⟨~ tasks⟩ **2** : MILD, LENIENT ⟨be ~ on him⟩ **3** : GRADUAL ⟨an ~ slope⟩ **4** : free from pain, trouble, or worry ⟨rest ~⟩ **5** : LEISURELY ⟨an ~ pace⟩ **6** : NATURAL ⟨an ~ manner⟩ **7** : COMFORTABLE ⟨an ~ chair⟩ — **eas·i·ly** \'ē-zə-lē\ *adv* — **eas·i·ness** \-zē-nəs\ *n*

easy·go·ing \,ē-zē-'gō-iŋ\ *adj* : relaxed and casual in style or manner

eat \'ēt\ *vb* **ate** \'āt\; **eat·en** \'ēt-ᵊn\; **eat·ing 1** : to take in as food : take food **2** : to use up : DEVOUR **3** : CORRODE — **eat·able** *adj or n* — **eat·er** *n*

eat·ery \'ē-tə-rē\ *n, pl* **-er·ies** : LUNCHEONETTE, RESTAURANT

eaves \'ēvz\ *n pl* : the overhanging lower edge of a roof

eaves·drop \'ēvz-,dräp\ *vb* : to listen secretly — **eaves·drop·per** *n*

¹ebb \'eb\ *n* **1** : the flowing back from shore of water brought in by the tide **2** : a point or state of decline

²ebb *vb* **1** : to recede from the flood **2** : DECLINE ⟨his fortunes ~ed⟩

EBCDIC \'eb-sə-,dik\ *n* [extended *b*inary *c*oded *d*ecimal *i*nterchange *c*ode] : a computer code for representing alphanumeric information

¹eb·o·ny \'e-bə-nē\ *n, pl* **-nies** : a hard heavy wood of Old World tropical trees related to the persimmon

²ebony *adj* **1** : made of or resembling ebony **2** : BLACK, DARK

ebul·lient \i-'bùl-yənt, -'bəl-\ *adj* **1** : BOILING, AGITATED **2** : EXUBERANT — **ebul·lience** \-yəns\ *n*

EC *abbr* European Community

ec·cen·tric \ik-'sen-trik\ *adj* **1** : deviating from a usual or accepted pattern **2** : deviating from a circular path ⟨~ orbits⟩ **3** : set with axis or support off center ⟨an ~ cam⟩; *also* : being off center **syn** erratic, queer, singular, curious, odd — **eccentric** *n* — **ec·cen·tri·cal·ly** \-tri-k(ə-)lē\ *adv* — **ec·cen·tric·i·ty** \,ek-,sen-'tri-sə-tē\ *n*

Eccles *abbr* Ecclesiastes

Ec·cle·si·as·tes \i-,klē-zē-'as-tēz\ *n* — see BIBLE table

ec·cle·si·as·tic \i-,klē-zē-'as-tik\ *n* : CLERGYMAN

ec·cle·si·as·ti·cal \-ti-kəl\ *or* **ec·cle·si·as·tic** \-tik\ *adj* : of or relating to a church esp. as an institution ⟨~ art⟩ — **ec·cle·si·as·ti·cal·ly** \-ti-k(ə-)lē\ *adv*

Ec·cle·si·as·ti·cus \i-,klē-zē-'as-ti-kəs\ *n* — see BIBLE table

Ecclus *abbr* Ecclesiasticus

ECG *abbr* electrocardiogram

ech·e·lon \'e-shə-,län\ *n* [F *échelon,* lit., rung of a lad-

der] **1** : a steplike arrangement (as of troops or airplanes) **2** : a level (as of authority or responsibility) within an organization

echi·no·derm \i-'kī-nə-,dərm\ *n* : any of a phylum of marine animals (as starfishes and sea urchins) having similar body parts (as the arms of a starfish) arranged around a central axis and often having a calcium-containing outer skeleton

echo \'e-kō\ *n, pl* **ech·oes** *also* **ech·os** : repetition of a sound caused by a reflection of the sound waves; *also* : the reflection of a radar signal by an object — **echo** *vb* — **echo·ic** \e-'kō-ik\ *adj*

echo·lo·ca·tion \,e-ko-lō-'kā-shən\ *n* : a process for locating distant or invisible objects by means of sound waves reflected back to the sender (as a bat) by the objects

éclair \ā-'klar\ *n* [F, lit., lightning] : an oblong shell of light pastry with whipped cream or custard filling

éclat \ā-'klä\ *n* [F] **1** : a dazzling effect or success **2** : ACCLAIM

eclec·tic \e-'klek-tik\ *adj* : selecting or made up of what seems best of varied sources — **eclectic** *n*

¹eclipse \i-'klips\ *n* **1** : the total or partial obscuring of one heavenly body by another; *also* : a passing into the shadow of a heavenly body **2** : a falling into obscurity or decline

²eclipse *vb* **eclipsed; eclips·ing** : to cause an eclipse of; *also* : SURPASS

eclip·tic \i-'klip-tik\ *n* : the great circle of the celestial sphere that is the apparent path of the sun

ec·logue \'ek-,lòg, -,läg\ *n* : a pastoral poem

ECM *abbr* European Common Market

ecol *abbr* ecological; ecology

ecol·o·gy \i-'kä-lə-jē, e-\ *n, pl* **-gies** [G *Ökologie,* fr. Gk *oikos* house + *logos* word] **1** : a branch of science concerned with the relationships between organisms and their environment **2** : the pattern of relations between one or more organisms and the environment — **eco·log·i·cal** \,ē-kə-'lä-ji-kəl, ,e-\ *also* **eco·log·ic** \-jik\ *adj* — **eco·log·i·cal·ly** \-ji-k(ə-)lē\ *adv* — **ecol·o·gist** \i-'kä-lə-jist, e-\ *n*

econ *abbr* economics; economist; economy

eco·nom·ic \,e-kə-'nä-mik, ,ē-\ *adj* : of or relating to the production, distribution, and consumption of goods and services

eco·nom·i·cal \-'nä-mi-kəl\ *adj* **1** : THRIFTY **2** : operating with little waste or at a saving **syn** frugal, sparing, provident — **ec·o·nom·i·cal·ly** \-k(ə-)lē\ *adv*

eco·nom·ics \,e-kə-'nä-miks, ,ē-\ *n* : a social science dealing with the production, distribution, and consumption of goods and services — **econ·o·mist** \i-'kä-nə-mist\ *n*

econ·o·mize \i-'kä-nə-,mīz\ *vb* **-mized; -miz·ing** : to practice economy : be frugal — **econ·o·miz·er** *n*

¹econ·o·my \i-'kä-nə-mē\ *n, pl* **-mies** [MF *yconomie,* fr. ML *oeconomia,* fr. Gk *oikonomia,* fr. *oikonomos* household manager, fr. *oikos* house + *nemein* to manage] **1** : thrifty and efficient use of resources; *also* : an instance of this **2** : manner of arrangement or functioning : ORGANIZATION **3** : an economic system ⟨a money ~⟩

²economy *adj* : ECONOMICAL ⟨~ cars⟩

eco·sys·tem \'ē-kō-,sis-təm, 'e-\ *n* : the complex of an ecological community and its environment functioning as a unit in nature

ecru \'e-krü, 'ā-\ *n* [F *écru,* lit., unbleached] : BEIGE — **ecru** *adj*

ec·sta·sy \'ek-stə-sē\ *n, pl* **-sies** : extreme and usu. rapturous emotional excitement — **ec·stat·ic** \ek-'statik, ik-\ *adj* — **ec·stat·i·cal·ly** \-ti-k(ə-)lē\ *adv*

Ecua *abbr* Ecuador

Ec·ua·dor·an \,e-kwə-'dòr-ən\ *or* **Ec·ua·dor·ean** *or* **Ec·ua·dor·ian** \-ē-ən\ *n* : a native or inhabitant of Ecuador — **Ecuadorean** *or* **Ecuadorian** *adj*

ec·u·men·i·cal \,e-kyü-'me-ni-kəl\ *adj* : general in extent or influence; *esp* : promoting or tending toward worldwide Christian unity — **ec•u•men•i•cal•ly** \-k(ə-)lē\ *adv*

ec•ze•ma \ig-ˈzē-mə, ˈeg-zə-mə, ˈek-sə-\ *n* : an itching skin inflammation with oozing and then crusted lesions — **ec•zem•a•tous** \ig-ˈze-mə-təs\ *adj*

ed *abbr* 1 edited; edition; editor 2 education

¹**-ed** \d *after a vowel or* b, g, j, l, m, n, ŋ, r, <u>th</u>, v, z, zh; əd, id *after* d, t; t *after other sounds*\ *vb suffix or adj suffix* 1 — used to form the past participle of regular weak verbs ⟨end*ed*⟩ ⟨fad*ed*⟩ ⟨tri*ed*⟩ ⟨patt*ed*⟩ 2 : having : characterized by ⟨cultur*ed*⟩ ⟨2-legg*ed*⟩; *also* : having the characteristics of ⟨bigot*ed*⟩

²**-ed** *vb suffix* — used to form the past tense of regular weak verbs ⟨judg*ed*⟩ ⟨deni*ed*⟩ ⟨dropp*ed*⟩

Edam \ˈē-dəm, -ˌdam\ *n* : a yellow Dutch pressed cheese made in balls

ed•dy \ˈe-dē\ *n, pl* **eddies** : WHIRLPOOL — **eddy** *vb*

edel•weiss \ˈād-ᵊl-ˌwīs, -ˌvīs\ *n* [G, fr. *edel* noble + *weiss* white] : a small perennial woolly composite herb that grows high in the Alps

ede•ma \i-ˈdē-mə\ *n* : abnormal accumulation of watery fluid in connective tissue or in a serous cavity — **edem•a•tous** \-ˈde-mə-təs\ *adj*

Eden \ˈēd-ᵊn\ *n* : PARADISE 2

¹**edge** \ˈej\ *n* 1 : the cutting side of a blade 2 : SHARPNESS; *also* : FORCE, EFFECTIVENESS 3 : the line where something begins or ends; *also* : the area adjoining such an edge 4 : ADVANTAGE — **edged** \ˈejd\ *adj*

²**edge** *vb* **edged; edg•ing** 1 : to give or form an edge 2 : to move or force gradually ⟨∼ into a crowd⟩ 3 : to defeat by a small margin ⟨*edged* out her opponent⟩ — **edg•er** *n*

edge•wise \ˈej-ˌwīz\ *adv* : SIDEWAYS

edg•ing \ˈe-jiŋ\ *n* : something that forms an edge or border ⟨a lace ∼⟩

edgy \ˈe-jē\ *adj* **edg•i•er; -est** 1 : SHARP ⟨an ∼ tone⟩ 2 : TENSE, NERVOUS — **edg•i•ness** *n*

ed•i•ble \ˈe-də-bəl\ *adj* : fit or safe to be eaten — **ed•i•bil•i•ty** \ˌe-də-ˈbi-lə-tē\ *n* — **edible** *n*

edict \ˈē-ˌdikt\ *n* : ORDER, DECREE

ed•i•fi•ca•tion \ˌe-də-fə-ˈkā-shən\ *n* : instruction and improvement esp. in morality — **ed•i•fy** \ˈe-də-ˌfī\ *vb*

ed•i•fice \ˈe-də-fəs\ *n* : a usu. large building

ed•it \ˈe-dət\ *vb* 1 : to revise, assemble, or prepare for publication or release (as a motion picture) 2 : to direct the publication and policies of (as a newspaper) 3 : DELETE — **ed•i•tor** \ˈe-də-tər\ *n* — **ed•i•tor•ship** *n* — **ed•i•tress** \-trəs\ *n*

edi•tion \i-ˈdi-shən\ *n* 1 : the form in which a text is published 2 : the total number of copies (as of a book) published at one time 3 : VERSION

¹**ed•i•to•ri•al** \ˌe-də-ˈtȯr-ē-əl\ *adj* 1 : of or relating to an editor or editing 2 : being or resembling an editorial — **ed•i•to•ri•al•ly** *adv*

²**editorial** *n* : an article (as in a newspaper) giving the views of the editors or publishers; *also* : an expression of opinion resembling an editorial ⟨a television ∼⟩

ed•i•to•ri•al•ize \ˌe-də-ˈtȯr-ē-ə-ˌlīz\ *vb* **-ized; -iz•ing** 1 : to express an opinion in an editorial 2 : to introduce opinions into factual reporting 3 : to express an opinion — **ed•i•to•ri•al•i•za•tion** \-ˌtȯr-ē-ə-lə-ˈzā-shən\ *n* — **ed•i•to•ri•al•iz•er** *n*

EDP *abbr* electronic data processing

EDT *abbr* Eastern daylight (saving) time

educ *abbr* education; educational

ed•u•ca•ble \ˈe-jə-kə-bəl\ *adj* : capable of being educated

ed•u•cate \ˈe-jə-ˌkāt\ *vb* **-cat•ed; -cat•ing** 1 : to provide with schooling 2 : to develop mentally and morally; *also* : to provide with information **syn** train, discipline, school, instruct, teach — **ed•u•ca•tor** \-ˌkā-tər\ *n*

ed•u•ca•tion \ˌe-jə-ˈkā-shən\ *n* 1 : the action or process of educating or being educated 2 : a field of study

dealing with methods of teaching and learning — **ed•u•ca•tion•al** \-shə-nəl\ *adj*

educational television *n* : PUBLIC TELEVISION

educe \i-ˈdüs, -ˈdyüs\ *vb* **educed; educ•ing** 1 : ELICIT, EVOKE 2 : DEDUCE **syn** extract, evince, extort

¹**-ee** \ˈē, (ˌ)ē\ *n suffix* 1 : one that receives or benefits from (a specified action or thing) ⟨grant*ee*⟩ ⟨patent*ee*⟩ 2 : a person who does (a specified action) ⟨escap*ee*⟩

²**-ee** *n suffix* 1 : a particular esp. small kind of ⟨boot*ee*⟩ 2 : one resembling or suggestive of ⟨goat*ee*⟩

EE *abbr* electrical engineer

EEC *abbr* European Economic Community

EEG *abbr* 1 electroencephalogram 2 electroencephalograph

eel \ˈēl\ *n* : any of numerous snakelike bony fishes with a smooth slimy skin

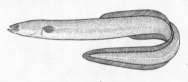

eel

EEO *abbr* equal employment opportunity

ee•rie *also* **ee•ry** \ˈir-ē\ *adj* **ee•ri•er; -est** : WEIRD, UNCANNY — **ee•ri•ly** \ˈir-ə-lē\ *adv*

eff *abbr* efficiency

ef•face \i-ˈfās, e-\ *vb* **ef•faced; ef•fac•ing** : to obliterate or obscure by or as if by rubbing out **syn** erase, delete, annul, cancel, expunge — **ef•face•able** *adj* — **ef•face•ment** *n*

¹**ef•fect** \i-ˈfekt\ *n* 1 : MEANING, INTENT 2 : RESULT 3 : APPEARANCE 4 : INFLUENCE 5 *pl* : GOODS, POSSESSIONS 6 : the quality or state of being operative : OPERATION **syn** consequence, outcome, upshot, aftermath, issue

²**effect** *vb* : to cause to happen ⟨∼ repairs⟩ ⟨∼ changes⟩

ef•fec•tive \i-ˈfek-tiv\ *adj* 1 : producing a decisive or desired effect 2 : IMPRESSIVE, STRIKING 3 : ready for service or action 4 : being in effect — **ef•fec•tive•ly** *adv* — **ef•fec•tive•ness** *n*

ef•fec•tu•al \i-ˈfek-chə-wəl\ *adj* : producing an intended effect : ADEQUATE — **ef•fec•tu•al•ly** *adv*

ef•fec•tu•ate \i-ˈfek-chə-ˌwāt\ *vb* **-at•ed; -at•ing** : BRING ABOUT, EFFECT

ef•fem•i•nate \ə-ˈfe-mə-nət\ *adj* : marked by qualities more typical of women than men — **ef•fem•i•na•cy** \-nə-sē\ *n*

ef•fen•di \e-ˈfen-dē\ *n* [Turk *efendi* master, fr. NGk *aphentēs*, alter. of Gk *authentēs*] : a man of property, authority, or education in an eastern Mediterranean country

ef•fer•ent \ˈe-fə-rənt\ *adj* : bearing or conducting outward from a more central part ⟨∼ nerves⟩

ef•fer•vesce \ˌe-fər-ˈves\ *vb* **-vesced; -vesc•ing** : to bubble and hiss as gas escapes; *also* : to be exhilarated — **ef•fer•ves•cence** \-ˈves-ᵊns\ *n* — **ef•fer•ves•cent** \-ᵊnt\ *adj* — **ef•fer•ves•cent•ly** *adv*

ef•fete \e-ˈfēt\ *adj* 1 : having lost character, vitality, or strength; *also* : DECADENT 2 : EFFEMINATE

ef•fi•ca•cious \ˌe-fə-ˈkā-shəs\ *adj* : producing an intended effect ⟨∼ remedies⟩ **syn** effectual, effective, efficient — **ef•fi•ca•cy** \ˈe-fi-kə-sē\ *n*

ef•fi•cient \i-ˈfi-shənt\ *adj* : productive of desired effects esp. without waste — **ef•fi•cien•cy** \-shən-sē\ *n* — **ef•fi•cient•ly** *adv*

ef•fi•gy \ˈe-fə-jē\ *n, pl* **-gies** : IMAGE; *esp* : a crude figure of a hated person

ef•flo•res•cence \ˌe-flə-ˈres-ᵊns\ *n* 1 : the period or state of flowering 2 : the action or process of developing 3 : fullness of development : FLOWERING

ef•flu•ence \ˈe-ˌflü-əns\ *n* : something that flows out

ef•flu•ent \ˈe-ˌflü-ənt\ *n* : something that flows out; *esp*

: a fluid (as sewage) discharged as waste — **effluent**
adj

ef·flu·vi·um \e-'flü-vē-əm\ *n, pl* **-via** \-vē-ə\ *or* **-vi·ums** [L, outflow] **1** : a usu. unpleasant emanation **2** : a by-product usu. in the form of waste

ef·fort \'e-fərt\ *n* **1** : EXERTION, ENDEAVOR; *also* : a product of effort **2** : active or applied force — **ef·fort·less** *adj* — **ef·fort·less·ly** *adv*

ef·fron·tery \i-'frən-tə-rē\ *n, pl* **-ter·ies** : shameless boldness : IMPUDENCE **syn** temerity, audacity, brass, gall, nerve, chutzpah

ef·ful·gence \i-'ful-jəns, -'fəl-\ *n* : radiant splendor : BRILLIANCE — **ef·ful·gent** \-jənt\ *adj*

ef·fu·sion \i-'fyü-zhən, e-\ *n* : a gushing forth; *also* : unrestrained utterance — **ef·fuse** \-'fyüz, e-\ *vb* — **ef·fu·sive** \i-'fyü-siv, e-\ *adj* — **ef·fu·sive·ly** *adv*

eft \'eft\ *n* : NEWT

EFT *or* **EFTS** *abbr* electronic funds transfer (system)

e.g. *abbr* [L *exempli gratia*] for example

Eg *abbr* Egypt; Egyptian

egal·i·tar·i·an·ism \i-ˌga-lə-'ter-ē-ə-ˌni-zəm\ *n* : a belief in human equality esp. in social, political, and economic affairs — **egal·i·tar·i·an** *adj or n*

¹egg \'eg\ *vb* [ME, fr. ON *eggja*; akin to OE *ecg* edge] : to urge to action — usu. used with *on*

²egg *n* [ME *egge*, fr. ON *egg*; akin to OE *æg* egg, L *ovum*] **1** : a rounded usu. hard-shelled reproductive body esp. of birds and reptiles from which the young hatches; *also* : the egg of the common domestic chicken as an article of food **2** : a germ cell produced by a female

egg·beat·er \'eg-ˌbē-tər\ *n* : a hand-operated kitchen utensil for beating, stirring, or whipping

egg cell *n* : EGG 2

egg·head \-ˌhed\ *n* : INTELLECTUAL, HIGHBROW

egg·nog \-ˌnäg\ *n* : a drink consisting of eggs beaten with sugar, milk or cream, and often alcoholic liquor

egg·plant \-ˌplant\ *n* : the edible usu. large and purplish fruit of a plant related to the potato; *also* : the plant

egg roll *n* : a thin egg-dough casing filled with minced vegetables and often bits of meat and usu. deep-fried

egg·shell \'eg-ˌshel\ *n* : the hard exterior covering of an egg

egis \'ē-jəs\ *var of* AEGIS

eg·lan·tine \'e-glən-ˌtīn, -ˌtēn\ *n* : SWEETBRIER

ego \'ē-gō\ *n, pl* **egos** [L, I] **1** : the self as distinguished from others **2** : the one of the three divisions of the psyche in psychoanalytic theory that is the organized conscious mediator between the person and reality

ego·cen·tric \ˌē-gō-'sen-trik\ *adj* : concerned or overly concerned with the self; *esp* : SELF-CENTERED

ego·ism \'ē-gō-ˌi-zəm\ *n* **1** : a doctrine holding self-interest to be the motive or the valid end of action **2** : excessive concern for oneself with or without exaggerated feelings of self-importance — **ego·ist** \-ist\ *n* — **ego·is·tic** \ˌē-gō-'is-tik\ *adj* — **ego·is·ti·cal·ly** *adv*

ego·tism \'ē-gə-ˌti-zəm\ *n* **1** : the practice of talking about oneself too much **2** : an exaggerated sense of self-importance : CONCEIT — **ego·tist** \-tist\ *n* — **ego·tis·tic** \ˌē-gə-'tis-tik\ *or* **ego·tis·ti·cal** \-ti-kəl\ *adj* — **ego·tis·ti·cal·ly** *adv*

ego trip *n* : an act that enhances and satisfies one's ego

egre·gious \i-'grē-jəs\ *adj* [L *egregius* outstanding, fr. *ex, e* out of + *greg-, grex* flock, herd] : notably bad : FLAGRANT — **egre·gious·ly** *adv* — **egre·gious·ness** *n*

egress \'ē-ˌgres\ *n* : a way out : EXIT

egret \'ē-grət, i-'gret\ *n* : any of various herons that bear long plumes during the breeding season

Egyp·tian \i-'jip-shən\ *n* **1** : a native or inhabitant of Egypt **2** : the language of the ancient Egyptians from earliest times to about the 3d century A.D. — **Egyptian** *adj*

ei·der \'ī-dər\ *n* : any of several northern sea ducks that yield a soft down

ei·der·down \-ˌdaún\ *n* **1** : the down of the eider **2** : a quilt filled with eiderdown

ei·do·lon \ī-'dō-lən\ *n, pl* **-lons** *or* **-la** \-lə\ **1** : PHANTOM **2** : IDEAL

eight \'āt\ *n* **1** : one more than seven **2** : the 8th in a set or series **3** : something having eight units — **eight** *adj or pron* — **eighth** \'ātth\ *adj or adv or n*

eight ball *n* : a black pool ball numbered 8 — **behind the eight ball** : in a highly disadvantageous position

eigh·teen \'āt-'tēn\ *n* : one more than 17 — **eighteen** *adj or pron* — **eigh·teenth** \-'tēnth\ *adj or n*

eighty \'ā-tē\ *n, pl* **eight·ies** : eight times 10 — **eight·i·eth** \'ā-tē-əth\ *adj or n* — **eighty** *adj or pron*

ein·stei·ni·um \īn-'stī-nē-əm\ *n* : an artificially produced radioactive element — see ELEMENT table

¹ei·ther \'ē-thər, 'ī-\ *adj* **1** : being the one and the other of two : EACH ⟨trees on ~ side⟩ **2** : being the one or the other of two ⟨take ~ road⟩

²either *pron* : the one or the other

³either *conj* — used as a function word before the first of two or more words or word groups of which the last is preceded by *or* to indicate that they represent alternatives ⟨a statement is ~ true or false⟩

ejac·u·late \i-'ja-kyə-ˌlāt\ *vb* **-lat·ed; -lat·ing 1** : to eject a fluid (as semen) **2** : to utter suddenly : EXCLAIM — **ejac·u·la·tion** \-ˌja-kyə-'lā-shən\ *n* — **ejac·u·la·to·ry** \-'ja-kyə-lə-ˌtōr-ē\ *adj*

eject \i-'jekt\ *vb* : to drive or throw out or off **syn** expel, oust, evict, dismiss — **ejec·tion** \-'jek-shən\ *n*

eke \'ēk\ *vb* **eked; ek·ing** : to gain, supplement, or extend usu. with effort — usu. used with *out* ⟨~ out a living⟩

EKG *abbr* [G *Elektrokardiogramm*] electrocardiogram; electrocardiograph

el *abbr* elevation

¹elab·o·rate \i-'la-bə-rət, -'la-brət\ *adj* **1** : planned or carried out with great care **2** : being complex and usu. ornate — **elab·o·rate·ly** *adv* — **elab·o·rate·ness** *n*

²elab·o·rate \i-'la-bə-ˌrāt\ *vb* **-rat·ed; -rat·ing 1** : to build up from simpler ingredients **2** : to work out in detail : develop fully — **elab·o·ra·tion** \-ˌla-bə-'rā-shən\ *n*

élan \ā-'läⁿ\ *n* [F] : ARDOR, SPIRIT

eland \'ē-lənd, -ˌland\ *n, pl* **eland** *also* **elands** [Afrikaans] : either of two large African antelopes with spirally twisted horns in both sexes

elapse \i-'laps\ *vb* **elapsed; elaps·ing** : to slip by : PASS

¹elas·tic \i-'las-tik\ *adj* **1** : SPRINGY **2** : FLEXIBLE, PLIABLE **3** : ADAPTABLE **syn** resilient, supple, stretch — **elas·tic·i·ty** \-ˌlas-'ti-sə-tē, ˌē-ˌlas-\ *n*

²elastic *n* **1** : elastic material **2** : a rubber band

elate \i-'lāt\ *vb* **elat·ed; elat·ing** : to fill with joy — **ela·tion** \-'lā-shən\ *n*

¹el·bow \'el-ˌbō\ *n* **1** : the joint of the arm; *also* : the outer curve of the bent arm **2** : a bend or joint resembling an elbow in shape

²elbow *vb* : to push aside with the elbow; *also* : to make one's way by elbowing

el·bow·room \'el-ˌbō-ˌrüm, -ˌrùm\ *n* : enough space for work or operation

¹el·der \'el-dər\ *n* : ELDERBERRY 2

²elder *adj* **1** : OLDER **2** : EARLIER, FORMER **3** : of higher rank : SENIOR

³elder *n* **1** : an older individual : SENIOR **2** : one having authority by reason of age and experience **3** : a church officer

el·der·ber·ry \'el-dər-ˌber-ē\ *n* **1** : the edible black or red fruit of a shrub or tree related to the honeysuckle and bearing flat clusters of small white or pink flowers **2** : a tree or shrub bearing elderberries

el·der·ly \'el-dər-lē\ *adj* **1** : rather old; *esp* : past middle age **2** : of, relating to, or characteristic of later life

el·dest \'el-dəst\ *adj* : of the greatest age

El Do·ra·do \₁el-də-ᵇrä-dō, -ᵇrä-\ *n* [Sp, lit., the gilded one] : a place of vast riches, abundance, or opportunity

elec *abbr* electric; electrical; electricity

¹**elect** \i-ᵇlekt\ *adj* **1** : CHOSEN, SELECT **2** : elected but not yet installed in office ⟨the president-*elect*⟩

²**elect** *n, pl* **elect 1** : a selected person **2** *pl* : a select or exclusive group

³**elect** *vb* **1** : to select by vote (as for office or membership) **2** : CHOOSE, PICK

elec·tion \i-ᵇlek-shən\ *n* **1** : an act or process of electing **2** : the fact of being elected

elec·tion·eer \i-₁lek-shə-ᵇnir\ *vb* : to work for the election of a candidate or party

¹**elec·tive** \i-ᵇlek-tiv\ *adj* **1** : chosen or filled by election **2** : permitting a choice : OPTIONAL

²**elective** *n* : an elective course or subject of study

elec·tor \i-ᵇlek-tər\ *n* **1** : one qualified to vote in an election **2** : one elected to an electoral college — **elec·tor·al** \i-ᵇlek-tə-rəl\ *adj*

electoral college *n* : a body of electors who elect the president and vice president of the U.S.

elec·tor·ate \i-ᵇlek-tə-rət\ *n* : a body of persons entitled to vote

elec·tric \i-ᵇlek-trik\ *adj* [NL *electricus* produced from amber by friction, electric, fr. ML, of amber, fr. L *electrum* amber, fr. Gk *ēlektron*] **1** *or* **elec·tri·cal** \-tri-kəl\ : of, relating to, operated by, or produced by electricity **2** : ELECTRIFYING, THRILLING — **elec·tri·cal·ly** *adv*

electrical storm *n* : THUNDERSTORM

electric chair *n* : a chair used to carry out the death penalty by electrocution

electric eye *n* : PHOTOELECTRIC CELL

elec·tri·cian \i-₁lek-ᵇtri-shən\ *n* : a person who installs, operates, or repairs electrical equipment

elec·tric·i·ty \i-₁lek-ᵇtri-sə-tē\ *n, pl* **-ties 1** : a form of energy that occurs in nature and is observable in natural phenomena (as lightning) and that can be produced by friction, chemical reaction, or mechanical effort **2** : electric current

elec·tri·fy \i-ᵇlek-trə-₁fī\ *vb* **-fied; -fy·ing 1** : to charge with electricity **2** : to equip for use of electric power **3** : THRILL — **elec·tri·fi·ca·tion** \i-₁lek-trə-fə-ᵇkā-shən\ *n*

elec·tro·car·dio·gram \i-₁lek-trō-ᵇkär-dē-ə-₁gram\ *n* : the tracing made by an electrocardiograph

elec·tro·car·dio·graph \-₁graf\ *n* : a device for recording the changes of electrical potential occurring during the heartbeat — **elec·tro·car·dio·graph·ic** \-₁kär-dē-ə-₁gra-fik\ *adj* — **elec·tro·car·di·og·ra·phy** \-dē-ᵇä-grə-fē\ *n*

elec·tro·chem·is·try \-ᵇke-mə-strē\ *n* : a branch of chemistry that deals with the relation of electricity to chemical changes — **elec·tro·chem·i·cal** \-ᵇke-mi-kəl\ *adj*

elec·tro·cute \i-ᵇlek-trə-₁kyüt\ *vb* **-cut·ed; -cut·ing** : to kill by an electric shock; *esp* : to kill (a criminal) in this way — **elec·tro·cu·tion** \-₁lek-trə-ᵇkyü-shən\ *n*

elec·trode \i-ᵇlek-₁trōd\ *n* : a conductor used to establish electrical contact with a nonmetallic part of a circuit

elec·tro·en·ceph·a·lo·gram \i-₁lek-trō-in-ᵇse-fə-lə-₁gram\ *n* : the tracing made by an electroencephalograph

elec·tro·en·ceph·a·lo·graph \-₁graf\ *n* : an apparatus for detecting and recording brain waves — **elec·tro·en·ceph·a·lo·graph·ic** \-₁se-fə-lə-ᵇgra-fik\ *adj* — **elec·tro·en·ceph·a·log·ra·phy** \-ᵇlä-grə-fē\ *n*

elec·trol·o·gist \i-₁lek-ᵇträ-lə-jist\ *n* : one that uses electrical means to remove hair, warts, moles, and birthmarks from the body

elec·trol·y·sis \i-₁lek-ᵇträ-lə-səs\ *n* **1** : the production of chemical changes by passage of an electric current through an electrolyte **2** : the destruction of hair roots

with an electric current — **elec·tro·lyt·ic** \-trə-ᵇli-tik\ *adj*

elec·tro·lyte \i-ᵇlek-trə-₁līt\ *n* : a nonmetallic electric conductor in which current is carried by the movement of ions; *also* : a substance whose solution or molten form is such a conductor

elec·tro·mag·net \i-₁lek-trō-ᵇmag-nət\ *n* : a core of magnetic material surrounded by a coil of wire through which an electric current is passed to magnetize the core

elec·tro·mag·net·ic \-mag-ᵇne-tik\ *adj* : of, relating to, or produced by electromagnetism — **elec·tro·mag·net·i·cal·ly** *adv*

electromagnetic radiation *n* : a series of electromagnetic waves

electromagnetic wave *n* : a wave (as a radio wave, an X ray, or a wave of visible light) that consists of associated electric and magnetic effects and that travels at the speed of light

elec·tro·mag·ne·tism \i-₁lek-trō-ᵇmag-nə-₁ti-zəm\ *n* **1** : magnetism developed by a current of electricity **2** : a natural force responsible for interactions between charged particles which result from their charge

elec·tro·mo·tive force \i-₁lek-trə-ᵇmō-tiv-\ *n* : the potential difference derived from an electrical source per unit quantity of electricity passing through the source

elec·tron \i-ᵇlek-₁trän\ *n* : a negatively charged elementary particle

elec·tron·ic \i-₁lek-ᵇträ-nik\ *adj* : of or relating to electrons or electronics — **elec·tron·i·cal·ly** \-ni-k(ə-)lē\ *adv*

electronic mail *n* : messages sent and received electronically

elec·tron·ics \i-₁lek-ᵇträ-niks\ *n* **1** : the physics of electrons and electronic devices **2** : electronic devices or equipment

electron microscope *n* : an instrument in which a focused beam of electrons is used to produce an enlarged image of a minute object

electron tube *n* : a device in which electrical conduction by electrons takes place within a sealed container and which is used for the controlled flow of electrons

elec·tro·pho·re·sis \i-₁lek-trə-fə-ᵇrē-səs\ *n* : the movement of suspended particles through a fluid by an electromotive force — **elec·tro·pho·ret·ic** \-ᵇrē-tik\ *adj*

elec·tro·plate \i-ᵇlek-trə-₁plāt\ *vb* : to coat (as with metal) by electrolysis

elec·tro·shock therapy \i-ᵇlek-trō-₁shäk-\ *n* : the treatment of mental disorder by the induction of coma with an electric current

elec·tro·stat·ics \i-₁lek-trə-ᵇsta-tiks\ *n* : physics dealing with the interactions of stationary electric charges

el·ee·mos·y·nary \₁e-li-ᵇmäs-ᵊn-₁er-ē\ *adj* : CHARITABLE

el·e·gance \ᵇe-li-gəns\ *n* **1** : refined gracefulness; *also* : tasteful richness (as of design) **2** : something marked by elegance — **el·e·gant** \-gənt\ *adj* — **el·e·gant·ly** *adv*

ele·giac \₁e-lə-ᵇjī-ək, -₁ak\ *adj* : of or relating to an elegy

el·e·gy \ᵇe-lə-jē\ *n, pl* **-gies** : a song, poem, or speech expressing grief for one who is dead; *also* : a reflective poem usu. melancholy in tone

elem *abbr* elementary

el·e·ment \ᵇe-lə-mənt\ *n* **1** *pl* : weather conditions; *esp* : severe weather ⟨boards exposed to the ∼s⟩ **2** : natural environment ⟨in her ∼⟩ **3** : a constituent part **4** *pl* : the simplest principles (as of an art or science) : RUDIMENTS **5** : a member of a mathematical set **6** : any of more than 100 fundamental substances that consist of atoms of only one kind **syn** component, ingredient, constituent — **el·e·men·tal** \₁e-lə-ᵇment-ᵊl\ *adj*

CHEMICAL ELEMENTS

ELEMENT	SYMBOL	ATOMIC NUMBER	ATOMIC WEIGHT (C = 12)
actinium	Ac	89	227.0278
aluminum	Al	13	26.98154
americium	Am	95	
antimony	Sb	51	121.75
argon	Ar	18	39.948
arsenic	As	33	74.9216
astatine	At	85	
barium	Ba	56	137.33
berkelium	Bk	97	
beryllium	Be	4	9.01218
bismuth	Bi	83	208.9804
boron	B	5	10.81
bromine	Br	35	79.904
cadmium	Cd	48	112.41
calcium	Ca	20	40.08
californium	Cf	98	
carbon	C	6	12.011
cerium	Ce	58	140.12
cesium	Cs	55	132.9054
chlorine	Cl	17	35.453
chromium	Cr	24	51.996
cobalt	Co	27	58.9332
copper	Cu	29	63.546
curium	Cm	96	
dysprosium	Dy	66	162.50
einsteinium	Es	99	
erbium	Er	68	167.26
europium	Eu	63	151.96
fermium	Fm	100	
fluorine	F	9	18.998403
francium	Fr	87	
gadolinium	Gd	64	157.25
gallium	Ga	31	69.72
germanium	Ge	32	72.59
gold	Au	79	196.9665
hafnium	Hf	72	178.49
helium	He	2	4.00260
holmium	Ho	67	164.9304
hydrogen	H	1	1.0079
indium	In	49	114.82
iodine	I	53	126.9045
iridium	Ir	77	192.22
iron	Fe	26	55.847
krypton	Kr	36	83.80
lanthanum	La	57	138.9055
lawrencium	Lr	103	
lead	Pb	82	207.2
lithium	Li	3	6.941
lutetium	Lu	71	174.967
magnesium	Mg	12	24.305
manganese	Mn	25	54.9380
mendelevium	Md	101	
mercury	Hg	80	200.59
molybdenum	Mo	42	95.94
neodymium	Nd	60	144.24
neon	Ne	10	20.179
neptunium	Np	93	237.0482
nickel	Ni	28	58.69
niobium	Nb	41	92.9064
nitrogen	N	7	14.0067
nobelium	No	102	
osmium	Os	76	190.2
oxygen	O	8	15.9994
palladium	Pd	46	106.42
phosphorus	P	15	30.97376
platinum	Pt	78	195.08
plutonium	Pu	94	
polonium	Po	84	
potassium	K	19	39.0983
praseodymium	Pr	59	140.9077
promethium	Pm	61	
protactinium	Pa	91	231.0359
radium	Ra	88	226.0254
radon	Rn	86	
rhenium	Re	75	186.207
rhodium	Rh	45	102.9055
rubidium	Rb	37	85.4678
ruthenium	Ru	44	101.07
samarium	Sm	62	150.36
scandium	Sc	21	44.9559
selenium	Se	34	78.96
silicon	Si	14	28.0855
silver	Ag	47	107.868
sodium	Na	11	22.98977
strontium	Sr	38	87.62
sulfur	S	16	32.06
tantalum	Ta	73	180.9479
technetium	Tc	43	
tellurium	Te	52	127.60
terbium	Tb	65	158.9254
thallium	Tl	81	204.383
thorium	Th	90	232.0381
thulium	Tm	69	168.9342
tin	Sn	50	118.69
titanium	Ti	22	47.88
tungsten	W	74	183.85
unnilhexium	Unh	106	
unnilpentium	Unp	105	
unnilquadium	Unq	104	
uranium	U	92	238.0289
vanadium	V	23	50.9415
xenon	Xe	54	131.29
ytterbium	Yb	70	173.04
yttrium	Y	39	88.9059
zinc	Zn	30	65.38
zirconium	Zr	40	91.22

el·e·men·ta·ry \ˌe-lə-ˈmen-trē, -tə-rē\ *adj* : SIMPLE, RU-DIMENTARY; *also* : of, relating to, or teaching the basic subjects of education

elementary particle *n* : a subatomic particle of matter and energy that does not appear to be made up of other smaller particles

elementary school *n* : a school usu. including the first six or the first eight grades

el·e·phant \ˈe-lə-fənt\ *n, pl* **elephants** *also* **elephant** : any of a family of huge thickset nearly hairless mammals that have the snout lengthened into a trunk and two long curving pointed ivory tusks

elephant

el·e·phan·ti·a·sis \ˌe-lə-fən-ˈtī-ə-səs\ *n, pl* **-a·ses** \-ˌsēz\ : enlargement and thickening of tissues in response esp. to infection by minute parasitic worms

el·e·phan·tine \ˌe-lə-ˈfan-ˌtēn, -ˌtīn, ˈe-lə-fən-\ *adj* **1** : of great size or strength **2** : CLUMSY, PONDEROUS

elev *abbr* elevation

el·e·vate \ˈe-lə-ˌvāt\ *vb* **-vat·ed; -vat·ing 1** : to lift up : RAISE **2** : EXALT, ENNOBLE **3** : ELATE

el·e·va·tion \ˌe-lə-ˈvā-shən\ *n* **1** : the height to which something is raised (as above sea level) **2** : a lifting up **3** : something (as a hill or swelling) that is elevated

el·e·va·tor \ˈe-lə-ˌvā-tər\ *n* **1** : a cage or platform for conveying people or things from one level to another **2** : a building for storing and discharging grain **3** : a movable surface on an airplane to produce motion up or down

elev·en \i-ˈle-vən\ *n* **1** : one more than 10 **2** : the 11th in a set or series **3** : something having 11 units; *esp* : a football team — **eleven** *adj or pron* — **elev·enth** \-vənth\ *adj or n*

elf \ˈelf\ *n, pl* **elves** \ˈelvz\ : a mischievous fairy — **elf·ish** \ˈel-fish\ *adj*

ELF *abbr* extremely low frequency

elf·in \ˈel-fən\ *adj* : of, relating to, or resembling an elf

elic·it \i-ˈli-sət\ *vb* : to draw out or forth **syn** evoke, educe, extract, extort

elide \i-ˈlīd\ *vb* **elid·ed; elid·ing** : to suppress or alter by elision

el·i·gi·ble \ˈe-lə-jə-bəl\ *adj* : qualified to participate or to be chosen — **el·i·gi·bil·i·ty** \ˌe-lə-jə-ˈbi-lə-tē\ *n* — **eligible** *n*

elim·i·nate \i-ˈli-mə-ˌnāt\ *vb* **-nat·ed; -nat·ing** [L *eliminatus,* pp. of *eliminare,* fr. *limen* threshold] **1** : REMOVE, ERADICATE **2** : to pass (wastes) from the body **3** : to leave out : IGNORE — **elim·i·na·tion** \-ˌli-mə-ˈnā-shən\ *n*

eli·sion \i-ˈli-zhən\ *n* : the omission of a final or initial sound or a word; *esp* : the omission of an unstressed vowel or syllable in a verse to achieve a uniform rhythm

elite \ā-ˈlēt, ē-\ *n* [F *élite*] **1** : the choice part; *also* : a superior group **2** : a typewriter type providing 12 characters to the inch — **elite** *adj*

elit·ism \-ˈlē-ˌti-zəm\ *n* : leadership or rule by an elite; *also* : advocacy of such elitism

elix·ir \i-ˈlik-sər\ *n* [ME, fr. ML, fr. Ar *al-iksīr* the elixir, fr. *al* the + *iksīr* elixir] **1** : a substance held capable of prolonging life indefinitely; *also* : PANACEA **2** : a sweetened alcoholic medicinal solution

Eliz·a·be·than \i-ˌli-zə-ˈbē-thən\ *adj* : of, relating to, or characteristic of Elizabeth I of England or her times

elk \ˈelk\ *n, pl* **elk** *or* **elks** **1** : MOOSE — used for one of the Old World **2** : a large gregarious deer of No. America, Europe, Asia, and northwestern Africa with curved antlers having many branches

¹ell \ˈel\ *n* : a former English cloth measure of 45 inches

²ell *n* : an extension at right angles to a building

el·lipse \i-ˈlips, e-\ *n* : a closed curve of oval shape

el·lip·sis \i-ˈlip-səs, e-\ *n, pl* **el·lip·ses** \-ˌsēz\ **1** : omission from an expression of a word clearly implied **2** : marks (as . . .) to show omission

el·lip·soid \i-ˈlip-ˌsȯid, e-\ *n* : a surface all plane sections of which are circles or ellipses — **el·lip·soi·dal** \-ˌlip-ˈsȯid-əl\ *also* **ellipsoid** *adj*

el·lip·ti·cal \i-ˈlip-ti-kəl, e-\ *or* **el·lip·tic** \-tik\ *adj* **1** : of, relating to, or shaped like an ellipse **2** : of, relating to, or marked by ellipsis — **el·lip·ti·cal·ly** \-ti-k(ə-)lē\ *adv*

elm \ˈelm\ *n* : any of a genus of large trees that have toothed leaves and nearly circular one-seeded winged fruits and are often grown as shade trees; *also* : the wood of an elm

el·o·cu·tion \ˌe-lə-ˈkyü-shən\ *n* : the art of effective public speaking — **el·o·cu·tion·ist** \-shə-nist\ *n*

elon·gate \i-ˈlȯŋ-ˌgāt\ *vb* **-gat·ed; -gat·ing** : to make or grow longer **syn** extend, lengthen, prolong, protract — **elon·ga·tion** \(ˌ)ē-ˌlȯŋ-ˈgā-shən\ *n*

elope \i-ˈlōp\ *vb* **eloped; elop·ing** : to run away esp. to be married — **elope·ment** *n* — **elop·er** *n*

el·o·quent \ˈe-lə-kwənt\ *adj* **1** : having or showing clear and forceful expression **2** : clearly showing some feeling or meaning — **el·o·quence** \-kwəns\ *n* — **el·o·quent·ly** *adv*

¹else \ˈels\ *adv* **1** : in a different or additional manner or place or at a different or additional time ⟨where ∼ can we meet⟩ **2** : OTHERWISE ⟨obey or ∼ you'll be sorry⟩

²else *adj* : OTHER; *esp* : being in addition ⟨what ∼ do you want⟩

else·where \-ˌhwer\ *adv* : in or to another place

elu·ci·date \i-ˈlü-sə-ˌdāt\ *vb* **-dat·ed; -dat·ing** : to make clear usu. by explanation **syn** clarify, explain, illuminate — **elu·ci·da·tion** \-ˌlü-sə-ˈdā-shən\ *n*

elude \ē-ˈlüd\ *vb* **elud·ed; elud·ing** **1** : EVADE **2** : to escape the notice of

elu·sive \ē-ˈlü-siv\ *adj* : tending to elude : EVASIVE — **elu·sive·ly** *adv* — **elu·sive·ness** *n*

el·ver \ˈel-vər\ *n* [alter. of *eelfare* migration of eels] : a young eel

elves *pl of* ELF

Ely·si·um \i-ˈli-zhē-əm, -zē-\ *n, pl* **-si·ums** *or* **-sia** \-zhē-ə, -zē-\ : PARADISE **2** — **Ely·sian** \-ˈli-zhən\ *adj*

em \ˈem\ *n* : a length approximately the width of the letter *M*

EM *abbr* **1** electromagnetic **2** electron microscope **3** enlisted man

ema·ci·ate \i-ˈmā-shē-ˌāt\ *vb* **-at·ed; -at·ing** : to become or cause to become very thin — **ema·ci·a·tion** \-ˌmā-shē-ˈā-shən, -sē-\ *n*

E-mail \ˈē-ˌmāl\ *n* : ELECTRONIC MAIL

emalangeni *pl of* LILANGENI

em·a·nate \ˈe-mə-ˌnāt\ *vb* **-nat·ed; -nat·ing** : to come out from a source **syn** proceed, spring, rise, arise, originate — **em·a·na·tion** \ˌe-mə-ˈnā-shən\ *n*

eman·ci·pate \i-ˈman-sə-ˌpāt\ *vb* **-pat·ed; -pat·ing** : to set free **syn** liberate, release, deliver, discharge — **eman·ci·pa·tion** \-ˌman-sə-ˈpā-shən\ *n* — **eman·ci·pa·tor** \-ˈman-sə-ˌpā-tər\ *n*

emas·cu·late \i-ˈmas-kyù-ˌlāt\ *vb* **-lat·ed; -lat·ing** : CASTRATE, GELD; *also* : WEAKEN — **emas·cu·la·tion** \-ˌmas-kyù-ˈlā-shən\ *n*

em·balm \im-ˈbäm, -ˈbälm\ *vb* : to treat (a corpse) so as to protect from decay — **em·balm·er** *n*

em·bank·ment \im-ˈbaŋk-mənt\ *n* : a raised structure (as of earth) to hold back water or carry a roadway

em·bar·go \im-ˈbär-gō\ *n, pl* **-goes** [Sp, fr. *embargar* to bar] : a prohibition on commerce — **embargo** *vb*

em·bark \im-ˈbärk\ *vb* **1** : to put or go on board a ship or airplane **2** : to make a start — **em·bar·ka·tion** \ˌem-ˌbär-ˈkā-shən\ *n*

em·bar·rass \im-ˈbar-əs\ *vb* **1** : CONFUSE, DISCONCERT **2** : to involve in financial difficulties **3** : to cause to experience self-conscious distress **4** : HINDER, IMPEDE — **em·bar·rass·ing·ly** *adv* — **em·bar·rass·ment** *n*

em·bas·sy \ˈem-bə-sē\ *n, pl* **-sies** **1** : a group of representatives headed by an ambassador **2** : the function, position, or mission of an ambassador **3** : the official residence and offices of an ambassador

em·bat·tle \im-ˈbat-əl\ *vb* : to arrange in order for battle; *also* : FORTIFY

em·bat·tled *adj* **1** : engaged in battle, conflict, or controversy **2** : being a site of battle, conflict, or controversy **3** : characterized by conflict or controversy

em·bed \im-ˈbed\ *vb* **em·bed·ded; em·bed·ding** **1** : to enclose closely in a surrounding mass **2** : to make something an integral part of

em·bel·lish \im-ˈbe-lish\ *vb* **1** : ADORN, DECORATE **2** : to add ornamental details to **syn** beautify, deck, bedeck, garnish, ornament, dress — **em·bel·lish·ment** *n*

em·ber \ˈem-bər\ *n* **1** : a glowing or smoldering fragment from a fire **2** *pl* : the smoldering remains of a fire

em·bez·zle \im-ˈbe-zəl\ *vb* **-zled; -zling** : to steal (as money) by falsifying records — **em·bez·zle·ment** *n* — **em·bez·zler** *n*

em·bit·ter \im-ˈbi-tər\ *vb* **1** : to arouse bitter feelings in **2** : to make bitter

em·bla·zon \-ˈblāz-ᵊn\ *vb* **1** : to adorn with heraldic devices **2** : to display conspicuously

em·blem \ˈem-bləm\ *n* : something (as an object or picture) suggesting another object or an idea : SYM-

BOL — **em·blem·at·ic** \,em-blə-'ma-tik\ *also* **em·blem·at·i·cal** \-ti-kəl\ *adj*

em·body \im-'bä-dē\ *vb* **em·bod·ied; em·body·ing 1** : INCARNATE **2** : to express in definite form **3** : to incorporate into a system or body **4** : PERSONIFY **syn** combine, integrate — **em·bodi·ment** \-di-mənt\ *n*

em·bold·en \im-'bōl-dən\ *vb* : to inspire with courage

em·bo·lism \'em-bə-,li-zəm\ *n* : the obstruction of a blood vessel by a foreign or abnormal particle

em·bon·point \än-bōⁿ-'pwäⁿ\ *n* [F] : plumpness of person : STOUTNESS

em·boss \im-'bäs, -'bós\ *vb* : to ornament with raised work

em·bou·chure \'äm-bu̇-,shu̇r, ,äm-bu̇-'shu̇r\ *n* [F, ultim. fr. *bouche* mouth] : the position and use of the lips, tongue, and teeth in playing a wind instrument

em·bow·er \im-'bau̇-ər\ *vb* : to shelter or enclose in a bower

¹**em·brace** \im-'brās\ *vb* **em·braced; em·brac·ing 1** : to clasp in the arms; *also* : CHERISH, LOVE **2** : ENCIRCLE **3** : TAKE UP, ADOPT; *also* : WELCOME **4** : INCLUDE **5** : to participate in an embrace **syn** comprehend, involve, encompass, embody

²**embrace** *n* : an encircling with the arms

em·bra·sure \im-'brā-zhər\ *n* **1** : an opening in a wall through which a cannon is fired **2** : a recess of a door or window

em·bro·ca·tion \,em-brə-'kā-shən\ *n* : LINIMENT

em·broi·der \im-'brȯi-dər\ *vb* **1** : to ornament with or do needlework **2** : to elaborate with exaggerated detail

em·broi·dery \im-'brȯi-də-rē\ *n, pl* **-der·ies 1** : the forming of decorative designs with needlework **2** : something embroidered

em·broil \im-'brȯil\ *vb* **1** : to throw into confusion or disorder **2** : to involve in conflict or difficulties — **em·broil·ment** *n*

em·bryo \'em-brē-,ō\ *n, pl* **embryos** : a living thing in its earliest stages of development — **em·bry·on·ic** \,em-brē-'ä-nik\ *adj*

em·bry·ol·o·gy \,em-brē-'ä-lə-jē\ *n* : a branch of biology dealing with embryos and their development — **em·bry·o·log·i·cal** \-brē-ə-'lä-ji-kəl\ *adj* — **em·bry·ol·o·gist** \-brē-'ä-lə-jist\ *n*

em·cee \em-'sē\ *n* : MASTER OF CEREMONIES — **emcee** *vb*

emend \ē-'mend\ *vb* : to correct usu. by altering the text of **syn** rectify, revise, amend — **emen·da·tion** \,ē-,men-'dā-shən\ *n*

emer *abbr* emeritus

¹**em·er·ald** \'em-rəld, 'e-mə-\ *n* : a green beryl prized as a gem

²**emerald** *adj* : brightly or richly green

emerge \i-'mərj\ *vb* **emerged; emerg·ing** : to rise, come forth, or come out into view — **emer·gence** \-'mər-jəns\ *n* — **emer·gent** \-jənt\ *adj*

emer·gen·cy \i-'mər-jən-sē\ *n, pl* **-cies** : an unforeseen event or condition requiring prompt action **syn** exigency, contingency, crisis, juncture

emergency room *n* : a hospital room for receiving and treating persons needing immediate medical care

emer·i·ta \i-'mer-ə-tə\ *adj* : EMERITUS — used of a woman

emer·i·tus \i-'mer-ə-təs\ *adj* [L] : retired from active duty ⟨professor ~⟩

em·ery \'e-mə-rē\ *n, pl* **em·er·ies** : a dark granular corundum used esp. for grinding and polishing

emet·ic \i-'me-tik\ *n* : an agent that induces vomiting — **emetic** *adj*

emf *n* [*electromotive force*] : POTENTIAL DIFFERENCE

em·i·grate \'e-mə-,grāt\ *vb* **-grat·ed; -grat·ing** : to leave a place (as a country) to settle elsewhere — **em·i·grant** \-mi-grənt\ *n* — **em·i·gra·tion** \,e-mə-'grā-shən\ *n*

émi·gré *also* **emi·gré** \'e-mi-,grā, ,e-mi-'grā\ *n* [F] : a person who emigrates esp. because of political conditions

em·i·nence \'e-mə-nəns\ *n* **1** : high rank or position; *also* : a person of high rank or attainments **2** : a lofty place

em·i·nent \'e-mə-nənt\ *adj* **1** : CONSPICUOUS, EVIDENT **2** : DISTINGUISHED, PROMINENT — **em·i·nent·ly** *adv*

eminent domain *n* : a right of a government to take private property for public use

emir \i-'mir, ā-\ *n* [Ar *amīr* commander] : a ruler, chief, or commander in Islamic countries — **emir·ate** \'e-mər-ət\ *n*

em·is·sary \'e-mə-,ser-ē\ *n, pl* **-sar·ies** : AGENT; *esp* : a secret agent

emis·sion \ē-'mi-shən\ *n* : something emitted; *esp* : substances discharged into the air

emit \ē-'mit\ *vb* **emit·ted; emit·ting 1** : to give off or out ⟨~ light⟩; *also* : EJECT **2** : EXPRESS, UTTER — **emit·ter** *n*

emol·lient \i-'mäl-yənt\ *adj* : making soft or supple; *also* : soothing esp. to the skin or mucous membrane — **emol·lient** *n*

emol·u·ment \i-'mäl-yə-mənt\ *n* [ME, fr. L *emolumentum* advantage, fr. *emolere* to produce by grinding] : the product (as salary or fees) of an employment

emote \i-'mōt\ *vb* **emot·ed; emot·ing** : to give expression to emotion in or as if in a play

emo·tion \i-'mō-shən\ *n* : a usu. intense feeling (as of love, hate, or despair) — **emo·tion·al** \-shə-nəl\ *adj* — **emo·tion·al·ly** *adv*

emp *abbr* emperor; empress

em·pa·thy \'em-pə-thē\ *n* : the experiencing as one's own of the feelings of another; *also* : the capacity for this — **em·path·ic** \em-'pa-thik\ *adj*

em·pen·nage \,äm-pə-'näzh, ,em-\ *n* [F] : the tail assembly of an airplane

em·per·or \'em-pər-ər\ *n* : the sovereign male ruler of an empire

em·pha·sis \'em-fə-səs\ *n, pl* **-pha·ses** \-,sēz\ : particular prominence given (as to a syllable in speaking or to a phase of action)

em·pha·size \-,sīz\ *vb* **-sized; -siz·ing** : to place emphasis on : STRESS

em·phat·ic \im-'fa-tik, em-\ *adj* : uttered with emphasis : STRESSED — **em·phat·i·cal·ly** \-'ti-k(ə-)lē\ *adv*

em·phy·se·ma \,em-fə-'zē-mə, -'sē-\ *n* : a condition marked esp. by abnormal expansion of the air spaces of the lungs and often by impairment of heart action

em·pire \'em-,pīr\ *n* **1** : a large state or a group of states under a single sovereign who is usu. an emperor; *also* : something resembling a political empire **2** : imperial sovereignty or dominion

em·pir·i·cal \im-'pir-i-kəl\ *also* **em·pir·ic** \-ik\ *adj* : based on observation; *also* : subject to verification by observation or experiment ⟨~ laws⟩ — **em·pir·i·cal·ly** \-i-k(ə-)lē\ *adv*

em·pir·i·cism \im-'pir-ə-,si-zəm, em-\ *n* : the practice of relying on observation and experiment esp. in the natural sciences — **em·pir·i·cist** \-sist\ *n*

em·place·ment \im-'plās-mənt\ *n* **1** : a prepared position for weapons or military equipment **2** : PLACEMENT

¹**em·ploy** \im-'plȯi\ *vb* **1** : to make use of **2** : to use the services of **3** : OCCUPY, DEVOTE — **em·ploy·er** *n*

²**em·ploy** \im-'plȯi; 'im-,plȯi, 'em-\ *n* : EMPLOYMENT

em·ploy·ee *or* **em·ploye** \im-,plȯi-'ē, ,em-; im-'plȯi-,ē, em-\ *n* : a person who works for another

em·ploy·ment \im-'plȯi-mənt\ *n* **1** : OCCUPATION, ACTIVITY **2** : the act of employing : the condition of being employed

em·po·ri·um \im-'pōr-ē-əm, em-\ *n, pl* **-ri·ums** *also* **-ria** \-ē-ə\ [L, fr. Gk *emporion*, fr. *emporos* traveler, trader] : a commercial center; *esp* : a store carrying varied articles

em·pow·er \im-'pau̇-ər\ *vb* : to give authority or power to; *also* : ENABLE — **em·pow·er·ment** \-mənt\ *n*

em·press \'em-prəs\ *n* **1** : the wife or widow of an emperor **2** : a sovereign female ruler of an empire

¹emp·ty \'emp-tē\ *adj* **emp·ti·er; -est 1** : containing nothing **2** : UNOCCUPIED, UNINHABITED **3** : lacking value, force, sense, or purpose **syn** vacant, blank, void, stark, vacuous — **emp·ti·ness** *n*

²empty *vb* **emp·tied; emp·ty·ing 1** : to make or become empty **2** : to discharge contents; *also* : to remove from what holds or encloses

³empty *n, pl* **empties** : an empty container or vehicle

emp·ty–hand·ed \,emp-tē-'han-dəd\ *adj* **1** : having or bringing nothing **2** : having acquired or gained nothing

em·py·re·an \,em-,pī-'rē-ən, -pə-\ *n* **1** : the highest heaven; *also* : FIRMAMENT **2** : an ideal place or state

EMT \,ē-(,)em-'tē\ *n* [*e*mergency *m*edical *t*echnician] : a specially trained medical technician licensed to provide basic medical services before and during transportation to a hospital

¹emu \'ē-myü, -mü\ *n* : a swift-running flightless Australian bird smaller than the related ostrich

²emu *abbr* electromagnetic unit

em·u·late \'em-yù-,lāt\ *vb* **-lat·ed; -lat·ing** : to strive to equal or excel : IMITATE — **em·u·la·tion** \,em-yù-'lā-shən\ *n* — **em·u·lous** \'em-yù-ləs\ *adj*

emul·si·fi·er \i-'məl-sə-,fī-ər\ *n* : a substance (as a soap) that helps to form and stabilize an emulsion

emul·si·fy \-,fī\ *vb* **-fied; -fy·ing** : to disperse (as an oil) in an emulsion — **emul·si·fi·ca·tion** \i-,məl-sə-fə-'kā-shən\ *n*

emul·sion \i-'məl-shən\ *n* **1** : a mixture of mutually insoluble liquids in which one is dispersed in droplets throughout the other ⟨an ∼ of oil in water⟩ **2** : a light-sensitive coating on photographic film or paper

en \'en\ *n* : a length approximately half the width of the letter *M*

¹-en *also* **-n** *adj suffix* : made of : consisting of ⟨earth*en*⟩

²-en *vb suffix* **1** : become or cause to be ⟨sharp*en*⟩ **2** : cause or come to have ⟨length*en*⟩

en·able \i-'nā-bəl\ *vb* **en·abled; en·abling 1** : to make able or feasible **2** : to give legal power, capacity, or sanction to

en·act \i-'nakt\ *vb* **1** : to make into law **2** : to act out — **en·act·ment** *n*

enam·el \i-'na-məl\ *n* **1** : a glasslike substance used to coat the surface of metal or pottery **2** : the hard outer layer of a tooth **3** : a usu. glossy paint that forms a hard coat — **enamel** *vb*

enam·el·ware \-,war\ *n* : metal utensils coated with enamel

en·am·or \i-'na-mər\ *vb* : to inflame with love

en·am·our *chiefly Brit var of* ENAMOR

en bloc \än-'bläk\ *adv or adj* : as a whole : in a mass

enc *or* **encl** *abbr* enclosure

en·camp \in-'kamp\ *vb* : to make camp — **en·camp·ment** *n*

en·cap·su·late \in-'kap-sə-,lāt\ *vb* **-lat·ed; -lat·ing 1** : to encase or become encased in a capsule **2** : SUMMARIZE — **en·cap·su·la·tion** \-,kap-sə-'lā-shən\ *n*

en·case \in-'kās\ *vb* : to enclose in or as if in a case

-ence *n suffix* **1** : action or process ⟨emerg*ence*⟩ : instance of an action or process ⟨refer*ence*⟩ **2** : quality or state ⟨depend*ence*⟩

en·ceinte \än-'sant\ *adj* : PREGNANT

en·ceph·a·li·tis \in-,se-fə-'lī-təs\ *n, pl* **-lit·i·des** \-'li-tə-,dēz\ : inflammation of the brain — **en·ceph·a·lit·ic** \-'li-tik\ *adj*

en·chain \in-'chān\ *vb* : FETTER, CHAIN

en·chant \in-'chant\ *vb* **1** : BEWITCH **2** : ENRAPTURE, FASCINATE — **en·chant·er** *n* — **en·chant·ing·ly** *adv* — **en·chant·ment** *n* — **en·chant·ress** \-'chan-trəs\ *n*

en·chi·la·da \,en-chə-'lä-də\ *n* : a rolled filled tortilla covered with chili sauce and usu. baked

en·ci·pher \in-'sī-fər, en-\ *vb* : ENCODE

en·cir·cle \in-'sər-kəl\ *vb* : to pass completely around : SURROUND — **en·cir·cle·ment** *n*

en·clave \'en-,klāv; 'än-,klāv\ *n* : a distinct territorial, cultural, or social unit enclosed within or as if within foreign territory

en·close \in-'klōz\ *vb* **1** : to shut up or in; *esp* : to surround with a fence **2** : to include along with something else in a parcel or envelope ⟨∼ a check⟩ — **en·clo·sure** \-'klō-zhər\ *n*

en·code \in-'kōd, en-\ *vb* : to convert (a message) into code

en·co·mi·um \en-'kō-mē-əm\ *n, pl* **-mi·ums** *or* **-mia** \-mē-ə\ : high or glowing praise

en·com·pass \in-'kəm-pəs\ *vb* **1** : ENCIRCLE **2** : ENVELOP, INCLUDE

¹en·core \'än-,kōr\ *n* : a demand for repetition or reappearance; *also* : a further performance (as of a singer) in response to such a demand

²encore *vb* **en·cored; en·cor·ing** : to request an encore from

¹en·coun·ter \in-'kaün-tər\ *vb* **1** : to meet as an enemy : FIGHT **2** : to meet usu. unexpectedly

²encounter *n* **1** : a hostile meeting; *esp* : COMBAT **2** : a chance meeting

en·cour·age \in-'kər-ij\ *vb* **-aged; -ag·ing 1** : to inspire with courage and hope **2** : STIMULATE, INCITE **3** : FOSTER — **en·cour·age·ment** *n* — **en·cour·ag·ing·ly** *adv*

en·croach \in-'krōch\ *vb* [ME *encrochen* to seize, fr. MF *encrochier*, fr. OF, fr. *croche* hook] : to enter gradually or stealthily upon another's property or rights — **en·croach·ment** *n*

en·crust \in-'krəst\ *vb* : to provide with or form a crust

en·crus·ta·tion \(,)in-,krəs-'tā-shən, ,en-\ *var of* INCRUSTATION

en·cum·ber \in-'kəm-bər\ *vb* **1** : to weigh down : BURDEN **2** : to hinder the function or activity of — **en·cum·brance** \-brəns\ *n*

ency *or* **encyc** *abbr* encyclopedia

-en·cy *n suffix* : quality or state ⟨despond*ency*⟩

¹en·cyc·li·cal \in-'si-kli-kəl, en-\ *adj* : addressed to all the individuals of a group

²encyclical *n* : an encyclical letter; *esp* : a papal letter to the bishops of the church

en·cy·clo·pe·dia *also* **en·cy·clo·pae·dia** \in-,sī-klə-'pē-dē-ə\ *n* [ML *encyclopaedia* course of general education, fr. Gk *enkyklios paideia* general education] : a work treating the various branches of learning — **en·cy·clo·pe·dic** \-'pē-dik\ *adj*

en·cyst \in-'sist, en-\ *vb* : to form or become enclosed in a cyst — **en·cyst·ment** *n*

¹end \'end\ *n* **1** : the part of an area that lies at the boundary; *also* : a point which marks the extent or limit of something or at which something ceases to exist **2** : a ceasing of a course (as of action or activity); *also* : DEATH **3** : the ultimate state; *also* : RESULT, ISSUE **4** : REMNANT **5** : PURPOSE, OBJECTIVE **6** : a player stationed at the extremity of a line (as in football) **7** : a share, operation, or aspect of an undertaking

²end *vb* **1** : to bring or come to an end **2** : DESTROY; *also* : DIE **3** : to form or be at the end of **syn** close, conclude, terminate, finish, complete

en·dan·ger \in-'dān-jər\ *vb* : to bring into danger; *also* : to create danger

en·dan·gered *adj* : being or relating to an endangered species

endangered species *n* : a species threatened with extinction

en·dear \in-'dir\ *vb* : to cause to become beloved or admired

en·dear·ment \-mənt\ *n* : a sign of affection : CARESS

en·deav·or \in-'de-vər\ *vb* : TRY, ATTEMPT — **endeavor** *n*

en·deav·our *chiefly Brit var of* ENDEAVOR

en·dem·ic \en-'de-mik, in-\ *adj* : restricted to a particular place ⟨∼ plants⟩ ⟨an ∼ disease⟩ — **endemic** *n*

end·ing \'en-diŋ\ *n* : something that forms an end; *esp* : SUFFIX

en·dive \'en-ˌdīv\ *n* **1** : an herb related to chicory and grown as a salad plant **2** : the blanched shoot of chicory

end·less \'end-ləs\ *adj* **1** : having or seeming to have no end : ETERNAL **2** : united at the ends : CONTINUOUS ⟨an ~ belt⟩ **syn** interminable, everlasting, unceasing, ceaseless, unending — **end·less·ly** *adv*

end·most \-ˌmōst\ *adj* : situated at the very end

end·note \-ˌnōt\ *n* : a note placed at the end of a text

en·do·crine \'en-də-krən, -ˌkrīn, -ˌkrēn\ *adj* : producing secretions that are distributed by way of the bloodstream ⟨~ glands⟩ — **endocrine** *n* — **en·do·cri·nol·o·gist** \-kri-'nä-lə-jist\ *n* — **en·do·cri·nol·o·gy** \-jē\ *n*

en·dog·e·nous \en-'dä-jə-nəs\ *adj* : caused or produced by factors inside the organism or system ⟨~ psychic depression⟩ — **en·dog·e·nous·ly** *adv*

en·dorse \in-'dòrs\ *vb* **en·dorsed**; **en·dors·ing 1** : to sign one's name on the back of (as a check) **2** : APPROVE, SANCTION — **en·dorse·ment** *n*

en·do·scope \'en-də-ˌskōp\ *n* : an instrument with which the interior of a hollow organ (as the rectum) may be visualized — **en·do·scop·ic** \ˌen-də-'skä-pik\ *adj* — **en·dos·co·py** \en-'däs-kə-pē\ *n*

en·do·ther·mic \ˌen-də-'thər-mik\ *adj* : characterized by or formed with absorption of heat

en·dow \in-'daù\ *vb* **1** : to furnish with funds for support ⟨~ a school⟩ **2** : to furnish with something freely or naturally — **en·dow·ment** *n*

en·due \in-'dü, -'dyü\ *vb* **en·dued; en·du·ing** : PROVIDE, ENDOW

en·dur·ance \in-'dùr-əns, -'dyùr-\ *n* **1** : DURATION **2** : the ability to withstand hardship or stress : FORTITUDE

en·dure \in-'dùr, -'dyùr\ *vb* **en·dured; en·dur·ing 1** : LAST, PERSIST **2** : to suffer firmly or patiently : BEAR **3** : TOLERATE — **en·dur·able** *adj*

end·ways \'end-ˌwāz\ *adv or adj* **1** : LENGTHWISE **2** : with the end forward **3** : on end

end·wise \-ˌwīz\ *adv or adj* : ENDWAYS

ENE *abbr* east-northeast

en·e·ma \'e-nə-mə\ *n, pl* **enemas** *also* **ene·ma·ta** \ˌe-nə-'mä-tə, 'e-nə-mə-tə\ : injection of liquid into the rectum; *also* : material so injected

en·e·my \'e-nə-mē\ *n, pl* **-mies** : one that attacks or tries to harm another : FOE; *esp* : a military opponent

en·er·get·ic \ˌe-nər-'je-tik\ *adj* : marked by energy : ACTIVE, VIGOROUS **syn** strenuous, lusty, dynamic, vital — **en·er·get·i·cal·ly** \-ti-k(ə-)lē\ *adv*

en·er·gize \'e-nər-ˌjīz\ *vb* **-gized; -giz·ing** : to give energy to

en·er·gy \'e-nər-jē\ *n, pl* **-gies 1** : vigorous action : EFFORT **2** : capacity for action **3** : capacity for performing work **4** : usable power (as heat or electricity); *also* : the resources for producing such power

energy level *n* : one of the stable states of constant energy that may be assumed by a physical system (as the electrons in an atom)

en·er·vate \'e-nər-ˌvāt\ *vb* **-vat·ed; -vat·ing** : to lessen the strength or vigor of : weaken in mind or body — **en·er·va·tion** \ˌe-nər-'vā-shən\ *n*

en·fee·ble \in-'fē-bəl\ *vb* **-bled; -bling** : to make feeble **syn** weaken, debilitate, sap, undermine, cripple — **en·fee·ble·ment** *n*

en·fi·lade \'en-fə-ˌlād, -ˌläd\ *n* : gunfire directed along the length of an enemy battle line — **enfilade** *vb*

en·fold \in-'fōld\ *vb* **1** : ENVELOP **2** : EMBRACE

en·force \in-'fōrs\ *vb* **1** : COMPEL ⟨~ obedience by threats⟩ **2** : to execute effectively ⟨~ the law⟩ — **en·force·able** *adj* — **en·force·ment** *n*

en·forc·er \in-'fōr-sər\ *n* : one that enforces; *esp* : an aggressive player (as in ice hockey) known for rough play

en·fran·chise \in-'fran-ˌchīz\ *vb* **-chised; -chis·ing 1** : to set free (as from slavery) **2** : to admit to citizenship; *also* : to grant the vote to — **en·fran·chise·ment** \-ˌchīz-mənt, -chəz-\ *n*

eng *abbr* engine; engineer; engineering

Eng *abbr* England; English

en·gage \in-'gāj\ *vb* **en·gaged; en·gag·ing 1** : PLEDGE; *esp* : to bind by a pledge to marry **2** : EMPLOY, HIRE **3** : to attract and hold esp. by interesting; *also* : to cause to participate **4** : to commence or take part in a venture **5** : to bring or enter into conflict **6** : to connect or interlock with : MESH; *also* : to cause to mesh

en·gage·ment \in-'gāj-mənt\ *n* **1** : APPOINTMENT **2** : EMPLOYMENT **3** : a mutual promise to marry **4** : a hostile encounter

en·gag·ing *adj* : ATTRACTIVE — **en·gag·ing·ly** *adv*

en·gen·der \in-'jen-dər\ *vb* **1** : BEGET **2** : BRING ABOUT, CREATE **syn** generate, breed, occasion, produce

en·gine \'en-jən\ *n* [ME *engin*, fr. OF, fr. L *ingenium* natural disposition, talent] **1** : a mechanical device **2** : a machine for converting energy into mechanical motion **3** : LOCOMOTIVE

¹en·gi·neer \ˌen-jə-'nir\ *n* **1** : a member of a military unit specializing in engineering work **2** : a designer or builder of engines **3** : one trained in engineering **4** : one that operates an engine

²engineer *vb* **1** : to lay out or manage as an engineer **2** : to guide the course of **syn** pilot, lead, steer

en·gi·neer·ing *n* : the practical applications of scientific and mathematical principles

En·glish \'iŋ-glish\ *n* **1** : the language of England, the U.S., and many areas now or formerly under British rule **2 English** *pl* : the people of England **3** : spin imparted to a ball that is driven or rolled — **English** *adj* — **En·glish·man** \-mən\ *n* — **En·glish·wom·an** \-ˌwù-mən\ *n*

English horn *n* : a woodwind instrument longer than and having a range lower than the oboe

English setter *n* : any of a breed of bird dogs with a flat silky coat of white or white with color

English sparrow *n* : HOUSE SPARROW

English system *n* : a system of weights and measures in which the foot is the principal unit of length and the pound is the principal unit of weight

engr *abbr* **1** engineer **2** engraved

en·gram \'en-ˌgram\ *n* : a hypothetical change in neural tissue postulated in order to account for persistence of memory

en·grave \in-'grāv\ *vb* **en·graved; en·grav·ing 1** : to produce (as letters or lines) by incising a surface **2** : to cut figures, letters, or designs on for printing; *also* : to print from an engraved plate **3** : PHOTOENGRAVE — **en·grav·er** *n*

en·grav·ing \in-'grā-viŋ\ *n* **1** : the art of one who engraves **2** : an engraved plate; *also* : a print made from it

en·gross \in-'grōs\ *vb* : to take up the whole interest or attention of **syn** monopolize, absorb, consume

en·gulf \in-'gəlf\ *vb* : to flow over and enclose

en·hance \in-'hans\ *vb* **en·hanced; en·hanc·ing** : to increase or improve (as in value or desirability) **syn** heighten, intensify, magnify — **en·hance·ment** *n*

enig·ma \i-'nig-mə\ *n* [L *aenigma*, fr. Gk *ainigma*, fr. *ainissesthai* to speak in riddles, fr. *ainos* fable] : something obscure or hard to understand

enig·mat·ic \ˌen-ig-'ma-tik\ *adj* : resembling an enigma **syn** obscure, cryptic, mystifying — **en·ig·mat·i·cal·ly** \-ti-k(ə-)lē\ *adv*

en·join \in-'jòin\ *vb* **1** : COMMAND, ORDER **2** : FORBID **syn** direct, bid, charge, command, instruct

en·joy \in-'jòi\ *vb* **1** : to have for one's benefit or use ⟨~ good health⟩ **2** : to take pleasure or satisfaction in ⟨~ed the concert⟩ — **en·joy·able** *adj* — **en·joy·ment** *n*

enl *abbr* **1** enlarged **2** enlisted

en·large \in-'lärj\ *vb* **en·larged; en·larg·ing 1** : to make or grow larger **2** : ELABORATE **syn** increase, augment, multiply, expand — **en·large·ment** *n*

en·light·en \in-ˈlīt-ᵊn\ vb **1** : INSTRUCT, INFORM **2** : to give spiritual insight to — **en·light·en·ment** n

en·list \in-ˈlist\ vb **1** : to secure the aid or support of **2** : to engage for service in the armed forces — **en·list·ee** \-ˌlis-ˈtē\ n — **en·list·ment** \-ˈlist-mənt\ n

en·list·ed \in-ˈlis-təd\ adj : of, relating to, or forming the part of a military force below commissioned or warrant officers

en·liv·en \in-ˈlī-vən\ vb : to give life, action, or spirit to : ANIMATE

en masse \än-ˈmas\ adv [F] : in a body : as a whole

en·mesh \in-ˈmesh\ vb : to catch or entangle in or as if in meshes

en·mi·ty \ˈen-mə-tē\ n, pl **-ties** : ILL WILL; esp : mutual hatred syn hostility, antipathy, animosity, rancor, antagonism

en·no·ble \i-ˈnō-bəl\ vb **-bled**; **-bling** : EXALT, ELEVATE; esp : to raise to noble rank — **en·no·ble·ment** n

en·nui \ˌän-ˈwē\ n [F] : BOREDOM

enor·mi·ty \i-ˈnȯr-mə-tē\ n, pl **-ties 1** : an outrageous, vicious, or immoral act **2** : great wickedness **3** : IMMENSITY

enor·mous \i-ˈnȯr-məs\ adj [L enormis, fr. e, ex out of + norma rule] **1** : exceedingly wicked **2** : great in size, number, or degree : HUGE syn immense, vast, gigantic, colossal, mammoth, elephantine

¹enough \i-ˈnəf\ adj : SUFFICIENT

²enough adv **1** : SUFFICIENTLY **2** : FULLY, QUITE **3** : TOLERABLY

³enough pron : a sufficient number, quantity, or amount

en·quire \in-ˈkwīr\, **en·qui·ry** \ˈin-kwīr-ē, in-ˈkwīr-; ˈin-kwə-rē, ˈiŋ-\ var of INQUIRE, INQUIRY

en·rage \in-ˈrāj\ vb : to fill with rage

en·rap·ture \in-ˈrap-chər\ vb **en·rap·tured**; **en·rap·tur·ing** : DELIGHT

en·rich \in-ˈrich\ vb **1** : to make rich or richer **2** : ORNAMENT, ADORN — **en·rich·ment** n

en·roll or **en·rol** \in-ˈrōl\ vb **en·rolled**; **en·roll·ing 1** : to enter or register on a roll or list **2** : to offer (oneself) for enrolling — **en·roll·ment** n

en route \än-ˈrüt, en-\ adv or adj : on or along the way

ENS abbr ensign

en·sconce \in-ˈskäns\ vb **en·sconced**; **en·sconc·ing 1** : SHELTER, CONCEAL **2** : to settle snugly or securely syn secrete, hide, cache, stash

en·sem·ble \än-ˈsäm-bəl\ n [F, fr. ensemble together, fr. L insimul at the same time] : a group (as of singers, dancers, or players) or a set (as of clothes) producing a single effect

en·sheathe \in-ˈshēth\ vb : to cover with or as if with a sheath

en·shrine \in-ˈshrīn\ vb **1** : to enclose in or as if in a shrine **2** : to cherish as sacred

en·shroud \in-ˈshraud\ vb : SHROUD, OBSCURE

en·sign \ˈen-sən, 1 also ˈen-ˌsīn\ n **1** : FLAG; also : BADGE, EMBLEM **2** : a commissioned officer in the navy ranking next below a lieutenant junior grade

en·slave \in-ˈslāv\ vb : to make a slave of — **en·slave·ment** n

en·snare \in-ˈsnar\ vb : SNARE, TRAP syn entrap, bag, catch, capture

en·sue \in-ˈsü\ vb **en·sued**; **en·su·ing** : to follow in time or as a result

en·sure \in-ˈshur\ vb **en·sured**; **en·sur·ing** : INSURE, GUARANTEE

en·tail \in-ˈtāl\ vb **1** : to limit the inheritance of (property) to the owner's lineal descendants or to a class thereof **2** : to include or involve as a necessary step or result — **en·tail·ment** n

en·tan·gle \in-ˈtaŋ-gəl\ vb : TANGLE, CONFUSE — **en·tan·gle·ment** n

en·tente \än-ˈtänt\ n [F understanding, agreement] : an understanding providing for joint action; also : parties linked by such an entente

en·ter \ˈen-tər\ vb **1** : to go or come in or into **2** : to become a member of : JOIN ⟨~ the ministry⟩ **3** : BEGIN **4** : to take part in : CONTRIBUTE **5** : to go into or upon and take possession **6** : to set down (as in a list) : REGISTER **7** : to place (a complaint) before a court; also : to put on record ⟨~ a complaint⟩

en·ter·itis \ˌen-tə-ˈrī-təs\ n : intestinal inflammation; also : a disease marked by this

en·ter·prise \ˈen-tər-ˌprīz\ n **1** : UNDERTAKING, PROJECT **2** : readiness for daring action : INITIATIVE **3** : a business organization

en·ter·pris·ing \-ˌprī-ziŋ\ adj : bold and vigorous in action : ENERGETIC

en·ter·tain \ˌen-tər-ˈtān\ vb **1** : to treat or receive as a guest **2** : AMUSE, DIVERT **3** : to hold in mind syn harbor, shelter, lodge, house, billet — **en·ter·tain·er** n — **en·ter·tain·ment** n

en·thrall or **en·thral** \in-ˈthrȯl\ vb **en·thralled**; **en·thrall·ing 1** : ENSLAVE **2** : to hold spellbound

en·throne \in-ˈthrōn\ vb **1** : to seat on or as if on a throne **2** : EXALT

en·thuse \in-ˈthüz, -ˈthyüz\ vb **en·thused**; **en·thus·ing 1** : to make enthusiastic **2** : to show enthusiasm

en·thu·si·asm \in-ˈthü-zē-ˌa-zəm, -ˈthyü-\ n [Gk enthousiasmos, fr. enthousiazein to be inspired, irreg. fr. entheos inspired, fr. theos god] **1** : strong warmth of feeling : keen interest : FERVOR **2** : a cause of fervor — **en·thu·si·ast** \-ˌast, -əst\ n — **en·thu·si·as·tic** \in-ˌthü-zē-ˈas-tik, -ˌthyü-\ adj — **en·thu·si·as·ti·cal·ly** \-ti-k(ə-)lē\ adv

en·tice \in-ˈtīs\ vb **en·ticed**; **en·tic·ing** : ALLURE, TEMPT — **en·tice·ment** n

en·tire \in-ˈtīr\ adj : COMPLETE, WHOLE syn sound, perfect, intact, undamaged — **en·tire·ly** adv

en·tire·ty \in-ˈtī-rə-tē, -ˈtīr-tē\ n, pl **-ties 1** : COMPLETENESS **2** : WHOLE, TOTALITY

en·ti·tle \in-ˈtīt-ᵊl\ vb **en·ti·tled**; **en·ti·tling 1** : NAME, DESIGNATE **2** : to give a right or claim to

en·ti·tle·ment \in-ˈtīt-ᵊl-mənt\ n : a government program providing benefits to members of a specified group

en·ti·ty \ˈen-tə-tē\ n, pl **-ties 1** : EXISTENCE, BEING **2** : something with separate and real existence

en·tomb \in-ˈtüm\ vb : to place in a tomb : BURY — **en·tomb·ment** n

en·to·mol·o·gy \ˌen-tə-ˈmä-lə-jē\ n : a branch of zoology that deals with insects — **en·to·mo·log·i·cal** \-mə-ˈlä-ji-kəl\ adj — **en·to·mol·o·gist** \-jist\ n

en·tou·rage \ˌän-tu-ˈräzh\ n [F] : RETINUE

en·tr'acte \ˈän-ˌtrakt\ n [F] **1** : something (as a dance) performed between two acts of a play **2** : the interval between two acts of a play

en·trails \ˈen-ˌtrālz\ n pl : VISCERA; esp : INTESTINES

¹en·trance \ˈen-trəns\ n **1** : permission or right to enter **2** : the act of entering **3** : a means or place of entry

²en·trance \in-ˈtrans\ vb **en·tranced**; **en·tranc·ing** : CHARM, DELIGHT

en·trant \ˈen-trənt\ n : one that enters esp. as a competitor

en·trap \in-ˈtrap\ vb : ENSNARE, TRAP — **en·trap·ment** n

en·treat \in-ˈtrēt\ vb : to ask urgently : BESEECH syn beg, implore, plead, supplicate — **en·treaty** \-ˈtrē-tē\ n

en·trée or **en·tree** \ˈän-ˌtrā\ n [F entrée] **1** : freedom of entry or access **2** : the main course of a meal in the U.S. syn admission, admittance, entrance

en·trench \in-ˈtrench\ vb **1** : to place within or surround with a trench esp. for defense; also : to establish solidly ⟨~ed customs⟩ **2** : ENCROACH, TRESPASS — **en·trench·ment** n

en·tre·pre·neur \ˌän-trə-prə-ˈnər, -ˈnu̇r, -ˈnyu̇r\ n [F, fr. OF, fr. entreprendre to undertake] : one who organizes and assumes the risk of a business or enterprise — **en·tre·pre·neur·ial** \-ˈnu̇r-ē-əl, -ˈnyu̇r-, -ˈnər-\ *adj*

en·tro·py \ˈen-trə-pē\ *n, pl* **-pies 1** : the degree of disorder in a system **2** : an ultimate state of inert uniformity

en·trust \in-ˈtrəst\ *vb* **1** : to commit something to as a trust **2** : to commit to another with confidence **syn** confide, consign, relegate, commend

en·try \ˈen-trē\ *n, pl* **entries 1** : ENTRANCE 2, 3; *also* : VESTIBULE 2 **2** : an entering in a record; *also* : an item so entered **3** : a headword with its definition or identification; *also* : VOCABULARY ENTRY **4** : one entered in a contest

en·twine \in-ˈtwīn\ *vb* : to twine together or around

enu·mer·ate \i-ˈnü-mə-ˌrāt, -ˈnyü-\ *vb* **-at·ed; -at·ing 1** : to determine the number of : COUNT **2** : LIST — **enu·mer·a·tion** \-ˌnü-mə-ˈrā-shən, -ˌnyü-\ *n*

enun·ci·ate \ē-ˈnən-sē-ˌāt\ *vb* **-at·ed; -at·ing 1** : to state definitely; *also* : ANNOUNCE, PROCLAIM **2** : PRONOUNCE, ARTICULATE — **enun·ci·a·tion** \-ˌnən-sē-ˈā-shən\ *n*

en·ure·sis \ˌen-yu̇-ˈrē-səs\ *n* : involuntary discharge of urine : BED-WETTING

env *abbr* envelope

en·vel·op \in-ˈve-ləp\ *vb* : to enclose completely with or as if with a covering — **en·vel·op·ment** *n*

en·ve·lope \ˈen-və-ˌlōp, ˈän-\ *n* **1** : a usu. paper container for a letter **2** : WRAPPER, COVERING

en·ven·om \in-ˈve-nəm\ *vb* **1** : to make poisonous **2** : EMBITTER

en·vi·able \ˈen-vē-ə-bəl\ *adj* : highly desirable — **en·vi·ably** \-blē\ *adv*

en·vi·ous \ˈen-vē-əs\ *adj* : feeling or showing envy — **en·vi·ous·ly** *adv* — **en·vi·ous·ness** *n*

en·vi·ron·ment \in-ˈvī-rən-mənt, -ˈvīrn-\ *n* **1** : SURROUNDINGS **2** : the whole complex of factors (as soil, climate, and living things) that influence the form and the ability to survive of a plant or animal or ecological community — **en·vi·ron·men·tal** \-ˌvī-rən-ˈment-əl, -ˌvīrn-\ *adj*

en·vi·ron·men·tal·ist \-ˌvī-rən-ˈment-əl-ist, -ˌvīrn-\ *n* : a person concerned about environmental quality esp. with respect to control of pollution

en·vi·rons \in-ˈvī-rənz\ *n pl* **1** : SUBURBS **2** : SURROUNDINGS; *also* : VICINITY

en·vis·age \in-ˈvi-zij\ *vb* **-aged; -ag·ing** : to have a mental picture of

en·vi·sion \in-ˈvi-zhən, en-\ *vb* : to picture to oneself ⟨∼s world peace⟩

en·voy \ˈen-ˌvȯi, ˈän-\ *n* **1** : a diplomatic agent **2** : REPRESENTATIVE, MESSENGER

¹**en·vy** \ˈen-vē\ *n, pl* **envies** [ME *envie*, fr. OF, fr. L *invidia*, fr. *invidus* envious, fr. *invidēre* to look askance at, envy, fr. *vidēre* to see] : painful or resentful awareness of another's advantages; *also* : an object of envy

²**envy** *vb* **en·vied; en·vy·ing** : to feel envy toward or on account of

en·zyme \ˈen-ˌzīm\ *n* : any of various complex proteins produced by living cells that catalyze specific biochemical reactions at body temperatures — **en·zy·mat·ic** \ˌen-zə-ˈma-tik\ *adj*

Eo·cene \ˈē-ə-ˌsēn\ *adj* : of, relating to, or being the epoch of the Tertiary between the Paleocene and the Oligocene — **Eocene** *n*

EOE *abbr* equal opportunity employer

eo·lian \ē-ˈō-lē-ən\ *adj* : borne, deposited, or produced by the wind

EOM *abbr* end of month

eon \ˈē-ən, ˈē-ˌän\ *var of* AEON

EP *abbr* European plan

EPA *abbr* Environmental Protection Agency

ep·au·let *also* **ep·au·lette** \ˌe-pə-ˈlet\ *n* [F *épaulette*, dim. of *épaule* shoulder] : a shoulder ornament esp. on a coat or military uniform

épée \ˈe-ˌpā, ā-ˈpā\ *n* [F] : a fencing or dueling sword

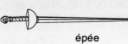

épée

Eph *or* **Ephes** *abbr* Ephesians

ephed·rine \i-ˈfe-drən\ *n* : a drug used in relieving hay fever, asthma, and nasal congestion

ephem·era \i-ˈfe-mər-ə\ *n pl* : collectibles (as posters or tickets) not intended to have lasting value

ephem·er·al \i-ˈfe-mə-rəl\ *adj* [Gk *ephēmeros* lasting a day, daily, fr. *epi-*on *hēmera* day] : SHORT-LIVED, TRANSITORY **syn** passing, fleeting, transient, evanescent

Ephe·sians \i-ˈfē-zhənz\ *n* — see BIBLE table

ep·ic \ˈe-pik\ *n* : a long poem in elevated style narrating the deeds of a hero — **epic** *adj*

epi·cen·ter \ˈe-pi-ˌsen-tər\ *n* : the point on the earth's surface directly above the point of origin of an earthquake

ep·i·cure \ˈe-pi-ˌkyu̇r\ *n* : a person with sensitive and discriminating tastes esp. in food and wine

ep·i·cu·re·an \ˌe-pi-kyu̇-ˈrē-ən, -ˈkyu̇r-ē-\ *n* : EPICURE — **epicurean** *adj*

¹**ep·i·dem·ic** \ˌe-pə-ˈde-mik\ *adj* : affecting many persons at one time ⟨∼ disease⟩; *also* : excessively prevalent

²**epidemic** *n* : an epidemic outbreak esp. of disease

epi·der·mis \ˌe-pə-ˈdər-məs\ *n* : an outer layer esp. of skin — **epi·der·mal** \-məl\ *adj*

epi·glot·tis \ˌe-pə-ˈglä-təs\ *n* : a thin plate of flexible tissue protecting the tracheal opening during swallowing

ep·i·gram \ˈe-pə-ˌgram\ *n* : a short witty poem or saying — **ep·i·gram·mat·ic** \ˌe-pə-grə-ˈma-tik\ *adj*

ep·i·lep·sy \ˈe-pə-ˌlep-sē\ *n, pl* **-sies** : a disorder typically marked by disturbed electrical rhythms of the central nervous system, by attacks of convulsions, and by loss of consciousness — **ep·i·lep·tic** \ˌe-pə-ˈlep-tik\ *adj or n*

ep·i·logue *also* **ep·i·log** \ˈe-pə-ˌlȯg, -ˌläg\ *n* : a speech addressed to the spectators by an actor at the end of a play

epi·neph·rine *also* **epi·neph·rin** \ˌe-pə-ˈne-frən\ *n* : an adrenal hormone used medicinally esp. as a heart stimulant, a muscle relaxant, and a vasoconstrictor

epiph·a·ny \i-ˈpi-fə-nē\ *n, pl* **-nies 1** *cap* : January 6 observed as a church festival in commemoration of the coming of the Magi to Jesus at Bethlehem **2** : a sudden striking understanding of something

epis·co·pa·cy \i-ˈpis-kə-pə-sē\ *n, pl* **-cies 1** : government of a church by bishops **2** : EPISCOPATE

epis·co·pal \i-ˈpis-kə-pəl\ *adj* **1** : of or relating to a bishop or episcopacy **2** *cap* : of or relating to the Protestant Episcopal Church

Epis·co·pa·lian \i-ˌpis-kə-ˈpāl-yən\ *n* : a member of the Protestant Episcopal Church

epis·co·pate \i-ˈpis-kə-pət, -ˌpāt\ *n* **1** : the rank, office, or term of a bishop **2** : a body of bishops

ep·i·sode \ˈe-pə-ˌsōd\ *n* [Gk *epeisodion*, fr. *epeisodios* coming in besides, fr. *eisodios* coming in, fr. *eis* into + *hodos* road, journey] **1** : a unit of action in a dramatic or literary work **2** : an incident in a course of events : OCCURRENCE ⟨a feverish ∼⟩ — **ep·i·sod·ic** \ˌe-pə-ˈsä-dik\ *adj*

epis·tle \i-ˈpi-səl\ *n* **1** *cap* : one of the letters of the New Testament **2** : LETTER — **epis·to·lary** \i-ˈpis-tə-ˌler-ē\ *adj*

ep·i·taph \ˈe-pə-ˌtaf\ *n* : an inscription in memory of a dead person

ep·i·tha·la·mi·um \ˌe-pə-thə-ˈlā-mē-əm\ *or* **ep·i·tha·la·mi·on** \-mē-ən\ *n pl* **-mi·ums** *or* **-mia** \-mē-ə\ : a song or poem in honor of a bride and bridegroom

ep·i·the·li·um \ˌe-pə-ˈthē-lē-əm\ *n, pl* **-lia** \-lē-ə\ : a cellular membrane covering a bodily surface or lining a cavity — **ep·i·the·li·al** \-lē-əl\ *adj*

ep·i·thet \'e-pə-ˌthet, -thət\ *n* : a characterizing and often abusive word or phrase

epit·o·me \i-'pi-tə-mē\ *n* **1** : ABSTRACT, SUMMARY **2** : EMBODIMENT — **epit·o·mize** \-ˌmīz\ *vb*

ep·och \'e-pək, -ˌpäk\ *n* : a usu. extended period : ERA, AGE — **ep·och·al** \-pə-kəl, -ˌpä-\ *adj*

ep·oxy \i-'päk-sē\ *vb* **ep·ox·ied** *or* **ep·oxyed; ep·oxy·ing** : to glue with epoxy resin

epoxy resin *n* : a synthetic resin used in coatings and adhesives

ep·si·lon \'ep-sə-län, -lən\ *n* : the 5th letter of the Greek alphabet — E or ε

Ep·som salts \'ep-səm-\ *n* : a bitter colorless or white magnesium salt with cathartic properties

eq *abbr* **1** equal **2** equation

equa·ble \'e-kwə-bəl, 'ē-\ *adj* : UNIFORM, EVEN; *esp* : free from unpleasant extremes — **eq·ua·bil·i·ty** \ˌe-kwə-'bi-lə-tē, ˌē-\ *n* — **equa·bly** \'e-kwə-blē, 'ē-\ *adv*

¹**equal** \'ē-kwəl\ *adj* **1** : of the same measure, quantity, value, quality, number, degree, or status as another **2** : IMPARTIAL **3** : free from extremes **4** : able to cope with a situation or task — **equal·i·ty** \i-'kwä-lə-tē\ *n* — **equal·ly** *adv*

²**equal** *vb* **equaled** *or* **equalled; equal·ing** *or* **equal·ling** : to be or become equal to; *also* : to be identical in value to

³**equal** *n* : one that is equal

equal·ize \'ē-kwə-ˌlīz\ *vb* **-ized; -iz·ing** : to make equal, uniform, or constant — **equal·i·za·tion** \ˌē-kwə-lə-'zā-shən\ *n* — **equal·iz·er** *n*

equals sign *or* **equal sign** *n* : a sign = indicating equivalence

equa·nim·i·ty \ˌē-kwə-'ni-mə-tē, ˌe-\ *n, pl* **-ties** : COMPOSURE

equate \i-'kwāt\ *vb* **equat·ed; equat·ing** : to make, treat, or regard as equal or comparable

equa·tion \i-'kwā-zhən\ *n* **1** : an act of equating : the state of being equated **2** : a usu. formal statement of equivalence esp. of mathematical expressions

equa·tor \i-'kwā-tər, 'ē-\ *n* : an imaginary circle around the earth that is everywhere equally distant from the two poles — **equa·to·ri·al** \ˌē-kwə-'tōr-ē-əl, ˌe-\ *adj*

equer·ry \'e-kwə-rē, i-'kwer-ē\ *n, pl* **-ries 1** : an officer in charge of the horses of a prince or noble **2** : a personal attendant of a member of the British royal family

¹**eques·tri·an** \i-'kwes-trē-ən\ *adj* : of or relating to horseback riding; *also* : representing a person on horseback ⟨an ∼ statue⟩

²**equestrian** *n* : one who rides a horse

eques·tri·enne \i-ˌkwes-trē-'en\ *n* : a female rider on horseback

equi·dis·tant \ˌē-kwə-'dis-tənt\ *adj* : equally distant

equi·lat·er·al \ˌē-kwə-'la-tə-rəl\ *adj* : having all sides or faces equal ⟨∼ triangles⟩

equi·lib·ri·um \ˌē-kwə-'li-brē-əm, ˌe-\ *n, pl* **-ri·ums** *or* **-ria** \-brē-ə\ : a state of intellectual or emotional balance; *also* : a state of balance between opposing forces or actions syn poise, balance, equipoise

equine \'ē-ˌkwīn, 'e-\ *adj* [L *equinus,* fr. *equus* horse] : of or relating to the horse — **equine** *n*

equi·noc·tial \ˌē-kwə-'näk-shəl, ˌe-\ *adj* : relating to an equinox

equi·nox \'ē-kwə-ˌnäks, 'e-\ *n* : either of the two times each year when the sun appears directly overhead at the equator and day and night are everywhere of equal length

equip \i-'kwip\ *vb* **equipped; equip·ping** : to supply with needed resources

eq·ui·page \'e-kwə-pij\ *n* : a horse-drawn carriage usu. with its servants

equip·ment \i-'kwip-mənt\ *n* **1** : things used in equip-

ping : SUPPLIES, OUTFIT **2** : the equipping of a person or thing : the state of being equipped

equi·poise \'e-kwə-ˌpȯiz, 'ē-\ *n* **1** : BALANCE, EQUILIBRIUM **2** : COUNTERBALANCE

eq·ui·ta·ble \'e-kwə-tə-bəl\ *adj* : JUST, FAIR — **eq·ui·ta·bly** \-blē\ *adv*

eq·ui·ta·tion \ˌe-kwə-'tā-shən\ *n* : the act or art of riding on horseback

equi·ty \'e-kwə-tē\ *n, pl* **-ties 1** : JUSTNESS, IMPARTIALITY **2** : value of a property or of an interest in it in excess of claims against it

equiv *abbr* equivalent

equiv·a·lent \i-'kwi-və-lənt\ *adj* : EQUAL; *also* : virtually identical — **equiv·a·lence** \-ləns\ *n* — **equivalent** *n*

equiv·o·cal \i-'kwi-və-kəl\ *adj* **1** : AMBIGUOUS **2** : UNCERTAIN, UNDECIDED **3** : SUSPICIOUS, DUBIOUS ⟨∼ behavior⟩ syn obscure, dark, vague, enigmatic — **equiv·o·cal·ly** *adv*

equiv·o·cate \i-'kwi-və-ˌkāt\ *vb* **-cat·ed; -cat·ing 1** : to use misleading language **2** : to avoid giving a definite answer — **equiv·o·ca·tion** \-ˌkwi-və-'kā-shən\ *n*

¹**-er** \ər\ *adj suffix or adv suffix* — used to form the comparative degree of adjectives and adverbs of one or two syllables ⟨hott*er*⟩ ⟨dri*er*⟩ ⟨silli*er*⟩ and sometimes of longer ones

²**-er** \ər\ *also* **-ier** \ē-ər, yər\ *or* **-yer** \yər\ *n suffix* **1** : a person occupationally connected with ⟨hatt*er*⟩ ⟨law*yer*⟩ **2** : a person or thing belonging to or associated with ⟨old-tim*er*⟩ **3** : a native of : resident of ⟨New Zealand*er*⟩ **4** : one that has ⟨double-deck*er*⟩ **5** : one that produces or yields ⟨pork*er*⟩ **6** : one that does or performs (a specified action) ⟨report*er*⟩ **7** : one that is a suitable object of (a specified action) ⟨broil*er*⟩ **8** : one that is ⟨foreign*er*⟩

Er *symbol* erbium

ER *abbr* emergency room

era \'ir-ə, 'er-ə, 'ē-rə\ *n* [LL *aera,* fr. L, counters, pl. of *aes* copper, money] **1** : a chronological order or system of notation reckoned from a given date as basis **2** : a period identified by some special feature **3** : any of the four major divisions of geologic time syn age, epoch, period, time

ERA *abbr* Equal Rights Amendment

erad·i·cate \i-'ra-də-ˌkāt\ *vb* **-cat·ed; -cat·ing** [L *eradicatus,* pp. of *eradicare,* fr. *e-* out + *radix* root] : UPROOT, ELIMINATE syn exterminate, annihilate, abolish, extinguish — **erad·i·ca·ble** \-di-kə-bəl\ *adj*

erase \i-'rās\ *vb* **erased; eras·ing** : to rub or scratch out (as written words); *also* : OBLITERATE syn cancel, efface, delete, expunge — **eras·er** *n* — **era·sure** \i-'rā-shər\ *n*

er·bi·um \'ər-bē-əm\ *n* : a rare metallic element found with yttrium — see ELEMENT table

¹**ere** \er\ *prep* : BEFORE

²**ere** *conj* : BEFORE

¹**erect** \i-'rekt\ *adj* **1** : not leaning or lying down : UPRIGHT **2** : being in a state of physiological erection

²**erect** *vb* **1** : BUILD **2** : to fix or set in an upright position **3** : SET UP; *also* : ESTABLISH, DEVELOP

erec·tile \i-'rekt-ᵊl, -'rek-ˌtīl\ *adj* : capable of becoming erect ⟨∼ tissue⟩ ⟨∼ feathers of a bird⟩

erec·tion \i-'rek-shən\ *n* **1** : the turgid state of a previously flaccid bodily part when it becomes dilated with blood **2** : CONSTRUCTION

ere·long \er-'lȯŋ\ *adv* : before long

er·e·mite \'er-ə-ˌmīt\ *n* : HERMIT

er·go \'er-gō, 'ər-\ *adv* [L] : THEREFORE

er·got \'ər-gət, -ˌgät\ *n* **1** : a disease of rye and other cereals caused by a fungus; *also* : this fungus **2** : a medicinal compound or preparation derived from an ergot fungus

Er·i·tre·an \ˌer-ə-'trē-ən, -'trā-\ *n* : a native or inhabitant of Eritrea — **Eritrean** *adj*

er·mine \'ər-mən\ *n, pl* **ermines 1** : any of several weasels with winter fur mostly white; *also* : the white fur of an ermine **2** : a rank or office whose official robe is ornamented with ermine

erode \i-'rōd\ *vb* **erod·ed; erod·ing** : to diminish or destroy by degrees; *esp* : to gradually eat into or wear away ⟨soil *eroded* by wind and water⟩ — **erod·ible** \-'rō-də-bəl\ *adj*

erog·e·nous \i-'rä-jə-nəs\ *adj* **1** : sexually sensitive ⟨∼ zones⟩ **2** : of, relating to, or arousing sexual feelings

ero·sion \i-'rō-zhən\ *n* : the process or state of being eroded — **ero·sion·al** \-'rō-zhə-nəl\ *adj* — **ero·sion·al·ly** *adv*

ero·sive \i-'rō-siv\ *adj* : tending to erode — **ero·sive·ness** *n*

erot·ic \i-'rä-tik\ *adj* : relating to or dealing with sexual love : AMATORY — **erot·i·cal·ly** \-ti-k(ə-)lē\ *adv* — **erot·i·cism** \-tə-ˌsi-zəm\ *n*

err \'ər, 'er\ *vb* : to be or do wrong

er·rand \'er-ənd\ *n* : a short trip taken to do something; *also* : the object or purpose of such a trip

er·rant \'er-ənt\ *adj* **1** : WANDERING ⟨an ∼ knight⟩ **2** : straying outside proper bounds **3** : deviating from an accepted pattern or standard

er·ra·ta \e-'rä-tə\ *n* : a list of corrigenda

er·rat·ic \i-'ra-tik\ *adj* **1** : having no fixed course **2** : INCONSISTENT; *also* : ECCENTRIC — **er·rat·i·cal·ly** \-ti-k(ə-)lē\ *adv*

er·ra·tum \e-'rä-təm\ *n, pl* **-ta** \-tə\ : CORRIGENDUM

er·ro·ne·ous \i-'rō-nē-əs, e-'rō-\ *adj* : INCORRECT — **er·ro·ne·ous·ly** *adv*

er·ror \'er-ər\ *n* **1** : a usu. ignorant or unintentional deviating from accuracy or truth ⟨made an ∼ in adding⟩ **2** : a defensive misplay in baseball **3** : the state of one that errs ⟨to be in ∼⟩ **4** : a product of mistake ⟨a typographical ∼⟩ — **er·ror·less** *adj*

er·satz \'er-ˌzäts\ *adj* [G *ersatz-*, fr. *Ersatz*, n., substitute] : being usu. an artificial and inferior substitute

erst \'ərst\ *adv, archaic* : ERSTWHILE

¹**erst·while** \-ˌhwīl\ *adv* : in the past : FORMERLY

²**erstwhile** *adj* : FORMER, PREVIOUS

er·u·di·tion \ˌer-ə-'di-shən, ˌer-yə-\ *n* : SCHOLARSHIP, LEARNING — **er·u·dite** \'er-ə-ˌdīt, 'er-yə-\ *adj*

erupt \i-'rəpt\ *vb* **1** : to burst forth or cause to burst forth : EXPLODE **2** : to break through a surface ⟨teeth ∼ing through the gum⟩ **3** : to break out with or as if with a skin rash — **erup·tion** \-'rəp-shən\ *n* — **erup·tive** \-tiv\ *adj*

-ery *n suffix* **1** : qualities collectively : character : -NESS ⟨snobb*ery*⟩ **2** : art : practice ⟨cook*ery*⟩ **3** : place of doing, keeping, producing, or selling ⟨the thing specified⟩ ⟨fish*ery*⟩ ⟨bak*ery*⟩ **4** : collection : aggregate ⟨fin*ery*⟩ **5** : state or condition ⟨slav*ery*⟩

ery·sip·e·las \ˌer-ə-'si-pə-ləs, ˌir-\ *n* : an acute bacterial disease marked by fever and severe skin inflammation

er·y·the·ma \ˌer-ə-'thē-mə\ *n* : abnormal redness of the skin due to capillary congestion (as in inflammation)

eryth·ro·cyte \i-'ri-thrə-ˌsīt\ *n* : RED BLOOD CELL

Es *symbol* einsteinium

¹**-es** \əz, iz *after* s, z, sh, ch; z *after* v *or a vowel*\ *n pl suffix* — used to form the plural of most nouns that end in *s* ⟨glass*es*⟩, *z* ⟨fuzz*es*⟩, *sh* ⟨bush*es*⟩, *ch* ⟨peach*es*⟩, or a final *y* that changes to *i* ⟨ladi*es*⟩ and of some nouns ending in *f* that changes to *v* ⟨loav*es*⟩

²**-es** *vb suffix* — used to form the third person singular present of most verbs that end in *s* ⟨bless*es*⟩, *z* ⟨fizz*es*⟩, *sh* ⟨hush*es*⟩, *ch* ⟨catch*es*⟩, or a final *y* that changes to *i* ⟨defi*es*⟩

es·ca·late \'es-kə-ˌlāt\ *vb* **-lat·ed; -lat·ing** : to increase in extent, volume, number, intensity, or scope — **es·ca·la·tion** \ˌes-kə-'lā-shən\ *n*

es·ca·la·tor \'es-kə-ˌlā-tər\ *n* : a moving set of stairs

es·cal·lop \is-'kä-ləp, -'ka-\ *var of* SCALLOP

es·ca·pade \'es-kə-ˌpād\ *n* [F, action of escaping] : a mischievous adventure

¹**es·cape** \is-'kāp\ *vb* **es·caped; es·cap·ing** [ME, fr. OF *escaper*, fr. (assumed) VL *excappare*, fr. L *ex-* out +

LL *cappa* head covering, cloak] **1** : to get free or away **2** : to avoid a threatening evil **3** : AVOID **2** ⟨∼ injury⟩ **4** : ELUDE ⟨his name ∼s me⟩ **5** : to be produced or uttered involuntarily by ⟨let a sob ∼ him⟩

²**escape** *n* **1** : flight from or avoidance of something unpleasant **2** : LEAKAGE **3** : a means of escape

³**escape** *adj* : providing a means or way of escape

es·cap·ee \is-ˌkā-'pē, ˌes-(ˌ)kā-\ *n* : one that has escaped esp. from prison

escape velocity *n* : the minimum velocity needed by a body (as a rocket) to escape from the gravitational field of a celestial body (as the earth)

es·cap·ism \is-'kā-ˌpi-zəm\ *n* : diversion of the mind to imaginative activity as an escape from routine — **es·cap·ist** \-pist\ *adj or n*

es·ca·role \'es-kə-ˌrōl\ *n* : ENDIVE 1

es·carp·ment \es-'kärp-mənt\ *n* **1** : a steep slope in front of a fortification **2** : a long cliff

es·chew \is-'chü\ *vb* : SHUN, AVOID

¹**es·cort** \'es-ˌkȯrt\ *n* : one (as a person or warship) accompanying another esp. as a protection or courtesy

²**es·cort** \is-'kȯrt, es-\ *vb* : to accompany as an escort

es·crow \'es-ˌkrō\ *n* : something (as a deed or a sum of money) delivered by one person to another to be delivered to a third party only upon the fulfillment of a condition; *also* : a fund or deposit serving as an escrow

es·cu·do \is-'kü-dō\ *n, pl* **-dos 1** — see MONEY table **2** : the peso of Guinea-Bissau

es·cutch·eon \is-'kə-chən\ *n* : the usu. shield≠shaped surface on which a coat of arms is shown

Esd *abbr* Esdras

Es·dras \'ez-drəs\ *n* — see BIBLE table

ESE *abbr* east-southeast

Es·ki·mo \'es-kə-ˌmō\ *n* **1** : a member of a group of peoples of northern Canada, Greenland, Alaska, and eastern Siberia **2** : any of the languages of the Eskimo peoples

Eskimo dog *n* : a sled dog of American origin

ESL *abbr* English as a second language

esoph·a·gus \i-'sä-fə-gəs\ *n, pl* **-gi** \-ˌgī, -ˌjī\ : a muscular tube that leads from the cavity behind the mouth to the stomach — **esoph·a·geal** \-ˌsä-fə-'jē-əl\ *adj*

es·o·ter·ic \ˌe-sə-'ter-ik\ *adj* **1** : designed for or understood only by the specially initiated **2** : PRIVATE, SECRET

esp *abbr* especially

ESP \ˌē-(ˌ)es-'pē\ *n* : EXTRASENSORY PERCEPTION

es·pa·drille \'es-pə-ˌdril\ *n* [F] : a flat sandal usu. having a fabric upper and a flexible sole

es·pal·ier \is-'pal-yər, -ˌyā\ *n* : a plant (as a fruit tree) trained to grow flat against a support — **espalier** *vb*

es·pe·cial \is-'pe-shəl\ *adj* : SPECIAL, PARTICULAR — **es·pe·cial·ly** *adv*

Es·pe·ran·to \ˌes-pə-'ran-tō, -'rän-\ *n* : an artificial international language based esp. on words common to the chief European languages

es·pi·o·nage \'es-pē-ə-ˌnäzh, -nij\ *n* [F *espionnage*] : the practice of spying

es·pla·nade \'es-plə-ˌnäd\ *n* : a level open stretch or area; *esp* : one for walking or driving along a shore

es·pous·al \i-'spaú-zəl\ *n* **1** : BETROTHAL; *also* : WEDDING **2** : a taking up (as of a cause) as a supporter — **es·pouse** \i-'spaúz\ *vb*

espres·so \e-'spre-sō\ *n, pl* **-sos** [It ⟨*caffè*⟩ *espresso*, lit., pressed out coffee] : coffee brewed by forcing steam through finely ground darkly roasted coffee beans

es·prit \i-'sprē\ *n* : sprightly wit

es·prit de corps \i-ˌsprē-də-'kȯr\ *n* [F] : the common spirit existing in the members of a group

es·py \i-'spī\ *vb* **es·pied; es·py·ing** : to catch sight of **syn** behold, see, view, descry

Esq *or* **Esqr** *abbr* esquire

es·quire \'es-ˌkwīr\ *n* [ME, fr. MF *esquier* squire, fr.

LL *scutarius,* fr. L *scutum* shield] **1** : a man of the English gentry ranking next below a knight **2** : a candidate for knighthood serving as attendant to a knight **3** — used as a title of courtesy

-ess \əs, ˌes\ *n suffix* : female ⟨author*ess*⟩

¹**es•say** \e-ˈsā, ˈe-ˌsā\ *vb* : ATTEMPT, TRY

²**es•say** *n* **1** \ˈe-ˌsā, e-ˈsā\ : ATTEMPT **2** \ˈe-ˌsā\ : a literary composition usu. dealing with a subject from a limited or personal point of view — **es•say•ist** \ˈe-ˌsā-ist\ *n*

es•sence \ˈes-ᵊns\ *n* **1** : fundamental nature or quality **2** : a substance distilled or extracted from another substance (as a plant or drug) and having the special qualities of the original substance **3** : PERFUME

¹**es•sen•tial** \i-ˈsen-chəl\ *adj* **1** : of, relating to, or constituting an essence ⟨voting is an ∼ right of citizenship⟩ ⟨∼ oils⟩ **2** : of the utmost importance : INDISPENSABLE **syn** imperative, necessary, necessitous — **es•sen•tial•ly** *adv*

²**essential** *n* : something essential

est *abbr* **1** established **2** estimate; estimated

EST *abbr* eastern standard time

¹**-est** \əst, ist\ *adj suffix or adv suffix* — used to form the superlative degree of adjectives and adverbs of one or two syllables ⟨fatt*est*⟩ ⟨lat*est*⟩ ⟨lucki*est*⟩ ⟨often*est*⟩ and less often of longer ones

²**-est** \əst, ist\ *or* **-st** \st\ *vb suffix* — used to form the archaic second person singular of English verbs (with *thou*) ⟨did*st*⟩

es•tab•lish \i-ˈsta-blish\ *vb* **1** : to institute permanently ⟨∼ a law⟩ **2** : FOUND ⟨∼ a settlement⟩; *also* : EFFECT **3** : to make firm or stable **4** : to put on a firm basis : SET UP ⟨∼ a son in business⟩ **5** : to gain acceptance or recognition of ⟨the movie ∼*ed* her as a star⟩; *also* : PROVE

es•tab•lish•ment \-mənt\ *n* **1** : something established **2** : a place of residence or business with its furnishings and staff **3** : an established ruling or controlling group ⟨the literary ∼⟩ **4** : the act or state of establishing or being established

es•tate \i-ˈstāt\ *n* **1** : STATE, CONDITION; *also* : social standing : STATUS **2** : a social or political class ⟨the three ∼s of nobility, clergy, and commons⟩ **3** : a person's possessions : FORTUNE **4** : a landed property

¹**es•teem** \i-ˈstēm\ *n* : high regard

²**esteem** *vb* **1** : REGARD **2** : to set a high value on **syn** respect, admire, revere

es•ter \ˈes-tər\ *n* : an often fragrant organic compound formed by the reaction of an acid and an alcohol

Esth *abbr* Esther

Es•ther \ˈes-tər\ *n* — see BIBLE table

esthete, esthetic, esthetics *var of* AESTHETE, AESTHETIC, AESTHETICS

es•ti•ma•ble \ˈes-tə-mə-bəl\ *adj* : worthy of esteem

¹**es•ti•mate** \ˈes-tə-ˌmāt\ *vb* **-mat•ed; -mat•ing** **1** : to give or form an approximation (as of value, size, or cost) **2** : JUDGE, CONCLUDE **syn** evaluate, value, rate, appraise, assay, assess — **es•ti•ma•tor** \-ˌmā-tər\ *n*

²**es•ti•mate** \ˈes-tə-mət\ *n* **1** : OPINION, JUDGMENT **2** : a rough or approximate calculation **3** : a statement of the cost of work to be done

es•ti•ma•tion \ˌes-tə-ˈmā-shən\ *n* **1** : JUDGMENT, OPINION **2** : ESTIMATE **3** : ESTEEM, HONOR

es•ti•vate \ˈes-tə-ˌvāt\ *vb* **-vat•ed; -vat•ing** : to pass the summer in an inactive or resting state — **es•ti•va•tion** \ˌes-tə-ˈvā-shən\ *n*

Es•to•nian \e-ˈstō-nē-ən\ *n* : a native or inhabitant of Estonia — **Estonian** *adj*

es•trange \i-ˈstrānj\ *vb* **es•tranged; es•trang•ing** : to alienate the affections or confidence of — **es•trange•ment** *n*

es•tro•gen \ˈes-trə-jən\ *n* : a substance (as a sex hormone) that tends to cause estrus and the development of female secondary sex characteristics — **es•tro•gen•ic** \ˌes-trə-ˈje-nik\ *adj*

estrous cycle *n* : the cycle of changes in the endocrine and reproductive systems of a female mammal from the beginning of one period of estrus to the beginning of the next

es•trus \ˈes-trəs\ *n* : a periodic state of sexual excitability during which the female of most mammals is willing to mate with the male and is capable of becoming pregnant : HEAT — **es•trous** \-trəs\ *adj*

es•tu•ary \ˈes-chù-ˌwer-ē\ *n, pl* **-ar•ies** : an arm of the sea at the mouth of a river

ET *abbr* eastern time

eta \ˈā-tə\ *n* : the 7th letter of the Greek alphabet — H or η

ETA *abbr* estimated time of arrival

et al \et-ˈal\ *abbr* [L *et alii* (masc.), *et aliae* (fem.), or *et alia* (neut.)] and others

etc *abbr* et cetera

et cet•era \et-ˈse-tə-rə, -ˈse-trə\ [L] and others esp. of the same kind

etch \ˈech\ *vb* [D *etsen,* fr. G *ätzen* to etch, corrode, fr. OHG *azzen* to feed] **1** : to produce (as a design) on a hard material by corroding its surface (as by acid) **2** : to delineate clearly — **etch•er** *n*

etch•ing *n* **1** : the action, process, or art of etching **2** : a design produced ones or print made from an etched plate

ETD *abbr* estimated time of departure

eter•nal \i-ˈtərn-ᵊl\ *adj* : EVERLASTING, PERPETUAL — **eter•nal•ly** *adv*

eter•ni•ty \i-ˈtər-nə-tē\ *n, pl* **-ties** **1** : infinite duration **2** : IMMORTALITY

¹**-eth** \əth, ith\ *or* **-th** \th\ *vb suffix* — used to form the archaic third person singular present of verbs ⟨do*th*⟩

²**-eth** — see ²-TH

eth•ane \ˈe-ˌthān\ *n* : a colorless odorless gaseous hydrocarbon found in natural gas and used esp. as a fuel

eth•a•nol \ˈe-thə-ˌnȯl\ *n* : ALCOHOL 1

ether \ˈē-thər\ *n* **1** : the upper regions of space; *also* : the gaseous element formerly held to fill these regions **2** : a light flammable liquid used as an anesthetic and solvent

ethe•re•al \i-ˈthir-ē-əl\ *adj* **1** : CELESTIAL, HEAVENLY **2** : exceptionally delicate : AIRY, DAINTY — **ethe•re•al•ly** *adv* — **ethe•re•al•ness** *n*

eth•i•cal \ˈe-thi-kəl\ *adj* **1** : of or relating to ethics **2** : conforming to accepted and esp. professional standards of conduct **syn** virtuous, moral, principled — **eth•i•cal•ly** *adv*

eth•ics \ˈe-thiks\ *n sing or pl* **1** : a discipline dealing with good and evil and with moral duty **2** : moral principles or practice

Ethi•o•pi•an \ˌē-thē-ˈō-pē-ən\ *n* : a native or inhabitant of Ethiopia — **Ethiopian** *adj*

¹**eth•nic** \ˈeth-nik\ *adj* [ME, heathen, fr. LL *ethnicus,* fr. Gk *ethnikos* national, gentile, fr. *ethnos* nation, people] : of or relating to races or large groups of people classed according to common traits and customs — **eth•ni•cal•ly** *adv*

²**ethnic** *n* : a member of a minority ethnic group who retains its customs, language, or social views

eth•nol•o•gy \eth-ˈnä-lə-jē\ *n* : a science dealing with the races of human beings, their origin, distribution, characteristics, and relations — **eth•no•log•i•cal** \ˌeth-nə-ˈlä-ji-kəl\ *adj* — **eth•nol•o•gist** \eth-ˈnä-lə-jist\ *n*

ethol•o•gy \ē-ˈthä-lə-jē\ *n* : the scientific and objective study of animal behavior — **etho•log•i•cal** \ˌē-thə-ˈlä-ji-kəl, ˌe-\ *adj* — **ethol•o•gist** \ē-ˈthä-lə-jist\ *n*

ethos \ˈē-ˌthäs\ *n* : the distinguishing character, sentiment, moral nature, or guiding beliefs of a person, group, or institution

ethyl alcohol *n* : ALCOHOL 1

eth•yl•ene \ˈe-thə-ˌlēn\ *n* : a colorless flammable gas found in coal gas or obtained from petroleum

eti•ol•o•gy \ˌē-tē-ˈä-lə-jē\ *n* : the causes of a disease or abnormal condition; *also* : a branch of medicine concerned with the causes and origins of diseases — **eti-**

o·log·ic \ˌē-tē-ə-'lä-jik\ *or* eti·o·log·i·cal \-ji-kəl\ *adj*

et·i·quette \'e-ti-kət, -ˌket\ *n* [F *étiquette*, lit., ticket] : the forms prescribed by custom or authority to be observed in social, official, or professional life **syn** propriety, decorum, decency, dignity

Etrus·can \i-'trəs-kən\ *n* **1** : the language of the Etruscans **2** : an inhabitant of ancient Etruria — **Etruscan** *adj*

et seq *abbr* [L *et sequens*] and the following one; [L *et sequentes* (masc. & fem. pl.) *or et sequentia* (neut. pl.)] and the following ones

-ette \'et, ˌet, ət, it\ *n suffix* **1** : little one ⟨din*ette*⟩ **2** : female ⟨usher*ette*⟩

étude \'ā-ˌtüd, -ˌtyüd\ *n* [F, lit., study] : a musical composition for practice to develop technical skill

et·y·mol·o·gy \ˌe-tə-'mä-lə-jē\ *n, pl* -gies **1** : the history of a linguistic form (as a word) shown by tracing its development and relationships **2** : a branch of linguistics dealing with etymologies — et·y·mo·log·i·cal \-mə-'lä-ji-kəl\ *adj* — et·y·mol·o·gist \-'mä-lə-jist\ *n*

Eu *symbol* europium

eu·ca·lyp·tus \ˌyü-kə-'lip-təs\ *n, pl* -ti \-ˌtī\ *or* -tus·es : any of a genus of mostly Australian evergreen trees widely grown for shade or their wood, oils, resins, and gums

Eu·cha·rist \'yü-kə-rəst\ *n* : COMMUNION 2 — eu·cha·ris·tic \ˌyü-kə-'ris-tik\ *adj, often cap*

¹eu·chre \'yü-kər\ *n* : a card game in which the side naming the trump must take three of five tricks to win

²euchre *vb* eu·chred; eu·chring : CHEAT, TRICK

eu·clid·e·an *also* eu·clid·i·an \yü-'kli-dē-ən\ *adj, often cap* : of or relating to the geometry of Euclid or a geometry based on similar axioms

eu·gen·ics \yü-'je-niks\ *n* : a science dealing with the improvement (as by selective breeding) of hereditary qualities esp. of human beings — eu·gen·ic \-nik\ *adj*

eu·lo·gy \'yü-lə-jē\ *n, pl* -gies **1** : a speech in praise of some person or thing **2** : high praise — eu·lo·gis·tic \ˌyü-lə-'jis-tik\ *adj* — eu·lo·gize \'yü-lə-ˌjīz\ *vb*

eu·nuch \'yü-nək\ *n* : a castrated man

eu·phe·mism \'yü-fə-ˌmi-zəm\ *n* [Gk *euphēmismos*, fr. *euphēmos* auspicious, sounding good, fr. *eu*- good + *phēmē* speech] : the substitution of a mild or pleasant expression for one offensive or unpleasant; *also* : the expression substituted — eu·phe·mis·tic \ˌyü-fə-'mis-tik\ *adj*

eu·pho·ni·ous \yü-'fō-nē-əs\ *adj* : pleasing to the ear — eu·pho·ni·ous·ly *adv*

eu·pho·ny \'yü-fə-nē\ *n, pl* -nies : the effect produced by words so combined as to please the ear

eu·pho·ria \yü-'fōr-ē-ə\ *n* : a marked feeling of well-being or elation — eu·phor·ic \-'fòr-ik\ *adj*

Eur *abbr* Europe; European

Eur·asian \yü-'rā-zhən, -shən\ *adj* **1** : of mixed European and Asian origin **2** : of or relating to Europe and Asia — Eurasian *n*

eu·re·ka \yü-'rē-kə\ *interj* [Gk *heurēka* I have found, fr. *heuriskein* to find; fr. the exclamation attributed to Archimedes on discovering a method for determining the purity of gold] — used to express triumph on a discovery

Eu·ro·bond \'yür-ō-ˌbänd\ *n* : a bond of a U.S. corporation that is sold outside the U.S. but that is valued and paid for in dollars and yields interest in dollars

Eu·ro·cur·ren·cy \ˌyür-ō-'kər-ən-sē\ *n* : moneys (as of the U.S. and Japan) held outside their countries of origin and used in the money markets of Europe

Eu·ro·dol·lar \'yür-ō-ˌdä-lər\ *n* : a U.S. dollar held as Eurocurrency

Eu·ro·pe·an \ˌyür-ə-'pē-ən\ *n* **1** : a native or inhabitant of Europe **2** : a person of European descent — European *adj*

European plan *n* : a hotel plan whereby the daily rates cover only the cost of the room

eu·ro·pi·um \yü-'rō-pē-əm\ *n* : a rare metallic chemical element — see ELEMENT table

eu·sta·chian tube \yü-'stā-shən-\ *n, often cap E* : a tube connecting the inner cavity of the ear with the throat and equalizing air pressure on both sides of the eardrum

eu·tha·na·sia \ˌyü-thə-'nā-zhə\ *n* [Gk, easy death, fr. *eu*- good + *thanatos* death] : MERCY KILLING

EVA *abbr* extravehicular activity

evac·u·ate \i-'va-kyə-ˌwāt\ *vb* -at·ed; -at·ing **1** : EMPTY **2** : to discharge wastes from the body **3** : to remove or withdraw from : VACATE — evac·u·a·tion \-ˌva-kyə-'wā-shən\ *n*

evac·u·ee \i-ˌva-kyə-'wē\ *n* : a person removed from a dangerous place

evade \i-'vād\ *vb* evad·ed; evad·ing : to manage to avoid esp. by dexterity or slyness : ELUDE, ESCAPE

eval·u·ate \i-'val-yü-ˌwāt\ *vb* -at·ed; -at·ing : APPRAISE, VALUE — eval·u·a·tion \-ˌval-yü-'wā-shən\ *n*

ev·a·nes·cent \ˌe-və-'nes-ᵊnt\ *adj* : tending to vanish like vapor **syn** passing, transient, transitory, momentary — ev·a·nes·cence \-ᵊns\ *n*

evan·gel·i·cal \ˌē-ˌvan-'je-li-kəl, ˌe-vən-\ *adj* [LL *evangelium* gospel, fr. Gk *evangelion*, fr. *eu*- good + *angelos* messenger] **1** : of or relating to the Christian gospel esp. as presented in the four Gospels **2** : of or relating to certain Protestant churches emphasizing the authority of Scripture and the importance of preaching as contrasted with ritual **3** : ZEALOUS ⟨∼ fervor⟩ — Evangelical *n* — Evan·gel·i·cal·ism \-kə-ˌli-zəm\ *n* — evan·gel·i·cal·ly *adv*

evan·ge·lism \i-'van-jə-ˌli-zəm\ *n* **1** : the winning or revival of personal commitments to Christ **2** : militant or crusading zeal — evan·ge·lis·tic \-ˌvan-jə-'lis-tik\ *adj* — evan·ge·lis·ti·cal·ly *adv*

evan·ge·list \i-'van-jə-list\ *n* **1** *often cap* : the writer of any of the four Gospels **2** : a person who evangelizes; *esp* : a Protestant minister or layman who preaches at special services

evan·ge·lize \i-'van-jə-ˌlīz\ *vb* -lized; -liz·ing **1** : to preach the gospel **2** : to convert to Christianity

evap *abbr* evaporate

evap·o·rate \i-'va-pə-ˌrāt\ *vb* -rat·ed; -rat·ing **1** : to pass off or cause to pass off in vapor **2** : to disappear quickly **3** : to drive out the moisture from (as by heat) — evap·o·ra·tion \-ˌva-pə-'rā-shən\ *n* — evap·o·ra·tor \-ˌrā-tər\ *n*

evap·o·rite \i-'va-pə-ˌrīt\ *n* : a sedimentary rock that originates by the evaporation of seawater in an enclosed basin

eva·sion \i-'vā-zhən\ *n* **1** : a means of evading **2** : an act or instance of evading — eva·sive \i-'vā-siv\ *adj* — eva·sive·ness *n*

eve \'ēv\ *n* **1** : EVENING **2** : the period just before some important event

¹even \'ē-vən\ *adj* **1** : LEVEL, FLAT **2** : REGULAR, SMOOTH **3** : EQUAL, FAIR **4** : BALANCED; *also* : fully revenged **5** : divisible by two **6** : EXACT — even·ly *adv* — even·ness *n*

²even *adv* **1** : EXACTLY, PRECISELY **2** : FULLY, QUITE **3** : at the very time **4** — used as an intensive to stress identity ⟨∼ I know that⟩ **5** — used as an intensive to emphasize something extreme or highly unlikely ⟨so simple ∼ a child can do it⟩ **6** — used as an intensive to stress the comparative degree ⟨did ∼ better⟩ **7** — used as an intensive to indicate a small or minimum degree ⟨didn't ∼ try⟩

³even *vb* : to make or become even

even·hand·ed \ˌē-vən-'han-dəd\ *adj* : FAIR, IMPARTIAL — even·hand·ed·ly *adv*

eve·ning \'ēv-niŋ\ *n* **1** : the end of the day and early part of the night **2** *chiefly Southern & Midland* : AFTERNOON

evening primrose *n* : a coarse biennial herb with yellow flowers that open in the evening

evening star *n* : a bright planet (as Venus) seen esp. in the western sky at or after sunset

even·song \'ē-vən-ˌsȯŋ\ *n, often cap* **1** : VESPERS **2** : evening prayer esp. when sung

event \i-'vent\ *n* [MF or L; MF, fr. L *eventus*, fr. *eve-nire* to happen, fr. *venire* to come] **1** : OCCURRENCE **2** : a noteworthy happening **3** : CONTINGENCY ⟨in the ∼ of rain⟩ **4** : a contest in a program of sports — **event·ful** *adj*

even·tide \'ē-vən-ˌtīd\ *n* : EVENING

even·tu·al \i-'ven-chù-wəl\ *adj* : coming at some later time : ULTIMATE — **even·tu·al·ly** *adv*

even·tu·al·i·ty \i-ˌven-chù-'wa-lə-tē\ *n, pl* **-ties** : a possible event or outcome

even·tu·ate \i-'ven-chù-ˌwāt\ *vb* **-at·ed; -at·ing** : to result finally

ev·er \'e-vər\ *adv* **1**·: ALWAYS **2** : at any time **3** : in any way : AT ALL

ev·er·glade \'e-vər-ˌglād\ *n* : a low-lying tract of swampy or marshy land

ev·er·green \-ˌgrēn\ *adj* : having foliage that remains green ⟨most coniferous trees are ∼⟩ — **evergreen** *n*

¹ev·er·last·ing \ˌe-vər-'las-tiŋ\ *adj* **1** : enduring forever : ETERNAL **2** : having or being flowers or foliage that retain form or color for a long time when dried — **ev·er·last·ing·ly** *adv*

²everlasting *n* **1** : ETERNITY ⟨from ∼⟩ **2** : a plant with everlasting flowers; *also* : its flower

ev·er·more \ˌe-vər-'mȯr\ *adv* : FOREVER

ev·ery \'ev-rē\ *adj* **1** : being each one of a group **2** : all possible ⟨given ∼ chance⟩; *also* : COMPLETE ⟨have ∼ confidence⟩

ev·ery·body \'ev-ri-ˌbä-dē, -bə-\ *pron* : every person

ev·ery·day \'ev-rē-ˌdā\ *adj* : encountered or used routinely : ORDINARY

ev·ery·one \-(ˌ)wən\ *pron* : EVERYBODY

ev·ery·thing \'ev-rē-ˌthiŋ\ *pron* **1** : all that exists **2** : all that is relevant

ev·ery·where \'ev-rē-ˌhwer\ *adv* : in every place or part

evg *abbr* evening

evict \i-'vikt\ *vb* **1** : to put (a person) out from a property by legal process **2** : EXPEL **syn** eject, oust, dismiss — **evic·tion** \-'vik-shən\ *n*

ev·i·dence \'e-və-dəns\ *n* **1** : an outward sign **2** : PROOF, TESTIMONY; *esp* : matter submitted in court to determine the truth of alleged facts

ev·i·dent \-dənt\ *adj* : clear to the vision and understanding **syn** manifest, distinct, obvious, apparent, plain

ev·i·dent·ly \'e-və-dənt-lē, ˌe-və-'dent-\ *adv* **1** : in an evident manner **2** : on the basis of available evidence

¹evil \'ē-vəl\ *adj* **evil·er** *or* **evil·ler; evil·est** *or* **evil·lest** **1** : WICKED **2** : causing or threatening distress or harm : PERNICIOUS — **evil·ly** *adv*

²evil *n* **1** : the fact of suffering, misfortune, and wrongdoing **2** : a source of sorrow or distress

evil·do·er \ˌē-vəl-'dü-ər\ *n* : one who does evil

evil–mind·ed \-'mīn-dəd\ *adj* : having an evil disposition or evil thoughts — **evil–mind·ed·ly** *adv*

evince \i-'vins\ *vb* **evinced; evinc·ing** : SHOW, REVEAL

evis·cer·ate \i-'vi-sə-ˌrāt\ *vb* **-at·ed; -at·ing 1** : to remove the entrails of **2** : to deprive of vital content or force — **evis·cer·a·tion** \-ˌvi-sə-'rā-shən\ *n*

evoke \i-'vōk\ *vb* **evoked; evok·ing** : to call forth or up — **evo·ca·tion** \ˌē-vō-'kā-shən, ˌe-və-\ *n* — **evoc·a·tive** \i-'vä-kə-tiv\ *adj*

evo·lu·tion \ˌe-və-'lü-shən\ *n* **1** : one of a set of prescribed movements (as in a dance) **2** : a process of change in a particular direction **3** : a theory that the various kinds of plants and animals are descended from other kinds that lived in earlier times and that the differences are due to inherited changes that occurred over many generations — **evo·lu·tion·ary** \-shə-ˌner-ē\ *adj* — **evo·lu·tion·ist** \-shə-nist\ *n*

evolve \i-'välv\ *vb* **evolved; evolv·ing** [L *evolvere* to unroll] : to develop or change by or as if by evolution

EW *abbr* enlisted woman

ewe \'yü\ *n* : a female sheep

ew·er \'yü-ər\ *n* : a water pitcher

¹ex \'eks\ *prep* [L] : out of : FROM

²ex *n* : a former spouse

³ex *abbr* **1** example **2** express **3** extra

Ex *abbr* Exodus

ex- \e *also occurs in this prefix where only* i *is shown below (as in* "express") *and* ks *sometimes occurs where only* gz *is shown (as in* "exact")\ *prefix* **1** : out of : outside **2** : former ⟨*ex*-president⟩

ex·ac·er·bate \ig-'za-sər-ˌbāt\ *vb* **-bat·ed; -bat·ing** : to make more violent, bitter, or severe — **ex·ac·er·ba·tion** \-ˌza-sər-'bā-shən\ *n*

¹ex·act \ig-'zakt\ *vb* **1** : to compel to furnish **2** : to call for as suitable or necessary — **ex·ac·tion** \-'zak-shən\ *n*

²exact *adj* : precisely accurate or correct — **ex·act·ly** *adv* — **ex·act·ness** *n*

ex·act·ing \ig-'zak-tiŋ\ *adj* **1** : greatly demanding ⟨an ∼ taskmaster⟩ **2** : requiring close attention and precision

ex·ac·ti·tude \ig-'zak-tə-ˌtüd, -ˌtyüd\ *n* : the quality or state of being exact

ex·ag·ger·ate \ig-'za-jə-ˌrāt\ *vb* **-at·ed; -at·ing** [L *exaggeratus*, pp. of *exaggerare*, lit., to heap up, fr. *agger* heap] : to enlarge (as a statement) beyond normal : OVERSTATE — **ex·ag·ger·at·ed·ly** *adv* — **ex·ag·ger·a·tion** \-ˌza-jə-'rā-shən\ *n* — **ex·ag·ger·a·tor** \-'za-jə-ˌrā-tər\ *n*

ex·alt \ig-'zȯlt\ *vb* **1** : to raise up esp. in rank, power, or dignity **2** : GLORIFY — **ex·al·ta·tion** \ˌeg-ˌzȯl-'tā-shən, ˌek-ˌsȯl-\ *n*

ex·am \ig-'zam\ *n* : EXAMINATION

ex·am·ine \ig-'za-mən\ *vb* **ex·am·ined; ex·am·in·ing 1** : to inspect closely **2** : QUESTION; *esp* : to test by questioning **syn** interrogate, query, quiz, catechize — **ex·am·i·na·tion** \-ˌza-mə-'nā-shən\ *n*

ex·am·ple \ig-'zam-pəl\ *n* **1** : something forming a model to be followed or avoided **2** : a representative sample **3** : a problem to be solved in order to show the application of some rule

ex·as·per·ate \ig-'zas-pə-ˌrāt\ *vb* **-at·ed; -at·ing** : VEX, IRRITATE — **ex·as·per·a·tion** \ig-ˌzas-pə-'rā-shən\ *n*

exc *abbr* **1** excellent **2** except

ex·ca·vate \'ek-skə-ˌvāt\ *vb* **-vat·ed; -vat·ing 1** : to hollow out; *also* : to form by hollowing out **2** : to dig out and remove (as earth) **3** : to reveal to view by digging away a covering — **ex·ca·va·tion** \ˌek-skə-'vā-shən\ *n* — **ex·ca·va·tor** \'ek-skə-ˌvā-tər\ *n*

ex·ceed \ik-'sēd\ *vb* **1** : to go or be beyond the limit of **2** : SURPASS

ex·ceed·ing·ly \-'sē-diŋ-lē\ *also* **ex·ceed·ing** *adv* : EXTREMELY, VERY

ex·cel \ik-'sel\ *vb* **ex·celled; ex·cel·ling** : SURPASS, OUTDO

ex·cel·lence \'ek-sə-ləns\ *n* **1** : the quality of being excellent **2** : an excellent or valuable quality : VIRTUE **3** : EXCELLENCY **2**

ex·cel·len·cy \-lən-sē\ *n, pl* **-cies 1** : EXCELLENCE **2** — used as a title of honor

ex·cel·lent \-lənt\ *adj* : very good of its kind : FIRST-CLASS — **ex·cel·lent·ly** *adv*

ex·cel·si·or \ik-'sel-sē-ər\ *n* : fine curled wood shavings used esp. for packing fragile items

¹ex·cept \ik-'sept\ *also* **ex·cept·ing** *prep* : with the exclusion or exception of ⟨daily ∼ Sundays⟩

²except *vb* **1** : to take or leave out **2** : OBJECT

³except *also* **excepting** *conj* **1** : UNLESS ⟨∼ you repent⟩ **2** : ONLY ⟨I'd go, ∼ it's too far⟩

ex·cep·tion \ik-'sep-shən\ *n* **1** : the act of excepting **2** : something excepted **3** : OBJECTION

ex·cep·tion·able \ik-'sep-shə-nə-bəl\ *adj* : OBJECTIONABLE

ex·cep·tion·al \ik-'sep-shə-nəl\ *adj* **1** : UNUSUAL **2** : SUPERIOR — **ex·cep·tion·al·ly** *adv*

ex·cerpt \'ek-ˌsərpt, 'eg-ˌzərpt\ *n* : a passage selected or copied : EXTRACT — **excerpt** \ek-ˈsərpt, eg-ˈzərpt; ˈek-ˌsərpt, ˈeg-ˌzərpt\ *vb*

ex·cess \ik-ˈses, ˈek-ˌses\ *n* **1** : SUPERFLUITY, SURPLUS **2** : the amount by which one quantity exceeds another **3** : INTEMPERANCE; *also* : an instance of intemperance — **excess** *adj* — **ex·ces·sive** \ik-ˈse-siv\ *adj* — **ex·ces·sive·ly** *adv*

exch *abbr* exchange; exchanged

¹**ex·change** \iks-ˈchānj\ *n* **1** : the giving or taking of one thing in return for another : TRADE **2** : a substituting of one thing for another **3** : interchange of valuables and esp. of bills of exchange or money of different countries **4** : a place where things and services are exchanged; *esp* : a marketplace for securities **5** : a central office in which telephone lines are connected for communication

²**exchange** *vb* **ex·changed; ex·chang·ing** : to transfer in return for some equivalent : BARTER, SWAP — **ex·change·able** \iks-ˈchān-jə-bəl\ *adj*

ex·che·quer \ˈeks-ˌche-kər\ *n* [ME *escheker*, fr. OF *eschequier* chessboard, counting table] : TREASURY; *esp* : a national treasury

ex·cise \ˈek-ˌsīz\ *n* : a tax on the manufacture, sale, or consumption of a commodity

ex·ci·sion \ik-ˈsi-zhən\ *n* : removal by or as if by cutting out esp. by surgical means — **ex·cise** \ik-ˈsīz\ *vb*

ex·cit·able \ik-ˈsī-tə-bəl\ *adj* : easily excited — **ex·cit·abil·i·ty** \-ˌsī-tə-ˈbi-lə-tē\ *n*

ex·cite \ik-ˈsīt\ *vb* **ex·cit·ed; ex·cit·ing 1** : to stir up the emotions of : ROUSE **2** : to increase the activity of : STIMULATE **syn** provoke, pique, quicken — **ex·ci·ta·tion** \ek-ˌsī-ˈtā-shən, ˌek-sə-\ *n* — **ex·cit·ed·ly** *adv* — **ex·cit·ing·ly** *adv*

ex·cite·ment \ik-ˈsīt-mənt\ *n* : AGITATION, STIR

ex·claim \iks-ˈklām\ *vb* : to cry out, speak, or utter sharply or vehemently — **ex·cla·ma·tion** \ˌeks-klə-ˈmā-shən\ *n* — **ex·clam·a·to·ry** \iks-ˈkla-mə-ˌtōr-ē\ *adj*

exclamation point *n* : a punctuation mark ! used esp. after an interjection or exclamation

ex·clude \iks-ˈklüd\ *vb* **ex·clud·ed; ex·clud·ing 1** : to prevent from using or participating : BAR **2** : to put out : EXPEL — **ex·clu·sion** \-ˈklü-zhən\ *n*

ex·clu·sive \iks-ˈklü-siv\ *adj* **1** : reserved for particular persons **2** : snobbishly aloof; *also* : STYLISH **3** : SOLE ⟨~ rights⟩; *also* : UNDIVIDED **syn** chic, modish, smart, swank, fashionable — **exclusive** *n* — **ex·clu·sive·ly** *adv* — **ex·clu·sive·ness** *n* — **ex·clu·siv·i·ty** \ˌeks-ˌklü-si-və-tē, iks-, -zi-\ *n*

exclusive of *prep* : not taking into account

ex·cog·i·tate \ek-ˈskä-jə-ˌtāt\ *vb* : to think out : DEVISE

ex·com·mu·ni·cate \ˌeks-kə-ˈmyü-nə-ˌkāt\ *vb* : to cut off officially from the rites of the church — **ex·com·mu·ni·ca·tion** \-ˌmyü-nə-ˈkā-shən\ *n*

ex·co·ri·ate \ek-ˈskōr-ē-ˌāt\ *vb* **-at·ed; -at·ing** : to criticize severely — **ex·co·ri·a·tion** \(ˌ)ek-ˌskōr-ē-ˈā-shən\ *n*

ex·cre·ment \ˈek-skrə-mənt\ *n* : waste discharged from the body and esp. from the alimentary canal — **ex·cre·men·tal** \ˌek-skrə-ˈmen-tᵊl\ *adj*

ex·cres·cence \ik-ˈskres-ᵊns\ *n* : OUTGROWTH; *esp* : an abnormal outgrowth (as a wart)

ex·cre·ta \ik-ˈskrē-tə\ *n pl* : waste matter separated or eliminated from an organism

ex·crete \ik-ˈskrēt\ *vb* **ex·cret·ed; ex·cret·ing** : to separate and eliminate wastes from the body esp. in urine or sweat — **ex·cre·tion** \-ˈskrē-shən\ *n* — **ex·cre·to·ry** \ˈek-skrə-ˌtōr-ē\ *adj*

ex·cru·ci·at·ing \ik-ˈskrü-shē-ˌā-tiŋ\ *adj* [L *excruciare*, fr. *cruciare* to crucify, fr. *crux* cross] : intensely painful or distressing **syn** agonizing, harrowing, torturous — **ex·cru·ci·at·ing·ly** *adv*

ex·cul·pate \ˈek-(ˌ)skəl-ˌpāt\ *vb* **-pat·ed; -pat·ing** : to clear from alleged fault or guilt **syn** absolve, exonerate, acquit, vindicate, clear

ex·cur·sion \ik-ˈskər-zhən\ *n* **1** : EXPEDITION; *esp* : a

pleasure trip **2** : DIGRESSION — **ex·cur·sion·ist** \-zhə-nist\ *n*

ex·cur·sive \-ˈskər-siv\ *adj* : constituting or characterized by digression

¹**ex·cuse** \ik-ˈskyüz\ *vb* **ex·cused; ex·cus·ing** [ME, fr. OF *excuser*, fr. L *excusare*, fr. *causa* cause, explanation] **1** : to make apology for **2** : PARDON **3** : to release from an obligation **4** : JUSTIFY — **ex·cus·able** *adj*

²**excuse** \ik-ˈskyüs\ *n* **1** : an act of excusing **2** : something that excuses or is a reason for excusing : JUSTIFICATION

exec *n* : EXECUTIVE

ex·e·cra·ble \ˈek-si-krə-bəl\ *adj* **1** : DETESTABLE **2** : very bad ⟨~ spelling⟩

ex·e·crate \ˈek-sə-ˌkrāt\ *vb* **-crat·ed; -crat·ing** [L *exsecratus*, pp. of *exsecrari* to put under a curse, fr. *ex-* out of + *sacer* sacred] : to denounce as evil or detestable; *also* : DETEST — **ex·e·cra·tion** \ˌek-sə-ˈkrā-shən\ *n*

ex·e·cute \ˈek-si-ˌkyüt\ *vb* **-cut·ed; -cut·ing 1** : to carry out fully : put completely into effect **2** : to do what is called for by (as a law) **3** : to put to death in accordance with a legal sentence **4** : to produce by carrying out a design **5** : to do what is needed to give validity to ⟨~ a deed⟩ — **ex·e·cu·tion** \ˌek-si-ˈkyü-shən\ *n* — **ex·e·cu·tion·er** *n*

¹**ex·ec·u·tive** \ig-ˈze-kyə-tiv\ *adj* **1** : of or relating to the enforcement of laws and the conduct of affairs **2** : designed for or related to carrying out plans or purposes

²**executive** *n* **1** : the branch of government with executive duties **2** : one having administrative or managerial responsibility

ex·ec·u·tor \ig-ˈze-kyə-tər\ *n* : the person named in a will to execute it

ex·ec·u·trix \ig-ˈze-kyə-ˌtriks\ *n, pl* **ex·ec·u·tri·ces** \-ˌze-kyə-ˈtrī-ˌsēz\ *or* **ex·ec·u·trix·es** \-ˈze-kyə-ˌtrik-səz\ : a woman who is an executor

ex·e·ge·sis \ˌek-sə-ˈjē-səs\ *n, pl* **-ge·ses** \-ˈjē-ˌsēz\ : explanation or critical interpretation of a text

ex·e·gete \ˈek-sə-ˌjēt\ *n* : one who practices exegesis — **ex·e·get·i·cal** \ˌek-sə-ˈje-ti-kəl\ *adj*

ex·em·plar \ig-ˈzem-ˌplär, -plər\ *n* **1** : one that serves as a model or example; *esp* : an ideal model **2** : a typical instance or example

ex·em·pla·ry \ig-ˈzem-plə-rē\ *adj* : serving as a pattern; *also* : COMMENDABLE

ex·em·pli·fy \ig-ˈzem-plə-ˌfī\ *vb* **-fied; -fy·ing** : to illustrate by example : serve as an example of — **ex·em·pli·fi·ca·tion** \-ˌzem-plə-fə-ˈkā-shən\ *n*

¹**ex·empt** \ig-ˈzempt\ *adj* : free from some liability to which others are subject

²**exempt** *vb* : to make exempt : EXCUSE — **ex·emp·tion** \ig-ˈzemp-shən\ *n*

¹**ex·er·cise** \ˈek-sər-ˌsīz\ *n* **1** : EMPLOYMENT, USE ⟨~ of authority⟩ **2** : exertion made for the sake of training or physical fitness **3** : a task or problem done to develop skill **4** *pl* : a public exhibition or ceremony

²**exercise** *vb* **-cised; -cis·ing 1** : EXERT ⟨~ control⟩ **2** : to train by or engage in exercise **3** : WORRY, DISTRESS — **ex·er·cis·er** *n*

ex·ert \ig-ˈzert\ *vb* : to bring or put into action ⟨~ influence⟩ ⟨~ed himself⟩ — **ex·er·tion** \-ˈzər-shən\ *n*

ex·hale \eks-ˈhāl\ *vb* **ex·haled; ex·hal·ing 1** : to breathe out **2** : to give or pass off in the form of vapor — **ex·ha·la·tion** \ˌeks-hə-ˈlā-shən\ *n*

¹**ex·haust** \ig-ˈzȯst\ *vb* **1** : to use up wholly **2** : to tire or wear out **3** : to draw off or let out completely; *also* : EMPTY **4** : to develop (a subject) completely

²**exhaust** *n* **1** : the escape of used vapor or gas from an engine; *also* : the gas that escapes **2** : a system of pipes through which exhaust escapes

ex·haus·tion \ig-ˈzȯs-chən\ *n* : extreme weariness : FATIGUE

ex·haus·tive \ig-ˈzȯ-stiv\ *adj* : covering all possibilities : THOROUGH — **ex·haus·tive·ly** *adv*

¹**ex·hib·it** \ig-ˈzi-bət\ *vb* **1** : to display esp. publicly **2** : to

present to a court in legal form **syn** display, show, parade, flaunt — **ex·hi·bi·tion** \ˌek-sə-ˈbi-shən\ *n* — **ex·hib·i·tor** \ig-ˈzi-bə-tər\ *n*

²**exhibit** *n* **1** : an act or instance of exhibiting; *also* : something exhibited **2** : something produced and identified in court for use as evidence

ex·hi·bi·tion·ism \ˌek-sə-ˈbi-shə-ˌni-zəm\ *n* **1** : a perversion marked by a tendency to indecent exposure **2** : the act or practice of behaving so as to attract attention to oneself — **ex·hi·bi·tion·ist** \-nist\ *n or adj*

ex·hil·a·rate \ig-ˈzi-lə-ˌrāt\ *vb* **-rat·ed; -rat·ing** : ENLIVEN, STIMULATE — **ex·hil·a·ra·tion** \-ˌzi-lə-ˈrā-shən\ *n*

ex·hort \ig-ˈzort\ *vb* : to urge, advise, or warn earnestly — **ex·hor·ta·tion** \ˌek-ˌsor-tā-shən, ˌeg-ˌzor-, -zər-\ *n*

ex·hume \ig-ˈzüm, iks-ˈhyüm\ *vb* **ex·humed; ex·huming** [F or ML; F *exhumer*, fr. ML *exhumare*, fr. L *ex* out of + *humus* earth] : DISINTER — **ex·hu·ma·tion** \ˌeks-hyü-ˈmā-shən, ˌeg-zü-\ *n*

ex·i·gen·cy \ˈek-sə-jən-sē, ig-ˈzi-jən-\ *n, pl* **-cies 1** *pl* : REQUIREMENTS **2** : urgent need — **ex·i·gent** \ˈek-sə-jənt\ *adj*

ex·ig·u·ous \ig-ˈzi-gyə-wəs\ *adj* : scanty in amount — **ex·i·gu·i·ty** \ˌeg-zi-ˈgyü-ə-tē\ *n*

¹**ex·ile** \ˈeg-ˌzīl, ˈek-ˌsīl\ *n* **1** : BANISHMENT; *also* : voluntary absence from one's country or home **2** : a person driven from his or her native place

²**exile** *vb* **ex·iled; ex·il·ing** : BANISH, EXPEL **syn** expatriate, deport, ostracize

ex·ist \ig-ˈzist\ *vb* **1** : to have being **2** : to continue to be : LIVE

ex·is·tence \ig-ˈzis-təns\ *n* **1** : continuance in living **2** : actual occurrence **3** : something existing — **ex·is·tent** \-tənt\ *adj*

ex·is·ten·tial \ˌeg-zis-ˈten-chəl, ˌek-sis-\ *adj* **1** : of or relating to existence **2** : EMPIRICAL **3** : having being in time and space **4** : of or relating to existentialism or existentialists

ex·is·ten·tial·ism \ˌeg-zis-ˈten-chə-ˌli-zəm\ *n* : a philosophy centered on individual existence and personal responsibility for acts of free will in the absence of certain knowledge of what is right or wrong — **ex·is·ten·tial·ist** \-list\ *adj or n*

ex·it \ˈeg-zət, ˈek-sət\ *n* **1** : a departure from a stage **2** : a going out or away; *also* : DEATH **3** : a way out of an enclosed space **4** : a point of departure from an expressway — **exit** *vb*

exo·bi·ol·o·gy \ˌek-sō-bī-ˈä-lə-jē\ *n* : biology concerned with life originating or existing outside the earth or its atmosphere — **exo·bi·ol·o·gist** \-jist\ *n*

exo·crine gland \ˈek-sə-krən-, -ˌkrīn-, -ˌkrēn-\ *n* : a gland (as a salivary gland) that releases a secretion externally by means of a canal or duct

Exod *abbr* Exodus

ex·o·dus \ˈek-sə-dəs\ *n* **1** *cap* — see BIBLE table **2** : a mass departure : EMIGRATION

ex of·fi·cio \ˌek-sə-ˈfi-shē-ˌō\ *adv or adj* : by virtue of or because of an office ⟨*ex officio* chairman⟩

ex·og·e·nous \ek-ˈsä-jə-nəs\ *adj* : caused or produced by factors outside the organism or system — **ex·og·e·nous·ly** *adv*

ex·on·er·ate \ig-ˈzä-nə-ˌrāt\ *vb* **-at·ed; -at·ing** [ME, fr. L *exoneratus*, pp. of *exonerare* to unburden, fr. *ex-* out + *onus* load] : to free from blame **syn** acquit, absolve, exculpate, vindicate — **ex·on·er·a·tion** \-ˌzä-nə-ˈrā-shən\ *n*

ex·or·bi·tant \ig-ˈzor-bə-tənt\ *adj* : exceeding what is usual or proper

ex·or·cise \ˈek-ˌsor-ˌsīz, -sər-\ *vb* **-cised; -cis·ing 1** : to get rid of by or as if by solemn command **2** : to free of an evil spirit — **ex·or·cism** \-ˌsi-zəm\ *n* — **ex·or·cist** \-ˌsist\ *n*

exo·sphere \ˈek-sō-ˌsfir\ *n* : the outermost region of the atmosphere

exo·ther·mic \ˌek-sō-ˈthər-mik\ *adj* : characterized by or formed with evolution of heat

ex·ot·ic \ig-ˈzä-tik\ *adj* **1** : introduced from another country **2** : strikingly, excitingly, or mysteriously different or unusual *n* — **exotic** *n* — **ex·ot·i·cal·ly** \-ti-k(ə-)lē\ *adv* — **ex·ot·i·cism** \-tə-ˌsi-zəm\ *n*

exp *abbr* **1** expense **2** experiment **3** export **4** express

ex·pand \ik-ˈspand\ *vb* **1** : to open up : UNFOLD **2** : ENLARGE **3** : to develop in detail **syn** amplify, swell, distend, inflate, dilate — **ex·pand·er** *n*

ex·panse \ik-ˈspans\ *n* : a broad extent (as of land or sea)

ex·pan·sion \ik-ˈspan-chən\ *n* **1** : the act or process of expanding **2** : the quality or state of being expanded **3** : an expanded part or thing

ex·pan·sive \ik-ˈspan-siv\ *adj* **1** : tending to expand or to cause expansion **2** : warmly benevolent, generous, or ready to talk **3** : of large extent or scope — **ex·pan·sive·ly** *adv* — **ex·pan·sive·ness** *n*

ex parte \eks-ˈpär-tē\ *adv or adj* [ML] : from a one-sided point of view

ex·pa·ti·ate \ek-ˈspā-shē-ˌāt\ *vb* **-at·ed; -at·ing** : to talk or write at length — **ex·pa·ti·a·tion** \ek-ˌspā-shē-ˈā-shən\ *n*

¹**ex·pa·tri·ate** \ek-ˈspā-trē-ˌāt\ *vb* **-at·ed; -at·ing** : EXILE — **ex·pa·tri·a·tion** \ek-ˌspā-trē-ˈā-shən\ *n*

²**ex·pa·tri·ate** \ek-ˈspā-trē-ˌāt, -trē-ət\ *adj* : living in a foreign country — **expatriate** *n*

ex·pect \ik-ˈspekt\ *vb* **1** : SUPPOSE, THINK **2** : to look forward to : ANTICIPATE **3** : to consider reasonable, due, or necessary **4** : to consider to be obliged

ex·pec·tan·cy \-ˈspek-tən-sē\ *n, pl* **-cies 1** : EXPECTATION **2** : the expected amount (as of years of life)

ex·pec·tant \-tənt\ *adj* : marked by expectation; *esp* : expecting the birth of a child — **ex·pec·tant·ly** *adv*

ex·pec·ta·tion \ˌek-ˌspek-ˈtā-shən\ *n* **1** : the act or state of expecting **2** : prospect of good or bad fortune — usu. used in pl. **3** : something expected

ex·pec·to·rant \ik-ˈspek-tə-rənt\ *n* : an agent that promotes the discharge or expulsion of mucus from the respiratory tract — **expectorant** *adj*

ex·pec·to·rate \-ˌrāt\ *vb* **-rat·ed; -rat·ing** : SPIT — **ex·pec·to·ra·tion** \-ˌspek-tə-ˈrā-shən\ *n*

ex·pe·di·ence \ik-ˈspē-dē-əns\ *n* : EXPEDIENCY

ex·pe·di·en·cy \-ən-sē\ *n, pl* **-cies 1** : fitness to some end **2** : use of expedient means and methods; *also* : something expedient

¹**ex·pe·di·ent** \-ənt\ *adj* [ME, fr. MF or L; MF, fr. L *expediens*, prp. of *expedire* to extricate, prepare, be useful, fr. *ex-* out + *ped-, pes* foot] **1** : adapted for achieving a particular end **2** : marked by concern with what is advantageous; *esp* : governed by self-interest

²**expedient** *n* : something expedient; *esp* : a temporary means to an end

ex·pe·dite \ˈek-spə-ˌdīt\ *vb* **-dit·ed; -dit·ing** : to carry out promptly; *also* : to speed up

ex·pe·dit·er \-ˌdī-tər\ *n* : one that expedites; *esp* : one employed to ensure efficient movement of goods or supplies in a business

ex·pe·di·tion \ˌek-spə-ˈdi-shən\ *n* **1** : a journey for a particular purpose; *also* : the persons making it **2** : efficient promptness

ex·pe·di·tion·ary \-ˈdi-shə-ˌner-ē\ *adj* : of, relating to, or constituting an expedition; *also* : sent on military service abroad

ex·pe·di·tious \-ˈdi-shəs\ *adj* : marked by or acting with prompt efficiency **syn** swift, fast, rapid, speedy

ex·pel \ik-ˈspel\ *vb* **ex·pelled; ex·pel·ling** : to drive or force out : EJECT

ex·pend \ik-ˈspend\ *vb* **1** : to pay out : SPEND **2** : UTILIZE; *also* : USE UP — **ex·pend·able** *adj*

ex·pen·di·ture \ik-ˈspen-di-chər, -ˌchùr\ *n* **1** : the act or process of expending **2** : something expended

ex·pense \ik-ˈspens\ *n* **1** : EXPENDITURE **2** : COST **3** : a cause of expenditure **4** : SACRIFICE

ex·pen·sive \ik-'spen-siv\ *adj* : COSTLY, DEAR — **ex·pen·sive·ly** *adv*

¹**ex·pe·ri·ence** \ik-'spir-ē-əns\ *n* **1** : observation of or participation in events resulting in or tending toward knowledge **2** : knowledge, practice, or skill derived from observation or participation in events; *also* : the length of such participation **3** : something encountered, undergone, or lived through (as by a person or community)

²**experience** *vb* **-enced; -enc·ing 1** : FIND OUT, DISCOVER **2** : to have experience of : UNDERGO

ex·pe·ri·enced *adj* : made capable through experience

¹**ex·per·i·ment** \ik-'sper-ə-mənt\ *n* : a controlled procedure carried out to discover, test, or demonstrate something; *also* : the process of testing — **ex·per·i·men·tal** \-ısper-ə-'ment-ə̇l\ *adj*

²**ex·per·i·ment** \-ıment\ *vb* : to make experiments — **ex·per·i·men·ta·tion** \ik-ısper-ə-mən-'tā-shən\ *n* — **ex·per·i·men·ter** *n*

¹**ex·pert** \'ek-ıspərt\ *adj* : showing special skill or knowledge — **ex·pert·ly** *adv* — **ex·pert·ness** *n*

²**ex·pert** \'ek-ıspərt\ *n* : an expert person : SPECIALIST

ex·per·tise \ıek-(ı)spər-'tēz\ *n* : the skill of an expert

expert system *n* : computer software that attempts to mimic the reasoning of a human specialist

ex·pi·ate \'ek-spē-ıāt\ *vb* **-at·ed; -at·ing** : to give satisfaction for : ATONE — **ex·pi·a·tion** \ıek-spē-'ā-shən\ *n*

ex·pi·a·to·ry \'ek-spē-ə-ıtōr-ē\ *adj* : serving to expiate

ex·pire \ik-'spīr, ek-\ *vb* **ex·pired; ex·pir·ing 1** : to breathe one's last breath : DIE **2** : to come to an end **3** : to breathe out from or as if from the lungs — **ex·pi·ra·tion** \ıek-spə-'rā-shən\ *n*

ex·plain \ik-'splān\ *vb* [ME *explanen*, fr. L *explanare*, lit., to make level, fr. *planus* level, flat] **1** : to make clear **2** : to give the reason for — **ex·pla·na·tion** \ıek-splə-'nā-shən\ *n* — **ex·plan·a·to·ry** \ik-'spla-nə-ıtōr-ē\ *adj*

ex·ple·tive \'ek-splə-tiv\ *n* : a usu. profane exclamation

ex·pli·ca·ble \ek-'spli-kə-bəl, 'ek- (ı)spli-\ *adj* : capable of being explained

ex·pli·cate \'ek-splə-ıkāt\ *vb* **-cat·ed; -cat·ing** : to give a detailed explanation of — **ex·pli·ca·tion** \ıek-spli-'kā-shən\ *n*

ex·plic·it \ik-'spli-sət\ *adj* : clearly and precisely expressed — **ex·plic·it·ly** *adv* — **ex·plic·it·ness** *n*

ex·plode \ik-'splōd\ *vb* **ex·plod·ed; ex·plod·ing** [L *explodere* to drive off the stage by clapping, fr. *ex-* out + *plaudere* to clap] **1** : DISCREDIT ⟨∼ a belief⟩ **2** : to burst or cause to burst violently and noisily ⟨∼ a bomb⟩ ⟨the boiler *exploded*⟩ **3** : to undergo a rapid chemical or nuclear reaction with production of heat and violent expansion of gas ⟨dynamite ∼s⟩ **4** : to give forth a sudden strong and noisy outburst of emotion **5** : to increase rapidly

ex·plod·ed *adj* : showing the parts separated but in correct relationship to each other ⟨an ∼ view of a carburetor⟩

¹**ex·ploit** \'ek-ısplȯit\ *n* : DEED; *esp* : a notable or heroic act

²**ex·ploit** \ik-'splȯit\ *vb* **1** : to make productive use of : UTILIZE **2** : to use unfairly for one's own advantage — **ex·ploi·ta·tion** \ıek-ısplȯi-'tā-shən\ *n*

ex·plore \ik-'splōr\ *vb* **ex·plored; ex·plor·ing 1** : to look into or travel over thoroughly **2** : to examine carefully ⟨∼ a wound⟩ — **ex·plo·ra·tion** \ıek-splə-'rā-shən\ *n* — **ex·plor·a·to·ry** \ik-'splōr-ə-ıtōr-ē\ *adj* — **ex·plor·er** *n*

ex·plo·sion \ik-'splō-zhən\ *n* : the act or an instance of exploding

ex·plo·sive \ik-'splō-siv\ *adj* **1** : relating to or able to cause explosion **2** : tending to explode — **explosive** *n* — **ex·plo·sive·ly** *adv*

ex·po \'ek-ıspō\ *n, pl* **expos** : EXPOSITION 2

ex·po·nent \ik-'spō-nənt, 'ek-ıspō-\ *n* **1** : a symbol written above and to the right of a mathematical expression (as ³ in *a*³) to signify how many times it is to be used as a factor **2** : INTERPRETER, EXPOUNDER **3** : ADVOCATE, CHAMPION — **ex·po·nen·tial** \ıek-spə-'nen-chəl\ *adj* — **ex·po·nen·tial·ly** *adv*

ex·po·nen·ti·a·tion \ıek-spə-ınen-chē-'ā-shen\ *n* : the mathematical operation of raising a quantity to a power

¹**ex·port** \ek-'spōrt, 'ek-ıspōrt\ *vb* : to send (as merchandise) to foreign countries — **ex·por·ta·tion** \ıek-spȯr-'tā-shən, -spər-\ *n* — **ex·port·er** *n*

²**ex·port** \'ek-ıspōrt\ *n* **1** : something exported esp. for trade **2** : the act of exporting

ex·pose \ik-'spōz\ *vb* **ex·posed; ex·pos·ing 1** : to deprive of shelter or protection **2** : to submit or subject to an action or influence; *esp* : to subject (as photographic film) to radiant energy (as light) **3** : to bring to light : DISCLOSE **4** : to cause to be open to view

ex·po·sé *or* **ex·po·se** \ıek-spō-'zā\ *n* : an exposure of something discreditable

ex·po·si·tion \ıek-spə-'zi-shən\ *n* **1** : a setting forth of the meaning or purpose (as of a writing); *also* : discourse designed to convey information **2** : a public exhibition

ex·pos·i·tor \ik-'spä-zə-tər\ *n* : one who explains : COMMENTATOR

ex post fac·to \ıeks-'pōst-ıfak-tō\ *adv or adj* : after the fact

ex·pos·tu·late \ik-'späs-chə-ılāt\ *vb* : to reason earnestly with a person esp. in dissuading : REMONSTRATE — **ex·pos·tu·la·tion** \-ıspäs-chə-'lā-shən\ *n*

ex·po·sure \ik-'spō-zhər\ *n* **1** : the fact or condition of being exposed **2** : the act or an instance of exposing **3** : the length of time for which a film is exposed **4** : a section of a photographic film for one picture

ex·pound \ik-'spaúnd\ *vb* **1** : STATE **2** : INTERPRET, EXPLAIN — **ex·pound·er** *n*

¹**ex·press** \ik-'spres\ *adj* **1** : EXPLICIT; *also* : EXACT, PRECISE **2** : SPECIFIC ⟨this ∼ purpose⟩ **3** : traveling at high speed and esp. with few stops ⟨an ∼ train⟩; *also* : adapted to high speed use ⟨∼ roads⟩ — **ex·press·ly** *adv*

²**express** *adv* : by express ⟨ship it ∼⟩

³**express** *n* **1** : a system for the prompt transportation of goods; *also* : a company operating such a service or the shipments so transported **2** : an express vehicle

⁴**express** *vb* **1** : to make known : SHOW, STATE ⟨∼ regret⟩; *also* : SYMBOLIZE **2** : to squeeze out : extract by pressing **3** : to send by express

ex·pres·sion \ik-'spre-shən\ *n* **1** : UTTERANCE **2** : something that represents or symbolizes : SIGN; *esp* : a mathematical symbol or combination of signs and symbols representing a quantity or operation **3** : a significant word or phrase; *also* : manner of expressing (as in writing or music) **4** : facial aspect or vocal intonation indicative of feeling — **ex·pres·sion·less** *adj*

ex·pres·sion·ism \ik-'spre-shə-ıni-zəm\ *n* : a theory or practice in art of seeking to depict the artist's subjective responses to objects and events — **ex·pres·sion·ist** \-nist\ *n or adj* — **ex·pres·sion·is·tic** \-ıspre-shə-'nis-tik\ *adj*

ex·pres·sive \ik-'spre-siv\ *adj* **1** : of or relating to expression **2** : serving to express — **ex·pres·sive·ly** *adv* — **ex·pres·sive·ness** *n*

ex·press·way \ik-'spres-ıwā\ *n* : a divided superhighway with limited access

ex·pro·pri·ate \ek-'sprō-prē-ıāt\ *vb* **-at·ed; -at·ing** : to deprive of possession or the right to own — **ex·pro·pri·a·tion** \(ı)ek-ısprō-prē-'ā-shən\ *n*

expt *abbr* experiment

ex·pul·sion \ik-'spəl-shən\ *n* : an expelling or being expelled : EJECTION

ex·punge \ik-'spənj\ *vb* **ex·punged; ex·pung·ing** [L *expungere* to mark for deletion by dots, fr. *ex-* out + *pungere* to prick] : OBLITERATE, ERASE

ex·pur·gate \'ek-spər-ıgāt\ *vb* **-gat·ed; -gat·ing** : to clear (as a book) of objectionable passages — **ex-pur-ga-tion** \ek-spər-'gā-shən\ n

ex-qui-site \ek-'skwi-zət, 'ek-(ˌ)skwi-\ adj [ME exquisit, fr. L exquisitus, pp. of exquirere to search out, fr. ex out quaerere to seek] **1** : marked by flawless form or workmanship **2** : keenly appreciative or sensitive **3** : pleasingly beautiful or delicate **4** : INTENSE

ext abbr **1** extension **2** exterior **3** external **4** extra **5** extract

ex-tant \'ek-stənt; ek-'stant\ adj : EXISTENT; esp : not lost or destroyed

ex-tem-po-ra-ne-ous \ek-ˌstem-pə-'rā-nē-əs\ adj : not planned beforehand : IMPROMPTU — **ex-tem-po-ra-ne-ous-ly** adv

ex-tem-po-rary \ik-'stem-pə-ˌrer-ē\ adj : EXTEMPORANEOUS

ex-tem-po-re \ik-'stem-pə-(ˌ)rē\ adv : EXTEMPORANEOUSLY

ex-tem-po-rize \ik-'stem-pə-ˌrīz\ vb **-rized; -riz-ing** : to do something extemporaneously

ex-tend \ik-'stend\ vb **1** : to spread or stretch forth or out (as in reaching) **2** : to exert or cause to exert to full capacity **3** : PROFFER (~ credit) **4** : PROLONG (~ a note) **5** : to make greater or broader (~ knowledge) (~ a business) **6** : to stretch out or reach across a distance, space, or time syn lengthen, elongate, protract — **ex-tend-able** also **ex-tend-ible** \-'sten-də-bəl\ adj

ex-ten-sion \ik-'sten-chən\ n **1** : an extending or being extended **2** : a program that geographically extends the educational resources of an institution **3** : an additional part; also : an extra telephone connected to a line

ex-ten-sive \ik-'sten-siv\ adj : of considerable extent : FAR-REACHING, BROAD — **ex-ten-sive-ly** adv

ex-tent \ik-'stent\ n **1** : the range or space over which something extends (a property of large ~) **2** : the point or degree to which something extends (to the fullest ~ of the law)

ex-ten-u-ate \ik-'sten-yù-ˌwāt\ vb **-at-ed; -at-ing** : to lessen the seriousness of — **ex-ten-u-a-tion** \-ˌsten-yù-'wā-shən\ n

¹ex-te-ri-or \ek-'stir-ē-ər\ adj **1** : EXTERNAL **2** : suitable for use on an outside surface (~ paint)

²exterior n : an exterior part or surface

ex-ter-mi-nate \ik-'stər-mə-ˌnāt\ vb **-nat-ed; -nat-ing** : to get rid of completely usu. by killing off syn extirpate, eradicate, abolish, annihilate — **ex-ter-mi-na-tion** \-ˌstər-mə-'nā-shən\ n — **ex-ter-mi-na-tor** \-'stər-mə-ˌnā-tər\ n

¹ex-ter-nal \ek-'stərn-ᵊl\ adj **1** : outwardly perceivable; also : SUPERFICIAL **2** : of, relating to, or located on the outside or an outer part **3** : arising or acting from without; also : FOREIGN (~ affairs) — **ex-ter-nal-ly** adv

²external n : an external feature

ex-tinct \ik-'stiŋkt\ adj **1** : EXTINGUISHED; also : no longer active (an ~ volcano) **2** : no longer existing or in use (dinosaurs are ~) (~ languages) — **ex-tinc-tion** \ik-'stiŋk-shən\ n

ex-tin-guish \ik-'stiŋ-gwish\ vb : to cause to stop burning; also : to bring to an end (as by destroying) — **ex-tin-guish-able** adj — **ex-tin-guish-er** n

ex-tir-pate \'ek-stər-ˌpāt\ vb **-pat-ed; -pat-ing** [L exstirpatus, pp. of exstirpare, fr. ex- out + stirps trunk, root] **1** : to destroy completely **2** : UPROOT syn exterminate, eradicate, abolish, annihilate — **ex-tir-pa-tion** \ek-stər-'pā-shən\ n

ex-tol also **ex-toll** \ik-'stōl\ vb **ex-tolled; ex-tol-ling** : to praise highly : GLORIFY

ex-tort \ik-'stórt\ vb [L extortus, pp. of extorquēre to wrench out, extort, fr. ex- out + torquēre to twist] : to obtain by force or improper pressure (~ a bribe) — **ex-tor-tion** \-'stór-shən\ n — **ex-tor-tion-er** n — **ex-tor-tion-ist** n

ex-tor-tion-ate \ik-'stór-shə-nət\ adj : EXCESSIVE, EXORBITANT — **ex-tor-tion-ate-ly** adv

¹ex-tra \'ek-strə\ adj **1** : ADDITIONAL **2** : SUPERIOR

²extra n **1** : a special edition of a newspaper **2** : an added charge **3** : an additional worker or performer (as in a motion picture)

³extra adv : beyond what is usual

¹ex-tract \ik-'strakt, esp for 3 'ek-ˌstrakt\ vb **1** : to draw out; esp : to pull out forcibly (~ a tooth) **2** : to withdraw (as a juice or a constituent) by a physical or chemical process **3** : to select for citation : QUOTE — **ex-tract-able** adj — **ex-trac-tion** \ik-'strak-shən\ n — **ex-trac-tor** \-tər\ n

²ex-tract \'ek-ˌstrakt\ n **1** : EXCERPT, CITATION **2** : a product (as a juice or concentrate) obtained by extracting

ex-tra-cur-ric-u-lar \ek-strə-kə-'ri-kyə-lər\ adj : lying outside the regular curriculum; esp : of or relating to school-connected activities (as sports) usu. carrying no academic credit

ex-tra-dite \'ek-strə-ˌdīt\ vb **-dit-ed; -dit-ing** : to obtain by or deliver up to extradition

ex-tra-di-tion \ek-strə-'di-shən\ n : the surrender of an alleged criminal to a different jurisdiction for trial

ex-tra-mar-i-tal \ek-strə-'mar-ət-ᵊl\ adj : of or relating to sexual intercourse by a married person with someone other than his or her spouse

ex-tra-mu-ral \-'myùr-əl\ adj : existing or functioning beyond the bounds of an organized unit

ex-tra-ne-ous \ek-'strā-nē-əs\ adj **1** : coming from without **2** : not forming a vital part; also : IRRELEVANT — **ex-tra-ne-ous-ly** adv

ex-traor-di-nary \ik-'stró̇rd-ᵊn-ˌer-ē, ˌek-strə-'ó̇rd-\ adj **1** : notably unusual or exceptional **2** : employed on special service — **ex-traor-di-nari-ly** \-ˌstró̇rd-ᵊn-'er-ə-lē, ˌek-strə-ó̇rd-\ adv

ex-trap-o-late \ik-'stra-pə-ˌlāt\ vb **-lat-ed; -lat-ing** : to infer (unknown data) from known data — **ex-trap-o-la-tion** \-ˌstra-pə-'lā-shən\ n

ex-tra-sen-so-ry \ek-strə-'sen-sə-rē\ adj : not acting or occurring through the known senses

extrasensory perception n : perception (as in telepathy) of events external to the self not gained through the senses and not deducible from previous experience

ex-tra-ter-res-tri-al \-tə-'res-trē-əl\ adj : originating or existing outside the earth or its atmosphere (~ life) — **extraterrestrial** n

ex-tra-ter-ri-to-ri-al \-ˌter-ə-'tōr-ē-əl\ adj : existing or taking place outside the territorial limits of a jurisdiction

ex-tra-ter-ri-to-ri-al-i-ty \-ˌtōr-ē-'a-lə-tē\ n : exemption from the application or jurisdiction of local law or tribunals (diplomats enjoy ~)

ex-trav-a-gant \ik-'stra-vi-gənt\ adj **1** : EXCESSIVE (~ claims) **2** : unduly lavish : WASTEFUL **3** : too costly syn immoderate, exorbitant, extreme, inordinate, undue — **ex-trav-a-gance** \-gəns\ n — **ex-trav-a-gant-ly** adv

ex-trav-a-gan-za \ik-ˌstra-və-'gan-zə\ n **1** : a literary or musical work marked by extreme freedom of style and structure **2** : a spectacular show

ex-tra-ve-hic-u-lar \ek-strə-vē-'hi-kyə-lər\ adj : taking place outside a vehicle (as a spacecraft) (~ activity)

¹ex-treme \ik-'strēm\ adj **1** : very great or intense (~ cold) **2** : very severe or radical (~ measures) **3** : going to great lengths or beyond normal limits (politically ~) **4** : most remote (the ~ end) **5** : UTMOST; also : MAXIMUM — **ex-treme-ly** adv

²extreme n **1** : something located at one end or the other of a range or series **2** : EXTREMITY **4**

extremely low frequency n : a radio frequency in the lowest range of the radio spectrum

ex-trem-ism \ik-'strē-ˌmi-zəm\ n : the quality or state of being extreme; esp : advocacy of extreme political measures — **ex-trem-ist** \-mist\ n or adj

ex-trem-i-ty \ik-'stre-mə-tē\ n, pl **-ties 1** : the most remote part or point **2** : a limb of the body; esp : a human hand or foot **3** : the greatest need or danger **4** : the utmost degree; *also* : a drastic or desperate measure

ex·tri·cate \'ek-strə-ˌkāt\ *vb* **-cat·ed; -cat·ing** [L *extricatus,* pp. of *extricare,* fr. *ex-* out + *tricae* trifles, perplexities] : to free from an entanglement or difficulty **syn** disentangle, untangle, disencumber — **ex·tri·ca·ble** \ik-'stri-kə-bəl, ek-; 'ek-(ˌ)stri-\ *adj* — **ex·tri·ca·tion** \ˌek-strə-'kā-shən\ *n*

ex·trin·sic \ek-'strin-zik, -sik\ *adj* **1** : not forming part of or belonging to a thing **2** : EXTERNAL — **ex·trin·si·cal·ly** \-zi-k(ə-)lē, -si-\ *adv*

ex·tro·vert *also* **ex·tra·vert** \'ek-strə-ˌvərt\ *n* : a gregarious and unreserved person — **ex·tro·ver·sion** *or* **ex·tra·ver·sion** \ˌek-strə-'vər-zhən\ *n* — **ex·tro·vert·ed** *also* **ex·tra·vert·ed** *adj*

ex·trude \ik-'strüd\ *vb* **ex·trud·ed; ex·trud·ing** **1** : to force, press, or push out **2** : to shape (as plastic) by forcing through a die — **ex·tru·sion** \-'strü-zhən\ *n* — **ex·trud·er** *n*

ex·u·ber·ant \ig-'zü-bə-rənt\ *adj* **1** : unrestrained in enthusiasm or style **2** : PROFUSE — **ex·u·ber·ance** \-rəns\ *n* — **ex·u·ber·ant·ly** *adv*

ex·ude \ig-'züd\ *vb* **ex·ud·ed; ex·ud·ing** [L *exsudare,* fr. *ex-* out + *sudare* to sweat] **1** : to discharge slowly through pores or cuts : OOZE **2** : to display conspicuously or abundantly ⟨∼s charm⟩ — **ex·u·date** \'ek-sù-ˌdāt, -syù-\ *n* — **ex·u·da·tion** \ˌek-sù-'dā-shən, -syù-\ *n*

ex·ult \ig-'zəlt\ *vb* : REJOICE, GLORY — **ex·ul·tant** \-'zəlt-ᵊnt\ *adj* — **ex·ul·tant·ly** *adv* — **ex·ul·ta·tion** \ˌek-(ˌ)səl-'tā-shən, ˌeg-(ˌ)zəl-\ *n*

ex·urb \'ek-ˌsərb, 'eg-ˌzərb\ *n* : a region outside a city and its suburbs inhabited chiefly by well-to-do families

ex·urb·an·ite \ek-'sər-bə-ˌnīt; eg-'zər-\ *n* : one who lives in an exurb

ex·ur·bia \ek-'sər-bē-ə, eg-'zer-\ *n* : the generalized region of exurbs

-ey — see -Y

¹eye \'ī\ *n* **1** : an organ of sight typically consisting in vertebrates of a globular structure that is located in a socket of the skull, is lined with a sensitive retina, and is normally paired **2** : VISION, PERCEPTION; *also* : faculty of discrimination ⟨an ∼ for bargains⟩ **3** : POINT OF VIEW, JUDGMENT — often used in pl. (in

the ∼s of the law) **4** : something suggesting an eye ⟨the ∼ of a needle⟩; *esp* : an undeveloped bud (as on a potato) **5** : the calm center of a cyclone — **eyed** \'īd\ *adj*

²eye *vb* **eyed; eye·ing** *or* **ey·ing** : to look at : WATCH

eye·ball \'ī-ˌbȯl\ *n* : the globular capsule of the vertebrate eye

eye·brow \-ˌbraù\ *n* : the ridge over the eye or the hair growing on it

eye·drop·per \-ˌdrä-pər\ *n* : DROPPER 2

eye·glass \-ˌglas\ *n* : a lens worn to aid vision; *also, pl* : GLASSES

eye·lash \-ˌlash\ *n* **1** : the fringe of hair edging the eyelid — usu. used in pl. **2** : a single hair of the eyelashes

eye·let \-lət\ *n* **1** : a small hole intended for ornament or for passage of a cord or lace **2** : a typically metal ring for reinforcing an eyelet : GROMMET

eye·lid \-ˌlid\ *n* : either of the movable folds of skin and muscle that can be closed over the eyeball

eye·lin·er \-ˌlī-nər\ *n* : makeup used to emphasize the contour of the eyes

eye–open·er \-ˌō-pə-nər\ *n* : something startling or surprising — **eye–open·ing** *adj*

eye·piece \-ˌpēs\ *n* : the lens or combination of lenses at the eye end of an optical instrument

eye shadow *n* : a colored cosmetic applied to the eyelids to accent the eyes

eye·sight \-ˌsīt\ *n* : SIGHT, VISION

eye·sore \-ˌsōr\ *n* : something offensive to view

eye·strain \-ˌstrān\ *n* : weariness or a strained state of the eye

eye·tooth \-'tüth\ *n* : a canine tooth of the upper jaw

eye·wash \-ˌwȯsh, -ˌwäsh\ *n* **1** : an eye lotion **2** : misleading or deceptive statements, actions, or procedures

eye·wit·ness \-'wit-nəs\ *n* : a person who actually sees something happen

ey·rie \'īr-ē, *or like* AERIE\ *var of* AERIE

ey·rir \'ā-ˌrir\ *n, pl* **au·rar** \'aù-ˌrär\ — see *krona* at MONEY table

Ez *or* **Ezr** *abbr* Ezra

Ezech *abbr* Ezechiel

Eze·chiel \i-'zē-kyəl\ *n* — see BIBLE table

Ezek *abbr* Ezekiel

Eze·kiel \i-'zē-kyəl\ *n* — see BIBLE table

Ez·ra \'ez-rə\ *n* — see BIBLE table

F

¹f \'ef\ *n, pl* **f's** *or* **fs** \'efs\ *often cap* **1** : the 6th letter of the English alphabet **2** : a grade rating a student's work as failing

²f *abbr, often cap* **1** Fahrenheit **2** false **3** family **4** farad **5** female **6** feminine **7** forte **8** French **9** frequency **10** Friday

³f *symbol* focal length

F *symbol* fluorine

FAA *abbr* Federal Aviation Administration

Fa·bi·an \'fā-bē-ən\ *adj* : of, relating to, or being a society of socialists organized in England in 1884 to spread socialist principles gradually — **Fabian** *n* — **Fa·bi·an·ism** *n*

fa·ble \'fā-bəl\ *n* **1** : a legendary story of supernatural happenings **2** : a narration intended to teach a lesson; *esp* : one in which animals speak and act like people **3** : FALSEHOOD

fa·bled \'fā-bəld\ *adj* **1** : FICTITIOUS **2** : told or celebrated in fable

fab·ric \'fa-brik\ *n* [MF *fabrique,* fr. L *fabrica* workshop, structure] **1** : STRUCTURE, FRAMEWORK ⟨the ∼ of society⟩ **2** : CLOTH; *also* : a material that resembles cloth

fab·ri·cate \'fa-bri-ˌkāt\ *vb* **-cat·ed; -cat·ing** **1** : INVENT, CREATE **2** : to make up for the sake of decep-

tion **3** : CONSTRUCT, MANUFACTURE — **fab·ri·ca·tion** \ˌfa-bri-'kā-shən\ *n*

fab·u·lous \'fa-byə-ləs\ *adj* **1** : resembling a fable; *also* : INCREDIBLE, MARVELOUS **2** : told in or based on fable — **fab·u·lous·ly** *adv*

fac *abbr* **1** facsimile **2** faculty

fa·cade *also* **fa·çade** \fə-'säd\ *n* [F *façade,* fr. It *facciata,* fr. *faccia* face] **1** : the principal face or front of a building **2** : a false, superficial, or artificial appearance ⟨a ∼ of composure⟩ **syn** mask, disguise, front, guise, pretense, veneer

¹face \'fās\ *n* **1** : the front part of the head **2** : PRESENCE ⟨in the ∼ of danger⟩ **3** : facial expression : LOOK ⟨put a sad ∼ on⟩ **4** : GRIMACE ⟨made a ∼⟩ **5** : outward appearance ⟨looks easy on the ∼ of it⟩ **6** : CONFIDENCE; *also* : BOLDNESS **7** : DIGNITY, PRESTIGE ⟨afraid to lose ∼⟩ **8** : SURFACE; *esp* : a front, principal, or bounding surface ⟨∼ of a cliff⟩ ⟨the ∼s of a cube⟩ — **faced** \'fāst, 'fā-səd\ *adj*

²face *vb* **faced; fac·ing** **1** : to confront brazenly **2** : to line near the edge esp. with a different material; *also* : to cover the front or surface of ⟨∼ a building with marble⟩ **3** : to meet or bring in direct contact or confrontation ⟨*faced* the problem⟩ **4** : to stand or sit with the face toward ⟨∼ the sun⟩ **5** : to have the front oriented toward ⟨a house *facing* the park⟩ **6** : to have as or be a prospect ⟨~ a grim future⟩ **7** : to turn the face or body in a specified direction — **face the music** : to meet the unpleasant consequences of one's actions

face·down \ˌfās-ˈdau̇n\ *adv* : with the face downward

face·less \-ləs\ *n* **1** : lacking a face **2** : lacking character or individuality

face–lift \ˈfās-ˌlift\ *n* **1** : a cosmetic surgical operation for removal of facial defects (as wrinkles) typical of aging **2** : MODERNIZATION — **face–lift** *vb*

face–off \ˈfās-ˌȯf\ *n* **1** : a method of beginning play by dropping a puck (as in ice hockey) between two opposing players each of whom attempts to control it **2** : CONFRONTATION

fac·et \ˈfa-sət\ *n* [F *facette*, dim. of *face*] **1** : a small plane surface of a cut gem **2** : ASPECT, PHASE

fa·ce·tious \fə-ˈsē-shəs\ *adj* **1** : joking often inappropriately **2** : JOCULAR, JOCOSE **syn** witty, humorous — **fa·ce·tious·ly** *adv* — **fa·ce·tious·ness** *n*

¹fa·cial \ˈfā-shəl\ *adj* **1** : of or relating to the face **2** : used to improve the appearance of the face

²facial *n* : a facial treatment

fac·ile \ˈfa-səl\ *adj* **1** : easily accomplished, handled, or attained **2** : SUPERFICIAL **3** : readily manifested and often insincere ⟨~ prose⟩ **4** : READY, FLUENT ⟨a ~ writer⟩

fa·cil·i·tate \fə-ˈsi-lə-ˌtāt\ *vb* **-tat·ed; -tat·ing** : to make easier

fa·cil·i·ty \fə-ˈsi-lə-tē\ *n, pl* **-ties** **1** : the quality of being easily performed **2** : ease in performance : APTITUDE **3** : PLIANCY **4** : something that makes easier an action, operation, or course of conduct; *also* : REST ROOM — often used in pl. **5** : something (as a hospital) built or installed for a particular purpose

fac·ing \ˈfā-siŋ\ *n* **1** : a lining at the edge esp. of a garment **2** *pl* : the collar, cuffs, and trimmings of a uniform coat **3** : an ornamental or protective layer **4** : material for facing

fac·sim·i·le \fak-ˈsi-mə-lē\ *n* [L *fac simile* make similar] **1** : an exact copy **2** : a system of transmitting and reproducing printed matter or pictures by means of signals sent over telephone lines

fact \ˈfakt\ *n* **1** : DEED; *esp* : CRIME ⟨accessory after the ~⟩ **2** : the quality of being actual **3** : something that exists or occurs **4** : a piece of information

fac·tion \ˈfak-shən\ *n* : a group or combination (as in a government) acting together within and usu. against a larger body : CLIQUE — **fac·tion·al·ism** \-shə-nə-ˌli-zəm\ *n*

fac·tious \ˈfak-shəs\ *adj* **1** : of, relating to, or caused by faction **2** : inclined to faction or the formation of factions : causing dissension **syn** insubordinate, contumacious, insurgent, seditious, rebellious

fac·ti·tious \fak-ˈti-shəs\ *adj* : ARTIFICIAL, SHAM ⟨a ~ display of grief⟩

¹fac·tor \ˈfak-tər\ *n* **1** : AGENT **2** : something that actively contributes to a result **3** : GENE **4** : any of the numbers or symbols in mathematics that when multiplied together form a product; *esp* : any of the integers that divide a given integer without a remainder

²factor *vb* **1** : to work as a factor **2** : to find the mathematical factors of and esp. the prime mathematical factors of

¹fac·to·ri·al \fak-ˈtōr-ē-əl\ *adj* : of, relating to, or being a factor

²factorial *n* : the product of all the positive integers from 1 to a given integer *n*

fac·to·ry \ˈfak-trē, -tə-rē\ *n, pl* **-ries** **1** : a trading post where resident brokers trade **2** : a building or group of buildings used for manufacturing

fac·to·tum \fak-ˈtō-təm\ *n* [NL, lit., do everything, fr. L *fac* do + *totum* everything] : a person (as a servant) having numerous or varied duties

facts of life : the physiological processes and behavior involved in sex and reproduction

fac·tu·al \ˈfak-chə-wəl\ *adj* : of or relating to facts; *also* : based on fact — **fac·tu·al·ly** *adv*

fac·ul·ty \ˈfa-kəl-tē\ *n, pl* **-ties** **1** : ability to act or do : POWER; *also* : natural aptitude **2** : one of the powers of the mind or body ⟨the ~ of hearing⟩ **3** : the teachers in a school or college or one of its divisions

fad \ˈfad\ *n* : a practice or interest followed for a time with exaggerated zeal : CRAZE — **fad·dish** *adj* — **fad·dist** *n*

fade \ˈfād\ *vb* **fad·ed; fad·ing** **1** : WITHER **2** : to lose or cause to lose freshness or brilliance of color **3** : VANISH **4** : to grow dim or faint

FADM *abbr* fleet admiral

fae·cal, fae·ces *var of* FECAL, FECES

fa·e·rie *also* **fa·ery** \ˈfā-rē, ˈfar-ē\ *n, pl* **fa·er·ies** **1** : FAIRYLAND **2** : FAIRY

¹fag \ˈfag\ *vb* **fagged; fag·ging** **1** : DRUDGE **2** : to act as a fag **3** : TIRE, EXHAUST

²fag *n* **1** : an English public-school boy who acts as servant to another **2** : MENIAL, DRUDGE

³fag *n* : CIGARETTE

fag end *n* **1** : REMNANT **2** : the extreme end **3** : the last part or coarser end of a web of cloth **4** : the untwisted end of a rope

fag·ot *or* **fag·got** \ˈfa-gət\ *n* : a bundle of sticks or twigs

fag·ot·ing *or* **fag·got·ing** *n* : an embroidery produced by tying threads in hourglass-shaped clusters

Fah *or* **Fahr** *abbr* Fahrenheit

Fahr·en·heit \ˈfar-ən-ˌhīt\ *adj* : relating to, conforming to, or having a thermometer scale with the boiling point of water at 212 degrees and the freezing point at 32 degrees above zero

fa·ience *or* **fa·ïence** \fā-ˈäns\ *n* [F] : earthenware decorated with opaque colored glazes

¹fail \ˈfāl\ *vb* **1** : to become feeble; *esp* : to decline in health **2** : to die away **3** : to stop functioning **4** : to fall short ⟨~ed in his duty⟩ **5** : to be or become absent or inadequate **6** : to be unsuccessful **7** : to become bankrupt **8** : DISAPPOINT **9** : NEGLECT

²fail *n* : FAILURE ⟨without ~⟩

¹fail·ing \ˈfā-liŋ\ *n* : WEAKNESS, SHORTCOMING

²failing *prep* : in the absence or lack of

faille \ˈfīl\ *n* : a somewhat shiny closely woven ribbed fabric (as silk)

fail–safe \ˈfāl-ˌsāf\ *adj* **1** : incorporating a counteractive feature for a possible source of failure **2** : having no chance of failure

fail·ure \ˈfāl-yər\ *n* **1** : a failing to do or perform **2** : a state of inability to perform a normal function adequately ⟨heart ~⟩ **3** : a fracturing or giving way under stress **4** : a lack of success **5** : BANKRUPTCY **6** : DEFICIENCY **7** : DETERIORATION, DECAY **8** : one that has failed

¹fain \ˈfān\ *adj* **1** *archaic* : GLAD; *also* : INCLINED **2** : being obliged or compelled

²fain *adv* **1** : with pleasure **2** : by preference

¹faint \ˈfānt\ *adj* [ME *faint, feint*, fr. OF, fr. *faindre, feindre* to feign, shirk] **1** : COWARDLY, SPIRITLESS **2** : weak, dizzy, and likely to faint **3** : lacking vigor or strength : FEEBLE ⟨~ praise⟩ **4** : INDISTINCT, DIM — **faint·ly** *adv* — **faint·ness** *n*

²faint *vb* : to lose consciousness

³faint *n* : the action of fainting; *also* : the resulting condition

faint·heart·ed \ˌfānt-ˈhär-təd\ *adj* : lacking courage : TIMID

¹fair \ˈfar\ *adj* **1** : pleasing in appearance : BEAUTIFUL **2** : superficially pleasing : SPECIOUS **3** : CLEAN, PURE **4** : CLEAR, LEGIBLE **5** : not stormy or cloudy **6** : JUST **7** : conforming with the rules : ALLOWED; *also* : being within the foul lines ⟨~ ball⟩ **8** : open to legitimate pursuit or attack ⟨~ game⟩ **9** : PROMISING, LIKELY ⟨a ~ chance of winning⟩ **10** : favorable to a ship's course ⟨a ~ wind⟩ **11** : light in complexion : BLOND **12** : ADEQUATE — **fair·ness** *n*

²fair *adv, chiefly Brit* : FAIRLY **4**

³fair *n* **1** : a gathering of buyers and sellers at a stated time and place for trade **2** : a competitive exhibition (as of farm products) **3** : a sale of assorted articles usu. for a charitable purpose

fair·ground \-₁graùnd\ *n* : an area where outdoor fairs, circuses, or exhibitions are held

fair·ing \ˈfar-iŋ\ *n* : a structure for producing a smooth outline and reducing drag (as on an airplane)

fair·ly \ˈfar-lē\ *adv* **1** : HANDSOMELY **2** : in a manner of speaking ⟨~ bursting with pride⟩ **3** : without bias **4** : to a full degree or extent : PLAINLY, DISTINCTLY **5** : SOMEWHAT, RATHER ⟨a ~ easy job⟩

fair-spo·ken \ˈfar-ˈspō-kən\ *adj* : pleasant and courteous in speech

fair–trade \-ˈtrād\ *adj* : of, relating to, or being an agreement between a producer and a seller that branded merchandise will be sold at or above a specified price — **fair–trade** *vb*

fair·way \-₁wā\ *n* : the mowed part of a golf course between tee and green

fairy \ˈfar-ē\ *n, pl* **fair·ies** [ME *fairie* fairyland, fairy people, fr. OF *faerie*, fr. *feie, fee* fairy, fr. L *Fata*, goddess of fate, fr. *fatum* fate] : an imaginary being of folklore and romance usu. having diminutive human form and magic powers — **fairy** *adj*

fairy·land \-₁land\ *n* **1** : the land of fairies **2** : a beautiful or charming place

fairy tale *n* **1** : a children's story about fairies **2** : FIB

fait ac·com·pli \ˈfāt-₁a-kōⁿ-ˈplē\ *n, pl* **faits accomplis** *same or* -ˈplēz\ [F, accomplished fact] : a thing accomplished and presumably irreversible

faith \ˈfāth\ *n, pl* **faiths** \ˈfāths, ˈfāthz\ [ME *feith*, fr. OF *feid, foi*, fr. L *fides*] **1** : allegiance to duty or a person : LOYALTY **2** : belief and trust in God **3** : complete trust **4** : a system of religious beliefs — **faith·ful** \-fəl\ *adj* — **faith·ful·ly** *adv* — **faith·ful·ness** *n*

faith·less \ˈfāth-ləs\ *adj* **1** : DISLOYAL **2** : not to be relied on **syn** false, traitorous, treacherous, unfaithful — **faith·less·ly** *adv* — **faith·less·ness** *n*

fa·ji·ta \fə-ˈhē-tə\ *n* : a marinated strip usu. of beef or chicken grilled or broiled and served usu. with a flour tortilla and savory fillings — usu. used in pl.

¹fake \ˈfāk\ *adj* : COUNTERFEIT, SHAM

²fake *n* **1** : IMITATION, FRAUD; *also* : IMPOSTOR **2** : a simulated move in sports (as a pretended pass)

³fake *vb* **faked; fak·ing 1** : to treat so as to falsify **2** : COUNTERFEIT **3** : to deceive (an opponent) in a sports contest by making a fake — **fak·er** *n*

fa·kir \fə-ˈkir\ *n* [Ar *faqīr*, lit., poor man] **1** : a Muslim mendicant : DERVISH **2** : a wandering Hindu ascetic

fal·con \ˈfal-kən, ˈfȯl-\ *n* **1** : a hawk trained for use in falconry **2** : any of various swift long-winged long-tailed hawks having a notched beak and usu. inhabiting open areas

fal·con·ry \ˈfal-kən-rē, ˈfȯl-\ *n* **1** : the art of training hawks to hunt in cooperation with a person **2** : the sport of hunting with hawks — **fal·con·er** *n*

¹fall \ˈfȯl\ *vb* **fell** \ˈfel\; **fall·en** \ˈfȯ-lən\; **fall·ing 1** : to descend freely by the force of gravity **2** : to hang freely **3** : to come or go as if by falling ⟨darkness *fell*⟩ **4** : to become uttered **5** : to lower or become lowered : DROP ⟨her eyes *fell*⟩ **6** : to leave an erect position suddenly and involuntarily **7** : STUMBLE, STRAY **8** : to drop down wounded or dead esp. in battle **9** : to become captured ⟨the city *fell* to the enemy⟩ **10** : to suffer ruin, defeat, or failure **11** : to commit an immoral act **12** : to move or extend in a downward direction **13** : SUBSIDE, ABATE **14** : to decline in quality, activity, quantity, or value **15** : to assume a look of shame or dejection ⟨her face *fell*⟩ **16** : to occur at a certain time **17** : to come by chance **18** : DEVOLVE ⟨the duties *fell* to him⟩ **19** : to have the proper place or station ⟨the accent ~s on the first syllable⟩ **20** : to come within the scope of something **21** : to pass from one condition to another ⟨*fell* ill⟩ **22** : to set about heartily or actively ⟨~ to work⟩ — **fall flat** : to produce no

response or result — **fall for 1** : to fall in love with **2** : to become a victim of — **fall foul** : to have a quarrel : CLASH — **fall from grace** : BACKSLIDE — **fall into line** : to comply with a certain course of action — **fall over oneself** *or* **fall over backward** : to display excessive eagerness — **fall short 1** : to be deficient **2** : to fail to attain

²fall *n* **1** : the act of falling **2** : a falling out, off, or away : DROPPING **3** : AUTUMN **4** : a thing or quantity that falls ⟨a ~ of snow⟩ **5** : COLLAPSE, DOWNFALL **6** : the surrender or capture of a besieged place **7** : departure from virtue or goodness **8** : SLOPE **9** : WATERFALL — usu. used in pl. **10** : a decrease in size, quantity, degree, or value ⟨a ~ in price⟩ **11** : the distance which something falls **12** : an act of forcing a wrestler's shoulders to the mat; *also* : a bout of wrestling

fal·la·cious \fə-ˈlā-shəs\ *adj* **1** : embodying a fallacy ⟨a ~ argument⟩ **2** : MISLEADING, DECEPTIVE

fal·la·cy \ˈfa-lə-sē\ *n, pl* **-cies 1** : a false or mistaken idea **2** : an often plausible argument using false or illogical reasoning

fall back *vb* : RETREAT, RECEDE

fall guy *n* **1** : one that is easily duped **2** : SCAPEGOAT

fal·li·ble \ˈfa-lə-bəl\ *adj* **1** : liable to be erroneous **2** : capable of making a mistake — **fal·li·bly** \-blē\ *adv*

fall·ing-out \ˈfȯ-liŋ-ˈaùt\ *n, pl* **fallings-out** *or* **falling-outs** : QUARREL

falling star *n* : METEOR

fal·lo·pi·an tube \fə-ˈlō-pē-ən-\ *n, often cap F* : either of the pair of anatomical tubes that carry the eggs from the ovary to the uterus

fall·out \ˈfȯ-₁laùt\ *n* **1** : the often radioactive particles that result from a nuclear explosion and descend through the air **2** : a secondary and often lingering effect or result

fall out *vb* : QUARREL

¹fal·low \ˈfa-(₁)lō\ *n* : fallow land; *also* : the state or period of being fallow — **fallow** *vb*

²fallow *adj* **1** : left without tilling or sowing after plowing **2** : DORMANT, INACTIVE ⟨a writer's ~ period⟩

false \ˈfȯls\ *adj* **fals·er; fals·est 1** : not genuine : ARTIFICIAL **2** : intentionally untrue **3** : adjusted or made so as to deceive ⟨~ scales⟩ **4** : tending to mislead : DECEPTIVE ⟨~ promises⟩ **5** : not true ⟨~ concepts⟩ **6** : not faithful or loyal : TREACHEROUS **7** : not essential or permanent ⟨~ front⟩ **8** : inaccurate in pitch **9** : based on mistaken ideas — **false·ly** *adv* — **false·ness** *n* — **fal·si·ty** \ˈfȯl-sə-tē\ *n*

false·hood \ˈfȯls-₁hùd\ *n* **1** : LIE **2** : absence of truth or accuracy **3** : the practice of lying

fal·set·to \fȯl-ˈse-tō\ *n, pl* **-tos** [It, fr. dim. of *falso* false] : an artificially high voice; *esp* : an artificial singing voice that overlaps and extends above the range of the full voice esp. of a tenor

fal·si·fy \ˈfȯl-sə-₁fī\ *vb* **-fied; -fy·ing 1** : to prove to be false **2** : to alter so as to deceive **3** : LIE; *also* : MISREPRESENT — **fal·si·fi·ca·tion** \₁fȯl-sə-fə-ˈkā-shən\ *n*

fal·ter \ˈfȯl-tər\ *vb* **1** : to move unsteadily : STUMBLE, TOTTER **2** : to hesitate in speech : STAMMER **3** : to hesitate in purpose or action : WAVER, FLINCH — **fal·ter·ing·ly** *adv*

fam *abbr* **1** familiar **2** family

fame \ˈfām\ *n* : public reputation : RENOWN — **famed** \ˈfāmd\ *adj*

fa·mil·ial \fə-ˈmil-yəl\ *adj* **1** : of, relating to, or suggestive of a family **2** : tending to occur in more members of a family than expected by chance alone ⟨a ~ disorder⟩

¹fa·mil·iar \fə-ˈmil-yər\ *n* **1** : COMPANION **2** : a spirit held to attend and serve or guard a person **3** : one who frequents a place

²familiar *adj* **1** : closely acquainted : INTIMATE **2** : of or relating to a family **3** : INFORMAL **4** : FORWARD, PRESUMPTUOUS **5** : frequently seen or experienced **6** : of everyday occurrence — **fa·mil·iar·ly** *adv*

fa·mil·iar·i·ty \fə-ˌmil-ˈyar-ə-tē, -ˌmi-lē-ˈar-\ *n, pl* **-ties** 1 : close friendship : INTIMACY 2 : INFORMALITY 3 : an unduly bold or forward act or expression : IMPROPRIETY 4 : close acquaintance with something

fa·mil·iar·ize \fə-ˈmil-yə-ˌrīz\ *vb* **-ized; -iz·ing** 1 : to make known or familiar 2 : to make thoroughly acquainted

fam·i·ly \ˈfam-lē, ˈfa-mə-\ *n, pl* **-lies** [ME *familie*, fr. L *familia* household, fr. *famulus* servant] 1 : a group of individuals living under one roof and under one head : HOUSEHOLD 2 : a group of persons of common ancestry : CLAN 3 : a group of things having common characteristics; *esp* : a group of related plants or animals ranking in biological classification above a genus and below an order 4 : a social unit usu. consisting of one or two parents and their children

family planning *n* : planning intended to determine the number and spacing of one's children by using birth control

family tree *n* : GENEALOGY; *also* : a genealogical diagram

fam·ine \ˈfa-mən\ *n* 1 : an extreme scarcity of food 2 : a great shortage

fam·ish \ˈfa-mish\ *vb* 1 : STARVE 2 : to suffer for lack of something necessary

fa·mous \ˈfā-məs\ *adj* 1 : widely known 2 : honored for achievement 3 : EXCELLENT, FIRST-RATE **syn** renowned, celebrated, noted, notorious, distinguished, eminent, illustrious

fa·mous·ly *adv* : SPLENDIDLY, EXCELLENTLY

¹fan \ˈfan\ *n* : a device (as a hand-waved triangular piece or a mechanism with blades) for producing a current of air

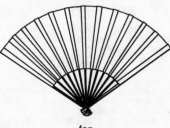

fan

²fan *vb* **fanned; fan·ning** 1 : to drive away the chaff from grain by winnowing 2 : to move (air) with or as if with a fan 3 : to direct a current of air upon ⟨∼ a fire⟩ 4 : to stir up to activity : STIMULATE 5 : to spread like a fan 6 : to strike out in baseball

³fan *n* : an enthusiastic follower or admirer

fa·nat·ic \fə-ˈna-tik\ *or* **fa·nat·i·cal** \-ti-kəl\ *adj* [L *fanaticus* inspired by a deity, frenzied, fr. *fanum* temple] : marked by excessive enthusiasm and often intense uncritical devotion — **fanatic** *n* — **fa·nat·i·cism** \-tə-ˌsi-zəm\ *n*

fan·ci·er \ˈfan-sē-ər\ *n* 1 : one that has a special liking or interest 2 : a person who breeds or grows some kind of animal or plant for points of excellence

fan·ci·ful \ˈfan-si-fəl\ *adj* 1 : marked by, existing in, or given to unrestrained imagination or whim rather than reason 2 : curiously made or shaped — **fan·ci·ful·ly** *adv*

¹fan·cy \ˈfan-sē\ *vb* **fan·cied; fan·cy·ing** 1 : LIKE 2 : IMAGINE 3 : to believe without evidence or certainty 4 : to visualize or interpret as

²fancy *n, pl* **fancies** [ME *fantasie, fantsy* fantasy, fancy, fr. MF *fantasie*, fr. L *phantasia*, fr. Gk, appearance, imagination] 1 : LIKING, INCLINATION; *also* : LOVE 2 : WHIM, NOTION, IDEA ⟨a passing ∼⟩ 3 : IMAGINATION 4 : TASTE, JUDGMENT **syn** caprice, crotchet, vagary

³fancy *adj* **fan·ci·er; -est** 1 : WHIMSICAL 2 : not plain : ORNAMENTAL, POSH 3 : of particular excellence 4 : bred esp. for a showy appearance 5 : EXCESSIVE 6 : executed with technical skill and style — **fan·ci·ly** \ˈfan-sə-lē\ *adv*

fancy dress *n* : a costume (as for a masquerade) chosen to suit a fancy

fan·cy–free \ˌfan-sē-ˈfrē\ *adj* : free from amorous attachment; *also* : free to imagine

fan·cy·work \ˈfan-sē-ˌwərk\ *n* : ornamental needlework (as embroidery)

fan·dan·go \fan-ˈdaŋ-gō\ *n, pl* **-gos** 1 : a lively Spanish or Spanish-American dance 2 : TOMFOOLERY

fane \ˈfān\ *n* 1 : TEMPLE 2 : CHURCH

fan·fare \ˈfan-ˌfar\ *n* 1 : a flourish of trumpets 2 : a showy display

fang \ˈfaŋ\ *n* : a long sharp tooth; *esp* : a grooved or hollow tooth of a venomous snake — **fanged** \ˈfaŋd\ *adj*

fan·light \ˈfan-ˌlīt\ *n* : a semicircular window with radiating bars like a fan that is set over a door or window

fan·tail \ˈfan-ˌtāl\ *n* 1 : a fan-shaped tail or end 2 : an overhang at the stern of a ship

fan·ta·sia \fan-ˈtā-zhə, -zhē-ə, -zē-ə, ˌfan-tə-ˈzē-ə\ *n* : a musical composition free and fanciful in form

fan·ta·size \ˈfan-tə-ˌsīz\ *vb* **-sized; -siz·ing** : IMAGINE, DAYDREAM

fan·tas·tic \fan-ˈtas-tik\ *also* **fan·tas·ti·cal** \-ti-kəl\ *adj* 1 : IMAGINARY, UNREAL 2 : conceived by unrestrained fancy 3 : exceedingly or unbelievably great 4 : ECCENTRIC **syn** chimerical, fanciful, imaginary — **fan·tas·ti·cal·ly** \-ti-k(ə-)lē\ *adv*

fan·ta·sy \ˈfan-tə-sē\ *n, pl* **-sies** 1 : IMAGINATION, FANCY 2 : a product of the imagination : ILLUSION 3 : FANTASIA — **fantasy** *vb*

¹far \ˈfär\ *adv* **far·ther** \-thər\ *or* **fur·ther** \ˈfər-\; **farthest** *or* **fur·thest** \-thəst\ 1 : at or to a considerable distance in space or time ⟨∼ from home⟩ 2 : by a broad interval : WIDELY, MUCH ⟨∼ better⟩ 3 : to or at a definite distance, point, or degree ⟨as ∼ as I know⟩ 4 : to an advanced point or extent ⟨go ∼ in his field⟩ — **by far** : by a considerable margin — **far and away** : DECIDEDLY — **so far** : until now

²far *adj* **farther** *or* **further; farthest** *or* **furthest** 1 : remote in space or time 2 : DIFFERENT 3 : LONG ⟨a ∼ journey⟩ 4 : being the more distant of two ⟨on the ∼ side of the lake⟩

far·ad \ˈfar-ˌad, -əd\ *n* : a unit of capacitance equal to the capacitance of a capacitor having a potential difference of one volt between its plates when it is charged with one coulomb of electricity

far·away \ˈfär-ə-ˌwā\ *adj* 1 : DISTANT, REMOTE 2 : DREAMY

farce \ˈfärs\ *n* 1 : a broadly satirical comedy with an improbable plot 2 : the humor characteristic of farce or pretense 3 : a ridiculous or empty display — **far·ci·cal** \ˈfär-si-kəl\ *adj*

¹fare \ˈfar\ *vb* **fared; far·ing** 1 : GO, TRAVEL 2 : GET ALONG, SUCCEED 3 : EAT, DINE

²fare *n* 1 : range of food : DIET; *also* : material provided for use, consumption, or enjoyment 2 : the price charged to transport a person 3 : a person paying a fare : PASSENGER

¹fare·well \far-ˈwel\ *vb imper* : get along well — used interjectionally to or by one departing

²farewell *n* 1 : a wish of well-being at parting : GOODBYE 2 : LEAVE-TAKING

³fare·well \ˈfar-ˌwel\ *adj* : PARTING, FINAL ⟨a ∼ concert⟩

far–fetched \ˈfär-ˈfecht\ *adj* : not easily or naturally deduced or introduced : IMPROBABLE ⟨∼ story⟩

far–flung \ˈfləŋ\ *adj* : widely spread or distributed

fa·ri·na \fə-ˈrē-nə\ *n* [L, meal, flour] : a fine meal (as of wheat) used in puddings or as a breakfast cereal

far·i·na·ceous \ˌfar-ə-ˈnā-shəs\ *adj* 1 : having a mealy texture or surface 2 : containing or rich in starch

¹**farm** \ˈfärm\ *n* [ME *ferme* rent, lease, fr. OF, lease, fr. *fermer* to fix, make a contract, fr. L *firmare* to make firm, fr. *firmus* firm] **1** : a tract of land used for raising crops or livestock **2** : a minor-league subsidiary of a major-league baseball team

²**farm** *vb* : to use (land) as a farm 〈∼ed 200 acres〉; *also* : to raise crops or livestock — **farm•er** *n*

farm•hand \ˈfärm-ˌhand\ *n* : a farm laborer

farm•house \-ˌhaús\ *n* : a dwelling on a farm

farm•ing \ˈfär-miŋ\ *n* : the occupation or business of a person who farms

farm•land \ˈfärm-ˌland\ *n* : land used or suitable for farming

farm out *vb* : to turn over (as a task) to another

farm•stead \ˈfärm-ˌsted\ *n* : a farm with its buildings

farm•yard \-ˌyärd\ *n* : land around or enclosed by farm buildings

far—off \ˈfär-ˈòf\ *adj* : remote in time or space : DISTANT

fa•rouche \fə-ˈrüsh\ *adj* [F] **1** : WILD **2** : marked by shyness and lack of polish

far—out \ˈfär-ˈaút\ *adj* : very unconventional 〈∼ clothes〉

far•ra•go \fə-ˈrä-gō, -ˈrä-\ *n, pl* **-goes** [L, mixed fodder, mixture] : a confused collection : MIXTURE

far—reach•ing \ˈfär-ˈrē-chiŋ\ *adj* : having a wide range or effect

far•ri•er \ˈfar-ē-ər\ *n* : a person who shoes horses

¹**far•row** \ˈfar-ō\ *vb* : to give birth to a litter of pigs

²**farrow** *n* : a litter of pigs

far•see•ing \ˈfär-ˌsē-iŋ\ *adj* : FARSIGHTED 1, 2

far•sight•ed \ˈfär-ˌsī-təd\ *adj* **1** : seeing or able to see to a great distance **2** : JUDICIOUS, WISE, SHREWD **3** : affected with an eye condition in which vision is better for distant than near objects — **far•sight•ed•ness** *n*

¹**far•ther** \ˈfär-thər\ *adv* **1** : at or to a greater distance or more advanced point **2** : to a greater degree or extent

²**farther** *adj* **1** : more distant **2** : ADDITIONAL

far•ther•most \-ˌmōst\ *adj* : FARTHEST

¹**far•thest** \ˈfär-thəst\ *adj* : most distant

²**farthest** *adv* **1** : to or at the greatest distance : REMOTEST **2** : to the most advanced point **3** : by the greatest degree or extent : MOST

far•thing \ˈfär-thiŋ\ *n* **1** : a former British monetary unit equal to ¼ of a penny; *also* : a coin representing this unit **2** : something of small value

fas•ci•cle \ˈfa-si-kəl\ *n* **1** : a small or slender bundle (as of pine needles or nerve fiber) **2** : one of the divisions of a book published in parts — **fas•ci•cled** \-kəld\ *adj*

fas•ci•nate \ˈfas-ᵊn-ˌāt\ *vb* **-nat•ed; -nat•ing** [L *fascinare*, fr. *fascinum* evil spell] **1** : to transfix and hold spellbound by an irresistible power **2** : ALLURE **3** : to be irresistibly attractive — **fas•ci•na•tion** \ˌfas-ᵊn-ˈā-shən\ *n*

fas•cism \ˈfa-ˌshi-zəm\ *n, often cap* : a political philosophy, movement, or regime that exalts nation and often race and stands for a centralized autocratic often militaristic government — **fas•cist** \-shist\ *n or adj, often cap* — **fas•cis•tic** \fa-ˈshis-tik\ *adj, often cap*

¹**fash•ion** \ˈfa-shən\ *n* **1** : the make or form of something **2** : MANNER, WAY **3** : a prevailing custom, usage, or style **4** : the prevailing style (as in dress) **syn** mode, vogue, rage, trend

²**fashion** *vb* **1** : MOLD, CONSTRUCT **2** : FIT, ADAPT

fash•ion•able \ˈfa-shə-nə-bəl\ *adj* **1** : dressing or behaving according to fashion : STYLISH **2** : of or relating to the world of fashion 〈∼ resorts〉 **syn** chic, modish, smart, swank — **fash•ion•ably** \-blē\ *adv*

¹**fast** \ˈfast\ *adj* **1** : firmly fixed **2** : tightly shut **3** : adhering firmly **4** : STUCK **5** : STAUNCH 〈∼ friends〉 **6** : characterized by quick motion, operation, or effect 〈a ∼ trip〉 〈a ∼ track〉 **7** : indicating ahead of the correct time 〈the clock is ∼〉 **8** : not easily disturbed : SOUND 〈a ∼ sleep〉 **9** : permanently dyed; *also* : being proof against fading 〈colors ∼ to sunlight〉 **10** : DISSIPATED, WILD **11** : sexually promiscuous **syn** rapid, swift, fleet, quick, speedy, hasty

²**fast** *adv* **1** : in a firm or fixed manner 〈stuck ∼ in the mud〉 **2** : SOUNDLY, DEEPLY 〈∼ asleep〉 **3** : SWIFTLY **4** : RECKLESSLY

³**fast** *vb* **1** : to abstain from food **2** : to eat sparingly or abstain from some foods

⁴**fast** *n* **1** : the act or practice of fasting **2** : a time of fasting

fast•back \ˈfast-ˌbak\ *n* : an automobile having a roof with a long slope to the rear

fast•ball \-ˌbòl\ *n* : a baseball pitch thrown at full speed

fas•ten \ˈfas-ᵊn\ *vb* **1** : to attach or join by or as if by pinning, tying, or nailing **2** : to make fast : fix securely **3** : to become fixed or joined **4** : to focus attention 〈∼ed onto the newest trends〉 — **fas•ten•er** *n*

fas•ten•ing *n* : something that fastens : FASTENER

fast—food \ˈfast-ˈfüd\ *adj* : specializing in food that is prepared and served quickly 〈a ∼ restaurant〉

fast—for•ward \-ˈfòr-wərd\ *n* **1** : a function of a tape player that advances tape rapidly **2** : a state of rapid advancement — **fast—forward** *vb*

fas•tid•i•ous \fa-ˈsti-dē-əs\ *adj* **1** : overly difficult to please **2** : showing a meticulous or demanding attitude 〈∼ workmanship〉 **syn** nice, finicky, fussy, particular, persnickety, squeamish — **fas•tid•i•ous•ly** *adv* — **fas•tid•i•ous•ness** *n*

fast•ness \ˈfast-nəs\ *n* **1** : the quality or state of being fast **2** : a fortified or secure place : STRONGHOLD

fast—talk \ˈfast-ˌtòk\ *vb* : to influence by persuasive and usu. deceptive talk

fast—track \ˈfast-ˌtrak\ *vb* : to speed up the processing or production of

fast track *n* : a course leading to rapid advancement or success

¹**fat** \ˈfat\ *adj* **fat•ter; fat•test** **1** : PLUMP, FLESHY **2** : OILY, GREASY **3** : well filled out : BIG **4** : well stocked : ABUNDANT **5** : richly rewarding — **fat•ness** *n*

²**fat** *n* **1** : animal tissue rich in greasy or oily matter **2** : any of numerous energy-rich esters that occur naturally in animal fats and in plants and are soluble in organic solvents (as ether) but not in water **3** : the best or richest portion 〈lived on the ∼ of the land〉 **4** : OBESITY **5** : excess matter

fa•tal \ˈfāt-ᵊl\ *adj* **1** : FATEFUL 〈that ∼ day〉 **2** : causing death or ruin 〈a ∼ mistake〉 — **fa•tal•ly** *adv*

fa•tal•ism \-ˌi-zəm\ *n* : the belief that events are determined by fate — **fa•tal•ist** \-ist\ *n* — **fa•tal•is•tic** \ˌfāt-ᵊl-ˈis-tik\ *adj* — **fa•tal•is•ti•cal•ly** \-ti-k(ə-)lē\ *adv*

fa•tal•i•ty \fā-ˈta-lə-tē, fə-\ *n, pl* **-ties** **1** : DEADLINESS **2** : FATE **3** : death resulting from a disaster or accident; *also* : one who suffers such a death

fat•back \ˈfat-ˌbak\ *n* : a fatty strip from the back of the hog usu. cured by salting and drying

fat cat *n* **1** : a wealthy contributor to a political campaign **2** : a wealthy privileged person

fate \ˈfāt\ *n* [ME, fr. MF or L; MF, fr. L *fatum*, lit., what has been spoken, fr. *fari* to speak] **1** : the cause or will that is held to determine events : DESTINY **2** : LOT, FORTUNE **3** : DISASTER; *esp* : DEATH **4** : END, OUTCOME **5** *cap, pl* : the three goddesses of classical mythology who determine the course of human life

fat•ed \ˈfā-təd\ *adj* : decreed, controlled, or marked by fate

fate•ful \ˈfāt-fəl\ *adj* **1** : OMINOUS, PROPHETIC **2** : IMPORTANT, DECISIVE **3** : DEADLY, DESTRUCTIVE **4** : determined by fate — **fate•ful•ly** *adv*

fath *abbr* fathom

fat•head \ˈfat-ˌhed\ *n* : a stupid person — **fat•head•ed** \-ˈhe-dəd\ *adj*

¹**fa•ther** \ˈfä-thər\ *n* **1** : a male parent **2** *cap* : God esp. as the first person of the Trinity **3** : FOREFATHER **4** : one deserving the respect and love given to a father **5** *often cap* : an early Christian writer accepted by the church as an authoritative witness to its teaching

and practice **6** : ORIGINATOR ⟨the ∼ of modern radio⟩; *also* : SOURCE **7** : PRIEST — used esp. as a title **8** : one of the leading men ⟨city ∼s⟩ — **fa·ther·hood** \-ˌhu̇d\ *n* — **fa·ther·less** *adj* — **fa·ther·ly** *adj*

²**father** *vb* **1** : BEGET **2** : to be the founder, producer, or author of **3** : to treat or care for as a father

father–in–law \ˈfä-thə-rən-ˌlȯ\ *n, pl* **fa·thers–in–law** \-thər-zən-\ : the father of one's husband or wife

fa·ther·land \ˈfä-thər-ˌland\ *n* **1** : the native land of one's ancestors **2** : one's native land

¹**fath·om** \ˈfa-thəm\ *n* [ME *fadme,* fr. OE *fæthm* outstretched arms, fathom] : a unit of length equal to 6 feet (about 1.8 meters) used esp. for measuring the depth of water

²**fathom** *vb* **1** : to measure by a sounding line **2** : PROBE **3** : to penetrate and come to understand — **fath·om·able** \ˈfa-thə-mə-bəl\ *adj*

fath·om·less \ˈfa-thəm-ləs\ *adj* : incapable of being fathomed

¹**fa·tigue** \fə-ˈtēg\ *n* [F] **1** : manual or menial work performed by military personnel **2** *pl* : the uniform or work clothing worn on fatigue and in the field **3** : weariness from labor or stress **4** : the tendency of a material to break under repeated stress

²**fatigue** *vb* **fa·tigued; fa·tigu·ing** : WEARY, TIRE

fat·ten \ˈfat-ᵊn\ *vb* : to make or grow fat

¹**fat·ty** \ˈfa-tē\ *adj* **fat·ti·er; -est 1** : containing fat esp. in unusual amounts **2** : GREASY

²**fatty** *n, pl* **fat·ties** : a fat person

fatty acid *n* : any of numerous acids that contain only carbon, hydrogen, and oxygen and that occur naturally in fats and various oils

fa·tu·ity \fə-ˈtü-ə-tē, -ˈtyü-\ *n, pl* **-ities** : FOOLISHNESS, STUPIDITY

fat·u·ous \ˈfa-chü-wəs\ *adj* : FOOLISH, INANE, SILLY — **fat·u·ous·ly** *adv*

fau·bourg \fō-ˈbu̇r\ *n* **1** : a suburb esp. of a French city **2** : a city quarter

fau·ces \ˈfȯ-ˌsēz\ *n pl* [L, throat] : the narrow passage located between the soft palate and the base of the tongue that joins the mouth to the pharynx

fau·cet \ˈfȯ-sət, ˈfä-\ *n* : a fixture for drawing off a liquid (as from a pipe)

¹**fault** \ˈfȯlt\ *n* **1** : a weakness in character : FAILING **2** : IMPERFECTION, IMPAIRMENT, DEFECT **3** : an error esp. in service in a net or racket game **4** : MISDEMEANOR; *also* : MISTAKE **5** : responsibility for something wrong **6** : a fracture in the earth's crust accompanied by a displacement of one side relative to the other — **fault·i·ly** \ˈfȯl-tə-lē\ *adv* — **fault·less** *adj* — **fault·less·ly** *adv* — **faulty** *adj*

²**fault** *vb* **1** : to commit a fault : ERR **2** : to fracture so as to produce a geologic fault **3** : to find a fault in

fault·find·er \ˈfȯlt-ˌfīn-dər\ *n* : a person who tends to find fault or complain **syn** critic, carper, caviler, complainer — **fault·find·ing** *n or adj*

faun \ˈfȯn\ *n* : a Roman god similar to but gentler than a satyr

fau·na \ˈfȯ-nə\ *n, pl* **faunas** *also* **fau·nae** \-ˌnē, -ˌnī\ [NL, fr. L *Fauna,* sister of Faunus (the Roman god of animals)] : animals or animal life esp. of a region, period, or environment — **fau·nal** \-nəl\ *adj*

fau·vism \ˈfō-ˌvi-zəm\ *n, often cap* : a movement in painting characterized by vivid colors, free treatment of form, and a vibrant and decorative effect — **fau·vist** \-vist\ *n, often cap*

faux pas \ˈfō-ˌpä, fō-ˈ\ *n, pl* **faux pas** *same or* -ˌpäz, -ˈpäz\ [F, lit., false step] : BLUNDER; *esp* : a social blunder

¹**fa·vor** \ˈfä-vər\ *n* **1** : friendly regard shown toward another esp. by a superior **2** : APPROVAL **3** : PARTIALITY **4** : POPULARITY **5** : gracious kindness; *also* : an act of such kindness **6** *pl* : effort in one's behalf : ATTENTION **7** : a token of love (as a ribbon) usu. worn conspicuously **8** : a small gift or decorative item given out at a party **9** : a special privilege **10** : sexual priv-

ileges — usu. used in pl. **11** *archaic* : LETTER **12** : BEHALF, INTEREST

²**favor** *vb* **1** : to regard or treat with favor **2** : OBLIGE **3** : ENDOW ⟨∼ed by nature⟩ **4** : to treat gently or carefully : SPARE ⟨∼ a lame leg⟩ **5** : PREFER **6** : SUPPORT, SUSTAIN **7** : FACILITATE ⟨darkness ∼s attack⟩ **8** : RESEMBLE ⟨he ∼s his father⟩

fa·vor·able \ˈfä-və-rə-bəl\ *adj* **1** : APPROVING **2** : HELPFUL, PROMISING, ADVANTAGEOUS ⟨∼ weather⟩ — **fa·vor·ably** \-blē\ *adv*

fa·vor·ite \ˈfä-və-rət, -vrət\ *n* **1** : a person or a thing that is favored above others **2** : a competitor regarded as most likely to win — **favorite** *adj*

favorite son *n* : a candidate supported by the delegates of his state at a presidential nominating convention

fa·vor·it·ism \ˈfä-və-rə-ˌti-zəm\ *n* : PARTIALITY, BIAS

fa·vour *chiefly Brit var of* FAVOR

¹**fawn** \ˈfȯn, ˈfän\ *vb* **1** : to show affection ⟨a dog ∼ing on its master⟩ **2** : to court favor by a cringing or flattering manner **syn** grovel, kowtow, toady, truckle

²**fawn** *n* **1** : a young deer **2** : a light grayish brown

fax \ˈfaks\ *n* **1** : FACSIMILE **2 2** : a device used to send or receive facsimile communications; *also* : such a communication — **fax** *vb*

fay \ˈfā\ *n* : FAIRY, ELF — **fay** *adj*

faze \ˈfāz\ *vb* **fazed; faz·ing** : to disturb the composure or courage of : DAUNT

FBI *abbr* Federal Bureau of Investigation

FCC *abbr* Federal Communications Commission

FD *abbr* fire department

FDA *abbr* Food and Drug Administration

FDIC *abbr* Federal Deposit Insurance Corporation

Fe *symbol* [L *ferrum*] iron

fe·al·ty \ˈfēl-tē\ *n, pl* **-ties** : LOYALTY, ALLEGIANCE **syn** fidelity, devotion, faithfulness, piety

¹**fear** \ˈfir\ *vb* **1** : to have a reverent awe of ⟨∼ God⟩ **2** : to be afraid of : have fear **3** : to be apprehensive

²**fear** *n* **1** : an unpleasant often strong emotion caused by expectation or awareness of danger; *also* : an instance of or a state marked by this emotion **2** : anxious concern : SOLICITUDE **3** : profound reverence esp. toward God **syn** dread, fright, alarm, panic, terror, trepidation

fear·ful \-fəl\ *adj* **1** : causing fear **2** : filled with fear **3** : showing or caused by fear **4** : extremely bad, intense, or large — **fear·ful·ly** *adv*

fear·less \-ləs\ *adj* : free from fear : BRAVE — **fear·less·ly** *adv* — **fear·less·ness** *n*

fear·some \-səm\ *adj* **1** : causing fear **2** : TIMID

fea·si·ble \ˈfē-zə-bəl\ *adj* **1** : capable of being done or carried out ⟨a ∼ plan⟩ **2** : SUITABLE **3** : REASONABLE, LIKELY **syn** possible, practicable, viable, workable — **fea·si·bil·i·ty** \ˌfē-zə-ˈbi-lə-tē\ *n* — **fea·si·bly** \ˈfē-zə-blē\ *adv*

¹**feast** \ˈfēst\ *n* **1** : an elaborate meal : BANQUET **2** : FESTIVAL 1

²**feast** *vb* **1** : to take part in a feast; *also* : to give a feast for **2** : to enjoy some unusual pleasure or delight **3** : DELIGHT, GRATIFY

feat \ˈfēt\ *n* : DEED, EXPLOIT, ACHIEVEMENT; *esp* : an act notable for courage, skill, endurance, or ingenuity

¹**feath·er** \ˈfe-thər\ *n* **1** : any of the light horny outgrowths that form the external covering of the body of a bird **2** : PLUME **3** : PLUMAGE **4** : KIND, NATURE ⟨birds of a ∼⟩ **5** : ATTIRE, DRESS ⟨in full ∼⟩ **6** : CONDITION, MOOD ⟨in fine ∼⟩ — **feath·ered** \-thərd\ *adj* — **feath·er·less** *adj* — **feath·ery** *adj* — **a feather in one's cap** : a mark of distinction : HONOR

²**feather** *vb* **1** : to furnish with a feather ⟨∼ an arrow⟩ **2** : to cover, clothe, line, or adorn with or as if with feathers — **feather one's nest** : to provide for oneself esp. while in a position of trust

feath·er·bed·ding \ˈfe-thər-ˌbe-diŋ\ *n* : the requiring of an employer usu. under a union rule or safety statute to employ more workers than are needed

feath·er·edge \-₁ej\ *n* : a very thin sharp edge

feath·er·weight \-₁wāt\ *n* : one that is very light in weight; *esp* : a boxer weighing more than 118 but not over 126 pounds

¹**fea·ture** \'fē-chər\ *n* 1 : the shape or appearance of the face or its parts 2 : a part of the face : LINEAMENT 3 : a prominent part or characteristic 4 : a special attraction (as in a newspaper) 5 : something offered to the public or advertised as particularly attractive — **fea·ture·less** *adj*

²**feature** *vb* 1 : to picture in the mind : IMAGINE 2 : to give special prominence to ⟨∼ a story in a newspaper⟩ 3 : to play an important part

feaze \'fēz, 'fāz\ *var of* FAZE

Feb *abbr* February

fe·brile \'fe-₁brīl\ *adj* : FEVERISH

Feb·ru·ary \'fe-b(y)ə-₁wer-ē, 'fe-brə-\ *n* [ME *Februarie*, fr. L *Februarius*, fr. *Februa*, pl., feast of purification] : the second month of the year having 28 and in leap years 29 days

fe·ces \'fē-₁sēz\ *n pl* : bodily waste discharged from the intestine — **fe·cal** \-kəl\ *adj*

feck·less \'fek-ləs\ *adj* 1 : WEAK, INEFFECTIVE 2 : WORTHLESS, IRRESPONSIBLE

fe·cund \'fe-kənd, 'fē-\ *adj* : FRUITFUL, PROLIFIC — **fe·cun·di·ty** \fi-'kən-də-tē, fe-\ *n*

fe·cun·date \'fe-kən-₁dāt, 'fē-\ *vb* **-dat·ed; -dat·ing** 1 : to make fecund 2 : IMPREGNATE — **fe·cun·da·tion** \₁fe-kən-'dā-shən, ₁fē-\ *n*

fed *abbr* federal; federation

fed·er·al \'fe-də-rəl, -drəl\ *adj* 1 : formed by a compact between political units that surrender individual sovereignty to a central authority but retain certain limited powers 2 : of or constituting a form of government in which power is distributed between a central authority and constituent territorial units 3 : of or relating to the central government of a federation 4 *cap* : FEDERALIST 5 *often cap* : of, relating to, or loyal to the federal government or the Union armies of the U.S. in the American Civil War — **fed·er·al·ly** *adv*

Federal *n* : a supporter of the U.S. government in the Civil War; *esp* : a soldier in the federal armies

federal district *n* : a district (as the District of Columbia) set apart as the seat of the central government of a federation

fed·er·al·ism \'fe-də-rə-li-zəm, -drə-\ *n* 1 *often cap* : the distribution of power in an organization (as a government) between a central authority and the constituent units 2 : support or advocacy of federalism 3 *cap* : the principles of the Federalists

fed·er·al·ist \-list\ *n* 1 : an advocate of federalism 2 *often cap* : an advocate of a federal union between the American colonies after the Revolution and of adoption of the U.S. Constitution 3 *cap* : a member of a major political party in the early years of the U.S. favoring a strong centralized national government — **federalist** *adj, often cap*

fed·er·al·ize \'fe-də-rə-₁līz, -drə-\ *vb* **-ized; -iz·ing** 1 : to unite in or under a federal system 2 : to bring under the jurisdiction of a federal government

fed·er·ate \'fe-də-₁rāt\ *vb* **-at·ed; -at·ing** : to join in a federation

fed·er·a·tion \₁fe-də-'rā-shən\ *n* 1 : the act of federating; *esp* : the forming of a federal union 2 : a federal government 3 : a union of organizations

fedn *abbr* federation

fe·do·ra \fi-'dōr-ə\ *n* : a low soft felt hat with the crown creased lengthwise

fed up *adj* : satiated, tired, or disgusted beyond endurance

fee \'fē\ *n* 1 : an estate in land held from a feudal lord 2 : an inherited or heritable estate in land 3 : a fixed charge; *also* : a charge for a service

fee·ble \'fē-bəl\ *adj* **fee·bler** \-bə-lər\; **fee·blest** \-bə-ləst\ [ME *feble*, fr. OF, fr. L *flebilis* lamentable,

wretched, fr. *flēre* to weep] 1 : DECREPIT, FRAIL 2 : INEFFECTIVE, INADEQUATE ⟨a ∼ protest⟩ — **fee·ble·ness** *n* — **fee·bly** \-blē\ *adv*

fee·ble·mind·ed \₁fē-bəl-'mīn-dəd\ *adj* : lacking normal intelligence — **fee·ble·mind·ed·ness** *n*

¹**feed** \'fēd\ *vb* **fed** \'fed\; **feed·ing** 1 : to give food to; *also* : to give as food 2 : EAT 1; *also* : PREY 3 : to furnish what is necessary to the growth or function of — **feed·er** *n*

²**feed** *n* 1 : a usu. large meal 2 : food for livestock 3 : a mechanism for feeding material to a machine

feed·back \'fēd-₁bak\ *n* 1 : the return to the input of a part of the output of a machine, system, or process 2 : response esp. to one in authority about an activity or policy

feed·lot \'fēd-₁lät\ *n* : land on which cattle are fattened for market

feed·stuff \-₁stəf\ *n* : FEED 2

¹**feel** \'fēl\ *vb* **felt** \'felt\; **feel·ing** 1 : to perceive or examine through physical contact : TOUCH, HANDLE 2 : EXPERIENCE; *also* : to suffer from 3 : to ascertain by cautious trial ⟨∼ out public sentiment⟩ 4 : to be aware of 5 : to be conscious of an inward impression, state of mind, or physical condition 6 : BELIEVE, THINK 7 : to search for something with the fingers : GROPE 8 : SEEM ⟨it ∼s like spring⟩ 9 : to have sympathy or pity

²**feel** *n* 1 : the sense of touch 2 : SENSATION, FEELING 3 : the quality of a thing as imparted through touch

feel·er \'fē-lər\ *n* 1 : one that feels; *esp* : a tactile organ (as on the head of an insect) 2 : a proposal or remark made to find out the views of other people

¹**feel·ing** \'fē-liŋ\ *n* 1 : the sense of touch; *also* : a sensation perceived by this 2 : a state of mind ⟨a ∼ of loneliness⟩ 3 *pl* : general emotional condition : SENSIBILITIES ⟨hurt their ∼s⟩ 4 : OPINION, BELIEF 5 : capacity to respond emotionally

²**feeling** *adj* 1 : SENSITIVE; *esp* : easily moved emotionally 2 : expressing emotion or sensitivity — **feel·ing·ly** *adv*

feet *pl of* FOOT

feign \'fān\ *vb* 1 : to give a false appearance of : SHAM ⟨∼ illness⟩ 2 : to assert as if true : PRETEND

feint \'fānt\ *n* : something feigned; *esp* : a mock blow or attack intended to distract attention from the real point of attack — **feint** *vb*

feld·spar \'feld-₁spär\ *n* : any of a group of crystalline minerals consisting of silicates of aluminum with another element (as potassium or sodium)

fe·lic·i·tate \fi-'li-sə-₁tāt\ *vb* **-tat·ed; -tat·ing** : CONGRATULATE — **fe·lic·i·ta·tion** \-₁li-sə-'tā-shən\ *n*

fe·lic·i·tous \fi-'li-sə-təs\ *adj* 1 : suitably expressed : APT 2 : PLEASANT, DELIGHTFUL — **fe·lic·i·tous·ly** *adv*

fe·lic·i·ty \fi-'li-sə-tē\ *n, pl* **-ties** 1 : the quality or state of being happy; *esp* : great happiness 2 : something that causes happiness 3 : a pleasing manner or quality esp. in art or language 4 : an apt expression

fe·line \'fē-₁līn\ *adj* [L *felinus*, fr. *felis* cat] 1 : of or relating to cats or their kin 2 : SLY, TREACHEROUS 3 : STEALTHY — **feline** *n*

¹**fell** \'fel\ *n* : SKIN, HIDE, PELT

²**fell** *vb* 1 : to cut, beat, or knock down; *also* : KILL 2 : to sew (a seam) by folding one raw edge under the other

³**fell** *past of* FALL

⁴**fell** *adj* : CRUEL, FIERCE; *also* : DEADLY

fel·lah \'fe-lə, fə-'lä\ *n, pl* **fel·la·hin** *or* **fel·la·heen** \₁fe-lə-'hēn\ : a peasant or agricultural laborer in Arab countries (as Egypt or Syria)

fel·la·tio \fə-'lä-shē-₁ō\ *also* **fel·la·tion** \-shən\ *n* : oral stimulation of the penis

fel·low \'fe-lō\ *n* [ME *felawe*, fr. OE *fēolaga*, fr. ON *fēlagi*, fr. *fēlag* partnership, fr. *fē* cattle, money + *lag* act of laying] 1 : COMRADE, ASSOCIATE 2 : EQUAL, PEER 3 : one of a pair : MATE 4 : a member of an incorporated literary or scientific society 5 : MAN, BOY 6 : BOYFRIEND 7 : a person granted a stipend for advanced study

fel·low·man \ˌfe-lō-'man\ *n* : a kindred human being

fel·low·ship \'fe-lō-ˌship\ *n* **1** : the condition of friendly relationship existing among persons : COMRADESHIP **2** : a community of interest or feeling **3** : a group with similar interests **4** : the position of a fellow (as of a university) **5** : the stipend granted a fellow

fellow traveler *n* : a person who sympathizes with and often furthers the ideals and program of an organized group (as the Communist party) without joining it

fel·on \'fe-lən\ *n* **1** : one who has committed a felony **2** : WHITLOW

fel·o·ny \'fe-lə-nē\ *n, pl* **-nies** : a serious crime punishable by a heavy sentence — **fe·lo·ni·ous** \fə-'lō-nē-əs\ *adj*

¹felt \'felt\ *n* **1** : a cloth made of wool and fur often mixed with natural or synthetic fibers **2** : a material resembling felt

²felt *past and past part of* FEEL

fem *abbr* **1** female **2** feminine

fe·male \'fē-ˌmāl\ *adj* [ME, alter. of *femel*, fr. MF *femelle*, fr. ML *femella*, fr. L girl, dim. of *femina* woman] : of, relating to, or being the sex that bears young; *also* : PISTILLATE **syn** feminine, womanly, womanlike, womanish, effeminate — **female** *n*

¹fem·i·nine \'fe-mə-nən\ *adj* **1** : of the female sex; *also* : characteristic of or appropriate or peculiar to women **2** : of, relating to, or constituting the gender that includes most words or grammatical forms referring to females — **fem·i·nin·i·ty** \ˌfe-mə-'ni-nə-tē\ *n*

²feminine *n* : a noun, pronoun, adjective, or inflectional form or class of the feminine gender; *also* : the feminine gender

fem·i·nism \'fe-mə-ˌni-zəm\ *n* **1** : the theory of the political, economic, and social equality of the sexes **2** : organized activity on behalf of women's rights and interests — **fem·i·nist** \-nist\ *n or adj*

femme fa·tale \ˌfem-fə-'tal\ *n, pl* **femmes fa·tales** *same or* -'talz\ [F, lit., disastrous woman] : a seductive woman

fe·mur \'fē-mər\ *n, pl* **fe·murs** *or* **fe·mo·ra** \'fe-mə-rə\ : the long thigh bone extending from the hip to the knee — **fem·o·ral** \'fe-mə-rəl\ *adj*

¹fen \'fen\ *n* : low swampy land

²fen \'fən\ *n, pl* **fen** — see *yuan* at MONEY table

¹fence \'fens\ *n* [ME *fens*, short for *defens* defense] **1** : a barrier (as of wood or wire) to prevent escape or entry or to mark a boundary **2** : a person who receives stolen goods; *also* : a place where stolen goods are disposed of — **on the fence** : in a position of neutrality or indecision

²fence *vb* **fenced; fenc·ing 1** : to enclose with a fence **2** : to keep in or out with a fence **3** : to practice fencing **4** : to use tactics of attack and defense esp. in debate — **fenc·er** *n*

fenc·ing *n* **1** : the art or practice of attack and defense with the foil, épée, or saber **2** : the fences of a property or region **3** : material used for building fences

fend \'fend\ *vb* **1** : to keep or ward off : REPEL **2** : SHIFT ⟨~ for yourself⟩

fend·er \'fen-dər\ *n* : a protective device (as a guard over the wheel of an automobile)

fen·es·tra·tion \ˌfe-nə-'strā-shən\ *n* : the arrangement and design of windows and doors in a building

Fe·ni·an \'fē-nē-ən\ *n* : a member of a secret 19th century Irish and Irish-American organization dedicated to overthrowing British rule in Ireland

fen·nel \'fen-ᵊl\ *n* : a garden plant related to the carrot and grown for its aromatic foliage and seeds

FEPC *abbr* Fair Employment Practices Commission

fe·ral \'fir-əl, 'fer-\ *adj* **1** : SAVAGE **2** : WILD **3** : having escaped from domestication and become wild

fer–de–lance \'fer-də-'läns\ *n, pl* **fer–de–lance** [F, lit., lance iron, spearhead] : a large venomous pit viper of Central and So. America

¹fer·ment \fər-'ment\ *vb* **1** : to cause or undergo fer-

mentation **2** : to be or cause to be in a state of agitation or intense activity

²fer·ment \'fər-ˌment\ *n* **1** : a living organism (as a yeast) causing fermentation by its enzymes; *also* : ENZYME **2** : AGITATION, TUMULT

fer·men·ta·tion \ˌfər-mən-'tā-shən, -ˌmen-\ *n* **1** : chemical decomposition of an organic substance (as in the souring of milk or the formation of alcohol from sugar) by enzymatic action in the absence of oxygen often with formation of gas **2** : FERMENT 2

fer·mi·um \'fer-mē-əm, 'fər-\ *n* : an artificially produced radioactive metallic chemical element — see ELEMENT table

fern \'fərn\ *n* : any of an order of vascular plants resembling seed plants in having roots, stems, and leaflike fronds but reproducing by spores instead of by flowers and seeds

fern·ery \'fər-nə-rē\ *n, pl* **-er·ies 1** : a place for growing ferns **2** : a collection of growing ferns

fe·ro·cious \fə-'rō-shəs\ *adj* **1** : FIERCE, SAVAGE **2** : extremely intense — **fe·ro·cious·ly** *adv* — **fe·ro·cious·ness** *n*

fe·roc·i·ty \fə-'rä-sə-tē\ *n* : the quality or state of being ferocious

¹fer·ret \'fer-ət\ *n* : a partially domesticated usu. white European mammal related to the weasels

²ferret *vb* **1** : to hunt game with ferrets **2** : to drive out of a hiding place **3** : to find and bring to light by searching ⟨~ out the truth⟩

fer·ric \'fer-ik\ *adj* : of, relating to, or containing iron

ferric oxide *n* : an oxide of iron found in nature as hematite and as rust and used as a pigment and for polishing

Fer·ris wheel \'fer-əs-\ *n* : an amusement device consisting of a large upright power-driven wheel with seats that remain horizontal around its rim

fer·ro·mag·net·ic \ˌfer-ō-mag-'ne-tik\ *adj* : of or relating to substances that are easily magnetized

fer·rous \'fer-əs\ *adj* : of, relating to, or containing iron

fer·rule \'fer-əl\ *n* : a metal ring or cap around a slender wooden shaft to prevent splitting

¹fer·ry \'fer-ē\ *vb* **fer·ried; fer·ry·ing** [ME *ferien*, fr. OE *ferian* to carry, convey] **1** : to carry by boat across a body of water **2** : to cross by a ferry **3** : to convey from one place to another

²ferry *n, pl* **ferries 1** : a place where persons or things are ferried **2** : FERRYBOAT

fer·ry·boat \'fer-ē-ˌbōt\ *n* : a boat used in ferrying

fer·tile \'fərt-ᵊl\ *adj* **1** : producing plentifully : PRODUCTIVE ⟨~ soils⟩ ⟨a ~ mind⟩ **2** : capable of developing or reproducing ⟨~ seed⟩ ⟨a ~ bull⟩ **syn** fruitful, prolific, fecund, productive — **fer·til·i·ty** \(ˌ)fər-'ti-lə-tē\ *n*

fer·til·ize \'fərt-ᵊl-ˌīz\ *vb* **-ized; -iz·ing 1** : to unite with in the process of fertilization ⟨a sperm ~s an egg⟩ **2** : to apply fertilizer to — **fer·til·iza·tion** \ˌfərt-ᵊl-ə-'zā-shən\ *n*

fer·til·iz·er \-ˌī-zər\ *n* : material (as manure or a chemical mixture) for enriching land

fer·ule \'fer-əl\ *n* : a rod or ruler used to punish children

fer·ven·cy \'fər-vən-sē\ *n, pl* **-cies** : FERVOR

fer·vent \'fər-vənt\ *adj* **1** : very hot : GLOWING **2** : marked by great intensity of feeling **syn** impassioned, ardent, fervid, fiery, passionate — **fer·vent·ly** *adv*

fer·vid \-vəd\ *adj* **1** : very hot **2** : ARDENT, ZEALOUS — **fer·vid·ly** *adv*

fer·vor \'fər-vər\ *n* **1** : intense heat **2** : intensity of feeling or expression

fer·vour *chiefly Brit var of* FERVOR

fes·tal \'fest-ᵊl\ *adj* : FESTIVE

fes·ter \'fes-tər\ *vb* **1** : to form pus **2** : PUTREFY, ROT **3** : RANKLE

fes·ti·val \'fes-tə-vəl\ *n* **1** : a time of celebration marked by special observances; *esp* : an occasion marked with religious ceremonies **2** : a periodic season or program of cultural events or entertainment ⟨a dance ∼⟩

fes·tive \\'fes-tiv\\ *adj* **1** : of, relating to, or suitable for a feast or festival **2** : JOYFUL, GAY — **fes·tive·ly** *adv*

fes·tiv·i·ty \\fes-'ti-və-tē\\ *n, pl* **-ties 1** : FESTIVAL 1 2 : the quality or state of being festive **3** : festive activity

¹fes·toon \\fes-'tün\\ *n* [F *feston,* fr. It *festone,* fr. *festa* festival] **1** : a decorative chain or strip hanging between two points **2** : a carved, molded, or painted ornament representing a decorative chain

²festoon *vb* **1** : to hang or form festoons on **2** : to shape into festoons

fe·tal \\'fēt-ᵊl\\ *adj* : of, relating to, or being a fetus

fetch \\'fech\\ *vb* **1** : to go or come after and bring or take back ⟨teach a dog to ∼ a stick⟩ **2** : to bring in (as a price) **3** : to cause to come : bring out ⟨∼ed tears from the eyes⟩ **4** : to give by striking ⟨∼ him a blow⟩

fetch·ing *adj* : ATTRACTIVE, PLEASING — **fetch·ing·ly** *adv*

¹fete *or* **fête** \\'fāt, 'fet\\ *n* [F *fête,* fr. OF *feste*] **1** : FESTIVAL **2** : a large elaborate entertainment or party

²fete *or* **fête** *vb* **fet·ed** *or* **fêt·ed; fet·ing** *or* **fêt·ing 1** : to honor or commemorate with a fete **2** : to pay high honor to

fet·id \\'fe-təd\\ *adj* : having an offensive smell : STINKING

fe·tish *also* **fe·tich** \\'fe-tish\\ *n* [F & Pg; F *fétiche,* fr. Pg *feitiço,* fr. *feitiço* artificial, false, fr. L *facticius* factitious] **1** : an object (as an idol or image) believed to have magical powers (as in curing disease) **2** : an object of unreasoning devotion or concern **3** : an object whose real or fantasied presence is psychologically necessary for sexual gratification

fe·tish·ism \\-ti-ˌshi-zəm\\ *n* **1** : belief in or devotion to fetishes **2** : the pathological transfer of sexual interest and gratification to a fetish — **fe·tish·ist** \\-shist\\ *n* — **fe·tish·is·tic** \\ˌfe-ti-'shis-tik\\ *adj*

fet·lock \\'fet-ˌläk\\ *n* : a projection on the back of a horse's leg above the hoof; *also* : a tuft of hair on this

fet·ter \\'fe-tər\\ *n* **1** : a chain or shackle for the feet **2** : something that confines : RESTRAINT — **fetter** *vb*

fet·tle \\'fet-ᵊl\\ *n* : a state of fitness or order : CONDITION ⟨in fine ∼⟩

fe·tus \\'fē-təs\\ *n* : an unborn or unhatched vertebrate esp. after its basic structure is laid down; *esp* : a developing human being in the uterus from usu. three months after pregnancy occurs to birth

feud \\'fyüd\\ *n* : a prolonged quarrel; *esp* : a lasting conflict between families or clans marked by violent attacks made for revenge — **feud** *vb*

feu·dal \\'fyüd-ᵊl\\ *adj* **1** : of, relating to, or having the characteristics of a medieval fee **2** : of, relating to, or characteristic of feudalism

feu·dal·ism \\'fyüd-ᵊl-ˌi-zəm\\ *n* : a system of political organization prevailing in medieval Europe in which a vassal renders service to a lord and receives protection and land in return; *also* : a similar political or social system — **feu·dal·is·tic** \\ˌfyüd-ᵊl-'is-tik\\ *adj*

¹feu·da·to·ry \\'fyü-də-ˌtōr-ē\\ *adj* : owing feudal allegiance

²feudatory *n, pl* **-ries 1** : FIEF **2** : a person who holds lands by feudal law or usage

fe·ver \\'fē-vər\\ *n* **1** : a rise in body temperature above the normal; *also* : a disease of which this is a chief symptom **2** : a state of heightened emotion or activity **3** : CRAZE — **fe·ver·ish** *adj* — **fe·ver·ish·ly** *adv*

¹few \\'fyü\\ *pron* : not many : a small number

²few *adj* **1** : consisting of or amounting to a small number **2** : not many but some ⟨caught a ∼ fish⟩ — **few·ness** *n* — **few and far between** : RARE

³few *n* **1** : a small number of units or individuals ⟨a ∼ of them⟩ **2** : a special limited number ⟨among the ∼⟩

few·er \\'fyü-ər\\ *pron* : a smaller number of persons or things

fey \\'fā\\ *adj* **1** *chiefly Scot* : fated to die; *also* : marked by a foreboding of death or calamity **2** : able to see into the future : VISIONARY **3** : marked by an otherworldly air or attitude **4** : CRAZY, TOUCHED

fez \\'fez\\ *n, pl* **fez·zes** *also* **fez·es** : a round red felt hat that has a flat top and a tassel but no brim

fez

ff *abbr* **1** folios **2** [following] and the following ones **3** fortissimo

FHA *abbr* Federal Housing Administration

fi·an·cé \\ˌfē-ˌän-'sā\\ *n* [F, fr. MF, fr. pp. of *fiancer* to promise, betroth, fr. OF *fiancier,* fr. *fiance* promise, trust, fr. *fier* to trust, ultim. fr. L *fidere*] : a man engaged to be married

fi·an·cée \\ˌfē-ˌän-'sā\\ *n* : a woman engaged to be married

fi·as·co \\fē-'as-kō\\ *n, pl* **-coes** [F] : a complete failure

fi·at \\'fē-ət, -ˌat, -ˌät; 'fī-ət, -ˌat\\ *n* [L, let it be done] : an authoritative and often arbitrary order or decree

¹fib \\'fib\\ *n* : a trivial or childish lie

²fib *vb* **fibbed; fib·bing** : to tell a fib — **fib·ber** *n*

fi·ber *or* **fi·bre** \\'fī-bər\\ *n* **1** : a threadlike substance or structure (as a muscle cell or fine root); *esp* : a natural (as wool or flax) or artificial (as rayon) filament capable of being spun or woven **2** : indigestible material in human food that stimulates the intestine to move its contents along **3** : an element that gives texture or substance **4** : basic toughness : STRENGTH — **fi·brous** \\-brəs\\ *adj*

fi·ber·board \\'fī-bər-ˌbōrd\\ *n* : a material made by compressing fibers (as of wood) into stiff sheets

fi·ber·fill \\-ˌfil\\ *n* : synthetic fibers used as a filling material (as for cushions)

fi·ber·glass \\-ˌglas\\ *n* : glass in fibrous form used in making various products (as insulation)

fiber optics *n* **1** *pl* : thin transparent fibers of glass or plastic that are enclosed by a less refractive material and that transmit light by internal reflection; *also* : a bundle of such fibers used in an instrument **2** : the technique of the use of fiber optics — **fiber–optic** *adj*

fi·bril \\'fī-brəl, 'fi-\\ *n* : a small fiber

fi·bril·la·tion \\ˌfi-brə-'lā-shən, ˌfī-\\ *n* : rapid irregular contractions of the heart muscle fibers resulting in a lack of synchronism between heartbeat and pulse — **fib·ril·late** \\'fi-brə-ˌlāt, 'fī-\\ *vb*

fi·brin \\'fī-brən\\ *n* : a white insoluble fibrous protein formed in the clotting of blood

fi·broid \\'fī-ˌbroid, 'fi-\\ *adj* : resembling, forming, or consisting of fibrous tissue ⟨∼ tumors⟩

fi·bro·sis \\fī-'brō-səs\\ *n* : a condition marked by abnormal increase of fiber-containing tissue

fib·u·la \\'fi-byə-lə\\ *n, pl* **-lae** \\-ˌlē, -ˌlī\\ *or* **-las** : the outer and usu. the smaller of the two bones between the knee and ankle — **fib·u·lar** \\-lər\\ *adj*

FICA *abbr* Federal Insurance Contributions Act

-fi·ca·tion *n comb form* : making : production ⟨simplification⟩

fiche \\'fēsh\\ *n, pl* **fiche** : MICROFICHE

fi·chu \\'fi-shü\\ *n* [F] : a woman's light triangular scarf draped over the shoulders and fastened in front

fick·le \\'fi-kəl\ *adj* : not firm or steadfast in disposition or character : INCONSTANT — **fick·le·ness** *n*

fic·tion \\'fik-shən\ *n* 1 : something (as a story) invented by the imagination 2 : fictitious literature (as novels) — **fic·tion·al** \-shə-nəl\ *adj* — **fic·tion·al·ly** *adv*

fic·ti·tious \fik-'ti-shəs\ *adj* 1 : of, relating to, or characteristic of fiction : IMAGINARY 2 : FEIGNED **syn** chimerical, fanciful, fantastic, unreal

¹fid·dle \\'fid-əl\ *n* : VIOLIN

²fiddle *vb* **fid·dled; fid·dling** 1 : to play on a fiddle 2 : to move the hands or fingers restlessly 3 : PUTTER 4 : MEDDLE, TAMPER — **fid·dler** *n*

fiddler crab *n* : any of a genus of burrowing crabs with one claw much enlarged in the male

fid·dle·stick \\'fid-əl-ˌstik\ *n* 1 *archaic* : a violin bow 2 *pl* : NONSENSE — used as an interjection

fi·del·i·ty \fə-'de-lə-tē, fī-\ *n, pl* **-ties** 1 : the quality or state of being faithful 2 : ACCURACY ⟨∼ in sound reproduction⟩ **syn** allegiance, loyalty, devotion, fealty

¹fidg·et \\'fi-jət\ *n* 1 *pl* : uneasiness or restlessness as shown by nervous movements 2 : one that fidgets — **fidg·ety** *adj*

²fidget *vb* : to move or cause to move or act restlessly or nervously

fi·du·ci·a·ry \fə-'dü-shē-ˌer-ē, -'dyü-, -shə-rē\ *adj* 1 : involving a confidence or trust 2 : held or holding in trust for another ⟨∼ accounts⟩ — **fiduciary** *n*

fie \\'fī\ *interj* — used to express disgust or disapproval

fief \\'fēf\ *n* : a feudal estate : FEE

¹field \\'fēld\ *n* 1 : open country 2 : a piece of cleared land for cultivation or pasture 3 : a piece of land yielding some special product 4 : the place where a battle is fought; *also* : BATTLE 5 : an area, division, or sphere of activity ⟨the ∼ of science⟩ ⟨salesmen in the ∼⟩ 6 : an area for military exercises 7 : an area for sports 8 : a background on which something is drawn or projected ⟨a flag with white stars on a ∼ of blue⟩ 9 : a region or space in which a given effect (as magnetism) exists — **field** *adj*

²field *vb* 1 : to handle a batted or thrown baseball while on defense 2 : to put into the field 3 : to answer satisfactorily ⟨∼ a tough question⟩ — **field·er** *n*

field day *n* 1 : a day devoted to outdoor sports and athletic competition 2 : a time of extraordinary pleasure or opportunity

field event *n* : a track-and-field event (as weight-throwing) other than a race

field glass *n* : a hand-held binocular telescope — usu. used in pl.

field hockey *n* : a field game played between two teams of 11 players each whose object is to knock a ball into the opponent's goal with a curved stick

field marshal *n* : an officer (as in the British army) of the highest rank

field–test \-ˌtest\ *vb* : to test (as a new product) in a natural environment — **field test** *n*

fiend \\'fēnd\ *n* 1 : DEVIL 1 2 : DEMON 3 : an extremely wicked or cruel person 4 : a person excessively devoted to a pursuit 5 : ADDICT ⟨dope ∼⟩ — **fiend·ish** *adj* — **fiend·ish·ly** *adv*

fierce \\'firs\ *adj* **fierc·er; fierc·est** 1 : violently hostile or aggressive in temperament 2 : PUGNACIOUS 3 : INTENSE 4 : furiously active or determined 5 : wild or menacing in appearance **syn** ferocious, barbarous, savage, cruel — **fierce·ly** *adv* — **fierce·ness** *n*

fi·ery \\'fī-ə-rē\ *adj* **fi·er·i·er; -est** 1 : consisting of fire 2 : BURNING, BLAZING 3 : FLAMMABLE 4 : hot like a fire : INFLAMED, FEVERISH 5 : RED 6 : full of emotion or spirit 7 : IRRITABLE — **fi·eri·ness** \-rē-nəs\ *n*

fi·es·ta \fē-'es-tə\ *n* [Sp] : FESTIVAL

fife \\'fīf\ *n* [G *Pfeife* pipe, fife] : a small flute

FIFO *abbr* first in, first out

fif·teen \fif-'tēn\ *n* : one more than 14 — **fifteen** *adj or pron* — **fif·teenth** \-'tēnth\ *adj or n*

fifth \\'fifth\ *n* 1 : one that is number five in a countable series 2 : one of five equal parts of something 3 : a unit of measure for liquor equal to ⅕ U.S. gallon (0.757 liter) — **fifth** *adj or adv*

fifth column *n* : a group of secret supporters of a nation's enemy that engage in espionage or sabotage within the country — **fifth columnist** *n*

fifth wheel *n* : one that is unnecessary and often burdensome

fif·ty \\'fif-tē\ *n, pl* **fifties** : five times 10 — **fif·ti·eth** \-tē-əth\ *adj or n* — **fifty** *adj or pron*

fif·ty–fif·ty \ˌfif-tē-'fif-tē\ *adj* 1 : shared equally ⟨a ∼ proposition⟩ 2 : half favorable and half unfavorable

¹fig \\'fig\ *n* : a usu. pear-shaped edible fruit of warm regions; *also* : a tree related to the mulberry that bears this fruit

fig: leaves and fruit

²fig *abbr* 1 figurative; figuratively 2 figure

¹fight \\'fīt\ *vb* **fought** \\'fȯt\; **fight·ing** 1 : to contend against another in battle or physical combat 2 : BOX 3 : to put forth a determined effort 4 : STRUGGLE, CONTEND 5 : to attempt to prevent the success or effectiveness of 6 : WAGE 7 : to gain by struggle

²fight *n* 1 : a hostile encounter : BATTLE 2 : a boxing match 3 : a verbal disagreement 4 : a struggle for a goal or an objective 5 : strength or disposition for fighting ⟨full of ∼⟩

fight·er \\'fī-tər\ *n* 1 : one that fights; *esp* : WARRIOR 2 : BOXER 3 : a fast maneuverable warplane for destroying enemy aircraft

fig·ment \\'fig-mənt\ *n* : something imagined or made up

fig·u·ra·tion \ˌfi-gyə-'rā-shən, -gə-\ *n* 1 : FORM, OUTLINE 2 : an act or instance of representation in figures and shapes

fig·u·ra·tive \\'fi-gyə-rə-tiv, -gə-\ *adj* 1 : EMBLEMATIC 2 : SYMBOLIC, METAPHORICAL ⟨∼ language⟩ — **fig·u·ra·tive·ly** *adv*

¹fig·ure \\'fi-gyər, -gər-\ *n* 1 : NUMERAL 2 *pl* : arithmetical calculations 3 : a written or printed character 4 : PRICE, SUM 5 : a combination of points, lines, or surfaces in geometry ⟨a circle is a closed plane ∼⟩ 6 : SHAPE, FORM, OUTLINE 7 : the graphic representation of a form esp. of a person 8 : a diagram or pictorial illustration of textual matter 9 : PATTERN, DESIGN 10 : appearance made or impression produced ⟨they cut quite a ∼⟩ 11 : a series of movements (as in a dance) 12 : PERSONAGE

²figure *vb* **fig·ured; fig·ur·ing** 1 : to represent by or as if by a figure or outline 2 : to decorate with a pattern 3 : to indicate or represent by numerals 4 : REGARD, CONSIDER 5 : to be or appear important or conspicuous 6 : COMPUTE, CALCULATE

fig·ure·head \\'fi-gyər-ˌhed, -gər-\ *n* 1 : a figure on the bow of a ship 2 : a head or chief in name only

figure of speech : a form of expression (as a simile or metaphor) that often compares or identifies one thing with another to convey meaning or heighten effect

figure out *vb* 1 : FIND OUT, DISCOVER 2 : SOLVE

fig·u·rine \\,fi-gyə-'rēn, -gə-\ *n* : a small carved or molded figure

Fi·ji·an \\'fē-jē-ən, fi-'jē-ən\ *n* : a native or inhabitant of the Pacific island country of Fiji — **Fijian** *adj*

fil·a·ment \\'fi-lə-mənt\ *n* : a fine thread or threadlike object, part, or process — **fil·a·men·tous** \\,fi-lə-'men-təs\ *adj*

fil·bert \\'fil-bərt\ *n* : the sweet thick-shelled nut of either of two European hazels; *also* : a shrub or small tree bearing filberts

filch \\'filch\ *vb* : to steal furtively

¹file \\'fīl\ *n* : a usu. steel tool with a ridged or toothed surface used esp. for smoothing a hard substance

²file *vb* **filed; fil·ing** : to rub, smooth, or cut away with a file

³file *vb* **filed; fil·ing** [ME, fr. MF *filer* to string documents on a string or wire, fr. *fil* thread, fr. L *filum*] **1** : to arrange in order **2** : to enter or record officially or as prescribed by law ⟨~ a lawsuit⟩ **3** : to send (copy) to a newspaper

⁴file *n* **1** : a device (as a folder or cabinet) by means of which papers may be kept in order **2** : a collection of papers or publications usu. arranged or classified **3** : a collection of data (as text) treated by a computer as a unit

⁵file *n* : a row of persons, animals, or things arranged one behind the other

⁶file *vb* **filed; fil·ing** : to march or proceed in file

fi·let mi·gnon \\,fi-(,)lā-mēn-'yōⁿ, fi-,lā-\ *n, pl* **filets mignons** \\-(,)lā-mēn-'yōⁿz, -,lā-\ [F, lit., dainty fillet] : a thick slice of beef cut from the narrow end of a beef tenderloin

fil·ial \\'fi-lē-əl, 'fil-yəl\ *adj* : of, relating to, or befitting a son or daughter

fil·i·bus·ter \\'fi-lə-,bəs-tər\ *n* [Sp *filibustero*, lit., freebooter] **1** : a military adventurer; *esp* : an American engaged in fomenting 19th century Latin American uprisings **2** : the use of delaying tactics (as extremely long speeches) esp. in a legislative assembly; *also* : an instance of this practice — **filibuster** *vb* — **fil·i·bus·ter·er** *n*

fil·i·gree \\'fi-lə-,grē\ *n* [F *filigrane*] : ornamental openwork (as of fine wire) — **fil·i·greed** \\-,grēd\ *adj*

fil·ing \\'fī-liŋ\ *n* **1** : the act or instance of using a file **2** : a small piece scraped off by a file ⟨iron ~s⟩

Fil·i·pi·no \\,fi-lə-'pē-nō\ *n, pl* **Filipinos** : a native or inhabitant of the Philippines — **Filipino** *adj*

¹fill \\'fil\ *vb* **1** : to make or become full **2** : to stop up : PLUG ⟨~ a cavity⟩ **3** : FEED, SATIATE **4** : SATISFY, FULFILL ⟨~ all requirements⟩ **5** : to occupy fully **6** : to spread through ⟨laughter ~ed the room⟩ **7** : OCCUPY ⟨~ the office of president⟩ **8** : to put a person in ⟨~ a vacancy⟩ **9** : to supply as directed ⟨~ a prescription⟩

²fill *n* **1** : a full supply; *esp* : a quantity that satisfies or satiates **2** : material used esp. for filling a low place

¹fill·er \\'fi-lər\ *n* **1** : one that fills **2** : a substance added to another substance (as to increase bulk or weight) **3** : a material used for filling cracks and pores in wood before painting

²fil·er \\'fi-,ler\ *n, pl* **fillers** *or* **filler** — see *forint* at MONEY table

¹fil·let \\'fil-ət, *in sense 2* fi-'lā, 'fi-(,)lā\ *also* **fi·let** \\fi-'lā, 'fi-(,)lā\ *n* [ME *filet*, fr. MF, dim. of *fil* thread] **1** : a narrow band, strip, or ribbon **2** : a piece or slice of boneless meat or fish; *esp* : the tenderloin of beef

²fil·let \\'fil-ət, *in sense 2 also* fi-'lā, 'fi-(,)lā\ *vb* **1** : to bind or adorn with or as if with a fillet **2** : to cut into fillets

fill in *vb* **1** : to provide necessary or recent information **2** : to serve as a temporary substitute

fill·ing \\'fi-liŋ\ *n* **1** : material used to fill something ⟨a ~ for a tooth⟩ **2** : the yarn interlacing the warp in a fabric **3** : a food mixture used to fill pastry or sandwiches

filling station *n* : SERVICE STATION

fil·lip \\'fi-ləp\ *n* **1** : a blow or gesture made by a flick or snap of the finger across the thumb **2** : something that serves to arouse or excite — **fillip** *vb*

fill–up \\'fil-,əp\ *n* : an act or instance of filling something

fil·ly \\'fi-lē\ *n, pl* **fillies** : a young female horse usu. less than four years old

¹film \\'film\ *n* **1** : a thin skin or membrane **2** : a thin coating or layer **3** : a flexible strip of chemically treated material used in taking pictures **4** : MOTION PICTURE — **filmy** *adj*

²film *vb* **1** : to cover with a film **2** : to make a motion picture of

film·dom \\'film-dəm\ *n* : the motion-picture industry

film·og·ra·phy \\fil-'mä-grə-fē\ *n, pl* **-phies** : a list of motion pictures featuring the work of a film figure or a particular topic

film·strip \\'film-,strip\ *n* : a strip of film bearing a sequence of images for projection as still pictures

fils \\'fils\ *n, pl* **fils** — see *dinar, dirham, rial* at MONEY table

¹fil·ter \\'fil-tər\ *n* **1** : a porous material through which a fluid is passed to separate out matter in suspension; *also* : a device containing such material **2** : a device for suppressing waves of certain frequencies; *esp* : one (as for a camera) that absorbs light of certain colors

²filter *vb* **1** : to remove by means of a filter **2** : to pass through a filter — **fil·ter·able** *also* **fil·tra·ble** \\-tə-rə-bəl, -trə-\ *adj* — **fil·tra·tion** \\fil-'trā-shən\ *n*

filth \\'filth\ *n* [ME, fr. OE *fȳlth*, fr. *fūl* foul] **1** : foul matter; *esp* : loathsome dirt or refuse **2** : moral corruption **3** : OBSCENITY — **filth·i·ness** *n* — **filthy** \\'fil-thē\ *adj*

fil·trate \\'fil-,trāt\ *n* : fluid that has passed through a filter

¹fin \\'fin\ *n* **1** : one of the thin external processes by which an aquatic animal (as a fish) moves through water **2** : a fin-shaped part (as on an airplane) **3** : FLIPPER 2 — **finned** \\'find\ *adj*

²fin *abbr* **1** finance; financial **2** finish

fi·na·gle \\fə-'nā-gəl\ *vb* **-gled; -gling 1** : to obtain by indirect or dishonest means : WANGLE **2** : to use devious dishonest methods to achieve one's ends — **fi·na·gler** *n*

¹fi·nal \\'fīn-ᵊl\ *adj* **1** : not to be altered or undone **2** : ULTIMATE **3** : relating to or occurring at the end or conclusion — **fi·nal·i·ty** \\fī-'na-lə-tē, fə-\ *n* — **fi·nal·ly** *adv*

²final *n* **1** : a deciding match or game — usu. used in pl. **2** : the last examination in a course — often used in pl.

fi·na·le \\fə-'na-lē, fi-'nä-\ *n* : the close or end of something; *esp* : the last section of a musical composition

fi·nal·ist \\'fīn-ᵊl-əst\ *n* : a contestant in the finals of a competition

fi·nal·ize \\'fīn-ᵊl-,īz\ *vb* **-ized; -iz·ing** : to put in final or finished form

¹fi·nance \\fə-'nans, 'fī-,nans\ *n* [ME, payment, ransom, fr. MF, fr. end, pay, fr. *fin* end, fr. L *finis* boundary, end] **1** *pl* : money resources available esp. to a government or business **2** : management of money affairs

²finance *vb* **fi·nanced; fi·nanc·ing 1** : to raise or provide funds for **2** : to furnish with necessary funds **3** : to sell or supply on credit

finance company *n* : a company that makes usu. small short-term loans usu. to individuals

fi·nan·cial \\fə-'nan-chəl, fī-\ *adj* : relating to finance or financiers — **fi·nan·cial·ly** *adv*

fi·nan·cier \\,fi-nən-'sir, ,fī-,nan-\ *n* **1** : a person skilled in managing public moneys **2** : a person who deals with large-scale finance and investment

finch \\'finch\ *n* : any of numerous songbirds with strong conical bills

¹find \\'fīnd\ *vb* **found** \\'faund\; **find·ing 1** : to meet

with either by chance or by searching or study : EN-
COUNTER, DISCOVER **2** : to obtain by effort or management ⟨∼ time to read⟩ **3** : to arrive at : REACH ⟨the
bullet *found* its mark⟩ **4** : EXPERIENCE, FEEL ⟨*found*
happiness⟩ **5** : to gain or regain the use of ⟨*found* his
voice again⟩ **6** : to determine and make a statement
about ⟨∼ a verdict⟩

²**find** *n* **1** : an act or instance of finding **2** : something
found; *esp* : a valuable item of discovery

find•er \'fīn-dər\ *n* : one that finds; *esp* : VIEWFINDER

fin de siè•cle \ˌfaⁿ-də-sē-'eklᵃ\ *adj* [F, end of century]
: of, relating to, or characteristic of the close of the
19th century

find•ing \'fīn-diŋ\ *n* **1** : the act of finding **2** : FIND 2 **3**
: the result of a judicial proceeding or inquiry

find out *vb* : to learn by study, observation, or search
: DISCOVER

¹**fine** \'fīn\ *n* : money exacted as a penalty for an offense

²**fine** *vb* **fined; fin•ing** : to impose a fine on : punish by
a fine

³**fine** *adj* **fin•er; fin•est 1** : free from impurity **2** : very
thin in gauge or texture **3** : not coarse **4** : SUBTLE,
SENSITIVE ⟨a ∼ distinction⟩ **5** : superior in quality or
appearance **6** : ELEGANT, REFINED — **fine•ly** *adv* —
fine•ness *n*

⁴**fine** *adv* : FINELY

fine art *n* : art (as painting, sculpture, or music) concerned primarily with the creation of beautiful objects — usu. used in pl.

fin•ery \'fī-nə-rē\ *n, pl* **-er•ies** : ORNAMENT, DECORA-
TION; *esp* : showy clothing and jewels

fine•spun \'fīn-'spən\ *adj* : developed with extremely
or excessively fine delicacy or detail

fi•nesse \fə-'nes\ *n* **1** : refinement or delicacy of workmanship, structure, or texture **2** : CUNNING, SUBTLE-
TY — **finesse** *vb*

fine–tune \'fīn-'tün\ *vb* : to adjust so as to bring to the
highest level of performance or effectiveness

fin•fish \'fin-ˌfish\ *n* : FISH 2

¹**fin•ger** \'fiŋ-gər\ *n* **1** : any of the five divisions at the
end of the hand; *esp* : one other than the thumb **2**
: something that resembles or does the work of a finger **3** : a part of a glove into which a finger is inserted

²**finger** *vb* **fin•gered; fin•ger•ing 1** : to touch or feel with
the fingers : HANDLE **2** : to perform with the fingers
or with a certain fingering **3** : to mark the notes of a
piece of music as a guide in playing **4** : to point out

fin•ger•board \'fiŋ-gər-ˌbōrd\ *n* : the part of a stringed
instrument against which the fingers press the strings
to vary the pitch

finger bowl *n* : a small water bowl for rinsing the fingers at the table

fin•ger•ing \'fiŋ-gə-riŋ\ *n* **1** : handling or touching with
the fingers **2** : the act or method of using the fingers
in playing an instrument **3** : the marking of the method of fingering

fin•ger•ling \'fiŋ-gər-liŋ\ *n* : a small fish

fin•ger•nail \'fiŋ-gər-ˌnāl\ *n* : the nail of a finger

fin•ger•print \-ˌprint\ *n* : the pattern of marks made by
pressing the tip of a finger or thumb on a surface; *esp*
: an ink impression of such a pattern taken for the
purpose of identification — **fingerprint** *vb*

fin•ger•tip \-ˌtip\ *n* : the tip of a finger

fin•ial \'fi-nē-əl\ *n* : an ornamental projection or end
(as on a spire)

fin•ick•ing \'fi-ni-kiŋ\ *adj* : FINICKY

fin•icky \'fi-ni-kē\ *adj* : excessively particular in taste
or standards

fi•nis \'fi-nəs\ *n* : END, CONCLUSION

¹**fin•ish** \'fi-nish\ *vb* **1** : TERMINATE **2** : to use or dispose
of entirely **3** : to bring to completion : ACCOMPLISH **4**
: to put a final coat or surface on **5** : to come to the
end of a course or undertaking — **fin•ish•er** *n*

²**finish** *n* **1** : END, CONCLUSION **2** : something that com-

pletes or perfects **3** : the final treatment or coating of
a surface

fi•nite \'fī-ˌnīt\ *adj* **1** : having definite or definable limits; *also* : having a limited nature or existence **2** : being less than some positive integer in number or
measure and greater than its negative **3** : showing distinction of grammatical person and number ⟨a ∼
verb⟩

fink \'fiŋk\ *n* **1** : a contemptible person **2** : STRIKE-
BREAKER **3** : INFORMER

Finn \'fin\ *n* : a native or inhabitant of Finland

fin•nan had•die \ˌfi-nən-'ha-dē\ *n* : smoked haddock

¹**Finn•ish** \'fi-nish\ *adj* : of or relating to Finland, the
Finns, or Finnish

²**Finnish** *n* : the language of Finland

fin•ny \'fi-nē\ *adj* : having or characterized by fins **2**
: relating to or being fish

fiord *var of* FJORD

fir \'fər\ *n* : any of a genus of erect evergreen trees related to the pines; *also* : the light soft wood of a fir

¹**fire** \'fīr\ *n* **1** : the light or heat and esp. the flame of
something burning **2** : ENTHUSIASM, ZEAL **3** : fuel that
is burning (as in a stove or fireplace) **4** : destructive
burning (as of a house) **5** : the firing of weapons —
fire•less *adj*

²**fire** *vb* **fired; fir•ing 1** : KINDLE, IGNITE ⟨∼ a house⟩ **2**
: STIR, ENLIVEN ⟨∼ the imagination⟩ **3** : to dismiss
from employment **4** : SHOOT ⟨∼ a gun⟩ ⟨∼ an arrow⟩
5 : BAKE ⟨*firing* pottery in a kiln⟩ **6** : to apply fire or
fuel to something ⟨∼ a furnace⟩

fire ant *n* : either of two small fiercely stinging South
American ants that are pests in the southeastern U.S.
esp. in fields used to grow crops

fire•arm \'fīr-ˌärm\ *n* : a weapon (as a pistol) from
which a shot is discharged by gunpowder

fire•ball \-ˌból\ *n* **1** : a ball of fire **2** : a very bright meteor **3** : the highly luminous cloud of vapor and dust
created by a nuclear explosion **4** : a highly energetic
person

fire•boat \-ˌbōt\ *n* : a boat equipped for fighting fires

fire•bomb \-ˌbäm\ *n* : an incendiary bomb — **fire-
bomb** *vb*

fire•box \-ˌbäks\ *n* **1** : a chamber (as of a furnace) that
contains a fire **2** : a box containing a fire alarm

fire•brand \-ˌbrand\ *n* **1** : a piece of burning wood **2** : a
person who creates unrest or strife : AGITATOR

fire•break \-ˌbrāk\ *n* : a barrier of cleared or plowed
land intended to check a forest or grass fire

fire•bug \-ˌbəg\ *n* : a person who deliberately sets destructive fires

fire•crack•er \-ˌkra-kər\ *n* : a paper tube containing an
explosive and a fuse and set off to make a noise

fire department *n* : an organization for preventing or
extinguishing fires; *also* : its members

fire engine *n* : a motor vehicle with equipment for extinguishing fires

fire escape *n* : a stairway or ladder for escape from a
burning building

fire•fight•er \'fīr-ˌfī-tər\ *n* : a person who fights fires;
esp : a member of a fire department

fire•fly \-ˌflī\ *n* : any of various small night-
flying beetles that produce flashes of light for courtship purposes

fire•house \-ˌhaús\ *n* : FIRE STATION

fire irons *n pl* : tools for tending a fire esp. in a fireplace

fire•man \'fīr-mən\ *n* **1** : STOKER **2** : FIREFIGHTER

fire off *vb* : to write and send

fire•place \-ˌplās\ *n* **1** : a framed opening made in a
chimney to hold an open fire **2** : an outdoor structure
of brick or stone for an open fire

fire•plug \-ˌpləg\ *n* : HYDRANT

fire•pow•er \-ˌpaú-ər\ *n* : the ability to deliver gunfire
or warheads on a target

¹**fire•proof** \-ˌprüf\ *adj* : resistant to fire

²**fireproof** *vb* : to make fireproof

fire screen *n* : a protective screen before a fireplace

¹fire·side \'fīr-ˌsīd\ *n* **1** : a place near the fire or hearth **2** : HOME

²fireside *adj* : having an informal or intimate quality

fire station *n* : a building housing fire engines and usu. firefighters

fire·storm \'fīr-ˌstȯrm\ *n* **1** : a large destructive very hot fire **2** : a sudden or violent outburst ⟨∼ of criticism⟩

fire tower *n* : a tower (as in a forest) from which a watch for fires is kept

fire·trap \'fīr-ˌtrap\ *n* : a building or place apt to catch on fire or difficult to escape from in case of fire

fire truck *n* : FIRE ENGINE

fire·wa·ter \'fīr-ˌwȯ-tər, -ˌwä-\ *n* : intoxicating liquor

fire·wood \-ˌwu̇d\ *n* : wood used for fuel

fire·work \-ˌwərk\ *n* : a device designed to produce a display of light, noise, and smoke by the burning of explosive or flammable materials

firing line *n* **1** : a line from which fire is delivered against a target **2** : the forefront of an activity

¹firm \'fərm\ *adj* **1** : securely fixed in place **2** : SOLID, VIGOROUS ⟨a ∼ handshake⟩ **3** : having a solid or compact texture **4** : not subject to change or fluctuation : STEADY ⟨∼ prices⟩ **5** : STEADFAST **6** : indicating firmness or resolution — **firm·ly** *adv* — **firm·ness** *n*

²firm *vb* : to make or become firm

³firm *n* [G *Firma*, fr. It. signature, ultim. fr. L *firmare* to make firm, confirm] **1** : the name under which a company transacts business **2** : a business partnership of two or more persons **3** : a business enterprise

fir·ma·ment \'fər-mə-mənt\ *n* : the arch of the sky : HEAVENS

firm·ware \'firm-ˌwar\ *n* : computer programs contained permanently in a hardware device

¹first \'fərst\ *adj* : preceding all others as in time, order, or importance

²first *adv* **1** : before any other **2** : for the first time **3** : in preference to something else

³first *n* **1** : number one in a countable series **2** : something that is first **3** : the lowest forward gear in an automotive vehicle **4** : the winning or highest place in a competition or examination

first aid *n* : emergency care or treatment given an injured or ill person

first·born \'fərst-ˌbȯrn\ *adj* : ELDEST — **firstborn** *n*

first class *n* : the best or highest group in a classification — **first–class** *adj or adv*

first·hand \'fərst-ˈhand\ *adj* : coming from direct personal observation or experience — **firsthand** *adv*

first lady *n, often cap F&L* : the wife or hostess of the chief executive of a political unit (as a country)

first lieutenant *n* : a commissioned officer (as in the army) ranking next below a captain

first·ling \'fərst-liŋ\ *n* : one that comes or is produced first

first·ly \-lē\ *adv* : in the first place : FIRST

¹first–rate \-ˈrāt\ *adj* : of the first order of size, importance, or quality

²first–rate *adv* : very well

first sergeant *n* **1** : a noncommissioned officer serving as the chief assistant to the commander of a military unit **2** : a rank in the army below a command sergeant major and in the marine corps below a sergeant major

first strike *n* : a preemptive nuclear attack

first–string \'fərst-ˈstriŋ\ *adj* : being a regular as distinguished from a substitute

firth \'fərth\ *n* [ME, fr. ON *fjǫrthr*] : ESTUARY

fis·cal \'fis-kəl\ *adj* [L *fiscalis*, fr. *fiscus* basket, treasury] **1** : of or relating to taxation, public revenues, or public debt **2** : of or relating to financial matters — **fis·cal·ly** *adv*

¹fish \'fish\ *n, pl* **fish** *or* **fish·es** **1** : a water-dwelling animal — usu. used in combination ⟨star*fish*⟩ ⟨shell*fish*⟩ **2** : any of numerous cold-blooded water-breathing vertebrates with fins, gills, and usu. scales that in-

clude the bony fishes and usu. the cartilaginous and jawless fishes **3** : the flesh of fish used as food

²fish *vb* **1** : to attempt to catch fish **2** : to seek something by roundabout means ⟨∼ for praise⟩ **3** : to search for something underwater **4** : to engage in a search by groping **5** : to draw forth

fish–and–chips *n pl* : fried fish and french fried potatoes

fish·bowl \'fish-ˌbōl\ *n* **1** : a bowl for the keeping of live fish **2** : a place or condition that affords no privacy

fish·er \'fi-shər\ *n* **1** : one that fishes **2** : a large dark brown No. American arboreal carnivorous mammal related to the weasels

fish·er·man \-mən\ *n* : a person engaged in fishing; *also* : a fishing boat

fish·ery \'fi-shə-rē\ *n, pl* **-er·ies** : the business of catching fish; *also* : a place for catching fish

fish·hook \'fish-ˌhu̇k\ *n* : a usu. barbed hook for catching fish

fish ladder *n* : an arrangement of pools in steps by which fish can pass over a dam

fish·net \'fish-ˌnet\ *n* **1** : netting for catching fish **2** : a coarse open-mesh fabric

fish·tail \-ˌtāl\ *vb* : to have the rear end slide from side to side out of control while moving forward

fish·wife \-ˌwīf\ *n* **1** : a woman who sells fish **2** : a vulgar abusive woman

fishy \'fi-shē\ *adj* **fish·i·er; -est** **1** : of or resembling fish **2** : QUESTIONABLE

fis·sion \'fi-shən, -zhən\ *n* [L *fissio*, fr. *findere* to split] **1** : a cleaving into parts **2** : a method of reproduction in which a living cell or body divides into two or more parts each of which grows into a whole new individual **3** : the splitting of an atomic nucleus resulting in the release of large amounts of energy — **fis·sion·able** \'fi-shə-nə-bəl, -zhə-\ *adj*

fis·sure \'fi-shər\ *n* : a narrow opening or crack

fist \'fist\ *n* **1** : the hand with fingers folded into the palm **2** : INDEX 6

fist·ful \'fist-ˌfu̇l\ *n* : HANDFUL

fist·i·cuffs \'fis-ti-ˌkəfs\ *n pl* : a fight with usu. bare fists

fis·tu·la \'fis-chə-lə\ *n, pl* **-las** *or* **-lae** : an abnormal passage leading from an abscess or hollow organ — **fis·tu·lous** \-ləs\ *adj*

¹fit \'fit\ *adj* **fit·ter; fit·test** **1** : adapted to a purpose : APPROPRIATE **2** : PROPER, RIGHT **3** : PREPARED, READY **4** : physically and mentally sound — **fit·ly** *adv* — **fit·ness** *n*

²fit *n* **1** : a sudden violent attack (as of bodily disorder) **2** : a sudden outburst

³fit *vb* **fit·ted** *also* **fit; fit·ting** **1** : to be suitable for or to **2** : to be correctly adjusted to or shaped for **3** : to insert or adjust until correctly in place **4** : to make a place or room for **5** : to be in agreement or accord with **6** : PREPARE **7** : ADJUST **8** : SUPPLY, EQUIP ⟨*fitted* out with gear⟩ **9** : BELONG — **fit·ter** *n*

⁴fit *n* : the fact, condition, or manner of fitting or being fitted

fit·ful \'fit-fəl\ *adj* : not regular : INTERMITTENT ⟨∼ sleep⟩ — **fit·ful·ly** *adv*

¹fit·ting \'fi-tiŋ\ *adj* : APPROPRIATE, SUITABLE — **fit·ting·ly** *adv*

²fitting *n* **1** : the action or act of one that fits; *esp* : a trying on of clothes being made or altered **2** : a small often standardized part ⟨a plumbing ∼⟩

five \'fīv\ *n* **1** : one more than four **2** : the 5th in a set or series **3** : something having five units; *esp* : a basketball team **4** : a 5-dollar bill — **five** *adj or pron*

¹fix \'fiks\ *vb* **1** : to make firm, stable, or fast **2** : to give a permanent or final form to **3** : AFFIX, ATTACH **4** : to hold or direct steadily ⟨∼*es* his eyes on the horizon⟩ **5** : ESTABLISH, SET **6** : ASSIGN ⟨∼ the blame⟩ **7** : to set in order : ADJUST **8** : PREPARE **9** : to make whole or sound again **10** : to get even with **11** : to influence by improper or illegal methods ⟨∼ a race⟩ — **fix·er** *n*

²**fix** *n* **1** : PREDICAMENT **2** : a determination of position (as of a ship) **3** : an accurate determination or understanding **4** : an act of improper influence **5** : a supply or dose of something (as an addictive drug) strongly desired or craved **6** : something that fixes or restores

fix·a·tion \fik-'sā-shən\ *n* : an obsessive or unhealthy preoccupation or attachment — **fix·ate** \'fik-₁sāt\ *vb*

fix·a·tive \'fik-sə-tiv\ *n* : something that stabilizes or sets

fixed \'fikst\ *adj* **1** : securely placed or fastened : STATIONARY **2** : not volatile **3** : SETTLED, FINAL **4** : INTENT, CONCENTRATED ⟨a ∼ stare⟩ **5** : supplied with a definite amount of something needed (as money) — **fixed·ly** \'fik-səd-lē\ *adv* — **fixed·ness** \'fik-səd-nəs\ *n*

fix·i·ty \'fik-sə-tē\ *n, pl* **-ties** : the quality or state of being fixed or stable

fix·ture \'fiks-chər\ *n* **1** : something firmly attached as a permanent part of some other thing **2** : a familiar feature in a particular setting; *esp* : a person associated with a place or activity

¹**fizz** \'fiz\ *vb* : to make a hissing or sputtering sound

²**fizz** *n* : an effervescent beverage

¹**fiz·zle** \'fi-zəl\ *vb* **fiz·zled; fiz·zling** **1** : FIZZ **2** : to fail after a good start — often used with *out*

²**fizzle** *n* : FAILURE

fjord \fē-'ȯrd\ *n* [Norw] : a narrow inlet of the sea between cliffs or steep slopes

fjord

fl *abbr* **1** [L *floruit*] flourished **2** fluid

FL *or* **Fla** *abbr* Florida

flab \'flab\ *n* : soft flabby body tissue

flab·ber·gast \'fla-bər-₁gast\ *vb* : ASTOUND

flab·by \'fla-bē\ *adj* **flab·bi·er; -est** : lacking firmness : FLACCID ⟨∼ muscles⟩ — **flab·bi·ness** \-bē-nəs\ *n*

flac·cid \'flak-səd\ *adj* : deficient in firmness ⟨∼ plant stems⟩

¹**flag** \'flag\ *n* : any of various irises; *esp* : a wild iris

²**flag** *n* **1** : a usu. rectangular piece of fabric of distinctive design that is used as a symbol (as of a nation) or as a signaling device **2** : something used like a flag to signal or attract attention **3** : one of the cross strokes of a musical note less than a quarter note in value

³**flag** *vb* **flagged; flag·ging** **1** : to signal with or as if with a flag; *esp* : to signal to stop ⟨∼ a taxi⟩ **2** : to put a flag on **3** : to call a penalty on

⁴**flag** *vb* **flagged; flag·ging** **1** : to hang loose or limp **2** : to become unsteady, feeble, or spiritless **3** : to decline in interest or attraction ⟨the topic *flagged*⟩

⁵**flag** *n* : a hard flat stone suitable for paving

flag·el·late \'fla-jə-₁lāt\ *vb* **-lat·ed; -lat·ing** : to punish by whipping — **flag·el·la·tion** \₁fla-jə-'lā-shən\ *n*

fla·gel·lum \flə-'je-ləm\ *n, pl* **-la** \-lə\ *also* **-lums** : a long whiplike process that is the primary organ of motion of many microorganisms — **fla·gel·lar** \-lər\ *adj*

fla·geo·let \₁fla-jə-'let, -'lā\ *n* [F] : a small woodwind instrument belonging to the flute class

fla·gi·tious \flə-'ji-shəs\ *adj* : grossly wicked : VILLAINOUS

flag·on \'fla-gən\ *n* : a container for liquids usu. with a handle, spout, and lid

flag·pole \'flag-₁pōl\ *n* : a pole on which to raise a flag

fla·grant \'flā-grənt\ *adj* [L *flagrans*, prp. of *flagrare* to burn] : conspicuously bad — **fla·grant·ly** *adv*

fla·gran·te de·lic·to \flə-₁gran-tē-di-'lik-tō\ *adv or adj* [ML, lit., while the crime is blazing] : in the very act of committing a misdeed; *also* : in the midst of sexual activity

flag·ship \'flag-₁ship\ *n* **1** : the ship that carries the commander of a fleet or subdivision thereof and flies his flag **2** : the most important one of a group

flag·staff \-₁staf\ *n* : FLAGPOLE

flag·stone \-₁stōn\ *n* : ⁵FLAG

¹**flail** \'flāl\ *n* : a tool for threshing grain by hand

²**flail** *vb* : to strike or swing with or as if with a flail

flair \'flar\ *n* [F, lit., sense of smell, fr. OF, odor, fr. *flairier* to give off an odor, fr. (assumed) VL *flagrare*, fr. L *fragrare*] **1** : ability to appreciate or make good use of something : BENT, TALENT **2** : a unique style

flak \'flak\ *n, pl* **flak** [G, fr. *Fliegerabwehrkanonen*, fr. *Flieger* flyer + *Abwehr* defense + *Kanonen* cannons] **1** : antiaircraft guns or bursting shells fired from them **2** : CRITICISM, OPPOSITION

¹**flake** \'flāk\ *n* **1** : a small loose mass or bit **2** : a thin flattened piece or layer : CHIP — **flaky** *adj*

²**flake** *vb* **flaked; flak·ing** : to form or separate into flakes

³**flake** *n* : a markedly eccentric person : ODDBALL — **flak·i·ness** \'flā-kē-nəs\ *n* — **flaky** *adj*

flam·beau \'flam-₁bō\ *n, pl* **flambeaux** \-₁bōz\ *or* **flambeaus** [F, fr. MF, fr. *flambe* flame] : a flaming torch

flam·boy·ant \flam-'bȯi-ənt\ *adj* : marked by or given to strikingly elaborate or colorful display or behavior — **flam·boy·ance** \-əns\ *n* — **flam·boy·an·cy** \-ən-sē\ *n* — **flam·boy·ant·ly** *adv*

flame \'flām\ *n* **1** : the glowing gaseous part of a fire **2** : a state of blazing combustion **3** : a flamelike condition **4** : burning zeal or passion **5** : BRILLIANCE **6** : SWEETHEART — **flame** *vb*

fla·men·co \flə-'meŋ-kō\ *n, pl* **-cos** [Sp, fr. *flamenco* of the Gypsies, lit., Flemish, fr. MD *Vlaminc* Fleming] : a vigorous rhythmic dance style of the Spanish Gypsies

flame·throw·er \'flām-₁thrō-ər\ *n* : a device that expels from a nozzle a burning stream of liquid or semiliquid fuel under pressure

fla·min·go \flə-'miŋ-gō\ *n, pl* **-gos** *also* **-goes** : any of several long-legged long-necked tropical water birds with scarlet wings and a broad bill bent downward

flam·ma·ble \'fla-mə-bəl\ *adj* : easily ignited and quick=burning — **flam·ma·bil·i·ty** \₁fla-mə-'bi-lə-tē\ *n* — **flammable** *n*

flange \'flanj\ *n* : a rim used for strengthening or guiding something or for attachment to another object

¹**flank** \'flaŋk\ *n* **1** : the fleshy part of the side between the ribs and the hip; *also* : the side of a quadruped **2** : SIDE **3** : the right or left of a formation

²**flank** *vb* **1** : to attack or threaten the flank of **2** : to be situated on the side of : BORDER

flank·er \'flaŋ-kər\ *n* : a football player stationed wide of the formation slightly behind the line of scrimmage as a pass receiver

flan·nel \'flan-ᵊl\ *n* **1** : a soft twilled wool or worsted fabric with a napped surface **2** : a stout cotton fabric napped on one side **3** *pl* : flannel underwear or trousers

¹**flap** \'flap\ *n* **1** : a stroke with something broad : SLAP **2** : something broad, limber, or flat and usu. thin that hangs loose **3** : the motion or sound of something broad and limber as it swings to and fro **4** : a state of excitement or confusion

²**flap** *vb* **flapped; flap·ping** **1** : to beat with something

broad and flat **2** : FLING **3** : to move (as wings) with a beating motion **4** : to sway loosely usu. with a noise of striking

flap·jack \'flap-ıjak\ *n* : PANCAKE

flap·per \'fla-pər\ *n* **1** : one that flaps **2** : a young woman of the 1920s who showed freedom from conventions (as in conduct)

¹flare \'flar\ *vb* **flared; flar·ing 1** : to flame with a sudden unsteady light **2** : to become suddenly excited or angry ⟨∼ up⟩ **3** : to spread outward

²flare *n* **1** : an unsteady glaring light **2** : a blaze of light used esp. to signal or illuminate; *also* : a device for producing such a blaze

flare–up \-ıəp\ *n* : a sudden outburst or intensification

¹flash \'flash\ *vb* **1** : to break forth in or like a sudden flame **2** : to appear or pass suddenly or with great speed **3** : to send out in or as if in flashes ⟨∼ a message⟩ **4** : to make a sudden display (as of brilliance or feeling) **5** : to gleam or glow intermittently **6** : to fill by a sudden rush of water **7** : to expose to view very briefly ⟨∼ a badge⟩ **syn** glance, glint, sparkle, twinkle — **flash·er** *n*

²flash *n* **1** : a sudden burst of light **2** : a movement of a flag or light in signaling **3** : a sudden and brilliant burst (as of wit) **4** : a brief time **5** : SHOW, DISPLAY; *esp* : ostentatious display **6** : one that attracts notice; *esp* : an outstanding athlete **7** : GLIMPSE, LOOK **8** : a first brief news report **9** : FLASHLIGHT **10** : a device for producing a brief and very bright flash of light for taking photographs **11** : a quick-spreading flame or momentary intense outburst of radiant heat

³flash *adj* **1** : of sudden origin and short duration **2** : involving brief exposure to an intense agent (as heat or cold)

flash·back \'flash-ıbak\ *n* **1** : interruption of the chronological sequence (as of a film or literary work) by an event of earlier occurrence **2** : a past event remembered vividly

flash back *vb* **1** : to vividly remember a past incident **2** : to employ a flashback

flash·bulb \-ıbəlb\ *n* : an electric bulb that can be used only once to produce a brief and very bright flash of light for taking photographs

flash card *n* : a card bearing words, numbers, or pictures briefly displayed usu. as a learning aid

flash·cube \'flash-ıkyüb\ *n* : a cubical device incorporating four flashbulbs

flash·gun \-ıgən\ *n* : a device for producing a bright flash of light for photography

flash·ing \'fla-shiŋ\ *n* : sheet metal used in waterproofing (as at the angle between a chimney and a roof)

flash·light \'flash-ılīt\ *n* : a battery-operated portable electric light

flashy \'fla-shē\ *adj* **flash·i·er; -est 1** : momentarily dazzling **2** : superficially attractive or impressive : SHOWY — **flash·i·ly** \-shə-lē\ *adv* — **flash·i·ness** \-shē-nəs\ *n*

flask \'flask\ *n* : a flattened bottle-shaped container ⟨a whiskey ∼⟩

¹flat \'flat\ *adj* **flat·ter; flat·test 1** : spread out along a surface; *also* : being or characterized by a horizontal line **2** : having a smooth, level, or even surface **3** : having a broad smooth surface and little thickness **4** : DOWNRIGHT, POSITIVE ⟨a ∼ refusal⟩ **5** : FIXED, UNCHANGING ⟨charge a ∼ rate⟩ **6** : EXACT, PRECISE ⟨in four minutes ∼⟩ **7** : DULL, UNINTERESTING; *also* : INSIPID **8** : DEFLATED **9** : lower than the true pitch; *also* : lower by a half step **10** : free from gloss **11** : lacking depth of characterization — **flat·ly** *adv* — **flat·ness** *n*

²flat *n* **1** : a level surface of land : PLAIN **2** : a flat part or surface **3** : a character ♭ that indicates that a specified note is to be lowered by a half step; *also* : the resulting note **4** : something flat **5** : an apartment on one floor **6** : a deflated tire

³flat *adv* **1** : FLATLY **2** : COMPLETELY ⟨∼ broke⟩ **3** : below the true musical pitch

⁴flat *vb* **flat·ted; flat·ting 1** : FLATTEN **2** : to lower in pitch esp. by a half step

flat·bed \'flat-ıbed\ *n* : a truck or trailer with a body in the form of a platform or shallow box

flat·boat \-ıbōt\ *n* : a flat-bottomed boat used esp. for carrying bulky freight

flat·car \-ıkär\ *n* : a railroad freight car without sides or roof

flat·fish \-ıfish\ *n* : any of an order of flattened marine bony fishes with both eyes on the upper side

flat·foot \-ıfut, -'fut\ *n, pl* **flat·feet** \-ıfēt, -'fēt\ : a condition in which the arch of the foot is flattened so that the entire sole rests upon the ground — **flat–foot·ed** \-'fu-təd\ *adj*

Flat·head \-ıhed\ *n, pl* **Flatheads** *or* **Flathead** : a member of an American Indian people of Montana

flat·iron \-ıīrn\ *n* : IRON 3

flat·land \-ıland\ *n* : land lacking significant variation in elevation

flat–out \'flat-ıaut\ *adj* **1** : being or going at maximum effort or speed **2** : OUT-AND-OUT, DOWNRIGHT ⟨it was a ∼ lie⟩

flat out *adv* **1** : BLUNTLY, DIRECTLY **2** : at top speed **3** *usu* **flat–out** : to the greatest degree : COMPLETELY ⟨is just *flat-out* confusing⟩

flat·ten \'flat-ən\ *vb* : to make or become flat

flat·ter \'fla-tər\ *vb* [ME *flateren*, fr. OF *flater* to lick, flatter] **1** : to praise too much or without sincerity **2** : to represent too favorably **3** : to display to advantage **4** : to judge (oneself) favorably or too favorably — **flat·ter·er** *n*

flat·tery \'fla-tə-rē\ *n, pl* **-ter·ies** : flattering speech or attentions : insincere or excessive praise

flat·top \'flat-ıtäp\ *n* **1** : AIRCRAFT CARRIER **2** : CREW CUT

flat·u·lent \'fla-chə-lənt\ *adj* **1** : full of gas ⟨a ∼ stomach⟩ **2** : INFLATED, POMPOUS — **flat·u·lence** \-ləns\ *n*

fla·tus \'flā-təs\ *n* : gas formed in the intestine or stomach

flat·ware \'flat-ıwar\ *n* : eating and serving utensils

flat·worm \-ıwurm\ *n* : any of a phylum of flattened mostly parasitic segmented worms (as trematodes and tapeworms)

flaunt \'flont\ *vb* **1** : to display oneself to public notice **2** : to wave or flutter showily **3** : to display ostentatiously or impudently : PARADE — **flaunt** *n*

flau·tist \'flo-tist, 'flau-\ *n* [It *flautista*] : FLUTIST

¹fla·vor \'flā-vər\ *n* **1** : the quality of something that affects the sense of taste or of taste and smell **2** : a substance that adds flavor **3** : characteristic or predominant quality — **fla·vored** \-vərd\ *adj* — **fla·vor·ful** *adj* — **fla·vor·less** *adj* — **fla·vor·some** *adj*

²flavor *vb* : to give or add flavor to

fla·vor·ing *n* : FLAVOR 2

fla·vour *chiefly Brit var of* FLAVOR

flaw \'flo\ *n* : a small often hidden defect — **flaw·less** *adj* — **flaw·less·ly** *adv* — **flaw·less·ness** *n*

flax \'flaks\ *n* : a fiber that is the source of linen; *also* : a blue-flowered plant grown for this fiber and its oily seeds

flax·en \'flak-sən\ *adj* **1** : made of flax **2** : resembling flax esp. in pale soft straw color

flay \'flā\ *vb* **1** : to strip off the skin or surface of **2** : to criticize harshly

fl dr *abbr* fluid dram

flea \'flē\ *n* : any of an order of small wingless leaping bloodsucking insects

flea·bane \'flē-ıbān\ *n* : any of various plants of the daisy family once believed to drive away fleas

flea–bit·ten \-ıbit-ən\ *adj* : bitten by or infested with fleas

flea market *n* : a usu. open-air market for secondhand articles and antiques

¹fleck \'flek\ *vb* : STREAK, SPOT

²fleck *n* **1** : SPOT, MARK **2** : FLAKE, PARTICLE

fledge \'flej\ *vb* **fledged; fledg·ing** : to develop the feathers necessary for flying

fledg·ling \'flej-liŋ\ *n* **1** : a young bird with flight feathers newly developed **2** : an immature or inexperienced person

flee \'flē\ *vb* **fled** \'fled\; **flee·ing 1** : to run away often from danger or evil **2** : VANISH **3** : to run away from : SHUN

¹fleece \'flēs\ *n* **1** : the woolly coat of an animal and esp. a sheep **2** : a soft or woolly covering — **fleecy** *adj*

²fleece *vb* **fleeced; fleec·ing 1** : to strip of money or property by fraud or extortion **2** : SHEAR

¹fleet \'flēt\ *vb* : to pass rapidly

²fleet *n* [ME *flete*, fr. OE *flēot* ship, fr. *flēotan* to float] **1** : a group of warships under one command **2** : a group (as of ships, planes, or trucks) under one management

³fleet *adj* **1** : SWIFT, NIMBLE **2** : not enduring : FLEETING — **fleet·ness** *n*

fleet admiral *n* : an admiral of the highest rank in the navy

fleet·ing \'flē-tiŋ\ *adj* : passing swiftly

Flem·ing \'fle-miŋ\ *n* : a member of a Germanic people inhabiting chiefly northern Belgium

Flem·ish \'fle-mish\ *n* **1** : the Dutch language as spoken by the Flemings **2 Flemish** *pl* : FLEMINGS — **Flemish** *adj*

flesh \'flesh\ *n* **1** : the soft parts of an animal's body; *esp* : muscular tissue **2** : MEAT **3** : the physical nature of humans as distinguished from the soul **4** : human beings; *also* : living beings **5** : STOCK, KINDRED **6** : fleshy plant tissue (as fruit pulp) — **fleshed** \'flesht\ *adj*

flesh fly *n* : a dipteran fly whose maggots feed on flesh

flesh·ly \'flesh-lē\ *adj* **1** : CORPOREAL, BODILY **2** : not spiritual : WORLDLY **3** : CARNAL, SENSUAL

flesh out *vb* : to make fuller or more nearly complete

flesh·pot \'flesh-ˌpät\ *n* **1** *pl* : bodily comfort : LUXURY **2** : a place of lascivious entertainment — usu. used in pl.

fleshy \'fle-shē\ *adj* **flesh·i·er; -est 1** : consisting of or resembling animal flesh **2** : PLUMP, FAT

flew *past of* ¹FLY

flex \'fleks\ *vb* : to bend esp. repeatedly — **flex** *n*

flex·i·ble \'flek-sə-bəl\ *adj* **1** : capable of being flexed : PLIANT **2** : yielding to influence : TRACTABLE **3** : readily changed or changing : ADAPTABLE **syn** elastic, supple, resilient, springy — **flex·i·bil·i·ty** \ˌflek-sə-ˈbi-lə-tē\ *n*

flex·ure \'flek-shər\ *n* : TURN, FOLD

flib·ber·ti·gib·bet \ˌfli-bər-tē-ˈji-bət\ *n* : a silly flighty person

¹flick \'flik\ *n* **1** : a light sharp jerky stroke or movement **2** : a sound produced by a flick **3** : ²FLICKER **4** : MOVIE — often used in pl.

²flick *vb* **1** : to strike lightly with a quick sharp motion **2** : FLUTTER, FLIT

¹flick·er \'fli-kər\ *vb* **1** : to move irregularly or unsteadily : FLUTTER **2** : to burn fitfully or with a fluctuating light — **flick·er·ing·ly** *adv*

²flicker *n* **1** : an act of flickering **2** : a sudden brief movement ⟨a ~ of an eyelid⟩ **3** : a momentary stirring ⟨a ~ of interest⟩ **4** : a slight indication : HINT **5** : a wavering light

³flicker *n* : a large barred and spotted No. American woodpecker with a brown back that occurs as an eastern form with yellow on the underside of the wings and tail and a western form with red in these areas

flied *past and past part of* ³FLY

fli·er \'flī-ər\ *n* **1** : one that flies; *esp* : PILOT **2** : a reckless or speculative undertaking **3** *usu* **fly·er** : an advertising circular

¹flight \'flīt\ *n* **1** : an act or instance of flying **2** : the ability to fly **3** : a passing through air or space **4** : the distance covered in a flight **5** : swift movement **6** : a trip made by or in an airplane or spacecraft **7** : a group of similar individuals (as birds or airplanes) flying as a unit **8** : a passing (as of the imagination) beyond ordinary limits **9** : a series of stairs from one landing to another — **flight·less** *adj*

²flight *n* : an act or instance of running away

flight bag *n* **1** : a lightweight traveling bag with zippered outside pockets **2** : a small canvas satchel

flight line *n* : a parking and servicing area for airplanes

flighty \'flī-tē\ *adj* **flight·i·er; -est 1** : easily upset : VOLATILE **2** : easily excited : SKITTISH **3** : CAPRICIOUS, SILLY — **flight·i·ness** \-tē-nəs\ *n*

flim·flam \'flim-ˌflam\ *n* : DECEPTION, FRAUD — **flim·flam·mery** \-ˌfla-mə-rē\ *n*

flim·sy \'flim-zē\ *adj* **flim·si·er; -est 1** : lacking strength or substance **2** : of inferior materials and workmanship **3** : having little worth or plausibility ⟨a ~ excuse⟩ — **flim·si·ly** \-zə-lē\ *adv* — **flim·si·ness** \-zē-nəs\ *n*

flinch \'flinch\ *vb* [MF *flenchir* to bend] : to shrink from or as if from pain : WINCE — **flinch** *n*

¹fling \'fliŋ\ *vb* **flung** \'fləŋ\; **fling·ing 1** : to move hastily, brusquely, or violently ⟨*flung* out of the room⟩ **2** : to kick or plunge vigorously **3** : to throw with force or recklessness; *also* : to cast as if by throwing **4** : to put suddenly into a state or condition

²fling *n* **1** : an act or instance of flinging **2** : a casual try : ATTEMPT **3** : a period of self-indulgence

flint \'flint\ *n* **1** : a hard quartz that produces a spark when struck by steel **2** : an alloy used for producing a spark in lighters — **flinty** *adj*

flint glass *n* : heavy glass containing an oxide of lead and used in lenses and prisms

flint·lock \'flint-ˌläk\ *n* **1** : a lock for a gun using a flint to ignite the charge **2** : a firearm fitted with a flintlock

¹flip \'flip\ *vb* **flipped; flip·ping 1** : to turn by tossing ⟨~ a coin⟩ **2** : to turn over; *also* : to leaf through **3** : FLICK, JERK ⟨~ a light switch⟩ **4** : to lose self-control — **flip** *n*

²flip *adj* : FLIPPANT, IMPERTINENT

flip·pant \'fli-pənt\ *adj* : lacking proper respect or seriousness — **flip·pan·cy** \'fli-pən-sē\ *n*

flip·per \'fli-pər\ *n* **1** : a broad flat limb (as of a seal) adapted for swimming **2** : a paddlelike shoe used in skin diving

flip side *n* : the reverse and usu. less popular side of a phonograph record

¹flirt \'flərt\ *vb* **1** : to move erratically : FLIT **2** : to behave amorously without serious intent **3** : to show casual interest ⟨~ed with the idea⟩; *also* : to come close to ⟨~ with danger⟩ — **flir·ta·tion** \ˌflər-ˈtā-shən\ *n* — **flir·ta·tious** \-shəs\ *adj*

²flirt *n* **1** : an act or instance of flirting **2** : a person who flirts

flit \'flit\ *vb* **flit·ted; flit·ting** : to pass or move quickly or abruptly from place to place : DART — **flit** *n*

flitch \'flich\ *n* : a side of cured meat; *esp* : a side of bacon

fliv·ver \'fli-vər\ *n* : a small cheap usu. old automobile

¹float \'flōt\ *n* **1** : something (as a raft) that floats **2** : a cork buoying up the baited end of a fishing line **3** : a hollow ball that floats at the end of a lever in a cistern or tank and regulates the liquid level **4** : a vehicle with a platform to carry an exhibit **5** : a soft drink with ice cream floating in it

²float *vb* **1** : to rest on the surface of or be suspended in a fluid **2** : to move gently on or through a fluid **3** : to cause to float **4** : WANDER **5** : to offer (securities) in order to finance an enterprise **6** : to finance by floating an issue of stocks or bonds **7** : to arrange for ⟨~ a loan⟩ — **float·er** *n*

¹flock \'fläk\ *n* **1** : a group of birds or mammals assembled or herded together **2** : a group of people under the guidance of a leader; *esp* : CONGREGATION **3** : a large number

²flock *vb* : to gather or move in a flock

floe \\'flō\ *n* : a flat mass of floating ice

flog \\'fläg\ *vb* **flogged; flog·ging 1** : to beat with or as if with a rod or whip **2** : SELL ⟨∼ encyclopedias⟩ — **flog·ger** *n*

¹flood \\'fləd\ *n* **1** : a great flow of water over the land **2** : the flowing in of the tide **3** : an overwhelming volume

²flood *vb* **1** : to cover or become filled with a flood **2** : to fill abundantly or excessively; *esp* : to supply (a carburetor) with too much fuel **3** : to pour forth in a flood — **flood·er** *n*

flood·gate \\'fləd-ˌgāt\ *n* : a gate for controlling a body of water : SLUICE

flood·light \-ˌlīt\ *n* : a lamp that throws a broad beam of light; *also* : the beam itself — **floodlight** *vb*

flood·plain \-ˌplān\ *n* : a plain along a river or stream subject to periodic flooding

flood tide *n* **1** : a rising tide **2** : an overwhelming quantity **3** : a high point

flood·wa·ter \\'fləd-ˌwȯ-tər, -ˌwä-\ *n* : the water of a flood

¹floor \\'flōr\ *n* **1** : the bottom of a room on which one stands **2** : a ground surface **3** : a story of a building **4** : a main level space (as in a legislative chamber) distinguished from a platform or gallery **5** : AUDIENCE **6** : the right to address an assembly **7** : a lower limit ⟨put a ∼ under wheat prices⟩ — **floor·ing** *n*

²floor *vb* **1** : to furnish with a floor **2** : to knock down **3** : AMAZE, DUMBFOUND **4** : to press (a vehicle's accelerator) to the floorboard esp. rapidly

floor·board \-ˌbȯrd\ *n* **1** : a board in a floor **2** : the floor of an automobile

floor leader *n* : a member of a legislative body who has charge of a party's organization and strategy on the floor

floor show *n* : a series of acts presented in a nightclub

floor·walk·er \\'flȯr-ˌwȯ-kər\ *n* : a person employed in a retail store to oversee the sales force and aid customers

floo·zy *or* **floo·zie** \\'flü-zē\ *n, pl* **floozies** : a usu. young woman of loose morals

flop \\'fläp\ *vb* **flopped; flop·ping 1** : FLAP **2** : to throw oneself down heavily, clumsily, or in a relaxed manner ⟨*flopped* into a chair⟩ **3** : FAIL — **flop** *n* — **flop** *adv* — **flop·per** *n*

flop·house \\'fläp-ˌhaus\ *n* : a cheap hotel

¹flop·py \\'flä-pē\ *adj* **flop·pi·er; -est** : tending to flop; *esp* : soft and flexible — **flop·pi·ly** \-pə-lē\ *adv*

²floppy *n, pl* **flop·pies** : FLOPPY DISK

floppy disk *n* : a small flexible disk with a magnetic coating on which computer data can be stored

flo·ra \\'flōr-ə\ *n, pl* **floras** *also* **flo·rae** \-ˌē, -ˌī\ [L *Flora*, Roman goddess of flowers] : plants or plant life esp. of a region or period

flo·ral \\'flōr-əl\ *adj* : of or relating to flowers or a flora

flo·res·cence \flȯ-ˈres-ᵊns, flə-\ *n* : a state or period of being in bloom or flourishing — **flo·res·cent** \-ᵊnt\ *adj*

flor·id \\'flȯr-əd\ *adj* **1** : very flowery in style : ORNATE ⟨∼ prose⟩ **2** : tinged with red : RUDDY **3** : marked by emotional or sexual fervor

flo·rin \\'flȯr-ən\ *n* **1** : an old gold coin first struck at Florence, Italy, in 1252 **2** : a gold coin of a European country patterned after the florin of Florence **3** : any of several modern silver coins issued in Commonwealth countries **4** : GULDEN

flo·rist \\'flȯr-ist\ *n* : a person who sells flowers or ornamental plants

¹floss \\'fläs\ *n* **1** : soft thread of silk or mercerized cotton for embroidery **2** : DENTAL FLOSS **3** : fluffy fibrous material

²floss *vb* : to use dental floss on (one's teeth) : use dental floss

flossy \\'flä-sē\ *adj* **floss·i·er; -est 1** : of, relating to, or having the characteristics of floss **2** : STYLISH, GLAMOROUS — **floss·i·ly** \-sə-lē\ *adv*

flo·ta·tion \flō-ˈtā-shən\ *n* : the process or an instance of floating

flo·til·la \flō-ˈti-lə\ *n* [Sp, dim. of *flota* fleet] : a fleet esp. of small ships

flot·sam \\'flät-səm\ *n* : floating wreckage of a ship or its cargo

¹flounce \\'flauns\ *vb* **flounced; flounc·ing 1** : to move with exaggerated jerky or bouncy motions **2** : to go with sudden determination

²flounce *n* : an act or instance of flouncing — **flouncy** \\'flaun-sē\ *adj*

³flounce *n* : a strip of fabric attached by one edge; *also* : a wide ruffle

¹floun·der \\'flaun-dər\ *n, pl* **flounder** *or* **flounders** : FLATFISH; *esp* : any of various important marine food fishes

²flounder *vb* **1** : to struggle to move or obtain footing **2** : to proceed clumsily ⟨∼ed through the speech⟩

¹flour \\'flaur\ *n* : finely ground and sifted meal of a grain (as wheat); *also* : a fine soft powder — **floury** *adj*

²flour *vb* : to coat with or as if with flour

¹flour·ish \\'flər-ish\ *vb* **1** : THRIVE, PROSPER **2** : to be in a state of activity or production ⟨∼ed about 1850⟩ **3** : to reach a height of development or influence **4** : to make bold and sweeping gestures **5** : BRANDISH

²flourish *n* **1** : a florid bit of speech or writing; *also* : an ornamental touch or decorative detail **2** : FANFARE **3** : WAVE ⟨with a ∼ of his cane⟩ **4** : showiness in doing something

¹flout \\'flaut\ *vb* : to treat with contemptuous disregard ⟨∼ the law⟩ — **flout·er** *n*

²flout *n* : TAUNT

¹flow \\'flō\ *vb* **1** : to issue or move in a stream **2** : RISE ⟨the tide ebbs and ∼s⟩ **3** : ABOUND **4** : to proceed smoothly and readily **5** : to have a smooth continuity **6** : to hang loose and billowing **7** : COME, ARISE **8** : MENSTRUATE

²flow *n* **1** : an act of flowing **2** : FLOOD 1, 2 **3** : a smooth uninterrupted movement **4** : STREAM; *also* : a mass of material that has flowed when molten **5** : the quantity that flows in a certain time **6** : MENSTRUATION **7** : a continuous transfer of energy — **flow·age** \\'flō-ij\ *n*

flow·chart \\'flō-ˌchärt\ *n* : a symbolic diagram showing step-by-step progression through a procedure

flow diagram *n* : FLOWCHART

¹flow·er \\'flau(-ə)r\ *n* **1** : a plant shoot modified for reproduction and bearing leaves specialized into floral organs; *esp* : one of a seed plant consisting of a calyx, corolla, stamens, and carpels **2** : a plant cultivated for its blossoms **3** : the best part or example **4** : the finest most vigorous period **5** : a state of blooming or flourishing — **flow·ered** \\'flau(-ə)rd\ *adj* — **flow·er·less** *adj*

²flower *vb* **1** : DEVELOP; *also* : FLOURISH **2** : to produce flowers : BLOOM

flower girl *n* : a little girl who carries flowers at a wedding

flower head *n* : a compact cluster of small flowers without stems suggesting a single flower

flowering plant *n* : any of a major group of vascular plants (as magnolias, grasses, or roses) that produce flowers and fruit and have the seeds enclosed in an ovary

flow·er·pot \\'flau(-ə)r-ˌpät\ *n* : a pot in which to grow plants

flow·ery \\'flau(-ə)r-ē\ *adj* **1** : of, relating to, or resembling flowers **2** : full of fine words or phrases — **flow·er·i·ly** \-ə-lē\ *adv* — **flow·er·i·ness** \-ē-nəs\ *n*

flown \\'flōn\ *past part of* ¹FLY

fl oz *abbr* fluid ounce

flu \\'flü\ *n* **1** : INFLUENZA **2** : any of several virus diseases marked esp. by respiratory symptoms

flub \\'fləb\ *vb* **flubbed; flub·bing** : BOTCH, BLUNDER — **flub** *n*

fluc·tu·ate \\'flək-chə-ˌwāt\ *vb* **-at·ed; -at·ing 1** : WA-

VER 2 : to move up and down or back and forth — **fluc·tu·a·tion** \ˌflək-chə-ˈwā-shən\ n

flue \ˈflü\ n : a passage (as in a chimney) for directing a current (as of smoke or gases)

flu·ent \ˈflü-ənt\ adj 1 : capable of flowing : FLUID 2 : ready or facile in speech ⟨~ in French⟩ 3 : effortlessly smooth and rapid ⟨~ speech⟩ — **flu·en·cy** \-ən-sē\ n — **flu·ent·ly** adv

flue pipe n : an organ pipe whose tone is produced by an air current striking the beveled opening of the pipe

¹**fluff** \ˈfləf\ n 1 : ⁷DOWN 1 ⟨~ from a pillow⟩ 2 : something fluffy 3 : something inconsequential 4 : BLUNDER; esp : an actor's lapse of memory

²**fluff** vb 1 : to make or become fluffy ⟨~ up a pillow⟩ 2 : to make a mistake

fluffy \ˈflə-fē\ adj **fluff·i·er; -est** 1 : covered with or resembling fluff 2 : being light and soft or airy ⟨a ~ omelet⟩ 3 : lacking in meaning or substance — **fluff·i·ly** \-fə-lē\ adv

¹**flu·id** \ˈflü-əd\ adj 1 : capable of flowing 2 : subject to change or movement 3 : showing a smooth easy style ⟨~ movements⟩ 4 : available for a different use; esp : LIQUID 5 ⟨~ assets⟩ — **flu·id·i·ty** \flü-ˈi-də-tē\ n — **flu·id·ly** adv

²**fluid** n : a substance (as a liquid or gas) tending to flow or take the shape of its container

fluid dram or **flu·i·dram** \ˌflü-ə-ˈdram\ n — see WEIGHT table

fluid ounce n — see WEIGHT table

¹**fluke** \ˈflük\ n : any of various trematode flatworms

²**fluke** n 1 : the part of an anchor that fastens in the ground 2 : a lobe of a whale's tail

³**fluke** n : a stroke of luck — **fluky** also **fluk·ey** \ˈflü-kē\ adj

flume \ˈflüm\ n 1 : an inclined channel for carrying water 2 : a ravine or gorge with a stream running through it

flung past and past part of FLING

flunk \ˈfləŋk\ vb : to fail esp. in an examination or course — **flunk** n

flun·ky or **flun·key** \ˈfləŋ-kē\ n, pl **flunkies** or **flunkeys** 1 : a liveried servant; also : one performing menial or miscellaneous duties 2 : YES-MAN

fluo·res·cence \flȯ-ˈres-ᵊns\ n : luminescence caused by radiation absorption that ceases almost immediately after the incident radiation has stopped; also : the emitted radiation — **fluo·resce** \-ˈres\ vb — **fluo·res·cent** \-ˈres-ᵊnt\ adj

fluorescent lamp n : a tubular electric lamp in which light is produced by the action of ultraviolet light on a fluorescent material that coats the inner surface of the lamp

fluo·ri·date \ˈflȯr-ə-ˌdāt\ vb **-dat·ed; -dat·ing** : to add a fluoride to (as drinking water) to reduce tooth decay — **fluo·ri·da·tion** \ˌflȯr-ə-ˈdā-shən\ n

fluo·ride \ˈflȯr-ˌīd\ n : a compound of fluorine

fluo·ri·nate \ˈflȯr-ə-ˌnāt\ vb **-nat·ed; -nat·ing** : to treat or cause to combine with fluorine or a compound of fluorine — **fluo·ri·na·tion** \ˌflȯr-ə-ˈnā-shən\ n

fluo·rine \ˈflȯr-ēn, -ən\ n : a pale yellowish flammable irritating toxic gaseous chemical element — see ELEMENT table

fluo·rite \ˈflȯr-ˌīt\ n : a mineral that consists of the fluoride of calcium used as a flux and in making glass

fluo·ro·car·bon \ˌflȯr-ō-ˈkär-bən\ n : a compound containing fluorine and carbon used chiefly as a lubricant, refrigerant, or nonstick coating; also : CHLOROFLUOROCARBON

fluo·ro·scope \ˈflȯr-ə-ˌskōp\ n : an instrument for observing the internal structure of an opaque object (as the living body) by means of X rays — **fluo·ro·scop·ic** \ˌflȯr-ə-ˈskä-pik\ adj — **fluo·ros·co·py** \-ˈä-skə-pē\ n

fluo·ro·sis \ˌflü-ˈrō-səs, ˌflȯ-\ n : an abnormal condition (as spotting of the teeth) caused by fluorine or its compounds

flur·ry \ˈflər-ē\ n, pl **flurries** 1 : a gust of wind 2 : a brief light snowfall 3 : COMMOTION, BUSTLE 4 : a brief outburst of activity ⟨a ~ of trading⟩ — **flurry** vb

¹**flush** \ˈfləsh\ vb : to cause (a bird) to take wing suddenly

²**flush** n : a hand of cards all of the same suit

³**flush** n 1 : a sudden flow (as of water) 2 : a surge esp. of emotion ⟨a ~ of triumph⟩ 3 : a tinge of red : BLUSH 4 : a fresh and vigorous state ⟨in the ~ of youth⟩ 5 : a passing sensation of extreme heat

⁴**flush** vb 1 : to flow and spread suddenly and freely 2 : to glow brightly 3 : BLUSH 4 : to wash out with a rush of fluid 5 : INFLAME, EXCITE 6 : to cause to blush

⁵**flush** adj 1 : of a ruddy healthy color 2 : full of life and vigor 3 : filled to overflowing 4 : AFFLUENT 5 : readily available : ABUNDANT 6 : having an unbroken or even surface 7 : directly abutting : immediately adjacent 8 : set even with an edge of a type page or column — **flush·ness** n

⁶**flush** adv 1 : in a flush manner 2 : SQUARELY ⟨a blow ~ on the chin⟩

⁷**flush** vb : to make flush

flus·ter \ˈfləs-tər\ vb : to put into a state of agitated confusion — **fluster** n

flute \ˈflüt\ n 1 : a hollow pipelike musical instrument 2 : a grooved pleat 3 : GROOVE — **flute** vb — **fluted** adj

flute 1

flut·ing n : fluted decoration

flut·ist \ˈflü-tist\ n : a flute player

¹**flut·ter** \ˈflə-tər\ vb [ME floteren to float, flutter, fr. OE floterian, fr. flotian to float] 1 : to flap the wings rapidly 2 : to move with quick wavering or flapping motions 3 : to vibrate in irregular spasms 4 : to move about or behave in an agitated aimless manner — **flut·tery** \-tə-rē\ adj

²**flutter** n 1 : an act of fluttering 2 : a state of nervous confusion 3 : FLURRY

¹**flux** \ˈfləks\ n 1 : an act of flowing 2 : a state of continuous change 3 : a substance used to aid in fusing metals

²**flux** vb : ¹FUSE

¹**fly** \ˈflī\ vb **flew** \ˈflü\; **flown** \ˈflōn\; **fly·ing** 1 : to move in or pass through the air with wings 2 : to move through the air or before the wind 3 : to float or cause to float, wave, or soar in the air 4 : FLEE 5 : to fade and disappear : VANISH 6 : to move or pass swiftly 7 : to become expended or dissipated rapidly 8 : to operate or travel in an aircraft or spacecraft 9 : to journey over by flying 10 : AVOID, SHUN 11 : to transport by flying

²**fly** n, pl **flies** 1 : the action or process of flying : FLIGHT 2 pl : the space over a theater stage 3 : a garment closing concealed by a fold of cloth 4 : the length of an extended flag from its staff or support 5 : a baseball hit high into the air 6 : the outer canvas of a tent with a double top — **on the fly** : while still in the air

³**fly** vb **flied; fly·ing** : to hit a fly in baseball

⁴**fly** n, pl **flies** 1 : a winged insect — usu. used in com-

bination ⟨butter*fly*⟩ **2** : any of a large order of insects mostly with one pair of functional wings and another pair that if present are reduced to balancing organs and often with larvae without a head, eyes, or legs; *esp* : one (as a housefly) that is large and stout= bodied **3** : a fishhook dressed to suggest an insect

fly·able \'flī-ə-bəl\ *adj* : suitable for flying or being flown

fly ball *n* : ²FLY 5

fly·blown \'flī-,blōn\ *adj* : not pure : TAINTED, COR- RUPT

fly·by \-,bī\ *n*, *pl* **flybys 1** : a usu. low-altitude flight by an aircraft over a public gathering **2** : a flight of a spacecraft past a heavenly body (as Jupiter) close enough to obtain scientific data

fly–by–night \-,bī-,nīt\ *adj* **1** : seeking a quick profit usu. by shady acts **2** : TRANSITORY, PASSING

fly casting *n* : the casting of artificial flies in fly= fishing or as a competitive sport

fly·catch·er \-,ka-chər, -,ke-\ *n* : any of various passer- ine birds that feed on insects caught in flight

fly·er *var of* FLIER

fly–fish·ing \'flī-,fi-shiŋ\ *n* : a method of fishing in which an artificial fly is used for bait

flying boat *n* : a seaplane with a hull designed for float- ing

flying buttress *n* : a projecting arched structure to sup- port a wall or building

flying fish *n* : any of numerous sea fishes capable of long gliding flights out of water by spreading their large fins like wings

flying saucer *n* : an unidentified flying object reported to be saucer-shaped or disk-shaped

flying squirrel *n* : any of several No. American squir- rels with folds of skin connecting the forelegs and hind legs that enable them to make long gliding leaps

fly·leaf \'flī-,lēf\ *n*, *pl* **fly·leaves** \-,lēvz\ : a blank leaf at the beginning or end of a book

fly·pa·per \-,pā-pər\ *n* : paper poisoned or coated with a sticky substance for killing or catching flies

fly·speck \-,spek\ *n* **1** : a speck of fly dung **2** : some- thing small and insignificant — **flyspeck** *vb*

fly·way \-,wā\ *n* : an established air route of migratory birds

fly·wheel \-,hwēl\ *n* : a heavy wheel for regulating the speed of machinery

fm *abbr* fathom

Fm *symbol* fermium

FM \'ef-,em\ *n* : a broadcasting system using frequen- cy modulation; *also* : a radio receiver of such a sys- tem

fn *abbr* footnote

fo *or* **fol** *abbr* folio

FO *abbr* foreign office

foal \'fōl\ *n* : a young horse or related animal; *esp* : one under one year — **foal** *vb*

¹foam \'fōm\ *n* **1** : a mass of bubbles formed on the sur- face of a liquid : FROTH, SPUME **2** : material (as rubber) in a lightweight cellular form — **foamy** *adj*

²foam *vb* : to form foam : FROTH

fob \'fäb\ *n* **1** : a short strap, ribbon, or chain attached esp. to a pocket watch **2** : a small ornament worn on a fob

FOB *abbr* free on board

fob off *vb* **1** : to put off with a trick, excuse, or inferior substitute **2** : to pass or offer as genuine **3** : to put aside

FOC *abbr* free of charge

focal length *n* : the distance of a focus from a lens or curved mirror

fo'·c'sle *var of* FORECASTLE

¹fo·cus \'fō-kəs\ *n*, *pl* **fo·ci** \-,sī\ *also* **fo·cus·es** [NL, fr. L, hearth] **1** : a point at which rays (as of light, heat, or sound) meet or diverge or appear to diverge; *esp* : the point at which an image is formed by a mirror, lens, or optical system **2** : FOCAL LENGTH **3** : adjust-

ment (as of eyes or eyeglasses) that gives clear vision **4** : central point : CENTER — **fo·cal** \'fō-kəl\ *adj* — **fo- cal·ly** *adv*

²focus *vb* **-cused** *also* **-cussed; -cus·ing** *also* **-cus·sing 1** : to bring or come to a focus ⟨~ rays of light⟩ **2** : CEN- TER ⟨~ attention on a problem⟩ **3** : to adjust the focus of

fod·der \'fä-dər\ *n* : coarse dry food (as cornstalks) for livestock

foe \'fō\ *n* [ME *fo*, fr. OE *fāh*, fr. *fāh* hostile] : ENEMY

FOE *abbr* Fraternal Order of Eagles

foehn *or* **föhn** \'fərn, 'fēn, 'fān\ *n* [G *Föhn*] : a warm dry wind blowing down a mountainside

foe·man \'fō-mən\ *n* : FOE

foe·tal, foe·tus *chiefly Brit var of* FETAL, FETUS

¹fog \'fȯg, 'fäg\ *n* **1** : fine particles of water suspended in the lower atmosphere **2** : mental confusion — **fog- gy** *adj*

²fog *vb* **fogged; fog·ging** : to obscure or be obscured with or as if with fog

fog·horn \'fȯg-,hȯrn, 'fäg-\ *n* : a horn sounded in a fog to give warning

fo·gy *also* **fo·gey** \'fō-gē\ *n*, *pl* **fogies** *also* **fogeys** : a person with old-fashioned ideas ⟨an old ~⟩

foi·ble \'fȯi-bəl\ *n* : a minor failing or weakness in char- acter or behavior

¹foil \'fȯil\ *vb* [ME, to trample, full cloth, fr. MF *fouler*] **1** : to prevent from attaining an end : DEFEAT **2** : to bring to naught : THWART

²foil *n* : a light fencing sword with a flexible blade ta- pering to a blunt point

³foil *n* [ME, leaf, fr. MF *foille, foil*, fr. L *folium*] **1** : a very thin sheet of metal ⟨aluminum ~⟩ **2** : one that serves as a contrast to another

foist \'fȯist\ *vb* : to pass off (something false or worthless) as genuine

¹fold \'fōld\ *n* **1** : an enclosure for sheep **2** : a group of people with a common faith, belief, or interest

²fold *vb* : to house (sheep) in a fold

³fold *vb* **1** : to lay one part over or against another part **2** : to clasp together **3** : EMBRACE **4** : to bend (as a lay- er of rock) into folds **5** : to incorporate into a mixture by overturning repeatedly without stirring or beating **6** : to become doubled or pleated **7** : FAIL, COLLAPSE

⁴fold *n* **1** : a doubling or folding over **2** : a part doubled or laid over another part

fold·away \'fōl-də-,wā\ *adj* : designed to fold out of the way or out of sight

fold·er \'fōl-dər\ *n* **1** : one that folds **2** : a folded printed circular **3** : a folded cover or large envelope for loose papers

fol·de·rol \'fäl-də-,räl\ *n* **1** : a useless trifle **2** : NON- SENSE

fold·out \'fōl-,daut\ *n* : a folded leaf (as in a magazine) larger in some dimension than the page

fo·liage \'fō-lē-ij\ *n* : a mass of leaves (as of a plant or forest)

fo·li·at·ed \'fō-lē-,ā-təd\ *adj* : composed of or separa- ble into layers

fo·lic acid \,fō-lik-\ *n* : a vitamin of the vitamin B com- plex used esp. to treat nutritional anemias

fo·lio \'fō-lē-,ō\ *n*, *pl* **fo·li·os 1** : a leaf of a book; *also* : a page number **2** : the size of a piece of paper cut two from a sheet **3** : a book printed on folio pages

¹folk \'fōk\ *n*, *pl* **folk** *or* **folks 1** : a group of people forming a tribe or nation; *also* : the largest number or most characteristic part of such a group **2** *pl* : PEO- PLE, PERSONS ⟨country⟩ ⟨old ~s⟩ **3** *folks pl* : the persons of one's own family

²folk *adj* : of, relating to, or originating among the com- mon people ⟨~ music⟩

folk·lore \'fōk-,lōr\ *n* : customs, beliefs, stories, and sayings of a people handed down from generation to generation — **folk·lor·ist** \-ist\ *n*

folk mass *n* : a mass in which traditional liturgical mu- sic is replaced by folk music

folk·sing·er \'fōk-ˌsiŋ-ər\ *n* : a singer of folk songs — **folk·sing·ing** *n*

folksy \'fōk-sē\ *adj* **folks·i·er; -est 1** : SOCIABLE, FRIENDLY **2** : informal, casual, or familiar in manner or style

folk·way \'fōk-ˌwā\ *n* : a way of thinking, feeling, or acting common to a given group of people; *esp* : a traditional social custom

fol·li·cle \'fä-li-kəl\ *n* **1** : a small anatomical cavity or gland ⟨a hair ∼⟩ **2** : a small fluid-filled cavity in the ovary of a mammal enclosing a developing egg

fol·low \'fä-lō\ *vb* **1** : to go or come after **2** : to proceed along **3** : to engage in as a way of life ⟨∼ the sea⟩ ⟨∼ a profession⟩ **4** : OBEY **5** : PURSUE **6** : to come after in order or rank or natural sequence **7** : to keep one's attention fixed on **8** : to result from **syn** succeed, ensue, supervene — **fol·low·er** *n* — **follow suit 1** : to play a card of the same suit as the card led **2** : to follow an example set

¹fol·low·ing \'fä-lə-wiŋ\ *adj* **1** : next after : SUCCEEDING **2** : that immediately follows

²following *n* : a group of followers, adherents, or partisans

³following *prep* : subsequent to : AFTER

follow–up \'fä-lə-ˌwəp\ *n* : a system or instance of pursuing an initial effort by supplementary action

fol·ly \'fä-lē\ *n, pl* **follies** [ME *folie*, fr. OF, fr. *fol* fool] **1** : lack of good sense **2** : a foolish act or idea : FOOLISHNESS **3** : an excessively costly or unprofitable undertaking

fo·ment \fō-'ment\ *vb* : INCITE

fo·men·ta·tion \ˌfō-mən-'tā-shən, -ˌmen-\ *n* **1** : a hot moist material (as a damp cloth) applied to the body to ease pain **2** : the act of fomenting : INSTIGATION

fond \'fänd\ *adj* [ME, fr. *fonne* fool] **1** : FOOLISH, SILLY ⟨∼ pride⟩ **2** : prizing highly : DESIROUS ⟨∼ of praise⟩ **3** : strongly attracted or predisposed ⟨∼ of music⟩ **4** : foolishly tender : INDULGENT; *also* : LOVING, AFFECTIONATE **5** : CHERISHED, DEAR ⟨his ∼*est* hopes⟩ — **fond·ly** *adv* — **fond·ness** *n*

fon·dant \'fän-dənt\ *n* : a creamy preparation of sugar used as a basis for candies or icings

fon·dle \'fänd-ᵊl\ *vb* **fon·dled; fon·dling** : to touch or handle lovingly : CARESS

fon·due *also* **fon·du** \fän-'dü, -'dyü\ *n* [F] : a preparation of melted cheese often flavored with white wine

¹font \'fänt\ *n* **1** : a receptacle for baptismal or holy water **2** : FOUNTAIN, SOURCE

²font *n* : an assortment of printing type of one size and style

food \'füd\ *n* **1** : material taken into an organism and used for growth, repair, and vital processes and as a source of energy; *also* : organic material produced by green plants and used by them as food **2** : nourishment in solid form **3** : something that nourishes, sustains, or supplies ⟨∼ for thought⟩

food chain *n* : a hierarchical arrangement of organisms in an ecological community such that each uses the next usu. lower member as a food source

food poisoning *n* : a digestive illness caused by bacteria or by chemicals in food

food·stuff \'füd-ˌstəf\ *n* : a substance with food value; *esp* : a specific nutrient (as fat or protein)

¹fool \'fül\ *n* [ME, fr. OF *fol*, fr. LL *follis*, fr. L, bellows, bag] **1** : a person who lacks sense or judgment **2** : JESTER **3** : DUPE **4** : IDIOT

²fool *vb* **1** : to spend time idly or aimlessly **2** : to meddle or tamper thoughtlessly or ignorantly **3** : JOKE **4** : DECEIVE **5** : FRITTER ⟨∼ed away his time⟩

fool·ery \'fü-lə-rē\ *n, pl* **-er·ies 1** : a foolish act, utterance, or belief **2** : foolish behavior

fool·har·dy \'fül-ˌhär-dē\ *adj* : foolishly daring : RASH — **fool·har·di·ness** \-dē-nəs\ *n*

fool·ish \'fü-lish\ *adj* **1** : showing or arising from folly or lack of judgment **2** : ABSURD, RIDICULOUS **3** : ABASHED — **fool·ish·ly** *adv* — **fool·ish·ness** *n*

fool·proof \'fül-ˌprüf\ *adj* : so simple or reliable as to leave no opportunity for error, misuse, or failure ⟨a ∼ plan⟩

fools·cap \'fül-ˌskap\ *n* [fr. the watermark of a fool's cap formerly applied to such paper] : a size of paper typically 16×13 inches

fool's gold *n* : PYRITE

¹foot \'fút\ *n, pl* **feet** \'fēt\ *also* **foot 1** : the end part of a leg below the ankle of a vertebrate animal **2** — see WEIGHT table **3** : a group of syllables forming the basic unit of verse meter **4** : something resembling an animal's foot in position or use **5** : the lowest part : BOTTOM **6** : the part at the opposite end from the head **7** : the part (as of a stocking) that covers the foot

²foot *vb* **1** : DANCE **2** : to go on foot **3** : to add up **4** : to pay or provide for paying

foot·age \'fú-tij\ *n* : length expressed in feet

foot·ball \'fút-ˌból\ *n* **1** : any of several games played by two teams on a rectangular field with goalposts at each end in which the object is to get the ball over the goal line or between goalposts by running, passing, or kicking **2** : the ball used in football

foot·board \-ˌbórd\ *n* **1** : a narrow platform on which to stand or brace the feet **2** : a board forming the foot of a bed

foot·bridge \-ˌbrij\ *n* : a bridge for pedestrians

foot·ed \'fú-təd\ *adj* : having a foot or feet of a specified kind or number ⟨flat-*footed*⟩ ⟨four-*footed*⟩

-foot·er \'fú-tər\ *comb form* : one that is a specified number of feet in height, length, or breadth ⟨a six= *footer*⟩

foot·fall \'fút-ˌfól\ *n* : the sound of a footstep

foot·hill \-ˌhil\ *n* : a hill at the foot of higher hills or mountains

foot·hold \-ˌhōld\ *n* **1** : a hold for the feet : FOOTING **2** : a position usable as a base for further advance

foot·ing *n* **1** : the placing of one's feet in a stable position **2** : the act of moving on foot **3** : a place or space for standing : FOOTHOLD **4** : position with respect to one another : STATUS **5** : BASIS

foot·less \'fút-ləs\ *adj* **1** : having no feet **2** : INEPT

foot·lights \-ˌlīts\ *n pl* **1** : a row of lights along the front of a stage floor **2** : the stage as a profession

foo·tling \'füt-liŋ\ *adj* **1** : INEPT **2** : TRIVIAL

foot·lock·er \'fút-ˌlä-kər\ *n* : a small trunk designed to be placed at the foot of a bed (as in a barracks)

foot·loose \-ˌlüs\ *adj* : having no ties : FREE, UNTRAMMELED

foot·man \-mən\ *n* : a male servant who attends a carriage, waits on table, admits visitors, and runs errands

foot·note \-ˌnōt\ *n* **1** : a note of reference, explanation, or comment placed usu. at the bottom of a page **2** : COMMENTARY

foot·pad \-ˌpad\ *n* : a round somewhat flat foot on the leg of a spacecraft for distributing weight to minimize sinking into a surface

foot·path \-ˌpath, -ˌpàth\ *n* : a narrow path for pedestrians

foot·print \-ˌprint\ *n* **1** : an impression of the foot **2** : the area on a surface covered by something

foot·race \-ˌrās\ *n* : a race run on foot

foot·rest \-ˌrest\ *n* : a support for the feet

foot·sore \-ˌsōr\ *adj* : having sore or tender feet (as from much walking)

foot·step \-ˌstep\ *n* **1** : the mark of the foot : TRACK **2** : TREAD **3** : distance covered by a step : PACE **4** : a step on which to ascend or descend **5** : a way of life, conduct, or action

foot·stool \-ˌstül\ *n* : a low stool to support the feet

foot·wear \-ˌwar\ *n* : apparel (as shoes or boots) for the feet

foot·work \-ˌwərk\ *n* : the management of the feet (as in boxing)

fop \'fäp\ *n* : DANDY 1 — **fop·pery** \'fä-pə-rē\ *n* — **fop·pish** *adj*

¹for \fər, 'for\ *prep* 1 : as a preparation toward ⟨dress ∼ dinner⟩ 2 : toward the purpose or goal of ⟨need time ∼ study⟩ ⟨money ∼ a trip⟩ 3 : so as to reach or attain ⟨run ∼ cover⟩ 4 : as being ⟨took him ∼ a fool⟩ 5 : because of ⟨cry ∼ joy⟩ 6 — used to indicate a recipient ⟨a letter ∼ you⟩ 7 : in support of ⟨fought ∼ his country⟩ 8 : directed at : AFFECTING ⟨a cure ∼ what ails you⟩ 9 — used with a noun or pronoun followed by an infinitive to form the equivalent of a noun clause ⟨∼ you to go would be silly⟩ 10 : in exchange as equal to : so as to return the value of ⟨a lot of trouble ∼ nothing⟩ ⟨pay $10 ∼ a hat⟩ 11 : CONCERNING ⟨a stickler ∼ detail⟩ 12 : CONSIDERING ⟨tall ∼ her age⟩ 13 : through the period of ⟨served ∼ three years⟩ 14 : in honor of

²for *conj* : BECAUSE

³for *abbr* 1 foreign 2 forestry

fora *pl of* FORUM

¹for·age \'for-ij\ *n* 1 : food for animals esp. when taken by browsing or grazing 2 : a search for food or supplies

²forage *vb* **for·aged; for·ag·ing** 1 : to collect forage from 2 : to search for food or supplies 3 : to get by foraging 4 : to make a search : RUMMAGE

for·ay \'for-ˌā, fò-'rā\ *vb* : to raid esp. in search of plunder — **foray** *n*

¹for·bear \for-'bar\ *vb* **-bore** \-'bōr\; **-borne** \-'bōrn\; **-bear·ing** 1 : to refrain from : ABSTAIN 2 : to be patient — **for·bear·ance** \-'bar-əns\ *n*

²forbear *var of* FOREBEAR

for·bid \fər-'bid\ *vb* **-bade** \-'bad, -'bād\ *or* **-bad** \-'bad\; **-bid·den** \-'bid-ᵊn\; **-bid·ding** 1 : to command against : PROHIBIT 2 : HINDER, PREVENT **syn** enjoin, interdict, inhibit, ban

for·bid·ding *adj* : DISAGREEABLE, REPELLENT

forbode *var of* FOREBODE

¹force \'fōrs\ *n* 1 : strength or energy esp. of an exceptional degree : active power 2 : capacity to persuade or convince 3 : military strength; *also, pl* : the whole military strength (as of a nation) 4 : a body (as of persons or ships) available for a particular purpose 5 : VIOLENCE, COMPULSION 6 : an influence (as a push or pull) that causes motion or a change of motion — **force·ful** \-fəl\ *adj* — **force·ful·ly** *adv* — **in force** 1 : in great numbers 2 : VALID, OPERATIVE

²force *vb* **forced; forc·ing** 1 : COMPEL, COERCE 2 : to cause through necessity ⟨forced to admit defeat⟩ 3 : to press, attain to, or effect against resistance or inertia ⟨∼ your way through⟩ 4 : to raise or accelerate to the utmost ⟨∼ the pace⟩ 5 : to produce with unnatural or unwilling effort ⟨forced a smile⟩ 6 : to hasten (as in growth) by artificial means

for·ceps \'for-səps\ *n, pl* **forceps** [L] : a hand=held instrument for grasping, holding, or pulling objects esp. for delicate operations (as by a surgeon)

forceps

forc·ible \'for-sə-bəl\ *adj* 1 : obtained or done by force 2 : showing force or energy : POWERFUL — **forc·i·bly** \-blē\ *adv*

¹ford \'fōrd\ *n* : a place where a stream may be crossed by wading

²ford *vb* : to cross (a body of water) by wading

¹fore \'fōr\ *adv* : in, toward, or adjacent to the front : FORWARD

²fore *adj* : being or coming before in time, order, or space

³fore *n* : something that occupies a front position

⁴fore *interj* — used by a golfer to warn anyone within range of the probable line of flight of the ball

fore–and–aft \ˌfōr-ə-'naft\ *adj* : lying, running, or acting along the length of a structure (as a ship)

¹fore·arm \(ˌ)fōr-'ärm\ *vb* : to arm in advance : PREPARE

²fore·arm \'fōr-ˌärm\ *n* : the part of the arm between the elbow and the wrist

fore·bear \-ˌbar\ *n* : ANCESTOR, FOREFATHER

fore·bode \fōr-'bōd\ *vb* 1 : to have a premonition esp. of misfortune 2 : FORETELL, PREDICT **syn** augur, bode, foreshadow, portend, promise — **fore·bod·ing** *n*

fore·cast \'fōr-ˌkast\ *vb* **-cast** *also* **-cast·ed; -cast·ing** 1 : PREDICT, CALCULATE ⟨∼ weather conditions⟩ 2 : to indicate as likely to occur — **forecast** *n* — **fore·cast·er** *n*

fore·cas·tle \'fōk-səl\ *n* 1 : the forward part of the upper deck of a ship 2 : the crew's quarters usu. in a ship's bow

fore·close \fōr-'klōz\ *vb* 1 : to shut out : PRECLUDE 2 : to take legal measures to terminate a mortgage and take possession of the mortgaged property

fore·clo·sure \-'klō-zhər\ *n* : the act of foreclosing; *esp* : the legal procedure of foreclosing a mortgage

fore·doom \fōr-'düm\ *vb* : to doom beforehand

fore·fa·ther \'fōr-ˌfä-thər\ *n* 1 : ANCESTOR 2 : a person of an earlier period and common heritage

forefend *var of* FORFEND

fore·fin·ger \-ˌfiŋ-gər\ *n* : the finger next to the thumb

fore·foot \-ˌfüt\ *n* : either of the front feet of a quadruped; *also* : the front part of the human foot

fore·front \-ˌfrənt\ *n* : the foremost part or place

fore·gath·er *var of* FORGATHER

¹fore·go \fōr-'gō\ *vb* **-went** \-'went\; **-gone** \-'gòn\; **-go·ing** : PRECEDE

²forego *var of* FORGO

fore·go·ing *adj* : PRECEDING

fore·gone \'fōr-ˌgòn\ *adj* : determined in advance ⟨a ∼ conclusion⟩

fore·ground \-ˌgraùnd\ *n* 1 : the part of a scene or representation that appears nearest to and in front of the spectator 2 : a position of prominence

fore·hand \-ˌhand\ *n* : a stroke (as in tennis) made with the palm of the hand turned in the direction in which the hand is moving; *also* : the side on which such a stroke is made — **forehand** *adj*

forehand

fore·hand·ed \(ˌ)fōr-'han-dəd\ *adj* : mindful of the future : PRUDENT

fore·head \'fōr-əd, 'fōr-ˌhed\ *n* : the part of the face above the eyes

for·eign \'fòr-ən\ *adj* [ME *forein*, fr. OF, fr. LL *foranus* on the outside, fr. L *foris* outside] 1 : situated outside a place or country and esp. one's own country 2 : born in, belonging to, or characteristic of some place or country other than the one under consideration ⟨∼ language⟩ **3** : not connected, pertinent, or characteristically present **4** : related to or dealing with other nations ⟨∼ affairs⟩ **5** : occurring in an abnormal situation in the living body ⟨a ∼ body in the eye⟩

for•eign•er \ˈfȯr-ə-nər\ *n* : a person belonging to or owing allegiance to a foreign country

foreign minister *n* : a governmental minister for foreign affairs

fore•know \fȯr-ˈnō\ *vb* **-knew** \-ˈnü, -ˈnyü\; **-known** \-ˈnōn\; **-know•ing** : to have previous knowledge of — **fore•knowl•edge** \ˈfȯr-ˌnä-lij, fȯr-ˈnä-\ *n*

fore•la•dy \ˈfȯr-ˌlā-dē\ *n* : FOREWOMAN

fore•leg \-ˌleg\ *n* : a front leg

fore•limb \-ˌlim\ *n* : either of an anterior pair of limbs (as wings, arms, or fins)

fore•lock \-ˌläk\ *n* : a lock of hair growing from the front part of the head

fore•man \-mən\ *n* **1** : a spokesperson of a jury **2** : a person in charge of a group of workers

fore•mast \-ˌmast\ *n* : the mast nearest the bow of a ship

fore•most \-ˌmōst\ *adj* : first in time, place, or order : most important : PREEMINENT — **foremost** *adv*

fore•name \-ˌnām\ *n* : a first name

fore•named \-ˌnāmd\ *adj* : previously named : AFORESAID

fore•noon \-ˌnün\ *n* : MORNING

¹**fo•ren•sic** \fə-ˈren-sik\ *adj* [L *forensis* public, forensic, fr. *forum* forum] **1** : belonging to, used in, or suitable to courts of law or to public speaking or debate **2** : relating to the application of scientific knowledge to legal problems ⟨∼ medicine⟩

²**forensic** *n* **1** : an argumentative exercise **2** *pl* : the art or study of argumentative discourse

fore•or•dain \fȯr-ȯr-ˈdān\ *vb* : to ordain or decree beforehand : PREDESTINE

fore•part \ˈfȯr-ˌpärt\ *n* **1** : the anterior part of something **2** : the earlier part of a period of time

fore•quar•ter \-ˌkwȯr-tər\ *n* : the front half of a lateral half of the body or carcass of a quadruped ⟨a ∼ of beef⟩

fore•run•ner \-ˌrə-nər\ *n* **1** : one that goes before to give notice of the approach of others : HARBINGER **2** : PREDECESSOR, ANCESTOR **syn** precursor, herald

fore•sail \-ˌsāl, -səl\ *n* **1** : the lowest sail on the foremast of a square-rigged ship or schooner **2** : the principal sail forward of the foremast (as of a sloop)

fore•see \fȯr-ˈsē\ *vb* **-saw** \-ˈsȯ\; **-seen** \-ˈsēn\; **-see•ing** : to see or realize beforehand : EXPECT **syn** foreknow, divine, apprehend, anticipate — **fore•see•able** *adj*

fore•shad•ow \-ˈsha-dō\ *vb* : to give a hint or suggestion of beforehand

fore•short•en \fȯr-ˈshȯrt-ᵊn\ *vb* : to shorten (a detail) in a drawing or painting so that it appears to have depth

fore•sight \ˈfȯr-ˌsīt\ *n* **1** : the act or power of foreseeing **2** : care or provision for the future : PRUDENCE **3** : an act of looking forward; *also* : a view forward — **fore•sight•ed** \-ˌsī-təd\ *adj* — **fore•sight•ed•ness** *n*

fore•skin \-ˌskin\ *n* : a fold of skin enclosing the end of the penis

for•est \ˈfȯr-əst\ *n* [ME, fr. OF, fr. LL *forestis* (*silva*) unenclosed (woodland), fr. L *foris* outside] : a large thick growth of trees and underbrush — **for•est•ed** \ˈfȯr-ə-stəd\ *adj* — **for•est•land** \ˈfȯr-əst-ˌland\ *n*

fore•stall \fȯr-ˈstȯl, fȯr-\ *vb* **1** : to keep out, hinder, or prevent by measures taken in advance **2** : ANTICIPATE

forest ranger *n* : a person in charge of the management and protection of a portion of a forest

for•est•ry \ˈfȯr-ə-strē\ *n* : the science of growing and caring for forests — **for•est•er** \ˈfȯr-ə-stər\ *n*

foreswear *var of* FORSWEAR

¹**fore•taste** \ˈfȯr-ˌtāst\ *n* : an advance indication, warning, or notion

²**fore•taste** \fȯr-ˈtāst\ *vb* : to taste beforehand : ANTICIPATE

fore•tell \fȯr-ˈtel\ *vb* **-told** \-ˈtōld\; **-tell•ing** : to tell of beforehand : PREDICT **syn** forecast, prophesy, prognosticate

fore•thought \ˈfȯr-ˌthȯt\ *n* **1** : PREMEDITATION **2** : consideration for the future

fore•to•ken \fȯr-ˈtō-kən\ *vb* : to indicate in advance

fore•top \ˈfȯr-ˌtäp\ *n* : a platform near the top of a ship's foremast

for•ev•er \fȯr-ˈe-vər\ *adv* **1** : for a limitless time **2** : at all times : ALWAYS

for•ev•er•more \-ˌe-vər-ˈmȯr\ *adv* : FOREVER

fore•warn \fȯr-ˈwȯrn\ *vb* : to warn beforehand

forewent *past of* FOREGO

fore•wing \ˈfȯr-ˌwiŋ\ *n* : either of the anterior wings of a 4-winged insect

fore•wom•an \ˈfȯr-ˌwu̇-mən\ *n* : a woman having the responsibilities of a foreman

fore•word \-ˌwərd\ *n* : PREFACE

¹**for•feit** \ˈfȯr-fət\ *n* **1** : something forfeited : PENALTY, FINE **2** : FORFEITURE **3** : something deposited and then redeemed on payment of a fine **4** *pl* : a game in which forfeits are exacted

²**forfeit** *vb* : to lose or lose the right to by some error, offense, or crime

for•fei•ture \ˈfȯr-fə-ˌchu̇r\ *n* **1** : the act of forfeiting **2** : something forfeited : PENALTY

for•fend \fȯr-ˈfend\ *vb* **1** : PREVENT **2** : PROTECT, PRESERVE

for•gath•er \fȯr-ˈga-thər\ *vb* **1** : to come together : ASSEMBLE **2** : to meet someone usu. by chance

¹**forge** \ˈfȯrj\ *n* [ME, fr. OF, fr. L *fabrica*, fr. *faber* smith] : a furnace or shop with its furnace where metal is heated and worked

²**forge** *vb* **forged; forg•ing 1** : to form (metal) by heating and hammering **2** : FASHION, SHAPE ⟨∼ an agreement⟩ **3** : to make or imitate falsely esp. with intent to defraud ⟨∼ a signature⟩ — **forg•er** *n* — **forg•ery** \ˈfȯr-jə-rē\ *n*

³**forge** *vb* **forged; forg•ing** : to move ahead steadily but gradually

for•get \fər-ˈget\ *vb* **for•got** \-ˈgät\; **for•got•ten** \-ˈgät-ᵊn\ *or* **for•got; for•get•ting 1** : to be unable to think of or recall **2** : to fail to become mindful of at the proper time **3** : NEGLECT, DISREGARD — **for•get•ful** \-ˈget-fəl\ *adj* — **for•get•ful•ly** *adv*

for•get—me—not \fər-ˈget-mē-ˌnät\ *n* : any of a genus of small herbs with bright blue or white flowers

forg•ing *n* : a piece of forged work

for•give \fər-ˈgiv\ *vb* **for•gave** \-ˈgāv\; **for•giv•en** \-ˈgi-vən\; **for•giv•ing 1** : to give up resentment of **2** : PARDON, ABSOLVE **3** : to grant relief from payment of — **for•giv•able** *adj* — **for•give•ness** *n*

for•giv•ing *adj* **1** : willing or able to forgive **2** : allowing room for error or weakness

for•go \fȯr-ˈgō\ *vb* **for•went** \-ˈwent\; **for•gone** \-ˈgȯn\; **for•go•ing** : to give up the enjoyment or advantage of : do without

fo•rint \ˈfȯr-int\ *n, pl* **forints** *also* **forint** — see MONEY table

¹**fork** \ˈfȯrk\ *n* **1** : an implement with two or more prongs for taking up (as in eating), pitching, or digging **2** : a forked part, tool, or piece of equipment **3** : a dividing into branches or a place where something branches; *also* : a branch of such a fork

²**fork** *vb* **1** : to divide into two or more branches **2** : to give the form of a fork to ⟨∼*ing* her fingers⟩ **3** : to raise or pitch with a fork ⟨∼ hay⟩ **4** : PAY, CONTRIBUTE — used with *over, out,* or *up*

forked \ˈfȯrkt, ˈfȯr-kəd\ *adj* : having a fork : shaped like a fork ⟨∼ lightning⟩

fork•lift \ˈfȯrk-ˌlift\ *n* : a machine for lifting heavy objects by means of steel fingers inserted under the load

for•lorn \fər-ˈlȯrn, fȯr-\ *adj* **1** : sad and lonely because of isolation or desertion **2** : WRETCHED **3** : nearly hopeless — **for·lorn·ly** adv — **for·lorn·ness** n

¹**form** \'form\ n **1** : SHAPE, STRUCTURE **2** : a body esp. of a person : FIGURE **3** : the essential nature of a thing **4** : established manner of doing or saying something **5** : FORMULA **6** : a document with blank spaces for insertion of information ⟨tax ∼⟩ **7** : CEREMONY **8** : manner of performing according to recognized standards **9** : a long seat : BENCH **10** : a model of the human figure used for displaying clothes **11** : MOLD ⟨a ∼ for concrete⟩ **12** : type or plates in a frame ready for printing **13** : MODE, KIND, VARIETY ⟨coal is a ∼ of carbon⟩ **14** : orderly method of arrangement; also : a particular kind or instance of such arrangement ⟨the sonnet ∼ in poetry⟩ **15** : the structural element, plan, or design of a work of art **16** : a bounded surface or volume **17** : a grade in a British school or in some American private schools **18** : RACING FORM **19** : known ability to perform; also : condition (as of an athlete) suitable for performing **20** : one of the ways in which a word is changed to show difference in use ⟨the plural ∼ of a noun⟩ — **form·less** adj

²**form** vb **1** : to give form or shape to : FASHION, MAKE **2** : TRAIN, INSTRUCT **3** : CONSTITUTE, COMPOSE **4** : DEVELOP, ACQUIRE ⟨∼ a habit⟩ **5** : to arrange in order ⟨∼ a battle line⟩ **6** : to take form : ARISE ⟨clouds are ∼ing⟩ **7** : to take a definite form, shape, or arrangement

¹**for·mal** \'for-məl\ adj **1** : according with conventional forms and rules ⟨a ∼ dinner party⟩ **2** : done in due or lawful form ⟨a ∼ contract⟩ **3** : CEREMONIOUS, PRIM ⟨a ∼ manner⟩ **4** : NOMINAL — **for·mal·ly** adv

²**formal** n : something (as a social event) formal in character

form·al·de·hyde \for-'mal-də-ˌhīd\ n : a colorless pungent gas used in water solution as a preservative and disinfectant

for·mal·ism \'for-mə-ˌli-zəm\ n : strict adherence to set forms

for·mal·i·ty \for-'ma-lə-tē\ n, pl **-ties 1** : compliance with formal or conventional rules **2** : the quality or state of being formal **3** : an established form that is required or conventional

for·mal·ize \'for-mə-ˌlīz\ vb **-ized; -iz·ing 1** : to give a certain or definite form to **2** : to make formal; also : to give formal status or approval to

¹**for·mat** \'for-ˌmat\ n **1** : the general composition or style of a publication **2** : the general plan or arrangement of something

²**format** vb **for·mat·ted; for·mat·ting** : to arrange (as material to be printed) in a particular format — **for·mat·ter** n

for·ma·tion \for-'mā-shən\ n **1** : a giving form to something : DEVELOPMENT **2** : something that is formed **3** : STRUCTURE, SHAPE **4** : an arrangement of persons or things in a prescribed manner or for a certain purpose

for·ma·tive \'for-mə-tiv\ adj **1** : giving or capable of giving form : CONSTRUCTIVE **2** : of, relating to, or characterized by important growth or formation ⟨a child's ∼ years⟩

for·mer \'for-mər\ adj **1** : PREVIOUS, EARLIER **2** : FOREGOING **3** : being first mentioned or in order of two or more things

for·mer·ly \-lē\ adv : in time past : PREVIOUSLY

form-fit·ting \'form-ˌfi-tiŋ\ adj : conforming to the outline of the body

for·mi·da·ble \'for-mə-də-bəl, for-'mi-\ adj **1** : exciting fear, dread, or awe **2** : imposing serious difficulties — **for·mi·da·bly** \-blē\ adv

form letter n **1** : a letter on a frequently recurring topic that can be sent to different people at different times **2** : a letter for mass circulation sent out in many printed copies

for·mu·la \'for-myə-lə\ n, pl **-las** or **-lae** \-ˌlē, -ˌlī\ **1** : a set form of words for ceremonial use **2** : RECIPE, PRESCRIPTION **3** : a milk mixture or substitute for a baby **4** : a group of symbols or figures joined to express in-

formation concisely **5** : a customary or set form or method

for·mu·late \-ˌlāt\ vb **-lat·ed; -lat·ing 1** : to express in a formula **2** : DESIGN, DEVISE ⟨∼ a policy⟩ **3** : to prepare according to a formula — **for·mu·la·tion** \ˌfor-myə-'lā-shən\ n

for·ni·ca·tion \ˌfor-nə-'kā-shən\ n : consensual sexual intercourse between two persons not married to each other — **for·ni·cate** \'for-nə-ˌkāt\ vb — **for·ni·ca·tor** \-ˌkā-tər\ n

for·sake \fər-'sāk, for-\ vb **for·sook** \-'suk\; **for·sak·en** \-'sā-kən\; **for·sak·ing** [ME, fr. OE forsacan, fr. sacan to dispute] : to renounce or turn away from entirely

for·sooth \fər-'süth\ adv : in truth : INDEED

for·swear \for-'swar\ vb **for·swore** \-'swor\; **for·sworn** \-'sworn\; **for·swear·ing 1** : to swear falsely : commit perjury **2** : to renounce earnestly or under oath **3** : to deny under oath

for·syth·ia \fər-'si-thē-ə\ n : any of a genus of shrubs related to the olive and having yellow bell-shaped flowers appearing before the leaves in early spring

fort \'fort\ n [ME forte, fr. MF fort, fr. fort strong, fr. L fortis] **1** : a fortified place **2** : a permanent army post

¹**forte** \'fort, 'for-ˌtā\ n [F fort, fr. fort, adj., strong] : one's strong point

²**for·te** \'for-ˌtā\ adv or adj [It, fr. forte strong] : LOUD — used as a direction in music

forth \'forth\ adv **1** : FORWARD, ONWARD ⟨from that day ∼⟩ **2** : out into view ⟨put ∼ leaves⟩

forth·com·ing \'forth-'kə-miŋ\ adj **1** : coming or available soon ⟨the ∼ holidays⟩ **2** : marked by openness and candor : OUTGOING

forth·right \'forth-ˌrīt\ adj : free from ambiguity or evasiveness : going straight to the point ⟨a ∼ answer⟩ — **forth·right·ly** adv — **forth·right·ness** n

forth·with \ˌforth-'with\ adv : IMMEDIATELY

for·ti·fy \'for-tə-ˌfī\ vb **-fied; -fy·ing 1** : to strengthen by military defenses **2** : to give physical strength or endurance to **3** : ENCOURAGE **4** : to strengthen or enrich with a material ⟨∼ bread with vitamins⟩ — **for·ti·fi·ca·tion** \ˌfor-tə-fə-'kā-shən\ n

for·tis·si·mo \for-'ti-sə-ˌmō\ adv or adj : very loud — used as a direction in music

for·ti·tude \'for-tə-ˌtüd, -ˌtyüd\ n : strength of mind that enables one to meet danger or bear pain or adversity with courage **syn** grit, backbone, pluck, guts

fort·night \'fort-ˌnīt\ n [ME fourtenight, alter. of fourtene night fourteen nights] : two weeks — **fort·night·ly** \-lē\ adj or adv

for·tress \'for-trəs\ n : FORT 1

for·tu·itous \for-'tü-ə-təs, -'tyü-\ adj **1** : happening by chance **2** : FORTUNATE

for·tu·ity \-ə-tē\ n, pl **-ities 1** : the quality or state of being fortuitous **2** : a chance event or occurrence

for·tu·nate \'for-chə-nət\ adj **1** : bringing some good thing not foreseen **2** : LUCKY

for·tu·nate·ly \-lē\ adv **1** : in a fortunate manner **2** : it is fortunate that

for·tune \'for-chən\ n **1** : prosperity attained partly through luck; also : CHANCE, LUCK **2** : what happens to a person : good or bad luck **3** : FATE, DESTINY **4** : RICHES, WEALTH

fortune hunter n : a person who seeks wealth esp. by marriage

for·tune–tell·er \-ˌte-lər\ n : a person who professes to tell future events — **for·tune–tell·ing** n or adj

for·ty \'for-tē\ n, pl **forties** : four times 10 — **for·ti·eth** \'for-tē-əth\ adj or n — **forty** adj or pron

for·ty–five \ˌfor-tē-'fīv\ n **1** : a .45 caliber handgun — usu. written .45 **2** : a phonograph record designed to be played at 45 revolutions per minute

for·ty–nin·er \-'nī-nər\ n : a person in the rush to California for gold in 1849

forty winks n sing or pl : a short sleep

fo·rum \ˈfōr-əm\ *n, pl* **forums** *also* **fo·ra** \-ə\ [L] **1** : the marketplace or central meeting place of an ancient Roman city **2** : a medium (as a publication) of open discussion **3** : COURT **4** : a public assembly, lecture, or program involving audience or panel discussion

¹for·ward \ˈfōr-wərd\ *adj* **1** : being near or at or belonging to the front **2** : EAGER, READY **3** : BRASH, BOLD **4** : notably advanced or developed : PRECOCIOUS **5** : moving, tending, or leading toward a position in front **6** : EXTREME, RADICAL **7** : of, relating to, or getting ready for the future — **for·ward·ness** *n*

²forward *adv* : to or toward what is ahead or in front

³forward *vb* **1** : to help onward : ADVANCE **2** : to send forward : TRANSMIT **3** : to send or ship onward

⁴forward *n* : a player who plays at the front of a team's offensive formation near the opponent's goal

for·ward·er \-wər-dər\ *n* : one that forwards; *esp* : an agent who forwards goods — **for·ward·ing** *n*

for·wards \ˈfōr-wərdz\ *adv* : FORWARD

¹fos·sil \ˈfä-səl\ *adj* [L *fossilis* obtained by digging, fr. *fodere* to dig] **1** : preserved from a past geologic age ⟨∼ plants⟩ **2** : of or relating to fossil fuels

²fossil *n* **1** : a trace or impression or the remains of a plant or animal of a past geologic age preserved in the earth's crust **2** : a person whose ideas are out=of-date — **fos·sil·ize** \ˈfä-sə-ˌliz\ *vb*

fossil fuel *n* : a fuel (as coal or oil) that is formed in the earth from plant or animal remains

¹fos·ter \ˈfòs-tər\ *adj* [ME, fr. OE *fōstor-*, fr. *fōstor* food, feeding] : affording, receiving, or sharing nourishment or parental care though not related by blood or legal ties ⟨∼ parent⟩ ⟨∼ child⟩

²foster *vb* **1** : to give parental care to : NURTURE **2** : to promote the growth or development of : ENCOURAGE

foster home *n* : a household in which an orphaned, neglected, or delinquent child is placed for care

fos·ter·ling \-tər-liŋ\ *n* : a foster child

Fou·cault pendulum \ˌfü-ˈkō-\ *n* : a device that consists of a heavy weight hung by a long wire and that swings in a constant direction which appears to change showing that the earth rotates

fought *past and past part of* FIGHT

¹foul \ˈfaül\ *adj* **1** : offensive to the senses : LOATHSOME; *also* : clogged with dirt **2** : ODIOUS, DETESTABLE **3** : OBSCENE, ABUSIVE **4** : DISAGREEABLE, STORMY ⟨∼ weather⟩ **5** : TREACHEROUS, DISHONORABLE, UNFAIR **6** : marking the bounds of a playing field ⟨∼ lines⟩; *also* : being outside the foul line ⟨∼ ball⟩ ⟨∼ territory⟩ **7** : containing marked-up corrections **8** : ENTANGLED — **foul·ly** *adv* — **foul·ness** *n*

²foul *n* **1** : an entanglement or collision in fishing or sailing **2** : an infraction of the rules in a game or sport; *also* : a baseball hit outside the foul line

³foul *vb* **1** : to make or become foul or filthy **2** : to entangle or become entangled **3** : OBSTRUCT, BLOCK **4** : to collide with **5** : to make or hit a foul

⁴foul *adv* : in a foul manner

fou·lard \fü-ˈlärd\ *n* : a lightweight silk of plain or twill weave usu. decorated with a printed pattern

foul·mouthed \ˈfaül-ˈmaüthd, -ˈmaütht\ *adj* : given to the use of obscene, profane, or abusive language

foul play *n* : VIOLENCE; *esp* : MURDER

foul-up \ˈfaül-ˌəp\ *n* **1** : a state of being fouled up **2** : a mechanical difficulty

foul up *vb* **1** : to spoil by mistakes or poor judgment **2** : to cause a foul-up : BUNGLE

¹found \ˈfaünd\ *past and past part of* FIND

²found *vb* **1** : to take the first steps in building **2** : to set or ground on something solid : BASE **3** : to establish (as an institution) often with provision for future maintenance — **found·er** *n*

foun·da·tion \faün-ˈdā-shən\ *n* **1** : the act of founding **2** : a basis upon which something stands or is supported ⟨suspicions without ∼⟩ **3** : funds given for the permanent support of an institution : ENDOWMENT;

also : an institution so endowed **4** : supporting structure : BASE **5** : CORSET — **foun·da·tion·al** \-shə-nəl\ *adj*

foun·der \ˈfaün-dər\ *vb* **1** : to make or become lame ⟨the horse ∼ed⟩ **2** : COLLAPSE **3** : SINK ⟨a ∼ing ship⟩ **4** : FAIL

found·ling \ˈfaünd-liŋ\ *n* : an infant found after its unknown parents have abandoned it

found·ry \ˈfaün-drē\ *n, pl* **foundries** : a building or works where metal is cast

fount \ˈfaünt\ *n* : SOURCE, FOUNTAIN

foun·tain \ˈfaünt-ᵊn\ *n* **1** : a spring of water **2** : SOURCE **3** : an artificial jet of water **4** : a container for liquid that can be drawn off as needed

foun·tain·head \-ˌhed\ *n* : SOURCE

fountain pen *n* : a pen with a reservoir that feeds the writing point with ink

four \ˈfōr\ *n* **1** : one more than three **2** : the 4th in a set or series **3** : something having four units — **four** *adj or pron*

four–flush \-ˌfləsh\ *vb* : to make a false claim : BLUFF — **four–flush·er** *n*

four·fold \-ˌfōld, -ˈfōld\ *adj* **1** : being four times as great or as many **2** : having four units or members — **four·fold** \-ˈfōld\ *adv*

4–H \ˈfōr-ˈāch\ *adj* [fr. the fourfold aim of improving the head, heart, hands, and health] : of or relating to a program set up by the U.S. Department of Agriculture to help young people become productive citizens — **4–H'·er** *n*

Four Hundred *or* **400** *n* : the exclusive social set of a community — used with *the*

four–in–hand \ˈfōr-ən-ˌhand\ *n* **1** : a team of four horses driven by one person; *also* : a vehicle drawn by such a team **2** : a necktie tied in a slipknot with long ends overlapping vertically in front

four–o'·clock \ˈfōr-ə-ˌkläk\ *n* : a garden plant with fragrant yellow, red, or white flowers without petals that open late in the afternoon

four–post·er \ˈfōr-ˈpō-stər\ *n* : a bed with tall corner posts orig. designed to support curtains or a canopy

four·score \ˈfōr-ˈskōr\ *adj* : being four times twenty : EIGHTY

four·some \ˈfōr-səm\ *n* **1** : a group of four persons or things **2** : a golf match between two pairs of partners

four·square \-ˈskwar\ *adj* **1** : SQUARE **2** : marked by boldness and conviction : FORTHRIGHT — **foursquare** *adv*

four·teen \fōr-ˈtēn\ *n* : one more than 13 — **fourteen** *adj or pron* — **four·teenth** \-ˈtēnth\ *adj or n*

fourth \ˈfōrth\ *n* **1** : one that is number four in a countable series **2** : one of four equal parts of something — **fourth** *adj or adv*

fourth estate *n, often cap F&E* : the public press

4WD *abbr* four-wheel drive

four–wheel \ˈfōr-ˌhwēl\ *or* **four·wheeled** \-ˌhwēld\ *adj* : acting on or by means of four wheels of a motor vehicle

¹fowl \ˈfaül\ *n, pl* **fowl** *or* **fowls** **1** : BIRD **2** : a cock or hen of the domestic chicken; *also* : the flesh of these used as food

²fowl *vb* : to hunt wildfowl

¹fox \ˈfäks\ *n, pl* **fox·es** *also* **fox** **1** : any of various flesh=eating mammals related to the wolves but smaller and with shorter legs and a more pointed muzzle; *also* : the fur of a fox **2** : a clever crafty person **3** *cap* : a member of an American Indian people formerly living in Wisconsin

²fox *vb* : TRICK, OUTWIT

fox·glove \ˈfäks-ˌgləv\ *n* : a common plant related to the snapdragons that is grown for its showy spikes of dotted white or purple tubular flowers and as a source of digitalis

fox·hole \-ˌhōl\ *n* : a pit dug for protection against enemy fire

fox·hound \-ˌhaünd\ *n* : any of various large swift powerful hounds used in hunting foxes

fox terrier *n* : a small lively terrier that occurs in varieties with smooth dense coats or with harsh wiry coats

fox–trot \\'fäks-ˌträt\ *n* **1** : a short broken slow trotting gait **2** : a ballroom dance in duple time

foxy \\'fäk-sē\ *adj* **fox·i·er; -est 1** : resembling or suggestive of a fox **2** : WILY **3** : physically attractive

foy·er \\'fȯi-ər, 'fȯi-ˌyā\ *n* [F, lit., fireplace, fr. (assumed) VL *focarium*, fr. L *focus* hearth] : LOBBY; *also* : an entrance hallway

fpm *abbr* feet per minute

FPO *abbr* fleet post office

fps *abbr* feet per second

fr *abbr* **1** father **2** franc **3** friar **4** from

¹**Fr** *abbr* **1** France; French **2** Friday

²**Fr** *symbol* francium

fra·cas \\'frā-kəs, 'fra-\ *n, pl* **fra·cas·es** \-kə-səz\ [F, din, row, fr. It *fracasso*, fr. *fracassare* to shatter] : BRAWL

frac·tal \\'frak-tᵊl\ *n* : an irregular curve or shape that repeats itself at any scale on which it is examined — **fractal** *adj*

frac·tion \\'frak-shən\ *n* **1** : a numerical representation (as ½, ¾, or 3.323) indicating the quotient of two numbers **2** : FRAGMENT **3** : PORTION — **frac·tion·al** \-shə-nəl\ *adj* — **frac·tion·al·ly** *adv*

frac·tious \\'frak-shəs\ *adj* **1** : tending to be troublesome : hard to handle or control **2** : QUARRELSOME, IRRITABLE

frac·ture \\'frak-chər\ *n* **1** : a breaking of something and esp. a bone **2** : CRACK, CLEFT — **fracture** *vb*

frag·ile \\'fra-jəl, -ˌjīl\ *adj* : easily broken : DELICATE — **fra·gil·i·ty** \frə-'ji-lə-tē\ *n*

¹**frag·ment** \\'frag-mənt\ *n* : a part broken off, detached, or incomplete

²**frag·ment** \-ˌment\ *vb* : to break into fragments — **frag·men·ta·tion** \ˌfrag-mən-'tā-shən, -mən-\ *n*

frag·men·tary \\'frag-mən-ˌter-ē\ *adj* : made up of fragments : INCOMPLETE

fra·grant \\'frā-grənt\ *adj* : sweet or agreeable in smell — **fra·grance** \-grəns\ *n* — **fra·grant·ly** *adv*

frail \\'frāl\ *adj* **1** : morally or physically weak **2** : FRAGILE, DELICATE

frail·ty \\'frāl-tē\ *n, pl* **frailties 1** : the quality or state of being frail **2** : a fault due to weakness

¹**frame** \\'frām\ *vb* **framed; fram·ing 1** : PLAN, CONTRIVE **2** : SHAPE, CONSTRUCT **3** : FORMULATE **4** : DRAW UP ⟨∼ a constitution⟩ **5** : to make appear guilty **6** : to fit or adjust for a purpose : ARRANGE **7** : to provide with or enclose in a frame — **fram·er** *n*

²**frame** *n* **1** : something made of parts fitted and joined together **2** : the physical makeup of the body **3** : an arrangement of structural parts that gives form or support **4** : a supporting or enclosing border or open case (as for a window or picture) **5** : one picture of a series (as on a length of film) **6** : FRAME-UP

³**frame** *adj* : having a wood frame

frame of mind *n* : mental attitude or outlook : MOOD

frame–up \\'frā-ˌməp\ *n* **1** : an act or series of actions in which someone is framed **2** : an action that is planned, contrived, or formulated

frame·work \\'frām-ˌwərk\ *n* : a basic supporting part or structure

franc \\'fraŋk\ *n* — see MONEY table

fran·chise \\'fran-ˌchīz\ *n* [ME, fr. MF, fr. *franchir* to free, fr. OF *franc* free] **1** : a special privilege granted to an individual or group ⟨a ∼ to operate a ferry⟩ **2** : a constitutional or statutory right or privilege; *esp* : the right to vote

fran·chi·see \ˌfran-ˌchī-'zē, -chə-\ *n* : one granted a franchise

fran·chis·er \\'fran-ˌchī-zər\ *n* **1** : FRANCHISEE **2** : FRANCHISOR

fran·chi·sor \ˌfran-ˌchī-'zȯr, -chə-\ *n* : one that grants a franchise

fran·ci·um \\'fran-sē-əm\ *n* : a radioactive metallic chemical element — see ELEMENT table

Fran·co–Amer·i·can \ˌfraŋ-kō-ə-'mer-ə-kən\ *n* : an American of French or esp. French-Canadian descent — **Franco–American** *adj*

fran·gi·ble \\'fran-jə-bəl\ *adj* : BREAKABLE — **fran·gi·bil·i·ty** \ˌfran-jə-'bi-lə-tē\ *n*

¹**frank** \\'fraŋk\ *adj* : marked by free, forthright, and sincere expression — **frank·ness** *n*

²**frank** *vb* : to mark (a piece of mail) with an official sign so that it can be mailed free; *also* : to mail free

³**frank** *n* **1** : the signature or mark on a piece of mail indicating free or paid postage **2** : the privilege of sending mail free

Fran·ken·stein \\'fraŋ-kən-ˌstīn\ *n* **1** : a monstrous creation that usu. ruins its originator **2** : a monster in the shape of a man

frank·furt·er \\'fraŋk-fər-tər, -ˌfər-\ *or* **frank·furt** \-fərt\ *n* : a seasoned sausage (as of beef or beef and pork)

frank·in·cense \\'fraŋ-kən-ˌsens\ *n* : a fragrant resin burned as incense

frank·ly \\'fraŋ-klē\ *adv* **1** : in a frank manner **2** : in truth : INDEED

fran·tic \\'fran-tik\ *adj* : marked by uncontrolled emotion or disordered anxious activity — **fran·ti·cal·ly** \-ti-k(ə-)lē\ *adv*

frap·pé \fra-'pā\ *or* **frappe** \same *or* 'frap\ [F *frappé*, fr. pp. of *frapper* to strike, chill] *n* **1** : an iced or frozen drink **2** : a thick milk shake — **frap·pé** \fra-'pā\ *adj*

fra·ter·nal \frə-'tərn-ᵊl\ *adj* **1** : of, relating to, or involving brothers **2** : of, relating to, or being a fraternity or society **3** : FRIENDLY, BROTHERLY — **fra·ter·nal·ly** *adv*

fra·ter·ni·ty \frə-'tər-nə-tē\ *n, pl* **-ties 1** : a social, honorary, or professional group; *esp* : a men's student organization **2** : BROTHERLINESS, BROTHERHOOD **3** : persons of the same class, profession, or tastes

frat·er·nize \\'fra-tər-ˌnīz\ *vb* **-nized; -niz·ing 1** : to mingle as friends **2** : to associate on close terms with members of a hostile group — **frat·er·ni·za·tion** \ˌfra-tər-nə-'zā-shən\ *n*

frat·ri·cide \\'fra-trə-ˌsīd\ *n* **1** : one that kills a sibling or countryman **2** : the act of a fratricide — **frat·ri·cid·al** \ˌfra-trə-'sīd-ᵊl\ *adj*

fraud \\'frȯd\ *n* **1** : DECEIT, TRICKERY **2** : TRICK **3** : IMPOSTOR, CHEAT

fraud·u·lent \\'frȯ-jə-lənt\ *adj* : characterized by, based on, or done by fraud : DECEITFUL — **fraud·u·lent·ly** *adv*

fraught \\'frȯt\ *adj* : full of or accompanied by something specified ⟨∼ with danger⟩

¹**fray** \\'frā\ *n* : FIGHT, STRUGGLE; *also* : QUARREL, DISPUTE

²**fray** *vb* **1** : to wear (as an edge of cloth) by rubbing **2** : to separate the threads at the edge of **3** : STRAIN, IRRITATE ⟨∼ed nerves⟩

fraz·zle \\'fra-zəl\ *vb* **fraz·zled; fraz·zling 1** : FRAY **2** : to put in a state of extreme physical or nervous fatigue — **frazzle** *n*

¹**freak** \\'frēk\ *n* **1** : WHIM, CAPRICE **2** : a strange, abnormal, or unusual person or thing **3** *slang* : a person who uses an illicit drug **4** : an ardent enthusiast — **freak·ish** *adj*

²**freak** *vb* **1** : to experience the effects (as hallucinations) of taking illicit drugs — often used with *out* **2** : to distress or become distressed — often used with *out* — **freak–out** \\'frē-ˌkaůt\ *n*

freck·le \\'fre-kəl\ *n* : a brownish spot on the skin — **freckle** *vb*

¹**free** \\'frē\ *adj* **fre·er; fre·est 1** : having liberty **2** : enjoying political or personal independence; *also* : not subject to or allowing slavery **3** : made or done voluntarily : SPONTANEOUS **4** : relieved from or lacking something unpleasant **5** : not subject to a duty, tax,

or charge **6** : not obstructed : CLEAR **7** : not being used or occupied **8** : not fastened **9** : LAVISH **10** : OPEN, FRANK **11** : given without charge **12** : not literal or exact **13** : not restricted by conventional forms — **free·ly** adv

²free vb **freed; free·ing 1** : to set free **2** : RELIEVE, RID **3** : DISENTANGLE, CLEAR syn release, liberate, discharge, emancipate, loose

³free adv **1** : FREELY **2** : without charge

free·base \ˈfrē-ˌbās\ n : purified cocaine smoked as crack or heated to produce vapors for inhalation — **freebase** vb

free·bie or **free·bee** \ˈfrē-bē\ n : something given without charge

free·board \ˈfrē-ˌbōrd\ n : the vertical distance between the waterline and the upper edge of the side of a boat

free·boo·ter \-ˌbü-tər\ n [D vrijbuiter, fr. vrijbuit plunder, fr. vrij free + buit booty] : PLUNDERER, PIRATE

free·born \-ˈbȯrn\ adj **1** : not born in vassalage or slavery **2** : of, relating to, or befitting one that is freeborn

freed·man \ˈfrēd-mən, -ˌman\ n : a man freed from slavery

free·dom \ˈfrē-dəm\ n **1** : the quality or state of being free : INDEPENDENCE **2** : EXEMPTION, RELEASE **3** : EASE, FACILITY **4** : FRANKNESS **5** : unrestricted use **6** : a political right; also : FRANCHISE, PRIVILEGE

free enterprise n : freedom of private business to operate with little regulation by the government

free-for-all \ˈfrē-fə-ˌrȯl\ n : a competition or fight open to all comers and usu. with no rules : BRAWL — **free-for-all** adj

free·hand \-ˌhand\ adj : done without mechanical aids or devices

free·hold \ˈfrē-ˌhōld\ n : ownership of an estate for life usu. with the right to bequeath it to one's heirs; also : an estate thus owned — **free·hold·er** n

free·lance \-ˌlans\ n : one who pursues a profession (as writing) without a long-term commitment to any one employer — **free·lance** adj or vb

free-living \ˈfrē-ˈli-viṅ\ adj **1** : unrestricted in pursuing personal pleasures **2** : being neither parasitic nor symbiotic ⟨∼ organisms⟩

free·load \ˈfrē-ˌlōd\ vb : to impose upon another's hospitality — **free·load·er** n

free love n : the practice of living openly with one of the opposite sex without marriage

free·man \ˈfrē-mən, -ˌman\ n **1** : one who has civil or political liberty **2** : one having the full rights of a citizen

Free·ma·son \-ˌmās-ᵊn\ n : a member of a secret fraternal society called Free and Accepted Masons — **Free·ma·son·ry** \-rē\ n

free·stand·ing \ˈfrē-ˈstan-diṅ\ adj : standing alone or on its own foundation free of support

free·stone \ˈfrē-ˌstōn\ n **1** : a stone that may be cut freely without splitting **2** : a fruit stone to which the flesh does not cling; also : a fruit (as a peach or cherry) having such a stone

free·think·er \-ˈthiṅ-kər\ n : one who forms opinions on the basis of reason independently of authority; esp : one who doubts or denies religious dogma — **free·think·ing** n or adj

free trade n : trade between nations without restrictions (as high taxes on imports)

free verse n : verse whose meter is irregular or whose rhythm is not metrical

free·way \ˈfrē-ˌwā\ n : an expressway without tolls

free·wheel \-ˈhwēl\ vb : to move, live, or play freely or irresponsibly

free·will \ˈfrē-ˌwil\ adj : VOLUNTARY

free will n : voluntary choice or decision

¹freeze \ˈfrēz\ vb **froze** \ˈfrōz\; **fro·zen** \ˈfrōz-ᵊn\; **freezing 1** : to harden or cause to harden into a solid (as ice) by loss of heat **2** : to withstand freezing **3** : to chill or become chilled with cold **4** : to damage by frost **5**

: to adhere solidly by or as if by freezing **6** : to become fixed, motionless, or incapable of speech **7** : to cause to grip tightly **8** : to become clogged with ice **9** : to fix at a certain stage or level

²freeze n **1** : an act or instance of freezing **2** : the state of being frozen **3** : a state of weather marked by low temperature

freeze-dry \ˈfrēz-ˈdrī\ vb : to dry in a frozen state under vacuum esp. for preservation — **freeze-dried** adj

freez·er \ˈfrē-zər\ n : a compartment, device, or room for freezing food or keeping it frozen

¹freight \ˈfrāt\ n **1** : payment for carrying goods **2** : CARGO **3** : BURDEN **4** : the carrying of goods by a common carrier **5** : a train that carries freight

²freight vb **1** : to load with goods for transportation **2** : BURDEN, CHARGE **3** : to ship or transport by freight

freight·er \ˈfrā-tər\ n : a ship or airplane used chiefly to carry freight

French \ˈfrench\ n **1** : the language of France **2** French pl : the people of France **3** : strong language — **French** adj — **French·man** \-mən\ n — **French·wom·an** \-ˌwu̇-mən\ n

French door n : a door with small panes of glass extending the full length

French dressing n **1** : a thin salad dressing usu. made of vinegar and oil with spices **2** : a creamy salad dressing flavored with tomatoes

french fry vb, often cap 1st F : to fry (as strips of potato) in deep fat until brown — **french fry** n, often cap 1st F

French horn n : a curved brass instrument with a funnel-shaped mouthpiece and a flaring bell

French toast n : bread dipped in a mixture of eggs and milk and fried at a low heat

fre·net·ic \fri-ˈne-tik\ adj : FRANTIC — **fre·net·i·cal·ly** \-ti-k(ə-)lē\ adv

fren·zy \ˈfren-zē\ n, pl **frenzies 1** : temporary madness or a violently agitated state **2** : intense often disordered activity — **fren·zied** \-zēd\ adj

freq abbr frequency; frequent; frequently

fre·quen·cy \ˈfrē-kwən-sē\ n, pl **-cies 1** : the fact or condition of occurring frequently **2** : rate of occurrence **3** : the number of cycles per second of an alternating current **4** : the number of waves (as of sound or electromagnetic energy) that pass a fixed point each second

frequency modulation n : variation of the frequency of a carrier wave according to another signal; also : FM

¹fre·quent \frē-ˈkwent, ˈfrē-kwənt\ vb : to associate with, be in, or resort to habitually — **fre·quent·er** n

²fre·quent \ˈfrē-kwənt\ adj **1** : happening often or at short intervals **2** : HABITUAL — **fre·quent·ly** adv

fres·co \ˈfres-kō\ n, pl **frescoes** [It, fr. fresco fresh] : the art of painting on fresh plaster; also : a painting done by this method

fresh \ˈfresh\ adj **1** : VIGOROUS, REFRESHED **2** : not containing salt **3** : not altered by processing (as freezing or canning) **4** : free from taint : PURE **5** : fairly strong : BRISK ⟨∼ breeze⟩ **6** : not stale, sour, or decayed ⟨∼ bread⟩ **7** : not faded **8** : not worn or rumpled **9** : experienced, made, or received newly or anew **10** : ADDITIONAL, ANOTHER ⟨made a ∼ start⟩ **11** : ORIGINAL, VIVID **12** : INEXPERIENCED **13** : newly come or arrived ⟨∼ from school⟩ **14** : IMPUDENT — **fresh·ly** adv — **fresh·ness** n

fresh·en \ˈfre-shən\ vb : to make, grow, or become fresh

fresh·et \ˈfre-shət\ n : an overflowing of a stream (as by heavy rains)

fresh·man \ˈfresh-mən\ n **1** : a 1st-year student **2** : BEGINNER, NEWCOMER

fresh·wa·ter \-ˌwȯ-tər, -ˌwä-\ n : water that is not salty — **freshwater** adj

¹fret \ˈfret\ vb **fret·ted; fret·ting** [ME, to devour, fret, fr. OE fretan to devour] **1** : WEAR, CORRODE; also

: FRAY 2 : RUB, CHAFE 3 : to make by wearing away 4 : to become irritated : WORRY, VEX 5 : GRATE; *also* : AGITATE

²fret *n* : an irritated or worried state ⟨in a ∼ about the interview⟩

³fret *n* : ornamental work esp. of straight lines in symmetrical patterns

⁴fret *n* : one of a series of ridges across the fingerboard of a stringed musical instrument — **fret·ted** *adj*

fret·ful \'fret-fəl\ *adj* : IRRITABLE — **fret·ful·ly** *adv* — **fret·ful·ness** *n*

fret·saw \-ˌsȯ\ *n* : a narrow-bladed saw used for cutting curved outlines

fret·work \-ˌwərk\ *n* 1 : decoration consisting of frets 2 : ornamental openwork or work in relief

Fri *abbr* Friday

fri·a·ble \'frī-ə-bəl\ *adj* : easily crumbled or pulverized ⟨∼ soil⟩

fri·ar \'frī-ər\ *n* [ME *frere, fryer,* fr. OF *frere,* lit., brother, fr. L *frater*] : a member of a religious order that orig. lived by alms

fri·ary \'frī-ər-ē\ *n, pl* **-ar·ies** : a monastery of friars

¹fric·as·see \'fri-kə-ˌsē, ˌfri-kə-'sē\ *n* : a dish made of meat (as chicken) cut into pieces, stewed in stock, and served in sauce

²fricassee *vb* **-seed; -see·ing** : to cook as a fricassee

fric·tion \'frik-shən\ *n* 1 : the rubbing of one body against another 2 : the force that resists motion between bodies in contact 3 : clash in opinions between persons or groups : DISAGREEMENT — **fric·tion·al** *adj*

friction tape *n* : a usu. cloth adhesive tape impregnated with insulating material and used esp. to protect and insulate electrical conductors

Fri·day \'frī-dē, -(ˌ)dā\ *n* : the sixth day of the week

fridge \'frij\ *n* : REFRIGERATOR

fried·cake \'frīd-ˌkāk\ *n* : DOUGHNUT, CRULLER

friend \'frend\ *n* 1 : one attached to another by respect or affection 2 : ACQUAINTANCE 3 : one who is not hostile 4 : one who supports or favors something ⟨a ∼ of art⟩ 5 *cap* : a member of the Society of Friends : QUAKER — **friend·less** *adj* — **friend·li·ness** \-lē-nəs\ *n* — **friend·ly** *adj* — **friend·ship** \-ˌship\ *n*

frieze \'frēz\ *n* : an ornamental often sculptured band extending around something (as a building or room)

frig·ate \'fri-gət\ *n* 1 : a square-rigged warship 2 : a warship smaller than a destroyer

fright \'frīt\ *n* 1 : sudden terror : ALARM 2 : something that is ugly or shocking

fright·en \'frīt-ᵊn\ *vb* 1 : to make afraid 2 : to drive away or out by frightening 3 : to become frightened — **fright·en·ing·ly** *adv*

fright·ful \'frīt-fəl\ *adj* 1 : TERRIFYING 2 : STARTLING 3 : EXTREME ⟨∼ thirst⟩ — **fright·ful·ly** *adv* — **fright·ful·ness** *n*

frig·id \'fri-jəd\ *adj* 1 : intensely cold 2 : lacking warmth or ardor : INDIFFERENT 3 : abnormally averse to or unable to achieve orgasm during sexual intercourse — used esp. of women — **fri·gid·i·ty** \fri-'ji-də-tē\ *n*

frigid zone *n* : the area or region between the arctic circle and the north pole or between the antarctic circle and the south pole

frill \'fril\ *n* 1 : a gathered, pleated, or ruffled edging 2 : something unessential — **frilly** *adj*

fringe \'frinj\ *n* 1 : an ornamental border consisting of short threads or strips hanging from an edge or band 2 : something that resembles a fringe : EDGE 3 : something that is additional or secondary to an activity, process, or subject — **fringe** *vb*

fringe benefit *n* 1 : an employment benefit paid for by an employer without affecting basic wage rates 2 : any additional benefit

frip·pery \'fri-pə-rē\ *n, pl* **-per·ies** [MF *friperie*] 1 : FINERY 2 : pretentious display

frisk \'frisk\ *vb* 1 : to leap, skip, or dance in a lively or playful way : GAMBOL 2 : to search (a person) esp.

for concealed weapons by running the hand rapidly over the clothing

frisky \'fris-kē\ *adj* **frisk·i·er; -est** : PLAYFUL — **frisk·i·ly** \-kə-lē\ *adv* — **frisk·i·ness** \-kē-nəs\ *n*

¹frit·ter \'fri-tər\ *n* : a small lump of fried batter often containing fruit or meat

²fritter *vb* 1 : to reduce or waste piecemeal 2 : to break into small fragments

fritz \'frits\ *n* : a state of disorder or disrepair ⟨the car is on the ∼⟩

friv·o·lous \'fri-və-ləs\ *adj* 1 : of little importance : TRIVIAL 2 : lacking in seriousness — **fri·vol·i·ty** \fri-'vä-lə-tē\ *n* — **friv·o·lous·ly** *adv*

frizz \'friz\ *vb* : to form into small tight curls — **frizz** *n* — **frizzy** *adj*

¹friz·zle \'fri-zəl\ *vb* **friz·zled; friz·zling** : FRIZZ, CURL — **frizzle** *n*

²frizzle *vb* **friz·zled; friz·zling** 1 : to fry until crisp and curled 2 : to cook with a sizzling noise

fro \'frō\ *adv* : BACK, AWAY — used in the phrase *to and fro*

frock \'fräk\ *n* 1 : an outer garment worn by monks and friars 2 : an outer garment worn esp. by men 3 : a woman's or girl's dress

frock coat *n* : a man's usu. double-breasted coat with knee-length skirts

frog \'frȯg, 'fräg\ *n* 1 : any of various largely aquatic smooth-skinned tailless leaping amphibians 2 : an ornamental braiding for fastening the front of a garment by a loop through which a button passes 3 : a condition in the throat causing hoarseness 4 : a small holder (as of metal, glass, or plastic) with perforations or spikes that is placed in a bowl or vase to keep cut flowers in position

frog·man \'frȯg-ˌman, 'fräg-, -mən\ *n* : a swimmer equipped to work underwater for long periods of time

¹frol·ic \'frä-lik\ *vb* **frol·icked; frol·ick·ing** 1 : to make merry 2 : to play about happily : ROMP

²frolic *n* 1 : a playful or mischievous action 2 : FUN, MERRIMENT — **frol·ic·some** \-səm\ *adj*

from \'frəm, 'främ\ *prep* 1 — used to show a starting point ⟨a letter ∼ home⟩ 2 — used to show removal or separation ⟨subtract 3 ∼ 9⟩ 3 — used to show a material, source, or cause ⟨suffering ∼ a cold⟩

frond \'fränd\ *n* : a usu. large divided leaf esp. of a fern or palm tree

¹front \'frənt\ *n* 1 : FOREHEAD; *also* : the whole face 2 : external and often feigned appearance 3 : a region of active fighting; *also* : a sphere of activity 4 : a political coalition 5 : the side of a building containing the main entrance 6 : the forward part or surface 7 : FRONTAGE 8 : a boundary between two dissimilar air masses 9 : a position directly before or ahead of something else 10 : a person, group, or thing used to mask the identity of the actual controlling agent

²front *vb* 1 : to have the principal side adjacent to something 2 : to serve as a front 3 : CONFRONT

front·age \'frən-tij\ *n* 1 : a piece of land lying adjacent (as to a street or the ocean) 2 : the length of a frontage 3 : the front side of a building

front·al \'frənt-ᵊl\ *adj* 1 : of, relating to, or next to the forehead 2 : of, relating to, or directed at the front ⟨a ∼ attack⟩ — **fron·tal·ly** *adv*

fron·tier \ˌfrən-'tir\ *n* 1 : a border between two countries 2 : a region that forms the margin of settled territory 3 : the outer limits of knowledge or achievement ⟨the ∼s of science⟩ — **fron·tiers·man** \-'tirz-mən\ *n*

fron·tis·piece \'frən-tə-ˌspēs\ *n* : an illustration preceding and usu. facing the title page of a book

front man *n* : a person serving as a front or figurehead

front·ward \'frənt-wərd\ *or* **front·wards** \-wərdz\ *adv or adj* : toward the front

¹frost \'frȯst\ *n* 1 : freezing temperature 2 : a covering of tiny ice crystals on a cold surface — **frosty** *adj*

²frost *vb* 1 : to cover with frost 2 : to put icing on (as a cake) **3** : to produce a slightly roughened surface on (as glass) **4** : to injure or kill by frost

¹frost·bite \'frost-₁bīt\ *vb* **-bit** \-₁bit\; **-bit·ten** \-₁bit-ᵊn\; **-bit·ing** : to injure by frost or frostbite

²frostbite *n* : the freezing or the local effect of a partial freezing of some part of the body

frost heave *n* : an upthrust of pavement caused by freezing of moist soil

frost·ing \'frȯ-stiŋ\ *n* **1** : ICING **2** : dull finish on metal or glass

froth \'frȯth\ *n, pl* **froths** \'frȯths, 'frȯthz\ **1** : bubbles formed in or on a liquid **2** : something light or worthless — **frothy** *adj*

frou·frou \'frü-₁frü\ *n* [F] **1** : a rustling esp. of a woman's skirts **2** : showy or frilly ornamentation

fro·ward \'frō-wərd\ *adj* : DISOBEDIENT, WILLFUL

frown \'fraùn\ *vb* **1** : to wrinkle the forehead (as in displeasure or thought) **2** : to look with disapproval **3** : to express with a frown — **frown** *n*

frow·sy *or* **frow·zy** \'fraù-zē\ *adj* **frow·si·er** *or* **frow·zi·er**; **-est** : having a slovenly or uncared-for appearance

froze *past of* FREEZE

fro·zen \'frōz-ᵊn\ *adj* **1** : treated, affected, or crusted over by freezing **2** : subject to long and severe cold **3** : incapable of being changed, moved, or undone : FIXED (~ wages) **4** : not available for present use (~ capital) **5** : expressing or characterized by cold unfriendliness

FRS *abbr* Federal Reserve System

frt *abbr* freight

fruc·ti·fy \'frək-tə-₁fī, 'frùk-\ *vb* **-fied; -fy·ing 1** : to bear fruit **2** : to make fruitful or productive

fru·gal \'frü-gəl\ *adj* : ECONOMICAL, THRIFTY — **fru·gal·i·ty** \frü-'ga-lə-tē\ *n* — **fru·gal·ly** *adv*

¹fruit \'früt\ *n* [ME, fr. OF, fr. L *fructus* fruit, use, fr. *frui* to enjoy, have the use of] **1** : a product of plant growth; *esp* : a usu. edible and sweet reproductive body (as a strawberry or apple) of a seed plant **2** : a product of fertilization in a plant; *esp* : the ripe ovary of a seed plant with its contents and appendages **3** : CONSEQUENCE, RESULT — **fruit·ed** \'frü-təd\ *adj*

²fruit *vb* : to bear or cause to bear fruit

fruit·cake \'früt-₁kāk\ *n* : a rich cake containing nuts, dried or candied fruits, and spices

fruit fly *n* : any of various small dipteran flies whose larvae feed on fruit or decaying vegetable matter

fruit·ful \'früt-fəl\ *adj* **1** : yielding or producing fruit **2** : very productive (a ~ soil); *also* : bringing results (a ~ idea) — **fruit·ful·ly** *adv* — **fruit·ful·ness** *n*

fru·ition \frü-'i-shən\ *n* **1** : ENJOYMENT **2** : the state of bearing fruit **3** : REALIZATION, ACCOMPLISHMENT

fruit·less \'früt-ləs\ *adj* **1** : not bearing fruit **2** : UNSUCCESSFUL (a ~ attempt) — **fruit·less·ly** *adv*

fruity \'frü-tē\ *adj* **fruit·i·er; -est** : resembling a fruit esp. in flavor

frumpy \'frəm-pē\ *adj* **frump·i·er; -est** : DOWDY, DRAB

frus·trate \'frəs-₁trāt\ *vb* **frus·trat·ed; frus·trat·ing 1** : to balk or defeat in an endeavor **2** : to induce feelings of insecurity, discouragement, or dissatisfaction in **3** : to bring to nothing — **frus·trat·ing·ly** *adv* — **frus·tra·tion** \₁frəs-'trā-shən\ *n*

frus·tum \'frəs-təm\ *n, pl* **frustums** *or* **frus·ta** \-tə\ : the part of a cone or pyramid formed by cutting off the top by a plane parallel to the base

frwy *abbr* freeway

¹fry \'frī\ *vb* **fried; fry·ing 1** : to cook in a pan or on a griddle over heat esp. with the use of fat **2** : to undergo frying

²fry *n, pl* **fries 1** : a social gathering where fried food is eaten **2** : a dish of something fried; *esp, pl* : FRENCH FRIES

³fry *n, pl* **fry 1** : recently hatched fishes; *also* : very small adult fishes **2** : members of a group or class (small ~)

fry·er \'frī-ər\ *n* **1** : something (as a young chicken)

suitable for frying **2** : a deep utensil for frying foods

FSLIC *abbr* Federal Savings and Loan Insurance Corporation

ft *abbr* **1** feet; foot **2** fort

FTC *abbr* Federal Trade Commission

fuch·sia \'fyü-shə\ *n* **1** : any of a genus of shrubs related to the evening primrose and grown for their showy nodding often red or purple flowers **2** : a vivid reddish purple color

fud·dle \'fəd-ᵊl\ *vb* **fud·dled; fud·dling** : MUDDLE, CONFUSE

fud·dy-dud·dy \'fə-dē-₁də-dē\ *n, pl* **-dies** : one that is old-fashioned, unimaginative, or conservative

¹fudge \'fəj\ *vb* **fudged; fudg·ing 1** : to exceed the proper bounds of something : CHEAT; *also* : FALSIFY **3** : to fail to come to grips with

²fudge *n* **1** : NONSENSE **2** : a soft candy of milk, sugar, butter, and flavoring

¹fu·el \'fyü-əl, 'fyül\ *n* : a material used to produce heat or power by burning; *also* : a material from which nuclear energy can be liberated

²fuel *vb* **-eled** *or* **-elled; -el·ing** *or* **-el·ling** : to provide with or take in fuel

fuel cell *n* : a device that continuously changes the chemical energy of a fuel directly into electrical energy

¹fu·gi·tive \'fyü-jə-tiv\ *n* **1** : one who flees or tries to escape **2** : something elusive or hard to find

²fugitive *adj* **1** : running away or trying to escape **2** : likely to vanish suddenly : not fixed or lasting

fugue \'fyüg\ *n* **1** : a musical composition in which different parts successively repeat the theme **2** : a disturbed state of consciousness characterized by acts that are not recalled upon recovery

füh·rer *or* **fueh·rer** \'fyur-ər, 'fir-\ *n* : LEADER; *esp* : TYRANT

¹-ful \fəl\ *adj suffix, sometimes* **-ful·ler;** *sometimes* **-ful·lest 1** : full of (pride*ful*) **2** : characterized by (peace*ful*) **3** : having the qualities of (master*ful*) **4** : tending, given, or liable to (help*ful*)

²-ful \₁ful\ *n suffix* : number or quantity that fills or would fill (room*ful*)

ful·crum \'fúl-krəm, 'fəl-\ *n, pl* **ful·crums** *or* **ful·cra** \-krə\ [LL, fr. L, bedpost] : the support on which a lever turns

F fulcrum

ful·fill *or* **ful·fil** \fúl-'fil\ *vb* **ful·filled; ful·fill·ing 1** : to put into effect **2** : to bring to an end **3** : SATISFY — **ful·fill·ment** *n*

¹full \'fúl\ *adj* **1** : FILLED **2** : complete esp. in detail, number, or duration **3** : having all the distinguishing characteristics (a ~ member) **4** : MAXIMUM **5** : rounded in outline (a ~ figure) **6** : possessing or containing an abundance (~ of wrinkles) **7** : having an abundance of material (a ~ skirt) **8** : satisfied esp. with food or drink **9** : having volume or depth of sound **10** : completely occupied with a thought or plan — **fullness** *also* **ful·ness** *n*

²full *adv* **1** : VERY, EXTREMELY **2** : ENTIRELY **3** : STRAIGHT, SQUARELY (hit him ~ in the face)

³full *n* **1** : the highest or fullest state or degree **2** : the utmost extent **3** : the requisite or complete amount

⁴full *vb* : to shrink and thicken (woolen cloth) by moistening, heating, and pressing — **full·er** *n*

full·back \'fül-ˌbak\ *n* : a football back stationed between the halfbacks

full–blood·ed \'fül-'blə-dəd\ *adj* : of unmixed ancestry : PUREBRED

full–blown \-'blōn\ *adj* **1** : being at the height of bloom **2** : fully mature or developed

full–bod·ied \-'bä-dēd\ *adj* : marked by richness and fullness

full dress *n* : the style of dress worn for ceremonial or formal occasions

full–fledged \'fül-'flejd\ *adj* **1** : fully developed **2** : having attained complete status ⟨a ~ lawyer⟩

full house *n* : a poker hand containing three of a kind and a pair

full moon *n* : the moon with its whole disk illuminated

full–scale \'fül-'skāl\ *adj* **1** : identical to an original in proportion and size ⟨~ drawing⟩ **2** : involving full use of available resources ⟨a ~ revolt⟩

full tilt *adv* : at high speed

full–time \'fül-'tīm\ *adj or adv* : involving or working a normal or standard schedule

ful·ly \'fü-lē\ *adv* **1** : in a full manner or degree : COMPLETELY **2** : at least

ful·mi·nate \'fül-mə-ˌnāt, 'fəl-\ *vb* **-nat·ed; -nat·ing** [ME, fr. ML *fulminare*, fr. L, to strike (of lightning), fr. *fulmen* lightning] : to utter or send out censure or invective : condemn severely — **ful·mi·na·tion** \ˌfül-mə-'nā-shən, ˌfəl-\ *n*

ful·some \'fül-səm\ *adj* **1** : COPIOUS, ABUNDANT ⟨~ detail⟩ **2** : generous in amount or extent ⟨a ~ victory⟩ **3** : excessively flattering ⟨~ praise⟩

fu·ma·role \'fyü-mə-ˌrōl\ *n* : a hole in a volcanic region from which hot gases issue

fum·ble \'fəm-bəl\ *vb* **fum·bled; fum·bling 1** : to grope about clumsily **2** : to fail to hold, catch, or handle properly — **fumble** *n*

¹fume \'fyüm\ *n* : a usu. irritating smoke, vapor, or gas

²fume *vb* **fumed; fum·ing 1** : to treat with fumes **2** : to give off fumes **3** : to express anger or annoyance

fu·mi·gant \'fyü-mi-gənt\ *n* : a substance used for fumigation

fu·mi·gate \'fyü-mə-ˌgāt\ *vb* **-gat·ed; -gat·ing** : to treat with fumes to disinfect or destroy pests — **fu·mi·ga·tion** \ˌfyü-mə-'gā-shən\ *n* — **fu·mi·ga·tor** \'fyü-mə-ˌgā-tər\ *n*

¹fun \'fən\ *n* [E dial. *fun* to hoax] **1** : something that provides amusement or enjoyment **2** : ENJOYMENT

²fun *adj* : full of fun ⟨a ~ person⟩ ⟨had a ~ time⟩

¹func·tion \'fəŋk-shən\ *n* **1** : OCCUPATION **2** : special purpose **3** : the particular purpose for which a person or thing is specially fitted or used or for which a thing exists ⟨the ~ of a hammer⟩; *also* : the natural or proper action of a bodily part in a living thing ⟨the ~ of the heart⟩ **4** : a formal ceremony or social affair **5** : a mathematical relationship that assigns to each element of a set one and only one element of the same or another set **6** : a variable (as a quality, trait, or measurement) that depends on and varies with another ⟨height is a ~ of age in children⟩ — **func·tion·al** \-shə-nəl\ *adj* — **func·tion·al·ly** *adv*

²function *vb* : to have or carry on a function

func·tion·ary \'fəŋk-shə-ˌner-ē\ *n, pl* **-ar·ies** : one who performs a certain function; *esp* : OFFICIAL

function word *n* : a word (as a preposition, auxiliary verb, or conjunction) expressing the grammatical relationship between other words

¹fund \'fənd\ *n* [L *fundus* bottom, country estate] **1** : a sum of money or resources intended for a special purpose **2** : STORE, SUPPLY **3** *pl* : available money **4** : an organization administering a special fund

²fund *vb* **1** : to provide funds for **2** : to convert (a short-term obligation) into a long-term interest-bearing debt

fun·da·men·tal \ˌfən-də-'ment-əl\ *adj* **1** : serving as an origin : PRIMARY **2** : BASIC, ESSENTIAL **3** : RADICAL ⟨~

change⟩ **4** : of central importance : PRINCIPAL — **fundamental** *n* — **fun·da·men·tal·ly** *adv*

fun·da·men·tal·ism \-ˌi-zəm\ *n*, **1** *often cap* : a Protestant religious movement emphasizing the literal infallibility of the Bible **2** : a movement or attitude stressing strict adherence to a set of basic principles — **fun·da·men·tal·ist** \-ist\ *adj or n*

¹fu·ner·al \'fyü-nə-rəl\ *adj* **1** : of, relating to, or constituting a funeral **2** : FUNEREAL 2

²funeral *n* : the ceremonies held for a dead person usu. before burial

fu·ner·ary \'fyü-nə-ˌrer-ē\ *adj* : of, used for, or associated with burial

fu·ne·re·al \fyü-'nir-ē-əl\ *adj* **1** : of or relating to a funeral **2** : suggesting a funeral

fun·gi·cide \'fən-jə-ˌsīd, 'fəŋ-jə-\ *n* : an agent that kills or checks the growth of fungi — **fun·gi·cid·al** \ˌfən-jə-'sīd-əl, ˌfən-gə-\ *adj*

fun·gus \'fəŋ-gəs\ *n, pl* **fun·gi** \'fən-ˌjī, 'fəŋ-ˌgī\ *also* **fun·gus·es** \'fəŋ-gə-səz\ : any of a major group of organisms (as molds, mildews, and mushrooms) that lack chlorophyll and are usu. classified as plants — **fun·gal** \-gəl\ *adj* — **fun·gous** \-gəs\ *adj*

fu·nic·u·lar \fyü-'ni-kyə-lər, fə-\ *n* : a cable railway ascending a mountain

funk \'fəŋk\ *n* : a depressed state of mind

funky \'fəŋ-kē\ *adj* **funk·i·er; -est 1** : having an earthy unsophisticated style and feeling; *esp* : having the style and feeling of older black American music **2** : odd or quaint in appearance or style

¹fun·nel \'fən-əl\ *n* **1** : a cone-shaped utensil with a tube used for catching and directing a downward flow (as of liquid) **2** : FLUE, SMOKESTACK

²funnel *vb* **-neled** *also* **-nelled; -nel·ing** *also* **-nel·ling 1** : to pass through or as if through a funnel **2** : to move to a central point or into a central channel

¹fun·ny \'fə-nē\ *adj* **fun·ni·er; -est 1** : AMUSING **2** : FACETIOUS **3** : PECULIAR 3 **4** : UNDERHANDED — **funny** *adv*

²funny *n, pl* **funnies** : a comic strip or a comic section (as of a newspaper)

funny bone *n* : a place at the back of the elbow where a blow easily compresses a nerve and causes a painful tingling sensation

¹fur \'fər\ *n* **1** : an article of clothing made of or with fur **2** : the hairy coat of a mammal esp. when fine, soft, and thick; *also* : this coat dressed for use — **fur** *adj* — **furred** \'fərd\ *adj*

²fur *abbr* furlong

fur·be·low \'fər-bə-ˌlō\ *n* **1** : FLOUNCE, RUFFLE **2** : showy trimming

fur·bish \'fər-bish\ *vb* **1** : to make lustrous : POLISH **2** : to give a new look to : RENOVATE

fu·ri·ous \'fyur-ē-əs\ *adj* **1** : FIERCE, ANGRY, VIOLENT **2** : BOISTEROUS **3** : INTENSE — **fu·ri·ous·ly** *adv*

furl \'fərl\ *vb* **1** : to wrap or roll (as a sail or a flag) close to or around something **2** : to curl in furls — **furl** *n*

fur·long \'fər-ˌlòŋ\ *n* [ME, fr. OE *furlang*, fr. *furh* furrow + *lang* long] : a unit of distance equal to 220 yards (about 201 meters)

fur·lough \'fər-lō\ *n* [D *verlof*, lit., permission] : a leave of absence from duty granted esp. to a soldier — **furlough** *vb*

fur·nace \'fər-nəs\ *n* : an enclosed structure in which heat is produced

fur·nish \'fər-nish\ *vb* **1** : to provide with what is needed : EQUIP **2** : SUPPLY, GIVE

fur·nish·ings \-ni-shiŋz\ *n pl* **1** : articles or accessories of dress **2** : FURNITURE

fur·ni·ture \'fər-ni-chər\ *n* : equipment that is necessary or desirable; *esp* : movable articles (as chairs or beds) for a room

fu·ror \'fyur-ˌòr\ *n* **1** : ANGER, RAGE **2** : a contagious excitement; *esp* : a fashionable craze **3** : UPROAR

fu·rore \-ˌòr\ *n* [It] : FUROR 2, 3

fur·ri·er \'fər-ē-ər\ *n* : one who prepares or deals in fur
fur·ring \'fər-iŋ\ *n* : wood or metal strips applied to a wall or ceiling to form a level surface or an air space
fur·row \'fər-ō\ *n* **1** : a trench in the earth made by a plow **2** : a narrow groove or wrinkle — **furrow** *vb*
fur·ry \'fər-ē\ *adj* **fur·ri·er; -est 1** : resembling or consisting of fur **2** : covered with fur
¹**fur·ther** \'fər-thər\ *adv* **1** : FARTHER 1 **2** : in addition : MOREOVER **3** : to a greater extent or degree
²**further** *vb* : to help forward — **fur·ther·ance** \'fər-thə-rəns\ *n*
³**further** *adj* **1** : FARTHER 1 **2** : ADDITIONAL
fur·ther·more \'fər-thər-ˌmōr\ *adv* : in addition to what precedes : BESIDES
fur·ther·most \-ˌmōst\ *adj* : most distant : FARTHEST
fur·thest \'fər-thəst\ *adv or adj* : FARTHEST
fur·tive \'fər-tiv\ *adj* [F or L; F *furtif*, fr. L *furtivus*, fr. *furtum* theft, fr. *fur* thief] : done by stealth : SLY — **fur·tive·ly** *adv* — **fur·tive·ness** *n*
fu·ry \'fyúr-ē\ *n, pl* **furies 1** : intense and often destructive rage **2** : extreme fierceness or violence **3** : FRENZY
furze \'fərz\ *n* : GORSE
¹**fuse** \'fyüz\ *vb* **fused; fus·ing 1** : MELT **2** : to unite by or as if by melting together — **fus·ible** *adj*
²**fuse** *n* : an electrical safety device having a metal wire or strip that melts and interrupts the circuit when the current becomes too strong
³**fuse** *n* **1** : a cord or cable that is set afire to ignite an explosive charge **2** *usu* **fuze** : a mechanical or electrical device for setting off the explosive charge of a projectile, bomb, or torpedo
⁴**fuse** *or* **fuze** \'fyüz\ *vb* **fused** *or* **fuzed; fus·ing** *or* **fuz·ing** : to equip with a fuse
fu·se·lage \'fyü-sə-ˌläzh, -zə-\ *n* : the central body portion of an aircraft
fu·sil·lade \'fyü-sə-ˌläd, -ˌläd\ *n* : a number of shots fired simultaneously or in rapid succession
fu·sion \'fyü-zhən\ *n* **1** : the act or process of melting or making plastic by heat **2** : union by or as if by melting **3** : the union of light atomic nuclei to form heavier nuclei with the release of huge quantities of energy
¹**fuss** \'fəs\ *n* **1** : needless bustle or excitement : COM-

MOTION **2** : effusive praise **3** : a state of agitation **4** : OBJECTION, PROTEST **5** : DISPUTE
²**fuss** *vb* : to make a fuss
fuss·bud·get \'fəs-ˌbə-jət\ *n* : one who fusses or is fussy about trifles
fussy \'fə-sē\ *adj* **fuss·i·er; -est 1** : IRRITABLE **2** : overly decorated **3** : requiring or giving close attention or concern to details or niceties — **fuss·i·ly** \-sə-lē\ *adv* — **fuss·i·ness** \-sē-nəs\ *n*
fus·tian \'fəs-chən\ *n* **1** : a strong usu. cotton fabric **2** : pretentious writing or speech — **fustian** *adj*
fus·ty \'fəs-tē\ *adj* **fus·ti·er; -est** [ME, fr. *fust* wine cask, fr. MF, club, cask, fr. L *fustis*] **1** : MUSTY **2** : OLD-FASHIONED
fut *abbr* future
fu·tile \'fyüt-əl, 'fyü-ˌtīl\ *adj* **1** : USELESS, VAIN **2** : FRIVOLOUS, TRIVIAL — **fu·til·i·ty** \fyü-'ti-lə-tē\ *n*
¹**fu·ture** \'fyü-chər\ *adj* **1** : of, relating to, or constituting a verb tense that expresses time yet to come **2** : coming after the present
²**future** *n* **1** : time that is to come **2** : what is going to happen **3** : an expectation of advancement or progressive development **4** : the future tense; *also* : a verb form in it
fu·tur·ism \'fyü-chə-ˌri-zəm\ *n* : a modern movement in art, music, and literature that tries esp. to express the energy and activity of mechanical processes — **fu·tur·ist** \'fyü-chə-rist\ *n*
fu·tur·is·tic \ˌfyü-chə-'ris-tik\ *adj* : of or relating to the future or to futurism; *also* : very modern
fu·tu·ri·ty \fyù-'túr-ə-tē, -'tyúr-\ *n, pl* **-ties 1** : FUTURE **2** : the quality or state of being future **3** *pl* : future events or prospects
fuze *var of* FUSE
fuzz \'fəz\ *n* : fine light particles or fibers (as of down or fluff)
fuzzy \'fə-zē\ *adj* **fuzz·i·er; -est 1** : having or resembling fuzz **2** : INDISTINCT — **fuzz·i·ness** \-zē-nəs\ *n*
fwd *abbr* forward
FWD *abbr* front-wheel drive
FY *abbr* fiscal year
-fy *vb suffix* : make : form into ⟨dandi*fy*⟩
FYI *abbr* for your information

G

¹**g** \'jē\ *n, pl* **g's** *or* **gs** \'jēz\ *often cap* **1** : the 7th letter of the English alphabet **2** : a unit of force equal to the force exerted by gravity on a body at rest and used to indicate the force to which a body is subjected when accelerated **3** *slang* : a sum of $1000
²**g** *abbr, often cap* **1** game **2** gauge **3** good **4** gram **5** gravity
ga *abbr* gauge
¹**Ga** *abbr* Georgia
²**Ga** *symbol* gallium
GA *abbr* **1** general assembly **2** general average **3** general of the army **4** Georgia
gab \'gab\ *vb* **gabbed; gab·bing** : to talk in a rapid or thoughtless manner : CHATTER — **gab** *n*
gab·ar·dine \'ga-bər-ˌdēn\ *n* **1** : GABERDINE 1 **2** : a firm durable twilled fabric having diagonal ribs and made of various fibers; *also* : a garment of gabardine
gab·ble \'ga-bəl\ *vb* **gab·bled; gab·bling** : JABBER, BABBLE
gab·by \'ga-bē\ *adj* **gab·bi·er; -est** : TALKATIVE, GARRULOUS
gab·er·dine \'ga-bər-ˌdēn\ *n* **1** : a long loose outer garment worn in medieval times and associated esp. with Jews **2** : GABARDINE 2
gab·fest \'gab-ˌfest\ *n* **1** : an informal gathering for general talk **2** : an extended conversation
ga·ble \'gā-bəl\ *n* : the vertical triangular end of a building formed by the sides of the roof sloping from

the ridge down to the eaves — **ga·bled** \-bəld\ *adj*
Gab·o·nese \ˌga-bə-'nēz, -'nēs\ *n* : a native or inhabitant of Gabon — **Gabonese** *adj*
gad \'gad\ *vb* **gad·ded; gad·ding** : to be constantly active without specific purpose — usu. used with *about* — **gad·der** *n*
gad·about \'ga-də-ˌbaút\ *n* : a person who flits about in social activity
gad·fly \'gad-ˌflī\ *n* **1** : a fly that bites or harasses livestock **2** : a person who annoys esp. by persistent criticism
gad·get \'ga-jət\ *n* : DEVICE, CONTRIVANCE — **gad·get·ry** \'ga-jə-trē\ *n*
gad·o·lin·i·um \ˌgad-əl-'i-nē-əm\ *n* : a magnetic metallic chemical element — see ELEMENT table
¹**Gael** \'gāl\ *n* : a Celtic inhabitant of Ireland or Scotland
²**Gael** *abbr* Gaelic
Gael·ic \'gā-lik\ *adj* : of or relating to the Gaels or their languages — **Gaelic** *n*
gaff \'gaf\ *n* **1** : a spear used in taking fish or turtles; *also* : a metal hook for holding or lifting heavy fish **2** : the spar supporting the top of a fore-and-aft sail **3** : rough treatment : ABUSE — **gaff** *vb*
gaffe \'gaf\ *n* : a social blunder
gaf·fer \'ga-fər\ *n* **1** : an old man **2** : a lighting electrician on a motion-picture or television set
¹**gag** \'gag\ *vb* **gagged; gag·ging 1** : to restrict use of the

mouth with a gag **2** : to prevent from speaking freely **3** : to retch or cause to retch **4** : OBSTRUCT, CHOKE **5** : BALK **6** : to make quips — **gag·ger** *n*

²**gag** *n* **1** : something thrust into the mouth esp. to prevent speech or outcry **2** : an official check or restraint on free speech **3** : a laugh-provoking remark or act **4** : PRANK, TRICK

¹**gage** \'gāj\ *n* **1** : a token of defiance; *esp* : a glove or cap cast on the ground as a pledge of combat **2** : SECURITY

²**gage** *var of* GAUGE

gag·gle \'ga-gəl\ *n* [ME *gagyll*, fr. *gagelen* to cackle] **1** : a flock of geese **2** : GROUP, CLUSTER

gai·ety \'gā-ə-tē\ *n, pl* **-eties 1** : festive activity : MERRYMAKING **2** : MERRIMENT **3** : FINERY **syn** mirth, festivity, glee, hilarity, jollity

gai·ly \'gā-lē\ *adv* : in a gay manner

¹**gain** \'gān\ *n* **1** : PROFIT **2** : ACQUISITION, ACCUMULATION **3** : INCREASE

²**gain** *vb* **1** : to get possession of : EARN **2** : WIN ⟨∼ a victory⟩ **3** : to increase in ⟨∼ momentum⟩ **4** : PERSUADE **5** : to arrive at **6** : ACHIEVE ⟨∼ strength⟩ **7** : to run fast ⟨the watch ∼s a minute a day⟩ **8** : PROFIT **9** : INCREASE **10** : to improve in health **syn** accomplish, attain, realize — **gain·er** *n*

gain·ful \'gān-fəl\ *adj* : PROFITABLE — **gain·ful·ly** *adv*

gain·say \gān-'sā\ *vb* **-said** \-'sed\, -'sād\; **-say·ing**; **-says** \-'sāz, -'sez\ [ME *gainsayen*, fr. *gain-* against + *-sayen* to say] **1** : DENY, DISPUTE **2** : to speak against **syn** contradict, contravene, impugn, negate — **gain·say·er** *n*

gait \'gāt\ *n* : manner of moving on foot; *also* : a particular pattern or style of such moving — **gait·ed** *adj*

gai·ter \'gā-tər\ *n* **1** : a leg covering reaching from the instep to ankle, mid-calf, or knee **2** : an overshoe with a fabric upper **3** : an ankle-high shoe with elastic gores in the sides

¹**gal** \'gal\ *n* : GIRL

²**gal** *abbr* gallon

Gal *abbr* Galatians

ga·la \'gā-lə, 'ga-, 'gä-\ *n* : a gay celebration : FESTIVITY — **gala** *adj*

ga·lac·tic \gə-'lak-tik\ *adj* : of or relating to a galaxy

Ga·la·tians \gə-'lā-shənz\ *n* — see BIBLE table

gal·axy \'ga-lək-sē\ *n, pl* **-ax·ies** [ME *galaxie, galaxias*, fr. LL *galaxias*, fr. Gk, fr. *galakt-, gala* milk] **1** *often cap* : MILKY WAY GALAXY — used with *the* **2** : a very large group of stars **3** : an assemblage of brilliant or famous persons or things

gale \'gāl\ *n* **1** : a strong wind **2** : an emotional outburst ⟨∼s of laughter⟩

ga·le·na \gə-'lē-nə\ *n* : a lustrous bluish gray mineral that consists of the sulfide of lead and is the chief ore of lead

¹**gall** \'gȯl\ *n* **1** : BILE **2** : something bitter to endure **3** : RANCOR **4** : IMPUDENCE **syn** effrontery, brass, cheek, chutzpah, audacity, presumption

²**gall** *n* : a skin sore caused by chafing

³**gall** *vb* **1** : CHAFE; *esp* : to become sore or worn by rubbing **2** : VEX, HARASS

⁴**gall** *n* : a swelling of plant tissue caused by parasites

¹**gal·lant** \gə-'lant, -'länt; 'ga-lənt\ *n* **1** : a young man of fashion **2** : a man who shows a marked fondness for the company of women and who is esp. attentive to them **3** : SUITOR

²**gal·lant** \'ga-lənt (*usual for 2, 3, 4*); gə-'lant, -'länt (*usual for 5*)\ *adj* **1** : showy in dress or bearing **2** : SMART **2** : SPLENDID, STATELY **3** : SPIRITED, BRAVE **4** : CHIVALROUS, NOBLE **5** : polite and attentive to women — **gal·lant·ly** *adv*

gal·lant·ry \'ga-lən-trē\ *n, pl* **-ries 1** *archaic* : gallant appearance **2** : an act of marked courtesy **3** : courteous attention to a woman **4** : conspicuous bravery **syn** heroism, valor, prowess

gall·blad·der \'gȯl-ˌbla-dər\ *n* : a membranous muscular sac attached to the liver and serving to store bile

gal·le·on \'ga-lē-ən\ *n* : a large square-rigged sailing ship formerly used esp. by the Spanish

galleon

gal·le·ria \ˌga-lə-'rē-ə\ *n* [It] : a roofed and usu. glass-enclosed promenade or court

gal·lery \'ga-lə-rē\ *n, pl* **-ler·ies 1** : an outdoor balcony; *also* : PORCH, VERANDA **2** : a long narrow passage, apartment, or hall **3** : a narrow passage (as one made underground by a miner or through wood by an insect) **4** : a room where works of art are exhibited; *also* : an organization dealing in works of art **5** : a balcony in a theater, auditorium, or church; *esp* : the highest one in a theater **6** : the spectators at a tennis or golf match **7** : a photographer's studio — **gal·ler·ied** \-rēd\ *adj*

gal·ley \'ga-lē\ *n, pl* **galleys 1** : a long low ship propelled esp. by oars and formerly used esp. in the Mediterranean Sea **2** : the kitchen esp. of a ship or airplane **3** : a proof of typeset matter esp. in a single column

Gal·lic \'ga-lik\ *adj* : of or relating to Gaul or France

gal·li·mau·fry \ˌga-lə-'mȯ-frē\ *n, pl* **-fries** [MF *galimafree* stew] : HODGEPODGE

gal·li·nule \'ga-lə-ˌnül, -ˌnyül\ *n* : any of several aquatic birds related to the rails

gal·li·um \'ga-lē-əm\ *n* : a rare bluish white metallic chemical element — see ELEMENT table

gal·li·vant \'ga-lə-ˌvant\ *vb* : to travel, roam, or move about for pleasure

gal·lon \'ga-lən\ *n* — see WEIGHT table

¹**gal·lop** \'ga-ləp\ *vb* **1** : to go or cause to go at a gallop **2** : to run fast — **gal·lop·er** *n*

²**gallop** *n* **1** : a bounding gait of a quadruped; *esp* : a fast 3-beat gait of a horse **2** : a ride or run at a gallop

gal·lows \'ga-lōz\ *n, pl* **gallows** *or* **gal·lows·es** : a frame usu. of two upright posts and a crosspiece from which criminals are hanged; *also* : the punishment of hanging

gall·stone \'gȯl-ˌstōn\ *n* : an abnormal concretion occurring in the gallbladder or bile passages

gal·lus·es \'ga-lə-səz\ *n pl* : SUSPENDERS

ga·lore \gə-'lȯr\ *adj* [Ir *go leor* enough] : ABUNDANT, PLENTIFUL

ga·losh \gə-'läsh\ *n* : a high overshoe

galv *abbr* galvanized

gal·va·nise *Brit var of* GALVANIZE

gal·va·nize \'gal-və-ˌnīz\ *vb* **-nized; -niz·ing 1** : to stimulate as if by an electric shock **2** : to coat (iron or steel) with zinc — **gal·va·ni·za·tion** \ˌgal-və-nə-'zā-shən\ *n* — **gal·va·niz·er** *n*

gal·va·nom·e·ter \ˌgal-və-'nä-mə-tər\ *n* : an instrument for detecting or measuring a small electric current

Gam·bi·an \'gam-bē-ən\ *n* : a native or inhabitant of Gambia — **Gambian** *adj*

gam·bit \'gam-bət\ *n* [It *gambetto*, lit., act of tripping someone, fr. *gamba* leg] **1** : a chess opening in which a player risks one or more minor pieces to gain an advantage in position **2** : a calculated move : STRATAGEM **syn** trick, artifice, gimmick, maneuver, play, ruse

¹**gam·ble** \'gam-bəl\ *vb* **gam·bled; gam·bling 1** : to play

a game for money or property **2** : BET, WAGER **3** : VENTURE, HAZARD — **gam·bler** n
²gamble n : a risky undertaking
gam·bol \'gam-bəl\ vb **-boled** or **-bolled; -bol·ing** or **-bol·ling** : to skip about in play : FRISK — **gambol** n
gam·brel roof \'gam-brəl-\ n : a roof with a lower steeper slope and an upper flatter one on each side
¹game \'gām\ n **1** : AMUSEMENT, DIVERSION **2** : SPORT, FUN **3** : SCHEME, PROJECT **4** : a line of work : PROFESSION **5** : CONTEST **6** : animals hunted for sport or food; also : the flesh of a game animal
²game vb **gamed; gam·ing** : to play for a stake : GAMBLE
³game adj : PLUCKY — **game·ly** adv — **game·ness** n
⁴game adj : LAME ⟨a ∼ leg⟩
game·cock \'gām-ˌkäk\ n : a rooster trained for fighting
game fish n : SPORT FISH
game·keep·er \'gām-ˌkē-pər\ n : a person in charge of the breeding and protection of game animals or birds in a private preserve
game·some \'gām-səm\ adj : MERRY **syn** playful, frolicsome, sportive, antic
game·ster \'gām-stər\ n : GAMBLER
gam·ete \'ga-ˌmēt\ n : a mature germ cell — **ga·met·ic** \gə-'me-tik\ adj
game theory n : the analysis of a situation involving conflicting interests (as in business) in terms of gains and losses among opposing players
gam·in \'ga-mən\ n [F] **1** : a boy who hangs around on the streets **2** : GAMINE 2
ga·mine \ga-'mēn\ n **1** : a girl who hangs around on the streets **2** : a small playfully mischievous girl
gam·ma \'ga-mə\ n : the 3d letter of the Greek alphabet — Γ or γ
gamma globulin n : a blood protein fraction rich in antibodies; also : a solution of this from human blood donors that is given to provide immunity against some infectious diseases (as measles)
gamma ray n : a photon emitted by a radioactive substance; also : a high-energy photon — used in pl.
gam·mer \'ga-mər\ n, archaic : an old woman
gam·mon \'ga-mən\ n, chiefly Brit : a cured ham or side of bacon
gam·ut \'ga-mət\ n : an entire range or series **syn** scale, spectrum
gamy or **gam·ey** \'gā-mē\ adj **gam·i·er; -est 1** : GAME, PLUCKY **2** : having the flavor of game esp. when near tainting **3** : SCANDALOUS; also : DISREPUTABLE — **gam·i·ness** \-mē-nəs\ n
¹gan·der \'gan-dər\ n : a male goose
²gander n : LOOK, GLANCE
¹gang \'gaŋ\ n **1** : a set of implements or devices arranged to operate together **2** : a group of persons working or associated together; esp : a group of criminals or young delinquents
²gang vb **1** : to attack in a gang — usu. used with up **2** : to form into or move or act as a gang
gang·land \'gaŋ-ˌland\ n : the world of organized crime
gan·gling \'gaŋ-gliŋ\ adj : loosely and awkwardly built : LANKY
gan·gli·on \'gaŋ-glē-ən\ n, pl **-glia** \-ə\ also **-gli·ons** : a mass of nerve cells outside the central nervous system; also : NUCLEUS 3 — **gan·gli·on·ic** \ˌgaŋ-glē-'ä-nik\ adj
gan·gly \'gaŋ-glē\ adj : GANGLING
gang·plank \'gaŋ-ˌplaŋk\ n : a movable bridge from a ship to the shore
gang·plow \-ˌplaü\ n : a plow that turns two or more furrows at one time
gan·grene \'gaŋ-ˌgrēn, gaŋ-'grēn\ n : the death of soft tissues in a local area of the body due to loss of the blood supply — **gangrene** vb — **gan·gre·nous** \'gaŋ-grə-nəs\ adj

gang·ster \'gaŋ-stər\ n : a member of a gang of criminals : RACKETEER
gang·way \'gaŋ-ˌwā\ n **1** : PASSAGEWAY; also : GANGPLANK **2** : clear passage through a crowd
gan·net \'ga-nət\ n, pl **gannets** also **gannet** : any of several large fish-eating usu. white and black marine birds that breed on offshore islands
gant·let \'gont-lət\ var of GAUNTLET
gan·try \'gan-trē\ n, pl **gantries** : a frame structure on side supports over or around something
GAO abbr General Accounting Office
gaol \'jāl\, **gaol·er** \'jā-lər\ chiefly Brit var of JAIL, JAILER
gap \'gap\ n **1** : BREACH, CLEFT **2** : a mountain pass **3** : a blank space; also : an incomplete or deficient area **4** : a wide difference in character or attitude **5** : a problem caused by a disparity ⟨credibility ∼⟩
gape \'gāp\ vb **gaped; gap·ing 1** : to open the mouth wide **2** : to open or part widely **3** : to stare with mouth open **4** : YAWN — **gape** n
¹gar \'gär\ n : any of several fishes that have a long body resembling that of a pike and long narrow jaws
²gar abbr garage
GAR abbr Grand Army of the Republic
¹ga·rage \gə-'räzh, -'räj\ n [F] : a shelter or repair shop for automobiles
²garage vb **ga·raged; ga·rag·ing** : to keep or put in a garage
garage sale n : a sale of used household or personal articles held on the seller's own premises
garb \'gärb\ n **1** : style of dress **2** : outward form : APPEARANCE — **garb** vb
gar·bage \'gär-bij\ n **1** : food waste **2** : unwanted or useless material — **gar·bage·man** \-ˌman\ n
gar·ble \'gär-bəl\ vb **gar·bled; gar·bling** [ME garbelen, fr. It garbellare to sift, fr. Ar gharbala] : to distort the meaning of ⟨∼ a story⟩
gar·çon \gär-'sōⁿ\ n, pl **garçons** \same or -'sōⁿz\ [F, boy, servant] : WAITER
¹gar·den \'gärd-ᵊn\ n **1** : a plot for growing fruits, flowers, or vegetables **2** : a public recreation area; esp : one for displaying plants or animals
²garden vb : to lay out or work in a garden — **gar·den·er** n
gar·de·nia \gär-'dē-nyə\ n [NL, genus name, fr. Alexander Garden †1791 Scot. naturalist] : the fragrant white or yellow flower of any of a genus of trees or shrubs related to the madder; also : one of these trees
garden–variety adj : COMMONPLACE, ORDINARY
gar·fish \'gär-ˌfish\ n : GAR
gar·gan·tuan \gär-'gan-chə-wən\ adj, often cap : of tremendous size or volume **syn** huge, colossal, gigantic, mammoth, monstrous, titanic
gar·gle \'gär-gəl\ vb **gar·gled; gar·gling** : to rinse the throat with liquid agitated by air forced through it from the lungs — **gargle** n
gar·goyle \'gär-ˌgȯil\ n **1** : a waterspout in the form of a grotesque human or animal figure projecting from the roof or eaves of a building **2** : a grotesquely carved figure
gar·ish \'gar-ish\ adj : FLASHY, GLARING, SHOWY, GAUDY
¹gar·land \'gär-lənd\ n : WREATH, CHAPLET
²garland vb : to form into or deck with a garland
gar·lic \'gär-lik\ n [ME garlek, fr. OE gārlēac, fr. gār spear + lēac leek] : an herb related to the lilies and grown for its pungent bulbs used in cooking; also : its bulb — **gar·licky** \-li-kē\ adj
gar·ment \'gär-mənt\ n : an article of clothing
gar·ner \'gär-nər\ vb **1** : to gather into storage **2** : to acquire by effort **3** : ACCUMULATE, COLLECT
gar·net \'gär-nət\ n [ME grenat, fr. MF, fr. grenat, adj., red like a pomegranate, fr. (pomme) grenate pomegranate] : a transparent deep red mineral sometimes used as a gem
gar·nish \'gär-nish\ vb **1** : DECORATE, EMBELLISH **2** : to

add decorative or savory touches to (food) **3** : GAR-NISHEE — **garnish** *n*

gar·nish·ee \ˌgär-nə-'shē\ *vb* **-eed; -ee·ing 1** : to serve with a garnishment **2** : to take (as a debtor's wages) by legal authority

gar·nish·ment \'gär-nish-mənt\ *n* **1** : GARNISH **2** : a legal warning concerning the attachment of property to satisfy a debt; *also* : the attachment of such property

gar·ni·ture \-ni-chər, -ˌchür\ *n* : EMBELLISHMENT, TRIMMING

gar·ret \'gar-ət\ *n* [ME *garette* watchtower, fr. MF *garite*] : the part of a house just under the roof : ATTIC

gar·ri·son \'gar-ə-sən\ *n* **1** : a military post; *esp* : a permanent military installation **2** : the troops stationed at a garrison — **garrison** *vb*

garrison state *n* : a state organized on a primarily military basis

gar·rote *or* **ga·rotte** \gə-'rät, -'rōt\ *n* [Sp *garrote*] **1** : a method of execution by strangulation; *also* : the apparatus used **2** : an implement (as a wire with handles) for strangulation — **garrote** *or* **garotte** *vb*

gar·ru·lous \'gar-ə-ləs\ *adj* : TALKATIVE, WORDY — **gar·ru·li·ty** \gə-'rü-lə-tē\ *n* — **gar·ru·lous·ly** *adv* — **gar·ru·lous·ness** *n*

gar·ter \'gär-tər\ *n* : a band or strap worn to hold up a stocking or sock

garter snake *n* : any of numerous harmless American snakes with longitudinal stripes on the back

¹gas \'gas\ *n, pl* **gas·es** *also* **gas·ses** [NL, alter. of L *chaos* space, chaos] **1** : a fluid (as hydrogen or air) that tends to expand indefinitely **2** : a gas or mixture of gases used as a fuel or anesthetic **3** : a substance that can be used to produce a poisonous, asphyxiating, or irritant atmosphere **4** : GASOLINE — **gas·eous** \'ga-sē-əs, -shəs\ *adj*

²gas *vb* **gassed; gas·sing 1** : to treat with gas; *also* : to poison with gas **2** : to fill with gasoline ⟨∼ up the car⟩

gash \'gash\ *n* : a deep long cut — **gash** *vb*

gas·ket \'gas-kət\ *n* : material (as rubber) or a part used to seal a joint

gas·light \'gas-ˌlīt\ *n* **1** : light made by burning illuminating gas **2** : a gas flame; *also* : a gas lighting fixture

gas mask *n* : a mask with a chemical air filter used to protect the face and lungs against poison gas

gas·o·line \'ga-sə-ˌlēn, ˌga-sə-'lēn\ *n* : a flammable liquid mixture made from petroleum and used esp. as a motor fuel

gasp \'gasp\ *vb* **1** : to catch the breath audibly (as with shock) **2** : to breathe laboriously : PANT **3** : to utter in a gasping manner — **gasp** *n*

gas·tric \'gas-trik\ *adj* : of or relating to the stomach

gastric juice *n* : the acid digestive secretion of the stomach

gas·tri·tis \gas-'trī-təs\ *n* : inflammation of the lining of the stomach

gas·tro·en·ter·ol·o·gy \ˌgas-trō-ˌen-tə-'rä-lə-jē\ *n* : a branch of medicine concerned with the structure, functions, and diseases of the stomach and intestines — **gas·tro·en·ter·ol·o·gist** \-jist\ *n*

gas·tro·in·tes·ti·nal \ˌgas-trō-in-'tes-tən-əl\ *adj* : of, relating to, affecting, or including both the stomach and intestine ⟨∼ tract⟩ ⟨∼ distress⟩

gas·tron·o·my \gas-'trä-nə-mē\ *n* [F *gastronomie,* fr. Gk *Gastronomia,* title of a 4th cent. B.C. poem, fr. *gastēr* belly + *-nomia* system of laws] : the art of good eating — **gas·tro·nom·ic** \ˌgas-trə-'nä-mik\ *also* **gas·tro·nom·i·cal** \-mi-kəl\ *adj*

gas·tro·pod \'gas-trə-ˌpäd\ *n* : any of a large class of mollusks (as snails and slugs) with a muscular foot and a spiral shell or none — **gastropod** *adj*

gas·works \'gas-ˌwərks\ *n sing or pl* : a plant for manufacturing gas

gate \'gāt\ *n* **1** : an opening for passage in a wall or fence **2** : a city or castle entrance often with defensive structures **3** : the frame or door that closes a gate **4** : a device (as a valve) for controlling the passage of

a fluid or signal **5** : the total admission receipts or the number of people at an event

-gate \ˌgāt\ *n comb form* [Water*gate,* scandal that resulted in the resignation of President Richard Nixon in 1974] : usu. political scandal often involving the concealment of wrongdoing

gate–crash·er \'gāt-ˌkra-shər\ *n* : a person who enters without paying admission or attends without invitation

gate·keep·er \-ˌkē-pər\ *n* : a person who tends or guards a gate

gate·post \-ˌpōst\ *n* : the post to which a gate is hung or the one against which it closes

gate·way \-ˌwā\ *n* **1** : an opening for a gate **2** : a means of entrance or exit

¹gath·er \'ga-thər\ *vb* **1** : to bring together : COLLECT **2** : PICK, HARVEST **3** : to pick up little by little **4** : to gain or win by gradual increase : ACCUMULATE ⟨∼ speed⟩ **5** : to summon up ⟨∼ courage to dive⟩ **6** : to draw about or close to something **7** : to pull (fabric) along a line of stitching into puckers **8** : GUESS, DEDUCE, INFER **9** : ASSEMBLE **10** : to swell out and fill with pus **11** : GROW, INCREASE syn congregate, forgather — **gath·er·er** *n*

²gather *n* : a puckering in cloth made by gathering

GATT \'gat\ *abbr* General Agreement on Tariffs and Trade

gauche \'gōsh\ *adj* [F, lit., left] **1** : lacking social experience or grace; *also* : not tactful **2** : crudely made or done syn clumsy, heavy-handed, inept, maladroit

gau·che·rie \ˌgō-shə-'rē\ *n* : a tactless or awkward action

gau·cho \'gaü-chō\ *n, pl* **gauchos** : a cowboy of the So. American pampas

gaud \'gȯd\ *n* : ORNAMENT, TRINKET

gaudy \'gȯ-dē\ *adj* **gaud·i·er; -est 1** : ostentatiously or tastelessly ornamented **2** : marked by showiness or extravagance syn garish, flashy, glaring, tawdry — **gaud·i·ly** \-də-lē\ *adv* — **gaud·i·ness** \-dē-nəs\ *n*

¹gauge *or* **gage** \'gāj\ *n* **1** : measurement according to some standard or system **2** : DIMENSIONS, SIZE **3** *usu* **gage** : an instrument for measuring, testing, or registering

²gauge *or* **gage** *vb* **gauged** *or* **gaged; gaug·ing** *or* **gag·ing 1** : MEASURE **2** : to determine the capacity or contents of **3** : ESTIMATE, JUDGE

gaunt \'gȯnt\ *adj* **1** : being thin and angular **2** : BARREN, DESOLATE syn bony, lank, lanky, lean, rawboned, skinny — **gaunt·ness** *n*

¹gaunt·let \'gȯnt-lət\ *n* **1** : a protective glove **2** : an open challenge (as to combat) **3** : a dress glove extending above the wrist

²gauntlet *n* **1** : ORDEAL **2** : a double file of men armed with weapons (as clubs) with which to strike at an individual who is made to run between them

gauze \'gȯz\ *n* : a very thin often transparent fabric used esp. for draperies and surgical dressings — **gauzy** *adj*

gave *past of* GIVE

gav·el \'ga-vəl\ *n* : the mallet of a presiding officer or auctioneer

ga·votte \gə-'vät\ *n* : a dance of French peasant origin marked by the raising rather than sliding of the feet

gawk \'gȯk\ *vb* : to gape or stare stupidly

gawky \'gȯ-kē\ *adj* **gawk·i·er; -est** : AWKWARD, CLUMSY — **gawk·i·ly** \-kə-lē\ *adv*

gay \'gā\ *adj* **1** : MERRY **2** : BRIGHT, LIVELY **3** : brilliant in color **4** : given to social pleasures; *also* : LICENTIOUS **5** : HOMOSEXUAL; *also* : of, relating to, or used by homosexuals

gay·ety, gay·ly *var of* GAIETY, GAILY

gaz *abbr* gazette

gaze \'gāz\ *vb* **gazed; gaz·ing** : to fix the eyes in a steady intent look syn gape, gawk, glare, goggle, peer, stare — **gaze** *n* — **gaz·er** *n*

ga·ze·bo \gə-ˈzē-bō\ *n, pl* **-bos 1** : BELVEDERE **2** : a free-standing roofed structure usu. open on the sides
ga·zelle \gə-ˈzel\ *n, pl* **gazelles** *also* **gazelle** : any of numerous small swift graceful antelopes

gazelle

ga·zette \gə-ˈzet\ *n* **1** : NEWSPAPER **2** : an official journal
gaz·et·teer \ˌga-zə-ˈtir\ *n* : a geographical dictionary
gaz·pa·cho \gəz-ˈpä-(ˌ)chō, gə-ˈspä-\ *n, pl* **-chos** [Sp] : a spicy soup usu. made from raw vegetables and served cold
GB *abbr* Great Britain
GCA *abbr* ground-controlled approach
gd *abbr* good
Gd *symbol* gadolinium
GDR *abbr* German Democratic Republic
Ge *symbol* germanium
gear \ˈgir\ *n* **1** : CLOTHING **2** : movable property : GOODS **3** : EQUIPMENT ⟨fishing ∼⟩ **4** : a mechanism that performs a specific function ⟨steering ∼⟩ **5** : a toothed wheel **6** : working adjustment of gears ⟨in ∼⟩ **7** : an adjustment of transmission gears (as of an automobile or bicycle) that determines speed and direction of travel — **gear** *vb*
gear·box \ˈgir-ˌbäks\ *n* : TRANSMISSION 3
gear·shift \-ˌshift\ *n* : a mechanism by which transmission gears are shifted
gear·wheel \-ˌhwēl\ *n* : GEAR 5
GED *abbr* **1** General Educational Development (tests) **2** general equivalency diploma
geek \ˈgēk\ *n* : a person often of an intellectual bent who is disapproved of — **geeky** *adj*
geese *pl of* GOOSE
gee·zer \ˈgē-zər\ *n* : an odd or eccentric person
Gei·ger counter \ˈgī-gər-\ *n* : an electronic instrument for detecting the presence of cosmic rays or radioactive substances
gei·sha \ˈgā-shə, ˈgē-\ *n, pl* **geisha** *or* **geishas** [Jp, fr. *gei* art + *-sha* person] : a Japanese girl or woman who is trained to provide entertaining company for men
gel \ˈjel\ *n* : a solid jellylike colloid (as gelatin dessert) — **gel** *vb*
gel·a·tin *also* **gel·a·tine** \ˈje-lət-ᵊn\ *n* : glutinous material and esp. protein obtained from animal tissues by boiling and used as a food, in dyeing, and in photography; *also* : an edible jelly formed with gelatin — **ge·lat·i·nous** \jə-ˈlat-ᵊn-əs\ *adj*
geld \ˈgeld\ *vb* : CASTRATE
geld·ing *n* : a castrated male horse
gel·id \ˈje-ləd\ *adj* : extremely cold
gem \ˈjem\ *n* **1** : JEWEL **2** : a usu. valuable stone cut and polished for ornament **3** : something valued for beauty or perfection
Gem·i·ni \ˈje-mə-(ˌ)nē, -ˌnī; ˈge-mə-nē\ *n* **1** : a zodiacal constellation between Taurus and Cancer usu. pictured as twins sitting together **2** : the 3d sign of the zodiac in astrology; *also* : one born under this sign

gem·ol·o·gy *or* **gem·mol·o·gy** \je-ˈmä-lə-jē, jə-\ *n* : the science of gems — **gem·olog·i·cal** \ˌje-mə-ˈlä-ji-kəl\ *adj* — **gem·ol·o·gist** *or* **gem·mol·o·gist** \-jist\ *n*
gem·stone \ˈjem-ˌstōn\ *n* : a mineral or petrified material that when cut and polished can be used in jewelry
gen *abbr* **1** general **2** genitive
Gen *abbr* Genesis
Gen AF *abbr* general of the air force
gen·darme \ˈzhän-ˌdärm, ˈjän-\ *n* [F, intended as sing. of *gensdarmes*, pl. of *gent d'armes*, lit., armed people] : a member of a body of soldiers esp. in France serving as an armed police force
gen·der \ˈjen-dər\ *n* **1** : any of two or more divisions within a grammatical class that determine agreement with and selection of other words or grammatical forms **2** : SEX 1
gene \ˈjēn\ *n* : a part of DNA or RNA that contains chemical information needed to make a particular protein (as an enzyme) controlling or influencing an inherited bodily trait or activity (as eye color) or that influences or controls the activity of another gene or genes — **gen·ic** \ˈjē-nik, ˈje-\ *adj*
ge·ne·al·o·gy \ˌjē-nē-ˈä-lə-jē, ˌje-, -ˈa-\ *n, pl* **-gies** : PEDIGREE, LINEAGE; *also* : the study of family pedigrees — **ge·ne·a·log·i·cal** \ˌjē-nē-ə-ˈlä-ji-kəl, ˌje-\ *adj* — **ge·ne·a·log·i·cal·ly** \-k(ə-)lē\ *adv* — **ge·ne·al·o·gist** \ˌjē-nē-ˈä-lə-jist, ˌje-; -ˈa-\ *n*
genera *pl of* GENUS
¹gen·er·al \ˈje-nə-rəl, ˈjen-rəl\ *adj* **1** : of or relating to the whole **2** : taken as a whole **3** : relating to or covering all instances **4** : not special or specialized **5** : common to many ⟨a ∼ custom⟩ **6** : not limited in meaning : not specific **7** : holding superior rank ⟨inspector ∼⟩ **syn** generic, universal
²general *n* **1** : something that involves or is applicable to the whole **2** : a commissioned officer ranking next below a general of the army or a general of the air force **3** : a commissioned officer of the highest rank in the marine corps — **in general** : for the most part
general assembly *n* **1** : a legislative assembly; *esp* : a U.S. state legislature **2** *cap G&A* : the supreme deliberative body of the United Nations
gen·er·a·lis·si·mo \ˌje-nə-rə-ˈli-sə-ˌmō\ *n, pl* **-mos** [It, fr. *generale* general] : the chief commander of an army
gen·er·al·i·ty \ˌje-nə-ˈra-lə-tē\ *n, pl* **-ties 1** : the quality or state of being general **2** : GENERALIZATION 2 **3** : a vague or inadequate statement **4** : the greatest part : BULK
gen·er·al·i·za·tion \ˌje-nə-rə-lə-ˈzā-shən, ˌjen-rə-\ *n* **1** : the act or process of generalizing **2** : a general statement, law, principle, or proposition
gen·er·al·ize \ˈje-nə-rə-ˌlīz, ˈjen-rə-\ *vb* **-ized; -iz·ing 1** : to make general **2** : to draw general conclusions from **3** : to reach a general conclusion esp. on the basis of particular instances **4** : to extend throughout the body
gen·er·al·ly \ˈjen-rə-lē, ˈjē-nə-\ *adv* **1** : in a general manner **2** : as a rule
general of the air force : a commissioned officer of the highest rank in the air force
general of the army : a commissioned officer of the highest rank in the army
general practitioner *n* : a physician or veterinarian whose practice is not limited to a specialty
gen·er·al·ship \ˈje-nə-rəl-ˌship, ˈjen-rəl-\ *n* **1** : office or tenure of office of a general **2** : LEADERSHIP **3** : military skill as a high commander
general store *n* : a retail store that carries a wide variety of goods but is not divided into departments
gen·er·ate \ˈje-nə-ˌrāt\ *vb* **-at·ed; -at·ing** : to bring into existence : PRODUCE **syn** create, originate, procreate, spawn
gen·er·a·tion \ˌje-nə-ˈrā-shən\ *n* **1** : a body of living beings constituting a single step in the line of descent

from an ancestor; *also* : the average period between generations **2** : PRODUCTION

gen·er·a·tive \'je-nə-rə-tiv, -ˌrā-tiv\ *adj* : having the power or function of generating, originating, producing, or reproducing ⟨∼ organs⟩

gen·er·a·tor \'je-nə-ˌrā-tər\ *n* : one that generates; *esp* : a machine by which mechanical energy is changed into electrical energy

ge·ner·ic \jə-'ner-ik\ *adj* **1** : not specific : GENERAL **2** : not protected by a trademark ⟨a ∼ drug⟩ **3** : of or relating to a biological genus — **generic** *n* — **ge·ner·i·cal·ly** \-i-k(ə-)lē\ *adv*

gen·er·ous \'je-nə-rəs\ *adj* **1** : free in giving or sharing **2** : HIGH-MINDED, NOBLE **3** : ABUNDANT, AMPLE, COPIOUS **syn** liberal, bountiful, munificent, openhanded — **gen·er·os·i·ty** \ˌje-nə-'rä-sə-tē\ *n* — **gen·er·ous·ly** \'je-nə-rəs-lē\ *adv* — **gen·er·ous·ness** *n*

gen·e·sis \'je-nə-səs\ *n, pl* **-e·ses** \-ˌsēz\ : the origin or coming into existence of something

Genesis *n* — see BIBLE table

gene–splic·ing \-ˌsplī-siŋ\ *n* : the technique by which recombinant DNA is produced and made to function in an organism

gene therapy *n* : the insertion of normal or altered genes into cells usu. to replace defective genes esp. in the treatment of genetic disorders

ge·net·ic \jə-'ne-tik\ *adj* : of or relating to the origin, development, or causes of something; *also* : of or relating to genetics — **ge·net·i·cal·ly** \-ti-k(ə-)lē\ *adv*

genetic code *n* : the chemical code that is the basis of genetic inheritance and consists of triplets of three linked chemical groups in DNA and RNA which specify particular amino acids used to make proteins or which start or stop the process of making proteins

genetic engineering *n* : the directed alteration of genetic material by intervention in genetic processes; *esp* : GENE-SPLICING — **genetically engineered** *adj*

ge·net·ics \jə-'ne-tiks\ *n* : a branch of biology dealing with heredity and variation — **ge·net·i·cist** \-tə-sist\ *n*

ge·nial \'jē-nyəl, 'jē-nē-əl\ *adj* **1** : favorable to growth or comfort ⟨∼ sunshine⟩ **2** : CHEERFUL, KINDLY ⟨a ∼ host⟩ **syn** affable, congenial, cordial, gracious, sociable — **ge·nial·i·ty** \ˌjē-nē-'a-lə-tē, jēn-'ya-\ *n* — **ge·nial·ly** *adv*

-gen·ic \'je-nik\ *adj comb form* **1** : producing : forming **2** : produced by : formed from **3** : suitable for production or reproduction by (such) a medium

ge·nie \'jē-nē\ *n, pl* **ge·nies** *also* **ge·nii** \-nē-ˌī\ [F *génie*, fr. Ar *jinnīy*] : a supernatural spirit that often takes human form usu. serving the person who calls on it

gen·i·tal \'je-nət-ᵊl\ *adj* **1** : concerned with reproduction ⟨∼ organs⟩ **2** : of, relating to, or characterized by the stage of psychosexual development in psychoanalytic theory in which oral and anal impulses are subordinated to adaptive interpersonal mechanisms — **gen·i·tal·ly** *adv*

gen·i·ta·lia \ˌje-nə-'tāl-yə\ *n pl* : reproductive organs; *esp* : the external genital organs — **gen·i·tal·ic** \-'ta-lik, -'tā-\ *adj*

gen·i·tals \'je-nət-ᵊlz\ *n pl* : GENITALIA

gen·i·tive \'je-nə-tiv\ *adj* : of, relating to, or constituting a grammatical case marking typically a relationship of possessor or source — **genitive** *n*

gen·i·to·uri·nary \ˌje-nə-tō-'yùr-ə-ˌner-ē\ *adj* : of or relating to the genital and urinary organs or functions

ge·nius \'jē-nyəs\ *n, pl* **ge·nius·es** *or* **ge·nii** \-nē-ˌī\ [L, tutelary spirit, natural inclinations, fr. *gignere* to beget] **1** *pl* **genii** : an attendant spirit of a person or place; *also* : a person who influences another for good or evil **2** : a strong leaning or inclination **3** : a peculiar or distinctive character or spirit (as of a nation or a language) **4** *pl usu* **genii** : SPIRIT, GENIE **5** *pl usu* **geniuses** : a single strongly marked capacity or aptitude **6** : extraordinary intellectual power; *also* : a person having such power **syn** gift, faculty, flair, knack, talent

genl *abbr* general

geno·cide \'je-nə-ˌsīd\ *n* : the deliberate and systematic destruction of a racial, political, or cultural group

-genous \jə-nəs\ *adj comb form* **1** : producing : yielding ⟨erogenous⟩ **2** : having (such) an origin ⟨endogenous⟩

genre \'zhän-rə, 'zhän-; 'zhänʳ; 'jän-rə\ *n* **1** : a distinctive type or category esp. of literary composition **2** : a style of painting in which everyday subjects are treated realistically

gens \'jenz, 'gens\ *n, pl* **gen·tes** \'jen-ˌtēz, 'gen-ˌtās\ : a Roman clan embracing the families of the same stock in the male line

gent *n* : GENTLEMAN

gen·teel \jen-'tēl\ *adj* **1** : ARISTOCRATIC **2** : ELEGANT, STYLISH **3** : POLITE, REFINED **4** : maintaining the appearance of superior social status **5** : marked by false delicacy, prudery, or affectation — **gen·teel·ly** *adv* — **gen·teel·ness** *n*

gen·tian \'jen-chən\ *n* : any of numerous herbs with opposite leaves and showy usu. blue flowers in the fall

gen·tile \'jen-ˌtīl\ *n* [LL *gentilis* heathen, pagan, fr. L *gent-, gens* clan, nation] **1** *often cap* : a person who is not Jewish; *esp* : a Christian as distinguished from a Jew **2** : HEATHEN, PAGAN — **gentile** *adj, often cap*

gen·til·i·ty \jen-'ti-lə-tē\ *n, pl* **-ties 1** : good birth and family **2** : the qualities characteristic of a well-bred person **3** : good manners **4** : superior social status shown in manners or mode of life

¹gen·tle \'jent-ᵊl\ *adj* **gen·tler** \'jent-lər, -ᵊl-ər\; **gen·tlest** \'jent-ləst, -ᵊl-əst\ **1** : belonging to a family of high social station **2** : of, relating to, or characteristic of a gentleman **3** : KIND, AMIABLE **4** : TRACTABLE, DOCILE **5** : not harsh, stern, or violent **6** : SOFT, DELICATE **7** : MODERATE — **gen·tle·ness** *n* — **gen·tly** *adv*

²gentle *vb* **gen·tled; gen·tling 1** : to make or become mild, docile, soft, or moderate **2** : MOLLIFY, PLACATE

gen·tle·folk \'jent-ᵊl-ˌfōk\ *also* **gen·tle·folks** \-ˌfōks\ *n* : persons of good family and breeding

gen·tle·man \-mən\ *n* **1** : a man of good family **2** : a well-bred man **3** : MAN — used in pl. as a form of address — **gen·tle·man·ly** *adj*

gen·tle·wom·an \-ˌwù-mən\ *n* **1** : a woman of good family **2** : a woman attending a lady of rank **3** : a woman with very good manners : LADY

gen·tri·fi·ca·tion \ˌjen-trə-fə-'kā-shən\ *n* : the process of renewal accompanying the influx of middle-class people into deteriorating areas that often displaces earlier usu. poorer residents — **gen·tri·fy** \'jen-trə-fī\ *vb*

gen·try \'jen-trē\ *n, pl* **gentries 1** : people of good birth, breeding, and education : ARISTOCRACY **2** : the class of English people between the nobility and the yeomanry **3** : persons of a designated class

gen·u·flect \'jen-yù-ˌflekt\ *vb* : to bend the knee esp. in worship — **gen·u·flec·tion** \ˌjen-yù-'flek-shən\ *n*

gen·u·ine \'jen-yə-wən\ *adj* **1** : AUTHENTIC, REAL **2** : SINCERE, HONEST **syn** bona fide, true, veritable — **gen·u·ine·ly** *adv* — **gen·u·ine·ness** *n*

ge·nus \'jē-nəs\ *n, pl* **gen·era** \'je-nə-rə\ [L, birth, race, kind] : a category of biological classification that ranks between the family and the species and contains related species

geo·cen·tric \ˌjē-ō-'sen-trik\ *adj* **1** : relating to or measured from the earth's center **2** : having or relating to the earth as a center

geo·chem·is·try \-'ke-mə-strē\ *n* : a branch of geology that deals with the chemical composition of and chemical changes in the earth — **geo·chem·i·cal** \-mi-kəl\ *adj* — **geo·chem·ist** \-mist\ *n*

ge·ode \'jē-ˌōd\ *n* : a nodule of stone having a cavity lined with mineral matter

¹geo·de·sic \ˌjē-ə-'de-sik\ *adj* : made of light straight structural elements ⟨a ∼ dome⟩

²geodesic *n* : the shortest line between two points on a surface

geo·det·ic \jē-ə-'de-tik\ *adj* : of, relating to, or being precise measurement of the earth and its features ⟨a ~ survey⟩

geog *abbr* geographic; geographical; geography

ge·og·ra·phy \jē-'ä-grə-fē\ *n, pl* **-phies 1** : a science that deals with the natural features of the earth and the climate, products, and inhabitants **2** : the natural features of a region — **ge·og·ra·pher** \-fər\ *n* — **geo·graph·ic** \jē-ə-'gra-fik\ *or* **geo·graph·i·cal** \-fi-kəl\ *adj* — **geo·graph·i·cal·ly** \-fi-k(ə-)lē\ *adv*

geol *abbr* geologic; geological; geology

ge·ol·o·gy \jē-'ä-lə-jē\ *n, pl* **-gies 1** : a science that deals with the history of the earth and its life esp. as recorded in rocks; *also* : a study of the features of a celestial body (as the moon) **2** : the geologic features of an area — **ge·o·log·ic** \jē-ə-'lä-jik\ *or* **ge·o·log·i·cal** \-ji-kəl\ *adj* — **geo·log·i·cal·ly** \-ji-k(ə-)lē\ *adv* — **ge·ol·o·gist** \jē-'ä-lə-jist\ *n*

geom *abbr* geometric; geometrical; geometry

geo·mag·net·ic \jē-ō-mag-'ne-tik\ *adj* : of or relating to the magnetism of the earth — **geo·mag·ne·tism** \-'mag-nə-₁ti-zəm\ *n*

geometric mean *n* : the *n*th root of the product of *n* numbers; *esp* : a number that is the second term of three consecutive terms of a geometric progression ⟨the *geometric mean* of 9 and 4 is 6⟩

geometric progression *n* : a progression (as 1, ½, ¼) in which the ratio of a term to its predecessor is always the same

ge·om·e·try \jē-'ä-mə-trē\ *n, pl* **-tries** [ultim. fr. Gk *geōmetria*, fr. *geōmetrein* to measure the earth, fr. *gē* earth + *metron* measure] : a branch of mathematics dealing with the relations, properties, and measurements of solids, surfaces, lines, points, and angles — **ge·om·e·ter** \-tər\ *n* — **ge·o·met·ric** \jē-ə-'me-trik\ *or* **ge·o·met·ri·cal** \-tri-kəl\ *adj*

geo·phys·ics \jē-ō-'fi-ziks\ *n* : the physics of the earth — **geo·phys·i·cal** \-zi-kəl\ *adj* — **geo·phys·i·cist** \-zə-sist\ *n*

geo·pol·i·tics \-'pä-lə-₁tiks\ *n* : a combination of political and geographic factors relating to a state

Geor·gian \'jȯr-jən\ *n* : a native or inhabitant of the Republic of Georgia — **Georgian** *adj*

geo·ther·mal \jē-ō-'thər-məl\ *adj* : of, relating to, or using the heat of the earth's interior

ger *abbr* gerund

Ger *abbr* German; Germany

ge·ra·ni·um \jə-'rä-nē-əm\ *n* [L, fr. Gk *geranion*, fr. *geranos* crane] **1** : any of a genus of herbs with usu. deeply cut leaves and pink, purple, or white flowers followed by long slender dry fruits **2** : any of a genus of herbs of the same family as the geraniums that have clusters of scarlet, pink, or white flowers with the sepals joined at the base into a hollow tube closed at one end

ger·bil *also* **ger·bile** \'jər-bəl\ *n* : any of numerous Old World burrowing desert rodents with long hind legs

ge·ri·at·ric \₁jer-ē-'a-trik\ *adj* **1** : of or relating to geriatrics or the process of aging **2** : of, relating to, or appropriate for elderly people **3** : OLD

ge·ri·at·rics \-triks\ *n* : a branch of medicine dealing with the problems and diseases of old age and aging

germ \'jərm\ *n* **1** : a bit of living matter capable of growth and development (as into an organism) **2** : SOURCE, RUDIMENTS **3** : MICROORGANISM; *esp* : one causing disease

Ger·man \'jər-mən\ *n* **1** : a native or inhabitant of Germany **2** : the language of Germany, Austria, and parts of Switzerland — **German** *adj* — **Ger·man·ic** \jər-'ma-nik\ *adj*

ger·mane \jər-'mān\ *adj* [ME *germain*, lit., having the same parents, fr. MF, fr. L *germanus*, fr. *germen* sprout, bud] : RELEVANT, APPROPRIATE **syn** applicable, material, pertinent

ger·ma·ni·um \jər-'mā-nē-əm\ *n* : a grayish white hard chemical element used as a semiconductor — see ELEMENT table

German measles *n sing or pl* : an acute contagious virus disease milder than typical measles but damaging to the fetus when occurring early in pregnancy

German shepherd *n* : any of a breed of intelligent responsive working dogs of German origin often used in police work and as guide dogs for the blind

germ cell *n* : an egg or sperm or one of their antecedent cells

ger·mi·cide \'jər-mə-₁sīd\ *n* : an agent that destroys germs — **ger·mi·cid·al** \₁jər-mə-'sīd-əl\ *adj*

ger·mi·nal \'jər-mə-nəl\ *adj* : of or relating to a germ or germ cell; *also* : EMBRYONIC

ger·mi·nate \'jər-mə-₁nāt\ *vb* **-nat·ed; -nat·ing 1** : to cause to develop : begin to develop : SPROUT **2** : to come into being : EVOLVE — **ger·mi·na·tion** \₁jər-mə-'nā-shən\ *n*

ger·on·tol·o·gy \₁jer-ən-'tä-lə-jē\ *n* : a scientific study of aging and the problems of the aged — **ge·ron·to·log·i·cal** \jə-₁ränt-əl-'ä-ji-kəl\ *adj* — **ger·on·tol·o·gist** \₁jer-ən-'tä-lə-jist\ *n*

ger·ry·man·der \'jer-ē-₁man-dər\ *vb* : to divide into election districts so as to give one political party an advantage — **gerrymander** *n*

ger·und \'jer-ənd\ *n* : a word having the characteristics of both verb and noun

ge·sta·po \gə-'stä-pō\ *n, pl* **-pos** [G, fr. *Geheime Staatspolizei*, lit., secret state police] : a usu. terrorist secret-police organization operating against persons suspected of disloyalty

ges·ta·tion \je-'stä-shən\ *n* : PREGNANCY, INCUBATION — **ges·tate** \'jes-₁tāt\ *vb*

ges·tic·u·late \je-'sti-kyə-₁lāt\ *vb* **-lat·ed; -lat·ing** : to make gestures esp. when speaking — **ges·tic·u·la·tion** \-₁sti-kyə-'lā-shən\ *n*

ges·ture \'jes-chər\ *n* **1** : a movement usu. of the body or limbs that expresses or emphasizes an idea, sentiment, or attitude **2** : something said or done by way of formality or courtesy, as a symbol or token, or for its effect on the attitudes of others — **ges·tur·al** \-chə-rəl\ *adj* — **gesture** *vb*

ge·sund·heit \gə-'zùnt-₁hīt\ *interj* [G, lit., health] — used to wish good health esp. to one who has just sneezed

¹get \'get\ *vb* **got** \'gät\; **got** *or* **got·ten** \'gät-ᵊn\; **get·ting 1** : to gain possession of (as by receiving, acquiring, earning, buying, or winning) : PROCURE, OBTAIN, FETCH **2** : to succeed in coming or going ⟨*got* away to the lake⟩ **3** : to cause to come or go ⟨*got* the car to the station⟩ **4** : BEGET **5** : to cause to be in a certain condition or position ⟨don't ~ wet⟩ **6** : BECOME ⟨~ sick⟩ **7** : PREPARE **8** : SEIZE **9** : to move emotionally; *also* : IRRITATE **10** : BAFFLE, PUZZLE **11** : KILL **12** : HIT **13** : to be subjected to ⟨~ the measles⟩ **14** : to receive as punishment **15** : to find out by calculation **16** : HEAR; *also* : UNDERSTAND **17** : PERSUADE, INDUCE **18** : HAVE ⟨he's *got* no money⟩ **19** : to have as an obligation or necessity ⟨you have *got* to come⟩ **20** : to establish communication with **21** : to be able ⟨finally *got* to go to med school⟩ **22** : to come to be ⟨*got* talking about old times⟩ **23** : to leave at once

²get \'get\ *n* : OFFSPRING, PROGENY

get along *vb* **1** : GET BY **2** : to be on friendly terms

get·away \'ge-tə-₁wā\ *n* **1** : ESCAPE **2** : START

get by *vb* : to meet one's needs

get–to·geth·er \'get-tə-₁ge-ᵺər\ *n* : an informal social gathering

get·up \'get-₁əp\ *n* **1** : OUTFIT, COSTUME **2** : general composition or structure

gew·gaw \'gü-₁gó, 'gyü-\ *n* : a showy trifle : BAUBLE, TRINKET

gey·ser \'gī-zər\ *n* [Icelandic *Geysir*, hot spring in Iceland] : a spring that intermittently shoots up hot water and steam

Gha·na·ian \gä-'nā-ən\ n : a native or inhabitant of Ghana — **Ghanaian** adj

ghast·ly \'gast-lē\ adj **ghast·li·er; -est 1** : HORRIBLE, SHOCKING **2** : resembling a ghost : DEATHLIKE, PALE syn gruesome, grim, lurid, grisly, macabre

ghat \'got\ n [Hindi] : a broad flight of steps on an Indian riverbank that provides access to the water

gher·kin \'gər-kən\ n **1** : a small prickly fruit of a vine related to the cucumber used to make pickles **2** : an immature cucumber

ghet·to \'ge-tō\ n, pl **ghettos** or **ghettoes** : a quarter of a city in which members of a minority group live because of social, legal, or economic pressure

¹**ghost** \'gōst\ n **1** : the seat of life : SOUL **2** : a disembodied soul; esp : the soul of a dead person believed to be an inhabitant of the unseen world or to appear in bodily form to living people **3** : SPIRIT, DEMON **4** : a faint trace (a ∼ of a smile) **5** : a false image in a photographic negative or on a television screen — **ghost·ly** adv

²**ghost** vb : GHOSTWRITE

ghost·write \-ˌrīt\ vb **-wrote** \-ˌrōt\; **-writ·ten** \-ˌrit-ᵊn\ : to write for and in the name of another — **ghost·writ·er** n

ghoul \'gül\ n [Ar ghūl] : a legendary evil being that robs graves and feeds on corpses — **ghoul·ish** adj

GHQ abbr general headquarters

gi abbr gill

¹**GI** \ˌjē-'ī\ adj [galvanized iron; fr. abbr. used in listing such articles as garbage cans, but taken as abbr. for government issue] **1** : provided by an official U.S. military supply department ⟨∼ shoes⟩ **2** : of, relating to, or characteristic of U.S. military personnel **3** : conforming to military regulations or customs ⟨a ∼ haircut⟩

²**GI** n, pl **GI's** or **GIs** \-'īz\ : a member or former member of the U.S. armed forces; esp : an enlisted man

³**GI** abbr **1** galvanized iron **2** gastrointestinal **3** general issue **4** government issue

gi·ant \'jī-ənt\ n **1** : a legendary humanlike being of great size and strength **2** : a living being or thing of extraordinary size or powers — **giant** adj

gi·ant·ess \'jī-ən-təs\ n : a female giant

gib·ber \'ji-bər\ vb : to speak rapidly, inarticulately, and often foolishly

gib·ber·ish \'ji-bə-rish\ n : unintelligible or confused speech or language

¹**gib·bet** \'ji-bət\ n : GALLOWS

²**gibbet** vb **1** : to hang on a gibbet **2** : to expose to public scorn **3** : to execute by hanging

gib·bon \'gi-bən\ n : any of several tailless apes of southeastern Asia

gib·bous \'ji-bəs, 'gi-\ adj **1** : rounded like the exterior of a sphere or circle **2** : seen with more than half but not all of the apparent disk illuminated ⟨∼ moon⟩ **3** : having a hump : HUMPBACKED

gibe \'jīb\ vb **gibed; gib·ing** : to utter taunting words : SNEER — **gibe** n

gib·lets \'jib-ləts\ n pl : the edible viscera of a fowl

Gib·son girl \'gib-sən-\ adj : of or relating to a style in women's clothing characterized by high necks, full sleeves, and slender waistlines

gid·dy \'gi-dē\ adj **gid·di·er; -est 1** : DIZZY **2** : causing dizziness **3** : not serious : FRIVOLOUS, SILLY — **gid·di·ness** \-dē-nəs\ n

gift \'gift\ n **1** : a special ability : TALENT **2** : something given : PRESENT **3** : the act or power of giving

gift·ed \'gif-təd\ adj : TALENTED

¹**gig** \'gig\ n **1** : a long light ship's boat **2** : a light 2-wheeled one-horse carriage

²**gig** n : a pronged spear for catching fish — **gig** vb

³**gig** n : a job for a specified time; esp : an entertainer's engagement

⁴**gig** n : a military demerit — **gig** vb

giga·byte \'ji-gə-ˌbīt, 'gi-\ n : a unit of computer storage capacity approximately equal to one billion bytes

gi·gan·tic \jī-'gan-tik\ adj : exceeding the usual (as in size or force)

gig·gle \'gi-gəl\ vb **gig·gled; gig·gling** : to laugh with repeated short catches of the breath — **giggle** n — **gig·gly** \-gə-lē\ adj

GIGO abbr garbage in, garbage out

gig·o·lo \'ji-gə-ˌlō\ n, pl **-los 1** : a man supported by a woman usu. in return for his attentions **2** : a professional dancing partner or male escort

Gi·la monster \'hē-lə-\ n : a large orange and black venomous lizard of the southwestern U.S.

¹**gild** \'gild\ vb **gild·ed** or **gilt** \'gilt\; **gild·ing 1** : to overlay with or as if with a thin covering of gold **2** : to give an attractive but often deceptive appearance to

²**gild** var of GUILD

¹**gill** \'jil\ n — see WEIGHT table

²**gill** \'gil\ n : an organ (as of a fish) for obtaining oxygen from water

¹**gilt** \'gilt\ adj : of the color of gold

²**gilt** n : gold or a substance resembling gold laid on the surface of an object

³**gilt** n : a young female swine

gim·crack \'jim-ˌkrak\ n : a showy object of little use or value

gim·let \'gim-lət\ n : a small tool with screw point and cross handle for boring holes

gim·mick \'gi-mik\ n **1** : CONTRIVANCE, GADGET **2** : an important feature that is not immediately apparent : CATCH **3** : a new and ingenious scheme — **gim·micky** \-mi-kē\ adj

gim·mick·ry \'gi-mi-krē\ n, pl **-ries** : an array of or the use of gimmicks

gimpy \'gim-pē\ adj : CRIPPLED, LAME

¹**gin** \'jin\ n [ME gin, modif. of OF engin] **1** : TRAP, SNARE **2** : a machine to separate seeds from cotton — **gin** vb

²**gin** n [by shortening & alter. fr. geneva, kind of gin] : a liquor distilled from a grain mash and flavored with juniper berries

gin·ger \'jin-jər\ n : the pungent aromatic rootstock of a tropical plant used esp. as a spice and in medicine; also : the spice or the plant

ginger ale n : a carbonated soft drink flavored with ginger

gin·ger·bread \'jin-jər-ˌbred\ n **1** : a cake made with molasses and flavored with ginger **2** : lavish or superfluous ornament

gin·ger·ly \'jin-jər-lē\ adj : very cautious or careful — **gingerly** adv

gin·ger·snap \-ˌsnap\ n : a thin brittle molasses cookie flavored with ginger

ging·ham \'giŋ-əm\ n : a clothing fabric usu. of yarn-dyed cotton in plain weave

gin·gi·vi·tis \ˌjin-jə-'vī-təs\ n : inflammation of the gums

gink·go also **ging·ko** \'giŋ-(ˌ)kō\ n, pl **ginkgoes** or **ginkgos** : a tree of eastern China with fan-shaped leaves often grown as a shade tree

gin·seng \'jin-ˌseŋ\ n : an aromatic root of a Chinese or No. American herb used esp. in Oriental medicine; also : one of these herbs

gi·raffe \jə-'raf\ n, pl **giraffes** [It giraffa, fr. Ar zirāfah] : an African ruminant mammal with a very long neck and a short coat with dark blotches

gird \'gərd\ vb **gird·ed** or **girt** \'gərt\; **gird·ing 1** : to encircle or fasten with or as if with a belt ⟨∼ on a sword⟩ **2** : to invest esp. with power or authority **3** : PREPARE, BRACE

gird·er \'gər-dər\ n : a horizontal main supporting beam

gir·dle \'gərd-ᵊl\ n **1** : something (as a belt or sash) that encircles or confines **2** : a woman's supporting undergarment that extends from the waist to below the hips — **girdle** vb

girl \'gərl\ n **1** : a female child **2** : a young woman **3** : SWEETHEART — **girl·hood** \-ˌhu̇d\ n — **girl·ish** adj

girl Friday *n* : a female assistant (as in an office) entrusted with a wide variety of tasks

girl·friend \'gərl-ˌfrend\ *n* **1** : a female friend **2** : a frequent or regular female companion of a boy or man

Girl Scout *n* : a member of any of the scouting programs of the Girl Scouts of the United States of America

girth \'gərth\ *n* **1** : a band around an animal by which something (as a saddle) may be fastened on its back **2** : a measure around something

gist \'jist\ *n* [MF, it lies, fr. *gesir* to lie, ultim. fr. L *jacēre*] : the main point or part

¹give \'giv\ *vb* **gave** \'gāv\; **giv·en** \'gi-vən\; **giv·ing 1** : to make a present of **2** : to bestow by formal action **3** : to accord or yield to another **4** : to yield to force, strain, or pressure **5** : to put into the possession or keeping of another **6** : PROFFER **7** : DELIVER 〈*gave* away the bride〉 **8** : to present in public performance or to view **9** : PROVIDE 〈~ a party〉 **10** : ATTRIBUTE **11** : to make, form, or yield as a product or result 〈cows ~ milk〉 **12** : PAY **13** : to deliver by some bodily action 〈*gave* me a push〉 **14** : to offer as a pledge 〈I ~ you my word〉 **15** : DEVOTE **16** : to cause to have or receive

²give *n* **1** : capacity or tendency to yield to force or strain **2** : the quality or state of being springy

give–and–take \ˌgiv-ən-'tāk\ *n* **1** : COMPROMISE **2** : a usu. good-natured exchange (as of remarks or ideas)

give·away \'gi-və-ˌwā\ *n* **1** : an unintentional revelation or betrayal **2** : something given away free; *esp* : PREMIUM

give in *vb* : SUBMIT, SURRENDER

¹giv·en \'gi-vən\ *adj* **1** : DISPOSED, INCLINED 〈~ to swearing〉 **2** : SPECIFIED, PARTICULAR 〈at a ~ time〉

²given *prep* : CONSIDERING

given name *n* : a name that precedes one's surname

give out *vb* **1** : EMIT **2** : BREAK DOWN **3** : to become exhausted : COLLAPSE

give up *vb* **1** : SURRENDER **2** : to abandon (oneself) to a feeling, influence, or activity **3** : QUIT

giz·mo *also* **gis·mo** \'giz-mō\ *n, pl* **gizmos** *also* **gismos** : GADGET

giz·zard \'gi-zərd\ *n* : the muscular usu. horny-lined enlargement of the alimentary canal of a bird used for churning and grinding up food

gla·cial \'glā-shəl\ *adj* **1** : extremely cold **2** : of or relating to glaciers **3** : being or relating to a past period of time when a large part of the earth was covered by glaciers **4** *cap* : PLEISTOCENE **5** : very slow 〈a ~ pace〉 — **gla·cial·ly** *adv*

gla·ci·ate \'glā-shē-ˌāt\ *vb* **-at·ed; -at·ing 1** : to subject to glacial action **2** : to produce glacial effects in or on — **gla·ci·a·tion** \ˌglā-shē-'ā-shən, -sē-\ *n*

gla·cier \'glā-shər\ *n* : a large body of ice moving slowly down a slope or spreading outward on a land surface

¹glad \'glad\ *adj* **glad·der; glad·dest 1** : experiencing pleasure, joy, or delight **2** : PLEASED **3** : very willing **4** : PLEASANT, JOYFUL **5** : CHEERFUL — **glad·ly** *adv* — **glad·ness** *n*

²glad *n* : GLADIOLUS

glad·den \'glad-ᵊn\ *vb* : to make glad

glade \'glād\ *n* : a grassy open space surrounded by woods

glad·i·a·tor \'gla-dē-ˌā-tər\ *n* **1** : a person engaged in a fight to the death for public entertainment in ancient Rome **2** : a person engaging in a public fight or controversy; *also* : PRIZEFIGHTER — **glad·i·a·to·ri·al** \ˌgla-dē-ə-'tōr-ē-əl\ *adj*

glad·i·o·lus \ˌgla-dē-'ō-ləs\ *n, pl* **-li** \-(ˌ)lē, -ˌlī\ [L, fr. dim. of *gladius* sword] : any of a genus of chiefly African plants related to the irises and having erect sword-shaped leaves and stalks of bright colored flowers

glad·some \'glad-səm\ *adj* : giving or showing joy : CHEERFUL

glad·stone \'glad-ˌstŏn\ *n, often cap* : a suitcase with flexible sides on a rigid frame that opens flat into two compartments

glam·or·ize *also* **glam·our·ize** \'gla-mə-ˌrīz\ *vb* **-ized; -iz·ing** : to make or look upon as glamorous

glam·our *or* **glam·or** \'gla-mər\ *n* [Sc *glamour* magic spell, alter. of E *grammar*; fr. the popular association of erudition with occult practices] : an exciting and often illusory and romantic attractiveness; *esp* : alluring personal attraction — **glam·or·ous** *also* **glam·our·ous** \-mə-rəs\ *adj*

¹glance \'glans\ *vb* **glanced; glanc·ing 1** : to strike and fly off to one side **2** : GLEAM **3** : to give a quick look

²glance *n* **1** : a quick intermittent flash or gleam **2** : a deflected impact or blow **3** : a quick look

gland \'gland\ *n* : a cell or group of cells that prepares and secretes a substance (as saliva or sweat) for further use in or discharge from the body

glan·du·lar \'glan-jə-lər\ *adj* : of, relating to, or involving glands

glans \'glanz\ *n, pl* **glan·des** \'glan-ˌdēz\ [L, lit., acorn] : a conical vascular body forming the extremity of the penis or clitoris

¹glare \'glar\ *vb* **glared; glar·ing 1** : to shine with a harsh dazzling light **2** : to stare fiercely or angrily

²glare *n* **1** : a harsh dazzling light **2** : an angry or fierce stare

glar·ing \'glar-iŋ\ *adj* : painfully obvious 〈a ~ error〉 — **glar·ing·ly** *adv*

glass \'glas\ *n* **1** : a hard brittle amorphous usu. transparent or translucent material consisting esp. of silica **2** : something made of glass; *esp* : TUMBLER **3** *pl* : a pair of lenses used to correct defects of vision : SPECTACLES **4** : the quantity held by a glass container — **glass** *adj* — **glass·ful** \-ˌfŭl\ *n* — **glassy** *adj*

glass·blow·ing \-ˌblō-iŋ\ *n* : the art of shaping a mass of glass that has been softened by heat by blowing air into it through a tube — **glass·blow·er** *n*

glass·ware \-ˌwar\ *n* : articles made of glass

glau·co·ma \glau̇-'kō-mə, glȯ-\ *n* : a disease of the eye marked by increased pressure within the eyeball resulting in damage to the retina and gradual loss of vision

¹glaze \'glāz\ *vb* **glazed; glaz·ing 1** : to furnish (as a window frame) with glass **2** : to apply glaze to

²glaze *n* : a glassy coating or surface

gla·zier \'glā-zhər\ *n* : a person who sets glass in window frames

¹gleam \'glēm\ *n* **1** : a transient subdued or partly obscured light **2** : GLINT **3** : a faint trace 〈a ~ of hope〉

²gleam *vb* **1** : to shine with subdued light or moderate brightness **2** : to appear briefly or faintly **syn** flash, glimmer, glisten, glitter, shimmer, sparkle

glean \'glēn\ *vb* **1** : to gather grain left by reapers **2** : to collect little by little or with patient effort — **glean·able** *adj* — **glean·er** *n*

glean·ings \'glē-niŋz\ *n pl* : things acquired by gleaning

glee \'glē\ *n* [ME, fr. OE *glēo* entertainment, music] **1** : JOY, HILARITY **2** : a part-song for three usu. male voices — **glee·ful** *adj*

glee club *n* : a chorus organized for singing usu. short choral pieces

glen \'glen\ *n* : a narrow hidden valley

glen·gar·ry \glen-'gar-ē\ *n, pl* **-ries** *often cap* : a woolen cap of Scottish origin

glib \'glib\ *adj* **glib·ber; glib·best** : speaking or spoken with careless ease — **glib·ly** *adv*

glide \'glīd\ *vb* **glid·ed; glid·ing 1** : to move smoothly and effortlessly **2** : to descend gradually without engine power 〈~ in an airplane〉 — **glide** *n*

glid·er \'glī-dər\ *n* **1** : one that glides **2** : an aircraft resembling an airplane but having no engine **3** : a porch seat suspended from an upright frame

¹glim·mer \'gli-mər\ *vb* : to shine faintly or unsteadily

²glimmer *n* **1** : a faint unsteady light **2** : INKLING **3** : a small amount : HINT

¹**glimpse** \'glimps\ *vb* **glimpsed; glimps·ing** : to take a brief look : see momentarily or incompletely

²**glimpse** *n* **1** : a faint idea : GLIMMER **2** : a short hurried look

glint \'glint\ *vb* **1** : to shine by reflection : SPARKLE, GLITTER, GLEAM **2** : to appear briefly or faintly — **glint** *n*

glis·san·do \gli-'sän-(ˌ)dō\ *n, pl* **-di** \-(ˌ)dē\ *or* **-dos** : a rapid sliding up or down the musical scale

¹**glis·ten** \'glis-ᵊn\ *vb* : to shine by reflection with a soft luster or sparkle

²**glisten** *n* : GLITTER, SPARKLE

glis·ter \'glis-tər\ *vb* : GLITTER

glitch \'glich\ *n* : MALFUNCTION; *also* : SNAG 2

¹**glit·ter** \'gli-tər\ *vb* **1** : to shine with brilliant or metallic luster : SPARKLE **2** : to shine with strong emotion : FLASH ⟨eyes ∼*ing* in anger⟩ **3** : to be brilliantly attractive esp. in a superficial way

²**glitter** *n* **1** : sparkling brilliancy, showiness, or attractiveness **2** : small glittering objects used for ornamentation — **glit·tery** \'gli-tə-rē\ *adj*

gloam·ing \'glō-miŋ\ *n* : TWILIGHT, DUSK

gloat \'glōt\ *vb* : to think about something with triumphant and often malicious delight

glob \'gläb\ *n* **1** : a small drop **2** : a large rounded mass

glob·al \'glō-bəl\ *adj* **1** : WORLDWIDE **2** : COMPREHENSIVE, GENERAL — **glob·al·ly** *adv*

globe \'glōb\ *n* **1** : BALL, SPHERE **2** : EARTH; *also* : a spherical representation of the earth

globe–trot·ter \'glōb-ˌträ-tər\ *n* : a person who travels widely — **globe–trot·ting** *n or adj*

glob·u·lar \'glä-byə-lər\ *adj* : having the shape of a globe or globule

glob·ule \'glä-(ˌ)byül\ *n* : a tiny globe or ball esp. of a liquid

glob·u·lin \'glä-byə-lən\ *n* : any of a class of simple proteins insoluble in pure water but soluble in dilute salt solutions that occur widely in plant and animal tissues

glock·en·spiel \'glä-kən-ˌshpēl, -ˌspēl\ *n* [G, fr. *Glocke* bell + *Spiel* play] : a percussion musical instrument consisting of a series of metal bars played with two hammers

gloom \'glüm\ *n* **1** : partial or total darkness **2** : lowness of spirits : DEJECTION **3** : an atmosphere of despondency — **gloom·i·ly** \'glü-mə-lē\ *adv* — **gloom·i·ness** \-mē-nəs\ *n* — **gloomy** \'glü-mē\ *adj*

glop \'gläp\ *n* : a messy mass or mixture

glo·ri·fy \'glōr-ə-ˌfī\ *vb* **-fied; -fy·ing** **1** : to raise to heavenly glory **2** : to light up brilliantly **3** : EXTOL **4** : to give glory to (as in worship) — **glo·ri·fi·ca·tion** \ˌglōr-ə-fə-'kā-shən\ *n*

glo·ri·ous \'glōr-ē-əs\ *adj* **1** : possessing or deserving glory : PRAISEWORTHY **2** : conferring glory **3** : RESPLENDENT, MAGNIFICENT **4** : DELIGHTFUL, WONDERFUL — **glo·ri·ous·ly** *adv*

¹**glo·ry** \'glōr-ē\ *n, pl* **glories** **1** : RENOWN **2** : honor and praise rendered in worship **3** : something that secures praise or renown **4** : a distinguishing quality or asset **5** : RESPLENDENCE, MAGNIFICENCE **6** : heavenly bliss **7** : a height of prosperity or achievement

²**glory** *vb* **glo·ried; glo·ry·ing** : to rejoice proudly : EXULT

¹**gloss** \'gläs, 'glòs\ *n* **1** : LUSTER, SHEEN, BRIGHTNESS **2** : outward show

²**gloss** *vb* **1** : to give a false appearance of acceptableness to ⟨∼ over inadequacies⟩ **2** : to deal with too lightly or not at all

³**gloss** *n* [alter. of *gloze*, fr. ME *glose*, fr. MF, fr. ML *glosa, glossa*, fr. Gk *glōssa, glōtta* tongue, language, unusual word] **1** : an explanatory note (as in the margin of a text) **2** : GLOSSARY **3** : an interlinear translation **4** : a continuous commentary accompanying a text

⁴**gloss** *vb* : to furnish glosses for

glos·sa·ry \'glä-sə-rē, 'glò-\ *n, pl* **-ries** : a collection of difficult or specialized terms with their meanings — **glos·sar·i·al** \glä-'sar-ē-əl, glò-\ *adj*

glos·so·la·lia \ˌglä-sə-'lā-lē-ə, ˌglò-\ *n* [Gk *glōssa* tongue, language + *lalia* chatter] : TONGUE 6

¹**glossy** \'glä-sē, 'glò-\ *adj* **gloss·i·er; -est** : having a surface luster or brightness — **gloss·i·ly** \-sə-lē\ *adv* — **gloss·i·ness** \-sē-nəs\ *n*

²**glossy** *n, pl* **gloss·ies** : a photograph printed on smooth shiny paper

glot·tis \'glä-təs\ *n, pl* **glot·tis·es** *or* **glot·ti·des** \-tə-ˌdēz\ : the slitlike opening between the vocal cords in the larynx — **glot·tal** \'glät-ᵊl\ *adj*

glove \'gləv\ *n* **1** : a covering for the hand having separate sections for each finger **2** : a padded leather covering for the hand for use in a sport

¹**glow** \'glō\ *vb* **1** : to shine with or as if with intense heat **2** : to have a rich warm usu. ruddy color : FLUSH, BLUSH **3** : to feel hot **4** : to show exuberance or elation ⟨∼ with pride⟩

²**glow** *n* **1** : brightness or warmth of color; *esp* : REDNESS **2** : warmth of feeling or emotion **3** : a sensation of warmth **4** : light such as is emitted from a heated substance

glow·er \'glaù-ər\ *vb* : to stare angrily : SCOWL — **glower** *n*

glow·worm \'glō-ˌwərm\ *n* : any of various insect larvae or adults that give off light

glox·in·ia \gläk-'si-nē-ə\ *n* : any of a genus of Brazilian herbs related to the African violets; *esp* : one with showy bell-shaped or slipper-shaped flowers

gloze \'glōz\ *vb* **glozed; gloz·ing** : to make appear right or acceptable : GLOSS

glu·cose \'glü-ˌkōs\ *n* **1** : a sugar known in two different forms; *esp* : DEXTROSE **2** : a sweet light-colored syrup made from cornstarch

glue \'glü\ *n* : a jellylike protein substance made from animal materials and used for sticking things together; *also* : any of various other strong adhesives — **glue** *vb* — **glu·ey** \'glü-ē\ *adj*

glum \'gləm\ *adj* **glum·mer; glum·mest** **1** : broodingly morose : SULLEN **2** : DREARY, GLOOMY **syn** crabbed, dour, saturnine, sulky

¹**glut** \'glət\ *vb* **glut·ted; glut·ting** **1** : OVERSUPPLY **2** : to fill esp. with food to satiety : SATIATE

²**glut** *n* : an excessive supply

glu·ten \'glüt-ᵊn\ *n* : a gluey protein substance that causes dough to be sticky

glu·ti·nous \'glüt-ᵊn-əs\ *adj* : STICKY

glut·ton \'glət-ᵊn\ *n* : one that eats to excess — **glut·ton·ous** \'glət-ᵊn-əs\ *adj* — **glut·tony** \'glət-ᵊn-ē\ *n*

glyc·er·in *or* **glyc·er·ine** \'gli-sə-rən\ *n* : GLYCEROL

glyc·er·ol \'gli-sə-ˌról, -ˌrōl\ *n* : a sweet syrupy alcohol usu. obtained from fats and used esp. as a solvent

gly·co·gen \'glī-kə-jən\ *n* : a white tasteless substance that is the chief storage carbohydrate of animals

gm *abbr* gram

GM *abbr* **1** general manager **2** guided missile

G–man \'jē-ˌman\ *n* : a special agent of the Federal Bureau of Investigation

GMT *abbr* Greenwich mean time

gnarled \'närld\ *adj* **1** : KNOTTY **2** : GLOOMY, SULLEN

gnash \'nash\ *vb* : to grind (as teeth) together

gnat \'nat\ *n* : any of various small usu. biting dipteran flies

gnaw \'nò\ *vb* **1** : to consume, wear away, or make by persistent biting or nibbling **2** : to affect as if by gnawing — **gnaw·er** *n*

gneiss \'nīs\ *n* : a layered rock similar in composition to granite

gnome \'nōm\ *n* : a dwarf of folklore who lives inside the earth and guards precious ore or treasure — **gnom·ish** *adj*

GNP *abbr* gross national product

gnu \'nü\ *n, pl* **gnu** *or* **gnus** : either of two large African antelopes with an oxlike head and horns and a horselike mane and tail

gnu

¹**go** \'gō\ *vb* **went** \'went\; **gone** \'gȯn, 'gän\; **go·ing; goes** \'gōz\ **1** : to move on a course : PROCEED ⟨~ slow⟩ **2** : LEAVE, DEPART **3** : to take a certain course or follow a certain procedure ⟨reports ~ through department channels⟩ **4** : EXTEND, RUN ⟨his land ~*es* to the river⟩; *also* : LEAD ⟨that door ~*es* to the cellar⟩ **5** : to be habitually in a certain state ⟨~*es* armed after dark⟩ **6** : to become lost, consumed, or spent; *also* : DIE **7** : ELAPSE, PASS **8** : to pass by sale ⟨*went* for a good price⟩ **9** : to become impaired or weakened **10** : to give way under force or pressure : BREAK **11** : to move along in a specified manner ⟨it *went* well⟩ **12** : to be in general or on an average ⟨cheap, as yachts ~⟩ **13** : to become esp. as the result of a contest ⟨the decision *went* against him⟩ **14** : to put or subject oneself ⟨~ to great expense⟩ **15** : RESORT ⟨*went* to court to recover damages⟩ **16** : to begin or maintain an action or motion ⟨here ~*es*⟩ **17** : to function properly ⟨the clock doesn't ~⟩ **18** : to be known ⟨~*es* by an alias⟩ **19** : to be or act in accordance ⟨a good rule to ~ by⟩ **20** : to come to be applied **21** : to pass by award, assignment, or lot **22** : to contribute to a result ⟨qualities that ~ to make a hero⟩ **23** : to be about, intending, or expecting something ⟨is ~*ing* to leave town⟩ **24** : to arrive at a certain state or condition ⟨~ to sleep⟩ **25** : to come to be ⟨the tire *went* flat⟩ **26** : to be capable of being sung or played ⟨the tune ~*es* like this⟩ **27** : to be suitable or becoming : HARMONIZE **28** : to be capable of passing, extending, or being contained or inserted ⟨this coat will ~ in the trunk⟩ **29** : to have a usual or proper place or position : BELONG ⟨these books ~ on the top shelf⟩ **30** : to be capable of being divided ⟨3 ~*es* into 6 twice⟩ **31** : to have a tendency ⟨that ~*es* to show that he is honest⟩ **32** : to be acceptable, satisfactory, or adequate **33** : to empty the bladder or bowels **34** : to proceed along or according to : FOLLOW **35** : TRAVERSE **36** : BET, BID ⟨willing to ~ $50⟩ **37** : to assume the function or obligation of ⟨~ bail for a friend⟩ **38** : to participate to the extent of ⟨~ halves⟩ **39** : WEIGH **40** : ENDURE, TOLERATE **41** : AFFORD ⟨can't ~ the price⟩ **42** : SAY — used chiefly in oral narration of speech **43** : to engage in ⟨don't ~ telling everyone⟩ — **go at 1** : ATTACK, ATTEMPT **2** : UNDERTAKE — **go back on 1** : ABANDON **2** : BETRAY **3** : FAIL — **go by the board** : to be discarded — **go down the line** : to give wholehearted support — **go for 1** : to pass for or serve as **2** : to try to secure **3** : FAVOR — **go one better** : OUTDO, SURPASS — **go over 1** : EXAMINE **2** : REPEAT **3** : STUDY, REVIEW — **go places** : to be on the way to success — **go steady** : to date one person exclusively — **go to bat for** : DEFEND, CHAMPION — **go to town 1** : to work or act efficiently **2** : to be very successful

²**go** *n, pl* **goes 1** : the act or manner of going **2** : the height of fashion ⟨boots are all the ~⟩ **3** : a turn of affairs : OCCURRENCE **4** : ENERGY, VIGOR **5** : ATTEMPT, TRY **6** : a spell of activity — **no go** : USELESS, HOPELESS — **on the go** : constantly active

³**go** *adj* : functioning properly

goad \'gōd\ *n* [ME *gode*, fr. OE *gād* spear, goad] **1** : a pointed rod used to urge on an animal **2** : something that urges **syn** stimulus, impetus, incentive, spur, stimulant — **goad** *vb*

go–ahead \'gō-ə-ˌhed\ *n* : authority to proceed

goal \'gōl\ *n* **1** : the mark set as limit to a race; *also* : an area to be reached safely in children's games **2** : AIM, PURPOSE **3** : an area or object toward which play is directed to score; *also* : a successful attempt to score

goal·ie \'gō-lē\ *n* : GOALKEEPER

goal·keep·er \'gōl-ˌkē-pər\ *n* : a player who defends the goal in various games

goal·post \-ˌpōst\ *n* : one of the two vertical posts with a crossbar that constitute the goal in various games

goat \'gōt\ *n, pl* **goats** *or* **goat** : any of various hollow-horned ruminant mammals related to the sheep that have backward-curving horns, a short tail, and usu. straight hair

goa·tee \gō-'tē\ *n* : a small trim pointed or tufted beard on a man's chin

goat·herd \'gōt-ˌhərd\ *n* : a person who tends goats

goat·skin \-ˌskin\ *n* : the skin of a goat or a leather made from it

¹**gob** \'gäb\ *n* : LUMP, MASS

²**gob** *n* : SAILOR

gob·bet \'gä-bət\ *n* : LUMP, MASS

¹**gob·ble** \'gä-bəl\ *vb* **gob·bled; gob·bling 1** : to swallow or eat greedily **2** : to take eagerly : GRAB

²**gobble** *vb* **gob·bled; gob·bling** : to make the natural guttural noise of a male turkey

gob·ble·dy·gook *also* **gob·ble·de·gook** \'gä-bəl-dē-ˌgùk, -ˌgük\ *n* : generally unintelligible jargon

gob·bler \'gä-blər\ *n* : a male turkey

go–be·tween \'gō-bə-ˌtwēn\ *n* : an intermediate agent : BROKER

gob·let \'gä-blət\ *n* : a drinking glass with a foot and stem

gob·lin \'gä-blən\ *n* : an ugly or grotesque sprite that is mischievous and sometimes evil and malicious

god \'gäd, 'gȯd\ *n* **1** *cap* : the supreme reality; *esp* : the Being worshiped as the creator and ruler of the universe **2** : a being or object believed to have supernatural attributes and powers and to require worship **3** : a person or thing of supreme value

god·child \'gäd-ˌchīld, 'gȯd-\ *n* : a person for whom another person stands as sponsor at baptism

god·daugh·ter \-ˌdȯ-tər\ *n* : a female godchild

god·dess \'gä-dəs, 'gȯ-\ *n* **1** : a female god **2** : a woman whose charm or beauty arouses adoration

god·fa·ther \'gäd-ˌfä-thər, 'gȯd-\ *n* **1** : a man who sponsors a person at baptism **2** : the leader of an organized crime syndicate

god·head \-ˌhed\ *n* **1** : divine nature or essence **2** *cap* : GOD 1; *also* : the nature of God esp. as existing in three persons

god·hood \-ˌhùd\ *n* : DIVINITY

god·less \-ləs\ *adj* : not acknowledging a deity or divine law — **god·less·ness** *n*

god·like \-ˌlīk\ *adj* : resembling or having the qualities of God or a god

god·ly \-lē\ *adj* **god·li·er; -est 1** : DIVINE **2** : PIOUS, DEVOUT — **god·li·ness** *n*

god·moth·er \-ˌmə-thər\ *n* : a woman who sponsors a person at baptism

god·par·ent \-ˌpar-ənt\ *n* : a sponsor at baptism

god·send \-ˌsend\ *n* : a desirable or needed thing or event that comes unexpectedly

god·son \-ˌsən\ *n* : a male godchild

God·speed \-'spēd\ *n* : a prosperous journey : SUCCESS ⟨bade him ~⟩

go·fer \'gō-fər\ *n* [alter. of *go for*] : an employee whose duties include running errands

go–get·ter \'gō-ˌge-tər\ *n* : an aggressively enterprising person — **go–get·ting** *adj or n*

gog·gle \'gä-gəl\ *vb* **gog·gled; gog·gling** : to stare with wide or protuberant eyes

gog·gles \\'gä-gəlz\\ *n pl* : protective glasses set in a flexible frame that fits snugly against the face

go–go \\'gō-ˌgō\\ *adj* **1** : related to, being, or employed to entertain in a disco ⟨~ dancers⟩ **2** : aggressively enterprising and energetic

go·ings–on \\ˌgō-iŋ-'zon, -'zän\\ *n pl* : ACTIONS, EVENTS

goi·ter \\'gȯi-tər\\ *n* : an abnormally enlarged thyroid gland visible as a swelling at the base of the neck — **goi·trous** \\-trəs, -tə-rəs\\ *adj*

goi·tre *chiefly Brit var of* GOITER

gold \\'gōld\\ *n* **1** : a malleable yellow metallic chemical element used esp. for coins and jewelry — see ELEMENT table **2** : gold coins; *also* : MONEY **3** : a yellow color

gold·brick \\'gōld-ˌbrik\\ *n* : a person who shirks assigned work — **goldbrick** *vb*

gold coast *n, often cap G&C* : an exclusive residential district

gold digger *n* : a person who uses charm to extract money or gifts from others

gold·en \\'gōl-dən\\ *adj* **1** : made of or relating to gold **2** : having the color of gold; *also* : BLOND **3** : SHINING, LUSTROUS **4** : SUPERB **5** : FLOURISHING, PROSPEROUS **6** : radiantly youthful and vigorous **7** : FAVORABLE, ADVANTAGEOUS ⟨a ~ opportunity⟩ **8** : MELLOW, RESONANT

gold·en–ag·er \\'gōl-dən-'ā-jər\\ *n* : an elderly and often retired person usu. engaging in club activities

golden hamster *n* : a small tawny hamster often kept as a pet

gold·en·rod \\'gōl-dən-ˌräd\\ *n* : any of numerous plants related to the daisies but having tall slender stalks with many tiny usu. yellow flower heads

gold·finch \\-ˌfinch\\ *n* **1** : a small largely red, black, and yellow Old World finch often kept in a cage **2** : any of three small American finches of which the males usu. become bright yellow and black in summer

gold·fish \\-ˌfish\\ *n* : a small usu. yellow or golden carp often kept as an aquarium or pond fish

gold·smith \\-ˌsmith\\ *n* : a person who makes or deals in articles of gold

golf \\'gälf, 'gȯlf\\ *n* : a game played with a small ball and various clubs on a course having 9 or 18 holes — **golf** *vb* — **golf·er** *n*

-gon \\ˌgän\\ *n comb form* : figure having (so many) angles ⟨hexa*gon*⟩

go·nad \\'gō-ˌnad\\ *n* : a sperm- or egg-producing gland : OVARY, TESTIS — **go·nad·al** \\gō-'nad-əl\\ *adj*

go·nad·o·trop·ic \\gō-ˌna-də-'trä-pik\\ *also* **go·nad·o·tro·phic** \\-'trō-fik,-'trä-\\ *adj* : acting on or stimulating the gonads ⟨~ hormones⟩

go·nad·o·tro·pin \\-'trō-pən\\ *also* **go·nad·o·tro·phin** \\-fən\\ *n* : a gonadotropic hormone

gon·do·la \\'gän-də-lə (*usual for 1*), gän-'dō-\\ *n* **1** : a long narrow boat used on the canals of Venice **2** : a railroad car used for hauling loose freight (as coal) **3** : an enclosure beneath an airship or balloon **4** : an enclosed car suspended from a cable and used esp. for transporting skiers

gondola 1

gon·do·lier \\ˌgän-də-'lir\\ *n* : a person who propels a gondola

¹gone \\'gȯn\\ *past part of* GO

²gone *adj* **1** : DEAD **2** : LOST, RUINED **3** : SINKING, WEAK **4** : INVOLVED, ABSORBED **5** : INFATUATED **6** : PREGNANT **7** : PAST

gon·er \\'gȯ-nər\\ *n* : one whose case is hopeless

gong \\'gäŋ, 'gȯŋ\\ *n* : a metallic disk that produces a resounding tone when struck

gono·coc·cus \\ˌgä-nə-'kä-kəs\\ *n, pl* **-coc·ci** \\-'käk-ˌsī, -(ˌ)sē, -'kä-ˌkī, -(ˌ)kē\\ : a pus-producing bacterium causing gonorrhea — **gono·coc·cal** \\-'kä-kəl\\ *adj*

gon·or·rhea \\ˌgä-nə-'rē-ə\\ *n* : a contagious sexually transmitted inflammation of the genital tract caused by a bacterium — **gon·or·rhe·al** \\-'rē-əl\\ *adj*

goo \\'gü\\ *n* **1** : a viscid or sticky substance **2** : sentimental tripe — **goo·ey** \\-ē\\ *adj*

goo·ber \\'gü-bər, 'gu-\\ *n, Southern & Midland* : PEANUT

¹good \\'gud\\ *adj* **bet·ter** \\'be-tər\\; **best** \\'best\\ **1** : of a favorable character or tendency **2** : BOUNTIFUL, FERTILE **3** : COMELY, ATTRACTIVE **4** : SUITABLE, FIT **5** : SOUND, WHOLE **6** : AGREEABLE, PLEASANT **7** : SALUTARY, WHOLESOME **8** : CONSIDERABLE, AMPLE **9** : FULL **10** : WELL-FOUNDED **11** : TRUE ⟨holds ~ for everybody⟩ **12** : legally valid or effectual **13** : ADEQUATE, SATISFACTORY **14** : conforming to a standard **15** : DISCRIMINATING **16** : COMMENDABLE, VIRTUOUS **17** : KIND **18** : UPPER-CLASS **19** : COMPETENT **20** : LOYAL, CLOSE — **good–heart·ed** \\-'här-təd\\ *adj* — **good·ish** *adj* — **good–look·ing** \\-'lu̇-kiŋ\\ *adj* — **good–tempered** \\-'tem-pərd\\ *adj*

²good *n* **1** : something good **2** : GOODNESS **3** : BENEFIT, WELFARE ⟨for the ~ of mankind⟩ **4** : something that has economic utility **5** *pl* : personal property **6** *pl* : CLOTH **7** *pl* : WARES, MERCHANDISE **8** : good persons ⟨the ~ die young⟩ **9** *pl* : proof of wrongdoing — **for good** : FOREVER, PERMANENTLY — **to the good** : in a position of net gain or profit ⟨$10 *to the good*⟩

³good *adv* : WELL

good–bye *or* **good–by** \\gud-'bī, gə-\\ *n* : a concluding remark at parting

good–for–noth·ing \\'gud-fər-ˌnə-thiŋ\\ *n* : an idle worthless person

Good Friday *n* : the Friday before Easter observed as the anniversary of the crucifixion of Christ

good·ly \\'gud-lē\\ *adj* **good·li·er; -est 1** : of pleasing appearance **2** : LARGE, CONSIDERABLE

good·man \\'gud-mən\\ *n, archaic* : MR.

good–na·tured \\'gud-'nā-chərd\\ *adj* : of a cheerful disposition — **good–na·tured·ly** \\-chərd-lē\\ *adv*

good·ness \\-nəs\\ *n* : EXCELLENCE, VIRTUE

good·wife \\-ˌwīf\\ *n, archaic* : MRS.

good·will \\-'wil\\ *n* **1** : BENEVOLENCE **2** : the value of the trade a business has built up over time **3** : cheerful consent **4** : willing effort

goody \\'gu-dē\\ *n, pl* **good·ies** : something that is good esp. to eat

goody–goody \\ˌgu-dē-'gu-dē\\ *adj* : affectedly good — **goody–goody** *n*

goof \\'güf\\ *vb* **1** : to spend time idly or foolishly **2** : BLUNDER — often used with *off* — **goof** *n*

goof·ball \\'güf-ˌbȯl\\ *n* **1** *slang* : a barbiturate sleeping pill **2** : a goofy person

go off *vb* **1** : EXPLODE **2** : to follow a course ⟨the party *went off* well⟩

goof–off \\'güf-ˌfȯf\\ *n* : one who evades work or responsibility

goofy \\'gü-fē\\ *adj* **goof·i·er; -est** : CRAZY, SILLY — **goof·i·ness** \\-fē-nəs\\ *n*

goon \\'gün\\ *n* : a man hired to terrorize or kill opponents

go on *vb* **1** : to continue in a course of action **2** : to take place : HAPPEN

goose \\'güs\\ *n, pl* **geese** \\'gēs\\ **1** : any of numerous long-necked web-footed birds related to the swans and ducks; *esp* : a female goose as distinguished from a gander **2** : a foolish person **3** *pl* **goos·es** : a tailor's smoothing iron

goose·ber·ry \\'güs-ˌber-ē, 'güz-, -bə-rē\\ *n* : the acid berry of any of several shrubs related to the currant and used esp. in jams and pies

goose bumps *n pl* : roughening of the skin caused usu. by cold, fear, or a sudden feeling of excitement

goose·flesh \-‚flesh\ *n* : GOOSE BUMPS

goose pimples *n pl* : GOOSE BUMPS

go out *vb* 1 : to become extinguished 2 : to become a candidate ⟨*went out* for the football team⟩

go over *vb* : SUCCEED

GOP *abbr* Grand Old Party (Republican)

go·pher \'gō-fər\ *n* 1 : a burrowing American land tortoise 2 : any of a family of No. American burrowing rodents with large cheek pouches opening beside the mouth 3 : any of several small ground squirrels of the prairie region of No. America

¹gore \'gōr\ *n* : BLOOD

²gore *n* : a tapering or triangular piece (as of cloth in a skirt)

³gore *vb* **gored; gor·ing** : to pierce or wound with something pointed

¹gorge \'górj\ *n* 1 : THROAT 2 : a narrow ravine 3 : a mass of matter that chokes up a passage

²gorge *vb* **gorged; gorg·ing** : to eat greedily : stuff to capacity : GLUT

gor·geous \'gór-jəs\ *adj* : resplendently beautiful

Gor·gon·zo·la \‚gór-gən-'zō-lə\ *n* : a blue cheese of Italian origin

go·ril·la \gə-'ri-lə\ *n* [NL, fr. Gk *Gorillai*, a tribe of hairy women in an account of a voyage around Africa] : an African anthropoid ape related to but much larger than the chimpanzee

gor·man·dize \'gór-mən-‚dīz\ *vb* **-dized; -diz·ing** : to eat ravenously — **gor·man·diz·er** *n*

gorp \'górp\ *n* : a snack consisting of high-calorie food (as raisins and nuts)

gorse \'górs\ *n* : a spiny yellow-flowered Old World evergreen shrub of the legume family

gory \'gōr-ē\ *adj* **gor·i·er; -est** 1 : BLOODSTAINED 2 : HORRIBLE, SENSATIONAL

gos·hawk \'gäs-‚hók\ *n* : any of several long-tailed hawks with short rounded wings

gos·ling \'gäz-liŋ, 'góz-\ *n* : a young goose

¹gos·pel \'gäs-pəl\ *n* [ME, fr. OE *gōdspel*, fr. *gōd* good + *spell* message, news] 1 : the teachings of Christ and the apostles 2 *cap* : any of the first four books of the New Testament 3 : something accepted as infallible truth

²gospel *adj* 1 : of, relating to, or emphasizing the gospel 2 : relating to or being American religious songs associated with evangelism

gos·sa·mer \'gä-sə-mər\ *n* [ME *gossomer*, fr. *gos* goose + *somer* summer] 1 : a film of cobwebs floating in the air 2 : something light, delicate, or tenuous

¹gos·sip \'gä-səp\ *n* 1 : a person who habitually reveals personal or sensational facts 2 : rumor or report of an intimate nature 3 : an informal conversation — **gos·sipy** *adj*

²gossip *vb* : to spread gossip

got *past and past part of* GET

Goth \'gäth\ *n* : a member of a Germanic people that early in the Christian era overran the Roman Empire

¹Goth·ic \'gä-thik\ *adj* 1 : of or relating to the Goths 2 : of or relating to a style of architecture prevalent in western Europe from the middle 12th to the early 16th century

²Gothic *n* 1 : the Germanic language of the Goths 2 : the Gothic architectural style or decoration

gotten *past part of* GET

Gou·da \'gü-də\ *n* : a mild Dutch milk cheese shaped in balls

¹gouge \'gaúj\ *n* 1 : a rounded troughlike chisel 2 : a hole or groove made with or as if with a gouge

²gouge *vb* **gouged; goug·ing** 1 : to cut holes or grooves in with or as if with a gouge 2 : DEFRAUD, CHEAT

gou·lash \'gü-‚läsh, -‚lash\ *n* [Hungarian *gulyás*] : a stew made with meat, assorted vegetables, and paprika

go under *vb* : to be overwhelmed, defeated, or destroyed : FAIL

gourd \'gōrd, 'gùrd\ *n* 1 : any of a family of tendril-bearing vines including the cucumber, squash, and melon 2 : the fruit of a gourd; *esp* : any of various inedible hard-shelled fruits used esp. for ornament or implements

gourde \'gùrd\ *n* — see MONEY table

gour·mand \'gùr-‚mänd\ *n* 1 : one who is excessively fond of eating and drinking 2 : GOURMET

gour·met \'gùr-‚mā, gùr-'mā\ *n* [F, fr. MF, alter. of *gromet* boy servant, vintner's assistant] : a connoisseur of food and drink

gout \'gaút\ *n* : a metabolic disease marked by painful inflammation and swelling of the joints — **gouty** *adj*

gov *abbr* 1 government 2 governor

gov·ern \'gə-vərn\ *vb* 1 : to control and direct the making and administration of policy in : RULE 2 : CONTROL, DIRECT, INFLUENCE 3 : DETERMINE, REGULATE 4 : RESTRAIN — **gov·er·nance** \-vər-nəns\ *n*

gov·ern·ess \'gə-vər-nəs\ *n* : a woman who teaches and trains a child esp. in a private home

gov·ern·ment \'gə-vərn-mənt\ *n* 1 : authoritative direction or control : RULE 2 : the making of policy 3 : the organization or agency through which a political unit exercises authority 4 : the complex of institutions, laws, and customs through which a political unit is governed 5 : the governing body — **gov·ern·men·tal** \‚gə-vərn-'ment-əl\ *adj*

gov·er·nor \'gə-vər-nər\ *n* 1 : one that governs; *esp* : a ruler, chief executive, or head of a political unit (as a state) 2 : an attachment to a machine for automatic control of speed — **gov·er·nor·ship** *n*

govt *abbr* government

gown \'gaún\ *n* 1 : a loose flowing outer garment 2 : an official robe worn esp. by a judge, clergyman, or teacher 3 : a woman's dress ⟨evening ∼s⟩ 4 : a loose robe — **gown** *vb*

gp *abbr* group

GP *abbr* general practitioner

GPO *abbr* 1 general post office 2 Government Printing Office

GQ *abbr* general quarters

gr *abbr* 1 grade 2 grain 3 gram 4 gravity 5 gross

grab \'grab\ *vb* **grabbed; grab·bing** : to take hastily : SNATCH — **grab** *n*

¹grace \'grās\ *n* 1 : unmerited help given to people by God (as in overcoming temptation) 2 : freedom from sin through divine grace 3 : a virtue coming from God 4 — used as a title for a duke, a duchess, or an archbishop 5 : a short prayer at a meal 6 : a temporary respite (as from the payment of a debt) 7 : APPROVAL, ACCEPTANCE ⟨in his good ∼s⟩ 8 : CHARM 9 : ATTRACTIVENESS, BEAUTY 10 : fitness or proportion of line or expression 11 : ease of movement 12 : a musical trill or ornament — **grace·ful** \-fəl\ *adj* — **grace·ful·ly** *adv* — **grace·ful·ness** *n* — **grace·less** *adj*

²grace *vb* **graced; grac·ing** 1 : HONOR 2 : ADORN, EMBELLISH

gra·cious \'grā-shəs\ *adj* 1 : marked by kindness and courtesy 2 : GRACEFUL 3 : characterized by charm and good taste 4 : MERCIFUL — **gra·cious·ly** *adv* — **gra·cious·ness** *n*

grack·le \'gra-kəl\ *n* : any of several American blackbirds with glossy iridescent plumage

grad *abbr* graduate; graduated

gra·da·tion \grā-'dā-shən, grə-\ *n* 1 : a series forming successive stages 2 : a step, degree, or stage in a series 3 : an advance by regular degrees 4 : the act or process of grading

¹grade \'grād\ *vb* **grad·ed; grad·ing** 1 : to arrange in grades : SORT 2 : to make level or evenly sloping ⟨∼ a highway⟩ 3 : to give a grade to ⟨∼ a pupil in history⟩ 4 : to assign a grade to

²grade *n* 1 : a degree or stage in a series, order, or ranking 2 : a position in a scale of rank, quality, or order

3 : a class of persons or things of the same rank or quality **4** : a division of the school course representing one year's work; *also* : the pupils in such a division **5** *pl* : the elementary school system **6** : a mark or rating esp. of accomplishment in school **7** : the degree of slope (as of a road); *also* : SLOPE

grad·er \'grā-dər\ *n* : a machine for leveling earth

grade school *n* : ELEMENTARY SCHOOL

gra·di·ent \'grā-dē-ənt\ *n* : SLOPE, GRADE

grad·u·al \'gra-jə-wəl\ *adj* : proceeding or changing by steps or degrees — **grad·u·al·ly** *adv*

grad·u·al·ism \-wə-ˌli-zəm\ *n* : the policy of approaching a desired end gradually

¹grad·u·ate \'gra-jə-wət\ *n* **1** : a holder of an academic degree or diploma **2** : a graduated container for measuring contents

²graduate *adj* **1** : holding an academic degree or diploma **2** : of or relating to studies beyond the first or bachelor's degree ⟨~ school⟩

³grad·u·ate \'gra-jə-ˌwāt\ *vb* **-at·ed; -at·ing 1** : to grant or receive an academic degree or diploma **2** : to divide into grades, classes, or intervals **3** : to admit to a particular standing or grade

grad·u·a·tion \ˌgra-jə-'wā-shən\ *n* **1** : a mark that graduates something **2** : an act or process of graduating **3** : COMMENCEMENT

graf·fi·to \gra-'fē-tō, grə-\ *n, pl* **-ti** \-(ˌ)tē\ : an inscription or drawing made on a public surface (as a wall)

¹graft \'graft\ *n* **1** : a grafted plant; *also* : the point of union in this **2** : material (as skin) used in grafting **3** : the getting of money or advantage dishonestly; *also* : the money or advantage so gained

graft 1

²graft *vb* **1** : to insert a shoot from one plant into another so that they join and grow; *also* : to join one thing to another as in plant grafting ⟨~ skin over a burn⟩ **2** : to get (as money) dishonestly — **graft·er** *n*

gra·ham cracker \'grā-əm-, 'gram-\ *n* : a slightly sweet cracker made chiefly of whole wheat flour

Grail \'grāl\ *n* : the cup or platter used according to medieval legend by Christ at the Last Supper and thereafter the object of knightly quests

grain \'grān\ *n* **1** : a seed or fruit of a cereal grass **2** : seeds or fruits of various food plants and esp. cereal grasses; *also* : a plant (as wheat) producing grain **3** : a small hard particle **4** : a unit of weight based on the weight of a grain of wheat — see WEIGHT table **5** : TEXTURE; *also* : the arrangement of fibers in wood **6** : natural disposition — **grained** \'grānd\ *adj*

grain alcohol *n* : ALCOHOL 1

grainy \'grā-nē\ *adj* **grain·i·er; -est 1** : resembling or having some characteristic of grain : not smooth or fine **2** *of a photograph* : appearing to be composed of grain-like particles

¹gram \'gram\ *n* [F *gramme*, fr. LL *gramma*, a small weight, fr. Gk *gramma* letter, writing, a small weight, fr. *graphein* to write] : a metric unit of mass and weight equal to ¹/₁₀₀₀ kilogram — see METRIC SYSTEM table

²gram *abbr* grammar; grammatical

-gram \ˌgram\ *n comb form* : drawing : writing : record ⟨tele*gram*⟩

gram·mar \'gra-mər\ *n* **1** : the study of the classes of words, their inflections, and their functions and relations in the sentence **2** : a study of what is to be pre-

ferred and what avoided in inflection and syntax **3** : speech or writing evaluated according to its conformity to grammatical rules — **gram·mar·i·an** \grə-'mer-ē-ən, -'mar-\ *n* — **gram·mat·i·cal** \-'ma-ti-kəl\ *adj* — **gram·mat·i·cal·ly** \-k(ə-)lē\ *adv*

grammar school *n* **1** : a secondary school emphasizing Latin and Greek in preparation for college; *also* : a British college preparatory school **2** : a school intermediate between the primary grades and high school **3** : ELEMENTARY SCHOOL

gramme \'gram\ *chiefly Brit var of* GRAM

gram·o·phone \'gra-mə-ˌfōn\ *n* : PHONOGRAPH

gra·na·ry \'grā-nə-rē, 'gra-\ *n, pl* **-ries 1** : a storehouse for grain **2** : a region producing grain in abundance

¹grand \'grand\ *adj* **1** : higher in rank or importance : FOREMOST, CHIEF **2** : great in size **3** : INCLUSIVE, COMPLETE ⟨a ~ total⟩ **4** : MAGNIFICENT, SPLENDID **5** : showing wealth or high social standing **6** : IMPRESSIVE, STATELY **7** : very good : FINE — **grand·ly** *adv* — **grand·ness** *n*

²grand *n, slang* : a thousand dollars

gran·dam \'gran-ˌdam, -dəm\ *or* **gran·dame** \-ˌdām, -dəm\ *n* : an old woman

grand·child \'grand-ˌchīld\ *n* : a child of one's son or daughter

grand·daugh·ter \'gran-ˌdȯ-tər\ *n* : a daughter of one's son or daughter

grande dame \grän-'däm\ *n, pl* **grandes dames** : a usu. elderly woman of great prestige or ability

gran·dee \gran-'dē\ *n* : a high-ranking Spanish or Portuguese nobleman

gran·deur \'gran-jər\ *n* **1** : the quality or state of being grand : MAGNIFICENCE **2** : something that is grand

grand·fa·ther \'grand-ˌfä-thər\ *n* : the father of one's father or mother; *also* : ANCESTOR

grandfather clock *n* : a tall clock that stands on the floor

gran·dil·o·quence \gran-'di-lə-kwəns\ *n* : pompous eloquence — **gran·dil·o·quent** \-kwənt\ *adj*

gran·di·ose \'gran-dē-ˌōs, ˌgran-dē-'ōs\ *adj* : IMPRESSIVE, IMPOSING; *also* : affectedly splendid — **gran·di·ose·ly** *adv* — **gran·di·os·i·ty** \ˌgran-dē-'ä-sə-tē\ *n*

grand jury *n* : a jury that examines accusations of crime against persons and makes formal charges on which the persons are later tried

grand mal \'grän-ˌmäl; 'grand-ˌmal\ *n* [F, lit., great illness] : severe epilepsy

grand·moth·er \'grand-ˌmə-thər\ *n* : the mother of one's father or mother; *also* : a female ancestor

grand·par·ent \-ˌpar-ənt\ *n* : a parent of one's father or mother

grand piano *n* : a piano with horizontal frame and strings

grand prix \grän-'prē\ *n, pl* **grand prix** *same or* -'prēz\ *often cap G&P* : a long-distance auto race over a road course

grand slam *n* **1** : a total victory or success **2** : a home run hit with three runners on base

grand·son \'grand-ˌsən\ *n* : a son of one's son or daughter

grand·stand \-ˌstand\ *n* : a usu. roofed stand for spectators at a racecourse or stadium

grange \'grānj\ *n* **1** : a farm or farmhouse with its various buildings **2** *cap* : one of the lodges of a national association originally made up of farmers; *also* : the association itself — **grang·er** \'grān-jər\ *n*

gran·ite \'gra-nət\ *n* : a hard granular igneous rock used esp. for building — **gra·nit·ic** \gra-'ni-tik\ *adj*

gran·ite·ware \'gra-nət-ˌwar\ *n* : ironware with mottled enamel

gra·no·la \grə-'nō-lə\ *n* : a cereal made of rolled oats and usu. raisins and nuts

¹grant \'grant\ *vb* **1** : to consent to : ALLOW, PERMIT **2** : GIVE, BESTOW **3** : to admit as true — **grant·ee** *n* — **grant·or** \'gran-tər, -ˌtȯr\ *n*

²grant *n* **1** : the act of granting **2** : something granted;

esp : a gift for a particular purpose ⟨a ∼ for study abroad⟩ **3** : a transfer of property by deed or writing; *also* : the instrument by which such a transfer is made **4** : the property transferred by grant — **grant·ee** \gran-ˈtē\ n

gran·u·lar \ˈgra-nyə-lər\ adj : consisting of or appearing to consist of granules — **gran·u·lar·i·ty** \ˌgra-nyə-ˈlar-ə-tē\ n

gran·u·late \ˈgra-nyə-ˌlāt\ vb **-lat·ed; -lat·ing** : to form into grains or crystals — **gran·u·la·tion** \ˌgra-nyə-ˈlā-shən\ n

gran·ule \ˈgra-nyül\ n : a small grain or particle

grape \ˈgrāp\ n [ME, fr. OF *crape, grape* hook, grape stalk, bunch of grapes, grape] **1** : a smooth-skinned juicy edible greenish white, deep red, or purple berry that is the chief source of wine **2** : any of numerous woody vines widely grown for their bunches of grapes

grape·fruit \ˈgrāp-ˌfrüt\ n **1** *pl* **grapefruit** *or* **grapefruits** : a large edible yellow-skinned citrus fruit **2** : a tree bearing grapefruit

grape hyacinth n : any of several small bulbous spring-flowering herbs with clusters of usu. blue flowers that are related to the lilies

grape·shot \ˈgrāp-ˌshät\ n : a cluster of small iron balls formerly fired at people from short range by a cannon

grape·vine \-ˌvīn\ n **1** : GRAPE 2 **2** : RUMOR; *also* : an informal means of circulating information or gossip

graph \ˈgraf\ n : a diagram that usu. by means of dots and lines shows change in one variable factor in comparison with one or more other factors — **graph** vb

-graph \ˌgraf\ n comb form **1** : something written ⟨auto*graph*⟩ **2** : instrument for making or transmitting records ⟨seismo*graph*⟩

¹graph·ic \ˈgra-fik\ *also* **graph·i·cal** \-fi-kəl\ adj **1** : being written, drawn, or engraved **2** : vividly described **3** : of or relating to the arts (**graphic arts**) of representation, decoration, and printing on flat surfaces — **graph·i·cal·ly** \-fi-k(ə-)lē\ adv

²graphic n **1** : a picture, map, or graph used for illustration **2** *pl* : a display (as of pictures or graphs) generated by a computer on a screen, printer, or plotter

graph·ics tablet \-fiks-\ n : a computer input device for entering pictorial information by drawing or tracing

graph·ite \ˈgra-ˌfīt\ n [G *Graphit*, fr. Gk *graphein* to write] : a soft black form of carbon used esp. for lead pencils and lubricants

grap·nel \ˈgrap-nəl\ n : a small anchor with usu. four claws used esp. in dragging or grappling operations

¹grap·ple \ˈgra-pəl\ n [MF *grappelle*, dim. of *grape* hook] : the act of grappling

²grapple vb **grap·pled; grap·pling** **1** : to seize or hold with or as if with a hooked implement **2** : to come to grips with : WRESTLE

¹grasp \ˈgrasp\ vb **1** : to make the motion of seizing **2** : to take or seize firmly **3** : to enclose and hold with the fingers or arms **4** : COMPREHEND

²grasp n **1** : HANDLE **2** : EMBRACE **3** : HOLD, CONTROL **4** : the reach of the arms **5** : the power of seizing and holding **6** : COMPREHENSION

grasp·ing adj : GREEDY, AVARICIOUS

grass \ˈgras\ n **1** : herbage for grazing animals **2** : any of a large family of plants (as wheat, bamboo, or sugarcane) with jointed stems and narrow leaves **3** : grass-covered land **4** : MARIJUANA — **grassy** adj

grass·hop·per \-ˌhä-pər\ n : any of numerous leaping plant-eating insects

grass·land \-ˌland\ n : land covered naturally or under cultivation with grasses and low-growing herbs

grass roots n pl : society at the local level as distinguished from the centers of political leadership

¹grate \ˈgrāt\ vb **grat·ed; grat·ing** **1** : to pulverize by rubbing against something rough **2** : to grind or rub against with a rasping noise **3** : IRRITATE — **grat·er** n — **grat·ing·ly** adv

²grate n **1** : GRATING **2** : a frame of iron bars for holding fuel while it burns

grate·ful \ˈgrāt-fəl\ adj **1** : THANKFUL, APPRECIATIVE; *also* : expressing gratitude **2** : PLEASING — **grate·ful·ly** adv — **grate·ful·ness** n

grat·i·fy \ˈgra-tə-ˌfī\ vb **-fied; -fy·ing** : to afford pleasure to — **grat·i·fi·ca·tion** \ˌgra-tə-fə-ˈkā-shən\ n

grat·ing \ˈgrā-tiŋ\ n : a framework with parallel bars or crossbars

gra·tis \ˈgra-təs, ˈgrā-\ adv or adj : without charge or recompense : FREE

grat·i·tude \ˈgra-tə-ˌtüd, -ˌtyüd\ n : THANKFULNESS

gra·tu·itous \grə-ˈtü-ə-təs, -ˈtyü\ adj **1** : done or provided without recompense : FREE **2** : UNWARRANTED

gra·tu·ity \-ə-tē\ n, pl **-ities** : ¹⁰TIP

gra·va·men \grə-ˈvā-mən\ n, pl **-va·mens** or **-vam·i·na** \-ˈva-mə-nə\ [LL, burden] : the basic or significant part of a grievance or complaint

¹grave \ˈgrāv\ vb **graved; grav·en** \ˈgrā-vən\ or **graved; grav·ing** : SCULPTURE, ENGRAVE

²grave n : an excavation in the earth as a place of burial; *also* : TOMB

³grave \ˈgrāv; 5 *also* ˈgräv\ adj **1** : IMPORTANT **2** : threatening great harm or danger **3** : DIGNIFIED, SOLEMN **4** : drab in color : SOMBER **5** : of, marked by, or being an accent mark having the form — **grave·ly** adv — **grave·ness** n

grav·el \ˈgra-vəl\ n : pebbles and small pieces of rock larger than grains of sand — **grav·el·ly** adj

grave·stone \ˈgrāv-ˌstōn\ n : a burial monument

grave·yard \-ˌyärd\ n : CEMETERY

grav·id \ˈgra-vəd\ adj [L *gravidus*, fr. *gravis* heavy] : PREGNANT

gra·vi·me·ter \gra-ˈvi-mə-tər, ˈgra-və-ˌmē-\ n : a device for measuring variations in a gravitational field

grav·i·tate \ˈgra-və-ˌtāt\ vb **-tat·ed; -tat·ing** : to move or tend to move toward something

grav·i·ta·tion \ˌgra-və-ˈtā-shən\ n **1** : a natural force of attraction that tends to draw bodies together and that occurs because of the mass of the bodies **2** : the action or process of gravitating — **grav·i·ta·tion·al** \-shə-nəl\ adj — **grav·i·ta·tion·al·ly** adv

grav·i·ty \ˈgra-və-tē\ n, pl **-ties** **1** : IMPORTANCE; *esp* : SERIOUSNESS **2** : ²MASS 5 **3** : the gravitational attraction of the mass of a celestial object (as earth) for bodies close to it; *also* : GRAVITATION 1

gra·vure \grə-ˈvyu̇r\ n [F] : PHOTOGRAVURE

gra·vy \ˈgrā-vē\ n, pl **gravies** **1** : a sauce made from the thickened and seasoned juices of cooked meat **2** : unearned or illicit gain : GRAFT

¹gray \ˈgrā\ adj **1** : of the color gray; *also* : dull in color **2** : having gray hair **3** : CHEERLESS, DISMAL **4** : intermediate in position or character — **gray·ish** adj — **gray·ness** n

²gray n **1** : something of a gray color **2** : a neutral color ranging between black and white

³gray vb : to make or become gray

gray·beard \ˈgrā-ˌbird\ n : an old man

gray·ling \ˈgrā-liŋ\ n, pl **grayling** *also* **graylings** : any of several slender freshwater food and sport fishes related to the trouts

gray matter n **1** : the grayish part of nervous tissue consisting mostly of nerve cell bodies **2** : INTELLIGENCE

gray wolf n : a large wolf of northern No. America and Asia that is usu. gray

¹graze \ˈgrāz\ vb **grazed; graz·ing** **1** : to feed on herbage or pasture **2** : to feed (livestock) on grass or pasture — **graz·er** n

²graze vb **grazed; graz·ing** **1** : to touch lightly in passing **2** : SCRATCH, ABRADE

¹grease \ˈgrēs\ n **1** : rendered animal fat **2** : oily material **3** : a thick lubricant — **greasy** \ˈgrē-sē, -zē\ adj

²grease \ˈgrēs, ˈgrēz\ vb **greased; greas·ing** : to smear or lubricate with grease

grease·paint \ˈgrēs-ˌpānt\ n : theater makeup

great \'grāt\ *adj* **1** : large in size : BIG **2** : ELABORATE, AMPLE **3** : large in number : NUMEROUS **4** : being beyond the average : MIGHTY, INTENSE ⟨a ~ weight⟩ ⟨in ~ pain⟩ **5** : EMINENT, GRAND **6** : long continued ⟨a ~ while⟩ **7** : MAIN, PRINCIPAL **8** : more distant in a family relationship by one generation ⟨a *great*-grandfather⟩ **9** : markedly superior in character, quality, or skill ⟨~ at bridge⟩ **10** : EXCELLENT, FINE ⟨had a ~ time⟩ — **great•ly** *adv* — **great•ness** *n*

great circle *n* : a circle on the surface of a sphere that has the same center as the sphere; *esp* : one on the surface of the earth an arc of which is the shortest travel distance between two points

great•coat \'grāt-ˌkōt\ *n* : a heavy overcoat

Great Dane *n* : any of a breed of tall massive powerful smooth-coated dogs

great•heart•ed \'grāt-'här-təd\ *adj* **1** : COURAGEOUS **2** : MAGNANIMOUS

great power *n, often cap G&P* : one of the nations that figure most decisively in international affairs

great white shark *n* : a large and dangerous shark of warm seas that is light colored below and darker above becoming dirty white in older and larger specimens

grebe \'grēb\ *n* : any of a family of lobe-toed diving birds related to the loons

Gre•cian \'grē-shən\ *adj* : GREEK

greed \'grēd\ *n* : acquisitive or selfish desire beyond reason — **greed•i•ly** \'grē-də-lē\ *adv* — **greed•i•ness** \-dē-nəs\ *n* — **greedy** \'grē-dē\ *adj*

¹Greek \'grēk\ *n* **1** : a native or inhabitant of Greece **2** : the ancient or modern language of Greece

²Greek *adj* **1** : of, relating to, or characteristic of Greece, the Greeks, or Greek **2** : ORTHODOX **3**

¹green \'grēn\ *adj* **1** : of the color green **2** : covered with verdure; *also* : consisting of green plants or of the leafy parts of plants ⟨a ~ salad⟩ **3** : UNRIPE; *also* : IMMATURE **4** : having a sickly appearance **5** : not fully processed or treated ⟨~ liquor⟩ ⟨~ hides⟩ **6** : INEXPERIENCED; *also* : NAIVE **7** : concerned with or supporting environmentalism — **green•ish** *adj* — **green•ness** *n*

²green *vb* : to make or become green

³green *n* **1** : a color between blue and yellow in the spectrum : the color of growing fresh grass or of the emerald **2** : something of a green color **3** : green vegetation; *esp, pl* : leafy herbs or leafy parts of a vegetable ⟨collard ~s⟩ ⟨beet ~s⟩ **4** : a grassy plot; *esp* : a smooth grassy area around the hole into which the ball must be played in golf

green•back \'grēn-ˌbak\ *n* : a U.S. legal-tender note

green bean *n* : a kidney bean that is used as a snap bean when the pods are colored green

green•belt \'grēn-ˌbelt\ *n* : a belt of parks or farmlands around a community

green•ery \'grē-nə-rē\ *n, pl* **-er•ies** : green foliage or plants

green—eyed \'grē-'nīd\ *adj* : JEALOUS

green•gro•cer \'grēn-ˌgrō-sər\ *n* : a retailer of fresh vegetables and fruit

green•horn \-ˌhȯrn\ *n* : an inexperienced person; *also* : NEWCOMER

green•house \-ˌhaus\ *n* : a glass structure for the growing of tender plants

greenhouse effect *n* : warming of a planet's atmosphere that occurs when the sun's radiation passes through the atmosphere, is absorbed by the planet, and is reradiated as radiation of longer wavelength that can be absorbed by atmospheric gases

green manure *n* : an herbaceous crop (as clover) plowed under when green to enrich the soil

green onion *n* : a young onion pulled before the bulb has enlarged and used esp. in salads; *also* : SCALLION

green pepper *n* : a sweet pepper before it turns red at maturity

green•room \'grēn-ˌrüm, -ˌrum\ *n* : a room in a theater or concert hall where actors or musicians relax before, between, or after appearances

green•sward \-ˌsword\ *n* : turf that is green with growing grass

green thumb *n* : an unusual ability to make plants grow

Green•wich mean time \'gri-nij-, 'gre-, -nich-\ *n* [*Greenwich,* England] : the time of the meridian of Greenwich used as the basis of worldwide standard time

Greenwich time *n* : GREENWICH MEAN TIME

green•wood \'grēn-ˌwùd\ *n* : a forest green with foliage

greet \'grēt\ *vb* **1** : to address with expressions of kind wishes **2** : to meet or react to in a specified manner **3** : to be perceived by — **greet•er** *n*

greet•ing *n* **1** : a salutation on meeting **2** *pl* : best wishes : REGARDS

greeting card *n* : a card that bears a message usu. sent on a special occasion

gre•gar•i•ous \gri-'gar-ē-əs\ *adj* [L *gregarius* of a flock or herd, fr. *greg-, grex* flock, herd] **1** : SOCIAL, COMPANIONABLE **2** : tending to flock together — **gre•gar•i•ous•ly** *adv* — **gre•gar•i•ous•ness** *n*

grem•lin \'grem-lən\ *n* : a cause of error or equipment malfunction conceived of as a small gnome

gre•nade \grə-'nād\ *n* [MF, pomegranate, fr. LL *granata,* fr. L, fem. of *granatus* seedy, fr. *granum* grain] : a small bomb that is thrown by hand or launched (as by a rifle)

gren•a•dier \ˌgre-nə-'dir\ *n* : a member of a European regiment formerly armed with grenades

gren•a•dine \ˌgre-nə-'dēn, 'gre-nə-ˌdēn\ *n* : a syrup flavored with pomegranates and used in mixed drinks

grew *past of* GROW

grey *var of* GRAY

grey•hound \'grā-ˌhaund\ *n* : any of a breed of tall slender dogs noted for speed and keen sight

greyhound

grid \'grid\ *n* **1** : GRATING **2** : a network of conductors for distributing electric power **3** : a network of horizontal and perpendicular lines (as for locating points on a map) **4** : GRIDIRON 2; *also* : FOOTBALL

grid•dle \'grid-əl\ *n* : a flat usu. metal surface for cooking food

griddle cake *n* : PANCAKE

grid•iron \'grid-ˌīrn, -ˌī-ərn\ *n* **1** : a grate for broiling food **2** : a football field

grid•lock \-ˌläk\ *n* : a traffic jam in which an intersection is so blocked that vehicles cannot move

grief \'grēf\ *n* **1** : emotional distress caused by or as if by bereavement; *also* : a cause of such distress **2** : MISHAP **3** : DISASTER

griev•ance \'grē-vəns\ *n* **1** : a cause of distress affording reason for complaint or resistance **2** : COMPLAINT

grieve \'grēv\ *vb* **grieved; griev•ing** [ME *greven,* fr. OF *grever,* fr. L *gravare* to burden, fr. *gravis* heavy, grave] **1** : to cause grief or sorrow to : DISTRESS **2** : to feel grief : SORROW

griev·ous \'grē-vəs\ *adj* **1** : causing suffering, grief, or sorrow : SEVERE (a ~ wound) **2** : OPPRESSIVE, ONEROUS **3** : SERIOUS, GRAVE — **griev·ous·ly** *adv*

¹**grill** \'gril\ *vb* **1** : to broil on a grill; *also* : to fry or toast on a griddle **2** : to question intensely

²**grill** *n* **1** : a cooking utensil of parallel bars on which food is grilled **2** : an informal restaurant

grille *or* **grill** \'gril\ *n* : a grating that forms a barrier or screen

grill·work \'gril-ˌwərk\ *n* : work constituting or resembling a grille

grim \'grim\ *adj* **grim·mer**; **grim·mest 1** : CRUEL, FIERCE **2** : harsh and forbidding in appearance **3** : ghastly or repellent in character **4** : RELENTLESS — **grim·ly** *adv* — **grim·ness** *n*

gri·mace \'gri-məs, gri-ˈmās\ *n* : a facial expression usu. of disgust or disapproval — **grimace** *vb*

grime \'grīm\ *n* : soot, smut, or dirt adhering to or embedded in a surface; *also* : accumulated dirtiness and disorder — **grimy** *adj*

grin \'grin\ *vb* **grinned**; **grin·ning** : to draw back the lips so as to show the teeth esp. in amusement — **grin** *n*

¹**grind** \'grīnd\ *vb* **ground** \'graund\; **grind·ing 1** : to reduce to small particles **2** : to wear down, polish, or sharpen by friction **3** : OPPRESS **4** : to press with a grating noise : GRIT ⟨~ the teeth⟩ **5** : to operate or produce by turning a crank **6** : DRUDGE; *esp* : to study hard **7** : to move with difficulty or friction ⟨gears ~ing⟩

²**grind** *n* **1** : dreary monotonous labor, routine, or study **2** : one who works or studies excessively

grind·er \'grīn-dər\ *n* **1** : MOLAR **2** *pl* : TEETH **3** : one that grinds **4** : SUBMARINE **2**

grind·stone \'grīnd-ˌstōn\ *n* : a flat circular stone of natural sandstone that revolves on an axle and is used for grinding, shaping, or smoothing

¹**grip** \'grip\ *vb* **gripped**; **grip·ping 1** : to seize or hold firmly **2** : to hold the interest of strongly

²**grip** *n* **1** : GRASP; *also* : strength in gripping **2** : a firm tenacious hold **3** : UNDERSTANDING **4** : a device for gripping **5** : TRAVELING BAG

gripe \'grip\ *vb* **griped**; **grip·ing 1** : IRRITATE, VEX **2** : to cause or experience spasmodic pains in the bowels **3** : COMPLAIN — **gripe** *n*

grippe \'grip\ *n* : INFLUENZA

gris–gris \'grē-ˌgrē\ *n, pl* **gris–gris** \-ˌgrēz\ [F] : an amulet or incantation used chiefly by people of black African ancestry

gris·ly \'griz-lē\ *adj* **gris·li·er**; **-est** : HORRIBLE, GRUESOME

grist \'grist\ *n* : grain to be ground or already ground

gris·tle \'gri-səl\ *n* : CARTILAGE — **gris·tly** \'gris-lē\ *adj*

grist·mill \'grist-ˌmil\ *n* : a mill for grinding grain

¹**grit** \'grit\ *n* **1** : a hard sharp granule (as of sand); *also* : material composed of such granules **2** : unyielding courage — **grit·ty** *adj*

²**grit** *vb* **grit·ted**; **grit·ting** : GRIND, GRATE

grits \'grits\ *n pl* : coarsely ground hulled grain ⟨hominy ~⟩

griz·zled \'gri-zəld\ *adj* : streaked or mixed with gray

griz·zly \'griz-lē\ *adj* **griz·zli·er**; **-est** : GRIZZLED

grizzly bear *n* : a large pale-coated bear of western No. America

gro *abbr* gross

groan \'grōn\ *vb* **1** : MOAN **2** : to make a harsh sound under sudden or prolonged strain ⟨the chair ~ed under his weight⟩ — **groan** *n*

groat \'grōt\ *n* : an old British coin worth four pennies

gro·cer \'grō-sər\ *n* [ME, fr. MF *grossier* wholesaler, fr. *gros* coarse, wholesale, fr. L *grossus* coarse] : a dealer esp. in staple foodstuffs — **gro·cery** \'grōs-rē, 'grōsh-, 'grō-sə-\ *n*

grog \'gräg\ *n* [*Old Grog*, nickname of Edward Vernon

†1757 Eng. admiral responsible for diluting the sailors' rum] : alcoholic liquor; *esp* : liquor (as rum) mixed with water

grog·gy \'grä-gē\ *adj* **grog·gi·er**; **-est** : weak and unsteady on the feet or in action — **grog·gi·ly** \-gə-lē\ *adv* — **grog·gi·ness** \-gē-nəs\ *n*

groin \'gróin\ *n* **1** : the juncture of the lower abdomen and inner part of the thigh; *also* : the region of this juncture **2** : the curved line or rib on a ceiling along which two vaults meet

grom·met \'grä-mət, 'grə-\ *n* **1** : a ring of rope **2** : an eyelet of firm material to strengthen or protect an opening

¹**groom** \'grüm, 'grum\ *n* **1** : a person responsible for the care of horses **2** : BRIDEGROOM

²**groom** *vb* **1** : to clean and care for (an animal) **2** : to make neat or attractive **3** : PREPARE

grooms·man \'grümz-mən, 'grumz-\ *n* : a male friend who attends a bridegroom at his wedding

groove \'grüv\ *n* **1** : a long narrow channel **2** : a fixed routine — **groove** *vb*

groovy \'grü-vē\ *adj* **groov·i·er**; **-est 1** : EXCELLENT **2** : HIP

grope \'grōp\ *vb* **groped**; **grop·ing 1** : to feel about or search for blindly or uncertainly ⟨~ for the right word⟩ **2** : to feel one's way by groping

gros·beak \'grōs-ˌbēk\ *n* : any of several finches of Europe or America with large stout conical bills

gro·schen \'grō-shən\ *n, pl* **groschen** — see *schilling* at MONEY table

gros·grain \'grō-ˌgrān\ *n* [F *gros grain* coarse texture] : a silk or rayon fabric with crosswise cotton ribs

¹**gross** \'grōs\ *adj* **1** : glaringly noticeable **2** : OUT-AND-OUT, UTTER **3** : BIG, BULKY; *esp* : excessively fat **4** : GENERAL, BROAD **5** : consisting of an overall total exclusive of deductions ⟨~ earnings⟩ **6** : CARNAL, EARTHY ⟨~ pleasures⟩ **7** : UNREFINED; *also* : crudely vulgar **8** : lacking knowledge — **gross·ly** *adv* — **gross·ness** *n*

²**gross** *n* : an overall total exclusive of deductions — **gross** *vb*

³**gross** *n, pl* **gross** : a total of 12 dozen things ⟨a ~ of pencils⟩

gross national product *n* : the total value of the goods and services produced in a nation during a year

gro·szy \'grō-shē\ *n, pl* **groszy** — see *zloty* at MONEY table

grot \'grät\ *n* : GROTTO

gro·tesque \grō-ˈtesk\ *adj* **1** : FANCIFUL, BIZARRE **2** : absurdly incongruous **3** : ECCENTRIC — **gro·tesque·ly** *adv*

grot·to \'grä-tō\ *n, pl* **grottoes** *also* **grottos 1** : CAVE **2** : an artificial cavelike structure

grouch \'grauch\ *n* **1** : a fit of bad temper **2** : an habitually irritable or complaining person — **grouch** *vb* — **grouchy** *adj*

¹**ground** \'graund\ *n* **1** : the bottom of a body of water **2** *pl* : sediment at the bottom of a liquid **3** : a basis for belief, action, or argument **4** : BACKGROUND **5** : the surface of the earth; *also* : SOIL **6** : an area with a particular use ⟨fishing ~s⟩ **7** *pl* : the area about and belonging to a building **8** : a conductor that makes electrical connection with the earth — **ground·less** *adj*

²**ground** *vb* **1** : to bring to or place on the ground **2** : to run or cause to run aground **3** : to provide a reason or justification for **4** : to furnish with a foundation of knowledge **5** : to connect electrically with a ground **6** : to restrict to the ground; *also* : prohibit from some activity

³**ground** *past and past part of* GRIND

ground ball *n* : a batted baseball that rolls or bounces along the ground

ground cover *n* : low plants that grow over and cover the soil; *also* : a plant suitable for use as ground cover

ground·er \'graun-dər\ *n* : GROUND BALL

ground·hog \'graund-ˌhȯg, -ˌhäg\ *n* : WOODCHUCK
ground·ling \'graund-liŋ\ *n* : a spectator in the pit of an Elizabethan theater
ground rule *n* **1** : a sports rule adopted to modify play on a particular field, court, or course **2** : a rule of procedure
ground squirrel *n* : any of various burrowing rodents of No. America and Eurasia that are related to the squirrels and live in colonies in open areas
ground swell *n* **1** : a broad deep ocean swell caused by an often distant gale or earthquake **2** *usu* **ground-swell** : a rapid spontaneous growth (as of political opinion)
ground·wa·ter \'graund-ˌwȯ-tər, -ˌwä-\ *n* : water within the earth that supplies wells and springs
ground·work \-ˌwərk\ *n* : FOUNDATION, BASIS
ground zero *n* : the point above, below, or at which a nuclear explosion occurs
¹group \'grüp\ *n* **1** : a number of individuals related by a common factor (as physical association, community of interests, or blood) **2** : a combination of atoms commonly found together in a molecule ⟨a methyl ∼⟩
²group *vb* : to associate in groups : CLUSTER, AGGREGATE
grou·per \'grü-pər\ *n, pl* **groupers** *also* **grouper** : any of numerous large solitary bottom fishes of warm seas
group·ie \'grü-pē\ *n* : a fan of a rock group who usu. follows the group around on concert tours; *also* : ENTHUSIAST, FAN
group therapy *n* : therapy in the presence of a therapist in which several patients discuss their personal problems
¹grouse \'graus\ *n, pl* **grouse** *or* **grouses** : any of numerous ground-dwelling game birds that have feathered legs and are usu. of reddish brown or other protective color
²grouse *vb* **groused; grous·ing** : COMPLAIN, GRUMBLE
grout \'graut\ *n* : material (as mortar) used for filling spaces — **grout** *vb*
grove \'grōv\ *n* : a small wood usu. without underbrush
grov·el \'grä-vəl, 'grə-\ *vb* **-eled** *or* **-elled; -el·ing** *or* **-el·ling 1** : to creep or lie with the body prostrate in fear or humility **2** : to abase oneself
grow \'grō\ *vb* **grew** \'grü\; **grown** \'grōn\; **grow·ing 1** : to spring up and develop to maturity **2** : to be able to grow : THRIVE **3** : to take on some relation through or as if through growth ⟨tree limbs *grown* together⟩ **4** : INCREASE, EXPAND **5** : to develop from a parent source **6** : BECOME **7** : to have an increasing influence **8** : to cause to grow — **grow·er** *n*
growl \'graul\ *vb* **1** : RUMBLE **2** : to utter a deep throaty sound **3** : GRUMBLE — **growl** *n*
grown–up \'grō-ˌnəp\ *adj* : not childish : ADULT — **grown–up** *n*
growth \'grōth\ *n* **1** : stage or condition attained in growing **2** : a process of growing esp. through progressive development or increase **3** : a result or product of growing ⟨a fine ∼ of hair⟩; *also* : an abnormal mass of tissue (as a tumor)
¹grub \'grəb\ *vb* **grubbed; grub·bing 1** : to clear or root out by digging **2** : to dig in the ground usu. for a hidden object **3** : to search about
²grub *n* **1** : a soft thick wormlike insect larva ⟨beetle ∼s⟩ **2** : DRUDGE; *also* : a slovenly person **3** : FOOD
grub·by \'grə-bē\ *adj* **grub·bi·er; -est** : DIRTY, SLOVENLY — **grub·bi·ness** \-bē-nəs\ *n*
grub·stake \'grəb-ˌstāk\ *n* : supplies or funds furnished a mining prospector in return for a share in his finds
¹grudge \'grəj\ *vb* **grudged; grudg·ing** : to be reluctant to give : BEGRUDGE
²grudge *n* : a feeling of deep-seated resentment or ill will
gru·el \'grü-əl\ *n* : a thin porridge

gru·el·ing *or* **gru·el·ling** \'grü-liŋ, 'grü-ə-\ *adj* : requiring extreme effort : EXHAUSTING
grue·some \'grü-səm\ *adj* [fr. earlier *growsome*, fr. E dial. *grow, grue* to shiver] : inspiring horror or repulsion
gruff \'grəf\ *adj* **1** : rough in speech or manner **2** : being deep and harsh : HOARSE — **gruff·ly** *adv*
grum·ble \'grəm-bəl\ *vb* **grum·bled; grum·bling 1** : to mutter in discontent **2** : GROWL, RUMBLE — **grumbler** *n*
grumpy \'grəm-pē\ *adj* **grump·i·er; -est** : moodily cross : SURLY — **grump·i·ly** \-pə-lē\ *adv* — **grump·i·ness** \-pē-nəs\ *n*
grun·gy \'grən-jē\ *adj* **grun·gi·er; -est** : shabby or dirty in character or condition
grun·ion \'grən-yən\ *n* : a fish of the California coast which comes inshore to spawn at nearly full moon
grunt \'grənt\ *n* : a deep throaty sound (as that of a hog) — **grunt** *vb*
GSA *abbr* **1** General Services Administration **2** Girl Scouts of America
G suit *n* [*gravity suit*] : a suit for a pilot or astronaut designed to counteract the physiological effects of acceleration
GSUSA *abbr* Girl Scouts of the United States of America
gt *abbr* great
Gt Brit *abbr* Great Britain
gtd *abbr* guaranteed
GU *abbr* Guam
gua·ca·mo·le \ˌgwä-kə-'mō-lē\ *n* [MexSp] : mashed and seasoned avocado
gua·nine \'gwä-ˌnēn\ *n* : a purine base that codes genetic information in the molecular chain of DNA and RNA
gua·no \'gwä-nō\ *n* [Sp, fr. Quechua (a South American Indian language) *wanu* fertilizer, dung] : a substance composed chiefly of the excrement of seabirds and used as a fertilizer
gua·ra·ni \ˌgwär-ə-'nē\ *n, pl* **guaranies** *also* **guaranis** — see MONEY table
¹guar·an·tee \ˌgar-ən-'tē\ *n* **1** : GUARANTOR **2** : GUARANTY 1 **3** : an agreement by which one person undertakes to secure another in the possession or enjoyment of something **4** : an assurance of the quality of or of the length of use to be expected from a product offered for sale **5** : GUARANTY 4
²guarantee *vb* **-teed; -tee·ing 1** : to undertake to answer for the debt, failure to perform, or faulty performance of (another) **2** : to undertake an obligation to establish, perform, or continue **3** : to give security to
guar·an·tor \ˌgar-ən-'tȯr\ *n* : one who gives a guarantee
¹guar·an·ty \'gar-ən-tē\ *n, pl* **-ties 1** : an undertaking to answer for another's failure to pay a debt or perform a duty **2** : GUARANTEE 3 **3** : GUARANTOR **4** : PLEDGE, SECURITY
²guaranty *vb* **-tied; -ty·ing** : GUARANTEE
¹guard \'gärd\ *n* **1** : a person or a body of persons on sentinel duty **2** *pl* : troops assigned to protect a sovereign **3** : a defensive position (as in boxing) **4** : the act or duty of protecting or defending **5** : PROTECTION **6** : a protective or safety device **7** : a football lineman playing between center and tackle; *also* : a basketball player stationed toward the rear — **on guard** : WATCHFUL, ALERT
²guard *vb* **1** : PROTECT, DEFEND **2** : to watch over **3** : to be on guard
guard·house \'gärd-ˌhaus\ *n* **1** : a building occupied by a guard or used as a headquarters by soldiers on guard duty **2** : a military jail
guard·ian \'gär-dē-ən\ *n* **1** : CUSTODIAN **2** : one who has the care of the person or property of another — **guard·ian·ship** *n*
guard·room \'gärd-ˌrüm\ *n* **1** : a room used by a mil-

itary guard while on duty **2** : a room where military prisoners are confined

guards·man \\'gärdz-mən\ *n* : a member of a military body called *guard* or *guards*

Gua·te·ma·lan \ˌgwä-tə-'mä-lən\ *n* : a native or inhabitant of Guatemala — **Guatemalan** *adj*

gua·va \\'gwä-və\ *n* : the sweet yellow or pink acid fruit of a shrubby tropical American tree used esp. for making jam and jelly; *also* : the tree

gu·ber·na·to·ri·al \ˌgü-bər-nə-'tōr-ē-əl\ *adj* : of or relating to a governor

guer·don \\'gərd-ᵊn\ *n* : REWARD, RECOMPENSE

Guern·sey \\'gərn-zē\ *n, pl* **Guernseys** : any of a breed of fawn and white dairy cattle that produce rich yellowish milk

guer·ril·la *or* **gue·ril·la** \gə-'ri-lə\ *n* [Sp *guerrilla*, fr. dim. of *guerra* war, of Gmc origin] : one who engages in irregular warfare esp. as a member of an independent unit

guess \\'ges\ *vb* **1** : to form an opinion from little or no evidence **2** : BELIEVE, SUPPOSE **3** : to conjecture correctly about : DISCOVER — **guess** *n*

guest \\'gest\ *n* **1** : a person to whom hospitality (as of a house or a club) is extended **2** : a patron of a commercial establishment (as a hotel) **3** : a person not a regular member of a cast who appears on a program

guf·faw \(ˌ)gə-'fo\ *n* : a loud burst of laughter — **guffaw** *vb*

guid·ance \\'gīd-ᵊns\ *n* **1** : the act or process of guiding **2** : ADVICE, DIRECTION

¹guide \\'gīd\ *n* **1** : one who leads or directs another's course **2** : one who shows and explains points of interest **3** : something that provides guiding information; *also* : SIGNPOST **4** : a device to direct the motion of something

²guide *vb* **guid·ed; guid·ing 1** : to act as a guide to **2** : MANAGE, DIRECT **3** : to superintend the training of — **guid·able** \\'gī-də-bəl\ *adj*

guide·book \\'gīd-ˌbuk\ *n* : a book of information for travelers

guided missile *n* : a missile whose course may be altered during flight

guide dog *n* : a dog trained to lead the blind

guide·line \\'gīd-ˌlīn\ *n* : an indication or outline of policy or conduct

guide word *n* : a term at the head of a page of an alphabetical reference work that indicates the alphabetically first and last words on that page

gui·don \\'gī-ˌdän, 'gīd-ᵊn\ *n* : a small flag (as of a military unit)

guild \\'gild\ *n* : an association of people with common aims and interests; *esp* : a medieval association of merchants or craftsmen — **guild·hall** \-ˌhol\ *n*

guil·der \\'gil-dər\ *n* : GULDEN

guile \\'gīl\ *n* : deceitful cunning : DUPLICITY — **guile·ful** *adj* — **guile·less·ness** *n*

guil·lo·tine \\'gi-lə-ˌtēn, ˌgē-ə-'tēn\ *n* [F, fr. Joseph *Guillotin* †1814 Fr. physician] : a machine for beheading persons — **guillotine** *vb*

guilt \\'gilt\ *n* **1** : the fact of having committed an offense esp. against the law **2** : BLAMEWORTHINESS **3** : a feeling of responsibility for wrongdoing — **guilt·less** *adj*

guilty \\'gil-tē\ *adj* **guilt·i·er; -est 1** : having committed a breach of conduct or a crime **2** : suggesting or involving guilt **3** : aware of or suffering from guilt — **guilt·i·ly** \-tə-lē\ *adv* — **guilt·i·ness** \-tē-nəs\ *n*

guin·ea \\'gi-nē\ *n* **1** : a British gold coin no longer issued worth 21 shillings **2** : a unit of value equal to 21 shillings

guinea fowl *n* : a gray and white spotted West African bird related to the pheasants and widely raised for food; *also* : any of several related birds

guinea hen *n* : a female guinea fowl; *also* : GUINEA FOWL

Guin·ean \\'gi-nē-ən\ *n* : a native or inhabitant of Guinea — **Guinean** *adj*

guinea pig *n* **1** : a small stocky short-eared and nearly tailless So. American rodent often kept as a pet or used in lab research **2** : a subject of research or testing

guise \\'gīz\ *n* **1** : a form or style of dress : COSTUME **2** : external appearance : SEMBLANCE

gui·tar \gi-'tär\ *n* : a musical instrument with usu. six strings plucked with a pick or with the fingers

gulch \\'gəlch\ *n* : RAVINE

gul·den \\'gül-dən, 'gül-\ *n, pl* **guldens** *or* **gulden** — see MONEY table

gulf \\'gəlf\ *n* [ME *goulf*, fr. MF *golfe*, fr. It *golfo*, fr. LL *colpus*, fr. Gk *kolpos* bosom, gulf] **1** : a part of an ocean or sea partly or mostly surrounded by land **2** : ABYSS, CHASM **3** : a wide separation

¹gull \\'gəl\ *n* : any of numerous mostly white or gray long-winged web-footed seabirds

²gull *vb* : to make a dupe of : DECEIVE — **gull·ible** \\'gə-lə-bəl\ *adj*

³gull *n* : DUPE

gul·let \\'gə-lət\ *n* : ESOPHAGUS; *also* : THROAT

gul·ly \\'gə-lē\ *n, pl* **gullies** : a trench worn in the earth by and often filled with running water after rains

gulp \\'gəlp\ *vb* **1** : to swallow hurriedly or greedily **2** : SUPPRESS ⟨~ down a sob⟩ **3** : to catch the breath as if in taking a long drink — **gulp** *n*

¹gum \\'gəm\ *n* : the oral tissue that surrounds the necks of the teeth

²gum *n* **1** : a sticky plant exudate; *esp* : one that hardens on drying **2** : a sticky substance **3** : a preparation usu. of a plant gum sweetened and flavored and used for chewing — **gum·my** *adj*

gum arabic *n* : a water-soluble gum obtained from several acacias and used esp. in making inks, adhesives, confections, and pharmaceuticals

gum·bo \\'gəm-bō\ *n* [AmerF *gombo*, of Bantu origin] : a rich thick soup usu. thickened with okra

gum·drop \\'gəm-ˌdräp\ *n* : a candy made usu. from corn syrup with gelatin and coated with sugar crystals

gump·tion \\'gəmp-shən\ *n* **1** : shrewd common sense **2** : ENTERPRISE, INITIATIVE

gum·shoe \\'gəm-ˌshü\ *n* : DETECTIVE — **gumshoe** *vb*

¹gun \\'gən\ *n* **1** : CANNON **2** : a portable firearm **3** : a discharge of a gun **4** : something suggesting a gun in shape or function **5** : THROTTLE — **gunned** \\'gənd\ *adj*

²gun *vb* **gunned; gun·ning 1** : to hunt with a gun **2** : SHOOT **3** : to open up the throttle of so as to increase speed

gun·boat \\'gən-ˌbōt\ *n* : a small lightly armed ship for use in shallow waters

gun·fight \-ˌfīt\ *n* : a duel with guns — **gun·fight·er** *n*

gun·fire \-ˌfīr\ *n* : the firing of guns

gung ho \\'gəŋ-'hō\ *adj* [*Gung ho!*, motto (taken to mean "work together") adopted by certain U.S. marines in World War II, fr. Chin *gōnghé*, short for *Zhōngguó Gōngyè Hézuò Shè* Chinese Industrial Cooperatives Society] : extremely zealous or enthusiastic

gun·man \-mən\ *n* : a man armed with a gun; *esp* : a professional killer

gun·ner \\'gə-nər\ *n* **1** : a soldier or airman who operates or aims a gun **2** : one who hunts with a gun

gun·nery \\'gə-nə-rē\ *n* : the use of guns; *esp* : the science of the flight of projectiles and effective use of guns

gunnery sergeant *n* : a noncommissioned officer in the marine corps ranking next below a first sergeant

gun·ny·sack \\'gə-nē-ˌsak\ *n* : a sack made of a coarse heavy fabric (as burlap)

gun·point \\'gən-ˌpoint\ *n* : the muzzle of a gun — **at gunpoint** : under a threat of death by being shot

gun·pow·der \-₁paù-dər\ *n* : an explosive powder used in guns and blasting

gun·shot \-₁shät\ *n* **1** : shot fired from a gun **2** : the range of a gun ⟨within ∼⟩

gun–shy \-₁shī\ *adj* **1** : afraid of a loud noise **2** : markedly distrustful

gun·sling·er \-₁sliŋ-ər\ *n* : a skilled gunman esp. in the old West

gun·smith \-₁smith\ *n* : one who designs, makes, or repairs firearms

gun·wale *also* **gun·nel** \ˈgən-əl\ *n* : the upper edge of a ship's or boat's side

gup·py \ˈgə-pē\ *n, pl* **guppies** [R.J.L. *Guppy* †1916 Trinidadian naturalist] : a small brightly colored tropical fish

gur·gle \ˈgər-gəl\ *vb* **gur·gled; gur·gling** : to make a sound like that of an irregularly flowing or gently splashing liquid — **gurgle** *n*

Gur·kha \ˈgùr-kə, ˈgər-\ *n* : a soldier from Nepal in the British or Indian army

gur·ney \ˈgər-nē\ *n, pl* **gurneys** : a wheeled cot or stretcher

gu·ru \ˈgùr-ü\ *n, pl* **gurus** [Hindi *gurū*, fr. Sanskrit *guru*, fr. *guru*, adj., heavy, venerable] **1** : a personal religious and spiritual teacher in Hinduism **2** : a teacher in matters of fundamental concern **3** : EXPERT ⟨a fitness ∼⟩

gush \ˈgəsh\ *vb* **1** : to issue or pour forth copiously or violently : SPOUT **2** : to make an effusive display of affection or enthusiasm

gush·er \ˈgə-shər\ *n* : one that gushes; *esp* : an oil well with a large natural flow

gushy \ˈgə-shē\ *adj* **gush·i·er; -est** : marked by effusive sentimentality

gus·set \ˈgə-sət\ *n* : a triangular insert (as in a seam of a sleeve) to give width or strength — **gusset** *vb*

gus·sy up \ˈgə-sē-\ *vb* : to dress up

¹gust \ˈgəst\ *n* **1** : a sudden brief rush of wind **2** : a sudden outburst : SURGE — **gusty** *adj*

²gust *vb* : to blow in gusts

gus·ta·to·ry \ˈgəs-tə-₁tōr-ē\ *adj* : relating to or associated with the sense of taste

gus·to \ˈgəs-tō\ *n, pl* **gustoes** : enthusiastic enjoyment; *also* : VITALITY 4

¹gut \ˈgət\ *n* **1** *pl* : BOWELS, ENTRAILS **2** : the alimentary canal or a part of it (as the intestine); *also* : BELLY, ABDOMEN **3** *pl* : the inner essential parts **4** *pl* : COURAGE, PLUCK

²gut *vb* **gut·ted; gut·ting** **1** : EVISCERATE **2** : to destroy the inside of

gutsy \ˈgət-sē\ *adj* **guts·i·er; -est** : marked by courage and determination

gut·ter \ˈgə-tər\ *n* : a groove or channel for carrying off esp. rainwater

gut·ter·snipe \-₁snīp\ *n* : a street urchin

gut·tur·al \ˈgə-tə-rəl\ *adj* **1** : sounded in the throat **2** : being or marked by an utterance that is strange, unpleasant, or disagreeable — **guttural** *n*

gut·ty \ˈgə-tē\ *adj* **gut·ti·er; -est** **1** : GUTSY **2** : having a vigorous challenging quality

gut–wrench·ing \ˈgət-₁ren-chiŋ\ *adj* : causing emotional anguish

¹guy \ˈgī\ *n* : a rope, chain, or rod attached to something as a brace or guide

²guy *vb* : to steady or reinforce with a guy

³guy *n* : MAN, FELLOW; *also, pl* : PERSONS ⟨all the ∼s came⟩

⁴guy *vb* : to make fun of : RIDICULE

Guy·a·nese \₁gī-ə-ˈnēz\ *n, pl* **Guyanese** : a native or inhabitant of Guyana — **Guyanese** *adj*

guz·zle \ˈgə-zəl\ *vb* **guz·zled; guz·zling** : to drink greedily

gym \ˈjim\ *n* : GYMNASIUM

gym·kha·na \jim-ˈkä-nə\ *n* : a meet featuring sports contests; *esp* : a contest of automobile-driving skill

gym·na·si·um *for 1* jim-ˈnä-zē-əm, -zhəm, *for 2* gim-ˈnä-zē-əm\ *n, pl* **-na·si·ums** *or* **-na·sia** \-ˈnä-zē-ə, -ˈnä-zhə; -ˈnä-zē-ə\ [L, exercise ground, school, fr. Gk *gymnasion*, fr. *gymnazein* to exercise naked, fr. *gymnos* naked] **1** : a room or building for indoor sports **2** : a European secondary school that prepares students for the university

gym·nas·tics \jim-ˈnas-tiks\ *n* : a competitive sport developed from physical exercises designed to demonstrate strength, balance, and body control — **gymnast** \ˈjim-₁nast\ *n* — **gym·nas·tic** *adj*

gym·no·sperm \ˈjim-nə-₁spərm\ *n* : any of a class or subdivision of woody vascular seed plants (as conifers) that produce naked seeds not enclosed in an ovary

gyn *or* **gynecol** *abbr* gynecology

gy·nae·col·o·gy *chiefly Brit var of* GYNECOLOGY

gy·ne·col·o·gy \₁gī-nə-ˈkä-lə-jē\ *n* : a branch of medicine dealing with the diseases and hygiene of women — **gy·ne·co·log·ic** \-ni-kə-ˈlä-jik\ *or* **gy·ne·co·log·i·cal** \-ji-kəl\ *adj* — **gy·ne·col·o·gist** \-nə-ˈkä-lə-jist\ *n*

gyp \ˈjip\ *n* **1** : CHEAT, SWINDLER **2** : FRAUD, SWINDLE — **gyp** *vb*

gyp·sum \ˈjip-səm\ *n* : a calcium-containing mineral used in making plaster of paris

Gyp·sy \ˈjip-sē\ *n, pl* **Gypsies** [by shortening & alter. fr. *Egyptian*] : a member of a traditionally traveling people coming orig. from India and living chiefly in Europe, Asia, and No. America; *also* : the language of the Gypsies

gypsy moth *n* : an Old World moth that was introduced into the U.S. where its caterpillar is a destructive defoliator of many trees

gy·rate \ˈjī-₁rāt\ *vb* **gy·rat·ed; gy·rat·ing** **1** : to revolve around a point or axis **2** : to oscillate with or as if with a circular or spiral motion — **gy·ra·tion** \jī-ˈrā-shən\ *n*

gyr·fal·con \ˈjər-₁fal-kən, -₁fòl-\ *n* : an arctic falcon with several color forms that is the largest of all falcons

gy·ro \ˈjī-rō\ *n, pl* **gyros** : GYROSCOPE

gy·ro·scope \ˈjī-rō-₁skōp\ *n* : a wheel or disk mounted to spin rapidly about an axis that is free to turn in various directions

Gy Sgt *abbr* gunnery sergeant

gyve \ˈjīv, ˈgīv\ *n* : FETTER — **gyve** *vb*

H

¹h \ˈāch\ *n, pl* **h's** *or* **hs** \ˈā-chəz\ *often cap* : the 8th letter of the English alphabet

²h *abbr, often cap* **1** hard; hardness **2** heroin **3** hit **4** husband

H *symbol* hydrogen

¹ha \ˈhä\ *interj* — used esp. to express surprise or joy

²ha *abbr* hectare

Hab *abbr* Habacuc; Habakkuk

Ha·ba·cuc \ˈha-bə-₁kək, hə-ˈba-kək\ *n* : HABAKKUK

Ha·bak·kuk \ˈha-bə-₁kək, hə-ˈba-kək\ *n* — see BIBLE table

ha·ba·ne·ra \₁hä-bə-ˈner-ə\ *n* [Sp *(danza) habanera*, lit., dance of Havana] : a Cuban dance in slow time; *also* : the music for this dance

ha·be·as cor·pus \ˈhā-bē-əs-ˈkòr-pəs\ *n* [ME, fr. ML, lit., you should have the body (the opening words of the writ)] : a writ issued to bring a party before a court

hab·er·dash·er \'ha-bər-ˌda-shər\ *n* : a dealer in men's clothing and accessories

hab·er·dash·ery \-ˌda-shə-rē\ *n, pl* **-er·ies** **1** : goods sold by a haberdasher **2** : a haberdasher's shop

ha·bil·i·ment \hə-'bi-lə-mənt\ *n* **1** *pl* : TRAPPINGS, EQUIPMENT **2** : DRESS; *esp* : the dress characteristic of an occupation or occasion — usu. used in pl.

hab·it \'ha-bət\ *n* **1** : DRESS, GARB **2** : BEARING, CONDUCT **3** : PHYSIQUE **4** : mental makeup **5** : a usual manner of behavior : CUSTOM **6** : a behavior pattern acquired by frequent repetition **7** : ADDICTION **8** : mode of growth or occurrence ⟨trees with a spreading ∼⟩

hab·it·able \'ha-bə-tə-bəl\ *adj* : capable of being lived in — **hab·it·abil·i·ty** \ˌha-bə-tə-'bi-lə-tē\ *n*

hab·i·tat \'ha-bə-ˌtat\ *n* [L, it inhabits] : the place or environment where a plant or animal naturally occurs

hab·i·ta·tion \ˌha-bə-'tā-shən\ *n* **1** : OCCUPANCY **2** : a dwelling place : RESIDENCE **3** : SETTLEMENT

hab·it–form·ing \'ha-bət-ˌfȯr-miŋ\ *adj* : causing addiction : ADDICTIVE

ha·bit·u·al \hə-'bi-chə-wəl\ *adj* **1** : CUSTOMARY **2** : doing, practicing, or acting by force of habit **3** : inherent in an individual — **ha·bit·u·al·ly** *adv* — **ha·bit·u·al·ness** *n*

ha·bit·u·ate \hə-'bi-chə-ˌwāt\ *vb* **-at·ed; -at·ing** **1** : ACCUSTOM **2** : to cause or undergo habituation

ha·bit·u·a·tion \hə-ˌbi-chə-'wā-shən\ *n* **1** : the process of making habitual **2** : psychological dependence on a drug after a period of use

ha·bi·tué *also* **ha·bi·tue** \hə-'bi-chə-ˌwā\ *n* [F] : one who may be regularly found in or at (as a place of entertainment)

ha·ci·en·da \ˌhä-sē-'en-də\ *n* **1** : a large estate in a Spanish-speaking country **2** : the main building of a farm or ranch

¹hack \'hak\ *vb* **1** : to cut or sever with repeated irregular blows **2** : to cough in a short dry manner **3** : to manage successfully; *also* : TOLERATE

²hack *n* **1** : an implement for hacking **2** : a short dry cough **3** : a hacking blow

³hack *n* **1** : a horse hired or used for varied work **2** : a horse worn out in service **3** : a light easy often 3-gaited saddle horse **4** : HACKNEY, TAXICAB **5** : a person who works solely for mercenary reasons; *esp* : a writer working solely for commercial success — **hack** *adj*

⁴hack *vb* : to operate a taxicab

hack·er \'ha-kər\ *n* **1** : one that hacks; *also* : a person unskilled at something **2** : an expert at using a computer **3** : a person who illegally gains access to and sometimes tampers with information in a computer system

hack·ie \'ha-kē\ *n* : a taxicab driver

hack·le \'ha-kəl\ *n* **1** : one of the long feathers on the neck or back of a bird **2** *pl* : hairs (as on a dog's neck) that can be erected **3** *pl* : TEMPER, DANDER

hack·man \'hak-mən\ *n* : HACKIE

¹hack·ney \'hak-nē\ *n, pl* **hackneys** **1** : a horse for riding or driving **2** : a carriage or automobile kept for hire

²hackney *vb* : to make trite

hack·neyed \'hak-nēd\ *adj* : lacking in freshness or originality

hack·saw \'hak-ˌsȯ\ *n* : a fine-tooth saw in a frame for cutting metal

hack·work \-ˌwərk\ *n* : work done on order usu. according to a formula

had *past and past part of* HAVE

had·dock \'ha-dək\ *n, pl* **haddock** *also* **haddocks** : an Atlantic food fish usu. smaller than the related cod

Ha·des \'hā-(ˌ)dēz\ *n* **1** : the abode of the dead in Greek mythology **2** *often not cap* : HELL

haf·ni·um \'haf-nē-əm\ *n* : a gray metallic chemical element — see ELEMENT table

haft \'haft\ *n* : the handle of a weapon or tool

hag \'hag\ *n* **1** : an ugly or evil-looking old woman **2** : WITCH 1

Hag *abbr* Haggai

Hag·gai \'ha-gē-ˌī, 'ha-ˌgī\ *n* — see BIBLE table

hag·gard \'ha-gərd\ *adj* : having a worn or emaciated appearance **syn** careworn, wasted, drawn — **hag·gard·ly** *adv* — **hag·gard·ness** *n*

hag·gis \'ha-gəs\ *n* : a traditionally Scottish dish made of the heart, liver, and lungs of a sheep or a calf minced with suet, onions, oatmeal, and seasonings

hag·gle \'ha-gəl\ *vb* **hag·gled; hag·gling** : to argue in bargaining — **hag·gler** *n*

Ha·gi·og·ra·pha \ˌha-gē-'ä-grə-fə, ˌhā-jē-\ *n pl* — see BIBLE table

ha·gi·og·ra·phy \ˌha-gē-'ä-grə-fē, ˌhā-jē-\ *n* **1** : biography of saints or venerated persons **2** : idealizing or idolizing biography — **ha·gi·og·ra·pher** \-fər\ *n*

hai·ku \'hī-(ˌ)kü\ *n, pl* **haiku** : an unrhymed Japanese verse form of three lines containing usu. 5, 7, and 5 syllables respectively; *also* : a poem in this form

¹hail \'hāl\ *n* **1** : precipitation in the form of small lumps of ice **2** : something that gives the effect of falling hail

²hail *vb* **1** : to precipitate hail **2** : to pour down and strike like hail

³hail *interj* [ME, fr. ON *heill*, fr. *heill* healthy] — used to express acclamation

⁴hail *vb* **1** : SALUTE, GREET **2** : SUMMON

⁵hail *n* **1** : an expression of greeting, approval, or praise **2** : hearing distance

Hail Mary *n* : a salutation and prayer to the Virgin Mary

hail·stone \'hāl-ˌstōn\ *n* : a pellet of hail

hail·storm \-ˌstȯrm\ *n* : a storm accompanied by hail

hair \'har\ *n* : a threadlike outgrowth esp. from the skin of a mammal; *also* : a covering or growth of hairs of an animal or a body part — **haired** \'hard\ *adj* — **hair·less** *adj*

hair·breadth \'har-ˌbredth\ *or* **hairs·breadth** \'harz-\ *n* : a very small distance or margin

hair·brush \-ˌbrəsh\ *n* : a brush for the hair

hair·cloth \-ˌklȯth\ *n* : a stiff wiry fabric used esp. for upholstery

hair·cut \-ˌkət\ *n* : the act, process, or style of cutting and shaping the hair

hair·do \-ˌdü\ *n, pl* **hairdos** : a way of wearing the hair

hair·dress·er \-ˌdre-sər\ *n* : one who dresses or cuts hair — **hair·dress·ing** *n*

hair·line \-ˌlīn\ *n* **1** : a very thin line **2** : the outline of the hair on the head

hair·piece \-ˌpēs\ *n* **1** : supplementary hair (as a switch) used in some women's hairdos **2** : TOUPEE

hair·pin \-ˌpin\ *n* **1** : a U-shaped pin to hold the hair in place **2** : a sharp U-shaped turn in a road — **hairpin** *adj*

hair–rais·ing \'har-ˌrā-ziŋ\ *adj* : causing terror or astonishment

hair·split·ter \-ˌspli-tər\ *n* : a person who makes excessively fine distinctions in reasoning — **hair·split·ting** \-ˌspli-tiŋ\ *adj or n*

hair·style \-ˌstīl\ *n* : HAIRDO — **hair·styl·ing** *n*

hair·styl·ist \-ˌstī-list\ *n* : HAIRDRESSER

hair–trig·ger *adj* : immediately responsive to the slightest stimulus

hairy \'har-ē\ *adj* **hair·i·er; -est** **1** : covered with or as if with hair **2** : tending to cause nervous tension ⟨a few ∼ moments⟩ — **hair·i·ness** \-ē-nəs\ *n*

hairy woodpecker *n* : a common No. American woodpecker with a white back that is larger than the similarly marked downy woodpecker

Hai·tian \'hā-shən\ *n* : a native or inhabitant of Haiti — **Haitian** *adj*

hajj \'haj\ *n* : the Islamic religious pilgrimage to Mecca

hajji \'ha-jē\ *n* : one who has made a pilgrimage to Mecca — often used as a title

hake \'hāk\ *n* : any of several marine food fishes related to the cod

ha·la·la \hə-'lä-lə\ *n, pl* **halala** *or* **halalas** — see *riyal* at MONEY table

hal·berd \'hal-bərd, 'hòl-\ *also* **hal·bert** \-bərt\ *n* : a weapon esp. of the 15th and 16th centuries consisting of a battle-ax and pike on a long handle

hal·cy·on \'hal-sē-ən\ *adj* [Gk *halkyōn*, a mythical bird believed to nest at sea and to calm the waves] : CALM, PEACEFUL

¹hale \'hāl\ *adj* : free from defect, disease, or infirmity **syn** healthy, sound, robust, well

²hale *vb* **haled; hal·ing 1** : HAUL, PULL **2** : to compel to go

ha·ler \'hä-lər\ *n, pl* **ha·le·ru** \'hä-lə-ˌrü\ — see *koruna* at MONEY table

¹half \'haf, 'hàf\ *n, pl* **halves** \'havz, 'hàvz\ **1** : either of two equal parts into which something is divisible **2** : one of a pair

²half *adj* **1** : being one of two equal parts **2** : amounting to nearly half **3** : PARTIAL, INCOMPLETE — **half** *adv*

half–and–half \ˌhaf-ən-'haf, ˌhàf-ən-'hàf\ *n* : something that is half one thing and half another

half–back \'haf-ˌbak, 'hàf-\ *n* **1** : a football back stationed on or near the flank **2** : a player stationed immediately behind the forward line

half–baked \-'bākt\ *adj* **1** : not thoroughly baked **2** : poorly planned; *also* : lacking common sense

half–breed \-ˌbrēd\ *n* : one of mixed racial descent — often used disparagingly — **half–breed** *adj*

half brother *n* : a brother related through one parent only

half–caste \'haf-ˌkast, 'hàf-\ *n* : HALF-BREED — **half–caste** *adj*

half–dol·lar \-'dä-lər\ *n* **1** : a coin representing one half of a dollar **2** : the sum of fifty cents

half–heart·ed \-'här-təd\ *adj* : lacking spirit or interest — **half·heart·ed·ly** *adv* — **half·heart·ed·ness** *n*

half–life \-ˌlīf\ *n* : the time required for half of something (as atoms or a drug) to undergo a process

half–mast \-'mast\ *n* : a point about halfway down from the top of a mast or staff

half note *n* : a musical note equal in time to one half of a whole note

half·pen·ny \'hāp-nē\ *n, pl* **half·pence** \'hā-pəns\ *or* **halfpennies** : a formerly used British coin representing one half of a penny

half–pint \'haf-ˌpīnt, 'hàf-\ *adj* : of less than average size — **half–pint** *n*

half sister *n* : a sister related through one parent only

half sole *n* : a shoe sole extending from the shank forward — **half–sole** *vb*

half–staff \'haf-ˌstaf, 'hàf-\ *n* : HALF-MAST

half step *n* : a musical interval equivalent to one twelfth of an octave

half·time \'haf-ˌtīm, 'hàf-\ *n* : an intermission between halves of a game

half–track \-ˌtrak\ *n* : a motor vehicle propelled by an endless chain-track drive system; *esp* : such a vehicle lightly armored for military use

half–truth \-ˌtrüth\ *n* : a statement that is only partially true; *esp* : one that deliberately mixes truth and falsehood

half·way \-'wā\ *adj* **1** : midway between two points **2** : PARTIAL 1 — **halfway** *adv*

half–wit \-ˌwit\ *n* : a foolish or imbecilic person — **half–wit·ted** \-'wi-təd\ *adj* — **half–wit·ted·ness** *n*

hal·i·but \'ha-lə-bət\ *n, pl* **halibut** *also* **halibuts** [ME *halybutte*, fr. *haly, holy* holy + *butte* flatfish; fr. its being eaten on holy days] : a large edible marine flatfish

ha·lite \'ha-ˌlīt, 'hā-\ *n* : ROCK SALT

hal·i·to·sis \ˌha-lə-'tō-səs\ *n* : the condition of having fetid breath

hall \'hòl\ *n* **1** : the residence of a medieval king or noble; *also* : the house of a landed proprietor **2** : a large public building **3** : a college or university building;

also : DORMITORY **4** : LOBBY; *also* : CORRIDOR **5** : AUDITORIUM

hal·le·lu·jah \ˌha-lə-'lü-yə\ *interj* [Heb *hallĕlūyāh* praise (ye) the Lord] — used to express praise, joy, or thanks

hall·mark \'hòl-ˌmärk\ *n* **1** : a mark put on an article to indicate origin, purity, or genuineness **2** : a distinguishing characteristic

hal·low \'ha-lō\ *vb* **1** : CONSECRATE **2** : REVERE — **hallowed** \-lōd, -lə-wəd\ *adj*

Hal·low·een *also* **Hal·low·e'en** \ˌha-lə-'wēn, ˌhä-\ *n* : the evening of October 31 observed esp. by children in merrymaking and masquerading

hal·lu·ci·nate \hə-'lüs-ᵊn-ˌāt\ *vb* **-nat·ed; -nat·ing** : to have hallucinations or experience as a hallucination

hal·lu·ci·na·tion \hə-ˌlüs-ᵊn-'ā-shən\ *n* : perception of objects with no reality due usu. to use of drugs or to disorder of the nervous system; *also* : something so perceived **syn** delusion, illusion, mirage — **hal·lu·ci·na·to·ry** \-ᵊn-ə-ˌtòr-ē\ *adj*

hal·lu·ci·no·gen \hə-'lüs-ᵊn-ə-jən\ *n* : a substance that induces hallucinations — **hal·lu·ci·no·gen·ic** \-ˌlüs-ᵊn-ə-'je-nik\ *adj or n*

hall·way \'hòl-ˌwā\ *n* **1** : an entrance hall **2** : CORRIDOR

ha·lo \'hā-lo\ *n, pl* **halos** *or* **haloes** [L *halos,* fr. Gk *halōs* threshing floor, disk, halo] **1** : a circle of light appearing to surround a shining body (as the sun) **2** : the aura of glory surrounding an idealized person or thing

hal·o·gen \'ha-lə-jən\ *n* : any of the five elements fluorine, chlorine, bromine, iodine, and astatine

¹halt \'hòlt\ *adj* : LAME

²halt *n* : STOP

³halt *vb* **1** : to stop marching or traveling **2** : DISCONTINUE, END

¹hal·ter \'hòl-tər\ *n* **1** : a rope or strap for leading or tying an animal; *also* : HEADSTALL **2** : NOOSE **3** : a brief blouse held in place by straps around the neck and across the back

²halter *vb* **hal·tered; hal·ter·ing 1** : to catch with or as if with a halter; *also* : to put a halter on (as a horse) **2** : HANG **3** : IMPEDE, RESTRAIN

halt·ing \'hòl-tiŋ\ *adj* : UNCERTAIN, FALTERING — **halt·ing·ly** *adv*

halve \'hav, 'hàv\ *vb* **halved; halv·ing 1** : to divide into two equal parts **2** : to reduce to one half

halv·ers \'ha-vərz, 'hà-\ *n pl* : half shares : HALVES

halves *pl of* HALF

hal·yard \'hal-yərd\ *n* : a rope or tackle for hoisting and lowering (as sails)

¹ham \'ham\ *n* **1** : a buttock with its associated thigh — usu. used in pl. **2** : a cut of meat and esp. pork from the thigh **3** : a showy performer **4** : an operator of an amateur radio station — **ham** *adj*

²ham *vb* **hammed; ham·ming** : to overplay a part : OVERACT

ham·burg·er \'ham-ˌbər-gər\ *or* **ham·burg** \-ˌbərg\ *n* [G *Hamburger* of Hamburg, Germany] **1** : ground beef **2** : a sandwich consisting of a ground-beef patty in a round roll

ham·let \'ham-lət\ *n* : a small village

¹ham·mer \'ha-mər\ *n* **1** : a hand tool used for pounding; *also* : something resembling a hammer in form or function **2** : the part of a gun whose striking action causes explosion of the charge **3** : a metal sphere hurled for distance in a track-and-field event (**hammer throw**) **4** : ACCELERATOR 2

²hammer *vb* **1** : to beat, drive, or shape with repeated blows of a hammer : POUND **2** : to produce or bring about as if by repeated blows — usu. used with *out*

ham·mer·head \'ha-mər-ˌhed\ *n* **1** : the striking part of a hammer **2** : any of a family of medium-sized sharks with eyes at the ends of lateral extensions of the flattened head

hammerhead 2

ham·mer·lock \-ˌläk\ *n* : a wrestling hold in which an opponent's arm is held bent behind the back

ham·mer·toe \-ˌtō\ *n* : a toe deformed by having one or more joints permanently flexed

¹**ham·mock** \'ha-mək\ *n* [Sp *hamaca*, of AmerInd origin] : a swinging couch hung by cords at each end

²**hammock** *n* : a fertile elevated area of the southern U.S. and esp. Florida with hardwood vegetation and soil rich in humus

¹**ham·per** \'ham-pər\ *vb* : IMPEDE; *also* : RESTRAIN **syn** trammel, clog, fetter, shackle

²**hamper** *n* : a large basket

ham·ster \'ham-stər\ *n* [G, fr. OHG *hamustro*, of Slavic origin] : any of a subfamily of small Old World rodents with large cheek pouches

¹**ham·string** \'ham-ˌstriŋ\ *n* : any of several muscles at the back of the thigh or tendons at the back of the knee

²**hamstring** *vb* **-strung** \-ˌstrəŋ\; **-string·ing** 1 : to cripple by cutting the leg tendons 2 : to make ineffective or powerless

¹**hand** \'hand\ *n* 1 : the end of a front limb when modified (as in humans) for grasping 2 : an indicator or pointer on a dial 3 : personal possession — usu. used in pl.; *also* : CONTROL 4 : SIDE 5 5 : a pledge esp. of betrothal 6 : HANDWRITING 7 : SKILL, ABILITY; *also* : a significant part 8 : ASSISTANCE; *also* : PARTICIPATION 9 : an outburst of applause 10 : a single round in a card game; *also* : the cards held by a player after a deal 11 : WORKER, EMPLOYEE; *also* : a member of a ship's crew — **hand·less** *adj* — **at hand** : near in time or place — **on hand** : in present possession or readily available

²**hand** *vb* 1 : to lead, guide, or assist with the hand 2 : to give, pass, or transmit with the hand

hand·bag \'hand-ˌbag\ *n* : a bag for carrying small personal articles and money

hand·ball \-ˌbȯl\ *n* : a game played by striking a small rubber ball against a wall with the hand

hand·bill \-ˌbil\ *n* : a small printed sheet for distribution by hand

hand·book \-ˌbük\ *n* : a concise reference book : MANUAL

hand·car \-ˌkär\ *n* : a small 4-wheeled railroad car propelled by hand or by a small motor

hand·clasp \-ˌklasp\ *n* : HANDSHAKE

hand·craft \-ˌkraft\ *vb* : to fashion by manual skill

¹**hand·cuff** \-ˌkəf\ *n* : a metal fastening that can be locked around a wrist and is usu. connected with another such fastening — usu. used in pl.

²**handcuff** *vb* : MANACLE

hand·ful \'hand-ˌfül\ *n, pl* **hand·fuls** \-ˌfülz\ *also* **hands·ful** \'handz-ˌfül\ 1 : as much or as many as the hand will grasp 2 : a small number 3 : as much as one can manage

hand·gun \-ˌgən\ *n* : a firearm held and fired with one hand

¹**hand·i·cap** \'han-di-ˌkap\ *n* [obs. E *handicap*, a game in which forfeits were held in a cap, fr. *hand in cap*] 1 : a contest in which an artificial advantage is given or disadvantage imposed on a contestant to equalize chances of winning; *also* : the advantage given or disadvantage imposed 2 : a disadvantage that makes achievement difficult

²**handicap** *vb* **-capped; -cap·ping** 1 : to give a handicap to 2 : to put at a disadvantage

hand·i·capped *adj* : having a physical or mental disability that limits activity

hand·i·cap·per \-ˌka-pər\ *n* : a person who predicts the winners in a horse race usu. for a publication

hand·i·craft \'han-di-ˌkraft\ *n* 1 : manual skill 2 : an occupation requiring manual skill 3 : the articles fashioned by those engaged in handicraft — **hand·i·craft·er** \-ˌkraf-tər\ *n* — **hand·i·crafts·man** \-ˌkrafts-mən\ *n*

hand in glove *or* **hand and glove** *adv* : in an extremely close relationship

hand·i·work \'han-di-ˌwərk\ *n* : work done personally or by the hands

hand·ker·chief \'haŋ-kər-chəf, -ˌchēf\ *n, pl* **-chiefs** \-chəfs, -ˌchēfs\ *also* **-chieves** \-ˌchēvz\ : a small piece of cloth used for various personal purposes (as the wiping of the face)

¹**han·dle** \'hand-ᵊl\ *n* : a part (as of a tool) designed to be grasped by the hand — **han·dled** \-ᵊld\ *adj* — **off the handle** : into a state of sudden and violent anger — usu. used with *fly*

²**handle** *vb* **han·dled; han·dling** 1 : to touch, hold, or manage with the hands 2 : to have responsibility for 3 : to deal or trade in 4 : to behave in a certain way when managed or directed ⟨a car that ∼s well⟩ — **han·dler** *n*

han·dle·bar \'hand-ᵊl-ˌbär\ *n* : a usu. bent bar with a grip at each end (as for steering a bicycle) — usu. used in pl.

hand·made \'hand-'mād\ *adj* : made by hand or by a hand process

hand·maid·en \-ˌmād-ᵊn\ *also* **hand·maid** \-ˌmād\ *n* : a female attendant

hand–me–down \-me-ˌdaun\ *adj* : used by one person after having been used by another — **hand–me–down** *n*

hand·out \'han-ˌdaut\ *n* 1 : a portion (as of food) given to a beggar 2 : a piece of printed information for free distribution; *also* : a prepared statement released to the press

hand·pick \'hand-'pik\ *vb* : to select personally ⟨a ∼ed candidate⟩

hand·rail \-ˌrāl\ *n* : a narrow rail for grasping as a support

hand·saw \-ˌsȯ\ *n* : a saw designed to be used with one hand

hands down *adv* 1 : with little effort 2 : without question

hand·sel \'han-səl\ *n* 1 : a gift made as a token of good luck 2 : a first installment : earnest money

hand·set \'hand-ˌset\ *n* : a combined telephone transmitter and receiver mounted on a handle

hand·shake \-ˌshāk\ *n* : a clasping usu. of right hands by two people

hands–off \'handz-'ȯf\ *adj* : characterized by noninterference

hand·some \'han-səm\ *adj* **hand·som·er; -est** [ME *handsom* easy to manipulate] 1 : SIZABLE, AMPLE 2 : GENEROUS, LIBERAL 3 : pleasing and usu. impressive in appearance **syn** beautiful, lovely, pretty, comely, fair — **hand·some·ly** *adv* — **hand·some·ness** *n*

hands–on \'handz-'ȯn, -'än\ *adj* 1 : being or providing direct practical experience in the operation of something 2 : characterized by active personal involvement ⟨∼ management⟩

hand·spring \'hand-ˌspriŋ\ *n* : an acrobatic feat in which the body turns in a full circle from a standing position and lands first on the hands and then on the feet

hand·stand \-ˌstand\ *n* : an act of supporting the body on the hands with the trunk and legs balanced in the air

hand–to–hand *adj* : involving physical contact or very close range ⟨∼ fighting⟩ — **hand to hand** *adv*

hand–to–mouth *adj* : having or providing nothing to spare

hand·wo·ven \'hand-ˌwō-vən\ adj : produced on a hand-operated loom

hand·writ·ing \-ˌrī-tiŋ\ n : writing done by hand; also : the form of writing peculiar to a person — **hand·writ·ten** \-ˌrit-ᵊn\ adj

handy \'han-dē\ adj **hand·i·er; -est** 1 : conveniently near 2 : easily used 3 : DEXTEROUS — **hand·i·ly** \-də-lē\ adv — **hand·i·ness** \-dē-nəs\ n

handy·man \-ˌman\ n 1 : one who does odd jobs 2 : one competent in a variety of small skills or repair work

¹hang \'haŋ\ vb **hung** \'həŋ\ also **hanged; hang·ing** 1 : to fasten or remain fastened to an elevated point without support from below; also : to fasten or be fastened so as to allow free motion on the point of suspension (~ a door) 2 : to suspend by the neck until dead; also : to die by hanging 3 : DROOP (hung his head in shame) 4 : to fasten to a wall (~ wallpaper) 5 : to prevent (a jury) from coming to a decision 6 : to display (pictures) in a gallery 7 : to remain stationary in the air 8 : to be imminent 9 : DEPEND 10 : to take hold for support 11 : to be burdensome 12 : to undergo delay 13 : to incline downward; also : to fit or fall from the figure in easy lines 14 : to be raptly attentive 15 : LINGER, LOITER — **hang·er** n

²hang n 1 : the manner in which a thing hangs 2 : an understanding of something

han·gar \'haŋ-ər\ n [F] : a covered and usu. enclosed area for housing and repairing aircraft

hang·dog \'haŋ-ˌdȯg\ adj 1 : ASHAMED, GUILTY 2 : ABJECT, COWED

hang·er–on \ˌhaŋ-ər-'ȯn, -'än\ n, pl **hangers–on** : one who hangs around a person or place esp. for personal gain

hang in vb : to persist tenaciously

hang·ing n 1 : an execution by strangling or snapping the neck by a suspended noose 2 : something hung

hang·man \'haŋ-mən\ n : a public executioner

hang·nail \-ˌnāl\ n : a bit of skin hanging loose at the edge of a fingernail

hang on vb 1 : HANG IN 2 : to keep a telephone connection open

hang·out \'haŋ-ˌaut\ n : a favorite place for spending time

hang·over \-ˌō-vər\ n 1 : something that remains from what is past 2 : disagreeable physical effects following heavy drinking

hang–up \'haŋ-ˌəp\ n : a source of mental or emotional difficulty

hang up vb 1 : to place on a hook or hanger 2 : to end a telephone conversation by replacing the receiver on the cradle 3 : to keep delayed or suspended

hank \'haŋk\ n : COIL, LOOP

han·ker \'haŋ-kər\ vb : to desire strongly or persistently — **han·ker·ing** n

han·kie or **han·ky** \'haŋ-kē\ n, pl **hankies** : HANDKERCHIEF

han·ky–pan·ky \ˌhaŋ-kē-'paŋ-kē\ n 1 : questionable or underhanded activity 2 : sexual dalliance

han·sel var of HANDSEL

han·som \'han-səm\ n : a 2-wheeled covered carriage with the driver's seat elevated at the rear

Ha·nuk·kah \'kä-nə-kə, 'hä-\ n [Heb ḥănukkāh dedication] : an 8-day Jewish holiday commemorating the rededication of the Temple of Jerusalem after its defilement by Antiochus of Syria

hap \'hap\ n 1 : HAPPENING 2 : CHANCE, FORTUNE

¹hap·haz·ard \hap-'ha-zərd\ n : CHANCE

²haphazard adj : marked by lack of plan or order — **hap·haz·ard·ly** adv — **hap·haz·ard·ness** n

hap·less \'hap-ləs\ adj : UNFORTUNATE — **hap·less·ly** adv — **hap·less·ness** n

hap·loid \'hap-ˌlȯid\ adj : having the number of chromosomes characteristic of gametic cells — **haploid** n

hap·ly \'hap-lē\ adv : by chance

hap·pen \'ha-pən\ vb 1 : to occur by chance 2 : to take place 3 : CHANCE 2

hap·pen·ing n 1 : OCCURRENCE 2 : an event that is especially interesting, entertaining, or important

hap·pi·ly \'ha-pə-lē\ adv 1 : LUCKILY 2 : in a happy manner or state (lived ~ ever after) 3 : APTLY, SUCCESSFULLY

hap·pi·ness \'ha-pē-nəs\ n 1 : a state of well-being and contentment; also : a pleasurable satisfaction 2 : APTNESS

hap·py \'ha-pē\ adj **hap·pi·er; -est** 1 : FORTUNATE 2 : APT, FELICITOUS 3 : enjoying well-being and contentment 4 : PLEASANT; also : PLEASED, GRATIFIED syn glad, cheerful, lighthearted, joyful, joyous

hap·py–go–lucky \ˌha-pē-gō-'lə-kē\ adj : CAREFREE

happy hour n : a period of time when the price of drinks at a bar is reduced

hara–kiri \ˌhar-i-'kir-ē, -'kar-ē\ n [Jp harakiri, fr. hara belly + kiri cutting] : ritual suicide by disembowelment

ha·rangue \hə-'raŋ\ n 1 : a ranting speech or writing 2 : LECTURE — **harangue** vb — **ha·rangu·er** n

ha·rass \hə-'ras, 'har-əs\ vb [F harasser, fr. MF, fr. harer to set a dog on, fr. OF hare, interj. used to incite dogs, of Gmc origin] 1 : EXHAUST, FATIGUE 2 : to worry and impede by repeated raids 3 : to annoy continually syn harry, plague, pester, tease, bedevil — **ha·rass·ment** n

har·bin·ger \'här-bən-jər\ n : one that announces or foreshadows what is coming : PRECURSOR; also : PORTENT

¹har·bor \'här-bər\ n 1 : a place of security and comfort 2 : a part of a body of water protected and deep enough to furnish anchorage : PORT

²harbor vb 1 : to give or take refuge : SHELTER 2 : to be the home or habitat of; also : LIVE 3 : to hold a thought or feeling (~ a grudge)

har·bor·age \'här-bə-rij\ n : HARBOR

har·bour chiefly Brit var of HARBOR

hard \'härd\ adj 1 : not easily penetrated : not easily yielding to pressure 2 : high in alcoholic content 3 : containing salts that prevent lathering with soap (~ water) 4 : stable in value (~ currency) 5 : physically fit 6 : FIRM, DEFINITE (~ agreement); also : based on clear fact (~ evidence) 7 : CLOSE, SEARCHING (~ look) 8 : REALISTIC (good ~ sense) 9 : OBDURATE, UNFEELING (~ heart) 10 : difficult to bear (~ times); also : HARSH, SEVERE 11 : RESENTFUL (~ feelings) 12 : STRICT, UNRELENTING (~ bargain) 13 : INCLEMENT (~ winter) 14 : intense in force or manner (~ blow) 15 : ARDUOUS, STRENUOUS (~ work) 16 : sounding as in arcing and geese respectively — used of c and g 17 : TROUBLESOME (~ problem) 18 : having difficulty in doing something (~ of hearing) 19 : addictive and gravely detrimental to health (~ drugs) 20 : of or relating to the natural sciences and esp. the physical sciences — **hard** adv — **hard·ness** n

hard–and–fast adj : rigidly binding : STRICT (a ~ rule)

hard·back \'härd-ˌbak\ n : a hardcover book

hard·ball \-ˌbȯl\ n 1 : BASEBALL 2 : forceful uncompromising methods

hard–bit·ten \-'bit-ᵊn\ adj : SEASONED, TOUGH (~ campaigners)

hard·board \-ˌbȯrd\ n : a very dense fiberboard

hard–boiled \-'bȯild\ adj 1 of an egg : boiled until both white and yolk have solidified 2 : lacking sentiment : TOUGH; also : HARDHEADED 2

hard·bound \-ˌbaund\ adj : HARDCOVER

hard copy n : copy of textual or graphic information (as from computer storage) produced on paper

hard–core \'härd-'kȯr\ adj 1 : extremely resistant to solution or improvement 2 : being the most determined or dedicated members of a specified group 3 : containing explicit depictions of sex acts — **hard core** n

hard·cov·er \-'kə-vər\ *adj* : having rigid boards on the sides covered in cloth or paper ⟨~ books⟩

hard disk *n* : a sealed rigid metal disk used as a computer storage device

hard·en \'härd-ᵊn\ *vb* **1** : to make or become hard or harder **2** : to confirm or become confirmed in disposition or action — **hard·en·er** *n*

hard·hack \'härd-ˌhak\ *n* : an American spirea with dense clusters of pink or white flowers and leaves having a hairy rusty yellow underside

hard hat *n* **1** : a protective hat worn esp. by construction workers **2** : a construction worker

hard·head·ed \'härd-'he-dəd\ *adj* **1** : STUBBORN, WILLFUL **2** : SOBER, REALISTIC — **hard·head·ed·ly** *adv* — **hard·head·ed·ness** *n*

hard·heart·ed \-'här-təd\ *adj* : PITILESS, CRUEL — **hard·heart·ed·ly** *adv* — **hard·heart·ed·ness** *n*

har·di·hood \'här-dē-ˌhu̇d\ *n* **1** : resolute courage and fortitude **2** : VIGOR, ROBUSTNESS

hard–line \'härd-'līn\ *adj* : advocating or involving a rigidly uncompromising course of action — **hard–lin·er** \-'lī-nər\ *n*

hard·ly \'härd-lē\ *adv* **1** : with force **2** : SEVERELY **3** : with difficulty **4** : only just : BARELY **5** : certainly not

hard–nosed \'härd-'nōzd\ *adj* : TOUGH, UNCOMPROMISING; *also* : HARDHEADED 2

hard palate *n* : the bony anterior part of the palate forming the roof of the mouth

hard·pan \'härd-ˌpan\ *n* : a compact layer in soil that is impenetrable by roots

hard–pressed \-'prest\ *adj* : HARD PUT; *esp* : being under financial strain

hard put *adj* **1** : barely able **2** : faced with difficulty or perplexity

hard rock *n* : rock music marked by a heavy beat, high amplification, and usu. frenzied performances

hard–shell \'härd-ˌshel\ *adj* : HIDEBOUND, UNCOMPROMISING ⟨a ~ conservative⟩

hard·ship \-ˌship\ *n* **1** : SUFFERING, PRIVATION **2** : something that causes suffering or privation

hard·tack \-ˌtak\ *n* : a saltless hard biscuit, bread, or cracker

hard·top \-ˌtäp\ *n* : an automobile having a permanent rigid top

hard·ware \-ˌwar\ *n* **1** : ware (as cutlery or tools) made of metal **2** : the physical components (as electronic devices) of a vehicle (as a spacecraft) or an apparatus (as a computer)

hard·wood \-ˌwu̇d\ *n* : the wood of a broad-leaved usu. deciduous tree as distinguished from that of a conifer; *also* : such a tree — **hardwood** *adj*

hard·work·ing \-'wər-kiŋ\ *adj* : INDUSTRIOUS

har·dy \'här-dē\ *adj* **har·di·er; -est 1** : BOLD, BRAVE **2** : AUDACIOUS, BRAZEN **3** : ROBUST; *also* : able to withstand adverse conditions (as of weather) ⟨~ shrubs⟩ — **har·di·ly** \-də-lē\ *adv* — **har·di·ness** \-dē-nəs\ *n*

hare \'har\ *n, pl* **hare** *or* **hares** : any of various swift timid long-eared mammals like the related rabbits but born with open eyes and fur

hare·bell \'har-ˌbel\ *n* : a slender herb with bright blue bell-shaped flowers

hare·brained \-'brānd\ *adj* : FOOLISH

hare·lip \-'lip\ *n* : a birth defect in which the upper lip is vertically split — **hare·lipped** \-'lipt\ *adj*

ha·rem \'har-əm\ *n* [Ar ḥarīm, lit., something forbidden & ḥaram, lit., sanctuary] **1** : a house or part of a house allotted to women in a Muslim household **2** : the women and servants occupying a harem **3** : a group of females associated with one male

hark \'härk\ *vb* : LISTEN

harken *var of* HEARKEN

har·le·quin \'här-li-kən, -kwən\ *n* **1** *cap* : a character (as in comedy) with a shaved head, masked face, variegated tights, and wooden sword **2** : CLOWN 2

har·lot \'här-lət\ *n* : PROSTITUTE

¹harm \'härm\ *n* **1** : physical or mental damage : INJU-

RY **2** : MISCHIEF, HURT — **harm·ful** \-fəl\ *adj* — **harm·ful·ly** *adv* — **harm·ful·ness** *n* — **harm·less** *adj* — **harm·less·ly** *adv* — **harm·less·ness** *n*

²harm *vb* : to cause harm to : INJURE

¹har·mon·ic \här-'mä-nik\ *adj* **1** : of or relating to musical harmony or harmonics **2** : pleasing to the ear — **har·mon·i·cal·ly** \-ni-k(ə-)lē\ *adv*

²harmonic *n* : a musical overtone

har·mon·i·ca \här-'mä-ni-kə\ *n* : a small wind instrument in which the sound is produced by metal reeds

har·mo·ni·ous \här-'mō-nē-əs\ *adj* **1** : musically concordant **2** : CONGRUOUS **3** : marked by accord in sentiment or action — **har·mo·ni·ous·ly** *adv* — **har·mo·ni·ous·ness** *n*

har·mo·ni·um \här-'mō-nē-əm\ *n* : a keyboard wind instrument in which the wind acts on a set of metal reeds

har·mo·nize \'här-mə-ˌnīz\ *vb* **-nized; -niz·ing 1** : to play or sing in harmony **2** : to be in harmony **3** : to bring into consonance or accord — **har·mo·ni·za·tion** \ˌhär-mə-nə-'zā-shən\ *n*

har·mo·ny \'här-mə-nē\ *n, pl* **-nies 1** : musical agreement of sounds; *esp* : the combination of tones into chords and progressions of chords **2** : a pleasing arrangement of parts; *also* : ACCORD **3** : internal calm

¹har·ness \'här-nəs\ *n* **1** : the gear other than a yoke of a draft animal **2** : something that resembles a harness

²harness *vb* **1** : to put a harness on; *also* : YOKE **2** : UTILIZE

¹harp \'härp\ *n* : a musical instrument consisting of a triangular frame set with strings plucked by the fingers — **harp·ist** \'här-pist\ *n*

²harp *vb* **1** : to play on a harp **2** : to dwell on a subject tiresomely — **harp·er** *n*

har·poon \här-'pün\ *n* : a barbed spear used esp. in hunting whales — **harpoon** *vb* — **har·poon·er** *n*

harp·si·chord \'härp-si-ˌkȯrd\ *n* : a keyboard instrument producing tones by the plucking of its strings with quills or with leather or plastic points

har·py \'här-pē\ *n, pl* **harpies** [L *Harpyia*, a mythical predatory monster having a woman's head and a bird's body, fr. Gk] **1** : a predatory person : LEECH **2** : a shrewish woman

har·ri·dan \'har-əd-ᵊn\ *n* : SHREW 2

¹har·ri·er \'har-ē-ər\ *n* **1** : any of a breed of medium-sized foxhounds **2** : a runner on a cross-country team

²harrier *n* : a slender long-legged hawk

¹har·row \'har-ō\ *n* : a cultivating tool that has spikes, spring teeth, or disks and is used esp. to pulverize and smooth the soil

²harrow *vb* **1** : to cultivate with a harrow **2** : TORMENT, VEX

har·ry \'har-ē\ *vb* **har·ried; har·ry·ing 1** : RAID, PILLAGE **2** : to torment by or as if by constant attack **syn** worry, annoy, plague, pester

harsh \'härsh\ *adj* **1** : disagreeably rough **2** : causing discomfort or pain **3** : unduly exacting : SEVERE — **harsh·ly** *adv* — **harsh·ness** *n*

hart \'härt\ *n, chiefly Brit* : STAG

har·um–scar·um \ˌhar-əm-'skar-əm\ *adj* : RECKLESS, IRRESPONSIBLE

¹har·vest \'här-vəst\ *n* **1** : the season for gathering in crops; *also* : the act of gathering in a crop **2** : a mature crop **3** : the product or reward of effort

²harvest *vb* **1** : to gather in a crop : REAP **2** : to gather, hunt, or kill (as deer) for human use or population control — **har·vest·er** *n*

has *pres 3d sing of* HAVE

has–been \'haz-ˌbin\ *n* : one that has passed the peak of ability, power, effectiveness, or popularity

¹hash \'hash\ *vb* [F *hacher*, fr. OF *hachier*, fr. *hache* battle-ax, of Gmc origin] **1** : to chop into small pieces **2** : to talk about

²hash *n* **1** : chopped meat mixed with potatoes and browned **2** : HODGEPODGE, JUMBLE

³hash *n* : HASHISH

hash browns *n pl* : boiled potatoes that have been diced, mixed with chopped onions and shortening, and fried

hash·ish \'ha-ˌshēsh, ha-'shēsh\ [Ar *ḥashīsh*] *n* : the concentrated resin from the flowering tops of the female hemp plant

hasp \'hasp\ *n* : a fastener (as for a door) consisting of a hinged metal strap that fits over a staple and is secured by a pin or padlock

hasp

has·sle \'ha-səl\ *n* **1** : WRANGLE; *also* : FIGHT **2** : an annoying or troublesome concern — **hassle** *vb*

has·sock \'ha-sək\ *n* : a cushion that serves as a seat or leg rest; *also* : a cushion to kneel on in prayer

haste \'hāst\ *n* **1** : rapidity of motion or action : SPEED **2** : rash or headlong action **3** : excessive eagerness — **hast·i·ly** \'hā-stə-lē\ *adv* — **hast·i·ness** \-stē-nəs\ *n* — **hasty** \'hā-stē\ *adj*

has·ten \'hās-ᵊn\ *vb* **1** : to urge on **2** : to move or act quickly : HURRY **syn** speed, accelerate, quicken

hat \'hat\ *n* : a covering for the head usu. having a shaped crown and brim

hat·box \'hat-ˌbäks\ *n* : a round piece of luggage esp. for carrying hats

¹hatch \'hach\ *n* **1** : a small door or opening **2** : a door or cover for access down into a compartment of a ship

²hatch *vb* **1** : to produce by incubation; *also* : INCUBATE **2** : to emerge from an egg or pupa; *also* : to give forth young **3** : ORIGINATE — **hatch·ery** \'ha-chə-rē\ *n*

hatch·back \'hach-ˌbak\ *n* : an automobile with a rear hatch that opens upward

hatch·et \'ha-chət\ *n* **1** : a short-handled ax with a hammerlike part opposite the blade **2** : TOMAHAWK

hatchet man *n* : a person hired for murder, coercion, or unscrupulous attack

hatch·ing \'ha-chiŋ\ *n* : the engraving or drawing of closely spaced fine lines chiefly to give an effect of shading; *also* : the pattern so created

hatch·way \'hach-ˌwā\ *n* : a hatch giving access usu. by a ladder or stairs

¹hate \'hāt\ *n* **1** : intense hostility and aversion **2** : an object of hatred — **hate·ful** \-fəl\ *adj* — **hate·ful·ly** *adv* — **hate·ful·ness** *n*

²hate *vb* **hat·ed; hat·ing 1** : to express or feel extreme enmity **2** : to find distasteful **syn** detest, abhor, abominate, loathe — **hat·er** *n*

ha·tred \'hā-trəd\ *n* : HATE; *also* : prejudiced hostility or animosity

hat·ter \'ha-tər\ *n* : one that makes, sells, or cleans and repairs hats

hau·berk \'hȯ-bərk\ *n* : a coat of mail

haugh·ty \'hȯ-tē\ *adj* **haugh·ti·er; -est** [obs. *haught*, fr. ME *haute*, fr. MF *haut*, lit., high, fr. L *altus*] : disdainfully proud **syn** insolent, lordly, overbearing, arrogant — **haugh·ti·ly** \-tə-lē\ *adv* — **haugh·ti·ness** \-tē-nəs\ *n*

¹haul \'hȯl\ *vb* **1** : to exert traction on : DRAW, PULL **2** : to furnish transportation : CART — **haul·er** *n*

²haul *n* **1** : PULL, TUG **2** : the result of an effort to obtain, collect, or win **3** : the length or course of a transportation route; *also* : LOAD

haul·age \'hȯ-lij\ *n* **1** : the act or process of hauling **2** : a charge for hauling

haunch \'hȯnch\ *n* **1** : ²HIP 1 **2** : HINDQUARTER 2 — usu. used in pl. **3** : HINDQUARTER 1

¹haunt \'hȯnt\ *vb* **1** : to visit often : FREQUENT **2** : to recur constantly and spontaneously to; *also* : to reappear continually in **3** : to visit or inhabit as a ghost — **haunt·er** *n* — **haunt·ing·ly** *adv*

²haunt \'hȯnt, 2 is usu 'hant\ *n* **1** : a place habitually frequented **2** *chiefly dial* : GHOST

haute cou·ture \ˌōt-kü-'tür\ *n* [F] : the establishments or designers that create exclusive and often trendsetting fashions for women; *also* : the fashions created

haute cui·sine \-kwi-'zēn\ *n* : artful or elaborate cuisine

hau·teur \hȯ-'tər, ō-, hō-\ *n* : ARROGANCE, HAUGHTINESS

¹have \'hav, həv, v; *in sense 2 before "to" usu* 'haf\ *vb* **had** \'had, həd\; **hav·ing; has** \'haz, həz, *in sense 2 before "to" usu* 'has\ **1** : to hold in possession; *also* : to hold in one's use, service, or regard **2** : to be compelled or forced ⟨~ to go now⟩ **3** : to stand in relationship to ⟨*has* many enemies⟩ **4** : OBTAIN; *also* : RECEIVE, ACCEPT **5** : to be marked by **6** : SHOW; *also* : USE, EXERCISE **7** : EXPERIENCE; *also* : TAKE ⟨~ a look⟩ **8** : to entertain in the mind ⟨~ an idea⟩ **9** : to cause to **10** : ALLOW **11** : to be competent in **12** : to hold in a disadvantageous position; *also* : TRICK **13** : BEGET **14** : to partake of **15** — used as an auxiliary with the past participle to form the present perfect, past perfect, or future perfect — **have at** : ATTACK — **have coming** : DESERVE — **have done with** : to be finished with — **have had it** : to have endured all one will permit or can stand — **have to do with** : to have in the way of relation with or effect on

²have \'hav\ *n* : one that has material wealth

ha·ven \'hā-vən\ *n* **1** : HARBOR, PORT **2** : a place of safety **3** : a place offering favorable conditions ⟨a tourist's ~⟩

have–not \'hav-ˌnät, -'nät\ *n* : one that is poor in material wealth

hav·er·sack \'ha-vər-ˌsak\ *n* [F *havresac*, fr. G *Habersack* bag for oats] : a bag similar to a knapsack but worn over one shoulder

hav·oc \'ha-vək\ *n* **1** : wide and general destruction **2** : great confusion and disorder

haw \'hȯ\ *n* : a hawthorn berry; *also* : HAWTHORN

Ha·wai·ian \hə-'wä-yən\ *n* : the Polynesian language of Hawaii

¹hawk \'hȯk\ *n* **1** : any of numerous mostly small or medium-sized day-flying birds of prey (as a falcon or kite) **2** : a supporter of a war or a warlike policy — **hawk·ish** *adj*

²hawk *vb* : to offer goods for sale by calling out in the street — **hawk·er** *n*

³hawk *vb* : to make a harsh coughing sound in or as if in clearing the throat; *also* : to raise by hawking

hawk·weed \'hȯk-ˌwēd\ *n* : any of several plants related to the daisies usu. having red or orange flower heads

haw·ser \'hȯ-zər\ *n* : a large rope for towing, mooring, or securing a ship

haw·thorn \'hȯ-ˌthȯrn\ *n* : any of a genus of spiny spring-flowering shrubs or trees related to the apple

¹hay \'hā\ *n* **1** : herbage (as grass) mowed and cured for fodder **2** : REWARD **3** *slang* : BED ⟨hit the ~⟩ **4** : a small amount of money

²hay *vb* : to cut, cure, and store for hay

hay·cock \'hā-ˌkäk\ *n* : a small conical pile of hay

hay fever *n* : an acute allergic reaction esp. to plant pollen that resembles a cold

hay·loft \'hā-ˌlȯft\ *n* : a loft for hay

hay·mow \-ˌmau̇\ *n* : a mow of or for hay

hay·rick \-ˌrik\ *n* : a large sometimes thatched outdoor stack of hay

hay·seed \-ˌsēd\ *n, pl* **hayseed** *or* **hayseeds 1** : clinging bits of straw or chaff from hay **2** : BUMPKIN, YOKEL

hay·stack \-ˌstak\ *n* : a stack of hay

hay·wire \-ˌwīr\ *adj* : being out of order or control : CRASY

¹**haz·ard** \ˈha-zərd\ *n* [ME, a dice game, fr. MF *hasard*, fr. Ar *az-zahr* the die] **1** : a source of danger **2** : CHANCE; *also* : ACCIDENT **3** : an obstacle on a golf course — **haz·ard·ous** *adj*

²**hazard** *vb* : VENTURE, RISK

¹**haze** \ˈhāz\ *n* **1** : fine dust, smoke, or light vapor causing lack of transparency in the air **2** : vagueness of mind or perception

²**haze** *vb* **hazed; haz·ing** : to harass by abusive and humiliating tricks usu. by way of initiation

ha·zel \ˈhā-zəl\ *n* **1** : any of a genus of shrubs or small trees related to the birches and bearing edible nuts (**ha·zel·nuts** \-ˌnəts\) **2** : a light brown color

hazy \ˈhā-zē\ *adj* **haz·i·er; -est 1** : obscured or darkened by haze **2** : VAGUE, INDEFINITE — **haz·i·ly** \-zə-lē\ *adv* — **haz·i·ness** \-zē-nəs\ *n*

Hb *abbr* hemoglobin

HBM *abbr* Her Britannic Majesty; His Britannic Majesty

H–bomb \ˈāch-ˌbäm\ *n* : HYDROGEN BOMB

HC *abbr* **1** Holy Communion **2** House of Commons

hd *abbr* head

HD *abbr* heavy-duty

hdbk *abbr* handbook

hdkf *abbr* handkerchief

HDL \ˌāch-(ˌ)dē-ˈel\ *n* [*high-density lipoprotein*] : a cholesterol-poor protein-rich lipoprotein of blood plasma correlated with reduced risk of atherosclerosis

hdwe *abbr* hardware

he \ˈhē\ *pron* **1** : that male one **2** : a person : the person ⟨~ who hesitates is lost⟩

He *symbol* helium

HE *abbr* **1** Her Excellency **2** His Eminence **3** His Excellency

¹**head** \ˈhed\ *n* **1** : the front or upper part of the body containing the brain, the chief sense organs, and the mouth **2** : MIND; *also* : natural aptitude **3** : POISE **4** : the obverse of a coin **5** : INDIVIDUAL; *also, pl* **head** : one of a number (as of cattle) **6** : the end that is upper or higher or opposite the foot; *also* : either end of something (as a drum) whose two ends need not be distinguished **7** : the source of a stream **8** : DIRECTOR, LEADER; *also* : a leading element (as of a procession) **9** : a projecting part; *also* : the striking part of a weapon **10** : the place of leadership or honor **11** : a separate part or topic **12** : the foam on a fermenting or effervescing liquid **13** : CRISIS — **head·ed** \ˈhe-dəd\ *adj* — **head·less** *adj*

²**head** *adj* : PRINCIPAL, CHIEF

³**head** *vb* **1** : to provide with or form a head; *also* : to form the head of **2** : LEAD, CONDUCT **3** : to get in front of esp. so as to stop; *also* : SURPASS **4** : to put or stand at the head **5** : to point or proceed in a certain direction

head·ache \ˈhe-ˌdāk\ *n* **1** : pain in the head **2** : a baffling situation or problem

head·band \ˈhed-ˌband\ *n* : a band worn on or around the head

head·board \-ˌbōrd\ *n* : a board forming the head (as of a bed)

head cold *n* : a common cold centered in the nasal passages and adjacent mucous tissues

head·dress \ˈhed-ˌdres\ *n* : an often elaborate covering for the head

head·first \-ˈfərst\ *adv* : HEADLONG 1 — **headfirst** *adj*

head·gear \-ˌgir\ *n* : a covering or protective device for the head

head–hunt·ing \-ˌhən-tiŋ\ *n* : the practice of seeking out and decapitating enemies and preserving their heads as trophies — **head·hunt·er** \-tər\ *n*

head·ing \ˈhe-diŋ\ *n* **1** : the compass direction in which

the longitudinal axis of a ship or airplane points **2** : something that forms or serves as a head

head·land \ˈhed-lənd, -ˌland\ *n* : PROMONTORY

head·light \-ˌlīt\ *n* : a light mounted on the front of a vehicle to illuminate the road ahead

head·line \-ˌlīn\ *n* : a head of a newspaper story or article usu. printed in large type

head·lock \-ˌläk\ *n* : a wrestling hold in which one encircles the opponent's head with one arm

¹**head·long** \-ˈlȯŋ\ *adv* **1** : with the head foremost **2** : RECKLESSLY **3** : without delay

²**head·long** \-ˌlȯŋ\ *adj* **1** : PRECIPITATE, RASH **2** : plunging with the head foremost

head·man \ˈhed-ˈman, -ˌman\ *n* : one who is a leader : CHIEF

head·mas·ter \-ˌmas-tər\ *n* : a man who is head of a private school

head·mis·tress \-ˌmis-trəs\ *n* : a woman who is head of a private school

head–on \ˈhed-ˈȯn, -ˈän\ *adj* : having the front facing in the direction of initial contact or line of sight ⟨~ collision⟩ — **head–on** *adv*

head·phone \-ˌfōn\ *n* : an earphone held on by a band over the head

head·piece \-ˌpēs\ *n* : a covering for the head

head·pin \-ˌpin\ *n* : a bowling pin that stands foremost in the arrangement of pins

head·quar·ters \-ˌkwȯr-tərz\ *n sing or pl* **1** : a place from which a commander exercises command **2** : the administrative center of an enterprise

head·rest \-ˌrest\ *n* **1** : a support for the head **2** : a pad at the top of the back of an automobile seat

head·room \-ˌrüm, -ˌrùm\ *n* : vertical space in which to stand, sit, or move

head·set \-ˌset\ *n* : a pair of headphones

head·ship \-ˌship\ *n* : the position, office, or dignity of a head

heads·man \ˈhedz-mən\ *n* : EXECUTIONER

head·stall \ˈhed-ˌstȯl\ *n* : a part of a bridle or halter that encircles the head

head·stone \-ˌstōn\ *n* : a memorial stone at the head of a grave

head·strong \-ˌstrȯŋ\ *adj* **1** : not easily restrained **2** : directed by ungovernable will **syn** unruly, intractable, willful, pertinacious, refractory, stubborn

head·wait·er \-ˈwā-tər\ *n* : the head of the dining-room staff of a restaurant or hotel

head·wa·ter \-ˌwȯ-tər, -ˌwä-\ *n* : the source of a stream — usu. used in pl.

head·way \-ˌwā\ *n* : forward motion; *also* : PROGRESS

head wind *n* : a wind blowing in a direction opposite to a course esp. of a ship or aircraft

head·word \ˈhed-ˌwərd\ *n* **1** : a word or term placed at the beginning **2** : a word qualified by a modifier

head·work \-ˌwərk\ *n* : mental work or effort : THINKING

heady \ˈhe-dē\ *adj* **head·i·er; -est 1** : WILLFUL, RASH; *also* : IMPETUOUS **2** : INTOXICATING **3** : SHREWD

heal \ˈhēl\ *vb* **1** : to make or become healthy, sound, or whole **2** : CURE, REMEDY — **heal·er** *n*

health \ˈhelth\ *n* **1** : sound physical or mental condition; *also* : overall condition of the body (in poor ~) **2** : WELL-BEING **3** : a toast to someone's health or prosperity

health·ful \ˈhelth-fəl\ *adj* **1** : beneficial to health **2** : HEALTHY — **health·ful·ly** *adv* — **health·ful·ness** *n*

health maintenance organization *n* : HMO

healthy \ˈhel-thē\ *adj* **health·i·er; -est 1** : enjoying or typical of good health : WELL **2** : evincing or conducive to health **3** : PROSPEROUS; *also* : CONSIDERABLE — **health·i·ly** \-thə-lē\ *adv* — **health·i·ness** \-thē-nəs\ *n*

¹**heap** \ˈhēp\ *n* : PILE; *also* : LOT

²**heap** *vb* **1** : to throw or lay in a heap **2** : to give in large quantities; *also* : to load heavily

hear \ˈhir\ *vb* **heard** \ˈhərd\; **hear·ing 1** : to perceive by the ear **2** : to gain knowledge of by hearing : LEARN **3** : HEED; *also* : ATTEND **4** : to give a legal hearing to or take testimony from — **hear·er** *n*

hear·ing *n* **1** : the process, function, or power of perceiving sound; *esp* : the special sense by which noises and tones are received as stimuli **2** : EARSHOT **3** : opportunity to be heard **4** : a listening to arguments (as in a court); *also* : a session of (as of a legislative committee) in which testimony is taken from witnesses

hear·ken \'här-kən\ *vb* : to give attention : LISTEN **syn** hear, hark, heed

hear·say \'hir-₁sā\ *n* : RUMOR

hearse \'hərs\ *n* : a vehicle for carrying the dead to the grave

heart \'härt\ *n* **1** : a hollow muscular organ that by rhythmic contraction keeps up the circulation of the blood in the body; *also* : something resembling a heart in shape **2** : any of a suit of playing cards marked with a red figure of a heart; *also, pl* : a card game in which the object is to avoid taking tricks containing hearts **3** : the whole personality; *also* : the emotional or moral as distinguished from the intellectual nature **4** : COURAGE **5** : one's innermost being **6** : CENTER; *also* : the essential part **7** : the younger central part of a compact leafy cluster (as of lettuce) — **heart·ed** \'här-təd\ *adj* — **by heart** : by rote or from memory

heart·ache \-₁āk\ *n* : anguish of mind

heart attack *n* : an acute episode of heart disease due to insufficient blood supply to the heart muscle

heart·beat \'härt-₁bēt\ *n* : one complete pulsation of the heart

heart·break \-₁brāk\ *n* : crushing grief

heart·break·ing \-₁brā-kiŋ\ *adj* : causing extreme sorrow or distress — **heart·break·er** \-₁brā-kər\ *n*

heart·bro·ken \-₁brō-kən\ *adj* : overcome by sorrow

heart·burn \-₁bərn\ *n* : a burning distress in the area of the heart usu. due to spasms of the esophagus or upper stomach

heart disease *n* : an abnormal organic condition of the heart or of the heart and circulation

heart·en \'härt-ᵊn\ *vb* : ENCOURAGE, CHEER

heart·felt \'härt-₁felt\ *adj* : deeply felt : SINCERE

hearth \'härth\ *n* **1** : an area (as of brick) in front of a fireplace; *also* : the floor of a fireplace **2** : HOME

hearth·stone \'härth-₁stōn\ *n* **1** : stone forming a hearth **2** : HOME

heart·less \'härt-ləs\ *adj* : CRUEL

heart·rend·ing \-₁ren-diŋ\ *adj* : HEARTBREAKING

heart·sick \-₁sik\ *adj* : very despondent — **heart·sick·ness** *n*

heart·strings \-₁striŋz\ *n pl* : the deepest emotions or affections

heart·throb \-₁thräb\ *n* **1** : the throb of a heart **2** : sentimental emotion **3** : SWEETHEART

heart–to–heart *adj* : SINCERE, FRANK

heart·warm·ing \'härt-₁wȯr-miŋ\ *adj* : inspiring sympathetic feeling

heart·wood \-₁wu̇d\ *n* : the older harder nonliving and usu. darker wood of the central part of a tree trunk

¹**hearty** \'här-tē\ *adj* **heart·i·er; -est 1** : giving full support; *also* : JOVIAL **2** : vigorously healthy **3** : ABUNDANT; *also* : NOURISHING **syn** sincere, wholehearted, unfeigned, heartfelt — **heart·i·ly** \-tə-lē\ *adv* — **heart·i·ness** \-tē-nəs\ *n*

²**hearty** *n, pl* **heart·ies** : an enthusiastic jovial fellow; *also* : SAILOR

¹**heat** \'hēt\ *vb* **1** : to make or become warm or hot **2** : EXCITE — **heat·ed·ly** *adv* — **heat·er** *n*

²**heat** *n* **1** : a condition of being hot : WARMTH **2** : a form of energy that when added to a body causes the body to rise in temperature, to fuse, to evaporate, or to expand **3** : high temperature **4** : intensity of feeling; *also* : sexual excitement esp. in a female mammal **5** : a preliminary race for narrowing the competition **6**

: pungency of flavor **7** *slang* : POLICE **8** : PRESSURE, COERCION; *also* : ABUSE, CRITICISM

heat exchanger *n* : a device (as an automobile radiator) for transferring heat from one fluid to another without allowing them to mix

heat exhaustion *n* : a condition marked by weakness, nausea, dizziness, and profuse sweating resulting from physical exertion in a hot environment

heath \'hēth\ *n* **1** : any of a large family of often evergreen shrubby plants (as a blueberry or heather) of wet acid soils **2** : a tract of wasteland — **heathy** *adj*

hea·then \'hē-thən\ *n, pl* **heathens** *or* **heathen 1** : an unconverted member of a people or nation that does not acknowledge the God of the Bible **2** : an uncivilized or irreligious person — **heathen** *adj* — **hea·then·dom** *n* — **hea·then·ish** *adj* — **hea·then·ism** *n*

heath·er \'he-thər\ *n* : a northern and alpine evergreen heath with usu. lavender flowers — **heath·ery** *adj*

heat lightning *n* : flashes of light without thunder ascribed to distant lightning reflected by high clouds

heat·stroke \'hēt-₁strōk\ *n* : a disorder marked esp. by high body temperature without sweating and by collapse that follows prolonged exposure to excessive heat

¹**heave** \'hēv\ *vb* **heaved** *or* **hove** \'hōv\; **heav·ing 1** : to rise or lift upward **2** : THROW **3** : to rise and fall rhythmically; *also* : PANT **4** : RETCH **5** : PULL, PUSH — **heav·er** *n*

²**heave** *n* **1** : an effort to lift or raise **2** : THROW, CAST **3** : an upward motion **4** *pl* : a chronic lung disease of horses marked by difficult breathing and persistent cough

heav·en \'he-vən\ *n* **1** : FIRMAMENT — usu. used in pl. **2** *often cap* : the abode of the Deity and of the blessed dead; *also* : a spiritual state of everlasting communion with God **3** *cap* : GOD 1 **4** : a place of supreme happiness — **heav·en·ly** *adj* — **heav·en·ward** *adv or adj*

¹**heavy** \'he-vē\ *adj* **heavi·er; -est 1** : having great weight **2** : hard to bear **3** : SERIOUS **4** : DEEP, PROFOUND **5** : burdened with something oppressive; *also* : PREGNANT **6** : SLUGGISH **7** : DRAB; *also* : DOLEFUL **8** : DROWSY **9** : greater than the average of its kind or class **10** : very rich and hard to digest; *also* : not properly raised or leavened **11** : producing goods (as steel) used in the production of other goods — **heavi·ly** \-və-lē\ *adv* — **heavi·ness** \-vē-nəs\ *n*

²**heavy** *n, pl* **heav·ies** : a theatrical role representing a dignified or imposing person; *also* : a villain esp. in a story

heavy–du·ty \₁he-vē-'dü-tē, -'dyü-\ *adj* : able to withstand unusual strain

heavy–hand·ed \-'han-dəd\ *adj* **1** : CLUMSY **2** : OPPRESSIVE, HARSH

heavy·heart·ed \-'här-təd\ *adj* : SADDENED, DESPONDENT

heavy metal *n* : energetic and highly amplified electronic rock music

heavy·set \₁he-vē-'set\ *adj* : stocky and compact in build

heavy water *n* : water enriched in deuterium

heavy·weight \'he-vē-₁wāt\ *n* : one above average in weight; *esp* : a boxer weighing over 175 pounds

Heb *abbr* Hebrews

He·bra·ism \'hē-brā-₁i-zəm\ *n* : the thought, spirit, or practice characteristic of the Hebrews — **He·bra·ic** \hi-'brā-ik\ *adj*

He·bra·ist \'hē-₁brā-ist\ *n* : a specialist in Hebrew and Hebraic studies

He·brew \'hē-brü\ *n* **1** : the language of the Hebrews **2** : a member of or descendant from a group of Semitic peoples; *esp* : ISRAELITE — **Hebrew** *adj*

He·brews \'hē-(₁)brüz\ *n* — see BIBLE table

hec·a·tomb \'he-kə-₁tōm\ *n* : an ancient Greek and Roman sacrifice of 100 oxen or cattle

heck·le \'he-kəl\ *vb* **heck·led; heck·ling** : to harass with questions or gibes : BADGER — **heck·ler** *n*

hect·are \'hek-ˌtar\ *n* — see METRIC SYSTEM table

hec·tic \'hek-tik\ *adj* **1** : being hot and flushed **2** : filled with excitement, activity, or confusion — **hec·ti·cal·ly** \-ti-k(ə-)lē\ *adv*

hec·to·gram \'hek-tə-ˌgram\ *n* — see METRIC SYSTEM table

hec·to·li·ter \'hek-tə-ˌlē-tər\ *n* — see METRIC SYSTEM table

hec·to·me·ter \'hek-tə-ˌmē-tər, hek-'tä-mə-tər\ *n* — see METRIC SYSTEM table

hec·tor \'hek-tər\ *vb* [*hector* bully, fr. *Hector*, champion of Troy in Greek legend] **1** : SWAGGER **2** : to intimidate by bluster or personal pressure

¹hedge \'hej\ *n* **1** : a fence or boundary formed of shrubs or small trees **2** : BARRIER **3** : a means of protection (as against financial loss)

²hedge *vb* **hedged; hedg·ing 1** : ENCIRCLE **2** : HINDER **3** : to protect oneself financially by a counterbalancing action **4** : to evade the risk of commitment — **hedg·er** *n*

hedge·hog \'hej-ˌhȯg, -ˌhäg\ *n* : a small Old World insect-eating mammal covered with spines; *also* : PORCUPINE

hedgehog

hedge·hop \-ˌhäp\ *vb* : to fly an airplane very close to the ground

hedge·row \-ˌrō\ *n* : a row of shrubs or trees bounding or separating fields

he·do·nism \'hēd-ᵊn-ˌi-zəm\ *n* [Gk *hēdonē* pleasure] : the doctrine that pleasure is the chief good in life; *also* : a way of life based on this — **he·do·nist** \-ist\ *n* — **he·do·nis·tic** \ˌhēd-ᵊn-'i-stik\ *adj*

¹heed \'hēd\ *vb* : to pay attention

²heed *n* : ATTENTION, NOTICE — **heed·ful** \-fəl\ *adj* — **heed·ful·ly** *adv* — **heed·ful·ness** *n* — **heed·less** *adj* — **heed·less·ly** *adv* — **heed·less·ness** *n*

¹heel \'hēl\ *n* **1** : the hind part of the foot **2** : one of the crusty ends of a loaf of bread **3** : a solid attachment forming the back of the sole of a shoe **4** : a rear, low, or bottom part **5** : a contemptible person

²heel *vb* : to tilt to one side : LIST

¹heft \'heft\ *n* : WEIGHT, HEAVINESS

²heft *vb* : to test the weight of by lifting

hefty \'hef-tē\ *adj* **heft·i·er; -est 1** : marked by bigness, bulk, and usu. strength **2** : impressively large

he·ge·mo·ny \hi-'je-mə-nē\ *n* : preponderant influence or authority over others : DOMINATION

he·gi·ra \hi-'jī-rə\ *n* [the *Hegira*, flight of Muhammad from Mecca in A.D. 622, fr. ML, fr. Ar *hijrah*, lit., flight] : a journey esp. when undertaken to escape a dangerous or undesirable environment

heif·er \'he-fər\ *n* : a young cow; *esp* : one that has not had a calf

height \'hīt\ *n* **1** : the highest part or point **2** : the distance from the bottom to the top of something standing upright **3** : ALTITUDE

height·en \'hīt-ᵊn\ *vb* **1** : to increase in amount or degree **2** : to make or become high or higher **syn** enhance, intensify, aggravate, magnify

Heim·lich maneuver \'hīm-lik-\ *n* [Henry J. *Heimlich* b1920 Am. surgeon] : the manual application of sud-

den upward pressure on the upper abdomen of a choking victim to force a foreign object from the windpipe

hei·nous \'hā-nəs\ *adj* [ME, fr. MF *haineus*, fr. *haine* hate, fr. *hair* to hate] : hatefully or shockingly evil — **hei·nous·ly** *adv* — **hei·nous·ness** *n*

heir \'ar\ *n* : one who inherits or is entitled to inherit property, rank, title, or office — **heir·ship** *n*

heir apparent *n, pl* **heirs apparent** : an heir whose right to succeed (as to a title) cannot be taken away if he or she survives the present holder

heir·ess \'ar-əs\ *n* : a female heir esp. to great wealth

heir·loom \'ar-ˌlüm\ *n* **1** : a piece of personal property that descends by inheritance **2** : something handed on from one generation to another

heir presumptive *n, pl* **heirs presumptive** : an heir whose present right to inherit could be lost through the birth of a nearer relative

heist \'hīst\ *vb, slang* : to commit armed robbery on; *also* : STEAL — **heist** *n, slang*

held *past and past part of* HOLD

he·li·cal \'he-li-kəl, 'hē-\ *adj* : SPIRAL

he·li·cop·ter \'he-lə-ˌkäp-tər, 'hē-\ *n* [F *hélicoptère*, fr. Gk *helix* spiral + *pteron* wing] : an aircraft that is supported in the air by one or more rotors revolving on substantially vertical axes

he·lio·cen·tric \ˌhē-lē-ō-'sen-trik\ *adj* : having or relating to the sun as center

he·lio·trope \'hē-lē-ə-ˌtrōp\ *n* [L *heliotropium*, fr. Gk *hēliotropion*, fr. *hēlios* sun + *tropos* turn; fr. its flowers' turning toward the sun] : any of a genus of herbs or shrubs related to the forget-me-not that have small white or purple flowers

he·li·port \'he-lə-ˌpȯrt\ *n* : a landing and takeoff place for a helicopter

he·li·um \'hē-lē-əm\ *n* [NL, fr. Gk *hēlios* sun] : a very light nonflammable gaseous chemical element occurring in various natural gases — see ELEMENT table

he·lix \'hē-liks\ *n, pl* **he·li·ces** \'he-lə-ˌsēz, 'hē-\ *also* **he·lix·es** \'hē-lik-səz\ : something spiral in form

hell \'hel\ *n* **1** : a nether world in which the dead continue to exist **2** : the realm of the devil in which the damned suffer everlasting punishment **3** : a place or state of torment or destruction — **hell·ish** *adj*

hell-bent \'hel-ˌbent\ *adj* : stubbornly determined

hell·cat \-ˌkat\ *n* **1** : WITCH **2 2** : a violently temperamental person; *esp* : an ill-tempered woman

hel·le·bore \'he-lə-ˌbōr\ *n* **1** : any of a genus of poisonous herbs related to the buttercups; *also* : the dried root of a hellebore **2** : a poisonous plant related to the lilies; *also* : its dried roots used in medicine and insecticides

Hel·lene \'he-ˌlēn\ *n* : GREEK

Hel·le·nism \'he-lə-ˌni-zəm\ *n* : a body of humanistic and classical ideals associated with ancient Greece — **Hel·len·ic** \he-'le-nik\ *adj* — **Hel·le·nist** \'he-lə-nist\ *n*

Hel·le·nis·tic \ˌhe-lə-'nis-tik\ *adj* : of or relating to Greek history, culture, or art after Alexander the Great

hell–for–leather *adv* : at full speed

hell·gram·mite \'hel-grə-ˌmīt\ *n* : an aquatic insect larva that is used as bait in fishing

hell·hole \'hel-ˌhōl\ *n* : a place of extreme misery or squalor

hell·ion \'hel-yən\ *n* : a troublesome or mischievous person

hel·lo \hə-'lō, he-\ *n, pl* **hellos** : an expression of greeting — used interjectionally

helm \'helm\ *n* **1** : a lever or wheel for steering a ship **2** : a position of control

hel·met \'hel-mət\ *n* : a protective covering for the head

helms·man \'helmz-mən\ *n* : the person at the helm : STEERSMAN

hel·ot \'he-lət\ *n* : SLAVE, SERF

¹**help** \'help\ *vb* 1 : AID, ASSIST 2 : IMPROVE, RELIEVE 3 : to be of use; *also* : PROMOTE 4 : to change for the better 5 : to refrain from; *also* : PREVENT 6 : to serve with food or drink ⟨∼ yourself⟩ — **help·er** *n*

²**help** *n* 1 : AID, ASSISTANCE; *also* : a source of aid 2 : REMEDY, RELIEF 3 : one who assists another 4 : EMPLOYEE — **help·ful** \-fəl\ *adj* — **help·ful·ly** *adv* — **help·ful·ness** *n* — **help·less** *adj* — **help·less·ly** *adv* — **help·less·ness** *n*

helper T cell *n* : a T cell of the immune system that has a protein on its surface to which HIV attaches and that is reduced to 20 percent or less of normal numbers in AIDS

help·ing *n* : a portion of food

help·mate \'help-ˌmāt\ *n* 1 : HELPER 2 : WIFE

help·meet \-ˌmēt\ *n* : HELPMATE

hel·ter–skel·ter \ˌhel-tər-'skel-tər\ *adv* 1 : in undue haste or disorder 2 : HAPHAZARDLY

helve \'helv\ *n* : a handle of a tool or weapon

Hel·ve·tian \hel-'vē-shən\ *adj* : SWISS — **Helvetian** *n*

¹**hem** \'hem\ *n* 1 : a border of an article (as of cloth) doubled back and stitched down 2 : RIM, MARGIN

²**hem** *vb* **hemmed; hem·ming** 1 : to make a hem in sewing; *also* : BORDER, EDGE 2 : to surround restrictively

he–man \'hē-ˌman\ *n* : a strong virile man

he·ma·tite \'hē-mə-ˌtīt\ *n* : a mineral that consists of an oxide of iron and that constitutes an important iron ore

he·ma·tol·o·gy \ˌhē-mə-'tä-lə-jē\ *n* : a branch of biology that deals with the blood and blood-forming organs — **he·ma·to·log·ic** \-tə-'lä-jik\ *also* **he·ma·to·log·i·cal** \-ji-kəl\ *adj* — **he·ma·tol·o·gist** \-'tä-lə-jist\ *n*

heme \'hēm\ *n* : the deep red iron-containing part of hemoglobin

hemi·sphere \'he-mə-ˌsfir\ *n* 1 : one of the halves of the earth as divided by the equator into northern and southern parts (**northern hemisphere, southern hemisphere**) or by a meridian into two parts so that one half (**eastern hemisphere**) to the east of the Atlantic ocean includes Europe, Asia, and Africa and the half (**western hemisphere**) to the west includes No. and So. America and surrounding waters 2 : either of two half spheres formed by a plane through the sphere's center — **hemi·spher·ic** \ˌhe-mə-'sfir-ik, -'sfer-\ *or* **hemi·spher·i·cal** \-'sfir-i-kəl, -'sfer-\ *adj*

hem·line \'hem-ˌlīn\ *n* : the line formed by the lower edge of a garment

hem·lock \'hem-ˌläk\ *n* 1 : any of several poisonous herbs related to the carrot 2 : an evergreen tree related to the pines; *also* : its soft light wood

he·mo·glo·bin \'hē-mə-ˌglō-bən\ *n* : an iron-containing compound found in red blood cells that carries oxygen from the lungs to the body tissues

he·mo·phil·ia \ˌhē-mə-'fi-lē-ə\ *n* : a hereditary blood defect usu. of males that slows blood clotting with resulting difficulty in stopping bleeding — **he·mo·phil·i·ac** \-lē-ˌak\ *adj or n*

hem·or·rhage \'hem-rij, 'he-mə-\ *n* : a large discharge of blood from the blood vessels — **hemorrhage** *vb* — **hem·or·rhag·ic** \ˌhe-mə-'ra-jik\ *adj*

hem·or·rhoid \'hem-ˌroid, 'he-mə-\ *n* : a swollen mass of dilated veins at or just within the anus — usu. used in pl.

hemp \'hemp\ *n* : a tall widely grown Asian herb related to the mulberry that is the source of a tough fiber used in rope and of marijuana and hashish from its flowers and leaves; *also* : the fiber — **hemp·en** \'hem-pən\ *adj*

hem·stitch \'hem-ˌstich\ *vb* : to embroider (fabric) by drawing out parallel threads and stitching the exposed threads in groups to form designs

hen \'hen\ *n* : a female chicken esp. over a year old; *also* : a female bird

hence \'hens\ *adv* 1 : AWAY 2 : from this time 3 : CONSEQUENTLY 4 : from this source or origin

hence·forth \hens-ˌfȯrth\ *adv* : from this point on

hence·for·ward \-'fȯr-wərd\ *adv* : HENCEFORTH

hench·man \'hench-mən\ *n* [ME *hengestman* groom, fr. *hengest* stallion] : a trusted follower or supporter

hen·na \'he-nə\ *n* 1 : an Old World tropical shrub with fragrant white flowers; *also* : a reddish brown dye obtained from its leaves and used esp. on hair 2 : the color of henna dye

hen·peck \'hen-ˌpek\ *vb* : to nag and boss one's husband

hep \'hep\ *adj* : HIP

hep·a·rin \'he-pə-rən\ *n* : a compound found esp. in liver that slows the clotting of blood and is used medically

he·pat·ic \hi-'pa-tik\ *adj* : of, relating to, or associated with the liver

he·pat·i·ca \hi-'pa-ti-kə\ *n* : any of a genus of herbs related to the buttercups that have lobed leaves and delicate white, pink, or bluish flowers

hep·a·ti·tis \ˌhe-pə-'tī-təs\ *n, pl* **-tit·i·des** \-'ti-tə-ˌdēz\ : inflammation of the liver; *also* : a virus disease of which this is a feature

hep·tam·e·ter \hep-'ta-mə-tər\ *n* : a line of verse containing seven metrical feet

¹**her** \'hər\ *adj* : of or relating to her or herself

²**her** *pron, objective case of* SHE

¹**her·ald** \'her-əld\ *n* 1 : an official crier or messenger 2 : HARBINGER 3 : ANNOUNCER 4 : ADVOCATE

²**herald** *vb* 1 : to give notice of 2 : HAIL, GREET; *also* : PUBLICIZE

he·ral·dic \he-'ral-dik, hə-\ *adj* : of or relating to heralds or heraldry

her·ald·ry \'her-əl-drē\ *n, pl* **-ries** 1 : the practice of devising and granting armorial insignia and of tracing genealogies 2 : INSIGNIA 3 : PAGEANTRY

herb \'ərb, 'hərb\ *n* 1 : a seed plant that lacks woody tissue and dies to the ground at the end of a growing season 2 : a plant or plant part valued for medicinal or savory qualities — **her·ba·ceous** \ˌər-'bā-shəs, ˌhər-\ *adj*

herb·age \'ər-bij, 'hər-\ *n* : green plants esp. when used or fit for grazing

herb·al·ist \'ər-bə-list, 'hər-\ *n* 1 : one who practices healing by the use of herbs 2 : one who collects or grows herbs

her·bar·i·um \ˌər-'bar-ē-əm, ˌhər-\ *n, pl* **-ia** \-ē-ə\ 1 : a collection of dried plant specimens 2 : a place that houses an herbarium

her·bi·cide \'ər-bə-ˌsīd, 'hər-\ *n* : an agent used to destroy or inhibit plant growth — **her·bi·cid·al** \ˌər-bə-'sīd-əl, ˌhər-\ *adj*

her·biv·o·rous \ˌər-'bi-və-rəs, ˌhər-\ *adj* : feeding on plants — **her·bi·vore** \'ər-bə-ˌvȯr, 'hər-\ *n*

her·cu·le·an \ˌhər-kyə-'lē-ən, hər-'kyü-lē-\ *adj, often cap* [*Hercules*, hero of Greek myth renowned for his strength] : of extraordinary power, size, or difficulty

¹**herd** \'hərd\ *n* 1 : a group of animals of one kind kept or living together 2 : a group of people with a common bond 3 : MOB

²**herd** *vb* : to assemble or move in a herd — **herd·er** *n*

herds·man \'hərdz-mən\ *n* : one who manages, breeds, or tends livestock

¹**here** \'hir\ *adv* 1 : in or at this place; *also* : NOW 2 : at or in this point, particular, or case 3 : in the present life or state 4 : to this place

²**here** *n* : this place ⟨get away from ∼⟩

here·abouts \'hir-ə-ˌbauts\ *or* **here·about** \-ˌbaut\ *adv* : in this vicinity

¹**here·af·ter** \hir-'af-tər\ *adv* 1 : after this in sequence or in time 2 : in some future time or state

²**hereafter** *n, often cap* 1 : FUTURE 2 : an existence beyond earthly life

here·by \hir-'bī\ *adv* : by means of this

he·red·i·tary \hə-'re-də-ˌter-ē\ *adj* 1 : genetically passed or passable from parent to offspring 2 : passing by inheritance; *also* : having title or possession through inheritance **3** : of a kind established by tradition

he·red·i·ty \-də-tē\ *n* : the qualities and potentialities genetically derived from one's ancestors; *also* : the passing of these from ancestor to descendant

Her·e·ford \'hər-fərd\ *n* : any of a breed of red=coated beef cattle with white faces and markings

here·in \hir-'in\ *adv* : in this

here·of \-'əv, -'äv\ *adv* : of this

here·on \-'ón, -'än\ *adv* : on this

her·e·sy \'her-ə-sē\ *n, pl* **-sies** [ME *heresie,* fr. OF, fr. LL *haeresis,* fr. LGk *hairesis,* fr. Gk, action of taking, choice, sect, fr. *hairein* to take] **1** : adherence to a religious opinion contrary to church dogma **2** : an opinion or doctrine contrary to church dogma **3** : dissent from a dominant theory, opinion, or practice — **her·e·tic** \-ˌtik\ *n* — **he·ret·i·cal** \hə-'re-ti-kəl\ *adj*

here·to \hir-'tü\ *adv* : to this document

here·to·fore \'hir-tə-ˌfōr\ *adv* : up to this time

here·un·der \hir-'ən-dər\ *adv* : under this or according to this writing

here·un·to \hir-'ən-tü\ *adv* : to this

here·upon \'hir-ə-ˌpón, -ˌpän\ *adv* : on this or immediately after this

here·with \'hir-'with, -'with\ *adv* **1** : with this **2** : HEREBY

her·i·ta·ble \'her-ə-tə-bəl\ *adj* : capable of being inherited

her·i·tage \'her-ə-tij\ *n* **1** : property that descends to an heir **2** : LEGACY **3** : BIRTHRIGHT

her·maph·ro·dite \(ˌ)hər-'ma-frə-ˌdīt\ *n* : an animal or plant having both male and female reproductive organs — **hermaphrodite** *adj* — **her·maph·ro·dit·ic** \(ˌ)hər-ˌma-frə-'di-tik-əl\ *adj*

her·met·ic \hər-'me-tik\ *also* **her·met·i·cal** \-ti-kəl\ *adj* : AIRTIGHT — **her·met·i·cal·ly** \-ti-k(ə-)lē\ *adv*

her·mit \'hər-mət\ *n* [ME *eremite,* fr. OF, fr. LL *eremita,* fr. LGk *erēmitēs,* fr. Gk, adj., living in the desert, fr. *erēmia* desert, fr. *erēmos* desolate] : one who lives in solitude esp. for religious reasons

her·mit·age \-mə-tij\ *n* **1** : the dwelling of a hermit **2** : a secluded dwelling

her·nia \'hər-nē-ə\ *n, pl* **-ni·as** *or* **-ni·ae** \-nē-ˌē, -nē-ˌī\ : a protrusion of a bodily part (as a loop of intestine) into a pouch of the weakened wall of a cavity in which it is normally enclosed — **her·ni·ate** \-nē-ˌāt\ *vb* — **her·ni·a·tion** \ˌhər-nē-'ā-shən\ *n*

he·ro \'hē-rō\ *n, pl* **heroes** **1** : a mythological or legendary figure of great strength or ability **2** : a man admired for his achievements and qualities **3** : the chief male character in a literary or dramatic work **4** *pl usu* **heros** : SUBMARINE **2** — **he·ro·ic** \hi-'rō-ik\ *adj* — **he·ro·i·cal·ly** \-i-k(ə-)lē\ *adv*

heroic couplet *n* : a rhyming couplet in iambic pentameter

he·ro·ics \hi-'rō-iks\ *n pl* : heroic or showy behavior

her·o·in \'her-ə-wən\ *n* : an illicit addictive narcotic drug made from morphine

her·o·ine \'her-ə-wən\ *n* **1** : a woman admired for her achievements and qualities **2** : the chief female character in a literary or dramatic work

her·o·ism \'her-ə-ˌwi-zəm\ *n* **1** : heroic conduct **2** : the qualities of a hero **syn** valor, prowess, gallantry

her·on \'her-ən\ *n, pl* **herons** *also* **heron** : any of various long-legged long-billed wading birds with soft plumage

her·pes \'hər-pēz\ *n* : any of several virus diseases characterized by the formation of blisters on the skin or mucous membranes

herpes sim·plex \-'sim-ˌpleks\ *n* : either of two virus diseases marked in one by watery blisters above the waist (as on the mouth and lips) and in the other on the sex organs

herpes zos·ter \-'zäs-tər\ *n* : SHINGLES

her·pe·tol·o·gy \ˌhər-pə-'tä-lə-jē\ *n* : a branch of zool-

ogy dealing with reptiles and amphibians — **her·pe·tol·o·gist** \ˌhər-pə-'tä-lə-jist\ *n*

her·ring \'her-iŋ\ *n, pl* **herring** *or* **herrings** : a valuable narrow-bodied food fish of the north Atlantic; *also* : a related fish of the north Pacific harvested esp. for its roe

her·ring·bone \'her-iŋ-ˌbōn\ *n* : a pattern made up of rows of parallel lines with adjacent rows slanting in reverse directions; *also* : a twilled fabric with this pattern

hers \'hərz\ *pron* : one or the ones belonging to her

her·self \hər-'self\ *pron* : SHE, HER — used reflexively, for emphasis, or in absolute constructions

hertz \'hərts, 'herts\ *n, pl* **hertz** : a unit of frequency equal to one cycle per second

hes·i·tant \'he-zə-tənt\ *adj* : tending to hesitate — **hes·i·tance** \-təns\ *n* — **hes·i·tan·cy** \-tən-sē\ *n* — **hes·i·tant·ly** *adv*

hes·i·tate \'he-zə-ˌtāt\ *vb* **-tat·ed; -tat·ing** **1** : to hold back (as in doubt) **2** : PAUSE **syn** waver, vacillate, falter, shilly-shally — **hes·i·ta·tion** \ˌhe-zə-'tā-shən\ *n*

het·ero·dox \'he-tə-rə-ˌdäks\ *adj* **1** : differing from an acknowledged standard **2** : holding unorthodox opinions — **het·ero·doxy** \-ˌdäk-sē\ *n*

het·er·o·ge·neous \ˌhe-tə-rə-'jē-nē-əs, -nyəs\ *adj* : consisting of dissimilar ingredients or constituents : MIXED — **het·er·o·ge·ne·ity** \-jə-'nē-ə-tē\ *n* — **het·er·o·ge·neous·ly** *adv*

het·ero·sex·u·al \ˌhe-tə-rō-ˌsek-shə-wəl\ *adj* **1** : of, relating to, or marked by sexual interest in the opposite sex; *also* : of, relating to, or involving sexual intercourse between members of opposite sex **2** : of or relating to different sexes — **heterosexual** *n* — **het·ero·sex·u·al·i·ty** \-ˌsek-shə-'wa-lə-tē\ *n*

hew \'hyü\ *vb* **hewed; hewed** *or* **hewn** \'hyün\; **hewing** **1** : to cut or fell with blows (as of an ax) **2** : to give shape to with or as if with an ax **3** : to conform strictly — **hew·er** *n*

HEW *abbr* Department of Health, Education, and Welfare

¹**hex** \'heks\ *vb* **1** : to practice witchcraft **2** : JINX

²**hex** *n* **1** : SPELL, JINX

³**hex** *adj* : HEXAGONAL

⁴**hex** *abbr* hexagon

hexa·gon \'hek-sə-ˌgän\ *n* : a polygon having six angles and six sides — **hex·ag·o·nal** \hek-'sa-gən-əl\ *adj*

hex·am·e·ter \hek-'sa-mə-tər\ *n* : a line of verse containing six metrical feet

hey·day \'hā-ˌdā\ *n* : a period of greatest strength, vigor, or prosperity

hf *abbr* half

Hf *symbol* hafnium

HF *abbr* high frequency

hg *abbr* hectogram

Hg *symbol* [NL *hydrargyrum,* lit., water silver] mercury

hgt *abbr* height

hgwy *abbr* highway

HH *abbr* **1** Her Highness **2** His Highness **3** His Holiness

HHS *abbr* Department of Health and Human Services

HI *abbr* **1** Hawaii **2** humidity index

hi·a·tus \hī-'ā-təs\ *n* [L, fr. *hiare* to yawn] **1** : a break in an object : GAP **2** : a lapse in continuity

hi·ba·chi \hi-'bä-chē\ *n* [Jp] : a charcoal brazier

hi·ber·nate \'hī-bər-ˌnāt\ *vb* **-nat·ed; -nat·ing** : to pass the winter in a torpid or resting state — **hi·ber·na·tion** \ˌhī-bər-'nā-shən\ *n* — **hi·ber·na·tor** \'hī-bər-ˌnā-tər\ *n*

hi·bis·cus \hī-'bis-kəs, hə-\ *n* : any of a genus of herbs, shrubs, and trees related to the mallows and noted for large showy flowers

hic·cup *also* **hic·cough** \'hi-(ˌ)kəp\ *n* : a spasmodic breathing movement checked by sudden closing of the glottis accompanied by a peculiar sound; *also, pl* : an attack of hiccuping — **hiccup** *vb*

hick \\'hik\ *n* [*Hick*, nickname for *Richard*] : an awkward provincial person — **hick** *adj*

hick·o·ry \\'hi-kə-rē\ *n*, *pl* **-ries** : any of a genus of No. American hardwood trees related to the walnuts; *also* : the wood of a hickory — **hickory** *adj*

hi·dal·go \hi-'dal-gō\ *n*, *pl* **-gos** *often cap* [Sp, fr. earlier *fijo dalgo*, lit., son of something] : a member of the lower nobility of Spain

hidden tax *n* **1** : a tax ultimately paid by someone other than the person on whom it is formally levied **2** : an economic injustice that reduces one's income or buying power

¹**hide** \\'hīd\ *vb* **hid** \\'hid\; **hid·den** \\'hid-ᵊn\ *or* **hid; hiding 1** : to put or remain out of sight **2** : to conceal for shelter or protection; *also* : to seek protection **3** : to keep secret **4** : to turn away in shame or anger — **hider** *n*

²**hide** *n* : the skin of an animal

hide–and–seek \\'hīd-ᵊn-'sēk\ *n* : a children's game in which everyone hides from one player who tries to find them

hide·away \\'hī-də-ˌwā\ *n* : HIDEOUT

hide·bound \\'hīd-ˌbaund\ *adj* : being inflexible or conservative

hid·eous \\'hi-dē-əs\ *adj* [ME *hidous*, fr. OF, fr. *hisde*, *hide* terror] **1** : offensive to one of the senses : UGLY **2** : morally offensive : SHOCKING **syn** ghastly, grisly, gruesome, horrible, lurid, macabre — **hid·eous·ly** *adv* — **hid·eous·ness** *n*

hide·out \\'hī-ˌdaut\ *n* : a place of refuge or concealment

hie \\'hī\ *vb* **hied; hy·ing** *or* **hie·ing** : HASTEN

hi·er·ar·chy \\'hī-ə-ˌrär-kē\ *n*, *pl* **-chies 1** : a ruling body of clergy organized into ranks **2** : persons or things arranged in a graded series — **hi·er·ar·chi·cal** \hī-ə-'rär-ki-kəl\ *adj* — **hi·er·ar·chi·cal·ly** \-k(ə-)lē\ *adv*

hi·er·o·glyph·ic \ˌhī-ə-rə-'gli-fik\ *n* [MF *hieroglyphique*, adj., ultim. fr. Gk *hieroglyphikos*, fr. *hieros* sacred + *glyphein* to carve] **1** : a character in a system of picture writing (as of the ancient Egyptians) **2** : a symbol or sign difficult to decipher

hieroglyphic 1

hi–fi \\'hī-'fī\ *n* **1** : HIGH FIDELITY **2** : equipment for reproduction of sound with high fidelity

hig·gle·dy–pig·gle·dy \ˌhi-gəl-dē-'pi-gəl-dē\ *adv* : in confusion

¹**high** \\'hī\ *adj* **1** : ELEVATED; *also* : TALL **2** : advanced toward fullness or culmination; *also* : slightly tainted **3** : advanced esp. in complexity ⟨~er mathematics⟩ **4** : long past **5** : SHRILL, SHARP **6** : far from the equator ⟨~ latitudes⟩ **7** : exalted in character **8** : of greater degree, size, or amount than average ⟨~ in cholesterol⟩ **9** : of relatively great importance **10** : FORCIBLE, STRONG ⟨~ winds⟩ **11** : showing elation or excitement **12** : INTOXICATED; *also* : excited or stupefied by or as if by a drug — **high·ly** *adv*

²**high** *adv* **1** : at or to a high place or degree **2** : LUXURIOUSLY ⟨living ~⟩

³**high** *n* **1** : an elevated place **2** : a region of high barometric pressure **3** : a high point or level **4** : the gear of a vehicle giving the highest speed **5** : an excited or stupefied state produced by or as if by a drug

high·ball \\'hī-ˌbȯl\ *n* : a usu. tall drink of liquor mixed with water or a carbonated beverage

high beam *n* : the long-range focus of a vehicle headlight

high·born \\'hī-'bȯrn\ *adj* : of noble birth

high·boy \-ˌbȯi\ *n* : a high chest of drawers mounted on a base with legs

high·bred \-'bred\ *adj* : coming from superior stock

high·brow \-ˌbrau\ *n* : a person of superior learning or culture — **highbrow** *adj* — **high·brow·ism** \-ˌbrau-ˌi-zəm\ *n*

high–density li·po·pro·tein \-ˌlī-pō-'prō-tēn, -ˌli-\ *n* : HDL

high·er–up \ˌhī-ər-'əp\ *n* : a superior officer or official

high–fa·lu·tin \ˌhī-fə-'lüt-ᵊn\ *adj* : PRETENTIOUS, POMPOUS

high fashion *n* **1** : HIGH STYLE **2** : HAUTE COUTURE

high fidelity *n* : the reproduction of sound or image with a high degree of faithfulness to the original

high five *n* : a slapping of upraised right hands by two people (as in celebration) — **high–five** *vb*

high–flown \\'hī-'flōn\ *adj* **1** : EXALTED **2** : BOMBASTIC

high frequency *n* : a radio frequency between 3 and 30 megahertz

high gear *n* **1** : HIGH 4 **2** : a state of intense or maximum activity

high–hand·ed \\'hī-'han-dəd\ *adj* : OVERBEARING — **high–hand·ed·ly** *adv* — **high–hand·ed·ness** *n*

high–hat \-'hat\ *adj* : SUPERCILIOUS, SNOBBISH — **high–hat** *vb*

high·land \\'hī-lənd\ *n* : elevated or mountainous land

high·land·er \-lən-dər\ *n* **1** : an inhabitant of a highland **2** *cap* : an inhabitant of the Scottish Highlands

¹**high·light** \-ˌlīt\ *n* : an event or detail of major importance

²**highlight** *vb* **1** : EMPHASIZE **2** : to constitute a highlight of

high–mind·ed \-'mīn-dəd\ *adj* : marked by elevated principles and feelings — **high–mind·ed·ness** *n*

high·ness \\'hī-nəs\ *n* **1** : the quality or state of being high **2** — used as a title (as for kings)

high–pres·sure \-'pre-shər\ *adj* : using or involving aggressive and insistent sales techniques

high–rise \-'rīz\ *adj* : having several stories and being equipped with elevators ⟨~ apartments⟩; *also* : of or relating to high-rise buildings

high road *n* : HIGHWAY

high school *n* : a school usu. including grades 9 to 12 or 10 to 12

high sea *n* : the open sea outside territorial waters — usu. used in pl.

high–sound·ing \\'hī-'saun-diŋ\ *adj* : POMPOUS, IMPOSING

high–spir·it·ed \-'spir-ə-təd\ *adj* : characterized by a bold or energetic spirit

high–strung \-'strəŋ\ *adj* : having an extremely nervous or sensitive temperament

high style *n* : the newest in fashion or design

high·tail \\'hī-ˌtāl\ *vb* : to retreat at full speed

high tech \-'tek\ *n* : HIGH TECHNOLOGY

high technology *n* : technology involving the use of advanced devices

high–ten·sion \\'hī-'ten-chən\ *adj* : having or using a high voltage

high–test \-'test\ *adj* : having a high octane number

high–toned \-'tōnd\ *adj* **1** : high in social, moral, or intellectual quality **2** : PRETENTIOUS, POMPOUS

high·way \\'hī-ˌwā\ *n* : a main direct road

high·way·man \-ˌwā-mən\ *n* : a person who robs travelers on a road

hi·jack *also* **high·jack** \\'hī-jak\ *vb* : to steal esp. by stopping a vehicle on the highway; *also* : to commandeer a flying airplane — **hijack** *n* — **hi·jack·er** *n*

¹**hike** \\'hīk\ *vb* **hiked; hik·ing 1** : to move or raise with a sudden motion **2** : to take a long walk — **hik·er** *n*

²**hike** *n* **1** : a long walk **2** : RISE, INCREASE

hi·lar·i·ous \hi-'lar-ē-əs, hī-\ *adj* : marked by or providing boisterous merriment — **hi·lar·i·ous·ly** *adv* — **hi·lar·i·ty** \-ə-tē\ *n*

hill \\'hil\ *n* **1** : a usu. rounded elevation of land **2** : a little heap or mound (as of earth) — **hilly** *adj*

hill·bil·ly \\'hil-ˌbi-lē\ *n*, *pl* **-lies** : a person from a backwoods area

hill·ock \'hi-lək\ *n* : a small hill
hill·side \'hil-ˌsīd\ *n* : the part of a hill between the summit and the foot
hill·top \-ˌtäp\ *n* : the top of a hill
hilt \'hilt\ *n* : a handle esp. of a sword or dagger
him \'him\ *pron, objective case of* HE
Hi·ma·la·yan \ˌhi-mə-'lā-ən, hi-'mäl-yən\ *adj* : of, relating to, or characteristic of the Himalaya mountains or the people living there
him·self \him-'self\ *pron* : HE, HIM — used reflexively, for emphasis, or in absolute constructions
¹hind \'hīnd\ *n, pl* **hinds** *also* **hind** : a female of a common Eurasian deer
²hind *adj* : REAR
¹hin·der \'hin-dər\ *vb* **1** : to impede the progress of **2** : to hold back **syn** obstruct, block, bar, impede
²hind·er \'hīn-dər\ *adj* : HIND
Hin·di \'hin-dē\ *n* : a literary and official language of northern India
hind·most \'hīnd-ˌmōst\ *adj* : farthest to the rear
hind·quar·ter \-ˌkwȯr-tər\ *n* **1** : one side of the back half of the carcass of a quadruped **2** *pl* : the part of the body of a quadruped behind the junction of hind limbs and trunk
hin·drance \'hin-drəns\ *n* **1** : the state of being hindered; *also* : the action of hindering **2** : IMPEDIMENT 1
hind·sight \'hīnd-ˌsīt\ *n* : understanding of an event after it has happened
Hindu–Arabic *adj* : relating to, being, or composed of Arabic numerals
Hin·du·ism \'hin-dü-ˌi-zəm\ *n* : a body of religious beliefs and practices native to India — **Hin·du** *n or adj*
hind wing *n* : either of the posterior wings of a 4-winged insect
¹hinge \'hinj\ *n* : a jointed device on which a swinging part (as a door, gate, or lid) turns
²hinge *vb* **hinged; hing·ing 1** : to attach by or furnish with hinges **2** : to be contingent on a single consideration
hint \'hint\ *n* **1** : an indirect or summary suggestion **2** : CLUE **3** : a very small amount **syn** dash, soupçon, suspicion, tincture, touch — **hint** *vb*
hin·ter·land \'hin-tər-ˌland\ *n* **1** : a region behind a coast **2** : a region remote from cities
¹hip \'hip\ *n* : the fruit of a rose
²hip *n* **1** : the part of the body on either side below the waist consisting of the side of the pelvis and the upper thigh **2** : HIP JOINT
³hip *adj* **hip·per; hip·pest** : keenly aware of or interested in the newest developments or styles — **hip·ness** *n*
⁴hip *vb* **hipped; hip·ping** : TELL, INFORM
hip·bone \'hip-'bōn, -ˌbōn\ *n* : the large flaring bone that makes a lateral half of the pelvis in mammals
hip joint *n* : the articulation between the femur and the hipbone
hipped \'hipt\ *adj* : having hips esp. of a specified kind ⟨broad-*hipped*⟩
hip·pie *or* **hip·py** \'hi-pē\ *n, pl* **hippies** : a usu. young person who rejects established mores, advocates nonviolence, and often uses psychedelic drugs or marijuana; *also* : a long-haired unconventionally dressed young person
hip·po·drome \'hi-pə-ˌdrōm\ *n* : an arena for equestrian performances
hip·po·pot·a·mus \ˌhi-pə-'pä-tə-məs\ *n, pl* **-mus·es** *or* **-mi** \-ˌmī\ [L, fr. Gk *hippopotamos*, alter. of *hippos potamios*, lit., river horse] : a large thick-skinned river mammal of sub-Saharan Africa that is related to the swine
¹hire \'hīr\ *n* **1** : payment for labor or personal services : WAGES **2** : EMPLOYMENT **3** : one who is hired
²hire *vb* **hired; hir·ing 1** : to employ for pay **2** : to engage the temporary use of for pay **3** : to take employment

hire·ling \'hīr-liŋ\ *n* : a hired person; *esp* : one with mercenary motives
hir·sute \'hər-ˌsüt, 'hir-\ *adj* : HAIRY
¹his \'hiz\ *adj* : of or relating to him or himself
²his *pron* : one or the ones belonging to him
His·pan·ic \hi-'spa-nik\ *adj* : of, relating to, or being a person of Latin-American descent living in the U.S. — **Hispanic** *n*
hiss \'his\ *vb* : to make a sharp sibilant sound; *also* : to express disapproval of by hissing — **hiss** *n*
hist *abbr* historian; historical; history
his·ta·mine \'his-tə-ˌmēn, -mən\ *n* : a compound widespread in animal tissues that plays a major role in allergic reactions (as hay fever)
his·to·gram \'his-tə-ˌgram\ *n* : a representation of statistical data by rectangles whose widths represent class intervals and whose heights usu. represent corresponding frequencies
his·to·ri·an \hi-'stȯr-ē-ən\ *n* : a student or writer of history
his·to·ric·i·ty \ˌhis-tə-'ri-sə-tē\ *n* : historical actuality
his·to·ri·og·ra·pher \hi-ˌstȯr-ē-'ä-grə-fər\ *n* : HISTORIAN
his·to·ry \'his-tə-rē\ *n, pl* **-ries** [L *historia*, fr. Gk, inquiry, history, fr. *histōr, istōr* knowing, learned] **1** : a chronological record of significant events often with an explanation of their causes **2** : a branch of knowledge that records and explains past events **3** : events that form the subject matter of history **4** : an established record ⟨a convict's ~ of violence⟩ — **his·tor·ic** \hi-'stȯr-ik\ *adj* — **his·tor·i·cal** \-i-kəl\ *adj* — **his·tor·i·cal·ly** \-k(ə-)lē\ *adv*
his·tri·on·ic \ˌhis-trē-'ä-nik\ *adj* [LL *histrionicus*, fr. L *histrio* actor] **1** : deliberately affected **2** : of or relating to actors, acting, or the theater — **his·tri·on·i·cal·ly** \-ni-k(ə-)lē\ *adv*
his·tri·on·ics \-niks\ *n pl* **1** : theatrical performances **2** : deliberate display of emotion for effect
¹hit \'hit\ *vb* **hit; hit·ting 1** : to reach with a blow : STRIKE; *also* : to arrive with a force like a blow ⟨the storm ~⟩ **2** : to make or bring into contact : COLLIDE **3** : to affect detrimentally ⟨was ~ by the flu⟩ **4** : to make a request of **5** : to come upon **6** : to accord with : SUIT **7** : REACH, ATTAIN **8** : to indulge in often to excess — **hit·ter** *n*
²hit *n* **1** : an act or instance of hitting or being hit **2** : a great success **3** : BASE HIT **4** : a dose of an illegal drug **5** : a murder committed by a gangster
¹hitch \'hich\ *vb* **1** : to move by jerks **2** : to catch or fasten esp. by a hook or knot **3** : HITCHHIKE
²hitch *n* **1** : JERK, PULL **2** : a sudden halt **3** : a connection between something towed and its mover **4** : KNOT
hitch·hike \'hich-ˌhīk\ *vb* : to travel by securing free rides from passing vehicles — **hitch·hik·er** *n*
¹hith·er \'hi-thər\ *adv* : to this place
²hither *adj* : being on the near or adjacent side
hith·er·to \-ˌtü\ *adv* : up to this time
HIV \ˌāch-(ˌ)ī-'vē\ *n* [*h*uman *i*mmunodeficiency *v*irus] : any of several retroviruses that infect and destroy helper T cells causing the great reduction in their numbers diagnostic of AIDS
hive \'hīv\ *n* **1** : a container for housing honeybees **2** : a colony of bees **3** : a place swarming with busy occupants — **hive** *vb*
hives \'hīvz\ *n sing or pl* : an allergic disorder marked by raised itching patches on the skin or mucous membranes
hl *abbr* hectoliter
HL *abbr* House of Lords
hm *abbr* hectometer
HM *abbr* **1** Her Majesty; Her Majesty's **2** His Majesty; His Majesty's
HMO \ˌāch-(ˌ)em-'ō\ *n* [*h*ealth *m*aintenance *o*rganization] : a comprehensive health-care organization financed by periodic fixed payments by voluntarily enrolled individuals and families

HMS *abbr* **1** Her Majesty's ship **2** His Majesty's ship

Ho *symbol* holmium

hoa·gie *also* **hoa·gy** \'hō-gē\ *n, pl* **hoagies** : SUBMARINE 2

hoard \'hōrd\ *n* : a hidden accumulation — **hoard** *vb* — **hoard·er** *n*

hoar·frost \'hōr-ˌfrȯst\ *n* : FROST 2

hoarse \'hōrs\ *adj* **hoars·er; hoars·est 1** : rough and harsh in sound **2** : having a grating voice — **hoarse·ly** *adv* — **hoarse·ness** *n*

hoary \'hōr-ē\ *adj* **hoar·i·er; -est 1** : gray or white with or as if with age **2** : ANCIENT — **hoar·i·ness** \'hōr-ē-nəs\ *n*

hoax \'hōks\ *n* : an act intended to trick or dupe; *also* : something accepted or established by fraud — **hoax** *vb* — **hoax·er** *n*

hob \'häb\ *n* : MISCHIEF, TROUBLE

¹hob·ble \'hä-bəl\ *vb* **hob·bled, hob·bling 1** : to limp along; *also* : to make lame **2** : FETTER

²hobble *n* **1** : a hobbling movement **2** : something used to hobble an animal

hob·by \'hä-bē\ *n, pl* **hobbies** : a pursuit or interest engaged in for relaxation — **hob·by·ist** \-ist\ *n*

hob·by·horse \'hä-bē-ˌhȯrs\ *n* **1** : a stick with a horse's head on which children pretend to ride **2** : a toy horse mounted on rockers **3** : a topic to which one constantly reverts

hob·gob·lin \'häb-ˌgäb-lən\ *n* **1** : a mischievous goblin **2** : BOGEY 1

hob·nail \-ˌnāl\ *n* : a short large-headed nail for studding shoe soles — **hob·nailed** \-ˌnāld\ *adj*

hob·nob \-ˌnäb\ *vb* **hob·nobbed; hob·nob·bing** : to associate familiarly

ho·bo \'hō-bō\ *n, pl* **hoboes** *also* **hobos** : TRAMP 2

¹hock \'häk\ *n* : a joint or region in the hind limb of a quadruped just above the foot and corresponding to the human ankle

²hock *n* [D *hok* pen, prison] : PAWN; *also* : DEBT 3 — **hock** *vb*

hock·ey \'hä-kē\ *n* **1** : FIELD HOCKEY **2** : ICE HOCKEY

ho·cus-po·cus \ˌhō-kəs-'pō-kəs\ *n* **1** : SLEIGHT OF HAND **2** : nonsense or sham used to conceal deception

hod \'häd\ *n* : a long-handled carrier for mortar or bricks

hodge·podge \'häj-ˌpäj\ *n* : a heterogeneous mixture : JUMBLE

hoe \'hō\ *n* : a long-handled implement with a thin flat blade used esp. for cultivating, weeding, or loosening the earth around plants — **hoe** *vb*

hoe·cake \-ˌkāk\ *n* : a small cornmeal cake

hoe·down \-ˌdaùn\ *n* **1** : SQUARE DANCE **2** : a gathering featuring hoedowns

¹hog \'hȯg, 'häg\ *n, pl* **hogs** *also* **hog 1** : a domestic swine esp. when grown **2** : a selfish, gluttonous, or filthy person — **hog·gish** *adj*

²hog *vb* **hogged; hog·ging** : to take or hold selfishly

ho·gan \'hō-ˌgän\ *n* : a Navajo Indian dwelling usu. made of logs and mud

hogan

hog·back \'hȯg-ˌbak, 'häg-\ *n* : a ridge with a sharp summit and steep sides

hog·nose snake \'hȯg-ˌnōz-, 'häg-\ *or* **hog·nosed snake** \-ˌnōzd-\ *n* : any of a genus of rather small harmless stout-bodied No. American snakes that seldom bite but hiss wildly and often play dead when disturbed

hogs·head \'hȯgz-ˌhed, 'hägz-\ *n* **1** : a large cask or barrel **2** : a liquid measure equal to 63 U.S. gallons

hog–tie \'hȯg-ˌtī, 'häg-\ *vb* **1** : to tie together the feet of ⟨~ a calf⟩ **2** : to make helpless

hog·wash \-ˌwȯsh, -ˌwäsh\ *n* **1** : SWILL, SLOP **2** : NONSENSE, BALONEY

hog–wild \-'wīld\ *adj* : lacking in restraint

hoi pol·loi \ˌhȯi-pə-'lȯi\ *n pl* [Gk, the many] : the general populace

¹hoist \'hȯist\ *vb* : RAISE, LIFT

²hoist *n* **1** : LIFT **2** : an apparatus for hoisting

hoke \'hōk\ *vb* **hoked; hok·ing** : FAKE — usu. used with *up*

hok·ey \'hō-kē\ *adj* **hok·i·er; -est** : CORNY; *also* : PHONY

ho·kum \'hō-kəm\ *n* : NONSENSE

¹hold \'hōld\ *vb* **held** \'held\; **hold·ing 1** : POSSESS; *also* : KEEP **2** : RESTRAIN **3** : to have a grasp on **4** : to support, remain, or keep in a particular situation or position **5** : SUSTAIN; *also* : RESERVE **6** : BEAR, COMPORT **7** : to maintain in being or action : PERSIST **8** : CONTAIN, ACCOMMODATE **9** : HARBOR, ENTERTAIN; *also* : CONSIDER, REGARD **10** : to carry on by concerted action; *also* : CONVOKE **11** : to occupy esp. by appointment or election **12** : to be valid **13** : HALT, PAUSE — **hold·er** *n* — **hold forth** : to speak at length — **hold to** : to adhere to : MAINTAIN — **hold with** : to agree with or approve of

²hold *n* **1** : STRONGHOLD **2** : CONFINEMENT; *also* : PRISON **3** : the act or manner of holding : GRIP **4** : a restraining, dominating, or controlling influence **5** : something that may be grasped as a support **6** : an order or indication that something is to be reserved or delayed — **on hold** : in a temporary state of waiting (as during a phone call); *also* : in a state of postponement ⟨plans *on hold*⟩

³hold *n* **1** : the interior of a ship below decks; *esp* : a ship's cargo deck **2** : an airplane's cargo compartment

hold·ing *n* **1** : land or other property owned **2** : a ruling of a court esp. on an issue of law

holding pattern *n* : a course flown by an aircraft waiting to land

hold out *vb* **1** : to continue to fight or work **2** : to refuse to come to an agreement — **hold·out** \-ˌdaùt\ *n*

hold·over \'hōl-ˌdō-vər\ *n* : one that is held over

hold·up \'hōl-ˌdəp\ *n* **1** : DELAY **2** : robbery at the point of a gun

hole \'hōl\ *n* **1** : an opening into or through something **2** : a hollow place (as a pit or cave) **3** : DEN, BURROW **4** : a wretched or dingy place **5** : a unit of play from tee to cup in golf **6** : an awkward position — **hole** *vb*

hol·i·day \'hä-lə-ˌdā\ *n* [ME, fr. OE *hāligdæg*, fr. *hālig* holy + *dæg* day] **1** : a day set aside for special religious observance **2** : a day of freedom from work; *esp* : one in commemoration of an event **3** : VACATION — **holiday** *vb*

ho·li·ness \'hō-lē-nəs\ *n* : the quality or state of being holy — used as a title for various high religious officials

ho·lis·tic \hō-'lis-tik\ *adj* : relating to or concerned with integrated wholes or complete systems rather than with the analysis or treatment of separate parts ⟨~ medicine⟩ ⟨~ ecology⟩

hol·ler \'hä-lər\ *vb* : to cry out : SHOUT — **holler** *n*

¹hol·low \'hä-lō\ *n* **1** : CAVITY, HOLE **2** : a surface depression

²hollow *adj* **hol·low·er** \'hä-lə-wər\; **hol·low·est** \-lə-wəst\ **1** : CONCAVE, SUNKEN **2** : having a cavity within **3** : lacking in real value, sincerity, or substance; *also* : FALSE **4** : MUFFLED ⟨a ~ sound⟩ — **hol·low·ness** *n*

³**hollow** *vb* : to make or become hollow

hol·low·ware *or* **hol·lo·ware** \'hä-lə-ˌwar\ *n* : vessels (as bowls or cups) with a significant depth and volume

hol·ly \'hä-lē\ *n, pl* **hollies** : either of two trees or shrubs with branches of usu. evergreen glossy spiny-margined leaves and red berries

hol·ly·hock \'hä-lē-ˌhäk, -ˌhòk\ *n* [ME *holihoc*, fr. *holi* holy + *hoc* mallow] : a perennial Chinese herb related to the mallows that is widely grown for its tall stalks of showy flowers

hol·mi·um \'hōl-mē-əm\ *n* : a metallic chemical element — see ELEMENT table

ho·lo·caust \'hä-lə-ˌkòst, 'hō-\ *n* **1** : a thorough destruction esp. by fire **2** *often cap* : the killing of European Jews by the Nazis during World War II; *also* : GENOCIDE

Ho·lo·cene \'hō-lə-ˌsēn\ *adj* : of, relating to, or being the present geologic epoch — **Holocene** *n*

ho·lo·gram \'hō-lə-ˌgram, 'hä-\ *n* : a three-dimensional image produced by an interference pattern of light (as laser light)

ho·lo·graph \'hō-lə-ˌgraf, 'hä-\ *n* : a document wholly in the handwriting of its author

ho·log·ra·phy \hō-'lä-grə-fē\ *n* : the process of making a hologram — **ho·lo·graph·ic** \ˌhō-lə-'gra-fik, ˌhä-\ *adj*

Hol·stein \'hōl-ˌstēn, -ˌstīn\ *n* : any of a breed of large black-and-white dairy cattle that produce large quantities of comparatively low-fat milk

Hol·stein–Frie·sian \-'frē-zhən\ *n* : HOLSTEIN

hol·ster \'hōl-stər\ *n* [D] : a usu. leather case for a firearm

ho·ly \'hō-lē\ *adj* **ho·li·er; -est 1** : worthy of absolute devotion **2** : SACRED **3** : having a divine quality **syn** hallowed, blessed, sanctified, consecrated — **ho·li·ly** \-lə-lē\ *adv*

Holy Spirit *n* : the third person of the Christian Trinity

ho·ly·stone \'hō-lē-ˌstōn\ *n* : a soft sandstone used to scrub a ship's decks — **holystone** *vb*

hom·age \'ä-mij, 'hä-\ *n* [ME, fr. OF *hommage*, fr. *homme* man, vassal, fr. L *homo* human being] : expression of high regard; *also* : TRIBUTE 3

hom·bre \'äm-brē, 'əm-, -ˌbrā\ *n* : GUY, FELLOW

hom·burg \'häm-bərg\ *n* [*Homburg*, Germany] : a man's felt hat with a stiff curled brim and a high crown creased lengthwise

¹**home** \'hōm\ *n* **1** : one's residence; *also* : HOUSE **2** : the social unit formed by a family living together **3** : a congenial environment; *also* : HABITAT **4** : a place of origin **5** : the objective in various games

²**home** *vb* **homed; hom·ing 1** : to go or return home **2** : to proceed to or toward a source of radiated energy used as a guide

home·body \'hōm-ˌbä-dē\ *n* : one whose life centers in the home

home·boy \-ˌbòi\ *n* **1** : a boy or man from one's neighborhood, hometown, or region **2** : a fellow member of a youth gang

home·bred \-'bred\ *adj* : produced at home : INDIGENOUS

home·com·ing \-ˌkə-miŋ\ *n* **1** : a return home **2** : the return of a group of people esp. on a special occasion to a place formerly frequented

home computer *n* : a small inexpensive microcomputer

home economics *n* : the theory and practice of homemaking

home·grown \'hōm-'grōn\ *adj* **1** : grown domestically **2** : LOCAL, INDIGENOUS

home·land \-ˌland\ *n* **1** : native land **2** : an area set aside to be a state for a people of a particular national, cultural, or racial origin

¹**home·less** \-ləs\ *adj* : having no home or permanent residence

²**homeless** *n, pl* : persons esp. in urban areas that have no home

home·ly \'hōm-lē\ *adj* **home·li·er; -est 1** : FAMILIAR **2** : unaffectedly natural **3** : lacking beauty or proportion — **home·li·ness** \-lē-nəs\ *n*

home·made \'hōm-ˌmād\ *adj* : made in the home, on the premises, or by one's own efforts

home·mak·er \-ˌmā-kər\ *n* : one who manages a household esp. as a wife and mother — **home·mak·ing** \-kiŋ\ *n*

ho·me·op·a·thy \ˌhō-mē-'ä-pə-thē\ *n* : a system of medical practice that treats disease esp. with minute doses of a remedy that would in healthy persons produce symptoms similar to those of the disease treated — **ho·meo·path** \'hō-mē-ə-ˌpath\ *n* — **ho·meo·path·ic** \ˌhō-mē-ə-'pa-thik\ *adj*

ho·meo·sta·sis \ˌhō-mē-ō-'stā-səs\ *n* : the maintence of a relatively stable state of equilibrium between interrelated physiological, psychological, or social factors characteristic of an individual or group — **ho·meo·stat·ic** \-'sta-tik\ *adj*

home plate *n* : a slab at the apex of a baseball diamond that a base runner must touch in order to score

hom·er \'hō-mər\ *n* : HOME RUN — **homer** *vb*

home·room \'hōm-ˌrüm, -ˌrum\ *n* : a classroom where pupils report at the beginning of each school day

home run *n* : a hit in baseball that enables the batter to go around all the bases and score a run

home·sick \'hōm-ˌsik\ *adj* : longing for home and family while absent from them — **home·sick·ness** *n*

home·spun \-ˌspən\ *adj* **1** : spun or made at home; *also* : made of a loosely woven usu. woolen or linen fabric **2** : SIMPLE, HOMELY

¹**home·stead** \-ˌsted\ *n* : the home and land occupied by a family

²**homestead** *vb* : to acquire or settle on public land — **home·stead·er** *n*

home·stretch \-'strech\ *n* **1** : the part of a racecourse between the last curve and the winning post **2** : a final stage (as of a project)

¹**home·ward** \-wərd\ *or* **home·wards** \-wərdz\ *adv* : toward home

²**homeward** *adj* : being or going toward home

home·work \-ˌwərk\ *n* **1** : an assignment given a student to be completed outside the classroom **2** : preparatory reading or research

hom·ey \'hō-mē\ *adj* **hom·i·er; -est** : characteristic of home

ho·mi·cide \'hä-mə-ˌsīd, 'hō-\ *n* [L *homicida* murderer & *homicidium* manslaughter; both fr. *homo* human being + *caedere* to cut, kill] **1** : a person who kills another **2** : a killing of one human being by another — **hom·i·cid·al** \ˌhä-mə-'sīd-əl\ *adj*

hom·i·ly \'hä-mə-lē\ *n, pl* **-lies** : SERMON — **hom·i·let·ic** \ˌhä-mə-'le-tik\ *adj*

homing pigeon *n* : a racing pigeon trained to return home

hom·i·nid \'hä-mə-nəd, -ˌnid\ *n* : any of a family of primate mammals that comprise all living humans and extinct ancestral and related forms — **hominid** *adj*

hom·i·ny \'hä-mə-nē\ *n* : hulled corn with the germ removed

ho·mo·ge·neous \ˌhō-mə-'jē-nē-əs, -nyəs\ *adj* : of the same or a similar kind; *also* : of uniform structure — **ho·mo·ge·ne·i·ty** \-jə-'nē-ə-tē\ *n* — **ho·mo·ge·neous·ly** *adv*

ho·mog·e·nize \hō-'mä-jə-ˌnīz, hə-\ *vb* **-nized; -nizing 1** : to make homogeneous **2** : to reduce the particles in (as milk) to uniform size and distribute them evenly throughout the liquid — **ho·mog·e·ni·za·tion** \-ˌmä-jə-nə-'zā-shən\ *n* — **ho·mog·e·niz·er** *n*

ho·mo·graph \'hä-mə-ˌgraf, 'hō-\ *n* : one of two or more words spelled alike but different in origin, meaning, or pronunciation (as the *bow* of a ship, a *bow* and arrow)

ho·mol·o·gy \hō-'mä-lə-jē, hə-\ *n, pl* **-gies 1** : structural likeness between corresponding parts of different plants or animals due to evolution from a common ancestor 2 : structural likeness between different parts of the same individual — **ho·mol·o·gous** \-ˈmä-lə-gəs\ *adj*

hom·onym \ˈhä-mə-ˌnim, ˈhō-\ *n* 1 : HOMOPHONE, HOMOGRAPH 2 : one of two or more words spelled and pronounced alike but different in meaning (as *pool* of water and *pool* the game)

ho·mo·phone \ˈhä-mə-ˌfōn, ˈhō-\ *n* : one of two or more words (as *to, too, two*) pronounced alike but different in meaning or derivation or spelling

Ho·mo sa·pi·ens \ˌhō-mō-ˈsä-pē-ənz, -ˈsa-\ *n* : HUMANKIND

ho·mo·sex·u·al \ˌhō-mō-ˈsek-shə-wəl\ *adj* : of, relating to, or marked by sexual interst in the same sex as oneself; *also* : of, relating to, or involving sexual intercourse between members of the same sex — **homosexual** *n* — **ho·mo·sex·u·al·i·ty** \-ˌsek-shə-ˈwa-lə-tē\ *n*

hon *abbr* honor; honorable; honorary

Hon·du·ran \hän-ˈdùr-ən\ *or* **Hon·du·ra·ne·an** *or* **Hon·du·ra·ni·an** \ˌhan-dù-ˈrā-nē-ən, -dyù-\ *n* : a native or inhabitant of Honduras — **Honduran** *or* **Honduranean** *or* **Honduranian** *adj*

hone \ˈhōn\ *n* : WHETSTONE — **hone** *vb* — **hon·er** *n*

hone in *vb* : to move toward or direct attention to an objective

¹hon·est \ˈä-nəst\ *adj* 1 : free from deception : TRUTHFUL; *also* : GENUINE, REAL 2 : REPUTABLE 3 : CREDITABLE 4 : marked by integrity 5 : FRANK **syn** upright, just, conscientious, honorable — **hon·est·ly** *adv* — **hon·es·ty** \-nə-stē\ *n*

²honest *adv* : HONESTLY; *also* : with all sincerity ⟨I didn't do it, ~⟩

hon·ey \ˈhə-nē\ *n, pl* **honeys** : a sweet sticky substance made by honeybees from the nectar of flowers

hon·ey·bee \ˈhə-nē-ˌbē\ *n* : a social and colonial 4-winged insect often kept in hives for the honey it produces

¹hon·ey·comb \-ˌkōm\ *n* : a mass of 6-sided wax cells built by honeybees; *also* : something of similar structure or appearance

²honeycomb *vb* : to make or become full of cavities like a honeycomb

hon·ey·dew \-ˌdü, -ˌdyü\ *n* : a sweetish deposit secreted on plants by aphids, scale insects, or fungi

honeydew melon *n* : a smooth-skinned muskmelon with sweet green flesh

honey locust *n* : a tall usu. spiny No. American leguminous tree with hard durable wood and long twisted pods

hon·ey·moon \ˈhə-nē-ˌmün\ *n* 1 : a period of harmony esp. just after marriage 2 : a holiday taken by a newly married couple — **honeymoon** *vb*

hon·ey·suck·le \ˈhə-nē-ˌsə-kəl\ *n* : any of a genus of shrubs or vines with tube-shaped flowers rich in nectar

honk \ˈhäŋk, ˈhòŋk\ *n* : the cry of a goose; *also* : a similar sound (as of a horn) — **honk** *vb* — **honk·er** *n*

hon·ky–tonk \ˈhäŋ-kē-ˌtäŋk, ˈhòŋ-kē-ˌtòŋk\ *n* : a tawdry nightclub or dance hall — **honky–tonk** *adj*

¹hon·or \ˈä-nər\ *n* 1 : good name : REPUTATION; *also* : outward respect 2 : PRIVILEGE 3 : a person of superior standing — used esp. as a title 4 : one who brings respect or fame 5 : an evidence or symbol of distinction 6 : CHASTITY, PURITY 7 : INTEGRITY **syn** homage, reverence, deference, obeisance

²honor *vb* 1 : to regard or treat with honor 2 : to confer honor on 3 : to fulfill the terms of; *also* : to accept as payment — **hon·or·ee** \ˌä-nə-ˈrē\ *n* — **hon·or·er** *n*

hon·or·able \ˈä-nə-rə-bəl\ *adj* 1 : deserving of honor 2 : of great renown 3 : accompanied with marks of honor 4 : doing credit to the possessor 5 : characterized

by integrity — **hon·or·able·ness** *n* — **hon·or·ably** \-blē\ *adv*

hon·o·rar·i·um \ˌä-nə-ˈrer-ē-əm\ *n, pl* **-ia** \-ē-ə\ *also* **-i·ums** : a reward usu. for services on which custom or propriety forbids a price to be set

hon·or·ary \ˈä-nə-ˌrer-ē\ *adj* 1 : having or conferring distinction 2 : conferred in recognition of achievement without the usual prerequisites ⟨~ degree⟩ 3 : UNPAID, VOLUNTARY — **hon·or·ari·ly** \ˌä-nə-ˈrer-ə-lē\ *adv*

hon·or·if·ic \ˌä-nə-ˈri-fik\ *adj* : conferring or conveying honor ⟨~ titles⟩

hon·our, hon·our·able *chiefly Brit var of* HONOR, HONORABLE

¹hood \ˈhùd\ *n* 1 : a covering for the head and neck and sometimes the face 2 : an ornamental fold (as at the back of an ecclesiastical vestment) 3 : a cover for parts of mechanisms; *esp* : the covering over an automobile engine — **hood·ed** \ˈhù-dəd\ *adj*

²hood \ˈhùd, ˈhüd\ *n* : HOODLUM

³hood \ˈhùd\ *n* : NEIGHBORHOOD 4

-hood \ˌhùd\ *n suffix* 1 : state : condition : quality : character ⟨boy*hood*⟩ ⟨hardi*hood*⟩ 2 : instance of a (specified) state or quality ⟨false*hood*⟩ 3 : individuals sharing a (specified) state or character ⟨brother*hood*⟩

hood·lum \ˈhüd-ləm, ˈhùd-\ *n* 1 : THUG 2 : a young ruffian

hoo·doo \ˈhü-dü\ *n, pl* **hoodoos** 1 : a body of magical practices traditional esp. among blacks in the southern U.S. 2 : something that brings bad luck — **hoodoo** *vb*

hood·wink \ˈhùd-ˌwiŋk\ *vb* : to deceive by false appearance

hoo·ey \ˈhü-ē\ *n* : NONSENSE

hoof \ˈhüf, ˈhùf\ *n, pl* **hooves** \ˈhùvz, ˈhüvz\ *or* **hoofs** : a horny covering that protects the ends of the toes of ungulate mammals (as horses or cattle); *also* : a hoofed foot — **hoofed** \ˈhüft, ˈhùft\ *adj*

¹hook \ˈhùk\ *n* 1 : a curved or bent device for catching, holding, or pulling 2 : something curved or bent like a hook 3 : a flight of a ball (as in golf) that curves in a direction opposite to the dominant hand of the player propelling it 4 : a short punch delivered with a circular motion and with the elbow bent and rigid

²hook *vb* 1 : CURVE, CROOK 2 : to seize or make fast with a hook 3 : STEAL 4 : to work as a prostitute

hoo·kah \ˈhù-kə, ˈhü-\ *n* [Ar *ḥuqqah* bottle of a water pipe] : WATER PIPE

hook·er \ˈhù-kər\ *n* 1 : one that hooks 2 : PROSTITUTE

hook·up \ˈhù-kəp\ *n* : an assemblage (as of apparatus or circuits) used for a specific purpose (as in radio)

hook·worm \ˈhùk-ˌwərm\ *n* : any of several parasitic intestinal nematode worms having hooks or plates around the mouth; *also* : infestation with or disease caused by hookworms

hoo·li·gan \ˈhü-li-gən\ *n* : RUFFIAN, HOODLUM

hoop \ˈhùp, ˈhüp\ *n* 1 : a circular strip used esp. for holding together the staves of a barrel 2 : a circular figure or object : RING 3 : a circle of flexible material for expanding a woman's skirt 4 : BASKETBALL — usu. used in pl.

hoop·la \ˈhüp-ˌlä, ˈhùp-\ *n* [F *houp-là*, interj.] : TO-DO; *also* : BALLYHOO

hoose·gow \ˈhüs-ˌgaù\ *n* [Sp *juzgado* panel of judges, courtroom] : JAIL

¹hoot \ˈhüt\ *vb* 1 : to shout or laugh usu. in contempt 2 : to make the natural throat noise of an owl — **hoot·er** *n*

²hoot *n* 1 : a sound of hooting 2 : the least bit ⟨don't give a ~⟩ 3 : something or someone amusing ⟨the play is a real ~⟩

¹hop \ˈhäp\ *vb* **hopped; hop·ping** 1 : to move by quick springy leaps 2 : to make a quick trip 3 : to ride on esp. surreptitiously and without authorization

²hop *n* 1 : a short brisk leap esp. on one leg 2 : DANCE 3 : a short trip by air

³**hop** n : a vine related to the mulberry whose ripe dried pistillate catkins are used esp. in flavoring malt liquors; *also, pl* : its pistillate catkins

¹**hope** \'hōp\ vb **hoped; hop·ing** : to desire with expectation of fulfillment

²**hope** n **1** : TRUST, RELIANCE **2** : desire accompanied by expectation of fulfillment; *also* : something hoped for **3** : one that gives promise for the future — **hope·ful** \-fəl\ adj — **hope·ful·ness** n — **hope·less** adj — **hope·less·ly** adv — **hope·less·ness** n

HOPE abbr Health Opportunity for People Everywhere

hope·ful·ly \'hōp-fə-lē\ adv **1** : in a hopeful manner **2** : it is hoped

Ho·pi \'hō-pē\ n, pl **Hopi** also **Hopis** : a member of an American Indian people of Arizona; *also* : the language of the Hopi people

hopped–up \'häpt-'əp\ adj **1** : being under the influence of a narcotic; *also* : full of enthusiasm or excitement **2** : having more power than usual ⟨a ∼ engine⟩

hop·per \'hä-pər\ n **1** : a usu. immature hopping insect (as a grasshopper) **2** : a usu. funnel-shaped container for delivering material (as grain) **3** : a freight car with hinged doors in a sloping bottom **4** : a box into which a bill to be considered by a legislative body is dropped **5** : a tank holding a liquid and having a device for releasing its contents through a pipe

hop·scotch \'häp-ıskäch\ n : a child's game in which a player tosses an object (as a stone) into areas of a figure drawn on the ground and hops through the figure to pick up the object

hor abbr horizontal

horde \'hōrd\ n : THRONG, SWARM

ho·ri·zon \hə-'rīz-°n\ n [Gk horizont-, horizōn, fr. prp. of horizein to bound, fr. horos limit, boundary] **1** : the apparent junction of earth and sky **2** : range of outlook or experience

hor·i·zon·tal \ıhor-ə-'zänt-°l\ adj : parallel to the horizon : LEVEL — **horizontal** n — **hor·i·zon·tal·ly** adv

hor·mon·al \hor-'mōn-°l\ adj : of, relating to, or effected by hormones

hor·mone \'hor-ımōn\ n [Gk hormōn, prp. of horman to stir up, fr. hormē impulse, assault] : a product of living cells that circulates in body fluids and has a specific effect on the activity of cells remote from its point of origin

horn \'horn\ n **1** : one of the hard projections of bone or keratin on the head of many hoofed mammals **2** : something resembling or suggesting a horn **3** : a brass wind instrument **4** : a usu. electrical device that makes a noise ⟨automobile ∼⟩ — **horned** \'hornd\ adj — **horn·less** adj

horn·book \'horn-ıbùk\ n **1** : a child's primer consisting of a sheet of parchment or paper protected by a sheet of transparent horn **2** : a rudimentary treatise

horned toad n : any of several small harmless insect-eating lizards with spines on the head resembling horns and spiny scales on the body

hor·net \'hor-nət\ n : any of the larger social wasps

horn in vb : to participate without invitation : INTRUDE

horn·pipe \'horn-ıpīp\ n : a lively folk dance of the British Isles

horny \'hor-nē\ adj **horn·i·er; -est 1** : of or made of horn; *also* : HARD, CALLOUS **2** : having horns **3** : desiring sexual gratification; *also* : excited sexually

ho·rol·o·gy \hə-'rä-lə-jē\ n : the science of measuring time or constructing time-indicating instruments — **hor·o·log·ic** \ıhor-ə-'lä-jik\ adj — **ho·rol·o·gist** \hə-'rä-lə-jist\ n

horo·scope \'hor-ə-ıskōp\ n [ME oruscope, fr. MF horoscope, fr. L horoscopus, fr. Gk hōroskopos, fr. hōra hour + skopos watcher] **1** : a diagram of the relative positions of planets and signs of the zodiac at a particular time for use by astrologers to foretell events of a person's life **2** : an astrological forecast

hor·ren·dous \ho-'ren-dəs\ adj : DREADFUL, HORRIBLE

hor·ri·ble \'hor-ə-bəl\ adj **1** : marked by or conducive to horror **2** : highly disagreeable — **hor·ri·ble·ness** n — **hor·ri·bly** \-blē\ adv

hor·rid \'hor-əd\ adj **1** : HIDEOUS **2** : REPULSIVE — **hor·rid·ly** adv

hor·ri·fy \'hor-ə-ıfī\ vb **-fied; -fy·ing** : to cause to feel horror **syn** appall, daunt, dismay

hor·ror \'hor-ər\ n **1** : painful and intense fear, dread, or dismay **2** : intense repugnance **3** : something that horrifies

hors de com·bat \ıor-də-kōⁿ-'bä\ adv or adj : in a disabled condition

hors d'oeuvre \or-'dərv\ n, pl **hors d'oeuvres** \same or -'dərvz\ also **hors d'oeuvre** [F hors-d'oeuvre, lit., outside of the work] : any of various savory foods usu. served as appetizers

horse \'hors\ n, pl **hors·es** also **horse 1** : a large solid-hoofed herbivorous mammal domesticated as a draft and saddle animal **2** : a supporting framework usu. with legs — **horse·less** adj

¹**horse·back** \'hors-ıbak\ n : the back of a horse

²**horseback** adv : on horseback

horse chestnut n : a large Asian tree with palmate leaves, erect conical clusters of showy flowers, and large glossy brown seeds enclosed in a prickly bur; *also* : its seed

horse·flesh \'hors-ıflesh\ n : horses for riding, driving, or racing

horse·fly \-ıflī\ n : any of a family of large dipteran flies with bloodsucking females

horse·hair \-ıhar\ n **1** : the hair of a horse esp. from the mane or tail **2** : cloth made from horsehair

horse·hide \-ıhīd\ n **1** : the dressed or raw hide of a horse **2** : the ball used in baseball

horse latitudes n pl : either of two calm regions near 30°N and 30°S latitude

horse·laugh \'hors-ılaf, -ılaf\ n : a loud boisterous laugh

horse·man \-mən\ n **1** : one who rides horseback; *also* : one skilled in managing horses **2** : a breeder or raiser of horses — **horse·man·ship** n

horse·play \-ıplā\ n : rough boisterous play

horse·play·er \-ər\ n : a bettor on horse races

horse·pow·er \'hors-ıpaù-ər\ n : a unit of power equal in the U.S. to 746 watts

horse·rad·ish \-ıra-dish\ n : a tall white-flowered herb related to the mustards whose pungent root is used as a condiment; *also* : the pungent condiment

horse·shoe \'hors-ıshü\ n **1** : a usu. U-shaped protective metal plate fitted to the rim of a horse's hoof **2** pl : a game in which horseshoes are pitched at a fixed object — **horse·shoe** vb — **horse·sho·er** n

horseshoe crab n : any of several marine arthropods with a broad crescent-shaped combined head and thorax

horse·tail \'hors-ıtāl\ n : any of a genus of primitive spore-producing plants with hollow jointed stems and leaves reduced to sheaths about the joints

horse·whip \-ıhwip\ vb : to flog with a whip made to be used on a horse

horse·wom·an \-ıwu-mən\ n : a woman skilled in riding horseback or in caring for or managing horses; *also* : a woman who breeds or raises horses

hors·ey or **horsy** \'hor-sē\ adj **hors·i·er; -est 1** : of, relating to, or suggesting a horse **2** : having to do with horses or horse racing

hort abbr horticultural; horticulture

hor·ta·tive \'hor-tə-tiv\ adj : giving exhortation

hor·ta·to·ry \'hor-tə-ıtōr-ē\ adj : HORTATIVE

hor·ti·cul·ture \'hor-tə-ıkəl-chər\ n : the science and art of growing fruits, vegetables, flowers, and ornamental plants — **hor·ti·cul·tur·al** \ıhor-tə-'kəl-chə-rəl\ adj — **hor·ti·cul·tur·ist** \-rist\ n

Hos abbr Hosea

ho·san·na \hō-'za-nə, -'zä-\ interj [Gk hōsanna, fr.

Heb *hōshī 'āh-nnā* pray, save (us)!] — used as a cry of acclamation and adoration — **hosanna** *n*

¹hose \'hōz\ *n, pl* **hose** *or* **hos•es 1** *pl* **hose** : STOCKING, SOCK; *also* : a close-fitting garment covering the legs and waist **2** : a flexible tube for conveying fluids (as from a faucet)

²hose *vb* **hosed; hos•ing** : to spray, water, or wash with a hose

Ho•sea \hō-'zā-ə, -'zē-\ *n* — see BIBLE table

ho•siery \'hō-zhə-rē, -zə-\ *n* : STOCKINGS, SOCKS

hosp *abbr* hospital

hos•pice \'häs-pəs\ *n* **1** : a lodging for travelers or for young persons or the underprivileged **2** : a facility or program for caring for dying persons

hos•pi•ta•ble \hä-'spi-tə-bəl, 'häs-(ˌ)pi-\ *adj* **1** : given to generous and cordial reception of guests **2** : readily receptive — **hos•pi•ta•bly** \-blē\ *adv*

hos•pi•tal \'häs-ˌpit-ᵊl\ *n* [ME, fr. OF, fr. ML *hospitale* hospice, guest house, fr neut. of L *hospitalis* of a guest, fr. *hospit-, hospes* guest, host] : an institution where the sick or injured receive medical or surgical care

hos•pi•tal•i•ty \ˌhäs-pə-'ta-lə-tē\ *n, pl* **-ties** : hospitable treatment, reception, or disposition

hos•pi•tal•ize \'häs-ˌpit-ᵊl-ˌīz\ *vb* **-ized; -iz•ing** : to place in a hospital as a patient — **hos•pi•tal•i•za•tion** \ˌhäs-ˌpit-ᵊl-ə-'zā-shən\ *n*

¹host \'hōst\ *n* [ME, fr. OF, fr. LL *hostis,* fr. L, stranger, enemy] **1** : ARMY **2** : MULTITUDE

²host *n* [ME *hoste* host, guest, fr. OF, fr. L *hospit-, hospes*] **1** : one who receives or entertains guests **2** : an animal or plant on or in which a parasite lives — **host** *vb*

³host *n, often cap* [ultim. fr. L *hostia* sacrifice] : the eucharistic bread

hos•tage \'häs-tij\ *n* **1** : a person kept as a pledge pending the fulfillment of an agreement **2** : a person taken by force to secure the taker's demands

hos•tel \'häst-ᵊl\ *n* [ME, fr. OF, fr. ML *hospitale* hospice] **1** : INN **2** : a supervised lodging for youth — **hos•tel•er** *n*

hos•tel•ry \-rē\ *n, pl* **-ries** : INN, HOTEL

host•ess \'hō-stəs\ *n* : a woman who acts as host

hos•tile \'häst-ᵊl, 'häs-ˌtīl\ *adj* : marked by usu. overt antagonism : UNFRIENDLY — **hostile** *n* — **hos•tile•ly** *adv*

hos•til•i•ty \hä-'sti-lə-tē\ *n, pl* **-ties 1** : an unfriendly state or action **2** *pl* : overt acts of war

hos•tler \'häs-lər, 'äs-\ *n* : one who takes care of horses or mules

hot \'hät\ *adj* **hot•ter; hot•test 1** : marked by a high temperature or an uncomfortable degree of body heat **2** : giving a sensation of heat or of burning **3** : ARDENT, FIERY **4** : sexually excited **5** : EAGER **6** : newly made or received **7** : PUNGENT **8** : unusually lucky or favorable ⟨~ dice⟩ **9** : recently and illegally obtained ⟨~ jewels⟩ — **hot** *adv* — **hot•ly** *adv* — **hot•ness** *n*

hot•bed \-ˌbed\ *n* **1** : a glass-covered bed of soil heated (as by fermenting manure) and used esp. for raising seedlings **2** : an environment that favors rapid growth or development

hot–blood•ed \-'blə-dəd\ *adj* : easily roused or excited

hot–box \-ˌbäks\ *n* : a bearing (as of a railroad car) overheated by friction

hot•cake \-ˌkāk\ *n* : PANCAKE

hot dog *n* : a cooked frankfurter usu. served in a long split roll

ho•tel \hō-'tel\ *n* [F *hôtel,* fr. OF *hostel,* fr. ML *hospitale* hospice] : a building where lodging and usu. meals, entertainment, and various personal services are provided for the public

hot flash *n* : a sudden brief flushing and sensation of heat usu. associated with menopausal endocrine imbalance

hot•head•ed \'hät-'he-dəd\ *adj* : FIERY, IMPETUOUS —

hot•head \-ˌhed\ *n* — **hot•head•ed•ly** *adv* — **hot•head•ed•ness** *n*

hot•house \-ˌhaus\ *n* : a heated greenhouse esp. for raising tropical plants

hot line *n* : a telephone line for emergency use (as between governments or to a counseling service)

hot plate *n* : a simple portable appliance for heating or for cooking

hot potato *n* : an embarrassing or controversial issue

hot rod *n* : an automobile modified for high speed and fast acceleration — **hot–rod•der** \-'rä-dər\ *n*

hots \'häts\ *n pl* : strong sexual desire — usu. used with *the*

hot seat *n* : a position of anxiety or embarrassment

hot•shot \'hät-ˌshät\ *n* : a showily skillful person

hot tub *n* : a large wooden tub of hot water in which bathers soak and usu. socialize

hot water *n* : TROUBLE, DIFFICULTY

hot–wire \'hät-ˌwīr\ *vb* : to start (an automobile) by short-circuiting the ignition system

¹hound \'haund\ *n* **1** : any of various long-eared hunting dogs that track prey by scent **2** : FAN, ADDICT

²hound *vb* : to pursue relentlessly

hour \'aur\ *n* **1** : the 24th part of a day : 60 minutes **2** : the time of day **3** : a particular or customary time **4** : a class session — **hour•ly** *adv or adj*

hour•glass \'aur-ˌglas\ *n* : a glass vessel for measuring time in which sand runs from an upper compartment to a lower compartment in an hour

hou•ri \'hur-ē\ *n* [F, fr. Per *hūri,* fr. Ar *ḥūrīyah*] : one of the beautiful maidens of the Muslim paradise

¹house \'haus\ *n, pl* **hous•es** \'hau-zəz\ **1** : a building for human habitation **2** : an animal shelter (as a den or nest) **3** : a building in which something is stored **4** : HOUSEHOLD; *also* : FAMILY **5** : a residence for a religious community or for students; *also* : those in residence **6** : a legislative body **7** : a place of business or entertainment **8** : a business organization **9** : the audience in a theater or concert hall — **house•ful** *n*

²house \'hauz\ *vb* **housed; hous•ing 1** : to provide with or take shelter : LODGE **2** : STORE

house•boat \'haus-ˌbōt\ *n* : a pleasure boat fitted for use as a dwelling or for leisurely cruising

house•boy \-ˌboi\ *n* : a boy or man hired to act as a household servant

house•break \-ˌbrāk\ *vb* **house•broke; house•bro•ken; house•break•ing** : to train in excretory habits acceptable in indoor living

house•break•ing \-ˌbrā-kiŋ\ *n* : the act of breaking into a dwelling with the intent of committing a felony

house•clean \-ˌklēn\ *vb* : to clean a house and its furniture — **house•clean•ing** *n*

house•coat \-ˌkōt\ *n* : a woman's often long-skirted informal garment for wear around the house

house•fly \-ˌflī\ *n* : a dipteran fly that is common about human habitations

¹house•hold \-ˌhōld\ *n* : those who dwell as a family under the same roof — **house•hold•er** *n*

²household *adj* **1** : DOMESTIC **2** : FAMILIAR, COMMON ⟨a ~ name⟩

house•keep•er \-ˌkē-pər\ *n* : a woman employed to take care of a house

house•keep•ing \-ˌkē-piŋ\ *n* : the care and management of a house or institutional property

house•lights \-ˌlīts\ *n pl* : the lights that illuminate the auditorium of a theater

house•maid \-ˌmād\ *n* : a female servant employed to do housework

house•moth•er \-ˌmə-thər\ *n* : a woman acting as hostess, chaperon, and often housekeeper in a group residence

house•plant \-ˌplant\ *n* : a plant grown or kept indoors

house sparrow *n* : a Eurasian sparrow widely introduced in urban and agricultural areas

house•top \'haus-ˌtäp\ *n* : ROOF

house·wares \-ˌwarz\ *n pl* : small articles of household equipment

house·warm·ing \-ˌwȯr-miŋ\ *n* : a party to celebrate the taking possession of a house or premises

house·wife \-ˌwīf\ *n* : a married woman in charge of a household — **house·wife·ly** *adj* — **house·wif·ery** \-ˌwī-fə-rē\ *n*

house·work \-ˌwərk\ *n* : the work of housekeeping

¹hous·ing \'haů-ziŋ\ *n* 1 : SHELTER; *also* : dwellings provided for people 2 : something that covers or protects

²housing *n* : CAPARISON 1

HOV *abbr* high-occupancy vehicle

hove *past and past part of* HEAVE

hov·el \'hə-vəl, 'hä-\ *n* : a small, wretched, and often dirty house : HUT

hov·er \'hə-vər, 'hä-\ *vb* **hov·ered; hov·er·ing** 1 : FLUTTER; *also* : to move to and fro 2 : to be in an uncertain state

hov·er·craft \-ˌkraft\ *n* : a vehicle that rides on a cushion of air over a surface

¹how \'haů\ *adv* 1 : in what way or manner ⟨∼ was it done⟩ 2 : with what meaning ⟨∼ do we interpret such behavior⟩ 3 : for what reason ⟨∼ could you have done such a thing⟩ 4 : to what extent or degree ⟨∼ deep is it⟩ 5 : in what state or condition ⟨∼ are you⟩ — **how about** : what do you say to or think of ⟨*how about* coming with me⟩ — **how come** : why is it that

²how *conj* 1 : in the way or manner in which ⟨remember ∼ they fought⟩ 2 : HOWEVER ⟨do it ∼ you like⟩

¹how·be·it \haů-'bē-ət\ *conj* : ALTHOUGH

²howbeit *adv* : NEVERTHELESS

how·dah \'haů-də\ *n* [Hindi *hauda*] : a seat or covered pavilion on the back of an elephant or camel

¹how·ev·er \haů-'e-vər\ *conj* : in whatever manner that

²however *adv* 1 : to whatever degree; *also* : in whatever manner 2 : in spite of that

how·it·zer \'haů-ət-sər\ *n* : a short cannon that shoots shells at a high angle

howl \'haůl\ *vb* 1 : to emit a loud long doleful sound characteristic of dogs 2 : to cry loudly — **howl** *n*

howl·er \'haů-lər\ *n* 1 : one that howls 2 : a humorous and ridiculous blunder

howl·ing *adj* 1 : DESOLATE, WILD 2 : very great ⟨a ∼ success⟩

how·so·ev·er \ˌhaů-sə-'we-vər\ *adv* : HOWEVER 1

hoy·den \'hȯid-ᵊn\ *n* : a girl or woman of saucy, boisterous, or carefree behavior — **hoy·den·ish** *adj*

hp *abbr* horsepower

HP *abbr* high pressure

HPF *abbr* highest possible frequency

HQ *abbr* headquarters

hr *abbr* 1 here 2 hour

HR *abbr* House of Representatives

HRH *abbr* 1 Her Royal Highness 2 His Royal Highness

hrzn *abbr* horizon

HS *abbr* high school

HST *abbr* Hawaiian standard time

ht *abbr* height

HT *abbr* 1 Hawaii time 2 high-tension

hua·ra·che \wə-'rä-chē\ *n* [MexSp] : a sandal with an upper made of interwoven leather strips

hub \'həb\ *n* 1 : the central part of a circular object (as a wheel) 2 : a center of activity; *esp* : an airport or city with heavy air traffic

hub·bub \'hə-bəb\ *n* : UPROAR; *also* : TURMOIL

hub·cap \'həb-ˌkap\ *n* : a removable metal cap over the end of an axle

hu·bris \'hyü-brəs\ *n* : exaggerated pride or self‑confidence

huck·le·ber·ry \'hə-kəl-ˌber-ē\ *n* 1 : an American shrub related to the blueberry; *also* : its edible dark blue berry 2 : BLUEBERRY

huck·ster \'hək-stər\ *n* : PEDDLER, HAWKER — **huckster** *vb*

HUD *abbr* Department of Housing and Urban Development

¹hud·dle \'həd-ᵊl\ *vb* **hud·dled; hud·dling** 1 : to crowd together 2 : CONFER

²huddle *n* 1 : a closely packed group 2 : MEETING, CONFERENCE

hue \'hyü\ *n* 1 : COLOR; *also* : gradation of color 2 : the attribute of colors that permits them to be classed as red, yellow, green, blue, or an intermediate color — **hued** \'hyüd\ *adj*

hue and cry *n* : a clamor of pursuit or protest

huff \'həf\ *n* : a fit of anger or pique — **huff** *vb* — **huffy** *adj*

hug \'həg\ *vb* **hugged; hug·ging** 1 : EMBRACE 2 : to stay close to — **hug** *n*

huge \'hyüj\ *adj* **hug·er; hug·est** : very large or extensive — **huge·ly** *adv* — **huge·ness** *n*

hug·ger–mug·ger \'hə-gər-ˌmə-gər\ *n* 1 : SECRECY 2 : CONFUSION, MUDDLE

Hu·gue·not \'hyü-gə-ˌnät\ *n* : a French Protestant of the 16th and 17th centuries

hu·la \'hü-lə\ *n* : a sinuous Polynesian dance usu. accompanied by chants

hulk \'həlk\ *n* 1 : a heavy clumsy ship 2 : an old ship unfit for service 3 : a bulky or unwieldy person or thing

hulk·ing \'həl-kiŋ\ *adj* : BURLY, MASSIVE

¹hull \'həl\ *n* 1 : the outer covering of a fruit or seed 2 : the frame or body esp. of a ship or boat

²hull *vb* : to remove the hulls of — **hull·er** *n*

hul·la·ba·loo \'hə-lə-bə-ˌlü\ *n, pl* **-loos** : a confused noise : UPROAR

hul·lo \ˌhə-'lō\ *chiefly Brit var of* HELLO

hum \'həm\ *vb* **hummed; hum·ming** 1 : to utter a sound like that of the speech sound \m\ prolonged 2 : DRONE 3 : to be busily active 4 : to run smoothly 5 : to sing with closed lips — **hum** *n* — **hum·mer** *n*

¹hu·man \'hyü-mən, 'yü-\ *adj* 1 : of, relating to, being, or characteristic of humans 2 : having human form or attributes — **hu·man·ly** *adv* — **hu·man·ness** *n*

²human *n* : any of a species of primate mammals comprising all living persons and their recent ancestors; *also* : HOMINID

hu·mane \hyü-'mān, yü-\ *adj* 1 : marked by compassion, sympathy, or consideration for others 2 : HUMANISTIC — **hu·mane·ly** *adv* — **hu·mane·ness** *n*

human immunodeficiency virus *n* : HIV

hu·man·ism \'hyü-mə-ˌni-zəm, 'yü-\ *n* 1 : devotion to the humanities; *also* : the revival of classical letters characteristic of the Renaissance 2 : a doctrine or way of life centered on human interests or values — **hu·man·ist** \-nist\ *n or adj* — **hu·man·is·tic** \ˌhyü-mə-'nis-tik, ˌyü-\ *adj*

hu·man·i·tar·i·an \hyü-ˌma-nə-'ter-ē-ən, yü-\ *n* : one who practices philanthropy — **humanitarian** *adj* — **hu·man·i·tar·i·an·ism** *n*

hu·man·i·ty \hyü-'ma-nə-tē, yü-\ *n, pl* **-ties** 1 : the quality or state of being human or humane 2 *pl* : the branches of learning dealing with human concerns (as philosophy) as opposed to natural processes (as physics) 3 : the human race

hu·man·ize \'hyü-mə-ˌnīz, 'yü-\ *vb* **-ized; -iz·ing** : to make human or humane — **hu·man·iza·tion** \ˌhyü-mə-nə-'zā-shən, ˌyü-\ *n* — **hu·man·iz·er** *n*

hu·man·kind \'hyü-mən-ˌkīnd, 'yü-\ *n* : the human race

hu·man·oid \'hyü-mə-ˌnȯid, 'yü-\ *adj* : having human form or characteristics — **humanoid** *n*

¹hum·ble \'həm-bəl\ *adj* **hum·bler** \-bə-lər\; **hum·blest** \-bə-ləst\ [ME, fr. OF, fr. L *humilis* low, humble, fr. *humus* earth] 1 : not proud or haughty 2 : not pretentious : UNASSUMING 3 : INSIGNIFICANT **syn** meek, modest, lowly — **hum·ble·ness** *n* — **hum·bly** *adv*

²humble *vb* **hum·bled; hum·bling** 1 : to make humble 2 : to destroy the power or prestige of — **hum·bler** *n*

¹**hum·bug** \'həm-ˌbəg\ *n* 1 : HOAX, FRAUD 2 : NONSENSE

²**humbug** *vb* **hum·bugged; hum·bug·ging** : DECEIVE

hum·ding·er \'həm-'diŋ-ər\ *n* : a person or thing of striking excellence

hum·drum \'həm-ˌdrəm\ *adj* : MONOTONOUS, DULL — **humdrum** *n*

hu·mer·us \'hyü-mə-rəs\ *n, pl* **hu·meri** \'hyü-mə-ˌrī, -ˌrē\ : the long bone extending from shoulder to elbow

hu·mid \'hyü-məd, 'yü-\ *adj* : containing or characterized by perceptible moisture : DAMP — **hu·mid·ly** *adv*

hu·mid·i·fy \hyü-'mi-də-ˌfī\ *vb* **-fied; -fy·ing** : to make humid — **hu·mid·i·fi·ca·tion** \-ˌmi-də-fə-'kā-shən\ *n* — **hu·mid·i·fi·er** \-'mi-də-ˌfī-ər\ *n*

hu·mid·i·ty \hyü-'mi-də-tē, yü-\ *n, pl* **-ties** : the amount of atmospheric moisture

hu·mi·dor \'hyü-mə-ˌdȯr, 'yü-\ *n* : a case (as for storing cigars) in which the air is kept properly humidified

hu·mil·i·ate \hyü-'mi-lē-ˌāt, yü-\ *vb* **-at·ed; -at·ing** : to injure the self-respect of : MORTIFY — **hu·mil·i·at·ing·ly** *adv* — **hu·mil·i·a·tion** \-ˌmi-lē-'ā-shən\ *n*

hu·mil·i·ty \hyü-'mi-lə-tē, yü-\ *n* : the quality or state of being humble

hum·ming·bird \'hə-miŋ-ˌbərd\ *n* : any of a family of tiny American birds related to the swifts

hum·mock \'hə-mək\ *n* : a rounded mound : KNOLL — **hum·mocky** \-mə-kē\ *adj*

hu·mon·gous \hyü-'məŋ-gəs, -'mäŋ-\ *adj* [perh. alter. of *huge* + *monstrous*] : extremely large

¹**hu·mor** \'hyü-mər, 'yü-\ *n* 1 : TEMPERAMENT 2 : MOOD 3 : WHIM 4 : a quality that appeals to a sense of the ludicrous or incongruous; *also* : a keen perception of the ludicrous or incongruous 5 : comical or amusing entertainment — **hu·mor·ist** \'hyü-mə-rist, 'yü-\ *n* — **hu·mor·less** \'hyü-mər-ləs, 'yü-\ *adj* — **hu·mor·less·ly** *adv* — **hu·mor·less·ness** *n* — **hu·mor·ous** \'hyü-mə-rəs, 'yü-\ *adj* — **hu·mor·ous·ly** *adv* — **hu·mor·ous·ness** *n*

²**humor** *vb* : to comply with the wishes or mood of

hu·mour *chiefly Brit var of* HUMOR

hump \'həmp\ *n* 1 : a rounded protuberance (as on the back of a camel) 2 : a difficult phase or obstacle ⟨over the ∼⟩ — **humped** *adj*

hump·back \'həmp-ˌbak; *1 also* -'bak\ *n* 1 : HUNCHBACK 2 : HUMPBACK WHALE — **hump·backed** *adj*

humpback whale *n* : a large baleen whale having very long flippers

hu·mus \'hyü-məs, 'yü-\ *n* : the dark organic part of soil formed from decaying matter

Hun \'hən\ *n* : a member of an Asian people that invaded Europe about A.D. 450

¹**hunch** \'hənch\ *vb* 1 : to thrust oneself forward 2 : to assume or cause to assume a bent or crooked posture

²**hunch** *n* 1 : PUSH 2 : a strong intuitive feeling about what will happen

hunch·back \'hənch-ˌbak\ *n* : a person with a crooked back; *also* : a back with a hump — **hunch·backed** *adj*

hun·dred \'hən-drəd\ *n, pl* **hundreds** *or* **hundred** : 10 times 10 — **hundred** *adj* — **hun·dredth** \-drədth\ *adj or n*

hun·dred·weight \-ˌwāt\ *n, pl* **hundredweight** *or* **hundredweights** — see WEIGHT table

¹**hung** *past and past part of* HANG

²**hung** *adj* : unable to reach a decision or verdict ⟨a ∼ jury⟩

Hung *abbr* Hungarian; Hungary

Hun·gar·i·an \ˌhəŋ-'ger-ē-ən\ *n* 1 : a native or inhabitant of Hungary 2 : the language of the Hungarians — **Hungarian** *adj*

hun·ger \'həŋ-gər\ *n* 1 : a craving or urgent need for food 2 : a strong desire — **hunger** *vb* — **hun·gri·ly** *adv* — **hun·gry** *adj*

hung·over \'həŋ-'ō-vər\ *adj* : having a hangover

hung up *adj* 1 : DELAYED 2 : ENTHUSIASTIC; *also* : PREOCCUPIED

hunk \'həŋk\ *n* 1 : a large piece 2 : an attractive well-built man — **hunky** *adj*

hun·ker \'həŋ-kər\ *vb* 1 : CROUCH, SQUAT — usu. used with *down* 2 : to settle in for a sustained period — used with *down*

hun·ky-do·ry \ˌhəŋ-kē-'dȯr-ē\ *adj* : quite satisfactory : FINE

¹**hunt** \'hənt\ *vb* 1 : to pursue for food or in sport; *also* : to take part in a hunt 2 : to try to find : SEEK 3 : to drive or chase esp. by harrying 4 : to traverse in search of prey — **hunt·er** *n*

²**hunt** *n* : an act, practice, or instance of hunting

hunt·ress \'hən-trəs\ *n* : a woman who hunts game

hunts·man \'hənts-mən\ *n* 1 : HUNTER 2 : a person who manages a hunt and looks after the hounds

hur·dle \'hərd-ᵊl\ *n* 1 : a barrier to leap over in a race 2 : OBSTACLE — **hurdle** *vb* — **hur·dler** *n*

hur·dy-gur·dy \ˌhər-dē-'gər-dē, 'hər-dē-ˌgər-dē\ *n, pl* **-gur·dies** : a musical instrument in which the sound is produced by turning a crank

hurl \'hərl\ *vb* 1 : to move or cause to move vigorously 2 : to throw down with violence 3 : FLING; *also* : PITCH — **hurl** *n* — **hurl·er** *n*

hur·ly-bur·ly \ˌhər-lē-'bər-lē\ *n* : UPROAR, TUMULT

Hu·ron \'hyür-ən, 'hyür-ˌän\ *n, pl* **Hurons** *or* **Huron** : a member of a confederacy of American Indian peoples formerly living between Georgian Bay and Lake Ontario

hur·rah \hù-'rȯ, -'rä\ *also* **hur·ray** \hù-'rā\ *interj* — used to express joy, approval, or encouragement

hur·ri·cane \'hər-ə-ˌkān\ *n* [Sp *huracán*, of AmerInd origin] : a tropical cyclone with winds of 74 miles (118 kilometers) per hour or greater that is usu. accompanied by rain, thunder, and lightning

¹**hur·ry** \'hər-ē\ *vb* **hur·ried; hur·ry·ing** 1 : to carry or cause to go with haste 2 : to impel to a greater speed 3 : to move or act with haste — **hur·ried·ly** *adv* — **hur·ried·ness** *n*

²**hurry** *n* : extreme haste or eagerness

¹**hurt** \'hərt\ *vb* **hurt; hurt·ing** 1 : to feel or cause to feel physical or emotional pain 2 : to do harm to : DAMAGE 3 : OFFEND 4 : HAMPER 5 : to be in need — usu. used with *for* — **hurt** *adj*

²**hurt** *n* 1 : a bodily injury or wound 2 : SUFFERING 3 : HARM, WRONG — **hurt·ful** *adj* — **hurt·ful·ness** *n*

hur·tle \'hərt-ᵊl\ *vb* **hur·tled; hur·tling** 1 : to move rapidly or forcefully 2 : HURL, FLING

¹**hus·band** \'həz-bənd\ *n* [ME *husbonde*, fr. OE *hūsbonda* master of a house, fr. ON *hūsbōndi*, fr. *hūs* house + *bōndi* householder] : a male partner in a marriage

²**husband** *vb* : to manage prudently

hus·band·man \'həz-bənd-mən\ *n* : FARMER

hus·band·ry \'həz-bən-drē\ *n* 1 : the control or judicious use of resources 2 : AGRICULTURE

¹**hush** \'həsh\ *vb* 1 : to make or become quiet or calm 2 : SUPPRESS

²**hush** *n* : SILENCE, QUIET

hush–hush \'həsh-ˌhəsh\ *adj* : SECRET, CONFIDENTIAL

¹**husk** \'həsk\ *n* 1 : a usu. thin dry outer covering of a seed or fruit 2 : an outer layer : SHELL

²**husk** *vb* : to strip the husk from — **husk·er** *n*

¹**hus·ky** \'həs-kē\ *adj* **hus·ki·er; -est** : HOARSE — **hus·ki·ly** \-kə-lē\ *adv* — **hus·ki·ness** \-kē-nəs\ *n*

²**husky** *adj* 1 : BURLY, ROBUST 2 : LARGE

³**husky** *n, pl* **huskies** : a heavy-coated working dog of the New World arctic

hus·sar \(ˌ)hə-'zär\ *n* [Hung *huszár*] : a member of any of various European cavalry units

hus·sy \'hə-zē, -sē\ *n, pl* **hussies** [alter. of *housewife*] 1 : a lewd or brazen woman 2 : a pert or mischievous girl

hus·tings \'həs-tiŋz\ *n pl* : a place where political campaign speeches are made; *also* : the proceedings in an election campaign

hus·tle \'hə-səl\ *vb* **hus·tled; hus·tling** 1 : JOSTLE,

SHOVE **2** : HASTEN, HURRY **3** : to work energetically — **hustle** *n* — **hus·tler** \'həs-lər\ *n*

hut \'hət\ *n* : a small and often temporary dwelling : SHACK

hutch \'həch\ *n* **1** : a chest or compartment for storage **2** : a cupboard usu. surmounted with open shelves **3** : a pen or coop for an animal **4** : HUT

huz·zah *or* **huz·za** \(ˌ)hə-'zä\ *n* : a shout of acclaim — often used interjectionally to express joy or approbation

HV *abbr* **1** high velocity **2** high voltage

HVAC *abbr* heating, ventilating and air-conditioning

hvy *abbr* heavy

HW *abbr* hot water

hwy *abbr* highway

hy·a·cinth \'hī-ə-(ˌ)sinth\ *n* : a bulbous Mediterranean herb related to the lilies that is widely grown for its spikes of fragrant bell-shaped flowers

hy·ae·na *var of* HYENA

hy·brid \'hī-brəd\ *n* **1** : an offspring of genetically differing parents (as members of different breeds or species) **2** : one of mixed origin or composition — **hybrid** *adj* — **hy·brid·i·za·tion** \ˌhī-brə-də-'zā-shən\ *n* — **hy·brid·ize** \'hī-brə-ˌdīz\ *vb* — **hy·brid·iz·er** *n*

hy·dra \'hī-drə\ *n* : any of numerous small tubular freshwater coelenterates that are polyps having at one end a mouth surrounded by tentacles

hy·dran·gea \hī-'drān-jə\ *n* : any of a genus of shrubs related to the currants and grown for their showy clusters of white or tinted flowers

hy·drant \'hī-drənt\ *n* : a pipe with a valve and spout at which water may be drawn from a main pipe

hy·drate \'hī-ˌdrāt\ *n* : a compound formed by union of water with some other substance — **hydrate** *vb*

hy·drau·lic \hī-'drȯ-lik\ *adj* **1** : operated, moved, or effected by means of water **2** : of or relating to hydraulics **3** : operated by the resistance offered or the pressure transmitted when a quantity of liquid is forced through a small orifice or through a tube **4** : hardening or setting under water

hy·drau·lics \-liks\ *n* : a science that deals with practical applications of liquid (as water) in motion

hydro \'hī-drō\ *n* : HYDROPOWER

hy·dro·car·bon \'hī-drō-ˌkär-bən\ *n* : an organic compound containing only carbon and hydrogen

hy·dro·ceph·a·lus \ˌhī-drō-'se-fə-ləs\ *n* : abnormal increase in the amount of fluid in the cranial cavity accompanied by enlargement of the skull and atrophy of the brain

hy·dro·chlo·ric acid \ˌhī-drə-ˌklȯr-ik-\ *n* : a sharp-smelling corrosive acid used in the laboratory and in industry and present in dilute form in gastric juice

hy·dro·dy·nam·ics \ˌhī-drō-dī-'na-miks\ *n* : a science that deals with the motion of fluids and the forces acting on moving bodies immersed in fluids — **hy·dro·dy·nam·ic** *adj*

hy·dro·elec·tric \ˌhī-drō-i-'lek-trik\ *adj* : of or relating to production of electricity by waterpower — **hy·dro·elec·tric·i·ty** \-ˌlek-'tri-sə-tē\ *n*

hy·dro·foil \'hī-drə-ˌfȯil\ *n* : a boat that has fins attached to the bottom by struts for lifting the hull clear of the water to allow faster speeds

hy·dro·gen \'hī-drə-jən\ *n* [F *hydrogène*, fr. Gk *hydōr* water + *-genēs* born; fr. the fact that water is generated by its combustion] : a gaseous colorless odorless highly flammable chemical element that is the lightest of the elements — **hy·drog·e·nous** \hī-'drä-jə-nəs\ *adj* — see ELEMENT table

hy·dro·ge·nate \hī-'drä-jə-ˌnāt, 'hī-drə-\ *vb* **-nat·ed; -nat·ing** : to combine or treat with hydrogen; *esp* : to add hydrogen to the molecule of — **hy·dro·ge·na·tion** \hī-ˌdrä-jə-'nā-shən, ˌhī-drə-\ *n*

hydrogen bomb *n* : a bomb whose violent explosive power is due to the sudden release of atomic energy resulting from the fusion of light nuclei (as of hydrogen atoms)

hydrogen peroxide *n* : an unstable compound of hydrogen and oxygen used esp. as an oxidizing and bleaching agent, an antiseptic, and a propellant

hy·dro·graph·ic \ˌhī-drə-'gra-fik\ *adj* : of or relating to the description and study of bodies of water — **hy·drog·ra·pher** *n* — **hy·drog·ra·phy** \hī-'drä-grə-fē\ *n*

hy·drol·o·gy \hī-'drä-lə-jē\ *n* : a science dealing with the properties, distribution, and circulation of water — **hy·dro·log·ic** \ˌhī-drə-'lä-jik\ *or* **hy·dro·log·i·cal** \-ji-kəl\ *adj* — **hy·drol·o·gist** \hī-'drä-lə-jist\ *n*

hy·dro·ly·sis \hī-'drä-lə-səs\ *n* : a chemical decomposition involving the addition of the elements of water

hy·drom·e·ter \hī-'drä-mə-tər\ *n* : a floating instrument for determining specific gravities of liquids and hence the strength (as of alcoholic liquors)

hy·dro·pho·bia \ˌhī-drə-'fō-bē-ə\ *n* [LL, fr. Gk, fr. *hydōr* water + *phobos* fear] : RABIES

hy·dro·phone \'hī-drə-ˌfōn\ *n* : an underwater listening device

¹hy·dro·plane \'hī-drə-ˌplān\ *n* **1** : a powerboat designed for racing that skims the surface of the water **2** : SEAPLANE

²hydroplane *vb* : to skid on a wet road due to loss of contact between the tires and road

hy·dro·pon·ics \ˌhī-drə-'pä-niks\ *n* : the growing of plants in nutrient solutions — **hy·dro·pon·ic** *adj*

hy·dro·pow·er \'hī-drə-ˌpaù-ər\ *n* : hydroelectric power

hy·dro·sphere \'hī-drə-ˌsfir\ *n* : the water (as vapor or lakes) of the earth

hy·dro·stat·ic \ˌhī-drə-'sta-tik\ *adj* : of or relating to fluids at rest or to the pressures they exert or transmit

hy·dro·ther·a·py \ˌhī-drə-'ther-ə-pē\ *n* : the use of water esp. externally in the treatment of disease or disability

hy·dro·ther·mal \ˌhī-drə-'thər-məl\ *adj* : of or relating to hot water

hy·drous \'hī-drəs\ *adj* : containing water

hy·drox·ide \hī-'dräk-ˌsīd\ *n* **1** : a negatively charged ion consisting of one atom of oxygen and one atom of hydrogen **2** : a compound of hydroxide with an element or group

hy·e·na \hī-'ē-nə\ *n* [L *hyaena*, fr. Gk *hyaina*, fr. *hys* hog] : any of several large nocturnal carnivorous mammals of Asia and Africa

hy·giene \'hī-jēn\ *n* **1** : a science concerned with establishing and maintaining good health **2** : conditions or practices conducive to health — **hy·gien·ic** \hī-'je-nik, -jē-\ *adj* — **hy·gien·i·cal·ly** \-ni-k(ə-)lē\ *adv* — **hy·gien·ist** \hī-'jē-nist, 'hī-ˌjē-, hī-'je-\ *n*

hy·grom·e·ter \hī-'grä-mə-tər\ *n* : any of several instruments for measuring the humidity of the atmosphere

hy·gro·scop·ic \ˌhī-grə-'skä-pik\ *adj* : readily taking up and retaining moisture

hying *pres part of* HIE

hy·men \'hī-mən\ *n* : a fold of mucous membrane partly closing the orifice of the vagina

hy·me·ne·al \ˌhī-mə-'nē-əl\ *adj* : NUPTIAL

hymn \'him\ *n* : a song of praise esp. to God — **hymn** *vb*

hym·nal \'him-nəl\ *n* : a book of hymns

hyp *abbr* hypothesis; hypothetical

¹hype \'hīp\ *vb* **hyped; hyp·ing 1** : STIMULATE — usu. used with *up* **2** : INCREASE — **hyped–up** *adj*

²hype *vb* **hyped; hyping 1** : DECEIVE **2** : PUBLICIZE

³hype *n* **1** : DECEPTION, PUT-ON **2** : PUBLICITY

hy·per \'hī-pər\ *adj* **1** : HIGH-STRUNG, EXCITABLE **2** : extremely active

hy·per·ac·id·i·ty \ˌhī-pər-ə-'si-də-tē\ *n* : the condition of containing excessive acid esp. in the stomach — **hy·per·ac·id** \-'a-səd\ *adj*

hy·per·ac·tive \-'ak-tiv\ *adj* : excessively or pathologically active — **hy·per·ac·tiv·i·ty** \-ˌak-'ti-və-tē\ *n*

hy·per·bar·ic \ˌhī-pər-ˈbar-ik\ adj : of, relating to, or utilizing greater than normal pressure (as of oxygen)

hy·per·bo·la \hī-ˈpər-bə-lə\ n, pl **-las** or **-lae** \-(ˌ)lē\ : a curve formed by the intersection of a double right circular cone with a plane that cuts both halves of the cone — **hy·per·bol·ic** \ˌhī-pər-ˈbä-lik\ adj

hy·per·bo·le \hī-ˈpər-bə-(ˌ)lē\ n : extravagant exaggeration used as a figure of speech

hy·per·crit·i·cal \ˌhī-pər-ˈkri-ti-kəl\ adj : excessively critical — **hy·per·crit·i·cal·ly** \-k(ə-)lē\ adv

hy·per·opia \ˌhī-pə-ˈrō-pē-ə\ n : a condition in which visual images come to focus behind the retina resulting esp. in defective vision for near objects — **hy·per·opic** \-ˈrō-pik, -ˈrä-\ adj

hy·per·sen·si·tive \-ˈsen-sə-tiv\ adj 1 : excessively or abnormally sensitive 2 : abnormally susceptible physiologically to a specific agent (as a drug) — **hy·per·sen·si·tive·ness** n — **hy·per·sen·si·tiv·i·ty** \-ˌsen-sə-ˈti-və-tē\ n

hy·per·ten·sion \ˈhī-pər-ˌten-chən\ n : high blood pressure — **hy·per·ten·sive** \ˌhī-pər-ˈten-siv\ adj or n

hy·per·thy·roid·ism \ˌhī-pər-ˈthī-ˌroi-di-zəm\ n : excessive activity of the thyroid gland; also : the resulting bodily condition — **hy·per·thy·roid** \-ˈthī-ˌroid\ adj

hy·per·tro·phy \hī-ˈpər-trə-fē\ n, pl **-phies** : excessive development of a body part — **hy·per·tro·phic** \ˌhī-pər-ˈtrō-fik\ adj — hypertrophy vb

hy·per·ven·ti·late \ˌhī-pər-ˈven-tə-ˌlāt\ vb : to breathe rapidly and deeply esp. to the point of losing an abnormal amount of carbon dioxide from the blood — **hy·per·ven·ti·la·tion** \-ˌven-tə-ˈlā-shən\ n

hy·phen \ˈhī-fən\ n : a punctuation mark - used esp. to divide or to compound words or word parts — **hyphen** vb

hy·phen·ate \ˈhī-fə-ˌnāt\ vb **-at·ed; -at·ing** : to connect or divide with a hyphen — **hy·phen·ation** \ˌhī-fə-ˈnā-shən\ n

hyp·no·sis \hip-ˈnō-səs\ n, pl **-no·ses** \-ˌsēz\ : an induced state that resembles sleep and in which the subject is responsive to suggestions of the inducer (**hyp·no·tist** \ˈhip-nə-tist\) — **hyp·no·tism** \ˈhip-nə-ˌti-zəm\ n — **hyp·no·tiz·able** \ˈhip-nə-ˌtī-zə-bəl\ adj — **hyp·no·tize** \-ˌtīz\ vb

¹**hyp·not·ic** \hip-ˈnä-tik\ adj 1 : inducing sleep : SOPORIFIC 2 : of or relating to hypnosis or hypnotism 3 : readily holding the attention — **hyp·not·i·cal·ly** \-ti-k(ə-)lē\ adv

²**hypnotic** n : a sleep-inducing drug

hy·po \ˈhī-pō\ n, pl hypos : SODIUM THIOSULFATE

hy·po·cen·ter \ˈhī-pə-ˌsen-tər\ n : the point of origin of an earthquake

hy·po·chon·dria \ˌhī-pə-ˈkän-drē-ə\ n [NL, fr. LL, pl.,

upper abdomen (formerly regarded as the seat of hypochondria), fr. Gk, lit., the parts under the cartilage (of the breastbone), fr. hypo- under + chondros cartilage] : depression of mind often centered on imaginary physical ailments — **hy·po·chon·dri·ac** \-drē-ˌak\ adj or n

hy·poc·ri·sy \hi-ˈpä-krə-sē\ n, pl **-sies** : a feigning to be what one is not or to believe what one does not; esp : the false assumption of an appearance of virtue or religion — **hyp·o·crite** \ˈhi-pə-ˌkrit\ n — **hyp·o·crit·i·cal** \ˌhi-pə-ˈkri-ti-kəl\ adj — **hyp·o·crit·i·cal·ly** \-k(ə-)lē\ adv

¹**hy·po·der·mic** \ˌhī-pə-ˈdər-mik\ adj : administered by or used in making an injection beneath the skin

²**hypodermic** n : HYPODERMIC SYRINGE; also : an injection made with this

hypodermic needle n : NEEDLE 3; also : HYPODERMIC SYRINGE

hypodermic syringe n : a small syringe with a hollow needle for injecting material into or through the skin

hy·po·gly·ce·mia \ˌhī-pō-glī-ˈsē-mē-ə\ n : abnormal decrease of sugar in the blood — **hy·po·gly·ce·mic** \-mik\ adj

hy·pot·e·nuse \hī-ˈpät-ᵊn-ˌüs, -ˌyüs, -ˌüz, -ˌyüz\ n : the side of a triangle having a right angle that is opposite the right angle; also : its length

hy·poth·e·sis \hī-ˈpä-thə-səs\ n, pl **-e·ses** \-ˌsēz\ : an assumption made esp. in order to test its logical or empirical consequences — **hy·po·thet·i·cal** \ˌhī-pə-ˈthe-ti-kəl\ adj — **hy·po·thet·i·cal·ly** \-k(ə-)lē\ adv

hy·poth·e·size \-ˌsīz\ vb **-sized; -siz·ing** : to adopt as a hypothesis

hy·po·thy·roid·ism \ˌhī-pō-ˈthī-ˌroi-di-zəm\ n : deficient activity of the thyroid gland; also : a resultant lowered metabolic rate and general loss of vigor — **hy·po·thy·roid** adj

hys·sop \ˈhi-səp\ n : a European mint sometimes used as a potherb

hys·ter·ec·to·my \ˌhis-tə-ˈrek-tə-mē\ n, pl **-mies** : surgical removal of the uterus

hys·te·ria \hi-ˈster-ē-ə, -ˈstir-\ n [NL, fr. E hysteric, adj., fr. L hystericus, fr. Gk hysterikos, fr. hystera womb; fr. the Greek notion that hysteria was peculiar to women and caused by disturbances in the uterus] 1 : a nervous disorder marked esp. by defective emotional control 2 : unmanageable fear or outburst of emotion — **hys·ter·ic** \-ˈster-ik\ n — **hys·ter·i·cal** \-ˈster-i-kəl\ also **hysteric** adj — **hys·ter·i·cal·ly** \-k(ə-)lē\ adv

hys·ter·ics \-ˈster-iks\ n pl : a fit of uncontrollable laughter or crying

Hz abbr hertz

I

¹**i** \ˈī\ n, pl **i's** or **is** \ˈīz\ often cap : the 9th letter of the English alphabet

²**i** abbr, often cap island; isle

¹**I** \ˈī, ə\ pron : the one speaking or writing

²**I** abbr interstate

³**I** symbol iodine

Ia or **IA** abbr Iowa

-ial adj suffix : ¹-AL (manorial)

iamb \ˈī-ˌam\ or **iam·bus** \ī-ˈam-bəs\ n, pl **iambs** \ˈī-ˌamz\ or **iam·bus·es** : a metrical foot of one unaccented syllable followed by one accented syllable — **iam·bic** \ī-ˈam-bik\ adj or n

-ian — see -AN

-i·at·ric \ē-ˈa-trik\ also **-i·at·ri·cal** \-tri-kəl\ adj comb form : of or relating to (such) medical treatment or healing (pediatric)

-i·at·rics \ē-ˈa-triks\ n pl comb form : medical treatment (pediatrics)

ib or **ibid** abbr ibidem

ibex \ˈī-ˌbeks\ n, pl **ibex** or **ibex·es** [L] : any of several Old World wild goats with large curved horns

ibi·dem \ˈi-bə-ˌdem, i-ˈbī-dəm\ adv [L] : in the same place

-ibility — see -ABILITY

ibis \ˈī-bəs\ n, pl **ibis** or **ibis·es** [L, fr. Gk, fr. Egypt hb] : any of various wading birds related to the herons but having a downwardly curved bill

-ible — see -ABLE

ibu·pro·fen \ˌī-byü-ˈprō-fən\ n : a nonsteroidal anti‑inflammatory drug used to relieve pain and fever

IC \ˌī-ˈsē\ n : INTEGRATED CIRCUIT

¹**-ic** \ik\ adj suffix 1 : of, relating to, or having the form of : being (panoramic) 2 : related to, derived from, or containing (alcoholic) 3 : in the manner of : like that of : characteristic of 4 : associated with or dealing with : utilizing (electronic) 5 : characterized by : exhibiting

⟨nostalg*ic*⟩ : affected with ⟨allerg*ic*⟩ **6** : caused by **7** : tending to produce ⟨analges*ic*⟩

²-ic *n suffix* : one having the character or nature of : one belonging to or associated with : one exhibiting or affected by : one that produces

-i·cal \i-kəl\ *adj suffix* : -IC ⟨symmet*rical*⟩ ⟨geolog*ical*⟩ — **-i·cal·ly** \i-kə-lē, -klē\ *adv suffix*

ICBM \ˌī-ˌsē-(ˌ)bē-ˈem\ *n, pl* **ICBM's** *or* **ICBMs** \-ˈemz\ : an intercontinental ballistic missile

ICC *abbr* Interstate Commerce Commission

¹ice \ˈīs\ *n* **1** : frozen water **2** : a substance resembling ice **3** : a state of coldness (as from formality or reserve) **4** : a flavored frozen dessert; *esp* : one containing no milk or cream

²ice *vb* **iced; ic·ing 1** : FREEZE **2** : CHILL **3** : to cover with or as if with icing

ice age *n* : a time of widespread glaciation

ice bag *n* : a waterproof bag to hold ice for local application of cold to the body

ice·berg \ˈīs-ˌbərg\ *n* : a large floating mass of ice broken off from a glacier

iceberg lettuce *n* : any of various crisp light green lettuces that form a compact head like a cabbage

ice·boat \ˈīs-ˌbōt\ *n* : a boatlike frame on runners propelled on ice by sails

ice·bound \-ˌbaùnd\ *adj* : surrounded, obstructed, or covered by ice

ice·box \-ˌbäks\ *n* : REFRIGERATOR

ice·break·er \-ˌbrā-kər\ *n* : a ship equipped to make a channel through ice

ice cap *n* : a glacier forming on relatively level land and flowing outward from its center

ice cream *n* : a frozen food containing sweetened or flavored cream or butterfat

ice hockey *n* : a game in which two teams of ice-skating players try to shoot a puck into the opponent's goal

ice·house \ˈīs-ˌhaùs\ *n* : a building in which ice is made or stored

Ice·land·er \-ˌlan-dər, -lən-\ *n* : a native or inhabitant of Iceland

¹Ice·lan·dic \īs-ˈlan-dik\ *adj* : of, relating to, or characteristic of Iceland, the Icelanders, or their language

²Icelandic *n* : the language of Iceland

ice·man \ˈīs-ˌman\ *n* : one who sells or delivers ice

ice milk *n* : a sweetened frozen food made of skim milk

ice pick *n* : a hand tool ending in a spike for chipping ice

ice–skate \ˈīs-ˌskāt\ *vb* : to skate on ice — **ice–skater** *n*

ice storm *n* : a storm in which falling rain freezes on contact

ice water *n* : chilled or iced water esp. for drinking

ich·thy·ol·o·gy \ˌik-thē-ˈä-lə-jē\ *n* : a branch of zoology dealing with fishes — **ich·thy·ol·o·gist** \-jist\ *n*

ici·cle \ˈī-ˌsi-kəl\ *n* : a hanging mass of ice formed by the freezing of dripping water

ic·ing \ˈī-siŋ\ *n* : a sweet usu. creamy mixture used to coat baked goods

ICJ *abbr* International Court of Justice

icky \ˈi-kē\ *adj* **ick·i·er; -est** : OFFENSIVE, DISTASTEFUL — **ick·i·ness** *n*

icon \ˈī-ˌkän\ *n* **1** : IMAGE; *esp* : a religious image painted on a wood panel **2** : a small picture on a computer display that suggests the purpose of an available function

icon·o·clasm \ī-ˈkä-nə-ˌkla-zəm\ *n* : the doctrine, practice, or attitude of an iconoclast

icon·o·clast \-ˌklast\ *n* [ML *iconoclastes*, fr. MGk *eikonoklastēs*, lit., image destroyer, fr. Gk *eikōn* image + *klan* to break] **1** : one who destroys religious images or opposes their veneration **2** : one who attacks cherished beliefs or institutions

-ics \iks\ *n sing or pl suffix* **1** : study : knowledge : skill : practice ⟨linguist*ics*⟩ ⟨electron*ics*⟩ **2** : characteristic actions or activities ⟨acrobat*ics*⟩ **3** : characteristic

qualities, operations, or phenomena ⟨mechan*ics*⟩

ic·tus \ˈik-təs\ *n* : the recurring stress or beat in a rhythmic or metrical series of sounds

ICU *abbr* intensive care unit

icy \ˈī-sē\ *adj* **ic·i·er; -est 1** : covered with, abounding in, or consisting of ice **2** : intensely cold **3** : being cold and unfriendly — **ic·i·ly** \ˈī-sə-lē\ *adv* — **ic·i·ness** \-sē-nəs\ *n*

¹id \ˈid\ *n* [L, it] : the part of the psyche in psychoanalytic theory that is completely unconscious and concerned with instinctual needs and drives

²id *abbr* idem

ID *abbr* **1** Idaho **2** identification

idea \ī-ˈdē-ə\ *n* **1** : a plan for action : DESIGN **2** : something imagined or pictured in the mind **3** : a central meaning or purpose **syn** concept, conception, notion, impression

¹ide·al \ī-ˈdēl\ *adj* **1** : existing only in the mind : IMAGINARY; *also* : lacking practicality **2** : of or relating to an ideal or to perfection : PERFECT

²ideal *n* **1** : a standard of excellence **2** : one regarded as a model worthy of imitation **3** : GOAL **syn** archetype, example, exemplar, paradigm, pattern

ide·al·ism \ī-ˈdē-ə-ˌli-zəm\ *n* : the practice of forming ideals or living under their influence; *also* : an idealized representation — **ide·al·ist** \-list\ *n* — **ide·al·istic** \ī-ˌdē-ə-ˈlis-tik\ *adj* — **ide·al·is·ti·cal·ly** \-ti-k(ə-)lē\ *adv*

ide·al·ize \ī-ˈdē-ə-ˌlīz\ *vb* **-ized; -iz·ing** : to think of or represent as ideal — **ide·al·i·za·tion** \-ˌdē-ə-lə-ˈzā-shən\ *n*

ide·al·ly \ī-ˈdē-lē, -ˈdē-ə-lē\ *adv* **1** : in idea or imagination : MENTALLY **2** : in agreement with an ideal : PERFECTLY

ide·a·tion \ˌī-dē-ˈā-shən\ *n* : the forming of ideas — **ide·ate** \ˈī-dē-ˌāt\ *vb* — **ide·a·tion·al** \ˌī-dē-ˈā-shə-nəl\ *adj*

idem \ˈī-ˌdem, ˈē-, ˈi-\ *pron* [L, same] : something previously mentioned

iden·ti·cal \ī-ˈden-ti-kəl\ *adj* **1** : being the same **2** : essentially alike **syn** equivalent, equal, tantamount

iden·ti·fi·ca·tion \ī-ˌden-tə-fə-ˈkā-shən\ *n* **1** : an act of identifying : the state of being identified **2** : evidence of identity **3** : an unconscious psychological process by which an individual models thoughts, feelings, and actions after another person or an object

iden·ti·fy \ī-ˈden-tə-ˌfī\ *vb* **-fied; -fy·ing 1** : to regard as identical **2** : ASSOCIATE **3** : to establish the identity of **4** : to practice psychological identification — **iden·ti·fi·able** \-ˌden-tə-ˈfī-ə-bəl\ *adj* — **iden·ti·fi·ably** \-blē\ *adv* — **iden·ti·fi·er** \-ˌfī(-ə)r\ *n*

iden·ti·ty \ī-ˈden-tə-tē\ *n, pl* **-ties 1** : sameness of essential character **2** : INDIVIDUALITY **3** : the fact of being the same person or thing as claimed

identity crisis *n* : psychological conflict esp. in adolescence involving confusion about one's social role and one's personality

ideo·gram \ˈī-dē-ə-ˌgram, ˈi-\ *n* **1** : a picture or symbol used in a system of writing to represent a thing or an idea **2** : a character or symbol used in a system of writing to represent an entire word

ide·ol·o·gy \ˌī-dē-ˈä-lə-jē, ˌi-\ *also* **ide·al·o·gy** \-ˈä-lə-jē, -ˈa-\ *n, pl* **-gies 1** : the body of ideas characteristic of a particular individual, group, or culture **2** : the assertions, theories, and aims that constitute a political, social, and economic program — **ide·o·log·i·cal** \ˌī-dē-ə-ˈlä-ji-kəl, ˌi-\ *adj* — **ide·ol·o·gist** \-dē-ˈä-lə-jist\ *n*

ides \ˈīdz\ *n sing or pl* : the 15th day of March, May, July, or October or the 13th day of any other month in the ancient Roman calendar

id·i·o·cy \ˈi-dē-ə-sē\ *n, pl* **-cies 1** : extreme mental retardation **2** : something notably stupid or foolish

id·i·om \ˈi-dē-əm\ *n* **1** : the language peculiar to a person or group **2** : the characteristic form or structure of a language **3** : an expression that cannot be understood from the meanings of its separate words (as *give way*) — **id·i·o·mat·ic** \ˌi-dē-ə-ˈma-tik\ *adj* — **id·i·o·mat·i·cal·ly** \-ti-k(ə-)lē\ *adv*

id·i·o·path·ic \ˌi-dē-ə-ˈpa-thik\ *adj* : arising spontaneously or from an obscure or unknown cause ⟨an ∼ disease⟩

id·i·o·syn·cra·sy \ˌi-dē-ə-ˈsiŋ-krə-sē\ *n, pl* **-sies** : personal peculiarity — **id·i·o·syn·crat·ic** \ˌi-dē-ō-sin-ˈkra-tik\ *adj* — **id·i·o·syn·crat·i·cal·ly** \-ˈkra-ti-k(ə-)lē\ *adv*

id·i·ot \ˈi-dē-ət\ *n* [ME, fr. L *idiota* ignorant person, fr. Gk *idiōtēs* one in a private station, ignorant person, fr. *idios* one's own, private] **1** : a mentally retarded person requiring complete custodial care **2** : a foolish or stupid person — **id·i·ot·ic** \ˌi-dē-ˈä-tik\ *adj* — **id·i·ot·i·cal·ly** \-ti-k(ə-)lē\ *adv*

¹idle \ˈīd-ᵊl\ *adj* **idler** \ˈī-də-lər\; **idlest** \ˈī-də-ləst\ **1** : GROUNDLESS, WORTHLESS, USELESS ⟨∼ talk⟩ **2** : not occupied or employed : INACTIVE **3** : LAZY — **idle·ness** *n* — **idly** \ˈīd-lē\ *adv*

²idle *vb* **idled; idling 1** : to spend time doing nothing **2** : to make idle **3** : to run without being connected so that power is not used for useful work — **idler** *n*

idol \ˈīd-ᵊl\ *n* **1** : an image worshiped as a god; *also* : a false god **2** : an object of passionate devotion

idol·a·ter *or* **idol·a·tor** \ī-ˈdä-lə-tər\ *n* : a worshiper of idols

idol·a·try \-trē\ *n, pl* **-tries 1** : the worship of a physical object as a god **2** : excessive devotion — **idol·a·trous** \-trəs\ *adj*

idol·ize \ˈīd-ᵊl-ˌīz\ *vb* **-ized; -iz·ing** : to make an idol of — **idol·iza·tion** \ˌīd-ᵊl-ə-ˈzā-shən\ *n*

idyll \ˈīd-ᵊl\ *n* **1** : a simple work of writing or poetry that describes country life or suggests a peaceful setting **2** : a fit subject for an idyll — **idyl·lic** \ī-ˈdi-lik\ *adj*

i.e. \ˈī-ˈē\ *abbr* [L *id est*] that is

IE *abbr* industrial engineer

-ier — see -ER

if \ˈif\ *conj* **1** : in the event that ⟨∼ he stays, I leave⟩ **2** : WHETHER ⟨ask ∼ he left⟩ **3** — used as a function word to introduce an exclamation expressing a wish ⟨∼ it would only rain⟩ **4** : even though ⟨an interesting ∼ untenable argument⟩

IF *abbr* intermediate frequency

if·fy \ˈi-fē\ *adj* : full of contingencies or unknown conditions

-i·fy \ə-ˌfī\ *vb suffix* : -FY

IG *abbr* inspector general

ig·loo \ˈi-glü\ *n, pl* **igloos** [Inuit (an Eskimo language) *iglu* house] : an Eskimo house or hut often made of snow blocks and in the shape of a dome

ig·ne·ous \ˈig-nē-əs\ *adj* **1** : FIERY **2** : formed by solidification of molten rock

ig·nite \ig-ˈnīt\ *vb* **ig·nit·ed; ig·nit·ing** : to set afire or catch fire — **ig·nit·able** \-ˈnī-tə-bəl\ *adj*

ig·ni·tion \ig-ˈni-shən\ *n* **1** : a setting on fire **2** : the process or means (as an electric spark) of igniting the fuel mixture in an engine

ig·no·ble \ig-ˈnō-bəl\ *adj* **1** : of common birth **2** : not honorable : BASE, MEAN **syn** despicable, scurvy, sordid, vile, wretched — **ig·no·bly** *adv*

ig·no·min·i·ous \ˌig-nə-ˈmi-nē-əs\ *adj* **1** : DISHONORABLE **2** : DESPICABLE **3** : HUMILIATING, DEGRADING **syn** disreputable, discreditable, disgraceful, inglorious — **ig·no·min·i·ous·ly** *adv* — **ig·no·mi·ny** \ˈig-nə-ˌmi-nē, ig-ˈnä-mə-nē\ *n*

ig·no·ra·mus \ˌig-nə-ˈrā-məs\ *n* [*Ignoramus,* ignorant lawyer in *Ignoramus* (1615), play by George Ruggle] : an utterly ignorant person

ig·no·rance \ˈig-nə-rəns\ *n* : the state of being ignorant

ig·no·rant \ˈig-nə-rənt\ *adj* **1** : lacking knowledge **2** : resulting from or showing lack of knowledge or intelligence **3** : UNAWARE, UNINFORMED **syn** benighted, illiterate, uneducated, unlettered, untutored — **ig·no·rant·ly** *adv*

ig·nore \ig-ˈnōr\ *vb* **ig·nored; ig·nor·ing** : to refuse to take notice of **syn** overlook, slight, neglect

igua·na \i-ˈgwä-nə\ *n* : any of various large tropical American lizards

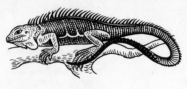

iguana

ihp *abbr* indicated horsepower

IHS \ˌī-ˌāch-ˈes\ [LL, part transliteration of Gk IHΣ, abbreviation for IHΣOYΣ *Iēsous* Jesus] — used as a Christian symbol and monogram for *Jesus*

ikon *var of* ICON

IL *abbr* Illinois

il·e·itis \ˌi-lē-ˈī-təs\ *n* : inflammation of the ileum

il·e·um \ˈi-lē-əm\ *n, pl* **il·ea** \-lē-ə\ : the part of the small intestine between the jejunum and the large intestine

il·i·ac \ˈi-lē-ˌak\ *adj* : of, relating to, or located near the ilium

il·i·um \ˈi-lē-əm\ *n* : the uppermost and largest of the three bones making up either side of the pelvis

ilk \ˈilk\ *n* : SORT, KIND

¹ill \ˈil\ *adj* **worse** \ˈwərs\; **worst** \ˈwərst\ **1** : attended or caused by an evil intent ⟨∼ deeds⟩ **2** : not normal or sound ⟨∼ health⟩; *also* : not in good health : SICK **3** : BAD, UNLUCKY ⟨∼ omen⟩ **4** : not right or proper ⟨∼ manners⟩ **5** : UNFRIENDLY, HOSTILE ⟨∼ feeling⟩

²ill *adv* **worse; worst 1** : with displeasure **2** : in a harsh manner **3** : HARDLY, SCARCELY ⟨can ∼ afford it⟩ **4** : BADLY, UNLUCKILY **5** : in a faulty way

³ill *n* **1** : EVIL **2** : MISFORTUNE, DISTRESS **3** : AILMENT, SICKNESS; *also* : TROUBLE

⁴ill *abbr* illustrated; illustration; illustrator

Ill *abbr* Illinois

ill–ad·vised \ˌil-əd-ˈvīzd\ *adj* : not well counseled ⟨∼ efforts⟩ — **ill–ad·vis·ed·ly** \-ˈvī-zəd-lē\ *adv*

ill–bred \-ˈbred\ *adj* : badly brought up : IMPOLITE

il·le·gal \il-ˈlē-gəl\ *adj* : not lawful; *also* : not sanctioned by official rules **syn** unlawful, criminal, illegitimate, illicit, wrongful — **il·le·gal·i·ty** \ˌi-li-ˈga-lə-tē\ *n* — **il·le·gal·ly** *adv*

il·leg·i·ble \il-ˈle-jə-bəl\ *adj* : not legible — **il·leg·i·bil·i·ty** \il-ˌle-jə-ˈbi-lə-tē\ *n* — **il·leg·i·bly** \il-ˈle-jə-blē\ *adv*

il·le·git·i·mate \ˌi-li-ˈji-tə-mət\ *adj* **1** : born of unmarried parents **2** : ILLOGICAL **3** : ILLEGAL — **il·le·git·i·ma·cy** \-ˈji-tə-mə-sē\ *n* — **il·le·git·i·mate·ly** *adv*

ill–fat·ed \ˈil-ˈfā-təd\ *adj* : UNFORTUNATE

ill–fa·vored \-ˈfā-vərd\ *adj* : UGLY, UNATTRACTIVE

ill–got·ten \-ˈgät-ᵊn\ *adj* : acquired by improper means ⟨∼ gains⟩

ill–hu·mored \-ˈhyü-mərd, -ˈyü-\ *adj* : SURLY, IRRITABLE

il·lib·er·al \il-ˈli-bə-rəl\ *adj* : not liberal : NARROW, BIGOTED

il·lic·it \il-ˈli-sət\ *adj* : not permitted : UNLAWFUL — **il·lic·it·ly** *adv*

il·lim·it·able \il-ˈli-mə-tə-bəl\ *adj* : BOUNDLESS, MEASURELESS — **il·lim·it·ably** \-blē\ *adv*

Il·li·nois \ˌi-lə-ˈnȯi *also* -ˈnȯiz\ *n, pl* **Illinois** : a member of an American Indian people of Illinois, Iowa, and Wisconsin

il·lit·er·ate \il-ˈli-tə-rət\ *adj* **1** : having little or no education; *esp* : unable to read or write **2** : showing a lack of familiarity with the fundamentals of a particular field of knowledge — **il·lit·er·a·cy** \-ˈli-tə-rə-sē\ *n* — **illiterate** *n*

ill–man·nered \'il-'ma-nərd\ *adj* : marked by bad manners : RUDE

ill–na·tured \-'nā-chərd\ *adj* : CROSS, SURLY — **ill–na·tured·ly** *adv*

ill·ness \'il-nəs\ *n* : SICKNESS

il·log·i·cal \il-'lä-ji-kəl\ *adj* : lacking sound reasoning; *also* : SENSELESS — **il·log·i·cal·ly** \-ji-k(ə-)lē\ *adv*

ill–starred \il-'stärd\ *adj* : UNLUCKY 1

ill–tem·pered \-'tem-pərd\ *adj* : CROSS

ill–treat \-'trēt\ *vb* : to treat cruelly or improperly : MALTREAT — **ill–treat·ment** *n*

il·lu·mi·nate \i-'lü-mə-ˌnāt\ *vb* **-nat·ed; -nat·ing** 1 : to supply or brighten with light : light up 2 : to make clear : ELUCIDATE 3 : to decorate (as a manuscript) with designs or pictures in gold or colors — **il·lu·mi·nat·ing·ly** *adv* — **il·lu·mi·na·tion** \-ˌlü-mə-'nā-shən\ *n* — **il·lu·mi·na·tor** \-'lü-mə-ˌnā-tər\ *n*

il·lu·mine \i-'lü-mən\ *vb* **-mined; -min·ing** : ILLUMINATE

ill–us·age \'il-'yü-sij\ *n* : harsh, unkind, or abusive treatment

ill–use \-'yüz\ *vb* : MALTREAT, ABUSE

il·lu·sion \i-'lü-zhən\ *n* [ME, fr. MF, fr. LL *illusio*, fr. L, action of mocking, fr. *illudere* to mock at, fr. *ludere* to play, mock] 1 : a mistaken idea : MISCONCEPTION 2 : a misleading visual image; *also* : HALLUCINATION

il·lu·sion·ist \i-'lü-zhə-nist\ *n* : one that produces illusions; *esp* : a sleight-of-hand performer

il·lu·sive \i-'lü-siv\ *adj* : DECEPTIVE

il·lu·so·ry \i-'lü-sə-rē, -zə-\ *adj* : DECEPTIVE

illust *or* **illus** *abbr* illustrated; illustration

il·lus·trate \'i-ləs-ˌtrāt\ *vb* **-trat·ed; -trat·ing** [L *illustrare*, fr. *lustrare* to purify, make bright] 1 : to explain by use of examples : CLARIFY; *also* : DEMONSTRATE 2 : to provide with pictures or figures that explain or decorate 3 : to serve to explain or decorate — **il·lus·tra·tor** \'i-lə-ˌstrā-tər\ *n*

il·lus·tra·tion \ˌi-lə-'strā-shən\ *n* 1 : the act of illustrating : the condition of being illustrated 2 : an example or instance that helps make something clear 3 : a picture or diagram that explains or decorates

il·lus·tra·tive \i-'ləs-trə-tiv, 'i-lə-ˌstrā-\ *adj* : serving, tending, or designed to illustrate — **il·lus·tra·tive·ly** *adv*

il·lus·tri·ous \i-'ləs-trē-əs\ *adj* : notably outstanding because of rank or achievement **syn** distinguished, eminent, famous, great, notable, prominent — **il·lus·tri·ous·ness** *n*

ill will *n* : unfriendly feeling

ILS *abbr* instrument landing system

¹**im·age** \'i-mij\ *n* 1 : a likeness or imitation of a person or thing; *esp* : STATUE 2 : a picture of an object formed by a device (as a mirror or lens) 3 : a person strikingly like another person ⟨he is the ∼ of his father⟩ 4 : a mental picture or conception : IMPRESSION, IDEA, CONCEPT 5 : a vivid representation or description

²**image** *vb* **im·aged; im·ag·ing** 1 : to call up a mental picture of 2 : to describe or portray in words 3 : to create a representation of 4 : REFLECT, MIRROR 5 : to make appear : PROJECT

im·ag·ery \'i-mij-rē\ *n* 1 : IMAGES; *also* : the art of making images 2 : figurative language 3 : mental images; *esp* : the products of imagination

imag·in·able \i-'ma-jə-nə-bəl\ *adj* : capable of being imagined : CONCEIVABLE — **imag·in·ably** *adv*

imag·i·nary \i-'ma-jə-ˌner-ē\ *adj* 1 : existing only in the imagination 2 : containing or relating to a quantity (**imaginary unit**) that is the positive square root of minus 1 ($\sqrt{-1}$)

imaginary number *n* : a complex number (as $2 + 3i$) with a nonzero term (**imaginary part**) containing the imaginary unit as a factor

imag·i·na·tion \i-ˌma-jə-'nā-shən\ *n* 1 : the act or power of forming a mental image of something not pres-

ent to the senses or not previously known or experienced 2 : creative ability 3 : RESOURCEFULNESS 4 : a mental image : a creation of the mind — **imag·i·na·tive** \i-'ma-jə-nə-tiv, -ˌnā-\ *adj* — **imag·i·na·tive·ly** *adv*

imag·ine \i-'ma-jən\ *vb* **imag·ined; imag·in·ing** 1 : to form a mental picture of something not present 2 : THINK, GUESS ⟨I ∼ it will rain⟩

im·ag·ism \'i-mi-ˌji-zəm\ *n, often cap* : a movement in poetry advocating free verse and the expression of ideas and emotions through clear precise images — **im·ag·ist** \-jist\ *n*

ima·go \i-'mā-gō, -'mä-\ *n, pl* **imagoes** *or* **ima·gi·nes** \-'mā-gə-ˌnēz, -'mä-\ [NL, fr. L, image] : an insect in its final adult stage — **ima·gi·nal** \i-'mā-gən-əl, -'mä-\ *adj*

im·bal·ance \'im-'ba-ləns\ *n* : lack of balance : the state of being out of equilibrium or out of proportion

im·be·cile \'im-bə-səl, -ˌsil\ *n* 1 : a mentally retarded person who needs help in routine personal care 2 : FOOL, IDIOT — **imbecile** *or* **im·be·cil·ic** \ˌim-bə-'si-lik\ *adj* — **im·be·cil·i·ty** \ˌim-bə-'si-lə-tē\ *n*

imbed *var of* EMBED

im·bibe \im-'bīb\ *vb* **im·bibed; im·bib·ing** 1 : to receive and retain in the mind 2 : DRINK 3 : to take in or up : ABSORB — **im·bib·er** *n*

im·bri·ca·tion \ˌim-brə-'kā-shən\ *n* 1 : an overlapping of edges (as of tiles) 2 : a pattern showing imbrication — **im·bri·cate** \'im-bri-kət\ *adj*

im·bro·glio \im-'brōl-yō\ *n, pl* **-glios** [It, fr. *imbrogliare* to entangle] 1 : a confused mass 2 : a complicated situation; *also* : a serious or embarrassing misunderstanding

im·brue \im-'brü\ *vb* **im·brued; im·bru·ing** : STAIN ⟨hands *imbrued* with blood⟩

im·bue \-'byü\ *vb* **im·bued; im·bu·ing** 1 : to permeate or influence as if by dyeing 2 : to tinge or dye deeply

IMF *abbr* International Monetary Fund

imit *abbr* imitative

im·i·ta·ble \'i-mə-tə-bəl\ *adj* : capable or worthy of being imitated or copied

im·i·tate \'i-mə-ˌtāt\ *vb* **-tat·ed; -tat·ing** 1 : to follow as a model : COPY 2 : RESEMBLE 3 : REPRODUCE 4 : MIMIC, COUNTERFEIT — **im·i·ta·tor** \-ˌtā-tər\ *n*

im·i·ta·tion \ˌi-mə-'tā-shən\ *n* 1 : an act of imitating 2 : COPY, COUNTERFEIT 3 : a literary work that reproduces the style of another author — **imitation** *adj*

im·i·ta·tive \'i-mə-ˌtā-tiv\ *adj* 1 : marked by imitation 2 : inclined to imitate 3 : COUNTERFEIT

im·mac·u·late \i-'ma-kyə-lət\ *adj* 1 : being without stain or blemish : PURE 2 : spotlessly clean ⟨∼ linen⟩ — **im·mac·u·late·ly** *adv*

im·ma·nent \'i-mə-nənt\ *adj* : having existence only in the mind — **im·ma·nence** \-nəns\ *n* — **im·ma·nen·cy** \-nən-sē\ *n*

im·ma·te·ri·al \ˌi-mə-'tir-ē-əl\ *adj* 1 : not consisting of matter : SPIRITUAL 2 : UNIMPORTANT, TRIFLING **syn** bodiless, disembodied, incorporeal, insubstantial, nonphysical — **im·ma·te·ri·al·i·ty** \-ˌtir-ē-'a-lə-tē\ *n*

im·ma·ture \ˌi-mə-'tür, -'tyür\ *adj* : lacking complete development : not yet mature — **im·ma·tu·ri·ty** \-'tür-ə-tē, -'tyür-\ *n*

im·mea·sur·able \(ˌ)i-'me-zhə-rə-bəl\ *adj* : not capable of being measured : indefinitely extensive : ILLIMITABLE — **im·mea·sur·ably** \-blē\ *adv*

im·me·di·a·cy \i-'mē-dē-ə-sē\ *n, pl* **-cies** 1 : the quality or state of being immediate 2 : something that is of immediate importance

im·me·di·ate \i-'mē-dē-ət\ *adj* 1 : acting directly and alone : DIRECT ⟨the ∼ cause of death⟩ 2 : being next in line or relation (members of the ∼ family) 3 : not distant : CLOSE 4 : made or done at once ⟨an ∼ response⟩ 5 : near to or related to the present time ⟨the ∼ future⟩ — **im·me·di·ate·ly** *adv*

im·me·mo·ri·al \ˌi-mə-'mȯr-ē-əl\ *adj* : extending beyond the reach of memory, record, or tradition

im·mense \i-'mens\ *adj* [MF, fr. L *immensus* immeasurable, fr. *mensus*, pp. of *metiri* to measure] **1** : very great in size or degree : VAST, HUGE **2** : EXCELLENT — **im·mense·ly** *adv* — **im·men·si·ty** \-'men-sə-tē\ *n*

im·merse \i-'mərs\ *vb* **im·mersed; im·mers·ing 1** : to plunge or dip esp. into a fluid **2** : ENGROSS, ABSORB **3** : to baptize by immersing — **im·mer·sion** \-'mər-zhən\ *n*

im·mi·grant \'i-mi-grənt\ *n* **1** : a person who immigrates **2** : a plant or animal that becomes established where it did not previously occur

im·mi·grate \'i-mə-ˌgrāt\ *vb* **-grat·ed; -grat·ing** : to come into a foreign country and take up residence — **im·mi·gra·tion** \ˌi-mə-'grā-shən\ *n*

im·mi·nent \'i-mə-nənt\ *adj* : ready to take place; *esp* : hanging threateningly over one's head — **im·mi·nence** \-nəns\ *n* — **im·mi·nent·ly** *adv*

im·mis·ci·ble \(ˌ)i-'mi-sə-bəl\ *adj* : incapable of mixing — **im·mis·ci·bil·i·ty** \-ˌmi-sə-'bi-lə-tē\ *n*

im·mo·bile \(ˌ)i-'mō-bəl\ *adj* : incapable of being moved : IMMOVABLE, FIXED — **im·mo·bil·i·ty** \ˌi-mō-'bi-lə-tē\ *n*

im·mo·bi·lize \i-'mō-bə-ˌlīz\ *vb* : to make immobile — **im·mo·bi·li·za·tion** \i-ˌmō-bə-lə-'zā-shən\ *n*

im·mod·er·ate \(ˌ)i-'mä-də-rət\ *adj* : lacking in moderation : EXCESSIVE — **im·mod·er·a·cy** \-rə-sē\ *n* — **im·mod·er·ate·ly** *adv*

im·mod·est \(ˌ)i-'mä-dəst\ *adj* : not modest : BRAZEN, INDECENT ⟨an ∼ dress⟩ ⟨∼ conduct⟩ — **im·mod·est·ly** *adv* — **im·mod·es·ty** \-də-stē\ *n*

im·mo·late \'i-mə-ˌlāt\ *vb* **-lat·ed; -lat·ing** [L *immolare*, fr. *mola* grits; fr. the custom of sprinkling victims with sacrificial meal] : to offer in sacrifice; *esp* : to kill as a sacrificial victim — **im·mo·la·tion** \ˌi-mə-'lā-shən\ *n*

im·mor·al \(ˌ)i-'mȯr-əl\ *adj* : not moral — **im·mor·al·ly** *adv*

im·mo·ral·i·ty \ˌi-mȯ-'ra-lə-tē, ˌi-mə-\ *n* **1** : WICKEDNESS; *esp* : UNCHASTITY **2** : an immoral act or practice

¹im·mor·tal \(ˌ)i-'mȯrt-ᵊl\ *adj* **1** : not mortal : exempt from death ⟨∼ gods⟩ **2** : destined to be remembered forever ⟨those ∼ words⟩ — **im·mor·tal·ly** *adv*

²immortal *n* **1** : one exempt from death **2** *pl, often cap* : the gods in Greek and Roman mythology **3** : a person whose fame is lasting ⟨an ∼ of baseball⟩

im·mor·tal·i·ty \ˌi-mȯr-'ta-lə-tē\ *n* : the quality or state of being immortal; *esp* : unending existence

im·mor·tal·ize \i-'mȯrt-ᵊl-ˌīz\ *vb* **-ized; -iz·ing** : to make immortal

im·mov·able \(ˌ)i-'mü-və-bəl\ *adj* **1** : firmly fixed, settled, or fastened : FAST, STATIONARY ⟨∼ mountains⟩ **2** : STEADFAST, UNYIELDING **3** : IMPASSIVE — **im·mov·abil·i·ty** \-ˌmü-və-'bi-lə-tē\ *n* — **im·mov·ably** \-blē\ *adv*

im·mune \i-'myün\ *adj* **1** : EXEMPT **2** : having a special capacity for resistance (as to a disease) **3** : containing or producing antibodies — **im·mu·ni·ty** \-'myü-nə-tē\ *n*

immune response *n* : a response of the body to an antigen resulting in the formation of antibodies and cells designed to react with the antigen and render it harmless

immune system *n* : the bodily system that protects the body from foreign substances, cells, and tissues by producing the immune response and that includes esp. the thymus, spleen, lymph nodes, and lymphocytes

im·mu·nize \'i-myə-ˌnīz\ *vb* **-nized; -niz·ing** : to make immune — **im·mu·ni·za·tion** \ˌi-myə-nə-'zā-shən\ *n*

im·mu·no·de·fi·cien·cy \ˌi-myə-nō-di-'fi-shən-sē\ *n* : inability to produce the normal number of antibodies or immunologically sensitized cells esp. in response to specific antigens — **im·mu·no·de·fi·cient** \-'fi-shənt\ *adj*

im·mu·no·glob·u·lin \ˌi-myə-nō-'glä-byə-lən\ *n* : ANTIBODY

im·mu·nol·o·gy \ˌi-myə-'nä-lə-jē\ *n* : a science that deals with the immune system, immunity, and the immune response — **im·mu·no·log·ic** \-nə-'lä-jik\ *or* **im·mu·no·log·i·cal** \-ji-kəl\ *adj* — **im·mu·no·log·i·cal·ly** \-ji-k(ə-)lē\ *adv* — **im·mu·nol·o·gist** \-'nä-lə-jist\ *n*

im·mu·no·sup·pres·sion \ˌi-myə-nō-sə-'pre-shən\ *n* : suppression (as by drugs) of natural immune responses — **im·mu·no·sup·press** \-'pres\ *vb* — **im·mu·no·sup·pres·sive** \-'pre-siv\ *adj*

im·mu·no·ther·a·py \-'ther-ə-pē\ *n* : treatment or prevention of disease by attempting to induce immunity

im·mure \i-'myur\ *vb* **im·mured; im·mur·ing 1** : to enclose within or as if within walls **2** : to build into a wall; *esp* : to entomb in a wall

im·mu·ta·ble \(ˌ)i-'myü-tə-bəl\ *adj* : UNCHANGEABLE, UNCHANGING — **im·mu·ta·bil·i·ty** \-ˌmyü-tə-'bi-lə-tē\ *n* — **im·mu·ta·bly** \-'myü-tə-blē\ *adv*

¹imp \'imp\ *n* **1** : a small demon : FIEND **2** : a mischievous child

²imp *abbr* **1** imperative **2** imperfect **3** imperial **4** import; imported

¹im·pact \im-'pakt\ *vb* **1** : to press together **2** : to have an impact on

²im·pact \'im-ˌpakt\ *n* **1** : a forceful contact, collision, or onset; *also* : the impetus communicated in or as if in a collision **2** : EFFECT

im·pact·ed \im-'pak-təd\ *adj* **1** : packed or wedged in **2** : wedged between the jawbone and another tooth

im·pair \im-'par\ *vb* : to diminish in quantity, value, excellence, or strength : DAMAGE, LESSEN — **im·pair·ment** *n*

im·paired \-'pard\ *adj* : being in a less than perfect or whole condition; *esp* : handicapped or functionally defective — often used in combination ⟨hearing∼ impaired⟩

im·pa·la \im-'pa-lə\ *n, pl* **impalas** *or* **impala** : a large brownish African antelope that in the male has slender curving horns

im·pale \im-'pāl\ *vb* **im·paled; im·pal·ing** : to pierce with or as if with something pointed — **im·pale·ment** *n*

im·pal·pa·ble \(ˌ)im-'pal-pə-bəl\ *adj* **1** : unable to be felt by touch : INTANGIBLE **2** : not easily seen or understood — **im·pal·pa·bly** \-blē\ *adv*

im·pan·el \im-'pan-ᵊl\ *vb* : to enter in or on a panel : ENROLL ⟨∼ a jury⟩

im·part \im-'pärt\ *vb* **1** : to give from one's store or abundance ⟨the sun ∼s warmth⟩ **2** : to make known

im·par·tial \(ˌ)im-'pär-shəl\ *adj* : not partial : UNBIASED, JUST — **im·par·tial·i·ty** \-ˌpär-shē-'a-lə-tē\ *n* — **im·par·tial·ly** *adv*

im·pass·able \(ˌ)im-'pa-sə-bəl\ *adj* : incapable of being passed, traversed, or crossed ⟨∼ roads⟩ — **im·pass·ably** \-blē\ *adv*

im·passe \'im-ˌpas\ *n* **1** : an impassable road or way **2** : a predicament from which there is no obvious escape

im·pas·si·ble \(ˌ)im-'pa-sə-bəl\ *adj* : incapable of feeling : IMPASSIVE

im·pas·sioned \im-'pa-shənd\ *adj* : filled with passion or zeal : showing great warmth or intensity of feeling **syn** passionate, ardent, fervent, fervid

im·pas·sive \(ˌ)im-'pa-siv\ *adj* : showing no signs of feeling, emotion, or interest : EXPRESSIONLESS, INDIFFERENT **syn** stoic, phlegmatic, apathetic, stolid — **im·pas·sive·ly** *adv* — **im·pas·siv·i·ty** \ˌim-ˌpa-'si-və-tē\ *n*

im·pas·to \im-'pas-tō, -'päs-\ *n* : the thick application of a pigment to a canvas or panel in painting; *also* : the body of pigment so applied

im·pa·tiens \im-'pā-shənz, -shəns\ *n* : any of a genus of annual herbs with usu. spurred flowers and seed capsules that readily split open

im·pa·tient \(ˌ)im-'pā-shənt\ *adj* **1** : not patient : restless or short of temper esp. under irritation, delay, or opposition **2** : INTOLERANT ⟨∼ of poverty⟩ **3**

: prompted or marked by impatience **4** : ANXIOUS —
im·pa·tience \-shəns\ *n* — **im·pa·tient·ly** *adv*
im·peach \im-'pēch\ *vb* [ME *empechen* to accuse, fr.
MF *empeechier* to hinder, fr. LL *impedicare* to fetter,
fr. L *pedica* fetter, fr. *ped-, pes* foot] **1** : to charge (a
public official) before an authorized tribunal with
misconduct in office **2** : to challenge the credibility or
validity of **3** : to remove from public office for misconduct — **im·peach·ment** *n*
im·pec·ca·ble \(₁)im-'pe-kə-bəl\ *adj* **1** : not capable of
sinning or wrongdoing **2** : FAULTLESS, IRREPROACH-
ABLE ⟨a man of ∼ character⟩ — **im·pec·ca·bil·i·ty**
\-₁pe-kə-'bi-lə-tē\ *n* — **im·pec·ca·bly** \-'pe-kə-blē\
adv
im·pe·cu·nious \₁im-pi-'kyü-nyəs, -nē-əs\ *adj* : having
little or no money — **im·pe·cu·nious·ness** *n*
im·ped·ance \im-'pēd-ᵊns\ *n* : the opposition in an
electrical circuit to the flow of an alternating current
im·pede \im-'pēd\ *vb* **im·ped·ed; im·ped·ing** [L *impe-
dire*, fr. *ped-, pes* foot] : to interfere with the progress
of
im·ped·i·ment \im-'pe-də-mənt\ *n* **1** : something that
impedes, hinders, or obstructs **2** : a speech defect
im·ped·i·men·ta \im-₁pe-də-'men-tə\ *n pl* : things that
impede
im·pel \im-'pel\ *vb* **im·pelled; im·pel·ling** : to urge or
drive forward or on : FORCE; *also* : PROPEL
im·pel·ler *also* **im·pel·lor** \im-'pe-lər\ *n* : a rotor esp.
in a pump
im·pend \im-'pend\ *vb* **1** : to hover or hang over
threateningly : MENACE **2** : to be about to occur
im·pen·e·tra·ble \(₁)im-'pe-nə-trə-bəl\ *adj* **1** : incapa-
ble of being penetrated or pierced ⟨an ∼ jungle⟩ **2** : incapable of being comprehended : INSCRUTABLE ⟨an ∼
mystery⟩ — **im·pen·e·tra·bil·i·ty** \-₁pe-nə-trə-'bi-lə-
tē\ *n* — **im·pen·e·tra·bly** \-'pe-nə-trə-blē\ *adv*
im·pen·i·tent \(₁)im-'pe-nə-tənt\ *adj* : not penitent : not
repenting of sin — **im·pen·i·tence** \-təns\ *n*
im·per·a·tive \im-'per-ə-tiv\ *adj* **1** : expressing a command, request, or encouragement ⟨∼ sentence⟩ **2**
: having power to restrain, control, or direct **3** : NEC-
ESSARY — **imperative** *n* — **im·per·a·tive·ly** *adv*
im·per·cep·ti·ble \₁im-pər-'sep-tə-bəl\ *adj* : not perceptible; *esp* : too slight to be perceived ⟨∼ changes⟩
— **im·per·cep·ti·bly** \-blē\ *adv*
im·per·cep·tive \₁im-pər-'sep-tiv\ *adj* : not perceptive
imperf *abbr* imperfect
¹im·per·fect \(₁)im-'pər-fikt\ *adj* **1** : not perfect : DEFEC-
TIVE, INCOMPLETE **2** : of, relating to, or being a verb
tense used to designate a continuing state or an incomplete action esp. in the past — **im·per·fect·ly** *adv*
²imperfect *n* : the imperfect tense; *also* : a verb form in
it
im·per·fec·tion \₁im-pər-'fek-shən\ *n* : the quality or
state of being imperfect; *also* : FAULT, BLEMISH
im·pe·ri·al \im-'pir-ē-əl\ *adj* **1** : of, relating to, or befitting an empire or an emperor; *also* : of or relating
to the United Kingdom or to the Commonwealth or
British Empire **2** : ROYAL, SOVEREIGN; *also* : REGAL,
IMPERIOUS **3** : of unusual size or excellence
im·pe·ri·al·ism \im-'pir-ē-ə-₁li-zəm\ *n* : the policy of
seeking to extend the power, dominion, or territories
of a nation — **im·pe·ri·al·ist** \-list\ *n or adj* — **im-
pe·ri·al·is·tic** \-₁pir-ē-ə-'lis-tik\ *adj* — **im·pe·ri·al·is-
ti·cal·ly** \-ti-k(ə-)lē\ *adv*
im·per·il \im-'per-əl\ *vb* **-iled** *or* **-illed; -il·ing** *or* **-il-
ling** : ENDANGER
im·pe·ri·ous \im-'pir-ē-əs\ *adj* **1** : COMMANDING, LORD-
LY **2** : ARROGANT, DOMINEERING **3** : IMPERATIVE, UR-
GENT — **im·pe·ri·ous·ly** *adv*
im·per·ish·able \(₁)im-'per-i-shə-bəl\ *adj* : not perish-
able or subject to decay
im·per·ma·nent \(₁)im-'pər-mə-nənt\ *adj* : not perma-
nent : TRANSIENT — **im·per·ma·nent·ly** *adv*
im·per·me·able \(₁)im-'pər-mē-ə-bəl\ *adj* : not permit-
ting passage (as of a fluid) through its substance

im·per·mis·si·ble \₁im-pər-'mi-sə-bəl\ *adj* : not permis-
sible
im·per·son·al \(₁)im-'pər-sə-nəl\ *adj* **1** : not referring to
any particular person or thing **2** : not involving human emotions — **im·per·son·al·i·ty** \-₁pər-sə-'na-lə-
tē\ *n* — **im·per·son·al·ly** *adv*
im·per·son·ate \im-'pər-sə-₁nāt\ *vb* **-at·ed; -at·ing** : to
assume or act the character of — **im·per·son·ation**
\-₁pər-sə-'nā-shən\ *n* — **im·per·son·ator** \-'pər-sə-
₁nā-tər\ *n*
im·per·ti·nent \(₁)im-'pərt-ᵊn-ənt\ *adj* **1** : IRRELEVANT
2 : not restrained within due or proper bounds
: RUDE, INSOLENT, SAUCY — **im·per·ti·nence** \-əns\ *n*
— **im·per·ti·nent·ly** *adv*
im·per·turb·able \₁im-pər-'tər-bə-bəl\ *adj* : marked by
extreme calm, impassivity, and steadiness : SERENE
im·per·vi·ous \(₁)im-'pər-vē-əs\ *adj* **1** : incapable of be-
ing penetrated (as by moisture) **2** : not capable of being affected or disturbed ⟨∼ to criticism⟩
im·pe·ti·go \₁im-pə-'tē-gō, -'tī-\ *n* : a contagious skin
disease characterized by vesicles, pustules, and yellowish crusts
im·pet·u·ous \im-'pe-chə-wəs\ *adj* **1** : marked by impulsive vehemence ⟨∼ temper⟩ **2** : marked by force
and violence ⟨with ∼ speed⟩ — **im·pet·u·os·i·ty**
\(₁)im-₁pe-chə-'wä-sə-tē\ *n* — **im·pet·u·ous·ly** *adv*
im·pe·tus \'im-pə-təs\ *n* [L, assault, impetus, fr. *impe-
tere* to attack, fr. *petere* to go to, seek] **1** : a driving
force : IMPULSE; *also* : INCENTIVE **2** : MOMENTUM
im·pi·e·ty \(₁)im-'pī-ə-tē\ *n, pl* **-ties** **1** : the quality or
state of being impious **2** : an impious act
im·pinge \im-'pinj\ *vb* **im·pinged; im·ping·ing** **1** : to
strike or dash esp. with a sharp collision **2** : EN-
CROACH, INFRINGE — **im·pinge·ment** *n*
im·pi·ous \'im-pē-əs, (₁)im-'pī-\ *adj* : not pious : IRREV-
ERENT, PROFANE
imp·ish \'im-pish\ *adj* : of, relating to, or befitting an
imp; *esp* : MISCHIEVOUS — **imp·ish·ly** *adv* — **imp-
ish·ness** *n*
im·pla·ca·ble \(₁)im-'pla-kə-bəl, -'plā-\ *adj* : not capa-
ble of being appeased, pacified, mitigated, or
changed ⟨an ∼ enemy⟩ — **im·pla·ca·bil·i·ty** \-₁pla-kə-
'bi-lə-tē, -₁plā-\ *n* — **im·pla·ca·bly** \-'pla-kə-blē\ *adv*
im·plant \im-'plant\ *vb* **1** : to set firmly or deeply **2** : to
fix in the mind or spirit **3** : to insert in a living site for
growth or absorption — **im·plant** \'im-₁plant\ *n* —
im·plan·ta·tion \₁im-₁plan-'tā-shən\ *n*
im·plau·si·ble \(₁)im-'plȯ-zə-bəl\ *adj* : not plausible —
im·plau·si·bil·i·ty \-₁plȯ-zə-'bi-lə-tē\ *n* — **im·plau-
si·bly** \-'plȯ-zə-blē\ *adv*
¹im·ple·ment \'im-plə-mənt\ *n* [ME, fr. LL *implemen-
tum* action of filling up, fr. L *implēre* to fill up] : TOOL,
UTENSIL, INSTRUMENT
²im·ple·ment \-₁ment\ *vb* **1** : CARRY OUT; *esp* : to put
into practice **2** : to provide implements for — **im-
ple·men·ta·tion** \₁im-plə-mən-'tā-shən\ *n*
im·pli·cate \'im-plə-₁kāt\ *vb* **-cat·ed; -cat·ing** **1** : IMPLY
2 : INVOLVE — **im·pli·ca·tion** \₁im-plə-'kā-shən\ *n*
im·plic·it \im-'pli-sət\ *adj* **1** : understood though not
directly stated or expressed : IMPLIED; *also* : POTEN-
TIAL **2** : COMPLETE, UNQUESTIONING, ABSOLUTE ⟨∼
faith⟩ — **im·plic·it·ly** *adv*
im·plode \im-'plōd\ *vb* **im·plod·ed; im·plod·ing** **1** : to
burst or collapse inward — **im·plo·sion** \-'plō-zhən\ *n*
— **im·plo·sive** \-siv\ *adj*
im·plore \im-'plȯr\ *vb* **im·plored; im·plor·ing** : BE-
SEECH, ENTREAT **syn** supplicate, beg, importune,
plead
im·ply \im-'plī\ *vb* **im·plied; im·ply·ing** **1** : to involve
or indicate by inference, association, or necessary
consequence rather than by direct statement ⟨war *im-
plies* fighting⟩ **2** : to express indirectly : hint at : SUG-
GEST
im·po·lite \₁im-pə-'līt\ *adj* : not polite : RUDE, DISCOUR-
TEOUS
im·pol·i·tic \(₁)im-'pä-lə-₁tik\ *adj* : not politic : RASH

im·pon·der·a·ble \(ˌ)im-ˈpän-də-rə-bəl\ *adj* : incapable of being weighed or evaluated with exactness — **imponderable** *n*

¹im·port \im-ˈpōrt\ *vb* **1** : MEAN, SIGNIFY **2** : to bring (as merchandise) into a place or country from a foreign or external source — **im·port·er** *n*

²im·port \ˈim-ˌpōrt\ *n* **1** : IMPORTANCE, SIGNIFICANCE **2** : MEANING, SIGNIFICATION **3** : something (as merchandise) brought in from another country

im·por·tance \im-ˈpȯrt-ᵊns\ *n* : the quality or state of being important : MOMENT, SIGNIFICANCE **syn** consequence, import, weight

im·por·tant \im-ˈpȯrt-ᵊnt\ *adj* **1** : marked by importance : SIGNIFICANT **2** : giving an impression of importance — **im·por·tant·ly** *adv*

im·por·ta·tion \ˌim-ˌpȯr-ˈtā-shən, -pər-\ *n* **1** : the act or practice of importing **2** : something imported

im·por·tu·nate \im-ˈpȯr-chə-nət\ *adj* **1** : troublesomely urgent or persistent **2** : BURDENSOME, TROUBLESOME

im·por·tune \ˌim-pər-ˈtün, -ˈtyün; im-ˈpȯr-chən\ *vb* **-tuned; -tun·ing** : to urge or beg with troublesome persistence — **im·por·tu·ni·ty** \-pər-ˈtü-nə-tē, ˈtyü-\ *n*

im·pose \im-ˈpōz\ *vb* **im·posed; im·pos·ing 1** : to establish or apply by authority ⟨~ a tax⟩; *also* : to establish by force ⟨*imposed* a government⟩ **2** : OBTRUDE ⟨*imposed* herself on others⟩ **3** : to take unwarranted advantage of something ⟨~ on her good nature⟩ — **im·po·si·tion** \ˌim-pə-ˈzi-shən\ *n*

im·pos·ing *adj* : impressive because of size, bearing, dignity, or grandeur — **im·pos·ing·ly** *adv*

im·pos·si·ble \(ˌ)im-ˈpä-sə-bəl\ *adj* **1** : incapable of being or of occurring **2** : enormously difficult **3** : extremely undesirable : UNACCEPTABLE — **im·pos·si·bil·i·ty** \-ˌpä-sə-ˈbi-lə-tē\ *n* — **im·pos·si·bly** \-ˈpä-sə-blē\ *adv*

¹im·post \ˈim-ˌpōst\ *n* : TAX, DUTY

²impost *n* : a block, capital, or molding from which an arch springs

im·pos·tor *or* **im·pos·ter** \im-ˈpäs-tər\ *n* : one that assumes an identity or title not one's own in order to deceive

im·pos·ture \im-ˈpäs-chər\ *n* : DECEPTION; *esp* : fraudulent impersonation

im·po·tent \ˈim-pə-tənt\ *adj* **1** : lacking in power or strength : HELPLESS **2** : unable to copulate; *also* : STERILE — **im·po·tence** \-təns\ *n* — **im·po·ten·cy** \-tən-sē\ *n* — **im·po·tent·ly** *adv*

im·pound \im-ˈpaünd\ *vb* **1** : CONFINE, ENCLOSE ⟨~ stray dogs⟩ **2** : to seize and hold in legal custody **3** : to collect in a reservoir ⟨~ water⟩ — **im·pound·ment** *n*

im·pov·er·ish \im-ˈpä-və-rish\ *vb* : to make poor; *also* : to deprive of strength, richness, or fertility — **im·pov·er·ish·ment** *n*

im·prac·ti·ca·ble \(ˌ)im-ˈprak-ti-kə-bəl\ *adj* : not practicable : incapable of being put into practice or use

im·prac·ti·cal \(ˌ)im-ˈprak-ti-kəl\ *adj* **1** : not practical **2** : IMPRACTICABLE

im·pre·cate \ˈim-pri-ˌkāt\ *vb* **-cat·ed; -cat·ing** : CURSE — **im·pre·ca·tion** \ˌim-pri-ˈkā-shən\ *n*

im·pre·cise \ˌim-pri-ˈsīs\ *adj* : not precise — **im·pre·cise·ly** *adv* — **im·pre·cise·ness** *n* — **im·pre·ci·sion** \-ˈsi-zhən\ *n*

im·preg·na·ble \im-ˈpreg-nə-bəl\ *adj* : incapable of being taken by assault : UNCONQUERABLE, UNASSAILABLE — **im·preg·na·bil·i·ty** \(ˌ)im-ˌpreg-nə-ˈbi-lə-tē\ *n*

im·preg·nate \im-ˈpreg-ˌnāt\ *vb* **-nat·ed; -nat·ing 1** : to fertilize or make pregnant **2** : to cause to be filled, permeated, or saturated — **im·preg·na·tion** \ˌim-ˌpreg-ˈnā-shən\ *n*

im·pre·sa·rio \ˌim-prə-ˈsär-ē-ˌō\ *n, pl* **-ri·os** [It, fr. *impresa* undertaking, fr. *imprendere* to undertake] **1** : the manager or conductor of an opera or concert company **2** : one who puts on an entertainment **3** : MANAGER, PRODUCER

¹im·press \im-ˈpres\ *vb* **1** : to apply with or produce (as a mark) by pressure : IMPRINT **2** : to press, stamp, or print in or upon **3** : to produce a vivid impression of **4** : to affect esp. forcibly or deeply — **im·press·ible** *adj*

²im·press \ˈim-ˌpres\ *n* **1** : a characteristic or distinctive mark **2** : IMPRESSION, EFFECT **3** : IMPRESSION 2 **4** : an image of something formed by or as if by pressure; *esp* : SEAL **5** : a product of pressure or influence

³im·press \im-ˈpres\ *vb* **1** : to force into naval service **2** : to get the aid or services of by forcible argument or persuasion — **im·press·ment** *n*

im·pres·sion \im-ˈpre-shən\ *n* **1** : a characteristic trait or feature resulting from influence : IMPRESS **2** : a stamp, form, or figure made by impressing : IMPRINT **3** : an esp. marked influence or effect on feeling, sense, or mind **4** : a single print or copy (as from type or from an engraved plate or book) **5** : all the copies of a publication (as a book) printed for one issue : PRINTING **6** : a usu. vague notion or remembrance **7** : an imitation in caricature of a noted personality as a form of entertainment

im·pres·sion·able \im-ˈpre-shə-nə-bəl\ *adj* : capable of being easily impressed : easily molded or influenced

im·pres·sion·ism \im-ˈpre-shə-ˌni-zəm\ *n, often cap* : a theory or practice in modern art of depicting the natural appearances of objects by dabs or strokes of primary unmixed colors in order to simulate actual reflected light — **im·pres·sion·is·tic** \-ˌpre-shə-ˈnis-tik\ *adj*

im·pres·sion·ist \im-ˈpre-shə-nist\ *n* **1** *often cap* : a painter who practices impressionism **2** : an entertainer who does impressions

im·pres·sive \im-ˈpre-siv\ *adj* : making or tending to make a marked impression ⟨an ~ speech⟩ — **im·pres·sive·ly** *adv* — **im·pres·sive·ness** *n*

im·pri·ma·tur \ˌim-prə-ˈmä-ˌtür\ *n* [NL, let it be printed] **1** : a license to print or publish; *also* : official approval of a publication by a censor **2** : SANCTION, APPROVAL

¹im·print \im-ˈprint, ˈim-ˌprint\ *vb* **1** : to stamp or mark by or as if by pressure : IMPRESS **2** : to fix firmly (as on the memory)

²im·print \ˈim-ˌprint\ *n* **1** : something imprinted or printed **2** : a publisher's name printed at the foot of a title page **3** : an indelible distinguishing effect or influence

im·pris·on \im-ˈpriz-ᵊn\ *vb* : to put in or as if in prison : CONFINE — **im·pris·on·ment** *n*

im·prob·a·ble \(ˌ)im-ˈprä-bə-bəl\ *adj* : unlikely to be true or to occur — **im·prob·a·bil·i·ty** \ˌprä-bə-ˈbi-lə-tē\ *n* — **im·prob·a·bly** \-ˈprä-bə-blē\ *adv*

im·promp·tu \im-ˈprämp-tü, -tyü\ *adj* [F, fr. *impromptu* extemporaneously, fr. L *in promptu* in readiness] **1** : made or done on or as if on the spur of the moment **2** : EXTEMPORANEOUS, UNREHEARSED — **impromptu** *adv or n*

im·prop·er \(ˌ)im-ˈprä-pər\ *adj* **1** : not proper, fit, or suitable **2** : INCORRECT, INACCURATE **3** : not in accord with propriety, modesty, or good manners — **im·prop·er·ly** *adv*

improper fraction *n* : a fraction whose numerator is equal to or larger than the denominator

im·pro·pri·ety \ˌim-prə-ˈprī-ə-tē\ *n, pl* **-ties 1** : an improper act or remark; *esp* : an unacceptable use of a word or of language **2** : the quality or state of being improper

im·prove \im-ˈprüv\ *vb* **im·proved; im·prov·ing 1** : to enhance or increase in value or quality **2** : to grow or become better ⟨your work is *improving*⟩ **3** : to make good use of ⟨~ the time by reading⟩ — **im·prov·able** \-ˈprü-və-bəl\ *adj*

im·prove·ment \im-ˈprüv-mənt\ *n* **1** : the act or process of improving **2** : increased value or excellence of something **3** : something that adds to the value or appearance of a thing

im·prov·i·dent \(ˌ)im-ˈprä-və-dənt\ *adj* : not providing for the future — **im·prov·i·dence** \-dəns\ *n*

im·pro·vise \'im-prə-ˌvīz\ *vb* **-vised; -vis·ing** [F *improviser*, fr. It *improvvisare*, fr. *improvviso* sudden, fr. L *improvisus*, lit., unforeseen] **1** : to compose, recite, play, or sing on the spur of the moment : EXTEMPORIZE ⟨~ on the piano⟩ **2** : to make, invent, or arrange offhand ⟨~ a sail out of shirts⟩ — **im·pro·vi·sa·tion** \im-ˌprä-və-'zā-shən, ˌim-prə-və-\ *n* — **im·pro·vis·er** *or* **im·pro·vi·sor** \ˌim-prə-'vī-zər, 'im-prə-ˌvī-\ *n*

im·pru·dent \(ˌ)im-'prüd-ənt\ *adj* : not prudent : lacking discretion — **im·pru·dence** \-əns\ *n*

im·pu·dent \'im-pyü-dənt\ *adj* : marked by contemptuous boldness or disregard of others — **im·pu·dence** \-dəns\ *n* — **im·pu·dent·ly** *adv*

im·pugn \im-'pyün\ *vb* [ME, to assail, ultim. fr. L *inpugnare*, fr. *pugnare* to fight] : to attack by words or arguments : oppose or attack as false or as lacking integrity

im·puis·sance \im-'pwis-əns, -'pyü-ə-səns\ *n* [ME, fr. MF] : the quality or state of being powerless : WEAKNESS

im·pulse \'im-ˌpəls\ *n* **1** : a force that starts a body into motion; *also* : the motion produced by such a force **2** : an arousing of the mind and spirit to some usu. unpremeditated action **3** : NERVE IMPULSE

im·pul·sion \im-'pəl-shən\ *n* **1** : the act of impelling : the state of being impelled **2** : a force that impels **3** : IMPULSE 2; *also* : COMPULSION 3

im·pul·sive \im-'pəl-siv\ *adj* **1** : having the power of or actually driving or impelling **2** : acting or prone to act on impulse ⟨~ buying⟩ — **im·pul·sive·ly** *adv* — **im·pul·sive·ness** *n*

im·pu·ni·ty \im-'pyü-nə-tē\ *n* [MF or L; MF *impunité*, fr. L *impunitas*, fr. *impune* without punishment, fr. *poena* penalty, punishment] : exemption from punishment, harm, or loss

im·pure \(ˌ)im-'pyür\ *adj* **1** : not pure : UNCHASTE, OBSCENE **2** : DIRTY, FOUL **3** : ADULTERATED, MIXED — **im·pu·ri·ty** \-'pyür-ə-tē\ *n*

im·pute \im-'pyüt\ *vb* **im·put·ed; im·put·ing 1** : to lay the responsibility or blame for often falsely or unjustly **2** : to credit to a person or a cause : ATTRIBUTE — **im·put·able** \-'pyü-tə-bəl\ *adj* — **im·pu·ta·tion** \ˌim-pyü-'tā-shən\ *n*

¹in \'in\ *prep* **1** — used to indicate physical surroundings ⟨swim ~ the lake⟩ **2** : INTO 1 ⟨ran ~ the house⟩ **3** : DURING ⟨~ the summer⟩ **4** : WITH ⟨written ~ pencil⟩ **5** — used to indicate one's situation or state of being ⟨~ luck⟩ ⟨~ love⟩ **6** — used to indicate manner or purpose ⟨~ a hurry⟩ ⟨said ~ reply⟩ **7** : INTO 2 ⟨broke ~ pieces⟩

²in *adv* **1** : to or toward the inside ⟨come ~⟩; *also* : to or toward some destination or place ⟨flew ~ from the South⟩ **2** : at close quarters : NEAR ⟨the enemy closed ~⟩ **3** : into the midst of something ⟨mix ~ the flour⟩ **4** : to or at its proper place ⟨fit a piece ~⟩ **5** : WITHIN ⟨locked ~⟩ **6** : in vogue or season **7** : in one's presence, possession, or control ⟨the results are ~⟩

³in *adj* **1** : located inside or within **2** : that is in position, operation, or power ⟨the ~ party⟩ **3** : directed inward : INCOMING ⟨the ~ train⟩ **4** : keenly aware of and responsive to what is new and smart ⟨the ~ crowd⟩; *also* : extremely fashionable ⟨the ~ thing to do⟩

⁴in *n* **1** : one who is in office or power or on the inside **2** : INFLUENCE, PULL ⟨he has an ~ with the owner⟩

⁵in *abbr* **1** inch **2** inlet

In *symbol* indium

IN *abbr* Indiana

in- \(ˌ)in\ *prefix* : not : absence of : NON-, UN-

inaccessibility	inadmissible
inaccessible	inadvisability
inaccuracy	inadvisable
inaccurate	inapparent
inaction	inapplicable
inactive	inapposite
inactivity	inapproachable
inadmissibility	inappropriate
inaptitude	ineffaceable
inarguable	inefficacious
inartistic	inefficacy
inattentive	inelastic
inaudible	inelasticity
inaudibly	inequitable
inauspicious	inequity
inauthentic	ineradicable
incautious	inerrant
incombustible	inexpedient
incomprehension	inexpensive
inconclusive	inexpressive
incongruent	inextinguishable
inconsistency	infeasible
inconsistent	inharmonious
incoordination	inhospitable
incurious	injudicious
indecipherable	inoffensive
indemonstrable	insanitary
indestructible	insensitive
indeterminable	insensitivity
indiscernible	insignificance
indistinguishable	insignificant
inedible	insolvable
ineducable	insusceptible

in·abil·i·ty \ˌi-nə-'bi-lə-tē\ *n* : the quality or state of being unable

in ab·sen·tia \ˌin-ab-'sen-chə, -chē-ə\ *adv* : in one's absence

in·ac·ti·vate \(ˌ)i-'nak-tə-ˌvāt\ *vb* : to make inactive — **in·ac·ti·va·tion** \(ˌ)i-ˌnak-tə-'vā-shən\ *n*

in·ad·e·quate \(ˌ)i-'na-di-kwət\ *adj* : not adequate : INSUFFICIENT — **in·ad·e·qua·cy** \-kwə-sē\ *n* — **in·ad·e·quate·ly** *adv* — **in·ad·e·quate·ness** *n*

in·ad·ver·tent \ˌi-nəd-'vərt-ənt\ *adj* **1** : HEEDLESS, INATTENTIVE **2** : UNINTENTIONAL — **in·ad·ver·tence** \-əns\ *n* — **in·ad·ver·ten·cy** \-ən-sē\ *n* — **in·ad·ver·tent·ly** *adv*

in·alien·able \(ˌ)i-'nāl-yə-nə-bəl, -'nā-lē-ə-\ *adj* : incapable of being alienated, surrendered, or transferred ⟨~ rights⟩ — **in·alien·abil·i·ty** \(ˌ)i-ˌnāl-yə-nə-'bi-lə-tē, -ˌnā-lē-ə-\ *n* — **in·alien·ably** *adv*

in·amo·ra·ta \i-ˌnä-mə-'rä-tə\ *n* : a woman with whom one is in love

inane \i-'nān\ *adj* **inan·er; -est** : EMPTY, INSUBSTANTIAL; *also* : SHALLOW, SILLY — **inan·i·ty** \i-'na-nə-tē\ *n*

in·an·i·mate \(ˌ)i-'na-nə-mət\ *adj* : not animate or animated : lacking the qualities of living things — **in·an·i·mate·ly** *adv* — **in·an·i·mate·ness** *n*

in·ap·pre·cia·ble \ˌi-nə-'prē-shə-bəl\ *adj* : too small to be perceived — **in·ap·pre·cia·bly** \-blē\ *adv*

in·apt \(ˌ)i-'napt\ *adj* **1** : not suitable **2** : INEPT — **in·apt·ly** *adv* — **in·apt·ness** *n*

in·ar·tic·u·late \ˌi-när-'ti-kyə-lət\ *adj* **1** : not understandable as spoken words **2** : MUTE **3** : incapable of being expressed by speech; *also* : UNSPOKEN **4** : not having the power of distinct utterance or effective expression — **in·ar·tic·u·late·ly** *adv*

in·as·much as \ˌi-nəz-'məch-\ *conj* : seeing that : SINCE

in·at·ten·tion \ˌi-nə-'ten-chən\ *n* : failure to pay attention : DISREGARD

¹in·au·gu·ral \i-'nȯ-gyə-rəl, -gə-\ *adj* **1** : of or relating to an inauguration **2** : marking a beginning

²inaugural *n* **1** : an inaugural address **2** : INAUGURATION

in·au·gu·rate \i-'nȯ-gyə-ˌrāt, -gə-\ *vb* **-rat·ed; -rat·ing 1** : to introduce into an office with suitable ceremonies : INSTALL **2** : to dedicate ceremoniously **3** : BEGIN, INITIATE — **in·au·gu·ra·tion** \-ˌnȯ-gyə-'rā-shən, -gə-\ *n*

in·board \'in-ˌbȯrd\ *adv* **1** : inside the hull of a ship **2** : close or closest to the center line of a vehicle or craft — **inboard** *adj*

in·born \'in-'bȯrn\ *adj* **1** : present from or as if from birth **2** : HEREDITARY, INHERITED **syn** innate, congenital, native

in·bound \'in-₁baůnd\ *adj* : inward bound ⟨~ traffic⟩

in·bred \'in-'bred\ *adj* **1** : ingrained in one's nature as deeply as if by heredity **2** : subjected to or produced by inbreeding

in·breed·ing \'in-₁brē-diŋ\ *n* **1** : the interbreeding of closely related individuals esp. to preserve and fix desirable characters of and to eliminate unfavorable characters from a stock **2** : confinement to a narrow range or a local or limited field of choice — **in·breed** \-'brēd\ *vb*

inc *abbr* **1** incomplete **2** incorporated **3** increase

In·ca \'iŋ-kə\ *n* [Sp, fr. Quechua (a So. American Indian language) *inka* ruler of the Inca empire] **1** : a noble or a member of the ruling family of an Indian empire of Peru, Bolivia, and Ecuador until the Spanish conquest **2** : a member of any people under Inca influence

in·cal·cu·la·ble \(₁)in-'kal-kyə-lə-bəl\ *adj* : not capable of being calculated; *esp* : too large or numerous to be calculated — **in·cal·cu·la·bly** \-blē\ *adv*

in·can·des·cent \₁in-kən-'des-ənt\ *adj* **1** : glowing with heat **2** : SHINING, BRILLIANT — **in·can·des·cence** \-ᵊns\ *n*

incandescent lamp *n* : a lamp in which an electrically heated filament emits light

in·can·ta·tion \₁in-₁kan-'tā-shən\ *n* : a use of spells or verbal charms spoken or sung as a part of a ritual of magic; *also* : a formula of words used in or as if in such a ritual

in·ca·pa·ble \(₁)in-'kā-pə-bəl\ *adj* : lacking ability or qualification for a particular purpose; *also* : UNQUALIFIED — **in·ca·pa·bil·i·ty** \-₁kā-pə-'bi-lə-tē\ *n*

in·ca·pac·i·tate \₁in-kə-'pa-sə-₁tāt\ *vb* **-tat·ed; -tat·ing** : to make incapable or unfit : DISQUALIFY, DISABLE

in·ca·pac·i·ty \₁in-kə-'pa-sə-tē\ *n, pl* **-ties** : the quality or state of being incapable

in·car·cer·ate \in-'kär-sə-₁rāt\ *vb* **-at·ed; -at·ing** : IMPRISON, CONFINE — **in·car·cer·a·tion** \(₁)in-₁kär-sə-'rā-shən\ *n*

in·car·na·dine \in-'kär-nə-₁dīn, -₁dēn\ *vb* **-dined; -din·ing** : REDDEN

in·car·nate \in-'kär-nət, -₁nāt\ *adj* **1** : having bodily and esp. human form and substance **2** : PERSONIFIED — **in·car·nate** \-₁nāt\ *vb*

in·car·na·tion \₁in-₁kär-'nā-shən\ *n* **1** : the embodiment of a deity or spirit in an earthly form **2** *cap* : the union of divine and human natures in Jesus Christ **3** : a person showing a trait or typical character to a marked degree **4** : the act of incarnating : the state of being incarnate

incase *var of* ENCASE

in·cen·di·ary \in-'sen-dē-₁er-ē\ *adj* **1** : of or relating to a deliberate burning of property **2** : tending to excite or inflame **3** : designed to start fires ⟨an ~ bomb⟩ — **incendiary** *n*

¹in·cense \'in-₁sens\ *n* **1** : material used to produce a fragrant odor when burned **2** : the perfume or smoke from some spices and gums when burned

²in·cense \in-'sens\ *vb* **in·censed; in·cens·ing** : to make extremely angry

in·cen·tive \in-'sen-tiv\ *n* [ME, fr. LL *incentivum*, fr. *incentivus* stimulating, fr. L, setting the tune, fr. *incinere* to set the tune, fr. *canere* to sing] : something that incites or is likely to incite to determination or action

in·cep·tion \in-'sep-shən\ *n* : BEGINNING, COMMENCEMENT

in·cer·ti·tude \(₁)in-'sər-tə-₁tüd, -₁tyüd\ *n* **1** : UNCERTAINTY, DOUBT, INDECISION **2** : INSECURITY, INSTABILITY

in·ces·sant \(₁)in-'ses-ᵊnt\ *adj* : continuing or flowing without interruption ⟨~ rains⟩ — **in·ces·sant·ly** *adv*

in·cest \'in-₁sest\ *n* [ME, fr. L *incestus* sexual impuri-

ty, fr. *incestus* impure, fr. *castus* pure] : sexual intercourse between persons so closely related that marriage is illegal — **in·ces·tu·ous** \in-'ses-chù-wəs\ *adj*

¹inch \'inch\ *n* [ME, fr. OE *ynce*, fr. L *uncia* twelfth part, inch, ounce] — see WEIGHT table

²inch *vb* : to move by small degrees

in·cho·ate \in-'kō-ət, 'in-kə-₁wāt\ *adj* : being only partly in existence or operation : INCOMPLETE, INCIPIENT

inch·worm \'inch-₁wərm\ *n* : LOOPER

in·ci·dence \'in-sə-dəns\ *n* : rate of occurrence or effect

¹in·ci·dent \-dənt\ *n* **1** : OCCURRENCE, HAPPENING **2** : an action likely to lead to grave consequences esp. in diplomatic matters

²incident *adj* **1** : occurring or likely to occur esp. in connection with some other happening **2** : falling or striking on something ⟨~ light rays⟩

¹in·ci·den·tal \₁in-sə-'dent-ᵊl\ *adj* **1** : subordinate, nonessential, or attendant in position or significance ⟨~ expenses⟩ **2** : CASUAL, CHANCE

²incidental *n* **1** *pl* : minor items (as of expense) that are not individually accounted for **2** : something incidental

in·ci·den·tal·ly \₁in-sə-'den-tə-lē, -'dent-lē\ *adv* **1** : in an incidental manner **2** : by the way

in·cin·er·ate \in-'si-nə-₁rāt\ *vb* **-at·ed; -at·ing** : to burn to ashes

in·cin·er·a·tor \in-'si-nə-₁rā-tər\ *n* : a furnace for burning waste

in·cip·i·ent \in-'si-pē-ənt\ *adj* : beginning to be or become apparent

in·cise \in-'sīz\ *vb* **in·cised; in·cis·ing** **1** : to cut into **2** : CARVE, ENGRAVE

in·ci·sion \in-'si-zhən\ *n* : CUT, GASH; *esp* : a surgical cut

in·ci·sive \in-'sī-siv\ *adj* : impressively direct and decisive — **in·ci·sive·ly** *adv*

in·ci·sor \in-'sī-zər\ *n* : a front tooth typically adapted for cutting

in·cite \in-'sīt\ *vb* **in·cit·ed; in·cit·ing** : to arouse to action : stir up — **in·cite·ment** *n* — **in·cit·er** *n*

in·ci·vil·i·ty \₁in-sə-'vi-lə-tē\ *n* **1** : RUDENESS, DISCOURTESY **2** : a rude or discourteous act

incl *abbr* include; included; including; inclusive

in·clem·ent \(₁)in-'kle-mənt\ *adj* : SEVERE, STORMY ⟨~ weather⟩ — **in·clem·en·cy** \-mən-sē\ *n*

in·cli·na·tion \₁in-klə-'nā-shən\ *n* **1** : PROPENSITY, BENT; *esp* : LIKING **2** : BOW, NOD ⟨an ~ of the head⟩ **3** : a tilting of something **4** : SLANT, SLOPE

¹in·cline \in-'klīn\ *vb* **in·clined; in·clin·ing** **1** : BOW, BEND **2** : to be drawn toward an opinion or course of action **3** : to deviate from the vertical or horizontal : SLOPE **4** : INFLUENCE, PERSUADE — **in·clin·er** *n*

²incline \'in-₁klīn\ *n* : SLOPE

inclose, inclosure *var of* ENCLOSE, ENCLOSURE

in·clude \in-'klüd\ *vb* **in·clud·ed; in·clud·ing** : to take in or comprise as a part of a whole ⟨the price ~s tax⟩ — **in·clu·sion** \in-'klü-zhən\ *n* — **in·clu·sive** \-'klü-siv\ *adj*

incog *abbr* incognito

¹in·cog·ni·to \₁in-₁käg-'nē-tō, in-'käg-nə-₁tō\ *n, pl* **-tos** **1** : one appearing or living incognito **2** : the state or disguise of an incognito

²incognito *adv or adj* [It, fr. L *incognitus* unknown, fr. *cognoscere* to know] : with one's identity concealed

in·co·her·ent \₁in-kō-'hir-ənt, -'her-\ *adj* **1** : not sticking closely or compactly together : LOOSE **2** : not clearly or logically connected : RAMBLING — **in·co·her·ence** \-əns\ *n* — **in·co·her·ent·ly** *adv*

in·come \'in-₁kəm\ *n* : a gain usu. measured in money that derives from labor, business, or property

income tax *n* : a tax on the net income of an individual or business concern

in·com·ing \'in-ˌkə-miŋ\ *adj* : coming in ⟨the ~ tide⟩ ⟨~ freshmen⟩

in·com·men·su·rate \ˌin-kə-'men-sə-rət, -'men-chə-\ *adj* : not commensurate; *esp* : INADEQUATE

in·com·mode \ˌin-kə-'mōd\ *vb* **-mod·ed; -mod·ing** : INCONVENIENCE, DISTURB

in·com·mu·ni·ca·ble \ˌin-kə-'myü-ni-kə-bəl\ *adj* : not communicable : not capable of being communicated or imparted; *also* : UNCOMMUNICATIVE

in·com·mu·ni·ca·do \ˌin-kə-ˌmyü-nə-'kä-dō\ *adv or adj* : without means of communication; *also* : in solitary confinement ⟨a prisoner held ~⟩

in·com·pa·ra·ble \(ˌ)in-'käm-pə-rə-bəl, -prə-\ *adj* 1 : eminent beyond comparison : MATCHLESS 2 : not suitable for comparison — **in·com·pa·ra·bly** \-blē\ *adv*

in·com·pat·i·ble \ˌin-kəm-'pa-tə-bəl\ *adj* : incapable of or unsuitable for association or use together ⟨~ colors⟩ ⟨temperamentally ~⟩ — **in·com·pat·i·bil·i·ty** \ˌin-kəm-ˌpa-tə-'bi-lə-tē\ *n*

in·com·pe·tent \(ˌ)in-'käm-pə-tənt\ *adj* 1 : not legally qualified 2 : not competent : lacking sufficient knowledge, skill, or ability — **in·com·pe·tence** \-təns\ *n* — **in·com·pe·ten·cy** \-tən-sē\ *n* — **incompetent** *n*

in·com·plete \ˌin-kəm-'plēt\ *adj* : lacking a part or parts : UNFINISHED, IMPERFECT — **in·com·plete·ly** *adv* — **in·com·plete·ness** *n*

in·com·pre·hen·si·ble \ˌin-ˌkäm-prē-'hen-sə-bəl\ *adj* : impossible to comprehend : UNINTELLIGIBLE

in·con·ceiv·able \ˌin-kən-'sē-və-bəl\ *adj* 1 : impossible to comprehend 2 : UNBELIEVABLE

in·con·gru·ous \(ˌ)in-'käŋ-grü-wəs\ *adj* : not consistent with or suitable to the surroundings or associations — **in·con·gru·i·ty** \ˌin-kən-'grü-ə-tē, -ˌkän-\ *n* — **in·con·gru·ous·ly** *adv*

in·con·se·quen·tial \ˌin-ˌkän-sə-'kwen-chəl\ *adj* 1 : ILLOGICAL; *also* : IRRELEVANT 2 : of no significance : UNIMPORTANT — **in·con·se·quence** \(ˌ)in-'kän-sə-ˌkwens\ *n* — **in·con·se·quen·tial·ly** *adv*

in·con·sid·er·able \ˌin-kən-'si-də-rə-bəl\ *adj* : SLIGHT, TRIVIAL

in·con·sid·er·ate \ˌin-kən-'si-də-rət\ *adj* : HEEDLESS, THOUGHTLESS; *esp* : not respecting the rights or feelings of others — **in·con·sid·er·ate·ly** *adv* — **in·con·sid·er·ate·ness** *n*

in·con·sol·able \ˌin-kən-'sō-lə-bəl\ *adj* : incapable of being consoled — **in·con·sol·ably** \-blē\ *adv*

in·con·spic·u·ous \ˌin-kən-'spi-kyə-wəs\ *adj* : not readily noticeable — **in·con·spic·u·ous·ly** *adv*

in·con·stant \(ˌ)in-'kän-stənt\ *adj* : not constant : CHANGEABLE **syn** fickle, capricious, mercurial, unstable, volatile — **in·con·stan·cy** \-stən-sē\ *n* — **in·con·stant·ly** *adv*

in·con·test·able \ˌin-kən-'tes-tə-bəl\ *adj* : not contestable : INDISPUTABLE — **in·con·test·ably** \-'tes-tə-blē\ *adv*

in·con·ti·nent \(ˌ)in-'känt-ᵊn-ənt\ *adj* 1 : lacking self-restraint 2 : unable to retain a bodily discharge (as urine) voluntarily — **in·con·ti·nence** \-əns\ *n*

in·con·tro·vert·ible \ˌin-ˌkän-trə-'vər-tə-bəl\ *adj* : not open to question : INDISPUTABLE ⟨~ evidence⟩ — **in·con·tro·vert·ibly** \-blē\ *adv*

¹**in·con·ve·nience** \ˌin-kən-'vē-nyəns\ *n* 1 : something that is inconvenient 2 : the quality or state of being inconvenient

²**inconvenience** *vb* : to subject to inconvenience

in·con·ve·nient \ˌin-kən-'vē-nyənt\ *adj* : not convenient : causing trouble or annoyance : INOPPORTUNE — **in·con·ve·nient·ly** *adv*

¹**in·cor·po·rate** \in-'kȯr-pə-ˌrāt\ *vb* **-rat·ed; -rat·ing** 1 : to unite closely or so as to form one body : BLEND 2 : to form, form into, or become a corporation 3 : to give material form to : EMBODY — **in·cor·po·ra·tion** \-ˌkȯr-pə-'rā-shən\ *n*

in·cor·po·re·al \ˌin-kȯr-'pōr-ē-əl\ *adj* : having no material body or form

in·cor·rect \ˌin-kə-'rekt\ *adj* 1 : INACCURATE, FAULTY 2 : not true : WRONG 3 : UNBECOMING, IMPROPER — **in·cor·rect·ly** *adv* — **in·cor·rect·ness** *n*

in·cor·ri·gi·ble \(ˌ)in-'kȯr-ə-jə-bəl\ *adj* : incapable of being corrected, amended, or reformed — **in·cor·ri·gi·bil·i·ty** \(ˌ)in-ˌkȯr-ə-jə-'bi-lə-tē\ *n* — **in·cor·ri·gi·bly** \-'kȯr-ə-jə-blē\ *adv*

in·cor·rupt·ible \ˌin-kə-'rəp-tə-bəl\ *adj* 1 : not subject to decay or dissolution 2 : incapable of being bribed or morally corrupted — **in·cor·rupt·ibil·i·ty** \-ˌrəp-tə-'bi-lə-tē\ *n* — **in·cor·rupt·ibly** \-'rəp-tə-blē\ *adv*

incr *abbr* increase; increased

¹**in·crease** \in-'krēs, 'in-ˌkrēs\ *vb* **in·creased; in·creas·ing** 1 : to become greater : GROW 2 : to multiply by the production of young ⟨rabbits ~ rapidly⟩ 3 : to make greater — **in·creas·ing·ly** \-'krē-siŋ-lē\ *adv*

²**in·crease** \'in-ˌkrēs, in-'krēs\ *n* 1 : addition or enlargement in size, extent, or quantity : GROWTH 2 : something that is added to an original stock or amount (as by growth)

in·cred·i·ble \(ˌ)in-'kre-də-bəl\ *adj* : too extraordinary and improbable to be believed; *also* : hard to believe — **in·cred·i·bil·i·ty** \(ˌ)in-ˌkre-də-'bi-lə-tē\ *n* — **in·cred·i·bly** \-'kre-də-blē\ *adv*

in·cred·u·lous \-'kre-jə-ləs\ *adj* 1 : SKEPTICAL 2 : expressing disbelief — **in·cre·du·li·ty** \ˌin-kri-'dü-lə-tē, -'dyü-\ *n* — **in·cred·u·lous·ly** *adv*

in·cre·ment \'iŋ-krə-mənt, 'in-\ *n* 1 : the action or process of increasing esp. in quantity or value : ENLARGEMENT; *also* : QUANTITY 2 : something gained or added; *esp* : one of a series of regular consecutive additions — **in·cre·men·tal** \ˌiŋ-krə-'ment-ᵊl, ˌin-\ *adj* — **in·cre·men·tal·ly** *adv*

in·crim·i·nate \in-'kri-mə-ˌnāt\ *vb* **-nat·ed; -nat·ing** : to charge with or prove involvement in a crime or fault : ACCUSE — **in·crim·i·na·tion** \-ˌkri-mə-'nā-shən\ *n* — **in·crim·i·na·to·ry** \-'kri-mə-nə-ˌtōr-ē\ *adj*

incrust *var of* ENCRUST

in·crus·ta·tion \ˌin-ˌkrəs-'tā-shən\ *n* 1 : CRUST; *also* : something resembling a crust ⟨~ of habits⟩ 2 : the act of encrusting : the state of being encrusted

in·cu·bate \'iŋ-kyù-ˌbāt, 'in-\ *vb* **-bat·ed; -bat·ing** : to sit on (eggs) to hatch by the warmth of the body; *also* : to keep (as an embryo) under conditions favorable for development — **in·cu·ba·tion** \ˌiŋ-kyù-'bā-shən, ˌin-\ *n*

in·cu·ba·tor \'iŋ-kyù-ˌbāt-ər, 'in-\ *n* : one that incubates; *esp* : an apparatus providing suitable conditions (as of warmth and moisture) for incubating something (as a premature baby)

in·cu·bus \'iŋ-kyə-bəs, 'in-\ *n, pl* **-bi** \-ˌbī, -ˌbē\ *also* **-bus·es** [ME, fr. LL, fr. L *incubare* to lie on] 1 : a spirit supposed to work evil on persons in their sleep 2 : NIGHTMARE 1 3 : one that oppresses like a nightmare

in·cul·cate \in-'kəl-ˌkāt, 'in-(ˌ)kəl-\ *vb* **-cat·ed; -cat·ing** [L *inculcare*, lit., to tread on, fr. *calcare* to trample, fr. *calx* heel] : to teach and impress by frequent repetitions or admonitions — **in·cul·ca·tion** \ˌin-(ˌ)kəl-'kā-shən\ *n*

in·cul·pa·ble \(ˌ)in-'kəl-pə-bəl\ *adj* : free from guilt : INNOCENT

in·cul·pate \in-'kəl-ˌpāt, 'in-(ˌ)kəl-\ *vb* **-pat·ed; -pat·ing** : INCRIMINATE

in·cum·ben·cy \in-'kəm-bən-sē\ *n, pl* **-cies** 1 : something that is incumbent 2 : the quality or state of being incumbent 3 : the office or period of office of an incumbent

¹**in·cum·bent** \in-'kəm-bənt\ *n* : the holder of an office or position

²**incumbent** *adj* 1 : imposed as a duty 2 : occupying a specified office 3 : lying or resting on something else

in·cu·nab·u·lum \ˌin-kyə-'na-byə-ləm, ˌin-\ *n, pl* **-la** \-lə\ [NL, fr. L *incunabula,* pl., bands holding the baby in a cradle, fr. *cunae* cradle] : a book printed before 1501

in·cur \in-ˈkər\ *vb* **in·curred; in·cur·ring** : to become liable or subject to : bring down upon oneself

in·cur·able \(ˌ)in-ˈkyur-ə-bəl\ *adj* **1** : not subject to cure **2** : not likely to be changed — **incurable** *n* — **in·cur·ably** \(ˌ)in-ˈkyur-ə-blē\ *adv*

in·cur·sion \in-ˈkər-zhən\ *n* **1** : a sudden hostile invasion : RAID **2** : an entering in or into (as an activity)

in·cus \ˈiŋ-kəs\ *n, pl* **in·cu·des** \iŋ-ˈkyü-(ˌ)dēz\ [NL, fr. L, anvil] : the middle bone of a chain of three small bones in the ear of a mammal

ind *abbr* **1** independent **2** index **3** industrial; industry

Ind *abbr* **1** Indian **2** Indiana

in·debt·ed \in-ˈde-təd\ *adj* **1** : owing gratitude or recognition to another **2** : owing money — **in·debt·ed·ness** *n*

in·de·cent \(ˌ)in-ˈdēs-ᵊnt\ *adj* : not decent; *esp* : morally offensive — **in·de·cen·cy** \-ᵊn-sē\ *n* — **in·de·cent·ly** *adv*

in·de·ci·sion \ˌin-di-ˈsi-zhən\ *n* : a wavering between two or more possible courses of action : IRRESOLUTION

in·de·ci·sive \ˌin-di-ˈsī-siv\ *adj* **1** : INCONCLUSIVE **2** : marked by or prone to indecision **3** : INDEFINITE — **in·de·ci·sive·ly** *adv* — **in·de·ci·sive·ness** *n*

in·de·co·rous \(ˌ)in-ˈde-kə-rəs; ˌin-di-ˈkōr-əs\ *adj* : not decorous **syn** improper, unseemly, indecent, unbecoming, indelicate — **in·de·co·rous·ly** *adv* — **in·de·co·rous·ness** *n*

in·deed \in-ˈdēd\ *adv* **1** : without any question : TRULY — often used interjectionally to express irony, disbelief, or surprise **2** : in reality **3** : all things considered

indef *abbr* indefinite

in·de·fat·i·ga·ble \ˌin-di-ˈfa-ti-gə-bəl\ *adj* : UNTIRING — **in·de·fat·i·ga·bly** \-blē\ *adv*

in·de·fea·si·ble \-ˈfē-zə-bəl\ *adj* : not capable of being annulled or voided — **in·de·fea·si·bly** \-blē\ *adv*

in·de·fen·si·ble \-ˈfen-sə-bəl\ *adj* **1** : incapable of being maintained as right or valid **2** : INEXCUSABLE **3** : incapable of being protected against physical attack

in·de·fin·able \-ˈfī-nə-bəl\ *adj* : incapable of being precisely described or analyzed — **in·de·fin·ably** \-blē\ *adv*

in·def·i·nite \(ˌ)in-ˈde-fə-nət\ *adj* **1** : not defining or identifying ⟨*an* is an ∼ article⟩ **2** : not precise : VAGUE **3** : having no fixed limit — **in·def·i·nite·ly** *adv* — **in·def·i·nite·ness** *n*

in·del·i·ble \in-ˈde-lə-bəl\ *adj* [ME, fr. ML *indelibilis,* alter. of L *indelebilis,* fr. *delēre* to delete, destroy] **1** : not capable of being removed or erased **2** : making marks that cannot be erased **3** : LASTING, UNFORGETTABLE — **in·del·i·bly** \in-ˈde-lə-blē\ *adv*

in·del·i·cate \(ˌ)in-ˈde-li-kət\ *adj* : not delicate; *esp* : IMPROPER, COARSE, TACTLESS **syn** indecent, unseemly, indecorous, unbecoming — **in·del·i·ca·cy** \in-ˈde-lə-kə-sē\ *n*

in·dem·ni·fy \in-ˈdem-nə-ˌfī\ *vb* **-fied; -fy·ing** [L *indemnis* unharmed, fr. *in-* not + *damnum* damage] **1** : to secure against hurt, loss, or damage **2** : to make compensation to for hurt, loss, or damage — **in·dem·ni·fi·ca·tion** \-ˌdem-nə-fə-ˈkā-shən\ *n*

in·dem·ni·ty \in-ˈdem-nə-tē\ *n, pl* **-ties** **1** : security against hurt, loss, or damage; *also* : exemption from incurred penalties or liabilities **2** : something that indemnifies

¹**in·dent** \in-ˈdent\ *vb* [ME, fr. MF *endenter,* fr. OF, fr. *dent* tooth, fr. L *dent-, dens*] **1** : to notch the edge of **2** : INDENTURE **3** : to set (as a line of a paragraph) in from the margin

²**indent** *vb* **1** : to force inward so as to form a depression **2** : to form a dent in

in·den·ta·tion \ˌin-ˌden-ˈtā-shən\ *n* **1** : NOTCH; also: a usu. deep recess (as in a coastline) **2** : the action of indenting : the condition of being indented **3** : DENT **4** : INDENTION 2

in·den·tion \in-ˈden-chən\ *n* **1** : INDENTATION 2 **2** : the blank space produced by indenting

¹**in·den·ture** \in-ˈden-chər\ *n* **1** : a written certificate or agreement; *esp* : a contract binding one person (as an apprentice) to work for another for a given period of time — usu. used in pl. **2** : INDENTATION 1 **3** : DENT

²**indenture** *vb* **in·den·tured; in·den·tur·ing** : to bind (as an apprentice) by indentures

in·de·pen·dence \ˌin-də-ˈpen-dəns\ *n* : the quality or state of being independent : FREEDOM

Independence Day *n* : July 4 observed as a legal holiday in commemoration of the adoption of the Declaration of Independence in 1776

in·de·pen·dent \ˌin-də-ˈpen-dənt\ *adj* **1** : SELF-GOVERNING; *also* : not affiliated with a larger controlling unit **2** : not requiring or relying on something else or somebody else ⟨an ∼ conclusion⟩ ⟨∼ of her parents⟩ **3** : not easily influenced : showing self-reliance and personal freedom ⟨an ∼ mind⟩ **4** : not committed to a political party ⟨an ∼ voter⟩ **5** : MAIN ⟨an ∼ clause⟩ — **independent** *n* — **in·de·pen·dent·ly** *adv*

in·de·scrib·able \ˌin-di-ˈskrī-bə-bəl\ *adj* **1** : that cannot be described **2** : being too intense or great for description — **in·de·scrib·ably** \-blē\ *adv*

in·de·ter·mi·nate \ˌin-di-ˈtər-mə-nət\ *adj* **1** : VAGUE; *also* : not known in advance **2** : not limited in advance; *also* : not leading to a definite end or result — **in·de·ter·mi·na·cy** \-nə-sē\ *n* — **in·de·ter·mi·nate·ly** *adv*

¹**in·dex** \ˈin-ˌdeks\ *n, pl* **in·dex·es** *or* **in·di·ces** \-də-ˌsēz\ **1** : POINTER **2** : SIGN, INDICATION ⟨an ∼ of character⟩ **3** : a guide for facilitating references; *esp* : an alphabetical list of items treated in a printed work with the page number where each item may be found **4** : a list of restricted or prohibited material **5** *pl usu* **indices** : a number or symbol or expression (as an exponent) associated with another to indicate a mathematical operation or use or position in an arrangement or expansion **6** : a character ☞ used to direct attention (as to a note) **7** : INDEX NUMBER

²**index** *vb* **1** : to provide with or put into an index **2** : to serve as an index of **3** : to regulate by indexation

in·dex·ation \ˌin-ˌdek-ˈsā-shən\ *n* : a system of economic control in which a body of variables (as wages and interest) rise or fall at the same rate as an index of the cost of living

index finger *n* : FOREFINGER

in·dex·ing *n* : INDEXATION

index number *n* : a number used to indicate change in magnitude (as of cost) as compared with the magnitude at some specified time usu. taken as 100

index of refraction *n* : the ratio of the speed of radiation in one medium to that in another medium

in·dia ink \ˈin-dē-ə-\ *n, often cap 1st I* **1** : a solid black pigment used in drawing **2** : a fluid made from india ink

In·di·an \ˈin-dē-ən\ *n* **1** : a native or inhabitant of the subcontinent of India **2** : a person of Indian descent **3** : AMERICAN INDIAN — **Indian** *adj*

Indian corn *n* : a tall widely grown American cereal grass bearing seeds on long ears; *also* : its ears or seeds

Indian meal *n* : CORNMEAL

Indian paintbrush *n* : any of a genus of herbaceous plants related to the snapdragon that have brightly colored bracts

Indian pipe *n* : a waxy white leafless saprophytic herb of Asia and the U.S.

Indian summer *n* : a period of mild weather in late autumn or early winter

In·dia paper \ˈin-dē-ə-\ *n* **1** : a thin absorbent paper used esp. for taking impressions (as of steel engravings) **2** : a thin tough opaque printing paper

indic *abbr* indicative

in·di·cate \ˈin-də-ˌkāt\ *vb* **-cat·ed; -cat·ing** **1** : to point out or to **2** : to show indirectly **3** : to state briefly — **in·di·ca·tion** \ˌin-də-ˈkā-shən\ *n* — **in·di·ca·tor** \ˈin-də-ˌkā-tər\ *n*

¹**in·dic·a·tive** \in-ˈdi-kə-tiv\ *adj* **1** : of, relating to, or being a verb form that represents an act or state as a fact ⟨∼ mood⟩ **2** : serving to indicate ⟨actions ∼ of fear⟩

²**indicative** *n* **1** : the indicative mood of a language **2** : a form in the indicative mood

in·di·cia \in-ˈdi-shə, -shē-ə\ *n pl* **1** : distinctive marks **2** : postal markings often imprinted on mail or mailing labels

in·dict \in-ˈdīt\ *vb* [alter. of earlier *indite*, fr. ME, fr. OF *enditer*, lit., to write down] **1** : to charge with a fault or offense **2** : to charge with a crime by the finding of a jury — **in·dict·able** *adj* — **in·dict·ment** *n*

in·dif·fer·ent \in-ˈdi-frənt, -fə-rənt\ *adj* **1** : UNBIASED, UNPREJUDICED **2** : of no importance one way or the other **3** : marked by no special liking for or dislike of something **4** : being neither excessive nor inadequate **5** : PASSABLE, MEDIOCRE **6** : being neither right nor wrong — **in·dif·fer·ence** \-frəns, -fə-rəns\ *n* — **in·dif·fer·ent·ly** *adv*

in·dig·e·nous \in-ˈdi-jə-nəs\ *adj* : produced, growing, or living naturally in a particular region

in·di·gent \ˈin-di-jənt\ *adj* : IMPOVERISHED, NEEDY — **in·di·gence** \-jəns\ *n*

in·di·gest·ible \ˌin-dī-ˈjes-tə-bəl, -də-\ *adj* : not readily digested

in·di·ges·tion \-ˈjes-chən\ *n* : inadequate or difficult digestion : DYSPEPSIA

in·dig·nant \in-ˈdig-nənt\ *adj* : filled with or marked by indignation — **in·dig·nant·ly** *adv*

in·dig·na·tion \ˌin-dig-ˈnā-shən\ *n* : anger aroused by something unjust, unworthy, or mean

in·dig·ni·ty \in-ˈdig-nə-tē\ *n, pl* **-ties** : an offense against personal dignity or self-respect; *also* : humiliating treatment

in·di·go \ˈin-di-ˌgō\ *n, pl* **-gos** *or* **-goes** [It dial., fr. L *indicum*, fr. Gk *indikon*, fr. *indikos* Indic, fr. *Indos* India] **1** : a blue dye obtained from plants or synthesized **2** : a deep reddish blue color

in·di·rect \ˌin-də-ˈrekt, -dī-\ *adj* **1** : not straight ⟨an ∼ route⟩ **2** : not straightforward and open ⟨∼ methods⟩ **3** : not having a plainly seen connection ⟨an ∼ cause⟩ **4** : not directly to the point ⟨an ∼ answer⟩ — **in·di·rec·tion** \-ˈrek-shən\ *n* — **in·di·rect·ly** *adv* — **in·di·rect·ness** *n*

in·dis·creet \ˌin-di-ˈskrēt\ *adj* : not discreet : IMPRUDENT — **in·dis·creet·ly** *adv*

in·dis·cre·tion \ˌin-di-ˈskre-shən\ *n* **1** : IMPUDENCE **2** : something marked by lack of discretion; *esp* : an act deviating from accepted morality

in·dis·crim·i·nate \ˌin-di-ˈskri-mə-nət\ *adj* **1** : not marked by discrimination or careful distinction **2** : HAPHAZARD, RANDOM **3** : UNRESTRAINED **4** : MOTLEY — **in·dis·crim·i·nate·ly** *adv*

in·dis·pens·able \ˌin-di-ˈspen-sə-bəl\ *adj* : absolutely essential : REQUISITE — **in·dis·pens·abil·i·ty** \-ˌspen-sə-ˈbi-lə-tē\ *n* — **indispensable** *n* — **in·dis·pens·ably** \-ˈspen-sə-blē\ *adv*

in·dis·posed \-ˈspōzd\ *adj* **1** : slightly ill **2** : AVERSE — **in·dis·po·si·tion** \ˌin-dis-pə-ˈzi-shən\ *n*

in·dis·put·able \ˌin-di-ˈspyü-tə-bəl, ˌ)in-ˈdis-pyə-\ *adj* : not disputable : UNQUESTIONABLE ⟨∼ proof⟩ — **in·dis·put·ably** \-blē\ *adv*

in·dis·sol·u·ble \ˌin-di-ˈsäl-yə-bəl\ *adj* : not capable of being dissolved, undone, or broken : PERMANENT

in·dis·tinct \ˌin-di-ˈstiŋkt\ *adj* **1** : not sharply outlined or separable : BLURRED, FAINT, DIM **2** : not readily distinguishable : UNCERTAIN — **in·dis·tinct·ly** *adv* — **in·dis·tinct·ness** *n*

in·dite \in-ˈdīt\ *vb* **in·dit·ed; in·dit·ing** : COMPOSE ⟨∼ a poem⟩; *also* : to put in writing ⟨∼ a letter⟩

in·di·um \ˈin-dē-əm\ *n* : a malleable silvery metallic chemical element — see ELEMENT table

indiv *abbr* individual

¹**in·di·vid·u·al** \ˌin-də-ˈvi-jə-wəl\ *adj* **1** : of, relating to, or associated with an individual ⟨∼ traits⟩ **2** : being

an individual : existing as an indivisible whole **3** : intended for one person **4** : SEPARATE ⟨∼ copies⟩ **5** : having marked individuality ⟨an ∼ style⟩ — **in·di·vid·u·al·ly** *adv*

²**individual** *n* **1** : a single member of a category : a particular person, animal, or thing **2** : PERSON ⟨a disagreeable ∼⟩

in·di·vid·u·al·ism \ˌin-də-ˈvi-jə-wə-ˌli-zəm\ *n* **1** : a doctrine that the interests of the individual are primary **2** : a doctrine holding that the individual has political or economic rights with which the state must not interfere **3** : INDIVIDUALITY

in·di·vid·u·al·ist \-list\ *n* **1** : one that pursues a markedly independent course in thought or action **2** : one that advocates or practices individualism — **individualist** *or* **in·di·vid·u·al·is·tic** \-ˌvi-jə-wə-ˈlis-tik\ *adj*

in·di·vid·u·al·i·ty \-ˌvi-jə-ˈwa-lə-tē\ *n, pl* **-ties 1** : the sum of qualities that characterize and distinguish an individual from all others; *also* : PERSONALITY **2** : separate or distinct existence **3** : INDIVIDUAL, PERSON

in·di·vid·u·al·ize \-ˈvi-jə-wə-ˌlīz\ *vb* **-ized; -iz·ing 1** : to make individual in character **2** : to treat or notice individually : PARTICULARIZE **3** : to adapt to the needs of an individual

individual retirement account *n* : IRA

in·di·vid·u·ate \ˌin-də-ˈvi-jə-ˌwāt\ *vb* **-at·ed; -at·ing** : to give individuality to : form into an individual — **in·di·vid·u·a·tion** \-ˌvi-jə-ˈwā-shən\ *n*

in·di·vis·i·ble \ˌin-də-ˈvi-zə-bəl\ *adj* : impossible to divide or separate — **in·di·vis·i·bil·i·ty** \-ˌvi-zə-ˈbi-lə-tē\ *n* — **in·di·vis·i·bly** *adv*

in·doc·tri·nate \in-ˈdäk-trə-ˌnāt\ *vb* **-nat·ed; -nat·ing 1** : to instruct esp. in fundamentals or rudiments : TEACH **2** : to teach the beliefs and doctrines of a particular group — **in·doc·tri·na·tion** \(ˌ)in-ˌdäk-trə-ˈnā-shən\ *n* — **in·doc·tri·na·tor** *n*

In·do-Eu·ro·pe·an \ˌin-dō-ˌyùr-ə-ˈpē-ən\ *adj* : of, relating to, or constituting a family of languages comprising those spoken in most of Europe and in the parts of the world colonized by Europeans since 1500 and also in Persia, the subcontinent of India, and some other parts of Asia

in·do·lent \ˈin-də-lənt\ *adj* [LL *indolens* insensitive to pain, fr. L *dolēre* to feel pain] **1** : slow to develop or heal ⟨∼ ulcers⟩ **2** : LAZY — **in·do·lence** \-ləns\ *n* — **in·do·lent·ly** *adv*

in·dom·i·ta·ble \in-ˈdä-mə-tə-bəl\ *adj* : UNCONQUERABLE ⟨∼ courage⟩ — **in·dom·i·ta·bly** \-blē\ *adv*

In·do·ne·sian \ˌin-də-ˈnē-zhən\ *n* : a native or inhabitant of the Republic of Indonesia — **Indonesian** *adj*

in·door \ˈin-ˌdōr\ *adj* **1** : of or relating to the inside of a building **2** : living, located, or carried on within a building

in·doors \in-ˈdōrz\ *adv* : in or into a building

indorse *var of* ENDORSE

in·du·bi·ta·ble \(ˌ)in-ˈdü-bə-tə-bəl, -ˈdyü-\ *adj* : UNQUESTIONABLE — **in·du·bi·ta·bly** \-blē\ *adv*

in·duce \in-ˈdüs, -ˈdyüs\ *vb* **in·duced; in·duc·ing 1** : PERSUADE, INFLUENCE **2** : BRING ABOUT **3** : to produce (as an electric current) by induction **4** : to determine by induction; *esp* : to infer from particulars — **in·duc·er** *n*

in·duce·ment \-mənt\ *n* **1** : something that induces : MOTIVE **2** : the act or process of inducing

in·duct \in-ˈdəkt\ *vb* **1** : to place in office **2** : to admit as a member **3** : to enroll for military training or service — **in·duct·ee** \-ˌdək-ˈtē\ *n*

in·duc·tance \in-ˈdək-təns\ *n* : a property of an electric circuit by which a varying current produces an electromotive force in that circuit or in a nearby circuit; *also* : the measure of this property

in·duc·tion \in-ˈdək-shən\ *n* **1** : the act or process of inducting; *also* : INITIATION **2** : the formality by which a civilian is inducted into military service **3** : inference of a generalized conclusion from particular instances; *also* : a conclusion so reached **4** : the act of causing or bringing on or about **5** : the process by which an electric current, an electric charge, or magnetism is produced in a body by the proximity of an electric or magnetic field

in·duc·tive \in-'dək-tiv\ *adj* : of, relating to, or employing induction

in·duc·tor \in-'dək-tər\ *n* : an electrical component that acts upon another or is itself acted upon by induction

in·dulge \in-'dəlj\ *vb* **in·dulged; in·dulg·ing 1** : to give free rein to : GRATIFY **2** : HUMOR **3** : to gratify one's taste or desire for ⟨∼ in alcohol⟩

in·dul·gence \in-'dəl-jəns\ *n* **1** : remission of temporal punishment due in Roman Catholic doctrine for sins whose eternal punishment has been remitted by reception of the sacrifice of penance **2** : the act of indulging : the state of being indulgent **3** : an indulgent act **4** : the thing indulged in **5** : SELF-INDULGENCE — **in·dul·gent** \-jənt\ *adj* — **in·dul·gent·ly** *adv*

in·du·rat·ed \'in-dyü-,rā-təd, -dü-\ *adj* : physically or emotionally hardened — **in·du·ra·tion** \,in-dyü-'rā-shən, -dü-\ *n*

in·dus·tri·al \in-'dəs-trē-əl\ *adj* **1** : of or relating to industry; *also* : HEAVY-DUTY **2** : characterized by highly developed industries — **in·dus·tri·al·ly** *adv*

in·dus·tri·al·ist \-ə-list\ *n* : a person owning or engaged in the management of an industry

in·dus·tri·al·ize \in-'dəs-trē-ə-,līz\ *vb* **-ized; -iz·ing** : to make or become industrial — **in·dus·tri·al·i·za·tion** \-,dəs-trē-ə-lə-'zā-shən\ *n*

in·dus·tri·ous \in-'dəs-trē-əs\ *adj* : DILIGENT, BUSY — **in·dus·tri·ous·ly** *adv* — **in·dus·tri·ous·ness** *n*

in·dus·try \'in-(,)dəs-trē\ *n, pl* **-tries 1** : DILIGENCE **2** : a department or branch of a craft, art, business, or manufacture; *esp* : one that employs a large personnel and capital **3** : a distinct group of productive enterprises **4** : manufacturing activity as a whole

in·dwell \(,)in-'dwel\ *vb* : to exist within as an activating spirit or force

¹ine·bri·ate \i-'nē-brē-,āt\ *vb* **-at·ed; -at·ing** : to make drunk : INTOXICATE — **ine·bri·a·tion** \-,nē-brē-'ā-shən\ *n*

²ine·bri·ate \-ət\ *n* : one that is drunk; *esp* : DRUNKARD

in·ef·fa·ble \(,)in-'e-fə-bəl\ *adj* **1** : incapable of being expressed in words : INDESCRIBABLE ⟨∼ joy⟩ **2** : UNSPEAKABLE ⟨∼ disgust⟩ **3** : not to be uttered : TABOO — **in·ef·fa·bly** \-blē\ *adv*

in·ef·fec·tive \,i-nə-'fek-tiv\ *adj* **1** : INEFFECTUAL **2** : not able to perform efficiently or as expected : INCAPABLE — **in·ef·fec·tive·ly** *adv* — **in·ef·fec·tive·ness** *n*

in·ef·fec·tu·al \-'fek-chə-wəl\ *adj* **1** : not producing the proper or usual effect **2** : INEFFECTIVE 2 — **in·ef·fec·tu·al·ly** *adv*

in·ef·fi·cient \,i-nə-'fi-shənt\ *adj* **1** : not producing the desired effect **2** : wasteful of time or energy **3** : INCAPABLE, INCOMPETENT — **in·ef·fi·cien·cy** \-'fi-shən-sē\ *n* — **in·ef·fi·cient·ly** *adv*

in·el·e·gant \(,)i-'ne-li-gənt\ *adj* : lacking in refinement, grace, or good taste — **in·el·e·gance** \-gəns\ *n* — **in·el·e·gant·ly** *adv*

in·el·i·gi·ble \(,)i-'ne-lə-jə-bəl\ *adj* : not qualified for an office or position — **in·el·i·gi·bil·i·ty** \(,)i-,ne-lə-jə-'bi-lə-tē\ *n*

in·eluc·ta·ble \,i-ni-'lək-tə-bəl\ *adj* : not to be avoided, changed, or resisted — **in·eluc·ta·bly** \-blē\ *adv*

in·ept \i-'nept\ *adj* **1** : lacking in fitness or aptitude : UNFIT **2** : FOOLISH **3** : being out of place : INAPPROPRIATE **4** : generally incompetent : BUNGLING — **in·ept·ly** *adv* — **in·ept·ness** *n*

in·ep·ti·tude \(,)i-'nep-ti-,tüd, -,tyüd\ *n* : the quality or state of being inept; *esp* : INCOMPETENCE

in·equal·i·ty \,i-ni-'kwä-lə-tē\ *n* **1** : the quality of being unequal or uneven; *esp* : UNEVENNESS, DISPARITY **2** : an instance of being unequal

in·ert \i-'nərt\ *adj* [L *inert-, iners* unskilled, idle, fr. *art-, ars* skill] **1** : powerless to move **2** : SLUGGISH **3** : lacking in active properties ⟨chemically ∼⟩ — **in·ert·ly** *adv* — **in·ert·ness** *n*

in·er·tia \i-'nər-shə, -shē-ə\ *n* **1** : a property of matter whereby it remains at rest or continues in uniform motion unless acted upon by some outside force **2** : INERTNESS, SLUGGISHNESS — **in·er·tial** \-shəl\ *adj*

in·es·cap·able \,i-nə-'skā-pə-bəl\ *adj* : incapable of being escaped : INEVITABLE — **in·es·cap·ably** \-blē\ *adv*

in·es·ti·ma·ble \(,)i-'nes-tə-mə-bəl\ *adj* **1** : incapable of being estimated or computed ⟨∼ errors⟩ **2** : too valuable or excellent to be fully appreciated — **in·es·ti·ma·bly** \-blē\ *adv*

in·ev·i·ta·ble \i-'ne-və-tə-bəl\ *adj* : incapable of being avoided or evaded : bound to happen — **in·ev·i·ta·bil·i·ty** \(,)i-,ne-və-tə-'bi-lə-tē\ *n*

in·ev·i·ta·bly \-blē\ *adv* **1** : in an inevitable way **2** : as is to be expected

in·ex·act \,i-nig-'zakt\ *adj* **1** : not precisely correct or true : INACCURATE **2** : not rigorous and careful — **in·ex·act·ly** *adv* — **in·ex·act·ness** *n*

in·ex·cus·able \,i-nik-'skyü-zə-bəl\ *adj* : being without excuse or justification — **in·ex·cus·ably** \-blē\ *adv*

in·ex·haust·ible \,i-nig-'zò-stə-bəl\ *adj* **1** : incapable of being used up ⟨an ∼ supply⟩ **2** : UNTIRING — **in·ex·haust·ibly** \-blē\ *adv*

in·ex·o·ra·ble \(,)i-'nek-sə-rə-bəl\ *adj* : not to be moved by entreaty : RELENTLESS — **in·ex·o·ra·bly** *adv*

in·ex·pe·ri·ence \,i-nik-'spir-ē-əns\ *n* : lack of experience or of knowledge gained by experience — **in·ex·pe·ri·enced** \-ənst\ *adj*

in·ex·pert \(,)i-'nek-,spərt\ *adj* : not expert : UNSKILLED — **in·ex·pert·ly** *adv*

in·ex·pi·a·ble \(,)i-'nek-spē-ə-bəl\ *adj* : not capable of being atoned for

in·ex·pli·ca·ble \,i-nik-'spli-kə-bəl, (,)i-'nek-(,)spli-\ *adj* : incapable of being explained or accounted for — **in·ex·pli·ca·bly** \-blē\ *adv*

in·ex·press·ible \-'spre-sə-bəl\ *adj* : not capable of being expressed — **in·ex·press·ibly** \-blē\ *adv*

in ex·tre·mis \,in-ik-'strā-məs, -'strē-\ *adv* : in extreme circumstances; *esp* : at the point of death

in·ex·tri·ca·ble \,i-nik-'stri-kə-bəl, (,)i-'nek-(,)stri-\ *adj* **1** : forming a maze or tangle from which it is impossible to get free **2** : incapable of being disentangled or untied — **in·ex·tri·ca·bly** \-blē\ *adv*

inf *abbr* **1** infantry **2** infinitive

in·fal·li·ble \(,)in-'fa-lə-bəl\ *adj* **1** : incapable of error : UNERRING **2** : SURE, CERTAIN ⟨an ∼ remedy⟩ — **in·fal·li·bil·i·ty** \(,)in-,fa-lə-'bi-lə-tē\ *n* — **in·fal·li·bly** \(,)in-'fa-lə-blē\ *adv*

in·fa·mous \'in-fə-məs\ *adj* **1** : having a reputation of the worst kind **2** : DISGRACEFUL — **in·fa·mous·ly** *adv*

in·fa·my \-mē\ *n, pl* **-mies 1** : evil reputation brought about by something grossly criminal, shocking, or brutal **2** : an extreme and publicly known criminal or evil act **3** : the state of being infamous

in·fan·cy \'in-fən-sē\ *n, pl* **-cies 1** : early childhood **2** : a beginning or early period of existence

in·fant \'in-fənt\ *n* [ME *enfaunt*, fr. MF *enfant*, fr. L *infant-, infans*, adj., incapable of speech, young, fr. *fant-, fans*, prp. of *fari* to speak] : BABY; *also* : a person who is a legal minor

in·fan·ti·cide \in-'fan-tə-,sīd\ *n* : the killing of an infant

in·fan·tile \'in-fən-,tīl, -t³l, -,tēl\ *adj* : of or relating to infants; *also* : CHILDISH

infantile paralysis *n* : POLIOMYELITIS

in·fan·try \'in-fən-trē\ *n, pl* **-tries** [MF & It; MF *infanterie*, fr. It *infanteria*, fr. *infante* boy, foot soldier] : soldiers trained, armed, and equipped to fight on foot — **in·fan·try·man** \-mən\ *n*

in·farct \'in-,färkt\ *n* [L *infarctus*, pp. of *infarcire* to stuff] : an area of dead tissue (as of the heart wall) caused by blocking of local blood circulation — **in-farc-tion** \in-'färk-shən\ *n*

in-fat-u-ate \in-'fa-chə-ˌwāt\ *vb* **-at-ed; -at-ing** : to inspire with a foolish or extravagant love or admiration — **in-fat-u-a-tion** \-ˌfa-chə-'wā-shən\ *n*

in-fect \in-'fekt\ *vb* **1** : to contaminate with disease=producing matter **2** : to communicate a germ or disease to **3** : to cause to share one's feelings

in-fec-tion \in-'fek-shən\ *n* **1** : a disease or condition caused by a germ or parasite; *also* : such a germ or parasite **2** : an act or process of infecting — **in-fec-tious** \-shəs\ *adj* — **in-fec-tive** \-'fek-tiv\ *adj*

infectious mononucleosis *n* : an acute infectious disease characterized by fever, swelling of lymph glands, and increased numbers of lymph cells in the blood

in-fe-lic-i-tous \in-fi-'li-sə-təs\ *adj* : not appropriate in application or expression — **in-fe-lic-i-ty** \-sə-tē\ *n*

in-fer \in-'fər\ *vb* **in-ferred; in-fer-ring 1** : to derive as a conclusion from facts or premises **2** : GUESS, SURMISE **3** : to lead to as a conclusion or consequence **4** : HINT, SUGGEST **syn** deduce, conclude, judge, gather — **in-fer-ence** \'in-frəns, -fə-rəns\ *n* — **in-fer-en-tial** \ˌin-fə-'ren-chəl\ *adj*

in-fe-ri-or \in-'fir-ē-ər\ *adj* **1** : situated lower down **2** : of low or lower degree or rank **3** : of lesser quality **4** : of little or less importance, value, or merit — **inferior** *n* — **in-fe-ri-or-i-ty** \(ˌ)in-ˌfir-ē-'òr-ə-tē\ *n*

in-fer-nal \in-'fərn-ᵊl\ *adj* **1** : of or relating to hell **2** : HELLISH, FIENDISH \(∼ schemes\) **3** : DAMNABLE \(an ∼ pest\) — **in-fer-nal-ly** *adv*

in-fer-no \in-'fər-nō\ *n*, *pl* **-nos** [It, hell, fr. LL *infernus* hell, fr. L, lower] : a place or a state that resembles or suggests hell; *also* : intense heat

in-fer-tile \(ˌ)in-'fərt-ᵊl\ *adj* : not fertile or productive : BARREN — **in-fer-til-i-ty** \ˌin-fər-'ti-lə-tē\ *n*

in-fest \in-'fest\ *vb* : to trouble by spreading or swarming in or over; *also* : to live in or on as a parasite — **in-fes-ta-tion** \ˌin-ˌfes-'tā-shən\ *n*

in-fi-del \'in-fəd-ᵊl, -fə-ˌdel\ *n* **1** : one who is not a Christian or opposes Christianity **2** : an unbeliever esp. with respect to a particular religion

in-fi-del-i-ty \ˌin-fə-'de-lə-tē, -fī-\ *n*, *pl* **-ties 1** : lack of belief in a religion **2** : UNFAITHFULNESS, DISLOYALTY **3** : marital unfaithfulness or an instance of it

in-field \'in-ˌfēld\ *n* : the part of a baseball field inside the baselines — **in-field-er** *n*

in-fight-ing \'in-ˌfī-tiŋ\ *n* **1** : fighting at close quarters **2** : dissension or rivalry among members of a group

in-fil-trate \in-'fil-ˌtrāt, 'in-(ˌ)fil-\ *vb* **-trat-ed; -trat-ing 1** : to enter or filter into or through something **2** : to pass into or through by or as if by filtering or permeating — **in-fil-tra-tion** \ˌin-(ˌ)fil-'trā-shən\ *n* — **in-fil-tra-tor** *n*

in-fi-nite \'in-fə-nət\ *adj* **1** : LIMITLESS, BOUNDLESS, ENDLESS \(∼ space\) \(∼ patience\) **2** : VAST, IMMENSE; *also* : INEXHAUSTIBLE \(∼ wealth\) **3** : greater than any preassigned finite value however large \(∼ number of positive integers\); *also* : extending to infinity \(∼ plane surface\) — **infinite** *n* — **in-fi-nite-ly** *adv*

in-fin-i-tes-i-mal \(ˌ)in-ˌfi-nə-'te-sə-məl\ *adj* : immeasurably or incalculably small — **in-fin-i-tes-i-mal-ly** *adv*

in-fin-i-tive \in-'fi-nə-tiv\ *n* : a verb form having the characteristics of both verb and noun and in English usu. being used with *to*

in-fin-i-tude \in-'fi-nə-ˌtüd, -ˌtyüd\ *n* **1** : the quality or state of being infinite **2** : something that is infinite esp. in extent

in-fin-i-ty \in-'fi-nə-tē\ *n*, *pl* **-ties 1** : the quality of being infinite **2** : unlimited extent of time, space, or quantity : BOUNDLESSNESS **3** : an indefinitely great number or amount

in-firm \in-'fərm\ *adj* **1** : deficient in vitality; *esp* : feeble from age **2** : weak of mind, will, or character : IRRESOLUTE **3** : not solid or stable : INSECURE

in-fir-ma-ry \in-'fər-mə-rē\ *n*, *pl* **-ries** : a place for the care of the infirm or sick

in-fir-mi-ty \in-'fər-mə-tē\ *n*, *pl* **-ties 1** : FEEBLENESS **2** : DISEASE, AILMENT **3** : a personal failing : FOIBLE

infl *abbr* influenced

in-flame \in-'flām\ *vb* **in-flamed; in-flam-ing 1** : KINDLE **2** : to excite to excessive or uncontrollable action or feeling; *also* : INTENSIFY **3** : to affect or become affected with inflammation

in-flam-ma-ble \in-'fla-mə-bəl\ *adj* **1** : FLAMMABLE **2** : easily inflamed, excited, or angered : IRASCIBLE

in-flam-ma-tion \ˌin-flə-'mā-shən\ *n* : a bodily response to injury in which an affected area becomes red, hot, and painful and congested with blood

in-flam-ma-to-ry \in-'fla-mə-ˌtòr-ē\ *adj* **1** : tending to excite the senses or to arouse anger, disorder, or tumult : SEDITIOUS **2** : causing or accompanied by inflammation \(an ∼ disease\)

in-flate \in-'flāt\ *vb* **in-flat-ed; in-flat-ing 1** : to swell with air or gas \(∼ a balloon\) **2** : to puff up : ELATE **3** : to expand or increase abnormally \(∼ prices\) — **in-flat-able** *adj*

in-fla-tion \in-'flā-shən\ *n* **1** : an act of inflating : the state of being inflated **2** : empty pretentiousness : POMPOSITY **3** : an increase in the volume of money and credit resulting in a continuing rise in the general price level

in-fla-tion-ary \-shə-ˌner-ē\ *adj* : of, characterized by, or productive of inflation

in-flect \in-'flekt\ *vb* **1** : to turn from a direct line or course : CURVE **2** : to vary a word by inflection **3** : to change or vary the pitch of the voice

in-flec-tion \in-'flek-shən\ *n* **1** : the act or result of curving or bending **2** : a change in pitch or loudness of the voice **3** : the change of form that words undergo to mark case, gender, number, tense, person, mood, or voice — **in-flec-tion-al** \-shə-nəl\ *adj*

in-flex-i-ble \(ˌ)in-'flek-sə-bəl\ *adj* **1** : UNYIELDING **2** : RIGID **3** : incapable of change — **in-flex-i-bil-i-ty** \-ˌflek-sə-'bi-lə-tē\ *n* — **in-flex-i-bly** \-'flek-sə-blē\ *adv*

in-flex-ion \in-'flek-shən\ *chiefly Brit var of* INFLECTION

in-flict \in-'flikt\ *vb* : AFFLICT; *also* : to give by or as if by striking — **in-flic-tion** \-'flik-shən\ *n*

in-flo-res-cence \ˌin-flə-'res-ᵊns\ *n* : the manner of development and arrangement of flowers on a stem; *also* : a flowering stem with its appendages : a flower cluster

in-flow \'in-ˌflō\ *n* : a flowing in

¹**in-flu-ence** \'in-ˌflü-əns\ *n* **1** : the act or power of producing an effect without apparent force or direct authority **2** : the power or capacity of causing an effect in indirect or intangible ways \(under the ∼ of liquor\) **3** : a person or thing that exerts influence — **in-flu-en-tial** \ˌin-flü-'en-chəl\ *adj*

²**influence** *vb* **-enced; -enc-ing 1** : to affect or alter by influence : SWAY **2** : to have an effect on the condition or development of : MODIFY

in-flu-en-za \ˌin-flü-'en-zə\ *n* [It, lit., influence, fr. ML *influentia;* fr. the belief that epidemics were due to the influence of the stars] : an acute and very contagious virus disease marked by fever, prostration, aches and pains, and respiratory inflammation; *also* : any of various feverish usu. virus diseases typically with respiratory symptoms

in-flux \'in-ˌfləks\ *n* : a coming in

in-fo \'in-(ˌ)fō\ *n* : INFORMATION

in-fold \in-'fōld\ *vb* **1** : ENFOLD **2** : to fold inward or toward one another

in-fo-mer-cial \'in-fō-ˌmər-shəl\ *n* : a television program that is an extended advertisement often including a discussion or demonstration

in-form \in-'fòrm\ *vb* **1** : to communicate knowledge to : TELL **2** : to give information or knowledge **3** : to act as an informer **syn** acquaint, apprise, advise, notify

in·for·mal \(ˌ)in-ˈfȯr-məl\ *adj* **1** : conducted or carried out without formality or ceremony ⟨an ~ party⟩ **2** : characteristic of or appropriate to ordinary, casual, or familiar use ⟨~ clothes⟩ — **in·for·mal·i·ty** \ˌin-fȯr-ˈma-lə-tē, -fər-\ *n* — **in·for·mal·ly** \(ˌ)in-ˈfȯr-mə-lē\ *adv*

in·for·mant \in-ˈfȯr-mənt\ *n* : a person who gives information : INFORMER

in·for·ma·tion \ˌin-fər-ˈmā-shən\ *n* **1** : the communication or reception of knowledge or intelligence **2** : knowledge obtained from investigation, study, or instruction : FACTS, DATA — **in·for·ma·tion·al** \-shə-nəl\ *adj*

in·for·ma·tive \in-ˈfȯr-mə-tiv\ *adj* : imparting knowledge : INSTRUCTIVE

in·formed \in-ˈfȯrmd\ *adj* **1** : having or based on information **2** : EDUCATED, KNOWLEDGEABLE

informed consent *n* : consent to a medical procedure by someone who understands what is involved

in·form·er \-ˈfȯr-mər\ *n* : one that informs; *esp* : a person who informs against others for illegalities esp. for financial gain

in·fo·tain·ment \ˌin-fō-ˈtān-mənt\ *n* : a television program that presents information (as news) in a manner intended to be entertaining

in·frac·tion \in-ˈfrak-shən\ *n* [ME, fr. ML *infractio*, fr. L, subduing, fr. *infringere* to break, crush] : the act of infringing : VIOLATION

in·fra dig \ˌin-frə-ˈdig\ *adj* [short for L *infra dignitatem*] : being beneath one's dignity

in·fra·red \ˌin-frə-ˈred\ *adj* : being, relating to, or using radiation having wavelengths longer than those of red light — **infrared** *n*

in·fra·struc·ture \ˈin-frə-ˌstrək-chər\ *n* **1** : the underlying foundation or basic framework (as of a system or organization) **2** : the system of public works of a country, state, or region; *also* : the resources (as buildings or equipment) required for an activity

in·fre·quent \(ˌ)in-ˈfrē-kwənt\ *adj* **1** : seldom happening : RARE **2** : placed or occurring at wide intervals in space or time **syn** uncommon, scarce, sporadic — **in·fre·quent·ly** *adv*

in·fringe \in-ˈfrinj\ *vb* **in·fringed; in·fring·ing 1** : VIOLATE, TRANSGRESS ⟨~ a patent⟩ **2** : ENCROACH, TRESPASS — **in·fringe·ment** *n*

in·fu·ri·ate \in-ˈfyu̇r-ē-ˌāt\ *vb* **-at·ed; -at·ing** : to make furious : ENRAGE — **in·fu·ri·at·ing·ly** *adv*

in·fuse \in-ˈfyüz\ *vb* **in·fused; in·fus·ing 1** : to instill a principle or quality in : INTRODUCE **2** : INSPIRE, ANIMATE **3** : to steep (as tea) without boiling — **in·fu·sion** \-ˈfyü-zhən\ *n*

¹-ing \iŋ\ *n suffix* **1** : action or process ⟨sleep*ing*⟩ : instance of an action or process ⟨a meet*ing*⟩ **2** : product or result of an action or process ⟨an engrav*ing*⟩ ⟨earn*ings*⟩ **3** : something used in an action or process ⟨a bed cover*ing*⟩ **4** : something connected with, consisting of, or used in making (a specified thing) ⟨scaffold*ing*⟩ **5** : something related to (a specified concept) ⟨off*ing*⟩

²-ing *n suffix* : one of a (specified) kind

³-ing *vb suffix or adj suffix* — used to form the present participle ⟨sail*ing*⟩ and sometimes to form an adjective resembling a present participle but not derived from a verb ⟨swashbuckl*ing*⟩

in·ga·ther \ˈin-ˌga-thər\ *vb* : to gather in : ASSEMBLE

in·ge·nious \in-ˈjēn-yəs\ *adj* **1** : marked by special aptitude at discovering, inventing, or contriving **2** : marked by originality, resourcefulness, and cleverness in conception or execution — **in·ge·nious·ly** *adv* — **in·ge·nious·ness** *n*

in·ge·nue *or* **in·gé·nue** \ˈan-jə-ˌnü, ˈän-; ˈaⁿ-zhə-, ˈäⁿ-\ *n* : a naive girl or young woman; *esp* : an actress portraying such a person

in·ge·nu·i·ty \ˌin-jə-ˈnü-ə-tē, -ˈnyü-\ *n, pl* **-ties** : skill or cleverness in planning or inventing : INVENTIVENESS

in·gen·u·ous \in-ˈjen-yə-wəs\ *adj* [L *ingenuus* native, freeborn, fr. *gignere* to beget] **1** : STRAIGHTFORWARD, FRANK **2** : NAIVE — **in·gen·u·ous·ly** *adv* — **in·gen·u·ous·ness** *n*

in·gest \in-ˈjest\ *vb* : to take in for or as if for digestion — **in·ges·tion** \-ˈjes-chən\ *n*

in·gle·nook \ˈiŋ-gəl-ˌnu̇k\ *n* : a nook by a large open fireplace; *also* : a bench occupying this nook

in·glo·ri·ous \(ˌ)in-ˈglȯr-ē-əs\ *adj* **1** : SHAMEFUL **2** : not glorious : lacking fame or honor — **in·glo·ri·ous·ly** *adv*

in·got \ˈiŋ-gət\ *n* : a mass of metal cast in a form convenient for storage or transportation

¹in·grain \(ˌ)in-ˈgrān\ *vb* : to work indelibly into the natural texture or mental or moral constitution — **in·grained** *adj*

²in·grain \ˈin-ˌgrān\ *adj* **1** : made of fiber that is dyed before being spun into yarn **2** : made of yarn that is dyed before being woven or knitted **3** : INNATE — **in·grain** *n*

in·grate \ˈin-ˌgrāt\ *n* : an ungrateful person

in·gra·ti·ate \in-ˈgrā-shē-ˌāt\ *vb* **-at·ed; -at·ing** : to gain favor by deliberate effort

in·gra·ti·at·ing *adj* **1** : capable of winning favor : PLEASING ⟨an ~ smile⟩ **2** : FLATTERING ⟨an ~ manner⟩

in·grat·i·tude \(ˌ)in-ˈgra-tə-ˌtüd, -ˌtyüd\ *n* : lack of gratitude : UNGRATEFULNESS

in·gre·di·ent \in-ˈgrē-dē-ənt\ *n* : one of the substances that make up a mixture or compound : CONSTITUENT

in·gress \ˈin-ˌgres\ *n* : ENTRANCE, ACCESS — **in·gres·sion** \in-ˈgre-shən\ *n*

in·grow·ing \ˈin-ˌgrō-iŋ\ *adj* : growing or tending inward

in·grown \-ˌgrōn\ *adj* : grown in; *esp* : having the free tip or edge embedded in the flesh ⟨~ toenail⟩

in·gui·nal \ˈiŋ-gwən-ᵊl\ *adj* : of, relating to, or situated in or near the region of the groin

in·hab·it \in-ˈha-bət\ *vb* : to live or dwell in — **in·hab·it·able** *adj*

in·hab·i·tant \in-ˈha-bə-tənt\ *n* : a permanent resident in a place

in·hal·ant \in-ˈhā-lənt\ *n* : something (as a medicine) that is inhaled

in·ha·la·tor \ˈin-hə-ˌlā-tər\ *n* : a device that provides a mixture of carbon dioxide and oxygen for breathing

in·hale \in-ˈhāl\ *vb* **in·haled; in·hal·ing** : to breathe in — **in·ha·la·tion** \ˌin-hə-ˈlā-shən\ *n*

in·hal·er \in-ˈhā-lər\ *n* : a device by means of which medicinal material is inhaled

in·here \in-ˈhir\ *vb* **in·hered; in·her·ing** : to be inherent

in·her·ent \in-ˈhir-ənt, -ˈher-\ *adj* : established as an essential part of something : INTRINSIC — **in·her·ent·ly** *adv*

in·her·it \in-ˈher-ət\ *vb* : to receive esp. from one's ancestors — **in·her·it·able** \-ə-tə-bəl\ *adj* — **in·her·i·tance** \-ə-təns\ *n* — **in·her·i·tor** \-ə-tər\ *n*

in·hib·it \in-ˈhi-bət\ *vb* **1** : PROHIBIT, FORBID **2** : to hold in check : RESTRAIN

in·hi·bi·tion \ˌin-hə-ˈbi-shən\ *n* **1** : PROHIBITION, RESTRAINT **2** : a usu. inner check on free activity, expression, or functioning

in-house \ˈin-ˌhau̇s, -ˈhau̇s\ *adj* : existing, originating, or carried on within a group or organization

in·hu·man \(ˌ)in-ˈhyü-mən, -ˈyü-\ *adj* **1** : lacking pity, kindness, or mercy : SAVAGE **2** : COLD, IMPERSONAL **3** : not worthy of or conforming to the needs of human beings **4** : of or suggesting a nonhuman class of beings — **in·hu·man·ly** *adv* — **in·hu·man·ness** *n*

in·hu·mane \ˌin-hyü-ˈmān, -yü-\ *adj* : not humane : INHUMAN 1

in·hu·man·i·ty \-ˈma-nə-tē\ *n, pl* **-ities 1** : the quality or state of being cruel or barbarous **2** : a cruel or barbarous act

in·im·i·cal \i-'ni-mi-kəl\ *adj* **1** : being adverse often by reason of hostility **2** : HOSTILE, UNFRIENDLY — **in·im·i·cal·ly** *adv*

in·im·i·ta·ble \(ˌ)i-'ni-mə-tə-bəl\ *adj* : not capable of being imitated

in·iq·ui·ty \i-'ni-kwə-tē\ *n, pl* **-ties** [ME *iniquite*, fr. MF *iniquité*, fr. L *iniquitas*, fr. *iniquus* uneven, fr. *aequus* equal] **1** : WICKEDNESS **2** : a wicked act — **in·iq·ui·tous** \-təs\ *adj*

¹in·i·tial \i-'ni-shəl\ *adj* **1** : of or relating to the beginning : INCIPIENT **2** : FIRST — **ini·tial·ly** *adv*

²initial *n* : the first letter of a word or name

³initial *vb* **-tialed** *or* **-tialled; -tial·ing** *or* **-tial·ling** : to affix an initial to

¹ini·ti·ate \i-'ni-shē-ˌāt\ *vb* **-at·ed; -at·ing** **1** : START, BEGIN **2** : to induct into membership by or as if by special ceremonies **3** : to instruct in the rudiments or principles of something — **ini·ti·a·tion** \-ˌni-shē-'ā-shən\ *n*

²ini·tiate \i-'ni-shē-ət\ *n* **1** : a person who is undergoing or has passed an initiation **2** : a person who is instructed or adept in some special field

ini·tia·tive \i-'ni-shə-tiv\ *n* **1** : an introductory step **2** : self-reliant enterprise ⟨showed great ∼⟩ **3** : a process by which laws may be introduced or enacted directly by vote of the people

ini·tia·to·ry \i-'ni-shē-ə-ˌtōr-ē\ *adj* **1** : INTRODUCTORY **2** : tending or serving to initiate ⟨∼ rites⟩

in·ject \in-'jekt\ *vb* **1** : to force into something ⟨∼ serum with a needle⟩ **2** : to introduce as an element into some situation or subject ⟨∼ a note of suspicion⟩ — **in·jec·tion** \-'jek-shən\ *n*

in·junc·tion \in-'jəŋk-shən\ *n* **1** : ORDER, ADMONITION **2** : a court writ whereby one is required to do or to refrain from doing a specified act

in·jure \'in-jər\ *vb* **in·jured; in·jur·ing** : WRONG, DAMAGE, HURT **syn** harm, impair, mar, spoil

in·ju·ry \'in-jə-rē\ *n, pl* **-ries** **1** : an act that damages or hurts : WRONG **2** : hurt, damage, or loss sustained — **in·ju·ri·ous** \in-'jùr-ē-əs\ *adj*

in·jus·tice \(ˌ)in-'jəs-təs\ *n* **1** : violation of a person's rights : UNFAIRNESS **2** : an unjust act or deed : WRONG

¹ink \'iŋk\ *n* [ME *enke*, fr. OF, fr. LL *encaustum*, fr. L *encaustus* burned in, fr. Gk *enkaustos*, fr. *enkaiein* to burn in] : a usu. liquid and colored material for writing and printing — **inky** *adj*

²ink *vb* : to put ink on; *esp* : SIGN

ink·blot test \'iŋk-ˌblät-\ *n* : any of several psychological tests based on the interpretation of irregular figures

ink·horn \-ˌhòrn\ *n* : a small bottle (as of horn) for holding ink

in–kind \'in-'kīnd\ *adj* : consisting of something (as goods) other than money

in·kling \'iŋ-kliŋ\ *n* **1** : HINT, INTIMATION **2** : a vague idea

ink·stand \'iŋk-ˌstand\ *n* : INKWELL; *also* : a pen and ink stand

ink·well \-ˌwel\ *n* : a container for ink

in·laid \'in-'lād\ *adj* : decorated with material set into a surface

¹in·land \'in-ˌland, -lənd\ *adj* **1** *chiefly Brit* : not foreign : DOMESTIC ⟨∼ revenue⟩ **2** : of or relating to the interior of a country

²inland *n* : the interior of a country

³inland *adv* : into or toward the interior

in–law \'in-ˌlò\ *n* : a relative by marriage

¹in·lay \(ˌ)in-'lā, 'in-ˌlā\ *vb* **in·laid** \-'lād\; **in·lay·ing** : to set (a material) into a surface or ground material esp. for decoration

²in·lay \'in-ˌlā\ *n* **1** : inlaid work **2** : a shaped filling cemented into a tooth

in·let \'in-ˌlet, -lət\ *n* **1** : a small or narrow bay **2** : an opening for intake esp. of a fluid

in·mate \'in-ˌmāt\ *n* : any of a group occupying a sin-

gle place of residence; *esp* : a person confined (as in a hospital or prison)

in me·di·as res \in-ˌmä-dē-əs-'rās\ *adv* [L, lit., into the midst of things] : in or into the middle of a narrative or plot

in me·mo·ri·am \ˌin-mə-'mōr-ē-əm\ *prep* [L] : in memory of

in·most \'in-ˌmōst\ *adj* : deepest within : INNERMOST

inn \'in\ *n* : HOTEL, TAVERN

in·nards \'i-nərdz\ *n pl* **1** : the internal organs of a human being or animal; *esp* : VISCERA **2** : the internal parts of a structure or mechanism

in·nate \i-'nāt\ *adj* **1** : existing in, belonging to, or determined by factors present in an individual from birth : NATIVE **2** : INHERENT, INTRINSIC — **in·nate·ly** *adv*

in·ner \'i-nər\ *adj* **1** : situated farther in ⟨the ∼ bark⟩ **2** : near a center esp. of influence ⟨the ∼ circle⟩ **3** : of or relating to the mind or spirit

inner city *n* : the usu. older, poorer, and more densely populated section of a city — **inner–city** *adj*

in·ner–di·rect·ed \ˌi-nər-də-'rek-təd, -(ˌ)dī-\ *adj* : directed in thought and action by one's own scale of values as opposed to external norms

inner ear *n* : the part of the ear that is most important for hearing, is located in a cavity in the temporal bone, and contains sense organs of hearing and of awareness of position in space

in·ner·most \'i-nər-ˌmōst\ *adj* : farthest inward : INMOST

in·ner·sole \'i-nər-'sōl\ *n* : INSOLE

in·ner·spring \'i-nər-'spriŋ\ *adj* : having coil springs inside a padded casing

inner tube *n* : an airtight rubber tube inside a tire to hold air under pressure

in·ning \'i-niŋ\ *n* **1** *sing or pl* : a division of a cricket match **2** : a baseball team's turn at bat; *also* : a division of a baseball game consisting of a turn at bat for each team

inn·keep·er \'in-ˌkē-pər\ *n* **1** : a proprietor of an inn **2** : a hotel manager

in·no·cence \'i-nə-səns\ *n* **1** : BLAMELESSNESS; *also* : freedom from legal guilt **2** : GUILELESSNESS, SIMPLICITY; *also* : IGNORANCE

in·no·cent \-sənt\ *adj* [ME, fr. MF, fr. L *innocens*, fr. *nocens* wicked, fr. *nocēre* to harm] **1** : free from guilt or sin : BLAMELESS **2** : harmless in effect or intention; *also* : CANDID **3** : free from legal guilt or fault : LAWFUL **4** : INGENUOUS **5** : UNAWARE — **innocent** *n* — **in·no·cent·ly** *adv*

in·noc·u·ous \i-'nä-kyə-wəs\ *adj* **1** : HARMLESS **2** : not offensive; *also* : INSIPID

in·nom·i·nate \i-'nä-mə-nət\ *adj* : having no name; *also* : ANONYMOUS

in·no·vate \'i-nə-ˌvāt\ *vb* **-vat·ed; -vat·ing** : to introduce as or as if new : make changes — **in·no·va·tive** \-ˌvā-tiv\ *adj* — **in·no·va·tor** \-ˌvā-tər\ *n*

in·no·va·tion \ˌi-nə-'vā-shən\ *n* **1** : the introduction of something new **2** : a new idea, method, or device

in·nu·en·do \ˌin-yə-'wen-dō\ *n, pl* **-dos** *or* **-does** [L, by hinting, fr. *innuere* to hint, fr. *nuere* to nod] : HINT, INSINUATION; *esp* : a veiled reflection on character or reputation

in·nu·mer·a·ble \i-'nü-mə-rə-bəl, -'nyü-\ *adj* : too many to be numbered

in·oc·u·late \i-'nä-kyə-ˌlāt\ *vb* **-lat·ed; -lat·ing** [ME, to insert a bud in a plant, fr. L *inoculare*, fr. *oculus* eye, bud] : to introduce something into; *esp* : to introduce a serum or antibody into (an organism) to treat or prevent a disease — **in·oc·u·la·tion** \-ˌnä-kyə-'lā-shən\ *n*

in·op·er·a·ble \(ˌ)i-'nä-pə-rə-bəl\ *adj* **1** : not suitable for surgery **2** : not operable

in·op·er·a·tive \-'nä-pə-rə-tiv, -'nä-pə-ˌrā-\ *adj* : not functioning

in·op·por·tune \(ˌ)i-ˌnä-pər-'tün, -'tyün\ *adj* : INCON-

VENIENT, INAPPROPRIATE — **in·op·por·tune·ly** *adv*

in·or·di·nate \i-'nord-ᵊn-ət\ *adj* : exceeding reasonable limits : IMMODERATE ⟨an ∼ curiosity⟩ — **in·or·di·nate·ly** *adv*

in·or·gan·ic \ˌi-nȯr-'ga-nik\ *adj* : being or composed of matter of other than plant or animal origin : MINERAL

in·pa·tient \'in-ˌpā-shənt\ *n* : a hospital patient who receives lodging and food as well as treatment

in·put \'in-ˌpu̇t\ *n* **1** : something put in **2** : power or energy put into a machine or system **3** : information fed into a computer or data processing system **4** : ADVICE, OPINION — **input** *vb*

in·quest \'in-ˌkwest\ *n* **1** : an official inquiry or examination esp. before a jury **2** : INQUIRY, INVESTIGATION

in·qui·etude \(ˌ)in-'kwī-ə-ˌtüd, -ˌtyüd\ *n* : UNEASINESS, RESTLESSNESS

in·quire \in-'kwīr\ *vb* **in·quired; in·quir·ing 1** : to ask about : ASK **2** : INVESTIGATE, EXAMINE — **in·quir·er** *n* — **in·quir·ing·ly** *adv*

in·qui·ry \'in-ˌkwīr-ē, in-'kwīr-ē; 'in-kwə-rē, 'iŋ-\ *n, pl* **-ries 1** : a request for information; *also* : RESEARCH **2** : a systematic investigation of a matter of public interest

in·qui·si·tion \ˌin-kwə-'zi-shən, ˌiŋ-\ *n* **1** : a judicial or official inquiry usu. before a jury **2** *cap* : a former Roman Catholic tribunal for the discovery and punishment of heresy **3** : a severe questioning — **in·quis·i·tor** \in-'kwi-zə-tər\ *n* — **in·quis·i·to·ri·al** \-ˌkwi-zə-'tȯr-ē-əl\ *adj*

in·quis·i·tive \in-'kwi-zə-tiv\ *adj* **1** : given to examination or investigation ⟨an ∼ mind⟩ **2** : unduly curious — **in·quis·i·tive·ly** *adv* — **in·quis·i·tive·ness** *n*

in re \in-'rā, -'rē\ *prep* : in the matter of

INRI *abbr* [L *Iesus Nazarenus Rex Iudaeorum*] Jesus of Nazareth, King of the Jews

in·road \'in-ˌrōd\ *n* **1** : INVASION, RAID **2** : ENCROACHMENT

in·rush \'in-ˌrəsh\ *n* : a crowding or flooding in

ins *abbr* **1** inches **2** insurance

INS *abbr* Immigration and Naturalization Service

in·sa·lu·bri·ous \ˌin-sə-'lü-brē-əs\ *adj* : UNWHOLESOME, NOXIOUS

ins and outs *n pl* **1** : characteristic peculiarities **2** : RAMIFICATIONS

in·sane \(ˌ)in-'sān\ *adj* **1** : exhibiting serious and debilitating mental disorder; *also* : used by or for the insane **2** : ABSURD — **in·sane·ly** *adv* — **in·san·i·ty** \in-'sa-nə-tē\ *n*

in·sa·tia·ble \(ˌ)in-'sā-shə-bəl\ *adj* : incapable of being satisfied — **in·sa·tia·bil·i·ty** \(ˌ)in-ˌsā-shə-'bi-lə-tē\ *n* — **in·sa·tia·bly** *adv*

in·sa·tiate \(ˌ)in-'sā-shē-ət, -shət\ *adj* : INSATIABLE — **in·sa·tiate·ly** *adv*

in·scribe \in-'skrīb\ *vb* **1** : to write, engrave, or print as a lasting record **2** : ENROLL **3** : to write, engrave, or print characters upon **4** : to dedicate to someone **5** : to draw within a figure so as to touch in as many places as possible — **in·scrip·tion** \-'skrip-shən\ *n*

in·scru·ta·ble \in-'skrü-tə-bəl\ *adj* : not readily comprehensible : MYSTERIOUS — **in·scru·ta·bly** \-blē\ *adv*

in·seam \'in-ˌsēm\ *n* : the seam on the inside of the leg of a pair of pants; *also* : the length of this seam

in·sect \'in-ˌsekt\ *n* [L *insectum*, fr. *insectus*, pp. of *insecare* to cut into, fr. *secare* to cut] : any of a class of small usu. winged arthropod animals (as flies, bees, beetles, and moths) with usu. three pairs of legs as adults

in·sec·ti·cide \in-'sek-tə-ˌsīd\ *n* : a preparation for destroying insects — **in·sec·ti·cid·al** \(ˌ)in-ˌsek-tə-'sīd-ᵊl\ *adj*

in·sec·tiv·o·rous \ˌin-sek-'ti-və-rəs\ *adj* : depending on insects as food

in·se·cure \ˌin-si-'kyu̇r\ *adj* **1** : UNCERTAIN **2** : not protected : UNSAFE **3** : LOOSE, SHAKY **4** : not highly stable; *also* : lacking assurance : ANXIOUS, FEARFUL —

in·se·cure·ly *adv* — **in·se·cu·ri·ty** \-'kyu̇r-ə-tē\ *n*

in·sem·i·nate \in-'se-mə-ˌnāt\ *vb* **-nat·ed; -nat·ing** : to introduce semen into the genital tract of (a female) — **in·sem·i·na·tion** \-ˌse-mə-'nā-shən\ *n*

in·sen·sate \(ˌ)in-'sen-ˌsāt, -sət\ *adj* **1** : lacking sense or understanding; *also* : FOOLISH **2** : INANIMATE **3** : BRUTAL, INHUMAN ⟨∼ rage⟩

in·sen·si·ble \(ˌ)in-'sen-sə-bəl\ *adj* **1** : IMPERCEPTIBLE; *also* : SLIGHT, GRADUAL **2** : INANIMATE **3** : UNCONSCIOUS **4** : lacking sensory perception or ability to react ⟨∼ to pain⟩ **5** : APATHETIC, INDIFFERENT; *also* : UNAWARE ⟨∼ of their danger⟩ **6** : MEANINGLESS **7** : lacking delicacy or refinement — **in·sen·si·bil·i·ty** \-ˌsen-sə-'bi-lə-tē\ *n* — **in·sen·si·bly** \-'sen-sə-blē\ *adv*

in·sen·tient \(ˌ)in-'sen-chē-ənt\ *adj* : lacking perception, consciousness, or animation — **in·sen·tience** \-chē-əns\ *n*

in·sep·a·ra·ble \(ˌ)in-'se-prə-bəl, -pə-rə-\ *adj* : incapable of being separated or disjoined — **in·sep·a·ra·bil·i·ty** \-ˌse-prə-'bi-lə-tē, -pə-rə-\ *n* — **inseparable** *n* — **in·sep·a·ra·bly** \-'se-prə-blē, -pə-rə-\ *adv*

¹in·sert \in-'sərt\ *vb* **1** : to put or thrust in ⟨∼ a key in a lock⟩ ⟨∼ a comma⟩ **2** : INTERPOLATE **3** : to set in (as a piece of fabric) and make fast

²in·sert \'in-ˌsərt\ *n* : something that is inserted or is for insertion; *esp* : written or printed material inserted (as between the leaves of a book)

in·ser·tion \in-'sər-shən\ *n* **1** : something that is inserted **2** : the act or process of inserting

in·set \'in-ˌset\ *vb* **inset** *or* **in·set·ted; in·set·ting** : to set in : INSERT — **inset** *n*

¹in·shore \'in-ˌshȯr\ *adj* **1** : situated, living, or carried on near shore **2** : moving toward shore

²inshore *adv* : to or toward shore

¹in·side \in-'sīd, 'in-ˌsīd\ *n* **1** : an inner side or surface : INTERIOR **2** : inward nature, thoughts, or feeling **3** *pl* : VISCERA, ENTRAILS **4** : a position of power, trust, or familiarity — **inside** *adj*

²inside *adv* **1** : on the inner side **2** : in or into the interior

³inside *prep* **1** : in or into the inside of **2** : WITHIN ⟨∼ an hour⟩

inside of *prep* : INSIDE

in·sid·er \in-'sī-dər\ *n* : a person who is in a position of power or has access to confidential information

in·sid·i·ous \in-'si-dē-əs\ *adj* [L *insidiosus*, fr. *insidiae* ambush, fr. *insidēre* to sit in, sit on, fr. *sedēre* to sit] **1** : SLY, TREACHEROUS **2** : SEDUCTIVE **3** : having a gradual and cumulative effect : SUBTLE — **in·sid·i·ous·ly** *adv* — **in·sid·i·ous·ness** *n*

in·sight \'in-ˌsīt\ *n* : the power, act, or result of seeing into a situation : UNDERSTANDING, PENETRATION — **in·sight·ful** \'in-ˌsīt-fəl, in-'sīt-\ *adj*

in·sig·nia \in-'sig-nē-ə\ *or* **in·sig·ne** \-(ˌ)nē\ *n, pl* **-nia** *or* **-ni·as** : a distinguishing mark esp. of authority or honor : BADGE

in·sin·cere \ˌin-sin-'sir\ *adj* : not sincere : HYPOCRITICAL — **in·sin·cere·ly** *adv* — **in·sin·cer·i·ty** \-'ser-ə-tē\ *n*

in·sin·u·ate \in-'sin-yə-ˌwāt\ *vb* **-at·ed; -at·ing** [L *insinuare*, fr. *sinuare* to bend, curve, fr. *sinus* curve] **1** : to introduce gradually or in a subtle, indirect, or artful way **2** : to imply in a subtle or devious way — **in·sin·u·a·tion** \(ˌ)in-ˌsin-yə-'wā-shən\ *n*

in·sin·u·at·ing *adj* **1** : winning favor and confidence by imperceptible degrees **2** : tending gradually to cause doubt, distrust, or change of outlook

in·sip·id \in-'si-pəd\ *adj* **1** : lacking taste or savor **2** : DULL, FLAT — **in·si·pid·i·ty** \ˌin-sə-'pi-də-tē\ *n*

in·sist \in-'sist\ *vb* [MF or L; MF *insister*, fr. L *insistere* to stand upon, persist, fr. *sistere* to take a stand] : to take a resolute stand

in·sis·tence \in-'sis-təns\ *n* : the act of insisting; *also* : an insistent attitude or quality : URGENCY

in·sis·tent \in-'sis-tənt\ *adj* : disposed to insist — **in·sis·tent·ly** *adv*

in si·tu \in-ˈsī-tü, -ˈsē-\ *adv or adj* [L, in position] : in the natural or original position

in·so·far as \ˌin-sə-ˈfär-\ *conj* : to the extent or degree that

insol *abbr* insoluble

in·so·la·tion \ˌin-(ˌ)sō-ˈlā-shən\ *n* : solar radiation that has been received

in·sole \ˈin-ˌsōl\ *n* **1** : an inside sole of a shoe **2** : a loose thin strip placed inside a shoe for warmth or comfort

in·so·lent \ˈin-sə-lənt\ *adj* : contemptuous, rude, disrespectful, or bold in behavior or language — **in·so·lence** \-ləns\ *n*

in·sol·u·ble \(ˌ)in-ˈsäl-yə-bəl\ *adj* **1** : having or admitting of no solution or explanation **2** : difficult or impossible to dissolve — **in·sol·u·bil·i·ty** \-ˌsäl-yə-ˈbil-ə-tē\ *n*

in·sol·vent \(ˌ)in-ˈsäl-vənt\ *adj* **1** : unable or insufficient to pay all debts ⟨an ∼ estate⟩ **2** : IMPOVERISHED, DEFICIENT — **in·sol·ven·cy** \-vən-sē\ *n*

in·som·nia \in-ˈsäm-nē-ə\ *n* : prolonged and usu. abnormal sleeplessness

in·so·much as \ˌin-sə-ˈməch-\ *conj* : INASMUCH AS

insomuch that *conj* : to such a degree that : SO

in·sou·ci·ance \in-ˈsü-sē-əns, aⁿ-süs-ˈyäⁿs\ *n* [F] : lighthearted unconcern — **in·sou·ci·ant** \in-ˈsü-sē-ənt, aⁿ-süs-ˈyäᵐ\ *adj*

insp *abbr* inspector

in·spect \in-ˈspekt\ *vb* : to view closely and critically : EXAMINE — **in·spec·tion** \-ˈspek-shən\ *n* — **in·spec·tor** \-tər\ *n*

inspector general *n* : the head of a system of inspection (as of an army)

in·spi·ra·tion \ˌin-spə-ˈrā-shən\ *n* **1** : the act or power of moving the intellect or emotions **2** : INHALATION **3** : the quality or state of being inspired; *also* : something that is inspired **4** : an inspiring agent or influence — **in·spi·ra·tion·al** \-shə-nəl\ *adj*

in·spire \in-ˈspīr\ *vb* **in·spired; in·spir·ing 1** : to influence, move, or guide by divine or supernatural inspiration **2** : exert an animating, enlivening, or exalting influence upon; *also* : AFFECT **3** : to communicate to an agent supernaturally; *also* : bring out or about **4** : INHALE **5** : INCITE **6** : to spread by indirect means — **in·spir·er** *n*

in·spir·it \in-ˈspir-ət\ *vb* : ENCOURAGE, HEARTEN

inst *abbr* **1** instant **2** institute; institution; institutional

in·sta·bil·i·ty \ˌin-stə-ˈbil-ə-tē\ *n* : lack of steadiness; *esp* : lack of emotional or mental stability

in·stall *or* **in·stal** \in-ˈstȯl\ *vb* **in·stalled; in·stall·ing 1** : to place formally in office : induct into an office, rank, or order **2** : to establish in an indicated place, condition, or status **3** : to set up for use or service — **in·stal·la·tion** \ˌin-stə-ˈlā-shən\ *n*

¹in·stall·ment *also* **in·stal·ment** \in-ˈstȯl-mənt\ *n* : INSTALLATION

²installment *also* **instalment** *n* **1** : one of the parts into which a debt or sum is divided for payment **2** : one of several parts presented at intervals

¹in·stance \ˈin-stəns\ *n* **1** : INSTIGATION, REQUEST **2** : EXAMPLE ⟨for ∼⟩ **3** : an event or step that is part of a process or series **syn** case, illustration, sample, specimen

²instance *vb* **in·stanced; in·stanc·ing** : to mention as a case or example

¹in·stant \ˈin-stənt\ *n* **1** : MOMENT ⟨the ∼ we met⟩ **2** : the present or current month

²instant *adj* **1** : URGENT **2** : PRESENT, CURRENT **3** : IMMEDIATE ⟨∼ relief⟩ **4** : premixed or precooked for easy final preparation ⟨∼ cake mix⟩; *also* : immediately soluble in water ⟨∼ coffee⟩

in·stan·ta·neous \ˌin-stən-ˈtā-nē-əs\ *adj* : done or occurring in an instant or without delay — **in·stan·ta·neous·ly** *adv*

in·stan·ter \in-ˈstan-tər\ *adv* : at once

in·stan·ti·ate \in-ˈstan-chē-ˌāt\ *vb* **-at·ed; -at·ing** : to

represent (an abstraction) by a concrete example — **in·stan·ti·a·tion** \-ˌstan-chē-ˈā-shən\ *n*

in·stant·ly \ˈin-stənt-lē\ *adv* : at once : IMMEDIATELY

in·state \in-ˈstāt\ *vb* : to establish in a rank or office : INSTALL

in·stead \in-ˈsted\ *adv* **1** : as a substitute or equivalent **2** : as an alternative : RATHER

instead of *prep* : as a substitute for or alternative to

in·step \ˈin-ˌstep\ *n* : the arched part of the human foot in front of the ankle joint; *esp* : its upper surface

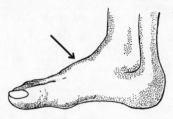
instep

in·sti·gate \ˈin-stə-ˌgāt\ *vb* **-gat·ed; -gat·ing** : to goad or urge forward : PROVOKE, INCITE ⟨∼ a revolt⟩ — **in·sti·ga·tion** \ˌin-stə-ˈgā-shən\ *n* — **in·sti·ga·tor** \ˈin-stə-ˌgā-tər\ *n*

in·still *also* **in·stil** \in-ˈstil\ *vb* **in·stilled; in·still·ing 1** : to cause to enter drop by drop **2** : to impart gradually

¹in·stinct \ˈin-ˌstiŋkt\ *n* **1** : a natural aptitude **2** : a largely inheritable and unalterable tendency of an organism to make a complex and specific response to environmental stimuli without involving reason; *also* : behavior originating below the conscious level — **in·stinc·tive** \in-ˈstiŋk-tiv\ *adj* — **in·stinc·tive·ly** *adv*

²in·stinct \in-ˈstiŋkt, ˈin-ˌstiŋkt\ *adj* : IMBUED, INFUSED

in·stinc·tu·al \in-ˈstiŋk-chə-wəl\ *adj* : of, relating to, or based on instinct

¹in·sti·tute \ˈin-stə-ˌtüt, -ˌtyüt\ *vb* **-tut·ed; -tut·ing 1** : to establish in a position or office **2** : ORGANIZE **3** : INAUGURATE, INITIATE

²institute *n* **1** : an elementary principle recognized as authoritative; *also, pl* : a collection of such principles and precepts **2** : an organization for the promotion of a cause : ASSOCIATION **3** : an educational institution **4** : a brief course of instruction on a particular field

in·sti·tu·tion \ˌin-stə-ˈtü-shən, -ˈtyü-\ *n* **1** : an act of originating, setting up, or founding **2** : an established practice, law, or custom **3** : a society or corporation esp. of a public character ⟨a charitable ∼⟩; *also* : ASYLUM **3** — **in·sti·tu·tion·al** \-ˈtü-shə-nəl, -ˈtyü-\ *adj* — **in·sti·tu·tion·al·ize** \-nə-ˌlīz\ *vb* — **in·sti·tu·tion·al·ly** *adv*

instr *abbr* **1** instructor **2** instrument; instrumental

in·struct \in-ˈstrəkt\ *vb* [ME, fr. L *instructus*, pp. of *instruere*, fr. *struere* to build] **1** : TEACH **2** : INFORM **3** : to give an order or a command to

in·struc·tion \in-ˈstrək-shən\ *n* **1** : LESSON, PRECEPT **2** : COMMAND, ORDER **3** *pl* : DIRECTIONS **4** : the action, practice, or profession of a teacher — **in·struc·tion·al** \-shə-nəl\ *adj*

in·struc·tive \in-ˈstrək-tiv\ *adj* : carrying a lesson : ENLIGHTENING

in·struc·tor \in-ˈstrək-tər\ *n* : one that instructs; *esp* : a college teacher below professorial rank — **in·struc·tor·ship** *n*

in·stru·ment \ˈin-strə-mənt\ *n* **1** : a device used to produce music **2** : a means by which something is done **3** : a device for doing work and esp. precision work **4** : a legal document (as a deed) **5** : a device used in navigating an airplane — **in·stru·ment** \-ˌment\ *vb*

in·stru·men·tal \ˌin-strə-ˈment-ᵊl\ *adj* **1** : acting as an agent or means **2** : of, relating to, or done with an instrument **3** : relating to, composed for, or performed on a musical instrument

in·stru·men·tal·ist \-'men-tə-list\ *n* : a player on a musical instrument

in·stru·men·tal·i·ty \in-strə-mən-'ta-lə-tē, -ımen-\ *n, pl* **-ties 1** : the quality or state of being instrumental **2** : MEANS, AGENCY

in·stru·men·ta·tion \in-strə-mən-'tā-shən, -ımen-\ *n* **1** : ORCHESTRATION **2** : instruments for a particular purpose

instrument panel *n* : DASHBOARD

in·sub·or·di·nate \in-sə-'bord-ºn-ət\ *adj* : disobedient to authority — **in·sub·or·di·na·tion** \-ıbord-ºn-'ā-shən\ *n*

in·sub·stan·tial \in-səb-'stan-chəl\ *adj* **1** : lacking substance or reality **2** : lacking firmness or solidity

in·suf·fer·able \(ı)in-'sə-fə-rə-bəl\ *adj* : not to be endured : INTOLERABLE (an ~ bore) — **in·suf·fer·ably** \-blē\ *adv*

in·suf·fi·cient \in-sə-'fi-shənt\ *adj* : not sufficient; *also* : INCOMPETENT — **in·suf·fi·cien·cy** \-shən-sē\ *n* — **in·suf·fi·cient·ly** *adv*

in·su·lar \'in-sə-lər, -syə-\ *adj* **1** : of, relating to, or forming an island **2** : dwelling or situated on an island **3** : NARROW-MINDED — **in·su·lar·i·ty** \in-sə-'lar-ə-tē, -syə-\ *n*

in·su·late \'in-sə-ılāt\ *vb* **-lat·ed; -lat·ing** [L *insula* island] : ISOLATE; *esp* : to separate a conductor of electricity, heat, or sound from other conducting bodies by means of a nonconductor — **in·su·la·tion** \in-sə-'lā-shən\ *n* — **in·su·la·tor** \'in-sə-ılā-tər\ *n*

in·su·lin \'in-sə-lən\ *n* : a pancreatic hormone essential esp. for the metabolism of carbohydrates and used in the control of diabetes mellitus

¹in·sult \in-'səlt\ *vb* [MF or L; MF *insulter*, fr. L *insultare*, lit., to spring upon, fr. *saltare* to leap] : to treat with insolence or contempt : AFFRONT — **in·sult·ing·ly** *adv*

²in·sult \'in-ısəlt\ *n* : a gross indignity

in·su·per·a·ble \(ı)in-'sü-pə-rə-bəl\ *adj* : incapable of being surmounted, overcome, passed over, or solved — **in·su·per·a·bly** \-blē\ *adv*

in·sup·port·able \in-sə-'pōr-tə-bəl\ *adj* **1** : UNENDURABLE **2** : UNJUSTIFIABLE

in·sur·able \in-'shù-rə-bəl\ *adj* : capable of being or proper to be insured

in·sur·ance \in-'shùr-əns\ *n* **1** : the business of insuring persons or property **2** : coverage by contract whereby one party agrees to guarantee another against a specified loss **3** : the sum for which something is insured **4** : a means of guaranteeing protection or safety

in·sure \in-'shùr\ *vb* **in·sured; in·sur·ing 1** : to provide or obtain insurance on or for : UNDERWRITE **2** : to make certain : ENSURE

in·sured \in-'shùrd\ *n* : a person whose life or property is insured

in·sur·er \in-'shùr-ər\ *n* : one that insures; *esp* : an insurance company

in·sur·gent \in-'sər-jənt\ *n* **1** : a person who revolts against civil authority or an established government : REBEL **2** : a member of a political party who rebels against it — **in·sur·gence** \-jəns\ *n* — **in·sur·gen·cy** \-jən-sē\ *n* — **in·sur·gent** *adj*

in·sur·mount·able \in-sər-maùn-tə-bəl\ *adj* : INSUPERABLE — **in·sur·mount·ably** \-blē\ *adv*

in·sur·rec·tion \in-sə-'rek-shən\ *n* : an act or instance of revolting against civil authority or an established government — **in·sur·rec·tion·ist** \-shə-nist\ *n*

int *abbr* **1** interest **2** interior **3** intermediate **4** internal **5** international **6** intransitive

in·tact \in-'takt\ *adj* : untouched esp. by anything that harms or diminishes

in·ta·glio \in-'tal-yō\ *n, pl* **-glios** [It] : an engraving cut deeply into the surface of a hard material (as stone)

in·take \'in-ıtāk\ *n* **1** : an opening through which fluid enters **2** : the act of taking in **3** : something taken in

in·tan·gi·ble \(ı)in-'tan-jə-bəl\ *adj* : incapable of being touched : IMPALPABLE — **intangible** *n* — **in·tan·gi·bly** \-blē\ *adv*

in·te·ger \'in-ti-jər\ *n* [L, adj., whole, entire] : a number (as 1, 2, 3, 12, 432) that is not a fraction and does not include a fraction, is the negative of such a number, or is 0

in·te·gral \'in-ti-grəl\ *adj* **1** : essential to completeness **2** : formed as a unit with another part **3** : composed of parts that make up a whole **4** : ENTIRE

integral calculus *n* : calculus concerned esp. with advanced methods of finding lengths, areas, and volumes

in·te·grate \'in-tə-ıgrāt\ *vb* **-grat·ed; -grat·ing 1** : to form, coordinate, or blend into a functioning whole : UNITE **2** : to incorporate into a larger unit **3** : to end the segregation of and bring into equal membership in society or an organization; *also* : DESEGREGATE — **in·te·gra·tion** \in-tə-'grā-shən\ *n*

integrated circuit *n* : a group of tiny electronic components and their connections that is produced in or on a small slice of material (as silicon)

in·teg·ri·ty \in-'te-grə-tē\ *n* **1** : adherence to a code of values : INCORRUPTIBILITY **2** : SOUNDNESS **3** : COMPLETENESS

in·teg·u·ment \in-'te-gyə-mənt\ *n* : a covering layer (as a skin or cuticle) of an organism

in·tel·lect \'int-ºl-ıekt\ *n* **1** : the power of knowing : the capacity for knowledge **2** : the capacity for rational or intelligent thought esp. when highly developed **3** : a person with great intellectual powers

in·tel·lec·tu·al \int-ºl-'ek-chə-wəl\ *adj* **1** : of, relating to, or performed by the intellect : RATIONAL **2** : given to study, reflection, and speculation **3** : engaged in activity requiring the creative use of the intellect — **intellectual** *n* — **in·tel·lec·tu·al·ly** *adv*

in·tel·lec·tu·al·ism \-chə-wə-ıli-zəm\ *n* : devotion to the exercise of intellect or to intellectual pursuits

in·tel·li·gence \in-'te-lə-jəns\ *n* **1** : ability to learn and understand or to deal with new or trying situations **2** : mental acuteness **3** : INFORMATION, NEWS **4** : an agency engaged in obtaining information esp. concerning an enemy or possible enemy; *also* : the information so gained

intelligence quotient *n* : a number often used as a measure of a person's intelligence

in·tel·li·gent \in-'te-lə-jənt\ *adj* [L *intelligens*, fr. *intelligere* to understand, fr. *inter* between + *legere* to select] : having or showing intelligence or intellect — **in·tel·li·gent·ly** *adv*

in·tel·li·gen·tsia \in-ıte-lə-'jent-sē-ə, -ıgent-\ *n* [Russ *intelligentsiya*, fr. L *intelligentia* intelligence] : intellectuals forming a vanguard or elite

in·tel·li·gi·ble \in-'te-lə-jə-bəl\ *adj* : capable of being understood or comprehended — **in·tel·li·gi·bil·i·ty** \-ıte-lə-jə-'bi-lə-tē\ *n* — **in·tel·li·gi·bly** \-'te-lə-jə-blē\ *adv*

in·tem·per·ance \(ı)in-'tem-pə-rəns\ *n* : lack of moderation; *esp* : habitual or excessive drinking of intoxicants — **in·tem·per·ate** \-pə-rət\ *adj* — **in·tem·per·ate·ness** *n*

in·tend \in-'tend\ *vb* [ME *entenden, intenden,* fr. MF *entendre* to purpose, fr. L *intendere* to stretch out, aim at, fr. *tendere* to stretch] **1** : to have in mind as a purpose or aim **2** : to design for a specified use or future

in·ten·dant \in-'ten-dənt\ *n* : an official (as a governor) esp. under the French, Spanish, or Portuguese monarchies

¹in·tend·ed *adj* **1** : expected to be such in the future; *esp* : BETROTHED **2** : INTENTIONAL

²intended *n* : an engaged person

in·tense \in-'tens\ *adj* **1** : existing in an extreme degree **2** : marked by great zeal, energy, or eagerness **3** : showing strong feeling; *also* : deeply felt — **in·tense·ly** *adv*

in·ten·si·fy \in-'ten-sə-ˌfī\ vb **-fied; -fy·ing 1** : to make or become intense or more intensive **2** : to make more acute : SHARPEN syn aggravate, heighten, enhance, magnify — **in·ten·si·fi·ca·tion** \-ˌten-sə-fə-'kā-shən\ n
in·ten·si·ty \in-'ten-sə-tē\ n, pl **-ties 1** : the quality or state of being intense; esp : degree of strength, energy, or force
¹in·ten·sive \in-'ten-siv\ adj **1** : highly concentrated **2** : serving to give emphasis — **in·ten·sive·ly** adv
²intensive n : an intensive word, particle, or prefix
intensive care n : special medical equipment and services for taking care of seriously ill patients ⟨an intensive care unit⟩
¹in·tent \in-'tent\ n **1** : the state of mind with which an act is done : VOLITION **2** : PURPOSE, AIM **3** : MEANING, SIGNIFICANCE
²intent adj **1** : directed with keen attention ⟨an ~ gaze⟩ **2** : ENGROSSED; also : DETERMINED — **in·tent·ly** adv — **in·tent·ness** n
in·ten·tion \in-'ten-chən\ n **1** : a determination to act in a certain way **2** : PURPOSE, AIM, END syn intent, design, object, objective, goal
in·ten·tion·al \in-'ten-chə-nəl\ adj : done by intention or design : INTENDED — **in·ten·tion·al·ly** adv
in·ter \in-'tər\ vb **in·terred; in·ter·ring** : BURY
in·ter·ac·tion \ˌin-tər-'ak-shən\ n : mutual or reciprocal action or influence — **in·ter·act** \-'akt\ vb
in·ter·ac·tive \-'ak-tiv\ adj **1** : mutually or reciprocally active **2** : allowing two-way electronic communications (as between a person and a computer) — **in·ter·ac·tive·ly** adv
in·ter alia \ˌin-tər-'ā-lē-ə, -'ä-\ adv : among other things
in·ter·atom·ic \ˌin-tər-ə-'tä-mik\ adj : existing or acting between atoms
in·ter·breed \-'brēd\ vb **-bred** \-'bred\; **-breed·ing** : to breed together
in·ter·ca·la·ry \in-'tər-kə-ˌler-ē\ adj **1** : INTERCALATED ⟨February 29 is an ~ day⟩ **2** : INTERPOLATED
in·ter·ca·late \-ˌlāt\ vb **-lat·ed; -lat·ing 1** : to insert (as a day) in a calendar **2** : to insert between or among existing elements or layers — **in·ter·ca·la·tion** \-ˌtər-kə-'lā-shən\ n
in·ter·cede \ˌin-tər-'sēd\ vb **-ced·ed; -ced·ing** : to act between parties with a view to reconciling differences
¹in·ter·cept \ˌin-tər-'sept\ vb **1** : to stop or interrupt the progress or course of **2** : to include (as part of a curve or solid) between two points, curves, or surfaces **3** : to gain possession of (an opponent's pass in football) — **in·ter·cep·tion** \-'sep-shən\ n
²in·ter·cept \'in-tər-ˌsept\ n : INTERCEPTION; esp : the interception of a target by an interceptor or missile
in·ter·cep·tor \ˌin-tər-'sep-tər\ n : a fighter plane designed for defense against attacking bombers
in·ter·ces·sion \ˌin-tər-'se-shən\ n **1** : MEDIATION **2** : prayer or petition in favor of another — **in·ter·ces·sor** \-'se-sər\ n — **in·ter·ces·so·ry** \-'se-sə-rē\ adj
¹in·ter·change \ˌin-tər-'chānj\ vb **1** : to put each in the place of the other **2** : EXCHANGE **3** : to change places mutually — **in·ter·change·able** \-'chān-jə-bəl\ adj — **in·ter·change·ably** \-blē\ adv
²in·ter·change \'in-tər-ˌchānj\ n **1** : EXCHANGE **2** : a highway junction that by separated levels permits passage between highways without crossing traffic streams
in·ter·col·le·giate \ˌin-tər-kə-'lē-jət\ adj : existing or carried on between colleges
in·ter·com \'in-tər-ˌkäm\ n : a two-way system for localized communication
in·ter·con·ti·nen·tal \-ˌkänt-ᵊn-'ent-ᵊl\ adj : extending among or carried on between continents ⟨~ trade⟩ **2** : capable of traveling between continents ⟨~ ballistic missiles⟩
in·ter·course \'in-tər-ˌkōrs\ n **1** : connection or dealings between persons or nations **2** : physical sexual

contact between individuals that involves the genitalia of at least one person ⟨oral ~⟩; esp : SEXUAL INTERCOURSE
in·ter·de·nom·i·na·tion·al \ˌin-tər-di-ˌnä-mə-'nā-shə-nəl\ adj : involving different denominations
in·ter·de·part·men·tal \ˌin-tər-di-ˌpärt-'ment-ᵊl, -ˌdē-\ adj : carried on between or involving different departments (as of a college)
in·ter·de·pen·dent \ˌin-tər-di-'pen-dənt\ adj : dependent upon one another — **in·ter·de·pen·dence** \-dəns\ n
in·ter·dict \ˌin-tər-'dikt\ vb **1** : to prohibit by decree **2** : to destroy, cut off, or damage (as an enemy line of supply) — **in·ter·dic·tion** \-'dik-shən\ n
in·ter·dis·ci·plin·ary \-'di-sə-plə-ˌner-ē\ adj : involving two or more academic, scientific, or artistic disciplines
¹in·ter·est \'in-trəst; 'in-tə-rəst, -ˌrest\ n **1** : right, title, or legal share in something **2** : a charge for borrowed money that is generally a percentage of the amount borrowed; also : the return received by capital on its investment **3** : WELFARE, BENEFIT; also : SELF-INTEREST **4** : CURIOSITY, CONCERN **5** : readiness to be concerned with or moved by an object or class of objects **6** : a quality in a thing that arouses interest
²interest vb **1** : to persuade to participate or engage **2** : to engage the attention of
in·ter·est·ing adj : holding the attention — **in·ter·est·ing·ly** adv
¹in·ter·face \'in-tər-ˌfās\ n **1** : a surface forming a common boundary of two bodies, spaces, or phases ⟨an oil-water ~⟩ **2** : the place at which two independent systems meet and act on or communicate with each other ⟨the man-machine ~⟩ **3** : the means by which interaction or communication is achieved at an interface — **in·ter·fa·cial** \ˌin-tər-'fā-shəl\ adj
²interface vb **-faced; -fac·ing 1** : to connect by means of an interface **2** : to serve as an interface
in·ter·faith \ˌin-tər-'fāth\ adj : involving persons of different religious faiths
in·ter·fere \ˌin-tər-'fir\ vb **-fered; -fer·ing** [MF (s') entreferir to strike one another, fr. OF, fr. entre between, among + ferir to strike, fr. L ferire] **1** : to come in collision or be in opposition : CLASH **2** : to enter into the affairs of others **3** : to affect one another
in·ter·fer·ence \-'fir-əns\ n **1** : the act or process of interfering **2** : something that interferes : OBSTRUCTION **3** : the mutual effect on meeting of two waves resulting in areas of increased and decreased amplitude **4** : the blocking of an opponent in football to make way for the ballcarrier **5** : the illegal hindering of an opponent in sports
in·ter·fer·om·e·ter \ˌin-tər-fə-'rä-mə-tər\ n : a device that uses the interference of waves (as of light) for making precise measurements — **in·ter·fer·om·e·try** \-fə-'rä-mə-trē\ n
in·ter·fer·on \ˌin-tər-'fir-ˌän\ n : any of a group of antiviral proteins of low molecular weight produced usu. by animal cells in response to a virus, a parasite in the cell, or a chemical
in·ter·ga·lac·tic \ˌin-tər-gə-'lak-tik\ adj : relating to or situated in the spaces between galaxies
in·ter·gla·cial \-'glā-shəl\ n : a warm period between successive glaciations
in·ter·gov·ern·men·tal \-ˌgə-vərn-'ment-ᵊl\ adj : existing or occurring between two governments or levels of government
in·ter·im \'in-tə-rəm\ n [L, adv., meanwhile, fr. inter between] : a time intervening : INTERVAL — **interim** adj
¹in·te·ri·or \in-'tir-ē-ər\ adj **1** : lying, occurring, or functioning within the limiting boundaries : INSIDE, INNER **2** : remote from the surface, border, or shore : INLAND
²interior n **1** : the inland part (as of a country) **2** : INSIDE

3 : the internal affairs of a state or nation **4** : a scene or view of the interior of a building

interior decoration *n* : INTERIOR DESIGN — **interior decorator** *n*

interior design *n* : the art or practice of planning and supervising the design and execution of architectural interiors and their furnishings — **interior designer** *n*

interj *abbr* interjection

in·ter·ject \in-tər-'jekt\ *vb* : to throw in between or among other things

in·ter·jec·tion \in-tər-'jek-shən\ *n* : an exclamatory word (as *ouch*) — **in·ter·jec·tion·al·ly** \-shə-nə-lē\ *adv*

in·ter·lace \in-tər-'lās\ *vb* **1** : to unite by or as if by lacing together : INTERWEAVE **2** : INTERSPERSE

in·ter·lard \in-tər-'lärd\ *vb* : to vary by inserting or interjecting something

in·ter·leave \in-tər-'lēv\ *vb* **-leaved; -leav·ing** : to arrange in alternate layers

in·ter·leu·kin \in-tər-'lü-kən\ *n* : any of several proteins of low molecular weight that are produced by cells of the body and regulate the immune system and immune responses

¹in·ter·line \in-tər-'līn\ *vb* : to insert between lines already written or printed

²interline *vb* : to provide (as a coat) with an interlining

in·ter·lin·ear \in-tər-'li-nē-ər\ *adj* : inserted between lines already written or printed ⟨an ∼ translation of a text⟩

in·ter·lin·ing \'in-tər-ılī-niŋ\ *n* : a lining (as of a coat) between the ordinary lining and the outside fabric

in·ter·link \in-tər-'liŋk\ *vb* : to link together

in·ter·lock \in-tər-'läk\ *vb* **1** : to engage or interlace together : lock together : UNITE **2** : to connect so that action of one part affects action of another part — **in·ter·lock** \'in-tər-ıläk\ *n*

in·ter·loc·u·tor \in-tər-'lä-kyə-tər\ *n* : one who takes part in dialogue or conversation

in·ter·loc·u·to·ry \-'tōr-ē\ *adj* : pronounced during the progress of a legal action and having only provisional force ⟨an ∼ decree⟩

in·ter·lope \in-tər-'lōp\ *vb* **-loped; -lop·ing 1** : to encroach on the rights (as in trade) of others **2** : INTRUDE, INTERFERE — **in·ter·lop·er** *n*

in·ter·lude \'in-tər-ılüd\ *n* **1** : a usu. short simple play or dramatic entertainment **2** : an intervening period, space, or event **3** : a piece of music inserted between the parts of a longer composition or a religious service

in·ter·mar·riage \in-tər-'mar-ij\ *n* **1** : marriage within one's own group as required by custom **2** : marriage between members of different groups

in·ter·mar·ry \-'mar-ē\ *vb* **1** : to marry each other **2** : to marry within a group **3** : to become connected by intermarriage

¹in·ter·me·di·ary \in-tər-'mē-dē-ıer-ē\ *adj* **1** : INTERMEDIATE **2** : acting as a mediator

²intermediary *n, pl* **-ar·ies** : MEDIATOR, GO-BETWEEN

¹in·ter·me·di·ate \in-tər-'mē-dē-ət\ *adj* : being or occurring at the middle place or degree or between extremes

²intermediate *n* **1** : one that is intermediate **2** : INTERMEDIARY

intermediate school *n* **1** : JUNIOR HIGH SCHOOL **2** : a school usu. comprising grades 4–6

in·ter·ment \in-'tər-mənt\ *n* : BURIAL

in·ter·mez·zo \in-tər-'met-sō, -'med-zō\ *n, pl* **-zi** \-sē, -zē\ *or* **-zos** [It, ultim. fr. L *intermedius* intermediate] : a short movement connecting major sections of an extended musical work (as a symphony); *also* : a short independent instrumental composition

in·ter·mi·na·ble \(ı)in-'tər-mə-nə-bəl\ *adj* : ENDLESS; *esp* : wearisomely protracted — **in·ter·mi·na·bly** \-blē\ *adv*

in·ter·min·gle \in-tər-'miŋ-gəl\ *vb* : to mingle or mix together

in·ter·mis·sion \in-tər-'mi-shən\ *n* **1** : INTERRUPTION,

BREAK **2** : a temporary halt esp. in a public performance

in·ter·mit \-'mit\ *vb* **-mit·ted; -mit·ting** : DISCONTINUE; *also* : to be intermittent

in·ter·mit·tent \-'mit-ənt\ *adj* : coming and going at intervals **syn** recurrent, periodic, alternate — **in·ter·mit·tent·ly** *adv*

in·ter·mix \in-tər-'miks\ *vb* : to mix together : INTERMINGLE — **in·ter·mix·ture** \-'miks-chər\ *n*

in·ter·mo·lec·u·lar \-mə-'le-kyə-lər\ *adj* : existing or acting between molecules

in·ter·mon·tane \in-tər-'män-ıtān\ *adj* : situated between mountains

¹in·tern \'in-ıtərn, in-'tərn\ *vb* : to confine or impound esp. during a war — **in·tern·ee** \(ı)in-ıtər-'nē\ *n* — **in·tern·ment** \in-'tərn-mənt\ *n*

²in·tern *or* **in·terne** \'in-ıtərn\ *n* : an advanced student or recent graduate (as in medicine) gaining supervised practical experience — **in·tern·ship** *n*

³in·tern \'in-ıtərn\ *vb* : to act as an intern

in·ter·nal \in-'tərn-əl\ *adj* **1** : INWARD, INTERIOR **2** : relating to or located in the inside of the body ⟨∼ pain⟩ **3** : of, relating to, or occurring within the confines of an organized structure ⟨∼ affairs⟩ **4** : of, relating to, or existing within the mind **5** : INTRINSIC, INHERENT — **in·ter·nal·ly** *adv*

internal combustion engine *n* : an engine in which the fuel is ignited within the engine cylinder

internal medicine *n* : a branch of medicine that deals with the diagnosis and treatment of diseases not requiring surgery

¹in·ter·na·tion·al \in-tər-'na-shə-nəl\ *adj* **1** : common to or affecting two or more nations ⟨∼ trade⟩ **2** : of, relating to, or constituting a group having members in two or more nations — **in·ter·na·tion·al·ly** *adv*

²international *n* : one that is international; *esp* : an organization of international scope

in·ter·na·tion·al·ise *Brit var of* INTERNATIONALIZE

in·ter·na·tion·al·ism \-'na-shə-nə-ıli-zəm\ *n* : a policy of cooperation among nations; *also* : an attitude favoring such a policy

in·ter·na·tion·al·ize \-'na-shə-nə-ılīz\ *vb* : to make international; *esp* : to place under international control

in·ter·ne·cine \in-tər-'ne-ısēn, -'nē-ısīn\ *adj* [L *internecinus*, fr. *internecare* to destroy, kill, fr. *necare* to kill, fr. *nec-, nex* violent death] **1** : DEADLY; *esp* : mutually destructive **2** : of, relating to, or involving conflict within a group ⟨∼ feuds⟩

in·ter·nist \'in-ıtər-nist\ *n* : a physician who specializes in internal medicine

in·ter·nun·cio \in-tər-'nən-sē-ıō, -'nun-\ *n* [It *internunzio*] : a papal legate of lower rank than a nuncio

in·ter·of·fice \-'ò-fəs\ *adj* : functioning or communicating between the offices of an organization

in·ter·per·son·al \-'pərs-ən-əl\ *adj* : being, relating to, or involving relations between persons — **in·ter·per·son·al·ly** *adv*

in·ter·plan·e·tary \in-tər-'pla-nə-ıter-ē\ *adj* : existing, carried on, or operating between planets ⟨∼ space⟩

in·ter·play \'in-tər-ıplā\ *n* : INTERACTION

in·ter·po·late \in-'tər-pə-ılāt\ *vb* **-lat·ed; -lat·ing 1** : to change (as a text) by inserting new or foreign matter **2** : to insert (as words) into a text or into a conversation **3** : to estimate values of (a function) between two known values — **in·ter·po·la·tion** \-ıtər-pə-'lā-shən\ *n*

in·ter·pose \in-tər-'pōz\ *vb* **-posed; -pos·ing 1** : to place between **2** : to thrust in : INTRUDE, INTERRUPT **3** : to inject between parts of a conversation or argument **4** : to come or be between **syn** interfere, intercede, intermediate, intervene — **in·ter·po·si·tion** \-pə-'zi-shən\ *n*

in·ter·pret \in-'tər-prət\ *vb* **1** : to explain the meaning of; *also* : to act as an interpreter : TRANSLATE **2** : to understand according to individual belief, judgment, or interest **3** : to represent artistically — **in·ter·pret·er** *n* — **in·ter·pre·tive** \-'tər-prə-tiv\ *adj*

in·ter·pre·ta·tion \in-₁tər-prə-'tā-shən\ *n* **1** : EXPLANATION **2** : an instance of artistic interpretation in performance or adaptation — **in·ter·pre·ta·tive** \-'tər-prə-₁tā-tiv\ *adj*

in·ter·ra·cial \-'rā-shəl\ *adj* : of, involving, or designed for members of different races

in·ter·reg·num \in-tə-'reg-nəm\ *n, pl* **-nums** *or* **-na** \-nə\ **1** : the time during which a throne is vacant between two successive reigns or regimes **2** : a pause in a continuous series

in·ter·re·late \in-tə-ri-'lāt\ *vb* : to bring into or have a mutual relationship — **in·ter·re·lat·ed·ness** \-lā-təd-nəs\ *n* — **in·ter·re·la·tion** \-'lā-shən\ *n* — **in·ter·re·la·tion·ship** *n*

interrog *abbr* interrogative

in·ter·ro·gate \in-'ter-ə-₁gāt\ *vb* **-gat·ed; -gat·ing** : to question esp. formally and systematically : ASK — **in·ter·ro·ga·tion** \-₁ter-ə-'gā-shən\ *n* — **in·ter·ro·ga·tor** \-'ter-ə-₁gā-tər\ *n*

in·ter·rog·a·tive \in-tə-'rä-gə-tiv\ *adj* : asking a question ⟨~ sentence⟩ — **interrogative** *n* — **in·ter·rog·a·tive·ly** *adv*

in·ter·rog·a·to·ry \in-tə-'rä-gə-₁tōr-ē\ *adj* : INTERROGATIVE

in·ter·rupt \in-tə-'rəpt\ *vb* **1** : to stop or hinder by breaking in **2** : to break the uniformity or continuity of **3** : to break in by speaking while another is speaking — **in·ter·rupt·er** *n* — **in·ter·rup·tion** \-'rəp-shən\ *n* — **in·ter·rup·tive** \-'rəp-tiv\ *adj*

in·ter·scho·las·tic \in-tər-skə-'las-tik\ *adj* : existing or carried on between schools

in·ter·sect \in-tər-'sekt\ *vb* **1** : to divide by passing through or across **2** : to meet and cross (as at a point); *also* : OVERLAP — **in·ter·sec·tion** \-'sek-shən\ *n*

in·ter·sperse \in-tər-'spərs\ *vb* **-spersed; -spers·ing 1** : to place something at intervals in or among **2** : to insert at intervals among other things — **in·ter·sper·sion** \-'spər-zhən\ *n*

¹in·ter·state \in-tər-'stāt\ *adj* : relating to, including, or connecting two or more states esp. of the U.S.

²in·ter·state \'in-tər-₁stāt\ *n* : an interstate highway

in·ter·stel·lar \in-tər-'ste-lər\ *adj* : located or taking place among the stars

in·ter·stice \in-'tər-stəs\ *n, pl* **-stic·es** \-stə-₁sēz, -stə-₁səz\ : a space that intervenes between things : CHINK — **in·ter·sti·tial** \in-tər-'sti-shəl\ *adj*

in·ter·tid·al \in-tər-'tīd-ᵊl\ *adj* : of, relating to, or being the area that is above low-tide mark but exposed to tidal flooding ⟨life in the ~ mud⟩

in·ter·twine \-'twīn\ *vb* : to twine or cause to twine about one another : INTERLACE — **in·ter·twine·ment** *n*

in·ter·twist \-'twist\ *vb* : INTERTWINE

in·ter·ur·ban \-'ər-bən\ *adj* : connecting cities or towns

in·ter·val \'in-tər-vəl\ *n* [ME *intervalle,* fr. MF, fr. L *intervallum* space between ramparts, interval, fr. *inter-* between + *vallum* rampart] **1** : a space of time between events or states : PAUSE **2** : a space between objects, units, or states **3** : the difference in pitch between two tones

in·ter·vene \in-tər-'vēn\ *vb* **-vened; -ven·ing 1** : to occur, fall, or come between points of time or between events **2** : to enter or appear as an unrelated feature or circumstance ⟨rain *intervened* and we postponed the trip⟩ **3** : to come in or between in order to stop, settle, or modify ⟨~ in a quarrel⟩ **4** : to occur or lie between two things — **in·ter·ven·tion** \-'ven-chən\ *n*

in·ter·ven·tion·ism \-'ven-chə-₁ni-zəm\ *n* : interference by one country in the political affairs of another — **in·ter·ven·tion·ist** \-'ven-chə-nist\ *n or adj*

in·ter·view \'in-tər-₁vyü\ *n* **1** : a formal consultation usu. to evaluate qualifications **2** : a meeting at which a writer or reporter obtains information from a per-

son; *also* : the recorded or written account of such a meeting — **interview** *vb* — **in·ter·view·ee** \in-tər-(₁)vyü-'ē\ *n* — **in·ter·view·er** *n*

in·ter·vo·cal·ic \in-tər-vō-'ka-lik\ *adj* : immediately preceded and immediately followed by a vowel

in·ter·weave \in-tər-'wēv\ *vb* **-wove** \-'wōv\ *also* **-weaved; -wo·ven** \-'wō-vən\ *also* **-weaved; -weav·ing** : to weave or blend together : INTERTWINE, INTERMINGLE — **interwoven** *adj*

in·tes·tate \in-'tes-₁tāt, -tət\ *adj* **1** : having made no valid will ⟨died ~⟩ **2** : not disposed of by will ⟨~ estate⟩

in·tes·tine \in-'tes-tən\ *n* : the tubular part of the alimentary canal that extends from stomach to anus and consists of a long narrow upper part (**small intestine**) followed by a broader shorter lower part (**large intestine**) — **in·tes·ti·nal** \-tən-ᵊl\ *adj*

¹in·ti·mate \'in-tə-₁māt\ *vb* **-mat·ed; -mat·ing 1** : ANNOUNCE, NOTIFY **2** : to communicate indirectly : HINT — **in·ti·ma·tion** \in-tə-mā-shən\ *n*

²in·ti·mate \'in-tə-mət\ *adj* **1** : INTRINSIC; *also* : INNERMOST **2** : marked by very close association, contact, or familiarity **3** : marked by a warm friendship **4** : suggesting informal warmth or privacy **5** : of a very personal or private nature — **in·ti·ma·cy** \'in-tə-mə-sē\ *n* — **in·ti·mate·ly** *adv*

³in·ti·mate \'in-tə-mət\ *n* : an intimate friend, associate, or confidant

in·tim·i·date \in-'ti-mə-₁dāt\ *vb* **-dat·ed; -dat·ing** : to make timid or fearful : FRIGHTEN; *esp* : to compel or deter by or as if by threats **syn** cow, bulldoze, bully, browbeat — **in·tim·i·dat·ing·ly** *adv* — **in·tim·i·da·tion** \-₁ti-mə-'dā-shən\ *n*

intl *or* **intnl** *abbr* international

in·to \'in-tü\ *prep* **1** : to the inside of ⟨ran ~ the house⟩ **2** : to the state, condition, or form of ⟨got ~ trouble⟩ **3** : AGAINST ⟨ran ~ a wall⟩

in·tol·er·a·ble \(₁)in-'tä-lə-rə-bəl\ *adj* **1** : UNBEARABLE **2** : EXCESSIVE — **in·tol·er·a·bly** \-blē\ *adv*

in·tol·er·ant \(₁)in-'tä-lə-rənt\ *adj* **1** : unable or unwilling to endure **2** : unwilling to grant equality, freedom, or other social rights : BIGOTED — **in·tol·er·ance** \-rəns\ *n*

in·to·na·tion \in-tō-'nā-shən\ *n* **1** : the act of intoning and esp. of chanting **2** : something that is intoned **3** : the manner of singing, playing, or uttering tones **4** : the rise and fall in pitch of the voice in speech

in·tone \in-'tōn\ *vb* **in·toned; in·ton·ing** : to utter in musical or prolonged tones : CHANT

in to·to \in-'tō-tō\ *adv* [L, on the whole] : TOTALLY, ENTIRELY

in·tox·i·cant \in-'täk-si-kənt\ *n* : something that intoxicates; *esp* : an alcoholic drink — **intoxicant** *adj*

in·tox·i·cate \-sə-₁kāt\ *vb* **-cat·ed; -cat·ing 1** : to affect by a drug (as alcohol or cocaine) esp. to the point of physical or mental impairment **2** : to excite to enthusiasm or frenzy — **in·tox·i·ca·tion** \-₁täk-sə-'kā-shən\ *n*

in·trac·ta·ble \(₁)in-'trak-tə-bəl\ *adj* : not easily controlled : OBSTINATE

in·tra·mu·ral \-'myür-əl\ *adj* : being or occurring within the walls or limits (as of a city or college) ⟨~ sports⟩

in·tra·mus·cu·lar \-'məs-kyə-lər\ *adj* : situated within, occurring in, or administered by entering a muscle — **in·tra·mus·cu·lar·ly** *adv*

intrans *abbr* intransitive

in·tran·si·gent \-jənt\ *adj* : UNCOMPROMISING; *also* : IRRECONCILABLE — **in·tran·si·gence** \-jəns\ *n* — **intransigent** *n*

in·tran·si·tive \(₁)in-'tran-sə-tiv, -zə-\ *adj* : not transitive; *esp* : not having or containing an object ⟨an ~ verb⟩ — **in·tran·si·tive·ly** *adv* — **in·tran·si·tive·ness** *n*

in·tra·state \in-trə-'stāt\ *adj* : existing or occurring within a state

in·tra·uter·ine device \-'yü-tə-rən-, -₁rīn-\ *n* : a device (as a spiral of plastic) inserted and left in the uterus to prevent pregnancy

in·tra·ve·nous \ˌin-trə-ˈvē-nəs\ *adj* : being within or entering by way of the veins; *also* : used in or using intravenous procedures — **in·tra·ve·nous·ly** *adv*

intrench *var of* ENTRENCH

in·trep·id \in-ˈtre-pəd\ *adj* : characterized by resolute fearlessness, fortitude, and endurance — **in·tre·pid·i·ty** \ˌin-trə-ˈpi-də-tē\ *n*

in·tri·cate \ˈin-tri-kət\ *adj* [ME, fr. L *intricatus*, pp. of *intricare* to entangle, fr. *tricae* trifles, complications] **1** : having many complexly interrelated parts : COMPLICATED **2** : difficult to follow, understand, or solve — **in·tri·ca·cy** \-tri-kə-sē\ *n* — **in·tri·cate·ly** *adv*

¹**in·trigue** \in-ˈtrēg\ *vb* **in·trigued**; **in·tri·gu·ing 1** : to accomplish by intrigue **2** : to carry on an intrigue; *esp* : PLOT, SCHEME **3** : to arouse the interest, desire, or curiosity of — **in·tri·gu·ing·ly** *adv*

²**in·trigue** \ˈin-ˌtrēg, in-ˈtrēg\ *n* **1** : a secret scheme : MACHINATION **2** : a clandestine love affair

in·trin·sic \in-ˈtrin-zik, -sik\ *adj* : belonging to the essential nature or constitution of a thing — **in·trin·si·cal·ly** \-zi-k(ə-)lē, -si-\ *adv*

introd *abbr* introduction

in·tro·duce \ˌin-trə-ˈdüs, -ˈdyüs\ *vb* **-duced**; **-duc·ing 1** : to lead or bring in esp. for the first time **2** : to bring into practice or use **3** : to cause to be acquainted **4** : to present for discussion **5** : PLACE, INSERT **syn** insinuate, interpolate, interpose, interject — **in·tro·duc·tion** \-ˈdək-shən\ *n* — **in·tro·duc·to·ry** \-ˈdək-tə-rē\ *adj*

in·troit \ˈin-ˌtroit, -ˌtrō-ət\ *n* **1** *often cap* : the first part of the traditional proper of the Mass **2** : a piece of music sung or played at the beginning of a worship service

in·tro·spec·tion \-ˈspek-shən\ *n* : a reflective looking inward : an examination of one's own thoughts or feelings — **in·tro·spect** \ˌin-trə-ˈspekt\ *vb* — **in·tro·spec·tive** \-ˈspek-tiv\ *adj* — **in·tro·spec·tive·ly** *adv*

in·tro·vert \ˈin-trə-ˌvərt\ *n* : a reserved or shy person — **in·tro·ver·sion** \ˌin-trə-ˈvər-zhən\ *n* — **introvert** *adj* — **in·tro·vert·ed** \ˈin-trə-ˌvər-təd\ *adj*

in·trude \in-ˈtrüd\ *vb* **in·trud·ed**; **in·trud·ing 1** : to thrust, enter, or force in or upon **2** : ENCROACH, TRESPASS — **in·trud·er** *n* — **in·tru·sion** \-ˈtrü-zhən\ *n* — **in·tru·sive** \-ˈtrü-siv\ *adj* — **in·tru·sive·ness** *n*

intrust *var of* ENTRUST

in·tu·it \in-ˈtü-ət, -ˈtyü-\ *vb* : to apprehend by intuition

in·tu·ition \ˌin-tü-ˈwi-shən, -tyü-\ *n* **1** : quick and ready insight **2** : the power or faculty of knowing things without conscious reasoning — **in·tu·i·tive** \in-ˈtü-ə-tiv, -ˈtyü-\ *adj* — **in·tu·i·tive·ly** *adv*

In·u·it \ˈi-nü-wət, ˈin-yü-\ *n* [Inuit *inuit*, pl. of *inuk* person] **1** : a member of the Eskimo people of No. America and Greenland **2** : the language of the Inuit people

in·un·date \ˈi-nən-ˌdāt\ *vb* **-dat·ed**; **-dat·ing** : to cover with or as if with a flood : OVERFLOW — **in·un·da·tion** \ˌi-nən-ˈdā-shən\ *n*

in·ure \i-ˈnu̇r, -ˈnyu̇r\ *vb* **in·ured**; **in·ur·ing** [ME *enuren*, fr. *en-* in + *ure*, n., use, custom, fr. MF *uevre* work, practice, fr. L *opera* work] **1** : to accustom to accept something undesirable **2** : to become of advantage

inv *abbr* **1** inventor **2** invoice

in vac·uo \in-ˈva-kyü-ˌwō\ *adv* [L] : in a vacuum

in·vade \in-ˈvād\ *vb* **in·vad·ed**; **in·vad·ing 1** : to enter for conquest or plunder **2** : to encroach upon **3** : to spread through and usu. harm (germs ∼ the tissues) — **in·vad·er** *n*

¹**in·val·id** \(ˌ)in-ˈva-ləd\ *adj* : being without foundation or force in fact, reason, or law — **in·va·lid·i·ty** \ˌin-və-ˈli-də-tē\ *n* — **in·val·id·ly** *adv*

²**in·va·lid** \ˈin-və-ləd\ *adj* : being in ill health : SICKLY

³**invalid** \ˈin-və-ləd\ *n* : a person in usu. chronic ill health — **in·va·lid·ism** \-lə-ˌdi-zəm\ *n*

⁴**in·va·lid** \ˈin-və-ləd, -ˌlid\ *vb* **1** : to remove from active

duty by reason of sickness or disability **2** : to make sickly or disabled

in·val·i·date \(ˌ)in-ˈva-lə-ˌdāt\ *vb* : to make invalid; *esp* : to weaken or make valueless — **in·val·i·da·tion** \in-ˌva-lə-ˈdā-shən\ *n*

in·valu·able \-ˈval-yə-bəl, -yə-wə-bəl\ *adj* : valuable beyond estimation

in·vari·able \-ˈver-ē-ə-bəl\ *adj* : not changing or capable of change : CONSTANT — **in·vari·ably** \-blē\ *adv*

in·va·sion \in-ˈvā-zhən\ *n* : an act or instance of invading; *esp* : entry of an army into a country for conquest

in·va·sive \in-ˈvā-siv, -ziv\ *adj* **1** : tending to spread ⟨∼ cancer cells⟩ **2** : involving entry into the living body (as by surgery) ⟨∼ therapy⟩

in·vec·tive \in-ˈvek-tiv\ *n* **1** : an abusive expression or speech **2** : abusive language — **invective** *adj*

in·veigh \in-ˈvā\ *vb* : to protest or complain bitterly or vehemently : RAIL

in·vei·gle \in-ˈvā-gəl, -ˈvē-\ *vb* **in·vei·gled**; **in·vei·gling** [modif. of MF *aveugler* to blind, hoodwink] **1** : to win over by flattery : ENTICE **2** : to acquire by ingenuity or flattery

in·vent \in-ˈvent\ *vb* **1** : to think up **2** : to create or produce for the first time — **in·ven·tor** \-ˈven-tər\ *n*

in·ven·tion \in-ˈven-chən\ *n* **1** : INVENTIVENESS **2** : a creation of the imagination; *esp* : a false conception **3** : a device, contrivance, or process originated after study and experiment **4** : the act or process of inventing

in·ven·tive \in-ˈven-tiv\ *adj* **1** : CREATIVE, INGENIOUS ⟨an ∼ composer⟩ **2** : characterized by invention ⟨an ∼ turn of mind⟩ — **in·ven·tive·ness** *n*

in·ven·to·ry \ˈin-vən-ˌtȯr-ē\ *n, pl* **-ries 1** : an itemized list of current goods or assets **2** : SURVEY, SUMMARY **3** : STOCK, SUPPLY **4** : the act or process of taking an inventory — **inventory** *vb*

¹**in·verse** \(ˌ)in-ˈvərs, ˈin-ˌvərs\ *adj* : opposite in order, nature, or effect : REVERSED — **in·verse·ly** *adv*

²**inverse** *n* : something inverse or resulting in or from inversion : OPPOSITE

in·ver·sion \in-ˈvər-zhən\ *n* **1** : a reversal of position, order, or relationship; *esp* : an increase of temperature with altitude through a layer of air **2** : the act or process of inverting

in·vert \in-ˈvərt\ *vb* **1** : to reverse in position, order, or relationship **2** : to turn upside down or inside out **3** : to turn inward

¹**in·ver·te·brate** \(ˌ)in-ˈvər-tə-brət, -ˌbrēt\ *adj* : lacking a backbone; *also* : of or relating to invertebrates

²**invertebrate** *n* : an invertebrate animal (as a jellyfish, insect, or worm)

¹**in·vest** \in-ˈvest\ *vb* **1** : to install formally in an office or honor **2** : to furnish with power or authority : VEST **3** : to cover completely : ENVELOP **4** : CLOTHE, ADORN **5** : BESIEGE **6** : to endow with a quality or characteristic

²**invest** *vb* **1** : to commit (money) in order to earn a financial return **2** : to expend for future benefits or advantages **3** : to make an investment — **in·ves·tor** \-ˈves-tər\ *n*

in·ves·ti·gate \in-ˈves-tə-ˌgāt\ *vb* **-gat·ed**; **-gat·ing** [L *investigare* to track, investigate, fr. *vestigium* footprint, track] : to study by close examination and systematic inquiry — **in·ves·ti·ga·tion** \-ˌves-tə-ˈgā-shən\ *n* — **in·ves·ti·ga·tive** \-ˈves-tə-ˌgā-tiv\ *adj* — **in·ves·ti·ga·tor** \-ˌgā-tər\ *n*

in·ves·ti·ture \in-ˈves-tə-ˌchu̇r, -chər\ *n* **1** : the act of ratifying or establishing in office **2** : something that covers or adorns

¹**in·vest·ment** \in-ˈvest-mənt\ *n* **1** : an outer layer : ENVELOPE **2** : INVESTITURE 1 **3** : BLOCKADE, SIEGE

²**investment** *n* : the outlay of money for income or profit; *also* : the sum invested or the property purchased

in·vet·er·ate \in-ˈve-tə-rət\ *adj* **1** : firmly established by age or long persistence **2** : confirmed in a habit

in·vi·a·ble \(ˌ)in-ˈvī-ə-bəl\ *adj* : incapable of surviving

in·vid·i·ous \in-ˈvi-dē-əs\ *adj* **1** : tending to cause discontent, animosity, or envy **2** : ENVIOUS **3** : OBNOXIOUS — **in·vid·i·ous·ly** *adv*

in·vig·o·rate \in-ˈvi-gə-ˌrāt\ *vb* **-rat·ed; -rat·ing** : to give life and energy to : ANIMATE — **in·vig·o·ra·tion** \-ˌvi-gə-ˈrā-shən\ *n*

in·vin·ci·ble \(ˌ)in-ˈvin-sə-bəl\ *adj* : incapable of being conquered, overcome, or subdued — **in·vin·ci·bil·i·ty** \-ˌvin-sə-ˈbi-lə-tē\ *n* — **in·vin·ci·bly** \-ˈvin-sə-blē\ *adv*

in·vi·o·la·ble \-ˈvī-ə-lə-bəl\ *adj* **1** : safe from violation or profanation **2** : UNASSAILABLE — **in·vi·o·la·bil·i·ty** \-ˌvī-ə-lə-ˈbi-lə-tē\ *n*

in·vi·o·late \-ˈvī-ə-lət\ *adj* : not violated or profaned : PURE

in·vis·i·ble \-ˈvi-zə-bəl\ *adj* **1** : incapable of being seen ⟨∼ to the naked eye⟩ **2** : HIDDEN **3** : IMPERCEPTIBLE, INCONSPICUOUS — **in·vis·i·bil·i·ty** \-ˌvi-zə-ˈbi-lə-tē\ *n* — **in·vis·i·bly** \-ˈvi-zə-blē\ *adv*

in·vi·ta·tion·al \ˌin-və-ˈtā-shə-nəl\ *adj* : limited to invited participants ⟨an ∼ tournament⟩ — **invitational** *n*

in·vite \in-ˈvīt\ *vb* **in·vit·ed; in·vit·ing 1** : ENTICE, TEMPT **2** : to increase the likelihood of **3** : to request the presence or participation of : ASK **4** : to request formally **5** : ENCOURAGE — **in·vi·ta·tion** \ˌin-və-ˈtā-shən\ *n*

in·vit·ing *adj* : ATTRACTIVE, TEMPTING

in vi·tro \in-ˈvē-trō, -ˈvī-, -ˈvi-\ *adv or adj* [NL, lit., in glass] : outside the living body and in an artificial environment ⟨*in vitro* fertilization⟩

in·vo·ca·tion \ˌin-və-ˈkā-shən\ *n* **1** : SUPPLICATION; *esp* : a prayer at the beginning of a service **2** : a formula for conjuring : INCANTATION

¹in·voice \ˈin-ˌvȯis\ *n* [modif. of MF *envois*, pl. of *envoi* message] : an itemized list of goods shipped usu. specifying the price and the terms of sale : BILL

²invoice *vb* **in·voiced; in·voic·ing** : to send an invoice to or for : BILL

in·voke \in-ˈvōk\ *vb* **in·voked; in·vok·ing 1** : to petition for help or support **2** : to appeal to or cite as authority ⟨∼ a law⟩ **3** : to call forth by incantation : CONJURE ⟨∼ spirits⟩ **4** : to make an earnest request for : SOLICIT **5** : to put into effect or operation **6** : to bring about : CAUSE

in·vol·un·tary \(ˌ)in-ˈvä-lən-ˌter-ē\ *adj* **1** : done contrary to or without choice **2** : COMPULSORY **3** : not controlled by the will : REFLEX ⟨∼ contractions⟩ — **in·vol·un·tar·i·ly** \-ˌvä-lən-ˈter-ə-lē\ *adv*

in·vo·lute \ˈin-və-ˌlüt\ *adj* : INVOLVED, INTRICATE

in·vo·lu·tion \ˌin-və-ˈlü-shən\ *n* **1** : the act or an instance of enfolding or entangling **2** : COMPLEXITY, INTRICACY

in·volve \in-ˈvälv\ *vb* **in·volved; in·volv·ing 1** : to draw in as a participant **2** : ENVELOP **3** : to occupy (as oneself) absorbingly; *esp* : to commit oneself emotionally **4** : to relate closely : CONNECT **5** : to have as part of itself : INCLUDE **6** : ENTAIL, IMPLY **7** : to have an effect on — **in·volve·ment** *n*

in·volved \-ˈvälvd\ *adj* : INTRICATE, COMPLEX ⟨an ∼ plot⟩

in·vul·ner·a·ble \(ˌ)in-ˈvəl-nə-rə-bəl\ *adj* **1** : incapable of being wounded, injured, or damaged **2** : immune to or proof against attack — **in·vul·ner·a·bil·i·ty** \-ˌvəl-nə-rə-ˈbi-lə-tē\ *n* — **in·vul·ner·a·bly** \-ˈvəl-nə-rə-blē\ *adv*

¹in·ward \ˈin-wərd\ *adj* **1** : situated on the inside **2** : MENTAL; *also* : SPIRITUAL **3** : directed toward the interior

²inward *or* **in·wards** \-wərdz\ *adv* **1** : toward the inside, center, or interior **2** : toward the inner being

in·ward·ly \ˈin-wərd-lē\ *adv* **1** : MENTALLY, SPIRITUALLY **2** : INTERNALLY ⟨bled ∼⟩ **3** : to oneself ⟨cursed ∼⟩

IOC *abbr* International Olympic Committee

io·dide \ˈī-ə-ˌdīd\ *n* : a compound of iodine with another element or group

io·dine \ˈī-ə-ˌdīn, -əd-ᵊn\ *n* **1** : a nonmetallic chemical element used esp. in medicine and photography — see ELEMENT table **2** : a solution of iodine used as a local antiseptic

io·dize \ˈī-ə-ˌdīz\ *vb* **io·dized; io·diz·ing** : to treat with iodine or an iodide

ion \ˈī-ən, ˈī-ˌän\ *n* [Gk, neut. of *iōn*, prp. of *ienai* to go; so called because in electrolysis it goes to one of the two poles] : an electrically charged particle, atom, or group of atoms — **ion·ic** \ī-ˈä-nik\ *adj*

-ion *n suffix* : act, process, state, or condition ⟨validation⟩

ion·ize \ˈī-ə-ˌnīz\ *vb* **ion·ized; ion·iz·ing 1** : to convert wholly or partly into ions **2** : to become ionized — **ion·iz·able** \ˌī-ə-ˈnī-zə-bəl\ *adj* — **ion·iza·tion** \ˌī-ə-nə-ˈzā-shən\ *n* — **ion·iz·er** \ˈī-ə-ˌnī-zər\ *n*

ion·o·sphere \ī-ˈä-nə-ˌsfir\ *n* : the part of the earth's atmosphere extending from about 30 miles (50 kilometers) to the exosphere that contains ionized atmospheric gases — **ion·o·spher·ic** \ī-ˌä-nə-ˈsfir-ik, -ˈsfer-\ *adj*

IOOF *abbr* Independent Order of Odd Fellows

io·ta \ī-ˈō-tə\ *n* [L, fr. Gk *iōta*] **1** : the 9th letter of the Greek alphabet — I or ι **2** : a very small quantity : JOT

IOU \ˌī-(ˌ)ō-ˈyü\ *n* : an acknowledgement of a debt

IP *abbr* innings pitched

ip·e·cac \ˈi-pi-ˌkak\ *n* [Pg *ipecacuanha*] : an emetic and expectorant drug used esp. as a syrup in treating accidental poisoning; *also* : either of two So. American plants or their rhizomes and roots used to make ipecac

ip·so fac·to \ˌip-sō-ˈfak-tō\ *adv* [NL, lit., by the fact itself] : by the very nature of the case

iq *abbr* [L *idem quod*] the same as

IQ \ˈī-ˈkyü\ *n* : INTELLIGENCE QUOTIENT

¹Ir *abbr* Irish

²Ir *symbol* iridium

IR *abbr* infrared

¹IRA \ˌī-(ˌ)är-ˈā; ˈī-rə\ *n* [*i*ndividual *r*etirement *a*ccount] : a savings account in which a person may make tax deductible deposits up to a stipulated amount each year with deposits and interest taxable after the person's retirement

²IRA *abbr* Irish Republican Army

Ira·ni·an \i-ˈrā-nē-ən *also* -ˈrä-\ *n* : a native or inhabitant of Iran — **Iranian** *adj*

Iraqi \i-ˈrä-kē, -ˈra-\ *n* : a native or inhabitant of Iraq — **Iraqi** *adj*

iras·ci·ble \i-ˈra-sə-bəl\ *adj* : marked by hot temper and easily provoked anger syn choleric, testy, touchy, cranky, cross — **iras·ci·bil·i·ty** \-ˌra-sə-ˈbi-lə-tē\ *n*

irate \ī-ˈrāt\ *adj* **1** : roused to ire **2** : arising from anger — **irate·ly** *adv*

ire \ˈīr\ *n* : ANGER, WRATH — **ire·ful** *adj*

Ire *abbr* Ireland

iren·ic \ī-ˈre-nik\ *adj* : favoring, conducive to, or operating toward peace or conciliation

ir·i·des·cence \ˌir-ə-ˈdes-ᵊns\ *n* : a rainbowlike play of colors — **ir·i·des·cent** \-ᵊnt\ *adj*

irid·i·um \ir-ˈi-dē-əm\ *n* : a hard brittle heavy metallic chemical element — see ELEMENT table

iris \ˈī-rəs\ *n, pl* **iris·es** *or* **iri·des** \ˈī-rə-ˌdēz, ˈir-ə-\ [ME, fr. L *iris* rainbow, iris plant, fr. Gk, rainbow, iris plant, iris of the eye] **1** : the colored part around the pupil of the eye **2** : any of a large genus of plants with linear basal leaves and large showy flowers

Irish \ˈīr-ish\ *n* **1 Irish** *pl* : the people of Ireland **2** : the Celtic language of Ireland — **Irish** *adj* — **Irish·man** \-mən\ *n* — **Irish·wom·an** \-ˌwu̇-mən\ *n*

Irish bull *n* : an incongruous statement (as "it was hereditary in his family to have no children")

Irish coffee *n* : hot sugared coffee with Irish whiskey and whipped cream

Irish moss *n* : the dried and bleached plants of two red algae; *also* : either of these red algae

Irish setter *n* : any of a breed of bird dogs with a mahogany-red coat

irk \'ərk\ *vb* : to make weary, irritated, or bored : ANNOY

irk·some \'ərk-səm\ *adj* : tending to irk : ANNOYING — **irk·some·ly** *adv*

¹**iron** \'īrn, 'ī-ərn\ *n* **1** : a heavy malleable magnetic metallic chemical element that rusts easily and is vital to biological processes — see ELEMENT table **2** : something made of metal and esp. iron; *also* : something (as handcuffs) used to bind or restrain ⟨put them in ~s⟩ **3** : a household device with a flat base that is heated and used for pressing cloth **4** : STRENGTH, HARDNESS

²**iron** *vb* **1** : to press or smooth with or as if with a heated iron **2** : to remove (as wrinkles) by ironing — **iron·er** *n*

¹**iron·clad** \-'klad\ *adj* **1** : sheathed in iron armor **2** : so firm or secure as to be unbreakable

²**iron·clad** \-ˌklad\ *n* : an armored naval vessel esp. of the 19th century

iron curtain *n* : a political, military, and ideological barrier that isolates an area; *esp, often cap* : one isolating an area under Soviet control

iron·ic \ī-'rä-nik\ *or* **iron·i·cal** \-ni-kəl\ *adj* **1** : of, relating to, or marked by irony **2** : given to irony

iron·i·cal·ly \-ni-k(ə-)lē\ *adv* **1** : in an ironic manner **2** : it is ironic

iron·ing *n* : clothes ironed or to be ironed

iron lung *n* : a device for artificial respiration that encloses the chest in a chamber in which changes of pressure force air into and out of the lungs

iron out *vb* : to remove or lessen difficulties in or extremes of

iron oxide *n* : FERRIC OXIDE

iron·stone \'īrn-ˌstōn, 'ī-ərn-\ *n* **1** : a hard iron-rich sedimentary rock **2** : a hard heavy durable pottery developed in England in the 19th century

iron·ware \-ˌwar\ *n* : articles made of iron

iron·weed \-ˌwēd\ *n* : any of several mostly weedy American plants related to the asters that have terminal heads of red or purple flowers

iron·wood \-ˌwud\ *n* : any of numerous trees or shrubs with exceptionally hard wood; *also* : the wood

iron·work \-ˌwərk\ *n* **1** : work in iron **2** *pl* : a mill or building where iron or steel is smelted or heavy iron or steel products are made — **iron·work·er** *n*

iro·ny \'ī-rə-nē\ *n*, *pl* **-nies** [L *ironia*, fr. Gk *eirōnia*, fr. *eirōn* dissembler] **1** : the use of words to express the opposite of what one really means **2** : incongruity between the actual result of a sequence of events and the expected result

Iro·quois \'ir-ə-ˌkwoi\ *n*, *pl* **Iroquois** *same or* -ˌkwoiz\ **1** *pl* : an American Indian confederacy of New York that consisted of the Cayuga, Mohawk, Oneida, Onondaga, and Seneca and later included the Tuscarora **2** : a member of any of the Iroquois peoples

ir·ra·di·ate \i-'rā-dē-ˌāt\ *vb* **-at·ed; -at·ing** **1** : ILLUMINATE **2** : ENLIGHTEN **3** : to treat by exposure to radiation **4** : RADIATE — **ir·ra·di·a·tion** \-ˌrā-dē-'ā-shən\ *n*

¹**ir·ra·tio·nal** \(ˌ)i-'ra-shə-nəl\ *adj* **1** : incapable of reasoning ⟨~ beasts⟩; *also* : defective in mental power ⟨~ with fever⟩ **2** : not based on reason ⟨~ fears⟩ **3** : being or numerically equal to an irrational number — **ir·ra·tio·nal·i·ty** \(ˌ)i-ra-shə-'na-lə-tē\ *n* — **ir·ra·tio·nal·ly** *adv*

²**irrational** *n* : IRRATIONAL NUMBER

irrational number *n* : a real number that cannot be expressed as the quotient of two integers

ir·rec·on·cil·able \(ˌ)i-re-kən-'sī-lə-bəl, -'re-kən-ˌsī-\ *adj* : impossible to reconcile, adjust, or harmonize — **ir·rec·on·cil·abil·i·ty** \(ˌ)i-re-kən-ˌsī-lə-'bi-lə-tē\ *n*

ir·re·cov·er·able \ir-i-'kə-və-rə-bəl\ *adj* : not capable of being recovered or rectified : IRREPARABLE — **ir·re·cov·er·ably** \-blē\ *adv*

ir·re·deem·able \ir-i-'dē-mə-bəl\ *adj* **1** : not redeemable; *esp* : not terminable by payment of the principal ⟨an ~ bond⟩ **2** : not convertible into gold or silver at the will of the holder **3** : being beyond remedy : HOPELESS

ir·re·den·tism \-'den-ˌti-zəm\ *n* : a principle or policy directed toward the incorporation of a territory historically or ethnically part of another into that other — **ir·re·den·tist** \-tist\ *n or adj*

ir·re·duc·ible \ir-i-'dü-sə-bəl, -'dyü-\ *adj* : not reducible — **ir·re·duc·ibly** \-blē\ *adv*

ir·re·fut·able \ir-i-'fyü-tə-bəl, (ˌ)i-'re-fyət-\ *adj* : impossible to refute

irreg *abbr* irregular

ir·reg·u·lar \(ˌ)i-'re-gyə-lər\ *adj* **1** : not regular : not natural or uniform **2** : not conforming to the normal or usual manner of inflection ⟨~ verbs⟩ **3** : not belonging to a regular or organized army ⟨~ troops⟩ — **irregular** *n* — **ir·reg·u·lar·ly** *adv*

ir·reg·u·lar·i·ty \(ˌ)i-ˌre-gyə-'lar-ə-tē\ *n*, *pl* **-ties** **1** : something that is irregular **2** : the quality or state of being irregular **3** : occasional constipation

ir·rel·e·vant \(ˌ)i-'re-lə-vənt\ *adj* : not relevant — **ir·rel·e·vance** \-vəns\ *n*

ir·re·li·gious \ir-i-'li-jəs\ *adj* : lacking religious emotions, doctrines, or practices

ir·re·me·di·able \ir-i-'mē-dē-ə-bəl\ *adj* : impossible to remedy or correct

ir·re·mov·able \-'mü-və-bəl\ *adj* : not removable

ir·rep·a·ra·ble \(ˌ)i-'re-pə-rə-bəl\ *adj* : impossible to make good, undo, repair, or remedy ⟨~ damage⟩

ir·re·place·able \ir-i-'plā-sə-bəl\ *adj* : not replaceable

ir·re·press·ible \-'pre-sə-bəl\ *adj* : impossible to repress or control

ir·re·proach·able \-'prō-chə-bəl\ *adj* : not reproachable : BLAMELESS

ir·re·sist·ible \ir-i-'zis-tə-bəl\ *adj* : impossible to successfully resist — **ir·re·sist·ibly** \-blē\ *adv*

ir·res·o·lute \(ˌ)i-'re-zə-ˌlüt\ *adj* : uncertain how to act or proceed : VACILLATING — **ir·res·o·lute·ly** \-'lüt-lē; (ˌ)i-ˌre-zə-'lüt-\ *adv* — **ir·res·o·lu·tion** \(ˌ)i-ˌre-zə-'lü-shən\ *n*

ir·re·spec·tive of \ir-i-'spek-tiv-\ *prep* : without regard to

ir·re·spon·si·ble \-'spän-sə-bəl\ *adj* : not responsible — **ir·re·spon·si·bil·i·ty** \-ˌspän-sə-'bi-lə-tē\ *n* — **ir·re·spon·si·bly** \-'spän-sə-blē\ *adv*

ir·re·triev·able \ir-i-'trē-və-bəl\ *adj* : not retrievable : IRRECOVERABLE

ir·rev·er·ence \(ˌ)i-'re-və-rəns\ *n* **1** : lack of reverence **2** : an irreverent act or utterance — **ir·rev·er·ent** \-rənt\ *adj*

ir·re·vers·ible \ir-i-'vər-sə-bəl\ *adj* : incapable of being reversed

ir·rev·o·ca·ble \(ˌ)i-'re-və-kə-bəl\ *adj* : incapable of being revoked or recalled — **ir·rev·o·ca·bly** \-blē\ *adv*

ir·ri·gate \'ir-ə-ˌgāt\ *vb* **-gat·ed; -gat·ing** : to supply (as land) with water by artificial means; *also* : to flush with liquid — **ir·ri·ga·tion** \ir-ə-'gā-shən\ *n*

ir·ri·ta·bil·i·ty \ir-ə-tə-'bi-lə-tē\ *n* **1** : the property of living things and of protoplasm that enables reaction to stimuli **2** : the quality or state of being irritable; *esp* : readiness to become annoyed or angry

ir·ri·ta·ble \'ir-ə-tə-bəl\ *adj* : capable of being irritated; *esp* : readily or easily irritated — **ir·ri·ta·bly** \-blē\ *adv*

ir·ri·tate \'ir-ə-ˌtāt\ *vb* **-tat·ed; -tat·ing** **1** : to excite to anger : EXASPERATE **2** : to make sore or inflamed — **ir·ri·tant** \'ir-ə-tənt\ *adj or n* — **ir·ri·tat·ing·ly** *adv* — **ir·ri·ta·tion** \ir-ə-'tā-shən\ *n*

ir·rupt \(ˌ)i-'rəpt\ *vb* **1** : to rush in forcibly or violently **2** : to increase suddenly in numbers ⟨rabbits ~ in cycles⟩ — **ir·rup·tion** \-'rəp-shən\ *n*

IRS *abbr* Internal Revenue Service
is *pres 3d sing of* BE
Isa *or* **Is** *abbr* Isaiah
Isa·iah \ī-'zā-ə\ *n* — see BIBLE table
Isa·ias \ī-'zā-əs\ *n* : ISAIAH
ISBN *abbr* International Standard Book Number
-ish \ish\ *adj suffix* **1** : of, relating to, or being ⟨Finn*ish*⟩ **2** : characteristic of ⟨boy*ish*⟩ ⟨mul*ish*⟩ **3** : inclined or liable to ⟨book*ish*⟩ **4** : having a touch or trace of : somewhat ⟨purpl*ish*⟩ **5** : having the approximate age of ⟨forty*ish*⟩
isin·glass \'īz-ᵊn-ˌglas, 'ī-ziŋ-\ *n* **1** : a gelatin obtained from various fish **2** : mica esp. in thin sheets
isl *abbr* island
Is·lam \is-'läm, iz-, -'lam, 'is-ˌ, 'iz-ˌ\ *n* [Ar *islām* submission (to the will of God)] : the religious faith of Muslims; *also* : the civilization built on this faith — **Is·lam·ic** \is-'lä-mik, iz-, -'la-\ *adj*
is·land \'ī-lənd\ *n* **1** : a body of land smaller than a continent surrounded by water **2** : something resembling an island in its isolation
is·land·er \'ī-lən-dər\ *n* : a native or inhabitant of an island
isle \'īl\ *n* : ISLAND; *esp* : a small island
is·let \'ī-lət\ *n* : a small island
ism \'i-zəm\ *n* : a distinctive doctrine, cause, or theory
-ism \ˌi-zəm\ *n suffix* **1** : act : practice : process ⟨critic*ism*⟩ **2** : manner of action or behavior characteristic of a (specified) person or thing ⟨fanatic*ism*⟩ **3** : state : condition : property ⟨dual*ism*⟩ **4** : abnormal state or condition ⟨alcohol*ism*⟩ **5** : doctrine : theory : cult ⟨Buddh*ism*⟩ **6** : adherence to a set of principles ⟨stoic*ism*⟩ **7** : prejudice or discrimination on the basis of a (specified) attribute ⟨rac*ism*⟩ ⟨sex*ism*⟩ **8** : characteristic or peculiar feature or trait ⟨colloquial*ism*⟩
iso·bar \'ī-sə-ˌbär\ *n* : a line on a map connecting places of equal barometric pressure — **iso·bar·ic** \ˌī-sə-'bär-ik, -'bar-\ *adj*
iso·late \'ī-sə-ˌlāt\ *vb* **-lat·ed; -lat·ing** [fr. *isolated* set apart, fr. F *isolé*, fr. It *isolato*, fr. *isola* island, fr. L *insula*] : to place or keep by itself : separate from others — **iso·la·tion** \ˌī-sə-'lā-shən\ *n*
iso·lat·ed *adj* **1** : occurring alone or once : UNIQUE **2** : SPORADIC
iso·la·tion·ism \ˌī-sə-'lā-shə-ˌni-zəm\ *n* : a policy of national isolation by abstention from international political and economic relations — **iso·la·tion·ist** \-shə-nist\ *n or adj*
iso·mer \'ī-sə-mər\ *n* : any of two or more chemical compounds that contain the same numbers of atoms of the same elements but differ in structural arrangement and properties — **iso·mer·ic** \ˌī-sə-'mer-ik\ *adj* — **isom·er·ism** \ī-'sä-mə-ˌri-zəm\ *n*
iso·met·rics \ˌī-sə-'me-triks\ *n sing or pl* : exercise involving a series of brief and intense contractions of muscles against each other or against an immovable resistance — **iso·met·ric** *adj*
iso·prene \'ī-sə-ˌprēn\ *n* : a hydrocarbon used esp. in making synthetic rubber
isos·ce·les \ī-'sä-sə-ˌlēz\ *adj* : having two equal sides ⟨an ∼ triangle⟩
iso·therm \'ī-sə-ˌthərm\ *n* : a line on a map connecting points having the same temperature
iso·ther·mal \ˌī-sə-'thər-məl\ *adj* : of, relating to, or marked by equality of temperature
iso·tope \'ī-sə-ˌtōp\ *n* [Gk *isos* equal + *topos* place] : any of the forms of a chemical element that differ chiefly in the number of neutrons in an atom — **iso·top·ic** \ˌī-sə-'tä-pik, -'tō-\ *adj* — **iso·top·i·cal·ly** \-'tä-pi-k(ə-)lē, -'tō-\ *adv*
Isr *abbr* Israel; Israeli
Is·rae·li \iz-'rā-lē\ *n, pl* **Israelis** *also* **Israeli** : a native or inhabitant of Israel — **Israeli** *adj*
Is·ra·el·ite \'iz-rē-ə-ˌlīt\ *n* : a member of the Hebrew people descended from Jacob

is·su·ance \'i-shù-wəns\ *n* : the act of issuing or giving out esp. officially
¹is·sue \'i-shü\ *n* **1** : the action of going, coming, or flowing out : EGRESS, EMERGENCE **2** : EXIT, OUTLET, VENT **3** : OFFSPRING, PROGENY **4** : OUTCOME, RESULT **5** : a point of debate or controversy; *also* : the point at which an unsettled matter is ready for a decision **6** : a discharge (as of blood) from the body **7** : something coming forth from a specified source **8** : the act of officially giving out or printing : PUBLICATION; *also* : the quantity of things given out at one time
²issue *vb* **is·sued; is·su·ing** **1** : to go, come, or flow out **2** : to come forth or cause to come forth : EMERGE, DISCHARGE, EMIT **3** : ACCRUE **4** : to descend from a specified parent or ancestor **5** : to result in **6** : to put forth or distribute officially **7** : PUBLISH **8** : EMANATE, RESULT — **is·su·er** *n*
¹-ist \ist\ *n suffix* **1** : one that performs a (specified) action ⟨cycl*ist*⟩ : one that makes or produces ⟨novel*ist*⟩ **2** : one that plays a (specified) musical instrument ⟨harp*ist*⟩ **3** : one that operates a (specified) mechanical instrument or contrivance ⟨machin*ist*⟩ **4** : one that specializes in a (specified) art or science or skill ⟨geolog*ist*⟩ **5** : one that adheres to or advocates a (specified) doctrine or system or code of behavior ⟨social*ist*⟩ or that of a (specified) individual ⟨Darwin*ist*⟩
²-ist *adj suffix* : -ISTIC
isth·mi·an \'is-mē-ən\ *adj* : of, relating to, or situated in or near an isthmus
isth·mus \'is-məs\ *n* : a narrow strip of land connecting two larger portions of land
-is·tic \'is-tik\ *or* **-is·ti·cal** \'is-ti-kəl\ *adj suffix* : of, relating to, or characteristic of ⟨altru*istic*⟩
¹it \'it\ *pron* **1** : that one — used of a lifeless thing, a plant, a person or animal, or an abstract entity ⟨∼'s a big building⟩ ⟨∼'s a shade tree⟩ ⟨who is ∼⟩ ⟨beauty is everywhere and ∼ is a source of joy⟩ **2** — used as a subject of an impersonal verb that expresses a condition or action without reference to an agent ⟨∼ is raining⟩ **3** — used as an anticipatory subject or object ⟨∼'s good to see you⟩
²it \'it\ *n* : the player in a game who performs the principal action of the game (as trying to find others in hide-and-seek)
It *abbr* Italian; Italy
ital *abbr* italic; italicized
Ital *abbr* Italian
Ital·ian \i-'tal-yən\ *n* **1** : a native or inhabitant of Italy **2** : the language of Italy — **Italian** *adj*
ital·ic \i-'ta-lik, ī-\ *adj* : relating to type in which the letters slope up toward the right (as in "*italic*") — **italic** *n*
ital·i·cize \i-'ta-lə-ˌsīz, ī-\ *vb* **-cized; -ciz·ing** : to print in italics
itch \'ich\ *n* **1** : an uneasy irritating skin sensation prob. related to sensing pain **2** : a skin disorder accompanied by an itch **3** : a persistent desire — **itch** *vb* — **itchy** *adj*
-ite \ˌīt\ *n suffix* **1** : native : resident ⟨suburban*ite*⟩ **2** : adherent : follower ⟨Lenin*ite*⟩ **3** : product ⟨metabol*ite*⟩ **4** : mineral : rock ⟨quartz*ite*⟩
item \'ī-təm\ *n* [L, likewise, also] **1** : a separate particular in a list, account, or series : ARTICLE **2** : a separate piece of news (as in a newspaper)
item·ize \'ī-tə-ˌmīz\ *vb* **-ized; -iz·ing** : to set down in detail : LIST — **item·i·za·tion** \ˌī-tə-mə-'zā-shən\ *n*
it·er·ate \'i-tə-ˌrāt\ *vb* **-at·ed; -at·ing** : REITERATE, REPEAT
it·er·a·tion \ˌi-tə-'rā-shən\ *n* **1** : REPETITION; *esp* : a computational process in which a series of operations is repeated until a condition is met **2** : one repetition of the series of operations in iteration
itin·er·ant \ī-'ti-nə-rənt, ə-\ *adj* : traveling from place to place; *esp* : covering a circuit ⟨an ∼ preacher⟩
itin·er·ary \ī-'ti-nə-ˌrer-ē, ə-\ *n, pl* **-ar·ies** **1** : the route

of a journey or the proposed outline of one **2** : a travel diary **3** : GUIDEBOOK

its ***'**its\\ *adj* : of or relating to it or itself

it·self \\it-**'**self\\ *pron* : that identical one — used reflexively, for emphasis, or in absolute constructions

-ity \\ə-tē\\ *n suffix* : quality : state : degree ⟨alkalin*ity*⟩

IUD \\ₐī-(ₐ)yü-**'**dē\\ *n* : INTRAUTERINE DEVICE

IV \\ₐī-**'**vē\\ *n* [*intravenous*] : an apparatus used to give an intravenous injection or feeding; *also* : such an injection or feeding

-ive \\iv\\ *adj suffix* : that performs or tends toward an (indicated) action ⟨correc*tive*⟩

ivo·ry **'**ī-vrē, -və-rē\\ *n, pl* **-ries** [ME *ivorie,* fr. OF *ivoire,* fr. L *eboreus* of ivory, fr. *ebur* ivory] **1** : the hard creamy-white material composing the tusks of an elephant or walrus **2** : a pale yellow color **3** : something made of ivory or of a similar substance

ivory tower *n* **1** : an impractical lack of concern with urgent problems **2** : a place of learning

ivy **'**ī-vē\\ *n, pl* **ivies** : a trailing woody evergreen vine with small black berries that is related to ginseng

IWW *abbr* Industrial Workers of the World

-ize \\ₐīz\\ *vb suffix* **1** : cause to be or conform to or resemble ⟨American*ize*⟩ : cause to be formed into ⟨union*ize*⟩ **2** : subject to a (specified) action ⟨satir*ize*⟩ **3** : saturate, treat, or combine with ⟨macadam*ize*⟩ **4** : treat like ⟨idol*ize*⟩ **5** : become : become like ⟨crystal*lize*⟩ **6** : be productive in or of : engage in a (specified) activity ⟨philosoph*ize*⟩ **7** : adopt or spread the manner of activity or the teaching of ⟨Christian*ize*⟩

J

¹j **'**jā\\ *n, pl* **j's** *or* **js** **'**jāz\\ *often cap* : the 10th letter of the English alphabet

²j *abbr, often cap* **1** jack **2** journal **3** judge **4** justice

¹jab **'**jab\\ *vb* **jabbed; jab·bing** : to thrust quickly or abruptly : POKE

²jab *n* : a usu. short straight punch

jab·ber **'**ja-bər\\ *vb* : to talk rapidly, indistinctly, or unintelligibly : CHATTER — **jabber** *n* — **jab·ber·er** *n*

jab·ber·wocky **'**ja-bər-ₐwä-kē\\ *n* : meaningless speech or writing

ja·bot \\zha-**'**bō, **'**ja-ₐbō\\ *n* : a ruffle worn down the front of a dress or shirt

jac·a·ran·da \\ₐja-kə-**'**ran-də\\ *n* : any of a genus of pinnate-leaved tropical American trees with clusters of showy blue flowers

¹jack **'**jak\\ *n* **1** : a mechanical device; *esp* : one used to raise a heavy body a short distance **2** : a male donkey **3** : a small target ball in lawn bowling **4** : a small national flag flown by a ship **5** : a small 6-pointed metal object used in a game (**jacks**) **6** : a playing card bearing the figure of a soldier or servant **7** : a socket into which a plug is inserted for connecting electric circuits

²jack *vb* **1** : to raise by means of a jack **2** : INCREASE ⟨∼ up prices⟩

jack·al **'**ja-kəl\\ *n* [Turk *çakal,* fr. Per *shagāl*] : any of several mammals of Asia and Africa related to the wolves

jack·a·napes **'**ja-kə-ₐnāps\\ *n* **1** : MONKEY, APE **2** : an impudent or conceited person

jack·ass **'**jak-ₐas\\ *n* **1** : DONKEY; *esp* : a male donkey **2** : a stupid person : FOOL

jack·boot \\-ₐbüt\\ *n* **1** : a heavy military boot of glossy black leather extending above the knee **2** : a laceless military boot reaching to the calf

jack·daw **'**jak-ₐdо̇\\ *n* : a black and gray Old World crowlike bird

jack·et **'**ja-kət\\ *n* [ME *jaket,* fr. MF *jaquet,* dim. of *jaque* short jacket, fr. *jacque* peasant, fr. the name *Jacques* James] **1** : a garment for the upper body usu. having a front opening, collar, and sleeves **2** : an outer covering or casing ⟨a book ∼⟩

Jack Frost *n* : frost or frosty weather personified

jack·ham·mer **'**jak-ₐha-mər\\ *n* : a pneumatic percussion tool for drilling rock or breaking pavement

jack–in–the–box *n, pl* **jack–in–the–boxes** *or* **jacks–in–the–box** : a toy consisting of a small box out of which a figure springs when the lid is raised

jack–in–the–pulpit *n, pl* **jack–in–the–pulpits** *or* **jacks–in–the–pulpit** : an American spring-flowering woodland herb having an upright club-shaped spadix arched over by a green and purple spathe

¹jack·knife **'**jak-ₐnīf\\ *n* **1** : a large pocketknife **2** : a dive in which the diver bends from the waist and touches the ankles before straightening out

²jackknife *vb* : to fold like a jackknife ⟨the trailer truck *jackknifed*⟩

jack·leg **'**jak-ₐleg\\ *adj* **1** : lacking skill or training **2** : MAKESHIFT

jack–of–all–trades *n, pl* **jacks–of–all–trades** : one who is able to do passable work at various tasks

jack–o'–lan·tern **'**ja-kə-ₐlan-tərn\\ *n* : a lantern made of a pumpkin cut to look like a human face

jack·pot **'**jak-ₐpät\\ *n* **1** : a large sum of money formed by the accumulation of stakes from previous play (as in poker) **2** : an impressive and often unexpected success or reward

jack·rab·bit \\-ₐra-bət\\ *n* : any of several large hares of western No. America with very long ears and hind legs

jack·straw \\-ₐstrо̇\\ *n* **1** *pl* : a game in which straws or thin sticks are let fall in a heap and each player in turn tries to remove them one at a time without disturbing the rest **2** : one of the straws or sticks in jackstraws

jack–tar \\-**'**tär\\ *n, often cap* : SAILOR

Ja·cob's ladder **'**jā-kəbz-\\ *n* : any of several perennial herbs related to phlox that have pinnate leaves and blue or white bell-shaped flowers

jac·quard **'**ja-ₐkärd\\ *n, often cap* : a fabric of intricate variegated weave or pattern

¹jade **'**jād\\ *n* **1** : a broken-down, vicious, or worthless horse **2** : a disreputable woman

²jade *vb* **jad·ed; jad·ing** **1** : to wear out by overwork or abuse **2** : to become weary **syn** exhaust, fatigue, tire

³jade *n* [F, fr. obs. Sp (*piedra de la*) *ijada,* lit., loin stone; fr. the belief that jade cures renal colic] : a usu. green gemstone that takes a high polish

jad·ed *adj* : dulled by a surfeit or excess

¹jag **'**jag\\ *n* : a sharp projecting part

²jag *n* : SPREE

jag·ged **'**ja-gəd\\ *adj* : sharply notched

jag·uar **'**ja-ₐgwär\\ *n* : a black-spotted tropical American cat that is larger and stockier than the Old World leopard

jaguar

jai alai **'**hī-ₐlī\\ *n* [Sp, fr. Basque, fr. *jai* festival + *alai* merry] : a court game played by usu. two or four players with a ball and a curved wicker basket strapped to the wrist

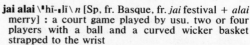

jail \'jāl\ *n* [ME *jaiole*, fr. OF, fr. LL *caveola*, dim. of L *cavea* cage] : PRISON; *esp* : one for persons held in lawful custody — **jail** *vb*

jail·bird \-ˌbərd\ *n* : an habitual criminal

jail·break \-ˌbrāk\ *n* : a forcible escape from jail

jail·er *or* **jail·or** \'jā-lər\ *n* : a keeper of a jail

jal·ap \'ja-ləp, 'jä-\ *n* : a powdered purgative drug from the root of a Mexican plant related to the morning glory; *also* : this root or plant

ja·la·pe·ño \ˌhä-lə-'pān-(ˌ)yō\ *n* : a Mexican hot pepper

ja·lopy \jə-'lä-pē\ *n, pl* **ja·lop·ies** : a dilapidated vehicle (as an automobile)

jal·ou·sie \'ja-lə-sē\ *n* [F, lit., jealousy] : a blind, window, or door with adjustable horizontal slats or louvers

¹jam \'jam\ *vb* **jammed; jam·ming 1** : to press into a close or tight position **2** : to cause to become wedged so as to be unworkable; *also* : to make or become unworkable through the jamming of a movable part **3** : to push forcibly ⟨~ on the brakes⟩ **4** : CRUSH, BRUISE **5** : to make unintelligible by sending out interfering signals or messages **6** : to take part in a jam session — **jam·mer** *n*

²jam *n* **1** : a crowded mass that impedes or blocks ⟨traffic ~⟩ **2** : a difficult state of affairs

³jam *n* : a food made by boiling fruit and sugar to a thick consistency

Jam *abbr* Jamaica

Ja·mai·can \jə-'mā-kən\ *n* : a native or inhabitant of Jamaica — **Jamaican** *adj*

jamb \'jam\ *n* [ME *jambe*, fr. MF, lit., leg] : an upright piece forming the side of an opening (as of a door)

jam·ba·laya \ˌjəm-bə-'lī-ə\ *n* [LaF] : rice cooked with ham, sausage, chicken, shrimp, or oysters and seasoned with herbs

jam·bo·ree \ˌjam-bə-'rē\ *n* : a large festive gathering

James \'jāmz\ *n* — see BIBLE table

jam–pack \'jam-'pak\ *vb* : to pack tightly or to excess

jam session *n* : an impromptu performance esp. by jazz musicians

Jan *abbr* January

jan·gle \'jaŋ-gəl\ *vb* **jan·gled; jan·gling** : to make a harsh or discordant sound — **jangle** *n*

jan·i·tor \'ja-nə-tər\ *n* [L, fr. *janua* door] : a person who has the care of a building — **jan·i·to·ri·al** \ˌja-nə-'tōr-ē-əl\ *adj*

Jan·u·ary \'ja-nyə-ˌwer-ē\ *n* [ME *Januarie*, fr. L *Januarius*, first month of the ancient Roman year, fr. *Janus*, two-faced god of gates and beginnings] : the 1st month of the year having 31 days

¹ja·pan \jə-'pan\ *n* : a varnish giving a hard brilliant finish

²japan *vb* **ja·panned; ja·pan·ning** : to cover with a coat of japan

Jap·a·nese \ˌja-pə-'nēz, -'nēs\ *n, pl* **Japanese 1** : a native or inhabitant of Japan **2** : the language of Japan — **Japanese** *adj*

Japanese beetle *n* : a small metallic green and brown scarab beetle introduced from Japan that is a pest on the roots of grasses as a grub and on foliage and fruits as an adult

¹jape \'jāp\ *vb* **japed; jap·ing 1** : JOKE **2** : MOCK

²jape *n* : JEST, GIBE

¹jar \'jär\ *vb* **jarred; jar·ring 1** : to make a harsh or discordant sound **2** : to have a harsh or disagreeable effect **3** : VIBRATE, SHAKE

²jar *n* **1** : a state of conflict **2** : a harsh discordant sound **3** : JOLT **4** : a painful effect : SHOCK

³jar *n* : a widemouthed container usu. of glass or earthenware

jar·di·niere \ˌjärd-ᵊn-'ir\ *n* : an ornamental stand for plants or flowers

jar·gon \'jär-gən\ *n* **1** : confused unintelligible language **2** : the special vocabulary of a particular group or activity **3** : obscure and often pretentious language

Jas *abbr* James

jas·mine \'jaz-mən\ *n* [F *jasmin*, fr. Ar *yāsamīn*] : any of various climbing shrubs with fragrant flowers

jas·per \'jas-pər\ *n* : a usu. red, yellow, or brown opaque quartz

jaun·dice \'jȯn-dəs\ *n* : yellowish discoloration of skin, tissues, and body fluids by bile pigments; *also* : an abnormal condition marked by jaundice

jaun·diced \-dəst\ *adj* **1** : affected with or as if with jaundice **2** : exhibiting envy, distaste, or hostility

jaunt \'jȯnt\ *n* : a short trip usu. for pleasure

jaun·ty \'jȯn-tē\ *adj* **jaun·ti·er; -est** : sprightly in manner or appearance : LIVELY — **jaun·ti·ly** \-tə-lē\ *adv* — **jaun·ti·ness** \-tē-nəs\ *n*

Ja·va·nese \ˌja-və-'nēz, ˌjä-, -'nēs\ *n* : a native or inhabitant of the Indonesian island of Java

jav·e·lin \'ja-və-lən\ *n* **1** : a light spear **2** : a slender shaft thrown for distance in a track-and-field contest

¹jaw \'jȯ\ *n* **1** : either of the bony or cartilaginous structures that support the soft tissues enclosing the mouth and that usu. bear teeth **2** : the parts forming the walls of the mouth and serving to open and close it — usu. used in pl. **3** : one of a pair of movable parts for holding or crushing something — **jawed** \'jȯd\ *adj*

²jaw *vb* : to talk abusively, indignantly, or at length

jaw·bone \-ˌbōn\ *n* : JAW 1

jaw·break·er \-ˌbrā-kər\ *n* **1** : a word difficult to pronounce **2** : a round hard candy

jay \'jā\ *n* : any of various noisy brightly colored often largely blue birds smaller than the related crows

jay·bird \'jā-ˌbərd\ *n* : JAY

jay·vee \ˌjā-'vē\ *n* **1** : JUNIOR VARSITY **2** : a member of a junior varsity team

jay·walk \'jā-ˌwȯk\ *vb* : to cross a street carelessly without regard for traffic regulations — **jay·walk·er** *n*

¹jazz \'jaz\ *n* **1** : American music characterized by improvisation, syncopated rhythms, and contrapuntal ensemble playing **2** : empty talk **3** : similar but unspecified things : STUFF

²jazz *vb* : ENLIVEN ⟨~ things up⟩

jazzy \'ja-zē\ *adj* **jazz·i·er; -est 1** : having the characteristics of jazz **2** : marked by unrestraint, animation, or flashiness

JCS *abbr* joint chiefs of staff

jct *abbr* junction

JD *abbr* **1** [L *juris doctor*] doctor of jurisprudence; doctor of law **2** [L *jurum doctor*] doctor of laws **3** justice department **4** juvenile delinquent

jeal·ous \'je-ləs\ *adj* **1** : demanding complete devotion **2** : suspicious of a rival or of one believed to enjoy an advantage **3** : VIGILANT — **jeal·ous·ly** *adv* — **jeal·ou·sy** \-lə-sē\ *n*

jeans \'jēnz\ *n pl* [pl. of *jean* twilled cloth, short for *jean fustian*, fr. ME *Gene* Genoa, Italy] : pants made of durable twilled cotton cloth

jeep \'jēp\ *n* [prob. fr. *g.p.* (abbr. of *general purpose*)] : a small four-wheel drive general-purpose motor vehicle used in World War II

¹jeer \'jir\ *vb* : to speak or cry out in derision : MOCK

²jeer *n* : TAUNT

Je·ho·vah \ji-'hō-və\ *n* : GOD 1

je·hu \'jē-hü, -hyü\ *n* : a driver of a coach or cab

je·june \ji-'jün\ *adj* [L *jejunus* empty of food, hungry, meager] : lacking interest or significance : DULL

je·ju·num \ji-'jü-nəm\ *n* [L] : the section of the small intestine between the duodenum and the ileum — **je·ju·nal** \-'jün-ᵊl\ *adj*

jell \'jel\ *vb* **1** : to come to the consistency of jelly **2** : to take shape

jel·ly \'je-lē\ *n, pl* **jellies 1** : a food with a soft elastic consistency due usu. to the presence of gelatin or pectin; *esp* : a fruit product made by boiling sugar and the juice of a fruit **2** : a substance resembling jelly — **jelly** *vb*

jelly bean *n* : a bean-shaped candy

jel·ly·fish \'je-lē-₁fish\ *n* : a coelenterate with a saucer=shaped jellylike body

jen·net \'je-nət\ *n* **1** : a small Spanish horse **2** : a female donkey

jen·ny \'je-nē\ *n, pl* **jennies** : a female bird or donkey

jeop·ar·dy \'je-pər-dē\ *n* [ME *jeopardie,* fr. OF *jeu parti* alternative, lit., divided game] : exposure to death, loss, or injury **syn** peril, hazard, risk, danger — **jeop·ar·dize** \-₁dīz\ *vb*

Jer *abbr* Jeremiah; Jeremias

jer·e·mi·ad \₁jer-ə-'mī-əd, -₁ad\ *n* : a prolonged lamentation or complaint; *also* : a cautionary or angry harangue

Jer·e·mi·ah \₁jer-ə-'mī-ə\ *n* — see BIBLE table

Jer·e·mi·as \₁jer-ə-'mī-əs\ *n* : JEREMIAH

¹jerk \'jərk\ *n* **1** : a short quick pull or twist : TWITCH **2** : an annoyingly stupid or foolish person — **jerk·i·ly** \'jər-kə-lē\ *adv* — **jerky** \'jər-kē\ *adj*

²jerk *vb* **1** : to give a sharp quick push, pull, or twist **2** : to move in short abrupt motions

jer·kin \'jər-kən\ *n* : a close-fitting usu. sleeveless jacket

jerk·wa·ter \'jərk-₁wȯ-tər, -₁wä-\ *adj* [fr. *jerkwater* rural train] : of minor importance : INSIGNIFICANT ⟨∼ towns⟩

jer·ry–built \'jer-ē-₁bilt\ *adj* : built cheaply and flimsily

jer·sey \'jər-zē\ *n, pl* **jerseys** [*Jersey,* one of the Channel islands] **1** : a plain weft-knitted fabric **2** : a close=fitting knitted shirt **3** *often cap* : any of a breed of small usu. fawn-colored dairy cattle

jess \'jes\ *n* : a leg strap by which a captive bird of prey may be controlled

jes·sa·mine \'je-sə-mən\ *var of* JASMINE

jest \'jest\ *n* **1** : an act intended to provoke laughter **2** : a witty remark **3** : a frivolous mood ⟨said in ∼⟩ — **jest** *vb*

jest·er \'jes-tər\ *n* : a retainer formerly kept to provide casual entertainment

¹jet \'jet\ *n* : a velvet-black coal that takes a good polish and is often used for jewelry

²jet *vb* **jet·ted; jet·ting** : to spout or emit in a stream

³jet *n* **1** : a forceful rush (as of liquid or gas) through a narrow opening; *also* : a nozzle for a jet of fluid **2** : a jet-propelled airplane

⁴jet *vb* **jet·ted; jet·ting** : to travel by jet

jet lag *n* : a condition that is marked esp. by fatigue and irritability and occurs following a long flight through several time zones — **jet–lagged** *adj*

jet·lin·er \'jet-₁li-nər\ *n* : a jet-propelled airliner

jet·port \-₁pȯrt\ *n* : an airport designed to handle jets

jet–propelled \₁jet-prə-'peld\ *adj* : driven by an engine (**jet engine**) that produces propulsion (**jet propulsion**) by the rearward discharge of a jet of fluid (as heated air and exhaust gases)

jet·sam \'jet-səm\ *n* : jettisoned goods; *esp* : such goods washed ashore

jet set *n* : an international group of wealthy people who frequent fashionable resorts

jet stream *n* : a long narrow high-altitude current of high-speed winds blowing generally from the west

jet·ti·son \'je-tə-sən\ *vb* **1** : to throw (goods) overboard to lighten a ship or aircraft in distress **2** : DISCARD — **jettison** *n*

jet·ty \'je-tē\ *n, pl* **jetties 1** : a pier built to influence the current or to protect a harbor **2** : a landing wharf

jeu d'es·prit \zhœ-des-'prē\ *n, pl* **jeux d'esprit** *same*\ [F, lit., play of the mind] : a witty comment or composition

Jew \'jü\ *n* **1** : ISRAELITE **2** : one whose religion is Judaism — **Jew·ish** *adj*

¹jew·el \'jü-əl\ *n* [ME *juel,* fr. OF, prob. dim. of *jeu* game, play, fr. L *jocus* game, joke] **1** : an ornament of precious metal **2** : GEMSTONE, GEM

²jewel *vb* **-eled** *or* **-elled; -el·ing** *or* **-el·ling** : to adorn or equip with jewels

jew·el·er *or* **jew·el·ler** \'jü-ə-lər\ *n* : a person who makes or deals in jewelry and related articles

jew·el·lery *chiefly Brit var of* JEWELRY

jew·el·ry \'jü-əl-rē\ *n* : JEWELS; *esp* : objects of precious metal set with gems and worn for personal adornment

Jew·ry \'jùr-ē, 'jù-ər-ē, 'jü-rē\ *n* : the Jewish people

jg *abbr* junior grade

¹jib \'jib\ *n* : a triangular sail set on a line running from the bow to the mast

²jib *vb* **jibbed; jib·bing** : to refuse to proceed further

jibe \'jīb\ *vb* **jibed; jib·ing** : to be in accord : AGREE

jif·fy \'ji-fē\ *n, pl* **jiffies** : MOMENT, INSTANT ⟨I'll be ready in a ∼⟩

¹jig \'jig\ *n* **1** : a lively dance in triple rhythm **2** : TRICK, GAME ⟨the ∼ is up⟩ **3** : a device used to hold work during manufacture or assembly

²jig *vb* **jigged; jig·ging** : to dance a jig

jig·ger \'ji-gər\ *n* : a measure usu. holding 1 to 2 ounces (30 to 60 milliliters) used in mixing drinks

jig·gle \'ji-gəl\ *vb* **jig·gled; jig·gling** : to move with quick little jerks — **jiggle** *n*

jig·saw \'jig-₁sò\ *n* : a machine saw with a narrow vertically reciprocating blade for cutting curved lines

jigsaw puzzle *n* : a puzzle consisting of small irregularly cut pieces to be fitted together to form a picture

ji·had \ji-'häd, -'had\ *n* **1** : a Muslim holy war **2** : CRUSADE 2

¹jilt \'jilt\ *vb* : to drop (a lover) capriciously or unfeelingly

²jilt *n* : one who jilts a lover

jim crow \'jim-'krō\ *n, often cap J&C* : discrimination against blacks esp. by legal enforcement or traditional sanctions — **jim crow** *adj, often cap J&C* — **jim crow·ism** \-'krō-₁i-zəm\ *n, often cap J&C*

jim–dan·dy \'jim-'dan-dē\ *n* : something excellent of its kind

jim·mies \'ji-mēz\ *n pl* : tiny rod-shaped bits of usu. chocolate-flavored candy often sprinkled on ice cream

¹jim·my \'ji-mē\ *n, pl* **jimmies** : a small crowbar

²jimmy *vb* **jim·mied; jim·my·ing** : to force open with a jimmy

jim·son·weed \'jim-sən-₁wēd\ *n, often cap* : a coarse poisonous weed related to the tomato that has large trumpet-shaped white or violet flowers

¹jin·gle \'jiŋ-gəl\ *vb* **jin·gled; jin·gling** : to make a light clinking or tinkling sound

²jingle *n* **1** : a light clinking or tinkling sound **2** : a short verse or song with catchy repetition

jin·go·ism \'jiŋ-gō-₁i-zəm\ *n* : extreme chauvinism or nationalism marked esp. by a belligerent foreign policy — **jin·go·ist** \-ist\ *n* — **jin·go·is·tic** \₁jiŋ-gō-'is-tik\ *adj*

jin·rik·sha \jin-'rik-₁shò\ *n* : RICKSHA

¹jinx \'jiŋks\ *n* : one that brings bad luck

²jinx *vb* : to foredoom to failure or misfortune

jit·ney \'jit-nē\ *n, pl* **jitneys** : a small bus that serves a regular route on a flexible schedule

jit·ter·bug \'ji-tər-₁bəg\ *n* : a dance in which couples two-step, balance, and twirl vigorously in standardized patterns — **jitterbug** *vb*

jit·ters \'ji-tərz\ *n pl* : extreme nervousness — **jit·tery** \-tə-rē\ *adj*

¹jive \'jīv\ *n* **1** : swing music or dancing performed to it **2** : glib, deceptive, or foolish talk **3** : the jargon of jazz enthusiasts

²jive *vb* **jived; jiv·ing 1** : KID, TEASE **2** : to dance to or play jive

Jn *or* **Jno** *abbr* John

Jo *abbr* Joel

¹job \'jäb\ *n* **1** : a piece of work **2** : something that has to be done : TASK **3** : a regular remunerative position — **job·less** *adj*

²job *vb* **jobbed; job·bing 1** : to do occasional pieces of work for hire **2** : to hire or let by the job

Job \\'jōb\ *n* — see BIBLE table
job action *n* : a protest action by workers to force compliance with demands
job·ber \\'jä-bər\ *n* **1** : a person who buys goods and then sells them to other dealers : MIDDLEMAN **2** : a person who does work by the job
job·hold·er \\'jäb-ˌhōl-dər\ *n* : one having a regular job
jock \\'jäk\ *n* [*jockstrap*] : ATHLETE; *esp* : a college athlete
¹**jock·ey** \\'jä-kē\ *n, pl* **jockeys** : one who rides a horse esp. as a professional in a race
²**jockey** *vb* **jock·eyed; jock·ey·ing** : to maneuver or manipulate by adroit or devious means
jock·strap \\'jäk-ˌstrap\ *n* [E slang *jock* penis] : ATHLETIC SUPPORTER
jo·cose \jō-'kōs\ *adj* : MERRY, HUMOROUS **syn** jocular, facetious, witty
joc·u·lar \\'jä-kyə-lər\ *adj* : marked by jesting : PLAYFUL — **joc·u·lar·i·ty** \ˌjäk-yə-'lar-ə-tē\ *n* — **joc·u·lar·ly** *adv*
jo·cund \\'jä-kənd\ *adj* : marked by mirth or cheerfulness
jodh·pur \\'jäd-pər\ *n* **1** *pl* : riding breeches loose above the knee and tight-fitting below **2** : an ankle-high boot fastened with a strap
Jo·el \\'jō-əl\ *n* — see BIBLE table
¹**jog** \\'jäg\ *vb* **jogged; jog·ging 1** : to give a slight shake or push to **2** : to go at a slow monotonous pace **3** : to run or ride at a slow trot — **jog·ger** *n*
²**jog** *n* **1** : a slight shake **2** : a jogging movement or pace
³**jog** *n* **1** : a projecting or retreating part of a line or surface **2** : a brief abrupt change in direction
jog·gle \\'jä-gəl\ *vb* **jog·gled; jog·gling** : to shake slightly — **joggle** *n*
john \\'jän\ *n* **1** : TOILET **2** : a prostitute's client
John \\'jän\ *n* — see BIBLE table
john·ny \\'jä-nē\ *n, pl* **johnnies** : a short-sleeved gown opening in the back that is worn by hospital patients
John·ny–jump–up \ˌjä-nē-'jəmp-ˌəp\ *n* : any of various small-flowered cultivated pansies
joie de vi·vre \ˌzhwä-də-'vēvrᵃ\ *n* [F] : keen enjoyment of life
¹**join** \\'jȯin\ *vb* **1** : to come or bring together so as to form a unit **2** : to come or bring into close association **3** : to become a member of **4** : ADJOIN **5** : to take part in a collective activity
join·er \\'jȯi-nər\ *n* **1** : a worker who constructs articles by joining pieces of wood **2** : a gregarious person who joins many organizations
¹**joint** \\'jȯint\ *n* **1** : the point of contact between bones of an animal skeleton with the parts that surround and support it **2** : a cut of meat suitable for roasting **3** : a place where two things or parts are connected **4** : ESTABLISHMENT; *esp* : a shabby or disreputable establishment **5** : a marijuana cigarette — **joint·ed** *adj*
²**joint** *adj* **1** : UNITED **2** : common to two or more — **joint·ly** *adv*
³**joint** *vb* **1** : to unite by or provide with a joint **2** : to separate the joints of
joist \\'jȯist\ *n* : any of the small beams ranged parallel from wall to wall in a building to support a floor or ceiling
¹**joke** \\'jōk\ *n* : something said or done to provoke laughter; *esp* : a brief narrative with a humorous climax
²**joke** *vb* **joked; jok·ing** : to make jokes — **jok·ing·ly** *adv*
jok·er \\'jō-kər\ *n* **1** : a person who jokes **2** : an extra card used in some card games **3** : a misleading part of an agreement that works to one party's disadvantage
jol·li·fi·ca·tion \ˌjä-li-fə-'kā-shən\ *n* : a festive celebration
jol·li·ty \\'jä-lə-tē\ *n, pl* **-ties** : GAIETY, MERRIMENT
jol·ly \\'jä-lē\ *adj* **jol·li·er; -est** : full of high spirits : MERRY

¹**jolt** \\'jōlt\ *vb* **1** : to give a quick hard knock or blow to **2** : to move with a sudden jerky motion — **jolt·er** *n*
²**jolt** *n* **1** : an abrupt jerky blow or movement **2** : a sudden shock
Jon *abbr* Jonah; Jonas
Jo·nah \\'jō-nə\ *n* — see BIBLE table
Jo·nas \\'jō-nəs\ *n* : JONAH
jon·gleur \zhōⁿ-'glər\ *n* : an itinerant medieval minstrel
jon·quil \\'jän-kwəl\ *n* [F *jonquille*, fr. Sp *junquillo*, dim. of *junco* reed, fr. L *juncus*] : a narcissus with fragrant clustered white or yellow flowers
Jor·da·ni·an \jȯr-'dā-nē-ən\ *n* : a native or inhabitant of Jordan — **Jordanian** *adj*
josh \\'jäsh\ *vb* : TEASE, JOKE
Josh *abbr* Joshua
Josh·ua \\'jä-shù-ə\ *n* — see BIBLE table
Joshua tree *n* : a tall branched yucca of the southwestern U.S.
jos·tle \\'jä-səl\ *vb* **jos·tled; jos·tling 1** : to come in contact or into collision **2** : to make one's way by pushing and shoving
Jos·ue \\'jä-shù-ē\ *n* : JOSHUA
¹**jot** \\'jät\ *n* : the least bit : IOTA
²**jot** *vb* **jot·ted; jot·ting** : to write briefly and hurriedly
jot·ting \\'jä-tiŋ\ *n* : a brief note
joule \\'jül\ *n* : a unit of work or energy equal to the work done by a force of one newton acting through a distance of one meter
jounce \\'jaúns\ *vb* **jounced; jounc·ing** : JOLT — **jounce** *n*
jour *abbr* **1** journal **2** journeyman
jour·nal \\'jərn-ᵊl\ *n* [ME, service book containing the day hours, fr. MF, fr. *journal* daily, fr. L *diurnalis*, fr. *dies* day] **1** : a brief account of daily events **2** : a record of proceedings (as of a legislative body) **3** : a periodical (as a newspaper) dealing esp. with current events **4** : the part of a rotating axle or spindle that turns in a bearing
jour·nal·ese \ˌjər-nə-'lēz, -'lēs\ *n* : a style of writing held to be characteristic of newspapers
jour·nal·ism \\'jər-nə-ˌli-zəm\ *n* **1** : the business of writing for, editing, or publishing periodicals (as newspapers) **2** : writing designed for or characteristic of newspapers — **jour·nal·ist** \-list\ *n* — **jour·nal·is·tic** \ˌjər-nə-'lis-tik\ *adj*
¹**jour·ney** \\'jər-nē\ *n, pl* **journeys** [ME, fr. OF *journee* day's journey, fr. *jour* day] : a traveling from one place to another
²**journey** *vb* **jour·neyed; jour·ney·ing** : to go on a journey : TRAVEL
jour·ney·man \-mən\ *n* **1** : a worker who has learned a trade and works for another person **2** : an experienced reliable worker
¹**joust** \\'jaúst\ *vb* : to engage in a joust
²**joust** *n* : a combat on horseback between two knights with lances esp. as part of a tournament
jo·vial \\'jō-vē-əl\ *adj* : marked by good humor — **jo·vi·al·i·ty** \ˌjō-vē-'a-lə-tē\ *n* — **jo·vi·al·ly** *adv*
¹**jowl** \\'jaúl\ *n* : loose flesh about the lower jaw or throat
²**jowl** *n* **1** : the lower jaw **2** : CHEEK
¹**joy** \\'jȯi\ *n* [ME, fr. OF *joie*, fr. L *gaudia*] **1** : a feeling of happiness that comes from success, good fortune, or a sense of well-being **2** : a source of happiness **syn** bliss, delight, enjoyment, pleasure — **joy·less** *adj*
²**joy** *vb* : REJOICE
joy·ful \-fəl\ *adj* : experiencing, causing, or showing joy — **joy·ful·ly** *adv*
joy·ous \\'jȯi-əs\ *adj* : JOYFUL — **joy·ous·ly** *adv* — **joy·ous·ness** *n*
joy·ride \\'jȯi-ˌrīd\ *n* : a ride for pleasure often marked by reckless driving — **joyride** *vb* — **joy·rid·er** *n* — **joy·rid·ing** *n*
joy·stick \-ˌstik\ *n* : a control device (as for a computer display) consisting of a lever capable of motion in two or more directions

JP *abbr* 1 jet propulsion 2 justice of the peace

Jr *abbr* junior

jt *or* **jnt** *abbr* joint

ju·bi·lant \'jü-bə-lənt\ *adj* [L *jubilans*, prp. of *jubilare* to rejoice] : EXULTANT — **ju·bi·lant·ly** *adv*

ju·bi·la·tion \,jü-bə-'lā-shən\ *n* : EXULTATION

ju·bi·lee \'jü-bə-ılē, ıjü-bə-'lē\ *n* [ME, fr. MF & LL; MF *jubilé*, fr. LL *jubilaeus*, fr. LGk *iōbēlaios*, fr. Heb *yōbhēl* ram's horn, trumpet, jubilee] 1 : a 50th anniversary 2 : a season or occasion of celebration

Jud *abbr* Judith

Ju·da·ic \jü-'dā-ik\ *also* **Ju·da·i·cal** \-'dā-ə-kəl\ *adj* : of, relating to, or characteristic of Jews or Judaism

Ju·da·ism \'jü-də-ıi-zəm, -dā-, -dē-\ *n* : a religion developed among the ancient Hebrews and marked by belief in one God and by the moral and ceremonial laws of the Old Testament and the rabbinic tradition

Jude \'jüd\ *n* — see BIBLE table

Judg *abbr* Judges

¹judge \'jəj\ *vb* **judged; judg·ing** 1 : to form an authoritative opinion 2 : to decide as a judge : TRY 3 : to form an estimate or evaluation about something : THINK **syn** conclude, deduce, gather, infer

²judge *n* 1 : a public official authorized to decide questions brought before a court 2 : UMPIRE 3 : one who gives an authoritative opinion : CRITIC — **judge·ship** *n*

Judges *n* — see BIBLE table

judg·ment *or* **judge·ment** \'jəj-mənt\ *n* 1 : a decision or opinion given after judging; *esp* : a formal decision given by a court 2 *cap* : the final judging of mankind by God 3 : the process of forming an opinion by discerning and comparing 4 : the capacity for judging : DISCERNMENT

judg·men·tal \ıjəj-'men-təl\ *adj* 1 : of, relating to, or involving judgment 2 : characterized by a tendency to judge harshly — **judg·men·tal·ly** *adv*

Judgment Day *n* : the day of the final judging of all human beings by God

ju·di·ca·ture \'jü-di-kə-ıchùr\ *n* 1 : the administration of justice 2 : JUDICIARY 1

ju·di·cial \jü-'di-shəl\ *adj* 1 : of or relating to the administration of justice or the judiciary 2 : ordered or enforced by a court 3 : CRITICAL — **ju·di·cial·ly** *adv*

ju·di·cia·ry \jü-'di-shē-ıer-ē, -shə-rē\ *n* 1 : a system of courts of law; *also* : the judges of these courts 2 : a branch of government in which judicial power is vested — **judiciary** *adj*

ju·di·cious \jü-'di-shəs\ *adj* : having, exercising, or characterized by sound judgment **syn** prudent, sage, sane, sensible, wise — **ju·di·cious·ly** *adv*

Ju·dith \'jü-dəth\ *n* — see BIBLE table

ju·do \'jü-dō\ *n* [Jp, fr. *jū* weakness + *dō* art] : a sport derived from jujitsu that emphasizes the use of quick movement and leverage to throw an opponent — **ju·do·ist** \-ist\ *n*

¹jug \'jəg\ *n* 1 : a large deep container with a narrow mouth and a handle 2 : JAIL, PRISON

²jug *vb* **jugged; jug·ging** : JAIL, IMPRISON

jug·ger·naut \'jə-gər-ınòt\ *n* [Hindi *Jagannāth*, title of Vishnu (a Hindu god), lit., lord of the world] : a massive inexorable force or object that crushes everything in its path

jug·gle \'jə-gəl\ *vb* **jug·gled; jug·gling** 1 : to keep several objects in motion in the air at the same time 2 : to manipulate esp. in order to achieve a desired end and often fraudulent end — **jug·gler** \'jə-glər\ *n*

jug·u·lar \'jə-gyə-lər\ *adj* : of, relating to, or situated in or on the throat or neck ⟨the ~ veins⟩

juice \'jüs\ *n* 1 : the extractable fluid contents of cells or tissues 2 *pl* : the natural fluids of an animal body 3 : something that supplies power; *esp* : ELECTRICITY 2

juic·er \'jü-sər\ *n* : an appliance for extracting juice (as from fruit)

juice up *vb* : to give life, energy, or spirit to

juicy \'jü-sē\ *adj* **juic·i·er; -est** 1 : SUCCULENT 2 : rich in interest; *also* : RACY — **juic·i·ly** \-sə-lē\ *adv* — **juic·i·ness** \-sē-nəs\ *n*

ju·jit·su *or* **ju·jut·su** \jü-'jit-sü\ *n* [Jp *jūjutsu*, fr. *jū* weakness + *jutsu* art, skill] : an art of fighting employing holds, throws, and paralyzing blows

ju·jube \'jü-ıjüb, 'jü-jü-ıbē\ *n* : a fruit-flavored gumdrop or lozenge

juke·box \'jük-ıbäks\ *n* : a coin-operated machine that automatically plays selected recordings

Jul *abbr* July

ju·lep \'jü-ləp\ *n* [ME, sweetened water, fr. MF, fr. Ar *julāb*, fr. Per *gulāb*, fr. *gul* rose + *āb* water] : a drink made of bourbon, sugar, and mint served over crushed ice

Ju·ly \jù-'lī\ *n* [ME *Julie*, fr. OE *Julius*, fr. L, fr. Gaius *Julius* Caesar] : the 7th month of the year having 31 days

¹jum·ble \'jəm-bəl\ *vb* **jum·bled; jum·bling** : to mix in a confused mass

²jumble *n* : a disorderly mass or pile

jum·bo \'jəm-bō\ *n, pl* **jumbos** [*Jumbo*, a huge elephant exhibited by P.T. Barnum] : a very large specimen of its kind — **jumbo** *adj*

¹jump \'jəmp\ *vb* 1 : to spring into the air : leap over 2 : to give a start 3 : to rise or increase suddenly or sharply 4 : to make a sudden attack 5 : ANTICIPATE ⟨~ the gun⟩ 6 : to leave hurriedly and often furtively ⟨~ town⟩ 7 : to act or move before (as a signal) — **jump bail** : to abscond after being released from custody on bail — **jump ship** 1 : to leave the company of a ship without authority 2 : to desert a cause

²jump *n* 1 : a spring into the air; *esp* : one made for height or distance in a track meet 2 : a sharp sudden increase 3 : an initial advantage

¹jump·er \'jəm-pər\ *n* : one that jumps

²jumper *n* 1 : a loose blouse 2 : a sleeveless one-piece dress worn usu. with a blouse 3 *pl* : a child's sleeveless coverall

jumping bean *n* : a seed of any of several Mexican shrubs that tumbles about because of the movements of a small moth larva inside it

jumping–off place *n* 1 : a remote or isolated place 2 : a place from which an enterprise is launched

jump–start \'jəmp-ıstärt\ *vb* : to start (an engine or vehicle) by connection to an external power source

jump·suit \'jəmp-ısüt\ *n* 1 : a coverall worn by parachutists in jumping 2 : a one-piece garment consisting of a blouse or shirt with attached trousers or shorts

jumpy \'jəm-pē\ *adj* **jump·i·er; -est** : NERVOUS, JITTERY

jun *abbr* junior

Jun *abbr* June

junc *abbr* junction

jun·co \'jəŋ-kō\ *n, pl* **juncos** *or* **juncoes** : any of a genus of small common pink-billed American finches that are largely gray with conspicuous white feathers in the tail

junc·tion \'jəŋk-shən\ *n* 1 : an act of joining 2 : a place or point of meeting

junc·ture \'jeŋk-chər\ *n* 1 : JOINT, CONNECTION 2 : UNION 3 : a critical time or state of affairs

June \'jün\ *n* [ME, fr. L *Junius*] : the 6th month of the year having 30 days

jun·gle \'jəŋ-gəl\ *n* 1 : a thick tangled mass of tropical vegetation; *also* : a tract overgrown with vegetation 2 : a place of ruthless struggle for survival

¹ju·nior \'jü-nyər\ *adj* 1 : YOUNGER 2 : lower in rank 3 : of or relating to juniors

²junior *n* 1 : a person who is younger or of lower rank than another 2 : a student in the next-to-last year before graduating

junior college *n* : a school that offers studies corresponding to those of the 1st two years of college

junior high school *n* : a school usu. including grades 7–9

junior varsity *n* : a team whose members lack the experience or qualifications required for the varsity

ju·ni·per \'jü-nə-pər\ *n* : any of numerous coniferous shrubs or trees with leaves like needles or scales and female cones like berries

¹**junk** \'jəŋk\ *n* **1** : old iron, glass, paper, or waste; *also* : discarded articles **2** : a shoddy product **3** *slang* : NARCOTICS; *esp* : HEROIN — **junky** *adj*

²**junk** *vb* : DISCARD, SCRAP

³**junk** *n* : a ship of eastern Asia with a high stern and 4-cornered sails

junk

junk·er \'jəŋ-kər\ *n* : something (as an old automobile) ready for scrapping

Jun·ker \'yùŋ-kər\ *n* [G] : a member of the Prussian landed aristocracy

jun·ket \'jəŋ-kət\ *n* **1** : a pudding of sweetened flavored milk set by rennet **2** : a trip made by an official at public expense

junk food *n* : food that is high in calories but low in nutritional content

junk·ie *also* **junky** \'jəŋ-kē\ *n, pl* **junkies 1** *slang* : a narcotics peddler or addict **2** : one that derives inordinate pleasure from or is dependent on something ⟨sugar ~⟩

jun·ta \'hùn-tə, 'jən-, 'hən-\ *n* [Sp, fr. *junto* joined, fr. L *junctus*, pp. of *jungere* to join] : a group of persons controlling a government esp. after a revolutionary seizure of power

Ju·pi·ter \'jü-pə-tər\ *n* : the largest of the planets and the one 5th in order of distance from the sun — see PLANET table

Ju·ras·sic \jù-'ra-sik\ *adj* : of, relating to, or being the period of the Mesozoic era between the Triassic and the Cretaceous that is marked esp. by the presence of dinosaurs — **Jurassic** *n*

ju·rid·i·cal \jù-'ri-di-kəl\ *or* **ju·rid·ic** \-dik\ *adj* **1** : of or relating to the administration of justice **2** : LEGAL — **ju·rid·i·cal·ly** \-di-k(ə-)lē\ *adv*

ju·ris·dic·tion \,jùr-əs-'dik-shən\ *n* **1** : the power, right, or authority to interpret and apply the law **2** : the authority of a sovereign power **3** : the limits or territory within which authority may be exercised — **ju·ris·dic·tion·al** \-shə-nəl\ *adj*

ju·ris·pru·dence \-'prüd-ᵊns\ *n* **1** : a system of laws **2** : the science or philosophy of law

ju·rist \'jùr-ist\ *n* : one having a thorough knowledge of law; *esp* : JUDGE

ju·ris·tic \jù-'ris-tik\ *adj* **1** : of or relating to a jurist or jurisprudence **2** : of, relating to, or recognized in law

ju·ror \'jùr-ər, -,ör\ *n* : a member of a jury

¹**ju·ry** \'jùr-ē\ *n, pl* **juries 1** : a body of persons sworn to inquire into a matter submitted to them and to give their verdict **2** : a committee for judging and awarding prizes

²**jury** *adj* : improvised for temporary use esp. in an emergency ⟨a ~ mast⟩

jury–rig \'jùr-ē-,rig\ *vb* : to construct or arrange in a makeshift fashion

¹**just** \'jəst\ *adj* **1** : having a basis in or conforming to fact or reason : REASONABLE ⟨~ comment⟩ **2** : CORRECT, PROPER ⟨~ proportions⟩ **3** : morally or legally right ⟨a ~ title⟩ **4** : DESERVED, MERITED ⟨~ punishment⟩ **syn** upright, honorable, conscientious, honest — **just·ly** *adv* — **just·ness** *n*

²**just** \'jəst, 'jist\ *adv* **1** : EXACTLY ⟨~ right⟩ **2** : very recently ⟨has ~ left⟩ **3** : BARELY ⟨~ too late⟩ **4** : DIRECTLY ⟨~ west of here⟩ **5** : ONLY ⟨~ last year⟩ **6** : QUITE ⟨~ wonderful⟩ **7** : POSSIBLY ⟨it ~ might work⟩

jus·tice \'jəs-təs\ *n* **1** : the administration of what is just (as by assigning merited rewards or punishments) **2** : JUDGE **3** : the administration of law **4** : FAIRNESS; *also* : RIGHTEOUSNESS

justice of the peace : a local magistrate empowered chiefly to try minor cases, to administer oaths, and to perform marriages

jus·ti·fy \'jəs-tə-,fī\ *vb* **-fied; -fy·ing 1** : to prove to be just, right, or reasonable **2** : to pronounce free from guilt or blame **3** : to adjust spaces in a line of printed text so the margins are even — **jus·ti·fi·able** *adj* — **jus·ti·fi·ca·tion** \,jəs-tə-fə-'kā-shən\ *n*

jut \'jət\ *vb* **jut·ted; jut·ting** : PROJECT, PROTRUDE

jute \'jüt\ *n* : a strong glossy fiber from either of two tropical plants used esp. for making sacks and twine

juv *abbr* juvenile

¹**ju·ve·nile** \'jü-və-,nīl, -nəl\ *adj* **1** : showing incomplete development **2** : of, relating to, or characteristic of children or young people

²**juvenile** *n* **1** : a young person; *esp* : one below the legally established age of adulthood **2** : a young animal (as a fish or a bird) or plant **3** : an actor or actress who plays youthful parts

juvenile delinquency *n* : violation of the law or antisocial behavior by a juvenile — **juvenile delinquent** *n*

jux·ta·pose \'jək-stə-,pōz\ *vb* **-posed; -pos·ing** : to place side by side — **jux·ta·po·si·tion** \,jək-stə-pə-'zi-shən\ *n*

JV *abbr* junior varsity

K

¹**k** \'kā\ *n, pl* **k's** *or* **ks** \'kāz\ **1** *often cap* : the 11th letter of the English alphabet **2** *cap* : STRIKEOUT

²**k** *abbr* **1** karat **2** kitchen **3** knit **4** kosher — often enclosed in a circle

¹**K** *abbr* Kelvin

²**K** *symbol* [NL *kalium*] potassium

ka·bob \kə-'bäb, 'kä-,bäb\ *n* : cubes of meat cooked with vegetables usu. on a skewer

Ka·bu·ki \kə-'bü-kē\ *n* : traditional Japanese popular drama with highly stylized singing and dancing

kad·dish \'kä-dish\ *n, often cap* : a Jewish prayer recited in the daily synagogue ritual and by mourners at public services after the death of a close relative

kaf·fee·klatsch \'kö-fē-,klach, 'kä-\ *n, often cap* [G] : an informal social gathering for coffee and conversation

kai·ser \'kī-zər\ *n* : EMPEROR; *esp* : the ruler of Germany from 1871 to 1918

kale \'kāl\ *n* : a hardy cabbage with curled leaves that do not form a head

ka·lei·do·scope \kə-'lī-də-,skōp\ *n* : a tube containing loose bits of colored material (as glass) and two mirrors at one end that shows many different patterns as it is turned — **ka·lei·do·scop·ic** \-,lī-də-'skä-pik\ *adj* — **ka·lei·do·scop·i·cal·ly** \-pi-k(ə-)lē\ *adv*

ka·ma·ai·na \,kä-mə-'ī-nə\ *n* [Hawaiian *kama'āina*, fr.

kama child + *'āina* land] : one who has lived in Hawaii for a long time

kame \'kām\ *n* [Sc, lit., comb] : a short ridge or mound of material deposited by water from a melting glacier

ka·mi·ka·ze \ˌkä-mi-'kä-zē\ *n* [Jp, lit., divine wind] : a member of a corps of Japanese pilots assigned to make a suicidal crash on a target; *also* : an airplane flown in such an attack

Kan *or* **Kans** *abbr* Kansas

kan·ga·roo \ˌkaŋ-gə-'rü\ *n, pl* **-roos** : any of various large leaping marsupial mammals of Australia and adjacent islands with powerful hind legs and a long thick tail

kangaroo court *n* : a court or an illegal self-appointed tribunal characterized by irresponsible, perverted, or irregular procedures

ka·o·lin \'kā-ə-lən\ *n* : a fine usu. white clay used in ceramics and refractories and for the treatment of diarrhea

ka·pok \'kā-ˌpäk\ *n* : silky fiber from the seeds of a tropical tree used esp. as a filling (as for life preservers)

Kap·o·si's sar·co·ma \'ka-pə-sēz-sär-'kō-mə\ *n* : a neoplastic disease associated esp. with AIDS that affects esp. the skin and mucous membranes and is characterized usu. by the formation of pink to reddish-brown or bluish plaques

kap·pa \'ka-pə\ *n* : the 10th letter of the Greek alphabet — K or κ

ka·put *also* **ka·putt** \kä-'put, kə-, -'püt\ *adj* [G, fr. F *capot* not having made a trick at piquet] **1** : utterly defeated or destroyed **2** : unable to function : USELESS

kar·a·kul \'kar-ə-kəl\ *n* : the dark tightly curled pelt of the newborn lamb of a hardy Asian breed of sheep

kar·at \'kar-ət\ *n* : a unit for expressing proportion of gold in an alloy equal to 1/24 part of pure gold

ka·ra·te \kə-'rä-tē\ *n* [Jp, lit., empty hand] : an art of self-defense in which an attacker is disabled by crippling kicks and punches

kar·ma \'kär-mə\ *n, often cap* [Skt] : the force generated by a person's actions held in Hinduism and Buddhism to perpetuate reincarnation and to determine the nature of the person's next existence — **kar·mic** \-mik\ *adj*

karst \'kärst\ *n* [G] : an irregular limestone region with sinks, underground streams, and caverns

ka·ty·did \'kā-tē-ˌdid\ *n* : any of several large green tree-dwelling American grasshoppers with long antennae

kay·ak \'kī-ˌak\ *n* : an Eskimo canoe made of a skin-covered frame with a small opening and propelled by a double-bladed paddle; *also* : a similar portable boat

kayo \(ˌ)kā-'ō, 'kā-ō\ *n* : KNOCKOUT — **kayo** *vb*

ka·zoo \kə-'zü\ *n, pl* **kazoos** : a toy musical instrument consisting of a tube with a membrane sealing one end and a side hole to sing or hum into

KB *abbr* kilobyte

kc *abbr* kilocycle

KC *abbr* **1** Kansas City **2** King's Counsel **3** Knights of Columbus

kc/s *abbr* kilocycles per second

KD *abbr* knocked down

ke·bab *or* **ke·bob** \kə-'bäb\ *var of* KABOB

kedge \'kej\ *n* : a small anchor

¹keel \'kēl\ *n* **1** : the chief structural member of a ship running lengthwise along the center of its bottom **2** : something (as a bird's breastbone) like a ship's keel in form or use — **keeled** \'kēld\ *adj*

²keel *vb* : FAINT, SWOON — usu. used with *over*

keel·boat \'kēl-ˌbōt\ *n* : a shallow covered keeled riverboat for freight that is usu. rowed, poled, or towed

keel·haul \-ˌhȯl\ *vb* : to haul under the keel of a ship as punishment

¹keen \'kēn\ *adj* **1** : SHARP (a ~ knife) **2** : SEVERE (a ~ wind) **3** : ENTHUSIASTIC (~ about swimming) **4** : men-

tally alert (a ~ mind) **5** : STRONG, ACUTE (~ eyesight) **6** : WONDERFUL, EXCELLENT — **keen·ly** *adv* — **keen·ness** *n*

²keen *n* : a lamentation for the dead uttered in a loud wailing voice or in a wordless cry — **keen** *vb*

¹keep \'kēp\ *vb* **kept** \'kept\; **keep·ing 1** : FULFILL, OBSERVE (~ a promise) (~ a holiday) **2** : GUARD (~ us from harm); *also* : to take care of (~ a neighbor's children) **3** : MAINTAIN (~ silence) **4** : to have in one's service or at one's disposal (~ a horse) **5** : to preserve a record in (~ a diary) **6** : to have in stock for sale **7** : to retain in one's possession (~ what you find) **8** : to carry on (as a business) : CONDUCT **9** : HOLD, DETAIN (~ him in jail) **10** : to refrain from revealing (~ a secret) **11** : to continue in good condition (meat will ~ in a freezer) **12** : ABSTAIN, REFRAIN — **keep·er** *n*

²keep *n* **1** : FORTRESS **2** : the means or provisions by which one is kept — **for keeps 1** : with the provision that one keep what one has won (play marbles *for keeps*) **2** : PERMANENTLY

keep·ing *n* : CONFORMITY (in ~ with good taste)

keep·sake \'kēp-ˌsāk\ *n* : MEMENTO

keep up *vb* **1** : to persevere in **2** : MAINTAIN, SUSTAIN **3** : to keep informed **4** : to continue without interruption

keg \'keg\ *n* : a small cask or barrel

keg·ler \'ke-glər\ *n* : ¹BOWLER

kelp \'kelp\ *n* : any of various coarse brown seaweeds; *also* : a mass of these or their ashes often used as fertilizer

Kelt \'kelt\ *var of* CELT

kel·vin \'kel-vən\ *n* : a unit of temperature equal to 1/273.16 of the Kelvin scale temperature of the triple point of water and equal to the Celsius degree

Kelvin *adj* : relating to, conforming to, or being a temperature scale according to which absolute zero is 0 K, the equivalent of −273.15°C

ken \'ken\ *n* **1** : range of vision : SIGHT **2** : range of understanding

ken·nel \'ken-ᵊl\ *n* : a shelter for a dog or cat; *also* : an establishment for the breeding or boarding of dogs or cats — **kennel** *vb*

ke·no \'kē-nō\ *n* : a game resembling bingo

Ken·tucky bluegrass *n* : a valuable pasture and meadow grass of both Europe and America

Ken·yan \'ke-nyən, 'kē-\ *n* : a native or inhabitant of Kenya — **Kenyan** *adj*

Ke·ogh plan \'kē-(ˌ)ō-\ *n* [Eugene James *Keogh* †1989 Am. politician] : an individual retirement account for the self-employed

ke·pi \'kā-pē, 'ke-\ *n* [F] : a military cap with a round flat top and a visor

ker·a·tin \'ker-ət-ᵊn\ *n* : any of various sulfur-containing proteins that make up hair and horny tissues

kerb \'kərb\ *n, Brit* : CURB 3

ker·chief \'kər-chəf, -ˌchēf\ *n, pl* **kerchiefs** \-chəfs, -ˌchēfs\ *also* **kerchieves** \-ˌchēvz\ [ME *courchef*, fr. OF *cuevrechief*, fr. *covrir* to cover + *chief* head] **1** : a square of cloth worn by women esp. as a head covering **2** : HANDKERCHIEF

kerf \'kərf\ *n* : a slit or notch made by a saw or cutting torch

ker·nel \'kərn-ᵊl\ *n* **1** : the inner softer part of a seed, fruit stone, or nut **2** : a whole seed of a cereal (a ~ of corn) **3** : a central or essential part : CORE

ker·o·sene *or* **ker·o·sine** \'ker-ə-ˌsēn, ˌker-ə-'sēn\ *n* : a flammable oil produced from petroleum and used for a fuel and as a solvent

ketch \'kech\ *n* : a large fore-and-aft rigged boat with two masts

ketch·up \'ke-chəp, 'ka-\ *n* : a seasoned tomato puree

ket·tle \'ket-ᵊl\ *n* : a metallic vessel for boiling liquids

ket·tle·drum \-ˌdrəm\ *n* : a brass, copper, or fiberglass drum with calfskin or plastic stretched across the top

¹key \ˈkē\ *n* **1** : a usu. metal instrument by which the bolt of a lock is turned; *also* : a device having the form or function of a key **2** : a means of gaining or preventing entrance, possession, or control **3** : EXPLANATION, SOLUTION **4** : one of the levers pressed by a finger in operating or playing an instrument **5** : a leading individual or principle **6** : a system of seven tones based on their relationship to a tonic; *also* : the tone or pitch of a voice **7** : a small switch for opening or closing an electric circuit ⟨a telegraph ∼⟩

²key *vb* **1** : SECURE, FASTEN **2** : to regulate the musical pitch of **3** : to bring into harmony or conformity **4** : to make nervous — usu. used with *up*

³key *adj* : BASIC, CENTRAL ⟨∼ issues⟩

⁴key *n* : a low island or reef (as off the southern coast of Florida)

⁵key *n, slang* : a kilogram esp. of marijuana or heroin

key•board \-ˌbōrd\ *n* **1** : a row of keys (as on a piano) **2** : an assemblage of keys for operating a machine

key club *n* : a private club serving liquor and providing entertainment

key•hole \ˈkē-ˌhōl\ *n* : a hole for receiving a key

¹key•note \-ˌnōt\ *n* **1** : the first and harmonically fundamental tone of a scale **2** : the central fact, idea, or mood

²keynote *vb* **1** : to set the keynote of **2** : to deliver the major address (as at a convention) — **key•not•er** *n*

key•punch \ˈkē-ˌpənch\ *n* : a machine with a keyboard used to cut holes or notches in punch cards — **key•punch** *vb* — **key•punch•er** *n*

key•stone \-ˌstōn\ *n* : the wedge-shaped piece at the crown of an arch that locks the other pieces in place

key•stroke \-ˌstrōk\ *n* : an act or instance of depressing a key on a keyboard

key word *n* : a word that is a key; *esp, usu* **key•word** : a significant word used as an indication of the content of or in searching (as a document or database)

kg *abbr* kilogram

KGB *abbr* [Russ *Komitet gosudarstvennoĭ bezopasnosti*] (Soviet) State Security Committee

kha•ki \ˈka-kē, ˈkä-\ *n* [Hindi *khaki* dust-colored, fr. *khāk* dust, fr. Per] **1** : a light yellowish brown color **2** : a khaki-colored cloth; *also* : a military uniform of this cloth

khan \ˈkän, ˈkan\ *n* : a Mongol leader; *esp* : a successor of Genghis Khan

khe•dive \kə-ˈdēv\ *n* : a ruler of Egypt from 1867 to 1914 governing as a viceroy of the sultan of Turkey

khoum \ˈküm\ *n* — see *ouguiya* at MONEY table

kHz *abbr* kilohertz

KIA *abbr* killed in action

kib•ble \ˈki-bəl\ *vb* **kib•bled; kib•bling** : to grind coarsely — **kibble** *n*

kib•butz \ki-ˈbu̇ts, -ˈbüts\ *n, pl* **kib•but•zim** \-ˌbu̇t-ˈsēm, -ˌbüt-\ [NHeb *qibbūṣ*] : a communal farm or settlement in Israel

ki•bitz•er \ˈki-bət-sər, kə-ˈbit-\ *n* : one who looks on and usu. offers unwanted advice esp. at a card game — **kib•itz** \ˈki-bəts\ *vb*

ki•bosh \ˈkī-ˌbäsh\ *n* : something that serves as a check or stop ⟨put the ∼ on his plan⟩

¹kick \ˈkik\ *vb* **1** : to strike out or hit with the foot; *also* : to score by kicking a ball **2** : to object strongly **3** : to recoil when fired — **kick•er** *n*

²kick *n* **1** : a blow or thrust with the foot; *esp* : a propelling of a ball with the foot **2** : the recoil of a gun **3** : a feeling or expression of objection **4** : stimulating effect esp. of pleasure

kick•back \ˈkik-ˌbak\ *n* **1** : a sharp violent reaction **2** : a secret return of a part of a sum received

kick in *vb* **1** : CONTRIBUTE **2** *slang* : DIE

kick•off \ˈkik-ˌȯf\ *n* **1** : a kick that puts the ball in play (as in football) **2** : COMMENCEMENT

kick off *vb* **1** : to start or resume play with a placekick **2** : to begin proceedings **3** *slang* : DIE

kick over *vb* : to begin or cause to begin to fire — used of an internal combustion engine

kick•shaw \ˈkik-ˌshȯ\ *n* [modif. of F *quelque chose* something] **1** : DELICACY **2** : TRINKET

kick•stand \ˈkik-ˌstand\ *n* : a swiveling metal bar attached to a 2-wheeled vehicle for holding it up when not in use

kicky \ˈki-kē\ *adj* : providing a kick or thrill : EXCITING

¹kid \ˈkid\ *n* **1** : a young goat **2** : the flesh, fur, or skin of a young goat; *also* : something made of kid **3** : CHILD, YOUNGSTER — **kid•dish** *adj*

²kid *vb* **kid•ded; kid•ding** **1** : FOOL **2** : TEASE — **kid•der** *n* — **kid•ding•ly** *adv*

kid•nap \ˈkid-ˌnap\ *vb* **kid•napped** *or* **kid•naped** \-ˌnapt\; **kid•nap•ping** *or* **kid•nap•ing** \-ˌna-piŋ\ : to hold or carry a person away by unlawful force or by fraud and against one's will — **kid•nap•per** *or* **kid•nap•er** \-ˌna-pər\ *n*

kid•ney \ˈkid-nē\ *n, pl* **kidneys** : either of a pair of organs lying near the backbone that excrete waste products of the body in the form of urine

kidney bean *n* **1** : an edible seed of the common cultivated bean; *esp* : one that is large and dark red **2** : a plant bearing kidney beans

kid•skin \ˈkid-ˌskin\ *n* : the skin of a young goat used for leather

kiel•ba•sa \kēl-ˈbä-sə, kil-\ *n, pl* **-basas** *also* **-ba•sy** \-ˈbä-sē\ [Pol *kiełbasa*] : a smoked sausage of Polish origin

¹kill \ˈkil\ *vb* **1** : to deprive of life **2** : to put an end to ⟨∼ competition⟩; *also* : DEFEAT ⟨∼ a proposed amendment⟩ **3** : USE UP ⟨∼ time⟩ **4** : to mark for omission **syn** slay, murder, assassinate, execute — **kill•er** *n*

²kill *n* **1** : an act of killing **2** : an animal or animals killed (as in a hunt); *also* : an aircraft, ship, or vehicle destroyed by military action

kill•deer \ˈkil-ˌdir\ *n, pl* **killdeers** *or* **killdeer** [imit.] : an American plover with a plaintive penetrating cry

killdeer

killer bee *n* : AFRICANIZED BEE

killer whale *n* : a small gregarious black and white flesh-eating whale with a white oval patch behind each eye

kill•ing *n* : a sudden notable gain or profit

kill•joy \ˈkil-ˌjȯi\ *n* : one who spoils the pleasures of others

kiln \ˈkil, ˈkiln\ *n* : a heated enclosure (as an oven) for processing a substance by burning, firing, or drying — **kiln** *vb*

ki•lo \ˈkē-lō\ *n, pl* **kilos** : KILOGRAM

ki•lo•byte \ˈki-lə-ˌbīt, ˈkē-\ *n* : 1024 bytes

kilo•cy•cle \ˈki-lə-ˌsī-kəl\ *n* : KILOHERTZ

ki•lo•gram \ˈkē-lə-ˌgram, ˈki-\ *n* **1** : the basic metric unit of mass that is nearly equal to the mass of 1000 cubic centimeters of water at its maximum density —

see METRIC SYSTEM table **2** : the weight of a kilogram mass under earth's gravity

ki·lo·hertz \'ki-lə-₁hərts, 'kē-, -₁herts\ *n* : 1000 hertz

kilo·li·ter \'ki-lə-₁lē-tər\ *n* — see METRIC SYSTEM table

ki·lo·me·ter \ki-'lä-mə-tər, 'ki-lə-₁mē-\ *n* — see METRIC SYSTEM table

ki·lo·ton \'ki-lə-₁tən, 'kē-lō-\ *n* **1** : 1000 tons **2** : an explosive force equivalent to that of 1000 tons of TNT

ki·lo·volt \-₁vōlt\ *n* : 1000 volts

kilo·watt \'ki-lə-₁wät\ *n* : 1000 watts

kilowatt–hour *n* : a unit of energy equal to that expended by one kilowatt in one hour

kilt \'kilt\ *n* : a knee-length pleated skirt usu. of tartan worn by men in Scotland

kil·ter \'kil-tər\ *n* : proper condition ⟨out of ∼⟩

ki·mo·no \kə-'mō-nə\ *n, pl* **-nos** **1** : a loose robe with wide sleeves traditionally worn with a wide sash as an outer garment by the Japanese **2** : a loose dressing gown or jacket

kin \'kin\ *n* **1** : an individual's relatives **2** : KINSMAN

ki·na \'kē-nə\ *n* — see MONEY table

¹kind \'kīnd\ *n* **1** : essential quality or character **2** : a group united by common traits or interests : CATEGORY; *also* : VARIETY **3** : goods or commodities as distinguished from money

²kind *adj* **1** : of a sympathetic, forbearing, or pleasant nature **2** : arising from sympathy or forbearance ⟨∼ deeds⟩ **syn** benevolent, benign, benignant, kindly — **kind·ness** *n*

kin·der·gar·ten \'kin-dər-₁gärt-ᵊn\ *n* [Ger., lit., children's garden] : a school or class for children usu. from four to six years old

kin·der·gart·ner \-₁gärt-nər\ *n* **1** : a kindergarten pupil **2** : a kindergarten teacher

kind·heart·ed \₁kīnd-'här-təd\ *adj* : marked by a sympathetic nature

kin·dle \'kind-ᵊl\ *vb* **kin·dled; kin·dling** **1** : to set on fire : start burning **2** : to stir up : AROUSE **3** : ILLUMINATE, GLOW

kin·dling \'kind-liŋ, 'kin-lən\ *n* : easily combustible material for starting a fire

¹kind·ly \'kīnd-lē\ *adj* **kind·li·er; -est** **1** : of an agreeable or beneficial nature **2** : of a sympathetic or generous nature — **kind·li·ness** *n*

²kindly *adv* **1** : READILY ⟨does not take ∼ to criticism⟩ **2** : SYMPATHETICALLY **3** : COURTEOUSLY, OBLIGINGLY

kind of *adv* : to a moderate degree ⟨it's *kind of* late to begin⟩

¹kin·dred \'kin-drəd\ *n* **1** : a group of related individuals **2** : one's relatives

²kindred *adj* : of a like nature or character

kine \'kīn\ *archaic pl of* COW

kin·e·ma \'ki-nə-mə\ *Brit var of* CINEMA

ki·ne·mat·ics \₁ki-nə-'ma-tiks\ *n* : a science that deals with motion apart from considerations of mass and force — **ki·ne·mat·ic** \-tik\ *or* **ki·ne·mat·i·cal** \-ti-kəl\ *adj*

kin·es·the·sia \₁ki-nəs-'thē-zhə, -zhē-ə\ *or* **kin·es·the·sis** \-'thē-səs\ *n, pl* **-thesias** *or* **-theses** \-₁sēz\ : a sense that perceives bodily movement, position, and weight and is mediated by nervous elements in tendons, muscles, and joints; *also* : sensory experience derived from this sense — **kin·es·thet·ic** \-'the-tik\ *adj*

ki·net·ic \kə-'ne-tik\ *adj* : of or relating to the motion of material bodies and the forces and energy (**kinetic energy**) associated with them

ki·net·ics \-tiks\ *n sing or pl* : a science that deals with the effects of forces upon the motions of material bodies or with changes in a physical or chemical system

kin·folk \'kin-₁fōk\ *or* **kinfolks** *n pl* : RELATIVES

king \'kiŋ\ *n* **1** : a male sovereign **2** : a chief among competitors ⟨home-run ∼⟩ **3** : the principal piece in the game of chess **4** : a playing card bearing the figure of a king **5** : a checker that has been crowned — **king·less** *adj* — **king·ly** *adj* — **king·ship** *n*

king crab *n* **1** : HORSESHOE CRAB **2** : a large crab of the north Pacific caught commercially for food

king·dom \'kiŋ-dəm\ *n* **1** : a country whose head is a king or queen **2** : a realm or region in which something or someone is dominant ⟨a cattle ∼⟩ **3** : one of the three primary divisions of lifeless material, plants, and animals into which natural objects are grouped; *also* : a biological category that ranks above the phylum

king·fish·er \-₁fi-shər\ *n* : any of numerous usu. bright-colored crested birds that feed chiefly on fish

king·pin \'kiŋ-₁pin\ *n* **1** : HEADPIN **2** : the leader in a group or undertaking

Kings *n* — see BIBLE table

king–size \'kiŋ-₁sīz\ *or* **king–sized** \-₁sīzd\ *adj* **1** : longer than the regular or standard size **2** : unusually large **3** : having dimensions of about 76 by 80 inches (1.9 by 2.0 meters) ⟨a ∼ bed⟩; *also* : of a size that fits a king-size bed

kink \'kiŋk\ *n* **1** : a short tight twist or curl **2** : a mental peculiarity : QUIRK **3** : CRAMP ⟨a ∼ in the back⟩ **4** : an imperfection likely to cause difficulties in operation — **kinky** *adj*

kin·ship \'kin-₁ship\ *n* : RELATIONSHIP

kins·man \'kinz-mən\ *n* : RELATIVE; *esp* : a male relative

kins·wom·an \-₁wu̇-mən\ *n* : a female relative

ki·osk \'kē-₁äsk\ *n* : a small structure with one or more open sides

Ki·o·wa \'kī-ə-₁wȯ, -₁wä, -₁wā\ *n, pl* **Kiowa** *or* **Kiowas** : a member of an American Indian people of Colorado, Kansas, New Mexico, Oklahoma, and Texas

kip \'kip, 'gip\ *n, pl* **kip** *or* **kips** — see MONEY table

kip·per \'ki-pər\ *n* : a fish (as a herring) preserved by salting and drying or smoking — **kipper** *vb*

kirk \'kərk, 'kirk\ *n, chiefly Scot* : CHURCH

kir·tle \'kərt-ᵊl\ *n* : a long gown or dress worn by women

kis·met \'kiz-₁met, -mət\ *n, often cap* [Turk, fr. Ar *qismah* portion, lot] : FATE

¹kiss \'kis\ *vb* **1** : to touch or caress with the lips as a mark of affection or greeting **2** : to touch gently or lightly

²kiss *n* **1** : a caress with the lips **2** : a gentle touch or contact **3** : a bite-size candy

kiss·er \'ki-sər\ *n* **1** : one that kisses **2** *slang* : MOUTH **3** *slang* : FACE

kit \'kit\ *n* **1** : a set of articles for personal use; *also* : a set of tools or implements or of parts to be assembled **2** : a container (as a case) for a kit

kitch·en \'ki-chən\ *n* **1** : a room with cooking facilities **2** : the personnel that prepares, cooks, and serves food

kitch·en·ette \₁ki-chə-'net\ *n* : a small kitchen or an alcove containing cooking facilities

kitchen police *n* **1** : KP **2** : the work of KPs

kitch·en·ware \'ki-chən-₁war\ *n* : utensils and appliances for kitchen use

kite \'kīt\ *n* **1** : any of various long-winged hawks often with deeply forked tails **2** : a light frame covered with paper or cloth and designed to be flown in the air at the end of a long string

kith \'kith\ *n* [ME, fr. OE *cȳthth*, fr. *cūth* known] : familiar friends, neighbors, or relatives ⟨∼ and kin⟩

kitsch \'kich\ *n* [G] : shoddy or cheap artistic or literary material — **kitschy** *adj*

kit·ten \'kit-ᵊn\ *n* : a young cat — **kit·ten·ish** *adj*

¹kit·ty \'ki-tē\ *n, pl* **kitties** : CAT; *esp* : KITTEN

²kitty *n, pl* **kitties** : a fund in a poker game made up of contributions from each pot; *also* : POOL

kit·ty–cor·ner *or* **kit·ty–cor·nered** *var of* CATER-CORNER

ki·wi \'kē-(₁)wē\ *n* : any of a small genus of flightless New Zealand birds

kiwi

ki·wi·fruit \-ˌfrüt\ *n* : a brownish hairy egg-shaped fruit of a subtropical vine that has sweet bright green flesh and small edible black seeds

KJV *abbr* King James Version

KKK *abbr* Ku Klux Klan

kl *abbr* kiloliter

klatch *or* **klatsch** \ˈklach\ *n* [G *Klatsch* gossip] : a gathering marked by informal conversation

klep·to·ma·nia \ˌklep-tə-ˈmā-nē-ə\ *n* : a persistent neurotic impulse to steal esp. without economic motive — **klep·to·ma·ni·ac** \-nē-ˌak\ *n*

klieg light *or* **kleig light** \ˈklēg-\ *n* : a very bright lamp used in making motion pictures

klutz \ˈkləts\ *n* [Yiddish *klots*, lit., wooden beam] : a clumsy person — **klutzy** *adj*

km *abbr* kilometer

kn *abbr* knot

knack \ˈnak\ *n* 1 : a clever way of doing something 2 : natural aptitude

knap·sack \ˈnap-ˌsak\ *n* : a bag (as of canvas) strapped on the back and used esp. for carrying supplies

knave \ˈnāv\ *n* 1 : ROGUE 2 : JACK 6 — **knav·ery** \ˈnā-və-rē\ *n* — **knav·ish** \ˈnā-vish\ *adj*

knead \ˈnēd\ *vb* : to work and press into a mass with the hands; *also* : MASSAGE — **knead·er** *n*

knee \ˈnē\ *n* : the joint in the middle part of the leg — **kneed** \ˈnēd\ *adj*

knee·cap \ˈnē-ˌkap\ *n* : a thick flat movable bone forming the front of the knee

knee·hole \-ˌhōl\ *n* : a space (as under a desk) for the knees

kneel \ˈnēl\ *vb* **knelt** \ˈnelt\ *or* **kneeled; kneel·ing** : to bend the knee : fall or rest on the knees

¹knell \ˈnel\ *vb* 1 : to ring esp. for a death or disaster 2 : to summon, announce, or proclaim by a knell

²knell *n* 1 : a stroke of a bell esp. when tolled (as for a funeral) 2 : an indication of the end or failure of something

knew *past of* KNOW

knick·ers \ˈni-kərz\ *n pl* : loose-fitting short pants gathered at the knee

knick·knack \ˈnik-ˌnak\ *n* : a small trivial article intended for ornament

¹knife \ˈnīf\ *n, pl* **knives** \ˈnīvz\ 1 : a cutting instrument consisting of a sharp blade fastened to a handle 2 : a sharp cutting tool in a machine

²knife *vb* **knifed; knif·ing** : to stab, slash, or wound with a knife

¹knight \ˈnīt\ *n* 1 : a mounted warrior of feudal times serving a king 2 : a man honored by a sovereign for merit and in Great Britain ranking below a baronet 3 : a man devoted to the service of a lady 4 : a member of an order or society 5 : a chess piece having an L-shaped move — **knight·ly** *adj*

²knight *vb* : to make a knight of

knight·hood \ˈnīt-ˌhud\ *n* 1 : the rank, dignity, or profession of a knight 2 : CHIVALRY 3 : knights as a class or body

knish \kə-ˈnish\ *n* [Yiddish] : a small round or square of dough stuffed with a filling (as of meat or fruit) and baked or fried

¹knit \ˈnit\ *vb* **knit** *or* **knit·ted; knit·ting** 1 : to link firmly or closely 2 : WRINKLE ⟨∼ her brows⟩ 3 : to form a fabric by interlacing yarn or thread in connected loops with needles 4 : to grow together — **knit·ter** *n*

²knit *n* 1 : a basic knitting stitch 2 : a knitted garment or fabric

knit·wear \-ˌwar\ *n* : knitted clothing

knob \ˈnäb\ *n* 1 : a rounded protuberance; *also* : a small rounded ornament or handle 2 : a rounded usu. isolated hill — **knobbed** \ˈnäbd\ *adj* — **knob·by** \ˈnä-bē\ *adj*

¹knock \ˈnäk\ *vb* 1 : to strike with a sharp blow 2 : BUMP, COLLIDE 3 : to make a pounding noise; *esp* : to have engine knock 4 : to find fault with

²knock *n* 1 : a sharp blow 2 : a pounding noise; *esp* : one caused by abnormal ignition in an automobile engine

knock·down \ˈnäk-ˌdaun\ *n* 1 : the action of knocking down 2 : something (as a blow) that knocks down 3 : something that can be easily assembled or disassembled

knock down *vb* 1 : to strike to the ground with or as if with as sharp blow 2 : to take apart : DISASSEMBLE 3 : to receive as income or salary : EARN 4 : to make a reduction in

knock·er \ˈnä-kər\ *n* : one that knocks; *esp* : a device hinged to a door for use in knocking

knock–knee \ˈnäk-ˌnē\ *n* : a condition in which the legs curve inward at the knees — **knock–kneed** \-ˌnēd\ *adj*

knock·off \ˈnäk-ˌof\ *n* : a copy or imitation of someone or something popular

knock off *vb* 1 : to stop doing something 2 : to do quickly, carelessly, or routinely 3 : to deduct from a price 4 : KILL 5 : ROB 6 : COPY, IMITATE

knock·out \ˈnäk-ˌaut\ *n* 1 : a blow that fells and immobilizes an opponent (as in boxing) 2 : something sensationally striking or attractive

knock out *vb* 1 : to defeat by a knockout 2 : to make unconscious or inoperative 3 : to tire out : EXHAUST

knock·wurst *or* **knack·wurst** \ˈnäk-ˌwərst, -ˌvürst\ *n* : a short thick heavily seasoned sausage

knoll \ˈnōl\ *n* : a small round hill

¹knot \ˈnät\ *n* 1 : an interlacing (as of string) forming a lump or knob and often used for fastening or tying together 2 : PROBLEM 3 : a bond of union; *esp* : the marriage bond 4 : a protuberant lump or swelling in tissue 5 : a rounded cross-grained area in lumber that is a section through the junction of a tree branch with the trunk; *also* : the woody tissue forming this junction in a tree 6 : GROUP, CLUSTER 7 : an ornamental bow of ribbon 8 : one nautical mile per hour; *also* : one nautical mile — **knot·ty** *adj*

²knot *vb* **knot·ted; knot·ting** 1 : to tie in or with a knot 2 : ENTANGLE

knot·hole \-ˌhōl\ *n* : a hole in a board or tree trunk where a knot has come out

knout \ˈnaut, ˈnüt\ *n* : a whip used for flogging

know \ˈnō\ *vb* **knew** \ˈnü, ˈnyü\; **known** \ˈnōn\; **know·ing** 1 : to perceive directly : have understanding or direct cognition of; *also* : to recognize the nature of 2 : to be acquainted or familiar with 3 : to be aware of the truth of 4 : to have a practical understanding of — **know·able** *adj* — **know·er** *n* — **in the know** : possessing confidential information

know–how \ˈnō-ˌhau\ *n* : knowledge of how to do something smoothly and efficiently

know·ing *adj* 1 : having or reflecting knowledge, intelligence, or information 2 : shrewdly and keenly alert 3 : DELIBERATE, INTENTIONAL **syn** clever, bright, smart — **know·ing·ly** *adv*

knowl·edge \ˈnä-lij\ *n* 1 : understanding gained by actual experience ⟨a ∼ of carpentry⟩ 2 : range of information ⟨to the best of my ∼⟩ 3 : clear perception of truth 4 : something learned and kept in the mind

knowl·edge·able \'nä-li-jə-bəl\ *adj* : having or showing knowledge or intelligence

knuck·le \'nə-kəl\ *n* : the rounded knob at a joint and esp. at a finger joint

knuckle down *vb* : to apply oneself earnestly

knuckle under *vb* : SUBMIT, SURRENDER

knurl \'nərl\ *n* **1** : KNOB **2** : one of a series of small ridges on a metal surface to aid in gripping — **knurled** \'nərld\ *adj* — **knurly** *adj*

¹KO \(,)kā-'ō, 'kā-ō\ *n* : KNOCKOUT

²KO *vb* **KO'd; KO'ing** : to knock out in boxing

ko·ala \kō-'ä-lə\ *n* : a gray furry Australian marsupial with large hairy ears that feeds on eucalyptus leaves

ko·bo \'kō-(,)bō\ *n, pl* **kobo** — see *naira* at MONEY table

K of C *abbr* Knights of Columbus

kohl·ra·bi \kōl-'rä-bē\ *n, pl* **-bies** [G, fr. It *cavolo rapa*, lit., cabbage turnip] : a cabbage that forms no head but has a swollen fleshy edible stem

ko·lin·sky \kə-'lin-skē\ *n, pl* **-skies** : the fur of various Asian minks

kook \'kük\ *n* : SCREWBALL 2

kooky *also* **kook·ie** \'kü-kē\ *adj* **kook·i·er; -est** : having the characteristics of a kook : CRAZY, ECCENTRIC — **kook·i·ness** *n*

ko·peck *or* **ko·pek** \'kō-,pek\ *n* [Russ *kopeĭka*] — see *ruble* at MONEY table

Ko·ran \kə-'ran, -'rän\ *n* [Ar *qur'ān*] : a sacred book of Islam that contains revelations made to Muhammad by Allah

Ko·re·an \kə-'rē-ən\ *n* : a native or inhabitant of Korea — **Korean** *adj*

ko·ru·na \'kȯr-ə-,nä\ *n, pl* **ko·ru·ny** \-ə-nē\ *or* **korunas** *or* **ko·rum** \'kȯr-əm\ — see MONEY table

ko·sher \'kō-shər\ *adj* [Yiddish, fr. Heb *kāshēr* fit, proper] **1** : ritually fit for use according to Jewish law **2** : selling or serving kosher food

kow·tow \kaȯ-'taȯ, 'kaȯ-,taȯ\ *vb* [Chin *kòutóu*, fr. *kòu* to knock + *tóu* head] **1** : to show obsequious deference **2** : to kneel and touch the forehead to the ground as a sign of homage or deep respect

KP \,kā-'pē\ *n* **1** : an enlisted man detailed to help the cooks in a military mess **2** : the work of KPs

kph *abbr* kilometers per hour

Kr *symbol* krypton

kraal \'kräl, 'krȯl\ *n* **1** : a native village in southern Africa **2** : an enclosure for domestic animals in southern Africa

kraut \'kraȯt\ *n* : SAUERKRAUT

Krem·lin \'krem-lən\ *n* : the Russian or Soviet government

Krem·lin·ol·o·gist \,krem-lə-'nä-lə-jist\ *n* : a specialist in the policies and practices of the Soviet government

¹kro·na \'krō-nə\ *n, pl* **kro·nor** \-,nȯr\ [Sw] — see MONEY table

²kro·na \'krō-nə\ *n, pl* **kro·nur** \-nər\ [Icel] — see MONEY table

kro·ne \'krō-nə\ *n, pl* **kro·ner** \-nər\ — see MONEY table

Kru·ger·rand \'krü-gər-,rand, -,ränd\ *n* : a 1-ounce gold coin of the Republic of South Africa

kryp·ton \'krip-,tän\ *n* : a gaseous chemical element used esp. in electric lamps — see ELEMENT table

KS *abbr* Kansas

kt *abbr* **1** karat **2** knight

ku·do \'kü-dō, 'kyü-\ *n, pl* **kudos** [fr. *kudos* (taken as pl.)] **1** : AWARD, HONOR **2** : COMPLIMENT, PRAISE

ku·dos \'kü-,däs, 'kyü-\ *n* : fame and renown resulting from achievement

kud·zu \'kùd-zü, 'kəd-\ *n* [Jp *kuzu*] : a creeping leguminous vine used for hay, forage, and erosion control

ku·lak \kü-'lak, kyü-, -'läk\ *n* [Russ, lit., fist] **1** : a wealthy peasant farmer in 19th century Russia **2** : a farmer characterized by Communists as too wealthy

kum·quat \'kəm-,kwät\ *n* : any of several small citrus fruits with sweet spongy rind and acid pulp

kung fu \,kəŋ-'fü, ,kùŋ-\ *n* : a Chinese art of self= defense resembling karate

ku·rus \kə-'rüsh\ *n, pl* **kurus** — see *lira* at MONEY table

Ku·waiti \kù-'wā-tē\ *n* : a native or inhabitant of Kuwait — **Kuwaiti** *adj*

kV *abbr* kilovolt

kvetch \'kvech, 'kfech\ *vb* : to complain habitually — **kvetch** *n*

kW *abbr* kilowatt

kwa·cha \'kwä-chə\ *n, pl* **kwacha** — see MONEY table

kwan·za \'kwän-zə\ *n, pl* **kwanzas** *or* **kwanza** — see MONEY table

kwash·i·or·kor \,kwä-shē-'ȯr-kȯr, -ȯr-'kȯr\ *n* : a disease of young children caused by deficient intake of protein

kWh *abbr* kilowatt-hour

Ky *or* **KY** *abbr* Kentucky

kyat \'chät\ *n* — see MONEY table

L

¹l \'el\ *n, pl* **l's** *or* **ls** \'elz\ *often cap* : the 12th letter of the English alphabet

²l *abbr, often cap* **1** lake **2** large **3** left **4** [L *libra*] pound **5** line **6** liter

¹La *abbr* Louisiana

²La *symbol* lanthanum

LA *abbr* **1** law agent **2** Los Angeles **3** Louisiana

lab \'lab\ *n* : LABORATORY

Lab *n* : LABRADOR RETRIEVER

¹la·bel \'lā-bəl\ *n* **1** : a slip attached to something for identification or description **2** : a descriptive or identifying word or phrase **3** : BRAND 3

²label *vb* **-beled** *or* **-belled; -bel·ing** *or* **-bel·ling** **1** : to affix a label to **2** : to describe or name with a label

la·bi·al \'lā-bē-əl\ *adj* : of or relating to the lips or labia

la·bia ma·jo·ra \'lā-bē-ə-mə-'jȯr-ə\ *n pl* : the outer fatty folds of the vulva

labia mi·no·ra \-mə-'nȯr-ə\ *n pl* : the inner highly vascular folds of the vulva

la·bile \'lā-,bīl, -bəl\ *adj* **1** : UNSTABLE **2** : ADAPTABLE

la·bi·um \'lā-bē-əm\ *n, pl* **la·bia** \-ə\ [NL, fr. L, lip] : any of the folds at the margin of the vulva

¹la·bor \'lā-bər\ *n* **1** : physical or mental effort; *also* : human activity that provides the goods or services in an economy **2** : the physical efforts of giving birth; *also* : the period of such labor **3** : TASK **4** : those who do manual labor or work for wages; *also* : labor unions or their officials

²labor *vb* **1** : WORK **2** : to move with great effort **3** : to be in the labor of giving birth **4** : to suffer from some disadvantage or distress ⟨~ under a delusion⟩ **5** : to treat or work out laboriously — **la·bor·er** *n*

lab·o·ra·to·ry \'la-brə-,tȯr-ē, -bə-rə-\ *n, pl* **-ries** : a place equipped for making scientific experiments or tests

Labor Day *n* : the 1st Monday in September observed as a legal holiday in recognition of the working people

la·bored \'lā-bərd\ *adj* : not freely or easily done ⟨~ breathing⟩

la·bo·ri·ous \lə-'bȯr-ē-əs\ *adj* **1** : INDUSTRIOUS **2** : requiring great effort — **la·bo·ri·ous·ly** *adv*

la·bor·sav·ing \'lā-bər-,sā-viŋ\ *adj* : designed to replace or decrease labor

labor union *n* : an organization of workers formed to advance its members' interest in respect to wages and working conditions

la·bour *chiefly Brit var of* LABOR
lab·ra·dor·ite \'la-brə-ˌdȯr-ˌīt\ *n* : an iridescent feldspar used in jewelry
Lab·ra·dor retriever \'la-brə-ˌdȯr-\ *n* : a strongly built retriever having a short dense black, yellow, or chocolate coat
la·bur·num \lə-'bər-nəm\ *n* : a leguminous shrub or tree with hanging clusters of yellow flowers
lab·y·rinth \'la-bə-ˌrinth\ *n* : a place constructed of or filled with confusing intricate passageways : MAZE
lab·y·rin·thine \ˌla-bə-'rin-thən, -ˌthīn, -ˌthēn\ *adj* : INTRICATE, INVOLVED
lac \'lak\ *n* : a resinous substance secreted by a scale insect and used chiefly in the form of shellac
¹lace \'lās\ *vb* **laced; lac·ing 1** : TIE **2** : to adorn with lace **3** : INTERTWINE **4** : BEAT, LASH **5** : to add to something to impart zest or savor to
²lace *n* [ME, fr. OF *laz*, fr. L *laqueus* snare, noose] **1** : a cord or string used for drawing together two edges **2** : an ornamental braid **3** : a fine openwork usu. figured fabric made of thread — **lacy** \'lā-sē\ *adj*
lac·er·ate \'la-sə-ˌrāt\ *vb* **-at·ed; -at·ing** : to tear roughly — **lac·er·a·tion** \ˌla-sə-'rā-shən\ *n*
lace·wing \'lās-ˌwiŋ\ *n* : any of various insects with delicate wing veins, long antennae, and often brilliant eyes
lach·ry·mal *or* **lac·ri·mal** \'la-krə-məl\ *adj* **1** *usu* lacrimal : of, relating to, or being glands that produce tears **2** : of, relating to, or marked by tears
lach·ry·mose \'la-krə-ˌmōs\ *adj* **1** : TEARFUL **2** : MOURNFUL
¹lack \'lak\ *vb* **1** : to be wanting or missing **2** : to be deficient in
²lack *n* : the fact or state of being wanting or deficient : NEED
lack·a·dai·si·cal \ˌla-kə-'dā-zi-kəl\ *adj* : lacking life, spirit, or zest — **lack·a·dai·si·cal·ly** \-k(ə-)lē\ *adv*
lack·ey \'la-kē\ *n, pl* **lackeys 1** : FOOTMAN, SERVANT **2** : TOADY
lack·lus·ter \'lak-ˌləs-tər\ *adj* : DULL
la·con·ic \lə-'kä-nik\ *adj* [L *laconicus* Spartan, fr. Gk *lakōnikos*; fr. the Spartan reputation for terseness of speech] : sparing of words : TERSE **syn** concise, curt, short, succinct, brusque — **la·con·i·cal·ly** \-ni-k(ə-)lē\ *adv*
lac·quer \'la-kər\ *n* : a clear or colored usu. glossy and quick-drying surface coating — **lacquer** *vb*
lac·ri·ma·tion \ˌla-krə-'mā-shən\ *n* : secretion of tears
la·crosse \lə-'krȯs\ *n* [CanF *la crosse*, lit., the crosier] : a goal game in which players use a long-handled triangular-headed stick having a mesh pouch for catching, carrying, and throwing the ball
lac·tate \'lak-ˌtāt\ *vb* **lac·tat·ed; lac·tat·ing** : to secrete milk — **lac·ta·tion** \lak-'tā-shən\ *n*
lac·tic \'lak-tik\ *adj* **1** : of or relating to milk **2** : obtained from sour milk or whey
lactic acid *n* : a syrupy acid present in blood and muscle tissue and used in food and medicine
lac·tose \'lak-ˌtōs\ *n* : a sugar present in milk
la·cu·na \lə-'kü-nə, -'kyü-\ *n, pl* **la·cu·nae** \-nē\ *or* **la·cu·nas** [L, pool, pit, gap, fr. *lacus* lake] : a blank space or missing part : GAP
lad \'lad\ *n* : YOUTH; *also* : FELLOW
lad·der \'la-dər\ *n* : a structure for climbing that consists of two parallel sidepieces joined at intervals by crosspieces
lad·die \'la-dē\ *n* : a young lad
lad·en \'lād-ᵊn\ *adj* : LOADED, BURDENED
lad·ing \'lā-diŋ\ *n* : CARGO, FREIGHT
la·dle \'lād-ᵊl\ *n* : a deep-bowled long-handled spoon used in taking up and conveying liquids — **ladle** *vb*
la·dy \'lā-dē\ *n, pl* **ladies** [ME, fr. OE *hlæfdige*, fr. *hlāf* bread + *-dīge* (akin to *dǣge* kneader of bread)] **1** : a woman of property, rank, or authority; *also* : a woman of superior social position or of refinement **2** : WOMAN **3** : WIFE

lady beetle *n* : LADYBUG
la·dy·bird \'lā-dē-ˌbərd\ *n* : LADYBUG
la·dy·bug \-ˌbəg\ *n* : any of various small nearly hemispherical and usu. brightly colored beetles that feed mostly on other insects
la·dy·fin·ger \-ˌfiŋ-gər\ *n* : a small finger-shaped sponge cake
lady–in–waiting *n, pl* **ladies–in–waiting** : a lady appointed to attend or wait on a queen or princess
la·dy·like \'lā-dē-ˌlīk\ *adj* : WELL-BRED
la·dy·ship \-ˌship\ *n* : the condition of being a lady : rank of lady
lady's slipper *or* **lady slipper** *n* : any of several No. American orchids with slipper-shaped flowers
¹lag \'lag\ *n* **1** : a slowing up or falling behind; *also* : the amount by which one lags **2** : INTERVAL
²lag *vb* **lagged; lag·ging 1** : to fail to keep up : stay behind **2** : to slacken gradually **syn** dawdle, dally, tarry, loiter
la·ger \'lä-gər\ *n* : a light-colored usu. dry beer
lag·gard \'la-gərd\ *adj* : tending to lag — **laggard** *n* — **lag·gard·ly** *adv or adj* — **lag·gard·ness** *n*
la·gniappe \'lan-ˌyap\ *n* : something given free esp. with a purchase
la·goon \lə-'gün\ *n* : a shallow sound, channel, or pond near or connected to a larger body of water
laid *past and past part of* LAY
laid–back \'lād-'bak\ *adj* : having a relaxed style or character ⟨~ music⟩
lain *past part of* ¹LIE
lair \'lar\ *n* : the resting or living place of a wild animal : DEN
laird \'lard\ *n, Scot* : a landed proprietor
lais·ser–faire *chiefly Brit var of* LAISSEZ-FAIRE
lais·sez–faire \ˌle-ˌsā-'far, ˌlā-, -ˌzā-\ *n* [F *laissez faire* let do] : a doctrine opposing governmental control of economic affairs beyond that necessary to maintain peace and property rights
la·ity \'lā-ə-tē\ *n* **1** : the people of a religious faith as distinct from its clergy **2** : the mass of people as distinct from those of a particular field
lake \'lāk\ *n* : an inland body of standing water of considerable size; *also* : a pool of liquid (as lava or pitch)
¹lam \'lam\ *vb* **lammed; lam·ming** : to flee hastily — **lam** *n*
²lam *abbr* laminated
Lam *abbr* Lamentations
la·ma \'lä-mə\ *n* : a Buddhist monk of Tibet or Mongolia
la·ma·sery \'lä-mə-ˌser-ē\ *n, pl* **-ser·ies** : a monastery for lamas
¹lamb \'lam\ *n* **1** : a young sheep; *also* : its flesh used as food **2** : an innocent or gentle person
²lamb *vb* : to bring forth a lamb
lam·baste *or* **lam·bast** \lam-'bāst, -'bast\ *vb* **1** : BEAT **2** : EXCORIATE **syn** castigate, flay, lash
lamb·da \'lam-də\ *n* : the 11th letter of the Greek alphabet — Λ or λ
lam·bent \'lam-bənt\ *adj* [L *lambens*, prp. of *lambere* to lick] **1** : FLICKERING **2** : softly radiant ⟨~ eyes⟩ **3** : marked by lightness or brilliance ⟨~ humor⟩ **syn** effulgent, incandescent, lucent, luminous — **lam·ben·cy** \-bən-sē\ *n* — **lam·bent·ly** *adv*
lamb·skin \'lam-ˌskin\ *n* : a lamb's skin or a small fine-grade sheepskin or the leather made from either
¹lame \'lām\ *adj* **lam·er; lam·est 1** : having a body part and esp. a limb so disabled as to impair freedom of movement; *also* : marked by stiffness and soreness **2** : lacking substance : WEAK — **lame·ly** *adv* — **lame·ness** *n*
²lame *vb* **lamed; lam·ing** : to make lame : CRIPPLE, DISABLE
la·mé \lä-'mā, la-\ *n* [F] : a brocaded clothing fabric with tinsel filling threads (as of gold or silver)
lame·brain \'lām-ˌbrān\ *n* : DOLT
lame duck *n* : an elected official continuing to hold of-

fice between an election and the inauguration of a successor — **lame–duck** *adj*

¹**la·ment** \lə-'ment\ *vb* **1** : to mourn aloud : WAIL **2** : to express sorrow or regret for : BEWAIL — **lam·en·ta·ble** \'la-mən-tə-bəl, lə-'men-tə-\ *adj* — **lam·en·ta·bly** \-blē\ *adv* — **lam·en·ta·tion** \₁la-mən-'tā-shən\ *n*

²**lament** *n* **1** : a crying out in grief : WAIL **2** : DIRGE, ELEGY **3** : COMPLAINT

Lamentations *n* — see BIBLE table

la·mia \'lā-mē-ə\ *n* : a female demon

lam·i·na \'la-mə-nə\ *n, pl* **-nae** \-₁nē\ *or* **-nas** : a thin plate or scale

¹**lam·i·nate** \'la-mə-₁nāt\ *vb* **-nat·ed; -nat·ing** : to make by uniting layers of one or more materials — **lam·i·na·tion** \₁la-mə-'nā-shən\ *n*

²**lam·i·nate** \-nət\ *n* : a product manufactured by laminating

lamp \'lamp\ *n* **1** : a vessel with a wick for burning a flammable liquid (as oil) to produce light **2** : a device for producing light or heat

lamp·black \-₁blak\ *n* : black soot used esp. as a pigment

lamp·light·er \-₁lī-tər\ *n* : one that lights a lamp

lam·poon \lam-'pün\ *n* : SATIRE; *esp* : a harsh satire directed against an individual — **lampoon** *vb*

lam·prey \'lam-prē\ *n, pl* **lampreys** : any of a family of eel-shaped jawless fishes that have well-developed eyes and a large disk-shaped sucking mouth armed with horny teeth

la·nai \lə-'nī\ *n* [Hawaiian *lānai*] : PORCH, VERANDA

¹**lance** \'lans\ *n* **1** : a spear carried by mounted soldiers **2** : any of various sharp-pointed implements; *esp* : LANCET

²**lance** *vb* **lanced; lanc·ing** : to pierce or open with a lance (~ a boil)

lance corporal *n* : an enlisted man in the marine corps ranking above a private first class and below a corporal

lanc·er \'lan-sər\ *n* : a cavalryman of a unit formerly armed with lances

lan·cet \'lan-sət\ *n* : a sharp-pointed and usu. 2-edged surgical instrument

¹**land** \'land\ *n* **1** : the solid part of the surface of the earth; *also* : a part of the earth's surface (fenced ~) (marshy ~) **2** : NATION **3** : REALM, DOMAIN — **land·less** *adj*

²**land** *vb* **1** : DISEMBARK; *also* : to touch at a place on shore **2** : to alight or cause to alight on a surface **3** : to bring to or arrive at a destination **4** : to catch and bring in (~ a fish); *also* : GAIN, SECURE (~ a job)

lan·dau \'lan-₁daů\ *n* : a 4-wheeled carriage with a top divided into two sections that can be lowered, thrown back, or removed

land·ed *adj* : having an estate in land (~ gentry)

land·er \'lan-dər\ *n* : a space vehicle designed to land on a celestial body

land·fall \'land-₁fól\ *n* : a sighting or making of land (as after a voyage); *also* : the land first sighted

land·fill \-₁fil\ *n* : a low-lying area on which refuse is buried between layers of earth

land·form \-₁fórm\ *n* : a natural feature of a land surface

land·hold·er \-₁hōl-dər\ *n* : a holder or owner of land — **land·hold·ing** \-diŋ\ *adj or n*

land·ing \'lan-diŋ\ *n* **1** : the action of one that lands **2** : a place for discharging or taking on passengers and cargo **3** : a level part of a staircase

landing gear *n* : the part that supports the weight of an aircraft when it is on the ground

land·la·dy \'land-₁lā-dē\ *n* : a woman who is a landlord

land·locked \-₁läkt\ *adj* **1** : enclosed or nearly enclosed by land (a ~ country) **2** : confined to fresh water by some barrier (~ salmon)

land·lord \-₁lórd\ *n* **1** : the owner of property leased or rented to another **2** : a person who rents lodgings : INNKEEPER

land·lub·ber \-₁lə-bər\ *n* : one who knows little of the sea or seamanship

land·mark \-₁märk\ *n* **1** : an object that marks a course or boundary or serves as a guide **2** : an event that marks a turning point **3** : a structure of unusual historical and usu. aesthetic interest

land·mass \-₁mas\ *n* : a large area of land

land mine *n* **1** : a mine placed on or just below the surface of the ground and designed to be exploded by the weight of someone or something passing over it **2** : a trap for the unwary

land·own·er \-₁ō-nər\ *n* : an owner of land

¹**land·scape** \-₁skāp\ *n* **1** : a picture of natural inland scenery **2** : a portion of land that can be seen in one glance

²**landscape** *vb* **land·scaped; land·scap·ing** : to modify (a natural landscape) by grading, clearing, or decorative planting

land·slide \-₁slīd\ *n* **1** : the slipping down of a mass of rocks or earth on a steep slope; *also* : the mass of material that slides **2** : an overwhelming victory esp. in a political contest

lands·man \'landz-mən\ *n* : a person who lives on land; *esp* : LANDLUBBER

land·ward \'land-wərd\ *adv or adj* : to or toward the land

lane \'lān\ *n* **1** : a narrow passageway (as between fences) **2** : a relatively narrow way or track (traffic ~)

lang *abbr* language

lan·guage \'laŋ-gwij\ *n* [ME, fr. OF, fr. *langue* tongue, language, fr. L *lingua*] **1** : the words, their pronunciation, and the methods of combining them used and understood by a community **2** : form or style of verbal expression **3** : a system of signs and symbols and rules for using them that is used to carry information

lan·guid \'laŋ-gwəd\ *adj* **1** : WEAK **2** : sluggish in character or disposition : LISTLESS **3** : SLOW — **lan·guid·ly** *adv* — **lan·guid·ness** *n*

lan·guish \'laŋ-gwish\ *vb* **1** : to become languid **2** : to become dispirited : PINE **3** : to appeal for sympathy by assuming an expression of grief

lan·guor \'laŋ-gər\ *n* **1** : a languid feeling **2** : listless indolence or inertia syn lethargy, lassitude, torpidity, torpor — **lan·guor·ous** *adj* — **lan·guor·ous·ly** *adv*

lank \'laŋk\ *adj* **1** : not well filled out **2** : hanging straight and limp

lanky \'laŋ-kē\ *adj* **lank·i·er; -est** : ungracefully tall and thin

lan·o·lin \'lan-əl-ən\ *n* : the fatty coating of sheep's wool esp. when refined for use in ointments and cosmetics

lan·ta·na \lan-'tä-nə\ *n* : any of a genus of tropical shrubs related to the vervains with showy heads of small bright flowers

lan·tern \'lan-tərn\ *n* **1** : a usu. portable light with a protective covering **2** : the chamber in a lighthouse containing the light **3** : a projector for slides

lan·tha·num \'lan-thə-nəm\ *n* : a soft malleable metallic chemical element — see ELEMENT table

lan·yard \'lan-yərd\ *n* : a piece of rope for fastening something in ships; *also* : any of various cords

Lao·tian \lā-'ō-shən, 'laů-shən\ *n* : a native or inhabitant of Laos — **Laotian** *adj*

¹**lap** \'lap\ *n* **1** : a loose panel of a garment **2** : the clothing that lies on the knees, thighs, and lower part of the trunk when one sits; *also* : the front part of the lower trunk and thighs of a seated person **3** : an environment of nurture (the ~ of luxury) **4** : CHARGE, CONTROL (in the ~ of the gods)

²**lap** *vb* **lapped; lap·ping 1** : FOLD **2** : WRAP **3** : to lay over or near so as to partly cover

³**lap** *n* **1** : the amount by which an object overlaps another; *also* : the part of an object that overlaps another **2** : an act or instance of going over a course (as a track or swimming pool)

⁴lap *vb* **lapped; lap•ping 1** : to scoop up food or drink with the tip of the tongue; *also* : DEVOUR — usu. used with *up* **2** : to splash gently (*lapping* waves)

⁵lap *n* **1** : an act or instance of lapping **2** : a gentle splashing sound

lap•dog \\'lap-ˌdȯg\\ *n* : a small dog that may be held in the lap

la•pel \\lə-'pel\\ *n* : the fold of the front of a coat that is usu. a continuation of the collar

¹lap•i•dary \\'la-pə-ˌder-ē\\ *n, pl* **-dar•ies** : a person who cuts, polishes, or engraves precious stones

²lapidary *adj* **1** : of, relating to, or suitable for engraved inscriptions **2** : of or relating to precious stones or the art of cutting them

lap•in \\'la-pən\\ *n* : rabbit fur usu. sheared and dyed

la•pis la•zu•li \\ˌla-pəs-'la-zə-lē, -zhə-\\ *n* : a usu. blue semiprecious stone often having sparkling bits of pyrite

Lapp \\'lap\\ *n* : a member of a people of northern Scandinavia, Finland, and the Kola peninsula of Russia

lap•pet \\'la-pət\\ *n* : a fold or flap on a garment

¹lapse \\'laps\\ *n* [L *lapsus,* fr. *labi* to slip] **1** : a slight error **2** : a fall from a higher to a lower state **3** : the termination of a right or privilege through failure to meet requirements **4** : INTERRUPTION **5** : APOSTASY **6** : a passage of time; *also* : INTERVAL **syn** blooper, blunder, boner, goof, mistake, slip

²lapse *vb* **lapsed; laps•ing 1** : to commit apostasy **2** : to sink or slip gradually : SUBSIDE **3** : CEASE

lap•top \\'lap-ˌtäp\\ *adj* : of a size that can be used conveniently on one's lap ⟨a ~ computer⟩ — **laptop** *n*

lap•wing \\'lap-ˌwiŋ\\ *n* : an Old World crested plover

lar•board \\'lär-bərd\\ *n* : ⁵PORT

lar•ce•ny \\'lär-sə-nē\\ *n, pl* **-nies** [ME, fr. MF *larcin* theft, fr. L *latrocinium* robbery, fr. *latro* mercenary soldier] : THEFT — **lar•ce•nous** \\-nəs\\ *adj*

larch \\'lärch\\ *n* : any of a genus of trees related to the pines that shed their needles in the fall

¹lard \\'lärd\\ *vb* **1** : to insert strips of usu. pork fat into (meat) before cooking; *also* : GREASE **2** *obs* : ENRICH

²lard *n* : a soft white fat obtained by rendering fatty tissue of the hog

lar•der \\'lär-dər\\ *n* : a place where foods (as meat) are kept

lar•es and pe•na•tes \\'lar-ēz . . . pə-'nä-tēz\\ *n pl* **1** : household gods **2** : personal or household effects

large \\'lärj\\ *adj* **larg•er; larg•est 1** : having more than usual power, capacity, or scope **2** : exceeding most other things of like kind in quantity or size **syn** big, great, oversize — **large•ness** *n* — **at large 1** : UNCONFINED **2** : as a whole

large•ly \\'lärj-lē\\ *adv* : to a large extent

lar•gesse *or* **lar•gess** \\lär-'zhes, -'jes\\ *n* **1** : liberal giving **2** : a generous gift

¹lar•go \\'lär-gō\\ *adv or adj* [It, slow, broad, fr. L *largus* abundant] : at a very slow tempo — used as a direction in music

²largo *n, pl* **largos** : a largo movement

lar•i•at \\'lar-ē-ət\\ *n* [AmerSp *la reata* the lasso, fr. Sp *la* the + AmerSp *reata* lasso, fr. Sp *reatar* to tie again] : a long rope used to catch or tether livestock : LASSO

¹lark \\'lärk\\ *n* : any of a family of small songbirds; *esp* : SKYLARK

²lark *n* : something done solely for fun or adventure

³lark *vb* : to engage in harmless fun or mischief — often used with *about*

lark•spur \\'lärk-ˌspər\\ *n* : DELPHINIUM; *esp* : any of the cultivated annual delphiniums

lar•va \\'lär-və\\ *n, pl* **lar•vae** \\-(ˌ)vē\\ *also* **larvas** [L, specter, mask] : the wingless often wormlike form in which insects hatch from the egg; *also* : any young animal (as a tadpole) that is fundamentally unlike its parent — **lar•val** \\-vəl\\ *adj*

lar•yn•gi•tis \\ˌlar-ən-'jī-təs\\ *n* : inflammation of the larynx

lar•ynx \\'lar-iŋks\\ *n, pl* **la•ryn•ges** \\lə-'rin-ˌjēz\\ *or* **lar•ynx•es** : the upper part of the trachea containing the vocal cords — **la•ryn•ge•al** \\lə-'rin-jəl\\ *adj*

la•sa•gna \\lə-'zän-yə\\ *n* [It] : boiled broad flat noodles baked with a sauce usu. of tomatoes, cheese, and meat

las•car \\'las-kər\\ *n* : an Indian sailor

las•civ•i•ous \\lə-'si-vē-əs\\ *adj* : LUSTFUL, LEWD **syn** licentious, lecherous, libidinous, salacious — **las•civ•i•ous•ness** *n*

la•ser \\'lā-zər\\ *n* [*l*ight *a*mplification by *s*timulated *e*mission of *r*adiation] : a device that produces an intense monochromatic beam of light

¹lash \\'lash\\ *vb* **1** : to move violently or suddenly **2** : WHIP **3** : to attack verbally

²lash *n* **1** : a stroke esp. with a whip; *also* : WHIP **2** : a stinging rebuke **3** : EYELASH

³lash *vb* : to bind with or as if with a line

lass \\'las\\ *n* : GIRL

lass•ie \\'la-sē\\ *n* : LASS

las•si•tude \\'la-sə-ˌtüd, -ˌtyüd\\ *n* **1** : WEARINESS, FATIGUE **2** : LANGUOR

las•so \\'la-sō, la-'sü\\ *n, pl* **lassos** *or* **lassoes** [Sp *lazo*] : a rope or long leather thong with a noose used for catching livestock — **lasso** *vb*

¹last \\'last\\ *vb* **1** : to continue in existence or operation **2** : to remain fresh or unimpaired : ENDURE **3** : to manage to continue **4** : to be enough for the needs of

²last *n* : a foot-shaped form on which a shoe is shaped or repaired

³last *vb* : to shape with a last

⁴last *adv* **1** : at the end **2** : most recently **3** : in conclusion

⁵last *adj* **1** : following all the rest : FINAL **2** : next before the present **3** : most up-to-date **4** : farthest from a specified quality, attitude, or likelihood ⟨the ~ thing we want⟩ **4** : CONCLUSIVE; *also* : SUPREME — **last•ly** *adv*

⁶last *n* : something that is last — **at last** : FINALLY

Last Supper *n* : the supper eaten by Jesus and his disciples on the night of his betrayal

lat *abbr* latitude

Lat *abbr* Latin

¹latch \\'lach\\ *vb* : to catch or get hold

²latch *n* : a catch that holds a door or gate closed

³latch *vb* : to make fast with a latch

latch•et \\'la-chət\\ *n* : a strap, thong, or lace for fastening a shoe or sandal

latch•key \\'lach-ˌkē\\ *n* : a key for opening a door latch esp. from the outside

latch•string \\-ˌstriŋ\\ *n* : a string on a latch that may be left hanging outside the door for raising the latch

¹late \\'lāt\\ *adj* **lat•er; lat•est 1** : coming or remaining after the due, usual, or proper time **2** : far advanced toward the close or end **3** : recently deceased **4** : made, appearing, or happening just previous to the present : RECENT — **late•ly** *adv* — **late•ness** *n*

²late *adv* **lat•er; lat•est 1** : after the usual or proper time; *also* : at or to an advanced point in time **2** : RECENTLY

late•com•er \\'lāt-ˌkə-mər\\ *n* : one who arrives late

la•teen \\lə-'tēn\\ *adj* : relating to or being a triangular sail extended by a long spar slung to a low mast

la•tent \\'lāt-ᵊnt\\ *adj* : present but not visible or active **syn** dormant, quiescent, potential — **la•ten•cy** \\-ᵊn-sē\\ *n*

¹lat•er•al \\'la-tə-rəl\\ *adj* : situated on, directed toward, or coming from the side — **lat•er•al•ly** *adv*

²lateral *n* **1** : a branch from the main part **2** : a football pass thrown parallel to the line of scrimmage or away from the opponent's goal

la•tex \\'lā-ˌteks\\ *n, pl* **la•ti•ces** \\'lā-tə-ˌsēz, 'la-\\ *or* **la•tex•es 1** : a milky juice produced by various plant cells (as of milkweeds, poppies, and the rubber tree) **2** : a water emulsion of a synthetic rubber or plastic used esp. in paint

lath \'lath, 'la̱th\ *n*, *pl* **laths** *or* **lath** : a thin narrow strip of wood used esp. as a base for plaster; *also* : a building material in sheets used for the same purpose — **lath** *vb*

lathe \'lā̱th\ *n* : a machine in which a piece of material is held and turned while being shaped by a tool

¹lath•er \'la-thər\ *n* **1** : a foam or froth formed when a detergent is agitated in water; *also* : foam from profuse sweating (as by a horse) **2** : DITHER

²lather *vb* : to spread lather over; *also* : to form a lather

Lat•in \'lat-ᵊn\ *n* **1** : the language of ancient Rome **2** : a member of any of the peoples whose languages derive from Latin — **Latin** *adj*

Latin American *n* : a native or inhabitant of any of the countries of No., Central, or So. America whose official language is Spanish or Portuguese — **Latin-American** *adj*

La•ti•no \lə-'tē-nō\ *n*, *pl* **-nos** : a native or inhabitant of Latin America; *also* : a person of Latin-American origin living in the U.S. — **Latino** *adj*

lat•i•tude \'la-tə-ˌtüd, -ˌtyüd\ *n* **1** : angular distance north or south from the earth's equator measured in degrees **2** : a region marked by its latitude **3** : freedom of action or choice

lat•i•tu•di•nar•i•an \ˌla-tə-ˌtü-də-'ner-ē-ən, -ˌtyü-\ *n* : a person who is liberal in religious belief and conduct

la•trine \lə-'trēn\ *n* : TOILET

lat•ter \'la-tər\ *adj* **1** : more recent; *also* : FINAL **2** : of, relating to, or being the second of two things referred to

lat•ter-day *adj* **1** : of present or recent times **2** : of a later or subsequent time

Latter-day Saint *n* : a member of a religious body founded by Joseph Smith in 1830 and accepting the Book of Mormon as divine revelation : MORMON

lat•ter•ly \'la-tər-lē\ *adv* **1** : LATER **2** : RECENTLY

lat•tice \'la-təs\ *n* **1** : a framework of crossed wood or metal strips; *also* : a window, door, or gate having a lattice **2** : a regular geometrical arrangement

lat•tice•work \-ˌwərk\ *n* : LATTICE; *also* : work made of lattices

Lat•vi•an \'lat-vē-ən\ *n* : a native or inhabitant of Latvia — **Latvian** *adj*

¹laud \'lȯd\ *n* : PRAISE, ACCLAIM

²laud *vb* : PRAISE, EXTOL **syn** celebrate, eulogize, glorify, magnify — **laud•able** *adj* — **laud•ably** *adv*

lau•da•num \'lȯd-ᵊn-əm\ *n* : a tincture of opium

lau•da•to•ry \'lȯ-də-ˌtȯr-ē\ *adj* : of, relating to, or expressive of praise

¹laugh \'laf, 'láf\ *vb* : to show mirth, joy, or scorn with a smile and chuckle or explosive sound; *also* : to become amused or derisive — **laugh•able** *adj* — **laugh•ing•ly** *adv*

²laugh *n* **1** : the act of laughing **2** : JOKE; *also* : JEER **3** *pl* : SPORT 1

laugh•ing•stock \'la-fiŋ-ˌstäk, 'lá-\ *n* : an object of ridicule

laugh•ter \'laf-tər, 'láf-\ *n* : the action or sound of laughing

¹launch \'lȯnch\ *vb* [ME, fr. OF *lancher*, fr. LL *lanceare* to wield a lance] **1** : THROW, HURL; *also* : to send off (~ a rocket) **2** : to set afloat **3** : to set in operation : START — **launch•er** *n*

²launch *n* : an act or instance of launching

³launch *n* : a small open or half-decked motorboat

launch•pad \'lȯnch-ˌpad\ *n* : a platform from which a rocket is launched

laun•der \'lȯn-dər\ *vb* **1** : to wash or wash and iron clothing and household linens **2** : to transfer (as money of an illegal origin) through an outside party to conceal the true source — **laun•der•er** *n*

laun•dress \'lȯn-drəs\ *n* : a woman who is a laundry worker

laun•dry \'lȯn-drē\ *n*, *pl* **laundries** [fr. obs. *launder* launderer, fr. MF *lavandier*, fr. ML *lavandarius*, fr. L *lavandus* needing to be washed, fr. *lavare* to wash] **1** : a place where laundering is done **2** : clothes or linens that have been or are to be laundered — **laun•dry•man** \-mən\ *n*

lau•re•ate \'lȯr-ē-ət\ *n* : the recipient of honor for achievement in an art or science — **lau•re•ate•ship** *n*

lau•rel \'lȯ-rəl\ *n* **1** : any of a genus of evergreen trees related to the sassafras and cinnamon; *esp* : a small tree of southern Europe **2** : MOUNTAIN LAUREL **3** : a crown of laurel : HONOR — usu. used in pl.

lav *abbr* lavatory

la•va \'lä-və, 'la-\ *n* [It] : melted rock coming from a volcano; *also* : such rock that has cooled and hardened

la•vage \lə-'väzh\ *n* [F] : WASHING; *esp* : the washing out (as of an organ) esp. for medicinal reasons

lav•a•to•ry \'la-və-ˌtȯr-ē\ *n*, *pl* **-ries** **1** : a fixed washbowl with running water and drainpipe **2** : BATHROOM

lave \'lāv\ *vb* **laved; lav•ing** : WASH

lav•en•der \'la-vən-dər\ *n* **1** : a Mediterranean mint or its dried leaves and flowers used to perfume clothing and bed linen **2** : a pale purple color

¹lav•ish \'la-vish\ *adj* [ME *lavas* abundance, fr. MF *lavasse* downpour, fr. *laver* to wash] **1** : expending or bestowing profusely **2** : expended or produced in abundance **3** : marked by excess — **lav•ish•ly** *adv* — **lav•ish•ness** *n*

²lavish *vb* : to expend or give freely

law \'lȯ\ *n* **1** : a rule of conduct or action established by custom or laid down and enforced by a governing authority; *also* : the whole body of such rules **2** : the control brought about by enforcing rules **3** *cap* : the revelation of the divine will set forth in the Old Testament; *also* : the first part of the Jewish scriptures — see BIBLE table **4** : a rule or principle of construction or procedure **5** : the science that deals with laws and their interpretation and application **6** : the profession of a lawyer **7** : a rule or principle stating something that always works in the same way under the same conditions

law•break•er \'lȯ-ˌbrā-kər\ *n* : one who violates the law

law•ful \'lȯ-fəl\ *adj* **1** : permitted by law **2** : RIGHTFUL — **law•ful•ly** *adv*

law•giv•er \-ˌgi-vər\ *n* : LEGISLATOR

law•less \'lȯ-ləs\ *adj* **1** : having no laws **2** : UNRULY, DISORDERLY (a ~ mob) — **law•less•ly** *adv* — **law•less•ness** *n*

law•mak•er \-ˌmā-kər\ *n* : LEGISLATOR

law•man \'lȯ-mən\ *n* : a law enforcement official (as a sheriff or marshal)

¹lawn \'lȯn\ *n* : ground (as around a house) covered with mowed grass

²lawn *n* : a fine sheer linen or cotton fabric

lawn bowling *n* : a bowling game played on a green with wooden balls which are rolled at a jack

law•ren•ci•um \lȯ-'ren-sē-əm\ *n* : a short-lived radioactive element — see ELEMENT table

law•suit \'lȯ-ˌsüt\ *n* : a suit in law

law•yer \'lȯ-yər\ *n* : one who conducts lawsuits for clients or advises as to legal rights and obligations in other matters — **law•yer•ly** *adj*

lax \'laks\ *adj* **1** : not strict (~ discipline) **2** : not tense or rigid **syn** remiss, negligent, neglectful, delinquent, derelict — **lax•i•ty** \'lak-sə-tē\ *n* — **lax•ly** *adv* — **lax•ness** *n*

¹lax•a•tive \'lak-sə-tiv\ *adj* : relieving constipation

²laxative *n* : a usu. mild laxative drug

¹lay \'lā\ *vb* **laid** \'lād\; **lay•ing** **1** : to beat or strike down **2** : to put on or set down : PLACE **3** : to produce and deposit eggs **4** : SETTLE; *also* : ALLAY **5** : SPREAD **6** : PREPARE, CONTRIVE **7** : WAGER **8** : to impose esp. as a duty or burden **9** : to set in order or position **10** : to bring to a specified condition **11** : to put forward : SUBMIT

²lay *n* : the way in which something lies or is laid in relation to something else

³lay *past of* ¹LIE

⁴lay *n* **1** : a simple narrative poem **2** : SONG

⁵lay *adj* **1** : of or relating to the laity **2** : not of a particular profession; *also* : lacking extensive knowledge of a particular subject

lay·away \'lā-ə-ˌwā\ *n* : a purchasing agreement by which a retailer agrees to hold merchandise secured by a deposit until the price is paid in full

lay·er \'lā-ər\ *n* **1** : one that lays **2** : one thickness, course, or fold laid or lying over or under another

lay·ette \lā-'et\ *n* [F, fr. MF, dim. of *laye* box] : an outfit of clothing and equipment for a newborn infant

lay·man \'lā-mən\ *n* : a person who is a member of the laity

lay·off \'lā-ˌôf\ *n* **1** : a period of inactivity **2** : the act of dismissing an employee usu. temporarily

lay·out \'lā-ˌaút\ *n* : the final arrangement, plan, or design of something

lay·over \-ˌō-vər\ *n* : STOPOVER

lay·per·son \-ˌpər-sən\ *n* : a member of the laity

lay·wom·an \'lā-ˌwú-mən\ *n* : a woman who is a member of the laity

la·zar \'la-zər, 'lā-\ *n* : LEPER

laze \'lāz\ *vb* **lazed; laz·ing** : to pass time in idleness or relaxation

la·zy \'lā-zē\ *adj* **la·zi·er; -est 1** : disliking activity or exertion **2** : encouraging idleness **3** : SLUGGISH **4** : DROOPY, LAX **5** : not rigorous or strict — **la·zi·ly** \-zə-lē\ *adv* — **la·zi·ness** \-zē-nəs\ *n*

la·zy·bones \-ˌbōnz\ *n sing or pl* : a lazy person

lazy Su·san \ˌlā-zē-'süz-ᵊn\ *n* : a revolving tray used for serving food

lb *abbr* [L *libra*] pound

lc *abbr* lowercase

LC *abbr* Library of Congress

¹LCD \ˌel-(ˌ)sē-'dē\ *n* [*liquid crystal display*] : a display (as of the time in a watch) that consists of segments of a liquid crystal whose reflectivity varies with the voltage applied to them

²LCD *abbr* least common denominator; lowest common denominator

LCDR *abbr* lieutenant commander

LCM *abbr* least common multiple; lowest common multiple

LCpl *abbr* lance corporal

LCS *abbr* League Championship Series

ld *abbr* **1** load **2** lord

LD *abbr* learning disabled; learning disability

LDC *abbr* less developed country

ldg *abbr* **1** landing **2** loading

LDL \ˌel-(ˌ)dē-'el\ *n* [*low-density lipoprotein*] : a cholesterol-rich protein-poor lipoprotein of blood plasma correlated with increased risk of atherosclerosis

L-do·pa \'el-'dō-pə\ *n* : an isomer of dopa used esp. in the treatment of Parkinson's disease

LDS *abbr* Latter-day Saints

lea \'lē, 'lā\ *n* : PASTURE, MEADOW

leach \'lēch\ *vb* : to pass a liquid (as water) through to carry off the soluble components; *also* : to dissolve out by such means ⟨∼ alkali from ashes⟩

¹lead \'lēd\ *vb* **led** \'led\; **lead·ing 1** : to guide on a way **2** : LIVE ⟨∼ a quiet life⟩ **3** : to direct the operations, activity, or performance of ⟨∼ an orchestra⟩ **4** : to go at the head of : be first ⟨∼ a parade⟩ **5** : to begin play with; *also* : BEGIN, OPEN **6** : to tend toward a definite result ⟨study ∼ing to a degree⟩ — **lead·er** *n* — **lead·er·less** *adj* — **lead·er·ship** *n*

²lead \'lēd\ *n* **1** : a position at the front; *also* : a margin by which one leads **2** : the privilege of leading in cards; *also* : the card or suit led **3** : EXAMPLE **4** : one that leads **5** : a principal role (as in a play); *also* : one who plays such a role **6** : INDICATION, CLUE **7** : an insulated electrical conductor

³lead \'led\ *n* **1** : a heavy malleable bluish white chemical element —see ELEMENT table **2** : an article made of lead; *esp* : a weight for sounding at sea **3** : a thin strip of metal used to separate lines of type in printing **4** : a thin stick of marking substance in or for a pencil

⁴lead \'led\ *vb* **1** : to cover, line, or weight with lead **2** : to fix (glass) in position with lead **3** : to treat or mix with lead or a lead compound

lead·en \'led-ᵊn\ *adj* **1** : made of lead; *also* : of the color of lead **2** : SLUGGISH, DULL

lead off *vb* : OPEN, BEGIN; *esp* : to bat first in an inning — **lead·off** \'lēd-ˌôf\ *n or adj*

¹leaf \'lēf\ *n, pl* **leaves** \'lēvz\ **1** : a usu. flat and green outgrowth of a plant stem that is a unit of foliage and functions esp. in photosynthesis; *also* : FOLIAGE **2** : something that is suggestive of a leaf — **leaf·less** *adj* — **leafy** *adj*

²leaf *vb* **1** : to produce leaves **2** : to turn the pages of a book

leaf·age \'lē-fij\ *n* : FOLIAGE

leafed \'lēft\ *adj* : LEAVED

leaf·hop·per \'lēf-ˌhä-pər\ *n* : any of a family of small leaping insects related to the cicadas that suck the juices of plants

leaf·let \'lē-flət\ *n* **1** : a division of a compound leaf **2** : PAMPHLET, FOLDER

leaf mold *n* : a compost or layer composed chiefly of decayed vegetable matter

leaf·stalk \'lēf-ˌstók\ *n* : PETIOLE

¹league \'lēg\ *n* : a unit of distance equal to about three miles (five kilometers)

²league *n* **1** : an association or alliance for a common purpose **2** : CLASS, CATEGORY — **league** *vb* — **leagu·er** \'lē-gər\ *n*

¹leak \'lēk\ *vb* **1** : to enter or escape through a leak **2** : to let a substance in or out through an opening **3** : to become or make known

²leak *n* **1** : a crack or hole that accidentally admits a fluid or light or lets it escape; *also* : something that secretly or accidentally permits the admission or escape of something else **2** : LEAKAGE — **leaky** *adj*

leak·age \'lē-kij\ *n* **1** : the act of leaking **2** : the thing or amount that leaks

¹lean \'lēn\ *vb* **1** : to bend from a vertical position : INCLINE **2** : to cast one's weight to one side for support **3** : to rely on for support **4** : to incline in opinion, taste, or desire — **lean** *n*

²lean *adj* **1** : lacking or deficient in flesh and esp. in fat **2** : lacking richness or productiveness **3** : low in fuel content — **lean·ness** *n*

leant \'lent\ *chiefly Brit past of* LEAN

lean-to \'lēn-ˌtü\ *n, pl* **lean-tos** \-ˌtüz\ : a wing or extension of a building having a roof of only one slope; *also* : a rough shed or shelter with a similar roof

¹leap \'lēp\ *vb* **leapt** \'lēpt, 'lept\ *or* **leaped; leap·ing** : to spring free from a surface or over an obstacle : JUMP

²leap *n* : JUMP

leap·frog \'lēp-ˌfròg, -ˌfräg\ *n* : a game in which a player bends down and is vaulted over by another — **leapfrog** *vb*

leap year *n* : a year containing 366 days with February 29 as the extra day

learn \'lərn\ *vb* **learned** \'lərnd, 'lərnt\; **learn·ing 1** : to gain knowledge, understanding, or skill by study or experience; *also* : MEMORIZE **2** : to find out : ASCERTAIN — **learn·er** *n*

learn·ed \'lər-nəd\ *adj* : SCHOLARLY, ERUDITE — **learn·ed·ly** *adv* — **learn·ed·ness** *n*

learn·ing \'lər-niŋ\ *n* : KNOWLEDGE, ERUDITION

learning disabled *adj* : having difficulty in learning a basic scholastic skill because of a disorder (as dyslexia) that interferes with the learning process — **learning disability** *n*

learnt \'lərnt\ *chiefly Brit past and past part of* LEARN

¹lease \'lēs\ *n* : a contract transferring real estate for a term of years or at will usu. for a specified rent

²lease *vb* **leased; leas·ing 1** : to grant by lease **2** : to hold under a lease **syn** let, charter, hire, rent

lease·hold \'lēs-ˌhōld\ *n* **1** : a tenure by lease **2** : land held by lease — **lease·hold·er** *n*

leash \'lēsh\ *n* [ME *lees, leshe,* fr. OF *laisse,* fr. *laissier* to let go, fr. L *laxare* to loosen, fr. *laxus* slack] : a line for leading or restraining an animal — **leash** *vb*

¹least \'lēst\ *adj* **1** : lowest in importance or position **2** : smallest in size or degree **3** : SLIGHTEST

²least *n* : one that is least

³least *adv* : in the smallest or lowest degree

least common denominator *n* : the least common multiple of two or more denominators

least common multiple *n* : the smallest common multiple of two or more numbers

least·wise \'lēst-ˌwīz\ *adv* : at least

leath·er \'le-thər\ *n* : animal skin dressed for use — **leath·ern** \-thərn\ *adj* — **leath·ery** *adj*

leath·er·neck \-ˌnek\ *n* : MARINE

¹leave \'lēv\ *vb* **left** \'left\; **leav·ing** **1** : to allow or cause to remain behind **2** : to have as a remainder **3** : BEQUEATH **4** : to let stay without interference **5** : to go away : depart from **6** : GIVE UP, ABANDON

²leave *n* **1** : PERMISSION; *also* : authorized absence from duty **2** : DEPARTURE

³leave *vb* **leaved; leav·ing** : LEAF

leaved \'lēvd\ *adj* : having leaves

¹leav·en \'le-vən\ *n* **1** : a substance (as yeast) used to produce fermentation (as in dough) **2** : something that modifies or lightens

²leaven *vb* : to raise (dough) with a leaven; *also* : to permeate with a modifying or vivifying element

leav·en·ing *n* : LEAVEN

leaves *pl of* LEAF

leave–tak·ing \'lēv-ˌtā-kiŋ\ *n* : DEPARTURE, FAREWELL

leav·ings \'lē-viŋz\ *n pl* : REMNANT, RESIDUE

Leb·a·nese \ˌle-bə-'nēz, -'nēs\ *n* : a native or inhabitant of Lebanon — **Lebanese** *adj*

lech·ery \'le-chə-rē\ *n* : inordinate indulgence in sexual activity — **lech·er** \'le-chər\ *n* — **lech·er·ous** \'le-chə-rəs\ *adj* — **lech·er·ous·ly** *adv* — **lech·er·ous·ness** *n*

lec·i·thin \'le-sə-thən\ *n* : any of several waxy phosphorus-containing substances that are common in animals and plants, form colloidal solutions in water, and have emulsifying and wetting properties

lect *abbr* lecture; lecturer

lec·tern \'lek-tərn\ *n* : a stand to support a book for a standing reader

lec·tor \-tər\ *n* : one whose chief duty is to read the lessons in a church service

lec·ture \'lek-chər\ *n* **1** : a discourse given before an audience esp. for instruction **2** : REPRIMAND — **lecture** *vb* — **lec·tur·er** *n* — **lec·ture·ship** *n*

led *past and past part of* LEAD

LED \ˌel-(ˌ)ē-'dē\ *n* [*light-*emitting *d*iode] : a semiconductor diode that emits light when a voltage is applied to it and is used esp. for electronic displays

le·der·ho·sen \'lā-dər-ˌhōz-ᵊn\ *n pl* : leather shorts often with suspenders worn esp. in Bavaria

ledge \'lej\ *n* [ME *legge* bar of a gate] **1** : a shelflike projection from a top or an edge **2** : REEF

led·ger \'le-jər\ *n* : a book containing accounts to which debits and credits are transferred in final form

lee \'lē\ *n* **1** : a protecting shelter **2** : the side (as of a ship) that is sheltered from the wind — **lee** *adj*

leech \'lēch\ *n* **1** : any of various segmented usu. freshwater worms that are related to the earthworms and have a sucker at each end **2** : a hanger-on who seeks gain

leek \'lēk\ *n* : an onionlike herb grown for its mildly pungent leaves and stalk

leer \'lir\ *n* : a suggestive, knowing, or malicious look — **leer** *vb*

leery \'lir-ē\ *adj* : SUSPICIOUS, WARY

lees \'lēz\ *n pl* : DREGS

¹lee·ward \'lē-wərd, 'lü-ərd\ *n* : the lee side

²leeward *adj* : situated away from the wind

lee·way \'lē-ˌwā\ *n* **1** : lateral movement of a ship when under way **2** : an allowable margin of freedom or variation

¹left \'left\ *adj* [ME, fr. OE, weak; fr. the left hand's being the weaker in most individuals] **1** : of, relating to, or being the side of the body in which the heart is mostly located; *also* : located nearer to this side than to the right **2** *often cap* : of, adhering to, or constituted by the political Left — **left** *adv*

²left *n* **1** : the left hand; *also* : the side or part that is on or toward the left side **2** *cap* : those professing political views marked by desire to reform the established order and usu. to give greater freedom to the common man

³left *past and past part of* LEAVE

left–hand *adj* **1** : situated on the left **2** : LEFT-HANDED

left–hand·ed \'left-'han-dəd\ *adj* **1** : using the left hand habitually or more easily than the right **2** : designed for or done with the left hand **3** : INSINCERE, BACKHANDED ⟨a ~ compliment⟩ **4** : COUNTERCLOCKWISE — **left–handed** *adv*

left·ism \'lef-ˌti-zəm\ *n* **1** : the principles and views of the Left **2** : advocacy of the doctrines of the Left — **left·ist** \-tist\ *n or adj*

left·over \'left-ˌō-vər\ *n* : something that remains unused or unconsumed

¹leg \'leg\ *n* **1** : a limb of an animal used esp. for supporting the body and in walking; *also* : the part of the vertebrate leg between knee and foot **2** : something resembling or analogous to an animal leg ⟨table ~⟩ **3** : the part of an article of clothing that covers the leg **4** : a portion of a trip — **legged** \'legd, 'le-gəd\ *adj* — **leg·less** *adj*

²leg *vb* **legged; leg·ging** : to use the legs in walking or esp. in running

³leg *abbr* **1** legal **2** legislative; legislature

leg·a·cy \'le-gə-sē\ *n, pl* **-cies** : INHERITANCE; *also* : something that has come from a predecessor or the past

le·gal \'lē-gəl\ *adj* **1** : of or relating to law or lawyers **2** : LAWFUL; *also* : STATUTORY **3** : enforced in courts of law — **le·gal·i·ty** \li-'ga-lə-tē\ *n* — **le·gal·ize** \'lē-gə-ˌlīz\ *vb* — **le·gal·ly** *adv*

le·gal·ism \'lē-gə-ˌli-zəm\ *n* **1** : strict, literal, or excessive conformity to the law or to a religious or moral code **2** : a legal term — **le·gal·is·tic** \ˌlē-gə-'lis-tik\ *adj*

leg·ate \'le-gət\ *n* : an official representative

leg·a·tee \ˌle-gə-'tē\ *n* : a person to whom a legacy is bequeathed

le·ga·tion \li-'gā-shən\ *n* **1** : a diplomatic mission headed by a minister **2** : the official residence and office of a minister in a foreign country

le·ga·to \li-'gä-tō\ *adv or adj* [It, lit., tied] : in a smooth and connected manner (as of music)

leg·end \'le-jənd\ *n* [ME *legende,* fr. MF & ML; MF *legende,* fr. ML *legenda,* fr. L *legere* to read] **1** : a story coming down from the past; *esp* : one popularly accepted as historical though not verifiable **2** : an inscription on an object; *also* : CAPTION **3** : an explanatory list of the symbols on a map or chart

leg·end·ary \'le-jən-ˌder-ē\ *adj* **1** : of, relating to, or characteristic of a legend **2** : FAMOUS — **leg·en·dari·ly** \-ˌder-ə-lē\ *adv*

leg·er·de·main \ˌle-jər-də-'mān\ *n* [ME, fr. MF *leger de main* light of hand] : SLEIGHT OF HAND

leg·ging *or* **leg·gin** \'le-gən, -giŋ\ *n* : a covering for the leg; *also* : TIGHTS

leg·gy \'le-gē\ *adj* **leg·gi·er; -est** **1** : having unusually long legs **2** : having long and attractive legs **3** : SPINDLY — used of a plant

leg·horn \'leg-ˌhorn, 'le-gərn\ *n* **1** : a fine plaited straw; *also* : a hat made of this straw **2** : any of a Mediterranean breed of small hardy fowls

leg·i·ble \'le-jə-bəl\ *adj* : capable of being read : CLEAR — **leg·i·bil·i·ty** \ˌle-jə-'bi-lə-tē\ *n* — **leg·i·bly** \'le-jə-blē\ *adv*

¹le·gion \'lē-jən\ *n* **1** : a unit of the Roman army comprising 3000 to 6000 soldiers **2** : MULTITUDE **3** : an association of ex-servicemen — **le·gion·ary** \-jə-ˌner-ē\ *n* — **le·gion·naire** \ˌlē-jə-'nar\ *n*

²legion *adj* : MANY, NUMEROUS

legis *abbr* legislation; legislative; legislature

leg·is·late \'le-jəs-ˌlāt\ *vb* **-lat·ed; -lat·ing** : to make or enact laws; *also* : to bring about by legislation — **leg·is·la·tor** \-ˌlā-tər\ *n*

leg·is·la·tion \ˌle-jəs-'lā-shən\ *n* **1** : the action of legislating **2** : laws made by a legislative body

leg·is·la·tive \'le-jəs-ˌlā-tiv\ *adj* **1** : having the power of legislating **2** : of or relating to a legislature or legislation

leg·is·la·ture \'le-jəs-ˌlā-chər\ *n* : an organized body of persons having the authority to make laws

le·git \li-'jit\ *adj, slang* : LEGITIMATE

¹le·git·i·mate \li-'ji-tə-mət\ *adj* **1** : lawfully begotten **2** : GENUINE **3** : LAWFUL **4** : conforming to recognized principles or accepted rules or standards — **le·git·i·ma·cy** \-mə-sē\ *n* — **le·git·i·mate·ly** *adv*

²le·git·i·mate \-ˌmāt\ *vb* : to make legitimate

le·git·i·mize \li-'ji-tə-ˌmīz\ *vb* **-mized; -miz·ing** : LEGITIMATE

leg·man \'leg-ˌman\ *n* **1** : a reporter assigned usu. to gather information **2** : an assistant who gathers information and runs errands

le·gume \'le-ˌgyüm, li-'gyüm\ *n* [F] **1** : any of a large family of plants having fruits that are dry pods and split when ripe and including important food and forage plants (as beans and clover); *also* : the part (as seeds or pods) of a legume used as food **2** : the pod of a legume — **le·gu·mi·nous** \li-'gyü-mə-nəs\ *adj*

¹lei \'lā, 'lā-ē\ *n* : a wreath or necklace usu. of flowers

²lei \'lā\ *pl of* LEU

lei·sure \'lē-zhər, 'le-, 'lā-\ *n* **1** : time free from work or duties **2** : EASE; *also* : CONVENIENCE **syn** relaxation, rest, repose — **lei·sure·ly** *adj or adv*

leit·mo·tiv *or* **leit·mo·tif** \'līt-mō-ˌtēf\ *n* [G *Leitmotiv,* fr. *leiten* to lead + *Motiv* motive] : a dominant recurring theme

lek \'lek\ *n, pl* **leks** *or* **le·ke** *also* **lek** *or* **le·ku** — see MONEY table

lem·ming \'le-miŋ\ *n* [Norw] : any of various short-tailed northern rodents; *esp* : one of Europe noted for recurrent mass migrations

lem·on \'le-mən\ *n* **1** : an acid yellow usu. nearly oblong citrus fruit; *also* : a citrus tree that bears lemons **2** : something (as an automobile) unsatisfactory or defective — **lem·ony** *adj*

lem·on·ade \ˌle-mə-'nād\ *n* : a beverage of lemon juice, sugar, and water

lem·pi·ra \lem-'pir-ə\ *n* — see MONEY table

le·mur \'lē-mər\ *n* : any of various arboreal mammals largely of Madagascar that are related to the mon-

lemur

keys and have large eyes, very soft woolly fur, and a long furry tail

lend \'lend\ *vb* **lent** \'lent\; **lend·ing** **1** : to give for temporary use on condition that the same or its equivalent be returned **2** : AFFORD, FURNISH **3** : ACCOMMODATE — **lend·er** *n*

lend–lease \-'lēs\ *n* : the transfer of goods and services to an ally to aid in a common cause with payment made by a return of the items or their use in the cause or by a similar transfer of other goods and services

length \'leŋth\ *n* **1** : the longer or longest dimension of an object; *also* : a measured distance **2** : duration or extent in time or space **3** : the length of something taken as a unit of measure **4** : a single piece of a series of pieces that may be joined together ⟨a ∼ of pipe⟩ — **at length** **1** : in full **2** : FINALLY

length·en \'leŋ-thən\ *vb* : to make or become longer **syn** extend, elongate, prolong, protract

length·wise \'leŋth-ˌwīz\ *adv* : in the direction of the length — **lengthwise** *adj*

lengthy \'leŋ-thē\ *adj* **length·i·er; -est** **1** : protracted excessively **2** : EXTENDED, LONG

le·nient \'lē-nē-ənt, -nyənt\ *adj* : of mild and tolerant disposition or effect **syn** indulgent, forbearing, merciful, tolerant — **le·ni·en·cy** \'lē-nē-ən-sē, -nyən-sē\ *n* — **le·ni·ent·ly** *adv*

len·i·tive \'le-nə-tiv\ *adj* : alleviating pain or harshness

len·i·ty \'le-nə-tē\ *n* : LENIENCY

lens \'lenz\ *n* [L *lent-, lens* lentil; so called fr. the shape of a convex lens] **1** : a curved piece of glass or plastic used singly or combined in an optical instrument for forming an image; *also* : a device for focusing radiation other than light **2** : a transparent body in the eye that focuses light rays on receptors at the back of the eye

Lent \'lent\ *n* : a 40-day period of penitence and fasting observed from Ash Wednesday to Easter by many churches — **Lent·en** \-ᵊn\ *adj*

len·til \'lent-ᵊl\ *n* : a Eurasian annual legume grown for its flat edible seeds and for fodder; *also* : its seed

Leo \'lē-ō\ *n* [L, lit., lion] **1** : a zodiacal constellation between Cancer and Virgo usu. pictured as a lion **2** : the 5th sign of the zodiac in astrology; *also* : one born under this sign

le·one \lē-'ōn\ *n, pl* **leones** *or* **leone** — see MONEY table

le·o·nine \'lē-ə-ˌnīn\ *adj* : of, relating to, or resembling a lion

leop·ard \'le-pərd\ *n* : a large usu. tawny and black-spotted cat of southern Asia and Africa

le·o·tard \'lē-ə-ˌtärd\ *n* : a close-fitting garment worn esp. by dancers and for exercise

lep·er \'le-pər\ *n* **1** : a person affected with leprosy **2** : OUTCAST

lep·re·chaun \'le-prə-ˌkän\ *n* : a mischievous elf of Irish folklore

lep·ro·sy \'le-prə-sē\ *n* : a chronic bacterial disease marked esp. if not treated by slow-growing swellings with deformity and loss of sensation of affected parts — **lep·rous** \-prəs\ *adj*

lep·ton \lep-'tän\ *n, pl* **lep·ta** \-'tä\ — see *drachma* at MONEY table

les·bi·an \'lez-bē-ən\ *n, often cap* [fr. the reputed homosexual group associated with the poet Sappho of Lesbos] : a female homosexual — **lesbian** *adj, often cap* — **les·bi·an·ism** \-ə-ˌni-zəm\ *n*

lèse ma·jes·té *or* **lese maj·es·ty** \'lāz-'ma-jə-stē, 'lez-, 'lēz-\ *n* [MF *lese majesté,* fr. L *laesa majestas,* lit., injured majesty] : an offense violating the dignity of a sovereign

le·sion \'lē-zhən\ *n* : an abnormal structural change in the body due to injury or disease; *esp* : one clearly marked off from healthy tissue around it

¹less \'les\ *adj, comparative of* ¹LITTLE **1** : FEWER ⟨∼ than six⟩ **2** : of lower rank, degree, or importance **3** : SMALLER; *also* : more limited in quantity

²less *adv, comparative of* ²LITTLE : to a lesser extent or degree

³less *n, pl* **less** 1 : a smaller portion 2 : something of less importance

⁴less *prep* : diminished by : MINUS

-less \ləs\ *adj suffix* 1 : destitute of : not having ⟨child*less*⟩ 2 : unable to be acted on or to act (in a specified way) ⟨daunt*less*⟩

les·see \le-'sē\ *n* : a tenant under a lease

less·en \'les-ᵊn\ *vb* : to make or become less **syn** decrease, diminish, dwindle, abate

less·er \'le-sər\ *adj, comparative of* ¹LITTLE : of less size, quality, or significance

les·son \'les-ᵊn\ *n* 1 : a passage from sacred writings read in a service of worship 2 : a reading or exercise to be studied by a pupil; *also* : something learned 3 : a period of instruction 4 : an instructive example

les·sor \'le-ᵢsȯr, le-'sȯr\ *n* : one who conveys property by a lease

lest \ᵢlest\ *conj* : for fear that

¹let \'let\ *n* [ME *lette*, fr. *letten* to delay, hinder, fr. OE *lettan*] 1 : HINDRANCE, OBSTACLE 2 : a shot or point in racket games that does not count

²let *vb* **let; let·ting** [ME *leten*, fr. OE *lǣtan*] 1 : to cause to : MAKE ⟨∼ it be known⟩ 2 : RENT, LEASE; *also* : to assign esp. after bids 3 : ALLOW, PERMIT ⟨∼ me go⟩

-let \lət\ *n suffix* 1 : small one ⟨book*let*⟩ 2 : article worn on ⟨wrist*let*⟩

let·down \'let-ᵢdau̇n\ *n* 1 : DISAPPOINTMENT 2 : a slackening of effort

le·thal \'lē-thəl\ *adj* : DEADLY, FATAL — **le·thal·ly** *adv*

leth·ar·gy \'le-thər-jē\ *n* 1 : abnormal drowsiness 2 : the quality or state of being lazy or indifferent **syn** languor, lassitude, torpor — **le·thar·gic** \li-'thär-jik\ *adj*

let on *vb* 1 : REVEAL 1 2 : PRETEND

¹let·ter \'le-tər\ *n* 1 : a symbol that stands for a speech sound and constitutes a unit of an alphabet 2 : a written or printed communication 3 *pl* : LITERATURE; *also* : LEARNING 4 : the literal meaning ⟨the ∼ of the law⟩ 5 : a single piece of type

²letter *vb* : to mark with letters : INSCRIBE — **let·ter·er** *n*

let·ter·head \'le-tər-ᵢhed\ *n* : stationery with a printed or engraved heading; *also* : the heading itself

let·ter–per·fect \ᵢle-tər-'pər-fikt\ *adj* : correct to the smallest detail

let·ter·press \'le-tər-ᵢpres\ *n* : printing done directly by impressing the paper on an inked raised surface

letters of marque \-'märk\ : a license granted to a private person by a government to fit out an armed ship to capture enemy shipping

letters patent *n pl* : a written grant from a government to a person in a form readily open for inspection by all

let·tuce \'le-təs\ *n* [ME *letuse*, fr. MF *laitues*, pl. of *laitue*, fr. L *lactuca*, fr. *lac* milk; fr. its milky juice] : a garden composite plant with crisp leaves used esp. in salads

let·up \'let-ᵢəp\ *n* : a lessening of effort

leu \'leu̇\ *n, pl* **lei** \'lā\ — see MONEY table

leu·kae·mia *chiefly Brit var of* LEUKEMIA

leu·ke·mia \lü-'kē-mē-ə\ *n* : a disease in which white blood cells increase greatly — **leu·ke·mic** \-mik\ *adj or n*

leu·ko·cyte \'lü-kə-ᵢsīt\ *n* : any of the white or colorless cells with a nucleus found in bodily tissues and esp. blood

lev \'lef\ *n, pl* **le·va** \'le-və\ — see MONEY table

Lev *or* **Levit** *abbr* Leviticus

¹le·vee \'le-vē; lə-'vē, -'vā\ *n* [F *lever* act of arising] : a reception held by or for a person of distinction

²lev·ee \'le-vē\ *n* : an embankment to prevent or confine flooding; *also* : a river landing place

¹lev·el \'le-vəl\ *n* 1 : a device for establishing a horizon-

tal line or plane 2 : horizontal condition 3 : a horizontal position, line, or surface often taken as an index of altitude; *also* : a flat area of ground 4 : height, position, rank, or size in a scale

²level *vb* **-eled** *or* **-elled; -el·ing** *or* **-el·ling** 1 : to make flat or level; *also* : to come to a level 2 : AIM, DIRECT 3 : EQUALIZE 4 : RAZE — **lev·el·er** *n*

³level *adj* 1 : having a flat even surface 2 : HORIZONTAL 3 : of the same height or rank; *also* : UNIFORM 4 : steady and cool in judgment — **lev·el·ly** *adv* — **lev·el·ness** *n*

lev·el·head·ed \ᵢle-vəl-'he-dəd\ *adj* : having sound judgment : SENSIBLE

le·ver \'le-vər, 'lē-\ *n* 1 : a bar used for prying or dislodging something; *also* : a means for achieving one's purpose 2 : a rigid piece turning about an axis and used for transmitting and changing force and motion

le·ver·age \'le-vrij, 'lē-, -və-rij\ *n* : the action or mechanical effect of a lever

le·vi·a·than \li-'vī-ə-thən\ *n* 1 : a large sea animal 2 : something large or formidable

lev·i·tate \'le-və-ᵢtāt\ *vb* **-tat·ed; -tat·ing** : to rise or cause to rise in the air in seeming defiance of gravitation — **lev·i·ta·tion** \ᵢle-və-'tā-shən\ *n*

Le·vit·i·cus \li-'vi-tə-kəs\ *n* — see BIBLE table

lev·i·ty \'le-və-tē\ *n* : lack of seriousness **syn** lightness, flippancy, frivolity

¹levy \'le-vē\ *n, pl* **lev·ies** 1 : the imposition or collection of an assessment; *also* : an amount levied 2 : the enlistment or conscription of men for military service; *also* : troops raised by levy

²levy *vb* **lev·ied; levy·ing** 1 : to impose or collect by legal authority 2 : to enlist for military service 3 : WAGE ⟨∼ war⟩ 4 : to seize property

lewd \'lüd\ *adj* [ME *lewed* vulgar, fr. OE *lǣwede* lay, ignorant] 1 : sexually unchaste 2 : OBSCENE, VULGAR — **lewd·ly** *adv* — **lewd·ness** *n*

lex·i·cog·ra·phy \ᵢlek-sə-'kä-grə-fē\ *n* 1 : the editing or making of a dictionary 2 : the principles and practices of dictionary making — **lex·i·cog·ra·pher** \-fər\ *n* — **lex·i·co·graph·i·cal** \-kō-'gra-fi-kəl\ *or* **lex·i·co·graph·ic** \-fik\ *adj*

lex·i·con \'lek-sə-ᵢkän\ *n, pl* **lex·i·ca** \-si-kə\ *or* **lexicons** 1 : DICTIONARY 2 : the vocabulary of a language, speaker, or subject

lg *abbr* 1 large 2 long

LH *abbr* 1 left hand 2 lower half

li *abbr* link

Li *symbol* lithium

LI *abbr* Long Island

li·a·bil·i·ty \ᵢlī-ə-'bi-lə-tē\ *n, pl* **-ties** 1 : the quality or state of being liable 2 *pl* : DEBTS 3 : DISADVANTAGE

li·a·ble \'lī-ə-bəl\ *adj* 1 : legally obligated : RESPONSIBLE 2 : LIKELY, APT ⟨∼ to fall⟩ 3 : SUSCEPTIBLE

li·ai·son \'lē-ə-ᵢzän, lē-'ā-\ *n* [F] 1 : a close bond : INTERRELATIONSHIP 2 : an illicit sexual relationship 3 : communication for mutual understanding (as between parts of an armed force); *also* : one that carries on a liaison

li·ar \'lī-ər\ *n* : a person who lies

¹lib \'lib\ *n* : LIBERATION

²lib *abbr* 1 liberal 2 librarian; library

li·ba·tion \lī-'bā-shən\ *n* 1 : an act of pouring a liquid as a sacrifice (as to a god); *also* : the liquid poured 2 : DRINK

¹li·bel \'lī-bəl\ *n* [ME, written declaration, fr. MF, fr. L *libellus*, dim. of *liber* book] 1 : a spoken or written statement or a representation that gives an unjustly unfavorable impression of a person or thing 2 : the action or crime of publishing a libel — **li·bel·ous** *or* **li·bel·lous** \-bə-ləs\ *adj*

²libel *vb* **-beled** *or* **-belled; -bel·ing** *or* **-bel·ling** : to make or publish a libel — **li·bel·er** *n* — **li·bel·ist** *n*

¹lib·er·al \'li-brəl, -bə-rəl\ *adj* [ME, fr. MF, fr. L *liberalis* suitable for a freeman, generous, fr. *liber* free] 1

: of, relating to, or based on the liberal arts **2** : GEN-EROUS, BOUNTIFUL **3** : not literal **4** : not narrow in opinion or judgment : TOLERANT; *also* : not orthodox **5** : not conservative — **lib·er·al·i·ty** \ˌli-bə-'ra-lə-tē\ *n* — **lib·er·al·ize** \'li-brə-ˌlīz, -bə-rə-\ *vb* — **lib·er·al·ly** *adv*

²liberal *n* : a person who holds liberal views

liberal arts *n pl* : the studies (as language, philosophy, history, literature, or abstract science) in a college or university intended to provide chiefly general knowledge and to develop the general intellectual capacities

lib·er·al·ism \'li-brə-ˌli-zəm, -bə-rə-\ *n* : liberal principles and theories

lib·er·ate \'li-bə-ˌrāt\ *vb* **-at·ed; -at·ing 1** : to free from bondage or restraint; *also* : to raise to equal rights and status **2** : to free (as a gas) from combination — **lib·er·a·tion** \ˌli-bə-'rā-shən\ *n* — **lib·er·a·tor** \'li-bə-ˌrā-tər\ *n*

lib·er·at·ed *adj* : freed from or opposed to traditional social and sexual attitudes or roles ⟨a ∼ marriage⟩

Li·be·ri·an \lī-'bir-ē-ən\ *n* : a native or inhabitant of Liberia — **Liberian** *adj*

lib·er·tar·i·an \ˌli-bər-'ter-ē-ən\ *n* **1** : an advocate of the doctrine of free will **2** : one who upholds the principles of unrestricted liberty

lib·er·tine \'li-bər-ˌtēn\ *n* : a person who leads a dissolute life

lib·er·ty \'li-bər-tē\ *n, pl* **-ties 1** : FREEDOM **2** : an action going beyond normal limits; *esp* : FAMILIARITY **3** : a short leave from naval duty

li·bid·i·nous \lə-'bid-ᵊn-əs\ *adj* **1** : LASCIVIOUS **2** : LIBIDINAL

li·bi·do \lə-'bē-dō, -'bī-\ *n, pl* **-dos** [NL, fr. L, desire, lust] **1** : psychic energy derived from basic biological urges **2** : sexual drive — **li·bid·i·nal** \lə-'bid-ᵊn-əl\ *adj*

Li·bra \'lē-brə\ *n* [L, lit., scales] **1** : a zodiacal constellation between Virgo and Scorpio usu. pictured as a balance scale **2** : the 7th sign of the zodiac in astrology; *also* : one born under this sign

li·brar·i·an \lī-'brer-ē-ən\ *n* : a specialist in the management of a library

li·brary \'lī-ˌbrer-ē\ *n, pl* **-brar·ies 1** : a place in which books and related materials are kept for use but not for sale **2** : a collection of books

li·bret·to \lə-'bre-tō\ *n, pl* **-tos** *or* **-ti** \-tē\ [It, dim. of *libro* book, fr. L *liber*] : the text esp. of an opera — **li·bret·tist** \-tist\ *n*

Lib·y·an \'li-bē-ən\ *n* : a native or inhabitant of Libya — **Libyan** *adj*

lice *pl of* LOUSE

li·cense *or* **li·cence** \'līs-ᵊns\ *n* **1** : permission to act **2** : a permission granted by authority to engage in an activity **3** : a document, plate, or tag providing proof of a license **4** : freedom used irresponsibly — **license** *vb*

licensed practical nurse *n* : a specially trained person who is licensed (as by a state) to provide routine care for the sick

licensed vocational nurse *n* : a licensed practical nurse licensed to practice in the states of California and Texas

li·cens·ee \ˌlīs-ᵊn-'sē\ *n* : a licensed person

licente *pl of* SENTE

li·cen·ti·ate \lī-'sen-chē-ət\ *n* : one licensed to practice a profession

li·cen·tious \lī-'sen-chəs\ *adj* : LEWD, LASCIVIOUS — **li·cen·tious·ly** *adv* — **li·cen·tious·ness** *n*

li·chee *var of* LITCHI

li·chen \'lī-kən\ *n* : any of various complex lower plants made up of an alga and a fungus growing as a unit on a solid surface — **li·chen·ous** *adj*

lic·it \'li-sət\ *adj* : LAWFUL

¹lick \'lik\ *vb* **1** : to draw the tongue over; *also* : to flicker over like a tongue **2** : THRASH; *also* : DEFEAT

²lick *n* **1** : a stroke of the tongue **2** : a small amount **3**

: a hasty careless effort **4** : BLOW **5** : a natural deposit of salt that animals lick

lick·e·ty–split \ˌli-kə-tē-'split\ *adv* : at great speed

lick·spit·tle \'lik-ˌspit-ᵊl\ *n* : a fawning subordinate : TOADY

lic·o·rice \'li-kə-rish, -rəs\ *n* [ME *licorice*, fr. OF, fr. LL *liquiritia*, alter. of L *glycyrrhiza*, fr. Gk *glykyrrhiza*, fr. *glykys* sweet + *rhiza* root] **1** : the dried root of a European leguminous plant; *also* : an extract from it used esp. as a flavoring and in medicine **2** : a candy flavored with licorice **3** : a plant yielding licorice

lid \'lid\ *n* **1** : a movable cover **2** : EYELID **3** : something that confines or suppresses — **lid·ded** \'li-dəd\ *adj*

li·do \'lē-dō\ *n, pl* **lidos** : a fashionable beach resort

¹lie \'lī\ *vb* **lay** \'lā\; **lain** \'lān\; **ly·ing** \'lī-iŋ\ **1** : to be in, stay at rest in, or assume a horizontal position; *also* : to be in a helpless or defenseless state **2** : EXTEND **3** : to occupy a certain relative position **4** : to have an effect esp. through mere presence

²lie *n* : the position in which something lies

³lie *vb* **lied; ly·ing** \'lī-iŋ\ : to tell a lie

⁴lie *n* : an untrue statement made with intent to deceive

lied \'lēt\ *n, pl* **lie·der** \'lē-dər\ [G] : a German song esp. of the 19th century

lie detector *n* : an instrument for detecting physiological evidence of the tension that accompanies lying

lief \'lēv, 'lēf\ *adv* : GLADLY, WILLINGLY

¹liege \'lēj\ *adj* : LOYAL, FAITHFUL

²liege *n* **1** : VASSAL **2** : a feudal superior

lien \'lēn, 'lē-ən\ *n* : a legal claim on the property of another for the satisfaction of a debt or duty

lieu \'lü\ *n, archaic* : PLACE, STEAD — **in lieu of** : in the place of

lieut *abbr* lieutenant

lieu·ten·ant \lü-'te-nənt\ *n* [ME, fr. MF, fr. *lieu* place + *tenant* holding, fr. *tenir* to hold, fr. L *tenēre*] **1** : a representative of another in the performance of duty **2** : FIRST LIEUTENANT; *also* : SECOND LIEUTENANT **3** : a commissioned officer in the navy ranking next below a lieutenant commander — **lieu·ten·an·cy** \-nən-sē\ *n*

lieutenant colonel *n* : a commissioned officer (as in the army) ranking next below a colonel

lieutenant commander *n* : a commissioned officer in the navy ranking next below a commander

lieutenant general *n* : a commissioned officer (as in the army) ranking next below a general

lieutenant governor *n* : a deputy or subordinate governor

lieutenant junior grade *n, pl* **lieutenants junior grade** : a commissioned officer in the navy ranking next below a lieutenant

life \'līf\ *n, pl* **lives** \'līvz\ **1** : the quality that distinguishes a vital and functional being from a dead body or inanimate matter; *also* : a state of an organism characterized esp. by capacity for metabolism, growth, reaction to stimuli, and reproduction **2** : the physical and mental experiences of an individual **3** : BIOGRAPHY **4** : a specific phase or period ⟨adult ∼⟩ **5** : the period from birth to death; *also* : a sentence of imprisonment for the remainder of a person's life **6** : a way of living **7** : PERSON **8** : ANIMATION, SPIRIT; *also* : LIVELINESS **9** : living beings ⟨forest ∼⟩ **10** : animate activity ⟨signs of ∼⟩ **11** : one providing interest and vigor ⟨∼ of the party⟩ — **life·less** *adj* — **life·like** *adj*

life·blood \'līf-ˌbləd\ *n* : a basic source of strength and vitality

life·boat \-ˌbōt\ *n* : a sturdy boat designed for use in saving lives at sea

life·guard \-ˌgärd\ *n* : a usu. expert swimmer employed to safeguard bathers

life·line \-ˌlīn\ *n* **1** : a line to which persons may cling for safety **2** : something considered vital for survival

life·long \-ˌlȯŋ\ *adj* : continuing through life

life preserver *n* : a buoyant device designed to save a person from drowning

lif·er \'lī-fər\ *n* **1** : a person sentenced to life imprisonment **2** : a person who makes a career in the armed forces

life raft *n* : a raft for use by people forced into the water

life·sav·ing \'līf-ˌsā-viŋ\ *n* : the skill or practice of saving or protecting lives esp. of drowning persons — **life·sav·er** \-ˌsā-vər\ *n*

life science *n* : a branch of science (as biology, medicine, anthropology, or sociology) that deals with living organisms and life processes — usu. used in pl. — **life scientist** *n*

life·style \'līf-ˌstīl\ *n* : a way of living

life·time \-ˌtīm\ *n* : the duration of an individual's existence

life·work \-'wərk\ *n* : the entire or principal work of one's lifetime; *also* : a work extending over a lifetime

LIFO *abbr* last in, first out

¹lift \'lift\ *vb* **1** : RAISE, ELEVATE; *also* : RISE, ASCEND **2** : to put an end to : STOP **3** : to pay off ⟨~ a mortgage⟩ — **lift·er** *n*

²lift *n* **1** : LOAD **2** : the action or an instance of lifting **3** : HELP; *also* : a ride along one's way **4** : RISE, ADVANCE **5** *chiefly Brit* : ELEVATOR **6** : an elevation of the spirits **7** : the upward force that is developed by a moving airfoil and that opposes the pull of gravity

lift·off \'lif-ˌtóf\ *n* : a vertical takeoff (as by a rocket)

lift truck *n* : a small truck for lifting and transporting loads

lig·a·ment \'li-gə-mənt\ *n* : a band of tough tissue that holds bones together or supports an organ in place

li·gate \'lī-ˌgāt\ *vb* **li·gat·ed; li·gat·ing** : to tie with a ligature — **li·ga·tion** \lī-'gā-shən\ *n*

lig·a·ture \'li-gə-ˌchùr, -chər\ *n* **1** : something that binds or ties; *also* : a thread used in surgery esp. for tying blood vessels **2** : a printed or written character consisting of two or more letters or characters (as æ) united

¹light \'līt\ *n* **1** : something that makes vision possible : electromagnetic radiation visible to the human eye; *also* : the sensation aroused by stimulation of the visual sense organs **2** : DAYLIGHT **3** : a source of light (as a candle) **4** : ENLIGHTENMENT; *also* : TRUTH **5** : public knowledge (facts brought to ~) **6** : a particular aspect presented to view ⟨saw the matter in a different ~⟩ **7** : WINDOW **8** *pl* : STANDARDS (according to his ~s) **9** : CELEBRITY **10** : LIGHTHOUSE, BEACON; *also* : TRAFFIC LIGHT **11** : a flame for lighting something

²light *adj* **1** : having light : BRIGHT **2** : PALE **2** ⟨~ blue⟩ — **light·ness** *n*

³light *vb* **lit** \'lit\ *or* **light·ed; light·ing** **1** : to make or become light **2** : to cause to burn : BURN **3** : to conduct with a light **4** : ILLUMINATE

⁴light *adj* **1** : not heavy **2** : not serious ⟨~ reading⟩ **3** : SCANTY ⟨~ rain⟩ **4** : easily disturbed ⟨a ~ sleeper⟩ **5** : GENTLE ⟨a ~ blow⟩ **6** : easily endurable ⟨a ~ cold⟩; *also* : requiring little effort ⟨~ exercise⟩ **7** : SWIFT, NIMBLE **8** : FRIVOLOUS **9** : DIZZY **10** : made with lower calorie content or less of some ingredient than usual ⟨~ salad dressing⟩ **11** : producing goods for direct consumption by the consumer ⟨~ industry⟩ — **light·ly** *adv* — **light·ness** *n*

⁵light *adv* **1** : LIGHTLY **2** : with little baggage ⟨travel ~⟩

⁶light *vb* **lit** \'lit\ *or* **light·ed; light·ing** **1** : SETTLE, ALIGHT **2** : to fall unexpectedly **3** : HAPPEN

light–emitting diode *n* : LED

¹light·en \'līt-ᵊn\ *vb* **1** : ILLUMINATE, BRIGHTEN **2** : to give out flashes of lightning

²lighten *vb* **1** : to relieve of a burden **2** : GLADDEN **3** : to become lighter

lighten up *vb* : to take things less seriously

¹light·er \'lī-tər\ *n* : a barge used esp. in loading or unloading ships

²light·er \'lī-tər\ *n* : one that lights; *esp* : a device for lighting

light·face \'līt-ˌfās\ *n* : a type having light thin lines — **light·faced** \-ˌfāst\ *adj*

light–head·ed \'līt-ˌhe-dəd\ *adj* **1** : feeling confused or dizzy **2** : lacking maturity or seriousness

light·heart·ed \-ˌhär-təd\ *adj* : free from worry — **light·heart·ed·ly** *adv* — **light·heart·ed·ness** *n*

light·house \-ˌhaús\ *n* : a structure with a powerful light for guiding sailors

light meter *n* : a usu. hand-held device for indicating correct photographic exposure

¹light·ning \'līt-niŋ\ *n* : the flashing of light produced by a discharge of atmospheric electricity; *also* : the discharge itself

²lightning *adj* : extremely fast

lightning bug *n* : FIREFLY

lightning rod *n* : a grounded metallic rod set up on a structure to protect it from lightning

light out *vb* : to leave in a hurry

light·proof \'līt-ˌprüf\ *adj* : impenetrable by light

lights \'līts\ *n pl* : the lungs esp. of a slaughtered animal

light·ship \'līt-ˌship\ *n* : a ship with a powerful light moored at a place dangerous to navigation

light show *n* : a kaleidoscopic display (as of colored lights)

light·some \'līt-səm\ *adj* **1** : free from care **2** : NIMBLE

¹light·weight \'līt-ˌwāt\ *n* : one of less than average weight; *esp* : a boxer weighing more than 126 but not over 135 pounds

²lightweight *adj* **1** : INCONSEQUENTIAL **2** : of less than average weight

light–year \'līt-ˌyir\ *n* **1** : an astronomical unit of distance equal to the distance that light travels in one year in a vacuum or about 5.88 trillion miles (9.46 trillion kilometers) **2** : an extremely large measure of comparison ⟨saw it ~s ago⟩

lig·nin \'lig-nən\ *n* : a substance related to cellulose that occurs in the woody cell walls of plants and in the cementing material between them

lig·nite \'lig-ˌnīt\ *n* : brownish black soft coal

¹like \'līk\ *vb* **liked; lik·ing** **1** : ENJOY ⟨~s baseball⟩ **2** : WANT **3** : CHOOSE ⟨does as she ~s⟩ — **lik·able** *or* **like·able** \'lī-kə-bəl\ *adj*

²like *n* : PREFERENCE

³like *adj* : SIMILAR **syn** alike, analogous, comparable, parallel, uniform

⁴like *prep* **1** : similar or similarly to ⟨it's ~ when we were kids⟩ **2** : typical of **3** : comparable to **4** : as though there would be ⟨looks ~ rain⟩ **5** : such as ⟨a subject ~ physics⟩

⁵like *n* **1** : COUNTERPART **2** : one that is similar to another — **and the like** : ET CETERA

⁶like *conj* : in the same way that

-like \ˌlīk\ *adj comb form* : resembling or characteristic of ⟨ladylike⟩ ⟨lifelike⟩

like·li·hood \'lī-klē-ˌhùd\ *n* : PROBABILITY

¹like·ly \'lī-klē\ *adj* **like·li·er; -est** **1** : very probable **2** : BELIEVABLE **3** : PROMISING ⟨a ~ place to fish⟩

²likely *adv* : in all probability

lik·en \'lī-kən\ *vb* : COMPARE

like·ness \'līk-nəs\ *n* **1** : COPY, PORTRAIT **2** : SEMBLANCE **3** : RESEMBLANCE

like·wise \-ˌwīz\ *adv* **1** : in like manner **2** : in addition : ALSO

lik·ing \'lī-kiŋ\ *n* : favorable regard; *also* : TASTE

li·ku·ta \li-'kü-tə\ *n, pl* **ma·ku·ta** \mä-\ — see *zaire* at MONEY table

li·lac \'lī-lək, -ˌlak, -ˌläk\ *n* [obs. F (now *lilas*), fr. Ar *līlak*, fr. Per *nīlak* bluish, fr. *nīl* blue, fr. Skt *nīla* dark blue] **1** : a shrub related to the olive that produces large clusters of fragrant grayish pink, purple, or white flowers **2** : a moderate purple color

lil·an·ge·ni \ˌli-lən-'ge-nē\ *n, pl* **em·a·lan·ge·ni** \ˌe-mə-lən-'ge-nē\ — see MONEY table

lil·li·pu·tian \ˌli-lə-ˈpyü-shən\ *adj, often cap* **1** : SMALL, MINIATURE **2** : PETTY

lilt \ˈlilt\ *n* **1** : a cheerful lively song or tune **2** : a rhythmical swing or flow

lily \ˈli-lē\ *n, pl* **lil·ies** : any of a genus of tall bulbous herbs with leafy stems and usu. funnel-shaped flowers; *also* : any of various related plants

lily of the valley : a low perennial herb related to the lilies that produces a raceme of fragrant nodding bell-shaped white flowers

li·ma bean \ˈlī-mə-\ *n* : a bushy or tall-growing bean widely cultivated for its flat edible usu. pale green or whitish seeds; *also* : the seed

limb \ˈlim\ *n* **1** : one of the projecting paired appendages (as legs, arms, or wings) used by an animal esp. in moving or grasping **2** : a large branch of a tree : BOUGH — **limb·less** *adj*

¹**lim·ber** \ˈlim-bər\ *adj* **1** : FLEXIBLE, SUPPLE **2** : LITHE, NIMBLE

²**limber** *vb* : to make or become limber

¹**lim·bo** \ˈlim-bō\ *n, pl* **limbos** [ME, fr. ML, abl. of *limbus* limbo, fr. L, border] **1** *often cap* : an abode of souls barred from heaven through no fault of their own **2** : a place or state of confinement, oblivion, or uncertainty

²**limbo** *n, pl* **limbos** : a West Indian acrobatic dance orig. for men

Lim·burg·er \ˈlim-bər-gər\ *n* : a pungent semisoft surface-ripened cheese

¹**lime** \ˈlīm\ *n* : a caustic powdery white solid that consists of calcium and oxygen, is obtained from limestone or shells, and is used in making cement and in fertilizer — **lime** *vb* — **limy** \ˈlī-mē\ *adj*

²**lime** *n* : a small yellowish green citrus fruit with juicy acid pulp

lime·ade \ˌlīm-ˈād, ˈlī-ˌmād\ *n* : a beverage of lime juice, sugar, and water

lime·light \ˈlīm-ˌlīt\ *n* **1** : a device in which flame is directed against a cylinder of lime formerly used in the theater to cast a strong white light on the stage **2** : the center of public attention

lim·er·ick \ˈli-mə-rik\ *n* : a light or humorous poem of 5 lines

lime·stone \ˈlīm-ˌstōn\ *n* : a rock that is formed by accumulation of organic remains (as shells), is used in building, and yields lime when burned

¹**lim·it** \ˈli-mət\ *n* **1** : something that restrains or confines; *also* : the utmost extent **2** : BOUNDARY; *also, pl* : BOUNDS **3** : a prescribed maximum or minimum — **lim·it·less** *adj* — **lim·it·less·ness** *n*

²**limit** *vb* **1** : to set limits to **2** : to reduce in quantity or extent — **lim·i·ta·tion** \ˌli-mə-ˈtā-shən\ *n*

lim·it·ed *adj* **1** : confined within limits **2** : offering faster service esp. by making fewer stops

limn \ˈlim\ *vb* **limned; limn·ing** \ˈli-miŋ, ˈlim-niŋ\ **1** : DRAW; *also* : PAINT **2** : DELINEATE **3** : DESCRIBE

limo \ˈli-(ˌ)mō\ *n, pl* **limos** : LIMOUSINE

li·mo·nite \ˈlī-mə-ˌnīt\ *n* : a ferric oxide that is a major ore of iron — **li·mo·nit·ic** \ˌlī-mə-ˈni-tik\ *adj*

lim·ou·sine \ˈli-mə-ˌzēn, ˌli-mə-ˈzēn\ *n* [F] **1** : a large luxurious often chauffeur-driven sedan **2** : a large vehicle for transporting passengers to and from an airport

¹**limp** \ˈlimp\ *vb* : to walk lamely; *also* : to proceed with difficulty

²**limp** *n* : a limping movement or gait

³**limp** *adj* **1** : having no defined shape; *also* : not stiff or rigid **2** : lacking in strength or firmness — **limp·ly** *adv* — **limp·ness** *n*

lim·pet \ˈlim-pət\ *n* : any of numerous gastropod sea mollusks with a conical shell that clings to rocks or timbers

lim·pid \ˈlim-pəd\ *adj* : CLEAR, TRANSPARENT

lin *abbr* **1** lineal **2** linear

lin·age \ˈlī-nij\ *n* : the number of lines of written or printed matter

linch·pin \ˈlinch-ˌpin\ *n* : a locking pin inserted crosswise (as through the end of an axle)

lin·den \ˈlin-dən\ *n* : any of a genus of trees with large heart-shaped leaves and clustered yellowish flowers rich in nectar

¹**line** \ˈlīn\ *n* **1** : CORD, ROPE, WIRE; *also* : a length of material used in measuring and leveling **2** : pipes for conveying a fluid ⟨a gas ∼⟩ **3** : a horizontal row of written or printed characters; *also* : VERSE **4** : NOTE **5** : the words making up a part in a drama — usu. used in pl. **6** : something distinct, long, and narrow; *also* : ROUTE **7** : a state of agreement **8** : a course of conduct, action, or thought; *also* : OCCUPATION **9** : LIMIT **10** : an arrangement of persons or objects of one kind in an orderly series ⟨waiting in ∼⟩ **11** : a transportation system **12** : the football players who are stationed on the line of scrimmage **13** : a long narrow mark; *also* : EQUATOR **14** : a geometric element that is the path of a moving point **15** : CONTOUR **16** : a general plan **17** : an indication based on insight or investigation

²**line** *vb* **lined; lin·ing** **1** : to mark with a line **2** : to place or form a line along **3** : ALIGN

³**line** *vb* **lined; lin·ing** : to cover the inner surface of

lin·eage \ˈli-nē-ij\ *n* : lineal descent from a common progenitor; *also* : FAMILY

lin·eal \ˈli-nē-əl\ *adj* **1** : LINEAR **2** : consisting of or being in a direct line of ancestry; *also* : HEREDITARY

lin·ea·ment \ˈli-nē-ə-mənt\ *n* : an outline, feature, or contour of a body and esp. of a face — usu. used in pl.

lin·ear \ˈli-nē-ər\ *adj* **1** : of, relating to, resembling, or having a graph that is a line and esp. a straight line : STRAIGHT **2** : composed of simply drawn lines with little attempt at pictorial representation ⟨∼ script⟩ **3** : being long and uniformly narrow

line·back·er \ˈlīn-ˌba-kər\ *n* : a defensive football player who lines up just behind the line of scrimmage

line drive *n* : a batted baseball hit in a flatter path than a fly ball

line·man \ˈlīn-mən\ *n* **1** : a person who sets up or repairs communication or power lines **2** : a player in the line in football

lin·en \ˈli-nən\ *n* **1** : cloth made of flax; *also* : thread or yarn spun from flax **2** : clothing or household articles made of linen cloth or similar fabric

line of scrimmage : an imaginary line in football parallel to the goal lines and tangent to the nose of the ball laid on the ground before a play

¹**lin·er** \ˈlī-nər\ *n* : a ship or airplane of a regular transportation line

²**liner** *n* : one that lines or is used as a lining — **lin·er·less** *adj*

line score *n* : a score of a baseball game giving the runs, hits, and errors made by each team

lines·man \ˈlīnz-mən\ *n* **1** : LINEMAN 1 **2** : an official who assists a referee

line·up \ˈlī-ˌnəp\ *n* **1** : a list of players taking part in a game (as of baseball) **2** : a line of persons arranged esp. for identification by police

ling \ˈliŋ\ *n* : any of various fishes related to the cod

-ling \liŋ\ *n suffix* **1** : one associated with ⟨nestling⟩ **2** : young, small, or minor one ⟨duckling⟩

lin·ger \ˈliŋ-gər\ *vb* : TARRY; *also* : PROCRASTINATE — **lin·ger·er** *n*

lin·ge·rie \ˌlän-jə-ˈrā, ˌlan-zhə-, -ˈrē\ *n* [F, fr. MF, fr. *linge* linen, fr. L *lineus* made of linen, fr. *linum* flax, linen] : women's intimate apparel

lin·go \ˈliŋ-gō\ *n, pl* **lingoes** : a usu. strange or incomprehensible language

lin·gua fran·ca \ˌliŋ-gwə-ˈfraŋ-kə\ *n, pl* **lingua francas** *or* **lin·guae fran·cae** \-gwē-ˈfraŋ-ˌkē\ [It] **1** *often cap* : a common language consisting of Italian mixed with French, Spanish, Greek, and Arabic that was formerly spoken in Mediterranean ports **2** : a common or commercial tongue among speakers of different languages

lin·gual \'liŋ-gwəl\ *adj* : of, relating to, or produced by the tongue

lin·guist \'liŋ-gwist\ *n* **1** : a person skilled in languages **2** : a person who specializes in linguistics

lin·guis·tics \liŋ-'gwis-tiks\ *n* : the study of human speech including the units, nature, structure, and modification of language — **lin·guis·tic** \-tik\ *adj*

lin·i·ment \'li-nə-mənt\ *n* : a liquid preparation rubbed on the skin esp. to relieve pain

lin·ing \'lī-niŋ\ *n* : material used to line esp. an inner surface

link \'liŋk\ *n* **1** : a connecting structure; *esp* : a single ring of a chain **2** : BOND, TIE — **link** *vb* — **link·er** *n*

link·age \'liŋ-kij\ *n* **1** : the manner or style of being united **2** : the quality or state of being linked **3** : a system of links

linking verb *n* : a word or expression (as a form of *be, become, feel,* or *seem*) that links a subject with its predicate

links \'liŋks\ *n pl* : a golf course

link·up \'liŋ-kəp\ *n* **1** : MEETING **2** : something that serves as a linking device or factor

lin·net \'li-nət\ *n* : an Old World finch

li·no·leum \lə-'nō-lē-əm\ *n* [L *linum* flax + *oleum* oil] : a floor covering with a canvas back and a surface of hardened linseed oil and a filler

lin·seed \'lin-ˌsēd\ *n* : the seeds of flax yielding a yellowish oil (**linseed oil**) used esp. in paints and linoleum

lin·sey–wool·sey \ˌlin-zē-'wul-zē\ *n* : a coarse sturdy fabric of wool and linen or cotton

lint \'lint\ *n* **1** : linen made into a soft fleecy substance **2** : fine ravels and short fibers of yarn or fabric **3** : the fibers that surround cotton seeds and form the cotton staple

lin·tel \'lint-ᵊl\ *n* : a horizontal piece across the top of an opening (as of a door) that carries the weight of the structure above it

li·on \'lī-ən\ *n, pl* **lions** : a large heavily-built cat of Africa and southern Asia with a shaggy mane in the male

li·on·ess \'lī-ə-nəs\ *n* : a female lion

li·on·heart·ed \ˌlī-ən-'här-təd\ *adj* : COURAGEOUS, BRAVE

li·on·ize \'lī-ə-ˌnīz\ *vb* **-ized; -iz·ing** : to treat as an object of great interest or importance — **li·on·i·za·tion** \ˌlī-ə-nə-'zā-shən\ *n*

lip \'lip\ *n* **1** : either of the two fleshy folds that surround the mouth; *also* : the margin of the human lip **2** : a part or projection suggesting a lip **3** : the edge of a hollow vessel or cavity — **lipped** \'lipt\ *adj*

lip·id \'li-pəd\ *n* : any of various substances (as fats and waxes) that with proteins and carbohydrates make up the principal structural parts of living cells

li·po·pro·tein \ˌlī-pō-'prō-ˌtēn, ˌli-\ *n* : a protein that is a complex of protein and lipid

li·po·suc·tion \'li-pə-ˌsək-shən, 'lī-\ *n* : surgical removal of local fat deposits (as in the thighs) esp. for cosmetic purposes

lip·read·ing \'lip-ˌrē-diŋ\ *n* : the interpreting of a speaker's words by watching lip and facial movements without hearing the voice

lip service *n* : an avowal of allegiance that is only verbal

lip·stick \'lip-ˌstik\ *n* : a waxy solid colored cosmetic in stick form for the lips — **lip·sticked** \-ˌstikt\ *adj*

liq *abbr* **1** liquid **2** liquor

liq·ue·fy *also* **liq·ui·fy** \'li-kwə-ˌfī\ *vb* **-fied; -fy·ing** : to make or become liquid — **liq·ue·fi·er** \-ˌfī-ər\ *n*

li·queur \li-'kər\ *n* [F] : a distilled alcoholic liquor flavored with aromatic substances and usu. sweetened

¹liq·uid \'li-kwəd\ *adj* **1** : flowing freely like water **2** : neither solid nor gaseous **3** : shining and clear (large ~ eyes) **4** : smooth and musical in tone; *also* : smooth and unconstrained in movement **5** : consist-

ing of or capable of ready conversion into cash ⟨~ assets⟩ — **li·quid·i·ty** \li-'kwi-də-tē\ *n*

²liquid *n* : a liquid substance

liq·ui·date \'li-kwə-ˌdāt\ *vb* **-dat·ed; -dat·ing 1** : to settle the accounts and distribute the assets of (as a business) **2** : to pay off ⟨~ a debt⟩ **3** : to get rid of; *esp* : KILL — **liq·ui·da·tion** \ˌli-kwə-'dā-shən\ *n*

liquid crystal *n* : an organic liquid that resembles a crystal in having ordered molecular arrays

liquid crystal display *n* : LCD

liquid measure *n* : a unit or series of units for measuring liquid capacity — see METRIC SYSTEM table, WEIGHT table

li·quor \'li-kər\ *n* : a liquid substance; *esp* : a distilled alcoholic beverage

li·quo·rice *chiefly Brit var of* LICORICE

li·ra \'lir-ə, 'lē-rə\ *n* — see MONEY table

lisente *pl of* SENTE

lisle \'līl\ *n* : a smooth tightly twisted thread usu. made of long-staple cotton

lisp \'lisp\ *vb* : to pronounce \s\ and \z\ imperfectly esp. by turning them into \th\ and \th̶\; *also* : to speak childishly — **lisp** *n* — **lisp·er** *n*

lis·some *also* **lis·som** \'li-səm\ *adj* **1** : easily flexed **2** : LITHE **2 3** : NIMBLE — **lis·some·ly** *adv*

¹list \'list\ *vb, archaic* : PLEASE; *also* : WISH

²list *vb, archaic* : LISTEN

³list *n* **1** : a simple series of words or numerals; *also* : an official roster **2** : CATALOG, CHECKLIST

⁴list *vb* : to make a list of; *also* : to include on a list — **list·ee** \li-'stē\ *n*

⁵list *vb* : TILT

⁶list *n* : a leaning to one side : TILT

lis·ten \'lis-ᵊn\ *vb* **1** : to pay attention in order to hear **2** : HEED — **lis·ten·er** *n*

lis·ten·er·ship \'lis-ᵊn-ər-ˌship\ *n* : the audience for a radio program or recording

list·ing \'lis-tiŋ\ *n* **1** : an act or instance of making or including in a list **2** : something that is listed

list·less \'list-ləs\ *adj* : SPIRITLESS, LANGUID — **list·less·ly** *adv* — **list·less·ness** *n*

list price *n* : the price of an item as published in a catalog, price list, or advertisement before being discounted

lists \'lists\ *n pl* : an arena for combat (as jousting)

¹lit \'lit\ *past and past part of* LIGHT

²lit *abbr* **1** liter **2** literal; literally **3** literary **4** literature

lit·a·ny \'lit-ᵊn-ē\ *n, pl* **-nies** [ME *letanie,* fr. OF, fr. LL *litania,* fr. LGk *litaneia,* fr. Gk, entreaty, fr. *litanos* suppliant] **1** : a prayer consisting of a series of supplications and responses said alternately by a leader and a group **2** : a lengthy recitation ⟨a ~ of complaints⟩

li·tchi \'lē-chē, 'lī-\ *n* [Chin (Beijing dialect) *lìzhī*] **1** : an oval fruit with a hard scaly outer covering, a small hard seed, and edible flesh **2** : an Asian tree bearing litchis

lite *var of* ³LIGHT 10

li·ter \'lē-tər\ *n* — see METRIC SYSTEM table

lit·er·al \'li-tə-rəl\ *adj* **1** : adhering to fact or to the ordinary or usual meaning (as of a word) **2** : UNADORNED; *also* : PROSAIC **3** : VERBATIM

lit·er·al·ism \-rə-ˌli-zəm\ *n* **1** : adherence to the explicit substance (as of an idea) **2** : fidelity to observable fact — **lit·er·al·ist** \-list\ *n* — **lit·er·al·is·tic** \ˌli-tə-rə-'lis-tik\ *adj*

lit·er·al·ly \'li-tə-rə-lē, 'li-trə-\ *adv* **1** : ACTUALLY ⟨was ~ insane⟩ **2** : VIRTUALLY ⟨~ poured out new ideas⟩

lit·er·ary \'li-tə-ˌrer-ē\ *adj* **1** : of or relating to literature **2** : WELL-READ

lit·er·ate \'li-trət, -tə-rət\ *adj* **1** : EDUCATED; *also* : able to read and write **2** : LITERARY; *also* : POLISHED, LUCID — **lit·er·a·cy** \'li-trə-sē, -tə-rə-\ *n* — **literate** *n*

lit·e·ra·ti \ˌli-tə-'rä-tē\ *n pl* **1** : the educated class **2** : persons interested in literature or the arts

lit·er·a·ture \'li-trə-ˌchur, -tə-rə-, -chər\ *n* **1** : the production of written works having excellence of form or expression and dealing with ideas of permanent interest **2** : the written works produced in a particular language, country, or age

lithe \'līth, 'līth\ *adj* **1** : SUPPLE **2** : characterized by effortless grace; *also* : athletically slim

lithe·some \'līth-səm, 'līth-\ *adj* : LISSOME

lith·i·um \'li-thē-əm\ *n* : a light silver-white metallic chemical element — see ELEMENT table

li·thog·ra·phy \li-'thä-grə-fē\ *n* : the process of printing from a plane surface (as a smooth stone or metal plate) on which the image to be printed is ink-receptive and the blank area ink-repellent — **lith·o·graph** \'li-thə-ˌgraf\ *vb* — **lithograph** *n* — **li·thog·ra·pher** \li-'thä-grə-fər, 'li-thə-ˌgra-fər\ *n* — **lith·o·graph·ic** \ˌli-thə-'gra-fik\ *adj* — **lith·o·graph·i·cal·ly** \-fi-k(ə-)lē\ *adv*

li·thol·o·gy \li-'thä-lə-jē\ *n, pl* **-gies** : the study of rocks — **lith·o·log·ic** \ˌli-thə-'lä-jik\ *or* **lith·o·log·i·cal** \-ji-kəl\ *adj*

lith·o·sphere \'li-thə-ˌsfir\ *n* : the outer part of the solid earth

Lith·u·a·nian \ˌli-thù-'wā-nē-ən, -thyù-\ *n* **1** : a native or inhabitant of Lithuania **2** : the language of the Lithuanians — **Lithuanian** *adj*

lit·i·gant \'li-ti-gənt\ *n* : a party to a lawsuit — **litigant** *adj*

lit·i·gate \-ˌgāt\ *vb* **-gat·ed; -gat·ing** : to carry on a legal contest by judicial process; *also* : to contest at law — **lit·i·ga·tion** \ˌli-tə-'gā-shən\ *n*

li·ti·gious \lə-'ti-jəs\ *adj* **1** : CONTENTIOUS **2** : prone to engage in lawsuits **3** : of or relating to litigation — **li·ti·gious·ly** *adv* — **li·ti·gious·ness** *n*

lit·mus \'lit-məs\ *n* : a coloring matter from lichens that turns red in acid solutions and blue in alkaline

litmus test *n* : a test in which a single factor (as an attitude) is decisive

Litt D *or* **Lit D** *abbr* [ML *litterarum doctor*] : doctor of letters; doctor of literature

¹lit·ter \'li-tər\ *n* [ME, fr. OF *litiere*, fr. *lit* bed, fr. L *lectus*] **1** : a covered and curtained couch with shafts that is used to carry a single passenger; *also* : a device (as a stretcher) for carrying a sick or injured person **2** : material used as bedding for animals; *also* : material used to absorb the urine and feces of animals **3** : the offspring of an animal at one birth **4** : RUBBISH

litter 1

²litter *vb* **1** : to give birth to young **2** : to strew or mark with scattered objects

lit·ter·bug \'li-tər-ˌbəg\ *n* : one who litters a public area

¹lit·tle \'lit-ᵊl\ *adj* **lit·tler** \'lit-ᵊl-ər\ *or* **less** \'les\ *or* **less·er** \'le-sər\; **lit·tlest** \'lit-ᵊl-əst\ *or* **least** \'lēst\ **1** : not big; *also* : YOUNG **2** : not important **3** : PETTY **3 4** : not much — **lit·tle·ness** *n*

²little *adv* **less** \'les\; **least** \'lēst\ **1** : SLIGHTLY; *also* : not at all **2** : INFREQUENTLY

³little *n* **1** : a small amount or quantity **2** : a short time or distance

Little Dipper *n* : the seven bright stars of Ursa Minor arranged in a form resembling a dipper

little theater *n* : a small theater for low-cost dramatic productions designed for a limited audience

lit·to·ral \'li-tə-rəl, ˌli-tə-'ral\ *adj* : of, relating to, or growing on or near a shore esp. of the sea — **littoral** *n*

lit·ur·gy \'li-tər-jē\ *n, pl* **-gies** : a rite or body of rites prescribed for public worship — **li·tur·gi·cal** \lə-'tər-ji-kəl\ *adj* — **li·tur·gi·cal·ly** \-k(ə-)lē\ *adv* — **lit·ur·gist** \'li-tər-jist\ *n*

liv·able *also* **live·able** \'li-və-bəl\ *adj* **1** : suitable for living in or with **2** : ENDURABLE — **liv·a·bil·i·ty** \ˌli-və-'bi-lə-tē\ *n*

¹live \'liv\ *vb* **lived; liv·ing 1** : to be or continue alive **2** : SUBSIST **3** : RESIDE **4** : to conduct one's life **5** : to remain in human memory or record

²live \'līv\ *adj* **1** : having life **2** : BURNING, GLOWING ⟨a ~ cigar⟩ **3** : connected to electric power ⟨a ~ wire⟩ **4** : UNEXPLODED ⟨a ~ bomb⟩ **5** : of continuing interest ⟨a ~ issue⟩ **6** : of or involving the actual presence of real people ⟨~ audience⟩; *also* : broadcast directly at the time of production ⟨a ~ radio program⟩ **7** : being in play ⟨a ~ ball⟩

lived–in \'livd-ˌin\ *adj* : of or suggesting long-term human habitation or use

live down *vb* : to live so as to wipe out the memory or effects of

live in *vb* : to live in one's place of employment — used of a servant — **live–in** \'liv-ˌin\ *adj*

live·li·hood \'līv-lē-ˌhùd\ *n* : means of support or subsistence

live·long \'liv-ˌlòn\ *adj* [ME *lef long*, fr. *lef* dear + *long* long] : WHOLE, ENTIRE ⟨the ~ day⟩

live·ly \'līv-lē\ *adj* **live·li·er; -est 1** : ANIMATED ⟨~ debate⟩ **2** : KEEN, VIVID ⟨~ interest⟩ **3** : showing activity or vigor ⟨a ~ manner⟩ **4** : quick to rebound ⟨a ~ ball⟩ **5** : full of life **syn** vivacious, sprightly, gay, spirited — **live·li·ness** *n* — **live·ly** *adv*

liv·en \'lī-vən\ *vb* : ENLIVEN

¹liv·er \'li-vər\ *n* **1** : a large glandular organ of vertebrates that secretes bile and is a center of metabolic activity **2** : the liver of an animal (as a calf or chicken) eaten as food

²liver *n* : one that lives esp. in a specified way ⟨a fast ~⟩

liv·er·ish \'li-və-rish\ *adj* **1** : resembling liver esp. in color **2** : BILIOUS **3** : PEEVISH — **liv·er·ish·ness** *adj*

liv·er·wort \'li-vər-ˌwərt\ *n* : any of a class of flowerless plants resembling the related mosses

liv·er·wurst \-ˌwərst, -ˌwùrst\ *n* [part trans. of G *Leberwurst*, fr. *Leber* liver + *Wurst* sausage] : a sausage consisting chiefly of liver

liv·ery \'li-və-rē\ *n, pl* **-er·ies 1** : a servant's uniform; *also* : distinctive dress **2** : the feeding, care, and stabling of horses for pay; *also* : an establishment (as a stable or business) keeping horses or vehicles for hire — **liv·er·ied** \-rēd\ *adj*

liv·ery·man \-mən\ *n* : the keeper of a livery

lives *pl of* LIFE

live·stock \'līv-ˌstäk\ *n* : farm animals kept for use and profit

live wire *n* : an alert, active, or aggressive person

liv·id \'li-vəd\ *adj* [F *livide*, fr. L *lividus*, fr. *livēre* to be blue] **1** : discolored by bruising **2** : ASHEN, PALLID **3** : REDDISH **4** : ENRAGED — **li·vid·i·ty** \li-'vi-də-tē\ *n*

¹liv·ing \'li-vin\ *adj* **1** : having life **2** : NATURAL **3** : full of life and vigor; *also* : VIVID

²living *n* **1** : the condition of being alive **2** : LIVELIHOOD **3** : manner of life

living room *n* : a room in a residence used for the common social activities of the occupants

living wage *n* : a wage sufficient to provide an acceptable standard of living

living will *n* : a document requesting that the signer

not be kept alive by artificial means unless there is a reasonable expectation of recovery

livre \ˈlēvrᵊ\ *n* : the pound of Lebanon

liz·ard \ˈli-zərd\ *n* : any of a group of 4-legged reptiles with long tapering tails

Lk *abbr* Luke

ll *abbr* lines

lla·ma \ˈlä-mə\ *n* [Sp] : any of a genus of wild or domesticated So. American mammals related to the camels but smaller and without a hump

lla·no \ˈlä-nō\ *n, pl* llanos : an open grassy plain esp. of Latin America

LLD *abbr* [NL *legum doctor*] doctor of laws

LNG *abbr* liquefied natural gas

¹load \ˈlōd\ *n* **1** : PACK; *also* : CARGO **2** : a mass of weight supported by something **3** : something that burdens the mind or spirits **4** : a large quantity — usu. used in pl. **5** : a standard, expected, or authorized burden

²load *vb* **1** : to put a load in or on; *also* : to receive a load **2** : to encumber with an obligation or something heavy or disheartening **3** : to increase the weight of by adding something **4** : to supply abundantly **5** : to put a charge in (as a firearm)

load·ed *adj* **1** *slang* : HIGH 12 **2** : having a large amount of money

load·stone *var of* LODESTONE

¹loaf \ˈlōf\ *n, pl* loaves \ˈlōvz\ : a shaped or molded mass esp. of bread

²loaf *vb* : to spend time in idleness : LOUNGE — **loaf·er** *n*

loam \ˈlōm, ˈlüm\ *n* : SOIL; *esp* : a loose soil of mixed clay, sand, and silt — **loamy** *adj*

¹loan \ˈlōn\ *n* **1** : money lent at interest; *also* : something lent for the borrower's temporary use **2** : the grant of temporary use

²loan *vb* : LEND

loan shark *n* : a person who lends money at excessive rates of interest — **loan·shark·ing** \ˈlōn-ˌshär-kiŋ\ *n*

loan·word \ˈlōn-ˌwərd\ *n* : a word taken from another language and at least partly naturalized

loath \ˈlōth, ˈlōth\ *also* **loathe** \ˈlōth, lōth\ *adj* : RELUCTANT

loathe \ˈlōth\ *vb* loathed; loath·ing : to dislike greatly **syn** abominate, abhor, detest, hate

loath·ing \ˈlō-thiŋ\ *n* : extreme disgust

loath·some \ˈlōth-səm, ˈlōth-\ *adj* : exciting loathing : REPULSIVE

lob \ˈläb\ *vb* lobbed; lob·bing : to throw, hit, or propel something in a high arc — **lob** *n*

¹lob·by \ˈlä-bē\ *n, pl* lobbies **1** : a corridor used esp. as a passageway or waiting room **2** : a group of persons engaged in lobbying

²lobby *vb* lob·bied; lob·by·ing : to try to influence public officials and esp. legislators — **lob·by·ist** *n*

lobe \ˈlōb\ *n* : a curved or rounded part esp. of a bodily organ — **lo·bar** \ˈlō-bər\ *adj* — **lobed** \ˈlōbd\ *adj*

lo·bot·o·my \lō-ˈbä-tə-mē\ *n, pl* -mies : surgical severance of certain nerve fibers in the brain for the relief of some mental disorders

lob·ster \ˈläb-stər\ *n* [ME, fr. OE *loppestre*, fr. *loppe* spider] : any of a family of edible marine crustaceans

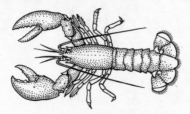

lobster

with two large pincerlike claws and four other pairs of legs; *also* : SPINY LOBSTER

¹lo·cal \ˈlō-kəl\ *adj* **1** : of, relating to, or occupying a particular place **2** : serving a particular limited district; *also* : making all stops ⟨a ~ train⟩ **3** : affecting a small part of the body ⟨~ infection⟩ — **lo·cal·ly** *adv*

²local *n* : one that is local

lo·cale \lō-ˈkal\ *n* : a place that is the setting for a particular event

lo·cal·i·ty \lō-ˈka-lə-tē\ *n, pl* -ties : a particular spot, situation, or location

lo·cal·ize \ˈlō-kə-ˌlīz\ *vb* -ized; -iz·ing : to fix in or confine to a definite place or locality — **lo·cal·i·za·tion** \ˌlō-kə- lə-ˈzā-shən\ *n*

lo·cate \ˈlō-ˌkāt, lō-ˈkāt\ *vb* lo·cat·ed; lo·cat·ing **1** : STATION, SETTLE **2** : to determine the site of **3** : to find or fix the place of in a sequence

lo·ca·tion \lō-ˈkā-shən\ *n* **1** : SITUATION, PLACE **2** : the process of locating **3** : a place outside a studio where a motion picture is filmed

loc cit *abbr* [L *loco citato*] in the place cited

loch \ˈläk, ˈläk̯\ *n, Scot* : LAKE; *also* : a bay or arm of the sea esp. when nearly landlocked

¹lock \ˈläk\ *n* : a tuft, strand, or ringlet of hair; *also* : a cohering bunch (as of wool or flax)

²lock *n* **1** : a fastening in which a bolt is operated **2** : the mechanism of a firearm by which the charge is exploded **3** : an enclosure (as in a canal) used in raising or lowering boats from level to level **4** : AIR LOCK **5** : a wrestling hold

³lock *vb* **1** : to fasten the lock of; *also* : to make fast with a lock **2** : to confine or exclude by means of a lock **3** : INTERLOCK **4** : to make or become motionless by the interlocking of parts

lock·er \ˈlä-kər\ *n* **1** : a drawer, cupboard, or compartment for individual storage use **2** : an insulated compartment for storing frozen food

lock·et \ˈlä-kət\ *n* : a small usu. metal case for a memento worn suspended from a chain or necklace

lock·jaw \ˈläk-ˌjȯ\ *n* : a symptom of tetanus marked by spasms of the jaw muscles and inability to open the jaws; *also* : TETANUS

lock·nut \-ˌnət\ *n* **1** : a nut screwed tight on another to prevent it from slacking back **2** : a nut designed to lock itself when screwed tight

lock·out \-ˌaȯt\ *n* : the suspension of work by an employer during a labor dispute in order to make employees accept the terms being offered

lock·smith \-ˌsmith\ *n* : one who makes or repairs locks

lock·step \-ˌstep\ *n* : a mode of marching in step by a body of men moving in a very close single file

lock·up \-ˌəp\ *n* : JAIL

lo·co \ˈlō-kō\ *adj* [Sp] *slang* : CRAZY, FRENZIED

lo·co·mo·tion \ˌlō-kə-ˈmō-shən\ *n* **1** : the act or power of moving from place to place **2** : TRAVEL

¹lo·co·mo·tive \ˌlō-kə-ˈmō-tiv\ *adj* : of or relating to locomotion or a locomotive

²locomotive *n* : a self-propelled vehicle used to move railroad cars

lo·co·mo·tor \ˌlō-kə-ˈmō-tər\ *adj* : of or relating to locomotion or organs used in locomotion

lo·co·weed \ˈlō-kō-ˌwēd\ *n* : any of several leguminous plants of western No. America that are poisonous to livestock

lo·cus \ˈlō-kəs\ *n, pl* lo·ci \ˈlō-ˌsī\ [L] **1** : PLACE, LOCALITY **2** : the set of all points whose location is determined by stated conditions

lo·cust \ˈlō-kəst\ *n* **1** : a usu. destructive migratory grasshopper **2** : CICADA **3** : any of various leguminous trees; *also* : the wood of a locust

lo·cu·tion \lō-ˈkyü-shən\ *n* : a particular form of expression; *also* : PHRASEOLOGY

lode \ˈlōd\ *n* : an ore deposit

lode·stone \-ˌstōn\ *n* : an iron-containing rock with magnetic properties

¹lodge \'läj\ *vb* **lodged; lodg·ing 1** : to provide quarters for; *also* : to settle in a place **2** : CONTAIN **3** : to come to a rest and remain **4** : to deposit for safekeeping **5** : to vest (as authority) in an agent **6** : FILE ⟨~ a complaint⟩

²lodge *n* **1** : a house set apart for residence in a special season or by an employee on an estate; *also* : INN **2** : a den or lair esp. of gregarious animals **3** : the meeting place of a branch of a fraternal organization; *also* : the members of such a branch

lodg·er \'lä-jər\ *n* : a person who occupies a rented room in another's house

lodg·ing \'lä-jiŋ\ *n* **1** : DWELLING **2** : a room or suite of rooms in another's house rented as a dwelling place — usu. used in pl.

lodg·ment *or* **lodge·ment** \'läj-mənt\ *n* **1** : a lodging place **2** : the act or manner of lodging **3** : DEPOSIT

loess \'les, 'ləs\ *n* : a usu. yellowish brown loamy deposit believed to be chiefly deposited by the wind

¹loft \'loft\ *n* [ME, fr. OE, air, sky, fr. ON *lopt*] **1** : ATTIC **2** : GALLERY ⟨organ ~⟩ **3** : an upper floor (as in a warehouse or barn) esp. when not partitioned **4** : the thickness of a fabric or insulated material (as of a sleeping bag)

²loft *vb* : to strike or throw a ball so that it rises high in the air

lofty \'lof-tē\ *adj* **loft·i·er; -est 1** : NOBLE; *also* : SUPERIOR **2** : extremely proud **3** : HIGH, TALL — **loft·i·ly** \'lof-tə-lē\ *adv* — **loft·i·ness** \-tē-nəs\ *n*

¹log \'log, 'läg\ *n* **1** : a bulky piece of unshaped timber **2** : an apparatus for measuring a ship's speed **3** : the daily record of a ship's progress; *also* : a regularly kept record of performance (as of an airplane)

²log *vb* **logged; log·ging 1** : to cut (trees) for lumber; *also* : to clear (land) of trees in lumbering **2** : to enter in a log **3** : to sail a ship or fly an airplane for (an indicated distance or period of time) **4** : to have (an indicated record) to one's credit : ACHIEVE — **log·ger** \'lo-gər, 'lä-\ *n*

³log *n* : LOGARITHM

lo·gan·ber·ry \'lō-gən-ˌber-ē\ *n* : a red-fruited upright-growing dewberry; *also* : its fruit

log·a·rithm \'lo-gə-ˌri-t͟həm, 'lä-\ *n* : the exponent that indicates the power to which a base is raised to produce a given number ⟨the ~ of 100 to base 10 is 2 since $10^2 = 100$⟩ — **log·a·rith·mic** \ˌlo-gə-ˈrith-mik, ˌlä-\ *adj*

loge \'lōzh\ *n* **1** : a small compartment; *also* : a box in a theater **2** : a small partitioned area; *also* : the forward section of a theater mezzanine

log·ger·head \'lo-gər-ˌhed, 'lä-\ *n* : a large sea turtle of subtropical and temperate waters — **at loggerheads** : in a state of quarrelsome disagreement

log·gia \'lō-jē-ə, 'lo-jä\ *n, pl* **loggias** \'lō-jē-əz, 'lo-jäz\ : a roofed open gallery

log·ic \'lä-jik\ *n* **1** : a science that deals with the rules and tests of sound thinking and proof by reasoning **2** : sound reasoning **3** : the arrangement of circuit elements for arithmetical computation in a computer — **log·i·cal** \-ji-kəl\ *adj* — **log·i·cal·ly** \-jik-(ə-)lē\ *adv* — **lo·gi·cian** \lō-ˈji-shən\ *n*

lo·gis·tics \lō-ˈjis-tiks\ *n sing or pl* : the procurement, maintenance, and transportation of matériel, facilities, and personnel — **lo·gis·tic** \-tik\ *adj*

log·jam \'log-ˌjam, 'läg-\ *n* **1** : a deadlocked jumble of logs in a watercourse **2** : DEADLOCK

logo \'lō-gō\ *n, pl* **log·os** \-gōz\ : an identifying symbol (as for advertising)

logo·type \'lō-gə-ˌtīp, 'lä-\ *n* : LOGO

log·roll·ing \-ˌrō-liŋ\ *n* : the trading of votes by legislators to secure favorable action on projects of individual interest

lo·gy \'lō-gē\ *also* **log·gy** \'lo-gē, 'lä-\ *adj* **lo·gi·er; -est** : deficient in vitality : SLUGGISH

loin \'loin\ *n* **1** : the part of the body on each side of the spinal column and between the hip and the lower ribs; *also* : a cut of meat from this part of an animal **2** *pl* : the pubic region; *also* : the organs of reproduction

loin·cloth \-ˌklóth\ *n* : a cloth worn about the loins often as the sole article of clothing in warm climates

loi·ter \'loi-tər\ *vb* **1** : LINGER **2** : to hang around idly **syn** dawdle, dally, procrastinate, lag, tarry — **loi·ter·er** *n*

loll \'läl\ *vb* **1** : DROOP, DANGLE **2** : LOUNGE

lol·li·pop *or* **lol·ly·pop** \'lä-li-ˌpäp\ *n* : a lump of hard candy on a stick

lol·ly·gag \'lä-lē-ˌgag\ *vb* **-gagged; -gag·ging** : DAWDLE

Lond *abbr* London

lone \'lōn\ *adj* **1** : SOLITARY ⟨a ~ sentinel⟩ **2** : SOLE, ONLY ⟨the ~ theater in town⟩ **3** : ISOLATED ⟨a ~ tree⟩

lone·ly \'lōn-lē\ *adj* **lone·li·er; -est 1** : being without company **2** : UNFREQUENTED ⟨a ~ spot⟩ **3** : LONESOME — **lone·li·ness** *n*

lon·er \'lō-nər\ *n* : one that avoids others

lone·some \'lōn-səm\ *adj* **1** : sad from lack of companionship **2** : REMOTE; *also* : SOLITARY — **lone·some·ly** *adv* — **lone·some·ness** *n*

¹long \'loŋ\ *adj* **lon·ger** \'loŋ-gər\; **lon·gest** \'loŋ-gəst\ **1** : extending for a considerable distance; *also* : TALL, ELONGATED **2** : having a specified length **3** : extending over a considerable time; *also* : TEDIOUS **4** : containing many items in a series **5** : being a syllable or speech sound of relatively great duration **6** : extending far into the future **7** : well furnished with something — used with *on*

²long *adv* : for or during a long time

³long *n* : a long period of time

⁴long *vb* **longed; long·ing** \'loŋ-iŋ\ : to feel a strong desire or wish **syn** yearn, hanker, pine, hunger, thirst

⁵long *abbr* longitude

long·boat \'loŋ-ˌbōt\ *n* : a large boat usu. carried by a merchant sailing ship

long·bow \-ˌbō\ *n* : a wooden bow drawn by hand and used esp. by medieval English archers

lon·gev·i·ty \län-ˈje-və-tē\ *n* [LL *longaevitas*, fr. L *longaevus* long-lived, fr. *longus* long + *aevum* age] : a long duration of individual life; *also* : length of life

long·hair \'loŋ-ˌhar\ *n* **1** : a lover of classical music **2** : HIPPIE **3** : a domestic cat having long outer fur — **long·haired** \-ˌhard\ *or* **long·hair** *adj*

long·hand \-ˌhand\ *n* : HANDWRITING

long·horn \-ˌhórn\ *n* : any of the cattle with long horns formerly common in the southwestern U.S.

long hundredweight *n, Brit* — see WEIGHT table

long·ing \'loŋ-iŋ\ *n* : a strong desire esp. for something unattainable — **long·ing·ly** *adv*

lon·gi·tude \'län-jə-ˌtüd, -ˌtyüd\ *n* : angular distance expressed usu. in degrees east or west from the prime meridian through Greenwich, England

lon·gi·tu·di·nal \ˌlän-jə-ˈtüd-ᵊn-əl, -ˈtyüd-\ *adj* **1** : extending lengthwise **2** : of or relating to length — **lon·gi·tu·di·nal·ly** *adv*

long·shore·man \'loŋ-ˌshór-mən\ *n* : a laborer at a wharf who loads and unloads cargo

long·suf·fer·ing \-ˈsə-friŋ, -fə-riŋ\ *n* : long and patient endurance of offense

long–term \'loŋ-ˈtərm\ *adj* **1** : extending over or involving a long period of time **2** : constituting a financial obligation based on a term usu. of more than 10 years ⟨~ bonds⟩

long·time \'loŋ-ˌtīm\ *adj* : of long duration ⟨~ friends⟩

long ton *n* — see WEIGHT table

lon·gueur \lōⁿ-ˈgœr\ *n, pl* **longueurs** \same or -ˈgœrz\ [F, lit., length] : a dull tedious passage or section

long–wind·ed \ˌloŋ-ˈwin-dəd\ *adj* : tediously long in speaking or writing

loo·fah \'lü-fə\ *n* : a sponge consisting of the fibrous skeleton of a gourd

¹look \'luk\ *vb* **1** : to exercise the power of vision : SEE **2** : EXPECT **3** : to have an appearance that befits ⟨~s the part⟩ **4** : SEEM ⟨~s thin⟩ **5** : to direct one's atten-

tion : HEED **6** : POINT, FACE **7** : to show a tendency —
look after : to take care of — **look for** : EXPECT
²**look** n **1** : the action of looking : GLANCE **2** : EXPRES-
SION; *also* : physical appearance **3** : ASPECT
look down *vb* : to regard with contempt — used with
on or *upon*
looking glass n : MIRROR
look·out \'lùk-ˌaùt\ n **1** : a person assigned to watch
(as on a ship) **2** : a careful watch **3** : VIEW **4** : a matter
of concern
look up *vb* **1** : IMPROVE ⟨business is *looking up*⟩ **2** : to
search for in or as if in a reference work **3** : to seek
out esp. for a brief visit
¹**loom** \'lüm\ n : a frame or machine for weaving together threads or yarns into cloth
²**loom** *vb* **1** : to come into sight in an unnaturally large,
indistinct, or distorted form **2** : to appear in an impressively exaggerated form
loon \'lün\ n : any of several web-footed black=
and-white fish-eating diving birds
loo·ny *or* **loo·ney** \'lü-nē\ adj **loo·ni·er; -est** : CRAZY,
FOOLISH
loony bin n : an insane asylum
loop \'lüp\ n **1** : a fold or doubling of a line through
which another line or hook can be passed; *also* : a
loop-shaped figure or course ⟨a ∼ in a river⟩ **2** : a circular airplane maneuver executed in the vertical
plane **3** : a piece of film or magnetic tape whose ends
are spliced together to project or play continuously
— **loop** *vb*
loop·er \'lü-pər\ n : any of numerous rather small hairless moth caterpillars that move with a looping movement
loop·hole \'lüp-ˌhōl\ n **1** : a small opening in a wall
through which firearms may be discharged **2** : a
means of escape; *esp* : an ambiguity or omission that
allows one to evade the intent of a law or contract
¹**loose** \'lüs\ adj **loos·er; loos·est 1** : not rigidly fastened
2 : free from restraint or obligation **3** : not dense or
compact in structure **4** : not chaste : LEWD **5** : SLACK
6 : not precise or exact — **loose·ly** adv — **loose·ness**
n
²**loose** *vb* **loosed; loos·ing 1** : RELEASE **2** : UNTIE **3** : DE-
TACH **4** : DISCHARGE **5** : RELAX, SLACKEN
³**loose** adv : LOOSELY
loos·en \'lüs-ⁿn\ *vb* **1** : FREE **2** : to make or become
loose **3** : to relax the severity of
loot \'lüt\ n [Hindi *lūṭ*; akin to Skt *luṇṭati* he plunders]
: goods taken in war or by robbery : PLUNDER — **loot**
vb — **loot·er** n
¹**lop** \'läp\ *vb* **lopped; lop·ping** : to cut branches or
twigs from : TRIM; *also* : to cut off
²**lop** *vb* **lopped; lop·ping** : to hang downward; *also* : to
flop or sway loosely
lope \'lōp\ n : an easy bounding gait — **lope** *vb*
lop·sid·ed \'läp-'sī-dəd\ adj **1** : leaning to one side **2**
: UNSYMMETRICAL — **lop·sid·ed·ly** adv — **lop·sid·ed·**
ness n
lo·qua·cious \lō-'kwā-shəs\ adj : excessively talkative
— **lo·quac·i·ty** \-'kwa-sə-tē\ n
¹**lord** \'lȯrd\ n [ME *loverd, lord*, fr. OE *hlāford*, fr. *hlāf*
loaf + *weard* keeper] **1** : one having power and authority over others; *esp* : a person from whom a feudal fee or estate is held **2** : a man of rank or high
position; *esp* : a British nobleman **3** *pl*, *cap* : the upper house of the British parliament **4** : a person of
great power in some field
²**lord** *vb* : to act like a lord; *esp* : to put on airs — usu.
used with *it*
lord chancellor n, *pl* **lords chancellor** : a British officer of state who presides over the House of Lords,
serves as head of the British judiciary, and is usu. a
leading member of the cabinet
lord·ly \-lē\ adj **lord·li·er; -est 1** : DIGNIFIED; *also* : NO-
BLE **2** : HAUGHTY
lord·ship \-ˌship\ n **1** : the rank or dignity of a lord —

used as a title **2** : the authority or territory of a lord
Lord's Supper n : COMMUNION
lore \'lȯr\ n : KNOWLEDGE; *esp* : traditional knowledge
or belief
lor·gnette \lȯrn-'yet\ n [F, fr. *lorgner* to take a sidelong
look at, fr. MF, fr. *lorgne* squinting] : a pair of eyeglasses or opera glasses with a handle
lorn \'lȯrn\ adj : FORSAKEN, DESOLATE
lor·ry \'lȯr-ē\ n, *pl* **lorries** *chiefly Brit* : MOTORTRUCK
lose \'lüz\ *vb* **lost** \'lȯst\; **los·ing** \'lü-ziŋ\ **1** : DESTROY
2 : to miss from a customary place : MISLAY **3** : to suffer deprivation of **4** : to fail to use : WASTE **5** : to fail
to win or obtain ⟨∼ the game⟩ **6** : to fail to keep or
maintain ⟨∼ his balance⟩ **7** : to wander from ⟨∼ her
way⟩ **8** : to get rid of — **los·er** n
loss \'lȯs\ n **1** : RUIN **2** : the harm resulting from losing
3 : something that is lost **4** *pl* : killed, wounded, or
captured soldiers **5** : failure to win **6** : an amount by
which the cost exceeds the selling price **7** : decrease
in amount or degree
loss leader n : an article sold at a loss in order to draw
customers
lost \'lȯst\ adj **1** : not used, won, or claimed **2** : no
longer possessed or known **3** : ruined or destroyed
physically or morally **4** : DENIED; *also* : HARDENED **5**
: unable to find the way; *also* : HELPLESS **6** : AB-
SORBED, RAPT **7** : not appreciated or understood ⟨his
jokes were ∼ on me⟩
lot \'lät\ n **1** : an object used in deciding something by
chance; *also* : the use of lots to decide something **2**
: SHARE, PORTION; *also* : FORTUNE, FATE **3** : a plot of
land **4** : a group of individuals : SET **5** : a considerable
quantity
loth \'lōth, 'lōth\ *var of* LOATH
lo·ti \'lō-tē\ n, *pl* **ma·lo·ti** \mə-'lō-tē\ — see MONEY table
lo·tion \'lō-shən\ n : a liquid preparation for cosmetic
and external medicinal use
lot·tery \'lä-tə-rē\ n, *pl* **-ter·ies 1** : a drawing of lots in
which prizes are given to the winning names or num-
bers **2** : a matter determined by chance
lo·tus \'lō-təs\ n **1** : a fruit held in Greek legend to
cause dreamy contentment and forgetfulness **2** : any
of various water lilies represented esp. in ancient
Egyptian and Hindu art **3** : any of several leguminous
forage plants
loud \'laùd\ adj **1** : marked by intensity or volume of
sound **2** : CLAMOROUS, NOISY **3** : obtrusive or offensive in color or pattern ⟨a ∼ suit⟩ — **loud** adv —
loud·ly adv — **loud·ness** n
loud·mouthed \-ˌmaùtht, -ˌmaùthd\ adj : given to loud
offensive talk
loud·speak·er \-ˌspē-kər\ n : a device that changes
electrical signals into sound
¹**lounge** \'laùnj\ *vb* **lounged; loung·ing** : to act or move
lazily or listlessly
²**lounge** n **1** : a room with comfortable furniture; *also* : a
room (as in a theater) with lounging, smoking, and
toilet facilities **2** : a long couch
lour \'laùr\, **loury** \'laùr-ē\ *var of* LOWER, LOWERY
louse \'laùs\ n, *pl* **lice** \'līs\ **1** : any of various small
wingless usu. flattened insects parasitic on warm=
blooded animals **2** : a plant pest (as an aphid) **3** : a
contemptible person
lousy \'laù-zē\ adj **lous·i·er; -est 1** : infested with lice
2 : POOR, INFERIOR **3** : amply supplied ⟨∼ with money⟩
— **lous·i·ly** \-zə-lē\ adv — **lous·i·ness** \-zē-nəs\ n
lout \'laùt\ n : a stupid awkward fellow — **lout·ish** adj
— **lout·ish·ly** adv
lou·ver *or* **lou·vre** \'lü-vər\ n **1** : an opening having parallel slanted slats to allow flow of air but to exclude
rain or sun or to provide privacy; *also* : a slat in such
an opening **2** : a device with movable slats for controlling the flow of air or light
¹**love** \'ləv\ n **1** : strong affection **2** : warm attachment
⟨∼ of the sea⟩ **3** : attraction based on sexual desire **4**

: a beloved person **5** : unselfish loyal and benevolent concern for others **6** : a score of zero in tennis — **love·less** *adj*

²**love** *vb* **loved; lov·ing 1** : CHERISH **2** : to feel a passion, devotion, or tenderness for **3** : CARESS **4** : to take pleasure in ⟨∼s to play bridge⟩ — **lov·able** \\'lə-və-bəl\\ *adj* — **lov·er** *n*

love·bird \\'ləv-ˌbərd\\ *n* : any of various small usu. gray or green parrots that seem to show caring behavior for their mates

love·lorn \\-ˌlȯrn\\ *adj* : deprived of love or of a lover

love·ly \\'ləv-lē\\ *adj* **love·li·er; -est** : BEAUTIFUL — **love·li·ly** \\'ləv-lə-lē\\ *adv* — **love·li·ness** *n* — **lovely** *adv*

love·mak·ing \\-ˌmā-kiŋ\\ *n* **1** : COURTSHIP **2** : sexual activity; *esp* : COPULATION

love·sick \\-ˌsik\\ *adj* **1** : YEARNING **2** : expressing a lover's longing — **love·sick·ness** *n*

lov·ing \\'lə-viŋ\\ *adj* **1** : AFFECTIONATE **2** : PAINSTAKING — **lov·ing·ly** *adv*

¹**low** \\'lō\\ *vb* : MOO

²**low** *n* : MOO

³**low** *adj* **low·er** \\'lō-ər\\; **low·est** \\'lō-əst\\ **1** : not high or tall ⟨∼ wall⟩; *also* : DÉCOLLETÉ **2** : situated or passing below the normal level or surface ⟨∼ ground⟩; *also* : marking a nadir **3** : not loud ⟨∼ voice⟩ **4** : being near the equator **5** : humble in status **6** : WEAK; *also* : DEPRESSED **7** : STRICKEN, PROSTRATE **8** : less than usual in number, amount, or value; *also* : of lesser degree than average **9** : falling short of a standard **10** : UNFAVORABLE — **low** *adv* — **low·ness** *n*

⁴**low** *n* **1** : something that is low **2** : a region of low barometric pressure **3** : the arrangement of gears in an automobile transmission that gives the slowest speed and greatest power

low beam *n* : the short-range focus of a vehicle headlight

low blow *n* : an unprincipled attack

low·brow \\'lō-ˌbraù\\ *n* : a person with little taste or intellectual interest

low–density lipoprotein *n* : LDL

low·down \\-ˌdaùn\\ *n* : pertinent and esp. guarded information

low–down \\-ˌdaùn\\ *adj* **1** : MEAN, CONTEMPTIBLE **2** : deeply emotional

low–end \\-ˌend\\ *adj* : of, relating to, or being the lowest-priced merchandise in a manufacturer's line

¹**low·er** \\'laù-ər\\ *vb* **1** : FROWN **2** : to become dark, gloomy, and threatening

²**low·er** \\'lō-ər\\ *adj* **1** : relatively low (as in rank) **2** : situated beneath the earth's surface **3** : constituting the popular and more representative branch of a bicameral legislative body

³**low·er** \\'lō-ər\\ *vb* **1** : DROP; *also* : DIMINISH **2** : to let descend by its own weight; *also* : to reduce the height of **3** : to reduce in value, number, or amount **4** : DEGRADE; *also* : HUMBLE

low·er·case \\ˌlō-ər-ˈkās\\ *adj* : being a letter that belongs to or conforms to the series a, b, c, etc., rather than A, B, C, etc. — **lowercase** *n*

lower class *n* : a social class occupying a position below the middle class and having the lowest status in a society — **lower–class** \\-ˈklas\\ *adj*

low·er·most \\'lō-ər-ˌmōst\\ *adj* : LOWEST

low·ery \\'laù-ə-rē\\ *adj* : GLOOMY, LOWERING

lowest common denominator *n* **1** : LEAST COMMON DENOMINATOR **2** : something designed to appeal to a lowbrow audience; *also* : such an audience

lowest common multiple *n* : LEAST COMMON MULTIPLE

low–key \\'lō-ˈkē\\ *also* **low–keyed** \\-ˈkēd\\ *adj* : of low intensity : RESTRAINED

low·land \\'lō-lənd, -ˌland\\ *n* : low and usu. level country

low·life \\'lō-ˌlīf\\ *n, pl* **low·lifes** \\-ˌlīfs\\ *also* **low·lives** \\-ˌlīvz\\ : a person of low social status or moral character

low·ly \\'lō-lē\\ *adj* **low·li·er; -est 1** : HUMBLE, MEEK **2**

: ranking low in some hierarchy — **low·li·ness** *n*

low–rise \\'lō-ˈrīz\\ *adj* **1** : having few stories and not equipped with elevators ⟨a ∼ building⟩ **2** : of, relating to, or characterized by low-rise buildings

low–tech \\'lō-ˈtek\\ *adj* : technologically simple or unsophisticated

¹**lox** \\'läks\\ *n* : liquid oxygen

²**lox** *n, pl* **lox** *or* **lox·es** : smoked salmon

loy·al \\'lȯi-əl\\ *adj* [MF, fr. OF *leial, leel,* fr. L *legalis* legal] **1** : faithful in allegiance to one's government **2** : faithful esp. to a cause or ideal : CONSTANT — **loy·al·ly** \\'lȯi-ə-lē\\ *adv* — **loy·al·ty** \\'lȯi-əl-tē\\ *n*

loy·al·ist \\'lȯi-ə-list\\ *n* : one who is or remains loyal to a political party, government, or sovereign

loz·enge \\'lä-zənj\\ *n* **1** : a diamond-shaped figure **2** : a small flat often medicated candy

LP *abbr* low pressure

LPG *abbr* liquefied petroleum gas

LPGA *abbr* Ladies Professional Golf Association

LPN \\ˈel-ˈpē-ˈen\\ *n* : LICENSED PRACTICAL NURSE

Lr *symbol* Lawrencium

LSD \\ˌel-(ˌ)es-ˈdē\\ *n* [G *Lysergsäure-Diäthylamid* lysergic acid diethylamide] : an illicit drug that causes psychotic symptoms similar to those of schizophrenia

lt *abbr* light

Lt *abbr* lieutenant

LT *abbr* long ton

LTC *or* **Lt Col** *abbr* lieutenant colonel

Lt Comdr *abbr* lieutenant commander

ltd *abbr* limited

LTG *or* **Lt Gen** *abbr* lieutenant general

LTJG *abbr* lieutenant, junior grade

ltr *abbr* letter

Lu *symbol* lutetium

lu·au \\'lü-ˌaù\\ *n* : a Hawaiian feast

lub *abbr* lubricant; lubricating

lub·ber \\'lə-bər\\ *n* **1** : LOUT **2** : an unskilled seaman — **lub·ber·ly** *adj*

lube \\'lüb\\ *n* : LUBRICANT; *also* : an application of a lubricant

lu·bri·cant \\'lü-bri-kənt\\ *n* : a material capable of reducing friction when applied between moving parts

lu·bri·cate \\'lü-brə-ˌkāt\\ *vb* **-cat·ed; -cat·ing** : to apply a lubricant to — **lu·bri·ca·tion** \\ˌlü-brə-ˈkā-shən\\ *n* — **lu·bri·ca·tor** \\'lü-brə-ˌkā-tər\\ *n*

lu·bri·cious \\lü-ˈbri-shəs\\ *or* **lu·bri·cous** \\'lü-bri-kəs\\ *adj* **1** : SMOOTH, SLIPPERY **2** : LECHEROUS; *also* : SALACIOUS — **lu·bric·i·ty** \\lü-ˈbri-sə-tē\\ *n*

lu·cent \\'lüs-ᵊnt\\ *adj* **1** : LUMINOUS **2** : CLEAR, LUCID — **lu·cent·ly** *adv*

lu·cerne \\lü-ˈsərn\\ *n, chiefly Brit* : ALFALFA

lu·cid \\'lü-səd\\ *adj* **1** : SHINING **2** : mentally sound **3** : easily understood — **lu·cid·i·ty** \\lü-ˈsi-də-tē\\ *n* — **lu·cid·ly** *adv* — **lu·cid·ness** *n*

Lu·ci·fer \\'lü-sə-fər\\ *n* [ME, the morning star, a fallen rebel archangel, the Devil, fr. OE, fr. L, the morning star, fr. *lucifer* light-bearing] : DEVIL, SATAN

¹**luck** \\'lək\\ *n* **1** : CHANCE, FORTUNE **2** : good fortune — **luck·less** *adj*

²**luck** *vb* **1** : to prosper or succeed esp. through chance or good fortune — usu. used with *out* **2** : to come upon something desirable by chance — usu. used with *out, on, onto,* or *into*

luck·i·ly \\'lə-kə-lē\\ *adv* **1** : in a lucky manner **2** : FORTUNATELY **2**

lucky \\'lə-kē\\ *adj* **luck·i·er; -est 1** : favored by luck : FORTUNATE **2** : FORTUITOUS **3** : seeming to bring good luck — **luck·i·ness** *n*

lu·cra·tive \\'lü-krə-tiv\\ *adj* : PROFITABLE — **lu·cra·tive·ly** *adv* — **lu·cra·tive·ness** *n*

lu·cre \\'lü-kər\\ *n* [ME, fr. L *lucrum*] : PROFIT; *also* : MONEY

lu·cu·bra·tion \\ˌlü-kyə-ˈbrā-shən, -kə-\\ *n* : laborious study : MEDITATION

lu·di·crous \'lü-də-krəs\ *adj* : LAUGHABLE, RIDICULOUS — **lu·di·crous·ly** *adv* — **lu·di·crous·ness** *n*

luff \'ləf\ *vb* : to turn the head of a ship toward the wind

¹lug \'ləg\ *vb* **lugged; lug·ging 1** : DRAG, PULL **2** : to carry laboriously

²lug *n* **1** : a projecting piece (as for fastening, support, or traction) **2** : a nut securing a wheel on an automobile

lug·gage \'lə-gij\ *n* : containers (as suitcases) for carrying personal belongings : BAGGAGE

lu·gu·bri·ous \lù-'gü-brē-əs\ *adj* : mournful often to an exaggerated degree — **lu·gu·bri·ous·ly** *adv* — **lu·gu·bri·ous·ness** *n*

Luke \'lük\ *n* — see BIBLE table

luke·warm \'lük-'wòrm\ *adj* **1** : moderately warm : TEPID **2** : not enthusiastic — **luke·warm·ly** *adv*

¹lull \'ləl\ *vb* **1** : SOOTHE, CALM **2** : to cause to relax vigilance

²lull *n* **1** : a temporary calm (as during a storm) **2** : a temporary drop in activity

lul·la·by \'lə-lə-,bī\ *n, pl* **-bies** : a song to lull children to sleep

lum·ba·go \,ləm-'bā-gō\ *n* : rheumatic pain in the lower back and loins

lum·bar \'ləm-bər, -,bär\ *adj* : of, relating to, or constituting the loins or the vertebrae between the thoracic vertebrae and sacrum ⟨∼ region⟩

¹lum·ber \'ləm-bər\ *vb* : to move heavily or clumsily

²lumber *n* **1** : surplus or disused articles that are stored away **2** : timber or logs esp. when dressed for use

³lumber *vb* : to cut logs; *also* : to saw logs into lumber — **lum·ber·man** \-mən\ *n*

lum·ber·jack \-,jak\ *n* : LOGGER

lum·ber·yard \-,yärd\ *n* : a place where lumber is kept for sale

lu·mi·nary \'lü-mə-,ner-ē\ *n, pl* **-nar·ies 1** : a very famous person **2** : a source of light; *esp* : a celestial body

lu·mi·nes·cence \,lü-mə-'nes-ᵊns\ *n* : the low-temperature emission of light (as by a chemical or physiological process); *also* : such light — **lu·mi·nes·cent** \-ᵊnt\ *adj*

lu·mi·nous \'lü-mə-nəs\ *adj* **1** : emitting light; *also* : LIGHTED **2** : CLEAR, INTELLIGIBLE — **lu·mi·nance** \-nəns\ *n* — **lu·mi·nos·i·ty** \,lü-mə-'nä-sə-tē\ *n* — **lu·mi·nous·ly** *adv*

lum·mox \'lə-məks\ *n* : a clumsy person

¹lump \'ləmp\ *n* **1** : a piece or mass of indefinite size and shape **2** : AGGREGATE, TOTALITY **3** : a usu. abnormal swelling — **lump·ish** *adj* — **lumpy** *adj*

²lump *vb* **1** : to heap together in a lump **2** : to form into lumps

³lump *adj* : not divided into parts ⟨a ∼ sum⟩

lu·na·cy \'lü-nə-sē\ *n, pl* **-cies 1** : INSANITY **2** : extreme folly

lu·nar \'lü-nər\ *adj* : of or relating to the moon

lu·na·tic \'lü-nə-,tik\ *adj* [ME *lunatik*, fr. LL *lunaticus*, fr. L *luna* moon; fr. the belief that lunacy fluctuated with the phases of the moon] **1** : INSANE; *also* : used for insane persons **2** : extremely foolish — **lunatic** *n*

¹lunch \'lənch\ *n* **1** : a light meal usu. eaten in the middle of the day **2** : the food prepared for a lunch

²lunch *vb* : to eat lunch

lun·cheon \'lən-chən\ *n* : a usu. formal lunch

lun·cheon·ette \,lən-chə-'net\ *n* : a small restaurant serving light lunches

lunch·room \'lənch-,rüm, -,rùm\ *n* **1** : LUNCHEONETTE **2** : a room (as in a school) where lunches are sold and eaten or lunches brought from home may be eaten

lu·nette \lü-'net\ *n* : something shaped like a crescent

lung \'ləŋ\ *n* **1** : one of the usu. paired baglike breathing organs in the chest of an air-breathing vertebrate **2** : a mechanical device to promote breathing and make it easier — **lunged** \'ləŋd\ *adj*

lunge \'lənj\ *n* **1** : a sudden thrust or pass (as with a sword) **2** : a sudden forward stride or leap — **lunge** *vb*

lu·pine \'lü-pən\ *n* : any of a genus of leguminous plants with long upright clusters of pealike flowers

lu·pus \'lü-pəs\ *n* [ML, fr. L, wolf] : any of several diseases characterized by skin lesions; *esp* : SYSTEMIC LUPUS ERYTHEMATOSUS

lurch \'lərch\ *n* : a sudden swaying or tipping movement — **lurch** *vb*

¹lure \'lùr\ *n* **1** : ENTICEMENT; *also* : APPEAL **2** : an artificial bait for catching fish

²lure *vb* **lured; lur·ing** : to draw on with a promise of pleasure or gain

lu·rid \'lùr-əd\ *adj* **1** : wan and ghostly pale in appearance **2** : shining with the red glow of fire seen through smoke or cloud **3** : GRUESOME; *also* : SENSATIONAL **syn** ghastly, grisly, grim, horrible, macabre — **lu·rid·ly** *adv*

lurk \'lərk\ *vb* **1** : to move furtively : SNEAK **2** : to lie concealed

lus·cious \'lə-shəs\ *adj* **1** : having a pleasingly sweet taste or smell **2** : sensually appealing — **lus·cious·ly** *adv* — **lus·cious·ness** *n*

¹lush \'ləsh\ *adj* : having or covered with abundant growth ⟨∼ pastures⟩

²lush *n* : an habitual heavy drinker

lust \'ləst\ *n* **1** : usu. intense or unbridled sexual desire : LASCIVIOUSNESS **2** : an intense longing — **lust** *vb* — **lust·ful** *adj*

lus·ter *or* **lus·tre** \'ləs-tər\ *n* **1** : a shine or sheen esp. from reflected light **2** : BRIGHTNESS, GLITTER **3** : GLORY, SPLENDOR — **lus·ter·less** *adj* — **lus·trous** \-trəs\ *adj*

lus·tral \'ləs-trəl\ *adj* : PURIFICATORY

lusty \'ləs-tē\ *adj* **lust·i·er; -est** : full of vitality : ROBUST — **lust·i·ly** \'ləs-tə-lē\ *adv* — **lust·i·ness** \-tē-nəs\ *n*

lute \'lüt\ *n* : a stringed musical instrument with a large pear-shaped body and a fretted fingerboard — **lu·te·nist** *or* **lu·ta·nist** \'lüt-ᵊn-ist\ *n*

lu·te·tium *also* **lu·te·cium** \lü-'tē-shē-əm, -shəm\ *n* : a metallic chemical element — see ELEMENT table

Lu·ther·an \'lü-thə-rən\ *n* : a member of a Protestant denomination adhering to the doctrines of Martin Luther — **Lu·ther·an·ism** \-rə-,ni-zəm\ *n*

lux·u·ri·ant \,ləg-'zhùr-ē-ənt, ,lək-'shùr-\ *adj* **1** : yielding or growing abundantly : LUSH, PRODUCTIVE **2** : abundantly rich and varied; *also* : FLORID **syn** exuberant, lavish, opulent, prodigal, profuse, riotous — **lux·u·ri·ance** \-ē-əns\ *n* — **lux·u·ri·ant·ly** *adv*

lux·u·ri·ate \-ē-,āt\ *vb* **-at·ed; -at·ing 1** : to grow profusely **2** : REVEL

lux·u·ry \'lək-shə-rē, 'ləg-zhə-\ *n, pl* **-ries 1** : great ease and comfort **2** : something adding to pleasure or comfort but not absolutely necessary — **lux·u·ri·ous** \,ləg-'zhùr-ē-əs, ,lək-'shùr-\ *adj* — **lux·u·ri·ous·ly** *adv*

lv *abbr* leave

LVN *n* : LICENSED VOCATIONAL NURSE

lwei \lə-'wā\ *n, pl* **lwei** — see *kwanza* at MONEY table

LWV *abbr* League of Women Voters

¹-ly \lē\ *adj suffix* **1** : like in appearance, manner, or nature ⟨queen*ly*⟩ **2** : characterized by regular recurrence in (specified) units of time : every ⟨hour*ly*⟩

²-ly *adv suffix* **1** : in a (specified) manner ⟨slow*ly*⟩ **2** : from a (specified) point of view ⟨grammatical*ly*⟩

ly·ce·um \lī-'sē-əm, 'lī-sē-\ *n* **1** : a hall for public lectures **2** : an association providing public lectures, concerts, and entertainments

lye \'lī\ *n* : a corrosive alkaline substance used esp. in making soap

ly·ing \'lī-iŋ\ *adj* : UNTRUTHFUL, FALSE

ly·ing–in \,lī-iŋ-'in\ *n, pl* **lyings–in** *or* **lying–ins** : the state during and consequent to childbirth : CONFINEMENT

Lyme disease \\'līm-\ *n* [*Lyme*, Connecticut, where it was first reported] : an acute inflammatory disease that is caused by a spirochete transmitted by ticks, is characterized esp. by chills and fever, and if left untreated may result in joint pain, arthritis, and cardiac and neurological disorders

lymph \\'limf\ *n* : a pale liquid consisting chiefly of blood plasma and white blood cells, circulating in thin-walled tubes (**lymphatic vessels**), and bathing the body tissues — **lym·phat·ic** \lim-'fa-tik\ *adj*

lymph·ade·nop·a·thy \,lim-,fad-ᵊn-'ä-pə-thē\ *n*, *pl* **-thies** : abnormal enlargement of the lymph nodes

lymph node *n* : any of the rounded masses of lymphoid tissue surrounded by a capsule

lym·pho·cyte \\'lim-fə-,sīt\ *n* : any of the weakly motile leukocytes produced in lymphoid tissue that are the typical cells in lymph and include the cellular mediators (as a B cell or a T cell) of immunity

lym·phoid \\'lim-,fȯid\ *adj* 1 : of, relating to, or being tissue (as of the lymph nodes) containing lymphocytes 2 : of, relating to, or resembling lymph

lym·pho·ma \lim-'fō-mə\ *n*, *pl* **-mas** *or* **-ma·ta** \-mə-tə\ : a tumor of lymphoid tissue

lynch \\'linch\ *vb* : to put to death by mob action without legal sanction or due process of law — **lyncher** *n*

lynx \\'liŋks\ *n*, *pl* **lynx** *or* **lynx·es** : any of several wildcats with a short tail, long legs, and usu. tufted ears

lynx

lyre \\'līr\ *n* : a stringed musical instrument of the harp class used by the ancient Greeks

¹**lyr·ic** \\'lir-ik\ *n* 1 : a lyric poem 2 *pl* : the words of a popular song — **lyr·i·cal** \-i-kəl\ *adj*

²**lyric** *adj* 1 : suitable for singing : MELODIC 2 : expressing direct and usu. intense personal emotion

ly·ser·gic acid di·eth·yl·am·ide \lə-'sər-jik . . . ,dī-,e-thə-'la-,mīd, lī-, -'la-məd\ *n* : LSD

LZ *abbr* landing zone

M

¹**m** \\'em\ *n*, *pl* **m's** *or* **ms** \\'emz\ *often cap* : the 13th letter of the English alphabet

²**m** *abbr, often cap* 1 Mach 2 male 3 married 4 masculine 5 medium 6 [L *meridies*] noon 7 meter 8 mile 9 [L *mille*] thousand 10 minute 11 month 12 moon

ma \\'mä, 'mȯ\ *n* : MOTHER

MA *abbr* 1 [ML *magister artium*] master of arts 2 Massachusetts 3 mental age

ma'am \\'mam, *after "yes" often* əm\ *n* : MADAM

Mac *abbr* Machabees

Mac *or* **Macc** *abbr* Maccabees

ma·ca·bre \mə-'käb; 'kä-brə, -bər\ *adj* [F] 1 : having death as a subject 2 : GRUESOME 3 : HORRIBLE

mac·ad·am \mə-'ka-dəm\ *n* : a roadway or pavement of small closely packed broken stone — **mac·ad·am·ize** \-də-,mīz\ *vb*

ma·caque \mə-'kak, -'käk\ *n* : any of a genus of short=tailed chiefly Asian monkeys

mac·a·ro·ni \,ma-kə-'rō-nē\ *n* 1 : pasta made chiefly of wheat flour and shaped in the form of slender tubes 2 *pl* **-nis** *or* **-nies** : FOP, DANDY

mac·a·roon \,ma-kə-'rün\ *n* : a small cookie made chiefly of egg whites, sugar, and ground almonds or coconut

ma·caw \mə-'kȯ\ *n* : any of numerous parrots of Central and So. America

Mac·ca·bees \\'ma-kə-,bēz\ *n* — see BIBLE table

¹**mace** \\'mās\ *n* : a spice made from the fibrous coating of the nutmeg

²**mace** *n* 1 : a heavy often spiked club used as a weapon esp. in the Middle Ages 2 : an ornamental staff carried as a symbol of authority

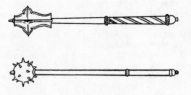

mace 1

Mac·e·do·nian \,ma-sə-'dō-nyən, -nē-ən\ *n* : a native or inhabitant of Macedonia — **Macedonian** *adj*

mac·er·ate \\'ma-sə-,rāt\ *vb* **-at·ed; -at·ing** 1 : to cause to waste away 2 : to soften by steeping or soaking so as to separate the parts — **mac·er·a·tion** \,ma-sə-'rā-shən\ *n*

mach *abbr* machine; machinery; machinist

Mach \\'mäk\ *n* : a speed expressed by a Mach number

Mach·a·bees \\'ma-kə-,bēz\ *n* : MACCABEES

ma·chete \mə-'she-tē\ *n* : a large heavy knife used for cutting sugarcane and underbrush and as a weapon

Ma·chi·a·vel·lian \,ma-kē-ə-'ve-lē-ən\ *adj* [Niccolò *Machiavelli*, †1527 Ital. political philosopher] : characterized by cunning, duplicity, and bad faith — **Ma·chi·a·vel·lian·ism** *n*

mach·i·na·tion \,ma-kə-'nā-shən, ,ma-shə-\ *n* : an act of planning esp. to do harm; *esp* : PLOT — **mach·i·nate** \\'ma-kə-,nāt, 'ma-shə-\ *vb*

¹**ma·chine** \mə-'shēn\ *n* 1 : CONVEYANCE, VEHICLE; *esp* : AUTOMOBILE 2 : a combination of mechanical parts that transmit forces, motion, and energy one to another 3 : an instrument (as a lever) for transmitting or modifying force or motion 4 : an electrical, electronic, or mechanical device for performing a task (a sewing ∼) 5 : a highly organized political group under the leadership of a boss or small clique

²**machine** *vb* **ma·chined; ma·chin·ing** : to shape or finish by machine-operated tools — **ma·chin·able** \-'shē-nə-bəl\ *adj*

machine gun *n* : an automatic gun capable of rapid continuous firing — **machine–gun** *vb* — **machine gunner** *n*

machine language *n* : the set of symbolic instruction codes used to represent operations and data in a machine (as a computer)

machine–readable *adj* : directly usable by a computer

ma·chin·ery \mə-'shē-nə-rē\ *n*, *pl* **-er·ies** 1 : MACHINES; *also* : the working parts of a machine 2 : the means by which something is done

ma·chin·ist \mə-'shē-nist\ *n* : a person who makes or works on machines

ma·chis·mo \mä-'chēz-(,)mō, -'chiz-\ *n* : a strong or exaggerated pride in one's masculinity

Mach number \\'mäk-\ *n* : a number representing the ratio of the speed of a body to the speed of sound in the surrounding atmosphere

ma·cho \\'mä-chō\ *adj* [Sp, lit., male, fr. L *masculus*] : characterized by machismo

mack·er·el \\'ma-kə-rəl\ *n*, *pl* **mackerel** *or* **mackerels**

: a No. Atlantic food fish greenish above and silvery below

mack·i·naw \\'ma-kə-ˌnȯ\ *n* : a short heavy plaid coat

mack·in·tosh *also* **mac·in·tosh** \\'ma-kən-ˌtäsh\ *n* **1** *chiefly Brit* : RAINCOAT **2** : a lightweight waterproof fabric

mac·ra·mé *also* **mac·ra·me** \\'ma-krə-ˌmā\ *n* [ultim. fr. Ar *miqramah* coverlet] : a coarse lace or fringe made by knotting threads or cords in a geometrical pattern

mac·ro \\'ma-(ˌ)krō\ *adj* : very large; *also* : involving large quantities or being on a large scale

mac·ro·bi·ot·ic \ˌma-krō-bī-ˈä-tik, -bē-\ *adj* : relating to or being a very restricted diet (as one containing chiefly whole grains)

mac·ro·cosm \\'ma-krə-ˌkä-zəm\ *n* : the great world : UNIVERSE

ma·cron \\'mā-ˌkrän, 'ma-\ *n* : a mark ‾ placed over a vowel (as in \mäk\) to show that the vowel is long

mac·ro·scop·ic \ˌma-krə-ˈskä-pik\ *adj* : visible to the naked eye — **mac·ro·scop·i·cal·ly** \-pi-k(ə-)lē\ *adv*

mad \\'mad\ *adj* **mad·der; mad·dest 1** : disordered in mind : INSANE **2** : being rash and foolish **3** : FURIOUS, ENRAGED **4** : carried away by enthusiasm **5** : RABID **6** : marked by wild gaiety and merriment **7** : FRANTIC — **mad·ly** *adv* — **mad·ness** *n*

Mad·a·gas·can \ˌma-də-ˈgas-kən\ *n* : a native or inhabitant of Madagascar

mad·am \\'ma-dəm\ *n* **1** *pl* **mes·dames** \mā-ˈdäm\ — used as a form of polite address to a woman **2** *pl* **madams** : the female head of a house of prostitution

ma·dame \\'dam, *before a surname also* 'ma-dəm\ *n, pl* **mes·dames** \mā-ˈdäm\ — MISTRESS — used as a title equivalent to *Mrs.* for a married woman not of English-speaking nationality

mad·cap \\'mad-ˌkap\ *adj* : WILD, RECKLESS — **mad·cap** *n*

mad·den \\'mad-ᵊn\ *vb* : to make mad — **mad·den·ing·ly** *adv*

mad·der \\'ma-dər\ *n* : a Eurasian herb with yellow flowers and fleshy red roots; *also* : its root or a dye prepared from it

made *past and past part of* MAKE

Ma·dei·ra \mə-ˈdir-ə\ *n* : an amber-colored dessert wine

ma·de·moi·selle \ˌma-də-mə-ˈzel, -mwə-, mam-ˈzel\ *n, pl* **ma·de·moi·selles** \-ˈzelz\ *or* **mes·de·moi·selles** \ˌmā-də-me-ˈzel, -mwe-\ : an unmarried girl or woman — used as a title for an unmarried woman not of English-speaking nationality

made–up \\'mā-ˈdəp\ *adj* **1** : fancifully conceived or falsely devised **2** : marked by the use of makeup

mad·house \\'mad-ˌhau̇s\ *n* **1** : a place for the detention and care of the insane **2** : a place of great uproar

mad·man \\'mad-ˌman, -mən\ *n* : LUNATIC

Ma·don·na \mə-ˈdä-nə\ *n* : a representation (as a picture or statue) of the Virgin Mary

ma·dras \\'ma-drəs; mə-ˈdras, -ˈdräs\ *n* [*Madras*, India] : a fine usu. cotton fabric with various designs (as plaid)

mad·ri·gal \\'ma-dri-gəl\ *n* [It *madrigale*] **1** : a short lyrical poem in a strict poetic form **2** : an elaborate part-song esp. of the 16th and 17th centuries

mad·wom·an \\'mad-ˌwu̇-mən\ *n* : a woman who is insane

mael·strom \\'māl-strəm\ *n* **1** : a violent whirlpool **2** : TUMULT

mae·stro \\'mī-strō\ *n, pl* **maestros** *or* **mae·stri** \-ˌstrē\ [It] : a master in an art; *esp* : an eminent composer, conductor, or teacher of music

Ma·fia \\'mä-fē-ə\ *n* [It] : a secret criminal society of Sicily or Italy; *also* : a similar organization elsewhere

ma·fi·o·so \ˌmä-fē-ˈō-(ˌ)sō\ *n, pl* **-si** \-(ˌ)sē\ : a member of the Mafia

¹mag \\'mag\ *n* : MAGAZINE

²mag *abbr* **1** magnetism **2** magneto **3** magnitude

mag·a·zine \\'ma-gə-ˌzēn\ *n* **1** : a storehouse esp. for military supplies **2** : a place for keeping gunpowder in a fort or ship **3** : a publication usu. containing stories, articles, or poems and issued periodically **4** : a container in a gun for holding cartridges; *also* : a chamber (as on a camera) for film

ma·gen·ta \mə-ˈjen-tə\ *n* : a deep purplish red color

mag·got \\'ma-gət\ *n* : the legless wormlike larva of a dipteran fly — **mag·goty** *adj*

ma·gi \\'mā- jī\ *n pl, often cap* : the three wise men from the East who paid homage to the infant Jesus

mag·ic \\'ma-jik\ *n* **1** : the use of means (as charms or spells) believed to have supernatural power over natural forces **2** : an extraordinary power or influence seemingly from a supernatural force **3** : SLEIGHT OF HAND — **magic** *adj* — **mag·i·cal** \-ji-kəl\ *adj* — **mag·i·cal·ly** \-ji-k(ə-)lē\ *adv*

ma·gi·cian \mə-ˈji-shən\ *n* : one skilled in magic

mag·is·te·ri·al \ˌma-jə-ˈstir-ē-əl\ *adj* **1** : AUTHORITATIVE **2** : of or relating to a magistrate or a magistrate's office or duties

ma·gis·tral \\'ma-jə-strəl\ *adj* : AUTHORITATIVE

mag·is·trate \\'ma-jə-ˌstrāt\ *n* : an official entrusted with administration of the laws — **mag·is·tra·cy** \-strə-sē\ *n*

mag·ma \\'mag-mə\ *n* : molten rock material within the earth — **mag·mat·ic** \mag-ˈma-tik\ *adj*

mag·nan·i·mous \mag-ˈna-nə-məs\ *adj* **1** : showing or suggesting a lofty and courageous spirit **2** : NOBLE, GENEROUS — **mag·na·nim·i·ty** \ˌmag-nə-ˈni-mə-tē\ *n* — **mag·nan·i·mous·ly** *adv* — **mag·nan·i·mous·ness** *n*

mag·nate \\'mag-ˌnāt\ *n* : a person of rank, influence, or distinction

mag·ne·sia \mag-ˈnē-shə, -zhə\ *n* [NL, fr. *magnes carneus*, a white earth, lit., flesh magnet] : a light white oxide of magnesium used as a laxative

mag·ne·sium \mag-ˈnē-zē-əm, -zhəm\ *n* : a silver-white light malleable metallic chemical element — see ELEMENT table

mag·net \\'mag-nət\ *n* **1** : LODESTONE **2** : a body that is able to attract iron **3** : something that attracts

mag·net·ic \mag-ˈne-tik\ *adj* **1** : having an unusual ability to attract ⟨a ∼ leader⟩ **2** : of or relating to a magnet or magnetism **3** : magnetized or capable of being magnetized — **mag·net·i·cal·ly** \-ti-k(ə-)lē\ *adv*

magnetic disk *n* : DISK 3

magnetic north *n* : the northerly direction in the earth's magnetic field indicated by the north-seeking pole of a compass needle

magnetic resonance imaging *n* : a noninvasive diagnostic technique that produces computerized images of internal body tissues based on electromagnetically induced activity of atoms within the body

magnetic tape *n* : a ribbon coated with a magnetic material on which information (as sound) may be stored

mag·ne·tism \\'mag-nə-ˌti-zəm\ *n* **1** : the power (as of a magnet) to attract iron **2** : the science that deals with magnetic phenomena **3** : an ability to attract

mag·ne·tise *Brit var of* MAGNETIZE

mag·ne·tite \\'mag-nə-ˌtīt\ *n* : a black mineral that is an important iron ore

mag·ne·tize \\'mag-nə-ˌtīz\ *vb* **-tized; -tiz·ing 1** : to induce magnetic properties in **2** : to attract like a magnet : CHARM — **mag·ne·tiz·able** *adj* — **mag·ne·ti·za·tion** \ˌmag-nə-tə-ˈzā-shən\ *n* — **mag·ne·tiz·er** *n*

mag·ne·to \mag-ˈnē-tō\ *n, pl* **-tos** : a generator used to produce sparks in an internal combustion engine

mag·ne·tom·e·ter \ˌmag-nə-ˈtä-mə-tər\ *n* : an instrument for measuring the strength of a magnetic field

mag·ne·to·sphere \mag-ˈnē-tə-ˌsfir, -ˈne-\ *n* : a region around a celestial object (as the earth) in which charged particles are trapped by its magnetic field — **mag·ne·to·spher·ic** \-ˌnē-tə-ˈsfir-ik, -ˈsfer-\ *adj*

mag·ni·fi·ca·tion \ˌmag-nə-fə-ˈkā-shən\ *n* **1** : the act of magnifying **2** : the amount by which an optical lens or instrument magnifies

mag·nif·i·cent \mag-ˈni-fə-sənt\ *adj* **1** : characterized by grandeur or beauty : SPLENDID **2** : EXALTED, NO-BLE syn imposing, stately, grand, majestic — **mag-nif·i·cence** \-səns\ *n* — **mag·nif·i·cent·ly** *adv*

mag·nif·i·co \mag-'ni-fi-ˌkō\ *n, pl* **-coes** *or* **-cos 1** : a nobleman of Venice **2** : a person of high position

mag·ni·fy \'mag-nə-ˌfī\ *vb* **-fied; -fy·ing 1** : EXTOL, LAUD; *also* : to cause to be held in greater esteem **2** : INTENSIFY; *also* : EXAGGERATE **3** : to enlarge in fact or in appearance ⟨a microscope *magnifies* an object⟩ — **mag·ni·fi·er** \'mag-nə-ˌfī-ər\ *n*

mag·nil·o·quent \mag-'ni-lə-kwənt\ *adj* : character-ized by an exalted and often bombastic style or man-ner — **mag·nil·o·quence** \-kwəns\ *n*

mag·ni·tude \'mag-nə-ˌtüd, -ˌtyüd\ *n* **1** : greatness of size or extent **2** : SIZE **3** : QUANTITY **4** : a number rep-resenting the brightness of a celestial body

mag·no·lia \mag-'nōl-yə\ *n* : any of a genus of usu. spring-flowering shrubs and trees with large often fragrant flowers

mag·num opus \'mag-nəm-'ō-pəs\ *n* [L] : the greatest achievement of an artist or writer

mag·pie \'mag-ˌpī\ *n* : any of various long-tailed often black-and-white birds related to the jays

Mag·yar \'mag-ˌyär, 'mäg-; 'mä-ˌjär\ *n* : a member of the dominant people of Hungary — **Magyar** *adj*

ma·ha·ra·ja *or* **ma·ha·ra·jah** \ˌmä-hə-'rä-jə\ *n* : a Hin-du prince ranking above a raja

ma·ha·ra·ni *or* **ma·ha·ra·nee** \-'rä-nē\ *n* **1** : the wife of a maharaja **2** : a Hindu princess ranking above a rani

ma·ha·ri·shi \ˌmä-hə-'rē-shē\ *n* : a Hindu teacher of mystical knowledge

ma·hat·ma \mə-'hät-mə, -'hat-\ *n* [Skt *mahātman*, fr. *mahātman* great-souled, fr. *mahat* great + *ātman* soul] : a person revered for high-mindedness, wis-dom, and selflessness

Ma·hi·can \mə-'hē-kən\ *n, pl* **Mahican** *or* **Mahicans** : a member of an American Indian people of the up-per Hudson River valley

ma·hog·a·ny \mə-'hä-gə-nē\ *n, pl* **-nies** : the reddish wood of any of various chiefly tropical trees that is used in furniture; *also* : a tree yielding this wood

ma·hout \mə-'haút\ *n* [Hindi *mahāut*] : a keeper and driver of an elephant

maid \'mād\ *n* **1** : an unmarried girl or young woman **2** : MAIDSERVANT

¹**maid·en** \'mād-ᵊn\ *n* : MAID 1 — **maid·en·ly** *adj*

²**maiden** *adj* **1** : UNMARRIED; *also* : VIRGIN **2** : of, relat-ing to, or befitting a maiden **3** : FIRST ⟨~ voyage⟩

maid·en·hair fern \-ˌhar-\ *n* : any of a genus of ferns with delicate feathery fronds

maid·en·head \'mād-ᵊn-ˌhed\ *n* **1** : VIRGINITY **2** : HY-MEN

maid·en·hood \-ˌhúd\ *n* : the condition or time of being a maiden

maid–in–waiting *n, pl* **maids–in–waiting** : a young woman appointed to attend a queen or princess

maid of honor : a bride's principal unmarried wedding attendant

maid·ser·vant \'mād-ˌsər-vənt\ *n* : a girl or woman who is a servant

¹**mail** \'māl\ *n* [ME *male* bag, fr. OF] **1** : something sent or carried in the postal system **2** : a nation's postal system — often used in pl.

²**mail** *vb* : to send by mail

³**mail** *n* [ME *maille*, fr. MF, fr. L *macula* spot, mesh] : armor made of metal links or plates

mail·box \'māl-ˌbäks\ *n* **1** : a public box for the col-lection of mail **2** : a private box for the delivery of mail

mail·man \-ˌman\ *n* : a man who delivers mail

maim \'mām\ *vb* : to mutilate, disfigure, or wound se-riously : CRIPPLE

¹**main** \'mān\ *n* **1** : FORCE ⟨with might and ~⟩ **2** : MAIN-LAND; *also* : HIGH SEA **3** : the chief part **4** : a principal pipe, duct, or circuit of a utility system

²**main** *adj* **1** : CHIEF, PRINCIPAL **2** : fully exerted ⟨~

force⟩ **3** : expressing the chief predication in a com-plex sentence ⟨the ~ clause⟩ — **main·ly** *adv*

main·frame \'mān-ˌfrām\ *n* : a large fast computer

main·land \-ˌland, -lənd\ *n* : a continuous body of land constituting the chief part of a country or continent

main·line \-ˌlīn\ *vb, slang* : to inject a narcotic drug into a vein

main line *n* : a principal highway or railroad line

main·mast \'mān-ˌmast, -məst\ *n* : the principal mast on a sailing ship

main·sail \-ˌsāl, -səl\ *n* : the largest sail on the main-mast

main·spring \-ˌspriŋ\ *n* **1** : the chief spring in a mech-anism (as of a watch) **2** : the chief motive, agent, or cause

main·stay \-ˌstā\ *n* **1** : a stay running from the head of the mainmast to the foot of the foremast **2** : a chief support

main·stream \-ˌstrēm\ *n* : a prevailing current or direc-tion of activity or influence — **mainstream** *adj*

main·tain \mān-'tān\ *vb* [ME *mainteinen*, fr. OF *main-tenir*, fr. ML *manutenēre*, fr. L *manu tenēre* to hold in the hand] **1** : to keep in an existing state (as of repair) **2** : to sustain against opposition or danger **3** : to continue in : CARRY ON **4** : to provide for : SUP-PORT **5** : ASSERT — **main·tain·abil·i·ty** \-ˌtā-nə-'bi-lə-tē\ *n* — **main·tain·able** \-'tā-nə-bəl\ *adj* — **main·te-nance** \'mānt-ᵊn-əns\ *n*

main·top \'mān-ˌtäp\ *n* : a platform at the head of the mainmast of a square-rigged ship

mai·son·ette \ˌmāz-ᵊn-'et\ *n* **1** : a small house **2** : an apartment often on two floors

maî·tre d' *or* **mai·tre d'** \ˌmā-trə-'dē, ˌme-\ *n, pl* **maî·tre d's** *or* **mai·tre d's** \-'dēz\ : MAÎTRE D'HÔTEL

maî·tre d'hô·tel \ˌmā-trə-dō-'tel, ˌme-\ *n, pl* **maîtres d'hôtel** *same*\ [F, lit., master of house] **1** : MAJOR-DOMO **2** : HEADWAITER

maize \'māz\ *n* : INDIAN CORN

Maj *abbr* major

maj·es·ty \'ma-jə-stē\ *n, pl* **-ties 1** : sovereign power, authority, or dignity; *also* : the person of a sovereign — used as a title **2** : GRANDEUR, SPLENDOR — **ma-jes·tic** \mə-'jes-tik\ *adj* — **ma·jes·ti·cal·ly** \-ti-k(ə-)lē\ *adv*

Maj Gen *abbr* Major General

ma·jol·i·ca \mə-'jä-li-kə\ *also* **ma·iol·i·ca** \-'yä-\ *n* : any of several faiences; *esp* : an Italian tin-glazed pottery

¹**ma·jor** \'mā-jər\ *adj* **1** : greater in number, extent, or importance ⟨a ~ poet⟩ **2** : notable or conspicuous in effect or scope ⟨a ~ improvement⟩ **3** : SERIOUS ⟨a ~ illness⟩ **4** : having half steps between the 3d and 4th and the 7th and 8th degrees ⟨~ scale⟩; *also* : based on a major scale ⟨~ key⟩ ⟨~ chord⟩

²**major** *n* **1** : a commissioned officer (as in the army) ranking next below a lieutenant colonel **2** : an aca-demic subject chosen as a field of specialization; *also* : a student specializing in such a field

³**major** *vb* : to pursue an academic major

ma·jor·do·mo \ˌmā-jər-'dō-mō\ *n, pl* **-mos** [Sp *mayor-domo* or obs. It *maiordomo*, fr. ML *major domus*, lit., chief of the house] : a head steward or butler

ma·jor·ette \ˌmā-jə-'ret\ *n* : DRUM MAJORETTE

major general *n* : a commissioned officer (as in the army) ranking next below a lieutenant general

ma·jor·i·ty \mə-'jór-ə-tē\ *n, pl* **-ties 1** : the age at which full civil rights are accorded; *also* : the status of one who has attained this age **2** : a number greater than half of a total; *also* : the excess of this greater number over the remainder **3** : the rank of a major

ma·jus·cule \'ma-jəs-ˌkyül, mə-'jəs-\ *n* : a large letter (as a capital)

¹**make** \'māk\ *vb* **made** \'mād\; **mak·ing** : to cause to exist, occur, or appear; *also* : DESTINE ⟨was *made* to be an actor⟩ **2** : FASHION ⟨~ a dress⟩; *also* : COMPOSE **3** : to formulate in the mind ⟨~ plans⟩ **4** : CONSTITUTE ⟨house *made* of stone⟩ **5** : to compute to be **6** : to set

in order : PREPARE ⟨∼ a bed⟩ **7** : to cause to be or become; *also* : APPOINT **8** : ENACT; *also* : EXECUTE ⟨∼ a will⟩ **9** : CONCLUDE ⟨didn't know what to ∼ of it⟩ **10** : CARRY OUT, PERFORM ⟨∼ a gesture⟩ **11** : COMPEL **12** : to assure the success of ⟨will ∼ us or break us⟩ **13** : to amount to in significance ⟨∼s no difference⟩ **14** : to be capable of developing or being fashioned into **15** : REACH, ATTAIN; *also* : GAIN **16** : to start out : GO **17** : to have weight or effect ⟨courtesy ∼s for safer driving⟩ **syn** form, shape, fabricate, manufacture — **mak·er** *n* — **make believe** : PRETEND — **make do** : to manage with the means at hand — **make fun of** : RIDICULE, MOCK — **make good 1** : INDEMNIFY ⟨*make good* the loss⟩; *also* : to carry out successfully ⟨*make good* his promise⟩ **2** : SUCCEED — **make way 1** : to give room for passing, entering, or occupying **2** : to make progress

²make *n* **1** : the manner or style of construction; *also* : BRAND **3 2** : MAKEUP **3** : the action of manufacturing — **on the make** : in search of wealth, social status, or sexual adventure

¹make–be·lieve \'māk-bə-₁lēv\ *n* : a pretending to believe : PRETENSE

²make–believe *adj* : IMAGINED, PRETENDED

make–do \-₁dü\ *adj* : MAKESHIFT

make out *vb* **1** : to draw up in writing ⟨*make out* a list⟩ **2** : to find or grasp the meaning of ⟨can you *make* that *out*⟩ **3** : to represent as being **4** : to pretend to be true **5** : DISCERN ⟨*make out* a ship in the fog⟩ **6** : GET ALONG, FARE ⟨*make out* well in life⟩ **7** : to engage in amorous kissing and caressing

make over *vb* : REMAKE, REMODEL — **make·over** \'mā-₁kō-vər\ *n*

make·shift \'māk-₁shift\ *n* : a temporary expedient — **makeshift** *adj*

make·up \'mā-₁kəp\ *n* **1** : the way in which something is put together; *also* : physical, mental, and moral constitution **2** : cosmetics esp. for the face; *also* : materials (as wigs and cosmetics) used in making up

make up *vb* **1** : FORM, COMPOSE **2** : to compensate for a deficiency **3** : SETTLE ⟨*made up* my mind⟩ **4** : INVENT, IMPROVISE **5** : to become reconciled **6** : to put on makeup (as for a play)

make–work \'māk-₁wərk\ *n* : BUSYWORK

mak·ings \'mā-kiŋz\ *n pl* : the material from which something is made

makuta *pl of* LIKUTA

Mal *abbr* Malachi

Mal·a·chi \'ma-lə-₁kī\ *n* — see BIBLE table

Mal·a·chi·as \₁ma-lə-'kī-əs\ *n* : MALACHI

mal·a·chite \'ma-lə-₁kīt\ *n* : a mineral that is a green carbonate of copper used for making ornamental objects

mal·adapt·ed \₁ma-lə-'dap-təd\ *adj* : poorly suited to a particular use, purpose, or situation

mal·ad·just·ed \₁ma-lə-'jəs-təd\ *adj* : poorly or inadequately adjusted (as to one's environment) — **mal·ad·just·ment** \-'jəst-mənt\ *n*

mal·adroit \₁ma-lə-'dròit\ *adj* : not adroit : INEPT

mal·a·dy \'ma-lə-dē\ *n, pl* **-dies** : a disease or disorder of body or mind

mal·aise \mə-'lāz, ma-\ *n* [F] : a hazy feeling of not being well

mal·a·mute \'ma-lə-₁myüt\ *n* : a dog often used to draw sleds esp. in northern No. America

mal·a·prop·ism \'ma-lə-₁prä-₁pi-zəm\ *n* : a usu. humorous misuse of a word

mal·ap·ro·pos \₁ma-₁la-prə-'pō, ma-₁la-prə-₁pō\ *adv* : in an inappropriate or inopportune way — **malapropos** *adj*

ma·lar·ia \mə-'ler-ē-ə\ *n* [It, fr. *mala aria* bad air] : a disease marked by recurring chills and fever and caused by a protozoan parasite of the blood that is transmitted by anopheles mosquitoes — **ma·lar·i·al** \-əl\ *adj*

ma·lar·key \mə-'lär-kē\ *n* : insincere or foolish talk

mal·a·thi·on \₁ma-lə-'thī-ən, -₁än\ *n* : an insecticide with a relatively low toxicity for mammals

Ma·la·wi·an \mə-'lä-wē-ən\ *n* : a native or inhabitant of Malawi — **Malawian** *adj*

Ma·lay \mə-'lā, 'mā-₁lā\ *n* **1** : a member of a people of the Malay Peninsula and Archipelago **2** : the language of the Malays — **Malay** *adj* — **Ma·lay·an** \mə-'lā-ən, 'mā-₁lā-\ *n or adj*

Ma·lay·sian \mə-'lā-zhən, -shən\ *n* : a native or inhabitant of Malaysia — **Malaysian** *adj*

mal·con·tent \₁mal-kən-'tent\ *adj* : marked by a dissatisfaction with the existing state of affairs : DISCONTENTED — **malcontent** *n*

mal de mer \₁mal-də-'mer\ *n* [F] : SEASICKNESS

¹male \'māl\ *adj* **1** : of, relating to, or being the sex that produces germ cells which fertilize the eggs of a female; *also* : STAMINATE **2** : MASCULINE — **male·ness** *n*

²male *n* : a male individual

male·dic·tion \₁ma-lə-'dik-shən\ *n* : CURSE, EXECRATION

male·fac·tor \'ma-lə-₁fak-tər\ *n* : EVILDOER; *esp* : one who commits an offense against the law — **male·fac·tion** \₁ma-lə-'fak-shən\ *n*

ma·lef·ic \mə-'le-fik\ *adj* **1** : BALEFUL **2** : MALICIOUS

ma·lef·i·cent \-fə-sənt\ *adj* : working or productive of harm or evil

ma·lev·o·lent \mə-'le-və-lənt\ *adj* : having, showing, or arising from ill will, spite, or hatred **syn** malignant, malign, malicious, spiteful — **ma·lev·o·lence** \-ləns\ *n*

mal·fea·sance \mal-'fēz-²ns\ *n* : wrongful conduct esp. by a public official

mal·for·ma·tion \₁mal-fòr-'mā-shən\ *n* : irregular or faulty formation or structure; *also* : an instance of this — **mal·formed** \mal-'fòrmd\ *adj*

mal·func·tion \mal-'fəŋk-shən\ *vb* : to fail to operate normally — **malfunction** *n*

Ma·li·an \'mä-lē-ən\ *n* : a native or inhabitant of Mali — **Malian** *adj*

mal·ice \'ma-ləs\ *n* : desire to cause injury or distress to another — **ma·li·cious** \mə-'li-shəs\ *adj* — **ma·li·cious·ly** *adv*

¹ma·lign \mə-'līn\ *adj* **1** : evil in nature, influence, or effect; *also* : MALIGNANT **2 2** : moved by ill will

²malign *vb* : to speak evil of : DEFAME

ma·lig·nant \mə-'lig-nənt\ *adj* **1** : INJURIOUS, MALIGN **2** : tending to produce death or deterioration ⟨a ∼ tumor⟩ — **ma·lig·nan·cy** \-nən-sē\ *n* — **ma·lig·nant·ly** *adv* — **ma·lig·ni·ty** \-nə-tē\ *n*

ma·lin·ger \mə-'liŋ-gər\ *vb* [F *malingre* sickly] : to pretend illness so as to avoid duty — **ma·lin·ger·er** *n*

mal·i·son \'ma-lə-sən, -zən\ *n* : CURSE

mall \'mòl, 'mal\ *n* **1** : a shaded walk : PROMENADE **2** : an urban shopping area featuring a variety of shops surrounding a concourse **3** : a usu. large enclosed suburban shopping area containing various shops

mal·lard \'ma-lərd\ *n, pl* **mallard** *or* **mallards** : a common wild duck that is the source of domestic ducks

mallard

mal·lea·ble \'ma-lē-ə-bəl\ *adj* **1** : capable of being extended or shaped by beating with a hammer or by the pressure of rollers **2** : ADAPTABLE, PLIABLE **syn** plastic, pliant, ductile, supple — **mal·le·a·bil·i·ty** \₁ma-lē-ə-'bi-lə-tē\ *n*

mal·let \'ma-lət\ *n* **1** : a tool with a large head for driving another tool or for striking a surface without marring it **2** : a long-handled hammerlike implement for striking a ball (as in croquet)

mal·le·us \'ma-lē-əs\ *n, pl* **mal·lei** \-lē-ıī, -lē-ıē\ [NL, fr. L, hammer] : the outermost of the three small bones of the mammalian middle ear

mal·low \'ma-lō\ *n* : any of a genus of herbs with lobed leaves, usu. showy flowers, and a disk-shaped fruit

malm·sey \'mälm-zē\ *n, often cap* : the sweetest variety of Madeira

mal·nour·ished \mal-'nər-isht\ *adj* : UNDERNOURISHED

mal·nu·tri·tion \ˌmal-nü-'tri-shən, -nyü-\ *n* : faulty and esp. inadequate nutrition

mal·oc·clu·sion \ˌma-lə-'klü-zhən\ *n* : faulty coming together of teeth in biting

mal·odor·ous \ma-'lō-də-rəs\ *adj* : ill-smelling — **mal·odor·ous·ly** *adv* — **mal·odor·ous·ness** *n*

ma·lo·ti \mə-'lō-tē\ *pl of* LOTI

mal·prac·tice \mal-'prak-təs\ *n* : a dereliction of professional duty or a failure of professional skill that results in injury, loss, or damage

malt \'mólt\ *n* **1** : grain and esp. barley steeped in water until it has sprouted and used in brewing and distilling **2** : liquor made with malt — **malty** *adj*

malted milk \'mól-təd-\ *n* : a powder prepared from dried milk and an extract from malt; *also* : a beverage of this powder in milk or other liquid

Mal·thu·sian \mal-'thü-zhən, -'thyü-\ *adj* : of or relating to a theory that population unless checked (as by war) tends to increase faster than its means of subsistence — **Malthusian** *n* — **Mal·thu·sian·ism** \-zhəˌni-zəm\ *n*

malt·ose \'mól-ıtōs\ *n* : a sugar formed esp. from starch by the action of enzymes

mal·treat \mal-'trēt\ *vb* : to treat cruelly or roughly : ABUSE — **mal·treat·ment** *n*

ma·ma *or* **mam·ma** \'mä-mə\ *n* : MOTHER

mam·bo \'mäm-bō\ *n, pl* **mambos** : a dance of Cuban origin related to the rumba — **mambo** *vb*

mam·mal \'ma-məl\ *n* : any of a class of warm-blooded vertebrates that includes humans and all other animals which nourish their young with milk and have the skin more or less covered with hair — **mam·ma·li·an** \mə-'mä-lē-ən, ma-\ *adj or n*

mam·ma·ry \'ma-mə-rē\ *adj* : of, relating to, or being the glands (**mammary glands**) that in female mammals secrete milk

mam·mo·gram \'ma-mə-ıgram\ *n* : an X-ray photograph of the breasts

mam·mog·ra·phy \ma-'mä-grə-fē\ *n* : X-ray examination of the breasts (as for early detection of cancer)

mam·mon \'ma-mən\ *n, often cap* : material wealth having a debasing influence

¹mam·moth \'ma-məth\ *n* : any of a genus of large hairy extinct elephants

²mammoth *adj* : of very great size : GIGANTIC **syn** colossal, enormous, immense, vast, elephantine

¹man \'man\ *n, pl* **men** \'men\ **1** : a human being; *esp* : an adult male **2** : the human race : MANKIND **3** : one possessing in high degree the qualities considered distinctive of manhood **4** : an adult male servant or employee **5** : the individual who can fulfill one's requirements ⟨he's your ∼⟩ **6** : one of the pieces with which various games (as chess) are played; *also* : one of the players on a team **7** *often cap* : white society or people

²man *vb* **manned; man·ning 1** : to supply with men ⟨∼ a fleet⟩ **2** : FORTIFY, BRACE

³man *abbr* manual

Man *abbr* Manitoba

man–about–town *n, pl* **men–about–town** : a worldly and socially active man

man·a·cle \'ma-ni-kəl\ *n* **1** : a shackle for the hand or wrist **2** : something used as a restraint

man·age \'ma-nij\ *vb* **man·aged; man·ag·ing 1** : HANDLE, CONTROL; *also* : to direct or carry on business or

affairs **2** : to make and keep compliant **3** : to treat with care : HUSBAND **4** : to achieve one's purpose : CONTRIVE — **man·age·abil·i·ty** \ˌma-ni-jə-'bi-lə-tē\ *n* — **man·age·able** \'ma-ni-jə-bəl\ *adj* — **man·age·able·ness** *n* — **man·age·ably** \-blē\ *adv*

man·age·ment \'ma-nij-mənt\ *n* **1** : the act or art of managing : CONTROL **2** : judicious use of means to accomplish an end **3** : the group of those who manage or direct an enterprise

man·ag·er \'ma-ni-jər\ *n* : one that manages — **man·a·ge·ri·al** \ˌma-nə-'jir-ē-əl\ *adj*

ma·ña·na \mən-'yä-nə\ [Sp, lit., tomorrow] *n* : an indefinite time in the future

man–at–arms *n, pl* **men–at–arms** : SOLDIER; *esp* : one who is heavily armed and mounted

man·a·tee \'ma-nə-ıtē\ *n* : any of a genus of chiefly tropical plant-eating aquatic mammals having a broad rounded tail

Man·chu·ri·an \man-'chúr-ē-ən\ *n* : a native or inhabitant of Manchuria, China — **Manchurian** *adj*

man·ci·ple \'man-sə-pəl\ *n* : a steward or purveyor esp. for a college or monastery

man·da·mus \man-'dā-məs\ *n* [L, we enjoin] : a writ issued by a superior court commanding that an official act or duty be performed

man·da·rin \'man-də-rən\ *n* **1** : a public official of high rank under the Chinese Empire **2** *cap* : the chief dialect group of China **3** : a yellow to reddish orange loose-skinned citrus fruit; *also* : a tree that bears mandarins

man·date \'man-ıdāt\ *n* **1** : an authoritative command **2** : an authorization to act given to a representative **3** : a commission granted by the League of Nations to a member nation for governing conquered territory; *also* : a territory so governed

man·da·to·ry \'man-də-ıtōr-ē\ *adj* **1** : containing or constituting a command : OBLIGATORY **2** : of or relating to a League of Nations mandate

man·di·ble \'man-də-bəl\ *n* **1** : JAW; *esp* : a lower jaw **2** : either segment of a bird's bill — **man·dib·u·lar** \man-'di-byə-lər\ *adj*

man·do·lin \ˌman-də-'lin, 'mand-ᵊl-ən\ *n* : a stringed musical instrument with a pear-shaped body and a fretted neck

man·drake \'man-ıdrāk\ *n* **1** : an Old World herb of the nightshade family or its large forked root superstitiously credited with human and medicinal attributes **2** : MAYAPPLE

man·drel *also* **man·dril** \'man-drəl\ *n* **1** : an axle or spindle inserted into a hole in a piece of work to support it during machining **2** : a metal bar used as a core around which material may be cast, shaped, or molded

man·drill \'man-drəl\ *n* : a large baboon of western central Africa

mane \'mān\ *n* : long heavy hair growing about the neck of some mammals (as a horse) — **maned** \'mānd\ *adj*

man–eat·er \'man-ıē-tər\ *n* : one (as a shark or cannibal) that has or is thought to have an appetite for human flesh — **man–eat·ing** *adj*

ma·nège \ma-'nezh, mə-\ *n* : the art of horsemanship or of training horses

ma·nes \'mä-ınās, 'mä-ınēz\ *n pl, often cap* : the spirits of the dead and gods of the lower world in ancient Roman belief

ma·neu·ver \mə-'nü-vər, -'nyü-\ *n* [F *manœuvre*, fr. OF *maneuvre* work done by hand, fr. ML *manuopera*, fr. L *manu operare* to work by hand] **1** : a military or naval movement; *also* : an armed forces training exercise — often used in pl. **2** : a procedure involving expert physical movement **3** : an evasive movement or shift of tactics; *also* : an action taken to gain a tactical end — **maneuver** *vb* — **ma·neu·ver·abil·i·ty** \-ınü-və-rə-'bi-lə-tē, -ınyü-\ *n* — **ma·neu·ver·able** \-'nü-və-rə-bəl, -'nyü-\ *adj*

man Friday *n* : an efficient and devoted aide or employee

man·ful \'man-fəl\ *adj* : having or showing courage and resolution — **man·ful·ly** *adv*

man·ga·nese \'maŋ-gə-ˌnēz, -ˌnēs\ *n* : a metallic chemical element resembling iron but not magnetic — see ELEMENT table

mange \'mānj\ *n* : any of several contagious itchy skin diseases esp. of domestic animals — **mangy** \'mān-jē\ *adj*

man·ger \'mān-jər\ *n* : a trough or open box for livestock feed or fodder

¹**man·gle** \'maŋ-gəl\ *vb* **man·gled; man·gling** 1 : to cut, bruise, or hack with repeated blows 2 : to spoil or injure esp. through ineptitude — **man·gler** *n*

²**mangle** *n* : a machine with heated rollers for ironing laundry

man·go \'maŋ-gō\ *n, pl* **mangoes** *also* **mangos** [Pg *manga*] : a usu. yellowish red slightly acid juicy tropical fruit borne by an evergreen tree related to the sumacs; *also* : this tree

man·grove \'man-ˌgrōv\ *n* : any of a genus of tropical maritime trees that send out many prop roots and form dense thickets important in coastal land building

man·han·dle \'man-ˌhand-əl\ *vb* : to handle roughly

man·hat·tan \man-'hat-ən\ *n, often cap* : a cocktail made of whiskey and vermouth

man·hole \'man-ˌhōl\ *n* : a hole through which a person may go esp. to gain access to an underground or enclosed structure

man·hood \-ˌhu̇d\ *n* 1 : the condition of being an adult male 2 : manly qualities : COURAGE 3 : MEN ⟨the nation's ∼⟩

man–hour \-'au̇r\ *n* : a unit of one hour's work by one person

man·hunt \-ˌhənt\ *n* : an organized hunt for a person and esp. for one charged with a crime

ma·nia \'mā-nē-ə, -nyə\ *n* 1 : excitement of psychotic proportions accompanied by disorganized behavior and elevated mood 2 : excessive enthusiasm

ma·ni·ac \'mā-nē-ˌak\ *n* : LUNATIC, MADMAN

ma·ni·a·cal \mə-'nī-ə-kəl\ *also* **ma·ni·ac** \'mā-nē-ak\ *adj* 1 : affected with or suggestive of madness 2 : FRANTIC

man·ic \'ma-nik\ *adj* : affected with, relating to, or resembling mania — **manic** *n* — **man·i·cal·ly** \-ni-k(ə-)lē\ *adv*

man·ic–de·pres·sive \ˌma-nik-di-'pre-siv\ *adj* : characterized by mania or by psychotic depression or by alternating mania and depression — **manic–depressive** *n*

¹**man·i·cure** \'ma-nə-ˌkyu̇r\ *n* 1 : MANICURIST 2 : a treatment for the care of the hands and nails

²**manicure** *vb* **-cured; -cur·ing** 1 : to do manicure work on 2 : to trim closely and evenly

man·i·cur·ist \-ˌkyu̇r-ist\ *n* : a person who gives manicure treatments

¹**man·i·fest** \'ma-nə-ˌfest\ *adj* [ME, fr. MF or L; MF *manifeste*, fr. L *manifestus*, caught in the act, flagrant, perh. fr. *manus* hand + *-festus* (akin to L in*festus* hostile)] 1 : readily perceived by the senses and esp. by the sight 2 : easily understood : OBVIOUS — **man·i·fest·ly** *adv*

²**manifest** *vb* : to make evident or certain by showing or displaying syn evince, demonstrate, exhibit

³**manifest** *n* : a list of passengers or an invoice of cargo for a ship or plane

man·i·fes·ta·tion \ˌma-nə-fə-'stā-shən\ *n* : DISPLAY, DEMONSTRATION

man·i·fes·to \ˌma-nə-'fes-tō\ *n, pl* **-tos** *or* **-toes** : a public declaration of intentions, motives, or views

¹**man·i·fold** \'ma-nə-ˌfōld\ *adj* 1 : marked by diversity or variety 2 : consisting of or operating many of one kind combined

²**manifold** *n* : a pipe fitting with several lateral outlets for connecting it with other pipes

³**manifold** *vb* 1 : MULTIPLY 2 : to make a number of copies of (as a letter)

man·i·kin *or* **man·ni·kin** \'ma-ni-kən\ *n* 1 : MANNEQUIN 2 : a little man : DWARF

Ma·nila hemp \mə-'ni-lə-\ *n* : a tough fiber from a Philippine plant related to the banana that is used for cordage

manila paper *n, often cap* M : a tough brownish paper made orig. from Manila hemp

man·i·oc \'ma-nē-ˌäk\ *n* : CASSAVA

ma·nip·u·late \mə-'ni-pyə-ˌlāt\ *vb* **-lat·ed; -lat·ing** 1 : to treat or operate manually or mechanically esp. with skill 2 : to manage or use skillfully 3 : to influence esp. with intent to deceive — **ma·nip·u·la·tion** \mə-ni-pyə-'lā-shən\ *n* — **ma·nip·u·la·tive** \-'ni-pyə-ˌlā-tiv\ *adj* — **ma·nip·u·la·tor** \-ˌlā-tər\ *n*

man·kind *n* 1 \'man-ˌkīnd\ : the human race 2 \-ˌkīnd\ : men as distinguished from women

¹**man·ly** \'man-lē\ *adj* **man·li·er; -est** : having qualities appropriate to or generally associated with a man : BOLD, RESOLUTE — **man·li·ness** *n*

²**manly** *adv* : in a manly manner

man–made \'man-ˌmād\ *adj* : made by humans rather than nature ⟨∼ systems⟩; *esp* : SYNTHETIC ⟨∼ fibers⟩

man·na \'ma-nə\ *n* 1 : food miraculously supplied to the Israelites in the wilderness 2 : something of value that comes unexpectedly : WINDFALL

manned \'mand\ *adj* : carrying or performed by a person ⟨∼ spaceflight⟩

man·ne·quin \'ma-ni-kən\ *n* 1 : a form representing the human figure used esp. for displaying clothes 2 : a person employed to model clothing

man·ner \'ma-nər\ *n* 1 : KIND, SORT 2 : a way of acting or proceeding ⟨worked in a brisk ∼⟩; *also* : normal behavior ⟨spoke bluntly as was his ∼⟩ 3 : a method of artistic execution 4 *pl* : social conduct; *also* : BEARING 5 *pl* : BEHAVIOR ⟨taught the child good ∼s⟩

man·nered \'ma-nərd\ *adj* 1 : having manners of a specified kind ⟨well-*mannered*⟩ 2 : having an artificial character ⟨a highly ∼ style⟩

man·ner·ism \'ma-nə-ˌri-zəm\ *n* 1 : ARTIFICIALITY, PRECIOSITY 2 : a peculiarity of action, bearing, or treatment syn pose, air, affectation

man·ner·ly \'ma-nər-lē\ *adj* : showing good manners : POLITE — **man·ner·li·ness** *n* — **mannerly** *adv*

man·nish \'ma-nish\ *adj* 1 : resembling or suggesting a man rather than a woman 2 : generally associated with or characteristic of a man — **man·nish·ly** *adv* — **man·nish·ness** *n*

ma·noeu·vre \mə-'nü-vər, -'nyü-\ *chiefly Brit var of* MANEUVER

man–of–war \ˌman-əv-'wȯr\ *n, pl* **men–of–war** \ˌmen-\ : WARSHIP

ma·nom·e·ter \mə-'nä-mə-tər\ *n* : an instrument for measuring the pressure of gases and vapors — **mano·met·ric** \ˌma-nə-'me-trik\ *adj*

man·or \'ma-nər\ *n* 1 : the house or hall of an estate; *also* : a landed estate 2 : an English estate of a feudal lord — **ma·no·ri·al** \mə-'nōr-ē-əl\ *adj* — **ma·no·ri·al·ism** \-ə-ˌli-zəm\ *n*

man power *n* 1 : power available from or supplied by the physical effort of human beings 2 *usu* **man·pow·er** : the total supply of persons available and fitted for service

man·qué \mäⁿ-'kā\ *adj* [F, fr. pp. of *manquer* to lack, fail] : short of or frustrated in the fulfillment of one's aspirations or talents ⟨a poet ∼⟩

man·sard \'man-ˌsärd, -sərd\ *n* : a roof having two slopes on all sides with the lower slope steeper than the upper one

manse \'mans\ *n* : the residence esp. of a Presbyterian minister

man·ser·vant \'man-ˌsər-vənt\ *n, pl* **men·ser·vants** \'men-ˌsər-vənts\ : a male servant

man·sion \\'man-chən\ *n* : a large imposing residence; *also* : a separate apartment in a large structure

man–size \\'man-ısīz\ *or* **man–sized** \-ısīzd\ *adj* : suitable for or requiring a man

man·slaugh·ter \-ıslȯ-tər\ *n* : the unlawful killing of a human being without express or implied malice

man·ta \\'man-tə\ *n* : a square piece of cloth or blanket used in southwestern U.S. and Latin America as a cloak or shawl

man·teau \man-'tō\ *n* : a loose cloak, coat, or robe

man·tel \\'mant-əl\ *n* : a beam, stone, or arch serving as a lintel to support the masonry above a fireplace; *also* : a shelf above a fireplace

man·tel·piece \\'mant-əl-ıpēs\ *n* : the shelf of a mantel

man·til·la \man-'tē-yə, -'ti-lə\ *n* : a light scarf worn over the head and shoulders esp. by Spanish and Latin-American women

man·tis \\'man-təs\ *n, pl* **man·tis·es** *or* **man·tes** \-ıtēz\ [NL, fr. Gk, lit., diviner, prophet] : any of a group of large usu. green insect-eating insects that hold their prey in forelimbs folded as if in prayer

man·tis·sa \man-'ti-sə\ *n* : the part of a logarithm to the right of the decimal point

¹man·tle \\'mant-əl\ *n* **1** : a loose sleeveless garment worn over other clothes **2** : something that covers, enfolds, or envelopes **3** : a lacy sheath that gives light by incandescence when placed over a flame **4** : the portion of the earth lying between the crust and the core **5** : MANTEL

²mantle *vb* **man·tled; man·tling 1** : to cover with a mantle **2** : BLUSH

man·tra \\'man-trə\ *n* : a mystical formula of invocation or incantation (as in Hinduism)

¹man·u·al \\'man-yə-wəl\ *adj* **1** : of, relating to, or involving the hands; *also* : worked by hand ⟨a ∼ pump⟩ **2** : requiring or using physical skill and energy — **man·u·al·ly** *adv*

²manual *n* **1** : a small book; *esp* : HANDBOOK **2** : the prescribed movements in the handling of a military item and esp. a weapon during a drill or ceremony ⟨the ∼ of arms⟩ **3** : a keyboard esp. of an organ

man·u·fac·to·ry \ıman-yə-'fak-tə-rē\ *n* : FACTORY

¹man·u·fac·ture \ıman-yə-'fak-chər\ *n* [MF, fr. ML *manufactura*, L *manu factus* made by hand] **1** : something made from raw materials **2** : the process of making wares by hand or by machinery; *also* : a productive industry using machinery

²manufacture *vb* **-tured; -tur·ing 1** : to make from raw materials by hand or by machinery; *also* : to engage in manufacture **2** : INVENT, FABRICATE; *also* : CREATE — **man·u·fac·tur·er** *n*

man·u·mit \ıman-yə-'mit\ *vb* **-mit·ted; -mit·ting** : to free from slavery — **man·u·mis·sion** \-'mi-shən\ *n*

¹ma·nure \mə-'nu̇r, -'nyu̇r\ *vb* **ma·nured; ma·nur·ing** : to fertilize land with manure

²manure *n* : FERTILIZER; *esp* : refuse from stables and barnyards — **ma·nu·ri·al** \-'nu̇r-ē-əl, -'nyu̇r-\ *adj*

man·u·script \\'man-yə-ıskript\ *n* [L *manu scriptus* written by hand] **1** : a written or typewritten composition or document; *also* : a document submitted for publication **2** : writing as opposed to print

Manx \\'manks\ *n pl* : the people of the Isle of Man — **Manx** *adj*

¹many \\'me-nē\ *adj* **more** \\'mȯr\; **most** \\'mōst\ : consisting of or amounting to a large but indefinite number ⟨∼ years ago⟩

²many *pron* : a large number ⟨∼ are called⟩

³many *n* : a large but indefinite number ⟨a good ∼ of them⟩

many·fold \ıme-nē-'fōld\ *adv* : by many times

many–sid·ed \-'sī-dəd\ *adj* **1** : having many sides or aspects **2** : VERSATILE

Mao·ism \\'mau̇-ı-zəm\ *n* : the theory and practice of Communism developed in China chiefly by Mao Tse≠tung — **Mao·ist** \\'mau̇-ist\ *n or adj*

Mao·ri \\'mau̇r-ē\ *n, pl* **Maori** *or* **Maoris** : a member of a Polynesian people native to New Zealand

¹map \\'map\ *n* [ML *mappa*, fr. L, napkin, towel] **1** : a representation usu. on a flat surface of the whole or part of an area **2** : a representation of the celestial sphere or part of it

²map *vb* **mapped; map·ping 1** : to make a map of **2** : to plan in detail ⟨∼ out a program⟩ — **map·pa·ble** \\'ma-pə-bəl\ *adj* — **map·per** *n*

MAP *abbr* modified American plan

ma·ple \\'mā-pəl\ *n* : any of a genus of trees or shrubs with 2-winged dry fruit and opposite leaves; *also* : the hard light-colored wood of a maple used esp. for floors and furniture

maple sugar *n* : sugar made by boiling maple syrup

maple syrup *n* : syrup made by concentrating the sap of maple trees and esp. the sugar maple

mar \\'mär\ *vb* **marred; mar·ring** : to detract from the wholeness or perfection of : SPOIL **syn** injure, hurt, harm, damage, impair, blemish

Mar *abbr* March

ma·ra·ca \mə-'rä-kə, -'ra-\ *n* [Pg *maracá*] : a rattle usu. made from a gourd and used as a percussion instrument

mar·a·schi·no cherry \ımar-ə-'skē-nō-, -'shē-\ *n, often cap M* : a cherry preserved in a sweet liqueur made from the juice of a bitter wild cherry

mar·a·thon \\'mar-ə-ıthän\ *n* [*Marathon*, Greece, site of a victory of Greeks over Persians in 490 B.C. the news of which was carried to Athens by a long-distance runner] **1** : a long-distance race esp. on foot **2** : an endurance contest

mar·a·thon·er \\'mar-ə-ıthä-nər\ *n* : a person who takes part in a marathon — **mar·a·thon·ing** *n*

ma·raud \mə-'rȯd\ *vb* : to roam about and raid in search of plunder : PILLAGE — **ma·raud·er** *n*

mar·ble \\'mär-bəl\ *n* **1** : a limestone that can be polished and used in fine building work **2** : something resembling marble (as in coldness) **3** : a small ball (as of glass) used in various games; *also, pl* : a children's game played with these small balls — **marble** *adj*

mar·bling \-bə-liŋ, -bliŋ\ *n* : an intermixture of fat through the lean of a cut of meat

mar·cel \mär-'sel\ *n* : a deep soft wave made in the hair by the use of a heated curling iron — **marcel** *vb*

¹march \\'märch\ *n* : a border region : FRONTIER

²march *vb* **1** : to move along in or as if in military formation **2** : to walk in a direct purposeful manner; *also* : PROGRESS, ADVANCE **3** : TRAVERSE ⟨∼ed 10 miles⟩ — **march·er** *n*

³march *n* **1** : the action of marching; *also* : the distance covered (as by a military unit) in a march **2** : a regular measured stride or rhythmic step used in marching **3** : forward movement **4** : a piece of music with marked rhythm suitable for marching to

March *n* [ME, fr. OF, fr. L *martius*, fr. *martius* of Mars fr. *Mart-, Mars*, Roman god of war] : the third month of the year having 31 days

mar·chio·ness \\'mär-shə-nəs\ *n* **1** : the wife or widow of a marquess **2** : a woman holding the rank of a marquess in her own right

Mar·di Gras \\'mär-dē-ıgrä\ *n* [F, lit., fat Tuesday] : the Tuesday before Ash Wednesday often observed with parades and merrymaking

¹mare \\'mar\ *n* : an adult female of the horse or a related mammal

²ma·re \\'mär-(ı)ā\ *n, pl* **ma·ria** \\'mär-ē-ə\ : any of several large dark areas on the surface of the moon or Mars

mar·ga·rine \\'mär-jə-rən\ *n* : a food product made usu. from vegetable oils churned with skimmed milk and used as a substitute for butter

mar·gin \\'mär-jən\ *n* **1** : the part of a page outside the main body of printed or written matter **2** : EDGE **3** : a spare amount, measure, or degree allowed for use if needed 4 : measure or degree of difference ⟨a one‑vote ∼⟩

mar·gin·al \-jə-nəl\ *adj* 1 : written or printed in the margin 2 : of, relating to, or situated at a margin or border 3 : close to the lower limit of quality or acceptability 4 : excluded from or existing outside the mainstream of society or a group — **mar·gin·al·ly** *adv*

mar·gi·na·lia \ˌmär-jə-ˈnā-lē-ə\ *n pl* : marginal notes

mar·grave \ˈmär-ˌgrāv\ *n* : the military governor esp. of a medieval German border province

ma·ri·a·chi \ˌmär-ē-ˈä-chē, ˌmar-\ *n* : a Mexican street band; *also* : a member of or the music of such a band

mari·gold \ˈmar-ə-ˌgōld, ˈmer-\ *n* : any of a genus of tropical American herbs related to the daisies that are grown for their double yellow, orange, or reddish flower heads

mar·i·jua·na *also* **mar·i·hua·na** \ˌmar-ə-ˈwä-nə, -ˈhwä-\ *n* [MexSp *marihuana*] : the dried leaves and flowering tops of the female hemp plant smoked usu. illegally for their intoxicating effect; *also* : HEMP

ma·rim·ba \mə-ˈrim-bə\ *n* : a xylophone of southern Africa and Central America; *also* : a modern version of it

ma·ri·na \mə-ˈrē-nə\ *n* : a dock or basin providing secure moorings for pleasure boats

mar·i·na·ra \ˌmar-ə-ˈnar-ə\ *adj* [It (*alla*) *marinara*, lit., in sailor style] : made with tomatoes, onions, garlic, and spices; *also* : served with marinara sauce

mar·i·nate \ˈmar-ə-ˌnāt\ *vb* **-nat·ed; -nat·ing** : to steep (as meat or fish) in a brine or pickle

¹ma·rine \mə-ˈrēn\ *adj* 1 : of or relating to the sea or its navigation or commerce 2 : of or relating to marines

²marine *n* 1 : the mercantile and naval shipping of a country 2 : any of a class of soldiers serving on shipboard or with a naval force

mar·i·ner \ˈmar-ə-nər\ *n* : SAILOR

mar·i·o·nette \ˌmar-ē-ə-ˈnet, ˌmer-\ *n* : a puppet moved by strings or by hand

mar·i·tal \ˈmar-ət-ᵊl\ *adj* : of or relating to marriage : CONJUGAL **syn** matrimonial, connubial, nuptial

mar·i·time \ˈmar-ə-ˌtīm\ *adj* 1 : of, relating to, or bordering on the sea 2 : of or relating to navigation or commerce of the sea

mar·jo·ram \ˈmär-jə-rəm\ *n* : any of various fragrant mints often used in cookery

¹mark \ˈmärk\ *n* 1 : something (as a line or fixed object) designed to record position; *also* : the starting line or position in a track event 2 : TARGET; *also* : GOAL, OBJECT 3 : an object of abuse or ridicule 4 : the question under discussion 5 : NORM ⟨not up to the ∼⟩ 6 : a visible sign : INDICATION; *also* : CHARACTERISTIC 7 : a written or printed symbol 8 : GRADE ⟨a ∼ of B+⟩ 9 : IMPORTANCE, DISTINCTION 10 : a lasting impression ⟨made his ∼ in the world⟩; *also* : a damaging impression left on a surface

²mark *vb* 1 : to set apart by a line or boundary 2 : to designate by a mark or make a mark on 3 : CHARACTERIZE ⟨the vehemence that ∼s his speeches⟩; *also* : SIGNALIZE ⟨this year ∼s our 50th anniversary⟩ 4 : to take notice of : OBSERVE — **mark·er** *n*

³mark *n* — see MONEY table

Mark \ˈmärk\ *n* — see BIBLE table

mark·down \ˈmärk-ˌdaun\ *n* 1 : a lowering of price 2 : the amount by which an original price is reduced

mark down *vb* : to put a lower price on

marked \ˈmärkt\ *adj* : NOTICEABLE — **mark·ed·ly** \ˈmär-kəd-lē\ *adv*

¹mar·ket \ˈmär-kət\ *n* 1 : a meeting together of people for trade by purchase and sale; *also* : a public place where such a meeting is held 2 : the rate or price offered for a commodity or security 3 : a geographical area of demand for commodities; *also* : extent of demand 4 : a retail establishment usu. of a specific kind

²market *vb* : to go to a market to buy or sell; *also* : SELL — **mar·ket·able** *adj*

mar·ket·place \ˈmär-kət-ˌplās\ *n* 1 : an open square in

a town where markets are held 2 : the world of trade or economic activity

mark·ka \ˈmär-ˌkä\ *n, pl* **mark·kaa** \ˈmär-ˌkä\ *or* **markkas** \-ˌkäz\ — see MONEY table

marks·man \ˈmärks-mən\ *n* : a person skillful at hitting a target — **marks·man·ship** *n*

mark·up \ˈmär-ˌkəp\ *n* 1 : a raising of price 2 : an amount added to the cost price of an article to determine the selling price

mark up *vb* : to put a higher price on

marl \ˈmärl\ *n* : an earthy deposit rich in lime used esp. as fertilizer — **marly** \ˈmär-lē\ *adj*

mar·lin \ˈmär-lən\ *n* : any of several large oceanic sport fishes related to sailfishes

mar·line·spike *also* **mar·lin·spike** \ˈmär-lən-ˌspīk\ *n* : a pointed iron tool used to separate strands of rope or wire (as in splicing)

mar·ma·lade \ˈmär-mə-ˌlād\ *n* : a clear jelly holding in suspension pieces of fruit and fruit rind

mar·mo·re·al \mär-ˈmōr-ē-əl\ *adj* : of, relating to, or suggestive of marble

mar·mo·set \ˈmär-mə-ˌset\ *n* : any of numerous small bushy-tailed tropical American monkeys

mar·mot \ˈmär-mət\ *n* : any of a genus of stout short‑legged burrowing No. American rodents

marmot

¹ma·roon \mə-ˈrün\ *vb* 1 : to put ashore (as on a desolate island) and leave to one's fate 2 : to leave in isolation and without hope of escape

²maroon *n* : a dark red color

mar·quee \mär-ˈkē\ *n* [modif. of F *marquise*, lit., marchioness] 1 : a large tent set up (as for an outdoor party) 2 : a usu. metal and glass canopy over an entrance (as of a theater)

mar·quess \ˈmär-kwəs\ *n* 1 : a nobleman of hereditary rank in Europe and Japan 2 : a member of the British peerage ranking below a duke and above an earl

mar·que·try \ˈmär-kə-trē\ *n* : inlaid work of wood, shell, or ivory (as on a table or cabinet)

mar·quis \ˈmär-kwəs, mär-ˈkē\ *n* : MARQUESS

mar·quise \mär-ˈkēz\ *n, pl* **mar·quises** *same or* -ˈkē-zəz\ : MARCHIONESS

mar·riage \ˈmar-ij\ *n* 1 : the state of being married 2 : a wedding ceremony and attendant festivities 3 : a close union — **mar·riage·able** *adj*

mar·row \ˈmar-ō\ *n* : a soft vascular tissue that fills the cavities of most bones

mar·row·bone \ˈmar-ə-ˌbōn, ˈmar-ō-\ *n* : a bone (as a shinbone) rich in marrow

mar·ry \ˈmar-ē\ *vb* **mar·ried; mar·ry·ing** 1 : to join as husband and wife according to law or custom 2 : to take as husband or wife : WED 3 : to enter into a close union — **mar·ried** *adj or n*

Mars \ˈmärz\ *n* : the planet 4th from the sun and conspicuous for its red color — see PLANET table

marsh \ˈmärsh\ *n* : a tract of soft wet land — **marshy** *adj*

¹mar·shal \ˈmär-shəl\ *n* 1 : a high official in a medieval household; *also* : a person in charge of the ceremonial aspects of a gathering **2** : a general officer of the highest military rank **3** : an administrative officer (as of a U.S. judicial district) having duties similar to a sheriff's **4** : the administrative head of a city police or fire department

²**marshal** *vb* **mar·shaled** *or* **mar·shalled; mar·shal·ing** *or* **mar·shal·ling 1** : to arrange in order, rank, or position **2** : to bring together **3** : to lead with ceremony — USHER

marsh gas *n* : METHANE

marsh·mal·low \'märsh-ˌme-lō, -ˌma-\ *n* : a light creamy confection made from corn syrup, sugar, albumen, and gelatin

marsh marigold *n* : a swamp herb related to the buttercups that has bright yellow flowers

mar·su·pi·al \mär-ˈsü-pē-əl\ *n* : any of an order of primitive mammals (as opossums, kangaroos, or wombats) that bear very immature young which are nourished in a pouch on the abdomen of the female — **marsupial** *adj*

mart \'märt\ *n* : MARKET

mar·ten \'märt-ᵊn\ *n, pl* **marten** *or* **martens** : a slender weasel-like mammal with fine gray or brown fur; *also* : this fur

mar·tial \'mär-shəl\ *adj* [L *martialis* of Mars, fr. *Mart-, Mars* Mars, Roman god of war] **1** : of, relating to, or suited for war or a warrior ⟨~ music⟩ **2** : of or relating to an army or military life **3** : WARLIKE

martial law *n* **1** : the law applied in occupied territory by the occupying military forces **2** : the established law of a country administered by military forces in an emergency when civilian law enforcement agencies are unable to maintain public order and safety

mar·tian \'mär-shən\ *adj, often cap* : of or relating to the planet Mars or its hypothetical inhabitants — **martian** *n, often cap*

mar·tin \'märt-ᵊn\ *n* : any of several small swallows and flycatchers

mar·ti·net \ˌmärt-ᵊn-ˈet\ *n* : a strict disciplinarian

mar·tin·gale \'märt-ᵊn-ˌgāl\ *n* : a strap connecting a horse's girth to the bit or reins so as to hold down its head

mar·ti·ni \mär-ˈtē-nē\ *n* : a cocktail made of gin or vodka and dry vermouth

¹**mar·tyr** \'mär-tər\ *n* [ME, fr. OE, fr. LL, fr. Gk *martyr-, martys*, lit., witness] **1** : a person who dies rather than renounce a religion; *also* : a person who makes a great sacrifice for the sake of principle **2** : a great or constant sufferer

²**martyr** *vb* **1** : to put to death for adhering to a belief **2** : TORTURE

mar·tyr·dom \'mär-tər-dəm\ *n* **1** : the suffering and death of a martyr **2** : TORTURE

¹**mar·vel** \'mär-vəl\ *n* **1** : something that causes wonder or astonishment **2** : intense surprise or interest

²**marvel** *vb* **mar·veled** *or* **mar·velled; mar·vel·ing** *or* **mar·vel·ling** : to feel surprise, wonder, or amazed curiosity

mar·vel·ous *or* **mar·vel·lous** \'mär-və-ləs\ *adj* **1** : causing wonder **2** : of the highest kind or quality — **mar·vel·ous·ly** *adv* — **mar·vel·ous·ness** *n*

Marx·ism \'märk-ˌsi-zəm\ *n* : the political, economic, and social principles and policies advocated by Karl Marx — **Marx·ist** \-sist\ *n or adj*

mar·zi·pan \'märt-sə-ˌpän, -ˌpan; 'mär-zə-ˌpan\ *n* [G] : a confection of almond paste, sugar, and egg whites

masc *abbr* masculine

mas·ca·ra \mas-ˈkar-ə\ *n* : a cosmetic esp. for coloring the eyelashes

mas·cot \'mas-ˌkät, -kət\ *n* [F *mascotte*, fr. Provençal *mascoto*, fr. *masco* witch, fr. ML *masca*] : a person, animal, or object believed to bring good luck

¹**mas·cu·line** \'mas-kyə-lən\ *adj* **1** : MALE; *also* : MANLY **2** : of, relating to, or constituting the gender that includes most words or grammatical forms referring to males — **mas·cu·lin·i·ty** \ˌmas-kyə-ˈli-nə-tē\ *n*

²**masculine** *n* : a noun, pronoun, adjective, or inflectional form or class of the masculine gender; *also* : the masculine gender

¹**mash** \'mash\ *n* **1** : a mixture of ground feeds for livestock **2** : crushed malt or grain steeped in hot water to make wort **3** : a soft pulpy mass

²**mash** *vb* **1** : to reduce to a soft pulpy state **2** : CRUSH, SMASH ⟨~ a finger⟩ — **mash·er** *n*

MASH *abbr* mobile army surgical hospital

¹**mask** \'mask\ *n* **1** : a cover for the face usu. for disguise or protection **2** : MASQUE **3** : a figure of a head worn on the stage in antiquity **4** : a copy of a face made by means of a mold ⟨death ~⟩ **5** : something that conceals or disguises **6** : the face of an animal

²**mask** *vb* **1** : to conceal from view : DISGUISE **2** : to cover for protection

mask·er \'mas-kər\ *n* : a participant in a masquerade

mas·och·ism \'ma-sə-ˌki-zəm, 'ma-zə-\ *n* **1** : a sexual perversion characterized by pleasure in being subjected to pain or humiliation **2** : pleasure in being abused or dominated — **mas·och·ist** \-kist\ *n* — **mas·och·is·tic** \ˌma-sə-ˈkis-tik, ˌma-zə-\ *adj*

ma·son \'mās-ᵊn\ *n* **1** : a skilled worker who builds with stone, brick, or concrete **2** *cap* : FREEMASON

Ma·son·ic \mə-ˈsä-nik\ *adj* : of or relating to Freemasons or Freemasonry

ma·son·ry \'mās-ᵊn-rē\ *n, pl* **-ries 1** : something constructed of materials used by masons **2** : the art, trade, or work of a mason **3** *cap* : FREEMASONRY

masque \'mask\ *n* **1** : MASQUERADE **2** : a short allegorical dramatic performance (as of the 17th century)

¹**mas·quer·ade** \ˌmas-kə-ˈrād\ *n* **1** : a social gathering of persons wearing masks; *also* : a costume for wear at such a gathering **2** : DISGUISE

²**masquerade** *vb* **-ad·ed; -ad·ing 1** : to disguise oneself : POSE **2** : to take part in a masquerade — **mas·quer·ad·er** *n*

¹**mass** \'mas\ *n* **1** *cap* : a sequence of prayers and ceremonies forming the eucharistic service of the Roman Catholic Church **2** *often cap* : a celebration of the Eucharist **3** : a musical setting for parts of the Mass

²**mass** *n* **1** : a quantity or aggregate of matter usu. of considerable size **2** : EXPANSE, BULK; *also* : MASSIVENESS **3** : the principal part **4** : AGGREGATE, WHOLE **5** : the quantity of matter that a body possesses as measured by its inertia **6** : a large quantity, amount, or number **7** : the great body of people — usu. used in pl. — **massy** *adj*

³**mass** *vb* : to form or collect into a mass

Mass *abbr* Massachusetts

mas·sa·cre \'ma-si-kər\ *n* **1** : the killing of many persons under cruel or atrocious circumstances **2** : a wholesale slaughter — **massacre** *vb*

¹**mas·sage** \mə-ˈsäzh, -ˈsäj\ *n* : manipulation of tissues (as by rubbing and kneading) esp. for therapeutic purposes

²**massage** *vb* **mas·saged; mas·sag·ing 1** : to subject to massage **2** : to treat flatteringly; *also* : MANIPULATE, DOCTOR ⟨~ data⟩

mas·seur \ma-ˈsər\ *n* : a man who practices massage

mas·seuse \-ˈsərz, -ˈsüz\ *n* : a woman who practices massage

mas·sif \ma-ˈsēf\ *n* : a principal mountain mass

mas·sive \'ma-siv\ *adj* **1** : forming or consisting of a large mass **2** : large in structure, scope, or degree — **mas·sive·ly** *adv* — **mas·sive·ness** *n*

mass·less \'mas-ləs\ *adj* : having no mass ⟨~ particles⟩

mass medium *n, pl* **mass media** : a medium of communication (as the newspapers or television) that is designed to reach the mass of the people

mass–pro·duce \ˌmas-prə-ˈdüs, -ˈdyüs\ *vb* : to produce in quantity usu. by machinery — **mass production** *n*

¹**mast** \'mast\ *n* **1** : a long pole or spar rising from the keel or deck of a ship and supporting the yards,

booms, and rigging **2** : a slender vertical structure — **mast·ed** \'mas-təd\ *adj*

²mast *n* : nuts (as acorns) accumulated on the forest floor and often serving as food for animals (as hogs)

mas·tec·to·my \ma-'stek-tə-mē\ *n, pl* **-mies** : surgical removal of the breast

¹mas·ter \'mas-tər\ *n* **1** : a male teacher; *also* : a person holding an academic degree higher than a bachelor's but lower than a doctor's **2** : one highly skilled (as in an art or profession) **3** : one having authority or control **4** : VICTOR, SUPERIOR **5** : the commander of a merchant ship **6** : a youth or boy too young to be called *mister* — used as a title **7** : an original from which copies are made

²master *vb* **1** : to become master of : OVERCOME **2** : to become skilled or proficient in **3** : to produce a master recording of (as a musical performance)

master chief petty officer *n* : a petty officer of the highest rank in the navy

mas·ter·ful \'mas-tər-fəl\ *adj* **1** : inclined and usu. competent to act as a master **2** : having or reflecting the skill of a master — **mas·ter·ful·ly** *adv* — **master·ful·ness** *n*

master gunnery sergeant *n* : a noncommissioned officer in the marine corps ranking above a master sergeant

master key *n* : a key designed to open several different locks

mas·ter·ly \'mas-tər-lē\ *adj* : indicating thorough knowledge or superior skill ⟨~ performance⟩ — **master·ly** *adv*

mas·ter·mind \-ˌmīnd\ *n* : a person who provides the directing or creative intelligence for a project — **mastermind** *vb*

master of ceremonies : a person who acts as host at a formal event or a program of entertainment

mas·ter·piece \'mas-tər-ˌpēs\ *n* : a work done with extraordinary skill

master plan *n* : an overall plan

mas·ter's \'mas-tərz\ *n* : a master's degree

master sergeant *n* **1** : a noncommissioned officer in the army ranking next below a sergeant major **2** : a noncommissioned officer in the air force ranking next below a senior master sergeant **3** : a noncommissioned officer in the marine corps ranking next below a master gunnery sergeant

mas·ter·stroke \'mas-tər-ˌstrōk\ *n* : a masterly performance or move

mas·ter·work \-ˌwərk\ *n* : MASTERPIECE

mas·tery \'mas-tə-rē\ *n* **1** : DOMINION; *also* : SUPERIORITY **2** : possession or display of great skill or knowledge

mast·head \'mast-ˌhed\ *n* **1** : the top of a mast **2** : the printed matter in a newspaper or periodical giving the title and details of ownership and rates of subscription or advertising

mas·tic \'mas-tik\ *n* : a pasty material used as a coating or cement

mas·ti·cate \'mas-tə-ˌkāt\ *vb* **-cat·ed; -cat·ing** : CHEW — **mas·ti·ca·tion** \ˌmas-tə-'kā-shən\ *n*

mas·tiff \'mas-təf\ *n* : any of a breed of large smooth-coated dogs used esp. as guard dogs

mast·odon \'mas-tə-ˌdän\ *n* [NL, fr. Gk *mastos* breast + *odōn, odous* tooth] : any of numerous huge extinct mammals related to the mammoths

mas·toid \'mas-ˌtóid\ *n* : a bony prominence behind the ear — **mastoid** *adj*

mas·tur·ba·tion \ˌmas-tər-'bā-shən\ *n* : stimulation of the genital organs apart from sexual intercourse, usu. to orgasm, and esp. by use of one's own hand — **mas·tur·bate** \'mas-tər-ˌbāt\ *vb* — **mas·tur·ba·to·ry** \'mas-tər-bə-ˌtōr-ē\ *adj*

¹mat \'mat\ *n* **1** : a piece of coarse woven or plaited fabric **2** : something made up of many intertwined strands **3** : a large thick pad used as a surface for wrestling and gymnastics

²mat *vb* **mat·ted; mat·ting** **1** : to provide with a mat **2** : to form into a tangled mass

³mat *vb* **mat·ted; mat·ting** **1** : to make (as a color) matte **2** : to provide (a picture) with a mat

⁴mat *var of* ²MATTE

⁵mat *or* **matt** *or* **matte** *n* : a border going around a picture between picture and frame or serving as the frame

mat·a·dor \'ma-tə-ˌdór\ *n* [Sp, fr. *matar* to kill] : a bullfighter whose role is to kill the bull in a bullfight

¹match \'mach\ *n* **1** : a person or thing equal or similar to another; *also* : one able to cope with another : RIVAL **2** : a suitable pairing of persons or objects **3** : a contest or game between two or more individuals **4** : a marriage union; *also* : a prospective marriage partner — **match·less** *adj*

²match *vb* **1** : to meet as an antagonist; *also* : PIT **2** : to provide with a worthy competitor; *also* : to set in comparison with **3** : MARRY **4** : to combine suitably or congenially; *also* : ADAPT, SUIT **5** : to provide with a counterpart

³match *n* : a short slender piece of flammable material (as wood) tipped with a combustible mixture that ignites through friction

match·book \'mach-ˌbùk\ *n* : a small folder containing rows of paper matches

match·lock \-ˌläk\ *n* : a musket with a slow-burning cord lowered over a hole in the breech to ignite the charge

match·mak·er \-ˌmā-kər\ *n* : one who arranges a match and esp. a marriage

match·wood \-ˌwùd\ *n* : small pieces of wood

¹mate \'māt\ *vb* **mat·ed; mat·ing** : CHECKMATE — **mate** *n*

²mate *n* **1** : ASSOCIATE, COMPANION; *also* : HELPER **2** : a deck officer on a merchant ship ranking below the captain **3** : one of a pair; *esp* : either member of a married couple or a breeding pair of animals

³mate *vb* **mat·ed; mat·ing** **1** : to join or fit together **2** : to come or bring together as mates **3** : COPULATE

¹ma·te·ri·al \mə-'tir-ē-əl\ *adj* **1** : PHYSICAL ⟨~ world⟩; *also* : BODILY ⟨~ needs⟩ **2** : of or relating to matter rather than form ⟨~ cause⟩; *also* : EMPIRICAL ⟨~ knowledge⟩ **3** : highly important : SIGNIFICANT **4** : of a physical or worldly nature ⟨~ progress⟩ — **ma·te·ri·al·ly** *adv*

²material *n* **1** : the elements or substance of which something is composed or made **2** : apparatus necessary for doing or making something

ma·te·ri·al·ise *Brit var of* MATERIALIZE

ma·te·ri·al·ism \mə-'tir-ē-ə-ˌli-zəm\ *n* **1** : a theory that everything can be explained as being or coming from matter **2** : a preoccupation with material rather than intellectual or spiritual things — **ma·te·ri·al·ist** \-list\ *n or adj* — **ma·te·ri·al·is·tic** \-ˌtir-ē-ə-'lis-tik\ *adj* — **ma·te·ri·al·is·ti·cal·ly** \-ti-k(ə-)lē\ *adv*

ma·te·ri·al·ize \mə-'tir-ē-ə-ˌlīz\ *vb* **-ized; -iz·ing** **1** : to give material form to; *also* : to assume bodily form **2** : to make an often unexpected appearance — **ma·te·ri·al·i·za·tion** \mə-ˌtir-ē-ə-lə-'zā-shən\ *n*

ma·té·ri·el *or* **ma·te·ri·el** \mə-ˌtir-ē-'el\ *n* [F *matériel*] : equipment, apparatus, and supplies used by an organization

ma·ter·nal \mə-'tərn-əl\ *adj* **1** : MOTHERLY **2** : related through or inherited or derived from a female parent — **ma·ter·nal·ly** *adv*

¹ma·ter·ni·ty \mə-'tər-nə-tē\ *n, pl* **-ties** **1** : the quality or state of being a mother; *also* : MOTHERLINESS **2** : a hospital facility for the care of women before and during childbirth and for newborn babies

²maternity *adj* **1** : designed for wear during pregnancy ⟨a ~ dress⟩ **2** : effective for the period close to and including childbirth ⟨~ leave⟩

¹math \'math\ *n* : MATHEMATICS

²math *abbr* mathematical; mathematician

math·e·mat·ics \ˌma-thə-'ma-tiks\ *n* : the science of

numbers and their properties, operations, and relations and with shapes in space and their structure and measurement — **math·e·mat·i·cal** \-ˈma-ti-kəl\ *adj* — **math·e·mat·i·cal·ly** \-ti-k(ə-)lē\ *adv* — **math·e·ma·ti·cian** \ˌma-thə-mə-ˈti-shən\ *n*

mat·i·nee *or* **mat·i·née** \ˌmat-ᵊn-ˈā\ *n* [F *matinée*, lit., morning, fr. OF, fr. *matin* morning, fr. L *matutinum*, fr. neut. of *matutinus* of the morning, fr. *Matuta*, goddess of morning] : a musical or dramatic performance in the daytime and esp. the afternoon

mat·ins \ˈmat-ᵊnz\ *n pl, often cap* 1 : special prayers said between midnight and 4 a.m. 2 : a morning service of liturgical prayer in Anglican churches

ma·tri·arch \ˈmā-trē-ˌärk\ *n* : a female who rules or dominates a family, group, or state — **ma·tri·ar·chal** \ˌmā-trē-ˈär-kəl\ *adj* — **ma·tri·ar·chy** \ˈmā-trē-ˌär-kē\ *n*

ma·tri·cide \ˈma-trə-ˌsīd, ˈmā-\ *n* : the murder of a mother by her child — **ma·tri·cid·al** \ˌma-trə-ˈsīd-ᵊl, ˌmā-\ *adj*

ma·tric·u·late \mə-ˈtri-kyə-ˌlāt\ *vb* **-lat·ed; -lat·ing** : to enroll as a member of a body and esp. of a college or university — **ma·tric·u·la·tion** \-ˌtri-kyə-ˈlā-shən\ *n*

mat·ri·mo·ny \ˈma-trə-ˌmō-nē\ *n* [ME, fr. MF *matremoine*, fr. L *matrimonium*, fr. *mater* mother, matron] : MARRIAGE — **mat·ri·mo·nial** \ˌma-trə-ˈmō-nē-əl\ *adj* — **mat·ri·mo·nial·ly** *adv*

ma·trix \ˈmā-triks\ *n, pl* **ma·tri·ces** \ˈmā-trə-ˌsēz, ˈma-\ *or* **ma·trix·es** \ˈmā-trik-səz\ 1 : something within or from which something else originates, develops, or takes form 2 : a mold from which a relief surface (as a piece of type) is made

ma·tron \ˈmā-trən\ *n* 1 : a married woman usu. of dignified maturity or social distinction 2 : a woman supervisor (as in a school or police station) — **ma·tron·ly** *adj*

Matt *abbr* Matthew

¹**matte** *or* **matt** \ˈmat\ *var of* ³MAT

²**matte** *also* **matt** \ˈmat\ *adj* : not shiny : DULL

¹**mat·ter** \ˈma-tər\ *n* 1 : a subject of interest or concern 2 *pl* : events or circumstances of a particular situation 3 : the subject of a discourse or writing 4 : TROUBLE, DIFFICULTY ⟨what's the ∼⟩ 5 : the substance of which a physical object is composed 6 : PUS 7 : an indefinite amount or quantity ⟨a ∼ of a few days⟩ 8 : something written or printed 9 : MAIL

²**matter** *vb* : to be of importance

mat·ter-of-fact \ˌma-tə-rəv-ˈfakt\ *adj* : adhering to fact; *also* : being plain, straightforward, or unemotional — **mat·ter-of-fact·ly** *adv* — **mat·ter-of-fact·ness** *n*

Mat·thew \ˈma-thyü\ *n* — see BIBLE table

mat·tins *often cap, chiefly Brit var of* MATINS

mat·tock \ˈma-tək\ *n* : a digging and grubbing tool with features of an adze and an ax or pick

mat·tress \ˈma-trəs\ *n* 1 : a fabric case filled with resilient material used as or for a bed 2 : an inflatable airtight sack for use as a mattress

mat·u·rate \ˈma-chə-ˌrāt\ *vb* **-rat·ed; -rat·ing** : MATURE

mat·u·ra·tion \ˌma-chə-ˈrā-shən\ *n* 1 : the process of becoming mature 2 : the emergence of personal and behavioral characteristics through growth processes — **mat·u·ra·tion·al** \-shə-nəl\ *adj*

¹**ma·ture** \mə-ˈtùr, -ˈtyùr\ *adj* **ma·tur·er; -est** 1 : based on slow careful consideration 2 : having attained a final or desired state 3 : of or relating to a condition of full development 4 : due for payment — **ma·ture·ly** *adv*

²**mature** *vb* **ma·tured; ma·tur·ing** : to reach or bring to maturity or completion

ma·tu·ri·ty \mə-ˈtùr-ə-tē, -ˈtyùr-\ *n* 1 : the quality or state of being mature; *esp* : full development 2 : the date when a note becomes due for payment

ma·tu·ti·nal \ˌma-chù-ˈtīn-ᵊl; mə-ˈtüt-ᵊn-əl, -ˈtyüt-\

adj : of, relating to, or occurring in the morning : EARLY

mat·zo \ˈmät-sə\ *n, pl* **mat·zoth** \-ˌsōt, -ˌsōth, -sōs\ *or* **mat·zos** [Yiddish *matse*, fr. Heb *maṣṣāh*] : unleavened bread eaten esp. at the Passover

maud·lin \ˈmȯd-lən\ *adj* [alter. of Mary *Magdalene;* fr. her depiction as a weeping, penitent sinner] 1 : drunk enough to be silly 2 : weakly and effusively sentimental

¹**maul** \ˈmȯl\ *n* : a heavy hammer often with a wooden head used esp. for driving wedges

²**maul** *vb* 1 : BEAT, BRUISE; *also* : MANGLE 2 : to handle roughly

maun·der \ˈmȯn-dər\ *vb* 1 : to wander slowly and idly 2 : to speak indistinctly or disconnectedly

mau·so·le·um \ˌmȯ-sə-ˈlē-əm, ˌmȯ-zə-\ *n, pl* **-leums** *or* **-lea** \-ˈlē-ə\ [L, fr. Gk *mausōleion*, fr. *Mausōlos* Mausolus † *ab* 353 B.C. ruler of Caria whose tomb was one of the seven wonders of the ancient world] : a large tomb; *esp* : a usu. stone building for entombment of the dead above ground

mauve \ˈmōv, ˈmȯv\ *n* : a moderate purple, violet, or lilac color

ma·ven *or* **ma·vin** \ˈmā-vən\ *n* [Yiddish *meyvn*, fr. LHeb *mēbhīn*] : EXPERT

mav·er·ick \ˈma-vrik, -və-rik\ *n* [perh. fr. Samuel A. *Maverick* † 1870 Am. pioneer who did not brand his calves] 1 : an unbranded range animal 2 : NONCONFORMIST

maw \ˈmȯ\ *n* 1 : STOMACH; *also* : the crop of a bird 2 : the throat, gullet, or jaws esp. of a voracious animal

mawk·ish \ˈmȯ-kish\ *adj* : sickly sentimental — **mawk·ish·ly** *adv* — **mawk·ish·ness** *n*

max *abbr* maximum

maxi \ˈmak-sē\ *n, pl* **max·is** : a long skirt, dress, or coat

maxi- *comb form* 1 : extra long ⟨*maxi*-kilt⟩ 2 : extra large ⟨*maxi*-problems⟩

max·il·la \mak-ˈsi-lə\ *n, pl* **max·il·lae** \-ˈsi-(ˌ)lē\ *or* **maxillas** : JAW 1; *esp* : an upper jaw — **max·il·lary** \ˈmak-sə-ˌler-ē\ *adj*

max·im \ˈmak-səm\ *n* : a proverbial saying

max·i·mal \ˈmak-sə-məl\ *adj* : MAXIMUM — **max·i·mal·ly** *adv*

max·i·mise *Brit var of* MAXIMIZE

max·i·mize \ˈmak-sə-ˌmīz\ *vb* **-mized; -miz·ing** 1 : to increase to a maximum 2 : to make the most of — **max·i·mi·za·tion** \ˌmak-sə-mə-ˈzā-shən\ *n*

max·i·mum \ˈmak-sə-məm\ *n, pl* **-ma** \-mə\ *or* **-mums** 1 : the greatest quantity, value, or degree 2 : an upper limit allowed by authority 3 : the largest of a set of numbers — **maximum** *adj*

may \ˈmā\ *verbal auxiliary, past* **might** \ˈmīt\; *pres sing & pl* **may** 1 : have permission or liberty to ⟨you ∼ go now⟩ 2 : be in some degree likely to ⟨you ∼ be right⟩ 3 — used as an auxiliary to express a wish, purpose, contingency, or concession

May \ˈmā\ *n* [ME, fr. OF *mai*, fr. L *Maius*, fr. *Maia*, Roman goddess] : the fifth month of the year having 31 days

Ma·ya \ˈmī-ə\ *n, pl* **Maya** *or* **Mayas** : a member of a group of peoples of Yucatán, Guatemala, and adjacent areas — **Ma·yan** \ˈmī-ən\ *n or adj*

may·ap·ple \ˈmā-ˌa-pəl\ *n* : a No. American woodland herb related to the barberry that has a poisonous root, one or two large leaves, and an edible but insipid yellow fruit

may·be \ˈmā-bē, ˈme-\ *adv* : PERHAPS

May Day \ˈmā-ˌdā\ *n* : May 1 celebrated as a springtime festival and in some countries as Labor Day

may·flow·er \ˈmā-ˌflaù-ər\ *n* : any of several spring blooming herbs (as the trailing arbutus or an anemone)

may·fly \ˈmā-ˌflī\ *n* : any of an order of insects with an aquatic nymph and a short-lived fragile adult having membranous wings

may·hem \'mā-ˌhem, 'mā-əm\ *n* **1** : willful and permanent crippling, mutilation, or disfigurement of a person **2** : needless or willful damage

may·on·naise \'mā-ə-ˌnāz\ *n* [F] : a dressing made of egg yolks, vegetable oil, and vinegar or lemon juice

may·or \'mā-ər\ *n* : an official elected to act as chief executive or nominal head of a city or borough — **may·or·al** \-əl\ *adj* — **may·or·al·ty** \-əl-tē\ *n*

may·pole \'mā-ˌpōl\ *n, often cap* : a tall flower=wreathed pole forming a center for May Day sports and dances

maze \'māz\ *n* : a confusing intricate network of passages — **mazy** *adj*

ma·zur·ka \mə-'zər-kə\ *n* : a Polish dance in moderate triple measure

MB *abbr* Manitoba

MBA *abbr* master of business administration

mc *abbr* megacycle

¹MC *n* : MASTER OF CEREMONIES

²MC *abbr* member of Congress

Mc·Coy \mə-'kȯi\ *n* : something that is neither imitation nor substitute ⟨the real ∼⟩

MCPO *abbr* master chief petty officer

¹Md *abbr* Maryland

²Md *symbol* mendelevium

MD *abbr* **1** [NL *medicinae doctor*] doctor of medicine **2** Maryland **3** muscular dystrophy

mdnt *abbr* midnight

mdse *abbr* merchandise

MDT *abbr* mountain daylight (saving) time

me \'mē\ *pron, objective case of* I

Me *abbr* Maine

ME *abbr* **1** Maine **2** mechanical engineer **3** medical examiner

¹mead \'mēd\ *n* : an alcoholic beverage brewed from water and honey, malt, and yeast

²mead *n, archaic* : MEADOW

mead·ow \'me-dō\ *n* : land in or mainly in grass; *esp* : a tract of moist low-lying usu. level grassland — **mead·ow·land** \-ˌland\ *n* — **mead·owy** \'me-də-wē\ *adj*

mead·ow·lark \'me-dō-ˌlärk\ *n* : any of several No. American songbirds related to the orioles that are streaked brown above and in northernmost forms have a yellow breast marked with a black crescent

mead·ow·sweet \-ˌswēt\ *n* : a No. American native or naturalized spirea

mea·ger *or* **mea·gre** \'mē-gər\ *adj* **1** : THIN **2** : lacking richness, fertility, or strength; *also* : POOR **syn** scanty, scant, spare, sparse — **mea·ger·ly** *adv* — **mea·ger·ness** *n*

¹meal \'mēl\ *n* **1** : an act or the time of eating a portion of food **2** : the portion of food eaten at a meal

²meal *n* **1** : usu. coarsely ground seeds of a cereal **2** : a product resembling seed meal — **mealy** *adj*

meal·time \'mēl-ˌtīm\ *n* : the usual time at which a meal is served

mealy·bug \'mē-lē-ˌbəg\ *n* : any of a family of scale insects with a white powdery covering that are destructive pests esp. of fruit trees

mealy·mouthed \'mē-lē-ˌmau̇thd, -ˌmau̇tht\ *adj* : not plain and straightforward : DEVIOUS

¹mean \'mēn\ *vb* **meant** \'ment\; **mean·ing 1** : to have in the mind as a purpose **2** : to serve to convey, show, or indicate : SIGNIFY **3** : to have importance to the degree of **4** : to direct to a particular individual

²mean *adj* **1** : HUMBLE **2** : lacking acumen : DULL **3** : SHABBY, CONTEMPTIBLE **4** : IGNOBLE, BASE **5** : STINGY **6** : pettily selfish or malicious **7** : VEXATIOUS **8** : EXCELLENT — **mean·ly** *adv* — **mean·ness** *n*

³mean *adj* **1** : occupying a middle position (as in space, order, or time) **2** : being a mean : AVERAGE ⟨a ∼ value⟩

⁴mean *n* **1** : a middle point between extremes **2** *pl* : something helpful in achieving a desired end **3** *pl*

: material resources affording a secure life **4** : ARITHMETIC MEAN

¹me·an·der \mē-'an-dər\ *n* [L *maeander*, fr. Gk *maiandros*, fr. *Maiandros* (now *Menderes*), river in Asia Minor] **1** : a winding course **2** : a winding of a stream — **me·an·drous** \-drəs\ *adj*

²meander *vb* **1** : to follow a winding course **2** : to wander aimlessly or casually

mean·ing *n* **1** : the thing one intends to convey esp. by language; *also* : the thing that is thus conveyed **2** : AIM **3** : SIGNIFICANCE; *esp* : implication of a hidden significance **4** : CONNOTATION; *also* : DENOTATION — **mean·ing·ful** \-fəl\ *adj* — **mean·ing·ful·ly** *adv* — **mean·ing·less** *adj*

¹mean·time \'mēn-ˌtīm\ *n* : the intervening time

²meantime *adv* : MEANWHILE

¹mean·while \-ˌhwīl\ *n* : MEANTIME

²meanwhile *adv* **1** : during the intervening time **2** : at the same time

meas *abbr* measure

mea·sles \'mē-zəlz\ *n pl* : an acute virus disease marked by fever and an eruption of distinct circular red spots

mea·sly \'mēz-lē, -zə-lē\ *adj* **mea·sli·er; -est** : contemptibly small or insignificant

¹mea·sure \'me-zhər, 'mā-\ *n* **1** : an adequate or moderate portion; *also* : a suitable limit **2** : the dimensions, capacity, or amount of something ascertained by measuring; *also* : an instrument for measuring **3** : a unit of measurement; *also* : a system of such units **4** : the act or process of measuring **5** : rhythmic structure or movement **6** : the part of a musical staff between two bars **7** : CRITERION **8** : a means to an end **9** : a legislative bill — **mea·sure·less** *adj*

²measure *vb* **mea·sured; mea·sur·ing 1** : to mark or fix in multiples of a specific unit ⟨∼ off five centimeters⟩ **2** : to find out the size, extent, or amount of **3** : to bring into comparison or competition **4** : to serve as a means of measuring **5** : to have a specified measurement — **mea·sur·able** \'me-zhə-rə-bəl, 'mā-\ *adj* — **mea·sur·ably** \-blē\ *adv* — **mea·sur·er** *n*

mea·sure·ment \'me-zhər-mənt, 'mā-\ *n* **1** : the act or process of measuring **2** : a figure, extent, or amount obtained by measuring

measure up *vb* **1** : to have necessary or fitting qualifications **2** : to equal esp. in ability

meat \'mēt\ *n* **1** : FOOD; *esp* : solid food as distinguished from drink **2** : animal and esp. mammal flesh considered as food **3** : the edible part inside a covering (as a shell or rind) — **meaty** *adj*

meat·ball \-ˌbȯl\ *n* : a small ball of chopped or ground meat

meat loaf *n* : a dish of ground meat seasoned and baked in the form of a loaf

mec·ca \'me-kə\ *n, often cap* [*Mecca*, Saudi Arabia, a destination of pilgrims in the Islamic world] : a center of activity sought as a goal by people sharing a common interest

mech *abbr* mechanical; mechanics

¹me·chan·ic \mi-'ka-nik\ *adj* : of or relating to manual work or skill

²mechanic *n* **1** : a manual worker **2** : MACHINIST; *esp* : one who repairs cars

me·chan·i·cal \mi-'ka-ni-kəl\ *adj* **1** : of or relating to machinery, to manual operations, or to mechanics **2** : done as if by a machine : AUTOMATIC **syn** instinctive, impulsive, spontaneous — **me·chan·i·cal·ly** \-k(ə-)lē\ *adv*

mechanical drawing *n* : drawing done with the aid of instruments

me·chan·ics \mi-'ka-niks\ *n sing or pl* **1** : a branch of physics that deals with energy and forces and their effect on bodies **2** : the practical application of mechanics (as to the operation of machines) **3** : mechanical or functional details

mech·a·nism \'me-kə-ˌni-zəm\ *n* **1** : a piece of machinery; *also* : a process or technique for achieving a result 2 : mechanical operation or action 3 : the fundamental processes involved in or responsible for a natural phenomenon ⟨the visual ∼⟩

mech·a·nis·tic \ˌme-kə-ˈnis-tik\ *adj* 1 : mechanically determined ⟨∼ universe⟩ 2 : MECHANICAL — **mech·a·nis·ti·cal·ly** \-ti-k(ə-)lē\ *adv*

mech·a·nize \ˈme-kə-ˌnīz\ *vb* **-nized; -niz·ing** 1 : to make mechanical 2 : to equip with machinery esp. in order to replace human or animal labor 3 : to equip with armed and armored motor vehicles — **mech·a·ni·za·tion** \ˌme-kə-nə-ˈzā-shən\ *n* — **mech·a·niz·er** *n*

med *abbr* 1 medical; medicine 2 medieval 3 medium

MEd *abbr* master of education

med·al \ˈmed-əl\ *n* [MF *medaille*, fr. OIt *medaglia* coin worth half a denarius, medal, fr. (assumed) VL *medalis* half, alter. of LL *medialis* middle, fr. L *medius*] 1 : a small usu. metal object bearing a religious emblem or picture 2 : a piece of metal issued to commemorate a person or event or to award excellence or achievement

med·al·ist *or* **med·al·list** \ˈmed-əl-ist\ *n* 1 : a designer or maker of medals 2 : a recipient of a medal as an award

me·dal·lion \mə-ˈdal-yən\ *n* 1 : a large medal 2 : a tablet or panel bearing a portrait or an ornament

med·dle \ˈmed-əl\ *vb* **med·dled; med·dling** : to interfere without right or propriety — **med·dler** \ˈmed-əl-ər\ *n*

med·dle·some \ˈmed-əl-səm\ *adj* : inclined to meddle

me·dia \ˈmē-dē-ə\ *n, pl* **me·di·as** : MEDIUM 4

me·di·al \ˈmē-dē-əl\ *adj* : occurring in or extending toward the middle

¹me·di·an \ˈmē-dē-ən\ *n* 1 : a value in an ordered set of values below and above which there are an equal number of values 2 : MEDIAN STRIP

²median *adj* 1 : being in the middle or in an intermediate position 2 : relating to or constituting a statistical median

median strip *n* : a strip dividing a highway into lanes according to the direction of travel

me·di·ate \ˈmē-dē-ˌāt\ *vb* **-at·ed; -at·ing** 1 : to act as an intermediary; *esp* : to work with opposing sides in order to resolve (as a dispute) or bring about (as a settlement) 2 : to bring about, influence, or transmit (as a physical process or effect) by acting as an intermediate or controlling agent or mechanism **syn** intercede, intervene, interpose, interfere — **me·di·a·tion** \ˌmē-dē-ˈā-shən\ *n* — **me·di·a·tor** \ˈmē-dē-ˌā-tər\ *n*

med·ic \ˈme-dik\ *n* : one engaged in medical work; *esp* : CORPSMAN

med·i·ca·ble \ˈme-di-kə-bəl\ *adj* : CURABLE

med·ic·aid \ˈme-di-ˌkād\ *n, often cap* : a program of financial assistance for medical care designed for those unable to afford regular medical service and financed jointly by the state and federal governments

med·i·cal \ˈme-di-kəl\ *adj* : of or relating to the science or practice of medicine or the treatment of disease — **med·i·cal·ly** \-k(ə-)lē\ *adv*

medical examiner *n* : a public officer who performs autopsies on bodies to find the cause of death

me·di·ca·ment \mi-ˈdi-kə-mənt, ˈme-di-kə-\ *n* : a substance used in therapy

medi·care \ˈme-di-ˌker\ *n, often cap* : a government program of financial assistance for medical care esp. for the aged

med·i·cate \ˈme-də-ˌkāt\ *vb* **-cat·ed; -cat·ing** : to treat with medicine

med·i·ca·tion \ˌme-də-ˈkā-shən\ *n* 1 : the act or process of medicating 2 : MEDICINE 1

me·dic·i·nal \mə-ˈdis-ən-əl\ *adj* : tending or used to cure disease or relieve pain — **me·dic·i·nal·ly** *adv*

med·i·cine \ˈme-də-sən\ *n* 1 : a substance or prepara-

tion used in treating disease 2 : a science and art dealing with the prevention and cure of disease

medicine ball *n* : a heavy stuffed leather ball used for conditioning exercises

medicine man *n* : a priestly healer or sorcerer esp. among the American Indians : SHAMAN

med·i·co \ˈme-di-ˌkō\ *n, pl* **-cos** : a medical practitioner or student

me·di·eval *or* **me·di·ae·val** \ˌmē-dē-ˈē-vəl, ˌme-, mē-ˈdē-vəl\ *adj* 1 : of, relating to, or characteristic of the Middle Ages 2 : extremely outmoded or antiquated — **me·di·e·val·ism** \-və-ˌli-zəm\ *n* — **me·di·e·val·ist** \-list\ *n*

me·di·o·cre \ˌmē-dē-ˈō-kər\ *adj* [ME, fr. MF, fr. L *mediocris*, fr. *medius* middle + *ocris* stony mountain] : of moderate or low quality : ORDINARY — **me·di·oc·ri·ty** \-ˈä-krə-tē\ *n*

med·i·tate \ˈme-də-ˌtāt\ *vb* **-tat·ed; -tat·ing** 1 : to muse over : CONTEMPLATE, PONDER 2 : INTEND, PLAN — **med·i·ta·tion** \ˌme-də-ˈtā-shən\ *n* — **med·i·ta·tive** \ˈme-də-ˌtā-tiv\ *adj* — **med·i·ta·tive·ly** *adv*

Med·i·ter·ra·nean \ˌme-də-tə-ˈrā-nē-ən, -ˈrā-nyən\ *adj* : of or relating to the Mediterranean Sea or to the lands or people around it

¹me·di·um \ˈmē-dē-əm\ *n, pl* **mediums** *or* **me·dia** \-dē-ə\ [L] 1 : something in a middle position; *also* : a middle position or degree 2 : a means of effecting or conveying something 3 : a surrounding or enveloping substance 4 : a channel or system of communication, information, or entertainment 5 : a mode of artistic expression 6 : an individual held to be a channel of communication between the earthly world and a world of spirits 7 : a condition or environment in which something may function or flourish

²medium *adj* : intermediate in amount, quality, position, or degree

me·di·um·is·tic \ˌmē-dē-ə-ˈmis-tik\ *adj* : of, relating to, or being a spiritualistic medium

med·ley \ˈmed-lē\ *n, pl* **medleys** 1 : HODGEPODGE 2 : a musical composition made up esp. of a series of songs

me·dul·la \mə-ˈdə-lə\ *n, pl* **-las** *or* **-lae** \-(ˌ)lē, -ˌlī\ : an inner or deep anatomical part; *also* : the posterior part (**medulla ob·lon·ga·ta** \-ˌä-ˌblȯṅ-ˈgä-tə\) of the vertebrate brain that is continuous with the spinal cord

meed \ˈmēd\ *n* : a fitting return

meek \ˈmēk\ *adj* 1 : characterized by patience and long-suffering 2 : deficient in spirit and courage 3 : MODERATE — **meek·ly** *adv* — **meek·ness** *n*

meer·schaum \ˈmir-shəm, -ˌshȯm\ *n* [G, fr. *Meer* sea + *Schaum* foam] : a tobacco pipe made of a light white clayey mineral

¹meet \ˈmēt\ *vb* **met** \ˈmet\; **meet·ing** 1 : to come upon : FIND 2 : JOIN, INTERSECT 3 : to appear to the perception of 4 : OPPOSE, FIGHT 5 : to join in conversation or discussion; *also* : ASSEMBLE 6 : to conform to 7 : to pay fully 8 : to cope with 9 : to provide for 10 : to be introduced to

²meet *n* : an assembling esp. for a hunt or for competitive sports

³meet *adj* : SUITABLE, PROPER

meet·ing \ˈmē-tiṅ\ *n* 1 : an act of coming together : ASSEMBLY 2 : JUNCTION, INTERSECTION

meet·ing·house \-ˌhaus\ *n* : a building for public assembly and esp. for Protestant worship

mega- *or* **meg-** *comb form* 1 : great : large ⟨*mega*hit⟩ 2 : million : multiplied by one million ⟨*mega*hertz⟩

mega·byte \ˈme-gə-ˌbīt\ *n* : a unit of computer storage capacity equal to 1,048,576 bytes

mega·cy·cle \-ˌsī-kəl\ *n* : MEGAHERTZ

mega·death \-ˌdeth\ *n* : one million deaths — used as a unit in reference to nuclear warfare

mega·hertz \ˈme-gə-ˌhərts, -ˌherts\ *n* : a unit of frequency equal to one million hertz

mega·lith \ˈme-gə-ˌlith\ *n* : a large stone used in prehistoric monuments — **mega·lith·ic** \ˌme-gə-ˈli-thik\ *adj*

meg·a·lo·ma·nia \ˌme-gə-lō-ˈmā-nē-ə, -nyə\ *n* : a mental disorder marked by feelings of personal omnipotence and grandeur — **meg·a·lo·ma·ni·ac** \-ˈmā-nē-ˌak\ *adj or n*

meg·a·lop·o·lis \ˌme-gə-ˈlä-pə-ləs\ *n* : a very large urban unit

mega·phone \ˈme-gə-ˌfōn\ *n* : a cone-shaped device used to intensify or direct the voice — **megaphone** *vb*

mega·ton \-ˌtən\ *n* : an explosive force equivalent to that of one million tons of TNT

mega·vi·ta·min \-ˌvī-tə-mən\ *adj* : relating to or consisting of very large doses of vitamins — **mega·vi·ta·mins** *n pl*

mei·o·sis \mī-ˈō-səs\ *n* : a process of cell division in gamete-producing cells in which the number of chromosomes is reduced to one half — **mei·ot·ic** \mī-ˈä-tik\ *adj*

mel·an·cho·lia \ˌme-lən-ˈkō-lē-ə\ *n* : a mental disorder marked by extreme depression often with delusions

mel·an·chol·ic \ˌme-lən-ˈkä-lik\ *adj* **1** : DEPRESSED **2** : of or relating to melancholia

mel·an·choly \ˈme-lən-ˌkä-lē\ *n, pl* **-chol·ies** [ME *malencolie*, fr. MF *melancolie*, fr. LL *melancholia*, fr. Gk, fr. *melan-*, *melas* black + *cholē* bile; so called fr. the former belief that it was caused by an excess of black bile, a substance supposedly secreted by the kidneys or spleen] : depression of spirits : DEJECTION — **melancholy** *adj*

Mel·a·ne·sian \ˌme-lə-ˈnē-zhən\ *n* : a member of the dominant native group of the Pacific island grouping of Melanesia — **Melanesian** *adj*

mé·lange \mā-ˈlä^nzh, -ˈlänj\ *n* : a mixture esp. of incongruous elements

mel·a·nin \ˈme-lə-nən\ *n* : a dark brown or black animal or plant pigment

mel·a·nism \ˈme-lə-ˌni-zəm\ *n* : an increased amount of black or nearly black pigmentation

mel·a·no·ma \ˌme-lə-ˈnō-mə\ *n, pl* **-mas** *also* **-ma·ta** \-mə-tə\ : a usu. malignant tumor containing dark pigment

¹meld \ˈmeld\ *vb* : to show or announce for a score in a card game

²meld *n* : a card or combination of cards that is or can be melded

me·lee \ˈmā-ˌlā, mā-ˈlā\ *n* [F *mêlée*] : a confused struggle **syn** fracas, row, brawl, donnybrook

me·lio·rate \ˈmēl-yə-ˌrāt, ˈmē-lē-ə-\ *vb* **-rat·ed; -rat·ing** : AMELIORATE — **me·lio·ra·tion** \ˌmēl-yə-ˈrā-shən, ˌmē-lē-ə-\ *n* — **me·lio·ra·tive** \ˈmēl-yə-ˌrā-tiv, ˈmē-lē-ə-\ *adj*

mel·lif·lu·ous \me-ˈli-flə-wəs, mə-\ *adj* [LL *mellifluus*, fr. L *mel* honey + *fluere* to flow] : sweetly flowing — **mel·lif·lu·ous·ly** *adv* — **mel·lif·lu·ous·ness** *n*

¹mel·low \ˈme-lō\ *adj* **1** : soft and sweet because of ripeness; *also* : well aged and pleasingly mild ⟨~ wine⟩ **2** : made gentle by age or experience **3** : being rich and full but not garish or strident ⟨~ colors⟩ **4** : of soft loamy consistency ⟨~ soil⟩ — **mel·low·ness** *n*

²mellow *vb* : to make or become mellow

me·lo·di·ous \mə-ˈlō-dē-əs\ *adj* : pleasing to the ear — **me·lo·di·ous·ly** *adv* — **me·lo·di·ous·ness** *n*

melo·dra·ma \ˈme-lə-ˌdrä-mə, -ˌdra-\ *n* : an extravagantly theatrical play in which action and plot predominate over characterization — **melo·dra·mat·ic** \ˌme-lə-drə-ˈma-tik\ *adj* — **melo·dra·mat·i·cal·ly** \-ti-k(ə-)lē\ *adv* — **melo·dra·ma·tist** \ˌme-lə-ˈdra-mə-tist, -ˈdrä-\ *n*

mel·o·dy \ˈme-lə-dē\ *n, pl* **-dies 1** : sweet or agreeable sound **2** : a particular succession of notes : TUNE, AIR — **me·lod·ic** \mə-ˈlä-dik\ *adj* — **me·lod·i·cal·ly** \-di-k(ə-)lē\ *adv*

mel·on \ˈme-lən\ *n* : any of various fruits (as a muskmelon or watermelon) of the gourd family usu. eaten raw

¹melt \ˈmelt\ *vb* **1** : to change from a solid to a liquid state usu. by heat **2** : DISSOLVE, DISINTEGRATE; *also* : to cause to disperse or disappear **3** : to make or become tender or gentle

²melt *n* : a melted substance

melt·down \ˈmelt-ˌdaůn\ *n* : the melting of the core of a nuclear reactor

melt·wa·ter \-ˌwȯ-tər, -ˌwä-\ *n* : water derived from the melting of ice and snow

mem *abbr* **1** member **2** memoir **3** memorial

mem·ber \ˈmem-bər\ *n* **1** : a part (as an arm, leg, leaf, or branch) of an animal or plant **2** : one of the individuals composing a group **3** : a constituent part of a whole

mem·ber·ship \-ˌship\ *n* **1** : the state or status of being a member **2** : the body of members

mem·brane \ˈmem-ˌbrān\ *n* : a thin pliable layer esp. of animal or plant origin — **mem·bra·nous** \-brə-nəs\ *adj*

me·men·to \mə-ˈmen-tō\ *n, pl* **-tos** *or* **-toes** [ME, fr. L, remember] : something that serves to warn or remind; *also* : SOUVENIR

memo \ˈme-mō\ *n, pl* **mem·os** : MEMORANDUM

mem·oir \ˈmem-ˌwär\ *n* **1** : MEMORANDUM **2** : AUTOBIOGRAPHY — usu. used in pl. **3** : an account of something noteworthy; *also, pl* : the record of the proceedings of a learned society

mem·o·ra·bil·ia \ˌme-mə-rə-ˈbi-lē-ə, -ˈbil-yə\ *n pl* [L] : things worthy of remembrance; *also* : MEMENTOS

mem·o·ra·ble \ˈme-mə-rə-bəl\ *adj* : worth remembering : NOTABLE — **mem·o·ra·bil·i·ty** \ˌme-mə-rə-ˈbi-lə-tē\ *n* — **mem·o·ra·ble·ness** *n* — **mem·o·ra·bly** \-blē\ *adv*

mem·o·ran·dum \ˌme-mə-ˈran-dəm\ *n, pl* **-dums** *or* **-da** \-də\ **1** : an informal record; *also* : a written reminder **2** : an informal written note

¹me·mo·ri·al \mə-ˈmȯr-ē-əl\ *adj* : serving to preserve remembrance

²memorial *n* **1** : something designed to keep remembrance alive; *esp* : MONUMENT **2** : a statement of facts often accompanied with a petition — **me·mo·ri·al·ize** *vb*

Memorial Day *n* : the last Monday in May or formerly May 30 observed as a legal holiday in honor of those who died in war

mem·o·rize \ˈme-mə-ˌrīz\ *vb* **-rized; -riz·ing** : to learn by heart — **mem·o·ri·za·tion** \ˌme-mə-rə-ˈzā-shən\ *n* — **mem·o·riz·er** *n*

mem·o·ry \ˈme-mə-rē\ *n, pl* **-ries 1** : the power or process of remembering **2** : the store of things remembered **3** : COMMEMORATION **4** : something remembered **5** : the time within which past events are remembered **6** : a device (as in a computer) in which information can be stored **syn** remembrance, recollection, reminiscence

men *pl of* MAN

¹men·ace \ˈme-nəs\ *n* **1** : THREAT **2** : DANGER; *also* : NUISANCE

²menace *vb* **men·aced; men·ac·ing 1** : THREATEN **2** : ENDANGER — **men·ac·ing·ly** *adv*

mé·nage \mā-ˈnäzh\ *n* [F] : HOUSEHOLD

me·nag·er·ie \mə-ˈna-jə-rē\ *n* : a collection of wild animals esp. for exhibition

¹mend \ˈmend\ *vb* **1** : to improve in manners or morals **2** : to put into good shape : REPAIR **3** : to improve in or restore to health : HEAL — **mend·er** *n*

²mend *n* **1** : an act of mending **2** : a mended place

men·da·cious \men-ˈdā-shəs\ *adj* : given to deception or falsehood : UNTRUTHFUL **syn** dishonest, deceitful — **men·da·cious·ly** *adv* — **men·dac·i·ty** \-ˈda-sə-tē\ *n*

men·de·le·vi·um \ˌmen-də-ˈlē-vē-əm, -ˈlā-\ *n* : a radioactive chemical element artificially produced — see ELEMENT table

men·di·cant \ˈmen-di-kənt\ *n* **1** : BEGGAR **2** *often cap* : FRIAR — **men·di·can·cy** \-kən-sē\ *n* — **mendicant** *adj*

men·folk \\'men-ˌfōk\\ *or* **men·folks** \\-ˌfōks\\ *n pl* **1** : men in general **2** : the men of a family or community

men·ha·den \\men-'hād-ᵊn, mən-\\ *n, pl* **-den** *also* **-dens** : a marine fish related to the herring that is abundant along the Atlantic coast of the U.S.

¹**me·nial** \\'mē-nē-əl, -nyəl\\ *adj* **1** : of or relating to servants **2** : HUMBLE; *also* : SERVILE — **me·ni·al·ly** *adv*

²**menial** *n* : a domestic servant

men·in·gi·tis \\ˌme-nən-'jī-təs\\ *n, pl* **-git·i·des** \\-'ji-tə-ˌdēz\\ : inflammation of the membranes enclosing the brain and spinal cord; *also* : a usu. bacterial disease marked by this

me·ninx \\'mē-niŋks, 'me-\\ *n, pl* **me·nin·ges** \\mə-'nin-(ˌ)jēz\\ : any of the three membranes that envelop the brain and spinal cord — **men·in·ge·al** \\ˌme-nən-'jē-əl\\ *adj*

me·nis·cus \\mə-'nis-kəs\\ *n, pl* **me·nis·ci** \\-'nis-ˌkī, -ˌkē\\ *also* **me·nis·cus·es** **1** : CRESCENT **2** : the curved upper surface of a column of liquid

meno·pause \\'me-nə-ˌpȯz\\ *n* : the period of life when menstruation stops naturally — **meno·paus·al** \\ˌme-nə-'pȯ-zəl\\ *adj*

me·no·rah \\mə-'nȯr-ə\\ *n* [Heb *měnōrāh* candlestick] : a candelabrum that is used in Jewish worship

men·ses \\'men-ˌsēz\\ *n pl* : the menstrual flow

men·stru·a·tion \\ˌmen-strə-'wā-shən, men-'strā-\\ *n* : a discharging of bloody matter at approximately monthly intervals from the uterus of breeding-age nonpregnant primate females; *also* : PERIOD 6 — **men·stru·al** \\'men-strə-wəl\\ *adj* — **men·stru·ate** \\'men-strə-ˌwāt, -ˌstrāt\\ *vb*

men·su·ra·ble \\'men-sə-rə-bəl, '-chə-\\ *adj* : MEASURABLE

men·su·ra·tion \\ˌmen-sə-'rā-shən, ˌmen-chə-\\ *n* : MEASUREMENT

-ment \\mənt\\ *n suffix* **1** : concrete result, object, or agent of a (specified) action ⟨embank*ment*⟩ ⟨entangle*ment*⟩ **2** : concrete means or instrument of a (specified) action ⟨entertain*ment*⟩ **3** : action : process ⟨encircle*ment*⟩ ⟨develop*ment*⟩ **4** : place of a (specified) action ⟨encamp*ment*⟩ **5** : state : condition ⟨amaze*ment*⟩

men·tal \\'ment-ᵊl\\ *adj* **1** : of or relating to the mind **2** : of, relating to, or affected with a disorder of the mind ⟨∼ illness⟩ — **men·tal·ly** *adv*

mental age *n* : a measure of a child's mental development in terms of the number of years it takes an average child to reach the same level

mental deficiency *n* : MENTAL RETARDATION

men·tal·i·ty \\men-'ta-lə-tē\\ *n, pl* **-ties** **1** : mental power or capacity **2** : mode or way of thought

mental retardation *n* : subaverage intellectual ability present from infancy that is characterized by an IQ of 70 or less and problems in development, learning, and social adjustment

men·thol \\'men-ˌthȯl, -ˌthōl\\ *n* : an alcohol occurring esp. in mint oils that has the odor and cooling properties of peppermint — **men·tho·lat·ed** \\-thə-ˌlā-təd\\ *adj*

¹**men·tion** \\'men-chən\\ *n* **1** : a brief or casual reference **2** : a formal citation for outstanding achievement

²**mention** *vb* **1** : to refer to : CITE **2** : to cite for superior achievement — **not to mention** : to say nothing of

men·tor \\'men-ˌtȯr, -tər\\ *n* : a trusted counselor or guide; *also* : TUTOR, COACH

menu \\'men-yü, 'mān-\\ *n, pl* **menus** [F, fr. *menu* small, detailed, fr. L *minutus* minute (adj.)] **1** : a list of the dishes available (as in a restaurant) for a meal; *also* : the dishes served **2** : a list of offerings or options

me·ow \\mē-'aù\\ *vb* : to make the characteristic cry of a cat — **meow** *n*

mer *abbr* meridian

mer·can·tile \\'mər-kən-ˌtēl, -ˌtīl\\ *adj* : of or relating to merchants or trading

¹**mer·ce·nary** \\'mərs-ᵊn-ˌer-ē\\ *n, pl* **-nar·ies** : a person who serves merely for wages; *esp* : a soldier hired into foreign service

²**mercenary** *adj* **1** : serving merely for pay or gain **2** : hired for service in a foreign army

mer·cer \\'mər-sər\\ *n, Brit* : a dealer in usu. expensive fabrics

mer·cer·ize \\'mər-sə-ˌrīz\\ *vb* **-ized; -iz·ing** : to treat cotton yarn or cloth with alkali so that it looks silky or takes a better dye

¹**mer·chan·dise** \\'mər-chən-ˌdīz, -ˌdīs\\ *n* : the commodities or goods that are bought and sold in business

²**mer·chan·dise** \\-ˌdīz\\ *vb* **-dised; -dis·ing** : to buy and sell in business : TRADE — **mer·chan·dis·er** *n*

mer·chant \\'mər-chənt\\ *n* **1** : a buyer and seller of commodities for profit **2** : STOREKEEPER

mer·chant·able \\'mər-chən-tə-bəl\\ *adj* : acceptable to buyers : MARKETABLE

mer·chant·man \\'mər-chənt-mən\\ *n* : a ship used in commerce

merchant marine *n* : the commercial ships of a nation

merchant ship *n* : MERCHANTMAN

mer·ci·ful·ly \\'mər-si-fə-lē\\ *adv* **1** : in a merciful manner **2** : FORTUNATELY 2

mer·cu·ri·al \\mər-'kyur-ē-əl\\ *adj* **1** : unpredictably changeable **2** : MERCURIC — **mer·cu·ri·al·ly** *adv* — **mer·cu·ri·al·ness** *n*

mer·cu·ric \\mər-'kyur-ik\\ *adj* : of, relating to, or containing mercury

mercuric chloride *n* : a poisonous compound of mercury and chlorine used as an antiseptic and fungicide

mer·cu·ry \\'mər-kyə-rē\\ *n, pl* **-ries** **1** : a heavy silver-white liquid metallic chemical element used esp. in scientific instruments — see ELEMENT table **2** *cap* : the planet nearest the sun — see PLANET table

mer·cy \\'mər-sē\\ *n, pl* **mercies** [ME, fr. OF *merci*, fr. ML *merced-, merces*, fr. L, price paid, wages, fr. *merc-, merx* merchandise] **1** : compassion shown to an offender; *also* : imprisonment rather than death for first-degree murder **2** : a blessing resulting from divine favor or compassion; *also* : a fortunate circumstance **3** : compassion shown to victims of misfortune — **mer·ci·ful** \\-si-fəl\\ *adj* — **mer·ci·less** \\-si-ləs\\ *adj* — **mer·ci·less·ly** *adv* — **mercy** *adj*

mercy killing *n* : the act or practice of killing or permitting the death of hopelessly sick or injured persons or animals with as little pain as possible for reasons of mercy

¹**mere** \\'mir\\ *n* : LAKE, POOL

²**mere** *adj, superlative* **mer·est** **1** : being nothing more than ⟨a ∼ child⟩ **2** : not diluted : PURE — **mere·ly** *adv*

mer·e·tri·cious \\ˌmer-ə-'tri-shəs\\ *adj* [L *meretricius*, fr. *meretrix* prostitute, fr. *merēre* to earn] : tawdrily attractive; *also* : SPECIOUS — **mer·e·tri·cious·ly** *adv* — **mer·e·tri·cious·ness** *n*

mer·gan·ser \\(ˌ)mər-'gan-sər\\ *n* : any of various fish-eating wild ducks with a usu. crested head and a slender bill hooked at the end and serrated along the margins

merge \\'mərj\\ *vb* **merged; merg·ing** **1** : to blend gradually **2** : to combine, unite, or coalesce into one **syn** mingle, amalgamate, fuse, interfuse, intermingle

merg·er \\'mər-jər\\ *n* **1** : the act or process of merging **2** : absorption by a corporation of one or more others

me·rid·i·an \\mə-'ri-dē-ən\\ *n* [ME, fr. MF *meridien*, fr. *meridien* of noon, fr. L *meridianus*, fr. *meridies* noon, south, irreg. fr. *medius* mid + *dies* day] **1** : the highest point : CULMINATION **2** : any of the imaginary circles on the earth's surface passing through the north and south poles — **meridian** *adj*

me·ringue \\mə-'raŋ\\ *n* [F] : a baked dessert topping of stiffly beaten egg whites and powdered sugar

me·ri·no \\mə-'rē-nō\\ *n, pl* **-nos** [Sp] **1** : any of a breed of sheep noted for fine soft wool **2** : a fine soft fabric or yarn of wool or wool and cotton

¹**mer·it** \\'mer-ət\\ *n* **1** : laudable or blameworthy traits or actions **2** : a praiseworthy quality; *also* : character or

conduct deserving reward or honor **3** *pl* : the intrinsic nature of a legal case; *also* : legal significance

²merit *vb* : EARN, DESERVE

mer·i·toc·ra·cy \ˌmer-ə-ˈtä-krə-sē\ *n, pl* **-cies** : a system in which the talented are chosen and moved ahead based on their achievement; *also* : leadership by the talented

mer·i·to·ri·ous \ˌmer-ə-ˈtōr-ē-əs\ *adj* : deserving honor or esteem — **mer·i·to·ri·ous·ly** *adv* — **mer·i·to·ri·ous·ness** *n*

mer·maid \ˈmər-ˌmād\ *n* : a legendary sea creature with a woman's upper body and a fish's tail

mer·man \-ˌman, -mən\ *n* : a legendary sea creature with a man's upper body and a fish's tail

mer·ri·ment \ˈmer-i-mənt\ *n* **1** : HILARITY **2** : FESTIVITY

mer·ry \ˈmer-ē\ *adj* **mer·ri·er; -est 1** : full of gaiety or high spirits **2** : marked by festivity **3** : BRISK ⟨a ∼ pace⟩ **syn** blithe, jocund, jovial, jolly, mirthful — **mer·ri·ly** \ˈmer-ə-lē\ *adv*

merry–go–round \ˈmer-ē-gō-ˌraund\ *n* **1** : a circular revolving platform with benches and figures of animals on which people sit for a ride **2** : a busy round of activities

mer·ry·mak·ing \ˈmer-ē-ˌmā-kiŋ\ *n* **1** : jovial or festive activity **2** : a festive occasion — **mer·ry·mak·er** \-ˌmā-kər\ *n*

me·sa \ˈmā-sə\ *n* [Sp, lit., table, fr. L *mensa*] : a flat-topped hill with steep sides

mes·cal \me-ˈskal, mə-\ *n* **1** : a small cactus that is the source of a stimulant used esp. by Mexican Indians **2** : a usu. colorless liquor distilled from the leaves of an agave; *also* : this agave

mes·ca·line \ˈmes-kə-lən, -ˌlēn\ *n* : a hallucinatory alkaloid from the mescal cactus

mesdames *pl of* MADAM *or of* MADAME *or of* MRS.

mesdemoiselles *pl of* MADEMOISELLE

¹mesh \ˈmesh\ *n* **1** : one of the openings between the threads or cords of a net; *also* : one of the similar spaces in a network **2** : the fabric of a net **3** : NETWORK **4** : working contact (as of the teeth of gears) ⟨in ∼⟩ — **meshed** \ˈmesht\ *adj*

²mesh *vb* **1** : to catch in or as if in a mesh **2** : to be in or come into mesh : ENGAGE **3** : to fit together properly

mesh·work \ˈmesh-ˌwərk\ *n* : NETWORK

me·si·al \ˈmē-zē-əl, -sē-\ *adj* : of, relating to, or being the surface of a tooth that is closest to the middle of the front of the jaw

mes·mer·ize \ˈmez-mə-ˌrīz\ *vb* **-ized; -iz·ing** : HYPNOTIZE — **mes·mer·ic** \mez-ˈmer-ik\ *adj* — **mes·mer·ism** \ˈmez-mə-ˌri-zəm\ *n*

Me·so·lith·ic \ˌme-zə-ˈli-thik\ *adj* : of, relating to, or being a transitional period of the Stone Age between the Paleolithic and the Neolithic periods

me·so·sphere \ˈme-zə-ˌsfir\ *n* : a layer of the atmosphere between the stratosphere and the thermosphere

Me·so·zo·ic \ˌme-zə-ˈzō-ik, ˌmē-\ *adj* : of, relating to, or being the era of geologic history between the Paleozoic and the Cenozoic and extending from about 230 million years ago to about 65 million years ago — **Mesozoic** *n*

mes·quite \mə-ˈskēt, me-\ *n* : any of several spiny leguminous trees and shrubs chiefly of the southwestern U.S. with sugar-rich pods important as fodder; *also* : mesquite wood used esp. in grilling food

¹mess \ˈmes\ *n* **1** : a quantity of food; *also* : enough food of a specified kind for a dish or meal ⟨a ∼ of beans⟩ **2** : a group of persons who regularly eat together; *also* : a meal eaten by such a group **3** : a place where meals are regularly served to a group **4** : a confused, dirty, or offensive state — **messy** *adj*

²mess *vb* **1** : to supply with meals; *also* : to take meals with a mess **2** : to make dirty or untidy; *also* : BUNGLE **3** : INTERFERE, MEDDLE **4** : PUTTER, TRIFLE

mes·sage \ˈme-sij\ *n* : a communication sent by one person to another

messeigneurs *pl of* MONSEIGNEUR

mes·sen·ger \ˈmes-ᵊn-jər\ *n* : one who carries a message or does an errand

messenger RNA *n* : an RNA that carries the code for a particular protein from DNA in the nucleus to a ribosome in the cytoplasm and acts as a template for the formation of that protein

Mes·si·ah \mə-ˈsī-ə\ *n* **1** : the expected king and deliverer of the Jews **2** : Jesus **3** *not cap* : a professed or accepted leader of a cause — **mes·si·an·ic** \ˌme-sē-ˈa-nik\ *adj*

messieurs *pl of* MONSIEUR

mess·mate \ˈmes-ˌmāt\ *n* : a member of a group who eat regularly together

Messrs. \ˈme-sərz\ *pl of* MR.

mes·ti·zo \me-ˈstē-zō\ *n, pl* **-zos** [Sp, fr. *mestizo* mixed, fr. LL *mixticius*, fr. L *mixtus*, pp. of *miscēre* to mix] : a person of mixed blood

¹met *past and past part of* MEET

²met *abbr* metropolitan

me·tab·o·lism \mə-ˈta-bə-ˌli-zəm\ *n* : the processes by which the substance of plants and animals incidental to life is built up and broken down; *also* : the processes by which a substance is handled in the body ⟨∼ of sugar⟩ — **met·a·bol·ic** \ˌme-tə-ˈbä-lik\ *adj* — **me·tab·o·lize** \mə-ˈta-bə-ˌlīz\ *vb*

me·tab·o·lite \-ˌlīt\ *n* **1** : a product of metabolism **2** : a substance essential to the metabolism of a particular organism or to a metabolic process

meta·car·pal \ˌme-tə-ˈkär-pəl\ *n* : any of usu. five more or less elongated bones of the part of the hand or forefoot between the wrist and the bones of the digits — **metacarpal** *adj*

meta·car·pus \-ˈkär-pəs\ *n* : the part of the hand or forefoot that contains the metacarpals

met·al \ˈmet-ᵊl\ *n* **1** : any of various opaque, fusible, ductile, and typically lustrous substances that are good conductors of electricity and heat **2** : METTLE; *also* : the material out of which a person or thing is made — **me·tal·lic** \mə-ˈta-lik\ *adj*

met·al·lur·gy \ˈmet-ᵊl-ˌər-jē\ *n* : the science and technology of metals — **met·al·lur·gi·cal** \ˌmet-ᵊl-ˈər-ji-kəl\ *adj* — **met·al·lur·gist** \ˈmet-ᵊl-ˌər-jist\ *n*

met·al·ware \ˈmet-ᵊl-ˌwar\ *n* : metal utensils for household use

met·al·work \-ˌwərk\ *n* : work and esp. artistic work made of metal — **met·al·work·er** \-ˌwər-kər\ *n* — **met·al·work·ing** *n*

meta·mor·phism \ˌme-tə-ˈmór-fi-zəm\ *n* : a change in the structure of rock; *esp* : a change to a more compact and more highly crystalline form produced by pressure, heat, and water — **meta·mor·phic** \-ˈmór-fik\ *adj*

meta·mor·pho·sis \ˌme-tə-ˈmór-fə-səs\ *n, pl* **-pho·ses** \-ˌsēz\ **1** : a change of physical form, structure, or substance esp. by supernatural means; *also* : a striking alteration (as in appearance or character) **2** : a fundamental change in form and often habits of an animal accompanying the transformation of a larva into an adult — **meta·mor·phose** \-ˌfōz, -ˌfōs\ *vb*

met·a·phor \ˈme-tə-ˌfór\ *n* : a figure of speech in which a word for one idea or thing is used in place of another to suggest a likeness between them (as in "the ship plows the sea") — **met·a·phor·i·cal** \ˌme-tə-ˈfór-i-kəl\ *adj*

meta·phys·ics \ˌme-tə-ˈfi-ziks\ *n* [ML *Metaphysica*, title of Aristotle's treatise on the subject, fr. Gk (*ta*) *meta* (*ta*) *physika*, lit., the (works) after the physical (works); fr. its position in his collected works] : the philosophical study of the ultimate causes and underlying nature of things — **meta·phys·i·cal** \-ˈfi-zi-kəl\ *adj* — **meta·phy·si·cian** \-fə-ˈzi-shən\ *n*

me·tas·ta·sis \mə-ˈtas-tə-səs\ *n, pl* **-ta·ses** \-ˌsēz\ : transfer of a health-impairing agency (as cancer cells) to a new site in the body; *also* : a secondary growth of a malignant tumor — **me·tas·ta·size** \-tə-ˌsīz\ *vb* — **met·a·stat·ic** \ˌme-tə-ˈsta-tik\ *adj*

meta·tar·sal \ˌme-tə-ˈtär-səl\ *n* : any of the bones of the foot between the tarsus and the bones of the digits that in humans include five more or less elongated bones — **metatarsal** *adj*

meta·tar·sus \-ˈtär-səs\ *n* : the part of the human foot or the hind foot in quadrupeds that contains the metatarsals

¹mete \ˈmēt\ *vb* **met·ed; met·ing 1** *archaic* : MEASURE **2** : ALLOT

²mete *n* : BOUNDARY ⟨∼s and bounds⟩

me·te·or \ˈmē-tē-ər, -ˌȯr\ *n* **1** : a small particle of matter in the solar system directly observable only by its glow from frictional heating on falling into the earth's atmosphere **2** : the streak of light produced by a meteor

me·te·or·ic \ˌmē-tē-ˈȯr-ik\ *adj* **1** : of, relating to, or resembling a meteor **2** : transiently brilliant ⟨a ∼ career⟩ — **me·te·or·i·cal·ly** \-i-k(ə-)lē\ *adv*

me·te·or·ite \ˈmē-tē-ə-ˌrīt\ *n* : a meteor that reaches the surface of the earth

me·te·or·oid \ˈmē-tē-ə-ˌrȯid\ *n* : a small particle of matter in the solar system

me·te·o·rol·o·gy \ˌmē-tē-ə-ˈrä-lə-jē\ *n* : a science that deals with the atmosphere and its phenomena and esp. with weather forecasting — **me·te·o·ro·log·ic** \ˌmē-tē-ˌȯr-ə-ˈlä-jik\ *or* **me·te·o·ro·log·i·cal** \-ˈlä-ji-kəl\ *adj* — **me·te·o·rol·o·gist** \ˌmē-tē-ə-ˈrä-lə-jist\ *n*

¹me·ter \ˈmē-tər\ *n* : rhythm in verse or music

²me·ter \ˈmē-tər\ *n* : the basic metric unit of length — see METRIC SYSTEM table

³me·ter \ˈmē-tər\ *n* : a measuring and sometimes recording instrument

⁴me·ter *vb* **1** : to measure by means of a meter **2** : to print postal indicia on by means of a postage meter ⟨∼ed mail⟩

meter–kilogram–second *adj* : of, relating to, or being a system of units based on the meter, the kilogram, and the second

meter maid *n* : a policewoman assigned to write tickets for parking violations

meth·a·done \ˈme-thə-ˌdōn\ *also* **meth·a·don** \-ˌdän\ *n* : a synthetic addictive narcotic drug used esp. as a substitute narcotic in the treatment of heroin addiction

meth·am·phet·amine \ˌme-tham-ˈfe-tə-ˌmēn, -thəm-, -mən\ *n* : a drug used medically in the form of its hydrochloride in the treatment of obesity and often illicitly as a stimulant

meth·ane \ˈme-ˌthān\ *n* : a colorless odorless flammable gas produced by decomposition of organic matter or from coal and used esp. as a fuel

meth·a·nol \ˈme-thə-ˌnȯl, -ˌnōl\ *n* : a volatile flammable poisonous liquid alcohol used esp. as a solvent and as an antifreeze

meth·aqua·lone \me-ˈtha-kwə-ˌlōn\ *n* : a sedative and hypnotic habit-forming drug that is not a barbiturate

meth·od \ˈme-thəd\ *n* [MF *methode*, fr. L *methodus*, fr. Gk *methodos*, fr. *meta* with + *hodos* way] **1** : a procedure or process for achieving an end **2** : orderly arrangement : PLAN **syn** mode, manner, way, fashion, system — **me·thod·i·cal** \mə-ˈthä-di-kəl\ *adj* — **me·thod·i·cal·ly** \-k(ə-)lē\ *adv* — **me·thod·i·cal·ness** *n*

Meth·od·ist \ˈme-thə-dist\ *n* : a member of a Protestant denomination adhering to the doctrines of John Wesley — **Meth·od·ism** \-ˌdi-zəm\ *n*

meth·od·ize \ˈme-thə-ˌdīz\ *vb* **-ized; -iz·ing** : SYSTEMATIZE

meth·od·ol·o·gy \ˌme-thə-ˈdä-lə-jē\ *n, pl* **-gies 1** : a body of methods and rules followed in a science or discipline **2** : the study of the principles or procedures of inquiry in a particular field

meth·yl \ˈme-thəl\ *n* : a chemical group consisting of carbon and hydrogen

methyl alcohol *n* : METHANOL

meth·yl·mer·cury \ˌme-thəl-ˈmər-kyə-rē\ *n* : any of various toxic compounds of mercury that often occur as pollutants which accumulate in animals esp. at the top of a food chain

met·i·cal \ˈme-ti-kəl\ *n* — see MONEY table

me·tic·u·lous \mə-ˈti-kyə-ləs\ *adj* [L *meticulosus* fearful, fr. *metus* fear] : extremely careful in attending to details — **me·tic·u·lous·ly** *adv* — **me·tic·u·lous·ness** *n*

mé·tier \ˈme-ˌtyā, me-ˈtyā\ *n* : an area of activity in which one is expert or successful

me·tre \ˈmē-tər\ *chiefly Brit var of* METER

met·ric \ˈme-trik\ *adj* **1** : of or relating to measurement; *esp* : of or relating to the metric system **2** : METRICAL 1

met·ri·cal \ˈme-tri-kəl\ *adj* **1** : of, relating to, or composed in meter **2** : METRIC 1 — **met·ri·cal·ly** \-k(ə-)lē\ *adv*

met·ri·ca·tion \ˌme-tri-ˈkā-shən\ *n* : the act or process of converting into or expressing in the metric system

met·ri·cize \ˈme-trə-ˌsīz\ *vb* **-cized; -ciz·ing** : to change into or express in the metric system

metric system *n* : a decimal system of weights and measures based on the meter and on the kilogram ☞ For table, see next page.

metric ton *n* — see METRIC SYSTEM table

¹me·tro \ˈme-trō\ *n, pl* **metros** : SUBWAY

²metro *adj* : of, relating to, or characteristic of a metropolis and sometimes including its suburbs

met·ro·nome \ˈme-trə-ˌnōm\ *n* : an instrument for marking exact time by a regularly repeated tick

me·trop·o·lis \mə-ˈträ-pə-ləs\ *n* [ME, fr. LL, fr. Gk *mētropolis*, fr. *mētēr* mother + *polis* city] : the chief or capital city of a country, state, or region — **met·ro·pol·i·tan** \ˌme-trə-ˈpä-lət-ᵊn\ *adj*

met·tle \ˈmet-ᵊl\ *n* **1** : SPIRIT, COURAGE **2** : quality of temperament

met·tle·some \ˈmet-ᵊl-səm\ *adj* : full of mettle : COURAGEOUS

MeV *abbr* million electron volts

¹mew \ˈmyü\ *vb* : MEOW — **mew** *n*

²mew *vb* : CONFINE

mews \ˈmyüz\ *n pl, chiefly Brit* : stables usu. with living quarters built around a court; *also* : a narrow street with dwellings converted from stables

Mex *abbr* Mexican; Mexico

Mex·i·can \ˈmek-si-kən\ *n* : a native or inhabitant of Mexico — **Mexican** *adj*

mez·za·nine \ˈmez-ᵊn-ˌēn, ˌmez-ᵊn-ˈēn\ *n* **1** : a low-ceilinged story between two main stories of a building **2** : the lowest balcony in a theater; *also* : the first few rows of such a balcony

mez·zo for·te \ˌmet-(ˌ)sō-ˈfȯr-ˌtā, ˌmed-(ˌ)zō-, -tē\ *adj or adv* [It] : moderately loud — used as a direction in music

mez·zo pia·no \-pē-ˈä-(ˌ)nō\ *adj or adv* [It] : moderately soft — used as a direction in music

mez·zo–so·pra·no \-sə-ˈpra-nō, -ˈprä-\ *n* : a woman's voice having a range between that of the soprano and contralto; *also* : a singer having such a voice

MFA *abbr* master of fine arts

mfr *abbr* manufacture; manufacturer

mg *abbr* milligram

Mg *symbol* magnesium

MG *abbr* **1** machine gun **2** major general **3** military government

mgr *abbr* **1** manager **2** monseigneur **3** monsignor

mgt *or* **mgmt** *abbr* management

MGy Sgt *abbr* master gunnery sergeant

MHz *abbr* megahertz

mi *abbr* **1** mile; mileage **2** mill

MI *abbr* **1** Michigan **2** military intelligence

MIA \ˌem-(ˌ)ī-ˈā\ *n* [*missing in action*] : a member of the armed forces whose whereabouts following a combat mission are unknown

Mi·ami \mī-ˈa-mē, -mə\ *n, pl* **Mi·ami** *or* **Mi·am·is** : a

METRIC SYSTEM[1]

LENGTH

unit	abbreviation	number of meters	approximate U.S. equivalent	
kilometer	km	1,000	0.62	mile
hectometer	hm	100	328.08	feet
dekameter	dam	10	32.81	feet
meter	m	1	39.37	inches
decimeter	dm	0.1	3.94	inches
centimeter	cm	0.01	0.39	inch
millimeter	mm	0.001	0.039	inch

AREA

unit	abbreviation	number of square meters	approximate U.S. equivalent	
square kilometer	sq km or km^2	1,000,000	0.3861	square mile
hectare	ha	10,000	2.47	acres
are	a	100	119.60	square yards
square centimeter	sq cm or cm^2	0.0001	0.155	square inch

VOLUME

unit	abbreviation	number of cubic meters	approximate U.S. equivalent	
cubic meter	m^3	1	1.307	cubic yards
cubic decimeter	dm^3	0.001	61.023	cubic inches
cubic centimeter	cu cm or cm^3 $also$ cc	0.000001	0.061	cubic inch

CAPACITY

unit	abbreviation	number of liters	approximate U.S. equivalent		
			cubic	dry	liquid
kiloliter	kl	1,000	1.31 cubic yards		
hectoliter	hl	100	3.53 cubic feet	2.84 bushels	
dekaliter	dal	10	0.35 cubic foot	1.14 pecks	2.64 gallons
liter	l	1	61.02 cubic inches	0.908 quart	1.057 quarts
deciliter	dl	0.1	6.1 cubic inches	0.18 pint	0.21 pint
centiliter	cl	0.01	0.61 cubic inch		0.338 fluid ounce
milliliter	ml	0.001	0.061 cubic inch		0.27 fluid dram

MASS AND WEIGHT

unit	abbreviation	number of grams	approximate U.S. equivalent	
metric ton	t	1,000,000	1.102	short tons
kilogram	kg	1,000	2.2046	pounds
hectogram	hg	100	3.527	ounces
dekagram	dag	10	0.353	ounce
gram	g	1	0.035	ounce
decigram	dg	0.1	1.543	grains
centigram	cg	0.01	0.154	grain
milligram	mg	0.001	0.015	grain

[1]For metric equivalents of U.S. units see Weights and Measures table

---

member of an American Indian people orig. of Wisconsin and Indiana

mi·as·ma \mī-'az-mə, mē-\ *n, pl* **-mas** *also* **-ma·ta** \-mə-tə\ **1** : a vapor from a swamp formerly believed to cause disease **2** : a harmful influence or atmosphere — **mi·as·mal** \-məl\ *adj* — **mi·as·mic** \-mik\ *adj*

Mic *abbr* Micah

mi·ca \'mī-kə\ *n* [NL, fr. L, grain, crumb] : any of various mineral silicates readily separable into thin transparent sheets

Mi·cah \'mī-kə\ *n* — see BIBLE table

mice *pl of* MOUSE

Mich *abbr* Michigan

Mi·che·as \'mī-kē-əs, mī-'kē-əs\ *n* : MICAH

Mic·mac \'mik-,mak\ *n, pl* **Micmac** *or* **Micmacs** : a member of an American Indian people of eastern Canada

micr- *or* **micro-** *comb form* **1** : small : minute 〈*micro*capsule〉 **2** : one millionth part of a specified unit 〈*mi*crosecond〉

¹mi·cro \'mī-krō\ *adj* **1** : very small; *esp* : MICROSCOPIC **2** : involving minute quantities or variations

²micro *n* : MICROCOMPUTER

mi·crobe \'mī-,krōb\ *n* : MICROORGANISM; *esp* : one causing disease — **mi·cro·bi·al** \mī-'krō-bē-əl\ *adj*

mi·cro·bi·ol·o·gy \,mī-krō-bī-'ä-lə-jē\ *n* : a branch of biology dealing esp. with microscopic forms of life —

mi·cro·bi·o·log·i·cal \-,bī-ə-'lä-ji-kəl\ *adj* — **mi·cro·bi·ol·o·gist** \-bī-'ä-lə-jist\ *n*

mi·cro·burst \'mī-krō-,bərst\ *n* : a violent short-lived localized downdraft that creates extreme wind shears at low altitudes

mi·cro·cap·sule \'mī-krō-,kap-səl, -,sül\ *n* : a tiny capsule containing material (as a medicine) released when the capsule is broken, melted, or dissolved

mi·cro·chip \-,chip\ *n* : INTEGRATED CIRCUIT

mi·cro·cir·cuit \-,sər-kət\ *n* : a compact electronic circuit

mi·cro·com·put·er \-kəm-,pyü-tər\ *n* : a very small computer that uses a microprocessor

mi·cro·cosm \'mī-krə-,kä-zəm\ *n* : an individual or community thought of as a miniature world or universe

mi·cro·elec·tron·ics \'mī-krō-i-,lek-'trä-niks\ *n* : a branch of electronics that deals with the miniaturization of electronic circuits and components — **mi·cro·elec·tron·ic** \-nik\ *adj*

mi·cro·en·cap·su·late \,mī-krō-in-'kap-sə-,lāt\ *vb* : to enclose (as a drug) in a microcapsule — **mi·cro·en·cap·su·la·tion** \-in-,kap-sə-'lā-shən\ *n*

mi·cro·fiche \'mī-krō-,fēsh, -,fish\ *n, pl* **-fiche** *or* **-fiches** *same or* -,fē-shəz, -,fi-\ : a sheet of microfilm containing rows of images of pages of printed matter

mi·cro·film \-,film\ *n* : a film bearing a photographic record (as of print) on a reduced scale — **microfilm** *vb*

mi·cro·graph \'mī-krə-ˌgraf\ *n* : a graphic reproduction of the image of an object formed by a microscope

mi·cro·me·te·or·ite \ˌmī-krō-'mē-tē-ə-ˌrīt\ *n* : a very small particle in interplanetary space

mi·crom·e·ter \mī-'krä-mə-tər\ *n* : an instrument used with a telescope or microscope for measuring minute distances

mi·cro·min·ia·tur·iza·tion \ˌmī-kro-ˌmi-nē-ə-ˌchur-ə-'zā-shən, -ˌmi-ni-ˌchur-, -chər-\ *n* : the process of producing things in a very small size and esp. in a size smaller than one considered miniature — **mi·cro·min·ia·tur·ized** \-'mi-nē-ə-chə-ˌrīzd, -'mi-ni-chə-\ *adj*

mi·cron \'mī-ˌkrän\ *n*, : one millionth of a meter

mi·cro·or·gan·ism \ˌmī-krō-'òr-gə-ˌni-zəm\ *n* : an organism (as a bacterium) too tiny to be seen by the unaided eye

mi·cro·phone \'mī-krə-ˌfōn\ *n* : an instrument for converting sound waves into variations of an electric current for transmitting or recording sound

mi·cro·pho·to·graph \ˌmī-krə-'fō-tə-ˌgraf\ *n* : PHOTOMICROGRAPH

mi·cro·pro·ces·sor \ˌmī-krō-'prä-ˌse-sər\ *n* : a computer processor contained on a microchip

mi·cro·scope \'mī-krə-ˌskōp\ *n* : an instrument for making magnified images of minute objects usu. using light — **mi·cros·co·py** \mī-'kräs-kə-pē\ *n*

mi·cro·scop·ic \ˌmī-krə-'skä-pik\ *also* **mi·cro·scop·i·cal** \-pi-kəl\ *adj* **1** : of, relating to, or involving the use of the microscope **2** : too tiny to be seen without the use of a microscope : very small — **mi·cro·scop·i·cal·ly** \-pi-k(ə-)lē\ *adv*

mi·cro·sec·ond \'mī-krō-ˌse-kənd\ *n* : one millionth of a second

mi·cro·sur·gery \ˌmī-krō-'sər-jə-rē\ *n* : minute dissection or manipulation (as by a laser beam) of living structures or tissue — **mi·cro·sur·gi·cal** \-'sər-ji-kəl\ *adj*

¹mi·cro·wave \'mī-krə-ˌwāv\ *n* **1** : a radio wave between one millimeter and one meter in wavelength **2** : MICROWAVE OVEN

²microwave *vb* : to heat or cook in a microwave oven — **mi·cro·wav·able** *or* **mi·cro·wave·able** \ˌmī-krə-'wā-və-bəl\ *adj*

microwave oven *n* : an oven in which food is cooked by the absorption of microwave energy by water molecules in the food

¹mid \'mid\ *adj* : MIDDLE

²mid *abbr* middle

mid·air \'mid-'ar\ *n* : a point or region in the air well above the ground

mid·day \'mid-ˌdā, -'dā\ *n* : NOON

mid·den \'mid-ᵊn\ *n* : a refuse heap

¹mid·dle \'mid-ᵊl\ *adj* **1** : equally distant from the extremes : MEDIAL, CENTRAL **2** : being at neither extreme : INTERMEDIATE **3** *cap* : constituting an intermediate period

²middle *n* **1** : a middle part, point, or position **2** : WAIST

middle age *n* : the period of life from about 40 to about 60 — **mid·dle-aged** \ˌmid-ᵊl-'ājd\ *adj*

Middle Ages *n pl* : the period of European history from about A.D. 500 to about 1500

mid·dle·brow \'mid-ᵊl-ˌbrau̇\ *n* : a person who is moderately but not highly cultivated — **middlebrow** *adj*

middle class *n* : a social class holding a position between the upper class and the lower class — **middleclass** *adj*

middle ear *n* : a small membrane-lined cavity of the ear through which sound waves are transmitted by a chain of tiny bones

middle finger *n* : the midmost of the five digits of the hand

mid·dle·man \'mid-ᵊl-ˌman\ *n* : INTERMEDIARY; *esp*

: one intermediate between the producer of goods and the retailer or consumer

middle-of-the-road *adj* : standing for or following a course of action midway between extremes; *esp* : being neither liberal nor conservative in politics — **middle-of-the-road·er** \-'rō-dər\ *n* — **mid·dle-of-the-road·ism** \-'rō-ˌdi-zəm\ *n*

middle school *n* : a school usu. including grades 5 to 8 or 6 to 8

mid·dle·weight \'mid-ᵊl-ˌwāt\ *n* : one of average weight; *esp* : a boxer weighing more than 147 but not over 160 pounds

mid·dling \'mid-liŋ, -lən\ *adj* **1** : of middle, medium, or moderate size, degree, or quality **2** : MEDIOCRE

mid·dy \'mi-dē\ *n, pl* **middies** : MIDSHIPMAN

midge \'mij\ *n* : a very small fly : GNAT

midg·et \'mi-jət\ *n* **1** : a very small person **2** : something (as an animal) very small for its kind

midi \'mi-dē\ *n* : a calf-length dress, coat, or skirt

mid·land \'mid-lənd, -ˌland\ *n* : the interior or central region of a country

mid·life \'mid-'līf\ *n* : MIDDLE AGE

midlife crisis *n* : a period of emotional turmoil in middle age characterized esp. by a strong desire for change

mid·most \-ˌmōst\ *adj* : being in or near the exact middle — **midmost** *adv*

mid·night \-ˌnīt\ *n* : 12 o'clock at night

mid·point \'mid-ˌpȯint, -'pȯint\ *n* : a point at or near the center or middle

mid·riff \'mi-ˌdrif\ *n* [ME *midrif*, fr. OE *midhrif*, fr. *midde* mid + *hrif* belly] **1** : DIAPHRAGM 1 **2** : the midregion of the human torso

mid·sec·tion \-ˌsek-shən\ *n* : a section midway between the extremes; *esp* : MIDRIFF 2

mid·ship·man \'mid-ˌship-mən, (ˌ)mid-'ship-\ *n* : a student in a naval academy

mid·ships \-ˌships\ *adv* : AMIDSHIPS

midst \'midst\ *n* **1** : the interior or central part or point **2** : a position of proximity to the members of a group ⟨in our ∼⟩ **3** : the condition of being surrounded or beset — **midst** *prep*

mid·stream \'mid-ˌstrēm, -'strēm\ *n* : the middle of a stream

mid·sum·mer \-'sə-mər, -ˌsə-\ *n* **1** : the middle of summer **2** : the summer solstice

mid·town \'mid-ˌtaün, -'taün\ *n* : a central section of a city; *esp* : one situated between sections called *downtown* and *uptown* — **midtown** *adj*

¹mid·way \'mid-ˌwā, -'wā\ *adv* : in the middle of the way or distance

²mid·way \-ˌwā\ *n* : an avenue (as at a carnival) for concessions and amusements

mid·week \-ˌwēk\ *n* : the middle of the week — **midweek·ly** \-ˌwē-klē, -'wē-\ *adj or adv*

mid·wife \'mid-ˌwīf\ *n* : a person who helps women in childbirth — **mid·wife·ry** \-ˌwī-fə-rē\ *n*

mid·win·ter \'mid-ˌwin-tər, -ˌwin-\ *n* **1** : the winter solstice **2** : the middle of winter

mid·year \-ˌyir\ *n* **1** : the middle of a year **2** : a midyear examination — **midyear** *adj*

mien \'mēn\ *n* **1** : air or bearing esp. as expressive of mood or personality : DEMEANOR **2** : APPEARANCE, ASPECT

miff \'mif\ *vb* : to put into an ill humor

¹might \'mīt\ *past of* MAY — used as an auxiliary to express permission or possibility in the past, a present condition contrary to fact, less probability or possibility than *may*, or as a polite alternative to *may*, *ought*, or *should*

²might *n* : the power, authority, or resources of an individual or a group

mighty \'mī-tē\ *adj* **might·i·er; -est 1** : very strong : POWERFUL **2** : GREAT, NOTABLE — **might·i·ly** \'mī-tə-lē\ *adv* — **might·i·ness** \-tē-nəs\ *n* — **mighty** *adv*

mi·gnon·ette \ˌmin-yə-'net\ *n* : an annual garden herb with spikes of tiny fragrant flowers

mi·graine \'mī-ˌgrān\ *n* [F, fr. LL *hemicrania* pain in one side of the head, fr. Gk *hēmikrania*, fr. *hēmi-* half + *kranion* cranium] : a condition marked by recurrent severe headache and often nausea; *also* : an attack of migraine

mi·grant \'mī-grənt\ *n* : one that migrates; *esp* : a person who moves in order to find work (as picking crops) — **migrant** *adj*

mi·grate \'mī-ˌgrāt\ *vb* **mi·grat·ed; mi·grat·ing 1** : to move from one country or place to another **2** : to pass usu. periodically from one region or climate to another for feeding or breeding — **mi·gra·tion** \mī-'grā-shən\ *n* — **mi·gra·to·ry** \'mī-grə-ˌtōr-ē\ *adj*

mi·ka·do \mə-'kä-dō\ *n, pl* **-dos** : an emperor of Japan

mike \'mīk\ *n* : MICROPHONE

¹mil \'mil\ *n* : a unit of length equal to ¹/₁₀₀₀ inch

²mil *abbr* military

milch \'milk, 'milch\ *adj* : giving milk ⟨∼ cow⟩

mild \'mīld\ *adj* **1** : gentle in nature or behavior **2** : moderate in action or effect **3** : TEMPERATE **syn** easy, complaisant, amiable, lenient — **mild·ly** *adv* — **mild·ness** *n*

mil·dew \'mil-ˌdü, -ˌdyü\ *n* : a superficial usu. whitish growth produced on organic matter and on plants by a fungus; *also* : a fungus producing this growth — **mildew** *vb*

mile \'mīl\ *n* [ME, fr. OE *mīl*, fr. L *milia* miles, fr. *milia passuum*, lit., thousands of paces] **1** — see WEIGHT table **2** : NAUTICAL MILE

mile·age \'mī-lij\ *n* **1** : an allowance for traveling expenses at a certain rate per mile **2** : distance in miles traveled (as in a day) **3** : the amount of service yielded (as by a tire) expressed in terms of miles of travel **4** : the average number of miles a car will travel on a gallon of gasoline

mile·post \'mīl-ˌpōst\ *n* : a post indicating the distance in miles from a given point

mile·stone \-ˌstōn\ *n* **1** : a stone serving as a milepost **2** : a significant point in development

mi·lieu \mēl-'yər, -'yü, -'yœ\ *n, pl* **mi·lieus** *or* **mi·lieux** *same or* -'yərz, -'yüz, -'yœz\ [F] : ENVIRONMENT, SETTING

mil·i·tant \'mi-lə-tənt\ *adj* **1** : engaged in warfare **2** : aggressively active esp. in a cause — **mil·i·tance** \-təns\ *n* — **mil·i·tan·cy** \-tən-sē\ *n* — **militant** *n* — **mil·i·tant·ly** *adv*

mil·i·ta·rism \'mi-lə-tə-ˌri-zəm\ *n* **1** : predominance of the military class or its ideals **2** : a policy of aggressive military preparedness — **mil·i·ta·rist** \-rist\ *n* — **mil·i·ta·ris·tic** \ˌmi-lə-tə-'ris-tik\ *adj*

mil·i·ta·rize \'mi-lə-tə-ˌrīz\ *vb* **-rized; -riz·ing 1** : to equip with military forces and defenses **2** : to give a military character to

¹mil·i·tary \'mi-lə-ˌter-ē\ *adj* **1** : of or relating to soldiers, arms, war, or the army **2** : performed by armed forces; *also* : supported by armed force **syn** martial, warlike — **mil·i·tar·i·ly** \ˌmi-lə-'ter-ə-lē\ *adv*

²military *n, pl* **military** *also* **mil·i·tar·ies 1** : the military, naval, and air forces of a nation **2** : military persons

mil·i·tate \'mi-lə-ˌtāt\ *vb* **-tat·ed; -tat·ing** : to have weight or effect

mi·li·tia \mə-'li-shə\ *n* : a part of the organized armed forces of a country liable to call only in emergency — **mi·li·tia·man** \-mən\ *n*

¹milk \'milk\ *n* **1** : a nutritive usu. whitish fluid secreted by female mammals for feeding their young **2** : a milklike liquid (as a plant juice) — **milk·i·ness** \'mil-kē-nəs\ *n* — **milky** *adj*

²milk *vb* **1** : to draw off the milk of ⟨∼ a cow⟩ **2** : to draw something from as if by milking

milk·maid \'milk-ˌmād\ *n* : DAIRYMAID

milk·man \-ˌman, -mən\ *n* : a person who sells or delivers milk

milk of magnesia : a milk-white mixture of hydroxide of magnesium and water used as an antacid and laxative

milk shake *n* : a thoroughly blended drink made of milk, a flavoring syrup, and often ice cream

milk·sop \'milk-ˌsäp\ *n* : an unmanly man

milk·weed \-ˌwēd\ *n* : any of a genus of herbs with milky juice and clustered flowers

Milky Way *n* **1** : a broad irregular band of light that stretches across the sky and is caused by the light of a very great number of faint stars **2** : MILKY WAY GALAXY

Milky Way galaxy *n* : the galaxy of which the sun is a member and which includes the stars that comprise the Milky Way

¹mill \'mil\ *n* **1** : a building with machinery for grinding grain into flour **2** : a machine used in processing (as by grinding, stamping, cutting, or finishing) raw material **3** : FACTORY

²mill *vb* **1** : to process in a mill **2** : to move in a circle or in an eddying mass

³mill *n* : one tenth of a cent

mill·age \'mi-lij\ *n* : a rate (as of taxation) expressed in mills

mil·len·ni·um \mə-'le-nē-əm\ *n, pl* **-nia** \-nē-ə\ *or* **-niums 1** : a period of 1000 years; *also* : a 1000th anniversary or its celebration **2** : the 1000 years mentioned in Revelation 20 when holiness is to prevail and Christ is to reign on earth **3** : a period of great happiness or perfect government

mill·er \'mi-lər\ *n* **1** : one that operates a mill and esp. a flour mill **2** : any of various moths having powdery wings

mil·let \'mi-lət\ *n* : any of several small-seeded cereal and forage grasses cultivated for grain or hay; *also* : the grain of a millet

mil·li·am·pere \ˌmi-lē-'am-ˌpir\ *n* : one thousandth of an ampere

mil·liard \'mil-ˌyärd, 'mi-lē-ˌärd\ *n, Brit* : a thousand millions

mil·li·bar \'mi-lə-ˌbär\ *n* : a unit of atmospheric pressure

mil·li·gram \-ˌgram\ *n* — see METRIC SYSTEM table

mil·li·li·ter \-ˌlē-tər\ *n* — see METRIC SYSTEM table

mil·lime \mə-'lēm\ *n* — see *dinar* at MONEY table

mil·li·me·ter \'mi-lə-ˌmē-tər\ *n* — see METRIC SYSTEM table

mil·li·ner \'mi-lə-nər\ *n* [irreg. fr. *Milan*, Italy; fr. importation of women's finery from Italy in the 16th century] : a person who designs, makes, trims, or sells women's hats

mil·li·nery \'mi-lə-ˌner-ē\ *n* **1** : women's apparel for the head **2** : the business or work of a milliner

mill·ing \'mi-liŋ\ *n* : a corrugated edge on a coin

mil·lion \'mil-yən\ *n, pl* **millions** *or* **million** : a thousand thousands — **million** *adj* — **mil·lionth** \-yənth\ *adj or n*

mil·lion·aire \ˌmil-yə-'ner, 'mil-yə-ˌner\ *n* : one whose wealth is estimated at a million or more (as of dollars or pounds)

mil·li·pede \'mi-lə-ˌpēd\ *n* : any of a class of arthropods related to the centipedes and having a long segmented body with a hard covering, two pairs of legs on most segments, and no poison fangs

mil·li·sec·ond \-ˌse-kənd\ *n* : one thousandth of a second

mil·li·volt \-ˌvōlt\ *n* : one thousandth of a volt

mill·pond \'mil-ˌpänd\ *n* : a pond made by damming a stream to produce a fall of water for operating a mill

mill·race \-ˌrās\ *n* : a canal in which water flows to and from a mill wheel

mill·stone \-ˌstōn\ *n* : either of two round flat stones used for grinding grain

mill·stream \-ˌstrēm\ *n* : a stream whose flow is used to run a mill; *also* : the stream in a millrace

mill wheel *n* : a waterwheel that drives a mill

mill·wright \'mil-ˌrīt\ *n* : a person who builds mills or sets up or maintains their machinery

milt \'milt\ *n* : the sperm-containing fluid of a male fish

mime \'mīm\ *n* 1 : MIMIC 2 : PANTOMIME — **mime** *vb*

mim·eo·graph \'mi-mē-ə-ˌgraf\ *n* : a machine for making many copies by means of a stencil through which ink is pressed — **mimeograph** *vb*

mi·me·sis \mə-'mē-səs, mī-\ *n* : IMITATION, MIMICRY

mi·met·ic \-'me-tik\ *adj* 1 : IMITATIVE 2 : relating to, characterized by, or exhibiting mimicry

¹mim·ic \'mi-mik\ *n* : one that mimics

²mimic *vb* **mim·icked** \-mikt\; **mim·ick·ing** 1 : to imitate closely 2 : to ridicule by imitation 3 : to resemble by biological mimicry

mim·ic·ry \'mi-mi-krē\ *n, pl* **-ries** 1 : an instance of mimicking 2 : a superficial resemblance of one organism to another or to natural objects among which it lives that gives it an advantage (as protection from predation)

mi·mo·sa \mə-'mō-sə, mī-, -zə\ *n* : any of a genus of leguminous trees, shrubs, and herbs of warm regions with ball-shaped heads of small white or pink flowers

min *abbr* 1 minim 2 minimum 3 mining 4 minister 5 minor 6 minute

min·a·ret \ˌmi-nə-'ret\ *n* [F, fr. Turk *minare*, fr. Ar *manārah* lighthouse] : a tall slender tower of a mosque from which a muezzin calls the faithful to prayer

1 minaret

mi·na·to·ry \'mi-nə-ˌtōr-ē, 'mī-\ *adj* : THREATENING, MENACING

mince \'mins\ *vb* **minced; minc·ing** 1 : to cut into very small pieces 2 : to restrain (words) within the bounds of decorum 3 : to walk in a prim affected manner

mince·meat \'mins-ˌmēt\ *n* : a finely chopped mixture esp. of raisins, apples, spices, and often meat used as a filling for a pie

¹mind \'mīnd\ *n* 1 : MEMORY 2 : the part of an individual that feels, perceives, thinks, wills, and esp. reasons 3 : INTENTION, DESIRE 4 : normal mental condition 5 : OPINION, VIEW 6 : MOOD 7 : mental qualities of a person or group 8 : intellectual ability

²mind *vb* 1 *chiefly dial* : REMEMBER 2 : to attend to closely : HEED, OBEY 4 : to be concerned about; *also* : DISLIKE 5 : to be careful or cautious 6 : to take charge of 7 : to regard with attention

mind–bend·ing \'mīnd-ˌben-diŋ\ *adj* : MIND-BLOWING

mind–blow·ing \-ˌblō-iŋ\ *adj* : PSYCHEDELIC 1; *also* : MIND-BOGGLING

mind–bog·gling \-ˌbä-gə-liŋ\ *adj* : mentally or emotionally exciting or overwhelming

mind·ed \'mīn-dəd\ *adj* 1 : INCLINED, DISPOSED 2 : having a mind of a specified kind or concerned with a specific thing — usu. used in combination 〈narrow-*minded*〉

mind·ful \'mīnd-fəl\ *adj* : bearing in mind : AWARE — **mind·ful·ly** *adv* — **mind·ful·ness** *n*

mind·less \-ləs\ *adj* 1 : marked by a lack of mind or consciousness; *esp* : marked by no use of the intellect

2 : not mindful : HEEDLESS — **mind·less·ly** *adv* — **mind·less·ness** *n*

¹mine \'mīn\ *pron* : that which belongs to me

²mine *n* 1 : an excavation in the earth from which minerals are taken; *also* : an ore deposit 2 : an underground passage beneath an enemy position 3 : an explosive device for destroying enemy personnel, vehicles, or ships 4 : a rich source of supply

³mine *vb* **mined; min·ing** 1 : to dig a mine 2 : UNDERMINE 3 : to get ore from the earth 4 : to place military mines in — **min·er** *n*

mine·field \'mīn-ˌfēld\ *n* 1 : an area set with mines 2 : something resembling a minefield esp. in having many dangers

mine·lay·er \-ˌlā-ər\ *n* : a naval vessel for laying underwater mines

min·er·al \'mi-nə-rəl\ *n* 1 : a crystalline substance (as diamond or quartz) of inorganic origin 2 : a naturally occurring substance (as coal, salt, or water) obtained usu. from the ground — **mineral** *adj*

min·er·al·ize \'mi-nə-rə-ˌlīz\ *vb* **-ized; -iz·ing** 1 : to impregnate or supply with minerals 2 : to change into mineral form — **min·er·al·i·za·tion** \-rə-lə-'zā-shən\ *n*

min·er·al·o·gy \ˌmi-nə-'rä-lə-jē, -'ra-\ *n* : a science dealing with minerals — **min·er·al·og·i·cal** \ˌmi-nə-rə-'lä-ji-kəl\ *adj* — **min·er·al·o·gist** \ˌmi-nə-'rä-lə-jist, -'ra-\ *n*

mineral oil *n* : an oil of mineral origin; *esp* : a refined petroleum oil used as a laxative

mineral water *n* : water infused with mineral salts or gases

min·e·stro·ne \ˌmi-nə-'strō-nē, -'strän\ *n* [It, fr. *minestra*, fr. *minestrare* to serve, dish up, fr. L *ministrare*, fr. *minister* servant] : a rich thick vegetable soup

mine·sweep·er \'mīn-ˌswē-pər\ *n* : a warship designed for removing or neutralizing underwater mines

min·gle \'miŋ-gəl\ *vb* **min·gled; min·gling** 1 : to bring or combine together : MIX 2 : ASSOCIATE; *also* : to move about (as in a group)

ming tree \'miŋ-\ *n* : a dwarfed usu. evergreen tree grown as bonsai; *also* : an artificial plant resembling this

mini \'mi-nē\ *n, pl* **min·is** : something small of its kind — **mini** *adj*

mini- *comb form* : smaller or briefer than usual, normal, or standard

min·ia·ture \'mi-nē-ə-ˌchùr, 'mi-ni-ˌchùr, -chər\ *n* [It *miniatura* art of illuminating a manuscript, fr. ML, fr. L *miniare* to color with red lead, fr. *minium* red lead] 1 : a copy on a much reduced scale; *also* : something small of its kind 2 : a small painting (as on ivory or metal) — **miniature** *adj* — **min·ia·tur·ist** \-ˌchùr-ist, -chər-\ *n*

min·ia·tur·ize \'mi-nē-ə-ˌchə-ˌrīz, 'mi-ni-\ *vb* **-ized; -iz·ing** : to design or construct in small size — **min·ia·tur·i·za·tion** \ˌmi-nē-ə-ˌchùr-ə-'zā-shən, ˌmi-ni-, -chər-\ *n*

mini·bike \'mi-nē-ˌbīk\ *n* : a small one-passenger motorcycle

mini·bus \-ˌbəs\ *n* : a small bus or van

mini·com·put·er \-kəm-ˌpyü-tər\ *n* : a computer between a mainframe and a microcomputer in size and speed

min·im \'mi-nəm\ *n* — see WEIGHT table

min·i·mal \'mi-nə-məl\ *adj* 1 : relating to or being a minimum : LEAST 2 : of or relating to minimalism or minimal art — **min·i·mal·ly** *adv*

minimal art *n* : abstract art consisting primarily of simple geometric forms executed in an impersonal style — **minimal artist** *n*

min·i·mal·ism \'mi-nə-mə-ˌli-zəm\ *n* : MINIMAL ART; *also* : a style (as in music or literature) marked by extreme spareness or simplicity — **min·i·mal·ist** \-list\ *n*

min·i·mize \'mi-nə-ˌmīz\ *vb* **-mized; -miz·ing** 1 : to reduce or keep to a minimum 2 : to underestimate intentionally; *also* : BELITTLE **syn** depreciate, decry, disparage

min·i·mum \'mi-nə-məm\ *n, pl* **-ma** \-mə\ *or* **-mums 1** : the least quantity assignable, admissible, or possible **2** : the least of a set of numbers **3** : the lowest degree or amount of variation (as of temperature) reached or recorded — **minimum** *adj*

min·ion \'min-yən\ *n* [MF *mignon* darling] **1** : a servile dependent, follower, or underling **2** : one highly favored **3** : a subordinate official

min·is·cule \'mi-nəs-ˌkyül\ *var of* MINUSCULE

mini·se·ries \'mi-nē-ˌsir-ēz\ *n* : a television story presented in sequential episodes

mini·skirt \-ˌskərt\ *n* : a skirt with the hemline several inches above the knee

¹min·is·ter \'mi-nə-stər\ *n* **1** : AGENT **2** : a member of the clergy esp. of a Protestant communion **3** : a high officer of state who heads a division of governmental activities **4** : a diplomatic representative to a foreign state — **min·is·te·ri·al** \ˌmi-nə-'stir-ē-əl\ *adj*

²minister *vb* **1** : to perform the functions of a minister of religion **2** : to give aid or service — **min·is·tra·tion** \ˌmi-nə-'strā-shən\ *n*

¹min·is·trant \'mi-nə-strənt\ *adj, archaic* : performing service as a minister

²ministrant *n* : one that ministers

min·is·try \'mi-nə-strē\ *n, pl* **-tries 1** : MINISTRATION **2** : the office, duties, or functions of a minister; *also* : the period of service or office **3** : CLERGY **4** : AGENCY **5** *often cap* : the body of ministers governing a nation or state; *also* : a government department headed by a minister

mini·van \'mi-nē-ˌvan\ *n* : a small van

mink \'miŋk\ *n, pl* **mink** *or* **minks** : either of two slender mammals resembling the related weasels; *also* : the soft lustrous typically dark brown fur of a mink

mink

Minn *abbr* Minnesota

min·ne·sing·er \'mi-ni-ˌsiŋ-ər, -ˌziŋ-\ *n* [G, fr. Middle High German, fr. *minne* love + *singer* singer] : any of a class of German lyric poets and musicians of the 12th to the 14th centuries

min·now \'mi-nō\ *n, pl* **minnows** *also* **minnow** : any of numerous small freshwater fishes

¹mi·nor \'mī-nər\ *adj* **1** : inferior in importance, size, or degree **2** : not having reached majority **3** : having the third, sixth, and sometimes the seventh degrees lowered by a half step ⟨∼ scale⟩; *also* : based on a minor scale ⟨∼ key⟩ **4** : not serious ⟨∼ illness⟩

²minor *n* **1** : a person who has not attained majority **2** : a subject of academic study chosen as a secondary field of specialization

³minor *vb* : to pursue an academic minor

mi·nor·i·ty \mə-'nȯr-ə-tē, mī-\ *n, pl* **-ties 1** : the period or state of being a minor **2** : the smaller in number of two groups; *esp* : a group having less than the number of votes necessary for control **3** : a part of a population differing from others (as in race); *also* : a member of a minority

mi·nox·i·dil \mə-'näk-sə-ˌdil\ *n* : a drug used orally to treat hypertension and topically in solution to promote hair regrowth in some forms of baldness

min·ster \'min-stər\ *n* : a large or important church

min·strel \'min-strəl\ *n* **1** : a medieval singer of verses; *also* : MUSICIAN, POET **2** : any of a group of performers usu. with blackened faces in a program of black

American songs, jokes, and impersonations ⟨a ∼ show⟩

min·strel·sy \-sē\ *n* : the singing and playing of a minstrel; *also* : a body of minstrels

¹mint \'mint\ *n* **1** : any of a large family of square-stemmed herbs and shrubs; *esp* : one (as spearmint) that is fragrant and is the source of a flavoring oil **2** : a mint-flavored piece of candy — **minty** *adj*

²mint *n* **1** : a place where coins are made **2** : a vast sum — **mint** *vb* — **mint·age** \-ij\ *n* — **mint·er** *n*

³mint *adj* : unmarred as if fresh from a mint ⟨in ∼ condition⟩

min·u·end \'min-yə-ˌwend\ *n* : a number from which another is to be subtracted

min·u·et \ˌmin-yə-'wet\ *n* : a slow graceful dance

¹mi·nus \'mī-nəs\ *prep* **1** : diminished by : LESS ⟨7 ∼ 3 equals 4⟩ **2** : LACKING, WITHOUT ⟨∼ his hat⟩

²minus *n* : a negative quantity or quality

³minus *adj* **1** : algebraically negative ⟨∼ quantity⟩ **2** : having negative qualities

¹mi·nus·cule \'mi-nəs-ˌkyül\ *n* : a lowercase letter

²minuscule *adj* : very small

minus sign *n* : a sign – used in mathematics to indicate subtraction or a negative quantity

¹min·ute \'mi-nət\ *n* **1** : a 60th part of an hour or of a degree : 60 seconds **2** : a short space of time **3** *pl* : the official record of the proceedings of a meeting

²mi·nute \mī-'nüt, mə-, -'nyüt\ *adj* **mi·nut·er; -est 1** : very small **2** : of little importance : TRIFLING **3** : marked by close attention to details **syn** diminutive, tiny, miniature, wee — **mi·nute·ly** *adv* — **mi·nute·ness** *n*

min·ute·man \'mi-nət-ˌman\ *n* : a member of a group of armed men pledged to take the field at a minute's notice during and immediately before the American Revolution

mi·nu·tia \mə-'nü-shə, -'nyü-, -shē-ə\ *n, pl* **-ti·ae** \-shē-ˌē\ [L] : a minute or minor detail — usu. used in pl.

minx \'miŋks\ *n* : a pert girl

Mio·cene \'mī-ə-ˌsēn\ *adj* : of, relating to, or being the epoch of the Tertiary between the Oligocene and the Pliocene — **Miocene** *n*

mir·a·cle \'mir-i-kəl\ *n* **1** : an extraordinary event manifesting divine intervention in human affairs **2** : an unusual event, thing, or accomplishment : WONDER, MARVEL — **mi·rac·u·lous** \mə-'ra-kyə-ləs\ *adj* — **mi·rac·u·lous·ly** *adv*

miracle drug *n* : a usu. newly discovered drug that elicits a dramatic response in a patient's condition

mi·rage \mə-'räzh\ *n* **1** : an illusion that often appears as a pool of water or a mirror in which distant objects are seen inverted, is sometimes seen at sea, in the desert, or over a hot pavement, and results from atmospheric conditions **2** : something illusory and unattainable

¹mire \'mīr\ *n* : heavy and often deep mud or slush — **miry** *adj*

²mire *vb* **mired; mir·ing** : to stick or sink in or as if in mire

¹mir·ror \'mir-ər\ *n* **1** : a polished or smooth surface (as of glass) that forms images by reflection **2** : a true representation

²mirror *vb* : to reflect in or as if in a mirror

mirth \'mərth\ *n* : gladness or gaiety accompanied with laughter **syn** glee, jollity, hilarity, merriment — **mirth·ful** \-fəl\ *adj* — **mirth·ful·ly** *adv* — **mirth·ful·ness** *n* — **mirth·less** *adj*

MIRV \'mərv\ *n* [*multiple independently targeted reentry vehicle*] : an ICBM with multiple warheads that have different targets — **MIRV** *vb*

mis·ad·ven·ture \ˌmi-səd-'ven-chər\ *n* : MISFORTUNE, MISHAP

mis·aligned \ˌmi-sə-'līnd\ *adj* : not properly aligned — **mis·align·ment** \-'līn-mənt\ *n*

mis·al·li·ance \ˌmi-sə-'lī-əns\ *n* : an improper or unsuitable marriage

mis·al·lo·ca·tion \mi-ˌsa-lə-ˈkā-shən\ *n* : faulty or improper allocation

mis·an·thrope \ˈmis-ᵊn-ˌthrōp\ *n* : one who hates mankind — **mis·an·throp·ic** \ˌmis-ᵊn-ˈthrä-pik\ *adj* — **mis·an·throp·i·cal·ly** \-pi-k(ə-)lē\ *adv* — **mis·an·thro·py** \mi-ˈsan-thrə-pē\ *n*

mis·ap·ply \ˌmi-sə-ˈplī\ *vb* : to apply wrongly — **mis·ap·pli·ca·tion** \ˌmi-ˌsa-plə-ˈkā-shən\ *n*

mis·ap·pre·hend \ˌmi-ˌsa-pri-ˈhend\ *vb* : MISUNDERSTAND — **mis·ap·pre·hen·sion** \-ˈhen-chən\ *n*

mis·ap·pro·pri·ate \ˌmi-sə-ˈprō-prē-ˌāt\ *vb* : to appropriate wrongly (as by embezzlement) — **mis·ap·pro·pri·a·tion** \-ˌprō-prē-ˈā-shən\ *n*

mis·be·got·ten \-bi-ˈgät-ᵊn\ *adj* : ILLEGITIMATE; *also* : ill-conceived

mis·be·have \ˌmis-bi-ˈhāv\ *vb* : to behave improperly — **mis·be·hav·er** *n* — **mis·be·hav·ior** \-ˈhā-vyər\ *n*

mis·be·liev·er \-bə-ˈlē-vər\ *n* : one who holds a false or unorthodox belief

mis·brand \mis-ˈbrand\ *vb* : to brand falsely or in a misleading manner

misc *abbr* miscellaneous

mis·cal·cu·late \mis-ˈkal-kyə-ˌlāt\ *vb* : to calculate wrongly — **mis·cal·cu·la·tion** \ˌmis-ˌkal-kyə-ˈlā-shən\ *n*

mis·call \mis-ˈkȯl\ *vb* : MISNAME

mis·car·riage \-ˈkar-ij\ *n* 1 : failure in the administration of justice 2 : spontaneous expulsion of a fetus before it is capable of independent life

mis·car·ry \-ˈkar-ē\ *vb* 1 : to have a miscarriage of a fetus 2 : to go wrong; *also* : to be unsuccessful

mis·ce·ge·na·tion \mi-se-jə-ˈnā-shən, ˌmi-si-jə-ˈnā-\ *n* [L *miscēre* to mix + *genus* race] : marriage or cohabitation between persons of different races

mis·cel·la·neous \ˌmi-sə-ˈlā-nē-əs\ *adj* 1 : consisting of diverse things or members 2 : having various traits; *also* : dealing with or interested in diverse subjects — **mis·cel·la·neous·ly** *adv* — **mis·cel·la·neous·ness** *n*

mis·cel·la·ny \ˈmi-sə-ˌlā-nē\ *n, pl* **-nies** 1 : a collection of writings on various subjects 2 : HODGEPODGE

mis·chance \mis-ˈchans\ *n* : bad luck; *also* : MISHAP

mis·chief \ˈmis-chəf\ *n* 1 : injury caused by a particular agent 2 : a source of harm or irritation 3 : action that annoys; *also* : MISCHIEVOUSNESS

mis·chie·vous \ˈmis-chə-vəs\ *adj* 1 : HARMFUL, INJURIOUS 2 : causing annoyance or minor injury 3 : irresponsibly playful — **mis·chie·vous·ly** *adv* — **mis·chie·vous·ness** *n*

mis·ci·ble \ˈmi-sə-bəl\ *adj* : capable of being mixed

mis·com·mu·ni·ca·tion \ˌmis-kə-ˌmyü-nə-ˈkā-shən\ *n* : failure to communicate clearly

mis·con·ceive \ˌmis-kən-ˈsēv\ *vb* : to interpret incorrectly — **mis·con·cep·tion** \-ˈsep-shən\ *n*

mis·con·duct \mis-ˈkän-(ˌ)dəkt\ *n* 1 : MISMANAGEMENT 2 : intentional wrongdoing 3 : improper behavior

mis·con·strue \ˌmis-kən-ˈstrü\ *vb* : MISINTERPRET — **mis·con·struc·tion** \-ˈstrək-shən\ *n*

mis·count \mis-ˈkaunt\ *vb* : to count incorrectly : MISCALCULATE

mis·cre·ant \ˈmis-krē-ənt\ *n* : one who behaves criminally or viciously — **miscreant** *adj*

mis·cue \mis-ˈkyü\ *n* : MISTAKE, ERROR — **miscue** *vb*

mis·deed \mis-ˈdēd\ *n* : a wrong deed

mis·de·mean·or \ˌmis-di-ˈmē-nər\ *n* 1 : a crime less serious than a felony 2 : MISDEED

mis·di·rect \ˌmis-də-ˈrekt, -dī-\ *vb* : to give a wrong direction to — **mis·di·rec·tion** \-ˈrek-shən\ *n*

mis·do·ing \mis-ˈdü-iŋ\ *n* : WRONGDOING — **mis·do** \-ˈdü\ *vb* — **mis·do·er** \-ˈdü-ər\ *n*

mise–en–scène \ˌmē-ˌzäⁿ-ˈsen, -ˈsän\ *n, pl* **mise–en–scènes** *same or* -ˈsenz, -ˈsänz\ [F] 1 : the arrangement of the scenery, property, and actors on a stage 2 : SETTING; *also* : ENVIRONMENT

mi·ser \ˈmī-zər\ *n* [L *miser* miserable] : a person who hoards and is stingy with money — **mi·ser·li·ness** \-lē-nəs\ *n* — **mi·ser·ly** *adj*

mis·er·a·ble \ˈmi-zə-rə-bəl, ˈmiz-rə-\ *adj* 1 : wretchedly deficient; *also* : causing extreme discomfort 2 : being in a state of distress 3 : SHAMEFUL — **mis·er·a·ble·ness** *n* — **mis·er·a·bly** \-blē\ *adv*

mis·ery \ˈmi-zə-rē\ *n, pl* **-er·ies** 1 : suffering and want caused by poverty or affliction 2 : a cause of suffering or discomfort 3 : emotional distress

mis·fea·sance \mis-ˈfēz-ᵊns\ *n* : the performance of a lawful action in an illegal or improper manner

mis·file \-ˈfīl\ *vb* : to file in the wrong place

mis·fire \-ˈfīr\ *vb* 1 : to fail to fire 2 : to miss an intended effect — **misfire** *n*

mis·fit \ˈmis-ˌfit, *sense 1 also* mis-ˈfit\ *n* 1 : something that fits badly 2 : one who is poorly adjusted to a situation or environment

mis·for·tune \mis-ˈfȯr-chən\ *n* 1 : bad luck 2 : an unfortunate condition or event

mis·giv·ing \-ˈgi-viŋ\ *n* : a feeling of doubt or suspicion esp. concerning a future event

mis·gov·ern \-ˈgə-vərn\ *vb* : to govern badly — **mis·gov·ern·ment** *n*

mis·guid·ance \mis-ˈgīd-ᵊns\ *n* : faulty guidance — **mis·guide** \-ˈgīd\ *vb*

mis·guid·ed \-ˈgī-dəd\ *adj* : led or prompted by wrong or inappropriate motives or ideals — **mis·guid·ed·ly** *adv*

mis·han·dle \-ˈhand-ᵊl\ *vb* 1 : MALTREAT 2 : to manage wrongly

mis·hap \ˈmis-ˌhap\ *n* : an unfortunate accident

mish·mash \ˈmish-ˌmash, -ˌmäsh\ *n* : HODGEPODGE, JUMBLE

mis·in·form \ˌmis-ᵊn-ˈfȯrm\ *vb* : to give false or misleading information to — **mis·in·for·ma·tion** \ˌmi-sin-fər-ˈmā-shən\ *n*

mis·in·ter·pret \ˌmis-ᵊn-ˈtər-prət\ *vb* : to understand or explain wrongly — **mis·in·ter·pre·ta·tion** \-ˌtər-prə-ˈtā-shən\ *n*

mis·judge \mis-ˈjəj\ *vb* 1 : to estimate wrongly 2 : to have an unjust opinion of — **mis·judg·ment** \mis-ˈjəj-mənt\ *n*

mis·la·bel \-ˈlā-bəl\ *vb* : to label incorrectly or falsely

mis·lay \mis-ˈlā\ *vb* **-laid** \-ˈlād\; **-lay·ing** : MISPLACE, LOSE

mis·lead \mis-ˈlēd\ *vb* **-led** \-ˈled\; **-lead·ing** : to lead in a wrong direction or into a mistaken action or belief — **mis·lead·ing·ly** *adv*

mis·like \-ˈlīk\ *vb* : DISLIKE — **mislike** *n*

mis·man·age \-ˈma-nij\ *vb* : to manage badly — **mis·man·age·ment** *n*

mis·match \-ˈmach\ *vb* : to match unsuitably or badly — **mis·match** \mis-ˈmach, ˈmis-ˌmach\ *n*

mis·name \-ˈnām\ *vb* : to name incorrectly : MISCALL

mis·no·mer \mis-ˈnō-mər\ *n* : a wrong name or designation

mi·sog·y·ny \mə-ˈsä-jə-nē\ *n* [Gk *misogynia*, fr. *misein* to hate + *gynē* woman] : a hatred of women — **mi·sog·y·nist** \-nist\ *n or adj* — **mi·sog·y·nis·tic** \mə-ˌsä-jə-ˈnis-tik\ *adj*

mis·ori·ent \mi-ˈsȯr-ē-ˌent\ *vb* : to orient improperly or incorrectly — **mis·ori·en·ta·tion** \mi-ˌsȯr-ē-ən-ˈtā-shən\ *n*

mis·place \mis-ˈplās\ *vb* 1 : to put in a wrong or unremembered place 2 : to set on a wrong object ⟨~ trust⟩

mis·play \-ˈplā\ *n* : a wrong or unskillful play — **mis·play** \mis-ˈplā, ˈmis-ˌplā\ *vb*

mis·print \ˈmis-ˌprint\ *n* : a mistake in printed matter — **misprint** \mis-ˈprint\ *vb*

mis·pro·nounce \ˌmis-prə-ˈnauns\ *vb* : to pronounce incorrectly — **mis·pro·nun·ci·a·tion** \-prə-ˌnən-sē-ˈā-shən\ *n*

mis·quote \mis-ˈkwōt\ *vb* : to quote incorrectly — **mis·quo·ta·tion** \ˌmis-kwō-ˈtā-shən\ *n*

mis·read \-ˈrēd\ *vb* **-read** \-ˈred\; **-read·ing** \-ˈrē-diŋ\ : to read or interpret incorrectly

mis·rep·re·sent \ˌmis-ˌre-pri-ˈzent\ *vb* : to represent falsely or unfairly — **mis·rep·re·sen·ta·tion** \-ˌzen-ˈtā-shən\ *n*

¹mis·rule \mis-ˈrül\ *vb* : MISGOVERN

²misrule *n* **1** : MISGOVERNMENT **2** : DISORDER

¹miss \ˈmis\ *vb* **1** : to fail to hit, reach, or contact **2** : to feel the absence of **3** : to fail to obtain **4** : AVOID ⟨just ~ed hitting the other car⟩ **5** : OMIT **6** : to fail to understand **7** : to fail to perform or attend; *also* : MISFIRE

²miss *n* **1** : a failure to hit or to attain a result **2** : MISFIRE

³miss *n* **1** *cap* — used as a title prefixed to the name of an unmarried woman or girl **2** : a young unmarried woman or girl

Miss *abbr* Mississippi

mis·sal \ˈmi-səl\ *n* : a book containing all that is said or sung at mass during the entire year

mis·send \mis-ˈsend\ *vb* : to send incorrectly ⟨*missent* mail⟩

mis·shap·en \-ˈshā-pən\ *adj* : badly shaped : having an ugly shape

mis·sile \ˈmi-səl\ *n* [L, fr. neut. of *missilis* capable of being thrown, fr. *mittere* to let go, send] : an object (as a stone, bullet, or rocket) thrown or projected usu. so as to strike a target

miss·ing \ˈmi-siŋ\ *adj* : ABSENT; *also* : LOST ⟨~ in action⟩

mis·sion \ˈmi-shən\ *n* **1** : a group of missionaries; *also* : a place where missionaries work **2** : a group of envoys to a foreign country; *also* : a team of specialists or cultural leaders sent to a foreign country **3** : TASK

¹mis·sion·ary \ˈmi-shə-ˌner-ē\ *adj* : of, relating to, or engaged in missions

²missionary *n*, *pl* **-ar·ies** : a person commissioned by a church to spread its faith or carry on humanitarian work

mis·sion·er \ˈmi-shə-nər\ *n* : MISSIONARY

Mis·sis·sip·pi·an \ˌmi-sə-ˈsi-pē-ən\ *adj* : of, relating to, or being the period of the Paleozoic era between the Devonian and the Pennsylvanian — **Mississippian** *n*

mis·sive \ˈmi-siv\ *n* : LETTER

mis·speak \mis-ˈspēk\ *vb* : to say imperfectly or incorrectly

mis·spell \-ˈspel\ *vb* : to spell incorrectly — **mis·spell·ing** *n*

mis·spend \-ˈspend\ *vb* **-spent** \-ˈspent\; **-spend·ing** : WASTE, SQUANDER ⟨my *misspent* youth⟩

mis·state \mis-ˈstāt\ *vb* : to state incorrectly — **mis·state·ment** *n*

mis·step \-ˈstep\ *n* **1** : a wrong step **2** : MISTAKE, BLUNDER

mist \ˈmist\ *n* **1** : water in the form of particles suspended or falling in the air **2** : something that obscures understanding — **mist** *vb*

mis·tak·able \mə-ˈstā-kə-bəl\ *adj* : capable of being misunderstood or mistaken

¹mis·take \mi-ˈstāk\ *vb* **-took** \-ˈstúk\; **-tak·en** \-ˈstā-kən\; **-tak·ing** **1** : to blunder in the choice of **2** : MISINTERPRET **3** : to make a wrong judgment of the character or ability of **4** : to confuse with another — **mis·tak·en·ly** *adv* — **mis·tak·er** *n*

²mistake *n* **1** : a wrong judgment : MISUNDERSTANDING **2** : a wrong action or statement : ERROR

¹mis·ter \ˈmis-tər\ *n* **1** *cap* — used sometimes instead of *Mr.* **2** : SIR — used without a name in addressing a man

²mist·er \ˈmis-tər\ *n* : a device for spraying mist

mis·tle·toe \ˈmi-səl-ˌtō\ *n* : a European parasitic green shrub with yellowish flowers and waxy white berries that grows on trees

mis·tral \ˈmis-trəl, mi-ˈsträl\ *n* [F, fr. Provençal, fr. *mistral* masterful, fr. LL *magistralis* of a teacher, fr. L *magister* master] : a strong cold dry northerly wind of southern France

mis·treat \mis-ˈtrēt\ *vb* : to treat badly : ABUSE — **mis·treat·ment** *n*

mis·tress \ˈmis-trəs\ *n* **1** : a woman who has power, authority, or ownership ⟨~ of the house⟩ **2** : something

personified as female that rules or dominates ⟨when Rome was ~ of the world⟩ **3** : a woman other than his wife with whom a married man has sexual relations; *also, archaic* : SWEETHEART **4** — used archaically as a title prefixed to the name of a married or unmarried woman

mis·tri·al \ˈmis-ˌtrīl\ *n* : a trial that has no legal effect

¹mis·trust \mis-ˈtrəst\ *n* : a lack of confidence : DISTRUST — **mis·trust·ful** \-fəl\ *adj* — **mis·trust·ful·ly** *adv* — **mis·trust·ful·ness** *n*

²mistrust *vb* : to have no trust or confidence in : SUSPECT

misty \ˈmis-tē\ *adj* **mist·i·er; -est** **1** : obscured by or as if by mist : INDISTINCT **2** : TEARFUL — **mist·i·ly** \-tə-lē\ *adv* — **mist·i·ness** \-tē-nəs\ *n*

mis·un·der·stand \ˌmi-ˌsən-dər-ˈstand\ *vb* **-stood** \-ˈstúd\; **-stand·ing** **1** : to fail to understand **2** : to interpret incorrectly

mis·un·der·stand·ing \-ˈstan-diŋ\ *n* **1** : MISINTERPRETATION **2** : DISAGREEMENT, QUARREL

mis·us·age \mis-ˈyü-sij\ *n* **1** : bad treatment : ABUSE **2** : wrong or improper use

mis·use \mis-ˈyüz\ *vb* **1** : to use incorrectly **2** : ABUSE, MISTREAT — **mis·use** \-ˈyüs\ *n*

mite \ˈmīt\ *n* **1** : any of numerous tiny arthropod animals related to the spiders that often live and feed on animals or plants **2** : a small coin or sum of money **3** : a small amount : BIT

¹mi·ter *or* **mi·tre** \ˈmī-tər\ *n* [ME *mitre*, fr. MF, fr. L *mitra* headband, turban, fr. Gk] **1** : a headdress worn by bishops and abbots **2** : MITER JOINT

²miter *or* **mitre** *vb* **mi·tered** *or* **mi·tred; mi·ter·ing** *or* **mi·tring** \ˈmī-tə-riŋ\ **1** : to match or fit together in a miter joint **2** : to bevel the ends of for making a miter joint

miter joint *n* : a joint made by fitting together two parts with the ends cut at an angle

mit·i·gate \ˈmi-tə-ˌgāt\ *vb* **-gat·ed; -gat·ing** **1** : to make less harsh or hostile **2** : to make less severe or painful — **mit·i·ga·tion** \ˌmi-tə-ˈgā-shən\ *n* — **mit·i·ga·tive** \ˈmi-tə-ˌgā-tiv\ *adj*

mi·to·sis \mī-ˈtō-səs\ *n*, *pl* **-to·ses** \-ˌsēz\ : a process that takes place in the nucleus of a dividing cell and results in the formation of two new nuclei each of which has the same number of chromosomes as the parent nucleus; *also* : cell division in which mitosis occurs — **mi·tot·ic** \-ˈtä-tik\ *adj*

mitt \ˈmit\ *n* **1** : a baseball catcher's or first baseman's glove **2** *slang* : HAND

mit·ten \ˈmit-ᵊn\ *n* : a covering for the hand having a separate section for the thumb only

¹mix \ˈmiks\ *vb* **1** : to combine into one mass **2** : ASSOCIATE **3** : to form by mingling components **4** : to produce (a recording) by electronically combining sounds from different sources **5** : HYBRIDIZE **6** : CONFUSE ⟨~es up the facts⟩ **7** : to become involved **syn** blend, merge, coalesce, amalgamate, fuse — **mix·able** *adj* — **mix·er** *n*

²mix *n* : a product of mixing; *esp* : a commercially prepared mixture of food ingredients

mixed number *n* : a number (as 5⅔) composed of an integer and a fraction

mixed–up \ˈmikst-ˈəp\ *adj* : CONFUSED

mixt *abbr* mixture

mix·ture \ˈmiks-chər\ *n* **1** : the act or process of mixing; *also* : the state of being mixed **2** : a product of mixing

mix–up \ˈmiks-ˌəp\ *n* **1** : an instance of confusion **2** : CONFLICT, FIGHT

miz·zen *also* **miz·en** \ˈmiz-ᵊn\ *n* **1** : a fore-and=aft sail set on the mizzenmast **2** : MIZZENMAST — **mizzen** *also* **mizen** *adj*

miz·zen·mast \-ˌmast, -məst\ *n* : the mast aft or next aft of the mainmast

mk *abbr* **1** mark **2** markka

Mk *abbr* Mark

mks *abbr* meter-kilogram-second

mkt *abbr* market

mktg *abbr* marketing

ml *abbr* milliliter

Mlle *abbr* [F] mademoiselle

Mlles *abbr* [F] mesdemoiselles

mm *abbr* millimeter

MM *abbr* [F] messieurs

Mme *abbr* [F] madame

Mmes *abbr* mesdames

Mn *symbol* manganese

MN *abbr* Minnesota

mne·mon·ic \nə-'mä-nik\ *adj* : assisting or designed to assist memory; *also* : of or relating to memory

mo *abbr* month

¹**Mo** *abbr* **1** Missouri **2** Monday

²**Mo** *symbol* molybdenum

MO *abbr* **1** mail order **2** medical officer **3** Missouri **4** modus operandi **5** money order

moan \'mōn\ *n* : a low prolonged sound indicative of pain or grief — **moan** *vb*

moat \'mōt\ *n* : a deep wide usu. water-filled trench around a castle

¹**mob** \'mäb\ *n* [L *mobile vulgus* vacillating crowd] **1** : MASSES, RABBLE **2** : a disorderly crowd **3** : a criminal gang

²**mob** *vb* **mobbed; mob·bing 1** : to crowd about and attack or annoy **2** : to crowd into or around ⟨shoppers *mobbed* the stores⟩

¹**mo·bile** \'mō-bəl, -ˌbīl, -ˌbēl\ *adj* **1** : capable of moving or being moved **2** : changeable in appearance, mood, or purpose; *also* : ADAPTABLE **3** : having the opportunity for or undergoing a shift in social status **4** : using vehicles for transportation ⟨∼ warfare⟩ — **mo·bil·i·ty** \mō-'bi-lə-tē\ *n*

²**mo·bile** \'mō-ˌbēl\ *n* : a construction or sculpture (as of wire and sheet metal) with parts that can be set in motion by air currents; *also* : a similar structure suspended so that it is moved by a current of air

mobile home *n* : a trailer used as a permanent dwelling

mo·bi·lize \'mō-bə-ˌlīz\ *vb* **-lized; -liz·ing 1** : to put into movement or circulation **2** : to assemble and make ready for action ⟨∼ army reserves⟩ — **mo·bi·li·za·tion** \ˌmō-bə-lə-'zā-shən\ *n* — **mo·bi·liz·er** \'mō-bə-ˌlī-zər\ *n*

mob·ster \'mäb-stər\ *n* : a member of a criminal gang

moc·ca·sin \'mä-kə-sən\ *n* **1** : a soft leather heelless shoe **2** : WATER MOCCASIN

mo·cha \'mō-kə\ *n* [*Mocha*, port in Yemen] **1** : choice coffee grown in Arabia **2** : a mixture of coffee and chocolate or cocoa **3** : a dark chocolate-brown color

¹**mock** \'mäk, 'mȯk\ *vb* **1** : to treat with contempt or ridicule **2** : DELUDE **3** : DEFY **4** : to mimic in sport or derision — **mock·er** *n* — **mock·ery** \'mä-kə-rē, 'mȯ-\ *n* — **mock·ing·ly** *adv*

²**mock** *adj* : SHAM, PSEUDO

mock–he·ro·ic \ˌmäk-hi-'rō-ik, ˌmȯk-\ *adj* : ridiculing or burlesquing heroic style, character, or action ⟨a ∼ poem⟩

mock·ing·bird \'mä-kiŋ-ˌbərd, 'mȯ-\ *n* : a grayish No. American songbird related to the catbirds and thrashers that mimics the calls of other birds

mock–up \'mä-ˌkəp, 'mȯ-\ *n* : a full-sized structural model built for study, testing, or display ⟨a ∼ of a car⟩

¹**mod** \'mäd\ *adj* **1** : of, relating to, or being the style of the 1960s British youth culture **2** : HIP, TRENDY

²**mod** *abbr* **1** moderate **2** modern **3** modification; modified

mode \'mōd\ *n* **1** : a particular form or variety of something; *also* : STYLE **2** : a manner of doing something **3** : the most frequent value of a set of data — **mod·al** \'mōd-ᵊl\ *adj*

¹**mod·el** \'mäd-ᵊl\ *n* **1** : structural design **2** : a miniature representation; *also* : a pattern of something to be made **3** : an example for imitation or emulation **4** : one who poses for an artist; *also* : MANNEQUIN **5** : TYPE, DESIGN

²**model** *vb* **mod·eled** *or* **mod·elled; mod·el·ing** *or* **mod·el·ling 1** : SHAPE, FASHION, CONSTRUCT **2** : to work as a fashion model

³**model** *adj* **1** : serving as or worthy of being a pattern ⟨a ∼ student⟩ **2** : being a miniature representation of something ⟨a ∼ airplane⟩

mo·dem \'mō-dəm, -ˌdem\ *n* : a device that converts signals from one device (as a computer) to a form compatible with another (as a telephone)

¹**mod·er·ate** \'mä-də-rət\ *adj* **1** : avoiding extremes; *also* : TEMPERATE **2** : AVERAGE; *also* : MEDIOCRE **3** : limited in scope or effect **4** : not expensive — **mod·erate** *n* — **mod·er·ate·ly** *adv* — **mod·er·ate·ness** *n*

²**mod·er·ate** \'mä-də-ˌrāt\ *vb* **-at·ed; -at·ing 1** : to lessen the intensity of : TEMPER **2** : to act as a moderator — **mod·er·a·tion** \ˌmä-də-'rā-shən\ *n*

mod·er·a·tor \'mä-də-ˌrā-tər\ *n* **1** : MEDIATOR **2** : one who presides over an assembly, meeting, or discussion

mod·ern \'mä-dərn\ *adj* [LL *modernus*, fr. L *modo* just now, fr. *modus* measure] : of, relating to, or characteristic of the present or the immediate past : CONTEMPORARY — **modern** *n* — **mo·der·ni·ty** \mə-'dər-nə-tē\ *n* — **mod·ern·ly** *adv* — **mod·ern·ness** *n*

mod·ern·ism \'mä-dər-ˌni-zəm\ *n* : a practice, movement, or belief peculiar to modern times

mod·ern·ize \'mä-dər-ˌnīz\ *vb* **-ized; -iz·ing** : to make or become modern — **mod·ern·i·za·tion** \ˌmä-dər-nə-'zā- shən\ *n* — **mod·ern·iz·er** *n*

mod·est \'mä-dəst\ *adj* **1** : having a moderate estimate of oneself; *also* : DIFFIDENT **2** : observing the proprieties of dress and behavior **3** : limited in size, amount, or scope — **mod·est·ly** *adv* — **mod·es·ty** \-də-stē\ *n*

mod·i·cum \'mä-di-kəm\ *n* : a small amount

modif *abbr* modification

mod·i·fy \'mä-də-ˌfī\ *vb* **-fied; -fy·ing 1** : MODERATE **2** : to limit the meaning of esp. in a grammatical construction **3** : CHANGE, ALTER — **mod·i·fi·ca·tion** \ˌmä-də-fə-'kä-shən\ *n* — **mod·i·fi·er** \'mä-də-ˌfī-ər\ *n*

mod·ish \'mō-dish\ *adj* : FASHIONABLE, STYLISH — **mod·ish·ly** *adv* — **mod·ish·ness** *n*

mo·diste \mō-'dēst\ *n* : a maker of fashionable dresses and hats

mod·u·lar \'mä-jə-lər\ *adj* : constructed with standardized units

mod·u·lar·ized \'mä-jə-lə-ˌrīzd\ *adj* : containing or consisting of modules

mod·u·late \'mä-jə-ˌlāt\ *vb* **-lat·ed; -lat·ing 1** : to tune to a key or pitch **2** : to keep in proper measure or proportion : TEMPER **3** : to vary the amplitude or frequency of a carrier wave for the transmission of intelligence (as in radio or television) — **mod·u·la·tion** \ˌmä-jə-'lä-shən\ *n* — **mod·u·la·tor** \'mä-jə-ˌlā-tər\ *n* — **mod·u·la·to·ry** \-lə-ˌtōr-ē\ *adj*

mod·ule \'mä-jül\ *n* **1** : any in a series of standardized units for use together **2** : an assembly of wired electronic parts for use with other such assemblies **3** : an independent unit that constitutes a part of the total structure of a space vehicle ⟨a propulsion ∼⟩

mo·dus ope·ran·di \ˌmō-dəs-ˌä-pə-'ran-dē, -ˌdī\ *n, pl* **mo·di operandi** \ˌmō-ˌdē-ˌäp-, 'mō-ˌdī-\ [NL] : a method of procedure

¹**mo·gul** \'mō-gəl, mō-'gəl\ *n* [fr. *Mogul*, member of a Muslim dynasty ruling northern India] : an important person : MAGNATE

²**mogul** \'mō-gəl\ *n* : a bump in a ski run

mo·hair \'mō-ˌhar\ *n* [modif. of obs. It *mocaiarro*, fr. Ar *mukhayyar*, lit., choice] : a fabric or yarn made wholly or in part from the long silky hair of the Angora goat; *also* : this goat hair

Mo·ham·med·an *var of* MUHAMMADAN

Mo·hawk \'mō-ˌhȯk\ *n, pl* **Mohawk** *or* **Mohawks** : a member of an American Indian people of the Mohawk River valley, New York; *also* : the language of the Mohawk people

Mo·he·gan \mō-'hē-gən, mə-\ *or* **Mo·hi·can** \-'hē-kən\ *n, pl* **Mohegan** *or* **Mohegans** *or* **Mohican** *or* **Mohicans** : a member of an American Indian people of southeastern Connecticut

Mo·hi·can \mō-'hē-kən, mə-\ *var of* MAHICAN

moi·e·ty \'mȯi-ə-tē\ *n, pl* **-ties** : one of two equal or approximately equal parts

moil \'mȯil\ *vb* : to work hard : DRUDGE — **moil** *n* — **moil·er** *n*

moi·ré \mȯ-'rā, mwä-\ *or* **moire** *same or* 'mȯir, 'mwär\ *n* : a fabric (as silk) having a watered appearance

moist \'mȯist\ *adj* : slightly or moderately wet — **moist·ly** *adv* — **moist·ness** *n*

moist·en \'mȯis-ᵊn\ *vb* : to make or become moist — **moist·en·er** *n*

mois·ture \'mȯis-chər\ *n* : the small amount of liquid that causes dampness

mois·tur·ize \'mȯis-chə-ˌrīz\ *vb* **-ized; -iz·ing** : to add moisture to — **mois·tur·iz·er** *n*

mol *abbr* molecular; molecule

mo·lar \'mō-lər\ *n* [ME *molares*, pl., fr. L *molaris*, fr. *molaris* of a mill, fr. *mola* millstone] : any of the broad teeth adapted to grinding food and located in the back of the jaw — **molar** *adj*

mo·las·ses \mə-'la-səz\ *n* : the thick brown syrup that is separated from raw sugar in sugar manufacture

¹mold \'mōld\ *n* : crumbly soil rich in organic matter

²mold *n* 1 : distinctive nature or character 2 : the frame on or around which something is constructed 3 : a cavity in which something is shaped; *also* : an object so shaped 4 : MOLDING

³mold *vb* 1 : to shape in or as if in a mold 2 : to ornament with molding — **mold·er** *n*

⁴mold *n* : a surface growth of fungus esp. on damp or decaying matter; *also* : a fungus that forms molds — **mold·i·ness** \'mōl-dē-nəs\ *n* — **moldy** *adj*

⁵mold *vb* : to become moldy

mold·board \'mōld-ˌbȯrd\ *n* : a curved iron plate attached above the plowshare to lift and turn the soil

mold·er \'mōl-dər\ *vb* : to crumble into small pieces

mold·ing \'mōl-diŋ\ *n* 1 : an act or process of shaping in a mold; *also* : an object so shaped 2 : a decorative surface, plane, or curved strip

¹mole \'mōl\ *n* : a small often pigmented spot or protuberance on the skin

²mole *n* : any of numerous small burrowing insect-eating mammals related to the shrews and hedgehogs

³mole *n* : a massive breakwater or jetty

molecular biology *n* : a branch of biology dealing with the ultimate physical and chemical organization of living matter and esp. with the molecular basis of inheritance and protein synthesis — **molecular biologist** *n*

molecular weight *n* : the mass of a molecule that is equal to the sum of the masses of all atoms contained in the molecule's formula

mol·e·cule \'mä-li-ˌkyül\ *n* : the smallest particle of matter that is the same chemically as the whole mass — **mo·lec·u·lar** \mə-'le-kyə-lər\ *adj*

mole·hill \'mōl-ˌhil\ *n* : a little ridge of earth thrown up by a mole

mole·skin \-ˌskin\ *n* 1 : the skin of the mole used as fur 2 : a heavy durable cotton fabric

mo·lest \mə-'lest\ *vb* 1 : ANNOY, DISTURB 2 : to make annoying sexual advances to; *esp* : to force physical and usu. sexual contact on — **mo·les·ta·tion** \ˌmō-ˌles-'tā-shən\ *n* — **mo·lest·er** *n*

moll \'mäl\ *n* : a gangster's girlfriend

mol·li·fy \'mä-lə-ˌfī\ *vb* **-fied; -fy·ing** 1 : to soothe in temper : APPEASE 2 : SOFTEN 3 : to reduce in intensity : ASSUAGE — **mol·li·fi·ca·tion** \ˌmä-lə-fə-'kā-shən\ *n*

mol·lusk *or* **mol·lusc** \'mä-ləsk\ *n* : any of a large phylum of usu. shelled and aquatic invertebrate animals

(as snails, clams, and squids) — **mol·lus·can** *also* **mol·lus·kan** \mə-'ləs-kən\ *adj*

¹mol·ly·cod·dle \'mä-lē-ˌkäd-ᵊl\ *n* : a pampered man or boy

²mollycoddle *vb* **mol·ly·cod·dled; mol·ly·cod·dling** : PAMPER

Mo·lo·tov cocktail \'mä-lə-ˌtȯf-, 'mȯ-\ *n* [Vyacheslav M. *Molotov* + 1986 Soviet foreign minister] : a crude bomb made of a bottle filled usu. with gasoline and fitted with a wick (as a saturated rag) that is ignited just prior to hurling

¹molt \'mōlt\ *vb* : to shed hair, feathers, outer skin, or horns periodically with the cast-off parts being replaced by new growth — **molt·er** *n*

²molt *n* : the act or process of molting

mol·ten \'mōlt-ᵊn\ *adj* 1 : fused or liquefied by heat 2 : GLOWING

mo·ly \'mō-lē\ *n* : a mythical herb with black root, white flowers, and magic powers

mo·lyb·de·num \mə-'lib-də-nəm\ *n* : a metallic chemical element used in strengthening and hardening steel — see ELEMENT table

mom \'mäm, 'məm\ *n* : MOTHER

mom—and—pop *adj* : being a small owner-operated business

mo·ment \'mō-mənt\ *n* 1 : a minute portion of time : INSTANT 2 : a time of excellence ⟨he has his ∼s⟩ 3 : IMPORTANCE **syn** consequence, significance, weight, import

mo·men·tari·ly \ˌmō-mən-'ter-ə-lē\ *adv* 1 : for a moment 2 *archaic* : INSTANTLY 3 : at any moment : SOON

mo·men·tary \'mō-mən-ˌter-ē\ *adj* 1 : continuing only a moment; *also* : EPHEMERAL 2 : recurring at every moment — **mo·men·tar·i·ness** \-ˌter-ē-nəs\ *n*

mo·men·tous \mō-'men-təs\ *adj* : very important — **mo·men·tous·ly** *adv* — **mo·men·tous·ness** *n*

mo·men·tum \mō-'men-təm\ *n, pl* **mo·men·ta** \-'men-tə\ *or* **momentums** : a property that a moving body has due to its mass and motion; *also* : IMPETUS

mom·my \'mä-mē, 'mə-\ *n, pl* **mom·mies** : MOTHER

Mon *abbr* Monday

mon·arch \'mä-nərk, -ˌnärk\ *n* 1 : a person who reigns over a kingdom or an empire 2 : one holding preeminent position or power 3 : MONARCH BUTTERFLY — **mo·nar·chi·cal** \mə-'när-ki-kəl\ *also* **mo·nar·chic** \-'när-kik\ *adj*

monarch butterfly *n* : a large orange and black migratory American butterfly whose larva feeds on milkweed

monarch butterfly

mon·ar·chist \'mä-nər-kist\ *n* : a believer in monarchical government — **mon·ar·chism** \-ˌki-zəm\ *n*

mon·ar·chy \'mä-nər-kē\ *n, pl* **-chies** : a nation or state governed by a monarch

mon·as·tery \'mä-nə-ˌster-ē\ *n, pl* **-ter·ies** : a house for persons under religious vows (as monks)

mo·nas·tic \mə-'nas-tik\ *adj* : of or relating to monasteries or to monks or nuns — **monastic** *n* — **mo·nas·ti·cal·ly** \-ti-k(ə-)lē\ *adv* — **mo·nas·ti·cism** \-tə-ˌsi-zəm\ *n*

mon·au·ral \mä-'nȯr-əl\ *adj* : MONOPHONIC — **mon·au·ral·ly** *adv*

Mon·day \ˈmən-dē, -ˌdā\ *n* : the second day of the week

mon·e·tary \ˈmä-nə-ˌter-ē, ˈmə-\ *adj* : of or relating to money or to the mechanisms by which it is supplied and circulated in the economy

mon·ey \ˈmə-nē\ *n, pl* **moneys** *or* **mon·ies** \ˈmə-nēz\ **1** : something (as metal currency) accepted as a medium of exchange **2** : wealth reckoned in monetary terms **3** : the 1st, 2d, and 3d places in a horse or dog race

MONEY

NAME	SUBDIVISIONS	COUNTRY
afghani	100 puls	Afghanistan
baht *or* tical	100 satang	Thailand
balboa	100 centesimos	Panama
birr	100 cents	Ethiopia
bolivar	100 centimos	Venezuela
boliviano	100 centavos	Bolivia
cedi	100 pesewas	Ghana
colón	100 centimos	Costa Rica
colón	100 centavos	El Salvador
cordoba	100 centavos	Nicaragua
cruzeiro	100 centavos	Brazil
dalasi	100 bututs	Gambia
deutsche mark	100 pfennig	Germany
dinar	100 centimes	Algeria
dinar	1000 fils	Bahrain
dinar	1000 fils	Iraq
dinar	1000 fils	Jordan
dinar	1000 fils	Kuwait
dinar	1000 dirhams	Libya
dinar	1000 millimes	Tunisia
dinar₁	1000 fils	Yemen
dinar	100 paras	Yugoslavia
dirham	100 centimes	Morocco
dirham	100 fils	United Arab Emirates
dobra	100 centimos	Sao Tome and Principe
dollar₂	100 cents	Antigua and Barbuda, Dominica, Grenada, St. Kitts-Nevis, St. Lucia, St. Vincent and the Grenadines
dollar	100 cents	Australia
dollar	100 cents	Bahamas
dollar	100 cents	Barbados
dollar	100 cents	Belize
dollar	100 cents	Bermuda
dollar	100 sen *or* cents	Brunei
dollar	100 cents	Canada
dollar *or* yuan	100 cents	China (Taiwan)
dollar	100 cents	Fiji
dollar	100 cents	Guyana
dollar	100 cents	Hong Kong
dollar	100 cents	Jamaica
dollar	100 cents	Liberia
dollar	100 cents	New Zealand
dollar	100 cents	Singapore
dollar	100 cents	Trinidad and Tobago
dollar	100 cents	United States
dollar	100 cents	Zimbabwe
dollar—see RINGGIT, below		
dong	100 xu	Vietnam
drachma	100 lepta	Greece
escudo	100 centavos	Cape Verde
escudo	100 centavos	Portugal
escudo—see PESO, below		
florin—see GULDEN, below		
forint	100 filler	Hungary

NAME	SUBDIVISIONS	COUNTRY
franc	100 centimes	Belgium
franc₃	100 centimes	Benin, Burkina Faso, Cameroon, Central African Republic, Chad, Congo, Equatorial Guinea, Gabon, Ivory Coast, Mali, Niger, Senegal, Togo
franc	100 centimes	Burundi
franc	100 centimes	Djibouti
franc	100 centimes	France
franc	100 centimes	Guinea
franc	100 centimes	Luxembourg
franc	100 centimes	Madagascar
franc	100 centimes	Rwanda
franc	100 centimes *or* rappen	Switzerland
gourde	100 centimes	Haiti
guarani	100 centimos	Paraguay
gulden *or* guilder *or* florin	100 cents	Netherlands
gulden *or* guilder *or* florin	100 cents	Suriname
kina	100 toea	Papua New Guinea
kip	100 at	Laos
koruna	100 haleru	Czech Republic
krona	100 aurar (*sing* eyrir)	Iceland
krona	100 ore	Sweden
krone	100 ore	Denmark
krone	100 ore	Norway
kwacha	100 tambala	Malawi
kwacha	100 ngwee	Zambia
kwanza	100 lwei	Angola
kyat	100 pyas	Myanmar
lek	100 qindarka	Albania
lempira	100 centavos	Honduras
leone	100 cents	Sierra Leone
leu	100 bani	Romania
lev	100 stotinki	Bulgaria
lilangeni	100 cents	Swaziland
(*pl* emalangeni)		
lira	100 centesimi₄	Italy
lira *or* pound	100 cents	Malta
lira	100 kurus	Turkey
livre—see POUND, below		
loti (*pl* maloti)	100 licente *or* lisente (*sing* sente)	Lesotho
mark—see DEUTSCHE MARK, above		
markka	100 pennia	Finland
metical	100 centavos	Mozambique
naira	100 kobo	Nigeria
ngultrum	100 chetrums	Bhutan
ouguiya	5 khoums	Mauritania
pa'anga	100 seniti	Tonga
pataca	100 avos	Macao
peseta	100 centimos	Spain
peso		Argentina
peso	100 centavos	Chile
peso	100 centavos	Colombia
peso	100 centavos	Cuba
peso	100 centavos	Dominican Republic
peso *or* escudo	100 centavos	Guinea-Bissau
peso	100 centavos	Mexico
peso *or* piso	100 sentimos *or* centavos	Philippines
peso	100 centesimos	Uruguay
pound	100 cents	Cyprus
pound	100 piastres	Egypt

NAME	SUBDIVISIONS	COUNTRY
pound	100 pence	Ireland
pound *or* livre	100 piastres	Lebanon
pound	100 piastres	Sudan
pound	100 piastres	Syria
pound	100 pence	United Kingdom
pound—see LIRA, above		
pula	100 thebe	Botswana
quetzal	100 centavos	Guatemala
rand	100 cents	South Africa
rial	100 dinars	Iran
rial	1000 baiza	Oman
rial¹	100 fils	Yemen
riel	100 sen	Cambodia
ringgit *or* dollar	100 sen	Malaysia
riyal	100 dirhams	Qatar
riyal	100 halala	Saudi Arabia
ruble	100 kopecks	Russia
rupee	100 paise	India
rupee	100 cents	Mauritius
rupee	100 paisa	Nepal
rupee	100 paisa	Pakistan
rupee	100 cents	Seychelles
rupee	100 cents	Sri Lanka
rupiah	100 sen	Indonesia
schilling	100 groschen	Austria
shekel *or* sheqel	100 agorot	Israel
shilling	100 cents	Kenya
shilling	100 cents	Somalia
shilling	100 cents	Tanzania
shilling	100 cents	Uganda
sol	100 centavos	Peru
sucre	100 centavos	Ecuador
taka	100 paisa *or* poisha	Bangladesh
tala	100 sene	Western Samoa
tical—see BAHT, above		
tugrik	100 mongo	Mongolia
won	100 chon	North Korea
won	100 chon	South Korea
yen	100 sen⁴	Japan
yuan	100 fen	China (mainland)
yuan—see DOLLAR, above		
zaire	100 makuta (*sing* likuta)	Zaire
zloty	100 groszy	Poland

1 The currencies of the formerly separate countries of Southern
 Yemen and the Yemen Arab Republic are both legal in unified
 Yemen.
2 Dollars issued by the Eastern Caribbean Central Bank, established to promote economic cooperation among the member
 nations.
3 Francs issued by the African Financial Community, established to promote economic cooperation among the member
 nations.
4 No longer minted; a subdivision in name only.

mon·eyed \'mə-nēd\ *adj* 1 : having money : WEALTHY
2 : consisting in or derived from money
mon·ey·lend·er \'mə-nē-ˌlen-dər\ *n* : one (as a bank or
pawnbroker) whose business is lending money
money market *n* : the trade in short-term negotiable
financial instruments
money of account : a denominator of value or basis of
exchange used in keeping accounts
money order *n* : an order purchased at a post office,
bank, or telegraph office directing another office to
pay a sum of money to a party named on it
mon·ger \'məŋ-gər, 'mäŋ-\ *n* 1 : DEALER 2 : one who
tries to stir up or spread something
mon·go \'mäŋ-(ˌ)gō\ *n, pl* mongo — see *tugrik* at MON-
EY table
Mon·gol \'mäŋ-gəl, 'män-ˌgōl\ *n* : a member of any of

several traditionally pastoral peoples of Mongolia —
Mongol *adj*
Mon·go·lian \män-'gōl-yən, mäŋ-, -'gō-lē-ən\ *n* 1 : a
native or inhabitant of Mongolia 2 : a member of the
Mongoloid racial stock — **Mongolian** *adj*
mon·gol·ism \'mäŋ-gə-ˌli-zəm\ *n* : DOWN'S SYNDROME
Mon·gol·oid \'mäŋ-gə-ˌlóid\ *adj* 1 : of or relating to a
major racial stock native to Asia that includes peoples of northern and eastern Asia, Malaysians, Eskimos, and often American Indians 2 *often not cap* : of,
relating to, or affected with Down's syndrome —
Mongoloid *n*
mon·goose \'män-ˌgüs, 'mäŋ-\ *n, pl* **mon·goos·es** *also*
mon·geese \-ˌgēs\ : any of a group of small agile Old
World mammals that are related to the civet cats and
feed on small animals and fruits
mon·grel \'mäŋ-grəl, 'məŋ-\ *n* : an offspring of parents
of different breeds; *esp* : one of uncertain ancestry
mo·nism \'mō-ˌni-zəm, 'mä-\ *n* : a view that reality is
basically one unitary organic whole — **mo·nist** \'mō-
nist, 'mä-\ *n*
mo·ni·tion \mō-'ni-shən, mə-\ *n* : WARNING, CAUTION
¹**mon·i·tor** \'mä-nə-tər\ *n* 1 : a student appointed to assist a teacher 2 : one that monitors; *esp* : a video display screen (as for a computer)
²**monitor** *vb* : to watch, check, or observe for a special
purpose
mon·i·to·ry \'mä-nə-ˌtōr-ē\ *adj* : giving admonition
: WARNING
¹**monk** \'məŋk\ *n* [ME, fr. OE *munuc*, fr. LL *mona-
chus*, fr. LGk *monachos*, fr. Gk, adj., single, fr.
monos single, alone] : a man belonging to a religious
order and living in a monastery — **monk·ish** *adj*
²**monk** *n* : MONKEY
¹**mon·key** \'məŋ-kē\ *n, pl* **monkeys** : a nonhuman primate mammal; *esp* : one of the smaller, longer=
tailed, and usu. more arboreal primates as contrasted
with the apes
²**monkey** *vb* **mon·keyed; mon·key·ing** 1 : FOOL, TRIFLE
2 : TAMPER
monkey bars *n pl* : a framework of bars on which children can play
mon·key·shine \'mən-kē-ˌshīn\ *n* : PRANK — usu. used
in pl.
monkey wrench *n* : a wrench with one fixed and one
adjustable jaw at right angles to a handle
monks·hood \'məŋks-ˌhùd\ *n* : any of a genus of poisonous plants related to the buttercups; *esp* : a tall
Old World plant with usu. purplish flowers
¹**mono** \'mä-nō\ *adj* : MONOPHONIC
²**mono** *n* : INFECTIOUS MONONUCLEOSIS
mono·chro·mat·ic \ˌmä-nə-krō-'ma-tik\ *adj* 1 : having
or consisting of one color 2 : consisting of radiation
(as light) of a single wavelength
mono·chrome \'mä-nə-ˌkrōm\ *adj* : involving or producing visual images in a single color or in varying
tones of a single color ⟨~ television⟩
mon·o·cle \'mä-ni-kəl\ *n* : an eyeglass for one eye
mono·clo·nal \ˌmä-nə-'klō-nəl\ *adj* : produced by, being, or composed of cells derived from a single cell
⟨~ antibodies⟩
mono·cot·y·le·don \ˌmä-nə-ˌkät-ºl-'ēd-ºn\ *n* : any of a
class or subclass of chiefly herbaceous seed plants
having an embryo with a single cotyledon and usu.
parallel-veined leaves
mon·o·dy \'mä-nə-dē\ *n, pl* **-dies** : ELEGY, DIRGE — **mo-
nod·ic** \mə-'nä-dik\ *or* **mo·nod·i·cal** \-di-kəl\ *adj* —
mon·o·dist \'mä-nə-dist\ *n*
mo·nog·a·my \mə-'nä-gə-mē\ *n* 1 : marriage with but
one person at a time 2 : the practice of having a single
mate during a period of time — **mo·nog·a·mist** \-mist\
n — **mo·nog·a·mous** \-məs\ *adj*
mono·gram \'mä-nə-ˌgram\ *n* : a sign of identity composed of the combined initials of a name — **monogram** *vb*

mono•graph \'mä-nə-ˌgraf\ *n* : a learned treatise on a small area of learning

mono•lin•gual \ˌmä-nə-'liŋ-gwəl\ *adj* : knowing or using only one language

mono•lith \'män-əl-ˌith\ *n* **1** : a single great stone often in the form of a monument or column **2** : something large and powerful that acts as a single unified force — **mono•lith•ic** \ˌmän-əl-'i-thik\ *adj*

mono•logue *also* **mono•log** \'män-əl-ˌóg\ *n* **1** : a dramatic soliloquy; *also* : a long speech monopolizing conversation **2** : the routine of a stand-up comic — **mono•logu•ist** \-ˌóg-ist\ *or* **mo•no•lo•gist** \mə-'nä-lə-jist; 'män-əl-ˌō-gist\ *n*

mono•ma•nia \ˌmä-nə-'mā-nē-ə, -nyə\ *n* **1** : mental disorder limited in expression to one area of thought **2** : excessive concentration on a single object or idea — **mono•ma•ni•ac** \-nē-ˌak\ *n or adj*

mono•mer \'mä-nə-mər\ *n* : a simple chemical compound that can be polymerized

mono•nu•cle•o•sis \ˌmä-nō-ˌnü-klē-'ō-səs, -ˌnyü-\ *n* : INFECTIOUS MONONUCLEOSIS

mono•phon•ic \ˌmä-nə-'fä-nik\ *adj* : of or relating to sound recording or reproduction involving a single transmission path

mono•plane \'mä-nə-ˌplān\ *n* : an airplane with only one set of wings

mo•nop•o•ly \mə-'nä-pə-lē\ *n, pl* **-lies** [L *monopolium*, fr. Gk *monopōlion*, fr. *monos* alone, single + *pōlein* to sell] **1** : exclusive ownership (as through command of supply) **2** : a commodity controlled by one party **3** : one that has a monopoly — **mo•nop•o•list** \-list\ *n* — **mo•nop•o•lis•tic** \mə-ˌnä-pə-'lis-tik\ *adj* — **mo•nop•o•li•za•tion** \-lə-'zā-shən\ *n* — **mo•nop•o•lize** \mə-'nä-pə-ˌlīz\ *vb*

mono•rail \'mä-nə-ˌrāl\ *n* : a single rail serving as a track for a vehicle; *also* : a vehicle traveling on such a track

mono•so•di•um glu•ta•mate \ˌmä-nə-ˌsō-dē-əm-'glü-tə-ˌmāt\ *n* : a crystalline salt used to enhance the flavor of food

mono•syl•la•ble \'mä-nə-ˌsi-lə-bəl\ *n* : a word of one syllable — **mono•syl•lab•ic** \ˌmä-nə-sə-'la-bik\ *adj* — **mono•syl•lab•i•cal•ly** \-bi-k(ə-)lē\ *adv*

mono•the•ism \'mä-nə-(ˌ)thē-ˌi-zəm\ *n* : a doctrine or belief that there is only one deity — **mono•the•ist** \-ˌthē-ist\ *n* — **mono•the•is•tic** \-ˌthē-'is-tik\ *adj*

mono•tone \'mä-nə-ˌtōn\ *n* : a succession of syllables, words, or sentences in one unvaried key or pitch

mo•not•o•nous \mə-'nät-ᵊn-əs\ *adj* **1** : uttered or sounded in one unvarying tone **2** : tediously uniform — **mo•not•o•nous•ly** *adv* — **mo•not•o•nous•ness** *n*

mo•not•o•ny \mə-'nät-ᵊn-ē\ *n* : tedious sameness or uniformity

mono•un•sat•u•rat•ed \ˌmä-nō-ˌən-'sa-chə-ˌrā-təd\ *adj* : containing one double or triple bond per molecule — used esp. of an oil or fatty acid

mon•ox•ide \mə-'näk-ˌsīd\ *n* : an oxide containing one atom of oxygen in a molecule

mon•sei•gneur \ˌmōⁿ-ˌsān-'yər\ *n, pl* **mes•sei•gneurs** \ˌmā-ˌsān-'yər, -'yərz\ : a French dignitary — used as a title

mon•sieur \məs-'yər, mə-'shər, *Fr* mə-'syœ̄\ *n, pl* **mes•sieurs** *same or* -'yərz, -'shərz\ : a Frenchman of high rank or station — used as a title equivalent to *Mister*

mon•si•gnor \män-'sē-nyər\ *n, pl* **monsignors** *or* **mon•si•gno•ri** \ˌmän-ˌsēn-'yōr-ē\ [It *monsignore*] : a Roman Catholic prelate — used as a title

mon•soon \män-'sün\ *n* [obs. Dutch *monssoen*, fr. Pg *monção*, fr. Ar *mawsim* time, season] **1** : a periodic wind esp. in the Indian Ocean and southern Asia **2** : the season of the southwest monsoon esp. in India **3** : rainfall associated with the monsoon

¹mon•ster \'män-stər\ *n* **1** : an abnormally developed plant or animal **2** : an animal of strange or terrifying shape; *also* : one unusually large of its kind **3** : an ex-

tremely ugly, wicked, or cruel person — **mon•stros•i•ty** \män-'strä-sə-tē\ *n* — **mon•strous** \'män-strəs\ *adj* — **mon•strous•ly** *adv*

²monster *adj* : very large : ENORMOUS

mon•strance \'män-strəns\ *n* : a vessel in which the consecrated Host is exposed for the adoration of the faithful

Mont *abbr* Montana

mon•tage \män-'täzh\ *n* [F] **1** : a composite photograph made by combining several separate pictures **2** : an artistic composition made up of several different kinds of elements **3** : a varied mixture : JUMBLE

month \'mənth\ *n, pl* **months** \'məns, 'mənths\ : one of the 12 parts into which the year is divided — **month•ly** *adv or adj or n*

month•long \'mənth-ˌlóŋ\ *adj* : lasting a month

mon•u•ment \'män-yə-mənt\ *n* **1** : a lasting reminder; *esp* : a structure erected in remembrance of a person or event **2** : NATIONAL MONUMENT

mon•u•men•tal \ˌmän-yə-'ment-ᵊl\ *adj* **1** : of or relating to a monument **2** : MASSIVE; *also* : OUTSTANDING **3** : very great — **mon•u•men•tal•ly** *adv*

moo \'mü\ *vb* : to make the natural throat noise of a cow — **moo** *n*

¹mood \'müd\ *n* **1** : a conscious state of mind or predominant emotion : FEELING **2** : a prevailing attitude : DISPOSITION **3** : a distinctive atmosphere

²mood *n* : distinction of form of a verb to express whether its action or state is conceived as fact or in some other manner (as wish)

moody \'mü-dē\ *adj* **mood•i•er; -est 1** : GLOOMY **2** : subject to moods : TEMPERAMENTAL — **mood•i•ly** \-də-lē\ *adv* — **mood•i•ness** \-dē-nəs\ *n*

¹moon \'mün\ *n* **1** : the earth's natural satellite **2** : SATELLITE 2

²moon *vb* : to engage in idle reverie

moon•beam \'mün-ˌbēm\ *n* : a ray of light from the moon

¹moon•light \-ˌlīt\ *n* : the light of the moon — **moon•lit** \-ˌlit\ *adj*

²moonlight *vb* **moon•light•ed; moon•light•ing** : to hold a second job in addition to a regular one — **moon•light•er** *n*

moon•scape \-ˌskāp\ *n* : the surface of the moon as seen or as pictured

moon•shine \-ˌshīn\ *n* **1** : MOONLIGHT **2** : empty talk **3** : intoxicating liquor usu. illegally distilled

moon•stone \-ˌstōn\ *n* : a transparent or translucent feldspar of pearly luster used as a gem

moon•struck \-ˌstrək\ *adj* **1** : mentally unbalanced **2** : romantically sentimental **3** : lost in fantasy

¹moor \'mùr\ *n* **1** *chiefly Brit* : an expanse of open rolling infertile land **2** : a boggy area; *esp* : one that is peaty and dominated by grasses and sedges

²moor *vb* : to make fast with or as if with cables, lines, or anchors

Moor \'mùr\ *n* : one of the Arab and Berber conquerors of Spain — **Moor•ish** *adj*

moor•ing \'mùr-iŋ\ *n* **1** : a place where or an object to which a craft can be made fast **2** : an established practice or stabilizing influence — usu. used in pl.

moor•land \-lənd, -ˌland\ *n* : land consisting of moors

moose \'müs\ *n, pl* **moose** : a large heavy-antlered ruminant mammal of the deer family with humped shoulders and long legs that inhabits northern New and Old World forested areas

¹moot \'müt\ *vb* : to bring up for discussion; *also* : DEBATE

²moot *adj* **1** : open to question; *also* : DISPUTED **2** : having no practical significance

¹mop \'mäp\ *n* : an implement made of absorbent material fastened to a handle and used esp. for cleaning floors

²mop *vb* **mopped; mop•ping** : to use a mop on : clean with a mop

mope \ˈmōp\ vb **moped; mop·ing 1** : to become dull, dejected, or listless **2** : DAWDLE

mo·ped \ˈmō-ˌped\ n : a light low-powered motorbike that can be pedaled

mop·pet \ˈmä-pət\ n [obs. E *mop* fool, child] : CHILD

mo·raine \mə-ˈrān\ n : an accumulation of earth and stones left by a glacier

¹mor·al \ˈmȯr-əl\ adj **1** : of or relating to principles of right and wrong **2** : conforming to a standard of right behavior; *also* : capable of right and wrong action **3** : probable but not proved ⟨a ∼ certainty⟩ **4** : having the effects of such on the mind, confidence, or will ⟨a ∼ victory⟩ syn virtuous, righteous, noble, ethical, principled — **mor·al·ly** adv

²moral n **1** : the practical meaning (as of a story) **2** pl : moral practices or teachings

mo·rale \mə-ˈral\ n **1** : MORALITY **2** : the mental and emotional attitudes of an individual to the tasks at hand; *also* : ESPRIT DE CORPS

mor·al·ist \ˈmȯr-ə-list\ n **1** : one who leads a moral life **2** : a thinker or writer concerned with morals **3** : one concerned with regulating the morals of others — **mor·al·is·tic** \ˌmȯr-ə-ˈlis-tik\ adj — **mor·al·is·ti·cal·ly** \-ti-k(ə-)lē\ adv

mo·ral·i·ty \mə-ˈra-lə-tē\ n, pl **-ties** : moral conduct : VIRTUE

mor·al·ize \ˈmȯr-ə-ˌlīz\ vb **-ized; -iz·ing** : to make moral reflections — **mor·al·i·za·tion** \ˌmȯr-ə-lə-ˈzā-shən\ n — **mor·al·iz·er** \ˈmȯr-ə-ˌlī-zər\ n

mo·rass \mə-ˈras\ n : SWAMP; *also* : something that entangles, impedes, or confuses

mor·a·to·ri·um \ˌmȯr-ə-ˈtȯr-ē-əm\ n, pl **-ri·ums** or **-ria** \-ē-ə\ [ultim. fr. L *mora* delay] : a suspension of activity

mo·ray \mə-ˈrā, ˈmȯr-ˌā\ n : any of numerous often brightly colored biting eels of warm seas

mor·bid \ˈmȯr-bəd\ adj **1** : of, relating to, or typical of disease; *also* : DISEASED, SICKLY **2** : characterized by gloomy or unwholesome ideas or feelings **3** : GRISLY, GRUESOME ⟨∼ details⟩ — **mor·bid·i·ty** \mȯr-ˈbi-də-tē\ n — **mor·bid·ly** adv — **mor·bid·ness** n

mor·dant \ˈmȯrd-ənt\ adj **1** : biting or caustic in manner or style **2** : BURNING, PUNGENT — **mor·dant·ly** adv

¹more \ˈmȯr\ adj **1** : GREATER **2** : ADDITIONAL

²more adv **1** : in addition **2** : to a greater or higher degree

³more n **1** : a greater quantity, number, or amount ⟨the ∼ the merrier⟩ **2** : an additional amount ⟨costs a little ∼⟩

⁴more pron : additional persons or things or a greater amount

mo·rel \mə-ˈrel\ n : any of several pitted edible fungi

more·over \mȯr-ˈō-vər\ adv : in addition : FURTHER

mo·res \ˈmȯr-ˌāz\ n pl [L, pl. of *mor-, mos* custom] **1** : the fixed morally binding customs of a group **2** : HABITS, MANNERS

Mor·gan \ˈmȯr-gən\ n : any of an American breed of lightly built horses

morgue \ˈmȯrg\ n : a place where the bodies of dead persons are kept until released for burial

mor·i·bund \ˈmȯr-ə-(ˌ)bənd\ adj : being in a dying condition

Mor·mon \ˈmȯr-mən\ n : a member of the Church of Jesus Christ of Latter-day Saints — **Mor·mon·ism** \-mə-ˌni-zəm\ n

morn \ˈmȯrn\ n : MORNING

morn·ing \ˈmȯr-niŋ\ n **1** : the early part of the day; *esp* : the time from the sunrise to noon **2** : BEGINNING

morning glory n : any of various twining plants related to the sweet potato that have often showy bell-shaped or funnel-shaped flowers

morning sickness n : nausea and vomiting that occur in the morning esp. during early pregnancy

morning star n : a bright planet (as Venus) seen in the eastern sky before or at sunrise

Mo·roc·can \mə-ˈrä-kən\ n : a native or inhabitant of Morocco

mo·roc·co \mə-ˈrä-kō\ n : a fine leather made of goatskins tanned with sumac

mo·ron \ˈmȯr-ˌän\ n **1** : a mentally retarded person having a potential mental age of between 8 and 12 years and capable of doing routine work under supervision **2** : a very stupid person — **mo·ron·ic** \mə-ˈrä-nik\ adj — **mo·ron·i·cal·ly** \-ni-k(ə-)lē\ adv

mo·rose \mə-ˈrōs\ adj [L *morosus* hard to please, exacting, fr. *mor-, mos* custom, disposition] : having a sullen disposition; *also* : GLOOMY — **mo·rose·ly** adv — **mo·rose·ness** n

mor·pheme \ˈmȯr-ˌfēm\ n : a meaningful linguistic unit that contains no smaller meaningful parts — **mor·phe·mic** \mȯr-ˈfē-mik\ adj

mor·phia \ˈmȯr-fē-ə\ n : MORPHINE

mor·phine \ˈmȯr-ˌfēn\ n [F, fr. Gk *Morpheus*, Greek god of dreams] : an addictive drug obtained from opium and used to ease pain or induce sleep

mor·phol·o·gy \mȯr-ˈfä-lə-jē\ n **1** : a branch of biology dealing with the form and structure of organisms **2** : a study and description of word formation in a language — **mor·pho·log·i·cal** \ˌmȯr-fə-ˈlä-ji-kəl\ adj — **mor·phol·o·gist** \mȯr-ˈfä-lə-jist\ n

mor·ris \ˈmȯr-əs\ n : a vigorous English dance traditionally performed by men wearing costumes and bells

mor·row \ˈmär-ō\ n : the next day

Morse code \ˈmȯrs-\ n : either of two codes consisting of dots and dashes or long and short sounds used for transmitting messages

mor·sel \ˈmȯr-səl\ n [ME, fr. OF, dim. of *mors* bite, fr. L *morsus*, fr. *mordēre* to bite] **1** : a small piece or quantity **2** : a tasty dish

mor·tal \ˈmȯrt-əl\ adj **1** : causing death : FATAL; *also* : leading to eternal punishment ⟨∼ sin⟩ **2** : subject to death ⟨∼ man⟩ **3** : implacably hostile ⟨∼ foe⟩ **4** : very great : EXTREME ⟨∼ fear⟩ **5** : HUMAN ⟨∼ limitations⟩ — **mortal** n — **mor·tal·i·ty** \mȯr-ˈta-lə-tē\ n — **mor·tal·ly** \ˈmȯrt-əl-ē\ adv

¹mor·tar \ˈmȯr-tər\ n **1** : a strong bowl in which substances are pounded or crushed with a pestle **2** : a short-barreled cannon used to fire shells at high angles

²mortar n : a building material (as a mixture of lime and cement with sand and water) that is spread between bricks or stones to bind them together as it hardens — **mortar** vb

mor·tar·board \ˈmȯr-tər-ˌbȯrd\ n **1** : a square board for holding mortar **2** : an academic cap with a flat square top

mort·gage \ˈmȯr-gij\ n [ME *morgage*, fr. MF, fr. OF, fr. *mort* dead + *gage* gage] : a transfer of rights to a piece of property usu. as security for the payment of a loan or debt that becomes void when the debt is paid — **mortgage** vb — **mort·gag·ee** \ˌmȯr-gi-ˈjē\ n — **mort·gag·or** \ˌmȯr-gi-ˈjȯr\ n

mor·ti·cian \mȯr-ˈti-shən\ n [L *mort-, mors* death + E *-ician* (as in *physician*)] : UNDERTAKER

mor·ti·fy \ˈmȯr-tə-ˌfī\ vb **-fied; -fy·ing 1** : to subdue (as the body) esp. by abstinence or self-inflicted pain **2** : HUMILIATE **3** : to become necrotic or gangrenous — **mor·ti·fi·ca·tion** \ˌmȯr-tə-fə-ˈkä-shən\ n

mor·tise also **mor·tice** \ˈmȯr-təs\ n : a hole cut in a piece of wood into which another piece fits to form a joint

mor·tu·ary \ˈmȯr-chə-ˌwer-ē\ n, pl **-ar·ies** : a place in which dead bodies are kept until burial

mos abbr months

mo·sa·ic \mō-ˈzā-ik\ n : a surface decoration made by inlaying small pieces (as of colored glass or stone) to form figures or patterns; *also* : a design made in mosaic — **mosaic** adj

mo·sey \ˈmō-zē\ vb **mo·seyed; mo·sey·ing** : SAUNTER

Mos·lem \ˈmäz-ləm\ var of MUSLIM

mosque \\'mäsk\ *n* : a building used for public worship by Muslims

mos·qui·to \mə-'skē-tō\ *n, pl* **-toes** *also* **-tos** : any of a family of dipteran flies the female of which sucks the blood of animals

mosquito net *n* : a net or screen for keeping out mosquitoes

moss \\'mȯs\ *n* : any of a class of green plants that lack flowers but have small leafy stems and often grow in clumps — **mossy** *adj*

moss·back \\'mȯs-ˌbak\ *n* : an extremely conservative person : FOGY

¹most \\'mōst\ *adj* **1** : GREATEST ⟨the ~ ability⟩ **2** : the majority of ⟨~ people⟩

²most *adv* **1** : to the greatest or highest degree ⟨~ beautiful⟩ **2** : to a very great degree ⟨a ~ careful driver⟩

³most *n* : the greatest amount ⟨the ~ I can do⟩

⁴most *pron* : the greatest number or part ⟨~ became discouraged⟩

-most \ˌmōst\ *adj suffix* : most ⟨inner*most*⟩ : most toward ⟨end*most*⟩

most·ly \\'mōst-lē\ *adv* : MAINLY

mot \\'mō\ *n, pl* **mots** *same or* \'mōz\ [F, word, saying, fr. LL *muttum* grunt] : a witty saying

mote \\'mōt\ *n* : a small particle

mo·tel \mō-'tel\ *n* [blend of *motor* and *hotel*] : a hotel in which the rooms are accessible from the parking area

mo·tet \mō-'tet\ *n* : a choral work on a sacred text for several voices usu. without instrumental accompaniment

moth \\'mȯth\ *n, pl* **moths** \\'mȯthz, 'mȯths\ : any of various insects belonging to the same order as the butterflies but usu. night-flying and with a stouter body and smaller wings

moth·ball \\'mȯth-ˌbȯl\ *n* **1** : a ball (as of naphthalene) used to keep moths out of clothing **2** *pl* : protective storage

¹moth·er \\'mə-thər\ *n* **1** : a female parent **2** : the superior of a religious community of women **3** : SOURCE, ORIGIN — **moth·er·hood** \-ˌhu̇d\ *n* — **moth·er·less** *adj* — **moth·er·li·ness** \-lē-nəs\ *n* — **moth·er·ly** *adj*

²mother *vb* **1** : to give birth to; *also* : PRODUCE **2** : to care for or protect like a mother

moth·er·board \\'mə-thər-ˌbȯrd\ *n* : the main circuit board esp. of a microcomputer

moth·er–in–law \\'mə-thər-ən-ˌlȯ\ *n, pl* **mothers–in–law** \\'mə-thərz-\ : the mother of one's spouse

moth·er·land \\'mə-thər-ˌland\ *n* **1** : the land of origin of something **2** : the native land of one's ancestors

moth·er–of–pearl \ˌmə-thər-əv-'pərl\ *n* : the hard pearly matter forming the inner layer of a mollusk shell

mo·tif \mō-'tēf\ *n* [F, motive, motif] : a dominant idea or central theme (as in a work of art)

mo·tile \\'mōt-əl, 'mō-ˌtīl\ *adj* : capable of spontaneous movement — **mo·til·i·ty** \mō-'ti-lə-tē\ *n*

¹mo·tion \\'mō-shən\ *n* **1** : an act, process, or instance of moving **2** : a proposal for action (as by a deliberative body) **3** *pl* : ACTIVITIES, MOVEMENTS — **mo·tion·less** *adj* — **mo·tion·less·ly** *adv* — **mo·tion·less·ness** *n*

²motion *vb* : to direct or signal by a movement

motion picture *n* : a series of pictures projected on a screen so rapidly that they produce a continuous picture in which persons and objects seem to move

motion sickness *n* : sickness induced by motion and characterized by nausea

mo·ti·vate \\'mō-tə-ˌvāt\ *vb* **-vat·ed; -vat·ing** : to provide with a motive : IMPEL — **mo·ti·va·tion** \ˌmō-tə-'vā-shən\ *n* — **mo·ti·va·tion·al** \-shə-nəl\ *adj* — **mo·ti·va·tor** \'mō-tə-ˌvā-tər\ *n*

¹mo·tive \\'mō-tiv, 2 *also* mō-'tēv\ *n* **1** : something (as a need or desire) that causes a person to act **2** : a recurrent theme in a musical composition **3** : MOTIF — **mo·tive·less** *adj*

²motive \\'mō-tiv\ *adj* **1** : moving to action **2** : of or relating to motion

mot·ley \\'mät-lē\ *adj* **1** : variegated in color **2** : made up of diverse often incongruous elements **syn** heterogeneous, miscellaneous, assorted, mixed, varied

¹mo·tor \\'mō-tər\ *n* **1** : one that imparts motion **2** : a machine that produces motion or power for doing work **3** : AUTOMOBILE

²motor *vb* : to travel or transport by automobile : DRIVE — **mo·tor·ist** *n*

mo·tor·bike \\'mō-tər-ˌbīk\ *n* : a small lightweight motorcycle

mo·tor·boat \-ˌbōt\ *n* : a boat propelled by a motor

mo·tor·cade \-ˌkād\ *n* : a procession of motor vehicles

mo·tor·car \-ˌkär\ *n* : AUTOMOBILE

mo·tor·cy·cle \\'mō-tər-ˌsī-kəl\ *n* : a 2-wheeled automotive vehicle — **mo·tor·cy·clist** \-k(ə-)list\ *n*

motor home *n* : a large motor vehicle equipped as living quarters

motor inn *n* : MOTEL

mo·tor·ize \\'mō-tə-ˌrīz\ *vb* **-ized; -iz·ing** **1** : to equip with a motor **2** : to equip with automobiles

mo·tor·man \\'mō-tər-mən\ *n* : an operator of a motor-driven vehicle (as a streetcar or subway train)

motor scooter *n* : a low 2- or 3-wheeled automotive vehicle resembling a child's scooter but having a seat

mo·tor·truck \\'mō-tər-ˌtrək\ *n* : an automotive truck

motor vehicle *n* : an automotive vehicle (as an automobile) not operated on rails

mot·tle \\'mät-əl\ *vb* **mot·tled; mot·tling** : to mark with spots of different color : BLOTCH

mot·to \\'mä-tō\ *n, pl* **mottoes** *also* **mottos** [It, fr. LL *muttum* grunt, fr. L *muttire* to mutter] **1** : a sentence, phrase, or word inscribed on something to indicate its character or use **2** : a short expression of a guiding rule of conduct

moue \\'mü\ *n* : a little grimace

mould \\'mōld\ *var of* MOLD

moult \\'mōlt\ *var of* MOLT

mound \\'mau̇nd\ *n* **1** : an artificial bank or hill of earth or stones **2** : KNOLL **3** : HEAP, PILE

¹mount \\'mau̇nt\ *n* : a high hill

²mount *vb* **1** : to increase in amount or extent; *also* : RISE, ASCEND **2** : to get up on something; *esp* : to seat oneself on (as a horse) for riding **3** : to put in position ⟨~ artillery⟩ **4** : to set on something that elevates **5** : to attach to a support **6** : to prepare esp. for examination or display — **mount·able** *adj* — **mount·er** *n*

³mount *n* **1** : FRAME, SUPPORT **2** : a means of conveyance; *esp* : SADDLE HORSE

moun·tain \\'mau̇nt-ən\ *n* : a landmass higher than a hill — **moun·tain·ous** \-ən-əs\ *adj* — **moun·tainy** \-ən-ē\ *adj*

mountain ash *n* : any of various trees related to the roses that have pinnate leaves and red or orange-red fruits

moun·tain·eer \ˌmau̇nt-ən-'ir\ *n* **1** : a native or inhabitant of a mountainous region **2** : one who climbs mountains for sport

mountain goat *n* : a ruminant mammal of mountain-

mountain goat

ous northwestern No. America that resembles a goat

mountain laurel *n* : a No. American evergreen shrub or small tree of the heath family with glossy leaves and clusters of rose-colored or white flowers

mountain lion *n* : COUGAR

moun·tain·side \'maùnt-ᵊn-ˌsīd\ *n* : the side of a mountain

moun·tain·top \-ˌtäp\ *n* : the summit of a mountain

moun·te·bank \'maùn-ti-ˌbaŋk\ *n* [It *montimbanco*, fr. *montare* to mount + *in* in, on + *banco, banca* bench] : QUACK, CHARLATAN

Mount·ie \'maùn-tē\ *n* : a member of the Royal Canadian Mounted Police

mount·ing \'maùn-tiŋ\ *n* : something that serves as a frame or support

mourn \'mōrn\ *vb* : to feel or express grief or sorrow — **mourn·er** *n*

mourn·ful \-fəl\ *adj* : expressing, feeling, or causing sorrow — **mourn·ful·ly** *adv* — **mourn·ful·ness** *n*

mourn·ing \'mōr-niŋ\ *n* 1 : an outward sign (as black clothes) of grief for a person's death 2 : a period of time during which signs of grief are shown

mouse \'maùs\ *n, pl* **mice** \'mīs\ 1 : any of numerous small rodents with pointed snout, long body, and slender tail 2 : a small manual device that controls cursor movement on a computer display

mous·er \'maù-sər\ *n* : a cat proficient at catching mice

mouse·trap \'maùs-ˌtrap\ *n* 1 : a trap for catching mice 2 : a stratagem that lures one to defeat or destruction — **mousetrap** *vb*

mousse \'müs\ *n* [F, lit., froth] 1 : a molded chilled dessert made with sweetened and flavored whipped cream or egg whites and gelatin 2 : a foamy preparation used in styling hair — **mousse** *vb*

mous·tache \'məs-ˌtash, (ˌ)məs-'tash\ *var of* MUSTACHE

mousy *or* **mous·ey** \'maù-sē, -zē\ *adj* **mous·i·er; -est** 1 : QUIET, STEALTHY 2 : TIMID 3 : grayish brown — **mous·i·ness** \'maù-sē-nəs, -zē-\ *n*

¹**mouth** \'maùth\ *n, pl* **mouths** \'maùthz, 'maùths\ 1 : the opening through which an animal takes in food; *also* : the cavity that encloses the tongue, lips, and teeth in the typical vertebrate 2 : something resembling a mouth (as in affording entrance) — **mouthed** \'maùthd, 'maùtht\ *adj* — **mouth·ful** *n*

²**mouth** \'maùth\ *vb* 1 : SPEAK; *also* : DECLAIM 2 : to repeat without comprehension or sincerity 3 : to form soundlessly with the lips

mouth·part \'maùth-ˌpärt\ *n* : a structure or appendage near the mouth (as of an insect) esp. when adapted for eating

mouth·piece \-ˌpēs\ *n* 1 : a part (as of a musical instrument) that goes in the mouth or to which the mouth is applied 2 : SPOKESMAN

mouth·wash \-ˌwȯsh, -ˌwäsh\ *n* : a usu. antiseptic liquid preparation for cleaning the mouth and teeth

mou·ton \'mü-ˌtän\ *n* : processed sheepskin that has been sheared or dyed to resemble beaver or seal

¹**move** \'müv\ *vb* **moved; mov·ing** 1 : to change or cause to change position or posture 2 : to go or cause to go from one point to another; *also* : DEPART 3 : to take or cause to take action 4 : to show marked activity 5 : to stir the emotions 6 : to make a formal request, application, or appeal 7 : to change one's residence 8 : EVACUATE 2 — **mov·able** *or* **move·able** \'mü-və-bəl\ *adj*

²**move** *n* 1 : an act of moving 2 : a calculated step taken to gain an objective 3 : a change of location 4 : an agile action esp. in sports

move·ment \'müv-mənt\ *n* 1 : the act or process of moving : MOVE 2 : a series of organized activities working toward an objective 3 : the moving parts of a mechanism (as of a watch) 4 : RHYTHM 5 : a section

of an extended musical composition 6 : an act of voiding the bowels; *also* : STOOL 4

mov·er \'mü-vər\ *n* : one that moves; *esp* : one that moves the belongings of others from one location to another

mov·ie \'mü-vē\ *n* 1 : MOTION PICTURE 2 *pl* : a showing of a motion picture 3 *pl* : the motion-picture industry

¹**mow** \'maù\ *n* : the part of a barn where hay or straw is stored

²**mow** \'mō\ *vb* **mowed; mowed** *or* **mown** \'mōn\; **mow·ing** 1 : to cut (as grass) with a scythe or machine 2 : to cut the standing herbage of ⟨∼ the lawn⟩ — **mow·er** *n*

Mo·zam·bi·can \ˌmō-zəm-'bē-kən\ *n* : a native or inhabitant of Mozambique

moz·za·rel·la \ˌmät-sə-'re-lə\ *n* [It] : a moist white unsalted unripened mild cheese of a smooth rubbery texture

MP *abbr* 1 melting point 2 member of parliament 3 metropolitan police 4 military police; military policeman

mpg *abbr* miles per gallon

mph *abbr* miles per hour

Mr. \'mis-tər\ *n, pl* **Messrs.** \'me-sərz\ — used as a conventional title of courtesy before a man's surname or his title of office

MRI *abbr* magnetic resonance imaging

Mrs. \'mi-səz, -səs, *esp Southern* 'mi-zəz, -zəs\ *n, pl* **Mes·dames** \mā-'däm, -'dam\ — used as a conventional title of courtesy before a married woman's surname

Ms. \'miz\ *n, pl* **Mss.** *or* **Mses.** \'mi-zez\ — used instead of *Miss* or *Mrs.*

MS *abbr* 1 manuscript 2 master of science 3 military science 4 Mississippi 5 motor ship 6 multiple sclerosis

msec *abbr* millisecond

msg *abbr* message

MSG *abbr* 1 master sergeant 2 monosodium glutamate

msgr *abbr* 1 monseigneur 2 monsignor

MSgt *abbr* master sergeant

MSS *abbr* manuscripts

MST *abbr* mountain standard time

mt *abbr* mount; mountain

Mt *abbr* Matthew

MT *abbr* 1 metric ton 2 Montana 3 mountain time

mtg *abbr* 1 meeting 2 mortgage

mtge *abbr* mortgage

mu \'myü, 'mü\ *n* : the 12th letter of the Greek alphabet — M or μ

¹**much** \'məch\ *adj* **more** \'mōr\; **most** \'mōst\ : great in quantity, amount, extent, or degree ⟨∼ money⟩

²**much** *adv* **more; most** 1 : to a great degree or extent ⟨∼ happier⟩ 2 : ALMOST, NEARLY ⟨looks ∼ as he did before⟩

³**much** *n* 1 : a great quantity, amount, extent, or degree 2 : something considerable or impressive

mu·ci·lage \'myü-sə-lij\ *n* : a watery sticky solution (as of a gum) used esp. as an adhesive — **mu·ci·lag·i·nous** \ˌmyü-sə-'la-jə-nəs\ *adj*

muck \'mək\ *n* 1 : soft moist barnyard manure 2 : FILTH, DIRT 3 : a dark richly organic soil; *also* : MUD, MIRE — **mucky** *adj*

muck·rake \-ˌrāk\ *vb* : to expose publicly real or apparent misconduct of a prominent individual or business — **muck·rak·er** *n*

mu·cus \'myü-kəs\ *n* : a slimy slippery protective secretion of membranes (**mucous membranes**) lining some body cavities — **mu·cous** \-kəs\ *adj*

mud \'məd\ *n* : soft wet earth : MIRE — **mud·di·ly** \'mə-də-lē\ *adv* — **mud·di·ness** \-dē-nəs\ *n* — **mud·dy** \'mə-dē\ *adj*

mud·dle \'məd-ᵊl\ *vb* **mud·dled; mud·dling** 1 : to make muddy 2 : to confuse esp. with liquor 3 : to mix up or make a mess of 4 : to think or act in a confused way

mud·dle·head·ed \ˌməd-əl-ˈhe-dəd\ *adj* **1** : mentally confused **2** : INEPT

mud·flat \ˈməd-ˌflat\ *n* : a level tract alternately covered and left bare by the tide

mud·guard \ˈməd-ˌgärd\ *n* : a guard over or a flap behind a wheel of a vehicle to catch or deflect mud

mud·room \-ˌrüm, -ˌrûm\ *n* : a room in a house for removing dirty or wet footwear and clothing

mud·sling·er \-ˌsliŋ-ər\ *n* : one who uses invective esp. against a political opponent — **mud·sling·ing** \-ˌsliŋ-iŋ\ *n*

Muen·ster \ˈmən-stər, ˈmün-, ˈmùn-\ *n* : a semisoft bland cheese

mu·ez·zin \mü-ˈez-ᵊn, myü-\ *n* : a Muslim crier who calls the hour of daily prayer

¹muff \ˈməf\ *n* : a warm tubular covering for the hands

²muff *n* : a bungling performance; *esp* : a failure to hold a ball in attempting a catch — **muff** *vb*

muf·fin \ˈmə-fən\ *n* : a small soft cake baked in a cup-shaped container

muf·fle \ˈmə-fəl\ *vb* **muf·fled; muf·fling** **1** : to wrap up so as to conceal or protect **2** : to wrap or pad with something to dull the sound of **3** : to keep down : SUPPRESS

muf·fler \ˈmə-flər\ *n* **1** : a scarf worn around the neck **2** : a device (as on a car's exhaust) to deaden noise

muf·ti \ˈməf-tē\ *n* : civilian clothes

¹mug \ˈməg\ *n* : a usu. metal or earthenware cylindrical drinking cup

²mug *vb* **mugged; mug·ging** **1** : to pose or make faces esp. to attract attention or for a camera **2** : PHOTOGRAPH

³mug *vb* **mugged; mug·ging** : to assault usu. with intent to rob — **mug·ger** *n*

mug·gy \ˈmə-gē\ *adj* **mug·gi·er; -est** : being warm and humid — **mug·gi·ness** \-gē-nəs\ *n*

mug·wump \ˈməg-ˌwəmp\ *n* [obs. slang *mugwump* kingpin, fr. Massachuset (a No. American Indian language) *mugquomp* war leader] : an independent in politics

Mu·ham·mad·an \mō-ˈha-mə-dən, -ˈhä-; mü-\ *n* : MUSLIM — **Mu·ham·mad·an·ism** \-də-ˌni-zəm\ *n*

mu·ja·hid·een *or* **mu·ja·hed·in** \mü-ˌja-hi-ˈdēn, -ˌjä-\ *n pl* [Ar *mujāhidīn*, pl. of *mujāhid*, lit., person who wages jihad] : Islamic guerrilla fighters esp. in the Middle East

muk·luk \ˈmək-ˌlək\ *n* **1** : an Eskimo boot of sealskin or reindeer skin **2** : a boot with a soft leather sole worn over several pairs of socks

mu·lat·to \mù-ˈla-tō, myù-, -ˈlä-\ *n, pl* **-toes** *or* **-tos** [Sp *mulato*, fr. *mulo* mule, fr. L *mulus*] : a first-generation offspring of a black person and a white person; *also* : a person of mixed white and black ancestry

mul·ber·ry \ˈməl-ˌber-ē\ *n* : any of a genus of trees with edible berrylike fruit and leaves used as food for silkworms; *also* : the fruit

mulch \ˈməlch\ *n* : a protective covering (as of straw or leaves) spread on the ground esp. to reduce evaporation or control weeds — **mulch** *vb*

¹mulct \ˈməlkt\ *n* : FINE, PENALTY

²mulct *vb* **1** : FINE **2** : CHEAT, DEFRAUD

¹mule \ˈmyül\ *n* **1** : a hybrid offspring of a male donkey and a female horse **2** : a very stubborn person — **mul·ish** \ˈmyü-lish\ *adj* — **mul·ish·ly** *adv* — **mu·lish·ness** *n*

²mule *n* : a slipper whose upper does not extend around the heel of the foot

mule deer *n* : a long-eared deer of western No. America

mu·le·teer \ˌmyü-lə-ˈtir\ *n* : one who drives mules

¹mull \ˈməl\ *vb* : PONDER, MEDITATE

²mull *vb* : to heat, sweeten, and flavor (as wine) with spices

mul·lein \ˈmə-lən\ *n* : a tall herb related to the snapdragons that has coarse woolly leaves and flowers in spikes

mul·let \ˈmə-lət\ *n, pl* **mullet** *or* **mullets** : any of a family of largely gray chiefly marine bony fishes including valuable food fishes

mul·li·gan stew \ˈmə-li-gən-\ *n* : a stew made from whatever ingredients are available

mul·li·ga·taw·ny \ˌmə-li-gə-ˈtò-nē\ *n* : a soup usu. of chicken stock seasoned with curry

mul·lion \ˈməl-yən\ *n* : a vertical strip separating windowpanes

multi- *comb form* **1** : many : multiple ⟨*multi*unit⟩ **2** : many times over ⟨*multi*millionaire⟩

mul·ti·col·ored \ˌməl-ti-ˈkə-lərd\ *adj* : having many colors

mul·ti·cul·tur·al \ˌməl-tē-ˈkəl-chə-rəl, -ˌtī-\ *adj* : of, relating to, reflecting, or adapted to diverse cultures ⟨a ∼ society⟩

mul·ti·di·men·sion·al \-ti-də-ˈmen-chə-nəl, -ˌtī-, -dī-\ *adj* : of, relating to, or having many facets or dimensions ⟨a ∼ problem⟩ ⟨∼ space⟩

mul·ti·fac·et·ed \-ˈfa-sə-təd\ *adj* : having several distinct facets

mul·ti·fam·i·ly \-ˈfam-lē, -ˈfa-mə-\ *adj* : designed for use by several families

mul·ti·far·i·ous \ˌməl-tə-ˈfar-ē-əs\ *adj* : having great variety : DIVERSE — **mul·ti·far·i·ous·ness** *n*

mul·ti·form \ˈməl-ti-ˌfòrm\ *adj* : having many forms or appearances — **mul·ti·for·mi·ty** \ˌməl-ti-ˈfòr-mə-tē\ *n*

mul·ti·lat·er·al \ˌməl-ti-ˈla-tə-rəl, -ˌtī-, -ˈla-trəl\ *adj* : having many sides or participants ⟨∼ treaty⟩ — **mul·ti·lat·er·al·ism** \-ˈla-tə-rə-ˌli-zəm\ *n*

mul·ti·lev·el \-ˈle-vəl\ *adj* : having several levels

mul·ti·lin·gual \-ˈliŋ-gwəl\ *adj* : knowing or using several languages — **mul·ti·lin·gual·ism** \-gwə-ˌli-zəm\ *n*

mul·ti·me·dia \-ˈmē-dē-ə\ *adj* : using, involving, or encompassing several media ⟨a ∼ advertising campaign⟩

mul·ti·mil·lion·aire \ˌməl-ti-ˌmil-yə-ˈnar, -ˌtī-, -ˈmil-yə-ˌnar\ *n* : a person worth several million dollars

mul·ti·na·tion·al \-ˈna-shə-nəl\ *adj* **1** : of or relating to several nationalities **2** : relating to or involving several nations **3** : having divisions in several countries ⟨a ∼ corporation⟩ — **multinational** *n*

¹mul·ti·ple \ˈməl-tə-pəl\ *adj* **1** : more than one; *also* : MANY **2** : VARIOUS

²multiple *n* : the product of a quantity by an integer ⟨35 is a ∼ of 7⟩

multiple–choice *adj* : having several answers given from which the correct one is to be chosen ⟨a ∼ question⟩

multiple personality *n* : a mental and emotional disorder which is a neurosis and in which the personality becomes separated into two or more parts each of which controls behavior part of the time

multiple sclerosis *n* : a disease marked by patches of hardened tissue in the brain or spinal cord and associated esp. with partial or complete paralysis and muscular tremor

mul·ti·pli·cand \ˌməl-tə-pli-ˈkand\ *n* : the number that is to be multiplied by another

mul·ti·pli·ca·tion \ˌməl-tə-plə-ˈkā-shən\ *n* **1** : INCREASE **2** : a short method of finding the result of adding a figure the number of times indicated by another figure

multiplication sign *n* **1** : TIMES SIGN **2** : a centered dot indicating multiplication

mul·ti·plic·i·ty \ˌməl-tə-ˈpli-sə-tē\ *n, pl* **-ties** : a great number or variety

mul·ti·pli·er \ˈməl-tə-ˌplī-ər\ *n* : one that multiplies; *esp* : a number by which another number is multiplied

mul·ti·ply \ˈməl-tə-ˌplī\ *vb* **-plied; -ply·ing** **1** : to increase in number (as by breeding) **2** : to find the product of by multiplication; *also* : to perform multiplication

mul·ti·pur·pose \ˌməl-ti-ˈpər-pəs, -ˌtī-\ *adj* : having or serving several purposes

mul·ti·ra·cial \-'rā-shəl\ *adj* : composed of, involving, or representing various races

mul·ti·sense \-ˌsens\ *adj* : having several meanings ⟨∼ words⟩

mul·ti·sto·ry \-ˌstōr-ē\ *adj* : having several stories ⟨∼ buildings⟩

mul·ti·tude \'məl-tə-ˌtüd, -ˌtyüd\ *n* : a great number — **mul·ti·tu·di·nous** \ˌməl-tə-'tüd-ᵊn-əs, -'tyüd-\ *adj*

mul·ti·unit \'məl-ti-ˌyü-nət, -ˌtī-\ *adj* : having several units

mul·ti·vi·ta·min \-'vī-tə-mən\ *adj* : containing several vitamins and esp. all known to be essential to health

¹**mum** \'məm\ *adj* : SILENT

²**mum** *n* : CHRYSANTHEMUM

³**mum** *chiefly Brit var of* MOM

mum·ble \'məm-bəl\ *vb* **mum·bled; mum·bling** : to speak in a low indistinct manner — **mumble** *n* — **mum·bler** *n* — **mum·bly** *adj*

mum·ble·ty–peg \'məm-bəl-tē-ˌpeg\ *also* **mum·ble-the–peg** \'məm-bəl-thə-\ *n* : a game in which the players try to flip a knife from various positions so that the blade will stick into the ground

mum·bo jum·bo \ˌməm-bō-'jəm-bō\ *n* 1 : a complicated ritual with elaborate trappings 2 : GIBBERISH, NONSENSE

mum·mer \'mə-mər\ *n* 1 : an actor esp. in a pantomime 2 : a person who goes merrymaking in disguise during festivals — **mum·mery** *n*

mum·my \'mə-mē\ *n, pl* **mummies** [ME *mummie* powdered parts of a mummified body used as a drug, fr. MF *momie*, fr. ML *mumia*, fr. Ar *mūmiyah* bitumen, mummy, fr. Per *mūm* wax] : a body embalmed for burial in the manner of the ancient Egyptians — **mum·mi·fi·ca·tion** \ˌmə-mi-fə-'kā-shən\ *n* — **mum·mi·fy** \'mə-mi-ˌfī\ *vb*

mumps \'məmps\ *n sing or pl* [fr. pl. of obs. *mump* grimace] : a virus disease marked by fever and swelling esp. of the salivary glands

mun *or* **munic** *abbr* municipal

munch \'mənch\ *vb* : to eat with a chewing action; *also* : to snack on

munch·ies \'mən-chēz\ *n pl* 1 : hunger pangs 2 : light snack foods

mun·dane \ˌmən-'dān, 'mən-ˌdān\ *adj* 1 : of or relating to the world 2 : concerned with the practical details of everyday life — **mun·dane·ly** *adv*

mu·nic·i·pal \myú-'ni-sə-pəl\ *adj* 1 : of, relating to, or characteristic of a municipality 2 : restricted to one locality — **mu·nic·i·pal·ly** *adv*

mu·nic·i·pal·i·ty \myú-ˌni-sə-'pa-lə-tē\ *n, pl* **-ties** : an urban political unit with corporate status and usu. powers of self-government

mu·nif·i·cent \myú-'ni-fə-sənt\ *adj* : liberal in giving : GENEROUS — **mu·nif·i·cence** \-səns\ *n*

mu·ni·tion \myú-'ni-shən\ *n* : ARMAMENT, AMMUNITION

¹**mu·ral** \'myúr-əl\ *adj* 1 : of or relating to a wall 2 : applied to and made part of a wall or ceiling surface

²**mural** *n* : a mural painting — **mu·ral·ist** *n*

¹**mur·der** \'mər-dər\ *n* 1 : the crime of unlawfully killing a person esp. with malice aforethought 2 : something unusually difficult or dangerous

²**murder** *vb* 1 : to commit a murder; *also* : to kill brutally 2 : to put an end to 3 : to spoil by performing poorly ⟨∼ a song⟩ — **mur·der·er** *n*

mur·der·ess \'mər-də-rəs\ *n* : a woman who murders

mur·der·ous \'mər-də-rəs\ *adj* 1 : having or appearing to have the purpose of murder 2 : marked by or causing murder or bloodshed ⟨∼ gunfire⟩ — **mur·der·ous·ly** *adv*

murk \'mərk\ *n* : DARKNESS, GLOOM — **murk·i·ly** \'mər-kə-lē\ *adv* — **murk·i·ness** \-kē-nəs\ *n* — **murky** *adj*

mur·mur \'mər-mər\ *n* 1 : a muttered complaint 2 : a low indistinct often continuous sound — **murmur** *vb* — **mur·mur·er** *n* — **mur·mur·ous** *adj*

mus *abbr* 1 museum 2 music; musical; musician

mus·ca·tel \ˌməs-kə-'tel\ *n* : a sweet fortified wine

¹**mus·cle** \'mə-səl\ *n* [ME, fr. MF, fr. L *musculus*, fr. dim. of *mus* mouse] 1 : a body tissue consisting of long cells that contract when stimulated and produce motion; *also* : an organ consisting of this tissue and functioning in moving a body part 2 : STRENGTH, BRAWN — **mus·cled** \'mə-səld\ *adj* — **mus·cu·lar** \'məs-kyə-lər\ *adj* — **mus·cu·lar·i·ty** \ˌməs-kyə-'lar-ə-tē\ *n*

²**muscle** *vb* **mus·cled; mus·cling** : to force one's way

mus·cle–bound \'mə-səl-ˌbaúnd\ *adj* : having some of the muscles abnormally enlarged and lacking in elasticity (as from excessive exercise)

muscular dystrophy *n* : any of a group of diseases characterized by progressive wasting of muscles

mus·cu·la·ture \'məs-kyə-lə-ˌchúr\ *n* : the muscles of the body or its parts

¹**muse** \'myüz\ *vb* **mused; mus·ing** [ME, fr. MF *muser* to gape, idle, muse, fr. *muse* mouth of an animal, fr. ML *musus*] : to become absorbed in thought — **mus·ing·ly** *adv*

²**muse** *n* [fr. *Muse* any of the nine sister goddesses of learning and the arts in Greek myth, fr. ME, fr. MF, fr. L *Musa*, fr. Gk *Mousa*] : a source of inspiration

mu·se·um \myú-'zē-əm\ *n* : an institution devoted to the procurement, care, and display of objects of lasting interest or value

¹**mush** \'məsh\ *n* 1 : cornmeal boiled in water 2 : sentimental drivel

²**mush** *vb* : to travel esp. over snow with a sled drawn by dogs

¹**mush·room** \'məsh-ˌrüm, -ˌrúm\ *n* : the fleshy usu. caplike spore-bearing organ of various fungi esp. when edible; *also* : such a fungus

²**mushroom** *vb* 1 : to collect wild mushrooms 2 : to spread out : EXPAND 3 : to grow rapidly

mushy \'mə-shē\ *adj* **mush·i·er; -est** 1 : soft like mush 2 : excessively sentimental

mu·sic \'myü-zik\ *n* 1 : the science or art of combining tones into a composition having structure and continuity; *also* : vocal or instrumental sounds having rhythm, melody, or harmony 2 : an agreeable sound

¹**mu·si·cal** \'myü-zi-kəl\ *adj* 1 : of or relating to music or musicians 2 : having the pleasing tonal qualities of music 3 : fond of or gifted in music — **mu·si·cal·ly** \-k(ə-)lē\ *adv*

²**musical** *n* : a film or theatrical production consisting of musical numbers and dialogue based on a unifying plot

mu·si·cale \ˌmyü-zi-'kal\ *n* : a usu. private social gathering featuring music

mu·si·cian \myú-'zi-shən\ *n* : a composer, conductor, or performer of music — **mu·si·cian·ly** *adj* — **mu·si·cian·ship** *n*

mu·si·col·o·gy \ˌmyü-zi-'kä-lə-jē\ *n* : the study of music as a field of knowledge or research — **mu·si·co·log·i·cal** \-kə-'lä-ji-kəl\ *adj* — **mu·si·col·o·gist** \-'kä-lə-jist\ *n*

musk \'məsk\ *n* : a substance obtained esp. from a small Asian deer (**musk deer**) and used as a perfume fixative — **musk·i·ness** \'məs-kē-nəs\ *n* — **musky** *adj*

mus·keg \'məs-ˌkeg\ *n* : BOG; *esp* : a mossy bog in northern No. America

mus·kel·lunge \'məs-kə-ˌlənj\ *n, pl* **muskellunge** : a large No. American pike that is a valuable sport fish

mus·ket \'məs-kət\ *n* [MF *mousquet*, fr. It *moschetto* arrow for a crossbow, musket, fr. dim. of *mosca* fly, fr. L *musca*] : a heavy large-caliber muzzle-loading shoulder firearm — **mus·ke·teer** \ˌməs-kə-'tir\ *n*

mus·ket·ry \'məs-kə-trē\ *n* 1 : MUSKETS 2 : MUSKETEERS 3 : musket fire

musk·mel·on \'məsk-ˌme-lən\ *n* : a small round to oval melon that has usu. a sweet edible green or orange flesh

musk ox *n* : a heavyset shaggy-coated wild ox of

Greenland and the arctic tundra of northern No. America

musk·rat \ˈməs-ˌkrat\ *n, pl* **muskrat** *or* **muskrats** : a large No. American aquatic rodent with webbed feet and dark brown fur; *also* : its fur

Mus·lim \ˈməz-ləm\ *n* : an adherent of Islam — **Muslim** *adj*

mus·lin \ˈməz-lən\ *n* : a plain-woven sheer to coarse cotton fabric

¹**muss** \ˈməs\ *n* : a state of disorder — **muss·i·ly** \ˈmə-sə-lē\ *adv* — **muss·i·ness** \-sē-nəs\ *n* — **mussy** *adj*

²**muss** *vb* : to make untidy : DISARRANGE

mus·sel \ˈmə-səl\ *n* **1** : a dark edible saltwater bivalve mollusk **2** : any of various freshwater bivalve mollusks of the central U.S. having shells with a pearly lining

¹**must** \ˈməst\ *vb* — used as an auxiliary esp. to express a command, requirement, obligation, or necessity

²**must** *n* **1** : an imperative duty **2** : an indispensable item

mus·tache \ˈməs-ˌtash, (ˌ)məs-ˈtash\ *n* : the hair growing on the human upper lip — **mus·tached** \-ˌtasht, -ˈtasht\ *adj*

mus·tang \ˈməs-ˌtaŋ\ *n* [MexSp *mestengo*, fr. Sp, stray, fr. *mesteño* strayed, fr. *mesta* annual roundup of cattle that disposed of strays, fr. ML *(animalia) mixta* mixed animals] : a small hardy naturalized horse of the western plains of America; *also* : BRONC

mus·tard \ˈməs-tərd\ *n* **1** : a pungent yellow powder of the seeds of an herb related to the cabbage and used as a condiment or in medicine **2** : a plant that yields mustard; *also* : a closely related plant — **mustardy** *adj*

mustard gas *n* : a poison gas used in warfare that has violent irritating and blistering effects

¹**mus·ter** \ˈməs-tər\ *n* **1** : an act of assembling (as for military inspection); *also* : critical examination **2** : an assembled group

²**muster** *vb* [ME *mustren* to show, muster, fr. OF *monstrer*, fr. L *monstrare* to show, fr. *monstrum* evil omen, monster] **1** : CONVENE, ASSEMBLE; *also* : to call the roll of **2** : ACCUMULATE **3** : to call forth : ROUSE **4** : to amount to : COMPRISE

muster out *vb* : to discharge from military service

musty \ˈməs-tē\ *adj* **mus·ti·er; -est** : MOLDY, STALE; *also* : tasting or smelling of damp or decay — **must·i·ly** \-tə-lē\ *adv* — **must·i·ness** \-tē-nəs\ *n*

mu·ta·ble \ˈmyü-tə-bəl\ *adj* **1** : prone to change : FICKLE **2** : capable of or liable to mutation : VARIABLE — **mu·ta·bil·i·ty** \ˌmyü-tə-ˈbi-lə-tē\ *n*

mu·tant \ˈmyüt-ᵊnt\ *adj* : of, relating to, or produced by mutation — **mu·tant** *n*

mu·tate \ˈmyü-ˌtāt\ *vb* **mu·tat·ed; mu·tat·ing** : to undergo or cause to undergo mutation — **mu·ta·tive** \ˈmyü-ˌtā-tiv, -tə-tiv\ *adj*

mu·ta·tion \myü-ˈtā-shən\ *n* **1** : CHANGE **2** : an inherited physical or biochemical change in genetic material; *also* : the process of producing a mutation **3** : an individual, strain, or trait resulting from mutation — **mu·ta·tion·al** *adj*

¹**mute** \ˈmyüt\ *adj* **mut·er; mut·est** **1** : unable to speak : DUMB **2** : SILENT — **mute·ly** *adv* — **mute·ness** *n*

²**mute** *n* **1** : a person who cannot or does not speak **2** : a device on a musical instrument that reduces, softens, or muffles the tone

³**mute** *vb* **mut·ed; mut·ing** : to muffle, reduce, or eliminate the sound of

mu·ti·late \ˈmyüt-ᵊl-ˌāt\ *vb* **-lat·ed; -lat·ing** **1** : to cut up or alter radically so as to make imperfect **2** : MAIM, CRIPPLE — **mu·ti·la·tion** \ˌmyüt-ᵊl-ˈā-shən\ *n* — **mu·ti·la·tor** \ˈmyüt-ᵊl-ˌā-tər\ *n*

mu·ti·ny \ˈmyüt-ᵊn-ē\ *n, pl* **-nies** : willful refusal to obey constituted authority; *esp* : revolt against a superior officer — **mu·ti·neer** \ˌmyüt-ᵊn-ˈir\ *n* — **mu·ti·nous** \ˈmyüt-ᵊn-əs\ *adj* — **mu·ti·nous·ly** *adv* — **mutiny** *vb*

mutt \ˈmət\ *n* : MONGREL, CUR

mut·ter \ˈmə-tər\ *vb* **1** : to speak indistinctly or with a low voice and lips partly closed **2** : GRUMBLE — **mutter** *n*

mut·ton \ˈmət-ᵊn\ *n* [ME *motoun*, fr. OF *moton* ram] : the flesh of a mature sheep used for food — **muttony** *adj*

mut·ton-chops \ˈmət-ᵊn-ˌchäps\ *n pl* : whiskers on the side of the face that are narrow at the temple and broad and round by the lower jaws

mu·tu·al \ˈmyü-chə-wəl\ *adj* **1** : given and received in equal amount ⟨∼ trust⟩ **2** : having the same feelings one for the other ⟨∼ enemies⟩ **3** : COMMON, JOINT ⟨a ∼ friend⟩ — **mu·tu·al·ly** *adv*

mutual fund *n* : an investment company that invests money of its shareholders in a usu. diversified group of securities of other corporations

muu·muu \ˈmü-ˌmü\ *n* : a loose dress of Hawaiian origin

¹**muz·zle** \ˈmə-zəl\ *n* **1** : the nose and jaws of an animal; *also* : a covering for the muzzle to prevent biting or eating **2** : the mouth of a gun

muzzle 1

²**muzzle** *vb* **muz·zled; muz·zling** **1** : to put a muzzle on **2** : to restrain from expression : GAG

mV *abbr* millivolt

MV *abbr* motor vessel

MVP *abbr* most valuable player

MW *abbr* megawatt

my \ˈmī\ *adj* **1** : of or relating to me or myself **2** — used interjectionally esp. to express surprise

my·col·o·gy \mī-ˈkä-lə-jē\ *n* : a branch of biology dealing with fungi — **my·co·log·i·cal** \ˌmī-kə-ˈlä-ji-kəl\ *adj* — **my·col·o·gist** \mī-ˈkä-lə-jist\ *n*

my·elo·ma \ˌmī-ə-ˈlō-mə\ *n, pl* **-mas** *or* **-ma·ta** \-mə-tə\ : a primary tumor of the bone marrow

my·nah *or* **my·na** \ˈmī-nə\ *n* : any of several Asian starlings; *esp* : a dark brown slightly crested bird sometimes taught to mimic speech

my·o·pia \mī-ˈō-pē-ə\ *n* : a condition in which visual images come to a focus in front of the retina resulting esp. in defective vision of distant objects — **my·o·pic** \-ˈō-pik, -ˈä-\ *adj* — **my·o·pi·cal·ly** \-pi-k(ə-)lē\ *adv*

¹**myr·i·ad** \ˈmir-ē-əd\ *n* [Gk *myriad-, myrias,* fr. *myrioi* countless, ten thousand] : an indefinitely large number

²**myriad** *adj* : consisting of a very great but indefinite number

myr·mi·don \ˈmər-mə-ˌdän\ *n* : a loyal follower; *esp* : one who executes orders without protest or pity

myrrh \ˈmər\ *n* : a fragrant aromatic plant gum used in perfumes and formerly for incense

myr·tle \ˈmərt-ᵊl\ *n* : an evergreen shrub of southern Europe with shiny leaves, fragrant flowers, and black berries; *also* : PERIWINKLE

my·self \mī-ˈself, mə-\ *pron* : I, ME — used reflexively, for emphasis, or in absolute constructions ⟨I hurt ∼⟩ ⟨I ∼ did it⟩ ⟨∼ busy, I sent him instead⟩

mys·tery \ˈmis-tə-rē\ *n, pl* **-ter·ies** **1** : a religious truth known by revelation alone **2** : something not understood or beyond understanding **3** : enigmatic quality or character **4** : a work of fiction dealing with the solution of a mysterious crime — **mys·te·ri·ous** \mis-'tir-ē-əs\ *adj* — **mys·te·ri·ous·ly** *adv* — **mys·te·ri·ous·ness** *n*

¹**mys·tic** \'mis-tik\ *adj* **1** : of or relating to mystics or mysticism **2** : MYSTERIOUS; *also* : MYSTIFYING

²**mystic** *n* : a person who follows, advocates, or experiences mysticism

mys·ti·cal \'mis-ti-kəl\ *adj* **1** : SPIRITUAL, SYMBOLIC **2** : of or relating to an intimate knowledge of or direct communion with God (as through contemplation or visions)

mys·ti·cism \'mis-tə-ˌsi-zəm\ *n* : the belief that direct knowledge of God or ultimate reality is attainable through immediate intuition or insight

mys·ti·fy \'mis-tə-ˌfī\ *vb* **-fied; -fy·ing 1** : to perplex the

mind of **2** : to make mysterious — **mys·ti·fi·ca·tion** \ˌmis-tə-fə-'kā-shən\ *n*

mys·tique \mi-'stēk\ *n* [F] **1** : an air or attitude of mystery and reverence developing around something or someone **2** : the special esoteric skill essential in a calling or activity

myth \'mith\ *n* **1** : a usu. legendary narrative that presents part of the beliefs of a people or explains a practice or natural phenomenon **2** : an imaginary or unverifiable person or thing — **myth·i·cal** \'mi-thi-kəl\ *adj*

my·thol·o·gy \mi-'thä-lə-jē\ *n, pl* **-gies** : a body of myths and esp. of those dealing with the gods and heroes of a people — **myth·o·log·i·cal** \ˌmi-thə-'lä-ji-kəl\ *adj* — **my·thol·o·gist** \mi-'thä-lə-jist\ *n*

N

¹**n** \'en\ *n, pl* **n's** *or* **ns** \'enz\ *often cap* **1** : the 14th letter of the English alphabet **2** : an unspecified quantity

²**n** *abbr, often cap* **1** net **2** neuter **3** noon **4** normal **5** north; northern **6** note **7** noun **8** number

N *symbol* nitrogen

-n — see -EN

Na *symbol* [NL *natrium*] sodium

NA *abbr* **1** no account **2** North America **3** not applicable **4** not available

NAACP \ˌen-ˌdə-bəl-ˌā-ˌsē-'pē, ˌen-ˌā-ˌā-ˌsē-\ *abbr* National Association for the Advancement of Colored People

nab \'nab\ *vb* **nabbed; nab·bing** : SEIZE; *esp* : ARREST

NAB *abbr* New American Bible

na·bob \'nā-ˌbäb\ *n* [Urdu *nawwāb*, provincial governor (in the Mogul empire), fr. Ar *nuwwāb*, pl. of *nā'ib* governor] : a man of great wealth or prominence

na·celle \nə-'sel\ *n* : an enclosure (as for an engine) on an aircraft

na·cre \'nā-kər\ *n* : MOTHER-OF-PEARL

na·dir \'nā-ˌdir, -dər\ *n* [ME, fr. MF, fr. Ar *naẓīr* opposite] **1** : the point of the celestial sphere that is directly opposite the zenith and directly beneath the observer **2** : the lowest point

¹**nag** \'nag\ *n* : HORSE; *esp* : an old or decrepit horse

²**nag** *vb* **nagged; nag·ging 1** : to find fault incessantly : COMPLAIN **2** : to irritate by constant scolding or urging **3** : to be a continuing source of annoyance (a *nagging* backache)

³**nag** *n* : one who nags habitually

Nah *abbr* Nahum

Na·huatl \'nä-ˌwät-ᵊl\ *n* : a group of American Indian languages of central and southern Mexico

Na·hum \'nā-həm, -əm\ *n* — see BIBLE table

NAIA *abbr* National Association of Intercollegiate Athletes

na·iad \'nā-əd, 'nī-, -ˌad\ *n, pl* **naiads** *or* **na·ia·des** \-ə-ˌdēz\ **1** : one of the nymphs in ancient mythology living in lakes, rivers, springs, and fountains **2** : an aquatic young of some insects (as a dragonfly)

¹**na·if** *or* **na·if** \nä-'ēf\ *adj* : NAIVE

²**naif** *or* **naif** *n* : a naive person

¹**nail** \'nāl\ *n* **1** : a horny sheath protecting the end of each finger and toe in humans and related primates **2** : a slender pointed fastener with a head designed to be pounded in

²**nail** *vb* : to fasten with or as if with a nail — **nail·er** *n*

nail down *vb* : to settle or establish clearly and unmistakably

nain·sook \'nān-ˌsuk\ *n* [Hindi *nainsukh*, fr. *nain* eye + *sukh* delight] : a soft lightweight muslin

nai·ra \'nī-rə\ *n* — see MONEY table

na·ive *or* **na·ïve** \nä-'ēv\ *adj* **na·iv·er; -est** [F *naïve*, fem. of *naïf*, fr. OF, inborn, natural, fr. L *nativus* na-

tive] **1** : marked by unaffected simplicity : ARTLESS, INGENUOUS **2** : CREDULOUS **syn** natural, innocent, simple, unaffected, unsophisticated, unstudied — **na·ive·ly** *adv* — **na·ive·ness** *n*

na·ïve·té *also* **na·ive·té** *or* **na·ive·te** \ˌnä-ˌē-və-'tā, nä-'ē-və-ˌtā\ *n* **1** : a naive remark or action **2** : the quality or state of being naive

na·ive·ty *also* **na·ïve·ty** \nä-'ē-və-tē\ *n, pl* **-ties** : NA-ÏVETÉ

na·ked \'nā-kəd\ *adj* **1** : having no clothes on : NUDE **2** : UNSHEATHED (a ~ sword) **3** : lacking a usual or natural covering (as of foliage or feathers) **4** : PLAIN, UNADORNED (the ~ truth) **5** : not aided by artificial means (seen by the ~ eye) — **na·ked·ly** *adv* — **na·ked·ness** *n*

nam·by–pam·by \ˌnam-bē-'pam-bē\ *adj* **1** : INSIPID **2** : WEAK, INDECISIVE **syn** bland, flat, inane, jejune, vapid, wishy-washy

¹**name** \'nām\ *n* **1** : a word or words by which a person or thing is known **2** : a disparaging epithet (call him ~s) **3** : REPUTATION; *esp* : distinguished reputation (made a ~ for herself) **4** : FAMILY, CLAN (was a disgrace to their ~) **5** : appearance as opposed to reality (a friend in ~ only)

²**name** *vb* **named; nam·ing 1** : to give a name to : CALL **2** : to mention or identify by name **3** : NOMINATE, APPOINT **4** : to decide on : CHOOSE **5** : to mention explicitly : SPECIFY (~ a price) — **name·able** *adj*

³**name** *adj* **1** : of, relating to, or bearing a name (~ tag) **2** : having an established reputation (~ brands)

name day *n* : the church feast day of the saint after whom one is named

name·less \'nām-ləs\ *adj* **1** : having no name **2** : not marked with a name (a ~ grave) **3** : not known by name (a ~ hero) **4** : too distressing to be described (~ fears) — **name·less·ly** *adv*

name·ly \-lē\ *adv* : that is to say : AS (the cat family, ~, lions, tigers, and similar animals)

name·plate \-ˌplāt\ *n* : a plate or plaque bearing a name (as of a resident)

name·sake \-ˌsāk\ *n* : one that has the same name as another; *esp* : one named after another

Na·mib·ian \nə-'mi-bē-ən, -byən\ *n* : a native or inhabitant of Namibia — **Namibian** *adj*

nan·keen \nan-'kēn\ *n* : a durable brownish yellow cotton fabric orig. woven by hand in China

nan·ny goat \'na-nē-\ *n* : a female domestic goat

nano·me·ter \'na-nə-ˌmē-tər\ *n* : one billionth of a meter

nano·sec·ond \-ˌse-kənd\ *n* : one billionth of a second

¹**nap** \'nap\ *vb* **napped; nap·ping 1** : to sleep briefly esp. during the day : DOZE **2** : to be off guard (was caught *napping*)

²**nap** *n* : a short sleep esp. during the day

narwhal

³nap *n* : a soft downy fibrous surface (as on yarn and cloth) — **nap·less** *adj* — **napped** \\'napt\\ *adj*

na·palm \\'nä-‚pälm, -‚päm\\ *n* [*naphthalene* + *palmitate*, salt of a fatty acid] **1** : a thickener used in jelling gasoline (as for incendiary bombs) **2** : fuel jelled with napalm

nape \\'nāp, 'nap\\ *n* : the back of the neck

na·pery \\'nā-pə-rē\\ *n* : household linen esp. for the table

naph·tha \\'naf-thə, 'nap-\\ *n* : any of various liquid hydrocarbon mixtures used chiefly as solvents

naph·tha·lene \\-‚lēn\\ *n* : a crystalline substance used esp. in organic synthesis and as a moth repellent

nap·kin \\'nap-kən\\ *n* **1** : a piece of material (as cloth) used at table to wipe the lips or fingers and protect the clothes **2** : a small cloth or towel

na·po·leon \\nə-'pōl-yən, -'pō-lē-ən\\ *n* : an oblong pastry with a filling of cream, custard, or jelly

Na·po·le·on·ic \\nə-‚pō-lē-'ä-nik\\ *adj* : of, relating to, or characteristic of Napoleon I or his family

narc *also* **nark** \\'närk\\ *n, slang* : a person (as a government agent) who investigates narcotics violations

nar·cis·sism \\'när-sə-‚si-zəm\\ *n* [G *Narzissismus*, fr. *Narziss* Narcissus, beautiful youth of Greek mythology who fell in love with his own image] **1** : undue dwelling on one's own self or attainments **2** : love of or sexual desire for one's own body — **nar·cis·sist** \\-sist\\ *n or adj* — **nar·cis·sis·tic** \\‚när-sə-'sis-tik\\ *adj*

nar·cis·sus \\när-'si-səs\\ *n, pl* **-cis·sus** *or* **-cis·si** \\-‚sī, -‚sē\\ *or* **-cis·sus·es** *or* : DAFFODIL; *esp* : one with short-tubed flowers usu. borne separately

nar·co·sis \\när-'kō-səs\\ *n, pl* **-co·ses** \\-‚sēz\\ : a state of stupor, unconsciousness, or arrested activity produced by the influence of chemicals (as narcotics)

nar·cot·ic \\när-'kä-tik\\ *n* [ME *narkotik*, fr. MF *narcotique*, fr. *narcotique*, adj., fr. ML *narcoticus*, fr. Gk *narkōtikos*, fr. *narkoun* to benumb, fr. *narkē* numbness] : a drug (as opium) that dulls the senses and induces sleep — **narcotic** *adj*

nar·co·tize \\'när-kə-‚tīz\\ *vb* **-tized; -tiz·ing 1** : to treat with or subject to a narcotic; *also* : to put into a state of narcosis **2** : to soothe to unconsciousness or unawareness

nard \\'närd\\ *n* : a fragrant ointment of the ancients

na·res \\'nar-(‚)ēz\\ *n pl* [L] : the pair of openings of the nose

Nar·ra·gan·set \\‚nar-ə-'gan-sət\\ *n, pl* **Narraganset** *or* **Narragansets** : a member of an American Indian people of Rhode Island

nar·rate \\'nar-‚āt\\ *vb* **nar·rat·ed; nar·rat·ing** : to recite the details of (as a story) : RELATE, TELL — **nar·ra·tion** \\na-'rā-shən\\ *n* — **nar·ra·tor** \\'nar-‚ā-tər\\ *n*

nar·ra·tive \\'nar-ə-tiv\\ *n* **1** : something that is narrated : STORY **2** : the art or practice of narrating

¹nar·row \\'nar-ō\\ *adj* **1** : of slender or less than standard width **2** : limited in size or scope : RESTRICTED **3** : not liberal in views : PREJUDICED **4** : interpreted or interpreting strictly **5** : CLOSE ⟨won by a ~ margin⟩; *also* : barely successful ⟨a ~ escape⟩ — **nar·row·ly** *adv* — **nar·row·ness** *n*

²narrow *n* : a narrow passage : STRAIT — usu. used in pl.

³narrow *vb* : to lessen in width or extent

nar·row–mind·ed \\‚nar-ō-'mīn-dəd\\ *adj* : not liberal or broad-minded **syn** illiberal, bigoted, hidebound, intolerant

nar·whal \\'när-‚hwäl, 'när-wəl\\ *n* : an arctic sea mammal about 20 feet (6 meters) long that is related to the dolphins and in the male has a long twisted ivory tusk

NAS *abbr* naval air station

NASA \\'na-sə\\ *abbr* National Aeronautics and Space Administration

¹na·sal \\'nā-zəl\\ *n* **1** : a nasal part **2** : a nasal consonant or vowel

²nasal *adj* **1** : of or relating to the nose **2** : uttered through the nose — **na·sal·ly** *adv*

na·sal·ize \\'nā-zə-‚līz\\ *vb* **-ized; -iz·ing** : to make nasal or pronounce as a nasal sound — **na·sal·i·za·tion** \\‚nā-zə-lə-'zā-shən\\ *n*

na·scent \\'nas-ᵊnt, 'nās-\\ *adj* : coming into existence : beginning to grow or develop — **na·scence** \\-ᵊns\\ *n*

nas·tur·tium \\nə-'stər-shəm, na-\\ *n* : either of two widely cultivated watery-stemmed herbs with showy spurred flowers and pungent seeds

nas·ty \\'nas-tē\\ *adj* **nas·ti·er; -est 1** : FILTHY **2** : INDECENT, OBSCENE **3** : HARMFUL, DANGEROUS ⟨took a ~ fall⟩ **4** : DISAGREEABLE ⟨~ weather⟩ **5** : MEAN, ILL-NATURED ⟨a ~ temper⟩ **6** : DIFFICULT, VEXATIOUS ⟨a ~ problem⟩ **7** : UNFAIR, DIRTY ⟨a ~ trick⟩ — **nas·ti·ly** \\'nas-tə-lē\\ *adv* — **nas·ti·ness** \\-tē-nəs\\ *n*

nat *abbr* **1** national **2** native **3** natural

na·tal \\'nāt-ᵊl\\ *adj* **1** : NATIVE **2** : of, relating to, or present at birth

na·ta·to·ri·um \\‚nā-tə-'tōr-ē-əm, ‚na-\\ *n* : a swimming pool esp. indoors

na·tion \\'nā-shən\\ *n* [ME *nacioun*, fr. MF *nation*, fr. L *nation-, natio* birth, race, nation, fr. *nasci* to be born] **1** : NATIONALITY 5; *also* : a politically organized nationality **2** : a community of people composed of one or more nationalities with its own territory and government **3** : the territory of a nation **4** : a federation of tribes (as of American Indians) — **na·tion·hood** *n*

¹na·tion·al \\'na-shə-nəl\\ *adj* **1** : of or relating to a nation **2** : comprising or characteristic of a nationality **3** : FEDERAL **3** — **na·tion·al·ly** *adv*

²national *n* **1** : one who owes allegiance to a nation **2** : a competition that is national in scope — usu. used in pl.

National Guard *n* **1** : a militia force recruited by each state of the U.S., equipped by the federal government, and jointly maintained subject to the call of either **2** *often not cap* : a military force serving as a national constabulary and defense force

na·tion·al·ism \\'na-shə-nə-‚li-zəm\\ *n* : devotion to national interests, unity, and independence

na·tion·al·ist \\-list\\ *n* **1** : an advocate of or believer in nationalism **2** *cap* : a member of a political party or group advocating national independence or strong national government — **nationalist** *adj, often cap* — **na·tion·al·is·tic** \\‚na-shə-nə-'lis-tik\\ *adj*

na·tion·al·i·ty \\‚na-shə-'na-lə-tē\\ *n, pl* **-ties 1** : national character **2** : a legal relationship involving allegiance of an individual and protection on the part of the state **3** : membership in a particular nation **4** : political independence or existence as a separate nation **5** : a people having a common origin, tradition, and language and capable of forming a state **6** : an ethnic group within a larger unit (as a nation)

na·tion·al·ize \\'na-shə-nə-‚līz\\ *vb* **-ized; -iz·ing 1** : to make national : make a nation of **2** : to remove from private ownership and place under government control — **na·tion·al·i·za·tion** \\‚na-shə-nə-lə-'zā-shən\\ *n*

national monument *n* : a place of historic, scenic, or scientific interest set aside for preservation usu. by presidential proclamation

national park *n* : an area of special scenic, historical, or scientific importance set aside and maintained by a national government esp. for recreation or study

national seashore *n* : a recreational area adjacent to a seacoast and maintained by the federal government

na·tion·wide \\‚nā-shən-'wīd\\ *adj* : extending throughout a nation

¹na·tive \'nā-tiv\ *adj* **1** : INBORN, NATURAL **2** : born in a particular place or country **3** : belonging to a person because of the place or circumstances of birth ⟨her ~ language⟩ **4** : grown, produced, or originating in a particular place : INDIGENOUS **syn** aboriginal, autochthonous, endemic

²native *n* : one that is native; *esp* : a person who belongs to a particular country by birth

Native American *n* : AMERICAN INDIAN

na·tiv·ism \'nā-ti-₁vi-zəm\ *n* **1** : a policy of favoring native inhabitants over immigrants **2** : the revival or perpetuation of a native culture esp. in opposition to acculturation

na·tiv·i·ty \nə-'ti-və-tē, nā-\ *n, pl* **-ties 1** : the process or circumstances of being born : BIRTH **2** *cap* : the birth of Christ

natl *abbr* national

NATO \'nā-(₁)tō\ *abbr* North Atlantic Treaty Organization

nat·ty \'na-tē\ *adj* **nat·ti·er; -est** : trimly neat and tidy : SMART — **nat·ti·ly** \-tə-lē\ *adv* — **nat·ti·ness** \-tē-nəs\ *n*

¹nat·u·ral \'na-chə-rəl\ *adj* **1** : determined by nature : INBORN, INNATE ⟨~ ability⟩ **2** : BORN ⟨a ~ fool⟩ **3** : ILLEGITIMATE **4** : HUMAN **5** : of or relating to nature **6** : not artificial **7** : being simple and sincere : not affected **8** : LIFELIKE **9** : being neither sharp nor flat **syn** ingenuous, naive, unsophisticated, artless, guileless — **nat·u·ral·ness** *n*

²natural *n* **1** : IDIOT **2** : a character ♮ placed on a line or space of the musical staff to nullify the effect of a preceding sharp or flat **3** : one obviously suitable for a purpose **4** : AFRO

natural childbirth *n* : a system of managing childbirth in which the mother prepares to remain conscious and assist in delivery with little or no use of drugs

natural gas *n* : a combustible gaseous mixture of hydrocarbons coming from the earth's crust and used chiefly as a fuel and raw material

natural history *n* **1** : a treatise on some aspect of nature **2** : the study of natural objects esp. from an amateur or popular point of view

nat·u·ral·ism \'na-chə-rə-₁li-zəm\ *n* **1** : action or thought based only on natural desires and instincts **2** : a doctrine that denies a supernatural explanation of the origin or development of the universe and holds that scientific laws account for all of nature **3** : realism in art and literature — **nat·u·ral·is·tic** \₁na-chə-rə-'lis-tik\ *adj*

nat·u·ral·ist \-list\ *n* **1** : one that advocates or practices naturalism **2** : a student of animals or plants esp. in the field

nat·u·ral·ize \-₁līz\ *vb* **-ized; -iz·ing 1** : to become or cause to become established as if native ⟨~ new forage crops⟩ **2** : to confer the rights of a citizen on — **nat·u·ral·iza·tion** \₁na-chə-rə-lə-'zā-shən\ *n*

nat·u·ral·ly \'na-chə-rə-lē, 'nach-rə-\ *adv* **1** : by nature : by natural character or ability **2** : as might be expected **3** : without artificial aid; *also* : without affectation **4** : REALISTICALLY

natural science *n* : a science (as physics, chemistry, or biology) that deals with matter, energy, and their interrelations and transformations or with objectively measurable phenomena — **natural scientist** *n*

natural selection *n* : the natural process that results in the survival of individuals or groups best adjusted to their environment

na·ture \'nā-chər\ *n* [ME, fr. MF, fr. L *natura*, fr. *natus*, pp. of *nasci* to be born] **1** : the inherent quality or basic constitution of a person or thing **2** : KIND, SORT **3** : DISPOSITION, TEMPERAMENT **4** : the physical universe **5** : one's natural instincts or way of life ⟨quirks of human ~⟩; *also* : primitive state ⟨a return to ~⟩ **6** : natural scenery or environment ⟨beauties of ~⟩

naught \'nȯt, 'nät\ *n* **1** : NOTHING **2** : the arithmetical symbol 0 : ZERO

naugh·ty \'nȯ-tē, 'nä-\ *adj* **naugh·ti·er; -est 1** : guilty of disobedience or misbehavior **2** : lacking in taste or propriety — **naugh·ti·ly** \-tə-lē\ *adv* — **naugh·ti·ness** \-tē-nəs\ *n*

nau·sea \'nȯ-zē-ə, -sē-; 'nȯ-zhə, -shə\ *n* [L, seasickness, nausea, fr. Gk *nautia, nausia*, fr. *nautēs* sailor] **1** : sickness of the stomach with a desire to vomit **2** : extreme disgust

nau·se·ate \'nȯ-zē-₁āt, -sē-, -zhē-, -shē-\ *vb* **-at·ed; -at·ing** : to affect or become affected with nausea — **nau·se·at·ing·ly** *adv*

nau·seous \'nȯ-shəs, -zē-əs\ *adj* **1** : causing nausea or disgust **2** : affected with nausea or disgust

naut *abbr* nautical

nau·ti·cal \'nȯ-ti-kəl\ *adj* : of or relating to sailors, navigation, or ships — **nau·ti·cal·ly** \-k(ə-)lē\ *adv*

nautical mile *n* : a unit of distance equal to about 6080 feet (1852 meters)

nau·ti·lus \'nȯt-ᵊl-əs\ *n, pl* **-lus·es** *or* **-li** \-ᵊl-₁ī, -₁ē\ : any of a genus of sea mollusks related to the octopuses but having a spiral chambered shell

nav *abbr* **1** naval **2** navigable; navigation

Na·va·jo *also* **Na·va·ho** \'na-və-₁hō, 'nä-\ *n, pl* **-jo** *or* **-jos** *also* **-ho** *or* **-hos** : a member of an American Indian people of northern New Mexico and Arizona; *also* : their language

na·val \'nā-vəl\ *adj* : of, relating to, or possessing a navy

naval stores *n pl* : products (as pitch, turpentine, or rosin) obtained from resinous conifers (as pines)

nave \'nāv\ *n* [ML *navis*, fr. L, ship] : the central part of a church running lengthwise

na·vel \'nā-vəl\ *n* : a depression in the middle of the abdomen that marks the point of attachment of fetus and mother

navel orange *n* : a seedless orange having a pit at the blossom end where the fruit encloses a small secondary fruit

nav·i·ga·ble \'na-vi-gə-bəl\ *adj* **1** : capable of being navigated ⟨a ~ river⟩ **2** : capable of being steered — **nav·i·ga·bil·i·ty** \₁na-vi-gə-'bi-lə-tē\ *n*

nav·i·gate \'na-və-₁gāt\ *vb* **-gat·ed; -gat·ing 1** : to sail on or through ⟨~ the Atlantic Ocean⟩ **2** : to steer or direct the course of a ship or aircraft **3** : MOVE; *esp* : WALK ⟨could hardly ~⟩ — **nav·i·ga·tion** \₁na-və-'gā-shən\ *n* — **nav·i·ga·tor** \'na-və-₁gā-tər\ *n*

na·vy \'nā-vē\ *n, pl* **navies 1** : FLEET; *also* : the warships belonging to a nation **2** *often cap* : a nation's organization for naval warfare

navy yard *n* : a yard where naval vessels are built or repaired

¹nay \'nā\ *adv* **1** : NO

²nay *n* : a negative vote; *also* : a person casting such a vote

³nay *conj* : not merely this but also : not only so but ⟨he was happy, ~, ecstatic⟩

nay·say·er \'nā-₁sā-ər\ *n* : one who denies, refuses, or opposes something

Na·zi \'nät-sē, 'nat-\ *n* [G, fr. *Nationalsozialist*, lit., national socialist] : a member of a German fascist party controlling Germany from 1933 to 1945 under Adolf Hitler — **Nazi** *adj* — **Na·zism** \'nät-₁si-zəm, 'nat-\ *or* **Na·zi·ism** \-sē-₁i-zəm\ *n*

Nb *symbol* niobium

NB *abbr* **1** New Brunswick **2** nota bene

NBA *abbr* **1** National Basketball Association **2** National Boxing Association

NBC *abbr* National Broadcasting Company

NBS *abbr* National Bureau of Standards

NC *abbr* **1** no charge **2** North Carolina

NCAA *abbr* National Collegiate Athletic Association

NCE *abbr* New Catholic Edition

NCO \₁en-₁sē-'ō\ *n* : NONCOMMISSIONED OFFICER

nd *abbr* no date

Nd *symbol* neodymium
ND *abbr* North Dakota
N Dak *abbr* North Dakota
Ne *symbol* neon
NE *abbr* **1** Nebraska **2** New England **3** northeast
Ne·an·der·thal \nē-'an-dər-ˌthȯl, nä-'än-dər-ˌtäl\ *adj* : of, relating to, or being an extinct Old World human; *also* : suggestive of a caveman — **Neanderthal** *n*
neap tide \'nēp-\ *n* : a tide of minimum range occurring at the first and third quarters of the moon
¹near \'nir\ *adv* **1** : at, within, or to a short distance or time **2** : ALMOST
²near *prep* : close to
³near *adj* **1** : closely related or associated; *also* : INTIMATE **2** : not far away; *also* : being the closer or left-hand member of a pair **3** : barely avoided ⟨a ~ accident⟩ **4** : DIRECT, SHORT ⟨by the ~*est* route⟩ **5** : STINGY **6** : not real but very like ⟨~ silk⟩ — **near·ly** *adv* — **near·ness** *n*
⁴near *vb* : APPROACH
near beer *n* : any of various malt liquors low in alcohol
near·by \nir-'bī, 'nir-ˌbī\ *adv or adj* : close at hand
near·sight·ed \'nir-'sī-təd\ *adj* : able to see near things more clearly than distant ones : MYOPIC — **near·sight·ed·ly** *adv* — **near·sight·ed·ness** *n*
neat \'nēt\ *adj* [MF *net*, fr. L *nitidus* bright, neat, fr. *nitēre* to shine] **1** : being orderly and clean **2** : not mixed or diluted ⟨~ brandy⟩ **3** : marked by tasteful simplicity **4** : PRECISE, SYSTEMATIC **5** : SKILLFUL, ADROIT **6** : FINE, ADMIRABLE **syn** shipshape, tidy, trig, trim — **neat** *adv* — **neat·ly** *adv* — **neat·ness** *n*
neath \'nēth\ *prep, dial* : BENEATH
neat's-foot oil \'nēts-ˌfùt-\ *n* [*neat* ox or cow] : a pale yellow fatty oil made esp. from the bones of cattle and used chiefly as a leather dressing
neb \'neb\ *n* **1** : the beak of a bird or tortoise; *also* : NOSE, SNOUT **2** : NIB
Neb *or* **Nebr** *abbr* Nebraska
NEB *abbr* New English Bible
neb·u·la \'ne-byə-lə\ *n, pl* **-lae** \-ˌlē, -ˌlī\ *also* **-las** [NL, fr. L, mist, cloud] **1** : any of numerous clouds of gas or dust in interstellar space **2** : GALAXY — **neb·u·lar** \-lər\ *adj*
neb·u·liz·er \'ne-byə-ˌlī-zər\ *n* : ATOMIZER
neb·u·lous \'ne-byə-ləs\ *adj* **1** : of or relating to a nebula **2** : HAZY, INDISTINCT
¹nec·es·sary \'ne-sə-ˌser-ē\ *n, pl* **-saries** : an indispensable item
²necessary *adj* **1** : INEVITABLE, INESCAPABLE; *also* : CERTAIN **2** : PREDETERMINED **3** : COMPULSORY **4** : positively needed : INDISPENSABLE **syn** imperative, necessitous, essential — **nec·es·sar·i·ly** \ˌne-sə-'ser-ə-lē\ *adv*
ne·ces·si·tate \ni-'se-sə-ˌtāt\ *vb* **-tat·ed; -tat·ing** : to make necessary
ne·ces·si·tous \ni-'se-sə-təs\ *adj* **1** : NEEDY, IMPOVERISHED **2** : URGENT **3** : NECESSARY
ne·ces·si·ty \ni-'se-sə-tē\ *n, pl* **-ties** **1** : conditions that cannot be changed **2** : WANT, POVERTY **3** : something that is necessary **4** : very great need
¹neck \'nek\ *n* **1** : the part of the body connecting the head and the trunk **2** : the part of a garment covering or near to the neck **3** : a relatively narrow part suggestive of a neck ⟨~ of a bottle⟩ ⟨~ of land⟩ **4** : a narrow margin esp. of victory ⟨won by a ~⟩ — **necked** \'nekt\ *adj*
²neck *vb* : to kiss and caress amorously
neck and neck *adv or adj* : very close (as in a race)
neck·er·chief \'ne-kər-chəf, -ˌchēf\ *n, pl* **-chiefs** \-chəfs, -ˌchēfs\ *also* **-chieves** \-ˌchēvz\ : a square of cloth worn folded about the neck like a scarf
neck·lace \'ne-kləs\ *n* : an ornament worn around the neck
neck·line \'nek-ˌlīn\ *n* : the outline of the neck opening of a garment

neck·tie \-ˌtī\ *n* : a strip of cloth worn around the neck and tied in front
ne·crol·o·gy \nə-'krä-lə-jē\ *n, pl* **-gies** **1** : OBITUARY **2** : a list of the recently dead
nec·ro·man·cy \'ne-krə-ˌman-sē\ *n* **1** : the art or practice of conjuring up the spirits of the dead for purposes of magically revealing the future **2** : MAGIC, SORCERY — **nec·ro·man·cer** \-sər\ *n*
ne·crop·o·lis \nə-'krä-pə-ləs, ne-\ *n, pl* **-lis·es** *or* **-les** \-ˌlēz\ *or* **-leis** \-ˌlās\ *or* **-li** \-ˌlī, -ˌlē\ : CEMETERY; *esp* : a large elaborate cemetery of an ancient city
ne·cro·sis \nə-'krō-səs, ne-\ *n, pl* **ne·cro·ses** \-ˌsēz\ : usu. local death of body tissue — **ne·crot·ic** \-'krä-tik\ *adj*
nec·tar \'nek-tər\ *n* **1** : the drink of the Greek and Roman gods; *also* : any delicious drink **2** : a sweet plant secretion that is the raw material of honey
nec·tar·ine \ˌnek-tə-'rēn\ *n* : a smooth-skinned peach
née *or* **nee** \'nā\ *adj* [F, lit., born] — used to identify a woman by her maiden family name
¹need \'nēd\ *n* **1** : OBLIGATION ⟨no ~ to hurry⟩ **2** : a lack of something requisite, desirable, or useful **3** : a condition requiring supply or relief ⟨when the ~ arises⟩ **4** : POVERTY **syn** necessity, exigency
²need *vb* **1** : to be in want **2** : to have cause or occasion for : REQUIRE ⟨he ~s advice⟩ **3** : to be under obligation or necessity ⟨we ~ to know the truth⟩
need·ful \'nēd-fəl\ *adj* : NECESSARY, REQUISITE
¹nee·dle \'nēd-əl\ *n* **1** : a slender pointed usu. steel implement used in sewing **2** : a slender rod (as for knitting, controlling a small opening, or transmitting vibrations to or from a recording) ⟨a phonograph ~⟩ **3** : a slender hollow instrument by which material is introduced into or withdrawn from the body **4** : a slender indicator on a dial **5** : a needle-shaped leaf (as of a pine)
²needle *vb* **nee·dled; nee·dling** : PROD, GOAD; *esp* : to incite to action by repeated gibes
nee·dle·point \'nēd-əl-ˌpȯint\ *n* **1** : lace worked with a needle over a paper pattern **2** : embroidery done on canvas across counted threads — **needlepoint** *adj*
need·less \'nēd-ləs\ *adj* : UNNECESSARY — **need·less·ly** *adv* — **need·less·ness** *n*
nee·dle·wom·an \'nēd-əl-ˌwù-mən\ *n* : a woman who does needlework; *esp* : SEAMSTRESS
nee·dle·work \-ˌwərk\ *n* : work done with a needle; *esp* : work (as embroidery) other than plain sewing
needs \'nēdz\ *adv* : of necessity : NECESSARILY ⟨must ~ be recognized⟩
needy \'nē-dē\ *adj* **need·i·er; -est** : being in want : POVERTY-STRICKEN
ne'er \'ner\ *adv* : NEVER
ne'er-do-well \'ner-dù-ˌwel\ *n* : an idle worthless person — **ne'er-do-well** *adj*
ne·far·i·ous \ni-'far-ē-əs\ *adj* [L *nefarius*, fr. *nefas* crime, fr. *ne-* not + *fas* right, divine law] : very wicked : EVIL **syn** bad, immoral, iniquitous, sinful, vicious — **ne·far·i·ous·ly** *adv*
neg *abbr* negative
ne·gate \ni-'gāt\ *vb* **ne·gat·ed; ne·gat·ing** **1** : to deny the existence or truth of **2** : to cause to be ineffective or invalid : NULLIFY
ne·ga·tion \ni-'gā-shən\ *n* **1** : the action or operation of negating or making negative **2** : a negative doctrine or statement
¹neg·a·tive \'ne-gə-tiv\ *adj* **1** : marked by denial, prohibition, or refusal ⟨a ~ reply⟩ **2** : not positive or constructive; *esp* : not affirming the presence of what is sought or suspected to be present ⟨test results were ~⟩ **3** : less than zero ⟨a ~ number⟩ **4** : being, relating to, or charged with electricity of which the electron is the elementary unit **5** : having the light and dark parts opposite to what they were in the original photographic subject — **neg·a·tive·ly** *adv* — **neg·a·tive·ness** *n* — **neg·a·tiv·i·ty** \ˌne-gə-'ti-və-tē\ *n*
²negative *n* **1** : a negative word or statement **2** : a neg-

ative vote or reply; *also* : REFUSAL **3** : something that is the opposite or negation of something else **4** : the side that votes or argues for the opposition (as in a debate) **5** : a negative number **6** : a negative photographic image on transparent material

³**negative** *vb* **-tived; -tiv•ing 1** : to refuse to accept or approve **2** : to vote against **3** : DISPROVE

negative income tax *n* : a system of federal subsidy payments to families with incomes below a stipulated level

neg•a•tiv•ism \'ne-gə-ti-₁vi-zəm\ *n* : an attitude of skepticism and denial of nearly everything affirmed or suggested by others

¹**ne•glect** \ni-'glekt\ *vb* [L *neglegere, neclegere*, fr. *nec-* not + *legere* to gather] **1** : DISREGARD **2** : to leave undone or unattended to esp. through carelessness **syn** omit, ignore, over-look, slight, forget, miss

²**neglect** *n* **1** : an act or instance of neglecting something **2** : the condition of being neglected — **ne•glect•ful** *adj*

neg•li•gee *also* **neg•li•gé** \₁ne-glə-'zhā\ *n* : a woman's long flowing dressing gown

neg•li•gent \'ne-gli-jənt\ *adj* : marked by neglect **syn** neglectful, remiss, delinquent, derelict — **neg•li•gence** \-jəns\ *n* — **neg•li•gent•ly** *adv*

neg•li•gi•ble \'ne-gli-jə-bəl\ *adj* : so small as to be neglected or disregarded

ne•go•tiant \ni-'gō-shē-ənt\ *n* : NEGOTIATOR

ne•go•ti•ate \ni-'gō-shē-₁āt\ *vb* **-at•ed; -at•ing** [L *negotiari* to carry on business, fr. *negotium* business, fr. *neg-* not + *otium* leisure] **1** : to confer with another so as to arrive at the settlement of some matter; *also* : to arrange for or bring about by such conferences ⟨∼ a treaty⟩ **2** : to transfer to another by delivery or endorsement in return for equivalent value ⟨∼ a check⟩ **3** : to get through, around, or over successfully ⟨∼ a turn⟩ — **ne•go•tia•ble** \-shə-bəl, -shē-ə-\ *adj* — **ne•go•ti•a•tion** \ni-₁gō-sē-'ā-shən, -shē-\ *n* — **ne•go•ti•a•tor** \-'gō-shē-₁ā-tər\ *n*

ne•gri•tude \'ne-grə-₁tüd, -₁tyüd, 'nē-\ *n* : a consciousness of and pride in one's African heritage

Ne•gro \'nē-grō\ *n, pl* **Negroes** [Sp or Pg, fr. *negro* black] : a member of the black race — **Negro** *adj* — **Ne•groid** \'nē-₁groid\ *n or adj, often not cap*

Neh *abbr* Nehemiah

Ne•he•mi•ah \₁nē-ə-'mī-ə\ *n* — see BIBLE table

neigh \'nā\ *n* : a loud prolonged cry of a horse — **neigh** *vb*

¹**neigh•bor** \'nā-bər\ *n* **1** : one living or located near another **2** : FELLOWMAN

²**neighbor** *vb* : to be next to or near to : border on

neigh•bor•hood \'nā-bər-₁hůd\ *n* **1** : NEARNESS **2** : a place or region near : VICINITY; *also* : a number or amount near ⟨costs in the ∼ of $10⟩ **3** : the people living near one another **4** : a section lived in by neighbors and usu. having distinguishing characteristics

neigh•bor•ly \-lē\ *adj* : befitting congenial neighbors; *esp* : FRIENDLY — **neigh•bor•li•ness** *n*

neigh•bour *chiefly Brit var of* NEIGHBOR

¹**nei•ther** \'nē-thər, 'nī-\ *pron* : neither one : not the one and not the other ⟨∼ of the two⟩

²**neither** *conj* **1** : not either ⟨∼ good nor bad⟩ **2** : NOR ⟨∼ did I⟩

³**neither** *adj* : not either ⟨∼ hand⟩

nel•son \'nel-sən\ *n* : a wrestling hold in which one applies leverage against an opponent's arm, neck, and head

nem•a•tode \'ne-mə-₁tōd\ *n* : any of a phylum of elongated cylindrical worms parasitic in animals or plants or free-living in soil or water

nem•e•sis \'ne-mə-səs\ *n, pl* **-e•ses** \-₁sēz\ [L *Nemesis*, goddess of divine retribution, fr. Gk] **1** : one that inflicts retribution or vengeance **2** : a formidable and usu. victorious rival **3** : an act or effect of retribution; *also* : CURSE

neo•clas•sic \₁nē-ō-'kla-sik\ *or* **neo•clas•si•cal** \-si-kəl\ *adj* : of or relating to a revival or adaptation of the classical style esp. in literature, art, or music

neo•co•lo•nial•ism \₁nē-ō-kə-'lō-nē-ə-₁li-zəm\ *n* : the economic and political policies by which a nation indirectly maintains or extends its influence over other areas or peoples — **neo•co•lo•nial** *adj* — **neo•co•lo•nial•ist** \-list\ *n or adj*

neo•con•ser•va•tive \-kən-'sər-və-tiv\ *n* : a former liberal espousing political conservatism — **neo•con•ser•va•tism** \-və-₁ti-zəm\ *n* — **neoconservative** *adj*

neo•dym•i•um \₁nē-ō-'di-mē-əm\ *n* : a yellow metallic chemical element — see ELEMENT table

neo•im•pres•sion•ism \₁nē-ō-im-'pre-shə-₁ni-zəm\ *n, often cap N&I* : a late 19th century French art movement that attempted to make impressionism more precise and to use a pointillist painting technique

Neo•lith•ic \₁nē-ə-'li-thik\ *adj* : of or relating to the latest period of the Stone Age characterized by polished stone implements

ne•ol•o•gism \nē-'ä-lə-₁ji-zəm\ *n* : a new word or expression

ne•on \'nē-₁än\ *n* [Gk, neut. of *neos* new] **1** : a gaseous colorless chemical element used in electric lamps — see ELEMENT table **2** : a lamp in which a discharge through neon gives a reddish glow — **neon** *adj*

neo•na•tal \₁nē-ō-'nāt-əl\ *adj* : of, relating to, or affecting the newborn — **neo•na•tal•ly** *adv*

ne•o•nate \'nē-ə-₁nāt\ *n* : a newborn child

neo•phyte \'nē-ə-₁fīt\ *n* **1** : a new convert : PROSELYTE **2** : NOVICE **3** : BEGINNER **syn** apprentice, freshman, newcomer, rookie, tenderfoot, tyro

neo•plasm \'nē-ə-₁pla-zəm\ *n* : a new growth of tissue serving no useful purpose in the body : TUMOR — **neo•plas•tic** \₁nē-ə-'plas-tik\ *adj*

neo•prene \'nē-ə-₁prēn\ *n* : a synthetic rubber used esp. for special-purpose clothing (as wet suits)

Ne•pali \nə-'pȯl-ē, -'päl-\ *n, pl* **Nepali** : a native or inhabitant of Nepal — **Nepali** *adj*

ne•pen•the \nə-'pen-thē\ *n* **1** : a potion used by the ancients to dull pain and sorrow **2** : something capable of making one forget grief or suffering

neph•ew \'ne-fyü, *chiefly Brit* -vyü\ *n* : a son of one's brother, sister, brother-in-law, or sister-in-law

ne•phrit•ic \ni-'fri-tik\ *adj* **1** : RENAL **2** : of, relating to, or affected with nephritis

ne•phri•tis \ni-'frī-təs\ *n, pl* **ne•phrit•i•des** \-'fri-tə-₁dēz\ : kidney inflammation

ne plus ul•tra \₁nē-₁pləs-'əl-trə\ *n* [NL, (go) no more beyond] : the highest point capable of being attained

nep•o•tism \'ne-pə-₁ti-zəm\ *n* [F *népotisme*, fr. It *nepotismo*, fr. *nepote* nephew, fr. L *nepot-, nepos* grandson, nephew] : favoritism shown to a relative (as in the granting of jobs)

Nep•tune \'nep-₁tün, -₁tyün\ *n* : the planet 8th in order from the sun — see PLANET table — **Nep•tu•ni•an** \nep-'tü-nē-ən, -'tyü-\ *adj*

nep•tu•ni•um \nep-'tü-nē-əm, -'tyü-\ *n* : a short-lived radioactive element — see ELEMENT table

nerd \'nərd\ *n* : an unstylish or socially inept person; *esp* : one slavishly devoted to intellectual pursuits — **nerdy** *adj*

Ne•re•id \'nir-ē-əd\ *n* : a sea nymph in Greek mythology

¹**nerve** \'nərv\ *n* **1** : SINEW, TENDON ⟨strain every ∼⟩ **2** : any of the strands of nervous tissue that carry nerve impulses between the brain and spinal cord and every part of the body **3** : power of endurance or control : FORTITUDE; *also* : BOLDNESS, DARING **4** *pl* : NERVOUSNESS **5** : a vein of a leaf or insect wing — **nerved** \'nərvd\ *adj* — **nerve•less** *adj*

²**nerve** *vb* **nerved; nerv•ing** : to give strength or courage to

nerve cell *n* : NEURON; *also* : the nucleus-containing central part of a neuron exclusive of its processes

nerve gas *n* : a chemical weapon damaging esp. to the nervous and respiratory systems

nerve impulse *n* : a physical and chemical change that moves along a process of a neuron after stimulation and carries a record of sensation or an instruction to act

nerve–rack·ing *or* **nerve–wrack·ing** \'nərv-ˌra-kiŋ\ *adj* : extremely trying on the nerves

ner·vous \'nər-vəs\ *adj* **1** : FORCIBLE, SPIRITED **2** : of, relating to, or made up of nerve cells or nerves **3** : easily excited or annoyed : JUMPY **4** : TIMID, APPREHENSIVE ⟨a ∼ smile⟩ **5** : UNEASY, UNSTEADY — **ner·vous·ly** *adv* — **ner·vous·ness** *n*

nervous breakdown *n* : an attack of mental or emotional disorder of sufficient severity to be incapacitating esp. when requiring hospitalization

nervous system *n* : a bodily system that in vertebrates is made up of the brain and spinal cord, nerves, ganglia, and parts of the sense organs and that receives and interprets stimuli and transmits nerve impulses

nervy \'nər-vē\ *adj* **nerv·i·er; -est 1** : showing calm courage **2** : marked by impudence or presumption ⟨a ∼ salesperson⟩ **3** : EXCITABLE, NERVOUS **syn** bold, cheeky, forward, fresh, impudent, saucy

-ness \nəs\ *n suffix* : state : condition : quality : degree ⟨good*ness*⟩

¹nest \'nest\ *n* **1** : the shelter prepared by a bird for its eggs and young **2** : a place where eggs (as of insects or fish) are laid and hatched **3** : a place of rest, retreat, or lodging **4** : DEN, HANGOUT ⟨a ∼ of thieves⟩ **5** : the occupants of a nest **6** : a series of objects (as bowls or tables) fitting inside or under one another

²nest *vb* **1** : to build or occupy a nest **2** : to fit compactly together or within one another

nest egg *n* : a fund of money accumulated as a reserve

nes·tle \'ne-səl\ *vb* **nes·tled; nes·tling 1** : to settle snugly or comfortably **2** : to press closely and affectionately : CUDDLE **3** : to settle, shelter, or house as if in a nest

nest·ling \'nest-liŋ\ *n* : a bird too young to leave its nest

¹net \'net\ *n* **1** : a meshed fabric twisted, knotted, or woven together at regular intervals **2** : a device made all or partly of net and used esp. to catch birds, fish, or insects **3** : something made of net used esp. for protecting, confining, carrying, or dividing ⟨a tennis ∼⟩ **4** : SNARE, TRAP

²net *vb* **net·ted; net·ting 1** : to cover or enclose with or as if with a net **2** : to catch in or as if in a net

³net *adj* : free from all charges or deductions ⟨∼ profit⟩ ⟨∼ weight⟩

⁴net *vb* **net·ted; net·ting** : to gain or produce as profit : CLEAR, YIELD ⟨his business *netted* $50,000 a year⟩

⁵net *n* : a net amount, profit, weight, or price

Neth *abbr* Netherlands

neth·er \'ne-thər\ *adj* : situated down or below ⟨the ∼ regions of the earth⟩

Neth·er·land·er \'ne-thər-ˌlan-dər\ *n* : a native or inhabitant of the Netherlands

neth·er·most \-ˌmōst\ *adj* : LOWEST

neth·er·world \-ˌwərld\ *n* **1** : the world of the dead **2** : UNDERWORLD

nett *Brit var of* NET

net·ting *n* **1** : NETWORK **2** : the act or process of making a net or network

¹net·tle \'net-əl\ *n* : any of a genus of coarse herbs with stinging hairs

²nettle *vb* **net·tled; net·tling** : PROVOKE, VEX, IRRITATE

net·tle·some \'net-əl-səm\ *adj* : causing vexation : IRRITATING

net·work \'net-ˌwərk\ *n* **1** : NET **2** : a system of elements (as lines or channels) that cross in the manner of the threads in a net **3** : a group or system of related or connected parts; *esp* : a chain of radio or television stations

net·work·ing \'net-ˌwər-kiŋ\ *n* : the exchange of information or services among individuals, groups, or institutions

neu·ral \'nur-əl, 'nyur-\ *adj* : of, relating to, or involving a nerve or the nervous system

neu·ral·gia \nu-'ral-jə, nyu-\ *n* : acute pain that follows the course of a nerve — **neu·ral·gic** \-jik\ *adj*

neur·as·then·ic \ˌnur-əs-'the-nik, ˌnyur-, -thē-\ *adj* : affected with or suggestive of mental disorder characterized esp. by fatiguing easily, lack of motivation, feelings of inadequacy, and psychosomatic symptoms — **neur·as·then·ia** \-'thē-nē-ə\ *n* — **neurasthenic** *n*

neu·ri·tis \-'rī-təs\ *n, pl* **-rit·i·des** \-'ri-tə-ˌdēz\ *or* **-ri·tis·es** : inflammation of a nerve — **neu·rit·ic** \-'ri-tik\ *adj or n*

neu·rol·o·gy \nu-'rä-lə-jē, nyu-\ *n* : the scientific study of the nervous system — **neu·ro·log·i·cal** \ˌnur-ə-'lä-ji-kəl, ˌnyur-\ *or* **neu·ro·log·ic** \-jik\ *adj* — **neu·ro·log·i·cal·ly** \-ji-k(ə-)lē\ *adv* — **neu·rol·o·gist** \nu-'rä-lə-jist, nyu-\ *n*

neu·ron \'nu-ˌrän, 'nyu-\ *also* **neu·rone** \-ˌrōn\ *n* : a cell with specialized processes that is the fundamental functional unit of nervous tissue

neu·ro·sci·ence \ˌnur-ō-'sī-əns, ˌnyur-\ *n* : a branch of the life sciences that deals with the anatomy, physiology, biochemistry, or molecular biology of nerves and nervous tissue and with their relation to behavior and learning — **neu·ro·sci·en·tist** \-ən-tist\ *n*

neu·ro·sis \nu-'rō-səs, nyu-\ *n, pl* **-ro·ses** \-ˌsēz\ : a mental and emotional disorder that is less serious than a psychosis, is not characterized by disturbance of the use of language, and is accompanied by various bodily and mental disturbances (as visceral symptoms, anxieties, or phobias)

neu·ro·sur·gery \-'sər-jə-rē\ *n* : surgery of nervous structures (as nerves, the brain, or the spinal cord)— **neu·ro·sur·geon** \-'sər-jən\ *n*

¹neu·rot·ic \nu-'rä-tik, nyu-\ *adj* : of, relating to, being, or affected with a neurosis; *also* : NERVOUS — **neu·rot·i·cal·ly** \-ti-k(ə-)lē\ *adv*

²neurotic *n* : an emotionally unstable or neurotic person

neu·ro·trans·mit·ter \ˌnur-ō-trans-'mi-tər, ˌnyur-, -tranz-\ *n* : a substance (as acetylcholine) that transmits nerve impulses across the gap between neurons

neut *abbr* neuter

¹neu·ter \'nü-tər, 'nyü-\ *adj* [ME *neutre*, fr. MF & L; MF *neutre*, fr. L *neuter*, lit., neither, fr. *ne-* not + *uter* which of two] **1** : of, relating to, or constituting the gender that includes most words or grammatical forms referring to things classed as neither masculine nor feminine **2** : having imperfectly developed or no sex organs

²neuter *n* **1** : a noun, pronoun, adjective, or inflectional form or class of the neuter gender; *also* : the neuter gender **2** : WORKER **2**; *also* : a spayed or castrated animal

³neuter *vb* : CASTRATE, SPAY

¹neu·tral \'nü-trəl, 'nyü-\ *n* **1** : one that is neutral **2** : a neutral color **3** : a position of disengagement (as of gears)

²neutral *adj* **1** : not favoring either side in a quarrel, contest, or war **2** : of or relating to a neutral state or power **3** : MIDDLING, INDIFFERENT **4** : having no hue : GRAY; *also* : not decided in color **5** : neither acid nor basic ⟨a ∼ solution⟩ **6** : not electrically charged

neu·tral·ism \'nü-trə-ˌli-zəm, 'nyü-\ *n* : a policy or the advocacy of neutrality esp. in international affairs

neu·tral·i·ty \nü-'tra-lə-tē, nyü-\ *n* : the quality or state of being neutral; *esp* : refusal to take part in a war between other powers

neu·tral·ize \'nü-trə-ˌlīz, 'nyü-\ *vb* **-ized; -iz·ing** : to make neutral; *esp* : COUNTERACT — **neu·tral·i·za·tion** \ˌnü-trə-lə-'zā-shən, ˌnyü-\ *n*

neu·tri·no \nü-'trē-nō, nyü-\ *n, pl* **-nos** : an uncharged elementary particle held to be massless or very light

neu·tron \'nü-ˌträn, 'nyü-\ *n* : an uncharged atomic particle that is nearly equal in mass to the proton

neutron bomb *n* : a nuclear bomb designed to produce lethal neutrons but less blast and fire damage than other nuclear bombs

neutron star *n* : a hypothetical dense celestial object that results from the collapse of a large star

Nev *abbr* Nevada

nev·er \'ne-vər\ *adv* **1** : not ever **2** : not in any degree, way, or condition

nev·er·more \₁ne-vər-'mōr\ *adv* : never again

nev·er–nev·er land \₁ne-vər-'ne-vər-\ *n* : an ideal or imaginary place

nev·er·the·less \₁ne-vər-*t͟h*ə-'les\ *adv* : in spite of that : HOWEVER

ne·vus \'nē-vəs\ *n, pl* **ne·vi** \-₁vī\ : a usu. pigmented birthmark

¹new \'nü, 'nyü\ *adj* **1** : not old : RECENT, MODERN **2** : recently discovered, recognized, or learned about ⟨~ drugs⟩ **3** : UNFAMILIAR **4** : different from the former **5** : not accustomed ⟨~ to the work⟩ **6** : beginning as a repetition of a previous act or thing ⟨a ~ year⟩ **7** : REFRESHED, REGENERATED ⟨rest made a ~ man of him⟩ **8** : being in a position or place for the first time ⟨a ~ member⟩ **9** *cap* : having been in use after medieval times : MODERN ⟨*New* Latin⟩ **syn** novel, new-fangled, fresh — **new·ish** *adj* — **new·ness** *n*

²new *adv* : NEWLY ⟨*new*-mown hay⟩

New Age *adj* **1** : of, relating to, or being a late 20th century social movement incorporating various untraditional concepts and practices relating esp. to spiritual, emotional, and physical well-being **2** : of, relating to, or being a soft soothing form of instrumental music

¹new·born \-₁bȯrn\ *adj* **1** : recently born **2** : born anew ⟨~ hope⟩

²newborn *n, pl* **newborn** *or* **newborns** : a newborn individual

new·com·er \-₁kə-mər\ *n* **1** : one recently arrived **2** : BEGINNER

New Deal *n* : the legislative and administrative program of President F. D. Roosevelt to promote economic recovery and social reform during the 1930s — **New Dealer** *n*

new·el \'nü-əl, 'nyü-\ *n* : a post about which the steps of a circular staircase wind; *also* : a post at the foot of a stairway or one at a landing

new·fan·gled \'nü-'faŋ-gəld, 'nyü-\ *adj* **1** : attracted to novelty **2** : of the newest style : NOVEL

new–fash·ioned \-'fa-shənd\ *adj* **1** : made in a new fashion or form **2** : UP-TO-DATE

new·found \-'faùnd\ *adj* : newly found

New Left *n* : a radical political movement originating in the 1960s

new·ly \'nü-lē, 'nyü-\ *adv* **1** : LATELY, RECENTLY **2** : ANEW, AFRESH

new·ly·wed \-₁wed\ *n* : one recently married

new moon *n* : the phase of the moon with its dark side toward the earth; *also* : the thin crescent moon seen for a few days after the new moon phase

news \'nüz, 'nyüz\ *n* **1** : a report of recent events : TIDINGS **2** : material reported in a newspaper or news periodical or on a newscast

news·boy \'nüz-₁bȯi, 'nyüz-\ *n* : one who delivers or sells newspapers

news·cast \-₁kast\ *n* : a radio or television broadcast of news — **news·cast·er** \-₁kas-tər\ *n*

news·let·ter \-₁le-tər\ *n* : a small newspaper containing news or information of interest chiefly to a special group

news·mag·a·zine \-₁ma-gə-₁zēn\ *n* : a usu. weekly magazine devoted chiefly to summarizing and analyzing news

news·man \-mən, -₁man\ *n* : one who gathers, reports, or comments on the news : REPORTER

news·pa·per \-₁pā-pər\ *n* : a paper that is published at regular intervals and contains news, articles of opinion, features, and advertising

news·pa·per·man \-₁pā-pər-₁man\ *n* : one who owns or is employed by a newspaper

news·print \-₁print\ *n* : paper made chiefly from wood pulp and used mostly for newspapers

news·reel \-₁rēl\ *n* : a short motion picture portraying current events

news·stand \-₁stand\ *n* : a place where newspapers and periodicals are sold

news·week·ly \-₁wēk-lē\ *n* : a weekly newspaper or newsmagazine

news·wom·an \-₁wu̇-mən\ *n* : a woman who gathers, reports, or comments on the news : REPORTER

news·wor·thy \-₁wər-*t͟h*ē\ *adj* : sufficiently interesting to the general public to warrant reporting (as in a newspaper)

newsy \'nü-zē, 'nyü-\ *adj* **news·i·er; -est** : filled with news; *esp* : TALKATIVE

newt \'nüt, 'nyüt\ *n* : any of various small chiefly aquatic salamanders

New Testament *n* : the second of the two chief divisions of the Bible — see BIBLE table

new·ton \'nüt-ᵊn, 'nyüt-\ *n* : the unit of force in the metric system equal to the force required to impart an acceleration of one meter per second per second to a mass of one kilogram

new wave *n, often cap N&W* : the latest and esp. the most outrageous style — **new–wave** *adj*

New World *n* : the western hemisphere; *esp* : the continental landmass of No. and So. America

New Year *n* **1** : NEW YEAR'S DAY; *also* : the first days of the year **2** : ROSH HASHANAH

New Year's Day *n* : January 1 observed as a legal holiday

New Zea·land·er \nü-'zē-lən-dər, nyü-\ *n* : a native or inhabitant of New Zealand

¹next \'nekst\ *adj* : immediately preceding or following : NEAREST

²next *prep* : nearest or adjacent to

³next *adv* **1** : in the time, place, or order nearest or immediately succeeding **2** : on the first occasion to come

nex·us \'nek-səs\ *n, pl* **nex·us·es** \-sə-səz\ *or* **nex·us** \-səs, -₁süs\ : CONNECTION, LINK

Nez Percé \'nez-₁pərs, *F* nā-per-sā\ *n* : a member of an American Indian people of Idaho, Washington, and Oregon; *also* : the language of the Nez Percé

NF *abbr* Newfoundland

NFC *abbr* National Football Conference

NFL *abbr* National Football League

Nfld *abbr* Newfoundland

NG *abbr* **1** National Guard **2** no good

ngul·trum \eŋ-'gül-trəm\ *n* — see MONEY table

ngwee \eŋ-'gwē\ *n, pl* **ngwee** — see *kwacha* at MONEY table

NH *abbr* New Hampshire

NHL *abbr* National Hockey League

Ni *symbol* nickel

ni·a·cin \'nī-ə-sən\ *n* : NICOTINIC ACID

nib \'nib\ *n* : POINT; *esp* : a pen point

¹nib·ble \'ni-bəl\ *vb* **nib·bled; nib·bling** : to bite gently or bit by bit

²nibble *n* : a small or cautious bite

Nic·a·ra·guan \₁ni-kə-'rä-gwən\ *n* : a native or inhabitant of Nicaragua — **Nicaraguan** *adj*

nice \'nīs\ *adj* **nic·er; nic·est** [ME, foolish, wanton, fr. OF, fr. L *nescius* ignorant, fr. *nescire* to not know] **1** : FASTIDIOUS, DISCRIMINATING **2** : marked by delicate discrimination or treatment **3** : PLEASING, AGREEABLE; *also* : well-executed **4** : WELL-BRED ⟨~ people⟩ **5** : VIRTUOUS, RESPECTABLE **syn** choosy, finicky, particular, persnickety, picky — **nice·ly** *adv* — **nice·ness** *n*

nice–nel·ly \'nīs-'ne-lē\ *adj, often cap 2d N* **1** : marked by euphemism **2** : PRUDISH — **nice nelly** *n, often cap 2d N* — **nice–nel·ly·ism** \-i-zəm\ *n, often cap 2d N*

nice•ty \\'nī-sə-tē\\ *n, pl* **-ties 1 :** a dainty, delicate, or elegant thing ⟨enjoy the *niceties* of life⟩ **2 :** a fine point or distinction ⟨*niceties* of workmanship⟩ **3 :** EXACTNESS, PRECISION, ACCURACY

niche \\'nich\\ *n* [F] **1 :** a recess in a wall esp. for a statue **2 :** a place, employment, or activity for which a person or thing is best fitted **3 :** the living space or role of an organism in an ecological community esp. with regard to food consumption

¹nick \\'nik\\ *n* **1 :** a small notch or groove **2 :** the final critical moment ⟨in the ∼ of time⟩

²nick *vb* : NOTCH, CHIP

nick•el \\'ni-kəl\\ *n* **1 :** a hard silver-white metallic chemical element capable of a high polish and used in alloys — see ELEMENT table **2 :** the U.S. 5-cent piece made of copper and nickel; *also* : the Canadian 5-cent piece

nick•el•ode•on \\ˌni-kə-'lō-dē-ən\\ *n* **1 :** an early movie theater to which admission cost five cents **2 :** JUKEBOX

nick•er \\'ni-kər\\ *vb* : NEIGH, WHINNY — **nicker** *n*

nick•name \\'nik-ˌnām\\ *n* [ME *nekename* additional name, alter. (from misdivision of *an ekename*) of *ekename*, fr. *eke* also + *name*] **1 :** a usu. descriptive name given instead of or in addition to the one belonging to a person, place, or thing **2 :** a familiar form of a proper name — **nickname** *vb*

nic•o•tine \\'ni-kə-ˌtēn\\ *n* : a poisonous and addictive substance in tobacco that is used as an insecticide

nic•o•tin•ic acid \\ˌni-kə-'tē-nik-, -'ti-\\ *n* : an organic acid of the vitamin B complex found in plants and animals and used against pellagra

niece \\'nēs\\ *n* : a daughter of one's brother, sister, brother-in-law, or sister-in-law

nif•ty \\'nif-tē\\ *adj* **nif•ti•er; -est** : very good : very attractive

Ni•ge•ri•an \\nī-'jir-ē-ən\\ *n* : a native or inhabitant of Nigeria — **Nigerian** *adj*

nig•gard \\'ni-gərd\\ *n* : a stingy person : MISER — **nig•gard•li•ness** \\-lē-nəs\\ *n* — **nig•gard•ly** *adj or adv*

nig•gling \\'ni-gə-liŋ\\ *adj* **1 :** PETTY **2 :** bothersome in a petty way **syn** inconsequential, measly, picayune, piddling, trifling, trivial

¹nigh \\'nī\\ *adv* **1 :** near in place, time, or relationship **2 :** NEARLY, ALMOST

²nigh *adj* : CLOSE, NEAR

³nigh *prep* : NEAR

night \\'nīt\\ *n* **1 :** the period between dusk and dawn **2 :** the darkness of night **3 :** a period of misery or unhappiness **4 :** NIGHTFALL — **night** *adj*

night blindness *n* : reduced visual capacity in faint light (as at night)

night•cap \\'nīt-ˌkap\\ *n* **1 :** a cloth cap worn with nightclothes **2 :** a usu. alcoholic drink taken at bedtime

night•clothes \\-ˌklōthz, -ˌklōz\\ *n pl* : garments worn in bed

night•club \\-ˌkləb\\ *n* : a place of entertainment open at night usu. serving food and liquor and providing music for dancing

night crawl•er \\-ˌkrò-lər\\ *n* : EARTHWORM; *esp* : a large earthworm found on the soil surface at night

night•dress \\'nīt-ˌdres\\ *n* : NIGHTGOWN

night•fall \\-ˌfòl\\ *n* : the coming of night

night•gown \\-ˌgaùn\\ *n* : a loose garment for wear in bed

night•hawk \\-ˌhòk\\ *n* : any of a genus of American birds related to and resembling the whippoorwill

night•in•gale \\'nīt-ᵊn-ˌgāl, 'nī-tiŋ-\\ *n* [ME, fr. OE *nihtegale*, fr. *niht* night + *galan* to sing] : any of several Old World thrushes noted for the sweet usu. nocturnal song of the male

night•life \\'nīt-ˌlīf\\ *n* : the activity of pleasure-seekers at night

night•ly \\'nīt-lē\\ *adj* **1 :** happening, done, or produced by night or every night **2 :** of or relating to the night or every night — **nightly** *adv*

night•mare \\'nīt-ˌmar\\ *n* **1 :** a frightening dream **2 :** a frightening or horrible experience — **nightmare** *adj* — **night•mar•ish** *adj*

night rider *n* : a member of a secret band who ride masked at night doing violence to punish or terrorize

night•shade \\'nīt-ˌshād\\ *n* : any of a large genus of herbs, shrubs, and trees that include poisonous forms (as belladonna) and important food plants (as the potato, tomato, and eggplant)

night•shirt \\-ˌshərt\\ *n* : a nightgown resembling a shirt

night soil *n* : human excrement used esp. for fertilizing the soil

night•stick \\'nīt-ˌstik\\ *n* : a police officer's club

night•time \\-ˌtīm\\ *n* : the time from dusk to dawn

night•walk•er \\-ˌwò-kər\\ *n* : a person who roves about at night esp. with criminal or immoral intent

ni•hil•ism \\'nī-ə-ˌli-zəm, 'nē-hə-\\ *n* **1 :** a viewpoint that traditional values and beliefs are unfounded and that existence is senseless and useless **2 :** ANARCHISM **3 :** TERRORISM — **ni•hil•ist** \\-list\\ *n or adj* — **ni•hil•is•tic** \\ˌnī-ə-'lis-tik, ˌnē-hə-\\ *adj*

nil \\'nil\\ *n* : ZERO, NOTHING

nim•ble \\'nim-bəl\\ *adj* **nim•bler; nim•blest** [ME *nimel*, fr. OE *numol* holding much, fr. *niman* to take] **1 :** quick and light in motion : AGILE ⟨a ∼ dancer⟩ **2 :** quick in understanding and learning : CLEVER ⟨a ∼ mind⟩ **syn** active, brisk, sprightly, spry, zippy — **nim•ble•ness** *n* — **nim•bly** \\-blē\\ *adv*

nim•bus \\'nim-bəs\\ *n, pl* **nim•bi** \\-ˌbī, -bē\\ *or* **nim•bus•es 1 :** a figure (as a disk) in an art work suggesting radiant light about the head of a divinity, saint, or sovereign **2 :** a rain cloud; *also* : THUNDERHEAD

NIMBY \\'nim-bē\\ *abbr* not in my backyard

nim•rod \\'nim-ˌräd\\ *n* : HUNTER

nin•com•poop \\'nin-kəm-ˌpüp\\ *n* : FOOL, SIMPLETON

nine \\'nīn\\ *n* **1 :** one more than eight **2 :** the 9th in a set or series **3 :** something having nine units; *esp* : a baseball team — **nine** *adj or pron* — **ninth** \\'nīnth\\ *adj or adv or n*

nine days' wonder *n* : something that creates a short-lived sensation

nine•pins \\'nīn-ˌpinz\\ *n* : tenpins played without the headpin

nine•teen \\'nīn-'tēn\\ *n* : one more than 18 — **nineteen** *adj or pron* — **nine•teenth** \\-'tēnth\\ *adj or n*

nine•ty \\'nīn-tē\\ *n, pl* **nineties** : nine times 10 — **nine•ti•eth** \\-tē-əth\\ *adj or n* — **ninety** *adj or pron*

nin•ja \\'nin-jə, -(ˌ)jä\\ *n, pl* **ninja** *or* **ninjas** [Jp] : a person trained in ancient Japanese martial arts and employed esp. for espionage and assassinations

nin•ny \\'ni-nē\\ *n, pl* **ninnies** : FOOL

ni•o•bi•um \\nī-'ō-bē-əm\\ *n* : a gray metallic chemical element used in alloys — see ELEMENT table

¹nip \\'nip\\ *vb* **nipped; nip•ping 1 :** to catch hold of and squeeze tightly between two surfaces, edges, or points **2 :** ³CLIP **3 :** to destroy the growth, progress, or fulfillment of ⟨*nipped* in the bud⟩ **4 :** to injure or make numb with cold : CHILL **5 :** SNATCH, STEAL

²nip *n* **1 :** a sharp stinging cold **2 :** a biting or pungent flavor **3 :** PINCH, BITE **4 :** a small portion : BIT

³nip *n* : a small quantity of liquor : SIP

⁴nip *vb* **nipped; nip•ping** : to take liquor in nips : TIPPLE

nip and tuck *adj or adv* : so close that the lead shifts rapidly from one contestant to another

nip•per \\'ni-pər\\ *n* **1 :** one that nips **2** *pl* : PINCERS **3** : CHILD; *esp* : a small boy

nip•ple \\'ni-pəl\\ *n* : the protuberance of a mammary gland through which milk is drawn off : TEAT; *also* : something resembling a nipple

nip•py \\'ni-pē\\ *adj* **nip•pi•er; -est 1 :** PUNGENT, SHARP **2 :** CHILLY

nir•va•na \\nir-'vä-nə\\ *n, often cap* [Skt *nirvāṇa*, lit., act of extinguishing, fr. *nis-* out + *vāti* it blows] **1 :** the final freeing of a soul from all that enslaves it; *esp* : the supreme happiness that according to Buddhism comes when all passion, hatred, and delusion die out and the soul is released from the necessity of further purification **2** : OBLIVION; *also* : PARADISE

ni·sei \nē-'sā, 'nē-ˌsā\ *n, pl* **nisei** *also* **niseis** : a son or daughter of immigrant Japanese parents who is born and educated in America

ni·si \'nī-ˌsī\ *adj* [L, unless, fr. *ne-* not + *si* if] : taking effect at a specified time unless previously modified or voided ⟨a divorce decree ∼⟩

nit \'nit\ *n* : the egg of a parasitic insect (as a louse); *also* : the young insect

nite *var of* NIGHT

ni·ter \'nī-tər\ *n* : POTASSIUM NITRATE

nit–pick·ing \'nit-ˌpi-kiŋ\ *n* : minute and usu. unjustified criticism — **nit·pick·er** *n*

¹**ni·trate** \'nī-ˌtrāt, -trət\ *n* **1** : a salt or ester of nitric acid **2** : sodium nitrate or potassium nitrate used as a fertilizer

²**ni·trate** \-ˌtrāt\ *vb* **ni·trat·ed; ni·trat·ing** : to treat or combine with nitric acid or a nitrate — **ni·tra·tion** \nī-'trā-shən\ *n*

ni·tre *chiefly Brit var of* NITER

ni·tric acid \'nī-trik-\ *n* : a corrosive liquid acid used esp. in making dyes, explosives, and fertilizers

ni·tri·fi·ca·tion \ˌnī-trə-fə-'kā-shən\ *n* : the oxidation (as by bacteria) of ammonium salts to nitrites and then to nitrates — **ni·tri·fy·ing** \'nī-trə-fī-iŋ\ *adj*

ni·trite \'nī-ˌtrīt\ *n* : a salt of nitrous acid

ni·tro \'nī-trō\ *n, pl* **nitros** : any of various nitrated products; *esp* : NITROGLYCERIN

ni·tro·gen \'nī-trə-jən\ *n* : a tasteless odorless gaseous chemical element constituting 78 percent of the atmosphere by volume — see ELEMENT table — **ni·trog·e·nous** \nī-'trä-jə-nəs\ *adj*

nitrogen narcosis *n* : a state of euphoria and exhilaration caused by nitrogen forced into a diver's bloodstream from atmospheric air under pressure

ni·tro·glyc·er·in *or* **ni·tro·glyc·er·ine** \ˌnī-trə-'gli-sə-rən\ *n* : a heavy oily explosive liquid used to make dynamite and in medicine to dilate blood vessels

ni·trous acid \'nī-trəs-\ *n* : an unstable nitrogen-containing acid known only in solution or in the form of its salts

nitrous oxide *n* : a colorless gas used esp. as an anesthetic in dentistry

nit·ty–grit·ty \'ni-tē-ˌgri-tē, ˌni-tē-'gri-tē\ *n* : what is essential and basic : specific practical details

nit·wit \'nit-ˌwit\ *n* : a scatterbrained or stupid person

¹**nix** \'niks\ *n* : NOTHING

²**nix** *vb* : VETO, REJECT

³**nix** *adv* : NO

NJ *abbr* New Jersey

NL *abbr* National League

NLRB *abbr* National Labor Relations Board

NM *abbr* **1** nautical mile **2** New Mexico

N Mex *abbr* New Mexico

NMI *abbr* no middle initial

NNE *abbr* north-northeast

NNW *abbr* north-northwest

¹**no** \'nō\ *adv* **1** — used to express the negative of an alternative ⟨shall we continue or ∼⟩ **2** : in no respect or degree ⟨he is ∼ better than the others⟩ **3** : not so ⟨∼, I'm not ready⟩ **4** — used with an adjective to imply a meaning opposite to the positive statement ⟨in ∼ uncertain terms⟩ **5** — used to introduce a more emphatic or explicit statement ⟨has the right, ∼, the duty to continue⟩ **6** — used as an interjection to express surprise or doubt ⟨∼—you don't say⟩ **7** — used in combination with a verb to form a compound adjective ⟨no-bake pie⟩

²**no** *adj* **1** : not any; *also* : hardly any **2** : not a ⟨she's ∼ expert⟩

³**no** \'nō\ *n, pl* **noes** *or* **nos** \'nōz\ **1** : REFUSAL, DENIAL **2** : a negative vote or decision; *also, pl* : persons voting in the negative

⁴**no** *abbr* **1** north; northern **2** [L *numero*, abl. of *numerus*] number

¹**No** *or* **Noh** \'nō\ *n, pl* **No** *or* **Noh** : classic Japanese dance-drama having a heroic theme, a chorus, and highly stylized action, costuming, and scenery

²**No** *symbol* nobelium

No·bel·ist \nō-'be-list\ *n* : a winner of a Nobel prize

no·bel·i·um \nō-'be-lē-əm\ *n* : a radioactive chemical element produced artificially — see ELEMENT table

No·bel prize \nō-'bel-, 'nō-ˌbel-\ *n* : any of various annual prizes (as in peace, literature, or medicine) established by the will of Alfred Nobel for the encouragement of persons who work for the interests of humanity

no·bil·i·ty \nō-'bi-lə-tē\ *n* **1** : the quality or state of being noble **2** : nobles considered as forming a class

¹**no·ble** \'nō-bəl\ *adj* **no·bler; no·blest** [ME, fr. OF, fr. L *nobilis* well known, noble, fr. *noscere* to come to know] **1** : ILLUSTRIOUS; *also* : FAMOUS, NOTABLE **2** : of high birth, rank, or station : ARISTOCRATIC **3** : EXCELLENT **4** : STATELY, IMPOSING ⟨a ∼ edifice⟩ **5** : of a superior nature **syn** august, baronial, grand, grandiose, magnificent, majestic — **no·ble·ness** *n* — **no·bly** \-blē\ *adv*

²**no·ble** *n* : a person of noble rank or birth

no·ble·man \'nō-bəl-mən\ *n* : a member of the nobility : PEER

no·blesse oblige \nō-ˌbles-ə-'blēzh\ *n* [F, lit., nobility obligates] : the obligation of honorable, generous, and responsible behavior associated with high rank or birth

no·ble·wom·an \'nō-bəl-ˌwu̇-mən\ *n* : a woman of noble rank : PEERESS

¹**no·body** \'nō-bä-dē, -bə-\ *pron* : no person

²**nobody** *n, pl* **no·bod·ies** : a person of no influence or importance

noc·tur·nal \näk-'tərn-ᵊl\ *adj* **1** : of, relating to, or occurring in the night **2** : active at night ⟨a ∼ bird⟩

noc·turne \'näk-ˌtərn\ *n* : a work of art dealing with night; *esp* : a dreamy pensive composition for the piano

noc·u·ous \'nä-kyə-wəs\ *adj* : HARMFUL — **noc·u·ous·ly** *adv*

nod \'näd\ *vb* **nod·ded; nod·ding** **1** : to bend the head downward or forward (as in bowing, going to sleep, or giving assent) **2** : to move up and down ⟨tulips *nodding* in the breeze⟩ **3** : to show by a nod of the head ⟨∼ agreement⟩ **4** : to make a slip or error in a moment of abstraction — **nod** *n*

nod·dle \'näd-ᵊl\ *n* : HEAD

nod·dy \'nä-dē\ *n, pl* **noddies** **1** : FOOL **2** : a stout-bodied tropical tern

node \'nōd\ *n* : a thickened, swollen, or differentiated area (as of tissue); *esp* : the part of a stem from which a leaf arises — **nod·al** \-ᵊl\ *adj*

nod·ule \'nä-jül\ *n* : a small lump or swelling — **nod·u·lar** \'nä-jə-lər\ *adj*

no·el \nō-'el\ *n* [F *noël* Christmas, carol, fr. L *natalis* birthday] **1** : a Christmas carol **2** *cap* : the Christmas season

noes *pl of* NO

no–fault \'nō-ˌfȯlt\ *adj* **1** : of, relating to, or being a motor vehicle insurance plan under which someone involved in an accident is compensated usu. up to a stipulated limit for actual losses by that person's own insurance company regardless of who is responsible **2** : of, relating to, or being a divorce law under which neither party is held responsible for the breakup of the marriage

nog·gin \'nä-gən\ *n* **1** : a small mug or cup; *also* : a small quantity of drink **2** : a person's head

no–good \'nō-ˌgu̇d\ *adj* : having no worth, virtue, use, or chance of success — **no–good** \'nō-ˌgu̇d\ *n*

Noh *var of* NO

no–hit·ter \(ˌ)nō-'hi-tər\ *n* : a baseball game or part of a game in which a pitcher allows no base hits

no·how \'nō-ˌhau̇\ *adv* : in no manner

¹**noise** \'nȯiz\ *n* [ME, fr. OF, strife, quarrel, noise, fr. L

nausea nausea] **1** : loud, confused, or senseless shouting or outcry **2** : SOUND; *esp* : one that lacks agreeable musical quality or is noticeably unpleasant **3** : unwanted electronic signal or disturbance — **noise·less** *adj* — **noise·less·ly** *adv*

²**noise** *vb* **noised; nois·ing** : to spread by rumor or report ⟨the story was *noised* abroad⟩

noise·mak·er \'nȯiz-ˌmā-kər\ *n* : one that makes noise; *esp* : a device used to make noise at parties

noise pollution *n* : annoying or harmful noise in an environment

noi·some \'nȯi-səm\ *adj* **1** : HARMFUL, UNWHOLESOME **2** : offensive to the senses (as smell) : DISGUSTING **syn** insalubrious, noxious, sickly, unhealthful, unhealthy

noisy \'nȯi-zē\ *adj* **nois·i·er; -est 1** : making loud noises **2** : full of noises : LOUD — **nois·i·ly** \-zə-lē\ *adv* — **nois·i·ness** \-zē-nəs\ *n*

nol·le pro·se·qui \ˌnä-lē-'prä-sə-ˌkwī\ *n* [L, to be unwilling to pursue] : an entry on the record of a legal action that the prosecutor or plaintiff will proceed no further in an action or suit or in some aspect of it

no·lo con·ten·de·re \ˌnō-lō-kən-'ten-də-rē\ *n* [L, I do not wish to contend] : a plea in a criminal prosecution that subjects the defendant to conviction but does not admit guilt or preclude denying the charges in another proceeding

nol–pros \'näl-'präs\ *vb* **nol–prossed; nol–pros·sing** : to discontinue by entering a nolle prosequi

nom *abbr* nominative

no·mad \'nō-ˌmad\ *n* **1** : a member of a people who have no fixed residence but move from place to place **2** : an individual who roams about aimlessly — **no·mad** *adj* — **no·mad·ic** \nō-'ma-dik\ *adj*

no–man's–land \'nō-manz-ˌland\ *n* **1** : an area of unowned, unclaimed, or uninhabited land **2** : an unoccupied area between opposing troops

nom de guerre \ˌnäm-di-'ger\ *n, pl* **noms de guerre** *same or* ˌnämz-\ [F, lit., war name] : PSEUDONYM

nom de plume \-'plüm\ *n, pl* **noms de plume** *same or* ˌnämz-\ [F, pen name; prob. coined in E] : PEN NAME

no·men·cla·ture \'nō-mən-ˌklā-chər\ *n* **1** : NAME, DESIGNATION **2** : a system of terms used in a science or art

nom·i·nal \'nä-mən-ᵊl\ *adj* **1** : being something in name or form only ⟨∼ head of a party⟩ **2** : TRIFLING ⟨a ∼ price⟩ — **nom·i·nal·ly** *adv*

nom·i·nate \'nä-mə-ˌnāt\ *vb* **-nat·ed; -nat·ing** : to choose as a candidate for election, appointment, or honor **syn** appoint, designate, name, tap — **nom·i·na·tion** \ˌnä-mə-'nā-shən\ *n*

nom·i·na·tive \'nä-mə-nə-tiv\ *adj* : of, relating to, or constituting a grammatical case marking typically the subject of a verb — **nominative** *n*

nom·i·nee \ˌnä-mə-'nē\ *n* : a person nominated for an office, duty, or position

non- \('\)nän *or* nän *before stressed syllables;* nän *elsewhere*\ *prefix* **1** : not : reverse of : absence of **2** : having no importance

nonabrasive	nonbelligerent
nonabsorbent	nonbreakable
nonacademic	noncancerous
nonacceptance	noncandidate
nonacid	noncellular
nonactivated	nonclerical
nonadaptive	noncoital
nonaddictive	noncombat
nonadhesive	noncombustible
nonadjacent	noncommercial
nonadjustable	noncommunist
nonaggression	noncompeting
nonalcoholic	noncompliance
nonappearance	noncompliance
nonaromatic	noncomplying
nonathletic	nonconducting
nonattendance	nonconflicting
nonbeliever	nonconformance

nonconforming	nonmagnetic
nonconstructive	nonmalignant
noncontagious	nonmaterial
noncontinuous	nonmember
noncorroding	nonmembership
noncorrosive	nonmigratory
noncritical	nonmilitary
noncrystalline	nonmoral
nondeductible	nonmotile
nondelivery	nonmoving
nondemocratic	nonnegotiable
nondenominational	nonobservance
nondepartmental	nonoccurrence
nondestructive	nonofficial
nondevelopment	nonoily
nondiscrimination	nonorthodox
nondiscriminatory	nonparallel
nondistinctive	nonparasitic
nondurable	nonparticipant
noneconomic	nonparticipating
noneducational	nonpathogenic
nonelastic	nonpaying
nonelection	nonpayment
nonelective	nonperformance
nonelectric	nonperishable
nonelectrical	nonphysical
nonemotional	nonpoisonous
nonenforcement	nonpolar
nonessential	nonpolitical
nonethical	nonporous
non-euclidean	nonpregnant
nonexclusive	nonproductive
nonexempt	nonprofessional
nonexistence	nonprotein
nonexistent	nonradioactive
nonexplosive	nonrandom
nonfarm	nonreactive
nonfatal	nonreciprocal
nonfattening	nonrecognition
nonfederated	nonrecurrent
nonferrous	nonrecurring
nonfiction	nonrefillable
nonfictional	nonreligious
nonfilamentous	nonrenewable
nonfilterable	nonresidential
nonflammable	nonrestricted
nonflowering	nonreturnable
nonfood	nonreversible
nonfreezing	nonruminant
nonfulfillment	nonsalable
nonfunctional	nonscientific
nongraded	nonscientist
nonhereditary	nonseasonal
nonhomogeneous	nonsectarian
nonhomologous	nonsegregated
nonhuman	nonselective
nonidentical	non-self-governing
nonimportation	nonsexist
nonindustrial	nonsexual
noninfectious	nonshrinkable
noninflammable	nonsinkable
nonintellectual	nonsmoker
nonintercourse	nonsmoking
noninterference	nonsocial
nonintoxicant	nonspeaking
nonintoxicating	nonspecialist
noninvasive	nonspecific
nonionizing	nonsteroidal
nonirritating	nonsuccess
nonlegal	nonsurgical
nonlethal	nontaxable
nonlife	nonteaching
nonlinear	nontechnical
nonliterary	nontemporal
nonliving	nontenured
nonlogical	nontheistic

nonthreatening
nontoxic
nontraditional
nontransferable
nontypical
nonuniform
nonuser
nonvascular
nonvenomous

nonviable
nonvisual
nonvocal
nonvolatile
nonvoter
nonvoting
nonworker
nonworking
nonzero

non·age \'nä-nij, 'nō-\ *n* **1** : legal minority **2** : a period of youth **3** : IMMATURITY

no·na·ge·nar·i·an \nō-nə-jə-'ner-ē-ən, nä-\ *n* : a person whose age is in the nineties

non·aligned \nän-ə-'līnd\ *adj* : not allied with other nations

non·book \'nän-ˌbůk\ *n* : a book of little literary merit that is often a compilation (as of pictures or speeches)

¹nonce \'näns\ *n* : the one, particular, or present occasion or purpose ⟨for the ∼⟩

²nonce *adj* : occurring, used, or made only once or for a special occasion ⟨a ∼ word⟩

non·cha·lant \nän-shə-'länt\ *adj* [F, fr. OF, fr. prp. of *nonchaloir* to disregard, fr. *non-* not + *chaloir* to concern, fr. L *calēre* to be warm] : giving an effect of unconcern or indifference **syn** collected, composed, cool, imperturbable, unflappable, unruffled — **non·cha·lance** \-'läns\ *n* — **non·cha·lant·ly** *adv*

non·com \'nän-ˌkäm\ *n* : NONCOMMISSIONED OFFICER

non·com·ba·tant \nän-kəm-'bat-ᵊnt, nän-'käm-bə-tənt\ *n* : a member (as a chaplain) of the armed forces whose duties do not include fighting; *also* : CIVILIAN — **noncombatant** *adj*

non·com·mis·sioned officer \nän-kə-'mi-shənd-\ *n* : a subordinate officer in the armed forces appointed from enlisted personnel

non·com·mit·tal \nän-kə-'mit-ᵊl\ *adj* : indicating neither consent nor dissent

non com·pos men·tis \nän-ˌkäm-pəs-'men-təs\ *adj* : not of sound mind

non·con·duc·tor \nän-kən-'dək-tər\ *n* : a substance that is a very poor conductor of heat, electricity, or sound

non·con·form·ist \-kən-'for-mist\ *n* **1** *often cap* : a person who does not conform to an established church and esp. the Church of England **2** : a person who does not conform to a generally accepted pattern of thought or action **syn** dissenter, dissident, heretic, schismatic, sectary, separatist — **non·con·for·mi·ty** \-'for-mə-tē\ *n*

non·co·op·er·a·tion \nän-kō-ˌä-pə-'rā-shən\ *n* : failure or refusal to cooperate; *esp* : refusal through civil disobedience of a people to cooperate with the government of a country

non·cred·it \(ˌ)nän-'kre-dət\ *adj* : not offering credit toward a degree

non·cus·to·di·al \nän-kə-'stō-dē-əl\ *adj* : of or being a parent who does not have legal custody of a child

non·dairy \'nän-ˌder-ē\ *adj* : containing no milk or milk products

non·de·script \nän-di-'skript\ *adj* **1** : not belonging to any particular class or kind **2** : lacking distinctive qualities

non·drink·er \-'driŋ-kər\ *n* : a person who abstains from alcohol

¹none \'nən\ *pron* **1** : not any ⟨∼ of them went⟩ **2** : not one ⟨∼ of the family⟩ **3** : not any such thing or person ⟨half a loaf is better than ∼⟩

²none *adj, archaic* : not any : NO

³none *adv* : by no means : not at all ⟨he got there ∼ too soon⟩

non·en·ti·ty \nän-'en-tə-tē\ *n* **1** : something that does not exist or exists only in the imagination **2** : one of no consequence or significance **syn** nobody, nothing, whippersnapper

nones \'nōnz\ *n sing or pl* : the 7th day of March, May, July, or October or the 5th day of any other month in the ancient Roman calendar

none·such \'nən-ˌsəch\ *n* : one without an equal — **nonesuch** *adj*

none·the·less \ˌnən-thə-'les\ *adv* : NEVERTHELESS

non·event \'nän-i-ˌvent\ *n* **1** : an event that fails to take place or to satisfy expectations **2** : a highly promoted event of little intrinsic interest

non·fat \-'fat\ *adj* : lacking fat solids : having fat solids removed ⟨∼ milk⟩

non·gono·coc·cal \nän-ˌgä-nə-'kä-kəl\ *adj* : not caused by a gonococcus

non·he·ro \'nän-ˌhē-rō\ *n* : ANTIHERO

non·in·ter·ven·tion \nän-ˌin-tər-'ven-chən\ *n* : refusal or failure to intervene (as in the affairs of other countries)

non·met·al \'nän-ˌmet-ᵊl\ *n* : a chemical element (as carbon) that lacks the characteristics of a metal — **non·me·tal·lic** \nän-mə-'ta-lik\ *adj*

non·neg·a·tive \-'ne-gə-tiv\ *adj* : not negative : being either positive or zero

non·nu·cle·ar \'nän-'nü-klē-ər\ *adj* **1** : not nuclear **2** : not having, using, or involving nuclear weapons

non·ob·jec·tive \nän-əb-'jek-tiv\ *adj* **1** : not objective **2** : representing no natural or actual object, figure, or scene ⟨∼ art⟩

¹non·pa·reil \-pə-'rel\ *adj* : having no equal : PEERLESS

²nonpareil *n* **1** : an individual of unequaled excellence : PARAGON **2** : a small flat disk of chocolate covered with white sugar pellets

non·par·ti·san \'nän-'pär-tə-zən\ *adj* : not partisan; *esp* : not influenced by political party spirit or interests

non·per·son \-'pərs-ᵊn\ *n* **1** : UNPERSON **2** : a person having no social or legal status

non·plus \'nän-'pləs\ *vb* **-plussed** *also* **-plused** \-'pləst\; **-plus·sing** *also* **-plus·ing** : PUZZLE, PERPLEX

non·pre·scrip·tion \nän-pri-'skrip-shən\ *adj* : available for sale legally without a doctor's prescription

non·prof·it \'nän-'prä-fət\ *adj* : not conducted or maintained for the purpose of making a profit ⟨a ∼ organization⟩

non·pro·lif·er·a·tion \ˌnän-prə-ˌli-fə-'rā-shən\ *adj* : providing for the stoppage of proliferation (as of nuclear arms) ⟨a ∼ treaty⟩

non·read·er \'nän-'rē-dər\ *n* : one who does not read

non·rep·re·sen·ta·tion·al \ˌnän-ˌre-pri-ˌzen-'tā-shə-nəl\ *adj* : NONOBJECTIVE 2

non·res·i·dent \nän-'re-zə-dənt\ *adj* : not living in a particular place — **non·res·i·dence** \-dəns\ *n* — **non·resident** *n*

non·re·sis·tance \nän-ri-'zis-təns\ *n* : the principles or practice of passive submission to authority even when unjust or oppressive

non·re·stric·tive \-ri-'strik-tiv\ *adj* **1** : not serving or tending to restrict **2** : not limiting the reference of the word or phrase modified ⟨a ∼ clause⟩

non·rig·id \nän-'ri-jəd\ *adj* : maintaining form by pressure of contained gas ⟨a ∼ airship⟩

non·sched·uled \'nän-'ske-jüld\ *adj* : licensed to carry passengers or freight by air without a regular schedule

non·sense \'nän-ˌsens, -səns\ *n* **1** : foolish or meaningless words or actions **2** : things of no importance or value — **non·sen·si·cal** \nän-'sen-si-kəl\ *adj* — **non·sen·si·cal·ly** \-k(ə-)lē\ *adv*

non se·qui·tur \nän-'se-kwə-tər\ *n* [L, it does not follow] : an inference that does not follow from the premises

non·sked \'nän-'sked\ *n* : a nonscheduled transport plane or airline

non·skid \'nän-'skid\ *adj* : designed to prevent skidding

non·slip \-'slip\ *adj* : designed to prevent slipping

non·stan·dard \nän-'stan-dərd\ *adj* **1** : not standard **2**

: not conforming to the usage characteristic of educated native speakers of a language

non·start·er \'nän-'stär-tər\ *n* 1 : one that does not start 2 : one that is not productive or effective

non·stick \-'stik\ *adj* : allowing easy removal of cooked food particles

non·stop \-'stäp\ *adj* : done or made without a stop — **nonstop** *adv*

non·sup·port \ˌnän-sə-'pōrt\ *n* : failure to support; *esp* : failure on the part of one under obligation to provide maintenance

non–U \ˌnän-'yü\ *adj* : not characteristic of the upper classes

non·union \-'yü-nyən\ *adj* 1 : not belonging to a trade union ⟨∼ carpenters⟩ 2 : not recognizing or favoring trade unions or their members ⟨∼ employers⟩

non·us·er \-'yü-zər\ *n* : one who does not make use of something (as drugs)

non·vi·o·lence \'nän-'vī-ə-ləns\ *n* 1 : abstention from violence as a matter of principle 2 : avoidance of violence 3 : nonviolent political demonstrations — **non·vi·o·lent** \-lənt\ *adj*

non·white \ˌnän-'hwīt, -'wīt\ *n* : a person whose features and esp. skin color are different from those of peoples of northwestern Europe — **nonwhite** *adj*

non·wo·ven \'nän-'wō-vən\ *adj* : made of fibers held together by interlocking or bonding (as by chemical or thermal means) — **nonwoven** *n*

noo·dle \'nüd-ᵊl\ *n* [G *Nudel*] : a food paste made with egg and shaped typically in ribbon form

nook \'nuk\ *n* 1 : an interior angle or corner formed usu. by two walls ⟨a chimney ∼⟩ 2 : a sheltered or hidden place ⟨searched every ∼ and cranny⟩

noon \'nün\ *n* : the middle of the day : 12 o'clock in the daytime — **noon** *adj*

noon·day \'nün-ˌdā\ *n* : NOON, MIDDAY

no one *pron* : NOBODY

noon·tide \'nün-ˌtīd\ *n* : NOON

noon·time \-ˌtīm\ *n* : NOON

noose \'nüs\ *n* : a loop with a running knot (as in a lasso) that binds closer the more it is drawn

nope \'nōp\ *adv* : NO

nor \'nȯr\ *conj* : and not ⟨not for you ∼ for me⟩ — used esp. to introduce and negate the second member and each later member of a series of items preceded by *neither* ⟨neither here ∼ there⟩

Nor *abbr* Norway; Norwegian

Nor·dic \'nȯr-dik\ *adj* 1 : of or relating to the Germanic peoples of northern Europe and esp. of Scandinavia 2 : of or relating to competitive ski events involving cross-country racing, ski jumping, or biathlon — **Nordic** *n*

nor·epi·neph·rine \ˌnȯr-ˌe-pə-'ne-frən\ *n* : a nitrogen-containing neurotransmitter in parts of the sympathetic and central nervous systems

norm \'nȯrm\ *n* [L *norma*, lit., carpenter's square] 1 : an authoritative standard or model; *esp* : a set standard of development or achievement usu. derived from the average or median achievement of a large group 2 : a typical or widespread practice, procedure, or custom **syn** average, mean, median, par

¹nor·mal \'nȯr-məl\ *adj* 1 : REGULAR, STANDARD, NATURAL 2 : of average intelligence; *also* : sound in mind and body — **nor·mal·cy** \-sē\ *n* — **nor·mal·i·ty** \nȯr-'ma-lə-tē\ *n* — **nor·mal·ly** *adv*

²normal *n* 1 : one that is normal 2 : the usual condition, level, or quantity

nor·mal·ize \'nȯr-mə-ˌlīz\ *vb* **-ized; -iz·ing** : to make or restore to normal — **nor·mal·i·za·tion** \ˌnȯr-mə-lə-'zā-shən\ *n*

Nor·man \'nȯr-mən\ *n* 1 : a native or inhabitant of Normandy 2 : one of the 10th century Scandinavian conquerors of Normandy 3 : one of the Norman-French conquerors of England in 1066 — **Norman** *adj*

nor·ma·tive \'nȯr-mə-tiv\ *adj* : of, relating to, or deter-

mining norms — **nor·ma·tive·ly** *adv* — **nor·ma·tive·ness** *n*

Norse \'nȯrs\ *n, pl* **Norse** 1 : NORWEGIAN; *also* : any of the western Scandinavian dialects or languages 2 *pl* : SCANDINAVIANS; *also* : NORWEGIANS

Norse·man \-mən\ *n* : any of the ancient Scandinavians

¹north \'nȯrth\ *adv* : to, toward, or in the north

²north *adj* 1 : situated toward or at the north 2 : coming from the north

³north *n* 1 : the direction to the left of one facing east 2 : the compass point directly opposite to south 3 *cap* : regions or countries north of a specified or implied point — **north·er·ly** \'nȯr-thər-lē\ *adv or adj* — **north·ern** \-thərn\ *adj* — **North·ern·er** \-thər-nər\ *n* — **north·ern·most** \-thərn-ˌmōst\ *adj* — **north·ward** \'nȯrth-wərd\ *adv or adj* — **north·wards** \-wərdz\ *adv*

north·east \nȯr-'thēst\ *n* 1 : the general direction between north and east 2 : the compass point midway between north and east 3 *cap* : regions or countries northeast of a specified or implied point — **northeast** *adj or adv* — **north·east·er·ly** \-'thē-stər-lē\ *adv or adj* — **north·east·ern** \-stərn\ *adj*

north·east·er \-'thēs-tər\ *n* 1 : a strong northeast wind 2 : a storm with northeast winds

north·er \'nȯr-thər\ *n* 1 : a strong north wind 2 : a storm with north winds

northern lights *n pl* : AURORA BOREALIS

north pole *n, often cap N&P* : the northernmost point of the earth

North Star *n* : the star toward which the northern end of the earth's axis points

north·west \nȯrth-'west\ *n* 1 : the general direction between north and west 2 : the compass point midway between north and west 3 *cap* : regions or countries northwest of a specified or implied point — **north·west** *adj or adv* — **north·west·er·ly** \-'we-stər-lē\ *adv or adj* — **north·west·ern** \-'we-stərn\ *adj*

Norw *abbr* Norway; Norwegian

Nor·we·gian \nȯr-'wē-jən\ *n* 1 : a native or inhabitant of Norway 2 : the language of Norway — **Norwegian** *adj*

nos *abbr* numbers

¹nose \'nōz\ *n* 1 : the part of the face or head containing the nostrils and covering the front of the nasal cavity 2 : the sense of smell 3 : something (as a point, edge, or projecting front part) that resembles a nose ⟨the ∼ of a plane⟩ — **nosed** \'nōzd\ *adj*

²nose *vb* **nosed; nos·ing** 1 : to detect by or as if by smell : SCENT 2 : to push or move with the nose 3 : to touch or rub with the nose : NUZZLE 4 : PRY 5 : to move ahead slowly ⟨the ship *nosed* into her berth⟩

nose·bleed \'nōz-ˌblēd\ *n* : a bleeding from the nose

nose cone *n* : a protective cone constituting the forward end of an aerospace vehicle

nose dive *n* 1 : a downward nose-first plunge (as of an airplane) 2 : a sudden extreme drop (as in prices)

nose·gay \'nōz-ˌgā\ *n* : a small bunch of flowers : POSY

nose out *vb* 1 : to discover often by prying 2 : to defeat by a narrow margin

nose·piece \-ˌpēs\ *n* 1 : a fitting at the lower end of a microscope tube to which the objectives are attached 2 : the bridge of a pair of eyeglasses

no–show \'nō-ˌshō\ *n* : a person who reserves space (as on an airplane or at a concert) but neither uses nor cancels the reservation

nos·tal·gia \nä-'stal-jə\ *n* [NL, fr. Gk *nostos* return home + *algos* pain, grief] 1 : HOMESICKNESS 2 : a wistful yearning for something past or irrecoverable — **nos·tal·gic** \-jik\ *adj*

nos·tril \'näs-trəl\ *n* [ME *nosethirl*, fr. OE *nosthyrl*, fr. *nosu* nose + *thyrel* hole] 1 : either of the nares usu. with the adjoining nasal wall and passage 2 : either fleshy lateral wall of the nose

nos·trum \'näs-trəm\ *n* [L, neut. of *noster* our, ours, fr. *nos* we] : a questionable medicine or remedy

nosy or **nos•ey** \'nō-zē\ adj **nos•i•er; -est** : INQUISITIVE, PRYING

not \'nät\ adv **1** — used to make negative a group of words or a word ⟨the boys are ∼ here⟩ **2** — used to stand for the negative of a preceding group of words ⟨sometimes hard to see and sometimes ∼⟩

no•ta be•ne \₁nō-tə-'bē-nē, -'be-\ [L, mark well] — used to call attention to something important

no•ta•bil•i•ty \₁nō-tə-'bi-lə-tē\ n, pl **-ties 1** : the quality or state of being notable **2** : NOTABLE

¹no•ta•ble \'nō-tə-bəl\ adj **1** : NOTEWORTHY, REMARKABLE ⟨a ∼ achievement⟩ **2** : DISTINGUISHED, PROMINENT ⟨two ∼ politicians made speeches⟩

²notable n : a person of note syn bigwig, eminence, nabob, personage, somebody, VIP

no•ta•bly \'nō-tə-blē\ adv **1** : in a notable manner **2** : ESPECIALLY, PARTICULARLY

no•tar•i•al \nō-'ter-ē-əl\ adj : of, relating to, or done by a notary public

no•ta•rize \'nō-tə-₁rīz\ vb **-rized; -riz•ing** : to acknowledge or make legally authentic as a notary public

no•ta•ry public \'nō-tə-rē-\ n, pl **notaries public** or **notary publics** : a public official who attests or certifies writings (as deeds) to make them legally authentic

no•ta•tion \nō-'tā-shən\ n **1** : ANNOTATION, NOTE **2** : the act, process, or method of representing data by marks, signs, figures, or characters; also : a system of symbols (as letters, numerals, or musical notes) used in such notation

¹notch \'näch\ n **1** : a V-shaped hollow in an edge or surface **2** : a narrow pass between two mountains

²notch vb **1** : to cut or make notches in **2** : to score or record by or as if by cutting a series of notches ⟨∼ed 20 points for the team⟩

notch•back \'näch-₁bak\ n : an automobile with a trunk whose lid forms a distinct deck

¹note \'nōt\ vb **not•ed; not•ing 1** : to notice or observe with care; also : to record or preserve in writing **2** : to make special mention of : REMARK

²note n **1** : a musical sound **2** : a cry, call, or sound esp. of a bird **3** : a special tone in a person's words or voice ⟨a ∼ of fear⟩ **4** : a character in music used to indicate duration of a tone by its shape and pitch by its position on the staff **5** : a characteristic feature : MOOD, QUALITY ⟨a ∼ of optimism⟩ **6** : MEMORANDUM **7** : a brief and informal record; also : a written or printed comment or explanation **8** : a written promise to pay a debt **9** : a piece of paper money **10** : a short informal letter **11** : a formal diplomatic or official communication **12** : DISTINCTION, REPUTATION ⟨an artist of∼⟩ **13** : OBSERVATION, NOTICE, HEED ⟨take ∼ of the time⟩

note•book \'nōt-₁bùk\ n : a book for notes or memoranda

not•ed \'nō-təd\ adj : well known by reputation : EMINENT, CELEBRATED

note•wor•thy \'nōt-₁wər-thē\ adj : worthy of note : REMARKABLE

¹noth•ing \'nə-thiŋ\ pron **1** : no thing ⟨leaves ∼ to the imagination⟩ **2** : no part **3** : one of no interest, value, or importance ⟨she's ∼ to me⟩

²nothing adv : not at all : in no degree

³nothing n **1** : something that does not exist **2** : ZERO **3** : a person or thing of little or no value or importance

⁴nothing adj : of no account : worthless

noth•ing•ness \'nə-thiŋ-nəs\ n **1** : the quality or state of being nothing **2** : NONEXISTENCE; also : utter insignificance **3** : something insignificant or valueless

¹no•tice \'nō-təs\ n **1** : WARNING, ANNOUNCEMENT **2** : notification of the termination of an agreement or contract at a specified time **3** : ATTENTION, HEED ⟨bring the matter to my ∼⟩ **4** : a written or printed announcement **5** : a short critical account or examination (as of a play) : REVIEW

²notice vb **no•ticed; no•tic•ing 1** : to make mention of

: remark on : NOTE **2** : to take notice of : OBSERVE, MARK

no•tice•able \'nō-tə-sə-bəl\ adj **1** : worthy of notice **2** : capable of being or likely to be noticed — **no•tice•ably** \-blē\ adv

no•ti•fy \'nō-tə-₁fī\ vb **-fied; -fy•ing 1** : to give notice of : report the occurrence of **2** : to give notice to — **no•ti•fi•ca•tion** \₁nō-tə-fə-'kā-shən\ n

no•tion \'nō-shən\ n **1** : IDEA, CONCEPTION ⟨have a ∼ of what he means⟩ **2** : a belief held : OPINION, VIEW **3** : WHIM, FANCY ⟨a sudden ∼ to go⟩ **4** pl : small useful articles (as pins, needles, or thread)

no•tion•al \'nō-shə-nəl\ adj **1** : existing in the mind only : IMAGINARY, UNREAL **2** : given to foolish or fanciful moods or ideas : WHIMSICAL

no•to•ri•ous \nō-'tōr-ē-əs\ adj : generally known and talked of; esp : widely and unfavorably known — **no•to•ri•ety** \₁nō-tə-'rī-ə-tē\ n — **no•to•ri•ous•ly** \nō-'tōr-ē-əs-lē\ adv

¹not•with•stand•ing \₁nät-with-'stan-diŋ, -with-\ prep : in spite of

²notwithstanding adv : NEVERTHELESS

³notwithstanding conj : ALTHOUGH

nou•gat \'nü-gət\ n [F, fr. Provençal, fr. Old Provençal nogat, fr. noga nut, ultim. fr. L nuc-, nux] : a confection of nuts or fruit pieces in a sugar paste

nought \'nòt, 'nät\ var of NAUGHT

noun \'naùn\ n : a word that is the name of a subject of discourse (as a person or place)

nour•ish \'nər-ish\ vb : to promote the growth or development of

nour•ish•ing adj : giving nourishment

nour•ish•ment \'nər-ish-mənt\ n **1** : FOOD, NUTRIENT **2** : the action or process of nourishing

nou•veau riche \₁nü-₁vō-'rēsh\ n, pl **nou•veaux riches** \same\ [F] : a person newly rich : PARVENU

Nov abbr November

no•va \'nō-və\ n, pl **novas** or **no•vae** \-(₁)vē, -₁vī\ [NL, fem. of L novus new] : a star that suddenly increases greatly in brightness and then within a few months or years grows dim again

¹nov•el \'nä-vəl\ adj **1** : having no precedent : NEW **2** : STRANGE, UNUSUAL

²novel n : a long invented prose narrative dealing with human experience through a connected sequence of events — **nov•el•ist** \-və-list\ n

nov•el•ette \₁nä-və-'let\ n : a brief novel or long short story

nov•el•ize \'nä-və-₁līz\ vb **-ized; -iz•ing** : to convert into the form of a novel — **nov•el•i•za•tion** \₁nä-və-lə-'zā-shən\ n

nov•el•la \nō-'ve-lə\ n, pl **novellas** or **no•vel•le** \-'ve-lē\ : NOVELETTE

nov•el•ty \'nä-vəl-tē\ n, pl **-ties 1** : something new or unusual **2** : NEWNESS **3** : a small manufactured article intended mainly for personal or household adornment — usu. in pl.

No•vem•ber \nō-'vem-bər\ n [ME Novembre, fr. OF, fr. L November (ninth month), fr. novem nine] : the 11th month of the year having 30 days

no•ve•na \nō-'vē-nə\ n : a Roman Catholic nine-day period of prayer

nov•ice \'nä-vəs\ n **1** : a new member of a religious order who is preparing to take the vows of religion **2** : one who is inexperienced or untrained

no•vi•tiate \nō-'vi-shət\ n **1** : the period or state of being a novice **2** : a house where novices are trained **3** : NOVICE

¹now \'naù\ adv **1** : at the present time or moment **2** : in the time immediately before the present **3** : IMMEDIATELY, FORTHWITH **4** — used with the sense of present time weakened or lost (as to express command, introduce an important point, or indicate a transition) ⟨∼ hear this⟩ **5** : SOMETIMES ⟨∼ one and ∼ another⟩ **6** : under the present circumstances **7** : at the time referred to

²**now** *conj* : in view of the fact ⟨~ that you're here, we'll start⟩

³**now** *n* : the present time or moment : PRESENT

⁴**now** *adj* **1** : of or relating to the present time ⟨the ~ president⟩ **2** : excitingly new ⟨~ clothes⟩; *also* : constantly aware of what is new ⟨~ people⟩

NOW *abbr* **1** National Organization for Women **2** negotiable order of withdrawal

now·a·days \'naù-ə-ˌdāz\ *adv* : at the present time

no·way \'nō-ˌwā\ *or* **no·ways** \-ˌwāz\ *adv* : NOWISE

no·where \-ˌhwer\ *adv* : not anywhere — **nowhere** *n*

nowhere near *adv* : not nearly

no·wise \'nō-ˌwīz\ *adv* : in no way

nox·ious \'näk-shəs\ *adj* : harmful esp. to health or morals

noz·zle \'nä-zəl\ *n* : a short tube constricted in the middle or at one end and used (as on a hose) to speed up or direct a flow of fluid

np *abbr* **1** no pagination **2** no place (of publication)

Np *symbol* neptunium

NP *abbr* notary public

NR *abbr* not rated

NRA *abbr* National Rifle Association

NS *abbr* **1** not specified **2** Nova Scotia

NSA *abbr* National Security Agency

NSC *abbr* National Security Council

NSF *abbr* **1** National Science Foundation **2** not sufficient funds

NSW *abbr* New South Wales

NT *abbr* **1** New Testament **2** Northern Territory **3** Northwest Territories

nth \'enth\ *adj* **1** : numbered with an unspecified or indefinitely large ordinal number ⟨for the ~ time⟩ **2** : EXTREME, UTMOST ⟨to the ~ degree⟩

NTP *abbr* normal temperature and pressure

nt wt *or* **n wt** *abbr* net weight

nu \'nü, 'nyü\ *n* : the 13th letter of the Greek alphabet— N or ν

NU *abbr* name unknown

nu·ance \'nü-ˌäns, 'nyü-, nü-'äns, nyü-\ *n* [F] : a shade of difference : a delicate variation (as in tone or meaning)

nub \'nəb\ *n* **1** : KNOB, LUMP **2** : GIST, POINT ⟨the ~ of the story⟩

nub·bin \'nə-bən\ *n* **1** : something (as an ear of Indian corn) that is small for its kind, stunted, undeveloped, or imperfect **2** : a small projecting bit

nu·bile \'nü-ˌbīl, 'nyü-, -bəl\ *adj* **1** : of marriageable condition or age **2** : sexually attractive ⟨~ young women⟩

nu·cle·ar \'nü-klē-ər, 'nyü-\ *adj* **1** : of, relating to, or constituting a nucleus **2** : of, relating to, or using the atomic nucleus or energy derived from it **3** : of, relating to, or being a weapon whose destructive power results from an uncontrolled nuclear reaction

nu·cle·ate \'nü-klē-ˌāt, 'nyü-\ *vb* **-at·ed; -at·ing** : to form, act as, or have a nucleus — **nu·cle·ation** \ˌnü-klē-'ā-shən, ˌnyü-\ *n*

nu·cle·ic acid \nü-'klē-ik, nyü-, -'klā-\ *n* : any of various complex organic acids (as DNA) found esp. in cell nuclei

nu·cle·us \'nü-klē-əs, 'nyü-\ *n, pl* **nu·clei** \-klē-ˌī\ *also* **nu·cle·us·es** [NL, fr. L, kernel, dim. of *nuc-, nux* nut] **1** : a central mass or part about which matter gathers or is collected : CORE **2** : a cell part that is characteristic of all living things except viruses, bacteria, and certain algae, that is necessary for heredity and for making proteins, that contains the chromosomes with their genes, and that is enclosed in a membrane **3** : a mass of gray matter or group of nerve cells in the central nervous system **4** : the central part of an atom that comprises nearly all of the atomic mass

¹**nude** \'nüd, 'nyüd\ *adj* **nud·er; nud·est** : BARE, NAKED, UNCLOTHED — **nu·di·ty** \'nü-də-tē, 'nyü-\ *n*

²**nude** *n* **1** : a nude human figure esp. as depicted in art **2** : the condition of being nude ⟨in the ~⟩

nudge \'nəj\ *vb* **nudged; nudg·ing** : to touch or push gently (as with the elbow) usu. in order to seek attention — **nudge** *n*

nud·ism \'nü-ˌdi-zəm, 'nyü-\ *n* : the practice of going nude esp. in mixed groups at specially secluded places — **nud·ist** \-dist\ *n*

nu·ga·to·ry \-gə-ˌtȯr-ē\ *adj* **1** : INCONSEQUENTIAL, WORTHLESS **2** : having no force : INEFFECTUAL

nug·get \'nə-gət\ *n* : a lump of precious metal (as gold)

nui·sance \'nüs-ᵊns, 'nyüs-\ *n* : an annoying or troublesome person or thing

nuisance tax *n* : an excise tax collected in small amounts directly from the consumer

¹**nuke** \'nük, 'nyük\ *n* **1** : a nuclear weapon **2** : a nuclear power plant

²**nuke** *vb* **nuked; nuk·ing 1** : to attack with nuclear weapons **2** : MICROWAVE

null \'nəl\ *adj* **1** : having no legal or binding force : INVALID, VOID **2** : amounting to nothing : INSIGNIFICANT — **nul·li·ty** \'nə-lə-tē\ *n*

null and void *adj* : having no force, binding power, or validity

nul·li·fy \'nə-lə-ˌfī\ *vb* **-fied; -fy·ing** : to make null or valueless; *also* : ANNUL — **nul·li·fi·ca·tion** \ˌnə-lə-fə-'kā-shən\ *n*

num *abbr* numeral

Num *or* **Numb** *abbr* Numbers

numb \'nəm\ *adj* : lacking sensation or emotion : BENUMBED — **numb** *vb* — **numb·ly** *adv* — **numb·ness** *n*

¹**num·ber** \'nəm-bər\ *n* **1** : the total of individuals or units taken together **2** : an indefinite total ⟨a small ~ of tickets remain unsold⟩ **3** : an ascertainable total ⟨the sands of the desert are without ~⟩ **4** : a distinction of word form to denote reference to one or more than one **5** : a unit belonging to a mathematical system and subject to its laws; *also, pl* : ARITHMETIC **6** : a symbol used to represent a mathematical number; *also* : such a number used to identify or designate ⟨a phone ~⟩ **7** : one in a series ⟨the best ~ on the program⟩
☞ For table, see next page.

²**number** *vb* **1** : COUNT, ENUMERATE **2** : to include with or be one of a group **3** : to restrict to a small or definite number **4** : to assign a number to **5** : to comprise in number : TOTAL

num·ber·less \-ləs\ *adj* : INNUMERABLE, COUNTLESS

Numbers *n* — see BIBLE table

nu·mer·al \'nü-mə-rəl, 'nyü-\ *n* : conventional symbol representing a number — **numeral** *adj*

nu·mer·ate \'nü-mə-ˌrāt, 'nyü-\ *vb* **-at·ed; -at·ing** : ENUMERATE

nu·mer·a·tor \-ˌrā-tər\ *n* : the part of a fraction above the line

nu·mer·ic \nü-'mer-ik, nyü-\ *adj* : NUMERICAL; *esp* : denoting a number or a system of numbers

nu·mer·i·cal \-'mer-i-kəl\ *adj* **1** : of or relating to numbers **2** : expressed in or involving numbers — **nu·mer·i·cal·ly** \-k(ə-)lē\ *adv*

nu·mer·ol·o·gy \ˌnü-mə-'rä-lə-jē, ˌnyü-\ *n* : the study of the occult significance of numbers — **nu·mer·ol·o·gist** \-jist\ *n*

nu·mer·ous \'nü-mə-rəs, 'nyü-\ *adj* : consisting of, including, or relating to a great number : MANY

nu·mis·mat·ics \ˌnü-məz-'ma-tiks, ˌnyü-\ *n* : the study or collection of monetary objects — **nu·mis·mat·ic** \-tik\ *adj* — **nu·mis·ma·tist** \nü-'miz-mə-tist, nyü-\ *n*

num·skull \'nəm-ˌskəl\ *n* : a stupid person : DUNCE

nun \'nən\ *n* : a woman belonging to a religious order; *esp* : one under solemn vows of poverty, chastity, and obedience

nun·cio \'nən-sē-ˌō, 'nún-\ *n, pl* **-ci·os** [It, fr. L *nuntius* messenger] : a permanent high-ranking papal representative to a civil government

nun·nery \'nə-nə-rē\ *n, pl* **-ner·ies** : a convent of nuns

TABLE OF NUMBERS

CARDINAL NUMBERS[1]			ORDINAL NUMBERS[4]	
NAME[2]	SYMBOL		NAME[5]	SYMBOL
	Hindu-Arabic	*Roman[3]*		
zero *or* naught *or* cipher	0		first	1st
one	1	I	second	2d *or* 2nd
two	2	II	third	3d *or* 3rd
three	3	III	fourth	4th
four	4	IV	fifth	5th
five	5	V	sixth	6th
six	6	VI	seventh	7th
seven	7	VII	eighth	8th
eight	8	VIII	ninth	9th
nine	9	IX	tenth	10th
ten	10	X	eleventh	11th
eleven	11	XI	twelfth	12th
twelve	12	XII	thirteenth	13th
thirteen	13	XIII	fourteenth	14th
fourteen	14	XIV	fifteenth	15th
fifteen	15	XV	sixteenth	16th
sixteen	16	XVI	seventeenth	17th
seventeen	17	XVII	eighteenth	18th
eighteen	18	XVIII	nineteenth	19th
nineteen	19	XIX	twentieth	20th
twenty	20	XX	twenty-first	21st
twenty-one	21	XXI	twenty-second	22d *or* 22nd
twenty-two	22	XXII	twenty-third	23d *or* 23rd
twenty-three	23	XXIII	twenty-fourth	24th
twenty-four	24	XXIV	twenty-fifth	25th
twenty-five	25	XXV	twenty-sixth	26th
twenty-six	26	XXVI	twenty-seventh	27th
twenty-seven	27	XXVII	twenty-eighth	28th
twenty-eight	28	XXVIII	twenty-ninth	29th
twenty-nine	29	XXIX	thirtieth	30th
thirty	30	XXX	thirty-first *etc*	31st
thirty-one *etc*	31	XXXI	fortieth	40th
forty	40	XL	fiftieth	50th
fifty	50	L	sixtieth	60th
sixty	60	LX	seventieth	70th
seventy	70	LXX	eightieth	80th
eighty	80	LXXX	ninetieth	90th
ninety	90	XC	hundredth *or*	100th
one hundred	100	C	one hundredth	
one hundred one *or*	101	CI	hundred and first *or*	101st
one hundred and one *etc*			one hundred and first *etc*	
two hundred	200	CC	two hundredth	200th
three hundred	300	CCC	three hundredth	300th
four hundred	400	CD	four hundredth	400th
five hundred	500	D	five hundredth	500th
six hundred	600	DC	six hundredth	600th
seven hundred	700	DCC	seven hundredth	700th
eight hundred	800	DCCC	eight hundredth	800th
nine hundred	900	CM	nine hundredth	900th
one thousand *or* ten hundred *etc*	1,000	M	thousandth *or* one thousandth	1,000th
			two thousandth *etc*	2,000th
two thousand *etc*	2,000	MM	five thousandth	5,000th
five thousand	5,000	$\overline{\text{V}}$	ten thousandth	10,000th
ten thousand	10,000	$\overline{\text{X}}$	hundred thousandth *or*	100,000th
one hundred thousand	100,000	$\overline{\text{C}}$	one hundred thousandth	
one million	1,000,000	$\overline{\text{M}}$	millionth *or* one millionth	1,000,000th

[1]The cardinal numbers are used in simple counting or in answer to "how many?" The words for these numbers may be used as nouns (I counted to *ten*), as pronouns (*ten* were found), or as adjectives (*ten* cows).

[2]In formal writing the numbers one to one hundred and in less formal writing the numbers one to nine are commonly written out, while larger numbers are given in numerals. A number occurring at the beginning of a sentence is usually written out. Except in very formal writing numerals are used for dates. Hindu-Arabic numerals from 1,000 to 9,999 are often written without commas (1000; 9999). Year numbers are always written without commas (1783).

[3]The Roman numerals are written either in capitals or in lowercase letters.

[4]The ordinal numbers are used to show the order in which such items as names, objects, and periods of time are considered (the *twelfth* month; the *fourth* row of seats; the *18th* century).

[5]Each of the names of the ordinal numbers except *first* and *second* is used for one of the equal parts into which a whole may be divided (a *fourth*; a *sixth*; a *tenth*) and also as the denominator in fractions (*one fourth*; *three fifths*). Fractions used as nouns are usually written as two words, but fractions used as adjectives are usually hyphenated (a *two-thirds* majority). When a two-word ordinal number is used as a noun to name a denominator, a hyphen is usually used to make sure that there is only one meaning (*six hundred ten-thousandths* means only 600/10,000 and not 610/1000). When fractions are written in numerals, the cardinal symbols are used ($\frac{1}{4}$, $\frac{3}{5}$, $\frac{4}{6}$).

¹**nup•tial** \'nəp-shəl\ *adj* : of or relating to marriage or a wedding

²**nuptial** *n* : MARRIAGE, WEDDING — usu. used in pl.

¹**nurse** \'nərs\ *n* [ME, fr. OF *nurice*, fr. LL *nutricia*, fr. L, fem. of *nutricius* nourishing] **1** : a girl or woman employed to take care of children **2** : a person trained to care for sick people

²**nurse** *vb* **nursed; nurs•ing 1** : SUCKLE **2** : to take charge of and watch over **3** : TEND ⟨∼ an invalid⟩ **4** : to treat with special care ⟨∼ a headache⟩ **5** : to hold in one's mind or consideration ⟨∼ a grudge⟩ **6** : to act or serve as a nurse

nurse•maid \'nərs-₁mād\ *n* : NURSE 1

nurse-prac•ti•tion•er \-prak-'ti-shə-nər\ *n* : a registered nurse who is qualified to assume some of the duties formerly assumed only by a physician

nurs•ery \'nər-sə-rē\ *n, pl* **-er•ies 1** : a room for children **2** : a place where children are temporarily cared for in their parents' absence **3** : a place where young plants are grown usu. for transplanting

nurs•ery•man \-mən\ *n* : a man who keeps or works in a plant nursery

nursery school *n* : a school for children under kindergarten age

nursing home *n* : a private establishment providing care for persons (as the aged or the chronically ill) who are unable to care for themselves

nurs•ling \'nərs-liŋ\ *n* **1** : one that is solicitously cared for **2** : a nursing child

¹**nur•ture** \'nər-chər\ *n* **1** : TRAINING, UPBRINGING; *also* : the influences that modify the expression of an individual's heredity **2** : FOOD, NOURISHMENT

²**nurture** *vb* **nur•tured; nur•tur•ing 1** : to care for : FEED, NOURISH **2** : EDUCATE, TRAIN **3** : FOSTER

nut \'nət\ *n* **1** : a dry fruit or seed with a hard shell and a firm inner kernel; *also* : its kernel **2** : a metal block with a hole through it that is fastened to a bolt or screw by means of a screw thread within the hole **3** : the ridge on the upper end of the fingerboard in a stringed musical instrument over which the strings pass **4** : a foolish, eccentric, or crazy person **5** : ENTHUSIAST

nut•crack•er \'nət-₁kra-kər\ *n* : an instrument for cracking nuts

nut•hatch \-₁hach\ *n* : any of various small tree-climbing chiefly insect-eating birds

nut•meg \-₁meg, -₁māg\ *n* [ME *notemuge*, ultim. fr. Old Provençal *noz muscada*, lit., musky nut] : a spice made by grinding the nutlike aromatic seed of a tropical tree; *also* : the seed or tree

nu•tria \'nü-trē-ə, 'nyü-\ *n* [Sp] **1** : the durable usu. light brown fur of a nutria **2** : a So. American aquatic rodent with webbed hind feet

¹**nu•tri•ent** \'nü-trē-ənt, 'nyü-\ *adj* : NOURISHING

²**nutrient** *n* : a nutritive substance or ingredient

nu•tri•ment \-trə-mənt\ *n* : NUTRIENT

nu•tri•tion \nú-'tri-shən, nyü-\ *n* : the act or process of nourishing; *esp* : the processes by which an individual takes in and utilizes food material — **nu•tri•tion•al** \-shə-nəl\ *adj* — **nu•tri•tious** \-shəs\ *adj* — **nu•tri•tive** \'nü-trə-tiv, 'nyü-\ *adj*

nuts \'nəts\ *adj* **1** : ENTHUSIASTIC, KEEN **2** : CRAZY, DEMENTED

nut•shell \'nət-₁shel\ *n* : the shell of a nut — **in a nutshell** : in a few words ⟨that's the story *in a nutshell*⟩

nut•ty \'nə-tē\ *adj* **nut•ti•er; -est 1** : containing or suggesting nuts ⟨a ∼ flavor⟩ **2** : mentally unbalanced

nuz•zle \'nə-zəl\ *vb* **nuz•zled; nuz•zling 1** : to root around, push, or touch with or as if with the nose **2** : NESTLE, SNUGGLE

NV *abbr* Nevada

NW *abbr* northwest

NWT *abbr* Northwest Territories

NY *abbr* New York

NYC *abbr* New York City

ny•lon \'nī-₁län\ *n* **1** : any of numerous strong tough elastic synthetic materials used esp. in textiles and plastics **2** *pl* : stockings made of nylon

nymph \'nimf\ *n* **1** : any of the lesser goddesses in ancient mythology represented as maidens living in the mountains, forests, meadows, and waters **2** : GIRL **3** : an immature insect resembling the adult but smaller, less differentiated, and usu. lacking wings

nym•pho•ma•nia \₁nim-fə-'mā-nē-ə, -nyə\ *n* : excessive sexual desire by a female — **nym•pho•ma•ni•ac** \-nē-₁ak\ *n or adj*

NZ *abbr* New Zealand

O

¹**o** \'ō\ *n, pl* **o's** *or* **os** \'ōz\ *often cap* **1** : the 15th letter of the English alphabet **2** : ZERO

²**o** *abbr, often cap* **1** ocean **2** Ohio **3** ohm

¹**O** \'ō\ *var of* OH

²**O** *symbol* oxygen

o/a *abbr* on or about

oaf \'ōf\ *n* : a stupid or awkward person — **oaf•ish** *adj*

oak \'ōk\ *n, pl* **oaks** *or* **oak** : any of a genus of trees or shrubs related to the beech and chestnut and having a rounded thin-shelled nut surrounded at the base by a hardened cup; *also* : the usu. tough hard durable wood of an oak — **oak•en** \'ō-kən\ *adj*

oa•kum \'ō-kəm\ *n* : loosely twisted hemp or jute fiber impregnated with tar and used esp. in caulking ships

oar \'ōr\ *n* : a long pole with a broad blade at one end used for propelling or steering a boat

oar•lock \'ōr-₁läk\ *n* : a U-shaped device for holding an oar in place

oars•man \'ōrz-mən\ *n* : one who rows esp. in a racing crew

OAS *abbr* Organization of American States

oa•sis \ō-'ā-səs\ *n, pl* **oa•ses** \-₁sēz\ : a fertile or green area in an arid region

oat \'ōt\ *n* : a cereal grass widely grown for its edible seed; *also* : this seed — **oat•en** \-ᵊn\ *adj*

oat•cake \'ōt-₁kāk\ *n* : a thin flat oatmeal cake

oath \'ōth\ *n, pl* **oaths** \'ōthz, 'ōths\ **1** : a solemn appeal to God to witness to the truth of a statement or the sacredness of a promise **2** : an irreverent or careless use of a sacred name

oat•meal \'ōt-₁mēl\ *n* **1** : ground or rolled oats **2** : porridge made from ground or rolled oats

Ob *or* **Obad** *abbr* Obadiah

Oba•di•ah \₁ō-bə-'dī-ə\ *n* — see BIBLE table

ob•bli•ga•to \₁ä-blə-'gä-tō\ *n, pl* **-tos** *also* **-ti** \-'gä-tē\ [It] : an accompanying part usu. played by a solo instrument

ob•du•rate \'äb-də-rət, -dyə-\ *adj* : stubbornly resistant : UNYIELDING **syn** inflexible, adamant, rigid, uncompromising — **ob•du•ra•cy** \-rə-sē\ *n*

obe•di•ent \ō-'bē-dē-ənt\ *adj* : submissive to the restraint or command of authority **syn** docile, tractable, amenable, biddable — **obe•di•ence** \-əns\ *n* — **obe•di•ent•ly** *adv*

obei•sance \ō-'bē-səns, -'bā-\ *n* : a bow made to show respect or submission; *also* : DEFERENCE, HOMAGE

obe•lisk \'ä-bə-₁lisk\ *n* [MF *obelisque*, fr. L *obeliscus*, fr. Gk *obeliskos*, fr. dim. of *obelos* spit, pointed pillar] : a 4-sided pillar that tapers toward the top and ends in a pyramid

obese \ō-'bēs\ *adj* [L *obesus*, fr. *ob-* against + *esus*, pp. of *edere* to eat] : excessively fat **syn** corpulent, fleshy, gross, overweight, portly, stout — **obe•si•ty** \-'bē-sə-tē\ *n*

obey \ō-ˈbā\ vb **obeyed; obey·ing 1** : to follow the commands or guidance of : behave obediently **2** : to comply with ⟨∼ orders⟩ **syn** conform, keep, mind, observe

ob·fus·cate \ˈäb-fə-ˌskāt\ vb **-cat·ed; -cat·ing 1** : to make dark or obscure **2** : CONFUSE — **ob·fus·ca·tion** \ˌäb-fəs-ˈkā-shən\ n

OB–GYN abbr obstetrician gynecologist; obstetrics gynecology

obi \ˈō-bē\ n [Jp] : a broad sash worn esp. with a Japanese kimono

obit \ō-ˈbit, ˈō-bət\ n : OBITUARY

obi·ter dic·tum \ō-bə-tər-ˈdik-təm\ n, pl **obiter dic·ta** \-tə\ [LL, lit., something said in passing] : an incidental remark or observation

obit·u·ary \ə-ˈbi-chə-ˌwer-ē\ n, pl **-ar·ies** : a notice of a person's death usu. with a short biographical account

obj abbr object; objective

¹**ob·ject** \ˈäb-jikt\ n **1** : something that may be seen or felt; also : something that may be perceived or examined mentally **2** : something that arouses an emotional response (as of affection or pity) **3** : AIM, PURPOSE **4** : a word or word group denoting that on or toward which the action of a verb is directed; also : a noun or noun equivalent in a prepositional phrase

²**ob·ject** \əb-ˈjekt\ vb **1** : to offer in opposition **2** : to oppose something; also : DISAPPROVE **syn** protest, remonstrate, expostulate — **ob·jec·tor** \-ˈjek-tər\ n

ob·jec·ti·fy \əb-ˈjek-tə-ˌfī\ vb **-fied; -fy·ing** : to make objective

ob·jec·tion \əb-ˈjek-shən\ n **1** : the act of objecting **2** : a reason for or a feeling of disapproval

ob·jec·tion·able \əb-ˈjek-shə-nə-bəl\ adj : UNDESIRABLE, OFFENSIVE — **ob·jec·tion·ably** \-blē\ adv

¹**ob·jec·tive** \əb-ˈjek-tiv\ adj **1** : of or relating to an object or end **2** : existing outside and independent of the mind **3** : of, relating to, or constituting a grammatical case marking typically the object of a verb or preposition **4** : treating or dealing with facts without distortion by personal feelings or prejudices — **ob·jec·tive·ly** adv — **ob·jec·tive·ness** n — **ob·jec·tiv·i·ty** \ˌäb-jek-ˈti-və-tē\ n

²**objective** n **1** : the lens (as in a microscope) nearest the object and forming an image of it **2** : an aim, goal, or end of action

ob·jet d'art \ȯb-ˌzhä-ˈdär\ n, pl **ob·jets d'art** \same\ [F] : an article of artistic worth; also : CURIO **syn** knickknack, bauble, bibelot, gewgaw, novelty, trinket

ob·jet trou·vé \ˈȯb-ˌzhä-trü-ˈvā\ n, pl **objets trouvés** \same\ [F, lit., found object] : a found natural object (as a piece of driftwood) held to have aesthetic value; also : an artifact not orig. intended as art but displayed as a work of art

ob·jur·ga·tion \ˌäb-jər-ˈgā-shən\ n : a harsh rebuke — **ob·jur·gate** \ˈäb-jər-ˌgāt\ vb

obl abbr **1** oblique **2** oblong

ob·late \ä-ˈblāt\ adj : flattened or depressed at the poles ⟨an ∼ spheroid⟩

ob·la·tion \ə-ˈblā-shən\ n : a religious offering

ob·li·gate \ˈä-blə-ˌgāt\ vb **-gat·ed; -gat·ing** : to bind legally or morally

ob·li·ga·tion \ˌä-blə-ˈgā-shən\ n **1** : an act of obligating oneself to a course of action **2** : something (as a promise or a contract) that binds one to a course of action **3** : INDEBTEDNESS; also : LIABILITY **4** : DUTY — **oblig·a·to·ry** \ə-ˈbli-gə-ˌtȯr-ē\ adj

oblige \ə-ˈblīj\ vb **obliged; oblig·ing** [ME, fr. OF obliger, fr. L obligare, lit., to bind to, fr. ob- toward + ligare to bind] **1** : FORCE, COMPEL **2** : to bind by a favor; also : to do a favor for or do something as a favor

oblig·ing adj : willing to do favors — **oblig·ing·ly** adv

oblique \ō-ˈblēk\ adj **1** : neither perpendicular nor parallel : SLANTING **2** : not straightforward : INDIRECT —

oblique·ly adv — **oblique·ness** n — **obliq·ui·ty** \-ˈbli-kwə-tē\ n

oblit·er·ate \ə-ˈbli-tə-ˌrāt\ vb **-at·ed; -at·ing** [L oblitterare, fr. ob in the way of + littera letter] **1** : to make undecipherable by wiping out or covering over **2** : to remove from recognition or memory **3** : CANCEL — **oblit·er·a·tion** \-ˌbli-tə-ˈrā-shən\ n

obliv·i·on \ə-ˈbli-vē-ən\ n **1** : the condition of being oblivious **2** : the condition or state of being forgotten

obliv·i·ous \ə-ˈbli-vē-əs\ adj **1** : lacking memory or mindful attention **2** : UNAWARE — **obliv·i·ous·ly** adv — **obliv·i·ous·ness** n

ob·long \ˈä-ˌblȯŋ\ adj : deviating from a square, circular, or spherical form by elongation in one dimension — **oblong** n

ob·lo·quy \ˈä-blə-kwē\ n, pl **-quies 1** : strongly condemnatory utterance or language **2** : bad repute : DISGRACE **syn** dishonor, shame, infamy, disrepute, ignominy

ob·nox·ious \äb-ˈnäk-shəs\ adj : REPUGNANT, OFFENSIVE — **ob·nox·ious·ly** adv — **ob·nox·ious·ness** n

oboe \ˈō-bō\ n [It, fr. F hautbois, fr. haut high + bois wood] : a woodwind instrument with a slender conical tube and a double reed mouthpiece — **obo·ist** \ˈo-ˌbō-ist\ n

oboe

ob·scene \äb-ˈsēn\ adj **1** : REPULSIVE **2** : deeply offensive to morality or decency; esp : designed to incite to lust or depravity **syn** gross, vulgar, coarse, crude, indecent — **ob·scene·ly** adv — **ob·scen·i·ty** \-ˈse-nə-tē\ n

ob·scu·ran·tism \ˌäb-ˈskyu̇r-ən-ˌti-zəm, ˌäb-skyu̇-ˈran-\ n **1** : opposition to the spread of knowledge **2** : deliberate vagueness or abstruseness — **ob·scu·ran·tist** \-tist\ n or adj

¹**ob·scure** \äb-ˈskyu̇r\ adj **1** : DIM, GLOOMY **2** : not readily understood : VAGUE **3** : REMOTE; also : HUMBLE **syn** dark, dusky, murky, tenebrous — **ob·scure·ly** adv — **ob·scu·ri·ty** \-ˈskyu̇r-ə-tē\ n

²**obscure** vb **ob·scured; ob·scur·ing 1** : to make dark, dim, or indistinct **2** : to conceal or hide by or as if by covering

ob·se·qui·ous \əb-ˈsē-kwē-əs\ adj : humbly or excessively attentive (as to a person in authority) : FAWNING, SYCOPHANTIC **syn** menial, servile, slavish, subservient — **ob·se·qui·ous·ly** adv — **ob·se·qui·ous·ness** n

ob·se·quy \ˈäb-sə-kwē\ n, pl **-quies** : a funeral or burial rite — usu. used in pl.

ob·serv·able \əb-ˈzər-və-bəl\ adj **1** : NOTEWORTHY **2** : capable of being observed — **ob·serv·abil·i·ty** \-ˌbi-lə-tē\ n

ob·ser·vance \əb-ˈzər-vəns\ n **1** : a customary practice or ceremony **2** : an act or instance of following a custom, rule, or law **3** : OBSERVATION

ob·ser·vant \-vənt\ adj **1** : WATCHFUL ⟨∼ spectators⟩ **2** : KEEN, PERCEPTIVE **3** : MINDFUL ⟨∼ of the amenities⟩

ob·ser·va·tion \ˌäb-sər-ˈvā-shən, -zər-\ n **1** : an act or instance of observing **2** : the gathering of information (as for scientific studies) by noting facts or occurrences **3** : a conclusion drawn from observing; also : REMARK, STATEMENT **4** : the fact of being observed

ob·ser·va·to·ry \əb-ˈzər-və-ˌtȯr-ē\ n, pl **-ries** : a place or institution equipped for observation of natural phenomena (as in astronomy)

ob·serve \əb-'zərv\ *vb* **ob·served; ob·serv·ing 1** : to conform one's action or practice to **2** : CELEBRATE **3** : to make a scientific observation of **4** : to see or sense esp. through careful attention **5** : to come to realize esp. through consideration of noted facts **6** : REMARK — **ob·serv·er** *n*

ob·sess \əb-'ses\ *vb* : to preoccupy intensely or abnormally

ob·ses·sion \äb-'se-shən\ *n* : a persistent disturbing preoccupation with an idea or feeling; *also* : an emotion or idea causing such a preoccupation — **ob·ses·sive** \-'se-siv\ *adj or n* — **ob·ses·sive·ly** *adv*

ob·sid·i·an \əb-'si-dē-ən\ *n* : a dark natural glass formed by the cooling of molten lava

ob·so·les·cent \ˌäb-sə-'les-ᵊnt\ *adj* : going out of use : becoming obsolete — **ob·so·les·cence** \-ᵊns\ *n*

ob·so·lete \ˌäb-sə-'lēt, 'äb-sə-ˌlēt\ *adj* : no longer in use; *also* : OLD-FASHIONED **syn** extinct, outworn, passé, superseded

ob·sta·cle \'äb-sti-kəl\ *n* : something that stands in the way or opposes

ob·stet·rics \əb-'ste-triks\ *n sing or pl* : a branch of medicine that deals with birth and with its antecedents and sequels — **ob·stet·ric** \-trik\ *or* **ob·stet·ri·cal** \-tri-kəl\ *adj* — **ob·ste·tri·cian** \ˌäb-stə-'tri-shən\ *n*

ob·sti·nate \'äb-stə-nət\ *adj* : fixed and unyielding (as in an opinion or course) despite reason or persuasion : STUBBORN — **ob·sti·na·cy** \-nə-sē\ *n* — **ob·sti·nate·ly** *adv*

ob·strep·er·ous \əb-'stre-pə-rəs\ *adj* **1** : uncontrollably noisy **2** : stubbornly resistant to control : UNRULY — **ob·strep·er·ous·ness** *n*

ob·struct \əb-'strəkt\ *vb* **1** : to block by an obstacle **2** : to impede the passage, action, or operation of **3** : to cut off from sight — **ob·struc·tive** \-'strək-tiv\ *adj* — **ob·struc·tor** \-tər\ *n*

ob·struc·tion \əb-'strək-shən\ *n* **1** : an act of obstructing : the state of being obstructed **2** : something that obstructs : HINDRANCE

ob·struc·tion·ist \-shə-nist\ *n* : a person who hinders progress or business esp. in a legislative body — **ob·struc·tion·ism** \-shə-ˌni-zəm\ *n*

ob·tain \əb-'tān\ *vb* **1** : to gain or attain usu. by planning or effort **2** : to be generally recognized or established **syn** procure, secure, win, earn, acquire — **ob·tain·able** *adj*

ob·trude \əb-'trüd\ *vb* **ob·trud·ed; ob·trud·ing 1** : to thrust out **2** : to thrust forward without warrant or request **3** : INTRUDE — **ob·tru·sion** \-'trü-zhən\ *n* — **ob·tru·sive** \-'trü-siv\ *adj* — **ob·tru·sive·ly** *adv* — **ob·tru·sive·ness** *n*

ob·tuse \äb-'tüs, -'tyüs\ *adj* **ob·tus·er; -est 1** : exceeding 90 degrees but less than 180 degrees (∼ angle) **2** : not pointed or acute : BLUNT **3** : not sharp or quick of wit — **ob·tuse·ly** *adv* — **ob·tuse·ness** *n*

obv *abbr* obverse

¹ob·verse \äb-'vərs, 'äb-ˌvərs\ *adj* **1** : facing the observer or opponent **2** : being a counterpart or complement — **ob·verse·ly** *adv*

²ob·verse \'äb-ˌvərs, äb-'vərs\ *n* **1** : the side (as of a coin) bearing the principal design and lettering **2** : a front or principal surface **3** : a counterpart having the opposite orientation or force

ob·vi·ate \'äb-vē-ˌāt\ *vb* **-at·ed; -at·ing** : to anticipate and prevent (as a situation) or make unnecessary (as an action) **syn** prevent, avert, forestall, forfend, preclude — **ob·vi·a·tion** \ˌäb-vē-'ā-shən\ *n*

ob·vi·ous \'äb-vē-əs\ *adj* [L *obvius*, fr. *obviam* in the way, fr. *ob* in the way of + *viam*, acc. of *via* way] : easily found, seen, or understood : PLAIN **syn** evident, manifest, patent, clear — **ob·vi·ous·ly** *adv* — **ob·vi·ous·ness** *n*

OC *abbr* officer candidate

oc·a·ri·na \ˌä-kə-'rē-nə\ *n* [It] : a wind instrument typically having an oval body with finger holes and a projecting mouthpiece

occas *abbr* occasionally

¹oc·ca·sion \ə-'kā-zhən\ *n* **1** : a favorable opportunity **2** : a direct or indirect cause **3** : the time of an event **4** : EXIGENCY **5** *pl* : AFFAIRS, BUSINESS **6** : a special event : CELEBRATION

²occasion *vb* : BRING ABOUT, CAUSE

oc·ca·sion·al \ə-'kā-zhə-nəl\ *adj* **1** : happening or met with now and then (∼ visits) **2** : used or designed for a special occasion (∼ verse) **syn** infrequent, rare, sporadic — **oc·ca·sion·al·ly** *adv*

oc·ci·den·tal \ˌäk-sə-'dent-ᵊl\ *adj, often cap* [fr. *Occident* West, fr. ME, fr. L *occident-, occidens*, fr. prp. of *occidere* to fall, set (of the sun)] : WESTERN — **Occidental** *n*

oc·clude \ə-'klüd\ *vb* **oc·clud·ed; oc·clud·ing 1** : OBSTRUCT (an *occluded* artery) **2** : to come together with opposing surfaces in contact — used of teeth — **oc·clu·sion** \-'klü-zhən\ *n* — **oc·clu·sive** \-'klü-siv\ *adj*

¹oc·cult \ə-'kəlt\ *adj* **1** : not revealed : SECRET **2** : ABSTRUSE, MYSTERIOUS **3** : of or relating to supernatural agencies, their effects, or knowledge of them — **oc·cult·ism** \-'kəl-ˌti-zəm\ *n* — **oc·cult·ist** \-tist\ *n*

²occult *n* : occult matters — used with *the*

oc·cu·pan·cy \'ä-kyə-pən-sē\ *n, pl* **-cies 1** : the act of occupying : the state of being occupied **2** : an occupied building or part of a building

oc·cu·pant \-pənt\ *n* : one who occupies something; *esp* : RESIDENT

oc·cu·pa·tion \ˌä-kyə-'pā-shən\ *n* **1** : an activity in which one engages; *esp* : VOCATION **2** : the taking possession of property; *also* : the taking possession of an area by a foreign military force — **oc·cu·pa·tion·al** \-shə-nəl\ *adj* — **oc·cu·pa·tion·al·ly** *adv*

occupational therapy *n* : therapy by means of activity; *esp* : creative activity prescribed for its effect in promoting recovery or rehabilitation — **occupational therapist** *n*

oc·cu·py \'ä-kyə-ˌpī\ *vb* **-pied; -py·ing 1** : to engage the attention or energies of **2** : to fill up (an extent in space or time) **3** : to take or hold possession of **4** : to reside in as owner or tenant — **oc·cu·pi·er** *n*

oc·cur \ə-'kər\ *vb* **oc·curred; oc·cur·ring** [L *occurrere*, fr. *ob-* in the way + *currere* to run] **1** : to be found or met with : APPEAR **2** : HAPPEN **3** : to come to mind

oc·cur·rence \ə-'kər-əns\ *n* **1** : something that takes place **2** : the action or process of occurring

ocean \'ō-shən\ *n* **1** : the whole body of salt water that covers nearly three fourths of the surface of the earth **2** : any of the large bodies of water into which the great ocean is divided — **ocean·ic** \ˌō-shē-'a-nik\ *adj*

ocean·ar·i·um \ˌō-shə-'nar-ē-əm\ *n, pl* **-iums** *or* **-ia** \-ē-ə\ : a large marine aquarium

ocean·front \'ō-shən-ˌfrənt\ *n* : a shore area on the ocean

ocean·go·ing \-ˌgō-iŋ\ *adj* : of, relating to, or suitable for travel on the ocean

ocean·og·ra·phy \ˌō-shə-'nä-grə-fē\ *n* : a science dealing with the ocean and its phenomena — **ocean·og·ra·pher** \-fər\ *n* — **ocean·o·graph·ic** \-nə-'gra-fik\ *adj*

oce·lot \'ä-sə-ˌlät, 'ō-\ *n* : a medium-sized American wildcat ranging southward from Texas to northern Argentina and having a tawny yellow or gray coat with black markings

ocher *or* **ochre** \'ō-kər\ *n* : an earthy usu. red or yellow iron ore used as a pigment; *also* : the color esp. of yellow ocher

o'clock \ə-'kläk\ *adv* : according to the clock

OCR *abbr* optical character reader; optical character recognition

OCS *abbr* officer candidate school

oct *abbr* octavo

Oct *abbr* October

oc·ta·gon \'äk-tə-ˌgän\ *n* : a polygon of eight angles

and eight sides — **oc·tag·o·nal** \äk-¹ta-gən-ᵊl\ *adj*

oc·tane \¹äk-ˌtān\ *n* : OCTANE NUMBER

octane number *n* : a number used to measure the antiknock properties of gasoline that increases as the likelihood of knocking decreases

oc·tave \¹äk-tiv\ *n* 1 : a musical interval embracing eight degrees; *also* : a tone or note at this interval or the whole series of notes, tones, or keys within this interval 2 : a group of eight

oc·ta·vo \äk-¹tā-vō, -¹tä-\ *n, pl* **-vos** 1 : the size of a piece of paper cut eight from a sheet 2 : a book printed on octavo pages

oc·tet \äk-¹tet\ *n* 1 : a musical composition for eight voices or eight instruments; *also* : the performers of such a composition 2 : a group or set of eight

Oc·to·ber \äk-¹tō-bər\ *n* [ME Octobre, fr. OF, fr. L October (eighth month), fr. octo eight] : the 10th month of the year having 31 days

oc·to·ge·nar·i·an \ˌäk-tə-jə-¹ner-ē-ən\ *n* : a person whose age is in the eighties

oc·to·pus \¹äk-tə-pəs\ *n, pl* **-pus·es** *or* **-pi** \-ˌpī\ : any of various sea mollusks with eight long arms furnished with suckers

octopus

oc·to·syl·lab·ic \ˌäk-tə-sə-¹la-bik\ *adj* : composed of verses having eight syllables — **octosyllabic** *n*

¹**oc·u·lar** \¹ä-kyə-lər\ *adj* 1 : VISUAL 2 : of or relating to the eye or the eyesight

²**ocular** *n* : EYEPIECE

oc·u·list \¹ä-kyə-list\ *n* 1 : OPHTHALMOLOGIST 2 : OPTOMETRIST

¹**OD** \ˌō-¹dē\ *n* : an overdose of a drug and esp. a narcotic

²**OD** *vb* **OD'd** *or* **ODed; OD'ing** : to become ill or die from an OD

³**OD** *abbr* 1 doctor of optometry 2 [L oculus dexter] right eye 3 officer of the day 4 olive drab 5 overdraft 6 overdrawn

odd \¹äd\ *adj* [ME odde, fr. ON oddi point of land, triangle, odd number] 1 : being only one of a pair or set ⟨an ~ shoe⟩ 2 : somewhat more than the number mentioned ⟨forty ~ years ago⟩ 3 : being an integer (as 1, 3, or 5) not divisible by two without leaving a remainder 4 : additional to what is usual ⟨~ jobs⟩ 5 : STRANGE ⟨an ~ way of behaving⟩ — **odd·ness** *n*

odd·ball \¹äd-ˌbȯl\ *n* : one that is eccentric — **oddball** *adj*

odd·i·ty \¹ä-də-tē\ *n, pl* **-ties** 1 : one that is odd 2 : the quality or state of being odd

odd·ly \¹äd-lē\ *adv* 1 : in an odd manner 2 : it is odd that

odd·ment \¹äd-mənt\ *n* : something left over : REMNANT

odds \¹ädz\ *n pl* 1 : a difference by which one thing is favored over another 2 : DISAGREEMENT — usu. used with *at* 3 : the ratio between the amount to be paid for a winning bet and the amount of the bet ⟨the horse went off at ~ of 6–1⟩

odds and ends *n pl* : miscellaneous things or matters

odds–on \¹ädz-¹ȯn, -¹än\ *adj* : having a better than even chance to win

ode \¹ōd\ *n* : a lyric poem that expresses a noble feeling with dignity

odi·ous \¹ō-dē-əs\ *adj* : causing or deserving hatred or repugnance — **odi·ous·ly** *adv* — **odi·ous·ness** *n*

odi·um \¹ō-dē-əm\ *n* 1 : merited loathing : HATRED 2 : DISGRACE

odom·e·ter \ō-¹dä-mə-tər\ *n* [F odomètre, fr. Gk hodometron, fr. hodos way, road + metron measure] : an instrument for measuring distance traveled (as by a vehicle)

odor \¹ō-dər\ *n* 1 : the quality of something that stimulates the sense of smell; *also* : a sensation resulting from such stimulation 2 : REPUTE, ESTIMATION — **odored** \¹ō-dərd\ *adj* — **odor·less** *adj* — **odor·ous** *adj*

odour *chiefly Brit var of* ODOR

od·ys·sey \¹ä-də-sē\ *n, pl* **-seys** [the *Odyssey*, epic poem attributed to Homer recounting the long wanderings of Odysseus] : a long wandering marked usu. by many changes of fortune

oe·cu·men·i·cal \ˌesp Brit ˌē-\ *var of* ECUMENICAL

OED *abbr* Oxford English Dictionary

oe·de·ma *chiefly Brit var of* EDEMA

oe·di·pal \¹e-də-pəl, ¹ē-\ *adj, often cap* : of, relating to, or resulting from the Oedipus complex

Oe·di·pus complex \-pəs-\ *n* : the positive sexual feelings of a child toward the parent of the opposite sex and hostile or jealous feelings toward the parent of the same sex that may be a source of adult personality disorder when unresolved

OEO *abbr* Office of Economic Opportunity

o'er \¹ȯr\ *adv or prep* : OVER

OES *abbr* Order of the Eastern Star

oe·soph·a·gus *chiefly Brit var of* ESOPHAGUS

oeu·vre \œvrᵊ\ *n, pl* **oeuvres** \same\ : a substantial body of work constituting the lifework of a writer, an artist, or a composer

of \¹əv, ¹äv\ *prep* 1 : FROM ⟨a man ~ the West⟩ 2 : having as a significant background or character element ⟨a man ~ noble birth⟩ ⟨a woman ~ ability⟩ 3 : owing to ⟨died ~ flu⟩ 4 : BY ⟨the plays ~ Shakespeare⟩ 5 : having as component parts or material, contents, or members ⟨a house ~ brick⟩ ⟨a glass ~ water⟩ ⟨a pack ~ fools⟩ 6 : belonging to or included by ⟨the front ~ the house⟩ ⟨a time ~ life⟩ ⟨one ~ you⟩ ⟨the best ~ its kind⟩ ⟨the son ~ a doctor⟩ 7 : ABOUT ⟨tales ~ the West⟩ 8 : connected with : OVER ⟨the queen ~ England⟩ 9 : that is : signified as ⟨the city ~ Rome⟩ 10 — used to indicate apposition of the words it joins ⟨that fool ~ a husband⟩ 11 : as concerns : FOR ⟨love ~ nature⟩ 12 — used to indicate the application of an adjective ⟨fond ~ candy⟩ 13 : BEFORE ⟨quarter ~ ten⟩

OF *abbr* outfield

¹**off** \¹ȯf\ *adv* 1 : from a place or position ⟨drove ~ in a new car⟩; *also* : ASIDE ⟨turned ~ into a side road⟩ 2 : at a distance in time or space ⟨stood ~ a few yards⟩ ⟨several years ~⟩ 3 : so as to be unattached or removed ⟨the lid blew ~⟩ 4 : to a state of discontinuance, exhaustion, or completion ⟨shut the radio ~⟩ 5 : away from regular work ⟨took time ~ for lunch⟩

²**off** *prep* 1 : away from ⟨just ~ the highway⟩ ⟨take it ~ the table⟩ 2 : to seaward of ⟨two miles ~ the coast⟩ 3 : FROM ⟨borrowed a dollar ~ me⟩ 4 : at the expense of ⟨lives ~ his parents⟩ 5 : not now engaged in ⟨~ duty⟩ 6 : abstaining from ⟨~ liquor⟩ 7 : below the usual level of ⟨~ his game⟩

³**off** *adj* 1 : more removed or distant 2 : started on the way 3 : not operating 4 : not correct 5 : REMOTE, SLIGHT 6 : INFERIOR 7 : provided for ⟨well ~⟩

⁴**off** *abbr* office; officer; official

of·fal \¹ȯ-fəl\ *n* : the waste or by-product of a process; *esp* : the viscera and trimmings of a butchered animal removed in dressing

off and on *adv* : INTERMITTENTLY

¹**off·beat** \¹ȯf-ˌbēt\ *n* : the unaccented part of a musical measure

²**offbeat** *adj* : ECCENTRIC, UNCONVENTIONAL

off–col·or \¹ȯf-¹kə-lər\ *or* **off–col·ored** \-lərd\ *adj* 1 : not having the right or standard color 2 : of doubtful propriety : verging on indecency ⟨~ stories⟩

of·fend \ə-¹fend\ *vb* 1 : SIN, TRANSGRESS 2 : to cause

discomfort or pain : HURT **3** : to cause dislike or vexation : ANNOY **syn** affront, insult, outrage — **of·fend·er** *n*

of·fense *or* **of·fence** \ə-'fens, *esp for 2 & 3* 'ä-ˌfens\ *n* **1** : something that outrages the senses **2** : ATTACK, ASSAULT **3** : the offensive team or members of a team playing offensive positions **4** : DISPLEASURE **5** : SIN, MISDEED **6** : an infraction of law : CRIME

¹of·fen·sive \ə-'fen-siv *esp for 1 & 2* 'ä-ˌfen-\ *adj* **1** : AGGRESSIVE **2** : of or relating to an attempt to score in a game; *also* : of or relating to a team in possession of the ball or puck **3** : OBNOXIOUS **4** : INSULTING — **of·fen·sive·ly** *adv* — **of·fen·sive·ness** *n*

²offensive *n* : ATTACK

¹of·fer \'ȯ-fər\ *vb* **of·fered; of·fer·ing 1** : SACRIFICE **2** : to present for acceptance : TENDER; *also* : to propose as payment **3** : PROPOSE, SUGGEST; *also* : to declare one's readiness **4** : to try or begin to exert ⟨~ resistance⟩ **5** : to place on sale — **of·fer·ing** *n*

²offer *n* **1** : PROPOSAL **2** : BID **3** : TRY

of·fer·to·ry \'ȯ-fər-ˌtȯr-ē\ *n, pl* **-ries** : the presentation of offerings at a church service; *also* : the musical accompaniment during it

off·hand \'ȯf-'hand\ *adv or adj* : without previous thought or preparation

off–hour \-ˌau̇(-ə)r\ *n* : a period of time other than a rush hour; *also* : a period of time other than business hours

of·fice \'ȯ-fəs\ *n* **1** : a special duty or position; *esp* : a position of authority in government ⟨run for ~⟩ **2** : a prescribed form or service of worship; *also* : RITE **3** : an assigned or assumed duty or role **4** : a place where a business is transacted or a service is supplied

of·fice·hold·er \'ȯ-fəs-ˌhōl-dər\ *n* : one holding a public office

of·fi·cer \'ȯ-fə-sər\ *n* **1** : one charged with the enforcement of law **2** : one who holds an office of trust or authority **3** : a person who holds a position of authority or command in the armed forces; *esp* : COMMISSIONED OFFICER

¹of·fi·cial \ə-'fi-shəl\ *n* : OFFICER 2

²official *adj* **1** : of or relating to an office or to officers **2** : AUTHORIZED, AUTHORITATIVE **3** : befitting or characteristic of a person in office — **of·fi·cial·ly** *adv*

of·fi·cial·dom \ə-'fi-shəl-dəm\ *n* : officials as a class

of·fi·cial·ism \ə-'fi-shə-ˌli-zəm\ *n* : lack of flexibility and initiative combined with excessive adherence to regulations

of·fi·ci·ant \ə-'fi-shē-ənt\ *n* : one (as a priest) who officiates at a religious rite

of·fi·ci·ate \ə-'fi-shē-ˌāt\ *vb* **-at·ed; -at·ing 1** : to perform a ceremony, function, or duty **2** : to act in an official capacity

of·fi·cious \ə-'fi-shəs\ *adj* : volunteering one's services where they are neither asked for nor needed — **of·fi·cious·ly** *adv* — **of·fi·cious·ness** *n*

off·ing \'ȯ-fiŋ\ *n* : the near or foreseeable future

off–line \'ȯf-'līn\ *adj or adv* : not connected to or controlled directly by a computer

off of *prep* : OFF

off·print \'ȯf-ˌprint\ *n* : a separately printed excerpt (as from a magazine)

off–road \-'rōd\ *adj* : of, relating to, or being a vehicle designed for use away from public roads

off–sea·son \-ˌsēz-ᵊn\ *n* : a time of suspended or reduced activity

¹off·set \-ˌset\ *n* **1** : a sharp bend (as in a pipe) by which one part is turned aside out of line **2** : a printing process in which an inked impression is first made on a rubber-blanketed cylinder and then transferred to the paper

²off·set *vb* **off·set; off·set·ting 1** : to place over against : BALANCE **2** : to compensate for **3** : to form an offset in (as a wall)

off·shoot \'ȯf-ˌshüt\ *n* **1** : a collateral or derived branch, descendant, or member **2** : a branch of a main stem (as of a plant)

¹off·shore \'ȯf-'shȯr\ *adv* **1** : at a distance from the shore **2** : outside the country : ABROAD

²off·shore \'ȯf-ˌshȯr\ *adj* **1** : moving away from the shore **2** : situated off the shore but within waters under a country's control

off·side \-'sīd\ *adv or adj* : illegally in advance of the ball or puck

off·spring \-ˌspriŋ\ *n, pl* **offspring** *also* **offsprings** : PROGENY, YOUNG

off·stage \'ȯf-'stāj, -ˌstāj\ *adv or adj* **1** : off or away from the stage **2** : out of the public view ⟨deals made ~⟩

off–the–record *adj* : given or made in confidence and not for publication

off–the–shelf *adj* : available as a stock item : not specially designed or made

off–the–wall *adj* : highly unusual : BIZARRE

off·track \'ȯf-ˌtrak\ *adv or adj* : away from a racetrack

off–white \'ȯf-'hwīt\ *n* : a yellowish or grayish white

off year *n* **1** : a year in which no major election is held **2** : a year of diminished activity or production

oft \'ȯft\ *adv* : OFTEN

of·ten \'ȯ-fən\ *adv* : many times : FREQUENTLY

of·ten·times \-ˌtīmz\ *or* **oft·times** \'ȯf-ˌtīmz, 'ȯft-\ *adv* : OFTEN

ogle \'ō-gəl\ *vb* **ogled; ogling** : to look at in a flirtatious way — **ogle** *n* — **ogler** *n*

ogre \'ō-gər\ *n* **1** : a monster of fairy tales and folklore that eats people **2** : a dreaded person or object

ogress \'ō-grəs\ *n* : a female ogre

oh \'ō\ *interj* **1** — used to express an emotion or in response to physical stimuli **2** — used in direct address

OH *abbr* Ohio

ohm \'ōm\ *n* : a unit of electrical resistance equal to the resistance of a circuit in which a potential difference of one volt produces a current of one ampere — **ohm·ic** \'ō-mik\ *adj*

ohm·me·ter \'ōm-ˌmē-tər\ *n* : an instrument for indicating resistance in ohms directly

¹oil \'ȯil\ *n* [ME *oile*, fr. OF, fr. L *oleum* olive oil, fr. Gk *elaion*, fr. *elaia* olive] **1** : any of numerous fatty or greasy liquid substances obtained from plants, animals, or minerals and used for fuel, food, medicines, and manufacturing **2** : PETROLEUM **3** : artists' colors made with oil; *also* : a painting in such colors — **oil·i·ness** \'ȯi-lē-nəs\ *n* — **oily** \'ȯi-lē\ *adj*

²oil *vb* : to put oil in or on — **oil·er** *n*

oil·cloth \'ȯil-ˌklȯth\ *n* : cloth treated with oil or paint and used for table and shelf coverings

oil pan *n* : the lower section of a crankcase used as an oil reservoir

oil shale *n* : a rock (as shale) from which oil can be recovered

oil·skin \'ȯil-ˌskin\ *n* **1** : an oiled waterproof cloth **2** : an oilskin raincoat **3** *pl* : an oilskin coat and trousers

oink \'ȯiŋk\ *n* : the natural noise of a hog — **oink** *vb*

oint·ment \'ȯint-mənt\ *n* : a salve for use on the skin

OJ *abbr* orange juice

Ojib·wa *or* **Ojib·way** \ō-'jib-ˌwä\ *n, pl* **Ojibwa** *or* **Ojibwas** *or* **Ojibway** *or* **Ojibways** : a member of an American Indian people of the region around Lake Superior and westward

OJT *abbr* on-the-job training

¹OK *or* **okay** \ō-'kā\ *adv or adj* : all right

²OK *or* **okay** *vb* **OK'd** *or* **okayed; OK'·ing** *or* **okay·ing** : APPROVE, AUTHORIZE — **OK** *or* **okay** *n*

³OK *abbr* Oklahoma

Okla *abbr* Oklahoma

okra \'ō-krə\ *n* : a tall annual plant related to the hollyhocks that has edible green pods; *also* : these pods

¹old \'ōld\ *adj* **1** : ANCIENT; *also* : of long standing **2** *cap* : belonging to an early period ⟨*Old* Irish⟩ **3** : having existed for a specified period of time **4** : of or relating to a past era **5** : advanced in years **6** : showing the effects of age or use **7** : no longer in use — **old·ish** \\'ōl-dish\\ *adj*

²old *n* : old or earlier time 〈days of ∼〉

old·en \\'ōl-dən\\ *adj* : of or relating to a bygone era

¹old–fash·ioned \\'ōld-'fa-shənd\\ *adj* **1** : OUT-OF-DATE, ANTIQUATED **2** : CONSERVATIVE

²old–fashioned *n* : a cocktail usu. made with whiskey, bitters, sugar, a twist of lemon peel, and water or soda water

old guard *n, often cap O&G* : the conservative members of an organization

old hat *adj* **1** : OLD-FASHIONED **2** : STALE, TRITE

old·ie \\'ōl-dē\\ *n* : something old; *esp* : a popular song from the past

old–line \\'ōld-'līn\\ *adj* **1** : ORIGINAL, ESTABLISHED 〈an ∼ business〉 **2** : adhering to old policies or practices

old maid *n* **1** : SPINSTER **2** : a prim fussy person — **old–maid·ish** \\'ōld-'mā-dish\\ *adj*

old man *n* **1** : HUSBAND **2** : FATHER

old·ster \\'ōld-stər\\ *n* : an old or elderly person

Old Testament *n* : the first of the two chief divisions of the Bible — see BIBLE table

old–time \\'ōld-'tīm\\ *adj* **1** : of, relating to, or characteristic of an earlier period **2** : of long standing

old–tim·er \\-'tī-mər\\ *n* VETERAN; *also* : OLDSTER

old–world \\-'wərld\\ *adj* : having old-fashioned charm

Old World *n* : the eastern hemisphere exclusive of Australia; *esp* : continental Europe

ole·ag·i·nous \\ō-lē-'a-jə-nəs\\ *adj* : OILY

ole·an·der \\'ō-lē-ın-dər\\ *n* : a poisonous evergreen shrub often grown for its fragrant white to red flowers

oleo \\'ō-lē-ıō\\ *n, pl* **oleos** : MARGARINE

oleo·mar·ga·rine \\ō-lē-ō-'mär-jə-rən\\ *n* : MARGARINE

ol·fac·to·ry \\äl-'fak-tə-rē, ōl-\\ *adj* : of or relating to the sense of smell

oli·gar·chy \\'ä-lə-ıgär-kē, 'ō-\\ *n, pl* **-chies 1** : a government in which power is in the hands of a few **2** : a state having an oligarchy; *also* : the group holding power in such a state — **oli·garch** \\-ıgärk\\ *n* — **oli·gar·chic** \\ıä-lə-'gär-kik, ıō-\\ *or* **oli·gar·chi·cal** \\-ki-kəl\\ *adj*

Oli·go·cene \\'ä-li-gō-ısēn, ə-'li-gə-ısēn\\ *adj* : of, relating to, or being the epoch of the Tertiary between the Eocene and the Miocene — **Oligocene** *n*

olio \\'ō-lē-ıō\\ *n, pl* **oli·os** : HODGEPODGE, MEDLEY

ol·ive \\'ä-liv\\ *n* **1** : an Old World evergreen tree grown in warm regions for its fruit that is a food and the source of an edible oil (**olive oil**) **2** : a dull yellow to yellowish green color

olive drab *n* **1** : a grayish olive color **2** : an olive drab wool or cotton fabric; *also* : a uniform of this fabric

ol·iv·ine \\'ä-lə-ıvēn\\ *n* : a usu. greenish mineral that is a complex silicate of magnesium and iron

Olym·pic Games \\ō-'lim-pik-\\ *n pl* : a modified revival of an ancient Greek festival consisting of international athletic contests that are held at separate winter and summer gatherings at four-year intervals

om \\'ōm\\ *n* : a mantra consisting of the sound "om" used in contemplating ultimate reality

Oma·ha \\'ō-mə-ıhä, -ıhȯ\\ *n, pl* **Omaha** *or* **Omahas** : a member of an American Indian people of northeastern Nebraska

om·buds·man \\'äm-ıbu̇dz-mən, äm-'bu̇dz-\\ *n, pl* **-men** \\-mən\\ **1** : a government official appointed to investigate complaints made by individuals against abuses or capricious acts of public officials **2** : one that investigates reported complaints (as from students or consumers)

ome·ga \\ō-'mā-gə\\ *n* : the 24th and last letter of the Greek alphabet — Ω or ω

om·elet *or* **om·elette** \\'äm-lət, 'ä-mə-\\ *n* [F *omelette*, alter. of MF *alumelle*, lit., knife blade, modif. of L *lamella*, dim. of *lamina* thin plate] : eggs beaten with milk or water, cooked without stirring until set, and folded over

omen \\'ō-mən\\ *n* : an event or phenomenon believed to be a sign or warning of a future occurrence

om·i·cron \\'ä-mə-ıkrän, 'ō-\\ *n* : the 15th letter of the Greek alphabet — O or o

om·i·nous \\'ä-mə-nəs\\ *adj* : foretelling evil : THREATENING — **om·i·nous·ly** *adv* — **om·i·nous·ness** *n*

omis·si·ble \\ō-'mi-sə-bəl\\ *adj* : that may be omitted

omis·sion \\ō-'mi-shən\\ *n* **1** : something neglected or left undone **2** : the act of omitting : the state of being omitted

omit \\ō-'mit\\ *vb* **omit·ted; omit·ting 1** : to leave out or leave unmentioned **2** : to fail to perform : NEGLECT

¹om·ni·bus \\'äm-ni-(ı)bəs\\ *n* : BUS

²omnibus *adj* : of, relating to, or providing for many things at once 〈an ∼ bill〉

om·nip·o·tent \\äm-'ni-pə-tənt\\ *adj* : having unlimited authority or influence : ALMIGHTY — **om·nip·o·tence** \\-əns\\ *n* — **om·nip·o·tent·ly** *adv*

om·ni·pres·ent \\ıäm-ni-'prez-ᵊnt\\ *adj* : present in all places at all times — **om·ni·pres·ence** \\-ᵊns\\ *n*

om·ni·scient \\äm-'ni-shənt\\ *adj* : having infinite awareness, understanding, and insight — **om·ni·science** \\-shəns\\ *n* — **om·ni·scient·ly** *adv*

om·ni·um–gath·er·um \\ıäm-nē-əm-'ga-thə-rəm\\ *n, pl* **omnium–gatherums** \\-ıa miscellaneous collection

om·niv·o·rous \\äm-'ni-və-rəs\\ *adj* : feeding on both animal and vegetable substances; *also* : AVID 〈an ∼ reader〉 — **om·niv·o·rous·ly** *adv*

¹on \\'ȯn, 'än\\ *prep* **1** : in or to a position over and in contact with 〈jumped ∼ his horse〉 **2** : touching the surface of 〈shadows ∼ the wall〉 **3** : AT, TO 〈∼ the right were the mountains〉 **4** : IN, ABOARD 〈went ∼ the train〉 **5** : during or at the time of 〈came ∼ Monday〉 〈every hour ∼ the hour〉 **6** : through the agency of 〈was cut ∼ a tin can〉 **7** : in a state or process of 〈∼ fire〉 〈∼ the wane〉 **8** : connected with as a member or participant 〈∼ a committee〉 〈∼ tour〉 **9** — used to indicate a basis, source, or standard of computation 〈has it ∼ good authority〉 〈10 cents ∼ the dollar〉 **10** : with regard to 〈a monopoly ∼ wheat〉 **11** : at or toward as an object 〈crept up ∼ her〉 **12** : ABOUT, CONCERNING 〈a book ∼ minerals〉

²on *adv* **1** : in or into a position of contact with or attachment to a surface **2** : FORWARD **3** : into operation

³on *adj* : being in operation or in progress

ON *abbr* Ontario

¹once \\'wəns\\ *adv* **1** : one time only **2** : at any one time **3** : FORMERLY **4** : by one degree of relationship

²once *n* : one single time — **at once 1** : at the same time **2** : IMMEDIATELY

³once *adj* : FORMER

⁴once *conj* : AS SOON AS

once–over \\'wəns-ıō-vər\\ *n* : a swift examination or survey

on·com·ing \\'ȯn-ıkə-miŋ, 'än-\\ *adj* : APPROACHING 〈∼ traffic〉

¹one \\'wən\\ *adj* **1** : being a single unit or thing 〈∼ person went〉 **2** : being one in particular 〈early ∼ morning〉 **3** : being the same in kind or quality 〈members of ∼ race〉; *also* : UNITED **4** : being not specified or fixed 〈∼ day soon〉

²one *n* **1** : the number denoting unity **2** : the 1st in a set or series **3** : a single person or thing — **one·ness** \\'wən-nəs\\ *n*

³one *pron* **1** : a certain indefinitely indicated person or thing 〈saw ∼ of his friends〉 **2** : a person in general 〈∼ never knows〉 **3** — used in place of a first-person pronoun

Onei·da \\ō-'nī-də\\ *n, pl* **Oneida** *or* **Oneidas** : a member of an American Indian people orig. of New York

oner·ous \\'ä-nə-rəs, 'ō-\\ *adj* : imposing or constituting a burden : TROUBLESOME **syn** oppressive, exacting, burdensome, weighty

one·self \\(ı)wən-'self\\ *also* **one's self** *pron* : one's own self — usu. used reflexively or for emphasis

one–sid·ed \\'wən-'sī-dəd\\ *adj* **1** : having or occurring on one side only; *also* : having one side prominent or more developed **2** : PARTIAL ⟨a ∼ interpretation⟩

one·time \-ˌtīm\ *adj* : FORMER

one–to–one \ˌwən-tə-'wən\ *adj* : pairing each element of a set uniquely with an element of another set

one up *adj* : being in a position of advantage ⟨was *one up* on the others⟩

one–way *adj* : moving, allowing movement, or functioning in only one direction ⟨∼ streets⟩

on·go·ing \'ȯn-ˌgō-iŋ, 'än-\ *adj* : continuously moving forward

on·ion \'ən-yən\ *n* : the pungent edible bulb of a cultivated plant related to the lilies; *also* : this plant

on·ion·skin \-ˌskin\ *n* : a thin strong translucent paper of very light weight

on–line *adj or adv* : connected to or controlled directly by a computer

on·look·er \'ȯn-ˌlu̇-kər, 'än-\ *n* : SPECTATOR

¹on·ly \'ōn-lē\ *adj* **1** : unquestionably the best **2** : SOLE

²only *adv* **1** : MERELY, JUST ⟨∼ $2⟩ **2** : SOLELY ⟨known ∼ to me⟩ **3** : at the very least ⟨was ∼ too true⟩ **4** : as a final result ⟨will ∼ make you sick⟩

³only *conj* : except that

on·o·mato·poe·ia \ˌä-nə-ˌmä-tə-'pē-ə\ *n* **1** : formation of words in imitation of natural sounds (as *buzz* or *hiss*) **2** : the use of words whose sound suggests the sense — **on·o·mato·poe·ic** \-'pē-ik\ *or* **on·o·mato·po·et·ic** \-pō-'e-tik\ *adj* — **on·o·mato·poe·i·cal·ly** \-'pē-ə-k(ə-)lē\ *or* **on·o·mato·po·et·i·cal·ly** \-pō-'e-ti-k(ə-)lē\ *adv*

On·on·da·ga \ˌä-nən-'dȯ-gə, -'dä-, -'dä\ *n, pl* **-ga** *or* **-gas** : a member of an American Indian people of New York and Canada

on·rush \'ȯn-ˌrəsh, 'än-\ *n* : a rushing onward — **on·rush·ing** *adj*

on·set \-ˌset\ *n* **1** : ATTACK **2** : BEGINNING

on·shore \-ˌshȯr\ *adj* **1** : moving toward the shore **2** : situated on or near the shore — **on·shore** \-'shȯr\ *adv*

on·slaught \'ȯn-ˌslȯt, 'än-\ *n* : a fierce attack; *also* : something resembling such an attack ⟨an ∼ of questions⟩

Ont *abbr* Ontario

on·to \'ȯn-tü, 'än-\ *prep* : to a position or point on

onus \'ō-nəs\ *n* **1** : BURDEN **2** : OBLIGATION **3** : BLAME

¹on·ward \'ȯn-wərd, 'än-\ *also* **on·wards** \-wərdz\ *adv* : FORWARD

²onward *adj* : directed or moving onward : FORWARD

on·yx \'ä-niks\ *n* [ME *onix*, fr. MF & L; MF, fr. L *onyx*, fr. Gk. lit., claw, nail] : a translucent chalcedony in parallel layers of different colors

oo·dles \'üd-ᵊlz\ *n pl* : a great quantity

oo·lite \'ō-ə-ˌlīt\ *n* : a rock consisting of small round grains cemented together — **oo·lit·ic** \ˌō-ə-'li-tik\ *adj*

¹ooze \'üz\ *n* **1** : a soft deposit (as of mud) on the bottom of a body of water **2** : soft wet ground : MUD — **oozy** \'ü-zē\ *adj*

²ooze *vb* **oozed; ooz·ing 1** : to flow or leak out slowly or imperceptibly **2** : EXUDE

³ooze *n* : something that oozes

op *abbr* **1** operation; operative; operator **2** opportunity **3** opus

OP *abbr* **1** observation post **2** out of print

opac·i·ty \ō-'pa-sə-tē\ *n, pl* **-ties 1** : the quality or state of being opaque **2** : obscurity of meaning **3** : mental dullness **4** : an opaque spot in a normally transparent structure

opal \'ō-pəl\ *n* : a mineral with iridescent colors that is used as a gem

opal·es·cent \ˌō-pə-'les-ᵊnt\ *adj* : IRIDESCENT — **opal·es·cence** \-ᵊns\ *n*

opaque \ō-'pāk\ *adj* **1** : blocking the passage of radiant energy and esp. light **2** : not easily understood **3** : OBTUSE — **opaque·ly** *adv* — **opaque·ness** *n*

op art \'äp-\ *n* : OPTICAL ART — **op artist** *n*

op cit *abbr* [L *opere citato*] in the work cited

ope \'ōp\ *vb* **oped; op·ing** *archaic* : OPEN

OPEC *abbr* Organization of Petroleum Exporting Countries

¹open \'ō-pən\ *adj* **open·er; open·est 1** : not shut or shut up ⟨an ∼ door⟩ **2** : not secret or hidden; *also* : FRANK **3** : not enclosed or covered ⟨an ∼ fire⟩; *also* : not protected **4** : free to be entered or used ⟨an ∼ tournament⟩ **5** : easy to get through or see ⟨∼ country⟩ **6** : spread out : EXTENDED **7** : not decided ⟨an ∼ question⟩ **8** : readily accessible and cooperative; *also* : GENEROUS **9** : having components separated by a space in writing and printing ⟨the name *Spanish moss* is an ∼ compound⟩ **10** : having openings, interruptions, or spaces ⟨an ∼ mesh⟩ **11** : ready to operate ⟨stores are ∼⟩ **12** : free from restraints or controls ⟨∼ season⟩ — **open·ly** *adv* — **open·ness** *n*

²open \'ō-pən\ *vb* **opened; open·ing 1** : to change or move from a shut position; *also* : to make open by clearing away obstacles **2** : to make accessible **3** : to make openings in **4** : to make or become functional ⟨∼ a store⟩ **5** : REVEAL; *also* : ENLIGHTEN **6** : BEGIN — **open·er** *n*

³open *n* **1** : OUTDOORS **2** : a contest or tournament open to all

open–air *adj* : OUTDOOR ⟨∼ theaters⟩

open·hand·ed \ˌō-pən-'han-dəd\ *adj* : GENEROUS — **open·hand·ed·ly** *adv*

open–heart *adj* : of, relating to, or performed on a heart temporarily relieved of circulatory function and laid open for inspection and treatment

open–hearth *adj* : of, relating to, or being a process of making steel in a furnace that reflects the heat from the roof onto the material

open·ing *n* **1** : an act or instance of making or becoming open **2** : BEGINNING **3** : something that is open **4** : OCCASION; *also* : an opportunity for employment

open–mind·ed \ˌō-pən-'mīn-dəd\ *adj* : free from rigidly fixed preconceptions

open sentence *n* : a statement (as in mathematics) containing at least one blank or unknown so that when the blank is filled or a quantity substituted for the unknown the statement becomes a complete statement that is either true or false

open shop *n* : an establishment having members and nonmembers of a labor union on the payroll

open·work \'ō-pən-ˌwərk\ *n* : work so made as to show openings through its substance ⟨a railing of wrought-iron ∼⟩ — **open–worked** \-ˌwərkt\ *adj*

¹opera *pl of* OPUS

²op·era \'ä-prə, -pə-rə\ *n* : a drama set to music — **op·er·at·ic** \ˌä-pə-'ra-tik\ *adj*

op·er·a·ble \'ä-pə-rə-bəl\ *adj* **1** : fit, possible, or desirable to use **2** : likely to result in a favorable outcome upon surgical treatment

opera glasses *n pl* : small binoculars for use in a theater

op·er·ate \'ä-pə-ˌrāt\ *vb* **-at·ed; -at·ing 1** : to perform work : FUNCTION **2** : to produce an effect **3** : to put or keep in operation **4** : to perform or subject to an operation — **op·er·a·tor** \-ˌrā-tər\ *n*

operating system *n* : software that controls the operation of a computer

op·er·a·tion \ˌä-pə-'rā-shən\ *n* **1** : a doing or performing of a practical work **2** : an exertion of power or influence; *also* : method or manner of functioning **3** : a surgical procedure **4** : a process of deriving one mathematical expression from others according to a rule **5** : a military action or mission — **op·er·a·tion·al** \-shə-nəl\ *adj*

¹op·er·a·tive \'ä-pə-rə-tiv, -ˌrā-\ *adj* **1** : producing an appropriate effect **2** : OPERATING ⟨an ∼ force⟩ **3** : having to do with physical operations; *also* : WORKING ⟨an ∼ craftsman⟩ **4** : based on or consisting of an operation ⟨∼ dentistry⟩

²operative *n* : OPERATOR; *esp* : a secret agent

op·er·et·ta \ˌä-pə-'re-tə\ *n* [It, dim. of *opera* opera] : a light musical-dramatic work with a romantic plot, spoken dialogue, and dancing scenes

oph·thal·mic \äf-'thal-mik, äp-\ adj [Gk ophthalmikos, fr. ophthalmos eye] : of, relating to, or located near the eye

oph·thal·mol·o·gy \,äf-thal-'mä-lə-jē, ,äp-\ n : a branch of medicine dealing with the structure, functions, and diseases of the eye — **oph·thal·mol·o·gist** \-jist\ n

oph·thal·mo·scope \äf-'thal-mə-,skōp, äp-\ n : an instrument for use in viewing the interior of the eye and esp. the retina

opi·ate \'ō-pē-ət, -pē-,ät\ n : a preparation or derivative of opium; also : a narcotic or a substance with similar activity — **opiate** adj

opine \ō-'pīn\ vb **opined; opin·ing** : to express an opinion : STATE

opin·ion \ə-'pin-yən\ n 1 : a belief stronger than impression and less strong than positive knowledge 2 : JUDGMENT 3 : a formal statement by an expert after careful study

opin·ion·at·ed \ə-'pin-yə-,nā-təd\ adj : obstinately adhering to personal opinions

opi·um \'ō-pē-əm\ n [ME, fr. L, fr. Gk opion, fr. dim. of opos sap] : an addictive narcotic drug that is the dried juice of a poppy

opos·sum \ə-'pä-səm\ n, pl **opossums** also **opossum** : a common omnivorous tree-dwelling marsupial mammal of the eastern U.S. that is active esp. at night

opp abbr opposite

op·po·nent \ə-'pō-nənt\ n : one that opposes : ADVERSARY

op·por·tune \,ä-pər-'tün, -'tyün\ adj [ME, fr. MF opportun, fr. L opportunus, fr. ob- toward + portus port, harbor] : SUITABLE — **op·por·tune·ly** adv

op·por·tun·ism \,ä-pər-'tü-,ni-zəm, -'tyü-\ n : a taking advantage of opportunities or circumstances esp. with little regard for principles or ultimate consequences — **op·por·tun·ist** \-nist\ n — **op·por·tu·nis·tic** \-tü-'nis-tik, -tyü-\ adj

op·por·tu·ni·ty \,ä-pər-'tü-nə-tē, -'tyü-\ n, pl **-ties 1** : a favorable combination of circumstances, time, and place **2** : a chance for advancement

op·pose \ə-'pōz\ vb **op·posed; op·pos·ing 1** : to place opposite or against something (as to provide resistance or contrast) **2** : to strive against : RESIST — **op·po·si·tion** \,ä-pə-'zi-shən\ n

¹**op·po·site** \'ä-pə-zət\ adj **1** : set over against something that is at the other end or side **2** : OPPOSED, HOSTILE; also : CONTRARY **3** : contrarily turned or moving — **op·po·site·ly** adv — **op·po·site·ness** n

²**opposite** n : one that is opposed or contrary

³**opposite** adv : on or to an opposite side

⁴**opposite** prep : across from and usu. facing ⟨the house ~ ours⟩

op·press \ə-'pres\ vb **1** : to crush by abuse of power or authority **2** : to weigh down : BURDEN **syn** aggrieve, wrong, persecute — **op·pres·sive** \-'pre-siv\ adj — **op·pres·sive·ly** adv — **op·pres·sor** \-'pre-sər\ n

op·pres·sion \ə-'pre-shən\ n **1** : unjust or cruel exercise of power or authority **2** : DEPRESSION — **op·pres·sive** \-'pre-siv\ adj

op·pro·bri·ous \ə-'prō-brē-əs\ adj : expressing or deserving opprobrium — **op·pro·bri·ous·ly** adv

op·pro·bri·um \-brē-əm\ n **1** : something that brings disgrace **2** : INFAMY

¹**opt** \'äpt\ vb : to make a choice; esp : to decide in favor of something

²**opt** abbr **1** optical; optician; optics **2** option; optional

op·tic \'äp-tik\ adj : of or relating to vision or the eye

op·ti·cal \'äp-ti-kəl\ adj **1** : relating to optics **2** : OPTIC **3** : of, relating to, or using light

optical art n : nonobjective art characterized by the use of geometric patterns often for an illusory effect

optical disk n : a disk on which information has been recorded digitally and which is read using a laser

optical fiber n : a single fiber-optic strand

op·ti·cian \äp-'ti-shən\ n **1** : a maker of or dealer in optical items and instruments **2** : a person who makes or orders eyeglass and contact lenses to prescription and sells glasses

op·tics \'äp-tiks\ n pl : a science that deals with the nature and properties of light

op·ti·mal \'äp-tə-məl\ adj : most desirable or satisfactory — **op·ti·mal·ly** adv

op·ti·mism \'äp-tə-,mi-zəm\ n [F optimisme, fr. L optimum, n., best, fr. neut. of optimus best] **1** : a doctrine that this world is the best possible world **2** : an inclination to anticipate the best possible outcome of actions or events — **op·ti·mist** \-mist\ n — **op·ti·mis·tic** \,äp-tə-'mis-tik\ adj — **op·ti·mis·ti·cal·ly** \-ti-k(ə-)lē\ adv

op·ti·mum \'äp-tə-məm\ n, pl **-ma** \-mə\ also **-mums** [L] : the amount or degree of something most favorable to an end; also : greatest degree attained under implied or specified conditions

op·tion \'äp-shən\ n **1** : the power or right to choose **2** : a right to buy or sell something at a specified price during a specified period **3** : something offered for choice — **op·tion·al** \-shə-nəl\ adj

op·tom·e·try \äp-'tä-mə-trē\ n : the art or profession of examining the eyes for defects of vision and of prescribing corrective lenses or exercises — **op·tom·e·trist** \-trist\ n

opt out vb : to choose not to participate

op·u·lence \'ä-pyə-ləns\ n **1** : WEALTH **2** : ABUNDANCE

op·u·lent \'ä-pyə-lənt\ adj **1** : WEALTHY **2** : richly abundant — **op·u·lent·ly** adv

opus \'ō-pəs\ n, pl **opera** \'ō-pə-rə, 'ä-\ also **opus·es** \'ō-pə-səz\ : WORK; esp : a musical composition

or \'ôr\ conj — used as a function word to indicate an alternative ⟨sink ~ swim⟩

OR abbr **1** operating room **2** Oregon

-or \ər\ n suffix : one that does a (specified) thing ⟨calculator⟩

or·a·cle \'ôr-ə-kəl\ n **1** : one held to give divinely inspired answers or revelations **2** : an authoritative or wise utterance; also : a person of great authority or wisdom — **orac·u·lar** \ò-'ra-kyə-lər\ adj

¹**oral** \'ôr-əl\ adj **1** : SPOKEN **2** : of or relating to the mouth **3** : of, relating to, or characterized by the first stage of psychosexual development in psychoanalytic theory in which libidinal gratification is derived from intake (as of food), by sucking, and later by biting **4** : relating to or characterized by personality traits of passive dependency and aggressiveness — **oral·ly** adv

²**oral** n : an oral examination — usu. used in pl.

orang \ə-'raŋ\ n : ORANGUTAN

or·ange \'ôr-inj\ n **1** : a juicy citrus fruit with reddish yellow rind; also : an evergreen tree with fragrant white flowers that bears this fruit **2** : a color between red and yellow

or·ange·ade \,ôr-in-'jād\ n : a beverage of orange juice, sugar, and water

orange hawkweed n : a weedy herb related to the daisies with bright orange-red flower heads

or·ange·ry \'ôr-inj-rē\ n, pl **-ries** : a protected place (as a greenhouse) for raising oranges in cool climates

orang·utan \ə-'raŋ-ə-,taŋ, -,tan\ n [Bazaar Malay (Malay-based pidgin), fr. Malay orang man + hutan forest] : a large reddish brown tree-living anthropoid ape of Borneo and Sumatra

orate \ò-'rāt\ vb **orat·ed; orat·ing** : to speak in a declamatory manner

ora·tion \ə-'rā-shən\ n : an elaborate discourse delivered in a formal and dignified manner

or·a·tor \'ôr-ə-tər\ n : one noted for skill and power as a public speaker

or·a·tor·i·cal \,ôr-ə-'tôr-i-kəl\ adj : of, relating to, or characteristic of an orator or oratory — **or·a·tor·i·cal·ly** \-'tôr-i-k(ə-)lē\ adv

or·a·to·rio \ˌȯr-ə-ˈtōr-ē-ˌō\ *n, pl* **-rios** : a lengthy choral work usu. on a scriptural subject

¹**or·a·to·ry** \ˈȯr-ə-ˌtōr-ē\ *n, pl* **-ries** : a private or institutional chapel

²**oratory** *n* : the art of speaking eloquently and effectively in public **syn** rhetoric, elocution

orb \ˈȯrb\ *n* : a spherical body; *also* : EYE

¹**or·bit** \ˈȯr-bət\ *n* [L *orbita,* lit., path, rut] **1** : a path described by one body in its revolution about another **2** : range or sphere of activity — **or·bit·al** \-ᵊl\ *adj*

²**orbit** *vb* **1** : CIRCLE **2** : to send up and make revolve in an orbit ⟨∼ a satellite⟩ — **or·bit·er** *n*

orch *abbr* orchestra

or·chard \ˈȯr-chərd\ *n* [ME, fr. OE *ortgeard,* fr. *ort-* (fr. L *hortus* garden) + *geard* yard] : a place where fruit trees, sugar maples, or nut trees are grown; *also* : the trees of such a place — **or·chard·ist** \-chər-dist\ *n*

or·ches·tra \ˈȯr-kə-strə\ *n* **1** : the front section of seats on the main floor of a theater **2** : a group of instrumentalists organized to perform ensemble music — **or·ches·tral** \ȯr-ˈkes-trəl\ *adj* — **or·ches·tral·ly** *adv*

or·ches·trate \ˈȯr-kə-ˌstrāt\ *vb* **-trat·ed; -trat·ing 1** : to compose or arrange for an orchestra **2** : to arrange so as to achieve a desired effect — **or·ches·tra·tion** \ˌȯr-kə-ˈstrā-shən\ *n*

or·chid \ˈȯr-kəd\ *n* : any of a large family of plants having often showy flowers with three petals of which the middle one is enlarged into a lip; *also* : a flower of an orchid

ord *abbr* **1** order **2** ordnance

or·dain \ȯr-ˈdān\ *vb* **1** : to admit to the ministry or priesthood by the ritual of a church **2** : DECREE, ENACT; *also* : DESTINE — **or·dain·ment** *n*

or·deal \ȯr-ˈdēl, ˈȯr-ˌdēl\ *n* : a severe trial or experience

¹**or·der** \ˈȯr-dər\ *vb* **1** : ARRANGE, REGULATE **2** : COMMAND **3** : to place an order

²**order** *n* **1** : a group of people formally united; *also* : a badge or medal of such a group **2** : any of the several grades of the Christian ministry; *also, pl* : ORDINATION **3** : a rank, class, or special group of persons or things **4** : a category of biological classification ranking above the family and below the class **5** : ARRANGEMENT, SEQUENCE; *also* : the prevailing state of things **6** : a customary mode of procedure; *also* : the rule of law or proper authority **7** : a specific rule, regulation, or authoritative direction **8** : a style of building; *also* : an architectural column forming the unit of a style **9** : condition esp. with regard to repair **10** : a written direction to pay money or to buy or sell goods; *also* : goods bought or sold

¹**or·der·ly** \ˈȯr-dər-lē\ *adj* **1** : arranged according to some order; *also* : NEAT, TIDY **2** : well behaved ⟨an ∼ crowd⟩ **syn** methodical, systematic, regular — **or·der·li·ness** *n*

²**orderly** *n, pl* **-lies 1** : a soldier who attends a superior officer **2** : a hospital attendant who does general work

¹**or·di·nal** \ˈȯrd-ᵊn-əl\ *n* : an ordinal number

²**ordinal** *adj* : indicating order or rank (as sixth) in a series

or·di·nance \ˈȯrd-ᵊn-əns\ *n* : an authoritative decree or law; *esp* : a municipal regulation

or·di·nary \ˈȯrd-ᵊn-ˌer-ē\ *adj* **1** : to be expected : USUAL **2** : of common quality, rank, or ability; *also* : POOR, INFERIOR **syn** customary, routine, normal, everyday — **or·di·nar·i·ly** \ˌȯrd-ᵊn-ˈer-ə-lē\ *adv* — **or·di·nar·i·ness** \ˈȯrd-ᵊn-ˌer-ē-nəs\ *n*

or·di·nate \ˈȯrd-ᵊn-ət, -ˌāt\ *n* : the coordinate of a point in a plane coordinate system that is the distance of the point from the horizontal axis found by measuring along a line parallel to the vertical axis

or·di·na·tion \ˌȯrd-ᵊn-ˈā-shən\ *n* : the act or ceremony by which a person is ordained

ord·nance \ˈȯrd-nəns\ *n* **1** : military supplies **2** : CANNON, ARTILLERY

Or·do·vi·cian \ˌȯr-də-ˈvi-shən\ *adj* : of, relating to, or being the period of the Paleozoic era between the Cambrian and the Silurian — **Ordovician** *n*

or·dure \ˈȯr-jər\ *n* : EXCREMENT

¹**ore** \ˈōr\ *n* : a mineral mined to obtain a substance that it contains

²**ore** \ˈər-ə\ *n, pl* **ore** — see *krona, krone* at MONEY table

Ore *or* **Oreg** *abbr* Oregon

oreg·a·no \ə-ˈre-gə-ˌnō\ *n* : a bushy perennial mint used as a seasoning and a source of oil

org *abbr* organization; organized

or·gan \ˈȯr-gən\ *n* **1** : a musical instrument having sets of pipes sounded by compressed air and controlled by keyboards; *also* : an instrument in which the sounds of the pipe organ are approximated by electronic devices **2** : a differentiated animal or plant structure (as a heart or a leaf) made up of cells and tissues and performing some bodily function **3** : a group that performs a specialized function ⟨the various ∼s of government⟩ **4** : PERIODICAL

or·gan·dy *also* **or·gan·die** \ˈȯr-gən-dē\ *n, pl* **-dies** [F *organdi*] : a fine transparent muslin with a stiff finish

or·gan·elle \ˌȯr-gə-ˈnel\ *n* : a specialized cell part that resembles an organ in having a special function

or·gan·ic \ȯr-ˈga-nik\ *adj* **1** : of, relating to, or arising in a bodily organ **2** : of, relating to, or derived from living things **3** : of, relating to, or containing carbon compounds **4** : of or relating to a branch of chemistry dealing with carbon compounds **5** : involving, producing, or dealing in foods produced without the use of laboratory-made fertilizers, growth substances, antibiotics, or pesticides **6** : ORGANIZED ⟨an ∼ whole⟩ — **or·gan·i·cal·ly** \-ni-k(ə-)lē\ *adv*

or·gan·ism \ˈȯr-gə-ˌni-zəm\ *n* : an individual living thing (as a person, animal, or plant) — **or·gan·is·mic** \ˌȯr-gə-ˈniz-mik\ *adj*

or·gan·ist \ˈȯr-gə-nist\ *n* : a person who plays an organ

or·ga·ni·za·tion \ˌȯr-gə-nə-ˈzā-shən\ *n* **1** : the act or process of organizing or of being organized; *also* : the condition or manner of being organized **2** : ASSOCIATION, SOCIETY **3** : an administrative structure (as a business or a political party) — **or·ga·ni·za·tion·al** \-shə-nəl\ *adj*

or·ga·nize \ˈȯr-gə-ˌnīz\ *vb* **-nized; -niz·ing 1** : to develop an organic structure **2** : to form into a complete and functioning whole **3** : to set up an administrative structure for **4** : to arrange by systematic planning and united effort **5** : to join in a union; *also* : UNIONIZE **syn** institute, found, establish, constitute — **or·ga·niz·er** *n*

or·gano·chlo·rine \ȯr-ˌga-nə-ˈklōr-ˌēn\ *adj* : of or relating to the chlorinated hydrocarbon pesticides (as DDT) — **organochlorine** *n*

or·gano·phos·phate \-ˈfäs-ˌfāt\ *n* : an organophosphorus pesticide — **organophosphate** *adj*

or·gano·phos·pho·rus \-ˈfäs-fə-rəs\ *also* **or·gano·phos·pho·rous** \-ˈfäs-ˈfōr-əs\ *adj* : of, relating to, or being a phosphorus-containing organic pesticide (as malathion)

or·gan·za \ȯr-ˈgan-zə\ *n* : a sheer dress fabric resembling organdy and usu. made of silk, rayon, or nylon

or·gasm \ˈȯr-ˌga-zəm\ *n* : the climax of sexual excitement — **or·gas·mic** \ȯr-ˈgaz-mik\ *adj*

or·gi·as·tic \ˌȯr-jē-ˈas-tik\ *adj* : of, relating to, or marked by orgies

or·gu·lous \ˈȯr-gyə-ləs, -gə-\ *adj* : PROUD

or·gy \ˈȯr-jē\ *n, pl* **orgies** : a gathering marked by unrestrained indulgence (as in sexual activity, alcohol, or drugs)

ori·el \ˈōr-ē-əl\ *n* : a window built out from a wall and usu. supported by a bracket

ori·ent \ˈōr-ē-ˌent\ *vb* **1** : to set in a definite position esp. in relation to the points of the compass **2** : to acquaint with an existing situation or environment **3** : to direct toward the interests of a particular group — **ori·en·ta·tion** \ˌōr-ē-ən-ˈtā-shən\ *n*

Orient *n* : EAST 3; *esp* : the countries of eastern Asia

ori·en·tal \ˌȯr-ē-'ent-əl\ *adj* [fr. *Orient* East, fr. ME, fr. MF, fr. L *orient-, oriens*, fr. prp. of *oriri* to rise] *often cap* : of or situated in the Orient — **Oriental** *n*

ori·en·tate \'ȯr-ē-ən-ˌtāt\ *vb* **-tat·ed; -tat·ing 1** : ORIENT **2** : to face east

or·i·fice \'ȯr-ə-fəs\ *n* : OPENING, MOUTH

ori·flamme \'ȯr-ə-ˌflam\ *n* : a brightly colored banner used as a standard or ensign in battle

orig *abbr* original; originally

ori·ga·mi \ˌȯr-ə-'gä-mē\ *n* : the art or process of Japanese paper folding

or·i·gin \'ȯr-ə-jən\ *n* **1** : ANCESTRY **2** : rise, beginning, or derivation from a source; *also* : CAUSE **3** : the intersection of coordinate axes

¹**orig·i·nal** \ə-'ri-jə-nəl\ *n* : something from which a copy, reproduction, or translation is made : PROTOTYPE

²**original** *adj* **1** : FIRST, INITIAL **2** : not copied from something else : FRESH **3** : INVENTIVE — **orig·i·nal·i·ty** \-ˌri-jə-'na-lə-tē\ *n* — **orig·i·nal·ly** \-'ri-jən-əl-ē\ *adv*

orig·i·nate \ə-'ri-jə-ˌnāt\ *vb* **-nat·ed; -nat·ing 1** : to give rise to : INITIATE **2** : to come into existence : BEGIN — **orig·i·na·tor** \-ˌnā-tər\ *n*

ori·ole \'ȯr-ē-ˌōl\ *n* : any of various New World birds of which the males are usu. black and yellow or black and orange

or·i·son \'ȯr-ə-sən\ *n* : PRAYER

or·mo·lu \'ȯr-mə-ˌlü\ *n* : a golden or gilded brass used for decorative purposes

¹**or·na·ment** \'ȯr-nə-mənt\ *n* : something that lends grace or beauty — **or·na·men·tal** \ˌȯr-nə-'ment-əl\ *adj*

²**or·na·ment** \-ˌment\ *vb* : to provide with ornament : ADORN — **or·na·men·ta·tion** \ˌȯr-nə-mən-'tā-shən\ *n*

or·nate \ȯr-'nāt\ *adj* : elaborately decorated — **or·nate·ly** *adv* — **or·nate·ness** *n*

or·nery \'ȯr-nə-rē, 'ä-nə-\ *adj* : having an irritable disposition

or·ni·thol·o·gy \ˌȯr-nə-'thä-lə-jē\ *n, pl* **-gies** : a branch of zoology dealing with birds — **or·ni·tho·log·i·cal** \-thə-'lä-ji-kəl\ *adj* — **or·ni·thol·o·gist** \-'thä-lə-jist\ *n*

oro·tund \'ȯr-ə-ˌtənd\ *adj* **1** : SONOROUS **2** : POMPOUS — **oro·tun·di·ty** \ˌȯr-ə-'tən-di-tē\ *n*

or·phan \'ȯr-fən\ *n* : a child deprived by death of one or usu. both parents — **orphan** *vb*

or·phan·age \'ȯr-fə-nij\ *n* : an institution for the care of orphans

or·tho·don·tia \ˌȯr-thə-'dän-chə, -chē-ə\ *n* : ORTHODONTICS

or·tho·don·tics \ˌȯr-thə-'dän-tiks\ *n* : a branch of dentistry concerned with the correction of faults in the arrangement and placing of the teeth — **or·tho·don·tist** \-'dän-tist\ *n*

or·tho·dox \'ȯr-thə-ˌdäks\ *adj* [MF or LL; MF *orthodoxe*, fr. LL *orthodoxus*, fr. LGk *orthodoxos*, fr. Gk *orthos* right + *doxa* opinion] **1** : conforming to established doctrine esp. in religion **2** : CONVENTIONAL **3** *cap* : of or relating to a Christian church originating in the church of the Eastern Roman Empire — **or·tho·doxy** \-ˌdäk-sē\ *n*

or·thog·ra·phy \ȯr-'thä-grə-fē\ *n* : SPELLING — **or·tho·graph·ic** \ˌȯr-thə-'gra-fik\ *adj*

or·tho·pe·dics \ˌȯr-thə-'pē-diks\ *n sing or pl* : a branch of medicine concerned with the correction or prevention of skeletal deformities — **or·tho·pe·dic** \-dik\ *adj* — **or·tho·pe·dist** \-dist\ *n*

-ory \ˌȯr-ē, ə-rē\ *adj suffix* **1** : of, relating to, or characterized by 〈anticipat*ory*〉 **2** : serving for, producing, or maintaining 〈illus*ory*〉

Os *symbol* osmium

OS *abbr* **1** [L *oculus sinister*] left eye **2** ordinary seaman **3** out of stock

Osage \ō-'sāj\ *n, pl* **Osag·es** *or* **Osage** : a member of an American Indian people orig. of Missouri

os·cil·late \'ä-sə-ˌlāt\ *vb* **-lat·ed; -lat·ing 1** : to swing backward and forward like a pendulum **2** : to move or travel back and forth between two points **3** : VARY, FLUCTUATE — **os·cil·la·tion** \ˌä-sə-'lā-shən\ *n* — **os·cil·la·tor** \'ä-sə-ˌlā-tər\ *n* — **os·cil·la·to·ry** \'ä-sə-lə-ˌtōr-ē\ *adj*

os·cil·lo·scope \ä-'si-lə-ˌskōp\ *n* : an instrument in which variations in current or voltage appear as a visible wave form on a fluorescent screen

os·cu·late \'äs-kyə-ˌlāt\ *vb* **-lat·ed; -lat·ing** : KISS — **os·cu·la·tion** \ˌäs-kyə-'lā-shən\ *n* — **os·cu·la·to·ry** \'äs-kyə-lə-ˌtōr-ē\ *adj*

Osee \'ō-ˌzē, ō-'zä-ə\ *n* : HOSEA

OSHA \'ō-shə\ *abbr* Occupational Safety and Health Administration

osier \'ō-zhər\ *n* : any of various willows with pliable twigs used esp. in making baskets and furniture; *also* : a twig from an osier

os·mi·um \'äz-mē-əm\ *n* : a heavy hard brittle metallic chemical element used esp. as a catalyst and in alloys — see ELEMENT table

os·mo·sis \äz-'mō-səs, äs-\ *n* : movement of a solvent through a semipermeable membrane into a solution of higher concentration that tends to equalize the concentrations of the solutions on either side of the membrane — **os·mot·ic** \-'mä-tik\ *adj*

os·prey \'äs-prē, -ˌprā\ *n, pl* **ospreys** : a large brown and white fish-eating hawk

os·si·fy \'ä-sə-ˌfi\ *vb* **-fied; -fy·ing** : to make or become hardened or set in one's ways — **os·si·fi·ca·tion** \ˌä-sə-fə-'kā-shən\ *n*

os·su·ary \'ä-shə-ˌwer-ē, -syə-\ *n, pl* **-ar·ies** : a depository for the bones of the dead

os·ten·si·ble \ä-'sten-sə-bəl\ *adj* : shown outwardly : PROFESSED, APPARENT — **os·ten·si·bly** \-blē\ *adv*

os·ten·ta·tion \ˌäs-tən-'tā-shən\ *n* : pretentious or excessive display — **os·ten·ta·tious** \-shəs\ *adj* — **os·ten·ta·tious·ly** *adv*

os·teo·path \'äs-tē-ə-ˌpath\ *n* : a practitioner of osteopathy

os·te·op·a·thy \ˌäs-tē-'ä-pə-thē\ *n* : a system of treating diseases emphasizing manipulation (as of joints) but not excluding other agencies (as the use of medicine and surgery) — **os·teo·path·ic** \ˌäs-tē-ə-'pa-thik\ *adj*

os·teo·po·ro·sis \ˌäs-tē-ō-pə-'rō-səs\ *n, pl* **-ro·ses** \-ˌsēz\ : a condition affecting esp. older women and characterized by fragile and porous bones

ost·mark \'ōst-ˌmärk, 'ȯst-\ *n* : the former East German mark

os·tra·cize \'äs-trə-ˌsīz\ *vb* **-cized; -ciz·ing** [Gk *ostrakizein* to banish by voting with potsherds, fr. *ostrakon* shell, potsherd] : to exclude from a group by common consent — **os·tra·cism** \-ˌsi-zəm\ *n*

os·trich \'äs-trich, 'ȯs-\ *n* : a very large swift-footed flightless bird of Africa and Arabia

Os·we·go tea \ä-'swē-gō-\ *n* : a No. American mint with showy scarlet flowers

OT *abbr* **1** occupational therapy **2** Old Testament **3** overtime

¹**oth·er** \'ə-thər\ *adj* **1** : being the one left; *also* : being the ones distinct from those first mentioned **2** : ALTERNATE 〈every ~ day〉 **3** : DIFFERENT **4** : ADDITIONAL **5** : recently past 〈the ~ night〉

²**other** *pron* **1** : remaining one or ones **2** : a different or additional one 〈something or ~〉

oth·er·wise \'ə-thər-ˌwīz\ *adv* **1** : in a different way **2** : in different circumstances **3** : in other respects **4** : if not **5** : NOT — **otherwise** *adj*

oth·er·world \-ˌwərld\ *n* : a world beyond death or beyond present reality

oth·er·world·ly \ˌə-thər-'wərld-lē\ *adj* : not worldly : concerned with spiritual, intellectual, or imaginative matters

oti·ose \'ō-shē-₁ōs, 'ō-tē-\ *adj* **1** : FUTILE **2** : IDLE **3** : USELESS

oto·lar·yn·gol·o·gy \₁ō-tō-₁lar-ən-'gä-lə-jē\ *n* : a medical specialty concerned esp. with the ear, nose, and throat — **oto·lar·yn·gol·o·gist** \-jist\ *n*

oto·rhi·no·lar·yn·gol·o·gy \₁ō-tō-₁rī-nō-₁lar-ən-'gä-lə-jē\ *n* : OTOLARYNGOLOGY — **oto·rhi·no·lar·yn·gol·o·gist** \-jist\ *n*

OTS *abbr* officers' training school

Ot·ta·wa \'ä-tə-wə, -₁wä, -₁wö\ *n, pl* **Ottawas** *or* **Ottawa** : a member of an American Indian people of Michigan and southern Ontario

ot·ter \'ä-tər\ *n, pl* **otters** *also* **otter** : any of various web-footed fish-eating mammals with dark brown fur that are related to the weasels; *also* : the fur

otter

ot·to·man \'ä-tə-mən\ *n* : an upholstered seat or couch usu. without a back; *also* : an overstuffed footstool

ou·bli·ette \₁ü-blē-'et\ *n* [F, fr. MF, fr. *oublier* to forget, ultim. fr. L *oblivisci*] : a dungeon with an opening at the top

ought \'ot\ *verbal auxiliary* — used to express moral obligation, advisability, natural expectation, or logical consequence

ou·gui·ya \ü-'gwē-ə, -'gē\ *n, pl* **ouguiya** — see MONEY table

ounce \'auns\ *n* [ME, fr. MF *unce*, fr. L *uncia* twelfth part, ounce, fr. *unus* one] **1** : a unit of avoirdupois, troy, and apothecaries' weight — see WEIGHT table **2** : FLUID OUNCE

our \är, ₁aúr\ *adj* : of or relating to us or ourselves

ours \'aúrz, 'ärz\ *pron* : that which belongs to us

our·selves \är-'selvz, aúr-\ *pron* : our own selves — used reflexively, for emphasis, or in absolute constructions ⟨we pleased ∼⟩ ⟨we'll do it ∼⟩ ⟨we were tourists ∼⟩

-ous \əs\ *adj suffix* : full of : abounding in : having : possessing the qualities of ⟨clamor*ous*⟩ ⟨poison*ous*⟩

oust \'aúst\ *vb* : to eject from or deprive of property or position : EXPEL **syn** evict, dismiss, banish, deport

oust·er \'aús-tər\ *n* : EXPULSION

¹out \'aút\ *adv* **1** : in a direction away from the inside or center **2** : beyond control **3** : to extinction, exhaustion, or completion **4** : in or into the open **5** : so as to retire a batter or base runner; *also* : so as to be retired

²out *vb* : to become known ⟨the truth will ∼⟩

³out *prep* **1** : out through ⟨looked ∼ the window⟩ **2** : outward on or along ⟨drive ∼ the river road⟩

⁴out *adj* **1** : situated outside or at a distance **2** : not in : ABSENT; *also* : not being in power **3** : not successful in reaching base **4** : not being in vogue or fashion : not up-to-date

⁵out *n* **1** : one who is out of office **2** : the retiring of a batter or base runner

out·age \'aú-tij\ *n* : a period or instance of interruption esp. of electricity

out–and–out *adj* : COMPLETE, THOROUGHGOING ⟨an ∼ fraud⟩

out·bid \aút-'bid\ *vb* : to make a higher bid than

¹out·board \'aút-₁bōrd\ *adj* **1** : situated outboard **2** : having or using an outboard motor

²outboard *adv* **1** : outside a ship's hull : away from the long axis of a ship **2** : in a position closer to the wing tip of an airplane

outboard motor *n* : a small internal combustion engine with propeller attached for mounting at the stern of a small boat

out·bound \'aút-₁baúnd\ *adj* : outward bound ⟨∼ traffic⟩

out·break \-₁brāk\ *n* **1** : a sudden increase in activity, incidence, or numbers **2** : INSURRECTION, REVOLT

out·build·ing \-₁bil-diŋ\ *n* : a building separate from but accessory to a main house

out·burst \-₁bərst\ *n* : ERUPTION; *esp* : a violent expression of feeling

out·cast \-₁kast\ *n* : one that is cast out by society

out·class \aút-'klas\ *vb* : SURPASS

out·come \'aút-₁kəm\ *n* : a final consequence : RESULT

out·crop \-₁kräp\ *n* : a coming out of bedrock to the surface of the ground; *also* : the part of a rock formation that thus appears — **outcrop** *vb*

out·cry \-₁krī\ *n* : a loud cry : CLAMOR

out·dat·ed \aút-'dā-təd\ *adj* : OUTMODED

out·dis·tance \-'dis-təns\ *vb* : to go far ahead of (as in a race) : OUTSTRIP

out·do \-'dü\ *vb* **-did** \-'did\; **-done** \-'dən\; **-do·ing**; **-does** \-'dəz\ : to go beyond in action or performance

out·door \'aút-₁dōr, -'dōr\ *also* **out·doors** \-₁dōrz, -'dōrz\ *adj* **1** : of or relating to the outdoors **2** : performed outdoors **3** : not enclosed (as by a roof)

¹out·doors \'aút-₁dōrz, -'dōrz\ *adv* : in or into the open air

²outdoors *n* **1** : the open air **2** : the world away from human habitation

out·draw \aút-'dró\ *vb* **-drew** \-'drü\; **-drawn** \-'drón\; **-draw·ing** **1** : to attract a larger audience than **2** : to draw a handgun more quickly than

out·er \'aú-tər\ *adj* **1** : EXTERNAL **2** : situated farther out; *also* : being away from a center

out·er·most \-₁mōst\ *adj* : farthest out

outer space *n* : SPACE 5

out·face \aút-'fās\ *vb* **1** : to cause to waver or submit **2** : DEFY

out·field \'aút-₁fēld\ *n* : the part of a baseball field beyond the infield and within the foul lines; *also* : players in the outfield — **out·field·er** \-₁fēl-dər\ *n*

out·fight \aút-'fīt\ *vb* : to surpass in fighting : DEFEAT

¹out·fit \'aút-₁fit\ *n* **1** : the equipment or apparel for a special purpose or occasion **2** : GROUP

²outfit *vb* **out·fit·ted; out·fit·ting** : EQUIP — **out·fit·ter** *n*

out·flank \aút-'flaŋk\ *vb* : to get around the flank of (an opposing force)

out·flow \'aút-₁flō\ *n* **1** : a flowing out **2** : something that flows out

out·fox \aút-'fäks\ *vb* : OUTWIT

out·go \'aút-₁gō\ *n, pl* **outgoes** : EXPENDITURES, OUTLAY

out·go·ing \-₁gō-iŋ\ *adj* **1** : going out ⟨∼ tide⟩ **2** : retiring from a place or position **3** : FRIENDLY

out·grow \aút-'grō\ *vb* **-grew** \-'grü\; **-grown** \-'grōn\; **-grow·ing** **1** : to grow faster than **2** : to grow too large for

out·growth \'aút-₁grōth\ *n* : a product of growing out : OFFSHOOT; *also* : CONSEQUENCE, RESULT

out·guess \aút-'ges\ *vb* : OUTWIT

out·gun \-'gən\ *vb* : to surpass in firepower

out·house \'aút-₁haús\ *n* : OUTBUILDING; *esp* : an outdoor toilet

out·ing \'aú-tiŋ\ *n* : a brief stay or trip in the open

out·land·ish \aút-'lan-dish\ *adj* **1** : of foreign appearance or manner; *also* : BIZARRE **2** : remote from civilization — **out·land·ish·ly** *adv*

out·last \-'last\ *vb* : to last longer than

¹out·law \'aút-₁ló\ *n* **1** : a person excluded from the protection of the law **2** : a lawless person

²outlaw *vb* **1** : to deprive of the protection of the law **2** : to make illegal — **out·law·ry** \'aút-₁lór-ē\ *n*

out·lay \'aút-₁lā\ *n* **1** : the act of spending **2** : EXPENDITURE

out·let \'aut-ˌlet, -lət\ *n* **1** : EXIT, VENT **2** : a means of release (as for an emotion) **3** : a market for a commodity **4** : a receptacle for the plug of an electrical device

¹out·line \'aut-ˌlīn\ *n* **1** : a line marking the outer limits of an object or figure **2** : a drawing in which only contours are marked **3** : SUMMARY, SYNOPSIS **4** : PLAN

²outline *vb* **1** : to draw the outline of **2** : to indicate the chief features or parts of

out·live \aut-'liv\ *vb* : to live longer than **syn** outlast, survive

out·look \'aut-ˌluk\ *n* **1** : a place offering a view; *also* : VIEW **2** : STANDPOINT **3** : the prospect for the future

out·ly·ing \-ˌlī-iŋ\ *adj* : distant from a center or main body

out·ma·neu·ver \ˌaut-mə-'nü-vər, -'nyü-\ *vb* : to defeat by more skillful maneuvering

out·mod·ed \aut-'mō-dəd\ *adj* **1** : no longer in style **2** : no longer acceptable or current

out·num·ber \-'nəm-bər\ *vb* : to exceed in number

out of *prep* **1** : out from within or behind ⟨walk *out of* the room⟩ ⟨look *out of* the window⟩ **2** : from a state of ⟨wake up *out of* a deep sleep⟩ **3** : beyond the limits of ⟨*out of* sight⟩ **4** : BECAUSE OF ⟨came *out of* curiosity⟩ **5** : FROM, WITH ⟨built it *out of* scrap⟩ **6** : in or into a state of loss or not having ⟨cheated him *out of* $5000⟩ ⟨we're *out of* matches⟩ **7** : from among ⟨one *out of* four⟩ — **out of it** : SQUARE, OLD-FASHIONED

out–of–bounds *adv or adj* : outside the prescribed boundaries or limits

out–of–date *adj* : no longer in fashion or in use : OUTMODED

out–of–door *or* **out–of–doors** *adj* : OUTDOOR

out–of–the–way *adj* **1** : UNUSUAL **2** : being off the beaten track

out·pa·tient \'aut-ˌpā-shənt\ *n* : a patient who visits a hospital or clinic for diagnosis or treatment without staying overnight

out·per·form \ˌaut-pər-'form\ *vb* : to perform better than

out·play \aut-'plā\ *vb* : to play more skillfully than

out·point \-'point\ *vb* : to win more points than

out·post \'aut-ˌpōst\ *n* **1** : a security detachment dispatched by a main body of troops to protect it from enemy surprise; *also* : a military base established (as by treaty) in a foreign country **2** : an outlying or frontier settlement

out·pour·ing \-ˌpōr-iŋ\ *n* : something that pours out or is poured out

out·pull \aut-'pul\ *vb* : OUTDRAW 1

¹out·put \'aut-ˌput\ *n* **1** : the amount produced (as by a machine or factory) : PRODUCTION **2** : the information produced by a computer

²output *vb* **out·put·ted** *or* **output; out·put·ting** : to produce as output

¹out·rage \'aut-ˌrāj\ *n* [ME, fr. MF, excess, outrage, fr. *outre* beyond, in excess, fr. L *ultra*] **1** : a violent or shameful act **2** : INJURY, INSULT **3** : the anger or resentment aroused by an outrage

²outrage *vb* **out·raged; out·rag·ing** **1** : RAPE **2** : to subject to violent injury or gross insult **3** : to arouse to extreme resentment

out·ra·geous \aut-'rā-jəs\ *adj* : extremely offensive, insulting, or shameful : SHOCKING — **out·ra·geous·ly** *adv*

out·rank \-'raŋk\ *vb* : to rank higher than

ou·tré \ü-'trā\ *adj* [F] : violating convention or propriety : BIZARRE

¹out·reach \aut-'rēch\ *vb* **1** : to surpass in reach **2** : to get the better of by trickery

²out·reach \'aut-ˌrēch\ *n* **1** : the act of reaching out **2** : the extent of reach **3** : the extending of services beyond usual limits

out·rid·er \-ˌrī-dər\ *n* : a mounted attendant

out·rig·ger \-ˌri-gər\ *n* **1** : a frame that extends from the side of a canoe or boat to prevent upsetting **2** : a craft equipped with an outrigger

¹out·right \aut-'rīt\ *adv* **1** : COMPLETELY **2** : INSTANTANEOUSLY

²out·right \'aut-ˌrīt\ *adj* **1** : being exactly what is stated ⟨an ~ lie⟩ **2** : given or made without reservation or encumbrance ⟨~ sale⟩

out·run \aut-'rən\ *vb* **-ran** \-'ran\; **-run; -run·ning** : to run faster than; *also* : EXCEED

out·sell \-'sel\ *vb* **-sold** \-'sōld\; **-sell·ing** : to exceed in sales

out·set \'aut-ˌset\ *n* : BEGINNING, START

out·shine \aut-'shīn\ *vb* **-shone** \-'shōn\ *or* **-shined; -shin·ing** **1** : to shine brighter than **2** : SURPASS

¹out·side \aut-'sīd, 'aut-ˌsīd\ *n* **1** : a place or region beyond an enclosure or boundary **2** : EXTERIOR **3** : the utmost limit or extent

²outside *adj* **1** : OUTER **2** : coming from without ⟨~ influences⟩ **3** : being apart from one's regular duties ⟨~ activities⟩ **4** : REMOTE ⟨an ~ chance⟩

³outside *adv* : on or to the outside

⁴outside *prep* **1** : on or to the outside of **2** : beyond the limits of **3** : EXCEPT

outside of *prep* **1** : OUTSIDE **2** : BESIDES

out·sid·er \aut-'sī-dər\ *n* : a person who does not belong to a group

out·size \'aut-ˌsīz\ *also* **out·sized** \-ˌsīzd\ *adj* : unusually large : extravagant in size or degree

out·skirts \-ˌskərts\ *n pl* : the outlying parts (as of a city) : BORDERS

out·smart \aut-'smärt\ *vb* : OUTWIT

out·sourc·ing \'aut-ˌsor-siŋ\ *n* : the subcontracting of manufacturing work to outside and esp. foreign and nonunion companies

out·spend \-'spend\ *vb* **1** : to exceed the limits of in spending ⟨~s his income⟩ **2** : to spend more than

out·spo·ken \aut-'spō-kən\ *adj* : direct and open in speech or expression — **out·spo·ken·ly** *adv* — **out·spo·ken·ness** *n*

out·spread \-'spred\ *vb* **-spread; -spread·ing** : to spread out

out·stand·ing \-'stan-diŋ\ *adj* **1** : PROJECTING **2** : UNPAID; *also* : UNRESOLVED **3** : publicly issued and sold **4** : CONSPICUOUS; *also* : DISTINGUISHED — **out·stand·ing·ly** *adv*

out·stay \-'stā\ *vb* **1** : OVERSTAY **2** : to surpass in endurance

out·stretched \-'strecht\ *adj* : stretched out : EXTENDED

out·strip \-'strip\ *vb* **1** : to go faster than **2** : EXCEL, SURPASS

out·take \'aut-ˌtāk\ *n* : something taken out; *esp* : a take that is not used in an edited version of a film or videotape

out·vote \-'vōt\ *vb* : to defeat by a majority of votes

¹out·ward \'aut-wərd\ *adj* **1** : moving or directed toward the outside **2** : showing outwardly

²outward *or* **out·wards** \-wərdz\ *adv* : toward the outside

out·ward·ly \-wərd-lē\ *adv* : on the outside : EXTERNALLY

out·wear \aut-'war\ *vb* **-wore** \-'wor\; **-worn** \-'worn\; **-wear·ing** : to wear longer than : OUTLAST

out·weigh \-'wā\ *vb* : to exceed in weight, value, or importance

out·wit \-'wit\ *vb* : to get the better of by superior cleverness

¹out·work \-'wərk\ *vb* : to outdo in working

²out·work \'aut-ˌwərk\ *n* : a minor defensive position outside a fortified area

out·worn \aut-'worn\ *adj* : OUTMODED

ou·zo \'ü-(ˌ)zō\ *n* : a colorless anise-flavored unsweetened Greek liqueur

ova *pl of* OVUM

oval \'ō-vəl\ *adj* [ML *ovalis*, fr. LL, of an egg, fr. L *ovum*] : egg-shaped; *also* : broadly elliptical — **oval** *n*

ova·ry \'ō-və-rē\ *n, pl* **-ries** **1** : one of the usu. paired female reproductive organs producing eggs and in vertebrates sex hormones **2** : the part of a flower in which seeds are produced — **ovar·i·an** \ō-'var-ē-ən, -'ver-\ *adj*

ovate \'ō-ˌvāt\ *adj* : egg-shaped

ova·tion \ō-'vā-shən\ *n* [L *ovation-, ovatio,* fr. *ovare* to exult] : an enthusiastic popular tribute

ov·en \'ə-vən\ *n* : a chamber (as in a stove) for baking, heating, or drying

oven·bird \-ˌbərd\ *n* : a large olive-green American warbler that builds its dome-shaped nest on the ground

¹over \'ō-vər\ *adv* **1** : across a barrier or intervening space **2** : across the brim ⟨boil ∼⟩ **3** : so as to bring the underside up **4** : out of a vertical position **5** : beyond some quantity, limit, or norm **6** : ABOVE **7** : at an end **8** : THROUGH; *also* : THOROUGHLY **9** : AGAIN ⟨do it ∼⟩

²over *prep* **1** : above in position, authority, or scope ⟨towered ∼ her⟩ ⟨obeyed those ∼ him⟩ **2** : more than ⟨cost ∼ $100⟩ **3** : ON, UPON ⟨a cape ∼ her shoulders⟩ **4** : along the length of ⟨∼ the road⟩ **5** : through the medium of : ON ⟨spoke ∼ TV⟩ **6** : all through ⟨showed me ∼ the house⟩ **7** : on or to the other side or beyond ⟨jump ∼ a ditch⟩ **8** : DURING ⟨∼ the past 25 years⟩ **9** : on account of ⟨trouble ∼ money⟩

³over *adj* **1** : UPPER, HIGHER **2** : REMAINING **3** : ENDED

over- *prefix* **1** : so as to exceed or surpass **2** : excessive; excessively

overabundance	overgraze
overabundant	overhasty
overactive	overheat
overaggressive	overindulge
overambitious	overindulgence
overanxious	overindulgent
overbid	overlarge
overbold	overlearn
overbuild	overload
overburden	overlong
overbuy	overmodest
overcapacity	overnice
overcapitalize	overoptimism
overcareful	overoptimistic
overcautious	overpay
overcompensation	overpraise
overconfidence	overproduce
overconfident	overproduction
overconscientious	overprotect
overcook	overprotective
overcritical	overrate
overcrowd	overreact
overdecorated	overreaction
overdependence	overrefinement
overdetermined	overrepresented
overdevelop	overripe
overdress	oversensitive
overeager	oversensitiveness
overeat	oversimple
overeducated	oversimplification
overemphasis	oversimplify
overemphasize	overspecialization
overenthusiastic	overspecialize
overestimate	overspend
overexcite	overstimulation
overexcited	overstock
overexert	oversubtle
overexertion	oversupply
overextend	overtax
overfatigued	overtired
overfeed	overtrain
overfill	overuse
overgeneralization	overvalue
overgeneralize	overzealous
overgenerous	

over·act \ˌō-vər-'akt\ *vb* : to exaggerate in acting

¹over·age \ˌō-vər-'āj\ *adj* **1** : too old to be useful **2** : older than is normal for one's position, function, or grade

²over·age \'ō-və-rij\ *n* : SURPLUS

over·all \ˌō-vər-'ol\ *adj* : including everything ⟨∼ expenses⟩

over·alls \'ō-vər-ˌolz\ *n pl* : trousers of strong material usu. with a piece extending up to cover the chest

over·arm \-ˌärm\ *adj* : done with the arm raised above the shoulder

over·awe \ˌō-vər-'o\ *vb* : to restrain or subdue by awe

over·bal·ance \-'ba-ləns\ *vb* **1** : OUTWEIGH **2** : to cause to lose balance

over·bear·ing \-'bar-iŋ\ *adj* : ARROGANT, DOMINEERING

over·blown \-'blōn\ *adj* **1** : PORTLY **2** : INFLATED, PRETENTIOUS

over·board \'ō-vər-ˌbord\ *adv* **1** : over the side of a ship into the water **2** : to extremes of enthusiasm

¹over·cast \'ō-vər-ˌkast\ *adj* : clouded over : GLOOMY

²overcast *n* : COVERING; *esp* : a covering of clouds

over·charge \ˌō-vər-'chärj\ *vb* **1** : to charge too much **2** : to fill or load too full — **over·charge** \'ō-vər-ˌchärj\ *n*

over·coat \'ō-vər-ˌkot\ *n* : a warm coat worn over indoor clothing

over·come \ˌō-vər-'kəm\ *vb* **-came** \-'kām\; **-come; -com·ing** **1** : CONQUER **2** : to make helpless or exhausted

over·do \ˌō-vər-'dü\ *vb* **-did** \-'did\; **-done** \-'dən\; **-do·ing; -does** \-'dəz\ **1** : to do too much; *also* : to tire oneself **2** : EXAGGERATE **3** : to cook too long

over·dose \'ō-vər-ˌdōs\ *n* : too great a dose (as of medicine); *also* : a lethal or toxic amount (as of a drug) — **over·dose** \-'dōs\ *vb*

over·draft \'ō-vər-ˌdraft, -ˌdraft\ *n* : an overdrawing of a bank account; *also* : the sum overdrawn

over·draw \ˌō-vər-'dro\ *vb* **-drew** \-'drü\; **-drawn** \-'dron\; **-draw·ing** **1** : to draw checks on a bank account for more than the balance **2** : EXAGGERATE

over·drive \'ō-vər-ˌdrīv\ *n* : an automotive transmission gear that transmits to the driveshaft a speed greater than the engine speed

over·dub \ˌō-vər-'dəb\ *vb* : to transfer (recorded sound) onto an earlier recording for a combined effect — **over·dub** \'ō-vər-ˌdəb\ *n*

over·due \-'dü, -'dyü\ *adj* **1** : unpaid when due; *also* : not appearing or presented on time **2** : more than ready

over·ex·pose \ˌō-vər-ik-'spōz\ *vb* : to expose (as film) for more time than is needed — **over·ex·po·sure** \-'spō-zhər\ *n*

¹over·flow \-'flō\ *vb* **1** : INUNDATE; *also* : to pour forth in a flood **2** : to flow over the brim or top of

²over·flow \'ō-vər-ˌflō\ *n* **1** : FLOOD; *also* : SURPLUS **2** : an outlet for surplus liquid

over·fly \ˌō-vər-'flī\ *vb* **-flew** \-'flü\; **-flown** \-'flōn\; **-fly·ing** : to fly over in an airplane or spacecraft — **over·flight** \'ō-vər-ˌflīt\ *n*

over·grow \ˌō-vər-'grō\ *vb* **-grew** \-'grü\; **-grown** \-'grōn\; **-grow·ing** **1** : to grow over so as to cover **2** : OUTGROW **3** : to grow excessively

over·hand \'ō-vər-ˌhand\ *adj* : made with the hand brought down from above — **overhand** *adv* — **overhand·ed** \-ˌhan-dəd\ *adv or adj*

¹over·hang \'ō-vər-ˌhaŋ, ˌō-vər-'haŋ\ *vb* **-hung** \-ˌhəŋ, -'həŋ\; **-hang·ing** **1** : to project over : jut out **2** : to hang over threateningly

²over·hang \'ō-vər-ˌhaŋ\ *n* : a part (as of a roof) that overhangs

over·haul \ˌō-vər-'hol\ *vb* **1** : to examine thoroughly and make necessary repairs and adjustments **2** : OVERTAKE

¹over·head \ˌō-vər-'hed\ *adv* : ALOFT

²over·head \'ō-vər-ˌhed\ *adj* : operating or lying above ⟨∼ door⟩

³over·head \\'ō-vər-‚hed\ *n* : business expenses not chargeable to a particular part of the work

over·hear \‚ō-vər-'hir\ *vb* **-heard** \-'hərd\; **-hear·ing** : to hear without the speaker's knowledge or intention

over·joyed \‚ō-vər-'jȯid\ *adj* : filled with great joy

over·kill \'ō-vər-‚kil\ *n* **1** : destructive capacity greatly exceeding that required for a target **2** : a large excess

over·land \'ō-vər-‚land, -lənd\ *adv or adj* : by, on, or across land

over·lap \‚ō-vər-'lap\ *vb* **1** : to lap over **2** : to have something in common — **over·lap** \'ō-vər-‚lap\ *n*

over·lay \‚ō-vər-'lā\ *vb* **-laid** \-'lād\; **-lay·ing** : to lay or spread over or across — **over·lay** \'ō-vər-‚lā\ *n*

over·leap \‚ō-vər-'lēp\ *vb* **-leaped** *or* **-leapt** \-'lēpt, -'lept\; **-leap·ing** **1** : to leap over or across **2** : to defeat (oneself) by going too far

over·lie \‚ō-vər-'lī\ *vb* **-lay** \-'lā\; **-lain** \-'lān\; **-ly·ing** : to lie over or upon

¹over·look \‚ō-vər-'lu̇k\ *vb* **1** : INSPECT **2** : to look down on from above **3** : to fail to see **4** : IGNORE; *also* : EXCUSE **5** : SUPERINTEND

²over·look \'ō-vər-‚lu̇k\ *n* : a place from which to look upon a scene below

over·lord \-‚lȯrd\ *n* : a lord who has supremacy over other lords

over·ly \'ō-vər-lē\ *adv* : EXCESSIVELY

over·match \‚ō-vər-'mach\ *vb* : to be more than a match for : DEFEAT

over·much \-'məch\ *adj or adv* : too much

¹over·night \-'nīt\ *adv* **1** : on or during the night **2** : SUDDENLY ⟨became famous ∼⟩

²overnight *adj* : of, lasting, or staying the night ⟨∼ guests⟩

over·pass \'ō-vər-‚pas\ *n* **1** : a crossing (as of two highways) at different levels by means of a bridge **2** : the upper level of an overpass

over·play \‚ō-vər-'plā\ *vb* **1** : EXAGGERATE; *also* : OVEREMPHASIZE **2** : to rely too much on the strength of

over·pop·u·la·tion \‚ō-vər-‚pä-pyə-'lā-shən\ *n* : the condition of having a population so dense as to cause a decline in population or in living conditions — **over·pop·u·lated** \-'pä-pyə-‚lā-təd\ *adj*

over·pow·er \-'pau̇-ər\ *vb* : to overcome by superior force

over·price \‚ō-vər-'prīs\ *vb* : to price too high

over·print \-'print\ *vb* : to print over with something additional — **over·print** \'ō-vər-‚print\ *n*

over·qual·i·fied \-'kwä-lə-‚fīd\ *adj* : having more education, training, or experience than a job calls for

over·reach \‚ō-vər-'rēch\ *vb* : to defeat (oneself) by too great an effort

over·ride \-'rīd\ *vb* **-rode** \-'rōd\; **-rid·den** \-'rid-ᵊn\; **-rid·ing** **1** : to ride over or across **2** : to prevail over; *also* : to set aside ⟨∼ a veto⟩

over·rule \-'rül\ *vb* **1** : to prevail over **2** : to rule against **3** : to set aside

¹over·run \-'rən\ *vb* **-ran** \-'ran\; **-run·ning** **1** : to defeat and occupy the positions of **2** : OVERSPREAD; *also* : INFEST **3** : to go beyond **4** : to flow over

²over·run \'ō-vər-‚rən\ *n* **1** : an act or instance of overrunning; *esp* : an exceeding of estimated costs **2** : the amount by which something overruns

over·sea \‚ō-vər-'sē, 'ō-vər-‚sē\ *adj or adv* : OVERSEAS

over·seas \‚ō-vər-'sēz, -‚sēz\ *adv or adj* : beyond or across the sea : ABROAD

over·see \‚ō-vər-'sē\ *vb* **-saw** \-'sȯ\; **-seen** \-'sēn\; **-see·ing** **1** : OVERLOOK **2** : INSPECT; *also* : SUPERVISE — **over·seer** \'ō-vər-‚sir\ *n*

over·sell \‚ō-vər-'sel\ *vb* **-sold**; **-sel·ling** : to sell too much to or too much of

over·sexed \‚ō-vər-'sekst\ *adj* : exhibiting excessive sexual drive or interest

over·shad·ow \-'sha-dō\ *vb* **1** : to cast a shadow over **2** : to exceed in importance

over·shoe \'ō-vər-‚shü\ *n* : a protective outer shoe; *esp* : GALOSH

over·shoot \‚ō-vər-'shüt\ *vb* **-shot** \-'shät\; **-shoot·ing** **1** : to pass swiftly beyond **2** : to shoot over or beyond

over·sight \'ō-vər-‚sīt\ *n* **1** : SUPERVISION **2** : an inadvertent omission or error

over·size \‚ō-vər-'sīz\ *or* **over·sized** \-'sīzd\ *adj* : of more than ordinary size

over·sleep \‚ō-vər-'slēp\ *vb* **-slept** \-'slept\; **-sleep·ing** : to sleep beyond the time for waking

over·spread \-'spred\ *vb* **-spread**; **-spread·ing** : to spread over or above

over·state \-'stāt\ *vb* : EXAGGERATE — **over·state·ment** *n*

over·stay \-'stā\ *vb* : to stay beyond the time or limits of

over·step \-'step\ *vb* : EXCEED

over·sub·scribe \-səb-'skrīb\ *vb* : to subscribe for more of than is available, asked for, or offered for sale

overt \ō-'vərt, 'ō-‚vərt\ *adj* [ME, fr. MF *ouvert*, *overt*, fr. pp. of *ouvrir* to open] : not secret — **overt·ly** *adv*

over·take \‚ō-vər-'tāk\ *vb* **-took** \-'tu̇k\; **-tak·en** \-'tā-kən\; **-tak·ing** : to catch up with; *also* : to catch up with and pass by

over–the–counter *adj* : sold lawfully without a prescription ⟨∼ drugs⟩

over·throw \‚ō-vər-'thrō\ *vb* **-threw** \-'thrü\; **-thrown** \-'thrōn\; **-throw·ing** **1** : UPSET **2** : to bring down : DEFEAT ⟨∼ a government⟩ **3** : to throw over or past — **over·throw** \'ō-vər-‚thrō\ *n*

over·time \'ō-vər-‚tīm\ *n* : time beyond a set limit; *esp* : working time in excess of a standard day or week — **overtime** *adv*

over·tone \-‚tōn\ *n* **1** : one of the higher tones in a complex musical tone **2** : IMPLICATION, SUGGESTION

over·trick \'ō-vər-‚trik\ *n* : a card trick won in excess of the number bid

over·ture \'ō-vər-‚chu̇r, -chər\ *n* [ME, lit., opening, fr. MF, fr. (assumed) VL *opertura*, alter. of L *apertura*] **1** : an opening offer **2** : an orchestral introduction to a musical dramatic work

over·turn \‚ō-vər-'tərn\ *vb* **1** : to turn over : UPSET **2** : INVALIDATE

over·view \'ō-vər-‚vyü\ *n* : a general survey : SUMMARY

over·ween·ing \‚ō-vər-'wē-niṅ\ *adj* **1** : ARROGANT **2** : IMMODERATE

over·weight \'ō-vər-‚wāt\ *n* **1** : weight above what is required or allowed **2** : bodily weight greater than normal — **overweight** *adj*

over·whelm \‚ō-vər-'hwelm\ *vb* **1** : OVERTHROW **2** : SUBMERGE **3** : to overcome completely

over·whelm·ing *adj* : EXTREME, GREAT ⟨∼ joy⟩ — **over·whelm·ing·ly** *adv*

over·win·ter \-'win-tər\ *vb* : to survive the winter

over·work \-'wərk\ *vb* **1** : to work or cause to work too hard or long **2** : to use too much — **overwork** *n*

over·wrought \‚ō-vər-'rȯt\ *adj* **1** : extremely excited **2** : elaborated to excess

ovi·duct \'ō-və-‚dəkt\ *n* : a tube that serves for the passage of eggs from an ovary

ovip·a·rous \ō-'vi-pə-rəs\ *adj* : reproducing by eggs that hatch outside the parent's body

ovoid \'ō-‚vȯid\ *or* **ovoi·dal** \ō-'vȯid-ᵊl\ *adj* : eggshaped : OVAL

ovu·la·tion \‚äv-yə-'lā-shən, ‚ōv-\ *n* : the discharge of a mature egg from the ovary — **ovu·late** \'äv-yə-‚lāt, 'ōv-\ *vb*

ovule \'äv-yül, 'ōv-\ *n* : any of the bodies in a plant ovary that after fertilization become seeds

ovum \'ō-vəm\ *n, pl* **ova** \-və\ : EGG 2

ow \'au̇\ *interj* — used esp. to express sudden pain

owe \'ō\ *vb* **owed**; **ow·ing** **1** : to be under obligation to pay or render **2** : to be indebted to or for; *also* : to be in debt

owing to *prep* : BECAUSE OF

owl \'aùl\ *n* : any of an order of chiefly nocturnal birds of prey with a large head and eyes and strong talons — **owl·ish** *adj* — **owl·ish·ly** *adv*

owl·et \'aù-lət\ *n* : a young or small owl

¹own \'ōn\ *adj* : belonging to oneself — used as an intensive after a possessive adjective ⟨her ∼ car⟩

²own *vb* **1** : to have or hold as property **2** : ACKNOWLEDGE; *also* : CONFESS — **own·er** *n* — **own·er·ship** *n*

³own *pron* : one or ones belonging to oneself

ox \'äks\ *n, pl* **ox·en** \'äk-sən\ *also* **ox** : any of the common large domestic cattle kept for milk, draft, and meat; *esp* : an adult castrated male ox

ox·blood \'äks-ˌbləd\ *n* : a moderate reddish brown

ox·bow \-ˌbō\ *n* **1** : a U-shaped collar worn by a draft ox **2** : a U-shaped bend in a river — **oxbow** *adj*

ox·ford \'äks-fərd\ *n* : a low shoe laced or tied over the instep

ox·i·dant \'äk-sə-dənt\ *n* : OXIDIZING AGENT — **oxidant** *adj*

ox·i·da·tion \ˌäk-sə-'dā-shən\ *n* : the act or process of oxidizing; *also* : the condition of being oxidized — **ox·i·da·tive** \'äk-sə-ˌdā-tiv\ *adj*

ox·ide \'äk-ˌsīd\ *n* : a compound of oxygen with another element or group

ox·i·dize \'äk-sə-ˌdīz\ *vb* **-dized; -diz·ing** : to combine with oxygen ⟨iron rusts because it is *oxidized* by exposure to the air⟩ — **ox·i·diz·er** *n*

oxidizing agent *n* : a substance (as oxygen or nitric acid) that oxidizes by taking up electrons

ox·y·gen \'äk-si-jən\ *n* [F *oxygène*, fr. Gk *oxys* acidic, lit., sharp + *-genēs* giving rise to; so called because it was once thought to be an essential element of all acids] : a colorless odorless gaseous chemical element that is found in the air, is essential to life, and is involved in combustion — see ELEMENT table

ox·y·gen·ate \'äk-si-jə-ˌnāt\ *vb* **-at·ed; -at·ing** : to impregnate, combine, or supply with oxygen — **ox·y·gen·a·tion** \ˌäk-si-jə-'nā-shən\ *n*

oxygen mask *n* : a device worn over the nose and mouth through which oxygen is supplied

oxygen tent *n* : a canopy which can be placed over a bedridden person and within which a flow of oxygen can be maintained

ox·y·mo·ron \ˌäk-sē-'mōr-ˌän\ *n* : a combination of contradictory words (as *cruel kindness*)

oys·ter \'ȯi-stər\ *n* : any of various marine mollusks with an irregular 2-valved shell that include commercially important edible shellfish and pearl producers — **oys·ter·ing** *n* — **oys·ter·man** \'ȯi-stər-mən\ *n*

oz *abbr* [It *onza* (now *oncia*)] ounce; ounces

ozone \'ō-ˌzōn\ *n* **1** : a bluish gaseous reactive form of oxygen that is formed naturally in the atmosphere and is used for disinfecting, deodorizing, and bleaching **2** : pure and refreshing air

ozone layer *n* : an atmospheric layer at heights of about 25 miles (40 kilometers) with high ozone content which blocks most solar ultraviolet radiation

P

¹p \'pē\ *n, pl* **p's** *or* **ps** \'pēz\ *often cap* : the 16th letter of the English alphabet

²p *abbr, often cap* **1** page **2** participle **3** past **4** pawn **5** pence; penny **6** per **7** petite **8** pint **9** pressure **10** purl

P *symbol* phosphorus

pa \'pä, 'pȯ\ *n* : FATHER

¹Pa *abbr* **1** pascal **2** Pennsylvania

²Pa *symbol* protactinium

¹PA \(ˌ)pē-'ā\ *n* : PHYSICIAN'S ASSISTANT

²PA *abbr* **1** Pennsylvania **2** per annum **3** power of attorney **4** press agent **5** private account **6** professional association **7** public address **8** purchasing agent

pa·'an·ga \pä-'äŋ-gə\ *n* — see MONEY table

pab·u·lum \'pa-byə-ləm\ *n* [L, food, fodder] : usu. soft digestible food

Pac *abbr* Pacific

PAC *abbr* political action committee

¹pace \'pās\ *n* **1** : rate of movement or progress (as in walking or working) **2** : a step in walking; *also* : a measure of length based on such a step **3** : GAIT; *esp* : a horse's gait in which the legs on the same side move together

²pace *vb* **paced; pac·ing** **1** : to go or cover at a pace or with slow steps **2** : to measure off by paces **3** : to set or regulate the pace of

³pa·ce \'pā-sē; 'pä-ˌkā, -ˌchä\ *prep* : contrary to the opinion of

pace·mak·er \'pās-ˌmā-kər\ *n* **1** : one that sets the pace for another **2** : a body part (as of the heart) that serves to establish and maintain a rhythmic activity **3** : an electrical device for stimulating or steadying the heartbeat

pac·er \'pā-sər\ *n* **1** : a horse that paces **2** : PACEMAKER

pachy·derm \'pa-ki-ˌdərm\ *n* [F *pachyderme*, fr. Gk *pachydermos* thick-skinned, fr. *pachys* thick + *derma* skin] : any of various thick-skinned hoofed mammals (as an elephant)

pach·ys·an·dra \ˌpa-ki-'san-drə\ *n* : any of a genus of low shrubby evergreen plants used as a ground cover

pa·cif·ic \pə-'si-fik\ *adj* **1** : tending to lessen conflict **2** : CALM, PEACEFUL

pac·i·fi·er \'pa-sə-ˌfī-ər\ *n* : one that pacifies; *esp* : a device for a baby to chew or suck on

pac·i·fism \'pa-sə-ˌfi-zəm\ *n* : opposition to war or violence as a means of settling disputes — **pac·i·fist** \-fist\ *n or adj* — **pac·i·fis·tic** \ˌpa-sə-'fis-tik\ *adj*

pac·i·fy \'pa-sə-ˌfī\ *vb* **-fied; -fy·ing** **1** : to allay anger or agitation in : SOOTHE **2** : SETTLE; *also* : SUBDUE — **pac·i·fi·ca·tion** \ˌpa-sə-fə-'kā-shən\ *n*

¹pack \'pak\ *n* **1** : a compact bundle; *also* : a flexible container for carrying a bundle esp. on the back **2** : a large amount : HEAP **3** : a set of playing cards **4** : a group or band of people or animals **5** : wet absorbent material for application to the body

²pack *vb* **1** : to stow goods in for transportation **2** : to fill in or surround so as to prevent passage of air, steam, or water **3** : to put into a protective container **4** : to load with a pack ⟨∼ a mule⟩ **5** : to crowd in **6** : to make into a pack **7** : to cause to go without ceremony ⟨∼ them off to school⟩ **8** : WEAR, CARRY ⟨∼ a gun⟩

³pack *vb* : to make up fraudulently so as to secure a desired result ⟨∼ a jury⟩

¹pack·age \'pa-kij\ *n* **1** : BUNDLE, PARCEL **2** : a group of related things offered as a whole

²package *vb* **pack·aged; pack·ag·ing** : to make into or enclose in a package

package deal *n* : an offer containing several items all or none of which must be accepted

package store *n* : a store that sells alcoholic beverages in sealed containers for consumption off the premises

pack·er \'pa-kər\ *n* : one that packs; *esp* : a wholesale food dealer

pack·et \'pa-kət\ *n* **1** : a small bundle or package **2** : a passenger boat carrying mail and cargo on a regular schedule

pack·horse \'pak-ˌhȯrs\ *n* : a horse used to carry goods or supplies

pack·ing \'pa-kiŋ\ *n* : material used to pack something

pack·ing·house \-ˌhaús\ *n* : an establishment for processing and packing food and esp. meat and its by-products

pack rat *n* : a bushy-tailed rodent of the Rocky Mountain area that hoards food and miscellaneous objects

pack·sad·dle \'pak-₁sad-ᵊl\ *n* : a saddle for supporting loads on the back of an animal

pack·thread \-₁thred\ *n* : strong thread for tying

pact \'pakt\ *n* : AGREEMENT, TREATY

¹pad \'pad\ *n* **1** : a cushioning part or thing : CUSHION **2** : the cushioned underside of the foot or toes of some mammals **3** : the floating leaf of a water plant **4** : a writing tablet **5** : LAUNCHPAD **6** : living quarters; *also* : BED

²pad *vb* **pad·ded; pad·ding 1** : to furnish with a pad or padding **2** : to expand with needless or fraudulent matter

pad·ding *n* : the material with which something is padded

¹pad·dle \'pad-ᵊl\ *vb* **pad·dled; pad·dling** : to move the hands and feet about in shallow water

²paddle *n* **1** : an implement with a flat blade used in propelling and steering a small craft (as a canoe) **2** : an implement used for stirring, mixing, or beating **3** : a broad board on the outer rim of a waterwheel or a paddle wheel

³paddle *vb* **pad·dled; pad·dling 1** : to move on or through water by or as if by using a paddle **2** : to beat or stir with a paddle

paddle wheel *n* : a wheel with paddles around its outer edge used to move a boat

paddle wheeler *n* : a steam-driven vessel propelled by a paddle wheel

pad·dock \'pad-ək\ *n* **1** : a usu. enclosed area for pasturing or exercising animals; *esp* : one where racehorses are saddled and paraded before a race **2** : an area at a racecourse where racing cars are parked

pad·dy \'pa-dē\ *n, pl* **paddies** : wet land where rice is grown

paddy wagon *n* : an enclosed motortruck for carrying prisoners

pad·lock \'pad-₁läk\ *n* : a removable lock with a curved piece that snaps into a catch — **padlock** *vb*

pa·dre \'pä-drā\ *n* [Sp or It or Pg, lit., father, fr. L *pater*] **1** : PRIEST **2** : a military chaplain

pae·an \'pē-ən\ *n* : an exultant song of praise or thanksgiving

pae·di·at·ric, pae·di·a·tri·cian, pae·di·at·rics *chiefly Brit var of* PEDIATRIC, PEDIATRICIAN, PEDIATRICS

pa·gan \'pā-gən\ *n* [ME, fr. LL *paganus,* fr. L, country dweller, fr. *pagus* country district] : HEATHEN — **pagan** *adj* — **pa·gan·ism** \-gə-₁ni-zəm\ *n*

¹page \'pāj\ *n* : ATTENDANT; *esp* : one employed to deliver messages

²page *vb* **paged; pag·ing** : to summon by repeatedly calling out the name of

³page *n* : a single leaf (as of a book); *also* : a single side of such a leaf

⁴page *vb* **paged; pag·ing** : to mark or number the pages of

pag·eant \'pa-jənt\ *n* [ME *pagyn, padgeant,* lit., scene of a play, fr. ML *pagina,* perh. fr. L, page] : an elaborate spectacle, show, or procession esp. with tableaux or floats — **pag·eant·ry** \-jən-trē\ *n*

page·boy \'pāj-₁bòi\ *n* [¹*page*] : an often shoulder= length hairdo with the ends of the hair turned smoothly under

pag·er \'pā-jər\ *n* : one that pages; *esp* : BEEPER

pag·i·nate \'pa-jə-₁nāt\ *vb* **-nat·ed; -nat·ing** : ⁴PAGE

pag·i·na·tion \₁pa-jə-'nā-shən\ *n* **1** : the paging of written or printed matter **2** : the number and arrangement of pages (as of a book)

pa·go·da \pə-'gō-də\ *n* : a tower with roofs curving upward at the division of each of several stories

paid *past and past part of* PAY

pail \'pāl\ *n* : a usu. cylindrical vessel with a handle — **pail·ful** \-₁fùl\ *n*

¹pain \'pān\ *n* **1** : PUNISHMENT, PENALTY **2** : suffering or distress of body or mind; *also* : a basic bodily sensation marked by discomfort (as throbbing or aching) **3** *pl* : great care — **pain·ful** \-fəl\ *adj* — **pain·ful·ly** *adv* — **pain·less** *adj* — **pain·less·ly** *adv*

²pain *vb* : to cause or experience pain

pain·kill·er \'pān-₁ki-lər\ *n* : something (as a drug) that relieves pain — **pain·kill·ing** *adj*

pains·tak·ing \-₁stā-kiŋ\ *adj* : taking pains : showing care — **pains·taking** *n* — **pains·tak·ing·ly** *adv*

¹paint \'pānt\ *vb* **1** : to apply color, pigment, or paint to **2** : to produce or portray in lines or colors on a surface; *also* : to practice the art of painting **3** : to decorate with colors **4** : to use cosmetics **5** : to describe vividly **6** : SWAB — **paint·er** *n*

²paint *n* **1** : something produced by painting **2** : MAKEUP **3** : a mixture of a pigment and a liquid that forms a thin adherent coating when spread on a surface; *also* : the dry pigment used in making this mixture **4** : an applied coating of paint

paint·brush \'pānt-₁brəsh\ *n* : a brush for applying paint

painting *n* **1** : a work (as a picture) produced by painting **2** : the art or occupation of painting

¹pair \'par\ *n, pl* **pairs** *also* **pair** [ME *paire,* fr. OF, fr. L *paria* equal things, fr. neut. pl. of *par* equal] **1** : two things of a kind designed for use together **2** : something made up of two corresponding pieces ⟨a ∼ of trousers⟩ **3** : a set of two people or animals

²pair *vb* **1** : to arrange in pairs **2** : to form a pair : MATCH **3** : to become associated with another

pai·sa \pī-'sä\ *n, pl* **paisa** *or* **pai·se** \-'sä\ — see *rupee, taka* at MONEY table

pais·ley \'pāz-lē\ *adj, often cap* : decorated with colorful curved abstract figures ⟨a ∼ shawl⟩

Pai·ute \'pī-₁üt, -₁yüt\ *n* : a member of an American Indian people orig. of Utah, Arizona, Nevada, and California

pa·ja·mas \pə-'jä-məz, -'ja-\ *n pl* : a loose suit for sleeping or lounging

Pak·i·stani \₁pa-ki-'sta-nē, ₁pä-ki-'stä-nē\ *n* : a native or inhabitant of Pakistan — **Pak·i·stani** *adj*

pal \'pal\ *n* : a close friend

pal·ace \'pa-ləs\ *n* [ME *palais,* fr. OF, fr. L *palatium,* fr. *Palatium,* the Palatine Hill in Rome where the emperors' residences were built] **1** : the official residence of a chief of state **2** : MANSION

pal·a·din \'pa-lə-dən\ *n* **1** : a trusted military leader (as for a medieval prince) **2** : a leading champion of a cause

pa·laes·tra \pə-'les-trə\ *n, pl* **-trae** \-(₁)trē\ : a school in ancient Greece or Rome for sports (as wrestling)

pa·lan·quin \₁pa-lən-'kēn\ *n* : an enclosed couch for one person borne on the shoulders of men by means of poles

pal·at·able \'pa-lə-tə-bəl\ *adj* : agreeable to the taste **syn** appetizing, savory, tasty, toothsome

pal·a·tal \'pa-lət-ᵊl\ *adj* **1** : of or relating to the palate **2** : pronounced with some part of the tongue near or touching the hard palate ⟨the \y\ in *yeast* and the \sh\ in *she* are ∼ sounds⟩

pal·a·tal·ize \'pa-lət-ᵊl-₁īz\ *vb* **-ized; -iz·ing** : to pronounce as or change into a palatal sound — **pal·a·tal·i·za·tion** \₁pa-lət-ᵊl-ə-'zā-shən\ *n*

pal·ate \'pa-lət\ *n* **1** : the roof of the mouth separating the mouth from the nasal cavity **2** : TASTE

pa·la·tial \pə-'lā-shəl\ *adj* **1** : of, relating to, or being a palace **2** : MAGNIFICENT

pa·lat·i·nate \pə-'lat-ᵊn-ət\ *n* : the territory of a palatine

¹pal·a·tine \'pa-lə-₁tīn\ *adj* **1** : possessing royal privileges; *also* : of or relating to a palatine or a palatinate **2** : of or relating to a palace : PALATIAL

²palatine *n* **1** : a feudal lord having sovereign power within his domains **2** : a high officer of an imperial palace

pa·la·ver \pə-'la-vər, -'lä-\ *n* [Pg *palavra* word,

speech, fr. LL *parabola* parable, speech] **1** : a long parley **2** : idle talk — **palaver** *vb*

¹pale \'pāl\ *n* **1** : a stake or picket of a fence **2** : an enclosed place; *also* : a district or territory within certain bounds or under a particular jurisdiction **3** : LIMITS, BOUNDS ⟨conduct beyond the ∼⟩

²pale *vb* **paled; pal·ing** : to enclose with or as if with pales : FENCE

³pale *adj* **pal·er; pal·est** **1** : deficient in color or intensity : WAN ⟨∼ face⟩ **2** : lacking in brightness : DIM ⟨∼ star⟩ **3** : not dark or intense in hue ⟨∼ blue⟩ — **pale·ness** *n*

⁴pale *vb* **paled; pal·ing** : to make or become pale

pale·face \'pāl-ˌfās\ *n* : a white person

Pa·leo·cene \'pā-lē-ə-ˌsēn\ *adj* : of, relating to, or being the earliest epoch of the Tertiary — **Paleocene** *n*

pa·le·og·ra·phy \ˌpā-lē-'ä-grə-fē\ *n* [NL *palaeographia*, fr. Gk *palaios* ancient + *graphein* to write] : the study of ancient writings and inscriptions — **pa·le·og·ra·pher** *n*

Pa·leo·lith·ic \ˌpā-lē-ə-'li-thik\ *adj* : of or relating to the earliest period of the Stone Age characterized by rough or chipped stone implements

pa·le·on·tol·o·gy \ˌpā-lē-ˌän-'tä-lə-jē\ *n* : a science dealing with the life of past geologic periods as known from fossil remains — **pa·le·on·tol·o·gist** \-ˌän-'tä-lə-jist, -ən-\ *n*

Pa·leo·zo·ic \ˌpā-lē-ə-'zō-ik\ *adj* : of, relating to, or being the era of geologic history extending from about 570 million years ago to about 245 million years ago — **Paleozoic** *n*

pal·ette \'pa-lət\ *n* : a thin often oval board that a painter holds and mixes colors on; *also* : the colors on a palette

pal·frey \'pȯl-frē\ *n, pl* **palfreys** *archaic* : a saddle horse that is not a warhorse; *esp* : one suitable for a woman

pa·limp·sest \'pa-ləmp-ˌsest\ *n* [L *palimpsestus*, fr. Gk *palimpsēstos* scraped again] : writing material (as a parchment) used after the erasure of earlier writing

pal·in·drome \'pa-lən-ˌdrōm\ *n* : a word, verse, or sentence (as "Able was I ere I saw Elba") or a number (as 1881) that reads the same backward or forward

pal·ing \'pā-liŋ\ *n* **1** : a fence of pales **2** : material for pales **3** : PALE, PICKET

pal·i·sade \ˌpa-lə-'sād\ *n* **1** : a high fence of stakes esp. for defense **2** : a line of steep cliffs

¹pall \'pȯl\ *vb* **1** : to lose in interest or attraction **2** : SATIATE, CLOY

²pall *n* **1** : a heavy cloth draped over a coffin **2** : something that produces a gloomy atmosphere

pal·la·di·um \pə-'lā-dē-əm\ *n* : a silver-white metallic chemical element used esp. as a catalyst and in alloys — see ELEMENT table

pall·bear·er \'pȯl-ˌbar-ər\ *n* : a person who attends the coffin at a funeral

¹pal·let \'pa-lət\ *n* : a small, hard, or makeshift bed

²pallet *n* : a portable platform for transporting and storing materials

pal·li·ate \'pa-lē-ˌāt\ *vb* **-at·ed; -at·ing** **1** : to ease (as a disease) without curing **2** : to cover by excuses and apologies — **pal·li·a·tion** \ˌpa-lē-'ā-shən\ *n* — **pal·li·a·tive** \'pa-lē-ˌā-tiv\ *adj or n*

pal·lid \'pa-ləd\ *adj* : PALE, WAN

pal·lor \'pa-lər\ *n* : PALENESS

¹palm \'päm, 'pälm\ *n* [ME, fr. OE, fr. L *palma* palm of the hand, palm tree; fr. the resemblance of the tree's leaves to the outstretched hand] **1** : any of a family of mostly tropical trees, shrubs, or vines usu. with a tall unbranched stem topped by a crown of large leaves **2** : a symbol of victory; *also* : VICTORY

²palm *n* : the underpart of the hand between the fingers and the wrist

³palm *vb* **1** : to conceal in or with the hand ⟨∼ a card⟩ **2** : to impose by fraud

pal·mate \'pal-ˌmāt, 'päl-\ *also* **pal·mat·ed** \-ˌmā-təd\ *adj* : resembling a hand with the fingers spread

pal·met·to \pal-'me-tō\ *n, pl* **-tos** *or* **-toes** : any of several usu. small palms with fan-shaped leaves

palm·ist·ry \'pä-mə-strē, 'päl-\ *n* : the practice of reading a person's character or future from the markings on the palms — **palm·ist** \'pä-mist, 'päl-\ *n*

Palm Sunday *n* : the Sunday preceding Easter and commemorating Christ's triumphal entry into Jerusalem

palmy \'pä-mē, 'päl-\ *adj* **palm·i·er; -est** **1** : abounding in or bearing palms **2** : FLOURISHING, PROSPEROUS

pal·o·mi·no \ˌpa-lə-'mē-nō\ *n, pl* **-nos** [AmerSp, fr. Sp, like a dove, fr. L *palumbinus*, fr. *palumbes*, a species of dove] : a horse with a pale cream to golden coat and cream or white mane and tail

pal·pa·ble \'pal-pə-bəl\ *adj* **1** : capable of being touched or felt : TANGIBLE **2** : OBVIOUS, PLAIN **syn** perceptible, sensible, appreciable, tangible, detectable — **pal·pa·bly** \-blē\ *adv*

pal·pate \'pal-ˌpāt\ *vb* **pal·pat·ed; pal·pat·ing** : to examine by touch esp. medically — **pal·pa·tion** \pal-'pā-shən\ *n*

pal·pi·tate \'pal-pə-ˌtāt\ *vb* **-tat·ed; -tat·ing** : to beat rapidly and strongly : THROB — **pal·pi·ta·tion** \ˌpal-pə-'tā-shən\ *n*

pal·sy \'pȯl-zē\ *n, pl* **palsies** **1** : PARALYSIS **2** : a condition marked by tremor — **pal·sied** \-zēd\ *adj*

pal·ter \'pȯl-tər\ *vb* **pal·tered; pal·ter·ing** **1** : to act insincerely : EQUIVOCATE **2** : HAGGLE

pal·try \'pȯl-trē\ *adj* **pal·tri·er; -est** **1** : TRASHY ⟨a ∼ pamphlet⟩ **2** : MEAN, DESPICABLE ⟨a ∼ trick⟩ **3** : TRIVIAL ⟨∼ excuses⟩ **4** : MEAGER, MEASLY ⟨∼ sum⟩

pam *abbr* pamphlet

pam·pas \'pam-pəz, 'päm-, -pəs\ *n pl* : wide grassy So. American plains

pam·per \'pam-pər\ *vb* : to treat with excessive attention : INDULGE **syn** coddle, humor, baby, spoil

pam·phlet \'pam-flət\ *n* [ME *pamflet* unbound booklet, fr. *Pamphilus seu De Amore* Pamphilus or On Love, popular Latin love poem of the 12th cent.] : an unbound printed publication

pam·phle·teer \ˌpam-flə-'tir\ *n* : a writer of pamphlets attacking something or urging a cause

¹pan \'pan\ *n* **1** : a usu. broad, shallow, and open container for domestic use; *also* : something resembling such a container **2** : a basin or depression in land **3** : HARDPAN

²pan *vb* **panned; pan·ning** **1** : to wash earth or gravel in a pan in searching for gold **2** : to criticize severely

Pan *abbr* Panama

pan·a·cea \ˌpa-nə-'sē-ə\ *n* : a remedy for all ills or difficulties : CURE-ALL

pa·nache \pə-'nash, -'näsh\ *n* [MF *pennache*, ultim. fr. LL *pinnaculum* small wing] **1** : an ornamental tuft (as of feathers) esp. on a helmet **2** : dash or flamboyance in style and action

pan·a·ma \'pa-nə-ˌmä, -ˌmȯ\ *n, often cap* : a handmade hat braided from strips of the leaves from a tropical American tree

Pan·a·ma·ni·an \ˌpa-nə-'mā-nē-ən\ *n* : a native or inhabitant of Panama — **Panamanian** *adj*

pan·a·tela \ˌpa-nə-'te-lə\ *n* [Sp, fr. AmerSp, a long thin biscuit, ultim. fr. L *panis* bread] : a long slender cigar with straight sides

pan·cake \'pan-ˌkāk\ *n* : a flat cake made of thin batter and fried on both sides

pan·chro·mat·ic \ˌpan-krō-'ma-tik\ *adj* : sensitive to all colors of visible light ⟨∼ film⟩

pan·cre·as \'paŋ-krē-əs, 'pan-\ *n* : a large compound gland of vertebrates that produces insulin and discharges enzymes into the intestine — **pan·cre·at·ic** \ˌpaŋ-krē-'a-tik, ˌpan-\ *adj*

pan·da \'pan-də\ *n* **1** : a long-tailed Himalayan mammal related to and resembling the racoon **2** : a large black-and-white mammal of western China usu. classified with the bears

panda: *A* panda 1, *B* panda 2

pan·dem·ic \pan-ˈde-mik\ *n* : a widespread outbreak of disease — **pandemic** *adj*

pan·de·mo·ni·um \ˌpan-də-ˈmō-nē-əm\ *n* : a wild uproar : TUMULT

¹pan·der \ˈpan-dər\ *n* **1** : a go-between in love intrigues **2** : PIMP **3** : someone who caters to or exploits others' desires or weaknesses

²pander *vb* : to act as a pander

P & I *abbr* principal and interest

P & L *abbr* profit and loss

pan·dow·dy \pan-ˈdaů-dē\ *n, pl* **-dies** : a deep-dish apple dessert spiced, sweetened, and covered with a crust

pane \ˈpān\ *n* : a sheet of glass (as in a door or window)

pan·e·gyr·ic \ˌpa-nə-ˈjir-ik\ *n* : a eulogistic oration or writing — **pan·e·gyr·ist** \-ˈjir-ist\ *n*

¹pan·el \ˈpan-əl\ *n* **1** : a list of persons appointed for special duty ⟨a jury ∼⟩; *also* : a group of people taking part in a discussion or quiz program **2** : a section of something (as a wall or door) often sunk below the level of the frame; *also* : a flat piece of construction material **3** : a flat piece of wood on which a picture is painted **4** : a mount for controls or dials

²panel *vb* **-eled** *or* **-elled; -el·ing** *or* **-el·ling** : to decorate with panels

paneling *n* : decorative panels

pan·el·ist \ˈpan-əl-ist\ *n* : a member of a discussion or quiz panel

panel truck *n* : a small motortruck with a fully enclosed body

pang \ˈpaŋ\ *n* : a sudden sharp spasm (as of pain) or attack (as of remorse)

¹pan·han·dle \ˈpan-ˌhand-əl\ *n* : a narrow projection of a larger territory (as a state) ⟨the Texas ∼⟩

²panhandle *vb* **-dled; -dling** : to ask for money on the street — **pan·han·dler** *n*

¹pan·ic \ˈpa-nik\ *n* : a sudden overpowering fright **syn** terror, consternation, dismay, alarm, dread, fear — **pan·icky** \-ni-kē\ *adj*

²panic *vb* **pan·icked** \-nikt\; **pan·ick·ing** : to affect or be affected with panic

pan·i·cle \ˈpa-ni-kəl\ *n* : a branched flower cluster (as of a lilac) in which each branch from the main stem has one or more flowers

pan·jan·drum \pan-ˈjan-drəm\ *n, pl* **-drums** *also* **-dra** \-drä\ : a powerful personage or pretentious official

pan·nier *also* **pan·ier** \ˈpan-yər\ *n* : a large basket esp. for bearing on the back

pan·o·ply \ˈpa-nə-plē\ *n, pl* **-plies** **1** : a full suit of armor **2** : a protective covering **3** : an impressive array

pan·ora·ma \ˌpa-nə-ˈra-mə, -ˈrä-\ *n* **1** : a picture unrolled before one's eyes **2** : a complete view in every direction — **pan·oram·ic** \-ˈra-mik\ *adj*

pan out *vb* : TURN OUT; *esp* : SUCCEED

pan·sy \ˈpan-zē\ *n, pl* **pansies** [ME *pensee*, fr. MF *pensée*, fr. *pensée* thought, fr. *penser* to think, fr. L *pensare* to ponder] : a low-growing garden herb related to the violet; *also* : its showy flower

¹pant \ˈpant\ *vb* [ME, fr. MF *pantaisier*, fr. (assumed) VL *phantasiare* to have hallucinations, fr. Gk *phantasioun*, fr. *phantasia* appearance, imagination] **1** : to breathe in a labored manner **2** : YEARN **3** : THROB

²pant *n* : a panting breath or sound

³pant *n* **1** : an outer garment covering each leg separately and usu. extending from the waist to the ankle — usu. used in pl. **2** *pl* : PANTIE

pan·ta·loons \ˌpan-tə-ˈlünz\ *n pl* **1** : close-fitting trousers of the 19th century usu. having straps passing under the instep **2** : loose-fitting usu. shorter than ankle-length trousers

pan·the·ism \ˈpan-thē-ˌi-zəm\ *n* : a doctrine that equates God with the forces and laws of the universe — **pan·the·ist** \-ist\ *n* — **pan·the·is·tic** \ˌpan-thē-ˈis-tik\ *adj*

pan·the·on \ˈpan-thē-ˌän, -ən\ *n* **1** : a temple dedicated to all the gods; *also* : the gods of a people **2** : a group of illustrious people

pan·ther \ˈpan-thər\ *n, pl* **panthers** *also* **panther 1** : LEOPARD; *esp* : a black one **2** : COUGAR **3** : JAGUAR

pant·ie *or* **panty** \ˈpan-tē\ *n, pl* **pant·ies** : a woman's or child's short underpants — usu. used in pl.

pan·to·mime \ˈpan-tə-ˌmīm\ *n* **1** : a play in which the actors use no words **2** : expression of something by bodily or facial movements only — **pantomime** *vb* — **pan·to·mim·ic** \ˌpan-tə-ˈmi-mik\ *adj*

pan·try \ˈpan-trē\ *n, pl* **pantries** : a storage room for food or dishes

pant·suit \ˈpant-ˌsüt\ *n* : a woman's outfit consisting usu. of a long jacket and pants of the same material

panty hose *n pl* : a one-piece undergarment for women consisting of hosiery combined with a pantie

panty·waist \ˈpan-tē-ˌwāst\ *n* : SISSY

pap \ˈpap\ *n* : soft food for infants or invalids

pa·pa \ˈpä-pə\ *n* : FATHER

pa·pa·cy \ˈpā-pə-sē\ *n, pl* **-cies** **1** : the office of pope **2** : a succession of popes **3** : the term of a pope's reign **4** *cap* : the system of government of the Roman Catholic Church

pa·pa·in \pə-ˈpā-ən, -ˈpī-ən\ *n* : an enzyme in papaya juice used esp. as a meat tenderizer and in medicine

pa·pal \ˈpā-pəl\ *adj* : of or relating to the pope or to the Roman Catholic Church

pa·paw *n* **1** \pə-ˈpȯ\ : PAPAYA **2** \ˈpä-ˌpȯ\ : a No. American tree with yellow edible fruit; *also* : its fruit

pa·pa·ya \pə-ˈpī-ə\ *n* : a tropical American tree with large yellow black-seeded edible fruit; *also* : its fruit

pa·per \ˈpā-pər\ *n* [ME *papir*, fr. MF *papier*, fr. L *papyrus* papyrus, paper, fr. Gk *papyros* papyrus] **1** : a pliable substance made usu. of vegetable matter and used to write or print on, to wrap things in, or to cover walls; *also* : a single sheet of this substance **2** : a printed or written document **3** : NEWSPAPER **4** : WALLPAPER — **paper** *adj or vb* — **pa·pery** \ˈpā-pə-rē\ *adj*

pa·per·back \-ˌbak\ *n* : a paper-covered book

pa·per·board \-ˌbȯrd\ *n* : a material made from cellulose fiber (as wood pulp) like paper but usu. thicker

pa·per·hang·er \ˈpā-pər-ˌhaŋ-ər\ *n* : one that applies wallpaper — **pa·per·hang·ing** *n*

pa·per·weight \-ˌwāt\ *n* : an object used to hold down loose papers by its weight

pa·pier–mâ·ché \ˌpā-pər-mə-ˈshā, ˌpa-ˌpyā-mə-, -ma-\ *n* [F, lit., chewed paper] : a molding material of wastepaper and additives (as glue) — **papier–mâché** *adj*

pa·pil·la \pə-ˈpi-lə\ *n, pl* **-lae** \-(ˌ)lē, -ˌlī\ [L, nipple] : a small projecting bodily part (as one of the nubs on the surface of the tongue) that resembles a tiny nipple in form — **pap·il·lary** \ˈpa-pə-ˌler-ē, pə-ˈpi-lə-rē\ *adj*

pa·poose \pa-'püs, pə-\ *n* : a young child of No. American Indian parents

pa·pri·ka \pə-'prē-kə, pa-\ *n* [Hung] : a mild red spice made from the fruit of various cultivated sweet peppers

Pap smear \'pap-\ *n* : a method for the early detection of cancer esp. of the uterine cervix

Pap test *n* : PAP SMEAR

pap·ule \'pa-pyül\ *n* : a small solid usu. conical lesion of the skin — **pap·u·lar** \-pyə-lər\ *adj*

pa·py·rus \pə-'pī-rəs\ *n, pl* **-rus·es** *or* **-ri** \-(ˌ)rē, -ˌrī\ **1** : a tall grassy sedge of the Nile valley **2** : paper made from papyrus pith

¹par \'pär\ *n* **1** : a stated value (as of a security) **2** : a common level : EQUALITY **3** : an accepted standard or normal condition **4** : the score standard set for each hole of a golf course — **par** *adj*

²par *abbr* **1** paragraph **2** parallel **3** parish

pa·ra \'pär-ə\ *n, pl* **paras** *or* **para** — see *dinar* at MONEY table

par·a·ble \'par-ə-bəl\ *n* : a simple story told to illustrate a moral truth

pa·rab·o·la \pə-'ra-bə-lə\ *n* : a plane curve formed by the intersection of a cone with a plane parallel to a straight line in its surface — **par·a·bol·ic** \ˌpar-ə-'bä-lik\ *adj*

para·chute \'par-ə-ˌshüt\ *n* [F, fr. *para-* (as in *parasol*) + *chute* fall] : a device for slowing the descent of a person or object through the air that consists of a usu. hemispherical canopy beneath which the person or object is suspended — **parachute** *vb* — **par·a·chut·ist** \-ˌshü-tist\ *n*

¹pa·rade \pə-'rād\ *n* **1** : a pompous display : EXHIBITION **2** : MARCH, PROCESSION; *esp* : a ceremonial formation and march **3** : a place for strolling

²parade *vb* **pa·rad·ed; pa·rad·ing 1** : to march in a parade **2** : PROMENADE **3** : SHOW OFF **4** : MASQUERADE

par·a·digm \'par-ə-ˌdīm, -ˌdim\ *n* **1** : MODEL, PATTERN **2** : a systematic inflection of a verb or noun showing a complete conjugation or declension — **par·a·dig·mat·ic** \ˌpar-ə-dig-'ma-tik\ *adj*

par·a·dise \'par-ə-ˌdīs, -ˌdīz\ *n* [ME *paradis*, fr. OF, fr. LL *paradisus*, fr. Gk *paradeisos*, lit., enclosed park, of Iranian origin] **1** : HEAVEN **2** : a place or state of bliss

par·a·di·si·a·cal \ˌpar-ə-də-'sī-ə-kəl\ *or* **par·a·dis·i·ac** \-'di-zē-ˌak, -sē-\ *adj* : of, relating to, or resembling paradise

par·a·dox \'par-ə-ˌdäks\ *n* : a statement that seems contrary to common sense and yet is perhaps true — **par·a·dox·i·cal** \ˌpar-ə-'däk-si-kəl\ *adj* — **par·a·dox·i·cal·ly** \-k(ə-)lē\ *adv*

par·af·fin \'par-ə-fən\ *n* : a waxy substance used esp. for making candles and sealing foods

par·a·gon \'par-ə-ˌgän, -gən\ *n* : a model of perfection : PATTERN

¹para·graph \'par-ə-ˌgraf\ *n* : a subdivision of a written composition that deals with one point or gives the words of one speaker; *also* : a character (as ¶) marking the beginning of a paragraph

²paragraph *vb* : to divide into paragraphs

Par·a·guay·an \ˌpar-ə-'gwī-ən, -'gwä-\ *n* : a native or inhabitant of Paraguay — **Paraguayan** *adj*

par·a·keet \'par-ə-ˌkēt\ *n* : any of numerous usu. small slender parrots with a long graduated tail

para·le·gal \ˌpar-ə-'lē-gəl\ *adj* : of, relating to, or being a paraprofessional who assists a lawyer — **paralegal** *n*

Par·a·li·pom·e·non \ˌpar-ə-lə-'pä-mə-ˌnän\ *n* : CHRONICLES

par·al·lax \'par-ə-ˌlaks\ *n* : the difference in apparent direction of an object as seen from two different points

¹par·al·lel \'par-ə-ˌlel\ *adj* [L *parallelus*, fr. Gk *parallēlos*, fr. *para* beside + *allēlōn* of one another, fr. *allos . . . allos* one . . . another, fr. *allos* other] **1** : lying or moving in the same direction but always the same

distance apart **2** : similar in essential parts — **par·al·lel·ism** \-ˌle-ˌli-zəm\ *n*

²parallel *n* **1** : a parallel line, curve, or surface **2** : one of the imaginary circles on the earth's surface that parallel the equator and mark the latitude **3** : something essentially similar to another **4** : SIMILARITY, LIKENESS

³parallel *vb* **1** : COMPARE **2** : to correspond to **3** : to extend in a parallel direction with

par·al·lel·o·gram \ˌpar-ə-'le-lə-ˌgram\ *n* : a 4-sided geometric figure with opposite sides equal and parallel

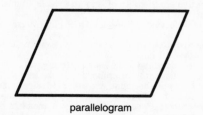

parallelogram

par·a·lyse *Brit var of* PARALYZE

pa·ral·y·sis \pə-'ra-lə-səs\ *n, pl* **-y·ses** \-ˌsēz\ : loss of function and esp. of feeling or the power of voluntary motion — **par·a·lyt·ic** \ˌpar-ə-'li-tik\ *adj or n*

par·a·lyze \'par-ə-ˌlīz\ *vb* **-lyzed; -lyz·ing 1** : to affect with paralysis **2** : to make powerless or inactive — **par·a·lyz·ing·ly** *adv*

par·a·me·cium \ˌpar-ə-'mē-shəm, -shē-əm, -sē-əm\ *n, pl* **-cia** \-shə, -shē-ə, -sē-ə\ *also* **-ci·ums** : any of a genus of slipper-shaped protozoans that move by cilia

para·med·ic \ˌpar-ə-'me-dik\ *also* **para·med·i·cal** \-di-kəl\ *n* **1** : a person who assists a physician in a paramedical capacity **2** : a specially trained medical technician licensed to provide a wide range of emergency services before or during transportation to a hospital

para·med·i·cal \ˌpar-ə-'me-di-kəl\ *also* **para·med·ic** \-'me-dik\ *adj* : concerned with supplementing the work of trained medical professionals

pa·ram·e·ter \pə-'ra-mə-tər\ *n* **1** : a quantity whose value characterizes a statistical population or a member of a system (as a family of curves) **2** : a physical property whose value determines the characteristics or behavior of a system **3** : a characteristic element : FACTOR — **par·a·met·ric** \ˌpar-ə-'me-trik\ *adj*

para·mil·i·tary \ˌpar-ə-'mi-lə-ˌter-ē\ *adj* : formed on a military pattern esp. as an auxiliary military force

par·a·mount \'par-ə-ˌmaunt\ *adj* : superior to all others : SUPREME **syn** preponderant, predominant, dominant, chief, sovereign

par·amour \'par-ə-ˌmur\ *n* : an illicit lover

para·noia \ˌpar-ə-'noi-ə\ *n* : a psychosis marked by delusions and irrational suspicion usu. without hallucinations — **par·a·noid** \'par-ə-ˌnoid\ *adj or n*

par·a·pet \'par-ə-pət, -ˌpet\ *n* **1** : a protecting rampart **2** : a low wall or railing (as at the edge of a bridge)

par·a·pher·na·lia \ˌpar-ə-fə-'nāl-yə, -fər-\ *n sing or pl* **1** : personal belongings **2** : EQUIPMENT, APPARATUS

para·phrase \'par-ə-ˌfrāz\ *n* : a restatement of a text giving the meaning in different words — **paraphrase** *vb*

para·ple·gia \ˌpar-ə-'plē-jə, -jē-ə\ *n* : paralysis of the lower trunk and legs — **para·ple·gic** \-jik\ *adj or n*

para·pro·fes·sion·al \-prə-'fe-shə-nəl\ *n* : a trained aide who assists a professional — **paraprofessional** *adj*

para·psy·chol·o·gy \ˌpar-ə-sī-'kä-lə-jē\ *n* : a field of study concerned with investigating telepathy and related subjects — **para·psy·chol·o·gist** \-jist\ *n*

par·a·site \'par-ə-ˌsīt\ *n* [MF, fr. L *parasitus*, fr. Gk *parasitos*, fr. *para-* beside + *sitos* grain, food] **1** : a plant or animal living in, with, or on another organism usu. to its harm **2** : one depending on another and not making adequate return — **par·a·sit·ic** \ˌpar-ə-ˈsi-tik\ adj — **par·a·sit·ism** \ˈpar-ə-sə-ˌti-zəm, -ˌsī-ˌti-\ n — **par·a·sit·ize** \-sə-ˌtīz\ vb

par·a·si·tol·o·gy \ˌpar-ə-sə-ˈtä-lə-jē\ n : a branch of biology dealing with parasites and parasitism esp. among animals — **par·a·si·tol·o·gist** \-jist\ n

para·sol \ˈpar-ə-ˌsȯl\ n [F, fr. It parasole, fr. parare to shield + sole sun, fr. L sol] : a lightweight umbrella used as a shield against the sun

para·sym·pa·thet·ic nervous system \ˌpar-ə-ˌsim-pə-ˈthe-tik-\ n : the part of the autonomic nervous system that tends to induce secretion, to increase the tone and contractility of smooth muscle, and to slow heart rate

para·thi·on \ˌpar-ə-ˈthī-ən, -ˌän\ n : an extremely toxic insecticide

para·thy·roid \-ˈthī-ˌrȯid\ n : PARATHYROID GLAND — **parathyroid** adj

parathyroid gland n : any of usu. four small endocrine glands adjacent to or embedded in the thyroid gland that produce a hormone (**parathyroid hormone**) concerned with calcium and phosphorus metabolism

para·troop·er \ˈpar-ə-ˌtrü-pər\ n : a member of the paratroops

para·troops \-ˌtrüps\ n pl : troops trained to parachute from an airplane

para·ty·phoid \ˌpar-ə-ˈtī-ˌfȯid\ n : a bacterial food poisoning resembling typhoid fever

par·boil \ˈpär-ˌbȯil\ vb : to boil briefly

¹par·cel \ˈpär-səl\ n 1 : a tract or plot of land 2 : COLLECTION, LOT 3 : a wrapped bundle : PACKAGE

²parcel vb -celed or -celled; -cel·ing or -cel·ling : to divide into portions

parcel post n 1 : a mail service handling parcels 2 : packages handled by parcel post

parch \ˈpärch\ vb 1 : to toast under dry heat 2 : to shrivel with heat

parch·ment \ˈpärch-mənt\ n : the skin of an animal prepared for writing on; also : a writing on such material

pard \ˈpärd\ n : LEOPARD

¹par·don \ˈpärd-ᵊn\ n : excuse of an offense without penalty; esp : an official release from legal punishment

²pardon vb : to free from penalty : EXCUSE, FORGIVE — **par·don·able** \ˈpärd-ᵊn-ə-bəl\ adj

par·don·er \ˈpärd-ᵊn-ər\ n 1 : a medieval preacher delegated to raise money for religious works by soliciting offerings and granting indulgences 2 : one that pardons

pare \ˈpar\ vb **pared; par·ing** 1 : to trim off an outside part (as the skin or rind) of 2 : to reduce as if by paring (~ expenses) — **par·er** n

par·e·gor·ic \ˌpar-ə-ˈgȯr-ik\ n : an alcoholic preparation of opium and camphor used esp. to relieve pain

par·ent \ˈpar-ənt\ n 1 : one that begets or brings forth offspring : FATHER, MOTHER 2 : one who brings up and cares for another 3 : SOURCE, ORIGIN — **parent·age** \-ən-tij\ n — **pa·ren·tal** \pə-ˈrent-ᵊl\ adj — **parent·hood** n

pa·ren·the·sis \pə-ˈren-thə-səs\ n, pl **-the·ses** \-ˌsēz\ 1 : a word, phrase, or sentence inserted in a passage to explain or modify the thought 2 : one of a pair of punctuation marks ( ) used esp. to enclose parenthetic matter — **par·en·thet·ic** \ˌpar-ən-ˈthe-tik\ or **par·en·thet·i·cal** \-ti-kəl\ adj — **par·en·thet·i·cal·ly** \-k(ə-)lē\ adv

pa·ren·the·size \pə-ˈren-thə-ˌsīz\ vb **-sized; -siz·ing** : to make a parenthesis of

par·ent·ing \ˈpar-ən-tiŋ, ˈper-\ n : the raising of a child by its parents

pa·re·sis \pə-ˈrē-səs, ˈpar-ə-\ n, pl **pa·re·ses** \-ˌsēz\ : a usu. incomplete paralysis; also : insanity caused by syphilitic alteration of the brain that leads to dementia and paralysis

par ex·cel·lence \ˌpär-ˌek-sə-ˈläⁿs\ adj [F, lit., by excellence] : being the best of a kind : PREEMINENT

par·fait \pär-ˈfā\ n [F, lit., something perfect] : a cold dessert made of layers of fruit, syrup, ice cream, and whipped cream

pa·ri·ah \pə-ˈrī-ə\ n : OUTCAST

pa·ri·etal \pə-ˈrī-ət-ᵊl\ adj 1 : of, relating to, or forming the walls of an anatomical structure 2 : of or relating to college living or its regulation

pari-mu·tu·el \ˌpar-i-ˈmyü-chə-wəl\ n : a betting system in which winners share the total stakes minus a percentage for the management

par·ing \ˈpar-iŋ\ n : a pared-off piece

pa·ri pas·su \ˌpar-i-ˈpa-sü\ adv or adj [L, with equal step] : at an equal rate or pace

par·ish \ˈpar-ish\ n 1 : a church district in the care of one pastor; also : the residents of such an area 2 : a local church community 3 : a civil division of the state of Louisiana : COUNTY

pa·rish·io·ner \pə-ˈri-shə-nər\ n : a member or resident of a parish

par·i·ty \ˈpar-ə-tē\ n, pl **-ties** : EQUALITY, EQUIVALENCE

¹park \ˈpärk\ n 1 : a tract of ground kept as a game preserve or recreation area 2 : a place where vehicles (as automobiles) are parked 3 : an enclosed stadium used esp. for ball games

²park vb 1 : to leave a vehicle temporarily (as in a parking lot or garage) 2 : to set and leave temporarily

par·ka \ˈpär-kə\ n : a very warm jacket with a hood

Par·kin·son's disease \ˈpär-kən-sənz-\ n : a chronic progressive nervous disease chiefly of later life marked by tremor and weakness of resting muscles and by a shuffling gait

Parkinson's law n : an observation in office organization: work expands so as to fill the time available for its completion

park·way \ˈpärk-ˌwā\ n : a broad landscaped thoroughfare

par·lance \ˈpär-ləns\ n 1 : SPEECH 2 : manner of speaking (military ~)

¹par·lay \ˈpär-ˌlā, -lē\ vb : to increase or change into something of much greater value

²parlay n : a series of bets in which the original stake plus its winnings are risked on successive wagers

par·ley \ˈpär-lē\ n, pl **parleys** : a conference usu. over matters in dispute : DISCUSSION — **parley** vb

par·lia·ment \ˈpär-lə-mənt\ n [ME, fr. OF parlement, fr. parler to speak, fr. ML parabolare, fr. LL parabola speech, parable] 1 : a formal governmental conference 2 cap : an assembly that constitutes the supreme legislative body of a country (as the United Kingdom) — **par·lia·men·ta·ry** \ˌpär-lə-ˈmen-tə-rē\ adj

par·lia·men·tar·i·an \ˌpär-lə-ˌmen-ˈter-ē-ən\ n 1 often cap : an adherent of the parliament during the English Civil War 2 : an expert in parliamentary procedure

par·lor \ˈpär-lər\ n 1 : a room for conversation or the reception of guests 2 : a place of business (beauty ~)

par·lour \ˈpär-lər\ chiefly Brit var of PARLOR

par·lous \ˈpär-ləs\ adj : full of danger or risk : PRECARIOUS — **par·lous·ly** adv

Par·me·san \ˈpär-mə-ˌzän, -ˌzhän, -ˌzan\ n : a hard dry cheese with a sharp flavor

par·mi·gia·na \ˌpär-mi-ˈjä-nə, ˌpär-mi-ˈzhän\ or **par·mi·gia·no** \-ˈjä-(ˌ)nō\ adj : made or covered with Parmesan cheese (veal ~)

pa·ro·chi·al \pə-ˈrō-kē-əl\ adj 1 : of or relating to a church parish 2 : limited in scope : NARROW, PROVINCIAL — **pa·ro·chi·al·ism** \-ə-ˌli-zəm\ n

parochial school n : a school maintained by a religious body

par·o·dy \ˈpar-ə-dē\ n, pl **-dies** [L parodia, fr. Gk parōidia, fr. para- beside + aidein to sing] : a humorous or satirical imitation — **parody** vb

pa·role \pə-ˈrōl\ n : a conditional release of a prisoner whose sentence has not expired — **parole** *vb* — **pa·rol·ee** \-ₗrō-ˈlē, -ˈrō-ₗlē\ *n*

par·ox·ysm \ˈpar-ək-ₗsi-zəm, pə-ˈräk-\ *n* : a sudden sharp attack (as of pain or coughing) : CONVULSION — **par·ox·ys·mal** \ₗpar-ək-ˈsiz-məl, pə-ₗräk-\ *adj*

par·quet \ˈpär-ₗkā, pär-ˈkā\ *n* [F] **1** : a flooring of parquetry **2** : the lower floor of a theater; *esp* : the forward part of the orchestra

par·que·try \ˈpär-kə-trē\ *n, pl* **-tries** : fine woodwork inlaid in patterns

par·ra·keet *var of* PARAKEET

par·ri·cide \ˈpar-ə-ₗsīd\ *n* **1** : one that murders a parent or a close relative **2** : the act of a parricide

par·rot \ˈpar-ət\ *n* : any of numerous bright-colored tropical birds that have a stout hooked bill

parrot fever *n* : an infectious disease of birds marked by diarrhea and wasting and transmissible to humans

par·ry \ˈpar-ē\ *vb* **par·ried; par·ry·ing 1** : to ward off a weapon or blow **2** : to evade esp. by an adroit answer — **parry** *n*

parse \ˈpärs *also* ˈpärz\ *vb* **parsed; pars·ing** : to give a grammatical description of a word or a group of words

par·sec \ˈpär-ₗsek\ *n* : a unit of measure for interstellar space equal to 3.26 light-years

par·si·mo·ny \ˈpär-sə-ₗmō-nē\ *n* : extreme or excessive frugality — **par·si·mo·ni·ous** \ₗpär-sə-ˈmō-nē-əs\ *adj* — **par·si·mo·ni·ous·ly** *adv*

pars·ley \ˈpär-slē\ *n* : a garden plant related to the carrot that has finely divided leaves used as a seasoning or garnish

pars·nip \ˈpär-snəp\ *n* : a garden plant related to the carrot that has a long edible usu. whitish root; *also* : this root

par·son \ˈpärs-ᵊn\ *n* [ME *persone*, fr. OF, fr. ML *persona*, lit., person, fr. L] : MINISTER 2, PASTOR

par·son·age \ˈpärs-ᵊn-ij\ *n* : a house provided by a church for its pastor

¹part \ˈpärt\ *n* **1** : a division or portion of a whole **2** : the melody or score for a particular voice or instrument **3** : a spare piece for a machine **4** : DUTY, FUNCTION **5** : one of the sides in a dispute **6** : ROLE; *also* : an actor's lines in a play **7** *pl* : TALENTS, ABILITY **8** : the line where one's hair divides (as in combing)

²part *vb* **1** : to take leave of someone **2** : to divide or break into parts : SEPARATE **3** : to go away : DEPART; *also* : DIE **4** : to give up possession ⟨~ed with her jewels⟩ **5** : APPORTION, SHARE

³part *abbr* **1** participial; participle **2** particular

par·take \pär-ˈtāk\ *vb* **-took** \-ˈtük\; **-tak·en** \-ˈtā-kən\; **-tak·ing 1** : to have a share or part **2** : to take a portion (as of food) — **par·tak·er** *n*

par·terre \pär-ˈter\ *n* [F, fr. MF, fr. *par terre* on the ground] **1** : an ornamental garden with paths between the flower beds **2** : the part of a theater floor behind the orchestra

par·the·no·gen·e·sis \ₗpär-thə-nō-ˈje-nə-səs\ *n* [NL, fr. Gk *parthenos* virgin + L *genesis* genesis] : development of a new individual from an unfertilized usu. female sex cell — **par·the·no·ge·net·ic** \-jə-ˈne-tik\ *adj*

par·tial \ˈpär-shəl\ *adj* **1** : not total or general : affecting a part only **2** : favoring one party over the other : BIASED **3** : markedly fond — used with *to* — **par·tial·i·ty** \ₗpär-shē-ˈa-lə-tē\ *n* — **par·tial·ly** *adv*

par·tic·i·pate \pär-ˈti-sə-ₗpāt\ *vb* **-pat·ed; -pat·ing 1** : to take part in something ⟨~ in a game⟩ **2** : SHARE — **par·tic·i·pant** \-pənt\ *adj or n* — **par·tic·i·pa·tion** \-ₗti-sə-ˈpā-shən\ *n* — **par·tic·i·pa·tor** \-ˈti-sə-ₗpā-tər\ *n* — **par·tic·i·pa·to·ry** \-ˈti-sə-pə-ₗtōr-ē\ *adj*

par·ti·ci·ple \ˈpär-tə-ₗsi-pəl\ *n* : a word having the characteristics of both verb and adjective — **par·ti·cip·i·al** \ₗpär-tə-ˈsi-pē-əl\ *adj*

par·ti·cle \ˈpär-ti-kəl\ *n* **1** : a very small bit of matter **2** : a unit of speech (as an article, preposition, or conjunction) expressing some general aspect of meaning or some connective or limiting relation

par·ti·cle·board \-ₗbōrd\ *n* : a board made of very small pieces of wood bonded together

par·ti—col·or \ₗpär-tē-ˈkə-lər\ *or* **par·ti—col·ored** \-lərd\ *adj* : showing different colors or tints; *esp* : having one main color broken by patches of one or more other colors

¹par·tic·u·lar \pər-ˈti-kyə-lər\ *adj* **1** : of or relating to a specific person or thing ⟨the laws of a ~ state⟩ **2** : DISTINCTIVE, SPECIAL ⟨the ~ point of his talk⟩ **3** : SEPARATE, INDIVIDUAL ⟨each ~ hair⟩ **4** : attentive to details : PRECISE **5** : hard to please : EXACTING — **par·tic·u·lar·i·ty** \-ₗti-kyə-ˈlar-ə-tē\ *n* — **par·tic·u·lar·ly** *adv*

²particular *n* : an individual fact or detail

par·tic·u·lar·ize \pər-ˈti-kyə-lə-ₗrīz\ *vb* **-ized; -iz·ing 1** : to state in detail : SPECIFY **2** : to go into details

par·tic·u·late \pər-ˈti-kyə-lət, pär-, -ₗlāt\ *adj* : relating to or existing as minute separate particles — **particulate** *n*

¹part·ing *n* : a place or point of separation or divergence

²parting *adj* : given, taken, or performed at parting ⟨a ~ kiss⟩

par·ti·san *also* **par·ti·zan** \ˈpär-tə-zən, -sən\ *n* **1** : one that takes the part of another : ADHERENT **2** : GUERRILLA — **partisan** *adj* — **par·ti·san·ship** *n*

par·tite \ˈpär-ₗtīt\ *adj* : divided into a usu. specified number of parts

par·ti·tion \pär-ˈti-shən\ *n* **1** : DIVISION **2** : something that divides or separates; *esp* : an interior dividing wall — **partition** *vb*

par·ti·tive \ˈpär-tə-tiv\ *adj* : of, relating to, or denoting a part

part·ly \ˈpärt-lē\ *adv* : in part : in some measure or degree

part·ner \ˈpärt-nər\ *n* **1** : ASSOCIATE, COLLEAGUE **2** : either of two persons who dance together **3** : one who plays on the same team with another **4** : SPOUSE **5** : one of two or more persons contractually associated as joint principals in a business — **part·ner·ship** *n*

part of speech : a class of words (as nouns or verbs) distinguished according to the kind of idea denoted and the function performed in a sentence

par·tridge \ˈpär-trij\ *n, pl* **partridge** *or* **par·tridg·es** : any of various stout-bodied game birds

part—song \ˈpärt-ₗsȯŋ\ *n* : a song with two or more voice parts

part—time \-ˈtīm\ *adj or adv* : involving or working less than a full or regular schedule — **part—tim·er** \-ˈtī-mər\ *n*

par·tu·ri·tion \ₗpär-tə-ˈri-shən, ₗpär-chə-, ₗpär-tyü-\ *n* : CHILDBIRTH

part·way \ˈpärt-ˈwā\ *adv* : to some extent : PARTLY

par·ty \ˈpär-tē\ *n, pl* **parties 1** : a person or group taking one side of a question; *esp* : a group of persons organized for the purpose of directing the policies of a government **2** : a person or group concerned in an action or affair : PARTICIPANT **3** : a group of persons detailed for a common task **4** : a social gathering

par·ve·nu \ˈpär-və-ₗnü, -ₗnyü\ *n* [F, fr. pp. of *parvenir* to arrive, fr. L *pervenire*, fr. *per* through + *venire* to come] : one who has recently or suddenly risen to wealth or power but has not yet secured the social position associated with it

pas \ˈpä\ *n, pl* **pas** *same or* ˈpäz\ : a dance step or combination of steps

pas·cal \pas-ˈkal\ *n* : a unit of pressure in the metric system equal to one newton per square meter

pas·chal \ˈpas-kəl\ *adj* : of, relating to, appropriate for, or used during Passover or Easter ceremonies

pa·sha \ˈpä-shə, ˈpa-; pə-ˈshä\ *n* : a man (as formerly a governor in Turkey) of high rank

¹pass \ˈpas\ *vb* **1** : MOVE, PROCEED **2** : to go away; *also* : DIE **3** : to move past, beyond, or over **4** : to allow to elapse : SPEND **5** : to go or make way through **6** : to go or allow to go unchallenged **7** : to undergo transfer **8** : to render a legal judgment **9** : OCCUR **10** : to secure the approval of (as a legislature) **11** : to go or cause to go through an inspection, test, or course of study successfully **12** : to be regarded **13** : CIRCULATE **14** : VOID **2 15** : to transfer the ball or puck to another player **16** : to decline to bid or bet on one's hand in a card game **17** : to give a base on balls to — **pass·er** *n*

²pass *n* : a gap in a mountain range

³pass *n* **1** : the act or an instance of passing **2** : REALIZATION, ACCOMPLISHMENT **3** : a state of affairs **4** : a written authorization to leave, enter, or move about freely **5** : a transfer of a ball or puck from one player to another **6** : BASE ON BALLS **7** : EFFORT, TRY **8** : a sexually inviting gesture or approach

⁴pass *abbr* **1** passenger **2** passive

pass·able \'pa-sə-bəl\ *adj* **1** : capable of being passed or traveled on **2** : just good enough : TOLERABLE — **pass·ably** \-blē\ *adv*

pas·sage \'pa-sij\ *n* **1** : a means (as a road or corridor) of passing **2** : the action or process of passing **3** : a voyage esp. by sea or air **4** : a right or permission to pass **5** : ENACTMENT **6** : a usu. brief portion or section (as of a book)

pas·sage·way \-ₗwā\ *n* : a way that allows passage

pass·book \'pas-ₗbŭk\ *n* : BANKBOOK

pas·sé \pa-'sā\ *adj* **1** : past one's prime **2** : not up-to-date : OUTMODED

pas·sel \'pa-səl\ *n* : a large number

pas·sen·ger \'pas-ⁿn-jər\ *n* : a traveler in a public or private conveyance

pass·er·by \'pa-sər-ₗbī\ *n, pl* **pass·ers·by** : one who passes by

pas·ser·ine \'pa-sə-ₗrīn\ *adj* : of or relating to the large order of birds comprising singing birds that perch

pas·sim \'pa-səm\ *adv* [L, fr. *passus* scattered, fr. pp. of *pandere* to spread] : here and there : THROUGHOUT

pass·ing *n* : the act of one that passes or causes to pass; *esp* : DEATH

pas·sion \'pa-shən\ *n* **1** *often cap* : the sufferings of Christ between the night of the Last Supper and his death **2** : strong feeling; *also, pl* : the emotions as distinguished from reason **3** : RAGE, ANGER **4** : LOVE; *also* : an object of affection or enthusiasm **5** : sexual desire — **pas·sion·ate** \'pa-shə-nət\ *adj* — **pas·sion·ate·ly** *adv* — **pas·sion·less** *adj*

pas·sion·flow·er \'pa-shən-ₗflaü-ər\ *n* [fr. the fancied resemblance of parts of the flower to the instruments of Christ's crucifixion] : any of a genus of chiefly tropical woody climbing vines or erect herbs with showy flowers and pulpy often edible berries (**passion fruit**)

pas·sive \'pa-siv\ *adj* **1** : not active : acted upon **2** : asserting that the grammatical subject is subjected to or affected by the action represented by the verb ⟨∼ voice⟩ **3** : making use of the sun's heat usu. without the aid of mechanical devices **4** : SUBMISSIVE, PATIENT — **passive** *n* — **pas·sive·ly** *adv* — **pas·siv·i·ty** \pa-'si-və-tē\ *n*

pass·key \'pas-ₗkē\ *n* : a key for opening two or more locks

pass out *vb* : to lose consciousness

Pass·over \'pas-ₗō-vər\ *n* [fr. the exemption of the Israelites from the slaughter of the firstborn in Egypt (Exod 12:23–27)] : a Jewish holiday celebrated in March or April in commemoration of the Hebrews' liberation from slavery in Egypt

pass·port \'pas-ₗpōrt\ *n* : an official document issued by a country upon request to a citizen requesting protection during travel abroad

pass up *vb* : DECLINE, REJECT

pass·word \'pas-ₗwərd\ *n* **1** : a word or phrase that must be spoken by a person before being allowed to pass a guard **2** : a sequence of characters required for access to a computer system

¹past \'past\ *adj* **1** : AGO ⟨10 years ∼⟩ **2** : just gone or elapsed ⟨the ∼ month⟩ **3** : having existed or taken place in a period before the present : BYGONE **4** : of, relating to, or constituting a verb tense that expresses time gone by

²past *prep or adv* : BEYOND

³past *n* **1** : time gone by **2** : something that happened or was done in a former time **3** : the past tense; *also* : a verb form in it **4** : a secret past life

pas·ta \'päs-tə\ *n* [It] **1** : a paste in processed form (as spaghetti) or in the form of fresh dough (as ravioli) **2** : a dish of cooked pasta

¹paste \'pāst\ *n* **1** : DOUGH **2** : a smooth food product made by evaporation or grinding ⟨tomato ∼⟩ **3** : a shaped dough (as spaghetti or ravioli) **4** : a preparation (as of flour and water) for sticking things together **5** : a brilliant glass used for artificial gems

²paste *vb* **past·ed; past·ing** : to cause to adhere by paste : STICK

paste·board \'pāst-ₗbōrd\ *n* : PAPERBOARD

¹pas·tel \pas-'tel\ *n* **1** : a paste made of powdered pigment; *also* : a crayon of such paste **2** : a drawing in pastel **3** : a pale or light color

²pastel *adj* **1** : of or relating to a pastel **2** : pale in color

pas·tern \'pas-tərn\ *n* : the part of a horse's foot extending from the fetlock to the top of the hoof

pas·teur·i·za·tion \ₗpas-chə-rə-'zā-shən, ₗpas-tə-\ *n* : partial sterilization of a substance (as milk) by heat or radiation — **pas·teur·ize** \'pas-chə-ₗrīz, 'pas-tə-\ *vb* — **pas·teur·iz·er** *n*

pas·tiche \pas-'tēsh\ *n* : a composition (as in literature or music) made up of selections from different works

pas·tille \pas-'tēl\ *n* : an aromatic or medicated lozenge

pas·time \'pas-ₗtīm\ *n* : DIVERSION; *esp* : something that serves to make time pass agreeably

pas·tor \'pas-tər\ *n* [ME *pastour*, fr. OF, fr. L *pastor*, herdsman, fr. *pascere* to feed, pasture, nurture] : a minister or priest serving a local church or parish — **pas·tor·ate** \-tə-rət\ *n*

¹pas·to·ral \'pas-tə-rəl\ *adj* **1** : of or relating to shepherds or to rural life **2** : of or relating to spiritual guidance esp. of a congregation **3** : of or relating to the pastor of a church

²pastoral *n* : a literary work dealing with shepherds or rural life

pas·to·rale \ₗpas-tə-'räl, -'ral\ *n* [It] : a musical composition having a pastoral theme

past participle *n* : a participle that typically expresses completed action, that is one of the principal parts of the verb, and that is used in the formation of perfect tenses in the active voice and of all tenses in the passive voice

pas·tra·mi \pə-'strä-mē\ *n* [Yiddish *pastrame*] : a highly seasoned smoked beef prepared esp. from shoulder cuts

pas·try \'pā-strē\ *n, pl* **pastries** : sweet baked goods made of dough or with a crust made of enriched dough

pas·tur·age \'pas-chə-rij\ *n* : PASTURE

¹pas·ture \'pas-chər\ *n* **1** : plants (as grass) for the feeding esp. of grazing livestock **2** : land or a plot of land used for grazing

²pasture *vb* **pas·tured; pas·tur·ing 1** : GRAZE **2** : to use as pasture

pasty \'pā-stē\ *adj* **past·i·er; -est** : resembling paste; *esp* : pallid and unhealthy in appearance

¹pat \'pat\ *n* **1** : a light tap esp. with the hand or a flat instrument; *also* : the sound made by it **2** : something (as butter) shaped into a small flat usu. square individual portion

²pat *adv* : in a pat manner : PERFECTLY

³pat *vb* **pat·ted; pat·ting 1** : to strike lightly with a flat instrument **2** : to flatten, smooth, or put into place or shape with a pat **3** : to tap gently or lovingly with the hand

⁴pat *adj* **1** : exactly suited to the occasion : APT **2** : memorized exactly **3** : UNYIELDING

PAT *abbr* point after touchdown

pa·ta·ca \pə-'tä-kə\ *n* — see MONEY table

¹patch \'pach\ *n* **1** : a piece used to cover a torn or worn place; *also* : one worn on a garment as an ornament or insignia **2** : a small area distinct from that about it **3** : a shield worn over the socket of an injured or missing eye

²patch *vb* **1** : to mend or cover with a patch **2** : to make of fragments **3** : to repair usu. in hasty fashion

patch test *n* : a test for allergic sensitivity made by applying to the unbroken skin small pads soaked with the allergen to be tested

patch·work \'pach-ˌwərk\ *n* : something made of pieces of different materials, shapes, or colors

patchy \'pa-chē\ *adj* **patch·i·er; -est** : marked by or consisting of patches; *also* : irregular in appearance or quality — **patch·i·ness** \-chē-nəs\ *n*

pate \'pāt\ *n* : HEAD; *esp* : the crown of the head

pâ·té *also* **pate** \pä-'tā\ *n* [F] **1** : a meat or fish pie or patty **2** : a spread of finely chopped or pureed seasoned meat

pa·tel·la \pə-'te-lə\ *n*, *pl* **-lae** \-'te-(ˌ)lē, -ˌlī\ *or* **-las** [L] : KNEECAP

pat·en \'pat-ᵊn\ *n* **1** : PLATE; *esp* : one of precious metal for the eucharistic bread **2** : a thin disk

¹pa·tent *l* & *4 are* 'pat-ᵊnt, *Brit also* 'pāt-, *2 & 3 are* 'pat-ᵊnt, 'pāt-\ *adj* **1** : open to public inspection — used chiefly in the phrase *letters patent* **2** : free from obstruction **3** : EVIDENT, OBVIOUS **4** : protected by a patent **syn** manifest, distinct, apparent, palpable, plain, clear — **pat·ent·ly** *adv*

²patent \'pat-ᵊnt, *Brit also* 'pāt-\ *n* **1** : an official document conferring a right or privilege **2** : a document securing to an inventor for a term of years exclusive right to his or her invention **3** : something patented

³patent *vb* : to secure by patent

pat·en·tee \ˌpat-ᵊn-'tē, *Brit also* 'pāt-\ *n* : one to whom a grant is made or a privilege secured by patent

pat·ent medicine \'pat-ᵊnt-\ *n* : a packaged nonprescription drug protected by a trademark; *also* : any proprietary drug

pa·ter·fa·mil·i·as \ˌpā-tər-fə-'mi-lē-əs\ *n*, *pl* **pa·tres·fa·mil·i·as** \pā-ˌtrēz-\ [L] : the father of a family : the male head of a household

pa·ter·nal \pə-'tərn-ᵊl\ *adj* **1** : FATHERLY **2** : related through or inherited or derived from a father — **pa·ter·nal·ly** *adv*

pa·ter·nal·ism \-ˌi-zəm\ *n* : a system under which an authority treats those under its control paternally (as by regulating their conduct and supplying their needs)

pa·ter·ni·ty \pə-'tər-nə-tē\ *n* **1** : FATHERHOOD **2** : descent from a father

¹path \'path, 'páth\ *n*, *pl* **paths** \'pathz, 'paths, 'páthz, 'páths\ **1** : a trodden way **2** : ROUTE, COURSE — **path·less** *adj*

²path *or* **pathol** *abbr* pathology

path·break·ing \'path-ˌbrā-kiŋ\ *adj* : TRAILBLAZING

pa·thet·ic \pə-'the-tik\ *adj* : evoking tenderness, pity, or sorrow **syn** pitiful, piteous, pitiable, poor — **pa·thet·i·cal·ly** \-ti-k(ə-)lē\ *adv*

path·find·er \'path-ˌfīn-dər, 'páth-\ *n* : one that discovers a way; *esp* : one that explores untraveled regions to mark out a new route

patho·gen \'pa-thə-jən\ *n* : a specific agent (as a bacterium) causing disease — **patho·gen·ic** \ˌpa-thə-'je-nik\ *adj* — **patho·ge·nic·i·ty** \-jə-'ni-sə-tē\ *n*

pa·thol·o·gy \pə-'thä-lə-jē\ *n*, *pl* **-gies** **1** : the study of the essential nature of disease **2** : the abnormality of structure and function characteristic of a disease — **path·o·log·i·cal** \ˌpa-thə-'lä-ji-kəl\ *adj* — **pa·thol·o·gist** \pə-'thä-lə-jist\ *n*

pa·thos \'pā-ˌthäs, -ˌthòs\ *n* : an element in experience or artistic representation evoking pity or compassion

path·way \'path-ˌwā, 'páth-\ *n* : PATH

pa·tience \'pā-shəns\ *n* **1** : the capacity, habit, or fact of being patient **2** *chiefly Brit* : SOLITAIRE 2

¹pa·tient \'pā-shənt\ *adj* **1** : bearing pain or trials without complaint **2** : showing self-control : CALM **3** : STEADFAST, PERSEVERING — **pa·tient·ly** *adv*

²patient *n* : one under medical care

pa·ti·na \'pa-tə-nə, pə-'tē-\ *n*, *pl* **pa·ti·nas** \-nəz\ *or* **pa·ti·nae** \'pa-tə-ˌnē, -ˌnī\ **1** : a green film formed on copper and bronze by exposure to moist air **2** : a superficial covering or exterior

pa·tio \'pa-tē-ˌō, 'pä-\ *n*, *pl* **pa·ti·os** **1** : COURTYARD **2** : an often paved area near a dwelling used esp. for outdoor dining

pa·tois \'pa-ˌtwä\ *n*, *pl* **pa·tois** \-ˌtwäz\ [F] **1** : a dialect other than the standard dialect; *esp* : uneducated or provincial speech **2** : JARGON 2

pa·tri·arch \'pā-trē-ˌärk\ *n* **1** : a man revered as father or founder (as of a tribe) **2** : a venerable old man **3** : an ecclesiastical dignitary (as the bishop of an Eastern Orthodox see) — **pa·tri·ar·chal** \ˌpā-trē-'är-kəl\ *adj* — **pa·tri·arch·ate** \'pā-trē-ˌär-kət, -ˌkät\ *n* — **pa·tri·ar·chy** \-ˌär-kē\ *n*

pa·tri·cian \pə-'tri-shən\ *n* : a person of high birth : ARISTOCRAT — **patrician** *adj*

pat·ri·cide \'pa-trə-ˌsīd\ *n* **1** : one who murders his or her own father **2** : the murder of one's own father

pat·ri·mo·ny \'pa-trə-ˌmō-nē\ *n* : something (as an estate) inherited or derived esp. from one's father : HERITAGE — **pat·ri·mo·ni·al** \ˌpa-trə-'mō-nē-əl\ *adj*

pa·tri·ot \'pā-trē-ət, -ˌät\ *n* [MF *patriote* compatriot, fr. LL *patriota*, fr. Gk *patriōtēs*, fr. *patria* lineage, fr. *patr-, patēr* father] : one who loves his or her country — **pa·tri·ot·ic** \ˌpā-trē-'ä-tik\ *adj* — **pa·tri·ot·i·cal·ly** \-ti-k(ə-)lē\ *adv* — **pa·tri·o·tism** \'pā-trē-ə-ˌti-zəm\ *n*

pa·tris·tic \pə-'tris-tik\ *adj* : of or relating to the church fathers or their writings

¹pa·trol \pə-'trōl\ *n* : the action of going the rounds (as of an area) for observation or the maintenance of security; *also* : a person or group performing such an action

²patrol *vb* **pa·trolled; pa·trol·ling** : to carry out a patrol

patrol car *n* : SQUAD CAR

pa·trol·man \pə-'trōl-mən\ *n* : a police officer assigned to a beat

patrol wagon *n* : PADDY WAGON

pa·tron \'pā-trən\ *n* [ME, fr. MF, fr. ML & L; ML *patronus* patron saint, patron of a benefice, pattern, fr. L, defender, fr. *patr-, pater* father] **1** : a person chosen or named as special protector **2** : a wealthy or influential supporter ⟨~ of poets⟩; *also* : BENEFACTOR **3** : a regular client or customer

pa·tron·age \'pa-trə-nij, 'pā-\ *n* **1** : the support or influence of a patron **2** : the trade of customers **3** : control of appointment to government jobs

pa·tron·ess \'pā-trə-nəs\ *n* : a woman who is a patron

pa·tron·ize \'pā-trə-ˌnīz, 'pa-\ *vb* **-ized; -iz·ing** **1** : to be a customer of **2** : to treat condescendingly, haughtily, or coolly

pat·ro·nym·ic \ˌpa-trə-'ni-mik\ *n* : a name derived from the name of one's father or a paternal ancestor usu. by the addition of an affix

pa·troon \pə-'trün\ *n* : the proprietor of a manorial estate esp. in New York under Dutch rule

pat·sy \'pat-sē\ *n*, *pl* **pat·sies** : a person who is easily duped or victimized

¹pat·ter \'pa-tər\ *vb* : to talk glibly or mechanically **syn** chatter, prate, chat, prattle, babble

²patter *n* **1** : a specialized lingo **2** : extremely rapid talk ⟨a comedian's ~⟩

³patter *vb* : to strike, pat, or tap rapidly

⁴patter *n* : a quick succession of taps or pats ⟨the ~ of rain⟩

¹pat·tern \'pa-tərn\ *n* [ME *patron*, fr. MF, fr. ML *patronus*, fr. L, defender, fr. *patr-, pater* father] **1** : an ideal model **2** : something used as a model for making things ⟨a dressmaker's ∼⟩ **3** : SAMPLE **4** : an artistic design **5** : CONFIGURATION

²**pattern** *vb* : to form according to a pattern

pat·ty *also* **pat·tie** \'pa-tē\ *n, pl* **patties 1** : a little pie **2** : a small flat cake esp. of chopped food

pau·ci·ty \'pȯ-sə-tē\ *n* : smallness of number or quantity

paunch \'pȯnch\ *n* : a usu. large belly : POTBELLY — **paunchy** *adj*

pau·per \'pȯ-pər\ *n* : a person without means of support except from charity — **pau·per·ism** \-pə-ˌri-zəm\ *n* — **pau·per·ize** \-pə-ˌrīz\ *vb*

¹**pause** \'pȯz\ *n* **1** : a temporary stop; *also* : a period of inaction **2** : a brief suspension of the voice **3** : a sign ⌒ or ⌣ above or below a musical note or rest to show it is to be prolonged **4** : a reason for pausing

²**pause** *vb* **paused; paus·ing** : to stop, rest, or linger for a time

pave \'pāv\ *vb* **paved; pav·ing** : to cover (as a road) with hard material in order to smooth or firm the surface

pave·ment \'pāv-mənt\ *n* **1** : a paved surface **2** : the material with which something is paved

pa·vil·ion \pə-'vil-yən\ *n* [ME *pavilon,* fr. OF *paveillon,* fr. L *papilion-, papilio* butterfly] **1** : a large tent **2** : a light structure (as in a park) used for entertainment or shelter

pav·ing \'pā-viŋ\ *n* : PAVEMENT

¹**paw** \'pȯ\ *n* : the foot of a quadruped (as a dog or lion) having claws

²**paw** *vb* **1** : to touch or strike with a paw; *also* : to scrape with a hoof **2** : to feel or handle clumsily or rudely **3** : to flail about or grab for with the hands

pawl \'pȯl\ *n* : a pivoted tongue or sliding bolt designed to fall into notches on another machine part to permit motion in one direction only

¹**pawn** \'pȯn\ *n* [ME *pown,* fr. MF *poon,* fr. ML *pedon-, pedo* foot soldier, fr. LL, one with broad feet, fr. L *ped-, pes* foot] : a chess piece of the least value

²**pawn** *n* **1** : something deposited as security for a loan; *also* : HOSTAGE **2** : the state of being pledged

³**pawn** *vb* : to deposit as a pledge

pawn·bro·ker \'pȯn-ˌbrō-kər\ *n* : one who lends money on goods pledged

Paw·nee \pȯ-'nē\ *n, pl* **Pawnee** *or* **Pawnees** : a member of an American Indian people orig. of Kansas and Nebraska

pawn·shop \'pȯn-ˌshäp\ *n* : a pawnbroker's place of business

paw·paw *var of* PAPAW

¹**pay** \'pā\ *vb* **paid** \'pād\ *also in sense 7* **payed; pay·ing** [ME, fr. OF *paier,* fr. L *pacare* to pacify, fr. *pac-, pax* peace] **1** : to make due return to for goods or services **2** : to discharge indebtedness for : SETTLE ⟨∼ a bill⟩ **3** : to give in forfeit ⟨∼ the penalty⟩ **4** : REQUITE **5** : to give, offer, or make freely or as fitting ⟨∼ attention⟩ **6** : to be profitable to : RETURN **7** : to make slack and allow to run out ⟨∼ out a rope⟩ — **pay·able** *adj* — **pay·ee** \pā-'ē\ *n* — **pay·er** *n*

²**pay** *n* **1** : something paid; *esp* : WAGES **2** : the status of being paid by an employer : EMPLOY

³**pay** *adj* **1** : containing something valuable (as gold) ⟨∼ dirt⟩ **2** : equipped to receive a fee for use ⟨∼ telephone⟩ **3** : requiring payment

pay·check \'pā-ˌchek\ *n* **1** : a check in payment of wages or salary **2** : WAGES, SALARY

pay·load \-ˌlōd\ *n* : the load carried by a vehicle in addition to what is necessary for its operation; *also* : the weight of such a load

pay·mas·ter \-ˌmas-tər\ *n* : one who distributes the payroll

pay·ment \'pā-mənt\ *n* **1** : the act of paying **2** : something paid

pay·off \-ˌȯf\ *n* **1** : PROFIT, REWARD; *also* : RETRIBUTION **2** : the climax of an incident or enterprise ⟨the ∼ of a story⟩

pay–per–view *n* : a cable television service by which customers can order access to a single airing of a TV feature

pay·roll \-ˌrōl\ *n* : a list of persons entitled to receive pay; *also* : the money to pay those on such a list

payt *abbr* payment

pay up *vb* : to pay what is due; *also* : to pay in full

Pb *symbol* [L *plumbum*] lead

PBS *abbr* Public Broadcasting Service

PBX \ˌpē-ˌbē-'eks\ *n* [*p*rivate *b*ranch *e*xchange] : a private telephone switchboard

¹**PC** \ˌpē-'sē\ *n, pl* **PCs** *or* **PC's 1** : PERSONAL COMPUTER **2** : MICROCOMPUTER

²**PC** *abbr* **1** Peace Corps **2** percent; percentage **3** politically correct **4** postcard **5** [L *post cibum*] after meals **6** professional corporation

PCB \ˌpē-ˌsē-'bē\ *n* : POLYCHLORINATED BIPHENYL

PCP \ˌpē-ˌsē-'pē\ *n* : PHENCYCLIDINE

pct *abbr* percent; percentage

pd *abbr* paid

Pd *symbol* palladium

PD *abbr* **1** per diem **2** police department **3** potential difference

PDQ \ˌpē-ˌdē-'kyü\ *adv, often not cap* [abbr. of *pretty damned quick*] : IMMEDIATELY

PDT *abbr* Pacific daylight (saving) time

PE *abbr* **1** physical education **2** printer's error **3** professional engineer

pea \'pē\ *n, pl* **peas** *also* **pease** \'pēz\ **1** : the round edible protein-rich seed borne in the pod of a widely grown leguminous vine; *also* : this vine **2** : any of various plants resembling or related to the pea

peace \'pēs\ *n* **1** : a state of calm and quiet; *esp* : public security under law **2** : freedom from disturbing thoughts or emotions **3** : a state of concord (as between persons or governments); *also* : an agreement to end hostilities — **peace·able** \'pē-sə-bəl\ *adj* — **peace·ably** \-blē\ *adv* — **peace·ful** *adj* — **peace·ful·ly** *adv*

peace·keep·ing \'pēs-ˌkē-piŋ\ *n* : the preserving of peace; *esp* : international enforcement and supervision of a truce — **peace·keep·er** *n*

peace·mak·er \-ˌmā-kər\ *n* : one who settles an argument or stops a fight

peace·time \-ˌtīm\ *n* : a time when a nation is not at war

peach \'pēch\ *n* [ME *peche,* fr. MF, fr. LL *persica,* fr. L (*malum*) *Persicum,* lit., Persian fruit] : a sweet juicy fruit of a low tree with pink blossoms related to the cherry and plums; *also* : this tree

pea·cock \'pē-ˌkäk\ *n* [ME *pecok,* fr. *pe-* (fr. OE *pēa* peafowl, fr. L *pavo* peacock) + *cok* cock] : the male peafowl that can spread its long tail feathers to make a colorful display

pea·fowl \-ˌfaul\ *n* : either of two large domesticated Asian pheasants

peafowl: *A* female, *B* male

pea·hen \-ˌhen\ *n* : the female peafowl

¹**peak** \ˈpēk\ *n* **1** : a pointed or projecting part **2** : the top of a hill or mountain; *also* : MOUNTAIN **3** : the front projecting part of a cap **4** : the narrow part of a ship's bow or stern **5** : the highest level or greatest degree — **peak** *adj*

²**peak** *vb* : to bring to or reach a maximum

peak·ed \ˈpē-kəd\ *adj* : THIN, SICKLY

¹**peal** \ˈpēl\ *n* **1** : the loud ringing of bells **2** : a set of tuned bells **3** : a loud sound or succession of sounds

²**peal** *vb* : to give out peals : RESOUND

pea·nut \ˈpē-(ˌ)nət\ *n* **1** : an annual herb related to the pea but having pods that ripen underground; *also* : this pod or one of the edible seeds it bears **2** *pl* : a very small amount

pear \ˈpar\ *n* : the fleshy fruit of a tree related to the apple; *also* : this tree

pearl \ˈpərl\ *n* **1** : a small hard often lustrous body formed within the shell of some mollusks and used as a gem **2** : one that is choice or precious ⟨∼s of wisdom⟩ **3** : a slightly bluish medium gray — **pearly** \ˈpər-lē\ *adj*

peas·ant \ˈpez-ənt\ *n* **1** : any of a class of small landowners or laborers tilling the soil **2** : a usu. uneducated person of low social status — **peas·ant·ry** \-ᵊn-trē\ *n*

pea·shoot·er \ˈpē-ˌshü-tər\ *n* : a toy blowgun for shooting peas

peat \ˈpēt\ *n* : a dark substance formed by partial decay of plants (as mosses) in water — **peaty** *adj*

peat moss *n* : SPHAGNUM

¹**peb·ble** \ˈpe-bəl\ *n* : a small usu. round stone — **peb·bly** \-b(ə-)lē\ *adj*

²**pebble** *vb* **peb·bled; peb·bling** : to produce a rough surface texture in ⟨∼ leather⟩

pec \ˈpek\ *n* : PECTORAL MUSCLE

pe·can \pi-ˈkän, -ˈkan; ˈpē-ˌkan\ *n* : the smooth-shelled edible nut of a large American hickory; *also* : this tree

pec·ca·dil·lo \ˌpe-kə-ˈdi-lō\ *n, pl* **-loes** *or* **-los** : a slight offense

pec·ca·ry \ˈpe-kə-rē\ *n, pl* **-ries** : any of several American chiefly tropical mammals resembling but smaller than the related pigs

peccary

pec·ca·vi \pe-ˈkä-ˌvē\ *n* [L, I have sinned, fr. *peccare* to sin] : an acknowledgment of sin

¹**peck** \ˈpek\ *n* — see WEIGHT table

²**peck** *vb* **1** : to strike or pierce with or as if with the bill **2** : to make (as a hole) by pecking **3** : to pick up with or as if with the bill

³**peck** *n* **1** : an impression made by pecking **2** : a quick sharp stroke

pecking order *also* **peck order** *n* : a basic pattern of social organization within a flock of poultry in which each bird pecks another lower in the scale without being pecked in return and submits to pecking by one of higher rank; *also* : a social hierarchy

pec·tin \ˈpek-tən\ *n* : any of various water-soluble plant substances that cause fruit jellies to set — **pec·tic** \-tik\ *adj*

pec·to·ral \ˈpek-tə-rəl\ *adj* : of or relating to the breast or chest

pectoral muscle *n* : either of two muscles on each side of the body which connect the front walls of the chest with the bones of the upper arm and shoulder

pe·cu·liar \pi-ˈkyül-yər\ *adj* [ME *peculier*, fr. L *peculiaris* of private property, special, fr. *peculium* private property, fr. *pecus* cattle] **1** : belonging exclusively to one person or group **2** : CHARACTERISTIC, DISTINCTIVE **3** : QUEER, ODD *syn* idiosyncratic, eccentric, singular, strange, weird — **pe·cu·liar·i·ty** \-ˌkyül-ˈyar-ə-tē, -ˌkyü-lē-ˈar-\ *n* — **pe·cu·liar·ly** *adv*

pe·cu·ni·ary \pi-ˈkyü-nē-ˌer-ē\ *adj* : of or relating to money : MONETARY

ped·a·gogue *also* **ped·a·gog** \ˈpe-də-ˌgäg\ *n* : TEACHER, SCHOOLMASTER

ped·a·go·gy \ˈpe-də-ˌgō-jē, -ˌgä-\ *n* : the art or profession of teaching; *esp* : EDUCATION **2** — **ped·a·gog·ic** \ˌpe-də-ˈgä-jik, -ˈgō-\ *or* **ped·a·gog·i·cal** \-ji-kəl\ *adj*

¹**ped·al** \ˈped-ᵊl\ *n* : a lever worked by the foot

²**ped·al** *adj* : of or relating to the foot

³**ped·al** \ˈped-ᵊl\ *vb* **ped·aled** *also* **ped·alled; ped·al·ing** *also* **ped·al·ling** **1** : to use or work a pedal (as of a piano or bicycle) **2** : to ride a bicycle

ped·ant \ˈped-ᵊnt\ *n* **1** : a person who makes a display of his learning **2** : a formal uninspired teacher — **pe·dan·tic** \pi-ˈdan-tik\ *adj* — **ped·ant·ry** \ˈped-ᵊn-trē\ *n*

ped·dle \ˈped-ᵊl\ *vb* **ped·dled; ped·dling** : to sell or offer for sale from place to place — **ped·dler** *also* **ped·lar** \ˈped-lər\ *n*

ped·er·ast \ˈpe-də-ˌrast\ *n* [Gk *paiderastēs*, lit., lover of boys] : one that practices anal intercourse esp. with a boy — **ped·er·as·ty** \ˈpe-də-ˌras-tē\ *n*

ped·es·tal \ˈpe-dəst-ᵊl\ *n* **1** : the support or foot of something (as a column, statue, or vase) that is upright **2** : a position of high regard

¹**pe·des·tri·an** \pə-ˈdes-trē-ən\ *adj* **1** : COMMONPLACE **2** : going on foot

²**pedestrian** *n* : WALKER

pe·di·at·rics \ˌpē-dē-ˈa-triks\ *n* : a branch of medicine dealing with the development, care, and diseases of children — **pe·di·at·ric** \-trik\ *adj* — **pe·di·a·tri·cian** \ˌpē-dē-ə-ˈtri-shən\ *n*

pedi·cab \ˈpe-di-ˌkab\ *n* : a pedal-driven tricycle with seats for a driver and two passengers

ped·i·cure \ˈpe-di-ˌkyúr\ *n* : care of the feet, toes, and nails; *also* : a single treatment of these parts — **ped·i·cur·ist** \-ˌkyúr-ist\ *n*

ped·i·gree \ˈpe-də-ˌgrē\ *n* [ME *pedegru*, fr. MF *pie de grue* crane's foot; fr. the shape made by the lines of a genealogical chart] **1** : a record of a line of ancestors **2** : an ancestral line — **ped·i·greed** \-ˌgrēd\ *adj*

ped·i·ment \ˈpe-də-mənt\ *n* : a low triangular gablelike decoration (as over a door or window) on a building

pe·dom·e·ter \pi-ˈdä-mə-tər\ *n* : an instrument that measures the distance one walks

pe·dun·cle \ˈpē-ˌdəŋ-kəl\ *n* : a narrow supporting stalk

peek \ˈpēk\ *vb* **1** : to look furtively **2** : to peer from a place of concealment **3** : GLANCE — **peek** *n*

¹**peel** \ˈpēl\ *vb* [ME *pelen*, fr. MF *peler*, fr. L *pilare* to remove the hair from, fr. *pilus* hair] **1** : to strip the skin, bark, or rind from **2** : to strip off (as a coat); *also* : to come off **3** : to lose the skin, bark, or rind

²**peel** *n* : a skin or rind esp. of a fruit

peel·ing \ˈpē-liŋ\ *n* : a peeled-off piece or strip (as of skin or rind)

peen \ˈpēn\ *n* : the usu. hemispherical or wedge-shaped end of the head of a hammer opposite the face

¹**peep** \ˈpēp\ *vb* : to utter a feeble shrill sound or the slightest sound

²**peep** *n* : a feeble shrill sound

³**peep** *vb* **1** : to look slyly esp. through an aperture : PEEK **2** : to begin to emerge — **peep·er** *n*

⁴peep *n* **1** : a first faint appearance **2** : a brief or furtive look

peep·hole \'pēp-ˌhōl\ *n* : a hole to peep through

¹peer \'pir\ *n* **1** : one of equal standing with another : EQUAL **2** : NOBLE — **peer·age** \-ij\ *n*

²peer *vb* **1** : to look intently or curiously **2** : to come slightly into view

peer·ess \'pir-əs\ *n* : a woman who is a peer

peer·less \'pir-ləs\ *adj* : having no equal : MATCHLESS **syn** supreme, unequalled, unparalleled, incomparable

¹peeve \'pēv\ *vb* **peeved; peev·ing** : to make resentful : ANNOY

²peeve *n* **1** : a feeling or mood of resentment **2** : a particular grievance

pee·vish \'pē-vish\ *adj* : querulous in temperament : FRETFUL **syn** irritable, petulant, huffy — **pee·vish·ly** *adv* — **pee·vish·ness** *n*

pee·wee \'pē-ˌwē\ *n* : one that is diminutive or tiny

¹peg \'peg\ *n* **1** : a small pointed piece (as of wood) used to pin down or fasten things or to fit into holes **2** : a projecting piece used as a support or boundary marker **3** : SUPPORT, PRETEXT **4** : STEP, DEGREE **5** : THROW

²peg *vb* **pegged; peg·ging 1** : to put a peg into : fasten, pin down, or attach with or as if with pegs **2** : to work hard and steadily : PLUG **3** : HUSTLE **4** : to mark by pegs **5** : to hold (as prices) at a set level or rate **6** : IDENTIFY **7** : THROW

PEI *abbr* Prince Edward Island

pei·gnoir \pān-'wär, pen-\ *n* [F, lit., garment worn while combing the hair, fr. MF, fr. *peigner* to comb the hair, fr. L *pectinare*, fr. *pectin-, pecten* comb] : NEGLIGEE

¹pe·jo·ra·tive \pi-'jȯr-ə-tiv\ *n* : a pejorative word or phrase

²pejorative *adj* : having negative connotations : DISPARAGING — **pe·jo·ra·tive·ly** *adv*

peke \'pēk\ *n, often cap* : PEKINGESE

Pe·king·ese *or* **Pe·kin·ese** \ˌpē-kə-'nēz, -'nēs; -kiŋ-'ēz, -'ēs\ *n, pl* **Pekingese** *or* **Pekinese** : any of a breed of Chinese origin of small short-legged long-haired dogs

pe·koe \'pē-ˌkō\ *n* : a black tea made from young tea leaves

pel·age \'pe-lij\ *n* : the hairy covering of a mammal

pe·lag·ic \pə-'la-jik\ *adj* : OCEANIC

pelf \'pelf\ *n* : MONEY, RICHES

pel·i·can \'pe-li-kən\ *n* : any of a genus of large web-footed birds having a pouched lower bill used to scoop in fish

pel·la·gra \pə-'la-grə, -'lā-\ *n* : a disease caused by a diet with too little nicotinic acid and protein and marked by a skin rash, disease of the digestive system, and nervous symptoms

pel·let \'pe-lət\ *n* **1** : a little ball (as of medicine) **2** : BULLET — **pel·let·al** \-lə-təl\ *adj* — **pel·let·ize** \-ˌtīz\ *vb*

pell–mell \ˌpel-'mel\ *adv* **1** : in mingled confusion **2** : HEADLONG

pel·lu·cid \pə-'lü-səd\ *adj* : extremely clear : LIMPID, TRANSPARENT **syn** translucent, lucid, lucent

¹pelt \'pelt\ *n* : a skin esp. of a fur-bearing animal

²pelt *vb* : to strike with a succession of blows or missiles

pel·vis \'pel-vəs\ *n, pl* **pel·vis·es** \-və-səz\ *or* **pel·ves** \-ˌvēz\ : a basin-shaped part of the vertebrate skeleton consisting of the large bone of each hip and the nearby bones of the spine — **pel·vic** \-vik\ *adj*

pem·mi·can *also* **pem·i·can** \'pe-mi-kən\ *n* : dried meat pounded fine and mixed with melted fat

¹pen \'pen\ *vb* **penned; pen·ning** : to shut in or as if in a pen

²pen *n* **1** : a small enclosure for animals **2** : a small place of confinement or storage

³pen *n* **1** : an implement for writing or drawing with ink or a similar fluid **2** : a writing instrument regarded as a means of expression

⁴pen *vb* **penned; pen·ning** : WRITE

⁵pen *n* : PENITENTIARY

⁶pen *abbr* peninsula

PEN *abbr* International Association of Poets, Playwrights, Editors, Essayists and Novelists

pe·nal \'pēn-əl\ *adj* : of or relating to punishment

pe·nal·ize \'pēn-əl-ˌīz, 'pen-\ *vb* **-ized; -iz·ing** : to put a penalty on

pen·al·ty \'pen-əl-tē\ *n, pl* **-ties 1** : punishment for crime or offense **2** : something forfeited when a person fails to do something agreed to **3** : disadvantage, loss, or hardship due to some action

pen·ance \'pe-nəns\ *n* **1** : an act performed to show sorrow or repentance for sin **2** : a sacrament (as in the Roman Catholic Church) consisting of confession, absolution, and a penance directed by the confessor

pence \'pens\ *pl of* PENNY

pen·chant \'pen-chənt\ *n* [F, fr. prp. of *pencher* to incline, fr. (assumed) VL *pendicare*, fr. L *pendere* to weigh] : a strong inclination : LIKING **syn** leaning, propensity, predilection, predisposition

¹pen·cil \'pen-səl\ *n* : a writing or drawing tool consisting of or containing a slender cylinder of a solid marking substance

²pencil *vb* **-ciled** *or* **-cilled; -cil·ing** *or* **-cil·ling** : to draw or write with a pencil

pen·dant *also* **pen·dent** \'pen-dənt\ *n* : a hanging ornament (as an earring)

pen·dent *or* **pen·dant** \'pen-dənt\ *adj* : SUSPENDED, OVERHANGING

¹pend·ing \'pen-diŋ\ *prep* **1** : DURING **2** : while awaiting

²pending *adj* **1** : not yet decided **2** : IMMINENT

pen·du·lous \'pen-jə-ləs, -də-\ *adj* : hanging loosely : DROOPING

pen·du·lum \-ləm\ *n* : a body that swings freely from a fixed point

pe·ne·plain *also* **pe·ne·plane** \'pē-ni-ˌplān\ *n* : a large almost flat land surface shaped by erosion

pen·e·trate \'pe-nə-ˌtrāt\ *vb* **-trat·ed; -trat·ing 1** : to enter into : PIERCE **2** : PERMEATE **3** : to see into : UNDERSTAND **4** : to affect deeply — **pen·e·tra·ble** \-trə-bəl\ *adj* — **pen·e·tra·tion** \ˌpe-nə-'trā-shən\ *n* — **pen·e·tra·tive** \'pe-nə-ˌtrā-tiv\ *adj*

pen·e·trat·ing *adj* **1** : having the power of entering, piercing, or pervading ⟨a ~ shriek⟩ ⟨a ~ odor⟩ **2** : ACUTE, DISCERNING ⟨a ~ look⟩

pen·guin \'pen-gwən, 'peŋ-\ *n* : any of various erect short-legged flightless seabirds of the southern hemisphere

pen·i·cil·lin \ˌpe-nə-'si-lən\ *n* : any of several antibiotics produced by molds or synthetically and used against various bacteria

pen·in·su·la \pə-'ni-nsə-lə\ *n* [L *paeninsula*, fr. *paene* almost + *insula* island] : a long narrow portion of land extending out into the water — **pen·in·su·lar** \-lər\ *adj*

pe·nis \'pē-nəs\ *n, pl* **pe·nes** \-ˌnēz\ *or* **pe·nis·es** : a male organ of copulation that in the human male also functions as the channel by which urine leaves the body

¹pen·i·tent \'pe-nə-tənt\ *adj* : feeling sorrow for sins or offenses : REPENTANT — **pen·i·tence** \-təns\ *n* — **pen·i·ten·tial** \ˌpe-nə-'ten-chəl\ *adj*

²penitent *n* : a penitent person

¹pen·i·ten·tia·ry \ˌpe-nə-'ten-chə-rē\ *n, pl* **-ries** : a state or federal prison

²penitentiary *adj* : of, relating to, or incurring confinement in a penitentiary

pen·knife \'pen-ˌnīf\ *n* : a small pocketknife

pen·light *or* **pen·lite** \-ˌlīt\ *n* : a small flashlight resembling a fountain pen in size or shape

pen·man \'pen-mən\ *n* **1** : COPYIST **2** : one skilled in penmanship **3** : AUTHOR

pen·man·ship \-ˌship\ *n* : the art or practice of writing with the pen

Penn *or* **Penna** *abbr* Pennsylvania

pen name *n* : an author's pseudonym

pen·nant \'pe-nənt\ n 1 : a tapering flag used esp. for signaling 2 : a flag symbolic of championship

pen·ni \'pe-nē\ n, pl **pen·nia** \-nē-ə\ or **pen·nis** \-nēz\ — see *markka* at MONEY table

pen·non \'pe-nən\ n 1 : a long narrow ribbonlike flag borne on a lance 2 : WING

Penn·syl·va·nian \,pen-səl-'vā-nyən\ adj : of, relating to, or being the period of the Paleozoic era between the Mississippian and the Permian — **Pennsylvanian** n

pen·ny \'pe-nē\ n, pl **pennies** \-nēz\ or **pence** \'pens\ 1 : a British monetary unit formerly equal to ¹⁄₁₂ shilling but now equal to ¹⁄₁₀₀ pound; *also* : a coin of this value — see *pound* at MONEY table 2 pl **pennies** : a cent of the U.S. or Canada — **pen·ni·less** \'pe-ni-ləs\ adj

pen·ny–pinch·ing \'pe-nē-,pin-chiŋ\ n : PARSIMONY — **pen·ny–pinch·er** n — **penny–pinching** adj

pen·ny·weight \-,wāt\ n — see WEIGHT table

pen·ny–wise \-,wīz\ adj : wise or prudent only in small matters

pe·nol·o·gy \pi-'nä-lə-jē\ n : a branch of criminology dealing with prisons and the treatment of offenders

¹pen·sion \'pen-chən\ n : a fixed sum paid regularly esp. to a person retired from service

²pension vb : to pay a pension to — **pen·sion·er** n

pen·sive \'pen-siv\ adj : musingly, dreamily, or sadly thoughtful **syn** reflective, speculative, contemplative, meditative — **pen·sive·ly** adv

pen·stock \'pen-,stäk\ n 1 : a sluice or gate for regulating a flow 2 : a pipe for carrying water

pent \'pent\ adj : shut up : CONFINED

pen·ta·gon \'pen-tə-,gän\ n : a polygon of five angles and five sides — **pen·tag·o·nal** \pen-'ta-gən-ᵊl\ adj

pen·tam·e·ter \pen-'ta-mə-tər\ n : a line of verse containing five metrical feet

Pen·te·cost \'pen-ti-,kȯst\ n : the 7th Sunday after Easter observed as a church festival commemorating the descent of the Holy Spirit on the apostles — **Pen·te·cos·tal** \,pen-ti-'käst-ᵊl\ adj

Pentecostal n : a member of a Christian religious body that stresses expressive worship, evangelism, and spiritual gifts — **Pen·te·cos·tal·ism** \,pen-ti-'käst-ᵊl-,i-zəm\ n

pent·house \'pent-,haus\ n [alter. of ME *pentis*, fr. MF *appentiz*, fr. *apent*, pp. of *apendre* to attach, hang against] 1 : a shed or sloping roof attached to a wall or building 2 : an apartment built on the roof of a building

pen·ul·ti·mate \pi-'nəl-tə-mət\ adj : next to the last ⟨∼ syllable⟩

pen·um·bra \pə-'nəm-brə\ n, pl **-brae** \-(,)brē\ or **-bras** : the partial shadow surrounding a complete shadow (as in an eclipse)

pe·nu·ri·ous \pə-'nur-ē-əs, -'nyur-\ adj 1 : marked by penury 2 : MISERLY **syn** stingy, close, tightfisted, parsimonious

pen·u·ry \'pe-nyə-rē\ n 1 : extreme poverty 2 : extreme frugality

pe·on \'pē-,än, -ən\ n, pl **peons** or **pe·o·nes** \pā-'ō-nēz\ 1 : a member of the landless laboring class in Spanish America 2 : one bound to service for payment of a debt — **pe·on·age** \-ə-nij\ n

pe·o·ny \'pē-ə-nē\ n, pl **-nies** : any of a genus of chiefly Eurasian plants with large often double red, pink, or white flowers; *also* : the flower

¹peo·ple \'pē-pəl\ n, pl **people** [ME *peple*, fr. OF *peuple*, fr. L *populus*] 1 pl : human beings making up a group or linked by a common characteristic or interest 2 pl : human beings — often used in compounds instead of *persons* ⟨sales*people*⟩ 3 pl : the mass of persons in a community : POPULACE; *also* : ELECTORATE ⟨the ∼'s choice⟩ 4 pl **peoples** : a body of persons (as a tribe, nation, or race) united by a common culture, sense of kinship, or political organization

²people vb **peo·pled; peo·pling** : to supply or fill with or as if with people

¹pep \'pep\ n : brisk energy or initiative — **pep·py** adj

²pep vb **pepped; pep·ping** : to put pep into : STIMULATE

¹pep·per \'pe-pər\ n 1 : either of two pungent condiments from the berry (**pep·per·corn** \-,kȯrn\) of an East Indian climbing plant; *also* : this plant 2 : a plant related to the tomato and widely grown for its hot or mild sweet fruit; *also* : this fruit

²pepper vb **pep·pered; pep·per·ing** 1 : to sprinkle or season with or as if with pepper 2 : to shower with missiles or rapid blows

pep·per·mint \-,mint, -mənt\ n : a pungent aromatic mint; *also* : candy flavored with its oil

pep·per·o·ni \,pe-pə-'rō-nē\ n : a highly seasoned beef and pork sausage

pep·pery \'pe-pə-rē\ adj 1 : having the qualities of pepper : PUNGENT, HOT 2 : having a hot temper 3 : FIERY

pep·sin \'pep-sən\ n : an enzyme of the stomach that promotes digestion by breaking down proteins; *also* : a preparation of this used medicinally

pep·tic \'pep-tik\ adj 1 : relating to or promoting digestion 2 : caused by digestive juices ⟨a ∼ ulcer⟩

Pe·quot \'pē-,kwät\ n : a member of an American Indian people of eastern Connecticut

¹per \'pər\ prep 1 : by means of 2 : to or for each 3 : ACCORDING TO

²per adv : for each : APIECE

³per abbr 1 period 2 person

¹per·ad·ven·ture \'pər-əd-,ven-chər\ adv, archaic : PERHAPS

²peradventure n 1 : DOUBT 2 : CHANCE 4

per·am·bu·late \pə-'ram-byə-,lāt\ vb **-lat·ed; -lat·ing** : to travel over esp. on foot — **per·am·bu·la·tion** \-,ram-byə-'lā-shən\ n

per·am·bu·la·tor \pə-'ram-byə-,lā-tər\ n, chiefly Brit : a baby carriage

per an·num \(,)pər-'a-nəm\ adv [ML] : in or for each year : ANNUALLY

per·cale \(,)pər-'kāl, 'pər-,; (,)pər-'kal\ n : a fine woven cotton cloth

per cap·i·ta \(,)pər-'ka-pə-tə\ adv or adj [ML, by heads] : by or for each person

per·ceive \pər-'sēv\ vb **per·ceived; per·ceiv·ing** 1 : to attain awareness : REALIZE 2 : to become aware of through the senses — **per·ceiv·able** adj

¹per·cent \pər-'sent\ adv [per + L centum hundred] : in each hundred

²percent n, pl **percent** or **percents** 1 : one part in a hundred : HUNDREDTH 2 : PERCENTAGE

per·cent·age \pər-'sen-tij\ n 1 : a part of a whole expressed in hundredths 2 : the result obtained by multiplying a number by a percent 3 : ADVANTAGE, PROFIT 4 : PROBABILITY; *also* : favorable odds

per·cen·tile \pər-'sen-,tīl\ n : a value on a scale of one hundred indicating the standing of a score or grade in terms of the percentage of scores or grades falling with or below it

per·cept \'pər-,sept\ n : an impression of an object obtained by use of the senses

per·cep·ti·ble \pər-'sep-tə-bəl\ adj : capable of being perceived — **per·cep·ti·bly** \-blē\ adv

per·cep·tion \pər-'sep-shən\ n 1 : an act or result of perceiving 2 : awareness of one's environment through physical sensation 3 : ability to understand : INSIGHT, COMPREHENSION **syn** penetration, discernment, discrimination

per·cep·tive \pər-'sep-tiv\ adj : capable of or exhibiting keen perception : OBSERVANT — **per·cep·tive·ly** adv

per·cep·tu·al \pər-'sep-chə-wəl\ adj : of, relating to, or involving sensory stimulus as opposed to abstract concept — **per·cep·tu·al·ly** adv

¹perch \'pərch\ n 1 : a roost for a bird 2 : a high station or vantage point

²perch vb : ROOST

³perch n, pl **perch** or **perch·es** : either of two small freshwater bony fishes used for food; *also* : any of various fishes resembling or related to these

per·chance \pər-ˈchans\ *adv* : PERHAPS

per·cip·i·ent \pər-ˈsi-pē-ənt\ *adj* : capable of or characterized by perception — **per·cip·i·ence** \-əns\ *n*

per·co·late \ˈpər-kə-ˌlāt\ *vb* **-lat·ed; -lat·ing 1** : to trickle or filter through a permeable substance **2** : to filter hot water through to extract the essence \∼ coffee\ — **per·co·la·tor** \-ˌlā-tər\ *n*

per con·tra \(ˌ)pər-ˈkän-trə\ *adv* [It, by the opposite side (of the ledger)] **1** : on the contrary **2** : by way of contrast

per·cus·sion \pər-ˈkə-shən\ *n* **1** : a sharp blow : IM-PACT; *esp* : a blow upon a cap (**percussion cap**) designed to explode the charge in a firearm **2** : the beating or striking of a musical instrument; *also* : instruments sounded by striking, shaking, or scraping

per di·em \pər-ˈdē-əm, -ˈdī-\ *adv* [ML] : by the day — **per diem** *adj or n*

per·di·tion \pər-ˈdi-shən\ *n* **1** : eternal damnation **2** : HELL

per·du·ra·ble \(ˌ)pər-ˈdùr-ə-bəl, -ˈdyùr-\ *adj* : very durable — **per·du·ra·bil·i·ty** \-ˌdùr-ə-ˈbi-lə-tē, -ˌdyùr-\ *n*

per·e·gri·na·tion \ˌper-ə-grə-ˈnā-shən\ *n* : a traveling about esp. on foot

per·e·grine \ˈper-ə-grən, -ˌgrēn\ *n* : a swift nearly cosmopolitan falcon that often nests in cities and is used in falconry

pe·remp·to·ry \pə-ˈremp-tə-rē\ *adj* **1** : barring a right of action or delay **2** : expressive of urgency or command : IMPERATIVE **3** : marked by arrogant self-assurance **syn** imperious, masterful, domineering, magisterial — **pe·remp·to·ri·ly** \-tə-rə-lē\ *adv*

¹**pe·ren·ni·al** \pə-ˈre-nē-əl\ *adj* **1** : present at all seasons of the year \∼ streams\ **2** : continuing to live from year to year \∼ plants\ **3** : recurring regularly : PER-MANENT \∼ problems\ **syn** lasting, perpetual, enduring, everlasting — **pe·ren·ni·al·ly** *adv*

²**perennial** *n* : a perennial plant

perf *abbr* **1** perfect **2** perforated

¹**per·fect** \ˈpər-fikt\ *adj* **1** : being without fault or defect **2** : EXACT, PRECISE **3** : COMPLETE **4** : relating to or being a verb tense that expresses an action or state completed at the time of speaking or at a time spoken of — **per·fect·ly** *adv* — **per·fect·ness** *n*

²**per·fect** \pər-ˈfekt\ *vb* : to make perfect

³**per·fect** \ˈpər-fikt\ *n* : the perfect tense; *also* : a verb form in it

per·fect·ible \pər-ˈfek-tə-bəl, ˈpər-fik-\ *adj* : capable of improvement or perfection — **per·fect·ibil·i·ty** \pər-ˌfek-tə-ˈbi-lə-tē, ˌpər-fik-\ *n*

per·fec·tion \pər-ˈfek-shən\ *n* **1** : the quality or state of being perfect **2** : the highest degree of excellence **3** : the act or process of perfecting

per·fec·tion·ist \-shə-nist\ *n* : a person who will not accept or be content with anything less than perfection

per·fec·to \pər-ˈfek-tō\ *n, pl* **-tos** : a cigar that is thick in the middle and tapers almost to a point at each end

per·fi·dy \ˈpər-fə-dē\ *n, pl* **-dies** [L *perfidia,* fr. *perfidus* faithless, fr. *per-* detrimental to + *fides* faith] : violation of faith or loyalty : TREACHERY — **per·fid·i·ous** \pər-ˈfi-dē-əs\ *adj* — **per·fid·i·ous·ly** *adv*

per·fo·rate \ˈpər-fə-ˌrāt\ *vb* **-rat·ed; -rat·ing** : to bore through : PIERCE; *esp* : to make a line of holes in to facilitate separation — **per·fo·ra·tion** \ˌpər-fə-ˈrā-shən\ *n*

per·force \pər-ˈfōrs\ *adv* : of necessity

per·form \pər-ˈfòrm\ *vb* **1** : FULFILL **2** : CARRY OUT, DO **3** : FUNCTION **4** : to do in a set manner **5** : to give a performance — **per·form·er** *n*

per·for·mance \pər-ˈfòr-məns\ *n* **1** : the act or process of performing **2** : DEED, FEAT **3** : a public presentation

¹**per·fume** \pər-ˈfyüm, ˈpər-ˌfyüm\ *n* **1** : a usu. pleasant odor : FRAGRANCE **2** : a preparation used for scenting

²**per·fume** \pər-ˈfyüm, ˈpər-ˌfyüm\ *vb* **per·fumed; per·fum·ing** : SCENT

per·fum·ery \ˌpər-ˈfyü-mə-rē\ *n* : PERFUMES

per·func·to·ry \pər-ˈfəŋk-tə-rē\ *adj* : done merely as a duty — **per·func·to·ri·ly** *adv*

per·go·la \ˈpər-gə-lə\ *n* [It] : a structure consisting of posts supporting an open roof in the form of a trellis

perh *abbr* perhaps

per·haps \pər-ˈhaps\ *adv* : possibly but not certainly

per·i·gee \ˈper-ə-ˌjē\ *n* [MF, fr. NL *perigeum,* fr. Gk *perigeion,* fr. *peri* around, near + *gē* earth] : the point at which an orbiting object is nearest the body (as the earth) being orbited

peri·he·lion \ˌper-ə-ˈhēl-yən\ *n, pl* **-he·lia** \-ˈhēl-yə\ : the point in the path of a celestial body (as a planet) that is nearest to the sun

per·il \ˈper-əl\ *n* : DANGER; *also* : a source of danger : RISK — **per·il·ous** *adj* — **per·il·ous·ly** *adv*

pe·rim·e·ter \pə-ˈri-mə-tər\ *n* **1** : the boundary of a closed plane figure; *also* : its length **2** : a line bounding or protecting an area

¹**pe·ri·od** \ˈpir-ē-əd\ *n* **1** : SENTENCE; *also* : the full pause closing the utterance of a sentence **2** : END, STOP **3** : a punctuation mark . used esp. to mark the end of a declarative sentence or an abbreviation **4** : an extent of time; *esp* : one regarded as a stage or division in a process or development **5** : a portion of time in which a recurring phenomenon completes one cycle and is ready to begin again **6** : a single cyclic occurrence of menstruation

²**period** *adj* : of or relating to a particular historical period \∼ furniture\

pe·ri·od·ic \ˌpir-ē-ˈä-dik\ *adj* **1** : occurring at regular intervals of time **2** : happening repeatedly **3** : of or relating to a sentence that has no trailing elements following full grammatical statement of the essential idea

¹**pe·ri·od·i·cal** \ˌpir-ē-ˈä-di-kəl\ *adj* **1** : PERIODIC **2** : published at regular intervals **3** : of or relating to a periodical — **pe·ri·od·i·cal·ly** \-k(ə-)lē\ *adv*

²**periodical** *n* : a periodical publication

periodic table *n* : an arrangement of chemical elements based on their atomic structure and on their properties

peri·odon·tal \ˌper-ē-ō-ˈdänt-ᵊl\ *adj* **1** : surrounding a tooth **2** : of or affecting periodontal tissues or regions \∼ disease\

per·i·pa·tet·ic \ˌper-ə-pə-ˈte-tik\ *adj* : performed or performing while moving about : ITINERANT

pe·riph·er·al \pə-ˈri-fər-əl\ *n* : a device connected to a computer to provide communication or auxiliary functions

peripheral nervous system *n* : the part of the nervous system that is outside the central nervous system and comprises the spinal nerves, the cranial nerves except the one supplying the retina, and the autonomic nervous system

pe·riph·ery \pə-ˈri-fə-rē\ *n, pl* **-er·ies 1** : the boundary of a rounded figure **2** : outward bounds : border area — **pe·riph·er·al** \-fə-rəl\ *adj*

pe·riph·ra·sis \pə-ˈri-frə-səs\ *n, pl* **-ra·ses** \-ˌsēz\ : CIR-CUMLOCUTION

peri·scope \ˈper-ə-ˌskōp\ *n* : a tubular optical instrument enabling an observer to see an otherwise blocked field of view

per·ish \ˈper-ish\ *vb* : to become destroyed or ruined : DIE

per·ish·able \ˈper-i-shə-bəl\ *adj* : easily spoiled \∼ foods\ — **perishable** *n*

peri·stal·sis \ˌper-ə-ˈstòl-səs, -ˈstal-\ *n, pl* **-stal·ses** : waves of contraction passing along the walls of a hollow muscular organ and esp. the intestine and forcing its contents onward — **per·i·stal·tic** \-ˈstòl-tik, -ˈstal-\ *adj*

peri·style \ˈper-ə-ˌstīl\ *n* : a row of columns surrounding a building or court

peri•to•ne•um \ˌper-ə-tə-ˈnē-əm\ *n, pl* **-ne•ums** *or* **-nea**
: the smooth transparent serous membrane that lines
the cavity of the abdomen — **peri•to•ne•al** \-ˈnē-əl\
adj

peri•to•ni•tis \ˌper-ə-tə-ˈnī-təs\ *n* : inflammation of the
peritoneum

peri•wig \ˈper-i-ˌwig\ *n* : WIG

¹**per•i•win•kle** \ˈper-i-ˌwiŋ-kəl\ *n* : a usu. blue-
flowered creeping plant cultivated as a ground cover

²**periwinkle** *n* : any of various small edible seashore
snails

per•ju•ry \ˈpər-jə-rē\ *n* : the voluntary violation of an
oath to tell the truth : lying under oath — **per•jure**
\ˈpər-jər\ *vb* — **per•jur•er** *n*

¹**perk** \ˈpərk\ *vb* 1 : to thrust (as the head) up impudently or jauntily 2 : to regain vigor or spirit 3 : to make
trim or brisk : FRESHEN — **perky** *adj*

²**perk** *vb* : PERCOLATE

³**perk** *n* : PERQUISITE — usu. used in pl.

per•lite \ˈpər-ˌlīt\ *n* : volcanic glass that when expanded by heat forms a lightweight material used esp. in
concrete and plaster and for potting plants

¹**perm** \ˈpərm\ *n* : PERMANENT

²**perm** *vb* : to give (hair) a permanent

³**perm** *abbr* permanent

per•ma•frost \ˈpər-mə-ˌfròst\ *n* : a permanently frozen
layer below the surface in frigid regions of a planet

¹**per•ma•nent** \ˈpər-mə-nənt\ *adj* : LASTING, STABLE —
per•ma•nence \-nəns\ *n* — **per•ma•nen•cy** \-nən-sē\ *n*
— **per•ma•nent•ly** *adv*

²**permanent** *n* : a long-lasting hair wave or straightening

permanent press *n* : the process of treating fabrics
with chemicals (as resin) and heat for setting the
shape and for aiding wrinkle resistance

per•me•able \ˈpər-mē-ə-bəl\ *adj* : having small openings that permit liquids or gases to seep through —
per•me•a•bil•i•ty \ˌpər-mē-ə-ˈbi-lə-tē\ *n*

per•me•ate \ˈpər-mē-ˌāt\ *vb* **-at•ed; -at•ing** 1 : PERVADE
2 : to seep through the pores of : PENETRATE — **per-
me•ation** \ˌpər-mē-ˈā-shən\ *n*

Perm•ian \ˈpər-mē-ən\ *adj* : of, relating to, or being the
latest period of the Paleozoic era — **Permian** *n*

per•mis•si•ble \pər-ˈmi-sə-bəl\ *adj* : that may be permitted : ALLOWABLE

per•mis•sion \pər-ˈmi-shən\ *n* : formal consent : AU-
THORIZATION

per•mis•sive \pər-ˈmi-siv\ *adj* : granting permission;
esp : INDULGENT — **per•mis•sive•ly** *adv* — **per•mis-
sive•ness** *n*

¹**per•mit** \pər-ˈmit\ *vb* **per•mit•ted; per•mit•ting** 1 : to
consent to : ALLOW 2 : to make possible

²**per•mit** \ˈpər-ˌmit, pər-ˈmit\ *n* : a written permission
: LICENSE

per•mu•ta•tion \ˌpər-myù-ˈtā-shən\ *n* 1 : a major or
fundamental change 2 : the act or process of changing
the order of an ordered set of objects **syn** innovation,
mutation, vicissitude

per•ni•cious \pər-ˈni-shəs\ *adj* [ME, fr. MF *pernicieus*,
fr. L *perniciosus*, fr. *pernicies* destruction, fr. *per-*
through + *nec-, nex* violent death] : very destructive
or injurious — **per•ni•cious•ly** *adv*

per•ora•tion \ˈper-ə-ˌrā-shən, ˈpər-\ *n* : the concluding
part of a speech

¹**per•ox•ide** \pə-ˈräk-ˌsīd\ *n* : an oxide containing a
large proportion of oxygen; *esp* : HYDROGEN PEROX-
IDE

²**peroxide** *vb* **-id•ed; -id•ing** : to bleach with hydrogen
peroxide

perp *abbr* 1 perpendicular 2 perpetrator

per•pen•dic•u•lar \ˌpər-pən-ˈdi-kyə-lər\ *adj* 1 : standing at right angles to the plane of the horizon 2 : forming a right angle with each other or with a given line
or plane — **perpendicular** *n* — **per•pen•dic•u•lar-
i•ty** \-ˌdi-kyə-ˈlar-ə-tē\ *n* — **per•pen•dic•u•lar•ly** *adv*

per•pe•trate \ˈpər-pə-ˌtrāt\ *vb* **-trat•ed; -trat•ing** : to

be guilty of : COMMIT — **per•pe•tra•tion** \ˌpər-pə-ˈtrā-
shən\ *n* — **per•pe•tra•tor** \ˈpər-pə-ˌtrā-tər\ *n*

per•pet•u•al \pər-ˈpe-chə-wəl\ *adj* 1 : continuing forever : EVERLASTING 2 : occurring continually : CON-
STANT ⟨~ annoyance⟩ **syn** ceaseless, unceasing,
continual, continuous, incessant, unremitting — **per-
pet•u•al•ly** *adv*

per•pet•u•ate \pər-ˈpe-chə-ˌwāt\ *vb* **-at•ed; -at•ing** : to
make perpetual : cause to last indefinitely — **per-
pet•u•a•tion** \-ˌpe-chə-ˈwā-shən\ *n*

per•pe•tu•i•ty \ˌpər-pə-ˈtü-ə-tē, -ˈtyü-\ *n, pl* **-ties** 1
: ETERNITY 1 2 : the quality or state of being perpetual

per•plex \pər-ˈpleks\ *vb* : to disturb mentally; *esp*
: CONFUSE — **per•plex•i•ty** \-ˈplek-sə-tē\ *n*

per•plexed \-ˈplekst\ *adj* 1 : filled with uncertainty
: PUZZLED 2 : full of difficulty : COMPLICATED — **per-
plexed•ly** \-ˈplek-səd-lē\ *adv*

per•qui•site \ˈpər-kwə-zət\ *n* : a privilege or profit beyond regular pay

pers *abbr* person; personal

per se \(ˌ)pər-ˈsā\ *adv* [L] : by, of, or in itself : as such

per•se•cute \ˈpər-si-ˌkyüt\ *vb* **-cut•ed; -cut•ing** : to pursue in such a way as to injure or afflict : HARASS; *esp*
: to cause to suffer because of belief — **per•se•cu-
tion** \ˌpər-si-ˈkyü-shən\ *n* — **per•se•cu•tor** \ˈpər-si-
ˌkyü-tər\ *n*

per•se•vere \ˌpər-sə-ˈvir\ *vb* **-vered; -ver•ing** : to persist (as in an undertaking) in spite of difficulties —
per•se•ver•ance \-ˈvir-əns\ *n*

Per•sian \ˈpər-zhən\ *n* 1 : a native or inhabitant of ancient Persia 2 : a member of one of the peoples of
modern Iran 3 : the language of the Persians

Persian cat *n* : any of a breed of stocky round-
headed domestic cats that have a long silky coat

Persian lamb *n* : a pelt that is obtained from lambs
that are older than those yielding broadtail and that
has very silky tightly curled fur

per•si•flage \ˈpər-si-ˌfläzh, ˈper-\ *n* [F, fr. *persifler* to
banter, fr. *per-* thoroughly + *siffler* to whistle, hiss,
boo, ultim. fr. L *sibilare*] : lightly jesting or mocking
talk

per•sim•mon \pər-ˈsi-mən\ *n* : either of two trees related to the ebony; *also* : the edible orange-red plum-
like fruit of a persimmon

per•sist \pər-ˈsist, -ˈzist\ *vb* 1 : to go on resolutely or
stubbornly in spite of difficulties 2 : to continue to exist — **per•sis•tence** \-ˈsis-təns, -ˈzis-\ *n* — **per•sis-
ten•cy** \-tən-sē\ *n* — **per•sis•tent** \-tənt\ *adj* — **per-
sis•tent•ly** *adv*

per•snick•e•ty \pər-ˈsni-kə-tē\ *adj* : fussy about small
details

per•son \ˈpər-sən\ *n* [ME, fr. OF *persone*, fr. L *persona*
actor's mask, character in a play, person, prob. fr.
Etruscan *phersu* mask, fr. Gk *prosōpa*, pl. of
prosōpon face, mask] 1 : a human being : INDIVIDUAL
— used in combination esp. by those who prefer to
avoid *man* in compounds applicable to both sexes
⟨chair*person*⟩ 2 : one of the three modes of being in
the Godhead as understood by Trinitarians 3 : the
body of a human being 4 : the individual personality
of a human being : SELF 5 : reference of a segment of
discourse to the speaker, to one spoken to, or to one
spoken of esp. as indicated by certain pronouns

per•son•able \ˈpər-sə-nə-bəl\ *adj* : pleasant in person
: ATTRACTIVE

per•son•age \ˈpər-sə-nij\ *n* : a person of rank, note, or
distinction

¹**per•son•al** \ˈpər-sə-nəl\ *adj* 1 : of, relating to, or affecting a person : PRIVATE ⟨~ correspondence⟩ 2 : done
in person ⟨a ~ inquiry⟩ 3 : relating to the person or
body ⟨~ injuries⟩ 4 : relating to an individual esp. in
an offensive way ⟨resented such ~ remarks⟩ 5 : of or
relating to temporary or movable property as distinguished from real estate 6 : denoting grammatical
person

²**personal** n 1 : a short newspaper paragraph relating to a person or group or to personal matters 2 : a short personal or private communication in the classified ads section of a newspaper

personal computer n : MICROCOMPUTER

per·son·al·i·ty \ˌpər-sə-'na-lə-tē\ n, pl **-ties** 1 : an offensively personal remark ⟨indulges in *personalities*⟩ 2 : the collection of emotional and behavioral traits that characterize a person 3 : distinction of personal and social traits 4 : a well-known person ⟨a TV ∼⟩ **syn** individuality, temperament, disposition, makeup

per·son·al·ize \'pər-sə-nə-ˌlīz\ vb **-ized; -iz·ing** : to make personal or individual; *esp* : to mark as belonging to a particular person

per·son·al·ly \-nə-lē\ adv 1 : in person 2 : as a person 3 : as far as oneself is concerned

per·son·al·ty \'pər-sə-nəl-tē\ n, pl **-ties** : personal property

per·so·na non gra·ta \pər-'sō-nə-ˌnän-'gra-tə, -'grä-\ adj [L] : being personally unacceptable or unwelcome

per·son·ate \'pər-sə-ˌnāt\ vb **-at·ed; -at·ing** : IMPERSONATE, REPRESENT

per·son·i·fy \pər-'sä-nə-ˌfī\ vb **-fied; -fy·ing** 1 : to think of or represent as a person 2 : to be the embodiment of : INCARNATE ⟨∼ the law⟩ — **per·son·i·fi·ca·tion** \-ˌsä-nə-fə-'kā-shən\ n

per·son·nel \ˌpər-sə-'nel\ n : a body of persons employed

per·spec·tive \pər-'spek-tiv\ n 1 : the science of painting and drawing so that objects represented have apparent depth and distance 2 : the aspect in which a subject or its parts are mentally viewed; *esp* : a view of things (as objects or events) in their true relationship or relative importance

per·spi·ca·cious \ˌpər-spə-'kā-shəs\ adj : having or showing keen understanding or discernment — **per·spi·cac·i·ty** \-'ka-sə-tē\ n

per·spic·u·ous \pər-'spi-kyə-wəs\ adj : plain to the understanding — **per·spi·cu·i·ty** \ˌpər-spə-'kyü-ə-tē\ n

per·spire \pər-'spīr\ vb **per·spired; per·spir·ing** : SWEAT — **per·spi·ra·tion** \ˌpər-spə-'rā-shən\ n

per·suade \pər-'swād\ vb **per·suad·ed; per·suad·ing** : to win over to a belief or course of action by argument or entreaty — **per·sua·sive** \-'swā-siv, -ziv\ adj — **per·sua·sive·ly** adv — **per·sua·sive·ness** n

per·sua·sion \pər-'swā-zhən\ n 1 : the act or process of persuading 2 : a system of religious beliefs; *also* : a group holding such beliefs

¹**pert** \'pərt\ adj [ME, open, bold, pert, modif. of OF *apert*, fr. L *apertus* open, fr. pp. of *aperire* to open] 1 : saucily free and forward : IMPUDENT 2 : stylishly trim : JAUNTY 3 : LIVELY

²**pert** abbr pertaining

per·tain \pər-'tān\ vb 1 : to belong to as a part, quality, or function ⟨duties ∼ing to the office⟩ 2 : to have reference : RELATE ⟨books ∼ing to birds⟩

per·ti·na·cious \ˌpər-tə-'nā-shəs\ adj 1 : holding resolutely to an opinion or purpose 2 : obstinately persistent ⟨a ∼ bill collector⟩ **syn** dogged, mulish, headstrong, perverse — **per·ti·nac·i·ty** \-'na-sə-tē\ n

per·ti·nent \'pərt-ᵊn-ənt\ adj : relating to the matter under consideration **syn** relevant, germane, applicable, apropos — **per·ti·nence** \-əns\ n

per·turb \pər-'tərb\ vb : to disturb greatly esp. in mind : UPSET — **per·tur·ba·tion** \ˌpər-tər-'bā-shən\ n

per·tus·sis \pər-'tə-səs\ n : WHOOPING COUGH

pe·ruke \pə-'rük\ n : WIG

pe·ruse \pə-'rüz\ vb **pe·rused; pe·rus·ing** : READ; *esp* : to read over attentively or leisurely — **pe·rus·al** \-'rü-zəl\ n

Pe·ru·vi·an \pə-'rü-vē-ən\ n : a native or inhabitant of Peru

per·vade \pər-'vād\ vb **per·vad·ed; per·vad·ing** : to

spread through every part of : PERMEATE, PENETRATE — **per·va·sive** \-ˌvā-siv, -ziv\ adj

per·verse \pər-'vərs\ adj 1 : turned away from what is right or good : CORRUPT 2 : obstinate in opposing what is reasonable or accepted — **per·verse·ly** adv — **per·verse·ness** n — **per·ver·si·ty** \-'vər-sə-tē\ n

per·ver·sion \pər-'vər-zhən\ n 1 : the action of perverting : the condition of being perverted 2 : a perverted form of something; *esp* : aberrant sexual behavior

¹**per·vert** \pər-'vərt\ vb 1 : to lead astray : CORRUPT ⟨∼ the young⟩ 2 : to divert to a wrong purpose : MISAPPLY ⟨∼ evidence⟩ **syn** deprave, debase, debauch, demoralize — **per·vert·er** n

²**per·vert** \'pər-ˌvərt\ n : one that is perverted; *esp* : one given to sexual perversion

pe·se·ta \pə-'sā-tə\ n — see MONEY table

pe·se·wa \pə-'sā-wə\ n — see *cedi* at MONEY table

pes·ky \'pes-kē\ adj **pes·ki·er; -est** : causing annoyance : TROUBLESOME

pe·so \'pā-sō\ n, pl **pesos** — see MONEY table

pes·si·mism \'pe-sə-ˌmi-zəm\ n [F *pessimisme*, fr. L *pessimus* worst] : an inclination to take the least favorable view (as of events) or to expect the worst — **pes·si·mist** \-mist\ n — **pes·si·mis·tic** \ˌpe-sə-'mis-tik\ adj

pest \'pest\ n 1 : a destructive epidemic disease : PLAGUE 2 : a plant or animal detrimental to humans 3 : one that pesters : NUISANCE — **pesty** adj

pes·ter \'pes-tər\ vb : to harass with petty irritations : ANNOY

pes·ti·cide \'pes-tə-ˌsīd\ n : an agent used to destroy pests

pes·tif·er·ous \pes-'ti-fə-rəs\ adj 1 : PESTILENT 2 : ANNOYING

pes·ti·lence \'pes-tə-ləns\ n : a destructive infectious swiftly spreading disease; *esp* : BUBONIC PLAGUE

pes·ti·lent \-lənt\ adj 1 : dangerous to life : DEADLY 2 : PERNICIOUS, HARMFUL 3 : TROUBLESOME 4 : INFECTIOUS, CONTAGIOUS

pes·ti·len·tial \ˌpes-tə-'len-chəl\ adj 1 : causing or tending to cause pestilence : DEADLY 2 : morally harmful

pes·tle \'pes-əl, 'pest-ᵊl\ n : an implement for grinding substances in a mortar — **pestle** vb

¹**pet** \'pet\ n 1 : FAVORITE, DARLING 2 : a domesticated animal kept for pleasure rather than utility

²**pet** adj 1 : kept or treated as a pet ⟨∼ dog⟩ 2 : expressing fondness ⟨∼ name⟩ 3 : particularly liked or favored

³**pet** vb **pet·ted; pet·ting** 1 : to stroke gently or lovingly 2 : to make a pet of : PAMPER 3 : to engage in amorous kissing and caressing

⁴**pet** n : a fit of peevishness, sulkiness, or anger — **pet·tish** adj

Pet abbr Peter

pet·al \'pet-ᵊl\ n : one of the modified leaves of a flower's corolla

pe·tard \pə-'tärd, -'tär\ n : a case containing an explosive to break down a door or gate or breach a wall

pe·ter \'pē-tər\ vb : to diminish gradually and come to an end ⟨his energy ∼ed out⟩

Pe·ter \'pē-tər\ n — see BIBLE table

pet·i·ole \'pe-tē-ˌōl\ n : a slender stem that supports a leaf

pe·tite \pə-'tēt\ adj [F] : small and trim of figure ⟨a ∼ woman⟩ — **petite** n

pe·tit four \ˌpe-tē-'for\ n, pl **petits fours** or **petit fours** \-'forz\ [F, lit., small oven] : a small cake cut from pound or sponge cake and frosted

¹**pe·ti·tion** \pə-'ti-shən\ n : an earnest request : ENTREATY; *esp* : a formal written request made to an authority

²**petition** vb : to make a request to or for — **pe·ti·tion·er** n

pe·trel \'pe-trəl\ *n* : any of numerous seabirds that fly far from land

pet·ri·fy \'pe-trə-ˌfī\ *vb* **-fied; -fy·ing 1** : to convert (organic matter) into stone or stony material **2** : to make rigid or inactive (as from fear or awe) — **pet·ri·fac·tion** \ˌpe-trə-'fak-shən\ *n*

pet·ro·chem·i·cal \ˌpe-trō-'ke-mi-kəl\ *n* : a chemical isolated or derived from petroleum or natural gas — **pet·ro·chem·is·try** \-'ke-mə-strē\ *n*

pet·rol \'pe-trəl\ *n, Brit* : GASOLINE

pet·ro·la·tum \ˌpe-trə-'lā-təm\ *n* : PETROLEUM JELLY

pe·tro·leum \pə-'trō-lē-əm\ *n* [ML, fr. Gk *petra* rock + L *oleum* oil] : an oily flammable liquid obtained from wells drilled in the ground and refined into gasoline, fuel oils, and other products

petroleum jelly *n* : a tasteless, odorless, and oily or greasy substance from petroleum that is used esp. in ointments and dressings

¹pet·ti·coat \'pe-tē-ˌkōt\ *n* **1** : a skirt worn under a dress **2** : an outer skirt

²petticoat *adj* : of, relating to, or exercised by women : FEMALE

pet·ti·fog \'pe-tē-ˌfóg, -ˌfäg\ *vb* **-fogged; -fog·ging 1** : to engage in legal trickery **2** : to quibble over insignificant details — **pet·ti·fog·ger** *n*

pet·ty \'pe-tē\ *adj* **pet·ti·er; -est** [ME *pety* small, minor, alter. of *petit*, fr. MF, small] **1** : having secondary rank : MINOR ⟨∼ prince⟩ **2** : of little importance : TRIFLING ⟨∼ faults⟩ **3** : marked by narrowness or meanness — **pet·ti·ly** \'pe-tə-lē\ *adv* — **pet·ti·ness** \-tē-nəs\ *n*

petty officer *n* : a subordinate officer in the navy or coast guard appointed from among the enlisted men

petty officer first class *n* : a petty officer ranking below a chief petty officer

petty officer second class *n* : a petty officer ranking below a petty officer first class

petty officer third class *n* : a petty officer ranking below a petty officer second class

pet·u·lant \'pe-chə-lənt\ *adj* : marked by capricious ill humor **syn** irritable, peevish, fretful, fractious, querulous — **pet·u·lance** \-ləns\ *n* — **pet·u·lant·ly** *adv*

pe·tu·nia \pi-'tün-yə, -'tyün-\ *n* : any of a genus of tropical American herbs related to the potato and having bright funnel-shaped flowers

pew \'pyü\ *n* [ME *pewe*, fr. MF *puie* balustrade, fr. L *podia*, pl. of *podium* parapet, podium, fr. Gk *podion* base, dim. of *pod-, pous* foot] : any of the benches with backs fixed in rows in a church

pe·wee \'pē-(ˌ)wē\ *n* : any of various small flycatchers

pew·ter \'pyü-tər\ *n* **1** : an alloy of tin used esp. for household utensils **2** : a bluish gray — **pewter** *adj* — **pew·ter·er** *n*

pey·o·te \pā-'ō-tē\ *also* **pey·otl** \-'ōt-əl\ *n* : a stimulant drug derived from an American cactus; *also* : this cactus

pf *abbr* **1** pfennig **2** preferred

PFC *or* **Pfc** *abbr* private first class

pfd *abbr* preferred

pfen·nig \'fe-nig\ *n, pl* **pfennig** *also* **pfennigs** *or* **pfen·ni·ge** \'fe-ni-gə\ — see *deutsche mark* at MONEY table

pg *abbr* page

PG *abbr* postgraduate

PGA *abbr* Professional Golfers' Association

pH \(ˌ)pē-'āch\ *n* : a value used to express acidity and alkalinity; *also* : the condition represented by such a value

PH *abbr* **1** pinch hit **2** public health

pha·eton \'fā-ət-ən\ *n* [F *phaéton*, fr. Gk *Phaethōn*, son of the sun god who persuaded his father to let him drive the chariot of the sun but who lost control of the horses with disastrous consequences] **1** : a light 4-wheeled horse-drawn vehicle **2** : an open automobile with two cross seats

phage \'fāj\ *n* : BACTERIOPHAGE

pha·lanx \'fā-ˌlaŋks\ *n, pl* **pha·lanx·es** *or* **pha·lan-**

phaeton 1

ges \fə-'lan-ˌjēz\ **1** : a group or body (as of troops) in compact formation **2** *pl* **phalanges** : one of the digital bones of the hand or foot of a vertebrate

phal·a·rope \'fa-lə-ˌrōp\ *n, pl* **-ropes** *also* **-rope** : any of a genus of small shorebirds related to sandpipers

phal·lic \'fa-lik\ *adj* **1** : of, relating to, or resembling a phallus **2** : relating to or being the stage of psychosexual development in psychoanalytic theory during which children become interested in their own sexual organs

phal·lus \'fa-ləs\ *n, pl* **phal·li** \'fa-ˌlī\ *or* **phal·lus·es** : PENIS; *also* : a symbolic representation of the penis

Phan·er·o·zo·ic \ˌfa-nə-rə-'zō-ik\ *adj* : of, relating to, or being an eon of geologic history comprising the Paleozoic, Mesozoic, and Cenozoic

phan·tasm \'fan-ˌta-zəm\ *n* : a product of the imagination : ILLUSION — **phan·tas·mal** \ˌfan-'taz-məl\ *adj*

phan·tas·ma·go·ria \fan-ˌtaz-mə-'gōr-ē-ə\ *n* : a constantly shifting complex succession of things seen or imagined; *also* : a scene that constantly changes or fluctuates

phantasy *var of* FANTASY

phan·tom \'fan-təm\ *n* **1** : something (as a specter) that is apparent to sense but has no substantial existence **2** : a mere show : SHADOW — **phantom** *adj*

pha·raoh \'fer-ō, 'fā-rō\ *n, often cap* : a ruler of ancient Egypt

phar·i·sa·ical \ˌfar-ə-'sā-ə-kəl\ *adj* : hypocritically self-righteous

phar·i·see \'far-ə-ˌsē\ *n* **1** *cap* : a member of an ancient Jewish sect noted for strict observance of rites and ceremonies of the traditional law **2** : a self-righteous or hypocritical person — **phar·i·sa·ic** \ˌfar-ə-'sā-ik\ *adj*

pharm *abbr* pharmaceutical; pharmacist; pharmacy

phar·ma·ceu·ti·cal \ˌfär-mə-'sü-ti-kəl\ *adj* : of, relating to, or engaged in pharmacy or the manufacture and sale of medicinal drugs — **pharmaceutical** *n*

phar·ma·col·o·gy \ˌfär-mə-'kä-lə-jē\ *n* **1** : the science of drugs esp. as related to medicinal uses **2** : the reactions and properties of one or more drugs — **phar·ma·co·log·i·cal** \-ji-kəl\ *also* **phar·ma·co·log·ic** \-kə-'lä-jik\ *adj* — **phar·ma·col·o·gist** \-'kä-lə-jist\ *n*

phar·ma·co·poe·ia *also* **phar·ma·co·pe·ia** \-kə-'pē-ə\ *n* **1** : a book describing drugs and medicinal preparations **2** : a stock of drugs

phar·ma·cy \'fär-mə-sē\ *n, pl* **-cies 1** : the art, practice, or profession of preparing and dispensing medical drugs **2** : DRUGSTORE — **phar·ma·cist** \-sist\ *n*

phar·ynx \'far-iŋks\ *n, pl* **pha·ryn·ges** \fə-'rin-ˌjēz\ *also* **phar·ynx·es** : the space just back of the mouth into which the nostrils, esophagus, and trachea open — **pha·ryn·ge·al** \fə-'rin-jəl, ˌfar-ən-'jē-əl\ *adj*

phase \'fāz\ *n* **1** : a particular appearance in a recurring series of changes ⟨∼s of the moon⟩ **2** : a stage or interval in a process or cycle ⟨first ∼ of an experiment⟩ **3** : an aspect or part under consideration — **pha·sic** \'fā-zik\ *adj*

phase in *vb* : to introduce in stages

phase·out \'fā-ˌzaút\ *n* : a gradual stopping of operations or production

phase out *vb* : to stop production or use of in stages

PhD *abbr* [L *philosophiae doctor*] doctor of philosophy

pheas·ant \'fez-ᵊnt\ *n, pl* **pheasant** *or* **pheasants** : any of numerous long-tailed brilliantly colored game birds related to the domestic chicken

pheasant

phen·cy·cli·dine \,fen-'sī-klə-,dēn\ *n* : a drug used esp. as a veterinary anesthetic and sometimes illicitly to induce vivid mental imagery

phe·no·bar·bi·tal \,fē-nō-'bär-bə-,tól\ *n* : a crystalline drug used as a hypnotic and sedative

phe·nol \'fē-,nòl\ *n* : a corrosive poisonous acidic compound present in coal and wood tars and used in solution as a disinfectant

phe·nom·e·non \fi-'nä-mə-,nän, -nən\ *n, pl* **-na** \-nə\ *or* **-nons** [LL *phaenomenon,* fr. Gk *phainomenon,* fr. neut. of *phainomenos,* prp. of *phainesthai* to appear] **1** *pl* **-na** : an observable fact or event **2** : an outward sign of the working of a law of nature **3** *pl* **-nons** : an extraordinary person or thing : PRODIGY — **phe·nom·e·nal** \-'nä-mən-ᵊl\ *adj* — **phe·nom·e·non·al·ly** *adv*

pher·o·mone \'fer-ə-,mōn\ *n* : a chemical substance that is produced by an animal and serves to stimulate a behavioral response in other individuals of the same species — **pher·o·mon·al** \,fer-ə-'mōn-ᵊl\ *adj*

phi \'fī\ *n* : the 21st letter of the Greek alphabet — Φ or φ

phi·al \'fī-əl\ *n* : VIAL

Phil *abbr* Philippians

phi·lan·der \fə-'lan-dər\ *vb* **1** : to make love without serious intent **2** : to have many love affairs — **phi·lan·der·er** *n*

phi·lan·thro·py \fə-'lan-thrə-pē\ *n, pl* **-pies 1** : goodwill toward all people; *esp* : effort to promote human welfare **2** : a charitable act or gift; *also* : an organization that distributes or is supported by donated funds — **phi·lan·throp·ic** \,fi-lən-'thrä-pik\ *adj* — **phi·lan·throp·i·cal·ly** \-pi-k(ə-)lē\ *adv* — **phi·lan·thro·pist** \fə-'lan-thrə-pist\ *n*

phi·lat·e·ly \fə-'lat-ᵊl-ē\ *n* : the collection and study of postage and imprinted stamps — **phi·lat·e·lic** \,fi-lə-'te-lik\ *adj* — **phi·lat·e·list** \-ᵊl-ist\ *n*

Phi·le·mon \fə-'lē-mən, fī-\ *n* — see BIBLE table

Phi·lip·pi·ans \fə-'li-pē-ənz\ *n* — see BIBLE table

phi·lip·pic \fə-'li-pik\ *n* : TIRADE

Phil·lips \'fi-ləps\ *adj* : of, relating to, or being a screw having a head with a cross slot or its corresponding screwdriver

phi·lis·tine \'fi-lə-,stēn; fə-'lis-tən\ *n, often cap* [*Philistine,* inhabitant of ancient Philistia (Palestine)] : a person who is smugly insensitive or indifferent to intellectual or artistic values — **philistine** *adj, often cap*

philo·den·dron \,fi-lə-'den-drən\ *n, pl* **-drons** *or* **-dra** \-drə\ [NL, fr. Gk, neut. of *philodendros* loving trees, fr. *philos* dear, friendly + *dendron* tree] : any of various plants of the arum family grown for their showy foliage

phi·lol·o·gy \fə-'lä-lə-jē\ *n* **1** : the study of literature and relevant fields **2** : LINGUISTICS; *esp* : historical and comparative linguistics — **phil·o·log·i·cal** \,fi-lə-'lä-ji-kəl\ *adj* — **phi·lol·o·gist** \fə-'lä-lə-jist\ *n*

philos *abbr* philosopher; philosophy

phi·los·o·pher \fə-'lä-sə-fər\ *n* **1** : a reflective thinker : SCHOLAR **2** : a student of or specialist in philosophy **3** : a person whose philosophical perspective makes it possible to meet trouble calmly

phi·los·o·phize \fə-'lä-sə-,fīz\ *vb* **-phized; -phiz·ing 1** : to reason like a philosopher : THEORIZE **2** : to expound a philosophy esp. superficially

phi·los·o·phy \fə-'lä-sə-fē\ *n, pl* **-phies 1** : sciences and liberal arts exclusive of medicine, law, and theology ⟨doctor of ∼⟩ **2** : a critical study of fundamental beliefs and the grounds for them **3** : a system of philosophical concepts ⟨Aristotelian ∼⟩ **4** : a basic theory concerning a particular subject or sphere of activity **5** : the sum of the ideas and convictions of an individual or group ⟨her ∼ of life⟩ **6** : calmness of temper and judgment — **phil·o·soph·ic** \,fi-lə-'sä-fik\ *or* **phil·o·soph·i·cal** \-fi-kəl\ *adj* — **phil·o·soph·i·cal·ly** \-k(ə-)lē\ *adv*

phil·ter *or* **phil·tre** \'fil-tər\ *n* **1** : a potion, drug, or charm held to arouse sexual passion **2** : a magic potion

phle·bi·tis \fli-'bī-təs\ *n* : inflammation of a vein

phle·bot·o·my \fli-'bä-tə-mē\ *n, pl* **-mies** : the opening of a vein esp. for removing or releasing blood

phlegm \'flem\ *n* : thick mucus secreted in abnormal quantity esp. in the nose and throat

phleg·mat·ic \fleg-'ma-tik\ *adj* : having or showing a slow and stolid temperament **syn** impassive, apathetic, stoic

phlo·em \'flō-,em\ *n* : a vascular plant tissue external to the xylem that carries dissolved food material and functions in support and storage

phlox \'fläks\ *n, pl* **phlox** *or* **phlox·es** : any of a genus of American herbs that have tall stalks with showy spreading terminal clusters of flowers

pho·bia \'fō-bē-ə\ *n* : an irrational persistent fear or dread

phoe·be \'fē-(,)bē\ *n* : a flycatcher of the eastern U.S. that has a slight crest and is grayish brown above and yellowish white below

phoe·nix \'fē-niks\ *n* : a legendary bird held to live for centuries and then to burn itself to death and rise fresh and young from its ashes

phon *abbr* phonetics

¹phone \'fōn\ *n* **1** : TELEPHONE **2** : EARPHONE

²phone *vb* **phoned; phon·ing** : TELEPHONE

pho·neme \'fō-,nēm\ *n* : one of the elementary units of speech that distinguish one utterance from another — **pho·ne·mic** \fō-'nē-mik\ *adj*

pho·net·ics \fə-'ne-tiks\ *n* : the study and systematic classification of the sounds made in spoken utterance — **pho·net·ic** \-tik\ *adj* — **pho·ne·ti·cian** \,fō-nə-'ti-shən\ *n*

pho·nic \'fä-nik\ *adj* **1** : of, relating to, or producing sound **2** : of or relating to the sounds of speech or to phonics — **pho·ni·cal·ly** \-ni-k(ə-)lē\ *adv*

pho·nics \'fä-niks\ *n* : a method of teaching people to read and pronounce words by learning the phonetic value of letters, letter groups, and esp. syllables

pho·no·graph \'fō-nə-,graf\ *n* : an instrument for reproducing sounds by means of the vibration of a needle following a spiral groove on a revolving disc

pho·nol·o·gy \fə-'nä-lə-jē\ *n* : a study and description of the sound changes in a language — **pho·no·log·i·cal** \,fō-nə-'lä-ji-kəl\ *adj* — **pho·nol·o·gist** \fə-'nä-lə-jist\ *n*

pho·ny *or* **pho·ney** \'fō-nē\ *adj* **pho·ni·er; -est** : marked by empty pretension : FAKE — **phony** *n*

phos·phate \'fäs-,fāt\ *n* : a salt of a phosphoric acid — **phos·phat·ic** \fäs-'fa-tik\ *adj*

phos·phor \'fäs-fər\ *n* : a phosphorescent substance

phos·pho·res·cence \,fäs-fə-'res-ᵊns\ *n* **1** : luminescence caused by radiation absorption followed by emission that continues after the incident radiation stops **2** : an enduring luminescence without sensible heat — **phos·pho·res·cent** \-ənt\ *adj* — **phos·pho·res·cent·ly** *adv*

phosphoric acid \ˌfäs-ˈfȯr-ik-, -ˈfär-\ *n* : any of several oxygen-containing acids of phosphorus

phos·pho·rus \ˈfäs-fə-rəs\ *n* [NL, fr. Gk *phōsphoros* light-bearing, fr. *phōs* light + *pherein* to carry, bring] : a nonmetallic chemical element that has characteristics similar to nitrogen and occurs widely esp. as phosphates — see ELEMENT table — **phos·phor·ic** \fäs-ˈfȯr-ik, -ˈfär-\ *adj* — **phos·pho·rous** \ˈfäs-fə-rəs; fäs-ˈfȯr-əs, -ˈfȯr-\ *adj*

phot- *or* **photo-** *comb form* **1** : light ⟨*photo*graphy⟩ **2** : photograph : photographic ⟨*photo*engraving⟩ **3** : photoelectric ⟨*photo*cell⟩

pho·to \ˈfō-tō\ *n, pl* **photos** : PHOTOGRAPH — **photo** *vb or adj*

pho·to·cell \ˈfō-tə-ˌsel\ *n* : PHOTOELECTRIC CELL

pho·to·chem·i·cal \ˌfō-tō-ˈke-mi-kəl\ *adj* : of, relating to, or resulting from the chemical action of radiant energy

pho·to·com·pose \-kəm-ˈpōz\ *vb* : to compose reading matter for reproduction by means of characters photographed on film — **pho·to·com·po·si·tion** \-ˌkäm-pə-ˈzi-shən\ *n*

pho·to·copy \ˈfō-tə-ˌkä-pē\ *n* : a photographic reproduction of graphic matter — **photocopy** *vb*

pho·to·elec·tric \ˌfō-tō-i-ˈlek-trik\ *adj* : relating to an electrical effect due to the interaction of light with matter — **pho·to·elec·tri·cal·ly** \-tri-k(ə-)lē\ *adv*

photoelectric cell *n* : a device whose electrical properties are modified by the action of light

pho·to·en·grave \ˌfō-tō-in-ˈgrāv\ *vb* : to make a photoengraving of

pho·to·en·grav·ing *n* : a process by which an etched printing plate is made from a photograph or drawing; *also* : a print made from such a plate

photo finish *n* : a race finish so close that a photograph of the finish is used to determine the winner

¹pho·tog \fə-ˈtäg\ *n* : PHOTOGRAPHER

²photog *abbr* photographic; photography

pho·to·gen·ic \ˌfō-tə-ˈje-nik\ *adj* : eminently suitable esp. aesthetically for being photographed

pho·to·graph \ˈfō-tə-ˌgraf\ *n* : a picture taken by photography — **photograph** *vb* — **pho·tog·ra·pher** \fə-ˈtä-grə-fər\ *n*

pho·tog·ra·phy \fə-ˈtä-grə-fē\ *n* : the art or process of producing images on a sensitized surface (as film in a camera) by the action of light — **pho·to·graph·ic** \ˌfō-tə-ˈgra-fik\ *adj* — **pho·to·graph·i·cal·ly** \-fi-k(ə-)lē\ *adv*

pho·to·gra·vure \ˌfō-tə-grə-ˈvyu̇r\ *n* : a process for making prints from an intaglio plate prepared by photographic methods

pho·to·li·thog·ra·phy \ˌfō-tō-li-ˈthä-grə-fē\ *n* : the process of photographically transferring a pattern to a surface for etching (as in making an integrated circuit)

pho·tom·e·ter \fō-ˈtä-mə-tər\ *n* : an instrument for measuring the intensity of light — **pho·to·met·ric** \ˌfō-tə-ˈme-trik\ *adj* — **pho·tom·e·try** \fō-ˈtä-mə-trē\ *n*

pho·to·mi·cro·graph \ˌfō-tə-ˈmī-krə-ˌgraf\ *n* : a photograph of a microscope image — **pho·to·mi·crog·ra·phy** \-mī-ˈkrä-grə-fē\ *n*

pho·ton \ˈfō-ˌtän\ *n* : a quantum of electromagnetic radiation

pho·to·play \ˈfō-tō-ˌplā\ *n* : MOTION PICTURE

pho·to·sen·si·tive \ˌfō-tō-ˈsen-sə-tiv\ *adj* : sensitive or sensitized to the action of radiant energy

pho·to·sphere \ˈfō-tə-ˌsfir\ *n* : the luminous surface of a star — **pho·to·spher·ic** \ˌfō-tə-ˈsfir-ik, -ˈsfer-\ *adj*

pho·to·syn·the·sis \ˌfō-tō-ˈsin-thə-səs\ *n* : the process by which chlorophyll-containing plants make carbohydrates from water and from carbon dioxide in the air in the presence of light — **pho·to·syn·the·size** \-ˌsīz\ *vb* — **pho·to·syn·thet·ic** \-sin-ˈthe-tik\ *adj*

phr *abbr* phrase

¹phrase \ˈfrāz\ *n* **1** : a brief expression **2** : a group of two or more grammatically related words that form a sense unit expressing a thought

²phrase *vb* **phrased; phras·ing** : to express in words

phrase·ol·o·gy \ˌfrā-zē-ˈä-lə-jē\ *n, pl* **-gies** : a manner of phrasing : STYLE

phras·ing *n* : style of expression

phre·net·ic \fri-ˈne-tik\ *adj* : FRENETIC

phren·ic \ˈfre-nik\ *adj* : of or relating to the diaphragm ⟨~ nerves⟩

phre·nol·o·gy \fri-ˈnä-lə-jē\ *n* : the study of the conformation of the skull based on the belief that it indicates mental faculties and character traits

phy·lac·tery \fə-ˈlak-tə-rē\ *n, pl* **-ter·ies** **1** : one of two small square leather boxes containing slips inscribed with scripture passages and traditionally worn on the left arm and forehead by Jewish men during morning weekday prayers **2** : AMULET

phy·lum \ˈfī-ləm\ *n, pl* **phy·la** \-lə\ [NL, fr. Gk *phylon* tribe, race] : a major division of the animal and in some classifications the plant kingdom; *also* : a group (as of people) apparently of common origin

phys *abbr* **1** physical **2** physics

¹phys·ic \ˈfi-zik\ *n* **1** : the profession of medicine **2** : MEDICINE; *esp* : PURGATIVE

²physic *vb* **phys·icked; phys·ick·ing** : PURGE 2

¹phys·i·cal \ˈfi-zi-kəl\ *adj* **1** : of or relating to nature or the laws of nature **2** : material as opposed to mental or spiritual **3** : of, relating to, or produced by the forces and operations of physics **4** : of or relating to the body — **phys·i·cal·ly** \-k(ə-)lē\ *adv*

²physical *n* : PHYSICAL EXAMINATION

physical education *n* : instruction in the development and care of the body ranging from simple calisthenics to training in hygiene, gymnastics, and the performance and management of athletic games

physical examination *n* : an examination of the bodily functions and condition of an individual

physical science *n* : any of the sciences (as physics and astronomy) that deal primarily with nonliving materials — **physical scientist** *n*

physical therapy *n* : the treatment of disease by physical and mechanical means (as massage, exercise, water, or heat) — **physical therapist** *n*

phy·si·cian \fə-ˈzi-shən\ *n* : a doctor of medicine

physician's assistant *n* : a person certified to provide basic medical care usu. under a licensed physician's supervision

phys·i·cist \ˈfi-zə-sist\ *n* : a scientist who specializes in physics

phys·ics \ˈfi-ziks\ *n* [L *physica*, pl., natural sciences, fr. Gk *physika*, fr. *physis* growth, nature, fr. *phyein* to bring forth] **1** : the science of matter and energy and their interactions **2** : the physical properties and composition of something

phys·i·og·no·my \ˌfi-zē-ˈäg-nə-mē\ *n, pl* **-mies** : facial appearance esp. as a reflection of inner character

phys·i·og·ra·phy \ˌfi-zē-ˈä-grə-fē\ *n* : geography dealing with physical features of the earth — **phys·io·graph·ic** \ˌfi-zē-ō-ˈgra-fik\ *adj*

phys·i·ol·o·gy \ˌfi-zē-ˈä-lə-jē\ *n* **1** : a branch of biology dealing with the functions and functioning of living matter and organisms **2** : functional processes in an organism or any of its parts — **phys·i·o·log·i·cal** \-zē-ə-ˈlä-ji-kəl\ *or* **phys·i·o·log·ic** \-jik\ *adj* — **phys·i·o·log·i·cal·ly** \-ji-k(ə-)lē\ *adv* — **phys·i·ol·o·gist** \-zē-ˈä-lə-jist\ *n*

phys·io·ther·a·py \ˌfi-zē-ō-ˈther-ə-pē\ *n* : PHYSICAL THERAPY — **phys·io·ther·a·pist** \-pist\ *n*

phy·sique \fə-ˈzēk\ *n* : the build of a person's body : bodily constitution

phy·to·plank·ton \ˈfī-tō-ˌplaŋk-tən\ *n* : plant life of the plankton

pi \ˈpī\ *n, pl* **pis** \ˈpīz\ **1** : the 16th letter of the Greek alphabet — Π *or* π **2** : the symbol π denoting the ratio of the circumference of a circle to its diameter; *also* : the ratio itself equal to approximately 3.1416

PI *abbr* private investigator

pi·a·nis·si·mo \ˌpē-ə-ˈni-sə-ˌmō\ *adv or adj* : very softly — used as a direction in music

pi·a·nist \pē-ˈa-nist, ˈpē-ə-\ *n* : one who plays the piano

¹pi·a·no \pē-ˈä-nō\ *adv or adj* : SOFTLY — used as a direction in music

²piano \pē-ˈa-nō\ *n, pl* **pianos** [It, short for *pianoforte*, fr. *gravicembalo col piano e forte*, lit., harpsichord with soft and loud; fr. the fact that its tones could be varied in loudness] : a musical instrument having steel strings sounded by felt-covered hammers operated from a keyboard

pi·a·no·forte \pē-ˌa-nō-ˈfȯr-ˌtā, -tē; pē-ˈa-nə-ˌfȯrt\ *n* : PIANO

pi·as·tre *also* **pi·as·ter** \pē-ˈas-tər\ *n* — see *pound* at MONEY table

pi·az·za \pē-ˈa-zə, *esp for 1* -ˈat-sə\ *n, pl* **piazzas** *or* **pi·az·ze** \-ˈat-(ˌ)sä, -ˈät-\ [It, fr. L *platea* broad street] **1** : an open square esp. in an Italian town **2** : a long hall with an arched roof **3** *dial* : VERANDA, PORCH

pi·broch \ˈpē-ˌbräk\ *n* : a set of variations for the bagpipe

pic \ˈpik\ *n, pl* **pics** *or* **pix** \ˈpiks\ **1** : PHOTOGRAPH **2** : MOTION PICTURE

pi·ca \ˈpī-kə\ *n* : a typewriter type with 10 characters to the inch

pi·ca·resque \ˌpi-kə-ˈresk, ˌpē-\ *adj* : of or relating to rogues ⟨~ fiction⟩

pic·a·yune \ˌpi-kē-ˈyün\ *adj* : of little value : TRIVIAL; *also* : PETTY

pic·ca·lil·li \ˌpi-kə-ˈli-lē\ *n* : a relish of chopped vegetables and spices

pic·co·lo \ˈpi-kə-ˌlō\ *n, pl* **-los** [It, short for *piccolo flauto* small flute] : a small shrill flute pitched an octave higher than the ordinary flute

pice \ˈpīs\ *n, pl* **pice** : PAISA

¹pick \ˈpik\ *vb* **1** : to pierce or break up with a pointed instrument **2** : to remove bit by bit; *also* : to remove covering matter from **3** : to gather by plucking ⟨~ apples⟩ **4** : CULL, SELECT **5** : ROB ⟨~ a pocket⟩ **6** : PROVOKE ⟨~ a quarrel⟩ **7** : to dig into or pull lightly at **8** : to pluck with fingers or a pick **9** : to loosen or pull apart with a sharp point ⟨~ wool⟩ **10** : to unlock with a wire **11** : to eat sparingly — **pick·er** *n*

²pick *n* **1** : the act or privilege of choosing **2** : the best or choicest one **3** : the part of a crop gathered at one time

³pick *n* **1** : a heavy wooden-handled tool pointed at one or both ends **2** : a pointed implement used for picking **3** : a small thin piece (as of plastic) used to pluck the strings of a stringed instrument

pick·a·back \ˈpi-gē-ˌbak, ˈpi-kə-\ *var of* PIGGYBACK

pick·ax \ˈpik-ˌaks\ *n* : ³PICK 1

pick·er·el \ˈpi-kə-rəl\ *n, pl* **pickerel** *or* **pickerels** : either of two bony fishes related to the pikes; *also* : WALLEYE 2

pickerel

pick·er·el·weed \-ˌwēd\ *n* : an American shallow-water herb that bears spikes of blue flowers

¹pick·et \ˈpi-kət\ *n* **1** : a pointed stake (as for a fence) **2** : a detached body of soldiers on outpost duty; *also* : SENTINEL **3** : a person posted by a labor union where workers are on strike; *also* : a person posted for a protest

²picket *vb* **1** : to guard with pickets **2** : TETHER **3** : to

post pickets at ⟨~ a factory⟩ **4** : to serve as a picket

pick·ings \ˈpi-kiŋz, -kənz\ *n pl* **1** : gleanable or eatable fragments : SCRAPS **2** : yield for effort expended : RETURN

pick·le \ˈpi-kəl\ *n* **1** : a brine or vinegar solution for preserving foods; *also* : a food (as a cucumber) preserved in a pickle **2** : a difficult situation : PLIGHT — **pickle** *vb*

pick·lock \ˈpik-ˌläk\ *n* **1** : BURGLAR, THIEF **2** : a tool for picking locks

pick·pock·et \ˈpik-ˌpä-kət\ *n* : one who steals from pockets

pick·up \ˈpik-ˌəp\ *n* **1** : a hitchhiker who is given a ride **2** : a temporary chance acquaintance **3** : a picking up **4** : revival of business activity **5** : ACCELERATION **6** : the conversion of mechanical movements into electrical impulses in the reproduction of sound; *also* : a device for making such conversion **7** : a light truck having an enclosed cab and an open body with low sides and a tailgate

pick up *vb* **1** : to take hold of and lift **2** : IMPROVE **3** : to put in order

picky \ˈpi-kē\ *adj* **pick·i·er; -est** : FUSSY, FINICKY

¹pic·nic \ˈpik-ˌnik\ *n* : an outing with food usu. provided by members of the group and eaten in the open

²picnic *vb* **pic·nicked; pic·nick·ing** : to go on a picnic : eat in picnic fashion

pi·cot \ˈpē-ˌkō\ *n* : one of a series of small loops forming an edging on ribbon or lace

pic·to·ri·al \pik-ˈtȯr-ē-əl\ *adj* : of, relating to, or consisting of pictures

¹pic·ture \ˈpik-chər\ *n* **1** : a representation made by painting, drawing, or photography **2** : a vivid description in words **3** : IMAGE, COPY **4** : a transitory visual image (as on a TV screen) **5** : MOTION PICTURE **6** : SITUATION

²picture *vb* **pic·tured; pic·tur·ing** **1** : to paint or draw a picture of **2** : to describe vividly in words **3** : to form a mental image of

pic·tur·esque \ˌpik-chə-ˈresk\ *adj* **1** : resembling a picture ⟨a ~ landscape⟩ **2** : CHARMING, QUAINT ⟨a ~ character⟩ **3** : GRAPHIC, VIVID ⟨a ~ account⟩ — **pic·tur·esque·ness** *n*

picture tube *n* : a cathode-ray tube on which the picture in a television set appears

pid·dle \ˈpid-ᵊl\ *vb* **pid·dled; pid·dling** : to act or work idly : DAWDLE

pid·dling \ˈpid-ᵊl-ən, -iŋ\ *adj* : TRIVIAL, PALTRY

pid·gin \ˈpi-jən\ *n* [fr. *pidgin English*, fr. Chinese Pidgin English *pidgin* business] : a simplified speech used for communication between people with different languages

pie \ˈpī\ *n* : a dish consisting of a pastry crust and a filling (as of fruit or meat)

¹pie·bald \ˈpī-ˌbȯld\ *adj* : of different colors; *esp* : blotched with white and black ⟨a ~ horse⟩

²piebald *n* : a piebald animal

¹piece \ˈpēs\ *n* **1** : a part of a whole : FRAGMENT **2** : one of a group, set, or mass ⟨chess ~⟩; *also* : a single item ⟨a ~ of news⟩ **3** : a length, weight, or size in which something is made or sold **4** : a product (as an essay) of creative work **5** : FIREARM **6** : COIN

²piece *vb* **pieced; piec·ing** **1** : to repair or complete by adding pieces : PATCH **2** : to join into a whole

pièce de ré·sis·tance \pē-ˌes-də-rä-ˈzē-ˈstäns\ *n, pl* **pièces de ré·sis·tance** *same*\ [F] **1** : the chief dish of a meal **2** : an outstanding item

piece·meal \ˈpēs-ˌmēl\ *adv or adj* : one piece at a time : GRADUALLY

piece·work \-ˌwərk\ *n* : work done and paid for by the piece — **piece·work·er** *n*

pie chart *n* : a circular chart that shows quantities or frequencies by parts of a circle shaped like pieces of pie

pied \ˈpīd\ *adj* : of two or more colors in blotches : VARIEGATED

pied–à–terre \pē-ıȧ-də-'ter\ n, pl **pieds-à-terre** \same\ [F, lit., foot to the ground] : a temporary or second lodging

pier \'pir\ n 1 : a support for a bridge span 2 : a structure built out into the water for use as a landing place or a promenade or to protect or form a harbor 3 : an upright supporting part (as a pillar) of a building or structure

pierce \'pirs\ vb **pierced; pierc·ing 1** : to enter or thrust into sharply or painfully : STAB **2** : to make a hole in or through : PERFORATE **3** : to force or make a way into or through : PENETRATE **4** : to see through : DISCERN

pies pl of PI or of PIE

pi·ety \'pī-ə-tē\ n, pl **pi·et·ies 1** : fidelity to natural obligations (as to parents) **2** : dutifulness in religion : DEVOUTNESS **3** : a pious act

pif·fle \'pi-fəl\ n : trifling talk or action

pig \'pig\ n 1 : SWINE; esp : a young swine **2** : PORK **3** : one that resembles a pig (as in dirtiness or greed) **4** : a crude casting of metal (as iron)

pi·geon \'pi-jən\ n : any of numerous stout-bodied short-legged birds with smooth thick plumage

¹pi·geon·hole \'pi-jən-ıhōl\ n : a small open compartment (as in a desk) for keeping letters or documents

²pigeonhole vb 1 : to place in or as if in a pigeonhole : FILE **2** : to lay aside 3 : CLASSIFY

pi·geon–toed \-ıtōd\ adj : having the toes turned in

pig·gish \'pi-gish\ adj 1 : GREEDY **2** : STUBBORN

pig·gy·back \'pi-gē-ıbak\ adv or adj 1 : up on the back and shoulders **2** : on a railroad flatcar

pig·head·ed \'pig-'he-dəd\ adj : OBSTINATE, STUBBORN

pig latin n, often cap L : a jargon that is made by systematic alteration of English

pig·let \'pi-glət\ n : a small usu. young swine

pig·ment \'pig-mənt\ n 1 : coloring matter **2** : a powder mixed with a liquid to give color (as in paints)

pig·men·ta·tion \ıpig-mən-'tā-shən\ n : coloration with or deposition of pigment; esp : an excessive deposition of bodily pigment

pig·my var of PYGMY

pig·nut \'pig-ınət\ n : the bitter nut of any of several hickory trees; also : any of these trees

pig·pen \-ıpen\ n 1 : a pen for pigs **2** : a dirty place

pig·skin \-ıskin\ n 1 : the skin of a swine or leather made of it **2** : FOOTBALL 2

pig·sty \-ıstī\ n : PIGPEN

pig·tail \-ıtāl\ n : a tight braid of hair

pi·ka \'pī-kə\ n : any of various small short-eared mammals related to the rabbits and occurring in rocky uplands of Asia and western No. America

¹pike \'pīk\ n : a sharp point or spike

²pike n, pl **pike** or **pikes** : a large slender long=snouted freshwater bony fish valued for food; also : any of various related fishes

³pike n : a long wooden shaft with a pointed steel head formerly used as a foot soldier's weapon

⁴pike n : TURNPIKE

pik·er \'pī-kər\ n 1 : one who does things in a small way or on a small scale **2** : TIGHTWAD, CHEAPSKATE

pike·staff \'pīk-ıstaf\ n : the staff of a foot soldier's pike

pi·laf or **pi·laff** \pi-'läf, 'pē-ıläf\ or **pi·lau** \pi-'lō, -'lȯ, 'pē-lō, -lȯ\ n : a dish of seasoned rice often with meat

pi·las·ter \pi-'las-tər, 'pī-ılas-tər\ n : an architectural support that looks like a rectangular column and projects slightly from a wall

pil·chard \'pil-chərd\ n : any of several fishes related to the herrings and often packed as sardines

¹pile \'pīl\ n : a long slender column (as of wood or steel) driven into the ground to support a vertical load

²pile n 1 : a quantity of things heaped together **2** : PYRE **3** : a great number or quantity : LOT

³pile vb **piled; pil·ing 1** : to lay in a pile : STACK **2** : to heap up : ACCUMULATE **3** : to press forward in a mass : CROWD

⁴pile n : a velvety surface of fine short hairs or threads (as on cloth) — **piled** \'pīld\ adj — **pile·less** adj

piles \'pīlz\ n pl : HEMORRHOIDS

pil·fer \'pil-fər\ vb : to steal in small quantities

pil·grim \'pil-grəm\ n [ME, fr. OF peligrin, fr. LL pelegrinus, alter. of L peregrinus foreigner, fr. peregrinus foreign, fr. peregri abroad, fr. per through + ager land] 1 : one who journeys in foreign lands : WAYFARER **2** : one who travels to a shrine or holy place as an act of devotion **3** cap : one of the English settlers founding Plymouth colony in 1620

pil·grim·age \-grə-mij\ n : a journey of a pilgrim esp. to a shrine or holy place

pil·ing \'pī-liŋ\ n : a structure of piles

pill \'pil\ n 1 : a medicine in a small rounded mass to be swallowed whole **2** : a disagreeable or tiresome person **3** often cap : an oral contraceptive — usu. used with the

pil·lage \'pi-lij\ vb **pil·laged; pil·lag·ing** : to take booty : LOOT, PLUNDER — **pillage** n — **pil·lag·er** n

pil·lar \'pi-lər\ n 1 : a strong upright support (as for a roof) **2** : a column or shaft standing alone esp. as a monument — **pil·lared** \-lərd\ adj

pill·box \'pil-ıbäks\ n 1 : a shallow round box for pills **2** : a low concrete emplacement esp. for machine guns

pil·lion \'pil-yən\ n 1 : a pad or cushion placed behind a saddle for an extra rider **2** chiefly Brit : a motorcycle or bicycle saddle for a passenger

¹pil·lo·ry \'pi-lə-rē\ n, pl **-ries** : a wooden frame for public punishment having holes in which the head and hands can be locked

²pillory vb **-ried; -ry·ing 1** : to set in a pillory **2** : to expose to public scorn

¹pil·low \'pi-lō\ n : a case filled with springy material (as feathers) and used to support the head of a resting person

²pillow vb : to rest or place on or as if on a pillow; also : to serve as a pillow for

pil·low·case \-ıkās\ n : a removable covering for a pillow

¹pi·lot \'pī-lət\ n 1 : HELMSMAN, STEERSMAN **2** : a person qualified and licensed to take ships into and out of a port **3** : GUIDE, LEADER **4** : one that flies an aircraft or spacecraft **5** : a television show filmed or taped as a sample of a proposed series — **pi·lot·less** adj

²pilot vb : CONDUCT, GUIDE; esp : to act as pilot of

³pilot adj : serving as a guiding or activating device or as a testing or trial unit ⟨a ∼ light⟩ ⟨a ∼ factory⟩

pi·lot·house \'pī-lət-ıhaȯs\ n : a shelter on the upper deck of a ship for the steering gear and the helmsman

pil·sner also **pil·sen·er** \'pilz-nər, 'pil-zə-\ n [G, lit., of Pilsen (Plzeň), city in the Czech Republic] 1 : a light beer with a strong flavor of hops **2** : a tall slender footed glass for beer

pi·men·to \pə-'men-tō\ n, pl **pimentos** or **pimento** [Sp pimienta allspice, pepper, fr. LL pigmenta, pl. of pigmentum plant juice, fr. L, pigment] 1 : ALLSPICE **2** : PIMIENTO

pi·mien·to \pə-'men-tō\ n, pl **-tos** : any of various mild red sweet pepper fruits used esp. to stuff olives and to make paprika

pimp \'pimp\ n : a man who solicits clients for a prostitute — **pimp** vb

pim·per·nel \'pim-pər-ınel, -nəl\ n : any of a genus of herbs related to the primroses

pim·ple \'pim-pəl\ n : a small inflamed swelling on the skin often containing pus — **pim·ply** \-p(ə-)lē\ adj

pin \'pin\ n 1 : a piece of wood or metal used esp. for fastening articles together or as a support by which one article may be suspended from another; esp : a small pointed piece of wire with a head used for fastening clothes or attaching papers **2** : an ornament or emblem fastened to clothing with a pin **3** : one of the wooden pieces constituting the target (as in bowling); *also* : the staff of the flag marking a hole on a golf course **4** : LEG

²**pin** *vb* **pinned; pin·ning 1** : to fasten, join, or secure with a pin **2** : to hold fast or immobile **3** : ATTACH, HANG ⟨*pinned* their hopes on one man⟩ **4** : to assign the blame for ⟨~ a crime on someone⟩ **5** : to define clearly : ESTABLISH ⟨~ down an idea⟩

PIN *abbr* personal identification number

pi·ña co·la·da \ˌpēn-yə-kō-ˈlä-də, ˌpē-nə-\ *n* [Sp, lit., strained pineapple] : a tall drink made of rum, cream of coconut, and pineapple juice mixed with ice

pin·afore \ˈpi-nə-ˌfȯr\ *n* : a sleeveless dress or apron fastened at the back

pince–nez \ˈpaⁿs-ˈnā\ *n, pl* **pince–nez** *same or* -ˈnāz\ [F, lit., pinch-nose] : eyeglasses clipped to the nose by a spring

pin·cer \ˈpin-sər\ *n* **1** *pl* : a gripping instrument with two handles and two grasping jaws **2** : a claw (as of a lobster) resembling pincers

¹**pinch** \ˈpinch\ *vb* **1** : to squeeze between the finger and thumb or between the jaws of an instrument **2** : to compress painfully **3** : CONTRACT, SHRIVEL **4** : to be miserly; *also* : to subject to strict economy **5** : to confine or limit narrowly **6** : STEAL **7** : ARREST

²**pinch** *n* **1** : a critical point : EMERGENCY **2** : painful effect **3** : an act of pinching **4** : a very small quantity **5** : ARREST

³**pinch** *adj* : SUBSTITUTE ⟨a ~ runner⟩

pinch–hit \ˌpinch-ˈhit\ *vb* **1** : to bat in the place of another player esp. when a hit is particularly needed **2** : to act or serve in place of another — **pinch hit** *n* — **pinch hitter** *n*

pin curl *n* : a curl made usu. by dampening a strand of hair, coiling it, and securing it by a hairpin or clip

pin·cush·ion \ˈpin-ˌku̇-shən\ *n* : a cushion for pins not in use

¹**pine** \ˈpīn\ *n* : any of a genus of evergreen cone-bearing trees; *also* : the light durable resinous wood of a pine

²**pine** *vb* **pined; pin·ing 1** : to lose vigor or health through distress **2** : to long for something intensely

pi·ne·al \ˈpī-nē-əl, pī-ˈnē-əl\ *n* : PINEAL GLAND — **pineal** *adj*

pineal gland *n* : a small usu. conical appendage of the brain of all vertebrates with a cranium that functions primarily as an endocrine organ

pine·ap·ple \ˈpīn-ˌa-pəl\ *n* : a tropical plant bearing an edible juicy fruit; *also* : its fruit

pin·feath·er \ˈpin-ˌfe-thər\ *n* : a new feather just coming through the skin

ping \ˈpiŋ\ *n* **1** : a sharp sound like that of a bullet striking **2** : engine knock

pin·hole \ˈpin-ˌhōl\ *n* : a small hole made by, for, or as if by a pin

¹**pin·ion** \ˈpin-yən\ *n* : the end section of a bird's wing; *also* : WING

²**pinion** *vb* : to restrain by binding the arms; *also* : SHACKLE

³**pinion** *n* : a gear with a small number of teeth designed to mesh with a larger wheel or rack

¹**pink** \ˈpiŋk\ *n* **1** : any of a genus of plants with narrow leaves often grown for their showy flowers **2** : the highest degree : HEIGHT ⟨the ~ of condition⟩

²**pink** *n* : a light tint of red

³**pink** *adj* **1** : of the color pink **2** : holding socialistic views — **pink·ish** *adj*

⁴**pink** *vb* **1** : to perforate in an ornamental pattern **2** : PIERCE, STAB **3** : to cut a saw-toothed edge on

pink elephants *n pl* : hallucinations arising esp. from heavy drinking or use of narcotics

pink·eye \ˈpiŋk-ˌī\ *n* : an acute contagious eye inflammation

pin·kie *or* **pin·ky** \ˈpiŋ-kē\ *n, pl* **pinkies** : the smallest finger of the hand

pin·nace \ˈpi-nəs\ *n* **1** : a light sailing ship **2** : a ship's boat

pin·na·cle \ˈpi-ni-kəl\ *n* [ME *pinacle*, fr. MF, fr. LL *pinnaculum* small wing, gable, fr. L *pinna* wing, battlement] **1** : a turret ending in a small spire **2** : a lofty peak **3** : ACME

pin·nate \ˈpi-ˌnāt\ *adj* : resembling a feather esp. in having similar parts arranged on each side of an axis ⟨a ~ leaf⟩ — **pin·nate·ly** *adv*

pi·noch·le \ˈpē-nə-kəl\ *n* : a card game played with a 48-card deck

pi·ñon *or* **pin·yon** \ˈpin-ˌyōn, -ˌyän\ *n, pl* **pi·ñons** *or* **pin·yons** *or* **pi·ño·nes** \-ˌyō-nēz\ [AmerSp *piñón*] : any of various low-growing pines of western No. America with edible seeds; *also* : the edible seed of a piñon

pin·point \ˈpin-ˌpȯint\ *vb* : to locate, hit, or aim with great precision

pin·prick \-ˌprik\ *n* **1** : a small puncture made by or as if by a pin **2** : a petty irritation or annoyance

pins and needles *n pl* : a pricking tingling sensation in a limb growing numb or recovering from numbness — **on pins and needles** : in a nervous or jumpy state of anticipation

pin·stripe \ˈpin-ˌstrīp\ *n* : a narrow stripe on a fabric; *also* : a suit with such stripes — **pin–striped** \-ˌstrīpt\ *adj*

pint \ˈpīnt\ *n* — see WEIGHT table

pin·to \ˈpin-ˌtō\ *n, pl* **pintos** *also* **pintoes** : a spotted horse or pony

pinto bean *n* : a spotted seed produced by a kind of kidney bean and used for food

pin·up \ˈpin-ˌəp\ *adj* : suitable or designed for hanging on a wall; *also* : suited (as by beauty) to be the subject of a pinup photograph

pin·wheel \-ˌhwēl, -ˌwēl\ *n* **1** : a fireworks device in the form of a revolving wheel of colored fire **2** : a toy consisting of lightweight vanes that revolve at the end of a stick

pin·worm \-ˌwərm\ *n* : a nematode worm parasitic in the human intestine

pin·yin \ˈpin-ˈyin\ *n, often cap* : a system for writing Chinese ideograms by using Roman letters to represent the sounds

¹**pi·o·neer** \ˌpī-ə-ˈnir\ *n* **1** : one that originates or helps open up a new line of thought or activity **2** : an early settler in a territory

²**pioneer** *vb* **1** : to act as a pioneer **2** : to open or prepare for others to follow; *also* : SETTLE

pi·ous \ˈpī-əs\ *adj* **1** : marked by reverence for deity : DEVOUT **2** : excessively or affectedly religious **3** : SACRED, DEVOTIONAL **4** : showing loyal reverence for a person or thing : DUTIFUL **5** : marked by sham or hypocrisy — **pi·ous·ly** *adv*

¹**pip** \ˈpip\ *n* : one of the dots used on dice and dominoes to indicate numerical value

²**pip** *n* : a small fruit seed (as of an apple)

¹**pipe** \ˈpīp\ *n* **1** : a tubular musical instrument played by forcing air through it **2** : BAGPIPE **3** : a tube designed to conduct something (as water, steam, or oil) **4** : a device for smoking having a tube with a bowl at one end and a mouthpiece at the other

²**pipe** *vb* **piped; pip·ing 1** : to play on a pipe **2** : to speak in a high or shrill voice **3** : to convey by or as if by pipes — **pip·er** *n*

pipe down *vb* : to stop talking or making noise

pipe dream *n* : an illusory or fantastic hope

pipe·line \ˈpīp-ˌlīn\ *n* **1** : a line of pipe with pumps, valves, and control devices for conveying fluids **2** : a channel for information

pi·pette *or* **pi·pet** \pī-ˈpet\ *n* : a device for measuring and transferring small volumes of liquid

pipe up *vb* : to speak loudly and distinctly; *also* : to express an opinion freely

pip·ing \ˈpī-piŋ\ *n* **1** : the music of pipes **2** : a narrow fold of material used to decorate edges or seams

piping hot *adj* : very hot

pip·pin \'pi-pən\ *n* : any of several yellowish apples

pip–squeak \'pip-ˌskwēk\ *n* : one that is small or insignificant

pi·quant \'pē-kənt\ *adj* 1 : pleasantly savory : PUNGENT 2 : engagingly provocative; *also* : having a lively charm — **pi·quan·cy** \-kən-sē\ *n*

¹**pique** \'pēk\ *n* [F] : a passing feeling of wounded vanity : RESENTMENT

²**pique** *vb* **piqued; piqu·ing** 1 : IRRITATE 1 2 : to arouse by a provocation or challenge : GOAD

pi·qué *or* **pi·que** \pi-'kā\ *n* : a durable ribbed clothing fabric

pi·quet \pi-'kā\ *n* : a 2-handed card game played with 32 cards

pi·ra·cy \'pī-rə-sē\ *n, pl* **-cies** 1 : robbery on the high seas; *also* : an act resembling such robbery 2 : the unauthorized use of another's production or invention

pi·ra·nha \pə-'rä-nə, -'rän-yə\ *n* [Pg, fr. Tupi (So. American Indian language) *piráya,* fr. *pira* fish + *áya* tooth] : any of various usu. small So. American fishes with sharp teeth that include some known to attack humans and large animals

pi·rate \'pī-rət\ *n* [ME, fr. MF or L; MF, fr. L *pirata,* fr. Gk *peiratēs,* fr. *peiran* to attempt, test] : one who commits piracy — **pirate** *vb* — **pi·rat·i·cal** \pə-'ra-ti-kəl, pī-\ *adj*

pir·ou·ette \ˌpir-ə-'wet\ *n* [F] : a rapid whirling about of the body; *esp* : a full turn on the toe or ball of one foot in ballet — **pirouette** *vb*

pis *pl of* PI

pis·ca·to·ri·al \ˌpis-kə-'tōr-ē-əl\ *adj* : of or relating to fishing

Pi·sces \'pī-sēz\ *n* [ME, fr. L, lit., fishes] 1 : a zodiacal constellation between Aquarius and Aries usu. pictured as a fish 2 : the 12th sign of the zodiac in astrology; *also* : one born under this sign

pis·mire \'pis-ˌmīr\ *n* : ANT

pi·so \'pē-(ˌ)sō\ *n* : the peso of the Philippines

pis·ta·chio \pə-'sta-shē-ˌō, -'stä-\ *n, pl* **-chios** : the greenish edible seed of a small Asian tree related to the sumacs; *also* : the tree

pis·til \'pist-ᵊl\ *n* : the female reproductive organ in a flower — **pis·til·late** \'pis-tə-ˌlāt\ *adj*

pis·tol \'pist-ᵊl\ *n* : a handgun whose chamber is integral with the barrel

pis·tol–whip \-ˌhwip\ *vb* : to beat with a pistol

pis·ton \'pis-tən\ *n* : a sliding piece that receives and transmits motion and that usu. consists of a short cylinder inside a large cylinder

¹**pit** \'pit\ *n* 1 : a hole, shaft, or cavity in the ground 2 : an often sunken area designed for a particular use; *also* : an enclosed place (as for cockfights) 3 : HELL; *also, pl* : WORST ⟨it's the ~s⟩ 4 : a natural hollow or indentation in a surface 5 : a small indented mark or scar (as from disease or corrosion) 6 : an area beside a racecourse where cars are fueled and repaired during a race

²**pit** *vb* **pit·ted; pit·ting** 1 : to form pits in or become marred with pits 2 : to match for fighting

³**pit** *n* : the stony seed of some fruits (as the cherry, peach, and date)

⁴**pit** *vb* **pit·ted; pit·ting** : to remove the pit from

pi·ta \'pē-tə\ *n* [NGk] : a thin flat bread

pit–a–pat \ˌpi-ti-'pat\ *n* : PITTER-PATTER — **pit–a–pat** *adv or adj*

pit bull *n* : a powerful compact short-haired dog developed for fighting

¹**pitch** \'pich\ *n* 1 : a dark sticky substance left over esp. from distilling tar or petroleum 2 : resin from various conifers — **pitchy** *adj*

²**pitch** *vb* 1 : to erect and fix firmly in place ⟨~ a tent⟩ 2 : THROW, FLING 3 : to deliver a baseball to a batter 4 : to toss (as coins) toward a mark 5 : to set at a particular level ⟨~ the voice low⟩ 6 : to fall headlong 7

: to have the front end (as of a ship) alternately plunge and rise 8 : to incline downward : SLOPE

³**pitch** *n* 1 : the action or a manner of pitching 2 : degree of slope ⟨~ of a roof⟩ 3 : the relative level of some quality or state ⟨high ~ of excitement⟩ 4 : highness or lowness of sound; *also* : a standard frequency for tuning instruments 5 : an often high-pressure sales talk 6 : the delivery of a baseball to a batter; *also* : the baseball delivered

pitch·blende \'pich-ˌblend\ *n* : a dark mineral that is the chief source of uranium

¹**pitch·er** \'pi-chər\ *n* : a container for liquids that usu. has a lip and a handle

²**pitcher** *n* : one that pitches esp. in a baseball game

pitcher plant *n* : any of various plants with leaves modified to resemble pitchers in which insects are trapped and digested

pitch·fork \'pich-ˌfork\ *n* : a long-handled fork used esp. in pitching hay

pitch in *vb* 1 : to begin to work 2 : to contribute to a common effort

pitch·man \'pich-mən\ *n* : SALESMAN; *esp* : one who sells merchandise on the streets or from a concession

pit·e·ous \'pi-tē-əs\ *adj* : arousing pity : PITIFUL — **pit·e·ous·ly** *adv*

pit·fall \'pit-ˌfol\ *n* 1 : TRAP, SNARE; *esp* : a covered pit used for capturing animals 2 : a hidden danger or difficulty

pith \'pith\ *n* 1 : loose spongy tissue esp. in the center of the stem of vascular plants 2 : the essential part : CORE

pithy \'pi-thē\ *adj* **pith·i·er; -est** 1 : consisting of or filled with pith 2 : having substance and point : CONCISE

piti·able \'pi-tē-ə-bəl\ *adj* : PITIFUL

piti·ful \'pi-ti-fəl\ *adj* 1 : arousing or deserving pity ⟨a ~ sight⟩ 2 : MEAN, MEAGER — **piti·ful·ly** *adv*

piti·less \'pi-ti-ləs\ *adj* : devoid of pity : MERCILESS — **pit·i·less·ly** *adv*

pi·ton \'pē-ˌtän\ *n* [F] : a spike, wedge, or peg that can be driven into a rock or ice surface as a support

pit·tance \'pit-ᵊns\ *n* : a small portion, amount, or allowance

pit·ted \'pi-təd\ *adj* : marked with pits

pit·ter–pat·ter \'pi-tər-ˌpa-tər, 'pi-tē-\ *n* : a rapid succession of light taps or sounds — **pitter–patter** \ˌpi-tər-'pa-tər, ˌpi-tē-\ *adv or adj* — **pitter–patter** \same as adv\ *vb*

pi·tu·itary \pə-'tü-ə-ˌter-ē, -'tyü-\ *n, pl* **-itar·ies** : PITUITARY GLAND — **pituitary** *adj*

pituitary gland *n* : a small oval endocrine gland attached to the brain which produces various hormones that affect most basic bodily functions

pit viper *n* : any of various mostly New World venomous snakes with a sensory pit on each side of the head and hollow perforated fangs

¹**pity** \'pi-tē\ *n, pl* **pit·ies** [ME *pite,* fr. OF *pité,* fr. L *pietas* piety, pity, fr. *pius* pious] 1 : sympathetic sorrow : COMPASSION 2 : something to be regretted

²**pity** *vb* **pit·ied; pity·ing** : to feel pity for

¹**piv·ot** \'pi-vət\ *n* : a fixed pin on which something turns — **pivot** *adj* — **piv·ot·al** \'pi-vət-ᵊl\ *adj*

²**pivot** *vb* : to turn on or as if on a pivot

pix *pl of* PIC

pix·el \'pik-səl, -ˌsel\ *n* : any of the small elements that together make up an image (as on a television screen)

pix·ie *or* **pixy** \'pik-sē\ *n, pl* **pix·ies** : FAIRY; *esp* : a mischievous sprite

piz·za \'pēt-sə\ *n* [It] : an open pie made of rolled bread dough spread with a spiced mixture (as of tomatoes, cheese, and ground meat) and baked

piz·zazz *or* **pi·zazz** \pə-'zaz\ *n* 1 : GLAMOUR 2 : VITALITY

piz·ze·ria \ˌpēt-sə-'rē-ə\ *n* : an establishment where pizzas are made and sold

piz·zi·ca·to \ˌpit-si-'kä-tō\ *adv or adj* [It] : by means of plucking instead of bowing — used as a direction in music

pj's \\'pē-ˌjāz\\ *n pl* : PAJAMAS

pk *abbr* **1** park **2** peak **3** peck **4** pike

pkg *abbr* package

pkt *abbr* **1** packet **2** pocket

pkwy *abbr* parkway

pl *abbr* **1** place **2** plate **3** plural

¹plac·ard \\'pla-kərd, -ˌkärd\\ *n* : a notice posted in a public place : POSTER

²plac·ard \\-ˌkärd, -kərd\\ *vb* **1** : to cover with or as if with placards **2** : to announce by or as if by posting

pla·cate \\'plā-ˌkāt, 'pla-\\ *vb* **pla·cat·ed; pla·cat·ing** : to soothe esp. by concessions : APPEASE — **pla·ca·ble** \\'pla-kə-bəl, 'plā-\\ *adj*

¹place \\'plās\\ *n* [ME, fr. OF, open space, fr. L *platea* broad street, fr. Gk *plateia (hodos)*, fr. fem. of *platys* broad, flat] **1** : SPACE, ROOM **2** : an indefinite region : AREA **3** : a building or locality used for a special purpose **4** : a center of population **5** : a particular part of a surface ; SPOT **6** : relative position in a scale or sequence; *also* : position at the end of a competition ⟨last ~⟩ **7** : ACCOMMODATION; *esp* : SEAT **8** : the position of a figure within a numeral ⟨12 is a two ~ number⟩ **9** : JOB; *esp* : public office **10** : a public square **11** : 2d place at the finish (as of a horse race)

²place *vb* **placed; plac·ing** **1** : to put in a particular place : SET **2** : to distribute in an orderly manner : ARRANGE **3** : IDENTIFY **4** : to give an order for ⟨~ a bet⟩ **5** : to earn a given spot in a competition; *esp* : to come in 2d

pla·ce·bo \\plə-'sē-ˌbō\\ *n, pl* **-bos** [L, I shall please] : an inert medication used for its psychological effect or for purposes of comparison in an experiment

place·hold·er \\'plās-ˌhōl-dər\\ *n* : a symbol in a mathematical or logical expression that may be replaced by the name of any element of a set

place·kick \\-ˌkik\\ *n* : the kicking of a ball placed or held on the ground — **placekick** *vb* — **place·kick·er** *n*

place·ment \\'plās-mənt\\ *n* : an act or instance of placing

pla·cen·ta \\plə-'sen-tə\\ *n, pl* **-tas** *or* **-tae** \\-(ˌ)tē\\ [NL, fr. L, flat cake] : the organ in most mammals by which the fetus is joined to the maternal uterus and is nourished — **pla·cen·tal** \\-'sent-ᵊl\\ *adj*

plac·er \\'pla-sər\\ *n* : a deposit of sand or gravel containing particles of valuable mineral (as gold)

plac·id \\'pla-səd\\ *adj* : UNDISTURBED, PEACEFUL **syn** tranquil, serene, calm — **pla·cid·i·ty** \\pla-'si-də-tē\\ *n* — **plac·id·ly** *adv*

plack·et \\'pla-kət\\ *n* : a slit in a garment

pla·gia·rize \\'plā-jə-ˌrīz\\ *vb* **-rized; -riz·ing** : to present the ideas or words of another as one's own — **pla·gia·rism** \\-ˌri-zəm\\ *n* — **pla·gia·rist** \\-rist\\ *n*

¹plague \\'plāg\\ *n* **1** : a disastrous evil or influx; *also* : NUISANCE **2** : PESTILENCE; *esp* : a destructive contagious bacterial disease (as bubonic plague)

²plague *vb* **plagued; plagu·ing** **1** : to afflict with or as if with disease or disaster **2** : TEASE, TORMENT, HARASS

plaid \\'plad\\ *n* **1** : a rectangular length of tartan worn esp. over the left shoulder as part of the Scottish national costume **2** : a twilled woolen fabric with a tartan pattern **3** : a pattern of unevenly spaced repeated stripes crossing at right angles — **plaid** *adj*

¹plain \\'plān\\ *n* : an extensive area of level or rolling treeless country

²plain *adj* **1** : lacking ornament ⟨a ~ dress⟩ **2** : free of extraneous matter **3** : OPEN, UNOBSTRUCTED ⟨~ view⟩ **4** : EVIDENT, OBVIOUS **5** : easily understood : CLEAR **6** : CANDID, BLUNT **7** : SIMPLE, UNCOMPLICATED ⟨~ cooking⟩ **8** : lacking beauty or ugliness — **plain·ly** *adv* — **plain·ness** *n*

plain·clothes·man \\'plān-'klōthz-mən, -'klōz-, -ˌman\\

n : a police officer who wears civilian clothes instead of a uniform while on duty : DETECTIVE

plain·spo·ken \\-'spō-kən\\ *adj* : FRANK

plaint \\'plānt\\ *n* **1** : LAMENTATION, WAIL **2** : PROTEST, COMPLAINT

plain·tiff \\'plān-təf\\ *n* : the complaining party in a lawsuit

plain·tive \\'plān-tiv\\ *adj* : expressive of suffering or woe : MELANCHOLY — **plain·tive·ly** *adv*

plait \\'plāt, 'plat\\ *n* **1** : PLEAT **2** : a braid esp. of hair or straw — **plait** *vb*

¹plan \\'plan\\ *n* **1** : a drawing or diagram showing the parts or details of something **2** : a method for accomplishing an objective; *also* : GOAL, AIM

²plan *vb* **planned; plan·ning** **1** : to form a plan of ⟨~ a new city⟩ **2** : INTEND ⟨planned to go⟩ — **plan·ner** *n*

¹plane \\'plān\\ *vb* **planed; plan·ing** **1** : to smooth or level off with or as if with a plane — **plan·er** *n*

²plane *n* : PLANE TREE

³plane *n* : a tool for smoothing or shaping a wood surface

⁴plane *n* **1** : a level or flat surface **2** : a level of existence, consciousness, or development **3** : AIRPLANE

⁵plane *adj* **1** : FLAT, LEVEL **2** : dealing with flat surfaces or figures ⟨~ geometry⟩

plane·load \\'plān-ˌlōd\\ *n* : a load that fills an airplane

plan·et \\'pla-nət\\ *n* [ME *planete*, fr. OF, fr. LL *planeta*, modif. of Gk *planēt-, planēs*, lit., wanderer, fr. *planasthai* to wander] : any of the large bodies in the solar system that revolve around the sun — **plan·e·tary** \\-nə-ˌter-ē\\ *adj*

☞ For table, see next page.

plan·e·tar·i·um \\ˌpla-nə-'ter-ē-əm\\ *n, pl* **-i·ums** *or* **-ia** \\-ē-ə\\ : a building or room housing a device to project images of celestial bodies

plan·e·tes·i·mal \\ˌpla-nə-'tes-ə-məl\\ *n* : any of numerous small solid celestial bodies which may have existed during the formation of the solar system

plan·e·toid \\'pla-nə-ˌtȯid\\ *n* : a body resembling a planet; *esp* : ASTEROID

plane tree *n* : any of a genus of trees (as a sycamore) with large lobed leaves and globe-shaped fruit

plan·gent \\'plan-jənt\\ *adj* **1** : having a loud reverberating sound **2** : having an expressive esp. plaintive quality — **plan·gen·cy** \\-jən-sē\\ *n*

¹plank \\'plaŋk\\ *n* **1** : a heavy thick board **2** : an article in the platform of a political party

²plank *vb* **1** : to cover with planks **2** : to set or lay down forcibly **3** : to cook and serve on a board

plank·ing \\'plaŋ-kiŋ\\ *n* : a quantity or covering of planks

plank·ton \\'plaŋk-tən\\ *n* [G, fr. Gk, neut. of *planktos* drifting] : the passively floating or weakly swimming animal and plant life of a body of water — **plank·ton·ic** \\plaŋk-'tä-nik\\ *adj*

¹plant \\'plant\\ *vb* **1** : to set in the ground to grow **2** : ESTABLISH, SETTLE **3** : to stock or provide with something **4** : to place firmly or forcibly **5** : to hide or arrange with intent to deceive

²plant *n* **1** : any of a kingdom of living things that usu. have no locomotor ability or obvious sense organs and have cellulose cell walls and usu. capacity for indefinite growth **2** : the land, buildings, and machinery used in carrying on a trade or business

¹plan·tain \\'plant-ᵊn\\ *n* [ME, fr. OF, fr. L *plantagin-, plantago*, fr. *planta* sole of the foot; fr. its broad leaves] : any of a genus of short-stemmed weedy herbs with spikes of tiny greenish flowers

²plantain *n* [Sp *plántano, plátano* plane tree, banana tree, fr. ML *plantanus* plane tree, alter. of L *platanus*] : a banana plant with starchy greenish fruit that are eaten cooked; *also* : its fruit

plan·tar \\'plan-tər, -ˌtär\\ *adj* : of or relating to the sole of the foot

plan·ta·tion \\plan-'tā-shən\\ *n* **1** : a large group of

PLANETS

SYMBOL	NAME	MEAN DISTANCE FROM THE SUN		PERIOD OF REVOLUTION IN DAYS OR YEARS	EQUATORIAL DIAMETER IN MILES
		astronomical units	million miles		
☿	Mercury	0.387	36.0	87.97 d.	3,032
♀	Venus	0.723	67.2	224.70 d.	7,523
⊕	Earth	1.000	92.9	365.26 d.	7,928
♂	Mars	1.524	141.5	686.98 d.	4,218
♃	Jupiter	5.203	483.4	11.86 y.	88,900
♄	Saturn	9.522	884.6	29.46 y.	74,900
♅	Uranus	19.201	1783.8	84.01 y.	31,800
♆	Neptune	30.074	2793.9	164.79 y.	30,800
♇	Pluto	39.725	3690.5	247.69 y.	1,400

plants and esp. trees under cultivation **2** : an agricultural estate usu. worked by resident laborers

plant·er **'**plan-tər\\ *n* **1** : one that plants or sows; *esp* : an owner or operator of a plantation **2** : a container for plants

plant louse *n* : APHID

plaque **'**plak\\ *n* [F] **1** : an ornamental brooch **2** : a flat thin piece (as of metal) used for decoration; *also* : a commemorative tablet **3** : a bacteria-containing film on a tooth

plash **'**plash\\ *n* : SPLASH — **plash** *vb*

plas·ma **'**plaz-mə\\ *n* **1** : the fluid part of blood, lymph, or milk **2** : a gas composed of ionized particles — **plas·mat·ic** \\plaz-**'**ma-tik\\ *adj*

¹plas·ter **'**plas-tər\\ *n* **1** : a dressing consisting of a backing spread with an often medicated substance that clings to the skin ⟨adhesive ∼⟩ **2** : a paste that hardens as it dries and is used for coating walls and ceilings

²plaster *vb* : to cover with or as if with plaster — **plaster·er** *n*

plas·ter·board **'**plas-tər-ˌbōrd\\ *n* : a wallboard consisting of fiberboard, paper, or felt over a plaster core

plaster of par·is \\-**'**par-əs\\ *often cap 2d P* : a white powder made from gypsum and used as a quick≠setting paste with water for casts and molds

¹plas·tic **'**plas-tik\\ *adj* [L *plasticus* of molding, fr. Gk *plastikos,* fr. *plassein* to mold, form] **1** : capable of being molded ⟨∼ clay⟩ **2** : characterized by or using modeling ⟨∼ arts⟩ **3** : made or consisting of a plastic **syn** pliable, pliant, ductile, malleable, adaptable — **plas·tic·i·ty** \\plas-**'**ti-sə-tē\\ *n*

²plastic *n* : a plastic substance; *esp* : a synthetic or processed material that can be formed into rigid objects or into films or filaments

plastic surgery *n* : surgery to repair, restore, or improve lost, injured, defective, or misshapen body parts — **plastic surgeon** *n*

¹plat **'**plat\\ *n* **1** : a small plot of ground **2** : a plan of a piece of land with actual or proposed features (as lots)

²plat *vb* **plat·ted; plat·ting** : to make a plat of

¹plate **'**plāt\\ *n* **1** : a flat thin piece of material **2** : domestic hollowware made of or plated with gold, silver, or base metals **3** : DISH **4** : HOME PLATE **5** : the molded metal or plastic cast of a page of type to be printed from **6** : a sheet of glass coated with a chemical sensitive to light and used in photography **7** : the part of a denture that fits to the mouth; *also* : DENTURE **8** : something printed from an engraving **9** : a huge mobile segment of the earth's crust

²plate *vb* **plat·ed; plat·ing** **1** : to overlay with metal (as gold or silver) **2** : to make a printing plate of

pla·teau \\pla-**'**tō\\ *n, pl* **plateaus** *or* **pla·teaux** \\-**'**tōz\\ [F] : a large level area of high land

plate glass *n* : rolled, ground, and polished sheet glass

plat·en **'**plat-ᵊn\\ *n* **1** : a flat plate; *esp* : one that exerts or receives pressure (as in a printing press) **2** : the roller of a typewriter or printer

plate tectonics *n* : a theory in geology that the lithosphere is divided into plates at the boundaries of which much of earth's seismic activity occurs

plat·form **'**plat-ˌfôrm\\ *n* **1** : a raised flooring or stage for speakers, performers, or workers **2** : a declaration of the principles on which a group of persons (as a political party) stands

plat·ing **'**plā-tiŋ\\ *n* : a coating of metal plates or plate ⟨the ∼ of a ship⟩

plat·i·num **'**plat-ᵊn-əm\\ *n* : a heavy grayish white metallic chemical element — see ELEMENT table

plat·i·tude **'**pla-tə-ˌtüd, -ˌtyüd\\ *n* : a flat or trite remark — **plat·i·tu·di·nous** \\-**'**tüd-ᵊn-əs, -**'**tyüd-\\ *adj*

pla·ton·ic love \\plə-**'**tä-nik-, plā-\\ *n, often cap P* : a close relationship between two persons without sexual desire

pla·toon \\plə-**'**tün\\ *n* [F *peloton* small detachment, lit., ball, fr. *pelote* little ball] **1** : a subdivision of a company-size military unit usu. consisting of two or more squads or sections **2** : a group of football players trained either for offense or for defense and sent into the game as a body

platoon sergeant *n* : a noncommissioned officer in the army ranking below a first sergeant

plat·ter **'**pla-tər\\ *n* **1** : a large serving plate **2** : a phonograph record

platy **'**pla-tē\\ *n, pl* **platy** *or* **plat·ys** *or* **plat·ies** : either of two small stocky often brilliantly colored bony fishes that are popular for tropical aquariums

platy·pus **'**pla-ti-pəs\\ *n, pl* **platy·pus·es** *also* **platy·pi** \\-ˌpī\\ [NL, fr. Gk *platypous* flat-footed, fr. *platys* broad, flat + *pous* foot] : a small aquatic egg≠laying marsupial mammal of Australia with webbed feet and a fleshy bill like a duck's

platypus

plau·dit **'**plȯ-dət\\ *n* : an act of applause

plau·si·ble **'**plȯ-zə-bəl\\ *adj* [L *plausibilis* worthy of applause, fr. *plausus,* pp. of *plaudere* to applaud]

: seemingly worthy of belief — **plau·si·bil·i·ty** \₁plȯ-zə-ˈbi-lə-tē\ *n* — **plau·si·bly** \ˈplȯ-zə-blē\ *adv*

¹**play** \ˈplā\ *n* **1** : brisk handling of something (as a weapon) **2** : the course of a game; *also* : a particular act or maneuver in a game **3** : recreational activity; *esp* : the spontaneous activity of children **4** : JEST ⟨said in ~⟩ **5** : the act or an instance of punning **6** : GAMBLING **7** : OPERATION ⟨bring extra force into ~⟩ **8** : a brisk or light movement **9** : free motion (as of part of a machine) **10** : scope for action **11** : PUBLICITY **12** : an effort to arouse liking ⟨made a ~ for her⟩ **13** : a stage representation of a drama; *also* : a dramatic composition — **play·ful** \-fəl\ *adj* — **play·ful·ly** *adv* — **play·ful·ness** *n* — **in play** : in condition or position to be played

²**play** *vb* **1** : to engage in recreation : FROLIC **2** : to handle or behave lightly or absentmindedly **3** : to make a pun ⟨~ on words⟩ **4** : to take advantage ⟨~ on fears⟩ **5** : to move or operate in a brisk or irregular manner ⟨a flashlight ~ed over the wall⟩ **6** : to perform music ⟨~ on a violin⟩; *also* : to perform (music) on an instrument ⟨~ a waltz⟩ **7** : to perform music upon ⟨~ the piano⟩; *also* : to sound in performance ⟨the organ is ~ing⟩ **8** : to cause to emit sounds ⟨~ a radio⟩ **9** : to act in a dramatic medium; *also* : to act in the character of ⟨~ the hero⟩ **10** : GAMBLE **11** : to behave in a specified way ⟨~ safe⟩; *also* : COOPERATE ⟨~ along with him⟩ **12** : to deal with; *also* : EMPHASIZE ⟨~ up her good qualities⟩ **13** : to perform for amusement ⟨~ a trick⟩ **14** : WREAK **15** : to contend with in a game; *also* : to fill (a certain position) on a team **16** : to make wagers on ⟨~ the races⟩ **17** : WIELD, PLY **18** : to keep in action — **play·er** *n*

play·act·ing \ˈplā-₁ak-tiŋ\ *n* **1** : performance in theatrical productions **2** : insincere or artificial behavior

play·back \-₁bak\ *n* : an act of reproducing a sound recording — **play back** *vb*

play·bill \-₁bil\ *n* : a poster advertising the performance of a play

play·book \-₁bu̇k\ *n* : a notebook containing diagrammed football plays

play·boy \-₁bȯi\ *n* : a man whose chief interest is the pursuit of pleasure

play·go·er \-₁gō-ər\ *n* : a person who frequently attends plays

play·ground \-₁grȧu̇nd\ *n* : an area used for games and play esp. by children

play·house \-₁hȧu̇s\ *n* **1** : THEATER **2** : a small house for children to play in

playing card *n* : any of a set of 24 to 78 cards marked to show its rank and suit and used to play a game of cards

play·let \ˈplā-lət\ *n* : a short play

play·mate \-₁māt\ *n* : a companion in play

play–off \-₁ȯf\ *n* : a contest or series of contests to break a tie or determine a championship

play·pen \-₁pen\ *n* : a portable enclosure in which a young child may play

play·suit \-₁süt\ *n* : a sports and play outfit for women and children

play·thing \-₁thiŋ\ *n* : TOY

play·wright \-₁rīt\ *n* : a writer of plays

pla·za \ˈpla-zə, ˈplä-\ *n* [Sp, fr. L *platea* broad street] **1** : a public square in a city or town **2** : a shopping center

PLC *abbr, Brit* public limited company

plea \ˈplē\ *n* **1** : a defendant's answer in law to a charge or indictment **2** : something alleged as an excuse **3** : ENTREATY, APPEAL

plead \ˈplēd\ *vb* **plead·ed** *or* **pled** \ˈpled\; **plead·ing 1** : to argue before a court or authority ⟨~ a case⟩ **2** : to answer to a charge or indictment ⟨~ guilty⟩ **3** : to argue for or against something ⟨~ for acquittal⟩ **4** : to appeal earnestly ⟨~s for help⟩ **5** : to offer as a plea (as in defense) ⟨~ed illness⟩ — **plead·er** *n*

pleas·ant \ˈplez-ᵊnt\ *adj* **1** : giving pleasure : AGREE-

ABLE ⟨a ~ experience⟩ **2** : marked by pleasing behavior or appearance ⟨a ~ person⟩ — **pleas·ant·ly** *adv* — **pleas·ant·ness** *n*

pleas·ant·ry \-ᵊn-trē\ *n, pl* **-ries** : a pleasant and casual act or speech

¹**please** \ˈplēz\ *vb* **pleased; pleas·ing 1** : to give pleasure or satisfaction to **2** : LIKE ⟨do as you ~⟩ **3** : to be the will or pleasure of ⟨may it ~ his Majesty⟩

²**please** *adv* — used as a function word to express politeness or emphasis in a request ⟨~ come in⟩

pleas·ing *adj* : giving pleasure — **pleas·ing·ly** *adv*

plea·sur·able \ˈple-zhə-rə-bəl\ *adj* : PLEASANT, GRATIFYING — **plea·sur·ably** \-blē\ *adv*

plea·sure \ˈple-zhər\ *n* **1** : DESIRE, INCLINATION ⟨await your ~⟩ **2** : a state of gratification : ENJOYMENT **3** : a source of delight or joy

¹**pleat** \ˈplēt\ *vb* **1** : FOLD; *esp* : to arrange in pleats **2** : BRAID

²**pleat** *n* : a fold (as in cloth) made by doubling material over on itself

plebe \ˈplēb\ *n* : a freshman at a military or naval academy

¹**ple·be·ian** \pli-ˈbē-ən\ *n* **1** : a member of the Roman plebs **2** : one of the common people

²**plebeian** *adj* **1** : of or relating to plebeians **2** : COMMON, VULGAR

pleb·i·scite \ˈple-bə-₁sīt, -sət\ *n* : a vote of the people (as of a country) on a proposal submitted to them

plebs \ˈplebz\ *n, pl* **ple·bes** \ˈplē-bēz\ **1** : the general populace **2** : the common people of ancient Rome

plec·trum \ˈplek-trəm\ *n, pl* **plec·tra** \-trə\ *or* **plec·trums** [L] : ³PICK 3

¹**pledge** \ˈplej\ *n* **1** : something given as security for the performance of an act **2** : the state of being held as a security or guaranty **3** : TOAST **4** : PROMISE, VOW

²**pledge** *vb* **pledged; pledg·ing 1** : to deposit as a pledge **2** : TOAST **3** : to bind by a pledge : PLIGHT **4** : PROMISE

Pleis·to·cene \ˈplī-stə-₁sēn\ *adj* : of, relating to, or being the earlier epoch of the Quaternary — **Pleistocene** *n*

ple·na·ry \ˈplē-nə-rē, ˈple-\ *adj* **1** : FULL ⟨~ power⟩ **2** : including all entitled to attend ⟨~ session⟩

pleni·po·ten·tia·ry \₁ple-nə-pə-ˈten-chə-rē, -ˈten-chē-₁er-ē\ *n, pl* **-ries** : a diplomatic agent having full authority — **plenipotentiary** *adj*

plen·i·tude \ˈple-nə-₁tüd, -₁tyüd\ *n* **1** : COMPLETENESS **2** : ABUNDANCE

plen·te·ous \ˈplen-tē-əs\ *adj* **1** : FRUITFUL **2** : existing in plenty

plen·ti·ful \ˈplen-ti-fəl\ *adj* **1** : containing or yielding plenty **2** : ABUNDANT — **plen·ti·ful·ly** *adv*

plen·ty \ˈplen-tē\ *n* : a more than adequate number or amount

ple·num \ˈple-nəm, ˈplē-\ *n, pl* **-nums** *or* **-na** \-nə\ : a general assembly of all members esp. of a legislative body

pleth·o·ra \ˈple-thə-rə\ *n* : an excessive quantity or fullness; *also* : PROFUSION

pleu·ri·sy \ˈplu̇r-ə-sē\ *n* : inflammation of the membrane that lines the chest and covers the lungs

plex·us \ˈplek-səs\ *n, pl* **plex·us·es** \-sə-səz\ : an interlacing network esp. of blood vessels or nerves

pli·able \ˈplī-ə-bəl\ *adj* **1** : FLEXIBLE **2** : yielding easily to others **syn** plastic, pliant, ductile, malleable, adaptable — **pli·a·bil·i·ty** \₁plī-ə-ˈbi-lə-tē\ *n*

pli·ant \ˈplī-ənt\ *adj* **1** : FLEXIBLE **2** : easily influenced : PLIABLE — **pli·an·cy** \-ən-sē\ *n*

pli·ers \ˈplī-ərz\ *n pl* : small pincers for bending or cutting wire or handling small objects

¹**plight** \ˈplīt\ *vb* : to put or give in pledge : ENGAGE

²**plight** *n* : an unfortunate, difficult, or precarious situation

plinth \ˈplinth\ *n* : the lowest part of the base of an architectural column

Plio·cene \ˈplī-ə-₁sēn\ *adj* : of, relating to, or being the latest epoch of the Tertiary — **Pliocene** *n*

PLO *abbr* Palestine Liberation Organization

plod \'pläd\ *vb* **plod·ded; plod·ding 1** : to walk heavily or slowly : TRUDGE **2** : to work laboriously and monotonously : DRUDGE — **plod·der** *n* — **plod·ding·ly** *adv*

plop \'pläp\ *vb* **plopped; plop·ping 1** : to fall or move with a sound like that of something dropping into water **2** : to set, drop, or throw heavily — **plop** *n*

¹plot \'plät\ *n* **1** : a small area of ground **2** : a ground plan (as of an area) **3** : the main story (as of a book or movie) **4** : a secret scheme : INTRIGUE

²plot *vb* **plot·ted; plot·ting 1** : to make a plot or plan of **2** : to mark on or as if on a chart **3** : to plan or contrive esp. secretly — **plot·ter** *n*

plo·ver \'plə-vər, 'plō-\ *n, pl* **plover** *or* **plovers** : any of a family of shore-inhabiting birds that differ from the sandpipers in having shorter stouter bills

¹plow *or* **plough** \'plaù\ *n* **1** : an implement used to cut, lift, turn over, and partly break up soil **2** : a device (as a snowplow) operating like a plow

²plow *or* **plough** *vb* **1** : to open, break up, or work with a plow **2** : to move through like a plow ⟨a ship ~ing the waves⟩ **3** : to proceed laboriously — **plow·able** *adj* — **plow·er** *n*

plow·boy \'plaù-,bòi\ *n* : a boy who leads the horse drawing a plow

plow·man \-mən, -,man\ *n* **1** : a man who guides a plow **2** : a farm laborer

plow·share \-,sher\ *n* : a part of a plow that cuts the earth

ploy \'plòi\ *n* : a tactic intended to embarrass or frustrate an opponent

¹pluck \'plək\ *vb* **1** : to pull off or out : PICK; *also* : to pull something from **2** : to play (an instrument) by pulling the strings **3** : TUG, TWITCH

²pluck *n* **1** : an act or instance of plucking **2** : SPIRIT, COURAGE

plucky \'plə-kē\ *adj* **pluck·i·er; -est** : COURAGEOUS, SPIRITED

¹plug \'pləg\ *n* **1** : STOPPER; *also* : an obstructing mass **2** : a cake of tobacco **3** : a poor or worn-out horse **4** : SPARK PLUG **5** : a lure with several hooks used in fishing **6** : a device on the end of a cord for making an electrical connection **7** : a piece of favorable publicity

²plug *vb* **plugged; plug·ging 1** : to stop, make tight, or secure by inserting a plug **2** : HIT, SHOOT **3** : to publicize insistently **4** : PLOD, DRUDGE

plum \'pləm\ *n* [ME, fr. OE *plūme*, modif. of L *prunum* plum, fr. Gk *proumnon*] **1** : a smooth-skinned juicy fruit borne by trees related to the peach and cherry; *also* : a tree bearing plums **2** : a raisin when used in desserts (as puddings) **3** : something excellent; *esp* : something desirable given in return for a favor

plum·age \'plü-mij\ *n* : the feathers of a bird — **plum·aged** \-mijd\ *adj*

¹plumb \'pləm\ *n* : a weight on the end of a line (**plumb line**) used esp. by builders to show vertical direction

²plumb *adv* **1** : VERTICALLY **2** : COMPLETELY **3** : EXACTLY; *also* : IMMEDIATELY

³plumb *vb* : to sound, adjust, or test with a plumb ⟨~ the depth of a well⟩

⁴plumb *adj* **1** : VERTICAL **2** : COMPLETE

plumb·er \'plə-mər\ *n* : a worker who fits or repairs pipes and fixtures

plumb·ing \'plə-miŋ\ *n* : a system of pipes in a building for supplying and carrying off water

¹plume \'plüm\ *n* : FEATHER; *esp* : a large, conspicuous, or showy feather — **plumed** \'plümd\ *adj* — **plumy** \'plü-mē\ *adj*

²plume *vb* **plumed; plum·ing 1** : to provide or deck with feathers **2** : to indulge (oneself) in pride

¹plum·met \'plə-mət\ *n* : PLUMB; *also* : PLUMB LINE

²plummet *vb* : to drop or plunge straight down

¹plump \'pləmp\ *vb* **1** : to drop or fall suddenly or heav-

ily **2** : to favor something strongly ⟨~ing for change⟩

²plump *n* : a sudden heavy fall or blow; *also* : the sound made by it

³plump *adv* **1** : straight down; *also* : straight ahead **2** : UNQUALIFIEDLY

⁴plump *adj* : having a full rounded usu. pleasing form **syn** fleshy, stout, roly-poly, rotund — **plump·ness** *n*

¹plun·der \'plən-dər\ *vb* : to take the goods of by force or wrongfully : PILLAGE — **plun·der·er** *n*

²plunder *n* : something taken by force or theft : LOOT

¹plunge \'plənj\ *vb* **plunged; plung·ing 1** : IMMERSE, SUBMERGE **2** : to enter or cause to enter a state or course of action suddenly or violently ⟨~ into war⟩ **3** : to cast oneself into or as if into water **4** : to gamble heavily and recklessly **5** : to descend suddenly

²plunge *n* : a sudden dive, leap, or rush

plung·er \'plən-jər\ *n* **1** : one that plunges **2** : a sliding piece driven by or against fluid pressure : PISTON **3** : a rubber cup on a handle pushed against an opening to free a waste outlet of an obstruction

plunk \'pləŋk\ *vb* **1** : to make or cause to make a hollow metallic sound **2** : to drop heavily or suddenly — **plunk** *n*

plu·per·fect \(,)plü-'pər-fikt\ *adj* [ME *pluperfyth*, modif. of LL *plusquamperfectus*, lit., more than perfect] : of, relating to, or constituting a verb tense that denotes an action or state as completed at or before a past time spoken of — **pluperfect** *n*

plu·ral \'plùr-əl\ *adj* [ME, fr. MF & L; MF *plurel*, fr. L *pluralis*, fr. *plur-, plus* more] : of, relating to, or constituting a word form used to denote more than one — **plural** *n*

plu·ral·i·ty \plù-'ra-lə-tē\ *n, pl* **-ties 1** : the state of being plural **2** : an excess of votes over those cast for an opposing candidate **3** : the greatest number of votes cast when not a majority

plu·ral·ize \'plùr-ə-,līz\ *vb* **-ized; -iz·ing** : to make plural or express in the plural form — **plu·ral·i·za·tion** \,plùr-ə-lə-'zā-shən\ *n*

¹plus \'pləs\ *adj* [L. more] **1** : mathematically positive **2** : having or being in addition to what is anticipated **3** : falling high in a specified range ⟨a grade of B ~⟩

²plus *n, pl* **plus·es** \'plə-səz\ *also* **plus·ses 1** : a sign + (**plus sign**) used in mathematics to indicate addition or a positive quantity **2** : an added quantity; *also* : a positive quality **3** : SURPLUS

³plus *prep* **1** : increased by : with the addition of ⟨3 ~ 4⟩ **2** : BESIDES

⁴plus *conj* : AND ⟨soup ~ salad and bread⟩

¹plush \'pləsh\ *n* : a fabric with a pile longer and less dense than velvet pile — **plushy** *adj*

²plush *adj* : notably luxurious — **plush·ly** *adv* — **plush·ness** *n*

Plu·to \'plü-tō\ *n* : the planet farthest from the sun — see PLANET table

plu·toc·ra·cy \plü-'tä-krə-sē\ *n, pl* **-cies 1** : government by the wealthy **2** : a controlling class of the wealthy — **plu·to·crat** \'plü-tə-,krat\ *n* — **plu·to·crat·ic** \,plü-tə-'kra-tik\ *adj*

plu·to·ni·um \plü-'tō-nē-əm\ *n* : a radioactive chemical element formed by the decay of neptunium — see ELEMENT table

plu·vi·al \'plü-vē-əl\ *adj* **1** : of or relating to rain **2** : characterized by abundant rain

¹ply \'plī\ *vb* **plied; ply·ing 1** : to use, practice, or work diligently ⟨~ a trade⟩ **2** : to keep supplying something to ⟨*plied* them with liquor⟩ **3** : to go or travel regularly esp. by sea

²ply *n, pl* **plies** : one of the folds, thicknesses, or strands of which something (as plywood or yarn) is made

³ply *vb* **plied; ply·ing** : to twist together ⟨~ yarns⟩

Plym·outh Rock \'pli-məth-\ *n* : any of an American breed of medium-sized single-combed domestic fowls

ply·wood \'plī-,wùd\ *n* : material made of thin sheets of wood glued and pressed together

pm *abbr* premium

Pm *symbol* promethium

PM *abbr* **1** paymaster **2** police magistrate **3** postmaster **4** post meridiem — often not cap. and often punctuated **5** postmortem **6** prime minister **7** provost marshal

pmk *abbr* postmark

PMS *abbr* premenstrual syndrome

pmt *abbr* payment

pneu•mat•ic \nü-'ma-tik, nyu̇-\ *adj* **1** : of, relating to, or using air or wind **2** : moved by air pressure **3** : filled with compressed air — **pneu•mat•i•cal•ly** \-ti-k(ə-)lē\ *adv*

pneu•mo•co•ni•o•sis \ˌnü-mō-ˌkō-nē-'ō-səs, ˌnyu̇-\ *n* : a disease of the lungs caused by habitual inhalation of irritant mineral or metallic particles

pneu•mo•nia \nu̇-'mō-nyə, nyu̇-\ *n* : an inflammatory disease of the lungs

Po *symbol* polonium

PO *abbr* **1** petty officer **2** post office

¹**poach** \'pōch\ *vb* [ME *pochen*, fr. MF *pocher*, fr. OF *pochier*, lit., to put into a bag, fr. *poche* bag, pocket, of Gmc origin] : to cook (as an egg or fish) in simmering liquid

²**poach** *vb* : to hunt or fish unlawfully — **poach•er** *n*

POB *abbr* post office box

pock \'päk\ *n* : a small swelling on the skin (as in smallpox); *also* : a spot suggesting this

¹**pock•et** \'pä-kət\ *n* **1** : a small bag open at the top or side inserted in a garment **2** : supply of money : MEANS **3** : RECEPTACLE, CONTAINER **4** : a small isolated area or group **5** : a small body of ore — **pock•et•ful** *n*

²**pocket** *vb* **1** : to put in or as if in a pocket **2** : STEAL

³**pocket** *adj* **1** : small enough to fit in a pocket; *also* : SMALL, MINIATURE **2** : carried in or paid from one's own pocket

¹**pock•et•book** \-ˌbu̇k\ *n* **1** : PURSE; *also* : HANDBAG **2** : financial resources

²**pocketbook** *adj* : relating to money

pocket gopher *n* : GOPHER 2

pock•et•knife \'pä-kət-ˌnīf\ *n* : a knife with a folding blade to be carried in the pocket

pocket veto *n* : an indirect veto of a legislative bill by an executive through retention of the bill unsigned until after adjournment of the legislature

pock•mark \'päk-ˌmärk\ *n* : a pit or scar caused by smallpox or acne — **pock•marked** \-ˌmärkt\ *adj*

po•co \'pō-kō, ˌpȯ-\ *adv* [It, little, fr. L *paucus*] : SOMEWHAT — used to qualify a direction in music ⟨∼ allegro⟩

po•co a po•co \ˌpō-kō-ä-'pō-kō, ˌpȯ-kō-ä-'pȯ-\ *adv* : little by little : GRADUALLY — used as a direction in music

pod \'päd\ *n* **1** : a dry fruit (as of a pea) that splits open when ripe **2** : an external streamlined compartment (as for a jet engine) on an airplane **3** : a compartment (as for personnel, a power unit, or an instrument) on a ship or craft

POD *abbr* pay on delivery

po•di•a•try \pə-'dī-ə-trē, pō-\ *n* : the medical care and treatment of the human foot — **po•di•a•trist** \pə-'dī-ə-trist, pō-\ *n*

po•di•um \'pō-dē-əm\ *n, pl* **podiums** *or* **po•dia** \-dē-ə\ **1** : a dais esp. for an orchestral conductor **2** : LECTERN

POE *abbr* port of entry

po•em \'pō-əm\ *n* : a composition in verse

po•esy \'pō-ə-zē\ *n* : POETRY

po•et \'pō-ət\ *n* [ME, fr. OF *poete*, fr. L *poeta*, fr. Gk *poiētēs* maker, poet, fr. *poiein* to make] : a writer of poetry; *also* : a creative artist of great sensitivity

po•et•as•ter \'pō-ə-ˌtas-tər\ *n* : an inferior poet

po•et•ess \'pō-ə-təs\ *n* : a girl or woman who is a poet

poetic justice *n* : an outcome in which vice is punished and virtue rewarded usu. in a manner peculiarly or ironically appropriate

po•et•ry \'pō-ə-trē\ *n* **1** : metrical writing **2** : POEMS — **po•et•ic** \pō-'e-tik\ *or* **po•et•i•cal** \-ti-kəl\ *adj*

po•grom \'pō-grəm, pō-'gräm\ *n* [Yiddish, fr. Russ, lit., devastation] : an organized massacre of helpless people and esp. of Jews

poi \'pȯi\ *n, pl* **poi** *or* **pois** : a Hawaiian food of taro root cooked, pounded, and kneaded to a paste and often allowed to ferment

poi•gnant \'pȯi-nyənt\ *adj* **1** : painfully affecting the feelings ⟨∼ grief⟩ **2** : deeply moving ⟨∼ scene⟩ — **poi•gnan•cy** \-nyən-sē\ *n*

poin•ci•ana \ˌpȯin-sē-'a-nə\ *n* : any of several ornamental tropical leguminous trees or shrubs with bright orange or red flowers

poin•set•tia \pȯin-'se-tē-ə\ *n* : any of several showy tropical American spurges with usu. scarlet bracts around their small greenish flowers

¹**point** \'pȯint\ *n* **1** : an individual detail; *also* : the most important essential **2** : PURPOSE **3** : a geometric element that has position but no size **4** : a particular place : LOCALITY **5** : a particular stage or degree **6** : a sharp end : TIP **7** : a projecting piece of land **8** : a punctuation mark; *esp* : PERIOD **9** : DECIMAL POINT **10** : one of the divisions of the compass **11** : a unit of counting (as in a game score) — **point•less** *adj* — **beside the point** : IRRELEVANT — **to the point** : RELEVANT, PERTINENT

²**point** *vb* **1** : to furnish with a point : SHARPEN **2** : PUNCTUATE **3** : to separate (a decimal fraction) from an integer by a decimal point — usu. used with *off* **4** : to indicate the position of esp. by extending a finger **5** : to direct attention to ⟨∼ out an error⟩ **6** : AIM, DIRECT **7** : to lie extended, aimed, or turned in a particular direction : FACE, LOOK

point–blank \'pȯint-'blaŋk\ *adj* **1** : so close to the target that a missile fired will travel in a straight line to the mark **2** : DIRECT, BLUNT — **point–blank** *adv*

point•ed \'pȯin-təd\ *adj* **1** : having a point **2** : being to the point : DIRECT **3** : aimed at a particular person or group; *also* : CONSPICUOUS, MARKED — **point•ed•ly** *adv*

point•er \'pȯin-tər\ *n* **1** : one that points out : INDICATOR **2** : a large short-haired hunting dog **3** : HINT, TIP

poin•til•lism \'pwaⁿ-tē-ˌyi-zəm, 'pȯint-ᵊl-ˌi-zəm\ *n* [F *pointillisme*, fr. *pointiller* to stipple, fr. *point* point] : the theory or practice in painting of applying small strokes or dots of color to a surface so that from a distance they blend together — **poin•til•list** *also* **poin•til•liste** \ˌpwaⁿ-tē-'yest, 'pȯint-ᵊl-ist\ *n or adj*

point of no return : a critical point at which turning back or reversal is not possible

point of view : a position from which something is considered or evaluated

¹**poise** \'pȯiz\ *n* **1** : BALANCE **2** : self-possessed calmness; *also* : a particular way of carrying oneself

²**poise** *vb* **poised; pois•ing** : BALANCE

poi•sha \'pȯi-shə\ *n, pl* **poisha** : the paisa of Bangladesh

¹**poi•son** \'pȯiz-ᵊn\ *n* [ME, fr. OF, drink, poisonous drink, poison, fr. L *potion-, potio* drink] : a substance that through its chemical action can injure or kill — **poi•son•ous** \-ᵊn-əs\ *adj*

²**poison** *vb* **1** : to injure or kill with poison **2** : to treat or taint with poison **3** : to affect destructively : CORRUPT ⟨∼ed her mind⟩ — **poi•son•er** *n*

poison hemlock *n* : a large branching poisonous herb with finely divided leaves and white flowers that is related to the carrot

poison ivy *n* **1** : a usu. climbing plant related to the sumacs that has leaves composed of three shiny leaflets and produces an irritating oil causing a usu. intensely itching skin rash; *also* : any of several related plants **2** : a skin rash caused by poison ivy

poison oak *n* : any of several shrubby plants closely related to poison ivy and having similar properties

poison sumac *n* : a smooth American swamp shrub

poison ivy 1

with pinnate leaves, greenish flowers, greenish white berries, and irritating properties like the related poison ivy

¹poke \'pōk\ *n* : BAG, SACK

²poke *vb* **poked; pok·ing 1** : PROD; *also* : to stir up by prodding **2** : to make a prodding or jabbing movement esp. repeatedly **3** : HIT, PUNCH **4** : to thrust forward obtrusively **5** : RUMMAGE **6** : MEDDLE, PRY **7** : DAWDLE — **poke fun at** : RIDICULE, MOCK

³poke *n* : a quick thrust; *also* : PUNCH

¹pok·er \'pō-kər\ *n* : a metal rod for stirring a fire

²po·ker \'pō-kər\ *n* : any of several card games in which the player with the highest hand at the end of the betting wins

poker: hands in descending value: *1* five of a kind, *2* royal flush, *3* straight flush, *4* four of a kind, *5* full house, *6* flush, *7* straight, *8* three of a kind, *9* two pairs, *10* one pair

poke·weed \'pōk-,wēd\ *n* : a coarse American perennial herb with clusters of white flowers and dark purple juicy berries

poky *or* **pok·ey** \'pō-kē\ *adj* **pok·i·er; -est 1** : small and cramped **2** : SHABBY, DULL **3** : annoyingly slow

pol \'päl\ *n* : POLITICIAN

po·lar \'pō-lər\ *adj* **1** : of or relating to a geographical pole **2** : of or relating to a pole (as of a magnet)

polar bear *n* : a large creamy-white bear that inhabits arctic regions

polar bear

Po·lar·is \pə-'lar-əs\ *n* : NORTH STAR

po·lar·i·ty \pō-'lar-ə-tē\ *n, pl* **-ties** : the condition of having poles and esp. magnetic or electrical poles

po·lar·i·za·tion \,pō-lə-rə-'zā-shən\ *n* **1** : the action of polarizing : the state of being polarized **2** : concentration about opposing extremes

po·lar·ize \'pō-lə-,rīz\ *vb* **-ized; -iz·ing 1** : to cause (light waves) to vibrate in a definite way **2** : to give physical polarity to **3** : to break up into opposing groups

pol·der \'pōl-dər, 'päl-\ *n* [D] : a tract of low land reclaimed from the sea

¹pole \'pōl\ *n* : a long slender piece of wood or metal ⟨telephone ∼⟩

²pole *vb* **poled; pol·ing** : to impel or push with a pole

³pole *n* **1** : either end of an axis esp. of the earth **2** : either of the terminals of an electric device (as a battery or generator) **3** : one of two or more regions in a magnetized body at which the magnetism is concentrated — **pole·ward** \'pōl-wərd\ *adj or adv*

Pole \'pōl\ *n* : a native or inhabitant of Poland

¹pole·ax \'pō-,laks\ *n* : a battle-ax with a short handle

²poleax *vb* : to attack or fell with or as if with a poleax

pole·cat \'pōl-,kat\ *n, pl* **polecats** *or* **polecat 1** : a European carnivorous mammal of which the ferret is considered a domesticated variety **2** : SKUNK

po·lem·ic \pə-'le-mik\ *n* : the art or practice of disputation — usu. used in pl. — **po·lem·i·cal** \-mi-kəl\ *also* **po·lem·ic** \-mik\ *adj* — **po·lem·i·cist** \-sist\ *n*

pole·star \'pōl-,stär\ *n* **1** : NORTH STAR **2** : a directing principle : GUIDE

pole vault *n* : a field contest in which each contestant uses a pole to vault for height over a crossbar — **pole–vault** *vb* — **pole–vault·er** *n*

¹po·lice \pə-'lēs\ *vb* **po·liced; po·lic·ing 1** : to control, regulate, or keep in order esp. by use of police ⟨∼ a highway⟩ **2** : to make clean and put in order

²police *n, pl* **police** [MF, government, fr. LL *politia*, fr. Gk *politeia*, fr. *politēs* citizen, fr. *polis* city, state] **1** : the department of government that keeps public order and safety and enforces the laws; *also* : the members of this department **2** : a private organization resembling a police force; *also* : its members **3** : military personnel detailed to clean and put in order

po·lice·man \-mən\ *n* : POLICE OFFICER

police officer *n* : a member of a police force

police state *n* : a state characterized by repressive, arbitrary, totalitarian rule by means of secret police

po·lice·wom·an \pə-'lēs-,wu̇-mən\ *n* : a woman who is a police officer

¹pol·i·cy \'pä-lə-sē\ *n, pl* **-cies** : a definite course or method of action selected to guide and determine present and future decisions

²policy *n, pl* **-cies** : a writing whereby a contract of insurance is made

pol·i·cy·hold·er \'pä-lə-sē-,hōl-dər\ *n* : one granted an insurance policy

po·lio \'pō-lē-,ō\ *n* : POLIOMYELITIS — **polio** *adj*

po·lio·my·eli·tis \-,mī-ə-'lī-təs\ *n* : an acute virus disease marked by inflammation of the nerve cells of the spinal cord

¹pol·ish \'pä-lish\ *vb* **1** : to make smooth and glossy usu. by rubbing **2** : to refine or improve in manners, condition, or style

²polish *n* **1** : a smooth glossy surface : LUSTER **2** : REFINEMENT, CULTURE **3** : the action or process of polishing **4** : a preparation used to produce a gloss

Pol·ish \'pō-lish\ *n* : the Slavic language of the Poles — **Polish** *adj*

polit *abbr* political; politician

po·lit·bu·ro \'pä-lət-,byu̇r-ō, 'pō-, pə-'lit-\ *n* [Russ *politbyuro*] : the principal policy-making committee of a Communist party

po·lite \pə-'līt\ *adj* **po·lit·er; -est 1** : REFINED, CULTIVATED ⟨∼ society⟩ **2** : marked by correct social conduct : COURTEOUS; *also* : CONSIDERATE, TACTFUL — **po·lite·ly** *adv* — **po·lite·ness** *n*

po·li·tesse \ˌpä-li-ˈtes\ *n* [F] : formal politeness

pol·i·tic \ˈpä-lə-ˌtik\ *adj* **1** : wise in promoting a policy ⟨a ~ statesman⟩ **2** : shrewdly tactful ⟨a ~ move⟩

po·lit·i·cal \pə-ˈli-ti-kəl\ *adj* **1** : of or relating to government or politics **2** : involving or charged or concerned with acts against a government or a political system ⟨~ prisoners⟩ — **po·lit·i·cal·ly** \-k(ə-)lē\ *adv*

politically correct *adj* : conforming to a belief that language and practices which could offend sensibilities (as in matters of sex or race) should be eliminated

pol·i·ti·cian \ˌpä-lə-ˈti-shən\ *n* : a person actively engaged in government or politics

pol·i·tick \ˈpä-lə-ˌtik\ *vb* : to engage in political discussion or activity

po·lit·i·co \pə-ˈli-ti-ˌkō\ *n, pl* **-cos** *also* **-coes** : POLITICIAN

pol·i·tics \ˈpä-lə-ˌtiks\ *n sing or pl* **1** : the art or science of government, of guiding or influencing governmental policy, or of winning and holding control over a government **2** : political affairs or business; *esp* : competition between groups or individuals for power and leadership **3** : political opinions

pol·i·ty \ˈpä-lə-tē\ *n, pl* **-ties** : a politically organized unit; *also* : the form or constitution of such a unit

pol·ka \ˈpōl-kə, ˈpō-kə\ *n* [Czech, fr. *Polka* Polish woman, fem. of *Polák* Pole] : a lively couple dance of Bohemian origin; *also* : music for this dance — **polka** *vb*

pol·ka dot \ˈpō-kə-ˌdät\ *n* : a dot in a pattern of regularly distributed dots — **polka–dot** *or* **polka–dot·ted** \-ˌdä-təd\ *adj*

¹poll \ˈpōl\ *n* **1** : HEAD **2** : the casting and recording of votes; *also* : the total vote cast **3** : the place where votes are cast — usu. used in pl. **4** : a questioning of persons to obtain information or opinions to be analyzed

²poll *vb* **1** : to cut off or shorten a growth or part of : CLIP, SHEAR **2** : to receive and record the votes of **3** : to receive (as votes) in an election **4** : to question in a poll

pol·lack *or* **pol·lock** \ˈpä-lək\ *n, pl* **pollack** *or* **pollock** : an important Atlantic food fish that is related to the cods; *also* : a related food fish of the north Pacific

pol·len \ˈpä-lən\ *n* [NL, fr. L, fine flour] : a mass of male spores of a seed plant usu. appearing as a yellow dust

pol·li·na·tion \ˌpä-lə-ˈnā-shən\ *n* : the carrying of pollen to the female part of a plant to fertilize the seed — **pol·li·nate** \ˈpä-lə-ˌnāt\ *vb* — **pol·li·na·tor** \-ˌnā-tər\ *n*

poll·ster \ˈpōl-stər\ *n* : one that conducts a poll or compiles data obtained by a poll

poll tax *n* : a tax of a fixed amount per person levied on adults

pol·lute \pə-ˈlüt\ *vb* **pol·lut·ed; pol·lut·ing** : to make impure; *esp* : to contaminate (an environment) esp. with man-made waste — **pol·lut·ant** \-ˈlüt-ᵊnt\ *n* — **pol·lut·er** *n* — **pol·lu·tion** \-ˈlü-shən\ *n*

pol·ly·wog *or* **pol·li·wog** \ˈpä-lē-ˌwäg\ *n* : TADPOLE

po·lo \ˈpō-lō\ *n* : a game played by two teams on horseback using long-handled mallets to drive a wooden ball

po·lo·ni·um \pə-ˈlō-nē-əm\ *n* [NL, fr. ML *Polonia* Poland, birthplace of its discoverer, Mme. Curie] : a radioactive metallic chemical element — see ELEMENT table

pol·ter·geist \ˈpōl-tər-ˌgīst\ *n* [G, fr. *poltern* to knock + *Geist* spirit] : a noisy usu. mischievous ghost held to be responsible for unexplained noises

pol·troon \päl-ˈtrün\ *n* : COWARD

poly- *comb form* **1** : many : several ⟨*poly*syllabic⟩ **2** : polymeric ⟨*poly*ester⟩

poly·chlo·ri·nat·ed bi·phe·nyl \ˌpä-li-ˌklōr-ə-ˌnā-təd-ˌbī-ˈfen-ᵊl, -ˈfēn-\ *n* : any of several industrial compounds that are poisonous environmental pollutants

poly·clin·ic \ˌpä-li-ˈkli-nik\ *n* : a clinic or hospital treating diseases of many sorts

poly·es·ter \ˈpä-lē-ˌes-tər\ *n* : a polymer composed of ester groups used esp. in making fibers or plastics

poly·eth·yl·ene \ˌpä-lē-ˈe-thə-ˌlēn\ *n* : a lightweight plastic resistant to chemicals and moisture and used chiefly in packaging

po·lyg·a·my \pə-ˈli-gə-mē\ *n* : the practice of having more than one wife or husband at one time — **po·lyg·a·mist** \-mist\ *n* — **po·lyg·a·mous** \-məs\ *adj*

poly·glot \ˈpä-li-ˌglät\ *adj* **1** : speaking or writing several languages **2** : containing or made up of several languages — **polyglot** *n*

poly·gon \ˈpä-li-ˌgän\ *n* : a closed plane figure bounded by straight lines — **po·lyg·o·nal** \pə-ˈli-gən-ᵊl\ *adj*

poly·graph \ˈpä-li-ˌgraf\ *n* : an instrument for recording variations of several bodily functions (as blood pressure) simultaneously — **po·lyg·ra·pher** \pə-ˈli-grə-fər, ˈpä-li-ˌgra-fər\ *n*

poly·he·dron \ˌpä-li-ˈhē-drən\ *n* : a solid formed by plane faces that are polygons — **poly·he·dral** \-drəl\ *adj*

poly·math \ˈpä-li-ˌmath\ *n* : a person of encyclopedic learning

poly·mer \ˈpä-lə-mər\ *n* : a chemical compound formed by union of small molecules and usu. consisting of repeating structural units — **poly·mer·ic** \ˌpä-lə-ˈmer-ik\ *adj*

po·lym·er·i·za·tion \pə-ˌli-mə-rə-ˈzā-shən\ *n* : a chemical reaction in which two or more small molecules combine to form polymers — **po·lym·er·ize** \pə-ˈli-mə-ˌrīz\ *vb*

Poly·ne·sian \ˌpä-lə-ˈnē-zhən\ *n* **1** : a member of any of the indigenous peoples of Polynesia **2** : a group of Austronesian languages spoken in Polynesia — **Polynesian** *adj*

poly·no·mi·al \ˌpä-lə-ˈnō-mē-əl\ *n* : an algebraic expression having one or more terms each of which consists of a constant multiplied by one or more variables raised to a nonnegative integral power — **polynomial** *adj*

pol·yp \ˈpä-ləp\ *n* **1** : an invertebrate animal (as a coral) that is a coelenterate having a hollow cylindrical body closed at one end **2** : a projecting mass of swollen and hypertrophied or tumorous membrane ⟨a rectal ~⟩

po·lyph·o·ny \pə-ˈli-fə-nē\ *n* : music consisting of two or more melodically independent but harmonizing voice parts — **poly·phon·ic** \ˌpä-li-ˈfä-nik\ *adj*

poly·pro·pyl·ene \ˌpä-lē-ˈprō-pə-ˌlēn\ *n* : any of various polymer plastics or fibers

poly·sty·rene \ˌpä-li-ˈstīr-ˌēn\ *n* : a rigid transparent nonconducting thermoplastic used esp. in molded products and foams

poly·syl·lab·ic \-sə-ˈla-bik\ *adj* **1** : having more than three syllables **2** : characterized by polysyllabic words

poly·syl·la·ble \ˈpä-li-ˌsi-lə-bəl\ *n* : a polysyllabic word

poly·tech·nic \ˌpä-li-ˈtek-nik\ *adj* : of, relating to, or instructing in many technical arts or applied sciences

poly·the·ism \ˈpä-li-thē-ˌi-zəm\ *n* : belief in or worship of many gods — **poly·the·ist** \-thē-ist\ *adj or n* — **poly·the·is·tic** \ˌpä-li-thē-ˈis-tik\ *adj*

poly·un·sat·u·rat·ed \ˌpä-lē-ˌən-ˈsa-chə-ˌrā-təd\ *adj* : having many double or triple bonds in a molecule — used esp. of an oil or fatty acid

poly·ure·thane \ˌpä-lē-ˈyùr-ə-ˌthān\ *n* : any of various polymers used esp. in foams and in resins (as for coatings)

poly·vi·nyl \ˌpä-li-ˈvīn-ᵊl\ *adj* : of, relating to, or being a polymerized vinyl compound, resin, or plastic — often used in combination

pome·gran·ate \ˈpä-mə-ˌgra-nət\ *n* [ME *poumgrenet*, fr. MF *pomme grenate*, lit., seedy apple] : a tropical reddish fruit with many seeds and an edible crimson pulp; *also* : the tree that bears it

¹pom·mel \'pə-məl, 'pä-\ *n* **1** : the knob on the hilt of a sword **2** : the knoblike bulge at the front and top of a saddlebow

²pom·mel \'pə-məl\ *vb* **-meled** *or* **-melled; -mel·ing** *or* **-mel·ling** : PUMMEL

pomp \'pämp\ *n* **1** : brilliant display : SPLENDOR **2** : OSTENTATION

pom·pa·dour \'päm-pə-ˌdōr\ *n* : a style of dressing the hair high over the forehead

pom·pa·no \'päm-pə-ˌnō, 'pəm-\ *n, pl* **-no** *or* **-nos** : a New World fish esp. of warmer Atlantic coasts

pom–pom \'päm-ˌpäm\ *n* **1** : an ornamental ball or tuft used on a cap or costume **2** : a fluffy ball flourished by cheerleaders

pom·pon \'päm-ˌpän\ *n* **1** : POM-POM **2** : a chrysanthemum or dahlia with small rounded flower heads

pomp·ous \'päm-pəs\ *adj* **1** : suggestive of pomp; *esp* : OSTENTATIOUS **2** : pretentiously dignified **3** : excessively elevated or ornate **syn** arrogant, magisterial, self-important — **pom·pos·i·ty** \päm-'pä-sə-tē\ *n* — **pomp·ous·ly** *adv*

pon·cho \'pän-chō\ *n, pl* **ponchos** [AmerSp, fr. Araucanian (American Indian language of Chile)] **1** : a blanket with a slit in the middle for the head so that it can be worn as a garment **2** : a waterproof garment resembling a poncho

pond \'pänd\ *n* : a small body of water

pon·der \'pän-dər\ *vb* **pon·dered; pon·der·ing 1** : to weigh in the mind **2** : to consider carefully

pon·der·o·sa pine \ˌpän-də-ˈrō-sə-, -zə-\ *n* : a tall pine of western No. America with long needles; *also* : its strong reddish wood

pon·der·ous \'pän-də-rəs\ *adj* **1** : of very great weight **2** : UNWIELDY, CLUMSY ⟨a ∼ weapon⟩ **3** : oppressively dull ⟨a ∼ speech⟩ **syn** cumbrous, cumbersome, weighty

pone \'pōn\ *n, Southern & Midland* : an oval-shaped cornmeal cake; *also* : corn bread in the form of pones

pon·iard \'pän-yərd\ *n* : DAGGER

pon·tiff \'pän-təf\ *n* : POPE — **pon·tif·i·cal** \pän-'ti-fi-kəl\ *adj*

¹pon·tif·i·cate \pän-'ti-fi-kət, -fə-ˌkāt\ *n* : the state, office, or term of office of a pontiff

²pon·tif·i·cate \pän-'ti-fə-ˌkāt\ *vb* **-cat·ed; -cat·ing** : to deliver dogmatic opinions

pon·toon \pän-'tün\ *n* **1** : a flat-bottomed boat **2** : a boat or float used in building a floating temporary bridge **3** : a float of a seaplane

po·ny \'pō-nē\ *n, pl* **ponies** : a small horse

po·ny·tail \-ˌtāl\ *n* : a style of arranging hair to resemble the tail of a pony

pooch \'püch\ *n* : DOG

poo·dle \'püd-ᵊl\ *n* [G *Pudel*, short for *Pudelhund*, fr. *pudeln* to splash + *Hund* dog] : a dog of any of three breeds of active intelligent heavy-coated solid-colored dogs

pooh–pooh \'pü-ˌpü\ *also* **pooh** \'pü\ *vb* **1** : to express contempt or impatience **2** : DERIDE, SCORN

¹pool \'pül\ *n* **1** : a small deep body of usu. fresh water **2** : a small body of standing liquid **3** : SWIMMING POOL

²pool *vb* : to form a pool

³pool *n* **1** : all the money bet on the result of a particular event **2** : any of several games of billiards played on a table having six pockets **3** : the amount contributed by the participants in a joint venture **4** : a combination between competing firms for mutual profit **5** : a readily available supply

⁴pool *vb* : to combine (as resources) in a common fund or effort

¹poop \'püp\ *n* : an enclosed superstructure at the stern of a ship

²poop *n, slang* : INFORMATION

poop deck *n* : a partial deck above a ship's main afterdeck

poor \'pùr\ *adj* **1** : lacking material possessions ⟨∼

people⟩ **2** : less than adequate : MEAGER ⟨∼ crop⟩ **3** : arousing pity ⟨you ∼ thing⟩ **4** : inferior in quality or value **5** : UNPRODUCTIVE, BARREN ⟨∼ soil⟩ **6** : fairly unsatisfactory ⟨∼ prospects⟩; *also* : UNFAVORABLE ⟨∼ opinion⟩ — **poor·ly** *adv*

poor boy \'pō-ˌbȯi, 'pȯr-\ *n* : SUBMARINE 2

poor·house \'pùr-ˌhaùs\ *n* : a publicly supported home for needy or dependent persons

poor–mouth \-ˌmaùth, -ˌmaùth\ *vb* : to plead poverty as a defense or excuse

¹pop \'päp\ *vb* **popped; pop·ping 1** : to go, come, enter, or issue forth suddenly or quickly ⟨∼ into bed⟩ **2** : to put or thrust suddenly ⟨∼ questions⟩ **3** : to burst or cause to burst with a sharp sound; *also* : to make a sharp sound **4** : to protrude from the sockets **5** : SHOOT **6** : to hit a pop-up

²pop *n* **1** : a sharp explosive sound **2** : SHOT **3** : SODA POP

³pop *n* : FATHER

⁴pop *adj* **1** : POPULAR ⟨∼ music⟩ **2** : of or relating to pop music ⟨∼ singer⟩ **3** : of or relating to the popular culture disseminated through the mass media ⟨∼ psychology⟩ **4** : of, relating to, or imitating pop art ⟨∼ painter⟩

⁵pop *n* : pop music or culture; *also* : POP ART

⁶pop *abbr* population

pop art *n* : art in which commonplace objects (as comic strips or soup cans) are used as subject matter — **pop artist** *n*

pop·corn \'päp-ˌkȯrn\ *n* : an Indian corn whose kernels burst open into a white starchy mass when heated; *also* : the burst kernels

pope \'pōp\ *n, often cap* : the head of the Roman Catholic Church

pop–eyed \'päp-ˌīd\ *adj* : having eyes that bulge (as from disease)

pop fly *n* : POP-UP

pop·gun \'päp-ˌgən\ *n* : a toy gun for shooting pellets with compressed air

pop·in·jay \'pä-pən-ˌjā\ *n* [ME *papejay* parrot, fr. MF *papegai, papejai*, fr. Ar *babghā'*] : a strutting supercilious person

pop·lar \'pä-plər\ *n* **1** : any of a genus of slender quick-growing trees (as a cottonwood) related to the willows **2** : the wood of a poplar

pop·lin \'pä-plən\ *n* : a strong plain-woven fabric with crosswise ribs

pop·over \'päp-ˌō-vər\ *n* : a hollow muffin made from a thin batter rich in egg

pop·per \'pä-pər\ *n* : a utensil for popping corn

pop·py \'pä-pē\ *n, pl* **poppies** : any of a genus of herbs with showy flowers including one that yields opium

pop·py·cock \-ˌkäk\ *n* : empty talk or writing : NONSENSE

pop·u·lace \'pä-pyə-ləs\ *n* **1** : the common people **2** : POPULATION

pop·u·lar \'pä-pyə-lər\ *adj* **1** : of or relating to the general public ⟨∼ government⟩ **2** : suited to the tastes of the general public ⟨∼ style⟩ **3** : INEXPENSIVE ⟨∼ rates⟩ **4** : frequently encountered or widely accepted ⟨∼ notion⟩ **5** : commonly liked or approved ⟨∼ teacher⟩ — **pop·u·lar·i·ty** \ˌpä-pyə-'lar-ə-tē\ *n* — **pop·u·lar·ize** \'pä-pyə-lə-ˌrīz\ *vb* — **pop·u·lar·ly** *adv*

pop·u·late \'pä-pyə-ˌlāt\ *vb* **-lat·ed; -lat·ing 1** : to have a place in : INHABIT **2** : PEOPLE

pop·u·la·tion \ˌpä-pyə-'lā-shən\ *n* **1** : the people or number of people in an area **2** : the organisms inhabiting a particular locality **3** : a group of individuals or items from which samples are taken for statistical measurement

population explosion *n* : a pyramiding of numbers of a biological population; *esp* : the recent great increase in human numbers resulting from increased survival and exponential population growth

pop·u·list \'pä-pyə-list\ *n* : a believer in or advocate of the rights, wisdom, or virtues of the common people — **pop·u·lism** \-ˌli-zəm\ *n*

pop·u·lous \\'pä-pyə-ləs\ *adj* **1** : densely populated; *also* : having a large population **2** : CROWDED — **pop·u·lous·ness** *n*

pop–up \\'päp-‚əp\ *n* : a short high fly in baseball

por·ce·lain \\'pȯr-sə-lən\ *n* : a fine-grained translucent ceramic ware

porch \\'pȯrch\ *n* : a covered entrance usu. with a separate roof

por·cine \\'pȯr-‚sīn\ *adj* : of, relating to, or suggesting swine

por·cu·pine \\'pȯr-kyə-‚pīn\ *n* [ME *porkepin*, fr. MF *porc espin*, fr. It *porcospino*, fr. L *porcus* pig + *spina* spine, prickle] : any of various mammals having stiff sharp spines mingled with their hair

¹**pore** \\'pȯr\ *vb* **pored; por·ing 1** : to read studiously or attentively ⟨~ over a book⟩ **2** : PONDER, REFLECT

²**pore** *n* : a tiny hole or space (as in the skin or soil) — **pored** \\'pȯrd\ *adj*

pork \\'pȯrk\ *n* : the flesh of swine dressed for use as food

pork barrel *n* : government projects or appropriations yielding rich patronage benefits

pork·er \\'pȯr-kər\ *n* : HOG; *esp* : a young pig suitable for use as fresh pork

por·nog·ra·phy \pȯr-'nä-grə-fē\ *n* : the depiction of erotic behavior intended to cause sexual excitement — **por·no·graph·ic** \‚pȯr-nə-'gra-fik\ *adj*

po·rous \\'pȯr-əs\ *adj* **1** : full of pores **2** : permeable to fluids : ABSORPTIVE — **po·ros·i·ty** \pə-'rä-sə-tē\ *n*

por·phy·ry \\'pȯr-fə-rē\ *n, pl* **-ries** : a rock consisting of feldspar crystals embedded in a compact fine-grained base material — **por·phy·rit·ic** \‚pȯr-fə-'ri-tik\ *adj*

por·poise \\'pȯr-pəs\ *n* [ME *porpoys*, fr. MF *porpois*, fr. ML *porcopiscis*, fr. L *porcus* pig + *piscis* fish] : any of a family of small gregarious toothed whales; *also* : DOLPHIN 1

por·ridge \\'pȯr-ij\ *n* : a soft food made by boiling meal of grains or legumes in milk or water

por·rin·ger \\'pȯr-ən-jər\ *n* : a low one-handled metal bowl or cup

¹**port** \\'pȯrt\ *n* **1** : HARBOR **2** : a city with a harbor **3** : AIRPORT

²**port** *n* **1** : an inlet or outlet (as in an engine) for a fluid **2** : PORTHOLE

³**port** *vb* : to turn or put a helm to the left

⁴**port** *n* : the left side of a ship or airplane looking forward — **port** *adj*

⁵**port** *n* : a sweet fortified wine

por·ta·ble \\'pȯr-tə-bəl\ *adj* : capable of being carried — **portable** *n*

¹**por·tage** \\'pȯr-tij, pȯr-'täzh\ *n* [ME, fr. MF, fr. *porter* to carry] : the carrying of boats and goods overland between navigable bodies of water; *also* : a route for such carrying

²**portage** *vb* **por·taged; por·tag·ing** : to carry gear over a portage

por·tal \\'pȯrt-ᵊl\ *n* : DOOR, ENTRANCE; *esp* : a grand or imposing one

portal–to–portal *adj* : of or relating to the time spent by a worker in traveling from the entrance to an employer's property to the worker's actual job site (as in a mine)

port·cul·lis \pȯrt-'kə-ləs\ *n* : a grating at the gateway of a castle or fortress that can be let down to stop entrance

porte co·chere \‚pȯrt-kō-'sher\ *n* [F *porte cochère*, lit., coach door] : a roofed structure extending from the entrance of a building over an adjacent driveway and sheltering those getting in or out of vehicles

por·tend \pȯr-'tend\ *vb* **1** : to give a sign or warning of beforehand **2** : INDICATE, SIGNIFY **syn** augur, prognosticate, foretell, predict, forecast, prophesy

por·tent \\'pȯr-‚tent\ *n* **1** : something that foreshadows a coming event : OMEN **2** : MARVEL, PRODIGY

por·ten·tous \pȯr-'ten-təs\ *adj* **1** : of, relating to, or constituting a portent **2** : PRODIGIOUS **3** : self-consciously solemn : POMPOUS

¹**por·ter** \\'pȯr-tər\ *n, chiefly Brit* : DOORKEEPER

²**porter** *n* **1** : a person who carries burdens; *esp* : one employed (as at a terminal) to carry baggage **2** : an attendant in a railroad car **3** : a dark heavy ale

por·ter·house \\'pȯr-tər-‚hau̇s\ *n* : a choice beefsteak with a large tenderloin

port·fo·lio \pȯrt-'fō-lē-‚ō\ *n, pl* **-li·os 1** : a portable case for papers or drawings **2** : the office and functions of a minister of state **3** : the securities held by an investor

port·hole \\'pȯrt-‚hōl\ *n* : an opening (as a window) in the side of a ship or aircraft

por·ti·co \\'pȯr-ti-‚kō\ *n, pl* **-coes** or **-cos** [It] : a row of columns supporting a roof around or at the entrance of a building

¹**por·tion** \\'pȯr-shən\ *n* **1** : one's part or share ⟨a ~ of food⟩ **2** : DOWRY **3** : an individual's lot **4** : a part of a whole ⟨a ~ of the sky⟩

²**portion** *vb* **1** : to divide into portions **2** : to allot to as a portion

port·land cement \\'pȯrt-lənd-\ *n* : a cement made by calcining and grinding a mixture of clay and limestone

port·ly \\'pȯrt-lē\ *adj* **port·li·er; -est** : somewhat stout

port·man·teau \pȯrt-'man-‚tō\ *n, pl* **-teaus** or **-teaux** \-‚tōz\ [MF *portemanteau*, fr. *porter* to carry + *manteau* mantle, fr. L *mantellum*] : a large traveling bag

port of call : an intermediate port where ships customarily stop for supplies, repairs, or transshipment of cargo

port of entry 1 : a place where foreign goods may be cleared through a customhouse **2** : a place where an alien may enter a country

por·trait \\'pȯr-trət, -‚trāt\ *n* : a picture (as a painting or photograph) of a person usu. showing the face

por·trait·ist \-trə-tist\ *n* : a maker of portraits

por·trai·ture \\'pȯr-trə-‚chùr\ *n* : the practice or art of making portraits

por·tray \pȯr-'trā\ *vb* **1** : to make a picture of : DEPICT **2** : to describe in words **3** : to play the role of — **por·tray·al** *n*

Por·tu·guese \\'pȯr-chə-‚gēz, -‚gēs; ‚pȯr-chə-'gēz, -'gēs\ *n, pl* **Portuguese 1** : a native or inhabitant of Portugal **2** : the language of Portugal and Brazil — **Portuguese** *adj*

Portuguese man–of–war *n* : any of several large colonial marine invertebrate animals related to the jellyfishes and having a large sac by which the colony floats at the surface

por·tu·laca \‚pȯr-chə-'la-kə\ *n* : a tropical succulent herb cultivated for its showy flowers

pos *abbr* **1** position **2** positive

¹**pose** \\'pōz\ *vb* **posed; pos·ing 1** : to assume or cause to assume a posture usu. for artistic purposes **2** : to set forth : PROPOSE ⟨~ a question⟩ **3** : to affect an attitude or character

²**pose** *n* **1** : a sustained posture; *esp* : one assumed by a model **2** : an attitude assumed for effect : PRETENSE

¹**pos·er** \\'pō-zər\ *n* : a puzzling question

²**poser** *n* : a person who poses

po·seur \pō-'zər\ *n* [F, lit., poser] : an affected or insincere person

posh \\'päsh\ *adj* : FASHIONABLE

pos·it \\'pä-zət\ *vb* : to assume the existence of : POSTULATE

po·si·tion \pə-'zi-shən\ *n* **1** : an arranging in order **2** : the stand taken on a question **3** : the point or area occupied by something : SITUATION **4** : a certain arrangement of bodily parts ⟨exercise in a sitting ~⟩ **5** : RANK, STATUS **6** : EMPLOYMENT, JOB — **position** *vb*

¹**pos·i·tive** \\'pä-zə-tiv\ *adj* **1** : expressed definitely ⟨her answer was a ~ no⟩ **2** : CONFIDENT, CERTAIN **3** : of, relating to, or constituting the degree of grammatical comparison that denotes no increase in quality, quan-

tity, or relation **4** : not fictitious : REAL **5** : active and effective in function ⟨~ leadership⟩ **6** : having the light and shade as existing in the original subject ⟨a ~ photograph⟩ **7** : numerically greater than zero ⟨a ~ number⟩ **8** : being, relating to, or charged with electricity of which the proton is the elementary unit **9** : AFFIRMATIVE ⟨a ~ response⟩ — **pos·i·tive·ly** *adv* — **pos·i·tive·ness** *n*

²**positive** *n* **1** : the positive degree or a positive form in a language **2** : a positive photograph

pos·i·tron \'pä-zə-ˌträn\ *n* : a positively charged particle having the same mass and magnitude of charge as the electron

poss *abbr* possessive

pos·se \'pä-sē\ *n* [ML *posse comitatus,* lit., power or authority of the county] : a body of persons organized to assist a sheriff in an emergency

pos·sess \pə-'zes\ *vb* **1** : to have as property : OWN **2** : to have as an attribute, knowledge, or skill **3** : to enter into and control firmly ⟨~ed by a devil⟩ — **pos·ses·sor** \-'ze-sər\ *n*

pos·ses·sion \-'ze-shən\ *n* **1** : control or occupancy of property **2** : OWNERSHIP **3** : something owned : PROPERTY **4** : domination by something (as an evil spirit, a passion, or an idea) **5** : SELF-CONTROL

pos·ses·sive \pə-'ze-siv\ *adj* **1** : of, relating to, or constituting a grammatical case denoting ownership **2** : showing the desire to possess ⟨a ~ nature⟩ — **possessive** *n* — **pos·ses·sive·ness** *n*

pos·si·ble \'pä-sə-bəl\ *adj* **1** : being within the limits of ability, capacity, or realization **2** : being something that may or may not occur ⟨~ dangers⟩ **3** : able or fitted to become ⟨a ~ site for a bridge⟩ — **pos·si·bil·i·ty** \ˌpä-sə-'bi-lə-tē\ *n* — **pos·si·bly** \'pä-sə-blē\ *adv*

pos·sum \'pä-səm\ *n* : OPOSSUM

¹**post** \'pōst\ *n* **1** : an upright piece of timber or metal serving esp. as a support : PILLAR **2** : a pole or stake set up as a mark or indicator

²**post** *vb* **1** : to affix to a usual place (as a wall) for public notices **2** : to publish or announce by or as if by a public notice ⟨~ grades⟩ **3** : to forbid (property) to trespassers by putting up a notice **4** : SCORE

³**post** *n* **1** *obs* : COURIER **2** *chiefly Brit* : ¹MAIL; *also* : POST OFFICE

⁴**post** *vb* **1** : to ride or travel with haste : HURRY **2** : MAIL ⟨~ a letter⟩ **3** : to enter in a ledger **4** : INFORM ⟨kept him ~ed on new developments⟩

⁵**post** *n* **1** : the place at which a soldier is stationed; *esp* : a sentry's beat or station **2** : a station or task to which a person is assigned **3** : the place at which a body of troops is stationed : CAMP **4** : OFFICE, POSITION **5** : a trading settlement or station

⁶**post** *vb* **1** : to station in a given place **2** : to put up (as bond)

post·age \'pōs-tij\ *n* : the fee for postal service; *also* : stamps representing this fee

post·al \'pōst-əl\ *adj* : of or relating to the mails or the post office

postal card *n* : POSTCARD

postal service *n* : a government agency or department handling the transmission of mail

post·card \'pōst-ˌkärd\ *n* : a card on which a message may be written for mailing without an envelope

post chaise *n* : a 4-wheeled closed carriage for two to four persons

post·con·so·nan·tal \ˌpōst-ˌkän-sə-'nant-əl\ *adj* : immediately following a consonant

post·date \ˌpōst-'dāt\ *vb* : to date with a date later than that of execution ⟨~ a check⟩

post·doc·tor·al \-'däk-tə-rəl\ *also* **post·doc·tor·ate** \-tə-rət\ *adj* : of, relating to, or engaged in advanced academic or professional work beyond a doctor's degree

post·er \'pō-stər\ *n* : a bill or placard for posting often in a public place

¹**pos·te·ri·or** \pō-'stir-ē-ər, pä-\ *adj* **1** : later in time **2** : situated behind

²**pos·te·ri·or** \pä-'stir-ē-ər, pō-\ *n* : the hinder bodily parts; *esp* : BUTTOCKS

pos·ter·i·ty \pä-'ster-ə-tē\ *n* **1** : the descendants from one ancestor **2** : all future generations

pos·tern \'pōs-tərn, 'päs-\ *n* **1** : a back door or gate **2** : a private or side entrance

post exchange *n* : a store at a military post that sells to military personnel and authorized civilians

post·grad·u·ate \(ˌ)pōst-'gra-jə-wət\ *adj* : of or relating to studies beyond the bachelor's degree — **postgraduate** *n*

post·haste \'pōst-'hāst\ *adv* : with all possible speed

post·hole \-ˌhōl\ *n* : a hole for a post and esp. a fence post

post·hu·mous \'päs-chə-məs\ *adj* **1** : born after the death of the father **2** : published after the death of the author — **post·hu·mous·ly** *adv*

post·hyp·not·ic \ˌpōst-hip-'nä-tik\ *adj* : of, relating to, or characteristic of the period following a hypnotic trance

pos·til·ion *or* **pos·til·lion** \pō-'stil-yən\ *n* : a rider on the left-hand horse of a pair drawing a coach

Post·im·pres·sion·ism \ˌpōst-im-'pre-shə-ˌni-zəm\ *n* : a late 19th century French theory or practice of art that stresses variously volume, picture structure, or expressionism

post·lude \'pōst-ˌlüd\ *n* : an organ solo played at the end of a church service

post·man \-mən, -ˌman\ *n* : MAILMAN

post·mark \-ˌmärk\ *n* : an official postal marking on a piece of mail; *esp* : the mark canceling the postage stamp — **postmark** *vb*

post·mas·ter \-ˌmas-tər\ *n* : a person who has charge of a post office

postmaster general *n, pl* **postmasters general** : an official in charge of a national postal service

post me·ri·di·em \ˌpōst-mə-'ri-dē-əm\ *adj* [L] : being after noon

post·mis·tress \'pōst-ˌmis-trəs\ *n* : a woman in charge of a post office

¹**post·mor·tem** \ˌpōst-'mòr-təm\ *adj* [L *post mortem* after death] **1** : done, occurring, or collected after death **2** : following the event

²**postmortem** *n* **1** : an analysis or discussion of an event after it is over **2** : AUTOPSY

post·na·sal drip \'pōst-ˌnā-zəl-\ *n* : flow of mucous secretion from the posterior part of the nasal cavity onto the wall of the pharynx

post·na·tal \(ˌ)pōst-'nāt-əl\ *adj* : occurring or being after birth; *esp* : of or relating to a newborn infant

post office *n* **1** : POSTAL SERVICE **2** : a local branch of a post office department

post·op·er·a·tive \(ˌ)pōst-'ä-prə-tiv, -pə-ˌrā-\ *adj* : following or having undergone a surgical operation ⟨~ care⟩

post·paid \'pōst-'pād\ *adv* : with the postage paid by the sender and not chargeable to the receiver

post·par·tum \(ˌ)pōst-'pär-təm\ *adj* [NL *post partum* after birth] : following parturition — **postpartum** *adv*

post·pone \pōst-'pōn\ *vb* **post·poned; post·pon·ing** : to put off to a later time — **post·pone·ment** *n*

post road *n* : a road over which mail is carried

post·script \'pōst-ˌskript\ *n* : a note added esp. to a completed letter

post time *n* : the designated time for the start of a horse race

pos·tu·lant \'päs-chə-lənt\ *n* : a probationary candidate for membership in a religious order

¹**pos·tu·late** \'päs-chə-ˌlāt\ *vb* **-lat·ed; -lat·ing** : to assume as true

²**pos·tu·late** \'päs-chə-lət, -ˌlāt\ *n* : a proposition taken for granted as true esp. as a basis for a chain of reasoning

¹**pos·ture** \'päs-chər\ *n* **1** : the position or bearing of the body or one of its parts **2** : STATE, CONDITION **3** : ATTITUDE

²**posture** *vb* **pos·tured; pos·tur·ing** : to strike a pose esp. for effect

post·war \'pōst-'wor\ *adj* : of or relating to the period after a war

po·sy \'pō-zē\ *n, pl* **posies 1** : a brief sentiment : MOTTO **2** : a bunch of flowers; *also* : FLOWER

¹**pot** \'pät\ *n* **1** : a rounded container used chiefly for domestic purposes **2** : the total of the bets at stake at one time **3** : RUIN ⟨go to ∼⟩ — **pot·ful** *n*

²**pot** *vb* **pot·ted; pot·ting 1** : to preserve or place in a pot **2** : SHOOT

³**pot** *n* : MARIJUANA

po·ta·ble \'pō-tə-bəl\ *adj* : suitable for drinking — **po·ta·bil·i·ty** \ˌpō-tə-'bi-lə-tē\ *n*

po·tage \pȯ-'täzh\ *n* : a thick soup

pot·ash \'pät-ˌash\ *n* [sing. of *pot ashes*] : potassium or any of its various compounds esp. as used in agriculture

po·tas·si·um \pə-'ta-sē-əm\ *n* : a silver-white soft metallic chemical element that occurs abundantly in nature — see ELEMENT table

potassium bromide *n* : a crystalline salt used as a sedative and in photography

potassium carbonate *n* : a white salt used in making glass and soap

potassium nitrate *n* : a soluble salt used in making gunpowder, as a fertilizer, and in medicine

po·ta·tion \pō-'tā-shən\ *n* : a usu. alcoholic drink; *also* : the act of drinking

po·ta·to \pə-'tā-tō\ *n, pl* **-toes** : the edible starchy tuber of a plant related to the tomato; *also* : this plant

potato beetle *n* : COLORADO POTATO BEETLE

potato bug *n* : COLORADO POTATO BEETLE

pot·bel·ly \'pät-ˌbe-lē\ *n* : a protruding abdomen — **pot·bel·lied** \-lēd\ *adj*

pot·boil·er \-ˌbȯi-lər\ *n* : a usu. inferior work of art or literature produced chiefly for profit

po·tent \'pōt-ᵊnt\ *adj* **1** : having authority or influence : POWERFUL **2** : chemically or medicinally effective **3** : able to copulate — used esp. of the male syn forceful, forcible, mighty, puissant — **po·ten·cy** \-ᵊn-sē\ *n*

po·ten·tate \'pōt-ᵊn-ˌtāt\ *n* : one who wields controlling power : RULER

¹**po·ten·tial** \pə-'ten-chəl\ *adj* : existing in possibility : capable of becoming actual ⟨a ∼ champion⟩ syn dormant, latent, quiescent — **po·ten·ti·al·i·ty** \pə-ˌten-chē-'a-lə-tē\ *n* — **po·ten·tial·ly** \-'ten-chə-lē\ *adv*

²**potential** *n* **1** : something that can develop or become actual ⟨a ∼ for violence⟩ **2** : the work required to move a unit positive charge from infinity to a point in question; *also* : POTENTIAL DIFFERENCE

potential difference *n* : the difference in potential between two points that represents the work involved in the transfer of a unit quantity of electricity from one point to the other

potential energy *n* : the energy an object has because of its position or the arrangement of its parts

po·ten·ti·ate \pə-'ten-chē-ˌāt\ *vb* **-at·ed; -at·ing** : to make potent; *esp* : to augment the activity of (as a drug) synergistically — **po·ten·ti·a·tion** \-ˌten-chē-'ā-shən\ *n*

pot·head \'pät-ˌhed\ *n* : a person who smokes marijuana

poth·er \'pä-thər\ *n* : a noisy disturbance; *also* : FUSS

pot·herb \'pät-ˌərb, -ˌhərb\ *n* : an herb whose leaves or stems are boiled for greens or used to season food

pot·hole \'pät-ˌhōl\ *n* : a large pit or hole (as in a road surface)

pot·hook \-ˌhůk\ *n* : an S-shaped hook for hanging pots and kettles over an open fire

po·tion \'pō-shən\ *n* : a mixture of liquids (as liquor or medicine)

pot·luck \'pät-'lək\ *n* : the regular meal available to a

guest for whom no special preparations have been made

pot·pie \-'pī\ *n* : pastry-covered meat and vegetables cooked in a deep dish

pot·pour·ri \ˌpō-pů-'rē\ *n* [F *pot pourri,* lit., rotten pot] **1** : a mixture of flowers, herbs, and spices used for scent **2** : a miscellaneous collection

pot·sherd \'pät-ˌshərd\ *n* : a pottery fragment

pot·shot \-ˌshät\ *n* **1** : a shot taken from ambush or at a random or easy target **2** : a critical remark made in a random or sporadic manner

pot·tage \'pä-tij\ *n* : a thick soup of vegetables and often meat

¹**pot·ter** \'pä-tər\ *n* : one that makes pottery

²**potter** *vb* : PUTTER

pot·tery \'pä-tə-rē\ *n, pl* **-ter·ies 1** : a place where earthen pots and dishes are made **2** : the art of the potter **3** : dishes, pots, and vases made from clay

¹**pouch** \'paůch\ *n* **1** : a small bag (as for tobacco) carried on the person **2** : a bag for storing or transporting goods ⟨mail ∼⟩ ⟨diplomatic ∼⟩ **3** : an anatomical sac; *esp* : one for carrying the young on the abdomen of a female marsupial (as a kangaroo)

²**pouch** *vb* : to put or form into or as if into a pouch

poult \'pōlt\ *n* : a young fowl; *esp* : a young turkey

poul·ter·er \'pōl-tər-ər\ *n* : one that deals in poultry

poul·tice \'pōl-təs\ *n* : a soft usu. heated and medicated mass spread on cloth and applied to a sore or injury — **poultice** *vb*

poul·try \'pōl-trē\ *n* : domesticated birds kept for eggs or meat — **poul·try·man** \-mən\ *n*

pounce \'paůns\ *vb* **pounced; pounc·ing** : to spring or swoop upon and seize something

¹**pound** \'paůnd\ *n, pl* **pounds** *also* **pound 1** : a unit of avoirdupois, troy, and apothecaries' weight — see WEIGHT table **2** — see MONEY table

²**pound** *n* : a public enclosure where stray animals are kept

³**pound** *vb* **1** : to crush to a powder or pulp by beating **2** : to strike or beat heavily or repeatedly **3** : DRILL 1 **4** : to move or move along heavily

pound·age \'paůn-dij\ *n* : POUNDS; *also* : weight in pounds

pound cake *n* : a rich cake made with a large proportion of eggs and shortening

pound–fool·ish \'paůnd-'fü-lish\ *adj* : imprudent in dealing with large sums or large matters

pour \'pōr\ *vb* **1** : to flow or cause to flow in a stream or flood **2** : to rain hard **3** : to supply freely and copiously

pour·boire \pür-'bwär\ *n* [F, fr. *pour boire* for drinking] : TIP, GRATUITY

pout \'paůt\ *vb* : to show displeasure by thrusting out the lips; *also* : to look sullen — **pout** *n*

pov·er·ty \'pä-vər-tē\ *n* [ME *poverte,* fr. OF *poverté,* fr. L *paupertat-, paupertas,* fr. *pauper* poor] **1** : lack of money or material possessions : WANT **2** : poor quality (as of soil)

poverty line *n* : a level of personal or family income below which one is classified as poor according to government standards

pov·er·ty–strick·en \'pä-vər-tē-ˌstri-kən\ *adj* : very poor : DESTITUTE

POW \ˌpē-(ˌ)ō-'də-bəl-(ˌ)yü\ *n* : PRISONER OF WAR

¹**pow·der** \'paů-dər\ *n* [ME *poudre,* fr. OF, fr. L *pulver-, pulvis* dust] **1** : dry material made up of fine particles; *also* : a usu. medicinal or cosmetic preparation in this form **2** : a solid explosive (as gunpowder) — **pow·dery** *adj*

²**powder** *vb* **1** : to sprinkle or cover with or as if with powder **2** : to reduce to powder

powder room *n* : a rest room for women

¹**pow·er** \'paů-ər\ *n* **1** : the ability to act or produce an effect **2** : a position of ascendancy over others : AUTHORITY **3** : one that has control or authority; *esp* : a sovereign state **4** : physical might; *also* : mental or

moral vigor **5** : the number of times as indicated by an exponent a number is to be multiplied by itself; *also* : the product itself **6** : force or energy used to do work; *also* : the time rate at which work is done or energy transferred **7** : MAGNIFICATION 2 — **pow·er·ful** \-fəl\ *adj* — **pow·er·ful·ly** *adv* — **pow·er·less** *adj*

²**power** *vb* : to supply with power and esp. motive power·er

pow·er·boat \-ˌbōt\ *n* : MOTORBOAT

pow·er·house \ˈpaů-ər-ˌhaůs\ *n* **1** : POWER PLANT 1 **2** : one having great drive, energy, or ability

power plant *n* **1** : a building in which electric power is generated **2** : an engine and related parts supplying the motive power of a self-propelled vehicle

pow·wow \ˈpaů-ˌwaů\ *n* **1** : a No. American Indian ceremony (as for victory in war) **2** : a meeting for discussion : CONFERENCE

pox \ˈpäks\ *n, pl* **pox** *or* **pox·es** : any of various diseases (as smallpox or syphilis) marked by a rash on the skin

pp *abbr* **1** pages **2** pianissimo

PP *abbr* **1** parcel post **2** past participle **3** postpaid **4** prepaid

ppd *abbr* **1** postpaid **2** prepaid

PPS *abbr* [L *post postscriptum*] an additional postscript

ppt *abbr* precipitate

PQ *abbr* Province of Quebec

pr *abbr* **1** pair **2** price

Pr *symbol* praseodymium

PR *abbr* **1** payroll **2** public relations **3** Puerto Rico

prac·ti·ca·ble \ˈprak-ti-kə-bəl\ *adj* : capable of being put into practice, done, or accomplished — **prac·ti·ca·bil·i·ty** \ˌprak-ti-kə-ˈbi-lə-tē\ *n*

prac·ti·cal \ˈprak-ti-kəl\ *adj* **1** : of, relating to, or shown in practice ⟨∼ questions⟩ **2** : VIRTUAL ⟨∼ control⟩ **3** : capable of being put to use ⟨a ∼ knowledge of French⟩ **4** : inclined to action as opposed to speculation ⟨a ∼ person⟩ **5** : qualified by practice ⟨a good ∼ mechanic⟩ — **prac·ti·cal·i·ty** \ˌprak-ti-ˈka-lə-tē\ *n* — **prac·ti·cal·ly** \-k(ə-)lē\ *adv*

practical joke *n* : a prank intended to trick or embarrass someone or cause physical discomfort

practical nurse *n* : a professional nurse without all of the qualifications of a registered nurse; *esp* : LICENSED PRACTICAL NURSE

¹**prac·tice** *or* **prac·tise** \ˈprak-təs\ *vb* **prac·ticed** *or* **prac·tised; prac·tic·ing** *or* **prac·tis·ing** **1** : CARRY OUT, APPLY ⟨∼ what you preach⟩ **2** : to perform or work at repeatedly so as to become proficient ⟨∼ tennis strokes⟩ **3** : to do or perform customarily ⟨∼ politeness⟩ **4** : to be professionally engaged in ⟨∼ law⟩

²**practice** *also* **practise** *n* **1** : actual performance or application **2** : customary action : HABIT **3** : systematic exercise for proficiency **4** : the exercise of a profession; *also* : a professional business

prac·ti·tion·er \prak-ˈti-shə-nər\ *n* : one who practices a profession

prae·tor \ˈprē-tər\ *n* : an ancient Roman magistrate ranking below a consul — **prae·to·ri·an** \prē-ˈtȯr-ē-ən, -ˈtȯr-\ *adj*

prag·mat·ic \prag-ˈma-tik\ *also* **prag·mat·i·cal** \-ti-kəl\ *adj* **1** : of or relating to practical affairs **2** : concerned with the practical consequences of actions or beliefs — **pragmatic** *n* — **prag·mat·i·cal·ly** \-ti-k(ə-)lē\ *adv*

prag·ma·tism \ˈprag-mə-ˌti-zəm\ *n* : a practical approach to problems and affairs

prai·rie \ˈprer-ē\ *n* : a broad tract of level or rolling grassland

prairie dog *n* : an American burrowing black-tailed rodent related to the squirrels and living in colonies

prairie schooner *n* : a covered wagon used by pioneers in cross-country travel

praise \ˈprāz\ *vb* **praised; prais·ing** **1** : to express approval of : COMMEND **2** : to glorify (a divinity or a saint) esp. in song — **praise** *n*

praise·wor·thy \-ˌwər-ˌthē\ *adj* : LAUDABLE

pra·line \ˈprä-ˌlēn, ˈprā-\ *n* [F] : a confection of nuts and sugar

pram \ˈpram\ *n, chiefly Brit* : PERAMBULATOR

prance \ˈprans\ *vb* **pranced; pranc·ing** **1** : to spring from the hind legs ⟨a *prancing* horse⟩ **2** : SWAGGER; *also* : CAPER — **prance** *n* — **pranc·er** *n*

prank \ˈpraŋk\ *n* : a playful or mildly mischievous act : TRICK

prank·ster \ˈpraŋk-stər\ *n* : a person who plays pranks

pra·seo·dym·i·um \ˌprä-zē-ō-ˈdi-mē-əm\ *n* : a yellowish white metallic chemical element — see ELEMENT table

prate \ˈprāt\ *vb* **prat·ed; prat·ing** : to talk long and idly : chatter foolishly

prat·fall \ˈprat-ˌfȯl\ *n* **1** : a fall on the buttocks **2** : a humiliating blunder

¹**prat·tle** \ˈprat-ᵊl\ *vb* **prat·tled; prat·tling** : PRATE, BABBLE

²**prattle** *n* : trifling or childish talk

prawn \ˈprȯn\ *n* : any of numerous edible shrimplike crustaceans; *also* : SHRIMP 1

pray \ˈprā\ *vb* **1** : ENTREAT, IMPLORE **2** : to ask earnestly for something **3** : to address God or a god esp. with supplication

prayer \ˈprar\ *n* **1** : a supplication or expression addressed to God or a god; *also* : a set order of words used in praying **2** : an earnest request or wish **3** : the act or practice of praying to God or a god **4** : a religious service consisting chiefly of prayers — often used in pl. **5** : something prayed for **6** : a slight chance

prayer book *n* : a book containing prayers and often directions for worship

prayer·ful \ˈprar-fəl\ *adj* **1** : DEVOUT **2** : EARNEST — **prayer·ful·ly** *adv*

praying mantis *n* : MANTIS

PRC *abbr* People's Republic of China

preach \ˈprēch\ *vb* **1** : to deliver a sermon **2** : to set forth in a sermon **3** : to advocate earnestly — **preach·er** *n* — **preach·ment** *n*

pre·ad·o·les·cence \ˌprē-ˌad-ᵊl-ˈes-ᵊns\ *n* : the period of human development just preceding adolescence — **pre·ad·o·les·cent** \-ᵊnt\ *adj or n*

pre·am·ble \ˈprē-ˌam-bəl\ *n* [ME, fr. MF *preambule*, fr. ML *preambulum*, fr. LL, neut. of *praeambulus* walking in front of, fr. L *prae* in front of + *ambulare* to walk] : an introductory part ⟨the ∼ to a constitution⟩

pre·ar·range \ˌprē-ə-ˈrānj\ *vb* : to arrange beforehand — **pre·ar·range·ment** *n*

pre·as·signed \ˌprē-ə-ˈsīnd\ *adj* : assigned beforehand

prec *abbr* preceding

Pre·cam·bri·an \ˈprē-ˈkam-brē-ən, -ˈkäm-\ *adj* : of, relating to, or being the era that is earliest in geologic history and is characterized esp. by the appearance of single-celled organisms — **Precambrian** *n*

pre·can·cel \(ˌ)prē-ˈkan-səl\ *vb* : to cancel (a postage stamp) in advance of use — **precancel** *n* — **pre·can·cel·la·tion** \ˌprē-ˌkan-sə-ˈlā-shən\ *n*

pre·can·cer·ous \(ˌ)prē-ˈkan-sə-rəs\ *adj* : likely to become cancerous

pre·car·i·ous \pri-ˈkar-ē-əs\ *adj* : dependent on uncertain conditions : dangerously insecure : UNSTABLE ⟨a ∼ foothold⟩ ⟨∼ prosperity⟩ **syn** delicate, sensitive, ticklish, touchy, tricky — **pre·car·i·ous·ly** *adv* — **pre·car·i·ous·ness** *n*

pre·cau·tion \pri-ˈkȯ-shən\ *n* : a measure taken beforehand to prevent harm or secure good — **pre·cau·tion·ary** \-shə-ˌner-ē\ *adj*

pre·cede \pri-ˈsēd\ *vb* **pre·ced·ed; pre·ced·ing** : to be, go, or come ahead or in front of (as in rank or time)

pre·ce·dence \ˈpre-sə-dəns, pri-ˈsēd-ᵊns\ *n* **1** : the act or fact of preceding **2** : consideration based on order of importance : PRIORITY

¹pre·ce·dent \pri-'sēd-³nt, 'pre-sə-dənt\ *adj* : prior in time, order, or significance

²prec·e·dent \'pre-sə-dənt\ *n* : something said or done that may serve to authorize or justify further words or acts of the same or a similar kind

pre·ced·ing \pri-'sē-diŋ\ *adj* : that precedes **syn** antecedent, foregoing, prior, former, anterior

pre·cen·tor \pri-'sen-tər\ *n* : a leader of the singing of a choir or congregation

pre·cept \'prē-₁sept\ *n* : a command or principle intended as a general rule of action or conduct

pre·cep·tor \pri-'sep-tər, 'prē-₁sep-\ *n* : TUTOR

pre·ces·sion \prē-'se-shən\ *n* : a slow gyration of the rotation axis of a spinning body (as the earth) — **pre·cess** \prē-'ses\ *vb* — **pre·ces·sion·al** \-'sə-shə-nəl\ *adj*

pre·cinct \'prē-₁siŋkt\ *n* **1** : an administrative subdivision (as of a city) : DISTRICT ⟨police ~⟩ ⟨electoral ~⟩ **2** : an enclosure bounded by the limits of a building or place — often used in pl. **3** *pl* : ENVIRONS

pre·ci·os·i·ty \₁pre-shē-'ä-sə-tē\ *n, pl* **-ties** : fastidious refinement

pre·cious \'pre-shəs\ *adj* **1** : of great value ⟨~ jewels⟩ **2** : greatly cherished : DEAR ⟨~ memories⟩ **3** : AFFECTED ⟨~ language⟩

prec·i·pice \'pre-sə-pəs\ *n* : a steep cliff

pre·cip·i·tan·cy \pri-'si-pə-tən-sē\ *n* : undue hastiness or suddenness

¹pre·cip·i·tate \pri-'si-pə-₁tāt\ *vb* **-tat·ed; -tat·ing** [L *praecipitare*, fr. *praecipit-, praeceps* headlong, fr. *prae* in front of + *caput* head] **1** : to throw violently **2** : to throw down **3** : to cause to happen quickly or abruptly ⟨~ a quarrel⟩ **4** : to cause to separate from solution or suspension **5** : to fall as rain, snow, or hail **syn** speed, accelerate, quicken, hasten, hurry

²pre·cip·i·tate \pri-'si-pə-tət, -₁tāt\ *n* : the solid matter that separates from a solution or suspension

³pre·cip·i·tate \pri-'si-pə-tət\ *adj* **1** : showing extreme or unwise haste : RASH **2** : falling with steep descent; *also* : PRECIPITOUS — **pre·cip·i·tate·ly** *adv* — **pre·cip·i·tate·ness** *n*

pre·cip·i·ta·tion \pri-₁si-pə-'tā-shən\ *n* **1** : rash haste **2** : the process of precipitating or forming a precipitate **3** : water that falls to earth esp. as rain or snow; *also* : the quantity of this water

pre·cip·i·tous \pri-'si-pə-təs\ *adj* **1** : PRECIPITATE **2** : having the character of a precipice : very steep ⟨a ~ slope⟩; *also* : containing precipices ⟨~ trails⟩ — **pre·cip·i·tous·ly** *adv*

pré·cis \prā-'sē\ *n, pl* **pré·cis** \-'sēz\ [F] : a concise summary of essentials

pre·cise \pri-'sīs\ *adj* **1** : exactly defined or stated : DEFINITE **2** : highly accurate : EXACT **3** : conforming strictly to a standard : SCRUPULOUS — **pre·cise·ly** *adv* — **pre·cise·ness** *n*

pre·ci·sion \pri-'si-zhən\ *n* : the quality or state of being precise

pre·clude \pri-'klüd\ *vb* **pre·clud·ed; pre·clud·ing** : to make impossible : BAR, PREVENT

pre·co·cious \pri-'kō-shəs\ *adj* [L *praecoc-, praecox*, lit., ripening early, fr. *prae-* ahead + *coquere* to cook] : early in development and esp. in mental development — **pre·co·cious·ly** *adv* — **pre·coc·i·ty** \pri-'kä-sə-tē\ *n*

pre·con·ceive \₁prē-kən-'sēv\ *vb* : to form an opinion of beforehand — **pre·con·cep·tion** \-'sep-shən\ *n*

pre·con·cert·ed \-'sər-təd\ *adj* : arranged or agreed on in advance

pre·con·di·tion \-'di-shən\ *vb* : to put in proper or desired condition or frame of mind in advance

pre·cook \₁prē-'kůk\ *vb* : to cook partially or entirely before final cooking or reheating

pre·cur·sor \pri-'kər-sər\ *n* : one that precedes and indicates the approach of another : FORERUNNER

pred *abbr* predicate

pre·da·ceous *or* **pre·da·cious** \pri-'dā-shəs\ *adj* : living by preying on others : PREDATORY

pre·date \'prē-'dāt\ *vb* : ANTEDATE

pre·da·tion \pri-'dā-shən\ *n* **1** : the act of preying or plundering **2** : a mode of life in which food is primarily obtained by killing and consuming animals

pred·a·tor \'pre-də-tər\ *n* : an animal that lives by predation

pred·a·to·ry \'pre-də-₁tōr-ē\ *adj* **1** : of or relating to plunder ⟨~ warfare⟩ **2** : disposed to exploit others **3** : preying upon other animals

pre·de·cease \₁prē-di-'sēs\ *vb* **-ceased; -ceas·ing** : to die before another person

pre·de·ces·sor \'pre-də-₁se-sər, 'prē-\ *n* : a previous holder of a position to which another has succeeded

pre·des·ig·nate \(₁)prē-'de-zig-₁nāt\ *vb* : to designate beforehand

pre·des·ti·na·tion \₁prē-₁des-tə-'nā-shən\ *n* : the act of foreordaining to an earthly lot or eternal destiny by divine decree; *also* : the state of being so foreordained — **pre·des·ti·nate** \prē-'des-tə-₁nāt\ *vb*

pre·des·tine \prē-'des-tən\ *vb* : to settle beforehand : FOREORDAIN

pre·de·ter·mine \₁prē-di-'tər-mən\ *vb* : to determine beforehand

pred·i·ca·ble \'pre-di-kə-bəl\ *adj* : capable of being predicated or affirmed

pre·dic·a·ment \pri-'di-kə-mənt\ *n* : a difficult or trying situation **syn** dilemma, pickle, quagmire, jam

¹pred·i·cate \'pre-di-kət\ *n* : the part of a sentence or clause that expresses what is said of the subject

²pred·i·cate \'pre-də-₁kāt\ *vb* **-cat·ed; -cat·ing** **1** : AFFIRM **2** : to assert to be a quality or attribute **3** : FOUND, BASE — **pred·i·ca·tion** \₁pre-də-'kā-shən\ *n*

pre·dict \pri-'dikt\ *vb* : to declare in advance — **pre·dict·abil·i·ty** \-₁dik-tə-'bi-lə-tē\ *n* — **pre·dict·able** \-'dik-tə-bəl\ *adj* — **pre·dict·ably** \-blē\ *adv* — **pre·dic·tion** \-'dik-shən\ *n*

pre·di·gest \₁prē-dī-'jest\ *vb* : to simplify for easy use; *also* : to subject to artificial or natural partial digestion

pre·di·lec·tion \₁pre-də-'lek-shən, ₁prē-\ *n* : an established preference for something

pre·dis·pose \₁prē-di-'spōz\ *vb* : to incline in advance : make susceptible — **pre·dis·po·si·tion** \₁prē-₁dis-pə-'zi-shən\ *n*

pre·dom·i·nant \pri-'dä-mə-nənt\ *adj* : greater in importance, strength, influence, or authority — **pre·dom·i·nance** \-nəns\ *n*

pre·dom·i·nant·ly \-nənt-lē\ *adv* : for the most part : MAINLY

pre·dom·i·nate \pri-'dä-mə-₁nāt\ *vb* : to be superior esp. in power or numbers : PREVAIL

pree·mie \'prē-mē\ *n* : a premature baby

pre·em·i·nent \prē-'e-mə-nənt\ *adj* : having highest rank : OUTSTANDING — **pre·em·i·nence** \-nəns\ *n* — **pre·em·i·nent·ly** *adv*

pre·empt \prē-'empt\ *vb* **1** : to settle upon (public land) with the right to purchase before others; *also* : to take by such right **2** : to seize upon before someone else can **3** : to take the place of **syn** usurp, confiscate, appropriate, expropriate — **pre·emp·tion** \-'emp-shən\ *n*

pre·emp·tive \prē-'emp-tiv\ *adj* : marked by the seizing of the initiative : initiated by oneself ⟨~ attack⟩

preen \'prēn\ *vb* **1** : to dress or smooth up : PRIMP **2** : to trim or dress with the bill — used of a bird **3** : to pride (oneself) for achievement

pre·ex·ist \₁prē-ig-'zist\ *vb* : to exist before — **pre·ex·is·tence** \-'zis-təns\ *n* — **pre·ex·is·tent** \-tənt\ *adj*

pref *abbr* **1** preface **2** preference **3** preferred **4** prefix

pre·fab \(₁)prē-'fab, 'prē-₁fab\ *n* : a prefabricated structure

pre·fab·ri·cate \(₁)prē-'fa-brə-₁kāt\ *vb* : to manufacture the parts of (a structure) beforehand for later assembly — **pre·fab·ri·ca·tion** \₁prē-₁fa-bri-'kā-shən\ *n*

¹pref·ace \'pre-fəs\ *n* : the introductory remarks of a speaker or writer — **pref·a·to·ry** \'pre-fə-₁tōr-ē\ *adj*

²**preface** \vb **pref·aced; pref·ac·ing** : to introduce with a preface

pre·fect \ˈprē-ˌfekt\ n 1 : a high official; esp : a chief officer or magistrate 2 : a student monitor

pre·fec·ture \ˈprē-ˌfek-chər\ n : the office, term, or residence of a prefect

pre·fer \pri-ˈfər\ vb **pre·ferred; pre·fer·ring** 1 : PROMOTE 2 : to like better 3 : to bring (as a charge) against a person — **pref·er·a·ble** \ˈpre-fə-rə-bəl\ adj — **pref·er·a·bly** \-blē\ adv

pref·er·ence \ˈpre-frəns, -fə-rəns\ n 1 : a special liking for one thing over another 2 : CHOICE, SELECTION — **pref·er·en·tial** \ˌpre-fə-ˈren-chəl\ adj

pre·fer·ment \pri-ˈfər-mənt\ n : PROMOTION, ADVANCEMENT

pre·fig·ure \prē-ˈfi-gyər\ vb 1 : FORESHADOW 2 : to imagine beforehand

¹**pre·fix** \ˈprē-ˌfiks, prē-ˈfiks\ vb : to place before ⟨∼ a title to a name⟩

²**pre·fix** \ˈprē-ˌfiks\ n : an affix occurring at the beginning of a word

pre·flight \ˌprē-ˈflīt\ adj : preparing for or preliminary to flight

pre·form \(ˌ)prē-ˈfȯrm, ˈprē-ˌfȯrm\ vb : to form or shape beforehand

preg·na·ble \ˈpreg-nə-bəl\ adj : vulnerable to capture ⟨a ∼ fort⟩

preg·nant \ˈpreg-nənt\ adj 1 : containing unborn young within the body 2 : rich in significance : MEANINGFUL — **preg·nan·cy** \-nən-sē\ n

pre·heat \ˌprē-ˈhēt\ vb : to heat beforehand; esp : to heat (an oven) to a designated temperature before using

pre·hen·sile \prē-ˈhen-səl, -ˌsīl\ adj : adapted for grasping esp. by wrapping around ⟨a monkey with a ∼ tail⟩

pre·his·tor·ic \ˌprē-his-ˈtȯr-ik\ or **pre·his·tor·i·cal** \-i-kəl\ adj : of, relating to, or existing in the period before written history began

pre·judge \(ˌ)prē-ˈjəj\ vb : to judge before full hearing or examination

¹**prej·u·dice** \ˈpre-jə-dəs\ n 1 : DAMAGE; esp : detriment to one's rights or claims 2 : an opinion made without adequate basis — **prej·u·di·cial** \ˌpre-jə-ˈdi-shəl\ adj

²**prejudice** vb **-diced; -dic·ing** 1 : to damage by a judgment or action esp. at law 2 : to cause to have prejudice

prel·ate \ˈpre-lət\ n : an ecclesiastic (as a bishop) of high rank — **prel·a·cy** \-lə-sē\ n

pre·launch \ˈprē-ˈlȯnch\ adj : preparing for or preliminary to launch

pre·lim \ˈprē-lim, pri-ˈlim\ n or adj : PRELIMINARY

¹**pre·lim·i·nary** \pri-ˈli-mə-ˌner-ē\ n, pl **-nar·ies** : something that precedes or introduces the main business or event

²**preliminary** adj : preceding the main discourse or business

pre·lude \ˈprel-ˌyüd; ˈpre-ˌlüd, ˈprā-\ n 1 : an introductory performance or event 2 : a musical section or movement introducing the main theme; also : an organ solo played at the beginning of a church service

prem abbr premium

pre·mar·i·tal \(ˌ)prē-ˈmar-ət-ᵊl\ adj : existing or occurring before marriage

pre·ma·ture \ˌprē-mə-ˈtur, -ˈtyur, -ˈchur\ adj : happening, coming, born, or done before the usual or proper time — **pre·ma·ture·ly** adv

¹**pre·med** \ˌprē-ˈmed\ n : a premedical student or course of study

²**premed** adj : PREMEDICAL

pre·med·i·cal \(ˌ)prē-ˈme-di-kəl\ adj : preceding and preparing for the professional study of medicine

pre·med·i·tate \pri-ˈme-də-ˌtāt\ vb : to consider and plan beforehand — **pre·med·i·ta·tion** \-ˌme-də-ˈtā-shən\ n

pre·men·stru·al \(ˌ)prē-ˈmen-strə-wəl\ adj : of, relating to, or occurring in the period just before menstruation

premenstrual syndrome n : a varying group of symptoms manifested by some women prior to menstruation

pre·mie var of PREEMIE

¹**pre·mier** \pri-ˈmir, -ˈmyir, ˈprē-mē-ər\ adj [ME primier, fr. MF premier first, chief, fr. L primarius of the first rank] : first in rank or importance : CHIEF; also : first in time : EARLIEST

²**premier** n : PRIME MINISTER — **pre·mier·ship** n

¹**pre·miere** \pri-ˈmyer, -ˈmir\ n : a first performance

²**premiere** or **pre·mier** \same as ¹PREMIERE\ vb **pre·miered; pre·mier·ing** : to give or receive a first public performance

prem·ise \ˈpre-məs\ n 1 : a statement of fact or a supposition made or implied as a basis of argument 2 pl : a piece of land with the structures on it; also : the place of business of an enterprise

pre·mi·um \ˈprē-mē-əm\ n [L praemium booty, reward, fr. prae before + emere to take, buy] 1 : REWARD, PRIZE 2 : a sum over and above the stated value 3 : something paid over and above a fixed wage or price 4 : something given with a purchase 5 : the sum paid for a contract of insurance 6 : an unusually high value

pre·mix \ˌprē-ˈmiks\ vb : to mix before use

¹**pre·mo·lar** \(ˌ)prē-ˈmō-lər\ adj : situated in front of or preceding the molar teeth

²**premolar** n : any of the double-pointed grinding teeth which are located between the canines and the true molars and of which there are two on each side of each human jaw

pre·mo·ni·tion \ˌprē-mə-ˈni-shən, ˌpre-\ n 1 : previous warning 2 : PRESENTIMENT — **pre·mon·i·to·ry** \pri-ˈmä-nə-ˌtȯr-ē\ adj

pre·na·tal \ˈprē-ˈnāt-ᵊl\ adj : occurring, existing, or taking place before birth

pre·oc·cu·pa·tion \prē-ˌä-kyə-ˈpā-shən\ n : complete absorption of the mind or interests; also : something that causes such absorption

pre·oc·cu·pied \prē-ˈä-kyə-ˌpīd\ adj 1 : lost in thought; also : absorbed in some preoccupation 2 : already occupied **syn** abstracted, absent, absentminded

pre·oc·cu·py \-ˌpī\ vb 1 : to occupy the attention of beforehand 2 : to take possession of before another

pre·op·er·a·tive \(ˌ)prē-ˈä-prə-tiv, -pə-ˌrā-\ adj : occurring before a surgical operation

pre·or·dain \ˌprē-ȯr-ˈdān\ vb : FOREORDAIN

pre·owned \(ˌ)prē-ˈōnd\ adj : SECONDHAND

prep abbr 1 preparatory 2 preposition

pre·pack·age \(ˌ)prē-ˈpa-kij\ vb : to package (as food) before offering for sale to the customer

preparatory school n 1 : a usu. private school preparing students primarily for college 2 Brit : a private elementary school preparing students primarily for public schools

pre·pare \pri-ˈpar\ vb **pre·pared; pre·par·ing** 1 : to make or get ready ⟨∼ dinner⟩ ⟨∼ a student for college⟩ 2 : to get ready beforehand 3 : to put together : COMPOUND ⟨∼ a prescription⟩ — **prep·a·ra·tion** \ˌpre-pə-ˈrā-shən\ n — **pre·par·a·to·ry** \pri-ˈpar-ə-ˌtȯr-ē\ adj

pre·pared·ness \pri-ˈpar-əd-nəs\ n : a state of adequate preparation

pre·pay \(ˌ)prē-ˈpā\ vb **-paid** \-ˈpād\; **-pay·ing** : to pay or pay the charge on in advance

pre·pon·der·ant \pri-ˈpän-də-rənt\ adj : having greater weight, force, influence, or frequency — **pre·pon·der·ance** \-rəns\ n — **pre·pon·der·ant·ly** adv

pre·pon·der·ate \pri-ˈpän-də-ˌrāt\ vb **-at·ed; -at·ing** [L praeponderare, fr. prae- ahead + ponder-, pondus weight] : to exceed in weight, force, influence, or frequency : PREDOMINATE

prep·o·si·tion \ˌpre-pə-ˈzi-shən\ n : a word that com-

bines with a noun or pronoun to form a phrase —
prep·o·si·tion·al \-'zi-shə-nəl\ adj
pre·pos·sess \ˌprē-pə-'zes\ vb **1** : to cause to be preoccupied **2** : to influence beforehand esp. favorably
pre·pos·sess·ing adj : tending to create a favorable impression ⟨a ~ manner⟩
pre·pos·ses·sion \-'ze-shən\ n **1** : PREJUDICE **2** : an exclusive concern with one idea or object
pre·pos·ter·ous \pri-'päs-tə-rəs\ adj : contrary to nature or reason : ABSURD
prep·py or **prep·pie** \'pre-pē\ n, pl **preppies 1** : a student at or a graduate of a preparatory school **2** : a
person deemed to dress or behave like a preppy
pre·puce \'prē-ˌpyüs\ n : FORESKIN
pre·quel \'prē-kwəl\ n : a literary or dramatic work
whose story precedes that of an earlier work
pre·re·cord·ed \ˌ(ˌ)prē-ri-'kór-dəd\ adj : recorded for
later broadcast
pre·req·ui·site \prē-'re-kwə-zət\ n : something required beforehand or for the end in view — **prereq-
uisite** adj
pre·rog·a·tive \pri-'rä-gə-tiv\ n : an exclusive or special right, power, or privilege
pres abbr **1** present **2** president
¹pres·age \'pre-sij\ n **1** : something that foreshadows a
future event : OMEN **2** : FOREBODING
²pre·sage \'pre-sij, pri-'sāj\ vb **pre·saged; pre·sag-
ing 1** : to give an omen or warning of : FORESHADOW
2 : FORETELL, PREDICT
pres·by·opia \ˌprez-bē-'ō-pē-ə\ n : a visual condition in
which loss of elasticity of the lens of the eye causes
defective accommodation and inability to focus
sharply for near vision — **pres·by·opic** \-'ō-pik, -'ä-\
adj or n
pres·by·ter \'prez-bə-tər\ n **1** : PRIEST, MINISTER **2** : an
elder in a Presbyterian church
¹Pres·by·te·ri·an \ˌprez-bə-'tir-ē-ən\ n : a member of a
Presbyterian church
²Presbyterian adj **1** often not cap : characterized by a
graded system of representative ecclesiastical bodies
(as presbyteries) exercising legislative and judicial
powers **2** : of or relating to a group of Protestant
Christian bodies that are presbyterian in government
— **Pres·by·te·ri·an·ism** \-ə-ˌni-zəm\ n
pres·by·tery \'prez-bə-ˌter-ē\ n, pl **-ter·ies 1** : the part
of a church reserved for the officiating clergy **2** : a
ruling body in Presbyterian churches consisting of
the ministers and representative elders of a district
¹pre·school \'prē-ˌskül\ adj : of or relating to the period
in a child's life from infancy to the age of five or six
— **pre·school·er** \-ˌskü-lər\ n
²preschool n : NURSERY SCHOOL
pre·science \'pre-shəns, 'prē-\ n : foreknowledge of
events; also : FORESIGHT — **pre·scient** \-shənt, -shē-
ənt\ adj
pre·scribe \pri-'skrīb\ vb **pre·scribed; pre·scrib·ing 1**
: to lay down as a guide or rule of action **2** : to direct
the use of (as a medicine) as a remedy
pre·scrip·tion \pri-'skrip-shən\ n **1** : the action of prescribing rules or directions **2** : a written direction for
the preparation and use of a medicine; also : a medicine prescribed
pres·ence \'prez-ᵊns\ n **1** : the fact or condition of being present **2** : the space immediately around a person
3 : one that is present **4** : the bearing of a person; esp
: stately bearing
¹pres·ent \'prez-ᵊnt\ n : something presented : GIFT
²pre·sent \pri-'zent\ vb **1** : to bring into the presence or
acquaintance of : INTRODUCE **2** : to bring before the
public ⟨~ a play⟩ **3** : to make a gift to **4** : to give formally **5** : to lay (as a charge) before a court for inquiry **6** : to aim or direct (as a weapon) so as to face
in a particular direction — **pre·sent·able** adj — **pre-
sen·ta·tion** \ˌprē-ˌzen-'tā-shən, ˌprez-ᵊn-\ n — **pre-
sent·ment** \pri-'zent-mənt\ n
³pres·ent \'prez-ᵊnt\ adj **1** : now existing or in progress

⟨~ conditions⟩ **2** : being in view or at hand ⟨~ at the
meeting⟩ **3** : under consideration ⟨the ~ problem⟩ **4**
: of, relating to, or constituting a verb tense that expresses present time or the time of speaking
⁴pres·ent \'prez-ᵊnt\ n **1** pl : the present legal document
2 : the present tense; also : a verb form in it **3** : the
present time
pres·ent–day \'prez-ᵊnt-ˌdā\ adj : now existing or occurring : CURRENT
pre·sen·ti·ment \pri-'zen-tə-mənt\ n : a feeling that
something is about to happen : PREMONITION
pres·ent·ly \'prez-ᵊnt-lē\ adv **1** : SOON **2** : NOW
present participle n : a participle that typically expresses present action and that in English is formed
with the suffix -ing and is used in the formation of the
progressive tenses
¹pre·serve \pri-'zərv\ vb **pre·served; pre·serv·ing 1** : to
keep safe : GUARD, PROTECT **2** : to keep from decaying; esp : to process food (as by canning or pickling)
to prevent spoilage **3** : MAINTAIN ⟨~ silence⟩ — **pres-
er·va·tion** \ˌprez-ər-'vā-shən\ n — **pre·ser·va·tive**
\pri-'zər-və-tiv\ adj or n — **pre·serv·er** n
²preserve n **1** : preserved fruit — often used in pl. **2** : an
area for the protection of natural resources (as
animals)
pre·set \ˌ(ˌ)prē-'set\ vb **-set; -set·ting** : to set beforehand
pre·shrunk \-'shrəŋk\ adj : subjected to a shrinking
process during manufacture usu. to reduce later
shrinking
pre·side \pri-'zīd\ vb **pre·sid·ed; pre·sid·ing** [L prae-
sidēre to guard, preside over, fr. prae in front of +
sedēre to sit] **1** : to exercise guidance or control **2** : to
occupy the place of authority; esp : to act as chairman
pres·i·dent \'pre-zə-dənt\ n **1** : one chosen to preside
⟨~ of the assembly⟩ **2** : the chief officer of an organization (as a corporation or society) **3** : an elected official serving as both chief of state and chief political
executive; also : a chief of state often with only minimal political powers — **pres·i·den·cy** \-dən-sē\ n —
pres·i·den·tial \ˌpre-zə-'den-chəl\ adj
pre·si·dio \pri-'sē-dē-ˌō, -'si-\ n, pl **-di·os** [Sp] : a military post or fortified settlement in areas currently or
orig. under Spanish control
pre·sid·i·um \pri-'si-dē-əm\ n, pl **-ia** \-dē-ə\ or **-iums**
[Russ prezidium, fr. L praesidium garrison] : a permanent executive committee that acts for a larger
body in a Communist country
¹pre·soak \ˌ(ˌ)prē-'sōk\ vb : to soak beforehand
²pre·soak \'prē-ˌsōk\ n **1** : an instance of presoaking **2**
: a preparation used in presoaking clothes
pre·sort \ˌ(ˌ)prē-'sórt\ vb : to sort (mail) by zip code
usu. before delivery to a post office
¹press \'pres\ n **1** : a crowded condition : THRONG **2** : a
machine for exerting pressure **3** : CLOSET, CUPBOARD
4 : PRESSURE **5** : the properly creased condition of a
freshly pressed garment **6** : PRINTING PRESS; also : the
act or the process of printing **7** : a printing or publishing establishment **8** : the media (as newspapers
and magazines) of public news and comment; also
: persons (as reporters) employed in these media **9**
: comment in newspapers and periodicals
²press vb **1** : to bear down upon : push steadily against
2 : ASSAIL, COMPEL **3** : to squeeze out the juice or contents of ⟨~ grapes⟩ **4** : to squeeze to a desired density,
shape, or smoothness; esp : IRON **5** : to try hard to
persuade : URGE **6** : to follow through : PROSECUTE **7**
: CROWD **8** : to force one's way **9** : to require haste or
speed in action — **press·er** n
press agent n : an agent employed to establish and
maintain good public relations through publicity
press·ing adj : URGENT
press·man \'pres-mən, -ˌman\ n : the operator of a
press and esp. a printing press
press·room \-ˌrüm, -ˌrum\ n **1** : a room in a printing

plant containing the printing presses **2** : a room for the use of reporters

¹pres·sure \'pre-shər\ *n* **1** : the burden of physical or mental distress **2** : the action of pressing; *esp* : the application of force to something by something else in direct contact with it **3** : the force exerted over a surface divided by its area **4** : the stress or urgency of matters demanding attention

²pressure *vb* **pres·sured; pres·sur·ing** : to apply pressure to

pressure group *n* : a group that seeks to influence governmental policy but not to elect candidates to office

pressure suit *n* : an inflatable suit for high-altitude flight or spaceflight to protect the body from low pressure

pres·sur·ize \'pre-shə-ˌrīz\ *vb* **-ized; -iz·ing 1** : to maintain higher pressure within than without; *esp* : to maintain normal atmospheric pressure within (as an airplane cabin) during high-altitude flight or spaceflight **2** : to apply pressure to **3** : to design to withstand pressure — **pres·sur·i·za·tion** \ˌpre-shə-rə-'zā-shən\ *n*

pres·ti·dig·i·ta·tion \ˌpres-tə-ˌdi-jə-'tā-shən\ *n* : SLEIGHT OF HAND

pres·tige \pres-'tēzh, -'tēj\ *n* [F, fr. MF, conjuror's trick, illusion, fr. LL *praestigium*, fr. L *praestigiae*, pl., conjuror's tricks, fr. *praestringere* to graze, blunt, constrict, fr. *prae-* in front of + *stringere* to bind tight] : standing or estimation in the eyes of people : REPUTATION **syn** influence, authority, weight, cachet — **pres·ti·gious** \-'ti-jəs, -'tē-\ *adj*

pres·to \'pres-tō\ *adv or adj* [It] **1** : suddenly as if by magic : IMMEDIATELY **2** : at a rapid tempo — used as a direction in music

pre·stress \(ˌ)prē-'stres\ *vb* : to introduce internal stresses into (as a structural beam) to counteract later load stresses

pre·sum·ably \pri-'zü-mə-blē\ *adv* : by reasonable assumption

pre·sume \pri-'züm\ *vb* **pre·sumed; pre·sum·ing 1** : to take upon oneself without leave or warrant : DARE **2** : to take for granted : ASSUME **3** : to act or behave with undue boldness — **pre·sum·able** \-'zü-mə-bəl\ *adj*

pre·sump·tion \pri-'zəmp-shən\ *n* **1** : presumptuous attitude or conduct : AUDACITY **2** : an attitude or belief dictated by probability; *also* : the grounds lending probability to a belief — **pre·sump·tive** \-tiv\ *adj*

pre·sump·tu·ous \pri-'zəmp-chə-wəs\ *adj* : overstepping due bounds : taking liberties — **pre·sump·tu·ous·ly** *adv*

pre·sup·pose \ˌprē-sə-'pōz\ *vb* **1** : to suppose beforehand **2** : to require beforehand as a necessary condition — **pre·sup·po·si·tion** \(ˌ)prē-sə-pə-'zi-shən\ *n*

pre·teen \'prē-'tēn\ *n* : a boy or girl not yet 13 years old — **preteen** *adj*

pre·tend \pri-'tend\ *vb* **1** : PROFESS (doesn't ∼ to be scientific) **2** : FEIGN (∼ to be angry) **3** : to lay claim (∼ to a throne) — **pre·tend·er** *n*

pre·tense *or* **pre·tence** \'prē-ˌtens, pri-'tens\ *n* **1** : CLAIM; *esp* : one not supported by fact **2** : mere display : SHOW **3** : an attempt to attain a certain condition (made a ∼ at discipline) **4** : false show : PRETEXT — **pre·ten·sion** \pri-'ten-chən\ *n*

pre·ten·tious \pri-'ten-chəs\ *adj* **1** : making or possessing usu. unjustified claims (as to excellence) (a ∼ literary style) **2** : making demands on one's ability or means : AMBITIOUS (too ∼ an undertaking) — **pre·ten·tious·ly** *adv* — **pre·ten·tious·ness** *n*

pret·er·it *or* **pret·er·ite** \'pre-tə-rət\ *adj* : PAST **3** — **preterit** *n*

pre·ter·nat·u·ral \ˌprē-tər-'na-chə-rəl\ *adj* **1** : exceeding what is natural **2** : inexplicable by ordinary means — **pre·ter·nat·u·ral·ly** *adv*

pre·text \'prē-ˌtekst\ *n* : a purpose stated or assumed to cloak the real intention or state of affairs

pret·ti·fy \'pri-ti-ˌfī\ *vb* **-fied; -fy·ing** : to make pretty — **pret·ti·fi·ca·tion** \ˌpri-ti-fə-'kā-shən\ *n*

pret·ty \'pri-tē\ *adj* **pret·ti·er; -est** [ME *praty, prety*, fr. OE *prættig* tricky, fr. *prætt* trick] **1** : pleasing by delicacy or grace : having conventionally accepted elements of beauty (∼ flowers) **2** : MISERABLE, TERRIBLE (a ∼ state of affairs) **3** : moderately large (a ∼ profit) **syn** comely, fair, beautiful, attractive, lovely — **pret·ti·ly** \-tə-lē\ *adv* — **pret·ti·ness** \-tē-nəs\ *n*

²pretty *adv* : in some degree : MODERATELY

³pretty *vb* **pret·tied; pret·ty·ing** : to make pretty

pret·zel \'pret-səl\ *n* [G *Brezel*, ultim. fr. L *brachiatus* having branches like arms, fr. *brachium* arm] : a brittle or chewy glazed usu. salted slender bread often shaped like a loose knot

prev *abbr* previous; previously

pre·vail \pri-'vāl\ *vb* **1** : to win mastery : TRIUMPH **2** : to be or become effective : SUCCEED **3** : to urge successfully (∼ed upon her to sing) **4** : to be frequent : PREDOMINATE — **pre·vail·ing·ly** *adv*

prev·a·lent \'pre-və-lənt\ *adj* : generally or widely existent : WIDESPREAD — **prev·a·lence** \-ləns\ *n*

pre·var·i·cate \pri-'var-ə-ˌkāt\ *vb* **-cat·ed; -cat·ing** : to deviate from the truth : EQUIVOCATE — **pre·var·i·ca·tion** \-ˌvar-ə-'kā-shən\ *n* — **pre·var·i·ca·tor** \-'var-ə-ˌkā-tər\ *n*

pre·vent \pri-'vent\ *vb* **1** : to keep from happening or existing (steps to ∼ war) **2** : to hold back : HINDER, STOP (∼ us from going) — **pre·vent·able** *also* **pre·vent·ible** \-'ven-tə-bəl\ *adj* — **pre·ven·tion** \-'ven-chən\ *n* — **pre·ven·tive** \-'ven-tiv\ *adj or n* — **pre·ven·ta·tive** \-'ven-tə-tiv\ *adj or n*

pre·ver·bal \ˌprē-'vər-bəl\ *adj* : having not yet acquired the faculty of speech

¹pre·view \'prē-ˌvyü\ *vb* : to see or discuss beforehand; *esp* : to view or show in advance of public presentation

²preview *n* **1** : an advance showing or viewing **2** *also* **pre·vue** \-ˌvyü\ : a showing of snatches from a motion picture advertised for future appearance **3** : FORETASTE

pre·vi·ous \'prē-vē-əs\ *adj* : going before : EARLIER, FORMER **syn** foregoing, prior, preceding, antecedent — **pre·vi·ous·ly** *adv*

pre·vi·sion \prē-'vi-zhən\ *n* **1** : FORESIGHT, PRESCIENCE **2** : FORECAST, PREDICTION

pre·war \'prē-'wȯr\ *adj* : occurring or existing before a war

¹prey \'prā\ *n, pl* **prey** *also* **preys 1** : an animal taken for food by a predator; *also* : VICTIM **2** : the act or habit of preying

²prey *vb* **1** : to raid for booty **2** : to seize and devour prey **3** : to have a harmful or wearing effect

prf *abbr* proof

¹price \'prīs\ *n* **1** *archaic* : VALUE **2** : the amount of money paid or asked for the sale of a specified thing; *also* : the cost at which something is obtained

²price *vb* **priced; pric·ing 1** : to set a price on **2** : to ask the price of **3** : to drive by raising prices (*priced* themselves out of the market)

price–fix·ing \'prīs-ˌfik-siŋ\ *n* : the setting of prices artificially (as by producers or government)

price·less \-ləs\ *adj* : having a value beyond any price : INVALUABLE **syn** precious, costly, expensive

price support *n* : artificial maintenance of prices of a commodity at a level usu. fixed through government action

price war *n* : a period of commercial competition in which prices are repeatedly cut by the competitors

pric·ey *also* **pricy** \'prī-sē\ *adj* **pric·i·er; -est** : EXPENSIVE

¹prick \'prik\ *n* **1** : a mark or small wound made by a pointed instrument **2** : something sharp or pointed **3** : an instance of pricking; *also* : a sensation of being pricked

²prick *vb* **1** : to pierce slightly with a sharp point; *also*

: to have or cause a pricking sensation **2** : to affect with anguish or remorse ⟨~s his conscience⟩ **3** : to outline with punctures ⟨~ out a pattern⟩ **4** : to stand or cause to stand erect ⟨the dog's ears ~ed up at the sound⟩ **syn** punch, puncture, perforate, bore, drill

prick·er \'pri-kər\ *n* : BRIAR; *also* : THORN

¹prick·le \'pri-kəl\ *n* **1** : a small sharp process (as on a plant) **2** : a slight stinging pain — **prick·ly** \'pri-klē\ *adj*

²prickle *vb* **prick·led; prick·ling 1** : to prick lightly **2** : TINGLE

prickly heat *n* : a red cutaneous eruption with intense itching and tingling caused by inflammation around the ducts of the sweat glands

prickly pear *n* : any of numerous cacti with usu. yellow flowers and prickly flat or rounded joints; *also* : the sweet pulpy pear-shaped edible fruit of various prickly pears

¹pride \'prīd\ *n* **1** : CONCEIT **2** : justifiable self-respect **3** : elation over an act or possession **4** : haughty behavior : DISDAIN **5** : ostentatious display — **pride·ful** *adj*

²pride *vb* **prid·ed; prid·ing** : to indulge (as oneself) in pride

priest \'prēst\ *n* [ME *preist*, fr. OE *prēost*, ultim. fr. LL *presbyter* elder, priest, fr. Gk *presbyteros*, fr. compar. of *presbys* old man, elder] : a person having authority to perform the sacred rites of a religion; *esp* : a member of the Anglican, Eastern, or Roman Catholic clergy ranking below a bishop and above a deacon — **priest·hood** *n* — **priest·li·ness** *n* — **priest·ly** *adj*

priest·ess \'prēs-təs\ *n* : a woman authorized to perform the sacred rites of a religion

prig \'prig\ *n* : one who irritates by rigid or pointed observance of proprieties — **prig·gish** \'pri-gish\ *adj* — **prig·gish·ly** *adv*

¹prim \'prim\ *adj* **prim·mer; prim·mest** : stiffly formal and precise — **prim·ly** *adv* — **prim·ness** *n*

²prim *abbr* **1** primary **2** primitive

pri·ma·cy \'prī-mə-sē\ *n* **1** : the state of being first (as in rank) **2** : the office, rank, or character of an ecclesiastical primate

pri·ma don·na \pri-mə-'dä-nə\ *n, pl* **prima donnas** [It, lit., first lady] **1** : a principal female singer (as in an opera company) **2** : an extremely sensitive, vain, or undisciplined person

pri·ma fa·cie \'prī-mə-'fā-shə, -sē, -shē\ *adj or adv* [L, at first view] **1** : based on immediate impression : APPARENT **2** : SELF-EVIDENT

pri·mal \'prī-məl\ *adj* **1** : ORIGINAL, PRIMITIVE **2** : first in importance

pri·mar·i·ly \prī-'mer-ə-lē\ *adv* **1** : FUNDAMENTALLY **2** : ORIGINALLY

¹pri·ma·ry \'prī-mer-ē, -mə-rē\ *adj* **1** : first in order of time or development; *also* : PREPARATORY **2** : of first rank or importance; *also* : FUNDAMENTAL **3** : not derived from or dependent on something else ⟨~ sources⟩

²primary *n, pl* **-ries** : a preliminary election in which voters nominate or express a preference among candidates usu. of their own party

primary color *n* : any of a set of colors from which all other colors may be derived

primary school *n* **1** : a school usu. including grades 1-3 and sometimes kindergarten **2** : ELEMENTARY SCHOOL

pri·mate \'prī-ˌmāt *or esp for 1* -mət\ *n* **1** *often cap* : the highest-ranking bishop of a province or nation **2** : any of an order of mammals including humans, apes, and monkeys

¹prime \'prīm\ *n* **1** : the earliest stage of something; *esp* : SPRINGTIME **2** : the most active, thriving, or successful stage or period (as of one's life) **3** : the best individual; *also* : the best part of something **4** : any integer other than 0, +1, or −1 that is not divisible without remainder by any integer except +1, −1,

and plus or minus itself; *esp* : any such integer that is positive

²prime *adj* **1** : standing first (as in time, rank, significance, or quality) ⟨~ requisite⟩ **2** : of, relating to, or being a number that is prime

³prime *vb* **primed; prim·ing 1** : FILL, LOAD **2** : to lay a preparatory coating upon (as in painting) **3** : to put in working condition **4** : to instruct beforehand : COACH

prime meridian *n* : the meridian of 0° longitude which runs through Greenwich, England, and from which other longitudes are reckoned east and west

prime minister *n* **1** : the chief minister of a ruler or state **2** : the chief executive of a parliamentary government

¹prim·er \'pri-mər\ *n* **1** : a small book for teaching children to read **2** : a small introductory book on a subject

²prim·er \'prī-mər\ *n* **1** : one that primes **2** : a device for igniting an explosive **3** : material for priming a surface

prime rate *n* : an interest rate announced by a bank to be the lowest available to its most credit-worthy customers

prime time *n* **1** : the time period when the television or radio audience is largest; *also* : prime-time television **2** : the choicest or busiest time

pri·me·val \prī-'mē-vəl\ *adj* : of or relating to the earliest ages : PRIMITIVE

¹prim·i·tive \'pri-mə-tiv\ *adj* **1** : ORIGINAL, PRIMARY **2** : of, relating to, or characteristic of an early stage of development **3** : ELEMENTAL, NATURAL **4** : of, relating to, or produced by a tribal people or culture **5** : SELF-TAUGHT; *also* : produced by a self-taught artist — **prim·i·tive·ly** *adv* — **prim·i·tive·ness** *n* — **prim·i·tiv·i·ty** \pri-mə-'ti-və-tē\ *n*

²primitive *n* **1** : something primitive **2** : a primitive artist **3** : a member of a primitive people

prim·i·tiv·ism \'pri-mə-ti-ˌvi-zəm\ *n* **1** : belief in the superiority of a simple way of life close to nature **2** : the style of art of primitive peoples or primitive artists

pri·mo·gen·i·tor \ˌprī-mō-'je-nə-tər\ *n* : ANCESTOR, FOREFATHER

pri·mo·gen·i·ture \-'je-nə-ˌchùr\ *n* **1** : the state of being the firstborn of a family **2** : an exclusive right of inheritance belonging to the eldest son

pri·mor·di·al \prī-'mor-dē-əl\ *adj* : first created or developed : existing in its original state : PRIMEVAL

primp \'primp\ *vb* : to dress in a careful or finicky manner

prim·rose \'prim-ˌrōz\ *n* : any of a genus of perennial herbs with large leaves arranged at the base of the stem and clusters of showy flowers on leafless stalks

prin *abbr* **1** principal **2** principle

prince \'prins\ *n* [ME, fr. OF, fr. L *princeps* leader, initiator, fr. *primus* first + *capere* to take] **1** : MONARCH, KING **2** : a male member of a royal family; *esp* : a son of the monarch **3** : a person of high standing (as in a class) — **prince·dom** \-dəm\ *n* — **prince·ly** *adj*

prince·ling \-liŋ\ *n* : a petty prince

prin·cess \'prin-səs, -ˌses\ *n* **1** : a female member of a royal family **2** : the consort of a prince

¹prin·ci·pal \'prin-sə-pəl\ *adj* : most important — **prin·ci·pal·ly** *adv*

²principal *n* **1** : a leading person (as in a play) **2** : the chief officer of an educational institution **3** : the person from whom an agent's authority derives **4** : a capital sum placed at interest or used as a fund

prin·ci·pal·i·ty \ˌprin-sə-'pa-lə-tē\ *n, pl* **-ties** : the position, territory, or jurisdiction of a prince

principal parts *n pl* : the inflected forms of a verb

prin·ci·ple \'prin-sə-pəl\ *n* **1** : a general or fundamental law, doctrine, or assumption **2** : a rule or code of conduct; *also* : devotion to such a code **3** : the laws or facts of nature underlying the working of an artificial device **4** : a primary source : ORIGIN; *also* : an underlying faculty or endowment **5** : the active part (as of a drug)

prin·ci·pled \-pəld\ *adj* : exhibiting, based on, or characterized by principle ⟨high-*principled*⟩

prink \'prink\ *vb* : PRIMP

¹print \'print\ *n* **1** : a mark made by pressure **2** : something stamped with an impression **3** : printed state or form **4** : printed matter **5** : a copy made by printing **6** : cloth with a pattern applied by printing

²print *vb* **1** : to stamp (as a mark) in or on something **2** : to produce impressions of (as from type) **3** : to write in letters like those of printer's type **4** : to make (a positive picture) from a photographic negative

print·able \'prin-tə-bəl\ *adj* **1** : capable of being printed or of being printed from **2** : worthy or fit to be published

print·er \'prin-tər\ *n* : one that prints; *esp* : a device that produces printout

print·ing *n* **1** : reproduction in printed form **2** : the art, practice, or business of a printer **3** : IMPRESSION 5

printing press *n* : a machine that produces printed copies

print·out \'print-ˌaut\ *n* : a printed output produced by a computer — **print out** *vb*

¹pri·or \'prī-ər\ *n* : the superior ranking next to the abbot or abbess of a religious house

²pri·or *adj* **1** : earlier in time or order **2** : taking precedence logically or in importance — **pri·or·i·ty** \prī-'òr-ə-tē\ *n*

pri·or·ess \'prī-ə-rəs\ *n* : a nun corresponding in rank to a prior

pri·or·i·tize \prī-'òr-ə-ˌtīz, 'prī-ə-rə-ˌtīz\ *vb* -tized; -tiz·ing : to list or rate in order of priority

prior to *prep* : in advance of : BEFORE

pri·o·ry \'prī-ə-rē\ *n, pl* -ries : a religious house under a prior or prioress

prise *chiefly Brit var of* ⁵PRIZE

prism \'pri-zəm\ *n* [LL *prisma*, fr. Gk., lit., anything sawed, fr. *priein* to saw] **1** : a solid whose sides are parallelograms and whose ends are parallel and alike in shape and size **2** : a usu. 3-sided transparent object that refracts light so that it breaks up into rainbow colors — **pris·mat·ic** \priz-'ma-tik\ *adj*

pris·on \'priz-ᵊn\ *n* : a place or state of confinement esp. for criminals

pris·on·er \'priz-ᵊn-ər\ *n* : a person deprived of his liberty; *esp* : one on trial or in prison

prisoner of war *n* : a person captured in war

pris·sy \'pri-sē\ *adj* **pris·si·er; -est** : being overly prim and precise : PRIGGISH — **pris·si·ness** \-sē-nəs\ *n*

pris·tine \'pris-ˌtēn, pri-'stēn\ *adj* **1** : PRIMITIVE **2** : having the purity of its original state : UNSPOILED

prith·ee \'pri-thē\ *interj, archaic* — used to express a wish or request

pri·va·cy \'prī-və-sē\ *n, pl* -cies **1** : the quality or state of being apart from others **2** : SECRECY

¹pri·vate \'prī-vət\ *adj* **1** : belonging to or intended for a particular individual or group ⟨∼ property⟩ **2** : restricted to the individual : PERSONAL ⟨∼ opinion⟩ **3** : carried on by the individual independently ⟨∼ study⟩ **4** : not holding public office ⟨a ∼ citizen⟩ **5** : withdrawn from company or observation ⟨a ∼ place⟩ **6** : not known publicly — **pri·vate·ly** *adv*

²private *n* : an enlisted man of the lowest rank in the marine corps or of one of the two lowest ranks in the army — **in private** : not openly or in public

pri·va·teer \prī-və-'tir\ *n* : an armed private ship licensed to attack enemy shipping; *also* : a sailor on such a ship

private first class *n* : an enlisted man ranking next below a corporal in the army and next below a lance corporal in the marine corps

pri·va·tion \prī-'vā-shən\ *n* **1** : DEPRIVATION 1 **2** : the state of being deprived; *esp* : lack of what is needed for existence

priv·et \'pri-vət\ *n* : a nearly evergreen shrub related to the olive and widely used for hedges

¹priv·i·lege \'priv-lij, 'pri-və-\ *n* [ME, fr. OF, fr. L *privilegium* law for or against a private person, fr. *privus* private + *leg-, lex* law] : a right or immunity granted as an advantage or favor esp. to some and not others

²privilege *vb* -leged; -leg·ing : to grant a privilege to

priv·i·leged *adj* **1** : having or enjoying one or more privileges ⟨∼ classes⟩ **2** : not subject to disclosure in a court of law ⟨a ∼ communication⟩

¹privy \'pri-vē\ *adj* **1** : PERSONAL, PRIVATE **2** : SECRET **3** : admitted as one sharing in a secret ⟨∼ to the conspiracy⟩ — **priv·i·ly** \'pri-və-lē\ *adv*

²privy *n, pl* **priv·ies** : TOILET; *esp* : OUTHOUSE

¹prize \'prīz\ *n* **1** : something offered or striven for in competition or in contests of chance **2** : something exceptionally desirable

²prize *adj* **1** : awarded or worthy of a prize ⟨a ∼ essay⟩; *also* : awarded as a prize ⟨a ∼ medal⟩ **2** : OUTSTANDING

³prize *vb* **prized; priz·ing** : to value highly : ESTEEM

⁴prize *n* : property (as a ship) lawfully captured in time of war

⁵prize *vb* **prized; priz·ing** : PRY

prize·fight \'prīz-ˌfīt\ *n* : a professional boxing match — **prize·fight·er** *n* — **prize·fight·ing** *n*

prize·win·ner \-ˌwi-nər\ *n* : a winner of a prize — **prize·win·ning** *adj*

¹pro \'prō\ *n, pl* **pros** : a favorable argument, person, or position

²pro *adv* : in favor : FOR

³pro *n or adj* : PROFESSIONAL

PRO *abbr* public relations officer

prob *abbr* **1** probable; probably **2** problem

prob·a·bil·i·ty \ˌprä-bə-'bi-lə-tē\ *n, pl* -ties **1** : the quality or state of being probable **2** : something probable **3** : a measure of how often a particular event will occur if something (as tossing a coin) is done repeatedly which results in any of a number of possible events

prob·a·ble \'prä-bə-bəl\ *adj* **1** : apparently or presumably true ⟨a ∼ hypothesis⟩ **2** : likely to be or become true or real ⟨a ∼ result⟩ — **prob·a·bly** \-bə-blē\ *adv*

¹pro·bate \'prō-ˌbāt\ *n* : the judicial determination of the validity of a will

²pro·bate *vb* **pro·bat·ed; pro·bat·ing** : to establish (a will) by probate as genuine and valid

pro·ba·tion \prō-'bā-shən\ *n* **1** : subjection of an individual to a period of testing and trial to ascertain fitness (as for a job) **2** : the action of giving a convicted offender freedom during good behavior under the supervision of a probation officer — **pro·ba·tion·ary** \-shə-ˌner-ē\ *adj*

pro·ba·tion·er \-shə-nər\ *n* **1** : a person (as a newly admitted student nurse) whose fitness is being tested during a trial period **2** : a convicted offender on probation

pro·ba·tive \'prō-bə-tiv\ *adj* **1** : serving to test or try **2** : serving to prove

¹probe \'prōb\ *n* **1** : a slender instrument for examining a cavity (as a wound) **2** : an information-gathering device sent into outer space **3** : a penetrating investigation **syn** inquiry, inquest, research, inquisition

²probe *vb* **probed; prob·ing 1** : to examine with a probe **2** : to investigate thoroughly

pro·bi·ty \'prō-bə-tē\ *n* : UPRIGHTNESS, HONESTY

prob·lem \'prä-bləm\ *n* **1** : a question raised for consideration or solution **2** : an intricate unsettled question **3** : a source of perplexity or vexation — **problem** *adj*

prob·lem·at·ic \ˌprä-blə-'ma-tik\ *or* **prob·lem·at·i·cal** \-ti-kəl\ *adj* **1** : difficult to solve or decide : PUZZLING **2** : DUBIOUS, QUESTIONABLE

pro·bos·cis \prə-'bä-səs, -'bäs-kəs\ *n, pl* -bos·cis·es *also* -bos·ci·des \-'bä-sə-ˌdēz\ [L, fr. Gk *proboskis*, fr. *pro-* before + *boskein* to feed] : a long flexible snout (as the trunk of an elephant)

proc *abbr* proceedings

pro·caine \'prō-ˌkān\ *n* : a drug used esp. as a local anesthetic

pro·ce·dure \prə-'sē-jər\ *n* **1** : a particular way of doing something ⟨democratic ∼⟩ **2** : a series of steps followed in a regular order ⟨surgical ∼⟩ — **pro·ce·dur·al** \-'sē-jə-rəl\ *adj*

pro·ceed \prō-'sēd\ *vb* **1** : to come forth : ISSUE **2** : to go on in an orderly way; *also* : CONTINUE **3** : to begin and carry on an action **4** : to take legal action **5** : to go forward : ADVANCE

pro·ceed·ing *n* **1** : PROCEDURE **2** *pl* : DOINGS **3** *pl* : legal action **4** : TRANSACTION **5** *pl* : an official record of things said or done

pro·ceeds \'prō-ˌsēdz\ *n pl* : the total amount or the profit arising from a business deal : RETURN

¹pro·cess \'prä-ˌses, 'prō-\ *n, pl* **pro·cess·es** \-ˌse-səz, -sə-səz, -sə-ˌsēz\ **1** : PROGRESS, ADVANCE **2** : something going on : PROCEEDING **3** : a natural phenomenon marked by gradual changes that lead toward a particular result ⟨the ∼ of growth⟩ **4** : a series of actions or operations directed toward a particular result ⟨a manufacturing ∼⟩ **5** : legal action **6** : a mandate issued by a court; *esp* : SUMMONS **7** : a projecting part of an organism or organic structure

²process *vb* : to subject to a special process

pro·ces·sion \prə-'se-shən\ *n* : a group of individuals moving along in an orderly often ceremonial way

pro·ces·sion·al \-'se-shə-nəl\ *n* **1** : music for a procession **2** : a ceremonial procession

pro·ces·sor \'prä-ˌse-sər, 'prō-\ *n* **1** : one that processes **2** : the part of a computer that operates on data

pro·choice \ˌprō-'chȯis\ *adj* : favoring the legalization of abortion

pro·claim \prō-'klām\ *vb* : to make known publicly : DECLARE

proc·la·ma·tion \ˌprä-klə-'mā-shən\ *n* : an official public announcement

pro·cliv·i·ty \prō-'kli-və-tē\ *n, pl* **-ties** : an inherent inclination esp. toward something objectionable

pro·con·sul \-'kän-səl\ *n* **1** : a governor or military commander of an ancient Roman province **2** : an administrator in a modern colony or occupied area — **pro·con·su·lar** \-sə-lər\ *adj*

pro·cras·ti·nate \prə-'kras-tə-ˌnāt, prō-\ *vb* **-nat·ed; -nat·ing** [L *procrastinare*, fr. *pro-* forward + *crastinus* of tomorrow, fr. *cras* tomorrow] : to put off usu. habitually doing something that should be done **syn** dawdle, delay — **pro·cras·ti·na·tion** \-ˌkras-tə-'nā-shən\ *n* — **pro·cras·ti·na·tor** \-'kras-tə-ˌnā-tər\ *n*

pro·cre·ate \'prō-krē-ˌāt\ *vb* **-at·ed; -at·ing** : to beget or bring forth offspring **syn** reproduce, breed, generate, propagate — **pro·cre·ation** \ˌprō-krē-'ā-shən\ *n* — **pro·cre·ative** \'prō-krē-ˌā-tiv\ *adj* — **pro·cre·ator** \-ˌā-tər\ *n*

pro·crus·te·an \prə-'krəs-tē-ən\ *adj, often cap* [fr. *Procrustes*, villain of Greek mythology who made victims fit his bed by stretching them or cutting off their legs] : marked by arbitrary often ruthless disregard of individual differences or special circumstances

proc·tor \'präk-tər\ *n* : one appointed to supervise students (as at an examination) — **proctor** *vb* — **proc·to·ri·al** \präk-'tȯr-ē-əl\ *adj*

proc·u·ra·tor \'prä-kyə-ˌrā-tər\ *n* : a Roman provincial administrator

pro·cure \prə-'kyu̇r\ *vb* **pro·cured; pro·cur·ing** **1** : to get possession of : OBTAIN **2** : to make women available for promiscuous sexual intercourse **3** : ACHIEVE **syn** secure, acquire, gain, win, earn — **pro·cur·able** \-'kyu̇r-ə-bəl\ *adj* — **pro·cure·ment** *n* — **pro·cur·er** *n*

¹prod \'präd\ *vb* **prod·ded; prod·ding** **1** : to thrust a pointed instrument into : GOAD **2** : INCITE, STIR — **prod** *n*

²prod *abbr* product; production

prod·i·gal \'prä-di-gəl\ *adj* **1** : recklessly extravagant; *also* : LUXURIANT **2** : WASTEFUL, LAVISH **syn** profuse, lush, opulent — **prodigal** *n* — **prod·i·gal·i·ty** \ˌprä-də-'ga-lə-tē\ *n*

pro·di·gious \prə-'di-jəs\ *adj* **1** : exciting wonder **2** : extraordinary in size or degree : ENORMOUS **syn** monstrous, tremendous, stupendous, monumental — **pro·di·gious·ly** *adv*

prod·i·gy \'prä-də-jē\ *n, pl* **-gies** **1** : something extraordinary : WONDER **2** : a highly talented child

¹pro·duce \prə-'düs, -'dyüs\ *vb* **pro·duced; pro·duc·ing** **1** : to present to view : EXHIBIT **2** : to give birth or rise to : YIELD **3** : EXTEND, PROLONG **4** : to give being or form to : BRING ABOUT, MAKE; *esp* : MANUFACTURE **5** : to cause to accrue ⟨∼ a profit⟩ — **pro·duc·er** *n*

²pro·duce \'prä-(ˌ)düs, 'prō- *also* -(ˌ)dyüs\ *n* : PRODUCT **2**; *also* : agricultural products and esp. fresh fruits and vegetables

prod·uct \'prä-(ˌ)dəkt\ *n* **1** : the number resulting from multiplication **2** : something produced

pro·duc·tion \prə-'dək-shən\ *n* **1** : something produced : PRODUCT **2** : the act or process of producing — **pro·duc·tive** \-'dək-tiv\ *adj* — **pro·duc·tive·ness** *n* — **pro·duc·tiv·i·ty** \(ˌ)prō-ˌdək-'ti-və-tē, ˌprä-(ˌ)dək-\ *n*

pro·em \'prō-ˌem\ *n* **1** : preliminary comment : PREFACE **2** : PRELUDE

prof *abbr* **1** professional **2** professor

¹pro·fane \prō-'fān\ *vb* **pro·faned; pro·fan·ing** **1** : to treat (something sacred) with irreverence or contempt **2** : to debase by an unworthy use — **prof·a·na·tion** \ˌprä-fə-'nā-shən\ *n*

²profane *adj* [ME *prophane*, fr. MF, fr. L *profanus*, fr. *pro-* before + *fanum* temple] **1** : not concerned with religion : SECULAR **2** : not holy because unconsecrated, impure, or defiled **3** : serving to debase what is holy : IRREVERENT ⟨∼ language⟩ — **pro·fane·ly** *adv* — **pro·fane·ness** *n*

pro·fan·i·ty \prō-'fa-nə-tē\ *n, pl* **-ties** **1** : the quality or state of being profane **2** : the use of profane language **3** : profane language

pro·fess \prə-'fes\ *vb* **1** : to declare or admit openly : AFFIRM **2** : to declare in words only : PRETEND **3** : to confess one's faith in **4** : to practice or claim to be versed in (a calling or occupation) — **pro·fess·ed·ly** \-'fe-səd-lē\ *adv*

pro·fes·sion \prə-'fe-shən\ *n* **1** : an open declaration or avowal of a belief or opinion **2** : a calling requiring specialized knowledge and often long academic preparation **3** : the whole body of persons engaged in a calling

¹pro·fes·sion·al \prə-'fe-shə-nəl\ *adj* **1** : of, relating to, or characteristic of a profession **2** : engaged in one of the professions **3** : participating for gain in an activity often engaged in by amateurs — **pro·fes·sion·al·ly** *adv*

²professional *n* : one that engages in an activity professionally

pro·fes·sion·al·ism \-nə-ˌli-zəm\ *n* **1** : the conduct, aims, or qualities that characterize or mark a profession or a professional person **2** : the following of a profession (as athletics) for gain or livelihood

pro·fes·sion·al·ize \-nə-ˌlīz\ *vb* **-ized; -iz·ing** : to give a professional nature to

pro·fes·sor \prə-'fe-sər\ *n* : a teacher at a university or college; *esp* : a faculty member of the highest academic rank — **pro·fes·so·ri·al** \ˌprō-fə-'sȯr-ē-əl, ˌprä-\ *adj* — **pro·fes·sor·ship** *n*

prof·fer \'prä-fər\ *vb* **prof·fered; prof·fer·ing** : to present for acceptance : OFFER — **proffer** *n*

pro·fi·cient \prə-'fi-shənt\ *adj* : well advanced in an art, occupation, or branch of knowledge **syn** adept, skillful, expert, masterful, masterly — **pro·fi·cien·cy** \-shən-sē\ *n* — **proficient** *n* — **pro·fi·cient·ly** *adv*

¹pro·file \'prō-ˌfīl\ *n* [It *profilo*, fr. *profilare* to draw in outline, fr. *pro-* forward (fr. L) + *filare* to spin, fr. LL, fr. L *filum* thread] **1** : a representation of something in outline; *esp* : a human head seen in side view

2 : a concise biographical sketch **3** : degree or level of public exposure ⟨keep a low ∼⟩

²profile *vb* **pro·filed; pro·fil·ing** : to write or draw a profile of

¹prof·it \'prä-fət\ *n* **1** : a valuable return : GAIN **2** : the excess of the selling price of goods over their cost — **prof·it·less** *adj*

²profit *vb* **1** : to be of use : BENEFIT **2** : to derive benefit : GAIN — **prof·it·able** \'prä-fə-tə-bəl\ *adj* — **prof·it·ably** \-blē\ *adv*

prof·i·teer \ˌprä-fə-'tir\ *n* : one who makes what is considered an unreasonable profit — **profiteer** *vb*

prof·li·gate \'prä-fli-gət, -flə-ˌgāt\ *adj* **1** : completely given up to dissipation and licentiousness **2** : wildly extravagant — **prof·li·ga·cy** \-gə-sē\ *n* — **profligate** *n* — **prof·li·gate·ly** *adv*

pro for·ma \(ˌ)prō-'for-mə\ *adj* : done or existing as a matter of form

pro·found \prə-'faund, prō-\ *adj* **1** : marked by intellectual depth or insight ⟨a ∼ thought⟩ **2** : coming from or reaching to a depth ⟨a ∼ sigh⟩ **3** : deeply felt : INTENSE ⟨∼ sympathy⟩ — **pro·found·ly** *adv* — **pro·fun·di·ty** \-'fən-də-tē\ *n*

pro·fuse \prə-'fyüs, prō-\ *adj* : pouring forth liberally : ABUNDANT **syn** lavish, prodigal, luxuriant, exuberant — **pro·fuse·ly** *adv* — **pro·fu·sion** \-'fyü-zhən\ *n*

prog *abbr* program

pro·gen·i·tor \prō-'je-nə-tər\ *n* **1** : a direct ancestor : FOREFATHER **2** : ORIGINATOR, PRECURSOR

prog·e·ny \'prä-jə-nē\ *n, pl* **-nies** : OFFSPRING, CHILDREN, DESCENDANTS

pro·ges·ter·one \prō-'jes-tə-ˌrōn\ *n* : a female hormone that causes the uterus to undergo changes so as to provide a suitable environment for a fertilized egg

prog·na·thous \'präg-nə-thəs\ *adj* : having the jaws projecting beyond the upper part of the face

prog·no·sis \präg-'nō-səs\ *n, pl* **-no·ses** \-ˌsēz\ **1** : the prospect of recovery from disease **2** : FORECAST

¹prog·nos·tic \präg-'näs-tik\ *n* **1** : PORTENT **2** : PROPHECY

²prognostic *adj* : of, relating to, or serving as ground for prognostication or a prognosis

prog·nos·ti·cate \präg-'näs-tə-ˌkāt\ *vb* **-cat·ed; -cat·ing** : to foretell from signs or symptoms — **prog·nos·ti·ca·tion** \-ˌnäs-tə-'kā-shən\ *n* — **prog·nos·ti·ca·tor** \-'näs-tə-ˌkā-tər\ *n*

¹pro·gram \'prō-ˌgram, -grəm\ *n* **1** : a brief outline of the order to be pursued or the subjects included (as in a public entertainment); *also* : PERFORMANCE **2** : a plan of procedure **3** : coded instructions for a computer — **pro·gram·mat·ic** \ˌprō-grə-'ma-tik\ *adj*

²program *also* **programme** *vb* **-grammed** *or* **-gramed; -gram·ming** *or* **-gram·ing** **1** : to enter in a program **2** : to provide (as a computer) with a program — **pro·gram·ma·bil·i·ty** \(ˌ)prō-ˌgra-mə-'bi-lə-tē\ *n* — **pro·gram·ma·ble** \'prō-ˌgra-mə-bəl\ *adj* — **pro·gram·mer** *also* **pro·gram·er** \'prō-ˌgra-mər, -grə-\ *n*

programme *chiefly Brit var of* PROGRAM

programmed instruction *n* : instruction through information given in small steps with each requiring a correct response by the learner before going on to the next step

pro·gram·ming *or* **pro·gram·ing** *n* **1** : the process of instructing or learning by means of an instruction program **2** : the process of preparing an instruction program

¹prog·ress \'prä-grəs, -ˌgres\ *n* **1** : a forward movement : ADVANCE **2** : a gradual betterment

²pro·gress \prə-'gres\ *vb* **1** : to move forward : PROCEED **2** : to develop to a more advanced stage : IMPROVE

pro·gres·sion \prə-'gre-shən\ *n* **1** : an act of progressing : ADVANCE **2** : a continuous and connected series

¹pro·gres·sive \prə-'gre-siv\ *adj* **1** : of, relating to, or characterized by progress ⟨a ∼ city⟩ **2** : moving forward or onward : ADVANCING **3** : increasing in extent or severity ⟨a ∼ disease⟩ **4** *often cap* : of or relating

to political Progressives **5** : of, relating to, or constituting a verb form that expresses action in progress at the time of speaking or a time spoken of — **pro·gres·sive·ly** *adv*

²progressive *n* **1** : one that is progressive **2** : a person believing in moderate political change and social improvement by government action; *esp, cap* : a member of a Progressive Party in the U.S.

pro·hib·it \prō-'hi-bət\ *vb* **1** : to forbid by authority **2** : to prevent from doing something

pro·hi·bi·tion \ˌprō-ə-'bi-shən\ *n* **1** : the act of prohibiting **2** : the forbidding by law of the sale or manufacture of alcoholic beverages — **pro·hi·bi·tion·ist** \-'bi-shə-nist\ *n* — **pro·hib·i·tive** \prō-'hi-bə-tiv\ *adj* — **pro·hib·i·tive·ly** *adv* — **pro·hib·i·to·ry** \-'hi-bə-ˌtōr-ē\ *adj*

¹proj·ect \'prä-ˌjekt, -jikt\ *n* **1** : a specific plan or design : SCHEME **2** : a planned undertaking ⟨a research ∼⟩

²pro·ject \prə-'jekt\ *vb* **1** : to devise in the mind : DESIGN **2** : to throw forward **3** : PROTRUDE **4** : to cause (light or shadow) to fall into space or (an image) to fall on a surface ⟨∼ a beam of light⟩ **5** : to attribute (a thought, feeling, or personal characteristic) to a person, group, or object — **pro·jec·tion** \-'jek-shən\ *n*

pro·jec·tile \prə-'jekt-ᵊl, -'jek-ˌtīl\ *n* **1** : a body hurled or projected by external force; *esp* : a missile for a firearm **2** : a self-propelling weapon

pro·jec·tion·ist \prə-'jek-shə-nist\ *n* : one that operates a motion-picture projector or television equipment

pro·jec·tor \-'jek-tər\ *n* : one that projects; *esp* : a device for projecting pictures on a screen

pro·le·gom·e·non \ˌprō-li-'gä-mə-ˌnän, -nən\ *n, pl* **-e·na** \-nə\ : prefatory remarks

pro·le·tar·i·an \ˌprō-lə-'ter-ē-ən\ *n* : a member of the proletariat — **proletarian** *adj*

pro·le·tar·i·at \-ē-ət\ *n* : the laboring class; *esp* : industrial workers who sell their labor to live

pro-life \(ˌ)prō-'līf\ *n* : ANTIABORTION

pro·lif·er·ate \prə-'li-fə-ˌrāt\ *vb* **-at·ed; -at·ing** : to grow or increase by rapid production of new units (as cells or offspring) — **pro·lif·er·a·tion** \-ˌli-fə-'rā-shən\ *n*

pro·lif·ic \prə-'li-fik\ *adj* **1** : producing young or fruit abundantly **2** : marked by abundant inventiveness or productivity ⟨a ∼ writer⟩ — **pro·lif·i·cal·ly** \-fi-k(ə-)lē\ *adv*

pro·lix \prō-'liks, 'prō-ˌliks\ *adj* : VERBOSE **syn** wordy, diffuse, redundant — **pro·lix·i·ty** \prō-'lik-sə-tē\ *n*

pro·logue *also* **pro·log** \'prō-ˌlog, -ˌläg\ *n* : PREFACE ⟨∼ of a play⟩

pro·long \prə-'lön\ *vb* **1** : to lengthen in time : CONTINUE ⟨∼ a meeting⟩ **2** : to lengthen in extent or range **syn** protract, extend, elongate, stretch — **pro·lon·ga·tion** \ˌprō-ˌlön-'gā-shən\ *n*

prom \'präm\ *n* : a formal dance given by a high school or college class

¹prom·e·nade \ˌprä-mə-'nād, -'näd\ *vb* **-nad·ed; -nad·ing** **1** : to take a promenade **2** : to walk about in or on

²promenade *n* [F, fr. *promener* to take for a walk, fr. L *prominare* to drive forward] **1** : a place for strolling **2** : a leisurely walk for pleasure or display **3** : an opening grand march at a formal ball

pro·me·thi·um \prə-'mē-thē-əm\ *n* : a metallic chemical element obtained from uranium or neodymium — see ELEMENT table

prom·i·nence \'prä-mə-nəns\ *n* **1** : something prominent **2** : the quality, state, or fact of being prominent or conspicuous **3** : a mass of cloudlike gas that arises from the sun's chromosphere

prom·i·nent \-nənt\ *adj* **1** : jutting out : PROJECTING **2** : readily noticeable : CONSPICUOUS **3** : DISTINGUISHED, EMINENT **syn** remarkable, outstanding, striking, salient — **prom·i·nent·ly** *adv*

pro·mis·cu·ous \prə-'mis-kyə-wəs\ *adj* **1** : consisting of various sorts and kinds : MIXED **2** : not restricted to one class or person **3** : having a number of sexual partners **syn** miscellaneous, assorted, heterogeneous, motley, varied — **pro·mis·cu·i·ty** \ˌprä-mis-'kyü-ə-tē, ˌprō-ˌmis-\ n — **pro·mis·cu·ous·ly** adv — **pro·mis·cu·ous·ness** n

¹**prom·ise** \'prä-məs\ n **1** : a pledge to do or not to do something specified **2** : ground for expectation of success or improvement **3** : something promised

²**promise** vb **prom·ised; prom·is·ing 1** : to engage to do, bring about, or provide ⟨∼ help⟩ **2** : to suggest beforehand ⟨dark clouds ∼ rain⟩ **3** : to give ground for expectation ⟨it ∼s to be a good game⟩

prom·is·ing adj : likely to succeed or yield good results — **prom·is·ing·ly** adv

prom·is·so·ry \'prä-mə-ˌsōr-ē\ adj : containing a promise

prom·on·to·ry \'prä-mən-ˌtōr-ē\ n, pl **-ries** : a point of land jutting into the sea : HEADLAND

pro·mote \prə-'mōt\ vb **pro·mot·ed; pro·mot·ing 1** : to advance in station, rank, or honor **2** : to contribute to the growth or prosperity of : FURTHER **3** : LAUNCH — **pro·mo·tion** \-'mō-shən\ n — **pro·mo·tion·al** \-shə-nəl\ adj

pro·mot·er \-'mō-tər\ n : one that promotes; esp : one that assumes the financial responsibilities of a sports event

¹**prompt** \'prämpt\ vb **1** : INCITE **2** : to assist (one acting or reciting) by suggesting the next words **3** : INSPIRE, URGE — **prompt·er** n

²**prompt** adj **1** : being ready and quick to act; also : PUNCTUAL **2** : performed readily or immediately ⟨∼ service⟩ — **prompt·ly** adv — **prompt·ness** n

prompt·book \-ˌbük\ n : a copy of a play with directions for performance used by a theater prompter

promp·ti·tude \'prämp-tə-ˌtüd, -ˌtyüd\ n : the quality or habit of being prompt : PROMPTNESS

pro·mul·gate \'prä-məl-ˌgāt; prō-'məl-\ vb **-gat·ed; -gat·ing** : to make known or put into force by open declaration — **prom·ul·ga·tion** \ˌprä-məl-'gā-shən, ˌprō-(ˌ)məl-\ n

pron abbr **1** pronoun **2** pronounced **3** pronunciation

prone \'prōn\ adj **1** : having a tendency or inclination : DISPOSED **2** : lying face downward; also : lying flat or prostrate ⟨on subject, exposed, open, liable, susceptible — **prone·ness** n

prong \'prȯŋ\ n : one of the sharp points of a fork : TINE; also : a slender projecting part (as of an antler) — **pronged** \'prȯŋd\ adj

prong·horn \'prȯŋ-ˌhȯrn\ n, pl **pronghorn** also **pronghorns** : a ruminant mammal of treeless parts of western No. America that resembles an antelope

pronghorn

pro·noun \'prō-ˌnau̇n\ n : a word used as a substitute for a noun

pro·nounce \prə-'nau̇ns\ vb **pro·nounced; pro·nounc·ing 1** : to utter officially or as an opinion ⟨∼ sentence⟩ **2** : to employ the organs of speech in order to produce ⟨∼ a word⟩; esp : to say or speak correctly

⟨she can't ∼ his name⟩ — **pro·nounce·able** adj — **pro·nun·ci·a·tion** \-ˌnən-sē-'ā-shən\ n

pro·nounced adj : strongly marked : DECIDED

pro·nounce·ment \prə-'nau̇ns-mənt\ n : a formal declaration of opinion; also : ANNOUNCEMENT

pron·to \'prän-ˌtō\ adv [Sp, fr. L promptus prompt] : QUICKLY

pro·nu·clear \'prō-'nü-klē-ər, -'nyü-\ adj : supporting the use of nuclear-powered electric generating stations

pro·nun·ci·a·men·to \prō-ˌnən-sē-ə-'men-tō\ n, pl **-tos** or **-toes** : PROCLAMATION, MANIFESTO

¹**proof** \'prüf\ n **1** : the evidence that compels acceptance by the mind of a truth or fact **2** : a process or operation that establishes validity or truth : TEST **3** : a trial impression (as from type) **4** : a trial print from a photographic negative **5** : alcoholic content (as of a beverage) indicated by a number that is twice the percent by volume of alcohol present ⟨whiskey of 90 ∼ is 45% alcohol⟩

²**proof** adj **1** : successful in resisting or repelling ⟨∼ against tampering⟩ ⟨waterproof⟩ **2** : of standard strength or quality or alcoholic content

proof·read \-ˌrēd\ vb : to read and mark corrections in — **proof·read·er** n

¹**prop** \'präp\ n : something that props

²**prop** vb **propped; prop·ping 1** : to support by placing something under or against **2** : SUSTAIN, STRENGTHEN

³**prop** n : PROPERTY 4

⁴**prop** n : PROPELLER

⁵**prop** abbr **1** property **2** proposition **3** proprietor

pro·pa·gan·da \ˌprä-pə-'gan-də, ˌprō-\ n [NL, fr. Congregatio de propaganda fide Congregation for propagating the faith, organization established by Pope Gregory XV] : the spreading of ideas or information to further or damage a cause; also : ideas or allegations spread for such a purpose — **pro·pa·gan·dist** \-dist\ n

pro·pa·gan·dize \-ˌdīz\ vb **-dized; -diz·ing** : to subject to or carry on propaganda

prop·a·gate \'prä-pə-ˌgāt\ vb **-gat·ed; -gat·ing 1** : to reproduce or cause to reproduce biologically : MULTIPLY **2** : to cause to spread — **prop·a·ga·tion** \ˌprä-pə-'gā-shən\ n

pro·pane \'prō-ˌpān\ n : a heavy flammable gas found in petroleum and natural gas and used esp. as a fuel

pro·pel \prə-'pel\ vb **pro·pelled; pro·pel·ling** : to drive forward or onward **syn** push, shove, thrust

pro·pel·lant also **pro·pel·lent** \-'pe-lənt\ n : something (as a fuel) that propels — **propellant** or **propellent** adj

pro·pel·ler \prə-'pe-lər\ n : a device consisting of a hub fitted with blades that is used to propel a vehicle (as a motorboat or an airplane)

pro·pen·si·ty \prə-'pen-sə-tē\ n, pl **-ties** : an often intense natural inclination or preference

¹**prop·er** \'prä-pər\ adj **1** : referring to one individual only ⟨∼ noun⟩ **2** : belonging characteristically to a species or individual : PECULIAR **3** : very satisfactory : EXCELLENT **4** : strictly limited to a specified thing ⟨the city ∼⟩ **5** : CORRECT ⟨the ∼ way to proceed⟩ **6** : strictly decorous : GENTEEL **7** : marked by suitability or rightness ⟨∼ punishment⟩ **syn** meet, appropriate, fitting, seemly — **prop·er·ly** adv

²**proper** n : the parts of the Mass that vary according to the liturgical calendar

prop·er·tied \'prä-pər-tēd\ adj : owning property and esp. much property

prop·er·ty \'prä-pər-tē\ n, pl **-ties 1** : a quality peculiar to an individual or thing **2** : something owned; esp : a piece of real estate **3** : OWNERSHIP **4** : an article or object used in a play or motion picture other than painted scenery and actor's costumes

proph·e·cy also **proph·e·sy** \'prä-fə-sē\ n, pl **-cies** also **-sies 1** : an inspired utterance of a prophet **2** : PREDICTION

proph·e·sy \-ˌsī\ *vb* **-sied; -sy·ing 1** : to speak or utter by divine inspiration **2** : PREDICT — **proph·e·si·er** *n*

proph·et \'prä-fət\ *n* [ME *prophete*, fr. OF, fr. L *propheta*, fr. Gk *prophētēs*, fr. *pro* for + *phanai* to speak] **1** : one who utters divinely inspired revelations **2** : one who foretells future events

proph·et·ess \'prä-fə-təs\ *n* : a woman who is a prophet

pro·phet·ic \prə-'fe-tik\ *or* **pro·phet·i·cal** \-ti-kəl\ *adj* : of, relating to, or characteristic of a prophet or prophecy — **pro·phet·i·cal·ly** \-ti-k(ə-)lē\ *adv*

Proph·ets \'prä-fəts\ *n pl* — see BIBLE table

¹pro·phy·lac·tic \ˌprō-fə-'lak-tik, ˌprä-\ *adj* **1** : preventing or guarding from disease **2** : PREVENTIVE

²prophylactic *n* : something prophylactic; *esp* : a device (as a condom) for preventing venereal infection or conception

pro·phy·lax·is \-'lak-səs\ *n, pl* **-lax·es** \-'lak-ˌsēz\ : measures designed to preserve health and prevent the spread of disease

pro·pin·qui·ty \prə-'piŋ-kwə-tē\ *n* **1** : KINSHIP **2** : nearness in place or time : PROXIMITY

pro·pi·ti·ate \prō-'pi-shē-ˌāt\ *vb* **-at·ed; -at·ing** : to gain or regain the favor of : APPEASE — **pro·pi·ti·a·tion** \-ˌpi-shē-'ā-shən\ *n* — **pro·pi·tia·to·ry** \-'pi-shē-ə-ˌtȯr-ē\ *adj*

pro·pi·tious \prə-'pi-shəs\ *adj* **1** : favorably disposed ⟨~ deities⟩ **2** : being of good omen ⟨~ circumstances⟩

prop·man \'präp-ˌman\ *n* : one who is in charge of stage properties

pro·po·nent \prə-'pō-nənt\ *n* : one who argues in favor of something

¹pro·por·tion \prə-'pȯr-shən\ *n* **1** : BALANCE, SYMMETRY **2** : SHARE, QUOTA **3** : the relation of one part to another or to the whole with respect to magnitude, quantity, or degree : RATIO **4** : SIZE, DEGREE — **in proportion** : PROPORTIONAL

²proportion *vb* **-tioned; -tion·ing 1** : to adjust (a part or thing) in size relative to other parts or things **2** : to make the parts of harmonious

pro·por·tion·al \prə-'pȯr-shə-nəl\ *adj* : corresponding in size, degree, or intensity; *also* : having the same or a constant ratio — **pro·por·tion·al·ly** *adv*

pro·por·tion·ate \prə-'pȯr-shə-nət\ *adj* : PROPORTIONAL — **pro·por·tion·ate·ly** *adv*

pro·pose \prə-'pōz\ *vb* **pro·posed; pro·pos·ing 1** : PLAN, INTEND ⟨~s to buy a house⟩ **2** : to make an offer of marriage **3** : to offer for consideration : SUGGEST ⟨~ a policy⟩ — **pro·pos·al** \-'pō-zəl\ *n* — **pro·pos·er** *n*

¹prop·o·si·tion \ˌprä-pə-'zi-shən\ *n* **1** : something proposed for consideration : PROPOSAL **2** : a request for sexual intercourse **3** : a statement of something to be discussed, proved, or explained **4** : SITUATION, AFFAIR ⟨a tough ~⟩ — **prop·o·si·tion·al** \-'zi-shə-nəl\ *adj*

²proposition *vb* **-tioned; -tion·ing** : to make a proposal to; *esp* : to suggest sexual intercourse to

pro·pound \prə-'pau̇nd\ *vb* : to set forth for consideration ⟨~ a doctrine⟩

pro·pri·e·tary \prə-'prī-ə-ˌter-ē\ *adj* **1** : of, relating to, or characteristic of a proprietor ⟨~ rights⟩ **2** : made and sold by one with the sole right to do so ⟨~ medicines⟩

pro·pri·e·tor \prə-'prī-ə-tər\ *n* : OWNER — **pro·pri·e·tor·ship** *n*

pro·pri·e·tress \-'prī-ə-trəs\ *n* : a woman who is a proprietor

pro·pri·e·ty \prə-'prī-ə-tē\ *n, pl* **-ties 1** : the standard of what is socially acceptable in conduct or speech **2** *pl* : the customs of polite society

pro·pul·sion \prə-'pəl-shən\ *n* **1** : the action or process of propelling **2** : something that propels — **pro·pul·sive** \-siv\ *adj*

pro ra·ta \(ˌ)prō-'rä-tə, -'rā-\ *adv* : in proportion to the share of each : PROPORTIONATELY

pro·rate \(ˌ)prō-'rāt\ *vb* **pro·rat·ed; pro·rat·ing** : to divide, distribute, or assess proportionately

pro·rogue \prə-'rōg\ *vb* **pro·rogued; pro·rogu·ing** : to suspend or end a session of (a legislative body) — **pro·ro·ga·tion** \ˌprō-rō-'gā-shən\ *n*

pros *pl of* PRO

pro·sa·ic \prō-'zā-ik\ *adj* : lacking imagination or excitement : DULL

pro·sce·ni·um \prō-'sē-nē-əm\ *n* **1** : the part of a stage in front of the curtain **2** : the wall containing the arch that frames the stage

pro·scribe \prō-'skrīb\ *vb* **pro·scribed; pro·scrib·ing 1** : OUTLAW **2** : to condemn or forbid as harmful — **pro·scrip·tion** \-'skrip-shən\ *n*

prose \'prōz\ *n* [ME, fr. MF, fr. L *prosa*, fr. fem. of *prorsus, prosus*, straightforward, being in prose, alter. of *proversus*, pp. of *provertere* to turn forward] : the ordinary language people use in speaking or writing

pros·e·cute \'prä-si-ˌkyüt\ *vb* **-cut·ed; -cut·ing 1** : to follow to the end ⟨~ an investigation⟩ **2** : to seek legal punishment of ⟨~ a forger⟩ — **pros·e·cu·tion** \ˌprä-si-'kyü-shən\ *n* — **pros·e·cu·tor** \'prä-si-ˌkyü-tər\ *n*

¹pros·e·lyte \'prä-sə-ˌlīt\ *n* : a new convert to a religion, belief, or party — **pros·e·ly·tism** \-ˌlī-ˌti-zəm\ *n*

²proselyte *vb* **-lyt·ed; -lyt·ing** : PROSELYTIZE

pros·e·ly·tize \'prä-sə-lə-ˌtīz\ *vb* **-tized; -tiz·ing 1** : to induce someone to convert to one's faith **2** : to recruit someone to join one's party, institution, or cause

pros·o·dy \'prä-sə-dē, -zə-\ *n, pl* **-dies** : the study of versification and esp. of metrical structure

¹pros·pect \'prä-ˌspekt\ *n* **1** : an extensive view; *also* : OUTLOOK **2** : the act of looking forward **3** : a mental vision of something to come **4** : something that is awaited or expected : POSSIBILITY **5** : a potential buyer or customer; *also* : a likely candidate — **pro·spec·tive** \prə-'spek-tiv, 'prä-ˌspek-\ *adj* — **pro·spec·tive·ly** *adv*

²pros·pect \'prä-ˌspekt\ *vb* : to explore esp. for mineral deposits — **pros·pec·tor** \-ˌspek-tər, prä-'spek-\ *n*

pro·spec·tus \prə-'spek-təs\ *n* : a preliminary statement that describes an enterprise and is distributed to prospective buyers or participants

pros·per \'prä-spər\ *vb* **pros·pered; pros·per·ing** : SUCCEED; *esp* : to achieve economic success

pros·per·i·ty \präs-'per-ə-tē\ *n* : thriving condition : SUCCESS; *esp* : economic well-being

pros·per·ous \'präs-pə-rəs\ *adj* **1** : FAVORABLE ⟨~ winds⟩ **2** : marked by success or economic well-being ⟨a ~ business⟩

pros·tate \'präs-ˌtāt\ *n* : PROSTATE GLAND — **pros·tat·ic** \prä-'sta-tik\ *adj*

prostate gland *n* : a glandular body about the base of the male urethra that produces a secretion which is a major part of the fluid ejaculated during an orgasm

pros·ta·ti·tis \ˌpräs-tə-'tī-təs\ *n* : inflammation of the prostate gland

pros·the·sis \präs-'thē-səs, 'präs-thə-\ *n, pl* **-the·ses** \-ˌsēz\ : an artificial replacement for a missing body part — **pros·thet·ic** \präs-'the-tik\ *adj*

pros·thet·ics \-'the-tiks\ *n pl* : the surgical or dental specialty concerned with the design, construction, and fitting of prostheses

¹pros·ti·tute \'präs-tə-ˌtüt, -ˌtyüt\ *vb* **-tut·ed; -tut·ing 1** : to offer indiscriminately for sexual activity esp. for money **2** : to devote to corrupt or unworthy purposes — **pros·ti·tu·tion** \ˌpräs-tə-'tü-shən, -'tyü-\ *n*

²prostitute *n* : one who engages in sexual activities for money

¹pros·trate \'prä-ˌstrāt\ *adj* **1** : stretched out with face on the ground in adoration or submission **2** : lying flat **3** : completely overcome ⟨~ with a cold⟩

²prostrate *vb* **pros·trat·ed; pros·trat·ing 1** : to throw or put into a prostrate position **2** : to reduce to a weak or powerless condition — **pros·tra·tion** \prä-'strā-shən\ *n*

prosy \'prō-zē\ *adj* **pros·i·er; -est 1** : PROSAIC **2** : TEDIOUS

Prot *abbr* Protestant

prot·ac·tin·i·um \ˌprō-tak-'ti-nē-əm\ *n* : a metallic radioactive chemical element of relatively short life — see ELEMENT table

pro·tag·o·nist \prō-'ta-gə-nist\ *n* 1 : the principal character in a drama or story 2 : a leader or supporter of a cause

pro·te·an \'prō-tē-ən\ *adj* : able to assume different shapes or roles

pro·tect \prə-'tekt\ *vb* : to shield from injury : GUARD

pro·tec·tion \prə-'tek-shən\ *n* 1 : the act of protecting : the state of being protected 2 : one that protects ⟨wear a helmet as a ∼⟩ 3 : the supervision or support of one that is smaller and weaker 4 : the freeing of producers from foreign competition in their home market by high duties on foreign competitive goods — **pro·tec·tive** \-'tek-tiv\ *adj*

pro·tec·tion·ist \-shə-nist\ *n* : an advocate of government economic protection for domestic producers through restrictions on foreign competitors — **pro·tec·tion·ism** \-shə-ˌni-zəm\ *n*

pro·tec·tor \prə-'tek-tər\ *n* 1 : one that protects : GUARDIAN 2 : a device used to prevent injury : GUARD 3 : REGENT 1

pro·tec·tor·ate \-tə-rət\ *n* 1 : government by a protector 2 : the relationship of superior authority assumed by one state over a dependent one; *also* : the dependent political unit in such a relationship

pro·té·gé \'prō-tə-ˌzhā\ *n* [F] : one who is protected, trained, or guided by an influential person

pro·tein \'prō-ˌtēn\ *n* [F *protéine,* fr. LGk *prōteios* primary, fr. Gk *prōtos* first] : any of numerous complex nitrogen-containing substances that consist of chains of amino acids, are present in all living cells, and are an essential part of the human diet

pro tem \prō-'tem\ *adv* : PRO TEMPORE

pro tem·po·re \prō-'tem-pə-rē\ *adv* [L] : for the time being

Pro·tero·zo·ic \ˌprä-tə-rə-'zō-ik, ˌprō-\ *adj* : of, relating to, or being the eon of geologic history between the Archean and the Phanerozoic — **Proterozoic** *n*

¹pro·test \'prō-ˌtest\ *n* 1 : the act of protesting; *esp* : an organized public demonstration of disapproval 2 : a complaint or objection against an idea, an act, or a course of action

²pro·test \prō-'test\ *vb* 1 : to assert positively : make solemn declaration of ⟨∼s his innocence⟩ 2 : to object strongly : make a protest against ⟨∼ a ruling⟩ — **pro·tes·ta·tion** \ˌprä-təs-'tā-shən\ *n* — **pro·test·er** *or* **pro·tes·tor** \-tər\ *n*

Prot·es·tant \'prä-təs-tənt, *3 also* prə-'tes-\ *n* 1 : a member or adherent of one of the Christian churches deriving from the Reformation 2 : a Christian not of a Catholic or Orthodox church 3 *not cap* : one who makes a protest — **Prot·es·tant·ism** \'prä-təs-tən-ˌti-zəm\ *n*

pro·tha·la·mi·on \ˌprō-thə-'lā-mē-ən\ *or* **pro·tha·la·mi·um** \-mē-əm\ *n, pl* **-mia** \-mē-ə\ : a song in celebration of a marriage

pro·to·col \'prō-tə-ˌkȯl\ *n* [MF *prothocole,* fr. ML *protocollum,* fr. LGk *prōtokollon* first sheet of a papyrus roll bearing data of manufacture, fr. Gk *prōtos* first + *kollan* to glue together, fr. *kolla* glue] 1 : an original draft or record 2 : a preliminary memorandum of diplomatic negotiation 3 : a code of diplomatic or military etiquette

pro·ton \'prō-ˌtän\ *n* [Gk *prōton,* neut. of *prōtos* first] : a positively charged atomic particle present in all atomic nuclei — **pro·ton·ic** \-'tä-nik\ *adj*

pro·to·plasm \'prō-tə-ˌpla-zəm\ *n* : the complex colloidal largely protein substance of living plant and animal cells — **pro·to·plas·mic** \ˌprō-tə-'plaz-mik\ *adj*

pro·to·type \'prō-tə-ˌtīp\ *n* : an original model : ARCHETYPE

pro·to·zo·an \ˌprō-tə-'zō-ən\ *n* : any of a phylum or subkingdom of unicellular lower invertebrate animals that include some pathogenic parasites of humans and domestic animals — **protozoan** *adj*

pro·tract \prō-'trakt\ *vb* : to prolong in time or space **syn** extend, lengthen, elongate, stretch

pro·trac·tor \-'trak-tər\ *n* : an instrument for drawing and measuring angles

pro·trude \prō-'trüd\ *vb* **pro·trud·ed; pro·trud·ing** : to stick out or cause to stick out : jut out — **pro·tru·sion** \-'trü-zhən\ *n*

pro·tu·ber·ance \prō-'tü-bə-rəns, -'tyü-\ *n* : something that protrudes

pro·tu·ber·ant \-rənt\ *adj* : extending beyond the surrounding surface in a bulge

proud \'praud\ *adj* 1 : having or showing excessive self-esteem : HAUGHTY 2 : highly pleased : EXULTANT 3 : having proper self-respect ⟨too ∼ to beg⟩ 4 : GLORIOUS ⟨a ∼ occasion⟩ 5 : SPIRITED ⟨a ∼ steed⟩ **syn** arrogant, insolent, overbearing, disdainful — **proud·ly** *adv*

prov *abbr* 1 province; provincial 2 provisional

Prov *abbr* Proverbs

prove \'prüv\ *vb* **proved; proved** *or* **prov·en** \'prü-vən\; **prov·ing** 1 : to test by experiment or by a standard 2 : to establish the truth of by argument or evidence 3 : to show to be correct, valid, or genuine 4 : to turn out esp. after trial or test ⟨the car *proved* to be a good choice⟩ — **prov·able** \'prü-və-bəl\ *adj*

prov·e·nance \'prä-və-nəns\ *n* : ORIGIN, SOURCE

Pro·ven·çal \ˌprō-vän-'säl, ˌprä-vən-\ *n* 1 : a native or inhabitant of Provence 2 : a Romance language spoken in southern France — **Provençal** *adj*

prov·en·der \'prä-vən-dər\ *n* 1 : dry food for domestic animals : FEED 2 : FOOD, VICTUALS

pro·ve·nience \prə-'vē-nyəns\ *n* : ORIGIN, SOURCE

prov·erb \'prä-ˌvərb\ *n* : a pithy popular saying : ADAGE

pro·ver·bi·al \prə-'vər-bē-əl\ *adj* 1 : of, relating to, or resembling a proverb 2 : commonly spoken of

Proverbs *n* — see BIBLE table

pro·vide \prə-'vīd\ *vb* **pro·vid·ed; pro·vid·ing** [ME, fr. L *providēre,* lit., to see ahead, fr. *pro-* forward + *vidēre* to see] 1 : to take measures beforehand ⟨∼ against inflation⟩ 2 : to make a proviso or stipulation 3 : to supply what is needed ⟨∼ for a family⟩ 4 : EQUIP 5 : to supply for use : YIELD — **pro·vid·er** *n*

pro·vid·ed *conj* : on condition that : IF

prov·i·dence \'prä-və-dəns\ *n* 1 *often cap* : divine guidance or care 2 *cap* : GOD 1 3 : the quality or state of being provident

prov·i·dent \-dənt\ *adj* 1 : making provision for the future : PRUDENT 2 : FRUGAL — **prov·i·dent·ly** *adv*

prov·i·den·tial \ˌprä-və-'den-chəl\ *adj* 1 : of, relating to, or determined by Providence 2 : OPPORTUNE, LUCKY

pro·vid·ing *conj* : PROVIDED

prov·ince \'prä-vəns\ *n* 1 : an administrative district or division of a country 2 *pl* : all of a country except the metropolises 3 : proper business or scope : SPHERE

pro·vin·cial \prə-'vin-chəl\ *adj* 1 : of or relating to a province 2 : limited in outlook : NARROW ⟨∼ ideas⟩ — **pro·vin·cial·ism** \-chə-ˌli-zəm\ *n*

proving ground *n* : a place for scientific experimentation or testing

¹pro·vi·sion \prə-'vi-zhən\ *n* 1 : the act or process of providing; *also* : a measure taken beforehand 2 : a stock of needed supplies; *esp* : a stock of food — usu. used in pl. 3 : PROVISO

²provision *vb* : to supply with provisions

pro·vi·sion·al \-'vi-zhə-nəl\ *adj* : provided for a temporary need : CONDITIONAL — **pro·vi·sion·al·ly** *adv*

pro·vi·so \prə-'vī-zō\ *n, pl* **-sos** *or* **-soes** [ME, fr. ML *proviso quod* provided that] : an article or clause that introduces a condition : STIPULATION

prov·o·ca·tion \ˌprä-və-'kā-shən\ *n* 1 : the act of provoking 2 : something that provokes

pro·voc·a·tive \prə-'vä-kə-tiv\ *adj* : serving to provoke or excite

pro·voke \prə-'vōk\ *vb* **pro·voked; pro·vok·ing 1** : to incite to anger : INCENSE **2** : to call forth : EVOKE ⟨a remark that *provoked* laughter⟩ **3** : to stir up on purpose ⟨~ an argument⟩ **syn** irritate, exasperate, aggravate, inflame, rile, pique — **pro·vok·er** *n*

pro·vo·lo·ne \₁prō-və-'lō-nē\ *n* : a usu. firm pliant often smoked Italian cheese

pro·vost \'prō-₁vōst, 'prä-vəst\ *n* : a high official : DIGNITARY; *esp* : a high-ranking university administrative officer

pro·vost mar·shal \'prō-₁vō-'mär-shəl\ *n* : an officer who supervises the military police of a command

prow \'prau̇\ *n* : the bow of a ship

prow·ess \'prau̇-əs\ *n* **1** : military valor and skill **2** : extraordinary ability

prowl \'prau̇l\ *vb* : to roam about stealthily — **prowl** *n* — **prowl·er** *n*

prox·i·mal \'präk-sə-məl\ *adj* **1** : next to or nearest the point of attachment or origin; *esp* : located toward the center of the body **2** : of, relating to, or being the mesial and distal surfaces of a tooth — **prox·i·mal·ly** *adv*

prox·i·mate \'präk-sə-mət\ *adj* **1** : DIRECT ⟨the ~ cause⟩ **2** : very near

prox·im·i·ty \präk-'si-mə-tē\ *n* : NEARNESS

prox·i·mo \'präk-sə-₁mō\ *adj* [L *proximo mense* in the next month] : of or occurring in the next month after the present

proxy \'präk-sē\ *n, pl* **prox·ies** : the authority or power to act for another; *also* : a document giving such authorization — **proxy** *adj*

prude \'prüd\ *n* : a person who shows or affects extreme modesty — **prud·ery** \'prü-də-rē\ *n* — **prud·ish** *adj* — **prud·ish·ly** *adv*

pru·dent \'prüd-ᵊnt\ *adj* **1** : shrewd in the management of practical affairs **2** : CAUTIOUS, DISCREET **3** : PROVIDENT, FRUGAL **syn** judicious, foresighted, sensible, sane — **pru·dence** \-ᵊns\ *n* — **pru·den·tial** \prü-'den-chəl\ *adj* — **pru·dent·ly** *adv*

¹prune \'prün\ *n* : a dried plum

²prune *vb* **pruned; prun·ing** : to cut off unwanted parts (as of a tree)

pru·ri·ent \'pru̇r-ē-ənt\ *adj* : LASCIVIOUS; *also* : exciting to lasciviousness — **pru·ri·ence** \-ē-əns\ *n*

¹pry \'prī\ *vb* **pried; pry·ing** : to look closely or inquisitively; *esp* : SNOOP

²pry *vb* **pried; pry·ing 1** : to raise, move, or pull apart with a pry or lever **2** : to detach or open with difficulty

³pry *n* : a tool for prying

Ps *or* **Psa** *abbr* Psalms

PS *abbr* **1** [L *postscriptum*] postscript **2** public school

PSA *abbr* public service announcement

psalm \'säm, 'sälm\ *n, often cap* [ME, fr. OE *psealm*, fr. LL *psalmus*, fr. Gk *psalmos*, lit., twanging of a harp, fr. *psallein* to pluck, play a stringed instrument] : a sacred song or poem; *esp* : one of the hymns collected in the Book of Psalms — **psalm·ist** *n*

psalm·o·dy \'sä-mə-dē, 'säl-\ *n* : the singing of psalms in worship

Psalms *n* — see BIBLE table

Psal·ter \'sȯl-tər\ *n* : the Book of Psalms; *also* : a collection of the Psalms arranged for devotional use

pseud *abbr* pseudonym; pseudonymous

pseu·do \'sü-dō\ *adj* : SPURIOUS, SHAM

pseu·do·nym \'sü-də-₁nim\ *n* : a fictitious name — **pseu·don·y·mous** \sü-'dä-nə-məs\ *adj*

PSG *abbr* platoon sergeant

¹psi \'sī, 'psī\ *n* : the 23d letter of the Greek alphabet — Ψ or ψ

²psi *abbr* pounds per square inch

pso·ri·a·sis \sə-'rī-ə-səs\ *n* : a chronic skin disease characterized by red patches covered with white scales

PST *abbr* Pacific standard time

¹psych *also* **psyche** \'sīk\ *vb* **psyched; psych·ing 1** : OUTWIT, OUTGUESS; *also* : to analyze beforehand **2** : INTIMIDATE; *also* : to prepare oneself psychologically ⟨get *psyched* up for the game⟩

²psych *abbr* psychology

psy·che \'sī-kē\ *n* : SOUL, SELF; *also* : MIND

psy·che·del·ic \₁sī-kə-'de-lik\ *adj* **1** : of, relating to, or causing abnormal psychic effects ⟨~ drugs⟩ **2** : relating to the taking of psychedelic drugs ⟨~ experience⟩ **3** : imitating, suggestive of, or reproducing the effects of psychedelic drugs ⟨~ art⟩ ⟨~ colors⟩ — **psychedelic** *n* — **psy·che·del·i·cal·ly** \-k(ə-)lē\ *adv*

psy·chi·a·try \sə-'kī-ə-trē, sī-\ *n* : a branch of medicine dealing with mental, emotional, and behavioral disorders — **psy·chi·at·ric** \₁sī-kē-'a-trik\ *adj* — **psy·chi·a·trist** \sə-'kī-ə-trist, sī-\ *n*

¹psy·chic \'sī-kik\ *also* **psy·chi·cal** \-ki-kəl\ *adj* **1** : of or relating to the psyche **2** : lying outside the sphere of physical science **3** : sensitive to nonphysical or supernatural forces — **psy·chi·cal·ly** \-k(ə-)lē\ *adv*

²psychic *n* : a person apparently sensitive to nonphysical forces; *also* : MEDIUM 6

psy·cho \'sī-kō\ *n, pl* **psychos** : a mentally disturbed person — **psycho** *adj*

psy·cho·ac·tive \₁sī-kō-'ak-tiv\ *adj* : affecting the mind or behavior

psy·cho·anal·y·sis \₁sī-kō-ə-'na-lə-səs\ *n* : a method of dealing with psychic disorders by having the patient talk freely about personal experiences and esp. about early childhood and dreams — **psy·cho·an·a·lyst** \-'an-ᵊl-ist\ *n* — **psy·cho·an·a·lyt·ic** \-₁an-ᵊl-'i-tik\ *adj* — **psy·cho·an·a·lyze** \-'an-ᵊl-₁īz\ *vb*

psy·cho·dra·ma \₁sī-kə-'drä-mə, -'dra-\ *n* **1** : an extemporized dramatization designed to afford catharsis for one or more of the participants from whose life the plot is taken **2** : a dramatic event or story with psychological overtones

psy·cho·gen·ic \-'je-nik\ *adj* : originating in the mind or in mental or emotional conflict

psychol *abbr* psychologist; psychology

psy·chol·o·gy \sī-'kä-lə-jē\ *n, pl* **-gies 1** : the science of mind and behavior **2** : the mental and behavioral characteristics of an individual or group — **psy·cho·log·i·cal** \₁sī-kə-'lä-ji-kəl\ *adj* — **psy·cho·log·i·cal·ly** \-ji-k(ə-)lē\ *adv* — **psy·chol·o·gist** \sī-'kä-lə-jist\ *n*

psy·cho·path \'sī-kō-₁path\ *n* : a mentally ill or unstable person; *esp* : one who has not lost contact with reality but who engages in abnormally aggressive and seriously irresponsible behavior with little or no feeling of guilt — **psy·cho·path·ic** \₁sī-kə-'pa-thik\ *adj*

psy·cho·sex·u·al \₁sī-kō-'sek-shə-wəl\ *adj* **1** : of or relating to the mental, emotional, and behavioral aspects of sexual development **2** : of or relating to the physiological psychology of sex

psy·cho·sis \sī-'kō-səs\ *n, pl* **-cho·ses** \-₁sēz\ : a serious mental illness (as schizophrenia) marked by loss of or greatly lessened ability to test whether what one is thinking and feeling about the real world is really true

psy·cho·so·mat·ic \₁sī-kō-sə-'ma-tik\ *adj* : of, relating to, involving, or concerned with bodily symptoms caused by mental or emotional disturbance

psy·cho·ther·a·py \₁sī-kō-'ther-ə-pē\ *n* : treatment of mental or emotional disorder or of related bodily ills by psychological means — **psy·cho·ther·a·pist** \-pist\ *n*

psy·chot·ic \sī-'kä-tik\ *adj* : of or relating to psychosis ⟨~ behavior⟩ — **psychotic** *n*

psy·cho·tro·pic \₁sī-kə-'trō-pik\ *adj* : acting on the mind ⟨~ drugs⟩

pt *abbr* **1** part **2** payment **3** pint **4** point **5** port

Pt *symbol* platinum

PT *abbr* **1** Pacific time **2** part-time **3** physical therapy **4** physical training

PTA *abbr* Parent-Teacher Association

ptar·mi·gan \'tär-mi-gən\ *n, pl* **-gan** *or* **-gans** : any of various grouses of northern regions with completely feathered feet

PT boat \(ˌ)pē-ˈtē-\ *n* [*patrol torpedo*] : a small fast patrol craft usu. armed with torpedos

pte *abbr, Brit* private

ptg *abbr* printing

PTO *abbr* **1** Parent-Teacher Organization **2** please turn over

pto·maine \ˈtō-ˌmān\ *n* : any of various chemical substances formed by bacteria in decaying matter (as meat) and including a few poisonous ones

PTV *abbr* public television

Pu *symbol* plutonium

¹pub \ˈpəb\ *n, chiefly Brit* **1** : PUBLIC HOUSE 2 **2** : TAVERN

²pub *abbr* **1** public **2** publication **3** published; publisher; publishing

pu·ber·ty \ˈpyü-bər-tē\ *n* : the condition of being or period of becoming first capable of reproducing sexually — **pu·ber·tal** \-bərt-ᵊl\ *adj*

pu·bes \ˈpyü-bēz\ *n, pl* **pubes 1** : the hair that appears upon the lower middle region of the abdomen at puberty **2** : the pubic region

pu·bes·cence \pyü-ˈbes-ᵊns\ *n* **1** : the quality or state of being pubescent **2** : a pubescent covering or surface

pu·bes·cent \-ᵊnt\ *adj* **1** : arriving at or having reached puberty **2** : covered with fine soft short hairs

pu·bic \ˈpyü-bik\ *adj* : of, relating to, or situated near the pubes or the pubis

pu·bis \ˈpyü-bəs\ *n, pl* **pu·bes** \-bēz\ : the ventral and anterior of the three principal bones composing either half of the pelvis

publ *abbr* **1** publication **2** published; publisher

¹pub·lic \ˈpə-blik\ *adj* **1** : exposed to general view ⟨the story became ∼⟩ **2** : of, relating to, or affecting the people as a whole ⟨∼ opinion⟩ **3** : CIVIC, GOVERNMENTAL ⟨∼ expenditures⟩ **4** : of, relating to, or serving the community ⟨∼ officials⟩ **5** : not private : SOCIAL ⟨∼ morality⟩ **6** : open to all ⟨∼ library⟩ **7** : well known : PROMINENT ⟨∼ figures⟩ — **pub·lic·ly** *adv*

²public *n* **1** : the people as a whole : POPULACE **2** : a group of people having common interests

pub·li·can \ˈpə-bli-kən\ *n* **1** : a Jewish tax collector for the ancient Romans **2** *chiefly Brit* : the licensee of a pub

pub·li·ca·tion \ˌpə-blə-ˈkā-shən\ *n* **1** : the act or process of publishing **2** : a published work

public house *n* **1** : INN **2** *chiefly Brit* : a licensed saloon or bar

pub·li·cist \ˈpə-blə-sist\ *n* : one that publicizes; *esp* : PRESS AGENT

pub·lic·i·ty \(ˌ)pə-ˈbli-sə-tē\ *n* **1** : information with news value issued to gain public attention or support **2** : public attention or acclaim

pub·li·cize \ˈpə-blə-ˌsīz\ *vb* **-cized; -ciz·ing** : to bring to public attention : ADVERTISE

public relations *n sing or pl* : the business of fostering public goodwill toward a person, firm, or institution; *also* : the degree of goodwill and understanding achieved

public school *n* **1** : an endowed secondary boarding school in Great Britain offering a classical curriculum and preparation for the universities or public service **2** : a free tax-supported school controlled by a local governmental authority

public–spirited *adj* : motivated by devotion to the general or national welfare

public television *n* : television supported by public funds and private contributions rather than by commercials

public works *n pl* : works (as schools or highways) constructed with public funds for public use

pub·lish \ˈpə-blish\ *vb* **1** : to make generally known : announce publicly **2** : to produce or release literature, information, musical scores or sometimes recordings, or art for sale to the public — **pub·lish·er** *n*

¹puck \ˈpək\ *n* : a mischievous sprite — **puck·ish** *adj* — **puck·ish·ly** *adv*

²puck *n* : a disk used in ice hockey

¹puck·er \ˈpə-kər\ *vb* **puck·ered; puck·er·ing** : to contract into folds or wrinkles

²pucker *n* : FOLD, WRINKLE

pud·ding \ˈpu̇-diŋ\ *n* : a soft, spongy, or thick creamy dessert

pud·dle \ˈpəd-ᵊl\ *n* : a very small pool of usu. dirty or muddy water

pu·den·dum \pyu̇-ˈden-dəm\ *n, pl* **-da** \-də\ [NL, fr. L *pudēre* to be ashamed] : the human external genital organs esp. of a woman

pudgy \ˈpə-jē\ *adj* **pudg·i·er; -est** : being short and plump : CHUBBY

pueb·lo \ˈpwe-blō, pü-ˈe-\ *n, pl* **-los** [Sp, village, lit., people, fr. L *populus*] **1** : an American Indian village of Arizona or New Mexico that consists of flat-roofed stone or adobe houses joined in groups sometimes several stories high **2** *cap* : a member of a group of American Indian peoples of the southwestern U.S.

pu·er·ile \ˈpyü-ə-rəl\ *adj* : CHILDISH, SILLY — **pu·er·il·i·ty** \ˌpyü-ə-ˈri-lə-tē\ *n*

pu·er·per·al \pyü-ˈər-pə-rəl\ *adj* : of, relating to, or occurring during childbirth or the period immediately following ⟨∼ infection⟩ ⟨∼ depression⟩

puerperal fever *n* : an abnormal condition that results from infection of the placental site following childbirth or abortion

Puer·to Ri·can \ˌpȯr-tə-ˈrē-kən, ˌpwer-\ *n* : a native or inhabitant of Puerto Rico — **Puerto Rican** *adj*

¹puff \ˈpəf\ *vb* **1** : to blow in short gusts **2** : PANT **3** : to emit small whiffs or clouds **4** : BLUSTER, BRAG **5** : INFLATE, SWELL **6** : to make proud or conceited **7** : to praise extravagantly

²puff *n* **1** : a short discharge (as of air or smoke); *also* : a slight explosive sound accompanying it **2** : a light fluffy pastry **3** : a slight swelling **4** : a fluffy mass; *also* : a small pad for applying cosmetic powder **5** : a laudatory notice or review — **puffy** *adj*

puff·ball \ˈpəf-ˌbȯl\ *n* : any of various globe-shaped and often edible fungi

puf·fin \ˈpə-fən\ *n* : any of several seabirds having a short neck and a deep grooved parti-colored bill

¹pug \ˈpəg\ *n* **1** : any of a breed of small stocky short-haired dogs with a wrinkled face **2** : a close coil of hair

pug

²pug *n* : ¹BOXER

pu·gil·ism \ˈpyü-jə-ˌli-zəm\ *n* : BOXING — **pu·gi·list** \-list\ *n* — **pu·gi·lis·tic** \ˌpyü-jə-ˈlis-tik\ *adj*

pug·na·cious \ˌpəg-ˈnā-shəs\ *adj* : having a quarrelsome or combative nature **syn** belligerent, bellicose, contentious, truculent — **pug·nac·i·ty** \-ˈna-sə-tē\ *n*

puis·sance \ˈpwi-səns, ˈpyü-ə-\ *n* : POWER, STRENGTH — **puis·sant** \-sənt\ *adj*

puke \ˈpyük\ *vb* **puked; puk·ing** : VOMIT — **puke** *n*

puk·ka \\'pə-kə\ *adj* [Hindi *pakkā* cooked, ripe, solid, fr. Skt *pakva*] : GENUINE, AUTHENTIC; *also* : FIRST= CLASS, COMPLETE

pul \\'pül\ *n, pl* **puls** \\'pülz\ *or* **pul** — see *afghani* at MONEY table

pu·la \\'pü-lə, 'pyü-\ *n, pl* **pula** — see MONEY table

pul·chri·tude \\'pəl-krə-₁tüd, -₁tyüd\ *n* : BEAUTY — **pul·chri·tu·di·nous** \₁pəl-krə-'tüd-ᵊn-əs, -'tyüd-\ *adj*

pule \\'pyül\ *vb* **puled; pul·ing** : WHINE, WHIMPER

¹**pull** \\'pül\ *vb* **1** : to exert force so as to draw (something) toward the force; *also* : MOVE ⟨~ out of a driveway⟩ **2** : PLUCK; *also* : EXTRACT ⟨~ a tooth⟩ **3** : STRETCH, STRAIN ⟨~ a tendon⟩ **4** : to draw apart : TEAR **5** : to make (as a proof) by printing **6** : REMOVE **7** : DRAW ⟨~ a gun⟩ **8** : to carry out esp. with daring ⟨~ a robbery⟩ **9** : PERPETRATE, COMMIT **10** : ATTRACT **11** : to express strong sympathy — **pull·er** *n*

²**pull** *n* **1** : the act or an instance of pulling **2** : the effort expended in moving **3** : ADVANTAGE; *esp* : special influence **4** : a device for pulling something or for operating by pulling **5** : a force that attracts or compels **6** : an injury from abnormal straining or stretching ⟨a muscle ~⟩

pull·back \\'pül-₁bak\ *n* : an orderly withdrawal of troops

pul·let \\'pü-lət\ *n* : a young hen esp. of the domestic chicken when less than a year old

pul·ley \\'pü-lē\ *n, pl* **pulleys** : a wheel used to transmit power by means of a belt, rope, or chain; *esp* : one with a grooved rim that forms part of a tackle for hoisting or for changing the direction of a force

Pull·man \\'pül-mən\ *n* : a railroad passenger car with comfortable furnishings esp. for night travel

pull off *vb* : to accomplish successfully

pull·out \\'pül-₁aüt\ *n* : PULLBACK

pull·over \\'pül-₁ō-vər\ *adj* : put on by being pulled over the head ⟨~ sweater⟩ — **pull·over** *n*

pull—up \\'pül-₁əp\ *n* : CHIN-UP

pull up *vb* : to bring or come to an often abrupt halt : STOP

pul·mo·nary \\'pül-mə-₁ner-ē, 'pəl-\ *adj* : of, relating to, or carried on by the lungs ⟨the ~ circulation⟩

pulp \\'pəlp\ *n* **1** : the soft juicy or fleshy part of a fruit or vegetable **2** : a soft moist mass **3** : the soft sensitive tissue that fills the central cavity of a tooth **4** : a material (as from wood) used in making paper **5** : a magazine using cheap paper and often dealing with sensational material — **pulpy** *adj*

pul·pit \\'pül-₁pit\ *n* : a raised platform or high reading desk used in preaching or conducting a worship service

pulp·wood \\'pəlp-₁wüd\ *n* : wood used in making pulp for paper

pul·sar \\'pəl-₁sär\ *n* : a celestial source of pulsating electromagnetic radiation (as radio waves)

pul·sate \\'pəl-₁sāt\ *vb* **pul·sat·ed; pul·sat·ing** : to expand and contract rhythmically : BEAT — **pul·sa·tion** \pəl-'sā-shən\ *n*

pulse \\'pəls\ *n* **1** : the regular throbbing in the arteries caused by the contractions of the heart **2** : rhythmical beating, vibrating, or sounding **3** : a brief change in electrical current or voltage — **pulse** *vb*

pul·ver·ize \\'pəl-və-₁rīz\ *vb* **-ized; -iz·ing** **1** : to reduce (as by crushing or grinding) or be reduced to very small particles **2** : DEMOLISH

pu·ma \\'pü-mə, 'pyü-\ *n, pl* **pumas** *also* **puma** : COUGAR

pum·ice \\'pə-məs\ *n* : a light porous volcanic glass used esp. for smoothing and polishing

pum·mel \\'pə-məl\ *vb* **-meled** *also* **-melled; -mel·ing** *also* **-mel·ling** : POUND, BEAT

¹**pump** \\'pəmp\ *n* : a device for raising, transferring, or compressing fluids esp. by suction or pressure

²**pump** *vb* **1** : to raise (as water) with a pump **2** : to draw fluid from with a pump; *also* : to fill by means of a

pump ⟨~ up a tire⟩ **3** : to force or propel in the manner of a pump — **pump·er** *n*

³**pump** *n* : a low shoe that grips the foot chiefly at the toe and heel

pum·per·nick·el \\'pəm-pər-₁ni-kəl\ *n* : a dark rye bread

pump·kin \\'pəmp-kən, 'pəŋ-kən\ *n* : the large usu. orange fruit of a vine of the gourd family that is widely used as food; *also* : this vine

pun \\'pən\ *n* : the humorous use of a word in a way that suggests two or more interpretations — **pun** *vb*

¹**punch** \\'pənch\ *vb* **1** : PROD, POKE; *also* : DRIVE, HERD ⟨~*ing* cattle⟩ **2** : to strike with the fist **3** : to emboss, perforate, or make with a punch **4** : to operate, produce, or enter (as data) by or as if by punching — **punch·er** *n*

²**punch** *n* **1** : a quick blow with or as if with the fist **2** : effective energy or forcefulness

³**punch** *n* : a tool for piercing, stamping, cutting, or forming

⁴**punch** *n* [perh. fr. Hindi *pāc* five, fr. Skt *pañca;* fr. the number of ingredients] : a drink usu. composed of wine or alcoholic liquor and nonalcoholic beverages; *also* : a drink composed of nonalcoholic beverages

punched card \\'pəncht-\ *n* : a card with holes punched in particular positions to represent data

pun·cheon \\'pən-chən\ *n* : a large cask

punch line *n* : the sentence or phrase in a joke that makes the point

punchy \\'pən-chē\ *adj* **punch·i·er; -est** **1** : having punch : FORCEFUL **2** : DAZED, CONFUSED

punc·til·io \pəŋk-'ti-lē-₁ō\ *n, pl* **-ios** **1** : a nice detail of conduct in a ceremony or in observance of a code **2** : careful observance of forms (as in social conduct)

punc·til·i·ous \₁pəŋk-'ti-lē-əs\ *adj* : marked by precise accordance with codes or conventions **syn** meticulous, scrupulous, careful, punctual

punc·tu·al \\'pəŋk-chə-wəl\ *adj* : being on time : PROMPT — **punc·tu·al·i·ty** \₁pəŋk-chə-'wa-lə-tē\ *n* — **punc·tu·al·ly** *adv*

punc·tu·ate \\'pəŋk-chə-₁wāt\ *vb* **-at·ed; -at·ing** **1** : to mark or divide (written matter) with punctuation marks **2** : to break into at intervals **3** : EMPHASIZE

punc·tu·a·tion \₁pəŋk-chə-'wā-shən\ *n* : the act, practice, or system of inserting standardized marks in written matter to clarify the meaning and separate structural units

¹**punc·ture** \\'pəŋk-chər\ *n* **1** : an act of puncturing **2** : a small hole or wound made by puncturing

²**puncture** *vb* **punc·tured; punc·tur·ing** **1** : to make a hole in : PIERCE **2** : to make useless as if by a puncture

pun·dit \\'pən-dət\ *n* **1** : a learned person : TEACHER **2** : AUTHORITY, CRITIC

pun·gent \\'pən-jənt\ *adj* **1** : having a sharp incisive quality : CAUSTIC ⟨a ~ editorial⟩ **2** : causing a sharp or irritating sensation; *esp* : ACRID ⟨~ smell of burning leaves⟩ — **pun·gen·cy** \-jən-sē\ *n* — **pun·gent·ly** *adv*

pun·ish \\'pə-nish\ *vb* **1** : to impose a penalty on for a fault or crime ⟨~ an offender⟩ **2** : to inflict a penalty for ⟨~ treason with death⟩ **3** : to inflict injury on : HURT **syn** chastise, castigate, chasten, discipline, correct — **pun·ish·able** *adj*

pun·ish·ment *n* **1** : retributive suffering, pain, or loss : PENALTY **2** : rough treatment

pu·ni·tive \\'pyü-nə-tiv\ *adj* : inflicting, involving, or aiming at punishment

¹**punk** \\'pəŋk\ *n* **1** : a young inexperienced person **2** : a petty hoodlum

²**punk** *adj* : very poor : INFERIOR

³**punk** *n* : dry crumbly wood useful for tinder; *also* : a substance made from fungi for use as tinder

pun·kin \\'pəŋ-kən\ *var of* PUMPKIN

pun·ster \\'pən-stər\ *n* : one who is given to punning

¹**punt** \\'pənt\ *n* : a long narrow flat-bottomed boat with square ends

²**punt** *vb* : to propel (as a punt) with a pole

³**punt** *vb* : to kick a football or soccer ball dropped from the hands before it touches the ground

⁴**punt** *n* : the act or an instance of punting a ball

pu·ny \'pyü-nē\ *adj* **pu·ni·er; -est** [MF *puisné* younger, lit., born afterward, fr. *puis* afterward (fr. L *post*) + *né* born, fr. L *natus*] : slight in power, size, or importance : WEAK

pup \'pəp\ *n* : a young dog; *also* : one of the young of some other animals

pu·pa \'pyü-pə\ *n, pl* **pu·pae** \-(ˌ)pē\ *or* **pupas** [NL, fr. L *pupa* doll] : a form of some insects (as a bee, moth, or beetle) between the larva and the adult that usu. has a protective covering (as a cocoon) — **pu·pal** \-pəl\ *adj*

¹**pu·pil** \'pyü-pəl\ *n* **1** : a child or young person in school or in the charge of a tutor **2** : DISCIPLE

²**pupil** *n* : the dark central opening of the iris of the eye

pup·pet \'pə-pət\ *n* [ME *popet*, fr. MF *poupette*, ultim. fr. L *pupa* doll] **1** : a small figure of a person or animal moved by hand or by strings or wires **2** : DOLL **3** : one whose acts are controlled by an outside force or influence

pup·pe·teer \ˌpə-pə-'tir\ *n* : one who manipulates puppets

pup·py \'pə-pē\ *n, pl* **puppies** : a young domestic dog

pur·blind \'pər-ˌblīnd\ *adj* **1** : partly blind **2** : lacking in insight : OBTUSE

¹**pur·chase** \'pər-chəs\ *vb* **pur·chased; pur·chas·ing** : to obtain by paying money or its equivalent : BUY — **pur·chas·able** \-chə-sə-bəl\ *adj* — **pur·chas·er** *n*

²**purchase** *n* **1** : an act or instance of purchasing **2** : something purchased **3** : a secure hold or grasp; *also* : advantageous leverage

pur·dah \'pər-də\ *n* : seclusion of women from public observation among Muslims and some Hindus esp. in India; *also* : a state of seclusion

pure \'pyùr\ *adj* **pur·er; pur·est 1** : unmixed with any other matter : free from taint ⟨∼ gold⟩ ⟨∼ water⟩ **2** : SHEER, ABSOLUTE ⟨∼ nonsense⟩ **3** : ABSTRACT, THEORETICAL ⟨∼ mathematics⟩ **4** : free from what vitiates, weakens, or pollutes ⟨speaks a ∼ French⟩ **5** : free from moral fault : INNOCENT **6** : CHASTE, CONTINENT — **pure·ly** *adv*

pure–blood·ed \-ˌblə-dəd\ *or* **pure–blood** \-ˌbləd\ *adj* : FULL-BLOODED — **pure–blood** *n*

pure·bred \-'bred\ *adj* : bred from members of a recognized breed, strain, or kind without crossbreeding over many generations — **pure·bred** *n*

¹**pu·ree** \pyù-'rā, -'rē\ *n* [F *purée*, fr. MF, fr. fem. of *puré*, pp. of *purer* to purify, strain, fr. L *purare* to purify] : a paste or thick liquid suspension usu. made from finely ground cooked food; *also* : a thick soup made of pureed vegetables

²**puree** *vb* **pu·reed; pu·ree·ing** : to make a puree of

pur·ga·tion \ˌpər-'gā-shən\ *n* : the act or result of purging

¹**pur·ga·tive** \'pər-gə-tiv\ *adj* : purging or tending to purge

²**purgative** *n* : a strong laxative : CATHARTIC

pur·ga·to·ry \'pər-gə-ˌtōr-ē\ *n, pl* **-ries 1** : an intermediate state after death for expiatory purification **2** : a place or state of temporary punishment — **pur·ga·tor·i·al** \ˌpər-gə-'tōr-ē-əl\ *adj*

¹**purge** \'pərj\ *vb* **purged; purg·ing 1** : to cleanse or purify esp. from sin **2** : to have or cause strong and usu. repeated emptying of the bowels **3** : to get rid of ⟨the leaders had been *purged*⟩

²**purge** *n* **1** : something that purges; *esp* : PURGATIVE **2** : an act or result of purging; *esp* : a ridding of persons regarded as treacherous or disloyal

pu·ri·fy \'pyùr-ə-ˌfī\ *vb* **-fied; -fy·ing** : to make or become pure — **pu·ri·fi·ca·tion** \ˌpyùr-ə-fə-'kā-shən\ *n* — **pu·ri·fi·ca·to·ry** \pyù-'ri-fi-kə-ˌtōr-ē\ *adj* — **pu·ri·fi·er** *n*

Pu·rim \'pùr-(ˌ)im\ *n* : a Jewish holiday celebrated in February or March in commemoration of the deliverance of the Jews from the massacre plotted by Haman

pu·rine \'pyùr-ˌēn\ *n* : any of a group of bases including several (as adenine or guanine) that are constituents of DNA or RNA

pur·ism \'pyùr-ˌi-zəm\ *n* : rigid adherence to or insistence on purity or nicety esp. in use of words — **pur·ist** \-ist\ *n* — **pu·ris·tic** \pyù-'ris-tik\ *adj*

pu·ri·tan \'pyùr-ət-ᵊn\ *n* **1** *cap* : a member of a 16th and 17th century Protestant group in England and New England opposing the ceremonies and government of the Church of England **2** : one who practices or preaches a stricter or professedly purer moral code than that which prevails — **pu·ri·tan·i·cal** \ˌpyùr-ə-'ta-ni-kəl\ *adj* — **pu·ri·tan·i·cal·ly** *adv*

pu·ri·ty \'pyùr-ə-tē\ *n* : the quality or state of being pure

¹**purl** \'pərl\ *vb* : to knit in purl stitch

²**purl** *n* : a stitch in knitting

³**purl** *n* : a gentle murmur or movement (as of purling water)

⁴**purl** *vb* **1** : EDDY, SWIRL **2** : to make a soft murmuring sound

pur·lieu \'pər-lü, 'pərl-yü\ *n* **1** : an outlying district : SUBURB **2** *pl* : ENVIRONS

pur·loin \(ˌ)pər-'lòin, 'pər-ˌlòin\ *vb* : STEAL, FILCH

¹**pur·ple** \'pər-pəl\ *adj* **pur·pler; pur·plest 1** : of the color purple **2** : highly rhetorical ⟨a ∼ passage⟩ **3** : PROFANE ⟨∼ language⟩ — **pur·plish** *adj*

²**purple** *n* **1** : a bluish red color **2** : a purple robe emblematic esp. of regal rank or authority

¹**pur·port** \'pər-ˌpōrt\ *n* : meaning conveyed or implied; *also* : GIST

²**pur·port** \(ˌ)pər-'pōrt\ *vb* : to convey or profess outwardly as the meaning or intention : CLAIM — **pur·port·ed·ly** \-'pōr-təd-lē\ *adv*

¹**pur·pose** \'pər-pəs\ *n* **1** : an object or result aimed at : INTENTION **2** : RESOLUTION, DETERMINATION — **pur·pose·ful** \-fəl\ *adj* — **pur·pose·ful·ly** *adv* — **pur·pose·less** *adj* — **pur·pose·ly** *adv*

²**purpose** *vb* **pur·posed; pur·pos·ing** : to propose as an aim to oneself

purr \'pər\ *n* : a low murmur typical of a contented cat — **purr** *vb*

¹**purse** \'pərs\ *n* **1** : a receptacle (as a pouch) to carry money and often other small objects in **2** : RESOURCES **3** : a sum of money offered as a prize or present

²**purse** *vb* **pursed; purs·ing** : PUCKER

purs·er \'pər-sər\ *n* : an official on a ship who keeps accounts and attends to the comfort of passengers

purs·lane \'pər-slən, -ˌslān\ *n* : a fleshy-leaved weedy trailing plant with tiny yellow flowers that is sometimes used in salads

pur·su·ance \pər-'sü-əns\ *n* : the act of carrying out or into effect

pur·su·ant to \-'sü-ənt-\ *prep* : in carrying out : ACCORDING TO

pur·sue \pər-'sü\ *vb* **pur·sued; pur·su·ing 1** : to follow in order to overtake or overcome : CHASE **2** : to seek to accomplish ⟨∼ a goal⟩ **3** : to proceed along ⟨∼ a course⟩ **4** : to engage in ⟨∼ a career⟩ — **pur·su·er** *n*

pur·suit \pər-'süt\ *n* **1** : the act of pursuing **2** : OCCUPATION, BUSINESS

pu·ru·lent \'pyùr-ə-lənt, -yə-\ *adj* : containing or accompanied by pus ⟨a ∼ discharge⟩ — **pu·ru·lence** \-ləns\ *n*

pur·vey \(ˌ)pər-'vā\ *vb* **pur·veyed; pur·vey·ing** : to supply (as provisions) usu. as a business — **pur·vey·ance** \-əns\ *n* — **pur·vey·or** \-ər\ *n*

pur·view \'pər-ˌvyü\ *n* **1** : the range or limit esp. of authority, responsibility, or intention **2** : range of vision, understanding, or cognizance

pus \'pəs\ *n* : thick yellowish white fluid matter (as in a boil) formed at a place of inflammation and infection (as an abscess) and containing germs, blood cells, and tissue debris

¹**push** \'push\ *vb* [ME *pusshen*, fr. OF *poulser* to beat, push, fr. L *pulsare*, fr. *pellere* to drive, strike] **1** : to press against with force in order to drive or impel **2** : to thrust forward, downward, or outward **3** : to urge on : press forward **4** : to cause to increase ⟨∼ prices to record levels⟩ **5** : to urge or press the advancement, adoption, or practice of; *esp* : to make aggressive efforts to sell **6** : to engage in the illicit sale of narcotics

²**push** *n* **1** : a vigorous effort : DRIVE **2** : an act of pushing : SHOVE **3** : vigorous enterprise : ENERGY

push–button *adj* **1** : operated or done by means of push buttons **2** : using or dependent on complex and more or less automatic mechanisms ⟨∼ warfare⟩

push button *n* : a small button or knob that when pushed operates something esp. by closing an electric circuit

push·cart \'push-ˌkärt\ *n* : a cart or barrow pushed by hand

push·er \'pu̇-shər\ *n* : one that pushes; *esp* : one that pushes illegal drugs

push·over \-ˌō-vər\ *n* **1** : an opponent easy to defeat **2** : SUCKER **3** : something easily accomplished

push–up \-ˌəp\ *n* : a conditioning exercise performed in a prone position by raising and lowering the body with the straightening and bending of the arms while keeping the back straight and supporting the body on the hands and toes

pushy \'pu̇-shē\ *adj* **push·i·er; -est** : aggressive often to an objectionable degree

pu·sil·lan·i·mous \ˌpyü-sə-'la-nə-məs\ *adj* [LL *pusill-animis*, fr. L *pusillus* very small (dim. of *pusus* boy) + *animus* spirit] : contemptibly timid : COWARDLY — **pu·sil·la·nim·i·ty** \ˌpyü-sə-lə-'ni-mə-tē\ *n*

¹**puss** \'pu̇s\ *n* : CAT

²**puss** *n* : FACE

¹**pussy** \'pu̇-sē\ *n, pl* **puss·ies** : CAT

²**pus·sy** \'pə-sē\ *adj* **pus·si·er; -est** : full of or resembling pus

pussy·cat \'pu̇-sē-ˌkat\ *n* : CAT

pussy·foot \-ˌfu̇t\ *vb* **1** : to tread or move warily or stealthily **2** : to refrain from committing oneself

pussy willow \'pu̇-sē-\ *n* : a willow having large silky catkins

pus·tule \'pəs-chül\ *n* : a pus-filled pimple

put \'pu̇t\ *vb* **put; put·ting 1** : to bring into a specified position : PLACE ⟨∼ the book on the table⟩ **2** : SEND, THRUST **3** : to throw with an upward pushing motion ⟨∼ the shot⟩ **4** : to bring into a specified state ⟨∼ the plan into effect⟩ **5** : SUBJECT ⟨∼ traitors to death⟩ **6** : IMPOSE **7** : to set before one for decision ⟨∼ the question⟩ **8** : EXPRESS, STATE **9** : TRANSLATE, ADAPT **10** : APPLY, ASSIGN ⟨∼ them to work⟩ **11** : ESTIMATE ⟨∼ the number at 20⟩ **12** : ATTACH, ATTRIBUTE ⟨∼ a high value on it⟩ **13** : to take a specified course ⟨the ship ∼ out to sea⟩

pu·ta·tive \'pyü-tə-tiv\ *adj* **1** : commonly accepted **2** : assumed to exist or to have existed

put–down \'pu̇t-ˌdau̇n\ *n* : a belittling remark

put in *vb* **1** : to come in with ⟨*put in* a good word for me⟩ **2** : to spend time at some occupation or job ⟨*put in* eight hours at the office⟩

put off *vb* : POSTPONE, DELAY

¹**put–on** \'pu̇t-ˌȯn, -ˌän\ *adj* : PRETENDED, ASSUMED

²**put–on** *n* **1** : a deliberate act of misleading someone **2** : PARODY, SPOOF

put·out \'pu̇t-ˌau̇t\ *n* : the retiring of a base runner or batter in baseball

put out *vb* **1** : EXTINGUISH **2** : ANNOY; *also* : INCONVENIENCE **3** : to cause to be out (as in baseball)

pu·tre·fy \'pyü-trə-ˌfī\ *vb* **-fied; -fy·ing** : to make or become putrid : ROT — **pu·tre·fac·tion** \ˌpyü-trə-'fak-shən\ *n* — **pu·tre·fac·tive** \-tiv\ *adj*

pu·tres·cent \pyü-'tres-ᵊnt\ *adj* : becoming putrid : ROTTING — **pu·tres·cence** \-ᵊns\ *n*

pu·trid \'pyü-trəd\ *adj* **1** : ROTTEN, DECAYED **2** : VILE, CORRUPT — **pu·trid·i·ty** \pyü-'tri-də-tē\ *n*

putsch \'pu̇ch\ *n* [G] : a secretly plotted and suddenly executed attempt to overthrow a government

putt \'pət\ *n* : a golf stroke made on the green to cause the ball to roll into the hole — **putt** *vb*

put·tee \ˌpə-'tē, 'pə-tē\ *n* [Hindi *paṭṭī* strip of cloth] **1** : a cloth strip wrapped around the lower leg **2** : a leather legging

¹**put·ter** \'pu̇-tər\ *n* : one that puts

²**putt·er** \'pə-tər\ *n* **1** : a golf club used in putting **2** : one that putts

³**put·ter** \'pə-tər\ *vb* **1** : to move or act aimlessly or idly **2** : TINKER

put·ty \'pə-tē\ *n, pl* **putties** [F *potée* potter's glaze, lit., potful, fr. OF, fr. *pot* pot] **1** : a doughlike cement used esp. to fasten glass in sashes **2** : one who is easily manipulated — **putty** *vb*

put up *vb* **1** : SHEATHE **2** : to prepare so as to preserve for later use **3** : to offer for public sale ⟨*put* the house *up* for auction⟩ **4** : ACCOMMODATE, LODGE **5** : BUILD **6** : to engage in ⟨*put up* a struggle⟩ **7** : CONTRIBUTE, PAY — **put up with** : TOLERATE **2**

¹**puz·zle** \'pə-zəl\ *vb* **puz·zled; puz·zling 1** : to bewilder mentally : PERPLEX **2** : to solve with difficulty or ingenuity ⟨∼ out a riddle⟩ **3** : to be in a quandary ⟨∼ over what to do⟩ **4** : to attempt a solution of a puzzle ⟨∼ over a person's words⟩ *syn* mystify, bewilder, nonplus, confound — **puz·zle·ment** *n* — **puz·zler** *n*

²**puzzle** *n* **1** : something that puzzles **2** : a question, problem, or contrivance designed for testing ingenuity

PVC *abbr* polyvinyl chloride

pvt *abbr* private

PW *abbr* prisoner of war

pwt *abbr* pennyweight

PX *abbr* post exchange

pya \pē-'ä\ *n* — see *kyat* at MONEY table

pyg·my \'pig-mē\ *n, pl* **pygmies** [ME *pigmei*, fr. L *pyg-maeus* of a pygmy, dwarfish, fr. Gk *pygmaios*, fr. *pygmē* fist, measure of length] **1** *cap* : any of a small people of equatorial Africa **2** : DWARF — **pygmy** *adj*

py·ja·mas \pə-'jä-məz\ *chiefly Brit var of* PAJAMAS

py·lon \'pī-ˌlän, -lən\ *n* **1** : a usu. massive gateway; *esp* : an Egyptian one flanked by flat-topped pyramids **2** : a tower that supports wires over a long span **3** : a post or tower marking the course in an airplane race

py·or·rhea \ˌpī-ə-'rē-ə\ *n* : an inflammation with pus of the sockets of the teeth

¹**pyr·a·mid** \'pir-ə-ˌmid\ *n* **1** : a massive structure with a square base and four triangular faces meeting at a point **2** : a geometrical solid having a polygon for its base and three or more triangles for its sides that meet at a point to form the top — **py·ra·mi·dal** \pə-'ra-məd-ᵊl, ˌpir-ə-'mid-\ *adj*

²**pyramid** *vb* **1** : to build up in the form of a pyramid : heap up **2** : to increase rapidly on a broadening base

pyre \'pīr\ *n* : a combustible heap for burning a dead body as a funeral rite

py·re·thrum \pī-'rē-thrəm\ *n* : an insecticide made from the dried heads of any of several Old World chrysanthemums

py·rim·i·dine \pī-'ri-mə-ˌdēn\ *n* : any of a group of bases including several (as cytosine, thymine, or uracil) that are constituents of DNA or RNA

py·rite \'pī-ˌrīt\ *n* : a mineral containing sulfur and iron that is brass-yellow in color

py·rol·y·sis \pī-'rä-lə-səs\ *n* : chemical change caused by the action of heat

py·ro·ma·nia \ˌpī-rō-'mā-nē-ə\ *n* : an irresistible impulse to start fires — **py·ro·ma·ni·ac** \-nē-ˌak\ *n*

py·ro·tech·nics \ˌpī-rə-ˈtek-niks\ *n pl* **1** : a display of fireworks **2** : a spectacular display (as of extreme virtuosity) — **py·ro·tech·nic** \-nik\ *also* **py·ro·tech·ni·cal** \-ni-kəl\ *adj*

Pyr·rhic \ˈpir-ik\ *adj* : achieved at excessive cost ⟨a ∼ victory⟩; *also* : costly to the point of outweighing expected benefits

Py·thag·o·re·an theorem \pī-ˌtha-gə-ˈrē-ən-\ *n* : a theorem in geometry: the square of the length of the hypotenuse of a right triangle equals the sum of the squares of the lengths of the other two sides

py·thon \ˈpī-ˌthän, -thən\ *n* [L, monstrous serpent killed by the god Apollo, fr. Gk *Pythōn*] : a large snake (as a boa) that squeezes and suffocates its prey; *esp* : any of the large Old World snakes that include the largest snakes living at the present time

pyx \ˈpiks\ *n* : a small case used to carry the Eucharist to the sick

Q

¹q \ˈkyü\ *n, pl* **q's** *or* **qs** \ˈkyüz\ *often cap* : the 17th letter of the English alphabet

²q *abbr, often cap* **1** quart **2** quarto **3** queen **4** query **5** question

QB *abbr* quarterback

QED *abbr* [L *quod erat demonstrandum*] which was to be demonstrated

qin·tar \kin-ˈtär\ *n, pl* **qin·dar·ka** \kin-ˈdär-kə\ *or* **qintar** — see *lek* at MONEY table

qi·vi·ut \ˈkē-vē-ˌüt\ *n* [Inuit] : the wool of the undercoat of the musk ox

Qld *abbr* Queensland

QM *abbr* quartermaster

QMC *abbr* quartermaster corps

QMG *abbr* quartermaster general

qq v *abbr* [L *quae vide*] which (*pl*) see

qr *abbr* quarter

qt *abbr* **1** quantity **2** quart

q.t. \ˌkyü-ˈtē\ *n, often cap Q&T* : QUIET — usu. used in the phrase *on the q.t.*

qto *abbr* quarto

qty *abbr* quantity

qu *or* **ques** *abbr* question

¹quack \ˈkwak\ *vb* : to make the characteristic cry of a duck

²quack *n* : a sound made by quacking

³quack *n* **1** : CHARLATAN **2** : a pretender to medical skill **syn** faker, impostor, mountebank — **quack** *adj* — **quack·ery** \ˈkwa-kə-rē\ *n* — **quack·ish** *adj*

¹quad \ˈkwäd\ *n* : QUADRANGLE

²quad *n* : QUADRUPLET

³quad *abbr* quadrant

quad·ran·gle \ˈkwä-ˌdraŋ-gəl\ *n* **1** : QUADRILATERAL **2** : a 4-sided courtyard or enclosure — **quad·ran·gu·lar** \kwä-ˈdraŋ-gyə-lər\ *adj*

quad·rant \ˈkwä-drənt\ *n* **1** : one quarter of a circle : an arc of 90° **2** : any of the four quarters into which something is divided by two lines intersecting each other at right angles

qua·drat·ic \kwä-ˈdra-tik\ *adj* : having or being a term in which the variable (as *x*) is squared but containing no term in which the variable is raised to a higher power than a square ⟨a ∼ equation⟩ — **quadratic** *n*

qua·dren·ni·al \kwä-ˈdre-nē-əl\ *adj* **1** : consisting of or lasting for four years **2** : occurring every four years

qua·dren·ni·um \-nē-əm\ *n, pl* **-ni·ums** *or* **-nia** \-nē-ə\ : a period of four years

¹quad·ri·lat·er·al \ˌkwä-drə-ˈla-tə-rəl\ *n* : a polygon of four sides

²quadrilateral *adj* : having four sides

qua·drille \kwä-ˈdril, kə-\ *n* : a square dance made up of five or six figures in various rhythms

quad·ri·par·tite \ˌkwä-drə-ˈpär-ˌtīt\ *adj* **1** : consisting of four parts **2** : shared by four parties or persons

qua·driv·i·um \kwä-ˈdri-vē-əm\ *n* : the four liberal arts of arithmetic, music, geometry, and astronomy in a medieval university

quad·ru·ped \ˈkwä-drə-ˌped\ *n* : an animal having four feet — **qua·dru·pe·dal** \kwä-ˈdrü-pəd-əl, ˌkwä-drə-ˈped-\ *adj*

¹qua·dru·ple \kwä-ˈdrü-pəl, -ˈdrə-; ˈkwä-drə-\ *vb* **qua·dru·pled; qua·dru·pling** : to make or become four times as great or as many

²quadruple *adj* : FOURFOLD

qua·dru·plet \kwä-ˈdrə-plət, -ˈdrü-; ˈkwä-drə-\ *n* **1** : one of four offspring born at one birth **2** : a group of four of a kind

¹qua·dru·pli·cate \kwä-ˈdrü-pli-kət\ *adj* **1** : repeated four times **2** : FOURTH

²qua·dru·pli·cate \-plə-ˌkāt\ *vb* **-cat·ed; -cat·ing 1** : QUADRUPLE **2** : to prepare in quadruplicate — **qua·dru·pli·ca·tion** \-ˌdrü-plə-ˈkā-shən\ *n*

³qua·dru·pli·cate \-ˈdrü-pli-kət\ *n* **1** : four copies all alike ⟨typed in ∼⟩ **2** : one of four like things

quaff \ˈkwäf, ˈkwaf\ *vb* : to drink deeply or repeatedly — **quaff** *n*

quag·mire \ˈkwag-ˌmīr, ˈkwäg-\ *n* **1** : soft miry land that yields under the foot **2** : PREDICAMENT

qua·hog \ˈkō-ˌhog, ˈkwo-, ˈkwō-, -ˌhäg\ *n* : a round thick-shelled edible No. American clam

quai \ˈkā\ *n* : QUAY

¹quail \ˈkwāl\ *n, pl* **quail** *or* **quails** [ME *quaille*, fr. MF, fr. ML *quaccula*, of imit. origin] : any of numerous small short-winged plump game birds (as a bobwhite) related to the domestic chicken

²quail *vb* [ME, to grow feeble, fr. MD *quelen*] : to lose heart : COWER **syn** recoil, shrink, flinch, wince, blanch

quaint \ˈkwānt\ *adj* : unusual or different in character or appearance; *esp* : pleasingly old-fashioned or unfamiliar **syn** odd, queer, curious, strange — **quaint·ly** *adv* — **quaint·ness** *n*

¹quake \ˈkwāk\ *vb* **quaked; quak·ing 1** : to shake usu. from shock or instability **2** : to tremble usu. from cold or fear

²quake *n* : a shaking or trembling; *esp* : EARTHQUAKE

Quak·er \ˈkwā-kər\ *n* : FRIEND 5

qual *abbr* quality

qual·i·fi·ca·tion \ˌkwä-lə-fə-ˈkā-shən\ *n* **1** : LIMITATION, MODIFICATION **2** : a special skill that fits a person for some work or position **3** : REQUIREMENT

qual·i·fied \ˈkwä-lə-ˌfīd\ *adj* **1** : fitted for a given purpose or job **2** : limited in some way

qual·i·fi·er \ˈkwä-lə-ˌfī-ər\ *n* **1** : one that satisfies requirements **2** : a word or word group that limits the meaning of another word or word group

qual·i·fy \ˈkwä-lə-ˌfī\ *vb* **-fied; -fy·ing 1** : to reduce from a general to a particular form : MODIFY **2** : to make less harsh **3** : to limit the meaning of (as a noun) **4** : to fit by skill or training for some purpose **5** : to give or have a legal right to do something **6** : to demonstrate the necessary ability ⟨∼ for the finals⟩ **syn** moderate, temper

qual·i·ta·tive \ˈkwä-lə-ˌtā-tiv\ *adj* : of, relating to, or involving quality — **qual·i·ta·tive·ly** *adv*

¹qual·i·ty \ˈkwä-lə-tē\ *n, pl* **-ties 1** : peculiar and essential character : NATURE **2** : degree of excellence **3** : high social status **4** : a distinguishing attribute

²quality *adj* : being of high quality

qualm \ˈkwäm, ˈkwälm\ *n* **1** : a sudden attack (as of nausea) **2** : a sudden feeling of doubt, fear, or uneasiness esp. in not following one's conscience or better judgment

qualm·ish \ˈkwä-mish, ˈkwäl-\ *adj* **1** : feeling qualms : NAUSEATED **2** : overly scrupulous : SQUEAMISH **3** : of, relating to, or producing qualms

quan·da·ry \'kwän-drē\ *n, pl* **-ries** : a state of perplex-ity or doubt

quan·ti·ta·tive \'kwän-tə-ˌtā-tiv\ *adj* : of, relating to, or involving quantity — **quan·ti·ta·tive·ly** *adv*

quan·ti·ty \'kwän-tə-tē\ *n, pl* **-ties 1** : AMOUNT, NUM-BER **2** : a considerable amount

quan·tize \'kwän-ˌtīz\ *vb* **quan·tized; quan·tiz·ing** : to subdivide (as energy) into small units

quan·tum \'kwän-təm\ *n, pl* **quan·ta** \-tə\ [L, neut. of *quantus* how much] **1** : QUANTITY, AMOUNT **2** : an el-emental unit of energy

quantum mechanics *n sing or pl* : a theory of matter based on the concept of possession of wave proper-ties by elementary particles — **quantum mechanical** *adj* — **quantum mechanically** *adv*

quantum theory *n* : a theory in physics based on the idea that radiant energy (as light) is composed of small separate packets of energy

quar *abbr* quarterly

quar·an·tine \'kwȯr-ən-ˌtēn\ *n* [modif. of It *quarante-na*, lit., period of forty days, fr. *quaranta* forty, fr. L *quadraginta*] **1** : a period during which a ship sus-pected of carrying contagious disease is forbidden contact with the shore **2** : a restraint on the move-ments of persons or goods to prevent the spread of pests or disease **3** : a place or period of quarantine **4** : a state of enforced isolation — **quarantine** *vb*

quark \'kwȯrk, 'kwärk\ *n* : a hypothetical elementary particle that carries a fractional charge and is held to be a constituent of heavier particles (as protons and neutrons)

¹**quar·rel** \'kwȯr-əl\ *n* **1** : a ground of dispute **2** : a ver-bal clash : CONFLICT — **quar·rel·some** \-səm\ *adj*

²**quarrel** *vb* **-reled** *or* **-relled; -rel·ing** *or* **-rel·ling 1** : to find fault **2** : to dispute angrily : WRANGLE

¹**quar·ry** \'kwȯr-ē\ *n, pl* **quarries** [ME *querre* entrails of game given to the hounds, fr. MF *cuiree*] **1** : game hunted with hawks **2** : PREY

²**quarry** *n, pl* **quarries** [ME *quarey*, alter. of *quarrere*, fr. MF *quarriere*, fr. (assumed) OF *quarre* squared stone, fr. L *quadrum* square] : an open excavation usu. for obtaining building stone or limestone — **quarry** *vb*

quart \'kwȯrt\ *n* — see WEIGHT table

¹**quar·ter** \'kwȯr-tər\ *n* **1** : one of four equal parts **2** : a fourth of a dollar; *also* : a coin of this value **3** : a dis-trict of a city **4** *pl* : LODGINGS (moved into new ~s) **5** : MERCY, CLEMENCY (gave no ~) **6** : a fourth part of the moon's period

²**quarter** *vb* **1** : to divide into four equal parts **2** : to pro-vide with shelter

¹**quar·ter·back** \-ˌbak\ *n* : a football player who calls the signals and directs the offensive play for the team

²**quarterback** *vb* **1** : to direct the offensive play of a football team **2** : LEAD, BOSS

quar·ter·deck \-ˌdek\ *n* : the stern area of a ship's up-per deck

quarter horse *n* : any of a breed of compact muscular saddle horses characterized by great endurance and by high speed for short distances

quarter horse

¹**quar·ter·ly** \'kwȯr-tər-lē\ *adv* : at 3-month intervals

²**quarterly** *adj* : occurring, issued, or payable at 3-month intervals

³**quarterly** *n, pl* **-lies** : a periodical published four times a year

quar·ter·mas·ter \-ˌmas-tər\ *n* **1** : a petty officer who attends to a ship's helm, binnacle, and signals **2** : an army officer who provides clothing and subsistence for troops

quar·ter·staff \-ˌstaf\ *n, pl* **-staves** \-ˌstavz, -ˌstāvz\ : a long stout staff formerly used as a weapon

quar·tet *also* **quar·tette** \kwȯr-'tet\ *n* **1** : a musical composition for four instruments or voices **2** : a group of four and esp. of four musicians

quar·to \'kwȯr-tō\ *n, pl* **quartos 1** : the size of a piece of paper cut four from a sheet **2** : a book printed on quarto pages

quartz \'kwȯrts\ *n* : a common often transparent crys-talline mineral that is a form of silica

quartz·ite \'kwȯrt-ˌsīt\ *n* : a compact granular rock composed of quartz and derived from sandstone

qua·sar \'kwā-ˌzär, -ˌsär\ *n* : any of a class of ex-tremely distant starlike celestial objects

¹**quash** \'kwäsh, 'kwȯsh\ *vb* : to suppress or extinguish summarily and completely : QUELL

²**quash** *vb* : to set aside by judicial action

qua·si \'kwā-ˌzī, -ˌsī; 'kwä-zē, -sē\ *adj* : being in some sense or degree (a ~ corporation)

quasi- *comb form* [L, as if, as it were, approximately, fr. *quam* as + *si* if] : in some sense or degree (*quasi-*historical)

Qua·ter·na·ry \'kwä-tər-ˌner-ē, kwə-'tər-nə-rē\ *adj* : of, relating to, or being the geologic period from the end of the Tertiary to the present — **Quaternary** *n*

qua·train \'kwä-ˌtrān\ *n* : a unit of four lines of verse

qua·tre·foil \'ka-tər-ˌfȯil, 'ka-trə-\ *n* : a stylized figure often of a flower with four petals

qua·ver \'kwā-vər\ *vb* **1** : TREMBLE, SHAKE **2** : TRILL **3** : to speak in tremulous tones **syn** shudder, quake, twitter, quiver, shiver — **quaver** *n*

quay \'kē, 'kwā, 'kā\ *n* : WHARF

Que *abbr* Quebec

quean \'kwēn\ *n* : PROSTITUTE

quea·sy \'kwē-zē\ *adj* **quea·si·er; -est** : NAUSEATED — **quea·si·ly** \-zə-lē\ *adv* — **quea·si·ness** \-zē-nəs\ *n*

queen \'kwēn\ *n* **1** : the wife or widow of a king **2** : a female monarch **3** : a woman notable for rank, power, or attractiveness **4** : the most powerful piece in the game of chess **5** : a playing card bearing the figure of a queen **6** : a fertile female of a social insect (as a bee or termite) — **queen·ly** *adj*

Queen Anne's lace \-'anz-\ *n* : a widely naturalized Eurasian herb from which the cultivated carrot orig-inated

queen consort *n, pl* **queens consort** : the wife of a reigning king

queen mother *n* : a dowager queen who is mother of the reigning sovereign

queen–size *adj* : having dimensions of approximately 60 inches by 80 inches (~ bed); *also* : of a size that fits a queen-size bed

¹**queer** \'kwir\ *adj* **1** : differing from the usual or normal : PECULIAR, STRANGE **2** : COUNTERFEIT **syn** weird, bi-zarre, eccentric, curious — **queer** *n* — **queer·ly** *adv* — **queer·ness** *n*

²**queer** *vb* : to spoil the effect of : DISRUPT (~ed our plans)

quell \'kwel\ *vb* **1** : to put an end to by force (~ a riot) **2** : CALM, PACIFY

quench \'kwench\ *vb* **1** : PUT OUT, EXTINGUISH **2** : SUB-DUE **3** : SLAKE, SATISFY (~ed his thirst) — **quench·able** *adj* — **quench·er** *n* — **quench·less** *adj*

quer·u·lous \'kwer-ə-ləs, -yə-\ *adj* **1** : constantly com-plaining **2** : FRETFUL, WHINING **syn** petulant, pettish, irritable, peevish, huffy — **quer·u·lous·ly** *adv* — **quer·u·lous·ness** *n*

que·ry \'kwir-ē, 'kwer-\ *n, pl* **queries** : QUESTION — **query** *vb*

quest \'kwest\ *n* : SEARCH — **quest** *vb*

¹ques·tion \'kwes-chən\ *n* **1** : an interrogative expression : QUERY **2** : a subject for debate; *also* : a proposition to be voted on **3** : INQUIRY **4** : DISPUTE

²question *vb* **1** : to ask questions **2** : DOUBT, DISPUTE **3** : to subject to analysis : EXAMINE **syn** interrogate, quiz, query — **ques·tion·er** *n*

ques·tion·able \'kwes-chə-nə-bəl\ *adj* **1** : not certain or exact : DOUBTFUL **2** : not believed to be true, sound, or moral **syn** dubious, problematical, moot, debatable — **ques·tion·ably** \-blē\ *adv*

question mark *n* : a punctuation mark ? used esp. at the end of a sentence to indicate a direct question

ques·tion·naire \₁kwes-chə-'nar\ *n* : a set of questions for obtaining information

quet·zal \ket-'säl, -'sal\ *n, pl* **quetzals** *or* **quet·za·les** \-'sä-läs, -'sa-\ **1** : a Central American bird with brilliant plumage **2** *pl* **quetzales** — see MONEY table

¹queue \'kyü\ *n* [F, lit., tail, fr. L *cauda, coda*] **1** : a braid of hair usu. worn hanging at the back of the head **2** : a waiting line (as of persons)

²queue *vb* **queued; queu·ing** *or* **queue·ing** : to line up in a queue

quib·ble \'kwi-bəl\ *n* **1** : an evasion of or shifting from the point at issue **2** : a minor objection or criticism — **quibble** *vb* — **quib·bler** *n*

¹quick \'kwik\ *adj* **1** : LIVING **2** : RAPID, SPEEDY ⟨∼ steps⟩ **3** : prompt to understand, think, or perceive : ALERT **4** : easily aroused ⟨a ∼ temper⟩ **5** : turning or bending sharply ⟨a ∼ turn in the road⟩ **syn** fleet, fast, hasty, expeditious — **quick** *adv* — **quick·ly** *adv* — **quick·ness** *n*

²quick *n* **1** : a sensitive area of living flesh **2** : a vital part : HEART

quick bread *n* : a bread made with a leavening agent that permits immediate baking of the dough or batter

quick·en \'kwi-kən\ *vb* **1** : to come to life : REVIVE **2** : AROUSE, STIMULATE **3** : to increase in speed : HASTEN **4** : to show vitality (as by growing or moving) **syn** animate, enliven, liven, vivify

quick–freeze \'kwik-'frēz\ *vb* **-froze** \-'frōz\; **-frozen** \-'frōz-ᵊn\; **-freez·ing** : to freeze (food) for preservation so rapidly that the natural juices and flavor are not lost

quick·ie \'kwi-kē\ *n* : something hurriedly done or made

quick·lime \'kwik-₁līm\ *n* : ¹LIME

quick·sand \-₁sand\ *n* : a deep mass of loose sand mixed with water

quick·sil·ver \-₁sil-vər\ *n* : MERCURY 1

quick·step \-₁step\ *n* : a spirited march tune or dance

quick–wit·ted \'kwik-'wi-təd\ *adj* : mentally alert **syn** clever, bright, smart, intelligent

quid \'kwid\ *n* : a lump of something chewable ⟨a ∼ of tobacco⟩

quid pro quo \₁kwid-₁prō-'kwō\ *n* [NL, something for something] : something given or received for something else

qui·es·cent \kwī-'es-ᵊnt\ *adj* : being at rest : QUIET **syn** latent, dormant, potential — **qui·es·cence** \-ᵊns\ *n*

¹qui·et \'kwī-ət\ *n* : REPOSE

²quiet *adj* **1** : marked by little motion or activity : CALM **2** : GENTLE, MILD ⟨a ∼ disposition⟩ **3** : enjoyed in peace and relaxation ⟨a ∼ cup of tea⟩ **4** : free from noise or uproar **5** : not showy : MODEST ⟨∼ clothes⟩ **6** : SECLUDED ⟨a ∼ nook⟩ — **quiet** *adv* — **qui·et·ly** *adv* — **qui·et·ness** *n*

³quiet *vb* **1** : CALM, PACIFY **2** : to become quiet ⟨∼ down⟩

qui·etude \'kwī-ə-₁tüd, -₁tyüd\ *n* : QUIETNESS, REPOSE

qui·etus \kwī-'ē-təs\ *n* [ME *quietus est*, fr. ML, he is quit, formula of discharge from obligation] **1** : final settlement (as of a debt) **2** : DEATH

quill \'kwil\ *n* **1** : a large stiff feather; *also* : the hollow tubular part of a feather **2** : one of the hollow sharp spines of a hedgehog or porcupine **3** : a pen made from a feather

¹quilt \'kwilt\ *n* : a padded bed coverlet

²quilt *vb* **1** : to fill, pad, or line like a quilt **2** : to stitch or sew in layers with padding in between **3** : to make quilts

quince \'kwins\ *n* : a hard yellow applelike fruit; *also* : a tree related to the roses that bears this fruit

qui·nine \'kwī-₁nīn\ *n* : a bitter white drug obtained from cinchona bark and used esp. in treating malaria

quint \'kwint\ *n* : QUINTUPLET

quin·tal \'kwint-ᵊl, 'kant-\ *n* : HUNDREDWEIGHT

quin·tes·sence \kwin-'tes-ᵊns\ *n* **1** : the purest essence of something **2** : the most typical example — **quint·es·sen·tial** \₁kwin-tə-'sen-chəl\ *adj* — **quin·tes·sen·tial·ly** *adv*

quin·tet *also* **quin·tette** \kwin-'tet\ *n* **1** : a musical composition for five instruments or voices **2** : a group of five and esp. of five musicians

¹quin·tu·ple \kwin-'tü-pəl, -'tyü-, -'tə-\ *adj* **1** : having five units or members **2** : being five times as great or as many — **quintuple** *n*

²quintuple *vb* **quin·tu·pled; quin·tu·pling** : to make or become five times as great or as many

quin·tu·plet \kwin-'tə-plət, -'tü-, -'tyu-\ *n* **1** : a group of five of a kind **2** : one of five offspring born at one birth

¹quin·tu·pli·cate \kwin-'tü-pli-kət, -'tyü-\ *adj* **1** : repeated five times **2** : FIFTH

²quintuplicate *n* **1** : one of five like things **2** : five copies all alike ⟨typed in ∼⟩

³quin·tu·pli·cate \-plə-₁kāt\ *vb* **-cat·ed; -cat·ing 1** : QUINTUPLE **2** : to provide in quintuplicate

quip \'kwip\ *n* : a clever remark : GIBE

²quip *vb* **quipped; quip·ping 1** : to make quips : GIBE **2** : to jest or gibe at

quire \'kwīr\ *n* : a set of 24 or sometimes 25 sheets of paper of the same size and quality

quirk \'kwərk\ *n* : a peculiarity of action or behavior — **quirky** *adj*

quirt \'kwərt\ *n* : a riding whip with a short handle and a rawhide lash

quis·ling \'kwiz-liŋ\ *n* [Vidkun *Quisling* †1945 Norw. politician who collaborated with the Nazis] : one who helps the invaders of one's own country

quit \'kwit\ *vb* **quit** *also* **quit·ted; quit·ting 1** : CONDUCT, BEHAVE ⟨∼ themselves well⟩ **2** : to depart from : LEAVE; *also* : to bring to an end **3** : to give up for good ⟨∼ smoking⟩ ⟨∼ my job⟩ **syn** acquit, comport, deport, demean — **quit·ter** *n*

quite \'kwīt\ *adv* **1** : COMPLETELY, WHOLLY **2** : to an extreme : POSITIVELY **3** : to a considerable extent : RATHER

quits \'kwits\ *adj* : even or equal with another ⟨call it ∼⟩

quit·tance \'kwit-ᵊns\ *n* : REQUITAL

¹quiv·er \'kwi-vər\ *n* : a case for carrying arrows

²quiver *vb* **quiv·ered; quiv·er·ing** : to shake with a slight trembling motion **syn** shiver, shudder, quaver, quake, tremble — **quiv·er·ing·ly** *adv*

³quiver *n* : the act or action of quivering : TREMOR

qui vive \kē-'vēv\ *n* [F *qui-vive*, fr. *qui vive?* long live who?, challenge of a French sentry] : ALERT ⟨on the *qui vive* for prowlers⟩

quix·ot·ic \kwik-'sä-tik\ *adj* [fr. Don *Quixote*, hero of the novel *Don Quixote de la Mancha* by Cervantes] : foolishly impractical esp. in the pursuit of ideals — **quix·ot·i·cal·ly** \-ti-kə-lē\ *adv*

¹quiz \'kwiz\ *n, pl* **quiz·zes 1** : an eccentric person **2** : PRACTICAL JOKE **3** : a short oral or written test

²quiz *vb* **quizzed; quiz·zing 1** : MOCK **2** : to look at inquisitively **3** : to question closely **syn** ask, interrogate, query

quiz·zi·cal \'kwi-zi-kəl\ *adj* **1** : comically quaint **2**

: mildly teasing or mocking **3** : expressive of puzzlement, curiosity, or disbelief

quoit *kwät, *kwȯit, *kȯit\ *n* **1** : a flattened ring of iron or circle of rope used in a throwing game **2** *pl* : a game in which quoits are thrown at an upright pin in an attempt to ring the pin

quon•dam *kwän-dəm, -₁dam\ *adj* [L, at one time, formerly, fr. *quom, cum* when] : FORMER

quo•rum *kwȯr-əm\ *n* : the number of members required to be present for business to be legally transacted

quot *abbr* quotation

quo•ta *kwō-tə\ *n* : a proportional part esp. when assigned : SHARE

quot•able *kwō-tə-bəl\ *adj* : fit for or worth quoting — **quot•abil•i•ty** \-₁bi-lə-tē\ *n*

quo•ta•tion \kwō-*tā-shən\ *n* **1** : the act or process of quoting **2** : the price currently bid or offered for something **3** : something that is quoted

quotation mark *n* : one of a pair of punctuation marks " " or ' ' used esp. to indicate the beginning and end

of a quotation in which exact phraseology is directly cited

quote *kwōt\ *vb* **quot•ed; quot•ing** [ML *quotare* to mark the number of, number references, fr. L *quotus* of what number or quantity, fr. *quot* how many, (as) many as] **1** : to speak or write a passage from another usu. with acknowledgment; *also* : to repeat a passage in substantiation or illustration **2** : to state the market price of a commodity, stock, or bond **3** : to inform a hearer or reader that matter following is quoted — **quote** *n*

quoth *kwōth\ *vb past* [ME, past of *quethen* to say, fr. OE *cwethan*] *archaic* : SAID — usu. used in the 1st and 3d persons with the subject following

quo•tid•i•an \kwō-*ti-dē-ən\ *adj* **1** : DAILY **2** : COMMONPLACE, ORDINARY

quo•tient *kwō-shənt\ *n* : the number obtained by dividing one number by another

qv *abbr* [L *quod vide*] which see

qy *abbr* query

R

¹r *är\ *n, pl* **r's** *or* **rs** *ärz\ *often cap* : the 18th letter of the English alphabet

²r *abbr, often cap* **1** rabbi **2** radius **3** rare **4** Republican **5** rerun **6** resistance **7** right **8** river **9** roentgen **10** rook **11** run

Ra *symbol* radium

RA *abbr* **1** regular army **2** Royal Academy

¹rab•bet *ra-bət\ *n* : a groove in the edge or face of a surface (as a board) esp. to receive another piece

²rabbet *vb* : to cut a rabbet in; *also* : to join by means of a rabbet

rab•bi *ra-₁bī\ *n* [LL, fr. Gk *rhabbi*, fr. Heb *rabbī* my master, fr. *rabh* master + -*ī* my] **1** : MASTER, TEACHER — used by Jews as a term of address **2** : a Jew trained and ordained for professional religious leadership — **rab•bin•ic** \rə-*bi-nik\ *or* **rab•bin•i•cal** \-ni-kəl\ *adj*

rab•bin•ate *ra-bə-nət, -₁nāt\ *n* **1** : the office of a rabbi **2** : the whole body of rabbis

rab•bit *ra-bət\ *n, pl* **rabbit** *or* **rabbits** : any of various long-eared burrowing mammals distinguished from the related hares by being blind, naked, and helpless at birth; *also* : the pelt of a rabbit

rabbit ears *n* : an indoor V-shaped television antenna

rab•ble *ra-bəl\ *n* **1** : MOB **2** **2** : the lowest class of people

rab•ble-rous•er *ra-bəl-₁rau̇-zər\ *n* : one that stirs up (as to hatred or violence) the masses of the people

ra•bid *ra-bəd\ *adj* **1** : VIOLENT, FURIOUS **2** : being fanatical or extreme **3** : affected with rabies — **ra•bid•ly** *adv*

ra•bies *rā-bēz\ *n, pl* **rabies** [NL, fr. L, madness] : an acute deadly virus disease of the nervous system transmitted by the bite of an affected animal

rac•coon \ra-*kün\ *n, pl* **raccoon** *or* **raccoons** : a gray No. American chiefly tree-dwelling mammal with a black mask, a bushy ringed tail, and nocturnal habits; *also* : its pelt

¹race *rās\ *n* **1** : a strong current of running water; *also* : its channel **2** : an onward course (as of time or life) **3** : a contest of speed **4** : a contest for a desired end (as election to office)

²race *vb* **raced; rac•ing 1** : to run in a race **2** : to run swiftly : RUSH **3** : to engage in a race with **4** : to drive or ride at high speed — **rac•er** *n*

³race *n* **1** : a family, tribe, people, or nation of the same stock; *also* : MANKIND **2** : a group of individuals within a biological species able to breed together — **ra•cial** *rā-shəl\ *adj* — **ra•cial•ly** *adv*

race•course *rās-₁kȯrs\ *n* : a course for racing

race•horse \-₁hȯrs\ *n* : a horse bred or kept for racing

ra•ceme \rā-*sēm\ *n* [L *racemus* bunch of grapes] : a flower cluster with flowers borne along a stem and blooming from the base toward the tip — **rac•e•mose** *ra-sə-₁mōs\ *adj*

race•track *rās-₁trak\ *n* : a usu. oval course on which races are run

race•way \-₁wā\ *n* **1** : a channel for a current of water **2** : RACECOURSE

ra•cial•ism *rā-shə-₁li-zəm\ *n* : RACISM — **ra•cial•ist** \-list\ *n* — **ra•cial•is•tic** \₁rā-shə-*lis-tik\ *adj*

racing form *n* : a paper giving data about racehorses for use by bettors

rac•ism *rā-₁si-zəm\ *n* : a belief that some races are by nature superior to others; *also* : discrimination based on such belief — **rac•ist** \-sist\ *n*

¹rack *rak\ *n* **1** : an instrument of torture on which a body is stretched **2** : a framework on or in which something may be placed (as for display or storage) **3** : a bar with teeth on one side to mesh with a pinion or worm gear

²rack *vb* **1** : to torture on or as if on a rack **2** : to stretch or strain by force **3** : TORMENT **4** : to place on or in a rack

¹rack•et *also* **rac•quet** *ra-kət\ *n* [MF *raquette*, ultim. fr. Ar *rāḥah* palm of the hand] : a light bat made of netting stretched in an oval open frame having a handle and used for striking a ball or shuttlecock

²racket *n* **1** : confused noise : DIN **2** : a fraudulent or dishonest scheme or activity

³racket *vb* : to make a racket

rack•e•teer \₁ra-kə-*tir\ *n* : a person who obtains money by an illegal enterprise usu. involving intimidation — **rack•e•teer•ing** *n*

rack up *vb* : ACCUMULATE, GAIN

ra•con•teur \₁ra-₁kän-*tər\ *n* : one good at telling anecdotes

racy *rā-sē\ *adj* **rac•i•er; -est 1** : full of zest **2** : PUNGENT, SPICY **3** : RISQUÉ, SUGGESTIVE — **rac•i•ly** *rā-sə-lē\ *adv* — **rac•i•ness** \-sē-nəs\ *n*

rad *abbr* **1** radical **2** radio **3** radius

ra•dar *rā-₁där\ *n* [*ra*dio *d*etecting *a*nd *r*anging] : a device that emits radio waves for detecting and locating an object by the reflection of the radio waves and that may use this reflection to determine the object's direction and speed

ra•dar•scope *rā-₁där-₁skōp\ *n* : a visual display for a radar receiver

¹ra•di•al *rā-dē-əl\ *adj* : arranged or having parts arranged like rays around a common center ⟨the ∼ form of a starfish⟩ — **ra•di•al•ly** *adv*

²**radial** *n* : a pneumatic tire with cords laid perpendicular to the center line

radial engine *n* : an internal combustion engine with cylinders arranged radially like the spokes of a wheel

ra·di·ant \'rā-dē-ənt\ *adj* **1** : SHINING, GLOWING **2** : beaming with happiness **3** : transmitted by radiation **syn** brilliant, bright, luminous, lustrous — **ra·di·ance** \-əns\ *n* — **ra·di·ant·ly** *adv*

radiant energy *n* : energy traveling as electromagnetic waves

ra·di·ate \'rā-dē-ˌāt\ *vb* **-at·ed; -at·ing 1** : to send out rays : SHINE, GLOW **2** : to issue in or as if in rays (light ∼s) **3** : to spread around as from a center — **ra·di·a·tion** \ˌrā-dē-'ā-shən\ *n*

radiation sickness *n* : sickness that results from exposure to radiation and is commonly marked by fatigue, nausea, vomiting, loss of teeth and hair, and in more severe cases by damage to blood-forming tissue

ra·di·a·tor \'rā-dē-ˌā-tər\ *n* : any of various devices (as a set of pipes or tubes) for transferring heat from a fluid within to an area or object outside

¹**rad·i·cal** \'ra-di-kəl\ *adj* [ME, fr. LL *radicalis*, fr. L *radic-, radix* root] **1** : FUNDAMENTAL, EXTREME, THOROUGHGOING **2** : of or relating to radicals in politics — **rad·i·cal·ism** \-kə-ˌli-zəm\ *n* — **rad·i·cal·ly** *adv*

²**radical** *n* **1** : a person who favors rapid and sweeping changes in laws and methods of government **2** : a group of atoms considered as a unit that remains unchanged during reactions **3** : a mathematical expression indicating a root by means of a radical sign; *also* : RADICAL SIGN

rad·i·cal·ize \-kə-ˌlīz\ *vb* **-ized; -iz·ing** : to make radical esp. in politics — **rad·i·cal·i·za·tion** \ˌra-di-kə-lə-'zā-shən\ *n*

radical sign *n* : the sign √‾ placed before a mathematical expression to indicate that its root is to be taken

radii *pl of* RADIUS

¹**ra·dio** \'rā-dē-ˌō\ *n, pl* **ra·di·os 1** : the wireless transmission or reception of signals using electromagnetic waves **2** : a radio receiving set **3** : the radio broadcasting industry — **radio** *adj*

²**radio** *vb* : to communicate or send a message to by radio

ra·dio·ac·tiv·i·ty \ˌrā-dē-ō-ˌak-'ti-və-tē\ *n* : the property that some elements or isotopes have of spontaneously emitting energetic particles by the disintegration of their atomic nuclei — **ra·dio·ac·tive** \-'ak-tiv\ *adj*

radio astronomy *n* : astronomy dealing with radio waves received from outside the earth's atmosphere

ra·dio·car·bon \ˌrā-dē-ō-'kär-bən\ *n* : CARBON 14

radio frequency *n* : an electromagnetic wave frequency intermediate between audio frequencies and infrared frequencies used esp. in radio and television transmission

ra·dio·gram \'rā-dē-ō-ˌgram\ *n* : a message transmitted by radio

ra·dio·graph \-ˌgraf\ *n* : a photograph made by some form of radiation other than light; *esp* : an X-ray photograph — **radiograph** *vb* — **ra·dio·graph·ic** \ˌrā-dē-ō-'gra-fik\ *adj* — **ra·dio·graph·i·cal·ly** \-fi-k(ə-)lē\ *adv* — **ra·di·og·ra·phy** \ˌrā-dē-'ä-grə-fē\ *n*

ra·dio·iso·tope \ˌrā-dē-ō-'ī-sə-ˌtōp\ *n* : a radioactive isotope

ra·di·ol·o·gy \ˌrā-dē-'ä-lə-jē\ *n* : the use of radiant energy (as X rays and radium radiations) in medicine — **ra·di·ol·o·gist** \-jist\ *n*

ra·dio·man \'rā-dē-ō-ˌman\ *n* : a radio operator or technician

ra·di·om·e·ter \ˌrā-dē-'ä-mə-tər\ *n* : an instrument for measuring the intensity of radiant energy — **ra·dio·met·ric** \ˌrā-dē-ō-'me-trik\ *adj* — **ra·di·om·e·try** \-mə-trē\ *n*

ra·dio·phone \'rā-dē-ə-ˌfōn\ *n* : RADIOTELEPHONE

ra·dio·sonde \'rā-dē-ō-ˌsänd\ *n* : a small radio transmitter carried aloft (as by balloon) and used to transmit meteorological data

ra·dio·tele·phone \ˌrā-dē-ō-'te-lə-ˌfōn\ *n* : a telephone that uses radio waves wholly or partly instead of connecting wires — **ra·dio·te·le·pho·ny** \-tə-'le-fə-nē, -'te-lə-ˌfō-nē\ *n*

radio telescope *n* : a radio receiver-antenna combination used for observation in radio astronomy

ra·dio·ther·a·py \ˌrā-dē-ō-'ther-ə-pē\ *n* : the treatment of disease by means of radiation (as X rays) — **ra·dio·ther·a·pist** \-pist\ *n*

rad·ish \'ra-dish\ *n* [ME, alter. of OE *rædic,* fr. L *radic-, radix* root, radish] : a pungent fleshy root usu. eaten raw; *also* : a plant related to the mustards that produces this root

ra·di·um \'rā-dē-əm\ *n* : a very radioactive metallic chemical element that is used in the treatment of cancer — see ELEMENT table

ra·di·us \'rā-dē-əs\ *n, pl* **ra·dii** \-ē-ˌī\ *also* **ra·di·us·es 1** : a straight line extending from the center of a circle or a sphere to the circumference or surface; *also* : the length of a radius **2** : the bone on the thumb side of the human forearm **3** : a circular area defined by the length of its radius **syn** range, reach, scope, compass

RADM *abbr* rear admiral

ra·don \'rā-ˌdän\ *n* : a heavy radioactive gaseous chemical element — see ELEMENT table

RAF *abbr* Royal Air Force

raf·fia \'ra-fē-ə\ *n* : fiber used esp. for making baskets and hats that is obtained from the stalks of the leaves of a Madagascar palm (**raffia palm**)

raff·ish \'ra-fish\ *adj* : jaunty or sporty esp. in a flashy or vulgar manner — **raff·ish·ly** *adv* — **raff·ish·ness** *n*

¹**raf·fle** \'ra-fəl\ *vb* **raf·fled; raf·fling** : to dispose of by a raffle

²**raffle** *n* : a lottery in which the prize is won by one of a number of persons buying chances

¹**raft** \'raft\ *n* **1** : a number of logs or timbers fastened together to form a float **2** : a flat structure for support or transportation on water

²**raft** *vb* **1** : to travel or transport by raft **2** : to make into a raft

³**raft** *n* : a large amount or number

raf·ter \'raf-tər\ *n* : any of the parallel beams that support a roof

¹**rag** \'rag\ *n* **1** : a waste piece of cloth **2** : NEWSPAPER

²**rag** *n* : a composition in ragtime

ra·ga \'rä-gə\ *n* **1** : a traditional melodic pattern or mode in Indian music **2** : an improvisation based on a raga

rag·a·muf·fin \'ra-gə-ˌmə-fən\ *n* [ME *Ragamuffyn,* name for a ragged, oafish person] : a ragged dirty person

¹**rage** \'rāj\ *n* **1** : violent and uncontrolled anger **2** : VOGUE, FASHION

²**rage** *vb* **raged; rag·ing 1** : to be furiously angry : RAVE **2** : to continue out of control (the fire *raged*)

rag·ged \'ra-gəd\ *adj* **1** : TORN, TATTERED; *also* : wearing tattered clothes **2** : done in an uneven way (a ∼ performance) — **rag·ged·ly** *adv* — **rag·ged·ness** *n*

rag·lan \'ra-glən\ *n* : an overcoat with sleeves (**raglan sleeves**) sewn in with seams slanting from neck to underarm

ra·gout \ra-'gü\ *n* [F *ragoût,* fr. *ragoûter* to revive the taste, fr. *re-* + *a-* to (fr. L *ad-*) + *goût* taste, fr. L *gustus*] : a highly seasoned meat stew with vegetables

rag·pick·er \'rag-ˌpi-kər\ *n* : one who collects rags and refuse for a living

rag·time \-ˌtīm\ *n* : music in which there is more or less continuous syncopation in the melody

rag·top \'rag-ˌtäp\ *n* : CONVERTIBLE

rag·weed \-ˌwēd\ *n* : any of several chiefly No. American weedy composite herbs with allergenic pollen

¹**raid** \'rād\ *n* : a sudden usu. surprise attack or invasion : FORAY

²**raid** *vb* : to make a raid on — **raid•er** *n*

¹**rail** \'rāl\ *n* [ME *raile*, fr. MF *reille* ruler, bar, fr. L *regula* ruler, fr. *regere* to keep straight, direct, rule] **1** : a bar extending from one support to another as a guard or barrier **2** : a bar of steel forming a track for wheeled vehicles **3** : RAILROAD

²**rail** *vb* : to provide with a railing

³**rail** *n, pl* **rail** *or* **rails** : any of numerous small wading birds often hunted as game birds

⁴**rail** *vb* [ME, fr. MF *railler* to mock, fr. OProv *ralhar* to babble, joke] : to complain angrily : SCOLD, REVILE — **rail•er** *n*

rail•ing \'rā-liŋ\ *n* : a barrier of rails

rail•lery \'rā-lə-rē\ *n, pl* **-ler•ies** : good-natured ridicule : BANTER

¹**rail•road** \'rāl-ˌrōd\ *n* : a permanent road with rails fixed to ties providing a track for cars; *also* : such a road and its assets constituting a property

²**railroad** *vb* **1** : to put through (as a law) too hastily **2** : to convict hastily or with insufficient or improper evidence **3** : to send by rail **4** : to work on a railroad — **rail•road•er** *n* — **rail•road•ing** *n*

rail•way \-ˌwā\ *n* : RAILROAD

rai•ment \'rā-mənt\ *n* : CLOTHING

¹**rain** \'rān\ *n* **1** : water falling in drops from the clouds **2** : a shower of objects ⟨a ~ of bullets⟩ — **rainy** *adj*

²**rain** *vb* **1** : to send down rain **2** : to fall as or like rain **3** : to pour down

rain•bow \-ˌbō\ *n* : an arc or circle of colors formed by the refraction and reflection of the sun's rays in rain, spray, or mist

rainbow trout *n* : a large stout-bodied fish of western No. America closely related to the salmons of the Pacific and usu. having red or pink stripes with black dots along its sides

rain check *n* **1** : a ticket stub good for a later performance when the scheduled one is rained out **2** : an assurance of a deferred extension of an offer

rain•coat \'rān-ˌkōt\ *n* : a waterproof or water-repellent coat

rain•drop \-ˌdräp\ *n* : a drop of rain

rain•fall \-ˌfȯl\ *n* **1** : amount of precipitation measured by depth **2** : a fall of rain

rain forest *n* : a tropical woodland having an annual rainfall of at least 100 inches (254 centimeters) and marked by lofty broad-leaved evergreen trees forming a continuous canopy

rain•mak•ing \'rān-ˌmā-kiŋ\ *n* : the action or process of producing or attempting to produce rain by artificial means — **rain•mak•er** *n*

rain out *vb* : to interrupt or prevent by rain

rain•storm \'rān-ˌstȯrm\ *n* : a storm of or with rain

rain•wa•ter \-ˌwȯ-tər, -ˌwä-\ *n* : water fallen as rain

¹**raise** \'rāz\ *vb* **raised; rais•ing 1** : to cause or help to rise : LIFT ⟨~ a window⟩ **2** : AWAKEN, AROUSE ⟨enough to ~ the dead⟩ **3** : BUILD, ERECT ⟨~ a monument⟩ **4** : PROMOTE ⟨was *raised* to captain⟩ **5** : END ⟨~ a siege⟩ **6** : COLLECT ⟨~ money⟩ **7** : BREED, GROW ⟨~ cattle⟩ ⟨~ corn⟩; *also* : BRING UP ⟨~ a family⟩ **8** : PROVOKE ⟨~ a laugh⟩ **9** : to bring to notice ⟨~ an objection⟩ **10** : INCREASE ⟨~ prices⟩; *also* : to bet more than **11** : to make light and spongy ⟨~ dough⟩ **12** : to multiply a quantity by itself a specified number of times **13** : to cause to form ⟨~ a blister⟩ **syn** lift, hoist, boost, elevate — **rais•er** *n*

²**raise** *n* : an increase in amount (as of a bid or bet); *also* : an increase in pay

rai•sin \'rāz-ᵊn\ *n* [ME, fr. MF, grape, fr. L *racemus* cluster of grapes or berries] : a grape dried for food

rai•son d'être \ˌrā-zōⁿ-ˈdetrᵊ\ *n* : reason or justification for existence

ra•ja *or* **ra•jah** \'rä-jə\ *n* [Hindi *rājā*, fr. Skt *rājan* king] : an Indian prince

¹**rake** \'rāk\ *n* : a long-handled garden tool having a crossbar with prongs

²**rake** *vb* **raked; rak•ing 1** : to gather, loosen, or smooth with or as if with a rake **2** : to sweep the length of (as a trench or ship) with gunfire

³**rake** *n* : inclination from either perpendicular or horizontal : SLANT

⁴**rake** *n* : a dissolute man : LIBERTINE

rake–off \'rāk-ˌȯf\ *n* : a percentage or cut taken

¹**rak•ish** \'rā-kish\ *adj* : DISSOLUTE — **rak•ish•ly** *adv* — **rak•ish•ness** *n*

²**rakish** *adj* **1** : having a trim appearance indicative of speed ⟨a ~ sloop⟩ **2** : JAUNTY, SPORTY ⟨~ clothes⟩ — **rak•ish•ly** *adv* — **rak•ish•ness** *n*

¹**ral•ly** \'ra-lē\ *vb* **ral•lied; ral•ly•ing 1** : to bring together for a common purpose; *also* : to bring back to order ⟨a leader ~*ing* his forces⟩ **2** : to arouse to activity or from depression or weakness **3** : to make a comeback **syn** stir, rouse, awaken, waken, kindle

²**rally** *n, pl* **rallies 1** : an act of rallying **2** : a mass meeting to arouse enthusiasm **3** : a competitive automobile event run over public roads

³**rally** *vb* **ral•lied; ral•ly•ing** : BANTER

¹**ram** \'ram\ *n* **1** : a male sheep **2** : BATTERING RAM

²**ram** *vb* **rammed; ram•ming 1** : to force or drive in or through **2** : CRAM, CROWD **3** : to strike against violently

RAM \'ram\ *n* : RANDOM-ACCESS MEMORY

¹**ram•ble** \'ram-bəl\ *vb* **ram•bled; ram•bling** : to go about aimlessly : ROAM, WANDER

²**ramble** *n* : a leisurely excursion; *esp* : an aimless walk

ram•bler \'ram-blər\ *n* **1** : a person who rambles **2** : any of various climbing roses with large clusters of small often double flowers

ram•bunc•tious \ram-ˈbəŋk-shəs\ *adj* : UNRULY

ra•mie \'rā-mē, 'ra-\ *n* : a strong lustrous bast fiber from an Asian nettle

ram•i•fi•ca•tion \ˌra-mə-fə-ˈkā-shən\ *n* **1** : the act or process of branching **2** : CONSEQUENCE, OUTGROWTH

ram•i•fy \'ra-mə-ˌfī\ *vb* **-fied; -fy•ing** : to branch out

ramp \'ramp\ *n* : a sloping passage or roadway connecting different levels

¹**ram•page** \'ram-ˌpāj, (ˌ)ram-ˈpāj\ *vb* **ram•paged; ram•pag•ing** : to rush about wildly

²**ram•page** \'ram-ˌpāj\ *n* : a course of violent or riotous action or behavior — **ram•pa•geous** \ram-ˈpā-jəs\ *adj*

ram•pant \'ram-pənt\ *adj* : unchecked in growth or spread : RIFE ⟨fear was ~ in the town⟩ — **ram•pan•cy** \-pən-sē\ *n* — **ram•pant•ly** *adv*

ram•part \'ram-ˌpärt\ *n* **1** : a protective barrier **2** : a broad embankment raised as a fortification

¹**ram•rod** \'ram-ˌräd\ *n* **1** : a rod used to ram a charge into a muzzle-loading gun **2** : a cleaning rod for small arms **3** : BOSS, OVERSEER

²**ramrod** *adj* : marked by rigidity or severity

³**ramrod** *vb* : to direct, supervise, and control

ram•shack•le \'ram-ˌsha-kəl\ *adj* : RICKETY, TUMBLE-DOWN

ran *past of* RUN

¹**ranch** \'ranch\ *n* [MexSp *rancho* small ranch, fr. Sp, camp, hut & Sp dial., small farm, fr. Old Spanish *ranchear (se)* to take up quarters, fr. MF *(se) ranger* to take up a position, fr. *ranger* to set in a row] **1** : an establishment for the raising and grazing of livestock (as cattle, sheep, or horses) **2** : a large farm devoted to a specialty **3** : RANCH HOUSE 2

²**ranch** *vb* : to live or work on a ranch — **ranch•er** *n*

ranch house *n* **1** : the main house on a ranch **2** : a one-story house typically with a low-pitched roof

ran•cho \'ran-chō, 'rän-\ *n, pl* **ranchos** : RANCH 1

ran•cid \'ran-səd\ *adj* **1** : having a rank smell or taste **2** : ROTTEN, SPOILED — **ran•cid•i•ty** \ran-ˈsi-də-tē\ *n*

ran•cor \'raŋ-kər\ *n* : bitter deep-seated ill will **syn** antagonism, animosity, antipathy, enmity, hostility — **ran•cor•ous** *adj*

ran•cour *Brit var of* RANCOR

rand \'rand, 'ränd, 'ränt\ *n, pl* **rand** — see MONEY table

R & B *abbr* rhythm and blues

R and D *n* : research and development

ran·dom \'ran-dəm\ *adj* : CHANCE, HAPHAZARD — **ran·dom·ly** *adv* — **ran·dom·ness** *n*

random–access *adj* : allowing access to stored data in any order the user desires

random–access memory *n* : a computer memory that provides the main internal storage for programs and data

ran·dom·ize \'ran-də-ˌmīz\ *vb* **-ized; -iz·ing** : to select, assign, or arrange in a random way — **ran·dom·i·za·tion** \ˌran-də-mə-'zā-shən\ *n*

R and R *abbr* rest and recreation; rest and recuperation

rang *past of* RING

¹**range** \'rānj\ *n* **1** : a series of things in a row **2** : a cooking stove having an oven and a flat top with burners **3** : open land where animals (as livestock) may roam and graze **4** : the act of ranging about **5** : the distance a weapon will shoot or is to be shot **6** : a place where shooting is practiced **7** : the space or extent included, covered, or used : SCOPE **8** : a variation within limits **syn** reach, compass, radius, circle

²**range** *vb* **ranged; rang·ing 1** : to set in a row or in proper order **2** : to set in place among others of the same kind **3** : to roam over or through : EXPLORE **4** : to roam at large or freely **5** : to correspond in direction or line **6** : to vary within limits **7** : to find the range of an object by instrument (as radar)

rang·er \'rān-jər\ *n* **1** : FOREST RANGER **2** : a member of a body of troops who range over a region **3** : an expert in close-range fighting and raiding tactics

rangy \'rān-jē\ *adj* **rang·i·er; -est** : being long-limbed and slender — **rang·i·ness** \'rān-jē-nəs\ *n*

ra·ni *or* **ra·nee** \rä-'nē, 'rä-ˌnē\ *n* : a raja's wife

¹**rank** \'raŋk\ *adj* **1** : strong and vigorous and usu. coarse in growth ⟨~ weeds⟩ **2** : unpleasantly strong-smelling — **rank·ly** *adv* — **rank·ness** *n*

²**rank** *n* **1** : ROW **2** : a line of soldiers ranged side by side **3** *pl* : the body of enlisted personnel ⟨rose from the ~s⟩ **4** : an orderly arrangement **5** : CLASS, DIVISION **6** : a grade of official standing (as in an army) **7** : position in a group **8** : superior position

³**rank** *vb* **1** : to arrange in lines or in regular formation **2** : RATE **3** : to rate above (as in official standing) **4** : to take or have a relative position

rank and file *n* : the general membership of a body as contrasted with its leaders

rank·ing \'raŋ-kiŋ\ *adj* **1** : having a high position : FOREMOST **2** : being next to the chairman in seniority

ran·kle \'raŋ-kəl\ *vb* **ran·kled; ran·kling** [ME *ranclen* to fester, fr. MF *rancler*, fr. OF *draoncler, raoncler*, fr. *draoncle, raoncle* festering sore, fr. (assumed) VL *dracunculus*, fr. L, dim. of *draco* serpent] : to cause anger, irritation, or bitterness

ran·sack \'ran-ˌsak\ *vb* : to search thoroughly; *esp* : to search through and rob

¹**ran·som** \'ran-səm\ *n* [ME *ransoun*, fr. OF *rançon*, fr. L *redemption-, redemptio* act of buying back, fr. *redimere* to buy back, redeem] **1** : something paid or demanded for the freedom of a captive **2** : the act of ransoming

²**ransom** *vb* : to free from captivity or punishment by paying a price — **ran·som·er** *n*

rant \'rant\ *vb* **1** : to talk loudly and wildly **2** : to scold violently — **rant·er** *n* — **rant·ing·ly** *adv*

¹**rap** \'rap\ *n* **1** : a sharp blow **2** : a sharp rebuke **3** : a negative often undeserved reputation ⟨a bum ~⟩ **4** : responsibility for or consequences of an action ⟨take the ~⟩

²**rap** *vb* **rapped; rap·ping 1** : to strike sharply : KNOCK **2** : to utter sharply **3** : to criticize sharply

³**rap** *vb* **rapped; rap·ping 1** : to talk freely and frankly **2** : to perform rap music

⁴**rap** *n* **1** : TALK, CONVERSATION **2** : a rhythmic chanting of usu. rhymed couplets to a musical accompaniment; *also* : a piece so performed

ra·pa·cious \rə-'pā-shəs\ *adj* **1** : excessively greedy or covetous **2** : living on prey **3** : RAVENOUS **2** — **ra·pa·cious·ly** *adv* — **ra·pa·cious·ness** *n* — **ra·pac·i·ty** \-'pa-sə-tē\ *n*

¹**rape** \'rāp\ *n* : a European herb related to the mustards that is grown as a forage crop and for its seeds (**rape·seed** \-ˌsēd\)

²**rape** *vb* **raped; rap·ing** : to commit rape on — **rap·er** *n* — **rap·ist** \'rā-pist\ *n*

³**rape** *n* **1** : a carrying away by force **2** : sexual intercourse by a man with a woman without her consent and chiefly by force or deception; *also* : unlawful sexual intercourse of any kind by force or threat

¹**rap·id** \'ra-pəd\ *adj* [L *rapidus* strong-flowing, rapid, fr. *rapere* to seize, carry away] : very fast : SWIFT **syn** fleet, quick, speedy — **ra·pid·i·ty** \rə-'pi-də-tē\ *n* — **rap·id·ly** *adv*

²**rapid** *n* : a place in a stream where the current flows very fast usu. over obstructions — usu. used in pl.

rapid eye movement *n* : rapid conjugate movement of the eyes associated with REM sleep

rapid transit *n* : fast passenger transportation (as by subway) in cities

ra·pi·er \'rā-pē-ər\ *n* : a straight 2-edged sword with a narrow pointed blade

rapier

rap·ine \'ra-pən, -ˌpīn\ *n* : PILLAGE, PLUNDER

rap·pel \ra-'pel, ra-\ *vb* **-pelled; -pel·ling** : to descend (as from a cliff) by sliding down a rope

rap·pen \'rä-pən\ *n, pl* **rappen** : the centime of Switzerland

rap·port \ra-'pōr\ *n* : RELATION; *esp* : relation characterized by harmony

rap·proche·ment \ˌra-ˌprōsh-'mäⁿ, ra-'prōsh-ˌmäⁿ\ *n* : the establishment of or a state of having cordial relations

rap·scal·lion \rap-'skal-yən\ *n* : RASCAL, SCAMP

rapt \'rapt\ *adj* **1** : carried away with emotion **2** : ABSORBED, ENGROSSED — **rapt·ly** \'rapt-lē\ *adv* — **rapt·ness** *n*

rap·ture \'rap-chər\ *n* : spiritual or emotional ecstasy — **rap·tur·ous** \-chə-rəs\ *adj* — **rap·tur·ous·ly** *adv*

rapture of the deep : NITROGEN NARCOSIS

ra·ra avis \ˌrar-ə-'ā-vəs\ *n* [L, rare bird] : a rare person or thing : RARITY

¹**rare** \'rar\ *adj* **rar·er; rar·est 1** : not thick or dense : THIN ⟨~ air⟩ **2** : unusually fine : EXCELLENT, SPLENDID **3** : seldom met with — **rare·ly** *adv* — **rare·ness** *n* — **rar·i·ty** \'rar-ə-tē\ *n*

²**rare** *adj* **rar·er; rar·est** : cooked so that the inside is still red ⟨~ beef⟩

rare·bit \'rar-bət\ *n* : WELSH RABBIT

rar·efac·tion \ˌrar-ə-'fak-shən\ *n* **1** : the action or process of rarefying **2** : the state of being rarefied

rar·efy *also* **rar·i·fy** \'rar-ə-ˌfī\ *vb* **-fied; -fy·ing** : to make or become rare, thin, or less dense

rar·ing \'rar-ən, -iŋ\ *adj* : full of enthusiasm or eagerness ⟨~ to go⟩

ras·cal \'ras-kəl\ *n* **1** : a mean or dishonest person **2** : a mischievous person — **ras·cal·i·ty** \ras-ˈka-lə-tē\ n — **ras·cal·ly** \ˈras-kə-lē\ adj

¹rash \ˈrash\ adj : having or showing little regard for consequences : too hasty in decision, action, or speech : RECKLESS syn daring, foolhardy, adventurous, venturesome — **rash·ly** adv — **rash·ness** n

²rash n : an eruption on the body

rash·er \ˈra-shər\ n : a thin slice of bacon or ham broiled or fried; also : a portion consisting of several such slices

¹rasp \ˈrasp\ vb 1 : to rub with or as if with a rough file 2 : to grate harshly on (as one's nerves) 3 : to speak in a grating tone

²rasp n : a coarse file with cutting points instead of ridges

rasp·ber·ry \ˈraz-ˌber-ē, -bə-rē\ n 1 : any of various edible usu. black or red berries produced by some brambles; also : such a bramble 2 : a sound of contempt made by protruding the tongue through the lips and expelling air forcibly

¹rat \ˈrat\ n 1 : any of numerous rodents larger than the related mice 2 : a contemptible person; esp : one that betrays friends or associates

²rat vb **rat·ted; rat·ting** 1 : to betray or inform on one's associates 2 : to hunt or catch rats

rat cheese n : CHEDDAR

ratch·et \ˈra-chət\ n : a device that consists of a bar or wheel having slanted teeth into which a pawl drops so as to allow motion in only one direction

ratchet wheel n : a toothed wheel held in position or turned by a pawl

¹rate \ˈrāt\ vb **rat·ed; rat·ing** : to scold violently

²rate n 1 : quantity, amount, or degree measured by some standard 2 : an amount (as of payment) measured by its relation to some other amount (as of time) 3 : a charge, payment, or price fixed according to a ratio, scale, or standard ⟨tax ∼⟩ 4 : RANK, CLASS

³rate vb **rat·ed; rat·ing** 1 : ESTIMATE 2 : CONSIDER, REGARD 3 : to settle the relative rank or class of 4 : to be classed : RANK 5 : to have a right to : DESERVE 6 : to be of consequence — **rat·er** n

rath·er \ˈra-thər, ˈrä-, ˈrə-\ adv [ME, fr. OE hrathor, compar. of hrathe quickly] 1 : more properly : PREFERABLY 3 : more correctly speaking 4 : to the contrary : INSTEAD 5 : SOMEWHAT

raths·kel·ler \ˈrät-ˌske-lər, ˈrat-\ n [obs. G (now Ratskeller), city-hall basement restaurant, fr. Rat council + Keller cellar] : a usu. basement tavern or restaurant

rat·i·fy \ˈra-tə-ˌfī\ vb **-fied; -fy·ing** : to approve and accept formally — **rat·i·fi·ca·tion** \ˌra-tə-fə-ˈkā-shən\ n

rat·ing \ˈrā-tiŋ\ n 1 : a classification according to grade : RANK 2 Brit : a naval enlisted man 3 : an estimate of the credit standing and business responsibility of a person or firm

ra·tio \ˈrā-shō, -shē-ō\ n, pl **ra·tios** 1 : the indicated quotient of two numbers or mathematical expressions 2 : the relationship in number, quantity, or degree between two or more things

ra·ti·o·ci·na·tion \ˌra-tē-ō-sə-ˈn-ˌā-shən, -shē-, -ˌäs-\ n : exact thinking : REASONING — **ra·ti·o·ci·nate** \-ˈōs-ᵊn-ˌāt, -ˌäs-\ vb — **ra·ti·o·ci·na·tive** \-ˈōs-ᵊn-ˌā-tiv, -ˈäs-\ adj — **ra·ti·o·ci·na·tor** \-ˈōs-ᵊn-ˌā-tər, -ˌäs-\ n

¹ra·tion \ˈra-shən, ˈrā-\ n 1 : a food allowance for one day 2 : FOOD, PROVISIONS, DIET — usu. used in pl. 3 : SHARE, ALLOTMENT

²ration vb 1 : to supply with or allot as rations 2 : to use or allot sparingly syn apportion, portion, prorate, parcel

¹ra·tio·nal \ˈra-shə-nəl\ adj 1 : having reason or understanding 2 : of or relating to reason 3 : relating to, consisting of, or being one or more rational numbers — **ra·tio·nal·ly** adv

²rational n : RATIONAL NUMBER

ra·tio·nale \ˌra-shə-ˈnal\ n : an explanation of principles controlling belief or practice 2 : an underlying reason

ra·tio·nal·ism \ˈra-shə-nə-ˌli-zəm\ n : the practice of guiding one's actions and opinions solely by what seems reasonable — **ra·tio·nal·ist** \-list\ n — **rationalist** or **ra·tio·nal·is·tic** \ˌra-shə-nə-ˈlis-tik\ adj

ra·tio·nal·i·ty \ˌra-shə-ˈna-lə-tē\ n, pl **-ties** : the quality or state of being rational

ra·tio·nal·ize \ˈra-shə-nə-ˌlīz\ vb **-ized; -iz·ing** 1 : to make (something irrational) appear rational or reasonable 2 : to provide a natural explanation of (as a myth) 3 : to justify (as one's behavior or weaknesses) esp. to oneself 4 : to find plausible but untrue reasons for conduct — **ra·tio·nal·i·za·tion** \ˌra-shə-nə-lə-ˈzā-shən\ n

rational number n : an integer or the quotient of an integer divided by a nonzero integer

rat race n : strenuous, tiresome, and usu. competitive activity or rush

rat·tan \ra-ˈtan, rə-\ n : a cane or switch made from one of the long stems of an Asian climbing palm; also : this palm

rat·ter \ˈra-tər\ n : a rat-catching dog or cat

¹rat·tle \ˈrat-ᵊl\ vb **rat·tled; rat·tling** 1 : to make or cause to make a series of clattering sounds 2 : to move with a clattering sound 3 : to say or do in a brisk lively fashion ⟨∼ off the answers⟩ 4 : CONFUSE, UPSET ⟨∼ a witness⟩

²rattle n 1 : a toy that produces a rattle when shaken 2 : a series of clattering and knocking sounds 3 : a rattling organ at the end of a rattlesnake's tail

rat·tler \ˈrat-lər\ n : RATTLESNAKE

rat·tle·snake \ˈrat-ᵊl-ˌsnāk\ n : any of various American pit vipers with a rattle at the end of the tail

rattlesnake

rat·tle·trap \ˈrat-ᵊl-ˌtrap\ n : something (as an old car) rickety and full of rattles

rat·tling \ˈrat-liŋ\ adj 1 : LIVELY, BRISK 2 : FIRST-RATE, SPLENDID

rat·trap \ˈrat-ˌtrap\ n 1 : a trap for rats 2 : a dilapidated building

rat·ty \ˈra-tē\ adj **rat·ti·er; -est** 1 : infested with rats 2 : of, relating to, or suggestive of rats 3 : SHABBY

rau·cous \ˈrȯ-kəs\ adj 1 : HARSH, HOARSE, STRIDENT 2 : boisterously disorderly — **rau·cous·ly** adv — **raucous·ness** n

raun·chy \ˈrȯn-chē, ˈrän-\ adj **raun·chi·er; -est** 1 : SLOVENLY, DIRTY 2 : OBSCENE, SMUTTY — **raun·chi·ness** \-chē-nəs\ n

¹rav·age \ˈra-vij\ n [F] : an act or result of ravaging : DEVASTATION

²ravage vb **rav·aged; rav·ag·ing** : to lay waste : DEVASTATE — **rav·ag·er** n

¹rave \ˈrāv\ vb **raved; rav·ing** [ME raven] 1 : to talk wildly in or as if in delirium : STORM, RAGE 2 : to talk with extreme enthusiasm

²rave n 1 : an act or instance of raving 2 : an extravagantly favorable criticism

¹rav·el \ˈra-vəl\ vb **-eled** or **-elled; -el·ing** or **-el·ling** 1 : UNRAVEL, UNTWIST 2 : TANGLE, CONFUSE

²**ravel** *n* **1** : something tangled **2** : something raveled out; *esp* : a loose thread

¹**ra·ven** \\'rā-vən\\ *n* : a large black bird related to the crow

²**raven** *adj* : black and glossy like a raven's feathers

³**rav·en** \\'ra-vən\\ *vb* **rav·ened; rav·en·ing 1** : to devour greedily **2** : DESPOIL, PLUNDER **3** : PREY

rav·en·ous \\'ra-və-nəs\\ *adj* **1** : RAPACIOUS, VORACIOUS **2** : eager for food : very hungry — **rav·en·ous·ly** *adv* — **rav·en·ous·ness** *n*

ra·vine \\rə-'vēn\\ *n* : a small narrow steep-sided valley larger than a gully

rav·i·o·li \\rä-vē-'ō-lē\\ *n* [It, fr. It dial., pl. of *raviolo*, lit., little turnip, dim. of *rava* turnip, fr. L *rapa*] : small cases of dough with a savory filling (as of meat or cheese)

rav·ish \\'ra-vish\\ *vb* **1** : to seize and take away by violence **2** : to overcome with emotion and esp. with joy or delight **3** : RAPE — **rav·ish·er** *n* — **rav·ish·ment** *n*

¹**raw** \\'rȯ\\ *adj* **raw·er** \\'rȯ-ər\\; **raw·est** \\'rȯ-əst\\ **1** : not cooked **2** : changed little from the original form : not processed ⟨∼ materials⟩ **3** : having the surface abraded or irritated ⟨a ∼ sore⟩ **4** : not trained or experienced ⟨∼ recruits⟩ **5** : VULGAR, COARSE **6** : disagreeably cold and damp ⟨a ∼ day⟩ **7** : UNFAIR ⟨∼ deal⟩ — **raw·ness** *n*

²**raw** *n* : a raw place or state; *esp* : NUDITY

raw·boned \\'rȯ-¡bōnd\\ *adj* **1** : LEAN, GAUNT **2** : having a heavy frame that seems to have little flesh

raw·hide \\'rȯ-¡hīd\\ *n* : the untanned skin of cattle; *also* : a whip made of this

¹**ray** \\'rā\\ *n* : any of an order of large flat catilaginous fishes that have the eyes on the upper surface and the hind end of the body slender and taillike

²**ray** *n* [ME, fr. MF *rai*, fr. L *radius* rod, ray] **1** : any of the lines of light that appear to radiate from a bright object **2** : a thin beam of radiant energy (as light) **3** : light from a beam **4** : a thin line like a beam of light **5** : an animal or plant structure resembling a ray **6** : a tiny bit : PARTICLE ⟨a ∼ of hope⟩

ray·on \\'rā-¡än\\ *n* : a fiber made from cellulose; *also* : a yarn, thread, or fabric made from such fibers

raze \\'rāz\\ *vb* **razed; raz·ing 1** : to scrape, cut, or shave off **2** : to destroy to the ground : DEMOLISH

ra·zor \\'rā-zər\\ *n* : a sharp cutting instrument used to shave off hair

ra·zor–backed \\'rā-zər-¡bakt\\ *or* **ra·zor·back** \\-¡bak\\ *adj* : having a sharp narrow back ⟨∼ horse⟩

razor clam *n* : any of a family of marine bivalve mollusks having a long narrow curved thin shell

¹**razz** \\'raz\\ *n* : RASPBERRY 2

²**razz** *vb* : RIDICULE, TEASE

Rb *symbol* rubidium

RBC *abbr* red blood cells; red blood count

RBI \\¡är-(¡)bē-'ī, 'ri-bē\\ *n, pl* **RBIs** *or* **RBI** [*r*un *b*atted *i*n] : a run in baseball that is driven in by a batter

RC *abbr* **1** Red Cross **2** Roman Catholic

RCAF *abbr* Royal Canadian Air Force

RCMP *abbr* Royal Canadian Mounted Police

RCN *abbr* Royal Canadian Navy

rct *abbr* recruit

rd *abbr* **1** road **2** rod **3** round

RD *abbr* rural delivery

RDA *abbr* recommended daily allowance; recommended dietary allowance

re \\'rā, 'rē\\ *prep* : with regard to

Re *symbol* rhenium

re- \\rē, ¡rē, 'rē\\ *prefix* **1** : again : for a second time **2** : anew : in a new or different form **3** : back : backward

reabsorb	readjust
reacquire	readjustment
reactivate	readmission
reactivation	readmit
readdress	reaffirm

reaffirmation	recondensation
realign	recondense
realignment	reconfirm
reallocate	reconfirmation
reallocation	reconnect
reanalysis	reconquer
reanalyze	reconquest
reanimate	reconsecrate
reanimation	reconsecration
reannex	recontact
reannexation	recontaminate
reappear	recontamination
reappearance	reconvene
reapplication	reconvert
reapply	recook
reappoint	recopy
reappointment	recross
reapportion	recrystallize
reapportionment	recut
reappraisal	redecorate
reappraise	redecoration
rearm	rededicate
rearmament	rededication
rearouse	redefine
rearrange	redefinition
rearrangement	redeposit
rearrest	redesign
reascend	redetermination
reassemble	redetermine
reassembly	redevelop
reassert	redevelopment
reassess	redirect
reassessment	rediscount
reassign	rediscover
reassignment	rediscovery
reassume	redissolve
reattach	redistill
reattachment	redistillation
reattain	redraft
reattempt	redraw
reauthorization	reecho
reauthorize	reedit
reawaken	reelect
rebaptism	reelection
rebaptize	reemerge
rebid	reemergence
rebind	reemphasis
reboil	reemphasize
rebroadcast	reemploy
reburial	reemployment
rebury	reenact
recalculate	reenactment
recalculation	reenergize
rechannel	reenlist
recharge	reenlistment
rechargeable	reenter
recharter	reequip
recheck	reestablish
rechristen	reestablishment
reclassification	reevaluate
reclassify	reevaluation
recoin	reexamination
recolonization	reexamine
recolonize	reexport
recolor	refashion
recombine	refight
recommence	refigure
recommission	refinish
recommit	refit
recompile	refix
recompose	refloat
recomputation	refold
recompute	reforge
reconceive	reformulate
reconcentrate	reformulation
reconception	refortify

refound
refreeze
refuel
refurnish
regain
regather
regild
regive
regrade
regrind
regrow
regrowth
rehandle
rehear
reheat
rehouse
reimpose
reimposition
reincorporate
reinsert
reinsertion
reintegrate
reinterpret
reinterpretation
reintroduce
reintroduction
reinvention
reinvest
reinvestment
reinvigorate
reinvigoration
reissue
rejudge
rekindle
reknit
relaunch
relearn
relight
reline
reload
remanufacture
remap
remarriage
remarry
rematch
remelt
remigration
remix
remold
rename
renegotiate
renegotiation
renominate
renomination
renumber
reoccupy
reoccur
reopen
reorder
reorganization
reorganize
reorient
reorientation
repack
repaint
repass
repeople
rephotograph
rephrase

replant
repopulate
reprice
reprocess
reprogram
republication
republish
repurchase
reradiate
reread
rereading
rerecord
reroute
reschedule
rescore
rescreen
reseal
reseed
resell
reset
resettle
resettlement
resew
reshow
resocialization
resow
respell
restaff
restart
restate
restatement
restock
restrengthen
restructure
restudy
restuff
restyle
resubmit
resummon
resupply
resurface
resurvey
resynthesis
resynthesize
retaste
retell
retest
retool
retrain
retransmission
retransmit
retrial
reunification
reunify
reunite
reusable
reuse
revaluate
revaluation
revalue
revisit
rewarm
rewash
reweave
rewed
reweigh
rewire
rezone

re·act \rē-**ˈ**akt\ *vb* **1** : to exert a return or counteracting influence **2** : to have or show a reaction **3** : to act in opposition to a force or influence **4** : to move or tend in a reverse direction **5** : to undergo chemical reaction

re·ac·tant \rē-**ˈ**ak-tənt\ *n* : a chemically reacting substance

re·ac·tion \rē-**ˈ**ak-shən\ *n* **1** : the act or process of reacting **2** : a counter tendency; *esp* : a tendency toward a former esp. outmoded political or social order or policy **3** : bodily, mental, or emotional response to a stimulus **4** : chemical change **5** : a process involving change in atomic nuclei

re·ac·tion·ary \rē-**ˈ**ak-shə-ˌner-ē\ *adj* : relating to, marked by, or favoring esp. political reaction — **reactionary** *n*

re·ac·tive \rē-**ˈ**ak-tiv\ *adj* : reacting or tending to react

re·ac·tor \rē-**ˈ**ak-tər\ *n* **1** : one that reacts **2** : a device for the controlled release of nuclear energy

¹read **ˈ**rēd\ *vb* **read** **ˈ**red\; **read·ing 1** : to understand language by interpreting written symbols for speech sounds **2** : to utter aloud written or printed words **3** : to learn by observing ⟨∼ nature's signs⟩ **4** : to study by a course of reading ⟨∼s law⟩ **5** : to discover the meaning of ⟨∼ the clues⟩ **6** : to recognize or interpret as if by reading **7** : to attribute (a meaning) to something ⟨∼ guilt in his manner⟩ **8** : INDICATE ⟨thermometer ∼s 10°⟩ **9** : to consist in phrasing or meaning ⟨the two versions ∼ differently⟩ — **read·abil·i·ty** \ˌrē-də-**ˈ**bi-lə-tē\ *n* — **read·able** **ˈ**rē-də-bəl\ *adj* — **read·ably** \-blē\ *adv* — **read·er** *n*

²read **ˈ**red\ *adj* : informed by reading ⟨widely ∼⟩

read·er·ship **ˈ**rē-dər-ˌship\ *n* : the mass or a particular group of readers

read·ing *n* **1** : something read or for reading **2** : a particular version **3** : data indicated by an instrument ⟨thermometer ∼⟩ **4** : a particular interpretation (as of a law) **5** : a particular performance (as of a musical work) **6** : an indication of a certain state of affairs

read—only memory *n* : a computer memory that contains special-purpose information (as a program) which cannot be altered

read·out **ˈ**rēd-ˌau̇t\ *n* : the process of removing information from an automatic device (as a computer) and displaying it in an understandable form; *also* : the information removed from such a device

read out *vb* **1** : to read aloud **2** : to expel from an organization

¹ready **ˈ**re-dē\ *adj* **read·i·er; -est 1** : prepared for use or action **2** : likely to do something indicated; *also* : willingly disposed : INCLINED **3** : spontaneously prompt ⟨her ∼ wit⟩ **4** : immediately available ⟨∼ cash⟩ — **read·i·ly** **ˈ**re-də-lē\ *adv* — **read·i·ness** \-dē-nəs\ *n* — **at the ready** : ready for immediate use

²ready *vb* **read·ied; ready·ing** : to make ready : PREPARE

ready—made \ˌre-dē-**ˈ**mād\ *adj* : already made up for general sale : not specially made — **ready—made** *n*

ready room *n* : a room in which pilots are briefed and await orders

re·agent \rē-**ˈ**ā-jənt\ *n* : a substance that takes part in or brings about a particular chemical reaction

¹re·al **ˈ**rēl\ *adj* [ME, real, relating to things (in law), fr. MF, fr. ML & LL; ML *realis* relating to things (in law), fr. LL, real, fr. L *res* thing, fact] **1** : of or relating to fixed or immovable things (as land) ⟨∼ property⟩ **2** : not artificial : GENUINE; *also* : not imaginary — **re·al·ness** *n* — **for real 1** : in earnest **2** : GENUINE

²real *adv* : VERY

real estate *n* : property in buildings and land

re·al·ism **ˈ**rē-ə-ˌli-zəm\ *n* **1** : the disposition to face facts and to deal with them practically **2** : true and faithful portrayal of nature and of people in art or literature — **re·al·ist** \-list\ *adj or n* — **re·al·is·tic** \ˌrē-ə-**ˈ**lis-tik\ *adj* — **re·al·is·ti·cal·ly** \-ti-k(ə-)lē\ *adv*

re·al·i·ty \rē-**ˈ**a-lə-tē\ *n, pl* **-ties 1** : the quality or state

¹reach **ˈ**rēch\ *vb* **1** : to stretch out **2** : to touch or attempt to touch or seize **3** : to extend to **4** : to communicate with **5** : to arrive at **syn** gain, realize, achieve, attain — **reach·able** *adj* — **reach·er** *n*

²reach *n* **1** : an unbroken stretch of a river **2** : the act of reaching **3** : a reachable distance; *also* : ability to reach **4** : a range of knowledge or comprehension

of being real **2** : something real **3** : the totality of real things and events

re·al·ize \'rē-ə-ˌlīz\ vb **-ized; -iz·ing 1** : to make actual : ACCOMPLISH **2** : to convert into money ⟨∼ assets⟩ **3** : OBTAIN, GAIN ⟨∼ a profit⟩ **4** : to be aware of : UNDERSTAND — **re·al·iz·able** adj — **re·al·i·za·tion** \ˌrē-ə-lə-ˈzā-shən\ n

re·al·ly \'rē-lē, 'ri-\ adv : in truth : in fact : ACTUALLY

realm \'relm\ n **1** : KINGDOM **2** : SPHERE, DOMAIN

real number n : any of the numbers (as −2, 3, ⅞, .25, π) that are rational or irrational

re·al·po·li·tik \rā-ˈäl-ˌpō-li-ˌtēk\ n [G] : politics based on practical and material factors rather than on theoretical or ethical objectives

real time n : the actual time during which something takes place — **real–time** adj

re·al·ty \'rēl-tē\ n : REAL ESTATE

¹ream \'rēm\ n [ME reme, fr. MF raime, fr. Ar rizmah, lit., bundle] : a quantity of paper that is variously 480, 500, or 516 sheets

²ream vb : to enlarge, shape, or clear with a reamer

ream·er \'rē-mər\ n : a tool with cutting edges that is used to enlarge or shape a hole

reap \'rēp\ vb **1** : to cut or clear with a scythe, sickle, or machine **2** : to gather by or as if by cutting : HARVEST ⟨∼ a reward⟩ — **reap·er** n

¹rear \'rir\ vb **1** : to erect by building **2** : to set or raise upright **3** : to breed and raise for use or market ⟨∼ livestock⟩ **4** : BRING UP, FOSTER **5** : to lift or rise up; esp : to rise on the hind legs

²rear n **1** : the unit (as of an army) or area farthest from the enemy **2** : BACK; also : the position at the back of something

³rear adj : being at the back

rear admiral n : a commissioned officer in the navy or coast guard ranking next below a vice admiral

¹rear·ward \'rir-wərd\ adj **1** : being at or toward the rear **2** : directed toward the rear

²rear·ward also **rear·wards** \-wərdz\ adv : at or toward the rear

reas abbr reasonable

¹rea·son \'rēz-ᵊn\ n [ME resoun, fr. OF raison, fr. L ration-, ratio reason, computation] **1** : a statement offered in explanation or justification **2** : GROUND, CAUSE **3** : the power to think : INTELLECT **4** : a sane or sound mind **5** : due exercise of the faculty of logical thought

²reason vb **1** : to talk with another to cause a change of mind **2** : to use the faculty of reason : THINK **3** : to discover or formulate by the use of reason — **rea·son·er** n — **rea·son·ing** n

rea·son·able \'rēz-ᵊn-ə-bəl\ adj **1** : being within the bounds of reason : not extreme **2** : INEXPENSIVE **3** : able to reason : RATIONAL — **rea·son·able·ness** n — **rea·son·ably** \-blē\ adv

re·as·sure \ˌrē-ə-ˈshùr\ vb **1** : to assure again **2** : to restore confidence to : free from fear — **re·as·sur·ance** \-ˈshùr-əns\ n — **re·as·sur·ing·ly** adv

¹re·bate \'rē-ˌbāt\ vb **re·bat·ed; re·bat·ing** : to make or give a rebate

²rebate n : a return of part of a payment **syn** deduction, abatement, discount

³re·bate \'ra-bət, 'rē-ˌbāt\ chiefly Brit var of RABBET

¹reb·el \'re-bəl\ adj [ME, fr. OF rebelle, fr. L rebellis, fr. re- + bellum war] : of or relating to rebels

²rebel n : one that rebels against authority

³re·bel \ri-ˈbel\ vb **re·belled; re·bel·ling 1** : to resist the authority of one's government **2** : to act in or show disobedience **3** : to feel or exhibit anger or revulsion

re·bel·lion \ri-ˈbel-yən\ n : resistance to authority; esp : defiance against a government through uprising or revolt

re·bel·lious \-yəs\ adj **1** : given to or engaged in rebellion **2** : inclined to resist authority — **re·bel·lious·ly** adv — **re·bel·lious·ness** n

re·birth \ˌrē-ˈbərth\ n **1** : a new or 2d birth **2** : RENAISSANCE, REVIVAL

re·born \-ˈbórn\ adj : born again : REGENERATED, REVIVED

¹re·bound \ˌrē-ˈbaùnd, 'rē-ˌbaùnd\ vb **1** : to spring back on or as if on striking another body **2** : to recover from a setback or frustration

²re·bound \'rē-ˌbaùnd\ n **1** : the action of rebounding **2** : a rebounding ball **3** : a reaction to setback or frustration

re·buff \ri-ˈbəf\ vb : to reject or criticize sharply : SNUB — **rebuff** n

re·build \(ˌ)rē-ˈbild\ vb **-built** \-ˈbilt\; **-build·ing 1** : REPAIR, RECONSTRUCT; also : REMODEL **2** : to build again

¹re·buke \ri-ˈbyük\ vb **re·buked; re·buk·ing** : to reprimand sharply : REPROVE

²rebuke n : a sharp reprimand

re·bus \'rē-bəs\ n [L, by things, abl. pl. of res thing] : a representation of syllables or words by means of pictures; also : a riddle composed of such pictures

re·but \ri-ˈbət\ vb **re·but·ted; re·but·ting** : to refute esp. formally (as in debate) by evidence and arguments **syn** disprove, controvert, confute — **re·but·ter** n

re·but·tal \ri-ˈbət-ᵊl\ n : the act of rebutting

rec abbr **1** receipt **2** record; recording **3** recreation

re·cal·ci·trant \ri-ˈkal-sə-trənt\ adj [LL recalcitrant-, recalcitrans, prp. of recalcitrare to be stubbornly disobedient, fr. L, to kick back, fr. re- back, again + calcitrare to kick, fr. calc-, calx heel] **1** : stubbornly resisting authority **2** : resistant to handling or treatment **syn** refractory, headstrong, willful, unruly, ungovernable — **re·cal·ci·trance** \-trəns\ n

¹re·call \ri-ˈkól\ vb **1** : to call back **2** : REMEMBER, RECOLLECT **3** : REVOKE, CANCEL

²re·call \ri-ˈkól, 'rē-ˌkól\ n **1** : a summons to return **2** : the procedure of removing an official by popular vote **3** : remembrance of things learned or experienced **4** : the act of revoking **5** : a call by a manufacturer for the return of a product that may be defective or contaminated

re·cant \ri-ˈkant\ vb : to take back (something one has said) publicly : make an open confession of error — **re·can·ta·tion** \ˌrē-ˌkan-ˈtā-shən\ n

¹re·cap \'rē-ˌkap, rē-ˈkap\ vb **re·capped; re·cap·ping** : RECAPITULATE — **recap** \'rē-ˌkap\ n

²recap vb **re·capped; re·cap·ping** : RETREAD — **recap** \'rē-ˌkap\ n

re·ca·pit·u·late \ˌrē-kə-ˈpi-chə-ˌlāt\ vb **-lat·ed; -lat·ing** : to restate briefly : SUMMARIZE — **re·ca·pit·u·la·tion** \-ˌpi-chə-ˈlā-shən\ n

re·cap·ture \(ˌ)rē-ˈkap-chər\ vb **1** : to capture again **2** : to experience again ⟨∼ happy times⟩

re·cast \(ˌ)rē-ˈkast\ vb **1** : to cast again **2** : REVISE, REMODEL ⟨∼ a sentence⟩

recd abbr received

re·cede \ri-ˈsēd\ vb **re·ced·ed; re·ced·ing 1** : to move back or away **2** : to slant backward **3** : DIMINISH, CONTRACT

¹re·ceipt \ri-ˈsēt\ n **1** : RECIPE **2** : the act of receiving **3** : something received — usu. used in pl. **4** : a written acknowledgment of something received

²receipt vb **1** : to give a receipt for **2** : to mark as paid

re·ceiv·able \ri-ˈsē-və-bəl\ adj **1** : capable of being received; esp : acceptable as legal ⟨∼ certificates⟩ **2** : subject to call for payment ⟨notes ∼⟩

re·ceive \ri-ˈsēv\ vb **re·ceived; re·ceiv·ing 1** : to take in or accept (as something sent or paid) : come into possession of : GET **2** : CONTAIN, HOLD **3** : to permit to enter : GREET, WELCOME **4** : to be at home to visitors **5** : to accept as true or authoritative **6** : to be the subject of : UNDERGO, EXPERIENCE ⟨∼ a shock⟩ **7** : to change incoming radio waves into sounds or pictures

re·ceiv·er \ri-ˈsē-vər\ n **1** : one that receives **2** : a person legally appointed to receive and have charge of property or money involved in a lawsuit **3** : a device for converting electromagnetic waves or signals into audio or visual form ⟨telephone ∼⟩

re·ceiv·er·ship \-ˌship\ *n* **1** : the office or function of a receiver **2** : the condition of being in the hands of a receiver

re·cen·cy \ˈrēs-ᵊn-sē\ *n* : RECENTNESS

re·cent \ˈrēs-ᵊnt\ *adj* **1** : of the present time or time just past ⟨∼ history⟩ **2** : having lately come into existence : NEW, FRESH **3** *cap* : HOLOCENE — **re·cent·ly** *adv* — **re·cent·ness** *n*

re·cep·ta·cle \ri-ˈsep-ti-kəl\ *n* **1** : something used to receive and hold something else : CONTAINER **2** : the enlarged end of a flower stalk upon which the parts of the flower grow **3** : an electrical fitting containing the live parts of a circuit

re·cep·tion \ri-ˈsep-shən\ *n* **1** : the act of receiving **2** : a social gathering at which guests are formally welcomed

re·cep·tion·ist \ri-ˈsep-shə-nist\ *n* : a person employed to greet callers

re·cep·tive \ri-ˈsep-tiv\ *adj* : able or inclined to receive; *esp* : open and responsive to ideas, impressions, or suggestions — **re·cep·tive·ly** *adv* — **re·cep·tive·ness** *n* — **re·cep·tiv·i·ty** \ˌrē-ˌsep-ˈti-və-tē\ *n*

re·cep·tor \ri-ˈsep-tər\ *n* **1** : one that receives; *esp* : SENSE ORGAN **2** : a chemical group or molecule in the outer cell membrane or in the cell interior that has an affinity for a specific chemical group, molecule, or virus

¹re·cess \ˈrē-ˌses, ri-ˈses\ *n* **1** : a secret or secluded place **2** : an indentation in a line or surface (as an alcove in a room) **3** : a suspension of business or procedure for rest or relaxation

²recess *vb* **1** : to put into a recess **2** : to make a recess in **3** : to interrupt for a recess **4** : to take a recess

re·ces·sion \ri-ˈse-shən\ *n* **1** : the act of receding : WITHDRAWAL **2** : a departing procession (as at the end of a church service) **3** : a period of reduced economic activity

re·ces·sion·al \ri-ˈse-shə-nəl\ *n* **1** : a hymn or musical piece at the conclusion of a service or program **2** : RECESSION 2

¹re·ces·sive \ri-ˈse-siv\ *adj* **1** : tending to recede **2** : producing or being a bodily characteristic that is masked or not expressed when a contrasting dominant gene or trait is present ⟨∼ genes⟩ ⟨∼ traits⟩

²recessive *n* : a recessive characteristic or gene; *also* : an individual that has one or more recessive characteristics

re·cher·ché \rə-ˌsher-ˈshā, -ˈsheər-ˌshā\ *adj* [F] **1** : CHOICE, RARE **2** : excessively refined

re·cid·i·vism \ri-ˈsi-də-ˌvi-zəm\ *n* : a tendency to relapse into a previous condition; *esp* : relapse into criminal behavior — **re·cid·i·vist** \-vist\ *n*

recip *abbr* reciprocal; reciprocity

reci·pe \ˈre-sə-(ˌ)pē\ *n* [L, take, imperative of *recipere* to take, receive, fr. *re-* back + *capere* to take] **1** : a set of instructions for making something from various ingredients **2** : a method of procedure : FORMULA

re·cip·i·ent \ri-ˈsi-pē-ənt\ *n* : one that receives

¹re·cip·ro·cal \ri-ˈsi-prə-kəl\ *adj* **1** : inversely related **2** : MUTUAL, SHARED **3** : serving to reciprocate **4** : mutually corresponding — **re·cip·ro·cal·ly** *adv*

²reciprocal *n* **1** : something in a reciprocal relationship to another **2** : one of a pair of numbers (as ⅔, 3/2) whose product is one

re·cip·ro·cate \-ˌkāt\ *vb* **-cat·ed; -cat·ing** **1** : to move backward and forward alternately **2** : to give and take mutually **3** : to make a return for something done or given — **re·cip·ro·ca·tion** \-ˌsi-prə-ˈkā-shən\ *n*

rec·i·proc·i·ty \ˌre-sə-ˈprä-sə-tē\ *n, pl* **-ties** **1** : the quality or state of being reciprocal **2** : mutual exchange of privileges (as trade advantages between countries)

re·cit·al \ri-ˈsīt-ᵊl\ *n* **1** : an act or instance of reciting : ACCOUNT **2** : a public reading or recitation ⟨a poetry ∼⟩ **3** : a concert given by a musician, dancer, or

dance troupe **4** : a public exhibition of skill given by music or dance pupils — **re·cit·al·ist** \-ᵊl-ist\ *n*

rec·i·ta·tion \ˌre-sə-ˈtā-shən\ *n* **1** : RECITING, RECITAL **2** : delivery before an audience usu. of something memorized **3** : a classroom exercise in which pupils answer questions on a lesson they have studied

re·cite \ri-ˈsīt\ *vb* **re·cit·ed; re·cit·ing** **1** : to repeat verbatim (as something memorized) **2** : to recount in some detail : RELATE **3** : to reply to a teacher's questions on a lesson — **re·cit·er** *n*

reck·less \ˈre-kləs\ *adj* : lacking caution : RASH **syn** hasty, brash, hotheaded, thoughtless — **reck·less·ly** *adv* — **reck·less·ness** *n*

reck·on \ˈre-kən\ *vb* **1** : COUNT, CALCULATE, COMPUTE **2** : CONSIDER, REGARD **3** *chiefly dial* : THINK, SUPPOSE, GUESS

reck·on·ing *n* **1** : an act or instance of reckoning **2** : a settling of accounts ⟨day of ∼⟩

re·claim \ri-ˈklām\ *vb* **1** : to recall from wrong conduct : REFORM **2** : to change from an undesirable to a desired condition ⟨∼ marshy land⟩ **3** : to obtain from a waste product or by-product **4** : to demand or obtain the return of — **re·claim·able** *adj* — **rec·la·ma·tion** \ˌre-klə-ˈmā-shən\ *n*

re·cline \ri-ˈklīn\ *vb* **re·clined; re·clin·ing** **1** : to lean or incline backward **2** : to lie down : REST

re·clin·er \ri-ˈklī-nər\ *n* : a chair with an adjustable back and footrest

re·cluse \ˈre-ˌklüs, ri-ˈklüs\ *n* : a person who leads a secluded or solitary life : HERMIT

rec·og·ni·tion \ˌre-kəg-ˈni-shən\ *n* **1** : the act of recognizing : the state of being recognized : ACKNOWLEDGMENT **2** : special notice or attention

re·cog·ni·zance \ri-ˈkäg-nə-zəns\ *n* : a promise recorded before a court or magistrate to do something (as to appear in court or to keep the peace) usu. under penalty of a money forfeiture

rec·og·nize \ˈre-kəg-ˌnīz\ *vb* **-nized; -niz·ing** **1** : to acknowledge (as a speaker in a meeting) as one entitled to be heard at the time **2** : to acknowledge the existence or the independence of (a country or government) **3** : to take notice of **4** : to acknowledge with appreciation **5** : to acknowledge acquaintance with **6** : to identify as previously known **7** : to perceive clearly : REALIZE — **rec·og·niz·able** \ˈre-kəg-ˌnī-zə-bəl\ *adj* — **rec·og·niz·ably** \-blē\ *adv*

¹re·coil \ri-ˈkȯil\ *vb* **1** : to draw back : RETREAT **2** : to spring back to or as if to a starting point **syn** shrink, flinch, wince, quail, blanch

²re·coil \ˈrē-ˌkȯil, ri-ˈkȯil\ *n* : the action of recoiling (as by a gun or spring)

re·coil·less \-ˌkȯil-ləs, -ˈkȯil-\ *adj* : venting expanding propellant gas before recoil is produced ⟨∼ gun⟩

rec·ol·lect \ˌre-kə-ˈlekt\ *vb* : to recall to mind : REMEMBER **syn** recall, remind, reminisce, bethink

rec·ol·lec·tion \ˌre-kə-ˈlek-shən\ *n* **1** : the act or power of recollecting **2** : something recollected

re·com·bi·nant DNA \(ˌ)rē-ˈkäm-bə- nənt-\ *n* : genetically engineered DNA prepared in vitro by joining together DNA fragments usu. from more than one species of organism

rec·om·mend \ˌre-kə-ˈmend\ *vb* **1** : to present as deserving of acceptance or trial **2** : to give in charge : COMMIT **3** : to make acceptable **4** : ADVISE, COUNSEL — **rec·om·mend·able** \-ˈmen-də-bəl\ *adj*

rec·om·men·da·tion \ˌre-kə-mən-ˈdā- shən\ *n* **1** : the act of recommending **2** : something recommended **3** : something that recommends

¹rec·om·pense \ˈre-kəm-ˌpens\ *vb* **-pensed; -pens·ing** **1** : to give compensation to : pay for **2** : to return in kind : REQUITE **syn** reimburse, indemnify, repay, compensate

²recompense *n* : COMPENSATION

rec·on·cile \ˈre-kən-ˌsīl\ *vb* **-ciled; -cil·ing** **1** : to cause to be friendly or harmonious again **2** : ADJUST, SETTLE ⟨∼ differences⟩ **3** : to bring to submission or acceptance **syn** conform, accommodate, harmonize, coordinate — **rec·on·cil·able** *adj* — **rec·on·cile·ment** *n* — **rec·on·cil·er** *n*

rec·on·cil·i·a·tion \re-kən-ˌsi-lē-ˈā-shən\ *n* **1** : the action of reconciling **2** : the Roman Catholic sacrament of penance

re·con·dite \ˈre-kən-ˌdīt\ *adj* **1** : hard to understand : PROFOUND, ABSTRUSE **2** : little known : OBSCURE

re·con·di·tion \ˌrē-kən-ˈdi-shən\ *vb* **1** : to restore to good condition (as by replacing parts) **2** : to condition anew

re·con·nais·sance \ri-ˈkä-nə-zəns, -səns\ *n* [F, lit., recognition] : a preliminary survey of an area; *esp* : an exploratory military survey of enemy territory

re·con·noi·ter *or* **re·con·noi·tre** \ˌrē-kə-ˈnȯi-tər, ˌre-\ *vb* **-noi·tered** *or* **-noi·tred; -noi·ter·ing** *or* **-noi·tring** : to make a reconnaissance of : engage in reconnaissance

re·con·sid·er \ˌrē-kən-ˈsi-dər\ *vb* : to consider again with a view to changing or reversing — **re·con·sid·er·a·tion** \-ˌsi-də-ˈrā-shən\ *n*

re·con·sti·tute \ˌrē-ˈkän-stə-ˌtüt, -ˌtyüt\ *vb* : to restore to a former condition by adding water (⟨∼ powdered milk⟩

re·con·struct \ˌrē-kən-ˈstrəkt\ *vb* : to construct again : REBUILD

re·con·struc·tion \ˌrē-kən-ˈstrək-shən\ *n* **1** : the action of reconstructing : the state of being reconstructed **2** *often cap* : the reorganization and reestablishment of the seceded states in the Union after the American Civil War **3** : something reconstructed

¹**re·cord** \ri-ˈkȯrd\ *vb* **1** : to set down in writing **2** : to register permanently **3** : INDICATE, READ **4** : to give evidence of **5** : to cause (as sound or visual images) to be registered (as on magnetic tape) in a form that permits reproduction

²**rec·ord** \ˈre-kərd\ *n* **1** : the act of being recorded **2** : a written account of proceedings **3** : known facts about a person; *also* : a collection of items of information (as in a database) treated as a unit **4** : an attested top performance **5** : something on which sound or visual images have been recorded

re·cord·er \ri-ˈkȯr-dər\ *n* **1** : a judge in some city courts **2** : one who records transactions officially **3** : a recording device **4** : a wind instrument with a whistle mouthpiece and eight fingerholes

re·cord·ing *n* : RECORD 5

re·cord·ist \ri-ˈkȯr-dist\ *n* : one who records sound esp. on film

¹**re·count** \ri-ˈkau̇nt\ *vb* : to relate in detail : TELL **syn** recite, rehearse, narrate, describe, state, report

²**re·count** \ˈrē-ˌkau̇nt, (ˌ)rē-ˈkau̇nt\ *vb* : to count again

³**re·count** \ˈrē-ˌkau̇nt, (ˌ)rē-ˈkau̇nt\ *n* : a second or fresh count

re·coup \ri-ˈküp\ *vb* : to get an equivalent or compensation for : make up for something lost

re·course \ˈrē-ˌkȯrs, ri-ˈkȯrs\ *n* **1** : a turning to someone or something for assistance or protection **2** : a source of aid : RESORT

re·cov·er \ri-ˈkə-vər\ *vb* **-ered; -er·ing 1** : to get back again : REGAIN, RETRIEVE **2** : to regain normal health, poise, or status **3** : to make up for : RECOUP ⟨∼ed all his losses⟩ **4** : RECLAIM ⟨∼ land from the sea⟩ **5** : to obtain a legal judgment in one's favor — **re·cov·er·able** *adj* — **re·cov·ery** \-ˈkə-və-rē\ *n*

re–cov·er \ˌrē-ˈkə-vər\ *vb* : to cover again

¹**rec·re·ant** \ˈre-krē-ənt\ *adj* [ME, fr. MF, fr. prp. of *recroire* to renounce one's cause in a trial by battle, fr. *re-* back + *croire* to believe, fr. L *credere*] **1** : COWARDLY **2** : UNFAITHFUL

²**recreant** *n* **1** : COWARD **2** : DESERTER

rec·re·ate \ˈre-krē-ˌāt\ *vb* **-at·ed; -at·ing 1** : to give new life or freshness to **2** : to take recreation — **rec·re·ative** \-ˌā-tiv\ *adj*

re–cre·ate \ˌrē-krē-ˈāt\ *vb* : to create again — **re–cre·ation** \-ˈā-shən\ *n* — **re–cre·ative** \-ˈā-tiv\ *adj*

rec·re·ation \ˌre-krē-ˈā-shən\ *n* : a refreshing of strength or spirits after work; *also* : a means of refreshment **syn** diversion, entertainment, amusement — **rec·re·ation·al** \-shə-nəl\ *adj*

recreational vehicle *n* : a vehicle designed for recreational use (as camping)

re·crim·i·na·tion \ri-ˌkri-mə-ˈnā-shən\ *n* : a retaliatory accusation — **re·crim·i·nate** \-ˈkri-mə-ˌnāt\ *vb* — **re·crim·i·na·tory** \-ˈkri-mə-nə-ˌtȯr-ē\ *adj*

re·cru·des·cence \ˌrē-krü-ˈdes-ᵊns\ *n* : a renewal or breaking out again esp. of something unhealthful or dangerous

¹**re·cruit** \ri-ˈkrüt\ *vb* **1** : to form or strengthen with new members ⟨∼ an army⟩ **2** : to enlist as a member of an armed service **3** : to secure the services of **4** : to seek to enroll **5** : to restore or increase in health or vigor ⟨resting to ∼ his strength⟩ — **re·cruit·er** *n* — **re·cruit·ment** *n*

²**recruit** *n* [F *recrute, recrue* fresh growth, new levy of soldiers, fr. MF, fr. *recroistre* to grow up again, fr. L *recrescere*] : a newcomer to an activity or field; *esp* : a newly enlisted member of the armed forces

rec sec *abbr* recording secretary

rect *abbr* **1** receipt **2** rectangle; rectangular **3** rectified

rec·tal \ˈrekt-ᵊl\ *adj* : of or relating to the rectum — **rec·tal·ly** *adv*

rect·an·gle \ˈrek-ˌtaŋ-gəl\ *n* : a 4-sided figure with four right angles; *esp* : one with adjacent sides of unequal length — **rect·an·gu·lar** \rek-ˈtaŋ-gyə-lər\ *adj*

rec·ti·fi·er \ˈrek-tə-ˌfī-ər\ *n* : one that rectifies; *esp* : a device for converting alternating current into direct current

rec·ti·fy \ˈrek-tə-ˌfī\ *vb* **-fied; -fy·ing** : to make or set right : CORRECT **syn** emend, amend, mend, right — **rec·ti·fi·ca·tion** \ˌrek-tə-fə-ˈkā-shən\ *n*

rec·ti·lin·ear \ˌrek-tə-ˈli-nē-ər\ *adj* **1** : moving in a straight line ⟨∼ motion⟩ **2** : characterized by straight lines

rec·ti·tude \ˈrek-tə-ˌtüd, -ˌtyüd\ *n* **1** : moral integrity **2** : correctness of procedure **syn** virtue, goodness, morality, probity

rec·to \ˈrek-tō\ *n, pl* **rectos** : a right-hand page

rec·tor \ˈrek-tər\ *n* **1** : a priest or minister in charge of a parish **2** : the head of a university or school — **rec·to·ri·al** \rek-ˈtȯr-ē-əl\ *adj*

rec·to·ry \ˈrek-tə-rē\ *n, pl* **-ries** : the residence of a rector or a parish priest

rec·tum \ˈrek-təm\ *n, pl* **rectums** *or* **rec·ta** \-tə\ [ME, fr. ML, fr. *rectum intestinum*, lit., straight intestine] : the last part of the intestine joining the colon and anus

re·cum·bent \ri-ˈkəm-bənt\ *adj* : lying down : RECLINING

re·cu·per·ate \ri-ˈkü-pə-ˌrāt-, -ˈkyü-\ *vb* **-at·ed; -at·ing** : to get back (as health or strength) : RECOVER — **re·cu·per·a·tion** \-ˌkü-pə-ˈrā-shən, -ˌkyü-\ *n* — **re·cu·per·a·tive** \-ˈkü-pə-ˌrā-tiv, -ˈkyü-\ *adj*

re·cur \ri-ˈkər\ *vb* **re·curred; re·cur·ring 1** : to go or come back in thought or discussion **2** : to occur or appear again esp. after an interval : occur time after time — **re·cur·rence** \-ˈkər-əns\ *n* — **re·cur·rent** \-ənt\ *adj*

re·cy·cle \rē-ˈsī-kəl\ *vb* **1** : to pass again through a cycle of changes or treatment **2** : to process (as liquid body waste, glass, or cans) in order to regain materials for human use — **re·cy·cla·ble** \-k(ə)lə-bəl\ *adj* — **recycle** *n*

¹**red** \ˈred\ *adj* **red·der; red·dest 1** : of the color red **2** : endorsing radical social or political change esp. by force **3** *often cap* : of or relating to the former U.S.S.R. or its allies — **red·ly** *adv* — **red·ness** *n*

²**red** *n* **1** : the color of blood or of the ruby **2** : a revolutionary in politics **3** *cap* : COMMUNIST **4** : the condition of showing a loss ⟨in the ∼⟩

re·dact \ri-ˈdakt\ *vb* **1** : to put in writing : FRAME **2** : EDIT — **re·dac·tor** \-ˈdak-tər\ *n*

re·dac·tion \-'dak-shən\ *n* **1** : an act or instance of re-dacting **2** : EDITION

red alga *n* : any of a group of reddish usu. marine algae

red blood cell *n* : any of the hemoglobin-containing cells that carry oxygen from the lungs to the tissues and are responsible for the red color of vertebrate blood

red·breast \'red-ˌbrest\ *n* : ROBIN

red–carpet *adj* : marked by ceremonial courtesy

red cedar *n* : an American juniper with fragrant close=grained red wood; *also* : its wood

red clover *n* : a Eurasian clover with globe-shaped heads of reddish flowers widely cultivated for hay and forage

red·coat \'red-ˌkōt\ *n* : a British soldier esp. during the Revolutionary War

red·den \'red-ᵊn\ *vb* : to make or become red or red-dish : FLUSH, BLUSH

red·dish \'re-dish\ *adj* : tinged with red — **red·dish·ness** *n*

re·deem \ri-'dēm\ *vb* [ME *redemen*, modif. of MF *red-imer*, fr. L *redimere*, fr. *re-*, *red-* re- + *emere* to take, buy] **1** : to recover (property) by discharging an ob-ligation **2** : to ransom, free, or rescue by paying a price **3** : to free from the consequences of sin **4** : to remove the obligation of by payment ⟨the govern-ment ~s savings bonds⟩; *also* : to convert into some-thing of value **5** : to make good (a promise) by performing : FULFILL **6** : to atone for — **re·deem·able** *adj* — **re·deem·er** *n*

re·demp·tion \ri-'demp-shən\ *n* : the act of redeeming : the state of being redeemed — **re·demp·tive** \-tiv\ *adj* — **re·demp·to·ry** \-tə-rē\ *adj*

re·de·ploy \ˌrē-di-'plȯi\ *vb* **1** : to transfer from one area or activity to another **2** : to relocate men or equipment — **re·de·ploy·ment** *n*

red–eye \'red-ˌī\ *n* **1** : cheap whiskey **2** : a late night or overnight flight

red fox *n* : a fox with orange-red to reddish brown fur

red fox

red giant *n* : a very large star with a relatively low sur-face temperature

red–hand·ed \'red-'han-dəd\ *adv or adj* : in the act of committing a misdeed

red·head \-ˌhed\ *n* : a person having red hair — **red-head·ed** \-ˌhe-dəd\ *adj*

red herring *n* : a diversion intended to distract atten-tion from the real issue

red–hot \'red-'hät\ *adj* **1** : extremely hot; *esp* : glow-ing with heat **2** : EXCITED, FURIOUS **3** : very new ⟨~ news⟩

re·dial \'rē-ˌdīl\ *n* : a telephone function that automat-ically repeats the dialing of the last number called — **redial** *vb*

re·dis·trib·ute \ˌrē-də-'stri-byüt\ *vb* **1** : to alter the dis-tribution of **2** : to spread to other areas — **re·dis·tri·bu·tion** \(ˌ)rē-dis-trə-'byü-shən\ *n*

re·dis·trict \ˌrē-'dis-(ˌ)trikt\ *vb* : to organize into new territorial and esp. political divisions

red–let·ter \'red-ˌle-tər\ *adj* : of special significance : MEMORABLE

red–light district *n* : a district with many houses of prostitution

re·do \(ˌ)rē-'dü\ *vb* : to do over or again; *esp* : REDEC-ORATE

red oak *n* : any of numerous American oaks with leaves usu. having spiny-tipped lobes and acorns that take two years to mature; *also* : the wood of a red oak

red·o·lent \'red-ᵊl-ənt\ *adj* **1** : FRAGRANT, AROMATIC **2** : having a specified fragrance ⟨a room ~ of cooked cabbage⟩ **3** : REMINISCENT, SUGGESTIVE — **red·o·lence** \-əns\ *n* — **red·o·lent·ly** *adv*

re·dou·ble \(ˌ)rē-'də-bəl\ *vb* : to make twice as great in size or amount; *also* : INTENSIFY

re·doubt \ri-'daùt\ *n* [F *redoute*, fr. It *ridotto*, fr. ML *reductus* secret place, fr. L, withdrawn, fr. *reducere* to lead back, fr. *re-* back + *ducere* to lead] : a small usu. temporary fortification

re·doubt·able \ri-'daù-tə-bəl\ *adj* [ME *redoutable*, fr. MF, fr. *redouter* to dread, fr. *re-* re- + *douter* to doubt] : arousing dread or fear : FORMIDABLE

re·dound \ri-'daùnd\ *vb* **1** : to have an effect **2** : to be-come added or transferred : ACCRUE

red pepper *n* : CAYENNE PEPPER

¹re·dress \ri-'dres\ *vb* **1** : to set right : REMEDY **2** : COM-PENSATE **3** : to remove the cause of (a grievance) **4** : AVENGE

²re·dress *n* **1** : relief from distress **2** : means or possi-bility of seeking a remedy **3** : compensation for loss or injury **4** : an act or instance of redressing

red·shift \'red-ˌshift\ *n* : displacement of the spectrum of a heavenly body toward longer wavelength

red snapper *n* : any of various reddish fishes including several food fishes

red spider *n* : SPIDER MITE

red squirrel *n* : a common American squirrel with the upper parts chiefly red

red–tailed hawk \'red-ˌtāld-\ *n* : a common rodent=eating hawk of eastern No. America with a rather short typically reddish tail

red tape *n* [fr. the red tape formerly used to bind legal documents in England] : official routine or procedure marked by excessive complexity which results in de-lay or inaction

red tide *n* : seawater discolored by the presence of large numbers of dinoflagellates which produce a tox-in that renders infected shellfish poisonous

re·duce \ri-'düs, -'dyüs\ *vb* **re·duced; re·duc·ing 1** : LESSEN **2** : to bring to a specified state or condition ⟨*reduced* them to tears⟩ **3** : to put in a lower rank or grade **4** : CONQUER ⟨~ a fort⟩ **5** : to bring into a cer-tain order or classification **6** : to correct (as a fracture) by restoration of displaced parts **7** : to less-en one's weight **syn** decrease, diminish, abate, dwin-dle, recede — **re·duc·er** *n* — **re·duc·ible** \-'dü-sə-bəl, -'dyü-\ *adj*

re·duc·tion \ri-'dək-shən\ *n* **1** : the act of reducing : the state of being reduced **2** : something made by reduc-ing **3** : the amount taken off in reducing something

re·dun·dan·cy \ri-'dən-dən-sē\ *n, pl* **-cies 1** : the qual-ity or state of being redundant : SUPERFLUITY **2** : something redundant or in excess **3** : the use of sur-plus words

re·dun·dant \-dənt\ *adj* : exceeding what is needed or normal : SUPERFLUOUS; *esp* : using more words than necessary — **re·dun·dant·ly** *adv*

red–winged blackbird \'red-ˌwiŋd-\ *n* : a No. Amer-ican blackbird of which the adult male is black with a patch of bright scarlet on the wings

red·wood \'red-ˌwùd\ *n* : a tall coniferous timber tree esp. of coastal California; *also* : its durable wood

reed \'rēd\ *n* **1** : any of various tall slender grasses of wet areas; *also* : a stem or growth of reed **2** : a mu-sical instrument made from the hollow stem of a reed **3** : an elastic tongue of cane, wood, or metal by which tones are produced in organ pipes and certain other wind instruments — **reedy** *adj*

re·ed·u·cate \(ˌ)rē-'e-jə-ˌkāt\ *vb* : to train again; *esp*

: to rehabilitate through education — **re·ed·u·ca·tion** *n*

¹reef \\ˈrēf\\ *n* **1** : a part of a sail taken in or let out in regulating the sail's size **2** : reduction in sail area by reefing

²reef *vb* : to reduce the area of a sail by rolling or folding part of it

³reef *n* : a ridge of rocks, sand or coral at or near the surface of the water

reef·er \\ˈrē-fər\\ *n* : a marijuana cigarette

¹reek \\ˈrēk\\ *n* : a strong or disagreeable fume or odor

²reek *vb* **1** : to give off or become permeated with a strong or offensive odor **2** : to give a strong impression of some constituent quality ⟨an excuse that ∼ed of falsehood⟩ — **reek·er** *n* — **reeky** \\ˈrē-kē\\ *adj*

¹reel \\ˈrēl\\ *n* : a revolvable device on which something flexible (as film or tape) is wound; *also* : a quantity of something wound on such a device

²reel *vb* **1** : to wind on or as if on a reel **2** : to pull or draw (as a fish) by reeling a line — **reel·able** *adj* — **reel·er** *n*

³reel *vb* **1** : WHIRL; *also* : to be giddy **2** : to waver or fall back (as from a blow) **3** : to walk or move unsteadily

⁴reel *n* : a reeling motion

⁵reel *n* : a lively Scottish dance or its music

reel off *vb* : to tell or recite rapidly and easily ⟨*reeled off* the right answers⟩

re·en·try \\rē-ˈen-trē\\ *n* **1** : a second or new entry **2** : the action of reentering the earth's atmosphere from space

reeve \\ˈrēv\\ *vb* **rove** \\ˈrōv\\ *or* **reeved; reev·ing** : to pass (as a rope) through a hole in a block or cleat

¹ref \\ˈref\\ *vb* & *n* : REFEREE 2

²ref *abbr* **1** reference **2** referred **3** reformed **4** refunding

re·fec·tion \\ri-ˈfek-shən\\ *n* **1** : refreshment esp. after hunger or fatigue **2** : food and drink together : REPAST

re·fec·to·ry \\ri-ˈfek-tə-rē\\ *n, pl* **-ries** : a dining hall (as in a monastery or college)

re·fer \\ri-ˈfər\\ *vb* **referred; re·fer·ring** **1** : to assign to a certain source, cause, or relationship **2** : to direct or send to some person or place (as for information or help) **3** : to submit to someone else for consideration or action **4** : to have recourse (as for information or aid) **5** : to have connection : RELATE **6** : to direct attention : speak of : MENTION, ALLUDE **syn** recur, repair, resort, apply, go, turn — **re·fer·able** \\ˈre-fə-rə-bəl, ri-ˈfər-ə-\\ *adj*

¹ref·er·ee \\ˌre-fə-ˈrē\\ *n* **1** : a person to whom an issue esp. in law is referred for investigation or settlement **2** : an umpire in certain games

²referee *vb* **-eed; -ee·ing** : to act as referee

ref·er·ence \\ˈre-frəns, -fə-rəns\\ *n* **1** : the act of referring **2** : RELATION, RESPECT **3** : ALLUSION, MENTION **4** : something that refers a reader to another passage or book **5** : consultation esp. for obtaining information ⟨books for ∼⟩ **6** : a person of whom inquiries as to character or ability can be made **7** : a written recommendation of a person for employment

ref·er·en·dum \\ˌre-fə-ˈren-dəm\\ *n, pl* **-da** \\-də\\ *or* **-dums** : the submitting of legislative measures to the voters for approval or rejection; *also* : a vote on a measure so submitted

ref·er·ent \\ˈre-frənt, -fə-rənt\\ *n* : one that refers or is referred to; *esp* : the thing a word stands for — **referent** *adj*

re·fer·ral \\ri-ˈfər-əl\\ *n* **1** : the act or an instance of referring **2** : one that is referred

¹re·fill \\ˌrē-ˈfil\\ *vb* : to fill again : REPLENISH — **re·fill·able** *adj*

²re·fill \\ˈrē-ˌfil\\ *n* : a new or fresh supply of something

re·fi·nance \\ˌrē-fə-ˈnans, (ˌ)rē-ˈfī-nans\\ *vb* : to renew or reorganize the financing of

re·fine \\ri-ˈfīn\\ *vb* **re·fined; re·fin·ing** **1** : to free from impurities or waste matter **2** : IMPROVE, PERFECT **3** : to free or become free of what is coarse or uncouth

4 : to make improvements by introducing subtle changes — **re·fin·er** *n*

re·fined \\ri-ˈfīnd\\ *adj* **1** : freed from impurities **2** : CULTURED, CULTIVATED **3** : SUBTLE

re·fine·ment \\ri-ˈfīn-mənt\\ *n* **1** : the action of refining **2** : the quality or state of being refined **3** : a refined feature or method; *also* : something intended to improve or perfect

re·fin·ery \\ri-ˈfī-nə-rē\\ *n, pl* **-er·ies** : a building and equipment for refining metals, oil, or sugar

refl *abbr* reflex; reflexive

re·flect \\ri-ˈflekt\\ *vb* [ME, fr. L *reflectere* to bend back, fr. *re-* back + *flectere* to bend] **1** : to bend or cast back (as light, heat, or sound) **2** : to give back a likeness or image of as a mirror does **3** : to bring as a result ⟨∼ed credit on him⟩ **4** : to cast reproach or blame ⟨their bad conduct ∼ed on their training⟩ **5** : PONDER, MEDITATE — **re·flec·tion** \\-ˈflek-shən\\ *n* — **re·flec·tive** \\-tiv\\ *adj* — **re·flec·tiv·i·ty** \\(ˌ)rē-ˌflek-ˈti-və-tē\\ *n*

re·flec·tor \\ri-ˈflek-tər\\ *n* : one that reflects; *esp* : a polished surface for reflecting radiation (as light)

¹re·flex \\ˈrē-ˌfleks\\ *n* **1** : an automatic and usu. inborn response to a stimulus not involving higher mental centers **2** *pl* : the power of acting or responding with enough speed ⟨an athlete with great ∼es⟩

²reflex *adj* **1** : bent or directed back **2** : of, relating to, or produced by a reflex — **re·flex·ly** *adv*

re·flex·ion *chiefly Brit var of* REFLECTION

¹re·flex·ive \\ri-ˈflek-siv\\ *adj* : of or relating to an action directed back upon the doer or the grammatical subject ⟨a ∼ verb⟩ ⟨the ∼ pronoun *himself*⟩ — **re·flex·ive·ly** *adv* — **re·flex·ive·ness** *n*

²reflexive *n* : a reflexive verb or pronoun

re·fo·cus \\(ˌ)rē-ˈfō-kəs\\ *vb* **1** : to focus again **2** : to change the emphasis or direction of ⟨∼ed her life⟩

re·for·es·ta·tion \\ˌrē-ˌfȯr-ə-ˈstā-shən\\ *n* : the action of renewing forest cover by planting seeds or young trees — **re·for·est** \\rē-ˈfȯr-əst\\ *vb*

¹re·form \\ri-ˈfȯrm\\ *vb* **1** : to make better or improve by removal of faults **2** : to correct or improve one's own character or habits **syn** correct, rectify, emend, remedy, redress, revise — **re·form·able** *adj* — **re·for·ma·tive** \\-ˈfȯr-mə-tiv\\ *adj*

²reform *n* : improvement or correction of what is corrupt or defective

re–form \\ˌrē-ˈfȯrm\\ *vb* : to form again

ref·or·ma·tion \\ˌre-fər-ˈmā-shən\\ *n* **1** : the act of reforming : the state of being reformed **2** *cap* : a 16th century religious movement marked by the establishment of the Protestant churches

¹re·for·ma·to·ry \\ri-ˈfȯr-mə-ˌtōr-ē\\ *adj* : aiming at or tending toward reformation : REFORMATIVE

²reformatory *n, pl* **-ries** : a penal institution for reforming esp. young or first offenders

re·form·er \\ri-ˈfȯr-mər\\ *n* **1** : one that works for or urges reform **2** *cap* : a leader of the Protestant Reformation

refr *abbr* refraction

re·fract \\ri-ˈfrakt\\ *vb* [L *refractus*, pp. of *refringere* to break open, break up, fr. *re-* back + *frangere* to break] : to subject to refraction

re·frac·tion \\ri-ˈfrak-shən\\ *n* : the bending of a ray (as of light) when it passes obliquely from one medium into another in which its speed is different — **re·frac·tive** \\-tiv\\ *adj*

re·frac·to·ry \\ri-ˈfrak-tə-rē\\ *adj* **1** : OBSTINATE, STUBBORN, UNMANAGEABLE **2** : capable of enduring high temperature ⟨∼ bricks⟩ **syn** recalcitrant, intractable, ungovernable, unruly, headstrong, willful — **re·frac·to·ri·ness** \\ri-ˈfrak-tə-rē-nəs\\ *n* — **refractory** *n*

¹re·frain \\ri-ˈfrān\\ *vb* : to hold oneself back : FORBEAR — **re·frain·ment** *n*

²refrain *n* : a phrase or verse recurring regularly in a poem or song

re·fresh \\ri-ˈfresh\\ *vb* **1** : to make or become fresh or fresher **2** : to revive by or as if by renewal of supplies ⟨∼ one's memory⟩ **3** : to freshen up **4** : to supply or take refreshment **syn** restore, rejuvenate, renovate, refurbish — **re·fresh·er** *n* — **re·fresh·ing·ly** *adv*

re·fresh·ment \-mənt\ *n* **1** : the act of refreshing : the state of being refreshed **2** : something that refreshes **3** *pl* : a light meal; *also* : assorted light foods

re·fried beans \'rē-ˌfrīd-\ *n pl* : beans cooked with seasonings, fried, then mashed and fried again

refrig *abbr* refrigerating; refrigeration

re·frig·er·ate \ri-'fri-jə-ˌrāt\ *vb* **-at·ed; -at·ing** : to make cool; *esp* : to chill or freeze (food) for preservation — **re·frig·er·ant** \-jə-rənt\ *adj or n* — **re·frig·er·a·tion** \-ˌfri-jə-'rā-shən\ *n* — **re·frig·er·a·tor** \-'fri-jə-ˌrā-tər\ *n*

ref·uge \'re-ˌfyüj\ *n* **1** : shelter or protection from danger or distress **2** : a place that provides protection

ref·u·gee \ˌre-fyu-'jē\ *n* : one who flees for safety esp. to a foreign country

re·ful·gence \ri-'ful-jəns, -'fəl-\ *n* : a radiant or resplendent quality or state — **re·ful·gent** \-jənt\ *adj*

¹re·fund \ri-'fənd, 'rē-ˌfənd\ *vb* : to give or put back (money) : REPAY — **re·fund·able** *adj*

²re·fund \'rē-ˌfənd\ *n* **1** : the act of refunding **2** : a sum refunded

re·fur·bish \ri-'fər-bish\ *vb* : to brighten or freshen up : RENOVATE

¹re·fuse \ri-'fyüz\ *vb* **re·fused; re·fus·ing** **1** : to decline to accept : REJECT **2** : to decline to do, give, or grant : DENY — **re·fus·al** \-'fyü-zəl\ *n*

²ref·use \'re-ˌfyüs, -ˌfyüz\ *n* : rejected or worthless matter : RUBBISH, TRASH

re·fute \ri-'fyüt\ *vb* **re·fut·ed; re·fut·ing** [L *refutare* to check, suppress, refute] : to prove to be false by argument or evidence — **ref·u·ta·tion** \ˌre-fyu-'tā-shən\ *n* — **re·fut·er** *n*

¹reg \'reg\ *n* : REGULATION

²reg *abbr* **1** region **2** register; registered; registration **3** regular

re·gal \'rē-gəl\ *adj* **1** : of, relating to, or befitting a king : ROYAL **2** : STATELY, SPLENDID — **re·gal·ly** *adv*

re·gale \ri-'gāl\ *vb* **re·galed; re·gal·ing** **1** : to entertain richly or agreeably **2** : to give pleasure or amusement to **syn** gratify, delight, please, rejoice, gladden

re·ga·lia \ri-'gāl-yə\ *n pl* **1** : the emblems, symbols, or paraphernalia of royalty (as the crown and scepter) **2** : the insignia of an office or order **3** : special costume : FINERY

¹re·gard \ri-'gärd\ *n* **1** : CONSIDERATION, HEED; *also* : CARE, CONCERN **2** : GAZE, GLANCE, LOOK **3** : RESPECT, ESTEEM **4** *pl* : friendly greetings implying respect and esteem **5** : an aspect to be considered : PARTICULAR — **re·gard·ful** *adj* — **re·gard·less** *adj*

²regard *vb* **1** : to think of : CONSIDER **2** : to pay attention to **3** : to show respect for : HEED **4** : to hold in high esteem : care for **5** : to look at : gaze upon **6** *archaic* : to relate to

re·gard·ing *prep* : CONCERNING

regardless of \ri-'gärd-ləs-\ *prep* : in spite of

re·gat·ta \ri-'gä-tə, -'ga-\ *n* : a boat race or a series of boat races

regd *abbr* registered

re·gen·cy \'rē-jən-sē\ *n, pl* **-cies** **1** : the office or government of a regent or body of regents **2** : a body of regents **3** : the period during which a regent governs

re·gen·er·a·cy \ri-'je-nə-rə-sē\ *n* : the state of being regenerated

¹re·gen·er·ate \ri-'je-nə-rət\ *adj* **1** : formed or created again **2** : spiritually reborn or converted

²re·gen·er·ate \ri-'je-nə-ˌrāt\ *vb* **1** : to subject to spiritual renewal **2** : to reform completely **3** : to replace (a body part) by a new growth of tissue **4** : to give new life to : REVIVE — **re·gen·er·a·tion** \-ˌje-nə-'rā-shən\ *n* — **re·gen·er·a·tive** \-'je-nə-ˌrā-tiv\ *adj* — **re·gen·er·a·tor** \-ˌrā-tər\ *n*

re·gent \'rē-jənt\ *n* **1** : a person who rules during the childhood, absence, or incapacity of the sovereign **2** : a member of a governing board (as of a state university) — **regent** *adj*

reg·gae \'re-ˌgā\ *n* : popular music of Jamaican origin that combines native styles with elements of rock and soul music

reg·i·cide \'re-jə-ˌsīd\ *n* **1** : one who murders a king **2** : murder of a king

re·gime *also* **ré·gime** \rā-'zhēm, ri-\ *n* **1** : REGIMEN **2** : a form or system of government **3** : a government in power; *also* : a period of rule

reg·i·men \'re-jə-mən\ *n* **1** : a systematic course of treatment or training ⟨a strict dietary ∼⟩ **2** : GOVERNMENT

¹reg·i·ment \'re-jə-mənt\ *n* : a military unit consisting usu. of a number of battalions — **reg·i·men·tal** \ˌre-jə-'ment-təl\ *adj*

²reg·i·ment \'re-jə-ˌment\ *vb* : to organize rigidly esp. for regulation or central control; *also* : to subject to order or uniformity — **reg·i·men·ta·tion** \ˌre-jə-mən-'tā-shən\ *n*

reg·i·men·tals \ˌre-jə-'men-təlz\ *n pl* **1** : a regimental uniform **2** : military dress

re·gion \'rē-jən\ *n* [ME, fr. MF, fr. L *region-, regio,* fr. *regere* to rule] : an often indefinitely defined part or area

re·gion·al \'rē-jə-nəl\ *adj* **1** : affecting a particular region : LOCALIZED **2** : of, relating to, characteristic of, or serving a region — **re·gion·al·ly** *adv*

¹reg·is·ter \'re-jə-stər\ *n* **1** : a record of items or details; *also* : a book or system for keeping such a record **2** : the range of a voice or instrument **3** : a device to regulate ventilation or heating **4** : an automatic device recording a number or quantity

²register *vb* **-tered; -ter·ing** **1** : to enter in a register (as in a list of guests) **2** : to record automatically **3** : to secure special care for (mail matter) by paying additional postage **4** : to convey an impression of : EXPRESS **5** : to make or adjust so as to correspond exactly

registered nurse *n* : a graduate trained nurse who has been licensed to practice by a state authority after passing qualifying examinations

reg·is·trant \'re-jə-strənt\ *n* : one that registers or is registered

reg·is·trar \-ˌsträr\ *n* : an official recorder or keeper of records (as at an educational institution)

reg·is·tra·tion \ˌre-jə-'strā-shən\ *n* **1** : the act of registering **2** : an entry in a register **3** : the number of persons registered : ENROLLMENT **4** : a document certifying an act of registering

reg·is·try \'re-jə-strē\ *n, pl* **-tries** **1** : ENROLLMENT, REGISTRATION **2** : a place of registration **3** : an official record book or an entry in one

reg·nant \'reg-nənt\ *adj* **1** : REIGNING **2** : DOMINANT **3** : of common or widespread occurrence

¹re·gress \'rē-ˌgres\ *n* **1** : an act or the privilege of going or coming back **2** : RETROGRESSION

²re·gress \ri-'gres\ *vb* : to go or cause to go back or to a lower level — **re·gres·sive** *adj* — **re·gres·sor** \-'gre-sər\ *n*

re·gres·sion \ri-'gre-shən\ *n* : the act or an instance of regressing; *esp* : reversion to an earlier mental or behavioral level

¹re·gret \ri-'gret\ *vb* **re·gret·ted; re·gret·ting** **1** : to mourn the loss or death of **2** : to be very sorry for **3** : to experience regret — **re·gret·ta·ble** \-'gre-tə-bəl\ *adj* — **re·gret·ter** *n*

²regret *n* **1** : sorrow caused by something beyond one's power to remedy **2** : an expression of sorrow **3** *pl* : a note politely declining an invitation — **re·gret·ful** \-fəl\ *adj* — **re·gret·ful·ly** *adv*

re·gret·ta·bly \-'gre-tə-blē\ *adv* **1** : to a regrettable extent **2** : it is to be regretted

re·group \(ˌ)rē-'grüp\ *vb* : to form into a new grouping

regt *abbr* regiment

¹reg·u·lar \'re-gyə-lər\ adj [ME reguler, fr. MF, fr. LL regularis regular, fr L, of a bar, fr. regula rule, straightedge, fr. regere to keep straight, rule] **1** : belonging to a religious order **2** : made, built, or arranged according to a rule, standard, or type; also : even or symmetrical in form or structure **3** : ORDERLY, METHODICAL ⟨∼ habits⟩; also : not varying : STEADY ⟨a ∼ pace⟩ **4** : made, selected, or conducted according to rule or custom **5** : properly qualified ⟨not a ∼ lawyer⟩ **6** : conforming to the normal or usual manner or inflection **7** : of, relating to, or constituting the permanent standing military force of a state — **reg·u·lar·i·ty** \ˌre-gyə-'lar-ə-tē\ n — **reg·u·lar·ize** \'re-gyə-lə-ˌrīz\ vb — **reg·u·lar·ly** adv

²regular n **1** : one that is regular (as in attendance) **2** : a member of the regular clergy **3** : a soldier in a regular army **4** : a player on an athletic team who is usu. in the starting lineup

reg·u·late \'re-gyə-ˌlāt\ vb -lat·ed; -lat·ing **1** : to govern or direct according to rule : CONTROL **2** : to bring under the control of law or authority **3** : to put in good order **4** : to fix or adjust the time, amount, degree, or rate of — **reg·u·la·tive** \-ˌlā-tiv\ adj — **reg·u·la·tor** \-ˌlā-tər\ n — **reg·u·la·to·ry** \-lə-ˌtōr-ē\ adj

reg·u·la·tion \ˌre-gyə-'lā-shən\ n **1** : the act of regulating : the state of being regulated **2** : a rule dealing with details of procedure **3** : an order issued by an executive authority of a government and having the force of law

re·gur·gi·tate \rē-'gər-jə-ˌtāt\ vb -tat·ed; -tat·ing [ML regurgitare, fr. L re- re- + LL gurgitare to engulf, fr. L gurgit-, gurges whirlpool] : to throw or be thrown back, up, or out ⟨∼ food⟩ — **re·gur·gi·ta·tion** \-ˌgər-jə-'tā-shən\ n

re·hab \'rē-ˌhab\ n **1** : REHABILITATION **2** : a rehabilitated building — **rehab** vb

re·ha·bil·i·tate \ˌrē-hə-'bi-lə-ˌtāt, ˌrē-ə-\ vb -tat·ed; -tat·ing **1** : to restore to a former capacity, rank, or right : REINSTATE **2** : to restore to good condition or health — **re·ha·bil·i·ta·tion** \-ˌbi-lə-'tā-shən\ n — **re·ha·bil·i·ta·tive** \-ˌtā-tiv\ adj

re·hash \rē-'hash\ vb : to present again in another form without real change or improvement — **rehash** n

re·hear·ing \ˌrē-'hir-iŋ\ n : a second or new hearing by the same tribunal

re·hears·al \ri-'hər-səl\ n **1** : something told again : RECITAL **2** : a private performance or practice session preparatory to a public appearance

re·hearse \ri-'hərs\ vb re·hearsed; re·hears·ing **1** : to say again : REPEAT **2** : to recount in order : ENUMERATE; also : RELATE 1 **3** : to give a rehearsal of **4** : to train by rehearsal **5** : to engage in a rehearsal — **re·hears·er** n

¹reign \'rān\ n **1** : the authority or rule of a sovereign **2** : the time during which a sovereign rules

²reign vb **1** : to rule as a sovereign **2** : to be predominant or prevalent

re·im·burse \ˌrē-əm-'bərs\ vb -bursed; -burs·ing [re- re- + obs. E imburse to put in the pocket, pay, fr. ML imbursare to put into a purse, fr. L in- in + ML bursa purse, fr. LL, hide of an ox, fr. Gk byrsa] : to pay back : make restitution : REPAY syn indemnify, recompense, requite, compensate — **re·im·burs·able** adj — **re·im·burse·ment** n

¹rein \'rān\ n **1** : a strap fastened to a bit by which a rider or driver controls an animal **2** : a restraining influence : CHECK **3** : controlling or guiding power **4** : complete freedom — usu. used in the phrase give rein to

²rein vb : to check or direct by reins

re·in·car·na·tion \ˌrē-(ˌ)in-(ˌ)kär-'nā-shən\ n : rebirth of the soul in a new body — **re·in·car·nate** \ˌrē-in-'kär-ˌnāt\ vb

rein·deer \'rān-ˌdir\ n [ME reindere, fr. ON hreinn reindeer + ME deer] : CARIBOU — used esp. for the Old World caribou

reindeer moss n : a gray, erect, tufted, and much-branched edible lichen of northern regions that is an important food of reindeer

re·in·fec·tion \ˌrē-in-'fek-shən\ n : infection following another infection of the same type

re·in·force \ˌrē-ən-'fōrs\ vb **1** : to strengthen with additional forces ⟨∼ our troops⟩ **2** : to strengthen with new force, aid, material, or support — **re·in·force·ment** n — **re·in·forc·er** n

re·in·state \ˌrē-in-'stāt\ vb -stat·ed; -stat·ing : to restore to a former position, condition, or capacity — **re·in·state·ment** n

re·in·vent \ˌrē-in-'vent\ vb **1** : to make as if for the first time something already invented ⟨∼ the wheel⟩ **2** : to remake completely

re·it·er·ate \rē-'i-tə-ˌrāt\ vb -at·ed; -at·ing : to state or do over again or repeatedly — **re·it·er·a·tion** \-ˌi-tə-'rā-shən\ n

¹re·ject \ri-'jekt\ vb **1** : to refuse to accept, consider, use, or submit to **2** : to refuse to hear, receive, or admit : REPEL **3** : to rebuff or withhold love from **4** : to throw out esp. as useless or unsatisfactory **5** : to subject to the immunological process of sloughing off (foreign tissue) — **re·jec·tion** \-'jek-shən\ n

²re·ject \'rē-ˌjekt\ n : a rejected person or thing

re·joice \ri-'jóis\ vb re·joiced; re·joic·ing **1** : to give joy to : GLADDEN **2** : to feel joy or great delight — **re·joic·er** n

re·join \(ˌ)rē-'jóin for 1, ri- for 2\ vb **1** : to join again **2** : to say in answer (as to a plaintiff's plea in court) : REPLY

re·join·der \ri-'join-dər\ n : REPLY; esp : an answer to a reply

re·ju·ve·nate \ri-'jü-və-ˌnāt\ vb -nat·ed; -nat·ing : to make young or youthful again : give new vigor to syn renew, refresh, renovate, restore — **re·ju·ve·na·tion** \-ˌjü-və-'nā-shən\ n

rel abbr **1** relating; relative **2** religion; religious

¹re·lapse \ri-'laps, 'rē-ˌlaps\ n **1** : the act or process of backsliding or worsening **2** : a recurrence of illness after a period of improvement

²re·lapse \ri-'laps\ vb re·lapsed; re·laps·ing : to slip or fall back into a former worse state (as of illness)

re·late \ri-'lāt\ vb re·lat·ed; re·lat·ing **1** : to give an account of : TELL, NARRATE **2** : to show or establish logical or causal connection between **3** : to have relationship or connection **4** : to have or establish relationship (the way a child ∼s to a teacher) **5** : to respond favorably — **re·lat·able** adj — **re·lat·er** or **re·la·tor** \-'lā-tər\ n

re·lat·ed adj **1** : connected by some understood relationship **2** : connected through membership in the same family — **re·lat·ed·ness** n

re·la·tion \ri-'lā-shən\ n **1** : NARRATION, ACCOUNT **2** : CONNECTION, RELATIONSHIP **3** : connection by blood or marriage : KINSHIP; also : RELATIVE **4** : REFERENCE, RESPECT ⟨in ∼ to⟩ **5** : the state of being mutually interested or involved (as in social or commercial matters) **6** pl : DEALINGS, AFFAIRS **7** pl : SEXUAL INTERCOURSE — **re·la·tion·al** \-shə-nəl\ adj

re·la·tion·ship \-ˌship\ n : the state of being related or interrelated

¹rel·a·tive \'re-lə-tiv\ n **1** : a word referring grammatically to an antecedent **2** : a thing having a relation to or a dependence upon another thing **3** : a person connected with another by blood or marriage

²relative adj **1** : introducing a subordinate clause qualifying an expressed or implied antecedent ⟨∼ pronoun⟩; also : introduced by such a connective ⟨∼ clause⟩ **2** : PERTINENT, RELEVANT **3** : not absolute or independent : COMPARATIVE **4** : expressed as the ratio of the specified quantity to the total magnitude or to the mean of all quantities involved **syn** dependent, contingent, conditional — **rel·a·tive·ly** *adv* — **rel·a·tive·ness** *n*

relative humidity *n* : the ratio of the amount of water vapor actually present in the air to the greatest amount possible at the same temperature

rel·a·tiv·is·tic \re-lə-ti-ˈvis-tik\ *adj* **1** : of, relating to, or characterized by relativity **2** : moving at a velocity that is a significant fraction of the speed of light so that effects predicted by the theory of relativity become evident ⟨a ∼ electron⟩ — **rel·a·tiv·is·ti·cal·ly** \-ti-k(ə-)lē\ *adv*

rel·a·tiv·i·ty \re-lə-ˈti-və-tē\ *n, pl* **-ties 1** : the quality or state of being relative **2** : a theory in physics that considers mass and energy to be equivalent and that predicts changes in mass, dimension, and time which are related to speed but are noticeable esp. at speeds approaching that of light

re·lax \ri-ˈlaks\ *vb* **1** : to make or become less firm, tense, or rigid **2** : to make less severe or strict **3** : to seek rest or recreation — **re·lax·er** *n*

¹re·lax·ant \ri-ˈlak-sənt\ *adj* : of, relating to, or producing relaxation

²relaxant *n* : a relaxing agent; *esp* : a drug that induces muscular relaxation

re·lax·ation \rē-lak-ˈsā-shən\ *n* **1** : the act of relaxing or state of being relaxed : a lessening of tension **2** : DIVERSION, RECREATION

¹re·lay \ˈrē-lā\ *n* **1** : a fresh supply (as of horses or men) arranged beforehand to relieve others **2** : a race between teams in which each team member covers a specified part of a course **3** : an electromagnetic device in which the opening or closing of one circuit activates another device (as a switch in another circuit) **4** : the act of passing along by stages

²re·lay \ˈrē-lā, ri-ˈlā\ *vb* **re·layed; re·lay·ing 1** : to place in or provide with relays **2** : to pass along by relays **3** : to control or operate by a relay

³re·lay \(ˌ)rē-ˈlā\ *vb* **-laid** \-ˈlād\; **-lay·ing** : to lay again

¹re·lease \ri-ˈlēs\ *vb* **re·leased; re·leas·ing 1** : to set free from confinement or restraint; *also* : DISMISS **2** : to relieve from something that oppresses, confines, or burdens **3** : RELINQUISH ⟨∼ a claim⟩ **4** : to permit publication, performance, exhibition, or sale of; *also* : to make available to the public **syn** emancipate, discharge, free, liberate

²release *n* **1** : relief or deliverance from sorrow, suffering, or trouble **2** : discharge from an obligation or responsibility **3** : an act of setting free : the state of being freed **4** : a document effecting a legal release **5** : a releasing for performance or publication; *also* : the matter released (as to the press) **6** : a device for holding or releasing a mechanism as required

rel·e·gate \ˈre-lə-ˌgāt\ *vb* **-gat·ed; -gat·ing 1** : to send into exile : BANISH **2** : to remove or dismiss to some less prominent position **3** : to assign to a particular class or sphere **4** : to submit to someone or something for appropriate action : DELEGATE **syn** commit, entrust, consign, commend — **rel·e·ga·tion** \re-lə-ˈgā-shən\ *n*

re·lent \ri-ˈlent\ *vb* **1** : to become less stern, severe, or harsh **2** : SLACKEN

re·lent·less \-ləs\ *adj* : showing or promising no abatement of severity, intensity, or pace ⟨∼ pressure⟩ — **re·lent·less·ly** *adv* — **re·lent·less·ness** *n*

rel·e·vance \ˈre-lə-vəns\ *n* : relation to the matter at hand; *also* : practical and esp. social applicability

rel·e·van·cy \-vən-sē\ *n* : RELEVANCE

rel·e·vant \ˈre-lə-vənt\ *adj* : bearing on the matter at hand : PERTINENT **syn** germane, material, applicable, apropos — **rel·e·vant·ly** *adv*

re·li·able \ri-ˈlī-ə-bəl\ *adj* : fit to be trusted or relied on : DEPENDABLE, TRUSTWORTHY — **re·li·abil·i·ty** \-ˌlī-ə-ˈbi-lə-tē\ *n* — **re·li·able·ness** *n* — **re·li·ably** \-ˈlī-ə-blē\ *adv*

re·li·ance \ri-ˈlī-əns\ *n* **1** : the act of relying **2** : the state of being reliant **3** : one relied on

re·li·ant \ri-ˈlī-ənt\ *adj* : having reliance on someone or something : DEPENDENT

rel·ic \ˈre-lik\ *n* **1** : an object venerated because of its association with a saint or martyr **2** : SOUVENIR, MEMENTO **3** *pl* : REMAINS, RUINS **4** : a remaining trace : VESTIGE

rel·ict \ˈre-likt\ *n* : WIDOW

re·lief \ri-ˈlēf\ *n* **1** : removal or lightening of something oppressive, painful, or distressing **2** : WELFARE **2 3** : military assistance to an endangered post or force **4** : release from a post or from performance of a duty; *also* : one that takes the place of another on duty **5** : legal remedy or redress **6** : projection of figures or ornaments from the background (as in sculpture) **7** : the elevations of a land surface

relief pitcher *n* : a baseball pitcher who takes over for another during a game

re·lieve \ri-ˈlēv\ *vb* **re·lieved; re·liev·ing 1** : to free partly or wholly from a burden or from distress **2** : to bring about the removal or alleviation of : MITIGATE **3** : to release from a post or duty; *also* : to take the place of **4** : to break the monotony of **5** : to discharge the bladder or bowels of (oneself) **syn** alleviate, lighten, assuage, allay — **re·liev·er** *n*

relig *abbr* religion

re·li·gion \ri-ˈli-jən\ *n* **1** : the service and worship of God or the supernatural **2** : devotion to a religious faith **3** : a personal set or institutionalized system of religious beliefs, attitudes, and practices **4** : a cause, principle, or belief held to with faith and ardor — **re·li·gion·ist** *n*

¹re·li·gious \ri-ˈli-jəs\ *adj* **1** : relating or devoted to an acknowledged ultimate reality or deity **2** : of or relating to religious beliefs or observances **3** : scrupulously and conscientiously faithful **4** : FERVENT, ZEALOUS — **re·li·gious·ly** *adv*

²religious *n, pl* **religious** : a member of a religious order under monastic vows

re·lin·quish \ri-ˈlin-kwish, -ˈlin-\ *vb* **1** : to withdraw or retreat from : ABANDON, QUIT **2** : GIVE UP ⟨∼ a title⟩ **3** : to let go of : RELEASE **syn** yield, leave, resign, surrender, cede, waive — **re·lin·quish·ment** *n*

rel·i·quary \ˈre-lə-ˌkwer-ē\ *n, pl* **-quar·ies** : a container for religious relics

¹rel·ish \ˈre-lish\ *n* [ME *reles* taste, fr. OF, something left behind, release, fr. *relessier* to relax, release, fr. L *relaxare*] **1** : characteristic flavor : SAVOR **2** : keen enjoyment or delight in something : GUSTO **3** : APPETITE, INCLINATION **4** : a highly seasoned sauce (as of pickles) eaten with other food to add flavor

²relish *vb* **1** : to add relish to **2** : to take pleasure in : ENJOY **3** : to eat with pleasure — **rel·ish·able** *adj*

re·live \(ˌ)rē-ˈliv\ *vb* : to live again or over again; *esp* : to experience again in the imagination

re·lo·cate \(ˌ)rē-ˈlō-ˌkāt, ˌrē-lō-ˈkāt\ *vb* **1** : to locate again **2** : to move to a new location — **re·lo·ca·tion** \ˌrē-lō-ˈkā-shən\ *n*

re·luc·tant \ri-ˈlək-tənt\ *adj* : feeling or showing aversion, hesitation or unwillingness ⟨∼ to get involved⟩ **syn** disinclined, indisposed, hesitant, loath, averse — **re·luc·tance** \-təns\ — **re·luc·tant·ly** *adv*

re·ly \ri-ˈlī\ *vb* **re·lied; re·ly·ing** [ME *relien* to rally, fr. MF *relier* to connect, rally, fr. L *religare* to tie back, fr. *re-* back + *ligare* to tie] : to place faith or confidence : DEPEND

REM \ˈrem\ *n* : RAPID EYE MOVEMENT

re·main \ri-ˈmān\ *vb* **1** : to be left after others have been removed, subtracted, or destroyed **2** : to be something yet to be shown, done, or treated ⟨it ∼*s* to be seen⟩ **3** : to stay after others have gone **4** : to continue unchanged

re·main·der \ri-ˈmān-dər\ *n* **1** : that which is left over : a remaining group, part, or trace **2** : the number left after a subtraction **3** : the number that is left over from the dividend after division and that is less than the divisor **4** : a book sold at a reduced price by the publisher after sales have slowed **syn** leavings, rest, balance, remnant, residue

re·mains \-'mānz\ *n pl* **1** : a remaining part or trace ⟨the ~ of a meal⟩ **2** : a dead body

¹re·make \(ˌ)rē-'māk\ *vb* **-made** \-'mād\; **-mak·ing** : to make anew or in a different form

²re·make \'rē-ˌmāk\ *n* : one that is remade; *esp* : a new version of a motion picture

re·mand \ri-'mand\ *vb* : to order back; *esp* : to return to custody pending trial or for further detention

¹re·mark \ri-'märk\ *n* **1** : the act of remarking : OBSERVATION, NOTICE **2** : a passing observation or comment

²remark *vb* **1** : to take notice of : OBSERVE **2** : to express as an observation or comment : SAY

re·mark·able \ri-'mär-kə-bəl\ *adj* : worthy of being or likely to be noticed : UNUSUAL, EXTRAORDINARY, NOTEWORTHY — **re·mark·able·ness** *n*

re·mark·ably \ri-'mär-kə-blē\ *adv* **1** : in a remarkable manner **2** : as is remarkable

re·me·di·a·ble \ri-'mē-dē-ə-bəl\ *adj* : capable of being remedied

re·me·di·al \ri-'mē-dē-əl\ *adj* : intended to remedy or improve

¹rem·e·dy \'re-mə-dē\ *n, pl* **-dies 1** : a medicine or treatment that cures or relieves a disease or condition **2** : something that corrects or counteracts an evil or compensates for a loss

²remedy *vb* **-died; -dy·ing** : to provide or serve as a remedy for

re·mem·ber \ri-'mem-bər\ *vb* **-bered; -ber·ing 1** : to bring to mind or think of again : RECOLLECT **2** : to keep from forgetting : keep in mind **3** : to convey greetings from **4** : COMMEMORATE

re·mem·brance \-brəns\ *n* **1** : an act of remembering : RECOLLECTION **2** : the ability to remember : MEMORY **3** : the period over which one's memory extends **4** : a memory of a person, thing, or event **5** : something that serves to bring to mind : REMINDER **6** : a greeting or gift recalling or expressing friendship or affection

re·mind \ri-'mīnd\ *vb* : to put in mind of something : cause to remember — **re·mind·er** *n*

rem·i·nisce \ˌre-mə-'nis\ *vb* **-nisced; -nisc·ing** : to indulge in reminiscence

rem·i·nis·cence \-'nis-ᵊns\ *n* **1** : a recalling or telling of a past experience **2** : an account of a memorable experience

rem·i·nis·cent \-ᵊnt\ *adj* **1** : of or relating to reminiscence **2** : marked by or given to reminiscence **3** : serving to remind : SUGGESTIVE — **rem·i·nis·cent·ly** *adv*

re·miss \ri-'mis\ *adj* **1** : negligent or careless in the performance of work or duty **2** : showing neglect or inattention **syn** lax, neglectful, delinquent, derelict — **re·miss·ly** *adv* — **re·miss·ness** *n*

re·mis·sion \ri-'mi-shən\ *n* **1** : the act or process of remitting **2** : a state or period during which something is remitted

re·mit \ri-'mit\ *vb* **re·mit·ted; re·mit·ting 1** : FORGIVE, PARDON **2** : to give or gain relief from (as pain) **3** : to refer for consideration, report, or decision **4** : to refrain from exacting or enforcing (as a penalty) **5** : to send (money) in payment of a bill

re·mit·tal \ri-'mit-ᵊl\ *n* : REMISSION

re·mit·tance \ri-'mit-ᵊns\ *n* **1** : a sum of money remitted **2** : transmittal of money (as to a distant place)

rem·nant \'rem-nənt\ *n* **1** : a usu. small part or trace remaining **2** : an unsold or unused end of fabrics that are sold by the yard

re·mod·el \ˌrē-'mäd-ᵊl\ *vb* : to alter the structure of : MAKE OVER

re·mon·strance \ri-'män-strəns\ *n* : an act or instance of remonstrating

re·mon·strant \-strənt\ *adj* : vigorously objecting or opposing — **remonstrant** *n* — **re·mon·strant·ly** *adv*

re·mon·strate \ri-'män-ˌstrāt\ *vb* **-strat·ed; -strat-**
ing : to plead in opposition to something : speak in protest or reproof **syn** expostulate, object, protest — **re·mon·stra·tion** \ri-ˌmän-'strā-shən, ˌre-mən-\ *n* — **re·mon·stra·tor** \ri-'män-ˌstrā-tər\ *n*

rem·o·ra \'re-mə-rə\ *n* : any of a family of marine bony fishes with sucking organs on the head by which they cling esp. to other fishes

re·morse \ri-'mórs\ *n* [ME, fr. MF *remors*, fr. ML *remorsus*, fr. LL, act of biting again, fr. L *remordēre* to bite again, fr. *re-* again + *mordēre* to bite] : a gnawing distress arising from a sense of guilt for past wrongs **syn** penitence, repentance, contrition — **re·morse·ful** *adj*

re·morse·less \-ləs\ *adj* **1** : MERCILESS **2** : PERSISTENT, RELENTLESS

¹re·mote \ri-'mōt\ *adj* **re·mot·er; -est 1** : far off in place or time : not near **2** : not closely related : DISTANT **3** : located out of the way : SECLUDED **4** : acting, acted on, or controlled indirectly or from a distance **5** : small in degree : SLIGHT ⟨a ~ chance⟩ **6** : distant in manner — **re·mote·ly** *adv* — **re·mote·ness** *n*

²remote *n* **1** : a radio or television program or a portion of a program originating outside the studio **2** : REMOTE CONTROL 2

remote control *n* **1** : control (as by radio signal) of operation from a point at some distance removed **2** : a device or mechanism for controlling something from a distance

¹re·mount \(ˌ)rē-'maunt\ *vb* **1** : to mount again **2** : to furnish remounts to

²re·mount \'rē-ˌmaunt\ *n* : a fresh horse to replace one disabled or exhausted

¹re·move \ri-'müv\ *vb* **re·moved; re·mov·ing 1** : to move from one place to another : TRANSFER **2** : to move by lifting or taking off or away **3** : DISMISS, DISCHARGE **4** : to get rid of : ELIMINATE ⟨~ a fire hazard⟩ **5** : to change one's residence or location **6** : to go away : DEPART **7** : to be capable of being removed — **re·mov·able** *adj* — **re·mov·al** \-'mü-vəl\ *n* — **re·mov·er** *n*

²remove *n* **1** : a transfer from one location to another : MOVE **2** : a degree or stage of separation

REM sleep *n* : a state of sleep associated esp. with rapid eye movements and dreaming and occurring approximately at 90-minute intervals

re·mu·ner·ate \ri-'myü-nə-ˌrāt\ *vb* **-at·ed; -at·ing** : to pay an equivalent for or to : RECOMPENSE — **re·mu·ner·a·tor** \-ˌrā-tər\ *n*

re·mu·ner·a·tion \ri-ˌmyü-nə-'rā-shən\ *n* : COMPENSATION, PAYMENT

re·mu·ner·a·tive \ri-'myü-nə-rə-tiv, -ˌrā-\ *adj* : serving to remunerate : GAINFUL

re·nais·sance \ˌre-nə-'säns, -'zäns\ *n* **1** *cap* : the cultural revival and beginnings of modern science in Europe in the 14th-17th centuries; *also* : the period of the Renaissance **2** *often cap* : a movement or period of vigorous artistic and intellectual activity **3** : REBIRTH, REVIVAL

re·nal \'rēn-ᵊl\ *adj* : of, relating to, or located in or near the kidneys

re·na·scence \ri-'nas-ᵊns, -'nās-\ *n, often cap* : RENAISSANCE

rend \'rend\ *vb* **rent** \'rent\; **rend·ing 1** : to remove by violence : WREST **2** : to tear forcibly apart : SPLIT

ren·der \'ren-dər\ *vb* **1** : to extract (as lard) by heating **2** : to give to another; *also* : YIELD **3** : to give in return **4** : to do (a service) for another ⟨~ aid⟩ **5** : to cause to be or become : MAKE **6** : to reproduce or represent by artistic or verbal means **7** : TRANSLATE ⟨~ into English⟩

¹ren·dez·vous \'rän-di-ˌvü, -dā-\ *n, pl* **ren·dez·vous** \-ˌvüz\ [MF, fr. *rendez vous* present yourselves] **1** : a place appointed for a meeting; *also* : a meeting at an appointed place **2** : a place of popular resort **3** : the process of bringing two spacecraft together

²rendezvous *vb* **-voused** \-ˌvüd\; **-vous·ing** \-ˌvü-iŋ\;

-vouses \-ˌvüz\ : to come or bring together at a rendezvous

ren·di·tion \ren-ˈdi-shən\ *n* : an act or a result of rendering ⟨first ∼ of the work into English⟩

ren·e·gade \ˈre-ni-ˌgād\ *n* [Sp *renegado*, fr. ML *renegatus*, fr. pp. of *renegare* to deny, fr. L *re-* re- + *negare* to deny] : a deserter from one faith, cause, principle, or party for another

re·nege \ri-ˈnig, -ˈneg, -ˈnēg, -ˈnāg\ *vb* **re·neged; re·neg·ing 1** : to go back on a promise or commitment **2** : to fail to follow suit when able in a card game in violation of the rules — **re·neg·er** *n*

re·new \ri-ˈnü, -ˈnyü\ *vb* **1** : to make or become new, fresh, or strong again **2** : to restore to existence : RECREATE, REVIVE **3** : to make or do again : REPEAT ⟨∼ a complaint⟩ **4** : to begin again : RESUME ⟨∼ed his efforts⟩ **5** : REPLACE ⟨∼ the lining of a coat⟩ **6** : to grant or obtain an extension of or on ⟨∼ a lease⟩ ⟨∼ a subscription⟩ — **re·new·er** *n*

re·new·able \ri-ˈnü-ə-bəl, -ˈnyü-\ *adj* **1** : capable of being renewed **2** : capable of being replaced by natural ecological cycles or sound management procedures ⟨∼ resources⟩

re·new·al \ri-ˈnü-əl, -ˈnyü-\ *n* **1** : the act of renewing : the state of being renewed **2** : something renewed

ren·net \ˈre-nət\ *n* **1** : the contents of the stomach of an unweaned animal (as a calf) or the lining membrane of the stomach used for curdling milk **2** : rennin or a substitute used to curdle milk

ren·nin \ˈre-nən\ *n* : a stomach enzyme that coagulates casein and is used commercially to curdle milk in the making of cheese

re·nounce \ri-ˈnaůns\ *vb* **re·nounced; re·nounc·ing 1** : to give up, refuse, or resign usu. by formal declaration **2** : to refuse further to follow, obey, or recognize : REPUDIATE — **re·nounce·ment** *n*

ren·o·vate \ˈre-nə-ˌvāt\ *vb* **-vat·ed; -vat·ing 1** : to make like new again : put in good condition : REPAIR **2** : to restore to vigor or activity — **ren·o·va·tion** \ˌre-nə-ˈvā-shən\ *n* — **ren·o·va·tor** \ˈre-nə-ˌvā-tər\ *n*

re·nown \ri-ˈnaůn\ *n* : a state of being widely acclaimed and honored : FAME, CELEBRITY **syn** honor, glory, reputation, repute — **re·nowned** \-ˈnaůnd\ *adj*

¹rent \ˈrent\ *n* **1** : money or the amount of money paid or due at intervals for the use of another's property **2** : property rented or for rent

²rent *vb* **1** : to give possession and use of in return for rent **2** : to take and hold under an agreement to pay rent **3** : to be for rent ⟨∼s for $100 a month⟩ — **rent·er** *n*

³rent *n* **1** : a tear in cloth **2** : a split in a party or organized group : SCHISM

¹rent·al \ˈren-təl\ *n* **1** : an amount paid or collected as rent **2** : something that is rented **3** : an act of renting

²rental *adj* : of or relating to rent

re·nun·ci·a·tion \ri-ˌnən-sē-ˈā-shən\ *n* : the act of renouncing : REPUDIATION

rep *abbr* **1** repair **2** repeat **3** report; reporter **4** representative **5** republic

Rep *abbr* Republican

re·pack·age \(ˌ)rē-ˈpa-kij\ *vb* : to package again or anew; *esp* : to put into a more attractive form

¹re·pair \ri-ˈpar\ *vb* [ME, fr. MF *repairier* to go back to one's country, fr. LL *repatriare*, fr. L *re-* re- + *patria* native country] : to make one's way : GO ⟨∼ed to the drawing room⟩

²repair *vb* [ME, fr. MF *reparer*, fr. L *reparare*, fr. *re-* re- + *parare* to prepare] **1** : to restore to good condition : FIX **2** : to restore to a healthy state **3** : REMEDY ⟨∼ a wrong⟩ — **re·pair·er** *n* — **re·pair·man** \-ˈman\ *n*

³repair *n* **1** : a result of repairing **2** : an act of repairing **3** : condition with respect to need of repairing ⟨in bad ∼⟩

rep·a·ra·tion \ˌre-pə-ˈrā-shən\ *n* **1** : the act of making amends for a wrong **2** : amends made for a wrong; *esp*

: money paid by a defeated nation in compensation for damages caused during hostilities — usu. used in pl. **syn** redress, restitution, indemnity

re·par·a·tive \ri-ˈpar-ə-tiv\ *adj* **1** : of, relating to, or effecting repairs **2** : serving to make amends

rep·ar·tee \ˌre-pər-ˈtē\ *n* **1** : a witty reply **2** : a succession of clever replies; *also* : skill in making such replies

re·past \ri-ˈpast, ˈrē-ˌpast\ *n* : a supply of food and drink served as a meal

re·pa·tri·ate \rē-ˈpā-trē-ˌāt\ *vb* **-at·ed; -at·ing** : to send or bring back to the country of origin or citizenship ⟨∼ prisoners of war⟩ — **re·pa·tri·ate** \-trē-ət, -trē-ˌāt\ *n* — **re·pa·tri·a·tion** \-ˌpā-trē-ˈā-shən\ *n*

re·pay \rē-ˈpā\ *vb* **-paid** \-ˈpād\; **-pay·ing 1** : to pay back : REFUND **2** : to give or do in return or requital **3** : to make a return payment to : RECOMPENSE, REQUITE **syn** remunerate, compensate, reimburse, indemnify — **re·pay·able** *adj* — **re·pay·ment** *n*

re·peal \ri-ˈpēl\ *vb* : to annul by authoritative and esp. legislative action — **repeal** *n* — **re·peal·er** *n*

¹re·peat \ri-ˈpēt\ *vb* **1** : to say again **2** : to do again **3** : to say over from memory — **re·peat·able** *adj* — **re·peat·er** *n*

²re·peat \ri-ˈpēt, ˈrē-ˌpēt\ *n* **1** : the act of repeating **2** : something repeated or to be repeated (as a radio or television program)

re·peat·ed \ri-ˈpē-təd\ *adj* : done or recurring again and again : FREQUENT — **re·peat·ed·ly** *adv*

re·pel \ri-ˈpel\ *vb* **re·pelled; re·pel·ling 1** : to drive away : REPULSE **2** : to fight against : RESIST **3** : to turn away : REJECT **4** : to cause aversion in : DISGUST

¹re·pel·lent *also* **re·pel·lant** \ri-ˈpe-lənt\ *adj* **1** : tending to drive away ⟨a mosquito-*repellent* spray⟩ **2** : causing disgust

²repellent *also* **repellant** *n* : something that repels; *esp* : a substance that repels insects

re·pent \ri-ˈpent\ *vb* **1** : to turn from sin and resolve to reform one's life **2** : to feel sorry for (something done) : REGRET — **re·pen·tance** \ri-ˈpent-ᵊns\ *n* — **re·pen·tant** \-ᵊnt\ *adj*

re·per·cus·sion \ˌrē-pər-ˈkə-shən, ˌre-\ *n* **1** : REVERBERATION **2** : a reciprocal action or effect **3** : a widespread, indirect, or unforeseen effect of something done or said

rep·er·toire \ˈre-pər-ˌtwär\ *n* [F] **1** : a list of plays, operas, pieces, or parts which a company or performer is prepared to present **2** : a list of the skills or devices possessed by a person or needed in his occupation

rep·er·to·ry \ˈre-pər-ˌtōr-ē\ *n, pl* **-ries 1** : REPOSITORY **2** : REPERTOIRE **3** : a company that presents its repertoire in the course of one season at one theater

rep·e·ti·tion \ˌre-pə-ˈti-shən\ *n* **1** : the act or an instance of repeating **2** : the fact of being repeated

rep·e·ti·tious \-ˈti-shəs\ *adj* : marked by repetition; *esp* : tediously repeating — **rep·e·ti·tious·ly** *adv* — **rep·e·ti·tious·ness** *n*

re·pet·i·tive \ri-ˈpe-ti-tiv\ *adj* : REPETITIOUS — **re·pet·i·tive·ly** *adv* — **re·pet·i·tive·ness** *n*

re·pine \ri-ˈpīn\ *vb* **re·pined; re·pin·ing 1** : to feel or express discontent or dejection **2** : to long for something

repl *abbr* replace; replacement

re·place \ri-ˈplās\ *vb* **1** : to restore to a former place or position **2** : to take the place of : SUPPLANT **3** : to put something new in the place of — **re·place·able** *adj* — **re·plac·er** *n*

re·place·ment \ri-ˈplās-mənt\ *n* **1** : the act of replacing : the state of being replaced **2** : one that replaces another esp. in a job or function

¹re·play \(ˌ)rē-ˈplā\ *vb* : to play again or over

²re·play \ˈrē-ˌplā\ *n* **1** : an act or instance of replaying **2** : the playing of a tape (as a videotape)

re·plen·ish \ri-ˈple-nish\ *vb* : to fill or build up again : stock or supply anew — **re·plen·ish·ment** *n*

re·plete \ri-ᵇplēt\ *adj* **1** : fully provided **2** : FULL; *esp* : full of food — **re·plete·ness** *n*

re·ple·tion \ri-ᵇplē-shən\ *n* : the state of being replete

rep·li·ca \ᵇre-pli-kə\ *n* [It. repetition, fr. *replicare* to repeat, fr. LL, fr. L, to fold back, fr. *re-* back + *plicare* to fold] **1** : an exact reproduction (as of a painting) executed by the original artist **2** : a copy exact in all details : DUPLICATE

¹**rep·li·cate** \ᵇre-plə-ˌkāt\ *vb* **-cat·ed; -cat·ing** : DUPLICATE, REPEAT

²**rep·li·cate** \-pli-kət\ *n* : one of several identical experiments or procedures

rep·li·ca·tion \ˌre-plə-ᵇkā-shən\ *n* **1** : ANSWER, REPLY **2** : precise copying or reproduction; *also* : an act or process of this

¹**re·ply** \ri-ᵇplī\ *vb* **re·plied; re·ply·ing** : to say or do in answer : RESPOND

²**reply** *n, pl* **replies** : ANSWER, RESPONSE

¹**re·port** \ri-ᵇpōrt\ *n* [ME, fr. MF, fr. OF, fr. *reporter* to report, fr. L *reportare*, fr. *re-* back + *portare* to carry] **1** : common talk : RUMOR **2** : FAME, REPUTATION **3** : a usu. detailed account or statement **4** : an explosive noise

²**report** *vb* **1** : to give an account of : RELATE, TELL **2** : to serve as carrier of (a message) **3** : to prepare or present (as an account of an event) for a newspaper or a broadcast **4** : to make a charge of misconduct against **5** : to present oneself (as for work) **6** : to make known to the authorities ⟨~ a fire⟩ **7** : to return or present (as a matter referred to a committee) with conclusions and recommendations — **re·port·able** *adj*

report·age \ri-ᵇpōr-tij, *esp for 2* ˌre-pər-ᵇtäzh, ˌre-ˌpór-ᵇ\ *n* [F] **1** : the act or process of reporting news **2** : writing intended to give an account of observed or documented events

report card *n* : a periodic report on a student's grades

re·port·ed·ly \ri-ᵇpōr-təd-lē\ *adv* : according to report

re·port·er \ri-ᵇpōr-tər\ *n* : one that reports; *esp* : a person who gathers and reports news for a news medium — **re·por·to·ri·al** \ˌre-pər-ᵇtōr-ē-əl\ *adj*

¹**re·pose** \ri-ᵇpōz\ *vb* **re·posed; re·pos·ing** **1** : to lay at rest **2** : to lie at rest **3** : to lie dead **4** : to take a rest **5** : to rest for support : LIE

²**repose** *n* **1** : a state of resting (as after exertion); *esp* : SLEEP **2** : eternal or heavenly rest **3** : CALM, PEACE **4** : cessation or absence of activity, movement, or animation **5** : composure of manner : POISE — **re·pose·ful** *adj*

³**repose** *vb* **re·posed; re·pos·ing** **1** : to place (as trust) in someone or something **2** : to place for control, management, or use

re·pos·i·to·ry \ri-ᵇpä-zə-ˌtōr-ē\ *n, pl* **-ries** **1** : a place where something is deposited or stored **2** : a person to whom something is entrusted

re·pos·sess \ˌrē-pə-ᵇzes\ *vb* **1** : to regain possession of **2** : to take possession in default of the payment of installments due — **re·pos·ses·sion** \-ᵇze-shən\ *n*

rep·re·hend \ˌre-pri-ᵇhend\ *vb* : to express disapproval of : CENSURE **syn** criticize, condemn, denounce, blame, pan — **rep·re·hen·sion** \-ᵇhen-chən\ *n*

rep·re·hen·si·ble \-ᵇhen-sə-bəl\ *adj* : deserving blame or censure : CULPABLE — **rep·re·hen·si·bly** \-blē\ *adv*

rep·re·sent \ˌre-pri-ᵇzent\ *vb* **1** : to present a picture or a likeness of : PORTRAY, DEPICT **2** : to serve as a sign or symbol of **3** : to act the role of **4** : to stand in the place of : act or speak for **5** : to be a member or example of : TYPIFY **6** : to serve as an elected representative of **7** : to describe as having a specified quality or character **8** : to state with the purpose of affecting judgment or action

rep·re·sen·ta·tion \ˌre-pri-zen-ᵇtā-shən\ *n* **1** : the act of representing **2** : one (as a picture or image) that represents something else **3** : the state of being represented in a legislative body; *also* : the body of persons representing a constituency **4** : a usu. formal statement made to effect a change

¹**rep·re·sen·ta·tive** \ˌre-pri-ᵇzen-tə-tiv\ *adj* **1** : serving to represent **2** : standing or acting for another **3** : founded on the principle of representation : carried on by elected representatives ⟨~ government⟩ — **rep·re·sen·ta·tive·ly** *adv* — **rep·re·sen·ta·tive·ness** *n*

²**representative** *n* **1** : a typical example of a group, class, or quality **2** : one that represents another; *esp* : one representing a district in a legislative body usu. as a member of a lower house

re·press \ri-ᵇpres\ *vb* **1** : CURB, SUBDUE **2** : RESTRAIN, SUPPRESS **3** : to exclude from consciousness — **re·pres·sion** \-ᵇpre-shən\ *n* — **re·pres·sive** \-ᵇpre-siv\ *adj*

¹**re·prieve** \ri-ᵇprēv\ *vb* **re·prieved; re·priev·ing** **1** : to delay the punishment or execution of **2** : to give temporary relief to

²**reprieve** *n* **1** : the act of reprieving : the state of being reprieved **2** : a formal temporary suspension of a sentence esp. of death **3** : a temporary respite

¹**rep·ri·mand** \ᵇre-prə-ˌmand\ *n* : a severe or formal reproof

²**reprimand** *vb* : to reprove severely or formally

¹**re·print** \(ˌ)rē-ᵇprint\ *vb* : to print again

²**re·print** \ᵇrē-ˌprint\ *n* : a reproduction of printed matter

re·pri·sal \ri-ᵇprī-zəl\ *n* : an act in retaliation for something done by another

re·prise \ri-ᵇprēz\ *n* : a recurrence, renewal, or resumption of an action; *also* : a musical repetition

¹**re·proach** \ri-ᵇprōch\ *n* **1** : an expression of disapproval **2** : DISGRACE, DISCREDIT **3** : the act of reproaching : REBUKE **4** : a cause or occasion of blame or disgrace — **re·proach·ful** \-fəl\ *adj* — **re·proach·ful·ly** *adv* — **re·proach·ful·ness** *n*

²**reproach** *vb* **1** : CENSURE, REBUKE **2** : to cast discredit on **syn** chide, admonish, reprove, reprimand — **re·proach·able** *adj*

rep·ro·bate \ᵇre-prə-ˌbāt\ *n* **1** : a person foreordained to damnation **2** : a thoroughly bad person : SCOUNDREL — **reprobate** *adj*

rep·ro·ba·tion \ˌre-prə-ᵇbā-shən\ *n* : strong disapproval : CONDEMNATION

re·pro·duce \ˌrē-prə-ᵇdüs, -ᵇdyüs\ *vb* **1** : to produce again or anew **2** : to produce offspring — **re·pro·duc·ible** \-ᵇdü-sə-bəl, -ᵇdyü-\ *adj* — **re·pro·duc·tion** \-ᵇdək-shən\ *n* — **re·pro·duc·tive** \-ᵇdək-tiv\ *adj*

re·proof \ri-ᵇprüf\ *n* : blame or censure for a fault

re·prove \ri-ᵇprüv\ *vb* **re·proved; re·prov·ing** **1** : to administer a rebuke to **2** : to express disapproval of **syn** reprimand, admonish, reproach, chide — **re·prov·er** *n*

rept *abbr* report

rep·tile \ᵇrep-təl, -ˌtīl\ *n* [ME *reptil*, fr. MF or LL; MF *reptile*, fr. LL *reptile*, fr. L *repere* to crawl] : any of a large class of air-breathing scaly vertebrates including snakes, lizards, alligators, turtles, and extinct related forms (as dinosaurs) — **rep·til·i·an** \rep-ᵇti-lē-ən\ *adj or n*

re·pub·lic \ri-ᵇpə-blik\ *n* [F *république*, fr. MF *republique*, fr. L *respublica*, fr. *res* thing, wealth + *publica*, fem. of *publicus* public] **1** : a government having a chief of state who is not a monarch and is usu. a president; *also* : a nation or other political unit having such a government **2** : a government in which supreme power is held by the citizens entitled to vote and is exercised by elected officers and representatives governing according to law; *also* : a nation or other political unit having such a form of government

¹**re·pub·li·can** \-bli-kən\ *adj* **1** : of, relating to, or resembling a republic **2** : favoring or supporting a republic **3** *cap* : of, relating to, or constituting one of the two major political parties in the U.S. evolving in the mid-19th century — **re·pub·li·can·ism** *n, often cap*

²**republican** *n* **1** : one that favors or supports a republican form of government **2** *cap* : a member of a re-

publican party and esp. of the Republican party of the U.S.

re·pu·di·ate \ri-'pyü-dē-ˌāt\ *vb* **-at·ed; -at·ing** [L *repudiare* to cast off, divorce, fr. *repudium* divorce] **1** : to cast off : DISOWN **2** : to refuse to have anything to do with : refuse to acknowledge, accept, or pay ⟨∼ a charge⟩ ⟨∼ a debt⟩ **syn** spurn, reject, decline — **re·pu·di·a·tion** \-ˌpyü-dē-'ā-shən\ *n* — **re·pu·di·a·tor** \-'pyü-dē-ˌā-tər\ *n*

re·pug·nance \ri-'pəg-nəns\ *n* **1** : the quality or fact of being contradictory or inconsistent **2** : strong dislike, distaste, or antagonism

re·pug·nant \-nənt\ *adj* **1** : marked by repugnance **2** : contrary to a person's tastes or principles : exciting distaste or aversion **syn** repellent, abhorrent, distasteful, obnoxious, revolting, loathsome — **re·pug·nant·ly** *adv*

¹re·pulse \ri-'pəls\ *vb* **repulsed; re·puls·ing 1** : to drive or beat back : REPEL **2** : to repel by discourtesy or denial : REBUFF **3** : to cause a feeling of repulsion in : DISGUST

²repulse *n* **1** : REBUFF, REJECTION **2** : the action of repelling an attacker : the fact of being repelled

re·pul·sion \ri-'pəl-shən\ *n* **1** : the action of repulsing : the state of being repulsed **2** : the force with which bodies, particles, or like forces repel one another **3** : a feeling of aversion

re·pul·sive \-siv\ *adj* **1** : serving or tending to repel or reject **2** : arousing aversion or disgust **syn** repugnant, revolting, loathsome, noisome — **re·pul·sive·ly** *adv* — **re·pul·sive·ness** *n*

rep·u·ta·ble \'re-pyə-tə-bəl\ *adj* : having a good reputation : ESTIMABLE — **rep·u·ta·bly** \-blē\ *adv*

rep·u·ta·tion \ˌre-pyu̇-'tā-shən\ *n* **1** : overall quality or character as seen or judged by people in general **2** : place in public esteem or regard

¹re·pute \ri-'pyüt\ *vb* **re·put·ed; re·put·ing** : CONSIDER, ACCOUNT

²repute *n* **1** : REPUTATION **2** : the state of being favorably known or spoken of

re·put·ed \ri-'pyü-təd\ *adj* **1** : REPUTABLE **2** : according to reputation : SUPPOSED — **re·put·ed·ly** *adv*

req *abbr* **1** request **2** require; required **3** requisition

¹re·quest \ri-'kwest\ *n* **1** : an act or instance of asking for something **2** : a thing asked for **3** : the condition of being asked for ⟨available on ∼⟩

²request *vb* **1** : to make a request to or of **2** : to ask for — **re·quest·er** *n*

re·qui·em \'re-kwē-əm, 'rā-\ *n* [ME, fr. L (first word of the requiem mass), acc. of *requies* rest, fr. *quies* quiet, rest] **1** : a mass for a dead person; *also* : a musical setting for this **2** : a musical service or hymn in honor of the dead

re·quire \ri-'kwīr\ *vb* **re·quired; re·quir·ing 1** : to demand as necessary or essential **2** : COMMAND, ORDER

re·quire·ment \-mənt\ *n* **1** : something (as a condition or quality) required ⟨entrance ∼s⟩ **2** : NECESSITY

req·ui·site \'re-kwə-zət\ *adj* : REQUIRED, NECESSARY — **requisite** *n*

req·ui·si·tion \ˌre-kwə-'zi-shən\ *n* **1** : formal application or demand (as for supplies) **2** : the state of being in demand or use — **requisition** *vb*

re·quite \ri-'kwīt\ *vb* **re·quit·ed; re·quit·ing 1** : to make return for : REPAY **2** : to make retaliation for : AVENGE **3** : to make return to — **re·quit·al** \-'kwīt-ᵊl\ *n*

rere·dos \'rer-ə-ˌdäs\ *n* : a usu. ornamental wood or stone screen or partition wall behind an altar

re·run \'rē-ˌrən, (ˌ)rē-'rən\ *n* : the act or an instance of running again or anew; *esp* : a showing of a motion picture or television program after its first run — **re·run** \(ˌ)rē-'rən\ *vb*

res *abbr* **1** research **2** reservation; reserve **3** reservoir **4** residence; resident **5** resolution

re·sale \'rē-ˌsāl, (ˌ)rē-'sāl\ *n* : the act of selling again

usu. to a new party — **re·sal·able** \(ˌ)rē-'sā-lə-bəl\ *adj*

re·scind \ri-'sind\ *vb* : REPEAL, CANCEL, ANNUL — **re·scis·sion** \-'si-zhən\ *n*

re·script \'rē-ˌskript\ *n* : an official or authoritative order or decree

res·cue \'res-kyü\ *vb* **res·cued; res·cu·ing** [ME, fr. MF *rescourre*, fr. OF, fr. *re-* re- + *escourre* to shake out, fr. L *excutere*] : to free from danger, harm, or confinement — **rescue** *n* — **res·cu·er** *n*

re·search \ri-'sərch, 'rē-ˌsərch\ *n* **1** : careful or diligent search **2** : studious inquiry or examination aimed at the discovery and interpretation of new knowledge **3** : the collecting of information about a particular subject — **research** *vb* — **re·search·er** *n*

re·sec·tion \ri-'sek-shən\ *n* : the surgical removal of part of an organ or structure

re·sem·blance \ri-'zem-bləns\ *n* : the quality or state of resembling

re·sem·ble \ri-'zem-bəl\ *vb* **-bled; -bling** : to be like or similar to

re·sent \ri-'zent\ *vb* : to feel or exhibit annoyance or indignation at — **re·sent·ful** \-fəl\ *adj* — **re·sent·ful·ly** *adv* — **re·sent·ment** *n*

re·ser·pine \ri-'sər-ˌpēn, -pən\ *n* : a drug used in treating high blood pressure and nervous tension

res·er·va·tion \ˌre-zər-'vā-shən\ *n* **1** : an act of reserving **2** : something (as a room in a hotel) arranged for in advance **3** : something reserved; *esp* : a tract of public land set aside for special use **4** : a limiting condition

¹re·serve \ri-'zərv\ *vb* **re·served; re·serv·ing 1** : to store for future or special use **2** : to hold back for oneself **3** : to set aside or arrange to have set aside or held for special use

²reserve *n* **1** : something reserved : STOCK, STORE **2** : a military force withheld from action for later use — usu. used in pl. **3** : the military forces of a country not part of the regular services; *also* : RESERVIST **4** : a tract set apart : RESERVATION **5** : an act of reserving **6** : restraint or caution in one's words or bearing **7** : money or its equivalent kept in hand or set apart to meet liabilities

re·served \ri-'zərvd\ *adj* **1** : restrained in words and actions **2** : set aside for future or special use — **re·serv·ed·ly** \-'zər-vəd-lē\ *adv* — **re·serv·ed·ness** \-vəd-nəs\ *n*

re·serv·ist \ri-'zər-vist\ *n* : a member of a military reserve

res·er·voir \'re-zə-ˌvwär, -zər-, -ˌvwȯr\ *n* [F] : a place where something is kept in store; *esp* : an artificial lake where water is collected as a water supply

re·shuf·fle \rē-'shə-fəl\ *vb* **1** : to shuffle again **2** : to reorganize usu. by redistribution of existing elements — **reshuffle** *n*

re·side \ri-'zīd\ *vb* **re·sid·ed; re·sid·ing 1** : to make one's home : DWELL **2** : to be present as a quality or vested as a right

res·i·dence \'re-zə-dəns\ *n* **1** : the act or fact of residing in a place as a dweller or in discharge of a duty or an obligation **2** : the place where one actually lives **3** : a building used as a home : DWELLING **4** : the period of living in a place

res·i·den·cy \'re-zə-dən-sē\ *n, pl* **-cies 1** : the residence of or the territory under a diplomatic resident **2** : a period of advanced training in a medical specialty

¹res·i·dent \-dənt\ *adj* **1** : RESIDING **2** : being in residence **3** : not migratory

²resident *n* **1** : one who resides in a place **2** : a diplomatic representative with governing powers (as in a protectorate) **3** : a physician serving a residency

res·i·den·tial \ˌre-zə-'den-chəl\ *adj* **1** : used as a residence or by residents **2** : occupied by or restricted to residences — **res·i·den·tial·ly** *adv*

¹re·sid·u·al \ri-'zi-jə-wəl\ *adj* : being a residue or remainder

²residual *n* **1** : a residual product or substance **2** : a payment (as to an actor or writer) for each rerun after an initial showing (as of a taped TV show)

re·sid·u·ary \ri-'zi-jə-ˌwer-ē\ *adj* : of, relating to, or constituting a residue esp. of an estate

res·i·due \'re-zə-ˌdü, -ˌdyü\ *n* : a part remaining after another part has been taken away : REMAINDER

re·sid·u·um \ri-'zi-jə-wəm\ *n*, *pl* **resid·ua** \-jə-wə\ [L] **1** : something remaining or residual after certain deductions are made **2** : a residual product

re·sign \ri-'zīn\ *vb* [ME, fr. MF *resigner*, fr. L *resignare*, lit., to unseal, cancel, fr. *signare* to sign, seal] **1** : to give up deliberately (as one's position) esp. by a formal act **2** : to give (oneself) over (as to grief or despair) without resistance — **re·sign·ed·ly** \-'zī-nəd-lē\ *adv*

re·sign \(ˌ)rē-'sīn\ *vb* : to sign again

res·ig·na·tion \ˌre-zig-'nā-shən\ *n* **1** : an act or instance of resigning; *also* : a formal notification of such an act **2** : the quality or state of being resigned

re·sil·ience \ri-'zil-yəns\ *n* **1** : the ability of a body to regain its original size and shape after being compressed, bent, or stretched **2** : an ability to recover from or adjust easily to change or misfortune

re·sil·ien·cy \-yən-sē\ *n* : RESILIENCE

re·sil·ient \-yənt\ *adj* : marked by resilience

res·in \'rez-ən\ *n* : any of various substances obtained from the gum or sap of some trees and used esp. in varnishes, plastics, and medicine; *also* : a comparable synthetic product — **res·in·ous** *adj*

¹re·sist \ri-'zist\ *vb* **1** : to fight against : OPPOSE ⟨∼ aggression⟩ **2** : to withstand the force or effect of ⟨∼ disease⟩ **syn** combat, repel — **re·sist·ible** \-'zis-tə-bəl\ *adj* — **re·sist·less** *adj*

²resist *n* : something (as a coating) that resists or prevents a particular action

re·sis·tance \ri-'zis-təns\ *n* **1** : the act or an instance of resisting : OPPOSITION **2** : the power or capacity to resist; *esp* : the inherent ability of an organism to resist harmful influences (as disease or infection) **3** : the opposition offered by a body to the passage through it of a steady electric current

re·sis·tant \-tənt\ *adj* : giving or capable of resistance

re·sis·tor \ri-'zis-tər\ *n* : a device used to provide resistance to the flow of an electric current in a circuit

res·o·lute \'re-zə-ˌlüt\ *adj* : firmly determined in purpose : RESOLVED **syn** steadfast, staunch, faithful, true, loyal — **res·o·lute·ly** *adv* — **res·o·lute·ness** *n*

res·o·lu·tion \ˌre-zə-'lü-shən\ *n* **1** : the act or process of resolving **2** : the action of solving; *also* : SOLUTION **3** : the quality of being resolute : FIRMNESS, DETERMINATION **4** : a formal statement expressing the opinion, will, or intent of a body of persons

¹re·solve \ri-'zälv\ *vb* **re·solved; re·solv·ing 1** : to break up into constituent parts : ANALYZE **2** : to distinguish between or make visible adjacent parts of **3** : to find an answer to : SOLVE **4** : DETERMINE, DECIDE **5** : to make or pass a formal resolution — **re·solv·able** *adj*

²resolve *n* **1** : fixity of purpose **2** : something resolved

res·o·nance \'re-zə-nəns\ *n* **1** : the quality or state of being resonant **2** : a reinforcement of sound in a vibrating body caused by waves from another body vibrating at nearly the same rate

res·o·nant \-nənt\ *adj* **1** : continuing to sound : RESOUNDING **2** : relating to or exhibiting resonance **3** : intensified and enriched by or as if by resonance — **res·o·nant·ly** *adv*

res·o·nate \-ˌnāt\ *vb* **-nat·ed; -nat·ing 1** : to produce or exhibit resonance **2** : REVERBERATE, RESOUND

res·o·na·tor \-ˌnā-tər\ *n* : something that resounds or exhibits resonance

re·sorp·tion \rē-'sorp-shən, -'zorp-\ *n* : the action or process of breaking down and assimilating something (as a tooth or an embryo)

¹re·sort \ri-'zort\ *n* [ME, fr. MF, resource, recourse, fr.

resortir to rebound, resort, fr. OF, fr. *sortir* to escape, sally] **1** : one looked to for help : REFUGE **2** : RECOURSE **3** : frequent or general visiting ⟨place of ∼⟩ **4** : a frequently visited place : HAUNT **5** : a place providing recreation esp. to vacationers

²resort *vb* **1** : to go often or habitually **2** : to have recourse ⟨∼ed to violence⟩

re·sound \ri-'zaùnd\ *vb* **1** : to become filled with sound : REVERBERATE, RING **2** : to sound loudly

re·sound·ing *adj* **1** : RESONATING, RESONANT **2** : impressively sonorous ⟨∼ name⟩ **3** : EMPHATIC, UNEQUIVOCAL ⟨a ∼ success⟩ — **re·sound·ing·ly** *adv*

re·source \'rē-ˌsors, ri-'sors\ *n* [F *ressource*, fr. OF *ressourse* relief, resource, fr. *resourdre* to relieve, lit., to rise again, fr. L *resurgere*, fr. *re-* again + *surgere* to rise] **1** : a source of supply or support — usu. used in pl. **2** *pl* : available funds **3** : a possibility of relief or recovery **4** : a means of spending leisure time **5** : ability to meet and handle situations — **re·source·ful** \ri-'sors-fəl\ *adj* — **re·source·ful·ness** *n*

resp *abbr* respective; respectively

¹re·spect \ri-'spekt\ *n* **1** : relation to something usu. specified : REGARD ⟨in ∼ to⟩ **2** : high or special regard : ESTEEM **3** *pl* : an expression of respect or deference **4** : DETAIL, PARTICULAR — **re·spect·ful** \-fəl\ *adj* — **re·spect·ful·ly** *adv* — **re·spect·ful·ness** *n*

²respect *vb* **1** : to consider deserving of high regard : ESTEEM **2** : to refrain from interfering with ⟨∼ another's privacy⟩ **3** : to have reference to : CONCERN — **re·spect·er** *n*

re·spect·able \ri-'spek-tə-bəl\ *adj* **1** : worthy of respect : ESTIMABLE **2** : decent or correct in conduct : PROPER **3** : fair in size, quantity, or quality : MODERATE, TOLERABLE **4** : fit to be seen : PRESENTABLE — **re·spect·a·bil·i·ty** \-ˌspek-tə-'bi-lə-tē\ *n* — **re·spect·ably** \-'spek-tə-blē\ *adv*

re·spect·ing *prep* : with regard to

re·spec·tive \-tiv\ *adj* : PARTICULAR, SEPARATE ⟨returned to their ∼ homes⟩

re·spec·tive·ly \-lē\ *adv* **1** : as relating to each **2** : each in the order given

res·pi·ra·tion \ˌres-pə-'rā-shən\ *n* **1** : an act or the process of breathing **2** : the physical and chemical processes (as breathing and oxidation) by which a living thing obtains oxygen and eliminates waste gases (as carbon dioxide) — **re·spi·ra·to·ry** \'res-pə-rə-ˌtor-ē, ri-'spī-rə-\ *adj* — **re·spire** \ri-'spīr\ *vb*

res·pi·ra·tor \'res-pə-ˌrā-tər\ *n* **1** : a device covering the mouth or nose esp. to prevent inhaling harmful vapors **2** : a device for artificial respiration

re·spite \'res-pət\ *n* **1** : a temporary delay **2** : an interval of rest or relief

re·splen·dent \ri-'splen-dənt\ *adj* : shining brilliantly : gloriously bright : SPLENDID — **re·splen·dence** \-dəns\ *n* — **re·splen·dent·ly** *adv*

re·spond \ri-'spänd\ *vb* **1** : ANSWER, REPLY **2** : REACT ⟨∼ed to a call for help⟩ **3** : to show favorable reaction ⟨∼ to medication⟩ — **re·spond·er** *n*

re·spon·dent \ri-'spän-dənt\ *n* : one who responds; *esp* : one who answers in various legal proceedings — **respondent** *adj*

re·sponse \ri-'späns\ *n* **1** : an act of responding **2** : something constituting a reply or a reaction

re·spon·si·bil·i·ty \ri-ˌspän-sə-'bi-lə-tē\ *n*, *pl* **-ties 1** : the quality or state of being responsible **2** : something for which one is responsible

re·spon·si·ble \ri-'spän-sə-bəl\ *adj* **1** : liable to be called upon to answer for one's acts or decisions : ANSWERABLE **2** : able to fulfill one's obligations : RELIABLE, TRUSTWORTHY **3** : able to choose for oneself between right and wrong **4** : involving accountability or important duties ⟨∼ position⟩ — **re·spon·si·ble·ness** *n* — **re·spon·si·bly** \-blē\ *adv*

re·spon·sive \-siv\ *adj* **1** : RESPONDING **2** : quick to respond : SENSITIVE **3** : using responses ⟨∼ readings⟩ — **re·spon·sive·ly** *adv* — **re·spon·sive·ness** *n*

¹rest \'rest\ *n* **1** : REPOSE, SLEEP **2** : freedom from work or activity **3** : a state of motionlessness or inactivity **4** : a place of shelter or lodging **5** : a silence in music equivalent in duration to a note of the same value; *also* : a character indicating this **6** : something used as a support — **rest·ful** \-fəl\ *adj* — **rest·ful·ly** *adv*

rest 5

²rest *vb* **1** : to get rest by lying down; *esp* : SLEEP **2** : to cease from action or motion **3** : to give rest to : set at rest **4** : to sit or lie fixed or supported **5** : to place on or against a support **6** : to remain based or founded **7** : to cause to be firmly fixed : GROUND **8** : to remain for action : DEPEND

³rest *n* : something left over

res·tau·rant \'res-trənt, -tə-ˌränt\ *n* [F, fr. prp. of *restaurer* to restore, fr. L *restaurare*] : a public eating place

res·tau·ra·teur \ˌres-tə-rə-'tər\ *also* **res·tau·ran·teur** \-ˌrän-\ *n* : the operator or proprietor of a restaurant

rest home *n* : an establishment that gives care for the aged or convalescent

res·ti·tu·tion \ˌres-tə-'tü-shən, -'tyü-\ *n* : the act of restoring : the state of being restored; *esp* : restoration of something to its rightful owner **syn** amends, redress, reparation, indemnity, compensation

res·tive \'res-tiv\ *adj* [ME, fr. MF *restif*, fr. *rester* to stop behind, remain, fr. L *restare*, fr. *re-* back + *stare* to stand] **1** : BALKY **2** : UNEASY, FIDGETY **syn** restless, impatient, nervous — **res·tive·ly** *adv* — **res·tive·ness** *n*

rest·less \'rest-ləs\ *adj* **1** : lacking or denying rest ⟨a ∼ night⟩ **2** : never resting or settled : always moving ⟨the ∼ sea⟩ **3** : marked by or showing unrest esp. of mind ⟨∼ pacing back and forth⟩ **syn** restive, impatient, nervous, fidgety — **rest·less·ly** *adv* — **rest·less·ness** *n*

res·tor·able \ri-'stōr-ə-bəl\ *adj* : fit for restoring or reclaiming

res·to·ra·tion \ˌres-tə-'rā-shən\ *n* **1** : an act of restoring : the state of being restored **2** : something (as a building) that has been restored

res·tor·ative \ri-'stōr-ə-tiv\ *n* : something that restores esp. to consciousness or health — **restorative** *adj*

re·store \ri-'stōr\ *vb* **re·stored; re·stor·ing 1** : to give back : RETURN **2** : to put back into use or service **3** : to put or bring back into a former or original state **4** : to put again in possession of something — **re·stor·er** *n*

re·strain \ri-'strān\ *vb* **1** : to prevent from doing something **2** : to limit, restrict, or keep under control : CURB **3** : to place under restraint or arrest — **re·strain·able** *adj* — **re·strain·er** *n*

re·strained \ri-'strānd\ *adj* : marked by restraint : DISCIPLINED — **re·strain·ed·ly** \-'strā-nəd-lē\ *adv*

restraining order *n* : a legal order directing one person to stay away from another

re·straint \ri-'strānt\ *n* **1** : an act of restraining : the state of being restrained **2** : a restraining force, agency, or device **3** : deprivation or limitation of liberty : CONFINEMENT **4** : control over one's feelings : RESERVE

re·strict \ri-'strikt\ *vb* **1** : to confine within bounds : LIMIT **2** : to place under restriction as to use — **re·stric·tive** *adj* — **re·stric·tive·ly** *adv*

re·stric·tion \ri-'strik-shən\ *n* **1** : something (as a law or rule) that restricts **2** : an act of restricting : the state of being restricted

rest room *n* : a room or suite of rooms that includes sinks and toilets

¹re·sult \ri-'zəlt\ *vb* [ME, fr. ML *resultare*, fr. L, to rebound, fr. *re-* re- + *saltare* to leap] : to come about as an effect or consequence — **re·sul·tant** \-'zəlt-ənt\ *adj or n*

²result *n* **1** : something that results : EFFECT, CONSEQUENCE **2** : beneficial or discernible effect **3** : something obtained by calculation or investigation

re·sume \ri-'züm\ *vb* **re·sumed; re·sum·ing 1** : to take or assume again **2** : to return to or begin again after interruption **3** : to take back to oneself — **re·sump·tion** \-'zəmp-shən\ *n*

ré·su·mé *or* **re·su·me** *or* **re·su·mé** \'re-zə-ˌmā, ˌre-zə-'mā\ *n* [F *résumé*] : SUMMARY; *esp* : a short account of one's career and qualifications usu. prepared by a job applicant

re·sur·gence \ri-'sər-jəns\ *n* : a rising again into life, activity, or prominence — **re·sur·gent** \-jənt\ *adj*

res·ur·rect \ˌre-zə-'rekt\ *vb* **1** : to raise from the dead **2** : to bring to attention or use again

res·ur·rec·tion \ˌre-zə-'rek-shən\ *n* **1** *cap* : the rising of Christ from the dead **2** *often cap* : the rising to life of all human dead before the final judgment **3** : REVIVAL

re·sus·ci·tate \ri-'sə-sə-ˌtāt\ *vb* **-tat·ed; -tat·ing** : to revive from apparent death or unconsciousness; *also* : REVITALIZE — **re·sus·ci·ta·tion** \ri-ˌsə-sə-'tā-shən, ˌrē-\ *n* — **re·sus·ci·ta·tor** \-ˌtā-tər\ *n*

ret *abbr* **1** retain **2** retired **3** return

¹re·tail \'rē-ˌtāl, *esp for 2 also* ri-'tāl\ *vb* **1** : to sell in small quantities directly to the ultimate consumer **2** : to tell in detail or to one person after another — **re·tail·er** *n*

²re·tail \'rē-ˌtāl\ *n* : the sale of goods in small amounts to ultimate consumers — **retail** *adj or adv*

re·tain \ri-'tān\ *vb* **1** : to hold in possession or use **2** : to engage (as a lawyer) by paying a fee in advance **3** : to keep in a fixed place or position **syn** detain, withhold, reserve

¹re·tain·er \ri-'tā-nər\ *n* **1** : one that retains **2** : a servant in a wealthy household; *also* : EMPLOYEE

²retainer *n* : a fee paid to secure services (as of a lawyer)

¹re·take \(ˌ)rē-'tāk\ *vb* **-took** \-'túk\; **-tak·en** \-'tā-kən\; **-tak·ing 1** : to take or seize again **2** : to photograph again

²re·take \'rē-ˌtāk\ *n* : a second photographing of a motion-picture scene

re·tal·i·ate \ri-'ta-lē-ˌāt\ *vb* **-at·ed; -at·ing** : to return like for like; *esp* : to get revenge — **re·tal·i·a·tion** \-ˌta-lē-'ā-shən\ *n* — **re·tal·ia·to·ry** \-'tal-yə-ˌtōr-ē\ *adj*

re·tard \ri-'tärd\ *vb* : to hold back : delay the progress of **syn** slow, slacken, detain — **re·tar·da·tion** \ˌrē-ˌtär-'dā-shən, ri-\ *n* — **re·tard·er** *n*

re·tard·ed *adj* : slow or limited in intellectual, emotional, or academic progress ⟨a ∼ child⟩

retch \'rech\ *vb* : to try to vomit; *also* : VOMIT

re·ten·tion \ri-'ten-chən\ *n* **1** : the act of retaining : the state of being retained **2** : the power of retaining esp. in the mind : RETENTIVENESS

re·ten·tive \-'ten-tiv\ *adj* : having the power of retaining; *esp* : retaining knowledge easily — **re·ten·tive·ness** *n*

re·think \(ˌ)rē-'thiŋk\ *vb* **-thought** \-'thòt\; **-think·ing** : to think about again : RECONSIDER

ret·i·cent \'re-tə-sənt\ *adj* **1** : tending not to talk or give out information **2** : RELUCTANT **syn** reserved, taciturn, closemouthed — **ret·i·cence** \-səns\ *n* — **ret·i·cent·ly** *adv*

ret·i·na \'ret-ən-ə\ *n, pl* **retinas** *or* **ret·i·nae** \-ən-ˌē\ : the sensory membrane lining the eye that receives the image formed by the lens — **ret·i·nal** \'ret-ən-əl\ *adj*

ret·i·nue \'ret-ᵊn-¡ü, -¡yü\ n : the body of attendants or followers of a distinguished person

re·tire \ri-'tīr\ vb **re·tired; re·tir·ing 1** : RETREAT **2** : to withdraw esp. for privacy **3** : to withdraw from one's occupation or position : conclude one's career **4** : to go to bed **5** : to cause to be out in baseball — **re·tire·ment** n

re·tired \ri-'tīrd\ adj **1** : SECLUDED, QUIET **2** : withdrawn from active duty or from one's career

re·tir·ee \ri-¡tī-'rē\ n : a person who has retired from a career

re·tir·ing adj : SHY, RESERVED

¹re·tort \ri-'tòrt\ vb [L retortus, pp. of retorquēre, lit., to twist back, hurl back, fr. re- back + torquēre to twist] **1** : to say in reply : answer back usu. sharply **2** : to answer (an argument) by a counter argument **3** : RETALIATE

²retort n : a quick, witty, or cutting reply

³re·tort \ri-'tòrt, 'rē-¡tòrt\ n [MF retorte, fr. ML retorta, fr. L, fem. of retortus, pp. of retorquēre to twist back; fr. its shape] : a vessel in which substances are distilled or broken up by heat

re·touch \(¡)rē-'təch\ vb : TOUCH UP; esp : to change (as a photographic negative) in order to produce a more desirable appearance

re·trace \(¡)rē-'trās\ vb : to go over again or in a reverse direction ⟨retraced his steps⟩

re·tract \ri-'trakt\ vb **1** : to draw back or in **2** : to withdraw (as a charge or promise) : DISAVOW — **re·tract·able** adj — **re·trac·tion** \-'trak-shən\ n

re·trac·tile \ri-'trakt-ᵊl, -'trak-¡tīl\ adj : capable of being drawn back or in ⟨∼ claws⟩

¹re·tread \(¡)rē-'tred\ vb **re·tread·ed; re·tread·ing** : to put a new tread on (a worn tire)

²re·tread \'rē-¡tred\ n **1** : a retreaded tire **2** : one pressed into service again; also : REMAKE

¹re·treat \ri-'trēt\ n **1** : an act of withdrawing esp. from something dangerous, difficult, or disagreeable **2** : a military signal for withdrawal; also : a military flag-lowering ceremony **3** : a place of privacy or safety : REFUGE **4** : a period of group withdrawal for prayer, meditation, and study

²retreat vb **1** : to make a retreat : WITHDRAW **2** : to slope backward

re·trench \ri-'trench\ vb [obs. F retrencher (now retrancher), fr. MF retrenchier, fr. re- + trenchier to cut] **1** : to cut down or pare away : REDUCE, CURTAIL **2** : to cut down expenses : ECONOMIZE — **re·trench·ment** n

ret·ri·bu·tion \¡re-trə-'byü-shən\ n : something administered or exacted in recompense; esp : PUNISHMENT **syn** reprisal, vengeance, revenge, retaliation — **re·trib·u·tive** \ri-'tri-byə-tiv\ adj — **re·trib·u·to·ry** \-byə-¡tōr-ē\ adj

re·trieve \ri-'trēv\ vb **re·trieved; re·triev·ing 1** : to search about for and bring in (killed or wounded game) **2** : RECOVER, RESTORE — **re·triev·able** adj — **re·triev·al** \-'trē-vəl\ n

re·triev·er \ri-'trē-vər\ n : one that retrieves; esp : a dog of any of several breeds used esp. for retrieving game

ret·ro·ac·tive \¡re-trō-'ak-tiv\ adj : made effective as of a date prior to enactment ⟨a ∼ pay raise⟩ — **ret·ro·ac·tive·ly** adv

ret·ro·fit \'re-tro-¡fit, ¡re-trō-'fit\ vb : to furnish (as an aircraft) with newly available equipment — **ret·ro·fit** \'re-tro-¡fit\ n

¹ret·ro·grade \'re-trə-¡grād\ adj **1** : moving or tending backward **2** : tending toward or resulting in a worse condition

²retrograde vb **1** : RETREAT **2** : DETERIORATE, DEGENERATE

ret·ro·gres·sion \¡re-trə-'gre-shən\ n : return to a former and less complex level of development or organization — **ret·ro·gress** \¡re-trə-'gres\ vb — **ret·ro·gres·sive** \¡re-trə-'gre-siv\ adj

ret·ro·rock·et \'re-trō-¡rä-kət\ n : an auxiliary rocket engine (as on a spacecraft) used to slow forward motion

ret·ro·spect \'re-trə-¡spekt\ n : a review of past events — **ret·ro·spec·tion** \¡re-trə-'spek-shən\ n — **ret·ro·spec·tive** \-'spek-tiv\ adj — **ret·ro·spec·tive·ly** adv

ret·ro·vi·rus \'re-trō-¡vī-rəs\ n : any of a group of RNA-containing viruses (as HIV) that make DNA using RNA instead of the reverse

¹re·turn \ri-'tərn\ vb **1** : to go or come back **2** : to pass, give, or send back to an earlier possessor **3** : to put back to or in a former place or state **4** : REPLY, ANSWER **5** : to report esp. officially **6** : to elect to office **7** : to bring in (as profit) : YIELD **8** : to give or perform in return — **re·turn·er** n

²return n **1** : an act of coming or going back to or from a former place or state **2** : RECURRENCE **3** : a report of the results of balloting **4** : a formal statement of taxable income **5** : the profit from labor, investment, or business : YIELD **6** : the act of returning something **7** : something that returns or is returned; also : a means for conveying something (as water) back to its starting point **8** : something given in repayment or reciprocation; also : ANSWER, RETORT **9** : an answering play — **return** adj

¹re·turn·able \ri-'tər-nə-bəl\ adj : capable of being returned (as for reuse or recycling); also : permitted to be returned

²returnable n : a returnable beverage container

re·turn·ee \ri-¡tər-'nē\ n : one who returns

re·union \rē-'yü-nyən\ n **1** : an act of reuniting : the state of being reunited **2** : a meeting of persons after separation

¹rev \'rev\ n : a revolution of a motor

²rev vb **revved; rev·ving** : to increase the revolutions per minute of (a motor)

³rev abbr **1** revenue **2** reverse **3** review; reviewed **4** revised; revision **5** revolution

Rev abbr **1** Revelation **2** Reverend

re·vamp \(¡)rē-'vamp\ vb : RECONSTRUCT, REVISE; also : RENOVATE

re·vanche \rə-'vänⁿsh\ n [F] : REVENGE; esp : a usu. political policy designed to recover lost territory or status

re·veal \ri-'vēl\ vb **1** : to make known **2** : to show plainly : open up to view

rev·eil·le \'re-və-lē\ n [modif. of F réveillez, imper. pl. of réveiller to awaken, fr. eveiller to awaken, fr. (assumed) VL exvigilare, fr. L vigilare to keep watch, stay awake] : a military signal sounded at about sunrise

¹rev·el \'re-vəl\ vb **-eled** or **-elled; -el·ing** or **-el·ling 1** : to take part in a revel **2** : to take great pleasure or satisfaction — **rev·el·er** or **rev·el·ler** n — **rev·el·ry** \-vəl-rē\ n

²revel n : a usu. wild party or celebration

rev·e·la·tion \¡re-və-'lā-shən\ n **1** : an act of revealing **2** : something revealed; esp : an enlightening or astonishing disclosure

Revelation n — see BIBLE table

¹re·venge \ri-'venj\ vb **re·venged; re·veng·ing** : to inflict harm or injury in return for (a wrong) : AVENGE — **re·veng·er** n

²revenge n **1** : a desire for revenge **2** : an act or instance of retaliation to get even **3** : an opportunity for getting satisfaction **syn** vengeance, retribution, reprisal — **re·venge·ful** adj

rev·e·nue \'re-və-¡nü, -¡nyü\ n [ME, fr. MF, fr. revenir to return, fr. L revenire, fr. re- back + venire to come] **1** : investment income **2** : money collected by a government (as through taxes)

rev·e·nu·er \'re-və-¡nü-ər, -¡nyü-\ n : a revenue officer or boat

re·verb \ri-'vərb, 'rē-¡vərb\ n : an electronically produced echo effect in recorded music; also : a device for producing reverb

re·ver·ber·ate \ri-'vər-bə-ˌrāt\ *vb* **-at·ed; -at·ing 1** : RE-FLECT ⟨∼ light or heat⟩ **2** : to resound in or as if in a series of echoes — **re·ver·ber·a·tion** \-ˌvər-bə-'rā-shən\ *n*

re·vere \ri-'vir\ *vb* **re·vered; re·ver·ing** : to show honor and devotion to : VENERATE **syn** reverence, worship, adore

¹rev·er·ence \'re-vrəns, -və-rəns\ *n* **1** : honor or respect felt or shown **2** : a gesture (as a bow or curtsy) of respect

²reverence *vb* **-enced; -enc·ing** : to regard or treat with reverence

¹rev·er·end \'re-vrənd, -və-rənd\ *adj* **1** : worthy of reverence : REVERED **2** : being a member of the clergy — used as a title

²reverend *n* : a member of the clergy

rev·er·ent \'re-vrənt, -və-rənt\ *adj* : expressing reverence — **rev·er·ent·ly** *adv*

rev·er·en·tial \ˌre-və-'ren-chəl\ *adj* : REVERENT

rev·er·ie *also* **rev·ery** \'re-və-rē\ *n, pl* **-er·ies 1** : DAY-DREAM **2** : the state of being lost in thought

re·ver·sal \ri-'vər-səl\ *n* : an act or process of reversing

¹re·verse \ri-'vərs\ *adj* **1** : opposite to a previous or normal condition ⟨in ∼ order⟩ **2** : acting or working in a manner opposite the usual **3** : bringing about reverse movement ⟨∼ gear⟩ — **re·verse·ly** *adv*

²reverse *vb* **re·versed; re·vers·ing 1** : to turn upside down or completely about in position or direction **2** : to set aside or change (as a legal decision) **3** : to change to the contrary ⟨∼ a policy⟩ **4** : to go or cause to go in the opposite direction **5** : to put (as a car) in reverse — **re·vers·ible** \-'vər-sə-bəl\ *adj*

³reverse *n* **1** : something contrary to something else : OPPOSITE **2** : an act or instance of reversing; *esp* : a change for the worse **3** : the back of something **4** : a gear that reverses something

re·ver·sion \ri-'vər-zhən\ *n* **1** : the right of succession or future possession (as to a title or property) **2** : return toward some former or ancestral condition; *also* : a product of this — **re·ver·sion·ary** \-zhə-ˌner-ē\ *adj*

re·vert \ri-'vərt\ *vb* **1** : to come or go back ⟨∼ed to savagery⟩ **2** : to return to a proprietor or his or her heirs **3** : to return to an ancestral type

¹re·view \ri-'vyü\ *n* **1** : an act of revising **2** : a formal military inspection **3** : a general survey **4** : INSPEC-TION, EXAMINATION; *esp* : REEXAMINATION **5** : a critical evaluation (as of a book) **6** : a magazine devoted to reviews and essays **7** : a renewed study of previously studied material **8** : REVUE

²review \ri-'vyü, *1 also* 'rē-\ *vb* **1** : to examine or study again; *esp* : to reexamine judicially **2** : to hold a review of ⟨∼ troops⟩ **3** : to write a critical examination of ⟨∼ a novel⟩ **4** : to look back over ⟨∼ed her accomplishments⟩ **5** : to study material again

re·view·er \ri-'vyü-ər\ *n* : one that reviews; *esp* : a writer of critical reviews

re·vile \ri-'vīl\ *vb* **re·viled; re·vil·ing** : to abuse verbally : rail at **syn** vituperate, berate, rate, upbraid, scold — **re·vile·ment** *n* — **re·vil·er** *n*

re·vise \ri-'vīz\ *vb* **re·vised; re·vis·ing 1** : to look over something written in order to correct or improve **2** : to make a new version of — **re·vis·able** *adj* — **re·vise** *n* — **re·vis·er** *or* **re·vi·sor** \-'vī-zər\ *n* — **re·vi·sion** \-'vi-zhən\ *n*

re·vi·tal·ize \ˌrē-'vīt-ᵊl-ˌīz\ *vb* **-ized; -iz·ing** : to give new life or vigor to — **re·vi·tal·i·za·tion** \(ˌ)rē-ˌvīt-ᵊl-ə-'zā-shən\ *n*

re·viv·al \ri-'vī-vəl\ *n* **1** : an act of reviving : the state of being revived **2** : a new publication or presentation (as of a book or play) **3** : an evangelistic meeting or series of meetings

re·vive \ri-'vīv\ *vb* **re·vived; re·viv·ing 1** : to bring back to life consciousness, or activity : make or become fresh or strong again **2** : to bring back into use — **re·viv·er** *n*

re·viv·i·fy \rē-'vi-və-ˌfī\ *vb* : REVIVE — **re·viv·i·fi·ca·tion** \-ˌvi-və-fə-'kā-shən\ *n*

re·vo·ca·ble \'re-və-kə-bəl *also* ri-'vō-kə-bəl\ *adj* : capable of being revoked

re·vo·ca·tion \ˌre-və-'kā-shən\ *n* : an act or instance of revoking

re·voke \ri-'vōk\ *vb* **re·voked; re·vok·ing 1** : to annul by recalling or taking back : REPEAL, RESCIND **2** : RE-NEGE **2** — **re·vok·er** *n*

¹re·volt \ri-'vōlt\ *vb* **1** : to throw off allegiance to a ruler or government : REBEL **2** : to experience disgust or shock **3** : to turn or cause to turn away with disgust or abhorrence — **re·volt·er** *n*

²revolt *n* : REBELLION, INSURRECTION

re·volt·ing *adj* : extremely offensive — **re·volt·ing·ly** *adv*

rev·o·lu·tion \ˌre-və-'lü-shən\ *n* **1** : the action by a heavenly body of going round in an orbit **2** : ROTA-TION **3** : a sudden, radical, or complete change; *esp* : the overthrow or renunciation of one ruler or government and substitution of another by the governed

¹rev·o·lu·tion·ary \-shə-ˌner-ē\ *adj* **1** : of or relating to revolution **2** : tending to or promoting revolution **3** : constituting or bringing about a major change

²revolutionary *n, pl* **-ar·ies** : one who takes part in a revolution or who advocates revolutionary doctrines

rev·o·lu·tion·ise *Brit var of* REVOLUTIONIZE

rev·o·lu·tion·ist \ˌre-və-'lü-shə-nist\ *n* : REVOLUTION-ARY — **revolutionist** *adj*

rev·o·lu·tion·ize \-ˌnīz\ *vb* **-ized; -iz·ing** : to change fundamentally or completely : make revolutionary — **rev·o·lu·tion·iz·er** *n*

re·volve \ri-'välv\ *vb* **re·volved; re·volv·ing 1** : to turn over in the mind : reflect upon : PONDER **2** : to move in an orbit; *also* : ROTATE — **re·volv·able** *adj*

re·volv·er \ri-'väl-vər\ *n* : a pistol with a revolving cylinder of several chambers

re·vue \ri-'vyü\ *n* : a theatrical production consisting typically of brief often satirical sketches and songs

re·vul·sion \ri-'vəl-shən\ *n* **1** : a strong sudden reaction or change of feeling **2** : a feeling of complete distaste or repugnance

revved *past and past part of* REV

revving *pres part of* REV

¹re·ward \ri-'word\ *vb* **1** : to give a reward to or for **2** : RECOMPENSE

²reward *n* **1** : something given in return for good or evil done or received; *esp* : something given or offered for some service or attainment **2** : a stimulus that is administered to an organism after a response and that increases the probability of occurrence of the response **syn** premium, prize, award

¹re·wind \(ˌ)rē-'wīnd\ *vb* **-wound; -wind·ing 1** : to wind again **2** : to reverse the winding of (as film)

²re·wind \'rē-ˌwīnd\ *n* **1** : something that rewinds **2** : an act of rewinding

re·work \(ˌ)rē-'wərk\ *vb* **1** : REVISE **2** : to reprocess for further use

¹re·write \(ˌ)rē-'rīt\ *vb* **-wrote; -writ·ten; -writ·ing** : to make a revision of : REVISE

²re·write \'rē-ˌrīt\ *n* : an instance or a piece of rewriting

RF *abbr* radio frequency

RFD *abbr* rural free delivery

Rh *symbol* rhodium

RH *abbr* right hand

rhap·so·dy \'rap-sə-dē\ *n, pl* **-dies** [L *rhapsodia* portion of an epic poem adapted for recitation, fr. Gk *rhapsōidia* recitation of selections from epic poetry, fr. *rhaptein* to sew, stitch together + *aidein* to sing] **1** : an expression of extravagant praise or ecstasy **2** : an instrumental composition of irregular form — **rhap·sod·ic** \rap-'sä-dik\ *adj* — **rhap·sod·i·cal·ly** \-di-k(ə-)lē\ *adv* — **rhap·so·dize** \'rap-sə-ˌdīz\ *vb*

rhea \'rē-ə\ *n* : either of two large flightless 3-toed So. American birds that resemble but are smaller than the African ostrich

rhe·ni·um \\'rē-nē-əm\ *n* : a rare heavy hard metallic chemical element — see ELEMENT table

rheo·stat \\'rē-ə-ˌstat\ *n* : a resistor for regulating an electric current by means of variable resistances — **rheo·stat·ic** \ˌrē-ə-ˈsta-tik\ *adj*

rhe·sus monkey \\'rē-səs-\ *n* : a pale brown Indian monkey often used in medical research

rhet·o·ric \\'re-tə-rik\ *n* [ME *rethorik*, fr. MF *rethorique*, fr. L *rhetorica*, fr. Gk *rhētorikē*, lit., art of oratory, fr. *rhētōr* public speaker, fr. *eirein* to speak] : the art of speaking or writing effectively — **rhe·tor·i·cal** \ri-ˈtȯr-i-kəl\ *adj* — **rhet·o·ri·cian** \ˌre-tə-ˈri-shən\ *n*

rheum \\'rüm\ *n* : a watery discharge from the mucous membranes esp. of the eyes or nose — **rheumy** *adj*

rheu·mat·ic fever \rü-ˈma-tik-\ *n* : an acute disease chiefly of children and young adults that is characterized by fever, by inflammation and pain in and around the joints, and by inflammation of the membranes surrounding the heart and the heart valves

rheu·ma·tism \\'rü-mə-ˌti-zəm, 'rü-\ *n* : any of various conditions marked by stiffness, pain, or swelling in muscles or joints — **rheu·mat·ic** \rü-ˈma-tik\ *adj*

rheu·ma·toid arthritis \-ˌtȯid-\ *n* : a progressive constitutional disease characterized by inflammation and swelling of joint structures

Rh factor \ˌär-ˈāch-\ *n* [*rh*esus monkey (in which it was first detected)] : any of one or more inherited substances in red blood cells that may cause dangerous reactions in some infants or in transfusions

rhine·stone \\'rīn-ˌstōn\ *n* : a colorless imitation stone of high luster made of glass, paste, or gem quartz

rhi·no \\'rī-nō\ *n, pl* **rhino** *or* **rhinos** : RHINOCEROS

rhi·noc·er·os \rī-ˈnä-sə-rəs\ *n, pl* **-noc·er·os·es** *or* **-noc·er·os** *or* **-noc·eri** \-ˈnä-sə-ˌrī\ [ME *rinoceros*, fr. L *rhinoceros*, fr. Gk *rhinokerōs*, fr. *rhin-, rhis* nose + *keras* horn] : any of a family of large thick-skinned mammals of Africa and Asia with one or two upright horns of keratin on the snout and three toes on each foot

rhi·zome \\'rī-ˌzōm\ *n* : a fleshy, rootlike, and usu. horizontal underground plant stem that forms shoots above and roots below — **rhi·zom·a·tous** \rī-ˈzä-mə-təs\ *adj*

Rh–neg·a·tive \ˌär-ˌāch-ˈne-gə-tiv\ *adj* : lacking Rh factors in the red blood cells

rho \\'rō\ *n* : the 17th letter of the Greek alphabet — P or ρ

rho·di·um \\'rō-dē-əm\ *n* : a hard ductile metallic chemical element — see ELEMENT table

rho·do·den·dron \ˌrō-də-ˈden-drən\ *n* : any of a genus of shrubs or trees of the heath family with clusters of large bright flowers

rhom·boid \\'räm-ˌbȯid\ *n* : a parallelogram with unequal adjacent sides and angles that are not right angles — **rhomboid** *or* **rhom·boi·dal** \räm-ˈbȯid-əl\ *adj*

rhom·bus \\'räm-bəs\ *n, pl* **rhom·bus·es** *or* **rhom·bi** \-ˌbī\ : a parallelogram having all four sides equal

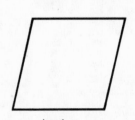

rhombus

Rh–pos·i·tive \ˌär-ˌāch-ˈpä-zə-tiv\ *adj* : containing one or more Rh factors in the red blood cells

rhu·barb \\'rü-ˌbärb\ *n* [ME *rubarbe*, fr. MF *reubarbe*, fr. ML *reubarbarum*, alter. of *rha barbarum*, lit., barbarian rhubarb] : a garden plant related to the buckwheat having leaves with thick juicy edible pink and red stems

¹rhyme \\'rīm\ *n* **1** : a composition in verse that rhymes; *also* : POETRY **2** : correspondence in terminal sounds (as of two lines of verse)

²rhyme *vb* **rhymed; rhym·ing 1** : to make rhymes; *also* : to write poetry **2** : to have rhymes : be in rhyme

rhythm \\'ri-thəm\ *n* **1** : regular rise and fall in the flow of sound in speech **2** : a movement or activity in which some action or element recurs regularly — **rhyth·mic** \\'rith-mik\ *or* **rhyth·mi·cal** \-mi-kəl\ *adj* — **rhyth·mi·cal·ly** \-k(ə-)lē\ *adv*

rhythm and blues *n* : popular music based on blues and black folk music

rhythm method *n* : birth control by refraining from sexual intercourse during the time when ovulation is most likely to occur

RI *abbr* Rhode Island

ri·al \rē-ˈȯl, -ˈäl\ *n* — see MONEY table

¹rib \\'rib\ *n* **1** : any of the series of curved bones of the chest of most vertebrates that are joined to the backbone in pairs and help to support the body wall and protect the organs inside **2** : something resembling a rib in shape or function **3** : any of the parallel ridges in a knitted or woven fabric

²rib *vb* **ribbed; rib·bing 1** : to furnish or strengthen with ribs **2** : to form ridges in knitting or weaving

³rib *vb* **ribbed; rib·bing** : to poke fun at : TEASE — **rib·ber** *n*

rib·ald \\'ri-bəld\ *adj* : coarse or indecent esp. in language ⟨~ jokes⟩ — **rib·ald·ry** \-bəl-drē\ *n*

rib·and \\'ri-bənd\ *n* : RIBBON

rib·bon \\'ri-bən\ *n* **1** : a narrow fabric typically of silk or velvet used for trimming and for badges **2** : a strip of inked cloth (as in a typewriter) **3** : TATTER, SHRED ⟨torn to ~s⟩

ri·bo·fla·vin \ˌrī-bə-ˈflā-vən, 'rī-bə-ˌflā-vən\ *n* : a growth-promoting vitamin of the vitamin B complex occurring in milk and liver

ri·bo·nu·cle·ic acid \ˌrī-bō-nù-ˌklē-ik-, -nyù-, -ˌklā-\ *n* : RNA

ri·bose \\'rī-ˌbōs\ *n* : a sugar with five carbon atoms and five oxygen atoms in each molecule that is part of RNA

ri·bo·some \\'rī-bə-ˌsōm\ *n* : any of the RNA-rich cytoplasmic granules in a cell that are sites of protein synthesis — **ri·bo·som·al** \ˌrī-bə-ˈsō-məl\ *adj*

rice \\'rīs\ *n* : the starchy seeds of an annual grass that are cooked and used for food; *also* : this widely cultivated grass of warm wet areas

rich \\'rich\ *adj* **1** : possessing or controlling great wealth : WEALTHY **2** : COSTLY, VALUABLE **3** : deep and pleasing in color or tone **4** : ABUNDANT **5** : containing much sugar, fat, or seasoning; *also* : high in combustible content **6** : FRUITFUL, FERTILE — **rich·ly** *adv* — **rich·ness** *n*

rich·es \\'ri-chəz\ *n pl* [ME, sing. or pl., fr. *richesse*, lit., richness, fr. OF, fr. *riche* rich] : things that make one rich : WEALTH

Rich·ter scale \\'rik-tər-\ *n* : a scale for expressing the magnitude of a seismic disturbance (as an earthquake) in terms of the energy dissipated in it

rick \\'rik\ *n* : a large stack (as of hay) in the open air

rick·ets \\'ri-kəts\ *n* : a childhood deficiency disease marked esp. by soft deformed bones and caused by inadequate sunlight or inadequate vitamin D

rick·ett·sia \ri-ˈket-sē-ə\ *n, pl* **-sias** *or* **-si·ae** \-sē-ˌē\ : any of a group of rod-shaped bacteria that cause various diseases (as typhus)

rick•ety \'ri-kə-tē\ *adj* **1** : affected with rickets **2** : SHAKY; *also* : in unsound physical condition

rick•sha *or* **rick•shaw** \'rik-ˌshò\ *n* : a small covered 2-wheeled carriage pulled by one person and used orig. in Japan

¹ric•o•chet \'ri-kə-ˌshā, *Brit also* -ˌshet\ *n* : a bouncing off at an angle (as of a bullet off a wall); *also* : an object that ricochets

²ricochet *vb* **-cheted** \-ˌshād\ *or* **-chet•ted** \-ˌshe-təd\; **-chet•ing** \-ˌshā-iŋ\ *or* **-chet•ting** \-ˌshe-tiŋ\ : to skip with or as if with glancing rebounds

rid \'rid\ *vb* **rid** *also* **rid•ded**; **rid•ding** : to make free : CLEAR, RELIEVE — **rid•dance** \'rid-ᵊns\ *n*

rid•den \'rid-ᵊn\ *adj* **1** : harassed, oppressed, or obsessed by ⟨debt-*ridden*⟩ **2** : excessively full of or supplied with ⟨slum-*ridden*⟩

¹rid•dle \'rid-ᵊl\ *n* : a puzzling question to be solved or answered by guessing

²riddle *vb* **rid•dled**; **rid•dling** **1** : EXPLAIN, SOLVE **2** : to speak in riddles

³riddle *n* : a coarse sieve

⁴riddle *vb* **rid•dled**; **rid•dling** **1** : to sift with a riddle **2** : to pierce with many holes **3** : PERMEATE

¹ride \'rīd\ *vb* **rode** \'rōd\; **rid•den** \'rid-ᵊn\; **rid•ing** **1** : to go on an animal's back or in a conveyance (as a boat, car, or airplane); *also* : to sit on and control so as to be carried along ⟨~ a bicycle⟩ **2** : to float or move on water ⟨~ at anchor⟩; *also* : to move like a floating object **3** : to bear along : CARRY ⟨*rode* her on their shoulders⟩ **4** : to travel over a surface ⟨car ~s well⟩ **5** : to proceed over on horseback **6** : to torment by nagging or teasing

²ride *n* **1** : an act of riding; *esp* : a trip on horseback or by vehicle **2** : a way (as a road or path) suitable for riding **3** : a mechanical device (as a merry-go-round) for riding on **4** : a means of transportation

rid•er \'rī-dər\ *n* **1** : one that rides **2** : an addition to a document often attached on a separate piece of paper **3** : a clause dealing with an unrelated matter attached to a legislative bill during passage — **rid•er•less** *adj*

¹ridge \'rij\ *n* **1** : a range of hills **2** : a raised line or strip **3** : the line made where two sloping surfaces (as of a roof) meet — **ridgy** *adj*

²ridge *vb* **ridged**; **ridg•ing** **1** : to form into a ridge **2** : to extend in ridges

¹rid•i•cule \'ri-də-ˌkyül\ *n* : the act of exposing to laughter : DERISION

²ridicule *vb* **-culed**; **-cul•ing** : to laugh at or make fun of mockingly or contemptuously **syn** deride, taunt, twit, mock

ri•dic•u•lous \rə-'di-kyə-ləs\ *adj* : arousing or deserving ridicule : ABSURD, PREPOSTEROUS **syn** laughable, ludicrous, farcical, risible — **ri•dic•u•lous•ly** *adv* — **ri•dic•u•lous•ness** *n*

ri•el \rē-'el\ *n* — see MONEY table

RIF *abbr* reduction in force

rife \'rīf\ *adj* : WIDESPREAD, PREVALENT, ABOUNDING — **rife** *adv* — **rife•ly** *adv*

riff \'rif\ *n* : a repeated phrase in jazz typically supporting a solo improvisation; *also* : a piece based on such a phrase — **riff** *vb*

riff•raff \'rif-ˌraf\ *n* [ME *riffe raffe*, fr. *rif and raf* every single one, fr. MF *rif et raf* completely] **1** : RABBLE **2** : REFUSE, RUBBISH

¹ri•fle \'rī-fəl\ *vb* **ri•fled**; **ri•fling** : to ransack esp. with the intent to steal — **ri•fler** *n*

²rifle *vb* **ri•fled**; **ri•fling** : to cut spiral grooves into the bore of ⟨*rifled* pipe⟩ — **rifling** *n*

³rifle *n* **1** : a shoulder weapon with a rifled bore **2** *pl* : soldiers armed with rifles — **ri•fle•man** \-fəl-mən\ *n*

rift \'rift\ *n* **1** : CLEFT, FISSURE **2** : FAULT 6 **3** : ESTRANGEMENT, SEPARATION — **rift** *vb*

¹rig \'rig\ *vb* **rigged**; **rig•ging** **1** : to fit out (as a ship) with rigging **2** : CLOTHE, DRESS **3** : EQUIP **4** : to set up esp. as a makeshift ⟨~ up a shelter⟩

²rig *n* **1** : the distinctive shape, number, and arrange-

ment of sails and masts of a ship **2** : a carriage with its horse **3** : CLOTHING, DRESS **4** : EQUIPMENT

³rig *vb* **rigged**; **rig•ging** **1** : to manipulate or control esp. by deceptive or dishonest means **2** : to fix in advance for a desired result — **rig•ger** *n*

rig•ging \'ri-giŋ, -gən\ *n* **1** : the ropes and chains that hold and move masts, sails, and spars of a ship **2** : a network (as in theater scenery) used for support and manipulation

¹right \'rīt\ *adj* **1** : RIGHTEOUS, UPRIGHT **2** : JUST, PROPER **3** : conforming to truth or fact : CORRECT **4** : APPROPRIATE, SUITABLE **5** : STRAIGHT ⟨a ~ line⟩ **6** : GENUINE, REAL **7** : of, relating to, or being the side of the body which is away from the heart and on which the hand is stronger and more skilled in most persons **8** : located nearer to the right hand; *esp* : being on the right when facing in the same direction as the observer **9** : made to be placed or worn outward ⟨~ side of a rug⟩ **10** : NORMAL, SOUND ⟨not in her ~ mind⟩ **syn** correct, accurate, exact, precise, nice — **right•ness** *n*

²right *n* **1** : qualities that constitute what is correct, just, proper, or honorable **2** : something (as a power or privilege) to which one has a just or lawful claim **3** : just action or decision : the cause of justice **4** : the side or part that is on or toward the right side **5** *cap* : political conservatives **6** *often cap* : a conservative position — **right•ward** \-wərd\ *adj*

³right *adv* **1** : according to what is right ⟨live ~⟩ **2** : EXACTLY, PRECISELY ⟨~ here and now⟩ **3** : DIRECTLY ⟨went ~ home⟩ **4** : according to fact or truth ⟨guess ~⟩ **5** : all the way : COMPLETELY ⟨~ to the end⟩ **6** : IMMEDIATELY ⟨~ after lunch⟩ **7** : QUITE, VERY ⟨~ nice weather⟩ **8** : on or to the right ⟨looked ~ and left⟩

⁴right *vb* **1** : to relieve from wrong **2** : to adjust or restore a proper state or position **3** : to bring or restore to an upright position **4** : to become upright — **right•er** *n*

right angle *n* : an angle whose measure is 90° : an angle whose sides are perpendicular to each other — **right–an•gled** \'rīt-ˌaŋ-gəld\ *or* **right–an•gle** \-gəl\ *adj*

right circular cone *n* : CONE 2

righ•teous \'rī-chəs\ *adj* : acting or being in accordance with what is just, honorable, and free from guilt or wrong : UPRIGHT **syn** virtuous, noble, moral, ethical — **right•eous•ly** *adv* — **right•eous•ness** *n*

right•ful \'rīt-fəl\ *adj* **1** : JUST; *also* : FITTING **2** : having or held by a legally just claim — **right•ful•ly** *adv* — **right•ful•ness** *n*

right–hand \'rīt-ˌhand\ *adj* **1** : situated on the right **2** : RIGHT-HANDED **3** : chiefly relied on ⟨his ~ man⟩

right–hand•ed \-'han-dəd\ *adj* **1** : using the right hand habitually or better than the left **2** : designed for or done with the right hand **3** : CLOCKWISE ⟨a ~ twist⟩ — **right–handed** *adv* — **right–hand•ed•ly** *adv* — **right–hand•ed•ness** *n*

right•ly \'rīt-lē\ *adv* **1** : FAIRLY, JUSTLY **2** : PROPERLY **3** : CORRECTLY, EXACTLY

right–of–way *n, pl* **rights–of–way** **1** : a legal right of passage over another person's ground **2** : the area over which a right-of-way exists **3** : the land on which a public road is built **4** : the land occupied by a railroad **5** : the land used by a public utility **6** : the right of traffic to take precedence over other traffic

right on *interj* — used to express agreement or give encouragement

right–to–life *adj* : ANTIABORTION — **right–to–lifer** *n*

right triangle *n* : a triangle having one right angle

rig•id \'ri-jəd\ *adj* **1** : lacking flexibility **2** : strictly observed **syn** severe, stern, rigorous, stringent — **ri•gid•i•ty** \rə-'ji-də-tē\ *n* — **rig•id•ly** *adv*

rig•ma•role \'ri-gə-mə-ˌrōl\ *n* [alter. of obs. *ragman roll* long list, catalog] **1** : confused or senseless talk **2** : a complex and ritualistic procedure

rig•or \'ri-gər\ *n* **1** : the quality of being inflexible or unyielding : STRICTNESS **2** : HARSHNESS, SEVERITY **3** : a tremor caused by a chill **4** : strict precision : EXACTNESS — **rig·or·ous** *adj* — **rig·or·ous·ly** *adv*

rig·or mor·tis \ˌri-gər-ˈmȯr-təs\ *n* [NL, stiffness of death] : temporary rigidity of muscles occurring after death

rig·our *chiefly Brit var of* RIGOR

rile \ˈrīl\ *vb* **riled; ril·ing 1** : to make angry **2** : ROIL 1

rill \ˈril\ *n* : a very small brook

¹rim \ˈrim\ *n* **1** : the outer part of a wheel **2** : an outer edge esp. of something curved : BORDER, MARGIN

²rim *vb* **rimmed; rim·ming 1** : to serve as a rim for : BORDER **2** : to run around the rim of

¹rime \ˈrīm\ *n* **1** : FROST **2** — **rimy** \ˈrī-mē\ *adj*

²rime *var of* RHYME

rind \ˈrīnd\ *n* : a usu. hard or tough outer layer ⟨lemon ∼⟩

¹ring \ˈriŋ\ *n* **1** : a circular band worn as an ornament or token or used for holding or fastening ⟨wedding ∼⟩ ⟨key ∼⟩ **2** : something circular in shape ⟨smoke ∼⟩ **3** : a place for contest or display ⟨boxing ∼⟩; *also* : PRIZEFIGHTING **4** : ANNUAL RING **5** : a group of people who work together for selfish or dishonest purposes — **ring·like** \ˈriŋ-ˌlīk\ *adj*

²ring *vb* **ringed; ring·ing** \ˈriŋ-iŋ\ **1** : ENCIRCLE **2** : to throw a ring over (a mark) in a game (as quoits) **3** : to move in a ring or spirally

³ring *vb* **rang** \ˈraŋ\; **rung** \ˈrəŋ\; **ring·ing** \ˈriŋ-iŋ\ **1** : to sound resonantly when struck; *also* : to feel as if filled with such sound **2** : to cause to make a clear metallic sound by striking **3** : to announce or call by or as if by striking a bell ⟨∼ an alarm⟩ **4** : to repeat loudly and persistently **5** : to summon esp. by a bell ⟨∼ for the butler⟩

⁴ring *n* **1** : a set of bells **2** : the clear resonant sound of vibrating metal **3** : resonant tone : SONORITY **4** : a sound or character expressive of a particular quality **5** : an act or instance of ringing; *esp* : a telephone call

¹ring·er \ˈriŋ-ər\ *n* **1** : one that sounds by ringing **2** : one that enters a competition under false representations **3** : one that closely resembles another

²ringer *n* : one that encircles or puts a ring around

ring finger *n* : the third finger of the left hand counting the forefinger as one

ring·git \ˈriŋ-git\ *n* — see MONEY table

ring·lead·er \ˈriŋ-ˌlē-dər\ *n* : a leader esp. of a group of troublemakers

ring·let \-lət\ *n* : a long curl

ring·mas·ter \-ˌmas-tər\ *n* : one in charge of performances in a circus ring

ring up *vb* **1** : to total and record esp. by means of a cash register **2** : ACHIEVE ⟨*rang up* many triumphs⟩

ring·worm \ˈriŋ-ˌwərm\ *n* : any of several contagious skin diseases caused by fungi and marked by ring-shaped discolored patches

rink \ˈriŋk\ *n* : a level extent of ice marked off for skating or various games; *also* : a similar surface (as of wood) marked off or enclosed for a sport or game ⟨roller-skating ∼⟩

¹rinse \ˈrins\ *vb* **rinsed; rins·ing** [ME *rincen*, fr. MF *rincer*, fr. (assumed) VL *recentiare*, fr. L *recent-, recens* fresh, recent] **1** : to wash lightly or in water only **2** : to cleanse (as of soap) with clear water **3** : to treat (hair) with a rinse — **rins·er** *n*

²rinse *n* **1** : an act of rinsing **2** : a liquid used for rinsing **3** : a solution that temporarily tints hair

ri·ot \ˈrī-ət\ *n* **1** *archaic* : disorderly behavior **2** : disturbance of the public peace; *esp* : a violent public disorder **3** : random or disorderly profusion ⟨a ∼ of color⟩ **4** : one that is wildly amusing ⟨the comedy is a ∼⟩ — **riot** *vb* — **ri·ot·er** *n* — **ri·ot·ous** *adj*

¹rip \ˈrip\ *vb* **ripped; rip·ping 1** : to cut or tear open **2** : to saw or split (wood) with the grain — **rip·per** *n*

²rip *n* : a rent made by ripping

RIP *abbr* [L *requiescat in pace*] may he rest in peace,

may she rest in peace; [L *requiescant in pace*] may they rest in peace

ri·par·i·an \rə-ˈper-ē-ən\ *adj* : of or relating to the bank of a stream, river, or lake

rip cord *n* : a cord that is pulled to release the pilot parachute which lifts a main parachute out of its container

ripe \ˈrīp\ *adj* **rip·er; rip·est 1** : fully grown and developed : MATURE ⟨∼ fruit⟩ **2** : fully prepared for some use or object : READY — **ripe·ly** *adv* — **ripe·ness** *n*

rip·en \ˈrī-pən\ *vb* **rip·ened; rip·en·ing 1** : to grow or make ripe **2** : to bring to completeness or perfection; *also* : to age or cure (cheese) to develop characteristic flavor, odor, body, texture, and color

rip–off \ˈrip-ˌȯf\ *n* **1** : an act of stealing : THEFT **2** : a cheap imitation — **rip off** *vb*

ri·poste \ri-ˈpōst\ *n* [F, modif. of It *risposta*, lit., answer] **1** : a fencer's return thrust after a parry **2** : a retaliatory maneuver or response; *esp* : a quick retort — **riposte** *vb*

rip·ple \ˈri-pəl\ *vb* **rip·pled; rip·pling 1** : to become lightly ruffled on the surface **2** : to make a sound like that of rippling water — **ripple** *n*

rip·saw \ˈrip-ˌsȯ\ *n* : a coarse-toothed saw used to cut wood in the direction of the grain

rip·stop \-ˌstäp\ *adj* : being a fabric woven in such a way that small tears do not spread ⟨∼ nylon⟩ — **rip·stop** *n*

¹rise \ˈrīz\ *vb* **rose** \ˈrōz\; **ris·en** \ˈriz-ᵊn\; **ris·ing 1** : to get up from sitting, kneeling, or lying **2** : to get up from sleep or from one's bed **3** : to return from death **4** : to take up arms **5** : to end a session : ADJOURN **6** : to appear above the horizon **7** : to move upward : ASCEND **8** : to extend above other objects **9** : to attain a higher level or rank **10** : to increase in quantity or in intensity **11** : to come into being : HAPPEN, BEGIN, ORIGINATE

²rise *n* **1** : a spot higher than surrounding ground **2** : an upward slope **3** : an act of rising : a state of being risen **4** : BEGINNING, ORIGIN **5** : the elevation of one point above another **6** : an increase in amount, number, or volume **7** : an angry reaction

ris·er \ˈrī-zər\ *n* **1** : one that rises **2** : the upright part between stair treads

ris·i·bil·i·ty \ˌri-zə-ˈbi-lə-tē\ *n, pl* **-ties** : the ability or inclination to laugh — often used in pl.

ris·i·ble \ˈri-zə-bəl\ *adj* **1** : able or inclined to laugh **2** : arousing laughter; *esp* : amusingly ridiculous

¹risk \ˈrisk\ *n* : exposure to possible loss or injury : DANGER, PERIL — **risk·i·ness** \ˈris-kē-nəs\ *n* — **risky** *adj*

²risk *vb* **1** : to expose to danger ⟨∼ed his life⟩ **2** : to incur the danger of

ris·qué \ris-ˈkā\ *adj* [F] : verging on impropriety or indecency

ri·tard \ri-ˈtärd\ *adv or adj* : with a gradual slackening in tempo — used as a direction in music

rite \ˈrīt\ *n* **1** : a set form for conducting a ceremony **2** : the liturgy of a church **3** : a ceremonial act or action

rit·u·al \ˈri-chə-wəl\ *n* **1** : the established form esp. for a religious ceremony **2** : a system of rites **3** : a ceremonial act or action **4** : a customarily repeated act or series of acts — **ritual** *adj* — **rit·u·al·ism** \-wə-ˌli-zəm\ *n* — **rit·u·al·is·tic** \ˌri-chə-wə-ˈlis-tik\ *adj* — **rit·u·al·is·ti·cal·ly** \-ti-k(ə-)lē\ *adv* — **rit·u·al·ly** *adv*

riv *abbr* river

¹ri·val \ˈrī-vəl\ *n* [MF or L; MF, fr. L *rivalis* one using the same stream as another, rival in love, fr. *rivalis* of a stream, fr. *rivus* stream] **1** : one of two or more trying to get what only one can have **2** : one striving for competitive advantage **3** : one that equals another esp. in desired qualities : MATCH, PEER

²rival *adj* : COMPETING

³rival *vb* **-valed** *or* **-valled; -val·ing** *or* **-val·ling 1** : to be in competition with **2** : to try to equal or excel **3** : to have qualities that approach or equal another's

ri·val·ry \'rī-vəl-rē\ *n, pl* **-ries** : COMPETITION

rive \'rīv\ *vb* **rived** \'rīvd\; **riv·en** \'ri-vən\ *also* **rived; riv·ing 1** : SPLIT, REND **2** : SHATTER

riv·er \'ri-vər\ *n* **1** : a natural stream larger than a brook **2** : a large stream or flow

riv·er·bank \-ˌbaŋk\ *n* : the bank of a river

riv·er·bed \-ˌbed\ *n* : the channel occupied by a river

riv·er·boat \-ˌbōt\ *n* : a boat for use on a river

riv·er·front \-ˌfrənt\ *n* : the land or area along a river

riv·er·side \-ˌsīd\ *n* : the side or bank of a river

¹riv·et \'ri-vət\ *n* : a metal bolt with a head at one end used to join parts by being put through holes in them and then being flattened on the plain end to make another head

²rivet *vb* : to fasten with or as if with a rivet — **riv·et·er** *n*

riv·u·let \'ri-vyə-lət, -və-\ *n* : a small stream

ri·yal \rē-'äl, -'al\ *n* — see MONEY table

rm *abbr* **1** ream **2** room

Rn *symbol* radon

¹RN \ˌär-'en\ *n* : REGISTERED NURSE

²RN *abbr* Royal Navy

RNA \ˌär-(ˌ)en-'ā\ *n* : any of various nucleic acids (as messenger RNA) that are found esp. in the cytoplasm of cells, have ribose as the 5-carbon sugar, and are associated with the control of cellular chemical activities

rnd *abbr* round

¹roach \'rōch\ *n, pl* **roach** *also* **roach·es** : any of various bony fishes related to the carp; *also* : any of several sunfishes

²roach *n* **1** : COCKROACH **2** : the butt of a marijuana cigarette

road \'rōd\ *n* **1** : ROADSTEAD — often used in pl. **2** : an open way for vehicles, persons, and animals : HIGHWAY **3** : ROUTE, PATH **4** : a series of scheduled visits (as games or performances) in several locations or the travel necessary to make these visits ⟨the team is on the ∼⟩

road·bed \'rōd-ˌbed\ *n* **1** : the foundation of a road or railroad **2** : the part of the surface of a road on which vehicles travel

road·block \-ˌbläk\ *n* **1** : a barricade on the road ⟨a police ∼⟩ **2** : an obstruction to progress

road·ie \'rō-dē\ *n* : one who works for traveling entertainers

road·kill \'rōd-ˌkil\ *n* : an animal that has been killed on a road by a motor vehicle

road·run·ner \-ˌrə-nər\ *n* : a largely terrestrial bird of the southwestern U.S. and Mexico that is a speedy runner

road·side \'rōd-ˌsīd\ *n* : the strip of land along a road — **roadside** *adj*

road·stead \-ˌsted\ *n* : an anchorage for ships usu. less sheltered than a harbor

road·ster \'rōd-stər\ *n* **1** : a driving horse **2** : an open automobile that seats two

road·way \-ˌwā\ *n* : ROAD; *esp* : ROADBED

road·work \-ˌwərk\ *n* **1** : work done in constructing or repairing roads **2** : conditioning for an athletic contest (as a boxing match) consisting mainly of long runs

roam \'rōm\ *vb* **1** : WANDER, ROVE **2** : to range or wander over or about

¹roan \'rōn\ *adj* : of dark color (as black, red, or brown) sprinkled with white ⟨a ∼ horse⟩

²roan *n* : an animal (as a horse) with a roan coat; *also* : its color

¹roar \'rōr\ *vb* **1** : to utter a full loud prolonged sound **2** : to make a loud confused sound (as of wind or waves) — **roar·er** *n*

²roar *n* : a sound of roaring

¹roast \'rōst\ *vb* **1** : to cook by dry heat (as before a fire or in an oven) **2** : to criticize severely or kiddingly

²roast *n* **1** : a piece of meat suitable for roasting **2** : an outing at which food is roasted ⟨corn ∼⟩ **3** : severe criticism or kidding

³roast *adj* : ROASTED

roast·er \'rō-stər\ *n* **1** : one that roasts **2** : a device for roasting **3** : something suitable for roasting

rob \'räb\ *vb* **robbed; rob·bing 1** : to steal from **2** : to deprive of something due or expected **3** : to commit robbery — **rob·ber** *n*

robber fly *n* : any of a family of predaceous flies

rob·bery \'rä-bə-rē\ *n, pl* **-ber·ies** : the act or practice of robbing; *esp* : theft of something from a person by use of violence or threat

¹robe \'rōb\ *n* **1** : a long flowing outer garment; *esp* : one used for ceremonial occasions **2** : a wrap or covering for the lower body (as for sitting outdoors)

²robe *vb* **robed; rob·ing 1** : to clothe with or as if with a robe **2** : DRESS

rob·in \'rä-bən\ *n* **1** : a small chiefly European thrush with a somewhat orange face and breast **2** : a large No. American thrush with a grayish back, a streaked throat, and a chiefly dull reddish breast

ro·bot \'rō-ˌbät, -bət\ *n* [Czech, fr. *robota* compulsory labor] **1** : a machine that looks and acts like a human being **2** : an efficient but insensitive person **3** : a device that automatically performs esp. repetitive tasks **4** : something guided by automatic controls — **ro·bot·ic** \rō-'bä-tik\ *adj*

ro·bot·ics \rō-'bä-tiks\ *n* : technology dealing with the design, construction, and operation of robots

ro·bust \rō-'bəst, 'rō-(ˌ)bəst\ *adj* [L *robustus* oaken, strong, fr. *robur* oak, strength] : strong and vigorously healthy — **ro·bust·ly** *adv* — **ro·bust·ness** *n*

ROC *abbr* Republic of China (Taiwan)

¹rock \'räk\ *vb* **1** : to move back and forth in or as if in a cradle **2** : to sway or cause to sway back and forth

²rock *n* **1** : a rocking movement **2** : popular music usu. played on electric instruments and characterized by a strong beat and much repetition

³rock *n* **1** : a mass of stony material; *also* : broken pieces of stone **2** : solid mineral deposits **3** : something like a rock in firmness **4** : GEM; *esp* : DIAMOND — **rock** *adj* — **rock·like** *adj* — **rocky** *adj*

rock and roll *n* : ²ROCK 2

rock·bound \'räk-ˌbaund\ *adj* : fringed or covered with rocks

rock·er \'rä-kər\ *n* **1** : one of the curved pieces on which something (as a chair or cradle) rocks **2** : a chair that rocks on rockers **3** : a device that works with a rocking motion **4** : a rock performer, song, or enthusiast

¹rock·et \'rä-kət\ *n* [It *rocchetta*, lit., small distaff] **1** : a firework that is propelled through the air by the discharge of gases produced by a burning substance **2** : a jet engine that operates on the same principle as a firework rocket but carries the oxygen needed for burning its fuel **3** : a rocket-propelled bomb or missile

²rocket *vb* **1** : to convey by means of a rocket **2** : to rise abruptly and rapidly

rock·et·ry \'rä-kə-trē\ *n* : the study or use of rockets

rocket ship *n* : a rocket-propelled spacecraft

rock·fall \'räk-ˌfol\ *n* : a mass of falling or fallen rocks

rock·fish \-ˌfish\ *n* : any of various market bony fishes that live among rocks or on rocky bottoms

rock salt *n* : common salt in rocklike masses or large crystals

Rocky Mountain sheep *n* : BIGHORN

ro·co·co \rə-'kō-kō\ *adj* [F, irreg. fr. *rocaille* style of ornament, lit., stone debris] : of or relating to an artistic style esp. of the 18th century marked by fanciful curved forms and elaborate ornamentation — **rococo** *n*

rod \'räd\ *n* **1** : a straight slender stick **2** : a stick or bundle of twigs used in punishing a person; *also* : PUNISHMENT **3** : a staff borne to show rank **4** — see WEIGHT table **5** : any of the rod-shaped receptor cells of the retina that are sensitive to faint light **6** *slang* : HANDGUN

rode *past of* RIDE

ro•dent \\'rōd-ᵊnt\\ *n* [ultim. fr. L *rodent-, rodens,* prp. of *rodere* to gnaw] : any of an order of relatively small mammals (as mice, squirrels, and beavers) with sharp front teeth used for gnawing

ro•deo \\'rō-dē-ˌō, rə-'dā-ō\\ *n, pl* **ro•de•os** [Sp, fr. *rodear* to surround, fr. *rueda* wheel, fr. L *rota*] 1 : ROUNDUP 1 2 : a public performance featuring cowboy skills (as riding and roping)

¹**roe** \\'rō\\ *n, pl* **roe** *or* **roes** : DOE

²**roe** *n* : the eggs of a fish esp. while bound together in a mass

roe•buck \\'rō-ˌbək\\ *n, pl* **roebuck** *or* **roebucks** : a male roe deer

roe deer *n* : either of two small nimble European or Asian deers

roe deer

roent•gen \\'rent-gən, 'rənt-, -jən\\ *n* : the international unit of measurement for X rays and gamma rays

rog•er \\'rä-jər\\ *interj* — used esp. in radio and signaling to indicate that a message has been received and understood

rogue \\'rōg\\ *n* 1 : a dishonest person : SCOUNDREL 2 : a mischievous person : SCAMP — **rogu•ery** \\'rō-gə-rē\\ *n* — **rogu•ish** *adj* — **rogu•ish•ly** *adv* — **rogu•ish•ness** *n*

roil \\'rȯil, *for 2 also* 'rīl\\ *vb* 1 : to make cloudy or muddy by stirring up 2 : RILE 1 — **roily** \\'rȯi-lē\\ *adj*

rois•ter \\'rȯi-stər\\ *vb* **rois•tered; rois•ter•ing** : to engage in noisy revelry : CAROUSE — **rois•ter•er** *n* — **rois•ter•ous** \\-stə-rəs\\ *adj*

ROK *abbr* Republic of Korea (South Korea)

role *also* **rôle** \\'rōl\\ *n* 1 : an assigned or assumed character; *also* : a part played (as by an actor) 2 : FUNCTION

role model *n* : a person whose behavior in a particular role is imitated by others

¹**roll** \\'rōl\\ *n* 1 : a document containing an official record 2 : an official list of names 3 : something (as a bun) that is rolled up or rounded as if rolled 4 : something that rolls : ROLLER

²**roll** *vb* 1 : to move by turning over and over 2 : to press with a roller 3 : to move on wheels 4 : to sound with a full reverberating tone 5 : to make a continuous beating sound (as on a drum) 6 : to utter with a trill 7 : to move onward as if by completing a revolution ⟨years ~ed by⟩ 8 : to flow or seem to flow in a continuous stream or with a rising and falling motion ⟨the river ~ed on⟩ 9 : to swing or sway from side to side 10 : to shape or become shaped in rounded form

³**roll** *n* 1 : a sound produced by rapid strokes on a drum 2 : a heavy reverberating sound 3 : a rolling movement or action 4 : a swaying movement (as of a ship) 5 : SOMERSAULT

roll•back \\'rōl-ˌbak\\ *n* : the act or an instance of rolling back

roll back *vb* 1 : to reduce (as a commodity price) on a national scale 2 : to cause to withdraw : push back

roll bar *n* : an overhead metal bar on an automobile designed to protect riders in case the automobile overturns

roll call *n* : the act or an instance of calling off a list of names (as of soldiers); *also* : a time for a roll call

roll•er \\'rō-lər\\ *n* 1 : a revolving cylinder used for moving, pressing, shaping, applying, or smoothing something 2 : a rod on which something is rolled up 3 : a long heavy ocean wave

roller coast•er \\'rō-lər-ˌkō-stər\\ *n* : an amusement ride consisting of an elevated railway having sharp curves and steep slopes

roller skate *n* : a skate with wheels instead of a runner — **roller–skate** *vb* — **roller skater** *n*

rol•lick \\'rä-lik\\ *vb* : ROMP, FROLIC

rol•lick•ing *adj* : full of fun and good spirits

roly–poly \\ˌrō-lē-'pō-lē\\ *adj* : ROTUND

Rom *abbr* 1 Roman 2 Romance 3 Romania; Romanian 4 Romans

ROM \\'räm\\ *n* : READ-ONLY MEMORY

ro•maine \\rō-'mān\\ *n* [F, lit., Roman] : a garden lettuce with a tall loose head of long crisp leaves

¹**Ro•man** \\'rō-mən\\ *n* 1 : a native or resident of Rome 2 *not cap* : roman letters or type

²**Roman** *adj* 1 : of or relating to Rome or the Romans and esp. the ancient Romans 2 *not cap* : relating to type in which the letters are upright (as in this definition) 3 : of or relating to the Roman Catholic Church

Roman candle *n* : a cylindrical firework that discharges balls of fire

Roman Catholic *adj* : of, relating to, or being a Christian church led by the pope and having a liturgy centered in the Mass — **Roman Catholicism** *n*

¹**ro•mance** \\rō-'mans, 'rō-ˌmans\\ *n* [ME *romauns,* fr. OF *romans* French, something written in French, tale in verse, fr. ML *Romanice* in a vernacular language, ultim. fr. L *Romanus* Roman] 1 : a medieval tale of knightly adventure 2 : a prose narrative dealing with heroic or mysterious events set in a remote time or place 3 : a love story 4 : a romantic attachment or episode between lovers — **ro•manc•er** *n*

²**romance** *vb* **ro•manced; ro•manc•ing** 1 : to exaggerate or invent detail or incident 2 : to have romantic fancies 3 : to carry on a romantic episode with

Romance \\rō-'mans, 'rō-ˌmans\\ *adj* : of or relating to any of several languages developed from Latin

Ro•ma•nian \\rů-'mä-nē-ən, rō-, -nyən\\ *n* 1 : a native or inhabitant of Romania 2 : the language of the Romanians

Roman numeral *n* : a numeral in a system of notation that is based on the ancient Roman system

Ro•ma•no \\rō-'mä-nō\\ *n* : a hard Italian cheese that is sharper than Parmesan

Ro•mans \\'rō-mənz\\ *n* — see BIBLE table

¹**ro•man•tic** \\rō-'man-tik\\ *n* : a romantic person; *esp* : a romantic writer, composer, or artist

²**romantic** *adj* 1 : IMAGINARY 2 : VISIONARY 3 : having an imaginative or emotional appeal 4 : of, relating to, or having the characteristics of romanticism — **ro•man•ti•cal•ly** \\-ti-k(ə-)lē\\ *adv*

ro•man•ti•cism \\rō-'man-tə-ˌsi-zəm\\ *n, often cap* : a literary movement (as in early 19th century England) marked esp. by emphasis on the imagination and the emotions and by the use of autobiographical material — **ro•man•ti•cist** \\-sist\\ *n, often cap*

romp \\'rämp\\ *vb* 1 : to play actively and noisily 2 : to win a contest easily — **romp** *n*

romp•er \\'räm-pər\\ *n* 1 : one that romps 2 : a child's one-piece garment with the lower part shaped like bloomers — usu. used in pl.

rood \\'rüd\\ *n* : CROSS, CRUCIFIX

¹**roof** \\'rüf, 'rů̇f\\ *n, pl* **roofs** \\'rüfs, 'rů̇fs; 'rüvz, 'rů̇vz\\ 1 : the upper covering part of a building 2 : something suggesting a roof of a building — **roofed** \\'rüft, 'rů̇ft\\ *adj* — **roof•ing** *n* — **roof•less** *adj*

²**roof** vb : to cover with a roof

roof·top \-ˌtäp\ n : a roof esp. of a house

¹**rook** \ˈrük\ n : a common Old World bird resembling the related crow

²**rook** vb : CHEAT, SWINDLE

³**rook** n : a chess piece that can move parallel to the sides of the board across any number of unoccupied squares

rook·ery \ˈrü-kə-rē\ n, pl -er·ies : a breeding ground or haunt of gregarious birds or mammals; also : a colony of such birds or mammals

rook·ie \ˈrü-kē\ n : BEGINNER, RECRUIT; esp : a first= year player in a professional sport

¹**room** \ˈrüm, ˈrùm\ n 1 : an extent of space occupied by or sufficient or available for something 2 : a par- titioned part of a building : CHAMBER; also : the peo- ple in a room 3 : OPPORTUNITY, CHANCE ⟨∼ to develop his talents⟩ — **room·ful** n — **roomy** adj

²**room** vb : to occupy lodgings : LODGE — **room·er** n

room·ette \rü-ˈmet, rù-\ n : a small private room on a railroad sleeping car

room·mate \ˈrüm-ˌmāt, ˈrùm-\ n : one of two or more persons sharing the same room or dwelling

¹**roost** \ˈrüst\ n : a support on which or a place where birds perch

²**roost** vb : to settle on or as if on a roost

roost·er \ˈrüs-tər, ˈrùs-\ n : an adult male domestic chicken : COCK

¹**root** \ˈrüt, ˈrùt\ n 1 : the leafless usu. underground part of a seed plant that functions in absorption, aer- ation, and storage or as a means of anchorage; also : an underground plant part esp. when fleshy and ed- ible 2 : something (as the basal part of a tooth or hair) resembling a root 3 : SOURCE, ORIGIN 4 : the essential core : HEART ⟨get to the ∼ of the matter⟩ 5 : a number that when taken as a factor an indicated number of times gives a specified number 6 : the lower part — **root·less** adj — **root·like** adj

²**root** vb 1 : to form roots 2 : to fix or become fixed by or as if by roots : ESTABLISH 3 : UPROOT

³**root** vb 1 : to turn up or dig with the snout ⟨pigs ∼ing⟩ 2 : to poke or dig around (as in search of something)

⁴**root** \ˈrüt\ vb 1 : to applaud or encourage noisily : CHEER 2 : to wish success or lend support to — **root·er** n

root beer n : a sweetened carbonated beverage fla- vored with extracts of roots and herbs

root·let \ˈrüt-lət, ˈrùt-\ n : a small root

root·stock \-ˌstäk\ n : an underground part of a plant that resembles a rhizome

¹**rope** \ˈrōp\ n 1 : a large strong cord made of strands of fiber 2 : a hangman's noose 3 : a thick string (as of pearls) made by twisting or braiding

²**rope** vb **roped; rop·ing** 1 : to bind, tie, or fasten to- gether with a rope 2 : to separate or divide by means of a rope 3 : LASSO

Ror·schach test \ˈrȯr-ˌshäk-\ n : a psychological test in which a subject interprets ink-blot designs in terms that reveal intellectual and emotional factors

ro·sa·ry \ˈrō-zə-rē\ n, pl -ries 1 often cap : a Roman Catholic devotion consisting of meditation on sacred mysteries during recitation of Hail Marys 2 : a string of beads used in praying

¹**rose** past of RISE

²**rose** \ˈrōz\ n 1 : any of a genus of usu. prickly often climbing shrubs with divided leaves and bright often fragrant flowers; also : one of these flowers 2 : some- thing resembling a rose in form 3 : a moderate pur- plish red color — **rose** adj

ro·sé \rō-ˈzā\ n [F] : a light pink wine

ro·se·ate \ˈrō-zē-ət, -zē-ˌāt\ adj 1 : resembling a rose esp. in color 2 : OPTIMISTIC ⟨a ∼ view of the future⟩

rose·bud \ˈrōz-ˌbəd\ n : the flower of a rose when it is at most partly open

rose·bush \-ˌbush\ n : a shrubby rose

rose·mary \ˈrōz-ˌmer-ē\ n, pl -mar·ies [ME rosma-

rine, fr. L rosmarinus, fr. ros dew + marinus of the sea, fr. mare sea] : a fragrant shrubby Old World mint; also : its leaves used as a seasoning

ro·sette \rō-ˈzet\ n [F] 1 : a usu. small badge or orna- ment of ribbon gathered in the shape of a rose 2 : a circular ornament filled with representations of leaves

rose·wa·ter \ˈrōz-ˌwȯ-tər, -ˌwä-\ n : a watery solution of the fragrant constituents of the rose used as a per- fume

rose·wood \-ˌwùd\ n : any of various tropical trees with dark red wood streaked with black; also : this wood

Rosh Ha·sha·nah \ˌräsh-hə-ˈshä-nə, ˌrȯsh-, -ˈshō-\ n [Heb rōsh hashshānāh, lit., beginning of the year] : the Jewish New Year observed as a religious holiday in September or October

ros·in \ˈräz-ən\ n : a brittle resin obtained esp. from pine trees and used esp. in varnishes and on violin bows

ros·ter \ˈräs-tər\ n 1 : a list of personnel; also : the per- sons listed on a roster 2 : an itemized list

ros·trum \ˈräs-trəm\ n, pl **rostrums** or **ros·tra** \-trə\ [L Rostra, pl., a platform for speakers in the Roman Fo- rum decorated with the beaks of captured ships, fr. pl. of rostrum beak, ship's beak, fr. rodere to gnaw] : a stage or platform for public speaking

rosy \ˈrō-zē\ adj **ros·i·er; -est** 1 : of the color rose 2 : HOPEFUL, PROMISING — **ros·i·ly** \ˈrō-zə-lē\ adv — **ros·i·ness** \-zē-nəs\ n

¹**rot** \ˈrät\ vb **rot·ted; rot·ting** : to undergo decomposi- tion : DECAY

²**rot** n 1 : DECAY 2 : any of various diseases of plants or animals in which tissue breaks down 3 : NONSENSE

¹**ro·ta·ry** \ˈrō-tə-rē\ adj 1 : turning on an axis like a wheel 2 : having a rotating part

²**rotary** n, pl -ries 1 : a rotary machine 2 : a one-way circular road junction

ro·tate \ˈrō-ˌtāt\ vb **ro·tat·ed; ro·tat·ing** 1 : to turn or cause to turn about an axis or a center : REVOLVE 2 : to alternate in a series **syn** turn, circle, spin, whirl, twirl — **ro·ta·tion** \rō-ˈtā-shən\ n — **ro·ta·tor** \ˈrō- ˌtā-tər\ n — **ro·ta·to·ry** \ˈrō-tə-ˌtōr-ē\ adj

ROTC abbr Reserve Officers' Training Corps

rote \ˈrōt\ n 1 : repetition from memory often without attention to meaning 2 : fixed routine or repetition — **rote** adj

ro·tis·ser·ie \rō-ˈti-sə-rē\ n [F] 1 : a restaurant special- izing in broiled and barbecued meats 2 : an appliance fitted with a spit on which food is rotated before or over a source of heat

ro·to·gra·vure \ˌrō-tə-grə-ˈvyùr\ n : PHOTOGRAVURE

ro·tor \ˈrō-tər\ n 1 : a part that rotates; esp : the ro- tating part of an electrical machine 2 : a system of ro- tating horizontal blades for supporting a helicopter

ro·to·till·er \ˈrō-tō-ˌti-lər\ n : an engine-powered ma- chine with rotating blades used to lift and turn over soil

rot·ten \ˈrät-ən\ adj 1 : having rotted 2 : CORRUPT 3 : extremely unpleasant or inferior — **rot·ten·ness** n

rot·ten·stone \ˈrät-ən-ˌstōn\ n : a decomposed sili- ceous limestone used for polishing

ro·tund \rō-ˈtənd\ adj : rounded out **syn** plump, chub- by, portly, stout — **ro·tun·di·ty** \-ˈtən-də-tē\ n

ro·tun·da \rō-ˈtən-də\ n 1 : a round building; esp : one covered by a dome 2 : a large round room

rou·ble \ˈrü-bəl\ var of RUBLE

roué \rü-ˈā\ n [F, lit., broken on the wheel, fr. pp. of rouer to break on the wheel, fr. ML rotare, fr. L, to rotate; fr. the feeling that such a person deserves this punishment] : a man devoted to a life of sensual pleasure : RAKE

rouge \ˈrüzh, ˈrüj\ n [F, lit., red] : a cosmetic used to give a red color to cheeks and lips — **rouge** vb

¹**rough** \ˈrəf\ adj **rough·er; rough·est** 1 : uneven in sur- face : not smooth 2 : SHAGGY 3 : not calm : TURBU-

LENT, TEMPESTUOUS **4** : marked by harshness or violence **5** : DIFFICULT, TRYING **6** : coarse or rugged in character or appearance **7** : marked by lack of refinement **8** : CRUDE, UNFINISHED **9** : done or made hastily or tentatively — **rough·ly** adv — **rough·ness** n

²rough n **1** : uneven ground covered with high grass esp. along a golf fairway **2** : a crude, unfinished, or preliminary state; also : something in such a state **3** : ROWDY, TOUGH

³rough vb **1** : ROUGHEN **2** : MANHANDLE **3** : to make or shape roughly esp. in a preliminary way — **rough·er** n

rough·age \'rə-fij\ n : FIBER **2**; also : food containing much indigestible material acting as fiber

rough–and–ready \,rə-fən-'re-dē\ adj : rude or unpolished in nature, method, or manner but effective in action or use

rough–and–tum·ble \-'təm-bəl\ n : rough unrestrained fighting or struggling — **rough–and–tumble** adj

rough·en \'rə-fən\ vb **rough·ened; rough·en·ing** : to make or become rough

rough–hewn \'rəf-'hyün\ adj **1** : being rough and unfinished ⟨∼ beams⟩ **2** : lacking smooth manners or social grace — **rough–hew** \-'hyü\ vb

rough·house \'rəf-,haus\ vb **rough·housed; rough·hous·ing** : to participate in rough noisy behavior — **roughhouse** n

rough·neck \'rəf-,nek\ n **1** : ROWDY, TOUGH **2** : a worker on a crew drilling oil wells

rough·shod \'rəf-shäd\ adv : with no consideration for the wishes or feelings of others ⟨rode ∼ over the opposition⟩

rou·lette \rü-'let\ n [F, lit., small wheel] **1** : a gambling game in which a whirling wheel is used **2** : a wheel or disk with teeth around the outside

¹round \'raund\ adj **1** : having every part of the surface or circumference the same distance from the center **2** : CYLINDRICAL **3** : COMPLETE, FULL **4** : approximately correct; esp : exact only to a specific decimal or place ⟨∼ numbers⟩ **5** : liberal or ample in size or amount **6** : BLUNT, OUTSPOKEN **7** : moving in or forming a circle **8** : having curves rather than angles — **round·ish** adj — **round·ness** n

²round prep or adv : AROUND

³round n **1** : something round (as a circle, globe, or ring) **2** : a curved or rounded part (as a rung of a ladder) **3** : an indirect path or course; also : a regularly covered route (as of a security guard) **4** : a series or cycle of recurring actions or events **5** : one shot fired by a soldier or a gun; also : ammunition for one shot **6** : a period of time or a unit of play in a game or contest **7** : a cut of meat (as beef) esp. between the rump and the lower leg — **in the round 1** : FREESTANDING **2** : with a center stage surrounded by an audience ⟨theater in the round⟩

⁴round vb **1** : to make or become round **2** : to go or pass around or part way around **3** : COMPLETE, FINISH **4** : to become plump or shapely **5** : to express as a round number — often used with off **6** : to follow a winding course : BEND

¹round·about \'raun-də-,baut\ adj : INDIRECT, CIRCUITOUS

²roundabout n, Brit : MERRY-GO-ROUND

roun·de·lay \'raun-də-,lā\ n **1** : a simple song with a refrain **2** : a poem with a recurring refrain

round·house \'raund-,haus\ n **1** : a circular building for housing and repairing locomotives **2** : a blow with the hand made with a wide swing

round·ly \'raund-lē\ adv **1** : in a complete manner; also : WIDELY **2** : in a blunt way **3** : with vigor

round–shoul·dered \-,shōl-dərd\ adj : having the shoulders stooping or rounded

round–trip n : a trip to a place and back

round·up \'raun-,dəp\ n **1** : the gathering together of cattle on the range by riding around them and driving

them in; also : the ranch hands and horses engaged in a roundup **2** : a gathering in of scattered persons or things **3** : SUMMARY ⟨news ∼⟩ — **round up** vb

round·worm \-,wərm\ n : NEMATODE

rouse \'rauz\ vb **roused; rous·ing 1** : to excite to activity : stir up **2** : to wake from sleep — **rous·er** n

roust·about \'raus-tə-,baut\ n : one who does heavy unskilled labor (as on a dock or in an oil field)

¹rout \'raut\ n **1** : MOB 1, 2 **2** : DISTURBANCE **3** : a fashionable gathering

²rout vb **1** : RUMMAGE **2** : to gouge out **3** : to expel by force

³rout n **1** : a state of wild confusion or disorderly retreat **2** : a disastrous defeat

⁴rout vb **1** : to put to flight **2** : to defeat decisively

¹route \'rüt, 'raut\ n **1** : a traveled way **2** : CHANNEL **3** : a line of travel

²route vb **rout·ed; rout·ing** : to send by a selected route : DIRECT

route·man \-mən, -,man\ n : one who sells and makes deliveries on an assigned route

rout·er \'rau-tər\ n : a machine with a revolving spindle and cutter for shaping a surface (as of wood)

rou·tine \rü-'tēn\ n [F, fr. MF, fr. route traveled way] **1** : a regular course of procedure **2** : an often repeated speech or formula **3** : a part fully worked out ⟨a comedy ∼⟩ **4** : a set of computer instructions that will perform a certain task — **routine** adj — **rou·tine·ly** adv — **rou·tin·ize** \-'tē-,nīz\ vb

¹rove \'rōv\ vb **roved; rov·ing** : to wander over or through — **rov·er** n

²rove past and past part of REEVE

¹row \'rō\ vb **1** : to propel a boat with oars **2** : to transport in a rowboat **3** : to pull an oar in a crew — **row·er** \'rō-ər\ n

²row n : an act or instance of rowing

³row n **1** : a number of objects in an orderly sequence **2** : WAY, STREET

⁴row \'rau\ n : a noisy quarrel

⁵row \'rau\ vb : to engage in a row

row·boat \'rō-,bōt\ n : a small boat designed to be rowed

row·dy \'rau-dē\ adj **row·di·er; -est** : coarse or boisterous in behavior : ROUGH — **row·di·ness** \'rau-dē-nəs\ n — **rowdy** n — **row·dy·ish** adj — **row·dy·ism** n

row·el \'rau-əl\ n : a small pointed wheel on a rider's spur — **rowel** vb

¹roy·al \'roi-əl\ adj **1** : of or relating to a sovereign : REGAL **2** : fit for a king or queen ⟨a ∼ welcome⟩ — **roy·al·ly** adv

²royal n : a person of royal blood

royal flush n : a straight flush having an ace as the highest card

roy·al·ist \'roi-ə-list\ n : an adherent of a king or of monarchical government

roy·al·ty \'roi-əl-tē\ n, pl **-ties 1** : the state of being royal **2** : royal persons **3** : a share of a product or profit (as of a mine or oil well) claimed by the owner for allowing another person to use the property **4** : a payment made to an author or composer for each copy of a work sold or to an inventor for each article sold under a patent

RP abbr **1** relief pitcher **2** Republic of the Philippines

rpm abbr revolutions per minute

rps abbr revolutions per second

rpt abbr **1** repeat **2** report

RR abbr **1** railroad **2** rural route

RS abbr **1** recording secretary **2** revised statutes **3** right side **4** Royal Society

RSV abbr Revised Standard Version

RSVP abbr [F répondez s'il vous plaît] please reply

rt abbr **1** right **2** route

RT abbr **1** radiotelephone **2** round-trip

rte abbr route

Ru symbol ruthenium

¹rub \'rəb\ *vb* **rubbed; rub·bing 1** : to use pressure and friction on a body or object **2** : to fret or chafe with friction **3** : to scour, polish, erase, or smear by pressure and friction

²rub *n* **1** : DIFFICULTY, OBSTRUCTION **2** : something grating to the feelings

¹rub·ber \'rə-bər\ *n* **1** : one that rubs **2** : ERASER **3** : a flexible waterproof elastic substance made from the milky juice esp. of a So. American tropical tree or made synthetically; *also* : something made of this material — **rubber** *adj* — **rub·ber·ize** \'rə-bə-ˌrīz\ *vb* — **rub·bery** *adj*

²rubber *n* **1** : a contest that consists of an odd number of games and is won by the side that takes a majority **2** : an extra game played to decide a tie

¹rub·ber·neck \-ˌnek\ *n* **1** : an idly or overly inquisitive person **2** : a person on a guided tour

²rubberneck *vb* : to look about, stare, or listen with excessive curiosity — **rub·ber·neck·er** *n*

rub·bish \'rə-bish\ *n* **1** : useless waste or rejected matter : TRASH **2** : something worthless or nonsensical

rub·ble \'rə-bəl\ *n* : broken fragments esp. of a destroyed building

ru·bel·la \rü-'be-lə\ *n* : GERMAN MEASLES

ru·bi·cund \'rü-bi-(ˌ)kənd\ *adj* : RED, RUDDY

ru·bid·i·um \rü-'bi-dē-əm\ *n* : a soft silvery metallic chemical element — see ELEMENT table

ru·ble \'rü-bəl\ *n* — see MONEY table

ru·bric \'rü-brik\ *n* [ME *rubrike* red ocher, heading in red letters of part of a book, fr. MF *rubrique*, fr. L *rubrica*, fr. *ruber* red] **1** : HEADING, TITLE; *also* : CLASS, CATEGORY **2** : a rule esp. for the conduct of a religious service

ru·by \'rü-bē\ *n, pl* **rubies** : a clear red precious stone — **ruby** *adj*

ru·by–throat·ed hummingbird \'rü-bē-ˌthrō-təd-\ *n* : a bright green and whitish hummingbird of eastern No. America with a red throat in the male

ruck·us \'rə-kəs\ *n* : ROW, DISTURBANCE

rud·der \'rə-dər\ *n* : a movable flat piece attached vertically at the rear of a ship or aircraft for steering

rud·dy \'rə-dē\ *adj* **rud·di·er; -est** : REDDISH; *esp* : of a healthy reddish complexion — **rud·di·ness** \'rə-dē-nəs\ *n*

rude \'rüd\ *adj* **rud·er; rud·est 1** : roughly made : CRUDE **2** : UNDEVELOPED, PRIMITIVE **3** : IMPOLITE **4** : UNSKILLED — **rude·ly** *adv* — **rude·ness** *n*

ru·di·ment \'rü-də-mənt\ *n* **1** : an elementary principle or basic skill — usu. used in pl. **2** : something not fully developed — usu. used in pl. — **ru·di·men·ta·ry** \ˌrü-də-'men-tə-rē\ *adj*

¹rue \'rü\ *n* : REGRET, SORROW — **rue·ful** \-fəl\ *adj* — **rue·ful·ly** *adv* — **rue·ful·ness** *n*

²rue *vb* **rued; ru·ing** : to feel regret, remorse, or penitence for

³rue *n* : a European strong-scented woody herb with bitter-tasting leaves

ruff \'rəf\ *n* **1** : a large round pleated collar worn about 1600 **2** : a fringe of long hair or feathers around the neck of an animal — **ruffed** \'rəft\ *adj*

ruf·fi·an \'rə-fē-ən\ *n* : a brutal person — **ruf·fi·an·ly** *adj*

¹ruf·fle \'rə-fəl\ *vb* **ruf·fled; ruf·fling 1** : to roughen the surface of **2** : IRRITATE, VEX **3** : to erect (as hair or feathers) in or like a ruff **4** : to flip through (as pages) **5** : to draw into or provide with plaits or folds

²ruffle *n* **1** : a strip of fabric gathered or pleated on one edge **2** : RUFF **2 3** : RIPPLE — **ruf·fly** \'rə-fə-lē, -flē\ *adj*

RU 486 \ˌär-ˌyü-ˌfōr-ˌā-tē-'siks\ *n* : a drug taken orally to induce abortion esp. early in pregnancy

rug \'rəg\ *n* **1** : a covering for the legs, lap, and feet **2** : a piece of heavy fabric usu. with a nap or pile used as a floor covering

rug·by \'rəg-bē\ *n, often cap* [*Rugby* School, Rugby, England, where it was first played] : a football game

in which play is continuous and interference and forward passing are not permitted

rug·ged \'rə-gəd\ *adj* **1** : having a rough uneven surface **2** : TURBULENT, STORMY **3** : HARSH, STERN **4** : ROBUST, STURDY — **rug·ged·ize** \'rə-gə-ˌdīz\ *vb* — **rug·ged·ly** *adv* — **rug·ged·ness** *n*

¹ru·in \'rü-ən\ *n* **1** : complete collapse or destruction **2** : the remains of something destroyed — usu. used in pl. **3** : a cause of destruction **4** : the action of destroying

²ruin *vb* **1** : DESTROY **2** : to damage beyond repair **3** : BANKRUPT

ru·in·ation \ˌrü-ə-'nā-shən\ *n* : RUIN, DESTRUCTION

ru·in·ous \'rü-ə-nəs\ *adj* **1** : RUINED, DILAPIDATED **2** : causing ruin — **ru·in·ous·ly** *adv*

¹rule \'rül\ *n* **1** : a guide or principle for governing action : REGULATION **2** : the usual way of doing something **3** : the exercise of authority or control : GOVERNMENT **4** : RULER **2**

²rule *vb* **ruled; rul·ing 1** : CONTROL; *also* : GOVERN **2** : to be supreme or outstanding in **3** : to give or state as a considered decision **4** : to mark on paper with or as if with a ruler

rul·er \'rü-lər\ *n* **1** : SOVEREIGN **2** : a straight strip of material (as wood or metal) marked off in units and used for measuring or as a straightedge

rum \'rəm\ *n* **1** : an alcoholic liquor made from molasses or sugarcane **2** : alcoholic liquor

Ru·ma·nian \rü-'mā-nē-ən, -nyən\ *n* : ROMANIAN — **Rumanian** *adj*

rum·ba \'rəm-bə, 'rüm-\ *n* : a dance of Cuban origin marked by strong rhythmic movements

¹rum·ble \'rəm-bəl\ *vb* **rum·bled; rum·bling** : to make a low heavy rolling sound; *also* : to move along with such a sound — **rum·bler** *n*

²rumble *n* **1** : a low heavy rolling sound **2** : a street fight esp. among gangs

rumble seat *n* : a folding seat in the back of an automobile that is not covered by the top

rum·bling \'rəm-bliŋ\ *n* **1** : RUMBLE **2** : widespread talk or complaints — usu. used in pl.

ru·men \'rü-mən\ *n, pl* **ru·mi·na** \-mə-nə\ *or* **rumens** : the large first compartment of the stomach of a ruminant (as a cow)

¹ru·mi·nant \'rü-mə-nənt\ *n* : a ruminant mammal

²ruminant *adj* **1** : chewing the cud; *also* : of or relating to a group of hoofed mammals (as cattle, deer, and camels) that chew the cud and have a complex usu. 4-chambered stomach **2** : MEDITATIVE

ru·mi·nate \'rü-mə-ˌnāt\ *vb* **-nat·ed; -nat·ing** [L *ruminari* to chew the cud, muse upon, fr. *rumin-, rumen* first stomach chamber of a ruminant] **1** : MEDITATE, MUSE **2** : to chew the cud — **ru·mi·na·tion** \ˌrü-mə-'nā-shən\ *n*

¹rum·mage \'rə-mij\ *vb* **rum·maged; rum·mag·ing** : to search thoroughly — **rum·mag·er** *n*

²rummage *n* **1** : a miscellaneous collection **2** : an act of rummaging

rum·my \'rə-mē\ *n* : any of several card games for two or more players

ru·mor \'rü-mər\ *n* **1** : common talk **2** : a statement or report current but not authenticated — **rumor** *vb*

ru·mour *chiefly Brit var of* RUMOR

rump \'rəmp\ *n* **1** : the rear part of an animal; *also* : a cut of meat (as beef) behind the upper sirloin **2** : a small or inferior remnant (as of a group)

rum·ple \'rəm-pəl\ *vb* **rum·pled; rum·pling** : TOUSLE, MUSS, WRINKLE — **rumple** *n* — **rum·ply** \'rəm-pə-lē\ *adj*

rum·pus \'rəm-pəs\ *n* : DISTURBANCE, RUCKUS

rumpus room *n* : a room usu. in the basement of a home that is used for games, parties, and recreation

¹run \'rən\ *vb* **ran** \'ran\; **run; run·ning 1** : to go faster than a walk **2** : to take to flight : FLEE **3** : to go without restraint ⟨let chickens ~ loose⟩ **4** : to go rapidly or hurriedly : HASTEN, RUSH **5** : to make a quick or casual trip or visit **6** : to contend in a race; *esp* : to enter an election **7** : to put forward as a candidate for office **8** : to move on or as if on wheels : pass or slide freely **9** : to go back and forth : PLY **10** : to move in large numbers esp. to a spawning ground ⟨shad are *running*⟩ **11** : FUNCTION, OPERATE ⟨left the motor *running*⟩ **12** : to continue in force ⟨two years to ∼⟩ **13** : to flow rapidly or under pressure : MELT, FUSE, DISSOLVE; *also* : DISCHARGE **7** ⟨my nose is *running*⟩ **14** : to tend to produce or to recur ⟨family ∼s to blonds⟩ **15** : to take a certain direction **16** : to be worded or written **17** : to be current ⟨rumors *running* wild⟩ **18** : to cause to run **19** : TRACE ⟨∼ down a rumor⟩ **20** : to perform or bring about by running **21** : to cause to pass ⟨∼ a wire from the antenna⟩ **22** : to cause to collide **23** : SMUGGLE **24** : MANAGE, CONDUCT, OPERATE ⟨∼ a business⟩ **25** : INCUR ⟨∼ a risk⟩ **26** : to permit to accumulate before settling ⟨∼ up a bill⟩

²**run** *n* **1** : an act or the action of running **2** : a migration of fish; *also* : the migrating fish **3** : a score in baseball **4** : BROOK, CREEK **5** : a continuous series esp. of similar things **6** : persistent heavy demands from depositors, creditors, or customers **7** : the quantity of work turned out in a continuous operation; *also* : a period of operation (as of a machine or plant) **8** : the usual or normal kind ⟨the ordinary ∼ of students⟩ **9** : the distance covered in continuous travel or sailing **10** : a regular course or trip **11** : freedom of movement in a place or area ⟨has the ∼ of the house⟩ **12** : an enclosure for animals **13** : an inclined course (as for skiing) **14** : a lengthwise ravel (as in a stocking) — **run·less** *adj*

run·about \'rə-nə-ˌbaůt\ *n* : a light wagon, automobile, or motorboat

run·a·gate \'rə-nə-ˌgāt\ *n* **1** : VAGABOND **2** : FUGITIVE

run·around \'rə-nə-ˌraůnd\ *n* : evasive or delaying action esp. in response to a request

¹**run·away** \'rə-nə-ˌwā\ *n* **1** : one that runs away : FUGITIVE **2** : the act of running away out of control; *also* : something (as a horse) that is running out of control

²**runaway** *adj* **1** : FUGITIVE **2** : won by a long lead; *also* : extremely successful **3** : subject to uncontrolled changes ⟨∼ inflation⟩ **4** : operating out of control ⟨a ∼ locomotive⟩

run·down \'rən-ˌdaůn\ *n* : an item-by-item report or review : SUMMARY

run·down \'rən-'daůn\ *adj* **1** : EXHAUSTED, WORN-OUT ⟨that ∼ feeling⟩ **2** : being in poor repair ⟨a ∼ farm⟩

run down *vb* **1** : to collide with and knock down **2** : to chase until exhausted or captured **3** : to find by search **4** : DISPARAGE **5** : to cease to operate for lack of motive power **6** : to decline in physical condition

rune \'rün\ *n* **1** : any of the characters of any of several alphabets formerly used by the Germanic peoples **2** : MYSTERY, MAGIC **3** : a poem esp. in Finnish or Old Norse — **ru·nic** \'rü-nik\ *adj*

¹**rung** *past part of* RING

²**rung** \'rəŋ\ *n* **1** : a rounded crosspiece between the legs of a chair **2** : one of the crosspieces of a ladder

run·in \'rən-ˌin\ *n* **1** : ALTERCATION, QUARREL **2** : something run in

run in *vb* **1** : to insert as additional matter **2** : to arrest esp. for a minor offense **3** : to pay a casual visit

run·nel \'rən-ᵊl\ *n* : BROOK, STREAMLET

run·ner \'rə-nər\ *n* **1** : one that runs **2** : BASE RUNNER **3** : BALLCARRIER **4** : a thin piece or part on which something (as a sled or an ice skate) slides **5** : the support of a drawer or a sliding door **6** : a horizontal branch from the base of a plant that produces new plants **7** : a plant producing runners **8** : a long narrow carpet **9** : a narrow decorative cloth cover for a table or dresser top

run·ner-up \'rə-nər-ˌəp\ *n, pl* **runners-up** *also*

runner-ups : the competitor in a contest who finishes second

¹**run·ning** *adj* **1** : FLOWING **2** : FLUID, RUNNY **3** : CONTINUOUS, INCESSANT **4** : measured in a straight line ⟨cost per ∼ foot⟩ **5** : of or relating to an act of running **6** : made or trained for running ⟨∼ horse⟩ ⟨∼ shoes⟩

²**running** *adv* : in succession

running light *n* : any of the lights carried by a vehicle (as a ship) at night

run·ny \'rə-nē\ *adj* : having a tendency to run ⟨a ∼ dough⟩ ⟨a ∼ nose⟩

run·off \'rən-ˌôf\ *n* : a final contest (as an election) to a previous indecisive contest

run-of-the-mill *adj* : not outstanding : AVERAGE

run on *vb* **1** : to talk at length **2** : to continue (matter in type) without a break or a new paragraph **3** : to place or add (as an entry in a dictionary) at the end of a paragraphed item — **run-on** \'rən-ˌôn, -ˌän\ *n*

runt \'rənt\ *n* : an unusually small person or animal : DWARF — **runty** *adj*

run·way \'rən-ˌwā\ *n* **1** : a beaten path made by animals; *also* : a passage for animals **2** : a paved strip of ground for the landing and takeoff of aircraft **3** : a narrow platform from a stage into an auditorium **4** : a support (as a track) on which something runs

ru·pee \rü-'pē, 'rü-ˌpē\ *n* — see MONEY table

ru·pi·ah \rü-'pē-ə\ *n, pl* **rupiah** *or* **rupiahs** — see MONEY table

¹**rup·ture** \'rəp-chər\ *n* : a breaking or tearing apart; *also* : HERNIA

²**rupture** *vb* **rup·tured; rup·tur·ing** : to cause or undergo rupture

ru·ral \'růr-əl\ *adj* : of or relating to the country, country people, or agriculture

ruse \'rüs, 'rüz\ *n* : a wily subterfuge : TRICK, ARTIFICE

¹**rush** \'rəsh\ *n* : any of various often tufted and hollow⸗stemmed grasslike marsh plants — **rushy** *adj*

²**rush** *vb* [ME *russhen*, fr. MF *ruser* to put to flight, deceive, fr. L *recusare* to refuse] **1** : to move forward or act with too great haste or eagerness or without preparation **2** : to perform in a short time or at high speed **3** : ATTACK, CHARGE — **rush·er** *n*

³**rush** *n* **1** : a violent forward motion **2** : unusual demand or activity **3** : a crowding of people to one place **4** : a running play in football **5** : a sudden feeling of pleasure

⁴**rush** *adj* : requiring or marked by special speed or urgency ⟨∼ orders⟩

rush hour *n* : a time when the amount of traffic or business is at a peak

rusk \'rəsk\ *n* : a sweet or plain bread baked, sliced, and baked again until dry and crisp

Russ *abbr* Russia; Russian

rus·set \'rə-sət\ *n* **1** : a coarse reddish brown cloth **2** : a reddish brown or yellowish brown color **3** : a baking potato — **russet** *adj*

Rus·sian \'rə-shən\ *n* **1** : a native or inhabitant of Russia **2** : a Slavic language of the Russian people — **Russian** *adj*

rust \'rəst\ *n* **1** : a reddish coating formed on iron when it is exposed to esp. moist air **2** : any of numerous plant diseases characterized by usu. reddish spots; *also* : a fungus causing rust **3** : a reddish brown color — **rust** *vb* — **rusty** *adj*

¹**rus·tic** \'rəs-tik\ *adj* : of, relating to, or suitable for the country or country people — **rus·ti·cal·ly** \-ti-k(ə-)lē\ *adv* — **rus·tic·i·ty** \ˌrəs-'ti-sə-tē\ *n*

²**rustic** *n* : a rustic person

rus·ti·cate \'rəs-ti-ˌkāt\ *vb* **-cat·ed; -cat·ing** : to go into or reside in the country — **rus·ti·ca·tion** \ˌrəs-ti-'kā-shən\ *n*

¹**rus·tle** \'rə-səl\ *vb* **rus·tled; rus·tling** **1** : to make or cause a rustle **2** : to cause to rustle ⟨∼ a newspaper⟩ **3** : to act or move with energy or speed; *also* : to procure in this way **4** : to forage food **5** : to steal cattle from the range — **rus·tler** *n*

²**rustle** *n* : a quick series of small sounds ⟨∼ of leaves⟩
¹**rut** \ˈrət\ *n* : state or period of sexual excitement esp. in male deer — **rut** *vb*
²**rut** *n* **1** : a track worn by wheels or by habitual passage of something **2** : a usual or fixed routine
ru•ta•ba•ga \ˌrü-tə-ˈbā-gə, ˌrü-\ *n* : a turnip with a large yellowish root
Ruth \ˈrüth\ *n* — see BIBLE table
ru•the•ni•um \rü-ˈthē-nē-əm\ *n* : a hard brittle metallic chemical element — see ELEMENT table
ruth•less \ˈrüth-ləs\ *adj* [fr. *ruth* compassion, pity, fr. ME *ruthe*, fr. *ruen* to rue, fr. OE *hrēowan*] : having no pity : MERCILESS, CRUEL — **ruth•less•ly** *adv* — **ruth•less•ness** *n*
¹**RV** \ˌär-ˈvē\ *n* : RECREATIONAL VEHICLE
²**RV** *abbr* Revised Version
R–value \ˈär-ˌval-yü\ *n* : a measure of resistance to the flow of heat through a substance (as insulation)
RW *abbr* **1** right worshipful **2** right worthy
rwy *or* **ry** *abbr* railway
-ry \rē\ *n suffix* : -ERY ⟨bigot*ry*⟩
rye \ˈrī\ *n* **1** : a hardy annual grass grown for grain or as a cover crop; *also* : its seed **2** : a whiskey distilled from a rye mash

S

¹**s** \ˈes\ *n, pl* **s's** *or* **ss** \ˈe-səz\ *often cap* : the 19th letter of the English alphabet
²**s** *abbr, often cap* **1** saint **2** second **3** senate **4** series **5** shilling **6** singular **7** small **8** son **9** south; southern
¹**-s** \s *after sounds* f, k, k̲, p, t, th; əz *after sounds* ch, j, s, sh, z, zh; z *after other sounds*\ *n pl suffix* — used to form the plural of most nouns that do not end in *s*, *z*, *sh*, *ch*, or postconsonantal *y* ⟨head*s*⟩ ⟨book*s*⟩ ⟨boy*s*⟩ ⟨belief*s*⟩, to form the plural of proper nouns that end in postconsonantal *y* ⟨Mary*s*⟩, and with or without a preceding apostrophe to form the plural of abbreviations, numbers, letters, and symbols used as nouns ⟨MC*s*⟩ ⟨4*s*⟩ ⟨ + #*s*⟩ ⟨B's⟩
²**-s** *adv suffix* — used to form adverbs denoting usual or repeated action or state ⟨works night*s*⟩
³**-s** *vb suffix* — used to form the third person singular present of most verbs that do not end in *s*, *z*, *sh*, *ch*, or postconsonantal *y* ⟨fall*s*⟩ ⟨take*s*⟩ ⟨play*s*⟩
S *symbol* sulfur
SA *abbr* **1** Salvation Army **2** seaman apprentice **3** sex appeal **4** [L *sine anno* without year] without date **5** South Africa **6** South America **7** subject to approval
Sab•bath \ˈsa-bəth\ *n* [ME *sabat*, fr. OF & OE, fr. L *sabbatum*, fr. Gk *sabbaton*, fr. Heb *shabbāth*, lit., rest] **1** : the 7th day of the week observed as a day of worship by Jews and some Christians **2** : Sunday observed among Christians as a day of worship
sab•bat•i•cal \sə-ˈba-ti-kəl\ *n* : a leave often with pay granted (as to a college professor) usu. every 7th year for rest, travel, or research
sa•ber *or* **sa•bre** \ˈsā-bər\ *n* [F *sabre*] : a cavalry sword with a curved blade and thick back
saber saw *n* : a portable electric saw with a pointed reciprocating blade
sa•ble \ˈsā-bəl\ *n, pl* **sables 1** : the color black **2** *pl* : mourning garments **3** : a dark brown mammal chiefly of northern Asia related to the weasels; *also* : its fur or pelt
¹**sab•o•tage** \ˈsa-bə-ˌtäzh\ *n* [F] **1** : deliberate destruction of an employer's property or hindering of production by workers **2** : destructive or hampering action by enemy agents or sympathizers in time of war
²**sabotage** *vb* **-taged; -tag•ing** : to practice sabotage on : WRECK
sab•o•teur \ˌsa-bə-ˈtər\ *n* : a person who practices sabotage
sac \ˈsak\ *n* : a pouch in an animal or plant often containing a fluid
SAC *abbr* Strategic Air Command
sac•cha•rin \ˈsa-kə-rən\ *n* : a white crystalline compound used as an artificial calorie-free sweetener
sac•cha•rine \ˈsa-kə-rən\ *adj* : nauseatingly sweet ⟨∼ poetry⟩
sac•er•do•tal \ˌsa-sər-ˈdōt-əl, -kər-\ *adj* : PRIESTLY
sac•er•do•tal•ism \-əl-ˌi-zəm\ *n* : a religious belief emphasizing the powers of priests as essential mediators between God and man

sa•chem \ˈsā-chəm\ *n* : a No. American Indian chief
sa•chet \sa-ˈshā\ *n* [F, fr. OF, dim. of *sac* bag] : a small bag filled with perfumed powder for scenting clothes
¹**sack** \ˈsak\ *n* **1** : a usu. rectangular-shaped bag (as of paper or burlap) **2** : a loose jacket or short coat
²**sack** *vb* : DISMISS, FIRE
³**sack** *n* [modif. of MF *sec* dry, fr. L *siccus*] : a white wine popular in England in the 16th and 17th centuries
⁴**sack** *vb* : to plunder a captured town
sack•cloth \-ˌklòth\ *n* : a rough garment worn as a sign of penitence
sac•ra•ment \ˈsa-krə-mənt\ *n* **1** : a formal religious act or rite; *esp* : one (as baptism or the Eucharist) held to have been instituted by Christ **2** : the elements of the Eucharist — **sac•ra•men•tal** \ˌsa-krə-ˈment-əl\ *adj*
sa•cred \ˈsā-krəd\ *adj* **1** : set apart for the service or worship of deity **2** : devoted exclusively to one service or use **3** : worthy of veneration or reverence **4** : of or relating to religion : RELIGIOUS *syn* blessed, divine, hallowed, holy, sanctified — **sa•cred•ly** *adv* — **sa•cred•ness** *n*
sacred cow *n* : one that is often unreasonably immune from criticism
¹**sac•ri•fice** \ˈsa-krə-ˌfīs\ *n* **1** : the offering of something precious to deity **2** : something offered in sacrifice **3** : LOSS, DEPRIVATION **4** : a bunt allowing a base runner to advance while the batter is put out; *also* : a fly ball allowing a runner to score after the catch — **sac•ri•fi•cial** \ˌsa-krə-ˈfi-shəl\ *adj* — **sac•ri•fi•cial•ly** *adv*
²**sac•ri•fice** *vb* **-ficed; -fic•ing 1** : to offer up or kill as a sacrifice **2** : to accept the loss or destruction of for an end, cause, or ideal **3** : to make a sacrifice in baseball
sac•ri•lege \ˈsa-krə-lij\ *n* [ME, fr. OF, fr. L *sacrilegium*, fr. *sacrilegus* one who steals sacred things, fr. *sacr-, sacer* sacred + *legere* to gather, steal] **1** : violation of something consecrated to God **2** : gross irreverence toward a hallowed person, place, or thing — **sac•ri•le•gious** \ˌsa-krə-ˈli-jəs, -ˈlē-\ *adj* — **sac•ri•le•gious•ly** *adv*
sac•ris•tan \ˈsa-krə-stən\ *n* **1** : a church officer in charge of the sacristy **2** : SEXTON
sac•ris•ty \ˈsa-krə-stē\ *n, pl* **-ties** : VESTRY
sac•ro•il•i•ac \ˌsa-krō-ˈi-lē-ˌak\ *n* : the joint between the upper part of the hipbone and the sacrum
sac•ro•sanct \ˈsa-krō-ˌsaŋkt\ *adj* : SACRED, INVIOLABLE
sa•crum \ˈsa-krəm, ˈsā-\ *n, pl* **sa•cra** \ˈsa-krə, ˈsā-\ : the part of the vertebral column that is directly connected with or forms a part of the pelvis and in humans consists of five fused vertebrae
sad \ˈsad\ *adj* **sad•der; sad•dest 1** : GRIEVING, MOURNFUL, DOWNCAST **2** : causing sorrow **3** : DULL, SOMBER — **sad•ly** *adv* — **sad•ness** *n*
sad•den \ˈsad-ən\ *vb* : to make sad

¹sad•dle \'sad-ᵊl\ *n* **1** : a usu. padded leather-covered seat (as for a rider on horseback) **2** : the upper back portion of a carcass (as of mutton)

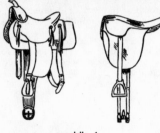

saddle 1

²saddle *vb* **sad•dled; sad•dling 1** : to put a saddle on **2** : OPPRESS, BURDEN

sad•dle•bow \'sad-ᵊl-ˌbō\ *n* : the arch in the front of a saddle

saddle horse *n* : a horse suited for or trained for riding

Sad•du•cee \'sa-jə-ˌsē, 'sa-dyə-\ *n* : a member of an ancient Jewish sect consisting of a ruling class of priests and rejecting certain doctrines — **Sad•du•ce•an** \ˌsa-jə-'sē-ən, ˌsa-dyə-\ *adj*

sad•iron \'sa-ˌdi-ərn\ *n* : a flatiron with a removable handle

sa•dism \'sā-ˌdi-zəm, 'sa-\ *n* : a sexual perversion in which gratification is obtained by inflicting physical or mental pain on others — **sa•dist** \'sā-dist, 'sa-\ *n* — **sa•dis•tic** \sə-'dis-tik\ *adj* — **sa•dis•ti•cal•ly** \-ti-k(ə-)lē\ *adv*

SAE *abbr* **1** self-addressed envelope **2** Society of Automotive Engineers **3** stamped addressed envelope

sa•fa•ri \sə-'fär-ē, -'far-\ *n* [Ar *safarīy* of a trip] **1** : a hunting expedition esp. in eastern Africa **2** : JOURNEY, TRIP

¹safe \'sāf\ *adj* **saf•er; saf•est 1** : free from harm or risk **2** : affording safety; *also* : secure from danger or loss **3** : RELIABLE — **safe•ly** *adv*

²safe *n* : a container for keeping articles (as valuables) safe

safe–con•duct \-'kän-(ˌ)dəkt\ *n* : a pass permitting a person to go through enemy lines

¹safe•guard \-ˌgärd\ *n* : a measure or device for preventing accident

²safeguard *vb* : to provide a safeguard for : PROTECT

safe•keep•ing \'sāf-'kē-piŋ\ *n* : a keeping or being kept in safety

safe sex *n* : sexual activity and esp. sexual intercourse in which various measures (as the use of latex condoms) are taken to avoid disease (as AIDS) transmitted by sexual contact

safe•ty \'sāf-tē\ *n, pl* **safeties 1** : freedom from danger : SECURITY **2** : a protective device **3** : a football play in which the ball is downed by the offensive team behind its own goal line **4** : a defensive football back in the deepest position — **safety** *adj*

safety glass *n* : shatter-resistant material formed of two sheets of glass with a sheet of clear plastic between them

safety match *n* : a match that ignites only when struck on a special surface

saf•flow•er \'sa-ˌflaù-ər\ *n* : a widely grown Old World herb related to the daisies that has large orange or red flower heads yielding a dyestuff and seeds rich in edible oil

saf•fron \'sa-frən\ *n* : a deep orange powder from the flower of a crocus used to color and flavor foods

sag \'sag\ *vb* **sagged; sag•ging 1** : to droop or settle from or as if from pressure **2** : to lose firmness or vigor — **sag** *n*

sa•ga \'sä-gə\ *n* [ON] : a narrative of heroic deeds; *esp* : one recorded in Iceland in the 12th and 13th centuries

sa•ga•cious \sə-'gā-shəs\ *adj* : of keen mind : SHREWD — **sa•gac•i•ty** \-'ga-sə-tē\ *n*

sag•a•more \'sa-gə-ˌmōr\ *n* : a subordinate No. American Indian chief

¹sage \'sāj\ *adj* [ME, fr. OF, fr. (assumed) VL *sapius*, fr. L *sapere* to taste, have good taste, be wise] : WISE, PRUDENT — **sage•ly** *adv*

²sage *n* : one who is distinguished for wisdom

³sage *n* [ME, fr. MF *sauge*, fr. L *salvia*, fr. *salvus* healthy; fr. its use as a medicinal herb] **1** : a mint with leaves used in flavoring **2** : SAGEBRUSH

sage•brush \'sāj-ˌbrəsh\ *n* : any of several low shrubby No. American composite plants; *esp* : one of the western U.S. with a sagelike odor

Sag•it•tar•i•us \ˌsa-jə-'ter-ē-əs\ *n* [L, lit., archer] **1** : a zodiacal constellation between Scorpio and Capricorn usu. pictured as a centaur archer **2** : the 9th sign of the zodiac in astrology; *also* : one born under this sign

sa•go \'sā-gō\ *n, pl* **sagos** : a dry granulated starch esp. from the pith of various tropical palms (**sago palm**)

sa•gua•ro \sə-'wär-ə, -'gwär-, -ō\ *n, pl* **-ros** [MexSp] : a desert cactus of the southwestern U.S. and Mexico with a tall columnar simple or sparsely branched trunk of up to 60 feet (18 meters)

said *past and past part of* SAY

¹sail \'sāl\ *n* **1** : a piece of fabric by means of which the wind is used to propel a ship **2** : a sailing ship **3** : something resembling a sail **4** : a trip on a sailboat

²sail *vb* **1** : to travel on a sailing ship **2** : to pass over in a ship **3** : to manage or direct the course of a ship **4** : to move with ease, grace, or nonchalance

sail•board \'sāl-ˌbōrd\ *n* : a modified surfboard having a mast and sailed by a standing person

sail•boat \-ˌbōt\ *n* : a boat propelled primarily by sail

sail•cloth \-ˌklöth\ *n* : a heavy canvas used for sails, tents, or upholstery

sail•fish \-ˌfish\ *n* : any of a genus of large marine bony fishes with a large dorsal fin that are related to marlins

sail•ing *n* : the sport of handling or riding in a sailboat

sail•or \'sā-lər\ *n* : one that sails; *esp* : a member of a ship's crew

sail•plane \'sāl-ˌplān\ *n* : a glider designed to rise in an upward air current

saint \'sānt, *before a name* (ˌ)sānt *or* sənt\ *n* **1** : one officially recognized as preeminent for holiness **2** : one of the spirits of the departed in heaven **3** : a holy or godly person — **saint•ed** \-'sān-təd\ *adj* — **saint•hood** \-ˌhùd\ *n*

Saint Ber•nard \-bər-'närd\ *n* : any of a Swiss alpine breed of tall powerful working dogs used esp. formerly in aiding lost travelers

Saint Bernard

saint·ly \'sānt-lē\ adj : relating to, resembling, or befitting a saint — **saint·li·ness** \-lē-nəs\ n

Saint Val·en·tine's Day \-'va-lən-ˌtīnz-\ n : February 14 observed in honor of St. Valentine and as a time for exchanging valentines

¹**sake** \'sāk\ n 1 : END, PURPOSE 2 : personal or social welfare, safety, or well-being

²**sa·ke** or **sa·ki** \'sä-kē\ n : a Japanese alcoholic beverage of fermented rice

sa·laam \sə-'läm\ n [Ar salām, lit., peace] 1 : a salutation or ceremonial greeting in the East 2 : an obeisance performed by bowing very low and placing the right palm on the forehead — **salaam** vb

sa·la·cious \sə-'lā-shəs\ adj 1 : arousing sexual desire or imagination 2 : LUSTFUL — **sa·la·cious·ly** adv — **sa·la·cious·ness** n

sal·ad \'sa-ləd\ n : a cold dish (as of lettuce, vegetables, fish, eggs, or fruit) served with dressing

sal·a·man·der \'sa-lə-ˌman-dər\ n : any of numerous amphibians that look like lizards but have scaleless usu. smooth moist skin

sa·la·mi \sə-'lä-mē\ n [It] : a highly seasoned sausage of pork and beef

sal·a·ry \'sa-lə-rē\ n, pl **-ries** [ME salarie, fr. L salarium pension, salary, fr. neut. of salarius of salt, fr. sal salt] : payment made at regular intervals for services

sale \'sāl\ n 1 : transfer of ownership of property from one person to another in return for money 2 : ready market : DEMAND 3 : AUCTION 4 : a selling of goods at bargain prices — **sal·able** or **sale·able** \'sā-lə-bəl\ adj

sales·girl \'sālz-ˌgərl\ n : SALESWOMAN

sales·man \-mən\ n : a person who sells in a store or to outside customers — **sales·man·ship** n

sales·per·son \-ˌpər-sən\ n : a salesman or saleswoman

sales·wom·an \-ˌwu̇-mən\ n : a woman who sells merchandise

sal·i·cyl·ic acid \ˌsa-lə-'si-lik-\ n : a crystalline organic acid used in the form of its salts and other derivatives to relieve pain and fever

¹**sa·lient** \'sāl-yənt, 'sā-lē-ənt\ adj : jutting forward beyond a line; also : PROMINENT **syn** conspicuous, striking, noticeable

²**salient** n : a projecting part in a line of defense

¹**sa·line** \'sā-ˌlēn, -ˌlīn\ adj : consisting of or containing salt : SALTY — **sa·lin·i·ty** \sā-'li-nə-tē, sə-\ n

²**saline** n 1 : a metallic salt esp. with a purgative action 2 : a saline solution

sa·li·va \sə-'lī-və\ n : a liquid secreted into the mouth that helps digestion — **sal·i·vary** \'sa-lə-ˌver-ē\ adj

sal·i·vate \'sa-lə-ˌvāt\ vb **-vat·ed; -vat·ing** : to produce saliva esp. in excess — **sal·i·va·tion** \ˌsa-lə-'vā-shən\ n

sal·low \'sa-lō\ adj : of a yellowish sickly color ⟨a ~ face⟩

sal·ly \'sa-lē\ n, pl **sallies** 1 : a rushing attack on besiegers by troops of a besieged place 2 : a witty remark or retort 3 : a brief excursion — **sally** vb

salm·on \'sa-mən\ n, pl **salmon** also **salmons** 1 : any of several bony fishes with pinkish flesh used for food that are related to the trouts 2 : a strong yellowish pink color

sal·mo·nel·la \ˌsal-mə-'ne-lə\ n, pl **-nel·lae** \-'ne-(ˌ)lē, -ˌlī\ or **-nellas** or **-nella** : any of a genus of rod-shaped bacteria that cause various illnesses (as food poisoning)

sa·lon \sə-'län, 'sa-ˌlän, sa-'lōⁿ\ n [F] : an elegant drawing room; also : a fashionable shop ⟨beauty ~⟩

sa·loon \sə-'lün\ n 1 : a large public cabin on a ship 2 : a place where liquors are sold and drunk : BARROOM 3 Brit : SEDAN 2

sal·sa \'sȯl-sə, 'säl-\ n : a spicy sauce of tomatoes, onions, and hot peppers

sal soda \'sal-'sō-də\ n : SODIUM CARBONATE

¹**salt** \'sȯlt\ n 1 : a white crystalline substance that consists of sodium and chlorine and is used in seasoning foods 2 : a saltlike cathartic substance (as Epsom salts) 3 : a compound formed usu. by action of an acid on metal 4 : SAILOR — **salt·i·ness** \'sȯl-tē-nəs\ n — **salty** \'sȯl-tē\ adj

²**salt** vb : to preserve, season, or feed with salt

³**salt** adj : preserved or treated with salt; also : SALTY

SALT abbr Strategic Arms Limitation Talks

salt away vb : to lay away safely : SAVE

salt·box \'sȯlt-ˌbäks\ n : a frame dwelling with two stories in front and one behind and a long sloping roof

salt·cel·lar \-ˌse-lər\ n : a small container for holding salt at the table

sal·tine \sȯl-'tēn\ n : a thin crisp cracker sprinkled with salt

salt lick n : LICK 5

salt·pe·ter \'sȯlt-'pē-tər\ n [ME salt petre, alter. of salpetre, fr. MF, fr. ML sal petrae, lit., salt of the rock] 1 : POTASSIUM NITRATE 2 : SODIUM NITRATE

salt·wa·ter \-ˌwȯ-tər, -ˌwä-\ adj : of, relating to, or living in salt water

sa·lu·bri·ous \sə-'lü-brē-əs\ adj : favorable to health

sal·u·tary \'sal-yə-ˌter-ē\ adj : health-giving; also : BENEFICIAL

sal·u·ta·tion \ˌsal-yə-'tā-shən\ n : an expression of greeting, goodwill, or courtesy usu. by word or gesture

sa·lu·ta·to·ri·an \sə-ˌlü-tə-'tōr-ē-ən\ n : the student having the 2nd highest rank in a graduating class who delivers the salutatory address

sa·lu·ta·to·ry \sə-'lü-tə-ˌtōr-ē\ adj : relating to or being the welcoming oration delivered at an academic commencement

¹**sa·lute** \sə-'lüt\ vb **sa·lut·ed; sa·lut·ing** 1 : GREET 2 : to honor by special ceremonies 3 : to show respect to (a superior officer) by a formal position of hand, rifle, or sword

²**salute** n 1 : GREETING 2 : the formal position assumed in saluting a superior

¹**sal·vage** \'sal-vij\ n 1 : money paid for saving a ship, its cargo, or passengers when the ship is wrecked or in danger 2 : the saving of a ship 3 : the saving of possessions in danger of being lost 4 : things saved from loss or destruction (as by a wreck or fire)

²**salvage** vb **sal·vaged; sal·vag·ing** : to rescue from destruction

sal·va·tion \sal-'vā-shən\ n 1 : the saving of a person from sin or its consequences esp. in the life after death 2 : the saving from danger, difficulty, or evil 3 : something that saves

¹**salve** \'sav, 'sȧv\ n 1 : a medicinal substance applied to the skin 2 : a soothing influence

²**salve** vb **salved; salv·ing** : EASE, SOOTHE

sal·ver \'sal-vər\ n [F salve, fr. Sp salva sampling of food to detect poison, tray, fr. salvar to save, sample food to detect poison, fr. LL salvare to save, fr. L salvus safe] : a small serving tray

sal·vo \'sal-vō\ n, pl **salvos** or **salvoes** : a simultaneous discharge of guns

Sam or **Saml** abbr Samuel

SAM \'sam, ˌes-ˌā-'em\ n [surface-to-air missile] : a guided missile for use against aircraft by ground units

sa·mar·i·um \sə-'mer-ē-əm\ n : a gray lustrous metallic chemical element — see ELEMENT table

¹**same** \'sām\ adj 1 : being the one referred to : not different 2 : SIMILAR — **same·ness** n

²**same** pron : the same one or ones

³**same** adv : in the same manner

Sa·mo·an \sə-'mō-ən\ n : a native or inhabitant of Samoa — **Samoan** adj

sam·o·var \'sa-mə-ˌvär\ n [Russ, fr. samo- self + varit' to boil] : an urn with a spigot at the base used esp. in Russia to boil water for tea

sam·pan \'sam-ˌpan\ n : a flat-bottomed skiff of the Far East usu. propelled by two short oars

¹**sam·ple** \'sam-pəl\ n : a representative piece, item, or

set of individuals that shows the quality or nature of the whole from which it was taken : EXAMPLE, SPECIMEN

²**sample** *vb* **sam·pled; sam·pling** : to judge the quality of by a sample

sam·pler \'sam-plər\ *n* : a piece of needlework; *esp* : one testing skill in embroidering

Sam·u·el \'sam-yə-wəl\ *n* — see BIBLE table

sam·u·rai \'sa-mə-ˌrī, 'sam-yə-\ *n, pl* **samurai** : a member of a Japanese feudal warrior class practicing a chivalric code

san·a·to·ri·um \ˌsa-nə-'tōr-ē-əm\ *n, pl* **-riums** *or* **-ria** \-ē-ə\ 1 : a health resort 2 : an establishment for the care esp. of convalescents or the chronically ill

sanc·ti·fy \'saŋk-tə-ˌfī\ *vb* **-fied; -fy·ing** 1 : to make holy : CONSECRATE 2 : to free from sin — **sanc·ti·fi·ca·tion** \ˌsaŋk-tə-fə-'kā-shən\ *n*

sanc·ti·mo·nious \ˌsaŋk-tə-'mō-nē-əs\ *adj* : hypocritically pious — **sanc·ti·mo·nious·ly** *adv*

¹**sanc·tion** \'saŋk-shən\ *n* 1 : authoritative approval 2 : a measure (as a threat or fine) designed to enforce a law or standard (economic ∼s)

²**sanction** *vb* : to give approval to : RATIFY **syn** endorse, accredit, certify, approve

sanc·ti·ty \'saŋk-tə-tē\ *n, pl* **-ties** 1 : GODLINESS 2 : SACREDNESS

sanc·tu·ary \'saŋk-chə-ˌwer-ē\ *n, pl* **-ar·ies** 1 : a consecrated place (as the part of a church in which the altar is placed) 2 : a place of refuge ⟨bird ∼⟩

sanc·tum \'saŋk-təm\ *n, pl* **sanctums** *also* **sanc·ta** \-tə\ : a private office or study : DEN ⟨an editor's ∼⟩

¹**sand** \'sand\ *n* : loose particles of hard broken rock — **sandy** *adj*

²**sand** *vb* 1 : to cover or fill with sand 2 : to scour, smooth, or polish with an abrasive (as sandpaper) — **sand·er** *n*

san·dal \'sand-ᵊl\ *n* : a shoe consisting of a sole strapped to the foot; *also* : a low or open slipper or rubber overshoe

san·dal·wood \-ˌwu̇d\ *n* : the fragrant yellowish heartwood of a parasitic tree of southern Asia that is much used in ornamental carving and cabinetwork; *also* : the tree

sand·bag \'sand-ˌbag\ *n* : a bag filled with sand and used in fortifications, as ballast, or as a weapon

sand·bank \-ˌbaŋk\ *n* : a deposit of sand (as in a bar or shoal)

sand·bar \-ˌbär\ *n* : a ridge of sand formed in water by tides or currents

sand·blast \-ˌblast\ *vb* : to treat with a stream of sand blown (as for cleaning stone) by compressed air — **sand·blast·er** *n*

sand dollar *n* : any of numerous flat circular sea urchins chiefly of sandy bottoms in shallow water

S & H *abbr* shipping and handling

sand·hog \'sand-ˌhȯg, -ˌhäg\ *n* : a laborer who builds underwater tunnels

sand·lot \-ˌlät\ *n* : a vacant lot esp. when used for the unorganized sports of children — **sand·lot** *adj* — **sand·lot·ter** *n*

sand·man \-ˌman\ *n* : the genie of folklore who makes children sleepy

sand·pa·per \-ˌpā-pər\ *n* : paper with abrasive (as sand) glued on one side used in smoothing and polishing surfaces — **sandpaper** *vb*

sand·pip·er \-ˌpī-pər\ *n* : any of numerous shorebirds with a soft-tipped bill longer than that of the related plovers

sand·stone \-ˌstōn\ *n* : rock made of sand united by a natural cement

sand·storm \-ˌstȯrm\ *n* : a windstorm that drives clouds of sand

sand trap *n* : a hazard on a golf course consisting of a hollow containing sand

¹**sand·wich** \'sand-(ˌ)wich\ *n* [after John Montagu, 4th Earl of *Sandwich* †1792 Eng. diplomat] 1 : two or more slices of bread with a layer (as of meat or cheese) spread between them 2 : something resembling a sandwich

²**sandwich** *vb* : to squeeze or crowd in

sane \'sān\ *adj* **san·er; san·est** : mentally sound and healthy; *also* : SENSIBLE, RATIONAL — **sane·ly** *adv*

sang *past of* SING

sang-froid \sän-'frwä\ *n* [F *sang-froid*, lit., cold blood] : self-possession or an imperturbable state esp. under strain

san·gui·nary \'saŋ-gwə-ˌner-ē\ *adj* : BLOODY ⟨∼ battle⟩

san·guine \'saŋ-gwən\ *adj* 1 : RUDDY 2 : CHEERFUL, HOPEFUL

sanit *abbr* sanitary; sanitation

san·i·tar·i·an \ˌsa-nə-'ter-ē-ən\ *n* : a specialist in sanitation and public health

san·i·tar·i·um \ˌsa-nə-'ter-ē-əm\ *n, pl* **-i·ums** *or* **-ia** \-ē-ə\ : SANATORIUM

san·i·tary \'sa-nə-ˌter-ē\ *adj* 1 : of or relating to health : HYGIENIC 2 : free from filth or infective matter

sanitary napkin *n* : a disposable absorbent pad used to absorb uterine flow (as during menstruation)

san·i·ta·tion \ˌsa-nə-'tā-shən\ *n* : the act or process of making sanitary; *also* : protection of health by maintenance of sanitary conditions

san·i·tize \'sa-nə-ˌtīz\ *vb* **-tized; -tiz·ing** 1 : to make sanitary 2 : to make more acceptable by removing unpleasant features

san·i·ty \'sa-nə-tē\ *n* : soundness of mind

sank *past of* SINK

sans \'sanz\ *prep* : WITHOUT

San·skrit \'san-ˌskrit\ *n* : an ancient language that is the classical language of India and of Hinduism — **Sanskrit** *adj*

San·ta Ana \ˌsan-tə-'a-nə\ *n* [*Santa Ana* Mountains in southern Calif.] : a hot dry wind from the north, northeast, or east in southern California

¹**sap** \'sap\ *n* 1 : a vital fluid; *esp* : a watery fluid that circulates through a vascular plant 2 : a foolish gullible person — **sap·less** *adj*

²**sap** *vb* **sapped; sap·ping** 1 : UNDERMINE 2 : to weaken gradually

sap·id \'sa-pəd\ *adj* : FLAVORFUL

sa·pi·ent \'sā-pē-ənt, 'sa-\ *adj* : WISE, DISCERNING — **sa·pi·ence** \-əns\ *n*

sap·ling \'sa-pliŋ\ *n* : a young tree

sap·phire \'sa-ˌfīr\ *n* : a hard transparent usu. rich blue gem

sap·py \'sa-pē\ *adj* **sap·pi·er; -est** 1 : full of sap 2 : overly sentimental 3 : SILLY, FOOLISH

sap·ro·phyte \'sa-prə-ˌfīt\ *n* : a living thing and esp. a plant living on dead or decaying organic matter — **sap·ro·phyt·ic** \ˌsa-prə-'fi-tik\ *adj*

sap·suck·er \'sap-ˌse-kər\ *n* : any of a genus of small No. American woodpeckers

sap·wood \-ˌwu̇d\ *n* : the younger active and usu. lighter and softer outer layer of wood (as of a tree trunk)

sar·casm \'sär-ˌka-zəm\ *n* 1 : a cutting or contemptuous remark 2 : ironic criticism or reproach — **sar·cas·tic** \sär-'kas-tik\ *adj* — **sar·cas·ti·cal·ly** \-ti-k(ə-)lē\ *adv*

sar·co·ma \sär-'kō-mə\ *n, pl* **-mas** *also* **-ma·ta** \-mə-tə\ : a malignant tumor esp. of connective tissue, bone, cartilage, or striated muscle

sar·coph·a·gus \sär-'kä-fə-gəs\ *n, pl* **-gi** \-ˌgī, -ˌjī\ *also* **-gus·es** [L *sarcophagus* (*lapis*) limestone used for coffins, fr. Gk (*lithos*) *sarkophagos*, lit., flesh-eating stone, fr. *sark-, sarx* flesh + *phagein* to eat] : a large stone coffin

sar·dine \sär-'dēn\ *n, pl* **sardines** *also* **sardine** : a young or small fish preserved for use as food

sar·don·ic \sär-'dä-nik\ *adj* : disdainfully or skeptically humorous : derisively mocking **syn** ironic, satiric, sarcastic — **sar·don·i·cal·ly** \-ni-k(ə-)lē\ *adv*

sa·ri *also* **sa·ree** \'sär-ē\ *n* [Hindi *sārī*] : a garment worn by women in southern Asia that consists of a long cloth draped around the body and head or shoulder

sa·rong \sə-'ròŋ, -'räŋ\ n : a loose garment wrapped around the body and worn by men and women of the Malay archipelago and the Pacific islands

sar·sa·pa·ril·la \ˌsas-ə-pə-'ri-lə, ˌsärs-\ n **1** : the dried roots of a tropical American smilax used esp. for flavoring; *also* : the plant **2** : a sweetened carbonated beverage flavored with sassafras and an oil from a birch

sar·to·ri·al \sär-'tōr-ē-əl\ adj : of or relating to a tailor or tailored clothes — **sar·to·ri·al·ly** adv

SASE abbr self-addressed stamped envelope

¹sash \'sash\ n : a broad band worn around the waist or over the shoulder

²sash n, pl **sash** also **sash·es** : a frame for panes of glass in a door or window; *also* : the movable part of a window

sa·shay \sa-'shā\ vb **1** : WALK, GLIDE, GO **2** : to strut or move about in an ostentatious manner **3** : to proceed in a diagonal or sideways manner

Sask abbr Saskatchewan

Sas·quatch \'sas-ˌkwach, -ˌkwäch\ n [Halkomelem (American Indian language of British Columbia) *sésqəc*] : a large hairy humanlike creature reported to exist in the northwestern U.S. and western Canada

sas·sa·fras \'sa-sə-ˌfras\ n [Sp *sasafrás*] : a No. American tree related to the laurel; *also* : its carcinogenic dried root bark

sassy \'sa-sē\ adj **sass·i·er; -est** : SAUCY

¹sat past and past part of SIT

²sat abbr saturate; saturated; saturation

Sat abbr Saturday

Sa·tan \'sāt-ᵊn\ n : DEVIL

sa·tang \sə-'täŋ\ n, pl **satang** or **satangs** — see *baht* at MONEY table

sa·tan·ic \sə-'ta-nik, sā-\ adj **1** : of or characteristic of Satan **2** : extremely malicious or wicked — **sa·tan·i·cal·ly** \-ni-k(ə-)lē\ adv

satch·el \'sa-chəl\ n : SUITCASE

sate \'sāt\ vb **sat·ed; sat·ing** : to satisfy to the full; *also* : SURFEIT, CLOT

sa·teen \sa-'tēn, sə-\ n : a cotton cloth finished to resemble satin

sat·el·lite \'sat-ᵊl-ˌīt\ n [F, fr. L *satelles* attendant] **1** : an obsequious follower of a distinguished person : TOADY **2** : a celestial body that orbits a larger body **3** : a manufactured object that orbits a celestial body

sa·ti·ate \'sā-shē-ˌāt\ vb **-at·ed; -at·ing** : to satisfy fully or to excess

sa·ti·ety \sə-'tī-ə-tē\ n : fullness to the point of excess

sat·in \'sat-ᵊn\ n : a fabric (as of silk) with a glossy surface — **sat·iny** adj

sat·in·wood \'sat-ᵊn-ˌwùd\ n : a hard yellowish brown wood of satiny luster; *also* : a tree yielding this wood

sat·ire \'sa-ˌtīr\ n : biting wit, irony, or sarcasm used to expose vice or folly; *also* : a literary work having these qualities — **sa·tir·ic** \sə-'tir-ik\ or **sa·tir·i·cal** \-i-kəl\ adj — **sa·tir·i·cal·ly** adv — **sat·i·rist** \'sa-tə-rist\ n — **sat·i·rize** \-tə-ˌrīz\ vb

sat·is·fac·tion \ˌsa-təs-'fak-shən\ n **1** : payment through penance of punishment incurred by sin **2** : CONTENTMENT, GRATIFICATION **3** : reparation for an insult **4** : settlement of a claim

sat·is·fac·to·ry \-'fak-tə-rē\ adj : giving satisfaction : ADEQUATE — **sat·is·fac·to·ri·ly** \-'fak-tə-rə-lē\ adv

sat·is·fy \'sa-təs-ˌfī\ vb **-fied; -fy·ing 1** : to answer or discharge (a claim) in full **2** : to make happy : GRATIFY **3** : to pay what is due to **4** : CONVINCE **5** : to meet the requirements of — **sat·is·fy·ing·ly** adv

sa·trap \'sā-ˌtrap, 'sa-\ n [ME, fr. L *satrapes*, fr. Gk *satrapēs*, fr. OPer *khshathrapāvan*, lit., protector of the dominion] : a petty prince : a subordinate ruler

sat·u·rate \'sa-chə-ˌrāt\ vb **-rat·ed; -rat·ing 1** : to soak thoroughly **2** : to treat or charge with something to

the point where no more can be absorbed, dissolved, or retained — **sat·u·ra·ble** \'sa-chə-rə-bəl\ adj — **sat·u·ra·tion** \ˌsa-chə-'rā-shən\ n

Sat·ur·day \'sa-tər-dē, -ˌdā\ n : the 7th day of the week

Saturday night special n : a cheap easily concealed handgun

Sat·urn \'sa-tərn\ n : the planet 6th in order from the sun — see PLANET table

sat·ur·nine \'sa-tər-ˌnīn\ adj : SULLEN, SARDONIC

sa·tyr \'sā-tər\ n **1** often cap : a woodland deity in Greek mythology having certain characteristics of a horse or goat **2** : a lecherous man

¹sauce \'sòs, 3 usu 'sas\ n **1** : a fluid dressing or topping for food **2** : stewed fruit **3** : IMPUDENCE

²sauce \'sòs, 2 usu 'sas\ vb **sauced; sauc·ing 1** : to put sauce on; *also* : to add zest to **2** : to be impudent to

sauce·pan \'sòs-ˌpan\ n : a small deep cooking pan with a handle

sau·cer \'sò-sər\ n : a rounded shallow dish for use under a cup

saucy \'sa-sē, 'sò-\ adj **sauc·i·er; -est** : IMPUDENT, PERT — **sauc·i·ly** \-sə-lē\ adv — **sauc·i·ness** \-sē-nəs\ n

Sau·di \'saü-dē, 'sò-; sä-'ü-dē\ n : SAUDI ARABIAN — **Saudi** adj

Saudi Arabian n : a native or inhabitant of Saudi Arabia — **Saudi Arabian** adj

sau·er·kraut \'saü-ər-ˌkraüt\ n [G, fr. *sauer* sour + *Kraut* greens] : finely cut cabbage fermented in brine

sau·na \'saü-nə\ n **1** : a Finnish steam bath in which the steam is provided by water thrown on hot stones **2** : a dry heat bath; *also* : a room or cabinet used for such a bath

saun·ter \'sòn-tər, 'sän-\ vb : STROLL

sau·ro·pod \'sòr-ə-ˌpäd\ n : any of a suborder of plant-eating dinosaurs (as a brontosaurus) with a long neck and tail and a small head — **sauropod** adj

sau·sage \'sò-sij\ n [ultim. fr. LL *salsicia*, fr. L *salsus* salted] : minced and highly seasoned meat (as pork) usu. enclosed in a tubular casing

S Aust abbr South Australia

sau·té \sò-'tā, sō-\ vb **sau·téed** or **sau·téd; sau·té·ing** [F] : to fry lightly in a little fat — **sauté** n

sau·terne \sō-'tərn, sò-\ n, often cap : a usu. semisweet American white wine

¹sav·age \'sa-vij\ adj [ME *sauvage*, fr. MF, fr. ML *salvaticus*, alter. of L *silvaticus* of the woods, wild, fr. *silva* wood, forest] **1** : WILD, UNTAMED **2** : UNCIVILIZED, BARBAROUS **3** : CRUEL, FIERCE — **sav·age·ly** adv — **sav·age·ness** n — **sav·age·ry** \-rē\ n

²savage n **1** : a member of a primitive human society **2** : a rude, unmannerly, or brutal person

sa·van·na or **sa·van·nah** \sə-'va-nə\ n [Sp *zavana*] : grassland containing scattered trees

sa·vant \sa-'vänt, sə-, 'sa-vənt\ n : a learned person : SCHOLAR

¹save \'sāv\ vb **saved; sav·ing 1** : to redeem from sin **2** : to rescue from danger **3** : to preserve or guard from destruction or loss **4** : to put aside as a store or reserve — **sav·er** n

²save n : a play that prevents an opponent from scoring or winning

³save prep : EXCEPT

⁴save conj : BUT

savings and loan association n : a cooperative association that holds savings of members in the form of dividend-bearing shares and that invests chiefly in mortgage loans

savings bank n : a bank that holds funds of individual depositors in interest-bearing accounts and makes long-term investments (as mortgage loans)

savings bond n : a registered U.S. bond issued in denominations of $50 to $10,000

sav·ior or **sav·iour** \'sāv-yər\ n **1** : one who saves **2** cap : Jesus Christ

sa·voir faire \ˌsav-ˌwär-'far\ n [F *savoir-faire*, lit., knowing how to do] : sureness in social behavior

¹sa·vor *also* sa·vour \'sā-vər\ *n* 1 : the taste and odor of something 2 : a special flavor or quality — sa·vory *adj*

²savor *also* savour *vb* 1 : to have a specified taste, smell, or quality 2 : to taste with pleasure

sa·vo·ry \'sā-və-rē\ *n, pl* -ries : either of two aromatic mints used in cooking

¹sav·vy \'sa-vē\ *vb* sav·vied; sav·vy·ing : UNDERSTAND, COMPREHEND

²savvy *n* : practical know-how ⟨political ∼⟩ — savvy *adj*

¹saw *past of* SEE

²saw \'so\ *n* : a cutting tool with a blade having a line of teeth along its edge

³saw *vb* sawed \'sod\; sawed *or* sawn \'son\; saw·ing : to cut or shape with or as if with a saw — saw·yer \-yər\ *n*

⁴saw *n* : a common saying : MAXIM

saw·dust \'so-(.)dəst\ *n* : fine particles made by a saw in cutting

saw·fly \-.flī\ *n* : any of numerous insects belonging to the same order as bees and wasps and including many whose larvae are plant-feeding pests

saw·horse \-.hors\ *n* : a rack on which wood is rested while being sawed by hand

saw·mill \-.mil\ *n* : a mill for sawing logs

saw palmetto *n* : any of several shrubby palms with spiny-toothed petioles

sax \'saks\ *n* : SAXOPHONE

sax·i·frage \'sak-sə-frij, -.frāj\ *n* [ME, fr. MF, fr. LL *saxifraga*, fr. L, fem. of *saxifragus*, breaking rocks] : any of a genus of plants with showy flowers and usu. with leaves growing in tufts close to the ground

sax·o·phone \'sak-sə-.fōn\ *n* : a musical instrument having a conical metal tube with a reed mouthpiece and finger keys — sax·o·phon·ist \-.fō-nist\ *n*

¹say \'sā\ *vb* said \'sed\; say·ing; says \'sez\ 1 : to express in words ⟨∼ what you mean⟩ 2 : to state as opinion or belief 3 : PRONOUNCE; *also* : RECITE, RE-PEAT ⟨∼ your prayers⟩ 4 : INDICATE ⟨the clock ∼s noon⟩

²say *n, pl* says \'sāz\ 1 : an expression of opinion 2 : power of decision

say·ing *n* : a commonly repeated statement

say-so \'sā-(.)sō\ *n* : an esp. authoritative assertion or decision; *also* : the right to decide

sb *abbr* substantive

Sb *symbol* [L *stibium*] antimony

SB *abbr* [NL *scientiae baccalaureus*] bachelor of science

SBA *abbr* Small Business Administration

sc *abbr* 1 scale 2 scene 3 science

Sc *symbol* scandium

SC *abbr* 1 South Carolina 2 supreme court

¹scab \'skab\ *n* 1 : scabies of domestic animals 2 : a protective crust over a sore or wound 3 : a worker who replaces a striker or works under conditions not authorized by a union 4 : any of various bacterial or fungus plant diseases marked by crusted spots on stems or leaves — scab·by *adj*

²scab *vb* scabbed; scab·bing 1 : to become covered with a scab 2 : to work as a scab

scab·bard \'ska-bərd\ *n* : a sheath for the blade of a weapon (as a sword)

sca·bies \'skā-bēz\ *n* [L] : contagious itch or mange caused by mites living as parasites under the skin

sca·brous \'ska-brəs, 'skā-\ *adj* 1 : DIFFICULT, KNOTTY 2 : rough to the touch : SCALY, SCURFY ⟨a ∼ leaf⟩ 3 : dealing with suggestive, indecent, or scandalous themes; *also* : SQUALID

scad \'skad\ *n* : a large number or quantity — usu. used in pl.

scaf·fold \'ska-fəld, -.fōld\ *n* 1 : a raised platform for workers to sit or stand on 2 : a platform on which a criminal is executed (as by hanging)

scaf·fold·ing *n* : a system of scaffolds; *also* : materials for scaffolds

scal·a·wag \'ska-li-.wag\ *n* : RASCAL

¹scald \'skold\ *vb* 1 : to burn with or as if with hot liquid or steam 2 : to heat to just below the boiling point

²scald *n* : a burn caused by scalding

¹scale \'skāl\ *n* 1 : either pan of a balance 2 : BALANCE — usu. used in pl. 3 : a weighing instrument

²scale *vb* scaled; scal·ing : WEIGH

³scale *n* 1 : one of the small thin plates that cover the body esp. of a fish or reptile 2 : a thin plate or flake 3 : a thin coating, layer, or incrustation 4 : SCALE IN-SECT — scaled \'skāld\ *adj* — scale·less \'skāl-ləs\ *adj* — scaly *adj*

⁴scale *vb* scaled; scal·ing : to strip of scales

⁵scale *n* [ME, fr. LL *scala* ladder, staircase, fr. L *scalae*, pl., stairs, rungs, ladder] 1 : something divided into regular spaces as a help in drawing or measuring 2 : a graduated series 3 : the size of a sample (as a model) in proportion to the size of the actual thing 4 : a standard of estimation or judgment 5 : a series of musical tones going up or down in pitch according to a specified scheme

⁶scale *vb* scaled; scal·ing 1 : to climb by or as if by a ladder 2 : to arrange in a graded series

scale insect *n* : any of numerous small insects with wingless scale-covered females that are related to aphids and live and are often pests on plants

scale·pan \'skāl-.pan\ *n* : ¹SCALE 1

scal·lion \'skal-yən\ *n* [ultim. fr. L *ascalonia* (*caepa*) onion of Ascalon (seaport in Palestine)] : an onion without an enlarged bulb

¹scal·lop \'skä-ləp, 'ska-\ *n* 1 : any of numerous marine bivalve mollusks with radially ridged shells; *also* : a large edible muscle of this mollusk 2 : one of a continuous series of rounded projections forming an edge

²scallop *vb* 1 : to bake in a casserole ⟨∼ed potatoes⟩ 2 : to shape, cut, or finish in scallops ⟨∼ed edges⟩

¹scalp \'skalp\ *n* : the part of the skin and flesh of the head usu. covered with hair

²scalp *vb* 1 : to remove the scalp from 2 : to resell at greatly increased prices ⟨∼ tickets⟩ — scalp·er *n*

scal·pel \'skal-pəl\ *n* : a small straight knife with a thin blade used esp. in surgery

scam \'skam\ *n* : a fraudulent or deceptive act or operation

scamp \'skamp\ *n* : RASCAL

scam·per \'skam-pər\ *vb* : to run nimbly and playfully — scamper *n*

scam·pi \'skam-pē\ *n, pl* scampi [It] : SHRIMP; *esp* : large shrimp prepared with a garlic-flavored sauce

¹scan \'skan\ *vb* scanned; scan·ning 1 : to read (verses) so as to show metrical structure 2 : to examine closely 3 : to examine with a sensing device esp. to obtain information 4 : to make a scan of (as the human body) — scan·ner *n*

²scan *n* 1 : the act or process of scanning 2 : a picture of the distribution of radioactive material in something; *also* : an image of a bodily part produced (as by computer) by combining radiographic data obtained from several angles or sections

Scand *abbr* Scandinavia; Scandinavian

scan·dal \'skand-ᵊl\ *n* [ME, fr. LL *scandalum* stumbling block, offense, fr. Gk *skandalon*] 1 : DISGRACE, DISHONOR 2 : malicious gossip : SLANDER — scan·dal·ize *vb* — scan·dal·ous *adj* — scan·dal·ous·ly *adv*

scan·dal·mon·ger \-.məŋ-gər, -.mäŋ-\ *n* : a person who circulates scandal

Scan·di·na·vian \.skan-də-'nā-vē-ən\ *n* : a native or inhabitant of Scandinavia — Scandinavian *adj*

scan·di·um \'skan-dē-əm\ *n* : a white metallic chemical element — see ELEMENT table

¹scant \'skant\ *adj* 1 : barely sufficient 2 : having scarcely enough syn scanty, skimpy, meager, sparse, exiguous

²scant *vb* 1 : SKIMP 2 : STINT

scant·ling \'skant-liŋ\ n : a small piece of lumber (as an upright in a house)

scanty \'skan-tē\ adj **scant·i·er; -est** : barely sufficient : SCANT — **scant·i·ly** \'skan-tə-lē\ adv — **scant·i·ness** \-tē-nəs\ n

scape·goat \'skāp-ˌgōt\ n : one that bears the blame for others

scape·grace \-ˌgrās\ n [*scape* (escape)] : an incorrigible rascal

scap·u·la \'ska-pyə-lə\ n, pl **-lae** \-ˌlē\ or **-las** [L] : SHOULDER BLADE

scap·u·lar \-lər\ n : a pair of small cloth squares worn on the breast and back under the clothing esp. for religious purposes

scar \'skär\ n : a mark left after injured tissue has healed — **scar** vb

scar·ab \'skar-əb\ n [MF *scarabee*, fr. L *scarabaeus*] : any of a family of large stout beetles; *also* : an ornament (as a gem) representing such a beetle

scarce \'skers\ adj **scarc·er; scarc·est 1** : deficient in quantity or number : not plentiful **2** : intentionally absent ⟨made himself ∼ at inspection time⟩ — **scar·ci·ty** \'sker-sə-tē\ n

scarce·ly \-lē\ adv **1** : BARELY **2** : almost not **3** : very probably not

¹scare \'sker\ vb **scared; scar·ing** : FRIGHTEN, STARTLE

²scare n : FRIGHT — **scary** adj

scare·crow \'sker-ˌkrō\ n : a crude figure set up to scare birds away from crops

¹scarf \'skärf\ n, pl **scarves** \'skärvz\ or **scarfs 1** : a broad band (as of cloth) worn about the shoulders, around the neck, over the head, or about the waist **2** : a long narrow cloth cover for a table or dresser top

²scarf vb [alter. of earlier *scoff* eat greedily] : to eat greedily

scar·i·fy \'skar-ə-ˌfī\ vb **-fied; -fy·ing 1** : to make scratches or small cuts in ⟨∼ skin for vaccination⟩ ⟨∼ seeds to help them germinate⟩ **2** : to lacerate the feelings of **3** : to break up and loosen the surface of (as a road) — **scar·i·fi·ca·tion** \ˌskar-ə-fə-ˈkā-shən\ n

scar·let \'skär-lət\ n : a bright red color — **scarlet** adj

scarlet fever n : an acute contagious disease marked by fever, sore throat, and red rash and caused by certain streptococci

scarp \'skärp\ n : a line of cliffs produced by faulting or erosion

scath·ing \'skā-thiŋ\ adj : bitterly severe ⟨a ∼ condemnation⟩

scat·o·log·i·cal \ˌska-tə-ˈlä-ji-kəl\ adj : concerned with obscene matters

scat·ter \'ska-tər\ vb **1** : to distribute or strew about irregularly **2** : DISPERSE

scat·ter·brain \'ska-tər-ˌbrān\ n : a silly careless person — **scat·ter·brained** \-ˌbrānd\ adj

scav·enge \'ska-vənj\ vb **scav·enged; scav·eng·ing** : to work or function as a scavenger

scav·en·ger \'ska-vən-jər\ n [alter. of earlier *scavager*, fr. ME *skawager* customs collector, fr. *skawage* customs, fr. OF *escauwage* inspection] : a person or animal that collects, eats, or disposes of refuse or waste

sce·nar·io \sə-ˈnar-ē-ˌō\ n, pl **-ios** : the plot or outline of a dramatic work; *also* : an account of a possible action

scene \'sēn\ n [MF, stage, fr. L *scena, scaena* stage, scene, prob. fr. Etruscan, fr. Gk *skēnē* temporary shelter, tent, building forming the background for a dramatic performance, stage] **1** : a division of one act of a play **2** : a single situation or sequence in a play or motion picture **3** : a stage setting **4** : VIEW, PROSPECT **5** : the place of an occurrence or action **6** : a display of strong feeling and esp. anger **7** : a sphere of activity ⟨the fashion ∼⟩ — **sce·nic** \'sē-nik\ adj

scen·ery \'sē-nə-rē\ n, pl **-er·ies 1** : the painted scenes or hangings and accessories used on a theater stage **2** : a picturesque view or landscape

¹scent \'sent\ n **1** : ODOR, SMELL **2** : sense of smell **3**

: course of pursuit : TRACK **4** : PERFUME **2** — **scent·ed** \'sen-təd\ adj — **scent·less** adj

²scent vb **1** : SMELL **2** : to imbue or fill with odor

scep·ter \'sep-tər\ n : a staff borne by a sovereign as an emblem of authority

scep·tic \'skep-tik\ var of SKEPTIC

scep·tre Brit var of SCEPTER

sch abbr school

¹sched·ule \'ske-jül, esp Brit ˈshe-dyül\ n **1** : a list of items or details **2** : TIMETABLE

²schedule vb **sched·uled; sched·ul·ing 1** : to make a schedule of; *also* : to enter on a schedule **2** : to appoint, assign, or designate for a fixed time

sche·mat·ic \ski-ˈma-tik\ adj : of or relating to a scheme or diagram : DIAGRAMMATIC — **schematic** n — **sche·mat·i·cal·ly** \-ti-k(ə-)lē\ adv

¹scheme \'skēm\ n **1** : a plan for doing something; *esp* : a crafty plot **2** : a systematic design

²scheme vb **schemed; schem·ing** : to form a plot : INTRIGUE — **schem·er** n

Schick test \'shik-\ n : a serological test for susceptibility to diphtheria

schil·ling \'shi-liŋ\ n — see MONEY table

schism \'si-zəm, 'ski-\ n **1** : DIVISION, SPLIT; *also* : DISCORD, DISSENSION **2** : a formal division in or separation from a religious body

schis·mat·ic \siz-ˈma-tik, ski-\ n : one who creates or takes part in schism — **schismatic** adj

schist \'shist\ n : a metamorphic crystalline rock

schizo·phre·nia \ˌskit-sə-ˈfrē-nē-ə\ n [NL, fr. Gk *schizein* to split + *phrēn* diaphragm, mind] : a psychotic mental illness that is characterized by a twisted view of the real world, by a greatly reduced ability to carry out one's daily tasks, and by abnormal ways of thinking, feeling, and behaving — **schiz·oid** \'skit-ˌsoid\ adj or n — **schizo·phren·ic** \ˌskit-sə-ˈfre-nik\ adj or n

schle·miel \shlə-ˈmēl\ n : an unlucky bungler : CHUMP

schlepp or **schlep** \'shlep\ vb [Yiddish *shlepn*] **1** : DRAG, HAUL **2** : to move slowly or awkwardly

schlock \'shläk\ or **schlocky** \'shlä-kē\ adj : of low quality or value — **schlock** n

schmaltz also **schmalz** \'shmōlts, 'shmälts\ n [Yiddish *shmalts*, lit., rendered fat] : sentimental or florid music or art — **schmaltzy** adj

schnau·zer \'shnaůt-sər, 'shnaů-zər\ n [G, fr. *Schnauze* snout] : a dog of any of three breeds that are characterized by a wiry coat, long head, small ears, heavy eyebrows, and long hair on the muzzle

schol·ar \'skä-lər\ n **1** : STUDENT, PUPIL **2** : a learned person : SAVANT — **schol·ar·ly** adj

schol·ar·ship \-ˌship\ n **1** : the qualities or learning of a scholar **2** : money awarded to a student to help pay for further education

scho·las·tic \skə-ˈlas-tik\ adj : of or relating to schools, scholars, or scholarship

¹school \'skül\ n **1** : an institution for teaching and learning; *also* : the pupils in attendance **2** : a body of persons of like opinions or beliefs ⟨the radical ∼⟩

²school vb : TEACH, TRAIN, DRILL

³school n : a large number of one kind of water animal swimming and feeding together

school·boy \-ˌbȯi\ n : a boy attending school

school·fel·low \-ˌfe-lō\ n : SCHOOLMATE

school·girl \-ˌgərl\ n : a girl attending school

school·house \-ˌhaůs\ n : a building used as a school

school·marm \-ˌmärm\ or **school·ma'am** \-ˌmäm, -ˌmam\ n **1** : a woman schoolteacher **2** : a person who exhibits characteristics popularly attributed to schoolteachers

school·mas·ter \-ˌmas-tər\ n : a male schoolteacher

school·mate \-ˌmāt\ n : a school companion

school·mis·tress \-ˌmis-trəs\ n : a woman schoolteacher

school·room \-ˌrüm, -ˌrům\ n : CLASSROOM

school·teach·er \-ₜtē-chər\ *n* : one who teaches in a school

schoo·ner \'skü-nər\ *n* : a fore-and-aft rigged sailing ship

schooner

schuss \'shús, 'shüs\ *vb* [G *Schuss*, n., lit., shot] : to ski down a slope at high speed — **schuss** *n*

sci *abbr* science; scientific

sci·at·i·ca \sī-'a-ti-kə\ *n* : pain in the region of the hips or along the course of the nerve at the back of the thigh

sci·ence \'sī-əns\ *n* [ME, fr. MF, fr. L *scientia*, fr. *scient-*, *sciens* having knowledge, fr. prp. of *scire* to know] 1 : an area of knowledge that is an object of study; *esp* : NATURAL SCIENCE 2 : knowledge covering general truths or the operation of general laws especially as obtained and tested through the scientific method — **sci·en·tif·ic** \ₛsī-ən-'ti-fik\ *adj* — **sci·en·tif·i·cal·ly** \-fi-k(ə-)lē\ *adv* — **sci·en·tist** \'sī-ən-tist\ *n*

science fiction *n* : fiction dealing principally with the impact of actual or imagined science on society or individuals

scientific method *n* : the rules and methods for the pursuit of knowledge involving the finding and stating of a problem, the collection of facts through observation and experiment, and the making and testing of ideas that need to be proven right or wrong

scim·i·tar \'si-mə-tər\ *n* : a curved sword used chiefly by Arabs and Turks

scin·til·la \sin-'ti-lə\ *n* : SPARK, TRACE

scin·til·late \'sint-ᵊl-ₜāt\ *vb* **-lat·ed; -lat·ing** : SPARKLE, GLEAM — **scin·til·la·tion** \ₛsint-ᵊl-'ā-shən\ *n*

sci·on \'sī-ən\ *n* 1 : a shoot of a plant joined to a stock in grafting 2 : DESCENDANT

scis·sors \'si-zərz\ *n pl* : a cutting instrument like shears but usu. smaller

scissors kick *n* : a swimming kick in which the legs move like scissors

scle·ro·sis \sklə-'rō-səs\ *n* : abnormal hardening of tissue (as of an artery); *also* : a disease characterized by this — **scle·rot·ic** \-'rä-tik\ *adj*

scoff \'skäf\ *vb* : MOCK, JEER — **scoff·er** *n*

scoff·law \-ₜlȯ\ *n* : a contemptuous law violator

¹**scold** \'skōld\ *n* : a person who scolds

²**scold** *vb* : to censure severely or angrily

sconce \'skäns\ *n* : a candlestick or an electric light fixture fastened to a wall

scone \'skōn, 'skän\ *n* : a biscuit (as of oatmeal) baked on a griddle

¹**scoop** \'sküp\ *n* 1 : a large shovel; *also* : a utensil with a shovellike or rounded end 2 : an act of scooping 3 : information of immediate interest

²**scoop** *vb* 1 : to take out or up or empty with or as if with a scoop 2 : to make hollow 3 : to report a news item in advance of

scoot \'süt\ *vb* : to move swiftly

scoot·er \'skü-tər\ *n* 1 : a child's vehicle consisting of a narrow board mounted between two wheels tandem

with an upright steering handle attached to the front wheel 2 : MOTOR SCOOTER

¹**scope** \'skōp\ *n* [It *scopo* purpose, goal, fr. Gk *skopos*] 1 : space or opportunity for action or thought 2 : extent covered : RANGE

²**scope** *n* : an instrument (as a microscope or radarscope) for viewing

scorch \'skȯrch\ *vb* : to burn the surface of; *also* : to dry or shrivel with heat ⟨~ed lawns⟩

¹**score** \'skȯr\ *n, pl* **scores** 1 *or pl* **score** : TWENTY 2 : CUT, SCRATCH, SLASH 3 : a record of points made (as in a game) 4 : DEBT 5 : REASON, GROUND 6 : the music of a composition or arrangement with different parts indicated 7 : success in obtaining something (as drugs) esp. illegally

²**score** *vb* **scored; scor·ing** 1 : RECORD 2 : to keep score in a game 3 : to mark with lines, grooves, scratches, or notches 4 : to gain or tally in or as if in a game ⟨*scored* a point⟩ 5 : to assign a grade or score to ⟨~ the tests⟩ 6 : to compose a score for 7 : SUCCEED — **score·less** *adj* — **scor·er** *n*

¹**scorn** \'skȯrn\ *n* : an emotion involving both anger and disgust : CONTEMPT — **scorn·ful** \-fəl\ *adj* — **scorn·ful·ly** *adv*

²**scorn** *vb* : to hold in contempt : DISDAIN — **scorn·er** *n*

Scor·pio \'skȯr-pē-ₜō\ *n* [L, lit., scorpion] 1 : a zodiacal constellation between Libra and Sagittarius usu. pictured as a scorpion 2 : the 8th sign of the zodiac in astrology; *also* : one born under this sign

scor·pi·on \'skȯr-pē-ən\ *n* : any of an order of arthropods related to the spiders that have a poisonous stinger at the tip of a long jointed tail

scorpion

¹**Scot** \'skät\ *n* : a native or inhabitant of Scotland

²**Scot** *abbr* Scotland; Scottish

Scotch \'skäch\ *n* 1 : SCOTS 2 **Scotch** *pl* : the people of Scotland 3 : a whiskey distilled in Scotland esp. from malted barley — **Scotch** *adj* — **Scotch·man** \-mən\ *n* — **Scotch·wom·an** \-ₜwu̇-mən\ *n*

Scotch pine *n* : a pine that is naturalized in the U.S. from northern Europe and Asia and is a valuable timber tree

Scotch terrier *n* : SCOTTISH TERRIER

scot—free \'skät-'frē\ *adj* : free from obligation, harm, or penalty

Scots \'skäts\ *n* : the English language of Scotland

Scots·man \'skäts-mən\ *n* : SCOT

Scots·wom·an \-ₜwu̇-mən\ *n* : a woman who is a Scot

Scot·tie \'skä-tē\ *n* : SCOTTISH TERRIER

Scot·tish \'skä-tish\ *adj* : of, relating to, or characteristic of Scotland, Scots, or the Scots

Scottish terrier *n* : any of an old Scottish breed of terrier with short legs, a large head with small erect ears, a broad deep chest, and a thick rough coat

scoun·drel \'skau̇n-drəl\ *n* : a disreputable person : VILLAIN

¹**scour** \'skau̇r\ *vb* 1 : to rub (as with a gritty substance) in order to clean 2 : to cleanse by or as if by rubbing

²**scour** *vb* 1 : to move rapidly through : RUSH 2 : to examine thoroughly

¹**scourge** \'skərj\ *n* 1 : LASH, WHIP 2 : PUNISHMENT; *also* : a cause of affliction (as a plague)

²**scourge** *vb* **scourged; scourg·ing 1** : LASH, FLOG **2** : to punish severely

¹**scout** \'skaut\ *vb* [ME, fr. MF *escouter* to listen, fr. L *auscultare*] **1** : to look around : RECONNOITER **2** : to inspect or observe to get information

²**scout** *n* **1** : a person sent out to get information; *also* : a soldier, airplane, or ship sent out to reconnoiter **2** : BOY SCOUT **3** : GIRL SCOUT — **scout·mas·ter** \-₁mas-tər\ *n*

³**scout** *vb* : SCORN, SCOFF

scow \'skau̇\ *n* : a large flat-bottomed boat with square ends

scowl \'skau̇l\ *vb* : to make a frowning expression of displeasure — **scowl** *n*

SCPO *abbr* senior chief petty officer

scrab·ble \'skra-bəl\ *vb* **scrab·bled; scrab·bling 1** : SCRAPE, SCRATCH **2** : CLAMBER, SCRAMBLE **3** : to work hard and long **4** : SCRIBBLE — **scrabble** *n* — **scrab·bler** *n*

scrag·gly \'skra-glē\ *adj* : IRREGULAR; *also* : RAGGED, UNKEMPT

scram \'skram\ *vb* **scrammed; scram·ming** : to go away at once

scram·ble \'skram-bəl\ *vb* **scram·bled; scram·bling 1** : to clamber clumsily around **2** : to struggle for or as if for possession of something **3** : to spread irregularly **4** : to mix together **5** : to cook (eggs) by stirring during frying — **scramble** *n*

¹**scrap** \'skrap\ *n* **1** : FRAGMENT, PIECE **2** : discarded material : REFUSE

²**scrap** *vb* **scrapped; scrap·ping 1** : to make into scrap ⟨~ a battleship⟩ **2** : to get rid of as useless

³**scrap** *n* : FIGHT

⁴**scrap** *vb* **scrapped; scrap·ping** : FIGHT, QUARREL — **scrap·per** *n*

scrap·book \'skrap-₁bu̇k\ *n* : a blank book in which mementos are kept

¹**scrape** \'skrāp\ *vb* **scraped; scrap·ing 1** : to remove by drawing a knife over; *also* : to clean or smooth by rubbing off the covering **2** : to damage or injure the surface of by contact with something rough **3** : to draw across a surface with a grating sound **4** : to get together (money) by strict economy **5** : to get along with difficulty — **scrap·er** *n*

²**scrape** *n* **1** : the act or the effect of scraping **2** : a bow accompanied by a drawing back of the foot **3** : an unpleasant predicament

¹**scrap·py** \'skra-pē\ *adj* **scrap·pi·er; -est** : DISCONNECTED, FRAGMENTARY

²**scrappy** *adj* **scrap·pi·er; -est 1** : QUARRELSOME **2** : having an aggressive and determined spirit

¹**scratch** \'skrach\ *vb* **1** : to scrape, dig, or rub with or as if with claws or nails ⟨a dog ~*ing* at the door⟩ ⟨~*ed* my arm⟩ **2** : SCRAPE 3 ⟨~*ed* his nails across the blackboard⟩ **3** : SCRAPE 4 **4** : to cancel or erase by or as if by drawing a line through **5** : to withdraw from a contest — **scratchy** *adj*

²**scratch** *n* **1** : a mark or injury made by or as if by scratching; *also* : a sound so made **2** : the starting line in a race **3** : a point at the beginning of a project at which nothing has been done ahead of time ⟨built from ~⟩

³**scratch** *adj* **1** : made as or used for a trial attempt ⟨~ paper⟩ **2** : made or done by chance ⟨a ~ hit⟩

scrawl \'skrȯl\ *vb* : to write hastily and carelessly — **scrawl** *n*

scraw·ny \'skrȯ-nē\ *adj* **scraw·ni·er; -est** : very thin : SKINNY

¹**scream** \'skrēm\ *vb* : to cry out loudly and shrilly

²**scream** *n* : a loud shrill cry

scream·ing *adj* : so striking as to attract notice as if by screaming ⟨~ headlines⟩

screech \'skrēch\ *vb* : SHRIEK — **screech** *n* — **screechy** \'skrē-chē\ *adj*

¹**screen** \'skrēn\ *n* **1** : a device or partition used to hide, restrain, protect, or decorate ⟨a window ~⟩; *also*

: something that shelters, protects, or conceals **2** : a sieve or perforated material for separating finer from coarser parts (as of sand) **3** : a surface on which an image is made to appear (as in television) **4** : the motion-picture industry

²**screen** *vb* **1** : to shield with or as if with a screen **2** : to separate with or as if with a screen **3** : to present (as a motion picture) on the screen

screen·ing \'skrē-niŋ\ *n* **1** : metal or plastic mesh (as for window screens) **2** : a showing of a motion picture

¹**screw** \'skrü\ *n* [ME, fr. MF *escroe* female screw, nut, fr. ML *scrofa*, fr. L, sow] **1** : a machine consisting of a solid cylinder with a spiral groove around it and a corresponding hollow cylinder into which it fits **2** : a naillike metal piece with a spiral groove and a head with a slot that is inserted into material by rotating and is used to fasten pieces of solid material together **3** : PROPELLER

²**screw** *vb* **1** : to fasten or close by means of a screw **2** : to operate or adjust by means of a screw **3** : to move or cause to move spirally; *also* : to close or set in position by such an action

screw·ball \'skrü-₁bȯl\ *n* **1** : a baseball pitch breaking in a direction opposite to a curve **2** : a whimsical, eccentric, or crazy person

screw·driv·er \-₁drī-vər\ *n* **1** : a tool for turning screws **2** : a drink made of vodka and orange juice

screw·worm \'skrü-₁wərm\ *n* : an American blowfly of warm regions whose larva matures in wounds or sores of mammals and may cause disease or death; *esp* : its larva

screwy \'skrü-ē\ *adj* **screw·i·er; -est 1** : crazily absurd, eccentric, or unusual **2** : CRAZY, INSANE

scrib·ble \'skri-bəl\ *vb* **scrib·bled; scrib·bling** : to write hastily or carelessly — **scribble** *n* — **scrib·bler** *n*

scribe \'skrīb\ *n* **1** : a scholar of Jewish law in New Testament times **2** : a person whose business is the copying of writing **3** : JOURNALIST

scrim \'skrim\ *n* : a light loosely woven cotton or linen cloth

scrim·mage \'skri-mij\ *n* : the play between two football teams beginning with the snap of the ball; *also* : practice play between two teams — **scrimmage** *vb*

scrimp \'skrimp\ *vb* : to economize greatly ⟨~ and save⟩

scrim·shaw \'skrim-₁shȯ\ *n* : carved or engraved articles made orig. by American whalers usu. from baleen or whale ivory — **scrimshaw** *vb*

scrip \'skrip\ *n* **1** : a certificate showing its holder is entitled to something (as stock or land) **2** : paper money issued for temporary use in an emergency

¹**script** \'skript\ *n* **1** : written matter (as lines for a play or broadcast) **2** : HANDWRITING

²**script** *abbr* scripture

scrip·ture \'skrip-chər\ *n* **1** *cap* : the books of the Bible — often used in pl. **2** : the sacred writings of a religion — **scrip·tur·al** \'skrip-chə-rəl\ *adj* — **scrip·tur·al·ly** *adv*

scriv·en·er \'skri-və-nər\ *n* : SCRIBE, COPYIST, WRITER

scrod \'skräd\ *n* : a young fish (as a cod or haddock); *esp* : one split and boned for cooking

scrof·u·la \'skrȯ-fyə-lə\ *n* : tuberculosis of lymph nodes esp. in the neck

¹**scroll** \'skrōl\ *n* : a roll of paper or parchment for writing a document; *also* : a spiral or coiled ornamental form suggesting a loosely or partly rolled scroll

²**scroll** *vb* : to move or cause to move text or graphics up, down, or across a display screen

scroll saw *n* : JIGSAW

scro·tum \'skrō-təm\ *n, pl* **scro·ta** \-tə\ *or* **scrotums** [L] : a pouch that in most male mammals contains the testes

scrounge \'skrau̇nj\ *vb* **scrounged; scroung·ing** : to collect by or as if by foraging

¹**scrub** \'skrəb\ *n* **1** : a thick growth of stunted trees or

shrubs; *also* : an area of land covered with scrub **2** : an inferior domestic animal **3** : a person of insignificant size or standing **4** : a player not on the first team — **scrub** *adj* — **scrub·by** *adj*

²scrub *vb* **scrubbed; scrub·bing 1** : to clean or wash by rubbing ⟨∼ clothes⟩ ⟨∼ out a spot⟩ **2** : CANCEL

³scrub *n* : an act or instance of scrubbing ⟨gave the clothes a good ∼⟩

scrub·ber \'skrə-bər\ *n* : one that scrubs; *esp* : an apparatus for removing impurities esp. from gases

scruff \'skrəf\ *n* : the loose skin of the back of the neck : NAPE

scruffy \'skrə-fē\ *adj* **scruff·i·er; -est** : UNKEMPT, SLOVENLY

scrump·tious \'skrəmp-shəs\ *adj* : DELIGHTFUL, EXCELLENT; *esp* : DELICIOUS — **scrump·tious·ly** *adv*

¹scru·ple \'skrü-pəl\ *n* [ME *scrupul*, MF *scrupule*, fr. L *scrupulus*, dim. of *scrupus* source of uneasiness, lit., sharp stone] **1** : a point of conscience or honor **2** : hesitation due to ethical considerations

²scruple *vb* **scru·pled; scru·pling** : to be reluctant on grounds of conscience : HESITATE

scru·pu·lous \'skrü-pyə-ləs\ *adj* **1** : having moral integrity **2** : PAINSTAKING — **scru·pu·lous·ly** *adv* — **scru·pu·lous·ness** *n*

scru·ti·nize \'skrüt-ə-nīz\ *vb* **-nized; -niz·ing** : to examine closely

scru·ti·ny \'skrüt-ᵊn-ē\ *n, pl* **-nies** [L *scrutinium*, fr. *scrutari* to search, examine, prob. fr. *scruta* trash] : a careful looking over **syn** inspection, examination, analysis

scu·ba \'skü-bə\ *n* [*self-contained underwater breathing apparatus*] : an apparatus for breathing while swimming underwater

scuba diver *n* : one who swims underwater with the aid of scuba gear

¹scud \'skəd\ *vb* **scud·ded; scud·ding** : to move speedily

²scud *n* : light clouds driven by the wind

¹scuff \'skəf\ *vb* **1** : to scrape the feet while walking : SHUFFLE **2** : to scratch or become scratched or worn away

²scuff *n* **1** : a mark or injury caused by scuffing **2** : a flat-soled slipper without heel strap

scuf·fle \'skə-fəl\ *vb* **scuf·fled; scuf·fling 1** : to struggle confusedly at close quarters **2** : to shuffle one's feet — **scuffle** *n*

¹scull \'skəl\ *n* **1** : an oar for use in sculling; *also* : one of a pair of short oars for a single oarsman **2** : a racing shell propelled by one or two persons using sculls

²scull *vb* : to propel (a boat) by an oar over the stern

scul·lery \'skə-lə-rē\ *n, pl* **-ler·ies** [ME, department of household in charge of dishes, fr. MF *escuelerie*, fr. *escuelle* bowl, fr. L *scutella* drinking bowl] : a small room near the kitchen used for cleaning dishes, cooking utensils, and vegetables

scul·lion \'skəl-yən\ *n* [ME *sculion*, fr. MF *escouillon* dishcloth, alter. of *escouvillon*, fr. *escouve* broom, fr. L *scopae*, lit., twigs bound together] : a kitchen helper

sculpt \'skəlpt\ *vb* : CARVE, SCULPTURE

sculp·tor \'skəlp-tər\ *n* : a person who produces works of sculpture

¹sculp·ture \'skəlp-chər\ *n* : the act, process, or art of carving or molding material (as stone, wood, or plastic); *also* : work produced this way — **sculp·tur·al** \'skəlp-chə-rəl\ *adj*

²sculpture *vb* **sculp·tured; sculp·tur·ing** : to form or alter as or as if a work of sculpture

scum \'skəm\ *n* **1** : a slimy or filmy covering on the surface of a liquid **2** : waste matter **3** : RABBLE

scup·per \'skə-pər\ *n* : an opening in the side of a ship through which water on deck is drained overboard

scurf \'skərf\ *n* : thin dry scales of skin (as dandruff); *also* : a scaly deposit or covering — **scurfy** \'skər-fē\ *adj*

scur·ri·lous \'skər-ə-ləs\ *adj* : coarsely jesting : OBSCENE, VULGAR

scur·ry \'skər-ē\ *vb* **scur·ried; scur·ry·ing** : SCAMPER

¹scur·vy \'skər-vē\ *n* : a disease marked by spongy gums, loosened teeth, and bleeding under the skin and caused by lack of vitamin C

²scurvy *adj* : MEAN, CONTEMPTIBLE — **scur·vi·ly** \'skər-və-lē\ *adv*

scutch·eon \'skə-chən\ *n* : ESCUTCHEON

¹scut·tle \'skət-ᵊl\ *n* : a pail for carrying coal

²scuttle *n* : a small opening with a lid esp. in the deck, side, or bottom of a ship

³scuttle *vb* **scut·tled; scut·tling** : to cut a hole in the deck, side, or bottom of (a ship) in order to sink

⁴scuttle *vb* **scut·tled; scut·tling** : SCURRY, SCAMPER

scut·tle·butt \'skət-ᵊl-ᵢbət\ *n* : GOSSIP

scythe \'sīth\ *n* : an implement for mowing (as grass or grain) by hand — **scythe** *vb*

SD *abbr* **1** South Dakota **2** special delivery

S Dak *abbr* South Dakota

SDI *abbr* Strategic Defense Initiative

Se *symbol* selenium

SE *abbr* southeast

sea \'sē\ *n* **1** : a large body of salt water **2** : OCEAN **3** : rough water; *also* : a large wave **4** : something likened to the sea esp. in vastness — **sea** *adj* — **at sea** : LOST, BEWILDERED

sea anemone *n* : any of numerous coelenterate polyps whose form, bright and varied colors, and cluster of tentacles superficially resemble a flower

sea·bird \'sē-ᵢbərd\ *n* : a bird (as a gull) frequenting the open ocean

sea·board \-ᵢbōrd\ *n* : SEACOAST; *also* : the land bordering a coast

sea·coast \-ᵢkōst\ *n* : the shore of the sea

sea·far·er \-ᵢfar-ər\ *n* : SEAMAN

sea·far·ing \-ᵢfar-iŋ\ *n* : the use of the sea for travel or transportation — **seafaring** *adj*

sea·food \-ᵢfüd\ *n* : edible marine fish and shellfish

sea·go·ing \-ᵢgō-iŋ\ *adj* : OCEANGOING

sea horse *n* : any of a genus of small marine fishes with the head and forepart of the body sharply flexed like the head and neck of a horse

¹seal \'sēl\ *n, pl* **seals** *also* **seal 1** : any of numerous large carnivorous sea mammals occurring chiefly in cold regions and having limbs adapted for swimming **2** : the pelt of a seal

²seal *vb* : to hunt seals

³seal *n* **1** : GUARANTEE, PLEDGE **2** : a device having a raised design that can be stamped on clay or wax; *also* : the impression made by stamping with such a device **3** : something that seals or closes up ⟨safety ∼⟩

⁴seal *vb* **1** : to affix a seal to; *also* : AUTHENTICATE **2** : to fasten with or as if with a seal to prevent tampering **3** : to close or make secure against access, leakage, or passage **4** : to determine irrevocably ⟨∼ed his fate⟩

sea–lane \'sē-ᵢlān\ *n* : an established sea route

seal·ant \'sē-lənt\ *n* : a sealing agent

seal·er \'sē-lər\ *n* : a coat applied to prevent subsequent coats of paint or varnish from sinking in

sea level *n* : the level of the surface of the sea esp. at its mean midway between mean high and low water

sea lion *n* : any of several large Pacific seals with external ears

seal·skin \'sēl-ᵢskin\ *n* **1** : ¹SEAL 2 **2** : a garment of sealskin

¹seam \'sēm\ *n* **1** : the line of junction of two edges and esp. of edges of fabric sewn together **2** : a layer of mineral matter **3** : WRINKLE — **seam·less** *adj*

²seam *vb* **1** : to join by or as if by sewing **2** : WRINKLE, FURROW

sea·man \'sē-mən\ *n* **1** : one who assists in the handling of ships : MARINER **2** : an enlisted man in the navy ranking next below a petty officer third class

seaman apprentice *n* : an enlisted man in the navy ranking next below a seaman

seaman recruit *n* : an enlisted man of the lowest rank in the navy

sea·man·ship \'sē-mən-ˌship\ *n* : the art or skill of handling a ship

sea·mount \'sē-ˌmaůnt\ *n* : an underwater mountain

seam·stress \'sēm-strəs\ *n* : a woman who does sewing

seamy \'sē-mē\ *adj* **seam·i·er; -est 1 :** UNPLEASANT **2 :** DEGRADED, SORDID

sé·ance \'sā-ˌäns\ *n* [F] : a meeting to receive communications from spirits

sea·plane \'sē-ˌplān\ *n* : an airplane that can take off from and land on water

sea·port \-ˌpŏrt\ *n* : a port for oceangoing ships

sear \'sir\ *vb* **1 :** WITHER **2 :** to burn or scorch esp. on the surface; *also* : BRAND — **sear** *n*

¹search \'sərch\ *vb* [ME *cerchen*, fr. MF *cerchier* to go about, survey, search, fr. LL *circare* to go about, fr. L *circum* round about] **1 :** to look through in trying to find something **2 :** SEEK **3 :** PROBE — **search·er** *n*

²search *n* : the act of searching

search·light \-ˌlīt\ *n* : an apparatus for projecting a powerful beam of light; *also* : the light projected

sea·scape \'sē-ˌskāp\ *n* **1 :** a view of the sea **2 :** a picture representing a scene at or of the sea

sea·shell \'sē-ˌshel\ *n* : the shell of a marine animal and esp. a mollusk

sea·shore \-ˌshŏr\ *n* : the shore of a sea

sea·sick \-ˌsik\ *adj* : nauseated by or as if by the motion of a ship — **sea·sick·ness** *n*

sea·side \'sē-ˌsīd\ *n* : SEASHORE

¹sea·son \'sē-zən\ *n* [ME, fr. OF *saison*, fr. L *sation-, satio* action of sowing, fr. *serere* to sow] **1 :** one of the divisions of the year (as spring or summer) **2 :** a special period (the Easter ~) — **sea·son·al** \-zə-nəl\ *adj* — **sea·son·al·ly** *adv*

²season *vb* **1 :** to make pleasant to the taste by use of salt, pepper, or spices **2 :** to make (as by aging or drying) suitable for use **3 :** to accustom or habituate to something (as hardship) **syn** harden, inure, acclimatize, toughen — **sea·son·er** *n*

sea·son·able \'sē-zə-nə-bəl\ *adj* : occurring at a good or proper time **syn** timely, propitious, opportune — **sea·son·ably** \-blē\ *adv*

sea·son·ing *n* : something that seasons : CONDIMENT

¹seat \'sēt\ *n* **1 :** a chair, bench, or stool for sitting on **2 :** a place which serves as a capital or center

²seat *vb* **1 :** to place in or on a seat **2 :** to provide seats for

seat belt *n* : straps designed to hold a person in a seat

SEATO \'sē-ˌtō\ *abbr* Southeast Asia Treaty Organization

seat–of–the–pants *adj* : employing or based on personal experience, judgment, and effort rather than technological aids (~ navigation)

sea urchin *n* : any of numerous spiny marine echinoderms having thin brittle globular shells

sea·wall \'sē-ˌwȯl\ *n* : an embankment to protect the shore from erosion

¹sea·ward \'sē-wərd\ *n* : the direction or side away from land and toward the open sea

²seaward *also* **sea·wards** \-wərdz\ *adv* : toward the sea

³seaward *adj* **1 :** directed or situated toward the sea **2 :** coming from the sea

sea·wa·ter \'sē-ˌwȯ-tər, -ˌwä-\ *n* : water in or from the sea

sea·way \-ˌwā\ *n* : an inland waterway that admits ocean shipping

sea·weed \-ˌwēd\ *n* : a marine alga (as a kelp); *also* : a mass of marine algae

sea·wor·thy \-ˌwər-thē\ *adj* : fit for a sea voyage (a ~ ship)

se·ba·ceous \si-'bā-shəs\ *adj* : of, relating to, or secreting fatty material

sec *abbr* **1** second; secondary **2** secretary **3** section **4** [L *secundum*] according to

SEC *abbr* Securities and Exchange Commission

se·cede \si-'sēd\ *vb* **se·ced·ed; se·ced·ing :** to withdraw from an organized body and esp. from a political body

se·ces·sion \si-'se-shən\ *n* : the act of seceding — **se·ces·sion·ist** *n*

se·clude \si-'klüd\ *vb* **se·clud·ed; se·clud·ing :** to keep or shut away from others

se·clu·sion \si-'klü-zhən\ *n* : the act of secluding : the state of being secluded — **se·clu·sive** \-siv\ *adj*

¹sec·ond \'se-kənd\ *adj* [ME, fr. OF, fr. L *secundus* second, following, favorable, fr. *sequi* to follow] **1 :** being number two in a countable series **2 :** next after the first **3 :** ALTERNATE (every ~ year) — **second** *or* **sec·ond·ly** *adv*

²second *n* **1 :** one that is second **2 :** one who assists another (as in a duel) **3 :** an inferior or flawed article (as of merchandise) **4 :** the second forward gear in a motor vehicle

³second *n* [ME *secunde*, fr. ML *secunda*, fr. L, fem. of *secundus* second; fr. its being the second division of a unit into 60 parts, as a minute is the first] **1 :** the 60th part of a minute of time or angular measure **2 :** an instant of time

⁴second *vb* **1 :** to encourage or give support to **2 :** to act as a second to **3 :** to support (a motion) by adding one's voice to that of a proposer

¹sec·ond·ary \'se-kən-ˌder-ē\ *adj* **1 :** second in rank, value, or occurrence : LESSER **2 :** belonging to a second or later stage of development **3 :** coming after the primary or elementary (~ schools) **syn** subordinate, collateral, dependent

²secondary *n, pl* **-ar·ies :** the defensive backfield of a football team

secondary sex characteristic *n* : a physical characteristic that appears in members of one sex at puberty or in seasonal breeders at breeding season and is not directly concerned with reproduction

second fiddle *n* : one that plays a supporting or subservient role

sec·ond–guess \ˌse-kənd-'ges\ *vb* **1 :** to think out other strategies or explanations for after the event **2 :** to seek to anticipate or predict

sec·ond·hand \-'hand\ *adj* **1 :** not original **2 :** not new : USED (~ clothes) **3 :** dealing in used goods

second lieutenant *n* : a commissioned officer (as in the army) ranking next below a first lieutenant

sec·ond–rate \ˌse-kənd-'rāt\ *adj* : INFERIOR

second–story man *n* : a burglar who enters by an upstairs window

sec·ond–string \'se-kənd-'striŋ\ *adj* : being a substitute (as on a team)

se·cre·cy \'sē-krə-sē\ *n, pl* **-cies 1 :** the habit or practice of being secretive **2 :** the condition of being hidden or concealed

¹se·cret \'sē-krət\ *adj* **1 :** HIDDEN, CONCEALED (a ~ staircase) **2 :** COVERT, STEALTHY; *also* : engaged in detecting or spying (a ~ agent) **3 :** kept from general knowledge — **se·cret·ly** *adv*

²secret *n* **1 :** MYSTERY **2 :** something kept from the knowledge of others

sec·re·tar·i·at \ˌse-krə-'ter-ē-ət\ *n* **1 :** the office of a secretary **2 :** the secretarial staff in an office **3 :** the administrative department of a governmental organization (the UN ~)

sec·re·tary \'se-krə-ˌter-ē\ *n, pl* **-tar·ies 1 :** a person employed to handle records, correspondence, and routine work for another person **2 :** an officer of a corporation or business who is in charge of correspondence and records **3 :** an official at the head of a department of government **4 :** a writing desk — **sec·re·tar·i·al** \ˌse-krə-'ter-ē-əl\ *adj* — **sec·re·tary·ship** \'se-krə-ˌter-ē-ˌship\ *n*

¹se·crete \si-ˈkrēt\ *vb* **se·cret·ed; se·cret·ing** : to form and give off (a secretion)

²se·crete \si-ˈkrēt, ˈsē-krət\ *vb* **se·cret·ed; se·cret·ing** : HIDE, CONCEAL

se·cre·tion \si-ˈkrē-shən\ *n* **1** : the process of secreting something **2** : a product of glandular activity; *esp* : one (as a hormone) useful in the organism **3** : the act of hiding something — **se·cre·to·ry** \ˈsē-krə-ˌtōr-ē\ *adj*

se·cre·tive \ˈsē-krə-tiv, si-ˈkrē-\ *adj* : tending to keep secrets or to act secretly — **se·cre·tive·ly** *adv* — **se·cre·tive·ness** *n*

¹sect \ˈsekt\ *n* **1** : a dissenting religious body **2** : a religious denomination **3** : a group adhering to a distinctive doctrine or to a leader

²sect *abbr* section; sectional

¹sec·tar·i·an \sek-ˈter-ē-ən\ *adj* **1** : of or relating to a sect or sectarian **2** : limited in character or scope — **sec·tar·i·an·ism** *n*

²sectarian *n* **1** : an adherent of a sect **2** : a narrow or bigoted person

sec·ta·ry \ˈsek-tə-rē\ *n, pl* **-ries** : a member of a sect

¹sec·tion \ˈsek-shən\ *n* **1** : a part cut off or separated **2** : a distinct part **3** : the appearance that a thing has or would have if cut straight through

²section *vb* **1** : to separate or become separated into sections **2** : to represent in sections

sec·tion·al \ˈsek-shə-nəl\ *adj* **1** : of, relating to, or characteristic of a section **2** : local or regional rather than general in character **3** : divided into sections — **sec·tion·al·ism** *n*

sec·tor \ˈsek-tər\ *n* **1** : a part of a circle between two radii **2** : an area assigned to a military leader to defend **3** : a subdivision of society

sec·u·lar \ˈse-kyə-lər\ *adj* **1** : not sacred or ecclesiastical **2** : not bound by monastic vows ⟨a ~ priest⟩

sec·u·lar·ism \ˈse-kyə-lə-ˌri-zəm\ *n* : indifference to or exclusion of religion — **sec·u·lar·ist** \-rist\ *n* — **sec·u·lar·ist** *or* **sec·u·lar·is·tic** \ˌse-kyə-lə-ˈris-tik\ *adj*

sec·u·lar·ize \ˈse-kyə-lə-ˌrīz\ *vb* **-ized; -iz·ing 1** : to make secular **2** : to transfer from ecclesiastical to civil or lay use, possession, or control — **sec·u·lar·i·za·tion** \ˌse-kyə-lə-rə-ˈzā-shən\ *n* — **sec·u·lar·iz·er** \ˈse-kyə-lə-ˌrī-zər\ *n*

¹se·cure \si-ˈkyúr\ *adj* **se·cur·er; -est** [L *securus* safe, secure, fr. *se* without + *cura* care] **1** : easy in mind : free from fear **2** : free from danger or risk of loss : SAFE **3** : CERTAIN, SURE — **se·cure·ly** *adv*

²secure *vb* **se·cured; se·cur·ing 1** : to make safe : GUARD **2** : to assure payment of by giving a pledge or collateral **3** : to fasten safely ⟨~ a door⟩ **4** : GET, ACQUIRE

se·cu·ri·ty \si-ˈkyúr-ə-tē\ *n, pl* **-ties 1** : SAFETY **2** : freedom from worry **3** : something given as pledge of payment ⟨a ~ deposit⟩ **4** *pl* : bond or stock certificates **5** : PROTECTION

secy *abbr* secretary

se·dan \si-ˈdan\ *n* **1** : a covered chair borne on poles by two men **2** : an automobile seating four or more people and usu. having a permanent top

¹se·date \si-ˈdāt\ *adj* : quiet and dignified in behavior **syn** staid, sober, serious, solemn — **se·date·ly** *adv*

²sedate *vb* **se·dat·ed; se·dat·ing** : to dose with sedatives — **se·da·tion** \si-ˈdā-shən\ *n*

¹sed·a·tive \ˈse-də-tiv\ *adj* : serving or tending to relieve tension

²sedative *n* : a sedative drug

sed·en·tary \ˈsed-ᵊn-ˌter-ē\ *adj* : characterized by or requiring much sitting

sedge \ˈsej\ *n* : any of a family of plants esp. of marshy areas that differ from the related grasses esp. in having solid stems — **sedgy** \ˈse-jē\ *adj*

sed·i·ment \ˈse-də-mənt\ *n* **1** : the material that settles to the bottom of a liquid **2** : material (as stones and sand) deposited by water, wind, or a glacier — **sed·i·men·ta·ry** \ˌse-də-ˈmen-tə-rē\ *adj* — **sed·i·men·ta·tion** \-mən-ˈtā-shən, -ˌmen-\ *n*

se·di·tion \si-ˈdi-shən\ *n* : the causing of discontent, insurrection, or resistance against a government — **se·di·tious** \-shəs\ *adj*

se·duce \si-ˈdüs, -ˈdyüs\ *vb* **se·duced; se·duc·ing 1** : to persuade to disobedience or disloyalty **2** : to lead astray **3** : to entice to sexual intercourse **syn** tempt, entice, inveigle, lure — **se·duc·er** *n* — **se·duc·tion** \-ˈdək-shən\ *n* — **se·duc·tive** \-tiv\ *adj*

sed·u·lous \ˈse-jə-ləs\ *adj* [L *sedulus*, fr. *sedulo* sincerely, diligently, fr. *se* without + *dolus* guile] : DILIGENT, PAINSTAKING

¹see \ˈsē\ *vb* **saw** \ˈsò\; **seen** \ˈsēn\; **see·ing 1** : to perceive by the eye; *also* : to have the power of sight **2** : EXPERIENCE **3** : UNDERSTAND **4** : to make sure ⟨~ that order is kept⟩ **5** : to meet with **6** : to keep company with esp. in dating **7** : ACCOMPANY, ESCORT **syn** behold, descry, espy, view, observe, note, discern

²see *n* : the authority or jurisdiction of a bishop

¹seed \ˈsēd\ *n, pl* **seed** *or* **seeds 1** : the grains of plants used for sowing **2** : a ripened ovule of a flowering plant that may develop into a new plant; *also* : a plant structure (as a spore or small dry fruit) capable of producing a new plant **3** : DESCENDANTS **4** : SOURCE, ORIGIN — **seed·less** *adj* — **go to seed** *or* **run to seed 1** : to develop seed **2** : DECAY

²seed *vb* **1** : SOW, PLANT ⟨~ land to grass⟩ **2** : to bear or shed seeds **3** : to remove seeds from — **seed·er** *n*

seed·bed \-ˌbed\ *n* : soil or a bed of soil prepared for planting seed

seed·ling \ˈsēd-liŋ\ *n* **1** : a young plant grown from seed **2** : a young tree before it becomes a sapling

seed·time \ˈsēd-ˌtīm\ *n* : the season for sowing

seedy \ˈsē-dē\ *adj* **seed·i·er; -est 1** : containing or full of seeds **2** : SHABBY

seek \ˈsēk\ *vb* **sought** \ˈsòt\; **seek·ing 1** : to search for **2** : to try to reach or obtain **3** : ATTEMPT — **seek·er** *n*

seem \ˈsēm\ *vb* **1** : to appear to the observation or understanding **2** : to give the impression of being : APPEAR

seem·ing *adj* : outwardly apparent — **seem·ing·ly** *adv*

seem·ly \ˈsēm-lē\ *adj* **seem·li·er; -est 1** : conventionally proper **2** : FIT

seep \ˈsēp\ *vb* : to flow or pass slowly through fine pores or cracks — **seep·age** \ˈsē-pij\ *n*

seer \ˈsir\ *n* : a person who foresees or predicts events : PROPHET

seer·suck·er \ˈsir-ˌsə-kər\ *n* [Hindi *śīrśaker*, fr. Per *shīr-o-shakar*, lit., milk and sugar] : a light fabric of linen, cotton, or rayon usu. striped and slightly puckered

see·saw \ˈsē-ˌsò\ *n* **1** : a contest in which now one side now the other has the lead **2** : a children's sport of riding up and down on the ends of a plank supported in the middle; *also* : the plank so used — **seesaw** *vb*

seethe \ˈsēth\ *vb* **seethed; seeth·ing** [archaic *seethe* boil] : to become violently agitated

seg·ment \ˈseg-mənt\ *n* **1** : a division of a thing : SECTION **2** : a part cut off from a geometrical figure (as a circle) by one or more points, lines, or planes — **seg·ment·ed** \-ˌmen-təd\ *adj*

seg·re·gate \ˈse-gri-ˌgāt\ *vb* **-gat·ed; -gat·ing** [L *segregare*, fr. *se-* apart + *greg-, grex* herd, flock] : to cut off from others; *esp* : to separate by races — **seg·re·ga·tion** \ˌse-gri-ˈgā-shən\ *n*

seg·re·ga·tion·ist \ˌse-gri-ˈgā-shə-nist\ *n* : one who believes in or practices the segregation of races

sei·gneur \sān-ˈyər\ *n, often cap* [MF, fr. ML *senior*, fr. L, adj., elder] : a feudal lord

¹seine \ˈsān\ *n* : a large weighted fishing net

²seine *vb* **seined; sein·ing** : to fish or catch with a seine — **sein·er** *n*

seis·mic \ˈsīz-mik, ˈsīs-\ *adj* : of, relating to, resembling, or caused by an earthquake — **seis·mi·cal·ly** \-mik(ə-)lē\ *adv* — **seis·mic·i·ty** \sīz-ˈmi-sə-tē, sīs-\ *n*

seis·mo·gram \'sīz-mə-ˌgram, 'sīs-\ *n* : the record of an earth tremor made by a seismograph

seis·mo·graph \-ˌgraf\ *n* : an apparatus to measure and record seismic vibrations — **seis·mo·graph·ic** \ˌsīz-mə-'gra-fik, ˌsīs-\ *adj* — **seis·mog·ra·phy** \sīz-'mä-grə-fē, sīs-\ *n*

seis·mol·o·gy \sīz-'mä-lə-jē, sīs-\ *n* : a science that deals with earthquakes — **seis·mo·log·i·cal** \ˌsīz-mə-'lä-ji-kəl, ˌsīs-\ *adj* — **seis·mol·o·gist** \sīz-'mä-lə-jist, sīs-\ *n*

seis·mom·e·ter \sīz-'mä-mə-tər, sīs-\ *n* : a seismograph measuring the actual movement of the ground

seize \'sēz\ *vb* **seized; seiz·ing 1** : to lay hold of or take possession of by force **2** : ARREST **3** : UNDERSTAND **4** : to attack or overwhelm physically : AFFLICT **syn** take, grasp, clutch, snatch, grab

sei·zure \'sē-zhər\ *n* **1** : the act of seizing : the state of being seized **2** : a sudden attack (as of disease)

sel *abbr* select; selected; selection

sel·dom \'sel-dəm\ *adv* : not often : RARELY

¹**se·lect** \sə-'lekt\ *adj* **1** : CHOSEN, PICKED; *also* : CHOICE **2** : judicious or restrictive in choice : DISCRIMINATING

²**select** *vb* : to choose from a number or group : pick out

se·lec·tion \sə-'lek-shən\ *n* **1** : the act or process of selecting **2** : something selected : CHOICE **3** : a natural or artificial process that tends to favor the survival and reproduction of individuals with certain traits but not those with others

se·lec·tive \sə-'lek-tiv\ *adj* : of or relating to selection : selecting or tending to select ⟨~ shoppers⟩

selective service *n* : a system for calling men up for military service : DRAFT

se·lect·man \si-'lekt-ˌman, -mən\ *n* : one of a board of officials elected in towns of most New England states to administer town affairs

se·le·ni·um \sə-'lē-nē-əm\ *n* : a nonmetallic chemical element — see ELEMENT table

self \'self\ *n, pl* **selves** \'selvz\ **1** : the essential person distinct from all other persons in identity **2** : a particular side of a person's character **3** : personal interest : SELFISHNESS

self- *comb form* **1** : oneself : itself **2** : of oneself or itself **3** : by oneself or itself; *also* : automatic **4** : to, for, or toward oneself

self-abasement	self-control
self-absorbed	self-correcting
self-absorption	self-created
self-accusation	self-criticism
self-acting	self-cultivation
self-addressed	self-deceit
self-adjusting	self-deception
self-administer	self-defeating
self-advancement	self-definition
self-aggrandizement	self-delusion
self-aggrandizing	self-denial
self-analysis	self-denying
self-appointed	self-deprecating
self-asserting	self-deprecation
self-assertion	self-depreciation
self-assertive	self-despair
self-assurance	self-destruct
self-assured	self-destruction
self-awareness	self-destructive
self-betrayal	self-determination
self-closing	self-discipline
self-conceit	self-distrust
self-concern	self-doubt
self-condemned	self-educated
self-confessed	self-employed
self-confidence	self-employment
self-confident	self-esteem
self-congratulation	self-examination
self-congratulatory	self-explaining
self-constituted	self-explanatory
self-contradiction	self-expression
self-contradictory	self-forgetful

self-giving	self-proclaimed
self-governing	self-propelled
self-government	self-propelling
self-hate	self-protection
self-help	self-realization
self-hypnosis	self-referential
self-identity	self-regard
self-image	self-reliance
self-importance	self-reliant
self-important	self-reproach
self-imposed	self-respect
self-improvement	self-respecting
self-incrimination	self-restraint
self-induced	self-revelation
self-indulgence	self-rule
self-indulgent	self-sacrifice
self-inflicted	self-sacrificing
self-interest	self-satisfaction
self-knowledge	self-satisfied
self-limiting	self-service
self-love	self-serving
self-lubricating	self-starting
self-luminous	self-styled
self-operating	self-sufficiency
self-perception	self-sufficient
self-perpetuating	self-supporting
self-pity	self-sustaining
self-portrait	self-taught
self-possessed	self-torment
self-possession	self-winding
self-preservation	self-worth

self–cen·tered \'self-'sen-tərd\ *adj* : concerned only with one's own self — **self–cen·tered·ness** *n*

self–com·posed \ˌself-kəm-'pōzd\ *adj* : having control over one's emotions

self–con·scious \'self-'kän-chəs\ *adj* : uncomfortably conscious of oneself as an object of observation by others — **self–con·scious·ly** *adv* — **self–con·scious-ness** *n*

self–con·tained \ˌself-kən-'tānd\ *adj* **1** : complete in itself **2** : showing self-control; *also* : reserved in manner

self–de·fense \'self-di-'fens\ *n* **1** : a plea of justification for the use of force or for homicide **2** : the act of defending oneself, one's property, or a close relative

self–ef·fac·ing \-ə-'fā-siŋ\ *adj* : RETIRING, SHY

self–ev·i·dent \ˌself-'e-və-dənt\ *adj* : evident without proof or reasoning

self–fer·til·iza·tion \ˌself-ˌfərt-ᵊl-ə-'zā-shən\ *n* : fertilization of a plant or animal by its own pollen or sperm

self–ful·fill·ing \ˌself-fül-'fi-liŋ\ *adj* : becoming real or true by virtue of having been predicted or expected ⟨a ~ prophecy⟩

self·ish \'sel-fish\ *adj* : concerned with one's own welfare excessively or without regard for others — **self·ish·ly** *adv* — **self·ish·ness** *n*

self·less \'self-ləs\ *adj* : UNSELFISH — **self·less·ness** *n*

self–made \'self-'mād\ *adj* : having achieved success or prominence by one's own efforts ⟨a ~ man⟩

self–pol·li·na·tion \ˌself-ˌpä-lə-'nā-shən\ *n* : pollination of a flower by its own pollen or sometimes by pollen from another flower on the same plant

self–reg·u·lat·ing \'self-'re-gyə-ˌlā-tiŋ\ *adj* : AUTOMATIC

self–righ·teous \-'rī-chəs\ *adj* : strongly convinced of one's own righteousness — **self–righ·teous·ly** *adv*

self·same \'self-ˌsām\ *adj* : precisely the same : IDENTICAL

self–seal·ing \'self-'sē-liŋ\ *adj* : capable of sealing itself (as after puncture)

self–seek·ing \'self-'sē-kiŋ\ *adj* : seeking only to further one's own interests — **self–seeking** *n*

self–start·er \-'stär-tər\ *n* : a person who has initiative

self–will \'self-'wil\ *n* : OBSTINACY

sell \'sel\ *vb* **sold** \'sōld\; **sell·ing 1** : to transfer (property) in return for money or something else of value **2** : to deal in as a business **3** : to be sold ⟨cars are ~*ing* well⟩ — **sell·er** *n*

sell out *vb* **1** : to dispose of entirely by sale; *esp* : to sell one's business **2** : BETRAY — **sell·out** \'sel-‚aüt\ *n*

selt·zer \'selt-sər\ *n* [modif. of G *Selterser (Wasser)* water of Selters, fr. Nieder *Selters,* Germany] : artificially carbonated water

sel·vage *or* **sel·vedge** \'sel-vij\ *n* : the edge of a woven fabric so formed as to prevent raveling

selves *pl of* SELF

sem *abbr* **1** semicolon **2** seminar **3** seminary

se·man·tic \si-'man-tik\ *also* **se·man·ti·cal** \-ti-kəl\ *adj* : of or relating to meaning in language

se·man·tics \si-'man-tiks\ *n sing or pl* : the study of meanings in language

sema·phore \'se-mə-‚fōr\ *n* **1** : a visual signaling apparatus with movable arms **2** : signaling by hand-held flags

semaphore 2: alphabet; 3 positions following Z: error, end of word, numerals follow; numerals 1,2,3,4,5,6,7,8,9,0 same as A through J

sem·blance \'sem-bləns\ *n* **1** : outward appearance **2** : IMAGE, LIKENESS

se·men \'sē-mən\ *n* [NL, fr. L, seed] : a sticky whitish fluid of the male reproductive tract that contains the sperm

se·mes·ter \sə-'mes-tər\ *n* [G, fr. L *semestris* half-yearly, fr. *sex* six + *mensis* month] **1** : half a year **2** : one of the two terms into which many colleges divide the school year

semi- \'se-mi, -‚mī\ *prefix* **1** : precisely half of **2** : half in quantity or value; *also* : half of or occurring halfway through a specified period **3** : partly : incompletely **4** : partial : incomplete **5** : having some of the characteristics of

semiannual
semiarid
semicentennial
semicircle
semicircular
semicivilized
semiclassical
semiconscious
semidarkness
semidivine
semiformal
semigloss
semi–independent
semiliquid
semiliterate
semimonthly

semiofficial
semipermanent
semipolitical
semiprecious
semiprivate
semiprofessional
semireligious
semiretired
semiskilled
semisoft
semisolid
semisweet
semitransparent
semiweekly
semiyearly

semi \'se-‚mī\ *n, pl* **sem·is** : SEMITRAILER

semi·au·to·mat·ic \‚se-mē-‚ȯ-tə-'ma-tik\ *adj, of a firearm* : reloading by mechanical means but requiring release and another press of the trigger to fire again

semi·co·lon \'se-mi-‚kō-lən\ *n* : a punctuation mark ; used esp. to separate major sentence elements

semi·con·duc·tor \‚se-mi-kən-'dək-tər\ *n* : a substance whose electrical conductivity is between that of a conductor and an insulator — **semi·con·duct·ing** *adj*

¹semi·fi·nal \‚se-mi-'fīn-əl\ *adj* : being next to the last in an elimination tournament

²semi·fi·nal \'se-mi-‚fīn-əl\ *n* : a semifinal round or match — **semi·fi·nal·ist** \-ist\ *n*

semi·lu·nar \-'lü-nər\ *adj* : shaped like a crescent

sem·i·nal \'se-mən-əl\ *adj* **1** : of, relating to, or consisting of seed or semen **2** : containing or contributing the seeds of later development : CREATIVE, ORIGINAL — **sem·i·nal·ly** *adv*

sem·i·nar \'se-mə-‚när\ *n* **1** : a course of study pursued by a group of advanced students doing original research under a professor **2** : CONFERENCE

sem·i·nary \'se-mə-‚ner-ē\ *n, pl* **-nar·ies** [ME, seedbed, nursery, fr. L *seminarium,* fr. *semen* seed] : an educational institution; *esp* : one that gives theological training — **sem·i·nar·i·an** \‚se-mə-'ner-ē-ən\ *n*

Sem·i·nole \'se-mə-‚nōl\ *n, pl* **Seminoles** *or* **Seminole** : a member of an American Indian people of Florida

semi·per·me·able \‚se-mi-'pər-mē-ə-bəl\ *adj* : partially but not freely or wholly permeable; *esp* : permeable to some usu. small molecules but not to other usu. larger particles ⟨a ~ membrane⟩ — **semi·per·me·abil·i·ty** \-‚pər-mē-ə-'bi-lə-tē\ *n*

Sem·ite \'se-‚mīt\ *n* : a member of any of a group of peoples (as the Hebrews or Arabs) of southwestern Asia — **Se·mit·ic** \sə-'mi-tik\ *adj*

semi·trail·er \'se-mi-‚trā-lər, -‚mī-\ *n* : a freight trailer that when attached is supported at its forward end by the truck tractor; *also* : a semitrailer with attached tractor

semp·stress \'semp-strəs\ *var of* SEAMSTRESS

¹sen \'sen\ *n, pl* **sen** — see *yen* at MONEY table

²sen *n, pl* **sen** — see *dollar, ringgit, rupiah* at MONEY table

³sen *n, pl* **sen** — see *riel* at MONEY table

⁴sen *abbr* **1** senate; senator **2** senior

sen·ate \'se-nət\ *n* : the second of two chambers of a legislature

sen·a·tor \'se-nə-tər\ *n* : a member of a senate — **sen·a·to·ri·al** \‚se-nə-'tōr-ē-əl\ *adj*

send \'send\ *vb* **sent** \'sent\; **send·ing** **1** : to cause to go **2** : EMIT **3** : to propel or drive esp. with force **4** : to put or bring into a certain condition — **send·er** *n*

send–off \'send-‚ȯf\ *n* : a demonstration of goodwill and enthusiasm at the start of a new venture (as a trip)

se·ne \'sā-(‚)nā\ *n, pl* **sene** — see *tala* at MONEY table

Sen·e·ca \'se-ni-kə\ *n, pl* **Seneca** *or* **Senecas** : a member of an American Indian people of western New York

Sen·e·ga·lese \‚se-ni-gə-'lēz, -'lēs\ *n, pl* **Senegalese** : a native or inhabitant of Senegal — **Senegalese** *adj*

se·nes·cence \si-'nes-əns\ *n* : the state of being old; *also* : the process of becoming old — **se·nes·cent** \-ənt\ *adj*

se·nile \'sē-‚nīl, 'se-\ *adj* : OLD, AGED; *esp* : exhibiting a loss of mental ability associated with old age — **se·nil·i·ty** \si-'ni-lə-tē\ *n*

¹se·nior \'sē-nyər\ *n* **1** : a person older or of higher rank than another **2** : a member of the graduating class of a high school or college

²senior *adj* [ME, fr. L, older, elder, compar. of *senex* old] **1** : ELDER **2** : more advanced in dignity or rank **3** : belonging to the final year of a school or college course

senior chief petty officer *n* : a petty officer in the navy or coast guard ranking next below a master chief petty officer

senior citizen *n* : an elderly person; *esp* : one who has retired

senior high school *n* : a school usu. including grades 10 to 12

se·nior·i·ty \sēn-'yȯr-ə-tē\ *n* **1** : the quality or state of being senior **2** : a privileged status owing to length of continuous service

senior master sergeant *n* : a noncommissioned officer in the air force ranking next below a chief master sergeant

sen·i·ti \'se-nə-tē\ *n, pl* **seniti** — see *pa'anga* at MONEY table

sen·na \'se-nə\ *n* **1** : CASSIA 2; *esp* : one used medicinally **2** : the dried leaflets or pods of a cassia used as a purgative

sen·sa·tion \sen-'sā-shən\ *n* **1** : awareness (as of noise or heat) or a mental process (as seeing or hearing) due to stimulation of a sense organ; *also* : an indefinite bodily feeling **2** : a condition of excitement; *also* : the thing that causes this condition

sen·sa·tion·al \-shə-nəl\ *adj* **1** : of or relating to sensation or the senses **2** : arousing an intense and usu. superficial interest or emotional reaction — **sen·sa·tion·al·ly** *adv*

sen·sa·tion·al·ism \-nə-₁li-zəm\ *n* : the use or effect of sensational subject matter or treatment — **sen·sa·tion·al·ist** \-nə-list\ *adj or n* — **sen·sa·tion·al·is·tic** \-₁sā-shə-nə-'lis-tik\ *adj*

sen·sa·tion·al·ize \-nə-₁līz\ *vb* **-ized; -iz·ing** : to present in a sensational manner

¹sense \'sens\ *n* **1** : semantic content : MEANING **2** : the faculty of perceiving by means of sense organs; *also* : a bodily function or mechanism (as sight, hearing, or smell) basically involving a stimulus and a sense organ **3** : SENSATION, AWARENESS **4** : INTELLIGENCE, JUDGMENT **5** : OPINION 〈the ~ of the meeting〉 — **sense·less** *adj* — **sense·less·ly** *adv*

²sense *vb* **sensed; sens·ing 1** : to be or become aware of 〈~ danger〉; *also* : to perceive by the senses **2** : to detect (as radiation) automatically

sense organ *n* : a bodily structure (as an eye or ear) that receives stimuli (as heat or light) which excite nerve cells to send information to the brain

sen·si·bil·i·ty \₁sen-sə-'bi-lə-tē\ *n, pl* **-ties** : delicacy of feeling : SENSITIVITY

sen·si·ble \'sen-sə-bəl\ *adj* **1** : capable of being perceived by the senses or the mind; *also* : capable of receiving sense impressions **2** : AWARE, CONSCIOUS **3** : REASONABLE, RATIONAL — **sen·si·bly** \-blē\ *adv*

sen·si·tive \'sen-sə-tiv\ *adj* **1** : subject to excitation by or responsive to stimuli **2** : having power of feeling **3** : of such a nature as to be easily affected **4** : TOUCHY 〈a ~ issue〉 — **sen·si·tive·ness** *n* — **sen·si·tiv·i·ty** \₁sen-sə-'ti-və-tē\ *n*

sensitive plant *n* : any of several mimosas with leaves that fold or droop when touched

sen·si·tize \'sen-sə-₁tīz\ *vb* **-tized; -tiz·ing** : to make or become sensitive or hypersensitive — **sen·si·ti·za·tion** \₁sen-sə-tə-'zā-shən\ *n*

sen·sor \'sen-₁sȯr, -sər\ *n* : a device that responds to a physical stimulus

sen·so·ry \'sen-sə-rē\ *adj* : of or relating to sensation or the senses

sen·su·al \'sen-shə-wəl\ *adj* **1** : relating to gratification of the senses **2** : devoted to the pleasures of the senses — **sen·su·al·ist** *n* — **sen·su·al·i·ty** \₁sen-shə-'wa-lə-tē\ *n* — **sen·su·al·ly** *adv*

sen·su·ous \'sen-shə-wəs\ *adj* **1** : relating to the senses or to things that can be perceived by the senses **2** : VOLUPTUOUS — **sen·su·ous·ly** *adv* — **sen·su·ous·ness** *n*

sent *past and past part of* SEND

sen·te \'sen-tē\ *n, pl* **li·cen·te** *or* **li·sen·te** \li-'sen-tē\ — see *loti* at MONEY table

¹sen·tence \'sent-ᵊns, -ᵊnz\ *n* [ME, fr. MF, fr. L *sententia*, lit., feeling, opinion, fr. *sentire* to feel] **1** : the punishment set by a court **2** : a grammatically self= contained speech unit that expresses an assertion, a question, a command, a wish, or an exclamation

²sentence *vb* **sen·tenced; sen·tenc·ing** : to impose a sentence on

sen·ten·tious \sen-'ten-chəs\ *adj* : using wise sayings or proverbs; *also* : using pompous language

sen·tient \'sen-chənt, -chē-ənt\ *adj* : capable of feeling : having perception

sen·ti·ment \'sen-tə-mənt\ *n* **1** : FEELING; *also* : thought and judgment influenced by feeling : emotional attitude **2** : OPINION, NOTION

sen·ti·men·tal \₁sen-tə-'ment-ᵊl\ *adj* **1** : influenced by tender feelings **2** : affecting the emotions **syn** bathetic, maudlin, mawkish, mushy — **sen·ti·men·tal·ism** *n* — **sen·ti·men·tal·ist** *n* — **sen·ti·men·tal·i·ty** \-₁men-'ta-lə-tē, -mən-\ *n* — **sen·ti·men·tal·ly** *adv*

sen·ti·men·tal·ize \-'ment-ᵊl-₁īz\ *vb* **-ized; -iz·ing 1** : to indulge in sentiment **2** : to look upon or imbue with sentiment — **sen·ti·men·tal·i·za·tion** \-₁ment-ᵊl-ə-'zā-shən\ *n*

sen·ti·mo \sen-'tē-(₁)mō\ *n, pl* **-mos** — see *peso* at MONEY table

sen·ti·nel \'sent-ᵊn-əl\ *n* [MF *sentinelle*, fr. It *sentinella*, fr. *sentina* vigilance, fr. *sentire* to perceive, fr. L] : one that watches or guards

sen·try \'sen-trē\ *n, pl* **sentries** : SENTINEL, GUARD

sep *abbr* separate, separated

Sep *abbr* September

SEP *abbr* simplified employee pension

se·pal \'sē-pəl, 'se-\ *n* : one of the modified leaves comprising a flower calyx

sep·a·ra·ble \'se-pə-rə-bəl\ *adj* : capable of being separated

¹sep·a·rate \'se-pə-₁rāt\ *vb* **-rat·ed; -rat·ing 1** : to set or keep apart : DISCONNECT, SEVER **2** : to keep apart by something intervening **3** : to cease to be together : PART

²sep·a·rate \'se-prət, -pə-rət\ *adj* **1** : not connected **2** : divided from each other **3** : SINGLE, PARTICULAR 〈the ~ pieces of the puzzle〉 — **sep·a·rate·ly** *adv*

³sep·a·rate *n* : an article of dress designed to be worn interchangeably with others to form various combinations

sep·a·ra·tion \₁se-pə-'rā-shən\ *n* **1** : the act or process of separating : the state of being separated **2** : a point, line, means, or area of division **3** : a formal separating of a married couple by agreement but without divorce

sep·a·rat·ist \'se-prə-tist, 'se-pə-₁rā-\ *n* : an advocate of separation (as from a political body) — **sep·a·rat·ism** \'se-prə-₁ti-zəm\ *n*

sep·a·ra·tive \'se-pə-₁rā-tiv, 'se-prə-tiv\ *adj* : tending toward, causing, or expressing separation

sep·a·ra·tor \'se-pə-₁rā-tər\ *n* : one that separates; *esp* : a device for separating cream from milk

se·pia \'sē-pē-ə\ *n* : a brownish gray to dark brown color

sep·sis \'sep-səs\ *n, pl* **sep·ses** \'sep-₁sēz\ : a toxic condition due to spread of bacteria or their products in the body

Sept *abbr* September

Sep·tem·ber \sep-'tem-bər\ *n* [ME *Septembre*, fr. OF & OE, both fr. L *September* (seventh month), fr. *septem* seven] : the 9th month of the year having 30 days

sep·tic \'sep-tik\ *adj* **1** : PUTREFACTIVE **2** : relating to or characteristic of sepsis

sep·ti·ce·mia \₁sep-tə-'sē-mē-ə\ *n* : BLOOD POISONING

septic tank *n* : a tank in which sewage is disintegrated by bacteria

sep·tu·a·ge·nar·i·an \sep-₁tü-ə-jə-'ner-ē-ən, -₁tyü-\ *n* : a person whose age is in the seventies — **septuagenarian** *adj*

Sep·tu·a·gint \sep-'tü-ə-jənt, -'tyü-\ *n* : a Greek version of the Old Testament prepared in the 3d and 2d centuries B.C. by Jewish scholars

sep·tum \'sep-təm\ *n, pl* **sep·ta** \-tə\ : a dividing wall or membrane esp. between bodily spaces or masses of soft tissue

se·pul·chral \sə-ˈpəl-krəl\ adj **1** : relating to burial or the grave **2** : GLOOMY

¹**sep·ul·chre** or **sep·ul·cher** \ˈse-pəl-kər\ n : a burial vault : TOMB

²**sepulchre** or **sepulcher** vb **-chred** or **-chered; -chring** or **-cher·ing** : BURY, ENTOMB

sep·ul·ture \ˈse-pəl-ˌchùr\ n **1** : BURIAL **2** : SEPULCHRE

seq abbr [L sequens, sequentes, sequentia] the following

seqq abbr [L sequentia] the following ones

se·quel \ˈsē-kwəl\ n **1** : logical consequence **2** : a literary or cinematic work continuing a story begun in a preceding one

se·quence \ˈsē-kwəns\ n **1** : SERIES **2** : chronological order of events **3** : RESULT, SEQUEL **syn** succession, chain, progression, train — **se·quen·tial** \si-ˈkwen-chəl\ adj — **se·quen·tial·ly** adv

se·quent \ˈsē-kwənt\ adj **1** : SUCCEEDING, CONSECUTIVE **2** : RESULTANT

se·ques·ter \si-ˈkwes-tər\ vb : to set apart : SEGREGATE

se·ques·trate \ˈsē-kwəs-ˌtrāt, si-ˈkwes-\ vb **-trat·ed; -trat·ing** : SEQUESTER — **se·ques·tra·tion** \ˌsē-kwəs-ˈtrā-shən, ˌse-\ n

se·quin \ˈsē-kwən\ n **1** : an old gold coin of Turkey and Italy **2** : a small metal or plastic plate used for ornamentation esp. on clothing

se·quoia \si-ˈkwói-ə\ n : either of two huge California coniferous trees

ser abbr **1** serial **2** series

sera pl of SERUM

se·ra·glio \sə-ˈral-yō\ n, pl **-glios** [It serraglio] : HAREM

se·ra·pe \sə-ˈrä-pē\ n : a colorful woolen shawl worn over the shoulders esp. by Mexican men

ser·aph \ˈser-əf\ n, pl **ser·a·phim** \-ə-ˌfim, -ˌfēm\ or **seraphs** : one of the 6-winged angels standing in the presence of God

ser·a·phim \ˈser-ə-ˌfim, -ˌfēm\ n pl **1** : the highest order of angels **2** sing, pl **seraphim** : SERAPH — **se·raph·ic** \sə-ˈra-fik\ adj

Serb \ˈsərb\ n : a native or inhabitant of Serbia

Ser·bo–Cro·a·tian \ˌsər-(ˌ)bō-krō-ˈā-shən\ n : a Slavic language spoken in Croatia, Bosnia and Herzegovina, Serbia, and Montenegro

sere \ˈsir\ adj : DRY, WITHERED

¹**ser·e·nade** \ˌser-ə-ˈnād\ n [F, fr. It serenata, fr. sereno clear, calm (of weather)] : music sung or played as a compliment esp. outdoors at night for a woman being courted

²**serenade** vb **-nad·ed; -nad·ing** : to entertain with or perform a serenade

ser·en·dip·i·ty \ˌser-ən-ˈdi-pə-tē\ n [fr. its possession by the heroes of the Persian fairy tale *The Three Princes of Serendip*] : the gift of finding valuable or agreeable things not sought for — **ser·en·dip·i·tous** \-təs\ adj

se·rene \sə-ˈrēn\ adj **1** : CLEAR ⟨∼ skies⟩ **2** : QUIET, CALM **syn** tranquil, peaceful, placid — **se·rene·ly** adv — **se·ren·i·ty** \sə-ˈre-nə-tē\ n

serf \ˈsərf\ n : a member of a servile class bound to the land and subject to the will of the landowner — **serf·dom** \-dəm\ n

serg or **sergt** abbr sergeant

serge \ˈsərj\ n : a twilled woolen cloth

ser·geant \ˈsär-jənt\ n [ME, servant, attendant, sergeant, fr. OF sergent, serjant, fr. L servient-, serviens, prp. of servire to serve] **1** : a noncommissioned officer (as in the army) ranking next below a staff sergeant **2** : an officer in a police force

sergeant first class n : a noncommissioned officer in the army ranking next below a master sergeant

sergeant major n, pl **sergeants major** or **sergeant majors 1** : a senior staff noncommissioned officer in the army or marine corps serving as advisor in matters related to enlisted personnel **2** : a noncommissioned

officer in the marine corps ranking above a first sergeant

¹**se·ri·al** \ˈsir-ē-əl\ adj **1** : appearing in parts that follow regularly ⟨a ∼ story⟩ **2** : effecting a series of similar acts over a period of time ⟨a ∼ killer⟩; also : occurring in such a series — **se·ri·al·ly** adv

²**serial** n : a serial story or other writing — **se·ri·al·ist** \-ə-list\ n

se·ries \ˈsir-ēz\ n, pl **series** : a number of things or events arranged in order and connected by being alike in some way **syn** succession, progression, sequence, chain, train, string

seri·graph \ˈser-ə-ˌgraf\ n : an original silk-screen print — **se·rig·ra·pher** \sə-ˈri-grə-fər\ n — **se·rig·ra·phy** \-fē\ n

se·ri·ous \ˈsir-ē-əs\ adj **1** : thoughtful or subdued in appearance or manner : SOBER **2** : requiring much thought or work **3** : EARNEST, DEVOTED **4** : DANGEROUS, HARMFUL **5** : excessive or impressive in quantity or degree ⟨making ∼ money⟩ **syn** grave, sedate, staid — **se·ri·ous·ly** adv — **se·ri·ous·ness** n

ser·mon \ˈsər-mən\ n [ME, fr. OF, fr. ML sermon, sermo, fr. L, speech, conversation, fr. serere to link together] **1** : a religious discourse esp. as part of a worship service **2** : a lecture on conduct or duty

se·rol·o·gy \sə-ˈrä-lə-jē\ n : a science dealing with serums and esp. their reactions and properties — **se·ro·log·i·cal** \ˌsir-ə-ˈlä-ji-kəl\ or **se·ro·log·ic** \-jik\ adj

se·rous \ˈsir-əs\ adj : of, relating to, resembling, or producing serum; esp : of thin watery constitution

ser·pent \ˈsər-pənt\ n : SNAKE

¹**ser·pen·tine** \ˈsər-pən-ˌtēn, -ˌtīn\ adj **1** : SLY, CRAFTY **2** : WINDING, TURNING

²**ser·pen·tine** \-ˌtēn\ n : a dull-green mineral having a mottled appearance

ser·rate \ˈser-ˌāt\ adj : having a saw-toothed edge ⟨a ∼ leaf⟩

ser·ried \ˈser-ēd\ adj : DENSE

se·rum \ˈsir-əm\ n, pl **serums** or **se·ra** \-ə\ [L, whey, wheylike fluid] : the clear yellowish antibody-containing fluid that can be separated from blood when it clots; also : a preparation of animal serum containing specific antibodies and used to prevent or cure disease

serv abbr service

ser·vant \ˈsər-vənt\ n : one that serves others; esp : a person employed for domestic or personal work

¹**serve** \ˈsərv\ vb **served; serv·ing 1** : to work as a servant **2** : to render obedience and worship to (God) **3** : to comply with the commands or demands of **4** : to work through or perform a term of service (as in the army) **5** : PUT IN ⟨served five years in jail⟩ **6** : to be of use : ANSWER ⟨pine boughs served for a bed⟩ **7** : BENEFIT **8** : to prove adequate or satisfactory for ⟨a pie that ∼s eight people⟩ **9** : to make ready and pass out ⟨∼ drinks⟩ **10** : to furnish or supply with something ⟨one power company serving the whole state⟩ **11** : to wait on ⟨∼ a customer⟩ **12** : to treat or act toward in a specified way **13** : to put the ball in play (as in tennis) — **serv·er** n

²**serve** n : the act of serving a ball (as in tennis)

¹**ser·vice** \ˈsər-vəs\ n **1** : the occupation of a servant **2** : HELP, BENEFIT **3** : a meeting for worship; also : a form followed in worship or in a ceremony ⟨burial ∼⟩ **4** : the act, fact, or means of serving **5** : performance of official or professional duties **6** : SERVE **7** : a set of dishes or silverware **8** : a branch of public employment; also : the persons in it ⟨civil ∼⟩ **9** : military or naval duty

²**service** vb **ser·viced; ser·vic·ing** : to do maintenance or repair work on or for

ser·vice·able \ˈsər-və-sə-bəl\ adj : prepared for service : USEFUL, USABLE

ser·vice·man \ˈsər-vəs-ˌman, -mən\ n **1** : a male member of the armed forces **2** : a man employed to repair or maintain equipment

service station *n* : a retail station for servicing motor vehicles

ser·vice·wom·an \\'sər-vəs-ˌwu̇-mən\\ *n* : a female member of the armed forces

ser·vile \\'sər-vəl, -ˌvīl\\ *adj* **1** : befitting a slave or servant **2** : behaving like a slave : SUBMISSIVE — **ser·vil·i·ty** \\sər-'vi-lə-tē\\ *n*

serv·ing \\'sər-viŋ\\ *n* : HELPING

ser·vi·tor \\'sər-və-tər\\ *n* : a male servant

ser·vi·tude \\'sər-və-ˌtüd, -ˌtyüd\\ *n* : SLAVERY, BONDAGE

ser·vo \\'sər-vō\\ *n, pl* **servos 1** : SERVOMOTOR **2** : SERVOMECHANISM

ser·vo·mech·a·nism \\'sər-vō-ˌme-kə-ˌni-zəm\\ *n* : a device for automatically correcting the performance of a mechanism

ser·vo·mo·tor \\-ˌmō-tər\\ *n* : a mechanism that supplements a primary control

ses·a·me \\'se-sə-mē\\ *n* : a widely cultivated annual herb of warm regions; *also* : its seeds that yield an edible oil (**sesame oil**) and are used in flavoring

ses·qui·cen·ten·ni·al \\ˌses-kwi-sen-'te-nē-əl\\ *n* [L *sesqui-* one and a half, half again] : a 150th anniversary or its celebration — **sesquicentennial** *adj*

ses·qui·pe·da·lian \\ˌses-kwə-pə-'dāl-yən\\ *adj* **1** : having many syllables : LONG **2** : using long words

ses·sile \\'se-ˌsīl, -səl\\ *adj* : permanently attached and not free to move about

ses·sion \\'se-shən\\ *n* **1** : a meeting or series of meetings of a body (as a court or legislature) for the transaction of business **2** : a meeting or period devoted to a particular activity

¹set \\'set\\ *vb* **set; set·ting 1** : to cause to sit **2** : PLACE **3** : ARRANGE, ADJUST **4** : to cause to be or do **5** : SETTLE, DECREE **6** : to fix in a frame **7** : to fix at a certain amount **8** : WAGER, STAKE **9** : to make or become fast or rigid **10** : to adapt (as words) to something (as music) **11** : to become fixed or firm or solid **12** : to be suitable : FIT **13** : BROOD **14** : to have a certain direction **15** : to pass below the horizon **16** : to defeat in bridge — **set about** : to begin to do — **set forth** : to begin a trip — **set off 1** : to start out on a course or a trip **2** : to cause to explode — **set out 1** : to begin a trip or undertaking — **set sail** : to begin a voyage — **set upon** : to attack usu. with violence

²set *n* **1** : a setting or a being set **2** : DIRECTION, COURSE; *also* : TENDENCY **3** : FORM, BUILD **4** : the fit of something (as a coat) **5** : an artificial setting for the scene of a play or motion picture **6** : a group of tennis games in which one side wins at least six **7** : a group of persons or things of the same kind or having a common characteristic usu. classed together **8** : a collection of things and esp. of mathematical elements (as numbers or points) **9** : an electronic apparatus ⟨a television ∼⟩

³set *adj* **1** : DELIBERATE, INTENT **2** : fixed by authority or custom **3** : RIGID **4** : PERSISTENT

set·back \\'set-ˌbak\\ *n* : a temporary defeat : REVERSE

set back *vb* **1** : HINDER, DELAY; *also* : REVERSE **2** : COST

set piece 1 : a composition (as in literature or music) executed in fixed or ideal form often with brilliant effect **2** : a scene, depiction, speech, or event obviously designed to have an imposing effect

set·screw \\'set-ˌskrü\\ *n* : a screw screwed through one part tightly upon or into another part to prevent relative movement

set·tee \\se-'tē\\ *n* : a bench or sofa with a back and arms

set·ter \\'se-tər\\ *n* : a large long-coated hunting dog

set·ting \\'se-tiŋ\\ *n* **1** : the frame in which a gem is set **2** : the time, place, and circumstances in which something occurs or develops; *also* : SCENERY **3** : music written for a text (as of a poem) **4** : the eggs that a fowl sits on for hatching at one time

set·tle \\'set-ᵊl\\ *vb* **set·tled; set·tling** [ME *settlen* to seat, bring to rest, come to rest, fr. OE *setlan*, fr. *setl* seat] **1** : to place so as to stay **2** : to establish in residence;

also : COLONIZE **3** : to make compact **4** : QUIET, CALM **5** : to establish or secure permanently **6** : to direct one's efforts **7** : to fix by agreement **8** : to give legally **9** : ADJUST, ARRANGE **10** : DECIDE, DETERMINE **11** : to make a final disposition of ⟨∼ an account⟩ **12** : to come to rest **13** : to reach an agreement on **14** : to sink gradually to a lower level **15** : to become clear by depositing sediment — **set·tler** *n*

set·tle·ment \\'set-ᵊl-mənt\\ *n* **1** : the act or process of settling **2** : BESTOWAL ⟨a marriage ∼⟩ **3** : payment or adjustment of an account **4** : COLONY **5** : a small village **6** : an institution providing various community services esp. to large city populations **7** : adjustment of doubts and differences

set–to \\'set-ˌtü\\ *n, pl* **set–tos** : FIGHT

set·up \\'set-ˌəp\\ *n* **1** : the manner or act of arranging **2** : glass, ice, and nonalcoholic beverage for mixing served to patrons who supply their own liquor **3** : something (as a plot) that has been constructed or contrived; *also* : FRAME-UP

set up *vb* **1** : to place in position; *also* : ASSEMBLE **2** : CAUSE **3** : FOUND, ESTABLISH **4** : FRAME **5**

sev·en \\'se-vən\\ *n* **1** : one more than six **2** : the 7th in a set or series **3** : something having seven units — **seven** *adj or pron* — **sev·enth** \\-vənth\\ *adj or adv or n*

sev·en·teen \\ˌse-vən-'tēn\\ *n* : one more than 16 — **seventeen** *adj or pron* — **sev·en·teenth** \\-'tēnth\\ *adj or n*

seventeen–year locust *n* : a cicada of the U.S. that has in the North a life of 17 years and in the South of 13 years of which most is spent underground as a nymph and only a few weeks as a winged adult

sev·en·ty \\'se-vən-tē\\ *n, pl* **-ties** : seven times 10 — **sev·en·ti·eth** \\-tē-əth\\ *adj or n* — **seventy** *adj or pron*

sev·en·ty–eight \\ˌse-vən-tē-'āt\\ *n* : a phonograph record designed to be played at 78 revolutions per minute

sev·er \\'se-vər\\ *vb* **sev·ered; sev·er·ing** : DIVIDE; *esp* : to separate by or as if by cutting — **sev·er·ance** \\'se-vrəns, 'se-və-\\ *n*

sev·er·al \\'sev-rəl, 'se-və-\\ *adj* [ME, fr. MF, fr. ML *separalis*, fr. L *separ* separate, fr. *separare* to separate] **1** : INDIVIDUAL, DISTINCT ⟨federal union of the ∼ states⟩ **2** : consisting of an indefinite number but yet not very many — **sev·er·al·ly** *adv*

severance pay *n* : extra pay given an employee upon termination of employment

se·vere \\sə-'vir\\ *adj* **se·ver·er; -est 1** : marked by strictness or sternness : AUSTERE **2** : strict in discipline **3** : causing distress and esp. physical discomfort or pain ⟨∼ weather⟩ ⟨a ∼ wound⟩ **4** : hard to endure ⟨∼ trials⟩ **5** : SERIOUS ⟨∼ depression⟩ **syn** stern, ascetic, astringent — **se·vere·ly** *adv* — **se·ver·i·ty** \\-'ver-ə-tē\\ *n*

sew \\'sō\\ *vb* **sewed; sewn** \\'sōn\\ *or* **sewed; sew·ing 1** : to unite or fasten by stitches **2** : to engage in sewing

sew·age \\'sü-ij\\ *n* : waste materials carried off by sewers

¹sew·er \\'sō-ər\\ *n* : one that sews

²sew·er \\'sü-ər\\ *n* : an artificial pipe or channel to carry off waste matter

sew·er·age \\'sü-ə-rij\\ *n* **1** : a system of sewers **2** : SEWAGE

sew·ing *n* **1** : the activity of one who sews **2** : material that has been or is to be sewed

sex \\'seks\\ *n* **1** : either of the two major forms that occur in many living things and are designated male or female according to their role in reproduction; *also* : the qualities by which these sexes are differentiated and which directly or indirectly function in reproduction involving two parents **2** : sexual activity or behavior; *also* : SEXUAL INTERCOURSE — **sexed** \\'sekst\\ *adj* — **sex·less** *adj*

sex·a·ge·nar·i·an \\ˌsek-sə-jə-'ner-ē-ən\\ *n* : a person whose age is in the sixties — **sexagenarian** *adj*

sex cell *n* : an egg cell or sperm cell

sex chromosome *n* : one of usu. a pair of chromosomes that are usu. similar in one sex but different in the other sex and are concerned with the inheritance of sex

sex hormone *n* : a hormone (as from the gonads or adrenal cortex) that affects the growth or function of the reproductive organs or the development of secondary sex characteristics

sex·ism \'sek-ˌsi-zəm\ *n* : prejudice or discrimination based on sex; *esp* : discrimination against women — **sex·ist** \'sek-sist\ *adj or n*

sex·pot \'seks-ˌpät\ *n* : a conspicuously sexy woman

sex symbol *n* : a usu. renowned person (as an entertainer) noted and admired for conspicuous attractiveness

sex·tant \'sek-stənt\ *n* [NL *sextant-, sextans* sixth part of a circle, fr. L, sixth part, fr. *sextus* sixth] : a navigational instrument for determining latitude

sex·tet \sek-'stet\ *n* 1 : a musical composition for six voices or instruments; *also* : the performers of such a composition 2 : a group or set of six

sex·ton \'sek-stən\ *n* : one who takes care of church property

sex·u·al \'sek-shə-wəl\ *adj* : of, relating to, or involving sex or the sexes ⟨a ∼ spore⟩ ⟨∼ relations⟩ — **sex·u·al·i·ty** \ˌsek-shə-'wa-lə-tē\ *n* — **sex·u·al·ly** \'sek-shə-wə-lē\ *adv*

sexual intercourse *n* 1 : intercourse between a male and a female in which the penis is inserted into the vagina 2 : intercourse between individuals involving genital contact other than insertion of the penis into the vagina

sexually transmitted disease *n* : a disease (as syphilis, gonorrhea, AIDS, or the genital form of herpes simplex) that is caused by a microorganism or virus usu. or often transmitted by direct sexual contact

sexual relations *n pl* : SEXUAL INTERCOURSE

sexy \'sek-sē\ *adj* **sex·i·er; -est** : sexually suggestive or stimulating : EROTIC

SF *abbr* 1 sacrifice fly 2 science fiction

SFC *abbr* sergeant first class

SG *abbr* 1 senior grade 2 sergeant 3 solicitor general 4 surgeon general

sgd *abbr* signed

Sgt *abbr* sergeant

Sgt Maj *abbr* sergeant major

sh *abbr* share

shab·by \'sha-bē\ *adj* **shab·bi·er; -est** 1 : dressed in worn clothes 2 : threadbare and faded from wear 3 : DESPICABLE, MEAN; *also* : UNFAIR ⟨∼ treatment⟩ — **shab·bi·ly** \'sha-bə-lē\ *adv* — **shab·bi·ness** \-bē-nəs\ *n*

shack \'shak\ *n* : HUT, SHANTY

¹shack·le \'sha-kəl\ *n* 1 : something (as a manacle or fetter) that confines the legs or arms 2 : a check on free action made as if by fetters 3 : a device for making something fast or secure

²shackle *vb* **shack·led; shack·ling** : to bind or fasten with shackles

shad \'shad\ *n, pl* **shad** : any of several sea fishes related to the herrings that swim up rivers to spawn and include some important food fishes

¹shade \'shād\ *n* 1 : partial obscurity 2 : space sheltered from the light esp. of the sun 3 : PHANTOM 4 : something that shelters from or intercepts light or heat; *also, pl* : SUNGLASSES 5 : a dark color or a variety of a color 6 : a small difference

²shade *vb* **shad·ed; shad·ing** 1 : to shelter from light and heat 2 : DARKEN, OBSCURE 3 : to mark with degrees of light or color 4 : to show slight differences esp. in color or meaning

shad·ing *n* : the color and lines representing darkness or shadow in a drawing or painting

¹shad·ow \'sha-dō\ *n* 1 : partial darkness in a space from which light rays are cut off 2 : SHELTER 3 : shade cast upon a surface by something intercepting rays from a light ⟨the ∼ of a tree⟩ 4 : PHANTOM 5 : a shaded

portion of a picture 6 : a small portion or degree : TRACE ⟨a ∼ of doubt⟩ 7 : a source of gloom or unhappiness — **shad·owy** *adj*

²shadow *vb* 1 : to cast a shadow on 2 : to represent faintly or vaguely 3 : to follow and watch closely : TRAIL

shad·ow·box \'sha-dō-ˌbäks\ *vb* : to box with an imaginary opponent esp. for training

shady \'shā-dē\ *adj* **shad·i·er; -est** 1 : affording shade 2 : of questionable honesty or reputation

¹shaft \'shaft\ *n, pl* **shafts** 1 : the long handle of a spear or lance 2 : SPEAR, LANCE 3 *or pl* **shaves** \'shavz\ : POLE; *esp* : one of two poles between which a horse is hitched to pull a vehicle 4 : something (as a column) long and slender 5 : a bar to support a rotating piece or to transmit power by rotation 6 : an inclined opening in the ground (as for finding or mining ore) 7 : a vertical opening (as for an elevator) through the floors of a building 8 : harsh or unfair treatment — usu. used with *the*

²shaft *vb* 1 : to fit with a shaft 2 : to treat unfairly or harshly

shag \'shag\ *n* : a shaggy tangled mass or covering (as of wool) : long coarse or matted fiber, nap, or pile

shag·gy \'sha-gē\ *adj* **shag·gi·er; -est** 1 : rough with or as if with long hair or wool 2 : tangled or rough in surface

shah \'shä, 'shò\ *n, often cap* : a sovereign of Iran until 1979

Shak *abbr* Shakespeare

¹shake \'shāk\ *vb* **shook** \'shùk\; **shak·en** \'shā-kən\; **shak·ing** 1 : to move or cause to move jerkily or irregularly 2 : BRANDISH, WAVE ⟨*shaking* his fist⟩ 3 : to disturb emotionally ⟨*shaken* by her death⟩ 4 : WEAKEN ⟨*shook* his faith⟩ 5 : to bring or come into a certain position, condition, or arrangement by or as if by moving jerkily 6 : to clasp (hands) in greeting or as a sign of goodwill or agreement **syn** tremble, quake, quaver, shiver, quiver — **shak·able** \'shā-kə-bəl\ *adj*

²shake *n* 1 : the act or result of shaking 2 : DEAL, TREATMENT ⟨a fair ∼⟩

shake·down \'shāk-ˌdaùn\ *n* 1 : an improvised bed 2 : EXTORTION 3 : a process or period of adjustment 4 : a test (as of a new ship or airplane) under operating conditions

shake down *vb* 1 : to take up temporary quarters 2 : to occupy a makeshift bed 3 : to become accustomed esp. to new surroundings or duties 4 : to settle down 5 : to give a shakedown test to 6 : to obtain money from in a deceitful or illegal manner 7 : to bring about a reduction of

shak·er \'shā-kər\ *n* 1 : one that shakes ⟨pepper ∼⟩ 2 *cap* : a member of a religious sect founded in England in 1747

shake–up \'shāk-ˌəp\ *n* : an extensive often drastic reorganization

shaky \'shā-kē\ *adj* **shak·i·er; -est** : UNSOUND, WEAK — **shak·i·ly** \'shā-kə-lē\ *adv* — **shak·i·ness** \-kē-nəs\ *n*

shale \'shāl\ *n* : a finely layered rock formed from clay, mud, or silt

shall \shəl, 'shal\ *vb, past* **should** \shəd, 'shùd\; *pres sing & pl* **shall** — used as an auxiliary to express a command, what seems inevitable or likely in the future, simple futurity, or determination

shal·lop \'sha-ləp\ *n* : a light open boat

shal·lot \shə-'lät, 'sha-lət\ *n* [modif. of F *échalote*] 1 : a small clustered bulb that is used in seasoning and is produced by a perennial herb belonging to a subspecies of the onion; *also* : this herb 2 : GREEN ONION

¹shal·low \'sha-lō\ *adj* 1 : not deep 2 : not intellectually profound

²shallow *n* : a shallow place in a body of water — usu. used in pl.

¹sham \'sham\ *n* 1 : an ornamental covering for a pillow 2 : COUNTERFEIT, IMITATION 3 : a person who shams

²**sham** *vb* **shammed; sham·ming** : FEIGN, PRETEND — **sham·mer** *n*

³**sham** *adj* : not genuine : FALSE, FEIGNED

sha·man \'shä-mən, 'shä-\ *n* [ultim. fr. Evenki (a language of Siberia) *šamān*] : a priest or priestess who uses magic to cure the sick, to divine the hidden, and to control events

sham·ble \'sham-bəl\ *vb* **sham·bled; sham·bling** : to shuffle along — **sham·ble** *n*

sham·bles \'sham-bəlz\ *n* **1** : a scene of great slaughter **2** : a scene or state of great destruction or disorder; *also* : MESS

¹**shame** \'shām\ *n* **1** : a painful sense of having done something wrong, improper, or immodest **2** : DISGRACE, DISHONOR **3** : a cause of feeling shame **4** : something to be regretted (it's a ∼ you'll miss the party) — **shame·ful** \-fəl\ *adj* — **shame·ful·ly** *adv* — **shame·less** *adj* — **shame·less·ly** *adv*

²**shame** *vb* **shamed; sham·ing 1** : DISGRACE **2** : to make ashamed

shame·faced \'shām-ˌfāst\ *adj* : ASHAMED, ABASHED — **shame·faced·ly** \-ˌfā-səd-lē, -ˌfāst-lē\ *adv*

¹**sham·poo** \sham-'pü\ *vb* [Hindi *čāpo*, imper. of *čāpnā* to press, shampoo] : to wash (as the hair) with soap and water or with a special preparation; *also* : to clean (as a rug) similarly

²**shampoo** *n, pl* **shampoos 1** : the act or an instance of shampooing **2** : a preparation for use in shampooing

sham·rock \'sham-ˌräk\ *n* [Ir *seamróg*, dim. of *seamar* clover] : a plant of folk legend with leaves composed of three leaflets that is associated with St. Patrick and Ireland

shang·hai \shaŋ-'hī\ *vb* **shang·haied; shang·hai·ing** [*Shanghai*, China] : to force aboard a ship for service as a sailor; *also* : to trick or force into an undesirable position

Shan·gri-la \ˌshaŋ-gri-'lä\ *n* [*Shangri-La*, imaginary land depicted in the novel *Lost Horizon* (1933) by James Hilton] : a remote idyllic hideaway

shank \'shaŋk\ *n* **1** : the part of the leg between the knee and the human ankle or a corresponding part of a quadruped **2** : a cut of meat from the leg **3** : the narrow part of the sole of a shoe beneath the instep **4** : the part of a tool or instrument (as a key or anchor) connecting the functioning part with a part by which it is held or moved

shan·tung \ˌshan-'təŋ\ *n* : a fabric in plain weave having a slightly irregular surface

shan·ty \'shan-tē\ *n, pl* **shanties** [prob. fr. CanF *chantier* lumber camp, hut, fr. F, gantry, fr. L *cantherius* rafter, trellis] : a small roughly built shelter or dwelling

¹**shape** \'shāp\ *vb* **shaped; shap·ing 1** : to form esp. in a particular shape **2** : DESIGN **3** : ADAPT, ADJUST **4** : REGULATE **syn** make, fashion, fabricate, manufacture, frame, mold

²**shape** *n* **1** : APPEARANCE **2** : surface configuration : FORM **3** : bodily contour apart from the head and face : FIGURE **4** : PHANTOM **5** : CONDITION — **shaped** \'shāpt\ *adj*

shape·less \'shā-pləs\ *adj* **1** : having no definite shape **2** : not shapely — **shape·less·ly** *adv* — **shape·less·ness** *n*

shape·ly \'shā-plē\ *adj* **shape·li·er; -est** : having a pleasing shape — **shape·li·ness** *n*

shard \'shärd\ *also* **sherd** \'shərd\ *n* : a broken piece : FRAGMENT

¹**share** \'shar\ *n* : PLOWSHARE

²**share** *n* **1** : a portion belonging to one person or group **2** : any of the equal interests into which the capital stock of a corporation is divided

³**share** *vb* **shared; shar·ing 1** : APPORTION **2** : to use or enjoy with others **3** : PARTICIPATE — **shar·er** *n*

share·crop·per \-ˌkrä-pər\ *n* : a farmer who works another's land in return for a share of the crop — **share·crop** *vb*

share·hold·er \-ˌhōl-dər\ *n* : STOCKHOLDER

¹**shark** \'shärk\ *n* : any of various active, usu. predaceous, and mostly large marine cartilaginous fishes

²**shark** *n* : a greedy crafty person

shark·skin \-ˌskin\ *n* **1** : the hide of a shark or leather made from it **2** : a fabric (as of cotton or rayon) woven from strands of many fine threads and having a sleek appearance and silky feel

¹**sharp** \'shärp\ *adj* **1** : having a thin cutting edge or fine point : not dull or blunt **2** : COLD, NIPPING (a ∼ wind) **3** : keen in intellect, perception, or attention **4** : BRISK, ENERGETIC **5** : IRRITABLE (a ∼ temper) **6** : causing intense distress (a ∼ pain) **7** : HARSH, CUTTING (a ∼ rebuke) **8** : affecting the senses as if cutting or piercing (a ∼ sound) (a ∼ smell) **9** : not smooth or rounded (∼ features) **10** : involving an abrupt or extreme change (a ∼ turn) **11** : CLEAR, DISTINCT (mountains in ∼ relief); *also* : easy to perceive (a ∼ contrast) **12** : higher than the true pitch; *also* : raised by a half step **13** : STYLISH (a ∼ dresser) **syn** keen, acute, quick-witted, penetrative — **sharp·ly** *adv* — **sharp·ness** *n*

²**sharp** *adv* **1** : in a sharp manner **2** : EXACTLY, PRECISELY (left at 8 ∼)

³**sharp** *n* **1** : a sharp edge or point **2** : a character ♯ which indicates that a specified note is to be raised by a half step; *also* : the resulting note **3** : SHARPER

⁴**sharp** *vb* : to raise in pitch by a half step

sharp·en \'shär-pən\ *vb* : to make or become sharp — **sharp·en·er** *n*

sharp·er \'shär-pər\ *n* : SWINDLER; *esp* : a cheating gambler

sharp·ie *or* **sharpy** \'shär-pē\ *n, pl* **sharp·ies 1** : SHARPER **2** : a person who is exceptionally keen or alert

sharp·shoot·er \'shärp-ˌshü-tər\ *n* : a good marksman — **sharp·shoot·ing** *n*

shat·ter \'sha-tər\ *vb* : to dash or burst into fragments — **shat·ter·proof** \'sha-tər-ˌprüf\ *adj*

¹**shave** \'shāv\ *vb* **shaved; shaved** *or* **shav·en** \'shā-vən\; **shav·ing 1** : to slice in thin pieces **2** : to make bare or smooth by cutting the hair from **3** : to cut or pare off by the sliding movement of a razor **4** : to skim along or near the surface of

²**shave** *n* **1** : any of various tools for cutting thin slices **2** : an act or process of shaving

shav·er \'shā-vər\ *n* **1** : an electric razor **2** : BOY, YOUNGSTER

shaves *pl of* SHAFT

shav·ing *n* **1** : the act of one that shaves **2** : something shaved off

shawl \'shol\ *n* : a square or oblong piece of fabric used esp. by women as a loose covering for the head or shoulders

Shaw·nee \sho-'nē, shä-\ *n, pl* **Shawnee** *or* **Shawnees** : a member of an American Indian people orig. of the central Ohio valley; *also* : their language

shd *abbr* should

she \'shē\ *pron* : that female one (who is ∼); *also* : that one regarded as feminine (∼'s a fine ship)

sheaf \'shēf\ *n, pl* **sheaves** \'shēvz\ **1** : a bundle of stalks and ears of grain **2** : a group of things bound together

¹**shear** \'shir\ *vb* **sheared; sheared** *or* **shorn** \'shorn\; **shear·ing 1** : to cut the hair or wool from : CLIP, TRIM **2** : to deprive by or as if by cutting **3** : to cut or break sharply

²**shear** *n* **1** : any of various cutting tools that consist of two blades fastened together so that the edges slide one by the other — usu. used in pl. **2** *chiefly Brit* : the act, an instance, or the result of shearing **3** : an action or stress caused by applied forces that causes two parts of a body to slide on each other

sheath \'shēth\ *n, pl* **sheaths** \'shēthz, 'shēths\ **1** : a case for a blade (as of a knife); *also* : an anatomical covering suggesting such a case **2** : a close-fitting dress usu. worn without a belt

sheathe \'shēth\ *also* **sheath** \'shēth\ *vb* **sheathed;**

sheath•ing 1 : to put into a sheath **2** : to cover with something that guards or protects

sheath•ing \\'shē-<u>thi</u>ŋ, -thiŋ\\ *n* : material used to sheathe something; *esp* : the first covering of boards or of waterproof material on the outside wall of a frame house or on a timber roof

sheave \\'shiv, 'shēv\\ *n* : a grooved wheel or pulley (as on a pulley block)

she•bang \\shi-'baŋ\\ *n* : CONTRIVANCE, AFFAIR, CONCERN (sold the whole ~)

¹shed \\'shed\\ *vb* **shed; shed•ding 1** : to cause to flow from a cut or wound (~ blood) **2** : to pour down in drops (~ tears) **3** : to give out (as light) : DIFFUSE **4** : to throw off (as a natural covering) : DISCARD

²shed *n* : a slight structure built for shelter or storage

sheen \\'shēn\\ *n* : a subdued luster

sheep \\'shēp\\ *n, pl* **sheep** : any of various cud-chewing mammals that are stockier than the related goats and lack a beard in the male; *esp* : one raised for meat or for its wool or skin **2** : a timid or defenseless person **3** : SHEEPSKIN

sheep dog *n* : a dog used to tend, drive, or guard sheep

sheep•fold \\'shēp-ˌfōld\\ *n* : a pen or shelter for sheep

sheep•herd•er \\-ˌhər-dər\\ *n* : a worker in charge of sheep esp. on open range — **sheep•herd•ing** *n*

sheep•ish \\'shē-pish\\ *adj* : BASHFUL, TIMID; *esp* : embarrassed by consciousness of a fault — **sheep•ish•ly** *adv*

sheep•skin \\'shēp-ˌskin\\ *n* **1** : the hide of a sheep or leather prepared from it; *also* : PARCHMENT **2** : DIPLOMA

¹sheer \\'shir\\ *vb* : to turn from a course

²sheer *adj* **1** : very thin or transparent **2** : UNQUALIFIED (~ folly) **3** : very steep **syn** pure, simple, absolute, unadulterated, unmitigated — **sheer** *adv*

¹sheet \\'shēt\\ *n* **1** : a broad piece of cloth (as for a bed); *also* : SAIL 1 **2** : a single piece of paper **3** : a broad flat surface (a ~ of ice) **4** : something broad and long and relatively thin

²sheet *n* : a rope used to trim a sail

sheet•ing \\'shē-tiŋ\\ *n* : material in the form of sheets or suitable for forming into sheets

sheikh *or* **sheik** \\'shēk, 'shāk\\ *n* : an Arab chief — **sheikh•dom** *or* **sheik•dom** \\-dəm\\ *n*

shek•el \\'she-kəl\\ *n* — see MONEY table

shelf \\'shelf\\ *n, pl* **shelves** \\'shelvz\\ **1** : a thin flat usu. long and narrow structure fastened horizontally (as on a wall) above the floor to hold things **2** : something (as a sandbar) that suggests a shelf

shelf life *n* : the period of storage time during which a material will remain useful

¹shell \\'shel\\ *n* **1** : a hard or tough often thin outer covering of an animal (as a beetle, turtle, or mollusk) or of an egg or a seed or fruit (as a nut); *also* : something that resembles a shell (a pastry ~) **2** : a light narrow racing boat propelled by oarsmen **3** : a case holding an explosive and designed to be fired from a cannon; *also* : a case holding the charge of powder and shot or bullet for small arms **4** : a plain usu. sleeveless blouse or sweater — **shelled** \\'sheld\\ *adj* — **shelly** \\'she-lē\\ *adj*

²shell *vb* **1** : to remove from a shell or husk **2** : BOMBARD — **shell•er** *n*

¹shel•lac \\shə-'lak\\ *n* **1** : a purified lac **2** : lac dissolved in alcohol and used as a wood filler or finish

²shellac *vb* **shel•lacked; shel•lack•ing 1** : to coat or treat with shellac **2** : to defeat decisively

shel•lack•ing *n* : a sound drubbing

shell bean *n* : a bean grown esp. for its edible seeds; *also* : its edible seed

shell•fish \\-ˌfish\\ *n* : an invertebrate water animal (as an oyster or lobster) with a shell

shell out *vb* : PAY

shell shock *n* : a psychological and nervous disorder of soldiers resulting from traumatic experience in combat — **shell–shocked** \\'shel-ˌshäkt\\ *adj*

¹shel•ter \\'shel-tər\\ *n* : something that gives protection : REFUGE

²shelter *vb* **shel•tered; shel•ter•ing** : to give protection or refuge to

shelve \\'shelv\\ *vb* **shelved; shelv•ing 1** : to slope gradually **2** : to store on shelves **3** : to dismiss from service or use **4** : to put aside : DEFER (~ a proposal)

shelv•ing \\'shel-viŋ\\ *n* : material for shelves; *also* : SHELVES

she•nan•i•gan \\shə-'na-ni-gən\\ *n* **1** : an underhand trick **2** : questionable conduct — usu. used in pl. **3** : high-spirited or mischievous activity — usu. used in pl.

¹shep•herd \\'she-pərd\\ *n* **1** : one who tends sheep **2** : GERMAN SHEPHERD

²shepherd *vb* : to tend as or in the manner of a shepherd

shep•herd•ess \\'she-pər-dəs\\ *n* : a woman who tends sheep

sheq•el \\'she-kəl\\ *n, pl* **sheq•a•lim** \\she-'kä-lim\\ *var of* SHEKEL

sher•bet \\'shər-bət\\ *n* [Turk *şerbet*, fr. Per *sharbat*, fr. Ar *sharbah* drink] **1** : a drink of sweetened diluted fruit juice **2** *or* **sher•bert** \\-bərt\\ : a frozen dessert of fruit juices, sugar, milk or water, and egg whites or gelatin

sherd *var of* SHARD

sher•iff \\'sher-əf\\ *n* [ME *shirreve*, fr. OE *scīrgerēfa*, lit., shire reeve (local official)] : a county officer charged with the execution of the law and the preservation of order

sher•ry \\'sher-ē\\ *n, pl* **sherries** [alter. of earlier *sherris* (taken as pl.), fr. *Xeres* (now *Jerez*), Spain] : a fortified wine with a nutty flavor

Shet•land pony \\'shet-lənd-\\ *n* : any of a breed of small stocky shaggy hardy ponies

shew \\'shō\\ *Brit var of* SHOW

shi•at•su *also* **shi•at•zu** \\shē-'ät-sü\\ *n* [short for Jp *shiatsuryōhō*] : a finger massage of those bodily areas used in acupuncture

shib•bo•leth \\'shi-bə-ləth\\ *n* [Heb *shibbōleth* stream; fr. the use of this word as a test to distinguish the men of Gilead from members of the tribe of Ephraim, who pronounced it *sibbōleth* (Judges 12:5, 6)] **1** : CATCHWORD 2 **2** : language that is a criterion for distinguishing members of a group

¹shield \\'shēld\\ *n* **1** : a broad piece of defensive armor carried on the arm **2** : something that protects or hides

²shield *vb* : to protect or hide with a shield **syn** protect, guard, safeguard

shier *comparative of* SHY

shiest *superlative of* SHY

¹shift \\'shift\\ *vb* **1** : EXCHANGE, REPLACE **2** : to change place, position, or direction : MOVE; *also* : to change gears **3** : GET BY, MANAGE

²shift *n* **1** : SCHEME, TRICK **2** : a woman's slip or loose-fitting dress **3** : a change in direction, emphasis, or attitude **4** : a group working together alternating with other groups **5** : TRANSFER **6** : GEARSHIFT

shift•less \\'shift-ləs\\ *adj* : LAZY, INEFFICIENT — **shift-less•ness** *n*

shifty \\'shif-tē\\ *adj* **shift•i•er; -est 1** : TRICKY; *also* : ELUSIVE **2** : indicative of a tricky nature (~ eyes)

shih tzu \\'shēd-'zü, 'shēt-'sü\\ *n, pl* **shih tzus** *also* **shih tzu** *often cap S&T* : any of a breed of small short-legged dogs of Chinese origin that have a short muzzle and a long dense coat

shill \\'shil\\ *n* : one who acts as a decoy (as for a pitchman) — **shill** *vb*

shil•le•lagh *also* **shil•la•lah** \\shə-'lā-lē\\ *n* [*Shillelagh*, town in Ireland] : CUDGEL, CLUB

shil•ling \\'shi-liŋ\\ *n* — see MONEY TABLE

shilly–shally \\'shi-lē-ˌsha-lē\\ *vb* **shilly–shall•ied; shilly–shally•ing 1** : to show hesitation or lack of decisiveness **2** : to waste time

shim \\'shim\\ *n* : a thin often tapered piece of wood, metal, or stone used (as in leveling) to fill in space

shim·mer \\'shi-mər\\ *vb* : to shine waveringly or tremulously : GLIMMER **syn** flash, gleam, glint, sparkle, glitter — **shimmer** *n* — **shim·mery** *adj*

shim·my \\'shi-mē\\ *n, pl* **shimmies** : an abnormal vibration esp. in the front wheels of a motor vehicle — **shimmy** *vb*

¹**shin** \\'shin\\ *n* : the front part of the leg below the knee

²**shin** *vb* **shinned; shin·ning** : to climb (as a pole) by gripping alternately with arms or hands and legs

shin·bone \\'shin-ˌbōn\\ *n* : TIBIA

¹**shine** \\'shīn\\ *vb* **shone** \\'shōn\\ *or* **shined; shin·ing** **1** : to give or cause to give light **2** : GLEAM, GLITTER **3** : to be eminent, conspicuous, or distinguished ⟨gave her a chance to ∼⟩ **4** : POLISH ⟨∼ your shoes⟩

²**shine** *n* **1** : BRIGHTNESS, RADIANCE **2** : LUSTER, BRILLIANCE **3** : fair weather : SUNSHINE ⟨rain or ∼⟩ **4** : LIKING, FANCY ⟨took a ∼ to them⟩ **5** : a polish given to shoes

shin·er \\'shī-nər\\ *n* **1** : a small silvery fish; *esp* : any of numerous small freshwater American fishes related to the carp **2** : a discoloration of the skin around the eye due to bruising

¹**shin·gle** \\'shiŋ-gəl\\ *n* **1** : a small thin piece of building material used in overlapping rows for covering a roof or outside wall **2** : a small sign

²**shingle** *vb* **shin·gled; shin·gling** : to cover with shingles

³**shingle** *n* : a beach strewn with gravel; *also* : coarse gravel (as on a beach)

shin·gles \\'shiŋ-gəlz\\ *n* : an acute inflammation of the spinal and cranial nerves caused by reactivation of the chicken pox virus and associated with eruptions and pain along the course of the affected nerves

shin·ny \\'shi-nē\\ *vb* **shin·nied; shin·ny·ing** : SHIN

shin·splints \\'shin-ˌsplints\\ *n sing or pl* : a condition marked by pain and sometimes tenderness and swelling in the shin caused by repeated small injuries to muscles and associated tissue esp. from running

Shin·to \\'shin-ˌtō\\ *n* : the indigenous religion of Japan consisting esp. in reverence of the spirits of natural forces and imperial ancestors — **Shin·to·ism** *n* — **Shin·to·ist** *n or adj*

shiny \\'shī-nē\\ *adj* **shin·i·er; -est** : BRIGHT, RADIANT; *also* : POLISHED

¹**ship** \\'ship\\ *n* **1** : a large oceangoing boat **2** : a ship's officers and crew **3** : AIRSHIP, AIRCRAFT, SPACECRAFT

²**ship** *vb* **shipped; ship·ping** **1** : to put or receive on board a ship for transportation **2** : to have transported by a carrier **3** : to take or draw into a boat ⟨∼ oars⟩ ⟨∼ water⟩ **4** : to engage to serve on a ship — **ship·per** *n*

-ship \\ˌship\\ *n suffix* **1** : state : condition : quality ⟨friend*ship*⟩ **2** : office : dignity : profession ⟨lord*ship*⟩ ⟨clerk*ship*⟩ **3** : art : skill ⟨horseman*ship*⟩ **4** : something showing, exhibiting, or embodying a quality or state ⟨town*ship*⟩ **5** : one entitled to a (specified) rank, title, or appellation ⟨his Lord*ship*⟩ **6** : the body of persons engaged in a specified activity ⟨reader*ship*⟩

ship·board \\'ship-ˌbōrd\\ *n* : SHIP

ship·build·er \\-ˌbil-dər\\ *n* : one who designs or builds ships

ship·fit·ter \\-ˌfi-tər\\ *n* **1** : one who constructs ships **2** : a naval enlisted man who works as a plumber

ship·mate \\-ˌmāt\\ *n* : a fellow sailor

ship·ment \\-mənt\\ *n* : the process of shipping; *also* : the goods shipped

ship·ping *n* **1** : SHIPS; *esp* : ships in one port or belonging to one country **2** : transportation of goods

ship·shape \\'ship-ˌshāp\\ *adj* : TRIM, TIDY

ship·worm \\-ˌwərm\\ *n* : any of various wormlike marine clams that burrow in wood and damage wooden ships and wharves

¹**ship·wreck** \\-ˌrek\\ *n* **1** : a wrecked ship **2** : destruction or loss of a ship **3** : total loss or failure : RUIN

²**shipwreck** *vb* : to cause or meet disaster at sea through destruction or foundering

ship·wright \\'ship-ˌrīt\\ *n* : a carpenter skilled in ship construction and repair

ship·yard \\-ˌyärd\\ *n* : a place where ships are built or repaired

shire \\'shīr, *in place-name compounds* ˌshir, shər\\ *n* : a county in Great Britain

shirk \\'shərk\\ *vb* : to avoid performing (duty or work) — **shirk·er** *n*

shirr \\'shər\\ *vb* **1** : to make shirring in **2** : to bake (eggs removed from the shell) until set

shirr·ing \\'shər-iŋ\\ *n* : a decorative gathering in cloth made by drawing up parallel lines of stitches

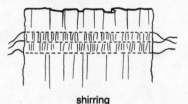

shirring

shirt \\'shərt\\ *n* **1** : a loose cloth garment usu. having a collar, sleeves, a front opening, and a tail long enough to be tucked inside trousers or a skirt **2** : UNDERSHIRT — **shirt·less** *adj*

shirt·ing \\'shir-tiŋ\\ *n* : cloth suitable for making shirts

shish ke·bab \\'shish-kə-ˌbäb\\ *n* [Turk *şiş kebabı*, fr. *şiş* spit + *kebap* roast meat] : kabob cooked on skewers

shiv \\'shiv\\ *n, slang* : KNIFE

¹**shiv·er** \\'shi-vər\\ *vb* : TREMBLE, QUIVER **syn** shudder, quaver, shake, quake

²**shiver** *n* : an instance of shivering — **shiv·ery** *adj*

¹**shoal** \\'shōl\\ *n* **1** : SHALLOW **2** : a sandbank or bar creating a shallow

²**shoal** *n* : a large group (as of fish)

shoat \\'shōt\\ *n* : a weaned young pig

¹**shock** \\'shäk\\ *n* : a pile of sheaves of grain or cornstalks set up in a field

²**shock** *n* [MF *choc*, fr. *choquer* to strike against] **1** : a sharp impact or violent shake or jar **2** : a sudden violent mental or emotional disturbance **3** : a state of bodily collapse caused esp. by crushing wounds, blood loss, or burns **4** : the effect of a charge of electricity passing through the body **5** : an attack of stroke or heart disease **6** : SHOCK ABSORBER — **shock·proof** \\-ˌprüf\\ *adj*

³**shock** *vb* **1** : to strike with surprise, horror, or disgust **2** : to subject to the action of an electrical discharge

⁴**shock** *n* : a thick bushy mass (as of hair)

shock absorber *n* : any of several devices for absorbing the energy of sudden shocks in machinery

shock·er \\'shä-kər\\ *n* : one that shocks; *esp* : a sensational work of fiction or drama

shock·ing *adj* : extremely startling and offensive — **shock·ing·ly** *adv*

shock therapy *n* : the treatment of mental disorder by induction of coma or convulsions by drugs or electricity

shock wave *n* : a wave formed by the sudden violent compression of the medium through which it travels

¹**shod·dy** \\'shä-dē\\ *n* **1** : wool reclaimed from old rags; *also* : a fabric made from it **2** : inferior or imitation material

²**shoddy** *adj* **shod·di·er; -est** **1** : made of shoddy **2** : poorly done or made — **shod·di·ly** \\'shä-də-lē\\ *adv* — **shod·di·ness** \\-dē-nəs\\ *n*

¹**shoe** \\'shü\\ *n* **1** : a covering for the human foot **2** : HORSESHOE **3** : the part of a brake that presses on the wheel

²**shoe** *vb* **shod** \\'shäd\\ *also* **shoed** \\'shüd\\; **shoe·ing** : to put a shoe or shoes on

shoe·lace \\'shü-ˌlās\\ *n* : a lace or string for fastening a shoe

shoe·mak·er \-ˌmā-kər\ *n* : one who makes or repairs shoes

shoe·string \-ˌstriŋ\ *n* **1** : SHOELACE **2** : a small sum of money

sho·gun \ˈshō-gən\ *n* [Jp *shōgun* general] : any of a line of military governors ruling Japan until the revolution of 1867–68

shone *past and past part of* SHINE

shook *past of* SHAKE

shook-up \(ˌ)shuk-ˈəp\ *adj* : nervously upset : AGITATED

¹shoot \ˈshüt\ *vb* **shot** \ˈshät\; **shoot·ing 1** : to drive (as an arrow or bullet) forward quickly or forcibly **2** : to hit, kill, or wound with a missile **3** : to cause a missile to be driven forth or forth from ⟨∼ a gun⟩ **4** : to send forth (as a ray of light) **5** : to thrust forward or out **6** : to pass rapidly along ⟨∼ the rapids⟩ **7** : PHOTOGRAPH, FILM **8** : to move swiftly : DART **9** : to grow by or as if by sending out shoots; *also* : MATURE, DEVELOP — **shoot·er** *n*

²shoot *n* **1** : a plant stem with its leaves and branches esp. when not yet mature **2** : an act of shooting **3** : a shooting match

shooting iron *n* : FIREARM

shooting star *n* : METEOR 2

shoot up *vb* : to inject a narcotic into a vein

¹shop \ˈshäp\ *n* [ME *shoppe*, fr. OE *sceoppa* booth] **1** : a place where things are made or worked on : FACTORY, MILL **2** : a retail store ⟨dress ∼⟩

²shop *vb* **shopped; shop·ping** : to visit stores for purchasing or examining goods — **shop·per** *n*

shop·keep·er \ˈshäp-ˌkē-pər\ *n* : a retail merchant

shop·lift \-ˌlift\ *vb* : to steal goods on display from a store — **shop·lift·er** *n*

shop·talk \-ˌtȯk\ *n* : talk about one's business or special interests

shop·worn \-ˌwȯrn\ *adj* : soiled or frayed from much handling in a store

¹shore \ˈshȯr\ *n* : land along the edge of a body of water — **shore·less** *adj*

²shore *vb* **shored; shor·ing** : to give support to : BRACE

³shore *n* : ¹PROP

shore·bird \-ˌbərd\ *n* : any of a suborder of birds (as the plovers and sandpipers) mostly found along the seashore

shore patrol *n* : a branch of a navy that exercises guard and police functions

shor·ing \ˈshȯr-iŋ\ *n* : a group of things that shore something up

shorn *past part of* SHEAR

¹short \ˈshȯrt\ *adj* **1** : not long or tall **2** : not great in distance **3** : brief in time **4** : not coming up to standard or to an expected amount **5** : CURT, ABRUPT **6** : insufficiently supplied **7** : made with shortening : FLAKY **8** : consisting of or relating to a sale of securities or commodities that the seller does not possess or has not contracted for at the time of the sale ⟨∼ sale⟩ — **short·ness** *n*

²short *adv* **1** : ABRUPTLY, CURTLY **2** : at some point before a goal aimed at

³short *n* **1** : something shorter than normal or standard **2** *pl* : drawers or trousers of less than knee length **3** : SHORT CIRCUIT

⁴short *vb* : SHORT-CIRCUIT

short·age \ˈshȯr-tij\ *n* : LACK, DEFICIT

short·cake \ˈshȯrt-ˌkāk\ *n* : a dessert consisting of short biscuit spread with sweetened fruit

short·change \-ˈchānj\ *vb* : to cheat esp. by giving less than the correct amount of change

short circuit *n* : a connection made between points in an electric circuit where current is not intended to flow — **short-circuit** *vb*

short·com·ing \ˈshȯrt-ˌkə-miŋ\ *n* : FAULT 1, FAILING

short·cut \-ˌkət\ *n* **1** : a route more direct than that usu. taken **2** : a quicker way of doing something

short·en \ˈshȯrt-ᵊn\ *vb* : to make or become short **syn** curtail, abbreviate, abridge, retrench

short·en·ing \ˈshȯrt-ᵊn-iŋ\ *n* : a substance (as lard or butter) that makes pastry tender and flaky

short·hand \ˈshȯrt-ˌhand\ *n* : a method of writing rapidly by using symbols and abbreviations for letters, words, or phrases : STENOGRAPHY

short·hand·ed \ˈshȯrt-ˈhan-dəd\ *adj* : short of the needed number of people

short·horn \ˈshȯrt-ˌhȯrn\ *n, often cap* : any of a breed of red, roan, or white cattle of English origin

short hundredweight *n* — see WEIGHT table

short–lived \ˈshȯrt-ˌlivd, -ˈlīvd\ *adj* : of short life or duration

short·ly \ˈshȯrt-lē\ *adv* **1** : in a few words **2** : in a short time : SOON

short order *n* : an order for food that can be quickly cooked

short shrift *n* **1** : a brief respite from death **2** : little consideration

short·sight·ed \ˈshȯrt-ˌsī-təd\ *adj* **1** : NEARSIGHTED **2** : lacking foresight — **short·sight·ed·ness** *n*

short·stop \-ˌstäp\ *n* : a baseball player defending the area between second and third base

short story *n* : a short work of fiction usu. dealing with a few characters and a single event

short–tem·pered \ˈshȯrt-ˈtem-pərd\ *adj* : having a quick temper

short–term \ˈshȯrt-ˌtərm\ *adj* **1** : occurring over or involving a relatively short period of time **2** : of or relating to a financial transaction based on a term usu. of less than a year

short ton *n* — see WEIGHT table

short·wave \ˈshȯrt-ˌwāv\ *n* : a radio wave with a wavelength between 10 and 100 meters

Sho·sho·ne *or* **Sho·sho·ni** \shə-ˈshō-nē\ *n, pl* **Shosho·nes** *or* **Shoshoni** : a member of an American Indian people orig. ranging through California, Idaho, Nevada, Utah, and Wyoming

¹shot \ˈshät\ *n* **1** : an act of shooting **2** : a stroke or throw in some games **3** : something that is shot : MISSILE, PROJECTILE; *esp* : small pellets forming a charge for a shotgun **4** : a metal sphere that is thrown for distance in the shot put **5** : RANGE, REACH **6** : MARKSMAN **7** : a single photographic exposure **8** : a single sequence of a motion picture or a television program made by one camera **9** : an injection (as of medicine) into the body **10** : a small serving of undiluted liquor

²shot *past and past part of* SHOOT

shot·gun \ˈshät-ˌgən\ *n* : a gun with a smooth bore used to fire shot at short range

shot put *n* : a field event in which a shot is heaved for distance

should \ˈshud, shəd\ *past of* SHALL — used as an auxiliary to express condition, obligation or propriety, probability, or futurity from a point of view in the past

¹shoul·der \ˈshōl-dər\ *n* **1** : the part of the body of a person or animal where the arm or foreleg joins the body **2** : either edge of a roadway **3** : a rounded or sloping part (as of a bottle) where the neck joins the body

²shoulder *vb* **1** : to push or thrust with the shoulder **2** : to bear on the shoulder **3** : to take the responsibility of

shoulder belt *n* : an automobile safety belt worn across the torso and over the shoulder

shoulder blade *n* : a flat triangular bone at the back of each shoulder

shout \ˈshaut\ *vb* : to utter a sudden loud cry — **shout** *n*

shove \ˈshəv\ *vb* **shoved; shov·ing** : to push along, aside, or away — **shove** *n*

¹shov·el \ˈshə-vəl\ *n* **1** : a broad long-handled scoop used to lift and throw material **2** : the amount a shovel will hold

²shovel *vb* **-eled** *or* **-elled; -el·ing** *or* **-el·ling 1** : to take up and throw with a shovel **2** : to dig or clean out with a shovel

¹show \'shō\ *vb* **showed** \'shōd\; **shown** \'shōn\ *or* **showed; show•ing 1** : to cause or permit to be seen : EXHIBIT ⟨∼ anger⟩ **2** : CONFER, BESTOW ⟨∼ mercy⟩ **3** : REVEAL, DISCLOSE ⟨∼*ed* courage in battle⟩ **4** : IN-STRUCT ⟨∼ me how⟩ **5** : PROVE ⟨∼*s* he was guilty⟩ **6** : APPEAR **7** : to be noticeable **8** : to be third in a horse race

²show *n* **1** : a demonstrative display **2** : outward appear-ance ⟨a ∼ of resistance⟩ **3** : SPECTACLE **4** : a theatrical presentation **5** : a radio or television program **6** : third place in a horse race

¹show•case \'shō-ˌkās\ *n* : a cabinet for displaying items (as in a store)

²showcase *vb* **show•cased; show•cas•ing** : EXHIBIT

show•down \'shō-ˌdaùn\ *n* : a decisive confrontation or contest; *esp* : the showing of poker hands to de-termine the winner of a pot

¹show•er \'shaù-ər\ *n* **1** : a brief fall of rain **2** : a party given by friends who bring gifts **3** : a bath in which water is showered on the person; *also* : a facility (as a stall) for such a bath — **show•ery** *adj*

²shower *vb* **1** : to rain or fall in a shower **2** : to bathe in a shower

show•man \'shō-mən\ *n* : one having a gift for dram-atization and visual effectiveness — **show•man•ship** *n*

show–off \'shō-ˌof\ *n* : one that seeks to attract atten-tion by conspicuous behavior

show off *vb* **1** : to display proudly **2** : to act as a show=off

show•piece \'shō-ˌpēs\ *n* : an outstanding example used for exhibition

show•place \-ˌplās\ *n* : an estate or building that is a showpiece

show up *vb* : ARRIVE

showy \'shō-ē\ *adj* **show•i•er; -est** : superficially im-pressive or striking — **show•i•ly** \'shō-ə-lē\ *adv* — **show•i•ness** \-ē-nəs\ *n*

shpt *abbr* shipment

shrap•nel \'shrap-nəl\ *n, pl* **shrapnel** : bomb, mine, or shell fragments

¹shred \'shred\ *n* : a narrow strip cut or torn off : a small fragment

²shred *vb* **shred•ded; shred•ding** : to cut or tear into shreds

shrew \'shrü\ *n* **1** : any of a family of very small mam-mals with velvety fur that are related to the moles **2** : a scolding woman

shrewd \'shrüd\ *adj* : CLEVER, ASTUTE — **shrewd-ly** *adv* — **shrewd•ness** *n*

shrew•ish \'shrü-ish\ *adj* : having an irritable disposi-tion : ILL-TEMPERED

shriek \'shrēk\ *n* : a shrill cry : SCREAM, YELL — **shriek** *vb*

shrift \'shrift\ *n, archaic* : the act of shriving

shrike \'shrīk\ *n* : any of numerous usu. largely gray-ish or brownish birds that often impale their usu. in-sect prey upon thorns before devouring it

¹shrill \'shril\ *vb* : to make a high-pitched piercing sound

²shrill *adj* : high-pitched : PIERCING ⟨∼ whistle⟩ — **shril•ly** *adv*

shrimp \'shrimp\ *n, pl* **shrimps** *or* **shrimp 1** : any of various small marine crustaceans related to the lob-sters **2** : a small or puny person

shrine \'shrīn\ *n* [ME, receptacle for the relics of a saint, fr. OE *scrīn*, fr. L *scrinium* case, chest] **1** : the tomb of a saint; *also* : a place where devotion is paid to a saint or deity **2** : a place or object hallowed by its associations

¹shrink \'shriŋk\ *vb* **shrank** \'shraŋk\ *also* **shrunk** \'shrəŋk\; **shrunk** *or* **shrunk•en** \'shrəŋ-kən\; **shrink•ing 1** : to draw back or away **2** : to become smaller or more compact **3** : to lessen in value **syn**

contract, constrict, compress, condense — **shrink-able** *adj*

²shrink *n* : a clinical psychiatrist or psychologist

shrink•age \'shriŋ-kij\ *n* **1** : the act of shrinking **2** : the amount lost by shrinkage

shrive \'shrīv\ *vb* **shrived** *or* **shrove** \'shrōv\; **shriv-en** \'shri-vən\ *or* **shrived** [ME, fr. OE *scrīfan* to pre-scribe, allot, shrive, fr. L *scribere* to write] : to min-ister the sacrament of penance to

shriv•el \'shri-vəl\ *vb* **-eled** *or* **-elled; -el•ing** *or* **-el-ling** : to shrink and draw into wrinkles : DWINDLE

¹shroud \'shraùd\ *n* **1** : something that covers or screens **2** : a cloth placed over a dead body **3** : any of the ropes leading from the masthead of a ship to the side to support the mast

²shroud *vb* : to veil or screen from view

shrub \'shrəb\ *n* : a low usu. several-stemmed woody plant — **shrub•by** *adj*

shrub•bery \'shrə-bə-rē\ *n, pl* **-ber•ies** : a planting or growth of shrubs

shrug \'shrəg\ *vb* **shrugged; shrug•ging** : to hunch (the shoulders) up to express aloofness, indifference, or uncertainty — **shrug** *n*

shrug off *vb* **1** : to brush aside : MINIMIZE **2** : to shake off **3** : to remove (a garment) by wriggling out

¹shuck \'shək\ *n* : SHELL, HUSK

²shuck *vb* : to strip of shucks

shud•der \'shə-dər\ *vb* : TREMBLE, QUAKE — **shudder** *n*

shuf•fle \'shə-fəl\ *vb* **shuf•fled; shuf•fling 1** : to mix in a disorderly mass **2** : to rearrange the order of (cards in a pack) by mixing two parts of the pack together **3** : to shift from place to place **4** : to move with a slid-ing or dragging gait **5** : to dance in a slow lagging manner — **shuffle** *n*

shuf•fle•board \'shə-fəl-ˌbōrd\ *n* : a game in which players use long-handled cues to shove disks into scoring areas marked on a smooth surface

shun \'shən\ *vb* **shunned; shun•ning** : to avoid delib-erately or habitually **syn** evade, elude, escape, duck

¹shunt \'shənt\ *vb* [ME, to flinch] : to turn off to one side; *esp* : to switch (a train) from one track to an-other

²shunt *n* **1** : a method or device for turning or thrusting aside **2** : a conductor joining two points in an elec-trical circuit forming an alternate path through which a portion of the current may pass

shut \'shət\ *vb* **shut; shut•ting 1** : CLOSE **2** : to forbid entrance into **3** : to lock up **4** : to fold together ⟨∼ a penknife⟩ **5** : to cease or suspend activity ⟨∼ down an assembly line⟩

shut•down \-ˌdaùn\ *n* : a temporary cessation of activ-ity (as in a factory)

shut–in \'shət-ˌin\ *n* : an invalid confined to home, a room, or bed

shut•out \'shət-ˌaùt\ *n* : a game or contest in which one side fails to score

shut out *vb* **1** : EXCLUDE **2** : to prevent (an opponent) from scoring in a game or contest

shut•ter \'shə-tər\ *n* **1** : a movable cover for a door or window : BLIND **2** : the part of a camera that opens and closes to expose the film

shut•ter•bug \'shə-tər-ˌbəg\ *n* : a photography enthu-siast

¹shut•tle \'shət-əl\ *n* **1** : an instrument used in weaving for passing the horizontal threads between the verti-cal threads **2** : a vehicle traveling back and forth over a short route ⟨a ∼ bus⟩ **3** : SPACE SHUTTLE

²shuttle *vb* **shut•tled; shut•tling** : to move back and forth frequently

shut•tle•cock \'shət-əl-ˌkäk\ *n* : a light conical object (as of cork or plastic) used in badminton

shut up *vb* : to cease or cause to cease talking

¹shy \'shī\ *adj* **shi•er** *or* **shy•er** \'shī-ər\; **shi•est** *or* **shy-est** \'shī-əst\ **1** : easily frightened : TIMID **2** : WARY **3**

: BASHFUL **4** : DEFICIENT, LACKING — **shy·ly** *adv* — **shy·ness** *n*

²shy *vb* **shied; shy·ing 1** : to show a dislike : RECOIL **2** : to start suddenly aside through fright ⟨the horse *shied*⟩

shy·ster \'shīs-tər\ *n* : an unscrupulous lawyer or politician

Si *symbol* silicon

Si·a·mese \ˌsī-ə-'mēz, -'mēs\ *n, pl* **Sia·mese** : THAI — **Siamese** *adj*

Siamese twin *n* [fr. Chang †1874 and Eng †1874 twins born in Siam with bodies united] : one of a pair of twins with bodies joined together at birth

¹sib·i·lant \'si-bə-lənt\ *adj* : having, containing, or producing the sound of or a sound resembling that of the *s* or the *sh* in *sash* — **sib·i·lant·ly** *adv*

²sibilant *n* : a sibilant speech sound (as English \s\, \z\, \sh\, \zh\, \ch (=tsh)\, or \j (=dzh)\)

sib·ling \'si-bliŋ\ *n* : a brother or sister considered irrespective of sex; *also* : one of two or more offspring having one common parent

sib·yl \'si-bəl\ *n, often cap* : PROPHETESS — **sib·yl·line** \-bə-ˌlīn, -ˌlēn\ *adj*

sic \'sik, 'sēk\ *adv* : intentionally so written — used after a printed word or passage to indicate that it exactly reproduces an original ⟨said he seed [∼] it all⟩

sick \'sik\ *adj* **1** : not in good health : ILL; *also* : of, relating to, or intended for use in sickness ⟨∼ pay⟩ **2** : NAUSEATED **3** : DISGUSTED **4** : PINING **5** : MACABRE, SADISTIC ⟨∼ jokes⟩ — **sick·ly** *adj*

sick·bed \'sik-ˌbed\ *n* : a bed on which one lies sick

sick·en \'si-kən\ *vb* : to make or become sick — **sick·en·ing·ly** *adv*

sick·le \'si-kəl\ *n* : a cutting tool consisting of a curved metal blade with a short handle

sickle–cell anemia *n* : an inherited anemia in which red blood cells tend to become crescent-shaped and cannot carry oxygen properly and which occurs esp. in individuals of African, Mediterranean, or southwest Asian ancestry

sick·ness \'sik-nəs\ *n* **1** : ill health; *also* : a specific disease **2** : NAUSEA

side \'sīd\ *n* **1** : the right or left part of the trunk of a body **2** : a place away from a central point or line **3** : a border of an object; *esp* : one of the longer borders as contrasted with an end **4** : an outer surface of an object **5** : a position regarded as opposite to another **6** : a body of contestants — **side** *adj*

side·arm \-ˌärm\ *adj* : made with a sideways sweep of the arm — **sidearm** *adv*

side arm *n* : a weapon worn at the side or in the belt

side·bar \'sīd-ˌbär\ *n* : a short news story accompanying a major story and presenting related information

side·board \-ˌbōrd\ *n* : a piece of dining-room furniture for holding articles of table service

side·burns \-ˌbərnz\ *n pl* : whiskers on the side of the face in front of the ears

side by side *adv* **1** : beside one another **2** : in the same place, time, or circumstance — **side–by–side** *adj*

side·car \-ˌkär\ *n* : a one-wheeled passenger car attached to the side of a motorcycle

side effect *n* : a secondary and usu. adverse effect (as of a drug)

side·kick \'sīd-ˌkik\ *n* : PAL, PARTNER

¹side·long \'sīd-ˌlȯŋ\ *adv* : in the direction of or along the side : OBLIQUELY

²sidelong *adj* : directed to one side ⟨∼ look⟩

side·man \'sīd-ˌman\ *n* : a member of a jazz or swing orchestra

side·piece \-ˌpēs\ *n* : a piece forming or contained in the side of something

si·de·re·al \sī-'dir-ē-əl, sə-\ *adj* [L *sidereus*, fr. *sider-*, *sidas* star, constellation] **1** : of or relating to the stars **2** : measured by the apparent motion of the stars

side·sad·dle \'sīd-ˌsad-ᵊl\ *n* : a saddle for women on

which the rider sits with both legs on the same side of the horse — **sidesaddle** *adv*

side·show \'sīd-ˌshō\ *n* **1** : a minor show offered in addition to a main exhibition (as of a circus) **2** : an incidental diversion

side·step \-ˌstep\ *vb* **1** : to step aside **2** : AVOID, EVADE

side·stroke \-ˌstrōk\ *n* : a swimming stroke which is executed on the side and in which the arms are swept backward and downward and the legs do a scissors kick

side·swipe \-ˌswīp\ *vb* : to strike with a glancing blow along the side — **sideswipe** *n*

¹side·track \-ˌtrak\ *n* : SIDING 1

²sidetrack *vb* **1** : to switch from a main railroad line to a siding **2** : to turn aside from a purpose

side·walk \'sīd-ˌwȯk\ *n* : a paved walk at the side of a road or street

side·wall \-ˌwȯl\ *n* **1** : a wall forming the side of something **2** : the side of an automobile tire

side·ways \-ˌwāz\ *adv or adj* **1** : from the side **2** : with one side to the front **3** : to, toward, or at one side

side·wind·er \-ˌwīn-dər\ *n* : a small pale-colored desert rattlesnake of the southwestern U.S.

sid·ing \'sī-diŋ\ *n* **1** : a short railroad track connected with the main track **2** : material (as boards) covering the outside of frame buildings

si·dle \'sīd-ᵊl\ *vb* **si·dled; si·dling** : to move sideways or with one side foremost

SIDS *abbr* sudden infant death syndrome

siege \'sēj\ *n* **1** : the placing of an army around or before a fortified place to force its surrender **2** : a persistent attack (as of illness)

sie·mens \'sē-mənz, 'zē-\ *n* : a unit of conductance equivalent to one ampere per volt

si·er·ra \sē-'er-ə\ *n* [Sp, lit., saw, fr. L *serra*] : a range of mountains esp. with jagged peaks

si·es·ta \sē-'es-tə\ *n* [Sp, fr. L *sexta (hora)* noon, lit., sixth hour] : a midday rest or nap

sieve \'siv\ *n* : a utensil with meshes or holes to separate finer particles from coarser or solids from liquids

sift \'sift\ *vb* **1** : to pass through a sieve **2** : to separate with or as if with a sieve **3** : to examine carefully **4** : to scatter by or as if by passing through a sieve — **sift·er** *n*

sig *abbr* **1** signal **2** signature

sigh \'sī\ *vb* **1** : to let out a deep audible breath (as in weariness or sorrow) **2** : GRIEVE, YEARN — **sigh** *n*

¹sight \'sīt\ *n* **1** : something seen or worth seeing **2** : the process or power of seeing; *esp* : the sense of which the eye is the receptor and by which qualities of appearance (as position, shape, and color) are perceived **3** : INSPECTION **4** : a device (as a small bead on a gun barrel) that aids the eye in aiming **5** : VIEW, GLIMPSE **6** : the range of vision — **sight·less** *adj*

²sight *vb* **1** : to get sight of **2** : to aim by means of a sight

sight·ed \'sī-təd\ *adj* : having sight

sight·ly \-lē\ *adj* : pleasing to the sight

sight–see·ing \'sīt-ˌsē-iŋ\ *adj* : engaged in or used for seeing sights of interest — **sight·seer** \-ˌsē-ər\ *n*

sig·ma \'sig-mə\ *n* : the 18th letter of the Greek alphabet — Σ or σ or ς

¹sign \'sīn\ *n* **1** : a gesture expressing a command, wish, or thought **2** : SYMBOL **3** : a notice publicly displayed for advertising purposes or for giving direction or warning **4** : OMEN, PORTENT **5** : TRACE, VESTIGE

²sign *vb* **1** : to mark with a sign **2** : to represent by a sign **3** : to make a sign or signal **4** : to write one's name on in token of assent or obligation **5** : to assign legally **6** : to use sign language — **sign·er** *n*

¹sig·nal \'sig-nəl\ *n* **1** : a sign agreed on as the start of some joint action **2** : a sign giving warning or notice of something **3** : the message, sound, or image transmitted in electronic communication (as radio)

²signal *vb* **-naled** *or* **-nalled; -nal·ing** *or* **-nal·ling 1** : to notify by a signal **2** : to communicate by signals

³**signal** *adj* : DISTINGUISHED ⟨a ∼ honor⟩ — **sig·nal·ly** *adv*

sig·nal·ize \'sig-nə-ˌlīz\ *vb* **-ized; -iz·ing** : to point out or make conspicuous — **sig·nal·i·za·tion** \ˌsig-nə-lə-'zā-shən\ *n*

sig·nal·man \'sig-nəl-mən, -ˌman\ *n* : a person who signals or works with signals

sig·na·to·ry \'sig-nə-ˌtōr-ē\ *n*, *pl* **-ries** : a person or government that signs jointly with others — **signatory** *adj*

sig·na·ture \'sig-nə-ˌchùr\ *n* **1** : the name of a person written by himself or herself **2** : the sign placed after the clef to indicate the key or the meter of a piece of music

sign·board \'sīn-ˌbōrd\ *n* : a board bearing a sign or notice

sig·net \'sig-nət\ *n* : a small intaglio seal (as in a ring)

sig·nif·i·cance \sig-'ni-fi-kəns\ *n* **1** : something signified : MEANING **2** : SUGGESTIVENESS **3** : CONSEQUENCE, IMPORTANCE

sig·nif·i·cant \-kənt\ *adj* **1** : having meaning; *esp* : having a hidden or special meaning **2** : having or likely to have considerable influence or effect : IMPORTANT — **sig·nif·i·cant·ly** *adv*

sig·ni·fy \'sig-nə-ˌfī\ *vb* **-fied; -fy·ing 1** : to show by a sign **2** : MEAN, IMPORT **3** : to have significance — **sig·ni·fi·ca·tion** \ˌsig-nə-fə-'kā-shən\ *n*

sign in *vb* : to make a record of arrival (as by signing a register)

sign language *n* : a formal system of hand gestures used for communication (as by the deaf)

sign off *vb* : to announce the end (as of a program or broadcast)

sign of the cross : a gesture of the hand forming a cross (as to invoke divine blessing)

sign on *vb* **1** : ENLIST **2** : to announce the start of broadcasting for the day

sign out *vb* : to make a record of departure (as by signing a register)

sign·post \'sīn-ˌpōst\ *n* : a post bearing a sign

Sikh \'sēk\ *n* : an adherent of a religion of India marked by rejection of caste — **Sikh·ism** *n*

si·lage \'sī-lij\ *n* : fodder fermented (as in a silo) to produce a rich moist animal feed

¹**si·lence** \'sī-ləns\ *n* **1** : the state of being silent **2** : STILLNESS **3** : SECRECY

²**silence** *vb* **si·lenced; si·lenc·ing 1** : to reduce to silence : STILL **2** : to cause to cease hostile firing or criticism

si·lenc·er \'sī-lən-sər\ *n* : a device for muffling the noise of a gunshot

si·lent \'sī-lənt\ *adj* **1** : not speaking : MUTE; *also* : TACITURN **2** : STILL, QUIET **3** : performed or borne without utterance **syn** reticent, reserved, closemouthed, close — **si·lent·ly** *adv*

¹**sil·hou·ette** \ˌsi-lə-'wet\ *n* [F] **1** : a representation of the outlines of an object filled in with black or some other uniform color **2** : OUTLINE ⟨∼ of a ship⟩

²**silhouette** *vb* **-ett·ed; -ett·ing** : to represent by a silhouette; *also* : to show against a light background

sil·i·ca \'si-li-kə\ *n* : a mineral that consists of silicon and oxygen

sil·i·cate \'si-lə-ˌkāt, 'si-li-kət\ *n* : a chemical salt that consists of a metal combined with silicon and oxygen

si·li·ceous *or* **si·li·cious** \sə-'li-shəs\ *adj* : of, relating to, or containing silica or a silicate

sil·i·con \'si-li-kən, 'si-lə-ˌkän\ *n* : a nonmetallic chemical element that occurs in combination as the most abundant element next to oxygen in the earth's crust and is used esp. in electronics — see ELEMENT table

sil·i·cone \'si-lə-ˌkōn\ *n* : an organic silicon compound used esp. for lubricants and varnishes

sil·i·co·sis \ˌsi-lə-'kō-səs\ *n* : a lung disease caused by prolonged inhaling of silica dusts

silk \'silk\ *n* **1** : a fine strong lustrous protein fiber produced by insect larvae usu. for their cocoons; *esp* : one from moth larvae (**silk·worms** \-ˌwərmz\) used

for cloth **2** : thread or cloth made from silk — **silk·en** \'sil-kən\ *adj* — **silky** *adj*

silk screen *n* : a stencil process in which coloring matter is forced through the meshes of a prepared silk or organdy screen; *also* : a print made by this process — **silk–screen** *vb*

sill \'sil\ *n* : a heavy crosspiece (as of wood or stone) that forms the bottom member of a window frame or a doorway; *also* : a horizontal supporting piece at the base of a structure

sil·ly \'si-lē\ *adj* **sil·li·er; -est** [ME *sely, silly* happy, innocent, pitiable, feeble, fr. OE *sælig*] : FOOLISH, ABSURD, STUPID — **sil·li·ness** *n*

si·lo \'sī-lō\ *n*, *pl* **silos** [Sp] **1** : a trench, pit, or esp. a tall cylinder for making and storing silage **2** : an underground structure for housing a guided missile

¹**silt** \'silt\ *n* **1** : fine earth; *esp* : particles of such soil floating in rivers, ponds, or lakes **2** : a deposit (as by a river) of silt — **silty** *adj*

²**silt** *vb* : to obstruct or cover with silt — **silt·ation** \sil-'tā-shən\ *n*

Si·lu·ri·an \sī-'lùr-ē-ən\ *adj* : of, relating to, or being the period of the Paleozoic era between the Ordovician and the Devonian marked by the appearance of the first land plants — **Silurian** *n*

¹**sil·ver** \'sil-vər\ *n* **1** : a white ductile metallic chemical element that takes a high polish and is a better conductor of heat and electricity than any other substance — see ELEMENT table **2** : coin made of silver **3** : FLATWARE **4** : a grayish white color — **sil·very** *adj*

²**silver** *adj* **1** : relating to, made of, or coated with silver **2** : SILVERY

³**silver** *vb* **sil·vered; sil·ver·ing** : to coat with or as if with silver — **sil·ver·er** *n*

silver bromide *n* : a light-sensitive compound used esp. in photography

sil·ver·fish \'sil-vər-ˌfish\ *n* : any of various small wingless insects found in houses and sometimes injurious esp. to sized paper and starched clothes

silver iodide *n* : a light-sensitive compound used in photography, rainmaking, and medicine

silver maple *n* : a No. American maple with deeply cut leaves that are green above and silvery white below

silver nitrate *n* : a soluble compound used in photography and as an antiseptic

sil·ver·ware \'sil-vər-ˌwar\ *n* : FLATWARE

sim·i·an \'si-mē-ən\ *n* : MONKEY, APE — **simian** *adj*

sim·i·lar \'si-mə-lər\ *adj* : marked by correspondence or resemblance **syn** alike, akin, comparable, parallel — **sim·i·lar·i·ty** \ˌsi-mə-'lar-ə-tē\ *n* — **sim·i·lar·ly** *adv*

sim·i·le \'si-mə-(ˌ)lē\ *n* [ME, fr. L, likeness, comparison, fr. neut. of *similis* like, similar] : a figure of speech in which two dissimilar things are compared by the use of *like* or *as* (as in "cheeks like roses")

si·mil·i·tude \sə-'mi-lə-ˌtüd, -ˌtyüd\ *n* : LIKENESS, RESEMBLANCE

sim·mer \'si-mər\ *vb* **sim·mered; sim·mer·ing 1** : to stew at or just below the boiling point **2** : to be on the point of bursting out with violence or emotional disturbance — **simmer** *n*

si·mo·nize \'sī-mə-ˌnīz\ *vb* **-nized; -niz·ing** : to polish with or as if with wax

si·mo·ny \'sī-mə-nē, 'si-\ *n* [ME *symonie*, fr. LL *simonia*, fr. L *Simon* Magus sorcerer of Samaria in Acts 8:9–24] : the buying or selling of a church office

sim·pa·ti·co \sim-'pä-ti-ˌkō, -'pa-\ *adj* : CONGENIAL, LIKABLE

sim·per \'sim-pər\ *vb* : to smile in a silly manner — **simper** *n*

sim·ple \'sim-pəl\ *adj* **sim·pler** \-pə-lər\; **sim·plest** \-pə-ləst\ [ME, fr. OF, plain, uncomplicated, artless, fr. L *simplus, simplex*, lit., single; L *simplus* fr. *sim-* one + *-plus* multiplied by; L *simplex* fr. *sim-* + *-plex* -fold] **1** : free from dishonesty or vanity : INNOCENT **2** : free from ostentation **3** : of humble origin or modest position **4** : STUPID **5** : not complex : PLAIN ⟨a ∼ melody⟩

⟨∼ directions⟩ **6** : lacking education, experience, or intelligence **7** : developing from a single ovary ⟨a ∼ fruit⟩ **syn** easy, facile, light, effortless — **sim·ple·ness** *n* — **sim·ply** *adv*

simple interest *n* : interest paid or computed on the original principal only of a loan or on the amount of an account

sim·ple·ton \'sim-pəl-tən\ *n* : FOOL

sim·plic·i·ty \sim-'pli-sə-tē\ *n* **1** : lack of complication : CLEARNESS **2** : CANDOR, ARTLESSNESS **3** : plainness in manners or way of life **4** : SILLINESS, FOLLY

sim·pli·fy \'sim-plə-ˌfī\ *vb* **-fied; -fy·ing** : to make less complex — **sim·pli·fi·ca·tion** \ˌsim-plə-fə-'kā-shən\ *n*

sim·plis·tic \sim-'plis-tik\ *adj* : excessively simple : tending to overlook complexities ⟨a ∼ solution⟩

sim·u·late \'sim-yə-ˌlāt\ *vb* **-lat·ed; -lat·ing** : to give or create the effect or appearance of : IMITATE; *also* : to make a simulation of — **sim·u·la·tor** \'sim-yə-ˌlā-tər\ *n*

sim·u·la·tion \ˌsim-yə-'lā-shən\ *n* **1** : the act or process of simulating **2** : an object that is not genuine **3** : the imitation by one system or process of the way in which another system or process works

si·mul·ta·ne·ous \ˌsī-məl-'tā-nē-əs, ˌsi-\ *adj* : occurring or operating at the same time — **si·mul·ta·ne·ous·ly** *adv* — **si·mul·ta·ne·ous·ness** *n*

¹**sin** \'sin\ *n* **1** : an offense esp. against God **2** : FAULT **3** : a weakened state of human nature in which the self is estranged from God — **sin·less** *adj*

²**sin** *vb* **sinned; sin·ning** : to commit a sin — **sin·ner** *n*

¹**since** \'sins\ *adv* **1** : from a past time until now **2** : backward in time : AGO **3** : after a time in the past

²**since** *conj* **1** : from the time when **2** : seeing that : BECAUSE

³**since** *prep* **1** : in the period after ⟨changes made ∼ the war⟩ **2** : continuously from ⟨has been here ∼ 1980⟩

sin·cere \sin-'sir\ *adj* **sin·cer·er; sin·cer·est** **1** : free from hypocrisy : HONEST **2** : GENUINE, REAL — **sin·cere·ly** *adv* — **sin·cer·i·ty** \-'ser-ə-tē\ *n*

si·ne·cure \'sī-ni-ˌkyùr, 'si-\ *n* : a paying job that requires little or no work

si·ne die \ˌsī-ni-'dī-ˌē, ˌsi-nā-'dē-ˌā\ *adv* [L, without day] : INDEFINITELY

si·ne qua non \ˌsi-ni-ˌkwä-'nän, -'nōn\ *n, pl* **sine qua nons** *also* **sine qui·bus non** \-ˌkwi-(ˌ)bùs-\ [LL, without which not] : something indispensable or essential

sin·ew \'sin-yü\ *n* **1** : TENDON **2** : physical strength — **sin·ewy** *adj*

sin·ful \'sin-fəl\ *adj* : marked by or full of sin : WICKED — **sin·ful·ly** *adv* — **sin·ful·ness** *n*

¹**sing** \'siŋ\ *vb* **sang** \'saŋ\ *or* **sung** \'səŋ\; **sung; sing·ing** **1** : to produce musical tones with the voice; *also* : to utter with musical tones **2** : to make a prolonged shrill sound ⟨locusts ∼*ing*⟩ **3** : to produce harmonious sustained sounds ⟨birds ∼*ing*⟩ **4** : CHANT, INTONE **5** : to write poetry; *also* : to celebrate in song or verse **6** : to give information or evidence — **sing·er** *n*

²**sing** *abbr* singular

Sin·ga·por·ean \ˌsiŋ-ə-'pōr-ē-ən\ *n* : a native or inhabitant of Singapore — **Singaporean** *adj*

singe \'sinj\ *vb* **singed; singe·ing** : to scorch lightly the outside of; *esp* : to remove the hair or down from (a plucked fowl) with flame

¹**sin·gle** \'siŋ-gəl\ *adj* **1** : UNMARRIED **2** : being alone : being the only one **3** : having only one feature or part **4** : made for one person **syn** sole, unique, lone, solitary, separate, particular — **sin·gle·ness** *n* — **sin·gly** *adv*

²**single** *vb* **sin·gled; sin·gling** **1** : to select (one) from a group **2** : to hit a single

³**single** *n* **1** : a separate person or thing; *also* : an unmarried person **2** : a hit in baseball that enables the batter to reach first base **3** *pl* : a tennis match with one player on each side

single bond *n* : a chemical bond in which one pair of electrons is shared by two atoms in a molecule

single–lens reflex *n* : a camera having a single lens that forms an image which is reflected to the viewfinder or recorded on film

sin·gle·tree \-ˌtrē\ *n* : WHIFFLETREE

sin·gu·lar \'siŋ-gyə-lər\ *adj* **1** : of, relating to, or constituting a word form denoting one person, thing, or instance **2** : OUTSTANDING, EXCEPTIONAL **3** : of unusual quality **4** : ODD, PECULIAR — **singular** *n* — **sin·gu·lar·i·ty** \ˌsiŋ-gyə-'lar-ə-tē\ *n* — **sin·gu·lar·ly** *adv*

sin·is·ter \'si-nəs-tər\ *adj* [ME, fr. L, on the left side, inauspicious] **1** : singularly evil or productive of evil **2** : accompanied by or leading to disaster **syn** baleful, malign, malefic, maleficent

¹**sink** \'siŋk\ *vb* **sank** \'saŋk\ *or* **sunk** \'səŋk\; **sunk; sink·ing** **1** : SUBMERGE **2** : to descend lower and lower **3** : to grow less in volume or height **4** : to slope downward **5** : to penetrate downward **6** : to fail in health or strength **7** : LAPSE, DEGENERATE **8** : to cause (a ship) to descend to the bottom **9** : to make (a hole or shaft) by digging, boring, or cutting **10** : INVEST — **sink·able** *adj*

²**sink** *n* **1** : DRAIN, SEWER **2** : a basin connected with a drain **3** : an extensive depression in the land surface

sink·er \'siŋ-kər\ *n* : a weight for sinking a fishing line or net

sink·hole \'siŋk-ˌhōl\ *n* : a hollow place in which drainage collects

sin tax *n* : a tax on substances or activities considered sinful or harmful

sin·u·ous \'sin-yə-wəs\ *adj* : bending in and out : WINDING — **sin·u·os·i·ty** \ˌsin-yə-'wä-sə-tē\ *n*

si·nus \'sī-nəs\ *n* [ME, fr. ML, fr. L, curve, hollow] **1** : any of several cavities of the skull usu. connecting with the nostrils **2** : a space forming a channel (as for the passage of blood)

si·nus·itis \ˌsī-nə-'sī-təs\ *n* : inflammation of a sinus of the skull

Sioux \'sü\ *n, pl* **Sioux** *same or* 'süz\ [F] : DAKOTA

sip \'sip\ *vb* **sipped; sip·ping** : to drink in small quantities — **sip** *n*

¹**si·phon** \'sī-fən\ *n* **1** : a bent tube through which a liquid can be transferred by means of air pressure up and over the edge of one container and into another container placed at a lower level **2** *usu* **sy·phon** : a bottle that ejects soda water through a tube when a valve is opened

siphon 1

²**siphon** *vb* **si·phoned; si·phon·ing** : to draw off by means of a siphon

sir \'sər\ *n* [ME *sire* sire, fr. OF, fr. L *senior*, compar. of *senex* old, old man] **1** : a man of rank or position — used as a title before the given name of a knight or baronet **2** — used as a usu. respectful form of address

Si·rach \'sī-rak, sə-'räk\ *n* — see BIBLE table

¹**sire** \'sīr\ *n* **1** : FATHER; *also, archaic* : FOREFATHER **2** *archaic* : LORD — used as a form of address and a title **3** : the male parent of an animal (as a horse or dog)

²**sire** *vb* **sired; sir·ing** : BEGET

si·ren \'sī-rən\ *n* **1** : a seductive or alluring woman **2** : an electrically operated device for producing a loud shrill warning signal — **siren** *adj*

sir·loin \'sər-ˌlȯin\ n [alter. of earlier *surloin*, modif. of MF *surlonge*, fr. *sur* over (fr. L *super*) + *longe* loin] : a cut of beef taken from the part in front of the round

sirup *var of* SYRUP

si·sal \'sī-səl, -zəl\ n : a strong cordage fiber from an agave; *also* : this agave

sis·sy \'sis-sē\ n, pl **sissies** : an effeminate boy or man; *also* : a timid or cowardly person

sis·ter \'sis-tər\ n 1 : a female having one or both parents in common with another individual 2 : a member of a religious order of women : NUN 3 *chiefly Brit* : NURSE 4 : a woman regarded as a comrade — **sis·ter·ly** *adj*

sis·ter·hood \-ˌhu̇d\ n 1 : the state of being a sister 2 : a community or society of sisters 3 : the solidarity of women based on shared conditions

sis·ter–in–law \'sis-tə-rən-ˌlȯ\ n, pl **sisters–in–law** : the sister of one's spouse; *also* : the wife of one's brother

sit \'sit\ vb **sat** \'sat\; **sit·ting** 1 : to rest upon the buttocks or haunches 2 : ROOST, PERCH 3 : to occupy a seat 4 : to hold a session 5 : to cover eggs for hatching : BROOD 6 : to pose for a portrait 7 : to remain quiet or inactive 8 : FIT 9 : to cause (oneself) to be seated 10 : to place in position 11 : to keep one's seat on ⟨~ a horse⟩ 12 : BABY-SIT — **sit·ter** n

si·tar \si-ˈtär\ n [Hindi *sitār*] : an Indian lute with a long neck and a varying number of strings

sit·com \'sit-ˌkäm\ n : SITUATION COMEDY

site \'sīt\ n : LOCATION

sit–in \'sit-ˌin\ n : an act of sitting in the seats or on the floor of an establishment as a means of organized protest

sit·u·at·ed \'si-chə-ˌwā-təd\ adj : LOCATED, PLACED

sit·u·a·tion \ˌsi-chə-ˈwā-shən\ n 1 : LOCATION, SITE 2 : JOB 3 : CONDITION, CIRCUMSTANCES

situation comedy n : a radio or television comedy series that involves a continuing cast of characters in a succession of episodes

sit–up \'sit-ˌəp\ n : an exercise performed from a supine position by raising the trunk to a sitting position without lifting the feet and returning to the original position

six \'siks\ n 1 : one more than five 2 : the 6th in a set or series 3 : something having six units — **six** *adj or pron* — **sixth** \'siksth\ *adj or adv or n*

six–gun \'siks-ˌgən\ n : a 6-chambered revolver

six–pack \-ˌpak\ n : six bottles or cans (as of beer) packaged and purchased together; *also* : the contents of a six-pack

six·pence \-pəns, *US also* -ˌpens\ n : the sum of six pence; *also* : an English silver coin of this value

six–shoot·er \'siks-ˌshü-tər\ n : SIX-GUN

six·teen \ˌsiks-ˈtēn\ n : one more than 15 — **sixteen** *adj or pron* — **six·teenth** \-ˈtēnth\ *adj or n*

six·ty \'siks-tē\ n, pl **sixties** : six times 10 — **six·ti·eth** \-tē-əth\ *adj or n* — **sixty** *adj or pron*

siz·able *or* **size·able** \'sī-zə-bəl\ *adj* : quite large — **siz·ably** \-blē\ *adv*

¹size \'sīz\ n : physical extent or bulk : DIMENSIONS; *also* : considerable proportions — **sized** \'sīzd\ *adj*

²size vb **sized; siz·ing** 1 : to grade or classify according to size 2 : to form a judgment of ⟨~ up the situation⟩

³size n : a gluey material used for filling the pores in paper, plaster, or textiles — **siz·ing** n

⁴size vb **sized; siz·ing** : to cover, stiffen, or glaze with size

siz·zle \'si-zəl\ vb **siz·zled; siz·zling** : to fry or shrivel up with a hissing sound — **sizzle** n

SJ *abbr* Society of Jesus

SK *abbr* Saskatchewan

ska \'skä\ n : popular music of Jamaican origin combining traditional Caribbean rhythms and jazz

¹skate \'skāt\ n, pl **skates** *also* **skate** : any of a family of rays with thick broad winglike fins

²skate n 1 : a metal frame and runner attached to a shoe and used for gliding over ice 2 : ROLLER SKATE — **skate** vb — **skat·er** n

skate·board \'skāt-ˌbȯrd\ n : a short board mounted on small wheels — **skate·board·er** n — **skate·board·ing** n

skeet \'skēt\ n : trapshooting in which clay targets are thrown in such a way that their angle of flight simulates that of a flushed game bird

skein \'skān\ n : a loosely twisted quantity of yarn or thread wound on a reel

skel·e·ton \'ske-lət-ᵊn\ n 1 : a usu. bony supporting framework of an animal body 2 : a bare minimum 3 : FRAMEWORK — **skel·e·tal** \-lət-ᵊl\ *adj*

skep·tic \'skep-tik\ n 1 : one who believes in skepticism 2 : a person disposed to skepticism esp. regarding religion — **skep·ti·cal** \-ti-kəl\ *adj*

skep·ti·cism \'skep-tə-ˌsi-zəm\ n 1 : a doubting state of mind 2 : a doctrine that certainty of knowledge cannot be attained 3 : doubt concerning religion

sketch \'skech\ n 1 : a rough drawing or outline 2 : a short or light literary composition (as a story or essay); *also* : a short comedy piece — **sketch** vb — **sketchy** *adj*

¹skew \'skyü\ vb : TWIST, SWERVE

²skew n : SLANT

skew·er \'skyü-ər\ n : a long pin for holding small pieces of meat and vegetables for broiling — **skewer** vb

¹ski \'skē\ n, pl **skis** [Norw, fr. ON *skīth* stick of wood, ski] : one of a pair of long strips (as of wood, metal or plastic) curving upward in front that are used for gliding over snow or water

²ski vb **skied** \'skēd\; **ski·ing** : to glide on skis — **ski·er** n

¹skid \'skid\ n 1 : a plank for supporting something above the ground 2 : a device placed under a wheel to prevent turning 3 : a timber or rail over or on which something is slid or rolled 4 : the act of skidding 5 : a runner on the landing gear of an aircraft 6 : ²PALLET

²skid vb **skid·ded; skid·ding** 1 : to slide without rotating ⟨a *skidding* wheel⟩ 2 : to slide sideways on the road ⟨the car *skidded* on ice⟩ 3 : SLIDE, SLIP

skid row n : a district of cheap saloons frequented by vagrants and alcoholics

skiff \'skif\ n : a small boat

ski jump n : a jump made by a person wearing skis; *also* : a course or track prepared for such jumping — **ski jump** vb — **ski jumper** n

skil·ful *chiefly Brit var of* SKILLFUL

ski lift n : a mechanical device (as a chairlift) for carrying skiers up a long slope

skill \'skil\ n 1 : ability to use one's knowledge effectively in doing something 2 : developed or acquired ability **syn** art, craft, cunning, dexterity, expertise, know-how — **skilled** \'skild\ *adj*

skil·let \'ski-lət\ n : a frying pan

skill·ful \'skil-fəl\ *adj* 1 : having or displaying skill : EXPERT 2 : accomplished with skill — **skill·ful·ly** *adv* — **skill·ful·ness** n

¹skim \'skim\ vb **skimmed; skim·ming** 1 : to take off from the top of a liquid; *also* : to remove (scum or cream) from ⟨~ milk⟩ 2 : to read rapidly and superficially 3 : to pass swiftly over — **skim·mer** n

²skim adj : having the cream removed

skimp \'skimp\ vb : to give insufficient attention, effort, or funds; *also* : to save by skimping

skimpy \'skim-pē\ adj **skimp·i·er; -est** : deficient in supply or execution

¹skin \'skin\ n 1 : the outer limiting layer of an animal body; *also* : the usu. thin tough tissue of which this is made 2 : an outer or surface layer (as a rind or peel) — **skin·less** adj — **skinned** adj

²skin vb **skinned; skin·ning** : to free from skin : remove the skin of

³skin adj : devoted to showing nudes ⟨~ magazines⟩

skin diving n : the sport of swimming under water with

a face mask and flippers and esp. without a portable breathing device — **skin–dive** *vb* — **skin diver** *n*

skin·flint \'skin-ˌflint\ *n* : a very stingy person

skin graft *n* : a piece of skin taken from one area to replace skin in another area — **skin grafting** *n*

¹**skin·ny** \'ski-nē\ *adj* **skin·ni·er; -est 1** : resembling skin **2** : very thin

²**skinny** *n* : inside information

skin·ny–dip·ping \-ˌdi-piŋ\ *n* : swimming in the nude

skin·tight \'skin-'tīt\ *adj* : closely fitted to the figure

¹**skip** \'skip\ *vb* **skipped; skip·ping 1** : to move with leaps and bounds **2** : to leap lightly over **3** : to pass from point to point (as in reading) disregarding what is in between **4** : to pass over without notice or mention

²**skip** *n* : a light bouncing step; *also* : a gait of alternate hops and steps

skip·jack \'skip-ˌjak\ *n* : a small sailboat with vertical sides and a bottom similar to a flat V

skip·per \'ski-pər\ *n* [ME, fr. MD *schipper*, fr. *schip* ship] : the master of a ship; *also* : the manager of a baseball team — **skipper** *vb*

skir·mish \'skər-mish\ *n* : a minor engagement in war; *also* : a minor dispute or contest — **skirmish** *vb*

¹**skirt** \'skərt\ *n* : a free-hanging garment or part of a garment extending from the waist down

²**skirt** *vb* **1** : to pass around the outer edge of **2** : BORDER **3** : EVADE

skit \'skit\ *n* : a brief dramatic sketch

ski tow *n* : SKI LIFT

skit·ter \'ski-tər\ *vb* : to glide or skip lightly or quickly : skim along a surface

skit·tish \'ski-tish\ *adj* **1** : CAPRICIOUS **2** : easily frightened ⟨a ~ horse⟩; *also* : WARY

ski·wear \'skē-ˌwar\ *n* : clothing suitable for wear while skiing

skosh \'skōsh\ *n* [Jp *sukoshi*] : a small amount : BIT

skul·dug·gery *or* **skull·dug·gery** \skəl-'də-gə-rē\ *n, pl* **-ger·ries** : underhanded or unscrupulous behavior

skulk \'skəlk\ *vb* : to move furtively : SNEAK, LURK — **skulk·er** *n*

skull \'skəl\ *n* : the skeleton of the head of a vertebrate that protects the brain and supports the jaws

skull and crossbones *n, pl* **skulls and crossbones** : a depiction of a human skull over crossbones usu. indicating a danger

skull·cap \'skəl-ˌkap\ *n* : a close-fitting brimless cap

¹**skunk** \'skəŋk\ *n, pl* **skunks** *also* **skunk 1** : any of various New World mammals related to the weasels that can forcibly eject an ill-smelling fluid when startled **2** : a contemptible person

²**skunk** *vb* : to defeat decisively; *esp* : to shut out in a game

skunk cabbage *n* : either of two No. American perennial herbs related to the arums that occur in shaded wet to swampy areas and have a fetid odor suggestive of a skunk

sky \'skī\ *n, pl* **skies 1** : the upper air **2** : HEAVEN — **sky·ey** \'skī-ē\ *adj*

sky·cap \-ˌkap\ *n* : a person employed to carry luggage at an airport

sky·div·ing \-ˌdī-viŋ\ *n* : the sport of jumping from an airplane and executing various body maneuvers before opening a parachute — **sky diver** *n*

sky·jack \-ˌjak\ *vb* : to commandeer an airplane in flight by threat of violence — **sky·jack·er** *n* — **sky·jack·ing** *n*

¹**sky·lark** \-ˌlärk\ *n* : a European lark noted for singing in steep upward flight

²**skylark** *vb* : FROLIC, SPORT

sky·light \'skī-ˌlīt\ *n* : a window in a roof or ceiling — **sky·light·ed** \-ˌli-təd\ *adj*

sky·line \-ˌlīn\ *n* **1** : HORIZON **2** : an outline against the sky

¹**sky·rock·et** \-ˌrä-kət\ *n* : ROCKET 1

²**skyrocket** *vb* : ROCKET 2

sky·scrap·er \-ˌskrā-pər\ *n* : a very tall building

sky·walk \-ˌwȯk\ *n* : an aerial walkway connecting two buildings

sky·ward \-wərd\ *adv* : toward the sky

sky·writ·ing \-ˌrī-tiŋ\ *n* : writing in the sky formed by smoke emitted from an airplane — **sky·writ·er** *n*

slab \'slab\ *n* : a thick flat piece or slice

¹**slack** \'slak\ *adj* **1** : CARELESS, NEGLIGENT **2** : SLUGGISH, LISTLESS **3** : not taut : LOOSE **4** : not busy or active **syn** lax, remiss, neglectful, delinquent, derelict — **slack·ly** *adv* — **slack·ness** *n*

²**slack** *vb* **1** : to make or become slack : LOOSEN, RELAX **2** : SLAKE 2

³**slack** *n* **1** : cessation of movement or flow : LETUP **2** : a part that hangs loose without strain ⟨~ of a rope⟩ **3** : trousers esp. for casual wear — usu. used in pl.

slack·en \'sla-kən\ *vb* : to make or become slack

slack·er \'sla-kər\ *n* : one that shirks work or evades military duty

slag \'slag\ *n* : the waste left after the melting of ores and the separation of metal from them

slain *past part of* SLAY

slake \'slāk, *for 2 also* 'slak\ *vb* **slaked; slak·ing 1** : to relieve or satisfy with or as if with refreshing drink ⟨~ thirst⟩ **2** : to cause (lime) to crumble by mixture with water

sla·lom \'slä-ləm\ *n* [Norw *slalåm*, lit., sloping track] : skiing in a zigzag course between obstacles

¹**slam** \'slam\ *n* : the winning of every trick or of all tricks but one in bridge

²**slam** *n* : a heavy jarring impact : BANG

³**slam** *vb* **slammed; slam·ming 1** : to shut violently and noisily **2** : to throw or strike with a loud impact

slam·mer \'sla-mər\ *n* : JAIL, PRISON

¹**slan·der** \'slan-dər\ *vb* : to utter slander against : DEFAME — **slan·der·er** *n*

²**slander** *n* [ME *sclaundre, slaundre*, fr. OF *esclandre*, fr. LL *scandalum* stumbling block, offense] : a false report maliciously uttered and tending to injure the reputation of a person — **slan·der·ous** *adj*

slang \'slaŋ\ *n* : an informal nonstandard vocabulary composed typically of invented words, arbitrarily changed words, and extravagant figures of speech — **slangy** *adj*

¹**slant** \'slant\ *n* **1** : a sloping direction, line, or plane **2** : a particular or personal viewpoint — **slant** *adj* — **slant·wise** \-ˌwīz\ *adv or adj*

²**slant** *vb* **1** : SLOPE **2** : to interpret or present in accordance with a special viewpoint or bias **syn** incline, lean, list, tilt, heel — **slant·ing·ly** *adv*

slap \'slap\ *vb* **slapped; slap·ping 1** : to strike sharply with the open hand **2** : REBUFF, INSULT — **slap** *n*

slap·stick \-ˌstik\ *n* : comedy stressing horseplay

¹**slash** \'slash\ *vb* **1** : to cut with sweeping strokes **2** : to cut slits in (a garment) **3** : to reduce sharply

²**slash** *n* **1** : GASH **2** : an ornamental slit in a garment

slat \'slat\ *n* : a thin narrow flat strip

¹**slate** \'slāt\ *n* **1** : a dense fine-grained rock that splits into thin layers **2** : a roofing tile or a writing tablet made from this rock **3** : a written or unwritten record ⟨start with a clean ~⟩ **4** : a list of candidates for election

²**slate** *vb* **slat·ed; slat·ing 1** : to cover with slate **2** : to designate for action or appointment

slath·er \'sla-thər\ *vb* : to spread with or on thickly or lavishly

slat·tern \'sla-tərn\ *n* : a slovenly woman — **slat·tern·ly** *adj*

¹**slaugh·ter** \'slȯ-tər\ *n* **1** : the butchering of livestock for market **2** : great destruction of lives esp. in battle

²**slaughter** *vb* **1** : to kill (animals) for food : BUTCHER **2** : to kill in large numbers or in a bloody way : MASSACRE

slaugh·ter·house \-ˌhaus\ *n* : an establishment where animals are butchered

Slav \'släv, 'slav\ *n* : a person speaking a Slavic language

¹slave \'slāv\ *n* [ME *sclave,* fr. OF or ML; OF *esclave,* fr. ML *sclavus,* fr. *Sclavus* Slav; fr. the enslavement of Slavs in eastern Europe in the Middle Ages] **1** : a person held in servitude as property **2** : a device (as the printer of a computer) that is directly responsive to another — **slave** *adj*

²slave *vb* **slaved; slav·ing** : to work like a slave : DRUDGE

¹sla·ver \'sla-vər, 'slā-\ *n* : SLOBBER — **slaver** *vb*

²slav·er \'slā-vər\ *n* : a ship or a person engaged in transporting slaves

slav·ery \'slāv-rē, 'slā-və-\ *n* **1** : wearisome drudgery **2** : the condition of being a slave **3** : the practice of owning slaves **syn** servitude, bondage, enslavement

¹Slav·ic \'sla-vik, 'slā-\ *n* : a branch of the Indo-European language family including various languages (as Russian or Polish) of eastern Europe

²Slavic *adj* : of or relating to the Slavs or their languages

slav·ish \'slā-vish\ *adj* **1** : SERVILE **2** : obeying or imitating with no freedom of judgment or choice — **slav·ish·ly** *adv*

slaw \'slȯ\ *n* : COLESLAW

slay \'slā\ *vb* **slew** \'slü\; **slain** \'slān\; **slay·ing** : KILL — **slay·er** *n*

sleaze \'slēz\ *n* : a sleazy quality, appearance, or behavior

slea·zy \'slē-zē\ *adj* **slea·zi·er; -est 1** : FLIMSY, SHODDY **2** : marked by cheapness of character or quality

¹sled \'sled\ *n* : a vehicle usu. on runners adapted esp. for sliding on snow

²sled *vb* **sled·ded, sled·ding** : to ride or carry on a sled

¹sledge \'slej\ *n* : SLEDGEHAMMER

²sledge *n* : a strong heavy sled

sledge·ham·mer \'slej-₁ha-mər\ *n* : a large heavy hammer wielded with both hands — **sledgehammer** *adj or vb*

¹sleek \'slēk\ *vb* **1** : to make smooth or glossy **2** : to gloss over

²sleek *adj* : having a smooth well-groomed look

¹sleep \'slēp\ *n* **1** : the natural periodic suspension of consciousness during which bodily powers are restored **2** : a state (as death or coma) suggesting sleep — **sleep·less** *adj* — **sleep·less·ness** *n*

²sleep *vb* **slept** \'slept\; **sleep·ing 1** : to rest or be in a state of sleep; *also* : to spend in sleep **2** : to have sexual intercourse — usu. used with *with* **3** : to provide sleeping space for

sleep·er \'slē-pər\ *n* **1** : one that sleeps **2** : a horizontal beam to support something on or near ground level **3** : SLEEPING CAR **4** : someone or something unpromising or unnoticed that suddenly attains prominence or value

sleeping bag *n* : a warmly lined bag for sleeping esp. outdoors

sleeping car *n* : a railroad car with berths for sleeping

sleeping pill *n* : a drug in tablet or capsule form taken to induce sleep

sleeping sickness *n* : a serious disease of tropical Africa that is marked by fever, lethargy, tremors, and loss of weight and is caused by protozoans transmitted by the tsetse fly

sleep·walk·er \'slēp-₁wȯ-kər\ *n* : one that walks while or as if while asleep — **sleep·walk** \-₁wȯk\ *vb*

sleepy \'slē-pē\ *adj* **sleep·i·er; -est 1** : ready for sleep **2** : quietly inactive — **sleep·i·ly** \'slē-pə-lē\ *adv* — **sleep·i·ness** \-pē-nəs\ *n*

sleet \'slēt\ *n* : frozen or partly frozen rain — **sleet** *vb* — **sleety** *adj*

sleeve \'slēv\ *n* **1** : a part of a garment covering an arm **2** : a tubular part designed to fit over another part — **sleeve·less** *adj*

¹sleigh \'slā\ *n* : an open usu. horse-drawn vehicle on runners for use on snow or ice

²sleigh *vb* : to drive or travel in a sleigh

sleight \'slīt\ *n* **1** : TRICK **2** : DEXTERITY

sleight of hand : a trick requiring skillful manual manipulation

slen·der \'slen-dər\ *adj* **1** : SLIM, THIN **2** : WEAK, SLIGHT **3** : MEAGER, INADEQUATE

slen·der·ize \-də-₁rīz\ *vb* **-ized; -iz·ing** : to make slender

sleuth \'slüth\ *n* [short for *sleuthhound* bloodhound, fr. ME, fr. *sleuth* track of an animal or person, fr. ON *slōth*] : DETECTIVE

¹slew \'slü\ *past of* SLAY

²slew *vb* : TURN, VEER, SKID

¹slice \'slīs\ *vb* **sliced; slic·ing 1** : to cut a slice from; *also* : to cut into slices **2** : to hit (a ball) so that a slice results

²slice *n* **1** : a thin flat piece cut from something **2** : a flight of a ball (as in golf) that curves in the direction of the dominant hand of the player hitting it

¹slick \'slik\ *vb* : to make smooth or sleek

²slick *adj* **1** : very smooth : SLIPPERY **2** : CLEVER, SMART

³slick *n* **1** : a smooth patch of water covered with a film of oil **2** : a popular magazine printed on coated paper

slick·er \'sli-kər\ *n* **1** : a long loose raincoat **2** : a sly tricky person **3** : a city dweller esp. of natty appearance or sophisticated mannerisms

¹slide \'slīd\ *vb* **slid** \'slid\; **slid·ing** \'slī-diŋ\ **1** : to move smoothly along a surface **2** : to fall by a loss of support **3** : to pass unobtrusively **4** : to move or pass smoothly; *also* : to pass unnoticed ⟨let it ∼ by⟩ **5** : to fall or dive toward a base in baseball

²slide *n* **1** : an act or instance of sliding **2** : something (as a cover or fastener) that operates by sliding **3** : a fall of a mass of earth or snow down a hillside **4** : a surface on which something slides **5** : a glass plate on which a specimen is mounted for examination under a microscope **6** : a small transparent photograph that can be projected on a screen

slid·er \'slī-dər\ *n* **1** : one that slides **2** : a baseball pitch that looks like a fastball but curves slightly

slide rule *n* : a manual device for calculation consisting of a ruler and a movable middle piece graduated with logarithmic scales

slier *comparative of* SLY

sliest *superlative of* SLY

¹slight \'slīt\ *adj* **1** : SLENDER; *also* : FRAIL **2** : UNIMPORTANT **3** : SCANTY, MEAGER — **slight·ly** *adv*

²slight *vb* **1** : to treat as unimportant **2** : to ignore discourteously **3** : to perform or attend to carelessly

³slight *n* : a humiliating discourtesy

¹slim \'slim\ *adj* **slim·mer; slim·mest** [D, bad, inferior, fr. MD, *slimp* crooked, bad] **1** : SLENDER, SLIGHT, THIN **2** : SCANTY, MEAGER

²slim *vb* **slimmed; slim·ming** : to make or become slender

slime \'slīm\ *n* **1** : sticky mud **2** : a slippery substance (as on the skin of a slug or catfish) — **slimy** *adj*

¹sling \'sliŋ\ *vb* **slung** \'sləŋ\; **sling·ing 1** : to throw forcibly : FLING **2** : to hurl with or as if with a sling

²sling *n* **1** : a short strap with strings attached for hurling stones or shot **2** : something (as a rope or chain) used to hoist, lower, support, or carry; *esp* : a bandage hanging from the neck to support an arm or hand

sling·shot \'sliŋ-₁shät\ *n* : a forked stick with elastic bands for shooting small stones or shot

slink \'sliŋk\ *vb* **slunk** \'sləŋk\ *also* **slinked** \'sliŋkt\; **slink·ing 1** : to move stealthily or furtively **2** : to move sinuously — **slinky** *adj*

¹slip \'slip\ *vb* **slipped; slip·ping 1** : to escape quietly or secretly **2** : to slide along or cause to slide along smoothly **3** : to make a mistake **4** : to pass unnoticed or undone **5** : to fall off from a standard or level

²slip *n* **1** : a ramp for repairing ships **2** : a ship's berth between two piers **3** : secret or hurried departure, escape, or evasion **4** : BLUNDER **5** : a sudden mishap **6** : a woman's one-piece garment worn under a dress **7** : PILLOWCASE

³slip *n* **1** : a shoot or twig from a plant for planting or grafting **2** : a long narrow strip; *esp* : one of paper used for a record ⟨deposit ∼⟩

⁴**slip** *vb* **slipped; slip·ping** : to take slips from (a plant)

slip·knot \'slip-ˌnät\ *n* : a knot that slips along the rope around which it is made

slipped disk *n* : a protrusion of one of the disks of cartilage between vertebrae with pressure on spinal nerves resulting esp. in low back pain

slip·per \'sli-pər\ *n* : a light low shoe that may be easily slipped on and off

slip·pery \'sli-pə-rē\ *adj* **slip·per·i·er; -est 1** : icy, wet, smooth, or greasy enough to cause one to fall or lose one's hold **2** : not to be trusted : TRICKY — **slip·per·i·ness** *n*

slip·shod \'slip-'shäd\ *adj* : SLOVENLY, CARELESS ⟨∼ work⟩

slip·stream \'slip-ˌstrēm\ *n* : a stream (as of air) driven aft by a propeller

slip·up \'slip-ˌəp\ *n* **1** : MISTAKE **2** : ACCIDENT

¹**slit** \'slit\ *vb* **slit; slit·ting 1** : SLASH **2** : to cut off or away

²**slit** *n* : a long narrow cut or opening

slith·er \'sli-thər\ *vb* : to slip or glide along like a snake — **slith·ery** *adj*

sliv·er \'sli-vər\ *n* : SPLINTER

slob \'släb\ *n* : a slovenly or boorish person

slob·ber \'slä-bər\ *vb* **slob·bered; slob·ber·ing** : to dribble saliva — **slobber** *n*

sloe \'slō\ *n* : the fruit of the blackthorn

slog \'släg\ *vb* **slogged; slog·ging 1** : to hit hard : BEAT **2** : to work hard and steadily

slo·gan \'slō-gən\ *n* [alter. of earlier *slogorn*, fr. ScGael *sluagh-ghairm*, fr. *sluagh* army, host + *gairm* cry] : a word or phrase expressing the spirit or aim of a party, group, or cause

sloop \'slüp\ *n* : a single-masted sailboat with a jib and a fore-and-aft mainsail

¹**slop** \'släp\ *n* **1** : thin tasteless drink or liquid food — usu. used in pl. **2** : food waste for animal feed : SWILL **3** : excreted body waste — usu. used in pl.

²**slop** *vb* **slopped; slop·ping 1** : SPILL **2** : to feed with slop ⟨∼ hogs⟩

¹**slope** \'slōp\ *vb* **sloped; slop·ing** : SLANT, INCLINE

²**slope** *n* **1** : upward or downward slant or degree of slant **2** : ground that forms an incline **3** : the part of a landmass draining into a particular ocean

slop·py \'slä-pē\ *adj* **slop·pi·er; -est 1** : MUDDY, SLUSHY **2** : SLOVENLY, MESSY

slosh \'släsh\ *vb* **1** : to flounder through or splash about in or with water, mud, or slush **2** : to move with a splashing motion

slot \'slät\ *n* **1** : a long narrow opening or groove **2** : a position in a sequence

slot car *n* : an electric toy racing car that runs on a grooved track

sloth \'slóth\ *n, pl* **sloths** \'slóths, 'slóthz\ **1** : LAZI-

sloth 2

NESS, INDOLENCE **2** : any of several slow-moving plant-eating arboreal mammals of So. and Central America — **sloth·ful** *adj*

slot machine *n* **1** : a machine whose operation is begun by dropping a coin into a slot **2** : a coin-operated gambling machine that pays off according to the matching of symbols on wheels spun by a handle

¹**slouch** \'slaúch\ *n* **1** : a lazy or incompetent person **2** : a loose or drooping gait or posture

²**slouch** *vb* : to walk, stand, or sit with a slouch : SLUMP

¹**slough** \'slü, 2 *usu* 'slaú\ *n* **1** : a wet and marshy or muddy place (as a swamp) **2** : a discouraged state of mind

²**slough** \'sləf\ *also* **sluff** *n* : something that has been or may be shed or cast off

³**slough** \'sləf\ *also* **sluff** *vb* : to cast off

Slo·vak \'slō-ˌväk, -ˌvak\ *n* : a member of a Slavic people of Slovakia — **Slovak** *adj* — **Slo·va·ki·an** \slō-'vä-kē-ən, -'va-\ *adj or n*

slov·en \'slə-vən\ *n* [ME *sloveyn* rascal, perh. fr. D dial. *sloovin* woman of low character] : an untidy person

Slo·vene \'slō-ˌvēn\ *n* : a member of a Slavic people living largely in Slovenia — **Slovene** *adj* — **Slo·ve·nian** \slō-'vē-nē-ən\ *adj or n*

slov·en·ly \'slə-vən-lē\ *adj* **1** : untidy in dress or person **2** : lazily or carelessly done : SLIPSHOD

¹**slow** \'slō\ *adj* **1** : SLUGGISH; *also* : dull in mind : STUPID **2** : moving, flowing, or proceeding at less than the usual speed **3** : taking more than the usual time **4** : registering behind the correct time **5** : not lively : BORING **syn** dilatory, laggard, deliberate, leisurely — **slow** *adv* — **slow·ly** *adv* — **slow·ness** *n*

²**slow** *vb* **1** : to make slow : hold back **2** : to go slower

slow motion *n* : motion-picture action photographed so as to appear much slower than normal — **slow-motion** *adj*

SLR *abbr* single-lens reflex

sludge \'sləj\ *n* : a slushy mass : OOZE; *esp* : solid matter produced by sewage treatment processes

slue *var of* ²SLEW

¹**slug** \'sləg\ *n* **1** : a small mass of metal; *esp* : BULLET **2** : a metal disk for use (as in a slot machine) in place of a coin **3** : any of numerous wormlike mollusks related to the snails **4** : a quantity of liquor drunk

²**slug** *vb* **slugged; slug·ging** : to strike forcibly and heavily — **slug·ger** *n*

slug·gard \'slə-gərd\ *n* : a lazy person

slug·gish \'slə-gish\ *adj* **1** : SLOTHFUL, LAZY **2** : slow in movement or flow **3** : STAGNANT, DULL — **slug·gish·ly** *adv* — **slug·gish·ness** *n*

¹**sluice** \'slüs\ *n* **1** : an artificial passage for water with a gate for controlling the flow; *also* : the gate so used **2** : a channel that carries off surplus water **3** : an inclined trough or flume for washing ore or floating logs

²**sluice** *vb* **sluiced; sluic·ing 1** : to draw off through a sluice **2** : to wash with running water : FLUSH

¹**slum** \'sləm\ *n* : a thickly populated area marked by poverty and dirty or deteriorated houses

²**slum** *vb* **slummed; slum·ming** : to visit slums esp. out of curiosity; *also* : to go somewhere or do something that might be considered beneath one's station

¹**slum·ber** \'sləm-bər\ *vb* **slum·bered; slum·ber·ing 1** : DOZE; *also* : SLEEP **2** : to be in a sluggish or torpid state

²**slumber** *n* : SLEEP

slum·ber·ous \'sləm-bə-rəs\ *or* **slum·brous** \-brəs\ *adj* **1** : SLUMBERING, SLEEPY **2** : PEACEFUL, INACTIVE

slum·lord \'sləm-ˌlórd\ *n* : a landlord who receives unusually large profits from substandard properties

slump \'sləmp\ *vb* **1** : to sink down suddenly : COLLAPSE **2** : SLOUCH **3** : to decline sharply — **slump** *n*

slung *past and past part of* SLING

slunk *past and past part of* SLINK

¹**slur** \'slər\ *vb* **slurred; slur·ring 1** : to slide or slip over

without due mention or emphasis **2** : to perform two or more successive notes of different pitch in a smooth or connected way

²**slur** *n* : a curved line connecting notes to be slurred; *also* : a group of slurred notes

³**slur** *n* : a slighting remark : ASPERSION

slurp \ˈslərp\ *vb* : to eat or drink noisily — **slurp** *n*

slur·ry \ˈslər-ē\ *n, pl* **slur·ries** : a watery mixture of insoluble matter

slush \ˈsləsh\ *n* **1** : partly melted or watery snow **2** : soft mud — **slushy** *adj*

slut \ˈslət\ *n* **1** : a slovenly woman **2** : a lewd woman — **slut·tish** *adj*

sly \ˈslī\ *adj* **sli·er** *also* **sly·er** \ˈslī-ər\; **sli·est** *also* **sly·est** \ˈslī-əst\ **1** : CRAFTY, CUNNING **2** : SECRETIVE, FURTIVE **3** : ROGUISH **syn** tricky, wily, artful, foxy, guileful — **sly·ly** *adv* — **sly·ness** *n*

sm *abbr* small

Sm *symbol* samarium

SM *abbr* sergeant major

SMA *abbr* sergeant major of the army

¹**smack** \ˈsmak\ *n* : characteristic flavor; *also* : a slight trace

²**smack** *vb* **1** : to have a taste **2** : to have a trace or suggestion

³**smack** *vb* **1** : to move (the lips) so as to make a sharp noise **2** : to kiss or slap with a loud noise

⁴**smack** *n* **1** : a sharp noise made by the lips **2** : a noisy slap

⁵**smack** *adv* : squarely and sharply

⁶**smack** *n* : a sailing ship used in fishing

⁷**smack** *n, slang* : HEROIN

SMaj *abbr* sergeant major

¹**small** \ˈsmȯl\ *adj* **1** : little in size or amount **2** : operating on a limited scale **3** : little or close to zero (as in number or value) **4** : made up of little things **5** : TRIFLING, UNIMPORTANT **6** : MEAN, PETTY **syn** diminutive, petite, wee, tiny, minute — **small·ish** *adj* — **small·ness** *n*

²**small** *n* : a small part or product ⟨the ∼ of the back⟩

small·pox \ˈsmȯl-ˌpäks\ *n* : a contagious virus disease of humans formerly common but now eradicated

small–time \ˈsmȯl-ˈtīm\ *adj* : insignificant in performance and standing : MINOR — **small–tim·er** *n*

¹**smart** \ˈsmärt\ *vb* **1** : to cause or feel a stinging pain **2** : to feel or endure distress — **smart** *n*

²**smart** *adj* **1** : making one smart ⟨a ∼ blow⟩ **2** : mentally quick : BRIGHT **3** : WITTY, CLEVER **4** : STYLISH **5** : being a guided missile **6** : containing a microprocessor for limited computing capability ⟨∼ terminal⟩ **syn** knowing, quick-witted, intelligent, brainy, sharp — **smart·ly** *adv* — **smart·ness** *n*

smart al·eck \ˈsmärt-ˌa-lik\ *n* : a person given to obnoxious cleverness

¹**smash** \ˈsmash\ *n* **1** : a smashing blow **2** : a hard, overhand stroke in tennis **3** : the act or sound of smashing **4** : collision of vehicles : CRASH **5** : COLLAPSE, RUIN; *esp* : BANKRUPTCY **6** : a striking success : HIT — **smash** *adj*

²**smash** *vb* **1** : to break or be broken into pieces **2** : to move forward with force and shattering effect **3** : to destroy utterly : WRECK

smat·ter·ing \ˈsma-tə-riŋ\ *n* **1** : superficial knowledge **2** : a small scattered number or amount

¹**smear** \ˈsmir\ *n* **1** : a spot left by an oily or sticky substance **2** : material smeared on a surface (as of a microscope slide)

²**smear** *vb* **1** : to overspread esp. with something oily or sticky **2** : SMUDGE, SOIL **3** : to injure by slander or insults

¹**smell** \ˈsmel\ *vb* **smelled** \ˈsmeld\ *or* **smelt** \ˈsmelt\; **smell·ing** **1** : to perceive the odor of by sense organs of the nose; *also* : to detect or seek with or as if with these organs **2** : to have or give off an odor

²**smell** *n* **1** : ODOR, SCENT **2** : the process or power of perceiving odor; *also* : the special sense by which one perceives odor **3** : an act of smelling — **smelly** *adj*

smelling salts *n pl* : an aromatic preparation used as a stimulant and restorative (as to relieve faintness)

¹**smelt** \ˈsmelt\ *n, pl* **smelts** *or* **smelt** : any of a family of small food fishes of coastal or fresh waters that are related to the trouts and salmons

²**smelt** *vb* : to melt or fuse (ore) in order to separate the metal; *also* : REFINE

smelt·er \ˈsmel-tər\ *n* **1** : one that smelts **2** : an establishment for smelting

smid·gen *also* **smid·geon** *or* **smid·gin** \ˈsmi-jən\ *n* : a small amount : BIT

smi·lax \ˈsmī-ˌlaks\ *n* **1** : any of various mostly climbing and prickly plants related to the lilies **2** : an ornamental plant related to the asparagus

¹**smile** \ˈsmīl\ *vb* **smiled**; **smil·ing** **1** : to look with a smile **2** : to be favorable **3** : to express by a smile

²**smile** *n* : a change of facial expression to express amusement, pleasure, or affection

smirch \ˈsmərch\ *vb* **1** : to make dirty or stained **2** : to bring disgrace on — **smirch** *n*

smirk \ˈsmərk\ *vb* : to wear a self-conscious or conceited smile : SIMPER — **smirk** *n*

smite \ˈsmīt\ *vb* **smote** \ˈsmōt\; **smit·ten** \ˈsmit-ᵊn\ *or* **smote**; **smit·ing** \ˈsmī-tiŋ\ **1** : to strike heavily; *also* : to kill by striking **2** : to affect as if by a heavy blow

smith \ˈsmith\ *n* : a worker in metals; *esp* : BLACKSMITH

smith·er·eens \ˌsmi-thə-ˈrēnz\ *n pl* [perh. fr. Ir *smidiríní*] : FRAGMENTS, BITS

smithy \ˈsmi-thē\ *n, pl* **smith·ies** : a smith's workshop

¹**smock** \ˈsmäk\ *n* : a loose garment worn over other clothes as a protection

²**smock** *vb* : to gather (cloth) in regularly spaced tucks — **smock·ing** *n*

smog \ˈsmäg, ˈsmȯg\ *n* [blend of *smoke* and *fog*] : a thick haze caused by the action of sunlight on air polluted by smoke and automobile exhaust fumes — **smog·gy** *adj*

¹**smoke** \ˈsmōk\ *n* **1** : the gas from burning material (as coal, wood, or tobacco) in which are suspended particles of soot **2** : a mass or column of smoke **3** : something (as a cigarette) to smoke; *also* : the act of smoking — **smoke·less** *adj* — **smoky** *adj*

²**smoke** *vb* **smoked**; **smok·ing** **1** : to emit smoke **2** : to inhale and exhale the fumes of burning tobacco; *also* : to use in smoking ⟨∼ a pipe⟩ **3** : to stupefy or drive away by smoke **4** : to discolor with smoke **5** : to cure (as meat) with smoke — **smok·er** *n*

smoke detector *n* : an alarm that sounds automatically when it detects smoke

smoke jumper *n* : a forest firefighter who parachutes to locations otherwise difficult to reach

smoke·stack \ˈsmōk-ˌstak\ *n* : a pipe or funnel through which smoke and gases are discharged

smol·der *or* **smoul·der** \ˈsmōl-dər\ *vb* **smol·dered** *or* **smoul·dered**; **smol·der·ing** *or* **smoul·der·ing** **1** : to burn and smoke without flame **2** : to burn inwardly — **smolder** *n*

smooch \ˈsmüch\ *vb* : KISS, PET — **smooch** *n*

¹**smooth** \ˈsmüth\ *adj* **1** : not rough or uneven **2** : not jarring or jolting **3** : BLAND, MILD **4** : fluent in speech and agreeable in manner — **smooth·ly** *adv* — **smooth·ness** *n*

²**smooth** *vb* **1** : to make smooth **2** : to free from trouble or difficulty

smooth muscle *n* : muscle with no cross striations that is typical of visceral organs (as the stomach and bladder) and is not under voluntary control

smor·gas·bord \ˈsmȯr-gəs-ˌbȯrd\ *n* [Sw *smörgåsbord*, fr. *smörgås* open sandwich + *bord* table] : a luncheon or supper buffet consisting of many foods

smote *past and past part of* SMITE

¹**smoth·er** \ˈsmə-thər\ *n* **1** : thick stifling smoke **2** : a

dense cloud (as of fog or dust) **3** : a confused multitude of things

²smother *vb* **smoth·ered; smoth·er·ing 1** : to be overcome by or die from lack of air **2** : to kill by depriving of air **3** : SUPPRESS **4** : to cover thickly

SMSgt *abbr* senior master sergeant

¹smudge \'sməj\ *vb* **smudged; smudg·ing** : to soil or blur by rubbing or smearing

²smudge *n* : a dirty or blurred spot — **smudgy** *adj*

smug \'sməg\ *adj* **smug·ger; smug·gest** : conscious of one's virtue and importance : SELF-SATISFIED — **smug·ly** *adv* — **smug·ness** *n*

smug·gle \'smə-gəl\ *vb* **smug·gled; smug·gling 1** : import or export secretly, illegally, or without paying the duties required by law **2** : to convey secretly — **smug·gler** \'smə-glər\ *n*

smut \'smət\ *n* **1** : something (as soot) that smudges; *also* : SMUDGE, SPOT **2** : any of various destructive diseases of plants caused by fungi; *also* : a fungus causing smut **3** : indecent language or matter — **smut·ty** *adj*

smutch \'sməch\ *n* : SMUDGE

Sn *symbol* [LL *stannum*] tin

SN *abbr* seaman

snack \'snak\ *n* : a light meal : BITE

snaf·fle \'sna-fəl\ *n* : a simple jointed bit for a horse's bridle

¹snag \'snag\ *n* **1** : a stump or piece of a tree esp. when under water **2** : an unexpected difficulty **syn** obstacle, obstruction, impediment, bar

²snag *vb* **snagged; snag·ging 1** : to become caught on or as if on a snag **2** : to seize quickly : SNATCH

snail \'snāl\ *n* : any of numerous small gastropod mollusks with a spiral shell into which they can withdraw

snake \'snāk\ *n* **1** : any of numerous long-bodied limbless reptiles : SERPENT **2** : a treacherous person **3** : something that resembles a snake — **snaky** *adj*

snake·bite \-ıbīt\ *n* : the bite of a snake and esp. a venomous snake

¹snap \'snap\ *vb* **snapped; snapping 1** : to grasp or slash at something with the teeth **2** : to get or buy quickly **3** : to utter sharp or angry words **4** : to break suddenly with a sharp sound **5** : to give a sharp cracking noise **6** : to throw with a quick motion **7** : FLASH ⟨her eyes *snapped*⟩ **8** : to put a football into play — **snap·per** *n* — **snap·pish** *adj* — **snap·py** *adj*

²snap *n* **1** : the act or sound of snapping **2** : something very easy to do : CINCH **3** : a short period of cold weather **4** : a catch or fastening that closes with a click **5** : a thin brittle cookie **6** : ENERGY, VIM; *also* : smartness of movement **7** : the putting of the ball into play in football

snap bean *n* : a bean grown primarily for its young tender pods that are usu. broken in pieces for cooking

snap·drag·on \'snap-ıdra-gən\ *n* : any of a genus of herbs with long spikes of showy flowers

snapping turtle *n* : either of two large American turtles with powerful jaws and a strong musky odor

snap·shot \'snap-ıshät\ *n* : a photograph taken usu. with an inexpensive hand-held camera

snare \'snar\ *n* : a trap often consisting of a noose for catching birds or mammals — **snare** *vb*

¹snarl \'snärl\ *vb* : to cause to become knotted and intertwined

²snarl *n* : TANGLE

³snarl *vb* : to growl angrily or threateningly

⁴snarl *n* : an angry ill-tempered growl

¹snatch \'snach\ *vb* **1** : to try to grasp something suddenly **2** : to seize or take away suddenly **syn** clutch, seize, grab, nab

²snatch *n* **1** : a short period **2** : an act of snatching **3** : something brief or fragmentary ⟨~es of song⟩

¹sneak \'snēk\ *vb* **sneaked** \'snēkt\ *or* **snuck** \'snək\; **sneak·ing** : to move, act, or take in a furtive manner — **sneak·ing·ly** *adv*

²sneak *n* **1** : one who acts in a furtive or shifty manner

2 : a stealthy or furtive move or escape — **sneak·i·ly** \'snē-kə-lē\ *adv* — **sneaky** *adj*

sneak·er \'snē-kər\ *n* : a sports shoe with a pliable rubber sole

sneer \'snir\ *vb* : to show scorn or contempt by curling the lip or by a jeering tone — **sneer** *n*

sneeze \'snēz\ *vb* **sneezed; sneez·ing** : to force the breath out suddenly and violently as a reflex act — **sneeze** *n*

SNF *abbr* skilled nursing facility

snick·er \'sni-kər\ *n* : a partly suppressed laugh — **snicker** *vb*

snide \'snīd\ *adj* **1** : MEAN, LOW ⟨a ~ trick⟩ **2** : slyly disparaging ⟨a ~ remark⟩

sniff \'snif\ *vb* **1** : to draw air audibly up the nose esp. for smelling **2** : to show disdain or scorn **3** : to detect by or as if by smelling — **sniff** *n*

snif·fle \'sni-fəl\ *n* **1** *pl* : a head cold marked by nasal discharge **2** : SNUFFLE — **sniffle** *vb*

¹snip \'snip\ *n* **1** : a fragment snipped off **2** : a simple stroke of the scissors or shears

²snip *vb* **snipped; snip·ping** : to cut off by bits : CLIP; *also* : to remove by cutting off

¹snipe \'snīp\ *n, pl* **snipes** *or* **snipe** : any of several long-billed game birds esp. of marshy areas that belong to the same family as the sandpipers

²snipe *vb* **sniped; snip·ing** : to shoot at an exposed enemy from a concealed position — **snip·er** *n*

snip·py \'sni-pē\ *adj* **snip·pi·er; -est** : CURT, SNAPPISH

snips \'snips\ *n pl* : hand shears used esp. for cutting sheet metal ⟨tin ~⟩

snitch \'snich\ *vb* **1** : INFORM, TATTLE **2** : PILFER, SNATCH

sniv·el \'sni-vəl\ *vb* **-eled** *or* **-elled; -el·ing** *or* **-el·ling 1** : to have a running nose; *also* : SNUFFLE **2** : to whine in a snuffling manner — **snivel** *n*

snob \'snäb\ *n* : one who seeks association with persons of higher social position and looks down on those considered inferior — **snob·bish** *adj* — **snob·bish·ly** *adv* — **snob·bish·ness** *n*

snob·bery \'snä-bə-rē\ *n, pl* **-ber·ies** : snobbish conduct

¹snoop \'snüp\ *vb* [D *snoepen* to buy or eat on the sly] : to pry in a furtive or meddlesome way

²snoop *n* : a prying meddlesome person

snooty \'snü-tē\ *adj* **snoot·i·er; -est** : DISDAINFUL, SNOBBISH

snooze \'snüz\ *vb* **snoozed; snooz·ing** : to take a nap : DOZE — **snooze** *n*

snore \'snōr\ *vb* **snored; snor·ing** : to breathe with a rough hoarse noise while sleeping — **snore** *n*

snor·kel \'snór-kəl\ *n* [G *Schnorchel*] : a tube projecting above the water used by swimmers for breathing with the face under water — **snorkel** *vb*

snort \'snórt\ *vb* **1** : to force air violently and noisily through the nose ⟨his horse ~ed⟩ **2** : INHALE — **snort** *n*

snot \'snät\ *n* : nasal mucus

snout \'snaút\ *n* **1** : a long projecting muzzle (as of a pig) **2** : a usu. large or grotesque nose

¹snow \'snō\ *n* **1** : crystals of ice formed from water vapor in the air **2** : a descent or shower of snow crystals

²snow *vb* **1** : to fall or cause to fall in or as snow **2** : to cover or shut in with or as if with snow

¹snow·ball \'snō-ıbòl\ *n* : a round mass of snow pressed into shape in the hand for throwing

²snowball *vb* **1** : to throw snowballs at **2** : to increase or expand at a rapidly accelerating rate

snow·bank \-ıbaŋk\ *n* : a mound or slope of snow

snow·belt \-ıbelt\ *n, often cap* : a region that receives an appreciable amount of annual snowfall

snow·blow·er \-ıblō-ər\ *n* : a machine in which a rotating spiral blade picks up and propels snow aside

snow·drift \-ıdrift\ *n* : a bank of drifted snow

snow·drop \-ıdräp\ *n* : a plant with narrow leaves and

a nodding white flower that blooms early in the spring

snow·fall \-ˌfȯl\ *n* : a fall of snow

snow fence *n* : a fence across the path of prevailing winds to protect something (as a road) from drifting snow

snow·field \ˈsnō-ˌfēld\ *n* : a mass of perennial snow at the head of a glacier

snow·mo·bile \ˈsnō-mō-ˌbēl\ *n* : any of various automotive vehicles for travel on snow — **snow·mo·bil·er** \-ˌbē-lər\ *n* — **snow·mo·bil·ing** \-liŋ\ *n*

snow pea *n* : a cultivated pea with flat edible pods

snow·plow \ˈsnō-ˌplaů\ *n* **1** : a device for clearing away snow **2** : a skiing maneuver in which the heels of both skis are slid outward for slowing down or stopping

¹snow·shoe \-ˌshü\ *n* : a light frame of wood strung with thongs that is attached to a shoe or boot to prevent sinking down into soft snow

²snowshoe *vb* **snow·shoed; snow·shoe·ing** : to travel on snowshoes

snow·storm \-ˌstȯrm\ *n* : a storm of falling snow

snow thrower *n* : SNOWBLOWER

snowy \ˈsnō-ē\ *adj* **snow·i·er; -est 1** : marked by snow **2** : white as snow

snub \ˈsnəb\ *vb* **snubbed; snub·bing** : to treat with disdain : SLIGHT — **snub** *n*

snub–nosed \ˈsnəb-ˌnōzd\ *adj* : having a nose slightly turned up at the end

snuck *past and past part of* SNEAK

¹snuff \ˈsnəf\ *vb* **1** : to pinch off the charred end of (a candle) **2** : to put out (a candle) — **snuff·er** *n*

²snuff *vb* **1** : to draw forcibly into or through the nose **2** : SMELL

³snuff *n* : SNIFF

⁴snuff *n* : pulverized tobacco

snuf·fle \ˈsnə-fəl\ *vb* **snuf·fled; snuf·fling 1** : to snuff or sniff audibly and repeatedly **2** : to breathe with a sniffing sound — **snuf·fle** *n*

snug \ˈsnəg\ *adj* **snug·ger; snug·gest 1** : fitting closely and comfortably **2** : CONCEALED — **snug·ly** *adv* — **snug·ness** *n*

snug·gle \ˈsnə-gəl\ *vb* **snug·gled; snug·gling** : to curl up or draw close comfortably : NESTLE

¹so \ˈsō\ *adv* **1** : in the manner indicated **2** : in the same way **3** : THUS **4** : FINALLY **5** : to the extent indicated **6** : THEREFORE

²so *conj* : for that reason ⟨he wanted it, ∼ he took it⟩

³so *pron* **1** : the same ⟨became chairman and remained ∼⟩ **2** : approximately that ⟨a dozen or ∼⟩

⁴so *abbr* south; southern

SO *abbr* strikeout

¹soak \ˈsōk\ *vb* **1** : to remain in a liquid **2** : WET, SATURATE **3** : to draw in by or as if by absorption **syn** drench, steep, impregnate

²soak *n* **1** : the act of soaking **2** : the liquid in which something is soaked **3** : DRUNKARD

soap \ˈsōp\ *n* : a cleansing substance made usu. by action of alkali on fat — **soap** *vb* — **soapy** *adj*

soap opera *n* [fr. its sponsorship by soap manufacturers] : a radio or television daytime serial drama

soap·stone \ˈsōp-ˌstōn\ *n* : a soft talc-containing stone with a soapy feel

soar \ˈsȯr\ *vb* : to fly upward or at a height on or as if on wings

sob \ˈsäb\ *vb* **sobbed; sob·bing** : to weep with convulsive heavings of the chest or contractions of the throat — **sob** *n*

so·ber \ˈsō-bər\ *adj* **so·ber·er** \-bər-ər\; **so·ber·est** \-bə-rəst\ **1** : temperate in the use of liquor **2** : not drunk **3** : serious or grave in mood or disposition **4** : having a quiet tone or color **syn** solemn, earnest, staid, sedate — **so·ber·ly** *adv* — **so·ber·ness** *n*

so·bri·ety \sō-ˈbrī-ə-tē\ *n* : the quality or state of being sober

so·bri·quet \ˈsō-bri-ˌkā, -ˌket\ *n* [F] : NICKNAME

soc *abbr* **1** social; society **2** sociology

so–called \ˈsō-ˈkȯld\ *adj* : commonly but often inaccurately so termed

soc·cer \ˈsä-kər\ *n* [by shortening & alter. fr. *association football*] : a game played on a field by two teams with a round inflated ball advanced by kicking

¹so·cia·ble \ˈsō-shə-bəl\ *adj* **1** : liking companionship : FRIENDLY **2** : characterized by pleasant social relations **syn** gracious, cordial, affable, genial — **so·cia·bil·i·ty** \ˌsō-shə-ˈbi-lə-tē\ *n* — **so·cia·bly** \ˈsō-shə-blē\ *adv*

²sociable *n* : SOCIAL

¹so·cial \ˈsō-shəl\ *adj* **1** : marked by pleasant companionship with one's friends **2** : naturally living and breeding in organized communities ⟨∼ insects⟩ **3** : of or relating to human society ⟨∼ institutions⟩ **4** : of, relating to, or based on rank in a particular society ⟨∼ circles⟩; *also* : of or relating to fashionable society — **so·cial·ly** *adv*

²social *n* : a social gathering

social disease *n* : VENEREAL DISEASE

so·cial·ism \ˈsō-shə-ˌli-zəm\ *n* : any of various social systems based on shared or government ownership and administration of the means of production and distribution of goods — **so·cial·ist** \ˈsō-shə-list\ *n or adj* — **so·cial·is·tic** \ˌsō-shə-ˈlis-tik\ *adj*

so·cial·ite \ˈsō-shə-ˌlīt\ *n* : a person prominent in fashionable society

so·cial·ize \ˈsō-shə-ˌlīz\ *vb* **-ized; -iz·ing 1** : to regulate according to the theory and practice of socialism **2** : to adapt to social needs or uses **3** : to participate actively in a social gathering — **so·cial·i·za·tion** \ˌsō-shə-lə-ˈzā-shən\ *n*

social science *n* : a science (as economics or political science) dealing with a particular aspect of human society — **social scientist** *n*

social work *n* : services, activities, or methods providing social services esp. to the economically underprivileged and socially maladjusted — **social worker** *n*

so·ci·e·ty \sə-ˈsī-ə-tē\ *n, pl* **-ties** [MF *societé*, fr. L *societat-, societas,* fr. *socius* companion] **1** : COMPANIONSHIP **2** : a voluntary association of persons for common ends **3** : a part of a community bound together by common interests and standards; *esp* : the group or set of fashionable people

so·cio·eco·nom·ic \ˌsō-sē-ō-ˌe-kə-ˈnä-mik, ˌsō-shē-, -ˌē-kə-\ *adj* : of, relating to, or involving both social and economic factors

sociol *abbr* sociologist; sociology

so·ci·ol·o·gy \ˌsō-sē-ˈä-lə-jē, ˌsō-shē-\ *n* : the science of society, social institutions, and social relationships — **so·cio·log·i·cal** \ˌsō-sē-ə-ˈlä-ji-kəl, ˌsō-shē-\ *adj* — **so·ci·ol·o·gist** \-ˈä-lə-jist\ *n*

¹sock \ˈsäk\ *n, pl* **socks** *or* **sox** \ˈsäks\ : a stocking with a short leg

²sock *vb* : to hit, strike, or apply forcefully

³sock *n* : a vigorous blow : PUNCH

sock·et \ˈsä-kət\ *n* : an opening or hollow that forms a holder for something

socket wrench *n* : a wrench usu. in the form of a bar and removable socket made to fit a bolt or nut

¹sod \ˈsäd\ *n* : TURF 1

²sod *vb* **sod·ded; sod·ding** : to cover with sod

so·da \ˈsō-də\ *n* **1** : SODIUM CARBONATE **2** : SODIUM BICARBONATE **3** : SODIUM **4** : SODA WATER **5** : SODA POP **6** : a sweet drink of soda water, flavoring, and often ice cream

soda pop *n* : a carbonated, sweetened, and flavored soft drink

soda water *n* : a beverage of water charged with carbon dioxide

sod·den \ˈsäd-ᵊn\ *adj* **1** : lacking spirit : DULLED **2** : SOAKED, DRENCHED **3** : heavy or doughy from being improperly cooked ⟨∼ biscuits⟩

so·di·um \ˈsō-dē-əm\ *n* : a soft waxy silver white metallic chemical element occurring in nature in combined form (as in salt) — see ELEMENT table

sodium bicarbonate *n* : a white weakly alkaline salt

used esp. in baking powders, fire extinguishers, and medicine

sodium carbonate *n* : a carbonate of sodium used esp. in washing and bleaching textiles

sodium chloride *n* : SALT 1

sodium fluoride *n* : a salt used chiefly in tiny amounts to prevent tooth decay

sodium hydroxide *n* : a white brittle caustic substance used in making soap and rayon and in bleaching

sodium nitrate *n* : a crystalline salt used as a fertilizer and in curing meat

sodium thiosulfate *n* : a hygroscopic crystalline salt used as a photographic fixing agent

sod·omy \'sä-də-mē\ *n* 1 : sexual intercourse with a member of the same sex or with an animal 2 : noncoital and esp. anal or oral sexual intercourse with a member of the opposite sex — **sod·om·ize** \'sä-də-ˌmīz\ *vb*

so·ev·er \sō-'e-vər\ *adv* 1 : in any degree or manner ⟨how bad ∼⟩ 2 : at all : of any kind ⟨any help ∼⟩

so·fa \'sō-fə\ *n* [Ar *suffah* long bench] : a couch usu. with upholstered back and arms

soft \'sȯft\ *adj* 1 : not hard or rough : NONVIOLENT 2 : RESTFUL, GENTLE, SOOTHING 3 : emotionally susceptible 4 : not prepared to endure hardship 5 : not containing certain salts that prevent lathering ⟨∼ water⟩ 6 : occurring at such a speed as to avoid destructive impact ⟨∼ landing of a spacecraft on the moon⟩ 7 : BIODEGRADABLE ⟨a ∼ detergent⟩ 8 : not alcoholic ⟨∼ drinks⟩ 9 : less detrimental than a hard narcotic ⟨∼ drugs⟩ — **soft·ly** *adv* — **soft·ness** *n*

soft·ball \'sȯft-ˌbȯl\ *n* : a game similar to baseball played with a ball larger and softer than a baseball; *also* : the ball used in this game

soft·bound \-ˌbau̇nd\ *adj* : not bound in hard covers ⟨∼ books⟩

soft coal *n* : BITUMINOUS COAL

soft·en \'sȯ-fən\ *vb* : to make or become soft — **soft·en·er** *n*

soft palate *n* : the fold at the back of the hard palate that partially separates the mouth and the pharynx

soft·ware \'sȯft-ˌwar\ *n* : the entire set of programs, procedures, and related documentation associated with a system; *esp* : computer programs

soft·wood \-ˌwu̇d\ *n* 1 : the wood of a coniferous tree as compared to that of a broad-leaved deciduous tree 2 : a tree that yields softwood — **softwood** *adj*

sog·gy \'sä-gē\ *adj* **sog·gi·er; -est** : heavy with water or moisture — **sog·gi·ly** \'sä-gə-lē\ *adv* — **sog·gi·ness** \-gē-nəs\ *n*

soi·gné *or* **soi·gnée** \swän-'yā\ *adj* : elegantly maintained; *esp* : WELL-GROOMED

¹**soil** \'sȯil\ *vb* 1 : CORRUPT, POLLUTE 2 : to make or become dirty 3 : STAIN, DISGRACE

²**soil** *n* 1 : STAIN, DEFILEMENT 2 : EXCREMENT, WASTE

³**soil** *n* 1 : firm land : EARTH 2 : the upper layer of earth in which plants grow 3 : COUNTRY, REGION

soi·ree *or* **soi·rée** \swä-'rā\ *n* [F *soirée* evening period, evening party, fr. MF, fr. *soir* evening, fr. L *sero* at a late hour] : an evening party

so·journ \'sō-ˌjərn, sō-'jərn\ *vb* : to dwell in a place temporarily — **so·journ** *n* — **so·journ·er** *n*

¹**sol** \'säl, 'sȯl\ *n* — see MONEY table

²**sol** *n* : a fluid colloidal system

³**sol** *abbr* 1 solicitor 2 soluble 3 solution

Sol \'säl\ *n* : SUN

¹**sol·ace** \'sä-ləs\ *n* : COMFORT

²**solace** *vb* **so·laced; so·lac·ing** : to give solace to : CONSOLE

so·lar \'sō-lər\ *adj* 1 : of, derived from, or relating to the sun 2 : measured by the earth's course in relation to the sun ⟨the ∼ year⟩ 3 : operated by or using the sun's light or heat ⟨∼ energy⟩

solar cell *n* : a photoelectric cell that converts light into electrical energy and is used as a power source

solar collector *n* : a device for the absorption of solar radiation for the heating of water or buildings or the production of electricity

solar flare *n* : a sudden temporary outburst of energy from a small area of the sun's surface

so·lar·i·um \sō-'lar-ē-əm\ *n, pl* **-ia** \-ē-ə\ *also* **-iums** : a room exposed to the sun; *esp* : a room (as in a hospital) for exposure of the body to sunshine

solar plexus *n* : the general area of the stomach below the sternum

solar system *n* : the sun together with the group of celestial bodies that revolve around it

solar wind *n* : plasma continuously ejected from the sun's surface

sold *past and past part of* SELL

sol·der \'sä-dər, 'sȯ-\ *n* : a metallic alloy used when melted to mend or join metallic surfaces — **solder** *vb*

soldering iron *n* : a metal device for applying heat in soldering

¹**sol·dier** \'sōl-jər\ *n* [ME *soudier*, fr. MF, fr. *soulde* pay, fr. LL *solidus* a Roman coin, fr. L, solid] : a person in military service; *esp* : an enlisted man or woman — **sol·dier·ly** *adj or adv*

²**soldier** *vb* **sol·diered; sol·dier·ing** 1 : to serve as a soldier 2 : to pretend to work while actually doing nothing

soldier of fortune : ADVENTURER 2

sol·diery \'sōl-jə-rē\ *n* : a body of soldiers

¹**sole** \'sōl\ *n* : any of various flatfishes marketed for food

²**sole** *n* 1 : the undersurface of the foot 2 : the bottom of a shoe

³**sole** *vb* **soled; sol·ing** : to furnish (a shoe) with a sole

⁴**sole** *adj* : SINGLE, ONLY — **sole·ly** \'sōl-lē\ *adv*

so·le·cism \'sä-lə-ˌsi-zəm, 'sō-\ *n* 1 : a mistake in grammar 2 : a breach of etiquette

sol·emn \'sä-ləm\ *adj* 1 : marked by or observed with full religious ceremony 2 : FORMAL, CEREMONIOUS 3 : highly serious 4 : SOMBER, GLOOMY — **so·lem·ni·ty** \sə-'lem-nə-tē\ *n* — **sol·emn·ly** \'sä-ləm-lē\ *adv*

sol·em·nize \'sä-ləm-ˌnīz\ *vb* **-nized; -niz·ing** 1 : to observe or honor with solemnity 2 : to celebrate (a marriage) with religious rites — **sol·em·ni·za·tion** \ˌsä-ləm-nə-'zā-shən\ *n*

so·le·noid \'sō-lə-ˌnȯid, 'sä-\ *n* : a coil of wire usu. in cylindrical form that when carrying a current acts like a magnet

so·lic·it \sə-'li-sət\ *vb* 1 : ENTREAT, BEG 2 : to approach with a request or plea 3 : TEMPT, LURE — **so·lic·i·ta·tion** \-ˌli-sə-'tā-shən\ *n*

so·lic·i·tor \sə-'li-sə-tər\ *n* 1 : one that solicits 2 : LAWYER; *esp* : a legal official of a city or state

so·lic·i·tous \sə-'li-sə-təs\ *adj* 1 : WORRIED, CONCERNED 2 : EAGER, WILLING **syn** avid, impatient, keen, anxious — **so·lic·i·tous·ly** *adv*

so·lic·i·tude \sə-'li-sə-ˌtüd, -ˌtyüd\ *n* : CONCERN, ANXIETY

¹**sol·id** \'sä-ləd\ *adj* 1 : not hollow; *also* : written as one word without a hyphen ⟨a ∼ compound⟩ 2 : having, involving, or dealing with three dimensions or with solids ⟨∼ geometry⟩ 3 : not loose or spongy : COMPACT ⟨a ∼ mass of rock⟩; *also* : neither gaseous nor liquid : HARD, RIGID ⟨∼ ice⟩ 4 : of good substantial quality or kind ⟨∼ comfort⟩ 5 : thoroughly dependable : RELIABLE ⟨a ∼ citizen⟩; *also* : serious in purpose or character ⟨∼ reading⟩ 6 : UNANIMOUS, UNITED ⟨∼ for pay increases⟩ 7 : of one substance or character — **solid** *adv* — **so·lid·i·ty** \sə-'li-də-tē\ *n* — **sol·id·ly** *adv* — **sol·id·ness** *n*

²**solid** *n* 1 : a geometrical figure (as a cube or sphere) having three dimensions 2 : a solid substance

sol·i·dar·i·ty \ˌsä-lə-'dar-ə-tē\ *n* : unity based on shared interests, objectives, or standards

so·lid·i·fy \sə-'li-də-ˌfī\ *vb* **-fied; -fy·ing** : to make or become solid — **so·lid·i·fi·ca·tion** \-ˌli-də-fə-'kā-shən\ *n*

solid–state *adj* **1** : relating to the structure and properties of solid material **2** : using semiconductor devices rather than vacuum tubes

so·lil·o·quize \sə-'li-lə-ˌkwīz\ *vb* **-quized; -quiz·ing** : to talk to oneself : utter a soliloquy

so·lil·o·quy \sə-'li-lə-kwē\ *n, pl* **-quies** [LL *soliloquium,* fr. L *solus* alone + *loqui* to speak] **1** : the act of talking to oneself **2** : a dramatic monologue that represents unspoken reflections by a character

sol·i·taire \'sä-lə-ˌtar\ *n* **1** : a single gem (as a diamond) set alone **2** : a card game for one person

sol·i·tary \'sä-lə-ˌter-ē\ *adj* **1** : being or living apart from others **2** : LONELY, SECLUDED **3** : SOLE, ONLY

sol·i·tude \'sä-lə-ˌtüd, -ˌtyüd\ *n* **1** : the state of being alone : SECLUSION **2** : a lonely place

soln *abbr* solution

¹so·lo \'sō-lō\ *n, pl* **solos** [It, fr. *solo* alone, fr. L *solus*] **1** : a piece of music for a single voice or instrument with or without accompaniment **2** : an action in which there is only one performer — **solo** *adj or vb* — **so·lo·ist** *n*

²solo *adv* : without a companion : ALONE

so·lon \'sō-lən\ *n* **1** : a wise and skillful lawgiver **2** : a member of a legislative body

sol·stice \'säl-stəs, 'sōl-\ *n* [ME, fr. OF, fr. L *solstitium,* fr. *sol* sun + *-stit-, -stes* standing] : the time of the year when the sun is farthest north of the equator (**summer solstice**) about June 22 or farthest south (**winter solstice**) about Dec. 22 — **sol·sti·tial** \säl-'sti-shəl, sōl-\ *adj*

sol·u·ble \'säl-yə-bəl\ *adj* **1** : capable of being dissolved in or as if in a liquid **2** : capable of being solved or explained — **sol·u·bil·i·ty** \ˌsäl-yə-'bi-lə-tē\ *n*

sol·ute \'säl-ˌyüt\ *n* : a dissolved substance

so·lu·tion \sə-'lü-shən\ *n* **1** : an action or process of solving a problem; *also* : an answer to a problem **2** : an act or the process by which one substance is homogenously mixed with another usu. liquid substance; *also* : a mixture thus formed

solve \'sälv\ *vb* **solved; solv·ing** : to find the answer to or a solution for — **solv·able** *adj*

sol·ven·cy \'säl-vən-sē\ *n* : the condition of being solvent

¹sol·vent \-vənt\ *adj* **1** : able or sufficient to pay all legal debts **2** : dissolving or able to dissolve

²solvent *n* : a usu. liquid substance capable of dissolving or dispersing one or more other substances

So·ma·lian \sō-'mäl-yən\ *n* : a native or inhabitant of Somalia — **Somalian** *adj*

so·mat·ic \sō-'ma-tik\ *adj* : of, relating to, or affecting the body in contrast to the mind or the sex cells and their precursors

som·ber *or* **som·bre** \'säm-bər\ *adj* **1** : DARK, GLOOMY **2** : GRAVE, MELANCHOLY — **som·ber·ly** *adv*

som·bre·ro \səm-'brer-ō\ *n, pl* **-ros** [Sp, fr. *sombra* shade] : a broad-brimmed felt hat worn esp. in the Southwest and in Mexico

sombrero

¹some \'səm\ *adj* **1** : one unspecified ⟨~ man called⟩ **2** : an unspecified or indefinite number of ⟨~ berries

are ripe⟩ **3** : at least a few or a little ⟨~ years ago⟩

²some *pron* : a certain number or amount ⟨~ of the berries are ripe⟩ ⟨~ of it is missing⟩

¹-some \səm\ *adj suffix* : characterized by a (specified) thing, quality, state, or action ⟨awe*some*⟩ ⟨burden*some*⟩

²-some *n suffix* : a group of (so many) members and esp. persons ⟨four*some*⟩

¹some·body \'səm-ˌbä-dē, -bə-\ *pron* : some person

²somebody *n* : a person of importance

some·day \'səm-ˌdā\ *adv* : at some future time

some·how \-ˌhaủ\ *adv* : by some means

some·one \-(ˌ)wən\ *pron* : some person

som·er·sault \'sə-mər-ˌsòlt\ *n* [MF *sombresaut* leap, ultim. fr. L *super* over + *saltus* leap, fr. *salire* to jump] : a leap or roll in which a person turns heels over head — **somersault** *vb*

som·er·set \-ˌset\ *n* : SOMERSAULT

some·thing \'səm-thiŋ\ *pron* : some undetermined or unspecified thing

some·time \-ˌtīm\ *adv* **1** : at a future time **2** : at an unknown or unnamed time

some·times \-ˌtīmz\ *adv* : OCCASIONALLY

¹some·what \-ˌhwät, -ˌhwət\ *pron* : SOMETHING

²somewhat *adv* : in some degree

some·where \-ˌhwer\ *adv* : in, at, or to an unknown or unnamed place

som·nam·bu·lism \säm-'nam-byə-ˌli-zəm\ *n* : performance of motor acts (as walking) during sleep; *also* : an abnormal condition of sleep characterized by this — **som·nam·bu·list** \-list\ *n*

som·no·lent \'säm-nə-lənt\ *adj* : SLEEPY, DROWSY — **som·no·lence** \-ləns\ *n*

son \'sən\ *n* **1** : a male offspring or descendant **2** *cap* : Jesus Christ **3** : a person deriving from a particular source (as a country, race, or school)

so·nar \'sō-ˌnär\ *n* [*sound navigation and ranging*] : a method or device for detecting and locating submerged objects (as submarines) by sound waves

so·na·ta \sə-'nä-tə\ *n* [It] : an instrumental composition with three or four movements differing in rhythm and mood but related in key

son·a·ti·na \ˌsä-nə-'tē-nə\ *n* [It, dim. of *sonata*] : a short usu. simplified sonata

song \'sòŋ\ *n* **1** : vocal music; *also* : a short composition of words and music **2** : poetic composition **3** : a distinctive or characteristic sound (as of a bird) **4** : a small amount ⟨sold for a ~⟩

song·bird \'sòŋ-ˌbərd\ *n* : a bird that utters a series of musical tones

Song of Sol·o·mon \-'sä-lə-mən\ *n* — see BIBLE table

Song of Songs *n* — see BIBLE table

song·ster \'sòŋ-stər\ *n* : one that sings

song·stress \-strəs\ *n* : a female singer

son·ic \'sä-nik\ *adj* : of or relating to sound waves or the speed of sound

sonic boom *n* : an explosive sound produced by an aircraft traveling at supersonic speed

son–in–law \'sən-ən-ˌlò\ *n, pl* **sons–in–law** : the husband of one's daughter

son·net \'sä-nət\ *n* : a poem of 14 lines usu. in iambic pentameter with a definite rhyme scheme

so·no·rous \sə-'nòr-əs, 'sä-nə-rəs\ *adj* **1** : giving out sound when struck **2** : loud, deep, or rich in sound : RESONANT **3** : high-sounding : IMPRESSIVE — **so·nor·i·ty** \sə-'nòr-ə-tē\ *n*

soon \'sün\ *adv* **1** : before long **2** : PROMPTLY, QUICKLY **3** *archaic* : EARLY **4** : WILLINGLY, READILY

soot \'sủt, 'sət, 'süt\ *n* : a fine black powder consisting chiefly of carbon that is formed when something burns and that colors smoke — **sooty** *adj*

sooth \'süth\ *n, archaic* : TRUTH

soothe \'süth̲\ *vb* **soothed; sooth·ing** **1** : to please by flattery or attention **2** : to calm down : COMFORT — **sooth·er** *n* — **sooth·ing·ly** *adv*

sooth·say·er \'süth-₁sā-ər\ *n* : one who foretells events — **sooth·say·ing** *n*

¹sop \'säp\ *n* : a conciliatory bribe, gift, or concession

²sop *vb* **sopped; sop·ping 1** : to steep or dip in or as if in a liquid **2** : to wet thoroughly : SOAK; *also* : to mop up (a liquid)

SOP *abbr* standard operating procedure; standing operating procedure

soph *abbr* sophomore

soph·ism \'sä-₁fi-zəm\ *n* **1** : an argument correct in form but embodying a subtle fallacy **2** : SOPHISTRY

soph·ist \'sä-fist\ *n* : PHILOSOPHER; *esp* : a captious or fallacious reasoner

so·phis·tic \sä-'fis-tik, sə-\ *or* **so·phis·ti·cal** \-ti-kəl\ *adj* : of or characteristic of sophists or sophistry **syn** fallacious, illogical, unreasonable, specious

so·phis·ti·cat·ed \sə-'fis-tə-₁kā-təd\ *adj* **1** : COMPLEX ⟨~ instruments⟩ **2** : made worldly-wise by wide experience **3** : intellectually appealing ⟨~ novel⟩ — **so·phis·ti·ca·tion** \-₁fis-tə-'kā-shən\ *n*

soph·ist·ry \'sä-fə-strē\ *n* : subtly deceptive reasoning or argument

soph·o·more \'säf-₁mȯr, 'sä-fə-\ *n* : a student in the second year of high school or college

soph·o·mor·ic \₁säf-'mȯr-ik, ₁sä-fə-\ *adj* **1** : being overconfident of knowledge but poorly informed and immature **2** : of, relating to, or characteristic of a sophomore ⟨a ~ prank⟩

So·pho·ni·as \₁sä-fə-'nī-əs, ₁sō-\ *n* : ZEPHANIAH

sop·o·rif·ic \₁sä-pə-'ri-fik\ *adj* **1** : causing sleep or drowsiness **2** : LETHARGIC

so·pra·no \sə-'pra-nō, -'prä-\ *n, pl* **-nos** [It, fr. *sopra* above, fr. L *supra*] **1** : the highest singing voice; *also* : a singer with this voice **2** : the highest part in a 4-part chorus — **soprano** *adj*

sor·bet \sȯr-'bā\ *n* : a fruit-flavored ice served for dessert or between courses as a palate refresher

sor·cery \'sȯr-sə-rē\ *n* [ME *sorcerie*, fr. OF, fr. *sorcier* sorcerer, fr. (assumed) VL *sortiarius*, fr. L *sort-, sors* chance, lot] : the use of magic : WITCHCRAFT — **sor·cer·er** \-rər\ *n* — **sor·cer·ess** \-rəs\ *n*

sor·did \'sȯr-dəd\ *adj* **1** : marked by baseness or grossness : VILE **2** : DIRTY, SQUALID — **sor·did·ly** *adv* — **sor·did·ness** *n*

¹sore \'sȯr\ *adj* **sor·er; sor·est 1** : causing pain or distress ⟨a ~ bruise⟩ **2** : painfully sensitive ⟨~ muscles⟩ **3** : SEVERE, INTENSE **4** : IRRITATED, ANGRY — **sore·ly** *adv* — **sore·ness** *n*

²sore *n* **1** : a sore spot on the body; *esp* : one (as an ulcer) with the tissues broken and usu. infected **2** : a source of pain or vexation

sore·head \'sȯr-₁hed, 'sȯr-\ *n* : a person easily angered or discontented

sore throat *n* : painful throat due to inflammation

sor·ghum \'sȯr-gəm\ *n* : a tall variable Old World tropical grass grown widely for its edible seed, for forage, or for its sweet juice which yields a syrup

so·ror·i·ty \sə-'rȯr-ə-tē\ *n, pl* **-ties** [ML *sororitas* sisterhood, fr. L *soror* sister] : a club of girls or women esp. at a college

¹sor·rel \'sȯr-əl\ *n* : a brownish orange to light brown color; *also* : a sorrel-colored animal (as a horse)

²sorrel *n* : any of various herbs having a sour juice

sor·row \'sär-ō\ *n* **1** : deep distress, sadness, or regret; *also* : resultant unhappy or unpleasant state **2** : a cause of grief or sadness **3** : a display of grief or sadness — **sor·row** *vb* — **sor·row·ful** \-fəl\ *adj* — **sor·row·ful·ly** \-f(ə-)lē\ *adv*

sor·ry \'sär-ē\ *adj* **sor·ri·er; -est 1** : feeling sorrow, regret, or penitence **2** : MOURNFUL, SAD **3** : causing sorrow, pity, or scorn : WRETCHED

¹sort \'sȯrt\ *n* **1** : a group of persons or things that have similar characteristics : CLASS **2** : WAY, MANNER **3** : QUALITY, NATURE **4** : an instance of sorting — **out of sorts 1** : somewhat ill **2** : GROUCHY, IRRITABLE

²sort *vb* **1** : to put in a certain place according to kind, class, or nature **2** : to be in accord : AGREE — **sort·er** *n*

sor·tie \'sȯr-tē, sȯr-'tē\ *n* **1** : a sudden issuing of troops from a defensive position against the enemy **2** : one mission or attack by one airplane

sort of *adv* : to a moderate degree

SOS \₁es-(₁)ō-'es\ *n* : a call or request for help or rescue

so–so \'sō-'sō\ *adv or adj* : PASSABLY

sot \'sät\ *n* : a habitual drunkard — **sot·tish** *adj* — **sot·tish·ly** *adv*

souf·flé \sü-'flā\ *n* [F, fr. *soufflé*, pp. of *souffler* to blow, puff up, fr. L *sufflare*, fr. *sub-* up + *flare* to blow] : a spongy dish made light in baking by stiffly beaten egg whites

sough \'saù, 'səf\ *vb* : to make a moaning or sighing sound — **sough** *n*

sought *past and past part of* SEEK

¹soul \'sōl\ *n* **1** : the immaterial essence of an individual life **2** : the spiritual principle embodied in human beings or the universe **3** : an active or essential part **4** : the moral and emotional nature of human beings **5** : spiritual or moral force **6** : PERSON ⟨a kindly ~⟩ **7** : a strong, positive feeling (as of intense sensitivity and emotional fervor) conveyed esp. by black American performers; *also* : NEGRITUDE — **souled** \'sōld\ *adj* — **soul·less** \'sōl-ləs\ *adj*

²soul *adj* **1** : of, relating to, or characteristic of black Americans or their culture ⟨~ food⟩ ⟨~ music⟩ **2** : designed for or controlled by blacks ⟨~ radio stations⟩

soul brother *n* : a black male

soul·ful \'sōl-fəl\ *adj* : full of or expressing deep feeling — **soul·ful·ly** *adv*

¹sound \'saùnd\ *adj* **1** : not diseased or sickly **2** : free from flaw or defect **3** : FIRM, STRONG **4** : free from error or fallacy : RIGHT **5** : LEGAL, VALID **6** : THOROUGH **7** : UNDISTURBED ⟨~ sleep⟩ **8** : showing good judgment — **sound·ly** *adv* — **sound·ness** *n*

²sound *n* **1** : the sensation of hearing; *also* : mechanical energy transmitted by longitudinal pressure waves (**sound waves**) (as in air) that is the stimulus to hearing **2** : something heard : NOISE, TONE; *also* : hearing distance : EARSHOT **3** : a musical style — **sound·less** *adj* — **sound·less·ly** *adv* — **sound·proof** \-₁prüf\ *adj or vb*

³sound *vb* **1** : to make or cause to make a sound **2** : to order or proclaim by a sound ⟨~ the alarm⟩ **3** : to convey a certain impression : SEEM **4** : to examine the condition of by causing to give out sounds — **sound·able** \'saùn-də-bəl\ *adj*

⁴sound *n* : a long passage of water wider than a strait often connecting two larger bodies of water ⟨Puget ~⟩

⁵sound *vb* **1** : to measure the depth of (water) esp. by a weighted line dropped from the surface : FATHOM **2** : PROBE **3** : to dive down suddenly ⟨the hooked fish ~ed⟩ — **sound·ing** *n*

sound·er \'saùn-dər\ *n* : one that sounds; *esp* : a device for making soundings

sound·stage \'saùnd-₁stāj\ *n* : the part of a motion-picture studio in which a production is filmed

soup \'süp\ *n* **1** : a liquid food with stock as its base and often containing pieces of solid food **2** : something having the consistency of soup **3** : an unfortunate predicament ⟨in the ~⟩

soup·çon \süp-'sōⁿ\ *n* [F, lit., suspicion] : a little bit : ¹TRACE 2

soup up *vb* : to increase the power of

soupy \'sü-pē\ *adj* **soup·i·er; -est 1** : having the consistency of soup **2** : densely foggy or cloudy

¹sour \'saùr\ *adj* **1** : having an acid or tart taste ⟨~ as vinegar⟩ **2** : SPOILED, PUTRID ⟨a ~ odor⟩ **3** : UNPLEASANT, DISAGREEABLE ⟨~ disposition⟩ — **sour·ish** *adj* — **sour·ly** *adv* — **sour·ness** *n*

²sour *vb* : to become or make sour

source \'sōrs\ *n* **1** : ORIGIN, BEGINNING **2** : a supplier of information **3** : the beginning of a stream of water

¹souse \'saús\ *vb* **soused; sous·ing 1** : PICKLE **2** : to plunge into a liquid **3** : DRENCH **4** : to make drunk

²souse *n* **1** : something (as pigs' feet) steeped in pickle **2** : a soaking in liquid **3** : DRUNKARD

¹south \'saúth\ *adv* : to or toward the south; *also* : into a state of decline

²south *adj* **1** : situated toward or at the south **2** : coming from the south

³south *n* **1** : the direction to the right of one facing east **2** : the compass point directly opposite to north **3** *cap* : regions or countries south of a specified or implied point; *esp* : the southeastern part of the U.S. — **south·er·ly** \'sə-thər-lē\ *adj or adv* — **south·ern** \'sə-thərn\ *adj* — **Sŏuth·ern·er** *n* — **south·ern·most** \-ˌmōst\ *adj* — **south·ward** \'saúth-wərd\ *adv or adj* — **south·wards** \-wərdz\ *adv*

South African *n* : a native or inhabitant of the Republic of South Africa — **South African** *adj*

south·east \saú-'thēst, *naut* saú-'ēst\ *n* **1** : the general direction between south and east **2** : the compass point midway between south and east **3** *cap* : regions or countries southeast of a specified or implied point — **southeast** *adj or adv* — **south·east·er·ly** *adv or adj* — **south·east·ern** \-'ēs-tərn\ *adj*

south·paw \'saúth-ˌpò\ *n* : a left-handed person; *esp* : a left-handed baseball pitcher — **southpaw** *adj*

south pole *n, often cap S&P* : the southernmost point of the earth

south·west \saúth-'west, *naut* saú-'west\ *n* **1** : the general direction between south and west **2** : the compass point midway between south and west **3** *cap* : regions or countries southwest of a specified or implied point — **southwest** *adj or adv* — **south·west·er·ly** *adv or adj* — **south·west·ern** \-'wes-tərn\ *adj*

sou·ve·nir \ˌsü-və-'nir\ *n* [F] : something serving as a reminder

sou'·west·er \saú-'wes-tər\ *n* : a long waterproof coat worn in storms at sea; *also* : a waterproof hat

¹sov·er·eign \'sä-vrən, -və-rən\ *n* **1** : one possessing the supreme power and authority in a state **2** : a gold coin of the United Kingdom

²sovereign *adj* **1** : EXCELLENT, FINE **2** : supreme in power or authority **3** : CHIEF, HIGHEST **4** : having independent authority

sov·er·eign·ty \-tē\ *n, pl* **-ties 1** : supremacy in rule or power **2** : power to govern without external control **3** : the supreme political power in a state

so·vi·et \'sō-vē-ˌet, 'sä-, -ət\ *n* **1** : an elected governmental council in a Communist country **2** *pl, cap* : the people and esp. the leaders of the U.S.S.R. — **soviet** *adj, often cap* — **so·vi·et·ize** *vb, often cap*

¹sow \'saú\ *n* : an adult female swine

²sow \'sō\ *vb* **sowed; sown** \'sōn\ *or* **sowed; sow·ing 1** : to plant seed esp. by scattering **2** : to strew with seed **3** : to scatter abroad — **sow·er** \'sō-ər\ *n*

sow bug \'saú-\ *n* : WOOD LOUSE

sox *pl of* SOCK

soy \'sòi\ *n* : a sauce made from soybeans fermented in brine

soy·bean \'sòi-ˌbēn\ *n* : an Asian legume widely grown for forage and for its edible seeds that yield a valuable oil (**soybean oil**); *also* : its seed

sp *abbr* **1** special **2** species **3** specimen **4** spelling **5** spirit

Sp *abbr* Spain

SP *abbr* **1** shore patrol; shore patrolman **2** shore police **3** specialist

spa \'spä\ *n* [*Spa*, watering place in Belgium] **1** : a resort with mineral springs **2** : a health and fitness facility **3** : a hot tub with a whirlpool device

¹space \'spās\ *n* **1** : a period of time **2** : some small measurable distance, area, or volume **3** : the limitless area in which all things exist and move **4** : an empty place **5** : the region beyond the earth's atmosphere **6** : a definite place (as a seat on a train or ship)

²space *vb* **spaced; spac·ing** : to place at intervals — **spac·er** *n*

space·age \'spās-ˌāj\ *adj* : of or relating to the age of space exploration

space·craft \-ˌkraft\ *n* : a vehicle for travel beyond the earth's atmosphere

space·flight \-ˌflīt\ *n* : flight beyond the earth's atmosphere

space heater *n* : a usu. portable device for heating a relatively small area

space·man \'spās-ˌman, -mən\ *n* : one who travels outside the earth's atmosphere

space·ship \-ˌship\ *n* : a vehicle used for space travel

space shuttle *n* : a reusable spacecraft designed to transport people and cargo between earth and space

space station *n* : a large artificial satellite serving as a base (as for scientific observation)

space suit *n* : a suit equipped to make life in space possible for its wearer

space walk *n* : a period of activity outside a spacecraft by an astronaut in space — **space·walk** \'spās-ˌwòk\ *vb* — **space·walk·er** *n*

spa·cious \'spā-shəs\ *adj* : very large in extent : ROOMY **syn** commodious, capacious, ample — **spa·cious·ly** *adv* — **spa·cious·ness** *n*

¹spade \'spād\ *n* : a shovel with a blade for digging — **spade·ful** *n*

²spade *vb* **spad·ed; spad·ing** : to dig with a spade — **spad·er** *n*

³spade *n* : any of a suit of playing cards marked with a black figure resembling an inverted heart with a short stem at the bottom

spa·dix \'spā-diks\ *n, pl* **spa·di·ces** \'spā-də-ˌsēz\ : a floral spike with a fleshy or succulent axis usu. enclosed in a spathe

spa·ghet·ti \spə-'ge-tē\ *n* [It, fr. pl. of *spaghetto*, dim. of *spago* cord, string] : thin solid pasta strings

¹span \'span\ *n* **1** : an English unit of length equal to nine inches (about 23 centimeters) **2** : a limited portion of time **3** : the spread (as of an arch) from one support to another

²span *vb* **spanned; span·ning 1** : MEASURE **2** : to extend across

³span *n* : a pair of animals (as mules) driven together

Span *abbr* Spanish

span·dex \'span-ˌdeks\ *n* : any of various elastic synthetic textile fibers

span·gle \'span-gəl\ *n* : a small disk of shining metal or plastic used esp. on a dress for ornament — **spangle** *vb*

Span·glish \'span-glish\ *n* : a combination of Spanish and English

Span·iard \'span-yərd\ *n* : a native or inhabitant of Spain

span·iel \'span-yəl\ *n* [ME *spaniell*, fr. MF *espaignol*, lit., Spaniard] : a dog of any of several breeds of mostly small and short-legged dogs usu. with long wavy hair and large drooping ears

spaniel

Span·ish \\'spa-nish\\ *n* **1** : the chief language of Spain and of the countries colonized by the Spanish **2** **Spanish** *pl* : the people of Spain — **Spanish** *adj*

Spanish American *n* : a resident of the U.S. whose native language is Spanish; *also* : a native or inhabitant of one of the countries of America in which Spanish is the national language — **Spanish–American** *adj*

Spanish fly *n* : a preparation of dried green European beetles noted as an aphrodisiac with often highly toxic side effects but not in reputable medical use

Spanish moss *n* : a plant related to the pineapple that grows in pendent tufts of grayish green filaments on trees from the southern U.S. to Argentina

Spanish rice *n* : rice cooked with onions, green peppers, and tomatoes

spank \\'spaŋk\\ *vb* : to hit on the buttocks with the open hand — **spank** *n*

spank·ing \\'spaŋ-kiŋ\\ *adj* : BRISK, LIVELY ⟨∼ breeze⟩ — **spanking** *adv*

span·ner \\'span-ər\\ *n, chiefly Brit* : WRENCH

¹spar \\'spär\\ *n* **1** : a stout pole **2** : a rounded wood or metal piece (as a mast, yard, boom, or gaff) for supporting sail rigging

²spar *vb* **sparred; spar·ring** : to box for practice without serious hitting; *also* : SKIRMISH, WRANGLE

¹spare \\'spar\\ *vb* **spared; spar·ing** **1** : to refrain from punishing or injuring : show mercy to ⟨∼d the prisoners⟩ **2** : to exempt from something ⟨∼ me the trouble⟩ **3** : to get along without ⟨can't ∼ a dime⟩ **4** : to use frugally or rarely ⟨don't ∼ the syrup⟩

²spare *adj* **spar·er; spar·est** **1** : held in reserve **2** : SUPERFLUOUS **3** : not liberal or profuse **4** : LEAN, THIN **5** : SCANTY **syn** meager, sparse, skimpy, exiguous, scant — **spare·ness** *n*

³spare *n* **1** : a duplicate kept in reserve; *esp* : a spare tire **2** : the knocking down of all the bowling pins with the first two balls

spar·ing \\'spar-iŋ\\ *adj* : SAVING, FRUGAL **syn** thrifty, economical, provident — **spar·ing·ly** *adv*

¹spark \\'spärk\\ *n* **1** : a small particle of a burning substance or a hot glowing particle struck from a mass (as by steel on flint) **2** : a short bright flash of electricity between two points **3** : SPARKLE **4** : a particle capable of being kindled or developed : GERM

²spark *vb* **1** : to emit or produce sparks **2** : to stir to activity : INCITE

³spark *vb* : WOO, COURT

¹spar·kle \\'spär-kəl\\ *vb* **spar·kled; spar·kling** **1** : FLASH, GLEAM **2** : to perform brilliantly **3** : EFFERVESCE — **spar·kler** *n*

²sparkle *n* **1** : GLEAM **2** : ANIMATION

spark plug *n* **1** : a device that produces a spark to ignite the fuel mixture in an engine cylinder **2** : one that begins something or drives something forward

spar·row \\'spar-ō\\ *n* : any of several small dull-colored singing birds

sparse \\'spärs\\ *adj* **spars·er; spars·est** : thinly scattered : SCANTY **syn** meager, spare, skimpy, exiguous, scant — **sparse·ly** *adv* — **sparse·ness** *n*

spasm \\'spa-zəm\\ *n* **1** : a sudden involuntary and abnormal muscular contraction **2** : a sudden, violent, and temporary effort, feeling, or outburst

spas·mod·ic \\spaz-'mä-dik\\ *adj* **1** : relating to or affected by or characterized by spasm ⟨∼ movements⟩; *also* : resembling a spasm **2** : INTERMITTENT — **spas·mod·i·cal·ly** \\-di-k(ə-)lē\\ *adv*

spas·tic \\'spas-tik\\ *adj* : of, relating to, marked by, or affected with muscular spasm ⟨∼ paralysis⟩ — **spastic** *n*

¹spat \\'spat\\ *past and past part of* SPIT

²spat *n, pl* **spat** *or* **spats** : a young bivalve mollusk (as an oyster)

³spat *n* : a gaiter covering instep and ankle

⁴spat *n* : a brief petty quarrel : DISPUTE

⁵spat *vb* **spat·ted; spat·ting** : to quarrel briefly

spat

spate \\'spāt\\ *n* : a sudden outburst

spathe \\'spāth\\ *n* : a sheathing bract or pair of bracts enclosing an inflorescence (as of the calla lily) and esp. a spadix on the same axis

spa·tial \\'spā-shəl\\ *adj* : of or relating to space — **spa·tial·ly** *adv*

spat·ter \\'spa-tər\\ *vb* **1** : to splash with drops of liquid **2** : to sprinkle around — **spatter** *n*

spat·u·la \\'spa-chə-lə\\ *n* : a flexible knifelike implement for scooping, spreading, or mixing soft substances

spav·in \\'spa-vən\\ *n* : a bony enlargement of the hock of a horse — **spav·ined** \\-vənd\\ *adj*

¹spawn \\'spón\\ *vb* [ME, fr. OF *espandre* to spread out, expand, fr. L *expandere*, fr. *ex-* out + *pandere* to spread] **1** : to produce eggs or offspring esp. in large numbers **2** : GENERATE — **spawn·er** *n*

²spawn *n* **1** : the eggs of water animals (as fishes or oysters) that lay many small eggs **2** : offspring esp. when produced in great quantities

spay \\'spā\\ *vb* **spayed; spay·ing** : to remove the ovaries of (a female animal)

SPCA *abbr* Society for the Prevention of Cruelty to Animals

SPCC *abbr* Society for the Prevention of Cruelty to Children

speak \\'spēk\\ *vb* **spoke** \\'spōk\\; **spo·ken** \\'spō-kən\\; **speak·ing** **1** : to utter words **2** : to express orally **3** : to mention in speech or writing **4** : to address an audience **5** : to use or be able to use (a language) in talking

speak·easy \\'spēk-ˌē-zē\\ *n, pl* **-eas·ies** : an illicit drinking place

speak·er \\'spē-kər\\ *n* **1** : one that speaks **2** : the presiding officer of a deliberative assembly **3** : LOUDSPEAKER

¹spear \\'spir\\ *n* **1** : a long-shafted weapon with a sharp point for thrusting or throwing **2** : a sharp-pointed instrument with barbs used in spearing fish — **spearman** \\-mən\\ *n*

²spear *vb* : to strike or pierce with or as if with a spear — **spear·er** *n*

³spear *n* : a usu. young blade, shoot, or sprout (as of asparagus)

spear·head \\-ˌhed\\ *n* : a leading force, element, or influence — **spearhead** *vb*

spear·mint \\-ˌmint\\ *n* : a common highly aromatic garden mint

spec *abbr* **1** special **2** specifically

spe·cial \\'spe-shəl\\ *adj* **1** : UNCOMMON, NOTEWORTHY **2** : particularly favored **3** : INDIVIDUAL, UNIQUE **4** : EXTRA, ADDITIONAL **5** : confined to or designed for a definite field of action, purpose, or occasion — **special** *n*

special delivery *n* : delivery of mail by messenger for an extra fee

special effects *n pl* : images in a television or film production added after filming is completed to enhance believability

Special Forces *n pl* : a branch of the army composed of soldiers specially trained in guerrilla warfare

spe·cial·ist \'spe-shə-list\ *n* **1** : a person who specializes in a particular branch of learning or activity **2** : any of four enlisted ranks in the army corresponding to the grades of corporal through sergeant first class

spe·cial·ize \'spe-shə-ˌlīz\ *vb* **-ized; -iz·ing** : to concentrate one's efforts in a special activity or field; *also* : to change in an adaptive manner — **spe·cial·i·za·tion** \ˌspe-shə-lə-'zā-shən\ *n*

spe·cial·ly \'spe-shə-lē\ *adv* **1** : in a special manner **2** : for a special purpose : in particular

spe·cial·ty \'spe-shəl-tē\ *n, pl* **-ties 1** : a particular quality or detail **2** : a product of a special kind or of special excellence **3** : something (as a discipline) in which one specializes

spe·cie \'spē-shē, -sē\ *n* : money in coin

spe·cies \'spē-shēz, -sēz\ *n, pl* **spe·cies** [ME, fr. L, appearance, kind, species, fr. *specere* to look] **1** : SORT, KIND **2** : a category of biological classification ranking just below the genus or subgenus and comprising closely related organisms potentially able to breed with one another

specif *abbr* specific; specifically

¹spe·cif·ic \spi-'si-fik\ *adj* **1** : having a unique effect or influence or reacting in only one way or with only one thing ⟨∼ antibodies⟩ ⟨∼ enzymes⟩ **2** : DEFINITE, EXACT **3** : of, relating to, or constituting a species — **spe·cif·i·cal·ly** \-fi-k(ə-)lē\ *adv*

²specific *n* : something specific : DETAIL, PARTICULAR — usu. used in pl.

spec·i·fi·ca·tion \ˌspe-sə-fə-'kā-shən\ *n* **1** : the act or process of specifying **2** : a description of work to be done and materials to be used (as in building) — usu. used in pl.

specific gravity *n* : the ratio of the density of a substance to the density of some substance (as water) taken as a standard when both densities are obtained by weighing in air

spec·i·fy \'spe-sə-ˌfī\ *vb* **-fied; -fy·ing** : to mention or name explicitly

spec·i·men \'spe-sə-mən\ *n* : an item or part typical of a group or whole

spe·cious \'spē-shəs\ *adj* : seeming to be genuine, correct, or beautiful but not really so ⟨∼ reasoning⟩

speck \'spek\ *n* **1** : a small spot or blemish **2** : a small particle — **speck** *vb*

speck·le \'spe-kəl\ *n* : a little speck — **speck·le** *vb*

¹specs \'speks\ *n pl* : GLASSES

²specs *n pl* : SPECIFICATIONS

spec·ta·cle \'spek-ti-kəl\ *n* **1** : an unusual or impressive public display **2** *pl* : GLASSES — **spec·ta·cled** \-kəld\ *adj*

spec·tac·u·lar \spek-'ta-kyə-lər\ *adj* : exciting to see : SENSATIONAL

spec·ta·tor \'spek-ˌtā-tər\ *n* : a person who looks on (as at a sports event) **syn** observer, witness, bystander, onlooker, eyewitness

spec·ter *or* **spec·tre** \'spek-tər\ *n* : a visible disembodied spirit : GHOST

spec·tral \'spek-trəl\ *adj* **1** : of, relating to, or resembling a specter **2** : of, relating to, or made by a spectrum

spec·tro·gram \'spek-trə-ˌgram\ *n* : a photograph or diagram of a spectrum

spec·tro·graph \-ˌgraf\ *n* : an instrument for dispersing radiation into a spectrum and photographing or mapping the spectrum — **spec·tro·graph·ic** \ˌspek-trə-'gra-fik\ *adj* — **spec·tro·graph·i·cal·ly** \-fi-k(ə-)lē\ *adv*

spec·trom·e·ter \spek-'trä-mə-tər\ *n* : an instrument for measuring spectra — **spec·tro·met·ric** \ˌspek-trə-'me-trik\ *adj* — **spec·trom·e·try** \spek-'trä-mə-trē\ *n*

spec·tro·scope \'spek-trə-ˌskōp\ *n* : an instrument that produces spectra esp. of visible electromagnetic radiation — **spec·tro·scop·ic** \ˌspek-trə-'skä-pik\ *adj* — **spec·tro·scop·i·cal·ly** \-pi-k(ə-)lē\ *adv* — **spec·tros-**

co·pist \spek-'träs-kə-pist\ *n* — **spec·tros·co·py** \-pē\ *n*

spec·trum \'spek-trəm\ *n, pl* **spec·tra** \-trə\ *or* **spec·trums** [NL, fr. L, appearance, fr. *specere* to look] **1** : a series of colors formed when a beam of white light is dispersed (as by a prism) so that its parts are arranged in the order of their wavelengths **2** : a series of radiations arranged in regular order **3** : a continuous sequence or range ⟨a wide ∼ of political opinions⟩

spec·u·late \'spe-kyə-ˌlāt\ *vb* **-lat·ed; -lat·ing** [L *speculari* to spy out, examine, fr. *specula* watchtower, fr. *specere* to look, look at] **1** : to think or wonder about a subject **2** : to take a business risk in hope of gain **syn** reason, think, deliberate, cogitate — **spec·u·la·tion** \ˌspe-kyə-'lā-shən\ *n* — **spec·u·la·tive** \'spe-kyə-ˌlā-tiv\ *adj* — **spec·u·la·tive·ly** *adv* — **spec·u·la·tor** \-ˌlā-tər\ *n*

speech \'spēch\ *n* **1** : the act of speaking **2** : TALK, CONVERSATION **3** : a public talk or lecture **4** : LANGUAGE, DIALECT **5** : an individual manner of speaking **6** : the power of speaking — **speech·less** *adj*

¹speed \'spēd\ *n* **1** *archaic* : SUCCESS **2** : SWIFTNESS, RAPIDITY **3** : rate of motion or performance **4** : a transmission gear (as of a bicycle) **5** : METHAMPHETAMINE; *also* : a related drug **syn** haste, hurry, dispatch, celerity — **speed·i·ly** \'spē-də-lē\ *adv* — **speedy** *adj*

²speed *vb* **sped** \'spēd\ *or* **speed·ed; speed·ing 1** *archaic* : PROSPER; *also* : GET ALONG, FARE **2** : to go fast; *esp* : to go at an excessive or illegal speed **3** : to cause to go faster — **speed·er** *n*

speed·boat \-ˌbōt\ *n* : a fast motorboat

speed bump *n* : a low raised ridge across a roadway (as in a parking lot) to limit vehicle speed

speed·om·e·ter \spi-'dä-mə-tər\ *n* : an instrument for indicating speed

speed·up \'spēd-ˌəp\ *n* : ACCELERATION

speed·way \-ˌwā\ *n* : a racecourse for motor vehicles

speed·well \'spēd-ˌwel\ *n* : a low creeping plant that bears spikes of small usu. bluish flowers and is related to the snapdragon

¹spell \'spel\ *vb* **spelled** \'speld, 'spelt\; **spell·ing 1** : to name, write, or print in order the letters of a word **2** : MEAN

²spell *n* [ME, talk, tale, fr. OE] **1** : a magic formula : INCANTATION **2** : a controlling influence

³spell *n* **1** : one's turn at work or duty **2** : a stretch of a specified kind of weather **3** : a period of bodily or mental distress or disorder : ATTACK

⁴spell *vb* **spelled** \'speld\; **spell·ing** : to take the place of for a time in work or duty : RELIEVE

spell·bind·er \-ˌbīn-dər\ *n* : a speaker of compelling eloquence

spell·bound \-ˌbau̇nd\ *adj* : held by or as if by a spell : FASCINATED

spell·er \'spe-lər\ *n* **1** : one who spells words **2** : a book with exercises for teaching spelling

spelt *chiefly Brit past and past part of* SPELL

spe·lunk·er \spi-'ləŋ-kər, 'spē-ˌləŋ-kər\ *n* [L *spelunca* cave, fr. Gk *spēlynx*] : one who makes a hobby of exploring caves — **spe·lunk·ing** *n*

spend \'spend\ *vb* **spent** \'spent\; **spend·ing 1** : to pay out : EXPEND **2** : WEAR OUT, EXHAUST; *also* : to consume wastefully **3** : to cause or permit to elapse : PASS — **spend·er** *n*

spend·thrift \'spend-ˌthrift\ *n* : one who spends wastefully or recklessly

spent \'spent\ *adj* : drained of energy

sperm \'spərm\ *n, pl* **sperm** *or* **sperms 1** : SEMEN **2** : a male gamete

sper·ma·to·zo·on \(ˌ)spər-ˌma-tə-'zō-ˌän, -'zō-ən\ *n, pl* **-zoa** \-'zō-ə\ : a motile male gamete of an animal usu. with a rounded or elongated head and a long posterior flagellum

sperm cell *n* : SPERM 2

sper·mi·cide \\'spər-mə-ˌsīd\ *n* : a preparation or substance used to kill sperm — **sper·mi·cid·al** \ˌspər-mə-'sī-dəl\ *adj*

sperm whale *n* : a whale with conical teeth, no whalebone, and a large fluid-containing cavity in the head

spew \\'spyü\ *vb* : VOMIT

SPF *abbr* sun protection factor

sp gr *abbr* specific gravity

sphag·num \\'sfag-nəm\ *n* : any of a genus of atypical mosses that grow in wet acid areas where their remains become compacted with other plant debris to form peat; *also* : a mass of these mosses

sphere \\'sfir\ *n* [ME *spere* globe, celestial sphere, fr. MF *espere*, fr. L *sphaera*, fr. Gk *sphaira*, lit., ball] **1** : a globe-shaped body : BALL **2** : a celestial body **3** : a solid figure so shaped that every point on its surface is an equal distance from the center **4** : range of action or influence — **spher·i·cal** \\'sfir-i-kəl, 'sfer-\ *adj* — **spher·i·cal·ly** \-i-k(ə-)lē\ *adv*

spher·oid \\'sfir-ˌoid, 'sfer-\ *n* : a figure similar to a sphere but not perfectly round — **sphe·roi·dal** \sfir-'oi-dəl\ *adj*

sphinc·ter \\'sfiŋk-tər\ *n* : a muscular ring that closes a bodily opening

sphinx \\'sfiŋks\ *n, pl* **sphinx·es** *or* **sphin·ges** \\'sfin-ˌjēz\ **1** : a winged monster in Greek mythology having a woman's head and a lion's body and noted for killing anyone unable to answer its riddle **2** : an enigmatic or mysterious person **3** : an ancient Egyptian image having the body of a lion and the head of a man, ram, or hawk

spice \\'spīs\ *n* **1** : any of various aromatic plant products (as pepper or nutmeg) used to season or flavor foods **2** : something that adds interest and relish — **spice** *vb* — **spicy** *adj*

spick–and–span *or* **spic–and–span** \ˌspik-ənd-'span\ *adj* : quite new; *also* : spotlessly clean

spic·ule \\'spi-kyül\ *n* : a slender pointed body esp. of calcium or silica ⟨sponge ∼s⟩

spi·der \\'spī-dər\ *n* **1** : any of an order of arachnids that have a 2-part body, eight legs, and two or more pairs of abdominal organs for spinning threads of silk used esp. in making webs for catching prey **2** : a castiron frying pan — **spi·dery** *adj*

spider mite *n* : any of several small web-spinning mites that attack forage and crop plants

spider plant *n* : a houseplant of the lily family having long green leaves usu. striped with white and producing tufts of small plants on long hanging stems

spi·der·web \\'spī-dər-ˌweb\ *n* : the web spun by a spider

spiel \\'spēl\ *vb* : to talk in a fast, smooth, and usu. colorful manner — **spiel** *n*

spig·ot \\'spi-gət, -kət\ *n* : FAUCET

¹spike \\'spīk\ *n* **1** : a very large nail **2** : any of various pointed projections (as on the sole of a shoe to prevent slipping) — **spiky** *adj*

²spike *vb* **spiked; spik·ing 1** : to fasten with spikes **2** : to put an end to : QUASH ⟨∼ a rumor⟩ **3** : to pierce with or impale on a spike **4** : to add alcoholic liquor to (a drink)

³spike *n* **1** : an ear of grain **2** : a long cluster of usu. stemless flowers

¹spill \\'spil\ *vb* **spilled** \\'spild, 'spilt\ *also* **spilt** \\'spilt\; **spill·ing 1** : to cause or allow to fall, flow, or run out esp. unintentionally **2** : to cause (blood) to flow **3** : to run out or over with resulting loss or waste **4** : to let out : DIVULGE — **spill·able** *adj*

²spill *n* **1** : an act of spilling; *also* : a fall from a horse or vehicle or an erect position **2** : something spilled

spill·way \-ˌwā\ *n* : a passage for surplus water to run over or around an obstruction (as a dam)

¹spin \\'spin\ *vb* **spun** \\'spən\; **spin·ning 1** : to draw out (fiber) and twist into thread; *also* : to form (thread) by such means **2** : to form thread by extruding a sticky quickly hardening fluid; *also* : to construct from such thread ⟨spiders ∼ their webs⟩ **3** : to produce slowly and by degrees ⟨∼ a story⟩ **4** : TWIRL **5** : WHIRL, REEL ⟨my head is *spinning*⟩ **6** : to move rapidly along — **spin·ner** *n*

²spin *n* **1** : a rapid rotating motion **2** : an excursion in a wheeled vehicle

spin·ach \\'spi-nich\ *n* : a dark green herb grown for its edible leaves

spi·nal \\'spīn-əl\ *adj* : of or relating to the backbone or spinal cord — **spi·nal·ly** *adv*

spinal column *n* : BACKBONE

spinal cord *n* : the thick cord of nervous tissue that extends from the brain along the back in the cavity of the backbone and carries nerve impulses to and from the brain

spinal nerve *n* : any of the paired nerves which arise from the spinal cord and pass to various parts of the body and of which there are normally 31 pairs in human beings

spin·dle \\'spind-əl\ *n* **1** : a round tapering stick or rod by which fibers are twisted in spinning **2** : a turned part of a piece of furniture ⟨the ∼s of a chair⟩ **3** : a slender pin or rod which turns or on which something else turns

spin·dling \\'spind-liŋ\ *adj* : SPINDLY

spin·dly \\'spind-lē\ *adj* : being long or tall and thin and usu. weak

spin·drift \\'spin-ˌdrift\ *n* : spray blown from waves

spine \\'spīn\ *n* **1** : BACKBONE **2** : a stiff sharp process esp. on a plant or animal **3** : the part of a book where the pages are attached — **spine·less** *adj* — **spiny** *adj*

spi·nel \spə-'nel\ *n* : a hard crystalline mineral of variable color used as a gem

spin·et \\'spi-nət\ *n* **1** : an early harpsichord having a single keyboard and only one string for each note **2** : a small upright piano

spin·na·ker \\'spi-ni-kər\ *n* : a large triangular sail set on a long light pole

spinning jen·ny \-'je-nē\ *n* : an early multiple-spindle machine for spinning wool or cotton

spinning wheel *n* : a small machine for spinning thread or yarn in which a large wheel drives a single spindle

spin–off \\'spin-ˌof\ *n* **1** : a usu. useful by-product **2** : something (as a TV show) derived from an earlier work — **spin off** *vb*

spin·ster \\'spin-stər\ *n* : an unmarried woman past the common age for marrying — **spin·ster·hood** \-ˌhud\ *n*

spiny lobster *n* : any of several edible crustaceans differing from the related lobster in lacking the large front claws and in having a very spiny carapace

¹spi·ral \\'spī-rəl\ *adj* : winding or coiling around a center or axis and usu. getting closer to or farther away from it — **spi·ral·ly** *adv*

²spiral *n* **1** : something that has a spiral form; *also* : a single turn in a spiral object **2** : a continuously spreading and accelerating increase or decrease

³spiral *vb* **-raled** *or* **-ralled; -ral·ing** *or* **-ral·ling 1** : to move and esp. to rise or fall in a spiral course **2** : to form into a spiral

spi·rant \\'spī-rənt\ *n* : a consonant (as \f\, \s\, \sh\) uttered with decided friction of the breath against some part of the oral passage — **spirant** *adj*

spire \\'spīr\ *n* **1** : a slender tapering stalk (as of grass) **2** : a pointed tip (as of an antler) **3** : STEEPLE — **spiry** *adj*

spi·rea *or* **spi·raea** \spī-'rē-ə\ *n* : any of a genus of shrubs related to the roses with dense clusters of small white or pink flowers

¹spir·it \\'spir-ət\ *n* [ME, fr. OF or L; OF, fr. L *spiritus*, lit., breath, fr. *spirare* to blow, breathe] **1** : a life-giving force; *also* : the animating principle : SOUL **2** *cap* : HOLY SPIRIT **3** : SPECTER, GHOST **4** : PERSON **5** : DISPOSITION, MOOD **6** : VIVACITY, ARDOR **7** : essential or real meaning : INTENT **8** : distilled alcoholic liquor **9** : LOYALTY ⟨school ∼⟩ — **spir·it·less** *adj*

²**spirit** *vb* : to carry off secretly or mysteriously

spir·it·ed \'spir-ə-təd\ *adj* 1 : ANIMATED, LIVELY 2 : COURAGEOUS

¹**spir·i·tu·al** \'spir-i-chəl, -chə-wəl\ *adj* 1 : of, relating to, consisting of, or affecting the spirit : INCORPOREAL 2 : of or relating to sacred matters 3 : ecclesiastical rather than lay or temporal — **spir·i·tu·al·i·ty** \spiri-chə-'wa-lə-tē\ *n* — **spir·i·tu·al·ize** \'spir-i-chə-,līz, -chə-wə-\ *vb* — **spir·i·tu·al·ly** *adv*

²**spiritual** *n* : a religious song originating among blacks of the southern U.S.

spir·i·tu·al·ism \'spir-i-chə-,li-zəm, -chə-wə-\ *n* : a belief that spirits of the dead communicate with the living usu. through a medium — **spir·i·tu·al·ist** \-list\ *n*, *often cap* — **spir·i·tu·al·is·tic** \,spir-i-chə-'lis-tik, -chə-wə-\ *adj*

spir·i·tu·ous \'spir-i-chəs, -chə-wəs; 'spir-ə-təs\ *adj* : containing alcohol

spi·ro·chete *also* **spi·ro·chaete** \'spī-rə-,kēt\ *n* : any of an order of spirally undulating bacteria including those causing syphilis and Lyme disease

spirt *var of* SPURT

¹**spit** \'spit\ *n* 1 : a thin pointed rod for holding meat over a fire 2 : a point of land that runs out into the water

²**spit** *vb* **spit·ted; spit·ting** : to pierce with or as if with a spit

³**spit** *vb* **spit** *or* **spat** \'spat\; **spit·ting** 1 : to eject (saliva) from the mouth 2 : to express by or as if by spitting 3 : to rain or snow lightly

⁴**spit** *n* 1 : SALIVA 2 : perfect likeness ⟨~ and image of his father⟩

spit·ball \'spit-,bȯl\ *n* 1 : paper chewed and rolled into a ball to be thrown as a missile 2 : a baseball pitch delivered after the ball has been moistened with saliva or sweat

¹**spite** \'spīt\ *n* : ill will with a wish to annoy, anger, or frustrate : petty malice **syn** malignity, spleen, grudge, malevolence — **spite·ful** \-fəl\ *adj* — **spite·ful·ly** *adv* — **spite·ful·ness** *n* — **in spite of** : in defiance or contempt of : NOTWITHSTANDING

²**spite** *vb* **spit·ed; spit·ing** : to treat maliciously : ANNOY, OFFEND

spit·tle \'spit-ᵊl\ *n* : SALIVA

spit·tle·bug \-,bəg\ *n* : any of a family of leaping insects with froth-secreting larvae that are related to aphids

spit·toon \spi-'tün\ *n* : a receptacle for spit

splash \'splash\ *vb* 1 : to dash a liquid about 2 : to scatter a liquid on : SPATTER 3 : to fall or strike with a splashing noise **syn** sprinkle, bespatter, douse, splatter — **splash** *n*

splash·down \'splash-,daȯn\ *n* : the landing of a manned spacecraft in the ocean — **splash down** *vb*

splat·ter \'spla-tər\ *vb* : SPATTER — **splatter** *n*

¹**splay** \'splā\ *vb* : to spread outward or apart — **splay** *n*

²**splay** *adj* 1 : spread out : turned outward 2 : AWKWARD, CLUMSY

spleen \'splēn\ *n* 1 : a vascular organ located near the stomach in most vertebrates that is concerned esp. with the filtration and storage of blood, destruction of red blood cells, and production of lymphocytes 2 : SPITE, MALICE **syn** malignity, grudge, malevolence, ill will, spitefulness

splen·did \'splen-dəd\ *adj* [L *splendidus*, fr. *splendēre* to shine] 1 : SHINING, BRILLIANT 2 : SHOWY, GORGEOUS 3 : ILLUSTRIOUS 4 : EXCELLENT **syn** resplendent, glorious, sublime, superb — **splen·did·ly** *adv*

splen·dor \'splen-dər\ *n* 1 : BRILLIANCE 2 : POMP, MAGNIFICENCE

splen·dour *chiefly Brit var of* SPLENDOR

sple·net·ic \spli-'ne-tik\ *adj* : marked by bad temper or spite

splen·ic \'sple-nik\ *adj* : of, relating to, or located in the spleen

splice \'splīs\ *vb* **spliced; splic·ing** 1 : to unite (as two ropes) by weaving the strands together 2 : to unite (as two lengths of film) by connecting the ends together — **splice** *n*

splint \'splint\ *n* 1 : a thin strip of wood interwoven with others to make something (as a basket) 2 : material or a device used to protect and keep in place an injured body part (as a broken arm)

¹**splin·ter** \'splin-tər\ *n* : a thin piece of something split off lengthwise : SLIVER

²**splinter** *vb* : to split into splinters

split \'split\ *vb* **split; split·ting** 1 : to divide lengthwise or along a grain or seam 2 : to burst or break in pieces 3 : to divide into parts or sections 4 : LEAVE **syn** rend, cleave, rip, tear — **split** *n*

split–lev·el \'split-'le-vəl\ *n* : a house divided so that the floor in one part is about halfway between two floors in the other

split personality *n* : SCHIZOPHRENIA; *also* : MULTIPLE PERSONALITY

split·ting *adj* : causing a piercing sensation ⟨~ headache⟩

splotch \'spläch\ *n* : BLOTCH

splurge \'splərj\ *vb* **splurged; splurging** : to spend more than usual esp. on oneself — **splurge** *n*

splut·ter \'splə-tər\ *n* : SPUTTER — **splutter** *vb*

¹**spoil** \'spȯil\ *n* : PLUNDER ⟨~s of war⟩

²**spoil** *vb* **spoiled** \'spȯild, 'spȯilt\ *or* **spoilt** \'spȯilt\; **spoil·ing** 1 : ROB, PILLAGE 2 : to damage seriously : RUIN 3 : to impair the quality or effect of 4 : to damage the disposition of by pampering; *also* : INDULGE, CODDLE 5 : DECAY, ROT 6 : to have an eager desire ⟨~ing for a fight⟩ **syn** injure, harm, hurt, mar — **spoil·age** \'spȯi-lij\ *n*

spoil·er \'spȯi-lər\ *n* 1 : one that spoils 2 : a device (as on an airplane or automobile) used to disrupt airflow and decrease lift

spoil·sport \'spȯil-,spȯrt\ *n* : one who spoils the fun of others

¹**spoke** \'spōk\ *past & archaic past part of* SPEAK

²**spoke** *n* : any of the rods extending from the hub of a wheel to the rim

spo·ken \'spō-kən\ *past part of* SPEAK

spokes·man \'spōks-mən\ *n* : a person who speaks as the representative of another or others

spokes·per·son \-,pər-sən\ *n* : SPOKESMAN

spokes·wom·an \-,wu̇-mən\ *n* : a woman who speaks as the representative of another or others

spo·li·a·tion \,spō-lē-'ā-shən\ *n* : the act of plundering : the state of being plundered

¹**sponge** \'spənj\ *n* 1 : an elastic porous water-absorbing mass of fibers that forms the skeleton of various primitive sea animals; *also* : any of a phylum of chiefly marine sea animals that are the source of natural sponges 2 : a spongelike or porous mass or material — **spongy** \'spən-jē\ *adj*

²**sponge** *vb* **sponged; spong·ing** 1 : to bathe or wipe with a sponge 2 : to live at another's expense 3 : to gather sponges — **spong·er** *n*

sponge cake *n* : a light cake made without shortening

sponge rubber *n* : a cellular rubber resembling natural sponge

spon·sor \'spän-sər\ *n* [LL, fr. L, guarantor, surety, fr. *spondēre* to promise] 1 : one who takes the responsibility for some other person or thing : SURETY 2 : GODPARENT 3 : a business firm that pays the cost of a radio or television program usu. in return for advertising time during its course — **sponsor** *vb* — **spon·sor·ship** *n*

spon·ta·ne·ous \spän-'tā-nē-əs\ *adj* [LL *spontaneus*, fr. L *sponte* of one's free will, voluntarily] 1 : done or produced freely or naturally 2 : acting or taking place without external force or cause **syn** impulsive, instinctive, automatic, unpremeditated — **spon·ta·ne·ity** \,spän-tə-'nē-ə-tē, -'nā-\ *n* — **spon·ta·ne·ous·ly** *adv*

spontaneous combustion *n* : a bursting into flame of material through heat produced within itself by chemical action (as oxidation)

spoof \'spüf\ *vb* **1** : DECEIVE, HOAX **2** : to make good-natured fun of — **spoof** *n*

¹**spook** \'spük\ *n* : GHOST, APPARITION — **spooky** *adj*

²**spook** *vb* : FRIGHTEN

spool \'spül\ *n* : a cylinder on which flexible material (as thread) is wound

spoon \'spün\ *n* [ME, fr. OE *spōn* splinter, chip] **1** : an eating or cooking implement consisting of a small shallow bowl with a handle **2** : a metal piece used on a fishing line as a lure — **spoon** *vb* — **spoon•ful** *n*

spoon•bill \'spün-‚bil\ *n* : any of several wading birds related to the ibises that have a bill with a broad flat tip

spoon–feed \-‚fēd\ *vb* **-fed** \-‚fed\; **-feed•ing** : to feed by means of a spoon

spoor \'spür, 'spōr\ *n* : a track, a trail, a scent, or droppings esp. of a wild animal

spo•rad•ic \spə-'ra-dik\ *adj* : occurring now and then **syn** occasional, rare, scarce, infrequent, uncommon — **spo•rad•i•cal•ly** \-di-k(ə-)lē\ *adv*

spore \'spōr\ *n* : a primitive usu. one-celled often environmentally resistant dormant or reproductive body produced by plants and some microorganisms

¹**sport** \'spōrt\ *vb* [ME, to divert, disport, short for *disporten*, fr. MF *desporter*, fr. *des-* (fr. L *dis-* apart) + *porter* to carry, fr. L *portare*] **1** : to amuse oneself : FROLIC **2** : SHOW OFF **1** — **sport•ive** *adj*

²**sport** *n* **1** : a source of diversion : PASTIME **2** : physical activity engaged in for pleasure **3** : JEST **4** : MOCKERY ⟨make ∼ of his efforts⟩ **5** : BUTT, LAUGHINGSTOCK **6** : one who accepts results cheerfully whether favorable or not **7** : an individual exhibiting marked deviation from its normal type esp. as a result of mutation **syn** play, frolic, fun, recreation — **sporty** *adj*

³**sport** *or* **sports** *adj* : of, relating to, or suitable for sport or casual wear ⟨∼ coats⟩

sport fish *n* : a fish noted for the sport it affords anglers

sports•cast \'spōrts-‚kast\ *n* : a broadcast dealing with sports events — **sports•cast•er** \-‚kas-tər\ *n*

sports•man \'spōrts-mən\ *n* **1** : a person who engages in sports (as in hunting or fishing) **2** : one who plays fairly and wins or loses gracefully — **sports•man•like** \-‚līk\ *adj* — **sports•man•ship** *n*

sports•wom•an \-‚wü-mən\ *n* : a woman who engages in sports

sports•writ•er \-‚rī-tər\ *n* : one who writes about sports esp. for a newspaper — **sports•writ•ing** *n*

¹**spot** \'spät\ *n* **1** : STAIN, BLEMISH **2** : a small part different (as in color) from the main part **3** : LOCATION, SITE — **spot•less** *adj* — **spot•less•ly** *adv* — **on the spot 1** : at the place of action **2** : in difficulty or danger

²**spot** *vb* **spot•ted; spot•ting 1** : to mark or disfigure with spots **2** : to pick out : RECOGNIZE, IDENTIFY

³**spot** *adj* **1** : being, done, or originating on the spot ⟨a ∼ broadcast⟩ **2** : paid upon delivery **3** : made at random or at a few key points ⟨a ∼ check⟩

spot–check \'spät-‚chek\ *vb* : to make a spot check of

spot•light \-‚līt\ *n* **1** : a circle of brilliant light projected upon a particular area, person, or object (as on a stage); *also* : the device that produces this light **2** : public notice — **spotlight** *vb*

spotted owl *n* : a rare large dark brown dark-eyed owl of humid old growth forests and thickly wooded canyons from British Columbia to southern California and central Mexico

spot•ter \'spä-tər\ *n* **1** : one that keeps watch : OBSERVER **2** : one that removes spots

spot•ty \'spä-tē\ *adj* **spot•ti•er; -est** : uneven in quality; *also* : sparsely distributed ⟨∼ attendance⟩

spou•sal \'spaü-zəl, -səl\ *n* : MARRIAGE **2**, WEDDING — usu. used in pl. — **spou•sal** \'spaü-zəl, -səl\ *adj*

spouse \'spaüs\ *n* : one's husband or wife

¹**spout** \'spaüt\ *vb* **1** : to eject or issue forth forcibly and freely ⟨wells ∼ing oil⟩ **2** : to speak pompously

²**spout** *n* **1** : a pipe or hole through which liquid spouts **2** : a jet of liquid; *esp* : WATERSPOUT **2**

spp *abbr, pl* species

¹**sprain** \'sprān\ *n* : a sudden or severe twisting of a joint with stretching or tearing of ligaments; *also* : a sprained condition

²**sprain** *vb* : to subject to sprain

sprat \'sprat\ *n* **1** : a small European herring **2** : a young herring

sprawl \'sprôl\ *vb* **1** : to lie or sit with limbs spread out awkwardly **2** : to spread out irregularly — **sprawl** *n*

¹**spray** \'sprā\ *n* : a usu. flowering branch; *also* : a decorative arrangement of flowers and foliage

²**spray** *n* **1** : liquid flying in small drops like water blown from a wave **2** : a jet of fine vapor (as from an atomizer) **3** : an instrument (as an atomizer) for scattering fine liquid

³**spray** *vb* **1** : to scatter or let fall in a spray **2** : to discharge spray on or into — **spray•er** *n*

spray can *n* : a pressurized container from which aerosols are sprayed

spray gun *n* : a device for spraying liquids (as paint or insecticide)

¹**spread** \'spred\ *vb* **spread; spread•ing 1** : to scatter over a surface **2** : to flatten out : open out **3** : to distribute over a period of time or among many persons **4** : to cover something with ⟨∼ rugs on the floor⟩ **5** : to prepare for a meal ⟨∼ a table⟩ **6** : to pass on from person to person **7** : to stretch, force, or push apart — **spread•er** *n*

²**spread** *n* **1** : the act or process of spreading **2** : EXPANSE, EXTENT **3** : a prominent display in a periodical **4** : a food to be spread on bread or crackers **5** : a cloth cover for a bed **6** : distance between two points : GAP

spread•sheet \'spred-‚shēt\ *n* : an accounting program for a computer

spree \'sprē\ *n* : an unrestrained outburst ⟨buying ∼⟩; *esp* : a drinking bout

sprig \'sprig\ *n* : a small shoot or twig

spright•ly \'sprīt-lē\ *adj* **spright•li•er; -est** : LIVELY, SPIRITED **syn** animated, vivacious, gay — **spright•li•ness** *n*

¹**spring** \'spriŋ\ *vb* **sprang** \'spraŋ\ *or* **sprung** \'sprəŋ\; **sprung; spring•ing 1** : to move suddenly upward or forward **2** : to grow quickly ⟨weeds *sprang* up overnight⟩ **3** : to come from by birth or descent **4** : to move quickly by elastic force **5** : WARP **6** : to develop (a leak) through the seams **7** : to cause to close suddenly ⟨∼ a trap⟩ **8** : to make known suddenly ⟨∼ a surprise⟩ **9** : to make lame : STRAIN

²**spring** *n* **1** : a source of supply; *esp* : an issuing of water from the ground **2** : SOURCE, ORIGIN; *also* : MOTIVE **3** : the season between winter and summer **4** : an elastic body or device that recovers its original shape when it is released after being distorted **5** : the act or an instance of leaping up or forward **6** : RESILIENCE — **springy** *adj*

spring•board \'spriŋ-‚bōrd\ *n* : a springy board used in jumping or vaulting or for diving

spring fever *n* : a lazy or restless feeling often associated with the onset of spring

spring tide *n* : a tide of greater-than-average range that occurs at each new moon and full moon

spring•time \'spriŋ-‚tīm\ *n* : the season of spring

¹**sprin•kle** \'spriŋ-kəl\ *vb* **sprin•kled; sprin•kling** : to scatter in small drops or particles — **sprin•kler** *n*

²**sprinkle** *n* : a light rainfall

sprin•kling *n* : SMATTERING

¹**sprint** \'sprint\ *vb* : to run at top speed esp. for a short distance — **sprint•er** *n*

²**sprint** *n* **1** : a short run at top speed **2** : a short distance race

sprite \'sprīt\ *n* **1** : GHOST, SPIRIT **2** : ELF, FAIRY

spritz *vb* : SPRAY

sprock·et \'sprä-kət\ *n* : a toothed wheel whose teeth engage the links of a chain

¹sprout \'spraùt\ *vb* : to send out new growth ⟨∼*ing* seeds⟩

²sprout *n* : a usu. young and growing plant shoot (as from a seed)

¹spruce \'sprüs\ *vb* **spruced; spruc·ing** : to make or become spruce

²spruce *adj* **spruc·er; spruc·est** : neat and smart in appearance **syn** stylish, fashionable, modish, dapper, natty

³spruce *n* : any of a genus of evergreen pyramid‑shaped trees related to the pines and having soft light wood; *also* : the wood of a spruce

sprung *past and past part of* SPRING

spry \'sprī\ *adj* **spri·er** *or* **spry·er** \'sprī-ər\; **spri·est** *or* **spry·est** \'sprī-əst\ : NIMBLE, ACTIVE **syn** agile, brisk, lively, sprightly

spud \'spəd\ *n* **1** : a sharp narrow spade **2** : POTATO

spume \'spyüm\ *n* : frothy matter on liquids : FOAM — **spumy** \'spyü-mē\ *adj*

spu·mo·ni *also* **spu·mo·ne** \spù-'mō-nē\ *n* [It *spumone*, fr. *spuma* foam] : ice cream in layers of different colors, flavors, and textures often with candied fruits and nuts

spun *past and past part of* SPIN

spun glass *n* : FIBERGLASS

spunk \'spəηk\ *n* [fr. *spunk* tinder, fr. ScGael *spong* sponge, tinder, fr. L *spongia* sponge] : PLUCK, COURAGE — **spunky** *adj*

¹spur \'spər\ *n* **1** : a pointed device fastened to a rider's boot and used to urge on a horse **2** : something that urges to action **3** : a stiff sharp spine (as on the leg of a cock); *also* : a hollow projecting appendage of a flower (as a columbine) **4** : a ridge extending sideways from a mountain **5** : a branch of railroad track extending from the main line **syn** goad, motive, impulse, incentive, inducement — **spurred** \'spərd\ *adj* — **on the spur of the moment** : on hasty impulse

²spur *vb* **spurred; spur·ring 1** : to urge a horse on with spurs **2** : INCITE

spurge \'spərj\ *n* : any of a genus of herbs and woody plants with bitter milky juice

spu·ri·ous \'spyùr-ē-əs\ *adj* [LL *spurius* false, fr. L, of illegitimate birth, fr. *spurius*, n., bastard] : not genuine : FALSE

spurn \'spərn\ *vb* **1** : to kick away or trample on **2** : to reject with disdain

¹spurt \'spərt\ *vb* : to gush out : SPOUT

²spurt *n* : a sudden gushing or spouting

³spurt *n* **1** : a sudden brief burst of effort or speed **2** : a sharp increase of activity ⟨∼ in sales⟩

⁴spurt *vb* : to make a spurt

sput·ter \'spə-tər\ *vb* **1** : to spit small scattered particles : SPLUTTER **2** : to utter words hastily or explosively in excitement or confusion **3** : to make small popping sounds — **sputter** *n*

spu·tum \'spyü-təm\ *n, pl* **spu·ta** \-tə\ [L] : material that is spit or coughed up and consists of saliva and mucus

¹spy \'spī\ *vb* **spied; spy·ing 1** : to watch or search for information secretly : act as a spy **2** : to get a momentary or quick glimpse of : SEE

²spy *n, pl* **spies 1** : one who secretly watches others **2** : a secret agent who tries to get information for one country in the territory of an enemy

spy·glass \'spī-ˌglas\ *n* : a small telescope

sq *abbr* **1** squadron **2** square

squab \'skwäb\ *n, pl* **squabs** *or* **squab** : a young bird and esp. a pigeon

squab·ble \'skwä-bəl\ *n* : a noisy altercation : WRANGLE **syn** quarrel, spat, row, tiff — **squabble** *vb*

squad \'skwäd\ *n* **1** : a small organized group of military personnel **2** : a small group engaged in a common effort

squad car *n* : a police car connected by two‑way radio with headquarters

squad·ron \'skwä-drən\ *n* : any of several units of military organization

squal·id \'skwä-ləd\ *adj* **1** : filthy or degraded through neglect or poverty **2** : SORDID, DEBASED **syn** nasty, foul, dirty, grubby

squall \'skwòl\ *n* : a sudden violent gust of wind often with rain or snow — **squally** *adj*

squa·lor \'skwä-lər\ *n* : the quality or state of being squalid

squan·der \'skwän-dər\ *vb* : to spend wastefully or foolishly

¹square \'skwar\ *n* **1** : an instrument used to lay out or test right angles **2** : a rectangle with all four sides equal **3** : something square **4** : the product of a number multiplied by itself **5** : an area bounded by four streets **6** : an open area in a city where streets meet **7** : a highly conventional person

²square *adj* **squar·er; squar·est 1** : having four equal sides and four right angles **2** : forming a right angle ⟨cut a ∼ corner⟩ **3** : multiplied by itself : SQUARED ⟨x^2 is the symbol for x ∼⟩ **4** : being a unit of square measure equal to a square each side of which measures one unit ⟨a ∼ foot⟩ **5** : being of a specified length in each of two dimensions ⟨an area 10 feet ∼⟩ **6** : exactly adjusted **7** : JUST, FAIR ⟨a ∼ deal⟩ **8** : leaving no balance ⟨make accounts ∼⟩ **9** : SUBSTANTIAL ⟨a ∼ meal⟩ **10** : highly conservative or conventional — **square·ly** *adv*

³square *vb* **squared; squar·ing 1** : to form with four equal sides and right angles or with flat surfaces ⟨∼ a timber⟩ **2** : to multiply (a number) by itself **3** : CONFORM, AGREE **4** : BALANCE, SETTLE ⟨∼ an account⟩

square dance *n* : a dance for four couples arranged to form a square

square measure *n* : a unit or system of units for measuring area — see METRIC SYSTEM table, WEIGHT table

square–rigged \'skwar-'rigd\ *adj* : having the chief sails extended on yards that are fastened to the masts horizontally and at their center

square–rig·ger \-ˌri-gər\ *n* : a square-rigged craft

square root *n* : either of the two numbers whose squares are equal to a given number ⟨the *square root* of 9 is +3 or −3⟩

¹squash \'skwäsh, 'skwòsh\ *vb* **1** : to beat or press into a pulp or flat mass **2** : QUASH, SUPPRESS

²squash *n* **1** : the impact of something soft and heavy; *also* : the sound of such impact **2** : a crushed mass **3** : a game played on a 4-wall court with a racket and rubber ball

³squash *n, pl* **squash·es** *or* **squash** : a fruit of any of various plants related to the gourds that is used esp. as a vegetable; *also* : a plant and esp. a vine bearing squashes

squash racquets *n* : SQUASH 3

¹squat \'skwät\ *vb* **squat·ted; squat·ting 1** : to sit down upon the hams or heels **2** : to settle on land without right or title; *also* : to settle on public land with a view to acquiring title — **squat·ter** *n*

²squat *n* : the act or posture of squatting

³squat *adj* **squat·ter; squat·test** : low to the ground; *also* : short and thick in stature **syn** thickset, stocky, heavyset, stubby

squaw \'skwò\ *n* : an American Indian woman

squawk \'skwòk\ *n* : a harsh loud cry; *also* : a noisy protest — **squawk** *vb*

squeak \'skwēk\ *vb* **1** : to utter or speak in a weak shrill tone **2** : to make a thin high-pitched sound — **squeak** *n* — **squeaky** *adj*

¹squeal \'skwēl\ *vb* **1** : to make a shrill sound or cry **2** : to betray a secret or turn informer **3** : COMPLAIN, PROTEST

²squeal *n* : a shrill sharp cry or noise

squea·mish \'skwē-mish\ *adj* **1** : easily nauseated; *also* : NAUSEATED **2** : easily disgusted **syn** fussy, nice, dainty, fastidious, persnickety — **squea·mish·ness** *n*

squee·gee \'skwē-ˌjē\ *n* : a blade set crosswise on a handle and used for spreading or wiping liquid on, across, or off a surface — **squeegee** *vb*

¹squeeze \'skwēz\ *vb* **squeezed; squeez·ing** **1** : to exert pressure on the opposite sides or parts of **2** : to obtain by pressure ⟨~ juice from a lemon⟩ **3** : to force, thrust, or cause to pass by pressure — **squeez·er** *n*

²squeeze *n* **1** : an act of squeezing **2** : a quantity squeezed out

squeeze bottle *n* : a flexible plastic bottle that dispenses its contents when it is squeezed

¹squelch \'skwelch\ *vb* **1** : to suppress completely : CRUSH **2** : to move in soft mud — **squelch** *n*

squib \'skwib\ *n* : a brief witty writing or speech

squid \'skwid\ *n, pl* **squid** *or* **squids** : any of an order of long-bodied sea mollusks having eight arms and two longer tentacles and usu. a slender internal shell

squint \'skwint\ *vb* **1** : to look or aim obliquely **2** : to look or peer with the eyes partly closed **3** : to be cross-eyed — **squint** *n or adj*

¹squire \'skwīr\ *n* [ME *squier,* fr. OF *esquier,* fr. LL *scutarius,* fr. L *scutum* shield] **1** : an armor-bearer of a knight **2** : a man gallantly devoted to a lady **3** : a member of the British gentry ranking below a knight and above a gentleman; *also* : a prominent landowner **4** : a local magistrate

²squire *vb* **squired; squir·ing** : to attend as a squire or escort

squirm \'skwərm\ *vb* : to twist about like a worm : WRIGGLE

¹squir·rel \'skwər-əl\ *n, pl* **squirrels** *also* **squirrel** [ME *squirel,* fr. MF *esquireul,* fr. (assumed) VL *scuriolus,* dim. of *scurius,* alter. of L *sciurus,* fr. Gk *skiouros,* prob. fr. *skia* shadow + *oura* tail] : any of various rodents usu. with a long bushy tail and strong hind legs; *also* : the fur of a squirrel

²squirrel *vb* **-reled** *or* **-relled; -rel·ing** *or* **-rel·ling** : to store up for future use

¹squirt \'skwərt\ *vb* : to eject liquid in a thin spurt

²squirt *n* **1** : an instrument (as a syringe) for squirting **2** : a small forcible jet of liquid

¹Sr *abbr* **1** senior **2** sister

²Sr *symbol* strontium

SR *abbr* seaman recruit

¹SRO \ˌes-(ˌ)är-'ō\ *n* [*single-room occupancy*] : a house or apartment building in which low-income tenants live in single rooms

²SRO *abbr* standing room only

SS *abbr* **1** saints **2** Social Security **3** steamship **4** sworn statement

SSA *abbr* Social Security Administration

SSE *abbr* south-southeast

SSG *or* **SSgt** *abbr* staff sergeant

SSI *abbr* supplemental security income

SSM *abbr* staff sergeant major

SSN *abbr* Social Security Number

ssp *abbr* subspecies

SSR *abbr* Soviet Socialist Republic

SSS *abbr* Selective Service System

SST \ˌes-(ˌ)es-'tē\ *n* [*supersonic transport*] : a supersonic passenger airplane

SSW *abbr* south-southwest

st *abbr* **1** stanza **2** state **3** stitch **4** stone **5** street

St *abbr* saint

ST *abbr* **1** short ton **2** standard time

-st — see -EST

sta *abbr* station; stationary

¹stab \'stab\ *n* **1** : a wound produced by a pointed weapon **2** : a quick thrust; *also* : a brief attempt

²stab *vb* **stabbed; stab·bing** : to pierce or wound with or as if with a pointed weapon; *also* : THRUST, DRIVE

sta·bile \'stā-ˌbēl\ *n* : an abstract sculpture or construction similar to a mobile but made to be stationary

sta·bi·lize \'stā-bə-ˌlīz\ *vb* **-lized; -liz·ing** **1** : to make

stable **2** : to hold steady ⟨~ prices⟩ — **sta·bi·li·za·tion** \ˌstā-bə-lə-'zā-shən\ *n* — **sta·bi·liz·er** \'stā-bə-ˌlī-zər\ *n*

¹sta·ble \'stā-bəl\ *n* : a building in which domestic animals are sheltered and fed — **sta·ble·man** \-mən, -ˌman\ *n*

²stable *vb* **sta·bled; sta·bling** : to put or keep in a stable

³stable *adj* **sta·bler; sta·blest** **1** : firmly established; *also* : mentally and emotionally healthy **2** : steady in purpose : CONSTANT **3** : DURABLE, ENDURING **4** : resistant to chemical or physical change **syn** lasting, permanent, perpetual, perdurable — **sta·bil·i·ty** \stə-'bi-lə-tē\ *n*

stac·ca·to \stə-'kä-tō\ *adj or adv* [It] : cut short so as not to sound connected ⟨~ notes⟩

¹stack \'stak\ *n* **1** : a large pile (as of hay or grain) **2** : an orderly pile (as of poker chips) **3** : a large quantity **4** : a vertical pipe : SMOKESTACK **5** : a rack with shelves for storing books

²stack *vb* **1** : to pile up **2** : to arrange (cards) secretly for cheating

stack up *vb* : MEASURE UP

sta·di·um \'stā-dē-əm\ *n, pl* **-dia** \-dē-ə\ *or* **-di·ums** : a structure with tiers of seats for spectators built around a field for sports events

¹staff \'staf\ *n, pl* **staffs** \'stafs, 'stavz\ *or* **staves** \'stavz, 'stāvz\ **1** : a pole, stick, rod, or bar used for supporting, for measuring, or as a symbol of authority; *also* : CLUB, CUDGEL **2** : something that sustains ⟨bread is the ~ of life⟩ **3** : the five horizontal lines on which music is written **4** : a body of assistants to an executive **5** : a group of officers holding no command but having duties concerned with planning and managing

²staff *vb* : to supply with a staff or with workers

staff·er \'sta-fər\ *n* : a member of a staff (as of a newspaper)

staff sergeant *n* : a noncommissioned officer ranking in the army next below a sergeant first class, in the air force next below a technical sergeant, and in the marine corps next below a gunnery sergeant

¹stag \'stag\ *n, pl* **stags** *or* **stag** : an adult male of various large deer

²stag *adj* : restricted to or intended for men ⟨a ~ party⟩ ⟨~ movies⟩

³stag *adv* : unaccompanied by a date

¹stage \'stāj\ *n* **1** : a raised platform on which an orator may speak or a play may be presented **2** : the acting profession : THEATER **3** : the scene of a notable action or event **4** : a station or resting place on a traveled road **5** : STAGECOACH **6** : a degree of advance in an undertaking, process, or development **7** : a propulsion unit in a rocket — **stagy** \'stā-jē\ *adj*

²stage *vb* **staged; stag·ing** : to produce or perform on or as if on a stage — **stage·able** *adj*

stage·coach \'stāj-ˌkōch\ *n* : a horse-drawn coach that runs regularly between stations

stag·fla·tion \ˌstag-'flā-shən\ *n* : inflation with stagnant economic activity and high unemployment

¹stag·ger \'sta-gər\ *vb* **1** : to reel from side to side : TOTTER **2** : to begin to doubt : WAVER **3** : to cause to reel or waver **4** : to arrange in overlapping or alternating positions or times ⟨~ working hours⟩ **5** : ASTONISH — **stag·ger·ing·ly** *adv*

²stagger *n* **1** *sing or pl* : an abnormal condition of domestic mammals and birds associated with damage to the central nervous system and marked by lack of coordination and a reeling unsteady gait **2** : a reeling or unsteady gait or stance

stag·ing \'stā-jiŋ\ *n* **1** : SCAFFOLDING **2** : the assembling of troops and matériel in transit in a particular place

stag·nant \'stag-nənt\ *adj* **1** : not flowing : MOTIONLESS ⟨~ water in a pond⟩ **2** : DULL, INACTIVE ⟨~ business⟩

stag·nate \'stag-ˌnāt\ *vb* **stag·nat·ed; stag·nat·ing** : to be or become stagnant — **stag·na·tion** \stag-'nā-shən\ *n*

staid \'stād\ *adj* : SOBER, SEDATE **syn** grave, serious, earnest

¹stain \'stān\ *vb* **1** : DISCOLOR, SOIL **2** : TAINT, CORRUPT **3** : DISGRACE **4** : to color (as wood, paper, or cloth) by processes affecting the material itself

²stain *n* **1** : a small soiled or discolored area **2** : a taint of guilt : STIGMA **3** : a preparation (as a dye or pigment) used in staining — **stain·less** *adj*

stainless steel *n* : steel alloyed with chromium that is highly resistant to stain, rust, and corrosion

stair \'star\ *n* **1** : a series of steps or flights of steps for passing from one level to another — often used in pl. **2** : one step of a stairway

stair·case \-ˌkās\ *n* : a flight of steps with their supporting framework, casing, and balusters

stair·way \-ˌwā\ *n* : one or more flights of stairs with connecting landings

stair·well \-ˌwel\ *n* : a vertical shaft in which stairs are located

¹stake \'stāk\ *n* **1** : a pointed piece of material (as of wood) driven into the ground as a marker or a support **2** : a post to which a person is bound for death by burning; *also* : such a death **3** : something that is staked for gain or loss **4** : the prize in a contest

²stake *vb* **staked; stak·ing 1** : to mark the limits of by or as if by stakes **2** : to tie to a stake **3** : to support or secure with stakes **4** : BET, WAGER

stake·out \'stāk-ˌaut\ *n* : a surveillance by police (as of a suspected criminal)

sta·lac·tite \stə-'lak-ˌtīt\ *n* [NL *stalactites*, fr. Gk *stalaktos* dripping] : an icicle-shaped deposit hanging from the roof or sides of a cavern

sta·lag·mite \stə-'lag-ˌmīt\ *n* [NL *stalagmites*, fr. Gk *stalagma* drop or *stalagmos* dripping] : a deposit resembling an inverted stalactite rising from the floor of a cavern

stale \'stāl\ *adj* **stal·er; stal·est 1** : having lost good taste and quality from age (⁓ bread) **2** : used or heard so often as to be dull (⁓ news) **3** : not as strong or effective as before (⁓ from lack of practice) — **stale·ness** *n*

stale·mate \'stāl-ˌmāt\ *n* : a drawn contest : DEADLOCK — **stalemate** *vb*

¹stalk \'stok\ *n* : a plant stem; *also* : any slender usu. upright supporting or connecting part — **stalked** \'stokt\ *adj*

²stalk *vb* **1** : to pursue (game) stealthily **2** : to walk stiffly or haughtily

¹stall \'stol\ *n* **1** : a compartment in a stable or barn for one animal **2** : a booth or counter where articles may be displayed for sale **3** : a seat in a church choir; *also* : a church pew **4** *chiefly Brit* : a front orchestra seat in a theater

²stall *vb* : to bring or come to a standstill unintentionally (⁓ an engine)

³stall *n* : the condition of an airfoil or aircraft in which lift is lost and the airfoil or aircraft tends to drop

⁴stall *n* [alter. of *stale* lure] : a ruse to deceive or delay

⁵stall *vb* : to hold off, divert, or delay by evasion or deception

stal·lion \'stal-yən\ *n* : a male horse

stal·wart \'stol-wərt\ *adj* : STOUT, STRONG; *also* : BRAVE, VALIANT

sta·men \'stā-mən\ *n* : an organ of a flower that produces pollen

stam·i·na \'sta-mə-nə\ *n* [L, pl. of *stamen* warp, thread of life spun by the Fates] : VIGOR, ENDURANCE

sta·mi·nate \'stā-mə-nət, 'sta-mə-, -ˌnāt\ *adj* **1** : having or producing stamens **2** : having stamens but no pistils

stam·mer \'sta-mər\ *vb* : to hesitate or stumble in speaking — **stammer** *n* — **stam·mer·er** *n*

¹stamp \'stamp; *for 2 also* 'stämp *or* 'stomp\ *vb* **1** : to pound or crush with a heavy instrument **2** : to strike or beat with the bottom of the foot **3** : IMPRESS, IM-

PRINT **4** : to cut out or indent with a stamp or die **5** : to attach a postage stamp to

²stamp *n* **1** : a device or instrument for stamping **2** : the mark made by stamping; *also* : a distinctive mark or quality **3** : the act of stamping **4** : a stamped or printed paper affixed to show that a charge has been paid (postage ⁓) (tax ⁓)

¹stam·pede \stam-'pēd\ *n* : a wild headlong rush or flight esp. of frightened animals

²stampede *vb* **stam·ped·ed; stam·ped·ing 1** : to flee or cause to flee in panic **2** : to act or cause to act together suddenly and heedlessly

stance \'stans\ *n* : a way of standing

¹stanch \'stonch, 'stanch\ *vb* : to check the flowing of (as blood); *also* : to cease flowing or bleeding

²stanch *var of* ²STAUNCH

stan·chion \'stan-chən\ *n* : an upright bar, post, or support

¹stand \'stand\ *vb* **stood** \'stud\; **stand·ing 1** : to take or be at rest in an upright or firm position **2** : to assume a specified position **3** : to remain stationary or unchanged **4** : to be steadfast **5** : to act in resistance (⁓ against a foe) **6** : to maintain a relative position or rank **7** : to gather slowly and remain (tears *stood* in her eyes) **8** : to set upright **9** : ENDURE, TOLERATE (I won't ⁓ for that) **10** : to submit to (⁓ trial) — **stand pat** : to oppose or resist change

²stand *n* **1** : an act of standing, staying, or resisting **2** : a stop made to give a performance **3** : POSITION, VIEWPOINT **4** : a place taken by a witness to testify in court **5** *pl* : tiered seats for spectators **6** : a raised platform (as for speakers) **7** : a structure for a small retail business **8** : a structure for supporting or holding something upright (music ⁓) **9** : a group of plants growing in a continuous area

stand-alone \'stan-də-ˌlōn\ *adj* : SELF-CONTAINED; *esp* : capable of operation independent of a computer system

stan·dard \'stan-dərd\ *n* **1** : a figure adopted as an emblem by a people **2** : the personal flag of a ruler; *also* : FLAG **3** : something set up as a rule for measuring or as a model to be followed **4** : an upright support (lamp ⁓) — **standard** *adj*

stan·dard–bear·er \-ˌbar-ər\ *n* : the leader of a cause

standard deviation *n* : a measure of dispersion in a set of data

stan·dard·ize \'stan-dər-ˌdīz\ *vb* **-ized; -iz·ing** : to make standard or uniform — **stan·dard·i·za·tion** \ˌstan-dər-də-'zā-shən\ *n*

standard of living : the necessities, comforts, and luxuries that a person or group is accustomed to

standard time *n* : the time established by law or by general usage over a region or country

¹stand·by \'stan-ˌbī\ *n, pl* **stand·bys** \-ˌbīz\ **1** : one that can be relied on **2** : a substitute in reserve — **on standby** : ready or available for immediate action or use

²standby *adj* **1** : ready for use **2** : relating to airline travel in which the passenger must wait for an available unreserved seat — **standby** *adv*

stand–in \'stan-ˌdin\ *n* **1** : someone employed to occupy an actor's place while lights and camera are readied **2** : SUBSTITUTE

¹stand·ing \'stan-diŋ\ *adj* **1** : ERECT **2** : not flowing : STAGNANT **3** : remaining at the same level or amount for an indefinite period (⁓ offer) **4** : PERMANENT **5** : done from a standing position (a ⁓ jump)

²standing *n* **1** : length of service; *also* : relative position in society or in a profession : RANK **2** : DURATION

stand·off \'stan-ˌdof\ *n* : TIE, DRAW

stand·off·ish \stan-'dô-fish\ *adj* : somewhat cold and reserved

stand·out \'stan-ˌdaut\ *n* : something conspicuously excellent

stand·pipe \'stand-ˌpīp\ *n* : a high vertical pipe or reservoir for water used to produce a uniform pressure

stand·point \-₁pȯint\ *n* : a position from which objects or principles are judged

stand·still \-₁stil\ *n* : a state of rest

stand–up \'stan-₁dəp\ *adj* : done or performing in a standing position ⟨a ∼ comic⟩ ⟨∼ comedy⟩

stank \'staŋk\ *past of* STINK

stan·za \'stan-zə\ *n* [It] : a group of lines forming a division of a poem

sta·pes \'stā-₁pēz\ *n, pl* **stapes** *or* **sta·pe·des** \'stā-pə-₁dēz\ : the small innermost bone of the ear of mammals

staph \'staf\ *n* : STAPHYLOCOCCUS

staph·y·lo·coc·cus \₁sta-fə-lō-'kä-kəs\ *n, pl* **-coc·ci** \-'kä-₁kī, -'käk-₁sī\ : any of various spherical bacteria including some pathogens of skin and mucous membranes — **staph·y·lo·coc·cal** \-'kä-kəl\ *adj*

¹**sta·ple** \'stā-pəl\ *n* : a U-shaped piece of metal or wire with sharp points to be driven into a surface or through thin layers (as paper) for attaching or holding together — **staple** *vb* — **sta·pler** *n*

²**staple** *n* **1** : a chief commodity or product **2** : a chief part of something ⟨a ∼ of their diet⟩ **3** : unmanufactured or raw material **4** : a textile fiber suitable for spinning into yarn

³**staple** *adj* **1** : regularly produced in large quantities **2** : PRINCIPAL, MAIN

¹**star** \'stär\ *n* **1** : a celestial body that appears as a fixed point of light; *esp* : such a body that is gaseous, self≈ luminous, and of great mass **2** : a planet or configuration of planets that is held in astrology to influence one's fortune — usu. used in pl. **3** *obs* : DESTINY, FORTUNE **4** : a conventional figure representing a star; *esp* : ASTERISK **5** : an actor or actress playing the leading role **6** : a brilliant performer — **star·dom** \'stär-dəm\ *n* — **star·less** *adj* — **star·like** *adj* — **star·ry** *adj*

²**star** *vb* **starred; star·ring 1** : to adorn with stars **2** : to mark with an asterisk **3** : to play the leading role

star·board \'stär-bərd\ *n* [ME *sterbord*, fr. OE *stēor-bord*, fr. *stēor-* steering oar + *bord* ship's side] : the right side of a ship or airplane looking forward — **starboard** *adj*

¹**starch** \'stärch\ *vb* : to stiffen with or as if with starch

²**starch** *n* : a complex carbohydrate that is stored in plants, is an important foodstuff, and is used in adhesives and sizes, in laundering, and in pharmacy — **starchy** *adj*

stare \'star\ *vb* **stared; star·ing** : to look fixedly with wide-open eyes — **stare** *n* — **star·er** *n*

star·fish \'stär-₁fish\ *n* : any of a class of echinoderms usu. having five arms arranged around a central disk and feeding largely on mollusks

star fruit *n* : CARAMBOLA 1

¹**stark** \'stärk\ *adj* **1** : rigid as if in death; *also* : STRICT **2** *archaic* : STRONG, ROBUST **3** : SHEER, UTTER **4** : BARREN, DESOLATE ⟨∼ landscape⟩; *also* : UNADORNED ⟨∼ realism⟩ **5** : sharply delineated — **stark·ly** *adv*

²**stark** *adv* : WHOLLY, ABSOLUTELY ⟨∼ naked⟩

star·light \'stär-₁līt\ *n* : the light given by the stars

star·ling \'stär-liŋ\ *n* : a dark brown or in summer glossy greenish black European bird related to the crows that is naturalized nearly worldwide and often considered a pest

¹**start** \'stärt\ *vb* **1** : to give an involuntary twitch or jerk (as from surprise) **2** : BEGIN, COMMENCE **3** : to set going **4** : to enter or cause to enter a game or contest; *also* : to be in the starting lineup — **start·er** *n*

²**start** *n* **1** : a sudden involuntary motion : LEAP **2** : a spasmodic and brief effort or action **3** : BEGINNING; *also* : the place of beginning

star·tle \'stärt-ᵊl\ *vb* **star·tled; star·tling** : to frighten or surprise suddenly : cause to start

star·tling *adj* : causing sudden fear, surprise, or anxiety

starve \'stärv\ *vb* **starved; starv·ing** [ME *sterven* to die, fr. OE *steorfan*] **1** : to die or cause to die from hunger **2** : to suffer extreme hunger or deprivation

⟨*starving* for affection⟩ **3** : to subdue by famine — **star·va·tion** \stär-'vā-shən\ *n*

starve·ling \'stärv-liŋ\ *n* : one that is thin from lack of nourishment

stash \'stash\ *vb* : to store in a secret place for future use — **stash** *n*

stat *abbr* **1** [L *statim*] immediately **2** statute

¹**state** \'stāt\ *n* [ME *stat*, fr. OF & L; OF *estat*, fr. L *status*, fr. *stare* to stand] **1** : mode or condition of being ⟨the four ∼s of matter⟩ **2** : condition of mind **3** : social position **4** : a body of people occupying a territory and organized under one government; *also* : the government of such a body of people **5** : one of the constituent units of a nation having a federal government — **state·hood** \-₁hud\ *n*

²**state** *vb* **stat·ed; stat·ing 1** : FIX ⟨*stated* intervals⟩ **2** : to express in words

state·craft \'stāt-₁kraft\ *n* : the art of conducting state affairs

state·house \-₁haus\ *n* : the building in which a state legislature meets

state·ly \'stāt-lē\ *adj* **state·li·er; -est 1** : having lofty dignity : HAUGHTY **2** : IMPRESSIVE, MAJESTIC **syn** magnificent, imposing, august — **state·li·ness** *n*

state·ment \'stāt-mənt\ *n* **1** : the act or result of presenting in words **2** : a summary of a financial account

state·room \'stāt-₁rüm, -₁rum\ *n* : a private room on a ship or railroad car

state·side \'stāt-₁sīd\ *adj* : of or relating to the U.S. as regarded from outside its continental limits — **state·side** *adv*

states·man \'stāts-mən\ *n* : a person engaged in fixing the policies and conducting the affairs of a government; *esp* : one wise and skilled in such matters — **states·man·like** *adj* — **states·man·ship** *n*

¹**stat·ic** \'sta-tik\ *adj* **1** : acting by mere weight without motion ⟨∼ pressure⟩ **2** : relating to bodies at rest or forces in equilibrium **3** : not moving : not active **4** : of or relating to stationary charges of electricity **5** : of, relating to, or caused by radio static

²**static** *n* : noise produced in a radio or television receiver by atmospheric or other electrical disturbances

¹**sta·tion** \'stā-shən\ *n* **1** : the place where a person or thing stands or is assigned to remain **2** : a regular stopping place on a transportation route : DEPOT **3** : a place where a fleet is assigned for duty **4** : a stock farm or ranch esp. in Australia or New Zealand **5** : social standing **6** : a complete assemblage of radio or television equipment for sending or receiving

²**station** *vb* : to assign to a station

sta·tion·ary \'stā-shə-₁ner-ē\ *adj* **1** : fixed in a station, course, or mode **2** : unchanging in condition

stationary front *n* : the boundary between two air masses neither of which is advancing

station break *n* : a pause in a radio or television broadcast to announce the identity of the network or station

sta·tio·ner \'stā-shə-nər\ *n* : one that sells stationery

sta·tio·nery \'stā-shə-₁ner-ē\ *n* : materials (as paper, pens, or ink) for writing; *esp* : letter paper with envelopes

station wagon *n* : an automobile having a passenger compartment which extends to the back of the vehicle and no trunk

sta·tis·tic \stə-'tis-tik\ *n* **1** : a single term or datum in a collection of statistics **2** : a quantity (as the mean) that is computed from a sample

sta·tis·tics \-tiks\ *n sing or pl* [G *Statistik* study of political facts and figures, fr. NL *statisticus* of politics, fr. L *status* state] : a branch of mathematics dealing with the collection, analysis, and interpretation of masses of numerical data; *also* : a collection of such numerical data — **sta·tis·ti·cal** \-ti-kəl\ *adj* — **sta·tis·ti·cal·ly** \-ti-k(ə-)lē\ *adv* — **stat·is·ti·cian** \₁sta-tə-'sti-shən\ *n*

stat·u·ary \'sta-chə-₁wer-ē\ *n, pl* **-ar·ies** **1** : the art of making statues **2** : STATUES

stat·ue \'sta-chü\ *n* : a likeness (as of a person or animal) sculptured, modeled, or cast in a solid substance

stat·u·esque \₁sta-chə-'wesk\ *adj* : tall and shapely

stat·u·ette \₁sta-chə-'wet\ *n* : a small statue

stat·ure \'sta-chər\ *n* **1** : natural height (as of a person) **2** : quality or status gained (as by achievement)

sta·tus \'stā-təs, 'sta-\ *n* **1** : the condition of a person in the eyes of others or of the law **2** : state of affairs

sta·tus quo \-'kwō\ *n* [L, state in which] : the existing state of affairs

stat·ute \'sta-chüt\ *n* : a law enacted by a legislative body

stat·u·to·ry \'sta-chə-₁tōr-ē\ *adj* : imposed by statute : LAWFUL

statutory rape *n* : sexual intercourse with a person who is below the statutory age of consent

¹staunch \'stȯnch\ *var of* ¹STANCH

²staunch *adj* **1** : WATERTIGHT ⟨a ~ ship⟩ **2** : FIRM, STRONG; *also* : STEADFAST, LOYAL **syn** resolute, constant, true, faithful — **staunch·ly** *adv*

¹stave \'stāv\ *n* **1** : CUDGEL, STAFF **2** : any of several narrow strips of wood placed edge to edge to make something (as a barrel) **3** : STANZA

²stave *vb* **staved** *or* **stove** \'stōv\; **stav·ing** **1** : to break in the staves of; *also* : to break a hole in **2** : to drive or thrust away ⟨~ off trouble⟩

staves *pl of* STAFF

¹stay \'stā\ *n* **1** : a strong rope or wire used to support a mast **2** : ¹GUY

²stay *vb* **stayed** \'stād\ *also* **staid** \'stād\; **stay·ing** **1** : PAUSE, WAIT **2** : REMAIN **3** : to stand firm **4** : LIVE, DWELL **5** : DELAY, POSTPONE **6** : to last out (as a race) **7** : STOP, CHECK **8** : to satisfy (as hunger) for a time **syn** remain, abide, linger, tarry

³stay *n* **1** : STOP, HALT **2** : a residence or sojourn in a place

⁴stay *n* **1** : PROP, SUPPORT **2** : CORSET — usu. used in pl.

⁵stay *vb* : to hold up : PROP

staying power *n* : STAMINA

stbd *abbr* starboard

std *abbr* standard

STD \₁es-(₁)tē-'dē\ *n* : SEXUALLY TRANSMITTED DISEASE

Ste *abbr* [F *sainte*] saint (female)

stead \'sted\ *n* **1** : ADVANTAGE ⟨stood him in good ~⟩ **2** : the place or function ordinarily occupied or carried out by another ⟨acted in her brother's ~⟩

stead·fast \'sted-₁fast\ *adj* **1** : firmly fixed in place **2** : not subject to change **3** : firm in belief, determination, or adherence : LOYAL **syn** resolute, true, faithful, staunch — **stead·fast·ly** *adv* — **stead·fast·ness** *n*

¹steady \'ste-dē\ *adj* **steadi·er; -est** **1** : direct or sure in movement; *also* : CALM **2** : FIRM, FIXED **3** : STABLE **4** : CONSTANT, RESOLUTE **5** : REGULAR **6** : RELIABLE, SOBER **syn** uniform, even — **steadi·ly** \-də-lē\ *adv* — **steadi·ness** \-dē-nəs\ *n* — **steady** *adv*

²steady *vb* **stead·ied; steady·ing** : to make or become steady

steak \'stāk\ *n* : a slice of meat and esp. beef; *also* : a slice of a large fish

¹steal \'stēl\ *vb* **stole** \'stōl\; **sto·len** \'stō-lən\; **steal·ing** **1** : to take and carry away without right or permission **2** : to come or go secretly or gradually **3** : to get for oneself slyly or by skill and daring ⟨~ a kiss⟩ ⟨~ the ball in basketball⟩ **4** : to gain or attempt to gain a base in baseball by running without the aid of a hit or an error **syn** pilfer, filch, purloin, swipe

²steal *n* **1** : an act of stealing **2** : BARGAIN

stealth \'stelth\ *n* **1** : secret or unobtrusive procedure **2** : an aircraft design intended to produce a weak radar return

stealthy \'stel-thē\ *adj* **stealth·i·er; -est** : done by stealth : FURTIVE, SLY **syn** secret, covert, clandes-

tine, surreptitious, underhanded — **stealth·i·ly** \'stel-thə-lē\ *adv*

¹steam \'stēm\ *n* **1** : the vapor into which water is changed when heated to the boiling point **2** : water vapor when compressed so that it supplies heat and power **3** : POWER, FORCE, ENERGY — **steamy** *adj*

²steam *vb* **1** : to pass off as vapor **2** : to emit vapor **3** : to move by or as if by the agency of steam — **steam·er** *n*

steam·boat \'stēm-₁bōt\ *n* : a boat driven by steam

steam engine *n* : a reciprocating engine having a piston driven by steam

steam·fit·ter \'stēm-₁fi-tər\ *n* : a worker who puts in or repairs equipment (as steam pipes) for heating, ventilating, or refrigerating systems

steam·roll·er \-₁rō-lər\ *n* : a machine for compacting roads or pavements — **steam·roll·er** *also* **steam·roll** \-₁rōl\ *vb*

steam·ship \-₁ship\ *n* : a ship driven by steam

steed \'stēd\ *n* : HORSE

¹steel \'stēl\ *n* **1** : iron treated with intense heat and mixed with carbon to make it hard and tough **2** : an article made of steel **3** : a quality (as hardness of mind) that suggests steel — **steel** *adj* — **steely** *adj*

²steel *vb* : to fill with courage or determination

steel wool *n* : long fine steel shavings used esp. for cleaning and polishing

¹steep \'stēp\ *adj* **1** : having a very sharp slope : PRECIPITOUS **2** : too great or too high ⟨~ prices⟩ — **steep·ly** *adv* — **steep·ness** *n*

²steep *n* : a steep slope

³steep *vb* **1** : to soak in a liquid; *esp* : to extract the essence of by soaking ⟨~ tea⟩ **2** : SATURATE ⟨~ed in learning⟩

stee·ple \'stē-pəl\ *n* : a tall tapering structure built on top of a church tower; *also* : a church tower

stee·ple·chase \-₁chās\ *n* [fr. the use of church steeples as landmarks to guide the riders] : a horse race across country; *also* : a race over a course obstructed by hurdles

¹steer \'stir\ *n* : a male bovine animal castrated before sexual maturity and usu. raised for beef

²steer *vb* **1** : to direct the course of (as by a rudder or wheel) **2** : GUIDE, CONTROL **3** : to pursue a course of action **4** : to be subject to guidance or direction — **steers·man** \'stirz-mən\ *n*

steer·age \'stir-ij\ *n* **1** : DIRECTION, GUIDANCE **2** : a section in a passenger ship for passengers paying the lowest fares

stego·sau·rus \₁ste-gə-'sȯr-əs\ *n* : any of a genus of plant-eating armored dinosaurs with a series of bony plates along the backbone

stein \'stīn\ *n* : an earthenware mug

stel·lar \'ste-lər\ *adj* : of or relating to stars : resembling a star

¹stem \'stem\ *n* **1** : the main stalk of a plant; *also* : a plant part that supports another part (as a leaf or fruit) **2** : the bow of a ship **3** : a line of ancestry : STOCK **4** : that part of an inflected word which remains unchanged throughout a given inflection **5** : something resembling the stem of a plant — **stem·less** *adj* — **stemmed** \'stemd\ *adj*

²stem *vb* **stemmed; stem·ming** : to have a specified source : DERIVE

³stem *vb* **stemmed; stem·ming** : to make headway against ⟨~ the tide⟩

⁴stem *vb* **stemmed; stem·ming** : to stop or check by or as if by damming

stench \'stench\ *n* : STINK

sten·cil \'sten-səl\ *n* [ME *stanselen* to ornament with sparkling colors, fr. MF *estanceler*, fr. *estancele* spark, fr. (assumed) VL *stincilla*, alter. of L *scintilla*] : an impervious material (as metal or paper) perforated with lettering or a design through which a substance (as ink or paint) is applied to a surface to be printed — **stencil** *vb*

ste·nog·ra·phy \stə-'nä-grə-fē\ *n* : the art or process of writing in shorthand — **ste·nog·ra·pher** \-fər\ *n* — **steno·graph·ic** \ste-nə-'gra-fik\ *adj*

sten·to·ri·an \sten-'tŏr-ē-ən\ *adj* : extremely loud and powerful

¹step \'step\ *n* **1** : a rest for the foot in ascending or descending : STAIR **2** : an advance made by raising one foot and putting it down elsewhere **3** : manner of walking **4** : a small space or distance **5** : a degree, rank, or plane in a series **6** : a sequential measure leading to a result

²step *vb* **stepped; step·ping 1** : to advance or recede by steps **2** : to go on foot : WALK **3** : to move along briskly **4** : to press down with the foot **5** : to measure by steps **6** : to construct or arrange in or as if in steps

step·broth·er \'step-ˌbrə-thər\ *n* : the son of one's stepparent by a former marriage

step·child \-ˌchīld\ *n* : a child of one's husband or wife by a former marriage

step·daugh·ter \-ˌdȯ-tər\ *n* : a daughter of one's wife or husband by a former marriage

step down *vb* **1** : RETIRE, RESIGN **2** : to lower (a voltage) by means of a transformer

step·fa·ther \-ˌfä-thər\ *n* : the husband of one's mother by a subsequent marriage

step·lad·der \'step-ˌla-dər\ *n* : a light portable set of steps in a hinged frame

step·moth·er \-ˌmə-thər\ *n* : the wife of one's father by a subsequent marriage

step·par·ent \-ˌpar-ənt\ *n* : one's stepfather or stepmother

steppe \'step\ *n* [Russ *step'*] : dry level grass-covered treeless land in regions of wide temperature range esp. in southeastern Europe and Asia

step·sis·ter \'step-ˌsis-tər\ *n* : the daughter of one's stepparent by a former marriage

step·son \-ˌsən\ *n* : a son of one's wife or husband by a former marriage

step up *vb* **1** : to increase (a voltage) by means of a transformer **2** : INCREASE, ACCELERATE **3** : to come forward — **step–up** \'step-ˌəp\ *n*

ster *abbr* sterling

ste·reo \'ster-ē-ˌō, 'stir-\ *n, pl* **ste·re·os 1** : stereophonic reproduction **2** : a stereophonic sound system — **stereo** *adj*

ste·reo·phon·ic \ster-ē-ə-'fä-nik, ˌstir-\ *adj* : of or relating to sound reproduction designed to create the effect of listening to the original — **ste·reo·phon·i·cal·ly** \-'fä-ni-k(ə-)lē\ *adv*

ster·e·o·scope \'ster-ē-ə-ˌskōp, 'stir-\ *n* [Gk *stereos* solid + *-skopion* means for viewing] : an optical instrument that blends two slightly different pictures of the same subject to give the effect of depth

ste·reo·scop·ic \ster-ē-ə-'skä-pik, ˌstir-\ *adj* **1** : of or relating to the stereoscope **2** : characterized by the seeing of objects in three dimensions ⟨~ vision⟩ — **ste·reo·scop·i·cal·ly** \-'skä-pi-k(ə-)lē\ *adv* — **ste·re·os·co·py** \ster-ē-'äs-kə-pē, ˌstir-\ *n*

ste·reo·type \'ster-ē-ə-ˌtīp, 'stir-\ *n* **1** : a metal printing plate cast from a mold made from set type **2** : something agreeing with a pattern; *esp* : an idea that many people have about a thing or a group and that may often be untrue or only partly true — **stereotype** *vb* — **ste·reo·typ·i·cal** \ster-ē-ə-'ti-pi-kəl\ *adj* — **ste·reo·typ·i·cal·ly** \-pi-k(ə-)lē\ *adv*

ste·reo·typed \-ˌtīpt\ *adj* : lacking originality or individuality **syn** trite, clichéd, commonplace, hackneyed, stale, threadbare

ster·ile \'ster-əl\ *adj* **1** : unable to bear fruit, crops, or offspring **2** : free from living things and esp. germs — **ste·ril·i·ty** \stə-'ri-lə-tē\ *n*

ster·il·ize \'ster-ə-ˌlīz\ *vb* **-ized; -iz·ing** : to make sterile; *esp* : to free from germs — **ster·il·i·za·tion** \ster-ə-lə-'zā-shən\ *n* — **ster·il·iz·er** \'ster-ə-ˌlī-zər\ *n*

¹ster·ling \'stər-liŋ\ *n* **1** : British money **2** : sterling silver

²sterling *adj* **1** : of, relating to, or calculated in terms of British sterling **2** : having a fixed standard of purity represented by an alloy of 925 parts of silver with 75 parts of copper **3** : made of sterling silver **4** : EXCELLENT

¹stern \'stərn\ *adj* **1** : SEVERE, AUSTERE **2** : STOUT, STURDY ⟨~ resolve⟩ — **stern·ly** *adv* — **stern·ness** *n*

²stern *n* : the rear end of a boat

ster·num \'stər-nəm\ *n, pl* **sternums** *or* **ster·na** \-nə\ : a long flat bone or cartilage at the center front of the chest connecting the ribs of the two sides

ste·roid \'stir-ˌȯid\ *n* : any of numerous compounds including various hormones (as anabolic steroids) and sugar derivatives — **steroid** *or* **ste·roi·dal** \stə-'rȯid-ᵊl\ *adj*

stetho·scope \'ste-thə-ˌskōp\ *n* : an instrument used to detect and listen to sounds produced in the body

ste·ve·dore \'stē-və-ˌdȯr\ *n* [Sp *estibador*, fr. *estibar* to pack, fr. L *stipare* to press together] : one who works at loading and unloading ships

¹stew \'stü, 'styü\ *n* **1** : a dish of stewed meat and vegetables served in gravy **2** : a state of agitation, worry, or resentment

²stew *vb* **1** : to boil slowly : SIMMER **2** : to be in a state of agitation, worry, or resentment

stew·ard \'stü-ərd, 'styü-\ *n* [ME, fr. OE *stīweard*, fr. *stī, stig* hall, sty + *weard* ward] **1** : one employed on a large estate to manage domestic concerns **2** : one who supervises the provision and distribution of food (as on a ship); *also* : an employee on a ship or airplane who serves passengers **3** : one actively concerned with the direction of the affairs of an organization — **stew·ard·ship** *n*

stew·ard·ess \'stü-ər-dəs, 'styü-\ *n* : a woman who is a steward esp. on an airplane

stg *abbr* sterling

¹stick \'stik\ *n* **1** : a cut or broken branch or twig; *also* : a long slender piece of wood **2** : ROD, STAFF **3** : something resembling a stick **4** : a dull uninteresting person **5** *pl* : remote usu. rural areas

²stick *vb* **stuck** \'stək\; **stick·ing 1** : STAB, PRICK **2** : IMPALE **3** : ATTACH, FASTEN **4** : to thrust or project in some direction or manner **5** : to be unable to proceed or move freely **6** : to hold fast by or as if by gluing : ADHERE **7** : to hold to something firmly or closely : CLING **8** : to become jammed or blocked

stick·er \'sti-kər\ *n* : one that sticks (as a bur) or causes sticking (as glue); *esp* : an adhesive label

stick insect *n* : any of various usu. wingless insects with a long round body resembling a stick

stick·ler \'sti-klər, -kə-lər\ *n* : one who insists on exactness or completeness

stick shift *n* : a manually operated automobile gearshift usu. mounted on the floor

stick–to–it·ive·ness \stik-'tü-ə-tiv-nəs\ *n* : dogged perseverance : TENACITY

stick up *vb* : to rob at gunpoint — **stick·up** \'stik-ˌəp\ *n*

sticky \'sti-kē\ *adj* **stick·i·er; -est 1** : ADHESIVE **2** : VISCOUS, GLUEY **3** : tending to stick ⟨~ valve⟩ **4** : DIFFICULT

¹stiff \'stif\ *adj* **1** : not pliant : RIGID **2** : not limber ⟨~ joints⟩; *also* : TENSE, TAUT **3** : not flowing or working easily ⟨~ paste⟩ **4** : not natural and easy : FORMAL **5** : STRONG, FORCEFUL ⟨~ breeze⟩ **6** : HARSH, SEVERE **syn** inflexible, inelastic — **stiff·ly** *adv* — **stiff·ness** *n*

²stiff *vb* : to refuse to pay or tip

stiff·en \'sti-fən\ *vb* : to make or become stiff — **stiff·en·er** *n*

stiff–necked \'stif-'nekt\ *adj* : STUBBORN, HAUGHTY

sti·fle \'stī-fəl\ *vb* **sti·fled; sti·fling 1** : to kill by depriving of or die from lack of oxygen or air : SMOTHER **2** : to keep in check by effort : SUPPRESS ⟨~ a sneeze⟩ — **sti·fling·ly** *adv*

stig·ma \'stig-mə\ *n, pl* **stig·ma·ta** \stig-'mä-tə, 'stig-mə-tə\ *or* **stigmas** [L] **1** : a mark of disgrace or discredit **2** *pl* : bodily marks resembling the wounds of the crucified Christ **3** : the upper part of the pistil of a flower that receives the pollen in fertilization — **stig·mat·ic** \stig-'ma-tik\ *adj*

stig·ma·tize \'stig-mə-ˌtīz\ *vb* **-tized; -tiz·ing 1** : to mark with a stigma **2** : to characterize as disgraceful

stile \'stīl\ *n* : steps used for crossing a fence or wall

sti·let·to \stə-'le-tō\ *n, pl* **-tos** *or* **-toes** [It. dim. of *stilo* stylus, dagger] : a slender dagger

¹still \'stil\ *adj* **1** : MOTIONLESS **2** : making no sound : SILENT — **still·ness** *n*

²still *vb* : to make or become still

³still *adv* **1** : without motion ⟨sit ∼⟩ **2** : up to and during this or that time **3** : in spite of that : NEVERTHELESS **4** : EVEN ⟨ran ∼ faster⟩ **5** : BESIDES, YET

⁴still *n* **1** : STILLNESS, SILENCE **2** : a static photograph esp. from a motion picture

⁵still *n* **1** : DISTILLERY **2** : apparatus used in distillation

still·birth \'stil-ˌbərth\ *n* : the birth of a dead fetus

still·born \-'bȯrn\ *adj* : born dead

still life *n, pl* **still lifes** : a picture of inanimate objects

stilt \'stilt\ *n* : one of a pair of poles for walking with each having a step or loop for the foot to elevate the wearer above the ground; *also* : a polelike support of a structure above ground or water level

stilt·ed \'stil-təd\ *adj* : not easy and natural ⟨∼ language⟩

Stil·ton \'stilt-ᵊn\ *n* : a blue cheese of English origin

stim·u·lant \'sti-myə-lənt\ *n* **1** : an agent (as a drug) that temporarily increases the activity of an organism or any of its parts **2** : STIMULUS **3** : an alcoholic beverage — **stimulant** *adj*

stim·u·late \-ˌlāt\ *vb* **-lat·ed; -lat·ing** : to make active or more active : ANIMATE, AROUSE *syn* excite, provoke, motivate, quicken — **stim·u·la·tion** \ˌsti-myə-'lā-shən\ *n* — **stim·u·la·tive** \'sti-myə-ˌlā-tiv\ *adj*

stim·u·lus \'sti-myə-ləs\ *n, pl* **-li** \-ˌlī\ [L] **1** : something that moves to activity **2** : an agent that directly influences the activity of a living organism or one of its parts

¹sting \'stiŋ\ *vb* **stung** \'stəŋ\; **sting·ing 1** : to prick painfully esp. with a sharp or poisonous process **2** : to cause to suffer acutely — **sting·er** *n*

²sting *n* **1** : an act of stinging; *also* : a resultant wound, sore, or pain **2** : a pointed often venom-bearing organ (as of a bee) : STINGER **3** : an elaborate confidence game; *esp* : one worked by undercover police to trap criminals

stin·gy \'stin-jē\ *adj* **stin·gi·er; -est** : not generous : giving or spending as little as possible — **stin·gi·ness** *n*

stink \'stiŋk\ *vb* **stank** \'staŋk\ *or* **stunk** \'stəŋk\; **stunk; stink·ing** : to give forth a strong and offensive smell; *also* : to be extremely bad in quality or repute — **stink** *n* — **stink·er** *n*

stink·bug \'stiŋk-ˌbəg\ *n* : any of various true bugs that emit a disagreeable odor

¹stint \'stint\ *vb* **1** : to be sparing or frugal **2** : to cut short in amount

²stint *n* **1** : an assigned amount of work **2** : RESTRAINT, LIMITATION **3** : a period of time spent at a particular activity

sti·pend \'stī-ˌpend, -pənd\ *n* [ME, alter. of *stipendy*, fr. L *stipendium*, fr. *stips* gift + *pendere* to weigh, pay] : a fixed sum of money paid periodically for services or to defray expenses

stip·ple \'sti-pəl\ *vb* **stip·pled; stip·pling 1** : to engrave by means of dots and light strokes **2** : to apply (as paint or ink) with small short touches — **stipple** *n*

stip·u·late \'sti-pyə-ˌlāt\ *vb* **-lat·ed; -lat·ing** : to make an agreement; *esp* : to make a special demand for something as a condition in an agreement — **stip·u·la·tion** \ˌsti-pyə-'lā-shən\ *n*

¹stir \'stər\ *vb* **stirred; stir·ring 1** : to move slightly **2** : AROUSE, EXCITE **3** : to mix, dissolve, or make by continued circular movement ⟨∼ eggs into cake bat-

ter⟩ **4** : to move to activity (as by pushing, beating, or prodding)

²stir *n* **1** : a state of agitation or activity **2** : an act of stirring

stir–fry \'stər-ˌfrī\ *vb* : to fry quickly over high heat while stirring continuously — **stir–fry** *n*

stir·ring \'stər-iŋ\ *adj* **1** : ACTIVE, BUSTLING **2** : ROUSING, INSPIRING

stir·rup \'stər-əp\ *n* [ME *stirop*, fr. OE *stigrāp*, lit., mounting rope] **1** : a light frame hung from a saddle to support the rider's foot **2** : STAPES

¹stitch \'stich\ *n* **1** : a sudden sharp pain esp. in the side **2** : one of the series of loops formed by or over a needle in sewing

²stitch *vb* **1** : to fasten or join with stitches **2** : to decorate with stitches **3** : SEW

stk *abbr* stock

stoat \'stōt\ *n, pl* **stoats** *also* **stoat** : the common Old and New World ermine esp. in its brown summer coat

¹stock \'stäk\ *n* **1** *archaic* : a block of wood **2** : a stupid person **3** : a wooden part of a thing serving as its support, frame, or handle **4** *pl* : a device for publicly punishing offenders consisting of a wooden frame with holes in which the feet and hands can be locked **5** : the original from which others derive; *also* : a group having a common origin : FAMILY **6** : LIVESTOCK **7** : a supply of goods **8** : the ownership element in a corporation divided to give the owners an interest and usu. voting power **9** : a company of actors playing at a particular theater and presenting a series of plays **10** : liquid in which meat, fish, or vegetables have been simmered that is used as a basis for soup, gravy, or sauce

stocks 4

²stock *vb* : to provide with stock

³stock *adj* : kept regularly for sale or use; *also* : commonly used : STANDARD

stock·ade \stä-'kād\ *n* [Sp *estacada*, fr. *estaca* stake, pale] : an enclosure (as of posts and stakes) for defense or confinement

stock·bro·ker \-ˌbrō-kər\ *n* : one who executes orders to buy and sell securities

stock car *n* : a racing car that is similar to a regular car

stock exchange *n* : a place where the buying and selling of securities is conducted

stock·hold·er \'stäk-ˌhōl-dər\ *n* : one who owns corporate stock

stock·i·nette *or* **stock·i·net** \ˌstä-kə-'net\ *n* : an elastic knitted fabric used esp. for infants' wear and bandages

stock·ing \'stä-kiŋ\ *n* : a close-fitting knitted covering for the foot and leg

stock market *n* **1** : STOCK EXCHANGE **2** : a market for stocks

stock·pile \'stäk-ˌpīl\ *n* : a reserve supply esp. of something essential — **stockpile** *vb*

stocky \'stä-kē\ *adj* **stock·i·er; -est** : being short and relatively thick : STURDY **syn** thickset, squat, heavyset, stubby

stock·yard \'stäk-ˌyärd\ n : a yard for stock; *esp* : one for livestock about to be slaughtered or shipped

stodgy \'stä-jē\ adj **stodg·i·er; -est 1** : HEAVY, DULL **2** : extremely old-fashioned

¹sto·ic \'stō-ik\ n [ME, fr. L *stoicus*, fr. Gk *stōïkos*, lit., of the portico, fr. *Stoa (Poikilē)* the Painted Portico, portico at Athens where the philosopher Zeno taught] : one who suffers without complaining

²stoic *or* **sto·i·cal** \-i-kəl\ adj : not affected by passion or feeling; *esp* : showing indifference to pain **syn** impassive, phlegmatic, apathetic, stolid — **sto·i·cal·ly** \-i-k(ə-)lē\ adv — **sto·icism** \'stō-ə-ˌsi-zəm\ n

stoke \'stōk\ vb **stoked; stok·ing 1** : to stir up a fire **2** : to tend and supply fuel to a furnace — **stok·er** n

STOL *abbr* short takeoff and landing

¹stole \'stōl\ *past of* STEAL

²stole n **1** : a long narrow band worn round the neck by some clergymen **2** : a long wide scarf or similar covering worn by women

stolen *past part of* STEAL

stol·id \'stä-ləd\ adj : not easily aroused or excited : showing little or no emotion **syn** phlegmatic, apathetic, impassive, stoic — **sto·lid·i·ty** \stä-'li-də-tē\ n — **stol·id·ly** adv

sto·lon \'stō-lən, -ˌlän\ n : RUNNER 6

¹stom·ach \'stə-mək\ n **1** : a saclike digestive organ of a vertebrate into which food goes from the mouth by way of the throat and which opens below into the intestine **2** : a cavity in an invertebrate animal that is analogous to a stomach **3** : ABDOMEN **4** : desire for food caused by hunger : APPETITE **5** : INCLINATION, DESIRE

²stomach vb : to bear without open resentment : put up with

stom·ach·ache \-ˌāk\ n : pain in or in the region of the stomach

stom·ach·er \'stə-mi-kər, -chər\ n : the front of a bodice often appearing between the laces of an outer garment (as in 16th century costume)

stomp \'stämp, 'stȯmp\ vb : STAMP — **stomp** n

¹stone \'stōn\ n **1** : hardened earth or mineral matter : ROCK **2** : a small piece of rock **3** : a precious stone : GEM **4** : CALCULUS 3 **5** : a hard stony seed (as of a date) or one (as of a plum) with a stony covering **6** pl usu **stone** : a British unit of weight equal to 14 pounds — **stony** *also* **ston·ey** \'stō-nē\ adj

²stone vb **stoned; ston·ing 1** : to pelt or kill with stones **2** : to remove the stones of (a fruit)

Stone Age n : the first known period of prehistoric human culture characterized by the use of stone tools

stoned \'stōnd\ adj **1** : DRUNK **2** : being under the influence of a drug

stone·wall \'stōn-ˌwȯl\ vb : to refuse to comply or cooperate with

stone·washed \'stōn-ˌwȯsht, -ˌwäsht\ adj : having been washed with stones during manufacture to create a softer fabric ⟨~ jeans⟩

stood *past and past part of* STAND

stooge \'stüj\ n **1** : a person who plays a subordinate or compliant role to a principal **2** : STRAIGHT MAN

stool \'stül\ n **1** : a seat usu. without back or arms **2** : FOOTSTOOL **3** : a seat used while urinating or defecating **4** : a discharge of fecal matter

stool pigeon n : DECOY, INFORMER

¹stoop \'stüp\ vb **1** : to bend forward and downward **2** : CONDESCEND **3** : to lower oneself morally

²stoop n **1** : an act of bending forward **2** : a bent position of head and shoulders

³stoop n : a porch or platform at a house door

¹stop \'stäp\ vb **stopped; stop·ping 1** : to close (an opening) by filling or covering closely **2** : BLOCK, HALT **3** : to cease to go on **4** : to bring activity or operation to an end **5** : STAY, TARRY **syn** quit, discontinue, desist, cease

²stop n **1** : END, CESSATION **2** : a set of organ pipes of one tone quality; *also* : a control knob for such a set **3** : OBSTRUCTION **4** : PLUG, STOPPER **5** : an act of stopping : CHECK **6** : a delay in a journey : STAY **7** : a place for stopping **8** *chiefly Brit* : any of several punctuation marks

stop·gap \'stäp-ˌgap\ n : something that serves as a temporary expedient

stop·light \-ˌlīt\ n : TRAFFIC LIGHT

stop·over \'stäp-ˌō-vər\ n **1** : a stop at an intermediate point in one's journey **2** : a stopping place on a journey

stop·page \'stä-pij\ n : the act of stopping : the state of being stopped

stop·per \'stä-pər\ n : something (as a cork) for sealing an opening

stop·watch \'stäp-ˌwäch\ n : a watch that can be started or stopped at will for exact timing

stor·age \'stȯr-ij\ n **1** : space for storing; *also* : cost of storing **2** : MEMORY 6 **3** : the act of storing; *esp* : the safekeeping of goods (as in a warehouse)

storage battery n : a group of connected rechargeable electrochemical cells used to provide electric current

¹store \'stȯr\ vb **stored; stor·ing 1** : to place or leave in a safe location for preservation or future use **2** : to provide esp. for a future need

²store n **1** : something accumulated and kept for future use **2** : a large or ample quantity **3** : STOREHOUSE **4** : a retail business establishment

store·house \-ˌhaus\ n : a building for storing goods or supplies; *also* : an abundant source or supply

store·keep·er \-ˌkē-pər\ n : one who operates a retail store

store·room \-ˌrüm, -ˌrum\ n : a room for storing goods or supplies

sto·ried \'stȯr-ēd\ adj : celebrated in story or history

stork \'stȯrk\ n : any of various large stout-billed Old World wading birds related to the herons and ibises

storm \'stȯrm\ n **1** : a heavy fall of rain, snow, or hail with high wind **2** : a violent outbreak or disturbance **3** : a mass attack on a defended position — **storm·i·ly** \'stȯr-mə-lē\ adv — **storm·i·ness** \-mē-nəs\ n — **stormy** adj

²storm vb **1** : to blow with violence; *also* : to rain, snow, or hail heavily **2** : to make a mass attack against **3** : to be violently angry : RAGE **4** : to rush along furiously

¹sto·ry \'stȯr-ē\ n, pl **stories 1** : NARRATIVE, ACCOUNT **2** : REPORT, STATEMENT **3** : ANECDOTE **4** : SHORT STORY **5** : LIE, FALSEHOOD **6** : a news article or broadcast **syn** untruth, tale, canard

²story *also* **sto·rey** \'stȯr-ē\ n, pl **stories** *also* **storeys** : a floor of a building or the space between two adjacent floor levels

sto·ry·tell·er \-ˌte-lər\ n : a teller of stories

sto·tin·ka \stō-'tiŋ-kə\ n, pl **-tin·ki** \-kē\ — see *lev* at MONEY table

¹stout \'staut\ adj **1** : BRAVE **2** : FIRM **3** : STURDY **4** : STAUNCH, ENDURING **5** : SOLID **6** : FORCEFUL, VIOLENT **7** : BULKY, THICKSET **syn** fleshy, fat, portly, corpulent, obese, plump — **stout·ly** adv — **stout·ness** n

²stout n : a dark heavy ale

¹stove \'stōv\ n : an apparatus that burns fuel or uses electricity to provide heat (as for cooking or heating)

²stove *past and past part of* STAVE

stow \'stō\ vb **1** : HIDE, STORE **2** : to pack in a compact mass

stow·away \'stō-ə-ˌwā\ n : one who hides on a vehicle to ride free

STP *abbr* standard temperature and pressure

strad·dle \'strad-əl\ vb **strad·dled; strad·dling 1** : to stand, sit, or walk with legs spread apart **2** : to favor or seem to favor two apparently opposite sides — **straddle** n

strafe \'strāf\ vb **strafed; straf·ing** [G *Gott strafe England* may God punish England, propaganda slogan during World War I] : to fire upon with machine guns from a low-flying airplane

strag·gle \'stra-gəl\ *vb* **strag·gled; strag·gling 1** : to wander from the direct course : ROVE, STRAY **2** : to become separated from others of the same kind — **strag·gler** *n* — **strag·gly** \'stra-g(ə-)lē\ *adj*

¹straight \'strāt\ *adj* **1** : free from curves, bends, angles, or irregularities **2** : not wandering from the main point or proper course ⟨~ thinking⟩ **3** : HONEST, UPRIGHT **4** : having the elements in correct order **5** : UNMIXED, UNDILUTED ⟨~ whiskey⟩ **6** : CONVENTIONAL, SQUARE; *also* : HETEROSEXUAL

²straight *adv* : in a straight manner

³straight *n* **1** : a straight line, course, or arrangement **2** : the part of a racetrack between the last turn and the finish **3** : a sequence of five cards in a poker hand

straight–arm \'strāt-ˌärm\ *n* : an act of warding off a football tackler with the arm fully extended — **straight–arm** *vb*

straight·away \'strā-tə-ˌwā\ *n* : a straight stretch (as at a racetrack)

straight·edge \'strāt-ˌej\ *n* : a piece of material with a straight edge for testing straight lines and surfaces or drawing straight lines

straight·en \'strāt-ᵊn\ *vb* : to make or become straight

straight flush *n* : a poker hand containing five cards of the same suit in sequence

straight·for·ward \strāt-'fȯr-wərd\ *adj* **1** : FRANK, CANDID, HONEST **2** : proceeding in a straight course or manner

straight man *n* : an entertainer who feeds lines to a comedian

straight·way \'strāt-'wā, -ˌwā\ *adv* : IMMEDIATELY

¹strain \'strān\ *n* [ME *streen* progeny, lineage, fr. OE *strēon* gain, acquisition] **1** : LINEAGE, ANCESTRY **2** : a group (as of people or plants) of presumed common ancestry **3** : an inherited or inherent character or quality ⟨a ~ of madness in the family⟩ **4** : STREAK, TRACE **5** : MELODY **6** : the general style or tone

²strain *vb* [ME, fr. MF *estraindre*, fr. L *stringere* to bind or draw tight, press together] **1** : to draw taut **2** : to exert to the utmost **3** : to strive violently **4** : to injure by improper or excessive use **5** : to filter or remove by filtering **6** : to stretch beyond a proper limit — **strain·er** *n*

³strain *n* **1** : excessive tension or exertion (as of body or mind) **2** : bodily injury from excessive tension, effort, or use; *esp* : one in which muscles or ligaments are unduly stretched usu. from a wrench or twist **3** : deformation of a material body under the action of applied forces

¹strait \'strāt\ *adj* [ME, fr. OF *estreit*, fr. L *strictus* strait, strict] **1** *archaic* : STRICT **2** *archaic* : NARROW **3** *archaic* : CONSTRICTED **4** : DIFFICULT, STRAITENED

²strait *n* **1** : a narrow channel connecting two bodies of water **2** *pl* : DISTRESS

strait·en \'strāt-ᵊn\ *vb* **1** : to hem in : CONFINE **2** : to make distressing or difficult

strait·jack·et *also* **straight·jack·et** \'strāt-ˌja-kət\ *n* : a cover or garment of strong material (as canvas) used to bind the body and esp. the arms closely in restraining a violent prisoner or patient — **straitjacket** *vb*

strait·laced *or* **straight·laced** \-'lāst\ *adj* : strict in manners, morals or opinion

¹strand \'strand\ *n* : SHORE, BEACH

²strand *vb* **1** : to run, drift, or drive upon the shore ⟨a ~ed ship⟩ **2** : to place or leave in a helpless position

³strand *n* **1** : one of the fibers twisted or plaited together into a cord, rope, or cable; *also* : a cord, rope, or cable made up of such fibers **2** : a twisted or plaited ropelike mass ⟨a ~ of pearls⟩ — **strand·ed** \'strandəd\ *adj*

strange \'strānj\ *adj* **strang·er; strang·est** [ME, fr. OF *estrange*, fr. L *extraneus*, lit., external, fr. *extra* outside] **1** : of external origin, kind, or character **2** : NEW, UNFAMILIAR **3** : DISTANT **6 4** : UNACCUSTOMED, INEX-

PERIENCED **syn** singular, peculiar, eccentric, erratic, odd, queer, quaint, curious — **strange·ly** *adv* — **strange·ness** *n*

strang·er \'strān-jər\ *n* **1** : FOREIGNER **2** : INTRUDER **3** : a person with whom one is unacquainted

stran·gle \'straŋ-gəl\ *vb* **stran·gled; stran·gling 1** : to choke to death : THROTTLE **2** : STIFLE, SUPPRESS — **stran·gler** *n*

stran·gu·late \'straŋ-gyə-ˌlāt\ *vb* **-lat·ed; -lat·ing 1** : STRANGLE, CONSTRICT **2** : to become so constricted as to stop circulation

stran·gu·la·tion \ˌstraŋ-gyə-'lā-shən\ *n* : the act or process of strangling or strangulating; *also* : the state of being strangled or strangulated

¹strap \'strap\ *n* : a narrow strip of flexible material used esp. for fastening, holding together, or wrapping

²strap *vb* **strapped; strap·ping 1** : to secure with a strap **2** : BIND, CONSTRICT **3** : to flog with a strap **4** : STROP

strap·less \-ləs\ *adj* : having no straps; *esp* : having no shoulder straps

¹strap·ping \'stra-piŋ\ *adj* : LARGE, STRONG, HUSKY

²strap·ping *n* : material for a strap

strat·a·gem \'stra-tə-jəm, -ˌjem\ *n* **1** : a trick to deceive or outwit the enemy; *also* : a deceptive scheme **2** : skill in deception

strat·e·gy \'stra-tə-jē\ *n, pl* **-gies** [Gk *stratēgia* generalship, fr. *stratēgos* general, fr. *stratos* camp, army + *agein* to lead] **1** : the science and art of military command aimed at meeting the enemy under conditions advantageous to one's own force **2** : a careful plan or method esp. for achieving an end — **stra·te·gic** \strə-'tē-jik\ *adj* — **strat·e·gist** \'stra-tə-jist\ *n*

strat·i·fy \'stra-tə-ˌfī\ *vb* **-fied; -fy·ing** : to form or arrange in layers — **strat·i·fi·ca·tion** \ˌstra-tə-fə-'kā-shən\ *n*

stra·tig·ra·phy \strə-'ti-grə-fē\ *n* : geology that deals with rock strata — **strati·graph·ic** \ˌstra-tə-'gra-fik\ *adj*

strato·sphere \'stra-tə-ˌsfir\ *n* : the part of the earth's atmosphere between about 7 miles (11 kilometers) and 31 miles (50 kilometers) above the earth — **strato·spher·ic** \ˌstra-tə-'sfir-ik, -'sfer-\ *adj*

stra·tum \'strā-təm, 'stra-\ *n, pl* **stra·ta** \'strā-tə, 'stra-\ [NL, fr. L, spread, bed, fr. neut. of *stratus*, pp. of *sternere* to spread out] **1** : a bed, layer, or sheetlike mass (as of one kind of rock lying between layers of other kinds of rock) **2** : a level of culture; *also* : a group of people representing one stage in cultural development

¹straw \'strȯ\ *n* **1** : stalks of grain after threshing; *also* : a single coarse dry stem (as of a grass) **2** : a thing of small worth : TRIFLE **3** : a tube (as of paper or plastic) for sucking up a beverage

²straw *adj* **1** : made of straw **2** : having no real force or validity ⟨a ~ vote⟩

straw·ber·ry \'strȯ-ˌber-ē, -bə-rē\ *n* : an edible juicy

strawberry

usu. red pulpy fruit of any of serveral low herbs with white flowers and long slender runners; *also* : one of these herbs

straw boss *n* : a foreman of a small group of workers

straw·flow·er \'strȯ-ˌflaü-ər\ *n* : any of several plants whose flowers can be dried with little loss of form or color

¹stray \'strā\ *n* **1** : a domestic animal wandering at large or lost **2** : WAIF

²stray *vb* **1** : to wander or roam without purpose **2** : DEVIATE

³stray *adj* **1** : having strayed : separated from the group or the main body **2** : occurring at random ⟨~ remarks⟩

¹streak \'strēk\ *n* **1** : a line or mark of a different color or texture from its background **2** : a narrow band of light; *also* : a lightning bolt **3** : a slight admixture : TRACE **4** : a brief run (as of luck); *also* : an unbroken series

²streak *vb* **1** : to form streaks in or on **2** : to move very swiftly

¹stream \'strēm\ *n* **1** : a body of water (as a river) flowing on the earth; *also* : any body of flowing fluid (as water or gas) **2** : a continuous procession ⟨a ~ of traffic⟩

²stream *vb* **1** : to flow in or as if in a stream **2** : to pour out streams of liquid **3** : to trail out in length **4** : to move forward in a steady stream

stream·bed \'strēm-ˌbed\ *n* : the channel occupied by a stream

stream·er \'strē-mər\ *n* **1** : a long narrow ribbonlike flag **2** : a long ribbon on a dress or hat **3** : a newspaper headline that runs across the entire sheet **4** *pl* : AURORA

stream·let \'strēm-lət\ *n* : a small stream

stream·lined \-ˌlīnd\ *adj* **1** : made with contours to reduce resistance to motion through water or air **2** : SIMPLIFIED **3** : MODERNIZED — **streamline** *vb*

street \'strēt\ *n* [ME *strete*, fr. OE *strǣt*, fr. LL *strata* paved road, fr. L, fem. of *stratus*, pp. of *sternere* to spread out] **1** : a thoroughfare esp. in a city, town, or village **2** : the occupants of the houses on a street

street·car \-ˌkär\ *n* : a passenger vehicle running on rails on city streets

street railway *n* : a company operating streetcars or buses

street·walk·er \'strēt-ˌwȯ-kər\ *n* : PROSTITUTE

strength \'streŋth\ *n* **1** : the quality of being strong : ability to do or endure : POWER **2** : TOUGHNESS, SOLIDITY **3** : power to resist attack **4** : INTENSITY **5** : force as measured in numbers ⟨the ~ of an army⟩

strength·en \'streŋ-thən\ *vb* : to make or become stronger — **strength·en·er** *n*

stren·u·ous \'stren-yə-wəs\ *adj* **1** : VIGOROUS, ENERGETIC **2** : requiring energy or stamina — **stren·u·ous·ly** *adv*

strep \'strep\ *n* : STREPTOCOCCUS

strep throat *n* : an infectious sore throat caused by streptococci and marked by fever, prostration, and toxemia

strep·to·coc·cus \ˌstrep-tə-'kä-kəs\ *n*, *pl* **-coc·ci** \-'kä-ˌkī, -'käk-ˌsī, -'kä-ˌkē, -'käk-ˌsē\ : any of various spherical bacteria that usu. grow in chains and include some causing serious diseases — **strep·to·coc·cal** \-kəl\ *adj*

strep·to·my·cin \-'mīs-ᵊn\ *n* : an antibiotic produced by soil bacteria and used esp. in treating tuberculosis

¹stress \'stres\ *n* **1** : PRESSURE, STRAIN; *esp* : a force that tends to distort a body **2** : a factor that induces bodily or mental tension; *also* : a state induced by such a stress **3** : EMPHASIS **4** : relative prominence of sound **5** : ACCENT; *also* : any syllable carrying the accent — **stress·ful** \'stres-fəl\ *adj*

²stress *vb* **1** : to put pressure or strain on **2** : to put emphasis on : ACCENT

¹stretch \'strech\ *vb* **1** : to spread or reach out : EXTEND

2 : to draw out in length or breadth : EXPAND **3** : to make tense : STRAIN **4** : EXAGGERATE **5** : to become extended without breaking ⟨rubber ~es easily⟩

²stretch *n* **1** : an act of extending or drawing out beyond ordinary or normal limits **2** : a continuous extent in length, area, or time **3** : the extent to which something may be stretched **4** : either of the straight sides of a racecourse

³stretch *adj* : easily stretched ⟨~ pants⟩

stretch·er \'stre-chər\ *n* **1** : one that stretches **2** : a device for carrying a sick, injured, or dead person

strew \'strü\ *vb* **strewed**; **strewed** *or* **strewn** \'strün\; **strew·ing 1** : to spread by scattering **2** : to cover by or as if by scattering something over or on **3** : DISSEMINATE

stria \'strī-ə\ *n*, *pl* **stri·ae** \'strī-ˌē\ **1** : STRIATION 3 **2** : a stripe or line (as in the skin)

stri·at·ed muscle \'strī-ˌā-təd-\ *n* : muscle tissue made up of long thin cells with many nuclei and alternate light and dark stripes that includes esp. the muscle of the heart and muscle that moves the vertebrate skeleton and is mostly under voluntary control

stri·a·tion \strī-'ā-shən\ *n* **1** : the state of being marked with stripes or lines **2** : arrangement of striations or striae **3** : a minute groove, scratch, or channel esp. when one of a parallel series

strick·en \'stri-kən\ *adj* **1** : afflicted by or as if by disease, misfortune, or sorrow **2** : WOUNDED

strict \'strikt\ *adj* **1** : allowing no evasion or escape : RIGOROUS ⟨~ discipline⟩ **2** : ACCURATE, PRECISE **syn** stringent, rigid — **strict·ly** *adv* — **strict·ness** *n*

stric·ture \'strik-chər\ *n* **1** : an abnormal narrowing of a bodily passage; *also* : the narrowed part **2** : hostile criticism : a critical remark

¹stride \'strīd\ *vb* **strode** \'strōd\; **strid·den** \'strid-ᵊn\; **strid·ing** : to walk or run with long regular steps — **strid·er** *n*

²stride *n* **1** : a long step **2** : a stage of progress **3** : manner of striding : GAIT

stri·dent \'strīd-ᵊnt\ *adj* : harsh sounding : GRATING, SHRILL

strife \'strīf\ *n* : CONFLICT, FIGHT, STRUGGLE **syn** discord, contention, dissension

¹strike \'strīk\ *vb* **struck** \'strək\; **struck** *also* **stricken** \'stri-kən\; **strik·ing 1** : to take a course : GO ⟨*struck* off through the brush⟩ **2** : to touch or hit sharply; *also* : to deliver a blow **3** : to produce by or as if by a blow ⟨*struck* terror in the foe⟩ **4** : to lower (as a flag or sail) **5** : to collide with; *also* : to injure or destroy by collision **6** : DELETE, CANCEL **7** : to produce by impressing ⟨*struck* a medal⟩; *also* : COIN ⟨~ a new cent⟩ **8** : to cause to sound ⟨~ a bell⟩ **9** : to afflict suddenly : lay low ⟨*stricken* with a high fever⟩ **10** : to appear to; *also* : to appear to as remarkable : IMPRESS **11** : to reach by reckoning ⟨~ an average⟩ **12** : to stop work in order to obtain a change in conditions of employment **13** : to cause (a match) to ignite by rubbing **14** : to come upon ⟨~ gold⟩ **15** : TAKE ON, ASSUME ⟨~ a pose⟩ — **strik·er** *n*

²strike *n* **1** : an act or instance of striking **2** : a sudden discovery of rich ore or oil deposits **3** : a pitched baseball that is swung at but not hit **4** : the knocking down of all the bowling pins with the 1st ball **5** : a military attack

strike·break·er \-ˌbrā-kər\ *n* : a person hired to replace a striking worker

strike·out \-ˌaüt\ *n* : an out in baseball as a result of a batter's being charged with three strikes

strike out *vb* **1** : to enter upon a course of action **2** : to start out vigorously **3** : to make an out in baseball by a strikeout

strike up *vb* **1** : to begin or cause to begin to sing or play **2** : BEGIN

strike zone *n* : the area over home plate through which a pitched baseball must pass to be called a strike

strik·ing \'strī-kiŋ\ *adj* : attracting attention : very noticeable **syn** arresting, salient, conspicuous, outstanding, remarkable, prominent — **strik·ing·ly** *adv*

¹**string** \'striŋ\ *n* **1** : a line usu. composed of twisted threads **2** : a series of things arranged as if strung on a cord **3** : a plant fiber (as a leaf vein) **4** *pl* : the stringed instruments of an orchestra **syn** succession, progression, sequence, chain, train

²**string** *vb* **strung** \'strəŋ\; **string·ing 1** : to provide with strings ⟨∼ a racket⟩ **2** : to make tense **3** : to thread on or as if on a string ⟨∼ pearls⟩ **4** : to hang, tie, or fasten by a string **5** : to take the strings out of ⟨∼ beans⟩ **6** : to extend like a string

string bean *n* : a bean of one of the older varieties of kidney bean that have stringy fibers on the lines of separation of the pods; *also* : SNAP BEAN

stringed \'striŋd\ *adj* **1** : having strings ⟨∼ instruments⟩ **2** : produced by strings

strin·gen·cy \'strin-jən-sē\ *n* **1** : STRICTNESS, SEVERITY **2** : SCARCITY ⟨∼ of money⟩ — **strin·gent** \-jənt\ *adj*

string·er \'striŋ-ər\ *n* **1** : a long horizontal member in a framed structure or a bridge **2** : a news correspondent paid by the amount of copy

stringy \'striŋ-ē\ *adj* **string·i·er; -est 1** : resembling string esp. in tough, fibrous, or disordered quality ⟨∼ meat⟩ ⟨∼ hair⟩ **2** : lean and sinewy in build

¹**strip** \'strip\ *vb* **stripped** \'stript\ *also* **stript; strip·ping 1** : to take the covering or clothing from **2** : to take off one's clothes **3** : to pull or tear off **4** : to make bare or clear (as by cutting or grazing) **5** : PLUNDER, PILLAGE **syn** divest, denude, deprive, dismantle — **strip·per** *n*

²**strip** *n* **1** : a long narrow flat piece **2** : AIRSTRIP

¹**stripe** \'strīp\ *vb* **striped** \'strīpt\; **strip·ing** : to make stripes on

²**stripe** *n* **1** : a line or long narrow division having a different color from the background **2** : a strip of braid (as on a sleeve) indicating military rank or length of service **3** : TYPE, CHARACTER — **striped** \'strīpt, 'strī-pəd\ *adj*

striped bass *n* : a large marine bony fish of the Atlantic and Pacific coasts of the U.S. that is an excellent food and sport fish

strip·ling \'stri-pliŋ\ *n* : YOUTH, LAD

strip mine *n* : a mine that is worked from the earth's surface by the stripping of the topsoil — **strip–mine** *vb*

strip·tease \'strip-ˌtēz\ *n* : a burlesque act in which a performer removes clothing piece by piece — **strip-teas·er** *n*

strive \'strīv\ *vb* **strove** \'strōv\ *also* **strived** \'strīvd\; **striv·en** \'stri-vən\ *or* **strived; striv·ing 1** : to make effort : labor hard **2** : to struggle in opposition : CONTEND **syn** endeavor, attempt, try, assay

strobe \'strōb\ *n* **1** : STROBOSCOPE **2** : a device for high-speed intermittent illumination (as in photography)

stro·bo·scope \'strō-bə-ˌskōp\ *n* : an instrument for studying rapid motion by means of a rapidly flashing light

strode *past of* STRIDE

¹**stroke** \'strōk\ *vb* **stroked; strok·ing 1** : to rub gently **2** : to flatter in a manner designed to persuade

²**stroke** *n* **1** : the act of striking : BLOW, KNOCK **2** : a sudden action or process producing an impact ⟨∼ of lightning⟩; *also* : an unexpected result **3** : sudden weakening or loss of consciousness or the power to move or feel caused by rupture or obstruction (as by a clot) of an artery of the brain **4** : one of a series of movements against air or water to get through or over it (the ∼ of a bird's wing) **5** : a rower who sets the pace for a crew **6** : a vigorous effort **7** : the sound of striking (as of a clock) **8** : a single movement with or as if with a tool or implement (as a pen)

stroll \'strōl\ *vb* : to walk in a leisurely or idle manner — **stroll** *n* — **stroll·er** *n*

strong \'strȯŋ\ *adj* **stron·ger** \'strȯŋ-gər\; **stron·gest**

\'strȯŋ-gəst\ **1** : POWERFUL, VIGOROUS **2** : HEALTHY, ROBUST **3** : of a specified number ⟨an army 10 thousand ∼⟩ **4** : not mild or weak **5** : VIOLENT ⟨∼ wind⟩ **6** : ZEALOUS **7** : not easily broken **8** : FIRM, SOLID **syn** stout, sturdy, stalwart, tough — **strong·ly** *adv*

strong–arm \'strȯŋ-ˌärm\ *adj* : having or using undue force ⟨∼ methods⟩

strong force *n* : the physical force responsible for binding together nucleons in the atomic nucleus

strong·hold \-ˌhōld\ *n* : a fortified place : FORTRESS

strong·man \-ˌman\ *n* : one who leads or controls by force of will and character or by military strength

stron·tium \'strän-chē-əm, 'strän-tē-əm\ *n* : a soft malleable metallic chemical element — see ELEMENT table

¹**strop** \'sträp\ *n* : STRAP; *esp* : one for sharpening a razor

²**strop** *vb* **stropped; strop·ping** : to sharpen a razor on a strop

stro·phe \'strō-fē\ *n* [Gk *strophē*, lit., act of turning] : a division of a poem — **stroph·ic** \'strä-fik\ *adj*

strove *past of* STRIVE

struck *past and past part of* STRIKE

¹**struc·ture** \'strək-chər\ *n* [ME, fr. L *structura*, fr. *structus*, pp. of *struere* to heap up, build] **1** : the action of building : CONSTRUCTION **2** : something built (as a house or a dam); *also* : something made up of interdependent parts in a definite pattern of organization **3** : arrangement or relationship of elements (as particles, parts, or organs) in a substance, body, or system — **struc·tur·al** *adj*

²**structure** *vb* **struc·tured; struc·tur·ing** : to make into a structure

stru·del \'strüd-əl, 'shtrüd-\ *n* [G, lit., whirlpool] : a pastry made of a thin sheet of dough rolled up with filling and baked ⟨apple ∼⟩

¹**strug·gle** \'strə-gəl\ *vb* **strug·gled; strug·gling 1** : to make strenuous efforts against opposition : STRIVE **2** : to proceed with difficulty or with great effort **syn** endeavor, attempt, try, assay

²**struggle** *n* **1** : CONTEST, STRIFE **2** : a violent effort or exertion

strum \'strəm\ *vb* **strummed; strum·ming** : to play on a stringed instrument by brushing the strings with the fingers ⟨∼ a guitar⟩

strum·pet \'strəm-pət\ *n* : PROSTITUTE

strung \'strəŋ\ *past and past part of* STRING

¹**strut** \'strət\ *vb* **strut·ted; strut·ting** : to walk with an affectedly proud gait

²**strut** *n* **1** : a bar or rod for resisting lengthwise pressure **2** : a haughty or pompous gait

strych·nine \'strik-ˌnīn, -nən, -ˌnēn\ *n* : a bitter poisonous plant alkaloid used as a poison (as for rats) and medicinally as a stimulant to the central nervous system

¹**stub** \'stəb\ *n* **1** : STUMP **2 2** : a short blunt end **3** : a small part of each leaf (as of a checkbook) kept as a memorandum of the items on the detached part

²**stub** *vb* **stubbed; stub·bing** : to strike (as one's toe) against something

stub·ble \'stə-bəl\ *n* **1** : the cut stem ends of herbs and esp. grasses left in the soil after harvest **2** : a rough surface or growth resembling stubble — **stub·bly** \-b(ə-)lē\ *adj*

stub·born \'stə-bərn\ *adj* **1** : FIRM, DETERMINED **2** : done or continued in a willful, unreasonable, or persistent manner **3** : not easily controlled or remedied ⟨a ∼ cold⟩ — **stub·born·ly** *adv* — **stub·born·ness** *n*

stub·by \'stə-bē\ *adj* : short, blunt, and thick like a stub

stuc·co \'stə-kō\ *n, pl* **stuccos** *or* **stuccoes** [It] : plaster for coating exterior walls — **stuc·coed** \'stə-kōd\ *adj*

stuck *past and past part of* STICK

stuck–up \'stək-'əp\ *adj* : CONCEITED

¹**stud** \'stəd\ *n* : a male animal and esp. a horse (**stud-horse** \-ˌhȯrs\) kept for breeding

²stud *n* **1** : one of the smaller uprights in a building to which the wall materials are fastened **2** : a removable device like a button used as a fastener or ornament ⟨shirt ~s⟩ **3** : a projecting nail, pin, or rod

³stud *vb* **stud·ded; stud·ding 1** : to supply with or adorn with studs **2** : DOT

⁴stud *abbr* student

stud·book \'stəd-ˌbủk\ *n* : an official record of the pedigree of purebred animals (as horses or dogs)

stud·ding \'stə-diŋ\ *n* : the studs in a building or wall

stu·dent \'stüd-ᵊnt, 'styüd-\ *n* : SCHOLAR, PUPIL; *esp* : one who attends a school

stud·ied \'stə-dēd\ *adj* : INTENTIONAL ⟨a ~ insult⟩ **syn** deliberate, considered, premeditated, designed

stu·dio \'stü-dē-ˌō, 'styü-\ *n, pl* **-dios 1** : a place where an artist works; *also* : a place for the study of an art **2** : a place where motion pictures are made **3** : a place equipped for the transmission of radio or television programs

stu·di·ous \'stü-dē-əs, 'styü-\ *adj* : devoted to study — **stu·di·ous·ly** *adv*

¹study \'stə-dē\ *n, pl* **stud·ies 1** : the use of the mind to gain knowledge **2** : the act or process of learning about something **3** : careful examination **4** : INTENT, PURPOSE **5** : a branch of learning **6** : a room esp. for reading and writing

²study *vb* **stud·ied; study·ing 1** : to engage in study or the study of **2** : to consider attentively or in detail **syn** consider, contemplate, weigh

¹stuff \'stəf\ *n* **1** : personal property **2** : raw material **3** : a finished textile fabric; *esp* : a worsted fabric **4** : writing, talk, or ideas of little or transitory worth **5** : an unspecified material substance or aggregate of matter **6** : fundamental material **7** : special knowledge or capability

²stuff *vb* **1** : to fill by packing things in : CRAM **2** : to eat greedily : GORGE **3** : to prepare (as meat) by filling with a stuffing **4** : to fill (as a cushion) with a soft material **5** : to stop up : PLUG

stuffed shirt \'stəft-\ *n* : a smug, conceited, and usu. pompous and inflexibly conservative person

stuff·ing *n* : material used to fill tightly; *esp* : a mixture of bread crumbs and spices used to stuff meat and poultry

stuffy \'stə-fē\ *adj* **stuff·i·er; -est 1** : STODGY **2** : lacking fresh air : CLOSE; *also* : blocked up ⟨a ~ nose⟩

stul·ti·fy \'stəl-tə-ˌfī\ *vb* **-fied; -fy·ing 1** : to cause to appear foolish or stupid **2** : to impair, invalidate, or make ineffective **3** : to have a dulling effect on — **stul·ti·fi·ca·tion** \ˌstəl-tə-fə-'kā-shən\ *n*

stum·ble \'stəm-bəl\ *vb* **stum·bled; stum·bling 1** : to blunder morally **2** : to trip in walking or running **3** : to walk unsteadily; *also* : to speak or act in a blundering or clumsy manner **4** : to happen by chance — **stum·ble** *n*

stumbling block *n* : an obstacle to belief, understanding, or progress

¹stump \'stəmp\ *n* **1** : the base of a bodily part (as a leg or tooth) left after the rest is removed **2** : the part of a plant and esp. a tree remaining with the root after the trunk is cut off **3** : a place or occasion for political public speaking — **stumpy** *adj*

²stump *vb* **1** : BAFFLE, PERPLEX **2** : to clear (land) of stumps **3** : to tour (a region) making political speeches **4** : to walk clumsily and heavily

stun \'stən\ *vb* **stunned; stun·ning 1** : to make senseless or dizzy by or as if by a blow **2** : BEWILDER, STUPEFY

stung *past and past part of* STING

stunk *past and past part of* STINK

stun·ning *adj* **1** : causing astonishment or disbelief **2** : strikingly beautiful — **stun·ning·ly** *adv*

¹stunt \'stənt\ *vb* : to hinder the normal growth or progress of

²stunt *n* : an unusual or spectacular feat

stu·pe·fy \'stü-pə-ˌfī, 'styü-\ *vb* **-fied; -fy·ing 1** : to make stupid, groggy, or insensible **2** : ASTONISH — **stu·pe·fac·tion** \ˌstü-pə-'fak-shən, ˌstyü-\ *n*

stu·pen·dous \stủ-'pen-dəs, styủ-\ *adj* : causing astonishment esp. because of great size or height **syn** tremendous, prodigious, monumental, monstrous — **stu·pen·dous·ly** *adv*

stu·pid \'stü-pəd, 'styü-\ *adj* [MF *stupide*, fr. L *stupidus*, fr. *stupēre* to be numb, be astonished] **1** : very dull in mind **2** : showing or resulting from dullness of mind — **stu·pid·i·ty** \stủ-'pi-də-tē, styủ-\ *n* — **stu·pid·ly** *adv*

stu·por \'stü-pər, 'styü-\ *n* **1** : a condition of greatly dulled or completely suspended sense or feeling **2** : a state of extreme apathy or torpor often following stress or shock — **stu·por·ous** *adj*

stur·dy \'stər-dē\ *adj* **stur·di·er; -est** [ME, brave, stubborn, fr. OF *estourdi* stunned, fr. pp. of *estourdir* to stun] **1** : RESOLUTE, UNYIELDING **2** : STRONG, ROBUST **syn** stout, stalwart, tough, tenacious — **stur·di·ly** \-də-lē\ *adv* — **stur·di·ness** \-dē-nəs\ *n*

stur·geon \'stər-jən\ *n* : any of a family of large bony fishes including some whose roe is made into caviar

sturgeon

stut·ter \'stə-tər\ *vb* : to speak with involuntary disruption or blocking of sounds — **stutter** *n*

¹sty \'stī\ *n, pl* **sties** : a pen or housing for swine

²sty *or* **stye** *n, pl* **sties** *or* **styes** : an inflamed swelling of a skin gland on the edge of an eyelid

¹style \'stīl\ *n* **1** : mode of address : TITLE **2** : a way of speaking or writing; *esp* : one characteristic of an individual, period, school, or nation ⟨ornate ~⟩ **3** : manner or method of acting, making, or performing; *also* : a distinctive or characteristic manner **4** : a slender pointed instrument or process; *esp* : STYLUS **5** : a fashionable manner or mode **6** : overall excellence, skill, or grace in performance, manner, or appearance **7** : the custom followed in spelling, capitalization, punctuation, and typography — **sty·lis·tic** \stī-'lis-tik\ *adj*

²style *vb* **styled; styl·ing 1** : NAME, DESIGNATE **2** : to make or design in accord with a prevailing mode

styl·ing \'stī-liŋ\ *n* : the way in which something is styled

styl·ish \'stī-lish\ *adj* : conforming to current fashion **syn** modish, smart, chic — **styl·ish·ly** *adv* — **styl·ish·ness** *n*

styl·ist \'stī-list\ *n* **1** : one (as a writer) noted for a distinctive style **2** : a developer or designer of styles

styl·ize \'stī-ˌlīz, 'stī-ə-\ *vb* **styl·ized; styl·iz·ing** : to conform to a style; *esp* : to represent or design according to a pattern or style rather than according to nature or tradition

sty·lus \'stī-ləs\ *n, pl* **sty·li** \'stī-ˌlī\ *also* **sty·lus·es** \'stī-lə-səz\ [L *stylus, stilus* spike, stylus] **1** : a pointed implement used by the ancients for writing on wax **2** : a phonograph needle

sty·mie \'stī-mē\ *vb* **sty·mied; sty·mie·ing** : BLOCK, FRUSTRATE

styp·tic \'stip-tik\ *adj* : tending to check bleeding — **styptic** *n*

suave \'swäv\ *adj* [MF, pleasant, sweet, fr. L *suavis*] : persuasively pleasing : smoothly agreeable **syn** urbane, smooth, bland — **suave·ly** *adv* — **sua·vi·ty** \'swä-və-tē\ *n*

¹sub \'səb\ *n* : SUBSTITUTE — **sub** *vb*

²sub *n* : SUBMARINE

³sub *abbr* **1** subtract **2** suburb

sub- \'səb\ *prefix* **1** : under : beneath **2** : subordinate

: secondary **3** : subordinate portion of : subdivision of **4** : with repetition of a process described in a simple verb so as to form, stress, or deal with subordinate parts or relations **5** : somewhat **6** : falling nearly in the category of : bordering on

subacute	subliterate
subagency	subminimal
subagent	subminimum
subaqueous	suboptimal
subarctic	suborder
subarea	subparagraph
subatmospheric	subparallel
subaverage	subphylum
subbasement	subplot
subcategory	subpopulation
subcellular	subproblem
subchapter	subprofessional
subclass	subprogram
subclassify	subregion
subcommittee	subroutine
subcontract	subsection
subcontractor	subsense
subculture	subsoil
subcutaneous	subspecies
subdiscipline	substage
subentry	substation
subfamily	subsystem
subfield	subteen
subfreezing	subthreshold
subgenre	subtopic
subgenus	subtotal
subgroup	subtreasury
subhead	subtype
subheading	subunit
subhuman	subvariety
subkingdom	subvisible
sublethal	subzero

sub·al·pine \ˌsəb-ˈal-ˌpīn\ *adj* **1** : of or relating to the region about the foot and lower slopes of the Alps **2** : of, relating to, or inhabiting high upland slopes esp. just below the timberline

sub·al·tern \sə-ˈbȯl-tərn\ *n* : SUBORDINATE; *esp* : a junior officer (as in the British army)

sub·as·sem·bly \ˌsəb-ə-ˈsem-blē\ *n* : an assembled unit to be incorporated with other units in a finished product

sub·atom·ic \ˌsəb-ə-ˈtä-mik\ *adj* : of or relating to the inside of the atom or to particles smaller than atoms

sub·clin·i·cal \ˌsəb-ˈkli-ni-kəl\ *adj* : not detectable by the usual clinical tests ⟨a ∼ infection⟩

sub·com·pact \ˈsəb-ˈkäm-ˌpakt\ *n* : an automobile smaller than a compact

¹sub·con·scious \səb-ˈkän-chəs, ˈsəb-\ *adj* : existing in the mind without entering conscious awareness — **sub·con·scious·ly** *adv* — **sub·con·scious·ness** *n*

²subconscious *n* : mental activities just below the threshold of consciousness

sub·con·ti·nent \ˌsəb-ˈkänt-ᵊn-ənt\ *n* : a major subdivision of a continent — **sub·con·ti·nen·tal** \ˌsəb-ˌkänt-ᵊn-ˈent- ᵊl\ *adj*

sub·di·vide \ˌsəb-də-ˈvīd, ˈsəb-də-ˌvīd\ *vb* : to divide the parts of into more parts; *esp* : to divide (a tract of land) into building lots — **sub·di·vi·sion** \-ˈvi-zhən, -ˌvi-\ *n*

sub·duc·tion \səb-ˈdək-shən\ *n* : the descent of the edge of one crustal plate beneath the edge of an adjacent plate

sub·due \səb-ˈdü, -ˈdyü\ *vb* **sub·dued; sub·du·ing 1** : to bring into subjection : VANQUISH **2** : to bring under control : CURB **3** : to reduce the intensity of

subj *abbr* **1** subject **2** subjunctive

¹sub·ject \ˈsəb-jikt\ *n* [ME, fr. MF, fr. L *subjectus* one under authority & *subjectum* subject of a proposition, fr. *subicere* to subject, lit., to throw under, fr. *sub-* under + *jacere* to throw] **1** : a person under the authority of another **2** : a person subject to a sover-

eign **3** : an individual that is studied or experimented on **4** : the person or thing discussed or treated : TOPIC, THEME **5** : a word or word group denoting that of which something is predicated

²subject *adj* **1** : being under the power or rule of another **2** : LIABLE, EXPOSED ⟨∼ to floods⟩ **3** : dependent on some act or condition ⟨appointment ∼ to senate approval⟩ **syn** subordinate, secondary, tributary, collateral, dependent

³sub·ject \səb-ˈjekt\ *vb* **1** : to bring under control : CONQUER **2** : to make liable **3** : to cause to undergo or endure — **sub·jec·tion** \-ˈjek-shən\ *n*

sub·jec·tive \(ˌ)səb-ˈjek-tiv\ *adj* **1** : of, relating to, or constituting a subject **2** : of, relating to, or arising within one's self or mind in contrast to what is outside : PERSONAL — **sub·jec·tive·ly** *adv* — **sub·jec·tiv·i·ty** \-ˌjek-ˈti-və-tē\ *n*

subject matter *n* : matter presented for consideration, discussion, or study

sub·join \(ˌ)səb-ˈjȯin\ *vb* : APPEND

sub ju·di·ce \(ˌ)süb-ˈyü-di-ˌkā, ˈsəb-ˈjü-də-(ˌ)sē\ *adv* [L] : before a judge or court : not yet legally decided

sub·ju·gate \ˈsəb-ji-ˌgāt\ *vb* **-gat·ed; -gat·ing** : CONQUER, SUBDUE; *also* : ENSLAVE **syn** reduce, overcome, overthrow, vanquish, defeat, beat — **sub·ju·ga·tion** \ˌsəb-ji-ˈgā-shən\ *n*

sub·junc·tive \səb-ˈjənk-tiv\ *adj* : of, relating to, or constituting a verb form that represents an act or state as contingent or possible or viewed emotionally (as with desire) ⟨the ∼ mood⟩ — **subjunctive** *n*

sub·lease \ˈsəb-ˈlēs, -ˌlēs\ *n* : a lease by a lessee of part or all of leased premises to another person with the original lessee retaining some right under the original lease — **sublease** *vb*

¹sub·let \ˈsəb-ˈlet\ *vb* **-let; -let·ting** : to let all or a part of (a leased property) to another; *also* : to rent (a property) from a lessee

²sublet \-ˈlet\ *n* : property and esp. housing obtained by or available through a sublease

sub·li·mate \ˈsə-blə-ˌmāt\ *vb* **-mat·ed; -mat·ing 1** : SUBLIME **2** : to direct the expression of (as a desire or impulse) from a primitive to a more socially and culturally acceptable form — **sub·li·ma·tion** \ˌsə-blə-ˈmā-shən\ *n*

¹sub·lime \sə-ˈblīm\ *vb* **sub·limed; sub·lim·ing** : to pass or cause to pass directly from the solid to the vapor state

²sublime *adj* **1** : EXALTED, NOBLE **2** : having awe-inspiring beauty or grandeur **syn** glorious, splendid, superb, resplendent, gorgeous — **sub·lime·ly** *adv* — **sub·lim·i·ty** \-ˈbli-mə-tē\ *n*

sub·lim·i·nal \(ˌ)səb-ˈli-mən-ᵊl, ˈsəb-\ *adj* **1** : inadequate to produce a sensation or mental awareness ⟨∼ stimuli⟩ **2** : existing or functioning below the threshold of consciousness ⟨the ∼ mind⟩ ⟨∼ advertising⟩

sub·ma·chine gun \ˌsəb-mə-ˈshēn-ˌgən\ *n* : an automatic firearm fired from the shoulder or hip

¹sub·ma·rine \ˈsəb-mə-ˌrēn, ˌsəb-mə-ˈrēn\ *adj* : UNDERWATER; *esp* : UNDERSEA

²submarine *n* **1** : a naval vessel designed to operate underwater **2** : a large sandwich made from a long split roll with any of a variety of fillings

sub·merge \səb-ˈmərj\ *vb* **sub·merged; sub·merg·ing 1** : to put or plunge under the surface of water **2** : INUNDATE — **sub·mer·gence** \-ˈmər-jəns\ *n*

sub·merse \səb-ˈmərs\ *vb* **sub·mersed; sub·mers·ing** : SUBMERGE — **sub·mer·sion** \-ˈmər-zhən\ *n*

¹sub·mers·ible \səb-ˈmər-sə-bəl\ *adj* : capable of being submerged

²submersible *n* : something that is submersible; *esp* : a small underwater craft used for deep-sea research

sub·mi·cro·scop·ic \ˌsəb-ˌmī-krə-ˈskä-pik\ *adj* : too small to be seen in an ordinary light microscope

sub·min·ia·ture \ˌsəb-ˈmi-nē-ə-ˌchur, ˈsəb-, -ˈmi-ni-ˌchur, -chər\ *adj* : very small

sub·mit \səb-ˈmit\ *vb* **sub·mit·ted; sub·mit·ting 1** : to commit to the discretion or decision of another or of others **2** : YIELD, SURRENDER **3** : to put forward as an opinion — **sub·mis·sion** \-'mi-shən\ *n* — **sub·mis·sive** \-'mi-siv\ *adj*

sub·nor·mal \ˌsəb-'nȯr-məl\ *adj* : falling below what is normal; *also* : having less of something and esp. intelligence than is normal — **sub·nor·mal·i·ty** \ˌsəb-nȯr-'ma-lə-tē\ *n*

sub·or·bit·al \ˌsəb-'ȯr-bət-əl, 'səb-\ *adj* : being or involving less than one orbit

¹sub·or·di·nate \sə-'bȯrd-ən-ət\ *adj* **1** : of lower class or rank **2** : INFERIOR **3** : submissive to authority **4** : subordinated to other elements in a sentence : DEPENDENT ⟨~ clause⟩ **syn** secondary, subject, tributary, collateral

²subordinate *n* : one that is subordinate

³sub·or·di·nate \sə-'bȯrd-ən-ˌāt\ *vb* **-nat·ed; -nat·ing 1** : to place in a lower rank or class **2** : SUBDUE — **sub·or·di·na·tion** \-ˌbȯrd-ən-'ā-shən\ *n*

sub·orn \sə-'bȯrn\ *vb* **1** : to induce secretly to do an unlawful thing **2** : to induce to commit perjury — **sub·or·na·tion** \ˌsə-bȯr-'nā-shən\ *n*

¹sub·poe·na \sə-'pē-nə\ *n* [ME *suppena*, fr. L *sub poena* under penalty] : a writ commanding the person named in it to attend court under penalty for failure to do so

²subpoena *vb* **-naed; -na·ing** : to summon with a subpoena

sub–Sa·ha·ran \ˌsəb-sə-'har-ən\ *adj* : of, relating to, or being the part of Africa south of the Sahara

sub·scribe \səb-'skrīb\ *vb* **sub·scribed; sub·scrib·ing 1** : to sign one's name to a document **2** : to give consent by or as if by signing one's name **3** : to promise to contribute by signing one's name with the amount promised **4** : to place an order by signing **5** : to receive a periodical or service regularly on order **6** : FAVOR, APPROVE **syn** agree, acquiesce, assent, accede — **sub·scrib·er** *n*

sub·script \'səb-ˌskript\ *n* : a symbol (as a letter or number) immediately below or below and to the right or left of another written character — **subscript** *adj*

sub·scrip·tion \səb-'skrip-shən\ *n* **1** : the act of subscribing : SIGNATURE **2** : a purchase by signed order

sub·se·quent \'səb-si-kwənt, -sə-ˌkwent\ *adj* : following after : SUCCEEDING — **sub·se·quent·ly** *adv*

sub·ser·vi·ence \səb-'sər-vē-əns\ *n* **1** : a subordinate place or condition **2** : SERVILITY — **sub·ser·vi·en·cy** \-ən-sē\ *n* — **sub·ser·vi·ent** \-ənt\ *adj*

sub·set \'səb-ˌset\ *n* : a set each of whose elements is an element of an inclusive set

sub·side \səb-'sīd\ *vb* **sub·sid·ed; sub·sid·ing** [L *subsidere*, fr. *sub-* under + *sidere* to sit down, sink] **1** : to settle to the bottom of a liquid **2** : to tend downward : DESCEND **3** : SINK, SUBMERGE **4** : to become quiet and tranquil **syn** abate, wane, moderate, slacken — **sub·sid·ence** \səb-'sīd-əns, 'səb-sə-dəns\ *n*

¹sub·sid·iary \səb-'si-dē-ˌer-ē\ *adj* : furnishing aid or support **2** : of secondary importance **3** : of or relating to a subsidy **syn** auxiliary, contributory, subservient, accessory

²subsidiary *n, pl* **-iar·ies** : one that is subsidiary; *esp* : a company controlled by another

sub·si·dize \'səb-sə-ˌdīz\ *vb* **-dized; -diz·ing** : to aid or furnish with a subsidy

sub·si·dy \'səb-sə-dē\ *n, pl* **-dies** [ME, fr. L *subsidium* reserve troops, support, assistance, fr. *sub-* near + *sedēre* to sit] : a gift of public money to a private person or company or to another government

sub·sist \səb-'sist\ *vb* **1** : EXIST, PERSIST **2** : to have the means (as food and clothing) of maintaining life; *esp* : to nourish oneself

sub·sis·tence \səb-'sis-təns\ *n* **1** : EXISTENCE **2** : means of subsisting : the minimum (as of food and clothing) necessary to support life

sub·son·ic \ˌsəb-'sä-nik, 'səb-\ *adj* : being or relating to a speed less than that of sound; *also* : moving at such a speed

sub·spe·cies \'səb-ˌspē-shēz, -ˌsēz\ *n* : a subdivision of a species; *esp* : a category in biological classification ranking just below a species that designates a geographic population genetically distinct from other such populations and potentially able to breed with them where its range overlaps theirs

sub·stance \'səb-stəns\ *n* **1** : essential nature : ESSENCE ⟨divine ~⟩; *also* : the fundamental or essential part or quality ⟨the ~ of the speech⟩ **2** : physical material from which something is made or which has discrete existence; *also* : matter of particular or definite chemical constitution **3** : material possessions : PROPERTY, WEALTH

substance abuse *n* : excessive use of a drug (as alcohol or cocaine) : use of a drug without medical justification

sub·stan·dard \ˌsəb-'stan-dərd\ *adj* : falling short of a standard or norm

sub·stan·tial \səb-'stan-chəl\ *adj* **1** : existing as or in substance : MATERIAL; *also* : not illusory : REAL **2** : IMPORTANT, ESSENTIAL **3** : NOURISHING, SATISFYING ⟨~ meal⟩ **4** : having means : WELL-TO-DO **5** : CONSIDERABLE ⟨~ profit⟩ **6** : STRONG, FIRM — **sub·stan·tial·ly** *adv*

sub·stan·ti·ate \səb-'stan-chē-ˌāt\ *vb* **-at·ed; -at·ing 1** : to give substance or body to **2** : VERIFY, PROVE — **sub·stan·ti·a·tion** \-ˌstan-chē-'ā-shən\ *n*

sub·stan·tive \'səb-stən-tiv\ *n* : NOUN; *also* : a word or phrase used as a noun

¹sub·sti·tute \'səb-stə-ˌtüt, -ˌtyüt\ *n* : a person or thing replacing another — **substitute** *adj*

²substitute *vb* **-tut·ed; -tut·ing 1** : to put or use in the place of another **2** : to serve as a substitute — **sub·sti·tu·tion** \ˌsəb-stə-'tü-shən, -'tyü-\ *n*

sub·strate \'səb-ˌstrāt\ *n* **1** : the base on which a plant or animal lives **2** : a substance acted upon (as by an enzyme)

sub·stra·tum \'səb-ˌstrā-təm, -ˌstra-\ *n, pl* **-stra·ta** \-tə\ : the layer or structure (as subsoil) lying underneath

sub·struc·ture \'səb-ˌstrək-chər\ *n* : FOUNDATION, GROUNDWORK

sub·sur·face \'səb-ˌsər-fəs\ *n* : earth material near the surface of the ground — **subsurface** *adj*

sub·ter·fuge \'səb-tər-ˌfyüj\ *n* : a trick or device used in order to conceal, escape, or evade **syn** fraud, deception, trickery

sub·ter·ra·nean \ˌsəb-tə-'rā-nē-ən\ *adj* **1** : lying or being underground **2** : SECRET, HIDDEN

sub·tile \'sət-əl\ *adj* **sub·til·er** \'sət-lər, -əl-ər\; **sub·til·est** \'sət-ləst, -əl-əst\ : SUBTLE

sub·ti·tle \'səb-ˌtīt-əl\ *n* **1** : a secondary or explanatory title (as of a book) **2** : printed matter projected on a motion-picture screen during or between the scenes

sub·tle \'sət-əl\ *adj* **sub·tler** \'sət-əl-ər\; **sub·tlest** \'sət-əl-əst\ **1** : hardly noticeable ⟨~ differences⟩ **2** : SHREWD, PERCEPTIVE **3** : CLEVER, SLY — **sub·tle·ty** \-tē\ *n* — **sub·tly** \'sət-əl-ē\ *adv*

sub·tract \səb-'trakt\ *vb* : to take away (as one part or number) from another; *also* : to perform the operation of deducting one number from another — **sub·trac·tion** \-'trak-shən\ *n*

sub·tra·hend \'səb-trə-ˌhend\ *n* : a number that is to be subtracted from another

sub·trop·i·cal \ˌsəb-'trä-pi-kəl, 'səb-\ *also* **sub·trop·ic** \-pik\ *adj* : of, relating to, or being regions bordering on the tropical zone — **sub·trop·ics** \-piks\ *n pl*

sub·urb \'sə-ˌbərb\ *n* **1** : an outlying part of a city; *also* : a small community adjacent to a city **2** *pl* : a residential area adjacent to a city — **sub·ur·ban** \sə-'bər-bən\ *adj or n* — **sub·ur·ban·ite** \sə-'bər-bə-ˌnīt\ *n*

sub·ur·bia \sə-'bər-bē-ə\ *n* **1** : SUBURBS **2** : suburban people or customs

sub·ven·tion \səb-'ven-chən\ *n* : SUBSIDY, ENDOWMENT

sub·vert \səb-'vərt\ *vb* **1** : OVERTHROW, RUIN **2** : COR-

RUPT — **sub·ver·sion** \-'vər-zhən\ n — **sub·ver·sive** \-'vər-siv\ adj

sub·way \'səb-ˌwā\ n : an underground way; esp : an underground electric railway

suc·ceed \sək-'sēd\ vb **1** : to follow next in order or next after another; esp : to inherit sovereignty, rank, title, or property **2** : to attain a desired object or end : be successful

suc·cess \sək-'ses\ n **1** : favorable or desired outcome **2** : the gaining of wealth and fame **3** : one that succeeds — **suc·cess·ful** \-fəl\ adj — **suc·cess·ful·ly** adv

suc·ces·sion \sək-'se-shən\ n **1** : the order, act, or right of succeeding to a property, title, or throne **2** : the act or process of following in order **3** : a series of persons or things that follow one after another **syn** progression, sequence, chain, train, string

suc·ces·sive \sək-'se-siv\ adj : following in order : CONSECUTIVE — **suc·ces·sive·ly** adv

suc·ces·sor \sək-'se-sər\ n : one that succeeds (as to a throne, title, estate, or office)

suc·cinct \(ˌ)sək-'siŋkt, sə-'siŋkt\ adj : BRIEF, CONCISE **syn** terse, laconic, summary, curt, short — **suc·cinct·ly** adv — **suc·cinct·ness** n

suc·cor \'sə-kər\ n [ME succur, fr. earlier sucurs, taken as pl., fr. OF sucors, fr. ML succursus, fr. L succurrere to run up, run to help] : AID, HELP, RELIEF — **succor** vb

suc·co·tash \'sə-kə-ˌtash\ n [Narraganset (American Indian language of Rhode Island) msíckquatash boiled corn kernels] : beans and corn kernels cooked together

suc·cour chiefly Brit var of SUCCOR

¹**suc·cu·lent** \'sə-kyə-lənt\ adj : full of juice : JUICY; also : having fleshy tissues that conserve moisture ⟨~ plants⟩ — **suc·cu·lence** \-ləns\ n

²**succulent** n : a succulent plant (as a cactus)

suc·cumb \sə-'kəm\ vb **1** : to yield to superior strength or force or overpowering appeal or desire **2** : DIE **syn** submit, capitulate, relent, defer

¹**such** \'səch, 'sich\ adj **1** : of this or that kind **2** : having a quality just specified or to be specified

²**such** pron **1** : such a one or ones ⟨he's a star, and acted as ~⟩ **2** : that or those similar or related thereto ⟨boards and nails and ~⟩

³**such** adv : to that degree : so

such·like \'səch-ˌlīk\ adj : SIMILAR

¹**suck** \'sək\ vb **1** : to draw in liquid and esp. mother's milk with the mouth **2** : to draw liquid from by action of the mouth ⟨~ an orange⟩ **3** : to take in or up or remove by or as if by suction

²**suck** n **1** : a sucking movement or force **2** : the act of sucking

suck·er \'sə-kər\ n **1** : one that sucks **2** : a part of an animal's body used for sucking or for clinging **3** : a fish with thick soft lips for sucking in food **4** : a shoot from the roots or lower part of a plant **5** : a person easily deceived **6** — used as a generalized term of reference

suck·le \'sə-kəl\ vb **suck·led**; **suck·ling** : to give or draw milk from the breast or udder; also : NURTURE

suck·ling \'sə-kliŋ\ n : a young unweaned mammal

su·cre \'sü-(ˌ)krā\ n — see MONEY table

su·crose \'sü-ˌkrōs, -ˌkrōz\ n : a sweet sugar obtained commercially esp. from sugarcane or sugar beets

suc·tion \'sək-shən\ n **1** : the act of sucking **2** : the act or process of drawing something (as liquid or dust) into a space (as in a vacuum cleaner or a pump) by partially exhausting the air in the space — **suc·tion·al** \-shə-nəl\ adj

suction cup n : a cup-shaped device in which a partial vacuum is produced when applied to a surface

Su·da·nese \ˌsüd-ə-n-'ēz, -'ēs\ n : a native or inhabitant of Sudan — **Sudanese** adj

sud·den \'səd-ᵊn\ adj [ME sodain, fr. MF, fr. L subitaneus, fr. subitus sudden, fr. pp. of subire to come up] **1** : happening or coming unexpectedly ⟨~ show-

er⟩; also : changing angle or character all at once ⟨~ turn⟩ ⟨~ descent⟩ **2** : HASTY, RASH ⟨~ decision⟩ **3** : made or brought about in a short time : PROMPT ⟨~ cure⟩ **syn** precipitate, headlong, impetuous — **sud·den·ly** adv — **sud·den·ness** n

sudden infant death syndrome n : death due to unknown causes of an apparently healthy infant usu. before one year of age and esp. during sleep

suds \'sədz\ n pl : soapy water esp. when frothy — **suds·y** \'səd-zē\ adj

sue \'sü\ vb **sued**; **su·ing** **1** : PETITION, SOLICIT **2** : to seek justice or right by bringing legal action

suede or **suède** \'swād\ n [F gants de Suède Swedish gloves] **1** : leather with a napped surface **2** : a fabric with a suedelike nap

su·et \'sü-ət\ n : the hard fat from beef and mutton that yields tallow

suff abbr **1** sufficient **2** suffix

suf·fer \'sə-fər\ vb **suf·fered**; **suf·fer·ing** **1** : to feel or endure pain **2** : EXPERIENCE, UNDERGO **3** : to bear loss, damage, or injury **4** : ALLOW, PERMIT **syn** endure, abide, tolerate, stand, brook, stomach — **suf·fer·able** \'sə-fə-rə-bəl\ adj — **suf·fer·er** n

suf·fer·ance \'sə-frəns, -fə-rəns\ n **1** : consent or approval implied by lack of interference or resistance **2** : ENDURANCE, PATIENCE

suf·fer·ing \'sə-friŋ, -fə-riŋ\ n : PAIN, MISERY, HARDSHIP

suf·fice \sə-'fīs\ vb **suf·ficed**; **suf·fic·ing** **1** : to satisfy a need : be sufficient **2** : to be capable or competent

suf·fi·cien·cy \sə-'fi-shən-sē\ n **1** : a sufficient quantity to meet one's needs **2** : ADEQUACY

suf·fi·cient \sə-'fi-shənt\ adj : adequate to accomplish a purpose or meet a need — **suf·fi·cient·ly** adv

¹**suf·fix** \'sə-ˌfiks\ n : an affix occurring at the end of a word

²**suf·fix** \'sə-ˌfiks, (ˌ)sə-'fiks\ vb : to attach as a suffix — **suf·fix·a·tion** \ˌsə-ˌfik-'sā-shən\ n

suf·fo·cate \'sə-fə-ˌkāt\ vb **-cat·ed**; **-cat·ing** : STIFLE, SMOTHER, CHOKE — **suf·fo·cat·ing·ly** adv — **suf·fo·ca·tion** \ˌsə-fə-'kā-shən\ n

suf·fra·gan \'sə-fri-gən\ n : an assistant bishop; esp : one not having the right of succession — **suffragan** adj

suf·frage \'sə-frij\ n [L suffragium] **1** : VOTE **2** : the right to vote : FRANCHISE

suf·frag·ette \ˌsə-fri-'jet\ n : a woman who advocates suffrage for women

suf·frag·ist \'səf-ri-jist\ n : one who advocates extension of the suffrage esp. to women

suf·fuse \sə-'fyüz\ vb **suf·fused**; **suf·fus·ing** : to spread over or through in the manner of a fluid or light **syn** infuse, imbue, ingrain, steep — **suf·fu·sion** \-'fyü-zhən\ n

¹**sug·ar** \'shù-gər\ n **1** : a sweet substance that is colorless or white when pure and is chiefly sucrose from sugarcane or sugar beets **2** : a water-soluble compound (as glucose) similar to sucrose — **sug·ary** adj

²**sugar** vb **sug·ared**; **sug·ar·ing** **1** : to mix, cover, or sprinkle with sugar **2** : SWEETEN ⟨~ advice with flattery⟩ **3** : to form sugar ⟨a syrup that ~s⟩ **4** : GRANULATE

sugar beet n : a large beet with a white root from which sugar is made

sug·ar·cane \'shù-gər-ˌkān\ n : a tall grass widely grown in warm regions for the sugar in its stalks

sugar daddy n **1** : a well-to-do usu. older man who supports or spends lavishly on a mistress or girlfriend **2** : a generous benefactor of a cause

sugar maple n : a maple with a sweet sap; esp : one of eastern No. America with sap that is the chief source of maple syrup and maple sugar

sugar pea n : SNOW PEA

sug·ar·plum \'shù-gər-ˌpləm\ n : a small ball of candy

sug·gest \səg-'jest, sə-\ vb **1** : to put (as a thought, plan, or desire) into a person's mind **2** : to remind or evoke by association of ideas **syn** imply, hint, intimate, insinuate, connote

sug·gest·ible \səg-'jes-tə-bəl, sə-\ *adj* : easily influenced by suggestion

sug·ges·tion \-'jes-chən\ *n* **1** : an act or instance of suggesting; *also* : something suggested **2** : a slight indication

sug·ges·tive \-'jes-tiv\ *adj* : tending to suggest something; *esp* : suggesting something improper or indecent — **sug·ges·tive·ly** *adv* — **sug·ges·tive·ness** *n*

sui·cide \'sü-ə-ˌsīd\ *n* **1** : the act of killing oneself purposely **2** : one that commits or attempts suicide — **sui·cid·al** \ˌsü-ə-'sīd-ᵊl\ *adj*

sui ge·ner·is \ˌsü-ī-'je-nə-rəs, ˌsü-ē-\ *adj* [L, of its own kind] : being in a class by itself : UNIQUE

¹suit \'süt\ *n* **1** : an action in court to recover a right or claim **2** : an act of suing or entreating; *esp* : COURTSHIP **3** : a number of things used together ⟨~ of clothes⟩ **4** : one of the four sets of playing cards in a pack

²suit *vb* **1** : to be appropriate or fitting **2** : to be becoming to **3** : to meet the needs or desires of : PLEASE

suit·able \'sü-tə-bəl\ *adj* : FITTING, PROPER, APPROPRIATE **syn** fit, meet, apt, happy — **suit·abil·i·ty** \ˌsü-tə-'bi-lə-tē\ *n* — **suit·able·ness** \'sü-tə-bəl-nəs\ *n* — **suit·ably** \-tə-blē\ *adv*

suit·case \'süt-ˌkās\ *n* : a bag or case carried by hand and designed to hold a traveler's clothing and personal articles

suite \'swēt, *for 4 also* 'süt\ *n* **1** : RETINUE **2** : a group of rooms occupied as a unit **3** : a modern instrumental composition in several movements of different character; *also* : a long orchestral concert arrangement in suite form of material drawn from a longer work **4** : a set of matched furniture for a room

suit·ing \'sü-tiŋ\ *n* : fabric for suits of clothes

suit·or \'sü-tər\ *n* **1** : one who sues or petitions **2** : one who seeks to marry a woman

su·ki·ya·ki \skē-'yä-kē, ˌsü-kē-'yä-\ *n* : thin slices of meat, bean curd, and vegetables cooked in soy sauce and sugar

sul·fa drug \'səl-fə-\ *n* : any of various synthetic organic bacteria-inhibiting drugs

sul·fate \'səl-ˌfāt\ *n* : a salt or ester of sulfuric acid

sul·fide \'səl-ˌfīd\ *n* : a compound of sulfur

sul·fur *also* **sul·phur** \'səl-fər\ *n* : a nonmetallic chemical element used esp. in the chemical and paper industries and in vulcanizing rubber — see ELEMENT table

sulfur di·ox·ide \-dī-'äk-ˌsīd\ *n* : a heavy pungent toxic gas that is used esp. in bleaching, as a preservative, and as a refrigerant, and is a major air pollutant

sul·fu·ric \ˌsəl-'fyùr-ik\ *adj* : of, relating to, or containing sulfur

sulfuric acid *or* **sul·phu·ric acid** \ˌsəl-'fyùr-ik-\ *n* : a heavy corrosive oily strong acid

sul·fu·rous *also* **sul·phu·rous** \'səl-fə-rəs, -fyə-, *also esp for 1* ˌsəl-'fyùr-əs\ *adj* **1** : of, relating to, or containing sulfur **2** : of or relating to brimstone or the fire of hell : INFERNAL **3** : FIERY, INFLAMED ⟨~ sermons⟩

¹sulk \'səlk\ *vb* : to be or become moodily silent or irritable

²sulk *n* : a sulky mood or spell

¹sulky \'səl-kē\ *adj* : inclined to sulk : MOROSE, MOODY **syn** surly, glum, sullen, gloomy — **sulk·i·ly** \'səl-kə-lē\ *adv* — **sulk·i·ness** \-kē-nəs\ *n*

²sulky *n, pl* **sulkies** : a light 2-wheeled horse-drawn vehicle with a seat for the driver and usu. no body

sul·len \'sə-lən\ *adj* **1** : gloomily silent : MOROSE **2** : DISMAL, GLOOMY ⟨a ~ sky⟩ **syn** glum, surly, dour, saturnine — **sul·len·ly** *adv* — **sul·len·ness** *n*

sul·ly \'sə-lē\ *vb* **sul·lied; sul·ly·ing** : SOIL, SMIRCH, DEFILE

sul·tan \'səlt-ᵊn\ *n* : a sovereign esp. of a Muslim state — **sul·tan·ate** \-ˌāt\ *n*

sul·ta·na \ˌsəl-'ta-nə\ *n* **1** : a female member of a sultan's family **2** : a pale seedless grape; *also* : a raisin of this grape

sul·try \'səl-trē\ *adj* **sul·tri·er; -est** [obs. E *sulter* to swelter, alter. of E *swelter*] : very hot and moist : SWELTERING; *also* : exciting sexual desire

¹sum \'səm\ *n* [ME *summe*, fr. OF, fr. L *summa*, fr. fem. of *summus* highest] **1** : a quantity of money **2** : the whole amount **3** : GIST **4** : the result obtained by adding numbers **5** : a problem in arithmetic

²sum *vb* **summed; sum·ming** : to find the sum of by adding or counting

su·mac *also* **su·mach** \'sü-ˌmak, 'shü-\ *n* : any of a genus of trees, shrubs, and woody vines with feathery compound leaves and spikes of red or whitish berries

sumac

sum·ma·rize \'sə-mə-ˌrīz\ *vb* **-rized; -riz·ing** : to tell in a summary

¹sum·ma·ry \'sə-mə-rē\ *adj* **1** : covering the main points briefly : CONCISE **2** : done without delay or formality ⟨~ punishment⟩ **syn** terse, succinct, laconic — **sum·mar·i·ly** \(ˌ)sə-'mer-ə-lē, 'sə-mə-rə-lē\ *adv*

²sum·ma·ry *n, pl* **-ries** : a concise statement of the main points

sum·ma·tion \(ˌ)sə-'mā-shən\ *n* : a summing up; *esp* : a speech in court summing up the arguments in a case

sum·mer \'sə-mər\ *n* : the season of the year in a region in which the sun shines most directly : the warmest period of the year — **sum·mery** *adj*

sum·mer·house \'sə-mər-ˌhaùs\ *n* : a covered structure in a garden or park to provide a shady retreat

summer squash *n* : any of various garden squashes (as zucchini) used as a vegetable while immature

sum·mit \'sə-mət\ *n* **1** : the highest point **2** : a conference of highest-level officials

sum·mon \'sə-mən\ *vb* [ME *somonen*, fr. OF *somondre*, fr. (assumed) VL *summonere*, alter. of L *summonēre* to remind secretly] **1** : to call to a meeting : CONVOKE **2** : to send for; *also* : to order to appear in court **3** : to evoke esp. by an act of the will ⟨~ up courage⟩ — **sum·mon·er** *n*

sum·mons \'sə-mənz\ *n, pl* **sum·mons·es 1** : an authoritative call to appear at a designated place or to attend to a duty **2** : a warning or citation to appear in court at a specified time to answer charges

sump·tu·ous \'səmp-shə-wəs, -chə-\ *adj* : LAVISH, LUXURIOUS

sum up *vb* : SUMMARIZE

¹sun \'sən\ *n* **1** : the shining celestial body around which the earth and other planets revolve and from which they receive light and heat **2** : a celestial body like the sun **3** : SUNSHINE — **sun·less** *adj* — **sun·ny** *adj*

²sun *vb* **sunned; sun·ning 1** : to expose to or as if to the rays of the sun **2** : to sun oneself

Sun *abbr* Sunday

sun·bath \'sən-ˌbath, -ˌbàth\ *n* : an exposure to sunlight or a sunlamp — **sun·bathe** \-ˌbāth\ *vb*

sun·beam \-ˌbēm\ *n* : a ray of sunlight

sun·block \'sən-ˌbläk\ *n* : a preparation for blocking out more of the sun's rays than a sunscreen

sun·bon·net \-ˌbä-nət\ *n* : a bonnet with a wide brim to shield the face and neck from the sun

¹**sun·burn** \-ˌbərn\ *vb* **-burned** \-ˌbərnd\ *or* **-burnt** \-ˌbərnt\; **-burn·ing** : to cause or become affected with sunburn

²**sunburn** *n* : a skin inflammation caused by overexposure to sunlight

sun·dae \'sən-(ˌ)dā, -dē\ *n* : ice cream served with topping

Sun·day \'sən-dē, -ˌdā\ *n* : the 1st day of the week : the Christian Sabbath

sun·der \'sən-dər\ *vb* : to force apart **syn** sever, part, disjoin, disunite

sun·di·al \-ˌdī(-ə)l\ *n* : a device for showing the time of day from the shadow cast on a plate by an object with a straight edge

sun·down \-ˌdaún\ *n* : SUNSET 2

sun·dries \'sən-drēz\ *n pl* : various small articles or items

sun·dry \'sən-drē\ *adj* : SEVERAL, DIVERS, VARIOUS

sun·fish \'sən-ˌfish\ *n* **1** : a huge marine fish with a deep flattened body **2** : any of numerous often brightly colored American freshwater fishes related to the perches and usu. having the body flattened from side to side

sun·flow·er \-ˌflaú-ər\ *n* : any of a genus of tall New World plants related to the daisies and often grown for the oil-rich seeds of their yellow-petaled dark= centered flower heads

sung *past and past part of* SING

sun·glasses \'sən-ˌgla-səz\ *n pl* : glasses to protect the eyes from the sun

sunk *past and past part of* SINK

sunk·en \'səŋ-kən\ *adj* **1** : SUBMERGED **2** : fallen in : HOLLOW ⟨~ cheeks⟩ **3** : lying in a depression ⟨~ garden⟩; *also* : constructed below the general floor level ⟨~ living room⟩

sun·lamp \'sən-ˌlamp\ *n* : an electric lamp designed to emit radiation of wavelengths from ultraviolet to infrared

sun·light \-ˌlīt\ *n* : SUNSHINE

sun·lit \-ˌlit\ *adj* : lighted by or as if by the sun

sun·rise \-ˌrīz\ *n* **1** : the apparent rising of the sun above the horizon **2** : the time at which the sun rises

sun·roof \-ˌrüf, -ˌrúf\ *n* : a panel in an automobile roof that can be opened

sun·screen \-ˌskrēn\ *n* : a substance used in suntan preparations to protect the skin

sun·set \-ˌset\ *n* **1** : the apparent descent of the sun below the horizon **2** : the time at which the sun sets

sun·shade \'sən-ˌshād\ *n* : something (as a parasol or awning) used as a protection from the sun's rays

sun·shine \-ˌshīn\ *n* : the direct light of the sun — **sun·shiny** *adj*

sun·spot \-ˌspät\ *n* : any of the dark spots that appear from time to time on the sun's surface

sun·stroke \-ˌströk\ *n* : heatstroke caused by direct exposure to the sun

sun·tan \-ˌtan\ *n* : a browning of the skin from exposure to the sun's rays

sun·up \-ˌəp\ *n* : SUNRISE 2

¹**sup** \'səp\ *vb* **supped; sup·ping** : to take or drink in swallows or gulps

²**sup** *n* : a mouthful esp. of liquor or broth; *also* : a small quantity of liquid

³**sup** *vb* **supped; sup·ping** **1** : to eat the evening meal **2** : to make one's supper ⟨*supped* on roast beef⟩

⁴**sup** *abbr* **1** superior **2** supplement; supplementary **3** supply **4** supra

¹**super** \'sü-pər\ *n* : SUPERINTENDENT

²**super** *adj* **1** : very fine : EXCELLENT **2** : EXTREME, EXCESSIVE

super- \ˌsü-pər\ *prefix* **1** : over and above : higher in quantity, quality, or degree than : more than **2** : in ad-

dition : extra **3** : exceeding a norm **4** : in excessive degree or intensity **5** : surpassing all or most others of its kind **6** : situated above, on, or at the top of **7** : next above or higher **8** : more inclusive than **9** : superior in status or position

superabsorbent	**superpatriotism**
superachiever	**superpremium**
superagency	**superrich**
superblock	**supersalesman**
superbomb	**supersecret**
supercity	**supersize**
superclean	**supersized**
superexpensive	**supersmart**
superfine	**supersophisticated**
superheat	**superspy**
superheavy	**superstar**
superhero	**superstate**
superhuman	**superstore**
superhumanly	**superstratum**
superindividual	**superstrength**
superliner	**superstrong**
superman	**supersubtle**
supermom	**supersystem**
supernormal	**supertanker**
superpatriot	**superthin**
superpatriotic	**superwoman**

su·per·abun·dant \ˌsü-pər-ə-'bən-dənt\ *adj* : more than ample — **su·per·abun·dance** \-dəns\ *n*

su·per·an·nu·ate \ˌsü-pər-'an-yə-ˌwāt\ *vb* **-at·ed; -at·ing** **1** : to make out-of-date **2** : to retire and pension because of age or infirmity — **su·per·an·nu·at·ed** *adj*

su·perb \sú-'pərb\ *adj* [L *superbus* excellent, proud, fr. *super* above] : marked to the highest degree by excellence, brilliance, or competence **syn** resplendent, glorious, gorgeous, sublime — **su·perb·ly** *adv*

su·per·charg·er \'sü-pər-ˌchär-jər\ *n* : a device for increasing the amount of air supplied to an internal combustion engine

su·per·cil·ious \ˌsü-pər-'si-lē-əs\ *adj* [L *superciliosus*, fr. *supercilium* eyebrow, haughtiness] : haughtily contemptuous **syn** disdainful, overbearing, arrogant, lordly, superior

su·per·com·pu·ter \'sü-pər-kəm-ˌpyü-tər\ *n* : a large very fast mainframe

su·per·con·duc·tiv·i·ty \ˌsü-pər-ˌkän-ˌdək-'ti-və-tē\ *n* : a complete disappearance of electrical resistance in a substance esp. at very low temperatures — **su·per·con·duc·tive** \-kən-'dək-tiv\ *adj* — **su·per·con·duc·tor** \-'dək-tər\ *n*

su·per·con·ti·nent \'sü-pər-ˌkänt-ᵊn-ənt\ *n* : a former large continent from which other continents are held to have broken off and drifted away

su·per·ego \ˌsü-pər-'ē-gō\ *n* : the one of the three divisions of the psyche in psychoanalytic theory that functions to reward and punish through a system of moral attitudes, conscience, and a sense of guilt

su·per·fi·cial \ˌsü-pər-'fi-shəl\ *adj* **1** : of or relating to the surface or appearance only **2** : not thorough : SHALLOW — **su·per·fi·ci·al·i·ty** \-ˌfi-shē-'a-lə-tē\ *n* — **su·per·fi·cial·ly** *adv*

su·per·flu·ous \sú-'pər-flə-wəs\ *adj* : exceeding what is sufficient or necessary : SURPLUS **syn** extra, spare, supernumerary — **su·per·flu·i·ty** \ˌsü-pər-'flü-ə-tē\ *n*

su·per·high·way \ˌsü-pər-'hī-ˌwā\ *n* : a broad highway designed for high-speed traffic

su·per·im·pose \-im-'pōz\ *vb* : to lay (one thing) over or above something else

su·per·in·tend \ˌsü-pə-rin-'tend\ *vb* : to have or exercise the charge and oversight of : DIRECT — **su·per·in·ten·dence** \-'ten-dəns\ *n* — **su·per·in·ten·den·cy** \-dən-sē\ *n* — **su·per·in·ten·dent** \-dənt\ *n*

¹**su·pe·ri·or** \sú-'pir-ē-ər\ *adj* **1** : situated higher up, over, or near the top; *also* : higher in rank or numbers **2** : of greater value or importance **3** : courageously indifferent (as to pain or misfortune) **4** : better than

most others of its kind **5** : ARROGANT, HAUGHTY —
su·pe·ri·or·i·ty \-ˌpir-ē-ˈȯr-ə-tē\ n
²superior n **1** : one who is above another in rank, office, or station; *esp* : the head of a religious house or order **2** : one higher in quality or merit

¹su·per·la·tive \su̇-ˈpər-lə-tiv\ adj **1** : of, relating to, or constituting the degree of grammatical comparison that denotes an extreme or unsurpassed level or extent **2** : surpassing others : SUPREME **syn** peerless, incomparable, superb — **su·per·la·tive·ly** adv
²superlative n **1** : the superlative degree or a superlative form in a language **2** : the utmost degree : ACME
su·per·mar·ket \ˈsü-pər-ˌmär-kət\ n : a self-service retail market selling foods and household merchandise
su·per·nal \su̇-ˈpər-nəl\ adj **1** : being or coming from on high **2** : of heavenly or spiritual character
su·per·nat·u·ral \ˌsü-pər-ˈna-chə-rəl\ adj : of or relating to phenomena beyond or outside of nature; *esp* : relating to or attributed to a divinity, ghost, or devil — **su·per·nat·u·ral·ly** adv
su·per·no·va \ˌsü-pər-ˈnō-və\ n : the explosion of a very large star
¹su·per·nu·mer·ary \-ˈnü-mə-ˌrer-ē, -ˈnyü-\ adj : exceeding the usual or required number : EXTRA **syn** surplus, superfluous, spare
²supernumerary n, pl **-ar·ies** : an extra person or thing; *esp* : an actor hired for a nonspeaking part
su·per·pose \ˌsü-pər-ˈpōz\ vb **-posed; -pos·ing** : SUPERIMPOSE — **su·per·po·si·tion** \-pə-ˈzi-shən\ n
su·per·pow·er \ˈsü-pər-ˌpau̇-ər\ n **1** : excessive or superior power **2** : one of a few politically and militarily dominant nations
su·per·sat·u·rat·ed \-ˈsa-chə-ˌrā-təd\ adj : containing an amount of a substance greater than that required for saturation
su·per·scribe \ˈsü-pər-ˌskrīb, ˌsü-pər-ˈskrīb\ vb **-scribed; -scrib·ing** : to write on the top or outside : ADDRESS — **su·per·scrip·tion** \ˌsü-pər-ˈskrip-shən\ n
su·per·script \ˈsü-pər-ˌskript\ n : a symbol (as a numeral or letter) written immediately above or above and to one side of another character
su·per·sede \ˌsü-pər-ˈsēd\ vb **-sed·ed; -sed·ing** [MF *superseder* to refrain from, fr. L *supersedēre* to be superior to, refrain from, fr. *super-* above + *sedēre* to sit] : to take the place of : REPLACE
su·per·son·ic \-ˈsä-nik\ adj **1** : ULTRASONIC **2** : being or relating to speeds from one to five times the speed of sound; *also* : capable of moving at such a speed ⟨a ∼ airplane⟩
su·per·sti·tion \ˌsü-pər-ˈsti-shən\ n **1** : beliefs or practices resulting from ignorance, fear of the unknown, or trust in magic or chance **2** : an unreasoning fear of nature, the unknown, or God resulting from superstition — **su·per·sti·tious** \-shəs\ adj
su·per·struc·ture \ˈsü-pər-ˌstrək-chər\ n : something built on a base or as a vertical extension
su·per·vene \ˌsü-pər-ˈvēn\ vb **-vened; -ven·ing** : to occur as something additional or unexpected
su·per·vise \ˈsü-pər-ˌvīz\ vb **-vised; -vis·ing** : OVERSEE, SUPERINTEND — **su·per·vi·sion** \ˌsü-pər-ˈvi-zhən\ n — **su·per·vi·sor** \ˈsü-pər-ˌvī-zər\ n — **su·per·vi·so·ry** \ˌsü-pər-ˈvī-zə-rē\ adj
su·pine \su̇-ˈpīn\ adj **1** : lying on the back or with the face upward **2** : LETHARGIC, SLUGGISH; *also* : ABJECT **syn** inactive, inert, passive, idle
supp or **suppl** abbr supplement; supplementary
sup·per \ˈsə-pər\ n : the evening meal esp. when dinner is taken at midday — **sup·per·time** \-ˌtīm\ n
sup·plant \sə-ˈplant\ vb **1** : to take the place of (another) esp. by force or trickery **2** : REPLACE
sup·ple \ˈsə-pəl\ adj **sup·pler; sup·plest 1** : COMPLIANT, ADAPTABLE **2** : capable of bending without breaking or creasing : LIMBER **syn** resilient, elastic, flexible
¹sup·ple·ment \ˈsə-plə-mənt\ n **1** : something that supplies a want or makes an addition **2** : a continuation

(as of a book) containing corrections or additional material — **sup·ple·men·tal** \ˌsə-plə-ˈment-ᵊl\ adj — **sup·ple·men·ta·ry** \-ˈmen-tə-rē\ adj
²sup·ple·ment \ˈsə-plə-ˌment\ vb : to fill up the deficiencies of : add to
sup·pli·ant \ˈsə-plē-ənt\ n : one who supplicates : PETITIONER, PLEADER
sup·pli·cant \ˈsə-pli-kənt\ n : SUPPLIANT
sup·pli·cate \ˈsə-plə-ˌkāt\ vb **-cat·ed; -cat·ing 1** : to make a humble entreaty; *esp* : to pray to God **2** : to ask earnestly and humbly : BESEECH **syn** implore, beg, entreat, plead — **sup·pli·ca·tion** \ˌsə-plə-ˈkā-shən\ n
¹sup·ply \sə-ˈplī\ vb **sup·plied; sup·ply·ing** [ME *supplien*, fr. MF *soupleier*, fr. L *supplēre* to fill up, supplement, supply, fr. *sub-* under, up to + *plēre* to fill] **1** : to add as a supplement **2** : to satisfy the needs of **3** : FURNISH, PROVIDE — **sup·pli·er** n
²supply n, pl **supplies 1** : the quantity or amount (as of a commodity) needed or available; *also* : PROVISIONS, STORES — usu. used in pl. **2** : the act or process of filling a want or need : PROVISION **3** : the quantities of goods or services offered for sale at a particular time or at one price
sup·ply–side \sə-ˈplī-ˌsīd\ adj : of, relating to, or being an economic theory that recommends the reduction of tax rates to expand economic activity
¹sup·port \sə-ˈpōrt\ vb **1** : BEAR, TOLERATE **2** : to take sides with : BACK, ASSIST **3** : to provide with food, clothing, and shelter **4** : to hold up or serve as a foundation for **syn** uphold, advocate, champion — **sup·port·able** adj — **sup·port·er** n
²support n **1** : the act of supporting : the state of being supported **2** : one that supports : PROP, BASE
support group n : a group of people with common experiences and concerns who provide emotional and moral support for one another
sup·pose \sə-ˈpōz\ vb **sup·posed; sup·pos·ing 1** : to assume to be true (as for the sake of argument) **2** : EXPECT ⟨I am *supposed* to go⟩ **3** : to think probable — **sup·pos·al** n
sup·posed \sə-ˈpōzd, -ˈpō-zəd\ adj : BELIEVED; *also* : mistakenly believed — **sup·pos·ed·ly** \-ˈpō-zəd-lē, -ˈpōzd-lē\ adv
sup·pos·ing conj : if by way of hypothesis : on the assumption that
sup·po·si·tion \ˌsə-pə-ˈzi-shən\ n **1** : something that is supposed : HYPOTHESIS **2** : the act of supposing
sup·pos·i·to·ry \sə-ˈpä-zə-ˌtōr-ē\ n, pl **-ries** [ML *suppositorium*, fr. LL, neut. of *suppositorius* placed beneath] : a small easily melted mass of usu. medicated material for insertion (as into the rectum)
sup·press \sə-ˈpres\ vb **1** : to put down by authority or force : SUBDUE ⟨∼ a revolt⟩ **2** : to keep from being known; *also* : to stop the publication or circulation of **3** : to hold back : REPRESS ⟨∼ anger⟩ ⟨∼ a cough⟩ — **sup·press·ible** \-ˈpre-sə-bəl\ adj — **sup·pres·sion** \-ˈpre-shən\ n
sup·pres·sant \sə-ˈpres-ᵊnt\ n : an agent (as a drug) suppressing rather than eliminating something ⟨a cough ∼⟩
sup·pu·rate \ˈsə-pyə-ˌrāt\ vb **-rat·ed; -rat·ing** : to form or give off pus — **sup·pu·ra·tion** \ˌsə-pyə-ˈrā-shən\ n
su·pra \ˈsü-prə, -ˌprä\ adv : earlier in this writing : ABOVE
su·pra·na·tion·al \ˌsü-prə-ˈna-shə-nəl, -ˌprä-\ adj : going beyond national boundaries, authority, or interests ⟨∼ organizations⟩
su·prem·a·cist \su̇-ˈpre-mə-sist\ n : an advocate of group supremacy
su·prem·a·cy \su̇-ˈpre-mə-sē\ n, pl **-cies** : supreme rank, power, or authority
su·preme \su̇-ˈprēm\ adj [L *supremus*, superl. of *superus* upper, fr. *super* over, above] **1** : highest in rank or authority **2** : highest in degree or quality ⟨∼ among poets⟩ **3** : ULTIMATE ⟨the ∼ sacrifice⟩ **syn** superlative,

surpassing, peerless, incomparable — **su·preme·ly** *adv* — **su·preme·ness** *n*

Supreme Being *n* : GOD 1

supt *abbr* superintendent

sur·cease \'sər-ˌsēs\ *n* : CESSATION, RESPITE

¹sur·charge \'sər-ˌchärj\ *vb* 1 : to fill to excess : OVER-LOAD 2 : to apply a surcharge to (postage stamps)

²surcharge *n* 1 : an extra fee or cost 2 : an excessive load or burden 3 : something officially printed on a postage stamp esp. to change its value

sur·cin·gle \'sər-ˌsiŋ-gəl\ *n* : a band put around a horse's body to make something (as a saddle) fast

¹sure \'shůr\ *adj* **sur·er; sur·est** [ME, fr. MF *sur*, fr. L *securus* secure] 1 : firmly established 2 : TRUSTWOR-THY, RELIABLE 3 : CONFIDENT 4 : not to be disputed : UNDOUBTED 5 : bound to happen 6 : careful to re-member or attend to something (be ∼ to lock the door) **syn** certain, cocksure, positive — **sure·ness** *n*

²sure *adv* : SURELY

sure·fire \'shůr-'fīr\ *adj* : certain to get results : DE-PENDABLE

sure·ly \'shůr-lē\ *adv* 1 : in a sure manner 2 : without doubt 3 : INDEED, REALLY

sure·ty \'shůr-ə-tē\ *n, pl* **-ties** 1 : SURENESS, CERTAINTY 2 : something that makes sure : GUARANTEE 3 : one who is a guarantor for another person

¹surf \'sərf\ *n* : waves that break upon the shore; *also* : the sound or foam of breaking waves

²surf *vb* : to ride the surf (as on a surfboard) — **surf·er** *n* — **surf·ing** *n*

¹sur·face \'sər-fəs\ *n* 1 : the outside of an object or body 2 : outward aspect or appearance — **surface** *adj*

²surface *vb* **sur·faced; sur·fac·ing** 1 : to give a surface to : make smooth 2 : to rise to the surface

surf·board \'sərf-ˌbōrd\ *n* : a buoyant board used in surfing

¹sur·feit \'sər-fət\ *n* 1 : EXCESS, SUPERABUNDANCE 2 : excessive indulgence (as in food or drink) 3 : disgust caused by excess

²surfeit *vb* : to feed, supply, or indulge to the point of surfeit : CLOY

surg *abbr* surgeon; surgery; surgical

¹surge \'sərj\ *vb* **surged; surg·ing** 1 : to rise and fall ac-tively : TOSS 2 : to move in waves 3 : to rise suddenly to an excessive or abnormal value

²surge *n* 1 : a sweeping onward like a wave of the sea ⟨a ∼ of emotion⟩ 2 : a large billow 3 : a transient sud-den increase of current or voltage in an electrical cir-cuit

sur·geon \'sər-jən\ *n* : a physician who specializes in surgery

sur·gery \'sər-jə-rē\ *n, pl* **-ger·ies** [ME *surgerie*, fr. OF *cirurgie, surgerie,* fr. L *chirurgia,* fr. Gk *cheirourgia,* fr. *cheirourgos* surgeon, fr. *cheirourgos* doing by hand, fr. *cheir* hand + *ergon* work] 1 : a branch of medicine concerned with the correction of physical defects, the repair of injuries, and the treatment of disease esp. by operations 2 : a room or area where surgery is performed 3 : the work done by a surgeon

sur·gi·cal \'sər-ji-kəl\ *adj* : of, relating to, or associated with surgeons or surgery — **sur·gi·cal·ly** \-k(ə-)lē\ *adv*

sur·ly \'sər-lē\ *adj* **sur·li·er; -est** [alter. of ME *sirly* lordly, imperious, fr. *sir*] : having a rude unfriendly disposition **syn** morose, glum, sullen, sulky, gloomy — **sur·li·ness** \-lē-nəs\ *n*

sur·mise \sər-'mīz\ *vb* **sur·mised; sur·mis·ing** : GUESS **syn** conjecture, presume, suppose — **surmise** *n*

sur·mount \sər-'maůnt\ *vb* 1 : to prevail over : OVER-COME 2 : to get to or lie at the top of

sur·name \'sər-ˌnām\ *n* 1 : NICKNAME 2 : the name borne in common by members of a family

sur·pass \sər-'pas\ *vb* 1 : to be superior to in quality, degree, or performance : EXCEL 2 : to go beyond the reach or powers of **syn** transcend, outdo, outstrip, exceed — **sur·pass·ing·ly** *adv*

sur·plice \'sər-pləs\ *n* : a loose white outer garment worn at church services

sur·plus \'sər-(ˌ)pləs\ *n* 1 : quantity left over : EXCESS 2 : the excess of assets over liabilities **syn** superfluity, overabundance, surfeit

¹sur·prise \sər-'prīz\ *n* 1 : an attack made without warning 2 : a taking unawares 3 : something that sur-prises 4 : AMAZEMENT, ASTONISHMENT

²surprise *also* **sur·prize** *vb* **sur·prised; sur·pris·ing** 1 : to come upon and attack unexpectedly 2 : to take unawares 3 : AMAZE 4 : to cause astonishment or sur-prise **syn** astonish, astound, dumbfound — **sur·pris·ing** *adj*

sur·pris·ing·ly \-'prī-ziŋ-lē\ *adv* 1 : in a surprising man-ner or degree 2 : it is surprising that

sur·re·al \sə-'rē-əl, -'rēl\ *adj* 1 : having the intense ir-rational reality of a dream 2 : of or relating to surre-alism

sur·re·al·ism \sə-'rē-ə-ˌli-zəm\ *n* : art, literature, or theater characterized by fantastic or incongruous im-agery or effects produced by unnatural juxtapositions and combinations — **sur·re·al·ist** \-list\ *n or adj* — **sur·re·al·is·tic** \sə-ˌrē-ə-'lis-tik\ *adj* — **sur·re·al·is·ti·cal·ly** \-ti-k(ə-)lē\ *adv*

¹sur·ren·der \sə-'ren-dər\ *vb* **-dered; -der·ing** 1 : to yield to the power of another : give up under com-pulsion 2 : RELINQUISH

²surrender *n* : the act of giving up or yielding oneself or the possession of something to another

sur·rep·ti·tious \ˌsər-əp-'ti-shəs\ *adj* : done, made, or acquired by stealth : CLANDESTINE **syn** underhand, covert, furtive — **sur·rep·ti·tious·ly** *adv*

sur·rey \'sər-ē\ *n, pl* **surreys** : a 2-seated horse= drawn carriage

surrey

sur·ro·ga·cy \'sər-ə-gə-sē\ *n* : SURROGATE MOTHER-HOOD

sur·ro·gate \'sər-ə-ˌgāt, -gət\ *n* 1 : DEPUTY, SUBSTI-TUTE 2 : a law officer in some states with authority in the probate of wills, the settlement of estates, and the appointment of guardians 3 : SURROGATE MOTHER

surrogate mother *n* : a woman who becomes pregnant (as by surgical implantation of a fertilized egg) in or-der to carry the fetus for another woman — **surro-gate motherhood** *n*

sur·round \sə-'raůnd\ *vb* 1 : to enclose on all sides : ENCIRCLE 2 : to enclose so as to cut off retreat or escape

sur·round·ings \sə-'raůn-diŋz\ *n pl* : conditions by which one is surrounded

sur·tax \'sər-ˌtaks\ *n* : an additional tax over and above a normal tax

sur·tout \(ˌ)sər-'tü\ *n* [F, fr. *sur* over (fr. L *super*) + *tout* all, fr. L *totus* whole] : a man's long close= fitting overcoat

surv *abbr* survey; surveying; surveyor

sur·veil·lance \sər-'vā-ləns\ *n* [F] : close watch; *also* : SUPERVISION

¹sur·vey \sər-'vā\ *vb* **sur·veyed; sur·vey·ing** 1 : to look over and examine closely 2 : to find and represent the contours, measurements, and position of a part of the earth's surface (as a tract of land) **3** : to view or study something as a whole **syn** scrutinize, examine, inspect, study — **sur·vey·or** \-ər\ n

²**sur·vey** \'sər-ˌvā\ n, pl **surveys** : the act or an instance of surveying; also : something that is surveyed

sur·vive \sər-'vīv\ vb **sur·vived; sur·viv·ing 1** : to remain alive or existent **2** : OUTLIVE, OUTLAST — **sur·viv·al** n — **sur·vi·vor** \-'vī-vər\ n

sus·cep·ti·ble \sə-'sep-tə-bəl\ adj **1** : of such a nature as to permit ⟨words ∼ of being misunderstood⟩ **2** : having little resistance to a stimulus or agency ⟨∼ to colds⟩ **3** : IMPRESSIONABLE, RESPONSIVE **syn** sensitive, subject, exposed, prone, liable, open — **sus·cep·ti·bil·i·ty** \-ˌsep-tə-'bi-lə-tē\ n

su·shi \'sü-shē\ n [Jp] : cold rice formed into various shapes and garnished esp. with bits of raw fish or seafood

¹**sus·pect** \'səs-ˌpekt, sə-'spekt\ adj : regarded with suspicion; also : QUESTIONABLE

²**sus·pect** \'səs-ˌpekt\ n : one who is suspected (as of a crime)

³**sus·pect** \sə-'spekt\ vb **1** : to have doubts of : MISTRUST **2** : to imagine to be guilty without proof **3** : SURMISE

sus·pend \sə-'spend\ vb **1** : to bar temporarily from a privilege, office, or function **2** : to stop temporarily : make inactive for a time **3** : to withhold (judgment) for a time **4** : HANG; esp : to hang so as to be free except at one point **5** : to keep from falling or sinking by some invisible support

sus·pend·er \sə-'spen-dər\ n : one of two supporting straps which pass over the shoulders and to which the trousers are fastened

sus·pense \sə-'spens\ n **1** : SUSPENSION **2** : mental uncertainty : ANXIETY **3** : excitement as to an outcome — **sus·pense·ful** adj

sus·pen·sion \sə-'spen-chən\ n **1** : the act of suspending : the state or period of being suspended **2** : the state of a substance when its particles are mixed with but undissolved in a fluid or solid; also : a substance in this state **3** : something suspended **4** : a device by which something is suspended

sus·pen·so·ry \sə-'spen-sə-rē\ adj **1** : SUSPENDED; also : fitted or serving to suspend something **2** : temporarily leaving undetermined

sus·pi·cion \sə-'spi-shən\ n **1** : the act or an instance of suspecting something wrong without proof **2** : TRACE, SOUPÇON **syn** mistrust, uncertainty, doubt, skepticism

sus·pi·cious \sə-'spi-shəs\ adj **1** : open to or arousing suspicion **2** : inclined to suspect **3** : showing suspicion — **sus·pi·cious·ly** adv

sus·tain \sə-'stān\ vb **1** : to provide with nourishment **2** : to keep going : PROLONG ⟨∼ed effort⟩ **3** : to hold up : PROP **4** : to hold up under : ENDURE **5** : SUFFER ⟨∼ a broken arm⟩ **6** : to support as true, legal, or valid **7** : PROVE, CORROBORATE — **sus·tain·able** \səs-'tā-nə-bəl\ adj

sus·te·nance \'səs-tə-nəns\ n **1** : FOOD, NOURISHMENT **2** : a supplying with the necessities of life **3** : something that sustains or supports

su·ture \'sü-chər\ n **1** : material or a stitch for sewing a wound together **2** : a seam or line along which two things or parts are joined by or as if by sewing

su·zer·ain \'sü-zə-rən, -ˌrān\ n [F] **1** : a feudal lord **2** : a nation that has political control over the foreign relations of another nation — **su·zer·ain·ty** \-tē\ n

svc or **svce** abbr service

svelte \'sfelt\ adj [F, fr. It svelto, fr. pp. of svellere to pluck out, modif. of L evellere, fr. e- out + vellere to pluck] : SLENDER, LITHE

svgs abbr savings

SW abbr **1** shortwave **2** southwest

¹**swab** \'swäb\ n **1** : MOP **2** : a wad of absorbent material esp. for applying medicine or for cleaning; also : a sample taken with a swab **3** : SAILOR

²**swab** vb **swabbed; swab·bing** : to use a swab on : MOP

swad·dle \'swäd-ᵊl\ vb **swad·dled; swad·dling 1** : to bind (an infant) in bands of cloth **2** : to wrap up : SWATHE

swaddling clothes n pl : bands of cloth wrapped around an infant

swag \'swag\ n : stolen goods : LOOT

swag·ger \'swa-gər\ vb **1** : to walk with a conceited swing or strut **2** : BOAST, BRAG — **swagger** n

Swa·hi·li \swä-'hē-lē\ n : a language that is a trade and governmental language over much of East Africa and the Congo region

swain \'swān\ n [ME swein boy, servant, fr. ON sveinn] **1** : RUSTIC; esp : SHEPHERD **2** : ADMIRER, SUITOR

SWAK abbr sealed with a kiss

¹**swal·low** \'swä-lō\ n : any of numerous small long-winged migratory birds that often have a deeply forked tail

²**swallow** vb **1** : to take into the stomach through the throat **2** : to envelop or take in as if by swallowing **3** : to accept or believe without question, protest, or anger

³**swallow** n **1** : an act of swallowing **2** : an amount that can be swallowed at one time

swal·low·tail \'swä-lō-ˌtāl\ n **1** : a deeply forked and tapering tail like that of a swallow **2** : TAILCOAT **3** : any of various large butterflies with the border of each hind wing usu. drawn out into a process resembling a tail — **swal·low–tailed** \-ˌtāld\ adj

swam past of SWIM

swa·mi \'swä-mē\ n [Hindi svāmī, fr. Skt svāmin owner, lord] : a Hindu ascetic or religious teacher

¹**swamp** \'swämp\ n : a spongy wetland — **swamp** adj — **swampy** adj

²**swamp** vb **1** : to fill or become filled with or as if with water **2** : OVERWHELM **3**

swamp·land \-ˌland\ n : SWAMP

swan \'swän\ n, pl **swans** also **swan** : any of various heavy-bodied long-necked mostly pure white swimming birds related to the geese

¹**swank** \'swaŋk\ or **swanky** \'swaŋ-kē\ adj **swanker** or **swank·i·er; -est** : showily smart and dashing; also : fashionably elegant

²**swank** n **1** : PRETENTIOUSNESS **2** : ELEGANCE

swans·down \'swänz-ˌdaùn\ n **1** : the very soft down of a swan used esp. for trimming **2** : a soft thick cotton flannel

swan song n : a farewell appearance, act, or pronouncement

swap \'swäp\ vb **swapped; swap·ping** : TRADE, EXCHANGE — **swap** n

sward \'sword\ n : the grassy surface of land

¹**swarm** \'sworm\ n **1** : a great number of honeybees leaving together from a hive with a queen to start a new colony; also : a hive of bees **2** : a large crowd

²**swarm** vb **1** : to form in a swarm and depart from a hive **2** : to throng together : gather in great numbers

swart \'swort\ adj : SWARTHY

swar·thy \'swor-thē, -thē\ adj **swar·thi·er; -est** : dark in color or complexion : dark-skinned

swash \'swäsh\ vb : to move about with a splashing sound — **swash** n

swash·buck·ler \-ˌbə-klər\ n : a swaggering or daring soldier or adventurer — **swash·buck·ling** adj

swas·ti·ka \'swäs-ti-kə\ n [Skt svastika, fr. svasti well-being, fr. su- well + as- to be] : a symbol or ornament in the form of a cross with the ends of the arms bent at right angles

swat \'swät\ vb **swat·ted; swat·ting** : to hit sharply ⟨∼ a fly⟩ ⟨∼ a ball⟩ — **swat** n — **swat·ter** n

SWAT abbr Special Weapons and Tactics

swatch \'swäch\ n : a sample piece (as of fabric) or a collection of samples

swath \'swäth, 'swoth\ or **swathe** \'swäth, 'swoth, 'swäth\ n [ME, fr. OE swæth footstep, trace] **1** : a row of cut grass or grain 2 : the sweep of a scythe or mowing machine or the path cut in mowing

swathe \'swäth, 'swóth, 'swäth\ *vb* **swathed; swathing** : to bind or wrap with or as if with a bandage

¹sway \'swā\ *n* 1 : a gentle swinging from side to side 2 : controlling influence or power : DOMINION

²sway *vb* 1 : to swing gently from side to side 2 : RULE, GOVERN 3 : to cause to swing from side to side 4 : BEND, SWERVE; *also* : INFLUENCE **syn** oscillate, fluctuate, vibrate, waver

sway·backed \'swā-ˌbakt\ *also* **sway·back** \-ˌbak\ *adj* : having an abnormally sagging back ⟨a ∼ mare⟩ — **swayback** *n*

swear \'swar\ *vb* **swore** \'swōr\; **sworn** \'swōrn\; **swear·ing** 1 : to make a solemn statement or promise under oath 2 : to assert or promise emphatically or earnestly 3 : to administer an oath to 4 : to bind by or as if by an oath 5 : to use profane or obscene language — **swear·er** *n*

swear in *vb* : to induct into office by administration of an oath

sweat \'swet\ *vb* **sweat** *or* **sweat·ed; sweat·ing** 1 : to excrete salty moisture from glands of the skin : PERSPIRE 2 : to form drops of moisture on the surface 3 : to work so that one sweats : TOIL 4 : to cause to sweat 5 : to draw out or get rid of by or as if by sweating 6 : to make a person overwork — **sweat** *n* — **sweaty** *adj*

sweat·er \'swe-tər\ *n* 1 : one that sweats 2 : a knitted or crocheted jacket or pullover

sweat·shirt \'swet-ˌshərt\ *n* : a loose collarless pullover usu. of heavy cotton jersey

sweat·shop \'swet-ˌshäp\ *n* : a shop or factory in which workers are employed for long hours at low wages and under unhealthy conditions

Swed *abbr* Sweden

swede \'swēd\ *n* 1 *cap* : a native or inhabitant of Sweden 2 *chiefly Brit* : RUTABAGA

Swed·ish \'swē-dish\ *n* 1 : the language of Sweden 2 **Swedish** *pl* : the people of Sweden — **Swedish** *adj*

¹sweep \'swēp\ *vb* **swept** \'swept\; **sweep·ing** 1 : to remove or clean by or as if by brushing 2 : to destroy completely; *also* : to remove or take with a single swift movement 3 : to remove from sight or consideration 4 : to move over with speed and force ⟨the tide *swept* over the shore⟩ 5 : to win an overwhelming victory in; *also* : to win all the games or contests of 6 : to move or extend in a wide curve — **sweep·er** *n*

²sweep *n* 1 : something (as a long oar) that operates with a sweeping motion 2 : a clearing off or away 3 : a winning of all the contests or prizes in a competition 4 : a sweeping movement 5 : CURVE, BEND 6 : RANGE, SCOPE

sweep·ing *adj* : EXTENSIVE ⟨∼ reforms⟩; *also* : indiscriminately inclusive ⟨∼ generalities⟩

sweep·ings \'swē-piŋz\ *n pl* : things collected by sweeping

sweep–sec·ond hand \'swēp-ˌse-kənd-\ *n* : a hand marking seconds on a timepiece

sweep·stakes \'swēp-ˌstāks\ *also* **sweep·stake** \-ˌstāk\ *n, pl* **sweepstakes** 1 : a race or contest in which the entire prize may go to the winner 2 : any of various lotteries

¹sweet \'swēt\ *adj* 1 : being or causing the one of the four basic taste sensations that is caused esp. by table sugar and is identified esp. by the taste buds at the front of the tongue; *also* : pleasing to the taste 2 : AGREEABLE 3 : pleasing to a sense other than taste ⟨a ∼ smell⟩ ⟨∼ music⟩ 4 : not stale or spoiled : WHOLESOME ⟨∼ milk⟩ 5 : not salted ⟨∼ butter⟩ — **sweet·ish** *adj* — **sweet·ly** *adv* — **sweet·ness** *n*

²sweet *n* 1 : something sweet : CANDY 2 : DARLING

sweet·bread \'swēt-ˌbred\ *n* : the pancreas or thymus of an animal (as a calf or lamb) used for food

sweet·bri·er *also* **sweet·bri·ar** \-ˌbrī-ər\ *n* : a thorny Old World rose with fragrant white to deep pink flowers

sweet clover *n* : any of a genus of erect legumes widely grown for soil improvement or hay

sweet corn *n* : an Indian corn with kernels rich in sugar and cooked as a vegetable while immature

sweet·en \'swēt-ᵊn\ *vb* **sweet·ened; sweet·en·ing** : to make sweet — **sweet·en·er** *n* — **sweet·en·ing** *n*

sweet·heart \'swēt-ˌhärt\ *n* : one who is loved

sweet·meat \-ˌmēt\ *n* : CANDY

sweet pea *n* : a garden plant of the legume family with climbing stems and fragrant flowers of many colors; *also* : its flower

sweet pepper *n* : a large mild thick-walled fruit of a pepper; *also* : a plant related to the potato that bears sweet peppers

sweet potato *n* : a tropical vine related to the morning glory; *also* : its sweet yellow edible root

sweet–talk \'swēt-ˌtök\ *vb* : FLATTER, COAX — **sweet talk** *n*

sweet tooth *n* : a craving or fondness for sweet food

sweet wil·liam \ˌswēt-'wil-yəm\ *n, often cap W* : a widely cultivated Old World pink with small white to deep red or purple flowers often showily spotted, banded, or mottled

¹swell \'swel\ *vb* **swelled; swelled** *or* **swol·len** \'swō-lən\; **swell·ing** 1 : to grow big or make bigger 2 : to expand or distend abnormally or excessively ⟨a *swollen* joint⟩; *also* : BULGE 3 : to fill or be filled with emotion (as pride) **syn** expand, amplify, distend, inflate, dilate — **swell·ing** *n*

²swell *n* 1 : a long crestless wave or series of waves in the open sea 2 : the condition of being protuberant 3 : a person dressed in the height of fashion; *also* : a person of high social position

³swell *adj* 1 : STYLISH; *also* : socially prominent 2 : EXCELLENT

swelled head *n* : an exaggerated opinion of oneself : SELF-CONCEIT

swell·head \'swel-ˌhed\ *n* : one who has a swelled head — **swell·head·ed** \-ˌhe-dəd\ *adj*

swel·ter \'swel-tər\ *vb* [ME *sweltren*, fr. *swelten* to die, be overcome by heat, fr. OE *sweltan* to die] 1 : to be faint or oppressed with the heat 2 : to become exceedingly hot

swept *past and past part of* SWEEP

swerve \'swərv\ *vb* **swerved; swerv·ing** : to move abruptly aside from a straight line or course — **swerve** *n*

¹swift \'swift\ *adj* 1 : moving or capable of moving with great speed 2 : occurring suddenly 3 : READY, ALERT — **swift·ly** *adv* — **swift·ness** *n*

²swift *n* : any of numerous small insect-eating birds with long narrow wings

swig \'swig\ *vb* **swigged; swig·ging** : to drink in long drafts — **swig** *n*

¹swill \'swil\ *vb* 1 : to swallow greedily : GUZZLE 2 : to feed (as hogs) on swill

²swill *n* 1 : food for animals composed of edible refuse mixed with liquid 2 : GARBAGE

¹swim \'swim\ *vb* **swam** \'swam\; **swum** \'swəm\; **swim·ming** 1 : to propel oneself along in water by natural means (as by hands and legs, by tail, or by fins) 2 : to glide smoothly along 3 : FLOAT 4 : to be covered with or as if with a liquid 5 : to be dizzy ⟨his head *swam*⟩ 6 : to cross or go over by swimming — **swim·mer** *n*

²swim *n* 1 : an act of swimming 2 : the main current of activity ⟨in the ∼⟩

swim·ming *n* : the action, art, or sport of swimming and diving

swimming pool *n* : a tank (as of concrete or plastic) designed for swimming

swim·suit \'swim-ˌsüt\ *n* : a suit for swimming or bathing

swin·dle \'swin-dᵊl\ *vb* **swin·dled; swin·dling** [fr. *swin-*

dler, fr. G *Schwindler* giddy person, fr. *schwindeln* to
be dizzy] : CHEAT, DEFRAUD — **swindle** n — **swindler** n

swine \'swīn\ n, pl **swine 1** : any of a family of stout
short-legged hoofed mammals with bristly skin and a
long flexible snout; *esp* : one widely raised as a meat
animal **2** : a contemptible person — **swin·ish** adj

¹**swing** \'swiŋ\ vb **swung** \'swəŋ\; **swing·ing 1** : to move
or cause to move rapidly in an arc **2** : to sway or
cause to sway back and forth **3** : to hang so as to
move freely back and forth or in a curve **4** : to be executed by hanging **5** : to move or turn on a hinge or
pivot **6** : to manage or handle successfully **7** : to
march or walk with free swaying movements **8** : to
have a steady pulsing rhythm; *also* : to play swing
music **9** : to be lively and up-to-date; *also* : to engage
freely in sex **syn** wield, manipulate, ply, maneuver —
swing·er n — **swing·ing** adj

²**swing** n **1** : the act of swinging **2** : a swinging blow,
movement, or rhythm **3** : the distance through which
something swings : FLUCTUATION **4** : progression of
an activity or process ⟨in full ∼⟩ **5** : a seat suspended
by a rope or chain for swinging back and forth for
pleasure **6** : jazz music played esp. by a large band
and marked by a steady lively rhythm, simple harmony, and a basic melody often submerged in improvisation

³**swing** adj **1** : of or relating to swing music **2** : that may
swing often decisively either way (as on an issue) ⟨∼
voters⟩

¹**swipe** \'swīp\ n : a strong sweeping blow

²**swipe** vb **swiped**; **swip·ing 1** : to strike or wipe with a
sweeping motion **2** : PILFER, SNATCH

swirl \'swərl\ vb : to move or cause to move with a
whirling motion — **swirl** n — **swirly** \'swər-lē\ adj

swish \'swish\ n **1** : a prolonged hissing sound **2** : a
light sweeping or brushing sound — **swish** vb

Swiss \'swis\ n, pl **Swiss** : a native or inhabitant of
Switzerland **2** : a hard cheese with large holes

Swiss chard n : a beet having large leaves and succulent stalks often cooked as a vegetable

¹**switch** \'swich\ n **1** : a slender flexible whip, rod, or
twig **2** : a blow with a switch **3** : a shift from one thing
to another; *also* : change from the usual **4** : a device
for adjusting the rails of a track so that a locomotive
or train may be turned from one track to another;
also : a railroad siding **5** : a device for making, breaking, or changing the connections in an electrical circuit **6** : a heavy strand of hair often used in addition
to a person's own hair for some coiffures

²**switch** vb **1** : to punish or urge on with a switch **2**
: WHISK ⟨a cow ∼ing her tail⟩ **3** : to shift or turn by
operating a switch **4** : CHANGE, EXCHANGE

switch·back \'swich-ˌbak\ n : a zigzag road, trail, or
section of railroad tracks for climbing a steep hill

switch·blade \-ˌblād\ n : a pocket-knife with a spring-
operated blade

switch·board \-ˌbōrd\ n : a panel for controlling the
operation of a number of electric circuits; *esp* : one
used to make and break telephone connections

switch–hit·ter \-ˈhi-tər\ n : a baseball player who bats
either right-handed or left-handed — **switch–hit**
\-ˈhit\ vb

switch·man \'swich-mən\ n : one who attends a railroad switch

Switz abbr Switzerland

¹**swiv·el** \'swi-vəl\ n : a device joining two parts so that
one or both can turn freely

²**swivel** vb **-eled** or **-elled**; **-el·ing** or **-el·ling** : to swing
or turn on or as if on a swivel

swiv·et \'swi-vət\ n : an agitated state

swiz·zle stick \'swi-zəl-\ n : a stick used to stir mixed
drinks

swollen past part of SWELL

swoon \'swün\ vb : FAINT — **swoon** n

swoop \'swüp\ vb : to move with a sweep ⟨the eagle
∼ed down on its prey⟩ — **swoop** n

swop chiefly Brit var of SWAP

sword \'sōrd\ n **1** : a weapon with a long blade for cutting or thrusting **2** : the use of force

sword·fish \-ˌfish\ n : a very large ocean fish used for
food that has the upper jaw prolonged into a long
swordlike beak

swordfish

sword·play \-ˌplā\ n : the art or skill of wielding a
sword

swords·man \'sōrdz-mən\ n : one skilled in swordplay;
esp : FENCER

sword·tail \'sōrd-ˌtāl\ n : a small brightly marked Central American fish

swore past of SWEAR

sworn past part of SWEAR

swum past part of SWIM

swung past and past part of SWING

syb·a·rite \'si-bə-ˌrīt\ n : a lover of luxury : VOLUPTU-
ARY — **syb·a·rit·ic** \ˌsi-bə-ˈri-tik\ adj

syc·a·more \'si-kə-ˌmōr\ n : a large spreading tree of
eastern and central No. America that has light brown
flaky bark and small round fruits hanging on long
stalks

sy·co·phant \'si-kə-fənt\ n : a servile flatterer — **syc-
o·phan·tic** \ˌsi-kə-ˈfan-tik\ adj

syl or **syll** abbr syllable

syl·lab·i·ca·tion \sə-ˌla-bə-ˈkā-shən\ n : the division of
words into syllables

syl·lab·i·fy \sə-ˈla-bə-ˌfī\ vb **-fied**; **-fy·ing** : to form or
divide into syllables — **syl·lab·i·fi·ca·tion** \-ˌla-bə-fə-
ˈkā-shən\ n

syl·la·ble \'si-lə-bəl\ n [ME, fr. MF *sillabe*, fr. L *sylla-
ba*, fr. Gk *syllabē*, fr. *syllambanein* to gather together,
fr. *syn* with + *lambanein* to take] : a unit of spoken
language consisting of an uninterrupted utterance
and forming either a whole word (as *cat*) or a commonly recognized division of a word (as *syl* in *syl≠
la-ble*); *also* : one or more letters representing such a
unit — **syl·lab·ic** \sə-ˈla-bik\ adj

syl·la·bus \'si-lə-bəs\ n, pl **-bi** \-ˌbī\ or **-bus·es** : a summary containing the heads or main topics of a speech,
book, or course of study

syl·lo·gism \'si-lə-ˌji-zəm\ n : a logical scheme of a formal argument consisting of a major and a minor
premise and a conclusion which must logically be
true if the premises are true — **syl·lo·gis·tic** \ˌsi-lə-
ˈjis-tik\ adj

sylph \'silf\ n **1** : an imaginary being inhabiting the air
2 : a slender graceful woman

syl·van \'sil-vən\ adj **1** : living or located in a wooded
area; *also* : of, relating to, or characteristic of forest
2 : abounding in woods or trees

sym abbr **1** symbol **2** symmetrical

sym·bi·o·sis \ˌsim-ˌbī-ˈō-səs, -bē-\ n, pl **-o·ses** \-ˌsēz\
: the living together in close association of two dissimilar organisms esp. when mutually beneficial —
sym·bi·ot·ic \-ˈä-tik\ adj

sym·bol \'sim-bəl\ n **1** : something that stands for
something else; *esp* : something concrete that represents or suggests another thing that cannot itself be
pictured ⟨the lion is a ∼ of bravery⟩ **2** : a letter, character, or sign used in writing or printing to represent
operations, quantities, elements, sounds, or other

ideas — **sym·bol·ic** \sim-'bä-lik\ *also* **sym·bol·i·cal** \-li-kəl\ *adj* — **sym·bol·i·cal·ly** \-k(ə-)lē\ *adv*

sym·bol·ism \'sim-bə-ˌli-zəm\ *n* : representation of abstract or intangible things by means of symbols

sym·bol·ize \'sim-bə-ˌlīz\ *vb* **-ized; -iz·ing 1** : to serve as a symbol of **2** : to represent by symbols — **sym·bol·i·za·tion** \ˌsim-bə-lə-'zā-shən\ *n*

sym·me·try \'si-mə-trē\ *n, pl* **-tries 1** : an arrangement marked by regularity and balanced proportions **2** : correspondence in size, shape, and position of parts that are on opposite sides of a dividing line or center — **sym·met·ri·cal** \sə-'me-tri-kəl\ *or* **sym·met·ric** \sə-'me-trik\ — **sym·met·ri·cal·ly** \-k(ə-)lē\ *adv*

sympathetic nervous system *n* : the part of the autonomic nervous system that is concerned esp. with preparing the body to react to situations of stress or emergency and that tends to decrease the tone and contractility of muscle not under direct voluntary control, increase the activity of the heart and the blood pressure, and cause the contraction of blood vessels

sym·pa·thize \'sim-pə-ˌthīz\ *vb* **-thized; -thiz·ing** : to feel or show sympathy — **sym·pa·thiz·er** *n*

sym·pa·thy \'sim-pə-thē\ *n, pl* **-thies 1** : a relationship between persons or things wherein whatever affects one similarly affects the other **2** : harmony of interests and aims **3** : FAVOR, SUPPORT **4** : the capacity for entering into and sharing the feelings or interests of another; *also* : COMPASSION, PITY **5** : an expression of sorrow for another's loss, grief, or misfortune — **sym·pa·thet·ic** \ˌsim-pə-'the-tik\ *adj* — **sym·pa·thet·i·cal·ly** \-ti-k(ə-)lē\ *adv*

sym·pho·ny \'sim-fə-nē\ *n, pl* **-nies 1** : harmony of sounds **2** : a large and complex composition for a full orchestra **3** : a large orchestra of a kind that plays symphonies — **sym·phon·ic** \sim-'fä-nik\ *adj*

sym·po·sium \sim-'pō-zē-əm\ *n, pl* **-sia** \-zē-ə\ *or* **-siums** : a conference at which a particular topic is discussed by various speakers; *also* : a collection of opinions about a subject

symp·tom \'simp-təm\ *n* [LL *symptoma,* fr. Gk *symptōma* happening, attribute, symptom, fr. *sympiptein* to happen, fr. *syn* with + *piptein* to fall] **1** : something that indicates the presence of disease or abnormality; *esp* : something (as a headache) that can be sensed only by the individual affected **2** : SIGN, INDICATION — **symp·tom·at·ic** \ˌsimp-tə-'ma-tik\ *adj*

syn *abbr* synonym; synonymous; synonymy

syn·a·gogue *or* **syn·a·gog** \'si-nə-ˌgäg\ *n* [ME *synagoge,* fr. OF, fr. LL *synagoga,* fr. Gk *synagōgē* assembly, synagogue, fr. *synagein* to bring together] **1** : a Jewish congregation **2** : the house of worship of a Jewish congregation

syn·apse \'si-ˌnaps, sə-'naps\ *n* : the point at which a nervous impulse passes from one neuron to another

¹**sync** *also* **synch** \'siŋk\ *vb* **synced** *also* **synched** \'siŋkt\; **sync·ing** *also* **synch·ing** \'siŋ-kiŋ\ : SYNCHRONIZE

²**sync** *also* **synch** *n* : SYNCHRONIZATION, SYNCHRONISM — **sync** *adj*

syn·chro·nize \'siŋ-krə-ˌnīz, 'sin-\ *vb* **-nized; -niz·ing 1** : to occur or cause to occur at the same instant **2** : to represent, arrange, or tabulate according to dates or time **3** : to cause to agree in time **4** : to make synchronous in operation — **syn·chro·nism** \-ni-zəm\ *n* — **syn·chro·ni·za·tion** \ˌsiŋ-krə-nə-'zā-shən, ˌsin-\ *n* — **syn·chro·niz·er** *n*

syn·chro·nous \'siŋ-krə-nəs, 'sin-\ *adj* **1** : happening at the same time; CONCURRENT **2** : working, moving, or occurring together at the same rate and at the proper time

syn·co·pa·tion \ˌsiŋ-kə-'pā-shən, ˌsin-\ *n* : a shifting of the regular musical accent : occurrence of accented notes on the weak beat — **syn·co·pate** \'siŋ-kə-ˌpāt, 'sin-\ *vb*

syn·co·pe \'siŋ-kə-(ˌ)pē, 'sin-\ *n* : the loss of one or

more sounds or letters in the interior of a word (as in *fo'c'sle* for *forecastle*)

¹**syn·di·cate** \'sin-di-kət\ *n* **1** : a group of persons who combine to carry out a financial or industrial undertaking **2** : a loose association of racketeers **3** : a business concern that sells materials for publication in many newspapers and periodicals at the same time

²**syn·di·cate** \-də-ˌkāt\ *vb* **-cat·ed; -cat·ing 1** : to combine into or manage as a syndicate **2** : to publish through a syndicate — **syn·di·ca·tion** \ˌsin-də-'kā-shən\ *n*

syn·drome \'sin-ˌdrōm\ *n* : a group of signs and symptoms that occur together and characterize a particular abnormality

syn·er·gism \'sin-ər-ˌji-zəm\ *n* : interaction of discrete agencies (as industrial firms), agents (as drugs), or conditions such that the total effect is greater than the sum of the individual effects — **syn·er·gist** \-jist\ *n* — **syn·er·gis·tic** \ˌsi-nər-'jis-tik\ *adj* — **syn·er·gis·ti·cal·ly** \-ti-k(ə-)lē\ *adv*

syn·fuel \'sin-ˌfyül\ *n* [*syn*thetic] : a fuel derived esp. from a fossil fuel

syn·od \'si-nəd\ *n* : COUNCIL, ASSEMBLY; *esp* : a religious governing body — **syn·od·al** \-nəd-ᵊl, -ˌnäd-ᵊl\ *adj* — **syn·od·ic** \-dik\ *or* **syn·od·i·cal** \sə-'nä-di-kəl\ *adj*

syn·onym \'si-nə-ˌnim\ *n* : one of two or more words in the same language which have the same or very nearly the same meaning — **syn·on·y·mous** \sə-'nä-nə-məs\ *adj* — **syn·on·y·my** \-mē\ *n*

syn·op·sis \sə-'näp-səs\ *n, pl* **-op·ses** \-ˌsēz\ : a condensed statement or outline (as of a treatise) : ABSTRACT

syn·op·tic \sə-'näp-tik\ *also* **syn·op·ti·cal** \-ti-kəl\ *adj* : characterized by or affording a comprehensive view

syn·tax \'sin-ˌtaks\ *n* : the way in which words are put together to form phrases, clauses, or sentences — **syn·tac·tic** \sin-'tak-tik\ *or* **syn·tac·ti·cal** \-ti-kəl\ *adj*

syn·the·sis \'sin-thə-səs\ *n, pl* **-the·ses** \-ˌsēz\ : the combination of parts or elements into a whole; *esp* : the production of a substance by union of chemically simpler substances — **syn·the·size** \-ˌsīz\ *vb* — **syn·the·siz·er** *n*

syn·thet·ic \sin-'the-tik\ *adj* : produced artificially esp. by chemical means; *also* : not genuine — **synthetic** *n* — **syn·thet·i·cal·ly** \-ti-k(ə-)lē\ *adv*

syph·i·lis \'si-fə-ləs\ *n* [NL, fr. *Syphilus,* hero of the poem *Syphilis sive Morbus Gallicus* (*Syphilis or the French disease*) (1530) by Girolamo Fracastoro †1553 Ital. physician] : an infectious usu. venereal disease caused by a spirochete — **syph·i·lit·ic** \ˌsi-fə-'li-tik\ *adj or n*

sy·phon *var of* SIPHON

Syr·i·an \'sir-ē-ən\ *n* : a native or inhabitant of Syria — **Syrian** *adj*

¹**sy·ringe** \sə-'rinj\ *n* : a device used esp. for injecting liquids into or withdrawing them from the body

²**syringe** *vb* **sy·ringed; sy·ring·ing** : to flush or cleanse with or as if with a syringe

syr·up \'sər-əp, 'sir-əp\ *n* **1** : a thick sticky solution of sugar and water often flavored or medicated **2** : the concentrated juice of a fruit or plant — **syr·upy** *adj*

syst *abbr* system

sys·tem \'sis-təm\ *n* **1** : a group of units so combined as to form a whole and to operate in unison **2** : the body as a functioning whole; *also* : a group of bodily organs (as the nervous system) that together carry on some vital function **3** : a definite scheme or method of procedure or classification **4** : regular method or order — **sys·tem·at·ic** \ˌsis-tə-'ma-tik\ *also* **sys·tem·at·i·cal** \-ti-kəl\ *adj* — **sys·tem·at·i·cal·ly** \-k(ə-)lē\ *adv*

sys·tem·atize \'sis-tə-mə-ˌtīz\ *vb* **-atized; -atiz·ing** : to make into a system : arrange methodically

¹**sys·tem·ic** \sis-'te-mik\ *adj* **1** : of, relating to, or affecting the whole body ⟨∼ disease⟩ **2** : of, relating to, or being a pesticide that when absorbed into the sap or

bloodstream makes the entire plant or animal toxic to a pest (as an insect or fungus)

²systemic *n* : a systemic pesticide

systemic lupus erythematosus *n* : a systemic disease esp. of women characterized by fever, skin rash, and arthritis, often by anemia, by small hemorrhages of the skin and mucous membranes, and in serious cases by involvement of various internal organs

sys·tem·ize \'sis-tə-ˌmīz\ *vb* **-ized; -iz·ing** : SYSTEMATIZE

systems analyst *n* : a person who studies a procedure or business to determine its goals or purposes and to discover the best ways to accomplish them — **systems analysis** *n*

sys·to·le \'sis-tə-(ˌ)lē\ *n* : a rhythmically recurrent contraction of the heart — **sys·tol·ic** \sis-'tä-lik\ *adj*

T

¹t \'tē\ *n, pl* **t's** *or* **ts** \'tēz\ *often cap* : the 20th letter of the English alphabet

²t *abbr, often cap* **1** metric ton **2** tablespoon **3** teaspoon **4** temperature **5** ton **6** transitive **7** troy **8** true

T *abbr* **1** toddler **2** T-shirt

Ta *symbol* tantalum

TA *abbr* teaching assistant

¹tab \'tab\ *n* **1** : a short projecting flap, loop, or tag; *also* : a small insert or addition **2** : close surveillance : WATCH ⟨keep ∼s on him⟩ **3** : BILL, CHECK

²tab *vb* **tabbed; tab·bing** : DESIGNATE

tab·by \'ta-bē\ *n, pl* **tabbies** : a usu. striped or mottled domestic cat; *also* : a female domestic cat

tab·er·na·cle \'ta-bər-ˌna-kəl\ *n* [ME, fr. OF, fr. LL *tabernaculum*, fr. L, tent, fr. *taberna* hut] **1** *often cap* : a tent sanctuary used by the Israelites during the Exodus **2** : a receptacle for the consecrated elements of the Eucharist **3** : a house of worship

¹ta·ble \'tā-bəl\ *n* **1** : a flat slab or plaque : TABLET **2** : a piece of furniture consisting of a smooth flat top fixed on legs **3** : a supply of food : BOARD, FARE **4** : a group of people assembled at or as if at a table **5** : an orderly arrangement of data usu. in rows and columns **6** : a short list ⟨∼ of contents⟩ — **ta·ble·top** \-ˌtäp\ *n*

²table *vb* **ta·bled; ta·bling 1** *Brit* : to place on the agenda **2** : to remove (a parliamentary motion) from consideration indefinitely

tab·leau \'ta-ˌblō\ *n, pl* **tab·leaux** \-ˌblōz\ *also* **tab·leaus** [F] : a scene or event usu. presented on a stage by costumed participants who remain silent and motionless

ta·ble·cloth \'tā-bəl-ˌkloth\ *n* : a covering spread over a dining table before the table is set

ta·ble d'hôte \ˌtä-bəl-'dōt\ *n* [F, lit., host's table] : a complete meal of several courses offered at a fixed price

ta·ble·land \'tā-bəl-ˌland\ *n* : PLATEAU

ta·ble·spoon \-ˌspün\ *n* **1** : a large spoon used esp. for serving **2** : a unit of measure equal to ½ fluid ounce (15 milliliters)

ta·ble·spoon·ful \-ˌfül\ *n, pl* **-spoonfuls** \-ˌfülz\ *also* **-spoons·ful** \-ˌspünz-ˌfül\ : TABLESPOON 2

tab·let \'ta-blət\ *n* **1** : a flat slab suited for or bearing an inscription **2** : a collection of sheets of paper glued together at one edge **3** : a compressed or molded block of material; *esp* : a usu. disk-shaped medicated mass

table tennis *n* : a game resembling tennis played on a tabletop with wooden paddles and a small hollow plastic ball

ta·ble·ware \'tā-bəl-ˌwar\ *n* : utensils (as of china or silver) for table use

¹tab·loid \'ta-ˌbloid\ *adj* : condensed into small scope

²tabloid *n* : a newspaper marked by small pages, condensation of the news, and usu. many photographs; *esp* : one characterized by sensationalism

¹ta·boo *also* **ta·bu** \tə-'bü, ta-\ *adj* [Tongan (a Polynesian language) *tabu*] : prohibited by a taboo

²taboo *also* **tabu** *n, pl* **taboos** *also* **tabus 1** : a prohibition against touching, saying, or doing something for fear of immediate harm from a supernatural force **2** : a prohibition imposed by social custom

ta·bor *also* **ta·bour** \'tā-bər\ *n* : a small drum used to accompany a pipe or fife played by the same person

tab·u·lar \'ta-byə-lər\ *adj* **1** : having a flat surface **2** : arranged in a table; *esp* : set up in rows and columns **3** : computed by means of a table

tab·u·late \-ˌlāt\ *vb* **-lat·ed; -lat·ing** : to put into tabular form — **tab·u·la·tion** \ˌta-byə-'lā-shən\ *n* — **tab·u·la·tor** \'ta-byə-ˌlā-tər\ *n*

TAC \'tak\ *abbr* Tactical Air Command

tach \'tak\ *n* : TACHOMETER

ta·chom·e·ter \ta-'kä-mə-tər, tə-\ *n* [ultim. fr. Gk *tachos* speed] : a device to indicate speed of rotation

tachy·car·dia \ˌta-ki-'kär-dē-ə\ *n* : relatively rapid heart action

tachy·on \'ta-kē-ˌän\ *n* : a hypothetical particle held to travel faster than light

tac·it \'ta-sət\ *adj* [F or L; F *tacite*, fr. L *tacitus* silent, fr. *tacēre* to be silent] **1** : expressed without words or speech **2** : implied or indicated but not actually expressed ⟨∼ consent⟩ — **tac·it·ly** *adv* — **tac·it·ness** *n*

tac·i·turn \'ta-sə-ˌtərn\ *adj* : disinclined to talk **syn** uncommunicative, reserved, reticent, closemouthed — **tac·i·tur·ni·ty** \ˌta-sə-'tər-nə-tē\ *n*

¹tack \'tak\ *vb* **1** : to fasten with tacks; *also* : to add on **2** : to change the direction of (a sailing ship) from one tack to another **3** : to follow a zigzag course

²tack *n* **1** : a small sharp nail with a broad flat head **2** : the direction toward the wind that a ship is sailing ⟨starboard ∼⟩; *also* : the run of a ship on one tack **3** : a change of course from one tack to another **4** : a zigzag course **5** : a course of action

³tack *n* : gear for harnessing a horse

¹tack·le \'ta-kəl, *naut often* 'tā-\ *n* **1** : GEAR, APPARATUS, EQUIPMENT **2** : the rigging of a ship **3** : an arrangement of ropes and pulleys for hoisting or pulling heavy objects **4** : the act or an instance of tackling; *also* : a football lineman playing between guard and end

²tackle *vb* **tack·led; tack·ling 1** : to attach and secure with or as if with tackle **2** : to seize, grapple with, or throw down with the intention of subduing or stopping **3** : to set about dealing with ⟨∼ a problem⟩ — **tack·ler** *n*

¹tacky \'ta-kē\ *adj* **tack·i·er; -est** : sticky to the touch

²tacky *adj* **tack·i·er; -est 1** : SHABBY, SEEDY **2** : marked by lack of style or good taste; *also* : cheaply showy

ta·co \'tä-kō\ *n, pl* **tacos** \-kōz\ [MexSp] : a usu. fried tortilla rolled up with or folded over a filling

tact \'takt\ *n* [F, sense of touch, fr. L *tactus*, fr. *tangere* to touch] : a keen sense of what to do or say to keep good relations with others — **tact·ful** \-fəl\ *adj* — **tact·ful·ly** *adv* — **tact·less** *adj* — **tact·less·ly** *adv*

tac·tic \'tak-tik\ *n* : a planned action for accomplishing an end

tac·tics \'tak-tiks\ *n sing or pl* **1** : the science of maneuvering forces in combat **2** : the skill of using available means to reach an end — **tac·ti·cal** \-ti-kəl\ *adj* — **tac·ti·cian** \tak-'ti-shən\ *n*

tac·tile \'takt-əl, 'tak-ˌtīl\ *adj* : of, relating to, or perceptible through the sense of touch

tad·pole \'tad-ˌpōl\ *n* [ME *taddepol*, fr. *tode* toad + *polle* head] : an aquatic larva of a frog or toad that has a tail and gills

tae kwon do \\'tī-'kwän-'dō\ *n* : a Korean martial art resembling karate

taf·fe·ta \\'ta-fə-tə\ *n* : a crisp lustrous fabric (as of silk or rayon)

taff·rail \\'taf-ˌrāl, -rəl\ *n* : the rail around a ship's stern

taf·fy \\'ta-fē\ *n, pl* **taffies** : a candy usu. of molasses or brown sugar stretched until porous and light‑colored

¹tag \\'tag\ *n* **1** : a metal or plastic binding on an end of a shoelace **2** : a piece of hanging or attached material **3** : a hackneyed quotation or saying **4** : a descriptive or identifying epithet

²tag *vb* **tagged; tag·ging 1** : to provide or mark with or as if with a tag; *esp* : IDENTIFY **2** : to attach as an addition **3** : to follow closely and persistently ⟨~s along everywhere we go⟩ **4** : to hold responsible for something

³tag *n* : a game in which one player chases others and tries to touch one of them

⁴tag *vb* **tagged; tag·ging 1** : to touch in or as if in a game of tag **2** : SELECT

TAG *abbr* the adjutant general

tag sale *n* : GARAGE SALE

Ta·hi·tian \tə-'hē-shən\ *n* **1** : a native or inhabitant of Tahiti **2** : the Polynesian language of the Tahitians — **Tahitian** *adj*

tai·ga \\'tī-gə\ *n* [Russ *taïga*] : a swampy coniferous subarctic forest extending south from the tundra

¹tail \\'tāl\ *n* **1** : the rear end or a process extending from the rear end of an animal **2** : something resembling an animal's tail **3** *pl* : full evening dress for men **4** : the back, last, lower, or inferior part of something; *esp* : the reverse of a coin **5** : one who follows or keeps watch on someone — **tailed** \\'tāld\ *adj* — **tail·less** \\'tāl-ləs\ *adj*

²tail *vb* : FOLLOW; *esp* : to follow for the purpose of surveillance

tail·coat \-'kōt\ *n* : a coat with tails; *esp* : a man's full‑dress coat with two long tapering skirts at the back

¹tail·gate \-ˌgāt\ *n* : a board or gate at the back end of a vehicle that can be let down (as for loading)

²tailgate *vb* **tail·gat·ed; tail·gat·ing 1** : to drive dangerously close behind another vehicle **2** : to hold a tailgate picnic

³tailgate *adj* : relating to or being a picnic set up on the tailgate esp. of a station wagon

tail·light \-ˌlīt\ *n* : a usu. red warning light mounted at the rear of a vehicle

¹tai·lor \\'tā-lər\ *n* [ME *taillour*, fr. OF *tailleur*, fr. *taillier* to cut, fr. LL *taliare*, fr. L *talea* twig, cutting] : a person whose occupation is making or altering garments

²tailor *vb* **1** : to make or fashion as the work of a tailor **2** : to make or adapt to suit a special purpose

tail pipe *n* : an outlet by which the exhaust gases are removed from an engine (as of an automobile)

tail·spin \\'tāl-ˌspin\ *n* : a rapid descent or downward spiral

tail wind *n* : a wind blowing in the same general direction as a course of movement (as of an aircraft)

¹taint \\'tānt\ *vb* **1** : CORRUPT, CONTAMINATE **2** : to affect or become affected with something bad (as putrefaction)

²taint *n* : a contaminating mark or influence

Tai·wan·ese \ˌtī-wə-'nēz, -'nēs\ *n* : a native or inhabitant of Taiwan — **Taiwanese** *adj*

ta·ka \\'tä-kə\ *n* — see MONEY table

¹take \\'tāk\ *vb* **took** \\'tu̇k\; **tak·en** \\'tā-kən\; **tak·ing 1** : to get into one's hands or possession : GRASP, SEIZE **2** : CAPTURE; *also* : DEFEAT **3** : to obtain or secure for use **4** : to catch or attack through the effect of a sudden force or influence ⟨*taken* ill⟩ **5** : CAPTIVATE, DELIGHT **6** : to bring into a relation ⟨~ a wife⟩ **7** : REMOVE, SUBTRACT **8** : to pick out : CHOOSE **9** : ASSUME, UNDERTAKE **10** : RECEIVE, ACCEPT **11** : to use for transportation ⟨~ a bus⟩ **12** : to become impregnated with : ABSORB ⟨~s a dye⟩ **13** : to receive into

one's body (as by swallowing) ⟨~ a pill⟩ **14** : ENDURE, UNDERGO **15** : to lead, carry, or cause to go along to another place **16** : NEED, REQUIRE **17** : to obtain as the result of a special procedure ⟨~ a snapshot⟩ **18** : to undertake and do, make, or perform ⟨~ a walk⟩ **19** : to take effect : ACT, OPERATE **syn** grab, clutch, snatch, seize, nab, grapple — **tak·er** *n* — **take advantage of 1** : to profit by **2** : EXPLOIT — **take after** : RESEMBLE — **take care** : to be careful — **take care of** : to care for : attend to — **take effect** : to become operative — **take exception** : OBJECT — **take for** : to suppose to be; *esp* : to mistake for — **take place** : HAPPEN — **take to 1** : to go to **2** : to apply or devote oneself to **3** : to conceive a liking for

²take *n* **1** : the number or quantity taken; *also* : PROCEEDS, RECEIPTS **2** : an act or the action of taking **3** : a television or movie scene filmed or taped at one time; *also* : a sound recording made at one time **4** : a distinct or personal point of view

take·off \\'tā-ˌkȯf\ *n* **1** : IMITATION; *esp* : PARODY **2** : an act or instance of taking off

take off *vb* **1** : REMOVE **2** : DEDUCT **3** : to set out : go away **4** : to leave the surface; *esp* : to begin flight

take on *vb* **1** : to begin to perform or deal with; *also* : to contend with as an opponent **2** : ENGAGE, HIRE **3** : to assume or acquire as or as if one's own **4** : to make an unusual show of one's feelings esp. of grief or anger

take over *vb* : to assume control or possession of or responsibility for — **take·over** \\'tā-ˌkō-vər\ *n*

take up *vb* **1** : PICK UP **2** : to begin to occupy **3** : to absorb or incorporate into itself ⟨plants ~ up nutrients⟩ **4** : to begin to engage in ⟨*took up* jogging⟩ **5** : to make tighter or shorter ⟨*take up* the slack⟩

tak·ings \\'tā-kiŋz\ *n pl* : receipts esp. of money

ta·la \\'tä-lə\ *n, pl* **tala** — see MONEY table

talc \\'talk\ *n* : a soft mineral with a soapy feel used esp. in making toilet powder (**tal·cum powder** \\'tal-kəm-\)

tale \\'tāl\ *n* **1** : a relation of a series of events **2** : a report of a confidential matter **3** : idle talk; *esp* : harmful gossip **4** : a usu. imaginative narrative **5** : FALSEHOOD **6** : COUNT, TALLY

tal·ent \\'ta-lənt\ *n* **1** : an ancient unit of weight and value **2** : the natural endowments of a person **3** : a special often creative or artistic aptitude **4** : mental power : ABILITY **5** : a person of talent **syn** genius, gift, faculty, aptitude, knack — **tal·ent·ed** *adj*

ta·ler \\'tä-lər\ *n* : any of numerous silver coins issued by German states from the 15th to the 19th centuries

tales·man \\'tālz-mən\ *n* : a person summoned for jury duty

tal·is·man \\'ta-ləs-mən, -ləz-\ *n, pl* **-mans** [F *talisman* or Sp *talismán* or It *talismano*, fr. Ar *tilsam*, fr. MGk *telesma*, fr. Gk, consecration, fr. *telein* to initiate into the mysteries, complete, fr. *telos* end] : an object thought to act as a charm

¹talk \\'tȯk\ *vb* **1** : to express in speech : utter words : SPEAK **2** : DISCUSS ⟨~ business⟩ **3** : to influence or cause by talking ⟨~ed him into going⟩ **4** : to use (a language) for communicating **5** : CONVERSE **6** : to reveal confidential information; *also* : GOSSIP **7** : to give a talk : LECTURE — **talk·er** *n* — **talk back** : to answer impertinently

²talk *n* **1** : the act of talking **2** : a way of speaking **3** : a formal discussion **4** : REPORT, RUMOR **5** : the topic of comment or gossip ⟨the ~ of the town⟩ **6** : an informal address or lecture

talk·ative \\'tȯ-kə-tiv\ *adj* : given to talking **syn** loquacious, chatty, gabby, garrulous — **talk·ative·ly** *adv* — **talk·ative·ness** *n*

talk·ing-to \\'tȯ-kiŋ-ˌtü\ *n* : REPRIMAND, REPROOF

tall \\'tȯl\ *adj* **1** : high in stature **syn** of a specified height ⟨six feet ~⟩ **2** : LARGE, FORMIDABLE ⟨a ~ order⟩ **3** : UNBELIEVABLE, IMPROBABLE ⟨a ~ story⟩ — **tall·ness** *n*

tal·low \\'ta-lō\ *n* : a hard white fat rendered usu. from cattle or sheep tissues and used esp. in candles

¹tal·ly \\'ta-lē\ *n, pl* **tallies** [ME *talye,* fr. ML *talea,* fr. L, twig, cutting] **1** : a device for visibly recording or accounting esp. business transactions **2** : a recorded account **3** : a corresponding part; *also* : CORRESPONDENCE

²tally *vb* **tal·lied; tal·ly·ing 1** : to mark on or as if on a tally **2** : to make a count of : RECKON; *also* : SCORE **3** : CORRESPOND, MATCH **syn** square, accord, harmonize, conform, jibe

tal·ly·ho \\ta-lē-'hō\ *n, pl* **-hos** : a call of a huntsman at sight of the fox

Tal·mud \\'täl-ˌmu̇d, 'tal-məd\ *n* [Late Heb *talmūdh,* lit., instruction] : the authoritative body of Jewish tradition — **Tal·mu·dic** \tal-'mü-dik, -'myü-, -'mə-; täl-'mu̇-\ *adj* — **Tal·mud·ist** \\'täl-ˌmu̇-dist, 'tal-mə-\ *n*

tal·on \\'ta-lən\ *n* : the claw of an animal and esp. of a bird of prey

ta·lus \\'tā-ləs, 'ta-\ *n* : rock debris at the base of a cliff

tam \\'tam\ *n* : TAM-O'-SHANTER

ta·ma·le \tə-'mä-lē\ *n* [MexSp *tamales,* pl. of *tamal* tamale, fr. Nahuatl *tamalli* (American Indian language) *tamalli* steamed cornmeal dough] : ground meat seasoned with chili, rolled in cornmeal dough, wrapped in corn husks, and steamed

tam·a·rack \\'ta-mə-ˌrak\ *n* : a larch of northern No. America; *also* : its hard resinous wood

tam·a·rind \\'ta-mə-rənd, -ˌrind\ *n* [Sp & Pg *tamarindo,* fr. Ar *tamr hindī,* lit., Indian date] : a tropical tree of the legume family with hard yellowish wood and feathery leaves; *also* : its acid fruit

tam·ba·la \täm-'bä-lə\ *n, pl* **-la** *or* **-las** — see *kwacha* at MONEY table

tam·bou·rine \ˌtam-bə-'rēn\ *n* : a small shallow drum with loose disks at the sides played by shaking or striking with the hand

¹tame \\'tām\ *adj* **tam·er; tam·est 1** : reduced from a state of native wildness esp. so as to be useful to humans : DOMESTICATED **2** : made docile : SUBDUED **3** : lacking spirit or interest : INSIPID **syn** submissive, domestic, domesticated — **tame·ly** *adv* — **tame·ness** *n*

²tame *vb* **tamed; tam·ing 1** : to make or become tame; *also* : to subject (land) to cultivation **2** : HUMBLE, SUBDUE — **tam·able** *or* **tame·able** \\'tā-mə-bəl\ *adj* — **tame·less** *adj* — **tam·er** *n*

tam—o'—shan·ter \\'ta-mə-ˌshan-tər\ *n* [fr. poem *Tam o' Shanter* (1790) by Robert Burns †1796 Scot. poet] : a Scottish woolen cap with a wide flat circular crown and usu. a pompon in the center

tamp \\'tamp\ *vb* : to drive down or in by a series of light blows

tam·per \\'tam-pər\ *vb* **1** : to carry on underhand negotiations (as by bribery) ⟨∼ with a witness⟩ **2** : to interfere so as to weaken or change for the worse ⟨∼ with a document⟩ **3** : to try foolish or dangerous experiments

tam·pon \\'tam-ˌpän\ *n* [F, lit., plug] : a plug (as of cotton) introduced into a body cavity usu. to absorb secretions (as from menstruation) or to arrest bleeding

¹tan \\'tan\ *vb* **tanned; tan·ning 1** : to change (hide) into leather esp. by soaking in a liquid containing tannin **2** : to make or become brown (as by exposure to the sun) **3** : WHIP, THRASH

²tan *n* **1** : a brown skin color induced by sun or weather **2** : a light yellowish brown color

³tan *abbr* tangent

tan·a·ger \\'ta-ni-jər\ *n* : any of numerous American birds that are often brightly colored

tan·bark \\'tan-ˌbärk\ *n* : bark (as of oak or sumac) that is rich in tannin and used in tanning

¹tan·dem \\'tan-dəm\ *n* [L, at last, at length (taken to mean "lengthwise"), fr. *tam* so] **1** : a 2-seated carriage with horses hitched tandem; *also* : its team **2** : a bicycle for two persons sitting one behind the other — **in tandem** : in a tandem arrangement

²tandem *adv* : one behind another

³tandem *adj* **1** : consisting of things arranged one behind the other **2** : working in conjunction with each other

tang \\'taŋ\ *n* **1** : a part in a tool that connects the blade with the handle **2** : a sharp distinctive flavor; *also* : a pungent odor — **tangy** *adj*

¹tan·gent \\'tan-jənt\ *adj* [L *tangent-, tangens,* prp. of *tangere* to touch] : TOUCHING; *esp* : touching a circle or sphere at only one point

²tangent *n* **1** : a tangent line, curve, or surface **2** : an abrupt change of course — **tan·gen·tial** \tan-'jen-chəl\ *adj*

tan·ger·ine \\'tan-jə-ˌrēn, ˌtan-jə-'rēn\ *n* : a deep orange loose-skinned citrus fruit; *also* : a tree that bears tangerines

¹tan·gi·ble \\'tan-jə-bəl\ *adj* **1** : perceptible esp. by the sense of touch : PALPABLE **2** : substantially real : MATERIAL ⟨∼ rewards⟩ **3** : capable of being appraised **syn** appreciable, perceptible, sensible, discernible — **tan·gi·bil·i·ty** \ˌtan-jə-'bi-lə-tē\ *n*

²tangible *n* : something tangible; *esp* : a tangible asset

¹tan·gle \\'taŋ-gəl\ *vb* **tan·gled; tan·gling 1** : to involve so as to hamper or embarrass; *also* : ENTRAP **2** : to unite or knit together in intricate confusion : ENTANGLE

²tangle *n* **1** : a tangled twisted mass **2** : a confusedly complicated state : MUDDLE

tan·go \\'taŋ-gō\ *n, pl* **tangos** : a dance of Latin-American origin — **tango** *vb*

tank \\'taŋk\ *n* **1** : a large artificial receptacle for liquids **2** : a heavily armed and armored combat vehicle that moves on tracks — **tank·ful** *n*

tan·kard \\'taŋ-kərd\ *n* : a tall one-handled drinking vessel

tank·er \\'taŋ-kər\ *n* : a vehicle equipped for transporting a liquid

tank top *n* : a sleeveless collarless pullover shirt with shoulder straps

tank town *n* : a small town

tan·ner \\'ta-nər\ *n* : one that tans hides

tan·nery \\'ta-nə-rē\ *n, pl* **-ner·ies** : a place where tanning is carried on

tan·nic acid \\'ta-nik-\ *n* : TANNIN

tan·nin \\'ta-nən\ *n* : any of various plant substances used esp. in tanning and dyeing, in inks, and as astringents

tan·sy \\'tan-zē\ *n, pl* **tansies** [ME *tanesey,* fr. MF *tanesie,* fr. ML *athanasia,* fr. Gk, immortality, fr. *athanatos* immortal, fr. *a-* not + *thanatos* death] : a common weedy herb related to the daisies with an aromatic odor and bitter-tasting finely divided leaves

tan·ta·lise *Brit var of* TANTALIZE

tan·ta·lize \\'tan-tə-ˌlīz\ *vb* **-lized; -liz·ing** [fr. *Tantalus,* king of Greek myth punished in Hades by having to stand up to his chin in water that receded as he bent to drink] : to tease or torment by presenting something desirable but keeping it out of reach — **tan·ta·liz·er** *n* — **tan·ta·liz·ing·ly** *adv*

tan·ta·lum \\'tan-tə-ləm\ *n* : a hard ductile metallic chemical element — see ELEMENT table

tan·ta·mount \\'tan-tə-ˌmau̇nt\ *adj* : equivalent in value or meaning

tan·trum \\'tan-trəm\ *n* : a fit of bad temper

Tan·za·ni·an \ˌtan-zə-'nē-ən\ *n* : a native or inhabitant of Tanzania — **Tanzanian** *adj*

Tao·ism \\'tau̇-ˌi-zəm, 'dau̇-\ *n* : a Chinese mystical philosophy; *also* : a religion developed from Taoist philosophy and Buddhism — **Tao·ist** \-ist\ *adj or n*

¹tap \\'tap\ *n* **1** : FAUCET, COCK **2** : liquor drawn through a tap **3** : the removing of fluid from a container or cavity by tapping **4** : a tool for forming an internal screw thread **5** : a point in an electric circuit where a connection may be made

²tap *vb* **tapped; tap·ping 1** : to release or cause to flow by piercing or by drawing a plug from a container or cavity **2** : to pierce so as to let out or draw off a fluid **3** : to draw from ⟨∼ resources⟩ **4** : to cut in on (a telephone wire) to get information; *also* : to cut in (an electrical circuit) on another circuit **5** : to form an internal screw thread in by means of a tap **6** : to connect (as a gas or water main) with a local supply — **tap·per** *n*

³tap *vb* **tapped; tap·ping 1** : to rap lightly **2** : to bring about by repeated light blows **3** : SELECT; *esp* : to elect to membership

⁴tap *n* **1** : a light blow or stroke; *also* : its sound **2** : a small metal plate for the sole or heel of a shoe

¹tape \'tāp\ *n* **1** : a narrow band of woven fabric **2** : a narrow flexible strip; *esp* : MAGNETIC TAPE

²tape *vb* **taped; tap·ing 1** : to fasten or support with tape **2** : to record on magnetic tape

tape deck *n* : a device used to play back magnetic tapes that usu. has to be connected to an audio system

tape measure *n* : a tape marked off in units (as inches) for measuring

¹ta·per \'tā-pər\ *n* **1** : a slender wax candle; *also* : a long waxed wick **2** : a gradual lessening of thickness or width in a long object

²taper *vb* **ta·pered; ta·per·ing 1** : to make or become gradually smaller toward one end **2** : to diminish gradually

tape–re·cord \ˌtā-pri-'kòrd\ *vb* : to make a recording of on magnetic tape — **tape recorder** *n* — **tape re·cording** *n*

tap·es·try \'ta-pə-strē\ *n, pl* **-tries** : a heavy reversible textile that has designs or pictures woven into it and is used esp. as a wall hanging

tape·worm \'tāp-ˌwərm\ *n* : any of a class of long flat segmented worms parasitic in vertebrate intestines

tap·i·o·ca \ˌta-pē-'ō-kə\ *n* : a usu. granular preparation of cassava starch used esp. in puddings; *also* : a dish (as pudding) that contains tapioca

ta·pir \'tā-pər\ *n, pl* **tapir** *or* **tapirs** : any of a genus of large harmless hoofed mammals of tropical America and Asia from Myanmar to Sumatra

tapir

tap·pet \'ta-pət\ *n* : a lever or projection moved by some other piece (as a cam) or intended to move something else

tap·room \'tap-ˌrüm, -ˌrùm\ *n* : BARROOM

tap·root \-ˌrüt, -ˌrùt\ *n* : a large main root growing straight down and giving off small side roots

taps \'taps\ *n sing or pl* : the last bugle call at night blown as a signal that lights are to be put out; *also* : a similar call blown at military funerals and memorial services

tap·ster \'tap-stər\ *n* : BARTENDER

¹tar \'tär\ *n* **1** : a thick dark sticky liquid distilled from organic material (as wood or coal) **2** : SAILOR, SEAMAN

²tar *vb* **tarred; tar·ring** : to cover or smear with or as if with tar

tar·an·tel·la \ˌtar-ən-'te-lə\ *n* : a lively folk dance of southern Italy in 6/8 time

ta·ran·tu·la \tə-'ran-chə-lə, -tə-lə\ *n, pl* **tarantulas** *also* **ta·ran·tu·lae** \-'ran-chə-ˌlē, -tə-ˌlē\ : any of a family of large hairy American spiders with a sharp bite that is not very poisonous to human beings

tar·dy \'tär-dē\ *adj* **tar·di·er; -est 1** : moving slowly : SLUGGISH **2** : LATE **syn** behindhand, overdue, belated — **tar·di·ly** \-də-lē\ *adv* — **tar·di·ness** \-dē-nəs\ *n*

¹tare \'tar\ *n* : a weed of grainfields

²tare *n* : a deduction from the gross weight of a substance and its container made in allowance for the weight of the container — **tare** *vb*

¹tar·get \'tär-gət\ *n* [ME, fr. MF *targette*, dim. of *targe* light shield, of Gmc origin] **1** : a mark to shoot at **2** : an object of ridicule or criticism **3** : a goal to be achieved

²target *vb* : to make a target of

tar·iff \'tar-əf\ *n* [It *tariffa*, fr. Ar *ta'rīf* notification] **1** : a schedule of duties imposed by a government esp. on imported goods; *also* : a duty or rate of duty imposed in such a schedule **2** : a schedule of rates or charges

tar·mac \'tär-ˌmak\ *n* : a surface paved with crushed stone covered with tar

tarn \'tärn\ *n* : a small mountain lake

tar·nish \'tär-nish\ *vb* : to make or become dull or discolored — **tarnish** *n*

ta·ro \'tär-ō, 'tar-\ *n, pl* **taros** : a tropical plant related to the arums that is grown for its edible starchy fleshy root; *also* : this root

tar·ot \'tar-ō\ *n* : one of a set of usu. 78 playing cards used esp. for fortune-telling

tar·pau·lin \tär-'pò-lən, 'tär-pə-\ *n* : a piece of material (as durable plastic) used for protecting exposed objects

tar·pon \'tär-pən\ *n, pl* **tarpon** *or* **tarpons** : a large silvery bony fish often caught for sport in the warm coastal waters of the Atlantic esp. off Florida

tar·ra·gon \'tar-ə-gən\ *n* : a small widely cultivated perennial wormwood with pungent leaves used as a flavoring; *also* : its leaves

¹tar·ry \'tar-ē\ *vb* **tar·ried; tar·ry·ing 1** : to be tardy : DELAY; *esp* : to be slow in leaving **2** : to stay in or at a place : SOJOURN **syn** remain, wait, linger, abide

²tar·ry \'tär-ē\ *adj* : of, resembling, or smeared with tar

tar sand *n* : sand or sandstone that is naturally soaked with the heavy sticky portions of petroleum

tar·sus \'tär-səs\ *n, pl* **tar·si** \-ˌsī\ [NL] : the part of a vertebrate foot between the metatarsus and the leg; *also* : the small bones that support this part — **tar·sal** \-səl\ *adj or n*

¹tart \'tärt\ *adj* **1** : agreeably sharp to the taste : PUNGENT **2** : BITING, CAUSTIC — **tart·ly** *adv* — **tart·ness** *n*

²tart *n* **1** : a small pie or pastry shell containing jelly, custard, or fruit **2** : PROSTITUTE

tar·tan \'tärt-ᵊn\ *n* : a twilled woolen fabric with a plaid design of Scottish origin consisting of stripes of varying width and color usu. patterned to designate a distinctive clan

tar·tar \'tär-tər\ *n* **1** : a substance in the juice of grapes deposited (as in wine casks) as a reddish crust or sediment **2** : a hard crust of saliva, food debris, and calcium salts on the teeth

tar·tar sauce *or* **tar·tare sauce** \'tär-tər-\ *n* : mayonnaise with chopped pickles, olives, or capers

¹task \'task\ *n* [ME *taske*, fr. OF *tasque*, fr. ML *tasca* tax or service imposed by a feudal superior, fr. *taxare* to tax] : a piece of assigned work **syn** job, duty, chore, stint, assignment

²task *vb* : to oppress with great labor

task force *n* : a temporary grouping to accomplish a particular objective

task·mas·ter \'task-ˌmas-tər\ n : one that imposes a task or burdens another with labor

¹**tas·sel** \'ta-səl, 'tä-\ n 1 : a hanging ornament made of a bunch of cords of even length fastened at one end 2 : something suggesting a tassel; esp : a male flower cluster of Indian corn

²**tassel** vb -seled or -selled; -sel·ing or -sel·ling : to adorn with or put forth tassels

¹**taste** \'tāst\ vb tast·ed; tast·ing 1 : EXPERIENCE, UNDERGO 2 : to try or determine the flavor of by taking a bit into the mouth 3 : to eat or drink esp. in small quantities : SAMPLE 4 : to have a specific flavor

²**taste** n 1 : a small amount tasted 2 : BIT; esp : a sample of experience 3 : the special sense that identifies sweet, sour, bitter, or salty qualities and is mediated by receptors in the taste buds of the tongue 4 : a quality perceptible to the sense of taste; also : a complex sensation involving true taste, smell, and touch 5 : individual preference 6 : critical judgment, discernment, or appreciation; also : aesthetic quality syn tang, relish, flavor, savor — **taste·ful** \-fəl\ adj — **taste·ful·ly** adv — **taste·less** adj — **taste·less·ly** adv — **tast·er** n

taste bud n : a sense organ mediating the sensation of taste

tasty \'tā-stē\ adj tast·i·er; -est : pleasing to the taste : SAVORY syn palatable, appetizing, toothsome, flavorsome — **tast·i·ness** \'tā-stē-nəs\ n

tat \'tat\ vb tat·ted; tat·ting : to work at or make by tatting

¹**tat·ter** \'ta-tər\ vb : to make or become ragged

²**tatter** n 1 : a part torn and left hanging 2 pl : tattered clothing

tat·ter·de·ma·lion \ˌta-tər-di-'māl-yən\ n : one that is ragged or disreputable

tat·ter·sall \'ta-tər-ˌsȯl, -səl\ n : a pattern of colored lines forming squares on solid background; also : a fabric in a tattersall pattern

tat·ting \'ta-tiŋ\ n : a delicate handmade lace formed usu. by looping and knotting with a single thread and a small shuttle; also : the act or process of making such lace

tat·tle \'tat-ᵊl\ vb tat·tled; tat·tling 1 : CHATTER, PRATE 2 : to tell secrets; also : to inform against another — **tat·tler** n

tat·tle·tale \'tat-ᵊl-ˌtāl\ n : one that tattles : INFORMER

¹**tat·too** \ta-'tü\ n, pl tattoos [alter. of earlier taptoo, fr. D taptoe, fr. the phrase tap toe! taps shut!] 1 : a call sounded before taps as notice to go to quarters 2 : a rapid rhythmic rapping

²**tattoo** vb : to mark (the skin) with tattoos

³**tattoo** n, pl tattoos [Tahitian tatau] : an indelible figure fixed upon the body esp. by insertion of pigment under the skin

tau \'tau̇, 'tȯ\ n : the 19th letter of the Greek alphabet— T or τ

taught past and past part of TEACH

¹**taunt** \'tȯnt\ n : a sarcastic challenge or insult

²**taunt** vb : to reproach or challenge in a mocking manner : jeer at syn mock, deride, ridicule, twit — **taunt·er** n

taupe \'tōp\ n : a brownish gray

Tau·rus \'tȯr-əs\ n [L, lit., bull] 1 : a zodiacal constellation between Aries and Gemini usu. pictured as a bull 2 : the 2d sign of the zodiac in astrology; also : one born under this sign

taut \'tȯt\ adj 1 : tightly drawn : not slack 2 : extremely nervous : TENSE 3 : TRIM, TIDY ⟨a ~ ship⟩ — **taut·ly** adv — **taut·ness** n

tau·tol·o·gy \tȯ-'tä-lə-jē\ n, pl -gies : needless repetition of an idea, statement, or word; also : an instance of such repetition — **tau·to·log·i·cal** \ˌtȯt-ᵊl-'ä-ji-kəl\ adj — **tau·to·log·i·cal·ly** \-ji-k(ə-)lē\ adv — **tau·tol·o·gous** \tȯ-'tä-lə-gəs\ adj — **tau·tol·o·gous·ly** adv

tav·ern \'ta-vərn\ n [ME taverne, fr. OF, fr. L taberna

hut, shop] 1 : an establishment where alcoholic liquors are sold to be drunk on the premises 2 : INN

taw \'tȯ\ n 1 : a marble used as a shooter 2 : the line from which players shoot at marbles

taw·dry \'tȯ-drē\ adj taw·dri·er; -est [tawdry lace a tie of lace for the neck, fr. St. Audrey (St. Etheldreda) †679 queen of Northumbria] : cheap and gaudy in appearance and quality syn garish, flashy, chintzy, meretricious — **taw·dri·ly** adv

taw·ny \'tȯ-nē\ adj taw·ni·er; -est : of a brownish orange color

¹**tax** \'taks\ vb 1 : to levy a tax on 2 : CHARGE, ACCUSE 3 : to put under pressure — **tax·able** \'tak-sə-bəl\ adj — **tax·a·tion** \tak-'sā-shən\ n

²**tax** n 1 : a charge usu. of money imposed by authority on persons or property for public purposes 2 : a heavy charge : STRAIN

¹**taxi** \'tak-sē\ n, pl tax·is \-sēz\ also tax·ies : TAXICAB; also : a similarly operated boat or aircraft

²**taxi** vb tax·ied; taxi·ing or taxy·ing; tax·is or tax·ies 1 : to move along the ground or on the water under an aircraft's own power when starting or after a landing 2 : to go by taxicab

taxi·cab \'tak-sē-ˌkab\ n : an automobile that carries passengers for a fare usu. based on the distance traveled

taxi·der·my \'tak-sə-ˌdər-mē\ n : the skill or occupation of preparing, stuffing, and mounting skins of animals — **taxi·der·mist** \-mist\ n

tax·on·o·my \tak-'sä-nə-mē\ n : classification esp. of animals or plants according to natural relationships — **tax·o·nom·ic** \ˌtak-sə-'nä-mik\ adj — **tax·on·o·mist** \tak-'sä-nə-mist\ n

tax·pay·er \'taks-ˌpā-ər\ n : one who pays or is liable for a tax — **tax·pay·ing** adj

Tay–Sachs disease \'tā-'saks-\ n : a hereditary disorder caused by the absence of an enzyme needed to break down fatty material, marked by buildup of lipids in nervous tissue, and causing death in childhood

tb abbr tablespoon; tablespoonful

Tb symbol terbium

TB \ˌtē-'bē\ n : TUBERCULOSIS

TBA abbr, often not cap to be announced

T–bar \'tē-ˌbär\ n : a ski lift with a series of T⸗shaped bars

tbs or **tbsp** abbr tablespoon; tablespoonful

Tc symbol technetium

TC abbr teachers college

T cell n : any of several lymphocytes (as a helper T cell) specialized esp. for activity in and control of immunity and the immune response

TD abbr 1 touchdown 2 Treasury Department

TDD abbr telecommunications device for the deaf

TDY abbr temporary duty

Te symbol tellurium

tea \'tē\ n 1 : the cured leaves and leaf buds of a shrub grown chiefly in China, Japan, India, and Sri Lanka; also : this shrub 2 : a drink made by steeping tea in boiling water 3 : refreshments usu. including tea served in late afternoon; also : a reception at which tea is served

teach \'tēch\ vb taught \'tȯt\; teach·ing 1 : to cause to know something : act as a teacher 2 : to show how ⟨~ a child to swim⟩ 3 : to make to know the disagreeable consequences of an action 4 : to guide the studies of 5 : to impart the knowledge of ⟨~ algebra⟩ — **teach·able** adj — **teach·er** n

teach·ing n 1 : the act, practice, or profession of a teacher 2 : something taught; esp : DOCTRINE

tea·cup \'tē-ˌkəp\ n : a small cup used with a saucer for hot beverages

teak \'tēk\ n : the hard durable yellowish brown wood of a tall East Indian timber tree related to the vervains; also : this tree

tea·ket·tle \'tē-ˌket-ᵊl\ n : a covered kettle with a handle and spout for boiling water

teal \\'tēl\ *n, pl* **teal** *or* **teals 1** : any of various small short-necked wild ducks **2** : a dark greenish blue color

teal 1

¹**team** \\'tēm\ *n* [ME *teme,* fr. OE *tēam* offspring, lineage, group of draft animals] **1** : two or more draft animals harnessed to the same vehicle or implement **2** : a number of persons associated in work or activity; *esp* : a group on one side in a match

²**team** *vb* **1** : to haul with or drive a team **2** : to form a team : join forces

³**team** *adj* : of or performed by a team; *also* : marked by devotion to teamwork ⟨a ∼ player⟩

team·mate \-ˌmāt\ *n* : a fellow member of a team

team·ster \\'tēm-stər\ *n* : one that drives a team or truck

team·work \-ˌwərk\ *n* : the work or activity of a number of persons acting in close association as members of a unit

tea·pot \\'tē-ˌpät\ *n* : a vessel with a spout for brewing and serving tea

¹**tear** \\'tir\ *n* : a drop of the salty liquid that moistens the eye and inner side of the eyelids; *also, pl* : an act of weeping or grieving — **tear·ful** \-fəl\ *adj* — **tear·ful·ly** *adv*

²**tear** \\'tir\ *vb* : to fill with or shed tears ⟨eyes ∼ing in the wind⟩

³**tear** \\'tar\ *vb* **tore** \\'tōr\; **torn** \\'tōrn\; **tear·ing 1** : to separate parts of or pull apart by force : REND **2** : LACERATE **3** : to disrupt by the pull of contrary forces **4** : to remove by force : WRENCH **5** : to move or act with violence, haste, or force **syn** rip, split, cleave, rend

⁴**tear** \\'tar\ *n* **1** : the act of tearing **2** : a hole or flaw made by tearing : RENT

tear gas \\'tir-\ *n* : a substance that on dispersion in the atmosphere blinds the eyes with tears — **tear gas** *vb*

tear·jerk·er \\'tir-ˌjər-kər\ *n* : an extravagantly pathetic story, song, play, movie, or broadcast

¹**tease** \\'tēz\ *vb* **teased; teas·ing 1** : to disentangle and lay parallel by combing or carding ⟨∼ wool⟩ **2** : to scratch the surface of (cloth) so as to raise a nap **3** : to annoy persistently esp. in fun by goading, coaxing, or tantalizing **4** : to comb (hair) by taking a strand and pushing the short hairs toward the scalp with the comb **syn** harass, worry, pester, annoy

²**tease** *n* **1** : the act of teasing or state of being teased **2** : one that teases

tea·sel \\'tē-zəl\ *n* : a prickly herb or its flower head covered with stiff bracts and used to raise the nap on cloth; *also* : an artificial device used for this purpose

tea·spoon \\'tē-ˌspün\ *n* **1** : a small spoon suitable for stirring beverages **2** : a unit of measure equal to ⅙ fluid ounce (5 milliliters)

tea·spoon·ful \-ˌfül\ *n, pl* **-spoonfuls** *also* **-spoons·ful** \-ˌspünz-ˌfül\ : TEASPOON 2

teat \\'tit, 'tēt\ *n* : the protuberance through which milk is drawn from an udder or breast

tech *abbr* **1** technical; technically; technician **2** technological; technology

tech·ne·tium \tek-'nē-shē-əm\ *n* : a metallic chemical element produced in certain nuclear reactions — see ELEMENT table

tech·nic \\'tek-nik, tek-'nēk\ *n* : TECHNIQUE 1

tech·ni·cal \\'tek-ni-kəl\ *adj* [Gk *technikos* of art, skillful, fr. *technē* art, craft, skill] **1** : having special knowledge esp. of a mechanical or scientific subject ⟨∼ experts⟩ **2** : of or relating to a particular and esp. a practical or scientific subject ⟨∼ training⟩ **3** : according to a strict interpretation of the rules **4** : of or relating to technique — **tech·ni·cal·ly** \-k(ə-)lē\ *adv*

tech·ni·cal·i·ty \ˌtek-nə-'ka-lə-tē\ *n, pl* **-ties 1** : a detail meaningful only to a specialist **2** : the quality or state of being technical

technical sergeant *n* : a noncommissioned officer in the air force ranking next below a master sergeant

tech·ni·cian \tek-'ni-shən\ *n* : a person who has acquired the technique of a specialized skill or subject

tech·nique \tek-'nēk\ *n* [F] **1** : the manner in which technical details are treated or basic physical movements are used **2** : technical methods

tech·noc·ra·cy \tek-'nä-krə-sē\ *n* : management of society by technical experts — **tech·no·crat** \\'tek-nə-ˌkrat\ *n* — **tech·no·crat·ic** \ˌtek-nə-'kra-tik\ *adj*

tech·nol·o·gy \tek-'nä-lə-jē\ *n, pl* **-gies** : ENGINEERING; *also* : a manner of accomplishing a task using technical methods or knowledge — **tech·no·log·i·cal** \ˌtek-nə-'lä-ji-kəl\ *adj*

tec·ton·ics \tek-'tä-niks\ *n sing or pl* **1** : geological structural features **2** : geology dealing esp. with the faulting and folding of a planet or moon — **tec·ton·ic** \-nik\ *adj*

ted·dy bear \\'te-dē-ˌbar\ *n* [*Teddy* Roosevelt; fr. a cartoon depicting the president sparing the life of a bear cub while hunting] : a stuffed toy bear

te·dious \\'tē-dē-əs\ *adj* : tiresome because of length or dullness **syn** boring, tiring, irksome — **te·dious·ly** *adv* — **te·dious·ness** *n*

te·di·um \\'tē-dē-əm\ *n* : TEDIOUSNESS; *also* : BOREDOM

¹**tee** \\'tē\ *n* : a small mound or peg on which a golf ball is placed to be hit at the beginning of play on a hole; *also* : the area from which the ball is hit to begin play

²**tee** *vb* **teed; tee·ing** : to place (a ball) on a tee

teem \\'tēm\ *vb* : to become filled to overflowing : ABOUND **syn** swarm, crawl, flow

teen *adj* : TEENAGE

teen·age \\'tē-ˌnāj\ *or* **teen·aged** \-ˌnājd\ *adj* : of, being, or relating to people in their teens — **teen·ag·er** \-ˌnā-jər\ *n*

teens \\'tēnz\ *n pl* : the numbers 13 to 19 inclusive; *esp* : the years 13 to 19 in a person's life

tee·ny \\'tē-nē\ *adj* **tee·ni·er; -est** : TINY

tee·pee *var of* TEPEE

tee shirt *var of* T-SHIRT

tee·ter \\'tē-tər\ *vb* **1** : to move unsteadily **2** : SEESAW — **teeter** *n*

teeth *pl of* TOOTH

teethe \\'tēth\ *vb* **teethed; teeth·ing** : to grow teeth : cut one's teeth

teeth·ing *n* : growth of the first set of teeth through the gums with its accompanying phenomena

tee·to·tal \\'tē-'tōt-əl, -ˌtōt-\ *adj* : of or relating to the practice of complete abstinence from alcoholic drinks — **tee·to·tal·er** *or* **tee·to·tal·ler** \-'tōt-əl-ər\ *n* — **tee·to·tal·ism** \-əl-ˌi-zəm\ *n*

TEFL *abbr* teaching English as a foreign language

tek·tite \\'tek-ˌtīt\ *n* : a glassy body of probably meteoric origin

tel *abbr* **1** telegram **2** telegraph **3** telephone

tele·cast \\'te-li-ˌkast\ *vb* **-cast** *also* **-cast·ed; -cast·ing** : to broadcast by television — **telecast** *n* — **tele·cast·er** *n*

tele·com·mu·ni·ca·tion \ˌte-li-kə-ˌmyü-nə-'kā-shən\ *n* : communication at a distance (as by telephone or radio)

tele·con·fer·ence \\'te-li-ˌkän-fə-rəns\ *n* : a conference among people remote from one another held using telecommunications — **tele·con·fer·enc·ing** *n*

teleg *abbr* telegraphy

tele·ge·nic \ˌte-lə-ˈje-nik, -ˈjē-\ *adj* : markedly attractive to television viewers

tele·gram \ˈte-lə-ˌgram\ *n* : a message sent by telegraph

¹**tele·graph** \-ˌgraf\ *n* : an electric apparatus or system for sending messages by a code over wires — **tele·graph·ic** \ˌte-lə-ˈgra-fik\ *adj*

²**telegraph** *vb* : to send or communicate by or as if by telegraph — **te·leg·ra·pher** \tə-ˈle-grə-fər\ *n*

te·leg·ra·phy \tə-ˈle-grə-fē\ *n* : the use or operation of a telegraph apparatus or system

tele·mar·ket·ing \ˌte-lə-ˈmär-kə-tiŋ\ *n* : the marketing of goods or services by telephone — **tele·mar·ket·er** \-tər\ *n*

te·lem·e·try \tə-ˈle-mə-trē\ *n* : the transmission esp. by radio of measurements made by automatic instruments to a distant station — **tele·me·ter** \ˈte-lə-ˌmē-tər\ *n*

te·lep·a·thy \tə-ˈle-pə-thē\ *n* : apparent communication from one mind to another by extrasensory means — **tele·path·ic** \ˌte-lə-ˈpa-thik\ *adj* — **tele·path·i·cal·ly** \-thi-k(ə-)lē\ *adv*

¹**tele·phone** \ˈte-lə-ˌfōn\ *n* : an instrument for sending and receiving sounds over long distances by electricity

²**telephone** *vb* **-phoned; -phon·ing** 1 : to send or communicate by telephone 2 : to speak to (a person) by telephone — **tele·phon·er** *n*

te·leph·o·ny \tə-ˈle-fə-nē, ˈte-lə-ˌfō-\ *n* : use or operation of apparatus for transmission of sounds between distant points — **tel·e·phon·ic** \ˌte-lə-ˈfä-nik\ *adj*

tele·pho·to \ˌte-lə-ˈfō-tō\ *adj* : being a camera lens giving a large image of a distant object — **tele·pho·tog·ra·phy** \-fə-ˈtä-grə-fē\ *n*

tele·play \ˈte-li-ˌplā\ *n* : a play written for television

tele·print·er \ˈte-lə-ˌprin-tər\ *n* : TELETYPEWRITER

¹**tele·scope** \ˈte-lə-ˌskōp\ *n* 1 : a cylindrical instrument equipped with lenses or mirrors for viewing distant objects 2 : RADIO TELESCOPE

²**telescope** *vb* **-scoped; -scop·ing** 1 : to slide or pass or cause to slide or pass one within another like the sections of a collapsible hand telescope 2 : COMPRESS, CONDENSE

tele·scop·ic \ˌte-lə-ˈskä-pik\ *adj* 1 : of or relating to a telescope 2 : seen only by a telescope 3 : able to discern objects at a distance 4 : having parts that telescope — **tele·scop·i·cal·ly** \-pi-k(ə-)lē\ *adv*

tele·text \ˈte-lə-ˌtekst\ *n* : a system for broadcasting text over a television signal and displaying it on a decoder-equipped television

tele·thon \ˈte-lə-ˌthän\ *n* : a long television program usu. to solicit funds for a charity

tele·type·writ·er \ˌte-lə-ˈtīp-ˌrī-tər\ *n* : a printing device resembling a typewriter used to send and receive signals over telephone lines

tele·vise \ˈte-lə-ˌvīz\ *vb* **-vised; -vis·ing** : to broadcast by television

tele·vi·sion \ˈte-lə-ˌvi-zhən\ *n* [F *télévision*, fr. Gk *tēle* far, at a distance + F *vision* vision] : a system for transmitting images and sound by converting them into electrical or radio waves which are converted back into images and sound by a receiver; *also* : a television receiving set

tell \ˈtel\ *vb* **told** \ˈtōld\; **tell·ing** 1 : COUNT, ENUMERATE 2 : to relate in detail : NARRATE 3 : SAY, UTTER 4 : to make known : REVEAL 5 : to report to : INFORM 6 : ORDER, DIRECT 7 : to find out by observing 8 : to have a marked effect 9 : to serve as evidence **syn** disclose, discover, betray

tell·er \ˈte-lər\ *n* 1 : one that relates : NARRATOR 2 : one that counts 3 : a bank employee handling money received or paid out

tell·ing \ˈte-liŋ\ *adj* : producing a marked effect : EFFECTIVE **syn** cogent, convincing, sound

tell off *vb* : REPRIMAND, SCOLD

tell·tale \ˈtel-ˌtāl\ *n* 1 : INFORMER, TATTLETALE 2

: something that serves to disclose : INDICATION — **telltale** *adj*

tel·lu·ri·um \tə-ˈlu̇r-ē-əm\ *n* : a chemical element used esp. in alloys — see ELEMENT table

tem·blor \ˈtem-blər\ *n* [Sp, lit., trembling] : EARTHQUAKE

te·mer·i·ty \tə-ˈmer-ə-tē\ *n, pl* **-ties** : rash or presumptuous daring : BOLDNESS **syn** audacity, effrontery, gall, nerve, cheek

¹**temp** \ˈtemp\ *n* 1 : TEMPERATURE 2 : a temporary worker

²**temp** *abbr* temporary

¹**tem·per** \ˈtem-pər\ *vb* 1 : to dilute or soften by the addition of something else ⟨~ justice with mercy⟩ 2 : to bring (as steel) to a desired hardness by reheating and cooling 3 : to toughen (glass) by gradual heating and cooling 4 : TOUGHEN 5 : TUNE

²**temper** *n* 1 : characteristic tone : TENDENCY 2 : the hardness or toughness of a substance ⟨~ of a knife blade⟩ 3 : a characteristic frame of mind : DISPOSITION 4 : calmness of mind : COMPOSURE 5 : state of feeling or frame of mind at a particular time 6 : heat of mind or emotion **syn** temperament, character, personality, makeup — **tem·pered** \ˈtem-pərd\ *adj*

tem·pera \ˈtem-pə-rə\ *n* [It] : a painting process using an albuminous or colloidal medium as a vehicle; *also* : a painting done in tempera

tem·per·a·ment \ˈtem-prə-mənt, -pər-mənt\ *n* 1 : characteristic or habitual inclination or mode of emotional response : DISPOSITION ⟨nervous ~⟩ 2 : excessive sensitiveness or irritability **syn** character, personality, nature, makeup — **tem·per·a·men·tal** \ˌtem-prə-ˈment-ᵊl, -pər-ˈment-\ *adj*

tem·per·ance \ˈtem-prəns, -pə-rəns\ *n* : habitual moderation in the indulgence of the appetites or passions; *esp* : moderation in or abstinence from the use of intoxicating drink

tem·per·ate \ˈtem-prət, -pə-rət\ *adj* 1 : not extreme or excessive : MILD 2 : moderate in indulgence of appetite or desire 3 : moderate in the use of intoxicating liquors 4 : having a moderate climate **syn** sober, continent, abstemious

temperate zone *n, often cap T&Z* : the region between the tropic of Cancer and the arctic circle or between the tropic of Capricorn and the antarctic circle

tem·per·a·ture \ˈtem-pər-ˌchu̇r, -prə-ˌchu̇r, -chər\ *n* 1 : degree of hotness or coldness of something (as air, water, or the body) as shown by a thermometer 2 : FEVER

tem·pest \ˈtem-pəst\ *n* [ME, fr. OF *tempeste*, ultim. fr. L *tempestas* season, weather, storm, fr. *tempus* time] : a violent storm

tem·pes·tu·ous \tem-ˈpes-chə-wəs\ *adj* : of, involving, or resembling a tempest : STORMY — **tem·pes·tu·ous·ly** *adv* — **tem·pes·tu·ous·ness** *n*

tem·plate *also* **tem·plet** \ˈtem-plət\ *n* : a gauge, mold, or pattern that functions as a guide to the form or structure of something being made

¹**tem·ple** \ˈtem-pəl\ *n* 1 : an edifice for the worship of a deity 2 : a place devoted to a special or exalted purpose

²**temple** *n* : the flattened space on each side of the forehead esp. of humans

tem·po \ˈtem-pō\ *n, pl* **tem·pi** \-(ˌ)pē\ *or* **tempos** [It, lit., time] 1 : the rate of speed of a musical piece or passage 2 : rate of motion or activity : PACE

¹**tem·po·ral** \ˈtem-pə-rəl\ *adj* 1 : of, relating to, or limited by time ⟨~ and spatial bounds⟩ 2 : of or relating to earthly life or secular concerns ⟨~ power⟩

²**temporal** *adj* : of or relating to the temples or the sides of the skull

¹**tem·po·rary** \ˈtem-pə-ˌrer-ē\ *adj* : lasting for a time only : TRANSITORY **syn** transient, ephemeral, momentary, impermanent — **tem·po·rar·i·ly** \ˌtem-pə-ˈrer-ə-lē\ *adv*

²**temporary** *n, pl* **-rar·ies** : one serving for a limited time

tem·po·rize \'tem-pə-ˌrīz\ *vb* **-rized; -riz·ing 1** : to adapt one's actions to the time or the dominant opinion : COMPROMISE **2** : to draw out matters so as to gain time — **tem·po·riz·er** *n*

tempt \'tempt\ *vb* **1** : to entice to do wrong by promise of pleasure or gain **2** : PROVOKE **3** : to risk the dangers of **4** : to induce to do something : INCITE **syn** inveigle, decoy, seduce, lure — **tempt·er** *n* — **tempt·ing·ly** *adv*

temp·ta·tion \temp-'tā-shən\ *n* **1** : the act of tempting : the state of being tempted **2** : something that tempts

temp·tress \'temp-trəs\ *n* : a woman who tempts

ten \'ten\ *n* **1** : one more than nine **2** : the 10th in a set or series **3** : something having 10 units — **ten** *adj or pron* — **tenth** \'tenth\ *adj or adv or n*

ten·a·ble \'te-nə-bəl\ *adj* : capable of being held, maintained, or defended — **ten·a·bil·i·ty** \ˌte-nə-'bi-lə-tē\ *n*

te·na·cious \tə-'nā-shəs\ *adj* **1** : not easily pulled apart : COHESIVE, TOUGH ⟨a ∼ metal⟩ **2** : holding fast ⟨∼ of his rights⟩ **3** : RETENTIVE ⟨a ∼ memory⟩ — **te·na·cious·ly** *adv* — **te·nac·i·ty** \tə-'na-sə-tē\ *n*

ten·an·cy \'te-nən-sē\ *n, pl* **-cies** : the temporary possession or occupancy of something (as a house) that belongs to another; *also* : the period of a tenant's occupancy

ten·ant \'te-nənt\ *n* **1** : one who rents or leases (as a house) from a landlord **2** : DWELLER, OCCUPANT — **tenant** *vb* — **ten·ant·less** *adj*

tenant farmer *n* : a farmer who works land owned by another and pays rent either in cash or in shares of produce

ten·ant·ry \'te-nən-trē\ *n, pl* **-ries** : the body of tenants esp. on a great estate

Ten Commandments *n pl* : the commandments of God given to Moses on Mount Sinai

¹**tend** \'tend\ *vb* **1** : to apply oneself ⟨∼ to your affairs⟩ **2** : to take care of ⟨∼ a plant⟩ **3** : to manage the operations of ⟨∼ a machine⟩

²**tend** *vb* **1** : to move or develop one's course in a particular direction **2** : to show an inclination or tendency

ten·den·cy \'ten-dən-sē\ *n, pl* **-cies 1** : DRIFT, TREND **2** : a proneness to or readiness for a particular kind of thought or action : PROPENSITY **syn** bent, leaning, disposition, inclination

ten·den·tious \ten-'den-chəs\ *adj* : marked by a tendency in favor of a particular point of view : BIASED — **ten·den·tious·ly** *adv* — **ten·den·tious·ness** *n*

¹**ten·der** \'ten-dər\ *adj* **1** : having a soft texture : easily broken, chewed, or cut **2** : physically weak : DELICATE; *also* : IMMATURE **3** : expressing or responsive to love or sympathy : LOVING, COMPASSIONATE **4** : SENSITIVE, TOUCHY **syn** sympathetic, warm, warmhearted — **ten·der·ly** *adv* — **ten·der·ness** *n*

²**tender** *n* **1** : an offer or proposal made for acceptance; *esp* : an offer of a bid for a contract **2** : something (as money) that may be offered in payment

³**tender** *vb* : to present for acceptance

⁴**tend·er** \'ten-dər\ *n* **1** : one that tends or takes care **2** : a boat carrying passengers and freight to a larger ship **3** : a car attached to a steam locomotive for carrying fuel and water

ten·der·foot \'ten-dər-ˌfùt\ *n, pl* **-feet** \-ˌfēt\ *also* **-foots** \-ˌfùts\ **1** : one not hardened to frontier or rough outdoor life **2** : an inexperienced beginner

ten·der·heart·ed \ˌten-dər-'här-təd\ *adj* : easily moved to love, pity, or sorrow

ten·der·ize \'ten-də-ˌrīz\ *vb* **-ized; -iz·ing** : to make (meat) tender — **ten·der·iz·er** \'ten-də-ˌrī-zər\ *n*

ten·der·loin \'ten-dər-ˌlòin\ *n* **1** : a tender strip of beef or pork from near the backbone **2** : a district of a city largely devoted to vice

ten·di·ni·tis *or* **ten·don·itis** \ˌten-də-'nī-təs\ *n* : inflammation of a tendon

ten·don \'ten-dən\ *n* : a tough cord of dense white fibrous tissue uniting a muscle with another part (as a bone) — **ten·di·nous** \-də-nəs\ *adj*

ten·dril \'ten-drəl\ *n* : a slender coiling organ by which some climbing plants attach themselves to a support

ten·e·brous \'te-nə-brəs\ *adj* : shut off from the light : GLOOMY, OBSCURE

ten·e·ment \'te-nə-mənt\ *n* **1** : a house used as a dwelling **2** : a building divided into apartments for rent to families; *esp* : one meeting only minimum standards of safety and comfort **3** : APARTMENT, FLAT

te·net \'te-nət\ *n* [L, he holds, fr. *tenēre* to hold] : one of the principles or doctrines held in common by members of a group (as a church or profession) **syn** doctrine, dogma, belief

ten·fold \'ten-ˌfōld, -'fōld\ *adj* : being 10 times as great or as many — **ten·fold** \-'fōld\ *adv*

ten–gallon hat *n* : a wide-brimmed hat with a large soft crown

Tenn *abbr* Tennessee

ten·nis \'te-nəs\ *n* : a game played with a ball and racket on a court divided by a net

ten·on \'te-nən\ *n* : a projecting part in a piece of material (as wood) for insertion into a mortise to make a joint

ten·or \'te-nər\ *n* **1** : the general drift of something spoken or written **2** : the highest natural adult male voice; *also* : a singer having this voice **3** : a continuing in a course, movement, or activity ⟨the ∼ of my life⟩

ten·our *chiefly Brit var of* TENOR

ten·pen·ny \'ten-'pe-nē\ *adj* : amounting to, worth, or costing 10 pennies

tenpenny nail *n* : a nail three inches (about 7.6 centimeters) long

ten·pin \'ten-ˌpin\ *n* : a bottle-shaped bowling pin set in groups of 10 and bowled at in a game (**tenpins**)

¹**tense** \'tens\ *n* [ME *tens* time, tense, fr. MF, fr. L *tempus*] : distinction of form of a verb to indicate the time of the action or state

²**tense** *adj* **tens·er; tens·est** [L *tensus*, fr. pp. of *tendere* to stretch] **1** : stretched tight : TAUT **2** : feeling or showing nervous tension **syn** stiff, rigid, inflexible — **tense·ly** *adv* — **tense·ness** *n* — **ten·si·ty** \'ten-sə-tē\ *n*

³**tense** *vb* **tensed; tens·ing** : to make or become tense

ten·sile \'ten-səl, -ˌsīl\ *adj* : of or relating to tension ⟨∼ strength⟩

ten·sion \'ten-chən\ *n* **1** : the act of straining or stretching; *also* : the condition of being strained or stretched **2** : a state of mental unrest often with signs of bodily stress **3** : a state of latent hostility or opposition

ten–speed \'ten-ˌspēd\ *n* : a bicycle with a derailleur having 10 possible combinations of gears

¹**tent** \'tent\ *n* **1** : a collapsible shelter of material stretched and supported by poles **2** : a canopy placed over the head and shoulders to retain vapors or oxygen given for medical reasons

²**tent** *vb* **1** : to lodge in tents **2** : to cover with or as if with a tent

ten·ta·cle \'ten-ti-kəl\ *n* : any of various long flexible projections about the head or mouth (as of an insect, mollusk, or fish) — **ten·ta·cled** \-kəld\ *adj* — **ten·tac·u·lar** \ten-'ta-kyə-lər\ *adj*

ten·ta·tive \'ten-tə-tiv\ *adj* **1** : not fully worked out or developed ⟨∼ plans⟩ **2** : HESITANT, UNCERTAIN ⟨a ∼ smile⟩ — **ten·ta·tive·ly** *adv*

ten·u·ous \'ten-yə-wəs\ *adj* **1** : not dense : RARE ⟨a ∼ fluid⟩ **2** : not thick : SLENDER ⟨a ∼ rope⟩ **3** : having little substance : FLIMSY, WEAK ⟨∼ influences⟩ **4** : lacking stability : SHAKY ⟨∼ reasoning⟩ — **te·nu·i·ty** \te-'nü-ə-tē, tə-, -'nyü-\ *n* — **ten·u·ous·ly** *adv* — **ten·u·ous·ness** *n*

ten·ure \'ten-yər\ *n* : the act, right, manner, or period of holding something (as a landed property, an office, or a position)

ten·ured \'ten-yərd\ *adj* : having tenure ⟨~ faculty members⟩

te·o·sin·te \ˌtā-ō-'sin-tē\ *n* : a tall annual grass of Mexico and Central America closely related to maize

te·pee \'tē-(ˌ)pē\ *n* [Dakota *thípi*, fr. *thi*- to dwell] : an American Indian conical tent usu. of skins

tep·id \'te-pəd\ *adj* 1 : moderately warm : LUKEWARM 2 : HALFHEARTED

te·qui·la \tə-'kē-lə, tā-\ *n* : a Mexican liquor made from mescal

ter *abbr* 1 terrace 2 territory

ter·bi·um \'tər-bē-əm\ *n* : a metallic chemical element — see ELEMENT table

ter·cen·te·na·ry \ˌtər-ˌsen-'te-nə-rē, tər-'sent-ᵊn-ˌer-ē\ *n, pl* **-ries** : a 300th anniversary or its celebration — **tercentenary** *adj*

ter·cen·ten·ni·al \ˌtər-ˌsen-'te-nē-əl\ *adj or n* : TERCENTENARY

te·re·do \tə-'rē-dō, -'rā-\ *n, pl* **teredos** *or* **te·red·i·nes** \-'red-ᵊn-ˌēz\ [L] : SHIPWORM

¹**term** \'tərm\ *n* 1 : END, TERMINATION 2 : DURATION; *esp* : a period of time fixed esp. by law or custom 3 : a mathematical expression connected with another by a plus or minus sign; *also* : an element (as a numerator) of a fraction or proportion 4 : a word or expression that has a precise meaning in some uses or is limited to a particular subject or field 5 *pl* : PROVISIONS, CONDITIONS ⟨~s of a contract⟩ 6 *pl* : mutual relationship ⟨on good ~s⟩ 7 : AGREEMENT, CONCORD

²**term** *vb* : to apply a term to : CALL

ter·ma·gant \'tər-mə-gənt\ *n* : an overbearing or nagging woman : SHREW

¹**ter·mi·nal** \'tər-mən-ᵊl\ *adj* 1 : of, relating to, or forming an end, limit, or terminus 2 : being or being in the final stages of a fatal disease ⟨a ~ patient⟩ ⟨~ illness⟩ **syn** final, concluding, last, latest — **ter·mi·nal·ly** *adv*

²**terminal** *n* 1 : EXTREMITY, END 2 : a device at the end of a wire or on electrical equipment for making a connection 3 : either end of a transportation line (as a railroad) with its offices and freight and passenger stations; *also* : a freight or passenger station 4 : a device (as in a computer system) for data entry and display

ter·mi·nate \'tər-mə-ˌnāt\ *vb* **-nat·ed; -nat·ing** : to bring or come to an end **syn** conclude, finish, complete — **ter·mi·na·ble** \-nə-bəl\ *adj* — **ter·mi·na·tion** \ˌtər-mə-'nā-shən\ *n* — **ter·mi·na·tor** \'tər-mə-ˌnā-tər\ *n*

ter·mi·nol·o·gy \ˌtər-mə-'nä-lə-jē\ *n, pl* **-gies** : the technical or special terms used in a business, art, science, or special subject

ter·mi·nus \'tər-mə-nəs\ *n, pl* **-ni** \-ˌnī\ *or* **-nus·es** [L] 1 : final goal : END 2 : either end of a transportation line or travel route; *also* : the station or city at such a place

ter·mite \'tər-ˌmīt\ *n* : any of numerous pale soft‑bodied social insects that feed on wood

tern \'tərn\ *n* : any of various chiefly marine birds with narrow wings and often a forked tail

ter·na·ry \'tər-nə-rē\ *adj* 1 : of, relating to, or proceeding by threes 2 : having three elements or parts

terr *abbr* territory

¹**ter·race** \'ter-əs\ *n* 1 : a flat roof or open platform 2 : a level area next to a building 3 : an embankment with level top 4 : a bank or ridge on a slope to conserve moisture and soil 5 : a row of houses on raised land; *also* : a street with such a row of houses 6 : a strip of park in the middle of a street

²**terrace** *vb* **ter·raced; ter·rac·ing** : to form into a terrace or supply with terraces

ter·ra–cot·ta \ˌter-ə-'kä-tə\ *n* [It *terra cotta*, lit., baked earth] : a reddish brown earthenware

terra fir·ma \-'fər-mə\ *n* [NL] : solid ground

ter·rain \tə-'rān\ *n* : the surface features of an area of land ⟨a rough ~⟩

ter·ra in·cog·ni·ta \ˌter-ə-ˌin-'käg-nē-tə\ *n, pl* **ter-**

rae in·cog·ni·tae \'ter-ˌī-ˌin-ˌkäg-'nē-tī\ [L] : an unexplored area or field of knowledge

ter·ra·pin \'ter-ə-pən\ *n* : any of various turtles of fresh or brackish water

ter·rar·i·um \tə-'rar-ē-əm\ *n, pl* **-ia** \-ē-ə\ *or* **-i·ums** : a usu. transparent enclosure for keeping or raising small plants and animals indoors

ter·res·tri·al \tə-'res-trē-əl\ *adj* 1 : of or relating to the earth or its inhabitants 2 : living or growing on land ⟨~ plants⟩ **syn** mundane, earthly, worldly

ter·ri·ble \'ter-ə-bəl\ *adj* 1 : exciting terror : FEARFUL, DREADFUL ⟨~ weapons⟩ 2 : hard to bear : DISTRESSING ⟨a ~ situation⟩ 3 : extreme in degree : INTENSE ⟨~ heat⟩ 4 : of very poor quality : AWFUL ⟨a ~ play⟩ **syn** frightful, horrible, shocking, appalling — **ter·ri·bly** \-blē\ *adv*

ter·ri·er \'ter-ē-ər\ *n* [F (*chien*) *terrier*, lit., earth dog, fr. *terrier* of earth, fr. ML *terrarius*, fr. L *terra* earth] : any of various usu. small dogs orig. used by hunters to drive small game animals from their holes

ter·rif·ic \tə-'ri-fik\ *adj* 1 : exciting terror 2 : EXTRAORDINARY, ASTOUNDING ⟨~ speed⟩ 3 : unusually good ⟨makes ~ chili⟩

ter·ri·fy \'ter-ə-ˌfī\ *vb* **-fied; -fy·ing** : to fill with terror : FRIGHTEN **syn** scare, terrorize, startle, alarm — **ter·ri·fy·ing·ly** *adv*

ter·ri·to·ry \'ter-ə-ˌtōr-ē\ *n, pl* **-ries** 1 : a geographical area belonging to or under the jurisdiction of a governmental authority 2 : a part of the U.S. not included within any state but organized with a separate legislature 3 : REGION, DISTRICT; *also* : a region in which one feels at home 4 : a field of knowledge or interest 5 : an assigned area 6 : an area occupied and defended by one or a group of animals — **ter·ri·to·ri·al** \ˌter-ə-'tōr-ē-əl\ *adj*

ter·ror \'ter-ər\ *n* 1 : a state of intense fear : FRIGHT 2 : one that inspires fear **syn** panic, consternation, dread, alarm, dismay, horror, trepidation

ter·ror·ism \'ter-ər-ˌi-zəm\ *n* : the systematic use of terror esp. as a means of coercion — **ter·ror·ist** \-ist\ *adj or n*

ter·ror·ize \'ter-ər-ˌīz\ *vb* **-ized; -iz·ing** 1 : to fill with terror : SCARE 2 : to coerce by threat or violence **syn** terrify, frighten, alarm, startle

ter·ry \'ter-ē\ *n, pl* **terries** : an absorbent fabric with a loose pile of uncut loops

terse \'tərs\ *adj* **ters·er; ters·est** [L *tersus* clean, neat, fr. pp. of *tergēre* to wipe off] : effectively brief : CONCISE — **terse·ly** *adv* — **terse·ness** *n*

ter·tia·ry \'tər-shē-ˌer-ē\ *adj* 1 : of third rank, importance, or value 2 *cap* : of, relating to, or being the earlier period of the Cenozoic era 3 : occurring in or being the third stage

Tertiary *n* : the Tertiary period

TESL *abbr* teaching English as a second language

TESOL *abbr* Teachers of English to Speakers of Other Languages

¹**test** \'test\ *n* [ME, vessel in which metals were assayed, fr. MF, fr. L *testum* earthen vessel] 1 : a critical examination or evaluation : TRIAL 2 : a means or result of testing

²**test** *vb* 1 : to put to test : TRY, EXAMINE 2 : to undergo or score on tests

tes·ta·ment \'tes-tə-mənt\ *n* 1 *cap* : either of two main divisions of the Bible 2 : EVIDENCE, WITNESS 3 : CREDO 4 : the legal instructions for the disposition of one's property after death : WILL — **tes·ta·men·ta·ry** \ˌtes-tə-'men-tə-rē\ *adj*

tes·tate \'tes-ˌtāt, -tət\ *adj* : having left a valid will

tes·ta·tor \'tes-ˌtā-tər, tes-'tā-\ *n* : a person who dies leaving a valid will

tes·ta·trix \tes-'tā-triks\ *n* : a female testator

¹**tes·ter** \'tēs-tər, 'tes-\ *n* : a canopy over a bed, pulpit, or altar

²**test·er** \'tes-tər\ *n* : one that tests

tes·ti·cle \'tes-ti-kəl\ *n* : TESTIS; *esp* : one of a higher mammal usu. with its enclosing structures

tes·ti·fy \'tes-tə-ˌfī\ *vb* **-fied; -fy·ing 1** : to make a statement based on personal knowledge or belief : bear witness **2** : to serve as evidence or proof

tes·ti·mo·ni·al \ˌtes-tə-'mō-nē-əl\ *n* **1** : a statement testifying to benefits received; *also* : a character reference **2** : an expression of appreciation : TRIBUTE — **testimonial** *adj*

tes·ti·mo·ny \'tes-tə-ˌmō-nē\ *n, pl* **-nies 1** : evidence based on observation or knowledge **2** : an outward sign : SYMBOL **3** : a solemn declaration made by a witness under oath esp. in a court **syn** evidence, confirmation, proof, testament

tes·tis \'tes-təs\ *n, pl* **tes·tes** \'tes-ˌtēz\ [L, witness, testis] : a typically paired male reproductive gland that produces sperm and in most mammals is contained within the scrotum at sexual maturity

tes·tos·ter·one \te-'stäs-tə-ˌrōn\ *n* : a male sex hormone causing development of the male reproductive system and secondary sex characteristics

test tube *n* : a glass tube closed at one end and used esp. in chemistry and biology

tes·ty \'tes-tē\ *adj* **tes·ti·er; -est** [ME *testif*, fr. Anglo-French (the French of medieval England), headstrong, fr. OF *teste* head, fr. LL *testa* skull, fr. L, shell] : easily annoyed; *also* : marked by ill humor

tet·a·nus \'tet-ᵊn-əs\ *n* : an infectious disease caused by bacterial poisons and marked by muscle stiffness and spasms esp. of the jaws — **tet·a·nal** \-ᵊl\ *adj*

tetchy \'te-chē\ *adj* **tetchi·er; -est** : irritably or peevishly sensitive

¹tête-à-tête \'tāt-ə-ˌtāt\ *n* [F, lit., head to head] : a private conversation between two persons

²tête-à-tête \ˌtāt-ə-'tāt\ *adv* : in private

³tête-à-tête \'tāt-ə-ˌtāt\ *adj* : being face-to-face : PRIVATE

¹teth·er \'te-thər\ *n* **1** : something (as a rope) by which an animal is fastened **2** : the limit of one's strength or resources

²tether *vb* : to fasten or restrain by or as if by a tether

tet·ra·eth·yl lead \ˌte-trə-'e-thəl-\ *n* : a heavy oily poisonous liquid used as an antiknock agent in gasoline

tet·ra·he·dron \-'hē-drən\ *n, pl* **-drons** *or* **-dra** \-drə\ : a polyhedron that has four faces — **tet·ra·he·dral** \-drəl\ *adj*

tet·ra·hy·dro·can·nab·i·nol \-ˌhī-drə-kə-'na-bə-ˌnȯl, -ˌnōl\ *n* : THC

te·tram·e·ter \te-'tra-mə-tər\ *n* : a line of verse consisting of four metrical feet

Teu·ton·ic \tü-'tä-nik, tyü-\ *adj* : GERMANIC

Tex *abbr* Texas

text \'tekst\ *n* **1** : the actual words of an author's work **2** : the main body of printed or written matter on a page **3** : a scriptural passage chosen as the subject esp. of a sermon **4** : THEME, TOPIC **5** : TEXTBOOK — **tex·tu·al** \'teks-chə-wəl\ *adj*

text·book \'tekst-ˌbuk\ *n* : a book used in the study of a subject

tex·tile \'tek-ˌstīl, 'tekst-ᵊl\ *n* : CLOTH; *esp* : a woven or knit cloth

tex·ture \'teks-chər\ *n* **1** : the visual or tactile surface characteristics and appearance of something ⟨a coarse ∼⟩ **2** : essential part **3** : basic scheme or structure : FABRIC **4** : overall structure

TGIF *abbr* thank God it's Friday

¹Th *abbr* Thursday

²Th *symbol* thorium

¹-th — see ¹-ETH

²-th *or* **-eth** *adj suffix* — used in forming ordinal numbers ⟨hundred*th*⟩

³-th *n suffix* **1** : act or process **2** : state or condition ⟨dear*th*⟩

Thai \'tī\ *n, pl* **Thai** *or* **Thais 1** : a native or inhabitant of Thailand **2** : the official language of Thailand — **Thai** *adj*

thal·a·mus \'tha-lə-məs\ *n, pl* **-mi** \-ˌmī\ [NL] : a subdivision of the brain that serves as a relay station to and from the cerebral cortex and functions in arousal and the integration of sensory information

thal·li·um \'tha-lē-əm\ *n* : a poisonous metallic chemical element — see ELEMENT table

¹than \'than, 'than\ *conj* **1** — used after a comparative adjective or adverb to introduce the second part of a comparison expressing inequality ⟨older ∼ I am⟩ **2** — used after *other* or a word of similar meaning to express a difference of kind, manner, or identity ⟨adults other ∼ parents⟩

²than *prep* : in comparison with ⟨older ∼ me⟩

thane \'thān\ *n* **1** : a free retainer of an Anglo-Saxon lord **2** : a Scottish feudal lord

thank \'thaŋk\ *vb* : to express gratitude to ⟨∼ed them for the present⟩

thank·ful \'thaŋk-fəl\ *adj* **1** : conscious of benefit received **2** : expressive of thanks **3** : GLAD — **thank·ful·ness** *n*

thank·ful·ly \-fə-lē\ *adv* **1** : in a thankful manner **2** : as makes one thankful

thank·less \'thaŋ-kləs\ *adj* **1** : UNGRATEFUL **2** : UNAPPRECIATED

thanks \'thaŋks\ *n pl* : an expression of gratitude

thanks·giv·ing \thaŋks-'gi-viŋ\ *n* **1** : the act of giving thanks **2** : a prayer expressing gratitude **3** *cap* : the 4th Thursday in November observed as a legal holiday for giving thanks for divine goodness

¹that \'that, thət\ *pron, pl* **those** \'thōz\ **1** : the one indicated, mentioned, or understood ⟨∼ is my house⟩ **2** : the one farther away or first mentioned ⟨this is an elm, ∼'s a maple⟩ **3** : what has been indicated or mentioned ⟨after ∼, we left⟩ **4** : the one or ones : IT, THEY ⟨*those* who wish to leave may do so⟩

²that \thət, 'that\ *conj* **1** : the following, namely ⟨he said ∼ he would⟩; *also* : which is, namely ⟨there's a chance ∼ it may fail⟩ **2** : to this end or purpose ⟨shouted ∼ all might hear⟩ **3** : as to result in the following, namely ⟨so heavy ∼ it can't be moved⟩ **4** : for this reason, namely : BECAUSE ⟨we're glad ∼ you came⟩

³that *adj, pl* **those 1** : being the one mentioned, indicated, or understood ⟨∼ boy⟩ ⟨*those* people⟩ **2** : being the one farther away or less immediately under discussion ⟨this chair or ∼ one⟩

⁴that \thət, 'that\ *pron* **1** : WHO, WHOM, WHICH ⟨the man ∼ saw you⟩ ⟨the man ∼ you saw⟩ ⟨the money ∼ was spent⟩ **2** : in, on, or at which ⟨the way ∼ he drives⟩ ⟨the day ∼ it rained⟩

⁵that \'that\ *adv* : to such an extent or degree ⟨I like it, but not ∼ much⟩

¹thatch \'thach\ *vb* : to cover with or as if with thatch — **thatch·er** *n*

²thatch *n* **1** : plant material (as straw) for use as roofing **2** : a mat of grass clippings accumulated next to the soil on a lawn **3** : a covering of or as if of thatch ⟨a ∼ of white hair⟩

thaw \'thȯ\ *vb* **1** : to melt or cause to melt **2** : to become so warm as to melt ice or snow **3** : to abandon aloofness or hostility — **thaw** *n*

THC \ˌtē-(ˌ)āch-'sē\ *n* [*tetra*hydro*c*annabinol] : a physiologically active chemical from hemp plant resin that is the chief intoxicant in marijuana

¹the \thə, *before vowel sounds usu* thē\ *definite article* **1** : that in particular **2** — used before adjectives functioning as nouns ⟨a word to ∼ wise⟩

²the *adv* **1** : to what extent ⟨∼ sooner, the better⟩ **2** : to that extent ⟨the sooner, ∼ better⟩

theat *abbr* theater; theatrical

the·ater *or* **the·atre** \'thē-ə-tər\ *n* [ME *theatre*, fr. MF, fr. L *theatrum*, fr. Gk *theatron*, fr. *theasthai* to view, fr. *thea* act of seeing] **1** : a building for dramatic performances; *also* : a building or area for showing motion pictures **2** : a place of enactment of significant events ⟨∼ of war⟩ **3** : a place (as a lecture room) resembling a theater **4** : dramatic literature or perform-ance

theater–in–the–round *n* : a theater with the stage in the center of the auditorium

the·at·ri·cal \thē-'a-tri-kəl\ *also* **the·at·ric** \-trik\ *adj* **1** : of or relating to the theater **2** : marked by artifici-ality of emotion : HISTRIONIC **3** : marked by extrav-agant display : SHOWY

the·at·ri·cals \-kəlz\ *n pl* : the performance of plays

the·at·rics \thē-'a-triks\ *n pl* **1** : THEATRICALS **2** : staged or contrived effects

the·be \'thä-bā\ *n, pl* **thebe** — see *pula* at MONEY table

thee \'thē\ *pron, archaic objective case of* THOU

theft \'theft\ *n* : the act of stealing

thegn \'thān\ *n* : THANE 1

their \thər, 'ther\ *adj* : of or relating to them or them-selves

theirs \'therz\ *pron* : their one : their ones

the·ism \'thē-i-zəm\ *n* : belief in the existence of a god or gods — **the·ist** \-ist\ *n or adj* — **the·is·tic** \thē-'is-tik\ *adj*

them \thəm, 'them\ *pron, objective case of* THEY

theme \'thēm\ *n* **1** : a subject or topic of discourse or of artistic representation **2** : a written exercise : COM-POSITION **3** : a melodic subject of a musical compo-sition or movement — **the·mat·ic** \thi-'ma-tik\ *adj*

them·selves \thəm-'selvz, them-\ *pron pl* : THEY, THEM — used reflexively, for emphasis, or in absolute con-structions ⟨they govern ∼⟩ ⟨they ∼ came⟩ ⟨∼ busy, they sent me⟩

¹then \'then\ *adv* **1** : at that time **2** : soon after that : NEXT **3** : in addition : BESIDES **4** : in that case **5** : CON-SEQUENTLY

²then *n* : that time ⟨since ∼⟩

³then *adj* : existing or acting at that time ⟨the ∼ attor-ney general⟩

thence \'thens, 'thens\ *adv* **1** : from that place **2** *ar-chaic* : THENCEFORTH **3** : from that fact : THEREFROM

thence·forth \-fōrth\ *adv* : from that time forward : THEREAFTER

thence·for·ward \thens-'fōr-wərd, thens-\ *also* **thence-for·wards** \-wərdz\ *adv* : onward from that place or time

the·oc·ra·cy \thē-'ä-krə-sē\ *n, pl* **-cies 1** : government by officials regarded as divinely inspired **2** : a state governed by a theocracy — **the·o·crat·ic** \thē-ə-'kra-tik\ *adj*

theol *abbr* theological; theology

the·ol·o·gy \thē-'ä-lə-jē\ *n, pl* **-gies 1** : the study of re-ligious faith, practice, and experience; *esp* : the study of God and of God's relation to the world **2** : a theory or system of theology — **the·o·lo·gian** \thē-ə-'lō-jən\ *n* — **the·o·log·i·cal** \-'lä-ji-kəl\ *adj*

the·o·rem \'thē-ə-rəm, 'thir-əm\ *n* **1** : a statement esp. in mathematics that has been or is to be proved **2** : an idea accepted or proposed as a demonstrable truth : PROPOSITION

the·o·ret·i·cal \thē-ə-'re-ti-kəl\ *also* **the·o·ret·ic** \-tik\ *adj* **1** : relating to or having the character of theory **2** : existing only in theory : HYPOTHETICAL — **the·o-ret·i·cal·ly** \-ti-k(ə-)lē\ *adv*

the·o·rize \'thē-ə-rīz\ *vb* **-rized; -riz·ing** : to form a theory : SPECULATE — **the·o·rist** \-rist\ *n*

the·o·ry \'thē-ə-rē, 'thir-ē\ *n, pl* **-ries 1** : abstract thought **2** : the general principles of a subject **3** : a plausible or scientifically acceptable general princi-ple offered to explain observed facts **4** : HYPOTHESIS, CONJECTURE

theory of games : GAME THEORY

the·os·o·phy \thē-'ä-sə-fē\ *n* : belief about God and the world held to be based on mystical insight — **theo-soph·i·cal** \thē-ə-'sä-fi-kəl\ *adj* — **the·os·o·phist** \thē-'ä-sə-fist\ *n*

ther·a·peu·tic \ther-ə-'pyü-tik\ *adj* [Gk *therapeutikos,* fr. *therapeuein* to attend, treat, fr. *theraps* attendant] : of, relating to, or dealing with healing and esp. with

remedies for diseases — **ther·a·peu·ti·cal·ly** \-ti-k(ə-)lē\ *adv*

ther·a·peu·tics \ther-ə-'pyü-tiks\ *n* : a branch of med-ical or dental science dealing with the use of remedies

ther·a·py \'ther-ə-pē\ *n, pl* **-pies** : treatment of bodily, mental, or behavioral disorders — **ther·a·pist** \-pist\ *n*

¹there \'ther, 'ther\ *adv* **1** : in or at that place — often used interjectionally **2** : to or into that place : THITH-ER **3** : in that matter or respect

²there \'ther, 'ther, thər\ *pron* — used as a function word to introduce a sentence or clause ⟨∼'s a pen here⟩

³there \'ther, 'ther\ *n* **1** : that place ⟨get away from ∼⟩ **2** : that point ⟨you take it from ∼⟩

there·abouts \ther-ə-'bauts, ther-; 'ther-ə-bauts, 'ther-\ *or* **there·about** \-'baut, -baut\ *adv* **1** : near that place or time **2** : near that number, degree, or quantity

there·af·ter \ther-'af-tər, ther-\ *adv* : after that : AFTER-WARD

there·at \-'at\ *adv* **1** : at that place **2** : at that occur-rence : on that account

there·by \ther-'bī, ther-, 'ther-bī, 'ther-bī\ *adv* **1** : by that : by that means **2** : connected with or with reference to that

there·for \ther-'fōr, ther-\ *adv* : for or in return for that

there·fore \'ther-fōr, 'ther-\ *adv* : for that reason : CONSEQUENTLY

there·from \ther-'frəm, ther-\ *adv* : from that or it

there·in \ther-'in, ther-\ *adv* **1** : in or into that place, time, or thing **2** : in that respect

there·of \-'əv, -'äv\ *adv* **1** : of that or it **2** : from that : THEREFROM

there·on \-'òn, -'än\ *adv* **1** : on that **2** *archaic* : THERE-UPON 3

there·to \ther-'tü, ther-\ *adv* : to that

there·un·to \ther-'ən-(,)tü; ,ther-ən-'tü, ,ther-\ *adv, archaic* : THERETO

there·upon \'ther-ə-,pòn, 'ther-, -,pän; ,ther-ə-'pòn, -'pän, ,ther-\ *adv* **1** : on that matter **2** : THEREFORE **3** : immediately after that : at once

there·with \ther-'with, ther-, -'with\ *adv* **1** : with that **2** *archaic* : THEREUPON, FORTHWITH

there·with·al \'ther-wi-,thòl, 'ther-, -,thòl\ *adv* **1** *ar-chaic* : BESIDES **2** : THEREWITH

therm *abbr* thermometer

ther·mal \'thər-məl\ *adj* **1** : of, relating to, or caused by heat **2** : designed to prevent the loss of body heat ⟨∼ underwear⟩ — **ther·mal·ly** *adv*

thermal pollution *n* : the discharge of heated liquid (as waste water from a factory) into natural waters at a temperature harmful to the environment

therm·is·tor \'thər-,mis-tər\ *n* : an electrical resistor whose resistance varies sharply with temperature

ther·mo·cline \'thər-mə-,klīn\ *n* : the region in a ther-mally stratified body of water that separates warmer surface water from cold deep water

ther·mo·cou·ple \'thər-mə-,kə-pəl\ *n* : a device for measuring temperature by measuring the temperature-dependent potential difference created at the junction of two dissimilar metals

ther·mo·dy·nam·ics \,thər-mə-dī-'na-miks\ *n* : physics that deals with the mechanical action or relations of heat — **ther·mo·dy·nam·ic** \-mik\ *adj* — **ther·mo-dy·nam·i·cal·ly** \-mi-k(ə-)lē\ *adv*

ther·mom·e·ter \thər-'mä-mə-tər\ *n* [F *thermomètre,* fr. Gk *thermē* heat + *metron* measure] : an instru-ment for measuring temperature typically by the rise or fall of a liquid (as mercury) in a thin glass tube — **ther·mo·met·ric** \,thər-mə-'me-trik\ *adj* — **ther·mo-met·ri·cal·ly** \-tri-k(ə-)lē\ *adv*

ther·mo·nu·cle·ar \,thər-mō-'nü-klē-ər, -'nyü-\ *adj* **1** : of or relating to changes in the nucleus of atoms of low atomic weight (as hydrogen) that require a very high temperature (as in the hydrogen bomb) **2** : utilizing or relating to a thermonuclear bomb ⟨∼ war⟩

ther·mo·plas·tic \ˌthər-mə-ˈplas-tik\ *adj* : capable of softening when heated and of hardening again when cooled ⟨∼ resins⟩ — **thermoplastic** *n*

ther·mos \ˈthər-məs\ *n* : a cylindrical container with a vacuum between an inner and an outer wall used to keep liquids hot or cold

ther·mo·sphere \ˈthər-mə-ˌsfir\ *n* : the part of the earth's atmosphere that lies above the mesosphere and that is characterized by steadily increasing temperature with height

ther·mo·stat \ˈthər-mə-ˌstat\ *n* : a device that automatically controls temperature — **ther·mo·stat·ic** \ˌthər-mə-ˈsta-tik\ *adj* — **ther·mo·stat·i·cal·ly** \-ti-k(ə-)lē\ *adv*

the·sau·rus \thi-ˈsor-əs\ *n, pl* **-sau·ri** \-ˈsor-ˌī\ *or* **-sau·rus·es** \-ˈsor-ə-səz\ [NL, fr. L, treasure, collection, fr. Gk *thēsauros*] : a book of words and their synonyms — **the·sau·ral** \-ˈsor-əl\ *adj*

these *pl of* THIS

the·sis \ˈthē-səs\ *n, pl* **the·ses** \ˈthē-ˌsēz\ **1** : a proposition that a person advances and offers to maintain by argument **2** : an essay embodying results of original research; *esp* : one written for an academic degree

¹thes·pi·an \ˈthes-pē-ən\ *adj, often cap* [fr. *Thespis*, 6th cent. B.C. Greek poet and reputed originator of tragedy] : relating to the drama : DRAMATIC

²thespian *n* : ACTOR

Thess *abbr* Thessalonians

Thes·sa·lo·nians \ˌthe-sə-ˈlō-nyənz, -nē-ənz\ *n* — see BIBLE table

the·ta \ˈthā-tə\ *n* : the 8th letter of the Greek alphabet — Θ or θ

thew \ˈthü, ˈthyü\ *n* : MUSCLE, SINEW — usu. used in pl.

they \ˈthā\ *pron* **1** : those individuals under discussion : the ones previously mentioned or referred to **2** : unspecified persons : PEOPLE

thi·a·mine \ˈthī-ə-mən, -ˌmēn\ *also* **thi·a·min** \-mən\ *n* : a vitamin of the vitamin B complex essential to normal metabolism and nerve function

¹thick \ˈthik\ *adj* **1** : having relatively great depth or extent from one surface to its opposite ⟨a ∼ plank⟩; *also* : heavily built : THICKSET **2** : densely massed : CROWDED; *also* : FREQUENT, NUMEROUS **3** : dense or viscous in consistency ⟨∼ syrup⟩ **4** : marked by haze, fog, or mist ⟨∼ weather⟩ **5** : measuring in thickness ⟨one meter ∼⟩ **6** : imperfectly articulated : INDISTINCT ⟨∼ speech⟩ **7** : STUPID, OBTUSE **8** : associated on close terms : INTIMATE **9** : EXCESSIVE **syn** compact, close, tight — **thick·ly** *adv*

²thick *n* **1** : the most crowded or active part **2** : the part of greatest thickness

thick·en \ˈthi-kən\ *vb* : to make or become thick — **thick·en·er** *n*

thick·et \ˈthi-kət\ *n* : a dense growth of bushes or small trees

thick·ness \-nəs\ *n* **1** : the smallest of three dimensions ⟨length, width, and ∼⟩ **2** : the quality or state of being thick **3** : LAYER, SHEET ⟨a single ∼ of canvas⟩

thick·set \ˈthik-ˈset\ *adj* **1** : closely placed or planted **2** : having a thick body : BURLY

thick–skinned \-ˈskind\ *adj* **1** : having a thick skin **2** : not easily bothered by criticism or insult

thief \ˈthēf\ *n, pl* **thieves** \ˈthēvz\ : one that steals esp. secretly

thieve \ˈthēv\ *vb* **thieved; thiev·ing** : STEAL, ROB **syn** filch, pilfer, purloin, swipe

thiev·ery \ˈthē-və-rē\ *n, pl* **-er·ies** : the act of stealing : THEFT

thigh \ˈthī\ *n* : the part of the vertebrate hind limb between the knee and the hip

thigh·bone \ˈthī-ˌbōn\ *n* : FEMUR

thim·ble \ˈthim-bəl\ *n* : a cap or guard worn on the finger to push the needle in sewing — **thim·ble·ful** *n*

¹thin \ˈthin\ *adj* **thin·ner; thin·nest 1** : having little extent from one surface through to its opposite : not thick : SLENDER **2** : not closely set or placed : SPARSE ⟨∼ hair⟩ **3** : not dense or not dense enough : more fluid or rarefied than normal ⟨∼ air⟩ ⟨∼ syrup⟩ **4** : lacking substance, fullness, or strength ⟨∼ broth⟩ **5** : FLIMSY — **thin·ly** *adv* — **thin·ness** *n*

²thin *vb* **thinned; thin·ning** : to make or become thin

thine \ˈthīn\ *pron, archaic* : one or the ones belonging to thee

thing \ˈthiŋ\ *n* **1** : a matter of concern : AFFAIR ⟨∼s to do⟩ **2** *pl* : state of affairs ⟨∼s are improving⟩ **3** : EVENT, CIRCUMSTANCE ⟨the crime was a terrible ∼⟩ **4** : DEED, ACT ⟨expected great ∼s of him⟩ **5** : a distinct entity : OBJECT **6** : an inanimate object distinguished from a living being **7** *pl* : POSSESSIONS, EFFECTS **8** : an article of clothing **9** : DETAIL, POINT **10** : IDEA, NOTION **11** : something one likes to do : SPECIALTY ⟨doing her ∼⟩

think \ˈthiŋk\ *vb* **thought** \ˈthot\; **think·ing 1** : to form or have in the mind **2** : to have as an opinion : BELIEVE **3** : to reflect on : PONDER **4** : to call to mind : REMEMBER **5** : REASON **6** : to form a mental picture of : IMAGINE **7** : to devise by thinking ⟨*thought* up a plan to escape⟩ **syn** conceive, fancy, realize, envisage — **think·er** *n*

think tank *n* : an institute, corporation, or group organized for interdisciplinary research (as in technological or social problems)

thin·ner \ˈthi-nər\ *n* : a volatile liquid (as turpentine) used to thin paint

thin–skinned \ˈthin-ˈskind\ *adj* **1** : having a thin skin **2** : extremely sensitive to criticism or insult

¹third \ˈthərd\ *adj* : next after the second — **third** *or* **third·ly** *adv*

²third *n* **1** : one of three equal parts of something **2** : one that is number three in a countable series **3** : the 3d forward gear in an automotive vehicle

third degree *n* : the subjection of a prisoner to mental or physical torture to force a confession

third dimension *n* **1** : thickness, depth, or apparent thickness or depth that confers solidity on an object **2** : a quality that confers reality — **third–dimensional** *adj*

third world *n, often cap T&W* : the aggregate of the underdeveloped nations of the world

¹thirst \ˈthərst\ *n* **1** : a feeling of dryness in the mouth and throat associated with a desire to drink; *also* : a bodily condition producing this **2** : an ardent desire : CRAVING ⟨a ∼ for knowledge⟩ — **thirsty** *adj*

²thirst *vb* **1** : to need drink : suffer thirst **2** : to have a strong desire : CRAVE

thir·teen \ˌthər-ˈtēn\ *n* : one more than 12 — **thirteen** *adj or pron* — **thir·teenth** \-ˈtēnth\ *adj or n*

thir·ty \ˈthər-tē\ *n, pl* **thirties** : three times 10 — **thir·ti·eth** \-tē-əth\ *adj or n* — **thirty** *adj or pron*

¹this \ˈthis\ *pron, pl* **these** \ˈthēz\ **1** : the one close or closest in time or space ⟨∼ is your book⟩ **2** : what is in the present or under immediate observation or discussion ⟨∼ is a mess⟩; *also* : what is happening or being done now ⟨after ∼ we'll leave⟩

²this *adj, pl* **these 1** : being the one near, present, just mentioned, or more immediately under observation ⟨∼ book⟩ **2** : constituting the immediate past or future ⟨friends all *these* years⟩

³this *adv* : to such an extent or degree ⟨we need a book about ∼ big⟩

this·tle \ˈthi-səl\ *n* : any of various tall prickly composite plants with often showy heads of tightly packed tubular flowers

this·tle·down \-ˌdaùn\ *n* : the down from the ripe flower head of a thistle

¹thith·er \ˈthi-thər\ *adv* : to that place

²thither *adj* : being on the farther side

thith·er·ward \-wərd\ *adv* : toward that place : THITHER

thole \\'thōl\\ *n* : a pin set in the gunwale of a boat to hold an oar in place

thong \\'thòŋ\\ *n* **1** : a strip esp. of leather or hide **2** : a sandal held on the foot by a thong between the toes

tho·rax \\'thōr-ˌaks\\ *n, pl* **tho·rax·es** *or* **tho·ra·ces** \\'thōr-ə-ˌsēz\\ **1** : the part of the body of a mammal between the neck and the abdomen; *also* : its cavity containing the heart and lungs **2** : the middle of the three main divisions of the body of an insect — **tho·rac·ic** \\thə-'ra-sik\\ *adj*

tho·ri·um \\'thōr-ē-əm\\ *n* : a radioactive metallic chemical element — see ELEMENT table

thorn \\'thòrn\\ *n* **1** : a woody plant bearing sharp processes **2** : a sharp rigid plant process that is usu. a modified leafless branch **3** : something that causes distress — **thorny** *adj*

thor·ough \\'thər-ō\\ *adj* **1** : COMPLETE, EXHAUSTIVE ⟨a ~ search⟩ **2** : very careful : PAINSTAKING ⟨a ~ scholar⟩ **3** : having full mastery — **thor·ough·ly** *adv* — **thor·ough·ness** *n*

¹thor·ough·bred \\'thər-ə-ˌbred\\ *adj* **1** : bred from the best blood through a long line **2** *cap* : of or relating to the Thoroughbred breed of horses **3** : marked by high-spirited grace

²thoroughbred *n* **1** *cap* : any of an English breed of light speedy horses kept chiefly for racing **2** : one (as a pedigreed animal) of excellent quality

Thoroughbred 1

thor·ough·fare \\-ˌfar\\ *n* : a public road or street

thor·ough·go·ing \\ˌthər-ə-'gō-iŋ\\ *adj* : marked by thoroughness or zeal

thorp \\'thòrp\\ *n, archaic* : VILLAGE

those *pl of* THAT

¹thou \\'thaù\\ *pron, archaic* : the person addressed

²thou \\'thaù\\ *n, pl* **thou** : a thousand of something (as dollars)

¹though \\'thō\\ *conj* **1** : despite the fact that ⟨~ the odds are hopeless, they fight on⟩ **2** : granting that ⟨~ it may look bad, still, all is not lost⟩

²though *adv* : HOWEVER, NEVERTHELESS ⟨not for long, ~⟩

¹thought \\'thòt\\ *past and past part of* THINK

²thought *n* **1** : the process of thinking **2** : serious consideration : REGARD **3** : reasoning power **4** : the power to imagine : CONCEPTION **5** : IDEA, NOTION **6** : OPINION, BELIEF

thought·ful \\'thòt-fəl\\ *adj* **1** : absorbed in thought **2** : marked by careful thinking ⟨a ~ essay⟩ **3** : considerate of others ⟨a ~ host⟩ — **thought·ful·ly** *adv* — **thought·ful·ness** *n*

thought·less \\-ləs\\ *adj* **1** : insufficiently alert : CARELESS ⟨a ~ worker⟩ **2** : RECKLESS ⟨a ~ act⟩ **3** : lacking concern for others : INCONSIDERATE ⟨~ remarks⟩ — **thought·less·ly** *adv* — **thought·less·ness** *n*

thou·sand \\'thaùz-ᵊnd\\ *n, pl* **thousands** *or* **thousand** : 10 times 100 — **thousand** *adj* — **thou·sandth** \\-ᵊnth\\ *adj or n*

thousands place *n* : the place four to the left of the decimal point in an Arabic number

thrall \\'thròl\\ *n* **1** : SLAVE, BONDMAN **2** : a state of servitude — **thrall·dom** *or* **thral·dom** \\'thròl-dəm\\ *n*

thrash \\'thrash\\ *vb* **1** : THRESH **1 2** : BEAT, WHIP; *also* : DEFEAT **3** : to move about violently **4** : to go over again and again ⟨~ over the matter⟩; *also* : to hammer out ⟨~ out a plan⟩

¹thrash·er \\'thra-shər\\ *n* : one that thrashes or threshes

²thrasher *n* : any of various long-tailed American songbirds related to the mockingbird

¹thread \\'thred\\ *n* **1** : a thin continuous strand of spun and twisted textile fibers **2** : something resembling a textile thread **3** : the ridge or groove that winds around a screw **4** : a train of thought **5** : a continuing element

²thread *vb* **1** : to pass a thread through the eye of (a needle) **2** : to pass (as film) through something **3** : to make one's way through or between **4** : to put together on a thread ⟨~ beads⟩ **5** : to form a screw thread on or in

thread·bare \\-ˌbar\\ *adj* **1** : having the nap worn off so that the thread shows : SHABBY **2** : TRITE

thready \\'thre-dē\\ *adj* **1** : consisting of or bearing fibers or filaments ⟨a ~ bark⟩ **2** : lacking in fullness, body, or vigor

threat \\'thret\\ *n* **1** : an expression of intent to do harm **2** : one that threatens

threat·en \\'thret-ᵊn\\ *vb* **1** : to utter threats against **2** : to give signs or warning of : PORTEND **3** : to hang over as a threat : MENACE — **threat·en·ing·ly** *adv*

threat·ened *adj* : having an uncertain chance of continued survival; *esp* : likely to become an endangered species

three \\'thrē\\ *n* **1** : one more than two **2** : the 3d in a set or series **3** : something having three units — **three** *adj or pron*

3–D \\'thrē-'dē\\ *n* : three-dimensional form

three–dimensional *adj* **1** : relating to or having three dimensions **2** : giving the illusion of varying distances ⟨a ~ picture⟩

three·fold \\'thrē-ˌfōld, -'fōld\\ *adj* **1** : having three parts : TRIPLE **2** : being three times as great or as many — **three·fold** \\-'fōld\\ *adv*

three·pence \\'thre-pəns, 'thri-, 'thrə-, *US also* 'thrē-pens\\ *n* **1** *pl* **threepence** *or* **three·penc·es** : a coin worth three pennies **2** : the sum of three British pennies

three·score \\'thrē-'skòr\\ *adj* : being three times twenty : SIXTY

three·some \\'thrē-səm\\ *n* : a group of three persons or things

thren·o·dy \\'thre-nə-dē\\ *n, pl* **-dies** : a song of lamentation : ELEGY

thresh \\'thrash, 'thresh\\ *vb* **1** : to separate (as grain from straw) mechanically **2** : THRASH — **thresh·er** *n*

thresh·old \\'thresh-ˌhōld\\ *n* **1** : the sill of a door **2** : a point or place of beginning or entering : OUTSET **3** : a point at which a physiological or psychological effect begins to be produced

threw *past of* THROW

thrice \\'thrīs\\ *adv* **1** : three times **2** : in a threefold manner or degree

thrift \\'thrift\\ *n* [ME, fr. ON, prosperity, fr. *thrīfask* to thrive] : careful management esp. of money : FRUGALITY — **thrift·i·ly** \\'thrif-tə-lē\\ *adv* — **thrift·less** *adj* — **thrifty** *adj*

thrill \\'thril\\ *vb* [ME *thirlen, thrillen* to pierce, fr. OE *thyrlian*, fr. *thyrel* hole, fr. *thurh* through] **1** : to have or cause to have sudden sharp feeling of excitement; *also* : TINGLE, SHIVER **2** : TREMBLE, VIBRATE — **thrill** *n* — **thrill·er** *n* — **thrill·ing·ly** *adv*

thrive \\'thrīv\\ *vb* **throve** \\'thrōv\\ *or* **thrived; thriv·en** \\'thri-vən\\ *also* **thrived; thriv·ing 1** : to grow luxuriantly : FLOURISH **2** : to gain in wealth or possessions : PROSPER

throat \\'thrōt\\ *n* : the part of the neck in front of the spinal column; *also* : the passage through it to the stomach and lungs — **throat·ed** *adj*

throaty \'thrō-tē\ *adj* **throat·i·er; -est 1** : uttered or produced from low in the throat ⟨a ~ voice⟩ **2** : heavy, thick, or deep as if from the throat ⟨~ notes of a horn⟩ — **throat·i·ly** \-tə-lē\ *adv* — **throat·i·ness** \-tē-nəs\ *n*

¹**throb** \'thräb\ *vb* **throbbed; throb·bing** : to pulsate or pound esp. with abnormal force or rapidity : BEAT, VIBRATE

²**throb** *n* : BEAT, PULSE

throe \'thrō\ *n* **1** : PANG, SPASM **2** *pl* : a hard or painful struggle

throm·bo·sis \thräm-'bō-səs\ *n, pl* **-bo·ses** \-ˌsēz\ : the formation or presence of a clot in a blood vessel — **throm·bot·ic** \-'bä-tik\ *adj*

throm·bus \'thräm-bəs\ *n, pl* **throm·bi** \-ˌbī\ : a clot of blood formed within a blood vessel and remaining attached to its place of origin

throne \'thrōn\ *n* **1** : the chair of state of a sovereign or high dignitary **2** : royal power : SOVEREIGNTY

¹**throng** \'thröŋ\ *n* **1** : MULTITUDE **2** : a crowding together of many persons

²**throng** *vb* **thronged; throng·ing** : CROWD

¹**throt·tle** \'thrät-ᵊl\ *vb* **throt·tled; throt·tling** [ME *throtlen*, fr. *throte* throat] **1** : CHOKE, STRANGLE **2** : SUPPRESS **3** : to reduce the speed of (an engine) by closing the throttle — **throt·tler** *n*

²**throttle** *n* : a valve regulating the flow of steam or fuel to an engine; *also* : the lever controlling this valve

¹**through** \'thrü\ *prep* **1** : into at one side and out at the other side of ⟨go ~ the door⟩ **2** : by way of ⟨entered ~ a skylight⟩ **3** : in the midst of ⟨a path ~ the trees⟩ **4** : by means of ⟨succeeded ~ hard work⟩ **5** : over the whole of ⟨rumors swept ~ the office⟩ **6** : during the whole of ⟨~ the night⟩ **7** : to and including ⟨Monday ~ Friday⟩

²**through** *adv* **1** : from one end or side to the other **2** : from beginning to end : to completion ⟨see it ~⟩ **3** : to the core : THOROUGHLY ⟨he was wet ~⟩ **4** : into the open : OUT ⟨break ~⟩

³**through** *adj* **1** : permitting free passage ⟨a ~ street⟩ **2** : going from point of origin to destination without change or transfer ⟨a ~ train⟩ **3** : coming from or going to points outside a local area ⟨~ traffic⟩ **4** : FINISHED ⟨~ with the job⟩

¹**through·out** \thrü-'aút\ *adv* **1** : EVERYWHERE **2** : from beginning to end

²**throughout** *prep* **1** : in or to every part of **2** : during the whole period of

through·put \'thrü-ˌpút\ *n* : OUTPUT, PRODUCTION ⟨the ~ of a computer⟩

throve *past of* THRIVE

¹**throw** \'thrō\ *vb* **threw** \'thrü\; **thrown** \'thrōn\; **throw·ing 1** : to propel through the air esp. with a forward motion of the hand and arm ⟨~ a ball⟩ **2** : to cause to fall or fall off **3** : to put suddenly in a certain position or condition ⟨~ into panic⟩ **4** : to put on or take off hastily ⟨~ on a coat⟩ **5** : to lose intentionally ⟨~ a game⟩ **6** : to move (a lever) so as to connect or disconnect parts of something (as a clutch) **7** : to act as host for ⟨~ a party⟩ **syn** toss, fling, pitch, sling — **throw·er** *n*

²**throw** *n* **1** : an act of throwing, hurling, or flinging; *also* : CAST **2** : the distance a missile may be thrown **3** : a light coverlet **4** : a woman's scarf or light wrap

throw·away \'thrō-ə-ˌwā\ *n* : something that is or is designed to be thrown away esp. after one use

throw·back \-ˌbak\ *n* : reversion to an earlier type or phase; *also* : an instance or product of this

throw up *vb* **1** : to build hurriedly **2** : VOMIT

thrum \'thrəm\ *vb* **thrummed; thrum·ming** : to play or pluck a stringed instrument idly : STRUM

thrush \'thrəsh\ *n* : any of numerous small or medium-sized songbirds that are mostly of a plain color often with spotted underparts

¹**thrust** \'thrəst\ *vb* **thrust; thrust·ing 1** : to push or drive with force : SHOVE **2** : STAB, PIERCE **3** : INTER-JECT **4** : to press the acceptance of upon someone

²**thrust** *n* **1** : a lunge with a pointed weapon **2** : ATTACK **3** : the pressure of one part of a construction against another (as of an arch against an abutment) **4** : the force produced by a propeller or jet or rocket engine that drives a vehicle (as an aircraft) forward **5** : a violent push : SHOVE

thrust·er *also* **thrust·or** \'thrəs-tər\ *n* : one that thrusts; *esp* : a rocket engine

thru·way \'thrü-ˌwā\ *n* : EXPRESSWAY

¹**thud** \'thəd\ *n* **1** : BLOW **2** : a dull sound

²**thud** *vb* **thud·ded; thud·ding** : to move or strike so as to make a thud

thug \'thəg\ *n* [Hindi *thag*, lit., thief] : a brutal ruffian or assassin — **thug·gish** *adj*

thu·li·um \'thü-lē-əm, 'thyü-\ *n* : a rare metallic chemical element — see ELEMENT table

¹**thumb** \'thəm\ *n* **1** : the short thick first digit of the human hand or a corresponding digit of a lower animal **2** : the part of a glove or mitten that covers the thumb

²**thumb** *vb* **1** : to leaf through (pages) with the thumb **2** : to wear or soil with the thumb by frequent handling **3** : to request or obtain (a ride) in a passing automobile by signaling with the thumb

thumb·nail \'thəm-ˌnāl\ *n* : the nail of the thumb

²**thumbnail** *adj* : BRIEF, CONCISE ⟨a ~ description⟩

thumb·print \-ˌprint\ *n* : an impression made by the thumb

thumb·screw \-ˌskrü\ *n* **1** : a screw with a head that may be turned by the thumb and forefinger **2** : a device of torture for squeezing the thumb

thumb·tack \-ˌtak\ *n* : a tack with a broad flat head for pressing with one's thumb into a board or wall

¹**thump** \'thəmp\ *vb* **1** : to strike with or as if with something thick or heavy so as to cause a dull sound **2** : POUND

²**thump** *n* : a blow with or as if with something blunt or heavy; *also* : the sound made by such a blow

¹**thun·der** \'thən-dər\ *n* **1** : the sound following a flash of lightning; *also* : a noise like such a sound **2** : a loud utterance or threat

²**thunder** *vb* **1** : to produce thunder **2** : ROAR, SHOUT

thun·der·bolt \-ˌbōlt\ *n* : a flash of lightning with its accompanying thunder

thun·der·clap \-ˌklap\ *n* : a crash of thunder

thun·der·cloud \-ˌklaúd\ *n* : a dark storm cloud producing lightning and thunder

thun·der·head \-ˌhed\ *n* : a large cumulus cloud often appearing before a thunderstorm

thun·der·ous \'thən-də-rəs\ *adj* : producing thunder; *also* : making a noise like thunder — **thun·der·ous·ly** *adv*

thun·der·show·er \'thən-dər-ˌshaú-ər\ *n* : a shower accompanied by thunder and lightning

thun·der·storm \-ˌstórm\ *n* : a storm accompanied by thunder and lightning

thun·der·struck \-ˌstrək\ *adj* : stunned as if struck by a thunderbolt

Thurs *or* **Thu** *abbr* Thursday

Thurs·day \'thərz-dē, -ˌdā\ *n* [ME, fr. OE *thursdæg*, fr. ON *thōrsdagr*, lit., day of Thor (Norse god)] : the 5th day of the week

thus \'thəs\ *adv* **1** : in this or that manner **2** : to this degree or extent : SO **3** : because of this or that : HENCE

¹**thwack** \'thwak\ *vb* : to strike with or as if with something flat or heavy

²**thwack** *n* : a heavy blow : WHACK

¹**thwart** \'thwórt\ *vb* **1** : FOIL, BAFFLE **2** : BLOCK, DE-FEAT **syn** balk, outwit, frustrate

²**thwart** \'thwórt, *naut often* 'thórt\ *adv* : ATHWART

³**thwart** *adj* : situated or placed across something else

⁴**thwart** \'thwȯrt\ *n* : a rower's seat extending across a boat

thy \'thī\ *adj, archaic* : of, relating to, or done by or to thee or thyself

thyme \'tīm, 'thīm\ *n* [ME, fr. MF *thym*, fr. L *thymum*, fr. Gk *thymon*, prob. fr. *thyein* to make a burnt offering, sacrifice] : a garden mint with aromatic leaves used esp. in seasoning; *also* : its leaves so used

thy·mine \'thī-ˌmēn\ *n* : a pyrimidine base that is one of the four bases coding genetic information in the molecular chain of DNA

thy·mus \'thī-məs\ *n* : a glandular organ of the neck region that is composed largely of lymphoid tissue, functions esp. in the development of the immune system, and tends to atrophy in the adult

thy·ris·tor \thī-'ris-tər\ *n* : a semiconductor device that acts as a switch, rectifier, or voltage regulator

thy·roid \'thī-ˌrȯid\ *also* **thy·roi·dal** \thī-'rȯid-ᵊl\ *adj* [NL *thyroides*, fr. Gk *thyreoeidēs* shield-shaped, thyroid, fr. *thyreos* shield shaped like a door, fr. *thyra* door] : of, relating to, or being a large endocrine gland that lies at the base of the neck and produces several iodine-containing hormones that affect growth, development, and metabolism — **thyroid** *n*

thy·rox·ine *or* **thy·rox·in** \thī-'räk-ˌsēn, -sən\ *n* : an iodine-containing hormone that is produced by the thyroid gland, increases metabolic rate, and is used to treat thyroid disorders

thy·self \thī-'self\ *pron, archaic* : YOURSELF

Ti *symbol* titanium

ti·ara \tē-'ar-ə, -'er-, -'är-\ *n* 1 : the pope's triple crown 2 : a decorative headband or semicircle for formal wear by women

Ti·bet·an \tə-'bet-ᵊn\ *n* : a native or inhabitant of Tibet — **Tibetan** *adj*

tib·ia \'ti-bē-ə\ *n, pl* **-i·ae** \-bē-ˌē\ *also* **-i·as** [L] : the inner of the two bones of the vertebrate hind limb between the knee and the ankle

tic \'tik\ *n* : a local and habitual twitching of muscles esp. of the face

ti·cal \ti-'käl, 'ti-kəl\ *n, pl* **ticals** *or* **tical** : BAHT

¹**tick** \'tik\ *n* : any of a large group of small blood=sucking arachnids

²**tick** *n* : the fabric case of a mattress or pillow; *also* : a mattress consisting of a tick and its filling

³**tick** *n* 1 : a light rhythmic audible tap or beat 2 : a small mark used to draw attention to or check something

⁴**tick** *vb* 1 : to make the sound of a tick or series of ticks 2 : to mark, count, or announce by or as if by ticking beats 3 : to mark or check with a tick 4 : to function as an operating mechanism : RUN

⁵**tick** *n* : CREDIT; *also* : a credit account

tick·er \'ti-kər\ *n* 1 : something (as a watch) that ticks 2 : a telegraph instrument that prints information (as stock prices) on paper tape 3 *slang* : HEART

ticker tape *n* : the paper ribbon on which a telegraphic ticker prints

¹**tick·et** \'ti-kət\ *n* [MF *etiquet, estiquette* notice attached to something, fr. *estiquier* to attach, fr. MD *steken* to stick] 1 : CERTIFICATE, LICENSE, PERMIT; *esp* : a certificate or token showing that a fare or admission fee has been paid 2 : TAG, LABEL 3 : SLATE 4 4 : a summons issued to a traffic offender

²**ticket** *vb* 1 : to attach a ticket to 2 : to furnish or serve with a ticket

tick·ing \'ti-kiŋ\ *n* : a strong fabric used in upholstering and as a mattress covering

tick·le \'ti-kəl\ *vb* **tick·led; tick·ling** 1 : to excite or stir up agreeably : PLEASE, AMUSE 2 : to have a tingling sensation 3 : to touch (as a body part) lightly so as to cause uneasiness, laughter, or spasmodic movements — **tickle** *n*

tick·lish \-kə-lish\ *adj* 1 : OVERSENSITIVE, TOUCHY 2 : UNSTABLE ⟨a ~ foothold⟩ 3 : requiring delicate handling ⟨~ subject⟩ 4 : sensitive to tickling — **tick·lish·ly** *adv* — **tick·lish·ness** *n*

tid·al wave \'tīd-ᵊl-\ *n* 1 : an unusually high sea wave that sometimes follows an earthquake 2 : an unusual rise of water alongshore due to strong winds

tid·bit \'tid-ˌbit\ *n* : a choice morsel

¹**tide** \'tīd\ *n* [ME, time, fr. OE *tīd*] 1 : the alternate rising and falling of the surface of the ocean 2 : something that fluctuates like the tides of the sea — **tid·al** \'tīd-ᵊl\ *adj*

²**tide** *vb* **tid·ed; tid·ing** : to carry through or help along as if by the tide ⟨a loan to ~ us over⟩

tide·land \'tīd-ˌland, -lənd\ *n* 1 : land overflowed during flood tide 2 : land under the ocean within a nation's territorial waters — often used in pl.

tide·wa·ter \-ˌwȯ-tər, -ˌwä-\ *n* 1 : water overflowing land at flood tide 2 : low-lying coastal land

tid·ings \'tī-diŋz\ *n pl* : NEWS, MESSAGE

¹**ti·dy** \'tī-dē\ *adj* **ti·di·er; -est** 1 : well ordered and cared for : NEAT 2 : LARGE, SUBSTANTIAL ⟨a ~ sum⟩ — **ti·di·ness** \'tī-dē-nəs\ *n*

²**tidy** *vb* **ti·died; ti·dy·ing** 1 : to put in order 2 : to make things tidy

³**tidy** *n, pl* **tidies** : a decorated covering used to protect the back or arms of a chair from wear or soil

¹**tie** \'tī\ *n* 1 : a line, ribbon, or cord used for fastening, uniting, or closing 2 : a structural element (as a beam or rod) holding two pieces together 3 : one of the cross supports to which railroad rails are fastened 4 : a connecting link : BOND ⟨family ~s⟩ 5 : an equality in number (as of votes or scores); *also* : an undecided or deadlocked contest 6 : NECKTIE

²**tie** *vb* **tied; ty·ing** *or* **tie·ing** 1 : to fasten, attach, or close by means of a tie 2 : to bring together firmly : UNITE 3 : to form a knot or bow in ⟨~ a scarf⟩ 4 : to restrain from freedom of action : CONSTRAIN 5 : to make or have an equal score with

tie·back \'tī-ˌbak\ *n* : a decorative strip for draping a curtain to the side of a window

tie–dye·ing \'tī-ˌdī-iŋ\ *n* : a method of producing patterns in textiles by tying parts of the fabric so that they will not absorb the dye — **tie–dyed** \-ˌdīd\ *adj*

tie–in \'tī-ˌin\ *n* : CONNECTION

tier \'tir\ *n* : ROW, LAYER; *esp* : one of two or more rows arranged one above another — **tiered** \'tird\ *adj*

tie–rod \'tī-ˌräd\ *n* : a rod used as a connecting member or brace

tie–up \-ˌəp\ *n* 1 : a slowing or stopping of traffic or business 2 : CONNECTION

tiff \'tif\ *n* : a petty quarrel — **tiff** *vb*

Tif·fa·ny \'ti-fə-nē\ *adj* : made of pieces of stained glass ⟨a ~ lamp⟩

ti·ger \'tī-gər\ *n* : a very large tawny black-striped Asian cat — **ti·ger·ish** *adj*

tiger

¹**tight** \'tīt\ *adj* 1 : so close in structure as to prevent passage of a liquid or gas 2 : strongly fixed or held : SECURE 3 : TAUT 4 : fitting usu. too closely ⟨~ shoes⟩ 5 : set close together : COMPACT ⟨a ~ formation⟩ 6 : DIFFICULT, TRYING ⟨get in a ~ spot⟩ 7 : STINGY, MISERLY 8 : evenly contested : CLOSE 9 : INTOXICATED 10 : low in supply : hard to get ⟨money is ~⟩ — **tight·ly** *adv* — **tight·ness** *n*

²**tight** *adv* 1 : TIGHTLY, FIRMLY 2 : SOUNDLY ⟨sleep ~⟩

tight·en \'tīt-ᵊn\ *vb* : to make or become tight
tight·fist·ed \'tīt-'fis-təd\ *adj* : STINGY
tight·rope \-ˌrōp\ *n* : a taut rope or wire for acrobats to perform on
tights \'tīts\ *n pl* : skintight garments covering the body esp. below the waist; *also, Brit* : PANTY HOSE
tight·wad \'tīt-ˌwäd\ *n* : a stingy person
ti·gress \'tī-grəs\ *n* : a female tiger
til·de \'til-də\ *n* [Sp, fr. ML *titulus* tittle] : a mark ˜ placed esp. over the letter *n* (as in Spanish *señor* sir) to denote the sound \nʸ\ or over vowels (as in Portuguese *irmã* sister) to indicate nasal quality
¹**tile** \'tīl\ *n* 1 : a flat or curved piece of fired clay, stone, or concrete used for roofs, floors, or walls; *also* : a pipe of earthenware or concrete used for a drain 2 : a thin piece (as of linoleum) used for covering walls or floors — **til·ing** \'tī-liŋ\ *n*
²**tile** *vb* **tiled; til·ing** : to cover with tiles — **til·er** *n*
¹**till** \'til\ *prep or conj* : UNTIL
²**till** *vb* : to work by plowing, sowing, and raising crops : CULTIVATE — **till·able** *adj*
³**till** *n* : DRAWER; *esp* : a money drawer in a store or bank
till·age \'ti-lij\ *n* 1 : the work of tilling land 2 : cultivated land
¹**til·ler** \'ti-lər\ *n* [OE *telgor, telgra* twig, shoot] : a sprout or stalk esp. from the base or lower part of a plant
²**till·er** \'ti-lər\ *n* : one that tills
³**til·ler** \'ti-lər\ *n* [ME *tiler* stock of a crossbow, fr. MF *telier*, lit., beam of a loom, fr. ML *telarium*, fr. L *tela* web] : a lever used for turning a boat's rudder from side to side
¹**tilt** \'tilt\ *n* 1 : a contest in which two combatants charging usu. with lances try to unhorse each other : JOUST; *also* : a tournament of tilts 2 : a verbal contest 3 : SLANT, TIP
²**tilt** *vb* 1 : to move or shift so as to incline : TIP 2 : to engage in or as if in combat with lances : JOUST, ATTACK
tilth \'tilth\ *n* 1 : TILLAGE 2 2 : the state of a soil esp. in relation to the suitability of its particle size and structure for growing crops
Tim *abbr* Timothy
tim·ber \'tim-bər\ *n* [ME, fr. OE, building, wood] 1 : growing trees or their wood — often used interjectionally to warn of a falling tree 2 : wood for use in making something 3 : a usu. large squared or dressed piece of wood
tim·bered \'tim-bərd\ *adj* : having walls framed by exposed timbers
tim·ber·land \'tim-bər-ˌland\ *n* : wooded land
tim·ber·line \'tim-bər-ˌlīn\ *n* : the upper limit of tree growth in mountains or high latitudes
timber rattlesnake *n* : a widely distributed rattlesnake of the eastern U.S.
timber wolf *n* : GRAY WOLF
tim·bre *also* **tim·ber** \'tam-bər, 'tim-\ *n* [F, fr. MF, bell struck by a hammer, fr. OF, drum, fr. MGk *tymbanon* kettledrum, fr. Gk *tympanon*] : the distinctive quality given to a sound by its overtones
tim·brel \'tim-brəl\ *n* : a small hand drum or tambourine
¹**time** \'tīm\ *n* 1 : a period during which an action, process, or condition exists or continues ⟨gone a long ∼⟩ 2 : LEISURE ⟨found ∼ to read⟩ 3 : a point or period when something occurs : OCCASION ⟨the last ∼ we met⟩ 4 : a set or customary moment or hour for something to occur ⟨arrived on ∼⟩ 5 : AGE, ERA 6 : state of affairs : CONDITIONS ⟨hard ∼s⟩ 7 : a rate of speed : TEMPO 8 : a moment, hour, day, or year as indicated by a clock or calendar ⟨what ∼ is it⟩ 9 : a system of reckoning time ⟨solar ∼⟩ 10 : one of a series of recurring instances; *also, pl* : added or accumulated quantities or examples ⟨five ∼s greater⟩ 11 : a person's experience during a particular period ⟨had a

good ∼⟩ 12 : the hours or days of one's work; *also* : an hourly pay rate ⟨straight ∼⟩ 13 : TIME-OUT
²**time** *vb* **timed; tim·ing** 1 : to arrange or set the time of : SCHEDULE ⟨∼s his calls conveniently⟩ 2 : to set the tempo or duration of ⟨∼ a performance⟩ 3 : to cause to keep time with 4 : to determine or record the time, duration, or rate of ⟨∼ a sprinter⟩ — **tim·er** *n*
time bomb *n* 1 : a bomb so made as to explode at a predetermined time 2 : something with a potentially dangerous delayed reaction
time clock *n* : a clock that records the time workers arrive and depart
time frame *n* : a period of time esp. with respect to some action or project
time–hon·ored \'tīm-ˌä-nərd\ *adj* : honored because of age or long usage
time·keep·er \-ˌkē-pər\ *n* 1 : a clerk who keeps records of the time worked by employees 2 : one appointed to mark and announce the time in an athletic game or contest
time·less \-ləs\ *adj* 1 : ETERNAL 2 : not limited or affected by time ⟨∼ works of art⟩ — **time·less·ly** *adv* — **time·less·ness** *n*
time·ly \-lē\ *adj* **time·li·er; -est** 1 : coming early or at the right time ⟨a ∼ arrival⟩ 2 : appropriate to the time ⟨a ∼ book⟩ — **time·li·ness** *n*
time–out \'tīm-ˌaut\ *n* : a brief suspension of activity esp. in an athletic game
time·piece \-ˌpēs\ *n* : a device (as a clock) to show the passage of time
times \'tīmz\ *prep* : multiplied by ⟨2 ∼ 2 is 4⟩
time–shar·ing \'tīm-ˌsher-iŋ\ *n* 1 : simultaneous use of a computer by many users 2 : joint onwership or rental of a vacation lodging by several persons with each taking turns using the place
times sign *n* : the symbol × used to indicate multiplication
time·ta·ble \'tīm-ˌtā-bəl\ *n* 1 : a table of the departure and arrival times (as of trains) 2 : a schedule showing a planned order or sequence
time warp *n* : an anomaly, discontinuity, or suspension held to occur in the progress of time
time·worn \-ˌwōrn\ *adj* 1 : worn by time 2 : HACKNEYED, STALE
tim·id \'ti-məd\ *adj* : lacking in courage or self-confidence : FEARFUL — **ti·mid·i·ty** \tə-'mi-də-tē\ *n* — **tim·id·ly** *adv*
tim·o·rous \'ti-mə-rəs\ *adj* : of a timid disposition : AFRAID — **tim·o·rous·ly** *adv* — **tim·o·rous·ness** *n*
tim·o·thy \'ti-mə-thē\ *n* : a grass with long cylindrical spikes widely grown for hay
Tim·o·thy \'ti-mə-thē\ *n* — see BIBLE table
tim·pa·ni \'tim-pə-nē\ *n sing or pl* [It] : a set of kettledrums played by one performer in an orchestra — **tim·pa·nist** \-nist\ *n*
¹**tin** \'tin\ *n* 1 : a soft white crystalline metallic chemical element malleable at ordinary temperatures that is used esp. in solders and alloys — see ELEMENT table 2 : a container (as a can) made of metal (as tinplate)
²**tin** *vb* **tinned; tin·ning** 1 : to cover or plate with tin 2 : to pack in tins
TIN *abbr* taxpayer identification number
tinct \'tiŋkt\ *n* : TINCTURE, TINGE
¹**tinc·ture** \'tiŋk-chər\ *n* 1 *archaic* : a substance that colors 2 : a slight admixture : TRACE 3 : an alcoholic solution of a medicinal substance **syn** touch, suggestion, suspicion, tinge
²**tincture** *vb* **tinc·tured; tinc·tur·ing** 1 : COLOR, TINGE 2 : AFFECT
tin·der \'tin-dər\ *n* 1 : a very flammable substance used as kindling 2 : something serving to incite or inflame
tin·der·box \'tin-dər-ˌbäks\ *n* 1 : a metal box for holding tinder and usu. flint and steel for striking a spark 2 : a highly flammable object or place

tine \'tīn\ *n* : a slender pointed part (as of a fork or an antler) : PRONG

tin·foil \'tin-ˌfȯil\ *n* : a thin metal sheeting usu. of aluminum or tin-lead alloy

¹tinge \'tinj\ *vb* **tinged; tinge·ing** *or* **ting·ing 1** : to color slightly : TINT **2** : to affect or modify esp. with a slight odor or taste

²tinge *n* : a slight coloring, flavor, or quality : TRACE **syn** touch, suggestion, suspicion, tincture, soupçon

tin·gle \'tiŋ-gəl\ *vb* **tin·gled; tin·gling 1** : to feel a prickling or thrilling sensation **2** : TINKLE — **tingle** *n*

¹tin·ker \'tiŋ-kər\ *n* **1** : a usu. itinerant mender of household utensils **2** : an unskillful mender : BUNGLER

²tinker *vb* : to repair or adjust something in an unskillful or experimental manner — **tin·ker·er** *n*

¹tin·kle \'tiŋ-kəl\ *vb* **tin·kled; tin·kling** : to make or cause to make a tinkle

²tinkle *n* : a series of short high ringing or clinking sounds

tin·ny \'ti-nē\ *adj* **tin·ni·er; -est 1** : abounding in or yielding tin **2** : resembling tin; *also* : LIGHT, CHEAP **3** : thin in tone ⟨a ∼ voice⟩ — **tin·ni·ly** \-nə-lē\ *adv* — **tin·ni·ness** \-nē-nəs\ *n*

tin·plate \'tin-ˈplāt\ *n* : thin sheet iron or steel coated with tin — **tin–plate** *vb*

tin·sel \'tin-səl\ *n* [MF *etincelle* spark, glitter] **1** : a thread, strip, or sheet of metal, paper, or plastic used to produce a glittering appearance **2** : something superficially attractive but of little worth

tin·smith \'tin-ˌsmith\ *n* : one that works with sheet metal (as tinplate)

¹tint \'tint\ *n* **1** : a slight or pale coloration : HUE **2** : any of various shades of a color

²tint *vb* : to impart a tint to : COLOR

tin·tin·nab·u·la·tion \ˌtin-tə-ˌna-byə-ˈlā-shən\ *n* **1** : the ringing of bells **2** : a tingling sound as if of bells

tin·ware \'tin-ˌwar\ *n* : articles and esp. utensils made of tinplate

ti·ny \'tī-nē\ *adj* **ti·ni·er; -est** : very small : MINUTE **syn** miniature, diminutive, wee, lilliputian

¹tip \'tip\ *vb* **tipped; tip·ping 1** : OVERTURN, UPSET **2** : LEAN, SLANT; *also* : to raise and tilt forward ⟨*tipped* his hat⟩

²tip *n* : the act or an instance of tipping

³tip *vb* **tipped; tip·ping 1** : to furnish with a tip **2** : to cover or adorn the tip of

⁴tip *n* **1** : the usu. pointed end of something **2** : a small piece or part serving as an end, cap, or point

⁵tip *n* : a light touch or blow

⁶tip *vb* **tipped; tip·ping** : to strike lightly : TAP

⁷tip *n* : a piece of advice or expert or confidential information : HINT

⁸tip *vb* **tipped; tip·ping** : to impart a piece of information about or to

⁹tip *vb* **tipped; tip·ping** : to give a gratuity to

¹⁰tip *n* : a gift or small sum given for a service performed or anticipated

tip–off \'tip-ˌȯf\ *n* : WARNING, TIP

tip·pet \'ti-pət\ *n* : a long scarf or shoulder cape

tip·ple \'ti-pəl\ *vb* **tip·pled; tip·pling** : to drink intoxicating liquor esp. habitually or excessively — **tipple** *n* — **tip·pler** *n*

tip·ster \'tip-stər\ *n* : a person who gives or sells tips esp. for gambling

tip·sy \'tip-sē\ *adj* **tip·si·er; -est** : unsteady or foolish from the effects of alcohol — **tip·si·ly** \-sə-lē\ *adv*

¹tip·toe \'tip-ˌtō\ *n* : the position of being balanced on the balls of the feet and toes with the heels raised; *also* : the ends of the toes

²tiptoe *adv or adj* : on or as if on tiptoe

³tiptoe *vb* **tip·toed; tip·toe·ing** : to walk or proceed on or as if on tiptoe

¹tip–top \'tip-ˈtäp\ *n* : the highest point

²tip–top *adj* : EXCELLENT, FIRST-RATE

ti·rade \'tī-ˌrād\ *n* [F, shot, tirade, fr. MF, fr. It *tirata*, fr. *tirare* to draw, shoot] : a prolonged speech of abuse or condemnation

¹tire \'tīr\ *vb* **tired; tir·ing 1** : to make or become weary : FATIGUE **2** : to wear out the patience of : BORE

²tire *n* **1** : a metal hoop that forms the tread of a wheel **2** : a rubber cushion usu. containing compressed air that encircles a wheel (as of a bike)

tired \'tīrd\ *adj* **1** : WEARY, FATIGUED **2** : HACKNEYED — **tired·ness** *n*

tire·less \'tīr-ləs\ *adj* : not tiring : UNTIRING, INDEFATIGABLE — **tire·less·ly** *adv* — **tire·less·ness** *n*

tire·some \-səm\ *adj* : tending to bore : WEARISOME, TEDIOUS — **tire·some·ly** *adv* — **tire·some·ness** *n*

tiro *chiefly Brit var of* TYRO

tis·sue \'ti-shü\ *n* [ME *tissu*, a rich fabric, fr. OF, fr. *tistre* to weave, fr. L *texere*] **1** : a fine lightweight often sheer fabric **2** : NETWORK, WEB **3** : a soft absorbent paper **4** : a mass or layer of cells forming a basic structural material of an animal or plant

¹tit \'tit\ *n* : TEAT

²tit *n* : TITMOUSE

Tit *abbr* Titus

ti·tan \'tīt-ᵊn\ *n* **1** *cap* : one of a family of giants overthrown by the gods of ancient Greece **2** : one gigantic in size or power

ti·tan·ic \tī-ˈta-nik\ *adj* : enormous in size, force, or power **syn** immense, gigantic, giant, colossal, mammoth

ti·ta·ni·um \tī-ˈtā-nē-əm\ *n* : a gray light strong metallic chemical element used esp. in alloys — see ELEMENT table

tit·bit \'tit-ˌbit\ *var of* TIDBIT

tithe \'tīth\ *n* : a 10th part paid or given esp. for the support of a church — **tithe** *vb* — **tith·er** *n*

tit·il·late \'tit-ᵊl-ˌāt\ *vb* **-lat·ed; -lat·ing 1** : to excite pleasurably **2** : TICKLE — **tit·il·la·tion** \ˌtit-ᵊl-ˈā-shən\ *n*

tit·i·vate *or* **tit·ti·vate** \'ti-tə-ˌvāt\ *vb* **-vat·ed; -vat·ing** : to dress up : spruce up — **tit·i·va·tion** \ˌti-tə-ˈvā-shən\ *n*

ti·tle \'tīt-ᵊl\ *n* **1** : CLAIM, RIGHT; *esp* : a legal right to the ownership of property **2** : the distinguishing name esp. of an artistic production (as a book) **3** : an appellation of honor, rank, or office **4** : CHAMPIONSHIP **syn** designation, denomination, appellation

ti·tled \'tīt-ᵊld\ *adj* : having a title esp. of nobility

title page *n* : a page of a book bearing the title and usu. the names of the author and publisher

tit·mouse \'tit-ˌmaůs\ *n, pl* **tit·mice** \-ˌmīs\ : any of numerous small long-tailed insect-eating birds

ti·tra·tion \tī-ˈtrā-shən\ *n* : a process of finding the concentration of a solution (as of an acid) by adding small portions of a second solution of known concentration (as of a base) to a fixed amount of the first until an expected change (as in color) occurs

tit·ter \'ti-tər\ *vb* : to laugh in an affected or in a nervous or half-suppressed manner : GIGGLE — **titter** *n*

tit·tle \'tit-ᵊl\ *n* : a tiny piece : JOT

tit·tle–tat·tle \'tit-ᵊl-ˌtat-ᵊl\ *n* : idle talk : GOSSIP — **tittle–tattle** *vb*

tit·u·lar \'ti-chə-lər\ *adj* **1** : existing in title only : NOMINAL ⟨∼ ruler⟩ **2** : of, relating to, or bearing a title ⟨∼ role⟩

Ti·tus \'tī-təs\ *n* — see BIBLE table

tiz·zy \'ti-zē\ *n, pl* **tizzies** : a highly excited and distracted state of mind

tk *abbr* **1** tank **2** truck

TKO \ˌtē-ˌkā-ˈō\ *n* [*technical knockout*] : the termination of a boxing match when a boxer is declared unable to continue the fight

tkt *abbr* ticket

Tl *symbol* thallium

TLC *abbr* tender loving care

T lymphocyte *n* : T CELL

Tm *symbol* thulium

TM *abbr* trademark

T-man \\'tē-₁man\ *n* : a special agent of the U.S. Treasury Department

tn *abbr* **1** ton **2** town

TN *abbr* Tennessee

tng *abbr* training

tnpk *abbr* turnpike

TNT \₁tē-(₁)en-'tē\ *n* : a flammable toxic compound used as a high explosive

¹to \tə, 'tü\ *prep* **1** : in the direction of and reaching ⟨drove ~ town⟩ **2** : in the direction of : TOWARD **3** : ON, AGAINST ⟨apply salve ~ a burn⟩ **4** : as far as ⟨can pay up ~ a dollar⟩ **5** : so as to become or bring about ⟨beaten ~ death⟩ ⟨broken ~ pieces⟩ **6** : BEFORE ⟨it's five minutes ~ six⟩ **7** : UNTIL ⟨from May ~ December⟩ **8** : fitting or being a part of : FOR ⟨key ~ the lock⟩ **9** : with the accompaniment of ⟨sing ~ the music⟩ **10** : in relation or comparison with ⟨similar ~ that one⟩ ⟨won 10 ~ 6⟩ **11** : in accordance with ⟨add salt ~ taste⟩ **12** : within the range of ⟨~ my knowledge⟩ **13** : contained, occurring, or included in ⟨two pints ~ a quart⟩ **14** : as regards ⟨agreeable ~ everyone⟩ **15** : affecting as the receiver or beneficiary ⟨whispered ~ her⟩ ⟨gave it ~ me⟩ **16** : for no one except ⟨a room ~ myself⟩ **17** : into the action of ⟨we got ~ talking⟩ **18** — used for marking the following verb as an infinitive ⟨wants ~ go⟩ and often used by itself at the end of a clause in place of an infinitive suggested by the preceding context ⟨goes to town whenever he wants ~⟩ ⟨can leave if you'd like ~⟩

²to \'tü\ *adv* **1** : in a direction toward ⟨run ~ and fro⟩ **2** : into contact esp. with the frame of a door ⟨the door slammed ~⟩ **3** : to the matter in hand ⟨fell ~ and ate heartily⟩ **4** : to a state of consciousness or awareness ⟨came ~ hours after the accident⟩

TO *abbr* turn over

toad \'tōd\ *n* : any of numerous tailless leaping amphibians differing typically from the related frogs in having a shorter stockier build, rough dry warty skin, and less aquatic habits

toad

toad·stool \-₁stül\ *n* : MUSHROOM; *esp* : one that is poisonous or inedible

toady \'tō-dē\ *n, pl* **toad·ies** : a person who flatters in the hope of gaining favors : SYCOPHANT — **toady** *vb*

to–and–fro \₁tü-ən-'frō\ *adj* : forward and backward — **to–and–fro** *n*

¹toast \'tōst\ *vb* **1** : to warm thoroughly **2** : to make (as bread) crisp, hot, and brown by heat **3** : to become toasted

²toast *n* **1** : sliced toasted bread **2** : someone or something in whose honor persons drink **3** : an act of drinking in honor of a toast

³toast *vb* : to propose or drink to as a toast

toast·er \'tō-stər\ *n* : an electrical appliance for toasting

toaster oven *n* : a portable electrical appliance that bakes, broils, and toasts

toast·mas·ter \'tōst-₁mas-tər\ *n* : a person who presides at a banquet and introduces the after-dinner speakers

toast·mis·tress \-₁mis-trəs\ *n* : a woman who acts as toastmaster

Tob *abbr* Tobit

to·bac·co \tə-'ba-kō\ *n, pl* **-cos** [Sp *tabaco*] **1** : a tall broad-leaved herb related to the potato; *also* : its leaves prepared for smoking or chewing or as snuff **2** : manufactured tobacco products; *also* : smoking as a practice

to·bac·co·nist \tə-'ba-kə-nist\ *n* : a dealer in tobacco

To·bi·as \tō-'bī-əs\ *n* : TOBIT

To·bit \'tō-bət\ *n* — see BIBLE table

¹to·bog·gan \tə-'bä-gən\ *n* : a long flat-bottomed light sled made of thin boards curved up at one end

²toboggan *vb* **1** : to coast on or as if on a toboggan **2** : to decline suddenly (as in value) — **to·bog·gan·er** *n*

toc·sin \'täk-sən\ *n* **1** : an alarm bell **2** : a warning signal

¹to·day \tə-'dā\ *adv* **1** : on or for this day **2** : at the present time

²today *n* : the present day, time, or age

tod·dle \'täd-ᵊl\ *vb* **tod·dled; tod·dling** : to walk with short tottering steps in the manner of a young child — **toddle** *n* — **tod·dler** *n*

tod·dy \'tä-dē\ *n, pl* **toddies** [Hindi *tāṛī* juice of a palm, fr. *tāṛ* a palm, fr. Skt *tāla*] : a drink made of liquor, sugar, spices, and hot water

to–do \tə-'dü\ *n, pl* **to–dos** \-'düz\ : BUSTLE, STIR, FUSS

¹toe \'tō\ *n* **1** : one of the jointed parts of the front end of a vertebrate's foot **2** : the front part of a foot or hoof

²toe *vb* **toed; toe·ing** : to touch, reach, or drive with the toes

toea \'toi-ə\ *n* — see **kina** at MONEY table

toe·hold \'tō-₁hōld\ *n* **1** : a place of support for the toes **2** : a slight footing

toe·nail \'tō-₁nāl\ *n* : a nail of a toe

tof·fee *or* **tof·fy** \'tò-fē, 'tä-\ *n, pl* **toffees** *or* **toffies** : candy of brittle but tender texture made by boiling sugar and butter together

to·fu \'tō-(₁)fü\ *n* [Jp *tōfu*] : a soft vegetable cheese made from soybeans

tog \'täg, 'tòg\ *vb* **togged; tog·ging** : to put togs on : DRESS

to·ga \'tō-gə\ *n* : the loose outer garment worn in public by citizens of ancient Rome — **to·gaed** \-gəd\ *adj*

¹to·geth·er \tə-'ge-thər\ *adv* **1** : in or into one place or group **2** : in or into contact or association ⟨mix ~⟩ **3** : at one time : SIMULTANEOUSLY ⟨talk and work ~⟩ **4** : in succession ⟨for days ~⟩ **5** : in or into harmony or coherence ⟨get ~ on a plan⟩ **6** : as a group : JOINTLY — **to·geth·er·ness** *n*

²together *adj* : composed in mind or manner

tog·gery \'tä-gə-rē, 'tò-\ *n* : CLOTHING

tog·gle switch \'tä-gəl-\ *n* : an electric switch operated by pushing a projecting lever through a small arc

To·go·lese \₁tō-gə-'lēz, -'lēs\ *n* : a native or inhabitant of Togo — **Togolese** *adj*

togs \'tägz, 'tògz\ *n pl* : CLOTHING; *esp* : clothes for a specified use ⟨riding ~⟩

¹toil \'tòil\ *n* **1** : laborious effort **2** : long fatiguing labor : DRUDGERY — **toil·ful** \-fəl\ *adj* — **toil·some** *adj*

²toil *vb* [ME, to argue, struggle, fr. OF *toeillier* to stir, disturb, dispute, fr. L *tudiculare* to crush, grind, fr. *tudicula* machine for crushing olives, dim. of *tudes* hammer] **1** : to work hard and long **2** : to proceed with great effort : PLOD — **toil·er** *n*

³toil *n* [ME *toile* cloth, net, fr. L *tela* cloth on a loom] : NET, TRAP — usu. used in pl.

toi·let \'tòi-lət\ *n* **1** : the act or process of dressing and grooming oneself **2** : BATHROOM **3** : a fixture for use in urinating and defecating; *esp* : one consisting essentially of a water-flushed bowl and seat — **toilet** *vb*

toi·let·ry \'tòi-lə-trē\ *n, pl* **-ries** : an article or preparation used in making one's toilet — usu. used in pl.

toi·lette \twä-'let\ *n* **1** : TOILET 1 **2** : formal attire; *also* : a particular costume

toilet training *n* : the process of training a child to control bladder and bowel movements and to use the toilet — **toilet train** *vb*

toil·worn \'tȯil-ˌwȯrn\ *adj* : showing the effects of toil

To·kay \tō-'kā\ *n* : naturally sweet wine from Hungary

toke \'tōk\ *n, slang* : a puff on a marijuana cigarette or pipe

¹to·ken \'tō-kən\ *n* **1** : an outward sign **2** : SYMBOL, EMBLEM **3** : SOUVENIR, KEEPSAKE **4** : a small part representing the whole **5** : a piece resembling a coin issued as money or for use by a particular group on specified terms

²token *adj* **1** : done or given as a token esp. in partial fulfillment of an obligation **2** : representing only a symbolic effort : MINIMAL, PERFUNCTORY

to·ken·ism \'tō-kə-ˌni-zəm\ *n* : the policy or practice of making only a symbolic effort (as to desegregate)

told *past and past part of* TELL

tole \'tōl\ *n* : sheet metal and esp. tinplate for use in domestic and ornamental wares

tol·er·a·ble \'tä-lə-rə-bəl\ *adj* **1** : capable of being borne or endured **2** : moderately good : PASSABLE — **tol·er·a·bly** \-blē\ *adv*

tol·er·ance \'tä-lə-rəns\ *n* **1** : the act or practice of tolerating; *esp* : sympathy or indulgence for beliefs or practices differing from one's own **2** : the allowable deviation from a standard (as of size) **3** : the body's ability to become less responsive over time to something (as a drug) — **tol·er·ant** *adj* — **tol·er·ant·ly** *adv*

tol·er·ate \'tä-lə-ˌrāt\ *vb* **-at·ed; -at·ing 1** : to exhibit physiological tolerance for (as a drug) **2** : to allow to be or to be done without hindrance **syn** abide, bear, suffer, stand, brook — **tol·er·a·tion** \ˌtä-lə-'rā-shən\ *n*

¹toll \'tōl\ *n* **1** : a tax paid for a privilege (as for passing over a bridge) **2** : a charge for a service (as for a long-distance telephone call) **3** : the cost in life, health, loss, or suffering

²toll *vb* **1** : to cause the slow regular sounding of (a bell) esp. by pulling a rope **2** : to give signal of : SOUND **3** : to sound with slow measured strokes **4** : to announce by tolling

³toll *n* : the sound of a tolling bell

toll·booth \'tōl-ˌbüth\ *n* : a booth where tolls are paid

toll·gate \-ˌgāt\ *n* : a point where vehicles stop to pay a toll

toll·house \-ˌhaús\ *n* : a house or booth where tolls are paid

tol·u·ene \'täl-yə-ˌwēn\ *n* : a liquid hydrocarbon used esp. as a solvent

tom \'täm\ *n* : the male of various animals (as a cat or turkey)

¹tom·a·hawk \'tä-mə-ˌhȯk\ *n* : a light ax used as a missile and as a hand weapon esp. by No. American Indians

²tomahawk *vb* : to strike or kill with a tomahawk

to·ma·to \tə-'mā-tō, -'mä-\ *n, pl* **-toes** : a usu. large, rounded, and red or yellow pulpy edible berry of a widely grown tropical herb related to the potato; *also* : this herb

tomb \'tüm\ *n* **1** : a place of burial : GRAVE **2** : a house, chamber, or vault for the dead — **tomb** *vb*

tom·boy \'täm-ˌbȯi\ *n* : a girl who behaves in a manner usu. considered boyish — **tom·boy·ish** *adj*

tomb·stone \'tüm-ˌstōn\ *n* : a stone marking a grave

tom·cat \'täm-ˌkat\ *n* : a male domestic cat

Tom Col·lins \ˌtäm-'kä-lənz\ *n* : a tall iced drink with a base of gin

tome \'tōm\ *n* : BOOK; *esp* : a large or weighty one

tom·fool·ery \täm-'fü-lə-rē\ *n* : playful or foolish behavior

tom·my gun \'tä-mē-ˌgən\ *n* : SUBMACHINE GUN — **tommy–gun** *vb*

to·mog·ra·phy \tō-'mä-grə-fē\ *n* : a method of producing a three-dimensional image of the internal structures of a solid object (as the human body or the earth) — **to·mo·graph·ic** \ˌtō-mə-'gra-fik\ *adj*

to·mor·row \tə-'mär-ō\ *adv* : on or for the day after today — **tomorrow** *n*

tom·tit \'täm-ˌtit, täm-'tit\ *n* : any of various small active birds

tom–tom \'täm-ˌtäm\ *n* : a small-headed drum beaten with the hands

ton \'tən\ *n, pl* **tons** *also* **ton 1** — see WEIGHT table **2** : a unit equal to the volume of a long ton weight of seawater used in reckoning the displacement of ships and equal to 35 cubic feet

to·nal·i·ty \tō-'na-lə-tē\ *n, pl* **-ties** : tonal quality

¹tone \'tōn\ *n* [ME, fr. L *tonus* tension, tone, fr. Gk *tonos*, lit., act of stretching; fr. the dependence of the pitch of a musical string on its tension] **1** : vocal or musical sound; *esp* : sound quality **2** : a sound of definite pitch **3** : WHOLE STEP **4** : accent or inflection expressive of an emotion **5** : the pitch of a word often used to express differences of meaning **6** : style or manner of expression **7** : color quality; *also* : SHADE, TINT **8** : the effect in painting of light and shade together with color **9** : healthy and vigorous condition of a living body or bodily part; *also* : the state of partial contraction characteristic of normal muscle **10** : general character, quality, or trend **syn** atmosphere, feeling, mood, vein — **ton·al** \'tōn-ᵊl\ *adj*

²tone *vb* **toned; ton·ing 1** : to give a particular intonation or inflection to **2** : to impart tone to **3** : SOFTEN, MELLOW **4** : to harmonize in color : BLEND

tone·arm *n* : the movable part of a record player that carries the pickup and the needle

tong \'täŋ, 'tȯŋ\ *n* : a Chinese secret society in the U.S.

tongs \'täŋz, 'tȯŋz\ *n pl* : a grasping device consisting of two pieces joined at one end by a pivot or hinged like scissors — **tong** *vb*

¹tongue \'təŋ\ *n* **1** : a fleshy movable process of the floor of the mouth used in tasting and in taking and swallowing food and in humans as a speech organ **2** : the flesh of a tongue (as of the ox) used as food **3** : the power of communication **4** : LANGUAGE 1 **5** : manner or quality of utterance; *also* : intended meaning **6** : ecstatic usu. unintelligible utterance accompanying religious excitation — usu. used in pl. **7** : something resembling an animal's tongue esp. in being elongated and fastened at one end only — **tongued** \'təŋd\ *adj* — **tongue·less** *adj*

²tongue *vb* **tongued; tongu·ing 1** : to touch or lick with the tongue **2** : to articulate notes on a wind instrument

tongue–in–cheek *adj* : characterized by insincerity, irony, or whimsical exaggeration — **tongue in cheek** *adv*

tongue–lash \'təŋ-ˌlash\ *vb* : CHIDE, REPROVE — **tongue–lash·ing** \-iŋ\ *n*

tongue–tied \-ˌtīd\ *adj* : unable or disinclined to speak clearly or freely (as from shyness or a tongue impairment)

tongue twister *n* : an utterance that is difficult to articulate because of a succession of similar consonants

¹ton·ic \'tä-nik\ *adj* **1** : of, relating to, or producing a healthy physical or mental condition : INVIGORATING **2** : relating to or based on the 1st tone of a scale — **to·nic·i·ty** \tō-'ni-sə-tē\ *n*

²tonic *n* **1** : something that invigorates, restores, or refreshes **2** : the 1st degree of a musical scale

tonic water *n* : a carbonated beverage flavored with a bit of quinine, lemon, and lime

¹to·night \tə-'nīt\ *adv* : on this present night or the coming night

²tonight *n* : the present or the coming night

ton·nage \'tə-nij\ *n* **1** : a duty on ships based on tons carried **2** : ships in terms of the number of tons registered or carried **3** : total weight in tons shipped, carried, or mined

ton·sil \'tän-səl\ *n* : either of a pair of oval masses of lymphoid tissue that lie one on each side of the throat at the back of the mouth

ton·sil·lec·to·my \ˌtän-sə-ˈlek-tə-mē\ *n, pl* **-mies** : the surgical removal of the tonsils

ton·sil·li·tis \-ˈlī-təs\ *n* : inflammation of the tonsils

ton·so·ri·al \tän-ˈsȯr-ē-əl\ *adj* : of or relating to a barber or a barber's work

ton·sure \ˈtän-chər\ *n* [ME, fr. ML *tonsura*, fr. L, act of shearing, fr. *tonsus*, pp. of *tondēre* to shear] **1** : the rite of admission to the clerical state by the clipping or shaving of the head **2** : the shaven crown or patch worn by clerics (as monks) — **tonsure** *vb*

too \ˈtü\ *adv* **1** : in addition : ALSO **2** : EXCESSIVELY **3** : to such a degree as to be regrettable **4** : VERY

took *past of* TAKE

¹tool \ˈtül\ *n* **1** : a hand instrument that aids in accomplishing a task **2** : the cutting or shaping part in a machine; *also* : a machine for shaping metal in any way **3** : something used in doing a job ⟨a scholar's books are his ∼s⟩; *also* : a means to an end **4** : a person used by another : DUPE **5** *pl* : natural ability

²tool *vb* **1** : to shape, form, or finish with a tool; *esp* : to letter or decorate (as a book cover) by means of hand tools **2** : to equip a plant or industry with machines and tools for production **3** : DRIVE, RIDE ⟨∼ing along at 60⟩

¹toot \ˈtüt\ *vb* **1** : to sound or cause to sound in short blasts **2** : to blow an instrument (as a horn) — **toot·er** *n*

²toot *n* : a short blast (as on a horn)

tooth \ˈtüth\ *n, pl* **teeth** \ˈtēth\ **1** : one of the hard bony structures borne esp. on the jaws of vertebrates and used for seizing and chewing food and as weapons; *also* : a hard sharp structure esp. around the mouth of an invertebrate **2** : something resembling an animal's tooth **3** : any of the projections on the edge of a wheel that fits into corresponding projections on another wheel — **toothed** \ˈtütht\ *adj* — **tooth·less** *adj*

tooth·ache \ˈtüth-ˌāk\ *n* : pain in or about a tooth

tooth·brush \-ˌbrəsh\ *n* : a brush for cleaning the teeth

tooth·paste \-ˌpāst\ *n* : a paste for cleaning the teeth

tooth·pick \-ˌpik\ *n* : a pointed instrument for removing food particles caught between the teeth

tooth powder *n* : a powder for cleaning the teeth

tooth·some \ˈtüth-səm\ *adj* **1** : AGREEABLE, ATTRACTIVE **2** : pleasing to the taste : DELICIOUS **syn** palatable, appetizing, savory, tasty

toothy \ˈtü-thē\ *adj* **tooth·i·er; -est** : having or showing prominent teeth

¹top \ˈtäp\ *n* **1** : the highest part, point, or level of something **2** : the stalks and leaves of a plant with edible roots ⟨beet ∼s⟩ **3** : the upper end, edge, or surface ⟨the ∼ of a page⟩ **4** : an upper piece, lid, or covering **5** : the highest degree, pitch, or rank

²top *vb* **topped; top·ping 1** : to remove or trim the top of : PRUNE ⟨∼ a tree⟩ **2** : to cover with a top or on the top : CROWN, CAP **3** : to be superior to : EXCEL, SURPASS **4** : to go over the top of **5** : to strike (a ball) above the center **6** : to make an end or conclusion ⟨∼ off a meal with coffee⟩

³top *adj* **1** : of, relating to, or being at the top : HIGHEST **2** : CHIEF

⁴top *n* : a child's toy that has a tapering point on which it is made to spin

to·paz \ˈtō-ˌpaz\ *n* : a hard silicate of aluminum; *esp* : a yellow transparent topaz used as a gem

top·coat \ˈtäp-ˌkōt\ *n* **1** : a lightweight overcoat **2** : a protective coating (as of paint)

top dollar *n* : the highest amount being paid for a commodity or service

top–dress \-ˌdres\ *vb* : to apply material to (as land) without working it in; *esp* : to scatter fertilizer over

top·dress·ing \-ˌdre-siŋ\ *n* : a material used to top-dress soil

top·flight \ˈtäp-ˈflīt\ *adj* : of, relating to, or being the highest level of excellence or rank — **top flight** *n*

top hat *n* : a tall-crowned hat usu. of beaver or silk

top–heavy \ˈtäp-ˌhe-vē\ *adj* : having the top part too heavy for the lower part

top·ic \ˈtä-pik\ *n* **1** : a heading in an outlined argument **2** : the subject of a discourse or a section of it : THEME

top·i·cal \-pi-kəl\ *adj* **1** : designed to be applied to or to work on a part (as of the body) **2** : of, relating to, or arranged by topics ⟨a ∼ outline⟩ **3** : relating to current or local events — **top·i·cal·ly** \-k(ə-)lē\ *adv*

top·knot \ˈtäp-ˌnät\ *n* **1** : an ornament (as a knot of ribbons) forming a headdress **2** : a crest of feathers or tuft of hair on the top of the head

top·less \-ləs\ *adj* **1** : wearing no clothing on the upper body **2** : featuring topless waitresses or entertainers

top·mast \ˈtäp-ˌmast, -məst\ *n* : the 2d mast above a ship's deck

top·most \ˈtäp-ˌmōst\ *adj* : highest of all : UPPERMOST

top–notch \-ˈnäch\ *adj* : of the highest quality : FIRST-RATE

to·pog·ra·phy \tə-ˈpä-grə-fē\ *n* **1** : the art of showing in detail on a map or chart the physical features of a place or region **2** : the outline of the form of a place showing its relief and the position of features (as rivers, roads, or cities) — **to·pog·ra·pher** \-fər\ *n* — **top·o·graph·ic** \ˌtä-pə-ˈgra-fik\ *or* **top·o·graph·i·cal** \-fi-kəl\ *adj*

top·ping \ˈtä-piŋ\ *n* : a food served on top of another to make it look or taste better

top·ple \ˈtä-pəl\ *vb* **top·pled; top·pling 1** : to fall from or as if from being top-heavy **2** : to push over : OVERTURN; *also* : OVERTHROW

tops \ˈtäps\ *adj* : topmost in quality or importance ⟨∼ in his field⟩

top·sail \ˈtäp-ˌsāl, -səl\ *also* **top·s'l** \-səl\ *n* : the sail next above the lowest sail on a mast in a square-rigged ship

top secret *adj* : demanding complete secrecy among those concerned

top·side \ˈtäp-ˈsīd\ *adv or adj* **1** : to or on the top or surface **2** : on deck

top·sides \-ˈsīdz\ *n pl* : the top portion of the outer surface of a ship on each side above the waterline

top·soil \ˈtäp-ˌsȯil\ *n* : surface soil usu. including the organic layer in which plants have most of their roots

top·sy–tur·vy \ˌtäp-sē-ˈtər-vē\ *adv* **1** : in utter confusion **2** : UPSIDE DOWN — **topsy–turvy** *adj*

toque \ˈtōk\ *n* : a woman's small hat without a brim

tor \ˈtȯr\ *n* : a high craggy hill

To·rah \ˈtȯr-ə\ *n* **1** : a scroll of the first five books of the Old Testament used in a synagogue; *also* : these five books **2** : the body of divine knowledge and law found in the Jewish scriptures and tradition

¹torch \ˈtȯrch\ *n* **1** : a flaming light made of something that burns brightly and usu. carried in the hand **2** : something that resembles a torch in giving light, heat, or guidance **3** *chiefly Brit* : FLASHLIGHT **4** : a portable burner for producing a hot flame

²torch *vb* : to set fire to

torch·bear·er \ˈtȯrch-ˌbar-ər\ *n* : one who carries a torch; *also* : one in the forefront (as of a political campaign)

torch·light \-ˌlīt\ *n* : light given by torches

torch song *n* : a popular sentimental song of unrequited love

tore *past of* TEAR

to·re·ador \ˈtȯr-ē-ə-ˌdȯr\ *n* : TORERO

to·re·ro \tə-ˈrer-ō\ *n, pl* **-ros** [Sp] : BULLFIGHTER

¹tor·ment \ˈtȯr-ˌment\ *n* **1** : extreme pain or anguish of body or mind **2** : a source of vexation or pain

²tor·ment \tȯr-ˈment\ *vb* **1** : to cause severe suffering of body or mind to **2** : DISTORT, TWIST **syn** rack, afflict, try, torture — **tor·men·tor** \-ˈmen-tər\ *n*

torn *past part of* TEAR

tor·na·do \tȯr-ˈnā-dō\ *n, pl* **-does** *or* **-dos** [modif of Sp *tronada* thunderstorm, fr. *tronar* to thunder, fr. L *ton-*

are] : a violent destructive whirling wind accompanied by a funnel-shaped cloud that moves over a narrow path

¹tor·pe·do \tȯr-'pē-dō\ *n, pl* **-does** : a thin cylindrical self-propelled underwater weapon

²torpedo *vb* **tor·pe·doed; tor·pe·do·ing** : to hit or destroy with or as if with a torpedo

torpedo boat *n* : a small very fast boat for firing torpedoes

tor·pid \'tȯr-pəd\ *adj* **1** : having lost motion or the power of exertion : DORMANT **2** : SLUGGISH **3** : lacking vigor : DULL — **tor·pid·i·ty** \tȯr-'pi-də-tē\ *n*

tor·por \'tȯr-pər\ *n* **1** : DULLNESS, APATHY **2** : extreme sluggishness : STAGNATION *syn* stupor, lethargy, languor, lassitude

¹torque \'tȯrk\ *n* : a force that produces or tends to produce rotation or torsion

²torque *vb* **torqued; torqu·ing** : to impart torque to : cause to twist (as about an axis)

tor·rent \'tȯr-ənt\ *n* [F, fr. L *torrent-, torrens,* fr. *torrent-, torrens* burning, seething, rushing, fr. prp. of *torrēre* to parch, burn] **1** : a tumultuous outburst **2** : a rushing stream (as of water)

tor·ren·tial \tȯ-'ren-chəl\ *adj* : relating to or resembling a torrent ⟨~ rains⟩

tor·rid \'tȯr-əd\ *adj* **1** : parched with heat esp. of the sun : HOT **2** : ARDENT

torrid zone *n* : the region of the earth between the tropic of Cancer and the tropic of Capricorn

tor·sion \'tȯr-shən\ *n* **1** : a wrenching by which one part of a body is under pressure to turn about a longitudinal axis while the other part is held fast or is under pressure to turn in the opposite direction **2** : a twisting of a bodily organ or part on its own axis — **tor·sion·al** \'tȯr-shə-nəl\ *adj* — **tor·sion·al·ly** *adv*

tor·so \'tȯr-sō\ *n, pl* **torsos** *or* **tor·si** \'tȯr-ˌsē\ [It, lit., stalk] : the trunk of the human body

tort \'tȯrt\ *n* : a wrongful act which does not involve a breach of contract and for which the injured party can recover damages in a civil action

tor·til·la \tȯr-'tē-ə\ *n* : a round thin cake of unleavened cornmeal or wheat flour bread

tor·toise \'tȯr-təs\ *n* : TURTLE; *esp* : any of a family of land turtles

tor·toise·shell \-ˌshel\ *n* : the mottled horny substance of the shell of some turtles used in inlaying and in making various ornamental articles — **tortoiseshell** *adj*

tor·to·ni \tȯr-'tō-nē\ *n* : rich ice cream often made with minced almonds and chopped cherries and flavored with rum

tor·tu·ous \'tȯr-chə-wəs\ *adj* **1** : marked by twists or turns : WINDING **2** : DEVIOUS, TRICKY

¹tor·ture \'tȯr-chər\ *n* **1** : anguish of body or mind **2** : the infliction of severe pain esp. to punish or coerce

²torture *vb* **tor·tured; tor·tur·ing 1** : to cause intense suffering to : TORMENT **2** : to punish or coerce by inflicting severe pain **3** : TWIST, DISTORT *syn* rack, harrow, afflict, try — **tor·tur·er** *n*

To·ry \'tȯr-ē\ *n, pl* **Tories 1** : a member of a chiefly 18th century British party upholding the established church and the traditional political structure **2** : an American supporter of the British during the American Revolution **3** *often not cap* : an extreme conservative — **Tory** *adj*

¹toss \'tȯs, 'täs\ *vb* **1** : to fling to and fro or up and down **2** : to throw with a quick light motion; *also* : BANDY **3** : to fling or lift with a sudden motion ⟨~ed her head angrily⟩ **4** : to move restlessly or turbulently ⟨~es on the waves⟩ **5** : to twist and turn repeatedly **6** : FLOUNCE **7** : to accomplish readily ⟨~ off an article⟩ **8** : to decide an issue by flipping a coin

²toss *n* : an act or instance of tossing; *esp* : TOSS-UP 1

toss–up \-ˌəp\ *n* **1** : a deciding by flipping a coin **2** : an even chance **3** : something that offers no clear basis for choice

¹tot \'tät\ *n* **1** : a small child **2** : a small drink of alcoholic liquor : SHOT

²tot *vb* **tot·ted; tot·ting** : to add up

³tot *abbr* total

¹to·tal \'tōt-ᵊl\ *adj* **1** : making up a whole : ENTIRE ⟨~ amount⟩ **2** : COMPLETE, UTTER ⟨a ~ failure⟩ **3** : involving a complete and unified effort esp. to achieve a desired effect — **to·tal·ly** *adv*

²total *n* **1** : SUM 4 **2** : the entire amount *syn* aggregate, whole, gross, totality

³total *vb* **to·taled** *or* **to·talled; to·tal·ing** *or* **to·tal·ling 1** : to add up : COMPUTE **2** : to amount to : NUMBER **3** : to make a total wreck of (a car)

to·tal·i·tar·i·an \tō-ˌta-lə-'ter-ē-ən\ *adj* : of, relating to, or advocating a political regime based on subordination of the individual to the state and strict control of all aspects of life esp. by coercive measures — **totalitarian** *n* — **to·tal·i·tar·i·an·ism** \-ē-ə-ˌni-zəm\ *n*

to·tal·i·ty \tō-'ta-lə-tē\ *n, pl* **-ties 1** : an aggregate amount : SUM, WHOLE **2** : ENTIRETY, WHOLENESS

to·tal·iza·tor *or* **to·tal·isa·tor** \'tōt-ᵊl-ə-ˌzā-tər\ *n* : a machine for registering and indicating the number of bets and the odds on a horse or dog race

¹tote \'tōt\ *vb* **tot·ed; tot·ing** : CARRY

²tote *vb* **tot·ed; tot·ing** : ADD, TOTAL — usu. used with *up*

to·tem \'tō-təm\ *n* : an object (as an animal or plant) serving as the emblem of a family or clan and often as a reminder of its ancestry; *also* : something usu. carved or painted to represent such an object

totem pole *n* : a pole that is carved with a series of totems and is erected before the houses of some northwest American Indians

tot·ter \'tä-tər\ *vb* **1** : to tremble or rock as if about to fall : SWAY **2** : to move unsteadily : STAGGER

tou·can \'tü-ˌkan\ *n* : any of a family of fruit-eating birds of tropical America with brilliant coloring and a very large beak

¹touch \'təch\ *vb* **1** : to bring a bodily part (as the hand) into contact with so as to feel **2** : to be or cause to be in contact **3** : to strike or push lightly esp. with the hand or foot **4** : DISTURB, HARM **5** : to make use of ⟨never ~es alcohol⟩ **6** : to induce to give or lend **7** : to get to : REACH **8** : to refer to in passing : MENTION **9** : to affect the interest of : CONCERN **10** : to leave a mark on; *also* : BLEMISH **11** : to move to sympathetic feeling **12** : to come close : VERGE **13** : to have a bearing : RELATE **14** : to make a usu. brief or incidental stop in port *syn* affect, influence, impress, strike, sway

²touch *n* **1** : a light stroke or tap **2** : the act or fact of touching or being touched **3** : the sense by which pressure or traction on the skin or mucous membrane is perceived; *also* : a particular sensation conveyed by this sense **4** : mental or moral sensitiveness : TACT **5** : a small quantity : HINT ⟨a ~ of spring in the air⟩ **6** : a manner of striking or touching esp. the keys of a keyboard instrument **7** : an improving detail ⟨add a few ~es to the painting⟩ **8** : distinctive manner or skill ⟨the ~ of a master⟩ **9** : the state of being in contact ⟨keep in ~⟩ *syn* suggestion, suspicion, tincture, tinge

touch·down \'təch-ˌdaún\ *n* : the act of scoring six points in American football by being lawfully in possession of the ball on, above, or behind an opponent's goal line

tou·ché \tü-'shā\ *interj* [F] — used to acknowledge a hit in fencing or the success of an argument, an accusation, or a witty point

touch football *n* : football in which touching is substituted for tackling

touch·ing *adj* : capable of stirring emotions *syn* moving, impressive, poignant, affecting

touch off *vb* **1** : to describe with precision **2** : to start by or as if by touching with fire

touch·stone \'təch-ˌstōn\ *n* : a test or criterion of genuineness or quality **syn** standard, gauge, benchmark, yardstick

touch up *vb* : to improve or perfect by small additional strokes or alterations — **touch–up** \'təch-ˌəp\ *n*

touchy \'təch-ē\ *adj* **touch·i·er; -est 1** : easily offended : PEEVISH **2** : calling for tact in treatment ⟨a ∼ subject⟩ **syn** irascible, cranky, cross, tetchy, testy

¹**tough** \'təf\ *adj* **1** : strong or firm in texture but flexible and not brittle **2** : not easily chewed **3** : characterized by severity and determination ⟨a ∼ policy⟩ **4** : capable of enduring strain or hardship : ROBUST **5** : hard to influence : STUBBORN **6** : difficult to accomplish, resolve, or cope with ⟨a ∼ problem⟩ **7** : ROWDYISH **syn** tenacious, stout, sturdy, stalwart — **tough·ly** *adv* — **tough·ness** *n*

²**tough** *n* : a tough person : ROWDY

tough·en \'tə-fən\ *vb* **tough·ened; tough·en·ing** : to make or become tough

tou·pee \tü-'pā\ *n* [F *toupet* forelock] : a small wig for a bald spot

¹**tour** \'tu̇r, *1 is also* 'tau̇r\ *n* **1** : one's turn : SHIFT **2** : a journey in which one returns to the starting point

²**tour** *vb* : to make a tour

tour de force \ˌtu̇r-də-'fōrs\ *n, pl* **tours de force** *same*\ [F] : a feat of strength, skill, or ingenuity

tour·ist \'tu̇r-ist\ *n* : one that makes a tour for pleasure or culture

tourist class *n* : economy accommodations (as on a ship)

tour·ma·line \'tu̇r-mə-lən, -ˌlēn\ *n* : a mineral that when transparent is valued as a gem

tour·na·ment \'tu̇r-nə-mənt, 'tər-\ *n* **1** : a medieval sport in which mounted armored knights contended with blunted lances or swords **2** : a championship series of games or athletic contests

tour·ney \-nē\ *n, pl* **tourneys** : TOURNAMENT

tour·ni·quet \'tu̇r-ni-kət, 'tər-\ *n* : a device (as a tight bandage) for stopping bleeding or blood flow

tou·sle \'tau̇-zəl\ *vb* **tou·sled; tou·sling** : to disorder by rough handling : DISHEVEL, MUSS

tout \'tau̇t, *2 is also* 'tüt\ *vb* **1** : to give a tip or solicit bets on a racehorse **2** : to praise or publicize loudly — **tout** *n*

¹**tow** \'tō\ *vb* : to draw or pull along behind

²**tow** *n* **1** : an act of towing or condition of being towed **2** : something (as a barge) that is towed

³**tow** *n* : short or broken fiber (as of flax or hemp) used esp. for yarn, twine, or stuffing

to·ward \'tōrd, 'tō-ərd, tə-'wȯrd\ *or* **to·wards** \'tōrdz, 'tō-ərdz, tə-'wȯrdz\ *prep* **1** : in the direction of ⟨heading ∼ the river⟩ **2** : along a course leading to ⟨efforts ∼ reconciliation⟩ **3** : in regard to ⟨tolerance ∼ minorities⟩ **4** : so as to face ⟨turn the chair ∼ the window⟩ **5** : close upon ⟨it was getting along ∼ sundown⟩ **6** : for part payment of ⟨here's $100 ∼ your tuition⟩

tow·boat \'tō-ˌbōt\ *n* : TUGBOAT

tow·el \'tau̇-əl\ *n* : an absorbent cloth or paper for wiping or drying

tow·el·ing *or* **tow·el·ling** *n* : a cotton or linen fabric for making towels

¹**tow·er** \'tau̇-ər\ *n* **1** : a tall structure either isolated or built upon a larger structure ⟨an observation ∼⟩ **2** : a towering citadel — **tow·ered** *adj*

²**tower** *vb* : to reach or rise to a great height

tow·er·ing *adj* **1** : LOFTY ⟨∼ pines⟩ **2** : reaching high intensity ⟨a ∼ rage⟩ **3** : EXCESSIVE ⟨∼ ambition⟩

tow·head \'tō-ˌhed\ *n* : a person having whitish blond hair — **tow·head·ed** \-ˌhe-dəd\ *adj*

to·whee \'tō-ˌhē, 'tō-(ˌ)ē, tō-'hē\ *n* : a common finch of eastern No. America having the male black, white, and reddish; *also* : any of several closely related finches

to wit *adv* : NAMELY

town \'tau̇n\ *n* **1** : a compactly settled area usu. larger than a village but smaller than a city **2** : CITY **3** : the inhabitants of a town **4** : a New England territorial

and political unit usu. containing both rural and urban areas; *also* : a New England community in which matters of local government are decided by a general assembly (**town meeting**) of qualified voters

town house *n* **1** : the city residence of a person having a country home **2** : a single-family house of two or sometimes three stories connected to another house by a common wall

town·ie *or* **towny** \'tau̇-nē\ *n, pl* **townies** : a permanent resident of a town as distinguished from a member of another group

towns·folk \'tau̇nz-ˌfōk\ *n pl* : TOWNSPEOPLE

town·ship \'tau̇n-ˌship\ *n* **1** : TOWN 4 **2** : a unit of local government in some states **3** : an unorganized subdivision of a county; *also* : an administrative division **4** : a division of territory in surveys of U.S. public land containing 36 square miles **5** : an area in the Republic of South Africa segregated for occupation by persons of non-European descent

towns·man \'tau̇nz-mən\ *n* **1** : a native or resident of a town or city **2** : a fellow citizen of a town

towns·peo·ple \-ˌpē-pəl\ *n pl* **1** : the inhabitants of a town or city **2** : town-bred persons

towns·wom·an \-ˌwu̇-mən\ *n* **1** : a woman who is a native or resident of a town or city **2** : a woman who is a fellow citizen of a town

tow·path \'tō-ˌpath, -ˌpȧth\ *n* : a path (as along a canal) traveled esp. by draft animals towing boats

tow truck *n* : a truck equipped for towing disabled vehicles

tox·emia \täk-'sē-mē-ə\ *n* : a bodily disorder associated with the presence of toxic substances in the blood

tox·ic \'täk-sik\ *adj* [LL *toxicus*, fr. L *toxicum* poison, fr. Gk *toxikon* arrow poison, fr. neut. of *toxikos* of a bow, fr. *toxon* bow, arrow] : of, relating to, or caused by poison or a toxin : POISONOUS — **tox·ic·i·ty** \täk-'si-sə-tē\ *n*

tox·i·col·o·gy \ˌtäk-sə-'kä-lə-jē\ *n* : a science that deals with poisons and esp. with problems of their use and control — **tox·i·co·log·i·cal** \-'lä-ji-kəl\ *or* **tox·i·co·log·ic** \ˌtäk-si-kə-'lä-jik\ *adj* — **tox·i·col·o·gist** \-'kä-lə-jist\ *n*

toxic shock syndrome *n* : an acute disease associated with the presence of a bacterium that is characterized by fever, diarrhea, nausea, diffuse erythema, and shock and occurs esp. in menstruating females using tampons

tox·in \'täk-sən\ *n* : a poisonous substance produced by metabolic activities of a living organism that is usu. unstable, very toxic when introduced into the tissues, and usu. capable of inducing antibodies

¹**toy** \'tȯi\ *n* **1** : something trifling **2** : a small ornament : BAUBLE **3** : something for a child to play with

²**toy** *vb* **1** : to deal with something lightly : TRIFLE **2** : FLIRT **3** : to amuse oneself as if with a plaything

³**toy** *adj* **1** : DIMINUTIVE **2** : designed for use as a toy

tp *abbr* **1** title page **2** township

tpk *or* **tpke** *abbr* turnpike

tr *abbr* **1** translated; translation; translator **2** transpose **3** troop

¹**trace** \'trās\ *n* **1** : a mark (as a footprint or track) left by something that has passed **2** : a minute or barely detectable amount

²**trace** *vb* **traced; trac·ing 1** : to mark out : SKETCH **2** : to form (as letters) carefully **3** : to copy (a drawing) by marking lines on transparent paper laid over the drawing to be copied **4** : to follow the trail of : track down **5** : to study out and follow the development of — **trace·able** *adj*

³**trace** *n* : either of two lines of a harness for fastening a draft animal to a vehicle

trac·er \'trā-sər\ *n* **1** : one that traces **2** : ammunition containing a chemical to mark the flight of projectiles by a trail of smoke or fire

trac·ery \'trā-sə-rē\ *n, pl* **-er·ies** : ornamental work having a design with branching or interlacing lines

tra·chea \'trā-kē-ə\ *n, pl* **-che·ae** \-kē-ˌē\ *also* **-che·as** : the main tube by which air enters the lungs of vertebrates : WINDPIPE — **tra·che·al** \-kē-əl\ *adj*

tra·che·ot·o·my \ˌtrā-kē-ˈä-tə-mē\ *n, pl* **-mies** : the surgical operation of cutting into the trachea esp. through the skin

trac·ing *n* **1** : the act of one that traces **2** : something that is traced **3** : a graphic record made by an instrument for measuring vibrations or pulsations

¹track \'trak\ *n* **1** : a mark left in passing **2** : PATH, ROUTE, TRAIL **3** : a course laid out for racing; *also* : track-and-field sports **4** : one of a series of paths along which material (as music) is recorded (as on magnetic tape) **5** : the course along which something moves; *esp* : a way made by two parallel lines of metal rails **6** : awareness of a fact or progression (lost ∼ of time) **7** : either of two endless metal belts on which a vehicle (as a bulldozer) travels

²track *vb* **1** : to follow the tracks or traces of : TRAIL **2** : to observe the moving path of (as a missile) **3** : to make tracks on **4** : to carry (as mud) on the feet and deposit — **track·er** *n*

track·age \'tra-kij\ *n* : lines of railway track

track–and–field *adj* : of or relating to athletic contests held on a running track or on the adjacent field

¹tract \'trakt\ *n* **1** : an area without precise boundaries (huge ∼s of land) **2** : a defined area of land **3** : a system of body parts or organs that act together to perform some function (the digestive ∼)

²tract *n* : a pamphlet of political or religious propaganda

trac·ta·ble \'trak-tə-bəl\ *adj* : easily controlled : DOCILE **syn** amenable, obedient, biddable

tract house *n* : any of many similar houses built on a tract of land

trac·tion \'trak-shən\ *n* **1** : the act of drawing : the state of being drawn **2** : the drawing of a vehicle by motive power; *also* : the particular form of motive power used **3** : the adhesive friction of a body on a surface on which it moves **4** : a pulling force applied to a skeletal structure (as a broken bone) by using a special device; *also* : a state of tension created by such a pulling force (a leg in ∼) — **trac·tion·al** \-shə-nəl\ *adj* — **trac·tive** \'trak-tiv\ *adj*

trac·tor \'trak-tər\ *n* **1** : an automotive vehicle used esp. for drawing farm equipment **2** : a truck for hauling a trailer

¹trade \'trād\ *n* **1** : one's regular business or work : OCCUPATION **2** : an occupation requiring manual or mechanical skill **3** : the persons engaged in a business or industry **4** : the business of buying and selling or bartering commodities **5** : an act of trading : TRANSACTION

²trade *vb* **trad·ed; trad·ing** **1** : to give in exchange for another commodity : BARTER **2** : to engage in the exchange, purchase, or sale of goods **3** : to deal regularly as a customer — **trade on** : EXPLOIT (*trades on* his family name)

trade–in \'trād-ˌin\ *n* : an item of merchandise traded in

trade in *vb* : to turn in as part payment for a purchase

¹trade·mark \'trād-ˌmärk\ *n* : a device (as a word or mark) that points distinctly to the origin or ownership of merchandise to which it is applied and that is legally reserved for the exclusive use of the owner; *also* : something that identifies a person or thing

²trademark *vb* : to secure the trademark rights for

trade name *n* : a name that is given by a manufacturer or merchant to a product to distinguish it as made or sold by him and that may be used and protected as a trademark

trad·er \'trā-dər\ *n* **1** : a person whose business is buying or selling **2** : a ship engaged in trade

trades·man \'trādz-mən\ *n* **1** : one who runs a retail store : SHOPKEEPER **2** : CRAFTSMAN

trades·peo·ple \-ˌpē-pəl\ *n pl* : people engaged in trade

trade union *n* : LABOR UNION

trade wind *n* : a wind blowing almost constantly in one direction

trading stamp *n* : a printed stamp given as a premium to a retail customer that when accumulated may be redeemed for merchandise

tra·di·tion \trə-ˈdi-shən\ *n* **1** : an inherited, established, or customary pattern of thought or action **2** : the handing down of beliefs and customs by word of mouth or by example without written instruction; *also* : a belief or custom thus handed down — **tra·di·tion·al** \-ˌdi-shə-nəl\ *adj* — **tra·di·tion·al·ly** *adv*

tra·duce \trə-ˈdüs, -ˈdyüs\ *vb* **tra·duced; tra·duc·ing** : to lower the reputation of : DEFAME, SLANDER **syn** malign, libel, calumniate — **tra·duc·er** *n*

¹traf·fic \'tra-fik\ *n* **1** : the business of bartering or buying and selling **2** : communication or dealings between individuals or groups **3** : the movement (as of vehicles) along a route; *also* : the vehicles, people, ships, or planes moving along a route **4** : the passengers or cargo carried by a transportation system

²traffic *vb* **traf·ficked; traf·fick·ing** : to carry on traffic — **traf·fick·er** *n*

traffic circle *n* : ROTARY 2

traffic light *n* : an electrically operated visual signal for controlling traffic

tra·ge·di·an \trə-ˈjē-dē-ən\ *n* **1** : a writer of tragedies **2** : an actor who plays tragic roles

tra·ge·di·enne \trə-ˌjē-dē-ˈen\ *n* [F] : an actress who plays tragic roles

trag·e·dy \'tra-jə-dē\ *n, pl* **-dies** [ME *tragedie,* fr. MF, fr. L *tragoedia,* fr. Gk *tragōidia,* fr. *tragos* goat + *aeidein* to sing] **1** : a serious drama with a sorrowful or disastrous conclusion **2** : a disastrous event : CALAMITY; *also* : MISFORTUNE **3** : tragic quality or element (the ∼ of life)

trag·ic \'tra-jik\ *also* **trag·i·cal** \-ji-kəl\ *adj* **1** : of, relating to, or expressive of tragedy **2** : appropriate to tragedy **3** : LAMENTABLE, UNFORTUNATE — **trag·i·cal·ly** \-ji-k(ə-)lē\ *adv*

¹trail \'trāl\ *vb* **1** : to hang down so as to drag along or sweep the ground **2** : to draw or drag along behind **3** : to extend over a surface in a straggling manner **4** : to lag behind **5** : to follow the track of : PURSUE **6** : DWINDLE (her voice ∼ed off)

²trail *n* **1** : something that trails or is trailed (a ∼ of smoke) **2** : a trace or mark left by something that has passed or been drawn along : SCENT, TRACK (a ∼ of blood) **3** : a beaten path; *also* : a marked path through woods

trail bike *n* : a small motorcycle for off-road use

trail·blaz·er \-ˌblā-zər\ *n* : PATHFINDER, PIONEER — **trail·blaz·ing** *adj or n*

trail·er \'trā-lər\ *n* **1** : one that trails; *esp* : a creeping plant (as an ivy) **2** : a vehicle that is hauled by another (as a tractor) **3** : a vehicle equipped to serve wherever parked as a dwelling or place of business

trailing arbutus *n* : a trailing spring-flowering plant of the heath family with fragrant pink or white flowers; *also* : its flower

¹train \'trān\ *n* **1** : a part of a gown that trails behind the wearer **2** : RETINUE **3** : a moving file of persons, vehicles, or animals **4** : a connected series (a ∼ of thought) **5** : AFTERMATH **6** : a connected line of railroad cars usu. hauled by a locomotive **syn** succession, sequence, procession, chain

²train *vb* **1** : to cause to grow as desired (∼ a vine on a trellis) **2** : to form by instruction, discipline, or drill **3** : to make or become prepared (as by exercise) for a test of skill **4** : to aim or point at an object (∼ guns on a fort) **syn** discipline, school, educate, instruct — **train·er** *n*

train·ee \trā-ˈnē\ *n* : one who is being trained esp. for a job

train·ing *n* **1** : the act, process, or method of one who

trains 2 : the skill, knowledge, or experience gained by one who trains

train·man \-mən\ *n* : a member of a train crew

traipse \ˈtrāps\ *vb* **traipsed; traips·ing** : TRAMP, WALK

trait \ˈtrāt\ *n* **1** : a distinguishing quality (as of personality) : PECULIARITY **2** : an inherited charactersitic

trai·tor \ˈtrā-tər\ *n* [ME *traitre*, fr. OF, fr. L *traditor*, fr. *tradere* to hand over, deliver, betray, fr. *transacross* + *dare* to give] **1** : one who betrays another's trust or is false to an obligation **2** : one who commits treason — **trai·tor·ous** *adj*

tra·jec·to·ry \trə-ˈjek-tə-rē\ *n, pl* **-ries** : the curve that a body (as a planet in its orbit) describes in space

tram \ˈtram\ *n* **1** : a boxlike car running on a railway (**tram·way** \-ˌwā\) in a mine **2** *chiefly Brit* : STREETCAR **3** : an overhead cable car

¹tram·mel \ˈtra-məl\ *n* [ME *tramayle*, a kind of net, fr. MF *tremail*, fr. LL *tremaculum*, fr. L *tres* three + *macula* mesh, spot] : something impeding activity, progress, or freedom

²trammel *vb* **-meled** *or* **-melled; -mel·ing** *or* **-mel·ling** **1** : to catch and hold in or as if in a net **2** : HAMPER **syn** clog, fetter, shackle, hobble

¹tramp \ˈtramp, *1 & 3 are also* ˈträmp, ˈtromp\ *vb* **1** : to walk, tread, or step heavily **2** : to walk about or through; *also* : HIKE **3** : to tread on forcibly and repeatedly

²tramp \ˈtramp, *5 is also* ˈträmp, ˈtromp\ *n* **1** : a foot traveler **2** : a begging or thieving vagrant **3** : an immoral woman; *esp* : PROSTITUTE **4** : a walking trip : HIKE **5** : the succession of sounds made by the beating of feet on a road **6** : a ship that does not follow a regular course but takes cargo to any port

tram·ple \ˈtram-pəl\ *vb* **tram·pled; tram·pling** **1** : to tread heavily so as to bruise, crush, or injure **2** : to inflict injury or destruction **3** : to press down or crush by or as if by treading — **trample** *n* — **tram·pler** *n*

tram·po·line \ˌtram-pə-ˈlēn, ˈtram-pə-ˌlēn\ *n* [It *trampolino* springboard] : a resilient sheet or web (as of nylon) supported by springs in a metal frame and used as a springboard in tumbling — **tram·po·lin·ist** \-nist\ *n*

trance \ˈtrans\ *n* [ME, fr. MF *transe*, fr. *transir* to pass away, swoon, fr. L *transire* to pass, pass away, fr. *trans-* across + *ire* to go] **1** : a living state in which the vital bodily and mental activities slow down greatly **2** : a sleeplike state (as of deep hypnosis) **3** : a state of very deep absorption

tran·quil \ˈtraŋ-kwəl, ˈtran-\ *adj* : free from agitation or disturbance : QUIET **syn** serene, placid, peaceful — **tran·quil·li·ty** *or* **tran·quil·i·ty** \tran-ˈkwi-lə-tē, traŋ-\ *n* — **tran·quil·ly** *adv*

tran·quil·ize *also* **tran·quil·lize** \ˈtraŋ-kwə-ˌlīz, ˈtran-\ *vb* **-ized** *also* **-lized; -iz·ing** *also* **-liz·ing** : to make or become tranquil; *esp* : to relieve of mental tension and anxiety by means of drugs

tran·quil·iz·er *also* **tran·quil·liz·er** \-ˌlī-zər\ *n* : a drug used to relieve mental disturbance (as tension and anxiety)

trans *abbr* **1** transaction **2** transitive **3** translated; translation; translator **4** transmission **5** transportation **6** transverse

trans·act \tran-ˈzakt, -ˈsakt\ *vb* : CARRY OUT, PERFORM; *also* : CONDUCT

trans·ac·tion \-ˈzak-shən, -ˈsak-\ *n* **1** : something transacted; *esp* : a business deal **2** : an act or process of transacting **3** *pl* : the records of the proceedings of a society or organization

trans·at·lan·tic \ˌtrans-ət-ˈlan-tik, ˌtranz-\ *adj* : crossing or extending across or situated beyond the Atlantic Ocean

trans·ax·le \trans-ˈak-səl\ *n* : a unit combining the transmission and the front axle of a front-wheel-drive automobile

trans·ceiv·er \tran-ˈsē-vər\ *n* : a radio transmitter

receiver that uses many of the same components for both transmission and reception

tran·scend \tran-ˈsend\ *vb* **1** : to rise above the limits of **2** : SURPASS **syn** exceed, outdo, outshine, outstrip

tran·scen·dent \-ˈsen-dənt\ *adj* **1** : exceeding usual limits : SURPASSING **2** : transcending material existence **syn** superlative, supreme, peerless, incomparable

tran·scen·den·tal \ˌtran-ˌsen-ˈdent-ᵊl, -sən-\ *adj* **1** : TRANSCENDENT **2 2** : of, relating to, or characteristic of transcendentalism; *also* : ABSTRUSE

tran·scen·den·tal·ism \-ᵊl-ˌi-zəm\ *n* : a philosophy holding that ultimate reality is unknowable or asserting the primacy of the spiritual over the material and empirical — **tran·scen·den·tal·ist** \-ᵊl-ist\ *adj or n*

trans·con·ti·nen·tal \ˌtrans-ˌkänt-ᵊn-ˈent-ᵊl\ *adj* : extending or going across a continent

tran·scribe \trans-ˈkrīb\ *vb* **tran·scribed; tran·scrib·ing** **1** : to write a copy of **2** : to make a copy of (dictated or recorded matter) in longhand or on a typewriter **3** : to represent (speech sounds) by means of phonetic symbols; *also* : to make a musical transcription of

tran·script \ˈtran-ˌskript\ *n* **1** : a written, printed, or typed copy **2** : an official copy esp. of a student's educational record

tran·scrip·tion \tran-ˈskrip-shən\ *n* **1** : an act or process of transcribing **2** : COPY, TRANSCRIPT **3** : an arrangement of a musical composition for some instrument or voice other than the original

tran·scrip·tion·ist \-shə-nist\ *n* : one that transcribes; *esp* : a typist who transcribes medical reports

trans·der·mal \trans-ˈdər-məl, ˈtranz-\ *adj* : relating to, being, or supplying a medication in a form for absorption through the skin ⟨∼ nicotine patch⟩

trans·duc·er \trans-ˈdü-sər, tranz-, -ˈdyü-\ *n* : a device that is actuated by power from one system and supplies power usu. in another form to a second system

tran·sept \ˈtran-ˌsept\ *n* : the part of a cruciform church that crosses at right angles to the greatest length; *also* : either of the projecting ends

¹trans·fer \trans-ˈfər, ˈtrans-ˌfər\ *vb* **trans·ferred; trans·fer·ring** **1** : to pass or cause to pass from one person, place, or situation to another : TRANSPORT, TRANSMIT **2** : to make over the possession of : CONVEY **3** : to print or copy from one surface to another by contact **4** : to change from one vehicle or transportation line to another — **trans·fer·able** \trans-ˈfər-ə-bəl\ *adj* — **trans·fer·al** \-ᵊl\ *n*

²trans·fer \ˈtrans-ˌfər\ *n* **1** : conveyance of right, title, or interest in property from one person to another **2** : an act or process of transferring **3** : one that transfers or is transferred **4** : a ticket entitling a passenger to continue a trip on another route

trans·fer·ence \trans-ˈfər-əns\ *n* : an act, process, or instance of transferring

trans·fig·ure \trans-ˈfi-gyər\ *vb* **-ured; -ur·ing** **1** : to change the form or appearance of **2** : EXALT, GLORIFY — **trans·fig·u·ra·tion** \ˌtrans-fi-gyə-ˈrā-shən, -gə-\ *n*

trans·fix \trans-ˈfiks\ *vb* **1** : to pierce through with or as if with a pointed weapon **2** : to hold motionless by or as if by piercing

trans·form \trans-ˈfórm\ *vb* : to change in structure, appearance, or character **syn** transmute, transfigure, transmogrify — **trans·for·ma·tion** \ˌtrans-fər-ˈmāshən\ *n*

trans·form·er \trans-ˈfór-mər\ *n* : one that transforms; *esp* : a device for converting variations of current in one circuit into variations of voltage and current in another circuit

trans·fuse \trans-ˈfyüz\ *vb* **trans·fused; trans·fus·ing** **1** : to cause to pass from one to another **2** : to diffuse into or through **3** : to transfer (as blood) into a vein of a person or animal — **trans·fu·sion** \-ˈfyüzhən\ *n*

trans·gress \trans-ˈgres, tranz-\ *vb* [F *transgresser*, fr. L *transgressus*, pp. of *transgredi* to step beyond or across, fr. *trans*- across + *gradi* to step] **1** : to go beyond the limits set by ⟨∼ the divine law⟩ **2** : to go beyond : EXCEED **3** : SIN — **trans·gres·sion** \-¹gre-shən\ *n* — **trans·gres·sor** \-¹gre-sər\ *n*

¹**tran·sient** \¹tran-shənt; -sē-ənt, -shē-, -zē-\ *adj* **1** : not lasting long : SHORT-LIVED **2** : passing through a place with only a brief stay **syn** transitory, passing, momentary, fleeting — **tran·sient·ly** *adv*

²**transient** *n* : one that is transient; *esp* : a transient guest

tran·sis·tor \tran-¹zis-tər, -¹sis-\ *n* [*transfer* + r*esistor*; fr. its transferring an electrical signal across a resistor] **1** : a small electronic semiconductor device used in electronic equipment **2** : a radio having transistors

tran·sis·tor·ized \-tə-¸rīzd\ *adj* : having or using transistors

tran·sit \¹tran-sət, -zət\ *n* **1** : a passing through, across, or over : PASSAGE **2** : conveyance of persons or things from one place to another **3** : usu. local transportation esp. of people by public conveyance **4** : a surveyor's instrument for measuring angles

tran·si·tion \tran-¹si-shən, -¹zi-\ *n* : passage from one state, place, stage, or subject to another : CHANGE — **tran·si·tion·al** \-¹si-shə-nəl, ¹zi-\ *adj*

tran·si·tive \¹tran-sə-tiv, -zə-\ *adj* **1** : having or containing an object required to complete the meaning **2** : TRANSITIONAL — **tran·si·tive·ly** *adv* — **tran·si·tive·ness** *n* — **tran·si·tiv·i·ty** \¸tran-sə-¹ti-və-tē, -zə-\ *n*

tran·si·to·ry \¹tran-sə-¸tōr-ē, -zə-\ *adj* : of brief duration : SHORT-LIVED, TEMPORARY **syn** transient, passing, momentary, fleeting

transl *abbr* translated; translation

trans·late \trans-¹lāt, tranz-\ *vb* **trans·lat·ed; trans·lat·ing 1** : to change from one place, state, or form to another **2** : to convey to heaven without death **3** : to turn into one's own or another language — **trans·lat·able** *adj* — **trans·la·tion** \-¹lā-shən\ *n* — **trans·la·tor** \-¹lā-tər\ *n*

trans·lit·er·ate \trans-¹li-tə-¸rāt, tranz-\ *vb* **-at·ed; -at·ing** : to represent or spell in the characters of another alphabet — **trans·lit·er·a·tion** \¸trans-¸li-tə-¹rā-shən, ¸tranz-\ *n*

trans·lu·cent \trans-¹lüs-ᵊnt, tranz-\ *adj* : not transparent but clear enough to allow light to pass through — **trans·lu·cence** \-ᵊns\ *n* — **trans·lu·cen·cy** \-ᵊn-sē\ *n* — **trans·lu·cent·ly** *adv*

trans·mi·grate \-¹mī-¸grāt\ *vb* : to pass at death from one body or being to another — **trans·mi·gra·tion** \¸trans-mī-¹grā-shən, ¸tranz-\ *n* — **trans·mi·gra·to·ry** \trans-¹mī-grə-¸tōr-ē\ *adj*

trans·mis·sion \-¹mi-shən\ *n* **1** : an act or process of transmitting **2** : the passage of radio waves between transmitting stations and receiving stations **3** : the gears by which power is transmitted from the engine of an automobile to the axle that propels the vehicle **4** : something transmitted

trans·mit \-¹mit\ *vb* **trans·mit·ted; trans·mit·ting 1** : to transfer from one person or place to another : FORWARD **2** : to pass on by or as if by inheritance **3** : to cause or allow to spread abroad or to another ⟨∼ a disease⟩ **4** : to cause (as light, electricity, or force) to pass through space or a medium **5** : to send out (radio or television signals) **syn** convey, communicate, impart — **trans·mis·si·ble** \-¹mi-sə-bəl\ *adj* — **trans·mit·ta·ble** \-¹mi-tə-bəl\ *adj* — **trans·mit·tal** \-¹mit-ᵊl\ *n*

trans·mit·ter \-¹mi-tər\ *n* : one that transmits; *esp* : an apparatus for transmitting telegraph, radio, or television signals

trans·mog·ri·fy \trans-¹mä-grə-¸fī, tranz-\ *vb* **-fied; -fy·ing** : to change or alter often with grotesque or humorous effect — **trans·mog·ri·fi·ca·tion** \-¸mä-grə-fə-¹kā-shən\ *n*

trans·mute \-¹myüt\ *vb* **trans·mut·ed; trans·mut·ing** : to change or alter in form, appearance, or nature **syn** transform, convert, transfigure, metamorphose

— **trans·mu·ta·tion** \¸trans-myu̇-¹tā-shən, ¸tranz-\ *n*

trans·na·tion·al \-¹na-shə-nəl\ *adj* : extending beyond national boundaries

trans·oce·an·ic \¸trans-¸ō-shē-¹a-nik, ¸tranz-\ *adj* **1** : lying or dwelling beyond the ocean **2** : crossing or extending across the ocean

tran·som \¹tran-səm\ *n* **1** : a piece (as a crossbar in the frame of a window or door) that lies crosswise in a structure **2** : a window above an opening (as a door) built on and often hinged to a horizontal crossbar

tran·son·ic *also* **trans–son·ic** \trans-¹sä-nik\ *adj* : being or relating to speeds near that of sound in air or about 741 miles (1185 kilometers) per hour

trans·pa·cif·ic \¸trans-pə-¹si-fik\ *adj* : crossing, extending across, or situated beyond the Pacific Ocean

trans·par·ent \trans-¹par-ənt\ *adj* **1** : clear enough to be seen through : SHEER, DIAPHANOUS ⟨a ∼ fabric⟩ **3** : readily understood : CLEAR; *also* : easily detected ⟨a ∼ lie⟩ **syn** lucid, translucent, lucent — **trans·par·en·cy** \-ən-sē\ *n* — **trans·par·ent·ly** *adv*

tran·spire \trans-¹pīr\ *vb* **tran·spired; tran·spir·ing** [MF *transpirer*, fr. L *trans*- across + *spirare* to breathe] **1** : to pass or give off (as water vapor) through pores or a membrane **2** : to become known **3** : to take place : HAPPEN — **tran·spi·ra·tion** \¸trans-pə-¹rā-shən\ *n*

¹**trans·plant** \trans-¹plant\ *vb* **1** : to dig up and plant elsewhere **2** : to remove from one place and settle or introduce elsewhere : TRANSPORT **3** : to transfer (an organ or tissue) from one part or individual to another — **trans·plan·ta·tion** \¸trans-¸plan-¹tā-shən\ *n*

²**trans·plant** \¹trans-¸plant\ *n* **1** : a person or thing transplanted **2** : the act or process of transplanting

trans·po·lar \trans-¹pō-lər\ *adj* : going or extending across either of the polar regions

trans·pon·der \tran-¹spän-dər\ *n* [*trans*mitter + re*sponder*] : a radio or radar set that upon receiving a certain signal emits a signal of its own and that is used esp. for the identification and location of objects

¹**trans·port** \trans-¹pōrt\ *vb* **1** : to convey from one place to another : CARRY **2** : to carry away by strong emotion : ENRAPTURE **3** : to send to a penal colony overseas **syn** bear, ferry — **trans·por·ta·tion** \¸trans-pər-¹tā-shən\ *n* — **trans·port·er** *n*

²**trans·port** \¹trans-¸pōrt\ *n* **1** : an act of transporting **2** : strong or intensely pleasurable emotion ⟨∼s of joy⟩ **3** : a ship used in transporting troops or supplies; *also* : a vehicle (as a truck or plane) used to transport persons or goods

trans·pose \trans-¹pōz\ *vb* **trans·posed; trans·pos·ing 1** : to change the position or sequence of ⟨∼ the letters in a word⟩ **2** : to write or perform (a musical composition) in a different key — **trans·po·si·tion** \¸trans-pə-¹zi-shən\ *n*

trans·sex·u·al \(¸)trans-¹sek-shə-wəl\ *n* : a person with a psychological urge to belong to the opposite sex that may be carried to the point of undergoing surgery to modify the sex organs to mimic the opposite sex

trans·ship \tran-¹ship, trans-\ *vb* : to transfer for further transportation from one ship or conveyance to another — **trans·ship·ment** *n*

tran·sub·stan·ti·a·tion \¸tran-səb-¸stan-chē-¹ā-shən\ *n* : the change in the eucharistic elements from the substance of bread and wine to the substance of the body of Christ with only the appearances of bread and wine remaining

trans·verse \trans-¹vərs, tranz-\ *adj* : lying across : set crosswise — **transverse** \¹trans-¸vərs, ¹tranz-\ *n* — **trans·verse·ly** *adv*

trans·ves·tite \trans-¹ves-¸tīt, tranz-\ *n* : a person and esp. a male who adopts the dress and often the behavior of the opposite sex — **transvestite** *adj* — **trans·ves·tism** \-¸ti-zəm\ *n*

¹**trap** \¹trap\ *n* **1** : a device for catching animals **2** : something by which one is caught unawares; *also* : a

situation from which escape is difficult or impossible **3** : a machine for throwing clay pigeons into the air; *also* : SAND TRAP **4** : a light one-horse carriage on springs **5** : a device to allow some one thing to pass through while keeping other things out ⟨a ∼ in a drainpipe⟩ **6** *pl* : a group of percussion instruments (as in a dance orchestra)

²**trap** *vb* **trapped; trap•ping 1** : to catch in or as if in a trap; *also* : CONFINE **2** : to provide or set (a place) with traps **3** : to set traps for animals esp. as a business **syn** snare, entrap, ensnare, bag, lure, decoy — **trap•per** *n*

trap•door \'trap-ˌdōr\ *n* : a lifting or sliding door covering an opening in a floor or roof

tra•peze \tra-'pēz\ *n* : a gymnastic apparatus consisting of a horizontal bar suspended by two parallel ropes

trap•e•zoid \'tra-pə-ˌzȯid\ *n* [NL *trapezoïdes*, fr. Gk *trapezoeidēs* trapezoidal, fr. *trapeza* table, fr. *tra-* four + *peza* foot] : a plane 4-sided figure with two and only two sides parallel — **trap•e•zoi•dal** \ˌtra-pə-'zȯid-ᵊl\ *adj*

trap•pings \'tra-piŋz\ *n pl* **1** : CAPARISON 1 **2** : outward decoration or dress; *also* : outward sign ⟨∼ of success⟩

traps \'traps\ *n pl* : personal belongings : LUGGAGE

trap•shoot•ing \'trap-ˌshü-tiŋ\ *n* : shooting at clay pigeons sprung from a trap into the air away from the shooter

¹**trash** \'trash\ *n* **1** : something of little worth : RUBBISH **2** : a worthless person; *also* : such persons as a group : RIFFRAFF — **trashy** *adj*

²**trash** *vb* **1** : VANDALIZE, DESTROY **2** : ATTACK **3** : SPOIL, RUIN **4** : to criticize or disparage harshly

trau•ma \'traú-mə, 'trȯ-\ *n, pl* **traumas** *also* **trau•ma•ta** \-mə-tə\ [Gk] : a bodily or mental injury usu. caused by an external agent; *also* : a cause of trauma — **trau•mat•ic** \trə-'ma-tik, trȯ-, traú-\ *adj*

¹**tra•vail** \trə-'vāl, 'tra-ˌvāl\ *n* **1** : painful work or exertion : TOIL **2** : AGONY, TORMENT **3** : CHILDBIRTH, LABOR

²**travail** *vb* : to labor hard : TOIL

¹**trav•el** \'tra-vəl\ *vb* **-eled** *or* **-elled; -el•ing** *or* **-el•ling** [ME *travailen* to labor, journey, fr. OF *travaillier* to torture, labor, fr. (assumed) VL *trepaliare* to torture, fr. LL *trepalium* instrument of torture] **1** : to go on or as if on a trip or tour : JOURNEY **2** : to move as if by traveling ⟨news ∼s fast⟩ **3** : ASSOCIATE **4** : to go from place to place as a sales representative **5** : to move from point to point ⟨light waves ∼ very fast⟩ **6** : to journey over or through ⟨∼ing the highways⟩ — **trav•el•er** *or* **trav•el•ler** *n*

²**travel** *n* **1** : the act of traveling : PASSAGE **2** : JOURNEY, TRIP — often used in pl. **3** : the number traveling : TRAFFIC **4** : the motion of a piece of machinery and esp. when to and fro

traveler's check *n* : a check paid for in advance that is signed when bought and signed again when cashed

traveling bag *n* : SUITCASE

trav•el•ogue *or* **trav•el•og** \'tra-və-ˌlȯg, -ˌläg\ *n* : a usu. illustrated lecture on travel

¹**tra•verse** \'tra-vərs\ *n* : something that crosses or lies across

²**tra•verse** \trə-'vərs, tra-'vərs *or* 'tra-vərs\ *vb* **tra•versed; tra•vers•ing 1** : to go or travel across or over **2** : to move or pass along or through **3** : to extend over **4** : SWIVEL

³**tra•verse** \'tra-ˌvərs\ *adj* : TRANSVERSE

trav•er•tine \'tra-vər-ˌtēn, -tən\ *n* : a crystalline mineral formed by deposition from spring waters

¹**trav•es•ty** \'tra-və-stē\ *vb* **-tied; -ty•ing** : to make a travesty of

²**travesty** *n, pl* **-ties** [obs. E *travesty* disguised, parodied, fr. F *travesti*, pp. of *travestir* to disguise, fr. It *travestire*, fr. *tra-* across (fr. L *trans-*) + *vestire* to

dress] : an imitation that makes crude fun of something; *also* : an inferior imitation

¹**trawl** \'trȯl\ *vb* : to fish or catch with a trawl — **trawl•er** *n*

²**trawl** *n* **1** : a large conical net dragged along the sea bottom in fishing **2** : a long heavy fishing line equipped with many hooks in series

tray \'trā\ *n* : an open receptacle with flat bottom and low rim for holding, carrying, or exhibiting articles

treach•er•ous \'tre-chə-rəs\ *adj* **1** : characterized by treachery **2** : UNTRUSTWORTHY, UNRELIABLE **3** : providing insecure footing or support **syn** traitorous, faithless, false, disloyal — **treach•er•ous•ly** *adv*

treach•ery \'tre-chə-rē\ *n, pl* **-er•ies** : violation of allegiance or trust

trea•cle \'trē-kəl\ *n* [ME *triacle* a medicinal compound, fr. MF, fr. L *theriaca*, fr. Gk *thēriakē* antidote against a poisonous bite, fr. *thērion* wild animal] *chiefly Brit* : MOLASSES — **treacly** \-k(ə-)lē\ *adj*

¹**tread** \'tred\ *vb* **trod** \'träd\; **trod•den** \'träd-ᵊn\ *or* **trod; tread•ing 1** : to step or walk on or over **2** : to move on foot : WALK; *also* : DANCE **3** : to beat or press with the feet

²**tread** *n* **1** : a mark made by or as if by treading **2** : the manner or sound of stepping **3** : the part of a wheel that makes contact with a road **4** : the horizontal part of a step

trea•dle \'tred-ᵊl\ *n* : a lever device pressed by the foot to drive a machine — **treadle** *vb*

tread•mill \'tred-ˌmil\ *n* **1** : a mill worked by persons who tread on steps around the edge of a wheel or by animals that walk on an endless belt **2** : a device with an endless belt on which a person walks or runs in place **3** : a wearisome routine

treas *abbr* treasurer; treasury

trea•son \'trēz-ᵊn\ *n* : the offense of attempting to overthrow the government of one's country or of assisting its enemies in war — **trea•son•able** \-ᵊn-ə-bəl\ *adj* — **trea•son•ous** \-ᵊn-əs\ *adj*

¹**trea•sure** \'tre-zhər, 'trā-\ *n* **1** : wealth stored up or held in reserve **2** : something of great value

²**treasure** *vb* **trea•sured; trea•sur•ing 1** : HOARD **2** : to keep as precious : CHERISH **syn** prize, value, appreciate, esteem

trea•sur•er *n* : an officer of a club, business, or government who has charge of money taken in and paid out

treasure trove \-ˌtrōv\ *n* **1** : treasure of unknown ownership found buried or hidden **2** : a valuable discovery

trea•sury \'tre-zhə-rē, 'trā-\ *n, pl* **-sur•ies 1** : a place in which stores of wealth are kept **2** : the place where collected funds are stored and paid out **3** *cap* : a governmental department in charge of finances

¹**treat** \'trēt\ *vb* **1** : NEGOTIATE **2** : to deal with esp. in writing; *also* : HANDLE **3** : to pay for the food or entertainment of **4** : to behave or act toward ⟨∼ them well⟩ **5** : to regard in a specified manner ⟨∼ as inferiors⟩ **6** : to give medical or surgical care to **7** : to subject to some action ⟨∼ soil with lime⟩

²**treat** *n* **1** : an entertainment given free to those invited **2** : a source of joy or amusement

trea•tise \'trē-təs\ *n* : a systematic written exposition or argument

treat•ment \'trēt-mənt\ *n* : the act or manner or an instance of treating someone or something; *also* : a substance or method used in treating

trea•ty \'trē-tē\ *n, pl* **treaties** : an agreement made by negotiation or diplomacy esp. between two or more states or governments

¹**tre•ble** \'tre-bəl\ *n* **1** : the highest of the four voice parts in vocal music : SOPRANO **2** : a high-pitched or shrill voice or sound **3** : the upper half of the musical pitch range

²**treble** *adj* **1** : triple in number or amount **2** : relating

to or having the range of a musical treble **3** : high=
pitched : SHRILL — **tre·bly** adv

³treble vb **tre·bled; tre·bling** : to make or become three
times the size, amount, or number

¹tree \'trē\ n **1** : a woody perennial plant usu. with a
single main stem and a head of branches and leaves
at the top **2** : a piece of wood adapted to a particular
use ⟨a shoe ∼⟩ **3** : something resembling a tree ⟨a genealogical ∼⟩ — **tree·less** adj

²tree vb **treed; tree·ing** : to drive to or up a tree ⟨∼ a
raccoon⟩

tree farm n : an area of forest land managed to ensure
continuous commercial production

tree line n : TIMBERLINE

tree of heaven : a Chinese ailanthus that is widely
grown as a shade and ornamental tree

tree surgery n : operative treatment of diseased trees
esp. for control of decay — **tree surgeon** n

tre·foil \'trē-ˌfoil, 'tre-\ n **1** : an herb (as clover) with
leaves with three leaflets **2** : a decorative design with
three leaflike parts

¹trek \'trek\ vb **trekked; trek·king 1** chiefly southern
Africa : to travel or migrate by ox wagon **2** : to make
one's way arduously

²trek n **1** chiefly southern Africa : a migration esp. of
settlers by ox wagon **2** : a slow or difficult journey

¹trel·lis \'tre-ləs\ n [ME trelis, fr. MF treliz fabric of
coarse weave, trellis, fr. (assumed) VL trilicius woven with triple thread, fr. L tres three + licium
thread] : a frame of latticework used esp. for climbing
plants

²trellis vb : to provide with a trellis; esp : to train (as a
vine) on a trellis

trem·a·tode \'tre-mə-ˌtōd\ n : any of a class of parasitic worms

¹trem·ble \'trem-bəl\ vb **trem·bled; trem·bling 1** : to
shake involuntarily (as with fear or cold) : SHIVER **2**
: to move, sound, pass, or come to pass as if shaken
or tremulous **3** : to be affected with fear or doubt

²tremble n : a spell of shaking or quivering

tre·men·dous \tri-'men-dəs\ adj **1** : causing dread,
awe, or terror : TERRIFYING **2** : unusually large, powerful, great, or excellent syn stupendous, monumental, monstrous — **tre·men·dous·ly** adv

trem·o·lo \'tre-mə-ˌlō\ n, pl **-los** [It] : a rapid fluttering
of a tone or alternating tones

trem·or \'tre-mər\ n **1** : a trembling or shaking esp.
from weakness, emotional stress, or disease **2** : a
quivering motion of the earth (as during an
earthquake)

trem·u·lous \'trem-yə-ləs\ adj **1** : marked by trembling
or tremors : QUIVERING **2** : TIMOROUS, TIMID — **trem·
u·lous·ly** adv

¹trench \'trench\ n [ME trenche track cut through a
wood, fr. MF, act of cutting, fr. trenchier to cut,
prob. fr. (assumed) VL trinicare to cut in three, fr. L
trini three each] **1** : a long narrow cut in the ground
: DITCH; esp : a ditch protected by banks of earth and
used to shelter soldiers **2** pl : a place or situation likened to trench warfare **3** : a long narrow steep=
sided depression in the ocean floor

²trench vb **1** : to cut or dig trenches in **2** : to protect
(troops) with trenches **3** : to come close : VERGE

tren·chant \'tren-chənt\ adj **1** : vigorously effective;
also : CAUSTIC **2** : sharply perceptive : KEEN **3**
: CLEAR-CUT, DISTINCT

tren·cher \'tren-chər\ n : a wooden platter for serving
food

tren·cher·man \'tren-chər-mən\ n : a hearty eater

trench foot n : a painful foot disorder resembling frostbite and resulting from exposure to cold and wet

trench mouth n : a progressive painful disease of the
mouth and adjacent parts that is marked by ulceration and associated with a great increase in certain
bacteria normally present in the mouth

¹trend \'trend\ vb **1** : to have or take a general direction
: TEND **2** : to show a tendency : INCLINE

²trend n **1** : a general direction taken (as by a stream or
mountain range) **2** : a prevailing tendency : DRIFT **3** : a
current style or preference : VOGUE

trendy \'tren-dē\ adj **trend·i·er; -est** : very fashionable; also : marked by superficial or faddish appeal or
taste

trep·i·da·tion \ˌtre-pə-'dā-shən\ n : nervous agitation
: APPREHENSION syn horror, terror, panic, consternation, dread, fright, dismay

¹tres·pass \'tres-pəs, -ˌpas\ n **1** : SIN, OFFENSE **2** : unlawful entry on someone else's land syn transgres-
sion, violation, infraction

²trespass vb **1** : to commit an offense : ERR, SIN **2** : IN-
TRUDE, ENCROACH; esp : to enter unlawfully upon the
land of another — **tres·pass·er** n

tress \'tres\ n : a long lock of hair — usu. used in pl.

tres·tle also **tres·sel** \'tre-səl\ n **1** : a supporting framework consisting usu. of a horizontal piece with
spreading legs at each end **2** : a braced framework of
timbers, piles, or steel for carrying a road or railroad
over a depression

trey \'trā\ n, pl **treys** : a card or the side of a die with
three spots

tri·ad \'trī-ˌad, -əd\ n : a union or group of three usu.
closely related persons or things

tri·age \trē-'äzh, 'trē-ˌäzh\ n [F, sorting] : the sorting
of and allocation of treatment to patients and esp.
battle or disaster victims according to a system of pri-
orities designed to maximize the number of survivors

tri·al \'trī-əl\ n **1** : the action or process of trying or
putting to the proof : TEST **2** : the hearing and judgment of a matter in issue before a competent tribunal
3 : a source of vexation or annoyance **4** : an experiment to test quality, value, or usefulness **5** : EFFORT,
ATTEMPT syn cross, ordeal, tribulation, affliction —
trial adj

tri·an·gle \'trī-ˌaŋ-gəl\ n **1** : a plane figure that has
three sides and three angles : a polygon having three
sides **2** : something shaped like a triangle — **tri·an·
gu·lar** \trī-'aŋ-gyə-lər\ adj — **tri·an·gu·lar·ly** adv

triangle 1: *1* equilateral, *2* isosceles, *3* right triangle

tri·an·gu·la·tion \(ˌ)trī-ˌaŋ-gyə-'lā-shən\ n : a method
using trigonometry to find the location of a point using bearings from two fixed points a known distance
apart — **tri·an·gu·late** \trī-'aŋ-gyə-ˌlāt\ vb

Tri·as·sic \trī-'a-sik\ adj : of, relating to, or being the
earliest period of the Mesozoic era marked by the
first appearance of the dinosaurs — **Triassic** n

trib abbr tributary

tribe \'trīb\ n **1** : a social group comprising numerous
families, clans, or generations **2** : a group of persons
having a common character, occupation, or interest **3**
: a group of related plants or animals ⟨the cat ∼⟩ —
trib·al \'trī-bəl\ adj

tribes·man \'trībz-mən\ n : a member of a tribe

trib·u·la·tion \ˌtri-byə-'lā-shən\ n [ME tribulacion, fr.
OF, fr. L tribulatio, fr. tribulare to press, oppress, fr.
tribulum drag used in threshing] : distress or suffering
resulting from oppression or persecution; also : a trying experience syn trial, affliction, cross, ordeal

tri·bu·nal \trī-'byün-əl, tri-\ n **1** : the seat of a judge **2**
: a court of justice **3** : something that decides or determines ⟨the ∼ of public opinion⟩

tri·bune \'tri-ˌbyün, tri-'byün\ n **1** : an official in ancient Rome with the function of protecting the inter-

ests of plebeian citizens from the patricians **2** : a defender of the people

¹trib·u·tary \'tri-byə-ˌter-ē\ *adj* **1** : paying tribute : SUBJECT **2** : flowing into a larger stream or a lake **syn** subordinate, secondary, dependent

²tributary *n, pl* **-tar·ies** **1** : a ruler or state that pays tribute **2** : a tributary stream

trib·ute \'tri-(ˌ)byüt, -byət\ *n* **1** : a payment by one ruler or nation to another as an act of submission or price of protection **2** : a usu. excessive tax, rental, or levy exacted by a sovereign or superior **3** : a gift or service showing respect, gratitude, or affection; *also* : PRAISE **syn** eulogy, citation, encomium, panegyric

trice \'trīs\ *n* : INSTANT, MOMENT

tri·ceps \'trī-ˌseps\ *n, pl* **triceps** : a large muscle along the back of the upper arm that is attached at its upper end by three main parts and acts to extend the forearm at the elbow joint

tri·cer·a·tops \(ˌ)trī-'ser-ə-ˌtäps\ *n, pl* **-tops** *also* **-topses** [NL, fr. Gk *tri-* three + *kerat-, keras* horn + *ōps* face] : any of a genus of large plant-eating Cretaceous dinosaurs with three horns, a bony crest on the neck, and hoofed toes

tri·chi·na \tri-'kī-nə\ *n, pl* **-nae** \-(ˌ)nē\ *also* **-nas** : a small slender nematode worm that in the larval state is parasitic in the voluntary muscles of flesh‑eating mammals (as the hog and humans)

trich·i·no·sis \ˌtri-kə-'nō-səs\ *n* : infestation with or disease caused by trichinae and marked esp. by pain, fever, and swelling

¹trick \'trik\ *n* **1** : a crafty procedure meant to deceive **2** : a mischievous action : PRANK **3** : a childish action **4** : a deceptive or ingenious feat designed to puzzle or amuse **5** : PECULIARITY, MANNERISM **6** : a quick or artful way of getting a result : KNACK **7** : the cards played in one round of a card game **8** : a tour of duty : SHIFT **syn** ruse, maneuver, artifice, wile, feint

²trick *vb* **1** : to deceive by cunning or artifice : CHEAT **2** : to dress ornately

trick·ery \'tri-kə-rē\ *n* : deception by tricks and stratagems

trick·le \'tri-kəl\ *vb* **trick·led; trick·ling** **1** : to run or fall in drops **2** : to flow in a thin gentle stream — **trickle** *n*

trick·ster \'trik-stər\ *n* : one who tricks or cheats

tricky \'tri-kē\ *adj* **trick·i·er; -est** **1** : inclined to trickery **2** : requiring skill or caution (a ~ situation to handle) **3** : UNRELIABLE (a ~ lock)

tri·col·or \'trī-ˌkə-lər\ *n* : a flag of three colors (the French ~)

tri·cy·cle \'trī-(ˌ)si-kəl\ *n* : a 3-wheeled vehicle usu. propelled by pedals

tri·dent \'trīd-ᵊnt\ *n* [L *trident-, tridens,* fr. *tri-* three + *dent-, dens* tooth] : a 3-pronged spear

tried \'trīd\ *adj* **1** : found trustworthy through testing **2** : subjected to trials

tri·en·ni·al \trī-'e-nē-əl\ *adj* **1** : occurring or being done every three years **2** : lasting for three years — **triennial** *n*

¹tri·fle \'trī-fəl\ *n* : something of little value or importance

²trifle *vb* **tri·fled; tri·fling** **1** : to talk in a jesting or mocking manner **2** : to treat someone or something as unimportant **3** : DALLY, FLIRT **4** : to handle idly : TOY — **tri·fler** *n*

tri·fling \'trī-fliŋ\ *adj* **1** : FRIVOLOUS **2** : TRIVIAL, INSIGNIFICANT **syn** petty, paltry, measly, inconsequential

tri·fo·cals \trī-'fō-kəlz\ *n pl* : eyeglasses with lenses having one part for close focus, one for intermediate focus, and one for distant focus

tri·fo·li·ate \trī-'fō-lē-ət\ *adj* : having three leaves or leaflets

¹trig \'trig\ *adj* : stylishly trim : SMART

²trig *n* : TRIGONOMETRY

¹trig·ger \'tri-gər\ *n* [alter. of earlier *tricker,* fr. D *trekker,* fr. MD *trecker* one that pulls, fr. *trecken* to pull]

: a movable lever that activates a device when it is squeezed; *esp* : the part of a firearm lock moved by the finger to fire a gun — **trigger** *adj* — **trig·gered** *adj*

²trigger *vb* **1** : to fire by pulling a trigger **2** : to initiate, actuate, or set off as if by a trigger

tri·glyc·er·ide *n* : any of a group of fats and oils that are derived from glycerol and fatty acids and are widespread in animal tissue

trig·o·nom·e·try \ˌtri-gə-'nä-mə-trē\ *n* : the branch of mathematics dealing with the properties of triangles and esp. with finding unknown angles or sides given the size or length of some angles or sides — **trig·o·no·met·ric** \-nə-'me-trik\ *also* **trig·o·no·met·ri·cal** \-tri-kəl\ *adj*

trike \'trīk\ *n* : TRICYCLE

¹trill \'tril\ *n* **1** : the alternation of two musical tones a scale degree apart **2** : WARBLE **3** : the rapid vibration of one speech organ against another (as of the tip of the tongue against the teeth)

²trill *vb* : to utter as or with a trill

tril·lion \'tril-yən\ *n* **1** : a thousand billions **2** *Brit* : a million billions — **trillion** *adj* — **tril·lionth** \-yənth\ *adj or n*

tril·li·um \'tri-lē-əm\ *n* : any of a genus of herbs of the lily family with an erect stem bearing a whorl of three leaves and a large solitary usu. spring-blooming flower with three petals

tril·o·gy \'tri-lə-jē\ *n, pl* **-gies** : a series of three dramas or literary or musical compositions that are closely related and develop one theme

¹trim \'trim\ *vb* **trimmed; trim·ming** [OE *trymian, trymman* to strengthen, arrange, fr. *trum* strong, firm] **1** : to put ornaments on : ADORN **2** : to defeat esp. resoundingly **3** : to make trim, neat, regular, or less bulky by or as if by cutting (~ a beard) (~ a budget) **4** : to cause (a boat) to assume a desired position in the water by arrangement of the load; *also* : to adjust (as a submarine or airplane) esp. for horizontal motion **5** : to adjust (a sail) to a desired position **6** : to change one's views for safety or expediency — **trim·ly** *adv* — **trim·mer** *n* — **trim·ness** *n*

²trim *adj* **trim·mer; trim·mest** : showing neatness, good order, or compactness (a ~ figure) **syn** tidy, trig, smart, spruce, shipshape

³trim *n* **1** : good condition : FITNESS **2** : material used for ornament or trimming; *esp* : the woodwork in the finish of a house esp. around doors and windows **3** : the position of a ship or boat esp. with reference to the horizontal; *also* : the relation between the plane of a sail and the direction of a ship **4** : the position of an airplane at which it will continue in level flight with no adjustments to the controls **5** : something that is trimmed off

tri·ma·ran \'trī-mə-ˌran, ˌtrī-mə-'ran\ *n* : a sailboat with three hulls

tri·mes·ter \trī-'mes-tər, 'trī-ˌmes-tər\ *n* **1** : a period of three or about three months (as in pregnancy) **2** : one of three terms into which an academic year is sometimes divided

trim·e·ter \'tri-mə-tər\ *n* : a line of verse consisting of three metrical feet

trim·ming \'tri-miŋ\ *n* **1** : DEFEAT **2** : the action of one that trims **3** : something that trims, ornaments, or completes

tri·month·ly \trī-'mənth-lē\ *adj* : occurring every three months

trine \'trīn\ *adj* : THREEFOLD, TRIPLE

Trin·i·da·di·an \ˌtri-nə-'dā-dē-ən, -'da-\ *n* : a native or inhabitant of the island of Trinidad — **Trinidadian** *adj*

Trin·i·tar·i·an \ˌtri-nə-'ter-ē-ən\ *n* : a believer in the doctrine of the Trinity — **Trin·i·tar·i·an·ism** \-ē-ə-ˌni-zəm\ *n*

Trin·i·ty \'tri-nə-tē\ *n* **1** : the unity of Father, Son, and

Holy Spirit as three persons in one Godhead **2** *not cap* : TRIAD

trin·ket \'triŋ-kət\ *n* **1** : a small ornament (as a jewel or ring) **2** : TRIFLE

trio \'trē-ō\ *n, pl* **tri·os** **1** : a musical composition for three voices or three instruments **2** : the performers of a trio **3** : a group or set of three

¹trip \'trip\ *vb* **tripped; trip·ping** **1** : to move with light quick steps **2** : to catch the foot against something so as to stumble or cause to stumble **3** : to make a mistake : SLIP; *also* : to detect in a misstep : EXPOSE **4** : to release (as a spring or switch) by moving a catch; *also* : ACTIVATE **5** : to get high on a drug and esp. a hallucinatory drug

²trip *n* **1** : JOURNEY, VOYAGE **2** : a quick light step **3** : a false step : STUMBLE; *also* : ERROR **4** : the action of tripping mechanically; *also* : a device for tripping **5** : an intense drug-induced hallucinatory experience **6** : absorption in an attitude or state of mind ⟨an ego ∼⟩

tri·par·tite \trī-'pär-ˌtīt\ *adj* **1** : divided into three parts **2** : having three corresponding parts or copies **3** : made between three parties ⟨a ∼ treaty⟩

tripe \'trīp\ *n* **1** : stomach tissue of a ruminant and esp. an ox used as food **2** : something poor, worthless, or offensive : TRASH

¹tri·ple \'tri-pəl\ *vb* **tri·pled; tri·pling** **1** : to make or become three times as great or as many **2** : to hit a triple

²triple *n* **1** : a triple quantity **2** : a group of three **3** : a hit in baseball that lets the batter reach third base

³triple *adj* **1** : being three times as great or as many **2** : having three units or members **3** : repeated three times

triple bond *n* : a chemical bond in which three pairs of electrons are shared by two atoms in a molecule

triple point *n* : the condition of temperature and pressure under which the gaseous, liquid, and solid forms of a substance can exist in equilibrium

trip·let \'tri-plət\ *n* **1** : a unit of three lines of verse **2** : a group of three of a kind **3** : one of three offspring born at one birth

tri·plex \'tri-ˌpleks, 'trī-\ *adj* : THREEFOLD, TRIPLE

¹trip·li·cate \'tri-pli-kət\ *adj* : made in three identical copies

²trip·li·cate \-plə-ˌkāt\ *vb* **-cat·ed; -cat·ing** **1** : TRIPLE **2** : to provide three copies of ⟨∼ a document⟩

³trip·li·cate \-pli-kət\ *n* : three copies all alike — used with *in* ⟨typed in ∼⟩

tri·ply \'tri-plē, 'tri-pə-lē\ *adv* : in a triple degree, amount, or manner

tri·pod \'trī-ˌpäd\ *n* : something (as a caldron, stool, or camera stand) that rests on three legs — **tripod** *or* **tri·po·dal** \'trī-pəd-ᵊl, 'trī-ˌpäd-\ *adj*

trip·tych \'trip-tik\ *n* : a picture or carving in three panels side by side

tri·reme \'trī-ˌrēm\ *n* : an ancient galley having three banks of oars

tri·sect \'trī-ˌsekt, trī-'sekt\ *vb* : to divide into three usu. equal parts — **tri·sec·tion** \'trī-ˌsek-shən\ *n*

trite \'trīt\ *adj* **trit·er; trit·est** [L *tritus*, fr. pp. of *terere* to rub, wear away] : used so commonly that the novelty is worn off : STALE **syn** hackneyed, stereotyped, commonplace, clichéd

tri·ti·um \'tri-tē-əm, 'tri-shē-\ *n* : a radioactive form of hydrogen with atoms of three times the mass of ordinary hydrogen atoms

tri·ton \'trīt-ᵊn\ *n* : any of various large marine gastropod mollusks with a heavy elongated conical shell; *also* : the shell of a triton

trit·u·rate \'tri-chə-ˌrāt\ *vb* **-rat·ed; -rat·ing** : to rub or grind to a fine powder

¹tri·umph \'trī-əmf\ *n, pl* **tri·umphs** **1** : the joy or exultation of victory or success **2** : VICTORY, CONQUEST — **tri·um·phal** \trī-'əm-fəl\ *adj*

²triumph *vb* **1** : to obtain victory : PREVAIL **2** : to celebrate victory or success exultantly — **tri·um·phant** \trī-'əm-fənt\ *adj* — **tri·um·phant·ly** *adv*

tri·um·vir \trī-'əm-vər\ *n, pl* **-virs** *also* **-vi·ri** \-və-ˌrī\ : a member of a triumvirate

tri·um·vi·rate \-və-rət\ *n* : a ruling body of three persons

tri·une \'trī-ˌün, -ˌyün\ *adj, often cap* : being three in one ⟨the ∼ God⟩

triv·et \'tri-vət\ *n* **1** : a 3-legged stand : TRIPOD **2** : a usu. metal stand with short feet for use under a hot dish

triv·ia \'tri-vē-ə\ *n sing or pl* : unimportant matters : TRIFLES

triv·i·al \'tri-vē-əl\ *adj* [L *trivialis* found everywhere, commonplace, fr. *trivium* crossroads, fr. *tri-* three + *via* way] : of little importance — **triv·i·al·i·ty** \ˌtri-vē-'a-lə-tē\ *n*

triv·i·um \'tri-vē-əm\ *n, pl* **triv·ia** \-vē-ə\ : the three liberal arts of grammar, rhetoric, and logic in a medieval university

tri·week·ly \trī-'wē-klē\ *adj* **1** : occurring or appearing three times a week **2** : occurring or appearing every three weeks — **triweekly** *adv*

tro·che \'trō-kē\ *n* : a medicinal lozenge

tro·chee \'trō-(ˌ)kē\ *n* : a metrical foot of one accented syllable followed by one unaccented syllable — **tro·cha·ic** \trō-'kā-ik\ *adj*

trod *past and past part of* TREAD

trod·den *past part of* TREAD

troi·ka \'troi-kə\ *n* [Russ *troĭka*, fr. *troe* three] : a group of three; *esp* : an administrative or ruling body of three

¹troll \'trōl\ *vb* **1** : to sing the parts of (a song) in succession **2** : to fish by trailing a lure or baited hook from a moving boat **3** : to sing or play jovially

²troll *n* : a lure used in trolling; *also* : the line with its lure

³troll *n* : a dwarf or giant in Scandinavian folklore inhabiting caves or hills

trol·ley *also* **trol·ly** \'trä-lē\ *n, pl* **trolleys** *also* **trollies** **1** : a device (as a grooved wheel on the end of a pole) to carry current from a wire to an electrically driven vehicle **2** : a streetcar powered electrically through a trolley **3** : a wheeled carriage running on an overhead rail or track

trol·ley·bus \'trä-lē-ˌbəs\ *n* : a bus powered electrically through a trolley

trolley car *n* : TROLLEY 2

trol·lop \'trä-ləp\ *n* : a disreputable woman; *esp* : one who engages in sex promiscuously

trom·bone \träm-'bōn, 'träm-ˌbōn\ *n* [It, lit., big trumpet, fr. *tromba* trumpet] : a brass wind instrument that consists of a long metal tube with two turns and a flaring end and that usu. has a movable slide to vary the pitch — **trom·bon·ist** \-'bō-nist, -ˌbō-\ *n*

trombone

tromp \'trämp, 'tromp\ *vb* **1** : TRAMP, MARCH **2** : to stamp with the foot **3** : DEFEAT

¹troop \'trüp\ *n* **1** : a cavalry unit corresponding to an infantry company **2** *pl* : armed forces : SOLDIERS **3** : a collection of people or things **4** : a unit of Girl Scouts or Boy Scouts under an adult leader

²troop *vb* : to move or gather in crowds

troop·er \'trü-pər\ *n* **1** : an enlisted cavalryman; *also* : a cavalry horse **2** : a mounted or a state police officer

troop·ship \'trüp-ˌship\ *n* : a ship for carrying troops

trope \'trōp\ *n* : a word or expression used in a figurative sense

tro·phy \'trō-fē\ *n, pl* **trophies** : something gained or given in conquest or victory esp. when preserved or mounted as a memorial

trop·ic \'trä-pik\ *n* [ME *tropik*, fr. L *tropicus* of the solstice, fr. Gk *tropikos*, fr. *tropē* turn] **1** : either of the two parallels of latitude approximately 23½ degrees north (**tropic of Can·cer** \-'kan-sər\) or south (**tropic of Cap·ri·corn** \-'ka-prə-ˌkórn\) of the equator where the sun is directly overhead when it reaches its most northerly or southerly point in the sky **2** *pl, often cap* : the region lying between the tropics — **trop·i·cal** \-pi-kəl\ *or* **tropic** *adj*

tro·pism \'trō-ˌpi-zəm\ *n* : an automatic movement by an organism in response to a source of stimulation; *also* : a reflex reaction involving this

tro·po·sphere \'trō-pə-ˌsfir, 'trä-\ *n* : the part of the atmosphere between the earth's surface and the stratosphere in which most weather changes occur — **tro·po·spher·ic** \ˌtrō-pə-'sfir-ik, ˌträ-, -'sfer-\ *adj*

¹trot \'trät\ *n* **1** : a moderately fast gait of a 4-footed animal (as a horse) in which the legs move in diagonal pairs **2** : a human jogging gait between a walk and a run

²trot *vb* **trot·ted; trot·ting 1** : to ride, drive, or go at a trot **2** : to proceed briskly : HURRY — **trot·ter** *n*

troth \'träth, 'trōth, 'tróth\ *n* **1** : pledged faithfulness **2** : one's pledged word; *also* : BETROTHAL

trou·ba·dour \'trü-bə-ˌdōr\ *n* [F, fr. OProv *trobador,* fr. *trobar* to compose] : any of a class of poet-musicians flourishing esp. in southern France and northern Italy during the 11th, 12th, and 13th centuries

¹trou·ble \'trə-bəl\ *vb* **trou·bled; trou·bling 1** : to agitate mentally or spiritually : DISTURB, WORRY **2** : to produce physical disorder in : AFFLICT **3** : to put to inconvenience **4** : RUFFLE ⟨∼ the waters⟩ **5** : to make an effort **syn** distress, ail, upset — **trou·ble·some** *adj* — **trou·ble·some·ly** *adv* — **trou·blous** \-bə-ləs\ *adj*

²trouble *n* **1** : the quality or state of being troubled esp. mentally **2** : an instance of distress or annoyance **3** : DISEASE, AILMENT ⟨heart ∼⟩ **4** : EXERTION, PAINS ⟨took the ∼ to phone⟩ **5** : a cause of disturbance or distress

trou·ble·mak·er \-ˌmā-kər\ *n* : a person who causes trouble

trou·ble·shoot·er \-ˌshü-tər\ *n* **1** : a worker employed to locate trouble and make repairs in equipment **2** : an expert in resolving disputes or problems — **trou·ble·shoot** *vb*

trough \'tróf, 'tróth, *by bakers often* 'trō\ *n, pl* **troughs** \'trófs, 'tróvz, 'tróths, 'tróthz, 'tróz\ **1** : a long shallow open boxlike container esp. for water or feed for livestock **2** : a gutter along the eaves of a house **3** : a long channel or depression (as between waves or hills) **4** : an elongated area of low barometric pressure

trounce \'traúns\ *vb* **trounced; trounc·ing 1** : to thrash or punish severely **2** : to defeat decisively

troupe \'trüp\ *n* : COMPANY; *esp* : a group of performers on the stage — **troup·er** *n*

trou·sers \'traú-zərz\ *n pl* [alter. of earlier *trouse,* fr. ScGael *triubhas*] : an outer garment covering each leg separately and usu. extending from the waist to the ankle — **trouser** *adj*

trous·seau \'trü-sō, trü-'sō\ *n, pl* **trousseaux** \-sōz, -'sōz\ *or* **trousseaus** [F] : the personal outfit of a bride

trout \'traút\ *n, pl* **trout** *also* **trouts** [ME, fr. OE *trūht,* fr. LL *tructa,* a fish with sharp teeth, fr. Gk *trōktēs,* lit., gnawer] : any of various mostly freshwater food and game fishes usu. smaller than the related salmons

trow \'trō\ *vb, archaic* : THINK, SUPPOSE

trow·el \'traú-əl\ *n* **1** : a hand tool used for spreading, shaping, or smoothing loose or plastic material (as mortar or plaster) **2** : a small flat or scooplike implement used in gardening — **trowel** *vb*

troy \'trói\ *adj* : expressed in troy weight ⟨∼ ounce⟩

troy weight *n* : a system of weights based on a pound of 12 ounces and an ounce of 480 grains (31 grams) — see WEIGHT table

tru·ant \'trü-ənt\ *n* [ME, vagabond, idler, fr. OF, vagrant] : a student who stays out of school without permission — **tru·an·cy** \-ən-sē\ *n* — **truant** *adj*

truce \'trüs\ *n* **1** : ARMISTICE **2** : a respite esp. from something unpleasant

¹truck \'trək\ *vb* **1** : EXCHANGE, BARTER **2** : to have dealings : TRAFFIC

²truck *n* **1** : BARTER **2** : small goods or merchandise; *esp* : vegetables grown for market **3** : DEALINGS

³truck *n* **1** : a wheeled vehicle (as a strong heavy automobile) designed for carrying heavy articles or hauling a trailer **2** : a swiveling frame with springs and one or more pairs of wheels used to carry and guide one end of a locomotive or railroad car

⁴truck *vb* **1** : to transport on a truck **2** : to be employed in driving a truck — **truck·er** *n*

truck farm *n* : a farm growing vegetables for market — **truck farmer** *n*

truck·le \'trə-kəl\ *vb* **truck·led; truck·ling** : to yield slavishly to the will of another : SUBMIT **syn** fawn, toady, cringe, cower

truc·u·lent \'trə-kyə-lənt\ *adj* **1** : feeling or showing ferocity : SAVAGE **2** : aggressively self-assertive : PUGNACIOUS — **truc·u·lence** \-ləns\ *n* — **truc·u·len·cy** \-lən-sē\ *n* — **truc·u·lent·ly** *adv*

trudge \'trəj\ *vb* **trudged; trudg·ing** : to walk or march steadily and usu. laboriously

¹true \'trü\ *adj* **tru·er; tru·est 1** : STEADFAST, LOYAL **2** : agreeing with facts or reality ⟨a ∼ description⟩ **3** : CONSISTENT ⟨∼ to expectations⟩ **4** : properly so called ⟨∼ love⟩ **5** : RIGHTFUL ⟨∼ and lawful king⟩ **6** : conformable to a standard or pattern; *also* : placed or formed accurately **syn** constant, staunch, resolute, steadfast

²true *adv* **1** : TRUTHFULLY **2** : ACCURATELY ⟨the bullet flew straight and ∼⟩; *also* : without variation from type ⟨breed ∼⟩

³true *n* **1** : TRUTH, REALITY — usu. used with *the* **2** : the state of being accurate (as in alignment) ⟨out of ∼⟩

⁴true *vb* **trued; true·ing** *also* **tru·ing** : to bring or restore to a desired precision

true–blue *adj* : marked by unswerving loyalty

true bug *n* : BUG 2

true·heart·ed \'trü-ˈhär-təd\ *adj* : FAITHFUL, LOYAL

truf·fle \'trə-fəl, 'trü-\ *n* **1** : the usu. dark and wrinkled edible fruit of any of several European underground fungi; *also* : one of these fungi **2** : a candy made of chocolate, butter, and sugar shaped into balls and coated with cocoa

tru·ism \'trü-ˌi-zəm\ *n* : an undoubted or self-evident truth **syn** commonplace, platitude, bromide, cliché

tru·ly \'trü-lē\ *adv* **1** : in all sincerity **2** : in agreement with fact **3** : ACCURATELY **4** : in a proper or suitable manner

¹trump \'trəmp\ *n* : TRUMPET

²trump *n* : a card of a designated suit any of whose cards will win over a card that is not of this suit; *also* : the suit itself — often used in pl.

³trump *vb* : to take with a trump

trumped–up \'trəmpt-'əp\ *adj* : fraudulently concocted : SPURIOUS

trum·pery \'trəm-pə-rē\ *n* **1** : NONSENSE **2** : trivial articles : JUNK

¹trum·pet \'trəm-pət\ *n* **1** : a wind instrument consisting of a long curved metal tube flaring at one end and with a cup-shaped mouthpiece at the other **2** : something that resembles a trumpet or its tonal quality **3** : a funnel-shaped instrument for collecting, directing, or intensifying sound

²trumpet *vb* **1** : to blow a trumpet **2** : to proclaim on or as if on a trumpet — **trum·pet·er** *n*

¹trun·cate \'trəŋ-ˌkāt, 'trən-\ *adj* : having the end square or blunt

²**trun·cate** *vb* **trun·cat·ed; trun·cat·ing** : to shorten by or as if by cutting : LOP — **trun·ca·tion** \ˌtrəŋ-ˈkā-shən\ *n*

trun·cheon \ˈtrən-chən\ *n* : a police officer's club

trun·dle \ˈtrənd-ᵊl\ *vb* **trun·dled; trun·dling** : to roll along : WHEEL

trundle bed *n* : a low bed that can be stored under a higher bed

trunk \ˈtrəŋk\ *n* 1 : the main stem of a tree 2 : the body of a person or animal apart from the head and limbs 3 : the main or central part of something 4 : a box or chest used to hold usu. clothes or personal effects (as of a traveler); *also* : the enclosed luggage space in the rear of an automobile 5 : the long muscular nose of an elephant 6 *pl* : men's shorts worn chiefly for sports 7 : a usu. major channel or passage

trunk line *n* : a system handling long-distance through traffic

¹**truss** \ˈtrəs\ *vb* 1 : to secure tightly : BIND 2 : to arrange for cooking by binding close the wings or legs of (a fowl) 3 : to support, strengthen, or stiffen by or as if by a truss

²**truss** *n* 1 : a collection of structural parts (as beams) forming a rigid framework (as in bridge or building construction) 2 : a device worn to reduce a hernia by pressure

¹**trust** \ˈtrəst\ *n* 1 : assured reliance on the character, strength, or truth of someone or something 2 : a basis of reliance, faith, or hope 3 : confident hope 4 : financial credit 5 : a property interest held by one person for the benefit of another 6 : a combination of firms formed by a legal agreement; *esp* : one that reduces competition 7 : something entrusted to one to be cared for in the interest of another 8 : CARE, CUSTODY **syn** confidence, dependence, faith, reliance

²**trust** *vb* 1 : to place confidence : DEPEND 2 : to be confident : HOPE 3 : ENTRUST 4 : to permit to stay or go or to do something without fear or misgiving 5 : to rely on or on the truth of : BELIEVE 6 : to extend credit to

trust·ee \ˌtrəs-ˈtē\ *n* 1 : a person to whom property is legally committed in trust 2 : a country charged with the supervision of a trust territory

trust·ee·ship \ˌtrəs-ˈtē-ˌship\ *n* 1 : the office or function of a trustee 2 : supervisory control by one or more nations over a trust territory

trust·ful \ˈtrəst-fəl\ *adj* : full of trust : CONFIDING — **trust·ful·ly** *adv* — **trust·ful·ness** *n*

trust territory *n* : a non-self-governing territory placed under a supervisory authority by the Trusteeship Council of the United Nations

trust·wor·thy \-ˌwər-thē\ *adj* : worthy of confidence : DEPENDABLE **syn** trusty, tried, reliable — **trust·wor·thi·ness** *n*

¹**trusty** \ˈtrəs-tē\ *adj* **trust·i·er; -est** : TRUSTWORTHY, DEPENDABLE

²**trusty** \ˈtrəs-tē, ˌtrəs-ˈtē\ *n, pl* **trust·ies** : a trusted person; *esp* : a convict considered trustworthy and allowed special privileges

truth \ˈtrüth\ *n, pl* **truths** \ˈtrüthz, ˈtrüths\ 1 : TRUTHFULNESS, HONESTY 2 : the real state of things : FACT 3 : the body of real events or facts : ACTUALITY 4 : a true or accepted statement or proposition ⟨the ∼s of science⟩ 5 : agreement with fact or reality : CORRECTNESS **syn** veracity, verity

truth·ful \ˈtrüth-fəl\ *adj* : telling or disposed to tell the truth — **truth·ful·ly** *adv* — **truth·ful·ness** *n*

truth serum *n* : a drug held to induce a subject under questioning to talk freely

¹**try** \ˈtrī\ *vb* **tried; try·ing** 1 : to examine or investigate judicially 2 : to conduct the trial of 3 : to put to test or trial 4 : to subject to strain, affliction, or annoyance 5 : to extract or clarify (as lard) by melting 6 : to make an effort to do something : ATTEMPT, ENDEAVOR **syn** essay, assay, strive, struggle

²**try** *n, pl* **tries** : an experimental trial

try·ing *adj* : severely straining the powers of endurance

try on *vb* : to put on (a garment) to test the fit and looks

try out *vb* : to participate in competition esp. for a position on an athletic team or a part in a play — **try·out** \ˈtrī-ˌaut\ *n*

tryst \ˈtrist\ *n* 1 : an agreement (as between lovers) to meet 2 : an appointed meeting or meeting place — **tryst** *vb* — **tryst·er** *n*

tsar \ˈzär, ˈtsär, ˈsär\ *var of* CZAR

tset·se fly \ˈtset-sē-, ˈtsēt-, ˈtet-, ˈtēt-, ˈset-, ˈsēt-\ *n* : any of several sub-Saharan African dipteran flies including the vector of sleeping sickness

TSgt *abbr* technical sergeant

T–shirt \ˈtē-ˌshərt\ *n* : a collarless short-sleeved or sleeveless cotton undershirt; *also* : an outer shirt of similar design — **T–shirt·ed** \-ˌshər-təd\ *adj*

tsp *abbr* teaspoon; teaspoonful

T square *n* : a ruler with a crosspiece at one end for making parallel lines

tsu·na·mi \su̇-ˈnä-mē, tsu̇-\ *n* [Jp] : a tidal wave caused by an underwater earthquake or volcanic eruption

TT *abbr* Trust Territories

TTY *abbr* teletypewriter

Tu *abbr* Tuesday

tub \ˈtəb\ *n* 1 : a wide low bucketlike vessel 2 : BATHTUB; *also* : BATH 3 : the amount that a tub will hold

tu·ba \ˈtü-bə, ˈtyü-\ *n* : a large low-pitched brass wind instrument

tub·al \ˈtü-bəl, ˈtyü-\ *adj* : of, relating to, or involving a tube and esp. a fallopian tube

tube \ˈtüb, ˈtyüb\ *n* 1 : any of various usu. cylindrical structures or devices; *esp* : one to convey fluids 2 : a slender hollow anatomical part (as a fallopian tube) functioning as a channel in a plant or animal body : DUCT 3 : a soft round container from which a paste is squeezed 4 : a tunnel for vehicular or rail travel 5 : INNER TUBE 6 : ELECTRON TUBE 7 : TELEVISION — **tubed** *adj* — **tube·less** *adj*

tu·ber \ˈtü-bər, ˈtyü-\ *n* : a short fleshy usu. underground stem (as of a potato plant) bearing minute scalelike leaves each with a bud at its base

tu·ber·cle \ˈtü-bər-kəl, ˈtyü-\ *n* 1 : a small knobby prominence or outgrowth esp. on an animal or plant 2 : a small abnormal lump in an organ or on the skin; *esp* : one caused by tuberculosis

tubercle bacillus *n* : a bacterium that is the cause of tuberculosis

tu·ber·cu·lar \tu̇-ˈbər-kyə-lər, tyü-\ *adj* 1 : TUBERCULOUS 2 : of, resembling, or being a tubercle

tu·ber·cu·lin \tu̇-ˈbər-kyə-lən, tyü-\ *n* : a sterile liquid extracted from the tubercle bacillus and used in the diagnosis of tuberculosis esp. in children and cattle

tu·ber·cu·lo·sis \tu̇-ˌbər-kyə-ˈlō-səs, tyü-\ *n, pl* **-lo·ses** \-ˌsēz\ : a communicable bacterial disease typically marked by wasting, fever, and formation of cheesy tubercles often in the lungs — **tu·ber·cu·lous** \-ˈbər-kyə-ləs\ *adj*

tube·rose \ˈtüb-ˌrōz, ˈtyüb-\ *n* : a bulbous herb related to the agaves and often grown for its spike of fragrant waxy-white flowers

tu·ber·ous \ˈtü-bə-rəs, ˈtyü-\ *adj* : of, resembling, or being a tuber

tub·ing \ˈtü-biŋ, ˈtyü-\ *n* 1 : material in the form of a tube; *also* : a length of tube 2 : a series or system of tubes

tu·bu·lar \ˈtü-byə-lər, ˈtyü-\ *adj* : having the form of or consisting of a tube; *also* : made with tubes

tu·bule \ˈtü-byül, ˈtyü-\ *n* : a small tube

¹**tuck** \ˈtək\ *n* 1 : a fold stitched into cloth to shorten, decorate, or control fullness 2 : a cosmetic surgical operation for the removal of excess skin or fat ⟨a tummy ∼⟩

²**tuck** *vb* 1 : to pull up into a fold ⟨∼ed up her skirt⟩ 2 : to make tucks in 3 : to put into a snug often con-

cealing place ⟨∼ a book under the arm⟩ **4** : to secure in place by pushing the edges under ⟨∼ in a blanket⟩ **5** : to cover by tucking in bedclothes

tuck·er \'tə-kər\ *vb* **tuck·ered; tuck·er·ing** : EXHAUST, FATIGUE

Tues *or* **Tue** *abbr* Tuesday

Tues·day \'tüz-dē, 'tyüz-, -dā\ *n* : the 3d day of the week

tu·fa \'tü-fə, 'tyü-\ *n* : a porous rock formed as a deposit from springs or streams

tuff \'təf\ *n* : a rock composed of volcanic detritus

¹tuft \'təft\ *n* **1** : a small cluster of long flexible outgrowths (as hairs); *also* : a bunch of soft fluffy threads cut off short and used as ornament **2** : CLUMP, CLUSTER — **tuft·ed** *adj*

²tuft *vb* **1** : to provide or adorn with a tuft **2** : to make (as a mattress) firm by stitching at intervals and sewing on tufts — **tuft·er** *n*

¹tug \'təg\ *vb* **tugged; tug·ging 1** : to pull hard **2** : to struggle in opposition : CONTEND **3** : to move by pulling hard : HAUL **4** : to tow with a tugboat

²tug *n* **1** : a harness trace **2** : an act of tugging : PULL **3** : a straining effort **4** : a struggle between opposing people or forces **5** : TUGBOAT

tug·boat \-ıbōt\ *n* : a strongly built boat used for towing or pushing

tug-of-war \ıtəg-əv-'wor\ *n, pl* **tugs-of-war 1** : a struggle for supremacy **2** : an athletic contest in which two teams pull against each other at opposite ends of a rope

tu·grik *or* **tu·ghrik** \'tü-grik\ *n* — see MONEY table

tu·ition \tü-'i-shən, tyü-\ *n* : money paid for instruction ⟨college ∼⟩

tu·la·re·mia \ıtü-lə-'rē-mē-ə, ıtyü-\ *n* : an infectious bacterial disease esp. of wild rabbits, rodents, humans, and some domestic animals that in humans is marked by symptoms (as fever) of toxemia

tu·lip \'tü-ləp, 'tyü-\ *n* [NL *tulipa*, fr. Turk *tülbent* turban] : any of a genus of Eurasian bulbous herbs related to the lilies and grown for their large showy erect cup-shaped flowers; *also* : a flower or bulb of a tulip

tulip tree *n* : a tall American timber tree with greenish tulip-shaped flowers and soft white wood that is related to the magnolias

tulle \'tül\ *n* : a sheer often stiffened silk, rayon, or nylon net ⟨a veil of ∼⟩

¹tum·ble \'təm-bəl\ *vb* **tum·bled; tum·bling** [ME, fr. *tumben* to dance, fr. OE *tumbian*] **1** : to fall or cause to fall suddenly and helplessly **2** : to fall into ruin **3** : to perform gymnastic feats of rolling and turning **4** : to roll over and over : TOSS **5** : to issue forth hurriedly and confusedly **6** : to come to understand **7** : to throw together in a confused mass

²tumble *n* **1** : a disorderly state **2** : an act or instance of tumbling

tum·ble·down \'təm-bəl-'daùn\ *adj* : DILAPIDATED, RAMSHACKLE

tum·bler \'təm-blər\ *n* **1** : one that tumbles; *esp* : ACROBAT **2** : a drinking glass without foot or stem **3** : a movable obstruction in a lock that must be adjusted to a particular position (as by a key) before the bolt can be thrown

tum·ble·weed \'təm-bəl-ıwēd\ *n* : a plant that breaks away from its roots in autumn and is driven about by the wind

tum·brel *or* **tum·bril** \'təm-brəl\ *n* **1** : CART **2** : a vehicle carrying condemned persons (as during the French Revolution) to a place of execution

tu·mid \'tü-məd, 'tyü-\ *adj* **1** : SWOLLEN, DISTENDED **2** : BOMBASTIC, TURGID

tum·my \'tə-mē\ *n, pl* **tummies** : BELLY, ABDOMEN, STOMACH

tu·mor \'tü-mər, 'tyü-\ *n* : an abnormal and functionless mass of tissue that is not inflammatory and arises from preexistent tissue — **tu·mor·ous** *adj*

tu·mour *chiefly Brit var of* TUMOR

tu·mult \'tü-ıməlt, 'tyü-\ *n* **1** : UPROAR **2** : violent agitation of mind or feelings

tu·mul·tu·ous \tù-'məl-chə-wəs, tyù-, -chəs\ *adj* **1** : marked by tumult **2** : tending to incite a tumult **3** : marked by violent upheaval

tun \'tən\ *n* : a large cask

tu·na \'tü-nə, 'tyü-\ *n, pl* **tuna** *or* **tunas** [Sp] : any of several mostly large marine fishes related to the mackerels and caught for food and sport; *also* : the flesh of a tuna

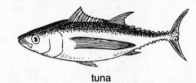

tuna

tun·able \'tü-nə-bəl, 'tyü-\ *adj* : capable of being tuned — **tun·abil·i·ty** \ıtü-nə-'bi-lə-tē, ıtyü-\ *n*

tun·dra \'tən-drə\ *n* [Russ] : a treeless plain of arctic and subarctic regions

¹tune \'tün, 'tyün\ *n* **1** : a succession of pleasing musical tones : MELODY **2** : correct musical pitch **3** : harmonious relationship : AGREEMENT ⟨in ∼ with the times⟩ **4** : general attitude ⟨changed his ∼⟩ **5** : AMOUNT, EXTENT ⟨in debt to the ∼ of millions⟩

²tune *vb* **tuned; tun·ing 1** : to adjust in musical pitch **2** : to bring or come into harmony : ATTUNE **3** : to put in good working order **4** : to adjust a radio or television receiver so as to receive a broadcast **5** : to adjust the frequency of the output of (a device) to a chosen frequency — **tun·er** *n*

tune·ful \-fəl\ *adj* : MELODIOUS, MUSICAL — **tune·ful·ly** *adv* — **tune·ful·ness** *n*

tune·less \-ləs\ *adj* **1** : UNMELODIOUS **2** : not producing music — **tune·less·ly** *adv*

tune-up \'tün-ıəp, 'tyün-\ *n* : an adjustment to ensure efficient functioning ⟨an engine ∼⟩

tung·sten \'təŋ-stən\ *n* [Sw, fr. *tung* heavy + *sten* stone] : a white hard heavy ductile metallic chemical element used esp. for electrical purposes and in alloys — see ELEMENT table

tu·nic \'tü-nik, 'tyü-\ *n* **1** : a usu. knee-length belted under or outer garment worn by ancient Greeks and Romans **2** : a hip-length or longer blouse or jacket

tuning fork *n* : a 2-pronged metal implement that gives a fixed tone when struck and is useful for tuning musical instruments

Tu·ni·sian \tü-'nē-zhən, tyü-, -'ni-\ *n* : a native or inhabitant of Tunisia — **Tunisian** *adj*

¹tun·nel \'tən-ᵊl\ *n* : an enclosed passage (as a tube or conduit); *esp* : one underground (as in a mine)

²tunnel *vb* **-neled** *or* **-nelled; -nel·ing** *or* **-nel·ling** : to make a tunnel through or under

tun·ny \'tə-nē\ *n, pl* **tunnies** *also* **tunny** : TUNA

tuque \'tük, 'tyük\ *n* [CanF] : a warm knitted cone꞊shaped cap

tur·ban \'tər-bən\ *n* **1** : a headdress worn esp. by Muslims and made of a cap around which is wound a long cloth **2** : a headdress resembling a turban; *esp* : a woman's close-fitting hat without a brim

tur·bid \'tər-bəd\ *adj* [L *turbidus* confused, turbid, fr. *turba* confusion, crowd] **1** : cloudy or discolored by suspended particles ⟨a ∼ stream⟩ **2** : CONFUSED, MUDDLED — **tur·bid·i·ty** \ıtər-'bi-də-tē\ *n*

tur·bine \'tər-bən, -ıbīn\ *n* [F, fr. L *turbin-, turbo* top, whirlwind, whirl] : an engine whose central driveshaft is fitted with curved vanes spun by the pressure of water, steam, or gas

tur·bo·fan \-ıfan\ *n* : a jet engine having a fan driven by a turbine for supplying air for combustion

tur·bo·jet \-ıjet\ *n* : an airplane powered by a jet engine (**turbojet engine**) having a turbine-driven air compressor supplying compressed air to the combustion chamber

tur·bo·prop \-ˌpräp\ *n* : an airplane powered by a jet engine (**turboprop engine**) having a turbine-driven propeller

tur·bot \'tər-bət\ *n, pl* **turbot** *also* **turbots** : a European flatfish that is a popular food fish; *also* : any of several similar flatfishes

tur·bu·lence \'tər-byə-ləns\ *n* : the quality or state of being turbulent

tur·bu·lent \-lənt\ *adj* **1** : causing violence or disturbance **2** : marked by agitation or tumult : TEMPESTU-OUS — **tur·bu·lent·ly** *adv*

tu·reen \tə-'rēn, tyù-\ *n* [F *terrine*, fr. MF, fr. fem. of *terrin* of earth] : a deep bowl from which foods (as soup) are served at table

¹turf \'tərf\ *n, pl* **turfs** \'tərfs\ *also* **turves** \'tərvz\ **1** : the upper layer of soil bound by grass and roots into a close mat; *also* : a piece of this **2** : an artificial substitute for turf (as on a playing field) **3** : a piece of peat dried for fuel **4** : a track or course for horse racing; *also* : horse racing as a sport or business

²turf *vb* : to cover with turf

tur·gid \'tər-jəd\ *adj* **1** : being in a swollen state **2** : excessively embellished in style or language : BOMBAS-TIC — **tur·gid·i·ty** \ˌtər-'ji-də-tē\ *n*

Turk \'tərk\ *n* : a native or inhabitant of Turkey

tur·key \'tər-kē\ *n, pl* **turkeys** [*Turkey*, country in western Asia and southeastern Europe; fr. confusion with the guinea fowl, supposed to be imported from Turkish territory] : a large American bird related to the domestic chicken and widely raised for food; *also* : its flesh

turkey buzzard *n* : TURKEY VULTURE

turkey vulture *n* : an American vulture with a red head and whitish bill

Turk·ish \'tər-kish\ *n* : the language of Turkey — **Turkish** *adj*

tur·mer·ic \'tər-mə-rik\ *n* : a spice or dyestuff obtained from the large aromatic deep-yellow rhizome of an East Indian perennial herb related to the ginger; *also* : this herb

tur·moil \'tər-ˌmóil\ *n* : an extremely confused or agitated condition

¹turn \'tərn\ *vb* **1** : to move or cause to move around an axis or center : ROTATE, REVOLVE ⟨∼ a wheel⟩ **2** : to effect a desired end by turning something ⟨∼ the oven on⟩ **3** : WRENCH ⟨∼ an ankle⟩ **4** : to change or cause to change position by moving through an arc of a circle ⟨∼ed her chair to the fire⟩ **5** : to cause to move around a center so as to show another side of ⟨∼ a page⟩ **6** : to revolve mentally : PONDER **7** : to become dizzy : REEL **8** : to reverse the sides or surfaces of ⟨∼ a pancake⟩ **9** : UPSET, DISORDER ⟨things were ∼ed topsy-turvy⟩ **10** : to set in another esp. contrary direction **11** : to change one's course or direction **12** : to go around ⟨∼ a corner⟩ **13** : BECOME ⟨my hair ∼ed gray⟩ ⟨∼ed twenty-one⟩ **14** : to direct toward or away from something; *also* : DEVOTE, APPLY **15** : to have recourse **16** : to become or make hostile **17** : to cause to become of a specified nature or appearance ⟨∼s the leaves yellow⟩ **18** : to make or become spoiled : SOUR **19** : to pass from one state to another ⟨water ∼s to ice⟩ **20** : CONVERT, TRANSFORM **21** : TRANSLATE, PARAPHRASE **22** : to give a rounded form to; *esp* : to shape by means of a lathe **23** : to gain by passing in trade ⟨∼ a quick profit⟩ — **turn color 1** : BLUSH **2** : to become pale — **turn loose** : to set free

²turn *n* **1** : a turning about a center or axis : REVOLU-TION, ROTATION **2** : the action or an act of giving or taking a different direction ⟨make a ∼ to the right⟩ **3** : a change of course or tendency ⟨a ∼ for the better⟩ **4** : a place at which something turns : BEND, CURVE **5** : a short walk or trip round about ⟨take a ∼ around the block⟩ **6** : an act affecting another ⟨did him a good

∼⟩ **7** : a place, time, or opportunity accorded in a scheduled order ⟨waited his ∼ in line⟩ **8** : a period of duty : SHIFT **9** : a short act esp. in a variety show **10** : a special purpose or requirement ⟨the job serves his ∼⟩ **11** : a skillful fashioning ⟨neat ∼ of phrase⟩ **12** : a single round (as of rope passed around an object) **13** : natural or special aptitude **14** : a usu. sudden and brief disorder of body or spirits; *esp* : a spell of nervous shock or faintness

turn·about \'tər-nə-ˌbaùt\ *n* **1** : a reversal of direction, trend, or policy **2** : RETALIATION

turn·buck·le \'tərn-ˌbə-kəl\ *n* : a link with a screw thread at one or both ends for tightening a rod or stay

turn·coat \-ˌkōt\ *n* : one who switches to an opposing side or party : TRAITOR

turn down *vb* : to decline to accept : REJECT — **turn·down** \'tərn-ˌdaùn\ *n*

turn·er \'tər-nər\ *n* **1** : one that turns or is used for turning **2** : one that forms articles with a lathe

turn·ery \'tər-nə-rē\ *n, pl* **-er·ies** : the work, products, or shop of a turner

turn in *vb* **1** : to deliver up **2** : to inform on **3** : to acquit oneself of ⟨*turn in* a good job⟩ **4** : to go to bed

turn·ing *n* **1** : the act or course of one that turns **2** : a place of a change of direction

tur·nip \'tər-nəp\ *n* **1** : a garden herb related to the cabbage with a thick edible usu. white root **2** : RU-TABAGA **3** : the root of a turnip

turn·key \'tərn-ˌkē\ *n, pl* **turnkeys** : one who has charge of a prison's keys

turn·off \'tərn-ˌóf\ *n* : a place for turning off esp. from an expressway

turn off *vb* **1** : to deviate from a straight course or a main road **2** : to stop the functioning or flow of **3** : to cause to lose interest; *also* : to evoke a negative feeling in

turn on *vb* **1** : to cause to flow, function, or operate **2** : to get high or cause to get high as a result of using a drug (as marijuana) **3** : EXCITE, STIMULATE

turn·out \'tərn-ˌaùt\ *n* **1** : an act of turning out **2** : the number of people who participate or attend an event **3** : a widened place in a highway for vehicles to pass or park **4** : manner of dress **5** : net yield : OUTPUT

turn out *vb* **1** : EXPEL, EVICT **2** : PRODUCE **3** : to come forth and assemble **4** : to get out of bed **5** : to prove to be in the end

¹turn·over \'tər-ˌnō-vər\ *n* **1** : UPSET **2** : SHIFT, REVER-SAL **3** : a filled pastry made by turning half of the crust over the other half **4** : the volume of business done **5** : movement (as of goods or people) into, through, and out of a place **6** : the number of persons hired within a period to replace those leaving or dropped **7** : an instance of a team's losing possession of the ball esp. through error

²turnover *adj* : capable of being turned over

turn over *vb* : TRANSFER ⟨*turn* the job *over* to her⟩

turn·pike \'tərn-ˌpīk\ *n* [ME *turnepike* revolving frame bearing spikes and serving as a barrier, fr. *turnen* to turn + *pike*] **1** : TOLLGATE; *also* : an expressway on which tolls are charged **2** : a main road

turn·stile \-ˌstīl\ *n* : a post with arms pivoted on the top set in a passageway so that persons can pass through only on foot one by one

turn·ta·ble \-ˌtā-bəl\ *n* : a circular platform that revolves (as for turning a locomotive or a phonograph record)

turn to *vb* : to apply oneself to work

turn up *vb* **1** : to come to light or bring to light : DIS-COVER, APPEAR **2** : to arrive at an appointed time or place **3** : to happen unexpectedly

tur·pen·tine \'tər-pən-ˌtīn\ *n* **1** : a mixture of oil and resin obtained from various cone-bearing trees (as pines) **2** : an oil distilled from turpentine or pine wood and used as a solvent and paint thinner

tur·pi·tude \'tər-pə-ˌtüd, -ˌtyüd\ *n* : inherent baseness : DEPRAVITY

tur·quoise *also* **tur·quois** \'tər-ˌkȯiz, -ˌkwȯiz\ *n* [ME *turkeis, turcas*, fr. MF *turquoyse*, fr. fem. of *turquoys* Turkish, fr. OF, fr. *Turc* Turk] **1** : a blue, bluish green, or greenish gray mineral that is valued as a gem **2** : a light greenish blue color

tur·ret \'tər-ət\ *n* **1** : a little tower often at an angle of a larger structure and merely ornamental **2** : a low usu. revolving structure (as on a tank or warship) in which one or more guns are mounted

¹tur·tle \'tərt-ᵊl\ *n, archaic* : TURTLEDOVE

²turtle *n, pl* **turtles** *also* **turtle** : any of an order of horny-beaked land, freshwater, or sea reptiles with the trunk enclosed in a bony shell

tur·tle·dove \'tərt-ᵊl-ˌdəv\ *n* : any of several small pigeons noted for plaintive cooing

tur·tle·neck \-ˌnek\ *n* : a high close-fitting turnover collar (as on a sweater); *also* : a sweater or shirt with a turtleneck — **tur·tle·necked** \-ˌnekt\ *adj*

turves *pl of* TURF

Tus·ca·ro·ra \ˌtəs-kə-'rōr-ə\ *n, pl* **Tuscarora** *or* **Tuscaroras** : a member of an American Indian people of No. Carolina and later of New York and Ontario

tusk \'təsk\ *n* : a long enlarged protruding tooth (as of an elephant, walrus, or boar) used esp. to dig up food or as a weapon — **tusked** \'təskt\ *adj*

tusk·er \'təs-kər\ *n* : an animal with tusks; *esp* : a male elephant with two normally developed tusks

¹tus·sle \'tə-səl\ *n* **1** : a physical struggle : SCUFFLE **2** : an intense argument, controversy, or struggle

²tussle *vb* **tus·sled; tus·sling** : to struggle roughly

tus·sock \'tə-sək\ *n* : a dense tuft esp. of grass or sedge; *also* : a hummock in a marsh or bog bound together by roots — **tus·socky** *adj*

tu·te·lage \'tüt-ᵊl-ij, 'tyüt-\ *n* **1** : an act of guarding or protecting **2** : the state of being under a guardian or tutor **3** : instruction esp. of an individual

tu·te·lary \'tüt-ᵊl-ˌer-ē, 'tyüt-\ *adj* : acting as a guardian ⟨∼ deity⟩

¹tu·tor \'tü-tər, 'tyü-\ *n* **1** : a person charged with the instruction and guidance of another **2** : a private teacher

²tutor *vb* **1** : to have the guardianship of **2** : to teach or guide individually : COACH ⟨∼ed her in Latin⟩ **3** : to receive instruction esp. privately

tu·to·ri·al \tü-'tōr-ē-əl, tyü-\ *n* : a class conducted by a tutor for one student or a small number of students

tut·ti \'tü-tē, 'tü-, -ˌtē\ *adj or adv* [It, pl. of *tutto* all] : with all voices and instruments playing together — used as a direction in music

tut·ti–frut·ti \ˌtü-ti-'frü-tē, ˌtü-\ *n* [It, lit., all fruits] : a confection or ice cream containing chopped usu. candied fruits

tux·e·do \ˌtək-'sē-dō\ *n, pl* **-dos** *or* **-does** [*Tuxedo* Park, N.Y.] **1** : a usu. black or blackish blue jacket **2** : semiformal evening clothes for men

TV \'tē-'vē\ *n* : TELEVISION

TVA *abbr* Tennessee Valley Authority

TV dinner *n* : a frozen packaged dinner that needs only heating before serving

twad·dle \'twäd-ᵊl\ *n* : silly idle talk : DRIVEL — **twad·dle** *vb*

twain \'twān\ *n* **1** : TWO **2** : PAIR

¹twang \'twaŋ\ *n* **1** : a harsh quick ringing sound like that of a plucked bowstring **2** : nasal speech or resonance **3** : the characteristic speech of a region

²twang *vb* **twanged; twang·ing 1** : to sound or cause to sound with a twang **2** : to speak with a nasal twang

tweak \'twēk\ *vb* : to pinch and pull with a sudden jerk and twitch — **tweak** *n*

tweed \'twēd\ *n* **1** : a rough woolen fabric made usu. in twill weaves **2** *pl* : tweed clothing; *esp* : a tweed suit

tweedy \'twē-dē\ *adj* **tweed·i·er; -est 1** : of or resembling tweed **2** : given to wearing tweeds **3** : suggestive of the outdoors in taste or habits

tween \'twēn\ *prep* : BETWEEN

tweet \'twēt\ *n* : a chirping note — **tweet** *vb*

tweet·er \'twē-tər\ *n* : a small loudspeaker that reproduces sounds of high pitch

twee·zers \'twē-zərz\ *n pl* [obs. E *tweeze*, n., case for small implements, short for obs. E *tweeze*, fr. pl. of obs. E *etwee*, fr. F *étui*] : a small pincerlike implement held between the thumb and forefinger for grasping something

twelve \'twelv\ *n* **1** : one more than 11 **2** : the 12th in a set or series **3** : something having 12 units — **twelfth** \'twelfth\ *adj or n* — **twelve** *adj or pron*

twelve·month \-ˌmənth\ *n* : YEAR

twen·ty \'twen-tē\ *n, pl* **twenties** : two times 10 — **twen·ti·eth** \-tē-əth\ *adj or n* — **twenty** *adj or pron*

twenty–twenty *or* **20/20** \ˌtwen-tē-'twen-tē\ *adj* : characterized by a visual capacity for seeing detail that is normal for the human eye ⟨∼ vision⟩

twice \'twīs\ *adv* **1** : on two occasions **2** : two times ⟨∼ two is four⟩

¹twid·dle \'twid-ᵊl\ *vb* **twid·dled; twid·dling 1** : to be busy with trifles; *also* : to play idly with something **2** : to rotate lightly or idly

²twiddle *n* : TURN, TWIST

twig \'twig\ *n* : a small branch — **twig·gy** *adj*

twi·light \'twī-ˌlīt\ *n* **1** : the light from the sky between full night and sunrise or between sunset and full night **2** : a state of imperfect clarity; *also* : a period of decline

twilight zone *n* **1** : TWILIGHT 2; *also* : an area just beyond ordinary legal or ethical limits **2** : a world of fantasy or unreality

twill \'twil\ *n* [ME *twyll*, fr. OE *twilic* having a double thread, part trans. of L *bilic-, bilix*, fr. *bi-* two + *licium* thread] **1** : a fabric with a twill weave **2** : a textile weave that gives an appearance of diagonal lines

twilled \'twild\ *adj* : made with a twill weave

¹twin \'twin\ *n* **1** : either of two offspring produced at a birth **2** : one of two persons or things closely related to or resembling each other

²twin *vb* **twinned; twin·ning 1** : to be coupled with another **2** : to bring forth twins

³twin *adj* **1** : born with one another or as a pair at one birth ⟨∼ brother⟩ ⟨∼ girls⟩ **2** : made up of two similar or related members or parts **3** : being one of a pair ⟨∼ city⟩

¹twine \'twīn\ *n* **1** : a strong thread of two or three strands twisted together **2** : an act of entwining or interlacing — **twiny** *adj*

²twine *vb* **twined; twin·ing 1** : to twist together; *also* : to form by twisting **2** : INTERLACE, WEAVE **3** : to coil about a support **4** : to stretch or move in a sinuous manner — **twin·er** *n*

¹twinge \'twinj\ *vb* **twinged; twing·ing** *or* **twinge·ing** : to affect with or feel a sharp sudden pain

²twinge *n* : a sudden sharp stab (as of pain or distress)

¹twin·kle \'twiŋ-kəl\ *vb* **twin·kled; twin·kling 1** : to shine or cause to shine with a flickering or sparkling light **2** : to appear bright with merriment **3** : to flutter or flit rapidly — **twin·kler** *n*

²twinkle *n* **1** : a wink of the eyelids; *also* : the duration of a wink **2** : an intermittent radiance **3** : a rapid flashing motion — **twin·kly** \'twiŋ-klē\ *adj*

twin·kling \'twiŋ-kliŋ\ *n* : the time required for a wink : INSTANT

¹twirl \'twərl\ *vb* : to turn or cause to turn rapidly ⟨∼ a baton⟩ **syn** revolve, rotate, circle, spin, swirl, pirouette — **twirl·er** *n*

²twirl *n* **1** : an act of twirling **2** : COIL, WHORL — **twirly** \'twər-lē\ *adj*

¹twist \'twist\ *vb* **1** : to unite by winding one thread or strand round another **2** : WREATHE, TWINE **3** : to turn so as to hurt ⟨∼ed her ankle⟩ **4** : to twirl into spiral shape **5** : to subject (as a shaft) to torsion **6** : to turn from the true form or meaning **7** : to pull off or break by torsion **8** : to follow a winding course **9** : to turn around

²twist *n* **1** : something formed by twisting or winding **2**

: an act of twisting : the state of being twisted **3** : a spiral turn or curve; *also* : SPIN **4** : a turning aside **5** : ECCENTRICITY **6** : a distortion of meaning **7** : an unexpected turn or development **8** : DEVICE, TRICK **9** : a variant approach or method

twist·er \'twis-tər\ *n* **1** : one that twists; *esp* : a ball with a forward and spinning motion **2** : TORNADO; *also* : WATERSPOUT 2

¹twit \'twit\ *n* : FOOL

²twit *vb* **twit·ted; twit·ting** : to ridicule as a fault; *also* : TAUNT **syn** deride, mock, razz

¹twitch \'twich\ *vb* **1** : to move or pull with a sudden motion : JERK **2** : to move jerkily : QUIVER

²twitch *n* **1** : an act or movement of twitching **2** : a short sharp contraction of muscle fibers

¹twit·ter \'twi-tər\ *vb* **1** : to make a succession of chirping noises **2** : to talk in a chattering fashion **3** : to tremble with agitation : FLUTTER

²twitter *n* **1** : a slight agitation of the nerves **2** : a small tremulous intermittent noise (as made by a swallow) **3** : a light chattering

twixt \'twikst\ *prep* : BETWEEN

two \'tü\ *n, pl* **twos 1** : one more than one **2** : the second in a set or series **3** : something having two units — **two** *adj or pron*

two cents *n* **1** : a sum or object of very small value **2** *or* **two cents worth** : an opinion offered on a topic under discussion

two–faced \'tü-'fāst\ *adj* **1** : DOUBLE-DEALING, FALSE **2** : having two faces

two·fold \'tü-ˌfōld, -'fōld\ *adj* **1** : having two units or members **2** : being twice as much or as many — **two·fold** \-'fōld\ *adv*

2,4–D \ˌtü-ˌfōr-'dē\ *n* : an irritant compound used esp. as a weed killer

2,4,5–T \-ˌfīv-'tē\ *n* : an irritant compound used esp. as an herbicide and defoliant

two·pence \'tə-pəns, *US also* 'tü-ˌpens\ *n* : the sum of two pence

two·pen·ny \'tə-pə-nē, *US also* 'tü-ˌpe-nē\ *adj* : of the value of or costing twopence

two–ply \'tü-'plī\ *adj* **1** : woven as a double cloth **2** : consisting of two strands or thicknesses

two·some \'tü-səm\ *n* **1** : a group of two persons or things : COUPLE **2** : a golf match between two players

two–step \'tü-ˌstep\ *n* : a ballroom dance performed with a sliding step in march or polka time; *also* : a piece of music for this dance — **two–step** *vb*

two–time \'tü-ˌtīm\ *vb* : to betray (a spouse or lover) by secret lovemaking with another — **two–tim·er** *n*

two–way *adj* : involving two elements or allowing movement or use in two directions or manners

2WD *abbr* two-wheel drive

twp *abbr* township

TWX *abbr* teletypewriter exchange

TX *abbr* Texas

-ty *n suffix* : quality : condition : degree ⟨real*ty*⟩

ty·coon \tī-'kün\ *n* [Jp *taikun*] **1** : a masterful leader (as in politics) **2** : a powerful businessman or industrialist

tying *pres part of* TIE

tyke \'tīk\ *n* : a small child

tym·pan·ic membrane \tim-'pa-nik-\ *n* : EARDRUM

tym·pa·num \'tim-pə-nəm\ *n, pl* **-na** \-nə\ *also* **-nums** : EARDRUM; *also* : MIDDLE EAR — **tym·pan·ic** \tim-'pa-nik\ *adj*

¹type \'tīp\ *n* [ME, fr. LL *typus*, fr. L & Gk; L *typus* image, fr. Gk *typos* blow, impression, model, fr. *typtein* to strike, beat] **1** : a person, thing, or event that foreshadows another to come : TOKEN, SYMBOL **2** : MODEL, EXAMPLE **3** : a distinctive stamp, mark, or sign : EMBLEM **4** : rectangular blocks usu. of metal each having a face so shaped as to produce a character when printed **5** : the letters or characters printed from or as if from type **6** : general character or form common to a number of individuals and setting them off as a distinguishable class ⟨horses of draft ∼⟩

7 : a class, kind, or group set apart by common characteristics ⟨a seedless ∼ of orange⟩; *also* : something distinguishable as a variety ⟨reactions of this ∼⟩ **syn** sort, nature, character, description

²type *vb* **typed; typ·ing 1** : to represent beforehand as a type **2** : to produce a copy of; *also* : REPRESENT, TYPIFY **3** : to write with a typewriter **4** : to identify as belonging to a type **5** : TYPECAST

type·cast \-ˌkast\ *vb* **-cast; -cast·ing 1** : to cast (an actor) in a part calling for characteristics possessed by the actor **2** : to cast repeatedly in the same type of role

type·face \-ˌfās\ *n* : all type of a single design

type·script \'tīp-ˌskript\ *n* : typewritten matter

type·set \-ˌset\ *vb* **-set; -set·ting** : to set in type : COMPOSE — **type·set·ter** *n*

type·write \-ˌrīt\ *vb* **-wrote** \-ˌrōt\; **-writ·ten** \-ˌrit-ᵊn\ : TYPE 3

type·writ·er \-ˌrī-tər\ *n* **1** : a machine for writing in characters similar to those produced by printers' type by means of types striking a ribbon to transfer ink or carbon impressions onto paper **2** : TYPIST

type·writ·ing \-ˌrī-tiŋ\ *n* : the use of a typewriter ⟨teach ∼⟩; *also* : writing produced with a typewriter

¹ty·phoid \'tī-ˌfȯid, tī-'fȯid\ *adj* : of, relating to, or being a communicable bacterial disease (**typhoid fever**) marked by fever, diarrhea, prostration, and intestinal inflammation

²typhoid *n* : TYPHOID FEVER

ty·phoon \tī-'fün\ *n* : a tropical cyclone in the region of the Philippines or the China sea

ty·phus \'tī-fəs\ *n* : a severe infectious disease transmitted esp. by body lice, caused by a rickettsia, and marked by high fever, stupor and delirium, intense headache, and a dark red rash

typ·i·cal \'ti-pi-kəl\ *adj* **1** : being or having the nature of a type **2** : exhibiting the essential characteristics of a group **3** : conforming to a type — **typ·i·cal·i·ty** \ˌti-pə-'ka-lə-tē\ *n* — **typ·i·cal·ness** *n*

typ·i·cal·ly \-pi-k(ə-)lē\ *adv* **1** : in a typical manner **2** : in typical circumstances

typ·i·fy \'ti-pə-ˌfī\ *vb* **-fied; -fy·ing 1** : to represent by an image, form, model, or resemblance **2** : to embody the essential or common characteristics of

typ·ist \'tī-pist\ *n* : one who operates a typewriter

ty·po \'tī-pō\ *n, pl* **typos** : an error in typing or in setting type

ty·pog·ra·pher \tī-'pä-grə-fər\ *n* : one who designs or arranges printing

ty·pog·ra·phy \tī-'pä-grə-fē\ *n* : the art of printing with type; *also* : the style, arrangement, or appearance of printed matter — **ty·po·graph·ic** \ˌtī-pə-'gra-fik\ *or* **ty·po·graph·i·cal** \-fi-kəl\ *adj* — **ty·po·graph·i·cal·ly** *adv*

ty·ran·ni·cal \tə-'ra-ni-kəl, tī-\ *also* **ty·ran·nic** \-nik\ *adj* : of or relating to a tyrant : DESPOTIC **syn** arbitrary, absolute, autocratic — **ty·ran·ni·cal·ly** \-ni-k(ə-)lē\ *adv*

tyr·an·nize \'tir-ə-ˌnīz\ *vb* **-nized; -niz·ing** : to act as a tyrant : rule with unjust severity — **tyr·an·niz·er** *n*

ty·ran·no·saur \tə-'ra-nə-ˌsȯr\ *n* : a very large American flesh-eating dinosaur of the Cretaceous that had small forelegs and walked on its hind legs

ty·ran·no·sau·rus \tə-ˌra-nə-'sȯr-əs\ *n* : TYRANNOSAUR

tyr·an·nous \'tir-ə-nəs\ *adj* : TYRANNICAL — **tyr·an·nous·ly** *adv*

tyr·an·ny \'tir-ə-nē\ *n, pl* **-nies 1** : oppressive power **2** : the rule or authority of a tyrant : government in which absolute power is vested in a single ruler **3** : a tyrannical act

ty·rant \'tī-rənt\ *n* **1** : an absolute ruler : DESPOT **2** : a ruler who governs oppressively or brutally **3** : one who uses authority or power harshly

tyre *chiefly Brit var of* TIRE

ty·ro \'tī-rō\ *n, pl* **tyros** [ML, fr. L *tiro* young soldier, tyro] : a beginner in learning : NOVICE

tzar \'zär, 'tsär, 'sär\ *var of* CZAR

U

¹**u** \'yü\ *n, pl* **u's** *or* **us** \'yüz\ *often cap* : the 21st letter of the English alphabet

²**u** *abbr, often cap* unit

¹**U** \'yü\ *adj* : characteristic of the upper classes

²**U** *abbr* **1** [abbr. of *Union of Orthodox Hebrew Congregations*] kosher certification — often enclosed in a circle **2** university **3** unsatisfactory

³**U** *symbol* uranium

UAE *abbr* United Arab Emirates

UAR *abbr* United Arab Republic

UAW *abbr* United Automobile Workers

ubiq·ui·tous \yü-'bi-kwə-təs\ *adj* : existing or being everywhere at the same time : OMNIPRESENT — **ubiq·ui·tous·ly** *adv* — **ubiq·ui·ty** \-kwə-tē\ *n*

U–boat \'yü-ˌbōt\ *n* [trans. of G *U-boot*, short for *Unterseeboot*, lit., undersea boat] : a German submarine

UC *abbr* uppercase

ud·der \'ə-dər\ *n* : an organ (as of a cow) consisting of two or more milk glands enclosed in a large hanging sac and each provided with a nipple

UFO \ˌyü-(ˌ)ef-'ō\ *n, pl* **UFO's** *or* **UFOs** \-'ōz\ : an unidentified flying object; *esp* : FLYING SAUCER

Ugan·dan \ü-'gan-dən, yü-, -'gän-\ *n* : a native or inhabitant of Uganda — **Ugandan** *adj*

ug·ly \'ə-glē\ *adj* **ug·li·er; -est** [ME, fr. ON *uggligr*, fr. *uggr* fear] **1** : FRIGHTFUL, DIRE **2** : offensive to the sight : HIDEOUS **3** : offensive or unpleasant to any sense **4** : morally objectionable : REPULSIVE **5** : likely to cause inconvenience or discomfort **6** : SURLY, QUARRELSOME ⟨an ∼ disposition⟩ — **ug·li·ness** \-glē-nəs\ *n*

UHF *abbr* ultrahigh frequency

UK *abbr* United Kingdom

ukase \yü-'kās, -'kāz\ *n* [F & Russ; F, fr. Russ *ukaz*, fr. *ukazat'* to show, order] : an edict esp. of a Russian emperor or government

Ukrai·ni·an \yü-'krā-nē-ən\ *n* : a native or inhabitant of Ukraine — **Ukrainian** *adj*

uku·le·le *also* **uke·le·le** \ˌyü-kə-'lā-lē\ *n* [Hawaiian *'ukulele*, fr. *'uku* flea + *lele* jumping] : a small usu. 4-stringed guitar popularized in Hawaii

ul·cer \'əl-sər\ *n* **1** : an open eroded sore of skin or mucous membrane often discharging pus **2** : something that festers and corrupts like an open sore — **ul·cer·ous** *adj*

ul·cer·ate \'əl-sə-ˌrāt\ *vb* **-at·ed; -at·ing** : to become affected with an ulcer — **ul·cer·ative** \'əl-sə-ˌrā-tiv\ *adj*

ul·cer·ation \ˌəl-sə-'rā-shən\ *n* **1** : the process of forming or state of having an ulcer **2** : ULCER 1

ul·na \'əl-nə\ *n* : the bone on the little-finger side of the human forearm; *also* : a corresponding bone of the forelimb of vertebrates above fishes

ul·ster \'əl-stər\ *n* : a long loose overcoat

ult *abbr* **1** ultimate **2** ultimo

ul·te·ri·or \ˌəl-'tir-ē-ər\ *adj* **1** : lying farther away : more remote **2** : situated beyond or on the farther side **3** : going beyond what is openly said or shown : HIDDEN ⟨∼ motives⟩

¹**ul·ti·mate** \'əl-tə-mət\ *adj* **1** : most remote in space or time : FARTHEST **2** : last in a progression : FINAL **3** : the best or most extreme of its kind **4** : arrived at as the last resort **5** : FUNDAMENTAL, ABSOLUTE, SUPREME ⟨∼ reality⟩ **6** : incapable of further analysis or division : ELEMENTAL **7** : MAXIMUM **syn** concluding, eventual, latest, terminal — **ul·ti·mate·ly** *adv*

²**ultimate** *n* : something ultimate

ul·ti·ma·tum \ˌəl-tə-'mā-təm, -'mä-\ *n, pl* **-tums** *or* **-ta** \-tə\ : a final condition or demand whose rejection will bring about a resort to forceful action

ul·ti·mo \'əl-tə-ˌmō\ *adj* [L *ultimo mense* in the last

month] : of or occurring in the month preceding the present

¹**ul·tra** \'əl-trə\ *adj* : going beyond others or beyond due limits : EXTREME

²**ultra** *n* : EXTREMIST

ul·tra·con·ser·va·tive \-kən-'sər-və-tiv\ *adj* : extremely conservative

ul·tra·high frequency \-'hī-\ *n* : a radio frequency between 300 and 3000 megahertz

¹**ul·tra·light** \'əl-trə-ˌlīt\ *adj* : extremely light esp. in weight

²**ultralight** *n* : a very light recreational aircraft typically carrying only one person

ul·tra·ma·rine \ˌəl-trə-mə-'rēn\ *n* **1** : a deep blue pigment **2** : a very bright deep blue color

ul·tra·mi·cro·scop·ic \-ˌmī-krə-'skä-pik\ *adj* : too small to be seen with an ordinary microscope

ul·tra·mod·ern \-'mä-dərn\ *adj* : extremely or excessively modern in idea, style, or tendency

ul·tra·mon·tane \-'män-ˌtān, -ˌmän-'tān\ *adj* **1** : of or relating to countries or peoples beyond the mountains (as the Alps) **2** : favoring greater or absolute supremacy of papal authority in the Roman Catholic Church — **ultramontane** *n, often cap* — **ul·tra·mon·tan·ism** \-'mänt-ən-ˌi-zəm\ *n*

ul·tra·pure \-'pyur\ *adj* : of the utmost purity

ul·tra·short \-'short\ *adj* **1** : having a wavelength below 10 meters **2** : very short in duration

ul·tra·son·ic \ˌəl-trə-'sä-nik\ *adj* : having a frequency too high to be heard by the human ear — **ul·tra·son·i·cal·ly** \-ni-k(ə-)lē\ *adv*

ul·tra·son·ics \-'sä-niks\ *n sing or pl* **1** : ultrasonic vibrations **2** : the science of ultrasonic phenomena

ul·tra·sound \-ˌsaund\ *n* **1** : ultrasonic vibrations **2** : the diagnostic or therapeutic use of ultrasound to form a two-dimensional image of internal body structures **3** : a diagnostic examination using ultrasound

ul·tra·vi·o·let \-'vī-ə-lət\ *adj* : having a wavelength shorter than those of visible light and longer than those of X rays ⟨∼ radiation⟩; *also* : producing or employing ultraviolet radiation — **ultraviolet** *n*

ul·tra vi·res \ˌəl-trə-'vī-rēz\ *adv or adj* [NL, lit., beyond power] : beyond the scope of legal power or authority

ul·u·late \'əl-yə-ˌlāt\ *vb* **-lat·ed; -lat·ing** : HOWL, WAIL

um·bel \'əm-bəl\ *n* : a flat-topped or rounded flower cluster in which the individual flower stalks all arise near one point on the main stem

um·ber \'əm-bər\ *n* : a brown earthy substance valued as a pigment either in its raw state or burnt — **umber** *adj*

umbilical cord *n* : a cord containing blood vessels that connects the navel of a fetus with the placenta of its mother

um·bi·li·cus \ˌəm-'bi-li-kəs, ˌəm-bə-'lī-\ *n, pl* **um·bi·li·ci** \ˌəm-'bi-lə-ˌkī; ˌəm-bə-'lī-ˌkī, -ˌsī\ *or* **um·bi·li·cus·es** : NAVEL — **um·bil·i·cal** \ˌəm-'bi-li-kəl\ *adj*

um·bra \'əm-brə\ *n, pl* **umbras** *or* **um·brae** \-(ˌ)brē, -ˌbrī\ **1** : SHADE, SHADOW **2** : the conical part of the shadow of a celestial body from which the sun's light is completely blocked

um·brage \'əm-brij\ *n* **1** : SHADE; *also* : FOLIAGE **2** : RESENTMENT, OFFENSE ⟨take ∼ at a remark⟩

um·brel·la \ˌəm-'bre-lə\ *n* **1** : a collapsible shade for protection against weather consisting of fabric stretched over hinged ribs radiating from a center pole **2** : something that resembles an umbrella in shape or purpose

umi·ak \'ü-mē-ˌak\ *n* : an open Eskimo boat made of a wooden frame covered with skins

☞ For illustration, see next page.

umiak

um•pire \\'əm-₁pīr\\ *n* [ME *oumpere*, alter. of *noumpere*
(the phrase *a noumpere* being understood as *an
oumpere*), fr. MF *nomper* not equal, not paired, fr.
non not + *per* equal, fr. L *par*] **1** : one having authority to decide finally a controversy or question between parties **2** : an official in a sport who rules on
plays — **umpire** *vb*
ump•teen \\'əmp-₁tēn\\ *adj* : very many : indefinitely
numerous — **ump•teenth** \\-₁tēnth\\ *adj*
UN *abbr* United Nations
un- \\₁ən, '\\'ən\\ *prefix* **1** : not : IN-, NON- **2** : opposite of
: contrary to

unabashed	unauthorized	uncomic	undirected
unabated	unavailable	uncommercial	undisciplined
unabsorbed	unavowed	uncompensated	undisclosed
unabsorbent	unawakened	uncomplaining	undiscovered
unacademic	unbaked	uncompleted	undiscriminating
unaccented	unbaptized	uncomplicated	undisguised
unacceptable	unbeloved	uncomplimentary	undismayed
unacclimatized	unbleached	uncompounded	undisputed
unaccommodating	unblemished	uncomprehending	undissolved
unaccredited	unblinking	unconcealed	undistinguished
unacknowledged	unbound	unconfined	undistributed
unacquainted	unbranched	unconfirmed	undisturbed
unadapted	unbranded	unconformable	undivided
unadjusted	unbreakable	uncongenial	undocumented
unadorned	unbridgeable	unconnected	undogmatic
unadventurous	unbruised	unconquered	undomesticated
unadvertised	unbrushed	unconsecrated	undone
unaesthetic	unbudging	unconsidered	undoubled
unaffiliated	unburied	unconsolidated	undramatic
unafraid	unburned	unconstrained	undraped
unaggressive	uncanceled	unconsumed	undreamed
unaided	uncanonical	unconsummated	undressed
unalike	uncap	uncontaminated	undrinkable
unaltered	uncapitalized	uncontested	undulled
unambiguous	uncared–for	uncontrolled	undutiful
unambiguously	uncataloged	uncontroversial	undyed
unambitious	uncaught	unconverted	uneager
unanchored	uncensored	unconvincing	uneatable
unannounced	uncensured	uncooked	uneaten
unanswerable	unchallenged	uncooperative	uneconomic
unanswered	unchangeable	uncoordinated	uneconomical
unanticipated	unchanged	uncorrected	unedifying
unapologetic	unchanging	uncorroborated	unedited
unapparent	unchaperoned	uncountable	uneducated
unappealing	uncharacteristic	uncreative	unembarrassed
unappeased	unchaste	uncredited	unemotional
unappetizing	unchastely	uncropped	unemphatic
unappreciated	unchasteness	uncrowded	unenclosed
unappreciative	unchastity	uncrowned	unencumbered
unapproachable	unchecked	uncrystallized	unendurable
unappropriated	unchivalrous	uncultivated	unenforceable
unapproved	unchristened	uncultured	unenforced
unarguable	unclad	uncured	unenlightened
unarguably	unclaimed	uncurious	unenterprising
unarmored	unclassified	uncurtained	unenthusiastic
unartistic	uncleaned	uncustomary	unenviable
unashamed	unclear	undamaged	unequipped
unasked	uncleared	undamped	unessential
unassertive	unclouded	undated	unethical
unassisted	uncluttered	undecided	unexamined
unathletic	uncoated	undecipherable	unexcelled
unattainable	uncollected	undeclared	unexceptional
unattended	uncolored	undecorated	unexcited
unattested	uncombed	undefeated	unexciting
unattractive	uncombined	undefended	unexpired
unauthentic	uncomely	undefiled	unexplained
		undefinable	unexploded
		undefined	unexplored
		undemanding	unexposed
		undemocratic	unexpressed
		undenominational	unexpurgated
		undependable	unfading
		undeserved	unfaltering
		undeserving	unfashionable
		undesired	unfashionably
		undetected	unfathomable
		undetermined	unfavorable
		undeterred	unfavorably
		undeveloped	unfeasible
		undifferentiated	unfeminine
		undigested	unfenced
		undignified	unfermented
		undiluted	unfertilized
		undiminished	unfilled
		undimmed	unfiltered
		undiplomatic	unfitted

unflagging	uninstructed	unostentatious	unrelated
unflattering	uninstructive	unowned	unreliable
unflavored	uninsured	unpaged	unrelieved
unfocused	unintended	unpaid	unremarkable
unfolded	unintentional	unpainted	unremembered
unforced	unintentionally	unpaired	unremovable
unforeseeable	uninteresting	unpalatable	unrepentant
unforeseen	uninvited	unpardonable	unreported
unforgivable	uninviting	unpasteurized	unrepresentative
unforgiving	unjointed	unpatriotic	unrepresented
unformulated	unjustifiable	unpaved	unrepressed
unfortified	unjustified	unpeeled	unresistant
unframed	unkept	unperceived	unresisting
unfree	unknowable	unperceptive	unresolved
unfulfilled	unknowledgeable	unperformed	unresponsive
unfunded	unlabeled	unpersuaded	unresponsiveness
unfunny	unladylike	unpersuasive	unrestful
unfurnished	unlamented	unperturbed	unrestricted
unfussy	unleavened	unplanned	unreturnable
ungentle	unlicensed	unplanted	unrewarding
ungentlemanly	unlighted	unpleasing	unrhymed
ungerminated	unlikable	unplowed	unrhythmic
unglamorous	unlimited	unpoetic	unripened
unglazed	unlined	unpolished	unromantic
ungoverned	unlit	unpolitical	unromantically
ungraceful	unliterary	unpolluted	unsafe
ungracefully	unlivable	unposed	unsaid
ungraded	unlovable	unpractical	unsalable
ungrammatical	unloved	unpredictable	unsalted
unground	unloving	unpredictability	unsanctioned
ungrudging	unmade	unprejudiced	unsanitary
unguided	unmalicious	unpremeditated	unsatisfactory
unhackneyed	unmanageable	unprepared	unsatisfied
unhampered	unmanned	unpreparedness	unscented
unhardened	unmapped	unprepossessing	unscheduled
unharmed	unmarked	unpressed	unscholarly
unharvested	unmarketable	unpretending	unsealed
unhatched	unmarred	unpretty	unseasoned
unhealed	unmarried	unprivileged	unseaworthy
unhealthful	unmasculine	unprocessed	unsegmented
unheated	unmatched	unproductive	unself–conscious
unheeded	unmeant	unprofessed	unself–consciously
unhelpful	unmeasurable	unprofessional	unsensational
unheralded	unmeasured	unprogrammed	unsentimental
unheroic	unmelodious	unprogressive	unserious
unhesitating	unmentioned	unpromising	unserviceable
unhindered	unmerited	unprompted	unsexual
unhistorical	unmilitary	unpronounceable	unshaded
unhonored	unmilled	unpropitious	unshakable
unhoused	unmixed	unprotected	unshaken
unhurried	unmodified	unproven	unshapely
unhurt	unmolested	unprovided	unshaven
unhygienic	unmotivated	unprovoked	unshorn
unidentifiable	unmounted	unpublished	unsifted
unidentified	unmovable	unpunished	unsigned
unidiomatic	unmoved	unquenchable	unsinkable
unimaginable	unmusical	unquestioned	unsmiling
unimaginative	unnameable	unraised	unsociable
unimpaired	unnamed	unrated	unsoiled
unimpassioned	unnecessary	unratified	unsold
unimpeded	unneeded	unreachable	unsoldierly
unimportant	unnewsworthy	unreadable	unsolicited
unimposing	unnoticeable	unready	unsolvable
unimpressed	unnoticed	unrealistic	unsolved
unimpressive	unobjectionable	unrealized	unsorted
unimproved	unobservant	unrecognizable	unspecified
unincorporated	unobserved	unrecognized	unspectacular
uninfected	unobstructed	unrecorded	unspent
uninfluenced	unobtainable	unrecoverable	unspiritual
uninformative	unofficial	unredeemable	unspoiled
uninformed	unofficially	unrefined	unspoken
uninhabitable	unopened	unreflecting	unsportsmanlike
uninhabited	unopposed	unreflective	unstained
uninitiated	unoriginal	unregistered	unstated
uninjured	unorthodox	unregulated	unsterile
uninspired	unorthodoxy	unrehearsed	unstructured

unstylish
unsubdued
unsubstantiated
unsubtle
unsuccessful
unsuccessfully
unsuitable
unsuited
unsullied
unsupervised
unsupportable
unsupported
unsure
unsurpassed
unsurprising
unsurprisingly
unsuspected
unsuspecting
unsuspicious
unsweetened
unsymmetrical
unsympathetic
unsystematic
untactful
untainted
untalented
untamed
untanned
untapped
untarnished
untaxed
unteachable
untenable
untenanted
untended
untested
unthrifty
untidy
untilled
untitled
untraceable
untraditional

untrained
untrammeled
untranslatable
untranslated
untraveled
untraversed
untreated
untrimmed
untrod
untroubled
untrustworthy
untruthful
untypical
unusable
unvaried
unvarying
unventilated
unverifiable
unverified
unversed
unvisited
unwanted
unwarranted
unwary
unwashed
unwavering
unweaned
unwearable
unwearied
unweathered
unwed
unwelcome
unwilling
unwillingly
unwillingness
unwomanly
unworkable
unworn
unworried
unwounded
unwoven

un·able \\ˌən-ˈā-bəl\ adj **1** : not able **2** : UNQUALIFIED, INCOMPETENT

un·abridged \\ˌən-ə-ˈbrijd\ adj **1** : not abridged ⟨an ∼ edition of Shakespeare⟩ **2** : complete of its class : not based on one larger ⟨an ∼ dictionary⟩

un·ac·com·pa·nied \\ˌən-ə-ˈkəm-pə-nēd\ adj : not accompanied; *esp* : being without instrumental accompaniment

un·ac·count·able \\ˌən-ə-ˈkaun-tə-bəl\ adj **1** : not to be accounted for : INEXPLICABLE **2** : not responsible — **un·ac·count·ably** \-blē\ adv

un·ac·count·ed \-ˈkaun-təd\ adj : not accounted ⟨the loss was ∼ for⟩

un·ac·cus·tomed \\ˌən-ə-ˈkəs-təmd\ adj **1** : not customary : not usual or common **2** : not accustomed or habituated ⟨∼ to noise⟩

un·adul·ter·at·ed \\ˌən-ə-ˈdəl-tə-ˌrā-təd\ adj : PURE, UNMIXED **syn** absolute, sheer, simple, unalloyed, undiluted, unmitigated

un·af·fect·ed \\ˌən-ə-ˈfek-təd\ adj **1** : not influenced or changed mentally, physically, or chemically **2** : free from affectation : NATURAL, GENUINE — **un·af·fect·ed·ly** adv

un·alien·able \-ˈāl-yə-nə-bəl, -ˈā-lē-ə-\ adj : INALIENABLE

un·aligned \\ˌən-ə-ˈlīnd\ adj : not associated with any one of competing international blocs ⟨∼ nations⟩

un·al·loyed \\ˌən-ə-ˈloid\ adj : UNMIXED, UNQUALIFIED, PURE ⟨∼ happiness⟩

un·al·ter·able \\ˌən-ˈol-tə-rə-bəl\ adj : not capable of being altered or changed — **un·al·ter·ably** \-blē\ adv

un–Amer·i·can \\ˌən-ə-ˈmer-ə-kən\ adj : not characteristic of or consistent with American customs or principles

unan·i·mous \yu̇-ˈna-nə-məs\ adj [L *unanimus,* fr. *unus* one + *animus* mind] **1** : being of one mind : AGREEING **2** : formed with or indicating the agreement of all — **una·nim·i·ty** \ˌyü-nə-ˈni-mə-tē\ n — **unan·i·mous·ly** adv

un·arm \ˌən-ˈärm\ vb : DISARM

un·armed \-ˈärmd\ adj : not armed or armored

un·as·sail·able \ˌən-ə-ˈsā-lə-bəl\ adj : not liable to doubt, attack, or question

un·as·sum·ing \ˌən-ə-ˈsü-miŋ\ adj : MODEST, RETIRING **syn** humble, lowly, meek

un·at·tached \ˌən-ə-ˈtacht\ adj **1** : not married or engaged **2** : not joined or united

un·avail·ing \ˌən-ə-ˈvā-liŋ\ adj : being of no avail — **un·avail·ing·ly** adv

un·avoid·able \ˌən-ə-ˈvoi-də-bəl\ adj : not avoidable : INEVITABLE **syn** certain, ineluctable, inescapable, necessary — **un·avoid·ably** \-blē\ adv

¹un·aware \ˌən-ə-ˈwar\ adv : UNAWARES

²unaware adj : not aware : IGNORANT — **un·aware·ness** n

un·awares \-ˈwarz\ adv **1** : without knowing : UNINTENTIONALLY **2** : without warning : by surprise ⟨taken ∼⟩

un·bal·anced \ˌən-ˈba-lənst\ adj **1** : not in a state of balance **2** : mentally disordered **3** : not adjusted so as to make credits equal to debits

un·bar \-ˈbär\ vb : UNBOLT, OPEN

un·bear·able \ˌən-ˈbar-ə-bəl\ adj : greater than can be borne ⟨∼ pain⟩ **syn** insufferable, insupportable, intolerable, unendurable, unsupportable — **un·bear·ably** \-blē\ adv

un·beat·able \-ˈbē-tə-bəl\ adj : not capable of being defeated **syn** indomitable, invincible, invulnerable, unconquerable

un·beat·en \-ˈbēt-ᵊn\ adj **1** : not pounded, beaten, or whipped **2** : UNTROD **3** : UNDEFEATED

un·be·com·ing \ˌən-bi-ˈkə-miŋ\ adj : not becoming : UNSUITABLE, IMPROPER **syn** indecorus, indecent, indelicate, unseemly — **un·be·com·ing·ly** adv

un·be·knownst \ˌən-bi-ˈnōnst\ *also* **un·be·known** \-ˈnōn\ adj : happening without one's knowledge

un·be·lief \ˌən-bi-ˈlēf\ n : the withholding or absence of belief : DOUBT — **un·be·liev·ing** \-ˈlē-viŋ\ adj

un·be·liev·able \-ˈlē-və-bəl\ adj : too improbable for belief; *also* : of such a superlative degree as to be hard to believe ⟨an ∼ catch for a touchdown⟩ **syn** inconceivable, unimaginable, unthinkable — **un·be·liev·ably** \-blē\ adv

un·be·liev·er \-ˈlē-vər\ n **1** : DOUBTER **2** : INFIDEL

un·bend \-ˈbend\ vb **-bent** \-ˈbent\; **-bend·ing 1** : to free from being bent : make or become straight **2** : UNTIE **3** : to make or become less stiff or more affable : RELAX

un·bend·ing adj : formal and distant in manner : INFLEXIBLE

un·bi·ased \ˌən-ˈbī-əst\ adj : free from bias; *esp* : UNPREJUDICED **syn** disinterested, dispassionate, impartial, nondiscriminatory, nonpartisan, objective, uncolored

un·bid·den \-ˈbid-ᵊn\ *also* **un·bid** \-ˈbid\ adj : not bidden : UNASKED

un·bind \-ˈbīnd\ vb **-bound** \-ˈbaund\; **-bind·ing 1** : to remove bindings from : UNTIE **2** : RELEASE

un·blessed *also* **un·blest** \ˌən-ˈblest\ adj **1** : not blessed **2** : EVIL

un·block \-ˈbläk\ vb : to free from being blocked

un·blush·ing \-ˈblə-shiŋ\ adj **1** : not blushing **2** : SHAMELESS — **un·blush·ing·ly** adv

un·bod·ied \-ˈbä-dēd\ adj **1** : having no body; *also* : DISEMBODIED **2** : FORMLESS

un·bolt \ˌən-ˈbōlt\ vb : to open or unfasten by withdrawing a bolt

un·bolt·ed \-ˈbōl-təd\ adj : not fastened by bolts

un·born \-ˈbȯrn\ adj : not yet born

un·bos·om \-ˈbu̇-zəm, -ˈbü-\ vb **1** : DISCLOSE, REVEAL **2**

: to disclose the thoughts or feelings of oneself

un·bound·ed \-'baün-dəd\ *adj* : having no bounds or limits ⟨∼ enthusiasm⟩ **syn** boundless, endless, immeasurable, limitless, measureless, unlimited

un·bowed \ˌən-'baúd\ *adj* 1 : not bowed down 2 : UNSUBDUED

un·bri·dled \-'brīd-ᵊld\ *adj* 1 : UNRESTRAINED 2 : not confined by a bridle

un·bro·ken \-'brō-kən\ *adj* 1 : not damaged 2 : not subdued or tamed 3 : not interrupted : CONTINUOUS

un·buck·le \-'bə-kəl\ *vb* : to loose the buckle of : UNFASTEN ⟨∼ a belt⟩

un·bur·den \-'bərd-ᵊn\ *vb* 1 : to free or relieve from a burden 2 : to relieve oneself of (as cares or worries)

un·but·ton \-'bət-ᵊn\ *vb* : to unfasten the buttons of ⟨∼ your coat⟩

un·called–for \ˌən-'kóld-ˌfór\ *adj* : not called for, needed, or wanted

un·can·ny \-'ka-nē\ *adj* 1 : GHOSTLY, MYSTERIOUS, EERIE 2 : suggesting superhuman or supernatural powers **syn** spooky, unearthly, weird — **un·can·ni·ly** \-'kan-ᵊl-ē\ *adv*

un·ceas·ing \-'sē-siŋ\ *adj* : never ceasing **syn** ceaseless, continuous, endless, interminable, unending, unremitting — **un·ceas·ing·ly** *adv*

un·cer·e·mo·ni·ous \ˌən-ˌser-ə-'mō-nē-əs\ *adj* : acting without or lacking ordinary courtesy : ABRUPT — **un·cer·e·mo·ni·ous·ly** *adv*

un·cer·tain \ˌən-'sərt-ᵊn\ *adj* 1 : not determined or fixed ⟨an ∼ quantity⟩ 2 : subject to chance or change : not dependable ⟨∼ weather⟩ 3 : not definitely known 4 : not sure ⟨∼ of the truth⟩ — **un·cer·tain·ly** *adv*

un·cer·tain·ty \-ᵊn-tē\ *n* 1 : lack of certainty : DOUBT 2 : something that is uncertain **syn** concern, doubt, dubiety, incertitude, skepticism, suspicion

un·chain \ˌən-'chān\ *vb* : to free by or as if by removing a chain

un·charged \ˌən-'chärjd\ *adj* : having no electrical charge

un·char·i·ta·ble \-'char-ə-tə-bəl\ *adj* : not charitable; *esp* : severe in judging others — **un·char·i·ta·ble·ness** *n* — **un·char·i·ta·bly** \-blē\ *adv*

un·chart·ed \-'chär-təd\ *adj* 1 : not recorded on a map, chart, or plan 2 : UNKNOWN

un·chris·tian \-'kris-chən\ *adj* 1 : not of the Christian faith 2 : contrary to the Christian spirit

un·churched \-'chərcht\ *adj* : not belonging to or connected with a church

un·cial \'ən-shəl, -chəl; 'ən-sē-əl\ *adj* : relating to or written in a form of script with rounded letters used esp. in early Greek and Latin manuscripts — **uncial** *n*

un·cir·cu·lat·ed \ˌən-'sər-kyə-ˌlā-təd\ *adj* : issued for use as money but kept out of circulation

un·cir·cum·cised \ˌən-'sər-kəm-ˌsīzd\ *adj* : not circumcised; *also* : HEATHEN

un·civ·il \ˌən-'si-vəl\ *adj* 1 : not civilized : BARBAROUS 2 : DISCOURTEOUS, ILL-MANNERED, IMPOLITE

un·civ·i·lized \-'si-və-ˌlīzd\ *adj* 1 : not civilized : BARBAROUS 2 : remote from civilization : WILD

un·clasp \-'klasp\ *vb* : to open by or as if by loosing the clasp

un·cle \'əŋ-kəl\ *n* [ME, fr. OF, fr. L *avunculus* mother's brother] : the brother of one's father or mother; *also* : the husband of one's aunt

un·clean \ˌən-'klēn\ *adj* 1 : morally or spiritually impure 2 : prohibited by ritual law for use or contact 3 : DIRTY, SOILED — **un·clean·li·ness** \-lē-nəs\ *n* — **un·clean·ly** *adj* — **un·clean·ness** *n*

un·clench \-'klench\ *vb* : to open from a clenched position : RELAX

Uncle Tom \-'täm\ *n* [fr. *Uncle Tom*, faithful slave in Harriet Beecher Stowe's novel *Uncle Tom's Cabin* (1851-52)] : a black eager to win the approval of whites

un·cloak \ˌən-'klōk\ *vb* 1 : to remove a cloak or cover from 2 : UNMASK, REVEAL

un·clog \-'kläg\ *vb* : to remove an obstruction from

un·close \-'klōz\ *vb* : OPEN — **un·closed** \-'klōzd\ *adj*

un·clothe \-'klōth\ *vb* : to strip of clothes or a covering — **un·clothed** \-'klōthd\ *adj*

un·coil \ˌən-'kóil\ *vb* : to release or become released from a coiled state

un·com·fort·able \ˌən-'kəmf-tə-bəl, -'kəm-fər-tə-\ *adj* 1 : causing discomfort 2 : feeling discomfort — **un·com·fort·ably** \-blē\ *adv*

un·com·mit·ted \ˌən-kə-'mi-təd\ *adj* : not committed; *esp* : not pledged to a particular belief, allegiance, or program

un·com·mon \ˌən-'kä-mən\ *adj* 1 : not ordinarily encountered : UNUSUAL, RARE 2 : REMARKABLE, EXCEPTIONAL **syn** extraordinary, phenomenal, singular, unique — **un·com·mon·ly** *adv*

un·com·mu·ni·ca·tive \ˌən-kə-'myü-nə-ˌkā-tiv, -ni-kə-\ *adj* : not inclined to talk or impart information : RESERVED **syn** closemouthed, reticent, silent, taciturn

un·com·pro·mis·ing \ˌən-'käm-prə-ˌmī-ziŋ\ *adj* : not making or accepting a compromise : UNYIELDING **syn** adamant, inflexible, obdurate, rigid, unbending

un·con·cern \ˌən-kən-'sərn\ *n* 1 : lack of care or interest : INDIFFERENCE 2 : freedom from excessive concern

un·con·cerned \-'sərnd\ *adj* 1 : not having any part or interest 2 : not anxious or upset : free of worry **syn** aloof, detached, incurious, remote, uncurious, uninterested — **un·con·cern·ed·ly** \-'sər-nəd-lē\ *adv*

un·con·di·tion·al \ˌən-kən-'di-shə-nəl\ *adj* : not limited in any way — **un·con·di·tion·al·ly** *adv*

un·con·di·tioned \-'di-shənd\ *adj* 1 : not subject to conditions 2 : not acquired or learned : NATURAL ⟨∼ responses⟩ 3 : producing an unconditioned response ⟨∼ stimuli⟩

un·con·quer·able \ˌən-'käŋ-kə-rə-bəl\ *adj* : incapable of being conquered or overcome : INDOMITABLE

un·con·scio·na·ble \-'kän-shə-nə-bəl\ *adj* 1 : not guided or controlled by conscience 2 : not in accordance with what is right or just **syn** unreasonable, undue, unjustifiable, unwarrantable, unwarranted — **un·con·scio·na·bly** \-blē\ *adv*

¹**un·con·scious** \ˌən-'kän-chəs, -shəs\ *adj* 1 : not knowing or perceiving : not aware 2 : not done consciously or on purpose 3 : having lost consciousness 4 : of or relating to the unconscious — **un·con·scious·ly** *adv* — **un·con·scious·ness** *n*

²**unconscious** *n* : the part of one's mental life of which one is not ordinarily aware but which is often a powerful force in controlling behavior

un·con·sti·tu·tion·al \ˌən-ˌkän-stə-'tü-shə-nəl, -'tyü-\ *adj* : not according to or consistent with the constitution of a state or society — **un·con·sti·tu·tion·al·i·ty** \-tü-shə-'na-lə-tē, -'tyü-\ *n* — **un·con·sti·tu·tion·al·ly** \-'tü-shə-nə-lē, -'tyü-\ *adv*

un·con·trol·la·ble \ˌən-kən-'trō-lə-bəl\ *adj* : incapable of being controlled : UNGOVERNABLE — **un·con·trol·la·bly** \-blē\ *adv*

un·con·ven·tion·al \-'ven-chə-nəl\ *adj* : not conventional : being out of the ordinary — **un·con·ven·tion·al·i·ty** \-ˌven-chə-'na-lə-tē\ *n* — **un·con·ven·tion·al·ly** \-'ven-chə-nə-lē\ *adv*

un·cork \ˌən-'kórk\ *vb* 1 : to draw a cork from 2 : to release from a sealed or pent-up state; *also* : to let go

un·count·ed \-'kaún-təd\ *adj* 1 : not counted 2 : INNUMERABLE

un·cou·ple \-'kə-pəl\ *vb* : DISCONNECT

un·couth \-'küth\ *adj* [ME, unfamiliar, fr. OE *uncūth*, fr. *un-* + *cūth* known] 1 : strange, awkward, and clumsy in shape or appearance 2 : vulgar in conduct or speech : RUDE **syn** discourteous, ill-mannered, impolite, ungracious, unmannered, unmannerly

un·cov·er \-'kə-vər\ *vb* 1 : to make known : DISCLOSE, REVEAL 2 : to expose to view by removing some covering **3** : to take the cover from **4** : to remove the hat from; *also* : to take off the hat as a token of respect — **un·covered** *adj*

un·crit·i·cal \ˌən-ˈkri-ti-kəl\ *adj* **1** : not critical : lacking in discrimination **2** : showing lack or improper use of critical standards or procedures — **un·crit·i·cal·ly** \-k(ə-)lē\ *adv*

un·cross \-ˈkrós\ *vb* : to change from a crossed position ⟨∼ed his legs⟩

unc·tion \ˈəŋk-shən\ *n* **1** : the act of anointing as a rite of consecration or healing **2** : exaggerated or insincere earnestness of language or manner

unc·tu·ous \ˈəŋk-chə-wəs\ *adj* [ME, fr. MF or ML; MF *unctueux*, fr. ML *unctuosus*, fr. L *unctus* act of anointing, fr. *unguere* to anoint] **1** : FATTY, OILY **2** : insincerely smooth in speech and manner — **unc·tu·ous·ly** *adv*

un·curl \ˌən-ˈkərl\ *vb* : to make or become straightened out from a curled or coiled position

un·cut \ˌən-ˈkət\ *adj* **1** : not cut down or into **2** : not shaped by cutting ⟨an ∼ diamond⟩ **3** : not having the folds of the leaves slit ⟨an ∼ book⟩ **4** : not abridged or curtailed ⟨the ∼ version of the film⟩ **5** : not diluted ⟨∼ heroin⟩

un·daunt·ed \-ˈdón-təd\ *adj* : not daunted : not discouraged or dismayed **syn** bold, brave, dauntless, fearless, intrepid, valiant — **un·daunt·ed·ly** *adv*

un·de·ceive \ˌən-di-ˈsēv\ *vb* : to free from deception, illusion, or error

un·de·mon·stra·tive \ˌən-di-ˈmän-strə-tiv\ *adj* : restrained in expression of feeling : RESERVED

un·de·ni·able \ˌən-di-ˈnī-ə-bəl\ *adj* **1** : plainly true : INCONTESTABLE **2** : unquestionably excellent or genuine **syn** incontrovertible, indisputable, indubitable, unquestionable — **un·de·ni·ably** \-blē\ *adv*

¹un·der \ˈən-dər\ *adv* **1** : in or into a position below or beneath something **2** : below some quantity, level, or limit ⟨$10 or ∼⟩ **3** : in or into a condition of subjection, subordination, or unconsciousness ⟨the ether put him ∼⟩

²un·der \ˈən-dər, ˈən-\ *prep* **1** : lower than and overhung, surmounted, or sheltered by ⟨∼ a tree⟩ **2** : subject to the authority or guidance of ⟨served ∼ him⟩ ⟨was ∼ contract⟩ **3** : subject to the action or effect of ⟨∼ the influence of alcohol⟩ **4** : within the division or grouping of ⟨items ∼ this heading⟩ **5** : less or lower than ⟨as in size, amount, or rank⟩ ⟨earns ∼ $5000⟩

³under \ˈən-dər\ *adj* **1** : lying below, beneath, or on the ventral side **2** : facing or protruding downward **3** : SUBORDINATE **4** : lower than usual, proper, or desired in amount, quality, or degree

un·der·achiev·er \ˌən-dər-ə-ˈchē-vər\ *n* : one who performs below an expected level of proficiency

un·der·act \-ˈakt\ *vb* : to perform feebly or with restraint

un·der·ac·tive \-ˈak-tiv\ *adj* : characterized by abnormally low activity ⟨∼ glands⟩ — **un·der·ac·tiv·i·ty** \-ˌak-ˈti-və-tē\ *n*

un·der·age \-ˈāj\ *adj* : of less than mature or legal age

un·der·arm \-ˈärm\ *adj* **1** : UNDERHAND **2** ⟨an ∼ throw⟩ **2** : placed under or on the underside of the arms ⟨∼ seams⟩ — **underarm** *adv or n*

un·der·bel·ly \ˈən-dər-ˌbe-lē\ *n* **1** : the underside of a body or mass **2** : a vulnerable area

un·der·bid \ˌən-dər-ˈbid\ *vb* **-bid; -bid·ding** **1** : to bid less than another **2** : to bid too low

un·der·body \ˈən-dər-ˌbä-dē\ *n* : the lower parts of the body of a vehicle

un·der·bred \ˌən-dər-ˈbred\ *adj* : marked by lack of good breeding

un·der·brush \ˈən-dər-ˌbrəsh\ *n* : shrubs, bushes, or small trees growing beneath large trees

un·der·car·riage \-ˌkar-ij\ *n* **1** : a supporting framework (as of an automobile) **2** *chiefly Brit* : the landing gear of an airplane

un·der·charge \ˌən-dər-ˈchärj\ *vb* : to charge (as a

person) too little — **undercharge** \ˈən-dər-ˌchärj\ *n*

un·der·class·man \ˌən-dər-ˈklas-mən\ *n* : a member of the freshman or sophomore class

un·der·clothes \ˈən-dər-ˌklōthz\ *n pl* : UNDERWEAR

un·der·cloth·ing \-ˌklō-thiŋ\ *n* : UNDERWEAR

un·der·coat \-ˌkōt\ *n* **1** : a coat worn under another **2** : a growth of short hair or fur partly concealed by the longer and usu. coarser hairs of a mammal **3** : a coat of paint under another

un·der·coat·ing \-ˌkō-tiŋ\ *n* : a special waterproof coating applied to the underside of a vehicle

un·der·cov·er \ˌən-dər-ˈkə-vər\ *adj* : acting or executed in secret; *esp* : employed or engaged in secret investigation ⟨an ∼ agent⟩

un·der·croft \ˈən-dər-ˌkróft\ *n* [ME, fr. *under* + *crofte* crypt, fr. MD, fr. ML *crupta*, fr. L *crypta*] : a vaulted chamber under a church

un·der·cur·rent \-ˌkər-ənt\ *n* **1** : a current below the surface **2** : a hidden tendency of feeling or opinion

un·der·cut \ˌən-dər-ˈkət\ *vb* **-cut; -cut·ting** **1** : to cut away the underpart of **2** : to offer to sell or to work at a lower rate than **3** : to strike (the ball) obliquely downward so as to give a backward spin or elevation to the shot — **un·der·cut** \ˈən-dər-ˌkət\ *n*

un·der·de·vel·oped \ˌən-dər-di-ˈve-ləpt\ *adj* **1** : not normally or adequately developed ⟨∼ muscles⟩ **2** : having a relatively low level of economic development ⟨the ∼ nations⟩

un·der·dog \ˈən-dər-ˌdóg\ *n* : the loser or predicted loser in a struggle

un·der·done \ˌən-dər-ˈdən\ *adj* : not thoroughly done or cooked : RARE

un·der·draw·ers \ˈən-dər-ˌdrórz, -ˌdró-ərz\ *n pl* : UNDERPANTS

un·der·em·pha·size \ˌən-dər-ˈem-fə-sīz\ *vb* : to emphasize inadequately — **un·der·em·pha·sis** \-səs\ *n*

un·der·em·ployed \-im-ˈplóid\ *adj* : having less than full-time or adequate employment

un·der·es·ti·mate \-ˈes-tə-ˌmāt\ *vb* : to set too low a value on

un·der·ex·pose \-ik-ˈspōz\ *vb* : to expose (a photographic plate or film) for less time than is needed — **un·der·ex·po·sure** \-ˈspō-zhər\ *n*

un·der·feed \ˌən-dər-ˈfēd\ *vb* **-fed** \-ˈfed\; **-feed·ing** : to feed with too little food

un·der·foot \-ˈfút\ *adv* **1** : under the feet ⟨flowers trampled ∼⟩ **2** : close about one's feet : in the way

un·der·fur \ˈən-dər-ˌfər\ *n* : an undercoat of fur esp. when thick and soft

un·der·gar·ment \-ˌgär-mənt\ *n* : a garment to be worn under another

un·der·gird \ˌən-dər-ˈgərd\ *vb* : to brace up : STRENGTHEN

un·der·go \ˌən-dər-ˈgō\ *vb* **-went** \-ˈwent\; **-gone** \-ˈgón, -ˈgän\; **-go·ing** **1** : to submit to : ENDURE **2** : to go through : EXPERIENCE

un·der·grad \ˈən-dər-ˌgrad\ *n* : UNDERGRADUATE

un·der·grad·u·ate \ˌən-dər-ˈgra-jə-wət, -jə-ˌwāt\ *n* : a student at a university or college who has not taken a first degree

¹un·der·ground \ˌən-dər-ˈgraúnd\ *adv* **1** : beneath the surface of the earth **2** : in or into hiding or secret operation

²un·der·ground \ˈən-dər-ˌgraúnd\ *n* **1** : a space under the surface of the ground; *esp* : SUBWAY **2** : a secret political movement or group; *esp* : an organized body working in secret to overthrow a government or an occupying power **3** : an avant-garde group or movement that operates outside the establishment

³underground \ˈən-dər-ˌgraúnd\ *adj* **1** : being, growing, operating, or located below the surface of the ground ⟨∼ stems⟩ **2** : conducted by secret means **3** : produced or published by the underground ⟨∼ publications⟩; *also* : of or relating to the avant-garde underground

un·der·growth \'ən-dər-ˌgrōth\ *n* : low growth (as of herbs and shrubs) on the floor of a forest

¹**un·der·hand** \'ən-dər-ˌhand\ *adv* 1 : in an underhanded or secret manner 2 : with an underhand motion

²**underhand** *adj* 1 : UNDERHANDED 2 : made with the hand kept below the level of the shoulder

¹**un·der·hand·ed** \ˌən-dər-'han-dəd\ *adv* : UNDERHAND

²**underhanded** *adj* : marked by secrecy and deception — **un·der·hand·ed·ly** *adv* — **un·der·hand·ed·ness** *n*

un·der·lie \-'lī\ *vb* **-lay** \-'lā\; **-lain** \-'lān\; **-ly·ing** \-'lī-iŋ\ 1 : to lie or be situated under 2 : to be at the basis of : form the foundation of : SUPPORT

un·der·line \'ən-dər-ˌlīn\ *vb* 1 : to draw a line under 2 : EMPHASIZE, STRESS — **underline** *n*

un·der·ling \'ən-dər-liŋ\ *n* : SUBORDINATE, INFERIOR

un·der·lip \ˌən-dər-'lip\ *n* : the lower lip

un·der·ly·ing \ˌən-dər-'lī-iŋ\ *adj* 1 : lying under or below 2 : FUNDAMENTAL, BASIC ⟨~ principles⟩

un·der·mine \-'mīn\ *vb* 1 : to excavate beneath 2 : to weaken or wear away secretly or gradually

un·der·most \'ən-dər-ˌmōst\ *adj* : lowest in relative position — **undermost** *adv*

¹**un·der·neath** \ˌən-dər-'nēth\ *prep* 1 : directly under 2 : under subjection to

²**underneath** *adv* 1 : below a surface or object : BENEATH 2 : on the lower side

un·der·nour·ished \ˌən-dər-'nər-isht\ *adj* : supplied with insufficient nourishment — **un·der·nour·ish·ment** \-'nər-ish-mənt\ *n*

un·der·pants \'ən-dər-ˌpants\ *n pl* : a usu. short undergarment for the lower trunk : DRAWERS

un·der·part \-ˌpärt\ *n* : a part lying on the lower side esp. of a bird or mammal

un·der·pass \-ˌpas\ *n* : a crossing of a highway and another way (as a road) at different levels; *also* : the lower level

un·der·pay \ˌən-dər-'pā\ *vb* : to pay too little

un·der·pin·ning \'ən-dər-ˌpi-niŋ\ *n* : the material and construction (as a foundation) used for support of a structure — **un·der·pin** \ˌən-dər-'pin\ *vb*

un·der·play \ˌən-dər-'plā\ *vb* : to treat or handle with restraint; *esp* : to play a role with subdued force

un·der·pop·u·lat·ed \ˌən-dər-'pä-pyə-ˌlā-təd\ *adj* : having a lower than normal or desirable density of population

un·der·priv·i·leged \-'priv-lijd, -'pri-və-lijd\ *adj* : having fewer esp. economic and social privileges than others

un·der·pro·duc·tion \ˌən-dər-prə-'dək-shən\ *n* : the production of less than enough to satisfy the demand or of less than the usual supply

un·der·rate \-'rāt\ *vb* : to rate or value too low

un·der·rep·re·sent·ed \-ˌre-pri-'zen-təd\ *adj* : inadequately represented

un·der·score \'ən-dər-ˌskōr\ *vb* 1 : to draw a line under : UNDERLINE 2 : EMPHASIZE — **underscore** *n*

¹**un·der·sea** \ˌən-dər-'sē\ *adj* : being, carried on, or used beneath the surface of the sea

²**undersea** *or* **un·der·seas** \-'sēz\ *adv* : beneath the surface of the sea

un·der·sec·re·tary \ˌən-dər-'se-krə-ˌter-ē\ *n* : a secretary immediately subordinate to a principal secretary ⟨~ of state⟩

un·der·sell \-'sel\ *vb* **-sold** \-'sōld\; **-sell·ing** : to sell articles cheaper than

un·der·sexed \-'sekst\ *adj* : deficient in sexual desire

un·der·shirt \'ən-dər-ˌshərt\ *n* : a collarless undergarment with or without sleeves

un·der·shoot \ˌən-dər-'shüt\ *vb* **-shot** \-'shät\; **-shoot·ing** 1 : to shoot short of or below (a target) 2 : to fall short of (a runway) in landing an airplane

un·der·shorts \'ən-dər-ˌshorts\ *n pl* : SHORT 2

un·der·shot \'ən-dər-ˌshät\ *adj* 1 : moved by water passing beneath ⟨an ~ waterwheel⟩ 2 : having the lower front teeth projecting beyond the upper when the mouth is closed

un·der·side \'ən-dər-ˌsīd, ˌən-dər-'sīd\ *n* : the side or surface lying underneath

un·der·signed \'ən-dər-ˌsīnd\ *n, pl* **undersigned** : one whose name is signed at the end of a document

un·der·sized \ˌən-dər-'sīzd\ *also* **un·der·size** \-'sīz\ *adj* : of a size less than is common, proper, or normal

un·der·skirt \'ən-dər-ˌskərt\ *n* : a skirt worn under an outer skirt; *esp* : PETTICOAT

un·der·staffed \ˌən-dər-'staft\ *adj* : inadequately staffed

un·der·stand \ˌən-dər-'stand\ *vb* **-stood** \-'stüd\; **-stand·ing** 1 : to grasp the meaning of : COMPREHEND 2 : to have thorough or technical acquaintance with or expertness in ⟨~ finance⟩ 3 : to have reason to believe ⟨I ~ you are leaving tomorrow⟩ 4 : INTERPRET ⟨we ~ this to be a refusal⟩ 5 : to have a sympathetic attitude 6 : to accept as settled ⟨it is *understood* that he will pay the expenses⟩ — **un·der·stand·able** \-'stan-də-bəl\ *adj*

un·der·stand·ably \-blē\ *adv* : as can be easily understood

¹**un·der·stand·ing** \ˌən-dər-'stan-diŋ\ *n* 1 : knowledge and ability to judge : INTELLIGENCE ⟨a person of ~⟩ 2 : agreement of opinion or feeling 3 : a mutual agreement informally or tacitly entered into

²**understanding** *adj* : endowed with understanding : TOLERANT, SYMPATHETIC

un·der·state \ˌən-dər-'stāt\ *vb* 1 : to represent as less than is the case 2 : to state with restraint esp. for effect — **un·der·state·ment** *n*

un·der·stood \ˌən-dər-'stüd\ *adj* 1 : agreed upon 2 : IMPLICIT

un·der·sto·ry \'ən-dər-ˌstōr-ē, -ˌstor-\ *n* : the vegetative layer between the top layer of a forest and the ground cover

un·der·study \'ən-dər-ˌstə-dē, ˌən-dər-'stə-dē\ *vb* : to study another actor's part in order to substitute in an emergency — **understudy** \'ən-dər-ˌstə-dē\ *n*

un·der·sur·face \'ən-dər-ˌsər-fəs\ *n* : UNDERSIDE

un·der·take \ˌən-dər-'tāk\ *vb* **-took** \-'tük\; **-tak·en** \-'tā-kən\; **-tak·ing** 1 : to take upon oneself : set about ⟨~ a task⟩ 2 : to put oneself under obligation 3 : GUARANTEE, PROMISE

un·der·tak·er \'ən-dər-ˌtā-kər\ *n* : one whose business is to prepare the dead for burial and to arrange and manage funerals

un·der·tak·ing \'ən-dər-ˌtā-kiŋ, ˌən-dər-'tā-kiŋ; *2 is* 'ən-dər-ˌtā-kiŋ *only*\ *n* 1 : the act of one who undertakes or engages in any project 2 : the business of an undertaker 3 : something undertaken 4 : PROMISE, GUARANTEE

under–the–counter *adj* : UNLAWFUL, ILLICIT ⟨~ sale of drugs⟩

un·der·tone \'ən-dər-ˌtōn\ *n* 1 : a low or subdued tone or utterance 2 : a subdued color (as seen through and modifying another color)

un·der·tow \-ˌtō\ *n* : the current beneath the surface that flows seaward when waves are breaking upon the shore

un·der·trick \-ˌtrik\ *n* : a trick by which a declarer in bridge falls short of making the contract

un·der·val·ue \ˌən-dər-'val-yü\ *vb* 1 : to value or estimate below the real worth 2 : to esteem lightly

un·der·wa·ter \ˌən-dər-'wȯ-tər, -'wä-\ *adj* : lying, growing, worn, or operating below the surface of the water — **un·der·wa·ter** *adv*

under way \-'wā\ *adv* 1 : into motion from a standstill 2 : in progress

un·der·wear \'ən-dər-ˌwar\ *n* : clothing or a garment worn next to the skin and under other clothing

un·der·weight \ˌən-dər-'wāt\ *n* : weight below what is normal, average, or necessary — **underweight** *adj*

un·der·world \'ən-dər-ˌwərld\ *n* 1 : the place of departed souls : HADES 2 : the side of the world opposite to one 3 : the world of organized crime

un·der·write \'ən-dər-ˌrīt, ˌən-dər-'rīt\ *vb* **-wrote**

\-ˌrōt, -ˈrōt\; **-writ·ten** \-ˌrit-ᵊn, -ˈrit-ᵊn\; **-writ·ing 1** : to write under or at the end of something else **2** : to set one's name to an insurance policy and thereby become answerable for a designated loss or damage **3** : to subscribe to : agree to **4** : to guarantee financial support of — **un·der·writ·er** n

un·de·sign·ing \ˌən-di-ˈzī-niŋ\ adj : having no artful, ulterior, or fraudulent purpose : SINCERE

un·de·sir·able \-ˈzī-rə-bəl\ adj : not desirable — **undesirable** n

un·de·vi·at·ing \ˌən-ˈdē-vē-ˌā-tiŋ\ adj : keeping a true course

un·dies \ˈən-dēz\ n pl : UNDERWEAR; esp : women's underwear

un·do \ˌən-ˈdü\ vb **-did** \-ˈdid\; **-done** \-ˈdən\; **-do·ing 1** : to make or become unfastened or loosened : OPEN **2** : to make null or as if not done : REVERSE **3** : to bring to ruin; also : UPSET

un·do·ing n : a cause of ruin

un·doubt·ed \-ˈdaù-təd\ adj : not doubted or called into question : CERTAIN — **un·doubt·ed·ly** adv

¹**un·dress** \ˌən-ˈdres\ vb : to remove the clothes or covering of : STRIP, DISROBE

²**undress** n **1** : informal dress; esp : a loose robe or dressing gown **2** : ordinary dress **3** : NUDITY

un·due \-ˈdü, -ˈdyü\ adj **1** : not due **2** : exceeding or violating propriety or fitness : EXCESSIVE

un·du·lant \ˈən-jə-lənt, ˈən-də-, -dyə-\ adj : UNDULATING

undulant fever n : a human disease caused by bacteria from infected domestic animals or their products and marked by intermittent fever, pain and swelling in the joints, and great weakness

un·du·late \-ˌlāt\ vb **-lated; -lating** [LL undula small wave, fr. L unda wave] **1** : to have a wavelike motion or appearance **2** : to rise and fall in pitch or volume

un·du·la·tion \ˌən-jə-ˈlā-shən, ˌən-də-, -dyə-\ n **1** : wavy or wavelike motion **2** : pulsation of sound **3** : a wavy appearance or outline — **un·du·la·to·ry** \ˈən-jə-lə-ˌtōr-ē, ˈən-də-, -dyə-\ adj

un·du·ly \ˌən-ˈdü-lē, ˈən-, -ˈdyü-\ adv : in an undue manner; esp : EXCESSIVELY

un·dy·ing \-ˈdī-iŋ\ adj : not dying : IMMORTAL, PERPETUAL

un·earned \-ˈərnd\ adj : not earned by labor, service, or skill ⟨∼ income⟩

un·earth \ˌən-ˈərth\ vb **1** : to dig up out of or as if out of the earth ⟨∼ buried treasure⟩ **2** : to bring to light : DISCOVER ⟨∼ a secret⟩

un·earth·ly \-lē\ adj **1** : not of or belonging to the earth **2** : SUPERNATURAL, WEIRD; also : ABSURD

un·easy \ˌən-ˈē-zē\ adj **1** : AWKWARD, EMBARRASSED ⟨∼ among strangers⟩ **2** : disturbed by pain or worry; also : RESTLESS **3** : UNSTABLE ⟨an ∼ truce⟩ — **un·eas·i·ly** \-ˈē-zə-lē\ adv — **un·eas·i·ness** \-ˈē-zē-nəs\ n

un·em·ployed \ˌən-im-ˈplóid\ adj : not being used; also : having no job

un·em·ploy·ment \-ˈplói-mənt\ n **1** : lack of employment **2** : money paid at regular intervals (as by a government agency) to an unemployed person

un·end·ing \ˌən-ˈen-diŋ\ adj : having no ending : ENDLESS

un·equal \ˌən-ˈē-kwəl\ adj **1** : not alike (as in size, amount, number, or value) **2** : not uniform : VARIABLE **3** : badly balanced or matched **4** : INADEQUATE, INSUFFICIENT ⟨∼ to the task⟩ — **un·equal·ly** adv

un·equaled or **un·equalled** \-kwəld\ adj : not equaled : UNPARALLELED

un·equiv·o·cal \ˌən-i-ˈkwi-və-kəl\ adj : leaving no doubt : CLEAR — **un·equiv·o·cal·ly** adv

un·err·ing \ˌən-ˈer-iŋ, ˌən-ˈər-\ adj : making no errors : CERTAIN, UNFAILING — **un·err·ing·ly** adv

UNES·CO \yü-ˈnes-kō\ abbr United Nations Educational, Scientific, and Cultural Organization

un·even \ˌən-ˈē-vən\ adj **1** : ODD **3** **2** : not even : not level or smooth : RUGGED, RAGGED **3** : IRREGULAR;

also : varying in quality — **un·even·ly** adv — **un·even·ness** n

un·event·ful \ˌən-i-ˈvent-fəl\ adj : lacking interesting or noteworthy incidents — **un·event·ful·ly** adv

un·ex·am·pled \ˌən-ig-ˈzam-pəld\ adj : UNPRECEDENTED, UNPARALLELED

un·ex·cep·tion·able \ˌən-ik-ˈsep-shə-nə-bəl\ adj : not open to exception or objection : beyond reproach

un·ex·pect·ed \ˌən-ik-ˈspek-təd\ adj : not expected : UNFORESEEN — **un·ex·pect·ed·ly** adv

un·fail·ing \ˌən-ˈfā-liŋ\ adj **1** : not failing, flagging, or waning : CONSTANT **2** : INEXHAUSTIBLE **3** : INFALLIBLE, SURE — **un·fail·ing·ly** adv

un·fair \-ˈfar\ adj **1** : marked by injustice, partiality, or deception : UNJUST **2** : not equitable in business dealings — **un·fair·ly** adv — **un·fair·ness** n

un·faith·ful \-ˈfāth-fəl\ adj **1** : not observant of vows, allegiance, or duty : DISLOYAL **2** : INACCURATE, UNTRUSTWORTHY — **un·faith·ful·ly** adv — **un·faith·ful·ness** n

un·fa·mil·iar \ˌən-fə-ˈmil-yər\ adj **1** : not well-known : STRANGE ⟨an ∼ place⟩ **2** : not well acquainted ⟨∼ with the subject⟩ — **un·fa·mil·iar·i·ty** \-ˌmi-lē-ˈar-, -ˌyar-\ n

un·fas·ten \ˌən-ˈfas-ᵊn\ vb : to make or become loose : UNDO, DETACH

un·feel·ing \-ˈfē-liŋ\ adj **1** : lacking feeling : INSENSATE **2** : HARDHEARTED, CRUEL — **un·feel·ing·ly** adv

un·feigned \-ˈfānd\ adj : not feigned : not hypocritical : GENUINE

un·fet·ter \-ˈfe-tər\ vb **1** : to free from fetters **2** : LIBERATE

un·fil·ial \ˌən-ˈfi-lē-əl, -ˈfil-yəl\ adj : not observing the obligations of a child to a parent : UNDUTIFUL

un·fin·ished \ˌən-ˈfi-nisht\ adj **1** : not brought to an end **2** : being in a rough or unpolished state

¹**un·fit** \-ˈfit\ adj : not fit or suitable; esp : physically or mentally unsound — **un·fit·ness** n

²**unfit** vb : DISABLE, DISQUALIFY

un·fix \-ˈfiks\ vb **1** : to loosen from a fastening : DETACH **2** : UNSETTLE

un·flap·pa·ble \-ˈfla-pə-bəl\ adj : not easily upset or panicked — **un·flap·pa·bly** adv

un·fledged \ˌən-ˈflejd\ adj : not feathered or ready for flight; also : IMMATURE, CALLOW

un·flinch·ing \-ˈflin-chiŋ\ adj : not flinching or shrinking : STEADFAST — **un·flinch·ing·ly** adv

un·fold \-ˈfōld\ vb **1** : to open the folds of : open up **2** : to lay open to view : DISCLOSE **3** : BLOSSOM, DEVELOP

un·for·get·ta·ble \ˌən-fər-ˈge-tə-bəl\ adj : incapable of being forgotten — **un·for·get·ta·bly** \-blē\ adv

un·formed \-ˈförmd\ adj : not regularly formed or ordered : UNDEVELOPED

un·for·tu·nate \-ˈför-chə-nət\ adj **1** : not fortunate : UNLUCKY **2** : attended with misfortune **3** : UNSUITABLE — **unfortunate** n

un·for·tu·nate·ly \-nət-lē\ adv **1** : in an unfortunate manner **2** : it is unfortunate

un·found·ed \ˌən-ˈfaùn-dəd\ adj : lacking a sound basis : GROUNDLESS

un·freeze \-ˈfrēz\ vb **-froze** \-ˈfrōz\; **-fro·zen** \-ˈfrōz-ᵊn\; **-freez·ing 1** : to cause to thaw **2** : to remove from a freeze ⟨∼ prices⟩

un·fre·quent·ed \ˌən-frē-ˈkwen-təd; ˌən-ˈfrē-kwən-\ adj : seldom visited or traveled over

un·friend·ly \ˌən-ˈfrend-lē\ adj **1** : not friendly or kind : HOSTILE **2** : UNFAVORABLE — **un·friend·li·ness** \-lē-nəs\ n

un·frock \-ˈfräk\ vb : DEFROCK

un·fruit·ful \-ˈfrüt-fəl\ adj **1** : not producing fruit or offspring : BARREN **2** : yielding no valuable result : UNPROFITABLE — **un·fruit·ful·ness** n

un·furl \-ˈfərl\ vb : to loose from a furled state : UNFOLD

un·gain·ly \-ˈgān-lē\ adj [un- + obs. gainly proper, becoming, fr. gain direct, handy, fr. ME geyn, fr. OE gēn, fr. ON *gegn*] : CLUMSY, AWKWARD — **un·gain·li·ness** \-lē-nəs\ *n*

un·gen·er·ous \ˌən-'je-nə-rəs\ *adj* : not generous or liberal : STINGY

un·glued \ˌən-'glüd\ *adj* : UPSET, DISORDERED

un·god·ly \ˌən-'gäd-lē, -'god-\ *adj* 1 : IMPIOUS, IRRELIGIOUS 2 : SINFUL, WICKED 3 : OUTRAGEOUS ⟨an ~ hour⟩ — **un·god·li·ness** \-lē-nəs\ *n*

un·gov·ern·able \-'gə-vər-nə-bəl\ *adj* : not capable of being governed, guided, or restrained : UNRULY

un·gra·cious \-'grā-shəs\ *adj* 1 : not courteous : RUDE 2 : not pleasing : DISAGREEABLE

un·grate·ful \ˌən-'grāt-fəl\ *adj* 1 : not thankful for favors 2 : DISAGREEABLE; *also* : THANKLESS — **un·grate·ful·ly** *adv* — **un·grate·ful·ness** *n*

un·guard·ed \-'gär-dəd\ *adj* 1 : UNPROTECTED 2 : DIRECT, INCAUTIOUS ⟨~ remarks⟩

un·guent \'əŋ-gwənt, 'ən-\ *n* : a soothing or healing salve : OINTMENT

¹**un·gu·late** \'əŋ-gyə-lət, 'ən-, -ˌlāt\ *adj* [LL *ungulatus*, fr. L *ungula* hoof, fr. *unguis* nail, hoof] : having hoofs

²**ungulate** *n* : a hoofed mammal (as a cow, horse, or rhinoceros)

Unh *symbol* unnilhexium

un·hal·lowed \ˌən-'ha-lōd\ *adj* 1 : not consecrated : UNHOLY 2 : IMPIOUS, PROFANE 3 : contrary to accepted standards : IMMORAL

un·hand \ˌən-'hand\ *vb* : to remove the hand from : let go

un·hand·some \-'han-səm\ *adj* 1 : not beautiful or handsome : HOMELY 2 : UNBECOMING 3 : DISCOURTEOUS, RUDE

un·handy \-'han-dē\ *adj* : INCONVENIENT; *also* : AWKWARD

un·hap·py \-'ha-pē\ *adj* 1 : UNLUCKY, UNFORTUNATE 2 : SAD, MISERABLE 3 : INAPPROPRIATE — **un·hap·pi·ly** \-'ha-pə-lē\ *adv* — **un·hap·pi·ness** \-pē-nəs\ *n*

un·har·ness \-'här-nəs\ *vb* : to remove the harness from (as a horse)

un·healthy \-'hel-thē\ *adj* 1 : not conducive to health : UNWHOLESOME 2 : SICKLY, DISEASED

un·heard \-'hərd\ *adj* 1 : not heard 2 : not granted a hearing

unheard—of *adj* : previously unknown; *esp* : UNPRECEDENTED

un·hinge \ˌən-'hinj\ *vb* 1 : to take from the hinges 2 : to make unstable esp. mentally

un·hitch \-'hich\ *vb* : UNFASTEN, LOOSE

un·ho·ly \-'hō-lē\ *adj* : not holy : PROFANE, WICKED — **un·ho·li·ness** \-lē-nəs\ *n*

un·hook \-'hůk\ *vb* : to loose from a hook

un·horse \-'hors\ *vb* : to dislodge from or as if from a horse

uni·cam·er·al \ˌyü-ni-'ka-mə-rəl\ *adj* : having a single legislative house or chamber

UNI·CEF \'yü-nə-ˌsef\ *abbr* [*United Nations International Children's Emergency Fund*, its former name] United Nations Children's Fund

uni·cel·lu·lar \ˌyü-ni-'sel-yə-lər\ *adj* : having or consisting of a single cell

uni·corn \'yü-nə-ˌkorn\ *n* [ME *unicorne*, fr. OF, fr. LL *unicornis*, fr. L, having one horn, fr. *unus* one + *cornu* horn] : a mythical animal with one horn in the middle of the forehead

uni·cy·cle \'yü-ni-ˌsī-kəl\ *n* : a vehicle that has a single wheel and is usu. propelled by pedals

uni·di·rec·tion·al \ˌyü-ni-də-'rek-shə-nəl, -dī-\ *adj* : having, moving in, or responsive in a single direction

uni·fi·ca·tion \ˌyü-nə-fə-'kā-shən\ *n* : the act, process, or result of unifying : the state of being unified

¹**uni·form** \'yü-nə-ˌform\ *adj* 1 : not varying 2 : of the same form with others ⟨~ procedures⟩ — **uni·form·ly** *adv*

²**uniform** *vb* : to clothe with a uniform

³**uniform** *n* : distinctive dress worn by members of a particular group (as an army or a police force)

uni·for·mi·ty \ˌyü-nə-'for-mə-tē\ *n, pl* **-ties** : the state of being uniform

uni·fy \'yü-nə-ˌfī\ *vb* **-fied; -fy·ing** : to make into a coherent whole : UNITE

uni·lat·er·al \ˌyü-nə-'la-tə-rəl\ *adj* : of, having, affecting, or done by one side only — **uni·lat·er·al·ly** *adv*

un·im·peach·able \ˌən-im-'pē-chə-bəl\ *adj* : not liable to accusation : BLAMELESS, IRREPROACHABLE

un·in·hib·it·ed \ˌən-in-'hi-bə-təd\ *adj* : free from inhibition; *also* : boisterously informal — **un·in·hib·it·ed·ly** *adv*

un·in·tel·li·gent \-'te-lə-jənt\ *adj* : lacking intelligence

un·in·tel·li·gi·ble \-jə-bəl\ *adj* : not intelligible : OBSCURE — **un·in·tel·li·gi·bly** \-blē\ *adv*

un·in·ter·est·ed \ˌən-'in-trəs-təd, -tə-rəs-, -tə-ˌres-\ *adj* : not interested : not having the mind or feelings engaged or aroused

un·in·ter·rupt·ed \ˌən-ˌin-tə-'rəp-təd\ *adj* : not interrupted : CONTINUOUS

union \'yü-nyən\ *n* 1 : an act or instance of uniting two or more things into one : the state of being so united : COMBINATION, JUNCTION 2 : a uniting in marriage 3 : something formed by a combining of parts or members; *esp* : a confederation of independent individuals (as nations or persons) for some common purpose 4 : an organization of workers (as a labor union or a trade union) formed to advance its members' interests esp. in respect to wages and working conditions 5 : a device emblematic of union used on or as a national flag; *also* : the upper inner corner of a flag 6 : a device for connecting parts (as of a machine); *esp* : a coupling for pipes

union·ism \'yü-nyə-ˌni-zəm\ *n* 1 : the principle or policy of forming or adhering to a union; *esp, cap* : adherence to the policy of a firm federal union before or during the U.S. Civil War 2 : the principles or system of trade unions — **union·ist** *n*

union·ize \'yü-nyə-ˌnīz\ *vb* **-ized; -iz·ing** : to form into or cause to join a labor union — **union·i·za·tion** \ˌyü-nyə-nə-'zā-shən\ *n*

union jack *n* 1 : a flag consisting of the part of a national flag that signifies union 2 *cap U&J* : the national flag of the United Kingdom

unique \yü-'nēk\ *adj* 1 : being the only one of its kind : SINGLE, SOLE 2 : very unusual : NOTABLE — **unique·ly** *adv* — **unique·ness** *n*

uni·sex \'yü-nə-ˌseks\ *adj* : not distinguishable as male or female; *also* : suitable or designed for both males and females — **unisex** *n*

uni·sex·u·al \ˌyü-nə-'sek-shə-wəl\ *adj* 1 : having only male or only female sex organs 2 : UNISEX

uni·son \'yü-nə-sən, -zən\ *n* [MF, fr. ML *unisonus* having the same sound, fr. L *unus* one + *sonus* sound] 1 : sameness or identity in musical pitch 2 : the condition of being tuned or sounded at the same pitch or in octaves ⟨sing in ~⟩ 3 : harmonious agreement or union : ACCORD

unit \'yü-nət\ *n* 1 : the smallest whole number greater than zero : ONE 2 : a definite amount or quantity used as a standard of measurement 3 : a single thing, person, or group that is a constituent of a whole; *also* : a part of a military establishment that has a prescribed organization — **unit** *adj*

Uni·tar·i·an \ˌyü-nə-'ter-ē-ən\ *n* : a member of a religious denomination stressing individual freedom of belief — **Uni·tar·i·an·ism** *n*

uni·tary \'yü-nə-ˌter-ē\ *adj* 1 : of or relating to a unit 2 : not divided — **uni·tar·i·ly** \ˌyü-nə-'ter-ə-lē\ *adv*

unite \yů-'nīt\ *vb* **unit·ed; unit·ing** 1 : to put or join together so as to make one : COMBINE, COALESCE 2 : to join by a legal or moral bond; *also* : to join in interest or fellowship 3 : AMALGAMATE, CONSOLIDATE 4 : to act in concert

unit·ed \yů-'nī-təd\ *adj* 1 : made one : COMBINED 2

: relating to or produced by joint action **3** : being in agreement : HARMONIOUS

unit·ize \'yü-nə-₁tīz\ *vb* **-ized; -iz·ing 1** : to form or convert into a unit **2** : to divide into units

uni·ty \'yü-nə-tē\ *n, pl* **-ties 1** : the quality or state of being or being made one : ONENESS **2** : a definite quantity or combination of quantities taken as one or for which 1 is made to stand in calculation **3** : CONCORD, ACCORD, HARMONY **4** : continuity without change ⟨~ of purpose⟩ **5** : reference of all the parts of a literary or artistic composition to a single main idea **6** : totality of related parts **syn** solidarity, union, integrity

univ *abbr* **1** universal **2** university

uni·valve \'yü-ni-₁valv\ *n* : a mollusk having a shell with only one piece; *esp* : GASTROPOD — **univalve** *adj*

uni·ver·sal \₁yü-nə-'vər-səl\ *adj* **1** : including, covering, or affecting the whole without limit or exception : UNLIMITED, GENERAL ⟨a ~ rule⟩ **2** : present or occurring everywhere **3** : used or for use among all ⟨a ~ language⟩ — **uni·ver·sal·ly** *adv*

uni·ver·sal·i·ty \-vər-sə-lə-tē\ *n* : the quality or state of being universal

uni·ver·sal·ize \-'vər-sə-₁līz\ *vb* **-ized; -iz·ing** : to make universal : GENERALIZE — **uni·ver·sal·i·za·tion** \-₁vər-sə-lə-'zā-shən\ *n*

universal joint *n* : a shaft coupling for transmitting rotation from one shaft to another not in a straight line with it

universal joint

Universal Product Code *n* : a combination of a bar code and numbers by which a scanner can identify a product and usu. assign a price

uni·verse \'yü-nə-₁vərs\ *n* [L *universum,* fr. neut. of *universus* entire, whole, fr. *unus* one + *versus* turned toward, fr. pp. of *vertere* to turn] : the whole body of things observed or assumed : COSMOS

uni·ver·si·ty \₁yü-nə-'vər-sə-tē\ *n, pl* **-ties** : an institution of higher learning authorized to confer degrees in various special fields (as theology, law, and medicine) as well as in the arts and sciences generally

un·just \₁ən-'jəst\ *adj* : characterized by injustice — **un·just·ly** *adv*

un·kempt \-'kempt\ *adj* **1** : lacking order or neatness; *also* : ROUGH, UNPOLISHED **2** : not combed : DISHEVELED

un·kind \-'kīnd\ *adj* : not kind or sympathetic ⟨an ~ remark⟩ — **un·kind·ly** *adv* — **un·kind·ness** *n*

un·kind·ly \-'kīnd-lē\ *adj* : UNKIND — **un·kind·li·ness** *n*

un·know·ing \₁ən-'nō-iŋ\ *adj* : not knowing — **un·know·ing·ly** *adv*

un·known \-'nōn\ *adj* : not known or not well-known — **unknown** *n*

un·lace \₁ən-'lās\ *vb* : to loose by undoing a lace

un·lade \-'lād\ *vb* **-lad·ed; -laded** *or* **-lad·en** \-'lād-ᵊn\ **-lad·ing** : to take the load or cargo from : UNLOAD

un·latch \-'lach\ *vb* **1** : to open or loose by lifting the latch **2** : to become loosed or opened

un·law·ful \₁ən-'lò-fəl\ *adj* **1** : not lawful : ILLEGAL **2** : ILLEGITIMATE — **un·law·ful·ly** *adv*

un·lead·ed \-'le-dəd\ *adj* : not treated or mixed with lead or lead compounds

un·learn \-'lərn\ *vb* : to put out of one's knowledge or memory; *also* : to discard the habit of

un·learned \-'lər-nəd *for 1;* -'lərnd *for 2*\ *adj* **1** : UN-

EDUCATED, ILLITERATE **2** : not gained by study or training

un·leash \-'lēsh\ *vb* : to free from or as if from a leash : let loose

un·less \ən-'les, 'ən-₁les\ *conj* : except on condition that ⟨won't go ~ you do⟩

un·let·tered \₁ən-'le-tərd\ *adj* : not educated : ILLITERATE

¹un·like \-'līk\ *adj* **1** : not like : DISSIMILAR, DIFFERENT **2** : UNEQUAL — **un·like·ness** *n*

²unlike *prep* **1** : different from ⟨she's quite ~ her sister⟩ **2** : unusual for ⟨it's ~ you to be late⟩ **3** : differently from ⟨behaves ~ his brother⟩

un·like·li·hood \₁ən-'lī-klē-₁hùd\ *n* : IMPROBABILITY

un·like·ly \-'lī-klē\ *adj* **1** : not likely : IMPROBABLE **2** : likely to fail

un·lim·ber \₁ən-'lim-bər\ *vb* : to get ready for action

un·list·ed \₁ən-'lis-təd\ *adj* **1** : not appearing on a list; *esp* : not appearing in a telephone book **2** : not listed on a stock exchange

un·load \-'lōd\ *vb* **1** : to take away or off : REMOVE ⟨~ cargo from a hold⟩; *also* : to get rid of **2** : to take a load from ⟨~ the ship⟩; *also* : to relieve or set free : UNBURDEN ⟨~ one's mind of worries⟩ **3** : to draw the charge from ⟨~ed the gun⟩ **4** : to sell in volume

un·lock \-'läk\ *vb* **1** : to open or unfasten through release of a lock **2** : RELEASE ⟨~ a flood of emotions⟩ **3** : DISCLOSE, REVEAL ⟨~ nature's secrets⟩

un·looked–for \-'lùkt-fór\ *adj* : UNEXPECTED

un·loose \₁ən-'lüs\ *vb* : to relax the strain of : set free; *also* : UNTIE

un·loos·en \-'lüs-ᵊn\ *vb* : UNLOOSE

un·love·ly \-'ləv-lē\ *adj* : having no charm or appeal : not amiable

un·luck·i·ly \-'lə-kə-lē\ *adv* : UNFORTUNATELY

un·lucky \-'lə-kē\ *adj* **1** : UNFORTUNATE, ILL-FATED **2** : likely to bring misfortune : INAUSPICIOUS **3** : REGRETTABLE

un·man \₁ən-'man\ *vb* **1** : to deprive of manly courage **2** : CASTRATE

un·man·ly \-'man-lē\ *adj* : not manly : COWARDLY; *also* : EFFEMINATE

un·man·ner·ly \-'ma-nər-lē\ *adj* : RUDE, IMPOLITE — **unmannerly** *adv*

un·mask \₁ən-'mask\ *vb* **1** : to strip of a mask or a disguise : EXPOSE **2** : to remove one's mask

un·mean·ing \-'mē-niŋ\ *adj* : having no meaning : SENSELESS

un·me·di·at·ed \₁ən-'mē-dē-₁ā-təd\ *adj* : not mediated : not communicated or transformed by an intervening agency

un·meet \-'mēt\ *adj* : not meet or fit : UNSUITABLE, IMPROPER

un·men·tion·able \-'men-chə-nə-bəl\ *adj* : not fit or proper to be talked about

un·mer·ci·ful \-'mər-si-fəl\ *adj* : not merciful : CRUEL, MERCILESS — **un·mer·ci·ful·ly** *adv*

un·mind·ful \-'mīnd-fəl\ *adj* : not mindful : CARELESS, UNAWARE

un·mis·tak·able \₁ən-mə-'stā-kə-bəl\ *adj* : not capable of being mistaken or misunderstood : CLEAR, OBVIOUS — **un·mis·tak·ably** \-blē\ *adv*

un·mit·i·gat·ed \₁ən-'mi-tə-₁gā-təd\ *adj* **1** : not softened or lessened **2** : ABSOLUTE, DOWNRIGHT ⟨an ~ liar⟩

un·moor \-'mùr\ *vb* : to loose from or as if from moorings

un·mor·al \-'mòr-əl\ *adj* : having no moral perception or quality : AMORAL — **un·mo·ral·i·ty** \₁ən-mə-'ra-lə-tē\ *n*

un·muz·zle \-'mə-zəl\ *vb* : to remove a muzzle from

un·nat·u·ral \₁ən-'na-chə-rəl\ *adj* : contrary to or acting contrary to nature or natural instincts; *also* : ABNORMAL — **un·nat·u·ral·ly** *adv* — **un·nat·u·ral·ness** *n*

un·nec·es·sar·i·ly \₁ən-₁ne-sə-'ser-ə-lē\ *adv* **1** : not by necessity **2** : to an unnecessary degree ⟨~ harsh⟩

un·nerve \ˌən-ˈnərv\ *vb* : to deprive of courage, strength, or steadiness; *also* : UPSET

un·nil·hex·i·um \ˌyün-əl-ˈhek-sē-əm\ *n* [NL. fr. *unnil-* (fr. L *unus* one + *nil* zero) + Gk *hex* six + NL *-ium*] : the chemical element of atomic number 106 — see ELEMENT table

un·nil·pen·ti·um \-ˈpen-tē-əm\ *n* : the chemical element of atomic number 105 — see ELEMENT table

un·nil·qua·di·um \-ˈkwä-dē-əm\ *n* : the chemical element of atomic number 104 — see ELEMENT table

un·num·bered \ˌən-ˈnəm-bərd\ *adj* : not numbered or counted : INNUMERABLE

un·ob·tru·sive \ˌən-əb-ˈtrü-siv\ *adj* : not obtrusive or forward : not bold : INCONSPICUOUS — **un·ob·tru·sive·ly** *adv*

un·oc·cu·pied \ˌən-ˈä-kyə-ˌpīd\ *adj* **1** : not busy : UNEMPLOYED **2** : not occupied : EMPTY, VACANT

un·or·ga·nized \-ˈȯr-gə-ˌnīzd\ *adj* **1** : not formed or brought into an integrated or ordered whole **2** : not organized into unions ⟨∼ labor⟩

Unp *symbol* unnilpentium

un·pack \ˌən-ˈpak\ *vb* **1** : to separate and remove things packed **2** : to open and remove the contents of

un·par·al·leled \ˌən-ˈpar-ə-ˌleld\ *adj* : having no parallel; *esp* : having no equal or match

un·par·lia·men·ta·ry \ˌən-ˌpär-lə-ˈmen-tə-rē\ *adj* : contrary to parliamentary practice

un·peg \ˌən-ˈpeg\ *vb* **1** : to remove a peg from **2** : to unfasten by or as if by removing a peg

un·per·son \ˈən-ˌpərs-ən, -ˌpərs-\ *n* : a person who usu. for political or ideological reasons is removed from recognition or consideration

un·pile \ˌən-ˈpīl\ *vb* : to take or disentangle from a pile

un·pin \-ˈpin\ *vb* : to remove a pin from : UNFASTEN

un·pleas·ant \-ˈplez-ənt\ *adj* : not pleasant : DISAGREEABLE — **un·pleas·ant·ly** *adv* — **un·pleas·ant·ness** *n*

un·plug \ˌən-ˈpləg\ *vb* **1** : UNCLOG **2** : to remove (a plug) from a receptacle; *also* : to disconnect from an electric circuit by removing a plug

un·plumbed \-ˈpləmd\ *adj* **1** : not tested or measured with a plumb line **2** : not thoroughly explored

un·pop·u·lar \ˌən-ˈpä-pyə-lər\ *adj* : not popular : looked upon or received unfavorably — **un·pop·u·lar·i·ty** \ˌən-ˌpä-pyə-ˈlar-ə-tē\ *n*

un·prec·e·dent·ed \ˌən-ˈpre-sə-ˌden-təd\ *adj* : having no precedent : NOVEL

un·pre·ten·tious \ˌən-pri-ˈten-chəs\ *adj* : not pretentious : MODEST

un·prin·ci·pled \ˌən-ˈprin-sə-pəld\ *adj* : lacking sound or honorable principles : UNSCRUPULOUS

un·print·able \-ˈprin-tə-bəl\ *adj* : unfit to be printed

un·prof·it·able \ˌən-ˈprä-fə-tə-bəl\ *adj* : not profitable : USELESS, VAIN

Unq *symbol* unnilquadium

un·qual·i·fied \ˌən-ˈkwä-lə-ˌfīd\ *adj* **1** : not having requisite qualifications **2** : not modified or restricted by reservations : COMPLETE — **un·qual·i·fied·ly** \-ˌfī-əd-lē\ *adv*

un·ques·tion·able \-ˈkwes-chə-nə-bəl\ *adj* : not questionable : INDISPUTABLE — **un·ques·tion·ably** \-blē\ *adv*

un·ques·tion·ing \-chə-niŋ\ *adj* : not questioning : accepting without examination or hesitation — **un·ques·tion·ing·ly** *adv*

un·qui·et \-ˈkwī-ət\ *adj* **1** : not quiet : AGITATED, DISTURBED **2** : physically, emotionally, or mentally restless : UNEASY

un·quote \ˈən-ˌkwōt\ *n* — used orally to indicate the end of a direct quotation

un·rav·el \ˌən-ˈra-vəl\ *vb* **1** : to separate the threads of **2** : SOLVE ⟨∼ a mystery⟩ **3** : to become unraveled

un·read \-ˈred\ *adj* **1** : not read; *also* : left unexamined **2** : lacking the benefits or the experience of reading

un·re·al \-ˈrēl\ *adj* : lacking in reality, substance, or genuineness — **un·re·al·i·ty** \ˌən-rē-ˈa-lə-tē\ *n*

un·rea·son·able \-ˈrēz-ən-ə-bəl\ *adj* **1** : not governed by

or acting according to reason; *also* : not conformable to reason : ABSURD **2** : exceeding the bounds of reason or moderation — **un·rea·son·able·ness** *n* — **un·rea·son·ably** *adv*

un·rea·soned \-ˈrēz-ənd\ *adj* : not based on reason or reasoning

un·rea·son·ing \-ˈrēz-ən-iŋ\ *adj* : not using or showing the use of reason as a guide or control

un·re·con·struct·ed \ˌən-rē-kən-ˈstrək-təd\ *adj* : not reconciled to some political, economic, or social change; *esp* : holding stubbornly to a particular belief, view, place, or style

un·reel \ˌən-ˈrēl\ *vb* **1** : to unwind from or as if from a reel **2** : to perform successfully

un·re·gen·er·ate \ˌən-ri-ˈje-nə-rət\ *adj* : not regenerated or reformed

un·re·lent·ing \-ˈlen-tiŋ\ *adj* **1** : not yielding in determination : STERN ⟨∼ leader⟩ **2** : not letting up or weakening in vigor or pace : CONSTANT — **un·re·lent·ing·ly** *adv*

un·re·mit·ting \-ˈmi-tiŋ\ *adj* : CONTINUOUS, INCESSANT, PERSEVERING — **un·re·mit·ting·ly** *adv*

un·re·quit·ed \ˌən-ri-ˈkwī-təd\ *adj* : not requited : not reciprocated or returned in kind ⟨∼ love⟩

un·re·served \-ˈzərvd\ *adj* **1** : not limited or partial ⟨∼ enthusiasm⟩ **2** : not cautious or reticent : FRANK, OPEN **3** : not set aside for special use — **un·re·served·ly** \-ˈzər-vəd-lē\ *adv*

un·rest \ˌən-ˈrest\ *n* : a disturbed or uneasy state : TURMOIL

un·re·strained \ˌən-ri-ˈstrānd\ *adj* **1** : IMMODERATE, UNCONTROLLED **2** : SPONTANEOUS

un·re·straint \-ri-ˈstrānt\ *n* : lack of restraint

un·rid·dle \ˌən-ˈrid-əl\ *vb* : to find the explanation of : SOLVE

un·righ·teous \-ˈrī-chəs\ *adj* **1** : SINFUL, WICKED **2** : UNJUST — **un·righ·teous·ness** *n*

un·ripe \-ˈrīp\ *adj* : not ripe : IMMATURE

un·ri·valed *or* **un·ri·valled** \ˌən-ˈrī-vəld\ *adj* : having no rival : SUPREME

un·robe \-ˈrōb\ *vb* : DISROBE, UNDRESS

un·roll \-ˈrōl\ *vb* **1** : to unwind a roll of : open out **2** : DISPLAY, DISCLOSE **3** : to become unrolled or spread out

un·roof \-ˈrüf, -ˈru̇f\ *vb* : to strip off the roof or covering of

un·ruf·fled \ˌən-ˈrə-fəld\ *adj* **1** : not agitated or upset **2** : not ruffled : SMOOTH ⟨∼ water⟩

un·ruly \-ˈrü-lē\ *adj* [ME *unreuly*, fr. *un-* + *reuly* disciplined, fr. *reule* rule, fr. OF, fr. L *regula* straightedge, rule, fr. *regere* to direct] : not submissive to rule or restraint : TURBULENT ⟨∼ passions⟩ — **un·rul·i·ness** \-ˈrü-lē-nəs\ *n*

un·sad·dle \ˌən-ˈsad-əl\ *vb* **1** : to remove the saddle from a horse **2** : UNHORSE

un·sat·u·rat·ed \-ˈsa-chə-ˌrā-təd\ *adj* **1** : capable of absorbing or dissolving more of something **2** : containing double or triple bonds between carbon atoms ⟨∼ fats or oils⟩ — **un·sat·u·rate** \-rət\ *n*

un·saved \ˌən-ˈsāvd\ *adj* : not saved; *esp* : not rescued from eternal punishment

un·sa·vory \-ˈsā-və-rē\ *adj* **1** : TASTELESS **2** : unpleasant to taste or smell **3** : morally offensive

un·say \-ˈsā\ *vb* **-said** \-ˈsed\; **-say·ing** : to take back (something said) : RETRACT, WITHDRAW

un·scathed \-ˈskāt͟hd\ *adj* : wholly unharmed : not injured

un·schooled \-ˈskül̇d\ *adj* : not schooled : UNTAUGHT, UNTRAINED

un·sci·en·tif·ic \ˌən-ˌsī-ən-ˈti-fik\ *adj* : not scientific : not in accord with the principles and methods of science

un·scram·ble \ˌən-ˈskram-bəl\ *vb* **1** : RESOLVE, CLARIFY **2** : to restore (as a radio message) to intelligible form

un·screw \-ˈskrü\ *vb* **1** : to draw the screws from **2** : to loosen by turning

un·scru·pu·lous \-ˈskrü-pyə-ləs\ *adj* : not scrupulous : UNPRINCIPLED — **un·scru·pu·lous·ly** *adv* — **un·scru·pu·lous·ness** *n*

un·seal \-ˈsēl\ *vb* : to break or remove the seal of : OPEN

un·search·able \-ˈsər-chə-bəl\ *adj* : not capable of being searched or explored

un·sea·son·able \-ˈsēz-ᵊn-ə-bəl\ *adj* : not seasonable : happening or coming at the wrong time : UNTIMELY — **un·sea·son·ably** \-blē\ *adv*

un·seat \-ˈsēt\ *vb* **1** : to throw from one's seat esp. on horseback **2** : to remove from political office

un·seem·ly \-ˈsēm-lē\ *adj* : not according with established standards of good form or taste; *also* : not suitable — **un·seem·li·ness** *n*

un·seen \ˌən-ˈsēn\ *adj* : not seen : INVISIBLE

un·seg·re·gat·ed \-ˈse-gri-ˌgā-təd\ *adj* : not segregated; *esp* : free from racial segregation

un·self·ish \-ˈsel-fish\ *adj* : not selfish : GENEROUS — **un·self·ish·ly** *adv* — **un·self·ish·ness** *n*

un·set·tle \ˌən-ˈset-ᵊl\ *vb* : to move or loosen from a settled position : DISPLACE, DISTURB

un·set·tled \-ˈset-ᵊld\ *adj* **1** : not settled : not fixed (as in position or character) **2** : not calm : DISTURBED **3** : not decided in mind : UNDETERMINED **4** : not paid ⟨~ accounts⟩ **5** : not occupied by settlers

un·shack·le \-ˈsha-kəl\ *vb* : to free from shackles

un·shaped \-ˈshāpt\ *adj* : not shaped; *esp* : not being in finished, final, or perfect form ⟨~ ideas⟩ ⟨~ timber⟩

un·sheathe \ˌən-ˈshēth\ *vb* : to draw from or as if from a sheath

un·ship \-ˈship\ *vb* **1** : to remove from a ship **2** : to remove or become removed from position ⟨~ an oar⟩

un·shod \ˌən-ˈshäd\ *adj* : not wearing or provided with shoes

un·sight·ly \ˌən-ˈsīt-lē\ *adj* : unpleasant to the sight : UGLY

un·skilled \-ˈskild\ *adj* **1** : not skilled; *esp* : not skilled in a specified branch of work **2** : not requiring skill

un·skill·ful \-ˈskil-fəl\ *adj* : lacking in skill or proficiency — **un·skill·ful·ly** *adv*

un·sling \-ˈsliŋ\ *vb* **-slung** \-ˈsləŋ\; **-sling·ing** : to remove from being slung

un·snap \-ˈsnap\ *vb* : to loosen or free by or as if by undoing a snap

un·snarl \-ˈsnärl\ *vb* : to remove snarls from : UNTANGLE

un·so·phis·ti·cat·ed \ˌən-sə-ˈfis-tə-ˌkā-təd\ *adj* **1** : not worldly-wise : lacking sophistication **2** : SIMPLE

un·sought \ˌən-ˈsȯt\ *adj* : not sought : not searched for or asked for : not obtained by effort ⟨~ honors⟩

un·sound \-ˈsau̇nd\ *adj* **1** : not healthy or whole; *also* : not mentally normal **2** : not valid **3** : not firmly made or fixed — **un·sound·ly** *adv* — **un·sound·ness** *n*

un·spar·ing \-ˈspar-iŋ\ *adj* **1** : HARD, RUTHLESS **2** : not frugal : LIBERAL, PROFUSE

un·speak·able \-ˈspē-kə-bəl\ *adj* **1** : impossible to express in words **2** : extremely bad — **un·speak·ably** \-blē\ *adv*

un·spot·ted \-ˈspä-təd\ *adj* : not spotted or stained; *esp* : free from moral stain

un·sprung \-ˈsprəŋ\ *adj* : not sprung; *esp* : not equipped with springs

un·sta·ble \-ˈstā-bəl\ *adj* **1** : not stable **2** : FICKLE, VACILLATING; *also* : lacking effective emotional control **3** : readily changing (as by decomposing) in chemical or physical composition or in biological activity ⟨an ~ atomic nucleus⟩

un·steady \ˌən-ˈste-dē\ *adj* : not steady : UNSTABLE — **un·stead·i·ly** \-ˈsted-ᵊl-ē\ *adv* — **un·stead·i·ness** \-ˈste-dē-nəs\ *n*

un·stint·ing \-ˈstin-tiŋ\ *adj* **1** : not restricting or holding back **2** : giving or being given freely or generously ⟨~ praise⟩

un·stop \-ˈstäp\ *vb* **1** : UNCLOG **2** : to remove a stopper from

un·stop·pa·ble \ˌən-ˈstä-pə-bəl\ *adj* : incapable of being stopped

un·strap \-ˈstrap\ *vb* : to remove or loose a strap from

un·stressed \ˌən-ˈstrest\ *adj* : not stressed; *esp* : not bearing a stress or accent

un·strung \-ˈstrəŋ\ *adj* **1** : having the strings loose or detached **2** : nervously tired or anxious

un·stud·ied \-ˈstə-dēd\ *adj* **1** : not acquired by study **2** : NATURAL, UNFORCED ⟨moved with ~ grace⟩

un·sub·stan·tial \ˌən-səb-ˈstan-chəl\ *adj* : INSUBSTANTIAL

un·sung \ˌən-ˈsəŋ\ *adj* **1** : not sung **2** : not celebrated in song or verse ⟨~ heroes⟩

un·swerv·ing \ˌən-ˈswer-viŋ\ *adj* **1** : not swerving or turning aside **2** : STEADY

un·tan·gle \-ˈtaŋ-gəl\ *vb* **1** : DISENTANGLE **2** : to straighten out : RESOLVE ⟨~ a problem⟩

un·taught \-ˈtȯt\ *adj* **1** : not instructed or taught : IGNORANT **2** : NATURAL, SPONTANEOUS ⟨~ kindness⟩

un·think·able \-ˈthiŋ-kə-bəl\ *adj* : not to be thought of or considered as possible ⟨~ cruelty⟩

un·think·ing \ˌən-ˈthiŋ-kiŋ\ *adj* : not thinking; *esp* : THOUGHTLESS, HEEDLESS — **un·think·ing·ly** *adv*

un·thought \ˌən-ˈthȯt\ *adj* : not anticipated : UNEXPECTED — often used with *of* ⟨*unthought*-of development⟩

un·tie \-ˈtī\ *vb* **-tied; -ty·ing** *or* **-tie·ing** **1** : to free from something that ties, fastens, or restrains : UNBIND **2** : DISENTANGLE, RESOLVE **3** : to become loosened or unbound

¹un·til \ˌən-ˈtil\ *prep* : up to the time of ⟨worked ~ 5 o'clock⟩

²until *conj* **1** : up to the time that ⟨wait ~ he calls⟩ **2** : to the point or degree that ⟨ran ~ she was breathless⟩

¹un·time·ly \ˌən-ˈtīm-lē\ *adv* : at an inopportune time : UNSEASONABLY; *also* : PREMATURELY

²untimely *adj* : PREMATURE ⟨~ death⟩; *also* : INOPPORTUNE, UNSEASONABLE

un·tir·ing \ˌən-ˈtī-riŋ\ *adj* : not becoming tired : INDEFATIGABLE — **un·tir·ing·ly** *adv*

un·to \ˈən-ˌtü\ *prep* : TO

un·told \ˌən-ˈtōld\ *adj* **1** : not counted : VAST, NUMBERLESS **2** : not told : not revealed

¹un·touch·able \ˌən-ˈtə-chə-bəl\ *adj* : forbidden to the touch

²untouchable *n* : a member of the lowest social class in India having in traditional Hindu belief the quality of defiling by contact a member of a higher caste

un·touched \ˌən-ˈtəcht\ *adj* **1** : not subjected to touching **2** : not described or dealt with **3** : not tasted **4** : being in a primeval state or condition **5** : UNAFFECTED

un·to·ward \ˌən-ˈtōrd, -ˈtō-ərd; ˌən-tə-ˈwȯrd\ *adj* **1** : difficult to manage : STUBBORN, WILLFUL ⟨an ~ child⟩ **2** : INCONVENIENT, TROUBLESOME ⟨an ~ encounter⟩

un·tried \ˌən-ˈtrīd\ *adj* : not tested or proved by experience or trial; *also* : not tried in court

un·true \-ˈtrü\ *adj* **1** : not faithful : DISLOYAL **2** : not according with a standard of correctness **3** : FALSE

un·truth \ˌən-ˈtrüth, ˈən-ˌtrüth\ *n* **1** : lack of truthfulness **2** : FALSEHOOD

un·tune \-ˈtün, -ˈtyün\ *vb* **1** : to put out of tune **2** : DISARRANGE, DISCOMPOSE

un·tu·tored \-ˈtü-tərd, -ˈtyü-\ *adj* : UNTAUGHT, UNLEARNED, IGNORANT

un·twine \-ˈtwīn\ *vb* : UNWIND, DISENTANGLE

un·twist \ˌən-ˈtwist\ *vb* **1** : to separate the twisted parts of : UNTWINE **2** : to become untwined

un·used \-ˈyüst, -ˈyüzd *for 1*; -ˈyüzd *for 2*\ *adj* **1** : UNACCUSTOMED **2** : not used

un·usu·al \-ˈyü-zhə-wəl\ *adj* : not usual : UNCOMMON, RARE — **un·usu·al·ly** *adv*

un·ut·ter·able \ˌən-ˈə-tə-rə-bəl\ *adj* : being beyond the powers of description : INEXPRESSIBLE — **un·ut·ter·ably** \-blē\ *adv*

un·var·nished \-ˈvär-nisht\ *adj* 1 : not varnished 2 : not embellished : PLAIN ⟨the ~ truth⟩

un·veil \ˌən-ˈvāl\ *vb* 1 : to remove a veil or covering from : DISCLOSE 2 : to remove a veil : reveal oneself

un·voiced \-ˈvȯist\ *adj* 1 : not verbally expressed : UN-SPOKEN 2 : VOICELESS

un·war·rant·able \-ˈwȯr-ən-tə-bəl\ *adj* : not justifiable : INEXCUSABLE — **un·war·rant·ably** \-blē\ *adv*

un·weave \-ˈwēv\ *vb* **-wove** \-ˈwōv\; **-wo·ven** \-ˈwō-vən\; **-weav·ing** : DISENTANGLE, RAVEL

un·well \ˌən-ˈwel\ *adj* : SICK, AILING

un·whole·some \-ˈhōl-səm\ *adj* 1 : harmful to physical, mental, or moral well-being 2 : CORRUPT, UNSOUND; *also* : offensive to the senses : LOATHSOME

un·wieldy \-ˈwēl-dē\ *adj* : not easily managed, handled, or used ⟨as because of bulk, weight, or complexity⟩ : AWKWARD ⟨an ~ tool⟩

un·wind \-ˈwīnd\ *vb* **-wound** \-ˈwaund\; **-wind·ing** 1 : to undo something that is wound : loose from coils 2 : to become unwound : be capable of being unwound 3 : RELAX

un·wise \ˌən-ˈwīz\ *adj* : not wise : FOOLISH — **un·wise·ly** *adv*

un·wit·ting \-ˈwi-tiŋ\ *adj* 1 : not knowing : UNAWARE 2 : not intended : INADVERTENT ⟨~ mistake⟩ — **un·wit·ting·ly** *adv*

un·wont·ed \-ˈwȯn-təd, -ˈwōn-\ *adj* 1 : RARE, UNUSUAL 2 : not accustomed by experience — **un·wont·ed·ly** *adv*

un·world·ly \-ˈwərld-lē\ *adj* 1 : not of this world; *esp* : SPIRITUAL 2 : NAIVE 3 : not swayed by worldly considerations — **un·world·li·ness** \-lē-nəs\ *n*

un·wor·thy \ˌən-ˈwər-thē\ *adj* 1 : BASE, DISHONORABLE 2 : not meritorious : not worthy : UNDESERVING 3 : not deserved : UNMERITED ⟨~ treatment⟩ — **un·wor·thi·ly** \-thə-lē\ *adv* — **un·wor·thi·ness** \-thē-nəs\ *n*

un·wrap \-ˈrap\ *vb* : to remove the wrapping from : DISCLOSE

un·writ·ten \-ˈrit-ᵊn\ *adj* 1 : not in writing : ORAL, TRA-DITIONAL ⟨an ~ law⟩ 2 : containing no writing : BLANK

un·yield·ing \ˌən-ˈyēl-diŋ\ *adj* 1 : characterized by lack of softness or flexibility 2 : characterized by firmness or obduracy

un·yoke \-ˈyōk\ *vb* : to remove a yoke from; *also* : SEP-ARATE, DISCONNECT

un·zip \-ˈzip\ *vb* : to zip open : open by means of a zipper

¹up \ˈəp\ *adv* 1 : in or to a higher position or level; *esp* : away from the center of the earth 2 : from beneath a surface ⟨as ground or water⟩ 3 : from below the horizon 4 : in or into an upright position; *esp* : out of bed 5 : with greater intensity ⟨speak ~⟩ 6 : in or into a better or more advanced state or a state of greater intensity or activity ⟨stir ~ a fire⟩ 7 : into existence, evidence, or knowledge ⟨the missing book turned ~⟩ 8 : into consideration ⟨brought the matter ~⟩ 9 : to or at bat 10 : into possession or custody ⟨gave himself ~⟩ 11 : ENTIRELY, COMPLETELY ⟨eat it ~⟩ 12 — used for emphasis ⟨clean ~ a room⟩ 13 : ASIDE, BY ⟨lay ~ supplies⟩ 14 : so as to arrive or approach ⟨ran ~ the path⟩ 15 : in a direction opposite to down 16 : in or into parts ⟨tear ~ paper⟩ 17 : to a stop ⟨pull ~ at the curb⟩ 18 : for each side ⟨the score was 15 ~⟩

²up *adj* 1 : risen above the horizon ⟨the sun is ~⟩ 2 : being out of bed ⟨~ by 6 o'clock⟩ 3 : relatively high ⟨prices are ~⟩ 4 : RAISED, LIFTED ⟨windows are ~⟩ 5 : BUILT, CONSTRUCTED ⟨the house is ~⟩ 6 : grown above a surface ⟨the corn is ~⟩ 7 : moving, inclining, or directed upward 8 : marked by agitation, excitement, or activity 9 : READY; *esp* : highly prepared 10 : going on : taking place ⟨find out what is ~⟩ 11 : EX-

PIRED, ENDED ⟨the time is ~⟩ 12 : well informed ⟨~ on the news⟩ 13 : being ahead or in advance of an opponent ⟨one hole ~ in a match⟩ 14 : presented for or being under consideration 15 : charged before a court ⟨~ for robbery⟩

³up *prep* 1 : to, toward, or at a higher point of ⟨~ a ladder⟩ 2 : to or toward the source of ⟨~ the river⟩ 3 : to or toward the northern part of ⟨~ the coast⟩ 4 : to or toward the interior of ⟨traveling ~ the country⟩ 5 : ALONG ⟨walk ~ the street⟩

⁴up *n* 1 : an upward course or slope 2 : a period or state of prosperity or success ⟨he had his ~s and downs⟩

⁵up *vb* upped \ˈəpt\ *or in 2* up; upped; up·ping; ups *or in 2* up 1 : to rise from a lying or sitting position 2 : to act abruptly or surprisingly ⟨she *upped* and left home⟩ 3 : to move or cause to move upward ⟨*upped* the prices⟩

Upa·ni·shad \ü-ˈpän-i-ˌshäd\ *n* : one of a set of Vedic philosophical treatises

¹up·beat \ˈəp-ˌbēt\ *n* : an unaccented beat in a musical measure; *esp* : the last beat of the measure

²upbeat *adj* : OPTIMISTIC, CHEERFUL

up·braid \ˌəp-ˈbrād\ *vb* : to criticize, reproach, or scold severely

up·bring·ing \ˈəp-ˌbriŋ-iŋ\ *n* : the process of bringing up and training

UPC *abbr* Universal Product Code

up·chuck \ˈəp-ˌchək\ *vb* : VOMIT

up·com·ing \ˈəp-ˌkə-miŋ\ *adj* : FORTHCOMING, AP-PROACHING

up·coun·try \ˈəp-ˌkən-trē\ *adj* : of or relating to the interior of a country or a region — **up–country** \ˈəp-ˈkən-\ *adv*

up·date \ˌəp-ˈdāt\ *vb* : to bring up to date — **update** \ˈəp-ˌdāt\ *n*

up·draft \ˈəp-ˌdraft, -ˌdråft\ *n* : an upward movement of gas ⟨as air⟩

up·end \ˌəp-ˈend\ *vb* : to set, stand, or rise on end; *also* : OVERTURN

up–front \ˈəp-ˌfrənt, ˌəp-ˈfrənt\ *adj* 1 : HONEST, CAN-DID 2 : ADVANCE ⟨~ payment⟩

up front *adv* : in advance ⟨paid *up front*⟩

¹up·grade \ˈəp-ˌgrād\ *n* 1 : an upward grade or slope 2 : INCREASE, RISE

²up·grade \ˈəp-ˌgrād, ˌəp-ˈgrād\ *vb* : to raise to a higher grade or position; *esp* : to advance to a job requiring a higher level of skill

up·growth \ˈəp-ˌgrōth\ *n* : the process of growing upward : DEVELOPMENT; *also* : a product or result of this

up·heav·al \ˌəp-ˈhē-vəl\ *n* 1 : the action or an instance of uplifting esp. of part of the earth's crust 2 : a violent agitation or change

¹up·hill \ˈəp-ˈhil\ *adv* : upward on a hill or incline; *also* : against difficulties

²up·hill \-ˌhil\ *adj* 1 : situated on elevated ground 2 : AS-CENDING 3 : DIFFICULT, LABORIOUS

up·hold \ˌəp-ˈhōld\ *vb* **-held** \-ˈheld\; **-hold·ing** 1 : to give support to 2 : to support against an opponent 3 : to keep elevated — **up·hold·er** *n*

up·hol·ster \ˌəp-ˈhōl-stər\ *vb* : to furnish with or as if with upholstery — **up·hol·ster·er** *n*

up·hol·stery \-stə-rē\ *n, pl* **-ster·ies** [ME *upholdester* upholsterer, fr. *upholden* to uphold, fr. *up + holden* to hold] : materials ⟨as fabrics, padding, and springs⟩ used to make a soft covering esp. for a seat

UPI *abbr* United Press International

up·keep \ˈəp-ˌkēp\ *n* : the act or cost of keeping up or maintaining; *also* : the state of being maintained

up·land \ˈəp-lənd, -ˌland\ *n* : high land esp. at some distance from the sea — **upland** *adj*

¹up·lift \ˌəp-ˈlift\ *vb* 1 : to lift or raise up : ELEVATE 2 : to improve the condition of esp. morally, socially, or intellectually

²up·lift \ˈəp-ˌlift\ *n* 1 : a lifting up; *esp* : an upheaval of the earth's surface **2** : moral or social improvement; *also* : a movement to make such improvement

up·mar·ket \ˌəp-ˈmär-kət\ *adj* : appealing to wealthy consumers

up·most \ˈəp-ˌmōst\ *adj* : UPPERMOST

up·on \ə-ˈpȯn, -ˈpän\ *prep* : ON

¹up·per \ˈə-pər\ *adj* **1** : higher in physical position, rank, or order **2** : constituting the smaller and more restricted branch of a bicameral legislature **3** *cap* : being a later part or formation of a specific geological period **4** : being toward the interior ⟨the ∼ Amazon⟩ **5** : NORTHERN ⟨∼ New York State⟩

²upper *n* : one that is upper; *esp* : the parts of a shoe or boot above the sole

up·per·case \ˌə-pər-ˈkās\ *adj* : CAPITAL 1 — **uppercase** *n*

upper class *n* : a social class occupying a position above the middle class and having the highest status in a society — **upper–class** *adj*

up·per·class·man \ˌə-pər-ˈklas-mən\ *n* : a junior or senior in a college or high school

upper crust *n* : the highest social class or group; *esp* : the highest circle of the upper class

up·per·cut \ˈə-pər-ˌkət\ *n* : a short swinging punch delivered (as in boxing) in an upward direction usu. with a bent arm

upper hand *n* : MASTERY, ADVANTAGE

up·per·most \ˈə-pər-ˌmōst\ *adv* : in or into the highest or most prominent position — **uppermost** *adj*

up·pish \ˈə-pish\ *adj* : UPPITY

up·pi·ty \ˈə-pə-tē\ *adj* : ARROGANT, PRESUMPTUOUS

up·raise \ˌəp-ˈrāz\ *vb* : to lift up : ELEVATE

¹up·right \ˈəp-ˌrīt\ *adj* **1** : PERPENDICULAR, VERTICAL **2** : erect in carriage or posture **3** : morally correct : JUST — **upright** *adv* — **up·right·ly** *adv* — **up·right·ness** *n*

²upright *n* **1** : the state of being upright : a vertical position **2** : something that stands upright

upright piano *n* : a piano whose strings run vertically

up·ris·ing \ˈəp-ˌrī-zin\ *n* : INSURRECTION, REVOLT, REBELLION

up·riv·er \ˈəp-ˈri-vər\ *adv or adj* : toward or at a point nearer the source of a river

up·roar \ˈəp-ˌrȯr\ *n* [D *oproer*, fr. MD, fr. *op* up + *roer* motion] : a state of commotion, excitement, or violent disturbance

up·roar·i·ous \ˌəp-ˈrȯr-ē-əs\ *adj* **1** : marked by uproar **2** : extremely funny — **up·roar·i·ous·ly** *adv*

up·root \ˌəp-ˈrüt, -ˈrüt\ *vb* : to remove by or as if by pulling up by the roots

¹up·set \ˌəp-ˈset\ *vb* **-set; -set·ting** **1** : to force or be forced out of the usual upright, level, or proper position **2** : to disturb emotionally : WORRY; *also* : to make somewhat ill **3** : UNSETTLE, DISARRANGE **4** : to defeat unexpectedly

²up·set \ˈəp-ˌset\ *n* **1** : an upsetting or being upset; *esp* : a minor illness **2** : a derangement of plans or ideas **3** : an unexpected defeat

³up·set \(ˌ)əp-ˈset\ *adj* : emotionally disturbed or agitated

up·shot \ˈəp-ˌshät\ *n* : the final result

¹up·side \ˈəp-ˌsīd\ *n* : the upper side

²up·side \ˌəp-ˈsīd\ *prep* : up on or against the side of ⟨knocked him ∼ the head⟩

upside down \ˌəp-ˌsīd-ˈdaun\ *adv* **1** : with the upper and the lower parts reversed in position **2** : in or into confusion or disorder — **upside–down** *adj*

up·si·lon \ˈüp-sə-ˌlän, ˈyüp-, ˈəp-\ *n* : the 20th letter of the Greek alphabet — Y or υ

¹up·stage \ˈəp-ˈstāj\ *adv or adj* : toward or at the rear of a theatrical stage

²up·stage \ˌəp-ˈstāj\ *vb* : to draw attention away from (as an actor)

¹up·stairs \ˌəp-ˈstarz\ *adv* **1** : up the stairs : to or on a higher floor **2** : to or at a higher position

²up·stairs \ˈəp-ˈstarz\ *adj* : situated above the stairs esp. on an upper floor ⟨∼ bedroom⟩

³up·stairs \ˈəp-ˈstarz, ˈəp-ˌstarz\ *n sing or pl* : the part of a building above the ground floor

up·stand·ing \ˌəp-ˈstan-din, ˈəp-\ *adj* **1** : ERECT **2** : STRAIGHTFORWARD, HONEST

¹up·start \ˌəp-ˈstärt\ *vb* : to jump up suddenly

²up·start \ˈəp-ˌstärt\ *n* : one that has risen suddenly; *esp* : one that claims more personal importance than is warranted — **up·start** \-ˈstärt\ *adj*

up·state \ˈəp-ˈstāt\ *adj* : of, relating to, or characteristic of a part of a state away from a large city and esp. to the north — **upstate** *adv* — **upstate** *n*

up·stream \ˈəp-ˈstrēm\ *adv* : at or toward the source of a stream — **upstream** *adj*

up·stroke \ˈəp-ˌstrōk\ *n* : an upward stroke (as of a pen)

up·surge \-ˌsərj\ *n* : a rapid or sudden rise

up·swept \ˈəp-ˌswept\ *adj* : swept upward ⟨∼ hairdo⟩

up·swing \ˈəp-ˌswin\ *n* : an upward swing; *esp* : a marked increase or rise (as in activity)

up·take \ˈəp-ˌtāk\ *n* **1** : UNDERSTANDING, COMPREHENSION ⟨quick on the ∼⟩ **2** : the process or an instance of absorbing and incorporating esp. into a living organism

up·thrust \ˈəp-ˌthrəst\ *n* : an upward thrust (as of the earth's crust) — **upthrust** *vb*

up·tight \ˈəp-ˈtīt\ *adj* **1** : TENSE, NERVOUS, UNEASY; *also* : ANGRY, INDIGNANT **2** : rigidly conventional

up–to–date *adj* **1** : extending up to the present time **2** : abreast of the times : MODERN — **up–to–date·ness** *n*

up·town \ˈəp-ˌtaun\ *n* : the upper part of a town or city; *esp* : the residential district — **up·town** \ˈəp-ˈtaun\ *adj or adv*

¹up·turn \ˈəp-ˌtərn, ˌəp-ˈtərn\ *vb* **1** : to turn (as earth) up or over **2** : to turn or direct upward

²up·turn \ˈəp-ˌtərn\ *n* : an upward turn esp. toward better conditions or higher prices

¹up·ward \ˈəp-wərd\ *or* **up·wards** \-wərdz\ *adv* **1** : in a direction from lower to higher **2** : toward a higher or better condition **3** : toward a greater amount or higher number, degree, or rate

²upward *adj* : directed or moving toward or situated in a higher place or level : ASCENDING — **up·ward·ly** *adv*

upwards of *also* **upward of** *adv* : more than : in excess of ⟨they cost *upwards of* $25 each⟩

up·well \ˌəp-ˈwel\ *vb* : to move or flow upward

up·well·ing \-ˈwe-lin\ *n* : a rising or an appearance of rising to the surface and flowing outward; *esp* : the movement of deep cold usu. nutrient-rich ocean water to the surface

up·wind \ˈəp-ˈwind\ *adv or adj* : in the direction from which the wind is blowing

ura·cil \ˈyur-ə-ˌsil\ *n* : a pyrimidine base that is one of the four bases coding genetic information in the molecular chain of RNA

ura·ni·um \yu-ˈrā-nē-əm\ *n* : a silvery heavy radioactive metallic chemical element used as a source of atomic energy — see ELEMENT table

Ura·nus \ˈyur-ə-nəs, yu-ˈrā-\ *n* [LL, the sky personified as a god, fr. Gk *Ouranos*, fr. *ouranos* sky, heaven] : the planet 7th in order from the sun — see PLANET table

ur·ban \ˈər-bən\ *adj* : of, relating to, characteristic of, or constituting a city

ur·bane \ˌər-ˈbān\ *adj* [L *urbanus* urban, urbane, fr. *urbs* city] : very polite and polished in manner : SUAVE

ur·ban·ite \ˈər-bə-ˌnīt\ *n* : a person who lives in a city

ur·ban·i·ty \ˌər-ˈba-nə-tē\ *n, pl* **-ties** : the quality or state of being urbane

ur·ban·ize \ˈər-bə-ˌnīz\ *vb* **-ized; -iz·ing** : to cause to take on urban characteristics — **ur·ban·i·za·tion** \ˌər-bə-nə-ˈzā-shən\ *n*

ur·chin \ˈər-chən\ *n* [ME, hedgehog, fr. MF *herichon*, ultim. fr. L *ericius*] : a pert or mischievous youngster

Ur•du \\'ùr-dü, 'ər-\ *n* [Hindi *urdū,* fr. Per *zabān-e-urdū-e-muallā* language of the Exalted Comp (the imperial bazaar in Delhi)] : an official language of Pakistan that is widely used by Muslims in urban areas of India

urea \yù-'rē-ə\ *n* : a soluble nitrogenous compound that is the chief solid constituent of mammalian urine

ure•mia \yù-'rē-mē-ə\ *n* : accumulation in the blood of materials normally passed off in the urine resulting in a poisoned condition — **ure•mic** \-mik\ *adj*

ure•ter \'yùr-ə-tər\ *n* : a duct that carries the urine from a kidney to the bladder

ure•thra \yù-'rē-thrə\ *n, pl* **-thras** *or* **-thrae** \-(,)thrē\ : the canal that in most mammals carries off the urine from the bladder and in the male also serves to carry semen from the body — **ure•thral** \-thrəl\ *adj*

ure•thri•tis \,yùr-i-'thrī-təs\ *n* : inflammation of the urethra

¹**urge** \'ərj\ *vb* **urged; urging 1** : to present, advocate, or demand earnestly **2** : to try to persuade or sway ⟨~ a guest to stay⟩ **3** : to serve as a motive or reason for **4** : to impress or impel to some course or activity ⟨the dog *urged* the sheep onward⟩

²**urge** *n* **1** : the act or process of urging **2** : a force or impulse that urges or drives

ur•gent \'ər-jənt\ *adj* **1** : calling for immediate attention : PRESSING **2** : urging insistently — **ur•gen•cy** \-jən-sē\ *n* — **ur•gent•ly** *adv*

uric \'yùr-ik\ *adj* : of, relating to, or found in urine

uric acid *n* : a nearly insoluble acid that is the chief nitrogenous excretory product of birds but is present in only small amounts in mammalian urine

uri•nal \'yùr-ən-°l\ *n* **1** : a receptacle for urine **2** : a place for urinating

uri•nal•y•sis \,yùr-ə-'na-lə-səs\ *n* : chemical analysis of urine

uri•nary \'yùr-ə-,ner-ē\ *adj* **1** : relating to, occurring in, or being organs for the formation and discharge of urine **2** : of, relating to, or for urine

urinary bladder *n* : a membranous sac in many vertebrates that serves for the temporary retention of urine and discharges by the urethra

uri•nate \'yùr-ə-,nāt\ *vb* **-nat•ed; -nat•ing** : to release or give off urine — **uri•na•tion** \,yùr-ə-'nā-shən\ *n*

urine \'yùr-ən\ *n* : a waste material from the kidneys that is usu. a yellowish watery liquid in mammals but is semisolid in birds and reptiles

urn \'ərn\ *n* **1** : a vessel that typically has the form of a vase on a pedestal and often is used to hold the ashes of the dead **2** : a closed vessel usu. with a spout for serving a hot beverage

uro•gen•i•tal \,yùr-ō-'je-nət-°l\ *adj* : of, relating to, or being the excretory and reproductive organs or functions

urol•o•gy \yù-'rä-lə-jē\ *n* : a branch of medical science dealing with the urinary or urogenital tract and its disorders — **uro•log•ic** \,yùr-ə-'lä-jik\ *or* **uro•log•i•cal** \-ji-kəl\ *adj* — **urol•o•gist** \yù-'rä-lə-jist\ *n*

Ur•sa Ma•jor \,ər-sə-'mā-jər\ *n* [L, lit., greater bear] : the northern constellation that contains the stars which form the Big Dipper

Ursa Mi•nor \-'mī-nər\ *n* [L, lit., lesser bear] : the constellation including the north pole of the heavens and the stars that form the Little Dipper with the North Star at the tip of the handle

ur•sine \'ər-,sīn\ *adj* : of, relating to, or resembling a bear

ur•ti•car•ia \,ər-tə-'kar-ē-ə\ *n* [NL, fr. L *urtica* nettle] : HIVES

Uru•guay•an \,ùr-ə-'gwī-ən, ,yùr-ə-'gwä-\ *n* : a native or inhabitant of Uruguay — **Uruguayan** *adj*

us \'əs\ *pron, objective case of* WE

US *abbr* United States

USA *abbr* **1** United States Army **2** United States of America

us•able *also* **use•able** \'yü-zə-bəl\ *adj* : suitable or fit for use — **us•abil•i•ty** \,yü-zə-'bi-lə-tē\ *n*

USAF *abbr* United States Air Force

us•age \'yü-sij, -zij\ *n* **1** : habitual or customary practice or procedure **2** : the way in which words and phrases are actually used **3** : the action or mode of using **4** : manner of treating

USCG *abbr* United States Coast Guard

USDA *abbr* United States Department of Agriculture

¹**use** \'yüs\ *n* **1** : the act or practice of using or employing something : EMPLOYMENT, APPLICATION **2** : the fact or state of being used **3** : the way of using **4** : USAGE, CUSTOM **5** : the privilege or benefit of using something **6** : the ability or power to use something (as a limb) **7** : the legal enjoyment of property that consists in its employment, occupation, or exercise; *also* : the benefit or profit esp. from property held in trust **8** : USEFULNESS, UTILITY; *also* : the end served : OBJECT, FUNCTION **9** : the occasion or need to employ ⟨he had no more ~ for it⟩ **10** : ESTEEM, LIKING ⟨had no ~ for modern art⟩

²**use** \'yüz\ *vb* **used** \'yüzd; "*used to*" *usu* 'yüs-tə\; **us•ing 1** : to put into action or service : EMPLOY **2** : to consume or take (as drugs) regularly **3** : UTILIZE ⟨~ tact⟩; *also* : MANIPULATE ⟨*used* his friends to get ahead⟩ **4** : to expend or consume by putting to use **5** : to behave toward : TREAT ⟨*used* the horse cruelly⟩ **6** : to benefit from ⟨house could ~ a coat of paint⟩ **7** — used in the past with *to* to indicate a former practice, fact, or state ⟨we *used* to work harder⟩ — **us•er** *n*

used \'yüzd\ *adj* **1** : having been used by another : SECONDHAND ⟨~ cars⟩ **2** : ACCUSTOMED, HABITUATED ⟨~ to the heat⟩

use•ful \'yüs-fəl\ *adj* : capable of being put to use : ADVANTAGEOUS; *esp* : serviceable for a beneficial end — **use•ful•ly** *adv* — **use•ful•ness** *n*

use•less \-ləs\ *adj* : having or being of no use : WORTHLESS — **use•less•ly** *adv* — **use•less•ness** *n*

USES *abbr* United States Employment Service

use up *vb* : to consume completely

¹**ush•er** \'ə-shər\ *n* [ME *ussher,* fr. MF *ussier,* fr. (assumed) VL *ustiarius* doorkeeper, fr. L *ostium, ustium* door, mouth of a river] **1** : an officer who walks before a person of rank **2** : one who escorts people to their seats (as in a church or theater)

²**usher** *vb* **1** : to conduct to a place **2** : to precede as an usher, forerunner, or harbinger **3** : INAUGURATE, INTRODUCE ⟨~ in a new era⟩

ush•er•ette \,ə-shə-'ret\ *n* : a girl or woman who is an usher (as in a theater)

USIA *abbr* United States Information Agency

USMC *abbr* United States Marine Corps

USN *abbr* United States Navy

USO *abbr* United Service Organizations

USP *abbr* United States Pharmacopeia

USPS *abbr* United States Postal Service

USS *abbr* United States ship

USSR *abbr* Union of Soviet Socialist Republics

usu *abbr* usual; usually

usu•al \'yü-zhə-wəl\ *adj* **1** : accordant with usage, custom, or habit : NORMAL **2** : commonly or ordinarily used **3** : ORDINARY **syn** customary, habitual, accustomed, routine — **usu•al•ly** \'yü-zhə-wə-lē, 'yü-zhə-lē\ *adv*

usu•fruct \'yü-zə-,frəkt\ *n* [L *ususfructus,* fr. *usus et fructus* use and enjoyment] : the legal right to use and enjoy the benefits and profits of something belonging to another

usu•rer \'yü-zhər-ər\ *n* : one that lends money esp. at an exorbitant rate

usu•ri•ous \yü-'zhùr-ē-əs\ *adj* : practicing, involving, or constituting usury ⟨a ~ rate of interest⟩

usurp \yù-'sərp, -'zərp\ *vb* [ME, fr. MF *usurper,* fr. L *usurpare,* lit., to take possession of without legal claim, fr. *usu* (abl. of *usus* use) + *rapere* to seize] : to seize and hold by force or without right ⟨~ a throne⟩

— **usur•pa•tion** \ˌyü-sər-ˈpā-shən, -zər-\ *n* — **usurp•er** \yu̇-ˈsər-pər, -ˈzər-\ *n*

usu•ry \ˈyü-zhə-rē\ *n, pl* **-ries 1** : the lending of money with an interest charge for its use **2** : an excessive rate or amount of interest charged; *esp* : interest above an established legal rate

UT *abbr* Utah

Ute \ˈyüt\ *n, pl* **Ute** *or* **Utes** : a member of an American Indian people orig. ranging through Utah, Colorado, Arizona, and New Mexico

uten•sil \yu̇-ˈten-səl\ *n* [ME, vessels for domestic use, fr. MF *utensile*, fr. L *utensilia*, fr. neut. pl. of *utensilis* useful, fr. *uti* to use] **1** : an instrument or vessel used in a household and esp. a kitchen **2** : a useful tool

uter•ine tube \ˈyü-tə-ˌrīn-, -rən-\ *n* : FALLOPIAN TUBE

uter•us \ˈyü-tə-rəs\ *n, pl* **uteri** \ˈyü-tə-ˌrī\ *also* **uter•us•es** : the muscular organ of a female mammal in which the young develop before birth — **uter•ine** \-ˌrīn, -rən\ *adj*

utile \ˈyüt-əl, ˈyü-ˌtīl\ *adj* : USEFUL

¹util•i•tar•i•an \yu̇-ˌti-lə-ˈter-ē-ən\ *n* : a person who believes in utilitarianism

²utilitarian *adj* **1** : of or relating to utilitarianism **2** : of or relating to utility : aiming at usefulness rather than beauty; *also* : serving a useful purpose

util•i•tar•i•an•ism \-ē-ə-ˌni-zəm\ *n* : a theory that the greatest good for the greatest number should be the main consideration in making a choice of actions

¹util•i•ty \yü-ˈti-lə-tē\ *n, pl* **-ties 1** : USEFULNESS **2** : something useful or designed for use **3** : a business organization performing a public service and subject to special governmental regulation **4** : a public service or a commodity (as electricity or water) provided by a public utility; *also* : equipment to provide such or a similar service

²utility *adj* **1** : capable of serving esp. as a substitute in various uses or positions ⟨a ∼ outfielder⟩ ⟨a ∼ knife⟩ **2** : being of a usable but poor quality ⟨∼ beef⟩

uti•lize \ˈyüt-əl-ˌīz\ *vb* **-lized; -liz•ing** : to make use of

: turn to profitable account or use — **uti•li•za•tion** \ˌyüt-əl-ə-ˈzā-shən\ *n*

ut•most \ˈət-ˌmōst\ *adj* **1** : situated at the farthest or most distant point : EXTREME **2** : of the greatest or highest degree, quantity, number, or amount — **utmost** *n*

uto•pia \yu̇-ˈtō-pē-ə\ *n* [*Utopia*, imaginary island described in Sir Thomas More's *Utopia*, fr. Gk *ou* not, no + *topos* place] **1** *often cap* : a place of ideal perfection esp. in laws, government, and social conditions **2** : an impractical scheme for social improvement

¹uto•pi•an \-pē-ən\ *adj, often cap* **1** : of, relating to, or resembling a utopia **2** : proposing ideal social and political schemes that are impractical **3** : VISIONARY

²utopian *n* **1** : a believer in the perfectibility of human society **2** : one that proposes or advocates utopian schemes

¹ut•ter \ˈə-tər\ *adj* [ME, remote, fr. OE *ūtera* outer, compar. adj. fr. *ūt* out, adv.] : ABSOLUTE, TOTAL ⟨∼ ruin⟩ — **ut•ter•ly** *adv*

²utter *vb* [ME *uttren*, fr. *utter* outside, adv., fr. OE *ūtor*, compar. of *ūt* out] **1** : to send forth as a sound : express in usu. spoken words : PRONOUNCE, SPEAK **2** : to put (as currency) into circulation — **ut•ter•er** *n*

ut•ter•ance \ˈə-tə-rəns\ *n* **1** : something uttered; *esp* : an oral or written statement **2** : the action of uttering with the voice : SPEECH **3** : power, style, or manner of speaking

ut•ter•most \ˈə-tər-ˌmōst\ *adj* : EXTREME, UTMOST ⟨the ∼ parts of the earth⟩ — **uttermost** *n*

U–turn \ˈyü-ˌtərn\ *n* : a turn resembling the letter U; *esp* : a 180-degree turn made by a vehicle in a road

UV *abbr* ultraviolet

uvu•la \ˈyü-vyə-lə\ *n, pl* **-las** *or* **-lae** \-ˌlē, -ˌlī\ : the fleshy lobe hanging at the back of the roof of the mouth — **uvu•lar** \-lər\ *adj*

UW *abbr* underwriter

ux•o•ri•ous \ˌək-ˈsȯr-ē-əs, ˌəg-ˈzȯr-\ *adj* : excessively devoted or submissive to a wife

V

¹v \ˈvē\ *n, pl* **v's** *or* **vs** \ˈvēz\ *often cap* : the 22d letter of the English alphabet

²v *abbr, often cap* **1** vector **2** velocity **3** verb **4** verse **5** versus **6** very **7** victory **8** vide **9** voice **10** voltage **11** volume **12** vowel

V *symbol* **1** vanadium **2** volt

Va *abbr* Virginia

VA *abbr* **1** Veterans Administration **2** vice admiral **3** Virginia

va•can•cy \ˈvā-kən-sē\ *n, pl* **-cies 1** : a vacating esp. of an office, position, or piece of property **2** : a vacant office, position, or tenancy; *also* : the period during which it stands vacant **3** : empty space : VOID **4** : the state of being vacant

va•cant \ˈvā-kənt\ *adj* **1** : not occupied ⟨∼ seat⟩ ⟨∼ room⟩ **2** : EMPTY ⟨∼ space⟩ **3** : free from business or care ⟨a few ∼ hours⟩ **4** : devoid of thought, reflection, or expression ⟨a ∼ smile⟩ — **va•cant•ly** *adv*

va•cate \ˈvā-ˌkāt\ *vb* **va•cat•ed; va•cat•ing 1** : to make void : ANNUL **2** : to make vacant (as an office or house); *also* : to give up the occupancy of

¹va•ca•tion \vā-ˈkā-shən, və-\ *n* : a period of rest from work : HOLIDAY

²vacation *vb* : to take or spend a vacation — **va•ca•tion•er** *n*

va•ca•tion•ist \-shə-nist\ *n* : a person taking a vacation

va•ca•tion•land \-shən-ˌland\ *n* : an area with recreational attractions and facilities for vacationists

vac•ci•nate \ˈvak-sə-ˌnāt\ *vb* **-nat•ed; -nat•ing** : to administer a vaccine to usu. by injection; *also* : to produce immunity to smallpox by inoculating (a person) with the related cowpox virus

vac•ci•na•tion \ˌvak-sə-ˈnā-shən\ *n* **1** : the act of vaccinating **2** : the scar left by vaccinating

vac•cine \vak-ˈsēn, ˈvak-ˌsēn\ *n* [L *vaccinus* of or from cows, fr. *vacca* cow; so called from the derivation of smallpox vaccine from cows] : material (as a preparation of killed or weakened virus or bacteria) used in vaccinating to induce immunity to a disease

vac•cin•ia \vak-ˈsi-nē-ə\ *n* : COWPOX

vac•il•late \ˈva-sə-ˌlāt\ *vb* **-lat•ed; -lat•ing 1** : SWAY, TOTTER; *also* : FLUCTUATE **2** : to incline first to one course or opinion and then to another : WAVER — **vac•il•la•tion** \ˌva-sə-ˈlā-shən\ *n*

va•cu•ity \va-ˈkyü-ə-tē\ *n, pl* **-ities 1** : an empty space **2** : the state, fact, or quality of being vacuous **3** : something that is vacuous

vac•u•ole \ˈva-kyə-ˌwōl\ *n* : a usu. fluid-filled cavity esp. in the cytoplasm of an individual cell — **vac•u•o•lar** \ˌva-kyə-ˈwō-lər, -ˌlär\ *adj*

vac•u•ous \ˈva-kyə-wəs\ *adj* **1** : EMPTY, VACANT, BLANK **2** : DULL, STUPID, INANE — **vac•u•ous•ly** *adv* — **vac•u•ous•ness** *n*

¹vac•u•um \ˈva-(ˌ)kyüm, -kyəm\ *n, pl* **vacuums** *or* **vac•ua** \-kyə-wə\ [L, fr. neut. of *vacuus* empty] **1** : a space entirely empty of matter **2** : a space from which most of the air has been removed (as by a pump) **3** : VOID, GAP **4** : VACUUM CLEANER — **vacuum** *adj*

²vacuum *vb* : to use a vacuum device (as a vacuum cleaner) on

vacuum bottle *n* : THERMOS

vacuum cleaner *n* : a household appliance for cleaning (as floors or rugs) by suction

vacuum–packed *adj* : having much of the air removed before being hermetically sealed

vacuum tube *n* : an electron tube from which most of the air has been removed

va·de me·cum \ˌvä-dē-ˈmē-kəm, ˌvä-dē-ˈmā-\ *n, pl* **vade mecums** [L, go with me] : something (as a handbook or manual) carried as a constant companion

VADM *abbr* vice admiral

¹**vag·a·bond** \ˈva-gə-ˌbänd\ *adj* **1** : WANDERING, HOMELESS **2** : of, characteristic of, or leading the life of a vagrant or tramp **3** : leading an unsettled or irresponsible life

²**vagabond** *n* : one leading a vagabond life; *esp* : TRAMP

va·gar·i·ous \vä-ˈger-ē-əs\ *adj* : marked by vagaries : CAPRICIOUS — **va·gar·i·ous·ly** *adv*

va·ga·ry \ˈvā-gə-rē, və-ˈger-ē\ *n, pl* **-ries** : an odd or eccentric idea or action : WHIM, CAPRICE

va·gi·na \və-ˈjī-nə\ *n, pl* **-nae** \-(ˌ)nē\ *or* **-nas** [L, lit., sheath] : a canal that leads from the uterus to the external opening of the female sex organs — **vag·i·nal** \ˈva-jən-ᵊl\ *adj*

vag·i·ni·tis \ˌva-jə-ˈnī-təs\ *n* : inflammation of the vagina

va·gran·cy \ˈvā-grən-sē\ *n, pl* **-cies** **1** : the quality or state of being vagrant; *also* : a vagrant act or notion **2** : the offense of being a vagrant

¹**va·grant** \ˈvā-grənt\ *n* : a person who has no job and wanders from place to place

²**vagrant** *adj* **1** : of, relating to, or characteristic of a vagrant **2** : following no fixed course : RANDOM, CAPRICIOUS ⟨~ thoughts⟩ — **va·grant·ly** *adv*

vague \ˈvāg\ *adj* **vagu·er; vagu·est** [MF, fr. L *vagus*, lit., wandering] **1** : not clear, definite, or distinct **2** : not clearly felt or analyzed ⟨a ~ unrest⟩ **syn** obscure, dark, enigmatic, ambiguous, equivocal — **vague·ly** *adv* — **vague·ness** *n*

vain \ˈvān\ *adj* [ME, fr. MF, fr. L *vanus* empty, vain] **1** : of no real value : IDLE, WORTHLESS **2** : FUTILE, UNSUCCESSFUL **3** : proud of one's looks or abilities **syn** conceited, narcissistic, vainglorious — **vain·ly** *adv*

vain·glo·ri·ous \ˌvān-ˈglȯr-ē-əs\ *adj* : marked by vainglory : BOASTFUL

vain·glo·ry \ˈvān-ˌglȯr-ē\ *n* **1** : excessive or ostentatious pride esp. in one's own achievements **2** : vain display : VANITY

val *abbr* value; valued

va·lance \ˈva-ləns, ˈvā-\ *n* **1** : drapery hanging from an edge (as of an altar, table, or bed) **2** : a drapery or a decorative frame across the top of a window

vale \ˈvāl\ *n* : VALLEY, DALE

vale·dic·tion \ˌva-lə-ˈdik-shən\ *n* [L *valedicere* to say farewell, fr. *vale* farewell + *dicere* to say] : an act or utterance of leave-taking : FAREWELL

vale·dic·to·ri·an \-ˌdik-ˈtȯr-ē-ən\ *n* : the student usu. of the highest rank in a graduating class who delivers the valedictory address at commencement

vale·dic·to·ry \-ˈdik-tə-rē\ *adj* : bidding farewell : delivered as a valediction ⟨a ~ address⟩ — **valedictory** *n*

va·lence \ˈvā-ləns\ *n* [LL *valentia* power, capacity, fr. L *valēre* to be strong] : the combining power of an atom as shown by the number of its electrons that are lost, gained, or shared in the formation of chemical bonds

Va·len·ci·ennes \və-ˌlen-sē-ˈen, ˌvä-lən-sē-, -ˈenz\ *n* : a fine handmade lace

val·en·tine \ˈva-lən-ˌtīn\ *n* : a sweetheart chosen or complimented on St. Valentine's Day; *also* : a greeting card sent on this day

Valentine's Day *also* **Valentine Day** *n* : SAINT VALENTINE'S DAY

¹**va·let** \ˈva-lət, -(ˌ)lā; va-ˈlā\ *n* **1** : a male servant who takes care of a man's clothes and performs personal services **2** : an attendant in a hotel who performs personal services for customers

²**valet** *vb* : to serve as a valet

val·e·tu·di·nar·i·an \ˌva-lə-ˌtüd-ᵊn-ˈer-ē-ən, -ˌtyüd-\ *n* : a person of a weak or sickly constitution; *esp* : one whose chief concern is being or becoming an invalid — **val·e·tu·di·nar·i·an·ism** \-ē-ə-ˌni-zəm\ *n*

val·iant \ˈval-yənt\ *adj* : having or showing valor : BRAVE, HEROIC **syn** valorous, doughty, courageous, bold, audacious, dauntless, undaunted, intrepid — **val·iant·ly** *adv*

val·id \ˈva-ləd\ *adj* **1** : having legal force ⟨a ~ contract⟩ **2** : founded on truth or fact : capable of being justified or defended : SOUND ⟨a ~ argument⟩ ⟨~ reasons⟩ — **va·lid·i·ty** \və-ˈli-də-tē\ *n* — **val·id·ly** *adv*

val·i·date \ˈva-lə-ˌdāt\ *vb* **-dat·ed; -dat·ing** **1** : to make legally valid **2** : to confirm the validity of **3** : VERIFY — **val·i·da·tion** \ˌva-lə-ˈdā-shən\ *n*

va·lise \və-ˈlēs\ *n* [F] : SUITCASE

val·ley \ˈva-lē\ *n, pl* **valleys** : a long depression between ranges of hills or mountains

val·or \ˈva-lər\ *n* [ME, fr. MF *valour*, fr. ML *valor* value, valor, fr. L *valēre* to be strong] : personal bravery **syn** heroism, prowess, gallantry — **val·or·ous** \ˈva-lə-rəs\ *adj*

val·o·ri·za·tion \ˌva-lə-rə-ˈzā-shən\ *n* : the support of commodity prices by any of various forms of government subsidy — **val·o·rize** \ˈva-lə-ˌrīz\ *vb*

val·our *chiefly Brit var of* VALOR

valse \ˈvals\ *n* [F] : WALTZ; *esp* : a concert waltz

¹**valu·able** \ˈval-yə-bəl, -yə-wə-bəl\ *adj* **1** : having money value **2** : having great money value **3** : of great use or service **syn** invaluable, priceless, costly, expensive, dear, precious

²**valuable** *n* : a usu. personal possession of considerable value ⟨their ~s were stolen⟩

val·u·ate \ˈval-yə-ˌwāt\ *vb* **-at·ed; -at·ing** : to place a value on : APPRAISE — **val·u·a·tor** \-ˌwā-tər\ *n*

val·u·a·tion \ˌval-yə-ˈwā-shən\ *n* **1** : the act or process of valuing; *esp* : appraisal of property **2** : the estimated or determined market value of a thing

¹**val·ue** \ˈval-yü\ *n* **1** : a fair return or equivalent in money, goods, or services for something exchanged **2** : the monetary worth of a thing; *also* : relative worth, utility, or importance ⟨nothing of ~ to say⟩ **3** : an assigned or computed numerical quantity ⟨the ~ of x in an equation⟩ **4** : relative lightness or darkness of a color : LUMINOSITY **5** : the relative length of a tone or note **6** : something (as a principle or ideal) intrinsically valuable or desirable ⟨human rather than material ~s⟩ — **val·ue·less** *adj*

²**value** *vb* **val·ued; val·u·ing** **1** : to estimate the monetary worth of : APPRAISE **2** : to rate in usefulness, importance, or general worth **3** : to consider or rate highly : PRIZE, ESTEEM — **val·u·er** *n*

val·ue–add·ed tax *n* : an incremental excise tax that is levied on the value added at each stage of the processing of a raw material or the production and distribution of a commodity

valve \ˈvalv\ *n* **1** : a structure (as in a vein) that temporarily closes a passage or that permits movement in one direction only **2** : a device by which the flow of a fluid material may be regulated by a movable part; *also* : the movable part of such a device **3** : a device in a brass wind instrument for quickly varying the tube length in order to change the fundamental tone by some definite interval **4** : one of the separate usu. hinged pieces of which the shell of some animals and esp. bivalve mollusks consists **5** : one of the pieces into which a ripe seed capsule or pod separates — **valved** \ˈvalvd\ *adj* — **valve·less** *adj*

val·vu·lar \ˈval-vyə-lər\ *adj* : of, relating to, or affecting a valve esp. of the heart ⟨~ heart disease⟩

va·moose \va-ˈmüs, və-\ *vb* **va·moosed; va·moos·ing** [Sp *vamos* let us go] : to leave or go away quickly

¹**vamp** \ˈvamp\ *vb* **1** : to provide with a new vamp **2** : to patch up with a new part **3** : INVENT, IMPROVISE ⟨~ up an excuse⟩

²**vamp** *n* **1** : the part of a boot or shoe upper covering

esp. the front part of the foot **2** : a short introductory musical passage often repeated

³vamp *n* : a woman who uses her charm or wiles to seduce and exploit men

⁴vamp *vb* : to practice seductive wiles on

vam·pire \'vam-ₚpīr\ *n* **1** : a night-wandering bloodsucking ghost **2** : a person who preys on other people; *esp* : a woman who exploits and ruins her lover **3** : VAMPIRE BAT

vampire bat *n* : any of various bats of Central and South America that feed on the blood of animals; *also* : any of several other bats that do not feed on blood but are sometimes reputed to do so

¹van \'van\ *n* : VANGUARD

²van *n* : a usu. enclosed wagon or motortruck for moving goods or animals; *also* : a versatile enclosed box-like motor vehicle

va·na·di·um \və-'nā-dē-əm\ *n* : a soft grayish ductile metallic chemical element used esp. to form alloys — see ELEMENT table

Van Al·len belt \van-'a-lən-\ *n* : a belt of intense radiation in the magnetosphere composed of charged particles trapped by earth's magnetic field

van·dal \'vand-ᵊl\ *n* **1** *cap* : a member of a Germanic people who sacked Rome in A.D. 455 **2** : a person who willfully mars or destroys property

van·dal·ise *Brit var of* VANDALIZE

van·dal·ism \-ᵢi-zəm\ *n* : willful or malicious destruction or defacement of public or private property

van·dal·ize \-ᵢīz\ *vb* **-ized; -iz·ing** : to subject to vandalism : DAMAGE

Van·dyke \van-'dīk\ *n* : a trim pointed beard

vane \'vān\ *n* [ME, fr. OE *fana* banner] **1** : a movable device attached to a high object for showing wind direction **2** : a thin flat or curved object that is rotated about an axis by a flow of fluid or that rotates to cause a fluid to flow or that redirects a flow of fluid ⟨the ∼s of a windmill⟩

van·guard \'van-ₚgärd\ *n* **1** : the troops moving at the front of an army **2** : the forefront of an action or movement

va·nil·la \və-'ni-lə\ *n* [NL, genus name, fr. Sp *vainilla* vanilla (plant and fruit), dim. of *vaina* sheath, fr. L *vagina*] : a flavoring extract obtained from the long beanlike pods (**vanilla beans**) of a tropical American climbing orchid or made synthetically; *also* : this orchid

van·ish \'va-nish\ *vb* : to pass from sight or existence : disappear completely — **van·ish·er** *n*

van·i·ty \'va-nə-tē\ *n, pl* **-ties** **1** : something that is vain, empty, or useless **2** : the quality or fact of being useless or futile : FUTILITY **3** : undue pride in oneself or one's appearance : CONCEIT **4** : a small case for cosmetics : COMPACT

vanity plate *n* : an automobile license plate bearing distinctive letters or numbers designated by the owner

van·quish \'vaŋ-kwish, 'van-\ *vb* **1** : to overcome in battle or in a contest **2** : to gain mastery over (as an emotion)

van·tage \'van-tij\ *n* **1** : superiority in a contest **2** : a position giving a strategic advantage or a commanding perspective

va·pid \'va-pəd, 'vā-\ *adj* : lacking spirit, liveliness, or zest : FLAT, INSIPID — **va·pid·i·ty** \va-'pi-də-tē\ *n* — **vap·id·ly** *adv* — **vap·id·ness** *n*

va·por \'vā-pər\ *n* **1** : fine separated particles (as fog or smoke) floating in the air and clouding it **2** : a substance in the gaseous state; *esp* : one that is liquid under ordinary conditions **3** : something insubstantial or fleeting **4** *pl* : a depressed or hysterical nervous condition

va·por·ing \'vā-pə-riŋ\ *n* : an idle, boastful, or high-flown expression or speech — usu. used in pl.

va·por·ise *Brit var of* VAPORIZE

va·por·ize \'vā-pə-ₚrīz\ *vb* **-ized; -iz·ing** : to convert into vapor — **va·por·i·za·tion** \ₚvā-pə-rə-'zā-shən\ *n*

va·por·iz·er \-ₚrī-zər\ *n* : a device that vaporizes something (as a medicated liquid)

vapor lock *n* : an interruption of flow of a fluid (as fuel in an engine) caused by the formation of vapor in the feeding system

va·por·ous \'vā-pə-rəs\ *adj* **1** : full of vapors : FOGGY, MISTY **2** : UNSUBSTANTIAL, VAGUE — **va·por·ous·ly** *adv* — **va·por·ous·ness** *n*

va·pory \'vā-pə-rē\ *adj* : MISTY

va·pour *chiefly Brit var of* VAPOR

va·que·ro \vä-'ker-ō\ *n, pl* **-ros** [Sp, fr. *vaca* cow, fr. L *vacca*] : a ranch hand : COWBOY

var *abbr* **1** variable **2** variant; variation **3** variety **4** various

¹var·i·able \'ver-ē-ə-bəl\ *adj* **1** : able or apt to vary : CHANGEABLE **2** : FICKLE **3** : not true to type : ABERRANT ⟨a ∼ wheat⟩ — **var·i·abil·i·ty** \ₚver-ē-ə-'bi-lə-tē, ₚvar-\ *n* — **var·i·ably** \-blē\ *adv*

²variable *n* **1** : a quantity that may take on any of a set of values; *also* : a mathematical symbol representing a variable **2** : something that is variable

var·i·ance \'ver-ē-əns\ *n* **1** : variation or a degree of variation : DEVIATION **2** : DISAGREEMENT, DISPUTE **3** : a license to do something contrary to the usual rule ⟨a zoning ∼⟩ **4** : the square of the standard deviation **syn** discord, contention, dissension, strife, conflict

¹var·i·ant \'ver-ē-ənt\ *adj* **1** : differing from others of its kind or class **2** : varying usu. slightly from the standard or type

²variant *n* **1** : one that exhibits variation from a type or norm **2** : one of two or more different spellings or pronunciations of a word

var·i·a·tion \ₚver-ē-'ā-shən\ *n* **1** : the act, process, or an instance of varying : a change in form, position, or condition : MODIFICATION, ALTERATION **2** : extent of change or difference **3** : divergence in the characteristics of an organism from those typical or usual for its group; *also* : one exhibiting such variation **4** : repetition of a musical theme with modifications in rhythm, tune, harmony, or key

vari·col·ored \'ver-i-ₚkə-lərd\ *adj* : having various colors : VARIEGATED

var·i·cose \'var-ə-ₚkōs\ *adj* : abnormally swollen and dilated ⟨∼ veins⟩ — **var·i·cos·i·ty** \ₚvar-ə-'kä-sə-tē\ *n*

var·ied \'ver-ēd\ *adj* **1** : having many forms or types : DIVERSE **2** : VARIEGATED — **var·ied·ly** *adv*

var·ie·gat·ed \'ver-ē-ə-ₚgā-təd\ *adj* **1** : having patches, stripes, or marks of different colors ⟨∼ flowers⟩ **2** : VARIED 1 — **var·ie·gate** \-ₚgāt\ *vb* — **var·ie·ga·tion** \ₚver-ē-ə-'gā-shən\ *n*

¹va·ri·etal \və-'rī-ət-ᵊl\ *adj* : of or relating to a variety; *esp* : of, relating to, or producing a varietal

²varietal *n* : a wine bearing the name of the principal grape from which it is made

va·ri·ety \və-'rī-ə-tē\ *n, pl* **-et·ies** **1** : the state of being varied or various : DIVERSITY **2** : a collection of different things : ASSORTMENT **3** : something varying from others of the same general kind **4** : any of various groups of plants or animals within a species distinguished by characteristics insufficient to separate species : SUBSPECIES **5** : entertainment such as is given in a stage presentation comprising a series of performances (as songs, dances, or acrobatic acts)

var·i·o·rum \ₚver-ē-'ōr-əm\ *n* : an edition or text of a work containing notes by various persons or variant readings of the text

var·i·ous \'ver-ē-əs\ *adj* **1** : VARICOLORED **2** : of differing kinds : MULTIFARIOUS **3** : UNLIKE ⟨animals as ∼ as the jaguar and the sloth⟩ **4** : having a number of different aspects **5** : NUMEROUS, MANY **6** : INDIVIDUAL, SEPARATE **syn** divergent, disparate, different, dissimilar, diverse, unalike — **var·i·ous·ly** *adv*

var·let \'vär-lət\ *n* **1** : ATTENDANT **2** : SCOUNDREL, KNAVE

var·mint \'vär-mənt\ *n* [alter. of *vermin*] **1** : an animal considered a pest; *esp* : one classed as vermin and unprotected by game law **2** : a contemptible person : RASCAL

¹var·nish \ˈvär-nish\ *n* **1** : a liquid preparation that is spread on a surface and dries into a hard glossy coating; *also* : the glaze of this coating **2** : something suggesting varnish by its gloss **3** : outside show : deceptive or superficial appearance

²varnish *vb* **1** : to cover with varnish **2** : to cover or conceal with something that gives a fair appearance : GLOSS

var·si·ty \ˈvär-sə-tē\ *n, pl* **-ties** [by shortening & alter. fr. *university*] **1** *Brit* : UNIVERSITY **2** : the principal team representing a college, school, or club

vary \ˈver-ē\ *vb* **var·ied; vary·ing 1** : ALTER, CHANGE **2** : to make or be of different kinds : introduce or have variety : DIVERSIFY, DIFFER **3** : DEVIATE, SWERVE **4** : to change in bodily structure or function away from what is usual for members of a group

vas·cu·lar \ˈvas-kyə-lər\ *adj* [NL *vascularis*, fr. L *vasculum* small vessel, dim. of *vas* vase, vessel] : of or relating to a channel or system of channels for the conveyance of a body fluid (as blood or sap); *also* : supplied with or containing such vessels and esp. blood vessels

vascular plant *n* : a plant having a specialized system for carrying fluids that includes xylem and phloem

vase \ˈvās, ˈvāz\ *n* : a usu. round vessel of greater depth than width used chiefly for ornament or for flowers

va·sec·to·my \və-ˈsek-tə-mē, vā-ˈzek-\ *n, pl* **-mies** : surgical excision of all or part of the sperm-carrying ducts of the testis usu. to induce sterility

va·so·con·stric·tion \ˌvas-ō-kən-ˈstrik-shən, ˌvāz-\ *n* : narrowing of the interior diameter of blood vessels

va·so·con·stric·tor \-tər\ *n* : an agent (as a nerve fiber or a drug) that initiates or induces vasoconstriction

vas·sal \ˈva-səl\ *n* **1** : a person under the protection of a feudal lord to whom he owes homage and loyalty : a feudal tenant **2** : one occupying a dependent or subordinate position — **vassal** *adj*

vas·sal·age \-sə-lij\ *n* **1** : the state of being a vassal **2** : the homage and loyalty due from a vassal **3** : SERVITUDE, SUBJECTION

¹vast \ˈvast\ *adj* : very great in size, amount, degree, intensity, or esp. extent **syn** enormous, huge, gigantic, colossal, mammoth — **vast·ly** *adv* — **vast·ness** *n*

²vast *n* : a great expanse : IMMENSITY

vasty \ˈvas-tē\ *adj* : VAST, IMMENSE

vat \ˈvat\ *n* : a large vessel (as a tub or barrel) esp. for holding liquids in manufacturing processes

VAT *abbr* value-added tax

vat·ic \ˈva-tik\ *adj* : PROPHETIC, ORACULAR

Vat·i·can \ˈva-ti-kən\ *n* **1** : the papal headquarters in Rome **2** : the papal government

vaude·ville \ˈvȯd-vəl, ˈväd-, ˈvōd-, -ˌvil\ *n* [F, fr. MF, satirical song, alter. of *vaudevire*, fr. *vau-de-Vire* valley of Vire, town in northwest France where such songs were composed] : a stage entertainment consisting of unrelated acts (as of acrobats, comedians, dancers, or singers)

¹vault \ˈvȯlt\ *n* **1** : an arched masonry structure usu. forming a ceiling or roof; *also* : something (as the sky) resembling a vault **2** : a room or space covered by a vault esp. when underground **3** : a room or compartment for the safekeeping of valuables **4** : a burial chamber; *also* : a usu. metal or concrete case in which a casket is enclosed at burial — **vaulty** *adj*

²vault *vb* : to form or cover with a vault

³vault *vb* : to leap vigorously esp. by aid of the hands or a pole — **vault·er** *n*

⁴vault *n* : an act of vaulting : LEAP

vault·ed *adj* **1** : built in the form of a vault : ARCHED **2** : covered with a vault

vault·ing *adj* : reaching for the heights ⟨∼ ambition⟩

vaunt \ˈvȯnt\ *vb* [ME, fr. MF *vanter*, fr. LL *vanitare*,

ultim. fr. L *vanus* vain] : BRAG, BOAST — **vaunt** *n*

vaunt·ed *adj* : much praised or boasted of

vb *abbr* verb; verbal

VCR \ˌvē-(ˌ)sē-ˈär\ *n* [videocassette recorder] : a videotape recorder that uses videocassettes

VD *abbr* venereal disease

VDT *abbr* video display terminal

veal \ˈvēl\ *n* : the flesh of a young calf

vec·tor \ˈvek-tər\ *n* **1** : a quantity that has magnitude and direction **2** : an organism (as a fly or tick) that transmits disease germs

Ve·da \ˈvā-də\ *n* [Skt, lit., knowledge] : any of a class of Hindu sacred writings — **Ve·dic** \ˈvā-dik\ *adj*

Ve·dan·ta \vā-ˈdän-tə, və-, -ˈdan-\ *n* : an orthodox Hindu philosophy based on the Upanishads

vee·jay \ˈvē-ˌjā\ *n* : an announcer of a program featuring music videos

veep \ˈvēp\ *n* : VICE PRESIDENT

veer \ˈvir\ *vb* : to shift from one direction or course to another **syn** turn, avert, deflect, divert — **veer** *n*

veg·an \ˈvē-gən, ˈvā-; ˈve-jən, -ˌjan\ *n* : a strict vegetarian who consumes no animal food or dairy products — **veg·an·ism** \ˈvē-gə-ˌni-zəm, ˈvā-, ˈve-\ *n*

¹veg·e·ta·ble \ˈvej-tə-bəl, ˈve-jə-\ *adj* [ME, fr. ML *vegetabilis* vegetative, fr. *vegetare* to grow, fr. L, to animate, fr. *vegetus* lively, fr. *vegēre* to enliven] **1** : of, relating to, or growing like plants ⟨the ∼ kingdom⟩ **2** : made or obtained from plants ⟨∼ oils⟩ **3** : suggesting that of a plant (as in inertness) ⟨a ∼ existence⟩

²vegetable *n* **1** : PLANT 1 **2** : a usu. herbaceous plant grown for an edible part that is usu. eaten as part of a meal; *also* : such an edible part

veg·e·tal \ˈve-jət-ᵊl\ *adj* **1** : VEGETABLE **2** : VEGETATIVE

veg·e·tar·i·an \ˌve-jə-ˈter-ē-ən\ *n* : one that believes in or practices living on a diet of vegetables, fruits, grains, nuts, and sometimes animal products (as milk and cheese) — **vegetarian** *adj* — **veg·e·tar·i·an·ism** \-ē-ə-ˌni-zəm\ *n*

veg·e·tate \ˈve-jə-ˌtāt\ *vb* **-tat·ed; -tat·ing** : to live or grow in the manner of a plant; *esp* : to lead a dull inert life

veg·e·ta·tion \ˌve-jə-ˈtā-shən\ *n* **1** : the act or process of vegetating; *also* : inert existence **2** : plant life or cover (as of an area) — **veg·e·ta·tion·al** \-shə-nəl\ *adj*

veg·e·ta·tive \ˈve-jə-ˌtā-tiv\ *adj* **1** : of or relating to nutrition and growth esp. as contrasted with reproduction **2** : of, relating to, or composed of vegetation **3** : VEGETABLE 3

veg out \ˈvej-\ *vb* **vegged out; vegging out** [short for *vegetate*] : to spend time idly or passively

ve·he·ment \ˈvē-ə-mənt\ *adj* **1** : marked by great force or energy **2** : marked by strong feeling or expression : PASSIONATE, FERVID — **ve·he·mence** \-məns\ *n* — **ve·he·ment·ly** *adv*

ve·hi·cle \ˈvē-ə-kəl, ˈvē-ˌhi-\ *n* **1** : a medium by which a thing is applied or administered ⟨linseed oil is a ∼ for pigments⟩ **2** : a medium through or by means of which something is conveyed or expressed **3** : a means of transporting persons or goods **syn** instrument, agent, agency, organ, channel — **ve·hic·u·lar** \vē-ˈhi-kyə-lər\ *adj*

¹veil \ˈvāl\ *n* **1** : a piece of often sheer or diaphanous material used to screen or curtain something or to cover the head or face **2** : the state of becoming a nun ⟨take the ∼⟩ **3** : something that hides or obscures like a veil

²veil *vb* : to cover with or as if with a veil : wear a veil

¹vein \ˈvān\ *n* **1** : a fissure in rock filled with mineral matter; *also* : a bed of useful mineral matter **2** : any of the tubular branching vessels that carry blood from the capillaries toward the heart **3** : any of the bundles of vascular vessels forming the framework of a leaf **4** : any of the thickened ribs that stiffen the wings of an insect **5** : something (as a wavy variegation in marble) suggesting veins **6** : a distinctive style of expression **7** : a distinctive element or quality

: STRAIN **8** : MOOD, HUMOR — **veined** \\'vānd\ *adj*
²**vein** *vb* : to pattern with or as if with veins — **vein-ing** *n*
vel *abbr* velocity
ve·lar \\'vē-lər\ *adj* : of or relating to a velum and esp. that of the soft palate
veld *or* **veldt** \\'velt, 'felt\ *n* [Afrikaans *veld*, fr. D. field] : an open grassland esp. in southern Africa usu. with few shrubs or trees
vel·lum \\'ve-ləm\ *n* [ME *velim*, fr. MF *veelin*, fr. *veelin*, adj., of a calf, fr. *veel* calf] **1** : a fine-grained lamb-skin, kidskin, or calfskin prepared for writing on or for binding books **2** : a strong cream-colored paper — **vellum** *adj*
ve·loc·i·pede \və-'lä-sə-,pēd\ *n* : an early bicycle
ve·loc·i·ty \və-'lä-sə-tē\ *n, pl* **-ties** : quickness of motion : SPEED (the ~ of light)
ve·lour *or* **ve·lours** \və-'lùr\ *n, pl* **velours** \-'lùrz\ : any of various textile fabrics with pile like that of velvet
ve·lum \\'vē-ləm\ *n, pl* **ve·la** \-lə\ : a membranous body part (as the soft palate) resembling a veil
vel·vet \\'vel-vət\ *n* [ME *veluet, velvet*, fr. MF *velu* shaggy, ultim. fr. L *villus* shaggy hair] **1** : a fabric having a short soft dense warp pile **2** : something resembling or suggesting velvet (as in softness or luster) **3** : the soft skin covering the growing antlers of deer — **velvet** *adj* — **velvety** *adj*
vel·ve·teen \,vel-və-'tēn\ *n* **1** : a fabric woven usu. of cotton in imitation of velvet **2** *pl* : clothes made of velveteen
Ven *abbr* venerable
ve·nal \\'vēn-əl\ *adj* : capable of being bought or bribed : MERCENARY, CORRUPT — **ve·nal·i·ty** \vi-'nal-ə-tē\ *n* — **ve·nal·ly** \\'vēn-əl-ē\ *adv*
ve·na·tion \ve-'nā-shən, vē-\ *n* : an arrangement or system of veins (the ~ of the hand) (leaf ~)

venation

vend \\'vend\ *vb* : SELL; *esp* : to sell as a hawker or peddler — **vend·ible** *adj*
vend·ee \ven-'dē\ *n* : one to whom a thing is sold : BUYER
ven·det·ta \ven-'de-tə\ *n* : a feud marked by acts of revenge
vending machine *n* : a coin-operated machine for selling merchandise
ven·dor \\'ven-dər, *for 1 also* ven-'dòr\ *n* **1** : one that vends : SELLER **2** : VENDING MACHINE
¹**ve·neer** \və-'nir\ *n* [G *Furnier*, fr. *furnieren* to veneer, fr. F *fournir* to furnish] **1** : a thin usu. superficial layer of material (brick ~); *esp* : a thin layer of fine wood glued over a cheaper wood **2** : superficial display : GLOSS
²**veneer** *vb* : to overlay with a veneer
ven·er·a·ble \\'ve-nə-rə-bəl\ *adj* **1** : deserving to be venerated — often used as a religious title **2** : made sacred by association
ven·er·ate \\'ve-nə-,rāt\ *vb* **-at·ed; -at·ing** : to regard

with reverential respect **syn** adore, revere, reverence, worship — **ven·er·a·tion** \,ve-nə-'rā-shən\ *n*
ve·ne·re·al \və-'nir-ē-əl\ *adj* : of or relating to sexual intercourse or to diseases transmitted by it (a ~ infection)
venereal disease *n* : a contagious disease (as gonorrhea or syphilis) usu. acquired by having sexual intercourse with someone who already has it
ve·ne·tian blind \və-'nē-shən-\ *n* : a blind having thin horizontal parallel slats that can be adjusted to admit a desired amount of light
Ven·e·zue·lan \,ve-nə-'zwā-lən\ *n* : a native or inhabitant of Venezuela — **Venezuelan** *adj*
ven·geance \\'ven-jəns\ *n* : punishment inflicted in retaliation for an injury or offense : REVENGE
venge·ful \\'venj-fəl\ *adj* : filled with a desire for revenge : VINDICTIVE — **venge·ful·ly** *adv*
ve·nial \\'vē-nē-əl\ *adj* : capable of being forgiven : EXCUSABLE (~ sin)
ve·ni·re \və-'nī-rē\ *n* : a panel from which a jury is drawn
ve·ni·re fa·ci·as \-'fā-shē-əs\ *n* [ME, fr. ML, you should cause to come] : a writ summoning persons to appear in court to serve as jurors
ve·ni·re·man \və-'nī-rē-mən, -'nir-ē-\ *n* : a member of a venire
ven·i·son \\'ven-ə-sən, -zən\ *n, pl* **venisons** *also* **venison** [ME, fr. OF *veneison* hunting, game, fr. L *venatio*, fr. *venari* to hunt, pursue] : the edible flesh of a deer
ven·om \\'ve-nəm\ *n* [ME *venim, venom*, fr. OF *venim*, ultim. fr. L *venenum* magic charm, drug, poison] **1** : poisonous material secreted by some animals (as snakes, spiders, or bees) and transmitted usu. by biting or stinging **2** : ILL WILL, MALEVOLENCE
ven·om·ous \\'ve-nə-məs\ *adj* **1** : full of venom : POISONOUS **2** : SPITEFUL, MALEVOLENT **3** : secreting and using venom (~ snakes) — **ven·om·ous·ly** *adv*
ve·nous \\'vē-nəs\ *adj* **1** : of, relating to, or full of veins **2** : being purplish red oxygen-deficient blood rich in carbon dioxide that is present in most veins
¹**vent** \\'vent\ *vb* **1** : to provide with a vent **2** : to serve as a vent for **3** : EXPEL, DISCHARGE **4** : to give vigorous or emotional expression to
²**vent** *n* **1** : an opportunity or way of escape or passage : OUTLET **2** : an opening for the escape of a gas or liquid or for the relief of pressure
³**vent** *n* : a slit in a garment esp. in the lower part of a seam (as of a jacket or skirt)
ven·ti·late \\'vent-əl-,āt\ *vb* **-lat·ed; -lat·ing 1** : to discuss freely and openly (~ a question) **2** : to give vent to (~ one's grievances) **3** : to cause fresh air to circulate through (as a room or mine) so as to replace foul air **4** : to provide with a vent or outlet **syn** express, vent, air, utter, voice, broach — **ven·ti·la·tor** \-əl-,ā-tər\ *n*
ven·ti·la·tion \,vent-əl-'ā-shən\ *n* **1** : the act or process of ventilating **2** : circulation of air (as in a room) **3** : a system or means of providing fresh air
ven·tral \\'ven-trəl\ *adj* **1** : of or relating to the belly : ABDOMINAL **2** : of, relating to, or located on or near the surface of the body that in humans is the front but in most other animals is the lower surface — **ven·tral·ly** *adv*
ven·tri·cle \\'ven-tri-kəl\ *n* **1** : a chamber of the heart that receives blood from the atrium of the same side and pumps it into the arteries **2** : any of the communicating cavities of the brain that are continuous with the central canal of the spinal cord
ven·tril·o·quism \ven-'tri-lə-,kwi-zəm\ *n* [LL *ventriloquus* ventriloquist, fr. L *venter* belly + *loqui* to speak; fr. the belief that the voice is produced from the ventriloquist's stomach] : the production of the voice in such a manner that the sound appears to come from a source other than the speaker — **ven·tril·o·quist** \-kwist\ *n*
ven·tril·o·quy \-kwē\ *n* : VENTRILOQUISM

¹ven·ture \'ven-chər\ *vb* ven·tured; ven·tur·ing 1 : to expose to hazard : RISK 2 : to undertake the risks of : BRAVE 3 : to offer at the risk of rebuff, rejection, or censure ⟨∼ an opinion⟩ 4 : to proceed despite danger : DARE

²venture *n* 1 : an undertaking involving chance or risk; *esp* : a speculative business enterprise 2 : something risked in a speculative venture : STAKE

ven·ture·some \'ven-chər-səm\ *adj* 1 : involving risk : DANGEROUS, HAZARDOUS 2 : inclined to venture : BOLD, DARING **syn** adventurous, venturous, rash, reckless, foolhardy — ven·ture·some·ly *adv* — ven·ture·some·ness *n*

ven·tur·ous \'ven-chə-rəs\ *adj* : VENTURESOME — ven·tur·ous·ly *adv* — ven·tur·ous·ness *n*

ven·ue \'ven-yü\ *n* : the place in which the alleged events from which a legal action arises took place; *also* : the place from which the jury is taken and where the trial is held

Ve·nus \'vē-nəs\ *n* : the planet 2d in order from the sun — see PLANET table

Ve·nu·sian \vi-'nü-zhən, -'nyü-\ *adj* : of or relating to the planet Venus

Ve·nus's–fly·trap \'vē-nə-səz-'flī-ˌtrap\ *or* Venus fly·trap *n* : an insect-eating plant of the Carolina coast that has the leaf tip modified into an insect trap

ve·ra·cious \və-'rā-shəs\ *adj* 1 : TRUTHFUL, HONEST 2 : TRUE, ACCURATE — ve·ra·cious·ly *adv*

ve·rac·i·ty \və-'ra-sə-tē\ *n, pl* -ties 1 : devotion to truth : TRUTHFULNESS 2 : conformity with fact : ACCURACY 3 : something true

ve·ran·da *or* ve·ran·dah \və-'ran-də\ *n* : a long open usu. roofed porch

verb \'vərb\ *n* : a word that is the grammatical center of a predicate and expresses an act, occurrence, or mode of being

¹ver·bal \'vər-bəl\ *adj* 1 : of, relating to, or consisting of words; *esp* : having to do with words rather than with the ideas to be conveyed 2 : expressed in usu. spoken words : not written : ORAL ⟨a ∼ contract⟩ 3 : of, relating to, or formed from a verb 4 : LITERAL, VERBATIM — ver·bal·ly *adv*

²verbal *n* : a word that combines characteristics of a verb with those of a noun or adjective

verbal auxiliary *n* : an auxiliary verb

ver·bal·ize \'vər-bə-ˌlīz\ *vb* -ized; -iz·ing 1 : to speak or write in wordy or empty fashion 2 : to express something in words : describe verbally 3 : to convert into a verb — ver·bal·i·za·tion \ˌvər-bə-lə-'zā-shən\ *n*

verbal noun *n* : a noun derived directly from a verb or verb stem and in some uses having the sense and constructions of a verb

ver·ba·tim \(ˌ)vər-'bā-təm\ *adv or adj* : in the same words : word for word

ver·be·na \(ˌ)vər-'bē-nə\ *n* : VERVAIN; *esp* : any of several garden plants of hybrid origin with showy spikes of bright often fragrant flowers

ver·biage \'vər-bē-ij, -bij\ *n* 1 : superfluity of words usu. of little or obscure content 2 : DICTION, WORDING

ver·bose \(ˌ)vər-'bōs\ *adj* : using more words than are needed : WORDY **syn** prolix, diffuse, redundant, windy — ver·bos·i·ty \-'bä-sə-tē\ *n*

ver·bo·ten \vər-'bōt-ᵊn, fər-\ *adj* [G] : forbidden usu. by dictate

ver·dant \'vərd-ᵊnt\ *adj* : green with growing plants — ver·dant·ly *adv*

ver·dict \'vər-(ˌ)dikt\ *n* [alter. of ME *verdit*, fr. Anglo-French (the French of medieval England), fr. OF *ver* true (fr. L *verus*) + *dit* saying, dictum, fr. L *dictum*, fr. *dicere* to say] 1 : the finding or decision of a jury 2 : DECISION, JUDGMENT

ver·di·gris \'vər-də-ˌgrēs, -ˌgris\ *n* : a green or bluish deposit that forms on copper, brass, or bronze surfaces

ver·dure \'vər-jər\ *n* : the greenness of growing vegetation; *also* : such vegetation

¹verge \'vərj\ *n* 1 : a staff carried as an emblem of authority or office 2 : something that borders or bounds : EDGE, MARGIN 3 : BRINK, THRESHOLD

²verge *vb* verged; verg·ing 1 : to be contiguous 2 : to be on the verge

³verge *vb* verged; verg·ing 1 : to move or extend in some direction or toward some condition : INCLINE 2 : to be in transition or change

verg·er \'vər-jər\ *n* 1 *chiefly Brit* : an attendant who carries a verge (as before a bishop) 2 : SEXTON

ve·rid·i·cal \və-'ri-di-kəl\ *adj* 1 : TRUTHFUL 2 : not illusory : GENUINE

ver·i·fy \'ver-ə-ˌfī\ *vb* -fied; -fy·ing 1 : to confirm in law by oath 2 : to establish the truth, accuracy, or reality of **syn** authenticate, corroborate, substantiate, validate — ver·i·fi·able *adj* — ver·i·fi·ca·tion \ˌver-ə-fə-'kā-shən\ *n*

ver·i·ly \'ver-ə-lē\ *adv* 1 : in very truth : CERTAINLY 2 : TRULY, CONFIDENTLY

veri·si·mil·i·tude \ˌver-ə-sə-'mi-lə-ˌtüd, -ˌtyüd\ *n* : the quality or state of appearing to be true

ver·i·ta·ble \'ver-ə-tə-bəl\ *adj* : ACTUAL, GENUINE, TRUE — ver·i·ta·bly *adv*

ver·i·ty \'ver-ə-tē\ *n, pl* -ties 1 : the quality or state of being true or real : TRUTH, REALITY 2 : something (as a statement) that is true 3 : HONESTY, VERACITY

ver·meil *n* [MF] 1 \'vər-məl, -ˌmäl\ : VERMILION 2 \verˈmā\ : gilded silver

ver·mi·cel·li \ˌvər-mə-'che-lē, -'se-\ *n* [It, fr. pl. of *vermicello*, dim. of *verme* worm] : a pasta made in thinner strings than spaghetti

ver·mic·u·lite \vər-'mi-kyə-ˌlīt\ *n* : any of various lightweight water-absorbent minerals derived from mica

ver·mi·form appendix \'vər-mə-ˌform-\ *n* : APPENDIX 2

ver·mil·ion *also* ver·mil·lion \vər-'mil-yən\ *n* : a bright reddish orange color; *also* : any of various red pigments

ver·min \'vər-mən\ *n, pl* vermin 1 : small common harmful or objectionable animals (as lice or mice) that are difficult to get rid of 2 : birds and mammals that prey on game — ver·min·ous *adj*

ver·mouth \vər-'müth\ *n* [F *vermout*, fr. G *Wermut* wormwood] : a dry or sweet wine flavored with herbs and often used in mixed drinks

¹ver·nac·u·lar \vər-'na-kyə-lər\ *adj* [L *vernaculus* native, fr. *verna* slave born in the master's house, native] 1 : of, relating to, or being a language or dialect native to a region or country rather than a literary, cultured, or foreign language 2 : of, relating to, or being the normal spoken form of a language 3 : applied to a plant or animal in common speech as distinguished from biological nomenclature ⟨∼ names⟩

²vernacular *n* 1 : a vernacular language 2 : the mode of expression of a group or class 3 : a vernacular name of a plant or animal

ver·nal \'vərn-ᵊl\ *adj* : of, relating to, or occurring in the spring

ver·ni·er \'vər-nē-ər\ *n* : a short scale made to slide along the divisions of a graduated instrument to indicate parts of divisions

ve·ron·i·ca \və-'rä-ni-kə\ *n* : SPEEDWELL

ver·sa·tile \'vər-sət-ᵊl\ *adj* : turning with ease from one thing or position to another; *esp* : having many aptitudes — ver·sa·til·i·ty \ˌvər-sə-'ti-lə-tē\ *n*

¹verse \'vərs\ *n* 1 : a line of poetry; *also* : STANZA 2 : metrical writing distinguished from poetry esp. by its lower level of intensity 3 : POETRY 4 : POEM 5 : one of the short divisions of a chapter in the Bible

²verse *vb* versed; vers·ing : to familiarize by experience, study, or practice ⟨well *versed* in the theater⟩

ver·si·cle \'vər-si-kəl\ *n* : a verse or sentence said or sung by a leader in public worship and followed by a response from the people

ver·si·fi·ca·tion \ˌvər-sə-fə-'kā-shən\ *n* 1 : the making of verses 2 : metrical structure

ver·si·fy \'vər-sə-ˌfī\ *vb* **-fied; -fy·ing 1** : to write verse **2** : to turn into verse — **ver·si·fi·er** \-ˌfī-ər\ *n*

ver·sion \'vər-zhən\ *n* **1** : TRANSLATION; *esp* : a translation of the Bible **2** : an account or description from a particular point of view esp. as contrasted with another **3** : a form or variant of a type or original

vers li·bre \ˌver-'lēbrᵊ\ *n, pl* **vers li·bres** *same*\ [F] : FREE VERSE

ver·so \'vər-sō\ *n, pl* **versos** : a left-hand page

ver·sus \'vər-səs\ *prep* **1** : AGAINST 1 ⟨the champion ∼ the challenger⟩ **2** : in contrast or as an alternative to ⟨free trade ∼ protection⟩

vert *abbr* vertical

ver·te·bra \'vər-tə-brə\ *n, pl* **-brae** \-ˌbrā, -ˌ(ˌ)brē\ *or* **-bras** [L] : one of the segments of bone or cartilage making up the backbone

ver·te·bral \(ˌ)vər-'tē-brəl, 'vər-tə-\ *adj* : of, relating to, or made up of vertebrae : SPINAL

vertebral column *n* : BACKBONE

¹ver·te·brate \'vər-tə-brət, -ˌbrāt\ *adj* **1** : having a backbone **2** : of or relating to the vertebrates

²vertebrate *n* : any of a large group of animals (as mammals, birds, reptiles, amphibians, or fishes) that have a backbone or in some primitive forms (as a lamprey) a flexible rod of cells and that have a tubular nervous system arranged along the back and divided into a brain and spinal cord

ver·tex \'vər-ˌteks\ *n, pl* **ver·ti·ces** \'vər-tə-ˌsēz\ *also* **ver·tex·es** [L *vertex, vortex* whirl, whirlpool, top of the head, summit, fr. *vertere* to turn] **1** : the point opposite to and farthest from the base of a geometrical figure **2** : the point where the sides of an angle or three or more edges of a polyhedron (as a cube) meet **3** : the highest point : TOP, SUMMIT

ver·ti·cal \'vər-ti-kəl\ *adj* **1** : of, relating to, or located at the vertex : directly overhead **2** : rising perpendicularly from a level surface : UPRIGHT — **vertical** *n* — **ver·ti·cal·i·ty** \ˌvər-tə-'ka-lə-tē\ *n* — **ver·ti·cal·ly** \-k(ə-)lē\ *adv*

ver·tig·i·nous \(ˌ)vər-'ti-jə-nəs\ *adj* : marked by, affected with, or tending to cause dizziness

ver·ti·go \'vər-ti-ˌgō\ *n, pl* **-goes** *or* **-gos** : DIZZINESS, GIDDINESS

ver·vain \'vər-ˌvān\ *n* : any of a genus of chiefly American herbs or low woody plants with often showy heads or spikes of tubular flowers

verve \'vərv\ *n* : liveliness of imagination; *also* : VIVACITY

¹very \'ver-ē\ *adj* **veri·er; -est** [ME *verray, verry,* fr. OF *verai,* ultim. fr. L *verax* truthful, fr. *verus* true] **1** : EXACT, PRECISE ⟨the ∼ heart of the city⟩ **2** : exactly suitable ⟨the ∼ tool for the job⟩ **3** : ABSOLUTE, UTTER ⟨the *veriest* nonsense⟩ **4** — used as an intensive esp. to emphasize identity ⟨before my ∼ eyes⟩ **5** : MERE, BARE ⟨the ∼ idea scared him⟩ **6** : SELFSAME, IDENTICAL ⟨the ∼ man I saw⟩

²very *adv* **1** : in actual fact : TRULY **2** : to a high degree : EXTREMELY

very high frequency *n* : a radio frequency of between 30 and 300 megahertz

ves·i·cant \'ve-si-kənt\ *n* : an agent that causes blistering — **vesicant** *adj*

ves·i·cle \'ve-si-kəl\ *n* : a membranous and usu. fluid-filled cavity in a plant or animal; *also* : BLISTER — **ve·sic·u·lar** \və-'si-kyə-lər\ *adj*

¹ves·per \'ves-pər\ *n* **1** *cap, archaic* : EVENING STAR **2** : a vesper bell **3** *archaic* : EVENING, EVENTIDE

²vesper *adj* : of or relating to vespers or the evening

ves·pers \-pərz\ *n pl, often cap* : a late afternoon or evening worship service

ves·sel \'ve-səl\ *n* **1** : a container (as a barrel, bottle, bowl, or cup) for holding something **2** : a person held to be the recipient of a quality (as grace) **3** : a craft bigger than a rowboat **4** : a tube in which a body fluid (as blood or sap) is contained and circulated

¹vest \'vest\ *vb* **1** : to place or give into the possession or discretion of some person or authority **2** : to grant or endow with a particular authority, right, or property **3** : to become legally vested **4** : to clothe with or as if with a garment; *esp* : to garb in ecclesiastical vestments

²vest *n* **1** : a man's sleeveless garment for the upper body usu. worn under a suit coat; *also* : a similar garment for women **2** *chiefly Brit* : a man's sleeveless undershirt **3** : a front piece of a dress resembling the front of a vest

¹ves·tal \'vest-ᵊl\ *adj* : CHASTE

²vestal *n* : VESTAL VIRGIN

vestal virgin *n* **1** : a virgin consecrated to the Roman goddess Vesta and to the service of watching the sacred fire perpetually kept burning on her altar **2** : a chaste woman

vest·ed *adj* : fully and unconditionally guaranteed as a legal right, benefit, or privilege

vested interest *n* : an interest (as in an existing political, economic, or social arrangement) to which the holder has a strong commitment; *also* : one (as a corporation) having a vested interest

ves·ti·bule \'ves-tə-ˌbyül\ *n* **1** : any of various bodily cavities forming or suggesting an entrance to some other cavity or space **2** : a passage or room between the outer door and the interior of a building — **ves·tib·u·lar** \ve-'sti-byə-lər\ *adj*

ves·tige \'ves-tij\ *n* [F, fr. L *vestigium* footprint, track, vestige] : a trace or visible sign left by something lost or vanished; *also* : a minute remaining amount — **ves·ti·gial** \ve-'sti-jē-əl, -jəl\ *adj* — **ves·ti·gial·ly** *adv*

vest·ing \'ves-tiŋ\ *n* : the conveying to an employee of inalienable rights to share in a pension fund; *also* : the right so conveyed

vest·ment \'vest-mənt\ *n* **1** : an outer garment; *esp* : a ceremonial or official robe **2** *pl* : CLOTHING, GARB **3** : a garment or insignia worn by a clergyman when officiating or assisting at a religious service

vest–pocket *adj* : very small ⟨a ∼ park⟩

ves·try \'ves-trē\ *n, pl* **vestries 1** : a room in a church for vestments, altar linens, and sacred vessels **2** : a room used for church meetings and classes **3** : a body administering the temporal affairs of an Episcopal parish

ves·try·man \-mən\ *n* : a member of a vestry

ves·ture \'ves-chər\ *n* **1** : a covering garment **2** : CLOTHING, APPAREL

¹vet \'vet\ *n* : VETERINARIAN

²vet *adj or n* : VETERAN

vetch \'vech\ *n* : any of a genus of twining herbs related to the garden pea including some grown for fodder and green manure

vet·er·an \'ve-trən, -tə-rən\ *n* [L *veteranus,* fr. *veteranus* old, of long experience, fr. *veter-, vetus* old] **1** : an old soldier of long service **2** : a former member of the armed forces **3** : a person of long experience in an occupation or skill — **veteran** *adj*

Veterans Day *n* : November 11 observed as a legal holiday in commemoration of the end of hostilities in 1918 and 1945

vet·er·i·nar·i·an \ˌve-trə-'ner-ē-ən, ˌve-tə-rə-\ *n* : one qualified and authorized to practice veterinary medicine

¹vet·er·i·nary \'ve-trə-ˌner-ē, 've-tə-rə-\ *adj* : of, relating to, or being the medical care of animals and esp. domestic animals

²veterinary *n, pl* **-nar·ies** : VETERINARIAN

¹ve·to \'vē-tō\ *n, pl* **vetoes** [L, I forbid] **1** : an authoritative prohibition **2** : a power of one part of a government to forbid the carrying out of projects attempted by another part; *esp* : a power vested in a chief executive to prevent the carrying out of measures adopted by a legislature **3** : the exercise of the power of veto

²veto *vb* **1** : FORBID, PROHIBIT **2** : to refuse assent to (a legislative bill) so as to prevent enactment or cause reconsideration — **ve•to•er** *n*

vex \'veks\ *vb* **vexed** *also* **vext; vex•ing 1** : to bring trouble, distress, or agitation to **2** : to annoy continually with little irritations

vex•a•tion \vek-'sā-shən\ *n* **1** : the act of vexing **2** : the quality or state of being vexed : IRRITATION **3** : a cause of trouble or annoyance

vex•a•tious \-shəs\ *adj* **1** : causing vexation : ANNOYING **2** : full of distress or annoyance : TROUBLED — **vex•a•tious•ly** *adv* — **vex•a•tious•ness** *n*

vexed \'vekst\ *adj* : fully debated or discussed ⟨a ∼ question⟩

VF *abbr* **1** video frequency **2** visual field

VFD *abbr* volunteer fire department

VFW *abbr* Veterans of Foreign Wars

VG *abbr* **1** very good **2** vicar-general

VHF *abbr* very high frequency

VI *abbr* Virgin Islands

via \'vī-ə, 'vē-ə\ *prep* **1** : by way of **2** : by means of

vi•a•ble \'vī-ə-bəl\ *adj* **1** : capable of living; *esp* : capable of surviving outside the mother's womb without artificial support ⟨a ∼ fetus⟩ **2** : capable of growing and developing ⟨∼ seeds⟩ **3** : capable of being put into practice : WORKABLE **4** : having a reasonable chance of succeeding ⟨a ∼ candidate⟩ — **vi•a•bil•i•ty** \,vī-ə-'bi-lə-tē\ *n* — **vi•a•bly** \'vī-ə-blē\ *adv*

via•duct \'vī-ə-,dəkt\ *n* : a long elevated roadway usu. consisting of a series of short spans supported on arches, piers, or columns

viaduct

vi•al \'vī-əl\ *n* : a small vessel for liquids

vi•and \'vī-ənd\ *n* : an article of food

vi•at•i•cum \vī-'a-ti-kəm, vē-\ *n, pl* **-cums** *or* **-ca** \-kə\ **1** : the Christian Eucharist given to a person in danger of death **2** : an allowance esp. in money for traveling needs and expenses

vibes \'vībz\ *n pl* **1** : VIBRAPHONE **2** : VIBRATIONS

vi•brant \'vī-brənt\ *adj* **1** : VIBRATING, PULSATING **2** : pulsating with vigor or activity **3** : readily set in vibration : RESPONSIVE **4** : sounding from vibration — **vi•bran•cy** \-brən-sē\ *n*

vi•bra•phone \'vī-brə-,fōn\ *n* : a percussion instrument like the xylophone but with metal bars and motor‑driven resonators

vi•brate \'vī-,brāt\ *vb* **vi•brat•ed; vi•brat•ing 1** : OSCILLATE **2** : to set in vibration **3** : to be in vibration **4** : WAVER, FLUCTUATE **5** : to respond sympathetically : THRILL

vi•bra•tion \vī-'brā-shən\ *n* **1** : a rapid to-and‑fro motion of the particles of an elastic body or medium (as a stretched cord) that produces sound **2** : an act of vibrating : a state of being vibrated : OSCILLATION **3** : a trembling motion **4** : VACILLATION **5** : a feeling or impression that someone or something gives off — usu. used in pl. ⟨good ∼s⟩ — **vi•bra•tion•al** \-shə-nəl\ *adj*

vi•bra•to \vi-'brä-tō\ *n, pl* **-tos** [It] : a slightly tremulous effect imparted to vocal or instrumental music

vi•bra•tor \'vī-,brā-tər\ *n* : one that vibrates or causes vibration; *esp* : a vibrating electrical device used in massage or for sexual stimulation

vi•bra•to•ry \'vī-brə-,tōr-ē\ *adj* : consisting of, capable of, or causing vibration

vi•bur•num \vī-'bər-nəm\ *n* : any of a genus of widely distributed shrubs or trees related to the honeysuckle and bearing small usu. white flowers in broad clusters

vic *abbr* vicinity

Vic *abbr* Victoria

vic•ar \'vi-kər\ *n* **1** : an administrative deputy **2** : a minister in charge of a church who serves under the authority of another minister — **vi•car•i•ate** \vī-'ker-ē-ət\ *n*

vic•ar•age \'vi-kə-rij\ *n* : a vicar's home

vicar–general *n, pl* **vicars–general** : an administrative deputy (as of a Roman Catholic or Anglican bishop)

vi•car•i•ous \vī-'ker-ē-əs, -'kar-\ *adj* **1** : acting for another **2** : done or suffered by one person on behalf of another or others ⟨a ∼ sacrifice⟩ **3** : sharing in someone else's experience through the use of the imagination or sympathetic feelings — **vi•car•i•ous•ly** *adv* — **vi•car•i•ous•ness** *n*

¹vice \'vīs\ *n* **1** : DEPRAVITY, WICKEDNESS **2** : a moral fault or failing **3** : a habitual usu. trivial fault **4** : an undesirable behavior pattern in a domestic animal

²vice *chiefly Brit var of* VISE

³vi•ce \'vī-sē\ *prep* : in the place of; *also* : rather than

vice admiral *n* : a commissioned officer in the navy or coast guard ranking above a rear admiral

vice•ge•rent \'vīs-'jir-ənt\ *n* : an administrative deputy of a king or magistrate — **vice•ge•ren•cy** \-ən-sē\ *n*

vi•cen•ni•al \vī-'se-nē-əl\ *adj* : occurring once every 20 years

vice presidency *n* : the office of vice president

vice president *n* **1** : an officer ranking next to a president and usu. empowered to act for the president during an absence or disability **2** : any of several of a president's deputies

vice•re•gal \'vīs-'rē-gəl\ *adj* : of or relating to a viceroy

vice•roy \'vīs-,ròi\ *n* : the governor of a country or province who rules as representative of the sovereign — **vice•roy•al•ty** \-əl-tē\ *n*

vice ver•sa \,vī-si-'vər-sə, 'vīs-'vər-\ *adv* : with the order reversed

vi•chys•soise \,vi-shē-'swäz, ,vē-\ *n* [F] : a soup made esp. from leeks or onions and potatoes, cream, and chicken stock and usu. served cold

vic•i•nage \'vis-ən-ij\ *n* : a neighboring or surrounding district : VICINITY

vi•cin•i•ty \və-'si-nə-tē\ *n, pl* **-ties** [MF *vicinité*, fr. L *vicinitas*, fr. *vicinus* neighboring, fr. *vicus* row of houses, village] **1** : NEARNESS, PROXIMITY **2** : a surrounding area : NEIGHBORHOOD

vi•cious \'vi-shəs\ *adj* **1** : having the quality of vice : WICKED, DEPRAVED **2** : DEFECTIVE, FAULTY; *also* : INVALID **3** : IMPURE, FOUL **4** : having a savage disposition; *also* : marked by violence or ferocity **5** : MALICIOUS, SPITEFUL **6** : worsened by internal causes that augment each other ⟨∼ wage-price spiral⟩ — **vi•cious•ly** *adv* — **vi•cious•ness** *n*

vi•cis•si•tude \və-'si-sə-,tüd, vī-, -,tyüd\ *n* : an irregular, unexpected, or surprising change

vic•tim \'vik-təm\ *n* **1** : a living being offered as a sacrifice in a religious rite **2** : an individual injured or killed (as by disease or accident) **3** : a person cheated, fooled, or injured ⟨a ∼ of circumstances⟩

vic•tim•ize \'vik-tə-,mīz\ *vb* **-ized; -iz•ing** : to make a victim of — **vic•tim•i•za•tion** \,vik-tə-mə-'zā-shən\ *n* — **vic•tim•iz•er** \'vik-tə-,mī-zər\ *n*

vic•tim•less *adj* : having no victim ⟨considered gambling to be a ∼ crime⟩

vic•tor \'vik-tər\ *n* : WINNER, CONQUEROR

vic·to·ria \vik-'tōr-ē-ə\ *n* : a low 4-wheeled carriage with a folding top and a raised driver's seat in front

¹Vic·to·ri·an \vik-'tōr-ē-ən\ *adj* **1** : of or relating to the reign of Queen Victoria of England or the art, letters, or tastes of her time **2** : typical of the standards, attitudes, or conduct of the age of Victoria esp. when considered prudish or narrow

²Victorian *n* **1** : a person and esp. an author of the Victorian period **2** : a typically large ornate house built during Queen Victoria's reign

vic·to·ri·ous \vik-'tōr-ē-əs\ *adj* **1** : having won a victory **2** : of, relating to, or characteristic of victory — **vic·to·ri·ous·ly** *adv*

vic·to·ry \'vik-tə-rē\ *n, pl* **-ries 1** : the overcoming of an enemy or an antagonist **2** : achievement of mastery or success in a struggle or endeavor

¹vict·ual \'vit-°l\ *n* **1** : food fit for humans **2** *pl* : food supplies

²victual *vb* **-ualed** *or* **-ualled; -ual·ing** *or* **-ual·ling 1** : to supply with food **2** : to store up provisions

vict·ual·ler *or* **vict·ual·er** \'vit-°l-ər\ *n* : one that supplies provisions (as to an army or a ship)

vi·cu·ña *or* **vi·cu·na** \vi-'kün-yə, vī-; vī-'kü-nə, -'kyü-\ *n* **1** : a So. American wild mammal related to the llama and alpaca; *also* : its wool **2** : a soft fabric woven from the wool of the vicuña; *also* : a sheep's wool imitation of this

vi·de \'vī-dē, 'vē-ˌdā\ *vb imper* [L] : SEE — used to direct a reader to another item

vi·de·li·cet \və-'de-lə-ˌset, vī-; vi-'dā-li-ˌket\ *adv* [ME, fr. L, fr. *vidēre* to see + *licet* it is permitted] : that is to say : NAMELY

¹vid·eo \'vi-dē-ˌō\ *n* **1** : TELEVISION **2** : VIDEOTAPE **3** : a videotaped performance ⟨music ∼s⟩

²video *adj* **1** : relating to or used in transmission or reception of the television image **2** : relating to or being images on a television screen or computer display ⟨a ∼ terminal⟩

vid·eo·cas·sette \ˌvi-dē-ō-kə-'set\ *n* **1** : a case containing videotape for use with a VCR **2** : a recording (as of a movie) on a videocassette

videocassette recorder *n* : VCR

vid·eo·disc *or* **vid·eo·disk** \'vi-dē-ō-ˌdisk\ *n* **1** : a disc similar in appearance and use to a phonograph record on which programs have been recorded for playback on a television set; *also* : OPTICAL DISK **2** : a recording (as of a movie) on a videodisc

video game *n* : an electronic game played on a video screen

vid·eo·phone \'vid-ē-ə-ˌfōn\ *n* : a telephone for transmitting both audio and video signals

¹vid·eo·tape \'vid-ē-ō-ˌtāp\ *n* : a recording of visual images and sound made on magnetic tape; *also* : the magnetic tape used for such a recording

²videotape *vb* : to make a videotape of

videotape recorder *n* : a device for recording and playing back videotapes

vie \'vī\ *vb* **vied; vy·ing** \'vī-iŋ\ : to compete for superiority : CONTEND — **vi·er** \'vī-ər\ *n*

Viet·cong \vē-'et-'käŋ, ˌvē-ət-, -'kòŋ\ *n, pl* **Vietcong** : a guerrilla soldier of the Vietnamese communist movement

Viet·nam·ese \vē-ˌet-nə-'mēz, ˌvē-ət-, -'mēs\ *n, pl* **Vietnamese** : a native or inhabitant of Vietnam — **Vietnamese** *adj*

¹view \'vyü\ *n* **1** : the act of seeing or examining : INSPECTION; *also* : SURVEY **2** : a way of looking at or regarding something **3** : ESTIMATE, JUDGMENT ⟨stated his ∼s⟩ **4** : a sight (as of a landscape) regarded for its pictorial quality **5** : extent or range of vision ⟨within ∼⟩ **6** : OBJECT, PURPOSE ⟨done with a ∼ to promotion⟩ **7** : a picture of a scene

²view *vb* **1** : to look at attentively : EXAMINE **2** : SEE, WATCH **3** : to examine mentally : CONSIDER — **view·er** *n*

view·er·ship \'vyü-ər-ˌship\ *n* : a television audience esp. with respect to size or makeup

view·find·er \'vyü-ˌfīn-dər\ *n* : a device on a camera for showing the view to be included in the picture

view·point \-ˌpòint\ *n* : POINT OF VIEW, STANDPOINT

vi·ges·i·mal \vī-'je-sə-məl\ *adj* : based on the number 20

vig·il \'vi-jəl\ *n* **1** : a religious observance formerly held on the night before a religious feast **2** : the day before a religious feast observed as a day of spiritual preparation **3** : evening or nocturnal devotions or prayers — usu. used in pl. **4** : an act or a time of keeping awake when sleep is customary; *esp* : WATCH 1

vig·i·lance \'vi-jə-ləns\ *n* : the quality or state of being vigilant

vigilance committee *n* : a committee of vigilantes

vig·i·lant \'vi-jə-lənt\ *adj* : alertly watchful esp. to avoid danger — **vig·i·lant·ly** *adv*

vig·i·lan·te \ˌvi-jə-'lan-tē\ *n* : a member of a volunteer committee organized to suppress and punish crime summarily (as when the processes of law appear inadequate); *also* : a self-appointed doer of justice — **vig·i·lan·tism** \-'lan-ˌti-zəm\ *n*

¹vi·gnette \vin-'yet\ *n* [F, fr. MF *vignete*, fr. dim. of *vigne* vine] **1** : a small decorative design **2** : a picture (as an engraving or a photograph) that shades off gradually into the surrounding ground **3** : a short descriptive literary sketch

²vignette *vb* **vi·gnett·ed; vi·gnett·ing 1** : to finish (as a photograph) in the manner of a vignette **2** : to describe briefly

vig·or \'vi-gər\ *n* **1** : active strength or energy of body or mind **2** : INTENSITY, FORCE

vig·or·ous \'vi-gə-rəs\ *adj* **1** : having vigor : ROBUST **2** : done with force and energy — **vig·or·ous·ly** *adv* — **vig·or·ous·ness** *n*

vig·our *chiefly Brit var of* VIGOR

Vi·king \'vī-kiŋ\ *n* [ON *vīkingr*] : any of the pirate Norsemen who raided or invaded the coasts of Europe in the 8th to 10th centuries

vil *abbr* village

vile \'vīl\ *adj* **vil·er; vil·est 1** : morally despicable **2** : physically repulsive : FOUL **3** : of little worth **4** : DEGRADING, IGNOMINIOUS **5** : utterly bad or contemptible ⟨∼ weather⟩ — **vile·ly** \'vīl-lē\ *adv* — **vile·ness** *n*

vil·i·fy \'vi-lə-ˌfī\ *vb* **-fied; -fy·ing** : to blacken the character of with abusive language : DEFAME **syn** malign, calumniate, slander, libel, traduce — **vil·i·fi·ca·tion** \ˌvi-lə-fə-'kā-shən\ *n* — **vil·i·fi·er** \'vi-lə-ˌfī-ər\ *n*

vil·la \'vi-lə\ *n* **1** : a country estate **2** : the rural or suburban residence of a wealthy person

vil·lage \'vi-lij\ *n* **1** : a settlement usu. larger than a hamlet and smaller than a town **2** : an incorporated minor municipality **3** : the people of a village

vil·lag·er \'vi-li-jər\ *n* : an inhabitant of a village

vil·lain \'vi-lən\ *n* **1** : VILLEIN **2** : an evil person : SCOUNDREL

vil·lain·ess \-lə-nəs\ *n* : a woman who is a villain

vil·lain·ous \-lə-nəs\ *adj* **1** : befitting a villain : WICKED, EVIL **2** : highly objectionable : DETESTABLE **syn** vicious, iniquitous, nefarious, infamous, corrupt, degenerate — **vil·lain·ous·ly** *adv* — **vil·lain·ous·ness** *n*

vil·lainy \-lə-nē\ *n, pl* **-lain·ies 1** : villainous conduct; *also* : a villainous act **2** : villainous character or nature

vil·lein \'vi-lən, -ˌlān\ *n* **1** : a free villager of Anglo-Saxon times **2** : an unfree peasant having the status of a slave to a feudal lord

vil·len·age \'vil-ə-nij\ *n* **1** : the holding of land at the will of a feudal lord **2** : the status of a villein

vil·lous \'vi-ləs\ *adj* : covered with fine hairs or villi

vil·lus \'vi-ləs\ *n, pl* **vil·li** \-ˌlī, -(ˌ)lē\ : a slender usu. vascular process; *esp* : one of the tiny projections of the mucous membrane of the small intestine that function in the absorption of food

vim \\'vim\ *n* : robust energy and enthusiasm : VITAL-ITY

VIN *abbr* vehicle identification number

vin·ai·grette \₁vi-ni-'gret\ *n* [F] : a sauce made typically of oil and vinegar, onions, parsley, and herbs

vin·ci·ble \'vin-sə-bəl\ *adj* : capable of being overcome or subdued

vin·di·cate \'vin-də-₁kāt\ *vb* -cat·ed; -cat·ing **1** : AVENGE **2** : EXONERATE, ABSOLVE **3** : CONFIRM, SUBSTANTIATE **4** : to provide defense for : JUSTIFY **5** : to maintain a right to : ASSERT — **vin·di·ca·tor** \-₁kā-tər\ *n*

vin·di·ca·tion \₁vin-də-'kā-shən\ *n* : a vindicating or being vindicated; *esp* : justification against denial or censure : DEFENSE

vin·dic·tive \vin-'dik-tiv\ *adj* **1** : disposed to revenge **2** : intended for or involving revenge **3** : VICIOUS, SPITEFUL — **vin·dic·tive·ly** *adv* — **vin·dic·tive·ness** *n*

vine \'vīn\ *n* [ME, fr. OF *vigne*, fr. L *vinea* vine, vineyard, fr. fem. of *vineus* of wine, fr. *vinum* wine] **1** : GRAPE **2 2** : a plant whose stem requires support and which climbs (as by tendrils) or trails along the ground; *also* : the stem of such a plant

vin·e·gar \'vi-ni-gər\ *n* [ME *vinegre*, fr. OF *vinaigre*, fr. *vin* wine + *aigre* keen, sour] : a sour liquid obtained by fermentation (as of cider, wine, or malt) and used in cookery and pickling

vin·e·gary \-gə-rē\ *adj* **1** : resembling vinegar : SOUR **2** : disagreeable in manner or disposition : CRABBED

vine·yard \'vin-yərd\ *n* **1** : a field of grapevines esp. to produce grapes for wine production **2** : a sphere of activity : field of endeavor

vi·nous \'vī-nəs\ *adj* **1** : of, relating to, or made with wine ⟨∼ medications⟩ **2** : showing the effects of the use of wine ⟨∼ bloodshot eyes⟩

¹vin·tage \'vin-tij\ *n* **1** : a season's yield of grapes or wine **2** : WINE; *esp* : a usu. superior wine which comes from a single year **3** : the act or period of gathering grapes or making wine **4** : a period of origin ⟨clothes of 1890 ∼⟩

²vintage *adj* **1** : of, relating to, or produced in a particular vintage **2** : of old, recognized, and enduring interest, importance, or quality : CLASSIC ⟨∼ cars⟩ **3** : of the best and most characteristic — used with a proper noun

vint·ner \'vint-nər\ *n* : a dealer in wines

vi·nyl \'vīn-ᵊl\ *n* **1** : a chemical derived from ethylene by the removal of one hydrogen atom **2** : a polymer of a vinyl compound or a product (as a textile fiber) made from one

vinyl chloride *n* : a flammable gaseous carcinogenic compound used esp. to make vinyl resins

vi·ol \'vī-əl\ *n* : a bowed stringed instrument chiefly of the 16th and 17th centuries having a fretted neck and usu. six strings

¹vi·o·la \vī-'ō-lə, 'vī-ə-lə\ *n* : VIOLET 1; *esp* : any of various hybrid garden plants with white, yellow, purple, or variously colored flowers that resemble but are smaller than the related pansies

²vi·o·la \vē-'ō-lə\ *n* : an instrument of the violin family slightly larger and tuned lower than a violin — **vi·o·list** \-list\ *n*

vi·o·la·ble \'vī-ə-lə-bəl\ *adj* : capable of being violated

vi·o·late \'vī-ə-₁lāt\ *vb* -lat·ed; -lat·ing **1** : BREAK, DISREGARD ⟨∼ a law⟩ ⟨∼ a frontier⟩ **2** : RAPE **3** : PROFANE, DESECRATE **4** : INTERRUPT, DISTURB ⟨*violated* his privacy⟩ — **vi·o·la·tor** \-₁lā-tər\ *n*

vi·o·la·tion \₁vī-ə-'lā-shən\ *n* : an act or instance of violating : the state of being violated **syn** breach, infraction, trespass, infringement, transgression

vi·o·lence \'vī-ləns, 'vī-ə-\ *n* **1** : exertion of physical force so as to injure or abuse **2** : injury by or as if by infringement or profanation **3** : intense or furious often destructive action or force **4** : vehement feeling or expression : INTENSITY **5** : jarring quality : DISCORDANCE **syn** compulsion, coercion, duress, constraint

vi·o·lent \-lənt\ *adj* **1** : marked by extreme force or sudden intense activity **2** : caused by or showing strong feeling ⟨∼ words⟩ **3** : EXTREME, INTENSE **4** : emotionally agitated to the point of loss of self-control **5** : caused by force : not natural ⟨∼ death⟩ — **vi·o·lent·ly** *adv*

vi·o·let \'vī-ə-lət\ *n* **1** : any of a genus of chiefly herbs usu. with heart-shaped leaves and both aerial and underground flowers; *esp* : one with small usu. solid-colored flowers **2** : a reddish blue color

vi·o·lin \₁vī-ə-'lin\ *n* : a bowed stringed instrument with four strings that has a shallow body, a fingerboard without frets, and a curved bridge — **vi·o·lin·ist** \-'li-nist\ *n*

violin

vi·o·lon·cel·lo \₁vī-ə-lən-'che-lō\ *n* [It] : CELLO — **vi·o·lon·cel·list** \-list\ *n*

VIP \₁vē-₁ī-'pē\ *n, pl* **VIPs** \-'pēz\ [*v*ery *i*mportant *p*erson] : a person of great influence or prestige; *esp* : a high official with special privileges

vi·per \'vī-pər\ *n* **1** : a common stout-bodied Eurasian venomous snake having a bite only rarely fatal to humans; *also* : any snake (as a pit viper) of the same family as the viper **2** : any venomous or reputedly venomous snake **3** : a vicious or treacherous person — **vi·per·ine** \-pə-₁rīn\ *adj*

vi·ra·go \və-'rä-gō, -'rā-\ *n, pl* -goes *or* -gos [ME, fr. L, strong or heroic woman, fr. *vir* man] **1** : a loud overbearing woman **2** : a woman of great strength and courage

vi·ral \'vī-rəl\ *adj* : of, relating to, or caused by a virus

vir·eo \'vir-ē-₁ō\ *n, pl* -e·os [L, a small bird, fr. *virēre* to be green] : any of various small insect-eating American songbirds mostly olive green and grayish in color

¹vir·gin \'vər-jən\ *n* **1** : an unmarried woman devoted to religion **2** : an unmarried girl or woman **3** *cap* : the mother of Jesus **4** : a person who has not had sexual intercourse

²virgin *adj* **1** : free from stain : PURE, SPOTLESS **2** : CHASTE **3** : befitting a virgin : MODEST **4** : FRESH, UNSPOILED; *esp* : not altered by human activity ⟨∼ forest⟩ **5** : INITIAL, FIRST

¹vir·gin·al \'vər-jən-ᵊl\ *adj* : of, relating to, or characteristic of a virgin or virginity — **vir·gin·al·ly** *adv*

²virginal *n* : a small rectangular spinet without legs popular in the 16th and 17th centuries

Vir·gin·ia creeper \vər-'jin-yə-\ *n* : a No. American vine related to the grapes that has leaves with five leaflets and bluish black berries

Virginia reel *n* : an American country-dance

vir·gin·i·ty \vər-'ji-nə-tē\ *n, pl* -ties **1** : the quality or state of being virgin; *esp* : MAIDENHOOD **2** : the unmarried life : CELIBACY

Vir·go \'vər-₁gō\ *n* [L, lit., virgin] **1** : a zodiacal constellation between Leo and Libra usu. pictured as a young woman **2** : the 6th sign of the zodiac in astrology; *also* : one born under this sign

vir·gule \'vər-gyül\ *n* : a mark / used typically to denote "or" (as in *and*/*or*) or "per" (as in *feet*/*second*)

vir·i·des·cent \₁vir-ə-'des-ᵊnt\ *adj* : slightly green : GREENISH

vir·ile \'vir-əl\ *adj* **1** : having the nature, powers, or qualities of a man **2** : MASCULINE, MALE **3** : MASTERFUL, FORCEFUL — **vi·ril·i·ty** \və-'ri-lə-tē\ *n*

vi·ri·on \'vī-rē-₁än, 'vir-ē-\ *n* : a complete virus particle consisting of an RNA or DNA core with a protein coat

vi·rol·o·gy \vī-'rä-lə-jē\ n : a branch of science that deals with viruses — **vi·rol·o·gist** \-jist\ n

vir·tu \vər-'tü, vir-\ n [It virtù, lit., virtue] **1** : a love of or taste for objects of art **2** : objects of art (as curios and antiques)

vir·tu·al \'vər-chə-wəl\ adj : being in essence or in effect though not formally recognized or admitted ⟨a ~ dictator⟩

vir·tu·al·ly \'vər-chə-wə-lē\ adv **1** : almost entirely : NEARLY **2** : for all practical purposes

vir·tue \'vər-chü\ n [ME virtu, fr. OF, fr. L virtus strength, manliness, virtue, fr. vir man] **1** : conformity to a standard of right : MORALITY **2** : a particular moral excellence **3** : manly strength or courage : VALOR **4** : a commendable quality : MERIT **5** : active power to accomplish a given effect : POTENCY, EFFICACY **6** : chastity esp. in a woman

vir·tu·os·i·ty \vər-chə-'wä-sə-tē\ n, pl -ties : great technical skill in the practice of a fine art

vir·tu·o·so \vər-chə-'wō-sō, -zō\ n, pl -sos or -si \-sē, -zē\ [It] **1** : one skilled in or having a taste for the fine arts **2** : one who excels in the technique of an art; esp : a highly skilled musical performer **syn** expert, adept, artist, doyen, master — **virtuoso** adj

vir·tu·ous \'vər-chə-wəs\ adj **1** : having or showing virtue and esp. moral virtue **2** : CHASTE — **vir·tu·ous·ly** adv

vir·u·lent \'vir-ə-lənt, 'vir-yə-\ adj **1** : highly infectious ⟨a ~ germ⟩; also : marked by a rapid, severe, and often deadly course ⟨a ~ disease⟩ **2** : extremely poisonous or venomous : NOXIOUS **3** : full of malice : MALIGNANT — **vir·u·lence** \-ləns\ n — **vir·u·lent·ly** adv

vi·rus \'vī-rəs\ n [L, venom, poisonous emanation] **1** : any of a large group of submicroscopic infectious agents that have an outside coat of protein around a core of RNA or DNA, that can grow and multiply only in living cells, and that cause important diseases in human beings, lower animals, and plants; also : a disease caused by a virus **2** : something (as a corrupting influence) that poisons the mind or spirit **3** : a computer program usu. hidden within another program that reproduces itself and inserts the copies into other programs and that usu. performs a malicious action (as destroying data)

vis abbr **1** visibility **2** visual

¹**vi·sa** \'vē-zə, -sə\ n [F] **1** : an endorsement by the proper authorities on a passport to show that it has been examined and the bearer may proceed **2** : a signature by a superior official signifying approval of a document

²**visa** vb **vi·saed** \-zəd, -səd\; **vi·sa·ing** \-zə-iŋ, -sə-\ : to give a visa to (a passport)

vis·age \'vi-zij\ n : the face or countenance of a person or sometimes an animal; also : LOOK, APPEARANCE

¹**vis-à-vis** \vēz-ə-'vē, vēs-\ prep [F, lit., face-to-face] **1** : face-to-face with : OPPOSITE **2** : in relation to **3** : as compared with

²**vis-à-vis** n, pl **vis-à-vis** \same or -'vēz\ **1** : one that is face-to-face with another **2** : ESCORT **3** : COUNTERPART **4** : TÊTE-À-TÊTE

³**vis-à-vis** adv : in company : TOGETHER

viscera pl of VISCUS

vis·cer·al \'vi-sə-rəl\ adj **1** : felt in or as if in the viscera **2** : not intellectual : INSTINCTIVE **3** : of or relating to the viscera — **vis·cer·al·ly** adv

vis·cid \'vi-səd\ adj : VISCOUS — **vis·cid·i·ty** \vi-'si-də-tē\ n

vis·cos·i·ty \vis-'kä-sə-tē\ n, pl -ties : the quality of being viscous; esp : the property of resistance to flow in a fluid

vis·count \'vī-kaunt\ n : a member of the British peerage ranking below an earl and above a baron

vis·count·ess \-kaun-təs\ n **1** : the wife or widow of a

viscount **2** : a woman who holds the rank of viscount in her own right

vis·cous \'vis-kəs\ adj [ME viscouse, fr. LL viscosus full of birdlime, viscous, fr. L viscum mistletoe, birdlime] **1** : having the sticky consistency of glue **2** : having or characterized by viscosity

vis·cus \'vis-kəs\ n, pl **vis·cera** \'vi-sə-rə\ : an internal organ of the body; esp : one (as the heart or liver) located in the cavity of the trunk

vise \'vīs\ n [MF vis something winding, fr. L vitis vine] : a tool with two jaws for holding work that typically close by a screw or lever

vis·i·bil·i·ty \vi-zə-'bi-lə-tē\ n, pl -ties **1** : the quality, condition, or degree of being visible **2** : the degree of clearness of the atmosphere

vis·i·ble \'vi-zə-bəl\ adj : capable of being seen ⟨~ stars⟩; also : MANIFEST, APPARENT ⟨has no ~ means of support⟩ — **vis·i·bly** \-blē\ adv

¹**vi·sion** \'vi-zhən\ n **1** : something seen otherwise than by ordinary sight (as in a dream or trance) **2** : a vivid picture created by the imagination **3** : the act or power of imagination **4** : unusual wisdom in foreseeing what is going to happen **5** : the act or power of seeing : SIGHT **6** : something seen; esp : a lovely sight

²**vision** vb : IMAGINE, ENVISION

¹**vi·sion·ary** \'vi-zhə-ner-ē\ adj **1** : of the nature of a vision : ILLUSORY, UNREAL **2** : not practical : UTOPIAN **3** : seeing or likely to see visions : given to dreaming or imagining **syn** imaginary, fantastic, chimerical, quixotic

²**visionary** n, pl -aries **1** : one whose ideas or projects are impractical : DREAMER **2** : one who sees visions

¹**vis·it** \'vi-zət\ vb **1** : to go to see in order to comfort or help **2** : to call on either as an act of courtesy or friendship **3** : to dwell with for a time as a guest **4** : to come to or upon as a reward, affliction, or punishment **5** : INFLICT **6** : to make a visit or regular or frequent visits **7** : CHAT, CONVERSE — **vis·it·able** adj

²**visit** n **1** : a short stay : CALL **2** : a brief residence as a guest **3** : a journey to and stay at a place **4** : a formal or professional call (as by a doctor)

vis·i·tant \'vi-zə-tənt\ n : VISITOR

vis·i·ta·tion \vi-zə-'tā-shən\ n **1** : VISIT; esp : an official visit **2** : a special dispensation of divine favor or wrath; also : a severe trial

visiting nurse n : a nurse employed to visit sick persons or perform public health services in a community

vis·i·tor \'vi-zə-tər\ n : one that visits

vi·sor \'vī-zər\ n **1** : the front piece of a helmet; esp : a movable upper piece **2** : VIZARD **3** : a projecting part (as on a cap) to shade the eyes — **vi·sored** \-zərd\ adj

vis·ta \'vis-tə\ n **1** : a distant view through or along an avenue or opening **2** : an extensive mental view over a series of years or events

VISTA abbr Volunteers in Service to America

¹**vi·su·al** \'vi-zhə-wəl\ adj **1** : of, relating to, or used in vision ⟨~ organs⟩ **2** : perceived by vision ⟨a ~ impression⟩ **3** : VISIBLE **4** : done by sight only ⟨~ navigation⟩ **5** : of or relating to instruction by means of sight ⟨~ aids⟩ — **vi·su·al·ly** adv

²**visual** n : something (as a picture, chart, or film) that appeals to the sight and is used for illustration, demonstration, or promotion — usu. used in pl.

vi·su·al·ize \'vi-zhə-wə-līz\ vb -ized; -iz·ing : to make visible; esp : to form a mental image of — **vi·su·al·i·za·tion** \vi-zhə-wə-lə-'zā-shən\ n — **vi·su·al·iz·er** n

vi·ta \'vē-tə, 'vī-\ n, pl **vi·tae** \'vē-tī, 'vī-tē\ [L, lit., life] : a brief autobiographical sketch

vi·tal \'vīt-ᵊl\ adj **1** : concerned with or necessary to the maintenance of life **2** : full of life and vigor : ANIMATED **3** : of, relating to, or characteristic of life or living beings **4** : FATAL, MORTAL ⟨~ wound⟩ **5** : FUNDAMENTAL, INDISPENSABLE — **vi·tal·ly** adv

vi·tal·i·ty \vī-'ta-lə-tē\ n, pl -ties **1** : the property distinguishing the living from the nonliving **2** : mental

and physical vigor **3** : enduring quality **4** : ANIMA-
TION, LIVELINESS

vi·tal·ize \'vīt-əl-ˌīz\ *vb* **-ized; -iz·ing** : to impart life or
vigor to : ANIMATE — **vi·tal·i·za·tion** \ˌvīt-əl-ə-'zā-
shən\ *n*

vi·tals \'vīt-əlz\ *n pl* **1** : vital organs (as the heart and
brain) **2** : essential parts

vital signs *n pl* : the pulse rate, respiratory rate, body
temperature, and often blood pressure of a person

vital statistics *n pl* : statistics dealing with births,
deaths, marriages, health, and disease

vi·ta·min \'vīt-ə-mən\ *n* : any of various organic substances that are essential in tiny amounts to the nutrition of most animals and some plants and are
mostly obtained from foods

vitamin A *n* : any of several vitamins (as from egg yolk
or fish-liver oils) required esp. for good vision

vitamin B *n* **1** : VITAMIN B COMPLEX **2** *or* **vitamin B₁**
: THIAMINE

vitamin B complex *n* : a group of vitamins that are
found widely in foods and are essential for normal
function of certain enzymes and for growth

vitamin B₆ \-'bē-ˌsiks\ *n* : any of several compounds
that are considered essential to vertebrate nutrition

vitamin B₁₂ \-'bē-'twelv\ *n* : a complex cobalt≈
containing compound that occurs esp. in liver and is
essential to normal blood formation, neural function,
and growth; *also* : any of several compounds of similar action

vitamin C *n* : a vitamin found esp. in fruits and vegetables that is needed by the body to prevent scurvy

vitamin D *n* : any or all of several vitamins that are
needed for normal bone and tooth structure and are
found esp. in fish-liver oils, egg yolk, and milk or are
produced by the body in response to ultraviolet light

vitamin E *n* : any of various oily fat-soluble liquid vitamins whose absence in the body is associated with
such ailments as infertility, the breakdown of muscles, and vascular problems and which are found esp.
in leaves and in seed germ oils

vitamin K *n* [Dan *k*oagulation coagulation] : any of
several vitamins needed for blood to clot properly

vi·ti·ate \'vi-shē-ˌāt\ *vb* **-at·ed; -at·ing** **1** : CONTAMI-
NATE, POLLUTE; *also* : DEBASE, PERVERT **2** : to make
legally ineffective : INVALIDATE — **vi·ti·a·tion** \ˌvi-
shē-'ā-shən\ *n* — **vi·ti·a·tor** \'vi-shē-ˌā-tər\ *n*

vi·ti·cul·ture \'vi-tə-ˌkəl-chər\ *n* : the growing of
grapes — **vi·ti·cul·tur·al** \ˌvi-tə-'kəl-chə-rəl\ *adj* —
vi·ti·cul·tur·ist \-rist\ *n*

vit·re·ous \'vi-trē-əs\ *adj* **1** : of, relating to, or resembling glass : GLASSY ⟨∼ rocks⟩ **2** : of, relating to, or
being the clear colorless transparent jelly (**vitreous
humor**) behind the lens in the eyeball

vit·ri·ol \'vi-trē-əl\ *n* : something resembling acid in being caustic, corrosive, or biting — **vit·ri·ol·ic** \ˌvi-trē-
'ä-lik\ *adj*

vit·tles \'vit-əlz\ *n pl* : VICTUALS

vi·tu·per·ate \vī-'tü-pə-ˌrāt, və-, -'tyü-\ *vb* **-at·ed; -at·
ing** : to abuse in words : SCOLD **syn** revile, berate,
rate, upbraid, rail, lash — **vi·tu·per·a·tive** \-'tü-pə-rə-
tiv, -'tyü-, -ˌrā-\ *adj* — **vi·tu·per·a·tive·ly** *adv*

vi·tu·per·a·tion \(ˌ)vī-tü-pə-'rā-shən, və-, -tyü-\ *n*
: lengthy harsh criticism or abuse

vi·va \'vē-və\ *interj* [It & Sp, long live] — used to express goodwill or approval

vi·va·ce \vē-'vä-chā\ *adv or adj* [It] : in a brisk spirited
manner — used as a direction in music

vi·va·cious \və-'vā-shəs, vī-\ *adj* : lively in temper,
conduct, or spirit : SPRIGHTLY — **vi·va·cious·ly** *adv* —
vi·va·cious·ness *n*

vi·vac·i·ty \-'va-sə-tē\ *n* : the quality or state of being
vivacious

vi·va vo·ce \ˌvī-və-'vō-sē, ˌvē-və-'vō-chä\ *adj* [ML,
with the living voice] : expressed or conducted by
word of mouth : ORAL — **viva voce** *adv*

viv·id \'vi-vəd\ *adj* **1** : having the appearance of vig-

orous life **2** : BRILLIANT, INTENSE ⟨a ∼ red⟩ **3** : producing a strong impression on the senses; *esp*
: producing distinct mental pictures ⟨a ∼ description⟩
— **viv·id·ly** *adv* — **viv·id·ness** *n*

viv·i·fy \'vi-və-ˌfī\ *vb* **-fied; -fy·ing** **1** : to put life into
: ANIMATE **2** : to make vivid — **viv·i·fi·ca·tion** \ˌvi-və-
fə-'kā-shən\ *n* — **viv·i·fi·er** *n*

vi·vip·a·rous \vī-'vi-pə-rəs, və-\ *adj* : producing living
young from within the body rather than from eggs —
vi·vi·par·i·ty \ˌvī-və-'par-ə-tē, ˌvi-\ *n*

vivi·sec·tion \ˌvi-və-'sek-shən, 'vi-və-ˌsek-\ *n* : the
cutting of or operation on a living animal; *also* : animal experimentation esp. if causing distress to the
subject

vix·en \'vik-sən\ *n* **1** : an ill-tempered scolding woman
2 : a female fox

viz *abbr* videlicet

viz·ard \'vi-zərd\ *n* : a mask for disguise or protection

vi·zier \və-'zir\ *n* : a high executive officer of many
Muslim countries

VJ *abbr* veejay

VOA *abbr* Voice of America

voc *abbr* **1** vocational **2** vocative

vocab *abbr* vocabulary

vo·ca·ble \'vō-kə-bəl\ *n* : TERM, NAME; *esp* : a word as
such without regard to its meaning

vo·cab·u·lary \vō-'ka-byə-ˌler-ē\ *n, pl* **-lar·ies** **1** : a list
or collection of words usu. alphabetically arranged
and defined or explained : LEXICON **2** : a stock of
words in a language used by a class or individual or
in relation to a subject

vocabulary entry *n* : a word (as the noun *book*), hy-
phened or open compound (as the verb *cross≈
refer* or the noun *boric acid*), word element (as the
affix *-an*), abbreviation (as *agt*), verbalized symbol
(as *Na*), or term (as *master of ceremonies*) entered alphabetically in a dictionary for the purpose of definition or identification or expressly included as an
inflected form (as the noun *mice* or the verb *saw*) or
as a derived form (as the noun *godlessness* or the adverb *globally*) or related phrase (as *in spite of*) run on
at its base word and usu. set in a type (as boldface)
readily distinguishable from that of the lightface running text which defines, explains, or identifies the entry

¹vo·cal \'vō-kəl\ *adj* **1** : uttered by the voice : ORAL **2**
: relating to, composed or arranged for, or sung by
the human voice ⟨∼ music⟩ **3** : given to expressing
oneself freely or insistently : OUTSPOKEN **4** : of or relating to the voice

²vocal *n* **1** : a vocal sound **2** : a vocal composition or its
performance

vocal cords *n pl* : either of two pairs of elastic folds of
mucous membrane that project into the cavity of the
larynx and function in the production of vocal sounds

vo·cal·ic \vō-'ka-lik\ *adj* : of, relating to, or functioning
as a vowel

vo·cal·ist \'vō-kə-list\ *n* : SINGER

vo·cal·ize \-ˌlīz\ *vb* **-ized; -iz·ing** **1** : to give vocal expression to : UTTER; *esp* : SING **2** : to make voiced
rather than voiceless — **vo·cal·iz·er** *n*

vo·ca·tion \vō-'kā-shən\ *n* **1** : a summons or strong inclination to a particular state or course of action ⟨re-
ligious ∼⟩ **2** : regular employment : OCCUPATION,
PROFESSION — **vo·ca·tion·al** \-shə-nəl\ *adj*

vo·ca·tion·al·ism \-shə-nə-ˌli-zəm\ *n* : emphasis on vocational training in education

voc·a·tive \'vä-kə-tiv\ *adj* : of, relating to, or constituting a grammatical case marking the one addressed —
vocative *n*

vo·cif·er·ate \vō-'si-fə-ˌrāt\ *vb* **-at·ed; -at·ing** [L *vocif-
erari*, fr. *voc-, vox* voice + *ferre* to bear] : to cry out
loudly : CLAMOR, SHOUT — **vo·cif·er·a·tion** \-ˌsi-fə-
'rā-shən\ *n*

vo·cif·er·ous \vō-'si-fə-rəs\ *adj* : making or given to loud outcry — **vo·cif·er·ous·ly** *adv* — **vo·cif·er·ous·ness** *n*

vod·ka \\'väd-kə\\ *n* [Russ. fr. *voda* water] : a colorless liquor distilled from a mash

vogue \\'vōg\\ *n* [MF, action of rowing, course, fashion, fr. It *voga*, fr. *vogare* to row] **1** : popular acceptance or favor : POPULARITY **2** : a period of popularity **3** : one that is in fashion at a particular time **syn** mode, fad, rage, craze, trend, fashion

vogu·ish \\'vō-gish\\ *adj* **1** : FASHIONABLE, SMART **2** : suddenly or temporarily popular

¹voice \\'vȯis\\ *n* **1** : sound produced through the mouth by vertebrates and esp. by human beings in speaking or shouting **2** : musical sound produced by the vocal cords : the power to produce such sound; *also* : one of the melodic parts in a vocal or instrumental composition **3** : the vocal organs as a means of tone production ⟨train the ∼⟩ **4** : sound produced by vibration of the vocal cords as heard in vowels and some consonants **5** : the power of speaking **6** : a sound suggesting a voice ⟨the ∼ of the sea⟩ **7** : an instrument or medium of expression **8** : a choice, opinion, or wish openly expressed; *also* : right of expression **9** : distinction of form of a verb to indicate the relation of the subject to the action expressed by the verb

²voice *vb* **voiced; voic·ing** : to give voice or expression to : UTTER ⟨∼ a complaint⟩ **syn** express, vent, air, ventilate

voice box *n* : LARYNX

voiced \\'vȯist\\ *adj* **1** : having a voice ⟨soft-*voiced*⟩ **2** : uttered with voice ⟨a ∼ consonant⟩ — **voiced·ness** \\'vȯist-nəs, 'vȯi-səd-nəs\\ *n*

voice·less \\'vȯis-ləs\\ *adj* **1** : having no voice **2** : not pronounced with voice — **voice·less·ly** *adv* — **voice·less·ness** *n*

voice mail *n* : an electronic communication system in which spoken messages are recorded for later playback to the intended recipient

voice–over *n* : the voice in a film or television program of a person who is heard but not seen or not seen talking

voice·print \\'vȯis-ˌprint\\ *n* : an individually distinctive pattern of voice characteristics that is spectrographically produced

¹void \\'vȯid\\ *adj* **1** : UNOCCUPIED, VACANT **2** : containing nothing : EMPTY **3** : LACKING, DEVOID ⟨proposals ∼ of sense⟩ **4** : VAIN, USELESS **5** : of no legal force or effect : NULL

²void *n* **1** : empty space : EMPTINESS, VACUUM **2** : a feeling of want or hollowness

³void *vb* **1** : to make or leave empty; *also* : VACATE, LEAVE **2** : DISCHARGE, EMIT ⟨∼ urine⟩ **3** : to render void : ANNUL, NULLIFY ⟨∼ a contract⟩ — **void·able** *adj* — **void·er** *n*

voi·là \\vwä-'lä\\ *interj* [F] — used to call attention or to express satisfaction or approval

voile \\'vȯil\\ *n* : a sheer fabric used for women's clothing and curtains

vol *abbr* **1** volume **2** volunteer

vol·a·tile \\'vä-lət-ᵊl\\ *adj* **1** : readily becoming a vapor at a relatively low temperature ⟨a ∼ liquid⟩ **2** : likely to change suddenly ⟨a ∼ temper⟩ — **vol·a·til·i·ty** \\ˌvä-lə-'ti-lə-tē\\ *n* — **vol·a·til·ize** \\'vä-lət-ᵊl-ˌīz\\ *vb*

vol·can·ic \\väl-'ka-nik\\ *adj* **1** : of, relating to, or produced by a volcano **2** : explosively violent

vol·ca·nism \\'väl-kə-ˌni-zəm\\ *n* : volcanic action or activity

vol·ca·no \\väl-'kā-nō\\ *n, pl* **-noes** *or* **-nos** [It *vulcano*, fr. L *Volcanus, Vulcanus* Roman god of fire and metalworking] : an opening in the earth's crust from which molten rock and steam issue; *also* : a hill or mountain composed of the ejected material

vol·ca·nol·o·gy \\ˌväl-kə-'nä-lə-jē\\ *n* : a branch of geology that deals with volcanic phenomena — **vol·ca·nol·o·gist** \\-kə-'nä-lə-jist\\ *n*

vole \\'vōl\\ *n* : any of various small rodents that are closely related to the lemmings and muskrats

vo·li·tion \\vō-'li-shən\\ *n* **1** : the act or the power of making a choice or decision : WILL **2** : a choice or decision made — **vo·li·tion·al** \\-'li-shə-nəl\\ *adj*

¹vol·ley \\'vä-lē\\ *n, pl* **volleys 1** : a flight of missiles (as arrows) **2** : simultaneous discharge of a number of missile weapons **3** : an act of volleying **4** : a burst of many things at once ⟨a ∼ of angry letters⟩

²volley *vb* **vol·leyed; vol·ley·ing 1** : to discharge or become discharged in or as if in a volley **2** : to hit an object of play in the air before it touches the ground

vol·ley·ball \\-ˌbȯl\\ *n* : a game played by volleying an inflated ball over a net; *also* : the ball used in this game

volt \\'vōlt\\ *n* : the meter-kilogram-second unit of electrical potential difference and electromotive force equal to the difference in potential between two points in a wire carrying a constant current of one ampere when the power dissipated between the points is equal to one watt

volt·age \\'vōl-tij\\ *n* : potential difference measured in volts

vol·ta·ic \\väl-'tā-ik, vōl-\\ *adj* : of, relating to, or producing direct electric current by chemical action

volte–face \\ˌvȯlt-'fäs, ˌvȯl-tə-\\ *n* : a reversal in policy : ABOUT-FACE

volt·me·ter \\'vōlt-ˌmē-tər\\ *n* : an instrument for measuring in volts the difference in potential between different points of an electrical circuit

vol·u·ble \\'väl-yə-bəl\\ *adj* : fluent and smooth in speech : GLIB **syn** garrulous, loquacious, talkative — **vol·u·bil·i·ty** \\ˌväl-yə-'bi-lə-tē\\ *n* — **vol·u·bly** \\'väl-yə-blē\\ *adv*

vol·ume \\'väl-yəm\\ *n* [ME, fr. MF, fr. L *volumen* roll, scroll, fr. *volvere* to roll] **1** : a series of printed sheets bound typically in book form; *also* : an arbitrary number of issues of a periodical **2** : space occupied as measured by cubic units ⟨the ∼ of a cylinder⟩ **3** : sufficient matter to fill a book ⟨her glance spoke ∼s⟩ **4** : AMOUNT ⟨increasing ∼ of business⟩ **5** : the degree of loudness of a sound **syn** body, bulk, mass

vo·lu·mi·nous \\və-'lü-mə-nəs\\ *adj* : having or marked by great volume or bulk : LARGE — **vo·lu·mi·nous·ly** *adv* — **vo·lu·mi·nous·ness** *n*

¹vol·un·tary \\'vä-lən-ˌter-ē\\ *adj* **1** : done, made, or given freely and without compulsion ⟨a ∼ sacrifice⟩ **2** : done on purpose : INTENTIONAL ⟨∼ manslaughter⟩ **3** : of, relating to, or regulated by the will ⟨∼ behavior⟩ **4** : having power of free choice **5** : provided or supported by voluntary action ⟨a ∼ organization⟩ **syn** deliberate, willful, willing, witting — **vol·un·tar·i·ly** \\ˌvä-lən-'ter-ə-lē\\ *adv*

²voluntary *n, pl* **-tar·ies** : an organ solo played in a religious service

voluntary muscle *n* : muscle (as most striated muscle) under voluntary control

¹vol·un·teer \\ˌvä-lən-'tir\\ *n* **1** : a person who voluntarily undertakes a service or duty **2** : a plant growing spontaneously esp. from seeds lost from a previous crop

²volunteer *vb* **1** : to offer or give voluntarily **2** : to offer oneself as a volunteer

vo·lup·tu·ary \\və-'ləp-chə-ˌwer-ē\\ *n, pl* **-ar·ies** : a person whose chief interest in life is the indulgence of sensual appetites

vo·lup·tuous \\-chə-wəs\\ *adj* **1** : giving sensual gratification **2** : given to or spent in enjoyment of luxury or pleasure **syn** luxurious, epicurean, sensuous — **vo·lup·tuous·ly** *adv* — **vo·lup·tuous·ness** *n*

vo·lute \\və-'lüt\\ *n* : a spiral or scroll-shaped decoration

¹vom·it \\'vä-mət\\ *n* : an act or instance of throwing up the contents of the stomach through the mouth; *also* : the matter thrown up

²vomit *vb* **1** : to throw up the contents of the stomach through the mouth **2** : to belch forth : GUSH

voo·doo \\'vü-dü\\ *n, pl* **voodoos 1** : a religion that is derived from African polytheism and is practiced chiefly in Haiti **2** : a person who deals in spells and necromancy; *also* : ¹SPELL 1 **3** : a charm used in voodoo — **voodoo** *adj*

voo·doo·ism \-ˌi-zəm\ *n* **1** : VOODOO 1 **2** : the practice of witchcraft

vo·ra·cious \vȯ-ˈrā-shəs, və-\ *adj* **1** : having a huge appetite : RAVENOUS **2** : very eager ⟨a ∼ reader⟩ **syn** gluttonous, ravening, rapacious — **vo·ra·cious·ly** *adv* — **vo·ra·cious·ness** *n* — **vo·rac·i·ty** \-ˈra-sə-tē\ *n*

vor·tex \ˈvȯr-ˌteks\ *n, pl* **vor·ti·ces** \ˈvȯr-tə-ˌsēz\ *also* **vor·tex·es** \ˈvȯr-ˌtek-səz\ : WHIRLPOOL; *also* : something resembling a whirlpool

vo·ta·ry \ˈvō-tə-rē\ *n, pl* **-ries 1** : ENTHUSIAST, DEVOTEE; *also* : a devoted adherent or admirer : a devout or zealous worshiper

¹vote \ˈvōt\ *n* [ME, fr. L *votum* vow, wish, fr. *vovēre* to vow] **1** : a choice or opinion of a person or body of persons expressed usu. by a ballot, spoken word, or raised hand; *also* : the ballot, word, or gesture used to express a choice or opinion **2** : the decision reached by voting **3** : the right of suffrage **4** : a group of voters with some common characteristics ⟨the big city ∼⟩ — **vote·less** *adj*

²vote *vb* **vot·ed; vot·ing 1** : to cast a vote **2** : to elect, decide, pass, defeat, grant, or make legal by a vote **3** : to declare by general agreement **4** : to offer as a suggestion : PROPOSE **5** : to cause to vote esp. in a given way — **vot·er** *n*

vo·tive \ˈvō-tiv\ *adj* : consisting of or expressing a vow, wish, or desire

vou *abbr* voucher

vouch \ˈvau̇ch\ *vb* **1** : PROVE, SUBSTANTIATE **2** : to verify by examining documentary evidence **3** : to give a guarantee **4** : to supply supporting evidence or testimony; *also* : to give personal assurance

vouch·er \ˈvau̇-chər\ *n* **1** : an act of vouching **2** : one that vouches for another **3** : a documentary record of a business transaction **4** : a written affidavit or authorization **5** : a form indicating a credit against future purchases or expenditures

vouch·safe \vau̇ch-ˈsāf\ *vb* **vouch·safed; vouch·saf·ing** : to grant or give as or as if a privilege or a special favor — **vouch·safe·ment** *n*

¹vow \ˈvau̇\ *n* : a solemn promise or statement; *esp* : one by which a person is bound to an act, service, or condition ⟨marriage ∼s⟩

²vow *vb* **1** : to make a vow or as a vow **2** : to bind or commit by a vow — **vow·er** *n*

vow·el \ˈvau̇-əl\ *n* **1** : a speech sound produced without obstruction or friction in the mouth **2** : a letter representing such a sound

vox po·pu·li \ˈväks-ˈpä-pyə-ˌlī\ *n* [L, voice of the people] : popular sentiment

¹voy·age \ˈvȯi-ij\ *n* [ME, fr. OF *voiage*, fr. LL *viaticum*, fr. L, traveling money, fr. neut. of *viaticus* of a journey, fr. *via* way] : a journey esp. by water from one place or country to another

²voyage *vb* **voy·aged; voy·ag·ing** : to take or make a voyage — **voy·ag·er** *n*

voya·geur \ˌvȯi-ə-ˈzhər, ˌvwä-yä-\ *n* [CanF] : a person employed by a fur company to transport goods to and from remote stations esp. in the Canadian Northwest

voy·eur \vwä-ˈyər, vȯi-ˈər\ *n* : one who habitually seeks sexual stimulation by visual means — **voy·eur·ism** \-ˌi-zəm\ *n*

VP *abbr* **1** verb phrase **2** vice president

vs *abbr* **1** verse **2** versus

vss *abbr* **1** verses **2** versions

V/STOL *abbr* vertical or short takeoff and landing

Vt *or* **VT** *abbr* Vermont

VTOL *abbr* vertical takeoff and landing

VTR *abbr* videotape recorder

vul·ca·nize \ˈvəl-kə-ˌnīz\ *vb* **-nized; -niz·ing** : to treat rubber or rubberlike material chemically to give useful properties (as elasticity and strength)

Vulg *abbr* Vulgate

vul·gar \ˈvəl-gər\ *adj* [ME, fr. L *vulgaris* of the mob, vulgar, fr. *vulgus* mob, common people] **1** : VERNACULAR ⟨the ∼ tongue⟩ **2** : of or relating to the common people : GENERAL, COMMON **3** : lacking cultivation or refinement : BOORISH; *also* : offensive to good taste or refined feelings **syn** gross, obscene, ribald, dirty, indecent, profane — **vul·gar·ly** *adv*

vul·gar·i·an \ˌvəl-ˈgar-ē-ən\ *n* : a vulgar person

vul·gar·ism \ˈvəl-gə-ˌri-zəm\ *n* **1** : VULGARITY **2** : a word or expression originated or used chiefly by illiterate persons **3** : a coarse expression : OBSCENITY

vul·gar·i·ty \ˌvəl-ˈgar-ə-tē\ *n, pl* **-ties 1** : something vulgar **2** : the quality or state of being vulgar

vul·gar·ize \ˈvəl-gə-ˌrīz\ *vb* **-ized; -iz·ing** : to make vulgar — **vul·gar·i·za·tion** \ˌvəl-gə-rə-ˈzā-shən\ *n* — **vul·gar·iz·er** \ˈvəl-gə-ˌrī-zər\ *n*

Vul·gate \ˈvəl-ˌgāt\ *n* [ML *vulgata*, fr. LL *vulgata editio* edition in general circulation] : a Latin version of the Bible used by the Roman Catholic Church

vul·ner·a·ble \ˈvəl-nə-rə-bəl\ *adj* **1** : capable of being wounded : susceptible to wounds **2** : open to attack **3** : liable to increased penalties in contract bridge — **vul·ner·a·bil·i·ty** \ˌvəl-nə-rə-ˈbi-lə-tē\ *n* — **vul·ner·a·bly** \ˈvəl-nə-rə-blē\ *adv*

vul·pine \ˈvəl-ˌpīn\ *adj* : of, relating to, or resembling a fox esp. in cunning

vul·ture \ˈvəl-chər\ *n* **1** : any of various large birds (as a turkey vulture) related to the hawks, eagles, and falcons but having weaker claws and the head usu. naked and living chiefly on carrion **2** : a rapacious person

vul·va \ˈvəl-və\ *n, pl* **vul·vae** \-ˌvē\ [NL, fr. L, womb, female genitals] : the external parts of the female genital organs

vv *abbr* **1** verses **2** vice versa

vy·ing *pres part of* VIE

W

¹w \ˈdə-bəl-(ˌ)yü\ *n, pl* **w's** *or* **ws** *often cap* : the 23d letter of the English alphabet

²w *abbr, often cap* **1** water **2** watt **3** week **4** weight **5** west; western **6** wide; width **7** wife **8** with

W *symbol* [G *Wolfram*] tungsten

WA *abbr* **1** Washington **2** Western Australia

wacky \ˈwa-kē\ *adj* **wack·i·er; -est** : ECCENTRIC, CRAZY

¹wad \ˈwäd\ *n* **1** : a little mass, bundle, or tuft ⟨∼s of clay⟩ **2** : a soft mass of usu. light fibrous material **3** : a pliable plug (as of felt) used to retain a powder charge (as in a cartridge) **4** : a considerable amount (as of money) **5** : a roll of paper money

²wad *vb* **wad·ded; wad·ding 1** : to push a wad into ⟨∼ a gun⟩ **2** : to form into a wad **3** : to hold in by a wad ⟨∼ a bullet in a gun⟩ **4** : to stuff or line with a wad : PAD

wad·ding \ˈwä-diŋ\ *n* **1** : WADS; *also* : material for making wads **2** : a soft mass or sheet of short loose fibers used for stuffing or padding

wad·dle \ˈwäd-ᵊl\ *vb* **wad·dled; wad·dling** : to walk with short steps swaying from side to side like a duck — **waddle** *n*

wade \ˈwād\ *vb* **wad·ed; wad·ing 1** : to step in or through a medium (as water) more resistant than air **2** : to move or go with difficulty or labor and often with determination ⟨∼ through a dull book⟩ — **wad·able** *or* **wade·able** \ˈwā-də-bəl\ *adj* — **wade** *n*

wad·er \'wā-dər\ *n* **1** : one that wades **2** : SHOREBIRD; *also* : WADING BIRD **3** *pl* : a waterproof garment consisting of pants with attached boots for wading

wa·di \'wä-dē\ *n* [Ar *wādiy*] : a streambed of southwest Asia and northern Africa that is dry except in the rainy season

wading bird *n* : any of an order of long-legged birds (as sandpipers, cranes, or herons) that wade in water in search of food

wa·fer \'wā-fər\ *n* **1** : a thin crisp cake or cracker **2** : a thin round piece of unleavened bread used in the Eucharist **3** : something (as a piece of candy) that resembles a wafer

waf·fle \'wä-fəl\ *n* : a soft but crisped cake of batter cooked in a special hinged metal utensil (**waffle iron**)

¹waft \'wäft, 'waft\ *vb* : to cause to move or go lightly by or as if by the impulse of wind or waves

²waft *n* **1** : a slight breeze : PUFF **2** : the act of waving

¹wag \'wag\ *vb* **wagged; wag·ging 1** : to sway or swing shortly from side to side or to-and-fro ⟨the dog *wagged* his tail⟩ **2** : to move in chatter or gossip ⟨scandal caused tongues to ~⟩

²wag *n* : an act of wagging : a wagging movement

³wag *n* : WIT, JOKER

¹wage \'wāj\ *n* **1** : payment for labor or services usu. according to contract **2** *pl* : RECOMPENSE, REWARD

²wage *vb* **waged; wag·ing 1** : to engage in : CARRY ON ⟨~ a war⟩ **2** : to be in process of being waged

¹wa·ger \'wā-jər\ *n* **1** : BET, STAKE **2** : something on which bets are laid : GAMBLE

²wager *vb* : BET — **wa·ger·er** *n*

wag·gery \'wa-gə-rē\ *n, pl* **-ger·ies 1** : mischievous merriment : PLEASANTRY **2** : JEST, TRICK

wag·gish \'wa-gish\ *adj* **1** : resembling or characteristic of a wag : MISCHIEVOUS **2** : SPORTIVE, HUMOROUS

wag·gle \'wa-gəl\ *vb* **wag·gled; wag·gling** : to move backward and forward or from side to side : WAG — **waggle** *n*

wag·gon *chiefly Brit var of* WAGON

wag·on \'wa-gən\ *n* **1** : a 4-wheeled vehicle; *esp* : one drawn by animals and used for freight or merchandise **2** : PADDY WAGON **3** : a child's 4-wheeled cart **4** : STATION WAGON

wag·on·er \'wa-gə-nər\ *n* : the driver of a wagon

wag·on·ette \₁wa-gə-'net\ *n* : a light wagon with two facing seats along the sides behind a cross seat in front

wa·gon–lit \₁va-gōⁿ-'lē\ *n, pl* **wagons–lits** *or* **wagon–lits** *same or* -'lēz\ [F, fr. *wagon* railroad car + *lit* bed] : a railroad sleeping car

wagon train *n* : a column of wagons traveling overland

wag·tail \'wag-₁tāl\ *n* : any of various slender-bodied mostly Old World birds with a long tail that jerks up and down

wa·hi·ne \wä-'hē-nä\ *n* **1** : a Polynesian woman **2** : a female surfer

wa·hoo \'wä-₁hü\ *n, pl* **wahoos** : a large vigorous food and sport fish related to the mackerel and found in warm seas

waif \'wāf\ *n* **1** : something found without an owner and esp. by chance **2** : a stray person or animal; *esp* : a homeless child

wail \'wāl\ *vb* **1** : LAMENT, WEEP **2** : to make a sound suggestive of a mournful cry **3** : COMPLAIN — **wail** *n*

wail·ful \-fəl\ *adj* : SORROWFUL, MOURNFUL **syn** melancholy, doleful, lugubrious, lamentable, plaintive, woeful — **wail·ful·ly** *adv*

wain \'wān\ *n* : a usu. large heavy farm wagon

wain·scot \'wān-skət, -₁skōt, -₁skät\ *n* **1** : a usu. paneled wooden lining of an interior wall of a room **2** : the lower part of an interior wall when finished differently from the rest — **wainscot** *vb*

wain·scot·ing *or* **wain·scot·ting** \-₁skō-tiŋ, -₁skä-, -skə-\ *n* : material for a wainscot; *also* : WAINSCOT

waist \'wāst\ *n* **1** : the narrowed part of the body be-

tween the chest and hips **2** : a part resembling the human waist esp. in narrowness or central position ⟨the ~ of a ship⟩ **3** : a garment or part of a garment (as a blouse or bodice) for the upper part of the body

waist·band \-₁band\ *n* : a band (as on trousers or a skirt) that fits around the waist

waist·coat \'wes-kət, 'wāst-₁kōt\ *n, chiefly Brit* : VEST 1

waist·line \'wāst-₁līn\ *n* **1** : a line around the waist at its narrowest part; *also* : the length of this **2** : the line at which the bodice and skirt of a dress meet

¹wait \'wāt\ *vb* **1** : to remain inactive in readiness or expectation : AWAIT ⟨~ for orders⟩ **2** : to delay serving (a meal) **3** : to act as attendant or servant ⟨~ on customers⟩ **4** : to attend as a waiter : SERVE ⟨~ tables⟩ ⟨~ at a banquet⟩ **5** : to be ready

²wait *n* **1** : a position of concealment usu. with intent to attack or surprise ⟨lie in ~⟩ **2** : an act or period of waiting

wait·er \'wā-tər\ *n* **1** : one that waits on another; *esp* : a person who waits tables **2** : TRAY

waiting game *n* : a strategy in which one or more participants withhold action in the hope of an opportunity for more effective action later

waiting room *n* : a room (as at a doctor's office) for the use of persons who are waiting

wait·per·son \'wāt-₁pər-sən\ *n* : a waiter or waitress

wait·ress \'wā-trəs\ *n* : a woman who waits tables

waive \'wāv\ *vb* **waived; waiv·ing** [ME *weiven*, fr. OF *weyver*, fr. *waif* lost, unclaimed] **1** : to give up claim to ⟨*waived* his right to a trial⟩ **2** : POSTPONE

waiv·er \'wā-vər\ *n* : the act of waiving right, claim, or privilege; *also* : a document containing a declaration of such an act

¹wake \'wāk\ *vb* **woke** \'wōk\ *also* **waked** \'wākt\; **woken** \'wō-kən\ *also* **waked** *or* **woke; wak·ing 1** : to be or remain awake; *esp* : to keep watch (as over a corpse) **2** : AWAKE, AWAKEN ⟨the baby *woke* up early⟩

²wake *n* **1** : the state of being awake **2** : a watch held over the body of a dead person prior to burial

³wake *n* : the track left by a ship in the water; *also* : a track left behind

wake·ful \'wāk-fəl\ *adj* : not sleeping or able to sleep : SLEEPLESS, ALERT — **wake·ful·ness** *n*

wak·en \'wā-kən\ *vb* : WAKE

wake–rob·in \'wāk-₁rä-bən\ *n* : TRILLIUM

wak·ing \'wā-kiŋ\ *adj* : passed in a conscious or alert state ⟨every ~ hour⟩

wale \'wāl\ *n* : a ridge esp. on cloth; *also* : the texture esp. of a fabric

¹walk \'wok\ *vb* [partly fr. ME *walken*, fr. OE *wealcan* to roll, toss and partly fr. ME *walkien*, fr. OE *wealcian* to roll up, muffle up] **1** : to move or cause to move on foot usu. at a natural unhurried gait ⟨~ to town⟩ ⟨~ a horse⟩ **2** : to pass over, through, or along by walking ⟨~ the streets⟩ **3** : to perform or accomplish by walking ⟨~ guard⟩ **4** : to follow a course of action or way of life ⟨~ humbly in the sight of God⟩ **5** : WALK OUT **6** : to receive a base on balls; *also* : to give a base on balls to — **walk·er** *n*

²walk *n* **1** : a going on foot ⟨go for a ~⟩ **2** : a place, path, or course for walking **3** : distance to be walked ⟨a quarter-mile ~ from here⟩ **4** : manner of living : CONDUCT, BEHAVIOR **5** : social or economic status ⟨various ~s of life⟩ **6** : manner of walking : GAIT; *esp* : a slow 4-beat gait of a horse **7** : BASE ON BALLS

walk·away \'wo-kə-₁wā\ *n* : an easily won contest

walk·ie–talk·ie \₁wo-kē-'to-kē\ *n* : a small portable radio transmitting and receiving set

¹walk–in \'wok-₁in\ *adj* : large enough to be walked into ⟨a ~ refrigerator⟩

²walk–in *n* **1** : an easy election victory **2** : one that walks in

walking papers *n pl* : DISMISSAL, DISCHARGE

walking stick *n* **1** : a stick used in walking **2** *usu* **walk-**

ing·stick : STICK INSECT; *esp* : one common in parts of the U.S.

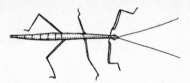

walking stick 2

walk–on \'wȯk-ˌȯn, -ˌän\ *n* : a small part in a dramatic production

walk·out \-ˌau̇t\ *n* 1 : a labor strike 2 : the action of leaving a meeting or organization as an expression of disapproval

walk out *vb* 1 : to leave suddenly often as an expression of disapproval 2 : to go on strike

walk·over \-ˌō-vər\ *n* : a one-sided contest : an easy victory

walk–up \'wȯk-ˌəp\ *n* : a building or apartment house without an elevator — **walk-up** *adj*

walk·way \-ˌwā\ *n* : a passage for walking

¹wall \'wȯl\ *n* [ME, fr. OE *weall*, fr. L *vallum* rampart, fr. *vallus* stake, palisade] 1 : a structure (as of stone or brick) intended for defense or security or for enclosing something 2 : one of the upright enclosing parts of a building or room 3 : the inside surface of a cavity or container ⟨the ∼ of a boiler⟩ 4 : something like a wall in appearance, function, or effect ⟨a tariff ∼⟩ — **walled** \'wȯld\ *adj*

²wall *vb* 1 : to provide, separate, or surround with or as if with a wall ⟨∼ in a garden⟩ 2 : to close (an opening) with or as if with a wall ⟨∼ up a door⟩

wal·la·by \'wä-lə-bē\ *n, pl* **wallabies** *also* **wallaby** : any of various small or medium-sized kangaroos

wall·board \'wȯl-ˌbȯrd\ *n* : a structural material (as of wood pulp or plaster) made in large sheets and used for sheathing interior walls and ceilings

wal·let \'wä-lət\ *n* 1 : a bag or sack for carrying things on a journey 2 : a pocketbook with compartments (as for personal papers and usu. unfolded money) : BILLFOLD

wall·eye \'wȯ-ˌlī\ *n* 1 : an eye with a whitish iris or an opaque white cornea 2 : a large vigorous No. American food and sport fish related to the perches — **wall·eyed** \-ˌlīd\ *adj*

wall·flow·er \'wȯl-ˌflau̇-ər\ *n* 1 : any of several Old World plants related to the mustards; *esp* : one with showy fragrant flowers 2 : a person who usu. from shyness or unpopularity remains alone (as at a dance)

Wal·loon \wä-'lün\ *n* : a member of a people of southern and southeastern Belgium and adjacent parts of France — **Walloon** *adj*

¹wal·lop \'wä-ləp\ *vb* [ME *walopen* to gallop, fr. OF *waloper*] 1 : to beat soundly : TROUNCE 2 : to hit hard : SOCK **syn** batter, beat, lambaste, pound, pummel, thrash

²wallop *n* 1 : a powerful blow or impact 2 : the ability to hit hard 3 : emotional, sensory, or psychological force : IMPACT

wal·lop·ing \'wä-lə-piŋ\ *adj* 1 : LARGE, WHOPPING 2 : exceptionally fine or impressive

¹wal·low \'wä-lō\ *vb* 1 : to roll oneself about sluggishly in or as if in deep mud ⟨hogs ∼ing in the mire⟩ 2 : to indulge oneself excessively ⟨∼ in luxury⟩ 3 : to become or remain helpless ⟨∼ in ignorance⟩ **syn** bask, indulge, luxuriate, revel, welter

²wallow *n* : a muddy or dust-filled area where animals wallow

wall·pa·per \'wȯl-ˌpā-pər\ *n* : decorative paper for the walls of a room — **wallpaper** *vb*

wall–to–wall *adj* 1 : covering the entire floor ⟨wall-to=

wall carpeting⟩ 2 : covering or filling one entire space or time ⟨crowds of *wall-to-wall* people⟩

wal·nut \'wȯl-(ˌ)nət\ *n* [ME *walnot*, fr. OE *wealhhnutu*, lit., foreign nut, fr. *Wealh* Welshman, foreigner + *hnutu* nut] 1 : a nut with a furrowed usu. rough shell and an adherent husk from any of a genus of trees related to the hickories; *esp* : the large edible nut of a Eurasian tree 2 : a tree that bears walnuts 3 : the usu. reddish to dark brown wood of a walnut used esp. in cabinetwork and veneers

wal·rus \'wȯl-rəs, 'wäl-\ *n, pl* **walrus** *or* **wal·rus·es** : a large mammal of northern seas related to the seals and having ivory tusks

¹waltz \'wȯlts\ *n* 1 : a gliding dance done to music having three beats to the measure 2 : music for or suitable for waltzing

²waltz *vb* [G *Walzer*, fr. *walzen* to roll, dance] 1 : to dance a waltz 2 : to move or advance easily, successfully, or conspicuously ⟨he ∼ed off with the championship⟩

wam·ble \'wäm-bəl\ *vb* **wam·bled; wam·bling** : to progress unsteadily or with a lurching shambling gait

wam·pum \'wäm-pəm\ *n* [short for *wampumpeag*, fr. Massachuset (a North American Indian language) *wampompeag*, fr. *wampan* white + *api* string + *-ag*, pl. suffix] 1 : beads made of shells strung in strands, belts, or sashes and used by No. American Indians as money and ornaments 2 *slang* : MONEY

wan \'wän\ *adj* **wan·ner; wan·nest** 1 : SICKLY, PALLID; *also* : FEEBLE 2 : DIM, FAINT 3 : LANGUID ⟨a ∼ smile⟩ **syn** ashen, blanched, doughy, livid, pale, waxen — **wan·ly** *adv* — **wan·ness** *n*

wand \'wänd\ *n* 1 : a slender staff carried in a procession 2 : the staff of a fairy, diviner, or magician

wan·der \'wän-dər\ *vb* 1 : to move about aimlessly or without a fixed course or goal : RAMBLE 2 : to go astray in conduct or thought; *esp* : to become delirious **syn** gad, gallivant, meander, range, roam, rove — **wan·der·er** *n*

wandering Jew *n* : either of two trailing or creeping plants cultivated for their showy and often white= striped foliage

wan·der·lust \'wän-dər-ˌləst\ *n* : strong longing for or impulse toward wandering

¹wane \'wän\ *vb* **waned; wan·ing** 1 : to grow gradually smaller or less ⟨the moon ∼s⟩ ⟨his strength *waned*⟩ 2 : to lose power, prosperity, or influence 3 : to draw near an end ⟨summer is *waning*⟩ **syn** abate, ebb, moderate, relent, slacken, subside

²wane *n* : a waning (as in size or power); *also* : a period in which something is waning

wan·gle \'waŋ-gəl\ *vb* **wan·gled; wan·gling** 1 : to obtain by sly or devious means; *also* : to use trickery or questionable means to achieve an end 2 : MANIPULATE; *also* : FINAGLE

wan·na–be \'wä-nə-ˌbē\ *n* : a person who wants or aspires to be someone or something else or who tries to look or act like someone else

¹want \'wȯnt, 'wänt\ *vb* 1 : to fail to possess : LACK ⟨they ∼ the necessities of life⟩ 2 : to feel or suffer the need of 3 : NEED, REQUIRE ⟨the house ∼s painting⟩ 4 : to desire earnestly : WISH

²want *n* 1 : a lack of a required or usual amount : SHORTAGE 2 : dire need : DESTITUTION 3 : something wanted : DESIRE 4 : personal defect : FAULT

¹want·ing \'wȯn-tiŋ, 'wän-\ *adj* 1 : not present or in evidence : ABSENT 2 : falling below standards or expectations 3 : lacking in ability or capacity : DEFICIENT (as in common sense)

²wanting *prep* 1 : LESS, MINUS ⟨a month ∼ two days⟩ 2 : WITHOUT ⟨a book ∼ a cover⟩

¹wan·ton \'wȯnt-ᵊn, 'wänt-\ *adj* [ME, undisciplined, fr. *wan-* deficient, wrong + *towen*, pp. of *teen* to draw, train, discipline] 1 : UNCHASTE, LEWD, LUSTFUL; *also* : SENSUAL 2 : having no regard for justice or for other persons' feelings, rights, or safety : MERCILESS, INHU-

MANE ⟨~cruelty⟩ **3** : having no just cause ⟨a ~ attack⟩ — **wan·ton·ly** *adv* — **wan·ton·ness** *n*

²wanton *n* : a wanton individual; *esp* : a lewd or immoral person

³wanton *vb* **1** : to be wanton : act wantonly **2** : to pass or waste wantonly

wa·pi·ti \'wä-pə-tē\ *n, pl* **wapiti** *or* **wapitis** : ELK 2

¹war \'wȯr\ *n* **1** : a state or period of usu. open and declared armed fighting between states or nations **2** : the art or science of warfare **3** : a state of hostility, conflict, or antagonism **4** : a struggle between opposing forces or for a particular end ⟨~ against disease⟩ — **war·less** \-ləs\ *adj*

²war *vb* **warred; war·ring** : to engage in warfare : be in conflict

³war *abbr* warrant

¹war·ble \'wȯr-bəl\ *n* **1** : a melodious succession of low pleasing sounds **2** : a musical trill

²warble *vb* **war·bled; war·bling** **1** : to sing or utter in a trilling manner or with variations **2** : to express by or as if by warbling

³warble *n* : a swelling under the hide esp. of the back of cattle, horses, and wild mammals caused by the maggot of a fly (**warble fly**); *also* : its maggot

war·bler \'wȯr-blər\ *n* **1** : SONGSTER **2** : any of various small slender-billed Old World singing birds related to the thrushes and noted for their song **3** : any of numerous small bright-colored American insect-eating birds with a usu. weak and unmusical song

war·bon·net \'wȯr-ıbä-nət\ *n* : a feathered American Indian ceremonial headdress

war cry *n* **1** : a cry used by fighters in war **2** : a slogan used esp. to rally people to a cause

¹ward \'wȯrd\ *n* **1** : a guarding or being under guard or guardianship; *esp* : CUSTODY **2** : a body of guards **3** : a division of a prison **4** : a division in a hospital **5** : a division of a city for electoral or administrative purposes **6** : a person (as a child) under the protection of a guardian or a law court **7** : a person or body of persons under the protection or tutelage of a government **8** : a means of defense : PROTECTION

²ward *vb* : to turn aside : DEFLECT — usu. used with *off* ⟨~ off a blow⟩

¹-ward \wərd\ *also* **-wards** \wərdz\ *adj suffix* **1** : that moves, tends, faces, or is directed toward ⟨wind*ward*⟩ **2** : that occurs or is situated in the direction of ⟨sea*ward*⟩

²-ward *or* **-wards** *adv suffix* **1** : in a (specified) direction ⟨up*wards*⟩ ⟨after*ward*⟩ **2** : toward a (specified) point, position, or area ⟨sky*ward*⟩

war dance *n* : a dance performed (as by American Indians) before going to war or in celebration of victory

war·den \'wȯrd-ᵊn\ *n* **1** : GUARDIAN, KEEPER **2** : the governor of a town, district, or fortress **3** : an official charged with special supervisory or enforcement duties ⟨game ~⟩ ⟨air raid ~⟩ **4** : an official in charge of the operation of a prison **5** : one of two ranking lay officers of an Episcopal parish **6** : any of various British college officials

ward·er \'wȯr-dər\ *n* : WATCHMAN, WARDEN

ward heel·er \-ıhē-lər\ *n* : a local worker for a political boss

ward·robe \'wȯr-ıdrōb\ *n* [ME *warderobe,* fr. OF, fr. *warder* to guard + *robe* robe] **1** : a room or closet where clothes are kept; *also* : CLOTHESPRESS **2** : a collection of wearing apparel ⟨his summer ~⟩

ward·room \-ıdrüm, -ıdrüm\ *n* : the dining area for officers aboard a warship

ward·ship \'wȯrd-ıship\ *n* **1** : GUARDIANSHIP **2** : the state of being under care of a guardian

ware \'war\ *n* **1** : manufactured articles or products of art or craft : GOODS ⟨glass*ware*⟩ **2** : an article of merchandise ⟨a peddler hawking his ~s⟩ **3** : items (as dishes) of fired clay : POTTERY

ware·house \-ıhaús\ *n* : a place for the storage of mer-

chandise or commodities : STOREHOUSE — **ware·house** *vb* — **ware·house·man** \-mən\ *n* — **ware·house·er** \-ıhaú-zər, -sər\ *n*

ware·room \'war-ırüm, -ırüm\ *n* : a room in which goods are exhibited for sale

war·fare \'wȯr-ıfar\ *n* **1** : military operations between enemies : WAR; *also* : an activity undertaken by one country to weaken or destroy another ⟨economic ~⟩ **2** : STRUGGLE, CONFLICT

war·fa·rin \'wȯr-fə-rən\ *n* : an anticoagulant compound used as a rodent poison and in medicine

war·head \'wȯr-ıhed\ *n* : the section of a missile containing the charge

war·horse \-ıhȯrs\ *n* **1** : a horse for use in war **2** : a veteran soldier or public person (as a politician)

war·like \-ılīk\ *adj* **1** : fond of war ⟨~ peoples⟩ **2** : of, relating to, or useful in war : MILITARY, MARTIAL ⟨~ supplies⟩ **3** : befitting or characteristic of war or of soldiers ⟨~ attitudes⟩

war·lock \-ıläk\ *n* [ME *warloghe,* fr. OE *wǣrloga* one that breaks faith, the Devil, fr. *wǣr* faith, troth + *-loga* (fr. *lēogan* to lie)] : SORCERER, WIZARD

war·lord \-ılȯrd\ *n* **1** : a high military leader **2** : a military commander exercising local civil power by force ⟨former Chinese ~s⟩

¹warm \'wȯrm\ *adj* **1** : having or giving out heat to a moderate or adequate degree ⟨~ milk⟩ ⟨a ~ stove⟩ **2** : serving to retain heat ⟨~ clothes⟩ **3** : feeling or inducing sensations of heat ⟨~ from exercise⟩ ⟨a ~ climb⟩ **4** : showing or marked by strong feeling : ARDENT ⟨~ support⟩ **5** : marked by tense excitement or hot anger ⟨a ~ campaign⟩ **6** : giving a pleasant impression of warmth, cheerfulness, or friendliness ⟨~ colors⟩ ⟨a ~ tone of voice⟩ **7** : marked by or tending toward injury, distress, or pain ⟨made things ~ for the enemy⟩ **8** : newly made : FRESH ⟨a ~ scent⟩ **9** : near to a goal ⟨getting ~ in a search⟩ — **warm·ly** *adv*

²warm *vb* **1** : to make or become warm **2** : to give a feeling of warmth or vitality to **3** : to experience feelings of affection or pleasure ⟨she ~ed to her guest⟩ **4** : to reheat for eating ⟨~ed over the roast⟩ **5** : to make ready for operation or performance by preliminary exercise or operation ⟨~ up the motor⟩ **6** : to become increasingly ardent, interested, or competent ⟨the speaker ~ed to his topic⟩ — **warm·er** *n*

warm—blood·ed \-'blə-dəd\ *adj* : able to maintain a relatively high and constant body temperature relatively independent of that of the surroundings

warmed—over \'wȯrmd-'ō-vər\ *adj* **1** : REHEATED ⟨~ cabbage⟩ **2** : not fresh or new ⟨~ ideas⟩

warm front *n* : an advancing edge of a warm air mass

warm·heart·ed \'wȯrm-'här-təd\ *adj* : marked by warmth of feeling : CORDIAL — **warm·heart·ed·ness** *n*

warming pan *n* : a long-handled covered pan filled with live coals and formerly used to warm a bed

war·mon·ger \'wȯr-ıməŋ-gər, -ımäŋ-\ *n* : one who urges or attempts to stir up war

warmth \'wȯrmth\ *n* **1** : the quality or state of being warm **2** : ZEAL, ARDOR, FERVOR

warm up *vb* : to engage in exercise or practice esp. before entering a game or contest — **warm—up** \'wȯrm-ıəp\ *n*

warn \'wȯrn\ *vb* **1** : to put on guard : CAUTION; *also* : ADMONISH, COUNSEL **2** : to notify esp. in advance : INFORM **3** : to order to go or keep away

¹warn·ing \'wȯr-niŋ\ *n* **1** : the act of warning : the state of being warned **2** : something that warns or serves to warn

²warning *adj* : serving as an alarm, signal, summons, or admonition ⟨~ bell⟩ — **warn·ing·ly** *adv*

¹warp \'wȯrp\ *n* **1** : the lengthwise threads on a loom or in a woven fabric **2** : a twist out of a true plane or straight line ⟨a ~ in a board⟩

²warp *vb* [ME, fr. OE *weorpan* to throw] **1** : to turn or twist out of shape; *also* : to become so twisted **2** : to lead astray : PERVERT; *also* : FALSIFY, DISTORT

war paint *n* : paint put on the face and body by American Indians as a sign of going to war

war·path \'wȯr-ˌpath, -ˌpȧth\ *n* : the course taken by a party of American Indians going on a hostile expedition — **on the warpath** : ready to fight or argue

war·plane \-ˌplān\ *n* : a military airplane; *esp* : one armed for combat

¹**war·rant** \'wȯr-ənt, 'wär-\ *n* **1** : AUTHORIZATION; *also* : JUSTIFICATION, GROUND **2** : evidence (as a document) of authorization; *esp* : a legal writ authorizing an officer to take action (as in making an arrest, seizure, or search) **3** : a certificate of appointment issued to an officer of lower rank than a commissioned officer

²**warrant** *vb* **1** : to guarantee security or immunity to : SECURE **2** : to declare or maintain positively ⟨I ~ this is so⟩ **3** : to assure (a person) of the truth of what is said **4** : to guarantee to be as it appears or as it is represented ⟨~ goods as of the first quality⟩ **5** : SANCTION, AUTHORIZE **6** : to give proof of : ATTEST; *also* : GUARANTEE **7** : JUSTIFY ⟨his need ~s the expenditure⟩

warrant officer *n* **1** : an officer in the armed forces ranking next below a commissioned officer **2** : a commissioned officer ranking below an ensign in the navy or coast guard and below a second lieutenant in the marine corps

war·ran·ty \'wȯr-ən-tē, 'wär-\ *n, pl* **-ties** : an expressed or implied statement that some situation or thing is as it appears to be or is represented to be; *esp* : a usu. written guarantee of the integrity of a product and of the maker's responsibility for the repair or replacement of defective parts

war·ren \'wȯr-ən, 'wär-\ *n* **1** : an area where rabbits breed; *also* : a structure where rabbits are bred or kept **2** : a crowded tenement or district

war·rior \'wȯr-yər; 'wȯr-ē-ər, 'wär-\ *n* : a man engaged or experienced in warfare

war·ship \'wȯr-ˌship\ *n* : a naval vessel

wart \'wȯrt\ *n* **1** : a small usu. horny projecting growth on the skin; *esp* : one caused by a virus **2** : a protuberance resembling a wart (as on a plant) — **warty** *adj*

wart·hog \'wȯrt-ˌhȯg, -ˌhäg\ *n* : a wild African hog which has large tusks and the males of which have two pairs of rough warty protuberances below the eyes

war·time \'wȯr-ˌtīm\ *n* : a period during which a war is in progress

wary \'war-ē\ *adj* **war·i·er; -est** : very cautious; *esp* : careful in guarding against danger or deception

was *past 1st & 3d sing of* BE

¹**wash** \'wȯsh, 'wäsh\ *vb* **1** : to clean with water and usu. soap or detergent ⟨~ clothes⟩ ⟨~ your hands⟩ **2** : to wet thoroughly : DRENCH **3** : to flow along the border of ⟨waves ~ the shore⟩ **4** : to pour or flow in a stream or current **5** : to move or remove by or as if by the action of water **6** : to cover or daub lightly with a liquid (as whitewash) **7** : to run water over (as gravel or ore) in order to separate valuable matter from refuse ⟨~ sand for gold⟩ **8** : to undergo laundering ⟨a dress that doesn't ~ well⟩ **9** : to stand a test ⟨that story will not ~⟩ **10** : to be worn away by water

²**wash** *n* **1** : the act or process or an instance of washing or being washed **2** : articles to be washed or being washed **3** : the flow or action of a mass of water (as a wave) **4** : erosion by waves (as of the sea) **5** *West* : the dry bed of a stream **6** : worthless esp. liquid waste : REFUSE, SWILL **7** : a thin coat of paint (as watercolor) **8** : a disturbance in the air caused by the passage of a wing or propeller

³**wash** *adj* : WASHABLE

Wash *abbr* Washington

wash·able \'wȯ-shə-bəl, 'wä-\ *adj* : capable of being washed without damage

wash–and–wear *adj* : of, relating to, or being a fabric or garment that needs little or no ironing after washing

wash·ba·sin \'wȯsh-ˌbās-ᵊn, 'wäsh-\ *n* : WASHBOWL

wash·board \-ˌbȯrd\ *n* : a grooved board to scrub clothes on

wash·bowl \-ˌbōl\ *n* : a large bowl for water for washing hands and face

wash·cloth \-ˌklȯth\ *n* : a cloth used for washing one's face and body

washed–out \'wȯsht-ˈaút, 'wäsht-\ *adj* **1** : faded in color **2** : EXHAUSTED ⟨felt ~ after working all night⟩

washed–up \-ˈəp\ *adj* : no longer successful, popular, skillful, or needed

wash·er \'wȯ-shər, 'wä-\ *n* **1** : a ring or perforated plate used around a bolt or screw to ensure tightness or relieve friction **2** : one that washes; *esp* : a machine for washing

wash·er·wom·an \-ˌwu̇-mən\ *n* : a woman whose occupation is washing clothes

wash·house \'wȯsh-ˌhaús, 'wäsh-\ *n* : a house or building for washing clothes

wash·ing \'wȯ-shiŋ, 'wä-\ *n* **1** : material obtained by washing **2** : articles washed or to be washed

washing soda *n* : SODIUM CARBONATE

Wash·ing·ton's Birthday \'wȯ-shiŋ-tənz-, 'wä-\ *n* : the 3d Monday in February observed as a legal holiday

wash·out \'wȯsh-ˌaút, 'wäsh-\ *n* **1** : the washing away of earth (as from a road); *also* : a place where earth is washed away **2** : a complete failure

wash·room \-ˌrüm, -ˌru̇m\ *n* : BATHROOM

wash·stand \-ˌstand\ *n* **1** : a stand holding articles needed for washing face and hands **2** : LAVATORY 1

wash·tub \-ˌtəb\ *n* : a tub for washing or soaking clothes

wash·wom·an \'wȯsh-ˌwu̇-mən, 'wäsh-\ *n* : WASHERWOMAN

washy \'wȯ-shē, 'wä-\ *adj* **wash·i·er; -est** **1** : WEAK, WATERY **2** : PALLID **3** : lacking in vigor, individuality, or definiteness

wasp \'wȧsp, 'wȯsp\ *n* : any of numerous social or solitary winged insects related to the bees and ants with biting mouthparts and in females and workers an often formidable sting

WASP *or* **Wasp** *n* [white *Anglo-Saxon Protestant*] : an American of northern European and esp. British ancestry and of Protestant background

wasp·ish \'wȧs-pish, 'wȯs-\ *adj* **1** : SNAPPISH, IRRITABLE **2** : resembling a wasp in form; *esp* : slightly built
syn fractious, fretful, huffy, peevish, petulant, querulous

wasp waist *n* : a very slender waist

¹**was·sail** \'wä-səl, wä-'sāl\ *n* [ME *wæs hæil*, fr. ON *ves heill* be well] **1** : an early English toast to someone's health **2** : a hot drink made with wine, beer, or cider, spices, sugar, and usu. baked apples and traditionally served at Christmas **3** : riotous drinking : REVELRY

²**wassail** *vb* **1** : CAROUSE **2** : to drink to the health of — **was·sail·er** *n*

Was·ser·mann test \'wä-sər-mən-, 'vä-\ *n* : a blood test for infection with syphilis

wast·age \'wā-stij\ *n* : WASTE 3

¹**waste** \'wāst\ *n* **1** : a sparsely settled or barren region : DESERT; *also* : uncultivated land **2** : the act or an instance of wasting : the state of being wasted **3** : gradual loss or decrease by use, wear, or decay **4** : material left over, rejected, or thrown away; *also* : an unwanted by-product of a manufacturing or chemical process **5** : refuse (as garbage) that accumulates about habitations **6** : material (as feces) produced but not used by a living organism — **waste·ful** \-fəl\ *adj* — **waste·ful·ly** *adv* — **waste·ful·ness** *n*

²**waste** *vb* **wast·ed; wast·ing** **1** : DEVASTATE **2** : to wear away or diminish gradually : CONSUME **3** : to spend or

use carelessly or uselessly : SQUANDER **4** : to lose or cause to lose weight, strength, or energy ⟨*wasting* away from fever⟩ **5** : to become diminished in bulk or substance : DWINDLE **syn** depredate, desolate, despoil, ravage, spoil, strip — **wast•er** *n*

³**waste** *adj* **1** : being wild and uninhabited : BARREN, DESOLATE; *also* : UNCULTIVATED **2** : being in a ruined condition **3** : discarded as worthless after being used ⟨~ water⟩ **4** : excreted from or stored in inert form in a living organism as a by-product of vital activity ⟨~ matter from birds⟩

waste•bas•ket \'wāst-₁bas-kət\ *n* : a receptacle for refuse

waste•land \-₁land, -lənd\ *n* : land that is barren or unfit for cultivation

waste•pa•per \-'pā-pər\ *n* : paper thrown away as used, not needed, or not fit for use

wast•rel \'wā-strəl\ *n* : one that wastes : SPENDTHRIFT

¹**watch** \'wäch, 'woch\ *vb* **1** : to be or stay awake intentionally : keep vigil ⟨~ed by the patient's bedside⟩ ⟨~ and pray⟩ **2** : to be on the lookout for danger : be on one's guard **3** : to keep guard ⟨~ outside the door⟩ **4** : OBSERVE ⟨~ a game⟩ **5** : to keep in view so as to prevent harm or warn of danger ⟨~ a brush fire carefully⟩ **6** : to keep oneself informed about ⟨~ his progress⟩ **7** : to lie in wait for esp. so as to take advantage of ⟨~ed her opportunity⟩ — **watch•er** *n*

²**watch** *n* **1** : the act of keeping awake to guard, protect, or attend; *also* : a state of alert and continuous attention **2** : a public weather alert ⟨tornado ~⟩ **3** : close observation **4** : LOOKOUT, WATCHMAN, GUARD **5** : a period during which a part of a ship's crew is on duty; *also* : the part of a crew on duty during a watch **6** : a portable timepiece carried on the person

watch•band \'wäch-₁band, 'woch-\ *n* : the bracelet or strap of a wristwatch

watch•dog \-₁dog\ *n* **1** : a dog kept to guard property **2** : one that guards or protects

watch•ful \-fəl\ *adj* : steadily attentive and alert esp. to danger : VIGILANT — **watch•ful•ly** *adv* — **watch•ful•ness** *n*

watch•mak•er \-₁mā-kər\ *n* : one that makes or repairs watches — **watch•mak•ing** \-₁mā-kiŋ\ *n*

watch•man \-mən\ *n* : a person assigned to watch : GUARD

watch night *n* : a devotional service lasting until after midnight esp. on New Year's Eve

watch•tow•er \'wäch-₁taú-ər, 'woch-\ *n* : a tower for a lookout

watch•word \-₁wərd\ *n* **1** : a secret word used as a signal or sign of recognition **2** : a word or motto used as a slogan or rallying cry

¹**wa•ter** \'wo-tər, 'wä-\ *n* **1** : the liquid that descends as rain and forms rivers, lakes, and seas **2** : a natural mineral water — usu. used in pl. **3** *pl* : the water occupying or flowing in a particular bed; *also* : a band of seawater bordering on and under the control of a country ⟨sailing Canadian ~s⟩ **4** : any of various liquids containing or resembling water; *esp* : a watery fluid (as tears, urine, or sap) formed or circulating in a living organism **5** : a specified degree of thoroughness or completeness ⟨a scoundrel of the first ~⟩

²**water** *vb* **1** : to supply with or get or take water ⟨~ horses⟩ ⟨the ship ~ed at each port⟩ **2** : to treat (as cloth) so as to give a lustrous appearance in wavy lines **3** : to dilute by or as if by adding water to **4** : to form or secrete water or watery matter ⟨her eyes ~ed⟩ ⟨my mouth ~ed⟩

water bed *n* : a bed whose mattress is a watertight bag filled with water

wa•ter•borne \-₁bōrn\ *adj* : supported or carried by water

water buffalo *n* : a common oxlike often domesticated Asian bovine

water chestnut *n* : a whitish crunchy vegetable used esp. in Chinese cooking that is the peeled tuber of a

water buffalo

widely cultivated Asian sedge; *also* : the tuber or the sedge itself

water closet *n* : a compartment or room with a toilet bowl : BATHROOM; *also* : a toilet bowl along with its accessories

wa•ter•col•or \'wo-tər-₁kə-lər, 'wä-\ *n* **1** : a paint whose liquid part is water **2** : the art of painting with watercolors **3** : a picture made with watercolors

wa•ter•course \-₁kōrs\ *n* : a stream of water; *also* : the bed of a stream

wa•ter•craft \-₁kraft\ *n* : a craft for water transport : SHIP, BOAT

wa•ter•cress \-₁kres\ *n* : a perennial European cress with white flowers that is naturalized in the U.S. and is used esp. in salads

wa•ter•fall \-₁fol\ *n* : a very steep descent of the water of a stream

wa•ter•fowl \'wo-tər-₁faul, 'wä-\ *n* **1** : a bird that frequents water **2** waterfowl *pl* : wild ducks and geese hunted as game

wa•ter•front \-₁frənt\ *n* : land or a section of a town fronting or abutting on a body of water

water gap *n* : a pass in a mountain ridge through which a stream runs

water glass *n* : a drinking glass

water hyacinth *n* : a showy floating aquatic plant of tropical America that often clogs waterways (as in the southern U.S.)

watering place *n* : a resort that features mineral springs or bathing

water lily *n* : any of various aquatic plants with floating roundish leaves and showy solitary flowers

wa•ter•line \'wo-tər-₁līn, 'wä-\ *n* : a line that marks the level of the surface of water on something (as a ship or the shore)

wa•ter•logged \-₁logd, -₁lägd\ *adj* : so filled or soaked with water as to be heavy or unmanageable ⟨a ~ boat⟩

wa•ter•loo \₁wo-tər-'lü, ₁wä-\ *n, pl* **-loos** [*Waterloo,* Belgium, scene of Napoleon's defeat in 1815] : a decisive or final defeat or setback

¹**wa•ter•mark** \'wo-tər-₁märk, 'wä-\ *n* **1** : a mark indicating height to which water has risen **2** : a marking in paper visible when the paper is held up to the light

²**watermark** *vb* : to mark (paper) with a watermark

wa•ter•mel•on \-₁me-lən\ *n* : a large roundish or oblong fruit with sweet juicy usu. red pulp; *also* : a widely grown African vine related to the squashes that produces watermelons

water moccasin *n* : a venomous pit viper chiefly of the southeastern U.S. that is related to the copperhead

water ou•zel \-'ü-zəl\ *n* : DIPPER 1

water pipe *n* : a pipe for smoking that has a long flexible tube whereby the smoke is cooled by passing through water

water polo *n* : a team game played in a swimming pool with a ball resembling a soccer ball

wa•ter•pow•er \'wo-tər-₁pau-ər, 'wä-\ *n* : the power of moving water used to run machinery

¹**wa•ter•proof** \'wo-tər-₁prüf, 'wä-\ *adj* : not letting wa-

ter through; *esp* : covered or treated with a material to prevent permeation by water — **wa•ter•proof•ing** *n*

²**waterproof** *n* **1** : a waterproof fabric **2** *chiefly Brit* : RAINCOAT

³**waterproof** *vb* : to make waterproof

wa•ter–re•pel•lent \ˌwȯ-tər-ri-ˈpe-lənt, ˌwä-\ *adj* : treated with a finish that is resistant to water penetration

wa•ter–re•sis•tant \-ri-ˈzis-tənt\ *adj* : WATER=REPELLENT

wa•ter•shed \ˈwȯ-tər-ˌshed, ˈwä-\ *n* **1** : a dividing ridge between two drainage areas **2** : the region or area drained by a particular body of water

wa•ter•side \-ˌsīd\ *n* : the land bordering a body of water

water ski *n* : a ski used on water when the wearer is towed — **wa•ter–ski** *vb* — **wa•ter–ski•er** \-ˌskē-ər\ *n*

wa•ter•spout \ˈwȯ-tər-ˌspau̇t, ˈwä-\ *n* **1** : a pipe for carrying water from a roof **2** : a funnel-shaped cloud extending from a cloud down to a spray torn up by whirling winds from an ocean or lake

water strider *n* : any of various long-legged bugs that move about swiftly on the surface of water

water table *n* : the upper limit of the portion of the ground wholly saturated with water

wa•ter•tight \ˌwȯ-tər-ˈtīt, ˌwä-\ *adj* **1** : constructed so as to keep water out **2** : allowing no possibility for doubt or uncertainty ⟨a ∼ case against the accused⟩

wa•ter•way \ˈwȯ-tər-ˌwā, ˈwä-\ *n* : a navigable body of water

wa•ter•wheel \-ˌhwēl\ *n* : a wheel made to turn by water flowing against it

water wings *n pl* : an air-filled device to give support to a person's body esp. when learning to swim

wa•ter•works \ˈwȯ-tər-ˌwərks, ˈwä-\ *n pl* : a system for supplying water (as to a city)

wa•tery \ˈwȯ-tə-rē, ˈwä-\ *adj* **1** : containing, full of, or giving out water ⟨∼ clouds⟩ **2** : being like water : THIN, WEAK ⟨∼ lemonade⟩; *also* : being soft and soggy ⟨∼ turnips⟩

WATS \ˈwäts\ *abbr* Wide-Area Telecommunications Service

watt \ˈwät\ *n* [James *Watt* †1819 Scottish engineer and inventor] : the metric unit of power equal to the work done at the rate of one joule per second or to the power produced by a current of one ampere across a potential difference of one volt

watt•age \ˈwä-tij\ *n* : amount of power expressed in watts

wat•tle \ˈwät-ᵊl\ *n* **1** : a framework of rods with flexible branches or reeds interlaced used esp. formerly in building; *also* : material for this framework **2** : a naked fleshy process hanging usu. from the head or neck (as of a bird) — **wat•tled** \-ᵊld\ *adj*

W Aust *abbr* Western Australia

¹**wave** \ˈwāv\ *vb* **waved; wav•ing 1** : FLUTTER ⟨flags *waving* in the breeze⟩ **2** : to motion with the hands or with something held in them in signal or salute **3** : to become moved or brandished to-and-fro; *also* : BRANDISH, FLOURISH ⟨∼ a sword⟩ **4** : to move before the wind with a wavelike motion ⟨fields of *waving* grain⟩ **5** : to curve up and down like a wave : UNDULATE

²**wave** *n* **1** : a moving ridge or swell on the surface of water **2** : a wavelike formation or shape ⟨a ∼ in the hair⟩ **3** : the action or process of making wavy or curly **4** : a waving motion; *esp* : a signal made by waving something **5** : FLOW, GUSH ⟨a ∼ of anger swept over her⟩ **6** : a peak of activity ⟨a ∼ of selling⟩ **7** : a disturbance that transfers energy progressively from point to point in a medium ⟨light travels in ∼s⟩ ⟨a sound ∼⟩ **8** : a period of hot or cold weather — **wavelike** *adj*

wave•length \ˈwāv-ˌleŋth\ *n* **1** : the distance in the line of advance of a wave from any one point (as a crest)

to the next corresponding point **2** : a line of thought that reveals a common understanding

wave•let \-lət\ *n* : a little wave : RIPPLE

wa•ver \ˈwā-vər\ *vb* **1** : to fluctuate in opinion, allegiance, or direction **2** : REEL, TOTTER; *also* : QUIVER, FLICKER ⟨∼*ing* flames⟩ **3** : FALTER **4** : to give an unsteady sound : QUAVER **syn** falter, hesitate, shilly-shally, vacillate — **waver** *n* — **wa•ver•er** *n* — **wa•ver•ing•ly** *adv*

wavy \ˈwā-vē\ *adj* **wav•i•er; -est** : having waves : moving in waves

¹**wax** \ˈwaks\ *n* **1** : a yellowish plastic substance secreted by bees for constructing the honeycomb **2** : any of various substances like beeswax

²**wax** *vb* : to treat or rub with wax

³**wax** *vb* **1** : to increase in size, numbers, strength, volume, or duration **2** : to increase in apparent size ⟨the moon ∼*es* toward the full⟩ **3** : to take on a quality or state : BECOME ⟨∼*ed* indignant⟩ ⟨the party ∼*ed* merry⟩

wax bean *n* : a kidney bean with pods that turn creamy yellow to bright yellow when mature enough to use as snap beans

wax•en \ˈwak-sən\ *adj* **1** : made of or covered with wax **2** : resembling wax (as in color or consistency)

wax myrtle *n* : any of a genus of shrubs or trees with aromatic leaves; *esp* : an evergreen shrub of the eastern U.S. that produces small hard berries with a thick coating of white wax used for candles

wax•wing \ˈwaks-ˌwiŋ\ *n* : any of a genus of chiefly brown to gray singing birds with a showy crest and red waxy material on the tips of some wing feathers

wax•work \-ˌwərk\ *n* **1** : an effigy usu. of a person in wax **2** *pl* : an exhibition of wax figures

waxy \ˈwak-sē\ *adj* **wax•i•er; -est 1** : made of or full of wax **2** : WAXEN 2

way \ˈwā\ *n* **1** : a thoroughfare for travel or passage : ROAD, PATH, STREET **2** : ROUTE **3** : a course of action ⟨chose the easy ∼⟩; *also* : opportunity, capability, or fact of doing as one pleases ⟨always had your own ∼⟩ **4** : a possible course : POSSIBILITY ⟨no two ∼s about it⟩ **5** : METHOD, MODE ⟨this ∼ of thinking⟩ ⟨a new ∼ of painting⟩ **6** : FEATURE, RESPECT ⟨a good worker in many ∼s⟩ **7** : the usual or characteristic state of affairs ⟨as is the ∼ with old people⟩; *also* : individual characteristic or peculiarity ⟨used to her ∼s⟩ **8** : DISTANCE ⟨a short ∼ from here⟩ ⟨a long ∼ from success⟩ **9** : progress along a course ⟨working my ∼ through college⟩ **10** : something having direction : LOCALITY ⟨out our ∼⟩ **11** : STATE, CONDITION ⟨the ∼ things are⟩ **12** *pl* : an inclined structure upon which a ship is built or is supported in launching **13** : CATEGORY, KIND ⟨get what you need in the ∼ of supplies⟩ **14** : motion or speed of a boat through the water — **by the way** : by way of interjection or digression — **by way of 1** : for the purpose of ⟨*by way of* illustration⟩ **2** : by the route through : VIA — **out of the way 1** : WRONG, IMPROPER **2** : SECLUDED, REMOTE

way•bill \ˈwā-ˌbil\ *n* : a paper that accompanies a freight shipment and gives details of goods, route, and charges

way•far•er \ˈwā-ˌfar-ər\ *n* : a traveler esp. on foot — **way•far•ing** \-ˌfar-iŋ\ *adj*

way•lay \ˈwā-ˌlā\ *vb* **-laid** \-ˌlād\; **-lay•ing** : to lie in wait for or attack from ambush

way–out \ˈwā-ˈau̇t\ *adj* : FAR-OUT

-ways \ˌwāz\ *adv suffix* : in (such) a way, course, direction, or manner ⟨side*ways*⟩

ways and means *n pl* : methods and resources esp. for raising revenues needed by a state; *also* : a legislative committee concerned with this function

way•side \ˈwā-ˌsīd\ *n* : the side of or land adjacent to a road or path

way station *n* : an intermediate station on a line of travel (as a railroad)

way•ward \ˈwā-wərd\ *adj* [ME, short for *awayward*

turned away, fr. *away*, adv. + *-ward* directed toward]
1 : following one's own capricious or wanton inclinations ⟨∼ children⟩ **2** : UNPREDICTABLE, IRREGULAR ⟨a ∼ act⟩

WBC *abbr* white blood cells

WC *abbr* **1** water closet **2** without charge

WCTU *abbr* Women's Christian Temperance Union

we \'wē\ *pron* **1** — used of a group that includes the speaker or writer **2** — used for the singular *I* by a monarch, editor, or writer

weak \'wēk\ *adj* **1** : lacking strength or vigor : FEEBLE **2** : not able to sustain or resist much weight, pressure, or strain **3** : deficient in vigor of mind or character; *also* : resulting from or indicative of such deficiency ⟨a ∼ policy⟩ ⟨a ∼ will⟩ ⟨weak-minded⟩ **4** : not supported by truth or logic ⟨a ∼ argument⟩ **5** : lacking skill or proficiency; *also* : indicative of a lack of skill or aptitude **6** : lacking vigor of expression or effect **7** : of less than usual strength ⟨∼ tea⟩ **8** : not having or exerting authority ⟨∼ government⟩; *also* : INEFFECTIVE, IMPOTENT **9** : of, relating to, or constituting a verb or verb conjugation that forms the past tense and past participle by adding *-ed* or *-d* or *-t* — **weak·ly** *adv*

weak·en \'wē-kən\ *vb* : to make or become weak **syn** enfeeble, debilitate, undermine, sap, cripple, disable

weak·fish \'wēk-ˌfish\ *n* [obs. D *weekvis*, fr. D *week* soft + *vis* fish; fr. its tender flesh] : a common marine fish of the Atlantic coast of the U.S. caught for food and sport; *also* : any of several related food fishes

weak force *n* : the physical force responsible for particle decay processes in radioactivity

weak–kneed \'wēk-ˈnēd\ *adj* : lacking willpower or resolution

weak·ling \'wē-kliŋ\ *n* : a person who is physically, mentally, or morally weak

weak·ly \'wē-klē\ *adj* : FEEBLE, WEAK

weak·ness \'wēk-nəs\ *n* **1** : the quality or state of being weak; *also* : an instance or period of being weak ⟨in a moment of ∼ he agreed to go⟩ **2** : FAULT, DEFECT **3** : an object of special desire or fondness ⟨chocolate is her ∼⟩

¹**weal** \'wēl\ *n* : WELL-BEING, PROSPERITY

²**weal** *n* : WELT

weald \'wēld\ *n* [The *Weald*, wooded district in England, fr. ME *Weeld* the Weald, fr. OE *weald* forest] **1** : FOREST **2** : WOLD

wealth \'welth\ *n* [ME *welthe* welfare, prosperity, fr. *wele* weal] **1** : abundance of possessions or resources : AFFLUENCE, RICHES **2** : abundant supply : PROFUSION ⟨a ∼ of detail⟩ **3** : all property that has a money or an exchange value; *also* : all objects or resources that have economic value **syn** fortune, property, substance, worth

wealthy \'wel-thē\ *adj* **wealth·i·er; -est** : having wealth : RICH

wean \'wēn\ *vb* **1** : to accustom (a young mammal) to take food by means other than nursing **2** : to free from a source of dependence; *also* : to free from a usu. unwholesome habit or interest

weap·on \'we-pən\ *n* **1** : something (as a gun, knife, or club) used to injure, defeat, or destroy **2** : a means of contending against another — **weap·on·less** \-ləs\ *adj*

weap·on·ry \-rē\ *n* : WEAPONS

¹**wear** \'war\ *vb* **wore** \'wōr\; **worn** \'wōrn\; **wear·ing 1** : to use as an article of clothing or adornment ⟨∼ a coat⟩ ⟨∼s earrings⟩; *also* : to carry on the person ⟨∼ a gun⟩ **2** : EXHIBIT, PRESENT ⟨∼ a smile⟩ **3** : to impair, diminish, or decay by use or by scraping or rubbing ⟨clothes *worn* to shreds⟩; *also* : to produce gradually by friction, rubbing, or wasting away ⟨∼ a hole in the rug⟩ **4** : to exhaust or lessen the strength of : WEARY, FATIGUE ⟨*worn* by care and toil⟩ **5** : to endure use : last under use or the passage of time ⟨this cloth ∼s well⟩ **6** : to diminish or fail with the passage of time ⟨the day ∼s on⟩ ⟨the effect of the drug *wore*

off⟩ **7** : to grow or become by attrition, use, or age ⟨the coin was *worn* thin⟩ — **wear·able** \'war-ə-bəl\ *adj* — **wear·er** *n*

²**wear** *n* **1** : the act of wearing : the state of being worn ⟨clothes for everyday ∼⟩ **2** : clothing usu. of a particular kind or for a special occasion or use ⟨children's ∼⟩ **3** : wearing or lasting quality ⟨the coat still has lots of ∼ in it⟩ **4** : the result of wearing or use : impairment due to use ⟨the suit shows ∼⟩

wear and tear *n* : the loss, injury, or stress to which something is subjected in the course of use; *esp* : normal depreciation

wear down *vb* : to weary and overcome by persistent resistance or pressure

wea·ri·some \'wir-ē-səm\ *adj* : causing weariness : TIRESOME — **wea·ri·some·ly** *adv* — **wea·ri·some·ness** *n*

wear out *vb* **1** : TIRE **2** : to make or become useless by wear

¹**wea·ry** \'wir-ē\ *adj* **wea·ri·er; -est 1** : worn out in strength, energy, or freshness **2** : expressing or characteristic of weariness ⟨a ∼ sigh⟩ **3** : having one's patience, tolerance, or pleasure exhausted ⟨∼ of war⟩ — **wea·ri·ly** \'wir-ə-lē\ *adv* — **wea·ri·ness** \-ē-nəs\ *n*

²**weary** *vb* **wea·ried; wea·ry·ing** : to become or make weary : TIRE

¹**wea·sel** \'wē-zəl\ *n, pl* **weasels** : any of various small slender flesh-eating mammals related to the minks

weasel

²**weasel** *vb* **wea·seled; wea·sel·ing 1** : to use weasel words : EQUIVOCATE **2** : to escape from or evade a situation or obligation — often used with *out*

weasel word *n* [fr. the weasel's reputed habit of sucking the contents out of an egg while leaving the shell superficially intact] : a word used to avoid a direct or forthright statement or position

¹**weath·er** \'we-thər\ *n* **1** : the state of the atmosphere with respect to heat or cold, wetness or dryness, calm or storm, clearness or cloudiness **2** : a particular and esp. a disagreeable atmospheric state : RAIN, STORM

²**weather** *vb* **1** : to expose to or endure the action of weather; *also* : to alter (as in color or texture) by such exposure **2** : to bear up against successfully ⟨∼ a storm⟩ ⟨∼ troubles⟩

³**weather** *adj* : WINDWARD

weath·er–beat·en \'we-thər-ˌbēt-ᵊn\ *adj* : worn or damaged by exposure to the weather; *also* : toughened or tanned by the weather ⟨∼ face⟩

weath·er·cock \-ˌkäk\ *n* : a weather vane shaped like a rooster

weath·er·ing \'we-thə-riŋ\ *n* : the action of the weather in altering the color, texture, composition, or form of exposed objects; *also* : alteration thus effected

weath·er·ize \'we-thə-ˌrīz\ *vb* **-ized; -iz·ing** : to make (as a house) better protected against winter weather (as by adding insulation)

weath·er·man \-ˌman\ *n* : one who reports and forecasts the weather : METEOROLOGIST

weath·er·per·son \-ˌpər-sən\ *n* : a person who reports and forecasts the weather : METEOROLOGIST

weath·er·proof \'we-thər-ˌprüf\ *adj* : able to withstand exposure to weather — **weatherproof** *vb*

weather stripping *n* : material used to seal a door or window at the edges

weather vane *n* : VANE 1

weath·er·worn \'we-thər-ˌwŏrn\ *adj* : worn by exposure to the weather

¹**weave** \'wēv\ *vb* **wove** \'wōv\ *or* **weaved; wo·ven** \'wō-vən\ *or* **weaved; weav·ing 1** : to form by interlacing strands of material; *esp* : to make on a loom by interlacing warp and filling threads ⟨∼ cloth⟩ **2** : to interlace (as threads) into a fabric and esp. cloth **3** : SPIN 2 **4** : to make as if by weaving together parts **5** : to insert as a part : work in **6** : to move in a winding or zigzag course esp. to avoid obstacles ⟨we *wove* our way through the crowd⟩ — **weav·er** *n*

²**weave** *n* : something woven; *also* : a pattern or method of weaving ⟨a loose ∼⟩

¹**web** \'web\ *n* **1** : a fabric on a loom or coming from a loom **2** : COBWEB; *also* : SNARE, ENTANGLEMENT ⟨caught in a ∼ of deceit⟩ **3** : an animal or plant membrane; *esp* : one uniting the toes (as in many birds) **4** : NETWORK ⟨a ∼ of highways⟩ **5** : the series of barbs on each side of the shaft of a feather — **webbed** \'webd\ *adj*

²**web** *vb* **webbed; web·bing 1** : to make a web **2** : to cover or provide with webs or a network **3** : ENTANGLE, ENSNARE

web·bing \'we-biŋ\ *n* : a strong closely woven tape designed for bearing weight and used esp. for straps, harness, or upholstery

web–foot·ed \'web-ˈfu̇-təd\ *adj* : having webbed feet

wed \'wed\ *vb* **wed·ded** *also* **wed; wed·ding 1** : to take, give, enter into, or join in marriage : MARRY **2** : to unite firmly

Wed *abbr* Wednesday

wed·ding \'we-diŋ\ *n* **1** : a marriage ceremony usu. with accompanying festivities : NUPTIALS **2** : a joining in close association **3** : a wedding anniversary or its celebration

¹**wedge** \'wej\ *n* **1** : a piece of wood or metal that tapers to a thin edge and is used to split logs or rocks or to raise heavy weights **2** : something (as an action or policy) that serves to open up a way for a breach, change, or intrusion **3** : a wedge-shaped object or part ⟨a ∼ of pie⟩

²**wedge** *vb* **wedged; wedg·ing 1** : to hold firm by or as if by driving in a wedge **2** : to force (something) into a narrow space

wed·lock \'wed-ˌläk\ *n* [ME *wedlok*, fr. OE *wedlāc* marriage bond, fr. *wedd* pledge + *-lāc*, suffix denoting activity] : the state of being married : MARRIAGE, MATRIMONY

Wednes·day \'wenz-dē, -(ˌ)dā\ *n* [ME, fr. OE *wōdens-dæg*, lit., day of Woden (supreme god of the pagan Anglo-Saxons)] : the 4th day of the week

wee \'wē\ *adj* [ME *we*, fr. *we*, n., little bit, fr. OE *wǣge* weight] **1** : very small : TINY **2** : very early ⟨∼ hours of the morning⟩

¹**weed** \'wēd\ *n* : a plant that tends to grow thickly where it is not wanted and to choke out more desirable plants

²**weed** *vb* **1** : to clear of or remove weeds or something harmful, inferior, or superfluous ⟨∼ a garden⟩ **2** : to get rid of ⟨∼ out the troublemakers⟩ — **weed·er** *n*

³**weed** *n* : mourning clothes — usu. used in pl. ⟨widow's ∼s⟩

weedy \'wē-dē\ *adj* **1** : full of weeds **2** : resembling a weed esp. in vigor of growth or spread **3** : noticeably lean and scrawny : LANKY

week \'wēk\ *n* **1** : seven successive days; *esp* : a calendar period of seven days beginning with Sunday and ending with Saturday **2** : the working or school days of the calendar week

week·day \'wēk-ˌdā\ *n* : a day of the week except Sunday or sometimes except Saturday and Sunday

¹**week·end** \-ˌend\ *n* : the period between the close of one working or business or school week and the beginning of the next

²**weekend** *vb* : to spend the weekend

¹**week·ly** \'wē-klē\ *adj* **1** : occurring, appearing, or done every week **2** : computed in terms of one week — **weekly** *adv*

²**weekly** *n, pl* **weeklies** : a weekly publication

ween \'wēn\ *vb, archaic* : SUPPOSE 3

wee·ny \'wē-nē\ *also* **ween·sy** \'wēn-sē\ *adj* : exceptionally small

weep \'wēp\ *vb* **wept** \'wept\; **weep·ing 1** : to express emotion and esp. sorrow by shedding tears : BEWAIL, CRY **2** : to give off fluid slowly : OOZE — **weep·er** *n*

weep·ing *adj* **1** : TEARFUL **2** : having slender drooping branches

weeping willow *n* : a willow with slender drooping branches

weepy \'wē-pē\ *adj* : inclined to weep

wee·vil \'wē-vəl\ *n* : any of a large group of mostly small beetles with a long head usu. curved into a snout and larvae that feed esp. in fruits or seeds — **wee·vily** *or* **wee·vil·ly** \'wē-və-lē\ *adj*

weft \'weft\ *n* **1** : a filling thread or yarn in weaving **2** : WEB, FABRIC; *also* : something woven

¹**weigh** \'wā\ *vb* [ME *weyen*, fr. OE *wegan* to move, carry, weigh] **1** : to find the heaviness of **2** : to have weight or a specified weight **3** : to consider carefully : PONDER **4** : to merit consideration as important : COUNT ⟨evidence ∼*ing* against him⟩ **5** : to raise before sailing ⟨∼ anchor⟩ **6** : to press down with or as if with a heavy weight

²**weigh** *n* [alter. of *way*] : WAY — used in the phrase *under weigh*

¹**weight** \'wāt\ *n* **1** : the amount that something weighs; *also* : the standard amount that something should weigh **2** : a quantity or object weighing a usu. specified amount **3** : a unit (as a pound or kilogram) of weight or mass; *also* : a system of such units **4** : a heavy object for holding or pressing something down; *also* : a heavy object for throwing or lifting in an athletic contest **5** : a mental or emotional burden **6** : IMPORTANCE; *also* : INFLUENCE ⟨threw his ∼ around⟩ **7** : overpowering force **8** : relative thickness (as of a textile) ⟨summer-*weight* clothes⟩ **syn** significance, moment, consequence, import, authority, prestige, credit

☞ For table, see next page.

²**weight** *vb* **1** : to load with or as if with a weight **2** : to oppress with a burden ⟨∼*ed* down with cares⟩

weight·less \'wāt-ləs\ *adj* : having little weight : lacking apparent gravitational pull — **weight·less·ly** *adv* — **weight·less·ness** *n*

weighty \'wā-tē\ *adj* **weight·i·er; -est 1** : of much importance or consequence : MOMENTOUS, SERIOUS ⟨∼ problems⟩ **2** : SOLEMN ⟨a ∼ manner⟩ **3** : HEAVY **4** : POWERFUL, TELLING ⟨∼ arguments⟩

weir \'war, 'wir\ *n* **1** : a fence set in a waterway for catching fish **2** : a dam in a stream to raise the water level or divert its flow

weird \'wird\ *adj* [ME *wird, werd* fate, destiny, fr. OE *wyrd*] **1** : MAGICAL **2** : UNEARTHLY, MYSTERIOUS **3** : ODD, UNUSUAL **syn** eerie, uncanny, spooky — **weird·ly** *adv* — **weird·ness** *n*

weirdo \'wir-(ˌ)dō\ *n, pl* **weird·os** : a person who is extraordinarily strange or eccentric

Welch \'welch\ *var of* WELSH

¹**wel·come** \'wel-kəm\ *vb* **wel·comed; wel·com·ing 1** : to greet cordially or courteously **2** : to accept, meet, or face with pleasure ⟨he ∼s criticism⟩

²**welcome** *adj* **1** : received gladly into one's presence ⟨a ∼ visitor⟩ **2** : giving pleasure : PLEASING ⟨∼ news⟩ **3** : willingly permitted or admitted ⟨all are ∼ to use the books⟩ **4** — used in the phrase "You're welcome" as a reply to an expression of thanks

³**welcome** *n* **1** : a cordial greeting or reception **2** : the state of being welcome ⟨overstayed their ∼⟩

WEIGHTS AND MEASURES[1]

UNIT	ABBREVIATION OR SYMBOL	EQUIVALENT IN OTHER U.S. UNITS	METRIC EQUIVALENT
WEIGHT			
avoirdupois (ordinary commodities)			
ton			
short ton		20 short hundredweight, 2000 pounds	0.907 metric ton
long ton		20 long hundredweight, 2240 pounds	1.016 metric tons
hundredweight	cwt		
short hundredweight		100 pounds, 0.05 short ton	45.359 kilograms
long hundredweight		112 pounds, 0.05 long ton	50.802 kilograms
pound	lb *or* lb avdp *also* #	16 ounces, 7000 grains (1.215 apothecaries' or troy pound)	0.454 kilogram
ounce	oz *or* oz avdp	16 drams, 437.5 grains (0.911 apothecaries' or troy ounce)	28.350 grams
dram	dr *or* dr avdp	27.344 grains, 0.0625 ounce	1.772 grams
grain	gr	0.037 dram, 0.002286 ounce	0.0648 gram
troy (precious metals, jewels)			
pound	lb t	12 ounces, 240 pennyweight, 5760 grains (0.823 avoirdupois pound, 1.0 apothecaries' pound)	0.373 kilogram
ounce	oz t	20 pennyweight, 480 grains (1.097 avoirdupois ounce, 1.0 apothecaries' ounce)	31.103 grams
pennyweight	dwt *also* pwt	24 grains, 0.05 ounce	1.555 grams
grain	gr	0.042 pennyweight, 0.002083 ounce	0.0648 gram
apothecaries' (drugs)			
pound	lb ap	12 ounces, 5760 grains (0.822 avoirdupois pound, 1.0 troy pound)	0.373 kilogram
ounce	oz ap *or* ℥	8 drams, 480 grains (1.097 avoirdupois ounce, 1.0 troy ounce)	31.103 grams
dram	dr ap *or* ℨ	0.125 ounce, 60 grains	3.888 grams
grain	gr	0.0166 dram, 0.002083 ounce	0.0648 gram
CAPACITY			
U.S. liquid measure			
gallon	gal	4 quarts (231 cubic inches)	3.785 liters
quart	qt	2 pints (57.75 cubic inches)	0.946 liter
pint	pt	4 gills (28.875 cubic inches)	0.473 liter
gill	gi	4 fluid ounces (7.219 cubic inches)	118.294 milliliters
fluid ounce	fl oz *or* f℥	8 fluid drams (1.805 cubic inches)	29.573 milliliters
fluid dram	fl dr *or* fℨ	60 minims (0.226 cubic inch)	3.697 milliliters
minim	min *or* ♍	1/60 fluid dram (0.003760 cubic inch)	0.061610 milliliter
U.S. dry measure			
bushel	bu	4 pecks (2150.42 cubic inches)	35.239 liters
peck	pk	8 quarts (537.605 cubic inches)	8.810 liters
quart	qt	2 pints (67.201 cubic inches)	1.101 liters
pint	pt	1/2 quart (33.600 cubic inches)	0.551 liter
LENGTH			
mile	mi	5280 feet, 320 rods, 1760 yards	1.609 kilometers
rod	rd	5.50 yards, 16.5 feet	5.029 meters
yard	yd	3 feet, 36 inches	0.9144 meter
foot	ft *or* '	12 inches, 0.333 yard	30.48 centimeters
inch	in *or* "	0.083 foot, 0.028 yard	2.54 centimeters
AREA			
square mile	sq mi *or* mi^2	640 acres, 102,400 square rods	2.590 square kilometers
acre		4840 square yards, 43,560 square feet	4047 square meters
square rod	sq rd *or* rd^2	30.25 square yards, 0.00625 acre	25.293 square meters
square yard	sq yd *or* yd^2	1296 square inches, 9 square feet	0.836 square meter
square foot	sq ft *or* ft^2	144 square inches, 0.111 square yard	0.093 square meter
square inch	sq in *or* in^2	0.0069 square foot, 0.00077 square yard	6.452 square centimeters
VOLUME			
cubic yard	cu yd *or* yd^3	27 cubic feet, 46.656 cubic inches	0.765 cubic meter
cubic foot	cu ft *or* ft^3	1728 cubic inches, 0.0370 cubic yard	0.028 cubic meter
cubic inch	cu in *or* in^3	0.00058 cubic foot, 0.000021 cubic yard	16.387 cubic centimeters

[1]For U.S. equivalents of metric units see Metric System table

¹**weld** \\'weld\ *vb* **1** : to unite (metal or plastic parts) either by heating and allowing the parts to flow together or by hammering or pressing together **2** : to unite closely or intimately ⟨∼ed together in friendship⟩ — **weld·er** *n*

²**weld** *n* **1** : a welded joint **2** : union by welding

wel·fare \\'wel-ˌfar\ *n* **1** : the state of doing well esp. in respect to happiness, well-being, or prosperity **2** : aid in the form of money or necessities for those in need; *also* : the agency through which the aid is given

welfare state *n* : a nation or state that assumes primary responsibility for the individual and social welfare of its citizens

wel·kin \\'wel-kən\ *n* : SKY; *also* : AIR

¹**well** \\'wel\ *n* **1** : a spring with its pool : FOUNTAIN; *also* : a source of supply ⟨a ∼ of information⟩ **2** : a hole sunk in the earth to obtain a natural deposit (as of water, oil, or gas) **3** : an open space (as for a staircase) extending vertically through floors of a structure **4** : something suggesting a well

²**well** *vb* : to rise up and flow out

³**well** *adv* **bet·ter** \\'be-tər\; **best** \\'best\ **1** : in a good or proper manner : RIGHTLY; *also* : EXCELLENTLY, SKILLFULLY **2** : SATISFACTORILY, FORTUNATELY ⟨the party turned out ∼⟩ **3** : ABUNDANTLY ⟨eat ∼⟩ **4** : with reason or courtesy : PROPERLY ⟨I cannot ∼ refuse⟩ **5** : COMPLETELY, FULLY, QUITE ⟨∼ worth the price⟩ ⟨*well*-hidden⟩ **6** : INTIMATELY, CLOSELY ⟨I know him ∼⟩ **7** : CONSIDERABLY, FAR ⟨∼ over a million⟩ ⟨∼ ahead⟩ **8** : without trouble or difficulty ⟨we could ∼ have gone⟩ **9** : EXACTLY, DEFINITELY ⟨remember it ∼⟩

⁴**well** *adj* **1** : PROSPEROUS; *also* : being in satisfactory condition or circumstances **2** : SATISFACTORY, PLEASING ⟨all is ∼⟩ **3** : ADVISABLE, DESIRABLE ⟨it is not ∼ to anger him⟩ **4** : free or recovered from ill health : HEALTHY **5** : FORTUNATE ⟨it is ∼ that this has happened⟩

well-ad·just·ed \ˌwel-ə-'jəs-təd\ *adj* : WELL-BALANCED 2

well-ad·vised \-əd-'vīzd\ *adj* **1** : PRUDENT **2** : resulting from, based on, or showing careful deliberation or wise counsel ⟨∼ plans⟩

well-ap·point·ed \-ə-'pȯin-təd\ *adj* : properly fitted out

well-ba·lanced \\'wel-'ba-lənst\ *adj* **1** : nicely or evenly balanced or arranged **2** : emotionally or psychologically untroubled

well-be·ing \-'bē-iŋ\ *n* : the state of being happy, healthy, or prosperous

well·born \-'bȯrn\ *adj* : born of noble or wealthy lineage

well·bred \-'bred\ *adj* : having or indicating good breeding : REFINED

well-de·fined \-di-'fīnd\ *adj* : having clearly distinguishable limits or boundaries

well-dis·posed \-di-'spōzd\ *adj* : disposed to be friendly, favorable, or sympathetic

well-done \\'wel-'dən\ *adj* **1** : rightly or properly performed **2** : cooked thoroughly

well-fa·vored \-'fā-vərd\ *adj* : GOOD-LOOKING, HANDSOME

well-fixed \-'fikst\ *adj* : WELL-HEELED

well-found·ed \-'faun-dəd\ *adj* : based on good reasons

well-groomed \-'grümd, -'grùmd\ *adj* : neatly dressed or cared for

well-ground·ed \-'graun-dəd\ *adj* **1** : having a firm foundation **2** : WELL-FOUNDED

well·head \-ˌhed\ *n* **1** : the source of a spring or a stream **2** : principal source **3** : the top of or a structure built over a well

well-heeled \-'hēld\ *adj* : financially well-off

well-known \-'nōn\ *adj* : fully or widely known

well-mean·ing \-'mē-niŋ\ *adj* : having or based on good intentions

well·ness \-nəs\ *n* : good health esp. as an actively

sought goal ⟨∼ clinics⟩ ⟨lifestyles that promote ∼⟩

well-nigh \-'nī\ *adv* : ALMOST, NEARLY

well-off \-'óf\ *adj* : being in good condition or circumstances; *esp* : WELL-TO-DO

well-or·dered \-'ȯr-dərd\ *adj* : having an orderly procedure or arrangement

well-read \-'red\ *adj* : well informed through reading

well-round·ed \-'raun-dəd\ *adj* **1** : broadly trained, educated, and experienced **2** : COMPREHENSIVE ⟨a ∼ program of activities⟩

well-spo·ken \\'wel-'spō-kən\ *adj* **1** : speaking well and esp. courteously **2** : spoken with propriety ⟨∼ words⟩

well·spring \-ˌspriŋ\ *n* : a source of continuous supply

well-timed \-'tīmd\ *adj* : TIMELY

well-to-do \ˌwel-tə-'dü\ *adj* : having more than adequate financial resources : PROSPEROUS

well-turned \\'wel-'tərnd\ *adj* **1** : pleasingly shaped ⟨a ∼ ankle⟩ **2** : pleasingly expressed ⟨a ∼ phrase⟩

well-wish·er \\'wel-ˌwi-shər\ *n* : one that wishes well to another — **well-wish·ing** *adj or n*

welsh \\'welsh, 'welch\ *vb* **1** : to avoid payment **2** : to break one's word ⟨∼ed on his promises⟩

Welsh \\'welsh\ *n* **1 Welsh** *pl* : the people of Wales **2** : the Celtic language of Wales — **Welsh** *adj* — **Welsh·man** \-mən\ *n*

Welsh cor·gi \-'kȯr-gē\ *n* [W *corgi*, fr. *cor* dwarf + *ci* dog] : a short-legged long-backed dog with foxy head of either of two breeds of Welsh origin

Welsh rabbit *n* : melted often seasoned cheese served over toast or crackers

Welsh rare·bit \-'rar-bət\ *n* : WELSH RABBIT

¹**welt** \\'welt\ *n* **1** : the narrow strip of leather between a shoe upper and sole to which other parts are stitched **2** : a doubled edge, strip, insert, or seam for ornament or reinforcement **3** : a ridge or lump raised on the skin usu. by a blow; *also* : a heavy blow

²**welt** *vb* **1** : to furnish with a welt **2** : to hit hard

¹**wel·ter** \\'wel-tər\ *vb* **1** : WRITHE, TOSS; *also* : WALLOW **2** : to rise and fall or toss about in or with waves **3** : to become deeply sunk, soaked, or involved **4** : to be in turmoil

²**welter** *n* **1** : TURMOIL **2** : a chaotic mass or jumble

wel·ter·weight \\'wel-tər-ˌwāt\ *n* : a boxer weighing more than 135 but not over 147 pounds

wen \\'wen\ *n* : an abnormal growth or a cyst protruding from a surface esp. of the skin

wench \\'wench\ *n* [ME *wenche*, short for *wenchel* child, fr. OE *wencel*] **1** : a young woman **2** : a female servant

wend \\'wend\ *vb* : to direct one's course : proceed on (one's way)

went *past of* GO

wept *past and past part of* WEEP

were *past 2d sing, past pl, or past subjunctive of* BE

were·wolf \\'wer-ˌwúlf, 'wir-, 'wər-\ *n, pl* **were·wolves** \-ˌwúlvz\ [ME, fr. OE *werwulf*, fr. *wer* man + *wulf* wolf] : a person transformed into a wolf or capable of assuming a wolf's form

wes·kit \\'wes-kət\ *n* : VEST 1

¹**west** \\'west\ *adv* : to or toward the west

²**west** *adj* **1** : situated toward or at the west **2** : coming from the west

³**west** *n* **1** : the general direction of sunset **2** : the compass point directly opposite to east **3** *cap* : regions or countries west of a specified or implied point **4** *cap* : Europe and the Americas — **west·er·ly** \\'wes-tər-lē\ *adv or adj* — **west·ward** *adv or adj* — **west·wards** *adv*

¹**west·ern** \\'wes-tərn\ *adj* **1** : lying toward or coming from the west **2** *cap* : of, relating to, or characteristic of a region conventionally designated West **3** *cap* : of or relating to the Roman Catholic or Protestant segment of Christianity — **West·ern·er** *n*

²**western** *n, often cap* : a novel, story, film, or radio or television show about life in the western U.S. during the latter half of the 19th century

west·ern·ize \'wes-tər-ˌnīz\ *vb* **-ized; -iz·ing** : to give western characteristics to

¹wet \'wet\ *adj* **wet·ter; wet·test 1** : consisting of or covered or soaked with liquid (as water) **2** : RAINY **3** : not dry ⟨~ paint⟩ **4** : permitting or advocating the manufacture and sale of alcoholic beverages ⟨a ~ town⟩ ⟨a ~ candidate⟩ **syn** damp, dank, moist, humid — **wet·ly** *adv* — **wet·ness** *n*

²wet *n* **1** : WATER; *also* : WETNESS, MOISTURE **2** : rainy weather : RAIN **3** : an advocate of a wet liquor policy

³wet *vb* **wet** *or* **wet·ted; wet·ting** : to make or become wet

wet blanket *n* : one that quenches or dampens enthusiasm or pleasure

weth·er \'we-thər\ *n* : a castrated male sheep or goat

wet·land \'wet-ˌland, -lənd\ *n* : land or areas (as swamps) containing much soil moisture — usu. used in pl.

wet nurse *n* : a woman who cares for and suckles children not her own

wet suit *n* : a rubber suit for swimmers that acts to retain body heat by keeping a layer of water against the body as insulation

wh *abbr* **1** which **2** white

¹whack \'hwak\ *vb* **1** : to strike with a smart or resounding blow **2** : to cut with or as if with a whack

²whack *n* **1** : a smart or resounding blow; *also* : the sound of such a blow **2** : PORTION, SHARE **3** : CONDITION, STATE ⟨the machine is out of ~⟩ **4** : an opportunity or attempt to do something : CHANCE **5** : a single action or occasion ⟨made three pies at a ~⟩

¹whale \'hwāl\ *n, pl* **whales 1** *or pl* **whale** : CETACEAN; *esp* : one (as a sperm whale or killer whale) of large size **2** : a person or thing impressive in size or quality ⟨a ~ of a story⟩

²whale *vb* **whaled; whal·ing** : to fish or hunt for whales

³whale *vb* **whaled; whal·ing 1** : THRASH **2** : to strike or hit vigorously

whale·boat \-ˌbōt\ *n* : a long narrow rowboat originally used by whalers

whale·bone \-ˌbōn\ *n* : BALEEN

whal·er \'hwā-lər\ *n* **1** : a person or ship that hunts whales **2** : WHALEBOAT

wham·my \'hwa-mē\ *n, pl* **wham·mies** : JINX, HEX

wharf \'hworf\ *n, pl* **wharves** \'hworvz\ *also* **wharfs** : a structure alongside which ships lie to load and unload

¹what \'hwät, 'hwət\ *pron* **1** — used to inquire about the identity or nature of a being, an object, or some matter or situation ⟨~ is he, a salesman⟩ ⟨~'s that⟩ ⟨~ happened⟩ **2** : that which ⟨I know ~ you want⟩ **3** : WHATEVER 1 ⟨take ~ you want⟩

²what *adv* **1** : in what respect : HOW ⟨~ does he care⟩ **2** — used with *with* to introduce a prepositional phrase that expresses cause ⟨kept busy ~ with school and work⟩

³what *adj* **1** — used to inquire about the identity or nature of a person, object, or matter ⟨~ books do you read⟩ **2** : how remarkable or surprising ⟨~ an idea⟩ **3** : WHATEVER

¹what·ev·er \hwät-'e-vər\ *pron* **1** : anything or everything that ⟨does ~ he wants to⟩ **2** : no matter what ⟨~ you do, don't cheat⟩ **3** : WHAT 1 — used as an intensive ⟨~ do you mean⟩

²whatever *adj* : of any kind at all ⟨no food ~⟩

¹what·not \'hwät-ˌnät\ *pron* : any of various other things that might also be mentioned ⟨needles, pins, and ~⟩

²whatnot *n* : a light open set of shelves for small ornaments

what·so·ev·er \ˌhwät-sō-'e-vər\ *pron or adj* : WHATEVER

wheal \'hwēl\ *n* : a rapidly formed flat slightly raised itching or burning patch on the skin; *also* : WELT

wheat \'hwēt\ *n* : a cereal grain that yields a fine white flour and is the chief breadstuff of temperate regions;

also : any of several grasses yielding wheat — **wheat·en** *adj*

wheat germ *n* : the vitamin-rich wheat embryo separated in milling

whee·dle \'hwēd-ᵊl\ *vb* **whee·dled; whee·dling 1** : to entice by flattery **2** : to gain or get by wheedling

¹wheel \'hwēl\ *n* **1** : a disk or circular frame that turns on a central axis **2** : a device whose main part is a wheel **3** : something resembling a wheel in shape or motion **4** : a curving or circular movement **5** : machinery that imparts motion : moving power ⟨the ~s of government⟩ **6** : a person of importance **7** *pl, slang* : AUTOMOBILE — **wheeled** \'hwēld\ *adj* — **wheel·less** *adj*

²wheel *vb* **1** : ROTATE, REVOLVE **2** : to change direction as if turning on a pivot **3** : to convey or move on wheels or in a vehicle

wheel·bar·row \-ˌbar-ō\ *n* : a vehicle with handles and usu. one wheel for carrying small loads

wheel·base \-ˌbās\ *n* : the distance in inches between the front and rear axles of an automotive vehicle

wheel·chair \-ˌcher\ *n* : a chair mounted on wheels esp. for the use of disabled persons

wheel·er \'hwē-lər\ *n* **1** : one that wheels **2** : WHEELHORSE **3** : something that has wheels — used in combination ⟨a side-*wheeler*⟩

wheel·er–deal·er \ˌhwē-lər-'dē-lər\ *n* : a shrewd operator esp. in business or politics

wheel·horse \'hwēl-ˌhors\ *n* **1** : a horse in a position nearest the front wheels of a wagon **2** : a steady and effective worker esp. in a political body

wheel·house \-ˌhaus\ *n* : PILOTHOUSE

wheel–thrown \'hwēl-ˌthrōn\ *adj* : made on a potter's wheel

wheel·wright \-ˌrīt\ *n* : a maker and repairer of wheels and wheeled vehicles

¹wheeze \'hwēz\ *vb* **wheezed; wheez·ing** : to breathe with difficulty usu. with a whistling sound

²wheeze *n* **1** : a sound of wheezing **2** : an often repeated and well-known joke **3** : a trite saying

wheezy \'hwē-zē\ *adj* **wheez·i·er; -est 1** : inclined to wheeze **2** : having a wheezing sound — **wheez·i·ly** \-zə-lē\ *adv* — **wheez·i·ness** \-zē-nəs\ *n*

whelk \'hwelk\ *n* : a large sea snail; *esp* : one much used as food in Europe

whelm \'hwelm\ *vb* : to overcome or engulf completely : OVERWHELM

¹whelp \'hwelp\ *n* : any of the young of various carnivorous mammals (as a dog)

²whelp *vb* : to give birth to (whelps); *also* : bring forth young

¹when \'hwen\ *adv* **1** : at what time ⟨~ will you return⟩ **2** : at or during which time ⟨a time ~ things were better⟩

²when *conj* **1** : at or during the time that ⟨leave ~ I do⟩ **2** : every time that ⟨they all clapped ~ he sang⟩ **3** : in the event that : IF ⟨disqualified ~ you cheat⟩ **4** : ALTHOUGH ⟨quit politics ~ he might have had a great career in it⟩

³when *pron* : what or which time ⟨since ~ have you been the boss⟩

⁴when *n* : the time of a happening

whence \'hwens\ *adv or conj* : from what place, source, or cause

when·ev·er \hwe-'ne-vər, hwə-\ *conj or adv* : at whatever time

when·so·ev·er \'hwen-sō-ˌe-vər\ *conj* : at whatever time

¹where \'hwer\ *adv* **1** : at, in, or to what place ⟨~ is it⟩ ⟨~ will we go⟩ **2** : at, in, or to what situation, position, direction, circumstances, or respect ⟨~ does this road lead⟩

²where *conj* **1** : at, in, or to what place ⟨knows ~ the house is⟩ **2** : at, in, or to what situation, position, direction, circumstances, or respect ⟨shows ~ the road leads⟩ **3** : WHEREVER ⟨goes ~ she likes⟩ **4** : at, in, or to which place ⟨the town ∼ we live⟩ **5** : at, in, or to the place at, in, or to which ⟨stay ∼ you are⟩ **6** : in a case, situation, or respect in which ⟨outstanding ∼ endurance is called for⟩

³**where** *n* : PLACE, LOCATION ⟨the ∼ and how of the accident⟩

¹**where•abouts** \-ə-₁baùts\ *also* **where•about** \-₁baùt\ *adv* : about where : near what place ⟨∼ does he live⟩

²**whereabouts** *n sing or pl* : the place where a person or thing is ⟨his present ∼ are unknown⟩

where•as \hwer-¹az\ *conj* **1** : while on the contrary; *also* : ALTHOUGH **2** : in view of the fact that : SINCE

where•at \-¹at\ *conj* **1** : at or toward which **2** : in consequence of which : WHEREUPON

where•by \-¹bī\ *conj* : by, through, or in accordance with which ⟨the means ∼ we achieved our goals⟩

¹**where•fore** \¹hwer-₁fòr\ *adv* **1** : for what reason or purpose : WHY **2** : THEREFORE

²**wherefore** *n* : an answer or statement giving an explanation : REASON

¹**where•in** \hwer-¹in\ *adv* : in what : in what respect ⟨∼ was I wrong⟩

²**wherein** *conj* **1** : in which : WHERE ⟨the city ∼ we live⟩ **2** : during which **3** : in what way : HOW ⟨showed me ∼ I was wrong⟩

where•of \-¹əv, -¹äv\ *conj* **1** : of what ⟨knows ∼ he speaks⟩ **2** : of which or whom ⟨books ∼ the best are lost⟩

where•on \-¹òn, -¹än\ *conj* : on which ⟨the base ∼ it rests⟩

where•so•ev•er \¹hwer-sō-₁e-vər\ *conj* : WHEREVER

where•to \¹hwer-₁tü\ *conj* : to which

where•up•on \¹hwer-ə-₁pòn, -₁pän\ *conj* **1** : on which **2** : closely following and in consequence of which

¹**wher•ev•er** \hwer-¹e-vər\ *adv* : where in the world ⟨∼ did he get that tie⟩

²**wherever** *conj* **1** : at, in, or to whatever place **2** : in any circumstance in which

where•with \¹hwer-₁with, -₁with\ *conj* : with or by means of which

where•with•al \¹hwer-wi-₁thòl, -₁thòl\ *n* : MEANS, RESOURCES; *esp* : MONEY

wher•ry \¹hwer-ē\ *n, pl* **wherries** : a long light rowboat sharp at both ends

whet \¹hwet\ *vb* **whet•ted; whet•ting 1** : to sharpen by rubbing on or with something abrasive ⟨as a whetstone⟩ **2** : to make keen : STIMULATE ⟨∼ the appetite⟩

wheth•er \¹hwe-thər\ *conj* **1** : if it is or was true that ⟨ask ∼ he is going⟩ **2** : if it is or was better ⟨uncertain ∼ to go or stay⟩ **3** : whichever is or was the case, namely that ⟨∼ we succeed or fail, we must try⟩ **4** : EITHER ⟨turned out well ∼ by accident or design⟩

whet•stone \¹hwet-₁stōn\ *n* : a stone for sharpening blades

whey \¹hwā\ *n* : the watery part of milk that separates after the milk sours and thickens

¹**which** \¹hwich\ *adj* **1** : being what one or ones out of a group ⟨∼ shirt should I wear⟩ **2** : WHICHEVER

²**which** *pron* **1** : which one or ones ⟨∼ is yours⟩ ⟨∼ are his⟩ ⟨it's in May or June, I'm not sure ∼⟩ **2** : WHICHEVER ⟨we have all kinds; take ∼ you like⟩ **3** — used to introduce a relative clause and to serve as a substitute therein for the noun modified by the clause ⟨the money ∼ is coming to me⟩

¹**which•ev•er** \hwich-¹e-vər\ *adj* : no matter which ⟨∼ way you go⟩

²**whichever** *pron* : whatever one or ones

which•so•ev•er \₁hwich-sō-¹e-vər\ *pron or adj* : WHICHEVER

whick•er \¹hwi-kər\ *vb* : NEIGH, WHINNY — **whicker** *n*

¹**whiff** \¹hwif\ *n* **1** : a quick puff or slight gust ⟨as of air⟩ **2** : an inhalation of odor, gas, or smoke **3** : a slight trace **4** : STRIKEOUT

²**whiff** *vb* **1** : to expel, puff out, or blow away in or as if in whiffs **2** : to inhale an odor **3** : STRIKE OUT 3

whif•fle•tree \¹hwi-fəl-(₁)trē\ *n* : the pivoted swinging bar to which the traces of a harness are fastened

Whig \¹hwig\ *n* [short for *Whiggamore*, member of a Scottish group that marched to Edinburgh in 1648 to oppose the court party] **1** : a member or supporter of a British political group of the late 17th through early 19th centuries seeking to limit royal authority and increase parliamentary power **2** : an American favoring independence from Great Britain during the American Revolution **3** : a member or supporter of an American political party formed about 1834 to oppose the Democrats

¹**while** \¹hwīl\ *n* **1** : a period of time ⟨stay a ∼⟩ **2** : the time and effort used : TROUBLE ⟨worth your ∼⟩

²**while** *conj* **1** : during the time that ⟨she called ∼ you were out⟩ **2** : AS LONG AS ⟨∼ there's life there's hope⟩ **3** : ALTHOUGH ⟨∼ he's respected, he's not liked⟩

³**while** *vb* **whiled; whil•ing** : to cause to pass esp. pleasantly ⟨∼ away an hour⟩

¹**whi•lom** \¹hwī-ləm\ *adv* [ME, lit., at times, fr. OE *hwīlum*, dat. pl. of *hwīl* time, while] *archaic* : FORMERLY

²**whilom** *adj* : FORMER ⟨his ∼ friends⟩

whilst \¹hwīlst\ *conj, chiefly Brit* : WHILE

whim \¹hwim\ *n* : a sudden wish, desire, or change of mind

whim•per \¹hwim-pər\ *vb* : to make a low whining plaintive or broken sound — **whimper** *n*

whim•si•cal \¹hwim-zi-kəl\ *adj* **1** : full of whims : CAPRICIOUS **2** : resulting from or characterized by whim or caprice : ERRATIC — **whim•si•cal•i•ty** \₁hwim-zə-¹ka-lə-tē\ *n* — **whim•si•cal•ly** \¹hwim-zi-k(ə-)lē\ *adv*

whim•sy *or* **whim•sey** \¹hwim-zē\ *n, pl* **whimsies** *or* **whimseys 1** : WHIM, CAPRICE **2** : a fanciful or fantastic device, object, or creation esp. in writing or art

whine \¹hwīn\ *vb* **whined; whin•ing** [ME, fr. OE *hwīnan* to whiz] **1** : to utter a usu. high-pitched plaintive or distressed cry; *also* : to make a sound similar to such a cry **2** : to complain with or as if with a whine — **whine** *n* — **whin•er** *n* — **whiny** *also* **whin•ey** \¹hwī-nē\ *adj*

¹**whin•ny** \¹hwi-nē\ *vb* **whin•nied; whin•ny•ing** : to neigh usu. in a low or gentle manner

²**whinny** *n, pl* **whinnies** : NEIGH

¹**whip** \¹hwip\ *vb* **whipped; whip•ping 1** : to move, snatch, or jerk quickly or forcefully ⟨∼ out a gun⟩ **2** : to strike with a slender lithe implement ⟨as a lash⟩ esp. as a punishment; *also* : SPANK **3** : to drive or urge on by or as if by using a whip **4** : to bind or wrap ⟨as a rope or rod⟩ with cord in order to protect and strengthen; *also* : to wind or wrap around something **5** : DEFEAT **6** : to stir up : INCITE ⟨∼ up enthusiasm⟩ **7** : to produce in a hurry ⟨∼ up a meal⟩ **8** : to beat ⟨as eggs or cream⟩ into a froth **9** : to proceed nimbly or briskly; *also* : to flap about forcefully ⟨flags *whipping* in the wind⟩ — **whip•per** *n* — **whip into shape** : to bring forcefully to a desired state or condition

²**whip** *n* **1** : a flexible instrument used for whipping **2** : a stroke or cut with or as if with a whip **3** : a dessert made by whipping a portion of the ingredients ⟨prune ∼⟩ **4** : a person who handles a whip **5** : a member of a legislative body appointed by a party to enforce party discipline **6** : a whipping or thrashing motion

whip•cord \-₁kòrd\ *n* **1** : a thin tough braided cord **2** : a strong cloth with fine diagonal cords or ribs

whip hand *n* : positive control : ADVANTAGE

whip•lash \¹hwip-₁lash\ *n* **1** : the lash of a whip **2** : injury resulting from a sudden sharp movement of the neck and head ⟨as of a person in a vehicle that is struck from the rear⟩

whip•per•snap•per \¹hwi-pər-₁sna-pər\ *n* : a small, insignificant, or presumptuous person

whip•pet \¹hwi-pət\ *n* : any of a breed of small swift slender dogs that are used for racing

whipping boy *n* : SCAPEGOAT

whip•ple•tree \¹hwi-pəl-(₁)trē\ *n* : WHIFFLETREE

whip·poor·will \\'hwip-pər-ˌwil\ *n* : an American insect-eating bird with dull variegated plumage whose call at nightfall and just before dawn is suggestive of its name

whippoorwill

whip·saw \\'hwip-ˌsȯ\ *vb* : to beset with two or more adverse conditions or situations at once

¹**whir** *also* **whirr** \\'hwər\ *vb* **whirred; whir·ring** : to move, fly, or revolve with a whir

²**whir** *also* **whirr** *n* : a continuous fluttering or vibratory sound made by something in rapid motion

¹**whirl** \\'hwərl\ *vb* **1** : to move or drive in a circle or curve esp. with force or speed **2** : to turn or cause to turn rapidly in circles **3** : to turn abruptly : WHEEL **4** : to move or go quickly **5** : to become dizzy or giddy : REEL

²**whirl** *n* **1** : a rapid rotating or circling movement; *also* : something whirling **2** : COMMOTION, BUSTLE ⟨the social ∼⟩ **3** : a state of mental confusion **4** : TRY ⟨gave it a ∼⟩

whirl·i·gig \\'hwər-li-ˌgig\ *n* [ME *whirlegigg*, fr. *whirlen* to whirl + *gigg* top] **1** : a child's toy having a whirling motion **2** : something that continuously whirls or changes

whirl·pool \\'hwərl-ˌpül\ *n* : water moving rapidly in a circle so as to produce a depression in the center into which floating objects may be drawn

whirl·wind \-ˌwind\ *n* **1** : a small whirling windstorm **2** : a confused rush **3** : a violent or destructive force

whirly·bird \\'hwər-lē-ˌbərd\ *n* : HELICOPTER

¹**whish** \\'hwish\ *vb* : to move with a whish or swishing sound

²**whish** *n* : a rushing sound : SWISH

¹**whisk** \\'hwisk\ *n* **1** : a quick light sweeping or brushing motion **2** : a usu. wire kitchen implement for beating food by hand **3** : WHISK BROOM

²**whisk** *vb* **1** : to move nimbly and quickly **2** : to move or convey briskly ⟨∼*ed* the children off to bed⟩ **3** : to beat or whip lightly ⟨∼ eggs⟩ **4** : to brush or wipe off lightly ⟨∼ a coat⟩

whisk broom *n* : a small broom with a short handle used esp. as a clothes brush

whis·ker \\'hwis-kər\ *n* **1** : one hair of the beard **2** *pl* : the part of the beard that grows on the sides of the face or on the chin **3** : one of the long bristles or hairs growing near the mouth of an animal (as a cat or mouse) — **whis·kered** \-kərd\ *adj*

whis·key *or* **whis·ky** \\'hwis-kē\ *n, pl* **whiskeys** *or* **whiskies** [Ir *uisce beathadh* & ScGael *uisge beatha*, lit., water of life] : a liquor distilled from the fermented mash of grain (as rye, corn, or barley)

¹**whis·per** \\'hwis-pər\ *vb* **1** : to speak very low or under the breath; *also* : to tell or utter by whispering ⟨∼ a secret⟩ **2** : to make a low rustling sound ⟨∼*ing* leaves⟩

²**whisper** *n* **1** : something communicated by or as if by whispering : HINT, RUMOR **2** : an act or instance of whispering

whist \\'hwist\ *n* : a card game played by four players in two partnerships with a deck of 52 cards

¹**whis·tle** \\'hwi-səl\ *n* **1** : a device by which a shrill sound is produced ⟨steam ∼⟩ ⟨tin ∼⟩ **2** : a shrill clear sound made by forcing breath out or air in through the puckered lips **3** : the sound or signal produced by

a whistle or as if by whistling **4** : the shrill clear note of an animal (as a bird)

²**whistle** *vb* **whis·tled; whis·tling** **1** : to utter a shrill clear sound by blowing or drawing air through the puckered lips **2** : to utter a shrill note or call resembling a whistle **3** : to make a shrill clear sound esp. by rapid movements ⟨the wind *whistled*⟩ **4** : to blow or sound a whistle **5** : to signal or call by a whistle **6** : to produce, utter, or express by whistling ⟨∼ a tune⟩ — **whis·tler** *n*

whis·tle–blow·er \\'hwi-səl-ˌblō-ər\ *n* : INFORMER

whis·tle–stop \-ˌstäp\ *n* : a brief personal appearance by a political candidate orig. on the rear platform of a touring train

whit \\'hwit\ *n* [prob. alter. of ME *wiht, wight* creature, thing, fr. OE *wiht*] : the smallest part or particle : BIT

¹**white** \\'hwīt\ *adj* **whit·er; whit·est** **1** : free from color **2** : of the color of new snow or milk; *esp* : of the color white **3** : light or pallid in color ⟨lips ∼ with fear⟩ **4** : SILVERY; *also* : made of silver **5** : of, relating to, or being a member of a group or race characterized by light-colored skin **6** : free from spot or blemish : PURE, INNOCENT **7** : BLANK 2 ⟨∼ space in printed matter⟩ **8** : not intended to cause harm ⟨a ∼ lie⟩ **9** : wearing white ⟨∼ friars⟩ **10** : marked by snow ⟨∼ Christmas⟩ **11** : consisting of a wide range of frequencies ⟨∼ light⟩ — **white·ness** \-nəs\ *n* — **whit·ish** \\'hwī-tish\ *adj*

²**white** *n* **1** : the color of maximal lightness that characterizes objects which both reflect and transmit light : the opposite of black **2** : a white or light-colored part or thing ⟨the ∼ of an egg⟩; *also, pl* : white garments **3** : the light-colored pieces in a 2-player board game; *also* : the person by whom these are played **4** : one that is or approaches the color white **5** : a person of a light-skinned race

white ant *n* : TERMITE

white blood cell *n* : a colorless blood cell (as a lymphocyte) that does not contain hemoglobin but does have a nucleus

white–bread \\'hwīt-ˈbred\ *adj* : being, typical of, or having qualities (as blandness) associated with the white middle class

white·cap \\'hwīt-ˌkap\ *n* : a wave crest breaking into white foam

white chocolate *n* : a whitish chocolate candy

white–col·lar \\'hwīt-ˈkä-lər\ *adj* : of, relating to, or constituting the class of salaried workers whose duties do not require the wearing of work clothes or protective clothing

white dwarf *n* : a small very dense whitish star of low luminosity

white elephant *n* **1** : an Indian elephant of a pale color that is sometimes venerated in India, Sri Lanka, Thailand, and Myanmar **2** : something requiring much care and expense and giving little profit or enjoyment

white feather *n* [fr. the superstition that a white feather in the plumage of a gamecock is a mark of a poor fighter] : a mark or symbol of cowardice

white·fish \\'hwīt-ˌfish\ *n* : any of various freshwater food fishes related to the salmons and trouts

white flag *n* : a flag of pure white used to signify truce or surrender

white gold *n* : a pale alloy of gold resembling platinum in appearance

white goods *n pl* : white fabrics or articles (as sheets or towels) typically made of cotton or linen

White·hall \\'hwīt-ˌhȯl\ *n* : the British government

white·head \-ˌhed\ *n* : a small whitish lump in the skin due to retention of secretion in an oil gland duct

white heat *n* : a temperature higher than red heat at which a body becomes brightly incandescent

white–hot *adj* **1** : being at or radiating white heat **2** : FERVID

White House \-ˌhaůs\ *n* **1** : the executive department of the U.S. government **2** : a residence of the president of the U.S.

white lead *n* : a heavy white poisonous carbonate of lead used esp. as a pigment in exterior paints

white matter *n* : whitish nerve tissue that consists largely of nerve-cell processes enclosed in a fatty material and that lies under the gray matter of the brain and spinal cord or is collected into nerves

whit·en \ˈhwīt-ᵊn\ *vb* : to make or become white **syn** blanch, bleach — **whit·en·er** *n*

white pine *n* : a tall-growing pine of eastern No. America with needles in clusters of five; *also* : its wood

white sale *n* : a sale on white goods

white shark *n* : GREAT WHITE SHARK

white slave *n* : a woman or girl held unwillingly for purposes of prostitution — **white slavery** *n*

white·tail \ˈhwīt-ˌtāl\ *n* : WHITE-TAILED DEER

white–tailed deer *n* : a No. American deer with a rather long tail white on the underside the males of which have forward-arching antlers

white·wall \ˈhwīt-ˌwol\ *n* : an automobile tire having a white band on the sidewall

¹white·wash \-ˌwosh, -ˌwäsh\ *vb* **1** : to whiten with whitewash **2** : to clear of a charge of wrongdoing by offering excuses, hiding facts, or conducting a perfunctory investigation **3** : SHUT OUT 2

²whitewash *n* **1** : a liquid mixture (as of lime and water) for whitening a surface **2** : a clearing of wrongdoing by whitewashing

white·wood \-ˌwud\ *n* : any of various trees and esp. a tulip tree having light-colored wood; *also* : such wood

¹whith·er \ˈhwi-thər\ *adv* **1** : to what place **2** : to what situation, position, degree, or end ⟨~ will this drive him⟩

²whither *conj* **1** : to the place at, in, or to which; *also* : to which place **2** : to whatever place

whith·er·so·ev·er \ˌhwi-thər-sō-ˈe-vər\ *conj* : to whatever place

¹whit·ing \ˈhwī-tiŋ\ *n* : any of several usu. light or silvery food fishes (as a hake) found mostly near seacoasts

²whiting *n* : calcium carbonate in powdered form used esp. as a pigment and in putty

whit·low \ˈhwit-ˌlō\ *n* : a deep inflammation of a finger or toe with pus formation

Whit·sun·day \ˈhwit-ˈsən-dē, -ˌsən-ˌdā\ *n* [ME *Whitsonday,* fr. OE *hwīta sunnandæg,* lit., white Sunday; prob. fr. the custom of wearing white robes by those newly baptized at this season] : PENTECOST

whit·tle \ˈhwit-ᵊl\ *vb* **whit·tled; whit·tling 1** : to pare or cut off chips from the surface of (wood) with a knife; *also* : to cut or shape by such paring **2** : to reduce as if by paring down ⟨~ down expenses⟩

¹whiz *or* **whizz** \ˈhwiz\ *vb* **whizzed; whiz·zing** : to hum, whir, or hiss like a speeding object (as an arrow or ball) passing through air

²whiz *or* **whizz** *n, pl* **whiz·zes** : a hissing, buzzing, or whizzing sound

³whiz *n, pl* **whiz·zes** : WIZARD 2

who \ˈhü\ *pron* **1** : what or which person or persons ⟨~ did it⟩ ⟨~ is he⟩ ⟨~ are they⟩ **2** : the person or persons that ⟨knows ~ did it⟩ **3** — used to introduce a relative clause and to serve as a substitute therein for the substantive modified by the clause ⟨the man ~ lives there is rich⟩

WHO *abbr* World Health Organization

whoa \ˈwō, ˈhwō, ˈhō\ *vb imper* — a command to an animal to stand still

who·dun·it *also* **who·dun·nit** \hü-ˈdə-nət\ *n* : a detective or mystery story

who·ev·er \hü-ˈe-vər\ *pron* : whatever person : no matter who

¹whole \ˈhōl\ *adj* [ME *hool* healthy, unhurt, entire, fr. OE *hāl*] **1** : being in healthy or sound condition : free from defect or damage **2** : having all its proper parts or elements ⟨~ milk⟩ **3** : constituting the total sum of : ENTIRE ⟨owns the ~ island⟩ **4** : each or all of the ⟨the ~ family⟩ **5** : not scattered or divided : CONCENTRATED ⟨gave me his ~ attention⟩ **6** : seemingly complete or total ⟨the ~ idea is to help, not hinder⟩ **syn** perfect, intact, sound — **whole·ness** *n*

²whole *n* **1** : a complete amount or sum **2** : something whole or entire — **on the whole 1** : in view of all the circumstances or conditions **2** : in general

whole·heart·ed \ˈhōl-ˈhär-təd\ *adj* : undivided in purpose, enthusiasm, or will : HEARTY, ZESTFUL, SINCERE

whole note *n* : a musical note equal to one measure of four beats

whole number *n* : any of the set of nonnegative integers; *also* : INTEGER

¹whole·sale \ˈhōl-ˌsāl\ *n* : the sale of goods in quantity usu. for resale by a retail merchant

²wholesale *adj* **1** : performed on a large scale without discrimination ⟨~ slaughter⟩ **2** : of, relating to, or engaged in wholesaling — **wholesale** *adv*

³wholesale *vb* **whole·saled; whole·sal·ing** : to sell at wholesale — **whole·sal·er** *n*

whole·some \ˈhōl-səm\ *adj* **1** : promoting mental, spiritual, or bodily health or well-being ⟨a ~ environment⟩ **2** : sound in body, mind, or morals : HEALTHY **3** : PRUDENT ⟨~ respect for the law⟩ — **whole·some·ness** *n*

whole step *n* : a musical interval comprising two half steps (as C–D or F♯–G♯)

whole wheat *adj* : made of ground entire wheat kernels

whol·ly \ˈhōl-lē\ *adv* **1** : COMPLETELY, TOTALLY **2** : SOLELY, EXCLUSIVELY

whom \ˈhüm\ *pron, objective case of* WHO

whom·ev·er \hü-ˈme-vər\ *pron, objective case of* WHOEVER

whom·so·ev·er \ˌhüm-sō-ˈe-vər\ *pron, objective case of* WHOSOEVER

¹whoop \ˈhwüp, ˈhwùp, ˈhüp, ˈhùp\ *vb* **1** : to shout or call loudly and vigorously **2** : to make the characteristic whoop of whooping cough **3** : to go or pass with a loud noise **4** : to utter or express with a whoop; *also* : to urge, drive, or cheer with a whoop

²whoop *n* **1** : a whooping sound or utterance : SHOUT, HOOT **2** : a crowing intake of breath after a fit of coughing in whooping cough

whooping cough *n* : an infectious bacterial disease esp. of children marked by convulsive coughing fits often followed by a shrill gasping intake of breath

whooping crane *n* : a large white nearly extinct No. American crane noted for its loud whooping call

whooping crane

whoop·la \ˈhwüp-ˌlä, ˈhwùp-\ *n* **1** : HOOPLA **2** : boisterous merrymaking

whop·per \ˈhwä-pər\ *n* : something unusually large or extreme of its kind; *esp* : a monstrous lie

whop·ping \ˈhwä-piŋ\ *adj* : extremely large

whore \ˈhōr\ *n* : PROSTITUTE

whorl \ˈhwórl, ˈhwərl\ *n* **1** : a group of parts (as leaves or petals) encircling an axis and esp. a plant stem **2** : something that whirls or coils around a center : COIL, SPIRAL **3** : one of the turns of a snail shell

whorled \'hwȯrld, 'hwərld\ *adj* : having or arranged in whorls

¹whose \'hüz\ *adj* : of or relating to whom or which esp. as possessor or possessors, agent or agents, or object or objects of an action ⟨asked ∼ bag it was⟩

²whose *pron* : whose one or ones ⟨∼ is this car⟩ ⟨∼ are those books⟩

who·so \'hü-ˌsō\ *pron* : WHOEVER

who·so·ev·er \ˌhü-sō-'e-vər\ *pron* : WHOEVER

whs *or* **whse** *abbr* warehouse

whsle *abbr* wholesale

¹why \'hwī\ *adv* : for what reason, cause, or purpose ⟨∼ did you do it?⟩

²why *conj* **1** : the cause, reason, or purpose for which ⟨that is ∼ you did it⟩ **2** : for which : on account of which ⟨knows the reason ∼ you did it⟩

³why *n, pl* **whys** : REASON, CAUSE ⟨the ∼s of racial prejudice⟩

⁴why \'wī, 'hwī\ *interj* — used to express surprise, hesitation, approval, disapproval, or impatience ⟨∼, here's what I was looking for⟩

WI *abbr* **1** West Indies **2** Wisconsin

WIA *abbr* wounded in action

wick \'wik\ *n* : a loosely bound bundle of soft fibers that draws up oil, tallow, or wax to be burned in a candle, oil lamp, or stove

wick·ed \'wi-kəd\ *adj* **1** : morally bad : EVIL, SINFUL **2** : FIERCE, VICIOUS **3** : ROGUISH ⟨a ∼ glance⟩ **4** : REPUGNANT, VILE ⟨a ∼ odor⟩ **5** : HARMFUL, DANGEROUS ⟨a ∼ attack⟩ **6** : impressively excellent ⟨throws a ∼ fastball⟩ — **wick·ed·ly** *adv* — **wick·ed·ness** *n*

wick·er \'wi-kər\ *n* **1** : a small pliant branch (as an osier or a withe) **2** : WICKERWORK — **wicker** *adj*

wick·er·work \-ˌwərk\ *n* : work made of osiers, twigs, or rods : BASKETRY

wick·et \'wi-kət\ *n* **1** : a small gate or door; *esp* : one forming a part of or placed near a larger one **2** : a window-like opening usu. with a grille or grate (as at a ticket office) **3** : a set of three upright rods topped by two crosspieces bowled at in cricket **4** : an arch or hoop in croquet

wick·i·up \'wi-kē-ˌəp\ *n* : a hut used by nomadic Indians of the western and southwestern U.S. with a usu. oval base and a rough frame covered with reed mats, grass, or brushwood

wid *abbr* widow, widower

¹wide \'wīd\ *adj* **wid·er; wid·est** **1** : covering a vast area **2** : measured across or at right angles to the length **3** : not narrow : BROAD; *also* : ROOMY **4** : opened to full width ⟨eyes ∼ with wonder⟩ **5** : not limited : EXTENSIVE ⟨∼ experience⟩ **6** : far from the goal, mark, or truth ⟨a ∼ guess⟩ — **wide·ly** *adv*

²wide *adv* **wid·er; wid·est** **1** : over a great distance or extent : WIDELY ⟨searched far and ∼⟩ **2** : over a specified distance, area, or extent **3** : so as to leave a wide space between ⟨∼ apart⟩ **4** : so as to clear by a considerable distance ⟨ran ∼ around left end⟩ **5** : COMPLETELY, FULLY ⟨opened her eyes ∼⟩

wide–awake \ˌwīd-ə-'wāk\ *adj* : fully awake; *also* : KNOWING, ALERT

wide–body \'wīd-ˌbä-dē\ *n* : a large jet aircraft

wide–eyed \'wīd-'īd\ *adj* **1** : having the eyes wide open esp. with wonder or astonishment **2** : NAIVE

wide–mouthed \-'maůthd, -'maůtht\ *adj* **1** : having one's mouth opened wide (as in awe) **2** : having a wide mouth ⟨∼ jars⟩

wid·en \'wīd-ᵊn\ *vb* : to increase in width, scope, or extent

wide·spread \'wīd-'spred\ *adj* **1** : widely scattered or prevalent **2** : widely extended or spread out ⟨∼ wings⟩

¹wid·ow \'wi-dō\ *n* : a woman who has lost her husband by death and has not married again — **wid·ow·hood** *n*

²widow *vb* : to cause to become a widow or widower

wid·ow·er \'wi-də-wər\ *n* : a man who has lost his wife by death and has not married again

width \'width\ *n* **1** : a distance from side to side : the measurement taken at right angles to the length : BREADTH **2** : largeness of extent or scope; *also* : FULLNESS **3** : a measured and cut piece of material ⟨a ∼ of calico⟩

wield \'wēld\ *vb* **1** : to use or handle esp. effectively ⟨∼ a broom⟩ **2** : to exert authority by means of : EMPLOY ⟨∼ influence⟩ — **wield·er** *n*

wie·ner \'wē-nər\ *n* [short for *wienerwurst*, fr. G, lit., Vienna sausage] : FRANKFURTER

wife \'wīf\ *n, pl* **wives** \'wīvz\ **1** *dial* : WOMAN **2** : a woman acting in a specified capacity — used in combination **3** : a female partner in a marriage — **wife·hood** *n* — **wife·less** *adj* — **wife·ly** *adj*

wig \'wig\ *n* [short for *periwig*, fr. MF *perruque*, fr. It *parrucca, perrucca* hair, wig] : a manufactured covering of natural or synthetic hair for the head; *also* : TOUPEE

wi·geon *or* **wid·geon** \'wi-jən\ *n, pl* **wigeon** *or* **wigeons** *or* **widgeon** *or* **widgeons** : any of several medium-sized freshwater ducks

wig·gle \'wi-gəl\ *vb* **wig·gled; wig·gling** **1** : to move to and fro with quick jerky or shaking movements : JIGGLE **2** : WRIGGLE — **wiggle** *n*

wig·gler \'wi-glər, -gə-lər\ *n* **1** : a larva or pupa of a mosquito **2** : one that wiggles

wig·gly \'wi-glē, -gə-lē\ *adj* **1** : tending to wiggle ⟨a ∼ worm⟩ **2** : WAVY ⟨∼ lines⟩

wight \'wīt\ *n* : a living being : CREATURE

wig·let \'wi-glət\ *n* : a small wig used esp. to enhance a hairstyle

¹wig·wag \'wig-ˌwag\ *vb* **1** : to signal by or as if by a flag or light waved according to a code **2** : to make or cause to make a signal (as with the hand or arm)

²wigwag *n* : the art or practice of wigwagging

wig·wam \'wig-ˌwäm\ *n* : a hut of the Indians of the eastern U.S. having typically an arched framework of poles overlaid with bark, rush mats, or hides

¹wild \'wīld\ *adj* **1** : living in a state of nature and not ordinarily tamed ⟨∼ ducks⟩ **2** : growing or produced without human aid or care ⟨∼ honey⟩ ⟨∼ plants⟩ **3** : WASTE, DESOLATE ⟨∼ country⟩ **4** : UNCONTROLLED, UNRESTRAINED, UNRULY ⟨∼ passions⟩ ⟨a ∼ young stallion⟩ **5** : TURBULENT, STORMY ⟨a ∼ night⟩ **6** : EXTRAVAGANT, FANTASTIC, CRAZY ⟨∼ ideas⟩ **7** : indicative of strong passion, desire, or emotion ⟨a ∼ stare⟩ **8** : UNCIVILIZED, SAVAGE **9** : deviating from the natural or expected course : ERRATIC ⟨a ∼ throw⟩ **10** : having a denomination determined by the holder ⟨deuces ∼⟩ — **wild·ly** *adv* — **wild·ness** *n*

²wild *adv* **1** : WILDLY **2** : without regulation or control ⟨running ∼⟩

³wild *n* **1** : WILDERNESS **2** : a natural or undomesticated state or existence

wild boar *n* : an Old World wild hog from which most domestic swine have been derived

wild carrot *n* : QUEEN ANNE'S LACE

¹wild·cat \'wīld-ˌkat\ *n, pl* **wildcats** **1** : any of various small or medium-sized cats (as a lynx or ocelot) **2** : a quick-tempered hard-fighting person

²wildcat *adj* **1** : not sound or safe ⟨∼ schemes⟩ **2** : initiated by a group of workers without formal union approval ⟨∼ strike⟩

³wildcat *vb* **wild·cat·ted; wild·cat·ting** : to drill an oil or gas well in a region not known to be productive

wil·de·beest \'wil-də-ˌbēst\ *n, pl* **wildebeests** *also* **wildebeest** [Afrikaans *wildebees*, fr. *wilde* wild + *bees* ox] : GNU

wil·der·ness \'wil-dər-nəs\ *n* [ME, fr. *wildern* wild, fr. OE *wilddēoren* of wild beasts] : an uncultivated and uninhabited region

wild·fire \'wīld-ˌfīr\ *n* : an uncontrollable fire — **like wildfire** : very rapidly

wild·fowl \-₁faúl\ *n* : a bird and esp. a waterfowl (as a wild duck or goose) hunted as game

wild–goose chase *n* : the pursuit of something unattainable

wild·life \'wīld-₁līf\ *n* : nonhuman living things and esp. wild animals living in their natural environment

wild oat *n* **1** : any of several wild grasses **2** *pl* : offenses and indiscretions attributed to youthful exuberance — usu. used in the phrase *sow one's wild oats*

wild rice *n* : a No. American aquatic grass; *also* : its edible seed

wild·wood \'wīld-₁wúd\ *n* : a wood unaltered or unfrequented by humans

¹wile \'wīl\ *n* **1** : a trick or stratagem intended to ensnare or deceive; *also* : a playful trick **2** : TRICKERY, GUILE

²wile *vb* **wiled; wil·ing** : LURE, ENTICE

¹will \'wil\ *vb, past* **would** \'wúd\; *pres sing & pl* **will** **1** : WISH, DESIRE ⟨call it what you ∼⟩ **2** — used as an auxiliary verb to express (1) desire, willingness, or in negative constructions refusal ⟨∼ you have another⟩ ⟨he *won't* do it⟩, (2) customary or habitual action ⟨∼ get angry over nothing⟩, (3) simple futurity ⟨tomorrow we ∼ go shopping⟩, (4) capability or sufficiency ⟨the back seat ∼ hold three⟩, (5) determination or willfulness ⟨I ∼ go despite them⟩, (6) probability ⟨that ∼ be the mailman⟩, (7) inevitability ⟨accidents ∼ happen⟩, or (8) a command ⟨you ∼ do as I say⟩

²will *n* **1** : wish or desire often combined with determination ⟨the ∼ to win⟩ **2** : something desired; *esp* : a choice or determination of one having authority or power **3** : the act, process, or experience of willing : VOLITION **4** : the mental powers manifested as wishing, choosing, desiring, or intending **5** : a disposition to act according to principles or ends **6** : power of controlling one's own actions or emotions ⟨a leader of iron ∼⟩ **7** : a legal document in which a person declares to whom his or her possessions are to go after death

³will *vb* **1** : to dispose of by or as if by a will : BEQUEATH **2** : to determine by an act of choice; *also* : DECREE, ORDAIN **3** : INTEND, PURPOSE; *also* : CHOOSE

will·ful *or* **wil·ful** \'wil-fəl\ *adj* **1** : governed by will without regard to reason : OBSTINATE **2** : INTENTIONAL ⟨∼ murder⟩ — **will·ful·ly** *adv*

wil·lies \'wi-lēz\ *n pl* : a fit of nervousness : JITTERS — used with *the*

will·ing \'wi-liŋ\ *adj* **1** : inclined or favorably disposed in mind : READY ⟨∼ to go⟩ **2** : prompt to act or respond ⟨∼ workers⟩ **3** : done, borne, or accepted voluntarily or without reluctance **4** : of or relating to the will : VOLITIONAL — **will·ing·ly** *adv* — **will·ing·ness** *n*

wil·li·waw \'wi-lē-₁wȯ\ *n* : a sudden violent gust of cold land air common along mountainous coasts of high latitudes

will-o'-the-wisp \₁wil-ə-thə-'wisp\ *n* **1** : a light that appears at night over marshy grounds **2** : a misleading or elusive goal or hope

wil·low \'wi-lō\ *n* **1** : any of a genus of quick-growing shrubs and trees with tough pliable shoots **2** : an object made of willow wood

wil·low·ware \-₁war\ *n* : dinnerware that is usu. blue and white and that is decorated with a storytelling design featuring a large willow tree by a little bridge

wil·lowy \'wi-lə-wē\ *adj* : PLIANT; *also* : gracefully tall and slender

will·pow·er \'wil-₁paú-ər\ *n* : energetic determination : RESOLUTENESS

wil·ly-nil·ly \₁wi-lē-'ni-lē\ *adv or adj* [alter. of *will I nill I* or *will ye nill ye* or *will he nill he*; *nill* fr. archaic *nill* to be unwilling, fr. ME *nilen*, fr. OE *nyllan*, fr. *ne* not + *wyllan* to wish] : without regard for one's choice : by compulsion ⟨they rushed us along ∼⟩

¹wilt \'wilt\ *vb* **1** : to lose or cause to lose freshness and

become limp esp. from lack of water : DROOP **2** : to grow weak or faint : LANGUISH

²wilt *n* : any of various plant disorders marked by wilting and often shriveling

wily \'wī-lē\ *adj* **wil·i·er; -est** : full of guile : TRICKY — **wil·i·ness** \-lē-nəs\ *n*

wimp \'wimp\ *n* : a weak, cowardly, or ineffectual person — **wimpy** \'wim-pē\ *adj*

¹wim·ple \'wim-pəl\ *n* : a cloth covering worn over the head and around the neck and chin by women esp. in the late medieval period and by some nuns

²wimple *vb* **wim·pled; wim·pling** **1** : to cover with or as if with a wimple **2** : to ripple or cause to ripple

¹win \'win\ *vb* **won** \'wən\; **win·ning** [ME *winnen*, fr. OE *winnan* to struggle] **1** : to get possession of esp. by effort : GAIN; *also* : to obtain by work : EARN **2** : to gain in or as if in battle or contest; *also* : to be the victor in ⟨won the war⟩ **3** : to solicit and gain the favor of; *esp* : to induce to accept oneself in marriage

²win *n* : VICTORY; *esp* : 1st place at the finish (as of a horse race)

wince \'wins\ *vb* **winced; winc·ing** : to shrink back involuntarily (as from pain) : FLINCH — **wince** *n*

winch \'winch\ *n* : a machine that has a drum on which is wound a rope or cable for hauling or hoisting — **winch** *vb*

¹wind \'wind\ *n* **1** : a movement of the air **2** : a prevailing force or influence : TENDENCY, TREND **3** : BREATH ⟨he had the ∼ knocked out of him⟩ **4** : gas produced in the stomach or intestines **5** : something insubstantial; *esp* : idle words **6** : air carrying a scent (as of game) **7** : INTIMATION ⟨they got ∼ of our plans⟩ **8** : WIND INSTRUMENTS; *also, pl* : players of wind instruments

²wind *vb* **1** : to get a scent of ⟨the dogs ∼ed the game⟩ **2** : to cause to be out of breath ⟨he was ∼ed from the climb⟩ **3** : to allow (as a horse) to rest so as to recover breath

³wind \'wīnd, 'wind\ *vb* **wind·ed** \'wīn-dəd, 'win-\ *or* **wound** \'waúnd\; **wind·ing** : to sound by blowing ⟨∼ a horn⟩

⁴wind \'wīnd\ *vb* **wound** \'waúnd\ *also* **wind·ed; wind·ing** **1** : ENTANGLE, INVOLVE **2** : to introduce stealthily : INSINUATE **3** : to encircle or cover with something pliable : WRAP, COIL, TWINE ⟨∼ a bobbin⟩ **4** : to hoist or haul by a rope or chain and a winch **5** : to tighten the spring of; *also* : CRANK **6** : to raise to a high level (as of excitement) **7** : to cause to move in a curving line or path **8** : to have a curving course or shape ⟨a river ∼ing through the valley⟩ **9** : to move or lie so as to encircle

⁵wind \'wīnd\ *n* : COIL, TURN

wind·age \'win-dij\ *n* : the influence of the wind in deflecting the course of a projectile through the air; *also* : the amount of such deflection

wind·bag \'wind-₁bag\ *n* : an overly talkative person

wind·blown \-₁blōn\ *adj* : blown by the wind; *also* : having the appearance of being blown by the wind

wind·break \-₁brāk\ *n* : a growth of trees or shrubs serving to break the force of the wind; *also* : a shelter from the wind

wind·break·er \-₁brā-kər\ *n* : a light jacket made of material that can resist the wind

wind–bro·ken \-₁brō-kən\ *adj* : having the power of breathing impaired by disease — used of a horse

wind·burned \-₁bərnd\ *adj* : irritated and inflamed by exposure to the wind — **wind·burn** \-₁bərn\ *n*

wind·chill \-₁chil\ *n* : a still-air temperature that would have the same cooling effect on exposed human skin as a given combination of temperature and wind speed

windchill factor *n* : WINDCHILL

wind·er \'wīn-dər\ *n* : one that winds

wind·fall \'wind-₁fȯl\ *n* **1** : something (as a tree or fruit) blown down by the wind **2** : an unexpected or sudden gift, gain, or advantage

wind·flow·er \-ˌflaů-ər\ *n* : ANEMONE

¹**wind·ing** \'wīn-diŋ\ *n* : material (as wire) wound or coiled about an object

²**winding** *adj* 1 : having a pronounced curve or spiral ⟨~ stairs⟩ 2 : having a course that winds ⟨a ~ road⟩

wind·ing–sheet \-ˌshēt\ *n* : SHROUD

wind instrument *n* : a musical instrument (as a flute or horn) sounded by wind and esp. by the breath

wind·jam·mer \'wind-ˌja-mər\ *n* : a sailing ship; *also* : one of its crew

wind·lass \'wind-ləs\ *n* [ME *wyndlas*, alter. of *wyndas*, fr. ON *vindāss*, fr. *vinda* to wind + *āss* pole] : a winch used esp. on ships for hoisting or hauling

wind·mill \'wind-ˌmil\ *n* : a mill or machine worked by the wind turning sails or vanes that radiate from a central shaft

win·dow \'win-dō\ *n* [ME *windowe*, fr. ON *vindauga*, fr. *vindr* wind + *auga* eye] 1 : an opening in the wall of a building to let in light and air; *also* : the framework with fittings that closes such an opening 2 : WINDOWPANE 3 : an opening resembling or suggesting that of a window in a building 4 : an interval of time during which certain conditions or an opportunity exists 5 : an area of a computer display on which different information may be displayed independently — **win·dow·less** *adj*

window box *n* : a box for growing plants in or by a window

window dressing *n* 1 : display of merchandise in a store window 2 : a showing made to create a deceptively favorable impression

win·dow·pane \'win-dō-ˌpān\ *n* : a pane in a window

win·dow–shop \-ˌshäp\ *vb* : to look at the displays in store windows without going inside the stores to make purchases — **win·dow–shop·per** *n*

win·dow·sill \-ˌsil\ *n* : the horizontal member at the bottom of a window

wind·pipe \'wind-ˌpīp\ *n* : the passage for the breath from the larynx to the lungs

wind·proof \-'prüf\ *adj* : impervious to wind ⟨a ~ jacket⟩

wind·row \'wind-ˌrō\ *n* 1 : hay raked up into a row to dry 2 : a row of something (as dry leaves) swept up by or as if by the wind

wind shear *n* : a radical shift in wind speed and direction that occurs over a very short distance

wind·shield \'wind-ˌshēld\ *n* : a transparent screen (as of glass) in front of the occupants of a vehicle

wind sock *n* : an open-ended truncated cloth cone mounted in an elevated position to indicate wind direction

wind·storm \-ˌstȯrm\ *n* : a storm with high wind and little or no rain

wind·surf·ing \-ˌsər-fiŋ\ *n* : the sport or activity of riding a sailboard — **wind·surf** \-ˌsərf\ *vb* — **wind·surf·er** *n*

wind·swept \'wind-ˌswept\ *adj* : swept by or as if by wind ⟨~ plains⟩

wind tunnel *n* : an enclosed passage through which air is blown to investigate air flow around an object

wind·up \'wīn-ˌdəp\ *n* 1 : CONCLUSION, FINISH 2 : a series of regular and distinctive motions made by a pitcher preliminary to delivering a pitch

wind up *vb* 1 : to bring or come to a conclusion : END 2 : to put in order for the purpose of bringing to an end 3 : to arrive in a place, situation, or condition at the end or as a result of a course of action ⟨*wound up* as paupers⟩ 4 : to make a pitching windup

¹**wind·ward** \'win-dwərd\ *n* : the side or direction from which the wind is blowing

²**windward** *adj* : being in or facing the direction from which the wind is blowing

windy \'win-dē\ *adj* **wind·i·er; -est** 1 : having wind : exposed to winds ⟨a ~ day⟩ ⟨a ~ prairie⟩ 2 : STORMY 3 : FLATULENT 4 : indulging in or characterized by useless talk : VERBOSE

¹**wine** \'wīn\ *n* 1 : fermented grape juice used as a beverage 2 : the usu. fermented juice of a plant product (as fruit) used as a beverage ⟨rice ~⟩

²**wine** *vb* **wined; win·ing** : to treat to or drink wine

wine cellar *n* : a room for storing wines; *also* : a stock of wines

wine·grow·er \-ˌgrō-ər\ *n* : one that cultivates a vineyard and makes wine

wine·press \-ˌpres\ *n* : a vat in which juice is pressed from grapes

¹**wing** \'wiŋ\ *n* 1 : one of the movable feathered or membranous paired appendages by means of which a bird, bat, or insect flies 2 : something suggesting a wing; *esp* : an airfoil that develops the lift which supports an aircraft in flight 3 : a plant or animal appendage or part likened to a wing 4 : a turned-back or extended edge on an article of clothing 5 : a means of flight or rapid progress 6 : the act or manner of flying : FLIGHT 7 *pl* : the area at the side of the stage out of sight 8 : one of the positions or players on either side of a center position or line 9 : either of two opposing groups within an organization : FACTION 10 : a unit in military aviation consisting of two or more squadrons — **wing·less** *adj* — **on the wing** : in flight : FLYING — **under one's wing** : in one's charge or care

²**wing** *vb* 1 : to fit with wings; *also* : to enable to fly easily 2 : to pass through in flight : FLY ⟨~ the air⟩ ⟨swallows ~*ing* southward⟩ 3 : to let fly : DISPATCH 4 : to wound in the wing ⟨~ a bird⟩; *also* : to wound without killing 5 : to perform without preparation : IMPROVISE ⟨~*ing* it⟩

wing·ding \'wiŋ-ˌdiŋ\ *n* : a wild, lively, or lavish party

winged \'wiŋd, 'wiŋ-əd, *in compounds* 'wiŋd\ *adj* 1 : having wings esp. of a specified character 2 : soaring with or as if with wings : ELEVATED 3 : SWIFT, RAPID

wing·span \'wiŋ-ˌspan\ *n* : the distance between the tips of a pair of wings

wing·spread \-ˌspred\ *n* : the spread of the wings; *esp* : the distance between the tips of the fully extended wings of a winged animal

¹**wink** \'wiŋk\ *vb* 1 : to close and open one eye quickly as a signal or hint 2 : to close and open the eyes quickly : BLINK 3 : to avoid seeing or noticing something ⟨~ at a traffic violation⟩ 4 : TWINKLE, FLICKER — **wink·er** \'wiŋ-kər\ *n*

²**wink** *n* 1 : a brief period of sleep : NAP 2 : an act of winking; *esp* : a hint or sign given by winking 3 : INSTANT ⟨dries in a ~⟩

win·ner \'wi-nər\ *n* : one that wins

¹**win·ning** \'wi-niŋ\ *n* 1 : VICTORY 2 : something won; *esp* : money won at gambling ⟨large ~s⟩

²**winning** *adj* 1 : successful esp. in competition 2 : ATTRACTIVE, CHARMING

win·now \'wi-nō\ *vb* 1 : to remove (as chaff) by a current of air; *also* : to free (as grain) from waste in this manner 2 : to sort or separate as if by winnowing

wino \'wī-nō\ *n, pl* **win·os** : one who is addicted to drinking wine

win·some \'win-səm\ *adj* [ME *winsum*, fr. OE *wynsum*, fr. *wynn* joy] 1 : generally pleasing and engaging 2 : CHEERFUL, GAY — **win·some·ly** *adv* — **win·some·ness** *n*

¹**win·ter** \'win-tər\ *n* : the season of the year in any region in which the noonday sun shines most obliquely : the coldest period of the year

²**winter** *adj* : sown in autumn for harvesting in the following spring or summer ⟨~ wheat⟩

win·ter·green \'win-tər-ˌgrēn\ *n* 1 : a low evergreen plant of the heath family with white bell-shaped flowers and spicy red berries 2 : an aromatic oil from the common wintergreen or its flavor or something flavored with it

win·ter·ize \'win-tə-ˌrīz\ *vb* **-ized; -iz·ing** : to make ready for winter

win·ter–kill \'win-tər-ˌkil\ *vb* : to kill or die by expo-sure to winter weather

winter squash *n* : any of various hard-shelled squash-es that keep well in storage

win·ter·tide \-ˌtīd\ *n* : WINTER

win·ter·time \-ˌtīm\ *n* : WINTER

win·try \'win-trē\ *also* **win·tery** \'win-tə-rē\ *adj* **win·tri·er; -est** 1 : of, relating to, or characteristic of win-ter 〈~ weather〉 2 : CHILLING, CHEERLESS 〈a ~ wel-come〉

¹wipe \'wīp\ *vb* **wiped; wip·ing** 1 : to clean or dry by rubbing 〈~ dishes〉 2 : to remove by or as if by rub-bing 〈~ away tears〉 3 : to erase completely : OBLIT-ERATE 4 : to pass or draw over a surface 〈*wiped* his hand across his face〉 — **wip·er** *n*

²wipe *n* 1 : an act or instance of wiping; *also* : BLOW, STRIKE, SWIPE 2 : something used for wiping

wipe out *vb* : to destroy completely

¹wire \'wīr\ *n* 1 : metal in the form of a thread or slen-der rod; *also* : a thread or rod of metal 2 : hidden or secret influences controlling the action of a person or organization — usu. used in pl. 〈pull ~s〉 3 : a line of wire for conducting electric current 4 : a telegraph or telephone wire or system 5 : TELEGRAM, CABLEGRAM 6 : the finish line of a race

²wire *vb* **wired; wir·ing** 1 : to provide or equip with wire 〈~ a house〉 2 : to bind, string, or mount with wire 3 : to send or send word to by telegraph

wire·hair \'wīr-ˌhar\ *n* : a wirehaired dog or cat

wire·haired \-'hard\ *adj* : having a stiff wiry outer coat of hair

¹wire·less \-ləs\ *adj* 1 : having no wire or wires 2 *chiefly Brit* : RADIO

²wireless *n* 1 : wireless telegraphy 2 *chiefly Brit* : RADIO

wire–pull·er \-ˌpu̇-lər\ *n* : one who uses secret or un-derhanded means to influence the acts of a person or organization — **wire–pull·ing** *n*

wire service *n* : a news agency that sends out syndi-cated news copy to subscribers by wire or satellite

wire·tap \-ˌtap\ *n* : the act or an instance of tapping a telephone or telegraph wire to get information; *also* : an electrical connection used for such tapping — **wiretap** *vb* — **wire·tap·per** \-ˌta-pər\ *n*

wire·worm \-ˌwərm\ *n* : any of various slender hard-coated beetle larvae esp. destructive to plant roots

wir·ing \'wīr-iŋ\ *n* : a system of wires

wiry \'wīr-ē\ *adj* **wir·i·er** \'wī-rē-ər\; **-est** 1 : made of or resembling wire 2 : slender yet strong and sinewy — **wir·i·ness** \'wī-rē-nəs\ *n*

Wis *or* **Wisc** *abbr* Wisconsin

Wisd *abbr* Wisdom

wis·dom \'wiz-dəm\ *n* [ME, fr. OE *wīsdom*, fr. *wīs* wise] 1 : accumulated philosophic or scientific learn-ing : KNOWLEDGE; *also* : INSIGHT 2 : good sense : JUDGMENT 3 : a wise attitude or course of action

Wisdom *n* — see BIBLE table

wisdom of Sol·o·mon \-'sä-lə-mən\ — see BIBLE table

wisdom tooth *n* : the last tooth of the full set on each half of each human jaw

¹wise \'wīz\ *n* : WAY, MANNER, FASHION 〈in no ~〉 〈in this ~〉

²wise *adj* **wis·er; wis·est** 1 : having wisdom : SAGE 2 : having or showing good sense or good judgment 3 : aware of what is going on : KNOWING; *also* : CRAFTY, SHREWD 4 : possessing inside information — **wise·ly** *adv*

-wise \-ˌwīz\ *adv comb form* : in the manner or direc-tion 〈slant*wise*〉

wise·acre \'wī-ˌzā-kər\ *n* [MD *wijssegger* soothsayer] : SMART ALECK

¹wise·crack \'wīz-ˌkrak\ *n* : a clever, smart, or flippant remark

²wisecrack *vb* : to make a wisecrack

¹wish \'wish\ *vb* 1 : to have a desire : long for 〈~ you were here〉 〈~ for a puppy〉 2 : to form or express a wish concerning 〈~ed him a happy birthday〉 3 : BID

〈he ~ed me good morning〉 4 : to request by express-ing a desire 〈I ~ you to go now〉

²wish *n* 1 : an act or instance of wishing or desire : WANT; *also* : GOAL 2 : an expressed will or desire

wish·bone \-ˌbōn\ *n* : a forked bone in front of the breastbone in most birds

wish·ful \'wish-fəl\ *adj* 1 : expressive of a wish; *also* : having a wish 2 : according with wishes rather than fact 〈~ thinking〉

wishy–washy \'wi-shē-ˌwȯ-shē, -ˌwä-\ *adj* : WEAK, IN-SIPID; *also* : morally feeble

wisp \'wisp\ *n* 1 : a small handful (as of hay or straw) 2 : a thin strand, strip, or fragment 〈a ~ of hair〉; *also* : a thready streak 〈a ~ of smoke〉 3 : something frail, slight, or fleeting 〈a ~ of a smile〉 — **wispy** *adj*

wis·te·ria \wis-'tir-ē-ə\ *or* **wis·tar·ia** \-'tir-ē-ə *also* -'ter-\ *n* : any of a genus of chiefly Asian mostly woody vines related to the peas and widely grown for their long showy clusters of blue, white, purple, or rose flowers

wist·ful \'wist-fəl\ *adj* : feeling or showing a timid de-sire — **wist·ful·ly** *adv* — **wist·ful·ness** *n*

wit \'wit\ *n* 1 : reasoning power : INTELLIGENCE 2 : mental soundness : SANITY — usu. used in pl. 3 : RE-SOURCEFULNESS, INGENUITY; *esp* : quickness and cleverness in handling words and ideas 4 : a talent for making clever remarks; *also* : a person noted for making witty remarks — **wit·ted** \'wi-təd\ *adj* — **at one's wit's end** : at a loss for a means of solving a problem

¹witch \'wich\ *n* 1 : a person believed to have magic power; *esp* : SORCERESS 2 : an ugly old woman : HAG 3 : a charming or alluring girl or woman

²witch *vb* : BEWITCH

witch·craft \'wich-ˌkraft\ *n* : the power or practices of a witch : SORCERY

witch doctor *n* : a person in a primitive society who uses magic to treat sickness and to fight off evil spir-its

witch·ery \'wi-chə-rē\ *n, pl* **-er·ies** 1 : SORCERY 2 : FAS-CINATION, CHARM

witch·grass \'wich-ˌgras\ *n* : any of several grasses that are weeds in cultivated areas

witch ha·zel \'wich-ˌhā-zəl\ *n* 1 : a shrub of eastern No. America bearing small yellow flowers in the fall 2 : a soothing alcoholic lotion made from witch hazel bark

witch–hunt \'wich-ˌhənt\ *n* 1 : a searching out and persecution of persons accused of witchcraft 2 : the searching out and deliberate harassment esp. of po-litical opponents

witch·ing \'wi-chiŋ\ *adj* : of, relating to, or suitable for sorcery or supernatural occurrences

with \'with, 'with\ *prep* 1 : AGAINST 〈a fight ~ his brother〉 2 : FROM 〈parting ~ friends〉 3 : in mutual re-lation to 〈talk ~ a friend〉 4 : in the company of 〈went there ~ her〉 5 : AS REGARDS, TOWARD 〈is patient ~ children〉 6 : compared to 〈on equal terms ~ another〉 7 : in support of 〈I'm ~ you all the way〉 8 : in the presence of : CONTAINING 〈tea ~ sugar〉 9 : in the opinion of : as judged by 〈their arguments had weight ~ her〉 10 : BECAUSE OF, THROUGH 〈pale ~ anger〉; *also* : by means of 〈hit him ~ a club〉 11 : in a manner indicating 〈work ~ a will〉 12 : GIVEN, GRANTED 〈~ your permission I'll leave〉 13 : HAVING 〈came ~ good news〉 〈stood there ~ his mouth open〉 14 : at the time of : right after 〈~ that we left〉 15 : DESPITE 〈~ all her cleverness, she failed〉 16 : in the direction of 〈swim ~ the tide〉

with·al \wi-'thȯl, -'thȯl\ *adv* 1 : together with this : BE-SIDES 2 : on the other hand : NEVERTHELESS

with·draw \with-'drȯ, with-\ *vb* **-drew** \-'drü\ **-drawn** \-'drȯn\ **-draw·ing** \-'drȯ-iŋ\ 1 : to take back or away : REMOVE 2 : to call back (as from consideration); *also* : RETRACT 3 : to go away : RETREAT, LEAVE 4 : to ter-minate one's participation in or use of something

with·draw·al \-'drȯ-əl\ n **1** : an act or instance of withdrawing **2** : the discontinuance of the use or administration of a drug and esp. an addicting drug; *also* : the period following such discontinuance marked by often painful physiological and psychological symptoms **3** : a pathological retreat from the real world (as in some schizophrenic states)

with·drawn \with-'drȯn\ adj **1** : ISOLATED, SECLUDED **2** : socially detached and unresponsive

withe \'with\ n : a slender flexible twig or branch

with·er \'wi-thər\ vb **1** : to shrivel from or as if from loss of bodily moisture and esp. sap **2** : to lose or cause to lose vitality, force, or freshness **3** : to cause to feel shriveled ⟨∼ed him with a glance⟩

with·ers \'wi-thərz\ n pl : the ridge between the shoulder bones of a horse; *also* : the corresponding part in other 4-footed animals

with·hold \with-'hōld, with-\ vb **-held** \-'held\; **-hold·ing 1** : to hold back : RESTRAIN; *also* : RETAIN **2** : to refrain from granting, giving, or allowing ⟨∼ permission⟩ ⟨∼ names⟩

withholding tax n : a tax on income withheld at the source

¹with·in \wi-'thin, -'thin-\ adv **1** : in or into the interior : INSIDE **2** : inside oneself : INWARDLY

²within prep **1** : inside the limits or influence of ⟨∼ call⟩ **2** : in the limits or compass of ⟨∼ a mile⟩ **3** : in or to the inner part of ⟨∼ the room⟩

with-it \'wi-thət, -thət\ adj : socially or culturally up-to-date

¹with·out \wi-'thaut, -'thaut\ prep **1** : OUTSIDE **2** : LACKING ⟨∼ hope⟩; *also* : not accompanied by or showing ⟨spoke ∼ thinking⟩

²without adv **1** : on the outside : EXTERNALLY **2** : with something lacking or absent ⟨has learned to do ∼⟩

with·stand \with-'stand, with-\ vb **-stood** \-'stud\; **-stand·ing** : to stand against : RESIST; *esp* : to oppose (as an attack) successfully

wit·less \'wit-ləs\ adj : lacking wit or understanding : FOOLISH — **wit·less·ly** adv — **wit·less·ness** n

¹wit·ness \'wit-nəs\ n [ME witnesse, fr. OE witnes knowledge, testimony, witness, fr. wit mind, intelligence] **1** : TESTIMONY ⟨bear ∼ to the fact⟩ **2** : one that gives evidence; *esp* : one who testifies in a cause or before a court **3** : one present at a transaction so as to be able to testify that it has taken place **4** : one who has personal knowledge or experience of something **5** : something serving as evidence or proof : SIGN

²witness vb **1** : to bear witness : TESTIFY **2** : to act as legal witness of **3** : to furnish proof of : BETOKEN **4** : to be a witness of **5** : to be the scene of ⟨this region has ∼ed many wars⟩

wit·ti·cism \'wi-tə-ˌsi-zəm\ n : a witty saying or phrase

wit·ting \'wi-tiŋ\ adj : done knowingly : INTENTIONAL — **wit·ting·ly** adv

wit·ty \'wi-tē\ adj **wit·ti·er; -est** : marked by or full of wit : AMUSING ⟨a ∼ writer⟩ ⟨a ∼ remark⟩ syn humorous, facetious, jocular, jocose — **wit·ti·ly** \-tə-lē\ adv — **wit·ti·ness** \-tē-nəs\ n

wive \'wīv\ vb **wived; wiv·ing** : to take a wife

wives pl of WIFE

wiz·ard \'wi-zərd\ n [ME wysard wise man, fr. wys wise] **1** : MAGICIAN, SORCERER **2** : a very clever or skillful person ⟨a ∼ at chess⟩

wiz·ard·ry \'wi-zər-drē\ n, pl **-ries 1** : magic skill : SORCERY **2** : great skill or cleverness in an activity

wiz·en \'wiz-ᵊn, 'wēz-\ vb : to become or cause to become dry, shrunken, or wrinkled

wk abbr **1** week **2** work

WL abbr wavelength

wmk abbr watermark

WNW abbr west-northwest

WO abbr warrant officer

w/o abbr without

woad \'wōd\ n : a European herb related to the mustards; *also* : a blue dyestuff made from its leaves

wob·ble \'wä-bəl\ vb **wob·bled; wob·bling 1** : to move or cause to move with an irregular rocking or side-to-side motion **2** : TREMBLE, QUAVER **3** : WAVER, VACILLATE — **wobble** n — **wob·bly** \-bə-lē\ adj

woe \'wō\ n **1** : deep suffering from misfortune, affliction, or grief **2** : TROUBLE, MISFORTUNE ⟨economic ∼s⟩

woe·be·gone \'wō-bi-ˌgȯn\ adj : exhibiting woe, sorrow, or misery; *also* : being in a sorry condition

woe·ful also **wo·ful** \'wō-fəl\ adj **1** : full of woe : AFFLICTED **2** : involving, bringing, or relating to woe **3** : DEPLORABLE — **woe·ful·ly** adv

wok \'wäk\ n : a bowl-shaped cooking utensil used esp. in stir-frying

woke past of WAKE

woken past part of WAKE

wold \'wōld\ n : an upland plain or stretch of rolling land without woods

¹wolf \'wulf\ n, pl **wolves** \'wulvz\ **1** : any of several large erect-eared bushy-tailed doglike predatory mammals that live and hunt in packs; *esp* : GRAY WOLF **2** : a fierce or destructive person — **wolf·ish** adj

²wolf vb : to eat greedily : DEVOUR

wolf·hound \-ˌhaund\ n : any of several large dogs orig. used in hunting wolves

wol·fram \'wul-frəm\ n : TUNGSTEN

wol·ver·ine \ˌwul-və-'rēn\ n, pl **wolverines** also **wolverine** : a dark shaggy-coated flesh-eating mammal of northern forests and associated tundra that is related to the weasels

wom·an \'wu-mən\ n, pl **wom·en** \'wi-mən\ [ME, fr. OE wīfman, fr. wīf woman, wife + man human being, man] **1** : an adult female person **2** : WOMANKIND **3** : feminine nature : WOMANLINESS **4** : a female servant or attendant

wom·an·hood \'wu-mən-ˌhud\ n **1** : the state of being a woman : the distinguishing qualities of a woman or of womankind **2** : WOMEN, WOMANKIND

wom·an·ish \'wu-mə-nish\ adj **1** : of, relating to, or characteristic of a woman **2** : suitable to a woman rather than to a man : EFFEMINATE

wom·an·kind \'wu-mən-ˌkīnd\ n : the females of the human race : WOMEN

wom·an·like \-ˌlīk\ adj : WOMANLY

wom·an·ly \-lē\ adj : having qualities characteristic of a woman — **wom·an·li·ness** \-lē-nəs\ n

woman suffrage n : possession and exercise of suffrage by women

womb \'wüm\ n **1** : UTERUS **2** : a place where something is generated

wom·bat \'wäm-ˌbat\ n : any of several stocky burrowing Australian marsupials that resemble small bears

wom·en·folk \'wi-mən-ˌfōk\ also **wom·en·folks** \-ˌfōks\ n pl : WOMEN

¹won \'wən\ past and past part of WIN

²won \'wȯn\ n, pl **won** — see MONEY table

¹won·der \'wən-dər\ n **1** : a cause of astonishment or surprise : MARVEL; *also* : MIRACLE **2** : the quality of exciting wonder (the charm and ∼ of the scene) **3** : a feeling (as of awed astonishment or uncertainty) aroused by something extraordinary or affecting

²wonder vb **1** : to feel surprise or amazement **2** : to feel curiosity or doubt

wonder drug n : MIRACLE DRUG

won·der·ful \'wən-dər-fəl\ adj **1** : exciting wonder : MARVELOUS, ASTONISHING **2** : unusually good : ADMIRABLE — **won·der·ful·ly** \-f(ə-)lē\ adv — **won·der·ful·ness** n

won·der·land \-ˌland, -lənd\ n **1** : an imaginary place of delicate beauty or magical charm **2** : a place that excites admiration or wonder

won·der·ment \-mənt\ n **1** : ASTONISHMENT, SURPRISE **2** : a cause of or occasion for wonder **3** : curiosity about something

won·drous \'wən-drəs\ *adj* : WONDERFUL, MARVELOUS — **won·drous·ly** *adv* — **won·drous·ness** *n*

¹wont \'wónt, 'wōnt\ *adj* [ME *woned, wont,* fr. pp. of *wonen* to dwell, be used to, fr. OE *wunian*] **1** : AC-CUSTOMED, USED ⟨as we are ~ to do⟩ **2** : INCLINED, APT

²wont *n* : CUSTOM, USAGE, HABIT ⟨according to her ~⟩

won't \'wōnt\ : will not

wont·ed \'wón-təd, 'wōn-\ *adj* : ACCUSTOMED, CUS-TOMARY ⟨his ~ courtesy⟩

woo \'wü\ *vb* **1** : to try to gain the love of : COURT **2** : SOLICIT, ENTREAT **3** : to try to gain or bring about ⟨~ public favor⟩ — **woo·er** *n*

¹wood \'wúd\ *n* **1** : a dense growth of trees usu. larger than a grove and smaller than a forest — often used in pl. **2** : a hard fibrous substance that is basically xy-lem and forms the bulk of trees and shrubs beneath the bark; *also* : this material fit or prepared for some use (as burning or building) **3** : something made of wood

²wood *adj* **1** : WOODEN **2** : suitable for holding, cutting, or working with wood **3** *or* **woods** \'wúdz\ : living or growing in woods

³wood *vb* **1** : to supply or load with wood esp. for fuel **2** : to cover with a growth of trees

wood alcohol *n* : METHANOL

wood·bine \'wúd-ˌbīn\ *n* : any of several honeysuck-les; *also* : VIRGINIA CREEPER

wood·block \-ˌbläk\ *n* : WOODCUT

wood·chop·per \-ˌchä-pər\ *n* : one engaged esp. in chopping down trees

wood·chuck \-ˌchək\ *n* : a thickset grizzled marmot of Alaska, Canada, and the northeastern U.S.

wood·cock \'wúd-ˌkäk\ *n, pl* **woodcocks** : a brown eastern No. American game bird with a short neck and long bill that is related to the snipe; *also* : a re-lated and similar Old World bird

wood·craft \-ˌkraft\ *n* **1** : skill and practice in matters relating to the woods and esp. in how to take care of oneself in them **2** : skill in shaping or constructing ar-ticles from wood

wood·cut \-ˌkət\ *n* **1** : a relief printing surface engraved on a block of wood **2** : a print from a woodcut

wood·cut·ter \-ˌkə-tər\ *n* : a person who cuts wood

wood·ed \'wú-dəd\ *adj* : covered with woods or trees ⟨~ slopes⟩

wood·en \'wú-dᵊn\ *adj* **1** : made of wood **2** : lacking flexibility : awkwardly stiff — **wood·en·ly** *adv* — **wood·en·ness** *n*

wood·en·ware \'wú-dᵊn-ˌwar\ *n* : articles made of wood for domestic use

wood·land \'wúd-lənd, -ˌland\ *n* : land covered with trees : FOREST — **woodland** *adj*

wood·lot \'wúd-ˌlät\ *n* : a restricted area of woodland usu. privately kept to meet fuel and timber needs ⟨a farm ~⟩

wood louse *n* : any of various small flat crustaceans that live esp. in ground litter and under stones and bark

wood·man \'wúd-mən\ *n* : WOODSMAN

wood·note \-ˌnōt\ *n* : verbal expression that is natural and artless

wood nymph *n* : a nymph living in the woods

wood·peck·er \'wúd-ˌpe-kər\ *n* : any of numerous usu. brightly marked climbing birds with stiff spiny tail feathers and a chisellike bill used to drill into trees for insects

wood·pile \-ˌpīl\ *n* : a pile of wood and esp. firewood

wood·shed \-ˌshed\ *n* : a shed for storing wood and esp. firewood

woods·man \'wúdz-mən\ *n* : a person who frequents or works in the woods; *esp* : one skilled in woodcraft

woodsy \'wúd-zē\ *adj* : relating to or suggestive of woods

wood·wind \'wúd-ˌwind\ *n* : one of a group of wind in-struments including flutes, clarinets, oboes, bas-soons, and sometimes saxophones

wood·work \-ˌwərk\ *n* : work made of wood; *esp* : in-terior fittings (as moldings or stairways) of wood

woody \'wú-dē\ *adj* **wood·i·er; -est 1** : abounding or overgrown with woods **2** : of or containing wood or wood fibers **3** : characteristic or suggestive of wood — **wood·i·ness** \'wú-dē-nəs\ *n*

woof \'wúf\ *n* [alter. of ME *oof,* fr. OE *ōwef,* fr. ō- (fr. *on* on) + *wefan* to weave] **1** : WEFT 1 **2** : a woven fab-ric; *also* : its texture

woof·er \'wú-fər\ *n* : a loudspeaker that reproduces sounds of low pitch

wool \'wúl\ *n* **1** : the soft wavy or curly hair of some mammals and esp. the domestic sheep; *also* : some-thing (as a textile or garment) made of wool **2** : ma-terial that resembles a mass of wool — **wooled** \'wúld\ *adj*

¹wool·en *or* **wool·len** \'wú-lən\ *adj* **1** : made of wool **2** : of or relating to the manufacture or sale of woolen products ⟨~ mills⟩

²woolen *or* **woollen** *n* **1** : a fabric made of wool **2** : gar-ments of woolen fabric — usu. used in pl.

wool·gath·er·ing \-ˌga-thə-riŋ\ *n* : idle daydreaming

¹wool·ly *also* **wooly** \'wú-lē\ *adj* **wool·li·er; -est 1** : of, relating to, or bearing wool **2** : consisting of or resem-bling wool **3** : mentally confused ⟨~ thinking⟩ **4** : marked by a lack of order or restraint ⟨the wild and ~ West⟩

²wool·ly *also* **wool·ie** *or* **wooly** \'wú-lē\ *n, pl* **wool·lies** : a garment made from wool; *esp* : underclothing of knitted wool — usu. used in pl.

woolly bear *n* : any of numerous very hairy moth cat-erpillars

woo·zy \'wü-zē\ *adj* **woo·zi·er; -est 1** : BEFUDDLED **2** : somewhat dizzy, nauseated, or weak — **woo·zi·ness** \'wü-zē-nəs\ *n*

¹word \'wərd\ *n* **1** : something that is said; *esp* : a brief remark **2** : a speech sound or series of speech sounds that communicates a meaning; *also* : a graphic rep-resentation of such a sound or series of sounds **3** : OR-DER, COMMAND **4** *often cap* : the 2d person of the Trinity; *also* : GOSPEL **5** : NEWS, INFORMATION **6** : PROMISE **7** *pl* : QUARREL, DISPUTE **8** : a verbal signal : PASSWORD — **word·less** *adj*

²word *vb* : to express in words : PHRASE

word·age \'wər-dij\ *n* **1** : WORDS **2** : number of words **3** : WORDING

word·book \'wərd-ˌbúk\ *n* : VOCABULARY, DICTION-ARY

word·ing \'wər-diŋ\ *n* : verbal expression : PHRASEOL-OGY

word of mouth : oral communication

word·play \'wərd-ˌplā\ *n* : verbal wit

word processing *n* : the production of typewritten doc-uments with automated and usu. computerized text-editing equipment — **word process** *vb*

word processor *n* : a keyboard-operated terminal for use in word processing; *also* : software to perform word processing

wordy \'wər-dē\ *adj* **word·i·er; -est** : using many words : VERBOSE **syn** prolix, diffuse, redundant — **word·i·ness** \-dē-nəs\ *n*

wore *past of* WEAR

¹work \'wərk\ *n* **1** : TOIL, LABOR; *also* : EMPLOYMENT ⟨out of ~⟩ **2** : TASK, JOB ⟨have ~ to do⟩ **3** : the energy used when a force is applied over a given distance **4** : DEED, ACHIEVEMENT **5** : a fortified structure **6** *pl* : engineering structures **7** *pl* : a place where industrial labor is done : PLANT, FACTORY **8** *pl* : the moving parts of a mechanism **9** : something produced by mental effort or physical labor; *esp* : an artistic pro-duction (as a book or needlework) **10** : WORKMANSHIP ⟨careless ~⟩ **11** : material in the process of manufac-ture **12** *pl* : everything possessed, available, or be-longing ⟨the whole ~s went overboard⟩; *also* : drastic treatment ⟨gave him the ∼s⟩ **syn** occupation, employment, business, pursuit, calling — **in the works** : in process of preparation

²work *adj* **1** : used for work ⟨∼ elephants⟩ **2** : suitable or styled for wear while working ⟨∼ clothes⟩

³work *vb* **worked** \'wərkt\ *or* **wrought** \'ròt\; **working 1** : to bring to pass : EFFECT **2** : to fashion or create a useful or desired product through labor or exertion **3** : to prepare for use (as by kneading) **4** : to bring into a desired form by a manufacturing process ⟨∼ cold steel⟩ **5** : to set or keep in operation : OPERATE ⟨a pump ∼ed by hand⟩ **6** : to solve by reasoning or calculation ⟨∼ out a problem⟩ **7** : to cause to toil or labor ⟨∼ed the men hard⟩; *also* : to make use of ⟨∼ a mine⟩ **8** : to pay for with labor or service ⟨∼ off a debt⟩ **9** : to bring or get into some position or condition by stages ⟨the stream ∼ed itself clear⟩ ⟨the knot ∼ed loose⟩ **10** : CONTRIVE, ARRANGE ⟨∼ it so you can leave early⟩ **11** : to practice trickery or cajolery on ⟨∼ed the management for a free ticket⟩ **12** : EXCITE, PROVOKE ⟨∼ed himself into a rage⟩ **13** : to exert oneself physically or mentally; *esp* : to perform work regularly for wages **14** : to function according to plan or design **15** : to produce a desired effect : SUCCEED ⟨the plan ∼ed⟩ **16** : to make way slowly and with difficulty ⟨he ∼ed forward through the crowd⟩ **17** : to permit of being worked ⟨this wood ∼s easily⟩ **18** : to be in restless motion; *also* : FERMENT 1 — **work on 1** : AFFECT **2** : to try to influence or persuade — **work upon** : to have effect upon : operate on : INFLUENCE

work·a·ble \'wər-kə-bəl\ *adj* **1** : capable of being worked **2** : PRACTICABLE, FEASIBLE — **work·a·ble·ness** *n*

work·a·day \'wər-kə-ˌdā\ *adj* **1** : relating to or suited for working days **2** : PROSAIC, ORDINARY

work·a·hol·ic \ˌwər-kə-'hò-lik, -'hä-\ *n* : a compulsive worker

work·bench \-ˌbench\ *n* : a bench on which work esp. of mechanics, machinists, and carpenters is performed

work·book \-ˌbùk\ *n* **1** : a worker's manual **2** : a student's book of problems to be answered directly on the pages

work·day \'wərk-ˌdā\ *n* **1** : a day on which work is done as distinguished from a day off **2** : the period of time in a day when work is performed

work·er \'wər-kər\ *n* **1** : one that works; *esp* : a person who works for wages **2** : any of the sexually undeveloped individuals of a colony of social insects (as bees, ants, or termites) that perform the work of the community

worker's compensation *n* : a system of insurance that reimburses an employer for damages paid to an employee who was injured while working

work ethic *n* : belief in work as a moral good

work farm *n* : a farm on which persons guilty of minor law violations are confined

work·horse \'wərk-ˌhòrs\ *n* **1** : a horse used for hard work **2** : a person who does most of the work of a group task **3** : a strong useful machine or vehicle

work·house \-ˌhaùs\ *n* **1** *Brit* : POORHOUSE **2** : a house of correction for persons guilty of minor law violations

¹work·ing \'wər-kiŋ\ *n* **1** : manner of functioning — usu. used in pl. **2** *pl* : an excavation made in mining or tunneling

²working *adj* **1** : engaged in work ⟨a ∼ journalist⟩ **2** : adequate to allow work to be done ⟨a ∼ majority⟩ ⟨a ∼ knowledge of French⟩ **3** : adopted or assumed to help further work or activity ⟨a ∼ model of the car⟩ **4** : spent at work ⟨∼ life⟩

work·ing·man \'wər-kiŋ-ˌman\ *n* : WORKER 1

work·man \'wərk-mən\ *n* **1** : WORKER 1 **2** : ARTISAN, CRAFTSMAN

work·man·like \-ˌlīk\ *adj* : worthy of a good workman : SKILLFUL

work·man·ship \-ˌship\ *n* : the art or skill of a workman : CRAFTSMANSHIP; *also* : the quality of a piece of work ⟨a vase of exquisite ∼⟩

work·out \'wərk-ˌaùt\ *n* **1** : a practice or exercise to test or improve one's fitness, ability, or performance **2** : a test or trial to determine ability or capacity or suitability

work out *vb* **1** : to bring about esp. by resolving difficulties **2** : DEVELOP, ELABORATE **3** : to prove effective, practicable, or suitable **4** : to amount to a total or calculated figure — used with *at* **5** : to engage in a workout

work·room \'wərk-ˌrüm, -ˌrùm\ *n* : a room used for work

work·shop \-ˌshäp\ *n* **1** : a shop where manufacturing or handicrafts are carried on **2** : a seminar emphasizing exchange of ideas and practical methods

work·sta·tion \-ˌstā-shən\ *n* : an area with equipment for the performance of a specialized task; *also* : an intelligent terminal or personal computer usu. connected to a computer network

world \'wərld\ *n* [ME, fr. OE *woruld* human existence, this world, age, fr. a prehistoric compound whose first constituent is represented by OE *wer* man and whose second constituent is akin to OE *eald* old] **1** : the earth with its inhabitants and all things upon it **2** : people in general : MANKIND **3** : human affairs ⟨withdraw from the ∼⟩ **4** : UNIVERSE, CREATION **5** : a state of existence : scene of life and action ⟨the ∼ of the future⟩ **6** : a distinctive class of persons or their sphere of interest ⟨the musical ∼⟩ **7** : a part or section of the earth or its inhabitants by itself **8** : a great number or quantity ⟨a ∼ of troubles⟩ **9** : a celestial body

world–beat·er \-ˌbē-tər\ *n* : one that excels all others of its kind : CHAMPION

world·ling \-liŋ\ *n* : a person absorbed in the concerns of the present world

world·ly \-lē\ *adj* **1** : of, relating to, or devoted to this world and its pursuits rather than to religion or spiritual affairs **2** : WORLDLY-WISE, SOPHISTICATED — **world·li·ness** \-lē-nəs\ *n*

world·ly–wise \-ˌwīz\ *adj* : possessing a practical and often shrewd understanding of human affairs

world·wide \'wərld-'wīd\ *adj* : extended throughout the entire world — **worldwide** *adv*

¹worm \'wərm\ *n* **1** : any of various small long usu. naked and soft-bodied round or flat invertebrate animals (as an earthworm, nematode, tapeworm, or maggot) **2** : a human being who is an object of contempt, loathing, or pity : WRETCH **3** : something that inwardly torments or devours **4** *pl* : infestation with or disease caused by parasitic worms **5** : a spiral or wormlike thing (as the thread of a screw) — **wormy** *adj*

²worm *vb* **1** : to move or cause to move or proceed slowly and deviously **2** : to insinuate or introduce (oneself) by devious or subtle means **3** : to obtain or extract by artful or insidious pleading, asking, or persuading ⟨∼ed the truth out of him⟩ **4** : to treat (an animal) with a drug to destroy or expel parasitic worms

worm–eat·en \'wərm-ˌēt-ⁿn\ *adj* : eaten or burrowed by worms

worm gear *n* : a mechanical linkage consisting of a short rotating screw whose threads mesh with the teeth of a gear wheel

worm·hole \'wərm-ˌhōl\ *n* : a hole or passage burrowed by a worm

worm·wood \-ˌwùd\ *n* **1** : any of a genus of aromatic woody plants (as a sagebrush); *esp* : one of Europe used in absinthe **2** : something bitter or grievous : BITTERNESS

worn *past part of* WEAR

worn–out \'wòrn-'aùt\ *adj* : exhausted or used up by or as if by wear

wor·ri·some \'wər-ē-səm\ *adj* 1 : causing distress or worry 2 : inclined to worry or fret

¹**wor·ry** \'wər-ē\ *vb* **wor·ried; wor·ry·ing** 1 : to shake and mangle with the teeth ⟨a terrier ∼*ing* a rat⟩ 2 : to make anxious or upset ⟨her poor health *worries* me⟩ 3 : to feel or express great care or anxiety : FRET — **wor·ri·er** *n*

²**worry** *n, pl* **worries** 1 : ANXIETY 2 : a cause of anxiety : TROUBLE

wor·ry·wart \'wər-ē-ˌwȯrt\ *n* : one who is inclined to worry unduly

¹**worse** \'wərs\ *adj, comparative of* BAD *or of* ILL 1 : bad or evil in a greater degree : less good 2 : more unfavorable, unpleasant, or painful; *also* : SICKER

²**worse** *n* 1 : one that is worse 2 : a greater degree of ill or badness ⟨a turn for the ∼⟩

³**worse** *adv, comparative of* BAD *or of* ILL : in a worse manner : to a worse extent or degree

wors·en \'wərs-ᵊn\ *vb* : to make or become worse

¹**wor·ship** \'wər-shəp\ *n* [ME *worship* worthiness, respect, reverence paid to a divine being, fr. OE *weorthscipe* worthiness, respect, fr. *weorth* worthy, worth + *-scipe* -ship, suffix denoting quality or condition] 1 *chiefly Brit* : a person of importance — used as a title for officials 2 : reverence toward a divine being or supernatural power; *also* : the expression of such reverence 3 : extravagant respect or admiration or devotion ⟨∼ of the dollar⟩

²**worship** *vb* **-shiped** *or* **-shipped; -ship·ing** *or* **-ship·ping** 1 : to honor or reverence as a divine being or supernatural power 2 : IDOLIZE 3 : to perform or take part in worship — **wor·ship·er** *or* **wor·ship·per** *n*

wor·ship·ful \'wər-shəp-fəl\ *adj* 1 *archaic* : NOTABLE, DISTINGUISHED 2 *chiefly Brit* — used as a title for various persons or groups of rank or distinction 3 : VENERATING, WORSHIPING

¹**worst** \'wərst\ *adj, superlative of* BAD *or of* ILL 1 : most bad, evil, ill, or corrupt 2 : most unfavorable, unpleasant, or painful; *also* : most unsuitable, faulty, or unattractive 3 : least skillful or efficient

²**worst** *adv, superlative of* ILL *or of* BAD *or* BADLY 1 : to the extreme degree of badness or inferiority : in the worst manner 2 : MOST ⟨those who need help ∼⟩

³**worst** *n* : one that is worst

⁴**worst** *vb* : DEFEAT

wor·sted \'wu̇s-təd, 'wər-stəd\ *n* [ME, fr. *Worsted* (now *Worstead*), England] : a smooth compact yarn from long wool fibers; *also* : a fabric made from such yarn

wort \'wərt, 'wȯrt\ *n* : a solution obtained by infusion from malt and fermented to form beer

¹**worth** \'wərth\ *n* 1 : monetary value; *also* : the equivalent of a specified amount or figure ⟨$5 ∼ of gas⟩ 2 : the value of something measured by its qualities 3 : MERIT, EXCELLENCE

²**worth** *prep* 1 : equal in value to; *also* : having possessions or income equal to 2 : deserving of ⟨well ∼ the effort⟩

worth·less \'wərth-ləs\ *adj* 1 : lacking worth : VALUELESS; *also* : USELESS 2 : LOW, DESPICABLE — **worth·less·ness** *n*

worth·while \'wərth-'hwīl\ *adj* : being worth the time or effort spent

¹**wor·thy** \'wər-thē\ *adj* **wor·thi·er; -est** 1 : having worth or value : ESTIMABLE 2 : HONORABLE, MERITORIOUS 3 : having sufficient worth ⟨∼ of the honor⟩ — **wor·thi·ly** \'wər-thə-lē\ *adv* — **wor·thi·ness** \-thē-nəs\ *n*

²**worthy** *n, pl* **worthies** : a worthy person

would \'wu̇d\ *past of* WILL 1 : wish for : WANT 2 : strongly desire : WISH ⟨I ∼ I were young again⟩ 3 — used as an auxiliary to express (1) preference ⟨∼ rather run than fight⟩, (2) wish, desire, or intent ⟨those who ∼ forbid gambling⟩, (3) habitual action ⟨we ∼ meet often for lunch⟩, (4) a contingency or possibility ⟨if he were coming, he ∼ be here by now⟩,

(5) probability ⟨∼ have won if he hadn't tripped⟩, or (6) a request ⟨∼ you help us⟩ 4 : COULD 5 : SHOULD

would–be \'wu̇d-'bē\ *adj* : desiring or pretending to be ⟨a ∼ artist⟩

¹**wound** \'wünd\ *n* 1 : an injury involving cutting or breaking of bodily tissue (as by violence, accident, or surgery) 2 : an injury or hurt to feelings or reputation

²**wound** *vb* : to inflict a wound to or in

³**wound** \'wau̇nd\ *past and past part of* WIND

wove *past of* WEAVE

woven *past part of* WEAVE

¹**wow** \'wau̇\ *n* : a striking success : HIT

²**wow** *vb* : to arouse enthusiastic approval

WP *abbr* word processing; word processor

WPM *abbr* words per minute

wpn *abbr* weapon

wrack \'rak\ *n* [ME, fr. OE *wræc* misery, punishment, something driven by the sea] : violent or total destruction

wraith \'rāth\ *n, pl* **wraiths** \'rāths, 'rāthz\ 1 : GHOST, SPECTER 2 : an insubstantial appearance : SHADOW

¹**wran·gle** \'raŋ-gəl\ *vb* **wran·gled; wran·gling** 1 : to quarrel angrily or peevishly : BICKER 2 : ARGUE 3 : to obtain by persistent arguing 4 : to herd and care for (livestock) on the range — **wran·gler** *n*

²**wrangle** *n* : an angry, noisy, or prolonged dispute; *also* : CONTROVERSY

¹**wrap** \'rap\ *vb* **wrapped; wrap·ping** 1 : to cover esp. by winding or folding 2 : to envelop and secure for transportation or storage 3 : to enclose wholly : ENFOLD 4 : to coil, fold, draw, or twine about something 5 : SURROUND, ENVELOP ⟨*wrapped* in mystery⟩ 6 : INVOLVE, ENGROSS ⟨*wrapped* up in a hobby⟩ 7 : to complete filming or videotaping

²**wrap** *n* 1 : WRAPPER, WRAPPING 2 : an article of clothing that may be wrapped around a person 3 *pl* : SECRECY ⟨kept under ∼s⟩ 4 : completion of filming or videotaping

wrap·around \'ra-pə-ˌrau̇nd\ *n* : a garment (as a dress) adjusted to the figure by wrapping around

wrap·per \'ra-pər\ *n* 1 : that in which something is wrapped 2 : one that wraps 3 : an article of clothing worn wrapped around the body

wrap·ping \'ra-piŋ\ *n* : something used to wrap an object : WRAPPER

wrap–up \'rap-ˌəp\ *n* : SUMMARY

wrap up *vb* 1 : SUMMARIZE, SUM UP 2 : to bring to a usu. successful conclusion

wrasse \'ras\ *n* : any of a large family of usu. brightly colored marine fishes including many food fishes

wrath \'rath\ *n* 1 : violent anger : RAGE 2 : divine punishment **syn** indignation, ire, fury, anger

wrath·ful \-fəl\ *adj* 1 : filled with wrath : very angry 2 : showing, marked by, or arising from anger — **wrath·ful·ly** *adv* — **wrath·ful·ness** *n*

wreak \'rēk\ *vb* 1 : to exact as a punishment : INFLICT ⟨∼ vengeance on an enemy⟩ 2 : to give free scope or rein to ⟨∼*ed* his wrath⟩ 3 : BRING ABOUT, CAUSE ⟨∼ havoc⟩

wreath \'rēth\ *n, pl* **wreaths** \'rēthz, 'rēths\ : something (as boughs or flowers) intertwined into a circular shape

wreathe \'rēth\ *vb* **wreathed; wreath·ing** 1 : to shape or take on the shape of a wreath 2 : to crown, decorate, or cover with or as if with a wreath ⟨a face *wreathed* in smiles⟩

¹**wreck** \'rek\ *n* 1 : something (as goods) cast up on the land by the sea after a shipwreck 2 : SHIPWRECK 3 : the action of breaking up or destroying something 4 : broken remains (as of a vehicle after a crash) 5 : something disabled or in a state of ruin; *also* : an individual broken in health or strength

²**wreck** *vb* 1 : SHIPWRECK 2 : to ruin or damage by breaking up : involve in disaster or ruin

wreck·age \'re-kij\ *n* 1 : the act of wrecking : the state of being wrecked : RUIN 2 : the remains of a wreck

wreck·er \'re-kər\ *n* **1** : one that searches for or works upon the wrecks of ships **2** : TOW TRUCK **3** : one that wrecks; *esp* : one whose work is the demolition of buildings

wren \'ren\ *n* : any of a family of small mostly brown singing birds with short wings and often a tail that points upward

¹**wrench** \'rench\ *vb* **1** : to move with a violent twist **2** : to pull, strain, or tighten with violent twisting or force **3** : to injure or disable by a violent twisting or straining **4** : to snatch forcibly : WREST

²**wrench** *n* **1** : a forcible twisting; *also* : an injury (as to one's ankle) by twisting **2** : a tool for holding, twisting, or turning (as nuts or bolts)

¹**wrest** \'rest\ *vb* **1** : to pull or move by a forcible twisting movement **2** : to gain with difficulty by or as if by force or violence ⟨∼ control of the government from the dictator⟩

²**wrest** *n* : a forcible twist : WRENCH

¹**wres·tle** \'re-səl, 'ra-\ *vb* **wres·tled; wres·tling 1** : to scuffle with and try to throw down an opponent **2** : to compete against in wrestling **3** : to struggle for control (as of something difficult) ⟨∼ with a problem⟩ — **wres·tler** \'res-lər, 'ras-\ *n*

²**wrestle** *n* : the action or an instance of wrestling : STRUGGLE

wres·tling \'res-liŋ\ *n* : the sport in which two opponents wrestle each other

wretch \'rech\ *n* [ME *wrecche,* fr. OE *wrecca* outcast, exile] **1** : a miserable unhappy person **2** : a base, despicable, or vile person

wretch·ed \'re-chəd\ *adj* **1** : deeply afflicted, dejected, or distressed : MISERABLE **2** : WOEFUL, GRIEVOUS ⟨a ∼ accident⟩ **3** : DESPICABLE ⟨a ∼ trick⟩ **4** : poor in quality or ability : INFERIOR ⟨∼ workmanship⟩ — **wretch·ed·ly** *adv* — **wretch·ed·ness** *n*

wrig·gle \'ri-gəl\ *vb* **wrig·gled; wrig·gling 1** : to twist or move to and fro like a worm : SQUIRM ⟨*wriggled* in his chair⟩ ⟨∼ your toes⟩; *also* : to move along by twisting and turning ⟨a snake *wriggled* along the path⟩ **2** : to extricate oneself as if by wriggling ⟨∼ out of difficulty⟩ — **wriggle** *n*

wrig·gler *n* **1** : one that wriggles **2** : WIGGLER 1

wring \'riŋ\ *vb* **wrung** \'rəŋ\; **wring·ing** \'riŋ-iŋ\ **1** : to squeeze or twist esp. so as to make dry or to extract moisture or liquid ⟨∼ wet clothes⟩ **2** : to get by or as if by twisting or pressing ⟨∼ the truth out of him⟩ **3** : to twist so as to strain or sprain : CONTORT ⟨∼ his neck⟩ **4** : to twist together as a sign of anguish ⟨*wrung* her hands⟩ **5** : to affect painfully as if by wringing : TORMENT ⟨her plight *wrung* my heart⟩

wring·er \'riŋ-ər\ *n* : one that wrings; *esp* : a device for squeezing out liquid or moisture ⟨clothes ∼⟩

¹**wrin·kle** \'riŋ-kəl\ *n* **1** : a crease or small fold on a surface (as in the skin or in cloth) **2** : a clever or new method, trick, or idea — **wrin·kly** \-k(ə-)lē\ *adj*

²**wrinkle** *vb* **wrin·kled; wrin·kling** : to develop or cause to develop wrinkles

wrist \'rist\ *n* : the joint or region between the hand and the arm; *also* : a corresponding part in a lower animal

wrist·band \-,band\ *n* : a band or the part of a sleeve encircling the wrist

wrist·let \-lət\ *n* : WRISTBAND; *esp* : a close-fitting knitted band attached to the top of a glove or the end of a sleeve

wrist·watch \-,wäch\ *n* : a small watch attached to a bracelet or strap to fasten about the wrist

writ \'rit\ *n* **1** : something written **2** : a written legal order signed by a court officer

write \'rīt\ *vb* **wrote** \'rōt\; **writ·ten** \'rit-ᵊn\ *also* **writ** \'rit\; **writ·ing** \'rī-tiŋ\ [ME, fr. OE *wrītan* to scratch, draw, inscribe] **1** : to form characters, letters, or words on a surface ⟨learn to read and ∼⟩ **2** : to form the letters or the words of ⟨∼ your name⟩ ⟨∼ a check⟩ **3** : to put down on paper : express in writing **4** : to

make up and set down for others to read ⟨∼ a book⟩ ⟨∼ music⟩ **5** : to write a letter to **6** : to communicate by letter : CORRESPOND

write–in \'rīt-,in\ *n* : a vote cast by writing in the name of a candidate; *also* : a candidate whose name is written in

write in *vb* : to insert (a name not listed on a ballot) in an appropriate space; *also* : to cast (a vote) in this manner

write off *vb* **1** : to reduce the estimated value of : DEPRECIATE **2** : CANCEL ⟨*write off* a bad debt⟩

writ·er \'rī-tər\ *n* : one that writes esp. as a business or occupation : AUTHOR

writer's cramp *n* : a painful spasmodic cramp of muscles of the hand or fingers brought on by excessive writing

write–up \'rīt-,əp\ *n* : a written account (as in a newspaper); *esp* : a flattering article

writhe \'rīth\ *vb* **writhed; writh·ing 1** : to twist and turn this way and that ⟨∼ in pain⟩ **2** : to suffer with shame or confusion

writ·ing *n* **1** : the act of one that writes; *also* : HANDWRITING **2** : something that is written or printed **3** : a style or form of composition **4** : the occupation of a writer

wrnt *abbr* warrant

¹**wrong** \'róŋ\ *n* **1** : an injurious, unfair, or unjust act **2** : a violation of the legal rights of another person **3** : something that is wrong : wrong principles, practices, or conduct ⟨know right from ∼⟩ **4** : the state, position, or fact of being wrong

²**wrong** *adj* **wrong·er** \'róŋ-ər\; **wrong·est** \'róŋ-əst\ **1** : SINFUL, IMMORAL **2** : not right according to a standard or code : IMPROPER **3** : INCORRECT ⟨a ∼ solution⟩ **4** : UNSATISFACTORY **5** : UNSUITABLE, INAPPROPRIATE **6** : constituting a surface that is considered the back, bottom, inside, or reverse of something ⟨iron only on the ∼ side of the fabric⟩ **syn** false, erroneous, incorrect, inaccurate, untrue — **wrong·ly** *adv*

³**wrong** *adv* **1** : INCORRECTLY **2** : in a wrong direction, manner, or relation

⁴**wrong** *vb* **wronged; wrong·ing** \'róŋ-iŋ\ **1** : to do wrong to : INJURE, HARM **2** : to treat unjustly : DISHONOR, MALIGN **syn** oppress, persecute, aggrieve

wrong·do·er \'róŋ-,dü-ər\ *n* : a person who does wrong and esp. moral wrong — **wrong·do·ing** \-,dü-iŋ\ *n*

wrong·ful \'róŋ-fəl\ *adj* **1** : WRONG, UNJUST **2** : UNLAWFUL — **wrong·ful·ly** *adv* — **wrong·ful·ness** *n*

wrong·head·ed \-'he-dəd\ *adj* : stubborn in clinging to wrong opinion or principles — **wrong·head·ed·ly** *adv* — **wrong·head·ed·ness** *n*

wrote *past of* WRITE

wroth \'róth, 'róth\ *adj* : filled with wrath : ANGRY

wrought \'rót\ *adj* [ME, fr. pp. of *worken* to work] **1** : FASHIONED, FORMED ⟨carefully ∼ essays⟩ **2** : ORNAMENTED **3** : beaten into shape by tools : HAMMERED ⟨∼ metals⟩ **4** : deeply stirred : EXCITED ⟨gets easily ∼ up⟩

wrought iron *n* : a commercial form of iron that is tough, malleable, and relatively soft — **wrought–iron** *adj*

wrung *past and past part of* WRING

wry \'rī\ *adj* **wry·er** \'rī-ər\; **wry·est** \'rī-əst\ **1** : having a bent or twisted shape ⟨a ∼ smile⟩; *esp* : turned abnormally to one side : CONTORTED ⟨a ∼ neck⟩ **2** : cleverly and often ironically humorous — **wry·ly** *adv* — **wry·ness** *n*

wry·neck \'rī-,nek\ *n* **1** : either of two Old World woodpeckers that differ from typical woodpeckers in having a peculiar manner of twisting the head and neck **2** : an abnormal twisting of the neck and head to one side caused by muscle spasms

WSW *abbr* west-southwest

wt *abbr* weight

wurst \'wərst, 'wu̇rst\ *n* : SAUSAGE

WV *or* **W Va** *abbr* West Virginia
WW *abbr* World War
w/w *abbr* wall-to-wall
WY *or* **Wyo** *abbr* Wyoming

WYS·I·WYG \'wi-zē-ˌwig\ *adj* [*what you see is what you get*] : of, relating to, or being a computer display that shows a document exactly as it will appear when printed out

X

¹x \'eks\ *n, pl* **x's** *or* **xs** \'ek-səz\ *often cap* **1** : the 24th letter of the English alphabet **2** : an unknown quantity
²x *vb* **x-ed** *also* **x'd** *or* **xed** \'ekst\; **x-ing** *or* **x'ing** \'ek-siŋ\ : to cancel or obliterate with a series of *x*'s — usu. used with *out*
³x *abbr* **1** ex **2** experimental
⁴x *symbol* **1** times ⟨3 x 2 is 6⟩ **2** by ⟨a 3 x 5 index card⟩ **3** *often cap* power of magnification
Xan·a·du \'za-nə-ˌdü, -ˌdyü\ *n* [fr. *Xanadu*, locality in *Kubla Khan* (1798), poem by Eng. poet Samuel Taylor Coleridge †1834] : an idyllic, exotic, or luxurious place
Xan·thip·pe \zan-'thi-pē, -'ti-\ *or* **Xan·tip·pe** \-'ti-pē\ *n* [Gk *Xanthippē*, shrewish wife of Socrates] : an ill-tempered woman
x–ax·is \'eks-ˌak-səs\ *n* : the axis of a graph or of a system of coordinates in a plane parallel to which abscissas are measured
X–C *abbr* cross-country
X chromosome *n* : a sex chromosome that usually occurs paired in each female cell and single in each male cell in organisms (as human beings) in which the male normally has two unlike sex chromosomes
Xe *symbol* xenon
xe·non \'zē-ˌnän, 'ze-\ *n* [Gk, neut. of *xenos* strange] : a heavy gaseous chemical element occurring in minute quantities in air — see ELEMENT table
xe·no·pho·bia \ˌze-nə-'fō-bē-ə, ˌzē-\ *n* : fear and hatred of strangers or foreigners or of what is strange or foreign — **xe·no·phobe** \'ze-nə-ˌfōb, 'zē-\ *n* — **xe·no·pho·bic** \ˌze-nə-'fō-bik, ˌzē-\ *adj*
xe·ric \'zir-ik, 'zer-\ *adj* : characterized by or requiring only a small amount of moisture ⟨a ∼ habitat⟩
xe·rog·ra·phy \zə-'rä-grə-fē\ *n* : a process for copying printed matter by the action of light on an electrically charged surface in which the latent image usu. is developed with a powder — **xe·ro·graph·ic** \ˌzir-ə-'gra-fik\ *adj*
xe·ro·phyte \'zir-ə-ˌfīt\ *n* : a plant adapted for growth with a limited water supply — **xe·ro·phyt·ic** \ˌzir-ə-'fi-tik\ *adj*
xi \'zī, 'ksī\ *n* : the 14th letter of the Greek alphabet — Ξ or ξ
XL *abbr* **1** extra large **2** extra long
Xmas \'kris-məs *also* 'eks-məs\ *n* [*X* (symbol for *Christ*, fr. the Gk letter chi (X), initial of *Christos* Christ) + *-mas* (in *Christmas*)] : CHRISTMAS
XO *abbr* executive officer
x–ra·di·a·tion \ˌeks-ˌrā-dē-'ā-shən\ *n, often cap* **1** : exposure to X rays **2** : radiation consisting of X rays
x–ray \'eks-ˌrā\ *vb, often cap* : to examine, treat, or photograph with X rays
X ray \'eks-ˌrā\ *n* **1** : a radiation of the same nature as light rays but of extremely short wavelength that is able to penetrate through various thicknesses of solids and to act on photographic film **2** : a photograph taken with X rays — **X–ray** *adj*
XS *abbr* extra small
xu \'sü\ *n, pl* **xu** — see *dong* at MONEY table
xy·lem \'zī-ləm, -ˌlem\ *n* : a woody tissue of vascular plants that transports water and dissolved materials upward, functions in support and storage, and lies central to the phloem
xy·lo·phone \'zī-lə-ˌfōn\ *n* [Gk *xylon* wood + *phōnē* voice, sound] : a musical instrument consisting of a series of wooden bars graduated in length to produce the musical scale, supported on belts of straw or felt, and sounded by striking with two small wooden hammers — **xy·lo·phon·ist** \-ˌfō-nist\ *n*

Y

¹y \'wī\ *n, pl* **y's** *or* **ys** \'wīz\ *often cap* : the 25th letter of the English alphabet
²y *abbr* **1** yard **2** year
¹Y \'wī\ *n* : YMCA, YWCA
²Y *symbol* yttrium
¹-y *also* **-ey** \ē\ *adj suffix* **1** : characterized by : full of ⟨dirt*y*⟩ ⟨clay*ey*⟩ **2** : having the character of : composed of ⟨ic*y*⟩ **3** : like : like that of ⟨home*y*⟩ ⟨wintr*y*⟩ ⟨stag*y*⟩ **4** : tending or inclined to ⟨sleep*y*⟩ ⟨chatt*y*⟩ **5** : giving occasion for (specified) action ⟨tear*y*⟩ **6** : performing (specified) action ⟨curl*y*⟩
²-y \ē\ *n suffix, pl* **-ies 1** : state : condition : quality ⟨beggar*y*⟩ **2** : activity, place of business, or goods dealt with ⟨laundr*y*⟩ **3** : whole body or group ⟨soldier*y*⟩
³-y *n suffix, pl* **-ies** : instance of a (specified) action ⟨entreat*y*⟩ ⟨inquir*y*⟩
YA *abbr* young adult
¹yacht \'yät\ *n* [obs. D *jaght*, fr. Middle Low German *jacht*, short for *jachtschip*, lit., hunting ship] : a usu. large recreational watercraft
²yacht *vb* : to race or cruise in a yacht
yacht·ing *n* : the sport of racing or cruising in a yacht
yachts·man \'yäts-mən\ *n* : a person who owns or sails a yacht
ya·hoo \'yā-hü, 'yä-\ *n, pl* **yahoos** [fr. *Yahoo*, one of a race of brutes having the form of men in Jonathan Swift's *Gulliver's Travels*] : a boorish, crass, or stupid person

Yah·weh \'yä-ˌwā\ *also* **Yah·veh** \-ˌvā\ *n* : GOD 1 — used esp. by the Hebrews
¹yak \'yak\ *n, pl* **yaks** *also* **yak** : a large long-haired wild or domesticated ox of Tibet and adjacent Asian uplands

yak

²yak *also* **yack** \'yak\ *n* : persistent or voluble talk — **yak** *also* **yack** *vb*
yam \'yam\ *n* **1** : the edible starchy root of a twining vine that largely replaces the potato as food in the tropics; *also* : a plant that produces yams **2** : a usu. deep orange sweet potato
yam·mer \'ya-mər\ *vb* [ME *yameren*, alter. of *yomeren* to murmur, be sad, fr. OE *gēomrian*] **1** : WHIMPER **2** : CHATTER — **yammer** *n*

¹**yank** \ˈyaŋk\ *n* : a strong sudden pull : JERK

²**yank** *vb* : to pull with a quick vigorous movement

Yank \ˈyaŋk\ *n* : YANKEE

Yan·kee \ˈyaŋ-kē\ *n* **1** : a native or inhabitant of New England; *also* : a native or inhabitant of the northern U.S. **2** : AMERICAN 2

yan·qui \ˈyän-kē\ *n, often cap* [Sp] : a citizen of the U.S. as distinguished from a Latin American

¹**yap** \ˈyap\ *vb* **yapped; yap·ping 1** : BARK, YELP **2** : GAB

²**yap** *n* **1** : a quick sharp bark **2** : CHATTER

¹**yard** \ˈyärd\ *n* [ME, fr. OE *geard* enclosure, yard] **1** : a small enclosed area open to the sky and adjacent to a building **2** : the grounds of a building **3** : the grounds surrounding a house usu. covered with grass **4** : an enclosure for livestock **5** : an area set aside for a particular business or activity **6** : a system of railroad tracks for storing cars and making up trains

²**yard** *n* [ME *yarde*, fr. OE *gierd* twig, measure, yard] **1** — see WEIGHT table **2** : a long spar tapered toward the ends that supports and spreads the head of a sail — **the whole nine yards** : all of a set of circumstances, conditions, or details

yard·age \ˈyär-dij\ *n* : an aggregate number of yards; *also* : the length, extent, or volume of something as measured in yards

yard·arm \ˈyärd-ˌärm\ *n* : either end of the yard of a square-rigged ship

yard·man \-mən, -ˌman\ *n* : a person employed in or about a yard

yard·mas·ter \-ˌmas-tər\ *n* : the person in charge of a railroad yard

yard·stick \-ˌstik\ *n* **1** : a graduated measuring stick three feet long **2** : a standard for making a critical judgment : CRITERION **syn** gauge, touchstone, benchmark, measure

yar·mul·ke *also* **yar·mel·ke** \ˈyä-mə-kə, ˈyär-, -məl-\ *n* : a skullcap worn esp. by Jewish males in the synagogue and the home

yarn \ˈyärn\ *n* **1** : a continuous often plied strand composed of fibers or filaments and used in weaving and knitting to form cloth **2** : STORY; *esp* : a tall tale

yar·row \ˈyar-ō\ *n* : a strong-scented herb related to the daisies that has white or pink flowers in flat clusters

yaw \ˈyo\ *vb* : to deviate erratically from a course ⟨the ship ∼ed in the heavy seas⟩ — **yaw** *n*

yawl \ˈyol\ *n* : a 2-masted sailboat with the shorter mast aft of the rudder

¹**yawn** \ˈyon\ *vb* : to open wide; *esp* : to open the mouth wide usu. as an involuntary reaction to fatigue or boredom — **yawn·er** *n*

²**yawn** *n* : a deep usu. involuntary intake of breath through the wide-open mouth

yawp *or* **yaup** \ˈyop\ *vb* **1** : to make a raucous noise : SQUAWK **2** : CLAMOR, COMPLAIN — **yawp·er** *n*

yaws \ˈyoz\ *n pl* : an infectious tropical disease caused by a spirochete closely resembling the causative agent of syphilis

y-ax·is \ˈwī-ˌak-səs\ *n* : the axis of a graph or of a system of coordinates in a plane parallel to which the ordinates are measured

Yb *symbol* ytterbium

YB *abbr* yearbook

Y chromosome *n* : a sex chromosome that is characteristic of male cells in organisms (as humans) in which the male typically has two unlike sex chromosomes

yd *abbr* yard

¹**ye** \ˈyē\ *pron* : YOU 1

²**ye** \yē, yə, *originally same as* THE\ *definite article, archaic* : THE — used by early printers to represent the manuscript word *þe* (*the*)

¹**yea** \ˈyā\ *adv* **1** : YES — used in oral voting **2** : INDEED, TRULY

²**yea** *n* : an affirmative vote; *also* : a person casting such a vote

year \ˈyir\ *n* **1** : the period of about 365¼ solar days required for one revolution of the earth around the sun **2** : a cycle of 365 or 366 days beginning with January 1; *also* : a calendar year specified usu. by a number **3** *pl* : a time of special significance ⟨their glory ∼s⟩ **4** *pl* : AGE ⟨advanced in ∼s⟩ **5** : a period of time other than a calendar year ⟨the school ∼⟩

year·book \-ˌbůk\ *n* **1** : a book published annually esp. as a report **2** : a school publication recording the history and activities of a graduating class

year·ling \ˈyir-liŋ, ˈyər-lən\ *n* **1** : one that is a year old **2** : a racehorse between January 1st of the year after the year in which it was born and the next January 1st

year·long \ˈyir-ˈloŋ\ *adj* : lasting through a year

¹**year·ly** \ˈyir-lē\ *adj* : ANNUAL

²**yearly** *adv* : every year

yearn \ˈyərn\ *vb* **1** : to feel a longing or craving **2** : to feel tenderness or compassion **syn** long, pine, hanker, hunger, thirst

yearn·ing *n* : a tender or urgent longing

year–round \ˈyir-ˈraůnd\ *adj* : effective, employed, or operating for the full year : not seasonal ⟨a ∼ resort⟩

yeast \ˈyēst\ *n* **1** : a surface froth or a sediment in sugary liquids (as fruit juices) that consists largely of cells of a tiny fungus and is used in making alcoholic liquors and as a leaven in baking **2** : a commercial product containing yeast plants in a moist or dry medium **3** : a minute one-celled fungus present and functionally active in yeast that reproduces by budding; *also* : any of several similar fungi **4** *archaic* : the foam of waves : SPUME **5** : something that causes ferment or activity

yeasty \ˈyē-stē\ *adj* **yeast·i·er; -est 1** : of, relating to, or resembling yeast **2** : UNSETTLED **3** : full of vitality; *also* : FRIVOLOUS

yegg \ˈyeg\ *n* : one that breaks open safes to steal; *also* : ROBBER

¹**yell** \ˈyel\ *vb* : to utter a loud cry or scream : SHOUT

²**yell** *n* **1** : SHOUT **2** : a cheer used esp. to encourage an athletic team (as at a college)

¹**yel·low** \ˈye-lō\ *adj* **1** : of the color yellow **2** : having a yellow complexion or skin **3** : SENSATIONAL ⟨∼ journalism⟩ **4** : COWARDLY — **yel·low·ish** \ˈye-lə-wish\ *adj*

²**yellow** *n* **1** : a color between green and orange in the spectrum : the color of ripe lemons or sunflowers **2** : something yellow; *esp* : the yolk of an egg **3** *pl* : any of several plant diseases marked by stunted growth and yellowing of foliage

³**yellow** *vb* : to make or turn yellow

yellow birch *n* : a No. American birch with thin lustrous gray or yellow bark; *also* : its strong hard wood

yellow fever *n* : an acute destructive virus disease marked by prostration, jaundice, fever, and often hemorrhage and transmitted by a mosquito

yellow jack *n* : YELLOW FEVER

yellow jacket *n* : any of various small social wasps having the body barred with bright yellow

yelp \ˈyelp\ *vb* [ME, to boast, cry out, fr. OE *gielpan* to boast, exult] : to utter a sharp quick shrill cry — **yelp** *n*

Ye·me·ni \ˈye-mə-nē\ *n* : YEMENITE — **Yemeni** *adj*

Ye·men·ite \ˈye-mə-ˌnīt\ *n* : a native or inhabitant of Yemen — **Yemenite** *adj*

¹**yen** \ˈyen\ *n, pl* **yen** — see MONEY table

²**yen** *n* [obs. E argot *yen-yen* craving for opium, fr. Chin (Guangdong dial.) *yīn-yáhn*, fr. *yīn* opium + *yáhn* craving] : a strong desire : LONGING

yeo·man \ˈyō-mən\ *n* **1** : an attendant or officer in a royal or noble household **2** : a naval petty officer who performs clerical duties **3** : a person who owns and cultivates a small farm; *esp* : one of a class of English freeholders below the gentry

yeo·man·ry \-rē\ *n* : the body of yeomen and esp. of small landed proprietors

-yer — see -ER

yoke 1

¹yes \'yes\ *adv* — used as a function word esp. to express assent or agreement or to introduce a more emphatic or explicit phrase

²yes *n* : an affirmative reply

ye·shi·va *or* **ye·shi·vah** \yə-'shē-və\ *n, pl* **yeshivas** *or* **ye·shi·voth** \-ˌshē-'vōt, -'vōth\ : a Jewish school esp. for religious instruction

yes–man \'yes-ˌman\ *n* : a person who endorses uncritically every opinion or proposal of a superior

¹yes·ter·day \'yes-tər-dē, -ˌdā\ *adv* 1 : on the day preceding today 2 : only a short time ago

²yesterday *n* 1 : the day last past 2 : time not long past

yes·ter·year \'yes-tər-ˌyir\ *n* 1 : last year 2 : the recent past

¹yet \'yet\ *adv* 1 : in addition : BESIDES; *also* : EVEN 6 2 : up to now; *also* : STILL 3 : so soon as now (not time to go ∼) 4 : EVENTUALLY 5 : NEVERTHELESS, HOWEVER

²yet *conj* : but nevertheless : BUT

ye·ti \'ye-tē, 'yā-\ *n* [Tibetan] : ABOMINABLE SNOWMAN

yew \'yü\ *n* 1 : any of a genus of evergreen trees and shrubs with dark stiff poisonous needles and fleshy fruits 2 : the wood of a yew; *esp* : that of an Old World yew

Yid·dish \'yi-dish\ *n* [Yiddish *yidish,* short for *yidish daytsh,* lit., Jewish German] : a language derived from medieval German and spoken by Jews esp. of eastern European origin — **Yiddish** *adj*

¹yield \'yēld\ *vb* 1 : to give as fitting, owed, or required 2 : GIVE UP; *esp* : to give up possession of on claim or demand 3 : to bear as a natural product 4 : PRODUCE, SUPPLY 5 : to bring in : RETURN 6 : to give way (as to force or influence) 7 : to give place **syn** relinquish, cede, waive, surrender

²yield *n* : something yielded; *esp* : the amount or quantity produced or returned

yield·ing \'yēl-diŋ\ *adj* 1 : not rigid or stiff : FLEXIBLE 2 : SUBMISSIVE, COMPLIANT

yikes \'yīks\ *interj* — used to express fear or astonishment

yip \'yip\ *vb* **yipped; yip·ping** : YAP

YMCA \ˌwī-ˌem-(ˌ)sē-'ā\ *n* : Young Men's Christian Association

YMHA \ˌwī-ˌem-ˌāch-'ā\ *n* : Young Men's Hebrew Association

yo \'yō\ *interj* — used to call attention, indicate attentiveness, or express affirmation

YOB *abbr* year of birth

yo·del \'yōd-əl\ *vb* **yo·deled** *or* **yo·delled; yo·del·ing** *or* **yo·del·ling** : to sing by suddenly changing from chest voice to falsetto and back; *also* : to shout or call in this manner — **yodel** *n* — **yo·del·er** *n*

yo·ga \'yō-gə\ *n* [Skt, lit., yoking, fr. *yunakti* he yokes] 1 *cap* : a Hindu theistic philosophy teaching the suppression of all activity of body, mind, and will in order that the self may realize its distinction from them and attain liberation 2 : a system of exercises for attaining bodily or mental control and well-being

yo·gi \'yō-gē\ *also* **yo·gin** \-gən, -ˌgin\ *n* 1 : a person who practices yoga 2 *cap* : an adherent of Yoga philosophy

yo·gurt *also* **yo·ghurt** \'yō-gərt\ *n* [Turk *yoğurt*] : a soured slightly acid often flavored semisolid milk food made of skimmed cow's milk and milk solids to which cultures of bacteria have been added

¹yoke \'yōk\ *n, pl* **yokes** 1 : a wooden bar or frame by which two draft animals (as oxen) are coupled at the heads or necks for working together; *also* : a frame fitted to a person's shoulders to carry a load in two equal portions 2 : a clamp that embraces two parts to hold or unite them in position 3 *pl usu* **yoke** : two animals yoked together 4 : SERVITUDE, BONDAGE 5 : TIE, LINK ⟨the ∼ of matrimony⟩ 6 : a fitted or shaped piece esp. at the shoulder of a garment **syn** couple, pair, brace

²yoke *vb* **yoked; yok·ing** 1 : to put a yoke on : couple

with a yoke 2 : to attach a draft animal to ⟨∼ a plow⟩ 3 : JOIN; *esp* : MARRY

yo·kel \'yō-kəl\ *n* : a naive or gullible country person

yolk \'yōk\ *n* 1 : the yellow rounded inner mass of the egg of a bird or reptile 2 : the stored food material of an egg consisting chiefly of proteins, lecithin, and cholesterol — **yolked** \'yōkt\ *adj*

Yom Kip·pur \ˌyōm-ki-'pu̇r, ˌyäm-, -'ki-pər\ *n* [Heb *yōm kippūr,* lit., day of atonement] : a Jewish holiday observed in September or October with fasting and prayer as a day of atonement

¹yon \'yän\ *adj* : YONDER

²yon *adv* 1 : YONDER 2 : THITHER ⟨ran hither and ∼⟩

¹yon·der \'yän-dər\ *adv* : at or to that place

²yonder *adj* 1 : more distant ⟨the ∼ side of the river⟩ 2 : being at a distance within view ⟨∼ hills⟩

yore \'yōr\ *n* [ME, fr. *yore,* adv., long ago, fr. OE *geāra,* fr. *gēar* year] : time long past ⟨in days of ∼⟩

York·ie \'yȯr-kē\ *n* : YORKSHIRE TERRIER

York·shire terrier \'yȯrk-ˌshir-, -shər-\ *n* : any of a breed of compact toy terriers with long straight silky hair

you \'yü\ *pron* 1 : the person or persons addressed ⟨∼ are a nice person⟩ ⟨∼ are nice people⟩ 2 : ONE 2 ⟨∼ turn this knob to open it⟩

¹young \'yəŋ\ *adj* **youn·ger** \'yəŋ-gər\; **youn·gest** \'yəŋ-gəst\ 1 : being in the first or an early stage of life, growth, or development 2 : having little experience 3 : recently come into being 4 : YOUTHFUL 5 *cap* : belonging to or representing a new or revived usu. political group or movement — **young·ish** \'yəŋ-ish\ *adj*

²young *n, pl* **young** : young persons; *also* : young animals

young·ling \'yəŋ-liŋ\ *n* : one that is young — **youngling** *adj*

young·ster \-stər\ *n* 1 : a young person 2 : CHILD

your \'yu̇r, 'yōr, yər\ *adj* : of or relating to you or yourself

yours \'yu̇rz, 'yōrz\ *pron* : one or the ones belonging to you

your·self \yər-'self\ *pron, pl* **yourselves** \-'selvz\ : YOU — used reflexively, for emphasis, or in absolute constructions ⟨you'll hurt ∼⟩ ⟨do it ∼⟩

youth \'yüth\ *n, pl* **youths** \'yüthz, 'yüths\ 1 : the period of life between childhood and maturity 2 : a young man; *also* : young persons 3 : YOUTHFULNESS

youth·ful \'yüth-fəl\ *adj* 1 : of, relating to, or appropriate to youth 2 : being young and not yet mature 3 : FRESH, VIGOROUS — **youth·ful·ly** *adv* — **youth·ful·ness** *n*

youth hostel *n* : HOSTEL 2

yowl \'yau̇l\ *vb* : to utter a loud long mournful cry : WAIL — **yowl** *n*

yo–yo \'yō-(ˌ)yō\ *n, pl* **yo–yos** : a thick grooved double disk with a string attached to its center which is made to fall and rise to the hand by unwinding and rewinding on the string

yr *abbr* 1 year 2 your

yrbk *abbr* yearbook

YT *abbr* Yukon Territory

yt·ter·bi·um \i-'tər-bē-əm\ *n* : a rare metallic chemical element — see ELEMENT table

yt·tri·um \'i-trē-əm\ *n* : a rare metallic chemical element — see ELEMENT table

yu·an \'yü-ən, yu̇-'än\ *n, pl* **yuan** 1 — see MONEY table 2 : the dollar of the Republic of China (Taiwan)

yuc·ca \\'yə-kə\ *n* : any of a genus of plants related to the agaves that grow esp. in warm dry regions and bear large clusters of white cup-shaped flowers atop a long stiff stalk

yuck \\'yək\ *interj* — used to express rejection or disgust

Yu·go·slav \\yü-gō-'släv, -'slav\ *n* : a native or inhabitant of Yugoslavia — **Yugoslav** *adj* — **Yu·go·sla·vi·an** \\-'slä-vē-ən\ *adj or n*

yule \\'yül\ *n, often cap* : CHRISTMAS

Yule log *n* : a large log formerly put onthe hearth on Christmas Eve as the foundation of the fire

yule·tide \\'yül-ˌtīd\ *n, often cap* : CHRISTMASTIDE

yum·my \\'yə-mē\ *adj* **yum·mi·er; -est** : highly attractive or pleasing

yup·pie \\'yə-pē\ *n* [prob. fr. *young urban professional* + *-ie* (as in hipp*ie*)] : a young college-educated adult employed in a well-paying profession and living and working in or near a large city

yurt \\'yùrt\ *n* : a light round tent of skins or felt stretched over a lattice framework used by pastoral peoples of inner Asia

YWCA \\ˌwī-ˌdə-bəl-yü-(ˌ)sē-'ā\ *n* : Young Women's Christian Association

YWHA \\-ˌäch-'ā\ *n* : Young Women's Hebrew Association

Z

¹z \\'zē\ *n, pl* **z's** *or* **zs** *often cap* : the 26th letter of the English alphabet

²z *abbr* **1** zero **2** zone

Z *symbol* atomic number

Zach *abbr* Zacharias

Zach·a·ri·as \\ˌza-kə-'rī-əs\ *n* : ZECHARIAH

zaire \\'zīr, zä-'ir\ *n, pl* **zaires** *or* **zaire** — see MONEY table

Zair·ian \\zä-'ir-ē-ən\ *n* : a native or inhabitant of Zaire — **Zairian** *adj*

Zam·bi·an \\'zam-bē-ən\ *n* : a native or inhabitant of Zambia — **Zambian** *adj*

¹za·ny \\'zā-nē\ *n, pl* **zanies** [It *zanni*, a traditional masked clown, fr. It dial. *Zanni*, nickname for It *Giovanni* John] **1** : CLOWN, BUFFOON **2** : a silly or foolish person

²zany *adj* **za·ni·er; -est 1** : characteristic of a zany **2** : CRAZY, FOOLISH — **za·ni·ly** \\'zā-nə-lē, 'zān-əl-ē\ *adv* — **za·ni·ness** \\'zā-nē-nəs\ *n*

zap \\'zap\ *vb* **zapped; zap·ping 1** : DESTROY, KILL **2** : to irradiate esp. with microwaves

zeal \\'zēl\ *n* : eager and ardent interest in the pursuit of something : FERVOR **syn** enthusiasm, passion, ardor

zeal·ot \\'ze-lət\ *n* : a zealous person; *esp* : a fanatical partisan **syn** enthusiast, bigot

zeal·ous \\'ze-ləs\ *adj* : filled with, characterized by, or due to zeal — **zeal·ous·ly** *adv* — **zeal·ous·ness** *n*

ze·bra \\'zē-brə\ *n, pl* **zebras** *also* **zebra** : any of several African mammals related to the horse but conspicuously striped with black or brown and white or buff

ze·bu \\'zē-bü, -byü\ *n* : an ox of any of various breeds developed in India that have a large fleshy hump over the shoulders, a dewlap, drooping ears, and marked resistance to heat and to insect attack

zebu

Zech *abbr* Zechariah

Zech·a·ri·ah \\ˌze-kə-'rī-ə\ *n* — see BIBLE table

zed \\'zed\ *n, chiefly Brit* : the letter *z*

zeit·geist \\'tsīt-ˌgīst, 'zīt-\ *n* [G, fr. *Zeit* time + *Geist* spirit] : the general intellectual, moral, and cultural state of an era

Zen \\'zen\ *n* : a Japanese Buddhist sect that teaches self-discipline, meditation, and attainment of enlightenment through direct intuitive insight

ze·na·na \\zə-'nä-nə\ *n* : HAREM

ze·nith \\'zē-nəth\ *n* **1** : the point in the heavens directly overhead **2** : the highest point : ACME **syn** culmination, pinnacle, apex

ze·o·lite \\'zē-ə-ˌlīt\ *n* : any of various feldsparlike silicates used esp. as water softeners

Zeph *abbr* Zephaniah

Zeph·a·ni·ah \\ˌze-fə-'nī-ə\ *n* — see BIBLE table

zeph·yr \\'ze-fər\ *n* : a breeze from the west; *also* : a gentle breeze

zep·pe·lin \\'ze-plən, -pə-lən\ *n* [Count Ferdinand von *Zeppelin* †1917 Ger. airship manufacturer] : a cylindrical rigid blimplike airship

¹ze·ro \\'zē-rō, 'zir-ō\ *n, pl* **zeros** *also* **zeroes** [ultim. fr. Ar *ṣifr*] **1** : the numerical symbol 0 **2** : the number represented by the symbol 0 **3** : the point at which the graduated degrees or measurements on a scale (as of a thermometer) begin **4** : the lowest point

²zero *adj* **1** : of, relating to, or being a zero **2** : having no magnitude or quantity **3** : ABSENT, LACKING; *esp* : having no modified inflectional form

³zero *vb* : to adjust the sights of a firearm to hit the point aimed at ⟨~ in⟩

zero hour *n* : the time at which an event (as a military operation) is scheduled to begin

zest \\'zest\ *n* **1** : a quality of enhancing enjoyment : PIQUANCY **2** : keen enjoyment : GUSTO — **zest·ful** \\-fəl\ *adj* — **zest·ful·ly** *adv* — **zest·ful·ness** *n*

ze·ta \\'zā-tə, 'zē-\ *n* : the 6th letter of the Greek alphabet — Z or ζ

zi·do·vu·dine \\zi-'dō-vyü-ˌdēn\ *n* : AZT

¹zig·zag \\'zig-ˌzag\ *n* : one of a series of short sharp turns, angles, or alterations in a course; *also* : something marked by such a series

²zigzag *adv* : in or by a zigzag path

³zigzag *adj* : having short sharp turns or angles

⁴zigzag *vb* **zig·zagged; zig·zag·ging** : to form into or proceed along a zigzag

zil·lion \\'zil-yən\ *n* : a large indeterminate number

Zim·ba·bwe·an \\zim-'bä-bwē-ən\ *n* : a native or inhabitant of Zimbabwe — **Zimbabwean** *adj*

zinc \\'ziŋk\ *n* : a bluish white crystalline metallic chemical element that is commonly found in minerals and is used esp. as a protective coating for iron and steel — see ELEMENT table

zinc ointment *n* : ZINC OXIDE OINTMENT

zinc oxide *n* : a white solid used esp. as a pigment, in compounding rubber, and in ointments

zinc oxide ointment *n* : an ointment containing zinc oxide and used for skin disorders

zing \\'ziŋ\ *n* **1** : a shrill humming noise **2** : VITALITY **4** — **zing** *vb*

zing·er \\'ziŋ-ər\ *n* : a pointed witty remark or retort

zin·nia \'zi-nē-ə, 'zēn-yə\ *n* : any of a small genus of tropical American herbs related to the daisies and widely grown for their showy long-lasting flower heads

Zi·on \'zī-ən\ *n* **1** : the Jewish people **2** : the Jewish homeland as a symbol of Judaism or of Jewish national aspiration **3** : HEAVEN **4** : UTOPIA

Zi·on·ism \'zī-ə-ˌni-zəm\ *n* : an international movement orig. for the establishment of a Jewish national or religious community in Palestine and later for the support of modern Israel — **Zi·on·ist** \-nist\ *adj or n*

¹zip \'zip\ *vb* **zipped; zip·ping** : to move, act, or function with speed or vigor

²zip *n* **1** : a sudden sharp hissing sound **2** : ENERGY, VIM

³zip *n* : NOTHING, ZERO

⁴zip *vb* **zipped; zip·ping** : to close or open with a zipper

zip code *n, often cap Z&I&P* [*zone improvement plan*] : a number that identifies each postal delivery area in the U.S.

zip·per \'zi-pər\ *n* : a fastener consisting of two rows of metal or plastic teeth on strips of tape and a sliding piece that closes an opening by drawing the teeth together

zip·py \'zi-pē\ *adj* **zip·pi·er; -est** : BRISK, SNAPPY

zir·con \'zər-ˌkän\ *n* : a zirconium-containing mineral transparent varieties of which are used as gems

zir·co·ni·um \ˌzər-'kō-nē-əm\ *n* : a gray corrosion-resistant metallic chemical element used esp. in alloys and ceramics — see ELEMENT table

zit \'zit\ *n* : PIMPLE

zith·er \'zi-thər, -thər\ *n* : a musical instrument having 30 to 40 strings played with plectrum and fingers

zi·ti \'zē-tē\ *n, pl* **ziti** [It] : medium-size tubular pasta

zlo·ty \'zlò-tē\ *n, pl* **zlo·tys** \-tēz\ *or* **zloty** — see MONEY table

Zn *symbol* zinc

zo·di·ac \'zō-dē-ˌak\ *n* [ME, fr. MF *zodiaque*, fr. L *zodiacus*, fr. Gk *zōidiakos*, fr. *zōidion* carved figure, sign of the zodiac, fr. dim. of *zōion* living being, figure] **1** : an imaginary belt in the heavens that encompasses the paths of most of the planets and that is divided into 12 constellations or signs **2** : a figure representing the signs of the zodiac and their symbols — **zo·di·a·cal** \zō-'dī-ə-kəl\ *adj*

zom·bie *also* **zom·bi** \'zäm-bē\ *n* : a person who is believed to have died and been brought back to life without speech or free will

zon·al \'zōn-ᵊl\ *adj* : of, relating to, or having the form of a zone — **zon·al·ly** *adv*

¹zone \'zōn\ *n* [ME, fr. L *zona* belt, zone, fr. Gk *zōnē*] **1** : any of five great divisions of the earth's surface made according to latitude and temperature and including the torrid zone about the equator, the two temperate zones lying between the torrid zone and the polar circles, and the two frigid zones lying between the polar circles and the poles **2** : an encircling band or girdle ⟨a ∼ of trees⟩ **3** : a section of an area or territory created for a particular purpose ⟨business ∼⟩ ⟨postal ∼⟩

²zone *vb* **zoned; zon·ing 1** : ENCIRCLE **2** : to arrange in or mark off into zones; *esp* : to divide (as a city) into sections reserved for different purposes

zonked \'zäŋkt\ *adj* : being or acting as if under the influence of alcohol or a drug : HIGH

zoo \'zü\ *n, pl* **zoos** : a zoological garden or collection of living animals usu. for public display

zoo·ge·og·ra·phy \ˌzō-ə-jē-'ä-grə-fē\ *n* : a branch of biogeography concerned with the geographical distri-

bution of animals — **zoo·ge·og·ra·pher** \-fər\ *n* — **zoo·geo·graph·ic** \-ˌjē-ə-'gra-fik\ *also* **zoo·geo·graph·i·cal** \-fi-kəl\ *adj*

zoo·keep·er \'zü-ˌkē-pər\ *n* : a person who cares for animals in a zoo

zool *abbr* zoological; zoology

zoological garden *n* : a garden or park where wild animals are kept for exhibition

zo·ol·o·gy \zō-'ä-lə-jē\ *n* : a branch of biology that deals with the classification and the properties and vital phenomena of animals — **zo·o·log·i·cal** \ˌzō-ə-'lä-ji-kəl\ *adj* — **zo·ol·o·gist** \zō-'ä-lə-jist\ *n*

zoom \'züm\ *vb* **1** : to move with a loud hum or buzz **2** : to gain altitude quickly **3** : to focus a camera or microscope using a special lens that permits the apparent distance of the object to be varied — **zoom** *n*

zoom lens *n* : a camera lens in which the image size can be varied continuously while the image remains in focus

zoo·mor·phic \ˌzō-ə-'mòr-fik\ *adj* **1** : having the form of an animal **2** : of, relating to, or being the representation of a deity in the form or with the attributes of an animal

zoo·plank·ton \ˌzō-ə-'plaŋk-tən, -ˌtän\ *n* : animal life of the plankton

zoo·spore \'zō-ə-ˌspòr\ *n* : a motile spore

zoot suit \'züt-\ *n* : a flashy suit of extreme cut typically consisting of a thigh-length jacket with wide padded shoulders and trousers that are wide at the top and narrow at the bottom — **zoot·suit·er** \-ˌsü-tər\ *n*

Zo·ro·as·tri·an·ism \ˌzòr-ə-'was-trē-ə-ˌni-zəm\ *n* : a religion founded by the Persian prophet Zoroaster — **Zo·ro·as·tri·an** \-trē-ən\ *adj or n*

Zou·ave \zu̇-'äv\ *n* : a member of a French infantry unit orig. composed of Algerians wearing a brilliant uniform and conducting a quick spirited drill; *also* : a member of a military unit modeled on the Zouaves

zounds \'zau̇ndz\ *interj* [euphemism for *God's wounds*] — used as a mild oath

zoy·sia \'zòi-shə, -zhə, -sē-ə, -zē-ə\ *n* : any of a genus of creeping perennial grasses having fine wiry leaves and including some used as lawn grasses

ZPG *abbr* zero population growth

Zr *symbol* zirconium

zuc·chet·to \zü-'ke-tō, tsü-\ *n, pl* **-tos** [It] : a small round skullcap worn by Roman Catholic ecclesiastics

zuc·chi·ni \zu̇-'kē-nē\ *n, pl* **-ni** *or* **-nis** [It] : a summer squash of bushy growth with smooth cylindrical dark green fruits; *also* : its fruit

Zu·lu \'zü-ˌlü\ *n, pl* **Zulu** *or* **Zulus** : a member of a Bantu-speaking people of South Africa; *also* : the Bantu language of the Zulus

Zu·ni \'zü-nē\ *or* **Zu·ñi** \-nyē\ *n, pl* **Zuni** *or* **Zunis** *or* **Zuñi** *or* **Zuñis** : a member of an American Indian people of western New Mexico; *also* : the language of the Zuni people

zwie·back \'swē-ˌbak, 'swī-, 'zwē-, 'zwī-, -ˌbäk\ *n* [G, lit., twice baked, fr. *zwie-* twice + *backen* to bake] : a usu. sweetened bread that is baked and then sliced and toasted until dry and crisp

Zwing·li·an \'zwiŋ-glē-ən, 'swiŋ-, -lē-; 'tsfiŋ-lē-\ *adj* : of or relating to the Swiss religious reformer Ulrich Zwingli or his teachings — **Zwinglian** *n*

zy·gote \'zī-ˌgōt\ *n* : a cell formed by the union of two sexual cells; *also* : the developing individual produced from such a cell — **zy·got·ic** \zī-'gä-tik\ *adj*

Common English Given Names

The following vocabulary presents given names that are most frequent in English use. The list is not exhaustive either of the names themselves or the variant spellings of those names which are entered. Compound or double names and surnames used as given names are not entered except in cases where long-continued or common use gives them an independent character.

Besides the pronunciations of the names, the list usually provides at least one of the following kinds of information at each entry: (1) etymology, indicating the language source but not the original form of the name, and (2) meaning where known or ascertainable with reasonable certainty.

Names of Men

Aar·on \'ar-ən, 'er-\ [Heb]
Abra·ham \'ā-brə-ˌham\ [Heb]
Ad·am \'ad-əm\ [Heb] man
Ad·di·son \'ad-ə-sən\ [fr. a surname]
Adolph \'ad-ˌälf, 'ā-ˌdälf\ [Gmc] noble wolf, i.e., noble hero
Adri·an \'ā-drē-ən\ [L] of Hadria, ancient town in central Italy
Al \al\ dim of ALAN, ALBERT. etc.
Al·an \'al-ən\ [Celt]
Al·bert \'al-bərt\ [Gmc] illustrious through nobility
Al·den \'ȯl-dən\ [OE] old friend
Al·ex \'al-iks\ or **Al·ec** \'al-ik\ dim of ALEXANDER
Al·ex·an·der \ˌal-ig-'zan-dər\ [Gk] a defender of men
Al·fred \'al-frəd, -fərd\ [OE] elf counsel, i.e., good counsel
Al·len or **Al·lan** or **Al·lyn** \'al-ən\ var of ALAN
Al·ton \'ȯlt-ᵊn, 'alt-\ [prob. fr. a surname]
Al·va or **Al·vah** \'al-və\ [Heb]
Al·vin \'al-vən\ [Gmc]
Amos \'ā-məs\ [Heb]
An·dre \'än-(ˌ)drā\ [F] var of ANDREW
An·drew \'an-(ˌ)drü\ [Gk] manly
An·dy \'an-dē\ dim of ANDREW
An·ge·lo \'an-jə-ˌlō\ [It, fr. Gk] angel, messenger
An·gus \'aŋ-gəs\ [Celt]
An·tho·ny \'an(t)-thə-nē, chiefly Brit 'an-tə-\ [L]
An·ton \'ant-ᵊn, 'an-ˌtän\ [G & Slav] var of ANTHONY
An·to·nio \an-'tō-nē-ˌō\ [It] var of ANTHONY
Ar·chi·bald \'är-chə-ˌbȯld, -bəld\ [Gmc]
Ar·chie \'är-chē\ dim of ARCHIBALD
Ar·den \'ärd-ᵊn\ [prob. fr. a surname]
Ar·len or **Ar·lin** \'är-lən\ [prob. fr. a surname]
Ar·lo \'är-(ˌ)lō\
Ar·mand \'är-ˌmänd, -mənd\ [F] var of HERMAN
Arne \'ärn\ [Scand] eagle
Ar·nold \'ärn-ᵊld\ [Gmc] power of an eagle
Art \'ärt\ dim of ARTHUR
Ar·thur \'är-thər\ [prob. L]
Au·brey \'ȯ-brē\ [Gmc] elf ruler
Au·gust \'ȯ-gəst\ [L] August, majestic
Aus·tin \'ȯs-tən, 'äs-\ alter of Augustine

Bai·ley \'bā-lē\ [fr. a surname]
Bar·clay \'bär-klē\ [fr. a surname]
Bar·net or **Bar·nett** \bär-'net\ [fr. a surname]
Bar·ney \'bär-nē\ dim of BERNARD
Bar·rett \'bar-ət\ [fr. a surname]
Bar·ry or **Bar·rie** \'bar-ē\ [Ir]
Bart \'bärt\ dim of Bartholomew
Bar·ton \'bärt-ᵊn\ [fr. a surname]
Ba·sil \'baz-əl, 'bäs-, 'bās-, 'bāz-\ [Gk] kingly, royal
Ben \'ben\ or **Ben·nie** or **Ben·ny** \'ben-ē\ dim of BENJAMIN
Ben·e·dict \'ben-ə-ˌdikt\ [L] blessed
Ben·ja·min \'benj-(ə-)mən\ [Heb] son of the right hand
Ben·nett \'ben-ət\ [OF] var of BENEDICT

Ben·ton \'bent-ᵊn\ [fr. a surname]
Ber·nard \'bər-nərd, (ˌ)bər-'närd\ or **Bern·hard** \'bərn-ˌhärd\ [Gmc] bold as a bear
Ber·nie \'bər-nē\ dim of BERNARD
Bert or **Burt** \'bərt\ dim of BERTRAM. ALBERT, etc.
Ber·tram \'bər-trəm\ [Gmc] bright raven
Bill \'bil\ or **Bil·ly** or **Bil·lie** \'bil-ē\ dim of WILLIAM
Blaine \'blān\ [fr. a surname]
Blair \'bla(ə)r, 'ble(ə)r\ [fr. a surname]
Bob·by \'bäb-ē\ or **Bob** \'bäb\ dim of ROBERT
Bo·ris \'bȯr-əs, 'bȯr-, 'bär-\ [Russ]
Boyd \'bȯid\ [fr. a surname]
Brad·ford \'brad-fərd\ [fr. a surname]
Brad·ley \'brad-lē\ [fr. a surname]
Bran·don \'bran-dən\ [fr. a surname]
Bren·dan \'bren-dən\ [Celt]
Brent \'brent\ [fr. a surname]
Brett or **Bret** \'bret\ [IrGael]
Bri·an or **Bry·an** \'brī-ən\ [Celt]
Brooks \'brüks\ [fr. a surname]
Bruce \'brüs\ [fr. a surname]
Bru·no \'brü-(ˌ)nō\ [It, fr. Gmc] brown
Bryce or **Brice** \'brīs\ [fr. a surname]
Bud·dy \'bəd-ē\ [prob. alter. of brother]
Bu·ford \'byü-fərd\ [fr. a surname]
Burke \'bərk\ [fr. a surname]
Bur·ton \'bərt-ᵊn\ [fr. a surname]
By·ron \'bī-rən\ [fr. a surname]

Cal·vin \'kal-vən\ [fr. a surname]
Cam·er·on \'kam-(ə-)rən\ [fr. a surname]
Carl \'kär(-ə)l\ var of KARL
Car·los \'kär-ləs, -ˌlōs\ [Sp] var of CHARLES
Carl·ton or **Carle·ton** \'kär(-ə)l-tən, 'kärlt-ᵊn\ [fr. a surname]
Car·lyle \kär-'lī(ə)l, 'kär-ˌ\ [fr. a surname]
Car·men \'kär-mən\ [Sp, fr. L] song
Car·roll \'kar-əl\ [fr. a surname]
Car·son \'kärs-ᵊn\ [fr. a surname]
Car·ter \'kärt-ər\ [fr. a surname]
Cary or **Car·ey** \'ka(ə)r-ē, 'ke(ə)r-ē\ [fr. a surname]
Ce·cil \'sē-səl, 'ses-əl\ [L]
Chad \'chad\ [Gmc]
Charles \'chär(-ə)lz\ [Gmc] man of the common people
Ches·ter \'ches-tər\ [fr. a surname]
Chris \'kris\ dim of CHRISTOPHER
Chris·tian \'kris(h)-chən\ [Gk] Christian (the believer)
Chris·to·pher \'kris-tə-fər\ [Gk] Christ bearer
Clar·ence \'klar-ən(t)s\ [fr. the English dukedom]
Clark or **Clarke** \'klärk\ [fr. a surname]
Claude or **Claud** \'klȯd\ [L]
Clay \'klā\ dim of CLAYTON
Clay·ton \'klāt-ᵊn\ [fr. a surname]
Clem \'klem\ dim of CLEMENT
Clem·ent \'klem-ənt\ [L] mild, merciful
Clif·ford \'klif-ərd\ [fr. a surname]
Clif·ton \'klif-tən\ [fr. a surname]
Clint \'klint\ dim of CLINTON
Clin·ton \'klint-ᵊn\ [fr. a surname]
Clyde \'klīd\ [fr. a surname]

Cole \'kōl\ [fr. a surname]
Co·lin \'käl-ən, 'kō-lən\ *or* **Col·lin** \'käl-ən\ *dim of* NICHOLAS
Con·rad \'kän-ˌrad, -rəd\ [Gmc] bold counsel
Con·stan·tine \'kän(t)-stən-ˌtēn, -ˌtīn\ [L]
Cor·ey \'kȯr-ē\ [fr. a surname]
Cor·ne·lius \kȯr-'nēl-yəs\ [L]
Craig \'krāg\ [fr. a surname]
Cur·tis \'kərt-əs\ [OF] courteous
Cyr·il \'sir-əl\ [Gk] lordly
Cy·rus \'sī-rəs\ [OPer]

Dale \'dā(ə)l\ [fr. a surname]
Dal·las \'dal-əs\ [fr. a surname]
Dal·ton \'dȯlt-ᵊn\ [fr. a surname]
Dan \'dan\ [Heb] judge
Da·na \'dā-nə\ [fr. a surname]
Dan·iel \'dan-yəl *also* 'dan-ᵊl\ [Heb] God has judged
Dan·ny \'dan-ē\ *dim of* DANIEL
Dar·old \'dar-əld\ *perh alter of* DARRELL
Dar·rell *or* **Dar·rel** *or* **Dar·ryl** *or* **Dar·yl** \'dar-əl\ [fr. a surname]
Dar·win \'där-wən\ [fr. a surname]
Dave \'dāv\ *dim of* DAVID
Da·vid \'dā-vəd\ [Heb] beloved
Da·vis \'dā-vəs\ [fr. a surname]
Dean *or* **Deane** \'dēn\ [fr. a surname]
Del·a·no \'del-ə-ˌnō\ [fr. a surname]
Del·bert \'del-bərt\ *dim of* Adalbert
Del·mar \'del-mər, -ˌmär\ *or* **Del·mer** \-mər\ [fr. a surname]
Den·nis *or* **Den·is** \'den-əs\ [OF, fr. Gk] belonging to Dionysus, god of wine
Den·ny \'den-ē\ *dim of* DENNIS
Den·ton \'dent-ᵊn\ [fr. a surname]
Der·ek \'der-ik\ [Middle Dutch, fr. Gmc] ruler of the people
Dew·ey \'d(y)ü-ē\ [fr. a surname]
De·witt \di-'wit\ [fr. a surname]
Dex·ter \'dek-stər\ [L] on the right hand, fortunate
Dick \'dik\ *dim of* RICHARD
Dirk \'dərk\ [Dutch] *var of* DEREK
Dom·i·nic *or* **Dom·i·nick** \'däm-ə-(ˌ)nik\ [L] belonging to the Lord
Don *or* **Donn** \'dän\ *dim of* DONALD
Don·al \'dän-ᵊl\ *var of* DONALD
Don·ald \'dän-ᵊld\ [ScGael] world ruler
Don·nie \'dän-ē\ *dim of* DON
Don·o·van \'dän-ə-vən, 'dən-\ [fr. a surname]
Doug \'dəg\ *dim of* DOUGLAS
Doug·las *or* **Doug·lass** \'dəg-ləs\ [fr. a surname]
Duane \dü-'ān, 'dwān\ [fr. a surname]
Dud·ley \'dəd-lē\ [fr. a surname]
Dun·can \'dəŋ-kən\ [ScGael] brown head
Dur·ward \'dər-wərd\ [fr. a surname]
Dwayne *or* **Dwaine** \'dwān\ [fr. a surname]
Dwight \'dwīt\ [fr. a surname]
Dy·lan \'dil-ən\ [W]

Earl *or* **Earle** \'ər(-ə)l\ [OE] warrior, noble
Ed \'ed\ *dim of* EDWARD. EDGAR. etc.
Ed·die *or* **Ed·dy** \'ed-ē\ *dim of* ED
Ed·gar \'ed-gər\ [OE] spear of wealth
Ed·mund *or* **Ed·mond** \'ed-mənd\ [OE] protector of wealth
Ed·son \'ed-sən\ [fr. a surname]
Ed·ward \'ed-wərd\ [OE] guardian of wealth
Ed·win \'ed-wən\ [OE] friend of wealth
El·bert \'el-bərt\ *var of* ALBERT
Eli \'ē-ˌlī\ [Heb] high
E·li·as \i-'lī-əs\ [Gk] *var of* Elijah
El·liott *or* **El·liot** *or* **El·iot** \'el-ē-ət, 'el-yət\ [fr. a surname]
El·lis \'el-əs\ *var of* ELIAS
Ells·worth \'elz-(ˌ)wərth\ [fr. a surname]
El·mer \'el-mər\ [fr. a surname]

El·mo \'el-(ˌ)mō\ [It, fr. Gk] lovable
El·ton \'elt-ᵊn\ [fr. a surname]
El·vin \'el-vən\ [fr. a surname]
El·wood *or* **Ell·wood** \'el-ˌwu̇d\ [fr. a surname]
Em·man·u·el *or* **Eman·u·el** \i-'man-yə(-wə)l\ [Heb] God with us
Em·er·son \'em-ər-sən\ [fr. a surname]
Emil \'ā-məl\ *or* **Emile** \ā-'mē(ə)l\ [L]
Em·mett \'em-ət\ [fr. a surname]
Em·o·ry *or* **Em·ery** \'em-(ə-)rē\ [Gmc]
Er·ic *or* **Er·ich** *or* **Er·ik** \'er-ik\ [Scand]
Er·nest *or* **Ear·nest** \'ər-nəst\ [G] earnestness
Er·nie \'ər-nē\ *dim of* ERNEST
Ernst \'ərn(t)st, 'e(ə)rn(t)st\ [G] *var of* ERNEST
Er·rol \'er-əl\ [prob. fr. a surname]
Ethan \'ē-thən\ [Heb] strength
Eu·gene \yu̇-'jēn, 'yü-\ [Gk] wellborn
Ev·an \'ev-ən\ [W] *var of* JOHN
Ev·er·ett \'ev-(ə-)rət\ [fr. a surname]

Fe·lix \'fē-liks\ [L] happy, prosperous
Fer·di·nand \'fərd-ᵊn-ˌand\ [Gmc]
Fer·nan·do \fər-'nan-(ˌ)dō\ [Sp] *var of* FERDINAND
Fletch·er \'flech-ər\ [fr. a surname]
Floyd \'flȯid\ [fr. a surname]
For·rest *or* **For·est** \'fȯr-əst, 'fär-\ [fr. a surname]
Fos·ter \'fȯs-tər, 'fäs-\ [fr. a surname]
Fran·cis \'fran(t)-səs\ [OIt & OF] Frenchman
Fran·cis·co \fran-'sis-(ˌ)kō\ [Sp] *var of* FRANCIS
Frank \'fraŋk\ [Gmc] freeman, Frank
Frank·lin *or* **Frank·lyn** \'fraŋ-klən\ [fr. a surname]
Fred \'fred\ *dim of* FREDERICK. ALFRED
Fred·die \'fred-ē\ *dim of* FREDERICK
Fred·er·ick *or* **Fred·er·ic** *or* **Fred·rick** *or* **Fred·ric** \'fred-(ə-)rik\ [Gmc] peaceful ruler
Free·man \'frē-mən\ [fr. a surname]
Fritz \'frits\ [G] *dim of* Friedrich

Ga·bri·el \'gā-brē-əl\ [Heb] man of God
Gar·land \'gär-lənd\ [fr. a surname]
Gar·rett \'gar-ət\ [fr. a surname]
Garth \'gärth\ [fr. a surname]
Gary \'gar-ē, 'ger-ē\ *or* **Gar·ry** \'gar-\ [prob. fr. a surname]
Gay·lord \'gā-ˌlȯ(ə)rd\ [fr. a surname]
Gene \'jēn\ *dim of* EUGENE
Geof·frey \'jef-rē\ [OF, fr. Gmc]
George \'jȯ(ə)rj\ [Gk] of or relating to a farmer
Ger·ald \'jer-əld\ [Gmc] spear dominion
Ge·rard \jə-'rärd, *chiefly Brit* 'jer-ˌärd, -ərd\ *or* **Ger·hard** \'ge(ə)r-ˌhärd\ [Gmc] strong with the spear
Ger·ry \'jer-ē\ *var of* JERRY
Gil·bert \'gil-bərt\ [Gmc] *prob* illustrious through hostages
Giles \'jī(ə)lz\ [OF, fr. LL]
Glenn *or* **Glen** \'glen\ [fr. a surname]
Gor·don \'gȯrd-ᵊn\ [fr. a surname]
Gra·ham \'grā-əm, 'gra(-ə)m\ [fr. a surname]
Grant \'grant\ [fr. a surname]
Gran·ville \'gran-ˌvil\ [fr. a surname]
Gray \'grā\ [fr. a surname]
Gregg *or* **Greg** \'greg\ *dim of* GREGORY
Greg·o·ry \'greg-(ə-)rē\ [LGk] vigilant
Gro·ver \'grō-vər\ [fr. a surname]
Gus \'gəs\ *dim of* Gustav *or* Augustus
Guy \'gī\ [OF, fr. Gmc]

Hal \'hal\ *dim of* HENRY
Hall \'hȯl\ [fr. a surname]
Ham·il·ton \'ham-əl-tən, -əlt-ᵊn\ [fr. a surname]
Hans \'hanz, 'hän(t)s\ [G] *dim of* Johannes
Har·lan \'här-lən\ *or* **Har·land** \-lənd\ [fr. a surname]
Har·ley \'här-lē\ [fr. a surname]
Har·low \'här-(ˌ)lō\ [fr. a surname]
Har·mon \'här-mən\ [fr. a surname]
Har·old \'har-əld\ [OE] army dominion

Har·ris \'har-əs\ [fr. a surname]
Har·ri·son \'har-ə-sən\ [fr. a surname]
Har·ry \'har-ē\ *dim of* HENRY
Har·vey \'här-vē\ [fr. a surname]
Hec·tor \'hek-tər\ [Gk] holding fast
Hel·mut \'hel-mət, -ˌmüt\ [G] helmet courage
Hen·ry \'hen-rē\ [Gmc] ruler of the home
Her·bert \'hər-bərt\ [Gmc] illustrious by reason of an
  army
Her·man *or* Her·mann \'hər-mən\ [Gmc] warrior
Her·schel *or* Her·shel \'hər-shəl\ [fr. a surname]
Hi·ram \'hī-rəm\ [Phoenician]
Ho·bart \'hō-bərt, -ˌbärt\ [fr. a surname]
Hol·lis \'häl-əs\ [fr. a surname]
Ho·mer \'hō-mər\ [Gk]
Hor·ace \'hȯr-əs, 'här-\ [L]
How·ard \'haů(-ə)rd\ [fr. a surname]
How·ell \'haů(-ə)l\ [W]
Hu·bert \'hyü-bərt\ [Gmc] bright in spirit
Hud·son \'həd-sən\ [fr. a surname]
Hugh \'hyü\ *or* Hu·go \'hyü-(ˌ)gō\ [Gmc] *prob* mind,
  spirit

Ian \'ē-ən\ [ScGael] *var of* JOHN
Ira \'ī-rə\ [Heb]
Ir·ving \'ər-viŋ\ *or* Ir·vin \-vən\ [fr. a surname]
Ir·win \'ər-wən\ [fr. a surname]
Isaac \'ī-zik, -zək\ [Heb] he laughs
Ivan \'ī-vən\ [Russ] *var of* JOHN

Jack \'jak\ *dim of* JOHN
Jack·son \'jak-sən\ [fr. a surname]
Ja·cob \'jā-kəb, -kəp\ [Heb] one who supplants
Jacques *or* Jacque \'zhäk\ [F] *var of* JAMES
Jake \'jāk\ *dim of* JACOB
James \'jāmz\ [OF, fr. LL *Jacobus*] *var of* JACOB
Ja·mie \'jā-mē\ *dim of* JAMES
Jan \'jan\ [Dutch & LG] *var of* JOHN
Jar·ed \'jar-əd, 'jer-\ [Heb] descent
Ja·son \'jās-ᵊn\ [Gk]
Jay \'jā\ [prob. fr. a surname]
Jed \'jed\ *dim of* Jedidiah
Jef·frey *or* Jeff·ery *or* Jef·fry \'jef-(ə-)rē\ *var of* GEOF-
  FREY
Jer·ald *or* Jer·old *or* Jer·rold \'jer-əld\ *var of* GERALD
Jer·e·my \'jer-ə-mē\ *or* Jer·e·mi·ah \ˌjer-ə-'mī-ə\ [Heb]
  prob Yahweh exalts
Je·rome \jə-'rōm, *Brit also* 'jer-əm\ [Gk] bearing a
  holy name
Jer·ry *or* Jere \'jer-ē\ *dim of* GERALD
Jes·se \'jes-ē\ [Heb]
Jim \'jim\ *or* Jim·my *or* Jim·mie \'jim-ē\ *dim of* JAMES
Jo·dy \'jō-dē\ *perh alter of* JOSEPH
Joe \'jō\ *dim of* JOSEPH
Jo·el \'jō-əl\ [Heb] Yahweh is God
John \'jän\ [Heb] Yahweh is gracious
Jon \'jän\ *var of* JOHN
Jo·nah \'jō-nə\ [Heb]
Jon·a·than \'jän-ə-thən\ [Heb] Yahweh has given
Jor·dan \'jȯrd-ᵊn\ [fr. a surname]
Jo·seph *or* Josef \'jō-zəf *also* -səf\ [Heb] he shall add
Josh·u·a \'jäsh-(ə-)wə\ [Heb] Yahweh saves
Judd \'jəd\ [fr. a surname]
Jud·son \'jəd-sən\ [fr. a surname]
Jules \'jülz\ [F] *var of* JULIUS
Ju·lian *or* Ju·lien \'jül-yən\ [L] sprung from or belong-
  ing to Julius
Ju·lius \'jül-yəs\ *or* Ju·lio \-(ˌ)yō\ [L]
Jus·tin \'jəs-tən\ *or* Jus·tus \-təs\ [L] just

Karl \'kär(-ə)l\ [G & Scand] *var of* CHARLES
Keith \'kēth\ [fr. a surname]
Kel·ly \'kel-ē\ [fr. a surname]
Ken \'ken\ *dim of* KENNETH
Ken·dall \'ken-dᵊl\ [fr. a surname]
Ken·neth \'ken-əth\ [ScGael]

Kent \'kent\ [prob. fr. a surname]
Ken·ton \'kent-ᵊn\ [fr. a surname]
Ker·mit \'kər-mət\ [prob. fr. a surname]
Ker·ry \'ker-ē\ [prob. fr. the county of Ireland]
Kev·in \'kev-ən\ [OIr]
Kir·by \'kər-bē\ [fr. a surname]
Kirk \'kərk\ [fr. a surname]
Klaus \'klaůs, 'klȯs\ [G] *dim of* Nikolaus
Kurt \'kərt, 'ků(ə)rt\ [G] *dim of* CONRAD
Kyle \'kī(ə)l\ [Celt]

La·mar \lə-'mär\ [fr. a surname]
Lance \'lan(t)s\ *dim of* Lancelot
Lane \'lān\ [fr. a surname]
Lan·ny \'lan-ē\ *prob dim of* LAWRENCE
Lar·ry \'lar-ē\ *dim of* LAWRENCE
Lars \'lärz\ [Sw] *var of* LAWRENCE
Law·rence *or* Lau·rence \'lȯr-ən(t)s, 'lär-\ [L] of Lau-
  rentum, ancient city in central Italy
Lee *or* Leigh \'lē\ [fr. a surname]
Leigh·ton *or* Lay·ton \'lāt-ᵊn\ [fr. a surname]
Le·land \'lē-lənd\ [fr. a surname]
Len \'len\ *dim of* LEONARD
Leo \'le-(ˌ)ō\ [L] lion
Le·on \'lē-ˌän, -ən\ [Sp] *var of* LEO
Leon·ard \'len-ərd\ [G] strong or brave as a lion
Le·roy \li-'rȯi, 'lē-ˌ\ [OF] royal
Les·lie \'les-lē, 'lez-\ [fr. a surname]
Les·ter \'les-tər\ [fr. a surname]
Lew·is \'lü-əs\ *var of* LOUIS
Li·am \'lē-əm\ [Ir]
Lin·coln \'liŋ-kən\ [fr. a surname]
Li·o·nel \'lī-ən-ᵊl, -ə-ˌnel\ [OF] young lion
Lloyd *or* Loyd \'lȯid\ [W] gray
Lo·gan \'lō-gən\ [fr. a surname]
Lon \'län\ *dim of* Alonzo
Lon·nie *or* Lon·ny \'län-ē\ *dim of* LON
Lo·ren \'lȯr-ən, 'lȯr-\ *dim of* Lorenzo
Lou·ie \'lü-ē\ *var of* LOUIS
Lou·is *or* Lu·is \'lü-əs, 'lü-ē\ [Gmc] famous warrior
Low·ell \'lō-əl\ [fr. a surname]
Lu·cian \'lü-shən\ [L]
Lud·wig \'ləd-(ˌ)wig, 'lüd-\ [G] *var of* LOUIS
Luke \'lük\ [Gk] *prob dim of* LUCIUS
Lu·ther \'lü-thər\ [fr. a surname]
Lyle \'lī(ə)l\ [fr. a surname]
Ly·man \'lī-mən\ [fr. a surname]
Lynn \'lin\ [fr. a surname]

Mack *or* Mac \'mak\ [fr. surnames beginning with *Mc*
  or *Mac*, fr. Gael *mac* son]
Mal·colm \'mal-kəm\ [ScGael] servant of (St.) Colum-
  ba
Man·fred \'man-frəd\ [Gmc] peace among men
Man·u·el \'man-yə(-wə)l\ [Sp & Pg] *var of* EMMANUEL
Mar·cus \'mär-kəs\ [L]
Ma·rio \'mär-ē-ˌō\ [It] *var of* MARIUS
Mar·i·on \'mer-ē-ən, 'mar-\ [fr. a surname]
Mark *or* Marc \'märk\ *var of* MARCUS
Mar·lin \'mär-lən\ [prob. fr. a surname]
Mar·shall *or* Mar·shal \'mär-shəl\ [fr. a surname]
Mar·tin \'märt-ᵊn\ [LL] of Mars
Mar·vin \'mär-vən\ [prob. fr. a surname]
Ma·son \'mās-ᵊn\ [fr. a surname]
Matt \'mat\ *dim of* MATTHEW
Mat·thew \'math-(ˌ)yü *also* 'math-(ˌ)ü\ [Heb] gift of
  Yahweh
Mau·rice \'mȯr-əs, 'mär-; mȯ-'rēs\ [LL] *prob* Moor-
  ish
Max \'maks\ *dim of* MAXIMILIAN
Max·well \'mak-ˌswel, -swəl\ [fr. a surname]
May·nard \'mā-nərd\ [Gmc] bold in strength
Mel·ville \'mel-ˌvil\ [fr. a surname]
Mel·vin *or* Mel·vyn \'mel-vən\ [prob. fr. a surname]
Mer·e·dith \'mer-əd-əth\ [W]
Merle \'mər(-ə)l\ [F] blackbird

Mer·lin *or* Mer·lyn \'mər-lən\ [Celt]
Mer·rill \'mer-əl\ [fr. a surname]
Mi·chael \'mī-kəl\ [Heb] who is like God?
Mick·ey \'mik-ē\ *dim of* MICHAEL
Mike \'mīk\ *dim of* MICHAEL
Mi·lan \'mī-lən\ [prob. fr. the city in Italy]
Miles *or* Myles \'mī(ə)lz\ [Gmc]
Mil·ford \'mil-fərd\ [fr. a surname]
Mil·lard \'mil-ərd, mil-'ärd\ [fr. a surname]
Mi·lo \'mī-(ˌ)lō\ [prob. L]
Mil·ton \'milt-ən\ [fr. a surname]
Mitch·ell \'mich-əl\ [fr. a surname]
Mon·roe \mən-'rō, 'mən-ˌ\ [fr. a surname]
Mon·te *or* Mon·ty \'mänt-ē\ *dim of* MONTAGUE
Mor·gan \'mȯr-gən\ [W] *prob* dweller on the sea
Mor·ris \'mȯr-əs, 'mär-\ *var of* MAURICE
Mor·ton \'mȯrt-ən\ [fr. a surname]
Mur·ray \'mər-ē, 'mə-rē\ [fr. a surname]
My·ron \'mī-rən\ [Gk]

Na·than \'nā-thən\ [Heb] given, gift
Na·than·iel \nə-'than-yəl\ [Heb] gift of God
Ned \'ned\ *dim of* EDWARD, EDWIN
Neil *or* Neal \'nē(ə)l\ [Celt]
Nel·son \'nel-sən\ [fr. a surname]
Nev·ille \'nev-əl\ [fr. a surname]
Nev·in \'nev-ən\ [fr. a surname]
New·ell \'n(y)ü-əl\ [fr. a surname]
New·ton \'n(y)üt-ən\ [fr. a surname]
Nich·o·las \'nik-(ə-)ləs\ [Gk] victorious among the people
Nick \'nik\ *dim of* NICHOLAS
Niles \'nī(ə)lz\ [fr. a surname]
Nils \'nils, 'nē(ə)ls\ [Scand]
No·ah \'nō-ə\ [Heb] rest
No·el \'nō-əl\ [F, fr. L] Christmas
No·lan \'nō-lən\ [fr. a surname]
Nor·man \'nȯr-mən\ [Gmc] Norseman, Norman
Nor·ris \'nȯr-əs, 'när-\ [fr. a surname]
Nor·ton \'nȯrt-ən\ [fr. a surname]

Ol·i·ver \'äl-ə-vər\ [OF]
Ol·lie \'äl-ē\ *dim of* OLIVER
Or·lan·do \ȯr-'lan-(ˌ)dō\ [It] *var of* ROLAND
Or·rin \'ȯr-ən, 'är-\ *or* Orin *or* Oren \'ȯr-, 'är-, 'ȯr-\ [prob. fr. a surname]
Or·ville *or* Or·val \'ȯr-vəl\ [prob. fr. a surname]
Os·car \'äs-kər\ [OE] spear of a deity
Otis \'ōt-əs\ [fr. a surname]
Ot·to \'ät-(ˌ)ō\ [Gmc]
Ow·en \'ō-ən\ [OW]

Palm·er \'päm-ər, 'päl-mər\ [fr. a surname]
Par·ker \'pär-kər\ [fr. a surname]
Pat \'pat\ *dim of* PATRICK
Pat·rick \'pa-trik\ [L] patrician
Paul \'pȯl\ [L] little
Pe·dro \'pē-(ˌ)drō, 'pā-\ [Sp] *var of* PETER
Per·cy \'pər-sē\ [fr. a surname]
Per·ry \'per-ē\ [fr. a surname]
Pete \'pēt\ *dim of* PETER
Pe·ter \'pēt-ər\ [Gk] rock
Phil \'fil\ *dim of* PHILIP
Phil·ip *or* Phil·lip \'fil-əp\ [Gk] lover of horses
Pierre \pē-'e(ə)r\ [F] *var of* PETER
Por·ter \'pȯrt-ər, 'pȯrt-\ [fr. a surname]
Pres·ton \'pres-tən\ [fr. a surname]

Quen·tin \'kwent-ən\ [LL] of or relating to the fifth

Ra·fa·el *or* Ra·pha·el \'raf-ē-əl, 'rä-fē-\ [Heb] God has healed
Ra·leigh \'rȯl-ē, 'räl-\ [fr. a surname]
Ralph \'ralf, *Brit also* 'räf\ [Gmc] wolf in counsel
Ra·mon \rə-'mōn, 'rä-mən\ [Sp] *var of* RAYMOND
Ran·dall *or* Ran·dal \'ran-dəl\ *var of* RANDOLPH

Ran·dolph \'ran-ˌdälf\ [Gmc] shield wolf
Ran·dy \'ran-dē\ *dim of* RANDOLPH
Ray \'rā\ *dim of* RAYMOND
Ray·mond \'rā-mənd\ [Gmc] wise protection
Reed *or* Reid \'rēd\ [fr. a surname]
Reg·gie \'rej-ē\ *dim of* REGINALD
Reg·i·nald \'rej-ən-əld\ [Gmc] wise dominion
Re·gis \'rē-jəs\ [fr. a proper name]
Re·ne \'ren-(ˌ)ā, rə-'nā, 'rä-nē, 'rē-nē\ [F, fr. L] reborn
Reu·ben *or* Ru·ben \'rü-bən\ [Heb]
Rex \'reks\ [L] king
Reyn·old \'ren-əld\ *var of* REGINALD
Rich·ard \'rich-ərd\ [Gmc] strong in rule
Rob·ert \'räb-ərt\ [Gmc] bright in fame
Ro·ber·to \rə-'bert-(ˌ)ō, rō-, -'bert-\ [Sp & It] *var of* ROBERT
Rob·in \'räb-ən\ *dim of* ROBERT
Rod·er·ick \'räd-(ə-)rik\ [Gmc] famous ruler
Rod·ney \'räd-nē\ [fr. a surname]
Rog·er *or* Rod·ger \'räj-ər\ [Gmc] famous spear
Rog·ers \'räj-ərz\ [fr. a surname]
Ro·land \'rō-lənd\ *or* Rol·land \'räl-ənd\ *or* Row·land \'rō-lənd\ [Gmc] famous land
Rolf \'rälf\ *var of* RUDOLPH
Rol·lin \'räl-ən\ *var of* ROLAND
Ron \'rän\ *dim of* RONALD
Ron·al \'rän-əl\ *var of* RONALD
Ron·ald \'rän-əld\ [ON] *var of* REGINALD
Ron·nie *or* Ron·ny \'rän-ē\ *dim of* RONALD
Ros·coe \'räs-(ˌ)kō, 'rȯs-\ [fr. a surname]
Ross \'rȯs\ [fr. a surname]
Roy \'rȯi\ [ScGael]
Roy·al \'rȯi(-ə)l\ [prob. fr. a surname]
Royce \'rȯis\ [fr. a surname]
Ru·dolph *or* Ru·dolf \'rü-ˌdälf\ [Gmc] famous wolf
Ru·dy \'rüd-ē\ *dim of* RUDOLPH
Ru·fus \'rü-fəs\ [L] red, red-haired
Ru·pert \'rü-pərt\ *var of* ROBERT
Rus·sell *or* Rus·sel \'rəs-əl\ [fr. a surname]
Ry·an \'rī-ən\ [IrGael]

Sal·va·tore \ˌsal-və-ˌtō(ə)r, -ˌtȯ(ə)r; ˌsal-və-'tōr-ē, -'tȯr-\ [It] savior
Sam \'sam\ *dim of* SAMUEL
Sam·my *or* Sam·mie \'sam-ē\ *dim of* SAM
Sam·u·el \'sam-yə(-wə)l\ [Heb] name of God
San·ford \'san-fərd\ [fr. a surname]
Saul \'sȯl\ [Heb] asked for
Scott \'skät\ [fr. a surname]
Sean \'shȯn\ [Ir] *var of* JOHN
Seth \'seth\ [Heb]
Sey·mour \'sē-ˌmō(ə)r, -ˌmȯ(ə)r\ [fr. a surname]
Shel·by \'shel-bē\ [fr. a surname]
Shel·don \'shel-dən\ [fr. a surname]
Sher·i·dan \'sher-əd-ən\ [fr. a surname]
Sher·man \'shər-mən\ [fr. a surname]
Sher·win \'shər-wən\ [fr. a surname]
Sher·wood \'shər-ˌwùd, 'she(ə)r-\ [fr. a surname]
Sid·ney *or* Syd·ney \'sid-nē\ [fr. a surname]
Sieg·fried \'sig-ˌfrēd, 'sēg-\ [Gmc] victorious peace
Sig·mund \'sig-mənd\ [Gmc] victorious protection
Si·mon \'sī-mən\ [Heb]
Sol·o·mon \'säl-ə-mən\ [Heb] peaceable
Spen·cer \'spen(t)-sər\ [fr. a surname]
Sta·cy *or* Sta·cey \'stā-sē\ [ML]
Stan \'stan\ *dim of* STANLEY
Stan·ford \'stan-fərd\ [fr. a surname]
Stan·ley \'stan-lē\ [fr. a surname]
Stan·ton \'stant-ən\ [fr. a surname]
Ste·fan \'stef-ən, -ˌän\ [Pol] *var of* STEPHEN
Ste·phen *or* Ste·ven *or* Ste·phan \'stē-vən\ [Gk] crown
Ster·ling \'stər-liŋ\ [fr. a surname]
Steve \'stēv\ *dim of* STEVEN
Stu·art *or* Stew·art \'st(y)ü-ərt, 'st(y)ü(-ə)rt\ [fr. a surname]

Syl·ves·ter \sil-'ves-tər\ [L] woodsy, of the woods

Tay·lor \'tā-lər\ [fr. a surname]
Ted \'ted\ or **Ted·dy** \'ted-ē\ dim of EDWARD. THEODORE
Ter·ence or **Ter·rance** or **Ter·rence** \'ter-ən(t)s\ [L]
Ter·rell or **Ter·rill** \'ter-əl\ [fr. a surname]
Ter·ry \'ter-ē\ dim of TERENCE
Thad \'thad\ dim of THADDEUS
Thad·de·us \'thad-ē-əs\ [Gk]
The·o·dore \'thē-ə-ˌdō(ə)r, -ˌdȯ(ə)r, -əd-ər\ [Gk] gift of God
Thom·as \'täm-əs\ [Aram] twin
Thur·man \'thər-mən\ [fr. a surname]
Tim \'tim\ dim of TIMOTHY
Tim·o·thy \'tim-ə-thē\ [Gk] revering God
To·by \'tō-bē\ dim of TOBIAS
Todd \'täd\ [prob. fr. a surname]
Tom \'täm\ or **Tom·my** or **Tom·mie** \'täm-ē\ dim of THOMAS
To·ny \'tō-nē\ dim of ANTHONY
Tra·cy \'trā-sē\ [fr. a surname]
Trav·is \'trav-əs\ [fr. a surname]
Trent \'trent\ [fr. a surname]
Tre·vor \'trev-ər\ [Celt]
Troy \'trȯi\ [prob. fr. a surname]
Tru·man \'trü-mən\ [fr. a surname]
Ty·ler \'tī-lər\ [fr. a surname]
Ty·rone \tī-ˌrōn, tī-'; tir-'ōn\ [prob. fr. the county in Ireland]

Val \'val\ dim of VALENTINE
Van \'van\ [fr. surnames beginning with Van, fr. Dutch van of]
Vance \'van(t)s\ [fr. a surname]
Vaughn \'vȯn, 'vän\ [fr. a surname]
Verne or **Vern** \'vərn\ prob alter of VERNON
Ver·non \'vər-nən\ [prob. fr. a surname]
Vic·tor \'vik-tər\ [L] conqueror
Vin·cent \'vin(t)-sənt\ [LL] of or relating to the conquering one
Vir·gil \'vər-jəl\ [L]

Wade \'wād\ [fr. a surname]
Wal·lace or **Wal·lis** \'wäl-əs\ [fr. a surname]
Walt \'wȯlt\ dim of WALTER
Wal·ter \'wȯl-tər\ [Gmc] army of dominion
Wal·ton \'wȯlt-ən\ [fr. a surname]
Ward \'wȯ(ə)rd\ [fr. a surname]
War·ner \'wȯr-nər\ [fr. a surname]
War·ren \'wȯr-ən, 'wär-\ [fr. a surname]
Wayne \'wān\ [fr. a surname]
Wel·don \'wel-dən\ [fr. a surname]
Wen·dell \'wen-dəl\ [fr. a surname]
Wer·ner \'wər-nər, 'we(ə)r-\ [Gmc] army of the Varini, a Germanic people
Wes·ley \'wes-lē also \'wez-\ [fr. a surname]
Wil·bur or **Wil·ber** \'wil-bər\ [fr. a surname]
Wi·ley or **Wy·lie** \'wī-lē\ [fr. a surname]
Wil·ford \'wil-fərd\ [fr. a surname]
Wil·fred \'wil-frəd\ [OE] desired peace
Will \'wil\ or **Wil·lie** \-ē\ dim of WILLIAM
Wil·lard \'wil-ərd\ [fr. a surname]
Wil·liam \'wil-yəm\ [Gmc] desired helmet
Wil·lis \'wil-əs\ [fr. a surname]
Wil·mer \'wil-mər\ [fr. a surname]
Wil·son \'wil-sən\ [fr. a surname]
Wil·ton \'wilt-ən\ [fr. a surname]
Win·field \'win-ˌfēld\ [fr. a surname]
Win·fred \'win-frəd\ [OE] prob joyous peace
Win·ston \'win(t)-stən\ [fr. a surname]
Win·ton \'wint-ən\ [fr. a surname]
Wood·row \'wüd-(ˌ)rō\ [fr. a surname]
Wy·att \'wī-ət\ [fr. a surname]

Yale \'yā(ə)l\ [fr. a surname]

Zach·a·ry \'zak-ə-rē\ dim of ZACHARIAH
Zane \'zān\ [fr. a surname]

Names of Women

Ab·by \'ab-ē\ dim of ABIGAIL
Ab·i·gail \'ab-ə-ˌgāl\ [Heb] prob source of joy
Ada \'ād-ə\ [Heb] prob ornament
Ad·di·son \'ad-ə-sən\ [fr. a surname]
Ad·e·laide \'ad-əl-ˌād\ [Gmc] of noble rank
Adele \ə-'del\ [Gmc] noble
Adri·enne \'ā-drē-ˌen, -ən\ [F] fem of ADRIEN
Ag·nes \'ag-nəs\ [LL]
Ai·leen \ī-'lēn\ [IrGael] var of HELEN
Al·ber·ta \al-'bərt-ə\ fem of ALBERT
Al·ex·an·dra \ˌal-ig-'zan-drə\ [Gk] fem of ALEXANDER
Alex·is \ə-'lek-səs\ [Gk]
Al·ice or **Al·yce** \'al-əs\ [OF] var of ADELAIDE
Ali·cia \ə-'lish-ə\ [ML] var of ADELAIDE
Al·i·son or **Al·li·son** \'al-ə-sən\ [OF] dim of ALICE
Al·ma \'al-mə\ [L] nourishing, cherishing
Al·va \'al-və\ [Sp, fr. L] white
Aman·da \ə-'man-də\ [L] worthy to be loved
Am·ber \'am-bər\ [E]
Ame·lia \ə-'mēl-yə\ [Gmc]
Amy \'ā-mē\ [L] beloved
An·as·ta·sia \ˌan-ə-'stā-zh(ē-)ə\ [LGk] of the resurrection
An·drea \'an-drē-ə, an-'drā-ə\ fem of ANDREW
An·ge·la \'an-jə-lə\ [It, fr. Gk] angel
An·gel·i·ca \an-'jel-i-kə\ var of ANGELA
An·ge·line \'an-jə-ˌlīn, -ˌlēn\ dim of ANGELA
Ani·ta \ə-'nēt-ə\ [Sp] dim of ANN
Ann or **Anne** \'an\ or **An·na** \'an-ə\ [Heb] grace
An·na·belle \'an-ə-ˌbel\ prob var of MABEL
An·nette \a-'net, ə-\ or **An·net·ta** \-'net-ə\ [F] dim of ANN
An·nie \'an-ē\ dim of ANN
An·toi·nette \ˌan-t(w)ə-'net\ [F] dim of ANTONIA
April \'ā-prəl\ [E] April (the month)
Ar·dell or **Ar·delle** \är-'del\ var of ADELE
Ar·lene or **Ar·leen** or **Ar·line** \är-'lēn\
Ash·ley \'ash-lē\ [OE] ash-tree meadow
As·trid \'as-trəd\ [Scand] beautiful as a deity
Au·dra \'ȯ-drə\ var of AUDREY
Au·drey \'ȯ-drē\ [OE] noble strength

Ba·bette \ba-'bet\ [F] dim of ELIZABETH
Bar·ba·ra \'bär-b(ə-)rə\ [Gk] foreign
Be·atrice \'bē-ə-trəs\ [It, fr. ML] she that makes happy
Becky \'bek-ē\ dim of REBECCA
Ber·na·dette \ˌbər-nə-'det\ [F] fem of BERNARD
Ber·na·dine \'bər-nə-ˌdēn\ fem of BERNARD
Ber·nice \(ˌ)bər-'nēs, 'bər-nəs\ [Gk] bringing victory
Ber·tha \'bər-thə\ [Gmc] bright
Ber·yl \'ber-əl\ [Gk] beryl (the mineral)
Bes·sie \'bes-ē\ dim of ELIZABETH
Beth \'beth\ dim of ELIZABETH
Bet·sy or **Bet·sey** \'bet-sē\ dim of ELIZABETH
Bet·ty or **Bet·te** or **Bet·tye** or **Bet·tie** \'bet-ē\ dim of ELIZABETH
Beu·lah \'byü-lə\ [Heb] married
Bev·er·ly or **Bev·er·ley** \'bev-ər-lē\ [prob. fr. a surname]
Bil·lie \'bil-ē\ fem of BILLY
Blair \'ble(ə)r\ [fr. a surname]
Blake \'blāk\ [fr. a surname]
Blanche \'blanch\ [OF, fr. Gmc] white
Bob·bie \'bäb-ē\ dim of ROBERTA
Bo·ni·ta \bə-'nēt-ə\ [Sp] pretty
Bon·nie \'bän-ē\ [ME] pretty
Bran·dy \'bran-dē\ [E]

Bren·da \'bren-də\ [Scand]
Bri·gitte \'brij-ət, brə-'jit\ [G] *var of* BRIDGET
Brit·tany \'brit-ᵊn-ē\ [E]
Brooke \'brŭk\ [OE] brook

Cait·lin \'kāt-lin\ [Ir] *var of* CATHERINE
Ca·mil·la \kə-'mil-ə\ [L] freeborn girl attendant at a sacrifice
Ca·mille \kə-'mē(ə)l\ [F] *var of* CAMILLA
Can·da·ce \'kan-dəs, kan-'dā-sē\ [Gk]
Car·la \'kär-lə\ [It] *fem of* Carlo
Car·lene \kär-'lēn\ *var of* CARLA
Car·lot·ta \kär-'lät-ə\ [It] *var of* CHARLOTTE
Car·men \'kär-mən\ *or* **Car·mine** \kär-'mēn, 'kär-mən\ [Sp, fr. L] song
Car·ol *or* **Car·ole** *or* **Car·yl** \'kar-əl\ *dim of* CAROLYN
Car·o·lyn \'kar-ə-lən\ *or* **Car·o·line** \-lən, -ˌlīn\ [It] *fem of* CHARLES
Car·rie \'kar-ē\ *dim of* CAROLINE
Cath·er·ine *or* **Cath·a·rine** \'kath-(ə-)rən\ [LGk]
Cath·leen \kath-'lēn\ [IrGael] *var of* CATHERINE
Cath·ryn \'kath-rən\ *var of* CATHERINE
Cathy *or* **Cath·ie** \'kath-ē\ *dim of* CATHERINE
Ce·cile \sə-'sē(ə)l\ *var of* CECILIA
Ce·ci·lia \sə-'sēl-yə, -'sil-\ *or* **Ce·ce·lia** \-'sēl-\ [L] *fem of* CECIL
Ce·leste \sə-'lest\ [L] heavenly
Ce·lia \'sēl-yə\ *dim of* CECILIA
Char·lene \shär-'lēn\ *fem of* CHARLES
Char·lotte \'shär-lət\ [F] *fem dim of* CHARLES
Cher·ie \'sher-ē\ [F] dear
Cher·ry \'cher-ē\ [E] cherry
Cher·yl \'cher-əl, 'sher-\ *prob var of* CHERRY
Chloe \'klō-ē\ [Gk] young verdure
Chris·tie \'kris-tē\ *dim of* CHRISTINE
Chris·tine \kris-'tēn\ *or* **Chris·ti·na** \-'tē-nə\ [Gk] Christian
Cin·dy \'sin-dē\ *dim of* LUCINDA
Claire *or* **Clare** \'kla(ə)r, 'kle(ə)r\ *var of* CLARA
Cla·ra \'klar-ə\ [L] bright
Cla·rice \'klar-əs, klə-'rēs\ *dim of* CLARA
Clau·dette \klȯ-'det\ [F] *fem of* CLAUDE
Clau·dia \'klȯd-ē-ə\ [L] *fem of* CLAUDE
Clau·dine \klȯ-'dēn\ [F] *fem of* CLAUDE
Cleo \'klē-(ˌ)ō\ *dim of* Cleopatra
Co·lette \kä-'let\ [OF] *fem dim of* NICHOLAS
Col·leen \kä-'lēn\ [IrGael] girl
Con·nie \'kän-ē\ *dim of* CONSTANCE
Con·stance \'kän(t)-stən(t)s\ [L] constancy
Co·ra \'kōr-ə, 'kȯr-\ [Gk] maiden
Cor·ey \'kȯr-ē\ [Ir]
Co·rinne *or* **Cor·rine** \kə-'rin, -'rēn\ [Gk] *dim of* CORA
Cor·ne·lia \kȯr-'nēl-yə\ [L] *fem of* CORNELIUS
Court·ney \'kȯ(ə)rt-nē, 'kȯ(ə)rt-\ [OE] of the court
Crys·tal \'kris-tᵊl\ [E]
Cyn·thia \'sin(t)-thē-ə\ [Gk] she of Mount Cynthus on the island of Delos

Dai·sy \'dā-zē\ [E] daisy
Dale \'dā(ə)l\ [E] valley
Da·na \'dā-nə\ [fr. a surname]
Dan·ielle \dăn-'yel\ [F] *fem of* DANIEL
Daph·ne \'daf-nē\ [Gk] laurel
Dar·la \'där-lə\ [deriv. of *darling*]
Dar·lene \där-'lēn\ [deriv. of *darling*]
Dawn \'dȯn, 'dän\ [E] dawn
De·an·na \dē-'an-ə\ *or* **De·anne** \-'an\ *var of* DIANA
Deb·bie *or* **Deb·by** \'deb-ē\ *dim of* DEBORAH
Deb·o·rah *or* **Deb·o·ra** \'deb-(ə-)rə\ [Heb] bee
Deb·ra \'deb-rə\ *var of* DEBORAH
Dee \'dē\ *prob dim of* EDITH
Deir·dre \'di(ə)r-drē, 'de(ə)r-\ [IrGael]
De·lia \'dēl-yə\ [Gk] she of Delos (i.e. the goddess Artemis)
Del·la \'del-ə\ *dim of* ADELAIDE. DELIA
De·lo·res \də-'lōr-əs, -'lȯr-\ *var of* DOLORES

De·na *or* **Dee·na** \'dē-nə\ *dim of* GERALDINE
De·nise \də-'nēz, -'nēs\ [F] *fem of* DENIS
Di·ana *or* **Di·an·na** \dī-'an-ə\ [L]
Di·ane *or* **Di·anne** *or* **Di·an** *or* **Di·ann** \dī-'an\ [F] *var of* DIANA
Di·na *or* **Di·nah** \'dī-nə\ [Heb] judged
Dix·ie \'dik-sē\ [E] *prob* Dixie (nickname for the southern states of the U.S.)
Do·lo·res \də-'lōr-əs, -'lȯr-\ [Sp, fr. L] sorrows (i.e. those of the Virgin Mary)
Don·na \'dän-ə\ *or* **Do·na** \'dän-ə, 'dō-nə\ [It, fr. L] lady
Do·ra \'dōr-ə, 'dȯr-\ *dim of* THEODORA. Eudora
Do·reen \dȯ-'rēn, də-\ [IrGael]
Dor·is \'dȯr-əs, 'där-\ [Gk] *prob* Dorian (a member of an ancient Hellenic race)
Dor·o·thy \'dȯr-ə-thē, 'där-\ *or* **Dor·o·thea** \ˌdȯr-ə-'thē-ə, ˌdär-\ [LGk] goddess of gifts
Dot·tie *or* **Dot·ty** \'dät-ē\ *dim of* DOROTHY

Edith *or* **Edythe** \'ēd-əth\ [OE]
Ed·na \'ed-nə\ [Aram]
Ed·wi·na \e-'dwē-nə, -'dwin-ə\ *fem of* EDWIN
Ef·fie \'ef-ē\ *dim of* Euphemia
Ei·leen \ī-'lēn\ [IrGael] *var of* HELEN
Elaine \i-'lān\ [OF] *var of* HELEN
El·ea·nor *or* **El·i·nor** *or* **Ele·a·nore** \'el-ə-nər, -ˌnȯ(ə)r, -ˌnŏ(ə)r\ [OProv] *var of* HELEN
Ele·na \'el-ə-nə, ə-'lē-nə\ [It] *var of* HELEN
Elise \ə-'lēz, -'lēs\ [F] *var of* ELIZABETH
Eliz·a·beth *or* **Elis·a·beth** \i-'liz-ə-bəth\ [Heb] God has sworn
El·la \'el-ə\ [OF]
El·len *or* **El·lyn** \'el-ən\ *var of* HELEN
El·o·ise \'el-ə-ˌwēz, ˌel-ə-'\ [OF, fr. Gmc]
El·sa \'el-sə\ [G] *dim of* ELIZABETH
El·sie \'el-sē\ *dim of* ELIZABETH
El·va \'el-və\ [Gmc] elf
Em·i·ly *or* **Em·i·lie** \'em-(ə-)lē\ [L] *fem of* EMIL
Em·ma \'em-ə\ [Gmc] *var of* ERMA
Enid \'ē-nəd\ [W]
Er·i·ka \'er-i-kə\ *fem of* ERIC
Er·in \'er-ən\ [IrGael]
Er·ma \'ər-mə\ [Gmc]
Er·nes·tine \'ər-nə-ˌstēn\ *fem of* ERNEST
Es·telle \e-'stel\ *or* **Es·tel·la** \e-'stel-ə\ [OProv, fr. L] star
Es·ther \'es-tər\ [prob. fr. Per] *prob* star
Eth·el \'eth-əl\ [OE] noble
Et·ta \'et-ə\ *dim of* HENRIETTA
Eu·ge·nia \yŭ-'jēn-yə\ *or* **Eu·ge·nie** \-'jē-nē\ *fem of* EUGENE
Eu·nice \'yü-nəs\ [Gk] having (i.e. bringing) happy victory
Eva \'ē-və\ *var of* EVE
Evan·ge·line \i-'van-jə-lən, -ˌlēn, -ˌlīn\ [Gk] bringing good news
Eve \'ēv\ [Heb] life, living
Ev·e·lyn \'ev-(ə-)lən, *chiefly Brit* 'ēv-\ [OF, fr. Gmc]

Faith \'fāth\ [E] faith
Faye *or* **Fay** \'fā\ *dim of* FAITH
Fe·lice \fə-'lēs\ [L] happiness
Fern *or* **Ferne** \'fərn\ [E] fern
Flo·ra \'flōr-ə, 'flȯr-\ [L] goddess of flowers
Flor·ence \'flȯr-ən(t)s, 'flär-\ [L] bloom, prosperity
Fran·ces \'fran(t)-səs, -ˌsəz\ *fem of* FRANCIS
Fran·cine \fran-'sēn\ [F] *prob dim of* FRANCES
Fre·da *or* **Frie·da** \'frēd-ə\ *dim of* WINIFRED
Fred·er·ic·ka *or* **Fred·er·i·ca** \ˌfred-(ə-)'rē-kə, -'rik-ə\ *fem of* FREDERICK

Gail *or* **Gayle** *or* **Gale** \'gā(ə)l\ *dim of* ABIGAIL
Gay \'gā\ [E] gay
Ge·ne·va \jə-'nē-və\ *var of* GENEVIEVE
Gen·e·vieve \'jen-ə-ˌvēv\ [prob. fr. Celt]

George·ann \ˌjȯr-ˈjan\ [*George* + *Ann*]
Geor·gette \ˌjȯr-ˈjet\ *fem of* GEORGE
Geor·gia \ˈjȯr-jə\ *fem of* GEORGE
Geor·gi·na \ˌjȯr-ˈjē-nə\ *fem of* GEORGE
Ger·al·dine \ˈjer-əl-ˌdēn\ *fem of* GERALD
Ger·trude \ˈgər-ˌtrüd\ [Gmc] spear strength
Gil·li·an \ˈjil-ē-ən\ *var of* JULIANA
Gin·ger \ˈjin-jər\ [E] ginger
Gi·sela \jə-ˈsel-ə, -ˈzel-\ [Gmc] pledge
Gi·selle \jə-ˈzel\ *var of* GISELA
Glad·ys \ˈglad-əs\ [W]
Glen·da \ˈglen-də\ *prob var of* GLENNA
Glen·na \ˈglen-ə\ *fem of* GLENN
Glo·ria \ˈglōr-ē-ə, ˈglȯr-\ [L] glory
Grace \ˈgrās\ [L] favor, grace
Gre·ta \ˈgrēt-ə, ˈgret-\ *dim of* MARGARET
Gretch·en \ˈgrech-ən\ [G] *dim of* MARGARET
Gwen \ˈgwen\ *dim of* GWENDOLYN
Gwen·do·lyn \ˈgwen-də-lən\ [W]

Han·nah \ˈhan-ə\ [Heb] *var of* ANN
Har·ri·et *or* Har·ri·ett *or* Har·ri·ette \ˈhar-ē-ət\ *var of* HENRIETTA
Hat·tie \ˈhat-ē\ *dim of* HARRIET
Ha·zel \ˈhā-zəl\ [E] hazel
Heath·er \ˈheth-ər\ [ME] heather (the shrub)
Hei·di \ˈhīd-ē\ [G] *dim of* ADELAIDE
He·laine \hə-ˈlān\ *var of* HELEN
Hel·en \ˈhel-ən\ *or* He·le·na \ˈhel-ə-nə, hə-ˈlē-nə\ [Gk]
He·lene \hə-ˈlēn\ [F] *var of* HELEN
Hel·ga \ˈhel-gə\ [Scand] holy
Hen·ri·et·ta \ˌhen-rē-ˈet-ə\ [MF] *fem of* HENRY
Her·mine \ˈhər-ˌmēn\ [G] *prob fem of* HERMAN
Hes·ter \ˈhes-tər\ *var of* ESTHER
Hil·ary *or* Hil·la·ry \ˈhil-ə-rē\ [L] cheerful
Hil·da \ˈhil-də\ [OE] battle
Hil·de·gard *or* Hil·de·garde \ˈhil-də-ˌgärd\ [Gmc] *prob* battle enclosure
Hol·ly \ˈhäl-ē\ [E] holly
Hope \ˈhōp\ [E] hope

Ida \ˈīd-ə\ [Gmc]
Ilene \ī-ˈlēn\ *var of* EILEEN
Imo·gene \ˈim-ə-ˌjēn, ˈī-mə-\
Ina \ˈī-nə\
Inez \ī-ˈnez, ˈī-nəz\ [Sp] *var of* AGNES
In·grid \ˈiŋ-grəd\ [Scand] beautiful as Ing (an ancient Germanic god)
Irene \ī-ˈrēn\ [Gk] peace
Iris \ˈī-rəs\ [Gk] rainbow
Ir·ma \ˈər-mə\ *var of* ERMA
Is·a·bel *or* Is·a·belle \ˈiz-ə-ˌbel\ [OProv] *var of* ELIZABETH

Jack·ie *or* Jacky \ˈjak-ē\ *dim of* JACQUELINE
Jac·que·line *or* Jac·que·lyn *or* Jac·que·lin \ˈjak-(w)ə-lən, -ˌlēn\ [OF] *fem of* JACOB
Ja·mie \ˈjā-mē\ *fem of* JAMES
Jan \ˈjan\ *dim of* JANET
Jane *or* Jayne \ˈjān\ [OF] *var of* JOAN
Ja·net *or* Ja·nette \ˈjan-ət, jə-ˈnet\ *dim of* JANE
Ja·nice \ˈjan-əs, jə-ˈnēs\ *or* Jan·is \ˈjan-əs\ *prob dim of* JANE
Ja·nie \ˈjā-nē\ *dim of* JANE
Jean *or* Jeanne \ˈjēn\ [OF] *var of* JOAN
Jea·nette *or* Jean·nette \jə-ˈnet\ [F] *dim of* JEANNE
Jean·nie *or* Jean·ie \ˈjē-nē\ *dim of* JEAN
Jean·nine *or* Jea·nine \jə-ˈnēn\ [F] *dim of* JEANNE
Jen·nie *or* Jen·ny \ˈjen-ē\ *dim of* JANE
Jen·ni·fer \ˈjen-ə-fər\ [Celt]
Jer·al·dine \ˈjer-əl-ˌdēn\ *var of* GERALDINE
Jer·i·lyn \ˈjer-ə-lən\ *var of* GERALDINE
Jer·ry *or* Jeri *or* Jer·rie \ˈjer-ē\ *dim of* GERALDINE
Jes·si·ca \ˈjes-i-kə\ [*prob.* Heb]
Jes·sie \ˈjes-ē\ [Sc] *dim of* JANET
Jew·el *or* Jew·ell \ˈjü(-ə)l, ˈju̇(-ə)l\ [E] jewel

Jill \ˈjil\ *dim of* JULIANA
Jo \ˈjō\ *dim of* JOSEPHINE
Joan *or* Joann *or* Joanne \ˈjō(-ə)n, jō-ˈan\ [Gk] *fem of* JOHN
Jo·an·na \jō-ˈan-ə\ *or* Jo·han·na \-ˈ(h)an-ə\ *var of* JOAN
Joc·e·lyn \ˈjäs-(ə-)lən\ [OF, fr. Gmc]
Jo·dy *or* Jo·die \ˈjō-dē\ *alter of* JUDITH
Jo·lene \jō-ˈlēn\ *prob dim of* JO
Jo·se·phine \ˈjō-zə-ˌfēn *also* ˈjō-sə-\ *fem of* JOSEPH
Joy \ˈjȯi\ [E] joy
Joyce \ˈjȯis\ [OF]
Jua·ni·ta \wä-ˈnēt-ə\ [Sp] *fem dim of* JOHN
Ju·dith \ˈjüd-əth\ [Heb] Jewess
Ju·dy *or* Ju·di *or* Ju·die \ˈjüd-ē\ *dim of* JUDITH
Ju·lia \ˈjül-yə\ [L] *fem of* JULIUS
Ju·li·ana \ˌjü-lē-ˈan-ə\ [LL] *fem of* JULIAN
Ju·li·anne *or* Ju·li·ann \ˌjü-lē-ˈan, jül-ˈyan\ *var of* JULIANA
Ju·lie \ˈjü-lē\ [MF] *var of* JULIA
Ju·liet \ˈjül-yət, -ē-ˌet, -ē-ət; ˌjül-ē-ˈet, jül-ˈyet, ˈjül-ˌyet\ [It] *dim of* JULIA
June \ˈjün\ [E] June (the month)
Jus·tine \ˌjəs-ˈtēn\ [F] *fem of* JUSTIN

Ka·ra \ˈkär-ə, ˈkar-ə\ *var of* CATHERINE
Kar·en *or* Kar·in *or* Kaa·ren \ˈkar-ən, ˈkär-\ [Scand] *var of* CATHERINE
Kar·la \ˈkär-lə\ *var of* CARLA
Kar·ol \ˈkar-əl\ *var of* CAROL
Kar·o·lyn \ˈkar-ə-lən\ *var of* CAROLYN
Kate \ˈkāt\ *dim of* CATHERINE
Kath·er·ine *or* Kath·a·rine *or* Kath·ryn \ˈkath-(ə-)rən\ *var of* CATHERINE
Kath·leen \kath-ˈlēn\ [IrGael] *var of* CATHERINE
Kathy \ˈkath-ē\ *dim of* CATHERINE
Ka·tie \ˈkāt-ē\ *dim of* KATE
Kay *or* Kaye \ˈkā\ *dim of* CATHERINE
Kel·ly \ˈkel-ē\ [fr. a surname]
Ker·ry \ˈker-ē\ [prob. fr. the county of Ireland]
Kim \ˈkim\ *prob dim of* KIMBERLY
Kim·ber·ly \ˈkim-bər-lē\ [OE]
Kit·ty \ˈkit-ē\ *dim of* CATHERINE
Kris·tin \ˈkris-tən\ [Scand] *var of* CHRISTINE
Kris·tine \kris-ˈtēn\ *var of* CHRISTINE

La·na \ˈlan-ə, ˈlän-ə, ˈlā-nə\
Lau·ra \ˈlȯr-ə, ˈlär-\ [ML] *prob fem of* LAWRENCE
Lau·rel \ˈlȯr-əl, ˈlär-\ [E] laurel
Lau·ren \ˈlȯr-ən, ˈlär-\ *var of* LAURA
Lau·rie \ˈlȯr-ē, ˈlär-\ *dim of* LAURA
La·verne *or* La·vern \lə-ˈvərn\
Le·ah \ˈlē-ə\ [Heb] *prob* wild cow
Le·anne \lē-ˈan\ [prob. fr. *Lee* + *Ann*]
Lee \ˈlē\ [fr. a surname]
Leigh \ˈlē\ *var of* LEE
Lei·la *or* Le·la \ˈlē-lə\ [Per] dark as night
Le·lia \ˈlēl-yə\ [L]
Le·na \ˈlē-nə\ [G] *dim of* HELENA. Magdalena
Le·nore \lə-ˈnō(ə)r, -ˈnȯ(ə)r\ *or* Le·no·ra \lə-ˈnȯr-ə, -ˈnȯr-\ *var of* LEONORA
Le·o·na \lē-ˈō-nə\ *fem of* LEON
Le·o·no·ra \ˌlē-ə-ˈnȯr-ə, -ˈnȯr-\ *var of* ELEANOR
Les·lie *or* Les·ley \ˈles-lē *also* ˈlez-\ [fr. a surname]
Le·ti·tia \li-ˈtish-ə, -ˈtē-shə\ [L] gladness
Lib·by \ˈlib-ē\ *dim of* ELIZABETH
Li·la \ˈlī-lə\ *var of* LEILA
Lil·lian \ˈlil-yən, ˈlil-ē-ən\ *prob dim of* ELIZABETH
Lil·lie \ˈlil-ē\ *dim of* LILLIAN
Lily \ˈlil-ē\ [E] lily
Lin·da *or* Lyn·da \ˈlin-də\ *dim of* MELINDA. Belinda
Lind·sey *or* Lind·say \ˈlin-zē\ [OE] linden isle
Li·sa \ˈlī-zə, ˈlē-\ *dim of* ELIZABETH
Lo·is \ˈlō-əs\ [Gk]
Lo·la \ˈlō-lə\ [Sp] *dim of* DOLORES
Lon·na \ˈlän-ə\ *fem of* LON
Lo·ra \ˈlōr-ə, ˈlȯr-\ *var of* LAURA

Lo·re·lei \'lōr-ə-ˌlī, 'lȯr-\ [G]
Lo·rene \lȯ-'rēn\ dim of LORA
Lo·ret·ta \lə-'ret-ə, lȯ-\ [ML] var of Lauretta
Lo·ri \'lōr-ē, 'lȯr-\ var of LAURA
Lor·na \'lȯr-nə\
Lor·raine or Lo·raine \lə-'rān, lȯ-\ [prob. fr. Lorraine, region in northeast France]
Lou \'lü\ dim of LOUISE
Lou·ise \lủ-'ēz\ or Lou·i·sa \-'ē-zə\ fem of LOUIS
Lu·anne \lü-'an\ [Lu- + Anne]
Lu·cille or Lu·cile \lü-'sē(ə)l\ [L] prob dim of LUCIA
Lu·cin·da \lü-'sin-də\ [L] var of LUCY
Lu·cre·tia \lü-'krē-shə\ [L]
Lu·cy \'lü-sē\ or Lu·cia \'lü-shə\ [L] fem of Lucius
Lu·el·la \lủ-'el-ə\ [prob. fr. Lou (dim. of Louise) + Ella]
Lyd·ia \'lid-ē-ə\ [Gk] woman of Lydia, ancient country in Asia Minor
Ly·nette \lə-'net\ [W]
Lynne or Lynn \'lin\ dim of CAROLYN. JACQUELYN. etc.

Ma·bel \'mā-bəl\ [L] lovable
Mac·ken·zie \mə-'ken-zē\ [fr. a surname]
Mad·e·line or Mad·e·leine or Mad·e·lyn \'mad-ᵊl-ən\ [Gk] woman of Magdala, ancient town in northern Palestine
Madge \'maj\ dim of MARGARET
Mal·lory \'mal-(ə-)rē\ [fr. a surname]
Ma·mie \'mā-mē\ dim of MARGARET
Ma·ra \'mär-ə\ var of MARY
Mar·cel·la \mär-'sel-ə\ [L] fem of Marcellus
Mar·cia \'mär-shə\ [L] fem of MARCUS
Mar·ga·ret \'mär-g(ə-)rət\ [Gk] pearl
Mar·gery \'märj-(ə-)rē\ [OF] var of MARGARET
Mar·gie \'mär-jē\ dim of MARGARET
Mar·go \'mär-(ˌ)gō\ var of MARGOT
Mar·got \'mär-(ˌ)gō, -gət\ dim of MARGARET
Mar·gue·rite \ˌmär-g(y)ə-'rēt\ [OF] var of MARGARET
Ma·ria \mə-'rē-ə also -'rī-\ var of MARY
Mar·i·an \'mer-ē-ən, 'mar-\ var of MARIANNE
Mar·i·anne \ˌmer-ē-'an, ˌmar-\ or Mar·i·an·na \-'an-ə\ [F] dim of MARY
Ma·rie \mə-'rē\ [OF] var of MARY
Mar·i·et·ta \ˌmer-ē-'et-ə, ˌmar-\ dim of MARY
Mar·i·lee \'mer-ə-(ˌ)lē, 'mar-\ [prob. fr. Mary + Lee]
Mar·i·lyn or Mar·i·lynn or Mar·y·lyn \'mer-ə-lən, 'mar-\ [prob. fr. Mary + -lyn]
Ma·ri·na \mə-'rē-nə\ [LGk]
Mar·i·on \'mer-ē-ən, 'mar-\ dim of MARY
Mar·jo·rie or Mar·jo·ry \'märj-(ə-)rē\ var of MARGERY
Mar·la \'mär-lə\ prob dim of MARLENE
Mar·lene \mär-'lēn(-ə), -'lā-nə\ [G] dim of Magdalene
Mar·lyn \'mär-lən\ prob var of MARLENE
Mar·sha \'mär-shə\ var of MARCIA
Mar·ta \'märt-ə\ [It] var of MARTHA
Mar·tha \'mär-thə\ [Aram] lady
Mar·va \'mär-və\ prob fem of MARVIN
Mary \'me(ə)r-ē, 'mā-rē\ [Gk, fr. Heb]
Mary·ann or Mary·anne \ˌmer-ē-'an, ˌmā-rē-\ [Mary + Ann]
Mary·el·len \ˌmer-ē-'el-ən, ˌmā-rē-\ [Mary + Ellen]
Mary·lon \'mer-ə-lən, 'mar-\ var of MARILYN
Maude \'mȯd\ [OF] var of Matilda
Mau·reen or Mau·rine \mȯ-'rēn\ [Ir] dim of MARY
Max·ine \mak-'sēn\ [F] fem dim of Maximilian
May or Mae \'mā\ dim of MARY
Me·gan \'meg-ən, 'mē-gən\ [Ir]
Mel·a·nie \'mel-ə-nē\ [Gk] blackness
Mel·ba \'mel-bə\ [E] woman of Melbourne, Australia
Me·lin·da \mə-'lin-də\ prob alter of Belinda
Me·lis·sa \mə-'lis-ə\ [Gk] bee
Mel·va \'mel-və\ prob fem of MELVIN
Mer·e·dith \'mer-əd-əth\ [W]
Merle \'mər(-ə)l\ [F] blackbird
Mer·ri·ly \'mer-ə-lē\ alter of MARILEE
Mer·ry \'mer-ē\ [E] merry

Mia \'mē-ə\ [It]
Mi·chele or Mi·chelle \mi-'shel\ [F] fem of MICHAEL
Mil·dred \'mil-drəd\ [OE] gentle strength
Mil·li·cent \'mil-ə-sənt\ [Gmc]
Mil·lie \'mil-ē\ dim of MILDRED
Min·nie \'min-ē\ [Sc] dim of MARY
Mir·an·da \mə-'ran-də\ [L] admirable
Mir·i·am \'mir-ē-əm\ [Heb] var of MARY
Mit·zi \'mit-sē\ prob dim of MARGARET
Mol·ly or Mol·lie \'mäl-ē\ dim of MARY
Mo·na \'mō-nə\ [IrGael]
Mon·i·ca \'män-i-kə\ [LL]
Mu·ri·el \'myủr-ē-əl\ [prob. Celt]
My·ra \'mī-rə\
Myr·na \'mər-nə\
Myr·tle \'mərt-ᵊl\ [Gk] myrtle

Na·dine \nā-'dēn, nə-\ [F, fr. Russ] hope
Nan \'nan\ dim of ANN
Nan·cy \'nan(t)-sē\ dim of ANN
Nan·nette or Na·nette \na-'net, nə-\ [F] dim of ANN
Na·o·mi \nā-'ō-mē\ [Heb] pleasant
Nat·a·lie \'nat-ᵊl-ē\ [LL] of or relating to Christmas
Nel·lie \'nel-ē\ or Nell \'nel\ dim of ELLEN. HELEN. ELEANOR
Net·tie \'net-ē\ [Sc] dim of JANET
Ni·cole \nē-'kȯl\ [F] fem of NICHOLAS
Ni·na \'nē-nə\ [Russ] dim of ANN
Ni·ta \'nēt-ə\ [Sp] dim of JUANITA
No·na \'nō-nə\ [L] ninth
No·ra \'nōr-ə, 'nȯr-\ dim of LEONORA. ELEANOR. Honora
No·reen \nō-'rēn\ [IrGael] dim of NORA
Nor·ma \'nȯr-mə\ [It]

Ol·ga \'äl-gə, 'ȯl-\ [Russ] var of HELGA
Ol·ive \'äl-iv, -əv\ or O·liv·ia \ə-'liv-ē-ə, ō-\ [L] olive
Opal \'ō-pəl\ [E] opal

Pam \'pam\ dim of PAMELA
Pa·me·la \'pam-ə-lə; pə-'mē-lə, pa-\
Pa·tri·cia \pə-'trish-ə, -'trē-shə\ [L] fem of PATRICK
Pat·sy \'pat-sē\ dim of PATRICIA
Pat·ty or Pat·ti or Pat·tie \'pat-ē\ dim of PATRICIA
Pau·la \'pȯ-lə\ [L] fem of PAUL
Pau·lette \pȯ-'let\ fem dim of PAUL
Pau·line \pȯ-'lēn\ fem dim of PAUL
Pearl \'pər(-ə)l\ [E] pearl
Peg·gy \'peg-ē\ dim of MARGARET
Pe·nel·o·pe \pə-'nel-ə-pē\ [Gk]
Pen·ny \'pen-ē\ dim of PENELOPE
Phoe·be \'fē-bē\ [Gk] shining
Phyl·lis \'fil-əs\ [Gk] green leaf
Pol·ly \'päl-ē\ dim of MARY
Por·tia \'pōr-shə, 'pȯr-\ [L]
Pris·cil·la \prə-'sil-ə\ [L]
Pru·dence \'prüd-ᵊn(t)s\ [E] prudence

Ra·chel \'rā-chəl\ [Heb] ewe
Rae \'rā\ dim of RACHEL
Ra·mo·na \rə-'mō-nə\ [Sp] fem of RAMON
Re·ba \'rē-bə\ dim of REBECCA
Re·bec·ca \ri-'bek-ə\ [Heb]
Re·gi·na \ri-'jē-nə, -'jī-\ [L] queen
Re·nee \rə-'nā, 'ren-(ˌ)ā, 'rā-nē, 'rē-nē\ [F] reborn
Rhea \'rē-ə\ [Gk]
Rho·da \'rōd-ə\ [Gk] rose
Ri·ta \'rēt-ə\ [It] dim of MARGARET
Ro·ber·ta \rə-'bərt-ə, rō-\ fem of ROBERT
Rob·in or Rob·yn \'räb-ən\ [E] robin
Ro·chelle \rō-'shel\ [prob. fr. a surname]
Ro·na or Rho·na \'rō-nə\
Ron·da \'rän-də\ var of Rhonda
Ron·nie \'rän-ē\ dim of VERONICA
Ro·sa·lie \'rō-zə-(ˌ)lē, 'räz-ə-\ [L] festival of roses
Ro·sa·lind \'räz-(ə-)lənd, 'rō-zə-lənd\ [Sp]
Rose \'rōz\ or Ro·sa \'rō-zə\ [L] rose

Rose•anne \rō-'zan\ [*Rose + Anne*]
Rose•mary \'rōz-ˌmer-ē\ *or* **Rose•ma•rie** \ˌrōz-mə-'rē\ [E] rosemary
Ro•set•ta \rō-'zet-ə\ *dim of* ROSE
Ros•lyn \'räz-lən\ *or* **Ro•sa•lyn** *or* **Ro•se•lyn** \'räz-(ə-)lən, 'rō-zə-lən\ *var of* ROSALIND
Ro•we•na \rə-'wē-nə\ [perh. fr. OE]
Rox•anne \räk-'san\ [OPer]
Ru•by \'rü-bē\ [E] ruby
Ruth \'rüth\ [Heb]
Ruth•ann \rü-'than\ [*Ruth + Ann*]

Sa•bra \'sā-brə\ *dim of* Sabrina
Sa•die \'sād-ē\ *dim of* SARA
Sal•ly *or* **Sal•lie** \'sal-ē\ *dim of* SARA
Sa•man•tha \sə-'man-thə\ [Aram]
San•dra \'san-drə, 'sän-\ *dim of* ALEXANDRA
San•dy \'san-dē\ *dim of* ALEXANDRA
Sar•ah *or* **Sara** \'ser-ə, 'sar-ə, 'sā-rə\ [Heb] princess
Sara•lee \'ser-ə-(ˌ)lē, 'sar-\ [prob. fr. *Sara + Lee*]
Saun•dra \'sȯn-drə, 'sän-\ *var of* SANDRA
Sel•ma \'sel-mə\ [Sw] *fem dim of* Anselm
Shari \'sha(ə)r-ē, 'she(ə)r-\ *dim of* SHARON
Shar•lene \shär-'lēn\ *var of* CHARLENE
Shar•on *or* **Shar•ron** \'shar-ən, 'sher-\ [Heb]
Shei•la \'shē-lə\ [IrGael] *var of* CECILIA
She•lia \'shēl-yə\ *var of* SHEILA
Shel•ley \'shel-ē\ [fr. a surname]
Sher•rill *or* **Sher•yl** \'sher-əl\ [prob. fr. a surname]
Sher•ry *or* **Sher•rie** *or* **Sheri** \'sher-ē\
Shir•ley \'shər-lē\ [fr. a surname]
Sig•rid \'sig-rəd\ [Scand] beautiful as victory
Son•dra \'sän-drə\ *var of* SANDRA
So•nia *or* **So•nya** *or* **So•nja** \'sō-nyə, 'sȯ-\ [Russ] *dim of* SOPHIA
So•phia \sə-'fē-ə, -'fī-\ *or* **So•phie** \'sō-fē\ [Gk] wisdom
Sta•cy *or* **Sta•cey** \'stā-sē\ *dim of* ANASTASIA
Stel•la \'stel-ə\ [L] star
Steph•a•nie \'stef-ə-nē\ *fem of* STEPHEN
Sue \'sü\ *or* **Su•sie** \'sü-zē\ *dim of* SUSAN
Su•el•len \sü-'el-ən\ [*Sue + Ellen*]
Su•san *or* **Su•zan** \'süz-ᵊn\ *dim of* SUSANNA
Su•san•na *or* **Su•san•nah** \sü-'zan-ə\ [Heb] lily
Su•zanne *or* **Su•sanne** *or* **Su•zann** \sü-'zan\ [F] *var of* SUSAN
Syb•il \'sib-əl\ [Gk] sibyl
Syl•via \'sil-vē-ə\ [L] she of the forest

Ta•mara \tə-'mar-ə\ [prob. fr. Georgian (language of the Soviet republic of Georgia)]
Tan•ya \'tan-yə\ [Russ] *dim of* TATIANA
Ta•ra \tăr-ə\ [IrGael]
Tat•i•ana \ˌtät-ē-'än-ə\ [Russ]
Te•re•sa \tə-'rē-sə\ *var of* THERESA
Ter•ry *or* **Ter•ri** \'ter-ē\ *dim of* THERESA
Thel•ma \'thel-mə\
The•o•do•ra \ˌthē-ə-'dōr-ə, -'dȯr-\ [LGk] *fem of* THEODORE
The•re•sa *or* **Te•re•sa** \tə-'rē-sə\ [LL]
The•rese \tə-'rēs\ *var of* THERESA
Tif•fa•ny \'tif-ə-nē\ [Gk]
Ti•na \'tē-nə\ *dim of* CHRISTINA
To•by \'tō-bē\
To•ni \'tō-nē\ *dim of* Antonia
Tra•cy \'trā-sē\ [fr. a surname]
Tru•dy \'trüd-ē\ *dim of* GERTRUDE

Ur•su•la \'ər-sə-lə\ [LL] little she-bear

Val•er•ie \'val-ə-rē\ [L] *prob* strong
Van•es•sa \və-'nes-ə\
Vel•ma \'vel-mə\
Ve•ra \'vir-ə\ [Russ] faith
Ver•na \'vər-nə\ *prob fem of* VERNON
Ve•ron•i•ca \və-'rän-i-kə\ [LL]
Vicki *or* **Vicky** *or* **Vick•ie** \'vik-ē\ *dim of* VICTORIA
Vic•to•ria \vik-'tōr-ē-ə, -'tȯr-\ [L] victory
Vi•da \'vēd-ə, 'vīd-\ *fem dim of* DAVID
Vi•o•la \vī-'ō-lə, vē-'ō-, 'vī-ə-, 'vē-ə-\ [L] violet
Vi•o•let \'vī-ə-lət\ [OF, fr. L] violet
Vir•gin•ia \vər-'jin-yə, -'jin-ē-ə\ [L]
Viv•i•an \'viv-ē-ən\ [LL]

Wan•da \'wän-də\ [Pol]
Wen•dy \'wen-dē\
Whit•ney \'hwit-nē, 'wit-\ [OE]
Wil•da \'wil-də\ *var of* WILLA
Wil•la \'wil-ə\ *or* **Wil•lie** \'wil-ē\ *prob fem dim of* WILLIAM
Wil•ma \'wil-mə\ *prob fem dim of* WILLIAM
Win•i•fred \'win-ə-frəd\ [W]

Yvette \i-'vet\ [F]
Yvonne \i-'vän\ [F]

Zel•da \'zel-də\ *dim of* Griselda

Foreign Words and Phrases

ab·eunt stu·dia in mo·res \ˈä-be-ˌu̇nt-ˈstü-dē-ˌä-in-ˈmō-ˌräs\ [L] : practices zealously pursued pass into habits

à bien·tôt \à-byaⁿ-tō\ [F] : so long

ab in·cu·na·bu·lis \ˌäb-ˌiŋ-kù-ˈnä-bù-ˌlēs\ [L] : from the cradle : from infancy

à bon chat, bon rat \à-bōⁿ-ˈshà-bōⁿ-ˈrà\ [F] : to a good cat, a good rat : retaliation in kind

à bouche ou·verte \à-bü-shü-vert\ [F] : with open mouth : eagerly : uncritically

ab ovo us·que ad ma·la \äb-ˈō-vō-ˌu̇s-kwe-ˌäd-ˈmä-lä\ [L] : from egg to apples : from soup to nuts : from beginning to end

à bras ou·verts \à-brà-zü-ver\ [F] : with open arms : cordially

ab·sit in·vi·dia \ˈäb-ˌsit-in-ˈwi-dē-ˌä\ [L] : let there be no envy or ill will

ab uno dis·ce om·nes \äb-ˈü-nō-ˌdis-ke-ˈòm-ˌnäs\ [L] : from one learn to know all

ab ur·be con·di·ta \äb-ˈu̇r-be-ˈkòn-di-ˌtä\ [L] : from the founding of the city (Rome, founded 753 B.C.) — used by the Romans in reckoning dates

ab·usus non tol·lit usum \ˈä-ˌbü-sùs-ˌnōn-ˌtò-lit-ˈü-süm\ [L] : abuse does not take away use, i.e., is not an argument against proper use

à compte \à-kōⁿt\ [F] : on account

à coup sûr \à-kü-sœ̄r\ [F] : with sure stroke : surely

acte gra·tuit \àk-tə-grà-twᵉe\ [F] : gratuitous impulsive act

ad ar·bi·tri·um \ˌad-är-ˈbi-trē-ùm\ [L] : at will : arbitrarily

ad as·tra per as·pe·ra \ad-ˈas-trə-ˌpər-ˈas-pə-rə\ [L] : to the stars by hard ways — motto of Kansas

ad ex·tre·mum \ˌad-ik-ˈstrē-məm\ [L] : to the extreme : at last

ad ka·len·das Grae·cas \ˌäd-kä-ˈlen-däs-ˈgrī-ˌkäs\ [L] : at the Greek calends : never (since the Greeks had no calends)

ad ma·jo·rem Dei glo·ri·am \ˌäd-mä-ˈyòr-ˌem-ˈde-ˌē-ˈglòr-ē-ˌäm\ [L] : to the greater glory of God — motto of the Society of Jesus

ad pa·tres \äd-ˈpä-ˌträs\ [L] : (gathered) to his fathers : deceased

ad re·fe·ren·dum \ˌäd-ˌre-fe-ˈren-dùm\ [L] : for reference : for further consideration by one having the authority to make a final decision

à droite \à-drwät\ [F] : to or on the right hand

ad un·guem \ˌäd-ˈu̇ŋ-ˌgwem\ [L] : to the fingernail : to a nicety : exactly (from the use of the fingernail to test the smoothness of marble)

ad utrum·que pa·ra·tus \ˌäd-ù-ˈtrùm-kwe-pä-ˈrä-tùs\ [L] : prepared for either (event)

ad vi·vum \ˌäd-ˈwē-ˌwùm\ [L] : to the life

ae·gri som·nia \ˈī-grē-ˈsóm-nē-ˌä\ [L] : a sick man's dreams

ae·quam ser·va·re men·tem \ˈī-kwäm-ser-ˈwä-rä-ˈmen-ˌtem\ [L] : to preserve a calm mind

ae·quo ani·mo \ˈī-ˌkwō-ˈä-ni-ˌmō\ [L] : with even mind : calmly

ae·re per·en·ni·us \ˈī-rä-pe-ˈre-nē-ˌùs\ [L] : more lasting than bronze

à gauche \à-gōsh\ [F] : to or on the left hand

age quod agis \ˈä-ge-ˌkwòd-ˈä-gis\ [L] : do what you are doing : to the business at hand

à grands frais \à-gräⁿ-fre\ [F] : at great expense

à huis clos \à-wᵉe-klō\ [F] : with closed doors

aide–toi, le ciel t'ai·dera \ed-twà-lə-ˈsyel-te-drà\ [F] : help yourself (and) heaven will help you

aî·né \e-nä\ [F] : elder : senior (masc.)

aî·née \e-nä\ [F] : elder : senior (fem.)

à l'aban·don \à-là-bäⁿ-dōⁿ\ [F] : carelessly : in disorder

à la belle étoile \à-là-bel-ä-twàl\ [F] : under the beautiful star : in the open air at night

à la bonne heure \à-là-bò-nœr\ [F] : at a good time : well and good : all right

à la fran·çaise \à-là-fräⁿ-sez\ [F] : in the French manner

à l'amé·ri·caine \à-là-mä-rē-ken\ [F] : in the American manner : of the American kind

à l'an·glaise \à-làⁿ-glez\ [F] : in the English manner

à la page \à-là-päzh\ [F] : at the page : up-to=the-minute

à la russe \à-là-rǖs\ [F] : in the Russian manner

alea jac·ta est \ˈä-lē-ˌä-ˌyäk-tä-ˈest\ [L] : the die is cast

à l'im·pro·viste \à-laⁿ-prò-vēst\ [F] : unexpectedly

ali·quan·do bo·nus dor·mi·tat Ho·me·rus \ˌä-li-ˈkwän-dō-ˌbò-nùs-dòr-ˈmē-tät-hō-ˈmer-ùs\ [L] : sometimes (even) good Homer nods

alis vo·lat pro·pri·is \ˈä-lēs-ˈwò-ˌlät-ˈprō-prē-ˌēs\ [L] : she flies with her own wings — motto of Oregon

al–ki \ˈal-ˌkī\ [Chinook Jargon] : by and by — motto of Washington

alo·ha oe \à-ˌlō-hä-ˈòi, -ˈō-ē\ [Hawaiian] : love to you : greetings : farewell

al·ter idem \ˌòl-tər-ˈī-ˌdem, ˌäl-ter-ˈē-\ [L] : second self

a max·i·mis ad mi·ni·ma \ä-ˈmäk-si-ˌmēs-ˌäd-ˈmi-ni-ˌmä\ [L] : from the greatest to the least

ami·cus hu·ma·ni ge·ne·ris \ä-ˌmē-kùs-hü-ˈmä-nē-ˈge-ne-ris\ [L] : friend of the human race

ami·cus us·que ad aras \ˌä-ˌu̇s-kwe-ˌäd-ˈär-äs\ [L] : a friend as far as to the altars, i.e., except in what is contrary to one's religion; *also* : a friend to the last extremity

ami de cour \à-mē-də-kùr\ [F] : court friend : insincere friend

amor pa·tri·ae \ˈä-ˌmòr-ˈpä-trē-ˌī\ [L] : love of one's country

amor vin·cit om·nia \ˈä-ˌmòr-ˈwiŋ-kit-ˈòm-nē-ä\ [L] : love conquers all things

an·cienne no·blesse \äⁿ-syen-nò-bles\ [F] : old-time nobility : the French nobility before the Revolution of 1789

an·guis in her·ba \ˈäŋ-gwis-in-ˈher-ˌbä\ [L] : snake in the grass

ani·mal bi·pes im·plu·me \ˈä-ni-mäl-ˈbi-ˌpäs-im-ˈplü-me\ [L] : two-legged animal without feathers (i.e., the human race)

ani·mis opi·bus·que pa·ra·ti \ˈä-ni-ˌmēs-ˌò-pi-ˈbùs-kwe-pä-ˈrä-tē\ [L] : prepared in mind and resources — one of the mottoes of South Carolina

an·no ae·ta·tis su·ae \ˈä-nō-ī-ˈtä-tis-ˈsü-ˌī\ [L] : in the (specified) year of his or her age

an·no mun·di \ˈä-nō-ˈmùn-dē\ [L] : in the year of the world — used in reckoning dates from the supposed period of the creation of the world, esp. as fixed by James Ussher at 4004 B.C. or by the Jews at 3761 B.C.

an·no ur·bis con·di·tae \ˈä-nō-ˈùr-bis-ˈkòn-di-ˌtī\ [L] : in the year of the founded city (Rome, founded 753 B.C.)

an·nu·it coep·tis \ˈä-nù-ˌwit-ˈkòip-ˌtēs\ [L] : He (God) has approved our beginnings — motto on the reverse of the Great Seal of the United States

à peu près \à-pœ-pre\ [F] : nearly : approximately

à pied \à-pyä\ [F] : on foot

après moi le déluge \à-pre-mwà-lə-dā-lūēzh\ *or* **après nous le déluge** \à-pre-nü-\ [F] : after me the deluge — attributed to Louis XV

à pro·pos de bottes \à-prə-pō-də-bót\ [F] : apropos of boots — used to change the subject

à pro·pos de rien \-ryaⁿ\ [F] : apropos of nothing

aqua et ig·ni in·ter·dic·tus \'äk-wä-et-'ig-nē-,in-ter-'dik-tús\ [L] : forbidden to be furnished with water and fire : outlawed

Ar·ca·des am·bo \'är-kä-,des-'äm-bō\ [L] : both Arcadians : two persons of like occupations or tastes; *also* : two rascals

ar·rec·tis au·ri·bus \ä-'rek-,tēs-'aú-ri-,bús\ [L] : with ears pricked up : attentively

ar·ri·ve·der·ci \ä-,rē-ve-'der-chē\ [It] : till we meet again : farewell

ars est ce·la·re ar·tem \'ärs-,est-kä-'lär-ā-'är-,tem\ [L] : it is (true) art to conceal art

ars lon·ga, vi·ta bre·vis \'ärs-'lóŋ-,gä-'wē-,tä-'bre-wis\ [L] : art is long, life is short

a ter·go \ä-'ter-(,)gō\ [L] : from behind

à tort et à tra·vers \à-,tór-ā-à-trà-'ver\ [F] : wrong and crosswise : at random : without rhyme or reason

au bout de son la·tin \ō-bü-də-sōⁿ-là-taⁿ\ [F] : at the end of one's Latin : at the end of one's mental resources

au con·traire \ō-kōⁿ-trer\ [F] : on the contrary

au·de·mus ju·ra nos·tra de·fen·de·re \aú-'dā-mùs-'yúr-ä-'nó-strä-dā-'fen-de-rä\ [L] : we dare defend our rights — motto of Alabama

au·den·tes for·tu·na ju·vat \aú-'den-,tās-fòr-'tü-nä-'yü-,wät\ [L] : fortune favors the bold

au·di al·ter·am par·tem \'aú-,dē-'äl-te-,räm-'pär-,tem\ [L] : hear the other side

au fait \ō-fet, -fe\ [F] : to the point : fully competent : fully informed : socially correct

au fond \ō-fōⁿ\ [F] : at bottom : fundamentally

au grand sé·rieux \ō-grän-sā-ryœ̄\ [F] : in all seriousness

au pays des aveugles les borgnes sont rois \ō-pā-ē-dā-zà-vœgl³-lā-bórn³-ə-sōⁿ-rwà\ [F] : in the country of the blind the one-eyed men are kings

au·rea me·dio·cri·tas \'aú-rē-ä-,me-dē-'ò-kri-,täs\ [L] : the golden mean

au reste \ō-rest\ [F] : for the rest : besides

aus·si·tôt dit, aus·si·tôt fait \ō-sē-tō-dē-ō-sē-tō-fe\ [F] : no sooner said than done

aut Cae·sar aut ni·hil \aút-'kī-sär-,aút-'ni-,hil\ [L] : either a Caesar or nothing

aut Caesar aut nul·lus \-'nü-lùs\ [L] : either a Caesar or a nobody

au·tres temps, au·tres mœurs \ō-trə-täⁿ-ō-trə-mœrs\ [F] : other times, other customs

aut vin·ce·re aut mo·ri \,aút-'wiŋ-ke-rä-,aút-'mò-,rē\ [L] : either to conquer or to die

aux armes \ō-zàrm\ [F] : to arms

avant la lettre \à-väⁿ-là-letr³\ [F] : before the letter : before a (specified) name existed

ave at·que va·le \'ä-,wā-,ät-kwe-'wä-,lā\ [L] : hail and farewell

à vo·tre san·té \à-vòt-säⁿ-tā, -vò-trə-\ [F] : to your health — used as a toast

beaux yeux \bō-zyœ̄\ [F] : beautiful eyes : beauty of face

bel·la fi·gu·ra \'bel-lä-fē-'gü-rä\ [It] : fine appearance or impression

belle laide \bel-led\ [F] : beautiful ugly woman : a woman who is attractive though not conventionally beautiful

bien en·ten·du \byaⁿ-näⁿ-täⁿ-dūē\ [F] : well understood : of course

bien—pen·sant \byaⁿ-päⁿ-säm\ [F] : right-minded : one who holds orthodox views

bien·sé·ance \byaⁿ-sā-äⁿs\ [F] : propriety

bis dat qui ci·to dat \'bis-,dät-kwē-'ki-tō-,dät\ [L] : he or she gives twice who gives promptly

bon ap·pé·tit \bó-nà-pā-tē\ [F] : good appetite : enjoy your meal

bon gré, mal gré \'bōⁿ-,grä-'màl-,grä\ [F] : whether with good grace or bad : willy-nilly

bo·nis avi·bus \'bó-,nēs-'ä-wi-,bùs\ [L] : under good auspices

bon·jour \bōⁿ-zhür\ [F] : good day : good morning

bonne foi \bón-fwä\ [F] : good faith

bon·soir \bōⁿ-swàr\ [F] : good evening

bru·tum ful·men \'brü-tùm-'fúl-men\ [L] : insensible thunderbolt : a futile threat or display of force

buon gior·no \bwòn-'jòr-nō\ [It] : good day

ca·dit quae·stio \'kä-dit-'kwī-stē-,ō\ [L] : the question drops : the argument collapses

cau·sa si·ne qua non \'kaú-,sä-si-nä-kwä-'nōn\ [L] : an indispensable cause or condition

ça va sans dire \sà-và-säⁿ-dēr\ [F] : it goes without saying

ca·ve ca·nem \'kä-wā-'kä-,nem\ [L] : beware the dog

ce·dant ar·ma to·gae \'kā-,dänt-'är-mə-'tō-,gī\ [L] : let arms yield to the toga : let military power give way to civil power — motto of Wyoming

ce n'est que le pre·mier pas qui coûte \snek-lə-prə-myä-pä-kē-küt\ [F] : it is only the first step that costs

c'est-à-dire \se-tà-dēr\ [F] : that is to say : namely

c'est au·tre chose \se-tōt-shōz, -tō-trə-\ [F] : that's a different thing

c'est la guerre \se-là-ger\ [F] : that's war : it cannot be helped

c'est la vie \se-là-vē\ [F] : that's life : that's how things happen

c'est plus qu'un crime, c'est une faute \se-plūē-kœⁿ-krēm-se-tūēn-fōt\ [F] : it is worse than a crime, it is a blunder

ce·te·ra de·sunt \'kä-te-rä-'dā-,sùnt\ [L] : the rest is missing

cha·cun à son goût \shà-kœⁿ-nà-sōⁿ-gü\ [F] : everyone to his or her taste

châ·teau en Es·pagne \shä-tō-äⁿ-nes-pán^y\ [F] : castle in Spain : a visionary project

cher·chez la femme \sher-shā-là-fàm\ [F] : look for the woman

che sa·rà, sa·rà \kā-sä-,rä-sä-'rä\ [It] : what will be, will be

che·val de ba·taille \shə-vàl-də-bà-tä^y\ [F] : war-horse : argument constantly relied on : favorite subject

co·gi·to, er·go sum \'kō-gi-,tō-'er-gō-'sùm\ [L] : I think, therefore I exist

co·mé·die hu·maine \kó-mā-dē-ūē-men\ [F] : human comedy : the whole variety of human life

comme ci, comme ça \kòm-sē-kòm-sà\ [F] : so-so

com·pa·gnon de voy·age \kōⁿ-pà-n^yōn- də-vwà-yàzh\ [F] : traveling companion

compte ren·du \kōⁿt-räⁿ-dūē\ [F] : report (as of proceedings in an investigation)

con·cor·dia dis·cors \kòn-'kòr-dē-ä-'dis-,kòrs\ [L] : discordant harmony

cor·rup·tio op·ti·mi pes·si·ma \kó-'rùp-tē-,ō-'äp-ti-,mē-'pe-si-,mä\ [L] : the corruption of the best is the worst of all

coup de maî·tre \küd-metr³, kü-də-\ [F] : masterstroke

coup d'es·sai \kü-dä-se\ [F] : experiment : trial

coûte que coûte \küt-kə-küt\ [F] : cost what it may

cre·do quia ab·sur·dum est \'krā-dō-'kwē-ä-äp-'sùr-dùm-'est\ [L] : I believe it because it is absurd

cres·cit eun·do \'kres-kit-'eùn-dō\ [L] : it grows as it goes — motto of New Mexico

crise de nerfs *or* **crise des nerfs** \krēz-də-ner\ [F] : crisis of nerves : nervous collapse : hysterical fit

crux cri·ti·co·rum \'krùks-,kri-ti-'kōr-ùm\ [L] : crux of critics

cuj·us re·gio, ej·us re·li·gio \\'kü-yùs-'re-gē-ō-'e-yùs-re-'li-gē-ō\\ [L] : whose region, his or her religion : subjects are to accept the religion of their ruler

cum gra·no sa·lis \\kùm-'grä-nō-'sä-lis\\ [L] : with a grain of salt

cur·sus ho·no·rum \\'kùr-sùs-hò-'nō-rùm\\ [L] : course of honors : succession of offices of increasing importance

cus·tos mo·rum \\'kùs-tōs-'mōr-ùm\\ [L] : guardian of manners or morals : censor

d'ac·cord \\dá-kór\\ [F] : in accord : agreed

dame d'hon·neur \\däm-dò-nœr\\ [F] : lady-in-waiting

dam·nant quod non in·tel·li·gunt \\'däm-nänt-kwòd-'nōn-in-'te-li-gùnt\\ [L] : they condemn what they do not understand

de bonne grâce \\də-bón-gräs\\ [F] : with good grace : willingly

de gus·ti·bus non est dis·pu·tan·dum \\dä-'gùs-ti-bùs-'nōn-est-dis-pù-'tän-dùm\\ [L] : there is no disputing about tastes

Dei gra·tia \\'de-ē-'grä-tē-ä\\ [L] : by the grace of God

de in·te·gro \\dä-'in-te-grō\\ [L] : anew : afresh

de l'au·dace, en·core de l'au·dace, et tou·jours de l'au·dace \\də-lō-däs-än-kór-də-lō-däs-ä-tü-zhür-də-lō-däs\\ [F] : audacity, more audacity, and ever more audacity

de·len·da est Car·tha·go \\dä-'len-dä-est-kär-'tä-gō\\ [L] : Carthage must be destroyed

de·li·ne·a·vit \\dä-lē-nä-'ä-wit\\ [L] : he or she drew it

de mal en pis \\də-mä-län-pē\\ [F] : from bad to worse

de mi·ni·mis non cu·rat lex \\dä-'mi-ni-mēs-nōn-'kü-rät-'leks\\ [L] : the law takes no account of trifles

de mor·tu·is nil ni·si bo·num \\dä-'mór-tù-wēs-nēl-ni-sē-'bò-nùm\\ [L] : of the dead (say) nothing but good

de nos jours \\də-nō-zhür\\ [F] : of our time : contemporary — used postpositively esp. after a proper name

Deo fa·ven·te \\dä-ō-fä-'ven-tā\\ [L] : with God's favor

Deo gra·ti·as \\dä-ō-'grä-tē-äs\\ [L] : thanks (be) to God

de pro·fun·dis \\dä-prō-'fùn-dēs\\ [L] : out of the depths

der Geist der stets ver·neint \\dər-'gīst-dər-shtäts-fer-'nīnt\\ [G] : the spirit that ever denies — applied originally to Mephistopheles

de·si·pe·re in lo·co \\dä-'si-pe-rä-in-'lō-kō\\ [L] : to indulge in trifling at the proper time

Deus vult \\'dä-ùs-'wùlt\\ [L] : God wills it — rallying cry of the First Crusade

di·es fau·stus \\'dē-äs-'faù-stùs\\ [L] : lucky day

dies in·fau·stus \\-'in-faù-stùs\\ [L] : unlucky day

dies irae \\-'ē-rī\\ [L] : day of wrath — used of the Judgment Day

Dieu et mon droit \\dyœ-ä-móⁿ-drwä\\ [F] : God and my right — motto on the British royal arms

Dieu vous garde \\dyœ-vü-gàrd\\ [F] : God keep you

di·ri·go \\'dē-ri-gō\\ [L] : I direct — motto of Maine

dis ali·ter vi·sum \\'dēs-'ä-li-ter-'wē-sùm\\ [L] : the Gods decreed otherwise

di·tat De·us \\'dē-tät-'dä-ùs\\ [L] : God enriches — motto of Arizona

di·vi·de et im·pe·ra \\'dē-wi-de-et-'im-pe-rä\\ [L] : divide and rule

do·cen·do dis·ci·mus \\dò-ken-dō-'dis-ki-mùs\\ [L] : we learn by teaching

Do·mi·ne di·ri·ge nos \\'dò-mi-ne-'dē-ri-ge-'nōs\\ [L] : Lord, direct us — motto of the City of London

Do·mi·nus vo·bis·cum \\'dò-mi-nùs-wō-'bēs-kùm\\ [L] : the Lord be with you

dul·ce et de·co·rum est pro pa·tria mo·ri \\'dùl-kä-et-de-'kór-ùm-est-prō-'pä-trē-ä-'mò-rē\\ [L] : it is sweet and seemly to die for one's country

dum spi·ro, spe·ro \\dùm-'spē-rō-'spä-rō\\ [L] : while I breathe I hope — one of the mottoes of South Carolina

dum vi·vi·mus vi·va·mus \\dùm-'wē-wē-mùs-wē-'wä-mùs\\ [L] : while we live, let us live

d'un certain âge \\dœn-ser-te-näzh\\ [F] : of a certain age : no longer young

dux fe·mi·na fac·ti \\'dùks-'fä-mi-nä-'fäk-tē\\ [L] : a woman was leader of the exploit

ec·ce sig·num \\'e-ke-'sig-nùm\\ [L] : behold the sign : look at the proof

e con·tra·rio \\ä-kòn-'trär-ē-ō\\ [L] : on the contrary

écra·sez l'in·fâme \\ä-krä-zä-laⁿ-fäm\\ [F] : crush the infamous thing

eheu fu·ga·ces la·bun·tur an·ni \\'ä-heù-fù-'gä-käs-lä-bùn-tùr-'än-ē\\ [L] : alas! the fleeting years glide on

ein' fes·te Burg ist un·ser Gott \\īn-fes-tə-'bùrk-ist-ùn-zər-'gòt\\ [G] : a mighty fortress is our God

em·bar·ras de ri·chesses *or* **embarras de ri·chesse** \\än-bä-rä-də-rē-shes\\ [F] : embarrassing surplus of riches : confusing abundance

em·bar·ras de choix \\än-bä-rä-də-shwä\\ *or* **embarras du choix** \\-dᵫ-shwä\\ [F] : embarrassing variety of choice

en ami \\äⁿ-nä-mē\\ [F] : as a friend

en ef·fet \\äⁿ-nä-fe\\ [F] : in fact : indeed

en fa·mille \\äⁿ-fä-mēy\\ [F] : in or with one's family : at home : informally

en·fant ché·ri \\äⁿ-fäⁿ-shä-rē\\ [F] : loved or pampered child : one that is highly favored

en·fant gâ·té \\äⁿ-fäⁿ-gä-tä\\ [F] : spoiled child

en·fants per·dus \\äⁿ-fäⁿ-per-dᵫ\\ [F] : lost children : soldiers sent to a dangerous post

en·fin \\äⁿ-faⁿ\\ [F] : in conclusion : in a word

en gar·çon \\äⁿ-gàr-sō^m\\ [F] : as or like a bachelor

en garde \\äⁿ-gàrd\\ [F] : on guard

en pan·tou·fles \\äⁿ-päⁿ-tüfl^ə\\ [F] : in slippers : at ease : informally

en plein air \\äⁿ-ple-ner\\ [F] : in the open air

en plein jour \\äⁿ-plaⁿ-zhür\\ [F] : in broad day

en règle \\äⁿ-regl^ə\\ [F] : in order : in due form

en re·tard \\äⁿ-rə-tàr\\ [F] : behind time : late

en re·traite \\äⁿ-rə-tret\\ [F] : in retreat : in retirement

en re·vanche \\äⁿ-rə-väⁿsh\\ [F] : in return : in compensation

en se·condes noces \\äⁿ-sə-gōnd-nós\\ [F] : in a second marriage

en·se pe·tit pla·ci·dam sub li·ber·ta·te qui·e·tem \\'en-se-pe-tit-'plä-ki-däm-sùb-'lē-ber-tä-te-kwē-'ä-tem\\ [L] : with the sword she seeks calm repose under liberty — by the sword we seek peace, but peace only under liberty — motto of Massachusetts

eo ip·so \\ä-ō-'ip-(.)sō\\ [L] : by that itself : by that fact alone

épa·ter le bour·geois \\ä-pá-tä-lə-bür-zhwä\\ [F] : to shock the middle classes

e plu·ri·bus unum \\ē-'plùr-ə-bəs-'yü-nəm, ä-'plùr-i-bùs-'ü-nùm\\ [L] : one out of many — used on the Great Seal of the U.S. and on several U.S. coins

ep·pur si muo·ve \\äp-'pür-sē-'mwò-vä\\ [It] : and yet it does move — attributed to Galileo after recanting his assertion of the earth's motion

Erin go bragh \\'er-ən-gə-'brò, -gō-'brä\\ [Ir *go brách* or *go bráth*, lit., till doomsday] : Ireland forever

er·ra·re hu·ma·num est \\e-'rär-e-hü-'mä-nùm-'est\\ [L] : to err is human

es·prit de l'es·ca·lier \\es-prēd-les-kà-lyä\\ *or* **es·prit d'es·ca·lier** \\-prē-des-\\ [F] : staircase wit : repartee thought of only too late

es·se quam vi·de·ri \\'e-sä-kwäm-wi-'dä-rē\\ [L] : to be rather than to seem — motto of North Carolina

est mo·dus in re·bus \\est-'mò-dùs-in-'rä-bùs\\ [L] : there is a proper measure in things, i.e., the golden mean should always be observed

es·to per·pe·tua \\'es-tō-per-'pe-tù-wä\\ [L] : may she endure forever — motto of Idaho

et hoc ge·nus om·ne \\et-'hōk-'ge-nùs-'òm-ne\\ *or* **et id genus omne** \\et-id-\\ [L] : and everything of this kind

et in Ar·ca·dia ego \ˌet-in-är-ˈkä-dē-ä-ˈe-gō\ [L] : I too (lived) in Arcadia

et sic de si·mi·li·bus \et-ˈsēk-dä-si-ˈmi-li-ˌbús\ [L] : and so of like things

et tu Bru·te \et-ˈtü-ˈbrü-te\ [L] : thou too, Brutus — exclamation attributed to Julius Caesar on seeing his friend Brutus among his assassins

eu·re·ka \yu̇-ˈrē-kə\ [Gk] : I have found it — motto of California

Ewig–Weib·li·che \ˌā-vik̲-ˈvīp-li-k̲ə\ [G] : eternal feminine

ex·al·té \eg-zȧl-tā\ [F] : emotionally excited or elated : fanatic

ex ani·mo \eks-ˈä-ni-ˌmō\ [L] : from the heart : sincerely

ex·cel·si·or \ik-ˈsel-sē-ər, eks-ˈkel-sē-ˌȯr\ [L] : still higher — motto of New York

ex·cep·tio pro·bat regu·lam de re·bus non ex·cep·tis \eks-ˈkep-tē-ō-ˈprō-bät-ˈrä-gu̇-ˌläm-dä-ˈrä-ˌbús-ˈnōn-eks-ˈkep-ˌtēs\ [L] : an exception establishes the rule as to things not excepted

ex·cep·tis ex·ci·pi·en·dis \eks-ˈkep-ˌtēs-eks-ˌki-pē-ˈen-ˌdēs\ [L] : with the proper or necessary exceptions

ex·i·tus ac·ta pro·bat \ˈek-si-ˌtús-ˈäk-tä-ˈprò-ˌbät\ [L] : the outcome justifies the deed

ex li·bris \eks-ˈlē-bris\ [L] : from the books of — used on bookplates

ex me·ro mo·tu \ˌeks-ˈmer-ō-ˈmō-tü\ [L] : out of mere impulse : of one's own accord

ex ne·ces·si·ta·te rei \ˌeks-ne-ˌke-si-ˈtä-te-ˈrä-ˌē\ [L] : from the necessity of the case

ex ni·hi·lo ni·hil fit \eks-ˈni-hi-ˌlō-ˈni-ˌhil-ˈfit\ [L] : from nothing nothing is produced

ex pe·de Her·cu·lem \eks-ˈpe-de-ˈher-ku̇-ˌlem\ [L] : from the foot (we may judge of the size of) Hercules : from a part we may judge of the whole

ex·per·to cre·de \eks-ˈper-tō-ˈkrä-de\ *or* **experto cre·di·te** \-ˈkrä-di-ˌte\ [L] : believe one who has had experience

ex un·gue le·o·nem \eks-ˈu̇ŋ-gwe-le-ˈō-ˌnem\ [L] : from the claw (we may judge of) the lion : from a part we may judge of the whole

ex vi ter·mi·ni \eks-ˈwē-ˈter-mi-ˌnē\ [L] : from the force of the term

fa·ci·le prin·ceps \ˈfä-ki-le-ˈpriŋ-ˌkeps\ [L] : easily first

fa·ci·lis de·scen·sus Aver·no \ˈfä-ki-ˌlis-dä-ˈskän-ˌsús-ä-ˈwer-nō\ *or* **facilis descensus Aver·ni** \-(ˌ)nē\ [L] : the descent to Avernus is easy : the road to evil is easy

fa·çon de par·ler \fȧ-sōⁿ-də-pȧr-lā\ [F] : manner of speaking : figurative or conventional expression

faire suivre \fer-swēēvrᵊ\ [F] : have forwarded : please forward

fas est et ab ho·ste do·ce·ri \ˈfäs-ˈest-et-äb-ˈhò-ste-dò-ˈkä-(ˌ)rē\ [L] : it is right to learn even from an enemy

Fa·ta vi·am in·ve·ni·ent \ˈfä-tä-ˈwē-ˌäm-in-ˈwe-nē-ˌent\ [L] : the Fates will find a way

fat·ti mas·chii, pa·ro·le fe·mi·ne \ˈfät-tē-ˈmäs-ˌkē-pä-ˈrò-lä-ˈfä-mē-ˌnä\ [It] : deeds are males, words are females : deeds are more effective than words — motto of Maryland, where it is generally interpreted as meaning "manly deeds, womanly words"

faux bon·homme \fō-bò-nóm\ [F] : pretended good fellow

faux–naïf \fō̅-nȧ-ēf\ [F] : spuriously or affectedly childlike : artfully simple

fe·lix cul·pa \ˈfā-liks-ˈkúl-pä\ [L] : fortunate fault — used esp. of original sin in relation to the consequent coming of Christ

femme de cham·bre \fäm-də-shäⁿbrᵊ\ [F] : chambermaid : lady's maid

fe·sti·na len·te \fe-ˈstē-nä-ˈlen-ˌtä\ [L] : make haste slowly

feux d'ar·ti·fice \fœ̅-dȧr-tē-fēs\ [F] : fireworks : display of wit

fi·at ex·pe·ri·men·tum in cor·po·re vi·li \ˈfē-ˌät-ek-ˌsper-ē-ˈmen-ˌtúm-in-ˈkòr-pò-re-ˈwē-lē\ [L] : let experiment be made on a worthless body

fi·at ju·sti·tia, ru·at cae·lum \ˈfē-ˌät-yús-ˈti-tē-ä-ˈrù-ˌät-ˈkī-ˌlúm\ [L] : let justice be done though the heavens fall

fi·at lux \ˈfē-ˌät-ˈlúks\ [L] : let there be light

Fi·dei De·fen·sor \ˈfi-de-ē-dä-ˈfän-ˌsòr\ [L] : Defender of the Faith — a title of the sovereigns of England

fi·dus Acha·tes \ˈfē-dús-ä-ˈkä-ˌtäs\ [L] : faithful Achates : trusty friend

fille de cham·bre \fēy-də-shäⁿbrᵊ\ [F] : lady's maid

fille d'hon·neur \fēy-dò-nœr\ [F] : maid of honor

fils \fēs\ [F] : son — used orig. after French and now also after other family names to distinguish a son from his father

fi·nem re·spi·ce \ˈfē-nem-ˈrä-spi-ˌke\ [L] : consider the end

fi·nis co·ro·nat opus \ˈfē-nis-kò-ˈrō-ˌnät-ˈō-ˌpús\ [L] : the end crowns the work

flo·re·at \ˈflō-rē-ˌät\ [L] : may (he, she, or it) flourish — usu. followed by a name

fluc·tu·at nec mer·gi·tur \ˈflúk-tú-ˌwät-ˌnek-ˈmer-gi-ˌtùr\ [L] : it is tossed by the waves but does not sink — motto of Paris

fo·lie de gran·deur *or* **fo·lie des gran·deurs** \fò-lē-də-grän-dœr\ [F] : delusion of greatness : megalomania

force de frappe \fòrs-də-fráp\ [F] : military striking force esp. with nuclear weapons

fors·an et haec olim me·mi·nis·se ju·va·bit \ˈfòr-ˌsän-et-ˈhīk-ˌō-lim-ˌme-mi-ˈni-se-yù-ˈwä-bit\ [L] : perhaps this too will be a pleasure to look back on one day

for·tes for·tu·na ju·vat \ˈfòr-ˌtäs-fòr-ˈtü-nä-ˈyù-ˌwät\ [L] : fortune favors the brave

fron·ti nul·la fi·des \ˈfrón-ˌtē-ˈnù-lä-ˈfi-ˌdäs\ [L] : no reliance can be placed on appearance

fu·it Ili·um \ˈfù-it-ˈi-lē-ùm\ [L] : Troy has been (i.e., is no more)

fu·ror lo·quen·di \ˈfúr-ˌòr-lò-ˈkwen-(ˌ)dē\ [L] : rage for speaking

furor po·e·ti·cus \-pò-ˈā-ti-kús\ [L] : poetic frenzy

furor scri·ben·di \-skrē-ˈben-(ˌ)dē\ [L] : rage for writing

Gal·li·ce \ˈgä-li-ˌke\ [L] : in French : after the French manner

gar·çon d'hon·neur \gȧr-sōⁿ-dò-nœr\ [F] : bridegroom's attendant

garde du corps \gȧrd-dᵫ-kòr\ [F] : bodyguard

gar·dez la foi \gȧr-dā-lȧ-fwä\ [F] : keep faith

gau·de·a·mus igi·tur \ˌgau̇d-ē-ˈä-mùs-ˈi-gi-ˌtùr\ [L] : let us then be merry

gens d'é·glise \zhäⁿ-dä-glēz\ [F] : church people : clergy

gens de guerre \zhäⁿ-də-ger\ [F] : military people : soldiery

gens du monde \zhäⁿ-dᵫ-mōⁿd\ [F] : people of the world : fashionable people

gno·thi se·au·ton \ˈgnō-thē-ˌse-au̇-ˈtòn\ [Gk] : know thyself

grand monde \grän-mōⁿd\ [F] : great world : high society

gros·so mo·do \ˈgròs-(ˌ)sō-ˈmō-(ˌ)dō\ [It] : roughly

guerre à ou·trance \ger-ȧ-ü-träⁿs\ [F] : war to the uttermost

gu·ten Tag \ˈgüt-ᵊn-ˈtäk\ [G] : good day

has·ta la vis·ta \ˈäs-tä-lä-ˈvēs-tä\ [Sp] : good-bye

haut goût \ō-gü\ [F] : high flavor : slight taint of decay

hic et nunc \ˈhēk-et-ˈnu̇ŋk\ [L] : here and now

hic et ubi·que \ˈhēk-et-ù-ˈbē-kwe\ [L] : here and everywhere

hic ja·cet \hik-ˈjä-sət, hēk-ˈyä-ket\ [L] : here lies — used preceding a name on a tombstone

hinc il·lae la·cri·mae \'hiŋk-'i-ɪlī-'lä-kri-ɪmī\ [L] : hence those tears

hoc age \hōk-'äg-e\ [L] : do this : apply yourself to what you are about

hoc opus, hic la·bor est \ɪhōk-'ȯ-ɪpüs-ɪhēk-'lä-ɪbȯr-'est\ [L] : this is the hard work, this is the toil

homme d'af·faires \ȯm-då-fer\ [F] : man of business : business agent

homme d'es·prit \-des-prē\ [F] : man of wit

homme moyen sen·suel \ȯm-mwȧ-yaⁿ-sän-swʸel\ [F] : the average nonintellectual man

ho·mo sum: hu·ma·ni nil a me ali·e·num pu·to \'hȯ-mō-ɪsùm-hü-'mä-nē-'nēl-ä-ɪmä-ɪä-lē-'ä-nùm-'pù-tō\ [L] : I am a human being: I regard nothing of human concern as foreign to my interests

ho·ni soit qui mal y pense \ȯ-nē-swȧ-kē-mȧl-ē-päⁿs\ [F] : shamed be he who thinks evil of it — motto of the Order of the Garter

hu·ma·num est er·ra·re \hü-'mä-nùm-ɪest-e-'rär-e\ [L] : to err is human

ich dien \iḵ-'dēn\ [G] : I serve — motto of the Prince of Wales

ici on parle fran·cais \ē-sē-ōⁿ-pȧrl-fräⁿ-se\ [F] : French is spoken here

idées re·çues \ē-dā-rə-sœ̄\ [F] : received ideas : conventional opinions

id est \id-'est\ [L] : that is

ig·no·ran·tia ju·ris ne·mi·nem ex·cu·sat \ɪig-nə-'rän-tē-ä-ɪyùr-is-'nä-mi-ɪnem-eks-'kü-ɪsät\ [L] : ignorance of the law excuses no one

ig·no·tum per ig·no·ti·us \ig-'nō-tùm-ɪper-ig-'nō-tē-ùs\ [L] : (explaining) the unknown by means of the more unknown

il faut cul·ti·ver no·tre jar·din \ēl-fō-kǖl-tē-vä-nȯtr-zhȧr-daⁿ, -nȯ-trə-zhȧr-\ [F] : we must cultivate our garden : we must tend to our own affairs

in ae·ter·num \ɪin-ī-'ter-ɪnùm\ [L] : forever

in du·bio \in-'dùb-ē-ɪō\ [L] : in doubt : undetermined

in fu·tu·ro \in-fù-'tùr-ō\ [L] : in the future

in hoc sig·no vin·ces \in-ɪhōk-'sig-nō-'wiŋ-ɪkās\ [L] : by this sign (the Cross) you will conquer

in li·mi·ne \in-'lē-mi-ɪne\ [L] : on the threshold : at the beginning

in om·nia pa·ra·tus \in-'ȯm-nē-ä-pä-'rä-ɪtùs\ [L] : ready for all things

in par·ti·bus in·fi·de·li·um \in-'pär-ti-ɪbùs-ɪin-fə-'dä-lē-ɪùm\ [L] : in the regions of the infidels — used of a titular bishop having no diocesan jurisdiction, usu. in non-Christian countries

in prae·sen·ti \ɪin-prī-'sen-ɪtē\ [L] : at the present time

in sae·cu·la sae·cu·lo·rum \in-'sī-kù-ɪlä-ɪsī-kù-'lȯr-ùm, -'sä-kù-ɪlä-ɪsä-\ [L] : for ages of ages : forever and ever

insh·al·lah \ɪin-shä-'lä\ [Ar] : if Allah wills : God willing

in sta·tu quo an·te bel·lum \in-'stä-ɪtü-kwō-'än-te-'be-lùm\ [L] : in the same state as before the war

in·te·ger vi·tae sce·le·ris·que pu·rus \'in-te-ɪger-'wē-ɪtī-ɪske-le-'ris-kwe-'pü-rùs\ [L] : upright of life and free from wickedness

in·ter nos \ɪin-tər-'nōs\ [L] : between ourselves

in·tra mu·ros \ɪin-trä-'mü-ɪrōs\ [L] : within the walls

in usum Del·phi·ni \in-'ü-sùm-del-'fē-ɪnē\ [L] : for the use of the Dauphin : expurgated

in utrum·que pa·ra·tus \ɪin-ü-'trùm-kwe-pä-'rä-ɪtùs\ [L] : prepared for either (event)

in·ve·nit \in-'wā-nit\ [L] : he or she devised it

in vi·no ve·ri·tas \in-'wē-nō-'wä-ri-ɪtäs\ [L] : there is truth in wine

in·vi·ta Mi·ner·va \in-'wē-ɪtä-mi-'ner-ɪwä\ [L] : Minerva being unwilling : without natural talent or inspiration

ip·sis·si·ma ver·ba \ip-'si-si-ɪmä-'wer-ɪbä\ [L] : the very words

ira fu·ror bre·vis est \'ē-rä-'fùr-ɪȯr-'bre-wis-'est\ [L] : anger is a brief madness

j'ac·cuse \zhȧ-kᵫz\ [F] : I accuse : bitter denunciation

jac·ta alea est \'yȧk-ɪtä-'ä-lē-ɪä-'est\ [L] : the die is cast

j'adoube \zhȧ-düb\ [F] : I adjust — used in chess when touching a piece without intending to move it

ja·nu·is clau·sis \ɪyä-nù-ɪwēs-'klaù-ɪsēs\ [L] : behind closed doors

je main·tien·drai \zhə-maⁿ-tyaⁿ-drā\ [F] : I will maintain — motto of the Netherlands

jeu de mots \zhœ̄-də-mō\ [F] : play on words : pun

Jo·an·nes est no·men eius \yō-'ä-näs-est-'nō-men-'ā-yùs\ [L] : John is his name — motto of Puerto Rico

jo·lie laide \zhȯ-lē-led\ [F] : good-looking ugly woman : woman who is attractive though not conventionally pretty

jour·nal in·time \zhür-nȧl-aⁿ-tēm\ [F] : intimate journal : private diary

jus di·vi·num \'yüs-di-'wē-ɪnùm\ [L] : divine law

jus·ti·tia om·ni·bus \yùs-'ti-tē-ä-'ȯm-ni-ɪbùs\ [L] : justice for all — motto of the District of Columbia

j'y suis, j'y reste \zhē-swʸē-zhē-rest\ [F] : here I am, here I remain

la belle dame sans mer·ci \lȧ-bel-dȧm-säⁿ-mer-sē\ [F] : the beautiful lady without mercy

la·bo·ra·re est ora·re \ɪlä-bō-'rär-ä-ɪest-'ō-ɪrär-ä\ [L] : to work is to pray

la·bor om·nia vin·cit \'lä-ɪbȯr-ɪȯm-nē-ä-'wiŋ-kit\ [L] : labor conquers all things — motto of Oklahoma

la·cri·mae re·rum \'lä-kri-ɪmī-'rä-ɪrùm\ [L] : tears for things : pity for misfortune; *also* : tears in things : tragedy in life

lais·sez–al·ler *or* **lais·ser–al·ler** \le-sä-ä-lä\ [F] : letting go : lack of restraint

lap·sus ca·la·mi \'läp-sùs-'kä-lä-ɪmē\ [L] : slip of the pen

lap·sus lin·guae \-'liŋ-ɪgwī\ [L] : slip of the tongue

la reine le veut \lȧ-ren-lə-vœ̄\ [F] : the queen wills it

la·scia·te ogni spe·ran·za, voi ch'en·tra·te \läsh-'shä-tä-ɪō-nʸē-spä-'rän-tsä-ɪvō-ē-kän-'trä-tä\ [It] : abandon all hope, ye who enter

lau·da·tor tem·po·ris ac·ti \laù-'dä-ɪtȯr-ɪtem-pȯ-ris-'äk-ɪtē\ [L] : one who praises past times

laus Deo \laùs-'dā-ō\ [L] : praise (be) to God

Le·bens·welt \'lā-bəns-ɪvelt\ [G] : life world : world of lived experience

le cœur a ses rai·sons que la rai·son ne con·naît point \lə-kœr-ä-sä-re-zōⁿk-lä-re-zōⁿ-nə-kȯ-ne-pwaⁿ\ [F] : the heart has its reasons that reason knows nothing of

le roi est mort, vive le roi \lə-rwä-e-mȯr-vēv-lə-rwä\ [F] : the king is dead, long live the king

le roi le veut \-lə-vœ̄\ [F] : the king wills it

le roi s'avi·se·ra \-sȧ-vēz-rä\ [F] : the king will consider

le style, c'est l'homme \lə-stēl-se-lȯm\ [F] : the style is the man

l'état, c'est moi \lā-tȧ-se-mwȧ\ [F] : the state, it is I

l'étoile du nord \lā-twȧl-dᵫ-nȯr\ [F] : the star of the north — motto of Minnesota

Lie·der·kranz \'lē-dər-ɪkränts\ [G] : wreath of songs : German singing society

lit·tera scrip·ta ma·net \'li-te-ɪrä-'skrip-tä-'mä-net\ [L] : the written letter abides

lo·cus in quo \'lȯ-kùs-in-'kwō\ [L] : place in which

l'union fait la force \lᵫ-nyōⁿ-fe-lȧ-fȯrs\ [F] : union makes strength — motto of Belgium

lu·sus na·tu·rae \'lü-sùs-nä-'tùr-ē, -'tùr-ɪī\ [L] : freak of nature

ma foi \mȧ-fwȧ\ [F] : my faith! : indeed

mag·na est ve·ri·tas et prae·va·le·bit \'mäg-nä-ɪest-'wä-ri-ɪtäs-et-ɪprī-wä-'lä-bit\ [L] : truth is mighty and will prevail

mag·ni no·mi·nis um·bra \'mäg-nē-'nō-mi-nis-'ùm-brä\ [L] : the shadow of a great name

ma·ha·lo \'mä-hä-lō\ [Hawaiian] : thank you

mai·son de san·té \mā-zōⁿ-də-sän-tä\ [F] : private hospital : asylum

ma·lade ima·gi·naire \mȧ-lȧd-ē-mȧ-zhē-ner\ [F]
: imaginary invalid : hypochondriac

ma·lis avi·bus \'mä-ˌlēs-'ä-wi-ˌbu̇s\ [L] : under evil
auspices

ma·no a ma·no \'mä-nō-ä-'mä-nō\ [Sp] : hand to hand
: in direct competition or confrontation

man spricht Deutsch \ˌmän-ˌshpri̇kt-'dȯich\ [G]
: German spoken

ma·riage de con·ve·nance \mȧ-ryäzh-də-kōⁿv-näⁿs\
[F] : marriage of convenience

mau·vaise honte \mȯ-vez-ōⁿt\ [F] : bad shame : bash-
fulness

mau·vais quart d'heure \mȯ-ve-kȧr-dœr\ [F] : bad
quarter hour : an uncomfortable though brief experience

me·dio tu·tis·si·mus ibis \'me-dē-ˌō-tü-'ti-si-mu̇s-'ē-
bis\ [L] : you will go most safely by the middle course

me ju·di·ce \mā-'yü-di-ke\ [L] : I being judge : in my
judgment

mens sa·na in cor·po·re sa·no \'mäns-'sä-nä-in-'kȯr-
pȯ-re-'sä-nō\ [L] : a sound mind in a sound body

me·um et tu·um \'mē-u̇m-ˌet-'tü-u̇m, 'mä-u̇m-\ [L]
: mine and thine : distinction of private property

mi·ra·bi·le vi·su \mi-'rä-bi-lā-'wē-sü\ [L] : wonderful
to behold

mi·ra·bi·lia \ˌmir-ä-'bi-lē-ä\ [L] : wonders : miracles

mœurs \mœr, mœrs\ [F] : mores : attitudes, customs,
and manners of a society

mo·le ru·it sua \'mō-le-'ru̇-it-'su̇-ä\ [L] : it collapses
from its own bigness

monde \mōⁿd\ [F] : world : fashionable world : society

mon·ta·ni sem·per li·be·ri \mȯn-'tä-nē-'sem-per-'lē-
be-ˌrē\ [L] : mountaineers are always free — motto
of West Virginia

mo·nu·men·tum ae·re per·en·ni·us \ˌmō-nu̇-'men-
tu̇m-ˌī-re-pe-'re-nē-u̇s\ [L] : a monument more lasting than bronze — used of an immortal work of art
or literature

mo·ri·tu·ri te sa·lu·ta·mus \ˌmȯr-i-'tu̇r-ē-ˌtä-sä-lu̇-
'tä-mu̇s\ or **morituri te sa·lu·tant** \-'sä-lu̇-ˌtänt\ [L]
: we (or those) who are about to die salute thee

mul·tum in par·vo \'mu̇l-tu̇m-in-'pär-vō\ [L] : much in
little

mu·ta·to no·mi·ne de te fa·bu·la nar·ra·tur \mü-'tä-tō-
'nō-mi-ne-ˌdä-'tä-'fä-bu̇-lä-nä-'rä-ˌtu̇r\ [L] : with the
name changed the story applies to you

my·ster·i·um tre·men·dum \mi-'ster-ē-ˌu̇m-tre-'men-
du̇m\ [L] : overwhelming mystery

**na·tu·ram ex·pel·las fur·ca, ta·men us·que re·cur·
ret** \nä-'tü-räm-ek-ˌspe-läs-'fu̇r-ˌkä-ˌtä-men-'u̇s-
kwe-re-'ku̇r-et\ [L] : you may drive nature out with
a pitchfork, but she will keep coming back

na·tu·ra non fa·cit sal·tum \nä-'tü-rä-ˌnōn-'fä-kit-
'säl-ˌtu̇m\ [L] : nature makes no leap

ne ce·de ma·lis \nä-'kä-de-'mä-ˌlēs\ [L] : yield not to
misfortunes

ne·mo me im·pu·ne la·ces·sit \'nä-mō-'mä-im-'pü-nä-
lä-'ke-sit\ [L] : no one attacks me with impunity —
motto of Scotland and of the Order of the Thistle

ne quid ni·mis \ˌnä-ˌkwid-'ni-mis\ [L] : not anything
in excess

n'est–ce pas? \nes-pä\ [F] : isn't it so?

nicht wahr? \ni̇kt-'vär\ [G] : not true? : isn't it so?

nil ad·mi·ra·ri \'nēl-ˌäd-mi-'rär-ē\ [L] : to be excited
by nothing : equanimity

nil de·spe·ran·dum \'nēl-ˌdä-spä-'rän-du̇m\ [L] : never despair

nil si·ne nu·mi·ne \'nēl-ˌsi-nä-'nü-mi-ne\ [L] : nothing
without the divine will — motto of Colorado

n'im·porte \naⁿ-pȯrt\ [F] : it's no matter

no·lens vo·lens \'nō-ˌlenz-'vō-ˌlenz\ [L] : unwilling
(or) willing : willy-nilly

non om·nia pos·su·mus om·nes \nōn-'ȯm-nē-ä-ˌpȯ-su̇-
mu̇s-'ȯm-ˌnäs\ [L] : we can't all (do) all things

non om·nis mo·ri·ar \nōn-'ȯm-nis-'mȯr-ē-ˌär\ [L] : I
shall not wholly die

non sans droict \nōⁿ-säⁿ-drwä\ [OF] : not without
right — motto on Shakespeare's coat of arms

non sum qua·lis eram \ˌnōn-ˌsu̇m-'kwä-lis-'er-ˌäm\
[L] : I am not what I used to be

nos·ce te ip·sum \'nȯs-ke-ˌtä-'ip-ˌsu̇m\ [L] : know thyself

nos·tal·gie de la boue \nȯs-täl-zhē-də-lä-bü\ [F]
: yearning for the mud : attraction to what is unworthy, crude, or degrading

nous avons chan·gé tout ce·la \nü-zä-vōⁿ-shäⁿ-zhä-tü-
sə-lä\ [F] : we have changed all that

nous ver·rons ce que nous ver·rons \nü-ve-rōⁿ-sə-kə-
nü-ve-rōⁿ\ [F] : we shall see what we shall see

no·vus ho·mo \'nō-wu̇s-'hȯ-mō\ [L] : new man : man
newly ennobled : upstart

no·vus or·do se·clo·rum \-'ȯr-ˌdō-sä-'klōr-u̇m\ [L] : a
new cycle of the ages — motto on the reverse of the
Great Seal of the United States

nu·gae \'nü-ˌgī\ [L] : trifles

nuit blanche \nwʸē-bläⁿsh\ [F] : white night : a sleepless night

nyet \'nyet\ [Russ] : no

ob·iit \'ȯ-bē-it\ [L] : he or she died

ob·scu·rum per ob·scu·ri·us \ȯb-'skyu̇r-u̇m-ˌper-ȯb-
'skyu̇r-ē-u̇s\ [L] : (explaining) the obscure by means
of the more obscure

ode·rint dum me·tu·ant \'ō-de-ˌrint-ˌdu̇m-'me-tu̇-
ˌwänt\ [L] : let them hate, so long as they fear

odi et amo \'ō-ˌdē-et-'ä-(ˌ)mō\ [L] : I hate and I love

omer·tà \ȯ-'mer-tä\ [It] : submission : code chiefly
among members of the criminal underworld that en-
joins private vengeance and the refusal to give information to outsiders (as the police)

om·ne ig·no·tum pro mag·ni·fi·co \'ȯm-ne-ig-'nō-
ˌtu̇m-prō-mäg-'ni-fi-ˌkō\ [L] : everything unknown
(is taken) as grand : the unknown tends to be exaggerated in importance or difficulty

om·nia mu·tan·tur, nos et mu·ta·mur in il·lis \'ȯm-nē-
ä-mü-'tän-ˌtu̇r-ˌnōs-et-mü-'tä-mu̇r-in-'i-ˌlēs\   [L]
: all things are changing, and we are changing with
them

om·nia vin·cit amor \'om-nē-ä-'wiŋ-kit-'ä-ˌmȯr\ [L]
: love conquers all

onus pro·ban·di \'ō-nu̇s-prō-'ban-ˌdī, -dē\ [L] : burden of proof

ora pro no·bis \'ō-rä-prō-'nō-ˌbēs\ [L] : pray for us

ore ro·tun·do \ˌȯr-ä-rō-'tu̇n-dō\ [L] : with round
mouth : eloquently

oro y pla·ta \'ȯr-ō-ē-'plä-tä\ [Sp] : gold and silver —
motto of Montana

o tem·po·ra! o mo·res! \ō-'tem-pȯ-rä-ō-'mō-ˌräs\ [L]
: oh the times! oh the manners!

oti·um cum dig·ni·ta·te \'ō-tē-ˌu̇m-ku̇m-ˌdig-ni-'tä-te\
[L] : leisure with dignity

où sont les neiges d'an·tan? \ü-sōⁿ-lä-nezh-däⁿ-täⁿ\ [F]
: where are the snows of yesteryear?

outre–mer \u̇tr²-mer\ [F] : overseas : distant lands

pal·li·da Mors \'pa-li-də-'mȯrz\ [L] : pale Death

pa·nem et cir·cen·ses \'pän-ˌem-et-kir-'kän-ˌsäs\ [L]
: bread and circuses : provision of the means of life
and recreation by government to appease discontent

pan·ta rhei \ˌpän-ˌtä-'rā\ [Gk] : all things are in flux

par avance \pär-ä-väⁿs\ [F] : in advance : by anticipation

par avion \pär-ä-vyōⁿ\ [F] : by airplane — used on airmail

par ex·em·ple \pär-äg-zäⁿplᵃ\ [F] : for example

pars pro to·to \'pärs-ˌprō-'tō-(ˌ)tō\ [L] : part (taken)
for the whole

par·tu·ri·unt mon·tes, nas·ce·tur ri·di·cu·lus mus
\pär-'tu̇r-ē-u̇nt-'mȯn-ˌtäs-näs-'kä-ˌtu̇r-ri-'di-ku̇-
lu̇s-'mu̇s\ [L] : the mountains are in labor, and a ridiculous mouse will be brought forth

pa·ter pa·tri·ae \'pä-ˌter-'pä-trē-ˌī\ [L] : father of his
country

pau·cis ver·bis \'pau̇-ˌkēs-'wer-ˌbēs\ [L] : in a few words

pax vo·bis·cum \'päks-vō-'bēs-ˌku̇m\ [L] : peace (be) with you

peine forte et dure \pen-fȯr-tā-dūer\ [F] : strong and hard punishment : torture

per an·gus·ta ad au·gus·ta \per-'än-ˌgu̇s-tä-äd-'au̇-ˌgu̇s-tä\ [L] : through difficulties to honors

père \per\ [F] : father — used orig. after French and now also after other family names to distinguish a father from his son

per·eant qui an·te nos nos·tra dix·e·runt \'per-e-ˌänt-kwē-ˌän-te-'nōs-'nȯs-trä-dēk-'sä-ˌru̇nt\ [L] : may they perish who have expressed our bright ideas before us

per·fide Al·bion \per-fēd-àl-byōᵐ\ [F] : perfidious Albion (England)

peu à peu \pœ̄-à-pœ̄\ [F] : little by little

peu de chose \pœ̄-də-shōz\ [F] : a trifle

pièce d'oc·ca·sion \pyes-dȯ-kä-zyōᵐ\ [F] : piece for a special occasion

pinx·it \'pink-sit\ [L] : he or she painted it

place aux dames \plàs-ō-dàm\ [F] : (make) room for the ladies

ple·no ju·re \'plä-nō-'yu̇r-e\ [L] : with full right

plus ça change, plus c'est la même chose \plū̄-sà-shäⁿzh-plū̄-se-là-mem-shōz\ [F] : the more that changes, the more it's the same thing — often shortened to *plus ça change*

plus roy·a·liste que le roi \plū̄-rwà-yà-lēst-kəl-rwà\ [F] : more royalist than the king

po·cas pa·la·bras \'pō-käs-pä-'lä-vräs\ [Sp] : few words

po·eta nas·ci·tur, non fit \pȯ-'ä-tä-'näs-ki-ˌtu̇r-nōn-'fit\ [L] : a poet is born, not made

pol·li·ce ver·so \'pȯ-li-ke-'ver-sō\ [L] : with thumb turned : with a gesture or expression of condemnation

post hoc, er·go prop·ter hoc \'pȯst-ˌhōk-ˌer-gō-'prȯp-ter-ˌhōk\ [L] : after this, therefore on account of it (a fallacy of argument)

post ob·itum \pȯst-'ȯ-bi-ˌtu̇m\ [L] : after death

pour ac·quit \pūr-à-kē\ [F] : received payment

pour le mé·rite \pūr-lə-mā-rēt\ [F] : for merit

pri·mum non no·ce·re \ˌprē-mu̇m-ˌnōn-nȯ-'kā-re\ [L] : the first thing (is) to do no harm

pro aris et fo·cis \prō-'ä-ˌrēs-et-'fȯ-ˌkēs\ [L] : for altars and firesides

pro bo·no pu·bli·co \prō-'bȯ-nō-'pü-bli-ˌkō\ [L] : for the public good

pro hac vi·ce \prō-'häk-'wi-ke\ [L] : for this occasion

pro pa·tria \prō-'pä-trē-ˌä\ [L] : for one's country

pro re·ge, le·ge, et gre·ge \prō-'rä-ge-'lä-ge-et-'gre-ˌge\ [L] : for the king, the law, and the people

pro re na·ta \ˌprō-'rä-'nä-tä\ [L] : for an occasion that has arisen : as needed — used in medical prescriptions

quand même \käⁿ-mem\ [F] : even so : all the same

quan·tum mu·ta·tus ab il·lo \'kwän-tu̇m-mü-'tä-tis-äb-'i-lō\ [L] : how changed from what he once was

quan·tum suf·fi·cit \'kwän-tu̇m-'sə-fi-ˌkit\ [L] : as much as suffices : a sufficient quantity — used chiefly in medical prescriptions

¿quién sa·be? \kyän-'sä-vä\ [Sp] : who knows?

qui fa·cit per ali·um fa·cit per se \kwē-'fä-kit-'per-'ä-lē-ˌu̇m-'fä-kit-'per-'sä\ [L] : he who does (something) through another does it through himself

quis cus·to·di·et ip·sos cus·to·des? \ˌkwis-ku̇s-'tō-dē-et-ip-ˌsōs-ku̇s-'tō-ˌdās\ [L] : who will keep the keepers themselves?

qui s'ex·cuse s'ac·cuse \kē-sek-skū̄z-sà-kū̄z\ [F] : he who excuses himself accuses himself

quis se·pa·ra·bit? \ˌkwis-sä-pä-'rä-bit\ [L] : who shall separate (us)? — motto of the Order of St. Patrick

qui trans·tu·lit sus·ti·net \kwē-'träns-tu̇-lit-'su̇s-ti-ˌnet\ [L] : He who transplanted sustains (us) — motto of Connecticut

qui va là? \kē-và-là\ [F] : who goes there?

quo·ad hoc \ˌkwȯ-'äd-'hōk\ [L] : as far as this : to this extent

quod erat de·mon·stran·dum \ˌkwȯd-'er-ˌät-ˌde-mȯn-'strän-du̇m\ [L] : which was to be proved

quod erat fa·ci·en·dum \-ˌfä-kē-'en-ˌdu̇m\ [L] : which was to be done

quod sem·per, quod ubi·que, quod ab om·ni·bus \ˌkwȯd-'sem-ˌper-kwȯd-'u̇-bi-ˌkwä-ˌkwȯd-äb-'ȯm-ni-ˌbu̇s\ [L] : what (has been held) always, everywhere, by everybody

quod vi·de \kwȯd-'wi-de\ [L] : which see

quo·rum pars mag·na fui \'kwȯr-u̇m-ˌpärs-'mäg-nə-'fu̇-ē\ [L] : in which I played a great part

quos de·us vult per·de·re pri·us de·men·tat \kwȯs-'de-u̇s-ˌwu̇lt-'per-de-ˌre-'prē-u̇s-dä-'men-ˌtät\ [L] : those whom a god wishes to destroy he first drives mad

quot ho·mi·nes, tot sen·ten·ti·ae \kwȯt-'hȯ-mi-ˌnäs-ˌtȯt-sen-'ten-tē-ˌī\ [L] : there are as many opinions as there are men

quo va·dis? \kwō-'vä-dis, -'wä-\ [L] : whither are you going?

rai·son d'état \re-zōⁿ-dä-tà\ [F] : reason of state

re·cu·ler pour mieux sau·ter \rə-kū̄-lä-pür-myœ̄-sō-tä\ [F] : to draw back in order to make a better jump

reg·nat po·pu·lus \'reg-ˌnät-'pȯ-pu̇-ˌlu̇s\ [L] : the people rule — motto of Arkansas

re in·fec·ta \'rä-in-ˌfek-tä\ [L] : the business being unfinished : without accomplishing one's purpose

re·li·gio lo·ci \re-'li-gē-ˌō-'lȯ-ˌkē\ [L] : religious sanctity of a place

rem acu te·ti·gis·ti \ˌrem-'ä-ˌkü-ˌte-ti-'gis-tē\ [L] : you have touched the point with a needle : you have hit the nail on the head

ré·pon·dez s'il vous plaît \rä-pōⁿ-dä-sēl-vü-ple\ [F] : reply, if you please

re·qui·es·cat in pa·ce \ˌre-kwē-'es-ˌkät-in-'pä-ˌke, ˌrä-kwē-'es-ˌkät-in-'pä-ˌchä\ [L] : may he or she rest in peace — used on tombstones

re·spi·ce fi·nem \'rä-spi-ˌke-'fē-ˌnem\ [L] : look to the end : consider the outcome

re·sur·gam \re-'sür-ˌgäm\ [L] : I shall rise again

re·te·nue \rət-nū̄\ [F] : self-restraint : reserve

re·ve·nons à nos mou·tons \rəv-nōⁿ-à-nō-mü-tōᵐ\ [F] : let us return to our sheep : let us get back to the subject

ruse de guerre \rū̄z-də-ger\ [F] : war stratagem

rus in ur·be \'rüs-in-'u̇r-ˌbe\ [L] : country in the city

sae·va in·dig·na·tio \'sī-wä-ˌin-dig-'nä-tē-ˌō\ [L] : fierce indignation

sal At·ti·cum \'sal-'a-ti-kəm\ [L] : Attic salt : wit

salle à man·ger \sàl-à-mäⁿ-zhä\ [F] : dining room

sa·lon des re·fu·sés \sà-lȯⁿ-dā-rə-fū̄-zä\ [F] : salon of the refused : exhibition of art that has been rejected by an official body

sa·lus po·pu·li su·pre·ma lex es·to \'säl-u̇s-'pȯ-pu̇-ˌlē-su̇-'prä-mä-ˌleks-'es-tō\ [L] : let the welfare of the people be the supreme law — motto of Missouri

sanc·ta sim·pli·ci·tas \ˌsäŋk-tä-sim-'pli-ki-ˌtäs\ [L] : holy simplicity — often used ironically in reference to another's naïveté

sans doute \säⁿ-düt\ [F] : without doubt

sans gêne \säⁿ-zhen\ [F] : without embarrassment or constraint

sans peur et sans re·proche \säⁿ-pœr-ä-säⁿ-rə-prȯsh\ [F] : without fear and without reproach

sans sou·ci \säⁿ-sü-sē\ [F] : without worry

sa·yo·na·ra \ˌsä-yō-'när-ä\ [Jp] : good-bye

sculp·sit \'sku̇lp-sit\ [L] : he or she carved it

scu·to bo·nae vo·lun·ta·tis tu·ae co·ro·nas·ti nos \'skü-tō-'bȯ-ˌnī-vȯ-lu̇n-'tä-tis-'tu̇-ˌī-ˌkȯr-ȯ-'näs-tē-'nōs\ [L] : Thou hast crowned us with the shield of Thy good will — a motto on the Great Seal of Maryland

se·cun·dum ar·tem \se-ˈkùn-dùm-ˈär-ˌtem\ [L] : according to the art : according to the accepted practice of a profession or trade

secundum na·tu·ram \-nä-ˈtü-ˌräm\ [L] : according to nature : naturally

se de·fen·den·do \ˈsā-ˌdā-ˌfen-ˈden-dō\ [L] : in self-defense

se ha·bla es·pa·ñol \sā-ˌäb-lä-ˌäs-pä-ˈnᵛòl\ [Sp] : Spanish spoken

sem·per ea·dem \ˈsem-ˌper-ˈe-ä-ˌdem\ [L] : always the same (fem.) — motto of Queen Elizabeth I

sem·per fi·de·lis \ˈsem-pər-fi-ˈdä-lis\ [L] : always faithful — motto of the U.S. Marine Corps

sem·per idem \ˈsem-ˌper-ˈē-ˌdem\ [L] : always the same (masc.)

sem·per pa·ra·tus \ˌsem-pər-pä-ˈrä-təs\ [L] : always prepared — motto of the U.S. Coast Guard

se non è ve·ro, è ben tro·va·to \sā-ˌnōn-e-ˈvä-rō-e-ˌben- trō-ˈvä-tō\ [It] : even if it is not true, it is well conceived

sic itur ad as·tra \ˌsēk-ˈi-ˌtùr-ˌäd-ˈäs-trä\ [L] : thus one goes to the stars : such is the way to immortality

sic sem·per ty·ran·nis \ˌsik-ˈsem-pər-ti-ˈra-nis\ [L] : thus ever to tyrants — motto of Virginia

sic trans·it glo·ria mun·di \ˌsēk-ˈträn-sit-ˈglòr-ē-ä-ˈmün-dē\ [L] : so passes away the glory of the world

si jeu·nesse sa·vait, si vieil·lesse pou·vait! \sē-zhœ-nes-sà-ve-sē-vye-yes-pü-ve\ [F] : if youth only knew, if age only could!

si·lent le·ges in·ter ar·ma \ˈsi-ˌlent-ˈlā-gäs-ˌin-ter-ˈär-mä\ [L] : the laws are silent in the midst of arms

s'il vous plaît \sēl-vü-ple\ [F] : if you please

si·mi·lia si·mi·li·bus cu·ran·tur \si-ˈmi-lē-ä-si-ˈmi-li-bùs-kü-ˈrän-ˌtùr\ [L] : like is cured by like

si·mi·lis si·mi·li gau·det \ˈsi-mi-lis-ˈsi-mi-lē-ˈgaù-ˌdet\ [L] : like takes pleasure in like

si mo·nu·men·tum re·qui·ris, cir·cum·spi·ce \sē-ˌmò-nù-ˈmen-tüm-re-ˈkwē-ris-kir-ˈkùm-spi-ke\ [L] : if you seek his monument, look around — epitaph of Sir Christopher Wren in St. Paul's, London, of which he was architect

sim·pliste \saⁿ-plēst\ [F] : simplistic : overly simple or naive

si quae·ris pen·in·su·lam amoe·nam, cir·cum·spi·ce \sē-ˈkwī-ris-pä-ˈnin-sù-ˌläm-ä-ˈmòi-ˌnäm-kir-ˈkùm-spi-ke\ [L] : if you seek a beautiful peninsula, look around — motto of Michigan

sis·te vi·a·tor \ˈsis-te-wē-ˈä-ˌtòr\ [L] : stop, traveler — used on Roman roadside tombs

si vis pa·cem, pa·ra bel·lum \sē-ˈwēs-ˈpä-kem-pä-rä-ˈbe-ˌlùm\ [L] : if you wish peace, prepare for war

sol·vi·tur am·bu·lan·do \ˈsòl-wi-ˌtùr-ˌäm-bü-ˈlän-dō\ [L] : it is solved by walking : the problem is solved by a practical experiment

splen·di·de men·dax \ˈsplen-di-ˌdā-ˈmen-ˌdäks\ [L] : nobly untruthful

spo·lia opi·ma \ˈspò-lē-ä-ō-ˈpē-mä\ [L] : rich spoils : the arms taken by the victorious from the vanquished general

sta·tus in quo \ˈstä-tùs-ˌin-ˈkwō\ [L] : state in which : the existing state

status quo an·te bel·lum \-kwō-ˌän-te-ˈbe-lùm\ [L] : the state existing before the war

sua·vi·ter in mo·do, for·ti·ter in re \ˈswä-wi-ˌter-in-ˈmò-dō-ˈfòr-ti-ˌter-in-ˈrä\ [L] : gently in manner, strongly in deed

sub ver·bo \ˌsùb-ˈwer-bō\ or **sub vo·ce** \ˌsùb-ˈwō-ke\ [L] : under the word — introducing a cross-reference in a dictionary or index

sunt la·cri·mae re·rum \ˌsùnt-ˌlä-kri-ˌmī-ˈrä-rùm\ [L] : there are tears for things : tears attend trials

suo ju·re \ˌsù-ō-ˈyùr-e\ [L] : in his or her own right

suo lo·co \-ˈlò-kō\ [L] : in its proper place

suo Mar·te \-ˈmär-te\ [L] : by one's own exertions

su·um cui·que \ˌsù-ùm-ˈkwi-kwe\ [L] : to each his own

tant mieux \tän-myœ̄\ [F] : so much the better

tant pis \-pē\ [F] : so much the worse : too bad

tem·po·ra mu·tan·tur, nos et mu·ta·mur in il·lis \ˈtem-pó-rä-mü-ˈtän-ˌtùr-ˈnòs-ˌet-mü-ˈtä-mùr-in-ˈi-ˌlēs\ [L] : the times are changing, and we are changing with them

tem·pus edax re·rum \ˈtem-pùs-ˌe-ˈdäks-ˈrä-rùm\ [L] : time, that devours all things

tem·pus fu·git \ˈtem-pəs-ˈfyü-jət, ˈtem-pùs-ˈfü-git\ [L] : time flies

ti·meo Da·na·os et do·na fe·ren·tes \ˈti-mē-ō-ˈdä-nä-ōs-ˌet-ˈdō-nä-fe-ˈren-tās\ [L] : I fear the Greeks even when they bring gifts

to·ti·dem ver·bis \ˈtò-ti-ˌdem-ˈwer-ˌbēs\ [L] : in so many words

to·tis vi·ri·bus \ˈtō-ˌtēs-ˈwē-ri-ˌbùs\ [L] : with all one's might

to·to cae·lo \ˈtò-tō-ˈkī-lō\ or **toto coe·lo** \-ˈkòi-lō\ [L] : by the whole extent of the heavens : diametrically

tou·jours per·drix \tü-zhür-per-drē\ [F] : always partridge : too much of a good thing

tour d'ho·ri·zon \tür-dò-rē-zōᵐ\ [F] : circuit of the horizon : general survey

tous frais faits \tü-fre-fe\ [F] : all expenses defrayed

tout à fait \tü-tà-fe\ [F] : altogether : quite

tout au con·traire \tü-tō-kōⁿ-trer\ [F] : quite the contrary

tout à vous \tü-tà-vü\ [F] : wholly yours : at your service

tout bien ou rien \tü-byaⁿ-nü-ryaᵐ\ [F] : everything well (done) or nothing (attempted)

tout com·pren·dre c'est tout par·don·ner \tü-kōⁿ-präⁿ-drə-se-tü-pár-dò-nä\ [F] : to understand all is to forgive all

tout court \tü-kür\ [F] : quite short : and nothing more : simply : just; also : brusquely

tout de même \tüt-mem\ [F] : all the same : nevertheless

tout de suite \tüt-swᵛēt\ [F] : immediately; also : all at once : consecutively

tout en·sem·ble \tü-tän-sänblᵃ\ [F] : all together : general effect

tout est per·du fors l'hon·neur \tü-te-per-dū̄-fòr-lò-nœr\ or **tout est perdu hors l'honneur** \-dū̄-òr-\ [F] : all is lost save honor

tout le monde \tül-mōⁿd\ [F] : all the world : everybody

tra·hi·son des clercs \trá-ē-zōⁿ-dä-klerk\ [F] : treason of the intellectuals

tranche de vie \träⁿsh-də-vē\ [F] : slice of life

trist·esse \trē-stes\ [F] : melancholy

tru·di·tur di·es die \ˈtrü-di-ˌtùr-ˈdi-ˌäs-ˈdi-ˌä\ [L] : day is pushed forth by day : one day hurries on another

tu·e·bor \tü-ˈä-ˌbòr\ [L] : I will defend — a motto on the Great Seal of Michigan

ua mau ke ea o ka ai·na i ka po·no \ˌù-ä-ˈmä-ù-ke-ˈe-ä-ō-kä-ˈä-ē-nä-ē-kä-ˈpō-nō\ [Hawaiian] : the life of the land is established in righteousness — motto of Hawaii

über alles [G] : above everything else

ue·ber·mensch \ˈū̄-bər-ˌmensh\ [G] : superman

ul·ti·ma ra·tio re·gum \ˈùl-ti-mä-ˌrä-tē-ō-ˈrä-gùm\ [L] : the final argument of kings, i.e., war

und so wei·ter \ˌùnt-zō-ˈvī-tər\ [G] : and so on

uno ani·mo \ˈü-nō-ˈä-ni-ˌmō\ [L] : with one mind : unanimously

ur·bi et or·bi \ˈùr-bē-ˌet-ˈòr-bē\ [L] : to the city (Rome) and the world : to everyone

uti·le dul·ci \ˈü-ti-le-ˈdùl-ˌkē\ [L] : the useful with the agreeable

ut in·fra \ˌùt-ˈin-frä\ [L] : as below

ut su·pra \ˌùt-ˈsü-prä\ [L] : as above

va·de re·tro me, Sa·ta·na \ˈwä-de-ˈrä-trō-ˌmä-ˈsä-tä-ˌnä\ [L] : get thee behind me, Satan

vae vic·tis \ˌwī-ˈwik-ˌtēs\ [L] : woe to the vanquished

va·ria lec·tio \\'wär-ē-ä-'lek-tē-ˌō\ *pl* **va·ri·ae lec·ti·o·nes** \\'wär-ē-ˌī-ˌlek-tē-'ō-ˌnäs\ [L] : variant reading

va·ri·um et mu·ta·bi·le sem·per fe·mi·na \\'wär-ē-ùm-ˌet-ˌmü-'tä-bi-le-'sem-ˌper-'fä-mi-nä\ [L] : woman is ever a fickle and changeable thing

ve·di Na·po·li e poi mo·ri \\'vä-dē-'nä-pō-lē-ä-ˌpò-ē-'mò-rē\ [It] : see Naples and then die

ve·ni, vi·di, vi·ci \\'wā-nē-'wē-dē-'wē- kē\ [L] : I came, I saw, I conquered

ven·tre à terre \\vän-trà-ter\ [F] : belly to the ground : at very great speed

ver·ba·tim ac lit·te·ra·tim \wer-'bä-tim- ˌäk-ˌli-te-'rä-tim\ [L] : word for word and letter for letter

ver·bum sat sa·pi·en·ti est \\'wer-bùm-'sät-ˌsä-pē-'en-tē-'est\ [L] : a word to the wise is sufficient

vieux jeu \vyœ̄-zhœ̄\ [F] : old game : old hat

vin·cit om·nia ve·ri·tas \\'wiŋ-ket-'òm-nē-ä-'wā-ri-ˌtäs\ [L] : truth conquers all things

vin·cu·lum ma·tri·mo·nii \\'wiŋ-kù-lùm-ˌmä-tri-'mō-nē-ˌē\ [L] : bond of marriage

vin du pays \vaⁿ-dǖ-pä-ē\ *or* **vin de pays** \vaⁿ-də-\ [F] : wine of the locality

vir·gi·ni·bus pu·e·ris·que \wir-'gi-ni- bùs-ˌpù-e-'rēs-kwe\ [L] : for girls and boys

vir·go in·tac·ta \\'vīr-ˌgō-in-'täk-tä\ [L] : untouched virgin

vir·tu·te et ar·mis \wir-'tü-te-ˌet-'är-mēs\ [L] : by valor and arms — motto of Mississippi

vis me·di·ca·trix na·tu·rae \\'wēs-ˌme-di-'kä-triks-nä-'tü-ˌrī\ [L] : the healing power of nature

vive la dif·fé·rence \vēv-lä-dē-fä-räⁿs\ [F] : long live the difference (between the sexes)

vive la reine \vēv-lá-ren\ [F] : long live the queen

vive le roi \vēv-lə-rwä\ [F] : long live the king

vix·e·re for·tes an·te Aga·mem·no·na \wik-'sä-re-'fòr-ˌtäs-ˌän-te-ä-gä-'mem-nò-ˌnä\ [L] : brave men lived before Agamemnon

vogue la ga·lère \vòg-là-gà-ler\ [F] : let the galley be kept rowing : keep on, whatever may happen

voi·là tout \vwà-là-tü\ [F] : that's all

vox et prae·te·rea ni·hil \\'wòks-et-prī-'ter-e-ä-'ni-ˌhil\ [L] : voice and nothing more

vox po·pu·li vox Dei \\'wòks-'pò-pù-ˌlē-'wòks-'de-ē\ [L] : the voice of the people is the voice of God

Wan·der·jahr \\'vän-dər-ˌyär\ [G] : year of wandering

wie geht's? \vē-'gāts\ [G] : how goes it?

wun·der·bar \\'vùn-dər-ˌbär\ [G] : wonderful

Biographical, Biblical, and Mythological Names

This section is a listing of the names of important figures from recorded history, biblical tradition, classical mythology, popular legend, and current events. Figures from the Bible, myth, or legend are clearly identified as such. In cases where figures have alternate names, they are entered under the name by which they are best known. The part of the name shown in boldface type is either the family name or the common shorter name for that figure. The dates following the name or pronunciation are the birth and death dates. Other dates in the entry refer to the dates of a particular office, honor, or achievement. Italicized names within an entry refer to a person's nickname, original name, title, or other name.

Aar·on \\ˈar-ən, ˈer-\\ brother of Moses and first high priest of the Hebrews in the Bible

Abel \\ˈā-bəl\\ son of Adam and Eve and brother of Cain in the Bible

Abra·ham \\ˈā-brə-ˌham\\ patriarch and founder of the Hebrew people in the Bible

Achil·les \\ə-ˈkil-ēz\\ Greek hero in the Trojan War in mythology

Ad·am \\ˈad-əm\\ the first man in the Bible

Ad·ams \\ˈad-əmz\\ Abigail 1744–1818 American writer; wife of John Adams

Adams John 1735–1826 2d president of the U.S. (1797–1801)

Adams John Quin·cy \\ˈkwin-zē, ˈkwin(t)-sē\\ 1767–1848 6th president of the U.S. (1825–29); son of John and Abigail Adams

Adams Samuel 1722–1803 patriot in the American Revolutionary War

Ad·dams \\ˈad-əmz\\ Jane 1860–1935 American social worker; Nobel Prize winner (1931)

Ado·nis \\ə-ˈdän-əs, -ˈdō-nəs\\ beautiful youth in Greek mythology who is loved by Aphrodite

Ae·ne·as \\i-ˈnē-əs\\ Trojan hero in Greek and Roman mythology

Ae·o·lus \\ˈē-ə-ləs\\ god of the winds in Greek mythology

Aes·chy·lus \\ˈes-kə-ləs, ˈēs-\\ 525–456 B.C. Greek dramatist

Aes·cu·la·pi·us \\ˌes-kyə-ˈlā-pē-əs\\ god of medicine in Roman mythology — compare ASCLEPIUS

Ae·sop \\ˈē-ˌsäp, -səp\\ legendary Greek writer of fables

Ag·a·mem·non \\ˌag-ə-ˈmem-ˌnän, -nən\\ leader of the Greeks during the Trojan War in Greek mythology

Ag·nes \\ˈag-nəs\\ Saint *died* 304 A.D. Christian martyr

Ahab \\ˈā-ˌhab\\ king of Israel in the 9th century B.C. and husband of Jezebel

Ajax \\ˈā-ˌjaks\\ hero in Greek mythology who kills himself because the armor of Achilles is awarded to Odysseus during the Trojan War

Alad·din \\ə-ˈlad-ᵊn\\ youth in the *Arabian Nights' Entertainments* who comes into possession of a magic lamp and ring

Al·cott \\ˈȯl-kət, ˈal-, -ˌkät\\ Louisa May 1832–1888 American author

Al·ex·an·der \\ˌal-ig-ˈzan-dər, ˌel-\\ name of eight popes: especially **VI** (Rodrigo Lanzol y Borja) 1431–1503 (pope 1492–1503)

Alexander III of Macedon 356–323 B.C. *the Great* king (336–323)

Al·fred \\ˈal-frəd, -fərd\\ 849–899 *the Great* king of the West Saxons (871–899)

Ali Ba·ba \\ˌal-ē-ˈbäb-ə\\ a woodcutter in the *Arabian Nights' Entertainments* who enters the cave of the Forty Thieves by using the password *Sesame*

Al·len \\ˈal-ən\\ Ethan 1738–1789 American Revolutionary soldier

Amerigo Vespucci — see VESPUCCI

Am·herst \\ˈam-(ˌ)ərst\\ Jeffrey 1717–1797 *Baron Amherst* British general in America

Amund·sen \\ˈäm-ən-sən\\ Roald 1872–1928 Norwegian explorer and discoverer of the South Pole (1911)

An·a·ni·as \\ˌan-ə-ˈnī-əs\\ early Christian struck dead for lying

An·der·sen \\ˈan-dər-sən\\ Hans Christian 1805–1875 Danish writer of fairy tales

An·der·son \\ˈan-dər-sən\\ Marian 1897–1993 American contralto

Anne \\ˈan\\ 1665–1714 queen of Great Britain (1702–14)

An·tho·ny \\ˈan(t)-thə-nē\\ Susan Brownell 1820–1906 American suffragist

An·tig·o·ne \\an-ˈtig-ə-nē\\ daughter of Oedipus and Jocasta in Greek mythology

An·to·ni·us \\an-ˈtō-nē-əs\\ Marcus *about* 82–30 B.C. *Mark* or *Marc An·to·ny* or *An·tho·ny* \\ˈan(t)-thə-nē, *chiefly British* ˈan-tə-nē\\ Roman general

Aph·ro·di·te \\ˌaf-rə-ˈdīt-ē\\ goddess of love and beauty in Greek mythology — compare VENUS

Apol·lo \\ə-ˈpäl-ō\\ god of sunlight, prophecy, music, and poetry in Greek and Roman mythology

Aqui·nas \\ə-ˈkwī-nəs\\ Saint Thomas 1224 (or 1225)–1274 Italian theologian

Ar·chi·me·des \\ˌär-kə-ˈmēd-ēz\\ *about* 287–212 B.C. Greek mathematician

Ares \\ˈa(ə)r-ˌēz, ˈe(ə)r-\\ god of war in Greek mythology — compare MARS

Ar·is·toph·a·nes \\ˌar-ə-ˈstäf-ə-ˌnēz\\ *about* 450– *about* 388 B.C. Greek dramatist

Ar·is·tot·le \\ˈar-ə-ˌstät-ᵊl\\ 384–322 B.C. Greek philosopher

Arm·strong \\ˈärm-ˌstrȯŋ\\ Louis 1901–1971 *Satchmo* \\ˈsach-ˌmō\\ American jazz musician

Armstrong Neil Alden 1930– American astronaut and first man on the moon (1969)

Ar·nold \\ˈärn-ᵊld\\ Benedict 1741–1801 American Revolutionary general and traitor

Ar·te·mis \\ˈärt-ə-məs\\ goddess of the moon, wild animals, and hunting in Greek mythology — compare DIANA

Ar·thur \\ˈär-thər\\ legendary king of the Britons whose story is based on traditions of a 6th century military leader — **Ar·thu·ri·an** \\är-ˈth(y)ùr-ē-ən\\ *adj*

Arthur Chester Alan 1829–1886 21st president of the U.S. (1881–85)

As·cle·pi·us \\ə-ˈsklē-pē-əs\\ god of medicine in Greek mythology — compare AESCULAPIUS

As·tor \\ˈas-tər\\ John Jacob 1763–1848 American (German-born) fur trader and capitalist

Athe·na \\ə-ˈthē-nə\\ *or* **Athe·ne** \\-nē\\ goddess of wisdom in Greek mythology — compare MINERVA

At·las \\ˈat-ləs\\ Titan in Greek mythology forced to bear the heavens on his shoulders

At·ti·la \\ə-ˈtil-ə, ˈat-ᵊl-ə\\ 406?–453 A.D. *the Scourge of God* king of the Huns

At·tucks \\'at-əks\ Crispus 1723?–1770 American patriot; one of five men killed in Boston Massacre

Au·du·bon \\'òd-ə-ˌbän, -bən\ John James 1785–1851 American (Haitian-born) artist and naturalist

Au·gus·tine \\'ò-gə-ˌstēn; ò-'gəs-tən, ə-\ Saint 354–430 A.D. church father; bishop of Hippo (396–430)

Au·gus·tus \ò-'gəs-təs, ə-\ *or* **Augustus Caesar** *or* **Oc·ta·vi·an** \äk-'tā-vē-ən\ 63 B.C.–14 A.D. 1st Roman emperor (27 B.C.–14 A.D.)

Aus·ten \\'òs-tən, 'äs-\ Jane 1775–1817 English author

Bac·chus \\'bak-əs\ — see DIONYSUS

Bach \\'bäk̲, 'bäk\ Johann Sebastian 1685–1750 German composer and organist

Ba·con \\'bā-kən\ Francis 1561–1626 English philosopher and author

Ba·den–Pow·ell \ˌbād-ᵊn-'pō-əl\ Robert Stephenson Smyth 1857–1941 English founder of Boy Scout movement

Baf·fin \\'baf-ən\ William *about* 1584–1622 English navigator

Bal·boa, de \bal-'bō-ə\ Vasco Núñez 1475–1519 Spanish explorer and discoverer of Pacific Ocean (1513)

Bal·ti·more \\'bòl-tə-ˌmō(ə)r, -ˌmó(ə)r\ Lord — see George CALVERT

Bal·zac, de \\'bòl-ˌzak, 'bal-\ Honoré 1799–1850 French author

Ba·rab·bas \bə-'rab-əs\ prisoner released in preference to Jesus at the demand of the multitude

Bar·num \\'bär-nəm\ Phineas Taylor 1810–1891 American show-business manager

Bar·rie \\'bar-ē\ Sir James Matthew 1860–1937 Scottish author

Bar·thol·di \bär-'täl-dē, -'tòl-, -'thäl-, -'thòl-\ Frédéric-Auguste 1834–1904 French sculptor who designed the Statue of Liberty

Bar·ton \\'bärt-ᵊn\ Clara 1821–1912 founder of American Red Cross Society

Beau·re·gard \\'bōr-ə-ˌgärd, 'bòr-\ Pierre Gustave Toutant 1818–1893 American Confederate general

Beck·et, à \ə-'bek-ət, ä-\ Saint Thomas *about* 1118–1170 archbishop of Canterbury (1162–1170)

Bee·tho·ven \\'bā-ˌtō-vən\ Ludwig van 1770–1827 German composer

Bell \\'bel\ Alexander Graham 1847–1922 American (Scottish-born) inventor of the telephone

Ben·e·dict \\'ben-ə-ˌdikt\ name of 15 popes: especially **XIV** (*Prospero Lambertini*) 1675–1758 (pope 1740–58); **XV** (*Giacomo della Chiesa*) 1854–1922 (pope 1914–22)

Be·nét \bə-'nā\ Stephen Vincent 1898–1943 American author

Ben·ja·min \\'benj-(ə-)mən\ youngest son of Jacob and ancestor of one of the 12 tribes of Israel in the Bible

Ben·ton \\'bent-ᵊn\ Thomas Hart 1889–1975 American painter

Be·o·wulf \\'bā-ə-ˌwùlf\ legendary warrior and hero of the Old English poem *Beowulf*

Be·ring \\'bi(ə)r-iŋ, 'be(ə)r-\ Vitus 1681–1741 Danish navigator; discovered Bering strait and Bering sea

Ber·lin \(ˌ)bər-'lin\ Irving 1888–1989 American (Russian-born) composer

Ber·ni·ni \bər-'nē-nē\ Gian Lorenzo 1598–1680 Italian sculptor, architect, and painter

Bes·se·mer \\'bes-ə-mər\ Sir Henry 1813–1898 English engineer and inventor

Be·thune \bə-'th(y)ün\ Mary 1875–1955 née *McLeod* American educator

Bi·zet \bē-'zā\ Alexandre-César-Léopold 1838–1875 called *Georges* French composer

Black Hawk \\'blak-ˌhòk\ 1767–1838 American Indian chief

Black·well \\'blak-ˌwel, -wəl\ Elizabeth 1821–1910 American (English-born) physician

Blake \\'blāk\ William 1757–1827 English poet and artist

Bloom·er \\'blü-mər\ Amelia Jenks 1818–1894 American social reformer

Boc·cac·cio \bō-'käch-(ē-ˌ)ō\ Giovanni 1313–1375 Italian author

Bohr \\'bō(ə)r, 'bò(ə)r\ Niels 1885–1962 Danish physicist

Bo·leyn \bù-'lin, 'bùl-ən\ Anne 1507?–1536 2d wife of Henry VIII and mother of Elizabeth I of England

Bo·lí·var Si·món \sē-ˌmōn-bə-'lē-ˌvär, ˌsī-mən-'bäl-ə-vər\ 1783–1830 South American liberator

Bon·i·face \\'bän-ə-fəs, -ˌfäs\ name of nine popes: especially **VIII** (*Benedetto Caetani*) *about* 1235 (or 1240)–1303 (pope 1294–1303)

Boone \\'bün\ Daniel 1734–1820 American pioneer

Booth \\'büth\ John Wilkes 1838–1865 assassin of Abraham Lincoln

Bo·re·as \\'bōr-ē-əs, 'bòr-\ god of the north wind in Greek mythology

Bot·ti·cel·li \ˌbät-ə-'chel-ē\ Sandro 1445–1510 Italian painter

Bow·ie \\'bü-ē, 'bō-\ James 1796–1836 hero of Texas revolution

Boyle \\'bòi(ə)l\ Robert 1627–1691 English physicist and chemist

Brad·bury \\'brad-ˌber-ē, -b(ə-)rē\ Ray Douglas 1920– American author

Brad·dock \\'brad-ək\ Edward 1695–1755 British general in America

Brad·ford \\'brad-fərd\ William 1590–1657 Pilgrim leader

Brad·street \\'brad-ˌstrēt\ Anne *about* 1612–1672 American poet

Bra·dy \\'brād-ē\ Mathew B. 1823?–1896 American photographer

Brah·ma \\'bräm-ə\ creator god of the Hindu sacred triad — compare SIVA, VISHNU

Brahms \\'brämz\ Johannes 1833–1897 German composer

Braille \\'brā(ə)l, 'brī\ Louis 1809–1852 French blind teacher of the blind

Braun \\'braùn\ Wernher von 1912–1977 American (German-born) engineer

Brezh·nev \\'brezh-ˌnef\ Leonid Ilyich 1906–1982 Russian politician; 1st secretary of Communist party (1964–82); president of the U.S.S.R. (1960–64; 1977–82)

Brid·ger \\'brij-ər\ James 1804–1881 American pioneer and scout

Bron·të \\'bränt-ē, 'brän-ˌtā\ family of English writers: Charlotte 1816–1855 and her sisters Emily 1818–1848 and Anne 1820–1849

Brooks \\'brùks\ Gwendolyn Elizabeth 1917– American poet

Brown \\'braùn\ John *Old Brown of Osa·wat·o·mie* \ˌō-sə-'wät- ə-mē\ 1800–1859 American abolitionist

Brow·ning \\'braù-niŋ\ Elizabeth Barrett 1806–1861 English poet; wife of Robert

Browning Robert 1812–1889 English poet; husband of Elizabeth

Bru·tus \\'brüt-əs\ Marcus Junius 85–42 B.C. Roman politician; one of Julius Caesar's assassins

Bry·an \\'brī-ən\ William Jennings 1860–1925 American lawyer and politician

Bu·chan·an \byü-'kan-ən, bə-\ James 1791–1868 15th president of the U.S. (1857–61)

Buck \\'bək\ Pearl 1892–1973 American author; Nobel Prize winner (1938)

Buddha — see GAUTAMA BUDDHA

Buffalo Bill — see William Frederick CODY

Bun·yan \\'bən-yən\ John 1628–1688 English preacher and author

Bur·bank \\'bər-ˌbaŋk\ Luther 1849–1926 American horticulturist

Bur·goyne \(ˌ)bər-'gòin, 'bər-ˌgòin\ John 1722–1792 British general in America

Burns \\'bərnz\ Robert 1759–1796 Scottish poet

Burn·side \\'bərn-ₗsīd\\ Ambrose Everett 1824–1881 American general

Burr \\'bər\\ Aaron 1756–1836 vice president of the U.S. (1801–05)

Bush \\'bush\\ George Herbert Walker 1924–   41st president of the U.S. (1989–93)

By·ron \\'bī-rən\\ Lord 1788–1824 *George Gordon Byron* English poet

Cab·ot \\'kab-ət\\ John *about* 1450–*about* 1499 Italian navigator; explored coast of North America for England

Cabot Sebastian 1476?–1557 English navigator; son of John Cabot

Ca·bri·ni \\kə-'brē-nē\\ Saint Frances Xavier 1850–1917 *Mother Cabrini* first American (Italian-born) saint (1946)

Cae·sar \\'sē-zər\\ Gaius Julius 100–44 B.C. Roman general, political leader, and writer

Cain \\'kān\\ brother of Abel in the Bible

Cal·houn \\kal-'hün\\ John Caldwell 1782–1850 vice president of the U.S. (1825–32)

Ca·lig·u·la \\kə-'lig-yə-lə\\ 12–41 A.D. *Gaius Caesar* Roman emperor (37–41)

Cal·li·ope \\kə-'lī-ə-ₗpē\\ muse of heroic poetry in Greek mythology

Cal·vert \\'kal-vərt\\ George 1580?–1632 1st Baron *Baltimore* English colonist in America

Cal·vin \\'kal-vən\\ John 1509–1564 French theologian and reformer

Ca·nute \\kə-'n(y)üt\\ *died* 1035 *the Great* king of England (1016–35); of Denmark (1018–35); of Norway (1028–35)

Car·ne·gie \\'kär-nə-gē, kär-'neg-ē\\ Andrew 1835–1919 American (Scottish-born) industrialist and philanthropist

Carroll Lewis — see Charles Lutwidge DODGSON

Car·son \\'kärs-ᵊn\\ Christopher 1809–1868 *Kit* American soldier and guide

Carson Rachel Louise 1907–1964 American scientist

Car·ter \\'kärt-ər\\ James Earl, Jr. 1924–   *Jimmy* 39th president of the U.S. (1977–81)

Car·tier \\kär-'tyā, 'kärt-ē-ₗā\\ Jacques 1491–1557 French navigator; discovered Saint Lawrence river

Ca·ru·so \\kə-'rü-sō, -zō\\ En·ri·co \\en-'rē-kō\\ 1873–1921 Italian tenor

Car·ver \\'kär-vər\\ George Washington *about* 1864–1943 American botanist

Ca·sa·no·va \\ₗkaz-ə-'nō-və, ₗkas-\\ Giovanni Giacomo 1725–1798 Italian adventurer

Cas·san·dra \\kə-'san-dra\\ daughter of Priam in Greek mythology who is endowed with the gift of prophecy but fated never to be believed

Cas·satt \\kə-'sat\\ Mary 1845–1926 American painter

Cas·tro \\'kas-trō, 'käs-\\ (Ruz) \\'rüs\\ Fi·del \\ fē-'del\\ 1926–   Cuban premier (1959–   )

Cath·er \\'kath-ər\\ Willa Sibert 1873–1947 American author

Cath·er·ine \\'kath-(ə-)rən\\ name of 1st, 5th, and 6th wives of Henry VIII of England: Catherine of Aragon 1485–1536; Catherine Howard 1520?–1542; Catherine Parr 1512–1548

Catherine I 1684–1727 wife of Peter the Great; empress of Russia (1725–27)

Catherine II 1729–1796 *the Great* empress of Russia (1762–96)

Cav·en·dish \\'kav-ən-(ₗ)dish\\ Henry 1731–1810 English scientist

Ce·ci·lia \\sə-'sēl-yə, -'sil-\\ Saint 2d or 3d century A.D. Roman martyr; patron saint of music

Ce·res \\'si(ə)r-ₗēz\\ the goddess of agriculture in Roman mythology — compare DEMETER

Cer·van·tes \\sər-'van-ₗtēz\\ Miguel de 1547–1616 Spanish author

Cé·zanne \\sā-'zan\\ Paul 1839–1906 French painter

Cha·gall \\shə-'gäl, -'gal\\ Marc 1887–1985 Russian painter

Cham·plain \\(')sham-'plān\\ Samuel de *about* 1567–1635 French explorer in America; founder of Quebec

Chap·lin \\'chap-lən\\ Sir Charles Spencer 1889–1977 British actor and producer

Chap·man \\'chap-mən\\ John 1774–1845 *Johnny Appleseed* \\'ap-əl-ₗsēd\\ American pioneer

Char·le·magne \\'shär-lə-ₗmān\\ 742–814 A.D. *Charles the Great* or *Charles I* Frankish king (768–814); emperor of the West (800–814)

Charles \\'chär(-ə)lz\\ name of 10 kings of France: especially **I** 823–877 A.D. (reigned 840–77) *the Bald*; Holy Roman emperor as *Charles II* (875–77); **IV** 1294–1328 (reigned 1322–28) *the Fair*; **V** 1337–1380 (reigned 1364–80) *the Wise*; **VI** 1368–1422 (reigned 1380–1422) *the Mad* or *the Beloved*; **VII** 1403–1461 (reigned 1422–61) *the Victorious*; **IX** 1550–1574 (reigned 1560–74); **X** 1757–1836 (reigned 1824–30)

Charles name of two kings of Great Britain: **I** 1600–1649 (reigned 1625–49) *Charles Stuart*; **II** 1630–1685 (reigned 1660–85) son of Charles I

Charles V 1500–1558 Holy Roman emperor (1519–56); king of Spain as *Charles I* (1516–56)

Charles Edward Stuart 1720–1788 *the Young Pretender*; *(Bonnie) Prince Charlie* English prince

Charles Mar·tel \\mär-'tel\\ *about* 688–741 A.D. Frankish ruler (719–41); grandfather of Charlemagne

Cha·ryb·dis \\kə-'rib-dəs, shə-, chə-\\ a whirlpool off the coast of Sicily personified in Greek mythology as a female monster

Chau·cer \\'chȯ-sər\\ Geoffrey *about* 1342–1400 English poet

Che·khov \\'chek-ₗȯf, -ₗȯv\\ Anton Pavlovich 1860–1904 Russian author

Cheops — see KHUFU

Ches·ter·ton \\'ches-tərt-ᵊn\\ Gilbert Keith 1874–1936 English author

Cho·pin \\'shō-ₗpan\\ Frédéric François 1810–1849 Polish pianist and composer

Chou En-lai \\'jō-'en-'lī\\ 1898–1976 Chinese Communist politician; premier (1949–76)

Christ Jesus — see JESUS

Chris·tie \\'kris-tē\\ Agatha 1890–1976 English author

Chur·chill \\'chər-ₗchil, 'chərch-ₗhil\\ Sir Winston Leonard Spencer 1874–1965 British prime minister (1940–45; 1951–55)

Clark \\'klärk\\ George Rogers 1752–1818 American soldier and pioneer

Clark William 1770–1838 American explorer

Clay \\'klā\\ Henry 1777–1852 American politician and orator

Clem·ens \\'klem-ənz\\ Samuel Langhorne 1835–1910 pseudonym *Mark Twain* \\'twān\\ American author

Cle·o·pa·tra \\ₗklē-ə-'pa-trə, -'pā-, -'pä-\\ 69–30 B.C. queen of Egypt (51–30)

Cleve·land \\'klēv-lənd\\ (Stephen) Grover 1837–1908 22d and 24th president of the U.S. (1885–89; 1893–97)

Clin·ton \\'klin-tᵊn\\ William Jefferson 1946–   42d president of the U.S. (1993–   )

Cly·tem·nes·tra \\ₗklīt-əm-'nes- trə\\ wife of Agamemnon in Greek mythology

Cobb \\'käb\\ Tyrus Raymond 1886–1961 *Ty* American baseball player

Co·chise \\kō-'chēs\\ 1812?–1874 Apache Indian chief

Co·dy \\'kōd-ē\\ William Frederick 1846–1917 *Buffalo Bill* American hunter, guide, and entertainer

Co·han \\'kō-ₗhan\\ George Michael 1878–1942 American actor and composer

Cole·ridge \\'kōl-rij, 'kō-lə-rij\\ Samuel Taylor 1772–1834 English poet

Co·lette \\kȯ-'let\\ Sidonie-Gabrielle 1873–1954 French author

Co·lum·bus \\kə-'ləm-bəs\\ Christopher 1451–1506 Italian navigator; discovered America for Spain (1492)

Con·fu·cius \\kən-'fyü-shəs\\ 551–479 B.C. Chinese philosopher

Con·rad \\'kän-₁rad\ Joseph 1857–1924 British (Ukrainian-born of Polish parents) author

Con·sta·ble \\'kən(t)-stə-bəl, 'kän(t)-\ John 1776–1837 English painter

Con·stan·tine \\'kän(t)-stən-₁tēn, -₁tīn\ *died* 337 A.D. *the Great* Roman emperor (306–37)

Cook \\'kůk\ Captain James 1728–1779 English navigator

Coo·lidge \\'kü-lij\ (John) Calvin 1872–1933 30th president of the U.S. (1923–29)

Coo·per \\'kü-pər, 'kůp-ər\ James Fen·i·more \\'fen-ə-₁mō(ə)r, -₁mó(ə)r\ 1789–1851 American author

Co·per·ni·cus \kō-'pər-ni-kəs\ Nicolaus 1473–1543 Polish astronomer

Cop·land \\'kō-plənd\ Aaron 1900–1990 American composer

Cop·ley \\'käp-lē\ John Sin·gle·ton \\'siŋ-gəl-tən\ 1738–1815 American portrait painter

Corn·wal·lis \kórn-'wäl-əs\ 1st Marquis 1738–1805 *Charles Cornwallis* British general in America

Co·ro·na·do \kór-ə-₁näd-ō, ₁kär-\ Francisco Vásquez de *about* 1510–1554 Spanish explorer of southwestern U.S.

Cor·tés \kór-'tez, 'kór-₁tez\ Hernán *or* Hernando 1485–1547 Spanish conqueror of Mexico

Cous·teau \kü-'stō\ Jacques-Yves 1910–   French marine explorer

Crane \\'krān\ Stephen 1871–1900 American author

Crazy Horse \\'krā-zē-₁hórs\ 1842–1877 Sioux Indian chief

Crock·ett \\'kräk-ət\ David 1786–1836 *Davy* American pioneer

Crom·well \\'kräm-₁wel, 'krəm-, -wəl\ Oliver 1599–1658 English general and political leader; lord protector of England (1653–58)

Cro·nus \\'krō-nəs, 'krän-əs\ a Titan in Greek mythology overthrown by his son Zeus

Cum·mings \\'kəm-iŋz\ Edward Estlin 1894–1962 known as *e. e. cummings* American poet

Cu·pid \\'kyü-pəd\ god of love in Roman mythology — compare EROS

Cu·rie \kyü-'rē, 'kyü(ə)r-ē\ Marie 1867–1934 French (Polish-born) chemist; Nobel Prize winner (1903–1911)

Curie Pierre 1859–1906 French chemist; Nobel Prize winner (1903)

Cus·ter \\'kəs-tər\ George Armstrong 1839–1876 American general

Cy·ra·no de Ber·ge·rac \₁sir-ə-₁nō-də-'ber-zhə-₁rak\ Savinien de 1619–1655 French poet and soldier

Dae·da·lus \\'ded-əl-əs, 'dēd-\ builder in Greek mythology of the Cretan labyrinth and inventor of wings by which he and his son Icarus escape from it

Dal·ton \\'dólt-ən\ John 1766–1844 English chemist and physicist

Da·na \\'dā-nə\ Richard Henry 1815–1882 American author

Dan·iel \\'dan-yəl\ a prophet in the Bible who is held captive in Babylon and delivered by God from a den of lions

Dan·te \\'dän-tā, 'dan-, -tē\ 1265–1321 Italian poet

Dare \\'da(ə)r, 'de(ə)r\ Virginia 1587–? first child born in America of English parents

Da·ri·us I \də-'rī-əs\ 550–486 B.C. *the Great* king of Persia (522–486)

Dar·row \\'dar-ō\ Clarence Seward 1857–1938 American lawyer

Dar·win \\'där-wən\ Charles Robert 1809–1882 English naturalist

Da·vid \\'dā-vəd\ a youth in the Bible who slays Goliath and succeeds Saul as king of Israel

Da·vis \\'dā-vəs\ Jefferson 1808–1889 president of the Confederate States of America (1861–65)

Dawes \\'dóz\ William 1745–1799 American patriot

Debs \\'debz\ Eugene Victor 1855–1926 American socialist

De·bus·sy \₁deb-yů-'sē, ₁däb-; də-'byü-sē\ (Achille-) Claude 1862–1918 French composer

De·ca·tur \di-'kāt-ər\ Stephen 1779–1820 American naval officer

De·foe \di-'fō\ Daniel 1660–1731 English author

De·gas \də-'gä\ (Hilaire-Germain-) Edgar 1834–1917 French painter

de Gaulle \di-'gōl, -'gól\ Charles-André-Joseph-Marie 1890–1970 French general; president of Fifth Republic (1958–69)

De·li·lah \di-'lī-lə\ mistress and betrayer of Samson in the Bible

De·me·ter \di-'mēt-ər\ goddess of agriculture in Greek mythology — compare CERES

de Mille \də-'mil\ Agnes George 1909?–1993 American dancer and choreographer

Des·car·tes \dā-'kärt\ René 1596–1650 French mathematician and philosopher

de So·to \di-'sōt-ō\ Hernando 1496 (or 1499 or 1500)–1542 Spanish explorer in America

Dew·ey \\'d(y)ü-ē\ George 1837–1917 American admiral

Dewey John 1859–1952 American philosopher and educator

Dewey Melvil 1851–1931 American librarian

Di·ana \dī-'an-ə\ goddess of the forest and of childbirth in ancient Italian mythology who was identified with Artemis by the Romans

Dick·ens \\'dik-ənz\ Charles John Huffam 1812–1870 pseudonym *Boz* \\'bäz, 'bōz\ English author

Dick·in·son \\'dik-ən-sən\ Emily Elizabeth 1830–1886 American poet

Di·do \\'dīd-ō\ legendary queen of Carthage who falls in love with Aeneas and kills herself when he leaves her

Di·o·ny·sus \₁dī-ə-'nī-səs, -'nē-\ god of wine and ecstasy in Greek mythology — **Di·o·ny·sian** \dī-ə-'nizh-ē-ən\ *adj*

Dis·ney \\'diz-nē\ Walter Elias 1901–1966 American film producer

Dis·rae·li \diz-'rā-lē\ Benjamin 1804–1881 1st Earl of *Bea·cons·field* \\'bē-kənz-₁fēld\ British prime minister (1868; 1874–80)

Dix \\'diks\ Dorothea Lynde 1802–1887 American social reformer

Dodg·son \\'däj-sən, 'däd-\ Charles Lut·widge \\'lət-wij\ 1832–1898 pseudonym *Lewis Car·roll* \\'kar-əl\ English author and mathematician

Donne \\'dən\ John 1572–1631 English poet and minister

Don Qui·xote \₁dän-kē-'(h)ōt-ē, ₁däŋ-; dän-'kwik-sət\ the idealistic and impractical hero of Cervantes' *Don Quixote*

Dos·to·yev·ski \₁däs-tə-'yef-skē, -'yev-\ Fyodor Mikhaylovich 1821–1881 Russian novelist

Doug·las \\'dəg-ləs\ Stephen Arnold 1813–1861 American politician

Doug·lass \\'dəg-ləs\ Frederick 1817–1895 American abolitionist

Doyle \\'dói(ə)l\ Sir Arthur Co·nan \\'kō-nən\ 1859–1930 British physician, novelist, and detective-story writer

Drake \\'drāk\ Sir Francis 1540 (or 1543)–1596 English navigator and admiral

Drei·ser \\'drī-sər, -zər\ Theodore 1871–1945 American author

Du Bois \d(y)ü-'bóis\ William Edward Burghardt 1868–1963 American educator and writer

Du·mas \d(y)ü-'mä, 'd(y)ü-₁mä\ Alexandre 1802–1870 *Dumas père* \\'pe(ə)r\ French author

Dumas Alexandre 1824–1895 *Dumas fils* \\'fēs\ French author

Dun·can \\'dəŋ-kən\ Isadora 1877–1927 American dancer

Dü·rer \\'d(y)ůr-ər\ Albrecht 1471–1528 German painter and engraver

Ea·kins \\'ā-kənz\ Thomas 1844–1916 American artist

Ear·hart \\'e(ə)r-₁härt, ₁'i(ə)r-\ Amelia 1897–1937 American aviator

Ed·dy \\'ed-ē\ Mary Baker 1821–1910 American founder of the Christian Science Church

Ed·i·son \\'ed-ə-sən\ Thomas Alva 1847–1931 American inventor

Ed·ward \\'ed-wərd\ name of eight post-Norman kings of England: **I** 1239–1307 (reigned 1272–1307) *Longshanks*; **II** 1284–1327 (reigned 1307–27); **III** 1312–1377 (reigned 1327–77); **IV** 1442–1483 (reigned 1461–70; 1471–83); **V** 1470–1483 (reigned 1483); **VI** 1537–1553 (reigned 1547–53) son of Henry VIII and Jane Seymour; **VII** 1841–1910 (reigned 1901–10) *Albert Edward* son of Queen Victoria; **VIII** 1894–1972 (reigned 1936; abdicated) *Duke of Windsor* son of George V

Ein·stein \\'īn-₁stīn\ Albert 1879–1955 American (German-born) physicist; Nobel Prize winner (1921)

Ei·sen·how·er \\'īz-ən-₁haů-(ə)r\ Dwight David 1890–1969 American general; 34th president of the U.S. (1953–61)

Elec·tra \i-'lek-trə\ sister of Orestes in Greek mythology who with her brother avenges their father's murder

Eli·jah \i-'lī-jə\ Hebrew prophet of the 9th century B.C.

El·iot \\'el-ē-ət, 'el-yət\ George 1819–1880 pseudonym of *Mary Ann Evans* English author

Eliot Thomas Stearns 1888–1965 British (American-born) poet and critic

Eliz·a·beth I \i-'liz-ə-bəth\ 1533–1603 daughter of Henry VIII and Anne Boleyn; queen of England (1558–1603)

Elizabeth II 1926– queen of the United Kingdom (1952–)

Em·er·son \\'em-ər-sən\ Ralph Waldo 1803–1882 American essayist and poet

En·dym·i·on \en-'dim-ē-ən\ beautiful youth in Greek mythology loved by the goddess of the moon

Ep·i·cu·rus \₁ep-i-'kyůr-əs\ 341–270 B.C. Greek philosopher

Er·ik \\'er-ik\ *the Red* 10th century Norwegian navigator; explored Greenland coast

Eriksson Leif — see LEIF ERIKSSON

Eros \\'e(ə)r-₁äs, 'i(ə)r-\ god of love in Greek mythology — compare CUPID

Esau \\'ē-(₁)sȯ\ son of Isaac and Rebekah and elder twin brother of Jacob in the Bible

Es·ther \\'es-tər\ Hebrew woman in the Bible who as the queen of Persia delivers her people from destruction

Eu·clid \\'yü-kləd\ *flourished about* 300 B.C. Greek mathematician

Eu·rip·i·des \yů-'rip-ə-₁dēz\ *about* 484–406 B.C. Greek dramatist

Eu·ro·pa \yů-'rō-pə\ a princess in Greek mythology who was carried off by Zeus disguised as a white bull

Eu·ryd·i·ce \yů-'rid-ə-sē\ the wife of Orpheus whom he attempts to bring back from Hades

Eve \\'ēv\ the first woman in the Bible

Eze·kiel \i-'zē-kyəl, -kē-əl\ Hebrew prophet of the 6th century B.C.

Fahr·en·heit \\'far-ən-₁hīt, 'fär-\ Daniel Gabriel 1686–1736 German physicist

Far·a·day \\'far-ə-₁dā, -əd-ē\ Michael 1791–1867 English chemist and physicist

Far·ra·gut \\'far-ə-gət\ David Glasgow 1801–1870 American admiral

Faulk·ner \\'fȯk-nər\ William 1897–1962 American author; Nobel Prize winner (1949)

Faust \\'faůst\ *or* **Fau·stus** \\'faů-stəs, 'fȯ-\ a legendary German magician who sells his soul to the devil

Fawkes \\'fȯks\ Guy 1570–1606 English conspirator

Fer·di·nand \\'fərd-ᵊn-₁and\ **II** of Aragon *or* **V** of Castile 1452–1516 *the Catholic* king of Castile (1474–

1504); of Aragon (1479–1516); of Naples (1504–16); founder of the Spanish monarchy

Fer·mi \\'fe(ə)r-mē\ Enrico 1901–1954 American (Italian-born) physicist; Nobel Prize winner (1938)

Fiel·ding \\'fē(ə)l-diṅ\ Henry 1707–1754 English author

Fill·more \\'fil-₁mō(ə)r, -₁mȯ(ə)r\ Millard 1800–1874 13th president of the U.S. (1850–53)

Fitz·ger·ald \fits-'jer-əld\ Francis Scott Key 1896–1940 American author

Flem·ing \\'flem-iṅ\ Sir Alexander 1881–1955 British bacteriologist; Nobel Prize winner (1945)

Flo·ra \\'flōr-ə, 'flȯr-\ goddess of flowers in Roman mythology

Flying Dutchman legendary Dutch mariner condemned to sail the seas until Judgment Day

Ford \\'fō(ə)rd, 'fȯ(ə)rd\ Gerald Rudolph 1913– 38th president of the U.S. (1974–77)

Ford Henry 1863–1947 American automobile manufacturer

Fos·ter \\'fȯs-tər, 'fäs-\ Stephen Collins 1826–1864 American songwriter

Francis \\'fran(t)-səs\ **of As·si·si** \ə-'sis-ē, -'sis-ē-ze, -'sē-sē, -'siz-ē\ Saint 1181 (or 1182)–1226 Italian friar; founder of Franciscan order

Frank·lin \\'fraṅ-klən\ Benjamin 1706–1790 American patriot, author, and inventor

Fred·er·ick I \\'fred-(ə-)rik\ *about* 1123–1190 *Frederick Bar·ba·ros·sa* \₁bär-bə-'räs-ə, -'rȯs-\ Holy Roman emperor (1152–90)

Frederick II 1712–1786 *the Great* king of Prussia (1740–86)

Fré·mont \\'frē-₁mänt\ John Charles 1813–1890 American general and explorer

French \\'french\ Daniel Chester 1850–1931 American sculptor

Freud \\'frȯid\ Sigmund 1856–1939 Austrian neurologist; founder of psychoanalysis

Frig·ga \\'frig-ə\ wife of Odin and goddess of married love and the hearth in Norse mythology

Frost \\'frȯst\ Robert Lee 1874–1963 American poet

Ful·ler \\'fůl-ər\ (Richard) Buckminster 1895–1983 American engineer

Fuller (Sarah) Margaret 1810–1850 American author and reformer

Ful·ton \\'fůlt-ᵊn\ Robert 1765–1815 American inventor

Ga·bri·el \\'gā-brē-əl\ one of the four archangels named in Hebrew tradition — compare MICHAEL, RAPHAEL, URIEL

Ga·ga·rin \gə-'gär-ən\ Yu·ry \'yů(ə)r-ē\ Alekseyevich 1934–1968 Russian astronaut; first man in space

Gage \\'gāj\ Thomas 1721–1787 British general in America

Gal·a·had \\'gal-ə-₁had\ knight of the Round Table who finds the Holy Grail

Gal·a·tea \₁gal-ə-'tē-ə\ a female figure sculpted by Pygmalion in Greek mythology and given life by Aphrodite in answer to the sculptor's prayer

Ga·len \\'gā-lən\ 129–*about* 199 A.D. Greek physician and writer

Gal·i·lei \₁gal-ə-'lā-ē\ Ga·li·leo \₁gal-ə-'lē-ō, -'lā-\ 1564–1642 usually called *Galileo* Italian astronomer and physicist — **Gal·i·le·an** \₁gal-ə-'lē-ən\ *adj*

Gall \\'gȯl\ 1840?–1894 Sioux Indian leader

Ga·ma, da \\'gam-ə, 'gäm-\ Vasco *about* 1460–1524 Portuguese navigator

Gan·dhi \\'gän-dē, 'gan-\ Mohandas Karamchand 1869–1948 *Ma·hat·ma* \mə-'hät-mə, -'hat-\ Indian leader

Gar·field \\'gär-₁fēld\ James Abram 1831–1881 20th president of the U.S. (1881)

Gar·i·bal·di \₁gar-ə-'bȯl-dē\ Giuseppe 1807–1882 Italian patriot

Gar·ri·son \\'gar-ə-sən\ William Lloyd 1805–1879 American abolitionist

Gau·guin \gō-gan\ (Eugène-Henri-) Paul 1848–1903 French painter

Gau·ta·ma Bud·dha \ˌgaut-ə-mə-ˈbüd-ə, -ˈbud-\ *about* 563–*about* 483 B.C. *The Buddha* Indian philosopher; founder of Buddhism

Gen·ghis Khan \ˌjeŋ-gə-ˈskän, ˌgeŋ-\ *about* 1162–1227 Mongol conqueror

George \ˈjȯ(ə)rj\ name of six kings of Great Britain: **I** 1660–1727 (reigned 1714–27); **II** 1683–1760 (reigned 1727–60); **III** 1738–1820 (reigned 1760–1820); **IV** 1762–1830 (reigned 1820–30); **V** 1865–1936 (reigned 1910–36); **VI** 1895–1952 (reigned 1936–52)

Ge·ron·i·mo \jə-ˈrän-ə-ˌmō\ 1829–1909 Apache Indian leader

Gersh·win \ˈgərsh-wən\ George 1898–1937 American composer

Gid·e·on \ˈgid-ē-ən\ Hebrew hero in the Bible

Gil·bert \ˈgil-bərt\ Sir William Schwenck 1836–1911 English librettist and poet; collaborator with Sir Arthur Sullivan

Glad·stone \ˈglad-ˌstōn, *chiefly British* -stən\ William Ewart 1809–1898 British prime minister (1868–74; 1880–85; 1886; 1892–94)

Glenn \ˈglen\ John Herschel 1921–   American astronaut and politician; first American to orbit the earth (1962)

Go·di·va \gə-ˈdī-və\ an English gentlewoman who in legend rode naked through Coventry to save its citizens from a tax

Goe·thals \ˈgō-thəlz\ George Washington 1858–1928 American general and engineer

Goe·the \ˈgə(r)-tə\ Johann Wolfgang von 1749–1832 German author

Gogh, van \van-ˈgō, -ˈgäk, -ˈk̲ȯk̲\ Vincent Willem 1853–1890 Dutch painter

Go·li·ath \gə-ˈlī-əth\ Philistine giant who is killed by David in the Bible

Gom·pers \ˈgäm-pərz\ Samuel 1850–1924 American (British-born) labor leader

Good·year \ˈgud-ˌyi(ə)r, ˈguj-ˌi(ə)r\ Charles 1800–1860 American inventor

Gor·gas \ˈgȯr-gəs\ William Crawford 1854–1920 American army surgeon

Gra·ham \ˈgrā-əm, ˈgra(-ə)m\ Martha 1893–1991 American dancer and choreographer

Grant \ˈgrant\ Ulysses 1822–1885 originally *Hiram Ulysses Grant* American general; 18th president of the U.S. (1869–77)

Gre·co, El \el-ˈgrek-ō\ 1541–1614 *Doménikos Theotokópoulos* Spanish (Cretan-born) painter

Gree·ley \ˈgrē-lē\ Horace 1811–1872 American journalist and politician

Greene \ˈgrēn\ Graham 1904–1991 British novelist

Greene Nathanael 1742–1786 American Revolutionary general

Greg·o·ry \ˈgreg-(ə-)rē\ name of 16 popes: especially **I** Saint *about* 540–604 *the Great* (pope 590–604); **VII** Saint *about* 1020–1085 (pope 1073–85); **XIII** 1502–1585 (pope 1572–85)

Grey \ˈgrā\ Lady Jane 1537–1554 English noblewoman beheaded as a possible rival for the throne of Mary I

Grey Zane 1875–1939 American novelist

Grimm \ˈgrim\ Jacob 1785–1863 and his brother Wilhelm 1786–1859 German philologists and folklorists

Guin·e·vere \ˈgwin-ə-ˌvi(ə)r\ wife of King Arthur and lover of Lancelot

Gu·ten·berg \ˈgüt-ᵊn-ˌbərg\ Johannes *about* 1390–1468 German inventor of printing from movable type

Ha·des \ˈhād-ˌēz\ — see PLUTO

Ha·dri·an \ˈhā-drē-ən\ 76–138 A.D. Roman emperor (117–138)

Ha·gar \ˈhā-ˌgär, -gər\ mistress of Abraham and mother of Ishmael in the Bible

Hai·le Se·las·sie \ˌhī-lē-sə-ˈlas-ē, -ˈläs-\ 1892–1975 emperor of Ethiopia (1930–36; 1941–74)

Hale \ˈhā(ə)l\ Edward Everett 1822–1909 American minister and author

Hale Nathan 1755–1776 American Revolutionary hero

Hal·ley \ˈhal-ē, ˈhā-lē\ Edmond *or* Edmund 1656–1742 English astronomer

Hal·sey \ˈhȯl-sē, -zē\ William Frederick 1882–1959 American admiral

Ham·il·ton \ˈham-əl-tən\ Alexander 1755–1804 American political leader

Ham·mu·ra·bi \ˌham-ə-ˈräb-ē\ *or* **Ham·mu·ra·pi** \-ˈräp-ē\ *died* 1750 B.C. king of Babylon (1792–50)

Han·cock \ˈhan-ˌkäk\ John 1737–1793 American Revolutionary patriot

Han·del \ˈhan-dᵊl\ George Frideric 1685–1759 British (German-born) composer

Han·dy \ˈhan-dē\ William Christopher 1873–1958 American blues musician

Han·ni·bal \ˈhan-ə-bəl\ 247–183 B.C. Carthaginian general

Har·ding \ˈhärd-iŋ\ Warren Gamaliel 1865–1923 29th president of the U.S. (1921–23)

Har·dy \ˈhärd-ē\ Thomas 1840–1928 English author

Har·ri·son \ˈhar-ə-sən\ Benjamin 1833–1901 23d president of the U.S. (1889–93); grandson of William Henry Harrison

Harte \ˈhärt\ Francis Brett 1836–1902 known as *Bret* American author

Har·vey \ˈhär-vē\ William 1578–1657 English physician and anatomist

Haw·thorne \ˈhȯ-ˌthȯ(ə)rn\ Nathaniel 1804–1864 American author

Hayes \ˈhāz\ Rutherford Birchard 1822–1893 19th president of the U.S. (1877–81)

Hearst \ˈhərst\ William Randolph 1863–1951 American newspaper publisher

Hec·tor \ˈhek-tər\ son of Priam and Trojan hero slain by Achilles in Greek mythology

Hec·u·ba \ˈhek-yə-bə\ wife of Priam in Greek mythology

Hel·en of Troy \ˌhel-ə-nəv-ˈtrȯi\ wife of Menelaus whose abduction by Paris in Greek mythology caused the Trojan War

He·li·os \ˈhē-lē-əs, -ōs\ god of the sun in Greek mythology

Hem·ing·way \ˈhem-iŋ-ˌwā\ Ernest Miller 1899–1961 American author; Nobel Prize winner (1954)

Hen·ry \ˈhen-rē\ name of eight kings of England: **I** 1068–1135 (reigned 1100–35); **II** 1133–1189 (reigned 1154–89); **III** 1207–1272 (reigned 1216–72); **IV** 1367–1413 (reigned 1399–1413); **V** 1387–1422 (reigned 1413–22); **VI** 1421–1471 (reigned 1422–61; 1470–71); **VII** 1457–1509 (reigned 1485–1509); **VIII** 1491–1547 (reigned 1509–47)

Henry name of 4 kings of France: **I** 1008–1060 (reigned 1031–60); **II** 1519–1559 (reigned 1547–59); **III** 1551–1589 (reigned 1574–89); **IV** 1553–1610 *Henry of Navarre* (reigned 1589–1610)

Henry O. — see William Sydney PORTER

Henry Patrick 1736–1799 American patriot and orator

He·phaes·tus \hi-ˈfes-təs, -ˈfēs-\ god of fire and of metalworking in Greek mythology — compare VULCAN

He·ra \ˈhir-ə, ˈhē-rə\ sister and wife of Zeus and goddess of women and marriage in Greek mythology — compare JUNO

Her·cu·les \ˈhər-kyə-ˌlēz\ *or* **Her·a·cles** \ˈher-ə-ˌklēz\ hero in Greek mythology noted for his strength and for performing 12 labors imposed on him by Hera

Her·maph·ro·di·tus \(ˌ)hər-ˌmaf-rə-ˈdīt-əs\ son of Hermes and Aphrodite who in Greek mythology is joined with a nymph into one body

Her·mes \ˈhər-ˌmēz\ god of commerce, eloquence, invention, travel, and theft who serves as herald and messenger of the other gods in Greek mythology

Her·od \ˈher-əd\ 73–4 B.C. *the Great* Roman king of Judea (37–4)

Herod An·ti·pas \ˈant-ə-ˌpas, -pəs\ 21 B.C.–39 A.D. Roman governor of Galilee (4 B.C.–39 A.D.); son of Herod the Great

Hey·er·dahl \'hā-ər-ˌdäl, 'hī-\ Thor 1914— Norwegian explorer and author

Hi·a·wa·tha \ˌhī-ə-'wò-thə, ˌhē-ə-, -'wäth-ə\ legendary Indian chief

Hick·ok \'hik-ˌäk\ James Butler 1837–1876 *Wild Bill* American scout and United States marshal

Hil·ton \'hilt-ᵊn\ James 1900–1954 English novelist

Hip·poc·ra·tes \hip-'äk-rə-ˌtēz\ *about* 460–*about* 377 B.C. *founder of medicine* Greek physician

Hi·ro·hi·to \ˌhir-ō-'hē-tō\ 1901–1989 emperor of Japan (1926–89)

Hit·ler \'hit-lər\ Adolf 1889–1945 German (Austrian-born) chancellor (1933–45)

Holmes \'hōmz, 'hōlmz\ Oliver Wendell 1809–1894 American physician and author

Holmes Oliver Wendell 1841–1935 American jurist; son of the preceding

Ho·mer \'hō-mər\ 9th–8th? century B.C. Greek epic poet — **Ho·mer·ic** \hō-'mer-ik\ *adj*

Homer Winslow 1836–1910 American painter

Hooke \'hùk\ Robert 1635–1703 English scientist

Hook·er \'hùk-ər\ Thomas 1586?–1647 English colonist; a founder of Connecticut

Hoo·ver \'hü-vər\ Herbert Clark 1874–1964 31st president of the U.S. (1929–33)

Hoover John Edgar 1895–1972 American criminologist; director of the Federal Bureau of Investigation (1924–72)

Hou·di·ni \hü-'dē-nē\ Harry 1874–1926 originally *Ehrich Weiss* American magician

Hous·ton \'(h)yü-stən\ Samuel 1793–1863 *Sam* American general; president of the Republic of Texas (1836–38; 1841–44)

Howe \'haù\ Elias 1819–1867 American inventor

Howe Julia 1819–1910 née *Ward* American suffragist and reformer

Hud·son \'həd-sən\ Henry *died* 1611 English navigator and explorer

Hughes \'hyüz *also* 'yüz\ (James) Langston 1902–1967 American author

Hus·sein I \hü-'sān\ 1935— king of Jordan (1952–)

Hutch·in·son \'həch-ə(n)-sən\ Anne 1591–1643 religious leader in America

Hutchinson Thomas 1711–1780 American colonial administrator

Hux·ley \'hək-slē\ Aldous Leonard 1894–1963 English author

Hy·men \'hī-mən\ god of marriage in Greek mythology

Ib·sen \'ib-sən, 'ip-\ Henrik 1828–1906 Norwegian dramatist and poet

Ic·a·rus \'ik-ə-rəs\ son of Daedalus who in Greek mythology falls into the sea when the wax of his artificial wings melts as he flies too near the sun

Ig·na·tius \ig-'nā-sh(ē-)əs \ *Saint Ignatius of Loy·o·la* \ˌlòi-'ō-lə\ 1491–1556 Spanish soldier and priest; founded the Society of Jesus

In·no·cent \'in-ə-sənt\ name of 13 popes: especially **II** *died* 1143 (pope 1130–43); **III** 1160 (or 1161)–1216 (pope 1198–1216); **IV** *died* 1254 (pope 1243–54); **XI** 1611–1689 (pope 1676–89)

Ir·ving \'ər-viŋ\ Washington 1783–1859 American author

Isaac \'ī-zik, -zək\ son of Abraham and father of Jacob in the Bible

Is·a·bel·la I \ˌiz-ə-'bel-ə\ 1451–1504 queen of Castile (1474–1504) and of Aragon (1479–1504); wife of Ferdinand V of Castile

Isa·iah \ī-'zā-ə\ Hebrew prophet of the 8th century B.C.

Ish·ma·el \'ish-(ˌ)mā-əl, -mē-\ outcast son of Abraham and Hagar in the Bible

Ives \'īvz\ Charles Edward 1874–1954 American composer

Jack·son \'jak-sən\ Andrew 1767–1845 American general; 7th president of the U.S. (1829–37)

Jackson Thomas Jonathan 1824–1863 *Stonewall* American Confederate general

Ja·cob \'jā-kəb\ son of Isaac and Rebekah and younger twin brother of Esau in the Bible

James \'jāmz\ one of the 12 apostles in the Bible

James *the Less* one of the 12 apostles in the Bible

James name of two kings of Great Britain: **I** 1566–1625 (reigned 1603–25); king of Scotland as *James VI* (reigned 1567–1603); **II** 1633–1701 (reigned 1685–88)

James Henry 1843–1916 British (American-born) author

Ja·nus \'jā-nəs\ god of gates and doors and of beginnings and endings in Roman mythology who is usually pictured as having two opposite faces

Ja·son \'jās-ᵊn\ hero in Greek mythology noted for his successful quest of the Golden Fleece

Jay \'jā\ John 1745–1829 American jurist and political leader; 1st chief justice of the U.S. Supreme Court (1789–95)

Jef·fer·son \'jef-ər-sən\ Thomas 1743–1826 3d president of the U.S. (1801–09) — **Jef·fer·so·nian** \ˌjef-ər-'sō-nē-ən, -nyən\ *adj*

Jer·e·mi·ah \ˌjer-ə-'mī-ə\ Hebrew prophet of the 6th and 7th centuries B.C.

Je·sus \'jē-zəs, -zəz\ *or* **Jesus Christ** \'krīst\ *or* **Christ** Jesus *about* 6 B.C.–*about* 30 A.D. source of the Christian religion and Savior in the Christian faith

Jez·e·bel \'jez-ə-ˌbel\ queen of Israel and wife of Ahab who was noted for her wickedness

Joan of Arc \ˌjō-nə-'värk\ Saint *about* 1412–1431 *the Maid of Orleans* French national heroine

Job \'jōb\ man in the Bible who has many sufferings but keeps his faith

Jo·cas·ta \jō-'kas-tə\ queen of Thebes in Greek mythology who unknowingly marries her son Oedipus

John \'jän\ *the Baptist* prophet and baptizer of Jesus in the Bible

John one of the 12 apostles believed to be the author of the fourth Gospel, three Epistles, and the Book of Revelation

John name of 21 popes: especially **XXIII** 1881–1963 (pope 1958–63)

John 1167–1216 *John Lack·land* \'lak-ˌland\ king of England (1199–1216)

John·son \'jän(t)-sən\ Andrew 1808–1875 17th president of the U.S. (1865–69)

Johnson Lyndon Baines 1908–1973 36th president of the U.S. (1963–69)

Johnson Samuel 1709–1784 *Dr. Johnson* English lexicographer and author

Jol·liet *or* **Jo·liet** \zhòl-'yā, ˌjō-lē-'et\ Louis 1645–1700 French explorer in America

Jo·nah \'jō-nə\ Hebrew prophet who in the Bible spends three days in the belly of a great fish

Jones \'jōnz\ John Paul 1747–1792 American (Scottish-born) naval officer

Jop·lin \'jäp-lən\ Scott 1868–1917 American pianist and composer

Jo·seph \'jō-zəf *also* -səf\ a son of Jacob in the Bible who rose to high office in Egypt after being sold into slavery by his brothers

Joseph *about* 1840–1904 Nez Percé Indian chief

Joseph *Saint* husband of Mary, the mother of Jesus, in the Bible

Josh·ua \'jäsh-(ə-)wə\ Hebrew leader in the Bible who succeeds Moses during the settlement of the Israelites in Canaan

Ju·dah \'jüd-ə\ son of Jacob and ancestor of one of the 12 tribes of Israel in the Bible

Ju·das \'jüd-əs\ *or* **Judas Is·car·i·ot** \-is-'kar-ē-ət\ one of the 12 apostles and the betrayer of Jesus in the Bible

Ju·no \'jü-nō\ the queen of heaven in Roman mythology, wife of Jupiter, and goddess of light, birth, women, and marriage — compare HERA

Ju·pi·ter \'jü-pət-ər\ the chief god in Roman mythology, husband of Juno, and the god of light, of the sky and weather, and of the state

Kalb \'kälp, 'kalb\ Johann 1721–1780 Baron *de Kalb* \di-'kalb\ German general in American Revolutionary army

Keats \'kēts\ John 1795–1821 English poet

Kel·ler \'kel-ər\ Helen Adams 1880–1968 American deaf and blind lecturer

Kel·vin \'kel-vən\ 1st Baron 1824–1907 *William Thomson* British mathematician and physicist

Ken·ne·dy \'ken-əd-ē\ John Fitzgerald 1917–1963 35th president of the U.S. (1961–63)

Kennedy Robert Francis 1925–1968 American politician; attorney general of the U.S. (1961–64); brother of John F. Kennedy

Ke·o·kuk \'kē-ə-,kək\ 1788?–?1848 American Indian chief

Key \'kē\ Francis Scott 1779–1843 American lawyer; author of "The Star-Spangled Banner"

Khayyám Omar — see OMAR KHAYYÁM

Khru·shchev \krüsh-'(ch)óf, -'(ch)óv, -'(ch)ef\ Nikita \nə-'kēt-ə\ Sergeyevich 1894–1971 premier of U.S.S.R. (1958–64)

Khu·fu \'kü-fü\ *or Greek* **Che·ops** \'kē-,äps\ 26th century B.C. king of Egypt and pyramid builder

Kidd \'kid\ William *about* 1645–1701 *Captain Kidd* Scottish pirate

King \'kiŋ\ Martin Luther, Jr. 1929–1968 American minister and civil rights leader; Nobel Prize winner (1964)

Kip·ling \'kip-liŋ\ Rud·yard \'rəd-yərd, 'rəj-ərd\ 1865–1936 English author

Kis·sin·ger \'kis-ən-jər\ Henry Alfred 1923– American (German-born) scholar and government official; U.S. secretary of state (1973–77); Nobel Prize winner (1973)

Knox \'näks\ John *about* 1514–1572 Scottish religious reformer

Koch \'kók, 'kök\ Robert 1843–1910 German bacteriologist; Nobel Prize winner (1905)

Koś·ciusz·ko \,käs-ē-'əs-,kō, kósh-'chùsh-kō\ Tadeusz 1746–1817 Polish patriot and general in American Revolutionary army

Krish·na \'krish-nə\ god worshipped in later Hinduism

Kriss Kringle — see SANTA CLAUS

Ku·blai Khan \,kü-blə-'kän, -,blī-\ 1215–1294 founder of Mongol dynasty in China

La·fa·yette \,läf-ē-'et, ,laf-\ Marquis de 1757–1834 French general in American Revolutionary army

La·ius \'lā-(y)əs, 'lī-əs\ king of Thebes who in Greek mythology is killed by his son Oedipus

Lan·ce·lot \'lan(t)-sə-,lät\ legendary knight of the Round Table and lover of Queen Guinevere

La Salle \lə-'sal\ Sieur de 1643–1687 French explorer in America

La·voi·sier \ləv-'wäz-ē-,ā\ Antoine-Laurent 1743–1794 French chemist

Law·rence \'lór-ən(t)s, 'lär-\ Thomas Edward 1888–1935 *Lawrence of Arabia* later surnamed *Shaw* British archaeologist, soldier, and author

Laz·a·rus \'laz-(ə-)rəs\ brother of Mary and Martha who in the Bible is raised by Jesus from the dead

Lazarus beggar in the biblical parable of the rich man and the beggar

Le·da \'lēd-ə\ a queen of Sparta in Greek mythology who is courted by Zeus in the form of a swan

Lee \'lē\ Ann 1736–1784 English mystic; founder of Shaker society in the U.S.

Lee Henry 1756–1818 *Light-Horse Harry* American general

Lee Robert Edward 1807–1870 American Confederate general

Leeu·wen·hoek \'lā-vən-,hùk\ Antonie van 1632–1723 Dutch naturalist

Leif Er·iks·son \,lā-'ver-ik-sən, ,lē-'fer-\ *or* **Er·ics·son** *flourished* 1000 Norwegian explorer; son of Erik the Red

Le·nin \'len-ən\ 1870–1924 originally *Vladimir Ilyich Ul·ya·nov* \ül-'yän-əf, -,óf,-,óv\ Russian Communist leader

Leo \'lē-ō\ name of 13 popes: especially **I** Saint *died* 461 (pope 440–61); **III** Saint *died* 816 (pope 795–816); **XIII** 1810–1903 (pope 1878–1903)

Le·o·nar·do da Vin·ci \,lē-ə-'närd-,ōd-ə-'vin-chē, ,lā-, -'vēn-\ 1452–1519 Italian painter, sculptor, architect, and engineer

Lew·is \'lü-əs\ John Llewellyn 1880–1969 American labor leader

Lewis Meriwether 1774–1809 American explorer (with William Clark)

Lewis (Harry) Sinclair 1885–1951 American author; Nobel Prize winner (1930)

Lin·coln \'liŋ-kən\ Abraham 1809–1865 16th president of the U.S. (1861–65)

Lind·bergh \'lin(d)-,bərg\ Charles Augustus 1902–1974 American aviator

Lin·nae·us \lə-'nē-əs, -'nā-\ Carolus 1707–1778 Swedish *Carl von Lin·né* \lə-'nā\ Swedish botanist

Lis·ter \'lis-tər\ Joseph 1827–1912 English surgeon

Liszt \'list\ Franz 1811–1886 Hungarian pianist and composer

Liv·ing·stone \'liv-iŋ-stən\ David 1813–1873 Scottish explorer in Africa

Long·fel·low \'lóŋ-,fel-ō\ Henry Wads·worth \'wädz-(,)wərth\ 1807–1882 American poet

Lou·is \'lü-ē, 'lü-əs\ name of 18 kings of France: especially **IX** Saint 1214–1270 (reigned 1226–70); **XI** 1423–1483 (reigned 1461–83); **XII** 1462–1515 (reigned 1498–1515); **XIII** 1601–1643 (reigned 1610–43); **XIV** 1638–1715 (reigned 1643–1715); **XV** 1710–1774 (reigned 1715–74); **XVI** 1754–1793 (reigned 1774–92; guillotined); **XVII** 1785–1795 (reigned in name 1793–95); **XVIII** 1755–1824 (reigned 1814–15; 1815–24)

Low \'lō\ Juliette Gordon 1860–1927 American founder of the Girl Scouts

Low·ell \'lō-əl\ Amy 1874–1925 American poet

Lowell James Russell 1819–1891 American author

Luke \'lük\ physician and companion of the apostle Paul believed to be the author of the third Gospel and the Book of Acts

Lu·ther \'lü-thər\ Martin 1483–1546 German Reformation leader

Ly·on \'lī-ən\ Mary 1797–1849 American educator

Mac·Ar·thur \mə-'kär-thər\ Douglas 1880–1964 American general

Mc·Car·thy \mə-'kär-thē\ Joseph Raymond 1908–1957 American politician

Mc·Clel·lan \mə-'klel-ən\ George Brinton 1826–1885 American general

Mc·Cor·mick \mə-'kór-mik\ Cyrus Hall 1809–1884 American inventor

Mc·Kin·ley \mə-'kin-lē\ William 1843–1901 25th president of the U.S. (1897–1901)

Ma·cy \'mā-sē\ Anne Sullivan 1866–1936 American educator; teacher of Helen Keller

Mad·i·son \'mad-ə-sən\ James 1751–1836 4th president of the U.S. (1809–17)

Ma·gel·lan \mə-'jel-ən\ Ferdinand *about* 1480–1521 Portuguese navigator

Mal·colm X \,mal-kə-'meks\ 1925–1965 American civil rights leader

Ma·net \ma-'nā, mä-\ Édouard 1832–1883 French painter

Mann \'man\ Horace 1796–1859 American educator

Mao Tse-tung \,maú(d)-zə-'dùŋ, ,maút-sə-\ 1893–1976 Chinese Communist; leader of People's Republic of China (1949–76)

Mar·co·ni \mär-'kō-nē\ Guglielmo 1874–1937 Italian physicist and inventor; Nobel Prize winner (1909)

Ma·rie An·toi·nette \mə-'rē-,an-t(w)ə-'net\ 1755–1793 wife of Louis XVI

Mar·i·on \'mer-ē-ən, 'mar-ē-\ Francis 1732?–1795 *the Swamp Fox* American commander in Revolution

Mark \\'märk\\ evangelist believed to be the author of the second Gospel

Mar·quette \\mär-'ket\\ Jacques 1637–1675 French-born Jesuit missionary and explorer in America

Mars \\'märz\\ the god of war in Roman mythology

Mar·shall \\'mär-shəl\\ George Catlett 1880–1959 American general and diplomat

Marshall John 1755–1835 American jurist; chief justice of the U.S. Supreme Court (1801–35)

Mar·tha \\'mär-thə\\ sister of Lazarus and Mary and friend of Jesus in the Bible

Mar·tin \\'märt-ᵊn\\ Saint *about* 316–397 *Martin of Tours* \\-'tü(ə)r\\ patron saint of France

Marx \\'märks\\ Karl 1818–1883 German political philosopher and socialist

Mary \\'me(ə)r-ē, 'ma(ə)r-ē, 'mä-rē\\ mother of Jesus

Mary sister of Lazarus and Martha in the Bible

Mary I 1516–1558 *Mary Tudor*; *Bloody Mary* queen of England (1553–58)

Mary II 1662–1694 joint British sovereign with William III (1689–94)

Mary Mag·da·lene \\-'mag-də-ᵢlən, -ᵢlēn\\ woman in the Bible who was healed of evil spirits by Jesus and who later saw the risen Christ

Mary Stuart 1542–1587 *Mary, Queen of Scots* queen of Scotland (1542–87)

Mas·sa·soit \\ᵢmas-ə-'soit\\ *died* 1661 Indian chief in eastern Massachusetts

Math·er \\'math-ər, 'math-\\ Cotton 1663–1728 American religious leader and author

Mather Increase 1639–1723 American minister and author; father of Cotton Mather

Mat·thew \\'math-yü\\ apostle believed to be the author of the first Gospel

Mau·pas·sant \\ᵢmō-pə-'sänt \\ (Henri-René-Albert-) Guy de 1850–1893 French short-story writer

Mead \\'mēd\\ Margaret 1901–1978 American anthropologist

Meade \\'mēd\\ George Gordon 1815–1872 American general

Mea·ny \\'mē-nē\\ George 1894–1980 American labor leader

Me·dea \\mə-'dē-ə\\ woman with magic powers in Greek mythology who helps Jason to win the Golden Fleece and who kills her children when he leaves her

Me·di·ci, de' \\'med-ə-chē\\ Catherine 1519–1589 French *Catherine de Médicis* \\ᵢmäd-ə-'sē(s)\\ queen of Henry II of France

Me·ir \\me-'i(ə)r\\ Golda 1898–1978 prime minister of Israel (1969–74)

Mel·ville \\'mel-ᵢvil\\ Herman 1819–1891 American author

Men·del \\'men-dᵊl\\ Gregor Johann 1822–1884 Austrian botanist

Men·e·la·us \\ᵢmen-ᵊl-'ā-əs\\ king of Sparta, brother of Agamemnon, and husband of Helen of Troy in Greek mythology

Meph·is·toph·e·les \\ᵢmef-ə-'stäf-ə-ᵢlēz\\ chief devil in the Faust legend

Mer·ca·tor \\(ᵢ)mər-'kāt-ər\\ Gerardus 1512–1594 Flemish mapmaker

Mer·cu·ry \\'mər-kyə-rē, -k(ə-)rē\\ god of commerce, eloquence, travel, and theft who serves as herald and messenger of the other gods in Roman mythology

Mer·lin \\'mər-lən\\ prophet and magician in the legend of King Arthur

Mi·chael \\'mī-kəl\\ one of the four archangels named in Hebrew tradition — compare GABRIEL, RAPHAEL, URIEL

Mi·chel·an·ge·lo \\ᵢmī-kə-'lan-jə-ᵢlō, ᵢmik-ə-'lan-, ᵢmē-kə-'län-\\ 1475–1564 Italian sculptor, painter, architect, and poet

Mi·das \\'mīd-əs\\ legendary king who was given the power to turn everything he touched into gold

Mil·lay \\mil-'ā\\ Edna St. Vincent 1892–1950 American poet

Mil·ler \\'mil-ər\\ Arthur 1915– American author

Mil·ton \\'milt-ᵊn\\ John 1608–1674 English poet

Mi·ner·va \\mə-'nər-və\\ goddess of wisdom in Roman mythology — compare ATHENA

Mi·no·taur \\'min-ə-ᵢtȯ(ə)r, 'mī-nə-\\ monster in Greek mythology shaped half like a man and half like a bull

Min·u·it \\'min-yə-wət\\ Peter 1580–1638 Dutch colonial administrator in America

Mitch·ell \\'mich-əl\\ Maria 1818–1889 American astronomer

Mo·lière \\mōl-'ye(ə)r, 'mōl-ᵢye(ə)r\\ 1622–1673 originally *Jean-Baptiste Poquelin* French actor and dramatist

Mo·net \\mō-'nā\\ Claude 1840–1926 French painter

Mon·roe \\mən-'rō\\ James 1758–1831 5th president of the U.S. (1817–25)

Mont·calm de Saint-Vé·ran \\mänt-'käm-də- ᵢsan-vā-'rän, -'kälm-\\ Marquis de 1712–1759 French field marshal in Canada

Mon·tes·so·ri \\ᵢmänt-ə-'sȯr-ē, -'sȯr\\ Maria 1870–1952 Italian physician and educator

Mon·te·zu·ma II \\ᵢmänt-ə-'zü-mə\\ 1466–1520 last Aztec emperor of Mexico (1502–20)

Moore \\'mō(ə)r, 'mȯ(ə)r, 'mù(ə)r\\ Marianne Craig 1887–1972 American poet

More \\'mō(ə)r, 'mȯ(ə)r\\ Sir Thomas 1478–1535 *Saint* English public official and author

Mor·gan \\'mȯr-gən\\ John Pierpont 1837–1913 American financier

Morse \\'mȯ(ə)rs\\ Samuel Finley Breese 1791–1872 American artist and inventor

Mo·ses \\'mō-zəz *also* -zəs\\ Hebrew prophet and lawgiver who in the Bible freed the Israelites from slavery in Egypt

Mott \\'mät\\ Lucretia 1793–1880 American reformer

Mo·zart \\'mōt-ᵢsärt\\ Wolfgang Amadeus 1756–1791 Austrian composer

Mu·h·am·mad \\mō-'ham-əd, -'häm- *also* mü-\\ *about* 570–632 Arab prophet and founder of Islam

Mus·so·li·ni \\ᵢmü-sə-'lē-nē, ᵢmüs-ə-\\ Be·ni·to \\bə-'nēt-ō\\ 1883–1945 *Il Du·ce* \\ēl-'dü-chā\\ Italian fascist premier (1922–43)

Na·po·leon I \\nə-'pōl-yən, -'pō-lē-ən\\ *or* **Napoleon Bo·na·parte** \\'bō-nə-ᵢpärt\\ 1769–1821 emperor of the French (1804–15) — **Na·po·le·on·ic** \\nə-ᵢpō-lē-'än-ik\\ *adj*

Nar·cis·sus \\när-'sis-əs\\ a beautiful youth in Greek mythology who pines away for love of his own reflection and is then turned into the narcissus flower

Nash \\'nash\\ Ogden 1902–1971 American poet

Na·tion \\'nā-shən\\ Car·ry \\'kar-ē\\ Amelia 1846–1911 American social reformer

Neb·u·cha·drez·zar II \\ᵢneb-(y)ə-kə-'drez-ər\\ *also* **Neb·u·chad·nez·zar** \\-kəd-'nez-\\ *about* 630–562 B.C. Chaldean king of Babylon (605–562)

Neh·ru \\'ne(ə)r-ü, 'nā-rü\\ Ja·wa·har·lal \\jə-'wä-hər-ᵢläl\\ 1889–1964 Indian nationalist; 1st prime minister (1947–64)

Nel·son \\'nel-sən\\ Horatio 1758–1805 Viscount *Nelson* British admiral

Nem·e·sis \\'nem-ə-səs\\ the goddess of reward and punishment in Greek mythology

Nep·tune \\'nep-ᵢt(y)ün\\ the god of the sea in Roman mythology

Ne·ro \\'nē-ᵢrō, 'ni(ə)r-ō\\ 37–68 A.D. Roman emperor (54–68)

New·ton \\'n(y)üt-ᵊn\\ Sir Isaac 1642–1727 English mathematician and physicist

Nich·o·las \\'nik-(ə-)ləs\\ Saint 4th century Christian bishop

Nicholas I 1796–1855 czar of Russia (1825–55)

Nicholas II 1868–1918 czar of Russia (1894–1917)

Night·in·gale \\'nīt-ᵊn-ᵢgäl, -iŋ-\\ Florence 1820–1910 English nurse and philanthropist

Ni·ke \\'nī-kē\\ the goddess of victory in Greek mythology

Ni·o·be \'nī-ə-bē\ a daughter of Tantalus in Greek mythology who while weeping for her slain children is turned into a stone from which her tears continue to flow

Nix·on \'nik-sən\ Richard Mil·hous \'mil-ˌhaús\ 1913–1994 37th president of the U.S. (1969–74)

No·ah \'nō-ə\ Old Testament builder of the ark in which he, his family, and living creatures of every kind survived the Flood

No·bel \nō-'bel\ Alfred Bernhard 1833–1896 Swedish manufacturer, inventor, and philanthropist

Oce·anus \ō-'sē-ə-nəs\ a Titan who rules over a great river encircling the earth in Greek mythology

Odin \'ōd-ᵊn\ or **Wo·den** \'wōd-ᵊn\ god of war and patron of heroes in Norse mythology

Odys·seus \ō-'dis-ē-əs, -'dis-yəs, -'dish-əs, -'dish-ˌüs\ or **Ulys·ses** \yü-'lis-ēz\ king of Ithaca and hero in Greek mythology who after the Trojan war wanders for 10 years before reaching home

Oe·di·pus \'ed-ə-pəs, 'ēd-\ son of Laius and Jocasta who in Greek mythology kills his father and marries his mother not knowing their identity

Ogle·thorpe \'ō-gəl-ˌthórp\ James Edward 1696–1785 English general and philanthropist; founder of Georgia

O'·Keeffe \ō-'kēf\ Georgia 1887–1986 American painter

Omar Khay·yám \ˌō-ˌmär-ˌkī-'(y)äm, ˌō-mər-, -'(y)am\ 1048?–1122 Persian poet and astronomer

O'·Neill \ō-'nē(ə)l\ Eugene Gladstone 1888–1953 American dramatist; Nobel Prize winner (1936)

Or·pheus \'ór-ˌfyüs, -fē-əs\ poet and musician in Greek mythology who almost rescues his wife Eurydice from Hades by charming Pluto and Persephone with his lyre

Or·well \'ór-ˌwel, -wəl\ George 1903–1950 pseudonym of *Eric Blair* English author — **Or·well·ian** \ór-'wel-ē-ən\ adj

Osce·o·la \ˌäs-ē-'ō-lə, ˌō-sē-\ about 1800–1838 Seminole Indian chief

Otis \'ōt-əs\ James 1725–1783 American Revolutionary patriot

Ov·id \'äv-əd\ 43 B.C.–17 A.D.? Roman poet

Ow·en \'ō-ən\ Robert 1771–1858 Welsh social reformer

Ow·ens \'ō-ənz\ Jesse 1913–1980 originally *James Cleveland* American athlete

Paine \'pān\ Thomas 1737–1809 American (English-born) political philosopher and author

Pan \'pan\ god of forests, pastures, flocks, and shepherds in Greek mythology who is represented as having the legs, ears, and horns of a goat

Pan·do·ra \pan-'dór-ə, -'dór-\ woman in Greek mythology who out of curiosity opened a box and let loose all of the evils that trouble humans

Par·is \'par-əs\ son of Priam whose abduction of Helen of Troy in Greek mythology led to the Trojan War

Park·man \'pärk-mən\ Francis 1823–1893 American historian

Pas·cal \pas-'kal\ Blaise 1623–1662 French mathematician and philosopher

Pas·ter·nak \'pas-tər-ˌnak\ Boris Leonidovich 1890–1960 Russian author; Nobel Prize winner (1958)

Pas·teur \pas-'tər\ Louis 1822–1895 French chemist and microbiologist

Pat·rick \'pa-trik\ Saint 5th century apostle and patron saint of Ireland

Pat·ton \'pat-ᵊn\ George Smith 1885–1945 American general

Paul \'pól\ Saint *died between 62 and 68* A.D. author of several New Testament epistles — **Pau·line** \'pó-ˌlīn\ adj

Paul name of six popes: especially **III** 1468–1549 (pope 1534–49); **V** 1552–1621 (pope 1605–21); **VI** 1897–1978 (pope 1963–78)

Paul Bun·yan \'pól-'bən-yən\ giant lumberjack in American folklore

Pau·ling \'pó-liŋ\ Linus Carl 1901– American chemist; Nobel Prize winner (1954, 1962)

Pav·lov \'päv-ˌlóf, 'pav-, -ˌlóv\ Ivan Petrovich 1849–1936 Russian physiologist; Nobel Prize winner (1904)

Pa·vlo·va \'pav-lə-və, pav-'lō-və\ Anna 1882–1931 Russian ballerina

Pea·ry \'pi(ə)r-ē\ Robert Edwin 1856–1920 American arctic explorer

Pe·cos Bill \ˌpā-kəs-'bil\ a cowboy in American folklore known for his extraordinary feats

Peg·a·sus \'peg-ə-səs\ winged horse in Greek mythology

Penn \'pen\ William 1644–1718 English Quaker; founder of Pennsylvania

Per·i·cles \'per-ə-ˌklēz\ about 495–429 B.C. Athenian political leader

Per·ry \'per-ē\ Matthew Calbraith 1794–1858 American commodore

Perry Oliver Hazard 1785–1819 American naval officer

Per·seph·o·ne \pər-'sef-ə-nē\ daughter of Zeus and Demeter who in Greek mythology is abducted by Pluto to rule with him over the underworld

Per·shing \'pər-shiŋ, -zhiŋ\ John Joseph 1860–1948 American general

Pe·ter \'pēt-ər\ Saint *died about* 64 A.D. *Si·mon Peter* \'sī-mən-\ one of the 12 apostles in the Bible

Peter I 1672–1725 *the Great* czar of Russia (1682–1725)

Phil·ip \'fil-əp\ one of the 12 apostles in the Bible

Philip 1639?–1676 American Indian chief

Philip name of six kings of France: espcially **II** or **Philip Augustus** 1165–1223 (reigned 1179–1223); **IV** 1268–1314 (reigned 1285–1314) *the Fair*; **VI** 1293–1350 (reigned 1328–50)

Philip name of five kings of Spain: especially **II** 1527–1598 (reigned 1556–98); **V** 1683–1746 (reigned 1700–46)

Philip II 382–336 B.C. king of Macedon (359–336); father of Alexander the Great

Pi·cas·so \pi-'käs-ō, -'kas-\ Pablo 1881–1973 Spanish painter and sculptor in France

Pick·ett \'pik-ət\ George Edward 1825–1875 American Confederate general

Pierce \'pi(ə)rs\ Franklin 1804–1869 14th president of the U.S. (1853–57)

Pi·late \'pī-lət\ Pon·tius \'pän-chəs, 'pən-chəs\ *died after* 36 A.D. Roman governor of Judea

Pitt \'pit\ William 1759–1806 English prime minister (1783–1801; 1804–6)

Pi·us \'pī-əs\ name of 12 popes: especially **VII** 1742–1823 (pope 1800–23); **IX** 1792–1878 (pope 1846–78); **X** 1835–1914 (pope 1903–14); **XI** 1857–1939 (pope 1922–39); **XII** 1876–1958 (pope 1939–58)

Pi·zar·ro \pə-'zär-ō\ Francisco *about* 1475–1541 Spanish conqueror of Peru

Pla·to \'plāt-ō\ *about* 428–348 (*or* 347) B.C. Greek philosopher

Plu·to \'plüt-ō\ god of the dead and the underworld in Greek mythology

Po·ca·hon·tas \ˌpō-kə-'hänt-əs\ *about* 1595–1617 American Indian princess

Poe \'pō\ Edgar Allan 1809–1849 American author

Polk \'pōk\ James Knox 1795–1849 11th president of the U.S. (1845–49)

Po·lo \'pō-lō\ Mar·co \'mär-kō\ 1254–1324 Venetian traveler

Poly·phe·mus \ˌpäl-ə-'fē-məs\ a Cyclops in Greek mythology who is blinded by Odysseus

Ponce de Le·ón \ˌpän(t)-sə-də-dā-lē-'ōn, ˌpän(t)s-də-'lē-ən\ Juan 1460–1521 Spanish explorer and discoverer of Florida (1513)

Pon·ti·ac \'pänt-ē-ˌak\ *about* 1720–1769 American Indian chief

Por·ter \\'pōrt-ər, 'pȯrt-\\ Cole Albert 1891–1964 American composer and songwriter

Porter David Dixon 1813–1891 American admiral

Porter Katherine Anne 1890–1980 American author

Porter William Sydney 1862–1910 pseudonym *O. Henry* \\(')ō-'hen-rē\\ American author

Po·sei·don \\pə-'sīd-ᵊn\\ god of the sea in Greek mythology — compare NEPTUNE

Pot·ter \\'pät-ər\\ Beatrix 1866–1943 British author and illustrator

Pow·ha·tan \\ˌpaú-ə-'tan, paú-'hat-ᵊn\\ 1550?–1618 American Indian chief

Pri·am \\'prī-əm, -ˌam\\ king of Troy during the Trojan War in Greek mythology

Pro·me·theus \\prə-'mē-th(y)üs, -thē-əs\\ a Titan in Greek mythology who is punished by Zeus for stealing fire from heaven and giving it to human beings

Pro·teus \\'prō-ˌt(y)üs, 'prōt-ē-əs\\ sea god in Greek mythology who is capable of assuming different forms

Puc·ci·ni \\pü-'chē-nē\\ Giacomo 1858–1924 Italian composer

Pu·las·ki \\pə-'las-kē, pyü-\\ Kazimierz 1747–1779 Polish soldier in American Revolutionary army

Pu·lit·zer \\'púl-ət-sər, 'pyü-lət-sər\\ Joseph 1847–1911 American (Hungarian-born) journalist

Pyg·ma·lion \\pig-'māl-yən, -'mā-lē-ən\\ a sculptor in Greek mythology who falls in love with a statue which is then brought to life

Py·thag·o·ras \\pə-'thag-ə-rəs, pī-\\ *about* 580–*about* 500 B.C. Greek philosopher and mathematician

Ra \\'rä, 'rȯ\\ god of the sun and chief deity of ancient Egypt

Ra·leigh *or* **Ra·legh** \\'rȯl-ē, 'räl- *also* 'ral-\\ Sir Walter 1554–1618 English navigator and historian

Ram·ses \\'ram-ˌsēz\\ *or* **Ram·es·es** \\'ram-ə-ˌsēz\\ name of 12 kings of Egypt: especially **II** (reigned 1304–1237 B.C.); **III** (reigned 1198–66 B.C.)

Ran·dolph \\'ran-ˌdälf\\ Asa Philip 1889–1979 American labor leader

Ra·pha·el \\'raf-ē-əl, 'rä-fē-\\ one of the four archangels named in Hebrew tradition — compare GABRIEL, MICHAEL, URIEL

Ra·pha·el \\'raf-ē-əl, 'rä-fē-, 'räf-ē-\\ 1483–1520 Italian painter

Ras·pu·tin \\ra-'sp(y)üt-ᵊn, -'spút-\\ Grigory Yefimovich 1872–1916 Russian mystic

Rea·gan \\'rā-gən *also* 'rē-\\ Ronald Wilson 1911– 40th president of the U.S. (1981–89)

Re·bek·ah *or* **Re·bec·ca** \\ri-'bek-ə\\ wife of Isaac in the Bible

Red Cloud \\'red-ˌklaúd\\ 1822–1909 American Indian chief

Reed \\'rēd\\ Walter 1851–1902 American army surgeon

Rem·brandt \\'rem-ˌbrant *also* -ˌbränt\\ 1606–1669 Dutch painter

Re·mus \\'rē-məs\\ son of Mars who in Roman mythology is killed by his twin brother Romulus

Re·noir \\'ren-ˌwär, rən-'wär\\ Pierre-Auguste 1841–1919 French painter

Re·vere \\ri-'vi(ə)r\\ Paul 1735–1818 American patriot and silversmith

Rich·ard \\'rich-ərd\\ name of three kings of England: **I** 1157–1199 (reigned 1189–99) *the Lion-Hearted*; **II** 1367–1400 (reigned 1377–99); **III** 1452–1485 (reigned 1483–85)

Rob·in Good·fel·low \\ˌräb-ən-'gúd-ˌfel-ō\\ mischievous elf in English folklore

Rob·in·son \\'räb-ən-sən\\ Edwin Arlington 1869–1935 American poet

Rob·in·son Cru·soe \\ˌräb-ə(n)-sən-'krü-sō\\ a shipwrecked sailor in Daniel Defoe's *Robinson Crusoe* who lives for many years on a desert island

Ro·cham·beau \\ˌrō-sham-'bō\\ Comte de 1725–1807 French general in American Revolution

Rocke·fel·ler \\'räk-i-ˌfel-ər, 'räk-ˌfel-\\ John Davison

father 1839–1937 and son 1874–1960 American oil magnates and philanthropists

Ro·ma·nov *or* **Ro·ma·noff** \\rō-'män-əf, 'rō-mə-ˌnäf\\ Michael 1596–1645 1st czar (1613–45) of Russian Romanov dynasty (1613–1917)

Rom·u·lus \\'räm-yə-ləs\\ son of Mars in Roman mythology who was the twin brother of Remus and the founder of Rome

Rönt·gen *or* **Roent·gen** \\'rent-gən, 'rənt-, -jən\\ Wilhelm Conrad 1845–1923 German physicist; Nobel Prize winner (1901)

Roo·se·velt \\'rō-zə-vəlt (*Roosevelts' usual pronunciation*), -ˌvelt *also* 'rü-\\ (Anna) Eleanor 1884–1962 American lecturer and writer; wife of Franklin Delano Roosevelt

Roosevelt Franklin Del·a·no \\'del-ə-ˌnō\\ 1882–1945 32d president of the U.S. (1933–45)

Roosevelt Theodore 1858–1919 26th president of the U.S. (1901–09); Nobel Prize winner (1906)

Ross \\'rȯs\\ Betsy 1752–1836 reputed maker of first American flag

Ros·si·ni \\rȯ-'sē-nē, rə-\\ Gioacchino Antonio 1792–1868 Italian composer

Ru·bens \\'rü-bənz\\ Peter Paul 1577–1640 Flemish painter

Rus·sell \\'rəs-əl\\ Bertrand Arthur William 1872–1970 English mathematician and philosopher; Nobel Prize winner (1950)

Ruth \\'rüth\\ woman in the Bible who was one of the ancestors of King David

Ruth George Herman 1895–1948 *Babe* American baseball player

Ruth·er·ford \\'rəth-ə(r)-fərd, 'rəth-\\ Ernest 1871–1937 1st Baron *Rutherford of Nelson* British physicist

Sa·bin \\'sā-bin\\ Albert Bruce 1906–1993 American physician

Sac·a·ga·wea \\ˌsak-ə-jə-'wē-ə, -ˌwä-ə\\ 1786?–1812 American Indian guide to Lewis and Clark

Sa·dat \\sə-'dat, -'dät\\ Anwar as- 1918–1981 president of Egypt (1970–81)

Saint Nicholas — see NICHOLAS, SANTA CLAUS

Sal·in·ger \\'sal-ən-jər\\ Jerome David 1919– American author

Salk \\'sȯk, 'sȯlk\\ Jonas Edward 1914– American physician

Sa·lo·me \\sə-'lō-mē\\ niece of Herod Antipas who in the Bible is given the head of John the Baptist as a reward for her dancing

Sa·mo·set \\'sam-ə-ˌset, sə-'mäs-ət\\ *died about* 1653 American Indian leader

Sam·son \\'sam(p)-sən\\ powerful Hebrew hero in the Bible who fought against the Philistines

Sam·u·el \\'sam-yə(-wə)l\\ Hebrew judge in the Bible who appointed Saul and then David king

Sand·burg \\'san(d)-ˌbərg\\ Carl 1878–1967 American author

San·ta Claus \\'sant-ē-ˌklȯz, 'sant-ə-\\ *or* **Saint Nich·o·las** \\ˌsānt-'nik-(ə-)ləs, sənt-\\ *or* **Kriss Krin·gle** \\'kris-'kriŋ-gəl\\ a fat jolly old man in modern folklore who delivers presents to good children at Christmastime

Sap·pho \\'saf-ō\\ *flourished about* 610–*about* 580 B.C. Greek poet

Sa·rah \\'ser-ə, 'sar-ə, 'sā-rə\\ wife of Abraham and mother of Isaac in the Bible

Sar·gent \\'sär-jənt\\ John Singer 1856–1925 American painter

Sat·urn \\'sat-ərn\\ a god of agriculture in Roman mythology

Saul \\'sȯl\\ first king of Israel in the Bible

Saul *or* **Saul of Tar·sus** \\-'tär-səs\\ the apostle Paul

Sche·her·a·zade \\shə-ˌher-ə-'zäd(-ə), -'zäd(-ē)\\ fictional oriental queen and narrator of the tales in the *Arabian Nights' Entertainments*

Schu·bert \\'shü-bərt, -ˌbərt\\ Franz Peter 1797–1828 Austrian composer

Schweit·zer \\'shwīt-sər, 'swīt-, 'shvīt-\\ Albert 1875–

1965 French Protestant minister, philosopher, physician, and music scholar; Nobel Prize winner (1952)

Scott \\'skät\\ Dred \\'dred\\ 1795?–1858 American slave

Scott Sir Walter 1771–1832 Scottish author

Scott Winfield 1786–1866 American general

Scyl·la \\'sil-ə\\ a nymph in Greek mythology who is changed into a monster and inhabits a cave opposite the whirlpool Charybdis off the coast of Sicily

Se·quoya \\si-'kwȯi-ə\\ *about* 1760–1843 Cherokee Indian leader

Ser·ra \\'ser-ə\\ Junípero 1713–1784 Spanish missionary in Mexico and California

Se·ton \\'sēt-ən\\ Saint Elizabeth Ann Bayley 1774–1821 *Mother Seton* American religious leader

Sew·ard \\'sü-ərd, 'sü(-ə)rd\\ William Henry 1801–1872 American politician; secretary of state (1861–69)

Shake·speare \\'shāk-ˌspi(ə)r\\ William 1564–1616 English dramatist and poet

Shaw \\'shȯ\\ George Bernard 1856–1950 British author

Shel·ley \\'shel-ē\\ Mary Woll·stone·craft \\'wûl-stən-ˌkraft\\ 1797–1851 English novelist; wife of Percy Bysshe Shelley

Shelley Percy Bysshe \\'bish\\ 1792–1822 English poet

Shep·ard \\'shep-ərd\\ Alan Bartlett 1923–   American astronaut; first American in space (1961)

Sher·i·dan \\'sher-əd-ən\\ Philip Henry 1831–1888 American general

Sher·lock Holmes \\'shər-ˌläk-'hōmz, -'hōlmz\\ detective in stories by Sir Arthur Conan Doyle

Sher·man \\'shər-mən\\ John 1823–1900 American politician

Sherman William Tecumseh 1820–1891 American general

Sieg·fried \\'sig-ˌfrēd, 'sēg-\\ hero in Germanic legend who kills a dragon guarding a gold hoard

Si·mon \\'sī-mən\\ *or* **Simon the Zealot** one of the 12 apostles

Sind·bad the Sailor \\'sin-ˌbad-\\ citizen of Baghdad whose adventures are narrated in the *Arabian Nights' Entertainments*

Sis·y·phus \\'sis-ə-fəs\\ king of Corinth who in Greek mythology is condemned to roll a heavy stone up a hill in Hades only to have it roll down again as it nears the top

Sit·ting Bull \\ˌsit-iŋ-'bùl\\ *about* 1831–90 Sioux Indian leader

Si·va \\'shiv-ə, 'siv-; 'shē-və, 'sē-\\ god of destruction in the Hindu sacred triad — compare BRAHMA, VISHNU

Smith \\'smith\\ Bessie 1894 (or 1898)–1937 American blues singer

Smith John *about* 1580–1631 English colonist in America

Smith Joseph 1805–1844 American founder of the Mormon Church

Soc·ra·tes \\'säk-rə-ˌtēz\\ *about* 470–399 B.C. Greek philosopher

Sol·o·mon \\'säl-ə-mən\\ son of David and 10th-century B.C. king of Israel noted for his wisdom

Soph·o·cles \\'säf-ə-ˌklēz\\ *about* 496–406 B.C. Greek dramatist

Sou·sa \\'sü-zə, 'sü-sə\\ John Philip 1854–1932 American bandmaster and composer

Spar·ta·cus \\'spärt-ə-kəs\\ *died* 71 B.C. Roman slave and gladiator; leader of a slave rebellion

Sphinx \\'sfiŋ(k)s\\ monster in Greek mythology having a lion's body, wings, and the head and bust of a woman

Squan·to \\'skwän-tō\\ *died* 1622 Indian friend of the Pilgrims

Sta·lin \\'stäl-ən, 'stal-, -ˌēn\\ Joseph 1879–1953 Soviet leader

Stan·dish \\'stan-dish\\ Myles *or* Miles 1584?–1656 American colonist

Stan·ley \\'stan-lē\\ Sir Henry Morton 1841–1904 British explorer in Africa

Stan·ton \\'stant-ən\\ Elizabeth Cady 1815–1902 American suffragist

Stein \\'stīn\\ Gertrude 1874–1946 American author

Stein·beck \\'stīn-ˌbek\\ John Ernst 1902–1968 American author; Nobel Prize winner (1962)

Steu·ben, von \\'st(y)ü-bən, 'shtȯi-\\ Baron Friedrich Wilhelm Ludolf Gerhard Augustin 1730–1794 Prussian-born general in American Revolution

Ste·ven·son \\'stē-vən-sən\\ Adlai Ewing 1900–1965 American politician

Stevenson Robert Louis Balfour 1850–1894 Scottish author

Stowe \\'stō\\ Harriet Elizabeth Beecher 1811–1896 American author

Stra·di·va·ri \\ˌstrad-ə-'vär-ē, -'var-, -'ver-\\ Antonio 1644–1737 Latin *Antonius Strad·i·var·i·us* \\ˌstrad-ə-'var-ē-əs, -'ver-\\ Italian violin maker

Strauss \\'straùs, 'shtraùs\\ Johann father 1804–1849 and his sons Johann 1825–1899 and Josef 1827–1870 Austrian composers

Stu·art \\'st(y)ü-ərt, 'st(y)ù(-ə)rt\\ — see CHARLES I, MARY STUART

Stuart Charles—CHARLES EDWARD STUART

Stuart Gilbert Charles 1755–1828 American painter

Stuart James Ewell Brown 1833–1864 *Jeb* American Confederate general

Stuy·ve·sant \\'stī-və-sənt\\ Peter *about* 1610–1672 Dutch colonial administrator in America

Sul·li·van \\'səl-ə-vən\\ Sir Arthur Seymour 1842–1900 English composer; collaborator with Sir William Gilbert

Sullivan Louis Henri 1856–1924 American architect

Sum·ner \\'səm-nər\\ Charles 1811–1874 American politician

Swift \\'swift\\ Jonathan 1667–1745 English author

Taft \\'taft\\ William Howard 1857–1930 27th president of the U.S. (1909–13); chief justice of the U.S. Supreme Court (1921–30)

Ta·ney \\'tȯ-nē\\ Roger Brooke 1777–1864 American jurist; chief justice of the U.S. Supreme Court (1836–64)

Tan·ta·lus \\'tant-əl-əs\\ king in Greek mythology who is condemned to stand up to his chin in a pool of water in Hades and beneath fruit-laden boughs only to have the water or fruit go out of reach at each attempt to drink or eat

Tay·lor \\'tā-lər\\ Zachary 1784–1850 12th president of the U.S. (1849–50)

Tchai·kov·sky \\chī-'kȯf-skē, chə-, -'kȯv-\\ Pyotr Ilich 1840–1893 Russian composer

Te·cum·seh \\tə-'kəm(p)-sə, -sē\\ 1768–1813 Shawnee Indian chief

Ten·ny·son \\'ten-ə-sən\\ Alfred 1809–1892 known as *Alfred, Lord Tennyson* English poet

Te·re·sa \\tə-'rā-zə, -'rē-sə\\ **of Ávi·la** \\'äv-i-lə\\ Saint 1515–1582 Spanish nun and mystic

The·seus \\'thē-ˌsüs, -sē-əs\\ hero in Greek mythology who kills the Minotaur and conquers the Amazons

Thom·as \\'täm-əs\\ apostle in the Bible who demanded proof of Christ's resurrection

Thomas à Becket — see BECKET, À

Thor \\'thȯ(ə)r\\ god of thunder, weather, and crops in Norse mythology

Tho·reau \\thə-'rō, thȯ-; 'thȯr-ō\\ Henry David 1817–1862 American author

Thur·ber \\'thər-bər\\ James Grover 1894–1961 American author

Ti·be·ri·us \\tī-'bir-ē-əs\\ 42 B.C.–37 A.D. Roman emperor (14–37)

Tocque·ville \\'tōk-ˌvil, 'tȯk-, 'täk-, -ˌvēl, -vəl\\ Alexis≠Charles-Henri Clérel de 1805–1859 French politician and author

Tol·kien \\'tȯl-ˌkēn, 'tōl-, 'täl-\\ John Ronald Reuel 1892–1973 English author

Tol·stoy \\tȯl-'stȯi, tōl-'stȯi, täl-'stȯi, 'tȯl-ˌstȯi, 'tōlₜstói, **'**täl-ₜstói\ Count Lev Nikolayevich 1828–1910 Russian author

Tri·ton **'**trīt-ᵊn\ sea god in Greek mythology who is half man and half fish

Trots·ky **'**trät-skē, **'**tròt-\ Leon 1879–1940 originally *Lev Davidovich Bronstein* Russian Communist

Tru·man **'**trü-mən\ Harry S 1884–1972 33d president of the U.S. (1945–53)

Truth **'**trüth\ Sojourner 1797?–1883 American abolitionist

Tub·man **'**təb-mən\ Harriet *about* 1820–1913 American abolitionist

Tut·ankh·a·men \ₜtü-ₜtaŋ-**'**käm-ən, -ₜtäŋ-\ *or* **Tut·ankh·a·ten** \-**'**kät-ᵊn\ *about* 1370–1352 B.C. king of Egypt (1361–1352 B.C.)

Twain Mark — see CLEMENS

Tweed **'**twēd\ William Marcy 1823–1878 *Boss Tweed* American politician

Ty·ler **'**tī-lər\ John 1790–1862 10th president of the U.S. (1841–45)

Ulysses — see ODYSSEUS

Ura·nus **'**yùr-ə-nəs, yù-**'**rā-\ the sky personified as a god and father of the Titans in Greek mythology

Ur·ban **'**ər-bən\ name of eight popes: especially **II** *about* 1035–1099 (pope 1088–99)

Uri·el **'**yùr-ē-əl\ one of the four archangels named in Hebrew tradition — compare GABRIEL, MICHAEL, RAPHAEL

Val·en·tine **'**val-ən-ₜtīn\ Saint 3d century Christian martyr

Van Bu·ren \van-**'**byùr-ən, vən-\ Martin 1782–1862 8th president of the U.S.(1837–41)

Van Dyck *or* **Van·dyke** \van-**'**dīk, vən-\ Sir Anthony 1599–1641 Flemish painter

Ve·láz·quez \və-**'**las-kəs\ Diego Rodríguez de Silva 1599–1660 Spanish painter

Ve·nus **'**vē-nəs\ the goddess of love and beauty in Roman mythology — compare APHRODITE

Ver·di **'**ve(ə)rd-ē\ Giuseppe Fortunio Francesco 1813–1901 Italian composer

Ver·meer \vər-**'**me(ə)r, -**'**mi(ə)r\ Jan 1632–1675 also called *Jan van der Meer van Delft* Dutch painter

Verne Jules **'**jülz-**'**vərn\ 1828–1905 French author

Ves·puc·ci \ve-**'**spü-chē\ Ame·ri·go \ₜäm-ə-**'**rē-gō\ 1454–1512 Latin *Amer·i·cus Ves·pu·cius* \ə-**'**mer-ə-kəs-ₜves-**'**pyü-sh(ē-)əs\ Italian navigator for whom America was named

Vic·to·ria \vik-**'**tōr-ē-ə, -**'**tòr-\ 1819–1901 *Alexandrina Victoria* queen of Great Britain (1837–1901)

Vinci, da Leonardo — see LEONARDO DA VINCI

Vir·gil *also* **Ver·gil** **'**vər-jəl\ 70–19 B.C. Roman poet

Vish·nu **'**vish-nü\ god of preservation in the Hindu sacred triad — compare BRAHMA, SIVA

Vol·ta **'**vōl-tə, **'**väl-, **'**vòl-\ Count Alessandro Giuseppe Antonio Anastasio 1745–1827 Italian physicist

Vol·taire \vōl-**'**ta(ə)r, vòl-, väl-, -**'**te(ə)r\ 1694–1778 originally *François-Marie Arouet* French author

Vul·can **'**vəl-kən\ the god of fire and metalworking in Roman mythology — compare HEPHAESTUS

Wag·ner **'**väg-nər\ (Wilhelm) Ri·chard **'**rik-ₜärt, **'**rik-\ 1813–1883 German composer

War·ren **'**wòr-ən, **'**wär-\ Earl 1891–1974 American jurist; chief justice of the U.S. Supreme Court (1953–69)

Wash·ing·ton **'**wòsh-iŋ-tən, **'**wäsh-\ Book·er **'**bùk-ər\ Tal·ia·ferro **'**täl-ə-vər\ 1856–1915 American educator

Washington George 1732–1799 American general; 1st president of the U.S. (1789–97)

Watt **'**wät\ James 1736–1819 Scottish inventor

Wayne **'**wān\ Anthony 1745–1796 *Mad Anthony* American general

Web·ster **'**web-stər\ Daniel 1782–1852 American politician

Webster Noah 1758–1843 American lexicographer

Wel·ling·ton **'**wel-iŋ-tən\ 1st Duke of 1769–1852 *Arthur Wellesley*; *the Iron Duke* British general and politician

Wells **'**welz\ Herbert George 1866–1946 English author and historian

Wes·ley **'**wes-lē, **'**wez-\ John 1703–1791 English founder of Methodism

Wes·ting·house **'**wes-tiŋ-ₜhaùs\ George 1846–1914 American inventor

Whar·ton **'**hwòrt-ᵊn, **'**wòrt-\ Edith Newbold 1862–1937 American author

Whis·tler **'**hwis-lər, **'**wis-\ James Abbott McNeill 1834–1903 American artist

Whit·man **'**hwit-mən, **'**wit-\ Walt 1819–1892 American poet

Whit·ney **'**hwit-nē, **'**wit-\ Eli 1765–1825 American inventor

Whit·ti·er **'**hwit-ē-ər, **'**wit-\ John Greenleaf 1807–1892 American poet

Wilde **'**wī(ə)ld\ Oscar Fingal O'Flahertie Wills 1854–1900 Irish author

Wil·der **'**wīl-dər\ Thornton Niven 1897–1975 American author

Wil·liam **'**wil-yəm\ name of four kings of England: **I** *(the Conqueror) about* 1028–1087 (reigned 1066–87); **II** *(Rufus* **'**rü-fəs\) *about* 1056–1100 (reigned 1087–1100); **III** 1650–1702 (reigned 1689–1702); **IV** 1765–1837 (reigned 1830–37)

Wil·liam Tell \ₜwil-yəm-**'**tel\ legendary Swiss patriot commanded to shoot an apple from his son's head

Wil·liams **'**wil-yəmz\ Roger 1603?–1683 English colonist; founder of Rhode Island

Williams Tennessee 1911–1983 originally *Thomas Lanier Williams* American dramatist

Wil·son **'**wil-sən\ (Thomas) Wood·row **'**wùd-ₜrō\ 1856–1924 28th president of the U.S. (1913–21); Nobel Prize winner (1919)

Win·throp **'**win(t)-thrəp\ John 1588–1649 1st governor of Massachusetts Bay Colony

Woden — see ODIN

Woolf **'**wùlf\ Virginia 1882–1941 English author

Words·worth **'**wərdz-(ₜ)wərth\ William 1770–1850 English poet

Wren **'**ren\ Sir Christopher 1632–1723 English architect

Wright **'**rīt\ Frank Lloyd 1867–1959 American architect

Wright Or·ville **'**òr-vəl\ 1871–1948 and his brother Wilbur 1867–1912 American pioneers in aviation

Wright Richard 1908–1960 American author

Wy·eth **'**wī-əth\ Andrew Newell 1917–   American painter

Yeats **'**yāts\ William Butler 1865–1939 Irish author

Young **'**yəŋ\ Brig·ham **'**brig-əm\ 1801–1877 American Mormon leader

Zech·a·ri·ah \ₜzek-ə-**'**rī-ə\ Hebrew prophet of the 6th century B.C.

Zeng·er **'**zeŋ-(g)ər\ John Peter 1697–1746 American (German-born) journalist and printer

Zeph·y·rus **'**zef-ə-rəs\ god of the west wind in Greek mythology

Zeus **'**züs\ chief god, ruler of the sky and weather (as lightning and rain), and husband of Hera in Greek mythology

Presidents of the United States

no.	name (pronunciation)	life dates	birthplace	term dates
1	George Washington \\'wȯsh-ing-tən, 'wäsh-\\	1732–1799	Va.	1789–1797
2	John Adams \\'ad-əmz\\	1735–1826	Mass.	1797–1801
3	Thomas Jefferson \\'jef-ər-sən\\	1743–1826	Va.	1801–1809
4	James Madison \\'mad-ə-sən\\	1751–1836	Va.	1809–1817
5	James Monroe \\mən-'rō\\	1758–1831	Va.	1817–1825
6	John Quincy Adams \\'ad-əmz\\	1767–1848	Mass.	1825–1829
7	Andrew Jackson \\'jak-sən\\	1767–1845	S. C.	1829–1837
8	Martin Van Buren \\van-'byu̇r-ən\\	1782–1862	N. Y.	1837–1841
9	William Henry Harrison \\'har-ə-sən\\	1773–1841	Va.	1841
10	John Tyler \\'tī-lər\\	1790–1862	Va.	1841–1845
11	James Knox Polk \\'pōk\\	1795–1849	N. C.	1845–1849
12	Zachary Taylor \\'tā-lər\\	1784–1850	Va.	1849–1850
13	Millard Fillmore \\'fil-ˌmōr\\	1800–1874	N. Y.	1850–1853
14	Franklin Pierce \\'piərs\\	1804–1869	N. H.	1853–1857
15	James Buchanan \\byü-'kan-ən\\	1791–1868	Penn.	1857–1861
16	Abraham Lincoln \\'ling-kən\\	1809–1865	Ky.	1861–1865
17	Andrew Johnson \\'jän-sən\\	1808–1875	N. C.	1865–1869
18	Ulysses S. Grant \\'grant\\	1822–1885	Ohio	1869–1877
19	Rutherford B. Hayes \\'hāz\\	1822–1893	Ohio	1877–1881
20	James A. Garfield \\'gär-ˌfēld\\	1831–1881	Ohio	1881
21	Chester A. Arthur \\'är-thər\\	1830–1886	Vt.	1881–1885
22	Grover Cleveland \\'klēv-lənd\\	1837–1908	N. J.	1885–1889
23	Benjamin Harrison \\'har-ə-sən\\	1833–1901	Ohio	1889–1893
24	Grover Cleveland \\'klēv-lənd\\	1837–1908	N. J.	1893–1897
25	William McKinley \\mə-'kin-lē\\	1843–1901	Ohio	1897–1901
26	Theodore Roosevelt \\'rō-zə-ˌvelt\\	1858–1919	N. Y.	1901–1909
27	William Howard Taft \\'taft\\	1857–1930	Ohio	1909–1913
28	Woodrow Wilson \\'wil-sən\\	1856–1924	Va.	1913–1921
29	Warren G. Harding \\'härd-ing\\	1865–1923	Ohio	1921–1923
30	Calvin Coolidge \\'kü-lij\\	1872–1933	Vt.	1923–1929
31	Herbert C. Hoover \\'hü-vər\\	1874–1964	Iowa	1929–1933
32	Franklin D. Roosevelt \\'rō-zə-ˌvelt\\	1882–1945	N. Y.	1933–1945
33	Harry S Truman \\'trü-mən\\	1884–1972	Miss.	1945–1953
34	Dwight D. Eisenhower \\'īz-n-ˌhau̇-ər\\	1890–1969	Texas	1953–1961
35	John F. Kennedy \\'ken-ə-dē\\	1917–1963	Mass.	1961–1963
36	Lyndon B. Johnson \\'jän-sən\\	1908–1973	Texas	1963–1969
37	Richard M. Nixon \\'nik-sən\\	1913–1994	Calif.	1969–1974
38	Gerald R. Ford \\'fōrd\\	1913–	Neb.	1974–1977
39	Jimmy Carter \\'kärt-ər\\	1924–	Ga.	1977–1981
40	Ronald W. Reagan \\'rā-gən\\	1911–	Ill.	1981–1989
41	George H. W. Bush \\'bu̇sh\\	1924–	Mass.	1989–1993
42	William J. Clinton \\'klin-tən\\	1946–	Ark.	1993–

Prime Ministers of Canada

no.	name (pronunciation)	life dates	term dates
1	John A. Macdonald \mək-ˈdän-ᵊld\	1815–1891	1867–1873
2	Alexander Mackenzie \mə-ˈken-zē\	1822–1892	1873–1878
3	John A. Macdonald \mək-ˈdän-ᵊld\	1815–1891	1878–1891
4	John J. C. Abbott \ˈab-ət\	1821–1893	1891–1892
5	John S. D. Thompson \ˈtäm(p)-sən\	1844–1894	1892–1894
6	Mackenzie Bowell \ˈbō(-ə)l\	1823–1917	1894–1896
7	Charles Tupper \ˈtəp-ər\	1821–1915	1896
8	Wilfrid Laurier \lȯr-yā, ˈlȯr-ē-ˌā\	1841–1919	1896–1911
9	Robert L. Borden \ˈbȯrd-ᵊn\	1854–1937	1911–1920
10	Arthur Meighen \ˈmē-ən\	1874–1960	1920–1921
11	W. L. Mackenzie King \ˈkiŋ\	1874–1950	1921–1926
12	Arthur Meighen \ˈmē-ən\	1874–1960	1926
13	W. L. Mackenzie King \ˈkiŋ\	1874–1950	1926–1930
14	Richard B. Bennett \ˈben-ət\	1870–1947	1930–1935
15	W. L. Mackenzie King \ˈkiŋ\	1874–1950	1935–1948
16	Louis Stephen St. Laurent \saⁿ-lȯ-räⁿ\	1882–1973	1948–1957
17	John George Diefenbaker \ˈdē-fən-ˌbā-kər\	1895–1979	1957–1963
18	Lester B. Pearson \ˈpi(ə)rs-ᵊn\	1897–1972	1963–1968
19	Pierre Elliott Trudeau \ˈtrü-(ˌ)dō, trü-ˈ\	1919–	1968–1979
20	Joe Clark \ˈklärk\	1939–	1979–1980
21	Pierre Elliott Trudeau \ˈtrü-(ˌ)dō, trü-ˈ\	1919–	1980–1984
22	John Turner \ˈtərn-ər\	1929–	1984
23	Brian Mulroney \məl-ˈrü-nē\	1939–	1984–1993
24	Kim Campbell \ˈkam-bəl\	1947–	1993
25	Jean Chrétien \krā-tyaⁿ\	1934–	1993–

Nations of the World

name and pronunciation	population
Afghanistan \af-ˈga-nə-ˌstan\	20,269,000
Albania \al-ˈbā-nē-ə\	3,422,000
Algeria \al-ˈjir-ē-ə\	27,029,000
Andorra \an-ˈdȯr-ə\	61,900
Angola \aŋ-ˈgō-lə, an-\	10,916,000
Antigua and Barbuda \an-ˈtē-gə...bär-ˈbü-də\	66,000
Argentina \ˌär-jen-ˈtē-nə\	33,507,000
Armenia \är-ˈmē-nē-ə\	3,550,000
Australia \ȯ-ˈstrāl-yə\	17,729,000
Austria \ˈȯs-trē-ə\	7,938,000
Azerbaijan \ˌä-zər-ˌbī-ˈjän\	7,398,000
Bahamas \bə-ˈhä-məz\	266,000
Bahrain \bä-ˈrān\	486,000
Bangladesh \ˌbäŋ-glə-ˈdesh, -ˈdāsh\	115,075,000
Barbados \bär-ˈbā-dəs, -(ˌ)dōz, -(ˌ)däs\	260,000
Belarus \ˌbye-lə-ˈrüs\	10,353,000
Belgium \ˈbel-jəm\	10,072,000
Belize \bə-ˈlēz\	204,000
Benin \bə-ˈnin\	5,091,000
Bhutan \bü-ˈtan, -ˈtän\	1,546,000
Bolivia \bə-ˈli-vē-ə\	7,715,000
Bosnia and Herzegovina \ˈbäz-nē-ə...ˌhert-sə-gō-ˈvē-nə, -ˈgō-və-nə\	4,422,000
Botswana \bät-ˈswä-nə\	1,406,000
Brazil \brə-ˈzil\	156,493,000
Brunei \brü-ˈnī\	275,000
Bulgaria \ˌbəl-ˈgar-ē-ə, bùl-\	8,466,000
Burkina Faso \bùr-ˈkē-nə-ˈfä-sō\	9,780,000
Burundi \bù-ˈrün-dē\	5,665,000
Cambodia \kam-ˈbō-dē-ə\	9,287,000
Cameroon \ka-mə-ˈrün\	13,103,000
Canada \ˈka-nə-də\	27,296,859
Cape Verde \ˌkāp-ˈvərd\	350,000
Central African Republic	2,998,000
Chad \ˈchad\	6,118,000
Chile \ˈchi-lē\	13,542,000
China, People's Republic of \-ˈchī-nə\	1,179,467,000
Colombia \kə-ˈləm-bē-ə\	33,951,000
Comoro Islands \ˈkä-mə-ˌrō-\	516,000
Congo \ˈkäŋ-go\	2,775,000
Costa Rica \ˌkäs-tə-ˈrē-kə\	3,199,000
Croatia \krō-ˈā-shə\	4,821,000
Cuba \ˈkyü-bə\	10,892,000
Cyprus \ˈsī-prəs\	764,000
Czech Republic \ˈchek-\	10,332,000
Denmark \ˈden-ˌmärk\	5,187,000
Djibouti \jə-ˈbü-tē\	565,000
Dominica \ˌdä-mə-ˈnē-kə\	74,000
Dominican Republic \də-ˈmi-ni-kən-\	7,634,000
Ecuador \ˈe-kwə-ˌdȯr\	10,985,000
Egypt \ˈē-jəpt\	57,109,000
El Salvador \el-ˈsal-və-ˌdȯr\	5,517,000
Equatorial Guinea \-ˈgi-nē\	377,000
Eritrea \ˌer-ə-ˈtrā-ə\	3,317,611
Estonia \e-ˈstō-nē-ə\	1,536,000
Ethiopia \ˌē-thē-ˈō-pē-ə\	52,078,000
Fiji \ˈfē-(ˌ)jē\	762,000
Finland \ˈfin-lənd\	5,058,000
France \ˈfrans\	57,690,000
Gabon \ga-ˈbōn\	1,280,000
Gambia \ˈgam-bē-ə\	1,033,000
Georgia \ˈjȯr-jə\	5,493,000
Germany \ˈjər-mə-nē\	81,187,000
Ghana \ˈgä-nə\	15,636,000
Greece \ˈgrēs\	10,310,000
Grenada \grə-ˈnä-də\	91,000
Guatemala \ˌgwä-tə-ˈmä-lə\	9,713,000
Guinea \ˈgi-nē\	7,418,000
Guinea-Bissau \-bi-ˈsaù\	1,036,000
Guyana \gī-ˈa-nə\	755,000
Haiti \ˈhā-tē\	6,902,000
Honduras \hän-ˈdùr-əs\	5,148,000
Hungary \ˈhəŋ-gə-rē\	10,296,000
Iceland \ˈīs-lənd, -ˌland\	264,000
India \ˈin-dē-ə\	896,567,000
Indonesia \ˌin-də-ˈnē-zhə\	188,216,000
Iran \i-ˈran, -ˈrän\	60,768,000
Iraq \i-ˈräk, -ˈrak\	19,435,000
Ireland \ˈīr-lənd\	3,516,000
Israel \ˈiz-rē-əl\	5,451,000
Italy \ˈi-tə-lē\	57,235,000
Ivory Coast	13,459,000
Jamaica \jə-ˈmā-kə\	2,472,000
Japan \jə-ˈpan\	124,670,000
Jordan \ˈjȯr-dən\	3,764,000
Kazakhstan \ˌkä-zäk-ˈstän\	17,186,000
Kenya \ˈken-yə, ˈkēn-\	28,113,000
Kiribati \ˈkir-ə-ˌbas\	76,900
Kuwait \kə-ˈwāt\	1,433,000
Kyrgyzstan \ˌkir-gi-ˈstän\	4,526,000
Laos \ˈlaùs, ˈlä-ōs\	4,533,000
Latvia \ˈlat-vē-ə\	2,596,000
Lebanon \ˈle-bə-nən\	2,909,000
Lesotho \lə-ˈsü-ˌtü\	1,903,000
Liberia \lī-ˈbir-ē-ə\	2,844,000
Libya \ˈli-bē-ə\	4,573,000
Liechtenstein \ˈlik-tən-ˌshtīn\	30,100
Lithuania \ˌli-thə-ˈwā-nē-ə\	3,753,000
Luxembourg \ˈlək-səm-ˌbərg, ˈlùk-səm-ˌbùrg\	392,000
Macedonia \ˌma-sə-ˈdō-nē-ə\	2,063,000
Madagascar \ˌma-də-ˈgas-kər\	13,255,000
Malawi \mə-ˈlä-wē\	10,581,000
Malaysia \mə-ˈlā-zhə\	19,077,000
Maldives \ˈmȯl-ˌdēvz, -ˌdīvz\	237,000
Mali \ˈmä-lē\	8,646,000
Malta \ˈmȯl-tə\	363,000
Mauritania \ˌmȯr-ə-ˈtā-nē-ə\	2,171,000
Mauritius \mȯ-ˈri-shē-əs\	1,103,000
Mexico \ˈmek-si-ˌkō\	89,955,000
Moldova \mäl-ˈdō-və\	4,362,000
Monaco \ˈmä-nə-ˌkō\	30,500
Mongolia \män-ˈgōl-yə\	2,256,000
Morocco \mə-ˈrä-kō\	26,494,000
Mozambique \ˌmō-zəm-ˈbēk\	15,243,000
Myanmar \ˈmyän-ˌmär\	44,613,000
Namibia \na-ˈmi-bē-ə\	1,537,000
Nauru \nä-ˈü-(ˌ)rü\	10,000
Nepal \nə-ˈpȯl\	19,264,000
Netherlands \ˈne-thər-ləndz\	15,302,000

New Zealand \-ˈzē-lənd\	3,520,000	Swaziland		
Nicaragua \ˌni-kə-ˈrä-gwə\	4,265,000	\ˈswä-zē-ˌland\	814,000	
Niger \ˈnī-jər\	8,516,000	Sweden \ˈswē-dən\	8,727,000	
Nigeria \nī-ˈjir-ē-ə\	91,549,000	Switzerland		
North Korea \-kə-ˈrē-ə\	22,646,000	\ˈswit-sər-lənd\	6,996,000	
Norway \ˈnȯr-ˌwā\	4,308,000	Syria \ˈsir-ē-ə\	13,398,000	
Oman \ō-ˈmän\	1,698,000	Taiwan (Republic of China)		
Pakistan \ˈpa-ki-ˌstan,		\tī-ˈwän\	20,926,000	
ˌpä-ki-ˈstän\	127,962,000	Tajikistan \tä-ˌji-ki-ˈstän\	5,705,000	
Panama \ˈpa-nə-ˌmä\	2,563,000	Tanzania \ˌtan-zə-ˈnē-ə\	26,542,000	
Papua New Guinea		Thailand \ˈtī-ˌland, -lənd\	57,829,000	
\ˈpä-pə-wə-\	3,918,000	Togo \ˈtō-gō\	3,810,000	
Paraguay \ˈpar-ə-ˌgwī, -ˌgwā\	4,613,000	Tonga \ˈtäŋ-gə\	99,100	
Peru \pə-ˈrü\	22,916,000	Trinidad and Tobago		
Philippines \ˌfi-lə-ˈpēnz,		\ˈtrin-ə-ˌdad...		
ˈfi-lə-ˌpēnz\	64,954,000	tə-ˈbā-gō\	1,249,000	
Poland \ˈpō-lənd\	38,521,000	Tunisia \tü-ˈnē-zhə\	8,530,000	
Portugal \ˈpōr-chi-gəl\	9,823,000	Turkey \ˈtər-kē\	59,869,000	
Qatar \ˈkä-tər\	539,000	Turkmenistan		
Romania \rù-ˈmā-nē-ə\	22,789,000	\ˌtərk-ˌme-nə-ˈstän\	4,294,000	
Russia \ˈrə-shə\	148,000,000	Tuvalu \tü-ˈvä-lü\	9,500	
Rwanda \rù-ˈän-də\	7,584,000	Uganda \yü-ˈgan-də\	17,741,000	
St. Kitts-Nevis \-ˈkits-ˈnē-vəs\	41,800	Ukraine \ˈyü-ˌkrān,		
St. Lucia \-ˈlü-shə\	136,000	ˌyü-ˈkrān\	52,344,000	
St. Vincent and the Grenadines		United Arab Emirates	1,986,000	
\-ˈvin-sənt...		United Kingdom of Great		
ˌgre-nə-ˈdēnz\	109,000	Britain and Northern		
San Marino		Ireland \-ˈbri-tən...ˈīr-lənd\	55,500,000	
\ˌsan-mə-ˈrē-nō\	24,100	England \ˈiŋ-glənd\	46,161,000	
Sao Tome and Principe		Northern Ireland	1,583,000	
\ˌsaù-tə-ˈmä...		Scotland \ˈskät-lənd\	4,957,000	
ˈprin-sə-pə\	125,000	Wales \ˈwālz\	2,799,000	
Saudi Arabia \ˌsaù-dē-ə-		United States of America		
ˈrā-bē-ə, sä-ˌü-dē-\	17,419,000	\-ə-ˈmer-i-kə\	249,632,692	
Senegal \ˌse-ni-ˈgȯl\	7,899,000	Uruguay \ˈür-ə-ˌgwī,		
Seychelles \sā-ˈchelz\	71,000	ˈyùr-ə-ˌgwä\	3,149,000	
Sierra Leone		Uzbekistan		
\sē-ˌer-ə-lē-ˈōn\	4,491,000	\ˌùz-ˌbe-ki-ˈstän\	21,901,000	
Singapore \ˈsiŋ-ə-ˌpȯr\	2,876,000	Vanuatu \ˌvan-ˌwä-ˈtü\	160,000	
Slovakia \slō-ˈvä-kē-ə\	5,329,000	Vatican City State		
Slovenia \slō-ˈvē-nē-ə\	1,997,000	\ˈva-ti-kən-\	1,800	
Solomon Islands		Venezuela		
\ˈsä-lə-mən-\	349,000	\ˌve-nə-ˈzwä-lə\	20,609,000	
Somalia \sō-ˈmä-lē-ə\	8,050,000	Vietnam \vē-ˈet-ˈnäm\	70,902,000	
South Africa, Republic of	33,071,000	Western Samoa		
South Korea \-kə-ˈrē-ə\	44,042,000	\-sə-ˈmō-ə\	163,000	
Spain \ˈspān\	39,141,000	Yemen \ˈye-mən\	12,519,000	
Sri Lanka \srē-ˈläŋ-kə,		Yugoslavia		
shrē-\	17,616,000	\ˌyü-gō-ˈslä-vē-ə\	10,561,000	
Sudan \sü-ˈdan\	25,000,000	Zaire \zä-ˈir\	42,473,000	
Suriname \ˌsùr-ə-ˈnä-mə\	405,000	Zambia \ˈzam-bē-ə\	8,504,000	
		Zimbabwe \zim-ˈbäb-wä\	10,123,000	

Population of Places in the United States

Having 19,000 or More Inhabitants in 1990

A

Aberdeen, S. Dak.	24,927
Abilene, Tex.	106,654
Addison, Ill.	32,058
Adrian, Mich.	22,097
Agawam, Mass.	27,323
Agoura Hills, Calif.	20,390
Aiken, S.C.	19,872
Akron, Ohio	223,019
Alameda, Calif.	76,459
Alamogordo, N. Mex.	27,596
Albany, Ga.	78,122
Albany, N.Y.	101,082
Albany, Oreg.	29,462
Albuquerque, N. Mex.	384,736
Alexandria, La.	49,188
Alexandria, Va.	111,183
Alhambra, Calif.	82,106
Alice, Tex.	19,788
Allen Park, Mich.	31,092
Allentown, Pa.	105,090
Alliance, Ohio	23,376
Altamonte Springs, Fla.	34,879
Alton, Ill.	32,905
Altoona, Pa.	51,881
Altus, Okla.	21,910
Alvin, Tex.	19,220
Amarillo, Tex.	157,615
Ames, Iowa	47,198
Amherst, Mass.	35,228
Amsterdam, N.Y.	20,714
Anaheim, Calif.	266,406
Anchorage, Alaska	226,338
Anderson, Ind.	59,459
Anderson, S.C.	26,184
Andover, Mass.	29,151
Annapolis, Md.	33,187
Ann Arbor, Mich.	109,592
Anniston, Ala.	26,623
Antioch, Calif.	62,195
Appleton, Wis.	65,695
Apple Valley, Calif.	46,079
Apple Valley, Minn.	34,598
Arcadia, Calif.	48,290
Ardmore, Okla.	23,079
Arlington, Mass.	44,630
Arlington, Tex.	261,721
Arlington Heights, Ill.	75,460
Arvada, Colo.	89,235
Asheville, N.C.	61,607
Ashland, Ky.	23,622
Ashland, Ohio	20,079
Ashtabula, Ohio	21,633
Atascadero, Calif.	23,138
Athens, Ga.	45,734
Athens, Ohio	21,265
Atlanta, Ga.	394,017
Atlantic City, N.J.	37,986
Attleboro, Mass.	38,383
Atwater, Calif.	22,282
Auburn, Ala.	33,830
Auburn, Me.	24,309
Auburn, N.Y.	31,258
Auburn, Wash.	33,102
Augusta, Ga.	44,639
Augusta, Me.	21,325
Aurora, Colo.	222,103
Aurora, Ill.	99,581
Austin, Minn.	21,907
Austin, Tex.	465,622
Azusa, Calif.	41,333

B

Bakersfield, Calif.	174,820
Baldwin, Pa.	21,923
Baldwin Park, Calif.	69,330
Ballwin, Mo.	21,816
Baltimore, Md.	736,014
Bangor, Me.	33,181
Banning, Calif.	20,570
Barberton, Ohio	27,623
Barnstable, Mass.	40,949
Barstow, Calif.	21,472
Bartlesville, Okla.	34,256
Bartlett, Ill.	19,373
Bartlett, Tenn.	26,989
Baton Rouge, La.	219,531
Battle Creek, Mich.	53,540
Bay City, Mich.	38,936
Bayonne, N.J.	61,444
Baytown, Tex.	63,850
Beaumont, Tex.	114,323
Beavercreek, Ohio	33,626
Beaverton, Oreg.	53,310
Bedford, Tex.	43,762
Bell, Calif.	34,365
Belleville, Ill.	42,785
Belleville, N.J.	34,213
Bellevue, Nebr.	30,982
Bellevue, Wash.	86,874
Bellflower, Calif.	61,815
Bell Gardens, Calif.	42,355
Bellingham, Wash.	52,179
Bellwood, Ill.	20,241
Belmont, Calif.	24,127
Belmont, Mass.	24,720
Beloit, Wis.	35,573
Benbrook, Tex.	19,564
Bend, Oreg.	20,469
Benicia, Calif.	24,437
Berea, Ohio	19,051
Bergenfield, N.J.	24,458
Berkeley, Calif.	102,724
Berwyn, Ill.	45,426
Bessemer, Ala.	33,497
Bethany, Okla.	20,075
Bethel Park, Pa.	33,823
Bethesda, Md.	62,936
Bethlehem, Pa.	71,428
Bettendorf, Iowa	28,132
Beverly, Mass.	38,195
Beverly Hills, Calif.	31,971
Biddeford, Me.	20,710
Big Spring, Tex.	23,093
Billerica, Mass.	37,609
Billings, Mont.	81,151

Biloxi, Miss.	46,319
Binghamton, N.Y.	53,008
Birmingham, Ala.	265,968
Birmingham, Mich.	19,997
Bismarck, N. Dak.	49,256
Blacksburg, Va.	34,590
Blaine, Minn.	38,975
Bloomfield, N.J.	45,061
Bloomington, Ill.	51,972
Bloomington, Ind.	60,633
Bloomington, Minn.	86,335
Blue Island, Ill.	21,203
Blue Springs, Mo.	40,153
Blytheville, Ark.	22,906
Boca Raton, Fla.	61,492
Boise, Idaho	125,738
Bolingbrook, Ill.	40,843
Bossier City, La.	52,721
Boston, Mass.	574,283
Boulder, Colo.	83,312
Bountiful, Utah	36,659
Bowie, Md.	37,589
Bowling Green, Ky.	40,641
Bowling Green, Ohio	28,176
Boynton Beach, Fla.	46,194
Bozeman, Mont.	22,660
Bradenton, Fla.	43,779
Braintree, Mass.	33,836
Branford, Conn.	27,603
Brea, Calif.	32,873
Bremerton, Wash.	38,142
Bridgeport, Conn.	141,686
Bristol, Conn.	60,640
Bristol, R.I.	21,625
Bristol, Tenn.	23,421
Brockton, Mass.	92,788
Broken Arrow, Okla.	58,043
Brookfield, Wis.	35,184
Brookline, Mass.	54,718
Brooklyn Center, Minn.	28,887
Brooklyn Park, Minn.	56,381
Brook Park, Ohio	22,865
Broomfield, Colo.	24,638
Brownsville, Tex.	98,962
Brunswick, Me.	20,906
Brunswick, Ohio	28,230
Bryan, Tex.	55,002
Buena Park, Calif.	68,784
Buffalo, N.Y.	328,123
Buffalo Grove, Ill.	36,427
Bullhead City, Ariz.	21,951
Burbank, Calif.	93,643
Burbank, Ill.	27,600
Burlingame, Calif.	26,801
Burlington, Iowa	27,208
Burlington, Mass.	23,302
Burlington, N.C.	39,498
Burlington, Vt.	39,127
Burnsville, Minn.	51,288
Burton, Mich.	27,617
Butte, Mont.	33,336

C

Calumet City, Ill.	37,840
Camarillo, Calif.	52,303
Cambridge, Mass.	95,802
Camden, N.J.	87,492
Campbell, Calif.	36,048
Canton, Ohio	84,161
Cape Coral, Fla.	74,991
Cape Girardeau, Mo.	34,438
Carbondale, Ill.	27,033
Carlsbad, Calif.	63,126
Carlsbad, N. Mex.	24,952
Carmel, Ind.	25,380

Carol Stream, Ill.	31,716
Carpentersville, Ill.	23,049
Carrollton, Tex.	82,169
Carson, Calif.	83,995
Carson City, Nev.	40,443
Carteret, N.J.	19,025
Cary, N.C.	43,858
Casa Grande, Ariz.	19,082
Casper, Wyo.	46,742
Cathedral City, Calif.	30,085
Cedar Falls, Iowa	34,298
Cedar Hill, Tex.	19,976
Cedar Rapids, Iowa	108,751
Centerville, Ohio	21,082
Ceres, Calif.	26,314
Cerritos, Calif.	53,240
Champaign, Ill.	63,502
Chandler, Ariz.	90,533
Chapel Hill, N.C.	38,719
Charleston, Ill.	20,398
Charleston, S.C.	80,414
Charleston, W. Va.	57,287
Charlotte, N.C.	395,934
Charlottesville, Va.	40,341
Chattanooga, Tenn.	152,466
Chelmsford, Mass.	32,383
Chelsea, Mass.	28,710
Chesapeake, Va.	151,976
Cheshire, Conn.	25,684
Chester, Pa.	41,856
Chesterfield, Mo.	37,991
Cheyenne, Wyo.	50,008
Chicago, Ill.	2,783,726
Chicago Heights, Ill.	33,072
Chico, Calif.	40,079
Chicopee, Mass.	56,632
Chillicothe, Ohio	21,923
Chino, Calif.	59,682
Chula Vista, Calif.	135,163
Cicero, Ill.	67,436
Cincinnati, Ohio	364,040
Claremont, Calif.	32,503
Clarksdale, Miss.	19,717
Clarksville, Ind.	19,833
Clarksville, Tenn.	75,494
Clearfield, Utah	21,435
Clearwater, Fla.	98,784
Cleburne, Tex.	22,205
Cleveland, Ohio	505,616
Cleveland, Tenn.	30,354
Cleveland Heights, Ohio	54,052
Cliffside Park, N.J.	20,393
Clifton, N.J.	71,742
Clinton, Iowa	29,201
Clinton, Miss.	21,847
Clovis, Calif.	50,323
Clovis, N. Mex.	30,954
Coconut Creek, Fla.	27,485
Coeur d'Alene, Idaho	24,563
College Park, Ga.	20,457
College Park, Md.	21,927
College Station, Tex.	52,456
Collinsville, Ill.	22,446
Colorado Springs, Colo.	281,140
Colton, Calif.	40,213
Columbia, Mo.	69,101
Columbia, S.C.	98,052
Columbia, Tenn.	28,583
Columbus, Ga.	179,278
Columbus, Ind.	31,802
Columbus, Miss.	23,799
Columbus, Nebr.	19,480
Columbus, Ohio	632,910
Compton, Calif.	90,454
Concord, Calif.	111,348
Concord, N.H.	36,006

Concord, N.C.	27,347
Conroe, Tex.	27,610
Conway, Ark.	26,481
Cookeville, Tenn.	21,744
Coon Rapids, Minn.	52,978
Cooper City, Fla.	20,791
Copperas Cove, Tex.	24,079
Coral Gables, Fla.	40,091
Coral Springs, Fla.	79,443
Corona, Calif.	76,095
Coronado, Calif.	26,540
Corpus Christi, Tex.	257,453
Corsicana, Tex.	22,911
Cortland, N.Y.	19,801
Corvallis, Oreg.	44,757
Costa Mesa, Calif.	96,357
Cottage Grove, Minn.	22,935
Council Bluffs, Iowa	54,315
Coventry, R.I.	31,083
Covina, Calif.	43,207
Covington, Ky.	43,264
Cranston, R.I.	76,060
Crystal, Minn.	23,788
Crystal Lake, Ill.	24,512
Cudahy, Calif.	22,817
Culver City, Calif.	38,793
Cumberland, Md.	23,706
Cumberland, R.I.	29,038
Cupertino, Calif.	40,263
Cuyahoga Falls, Ohio	48,950
Cypress, Calif.	42,655

D

Dallas, Tex.	1,006,877
Dalton, Ga.	21,761
Daly City, Calif.	92,311
Dana Point, Calif.	31,896
Danbury, Conn.	65,585
Danvers, Mass.	24,174
Danville, Calif.	31,306
Danville, Ill.	33,828
Danville, Va.	53,056
Dartmouth, Mass.	27,244
Davenport, Iowa	95,333
Davie, Fla.	47,217
Davis, Calif.	46,209
Dayton, Ohio	182,044
Daytona Beach, Fla.	61,921
Dearborn, Mich.	89,286
Dearborn Heights, Mich.	60,838
Decatur, Ala.	48,761
Decatur, Ill.	83,885
Dedham, Mass.	23,782
Deerfield Beach, Fla.	46,325
Deer Park, Tex.	27,652
De Kalb, Ill.	34,925
Delano, Calif.	22,762
Delaware, Ohio	20,030
Del City, Okla.	23,928
Delray Beach, Fla.	47,181
Del Rio, Tex.	30,705
Denison, Tex.	21,505
Denton, Tex.	66,270
Denver, Colo.	467,610
Derry, N.H.	29,603
Des Moines, Iowa	193,187
De Soto, Tex.	30,544
Des Plaines, Ill.	53,223
Detroit, Mich.	1,027,974
Diamond Bar, Calif.	53,672
Dodge City, Kans.	21,129
Dolton, Ill.	23,930
Dothan, Ala.	53,589
Dover, Del.	27,630
Dover, N.H.	25,042

Downers Grove, Ill.	46,858
Downey, Calif.	91,444
Dracut, Mass.	25,594
Duarte, Calif.	20,688
Dublin, Calif.	23,229
Dubuque, Iowa	57,546
Duluth, Minn.	85,493
Duncan, Okla.	21,732
Duncanville, Tex.	35,748
Dunedin, Fla.	34,012
Durham, N.C.	136,611

E

Eagan, Minn.	47,409
Eagle Pass, Tex.	20,651
East Chicago, Ind.	33,892
East Cleveland, Ohio	33,096
East Detroit, Mich.	35,283
East Hartford, Conn.	50,452
East Haven, Conn.	26,144
Eastlake, Ohio	21,161
East Lansing, Mich.	50,677
East Moline, Ill.	20,147
Easton, Mass.	19,807
Easton, Pa.	26,276
East Orange, N.J.	73,552
East Palo Alto, Calif.	23,451
East Peoria, Ill.	21,378
East Point, Ga.	34,402
East Providence, R.I.	50,380
East Ridge, Tenn.	21,101
East St. Louis, Ill.	40,944
Eau Claire, Wis.	56,856
Eden Prairie, Minn.	39,311
Edina, Minn.	46,070
Edinburg, Tex.	29,885
Edmond, Okla.	52,315
Edmonds, Wash.	30,744
El Cajon, Calif.	88,693
El Centro, Calif.	31,384
El Cerrito, Calif.	22,869
El Dorado, Ark.	23,146
Elgin, Ill.	77,010
Elizabeth, N.J.	110,002
Elk Grove Village, Ill.	33,429
Elkhart, Ind.	43,627
Elmhurst, Ill.	42,029
Elmira, N.Y.	33,724
El Monte, Calif.	106,209
Elmwood Park, Ill.	23,206
El Paso, Tex.	515,342
Elyria, Ohio	56,746
Emporia, Kans.	25,512
Encinitas, Calif.	55,386
Enfield, Conn.	45,532
Englewood, Colo.	29,387
Englewood, N.J.	24,850
Enid, Okla.	45,309
Enterprise, Ala.	20,123
Erie, Pa.	108,718
Escondido, Calif.	108,635
Euclid, Ohio	54,875
Eugene, Oreg.	112,669
Euless, Tex.	38,149
Eureka, Calif.	27,025
Evanston, Ill.	73,233
Evansville, Ind.	126,272
Everett, Mass.	35,701
Everett, Wash.	69,961
Evergreen Park, Ill.	20,874

F

Fairbanks, Alaska	30,843
Fairborn, Ohio	31,300

Fairfax, Va.	19,622	Gilroy, Calif.	31,487
Fairfield, Calif.	77,211	Gladstone, Mo.	26,243
Fairfield, Conn.	53,418	Glastonbury, Conn.	27,901
Fairfield, Ohio	39,729	Glen Cove, N.Y.	24,149
Fair Lawn, N.J.	30,548	Glendale, Ariz.	148,134
Fairmont, W. Va.	20,210	Glendale, Calif.	180,038
Fall River, Mass.	92,703	Glendale Heights, Ill.	27,973
Falmouth, Mass.	27,960	Glendora, Calif.	47,828
Fargo, N. Dak.	74,111	Glen Ellyn, Ill.	24,944
Farmers Branch, Tex.	24,250	Glenview, Ill.	37,093
Farmington, N. Mex.	33,997	Gloucester, Mass.	28,716
Farmington Hills, Mich.	74,652	Golden Valley, Minn.	20,971
Fayetteville, Ark.	42,099	Goldsboro, N.C.	40,709
Fayetteville, N.C.	75,695	Goose Creek, S.C.	24,692
Ferguson, Mo.	22,286	Goshen, Ind.	23,797
Ferndale, Mich.	25,084	Grand Forks, N. Dak.	49,425
Findlay, Ohio	35,703	Grand Island, Nebr.	39,386
Fitchburg, Mass.	41,194	Grand Junction, Colo.	29,034
Flagstaff, Ariz.	45,857	Grand Prairie, Tex.	99,616
Flint, Mich.	140,761	Grand Rapids, Mich.	189,126
Florence, Ala.	36,426	Grandview, Mo.	24,967
Florence, S.C.	29,813	Granite City, Ill.	32,862
Florissant, Mo.	51,206	Grapevine, Tex.	29,202
Folsom, Calif.	29,802	Great Falls, Mont.	55,097
Fond du Lac, Wis.	37,757	Greeley, Colo.	60,536
Fontana, Calif.	87,535	Green Bay, Wis.	96,466
Fort Collins, Colo.	87,758	Greenbelt, Md.	21,096
Fort Dodge, Iowa	25,894	Greenfield, Wis.	33,403
Fort Lauderdale, Fla.	149,377	Greensboro, N.C.	183,521
Fort Lee, N.J.	31,997	Greenville, Miss.	45,226
Fort Myers, Fla.	45,206	Greenville, N.C.	44,972
Fort Pierce, Fla.	36,830	Greenville, S.C.	58,282
Fort Smith, Ark.	72,798	Greenville, Tex.	23,071
Fort Walton Beach, Fla.	21,471	Greenwich, Conn.	58,441
Fort Wayne, Ind.	173,072	Greenwood, Ind.	26,265
Fort Worth, Tex.	447,619	Greenwood, S.C.	20,807
Foster City, Calif.	28,176	Gresham, Oreg.	68,235
Fountain Valley, Calif.	53,691	Griffin, Ga.	21,347
Framingham, Mass.	64,989	Groton, Conn.	45,144
Frankfort, Ky.	25,968	Grove City, Ohio	19,661
Franklin, Mass.	22,095	Guilford, Conn.	19,848
Franklin, Tenn.	20,098	Gulfport, Miss.	40,775
Franklin, Wis.	21,855		
Frederick, Md.	40,148	**H**	
Fredericksburg, Va.	19,027		
Freeport, Ill.	25,840	Hackensack, N.J.	37,049
Freeport, N.Y.	39,894	Hagerstown, Md.	35,445
Fremont, Calif.	173,339	Hallandale, Fla.	30,996
Fremont, Nebr.	23,680	Haltom City, Tex.	32,856
Fresno, Calif.	354,202	Hamden, Conn.	52,434
Fridley, Minn.	28,335	Hamilton, Ohio	61,368
Friendswood, Tex.	22,814	Hammond, Ind.	84,236
Fullerton, Calif.	114,144	Hampton, Va.	133,793
		Hanford, Calif.	30,897
G		Hanover Park, Ill.	32,895
		Harlingen, Tex.	48,735
Gadsden, Ala.	42,523	Harrisburg, Pa.	52,376
Gahanna, Ohio	27,791	Harrison, N.Y.	23,308
Gainesville, Fla.	84,770	Harrisonburg, Va.	30,707
Gaithersburg, Md.	39,542	Hartford, Conn.	139,739
Galesburg, Ill.	33,530	Harvey, Ill.	29,771
Gallup, N. Mex.	19,154	Hastings, Nebr.	22,837
Galveston, Tex.	59,070	Hattiesburg, Miss.	41,882
Gardena, Calif.	49,847	Havelock, N.C.	20,268
Garden City, Kans.	24,097	Haverhill, Mass.	51,418
Garden City, Mich.	31,846	Hawthorne, Calif.	71,349
Garden City, N.Y.	21,686	Hayward, Calif.	111,498
Garden Grove, Calif.	143,050	Hazel Park, Mich.	20,051
Gardner, Mass.	20,125	Hazleton, Pa.	24,730
Garfield, N.J.	26,727	Helena, Mont.	24,569
Garfield Heights, Ohio	31,739	Hemet, Calif.	36,094
Garland, Tex.	180,650	Hempstead, N.Y.	49,453
Gary, Ind.	116,646	Henderson, Ky.	25,945
Gastonia, N.C.	54,732	Henderson, Nev.	64,942
Germantown, Tenn.	32,893	Hendersonville, Tenn.	32,188
Gilbert, Ariz.	29,188	Hesperia, Calif.	50,418

Hialeah, Fla.	188,004
Hickory, N.C.	28,301
Highland, Calif.	34,439
Highland, Ind.	23,696
Highland Park, Ill.	30,575
Highland Park, Mich.	20,121
High Point, N.C.	69,496
Hillsboro, Oreg.	37,520
Hilo, Hawaii	37,808
Hilton Head Island, S.C.	23,694
Hinesville, Ga.	21,603
Hingham, Mass.	19,821
Hobart, Ind.	21,822
Hobbs, N. Mex.	29,115
Hoboken, N.J.	33,397
Hoffman Estates, Ill.	46,561
Holland, Mich.	30,745
Hollister, Calif.	19,212
Hollywood, Fla.	121,697
Holyoke, Mass.	43,704
Homestead, Fla.	26,866
Homewood, Ala.	22,922
Homewood, Ill.	19,278
Honolulu, Hawaii	365,272
Hoover, Ala.	39,788
Hopewell, Va.	23,101
Hopkinsville, Ky.	29,809
Hot Springs, Ark.	32,462
Houma, La.	30,495
Houston, Tex.	1,630,553
Huber Heights, Ohio	38,696
Huntington, W. Va.	54,844
Huntington Beach, Calif.	181,519
Huntington Park, Calif.	56,065
Huntsville, Ala.	159,789
Huntsville, Tex.	27,925
Hurst, Tex.	33,574
Hutchinson, Kans.	39,308

I

Idaho Falls, Idaho	43,929
Imperial Beach, Calif.	26,512
Independence, Mo.	112,301
Indianapolis, Ind.	741,952
Indio, Calif.	36,793
Inglewood, Calif.	109,602
Inkster, Mich.	30,772
Inver Grove Heights, Minn.	22,477
Iowa City, Iowa	59,738
Irvine, Calif.	110,330
Irving, Tex.	155,037
Ithaca, N.Y.	29,541

J

Jackson, Mich.	37,446
Jackson, Miss.	196,637
Jackson, Tenn.	48,949
Jacksonville, Ark.	29,101
Jacksonville, Fla.	672,971
Jacksonville, Ill.	19,324
Jacksonville, N.C.	30,013
Jamestown, N.Y.	34,681
Janesville, Wis.	52,133
Jefferson City, Mo.	35,481
Jeffersontown, Ky.	23,221
Jeffersonville, Ind.	21,841
Jersey City, N.J.	228,537
Johnson City, Tenn.	49,381
Johnston, R.I.	26,542
Johnstown, Pa.	28,134
Joliet, Ill.	76,836
Jonesboro, Ark.	46,535
Joplin, Mo.	40,961
Junction City, Kans.	20,604

Juneau, Alaska	26,751
Jupiter, Fla.	24,986

K

Kailua, Hawaii	36,818
Kalamazoo, Mich.	80,277
Kaneohe, Hawaii	35,448
Kankakee, Ill.	27,575
Kannapolis, N.C.	29,696
Kansas City, Kans.	149,767
Kansas City, Mo.	435,146
Kearney, Nebr.	24,396
Kearny, N.J.	34,874
Keene, N.H.	22,430
Keizer, Oreg.	21,884
Kenner, La.	72,033
Kennewick, Wash.	42,155
Kenosha, Wis.	80,352
Kent, Ohio	28,835
Kent, Wash.	37,960
Kentwood, Mich.	37,826
Kettering, Ohio	60,569
Key West, Fla.	24,832
Killeen, Tex.	63,535
Kingsport, Tenn.	36,365
Kingston, N.Y.	23,095
Kingsville, Tex.	25,276
Kinston, N.C.	25,295
Kirkland, Wash.	40,052
Kirkwood, Mo.	27,291
Kissimmee, Fla.	30,050
Knoxville, Tenn.	165,121
Kokomo, Ind.	44,962

L

La Canada Flintridge, Calif.	19,378
Lacey, Wash.	19,279
Lackawanna, N.Y.	20,585
La Crosse, Wis.	51,003
Lafayette, Calif.	23,501
Lafayette, Ind.	43,764
Lafayette, La.	94,440
La Grange, Ga.	25,597
Laguna Beach, Calif.	23,170
Laguna Niguel, Calif.	44,400
La Habra, Calif.	51,266
Lake Charles, La.	70,580
Lake Havasu City, Ariz.	24,363
Lake Jackson, Tex.	22,776
Lakeland, Fla.	70,576
Lake Oswego, Oreg.	30,576
Lakeville, Minn.	24,854
Lakewood, Calif.	73,557
Lakewood, Colo.	126,481
Lakewood, Ohio	59,718
Lake Worth, Fla.	28,564
La Mesa, Calif.	52,931
La Mirada, Calif.	40,452
Lancaster, Calif.	97,291
Lancaster, Ohio	34,507
Lancaster, Pa.	55,551
Lancaster, Tex.	22,117
Lansing, Ill.	28,086
Lansing, Mich.	127,321
La Porte, Ind.	21,507
La Porte, Tex.	27,910
La Puente, Calif.	36,955
Laramie, Wyo.	26,687
Laredo, Tex.	122,899
Largo, Fla.	65,674
Las Cruces, N. Mex.	62,126
Las Vegas, Nev.	258,295
Lauderdale Lakes, Fla.	27,341
Lauderhill, Fla.	49,708

Laurel, Md.	19,438	Manhattan, Kans.	37,712
La Verne, Calif.	30,897	Manhattan Beach, Calif.	32,063
Lawndale, Calif.	27,331	Manitowoc, Wis.	32,520
Lawrence, Ind.	26,763	Mankato, Minn.	31,477
Lawrence, Kans.	65,608	Mansfield, Conn.	21,103
Lawrence, Mass.	70,207	Mansfield, Ohio	50,627
Lawton, Okla.	80,561	Manteca, Calif.	40,773
Layton, Utah	41,784	Maple Grove, Minn.	38,736
League City, Tex.	30,159	Maple Heights, Ohio	27,089
Leavenworth, Kans.	38,495	Maplewood, Minn.	30,954
Leawood, Kans.	19,693	Marblehead, Mass.	19,971
Lebanon, Pa.	24,800	Margate, Fla.	42,985
Lee's Summit, Mo.	46,418	Marietta, Ga.	44,129
Lemon Grove, Calif.	23,984	Marina, Calif.	26,436
Lenexa, Kans.	34,034	Marion, Ind.	32,618
Leominster, Mass.	38,145	Marion, Iowa	20,403
Lewiston, Idaho	28,082	Marion, Ohio	34,075
Lewiston, Me.	39,757	Marlborough, Mass.	31,813
Lewisville, Tex.	46,521	Marquette, Mich.	21,977
Lexington, Ky.	225,366	Marshall, Tex.	23,682
Lexington, Mass.	28,974	Marshalltown, Iowa	25,178
Liberty, Mo.	20,459	Marshfield, Mass.	21,531
Libertyville, Ill.	19,174	Marshfield, Wis.	19,291
Lima, Ohio	45,549	Martinez, Calif.	31,808
Lincoln, Nebr.	191,972	Maryland Heights, Mo.	25,407
Lincoln Park, Mich.	41,832	Maryville, Tenn.	19,208
Linden, N.J.	36,701	Mason City, Iowa	29,040
Lindenhurst, N.Y.	26,879	Massillon, Ohio	31,007
Lisle, Ill.	19,512	Mayfield Heights, Ohio	19,847
Little Rock, Ark.	175,795	Maywood, Calif.	27,850
Littleton, Colo.	33,685	Maywood, Ill.	27,139
Livermore, Calif.	56,741	Medford, Mass.	57,407
Livonia, Mich.	100,850	Medford, Oreg.	46,951
Lockport, N.Y.	24,426	Melbourne, Fla.	59,646
Lodi, Calif.	51,874	Melrose, Mass.	28,150
Lodi, N.J.	22,355	Melrose Park, Ill.	20,859
Logan, Utah	32,762	Memphis, Tenn.	610,337
Lombard, Ill.	39,408	Menlo Park, Calif.	28,040
Lomita, Calif.	19,382	Menomonee Falls, Wis.	26,840
Lompoc, Calif.	37,649	Mentor, Ohio	47,358
Long Beach, Calif.	429,433	Merced, Calif.	56,216
Long Beach, N.Y.	33,510	Mercer Island, Wash.	20,816
Long Branch, N.J.	28,658	Meriden, Conn.	59,479
Longmont, Colo.	51,555	Meridian, Miss.	41,036
Longview, Tex.	70,311	Merrillville, Ind.	27,257
Longview, Wash.	31,499	Mesa, Ariz.	288,091
Lorain, Ohio	71,245	Mesquite, Tex.	101,484
Los Altos, Calif.	26,303	Methuen, Mass.	39,990
Los Angeles, Calif.	3,485.398	Miami, Fla.	358,548
Los Gatos, Calif.	27,357	Miami Beach, Fla.	92,639
Louisville, Ky.	269,063	Michigan City, Ind.	33,822
Loveland, Colo.	37,352	Middletown, Conn.	42,762
Lowell, Mass.	103,439	Middletown, N.Y.	24,160
Lubbock, Tex.	186,206	Middletown, Ohio	46,022
Lufkin, Tex.	30,206	Middletown, R.I.	19,460
Lynbrook, N.Y.	19,208	Midland, Mich.	38,053
Lynchburg, Va.	66,049	Midland, Tex.	89,443
Lynn, Mass.	81,245	Midwest City, Okla.	52,267
Lynnwood, Wash.	28,695	Milford, Conn.	49,938
Lynwood, Calif.	61,945	Milford, Mass.	25,355
		Mililani Town, Hawaii	29,359
M		Millbrae, Calif.	20,412
		Millville, N.J.	25,992
McAllen, Tex.	84,021	Milpitas, Calif.	50,686
Machesney Park, Ill.	19,033	Milton, Mass.	25,725
McKeesport, Pa.	26,016	Milwaukee, Wis.	628,088
McKinney, Tex.	21,283	Minneapolis, Minn.	368,383
Macomb, Ill.	19,952	Minnetonka, Minn.	48,370
Macon, Ga.	106,612	Minot, N. Dak.	34,544
Madera, Calif.	29,281	Miramar, Fla.	40,663
Madison, Wis.	191,262	Mishawaka, Ind.	42,608
Madison Heights, Mich.	32,196	Mission, Tex.	28,653
Malden, Mass.	53,884	Mission Viejo, Calif.	72,820
Manassas, Va.	27,957	Missoula, Mont.	42,918
Manchester, Conn.	51,618	Missouri City, Tex.	36,176
Manchester, N.H.	99,567	Mobile, Ala.	196,278

Modesto, Calif.	164,730	Newton, Mass.	82,585
Moline, Ill.	43,202	Newtown, Conn.	20,779
Monroe, La.	54,909	New York City, N.Y.	7,322,564
Monroe, Mich.	22,902	Bronx	1,203,789
Monroeville, Pa.	29,169	Brooklyn	2,300,664
Monrovia, Calif.	35,761	Manhattan	1,487,536
Montclair, Calif.	28,434	Queens	1,951,598
Montclair, N.J.	37,729	Richmond	378,977
Montebello, Calif.	59,564	Niagara Falls, N.Y.	61,840
Monterey, Calif.	31,954	Niles, Ill.	28,284
Monterey Park, Calif.	60,738	Niles, Ohio	21,128
Montgomery, Ala.	187,106	Nogales, Ariz.	19,489
Moore, Okla.	40,318	Norco, Calif.	28,302
Moorhead, Minn.	32,295	Norfolk, Nebr.	21,476
Moorpark, Calif.	25,494	Norfolk, Va.	261,229
Moreno Valley, Calif.	118,779	Normal, Ill.	40,023
Morgan Hill, Calif.	23,928	Norman, Okla.	80,071
Morgantown, W. Va.	25,879	Norristown, Pa.	30,749
Morristown, Tenn.	21,385	Northampton, Mass.	29,289
Morton Grove, Ill.	22,408	North Andover, Mass.	22,792
Mountain Brook, Ala.	19,810	North Attleboro, Mass.	25,038
Mountain View, Calif.	67,460	Northbrook, Ill.	32,308
Mountlake Terrace, Wash.	19,320	North Charleston, S.C.	70,218
Mount Pleasant, Mich.	23,285	North Chicago, Ill.	34,978
Mount Pleasant, S.C.	30,108	Northglenn, Colo.	27,195
Mount Prospect, Ill.	53,170	North Haven, Conn.	22,247
Mount Vernon, N.Y.	67,153	North Kingstown, R.I.	23,786
Muncie, Ind.	71,035	North Las Vegas, Nev.	47,707
Mundelein, Ill.	21,215	North Lauderdale, Fla.	26,506
Munster, Ind.	19,949	North Little Rock, Ark.	61,741
Murfreesboro, Tenn.	44,922	North Miami, Fla.	49,998
Murray, Utah	31,282	North Miami Beach, Fla.	35,359
Muscatine, Iowa	22,881	North Olmsted, Ohio	34,204
Muskegon, Mich.	40,283	North Platte, Nebr.	22,605
Muskogee, Okla.	37,708	North Providence, R.I.	32,090
Myrtle Beach, S.C.	24,848	North Richland Hills, Tex.	45,895
		North Ridgeville, Ohio	21,564
N		North Royalton, Ohio	23,197
		North Tonawanda, N.Y.	34,989
Nacogdoches, Tex.	30,872	Norton Shores, Mich.	21,755
Nampa, Idaho	28,365	Norwalk, Calif.	94,279
Napa, Calif.	61,842	Norwalk, Conn.	78,331
Naperville, Ill.	85,351	Norwich, Conn.	37,391
Naples, Fla.	19,505	Norwood, Mass.	28,700
Nashua, N.H.	79,662	Norwood, Ohio	23,674
Nashville, Tenn.	510,784	Novato, Calif.	47,585
Natchez, Miss.	19,460	Novi, Mich.	32,998
Natick, Mass.	30,510	Nutley, N.J.	27,099
National City, Calif.	54,249		
Naugatuck, Conn.	30,625	**O**	
Needham, Mass.	27,557		
Neenah, Wis.	23,219	Oak Creek, Wis.	19,513
New Albany, Ind.	36,322	Oak Forest, Ill.	26,203
Newark, Calif.	37,861	Oakland, Calif.	372,242
Newark, Del.	25,098	Oakland Park, Fla.	26,326
Newark, N.J.	275,221	Oak Lawn, Ill.	56,182
Newark, Ohio	44,389	Oak Park, Ill.	53,648
New Bedford, Mass.	99,922	Oak Park, Mich.	30,462
New Berlin, Wis.	33,592	Oak Ridge, Tenn.	27,310
New Braunfels, Tex.	27,334	Ocala, Fla.	42,045
New Brighton, Minn.	22,207	Oceanside, Calif.	128,398
New Britain, Conn.	75,491	Odessa, Tex.	89,699
New Brunswick, N.J.	41,711	Ogden, Utah	63,909
Newburgh, N.Y.	26,454	Oklahoma City, Okla.	444,719
New Castle, Pa.	28,334	Olathe, Kans.	63,352
New Haven, Conn.	130,474	Olympia, Wash.	33,840
New Hope, Minn.	21,853	Omaha, Nebr.	335,795
New Iberia, La.	31,828	Ontario, Calif.	133,179
Newington, Conn.	29,208	Opelika, Ala.	22,122
New London, Conn.	28,540	Orange, Calif.	110,658
New Milford, Conn.	23,629	Orange, N.J.	29,925
New Orleans, La.	496,938	Orange, Tex.	19,381
Newport, R.I.	28,227	Orem, Utah	67,561
Newport Beach, Calif.	66,643	Orlando, Fla.	164,693
Newport News, Va.	170,045	Orland Park, Ill.	35,720
New Rochelle, N.Y.	67,265	Ormond Beach, Fla.	29,721

Oshkosh, Wis.	55,006	Pontiac, Mich.	71,166
Ossining, N.Y.	22,582	Portage, Ind.	29,060
Oswego, N.Y.	19,195	Portage, Mich.	41,042
Ottumwa, Iowa	24,488	Port Arthur, Tex.	58,724
Overland Park, Kans.	111,790	Port Chester, N.Y.	24,728
Owatonna, Minn.	19,386	Porterville, Calif.	29,563
Owensboro, Ky.	53,549	Port Hueneme, Calif.	20,319
Oxnard, Calif.	142,216	Port Huron, Mich.	33,694
		Portland, Me.	64,358

P

		Portland, Oreg.	437,319
		Port Orange, Fla.	35,317
Pacifica, Calif.	37,670	Port St. Lucie, Fla.	55,866
Paducah, Ky.	27,256	Portsmouth, N.H.	25,925
Palatine, Ill.	39,253	Portsmouth, Ohio	22,676
Palm Bay, Fla.	62,632	Portsmouth, Va.	103,907
Palm Springs, Calif.	40,181	Pottstown, Pa.	21,831
Palo Alto, Calif.	55,900	Poughkeepsie, N.Y.	28,844
Pampa, Tex.	19,959	Poway, Calif.	43,516
Panama City, Fla.	34,378	Prairie Village, Kans.	23,186
Paradise, Calif.	25,408	Prattville, Ala.	19,587
Paramount, Calif.	47,669	Prescott, Ariz.	26,455
Paramus, N.J.	25,067	Prichard, Ala.	34,311
Paris, Tex.	24,699	Providence, R.I.	160,728
Parkersburg, W. Va.	33,862	Provo, Utah	86,835
Park Forest, Ill.	24,646	Pueblo, Colo.	98,640
Park Ridge, Ill.	36,175	Pullman, Wash.	23,478
Parma, Ohio	87,876	Puyallup, Wash.	23,875
Parma Heights, Ohio	21,448		
Pasadena, Calif.	119,363		
Pasadena, Tex.	131,591	**Q**	
Pascagoula, Miss.	25,899		
Pasco, Wash.	20,337	Quincy, Ill.	39,681
Passaic, N.J.	58,041	Quincy, Mass.	84,985
Paterson, N.J.	140,891		
Pawtucket, R.I.	72,644	**R**	
Peabody, Mass.	47,039		
Peachtree City, Ga.	19,027	Racine, Wis.	84,298
Pearl, Miss.	19,588	Radcliff, Ky.	19,772
Pearl City, Hawaii	30,993	Rahway, N.J.	25,325
Peekskill, N.Y.	19,536	Raleigh, N.C.	207,951
Pekin, Ill.	32,254	Rancho Cucamonga, Calif.	101,409
Pembroke Pines, Fla.	65,452	Rancho Palos Verdes, Calif.	41,659
Pensacola, Fla.	58,165	Randolph, Mass.	30,093
Peoria, Ariz.	50,618	Rapid City, S. Dak.	54,523
Peoria, Ill.	113,504	Raytown, Mo.	30,601
Perris, Calif.	21,460	Reading, Mass.	22,539
Perth Amboy, N.J.	41,967	Reading, Pa.	78,380
Petaluma, Calif.	43,184	Redding, Calif.	66,462
Petersburg, Va.	38,386	Redlands, Calif.	60,394
Pharr, Tex.	32,921	Redmond, Wash.	35,800
Phenix City, Ala.	25,312	Redondo Beach, Calif.	60,167
Philadelphia, Pa.	1,585,577	Redwood City, Calif.	66,072
Phoenix, Ariz.	983,403	Reno, Nev.	133,850
Pico Rivera, Calif.	59,177	Renton, Wash.	41,688
Pine Bluff, Ark.	57,140	Revere, Mass.	42,786
Pinellas Park, Fla.	43,426	Reynoldsburg, Ohio	25,748
Piqua, Ohio	20,612	Rialto, Calif.	72,388
Pittsburg, Calif.	47,564	Richardson, Tex.	74,840
Pittsburgh, Pa.	369,879	Richfield, Minn.	35,710
Pittsfield, Mass.	48,622	Richland, Wash.	32,315
Placentia, Calif.	41,259	Richmond, Calif.	87,425
Plainfield, N.J.	46,567	Richmond, Ind.	38,705
Plainview, Tex.	21,700	Richmond, Ky.	21,155
Plano, Tex.	128,713	Richmond, Va.	203,056
Plantation, Fla.	66,692	Ridgecrest, Calif.	27,725
Plant City, Fla.	22,754	Ridgefield, Conn.	20,919
Plattsburgh, N.Y.	21,255	Ridgewood, N.J.	24,152
Pleasant Hill, Calif.	31,585	Rio Rancho, N. Mex.	32,505
Pleasanton, Calif	50,553	Riverside, Calif.	226,505
Plum, Pa.	25,609	Riviera Beach, Fla.	27,639
Plymouth, Mass.	45,608	Roanoke, Va.	96,397
Plymouth, Minn.	50,889	Rochester, Minn.	70,745
Pocatello, Idaho	46,080	Rochester, N.H.	26,630
Pomona, Calif.	131,723	Rochester, N.Y.	231,636
Pompano Beach, Fla.	72,411	Rochester Hills, Mich.	61,766
Ponca City, Okla.	26,359	Rockford, Ill.	139,426
		Rock Hill, S.C.	41,643

Rock Island, Ill.	40,552
Rocklin, Calif.	19,033
Rock Springs, Wyo.	19,050
Rockville, Md.	44,835
Rockville Centre, N.Y.	24,727
Rocky Mount, N.C.	48,997
Rocky River, Ohio	20,410
Rogers, Ark.	24,692
Rohnert Park, Calif.	36,326
Rolling Meadows, Ill.	22,591
Rome, Ga.	30,326
Rome, N.Y.	44,350
Romulus, Mich.	22,897
Roselle, Ill.	20,819
Roselle, N.J.	20,314
Rosemead, Calif.	51,638
Rosenberg, Tex.	20,183
Roseville, Calif.	44,685
Roseville, Mich.	51,412
Roseville, Minn.	33,485
Roswell, Ga.	47,923
Roswell, N. Mex.	44,654
Round Rock, Tex.	30,923
Rowlett, Tex.	23,260
Roy, Utah	24,603
Royal Oak, Mich.	65,410
Russellville, Ark.	21,260
Ruston, La.	20,027

S

Sacramento, Calif.	369,365
Saginaw, Mich.	69,512
St. Charles, Ill.	22,501
St. Charles, Mo.	54,555
St. Clair Shores, Mich.	68,107
St. Cloud, Minn.	48,812
St. George, Utah	28,502
St. Joseph, Mo.	71,852
St. Louis, Mo.	396,685
St. Louis Park, Minn.	43,787
St. Paul, Minn.	272,235
St. Peters, Mo.	45,779
St. Petersburg, Fla.	238,629
Salem, Mass.	38,091
Salem, N.H.	25,746
Salem, Oreg.	107,786
Salem, Va.	23,756
Salina, Kans.	42,303
Salinas, Calif.	108,777
Salisbury, Md.	20,592
Salisbury, N.C.	23,087
Salt Lake City, Utah	159,936
San Angelo, Tex.	84,474
San Antonio, Tex.	935,933
San Benito, Tex.	20,125
San Bernardino, Calif.	164,164
San Bruno, Calif.	38,961
San Carlos, Calif.	26,167
San Clemente, Calif.	41,100
San Diego, Calif.	1,110,549
San Dimas, Calif.	32,397
Sandusky, Ohio	29,764
Sandy, Utah	75,058
San Fernando, Calif.	22,580
Sanford, Fla.	32,387
Sanford, Me.	20,463
San Francisco, Calif.	723,959
San Gabriel, Calif.	37,120
San Jose, Calif.	782,248
San Juan Capistrano, Calif.	26,183
San Leandro, Calif.	68,223
San Luis Obispo, Calif.	41,958
San Marcos, Calif.	38,974
San Marcos, Tex.	28,743
San Mateo, Calif.	85,486

San Pablo, Calif.	25,158
San Rafael, Calif.	48,404
San Ramon, Calif.	35,303
Santa Ana, Calif.	293,742
Santa Barbara, Calif.	85,571
Santa Clara, Calif.	93,613
Santa Clarita, Calif.	110,642
Santa Cruz, Calif.	49,040
Santa Fe, N. Mex.	55,859
Santa Maria, Calif.	61,284
Santa Monica, Calif.	86,905
Santa Paula, Calif.	25,062
Santa Rosa, Calif.	113,313
Santee, Calif.	52,902
Sarasota, Fla.	50,961
Saratoga, Calif.	28,061
Saratoga Springs, N.Y.	25,001
Saugus, Mass.	25,549
Savannah, Ga.	137,560
Sayreville, N.J.	34,986
Schaumburg, Ill.	68,586
Schenectady, N.Y.	65,566
Schererville, Ind.	19,926
Schofield Barracks, Hawaii	19,597
Scottsdale, Ariz.	130,069
Scranton, Pa.	81,805
Seal Beach, Calif.	25,098
Seaside, Calif.	38,901
Seattle, Wash.	516,259
Sedalia, Mo.	19,800
Selma, Ala.	23,755
Shaker Heights, Ohio	30,831
Shawnee, Kans.	37,993
Shawnee, Okla.	26,017
Sheboygan, Wis.	49,676
Shelton, Conn.	35,418
Sherman, Tex.	31,601
Shoreview, Minn.	24,587
Shreveport, La.	198,525
Shrewsbury, Mass.	24,146
Sierra Vista, Ariz.	32,983
Simi Valley, Calif.	100,217
Simsbury, Conn.	22,023
Sioux City, Iowa	80,505
Sioux Falls, S. Dak.	100,814
Skokie, Ill.	59,432
Slidell, La.	24,124
Smithfield, R.I.	19,163
Smyrna, Ga.	30,981
Socorro, Tex.	22,995
Somerville, Mass.	76,210
South Bend, Ind.	105,511
South El Monte, Calif.	20,850
South Euclid, Ohio	23,866
Southfield, Mich.	75,728
South Gate, Calif.	86,284
Southgate, Mich.	30,771
South Holland, Ill.	22,105
Southington, Conn.	38,518
South Kingstown, R.I.	24,631
South Lake Tahoe, Calif.	21,586
South Milwaukee, Wis.	20,958
South Pasadena, Calif.	23,936
South Plainfield, N.J.	20,489
South Portland, Me.	23,163
South St. Paul, Minn.	20,197
South San Francisco, Calif.	54,312
South Windsor, Conn.	22,090
Sparks, Nev.	53,367
Spartanburg, S.C.	43,467
Spokane, Wash.	177,196
Springdale, Ark.	29,941
Springfield, Ill.	105,227
Springfield, Mass.	156,983

Springfield, Mo.	140,494
Springfield, Ohio	70,487
Springfield, Oreg.	44,683
Spring Valley, N.Y.	21,802
Stamford, Conn.	108,056
Stanton, Calif.	30,491
State College, Pa.	38,923
Staunton, Va.	24,461
Sterling Heights, Mich.	117,810
Steubenville, Ohio	22,125
Stevens Point, Wis.	23,006
Stillwater, Okla.	36,676
Stockton, Calif.	210,943
Stoneham, Mass.	22,203
Stoughton, Mass.	26,777
Stow, Ohio	27,702
Stratford, Conn.	49,389
Streamwood, Ill.	30,987
Strongsville, Ohio	35,308
Suffolk, Va.	52,141
Sugar Land, Tex.	24,529
Suisun City, Calif.	22,686
Sulphur, La.	20,125
Summerville, S.C.	22,519
Summit, N.J.	19,757
Sumter, S.C.	41,943
Sunnyvale, Calif.	117,229
Sunrise, Fla.	64,407
Superior, Wis.	27,134
Syracuse, N.Y.	163,860

T

Tacoma, Wash.	176,664
Tallahassee, Fla.	124,773
Tamarac, Fla.	44,822
Tampa, Fla.	280,015
Taunton, Mass.	49,832
Taylor, Mich.	70,811
Temecula, Calif.	27,099
Tempe, Ariz.	141,865
Temple, Tex.	46,109
Temple City, Calif.	31,100
Terre Haute, Ind.	57,483
Tewksbury, Mass.	27,266
Texarkana, Ark.	22,631
Texarkana, Tex.	31,656
Texas City, Tex.	40,822
The Colony, Tex.	22,113
Thornton, Colo.	55,031
Thousand Oaks, Calif.	104,352
Tigard, Oreg.	29,344
Tinley Park, Ill.	37,121
Titusville, Fla.	39,394
Toledo, Ohio	332,943
Topeka, Kans.	119,883
Torrance, Calif.	133,107
Torrington, Conn.	33,687
Tracy, Calif.	33,558
Trenton, Mich.	20,586
Trenton, N.J.	88,675
Troy, Mich.	72,884
Troy, N.Y.	54,269
Troy, Ohio	19,478
Trumbull, Conn.	32,016
Tucson, Ariz.	405,390
Tulare, Calif.	33,249
Tulsa, Okla.	367,302
Tupelo, Miss.	30,685
Turlock, Calif.	42,198
Tuscaloosa, Ala.	77,759
Tustin, Calif.	50,689
Twin Falls, Idaho	27,591
Tyler, Tex.	75,450

U

Union City, Calif.	53,762
Union City, N.J.	58,012
University City, Mo.	40,087
University Park, Tex.	22,259
Upland, Calif.	63,374
Upper Arlington, Ohio	34,128
Urbana, Ill.	36,344
Urbandale, Iowa	23,500
Utica, N.Y.	68,637

V

Vacaville, Calif.	71,479
Valdosta, Ga.	39,806
Vallejo, Calif.	109,199
Valley Stream, N.Y.	33,946
Valparaiso, Ind.	24,414
Vancouver, Wash.	46,380
Ventura (San Buenaventura), Calif.	92,575
Vernon, Conn.	29,841
Vestavia Hills, Ala.	19,749
Vicksburg, Miss.	20,908
Victoria, Tex.	55,076
Victorville, Calif.	40,674
Villa Park, Ill.	22,253
Vincennes, Ind.	19,859
Vineland, N.J.	54,870
Virginia Beach, Va.	393,069
Visalia, Calif.	75,636
Vista, Calif.	71,872

W

Waco, Tex.	103,590
Waipahu, Hawaii	31,435
Wakefield, Mass.	24,825
Walla Walla, Wash.	26,478
Wallingford, Conn.	40,822
Walnut, Calif.	29,105
Walnut Creek, Calif.	60,569
Walpole, Mass.	20,212
Waltham, Mass.	57,878
Wareham, Mass.	19,232
Warner Robins, Ga.	43,726
Warren, Mich.	144,864
Warren, Ohio	50,793
Warwick, R.I.	85,427
Washington, D.C.	609,909
Watauga, Tex.	20,009
Waterbury, Conn.	108,961
Waterloo, Iowa	66,467
Watertown, Conn.	20,456
Watertown, Mass.	33,284
Watertown, N.Y.	29,429
Watertown, Wis.	19,142
Watsonville, Calif.	31,099
Waukegan, Ill.	69,392
Waukesha, Wis.	56,958
Wausau, Wis.	37,060
Wauwatosa, Wis.	49,366
Wayne, Mich.	19,899
Webster Groves, Mo.	22,987
Weirton, W. Va.	22,124
Wellesley, Mass.	26,615
Wenatchee, Wash.	21,756
Weslaco, Tex.	21,877
West Allis, Wis.	63,221
West Bend, Wis.	23,916
West Covina, Calif.	96,086
West Des Moines, Iowa	31,702
Westerly, R.I.	21,605
Westerville, Ohio	30,269
Westfield, Mass.	38,372
Westfield, N.J.	28,870

West Hartford, Conn.	60,110
West Haven, Conn.	54,021
West Hollywood, Calif.	36,118
West Jordan, Utah	42,892
West Lafayette, Ind.	25,907
Westlake, Ohio	27,018
Westland, Mich.	84,724
West Memphis, Ark.	28,259
West Mifflin, Pa.	23,644
Westminster, Calif.	78,118
Westminster, Colo.	74,625
Westmont, Ill.	21,228
West New York, N.J.	38,125
West Orange, N.J.	39,103
West Palm Beach, Fla.	67,643
Westport, Conn.	24,410
West Sacramento, Calif.	28,898
West St. Paul, Minn.	19,248
West Springfield, Mass.	27,537
West Valley City, Utah	86,976
West Warwick, R.I.	29,268
Wethersfield, Conn.	25,651
Weymouth, Mass.	54,063
Wheaton, Ill.	51,464
Wheat Ridge, Colo.	29,419
Wheeling, Ill.	29,911
Wheeling, W. Va.	34,882
White Bear Lake, Minn.	24,704
Whitehall, Ohio	20,572
White Plains, N.Y.	48,718
Whittier, Calif.	77,671
Wichita, Kans.	304,011
Wichita Falls, Tex.	96,259
Wilkes-Barre, Pa.	47,523
Wilkinsburg, Pa.	21,080
Williamsport, Pa.	31,933
Willoughby, Ohio	20,510
Wilmette, Ill.	26,690
Wilmington, Del.	71,529
Wilmington, N.C.	55,530
Wilson, N.C.	36,930
Winchester, Mass.	20,267
Winchester, Va.	21,947
Windham, Conn.	22,039
Windsor, Conn.	27,817
Winona, Minn.	25,399
Winston-Salem, N.C.	143,485
Winter Haven, Fla.	24,725
Winter Park, Fla.	22,242
Winter Springs, Fla.	22,151
Woburn, Mass.	35,943
Woodbury, Minn.	20,075
Woodland, Calif.	39,802
Woodridge, Ill.	26,256
Woonsocket, R.I.	43,877
Wooster, Ohio	22,191
Worcester, Mass.	169,759
Wyandotte, Mich.	30,938
Wyoming, Mich.	63,891

X

Xenia, Ohio	24,664

Y

Yakima, Wash.	54,827
Yarmouth, Mass.	21,174
Yonkers, N.Y.	188,082
Yorba Linda, Calif.	52,422
York, Pa.	42,192
Youngstown, Ohio	95,732
Ypsilanti, Mich.	24,846
Yuba City, Calif.	27,437
Yucaipa, Calif.	32,824
Yukon, Okla.	20,935
Yuma, Ariz.	54,923

Z

Zanesville, Ohio	26,778
Zion, Ill.	19,775

Population of the United States in 1990

SUMMARY BY STATES AND DEPENDENCIES
(Figures in parentheses give rank of states in population)

THE STATES AND THE DISTRICT OF COLUMBIA

Alabama .... (22)	4,040,587
Alaska .... (49)	550,043
Arizona .... (24)	3,665,228
Arkansas .... (33)	2,350,725
California ...... (1)	29,760,020
Colorado .... (26)	3,294,394
Connecticut ..... (27)	3,287,116
Delaware .... (46)	666,168
District of Columbia	606,900
Florida .... (4)	12,937,926
Georgia .... (11)	6,478,216
Hawaii .... (41)	1,108,229
Idaho .... (42)	1,006,749
Illinois .... (6)	11,430,602
Indiana .... (14)	5,544,159
Iowa .... (30)	2,776,755
Kansas .... (32)	2,477,574
Kentucky .... (23)	3,685,296
Louisiana .... (21)	4,219,973
Maine .... (38)	1,227,928
Maryland .... (19)	4,781,468
Massachusetts .. (13)	6,016,425
Michigan .... (8)	9,295,297
Minnesota ...... (20)	4,375,099
Mississippi ..... (31)	2,573,216
Missouri .... (15)	5,117,073
Montana .... (44)	799,065
Nebraska .... (36)	1,578,385
Nevada .... (39)	1,201,833
New Hampshire .... (40)	1,109,252
New Jersey ..... (9)	7,730,188
New Mexico .... (37)	1,515,069
New York ...... (2)	17,990,456
North Carolina . (10)	6,628,637
North Dakota .. (47)	638,800
Ohio .... (7)	10,847,115
Oklahoma ...... (28)	3,145,585
Oregon .... (29)	2,842,321
Pennsylvania ... (5)	11,881,643
Rhode Island ... (43)	1,003,464
South Carolina . (25)	3,486,703
South Dakota ... (45)	696,004
Tennessee ...... (17)	4,877,185
Texas .... (3)	16,986,510
Utah .... (35)	1,722,850
Vermont .... (48)	562,758
Virginia .... (12)	6,187,358
Washington ..... (18)	4,866,692
West Virginia ... (34)	1,793,477
Wisconsin ...... (16)	4,891,769
Wyoming .... (50)	453,588
Total	249,632,692

DEPENDENCIES

American Samoa	46,773
Belau	15,122
Guam	133,152
Northern Mariana Islands	43,345
Puerto Rico	3,522,037
Virgin Islands of the U.S.	101,809

Population of Places in Canada

Having 21,500 or More Inhabitants in 1991

Ajax, Ont.	57,350
Alma, Que.	25,910
Ancaster, Ont.	21,988
Anjou, Que.	37,210
Aurora, Ont.	29,454
Aylmer, Que.	32,244
Baie-Comeau, Que.	26,012
Barrie, Ont.	62,728
Beauport, Que.	69,158
Belleville, Ont.	37,243
Blainville, Que.	22,679
Boucherville, Que.	33,796
Brampton, Ont.	234,445
Brandon, Man.	38,567
Brantford, Ont.	81,997
Brockville, Ont.	21,582
Brossard, Que.	64,793
Burlington, Ont.	129,575
Burnaby, B.C.	158,858
Caledon, Ont.	34,965
Calgary, Alta.	710,677
Cambridge, Ont.	92,772
Cap-de-la-Madeleine, Que.	33,716
Charlesbourg, Que.	70,788
Châteauguay, Que.	39,833
Chatham, Ont.	43,557
Chicoutimi, Que.	62,670
Chilliwack, B.C.	49,531
Coquitlam, B.C.	84,021
Corner Brook, Nfld.	22,410
Cornwall, Ont.	47,137
Côte-St-Luc, Que.	28,700
Cumberland, Ont.	40,697
Dartmouth, N.S.	67,798

Delta, B.C.	88,978	Owen Sound, Ont.	21,674
Dollard-des-Ormeaux, Que.	46,922	Penticton, B.C.	27,258
Drummondville, Que.	35,462	Peterborough, Ont.	68,371
Dundas, Ont.	21,868	Pickering, Ont.	68,631
East York, Ont.	102,696	Pierrefonds, Que.	48,735
Edmonton, Alta.	616,741	Pointe-Claire, Que.	27,647
Etobicoke, Ont.	309,993	Port Coquitlam, B.C.	36,773
Flamborough, Ont.	29,616	Prince Albert, Sask.	34,181
Fort Erie, Ont.	26,006	Prince George, B.C.	69,653
Fort McMurray, Alta.	34,706	Quebec, Que.	167,517
Fredericton, N.B.	46,466	Red Deer, Alta.	58,134
Gatineau, Que.	92,284	Regina, Sask.	179,178
Georgina, Ont.	29,746	Repentigny, Que.	49,630
Gloucester, Ont.	101,677	Richmond Hill, Ont.	80,142
Granby, Que.	42,804	Rimouski, Que.	30,873
Grande Prairie, Alta.	28,271	Rouyn-Noranda, Que.	26,448
Guelph, Ont.	87,976	Saanich, B.C.	95,577
Halifax, N.S.	114,455	St. Albert, Alta.	42,146
Halton Hills, Ont.	36,816	St-Bruno-de-Montarville, Que.	23,849
Hamilton, Ont.	318,499	St. Catharines, Ont.	129,300
Hull, Que.	60,707	Ste-Foy, Que.	71,133
Innisfil, Ont.	21,667	Ste-Thérèse, Que.	24,158
Jonquière, Que.	57,933	St. Eustache, Que.	37,278
Kamloops, B.C.	67,057	St-Hubert, Que.	74,027
Kanata, Ont.	37,344	St-Hyacinthe, Que.	39,292
Kelowna, B.C.	75,950	St-Jean-sur-Richelieu, Que.	37,607
Kingston, Ont.	56,597	St-Jerôme, Que.	23,384
Kitchener, Ont.	168,282	Saint John, N.B.	74,969
Lachine, Que.	35,266	St. John's, Nfld.	95,770
Langley, B.C.	66,040	St-Laurent, Que.	72,402
LaSalle, Que.	73,804	St-Léonard, Que.	73,120
Laval, Que.	314,398	St. Thomas, Ont.	29,990
Lethbridge, Alta.	60,974	Salaberry-de-Valleyfield, Que.	27,598
Lévis-Lauzon, Que.	39,452	Sarnia-Clearwater, Ont.	74,376
London, Ont.	303,165	Saskatoon, Sask.	186,058
Longueuil, Que.	129,874	Sault Ste. Marie, Ont.	81,476
Lunenburg, N.S.	25,720	Scarborough, Ont.	524,598
Maple Ridge, B.C.	48,422	Sept-Iles, Que.	24,848
Markham, Ont.	153,811	Sherbrooke, Que.	76,429
Mascouche, Que.	25,828	Stoney Creek, Ont.	49,968
Matsqui, B.C.	68,064	Stratford, Ont.	27,666
Medicine Hat, Alta.	43,625	Sudbury, Ont.	92,884
Milton, Ont.	32,075	Surrey, B.C.	245,173
Mission, B.C.	26,202	Sydney, N.S.	26,063
Mississauga, Ont.	463,388	Terrebonne, Que.	39,678
Moncton, N.B.	57,010	Thunder Bay, Ont.	113,946
Montreal, Que.	1,017,666	Timmins, Ont.	47,461
Montreal North, Que.	85,516	Toronto, Ont.	635,395
Moose Jaw, Sask.	33,593	Trois-Rivières, Que.	49,426
Mount Pearl, Nfld.	23,689	Val-d'Or, Que.	23,842
Nanaimo, B.C.	60,129	Valley East, Ont.	21,939
Nanticoke, Ont.	22,727	Vancouver, B.C.	471,844
Nepean, Ont.	107,627	Vaughan, Ont.	111,359
Newcastle, Ont.	49,479	Verdun, Que.	61,307
Newmarket, Ont.	45,474	Vernon, B.C.	23,514
New Westminster, B.C.	43,585	Victoria, B.C.	71,228
Niagara Falls, Ont.	75,399	Waterloo, Ont.	71,181
North Bay, Ont.	55,405	Welland, Ont.	47,914
North Vancouver, B.C.	38,436	West Vancouver, B.C.	38,783
North York, Ont.	562,564	Whitby, Ont.	61,281
Oakville, Ont.	114,670	Windsor, Ont.	191,435
Orillia, Ont.	25,925	Winnipeg, Man.	616,790
Oshawa, Ont.	129,344	Woodstock, Ont.	30,075
Ottawa, Ont.	313,987	York, Ont.	140,525
Outremont, Que.	22,935		

Population of Canada in 1991

Summary by Provinces and Territories

Alberta	2,545,553	Prince Edward Island		129,765
British Columbia	3,282,061	Quebec		6,895,963
Manitoba	1,091,942	Saskatchewan		988,928
New Brunswick	723,900	Yukon Territory		27,797
Newfoundland	568,474	Northwest Territories		57,649
Nova Scotia	899,942	TOTAL		27,296,859
Ontario	10,084,885			

Signs and Symbols

Astronomy

⊙ the sun; Sunday
◑, ☾, or ☽ the moon; Monday
● new moon
☽, ◑, ☽, ☽ first quarter
○ or ☺ full moon
☾, ◑, ☾, ☾ last quarter
☿ Mercury; Wednesday
♀ Venus; Friday

⊕, ⊖, or ♁ the earth
♂ Mars; Tuesday
♃ Jupiter; Thursday
♄ or ♄ Saturn; Saturday
♁, ♅, or ♅ Uranus
♆, ♆, or ♆ Neptune
♇ Pluto
☄ comet
✳ or ✳ fixed star

Business

a/c account ⟨in a/c with⟩
@ at; each ⟨4 apples @ 5¢ = 20¢⟩
/ or ⅌ per
c/o care of
number if it precedes a numeral ⟨track #3⟩; pounds if it follows ⟨a 5# sack of sugar⟩
℔ pound; pounds

% percent
‰ per thousand
$ dollars
¢ cents
£ pounds
/ shillings
© copyrighted
® registered trademark

Mathematics

+ plus; positive ⟨a+b=c⟩—used also to indicate omitted figures or an approximation

− minus; negative

± plus or minus ⟨the square root of 4a² is ± 2a⟩

× multiplied by; times ⟨6×4=24⟩—also indicated by placing a dot between the factors ⟨6·4=24⟩ or by writing the factors one after the other, often enclosed in parentheses, without explicitly indicating multiplication ⟨(4)(5)(3)=60⟩ ⟨−4abc⟩

÷ or : divided by ⟨24÷6=4⟩—also indicated by writing the divisor under the dividend with a line between ⟨$\frac{24}{6}$=4⟩ or by writing the divisor after the dividend with an oblique line between ⟨3/8⟩

= equals ⟨6+2=8⟩

≠ or ≠ is not equal to

> is greater than ⟨6>5⟩

< is less than ⟨3<4⟩

≧ or ≥ is greater than or equal to

≦ or ≤ is less than or equal to

∝ varies directly as; is proportional to

: is to; the ratio of

∴ therefore

∞ infinity

∠ angle; the angle ⟨∠ABC⟩

∟ right angle ⟨∟ABC⟩

⊥ the perpendicular; is perpendicular to ⟨AB⊥CD⟩

$\parallel$	parallel; is parallel to $\langle AB \parallel CD \rangle$
$\odot$ *or* $\bigcirc$	circle
$\frown$	arc of a circle
$\triangle$	triangle
$\square$	square
$\square$	rectangle
$\sqrt{}$ *or* $\sqrt{}$	root—used without a figure to indicate a square root (as in $\sqrt{4}=2$) or with an index above the sign to indicate a higher degree (as in $\sqrt[3]{3},\sqrt[5]{7}$); also denoted by a fractional index at the right of a number whose denominator expresses the degree of the root $\langle 3^{1/3}=\sqrt[3]{3}\rangle$
( )	parenthesis $\left.\begin{array}{l}\\ \\ \end{array}\right\}$ indicate that the quantities
[ ]	brackets enclosed by them are to be
{ }	braces taken together
s	standard deviation of a sample taken from a population
σ	standard deviation of a population
$\bar{x}$	arithmetic mean of a sample of a variable x
μ	arithmetic mean of a population
μ_2 *or* σ^2	variance
π	pi; the number $3.14159265+$; the ratio of the circumference of a circle to its diameter
$\circ$	degree $\langle 60° \rangle$
$'$	minute; foot $\langle 30' \rangle$—used also to distinguish between different values of the same variable or between different variables (as a', a'', a''', usually read a prime, a double prime, a triple prime)
$''$	second; inch $\langle 30'' \rangle$
$^0, ^1, ^2, ^3$, etc.	—used as exponents placed above and at the right of an expression to indicate that it is raised to a power whose degree is indicated by the figure $\langle a^0$ equals $1 \rangle$ $\langle a^1$ equals $a \rangle$ $\langle a^2$ is the square of $a \rangle$
$^{-1}, ^{-2}, ^{-3}$, etc.	—used as exponents placed above and at the right of an expression to indicate that the reciprocal of the expression is raised to the power whose degree is indicated by the figure $\langle a^{-1}$ equals $1/a \rangle$ $\langle a^{-2}$ equals $1/a^2 \rangle$
$!$	factorial $\langle n! = n\,(n\text{-}1)(n\text{-}2) \ldots 1 \rangle$
n	an unspecified number esp. when an integer
$\subset$	is included in, is a subset of
$\supset$	contains as a subset
$\in$ *or* ϵ	is an element of
$\notin$	is not an element of

Medicine

$\overline{\text{AA}}$, $\bar{\text{A}}$, *or* āā	of each
$\text{R\!\!\!/}$	take—used on prescriptions; prescription; treatment
☠	poison

Miscellaneous

&	and
&c	et cetera; and so forth
" *or* "	ditto marks
/	virgule; used to mean "or" (as in *and/or*), "and/or" (as in *dead/wounded*), "per" (as in *feet/second*), indicates end of a line of verse; separates the figures of a date (4/8/74)
☞	index *or* fist

<	derived from
>	whence derived
+	and

} used in linguistics

*	hypothetical, ungrammatical
†	died—used esp. in genealogies
✚	cross
☧	monogram from Greek XP signifying Christ
卐	swastika
✡	Judaism
☥	ankh
℣	versicle
℟	response
∗	—used in Roman Catholic and Anglican service books to divide each verse of a psalm, indicating where the response begins
✠ *or* +	—used in some service books to indicate where the sign of the cross is to be made; also used by certain Roman Catholic and Anglican prelates as a sign of the cross preceding their signatures
LXX	Septuagint
fl or f:	relative aperture of a photographic lens
⊕	civil defense
☮	peace

Reference marks

*	asterisk *or* star		§	section *or* numbered clause
†	dagger		‖	parallels
‡	double dagger		¶ *or* ℙ	paragraph

Stamps and stamp collecting

★ *or* *	unused
★★ *or* **	unused with original gum intact and never mounted with a stamp hinge
⊙ *or* ○ *or* 0	used
⊞	block of four or more
⊠	entire cover or card

Weather

H *or* Ⓗ	high pressure region		∞	haze
L *or* Ⓛ	low pressure region		◕	hurricane
◎	calm		ↄ	tropical storm
○	clear		•	rain
◑	cloudy (partly)		✶	rain and snow
●	cloudy (completely overcast)		⩎	frost
⇾	drifting or blowing snow		⑊	sandstorm or dust storm
ꝯ	drizzle		▽	shower(s)
≡	fog		⩒	shower of rain
∾	freezing rain		⩟	shower of hail
▲▲▲▲	cold front		△	sleet
⌒⌒⌒	warm front		✳	snow
⌒∿	stationary front		ꝶ	thunderstorm
)(	funnel clouds		⌒∿	visibility reduced by smoke

A Handbook of Style

Punctuation

The English writing system uses punctuation marks to separate groups of words for meaning and emphasis; to convey an idea of the variations of pitch, volume, pauses, and intonations of speech; and to help avoid contextual ambiguity. The use of the standard English punctuation marks is discussed in the following pages; examples are provided to illustrate the general rules.

Apostrophe   '

1. Indicates the possessive case of nouns and indefinite pronouns. The possessive case of almost all singular nouns may be formed by adding 's. Traditionally, however, only the apostrophe is added when the s would not be pronounced in normal speech. The possessive case of plural nouns ending in s or in an \s\ or \z\ sound is generally formed by adding an apostrophe only; the possessive of irregular plurals is formed by adding 's.

> her mother-in-law's car
> anyone's guess
> the boy's mother
> the boys' mothers
> Degas's drawings
> Knox's products
> Aristophanes' play
> for righteousness' sake
> the Stephenses' house
> children's laughter

2. Marks omission of letters in contracted words.
> didn't
> o'clock
> hang 'em up

3. Marks omission of digits in numbers.
> class of '83

4. Is often used to form plurals of letters, figures, punctuated abbreviations, symbols, and words referred to as words.
> Dot your *i*'s and cross your *t*'s.
> Two of the junior faculty have Ph.D's.
> She has trouble pronouncing her *the*'s.

Brackets   [   ]

1. Set off interpolated editorial matter within quoted material.

> He wrote, "I ain't [sic] going."
> Vaulting ambition, which o'erleaps itself
> And falls on the other [side].
>   —Shakespeare

2. Function as parentheses within parentheses.
> Bowman Act (22 Stat., ch. 4, § [or sec.] 4, p. 50)

3. Set off phonetic symbols and transcriptions.
> [t] in British *duty*
> the word is pronounced [ˈek-sə-jənt]

Colon   :

1. Introduces a clause or phrase that explains, illustrates, amplifies, or restates what has gone before.
> The sentence was poorly constructed: it lacked both unity and coherence.

2. Directs attention to an appositive.
> He had only one pleasure: eating.

3. Introduces a series.
> Three abstained: England, France, and Belgium.

4. Introduces lengthy quoted material set off from the rest of a text by indentation but not by quotation marks.
> I quote from the text of Chapter One:

5. Separates elements in page references, in bibliographical and biblical citations, and in set formulas used to express ratios and time.
> *Journal of the American Medical Association* 48:356
> Stendhal, *Love* (New York: Penguin, 1975)
> John 4:10
> a ratio of 3:5
> 8:30 a.m.

6. Separates titles and subtitles (as of books).

Battle Cry of Freedom: The Era of the Civil War

7. Follows the salutation in formal correspondence.

Dear Sir or Madam:

Ladies and Gentlemen:

8. Punctuates headings in memorandums and formal correspondence.

TO: VIA:
SUBJECT: REFERENCE:

, Comma

1. Separates main clauses joined by a coordinating conjunction (such as *and, but, or, nor,* or *for*) and sometimes short parallel clauses not joined by conjunctions.

She knew very little about him, and he volunteered nothing.

I came, I saw, I conquered.

2. Sets off an adverbial clause or a long adverbial phrase that precedes or interrupts the main clause.

When she discovered the answer, she reported it to us.

The report, after being read aloud, was put up for consideration.

3. Sets off transitional words and expressions (such as *on the contrary, on the other hand*), conjunctive adverbs (such as *consequently, furthermore, however*), and expressions that introduce an illustration or example (such as *namely, for example*).

My partner, on the other hand, remains unconvinced.

The regent's whim, however, threw the negotiations into chaos.

She responded as completely as she could; that is, she answered each individual question specifically.

4. Sets off contrasting and opposing expressions within sentences.

The cost is not $65.00, but $56.65.

He changed his style, not his ethics.

5. Separates words, phrases, or clauses in series. (Many omit the comma before the conjunction introducing the last item in a series when no ambiguity results.)

He was young, eager, and restless.

It requires one to travel constantly, to have no private life, and to live on almost nothing.

Be sure to pack a flashlight, a sweater and an extra pair of socks.

6. Separates coordinate adjectives modifying a noun. However, a comma is not used between two adjectives when the first modifies the combination of the second adjective and the word or phrase it modifies.

The harsh, damp, piercing wind cut through his jacket.

a low common denominator

7. Sets off parenthetical elements such as nonrestrictive clauses and phrases.

Our guide, who wore a blue beret, was an experienced traveler.

We visited Gettysburg, site of the famous battle.

The book's author, Marie Jones, was an accomplished athlete.

8. Introduces a direct quotation, terminates a direct quotation that is neither a question nor an exclamation, and sets off split quotations. The comma is not used with quotations that are tightly integrated into the sentences in which they appear (e.g., as subject or predicate nominatives) or those that do not represent actual dialogue.

Mary said, "I am leaving."

"I am leaving," Mary said.

"I am leaving," Mary said with determination, "even if you want me to stay."

"The computer is down" was the reply she feared.

The fact that he said he was about to "faint from hunger" doesn't mean he actually fainted.

9. Sets off words in direct address, absolute phrases, and mild interjections.

You may go, John, if you wish.

I fear their encounter, his temper being what it is.

Ah, that's my idea of an excellent dinner.

10. Separates a tag question from the rest of the sentence.

It's a fine day, isn't it?

11. Indicates the omission of a word or words used in a parallel construction earlier in the sentence. When the meaning of the sentence is quite clear without the comma, the comma is omitted.

Common stocks are preferred by some investors; bonds, by others.

He was in love with her and she with him.

12. Is used to avoid ambiguity that might arise from adjacent words.

To Mary, Jane was someone special.

13. Is used to to divide digits in numbers into groups of three; however, it is generally not used in pagination, in dates, or in street numbers, and sometimes not used in numbers with four digits.

Smithville, pop. 100,000

4,550 cars

but

page 1411   4507 Main St.
3600 rpm   the year 1983

14. Punctuates an inverted name.

    Morton, William A.

15. Separates a surname from a following title or degree and often from the words "Junior" and "Senior" and their abbreviations.

    Sandra H. Cobb, Vice President

    Jesse Ginsburg, D.D.M.

16. Sets off geographical names (such as state or country from city), elements of dates, and addresses. When just the month and the year are given in a date, the comma is usually omitted.

    Shreveport, Louisiana, is the site of a large air base.

    On Sunday, June 23, 1940, he was wounded.

    Number 10 Downing Street, London, is a famous address.

    She began her career in April 1993 at a modest salary.

17. Follows the salutation in informal correspondence, and follows the complimentary close of a letter.

    Dear Mark,

    Affectionately,

    Very truly yours,

Dash   —

1. Usually marks an abrupt change or break in the continuity of a sentence.

    When in 1960 the stockpile was sold off—indeed, dumped as surplus—natural rubber sales were hard hit.—Barry Commoner.

2. Is sometimes used in place of commas or parentheses when special emphasis is required.

    The presentations—and especially the one by Ms. Dow—impressed the audience.

3. Introduces a statement that explains, summarizes, or expands on what precedes it.

    Oil, steel, and wheat—these are the sinews of industrialization.

    The motion was then tabled—that is, removed indefinitely from consideration.

4. Often precedes the attribution of a quotation.

    My foot is on my native heath. . .

                —Sir Walter Scott

5. Sets off an interrupting clause or phrase. The dash takes the place of a comma that would ordinarily set off the clause, but an exclamation point or question mark is retained.

    If we don't succeed—and the critics say we won't—then the whole project is in jeopardy.

    They are demanding that everything—even the marshland!—be transferred to the new trust.

    Your question—it was *your* question, wasn't it, Mr. Jones?—just can't be answered.

Ellipsis (or Suspension Points) . . . .

1. Indicates the omission of one or more words within a quoted passage. When four dots are used, the ellipsis indicates the omission of one or more sentences within the passage or the omission of words at the end of a sentence. The first or the last of the four dots is a period.

    In the little world in which children have their existence, . . . there is nothing so finely perceived and so finely felt as injustice.—Charles Dickens

    Security is mostly a superstition. . . . Avoiding danger is no safer in the long run than outright exposure. . . . Life is either a daring adventure or nothing.—Helen Keller

2. Usually indicates omission of one or more lines of poetry when ellipsis is extended the length of the line.

    I think that I shall never see

    A poem lovely as a tree

    . . . .

    Poems are made by fools like me,

    But only God can make a tree.

                —Joyce Kilmer

3. Indicates halting speech or an unfinished sentence in dialogue.

    "I'd like to. . . that is. . . if you don't mind. . . ."

Exclamation Point   !

1. Ends an emphatic phrase or sentence.

    Get out of here!

    Her notorious ostentation—she flew her friends to Bangkok for her birthday parties!—was feasted on by the popular press.

2. Ends an emphatic interjection.

    Encore!

    All of this proves—at long last!—that we were right from the start.

Hyphen   -

The hyphen is often used between parts of a compound. The styling of such words varies; when in doubt, see the entry in the dictionary at its own place or in a list of undefined words at an individual prefix. For unentered compounds, advice will be found in *Webster's Standard American Style Manual* or a comparable guide.

1. Is often used between a prefix and root, especially whenever the root is capitalized, when two identical vowels come together, or when the resulting word could be confused with another identically spelled word.

pre-Renaissance   co-opted

anti-inflationary

re-cover a sofa

but

recover from an illness

2. Is used in some compounds, especially those containing prepositions.

president-elect   sister-in-law

good-for-nothing   over-the-counter

falling-out   write-off

3. Is often used in compound modifiers in attributive position.

traveling in a fast-moving van

She has gray-green eyes.

a come-as-you-are party

4. Suspends the first element of a hyphenated compound or a prefix (hyphenated or not) when the second element or base word is part of a following hyphenated compound or derived form.

a six- or eight-cylinder engine

pre- and postadolescent trauma

5. Marks division of a word at the end of a line.

The ruling pas-
sion of his life

6. Is used in writing out compound numbers between 21 and 99.

thirty-four

one hundred and thirty-eight

7. Is often used between the numerator and the denominator in writing out fractions, especially when they are used as modifiers. However, fractions used as nouns are often written as open compounds, especially when either the numerator or the denominator already contains a hyphen.

a two-thirds majority of the vote

three fifths of her paycheck

one seventy-second of an inch

8. Serves as an equivalent of *through* or (*up*) *to and including* when used between indicators of range such as numbers and dates. (In typeset material the longer en dash is used.)

pages 40–98

the years 1980–89

9. Serves as the equivalent of *to, and,* or *versus* in indicating linkage or opposition. (In typeset material the longer en dash is used.)

the New York–Paris flight

the Hardy–Weinberg law

the Lincoln–Douglas Debates

The final score was 7–2.

 # Hyphen, Double

Is used at the end-of-line division of a hyphenated compound to indicate that the compound is hyphenated and not closed.

self= [end of line] seeker

but

self- [end of line] same

( ) Parentheses

1. Enclose words, numbers, phrases, or clauses that provide examples, explanations, or supplementary material that does not essentially alter the meaning of the sentence.

Three old destroyers (all now out of commission) will be scrapped.

He has followed the fortunes of the modern renaissance (*al-Nahdad*) in the Arabic-speaking world.

2. Enclose numerals that confirm a written number in a text.

Delivery will be made in thirty (30) days.

3. Enclose numbers or letters in a series.

We must set forth (1) our long-term goals, (2) our immediate objectives, and (3) the means at our disposal.

4. Enclose abbreviations that follow their spelled-out forms or spelled-out forms that follow their abbreviations.

a ruling by the Federal Communications Commission (FCC)

the manufacture and disposal of PVC (polyvinyl chloride)

5. Indicate alternative terms.

Please indicate the lecture(s) you would like to attend.

6. Enclose publication data in footnotes and endnotes.

Marguerite Yourcenar, *The Dark Brain of Piranesi and Other Essays* (New York: Farrar, Straus and Giroux, 1985), p. 9.

7. Are used with other punctuation marks in the following ways:

If the parenthetic expression is an independent sentence standing alone, its first word is capitalized and a period is included *inside* the last parenthesis. However, if the parenthetic expression, even if it could stand alone as a sentence, occurs within a sentence, it is uncapitalized and has no sentence period but may have an exclamation point, a question mark, a period for an abbreviation, or quotation marks within the closing parenthesis.

The discussion was held in the boardroom. (The results are still confidential.)

Although we liked the restaurant (their Italian food was the best), we seldom went there.

After waiting in line for an hour (why do we do these things?), we finally left.

Years ago, someone (I wish I could remember who!) told me about it.

What was once informally known as A.B.D. status is now often recognized by the degree of Master of Philosophy (M. Phil.).

He was depressed ("I must resign") and refused to do anything.

No punctuation mark should be placed directly before parenthetical material in a sentence; if a break is required, punctuation should be placed *after* the final parenthesis.

I'll get back to you tomorrow (Friday), when I have more details.

Period   .

1. Ends sentences or sentence fragments that are neither interrogatory nor exclamatory.

Not bad.

Give it your best.

I gave it my best.

He asked if she had given it her best.

2. Follows some abbreviations and contractions.

Dr.   A.D.   ibid.   i.e.

Jr.   etc.   cont.

3. Is normally used with an individual's initials.

F. Scott Fitzgerald

T. S. Eliot

4. Is used after numerals and letters in vertical enumerations and outlines.

Required skills are:
1. Shorthand
2. Typing
3. Transcription
I. Objectives
A. Economy
1. low initial cost
2. low maintenance cost
B. Ease of operation

Question Mark   ?

1. Ends a direct question.

How did she do it?

"How did she do it?" he asked.

2. Ends a question that is part of a larger sentence, but not an indirect question.

How did she do it? was the question on each person's mind.

He wondered, Will it work?

He wondered whether it would work.

3. Indicates the writer's ignorance or uncertainty.

Geoffrey Chaucer, English poet (1342?–1400)

Quotation Marks, Double   " "

1. Enclose direct quotations but not indirect quotations.

She said, "I am leaving."

She said that she was leaving.

2. Enclose words or phrases borrowed from others, words used in a special way, and words of marked informality when introduced into formal writing.

Much of the population in the hellish future he envisions is addicted to "derms," patches that deliver potent drug doses instantaneously through the skin.

He called himself "emperor," but he was really just a dictator.

He was arrested for smuggling "smack."

3. Enclose titles of poems, short stories, articles, lectures, chapters of books, short musical compositions, and radio and TV programs.

Robert Frost's "After Apple-Picking"

Cynthia Ozick's "Rosa"

The third chapter of *Treasure Island* is entitled "The Black Spot."

"All the Things You Are"

Debussy's "Clair de lune"

NBC's "Today Show"

4. Are used with other punctuation marks in the following ways:

The period and the comma fall *within* the quotation marks.

"I am leaving," she said.

It was unclear how she maintained such an estate on "a small annuity."

The colon and semicolon fall *outside* the quotation marks.

There was only one thing to do when he said, "I may not run": promise him a large campaign contribution.

He spoke of his "little cottage in the country"; he might better have called it a mansion.

The dash, the question mark, and the exclamation point fall *within* the quotation marks when they refer to the quoted matter only; they fall *outside* when they refer to the whole sentence.

"I can't see how—" he started to say.

He asked, "When did she leave?"

What is the meaning of "the open door"?

The sergeant shouted "Halt!"

Save us from his "mercy"!

5. Are not used with *yes* or *no* except in direct discourse.

She said yes to all our requests.

6. Are not used with lengthy quotations set off from the text.

He took the title for his biography of Thoreau from a passage in *Walden*:

I long ago lost a hound, a bay horse, and a turtledove, and am still on their trail. . . . I have met one or two who had heard the hound, and the tramp of the horse, and even seen the dove disappear behind a cloud, and they seemed as anxious to recover them as if they had lost them themselves.

However, the title *A Hound, a Bay Horse, and a Turtle-Dove* probably puzzled some readers.

' ' Quotation Marks, Single

1. Enclose a quotation within a quotation in American usage. When both single and double quotation marks occur at the end of a sentence, the period typically falls within *both* sets of marks.

The witness said, "I distinctly heard him say, 'Don't be late,' and then heard the door close."

The witness said, "I distinctly heard him say, 'Don't be late.'"

2. Are sometimes used in place of double quotation marks especially in British usage. In this case a quotation within a quotation is set off by double quotation marks.

The witness said, 'I distinctly heard him say, "Don't be late," and then heard the door close.'

Semicolon ;

1. Links independent clauses not joined by a coordinating conjunction.

Some people have the ability to write well; others do not.

2. Links clauses joined by a conjunctive adverb (such as *consequently, furthermore, however*).

Speeding is illegal; furthermore, it is very dangerous.

3. Often occurs before expressions that introduce expansions or series (such as *for example, for instance, that is, e.g.,* or *i.e.*).

As a manager she tried to do the best job she could; that is, to keep her project on schedule and under budget.

4. Separates phrases that contain commas.

The country's resources consist of large ore deposits; lumber, waterpower, and fertile soils; and a strong, rugged people.

Send copies to our offices in Portland, Maine; Springfield, Illinois; and Savannah, Georgia.

5. Is placed outside quotation marks and parentheses.

They again demanded "complete autonomy"; the demand was again rejected.

/ Virgule (or Slash)

1. Separates alternatives.

high-heat and/or high-speed applications

. . . sit hour after hour. . . and finally year after year in a catatonic/frenzied trance rewriting the Bible —William Saroyan

2. Replaces the word *to* or *and* between related terms that are compounded.

the fiscal year 1983/1984

in the May/June issue

3. Divides run-in lines of poetry.

Say, sages, what's the charm on earth/Can turn death's dart aside?—Robert Burns

4. Divides elements in dates and divides numerators and denominators in fractions.

offer expires 5/19/94

Fifteen and 44/100 dollars

5. Often represents *per* or *to* when used with units of measure or to indicate the terms of a ratio.

9 ft/sec

risk/reward trade-off

6. Sets off phonemes of phonemic transcription.

/b/ as in *but*

Capitalization

Capitals are used for two broad purposes in English: they mark a beginning (as of a sentence) and they signal a proper noun, pronoun, or adjective. The following principles, each with examples, describe the most common uses of capital letters.

Beginnings

1. The first word of a sentence or sentence fragment is capitalized.

> The play lasted nearly three hours.
>
> How are you feeling?
>
> Bravo!

2. The first word of a sentence contained within parentheses is capitalized if it does not occur within another sentence. The first word of a parenthetical sentence within another sentence is not capitalized.

> The discussion was held in the boardroom. (The results are still confidential.)
>
> Although we liked the restaurant (their Italian food was the best), we seldom ate there.
>
> After waiting in line for an hour (why do we do these things?), we finally left.

3. The first word of a direct quotation is capitalized. However, if the quotation is interrupted in the middle of a sentence, the second part does not begin with a capital. When a quotation, whether a sentence fragment or a complete sentence, is syntactically dependent on the sentence in which it occurs, the quotation does not begin with a capital.

> The President said, "We have rejected this report entirely."
>
> "We have rejected this report entirely," the President said, "and we will not comment on it further."
>
> The President made it clear that "there is no room for compromise."

4. The first word of a sentence within a sentence is usually capitalized when it represents a direct question, a motto or aphorism, or spoken or unspoken dialogue. The first word following a colon may be either lowercased or capitalized if it introduces a complete sentence. While the former is more usual, the latter is common when the sentence is fairly lengthy and distinctly separate from the preceding clause.

> That question, as Disraeli said, is this: Is man an ape or an angel?
>
> My first thought was, How can I avoid this assignment?
>
> The advantage of this particular system is clear: it's inexpensive.
>
> The situation is critical: This company cannot hope to recoup the fourth-quarter losses that were sustained in five operating divisions.

5. The first word of a line of poetry is traditionally capitalized; however, in much twentieth-century poetry the line beginnings are lowercased.

> The best lack all conviction, while the worst
> Are full of passionate intensity.
> —W. B. Yeats

6. The first words of run-in enumerations that form complete sentences are capitalized, as are usually the first words of vertical lists and enumerations. However, enumerations of words or phrases run in with the introductory text are generally lowercased.

> Do the following tasks at the end of the day: 1. Clear your desktop of papers. 2. Cover office machines. 3. Straighten the contents of your desk drawers, cabinets, and bookcases.
>
> This is the agenda:
> Call to order
> Roll call
> Minutes of the previous meeting
> Treasurer's report
>
> On the agenda will be (1) call to order, (2) roll call, (3) minutes of the previous meeting, (4) treasurer's report. . . .

7. The first word in an outline heading is capitalized.

> I. Editorial tasks
> II. Production responsibilities
>   A. Cost estimates
>   B. Bids

8. The first word of the salutation of a letter and the first word of a complimentary close are capitalized.

> Dear Mary,
>
> Ladies and Gentlemen:
>
> Sincerely yours,

Proper Nouns, Pronouns, and Adjectives

Capitals are used with almost all proper nouns—that is, nouns that name particular persons, places, or things (including abstract entities), distinguishing them from others of the same class—and proper adjectives—that is, adjectives that take their meaning from what is named by the proper noun. The essential distinction in the use of capitals and lowercase letters at the beginnings of words lies in this individualizing significance of capitals as against the generalizing significance of lowercase. The following subject headings are in alphabetical order.

ARMED FORCES

1. Branches and units of the armed forces are capitalized, as are easily recognized short forms of full branch and unit designations. However, the words *army, navy,* etc., are lowercased when used in their plural forms or when they are not part of an official title.

> United States Army
> a contract with the Army
> Corps of Engineers
> a bridge built by the Engineers
> allied armies

AWARDS

2. Names of awards and prizes are capitalized.

> the Nobel Prize in Chemistry
> Distinguished Service Cross
> Academy Award

DERIVATIVES OF PROPER NAMES

3. Derivatives of proper names are capitalized when used in their primary sense. However, if the derived term has taken on a specialized meaning, it is usually not capitalized.

> Roman customs
> Shakespearean comedies
> Edwardian era
> > *but*
> quixotic
> herculean
> bohemian tastes

GEOGRAPHICAL REFERENCES

4. Divisions of the earth's surface and names of distinct areas, regions, places, or districts are capitalized, as are most derivative adjectives and some derivative nouns and verbs.

> The Eastern Hemisphere
> Midwest
> Tropic of Cancer
> Springfield, Massachusetts
> the Middle Eastern situation
> an Americanism
> > *but*
> french fries
> a japan finish
> manila envelope

5. Popular names of localities are capitalized.

> the Corn Belt   the Loop
> The Big Apple   the Gold Coast
> the Pacific Rim

6. Words designating global, national, regional, or local political divisions are capitalized when they are essential elements of specific names. However, they are usually lowercased when they precede a proper name or stand alone. (In legal documents, these words are often capitalized regardless of position.)

> the British Empire   Washington State
> New York City   Ward 1
> > *but*
> the fall of the empire the state of
>   Washington
> the city of New York fires in three wards

7. Generic geographical terms (such as *lake, mountain, river, valley*) are capitalized if they are part of a specific proper name.

> Hudson Bay   Long Island
> Niagara Falls   Crater Lake
> the Shenandoah Valley

8. Generic terms preceding names are usually capitalized.

> Lakes Michigan and Superior
> Mounts Whitney and Rainier

9. Generic terms following names are usually lowercased, as are singular or plural generic terms that are used descriptively or alone.

> the Himalaya and Andes mountains
> the Atlantic coast of Labrador
> the Hudson valley
> the river valley
> the valley

10. Compass points are capitalized when they refer to a geographical region or when they are part of a street name, but they are lowercased when they refer to simple direction.

> up North
> back East
> the Northwest
> West Columbus Avenue
> Park Avenue South
> > *but*
> west of the Rockies
> the east coast of Florida

11. Adjectives derived from compass points and nouns designating the inhabitants of some geographical regions are capitalized. When in doubt, see the entry in the dictionary.

> a Southern accent
> Northerners

12. Terms designating public places are capitalized if they are part of a proper name.

> Brooklyn Bridge
> Lincoln Park

the St. Regis Hotel

Independence Hall

but

Wisconsin and Connecticut avenues

the Plaza and St. Regis hotels

GOVERNMENTAL AND JUDICIAL BODIES

13. Full names of legislative, deliberative, executive, and administrative bodies are capitalized, as are short forms of these names. However, nonspecific noun and adjective references to them are usually lowercased.

the U.S. House of Representatives

the House

the Federal Bureau of Investigation

but

both houses of Congress

a federal agency

14. Names of international courts, the U.S. Supreme Court, and other higher courts are capitalized. However, names of city and county courts are usually lowercased.

The International Court of Arbitration

the Supreme Court of the United States

the Supreme Court

the United States Court of Appeals for the Second Circuit

the Michigan Court of Appeals

Lawton municipal court

Newark night court

HISTORICAL PERIODS AND EVENTS

15. Names of congresses, councils, and expositions are capitalized.

the Yalta Conference

the Republican National Convention

16. Names of historical events, some historical periods, and some cultural periods and movements are capitalized. When in doubt, consult the entry in the dictionary, especially for periods.

the Boston Tea Party

Renaissance

Prohibition

the Augustan Age

the Enlightenment

but

the space age

neoclassicism

17. Numerical designations of historical time periods are capitalized when they are part of a proper name; otherwise they are lowercased.

the Third Reich

the Roaring Twenties

but

the eighteenth century

the eighties

18. Names of treaties, laws, and acts are capitalized.

Treaty of Versailles

The Clear Air Act of 1990

ORGANIZATIONS

19. Names of firms, corporations, schools, and organizations and their members are capitalized. However, common nouns occurring after the names of two or more organizations are lowercased. The word *the* at the beginning of such names is only capitalized when the full legal name is used.

Thunder's Mouth Press

University of Wisconsin

European Community

Rotary International

Kiwanians

American and United airlines

20. Words such as *group, division, department, office*, or *agency* that designate a corporate and organizational unit are capitalized only when used with its specific name.

in the Editorial Department of Merriam-Webster

but

a notice to all department heads

PEOPLE

21. Names of persons are capitalized. However, the capitalization of particles such as *de, della, der, du, l', la, ten*, and *van* varies widely, especially in names of people in English-speaking countries.

Noah Webster

W.E.B. Du Bois

Daphne du Maurier

Werner Von Braun

Anthony Van Dyck

22. Titles preceding the name of a person and epithets used instead of a name are capitalized. However, titles following a name or used alone are usually lowercased.

President Roosevelt

Professor Kaiser

Queen Elizabeth

Old Hickory

the Iron Chancellor

but

Henry VIII, king of England

23. Corporate titles are capitalized when used with an individual's name; otherwise, they are lowercased.

Lisa Dominguez, Vice President

The sales manager called me.

24. Words of family relationship preceding or used in place of a person's name are capitalized; how-

ever, these words are lowercased if they are part of a noun phrase used in place of a name.

> Cousin Julia
>
> I know when Mother's birthday is.
>
> > *but*
>
> I know when my mother's birthday is.

25. Words designating peoples, nationalities, religious groups, tribes, races, and languages are capitalized. Other terms used to refer to groups of people are often lowercased. Designations based on color are usually lowercased.

Canadians	Iroquois
Ibo	African-American
Latin	Indo-European

highlander (an inhabitant of a highland)

Highlander (an inhabitant of the Highlands of Scotland)

black	white

PERSONIFICATIONS

26. Personifications are capitalized.

> She dwells with Beauty—Beauty, that must die;
> And Joy, whose hand is ever at his lips Bidding adieu.
>
> > —John Keats

obey the commands of Nature

PRONOUNS

27. The pronoun *I* is capitalized. For pronouns referring to the Deity, see rule 29 below.

> . . . no one but I myself had yet printed any of my work.—Paul Bowles

RELIGIOUS TERMS

28. Words designating the Deity are capitalized.

> An anthropomorphic, vengeful Jehovah became a spiritual, benevolent Supreme Being.—A. R. Katz

29. Personal pronouns referring to the Deity are usually capitalized, even when they closely follow their antecedent. However, many writers never capitalize such pronouns.

> All Thy works, O Lord, shall bless Thee.
> > —*Oxford American Hymnal*
>
> God's in his heaven—
> All's right with the world!
> > —Robert Browning

30. Traditional designations of revered persons, such as prophets, apostles, and saints, are often capitalized.

> our Lady
> the Prophet
> the Lawgiver

31. Names of religions, creeds and confessions, denominations, and religious orders are capitalized, as is the word *Church* when used as part of a proper name.

Judaism

Apostles' Creed

the Thirty-nine Articles of the Church of England

Society of Jesus

Hunt Memorial Church

> *but*

the local Baptist church

32. Names for the Bible or parts, versions, or editions of it and names of other sacred books are capitalized but not italicized. Adjectives derived from the names of sacred books are irregularly capitalized or lowercased; when in doubt, see the entry in the dictionary.

Authorized Version	New English Bible
Old Testament	Pentateuch
Apocrypha	Gospel of Saint Mark
Talmud	Koran
biblical	Koranic

SCIENTIFIC TERMS

33. Names of planets and their satellites, asteroids, stars, constellations and groups of stars, and other unique celestial objects are capitalized. However, the words *sun, earth,* and *moon* are usually lowercased unless they occur with other astronomical names.

Venus	Ganymede
Sirius	Pleiades

the Milky Way

enjoying the beauty of the moon

probes heading for the Moon and Mars

34. New Latin genus names in zoology and botany are capitalized; the second term in binomial scientific names, identifying the species, is not.

> a cabbage butterfly (*Pieris rapae*)
>
> a common buttercup (*Ranunculus acris*)

35. New Latin names of all groups above genus in zoology and botany (such as class or family) are capitalized; however, their derivative adjectives and nouns are not.

Gastropoda *but* gastropod

Mantidae *but* mantid

36. Names of geological eras, periods, epochs, and strata and names of prehistoric divisions are capitalized.

Silurian period	Pleistocene epoch
Age of Reptiles	Neolithic age

SEASONS, MONTHS, DAYS

37. Names of months, days of the week, and holidays and holy days are capitalized.

January	Ramadan
Tuesday	Thanksgiving
Yom Kippur	Easter

38. Names of seasons are not capitalized except when personified.

>   last spring
>   the sweet breath of Spring

TITLES OF PRINTED MATTER AND WORKS OF ART

39. Words in titles are capitalized, with the exception of internal conjunctions, prepositions, and articles. In some publications, prepositions of five or more letters are capitalized also.

>   *Of Mice and Men*
>   "The Man Who Would Be King"
>   "To His Coy Mistress"
>   *Slouching Toward Bethlehem*

40. Capitalization of the titles of movies, plays, paintings, sculpture, and musical compositions follow similar conventions. For more details, see the Italicization section below.

41. Major sections of books, long articles, or reports are capitalized when they are referred to within the same material.

>   See the Appendix for further information.

The Introduction explains the scope of this book.

discussed later in Chapter 4

42. Nouns used with numbers or letters to designate major reference headings are capitalized. Nouns designating minor elements are typically lowercased.

>   Volume V   Table 3
>   page 101   note 10

TRADEMARKS

43. Registered trademarks and service marks are capitalized.

>   Express Mail   Orlon
>   Kleenex   Walkman

VEHICLES

44. Names of ships, aircraft, and spacecraft are capitalized.

>   *Titanic*
>   Lindbergh's *Spirit of St. Louis*
>   *Apollo 13*

Italicization

The following are usually italicized in print and underlined in manuscript and typescript.

1. Words and passages that are to be emphasized.

   This was their fatal error: there *was* no cache of supplies in the now-abandoned depot.

2. Titles of books, magazines, newspapers, plays, long poems, movies, paintings, sculpture, and long musical compositions (but not musical compositions identified by the name of their genre).

   Dickens's *Bleak House*

   National Geographic

   Christian Science Monitor

   Shakespeare's *Othello*

   Eliot's *The Waste Land*

   the movie *Back to the Future*

   Gainsborough's *Blue Boy*

   Mozart's *Don Giovanni*

   but

   Schubert's Sonata in B-flat Major, D. 960

   NOTE: In the plurals of such italicized titles, the *s* or *es* endings are usually in roman type.

   hidden under a stack of *New Yorker*s

3. Names of ships, aircraft, and spacecraft.

   Titanic

   Lindbergh's *Spirit of St. Louis*

   Apollo 13

4. Words, letters, and figures when referred to as such.

   The *g* in *align* is silent.

   The first *2* and the last *0* are barely legible.

5. Unfamiliar words when first introduced and defined in a text.

   Heart failure is often accompanied by *edema*, an accumulation of fluid which tends to produce swelling of the lower extremities.

6. Foreign words and phrases that have not been naturalized in English. In general, any word entered in the main A–Z vocabulary of this dictionary need not be italicized.

   c'est la vie

   aere perennius

   che sarà, sarà

   sans peur et sans reproche

   but

   pasta   ad hoc   ex officio

7. New Latin scientific names of genera, species, subspecies, races, and varieties (but not groups of higher rank, such as phyla, classes, or orders) in botanical or zoological names.

   a thick-shelled American clam (*Mercenaria mercenaria*)

   a mallard (*Anas platyrhynchos*)

   but

   the family Hominidae

8. Case titles in legal citations, both in full and shortened form; "v" for "versus" is set in either roman or italic.

   Jones v. Ohio

   Smith et al v. Jones

   the *Jones* case

   Jones

Documentation of Sources

Writers and editors use various methods to indicate the source of a quotation or piece of information borrowed from another work. In works published for the general public and traditionally in scholarly works in the humanities, footnotes or endnotes have been preferred. In this system, sequential numbers within the text refer the reader to notes at the bottom of the page or at the end of the article, chapter, or book; these notes contain full bibliographical information of the works cited. In scholarly works in the social and natural sciences, and increasingly in the humanities as well, parenthetical references within the text refer the reader to an alphabetically arranged list of sources at the end of the work. The system of footnotes or endnotes is the more flexible, in that it allows for commentary on the work or subject and can also be used for brief peripheral discussions not tied to any specific work. However, style manuals tend to encourage the use of parenthetical references in addition to or instead of footnotes or endnotes, since for most kinds of material they are efficient and convenient for both writer and reader. In a carefully documented work, a bibliography or list of sources normally follows the entire text (including any endnotes) regardless of which system is used.

Though different publishers and journals have adopted slightly varying styles, the following examples illustrate standard styles for references, notes, and bibliographic entries. For more extensive treatment than can be provided here, *Webster's Standard American Style Manual, The Chicago Manual of Style, The MLA Style Manual,* or the *Publication Manual of the American Psychological Association* may be consulted.

Footnotes and Endnotes

Footnotes and endnotes are indicated by superscript Arabic numerals placed immediately after the material to be documented. The numbering is consecutive throughout an article or monograph; in a book, it usually starts over with each new chapter or section. Footnotes appear at the bottom of the page; endnotes, which take the same form as footnotes, are gathered at the end of the article, chapter, or book. Endnotes are generally preferred over footnotes by writers and publishers because they are easier to handle when preparing both manuscript and printed pages, though they can be less convenient for the reader. All of the examples shown reflect humanities citation style. All of the cited works appear again in the Lists of Sources section below.

Books

One author	[1]Elizabeth Bishop, *The Complete Poems: 1927–1979* (New York: Farrar, Straus & Giroux, 1983), 46.
Two or more authors	[2]Bert Holldobler and Edward O. Wilson, *The Ants* (Cambridge, Mass.: Belknap–Harvard Univ. Press, 1990), 119.
	[3]Randolph Quirk et al., *A Comprehensive Grammar of the English Language* (London: Longman, 1985), 135.
Edition and/or translation	[4]Arthur S. Banks, ed. *Political Handbook of the World: 1992* (Binghamton, N.Y.: CSA Publications, 1992), 293–95.

[5]Simone de Beauvoir, *The Second Sex,* trans. and ed. H.M. Parshley (New York: Knopf, 1953; Random House, 1974), 446.

Second or later edition

[6]Albert C. Baugh and Thomas Cable, *A History of the English Language,* 3d ed. (Englewood Cliffs, N.J.: Prentice Hall, 1978), 14.

Article in a collection or festschrift

[7]Ernst Mayr, "Processes of Speciation in Animals," in *Mechanisms of Speciation,* ed. C. Barigozzi (New York: Alan R. Liss, 1982), 1–3.

Work in two or more volumes

[8]Ronald M. Nowak, *Walker's Mammals of the World,* 5th ed. (Baltimore: Johns Hopkins Univ. Press, 1991), 2:661.

Corporate author

[9]Commission of the Humanities. *The Humanities in American Life* (Berkeley: Univ. of California Press, 1980), 46.

Book lacking publication data

[10]*Photographic View Album of Cambridge* [England], n.p., n.d., n.pag.

Subsequent reference

[11]Baugh and Cable, 18–19.

Articles

Journal paginated consecutively throughout annual volume

[12]Stephen Jay Gould and Niles Eldredge, "Punctuated Equilibria: The Tempo and Mode of Evolution Reconsidered," *Paleobiology* 3 (1977): 121.

Journal paginated consecutively only within each issue

[13]Roseann Duenas Gonzalez, "Teaching Mexican American Students to Write: Capitalizing on the Culture," *English Journal* 71.7 (Nov. 1982): 22–24.

Monthly magazine

[14]John Lukacs, "The End of the Twentieth Century," *Harper's,* Jan. 1993: 40.

Weekly magazine

[15]Richard Preston, "A Reporter at Large: Crisis in the Hot Zone," *New Yorker,* 26 Oct. 1992: 58.

Newspaper

[16]William J. Broad, "Big Science Squeezes Small-Scale Researchers," *New York Times,* 29 Dec. 1992: C1.

Signed review

[17]George Steiner, review of *Oeuvres en Prose Complètes, Tome 3,* by Charles Péguy, *Times Literary Supplement,* 25 Dec. 1992: 3.

Parenthetical References

Parenthetical references are highly abbreviated bibliographical citations that appear within the text itself, enclosed in parentheses. Such references direct the reader to a detailed bibliography or list of sources at the end of the work, often removing the need for footnotes or endnotes. The parenthetical references usually include only the author's last name and a page reference. (In the social and natural sciences, the year of publication is included after the author's name, and the page number is often omitted.) Any element of the reference that is clear from the context may be omitted. To distinguish among cited works published by the same author, the author's name may be followed by the specific work's title, which is usually shortened. (If the author-date system is being used, a lowercase letter can be added after the year—e.g., 1992a, 1992b—to distinguish between works published in the same year.) Each of the following references is keyed to an entry in the Lists of Sources section below.

Humanities style

(Quirk et al., 135)
(Baugh and Cable, *History,* 14)
(Commission on the Humanities, 46)

Sciences style   (Mayr 1982, 1–3)
                                  (Nowak 1991, 2:661)
                                  (Gould and Eldredge 1977)

Lists of Sources

A bibliography or list of sources in alphabetical order usually appears at the
end of the work. The following lists of cited works illustrate standard styles
employed in, respectively, the humanities and the social and natural sciences. The principal differences between the two styles are these. In the sciences, (1) an initial is generally used instead of the author's first name, (2)
the date is placed directly after the author's name, (3) all words in titles are
lowercased except the first word and the first word of any subtitle as well
as proper nouns and adjectives, and (4) article titles are not set off by quotation marks. (In some scientific publications, book and journal titles are not
italicized.)

Humanities style   Baugh, Albert C., and Thomas Cable. *A History of the English
                                  Language*. 3d ed. Englewood Cliffs, N.J.: Prentice Hall, 1978.

                                  Beauvoir, Simone de. *The Second Sex*. Trans. and ed. H. M.
                                  Parshley. New York: Alfred A. Knopf, 1953. Reprint. New York:
                                  Random House, 1974.

                                  Bishop, Elizabeth. *The Complete Poems: 1927–1979*. New York:
                                  Farrar, Straus & Giroux, 1983.

                                  Commission on the Humanities. *The Humanities in American Life*.
                                  Berkeley: University of California Press, 1980.

                                  Gonzalez, Roseann Duenas. "Teaching Mexican American Students
                                  to Write: Capitalizing on the Culture." *English Journal* 71.7
                                  (November 1982): 22–24.

                                  Lukacs, John. "The End of the Twentieth Century." *Harper's*,
                                  January 1993: 39–58.

                                  Photographic View Album of Cambridge [England]. N.d., n.p., n.
                                  pag.

                                  Quirk, Randolph, Sidney Greenbaum, Geoffrey Leech, and Jan
                                  Svartvik. *A Comprehensive Grammar of the English Language*.
                                  London: Longman, 1985.

                                  Steiner, George. Review of *Oeuvres en Prose Complètes, Tome 3*, by
                                  Charles Péguy. *Times Literary Supplement*, 25 December 1992: 3–4.

Sciences style   Banks, A. S., ed. 1992. *Political handbook of the world: 1992*.
                                  Binghamton, N.Y.: CSA Publications.

                                  Broad, W. J. 1992. Big science squeezes small-scale researchers.
                                  New York Times, 29 Dec.: C1+.

                                  Gould, S. J., and N. Eldredge. 1977. Punctuated equilibria: The tempo
                                  and mode of evolution reconsidered. *Paleobiology* 3: 115–151.

                                  Holldobler, B., and E. O. Wilson. 1990. *The ants*. Cambridge,
                                  Mass.: Belknap–Harvard Univ. Press.

                                  Mayr, E. 1982. Processes of speciation in animals. In C. Barigozzi,
                                  ed., *Mechanisms of speciation*. New York: Alan R. Liss: 1–19.

                                  Nowak, R.M. 1991. *Walker's mammals of the world*. 5th ed. 2 vols.
                                  Baltimore: Johns Hopkins Univ. Press.

                                  Preston, R. 1992. A reporter at large: Crisis in the hot zone. *New
                                  Yorker*, 26 Oct.: 58–81.

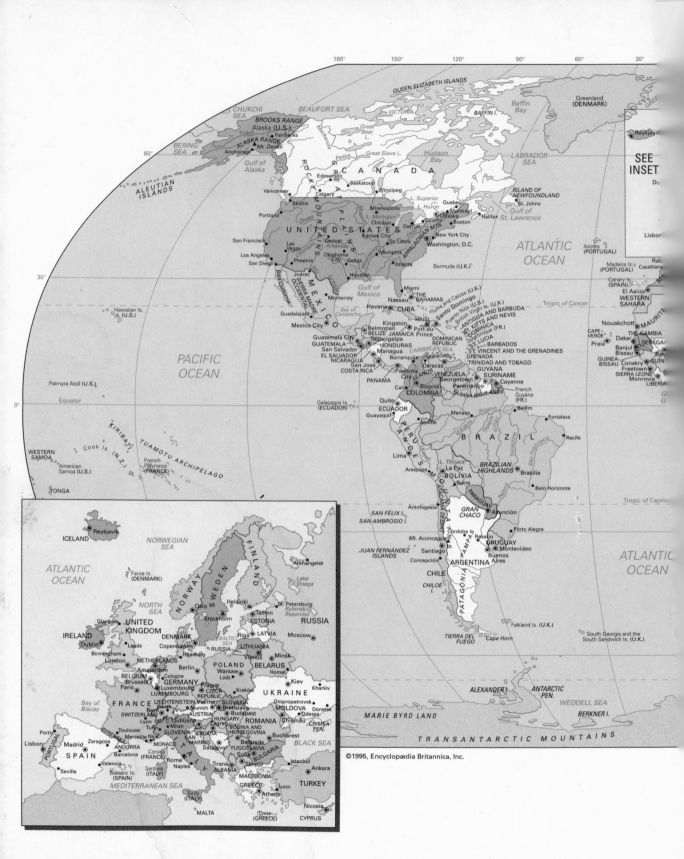

180°   150°   120°   90°   60°   30°

QUEEN ELIZABETH ISLANDS

Greenland
(DENMARK)

CHUKCHI SEA   BEAUFORT SEA   VICTORIA   Baffin
                                          Bay   BAFFIN I.

BROOKS RANGE
Alaska (U.S.)   Great
Fairbanks   Bear L.
ALASKA RANGE   Yukon
Mt. Denali   Great Slave L.   Hudson   LABRADOR
Anchorage   Peace   Bay   SEA
60°   BERING   Gulf of   Edmonton   C A N A D A
SEA   Alaska   Saskatoon   ISLAND OF
ALEUTIAN   Vancouver   Calgary   Winnipeg   NEWFOUNDLAND
ISLANDS   Seattle   L. Superior   Quebec   St. Johns
Portland   Minneapolis   L. Huron   Montreal   Gulf of
Chicago   Detroit   Ottawa   St. Lawrence   Halifax
U N I T E D   S T A T E S   Toronto   Boston   ATLANTIC
San Francisco   Denver   St. Louis   New York City   OCEAN
Las Vegas   Kansas City   Washington, D.C.
Los Angeles   Oklahoma   Memphis   Azores   PORTUGAL
San Diego   Phoenix   City   Dallas   Atlanta   Bermuda (U.K.)   (PORTUGAL)
Juárez   Houston   Madeira Is.   Casablanca
30°   Monterrey   Gulf of   Miami   (PORTUGAL)   Rab
MEXICO   Mexico   THE   Canary Is.   El Aaiún
Guadalajara   Bay of   Nassau   BAHAMAS   Tropic of Cancer   (SPAIN)   WESTERN
Campeche   Havana   CUBA   Turks and Caicos (U.K.)   SAHARA
Mexico City   Kingston   HAITI   Santo Domingo   Nouakchott   MAURIT
PACIFIC   Guatemala City   Belmopan   Port-au-   Puerto Rico (U.S.)   CAPE   THE GAMBIA
OCEAN   GUATEMALA   BELIZE   JAMAICA   Prince   British Virgin Is.   VERDE   Dakar   SENEGA
HONDURAS   Tegucigalpa   DOMINICAN   ANTIGUA AND BARBUDA   Praia   Bissau   GUIN
EL SALVADOR   Managua   REPUBLIC   ST. KITTS AND NEVIS   GUINEA-   Banjul
San Salvador   Barranquilla   DOMINICA   Martinique (FR.)   BISSAU   Conakry   Bay
NICARAGUA   Maracaibo   ST. LUCIA   Freetown   GUIN
San José   Caracas   BARBADOS   SIERRA LEONE   Monrovia
0°   Equator   COSTA RICA   Panama   GRENADA   LIBERIA
Palmyra Atoll (U.S.)   PANAMA   VENEZUELA   TRINIDAD AND TOBAGO
Cali   Georgetown   GUYANA
Galapagos Is.   Bogotá   Paramaribo   SURINAME
(ECUADOR)   COLOMBIA   GUIANA HIGHLANDS   Cayenne   French
Quito   Guiana (FR.)
WESTERN   ECUADOR   Manaus   Belém
SAMOA   Guayaquil   Iquitos   Fortaleza
American   Cook Is. (N.Z.)   KIRIBATI   B R A Z I L
Samoa (U.S.)   TUAMOTU ARCHIPELAGO   P E R U   Recife
French   Lima   BRAZILIAN
Polynesia   La Paz   HIGHLANDS   Brasília
TONGA   (FRANCE)   Arequipa   BOLIVIA
Sucre   Belo Horizonte
Antofagasta   GRAN   Asunción
SAN FÉLIX   CHACO   PARAGUAY   Tropic of Capric
SAN AMBROSIO I.   Córdoba   Pôrto Alegre
JUAN FERNÁNDEZ   Mt. Aconcagua   Rosario   URUGUAY
ISLANDS   Santiago   PAMPAS   Montevideo
Concepción   A R G E N T I N A   Buenos   ATLANTIC
CHILE   Aires   OCEAN
CHILOÉ I.
Falkland Is. (U.K.)   South Georgia and the
TIERRA DEL   South Sandwich Is. (U.K.)
FUEGO   Cape Horn
ALEXANDER I.   ANTARCTIC
PEN.
MARIE BYRD LAND   WEDDELL SEA   BERKNER I.

T R A N S A N T A R C T I C   M O U N T A I N S

©1995, Encyclopædia Britannica, Inc.

ICELAND   Reykjavík   NORWEGIAN
SEA
ATLANTIC   Faroe Is.   Arkhangelsk
OCEAN   (DENMARK)
FINLAND   Lake
NORTH   Helsinki   Onega
SEA   SWEDEN   St. Petersburg
Glasgow   UNITED   Oslo   Rybinsk
IRELAND   KINGDOM   Stockholm   Tallinn   Reservoir   RUSSIA
Dublin   Leeds   DENMARK   Riga   ESTONIA   Moscow
Birmingham   Copenhagen   LATVIA
London   NETHERLANDS   Hamburg   RUSSIA   LITHUANIA
Amsterdam   Berlin   Vilnius   Minsk
BELGIUM   Cologne   POLAND   BELARUS
Brussels   GERMANY   Warsaw   Homel
Paris   Luxembourg   Prague   Łódź   Kiev
LUXEMBOURG   CZECH   Kraków   Kharkiv
Bay of   LIECHTENSTEIN   Vienna   REPUBLIC   SLOVAKIA   U K R A I N E
Biscay   FRANCE   Zürich   Munich   Bratislava   MOLDOVA
SWITZERLAND   AUSTRIA   Budapest   Chişinău   Donetsk
Lyon   ALPS   Ljubljana   HUNGARY   CRIMEA
Toulouse   Turin   Milan   SLOVENIA   Zagreb   ROMANIA   PEN.
Porto   Marseille   Nice   CROATIA   Bucharest
PORTUGAL   PYRENEES   MONACO   SAN   BOSNIA AND   BLACK SEA
Lisbon   Madrid   Zaragoza   ANDORRA   Corsica   MARINO   HERZEGOVINA   YUGOSLAVIA
Barcelona   (FRANCE)   Sarajevo   Belgrade   BULGARIA
SPAIN   Valencia   Rome   Naples   Tiranë   Sofia   Skopje   Istanbul
Seville   Balearic Is.   Sardinia   I T A L Y   ALBANIA   MACEDONIA   Ankara
(SPAIN)   (ITALY)   GREECE   Izmir   TURKEY
MEDITERRANEAN SEA   Sicily   Athens   Nicosia
(ITALY)   Crete   CYPRUS
MALTA   (GREECE)